THE
BRITISH
FILM
CATALOGUE
1895-1970

WORKS BY DENIS GIFFORD

BOOKS

Cinema Britanico
British Cinema
Movie Monsters
Science Fiction Film
Discovering Comics
Stap Me! The British Newspaper Strip
Test Your Nostalgia Quotient
Fifty Years of Radio Comedy
A Pictorial History of Horror Movies
Karloff: The Man, The Monster, The Movies

COMPILATION FILMS

Highlight: The Singing Cinema
The Sporting Year

EDITOR

Streamline Comics
Fizz
Roy Regan
Fido
Star Comic
Six Comics of World War One
Film Pictorial Souvenir 1933

RADIO

Cartunes
People Are Funny
Sounds Familiar

SCREENPLAYS

The Handy Manns
The Glass-and-a-half Day
Carry On Spaceman (unproduced)

STORIES

Pip Pippin

STRIP CARTOONS

South London Sam
Streamline
Steadfast McStaunch
Sammy Sprockett and his Pocket Rocket
Telestrip
Koo Koo Klub
Scatty Scrapbook
Tellytoon

TELEVISION

The Alberts' Channel, Too
Elstree: Studio of the Stars
Looks Familiar

THE BRITISH FILM CATALOGUE 1895-1970

A Reference Guide

DENIS GIFFORD

McGRAW–HILL BOOK COMPANY

NEW YORK   ST. LOUIS   SAN FRANCISCO
DÜSSELDORF / JOHANNESBURG / KUALA LUMPUR
LONDON / MEXICO / MONTREAL
NEW DELHI / PANAMA / RIO DE JANEIRO
SINGAPORE / SYDNEY / TORONTO

Library of Congress Cataloging in Publication Data

Gifford, Denis.
    The British film catalogue, 1895-1970.

    1. Moving-pictures — Great Britain. I. Title.
PN 1993.5.G7G5   791.43'0942   72-7861
ISBN 0-07-023205-9

Contents

1758535

FOR FITZ
And Pandora Jane
They would have loved each other

Preface

THIS IS the first complete catalogue of every British film produced for public entertainment since the invention of cinematography. British film producers, unlike their American counterparts, have never been required to register their films for purposes of copyright, and so no national British register exists to compare with that held and published in book form by the Library of Congress in Washington. It is a complete catalogue in that it includes every traceable British entertainment film. Since the introduction of the Cinematograph Films Act of 1927, British companies have been required to register title and footage information with the Board of Trade. Every film so registered is included in this book, but the inclusion of British films produced before the Act cannot be guaranteed. However, every available piece of published information on British films has been studied, including trade papers, fan magazines, and company catalogues preserved in the archives of the British Film Institute and the British Museum. In addition, every last pioneer of the British film industry — producer, director, writer, photographer, or actor — has been personally interviewed.

The term 'British Film' was defined by the 1927 Act, Part IV paragraph 2, as follows:

> For the purposes of this Act a film shall be deemed to be a British film if it complies with all the following requirements: 1. It must be made by a person who was at the time a British subject, or by two or more persons each of whom was a British subject, or by a British Company; 2. The studio scenes must have been photographed in a studio in the British Empire; 3. The author of the scenario must be a British subject; 4. Not less than seventy-five per cent of the salaries, wages and payments for labour and services (exclusive of payments for copyright and salary to one foreign actor or actress or producer, but inclusive of payments to the scenario author) has been paid to British subjects or persons domiciled in the British Empire. The expression 'British Company' means a company registered under the laws of any part of the British Empire, the majority of the directors of which are British subjects.

While useful as a basic yardstick, this definition had to be both narrowed and broadened for this book. The Board of Trade classified as 'British' the native product of Australia, Canada, India, New Zealand and the West Indies. None of these productions has been included in this catalogue, although all films known to have been made in Ireland, Scotland and Wales are. The BOT classified as 'Foreign' a number of British-made films, such as Herbert Wilcox's *Madame Pompadour,* and films such as these are included.

More genuinely 'foreign' films included in this catalogue are those produced by British companies in co-operative arrangements with studios in France, Germany, Holland, Italy and even Hollywood. During the early sound period, two or more versions of the same film would be made with English and foreign casts, sometimes in a British studio, sometimes abroad. Where the latter situation arises, the film has been included despite a BOT 'Foreign' registration, with a note in brackets as to the place of production. Films produced in the British Isles by American companies on location, ranging from early visits by Kalem and Edison to such apparently native American productions as *The Dirty Dozen,* are also included.

This is a catalogue of British films 'produced for public entertainment'; in other words it includes films completed but not necessarily exhibited. Some of the films made in the silent period were never shown to the paying public, either because of the arrival of sound or because they were just inferior. Some of the films produced in recent years are still awaiting release, others never reached the cinema but eventually attained a showing on television; all these films have been included. Films not included are those made specifically for television, even when they have been exhibited in cinemas as shorts, featurettes, or joined together into features. These must await the compilation of a separate catalogue of British television films. A further amplification of the phrase 'produced for public entertainment' is that films in this catalogue are all professional productions; the exceptions are a few amateur films made on sub-standard 16mm stock, which were blown up to 35mm for release to cinemas.

Originally this book was to have catalogued what is generally termed the 'Fiction Film'. It was found, however, that if this definition was applied strictly, too many fringe subjects would have to be omitted. Many early films are simply recordings of Music Hall stars in performance of their theatrical acts; others are staged reconstructions of Boer War and Russo-Japanese War incidents, which were fraudulently marketed as actualities. Such films are too important in the development of the cinema to exclude as non-fiction, and so the term 'entertainment film' was selected. This neatly allows the exclusion of all news-reels, documentaries, and films of pure actuality, advertisement, education, information, propaganda, and travel. Also excluded are films of the animation variety which do not employ the live actor. There are more than enough of these to fill a companion volume, and perhaps one day they will.

It is usual for a catalogue of films to be arranged in alphabetical order. This is ideal for the enquirer who knows the title of the film but over fourteen thousand titles are dealt with here and many could be known only to an eighty-year old expert. Rather than let these many rediscoveries return to alphabetical oblivion, it was decided that a chronological listing in order of exhibition would enable both casual enquirer and expert to survey the entire history of the British film industry in a way not possible with the standard type of catalogue. To browse through a chosen year or to scan the pages is to catch a moment in time: perhaps a favourite star making a debut in a small role, or a once-great name on the wane; a famous director starting out as a writer, or a producer playing a bit part to make ends meet; perhaps sound films are coming in and silent films are fading out, or the first three-reel features are appearing among the mass of one-reel dramas and half-reel comedies; the first close-up is being cut in, or the first Academy Award being won. Between the lines of names and titles lies the history of the British film, with its almost annual booms and crises, echoed by the waxing and waning of stars and directors and the changes in fashion of stories and themes. It is hoped that in this way the catalogue will prove a useful source book, not only for the growing army of film students, but for the social historian as well as the casual reader seeking interesting entertainment.

An alphabetical index of film titles is provided for those who know what film they are looking for. Finally, may I recommend that the reader initially studies the section 'How to Use The Catalogue', which, together with the Acknowledgements, should add considerably to the enjoyment of the book.

Denis Gifford 1972

How to use the Book

TO FIND full information on any British entertainment film, whether short or feature, silent or sound, locate the title in the alphabetical *Title Index* at the back of the book. Immediately preceding the title is the *Catalogue Number* of the film. The main entries for the films run chronologically from 1895 to 1970, the catalogue numbers running from 00001 to 14161. The position of a film in the book can be found by checking the catalogue numbers at the top left hand corner of each spread.

To survey a typical year's film production, choose the year and turn to it. The chronological arrangement is divided by years and then by months; in addition, the top right-hand corner of each page shows the year featured on that spread.

INFORMATION

As much information as could be discovered from available published sources (see *Bibliography*) is given for each film, information on early films being naturally less than with more recent productions. However, a good deal of 'new' information has been uncovered and is published here for the first time. The elements which constitute a perfect catalogue entry appear in the following order, but it should be borne in mind that a great many entries will contain only some of the following elements.

1. Date

Films are catalogued chronologically in order of their initial exhibition. This is decided in one of several ways: by date of first advertisement, first review, notice, or listing in contemporary publications; by date of first Trade Show; by date of showing to the British Board of Film Censors (from January 1913); by date of compulsory registration with the Board of Trade (from January 1928); by date of completion in the case of films as yet unshown. Where several alternative dates exist, the earliest is used.

It is common for films to be dated by their dates of release. This practice has not been followed here, as in the British cinema a release date can follow a first show date by one, five, or, in one case, fourteen years. Where no date could be ascertained the film is included at a deduced date with the phrase 'Date Uncertain' in brackets, following the summary.

The Catalogue is divided into years, and then into months. Days of the month are not shown, and the films should not be taken as chronologically arranged within the monthly divisions. However, in the silent period, films by prolific production companies are grouped together in chronological order under the monthly divisions.

2. Catalogue Number

The number which appears immediately preceding each title is the catalogue number of the film. These numbers run chronologically through the main entries from 00001 for the first film of 1895 to 14161 for the last film of 1970. These numbers are provided purely for the speedy location of a film known only by the title, and are used in conjunction with the Alphabetical Index. The Catalogue Numbers are allocated by the compiler.

3. Title

The main title given for each film is the original title used at the first showing of the film. It is followed by any subsequent change of title in the English language. Also provided are alternative titles in contemporary listings, the subsequent change of title for later revival or reissue, the change of title for public showing or release and the change of title for American distribution.

4. Length

The length of each film is given in one of two ways: *Silent films* as actual footage, *Sound films* as running time in minutes. Both figures are given in brackets following the main title of the film. The original intention to standardise all lengths as running time in minutes proved impossible. Although it is generally accepted that silent films were made to be projected at an average speed of one foot per second, in practice this was not so. By the last years of the silent era projection speed almost matched that of the new sound film standard, at 1.5 feet per second. Silent films made in the Kinemacolor system ran at twice the normal speed, and so published footages have been halved in this catalogue to give a correct comparison with normal films. Where silent film footage is given in rounded thousands (1000, 2000, etc), this should be taken as an approximate figure, as more accurate footage cannot be traced. 1000 feet is the standard length of one reel of film.

5. Censor's Certificate

This information is given for all films passed by the British Board of Film Censors since January 1913. The type of certificate awarded (A, AA, H, U, X) is shown in brackets immediately following the film's length. For explanation of the various certificates, see *Abbreviations*.

6. Silent or Sound

Experiments with synchronised sound began in the early days of film making. Actors were photographed miming to gramophone recordings, and all traceable examples of these have been included. Unfortunately, the Hepworth Vivaphone productions were never advertised or listed by title, except in the case of special dramatised productions such as *Faust*. Consequently, the twice-weekly Vivaphone releases cannot be listed here.

The main entries to the catalogue are divided into two parts, Silent Films and Sound Films. The division is made between December 1928 and January 1929. Before January 1929, all films catalogued are classed as silent, except where the word *sound* is shown following the title, length, and certificate. These are generally experimental or short productions.

After December 1928, all films catalogued are classed as sound films, except where the word *silent* follows the title, length, and certificate. There were naturally many silent releases during the first year or so of sound production. Where a film produced as a silent film has later had a sound track added to it for release or reissue, this information is given together with the date in brackets following the plot summary.

Where a sound film is produced in more than one language version, note is made following title, length, and certificate by the words bilingual, trilingual and multilingual.

7. Colour Systems

Any colour system used in the film, either throughout or in sequences, is noted next. See *Abbreviations* for the full list of colour systems. A note on Kinemacolour films appears in section 4 above.

8. Screen Ratio

The only screen ratio noted is that of Cinemascope, which is shown by the abbreviation *scope*. The many different processes providing similar proportions (Dylaiscope, Hammerscope, Nudiscope, etc) are not differentiated but are included under this term.

9. Stereoscopy

Films photographed (but not necessarily exhibited) in any stereoscopic process are indicated by the term 3D, given in brackets.

10. Production Company

The name of each film's production company is given next, underneath the title. This is given in shortened form, the words Films, Productions, Producing Company, and so on, having been eliminated. Some companies are given in abbreviated or initial form; full names of these will be found under *Abbreviations*. In the case of co-productions, names of companies are joined by a hyphen.

11. Distribution Company

The name of each film's distributor is given in abbreviated form in brackets following the Production company. Included here as distributors are such early variants as publisher, agent, selling agent, and renter. Where no distributor appears, the production company is also the distributor.

12. Reissue

Note is made of every film which has been generally

reissued or re-released some time after its original release. After the word *reissue*, the year or years are given, followed by any change of title and, in brackets, any change of distributor, length or running time.

13. Producer

Production credits now appear beneath the production-distribution information. The name of the film's producer is given following the abbreviation 'P'. Included in this category are such early terms as Supervisor, and Director General of Productions. No separate divisions are made for Executive Producer, Executive in Charge of Production, Production Executive, and similar credits, but their names are generally included here. Where the actual producer of the film is credited as Associate Producer, his name follows the abbreviation 'AP'.

14. Director

The name of the film's director is given following the abbreviation 'D'. The earliest film directors were called Stage Managers; later they were known as Producers. The American term Director did not come into general use in England until the twenties. To avoid confusion, only the term Director is used in this catalogue, but historians should bear these subtleties in mind.

Director's names which are given within brackets have been supplied by the compiler from sources unconfirmed by documentary evidence.

15. Story Source

The name of the author of the original story of the film is given following the abbreviation 'S'. The story may be taken as original to the film where no qualification precedes the author's name. Where the story is not original to the film, the form of the source is given in brackets, immediately following the 'S'.

Book	Work of non-fiction
Cartoon	Cartoon or comic strip
Novel	Book-length fictional work
Opera	Opera, operetta, or comic opera
Poem	Work of poetry
Play	Full length theatrical play
Sketch	Short playlet or music hall sketch
Story	Short story

The original title of the work, where this differs

from the title of the film, is given in brackets following the name of the author.

Included under this heading are authors whose actual credits on the film may vary from Story, Original Story, Original Screenplay, Screen Original, Script, Scenario, Photoplay, Written By, Specially Written For The Screen By, and just plain By.

16. Screenplay

The abbreviation 'SC', which directly follows 'S', is generally used for authors of adaptions from another form of story. All original film screenplays and scripts are included under the heading 'S'.

Earlier terms for film writing are not listed separately. These include Adaptation, Continuity, Photoplay, Picturization, and Scenario. Other writing credits such as Additional Dialogue, Additional Material, Dialogue, Script Associate, Script Contribution, Treatment, etc, are not distinguished but are included under this heading.

17. Narrator

The abbreviation 'N' includes all 'voices over' provided by unseen actors or commentators, whether credited in the film to a Commentator, Narrator, Prologue, or indeed uncredited.

18. Cast and Characters

Players' names appear in the left-hand column, the names of the characters they are portraying in the right. In the case of early films it has not always been possible to determine character names. In the case of films of the class Revue and occasionally Musical, where all performers appear as themselves, the right-hand column is also used for performers' names. Otherwise performers appearing as themselves are generally listed at the foot of the cast.

No real standard exists for published cast lists: some casts give actors in order of appearance, others in order of importance, alphabetical order, or even in the old theatrical tradition of separated sexes. By going to the original advertising or billing of the films, and where possible the original credit titles, an attempt has been made to arrange players' names in order of importance or stardom.

Pressure of space prevents the publication of complete casts for every film. Full casts often run to fifty or more names, from leading player down to such credits as 'Third Virgin at Orgy'. To include all names would have resulted in a book almost twice as long as this and so some discretion has therefore been used in the elimination of minor players and characters. However, all names of special interest have been retained: early appearances of actors who later attained stature, minor appearances of former stars, and unusual personalities in special but small roles. In the case of early films, however, every discoverable name has been included.

19. Subject

Each film is now given a single descriptive key word in capital letters, immediately preceding the summary. This instantly classifies the content of the film into one of the following twenty-three different categories.

ACT	Stage performer reproducing a stage performance for the camera.
ADVENTURE	Dramatic story with action, generally set in a foreign location or in historical time.
ADVERT	Sponsored film made to advertise a commercial product. (Early examples only are included.)
ANIMAL	Dramatic, humorous or adventure story in which the key figure is an animal.
CHASE	Popular form of early comedy or drama in which one party pursues another for the greater part of the film.
CHILDREN	Film made specifically for a juvenile audience.
COMEDY	Humorous story including all styles of comedy: slapstick, farce, etc.
COMPILATION	Film composed of extracts from earlier films.
CRIME	Dramatic plot turning on any aspect of crime, including mystery, murder, detection, violence.
DRAMA	General term for any serious story which cannot be classified under a more particular heading.
FACIAL	Early form of short comedy concentrating on facial expressions in close-up.
FANTASY	Dramatic or humorous film with a fantastic or impossible story, including science fiction.
HISTORY	Drama founded on historical fact or involving the representation of actual persons, living or dead. This category includes biographical films, but not costume adventures or religious stories.
HORROR	Dramatic film, often fantasy, but with elements calculated to horrify or frighten the audience.
MUSICAL	Comedy, drama, or romance with an above-average quota of songs or dances. This category includes ballet, dance, opera, and early song films, both mimed and dramatised.
NUDIST	Comedy, drama or romance in which one or more performers appear naked. Usually set in a nudist camp.
PATHOS	The 'pathetic' was a popular form of early drama, and usually implies a story of tragedy ending in death.
RELIGION	Dramatic story based on Christian history or a religious theme.
ROMANCE	Story, generally dramatic, occasionally humorous, concentrating on the theme of love.
SPORT	Dramatic film, usually involving crime, in which the central theme is a sport such as boxing, football, horse racing, etc.

TRICK	Early form of comedy in which trick photography dominates the action, rather than serving the plot.
WAR	Dramatic story in a wartime setting, or reconstruction of a wartime incident.
WESTERN	Dramatic action film made in imitation of the familiar American cowboy story.

20. Summary

The plot or content of each film is summarised in a single sentence, following the Subject heading. Where applicable, the plotline is preceded by the setting, date or period of the story. The word Ruritania is used throughout to locate all stories set in imaginary countries.

Where no published plot of an early film can be traced, an extract from an advertisement or contemporary review is given instead, enclosed by quotation marks. Where no plotline or quote appears, no published description of the film has been found.

21. Awards

Any awards won by the film are given within brackets, following the summary. These are noted in abbreviation, with the year of award in full. A full list of awards included appears under the *Abbreviations*

section. Royal Film performances are included under this heading.

22. Additional Information

The development of the film as an art is noted, where known, by the inclusion within brackets of special information relating to the structure of the film. For example, where it is usual at the time for films to be of one single scene, the first films to contain more are noted thus: (2 scenes), (3 scenes), etc. The first discovered close-ups, cut-in close-ups, double exposures, and other important steps, are also noted. Any other important information appears within brackets following the summary.

23. Series and Serials

Films made in groups as series and in episodes as serials are first noted as either in brackets following the main title. Separate episode titles with their episode numbers are listed following the cast. Lengths are given for each episode, and also censor certificates. Each episode is given a separate catalogue number.

Index

The index lists film titles in alphabetical order, including all alternative titles, title changes for reissue, title changes for American release, and series and serial episode titles. The Catalogue Number appears before each title.

Abbreviations

Awards

AA	Academy of Motion Picture Arts and Sciences (1928-70)
BFA	British Film Academy (1947-70)
DEFA	Daily Express Film Award (1947-50)
DMNFA	Daily Mail National Film Award (1946-51)
FWA	Film Weekly Award (1929-39)
PGAA	Picturegoer Annual Award (1933-59)
RFP	Royal Film Performance (1946-70)
Top Moneymaker	British film taking the greatest amount at the Nation's box offices during the year, according to the Kinematograph Weekly (1936-70)

Censor's Certificates

(A)	Jan 1913-June 1970: Adult; children accompanied by a responsible adult. July-December 1970: Parents advised that film may be unsuitable for children under 14.
(AA)	Children under 14 not admitted.
(H)	Horrific; persons over 16 only.
(U)	Universal; unrestricted admission.
(X)	Adult; persons under 16 not admitted. From July 1970, persons under 18 not admitted.

Colour Systems

ansco	Anscocolor
chemi	Chemicolor
colour	Unspecified system
dufay	Dufaycolor
eastman	Eastmancolor
ferrania	Ferraniacolor
harmoni	Harmonicolor
kinema	Kinemacolor
metro	Metrocolor
pathe	Pathecolor
prizma	Prizmacolor
raycol	Raycolcolor
spectra	Spectracolor
tru	Trucolor
warner	Warnercolor

Credits

AP	Associate Producer
D	Director
N	Narrator
P	Producer
S	Story; source; screenplay
SC	Screenplay (adaptation)

Miscellaneous

also	Alternative release title
BBFC	British Board of Film Censors
BOT	Board of Trade
B/W	Black and white
bilingual	Film made in two language versions
DORA	Defence of the Realm Act
dir	Director
doc	Documentary
ft	Feet
mins	Minutes
multilingual	Film made in more than three language versions
pho	Photography

scope	Cinemascope or any other system giving similar proportions
seq	Sequence
3D	Stereoscopic
trilingual	Film made in three language versions
USA	American release title

Standard abbreviations used in the text include capt (captain), cpl (corporal), dr (doctor), insp (inspector), pte (private), supt (superintendent), tec (detective), WC (wing-commander).

Production and Distribution Companies

AA	Anglo-Amalgamated Film Distributors
AB	Associated British
ABFD	Associated British Film Distributors
ABPC	Associated British Picture Corporation
ACT	Association of Cinema Technicians
AEMI	Anglo-EMI Film Distributors
AF	Audible Filmcraft
AFM	Allied Film Makers
AIP	American International Pictures
AP&D	Associated Producers and Distributors
ASFI	Associated Sound Film Industries
ATP	Associated Talking Pictures
Amb	Ambassador Film Productions
BAP	British Aviation Pictures
B&C	British and Colonial Kinematograph Company
B&D	British and Dominions Film Corporation
BBC	British Broadcasting Corporation
BEF	British Exhibitors' Films
BFI	British Film Institute
BFM	British Film Makers
BHE	British Home Entertainments
BIED	British Independent Exhibitors' Distributors
BIF	British Instructional Films
BIP	British International Pictures
BL	British Lion Film Corporation
BLPA	British Lion Production Assets
BSFP	British Sound Film Productions
BSS	British Screen Service
Bry	Bryanston Films
Butch	Butcher's Film Service
C&M	Cricks and Martin Films
CFF	Children's Film Foundation
CUE	Commonwealth United Entertainment
Col	Columbia Pictures Corporation
Cosmo	Cosmopolitan Films
DFSA	Davison Film Sales Agency
DUK	Do-U-Know Film Productions
EB	Equity British Film Productions
EL	Eagle-Lion Film Distributors
EMI	Electrical and Musical Industries
Eal	Ealing Studios
Ex	Exclusive Films
FBO	Film Booking Offices
FN	First National Pictures
FNP	First National-Pathe
Fed	Federated Film Corporation
Fox	Fox Film Company
GAS	George Albert Smith Films
G&S	Greenspan and Seligman Enterprises
GEF	Golden Era Film Distributors
GFD	General Film Distributors
GHW	Gregory, Hake and Walker
GN	Grand National Pictures
Gau	Gaumont Company
IFD	Independent Film Distributors
IFR	International Film Renters
IP	Independent Producers
IVTA	International Variety Theatres Agency
JMG	Jury-Metro-Goldwyn
JPD	Jack Phillips Distributors
KTC	Kinematograph Trading Company
Kin-Ex	Kinema Exclusives
LIP	London Independent Producers
Lib	Liberty Films
MGM	Metro-Goldwyn-Mayer Pictures
MOI	Ministry of Information
MP	Moving Pictures Sales Agency
MRA	Moral Rearmament

Mon	Monarch Film Corporation	TC	Two Cities Films
NA	New Agency	TFD	Twickenham Film Distributors
NofE	North of England Films	20	Twentieth Century Fox Film Corporation
NPFD	National Provincial Film Distributors	U	Universal Pictures
NR	New Realm Pictures	UA	United Artists Film Corporation
NSS	National Screen Service	UFA	Universum Film Aktiengesells- chaft
P&C	Phillips and Carroll	UI	Universal International Pictures
PDC	Producers Distributing Corporation	UK	United Kingdom Photoplays
Par	Paramount Pictures Corporation	W&F	Woolf and Freedman Film Service
Pi	Pioneer Exclusives		
RFD	Rank Film Distributors	WB	Warner Brothers Pictures
RFI	Regal Films International	WB-FN	Warner Brothers-First National
RKO	RKO-Radio Pictures	WI	Western Import
Ren	Renown Pictures Corporation	WP	Williams and Pritchard Films
Rom	Romulus Films	YCC	Yorkshire Cinematograph Co
SC	Sound City Films	YSA	Yorkshire Sales Agency

Bibliography

Main references arranged chronologically

Trade Journals, Fan Magazines, Newspapers

1894-1905	The Photogram
1894-1902	The Optical Magic Lantern Journal
1896	The Entr'acte
1896-1920	The Stage
1896-1932	The Era
1898-1906	Music Hall and Theatre Review
1900-2	The Showman
1902-8	The Music Hall
1904	The Talking Machine News and Cinematograph Journal
1904-7	The Optical Lantern and Kinematograph Journal
1907-8	The World's Fair
1907-70	The Kinematograph Weekly
1908-32	The Bioscope
1910-12	The Film House Record
1910-12	The Picture Theatre News
1911-12	The Pictures
1911-14	The Talbot Tattler
1911-20	The Moving Picture World
1912-13	The Top-Line Indicator
1912-14	The Evening News
1912-16	The Film Censor
1912-22	The Kinematograph Monthly Film Record
1912-70	The Cinema News and Property Gazette/Daily Cinema
1913-14	Pictures and Pleasures
1913-15	Illustrated Films Monthly
1913-15	Pathe Cinema Journal/ Pathe Weekly Bulletin
1913-60	Pictures and the Picturegoer /Picturegoer
1914	The Cinematograph Exhibitors' Mail
1914-18	The Film Renter
1915-17	The Picture Palace News
1919-20	Cinema Chat
1919-20	The Trade Show Critic
1919-24	Stoll Editorial News
1919-40	Boys' Cinema
1919-60	Picture Show
1921-24	Motion Picture Studio
1928-39	Film Weekly
1928-70	Board of Trade Journal
1932-35	Film Star Weekly
1932-39	Film Pictorial
1932-70	Sight and Sound
1934-70	Monthly Film Bulletin
1935	The London Reporter
1935-70	The Motion Picture Herald
1935-70	The Cine-Technician/Film and TV Technician
1950-70	Variety
1954-70	Films and Filming

Reference Books

1894-1912	*Motion Pictures from the Library of Congress Paper Print Collection 1894-1912* (Kemp R. Niver)
1894-1949	*Motions Pictures: Catalogues of Copyright Entries* 3 vol (Library of Congress)
1914-70	*Kinematograph Year Book*
1927-34	*Spotlight Casting Directory*
1944-70	*Film Review* (F. Maurice Speed)
1946-70	*The British Film (And Television) Year Book* (Peter Noble)

Catalogues

1895-1913	W. Butcher; Cinematograph Company; Cricks and Martin; Cricks and Sharp; Edison Manufacturing Co; Gaumont Co; Hepwix Films; Jury's Imperial Pictures; Kinemacolor Films; R.W. Paul; Sheffield Photo Co; G.A. Smith; Charles Urban Trading Company; Walturdaw; Warwick Trading Co; Williamson Kinematograph Co.
1895-1934	*National Film Archive Catalogue* Parts I-III

Biographies

Arranged alphabetically by personality.

Ackland, Rodney and Elspeth Grant, *The Celluloid Mistress* (1954)

Anderson, Lindsay, *Lindsay Anderson* by Elizabeth Sussex (1969)

Arliss, George, *George Arliss by Himself* (1940)

Balcon, Michael, *Michael Balcon Presents a Lifetime of Films* (1969)
Michael Balcon's 25 Years in Films by Monja Danischewsky (1947)

Barkas, Geoffrey, *Behind the Camera* by Natalie Barkas (1934)

The Beatles, by Hunter Davies (1968)

Brunel, Adrian, *Nice Work* (1949)

Bull, Peter, *I Know the Face But. . .* (1963)
I Say, Look Here! (1965)

Burton, Richard, *Richard Burton* by Ruth Waterbury (1965)

Carstairs, John Paddy, *Hadn't We the Gaiety* (1940) *Honest Injun* (1942)

Connery, Sean, *Gilt-Edged Bond* by Richard Gant (1967)

Cooper, Gladys, *Without Veils* by Sewell Stokes (1953)

Courtneidge, Cicely, *Cicely* (1953)

Coward, Noel, *Theatrical Companion to Coward* by Raymond Mander and Joe Mitchenson (1953)
Future Indefinite (1954)

Daniels, Bebe and Ben Lyon, *Life With the Lyons* (1953)

Desmond, Florence, *Florence Desmond by Herself* (1953)

Dietrich, Marlene, *Blonde Venus* by Leslie Frewin (1955)

Donat, Robert, *Robert Donat* by J.C. Trewin (1968)

Donlan, Yolande, *Sand in My Mink* (1955)

Dors, Diana, *Swingin' Dors* (1960)

East, John M, *'Neath the Mask* by John East (1967)

Emney, Fred, *The Fred Emney Story* by Gerard Fairlie (1960)

Fairbanks jr, Douglas, *Knight Errant* by Brian Connell (1955)

Fairlie, Gerard, *With Prejudice* (1952)

Faith, Adam, *Poor Me* (1961)

Farrar, David, *No Royal Road* (1947)

Fields, Gracie, *Sing As We Go* (1960)

Flaherty, Robert, *The Innocent Eye* by Arthur Calder-Marshall (1963)
The Odyssey of a Film Maker by Frances Flaherty (1960)
The World of Robert Flaherty by Richard Griffith (1953)

Flanagan, Bud, *My Crazy Life* (1961)

Friese-Greene, William, *Close-Up of an Inventor* by Ray Allister (1948)

Gielgud, John, *John Gielgud* by Hallam Fordham (1952)

Glyn, Elinor, *Elinor Glyn* by Anthony Glyn (1955)

Grantley, Lord, *Silver Spoon* by Mary & Alan Wood (1954)

Hall, Henry, *Here's To the Next Time* (1955)

Hancock, Tony, *Hancock,* by Freddie Hancock & David Nathan (1969)

Hardwicke, Cedric, *A Victorian in Orbit* (1961)

Hare, Robertson, *Yours Indubitably* (1956)

Henderson-Bland, R, *Actor, Soldier, Poet* (1959)

Henrey, Bobby, *A Film Star in Belgrave Square* by Robert Henrey (1948)

Henry, Leonard, *My Laugh Story* (1938)

Henson, Leslie, *Yours Faithfully* (1946)

Hepworth, Cecil M., *Came the Dawn* (1951)

Hitchcock, Alfred, *The Films of Alfred Hitchcock* by George Perry (1965)
Hitchcock by Francois Truffaut (1968)
Hitchcock's Films by Robin Wood (1965)

Holloway, Stanley, *Wiv a Little Bit of Luck* by Dick Richards (1967)

Hopkinson, Peter, *Split Focus* (1969)

Howard, Leslie, *A Quite Remarkable Father* by Leslie Ruth Howard (1959)
Flight 777 by Ian Colvin (1957)

June, *The Glass Ladder* (1960)

Karno, Fred, *Remember Fred Karno* Edwin Adeler, Con West (1939)

Kendall, Henry, *I Remember Romano's* (1960)

Korda, Alexander, *Alexander Korda* by Paul Tabori (1959)

Lane, Lupino, *Born to Star* by James Dillon White (1957)
How to Be a Comedian (1965)

Lang, Matheson, *Mr Wu Looks Back* (1940)

Laughton, Charles, *Charles Laughton and I* by Elsa Lanchester (1938)
The Charles Laughton Story by Kurt Singer (1954)

Lawrence, Gertrude, *A Star Danced* (1945)

Laye, Evelyn, *Boo to My Friends* (1958)

Lee, Norman, *Log of a Film Director* (1949)

Leigh, Vivien, *Light of a Star* by Gwen Robyns (1968)

Lejeune, C.A., *Thank You for Having Me* (1964)

Levy, Louis, *Music for the Movies* (1948)
Lucky Star (1955)

Lockwood, Margaret, *My Life and Films* (1948)

Losey, Joseph, *Losey on Losey* by Tom Milne (1967)

Lupino, Stanley, *From the Stocks to the Stars* (1934)

MaLaglen, Victor, *Express to Hollywood* (1934)

Malins, Geoffrey, *How I Filmed the War* (1919)

Maltby, H.F., *Ring Up the Curtain* (1950)

Marks, Harrison, *The Naked Truth About Harrison Marks* by Franklyn Wood (1967)

Maschwitz, Eric, *No Chip on My Shoulder* (1957)

Mason, James, *James Mason* by Jno P. Monaghan (1947)

Matthews, A.E., *Matty* (1952)

Maugham, Somerset, *Theatrical Companion Companion to Maugham* by Raymond Mander, Joe Mitchenson (1955)

Miller, Ruby, *Champagne From My Slipper* (1962)

Mitchell, Yvonne, *Actress* (1957)

More, Kenneth, *Happy Go Lucky* (1959)

Morley, Robert, *Robert Morley, Responsible Gentleman* by Sewell Stokes (1966)

Mills, John, *What Shall We Do Tomorrow* by Mary Hayley Bell (1968)

Nares, Owen, *Myself and Some Others* (1925)

Nathan, *Costumes by Nathan* by Archie Nathan (1960)

Neagle, Anna, *It's Been Fun* (1949)

Noble, Peter, *Reflected Glory* (1958)

Noble, Ronnie, *Shoot First* (1955)

Novello, Ivor, *Ivor* by W. Mcqueen-Pope (1952) *Ivor Novello* by Peter Noble (1951)

Olivier, Laurence, *Laurence Olivier* by W. A. Darlington (1968) *Cry God for Larry* by Virginia Fairweather (1969) *The Oliviers* by Felix Barker (1953)

Oliver, Vic, *Mr Showbusiness* (1964

Pearson, George, *Flashback* (1957)

Pertwee, Roland, *Master of None* (1940)

Powell, Michael, *20,000 Feet on Foula* (1938)

Rank, J. Arthur, *Mr Rank* by Alan Wood (1952)

Redgrave, Michael, *The Actor's Ways and Means* (1953) *Mask or Face* (1958) *Michael Redgrave, Actor* by Richard Findlater (1956)

Richard, Cliff, *New Singer, New Song* by David Winter (1967) *The Wonderful World of Cliff Richard* by Bob Ferrier (1964)

Richardson, Ralph, *Ralph Richardson* by Harold Hobson (1958)

Robeson, Paul, *Paul Robeson* by Marie Seton (1958) *Paul Robeson* by Edwin Hoyt (1968)

Robey, George, *Looking Back on Life* (1933)

Robson, Flora, *Flora Robson* by Janet Dunbar (1960)

Sanders, George, *Memoirs of a Professional Cad* (1960)

Scott, Janette, *Act One* (1953)

Scruffy, *Scruffy* by Claude Burbidge (1937)

Sellers, Peter, *The Mask Behind the Mask* by Peter Evans (1969)

Shaw, George Bernard, *Theatrical Companion to Shaw* by Raymond Mander, Joe Mitchenson (1957)

Steele, Tommy, *Tommy Steele* by John Kennedy (1958)

Tauber, Richard, *Richard Tauber* by Diana Napier Tauber (1949) *My Heart and I* by Diana Napier Tauber (1959)

Thesiger, Ernest, *Practically True* (1927)

Thorndike, Sybil, *Sybil Thorndike* by J. C. Trewin (1955)

Train, Jack, *Up and Down the Line* (1956)

Travers, Ben, *Vale of Laughter* (1957)

Van Damm, Vivian, *Tonight and Every Night* (1952)

Wallace, Edgar, *Edgar Wallace* by Ethel Wallace (1932) *Edgar Wallace* by Margaret Lane (1938)

Warren, Low, *The Film Game* (1937)

Wells, Ingeborg, *Enough No More* (1948)

Wilcox, Herbert, *Twenty Five Thousand Sunsets* (1967)

Williams, Emlyn, *Emlyn Williams* by Richard Findlater (1956)

Wood, Georgie, *I Had to be Wee* (1948)

Ziegler, Anne and Webster Booth, *Duet* (1951)

British Screen Stars by Peter Noble (Yearbooks; 1946; 1947)

Life Stories of the Stars by Leslie Wood (1946)

Stars of the Screen by Cedric Bermingham (1930-32)

Who's Who in Filmland by Langford Reed and Hetty Spiers (1924; 1929; 1931)

General Works

Anstey, E. etc *Shots in the Dark* (1951)

Balcon, M. etc *Twenty Years of British Films* (1947)

Ball, R. H. *Shakespeare on Silent Film* (1968)

Barry, I. *Let's Go to the Pictures* (1926)

Betts, E. *Heraclitus, or the Future of Films* (1928)

Bird, J. H. *Cinema Parade* (1947)

Blakeston, O. *Working for the Films* (1947)

Boughey, D. *The Film Industry* (1921)

The British Film Industry (1952, 1958)
Brunel, A. *Film Script* (1948)
Carrick, E. *Art and Design in the British Film* (1949)
Carstairs, J. P. *Movie Merry-go-Round* (1937)
Ceram, C.W. *Archaeology of the Cinema* (1965)
Cook, O. *Movement in Two Dimensions* (1963)
Davy, C. *Footnotes to the Film* (1937)
Deans, M. *Meeting at the Sphinx* (1946)
Dickinson, T. *A Discovery of Cinema* (1971)
Durgnat, R. *Eros in the Cinema* (1966)
Durgnat, R. *A Mirror for England* (1970)
The Elstree Story (1948)
Enser, A. G. S. *Filmed Books and Plays* (1968)
Fawcett, L. E. *Films: Facts and Forecasts* (1927)
Fawcett, L. E. *Writing for the Films* (1932)
Field, M. *Good Company* (1952)
The Film in National Life (1932)
Forman, D. *Films 1945-50* (1952
Furniss, H. *Our Lady Cinema* (1914)
Gifford, D. *British Cinema* (1968)
Gifford, D. *Movie Monsters* (1969)
Gifford, D. *Science Fiction Film* (1971)
Halliwell, L. *The Filmgoers Companion* (1965)
Hardy, F. *Grierson on Documentary* (1946)
Hepworth, M. *Animated Photography* (1897)
Herring, R. *Films of the Year 1927-28* (1928)
Hopwood, H. *Living Pictures* (1899)
Huntley, J. *British Film Music* (1947)
Huntley, J. *Railways in the Cinema* (1969)
Jackson, A. *Writing for the Screen* (1919)
Knight, D., Porter, V. *A Long Look at Short Films* (1967)
Knowles, D. *The Censor, the Drama and the Film* (1934)
Lee, N. *A Film is Born* (1955)
Lee, N. *Money For Film Stories* (1937)
Lejeune, C. A. *Chestnuts in Her Lap* (1947)
Leyda, J. *Films Beget Films* (1964)
Lindgren, E. *Picture History of the Cinema* (1960) *The Art of the Film* (1950)
Lomas, H. M. *Picture Play Photography* (1914)
Lore, C. *The Modern Photoplay* (1928)
Low, R. *The History of the British Film* (4 vols) (1948-1971)

Manvell, R. *Film* (1944)
Manvell, R. *A Seat at the Cinema* (1951)
Manvell, R., Huntley, J. *The Technique of Film Music* (1957)
Margrave, S. *Successful Screen Writing* (1936)
Mayer, J. P. *British Cinemas and Their Audiences* (1948)
Messel, R. *This Film Business* (1928)
Miller, M. *Winchester's Screen Encyclopaedia* (1948)
Montague, I. *Film World* (1964)
Montgomery, J. *Comedy Films* (1954)
Museum of Modern Art *The Film Index* (1941)
Noble, P. *Films of the Year 1955-56* (1956)
Noble, P. *The Negro in Films* (1949)
Noble, P. *Spotlight on Filmland* (1947)
Oakley, C. *Where We Came In* (1964)
O'Leary, L. *The Silent Cinema* (1965)
Picturegoer Who's Who and Encyclopaedia (1933)
Powell, D. *Films Since 1939* (1947)
Quigley, M. *Magic Shadows* (1960)
Ramsaye, T. *A Million and One Nights* (1926)
Robinson, D. *The Great Funnies* (1969)
Rotha, P. *Documentary Film* (1952)
Rotha, P. *The Film Till Now* (1930)
Rotha, P., Griffiths, R. *The Film Till Now* (1945)
Rotha, P. *Movie Parade* (1936)
Sharp, D. *The Picture Palace* (1969)
Speed, F. M. *Movie Cavalcade* (1942)
Spraos, J. *The Decline of the Cinema* (1962)
Steer, V. *The Romance of the Cinema* (1913)
Steer, V. *Secrets of the Cinema* (1920)
Talbot, F. A. *Moving Pictures, How They are Made and Worked* (1912)
Thomas, D. B. *The Origins of the Motion Picture* (1964)
Towers, H. A., Mitchell, L. *March of the Movies* (1947)
Truby, J. *Daily Mail Film Award Annual* (1948-9)
Weston, H. *The Art of Photoplay Writing* (1916)
Wilson, A. E. *Movie Review* (1949)
Winchester, C. *World Film Encyclopaedia* (1933)
Winnington, R. *Drawn and Quartered* (1948)
Wideman, T. *Cinema* (1964)
Wood, L. *The Miracle of the Movies* (1947)
Wood, L. *The Romance of the Movies* (1937)

Acknowledgements

Much of the information on early British films, here published for the first time, was obtained from personal interviews with, or letters written by, film veterans and their relatives. Unhappily, many of these willing helpers have died before they could see their contributions to cinema history recorded in print.

First, my special thanks to the following people directly concerned with the production of British films. Sidney Birt Acres, son of the pioneer; the late James Anderson, editor and compilation maker; the late Dave Aylott, actor-writer-director; the late Charles Barnett, writer-director; Miss Dorothy Batley, actress daughter of the late actor-writer-director team of Ernest G. and Ethyle Batley; Miss Dorothy Bellew (Mrs Burke), actress; the late Wally Bosco, actor; Miss Billie Bristow (Mrs Pleydell-Bouverie), writer; Miss Estelle Brody, actress; Clive Brook, actor; William Carrington, boy actor; Hubert S. Chambers; May Clark (Mrs Mabel French), actress; the late Arthur Melbourne Cooper, director; Mrs Annie Cooling, actress; the late R. Howard Cricks, boy actor; Gerald de Beaurepaire, writer; Miss Margot Drake, actress; Edward Dryhurst, writer-director; the late Maurice Elvey, director; the late Joe Evans, writer-comedian; Stanley J. Faithfull, photographer; Miss Lenore Fisher (Mrs Corbett), actress; the late Lewin Fitzhamon, actor-writer-director; the late Kenelm Foss, actor-writer-director; Sidney Gilliat, writer-director; Ken Gordon, cameraman; the late Frank R. Growcott, actor-stage manager; Miss Lillian Haggar (Mrs Richards), actress; the late Charles B. Heath; Baynham Honri, technician; the late Edward Horder, distributor; Miss Elsie Hughes, cashier; Miss Winifred Jackson, actress; Clifford Jeapes, cameraman; Frank Launder, writer-director; the late Patrick L. Mannock, writer; Hubert Marno, musician; Miss Helena Millais, actress; Miss Joan Morgan, actress; Frank Orford, technician; the late F. Oswell-Jones, scenic designer; the late Harry Broughton Parkinson, producer-director; the late Wally Patch, actor; Miss Lettie Paxton, actress; the late Douglas Payne, actor; George Pearson, director; the late Roland Pertwee, writer; the late Edward Hay Plumb, actor-director; Albert Potter and Miss Gertie Potter, actors; Miss Mabel Poulton, actress; the late Mrs Hetty Langford Reed; the late Stewart Rome, actor; Don Saunders, technician; Leslie Seldon-Truss, writer-director; the late Miss Connie Somers-Clarke (Mrs Veltom), actress; John Stuart, actor; Miss Alma Taylor, actress; the late Warwick Ward, actor; Ewart Wheeler, actor; Miss Chrissie White, actress; Herbert Wilcox, producer-director; the late Miss Florence Williamson (Mrs Hunter) and Thomas H. Williamson, children of the late James Williamson; the late Herbert Wynne, actor-director.

Particular thanks are due to the following collectors, enthusiasts, experts and historians: Professor Robert H. Ball, John Barnes, Kevin Brownlow, Geoff N. Donaldson, John M. East, David Grenfell, Tony Hawes, Thomas Johnson, Bert Langdon, Raymond Mander, Joe Mitchenson, Kemp R. Niver, Liam O'Leary, Michael Poynter, Ray Selfe, Maurice Trace and Mrs Audrey Wadowska.

Research was carried out at the following places: the Barnes Museum of Cinematography, the British Board of Film Censors, the British Film Institute Information Department and Library, the British Museum Library and Newspaper Library, the Kinematograph Weekly offices, the Raymond Mander and Joe Mitchenson Theatre Collection, the National Film Archive Cataloguing Department, the Stage offices, the Victoria and Albert Museum Gabrielle Endtoven Collection, and through the National Lending Library for Science and Technology.

THE
BRITISH
FILM
CATALOGUE
1895-1970

1895

MAR

00001
UNTITLED KINETOSCOPE COMEDY
R.W. Paul
D: Birt Acres
COMEDY (Taken for showing in the Edison
Kinetoscope; projected later in the year.)

DEC

00002
TOM MERRY, LIGHTNING CARTOONIST
(40)
Birt Acres
D: Birt Acres
Tom Merry
ACT Stage cartoonist sketches Kaiser Wilhelm.
(Date uncertain)

00003
TOM MERRY, LIGHTNING CARTOONIST
(40)
Birt Acres
D: Birt Acres
Tom Merry
ACT Stage cartoonist sketches Bismarck.
(Date uncertain)

1896

JAN

00004
THE BOXING KANGAROO (40)
Birt Acres
D: Birt Acres
ACT Boxing bout between man and kangaroo.

00005
BOXING MATCH; OR, GLOVE CONTEST (40)
Birt Acres
D: Birt Acres
Sgt-Instr Barrett
Sgt Pope
SPORT Staged boxing match: round, interval, knockout.

FEB

00006
THE WANDERING NEGRO MINSTRELS (53)
Lumiere's Cinematographe
ACT Five London buskers dance and play banjos, tambourines and bones.

MAR

00007
TOM MERRY, LIGHTNING CARTOONIST (40)
Birt Acres
D: Birt Acres
Tom Merry
ACT Stage cartoonist sketches Lord Salisbury.

00008
TOM MERRY, LIGHTNING CARTOONIST (40)
Birt Acres
D: Birt Acres
Tom Merry
ACT Stage cartoonist sketches William Gladstone.

00009
DANCING GIRLS (40) *colour*
R. W. Paul
Alhambra Girls
ACT Dancers perform a nautch dance. (Hand coloured by Mr Doubell).

00010
CONTORTIONIST (40)
R.W. Paul
ACT Girl puts apparatus into mouth and spins around.

APR

00011
TRILBY BURLESQUE (40)
R.W. Paul
Alhambra Girls
ACT Dance scene from Alhambra Theatre production.

MAY

00012
GOLFING EXTRAORDINARY, FIVE GENTLEMEN (40)
Birt Acres
D: Birt Acres
COMEDY Five golfers; one misses his ball and falls down.

00013
THE ARREST OF A PICKPOCKET (40)
Birt Acres
D: Birt Acres
CRIME Policeman catches pickpocket, who slips from jacket but is caught by sailor.

00014
THE ARREST OF A BOOKMAKER (40)
R.W. Paul
CRIME Bookmaker struggles with police and is arrested.

00015
THE SOLDIER'S COURTSHIP (80)
R.W. Paul
D: Alfred Moul
Fred Storey.....Soldier
COMEDY Fat woman interupts courting couple who tip her off park bench

JUN

00016
THE MYSTERIOUS RABBIT (40)
R.W. Paul
David Devant
ACT Conjuror produces rabbit from hat and duplicates it.

00017
THE EGG-LAYING MAN (50)
R.W. Paul
David Devant
ACT Conjuror produces eggs from head and arms.

00018
DEVANT'S EXHIBITION OF PAPER FOLDING (40)
R.W. Paul
David Devant
ACT Conjuror rapidly forms number of objects from large sheet of paper.

00019
DEVANT'S HAND SHADOWS (80)
R.W. Paul
David Devant
ACT Two scenes of conjuror demonstrating shadowgraphy.

00020
CHIRGWIN IN HIS HUMOROUS BUSINESS (40)
R.W. Paul
G.H. Chirgwin
ACT 'The White Eyed Kaffir' performs with top hat.

00021
CHIRGWIN PLAYS A SCOTCH REEL (40)
R.W. Paul
G.H. Chirgwin
ACT 'The White Eyed Kaffir' performs a sword dance with tobacco pipes.

00022
LANDING AT LOW TIDE (40)
R.W. Paul — Birt Acres
D: Birt Acres
COMEDY Brighton. Landing of party from small boat with comic incidents.

00023
THE TEA PARTY (40)
R.W. Paul
COMEDY Ladies and gentlemen have tea and one upsets table.

JUL

00024
MR MASKELEYNE SPINNING PLATES AND BASINS (40)
R.W. Paul
Nevil Maskeleyne
ACT Conjuror spins plates and basins.

00025
UP THE RIVER (40)
R.W. Paul
DRAMA Passenger drops child from steam launch; it is rescued by swimmer from river bank.

AUG

00026
A SURREY GARDEN (40)
Birt Acres
D: Birt Acres
COMEDY Boy tricks gardener by stepping on his hose, then releasing water.

00027
THE TWINS' TEA PARTY (40)
R.W. Paul
COMEDY Two babies laughing, playing, and crying over tea.
Paul Clerget .... Husband
Miss Ross-Selwicke ..... Wife
COMEDY Drunk comes home late and wakes his wife.

00028
TWO AM; OR, THE HUSBAND'S RETURN (40)
R.W. Paul
S: (PLAY) Paul Clerget
Auguste Van Biene ..... Paul Borinski
Mrs Van Biene .... Vera Borinski

SEP

00029
CRONIN, AMERICAN CLUB MANIPULATOR (40)
R.W. Paul
Morris Cronin
ACT Juggler performs with Indian clubs.

00030
CRONIN WITH THREE CLUBS (40)
R.W. Paul
Morris Cronin
ACT Juggler performs with Indian clubs.

00031
THE SISTERS HENGLER SPECIALTY DANCERS (40)
R.W. Paul
May & Flora Hengler
ACT Sisters perform specialty dance.

OCT

00032
THE BROKEN MELODY (40)
Esme Collings
D: Esme Collings
S: (PLAY) James Tanner, Herbert Keene
DRAMA Servant persuades cellist to play and his errant wife returns.

00033
CHILDREN IN THE NURSERY (40)
R.W. Paul
COMEDY Children fight with pillows.

00034
YOU DIRTY BOY (40)
R.W. Paul
COMEDY 'Famous statue brought to life'.

1897

1758535

JAN

00035
AN UNFRIENDLY CALL (40)
Birt Acres
D: Birt Acres
COMEDY

MAR

00036
PIERROT AND PIERRETTE (40)
Birt Acres
D: Birt Acres
COMEDY Pierrette loses game of cards and
kisses her partner.

JUN

00037
BOLSTER FIGHT (50)
Chard's Vitagraph
COMEDY Girls fight with pillows and bolsters.

JUL

00038
THE MILLER AND THE SWEEP (50)
G.A. Smith
D: G.A. Smith
COMEDY Miller and sweep fight with sacks
of flour and soot until the sweep turns white
and the miller black.

AUG

00039
THE MAID IN THE GARDEN (50)
G.A. Smith
D: G.A. Smith
Tom Green .... The Master
Nellie Green .... The Mistress
COMEDY Master kisses maid behind blanket on
clothes line and is seen by his wife.

SEP

00040
CHILDREN PADDLING AT THE SEASIDE
(50)
G.A. Smith
D: G.A. Smith
COMEDY Southwick. 'Comic fat old lady and
lovers.'

00041
NURSING THE BABY (50)
G.A. Smith
D: G.A. Smith
COMEDY 'Three figures: humorous.'

00042
GYMNASTICS — INDIAN CLUB PERFORMER
(50)
G.A. Smith
D: G.A. Smith
ACT Gymnastics instructor demonstrates
Indian clubs.

00043
COMIC SHAVING (50) also: COMIC BARBER
G.A. Smith
D: G.A. Smith
Tom Green
W. Carlile
COMEDY Barber shaves customer.

00044
THE MILLER AND THE SWEEP (52)
G.A. Smith   reissue: 1900 (WTC)
D: G.A. Smith
COMEDY Second version of 00038.

00045
COMIC FACE (50) also: MAN DRINKING
G.A. Smith
D: G.A. Smith
Tom Green
FACIAL Close view of man enjoying glass of
beer. (First 'close-up'.)

00046
WEARY WILLIE (50)
G.A. Smith   reissue: 1900 (WTC)
D: G.A. Smith
Tom Green
COMEDY Tramp hired to beat carpet
accidentally beats housewife.

00047
MOUNTAINOUS (40)
R.W. Paul
S: (PLAY) Owen Hall (THE GEISHA)
DRAMA Scene from play. (See 00048)

00048
MARQUIS (40)
R.W. Paul
S: (PLAY) Owen Hall (THE GEISHA)
DRAMA Scene from play. (See 00047)

00049
THE MILLER AND THE SWEEP (40)
R.W. Paul
COMEDY Sweep flirts with girls, then fights
her miller father. (Date uncertain).

00050
CUPID AT THE WASHTUB (40)
R.W. Paul
COMEDY Groom flirts with laundress who
ducks him in tub of suds. (Date uncertain.)

00051
THE GAMBLERS (40)
R.W. Paul
COMEDY Boy and girl quarrel over card game.
(Date uncertain.)

00052
THE YOUNG RIVALS (40)
R.W. Paul
COMEDY Two boys quarrel over girl at
birthday party. (Date uncertain.)

00053
THE RIVAL BILL-STICKERS (40)
R.W. Paul
COMEDY Rival poster men fight with brushes
and paste. (Date uncertain.)

00054
A LIVELY DISPUTE (40)
R.W. Paul
COMEDY City gent bumps into old man and
they fight. (Date uncertain.)

00055
THEFT (40)
R.W. Paul
COMEDY Two tramps steal a goose and are
chased by farmer's wife. (Date uncertain.)
(See 00056)

00056
TRAMPS (40)
R.W. Paul
COMEDY Two tramps pluck a stolen goose and
cook it. (Date uncertain.) (See 00055)

00057
SPREE (40)
R.W. Paul

COMEDY Corporal catches soldiers in public
house and joins them for drink. (See 00058)
(Date uncertain.)

00058
GOAT (40)
R.W. Paul
COMEDY Soldiers dress goat in their uniforms
and it butts them. (Date uncertain.) (See 00057)

00059
QUARRELSOME NEIGHBOURS (40)
R.W. Paul
COMEDY Neighbours fight over fence with
soot and whitewash. (Date uncertain.)

00060
ROBBERY (60)
R.W. Paul
COMEDY Robber forces wayfarer to undress.
(Date uncertain.)

00061
JEALOUSY (80)
R.W. Paul
CRIME 'Dramatic scene in gardens — jealous
husband shot.' (Date uncertain.)

00062
THE VILLAGE BLACKSMITH (60)
R.W. Paul
S: (POEM) Henry Wadsworth Longfellow
Mel B. Spurr
FACIAL Comedian pulls faces as he recites
poem. (Date uncertain.)

00063
FUN ON THE CLOTHESLINE (60)
R.W. Paul
Harry Lamore
COMEDY Wire-walker performs on woman's
clothesline. (Date uncertain.)

00064
THE VANISHING LADY (40)
R.W. Paul
Charles Bertram
ACT Conjuror makes girl disappear.
(Date uncertain.)

00065
HAIL BRITANNIA! (60)
R.W. Paul
Charles Bertram
ACT Conjuror produces flags and changes them
into Britannia. (Date uncertain.)

OCT

00066
X-RAYS (54) also: THE X-RAY FIEND
G.A. Smith
D: G.A. Smith
TRICK Professor turns X-ray machine on
courters and reveals their embracing skeletons.

00067
THE DEATH OF NELSON (150)
Philip Wolff
S: (SONG) Braham
MUSICAL Three separate scenes illustrating
the ballad to be shown while it is sung.

00068
THE WRITING ON THE WALL (40)
Walter D. Welford
D: S: Walter D. Welford
ADVERT Tottenham. Man chalks 'Ride Smith
Tyres' on a brick wall.

00069
SERPENTELLO (50)
Velograph Syndicate
ACT Female contortionist.

NOV

00070
SUNLIGHT SOAP WASHING COMPETITION
Nestles and Lever Brothers
ADVERT (Supplied free with films booked
from film agency.)

00071
THE SIGN WRITER (50) also: THE
AWKWARD SIGN WRITER
G.A. Smith
D: G.A. Smith
TRICK Man paints 'This house to let' and then
the film is reversed.

00072
TIPSY—TOPSY—TURVY (50)
G.A. Smith

D: G.A. Smith
TRICK Drunk returns from club, undresses and
the film is reversed.

DEC

00073
THE HAUNTED CASTLE (50)
G.A. Smith
D: G.A. Smith
TRICK

00074
MAKING SAUSAGES (50) also: THE END OF
ALL THINGS
G.A. Smith
D: G.A. Smith
TRICK Four cooks make sausages from cats,
dogs, ducks, and old boots.

00075
REPAIRING A PUNCTURE (40)
Walter D. Welford
D: S: Walter D. Welford

TRICK Crystal Palace. Speeded action of
racing cyclist mending tyre.

00076
A STORY WITHOUT WORDS (50)
Prestwich Mfg Co
COMEDY Policeman flirts with housewife and
is caught by her husband. (Date uncertain.)

00077
THE ARTIST'S MODEL (75)
Prestwich Mfg Co
COMEDY Model cuts hole in artist's painting
and sticks head through. (Date uncertain.)

00078
PROFESSOR GARLAND THE CONJUROR
(50)
Prestwich Mfg Co
Prof. Garland
ACT Conjuror produces articles from hat.
(Date uncertain.)

1898

FEB

00079
SAILOR'S HORNPIPE (70)
Levi, Jones & Co
Daisy Quartette
ACT Four sailors dance hornpipe.

00080
SCOTCH REEL (70)
Levi, Jones & Co
Daisy Quartette·
ACT Four Scotsmen dance reel.

00081
IRISH JIG (70)
Levi, Jones & Co
Daisy Quartette
ACT Four Irishmen dance jig.

00082
DANCE BY THE DAISY QUARTETTE (70)
Levi, Jones & Co
Daisy Quartette
ACT Four people dance specialty.

00083
CLOG DANCING (120)
R.W. Paul
Mr Burns
ACT Clog dancing contest winner dances on dinner plate.

00084
GOOD NIGHT
Mutoscope & Biograph Co
Charles Morton
ACT Alhambra Theatre manager bows before the entwined flags of Britain and America.

MAR

00085
THE VILLAGE BLACKSMITH (75)
Birt Acres
D: Arthur Cooper
COMEDY

00086
FREGOLI THE PROTEAN ARTISTE (400)
R.W. Paul
Leopoldo Fregoli
ACT Impersonations of conductors including Rossini and Verdi.

00087
THE RUNAWAY KNOCK (50)
G.A.S. Films *reissue:* 1900 (WTC)
D: G.A. Smith
COMEDY Old gentleman knocks on door for boy and gets doused.

00088
A PRACTICAL JOKE (50) *also:* A JOKE ON THE GARDENER
G.A.S. Films
D: G.A. Smith
COMEDY Boy treads on gardeners hose, then releases the water.

00089
UNTITLED COMEDY
Walter D. Welford
D: S: Walter D. Welford
A Conjuror..........The Lover
A Singer.............The Girl
A Baggage Man...The Wicked Cyclist
His Wife..............The Woman
Mrs Welford........The Visitor
A Demonstrater..Her Admirer
COMEDY Paignton. Cyclist rides into courters and causes a fight.

APR

00090
THE MASCOTS (60)
Chard's Vitagraph
Tiller Girls
ACT 'The celebrated Tiller troupe in all their finest dances'.

00091
GIRLS PLAYING LEAPFROG (60)
Chard's Vitagraph
Tiller Girls
COMEDY Girl dancers play game of leapfrog.

00092
TRICK BICYCLISTS (70)
Haydon & Urry
The Brothers Henry
ACT Brothers demonstrate trick cycling.

JUL

00093
THE POLICEMAN THE COOK AND THE COPPER (75)
G.A.S. Films
D: G.A. Smith
S: (PLAY) Tom Green (THE AREA BELLE)
Tom Green.....Policeman
COMEDY Cook hides PC in copper and her mistress lights it.

00094
TWO NAUGHTY BOYS UPSETTING THE SPOONS (75)
Williamson
D: S: James Williamson
Alan Williamson.....Boy
Colin Williamson....Boy
COMEDY Boy's joke on their aunt's suitor causes him to fall.

00095
TWO NAUGHTY BOYS SPRINKLING THE SPOONS (66)
Williamson
D: S: James Williamson
Alan Williamson.....Boy
Colin Williamson....Boy
COMEDY Boys hand their aunt's suitor a hosepipe instead of his cane.

00096
TWO NAUGHTY BOYS TEASING THE COBBLER (68)
Williamson
D: S: James Williamson
Alan Williamson.....Boy
Colin Williamson....Boy
COMEDY Boys blow peas at cobbler, who throws a boot and hits a woman.

00097
WASHING THE SWEEP (75)
Williamson
D: S: James Williamson
Marie Mayhew.....The Maid
COMEDY Sweep dirties maid's washing and is scrubbed.

00098
WINNING THE GLOVES (75)
Williamson
D: S: James Williamson
James Williamson.....The Man
COMEDY Man feigns sleep so a girl will kiss him, and she tricks him with a donkey.

00099
THE FORBIDDEN LOVER (65)
Williamson
D: S: James Wiliiamson
James Williamson.....Father
COMEDY Girl's suitor poses as a chair to elude her father, and is sat on.

00100
SLOPER'S VISIT TO BRIGHTON (210)
Williamson
D: SC: James Williamson
S: (Cartoons) Charles Ross
COMEDY 3 scenes: Donkey riding; Bathing; Chucked out.

AUG

00101
A STUDY IN FACIAL EXPRESSION (60)
R.W. Paul
FACIAL Man laughs at naughty story and has to show his wife.

00102
THE STOCKBROKER (60)
R.W. Paul
FACIAL Ruined broker tries to shoot himself but smashes a mirror.

00103
BIRDSNESTING (60)
R.W. Paul
COMEDY Boy climbs tree, falls on farmer and is chased.

00104
WHEN THE CAT'S AWAY (60)
R.W. Paul
COMEDY Boy plays tricks in class until teacher returns.

00105
PHOTOGRAPHY (60)
R.W. Paul
COMEDY Pests prevent photographer from taking picture.

00106
THE SAILOR'S DEPARTURE (60)
R.W. Paul
DRAMA Sailor says farewell to his wife. (See 00107)

00107
THE SAILOR'S RETURN (60)
R.W. Paul
DRAMA Sailor returns to his wife and sees their baby. (See 00106)

00108
THE MONKS (60)
R.W. Paul
COMEDY Monk smokes a cigar and accidentally burns his sleeping friend.

00109
THE JOVIAL MONKS IN THE REFECTORY (80)
R.W. Paul
COMEDY Novice gets drunk while tolling bell.

00110
MR BUMBLE THE BEADLE (60)
R.W. Paul
S: (NOVEL) Charles Dickens (OLIVER TWIST)
COMEDY Period. Beadle courts a workhouse matron.

00111
OLD TIME SCENE IN THE VILLAGE STOCKS (80)
R.W. Paul
COMEDY Period. Villagers pelt couple in stocks.

00112
THE BREADWINNER (80)
R.W. Paul
DRAMA Poor mother dresses child as pantomime
fairy. (See 00113)

00113
THE FAIRY (60)
R.W. Paul
DRAMA 'Similar to *The Breadwinner* but
shorter'. (See 00112)

00114
TOMMY ATKINS IN THE PARK (80)
R.W. Paul
COMEDY Fat woman interrupts courters and
is tipped off park bench.

00115
A FAVOURITE NURSERY SCENE (80)
R.W. Paul
COMEDY Girl tickles her two brothers, hides
under bed and causes pillow fight.

00116
RESCUE FROM DROWNING (80)
R.W. Paul
DRAMA Several drowning persons are saved
by rowboat.

00117
THE LODGER (80)
R.W. Paul
COMEDY Lodger in boarding-house is attacked
by fleas.

00118
IN THE NAME OF THE QUEEN (80)
R.W. Paul
DRAMA Deserter hidden by his mother is
found by army police.

00119
COME ALONG DO! (80)
R.W. Paul
COMEDY (2 scenes) Country pair enter art
gallery and laugh at statues. (First use of edited
scenes.)

00120
OUR NEW GENERAL SERVANT (320)
R.W. Paul
COMEDY (4 scenes) Wife hires maid at
registry; husband flirts in parlour; wife sees
them kiss in garden; wife sacks maid in kitchen.
(First use of subtitles).

00121
THE BAKER AND THE SWEEP (75)
G.A.S. Films
D: G.A. Smith
COMEDY Baker and sweep fight with flour
and soot and get doused.

00122
THE LADY BARBER (75)
G.A.S. Films
D: G.A. Smith
COMEDY Suffragette takes over gentleman's
barber shop.

00123
THE CORSICAN BROTHERS (75)
G.A.S. Films
D: G.A. Smith
S: (NOVEL) Alexandre Dumas
TRICK Period. Ghost of man's twin shows him
vision of how he was killed in duel. (First
double exposure.)

00124
CINDERELLA AND THE FAIRY GODMOTHER
(75)
G.A.S. Films
D: G.A. Smith
Laura Bayley.....Cinderella
TRICK Fairy conjures vision of prince's ball,
changes drudge's rags to gown, and flies up
chimney. (First double exposure and stop
action.)

00125
FAUST AND MEPHISTOPHELES (75)
G.A.S. Films
D: G.A. Smith
TRICK Satan conjures vision of girl, for whom
old man signs pact and is made young.

00126
PHOTOGRAPHING A GHOST (76)
G.A.S. Films
D: G.A. Smith
TRICK Photographer tries to take picture of
a ghost, but it won't keep still and then vanishes.

00127
THE UNGALLANT LOVER (50)
Warwick Trading Co
COMEDY Brighton. Couple kiss and fall
backwards into boat.

00128
HE AND SHE
British Mutoscope & Biograph Co
S: (SKETCH) Roma T. Roma
Roma T. Roma.....She
Frank Wood.........He
COMEDY 'Graceful she is shown in lively mood
with speechless he'.

00129
GOOD NIGHT (54)
C. Goodwin Norton
D: C. Goodwin Norton
COMEDY Shopman closes shutters on which
is written 'Good Night'.

00130
THE JEALOUS PAINTER (60)
Williamson
D: James Williamson
COMEDY Painter pours whitewash over his
rival.

00131
THE CLOWN BARBER (70)
Williamson
D: James Williamson
TRICK Clown cuts off customer's head and
replaces it.

00132
THE FRAUDULENT BEGGAR (65)
Williamson
D: James Williamson
COMEDY PC catches blind beggar reading
story to his deaf colleague.

00133
NORAH MAYER THE QUICK-CHANGE
DANCER (75; 75; 75)
Williamson
D: James Williamson
Norah Mayer
ACT Eccentric dances; National dances;
Spanish and Japanese dances.

SEP
00134
AN OVERFUL SEAT (75) *also*: WEARY
WILLIE
Riley Brothers
COMEDY Tramp frightens four people off
park bench.

00135
PILLOW FIGHT (75)
Riley Brothers
COMEDY Four girls fight with pillows in
bedroom.

00136
THE NURSEMAID'S SURPRISE (75)
Riley Brothers — Bamforth
COMEDY Tramp changes places with baby and
is caressed by its nurse. (Date uncertain.)

00137
THE SCHOOLMASTER'S PORTRAIT (60)
Riley Brothers — Bamforth
COMEDY Boy draws caricature of his teacher
on blackboard, and is caned. (Date uncertain.)

00138
THE RUNAWAY KNOCK AND THE
SUFFERING MILKMAN (57)
Riley Brothers — Bamforth
COMEDY Boys knock at door and run away
so milkman takes blame. (Date uncertain.)

00139
SANTA CLAUS (75) *also*: THE VISIT OF
SANTA CLAUS
G.A.S. Films
D. G.A. Smith
TRICK Children dream of Santa Claus coming
down chimney.

00140
THE MESMERIST (75)
G.A.S. Films
D: G.A. Smith
TRICK Professor draws the spirit from a girl's
body, and returns it.

00141
FENCING CONTEST FROM 'THE THREE
MUSKETEERS'
Mutoscope & Biograph Co
S: (NOVEL) Alexandre Dumas
DRAMA Fencing scene from stage production.

00142
THE FATAL LETTER
Mutoscope & Biograph Co
Ben Nathan
FACIAL Close view of beneficiary reading of
his aunt's death.

00143
AN INTERRUPTED PICNIC (50)
Hepworth (WTC)
D: Cecil Hepworth
Cecil Hepworth
COMEDY Tramp orders picnickers to leave
but they throw him in the river.

00144
EXCHANGE IS NO ROBBERY (50)
Hepworth (WTC)
D: Cecil Hepworth
Cecil Hepworth .... Swimmer
COMEDY Tramp steals swimmer's clothes and
leaves his own in exchange.

00145
THE IMMATURE PUNTER (50)
Hepworth (WTC)
D: Cecil Hepworth
Cecil Hepworth.....Punter
COMEDY Punter's pole sticks in the mud and
he is left hanging.

00146
THE QUARRELSOME ANGLERS (50) *also*:
THE STOLEN DRINK
Hepworth (WTC)
D: Cecil Hepworth
Cecil Hepworth.....Fisherman
COMEDY Fishermen in punt quarrel over jar
of drink and fall in river.

00147
TWO FOOLS IN A CANOE (50) *also*: TWO
COCKNEYS IN A CANOE
Hepworth (WTC)
D: Cecil Hepworth
Cecil Hepworth.....Canoer
COMEDY Two men in canoe splash each other
until it capsizes.

OCT

00148
ALLY SLOPER (75)
G.A.S. Films
D: G.A. Smith
S: (CARTOONS) Charles Ross
TRICK Man dresses up as woman, and the film
is reversed.

00149
ANIMATED CLOWN PORTRAIT (75)
G.A.S. Films   *reissue*: 1900 (WTC)
D: G.A. Smith
TRICK Picture of clown comes to life.

00150
PUNCH AND JUDY (65; 65)
European Blair Camera Co
ACT (2 scenes) Puppet performance.

00151
LITTLE STANLEY, LIGHTNING
CARTOONIST (53)
Cinematograph Co
ACT Boy cartoonist draws with crayon.

00152
CASTINET DANCE (53)
Cinematograph Co
Senorita Velasco
ACT Dance.

00153
HAT DANCE (53)
Cinematograph Co
Senorita Velasco
ACT Dance.

00154
JUGGLER (53)
Cinematograph Co
Ala Coma
ACT Three juggling tricks.

00155
MOCCESSEN THE HUMAN SNAKE (53)
Cinematograph Co
ACT Contortionist.

00156
FLIRTATION IN A BOAT (53)
Cinematograph Co
COMEDY

00157
TWO TIPSY FELLOWS IN A BOAT (53)
Cinematograph Co
COMEDY

00158
A FISHING CATASTROPHE (53)
Cinematograph Co
COMEDY

00159
MARIONETTES (53)
Cinematograph Co

ACT Lively skeleton; Clown; Acrobat
and chairs.

00160
THE INEBRIATED PHOTOGRAPHER (53)
Cinematograph Co
COMEDY

00161
A LIVELY CARD PARTY (53)
Cinematograph Co
COMEDY

00162
THE CLUB RAID (53)
Cinematograph Co
COMEDY

00163
CLUB PARTY AND POLICE (53)
Cinematograph Co
COMEDY

00164
SKIRT DANCE (53)
Cinematograph Co
ACT Dance.

NOV

00165
SANTA CLAUS AND THE CHILDREN (60)
R.W. Paul
COMEDY Santa Claus comes down chimney
and delivers toys to children.

DEC

00166
THE BRIDE'S FIRST NIGHT (75)
Haydon & Urry
COMEDY (See 00167)

00167
TWELVE MONTHS AFTER (75)
Haydon & Urry
COMEDY Sequel to *The Bride's First Night.*
(See 00166)

1899

JAN

00168
SIMON THE CELLARER (150)
Philipp Wolff
S: (SONG)
MUSICAL Three scenes illustrating song; to be shown while it is sung.

00169
THE BLACK CAT AND THE DINNER FOR TWO
Mutoscope & Biograph
COMEDY Cat eats owner's dinner.

00170
MAN OVERBOARD (150)
Warwick Trading Co
DRAMA (3 scenes) Man falls from 'SS Tantallen Castle', is saved and resuscitated.

MAR

00171
SENSATIONAL FISHING SCENE (75)
Haydon & Urry
COMEDY (Trick?)

00172
A TRICK ON THE BOATMAN (75)
Haydon & Urry
COMEDY

00173
THE IMPROMPTU BATH (75)
Haydon & Urry
COMEDY

00174
LANDING AT LOW TIDE (75)
Haydon & Urry
COMEDY Boatman carries fat woman ashore and they fall in the sea.

00175
ON THE BENCHES IN THE PARK (75)
Haydon & Urry
COMEDY 'Courtship scene'.

00176
THE KISSING DUET (75)
Haydon & Urry
FACIAL Close view of a couple kissing.

00177
FIRE CALL AND RESCUE BY FIRE ESCAPES (175)
Warwick Trading Co
Commander Wells
DRAMA Man sees smoke, gives alarm, and firemen rescue two.

APR

00178
HE GOT MORE THAN HE BARGAINED FOR
Mutoscope & Biograph
COMEDY

00179
COMIC BOXING MATCH (150)
Warwick Trading Co
COMEDY (3 scenes) Tall man boxes short man aboard 'SS Carisbrooke Castle'.

MAY

00180
HARRY TATE GRIMACES (50)
Warwick Trading Co
Harry Tate
FACIAL Comedian pulls faces.

00181
HARRY TATE IMPERSONATIONS (100)
Warwick Trading Co
Harry Tate
ACT Comedian impersonates George Beauchamp, George Robey, Gus Elen, Dan Leno, Joe Elvin, R.G. Knowles.

JUN

00182
AN AFFAIR OF HONOUR (150)
Warwick Trading Co
DRAMA Dueller kills opponent and is arrested.

00183
THE INTOXICATED ARTIST (50)
Warwick Trading Co
COMEDY Theatrical agent ejects cheeky drunk.

00184
THE HALL PORTER'S INDISCRETION (50)
Warwick Trading Co
COMEDY Drunk porter squirts agent with syphon.

00185
THE SOUBRETTE'S CREDENTIALS (50)
Warwick Trading Co
COMEDY Theatrical agent makes soubrette verify claimed proportions.

00186
THE INTERRUPTED COURTSHIP (50)
Warwick Trading Co
COMEDY Couple try to steal kiss in busy hotel lounge.

00187
THEY DO SUCH THINGS AT BRIGHTON (50)
Warwick Trading Co
Will Evans
COMEDY Comedian relives courting days.

00188
FOUR TO ONE (75)
Warwick Trading Co
COMEDY Scene painters get drunk and paint policeman.

00189
THE LEGACY (75)
G.A.S. Films
D: G.A. Smith
FACIAL Beneficiary's expressions as he reads of death and legacy.

00190
EXPRESSIONS (75)
C. Goodwin Norton
D: C. Goodwin Norton
FACIAL Comedian pulls faces.

00191
DANCING NIGGERS (75)
C. Goodwin Norton
D: C. Goodwin Norton
ACT Minstrels dance.

JUL

00192
A GOOD JOKE (75)
G.A.S. Films
D: G.A. Smith
Tom Green
Mr Hunter
FACIAL Two men laugh over naughty story in magazine.

00193
ON FORBIDDEN LAND (75)
Warwick Trading Co
COMEDY Picnic party chased by bull.

00194
FISHERMAN'S LUCK (75)
Warwick Trading Co
COMEDY Three anglers hook large fish which pulls them into sea.

00195
FAMILY JARS (75)
Warwick Trading Co
COMEDY Boy scrubs poodle andis attacked by pet monkey.

00196
A HAPPY FAMILY (75)
Warwick Trading Co
COMEDY Family's pet monkey steals fruit.

00197
TEASING THE MONKEY (50)
Warwick Trading Co
COMEDY Monkey fights back when family pulls tail.

00198
THE MONKEY'S REVENGE (50)
Warwick Trading Co
COMEDY 'The boy, the poodle, the monkey, and the washtub.'

00199
THE MUSICAL ECCENTRIC (75) also: WILL EVANS THE LIVING CATHERINE WHEEL
Warwick Trading Co
Will Evans
ACT Comedian turns somersaults, etc.

00200
LET' EM ALL COME (50)
Warwick Trading Co
Will Evans
ACT Sundry objects flung at comedian playing cornet.

00201
MY PAL (75)
Warwick Trading Co
Fred Poplar
COMEDY Drunk gets involved with tailor's dummy.

AUG

00202
A HIGH OLD TIME (200)
Warwick Trading Co
COMEDY Drunks invite girls to join them for drink and dance.

00203
A LOVERS' QUARREL (100)
Warwick Trading Co
ROMANCE Man drops letter, girl reads it, they quarrel, man gives girl ring, they kiss.

00204
SKIRMISH BY THE CYCLE CORPS (50)
Warwick Trading Co
WAR Eight cyclists ride up, jump off cycles, shoot, and ride off.

00205
THE LIGHTFOOTED DARKEY (50)
Warwick Trading Co
ACT Crystal Palace. Minstrel dances in Derby race course setting.

00206
DANCE AT THE RACES (50)
Warwick Trading Co
ACT Crystal Palace. Crowds join in minstrel's dance.

00207
FANCY STEP JIG (75)
Warwick Trading Co
ACT Crystal Palace. Solo and chorus dance by Terpsichorean Islanders.

00208
SPECIALTY DANCE BY WILLIAM VOKES (50)
Warwick Trading Co
ACT Crystal Palace. Solo and corps de ballet.

00209
SPORTS AND NATIONS' DANCE, GRAND FINALE AND CURTAIN (150)
Warwick Trading Co
ACT Crystal Palace. Britannia's tea party to the Powers.

00210
THE SANDWICHES (75) also: THE HUNGRY COUNTRYMAN
G.A.S. Films
D: G.A. Smith
TRICK Man eats sandwiches and refuses to pay; the film then reverses

00211
FIGHT BETWEEN A MILLER AND A SWEEP (50)
Birt Acres
D: Arthur Cooper
COMEDY Miller and sweep fight with sacks of flour and soot.

00212
SOLDIER, POLICEMAN AND COOK (80) also: THE AMOROUS COOK
Birt Acres
D: Arthur Cooper
COMEDY Cook hides soldier sweetheart when PC calls.

00213
THE FIREMAN'S SNAPSHOT (80)
Birt Acres
D: Arthur Cooper
COMEDY Photographer tries to snap fireman, and gets hosed.

SEP

00214
BERTIE'S BIKE; OR, THE MERRY MADCAPS (50)
R.W. Paul
COMEDY Girl tries to ride man's bicycle, and falls off.

00215
THE COUNTRY WAITER; OR, THE TALE OF A CRUSHED HAT (70)
R.W. Paul
COMEDY Cloakroom attendant tries to flatten a top hat. (Date uncertain.)

00216
TWO TIPSY PALS AND THE TAILOR'S DUMMY (60)
R.W. Paul
COMEDY Drunk fights tailor's dummy in mistake for friend. (Date uncertain.)

00217
A GRETNA GREEN WEDDING (60)
R.W. Paul
COMEDY Period. Girl's father arrives late at church. (Date uncertain.)

00218
THE BRICKLAYER AND HIS MATE; OR, A JEALOUS MAN'S CRIME (50)
R.W. Paul
DRAMA Jealous workman throws mate from ladder to the ground. (Date uncertain.)

00219
THRILLING FIGHT ON A SCAFFOLD (100)
R.W. Paul
DRAMA Builders fight on the scaffold of Paul's new studio until one falls and is injured. (Date uncertain.)

00220
THE MISER'S DOOM (45)
R.W. Paul
D: Walter Booth
TRICK Miser dies of shock when ghost of poor woman appears. (Date uncertain.)

00221
ON A RUNAWAY MOTOR CAR THROUGH PICADILLY CIRCUS (80)
R.W. Paul
TRICK Speeded 'phantom ride' through busy London traffic.

00222
UPSIDE DOWN; OR, THE HUMAN FLIES (80)
R.W. Paul
D: Walter Booth
TRICK Spiritualist causes group of table-turners to walk upside down on ceiling.

00223
AN UNEXPECTED VISIT; OR, OUR FLAT (70)
R.W. Paul
COMEDY Poor couple fake chair for their visitor; it collapses.

00224
CAUGHT FLIRTING (100)
R.W. Paul
COMEDY Girl's father sets dog on rival suitors.

00225
MAN OVERBOARD
Mutoscope & Biograph
DRAMA Man falls from boat and is rescued.

00226
KING JOHN
Mutoscope & Biograph
S: (PLAY) William Shakespeare
Beerbohm Tree ....King John
Julia Neilson ....Constance
Lewis Walker ....Phillip
Norman McKinnel ....Lymoges
HISTORY (Scene from Her Majesty's Theatre production.)

00227
MAJOR WILSON'S LAST STAND (125)
Warwick Trading Co
S: (SHOW) Frank E. Fillis (SAVAGE SOUTH AFRICA)
WAR Savages attack soldiers in laager.

00228
SAVAGE ATTACK AND REPULSE (75)
Warwick Trading Co
S: (SHOW) Frank E. Fillis (SAVAGE SOUTH AFRICA)
WAR Attacking Impi mown down by soldiers with Maxim guns.

00229
A SUDDEN ALARM (75)
Warwick Trading Co
S: (SHOW) Frank E. Fillis (SAVAGE SOUTH AFRICA)
WAR The scene of 00227 photographed from different angle.

00230
TILLER'S SIX DIAMONDS (200)
Warwick Trading Co
ACT Crystal Palace. Six dancing girls in three skipping scenes.

00231
SPECIALTY DANCE BY FRED STOREY (50)
Warwick Trading Co
ACT Crystal Palace. Eccentric dance.

00232
RITCHIE, TRAMP CYCLIST (100)
Warwick Trading Co
W.E. Ritchie
ACT Comedian tries to ride one-wheeled cycle.

OCT

00233
GOOD STORIES (100)
G.A.S. Films (WTC)
D: G.A. Smith
Tom Green
Mr Hunter
FACIAL Two men laugh at jokes.

00234
THE HAUNTED PICTURE GALLERY (75)
G.A.S. Films (WTC)
D: G.A. Smith
TRICK Gainsborough painting comes alive and dances minuet.

00235
A GAME OF CHESS AND KISSES (75)
G.A.S. Films (WTC)
D: G.A. Smith
COMEDY Chess player dons bonnet and is kissed by opponent.

00236
THE GAMBLER'S WIFE (75)
G.A.S. Films (WTC)
D: G.A. Smith
TRICK Gambler is stopped from shooting himself by wife's spirit.

00237
THE INEXHAUSTIBLE CAB (75)
G.A.S. Films (WTC)
D: G.A. Smith
TRICK Clown puts dozen people into small cab and vanishes it.

00238
THE JOVIAL MONKS No. I (72)
Williamson
D: James Williamson
D. Philippe.....Monk
FACIAL Monk tricks brother into drinking bad wine. (Date uncertain.)

00239
THE JOVIAL MONKS No. 2 — TIT FOR TAT (54)
Williamson
D: James Williamson

D. Philippe.....Monk
FACIAL Tricked monk tricks brother into drinking bad wine. (Date uncertain.)

00240
COURTSHIP UNDER DIFFICULTIES (67)
Williamson
D: James Williamson
Florence Williamson
COMEDY Small girl ties sister's suitor to chair. (Date uncertain.)

00241
THE SLEEPING LOVERS (60)
Williamson
D: James Williamson
COMEDY Suitor awakens to find man has taken sweetheart's place. (Date uncertain.)

NOV

00242
ALADDIN AND THE WONDERFUL LAMP (75)
G.A.S. Films
D: G.A. Smith
TRICK China. Genie gives boy fine clothes and palatial apartment.

00243
DICK WHITTINGTON (75)
G.A.S. Films
D: G.A. Smith
TRICK Fairy shows sleeping youth three visions of future.

00244
THE KISS IN THE TUNNEL (40)
G.A. Smith
D: G.A. Smith
G.A. Smith.....Passenger
COMEDY 'To be joined into tunnel portion of a Phantom Ride'.

00245
THE BATHERS DISTURBED; OR, THE LOVERS' SURPRISE (50)
Philipp Wolff
COMEDY

00246
D.T.s; OR, THE HORRORS OF DRINK (50)
Philipp Wolff
TRICK

00247
PEEPING TOM (50)
Philipp Wolff
COMEDY

00248
SHOOTING A BOER SPY (60)
R.W. Paul
D: Sir Robert Ashe
WAR Spy rejects bandage and is shot by firing squad.

00249
THE BOMBARDMENT OF MAFEKING (60)
R.W. Paul
D: Sir Robert Ashe
WAR Soldiers play cards and jeer as shells burst around them.

00250
THE BATTLE OF GLENCOE (80)
R.W. Paul
D: Sir Robert Ashe
WAR Soldiers use Maxim gun to drive Boers over hill.

00251
SURPRISING A PICKET (40) also: ATTACK ON A PICQUET
R.W. Paul
D: Sir Robert Ashe
WAR Boers kill dozing sentry, attack camp and rob dead soldiers.

DEC

00252
BRITISH CAPTURING A MAXIM GUN (60)
R.W. Paul
D: Sir Robert Ashe
WAR British soldiers capture Maxim gun from Boers.

00253
NURSES ATTENDING THE WOUNDED (60) also: NURSES ON THE BATTLEFIELD
R.W. Paul
D: Sir Robert Ashe
WAR Nurses and stretcher party attend to wounded after battle.

00254
THE VICTORY (60)
R.W. Paul
D: Sir Robert Ashe
WAR

00255
WRECKING AN ARMOURED TRAIN (100)
R.W. Paul
D: Sir Robert Ashe
WAR Britons defend train but are forced to surrender.

00256
HOW TOMMY WON THE VICTORIA CROSS (100)
Warwick Trading Co
WAR Cavalry trooper rescues scout from dervish ambush.

00257
A REMINISCENCE OF THE WAR
C. Goodwin Norton
WAR (Date uncertain.)

00258
THE BILL POSTER
C. Goodwin Norton
COMEDY Boy and bill poster fight with paste. (Date uncertain.)

00259
A GAME OF SNOWBALLING
C. Goodwin Norton
COMEDY (Date uncertain.)

00260
THE DISTRACTED BATHER
C. Goodwin Norton
COMEDY (Date uncertain.)

00261
THE BUTCHER AND THE TRAMP
C. Goodwin Norton
COMEDY (Date uncertain.)

00262
THE POSTMAN AND THE NURSEMAID
C. Goodwin Norton
COMEDY (Date uncertain.)

00263
THE TRAMP'S SURPRISE
Mitchell & Kenyon
COMEDY 'Very funny'.

00264
THE TRAMPS AND THE ARTIST
Mitchell & Kenyon
COMEDY 'Most laughable'.

00265
KIDNAPPING BY INDIANS
Mitchell & Kenyon
WESTERN 'Exciting'.

00266
THE HONEYMOON (62)
Riley Brothers — Bamforth
COMEDY Friends see newlyweds off on train. (Date uncertain.)

00267
THE KISS IN THE TUNNEL (78)
Riley Brothers — Bamforth
COMEDY Newlyweds kiss when their railway carriage enters tunnel. (Date uncertain. Studio scene edited into location scenes.)

00268
THE BITER BIT (68)
Riley Brothers — Bamforth
COMEDY Youth grips gardener's hose, then releases water. (Date uncertain.)

00269
THE TRAMP AND THE BABY'S BOTTLE (72)
Riley Brothers — Bamforth
COMEDY Tramp steal baby's bottle and is caught by policeman. (Date uncertain.)

00270
CATCHING THE MILK THIEF (50)
Riley Brothers — Bamforth
COMEDY Tramp drinks from Nestle's Milk churn and is caught by yokel. (Date uncertain.)

00271
THE WOULD-BE CONJUROR (65)
Riley Brothers — Bamforth
COMEDY Yokel helps conjuror and tries tricks on wife. (Date uncertain.)

1900

JAN

00272
BRITON V. BOER
Birt Acres
WAR Staged war scenes combined with actuality scenes.

00273
WIPING SOMETHING OFF THE SLATE (75)
Hepworth
D: Cecil Hepworth
Cecil Hepworth.....Soldier
WAR Soldier wipes 'Majuba' off slate and is shot.

00274
THE CONJURER AND THE BOER (75)
Hepworth
D: Cecil Hepworth
Cecil Hepworth
TRICK Conjurer changes Boer soldier into Britannia

00275
SNOWBALLING OOM PAUL (40)
R.W. Paul
COMEDY Children make snowman resembling Kruger, then destroy it.

FEB

00276
A JOLLY OLD COUPLE (75)
G.A.S. Films (WTC)
D: G.A. Smith
Tom Green
FACIAL Man smokes pipe and drinks beer; woman plays with cat and sews.

00277
THE TWO OLD SPORTS (75)
G.A.S. Films (WTC)
D: G.A. Smith
Tom Green
Mr Hunter
FACIAL Two men chuckle over picture of actress.

00278
TWO GRINNING YOKELS (50)
G.A.S. Films (WTC)
D: G.A. Smith
FACIAL Two country yokels grin through horsecollars for beer.

00279
THE CONJURER (50)
G.A.S. Films (WTC)
D: G.A. Smith
TRICK Conjuror vanishes girl and produces kittens from handkerchief.

00280
AN INCIDENT ON BRIGHTON PIER (50)
G.A.S. Films (WTC)
D: G.A. Smith
COMEDY 'The masher mashed'.

00281
THE RIVAL CLOTHIERS (75)
Warwick Trading Co.
COMEDY Jewish rivals cut prices until one buys the other's stock.

00282
A CONVENIENT CIGAR LIGHTER (50)
Warwick Trading Co.
COMEDY Strong man bends lamp post to light cigar.

MAR

00283
PRIZE FIGHT OR GLOVE CONTEST BETWEEN JOHN BULL AND PRESIDENT KRUGER (200)
John Sloane Barnes
WAR Symbolic boxing match.

00284
PLUCKED FROM THE BURNING (100)
R.W. Paul
D: Walter Booth
DRAMA Fireman rescues mother and child just before ceiling falls.

00285
THE HAIRBREADTH ESCAPE OF JACK SHEPPARD (100)
R.W. Paul
D: Walter Booth
CRIME Thief chased by watchman crosses roof on plank.

00286
DIVING FOR TREASURE (45)
R.W. Paul
D: Walter Booth
TRICK Divers enter water and are shown finding treasure under sea.

00287
A RAILWAY COLLISION (40)
R.W. Paul
D: Walter Booth
TRICK Express train crashes into goods train and plunges down embankment.

00288
THE BRUTAL BURGLAR
P.W. Paul
CRIME

00289
A MORNING AT BOW STREET
R.W. Paul
COMEDY 'Four lively cases in the dock'.

00290
THE WORRIED GERMAN (90)
R.W. Paul
COMEDY Boy inverts barrel so that tormentor's lunch falls in. (Date uncertain.)

00291
HIGH LIFE BELOW STAIRS (80)
R.W. Paul
COMEDY Mistress finds maid's lover in hiding and calls PC. (Date uncertain.)

MAY

00292
KRUGER'S DREAM OF EMPIRE (65)
R.W. Paul
D: Walter Booth
TRICK Oom Paul dreams Chamberlain offers him England's crown and is changed into Britannia by soldier.

00293
A NAUGHTY STORY (60)
R.W. Paul
FACIAL Man chuckles over story in magazine and shows it to friend.

00294
SAN TOY
Mutoscope & Biograph
S: (PLAY) Edward Morton

Marie Tempest ....San Toy
Hayden Coffin ....Capt Preston
Huntley Wright Li
Rutland Barrington ......Yen How
COMEDY Scene from 'Daly's Theatre' production.

JUL

00295
THE RATS (275)
Warwick Trading Co
Dan Leno ....Herbert Campbell
Joe Elvin ....Will Evans
George Robey ....Harry Randall
COMEDY (3 scenes) Off for Picnic; At Play; At Dinner. (Impromptu antics of London Music Hall Society.)

00296
MERRY SCHOOLDAYS (50)
Warwick Trading Co
COMEDY (2 scenes) Schoolboys enter class reluctantly; then rush home.

00297
THE PUNTER'S MISHAP (75)
Hepworth
D: Cecil M. Hepworth
Cecil Hepworth.....Punter
COMEDY Punter's pole sticks in mud and he falls into river.

00298
THE GUNPOWDER PLOT (50)
Hepworth
D: Cecil M. Hepworth
Cecil Hepworth.....Father
TRICK Boy puts firework under father's chair and blows him to pieces.

00299
THE EXPLOSION OF A MOTOR CAR (100)
Hepworth USA: THE DELIGHTS OF AUTO—MOBILING
D: Cecil M. Hepworth
Cecil Hepworth........Driver
Henry Lawley..........Passenger
TRICK Car explodes and blows its passengers to pieces (in THROUGH THREE REIGNS 1922.)

00300
THE EGG-LAYING MAN (75)
Hepworth
D: Cecil M. Hepworth
Cecil Hepworth.....The Man
TRICK Close shot of man taking five eggs from his mouth, the last one smelling bad.

00301
CLOWN AND POLICEMAN (100)
Hepworth
D: Cecil M. Hepworth
Cecil Hepworth.....Clown
TRICK Clown blows PC to pieces and fits him together again.

00302
LEAPFROG AS SEEN BY THE FROG (50)
Hepworth
D: Cecil M. Hepworth
COMEDY Boys run towards camera and leap over it.

00303
HOW IT FEELS TO BE RUN OVER (50)
Hepworth
D: Cecil M. Hepworth

Cecil Hepworth.......Driver
May Clark...............Passenger
TRICK Motor car drives straight at camera and crashes into it.

00304
THE PLEASURES OF PHOTOGRAPHY (50)
Warwick Trading Co
COMEDY Photographer snaps firemen and they squirt him with hose.

00305
BRITON VS. BOER (100)
R.W. Paul
D: S: Lewin Fitzhamon
Lewin Fitzhamon.........Boer Field Cornet
Henry G. Shaw.............Colonial Officer
WAR Fight between Briton and Boer: Briton wins.

00306
HIS MOTHER'S PORTRAIT; OR, THE SOLDIER'S VISION (100)
R.W. Paul
D: Lewin Fitzhamon
WAR Wounded soldier dreams of mother whose framed miniature deflects bullet from heart.

00307
PUNISHED (40)
R.W. Paul
COMEDY Music Hall agent's wife tears up picture of girl client.

00308
THE LAST DAYS OF POMPEII (80)
R.W. Paul
D: Walter Booth
DRAMA Vesuvius erupts and people escape from room as ceiling falls.

00309
ATTACK ON A MISSION STATION (87)
Mitchell & Kenyon
WAR Missionary barricades house against Boxers and is saved by marines.

00310
ATTEMPTED CAPTURE OF AN ENGLISH NURSE AND CHILDREN (60)
Mitchell & Kenyon
WAR Nurse screams for help when Boxer throws baby on head.

00311
THE ASSASSINATION OF A BRITISH SENTRY (91)
Mitchell & Kenyon
WAR Boxer stabs sentry whose gun fires and brings soldiers.

00312
THE CLEVER CORRESPONDENT (54)
Mitchell & Kenyon
WAR Artist lures Boxers, then turns on them and throws them.

00313
WASHING A BOER PRISONER IN CAMP (63)
Mitchell & Kneyon
WAR Soldiers scrub dirty Boer. (Date uncertain.)

00314
THE DISPATCH BEARER (74)
Mitchell & Kenyon
WAR Dispatch rider gets through Boer ambush. (Date uncertain.)

00315
WINNING THE V.C. (69)
Mitchell & Kenyon

WAR British soldier's brave deed. (Date uncertain.)

00316
WHITE FLAG TREACHERY (75)
Mitchell & Kenyon
WAR Boers pretend to surrender, then shoot Britons. (Date uncertain.)

00317
THE NURSE'S BROTHER (57)
Mitchell & Kenyon
WAR Nurse saves wounded man who recognises her as sister. (Date uncertain.)

00318
SHELLING THE RED CROSS (72)
Mitchell & Kenyon
WAR Boer throws bomb into British Red Cross tent and wounds nurse. (Date uncertain.)

AUG
00319
BOXERS SACKING A MISSION STATION
Harrison
WAR Staged topical of Boxer rebellion.

00320
A QUICK SHAVE AND BRUSH UP (50)
G.A.S. Films (WTC)
D: G.A. Smith
FACIAL Man attempts to shave with blunt razor.

00321
LET ME DREAM AGAIN (75)
G.A.S. Films (WTC)
D: G.A. Smith
COMEDY Old man flirts at ball, and wakes in bed with wife.

00322
BURLESQUE ATTACK ON A SETTLER'S CABIN (50)
Warwick Trading Co
Dan Leno
Herbert Campbell
Joe Elvin
COMEDY Music Hall scene.

00323
DAN LENO'S ATTEMPT TO MASTER THE CYCLE (50)
Warwick Trading Co
Dan Leno
COMEDY Comedian tries to ride a bicycle.

00324
BURLESQUE FOX HUNT (50)
Warwick Trading Co
Dan Leno
Herbert Campbell
COMEDY Music Hall scene.

SEP
00325
DAN LENO'S CRICKET MATCH (100)
Birt Acres
Dan Leno
COMEDY Comedian's antics at cricket match.

00326
THE CLOWN AND THE ENCHANTED CANDLE (50)
Warwick Trading Co
TRICK Candle grows large and shrinks as clown reads book.

00327
THE DULL RAZOR (75)
G.A.S. Films (WTC)
D: G.A. Smith
FACIAL Man shaves, back to camera, face reflected in mirror.

00328
SNAPSHOTTING AN AUDIENCE (75)
G.A.S. Films (WTC)
D: G.A. Smith
COMEDY Photographer facing camera poses audience for snapshot.

00329
GRANDMA THREADING HER NEEDLE (75)
G.A.S. Films (WTC)
D: G.A. Smith
Eva Bayley.....Grandma
FACIAL Grandmother eventually succeeds in threading needle.

00330
SCANDAL OVER THE TEACUPS (75)
G.A.S. Films (WTC)
D: G.A. Smith
Eva Bayley.....Spinster
FACIAL Two spinsters gossip while drinking tea.

00331
THE OLD MAID'S VALENTINE (50) also: THE VALENTINE
G.A.S. Films (WTC)
D: G.A. Smith
FACIAL Spinster receives an insulting valentine card.

00332
THE TWO OLD SPORTS' POLITICAL DISCUSSION (75)
G.A.S. Films (WTC)
D: G.A. Smith
Tom Green
Mr Hunter
FACIAL Two men argue over their newspapers.

00333
THE TWO OLD SPORTS' GAME OF NAP (125) also: THE WINNING HAND
G.A.S. Films (WTC)
D: G.A. Smith
Tom Green
Mr Hunter
FACIAL (2 parts) Two men argue over card game.

00334
A BAD CIGAR (75)
G.A.S. Films (WTC)
D: G.A. Smith
FACIAL Man tries to smoke bad cigar.

00335
THE HOUSE THAT JACK BUILT (50)
G.A.S. Films (WTC)
D: G.A. Smith
TRICK Boy knocks down girl's toy house, and the film is reversed.

00336
GRANDMA'S READING CLASS (100)
G.A.S. Films (WTC)
D: G.A. Smith
TRICK Boy looks at various objects which are shown in cut-in closeups.

00337
AS SEEN THROUGH THE TELESCOPE (75)
G.A.S. Films (WTC)

D: G.A. Smith
COMEDY Man looks through telescope at girl tying shoelace which is shown in closeup.

00338
HINDOO JUGGLERS (70)
R.W. Paul
D: Walter Booth
TRICK Indian juggler passes swords through boy in basket.

00339
CHINESE MAGIC (100) *also*: YELLOW PERIL
R.W. Paul
D: Walter Booth
TRICK Chinese conjurer changes girl into butterfly, and himself into giant bat.

00340
ARMY LIFE; OR, HOW SOLDIERS ARE MADE (series)
R.W. Paul
Documentary series including the following staged scenes (00341 – 00345):

00341
JOINING THE ARMY (160)
R.W. Paul
DRAMA Recruit enlists, is examined, sworn in, and marched to depot.

00342
WORK AND PLAY AT THE DEPOT (80)
R.W. Paul
DRAMA Fatigue party rushes to canteen, and soldier cheats at cards and is punished.

00343
A LARK IN CAMP (60)
R.W. Paul
COMEDY Soldier teases mates with broom and is tossed in blanket.

00344
LEAVING THE ARMY (60)
R.W. Paul
DRAMA Old soldier's kit auctioned and he joins Commissionaire Corps.

00345
DEFENDING A REDOUBT (60)
R.W. Paul
WAR Soldiers fire on enemy and then charge.

00346
BRITAIN'S WELCOME TO HER SONS (100)
R.W. Paul
D: Walter Booth
TRICK Britannia shows soldiers winning VCs, returning home, etc.

00347
A WET DAY AT THE SEASIDE (50)
R.W. Paul
COMEDY Children make 'seaside' in their bathroom.

00348
THE DRENCHED LOVER (70)
R.W. Paul
COMEDY Girl's parents chase suitor into pond.

00349
JIMMY GLOVER CONDUCTING HIS FAMOUS ORCHESTRA (50)
Gibbons' Bio-Tableaux
FACIAL Bexhill. Conductor pulls faces and waves arms.

00350
A FUNNY STORY (50)
Gibbons' Bio-Tableaux

D: Jack Smith
Walter Gibbons
Jack Smith
DACIAL Two men laugh at joke in magazine, and fall down.

00351
LIVING STATUES (120)
Gibbons' Bio-Tableaux
D: Jack Smith
TRICK Gallery attendant breaks statue and film reverses.

00352
FISHERMAN'S LUCK (120)
Gibbons' Bio-Tableaux
D: Jack Smith
TRICK Fisherman is pulled into water, rescuer dives in, and film reverses.

00353
A MORNING WASH (90)
Gibbons' Bio-Tableaux
D: Jack Smith
Walter Gibbons.....Man
Jack Smith..........Friend
COMEDY Man exchanges shoe blacking for friend's soap.

00354
SCENES BETWEEN TWO WELL-KNOWN COMEDIANS (80:50;70)
Gibbons' Bio-Tableaux
D: Jack Smith
COMEDY (3 scenes) Trick chair; staircase; cheating at cards.

00355
ENGLISH NELL
Mutoscope & Biograph
S: (PLAY) Anthony Hope, Edward Rose
Marie Tempest.........Nell Gwynne
Ben Webster.............Simon Dale
H.B. Warner.............Duke of Monmouth
Frank Cooper..........Charles II
HISTORY Scene from second act of 'Prince of Wales Theatre' production.

00356
A GALLANT RESCUE (100)
Harrison
TRICK Man falls off barge and lock-keeper dives in; then film reverses.

OCT

00357
IT'S NO USE CRYING OVER SPILT MILK (100)
Birt Acres
D: Arthur Cooper
COMEDY Yokel carrying milk is run into by lady cyclist and aunt.

00358
FARMER GILES AND HIS PORTRAIT (100)
Birt Acres
D: Arthur Cooper
COMEDY Farmer and wife cause trouble in photographer's studio.

00359
THE FLYING SCOTS (175)
Warwick Trading Co
The Three Missouris
ACT Comic acrobats dressed as Scotsmen in their scena 'More Rosin'.

00360
THE UNFORTUNATE EGG MERCHANT (75)
Warwick Trading Co
COMEDY Couple tip man off bench and pelt him with eggs.

00361
THE YOKELS' DINNER (75)
Warwick Trading Co
TRICK Yokels eat pudding, then film reverses.

NOV

00362
TWO JOLLY OLD FELLOWS (100) *also*: they THEY ARE JOLLY GOOD FELLOWS
G.A.S. Films (WTC)
D: G.A. Smith
Tom Green
Mr Hunter
FACIAL Two men hold whispered conversion..

00363
CLEVER AND COMIC CYCLE ACT (100)
Williamson
D: James Williamson
Lotto, Lilo and Otto
ACT Comedy cyclists. (Date uncertain.)

00364
THE DISABLED MOTOR (70)
Williamson
D: James Williamson
COMEDY Horse tows car containing bandaged driver.

00365
ATTACK ON A CHINESE MISSION —
BLUEJACKETS TO THE RESCUE (230)
Williamson
D: S: James Williamson
Florence Williamson .... The Girl
Mr Lepard .... The Missionary
Mr James .... The Officer
Three Acrobats .... The Sailors
WAR (4 scenes) China. Boxers break through gates; missionary killed as wife waves for help; sailors see signal; sailors arrive and defeat Boxers.

00366
THE ECCENTRIC DANCER (50)
Hepworth
D: Cecil Hepworth
TRICK Clown performs impossible dance.

00367
THE BATHERS (100)
Hepworth
D: Cecil Hepworth
Cecil Hepworth.....Bather
TRICK Couple undress and dive into river; then film reverses.

00368
THE SLUGGARD'S SURPRISE (75)
Hepworth
D: Cecil Hepworth
COMEDY Lazy man gets surprise.

00369
THE ELECTRICTY CURE (75)
Hepworth
D: Cecil Hepworth
COMEDY Man gets electric shock.

00370
THE BEGGAR'S DECEIT (50)
Hepworth
D: Cecil Hepworth
COMEDY Fat policeman finds crippled beggar is fraud, and chases him.

00371
THE BURNING STABLE (100)
Hepworth
D; Cecil Hepworth
William Clark.....Stableman
Sydney Clark.....Stableman
DRAMA Men rescue horses from burning stable.

00372
TOPSY-TURVY VILLA (75)
Hepworth
D: Cecil Hepworth
Cecil Hepworth.......Policeman
May Clark...............Cook
TRICK PC, cook and boy walk about on ceiling.

00373
PHONO-BIO-TABLEAUX FILMS (series)
sound
Gibbons' Bio-Tableaux
D: Walter Gibbons

00374
THE MIDNIGHT SON (3)
Vesta Tilley

00375
ALGY THE PICCADILLY JOHNNY (3)
Vesta Tilley

00376
LOUISIANA LOU (3)
Vesta Tilley

00377
KITTY MAHONE (3)
Lil Hawthorne

00378
THE LAMBETH WALK (3)
Alec Hurley

00379
SALLY IN OUR ALLEY (3)
American Comedy Four.

00380
THE BLIND BOY (3)
G.H. Chirgwin

00381
THE CORNFIELDS QUARTETTE (3)

00382
TURN OUT OF THE FIRE BRIGADE (3)
(Synchronised sound effects)
MUSICAL Synchronised to gramophone
recordings. (First synchronised sound films.)

DEC

00383
THE VILLAGE CHOIR (75)
G.A.S. Films (WTC)
D: G.A. Smith
FACIAL Several singers in discordant song.

00384
WHERE DID YOU GET IT? (75)
G.A.S. Films (WTC)
D: G.A. Smith
FACIAL Four men pass naughty photograph
around.

00385
LEAPFROG (75)
Riley Brothers
COMEDY Players run towards camera and jump
over it.

00386
WOMENS' RIGHTS (75)
Riley Brothers
COMEDY Suffragettes.

00387
THE CARPENTER AND THE COOK (50)
Warwick Trading Co — Biokam
COMEDY (Date uncertain.)

00388
THE UP-TO-DATE CONJURER (50)
Warwick Trading Co — Biokam
TRICK (Date uncertain.)

00389
THE DEATH OF POOR JOE (50)
Warwick Trading Co — Biokam
PATHOS Child-crossing sweeper dies in the
snow. (Date uncertain.)

00390
AUNT SELINA (50)
Warwick Trading Co — Biokam
FACAIL Old lady takes snuff and sews. (Date
uncertain.)

00391
STUMP SPEECH (50)
Warwick Trading Co — Biokam
FACAIL Negro minstrel makes speech. (Date
uncertain.)

00392
LADY AT HER MORNING TOILET (50)
Warwick Trading Co — Biokam
FACIAL (Date uncertain.)

00393
AN INCIDENT IN THE BOER WAR
George Green
D: George Green
WAR (Date uncertain.)

00394
THE CHILDREN AND THE LIONS
George Green
D: George Green
DRAMA (Date uncertain.)

1901

JAN

00395
THE SNOWMAN (65)
Mitchell & Kenyon
COMEDY

FEB

00396
THE LLOYD BROTHERS DOUBLE ROPE
ACT (125)
Warwick Trading Co
ACT Acrobats play violins while balancing
outside circus tent.

MAR

00397
WHISKEY VERSUS BULLETS (50)
G.A.S. Films (WTC)
D: G.A. Smith
FACIAL Man tries to shoot himself but drinks
whiskey instead.

00398
CANNON BALL JUGGLING (75)
Warwick Trading Co
Paul Cinquevalli
ACT Juggler performs with cannon balls.

00399
THE TILLER GROUP OF DANCERS (50)
Warwick Trading Co
ACT Ten girls perform high kick dance.

00400
GIRLS INDULGING IN A PILLOW FIGHT (50)
Warwick Trading Co
COMEDY Four schoolgirls in night dresses
fight with pillows.

00401
SET-TO BETWEEN JOHN BULL AND PAUL
KRUGER (200)
Warwick Trading Co
WAR Symbolic fight.

MAY

00402
THE BILL POSTER'S REVENGE (50)
G.A.S. Films (WTC)·
D: G.A. Smith
COMEDY Bill poster changes halves of his
rival's posters.

00403
THE MONOCLE — ME AND JOE
CHAMBERLAIN (50)
G.A.S. Films (WTC)
D: G.A. Smith
FACIAL Man tries to look like cartoon of
prime minister.

JUN

00404
THE KITTEN NURSERY (100)
G.A.S. Films (WTC)
D: G.A. Smith
COMEDY Boy gives spoonful of milk to
kitten. (Cut in closeup.)

00405
THE LITTLE DOCTOR AND THE SICK
KITTEN (50)
G.A.S. Films (WTC)
D: G.A. Smith
COMEDY Girl gives spoonful of milk to
kitten. (Cut in closeup.)

00406
THE LAST GLASS OF THE TWO OLD
SPORTS (50) also: THE LAST BOTTLE AT
THE CLUB
G.A.S. Films (WTC)
D: G.A. Smith
Tom Green
Mr Hunter
FACIAL Old clubmen toast each other and
drink.

00407
TALLY HO!
Gibbons' Bio-Tableaux
D: Frank Parker
S: (PLAY) W.H. Risque
Charles Rock...............Squire Oldbuck
Hetty Chattell.............Kate Oldbuck
Douglas Gordon...........Jack Ferrers
Fitzroy Morgan...........Herbert Fitzherbert
James Campbell..........Rev Milford
Windham Guise...........Peters
Nellie Dade.................Dame
Hugh Seton.................Cholmondeley
Hengler's Plunging Horses; Herbert's Dogs
COMEDY (4 scenes) Man dons disguise to elope
with squire's daughter. ('London Hippodrome'
stage performance.)

JUL

00408
DAN LENO'S DAY OUT (100)
Warwick Trading Co
COMEDY Stamford Bridge. Comedian's
impromptu antics on cricket ground

00409
DAN LENO, MUSICAL DIRECTOR (50)
Warwick Trading Co
COMEDY Stamford Bridge. Comedian conducts
Metropolitan Police band in 'A Little Bit Off the
Top'.

AUG

00410
MADEMOISELLE ROSIE AQUINALDO
(300)
Warwick Trading Co
ACT (3 parts) Fifteen-year old Australian
contortioniste.

00411
A GOOD STORY (50)
G.A.S. Films (WTC)
D: G.A. Smith
FACIAL Monk tells brother naughty story.

00412
PHOTOGRAPH FROM AN AREA WINDOW
(100)
G.A.S. Films (WTC)
D: G.A. Smith
COMEDY Close view of legs and feet passing a
basement window.

00413
HOW THE BURGLAR TRICKED THE BOBBY
(100)
Hepworth
D: Cecil Hepworth
Cecil Hepworth.....Burglar
COMEDY (3 scenes) Burglar traps PC in cottage
door, and escapes.

00414
THE INDIAN CHIEF AND THE SEIDLITZ
POWDER (90)
Hepworth
D: Cecil Hepworth
TRICK Red Indian takes powders in wrong
order, swells and bursts.

00415
THE COMIC GRIMACER (50)
Hepworth
D: Cecil Hepworth
FACIAL Close view of man with 'india rubber
face.

00416
INTERIOR OF A RAILWAY CARRIAGE —
BANK HOLIDAY (75)
Hepworth
D: Cecil Hepworth
Cecil Hepworth
May Clark
Henry Lawley
Sydney Clark
COMEDY Fun in crowded railway train
compartment.

00417
ACROBATIC PERFORMANCE — SELLS
AND YOUNG (150)
R.W. Paul
Emilie Sells & Fritz Young
ACT 'The boneless lady and the funny clown'.
(Date uncertain.)

00418
THE DEONZO BROTHERS (120)
R.W. Paul
ACT Tub jumpers. (Date uncertain.)

00419
THE CAPTAIN'S BIRTHDAY (100)
R.W. Paul
D: Walter Booth
Fred Farren.....Captain Kettle
COMEDY Fancy dress dance aboard ship.
(Date uncertain.)

00420
AN OVER-INCUBATED BABY (80)
R.W. Paul
D: Walter Booth
COMEDY Child put into professor's
incubator comes out old man. (Date uncertain.)

00421
GARTERS VERSUS BRACES; OR, ALGY IN
A FIX (90)
R.W. Paul
COMEDY When man demands return of gift
garters, fiancee demands return of braces.
(Date uncertain.)

00422
THE ARTIST AND THE FLOWER GIRL (80)
R.W. Paul
ROMANCE Artist saves girl from snow, hides
her from friends, and she creeps away. (Date
uncertain.)

00423
THE AUTOMATIC MACHINE; OR, OH WHAT
A SURPRISE (100)
R.W. Paul
COMEDY Customers angered by fraudulent
prizes find man inside slot machine. (Date
uncertain.)

00424
HANDY ANDY THE CLUMSY SERVANT
(100)
R.W. Paul
COMEDY Clumsy servant's mistakes cause
trouble. (Date uncertain.)

00425
HIS BRAVE DEFENDER (100)
R.W. Paul
COMEDY Burglar ties up woman while
husband hides under bed. (Date uncertain.)

00426
AN INTERRUPTED REHEARSAL; OR,
MURDER WILL OUT (100)
R.W. Paul
COMEDY PC mistakes rehearsing actors for
murderers. (Date uncertain.)

00427
THE MUDDLED BILL POSTER (120)
R.W. Paul
COMEDY Tramps paste posters on sleeping
bill-poster. (Date uncertain.)

00428
WILLIAM TELL (100)
R.W. Paul
HISTORY Austria. Archer shoots apple off
son's head. (Date uncertain.)

00429
THE DEVIL IN THE STUDIO (100)
R.W. Paul
D: (W.R. Booth)
TRICK Mephistopheles causes artist's model
to disappear. (Date uncertain.)

00430
THE HAUNTED CURIOSITY SHOP (140)
R.W. Paul
D: (W.R. Booth)
TRICK Egyptian mummy revives and frightens
curio dealer. (Date uncertain.)

00431
UNDRESSING EXTRAORDINARY; OR, THE
TROUBLES OF A TIRED TRAVELLER (200)
R.W. Paul
D: (W.R. Booth)
TRICK Seaside lodger finds lively skeleton in
bed. (Date uncertain.)

00432
THE CHEESE MITES; OR, LILLIPUTIANS
IN A LONDON RESTAURANT (70)
R.W. Paul
D: (W.R. Booth)
TRICK Six-inch high sailors dance upon
diner's cheese.

00433
THE DRUNKARD'S CONVERSION (80)
retitled: THE HORRORS OF DRINK
R.W. Paul
D: (W.R. Booth)
TRICK Drunk sees gnome, snake and Spirit of
Temperance.

00434
THE TRAMP AT THE SPINSTERS' PICNIC
(70)
R.W. Paul
COMEDY Undressed tramp hides in tree and
falls into girl's pie.

SEP

00435
'ARRY ON THE STEAMBOAT (180)
R.W. Paul
D: (W.R. Booth)
S: (SONG) E. Lonnen
MUSICAL Coster couple's boat trip to
Greenwich. (Shown while song is sung.)

00436
ORA PRO NOBIS; OR, THE POOR ORPHAN'S
LAST PRAYER (100)
R.W. Paul
D: (W.R. Booth)
S: (SONG)
MUSICAL Orphan dies in snow and angels bear
spirit to heaven. (Shown while song is sung.)

00437
THE WAIF AND THE WIZARD; OR, THE
HOME MADE HAPPY (90)
R.W. Paul
D: (W.R. Booth)
S: (SONG)
MUSICAL Conjurer changes bailiff into waiter
with food. (Shown while song is sung.)

00438
BRITAIN'S TRIBUTE TO HER SONS (150)
R.W. Paul
D: (W.R. Booth)
S: (SONG) Clarence Hunt
MUSICAL Tribute to Empire soldiers. (Shown
while song is sung.)

00439
THE LOST SCOUT ON THE VELDT
Mitchell & Kenyon
WAR (Date uncertain.)

00440
TOMMY'S REVENGE
Mitchell & Kenyon
WAR (Date uncertain.)

00441
BLOWING UP THE POWDER MAGAZINE
Mitchell & Kenyon
WAR (Date uncertain.)

00442
HANDS OFF THE FLAG (113)
Mitchell & Kenyon
WAR Settler sees Boer pull down flag and
returns home in time to save wife.

00443
TOMMY'S LAST SHOT (95)
Mitchell & Kenyon
WAR Wounded soldier killed as he writes
letter.

00444
POISONING THE WELL (91)
Mitchell & Kenyon
WAR Boer stabs sentry but is caught before
he can poison well.

00445
SAVED BY A WOMAN (83)
Mitchell & Kenyon
WAR Girl holds Boer at bay while friend helps
wounded man.

00446
THE FIGHT FOR THE GUN (65)
Mitchell & Kenyon
WAR Soldiers recapture machine gun from
Boers.

00447
A TIGHT CORNER (232)
Mitchell & Kenyon
WAR (4 scenes) A dash for help; through the
enemy's lines; The message delivered; Just in
time.

00448
THE SNEAKY BOER (82)

Mitchell & Kenyon
WAR Two Boers shoot and rob sentry.

00449
THE SURPRISE OF A BOER CAMP (90)
Mitchell & Kenyon
WAR Britons capture Boer camp after brief
struggle.

00450
CHASING DE WET (108)
Mitchell & Kenyon
TRICK Two soldiers try to chase Boer leader
but he gets away.

00451
THE ADRIAN TROUPE OF CYCLISTS (150)
G.A.S. Films (WTC)
D: G.A. Smith
ACT Trick bicyclists on 'teacup track'.

OCT

00452
IN THE GREEN ROOM (100)
G.A.S.Films (WTC)
D: G.A. Smith
ACT Actor dresses for role of giant in 'Jack
the Giant Killer'.

00453
IRENE LATOUR, CONTORTIONIST (150)
Warwick Trading Co
ACT Contortionist and her little dog Zaza.

00454
THE BIG SWALLOW (60)
Williamson
D: James Williamson
Sam Dalton
TRICK Man comes closer until mouth so large
that cameraman falls in. (Date uncertain.)

00455
THE MAGIC EXTINGUISHER (110)
Williamson
D: James Williamson
Sam Dalton
TRICK Conjurer vanishes animals, then
vanishes himself. (Date uncertain.)

00456
THE ELIXIR OF LIFE (90)
Williamson
D: James Williamson
Sam Dalton
FACIAL Old man drinks elixir and becomes
young. (Date uncertain.)

00457
STOP THIEF ! (115)
Williamson
D: James Williamson
CHASE (3 scenes) Tramp steals joint from
butcher, is chased by dogs into tub, and is
eaten. (Date uncertain.)

00458
OVER THE GARDEN WALL (65)
Williamson
D: James Williamson
COMEDY Boy hides under basket upon which
maid stands to kiss PC. (Date uncertain.)

00459
THE MARVELLOUS HAIR RESTORER (105)
Williamson
D: James Williamson
Sam Dalton
TRICK Bald man grows hair and so does table
he splashes. (Date uncertain.)

00460
ARE YOU THERE? (75)
Williamson
D: James Williamson
Sam Dalton
COMEDY Girl's father overhears telephone appointment and takes her place. (Date uncertain.)

00461
THE PUZZLED BATHER AND HIS ANIMATED CLOTHES (80)
Williamson
D: James Williamson
TRICK The more clothes bather removes, the more appear. (Date uncertain.)

00462
TEASING GRANDPA (92)
Williamson
D: James Williamson
Alan Williamson............Boy
Colin Williamson...........Boy
COMEDY Boys stick dead fly on Grandpa's spectacles. (Date uncertain.)

00463
TOMORROW WILL BE FRIDAY (95)
Williamson
D: James Williamson
S: (SONG)
John Macauley..........Monk
COMEDY Fishing monk drains his bottle and drinks brother's. (Date uncertain.)

00464
CYCLIST SCOUTS IN ACTION (150)
Williamson
D: James Williamson
WAR Boer shoots cyclist scout and is himself shot. (Date uncertain.)

00465
FIRE! (280)
Williamson (Gaumont)
D: James Williamson
DRAMA (5 scenes) PC sees burning house; summons brigade; engines rush down street; fireman carries man through bedroom window; outside, he returns for family.

00466
THE COUNTRYMAN AND THE CINEMATOGRAPH (50)
R.W. Paul
COMEDY Film of train scares yokel, who tears down screen and fights the projectionist.

00467
PUNCH AND JUDY
R.W. Paul
COMEDY 'Life size' puppet performance.

00468
ARTISTIC CREATION (85)
R.W. Paul

D: (W.R. Booth)
TRICK Pierrot draws lady in sections, and parts come alive.

00469
THE FAMOUS ILLUSION OF DE KOLTA (120)
R.W. Paul
D: (W.R. Booth)
TRICK Pierrot draws silkworm, which becomes girl butterfly.

00470
HAIR SOUP; OR, A DISGRUNTLED DINER (60)
R.W. Paul
FACIAL Diner finds hair in his soup.

00471
THE TRAMP AND THE TURPENTINE BOTTLE; OR, GREEDINESS PUNISHED (70)
R.W. Paul
FACIAL Tramp drinks turpentine in mistake for beer.

NOV

00472
THE GAMBLER'S FATE; OR, THE ROAD TO RUIN (200)
R.W. Paul
CRIME (2 scenes) Gambler shoots cardsharper; police arrest gambler.

00473
MR PICKWICK'S CHRISTMAS AT WARDLE'S (140)
R.W. Paul
D: (W.R. Booth)
S: (NOVEL) Charles Dickens (PICKWICK PAPERS)
COMEDY Period. Dances, games and waits.

00474
THE MAGIC SWORD; OR, A MEDIAEVAL MYSTERY (180)
R.W. Paul
D: S: W.R. Booth
FANTASY Mediaeval knight saves lady from ogre and witch.

00475
SCROOGE; OR, MARLEY'S GHOST (620)
R.W. Paul
D: W.R. Booth
S: (NOVEL) Charles Dickens (A CHRISTMAS CAROL)
FANTASY (13 scenes) Miser reforms after visions of past, present and future.

00476
THE KING AND THE JESTER (50)
Warwick Trading Co
COMEDY 'A cracked crown'.

00477
THE FAMOUS WILLE BROTHERS (150)
Warwick Trading Co
ACT Balancing act.

00478
THE MISER'S AVARICE (50)
Warwick Trading Co
DRAMA 'The glitter of gold'.

00479
THE MYSTERIOUS BAG (150)
Warwick Trading Co
ACT 'Music Hall turn'.

00480
TAKE YOUR PHOTOGRAPH SIR? (175)
Warwick Trading Co
COMEDY

00481
THE AUTOMATIC SLOT MACHINE (125)
Warwick Trading Co
COMEDY Swindled customers find man inside slot machine.

00482
WILLIAM TELL (150)
Warwick Trading Co
COMEDY 'The row about an apple'.

00483
THE LASSIE AND HER DOG (150)
Warwick Trading Co
COMEDY 'Where patience is a virtue.'

00484
THE GLUTTON'S NIGHTMARE (150)
Hepworth
D: Percy Stow
TRICK Glutton dreams of cats in rabbit pie, and dogs in sausages.

DEC
00485
DOLLY'S TOYS (80)
R.W. Paul
D: (Arthur Cooper)
TRICK Child dreams toys come to life.

00486
HARLEQUINADE —WHAT THEY FOUND IN THE LAUNDRY BASKET (240)
Williamson (Gaumont)
D: James Williamson
TRICK Clown's basket causes people to disappear.

00487
THE THIRD CUP (50)
Warwick Trading Co
ADVERT Bird's Custard Powder. (Date uncertain.)

00488
STEPPING STONE TO HAPPINESS (50)
ADVERT Swan Soap. (Date uncertain).

1902

JAN

00489
ARMANDUS , QUICK CHANGE ARTISTE (100)
Warwick Trading Co
ACT

00490
THE MONK IN THE MONASTERY WINE CELLARS (50)
G.A.S. Films (WTC)
D: G.A. Smith
COMEDY Monk gets drunk.

00491
THE TWO OLD SPORTS AT THE MUSIC HALL (75)
G.A.S. Films (WTC)
D: G.A. Smith
Tom Green
Mr Hunter
COMEDY Men in box watch tenor and dancing girl.

00492
TOO MUCH OF A GOOD THING (50)
G.A.S. Films (WTC)
D: G.A. Smith
COMEDY Nurse brings triplets to father, who flees.

00493
OH THAT COLLAR BUTTON! (50)
G.A.S. Films (WTC)
D: G.A. Smith
FACIAL Man's difficulty in buttoning tight collar.

00494
THE COMEDIAN AND THE FLYPAPER (75)
G.A.S. Films (WTC)
D: G.A. Smith
Mat Melrose
COMEDY Man tries to throw away sticky flypaper.

00495
THE CAKEWALK (75)
G.A.S. Films (WTC)
D: G.A. Smith
Melrose Trio
ACT Crystal Palace. Three dancers demonstrate latest craze.

00496
PERMAN'S EQUESTRIAN BEAR (100)
Warwick Trading Co
ACT Crystal Palace. Bear does tricks riding a horse.

FEB

00497
MLLE AIDA AND HER TROUPE OF PERFORMING DOGS (125)
Warwick Trading Co
ACT

00498
THE COCKFIGHT (50)
R.W. Paul
COMEDY Coster and gentleman bet on cocks, then fight each other.

00499
AN IMAGINARY LOVE SCENE
Mutoscope & Biograph
COMEDY

MAR

00500
WHERE ARE YOU GOING TO, MY PRETTY MAID? (150)
Warwick Trading Co
COMEDY 'A skit'.

00501
THE INTERRUPTED PRIZE FIGHT (75)
Warwick Trading Co
COMEDY

00502
BLUEBEARD (100)
Warwick Trading Co
S: (PANTOMIME)
Dan Leno......................Sister Anne
Arthur Conquest..........Mechanical Head
COMEDY Scene from 'Drury Lane Theatre' production.

00503
VESTA VICTORIA AS GRACE DARLING (100)
Warwick Trading Co
Vesta Victoria .... Grace Darling
ACT Comic song and dance.

00504
THE BREWSTER TRIO (75)
Warwick Trading Co
ACT Dance and juggling with banjos.

00505
THE BREWSTER TRIO OF HIGH KICKERS AND DANCERS (125)
Warwick Trading Co
ACT Dancers.

00506
HARRY WATSON'S PONY TUMBLING ACT (60)
Warwick Trading Co
ACT Small gymnast turns two back somersaults over pony.

00507
WATSON'S CLOWN AND DOGS TUG-OF-WAR (50)
Warwick Trading Co
ACR Trained dogs perform tug-of-war.

00508
THE CALL TO ARMS (150)
Hepworth
D: Cecil M. Hepworth
Sydney Clark................The Gentleman
May Clark.....................His Wife
William Clark...............The Doctor
Cecil Hepworth............A Soldier
WAR (5 scenes) Volunteer, wounded in Africa, returns home to his family.

APR

00509
DAN LENO AND HERBERT CAMPBELL EDIT 'THE SUN'
Mutoscope & Biograph
COMEDY Comedians take over newspaper as advertising stunt.

00510
LITTLE MISS LILLIAN (150) USA: LITTLE LILLIAN, TOE DANSEUSE
Warwick Trading Co
ACT Eight-year old toe-dancer in five character dances.

MAY

00511
THE THREE MISSOURIS (350)
Warwick Trading
ACT Acrobats perform with beam.

00512
THE IRISHMAN AND THE BUTTON (50)
G.A.S. Films (WTC)
D: G.A. Smith
FACIAL

00513
THE DONKEY AND THE SERPENTINE DANCER (75)
G.A.S. Films (WTC)
D: G.A. Smith
ACT Coster and donkey perform serpentine dance.

00514
TOMMY ATKINS AND HIS HARRIET ON A BANK HOLIDAY (50)
G.A.S. Films (WTC)
D: G.A. Smith
COMEDY Coster couple dance.

00515
PING-PONG (90)
Williamson
D: James Williamson
COMEDY Builders play ping-pong in lunch break and start fight.

00516
BURLESQUE OF POPULAR COMPOSERS (150)
Williamson
D: James Williamson
Mr Hanson
ACT Impersonations of Strauss, General Booth, etc.

JUN

00517
THE SOLDIER'S RETURN (185)
Williamson
D: James Williamson
DRAMA (5 scenes) Soldier returns in time to save mother from poor house.

00518
A WORKMAN'S PARADISE (170)
Williamson
D: James Williamson
TRICK Builder looks on as house builds itself.

00519
ELDRED'S GREAT EQUESTRIAN ACT (100)
Warwick Trading Co
ACT Triple simultaneous jump onto galloping horse.

00520
THE CORONATION OF THEIR MAJESTIES KING EDWARD VII AND QUEEN ALEXANDRIA (330)
Warwick Trading Co — Star Films
D: George S. Melies, G. A. Smith
HISTORY (10 scenes) Staged topical; made in France with British supervision.

00521
TOMMY AND THE MOUSE IN THE ART SCHOOL (50) also: LITTLE WILLIE AND THE MOUSE
G.A.S. Films (WTC)

D: G.A. Smith
COMEDY Boy releases mouse and frightens model.

00522
TOPSY-TURVY DANCE BY THREE QUAKER MAIDENS (125)
G.A.S. Films (WTC)
D: G.A. Smith
ACT Flag is removed to reveal girls' legs are their arms.

00523
THE MARCH OF THE AMAZONS (75)
G.A.S. Films (WTC)
D: G.A. Smith
ACT 16 girls marching and dancing.

00524
TAMBOURINE DANCING QUARTETTE (135)
G.A.S. Films (WTC)
D: G.A. Smith
ACT 4 high-kicking girls.

00525
A CONVICT'S DARING (260) reissue: 1907
R.W. Paul
CRIME (4 scenes) Convict, wounded while escaping, has vision of home. (Extract in BLOODHOUNDS TRACKING CONVICT 1903.)

00526
LOVE'S ARDOUR SUDDENLY COOLED (53)
R.W. Paul
COMEDY

00527
LITTLE WILLIE'S CORONATION CELEBRATIONS (75)
R.W. Paul
COMEDY

00528
FACIAL EXPRESSIONS (80)
R.W. Paul
FACIAL Actor makes up as old man and old woman.

00529
THE HOTEL MYSTERY (85)
R.W. Paul
TRICK 'Don't blow out the gas, or what happened to a visitor'.

00530
THAT ETERNAL PING-PONG (100)
Hepworth
D: Percy Stow
May Clark.....Girl
TRICK Boy and girl start table tennis game in 1900; their skeletons are still playing in 2000. (Date uncertain.)

00531
THE QUARRELSOME COUPLE (50)
Hepworth
D: Percy Stow
COMEDY Angry wife throws soup over preoccupied husband. (Date uncertain.)

00532
THE COUNTRYMAN AND THE FLUTE (50)
Hepworth
D: Percy Stow
COMEDY Yokel's flute playing annoys fat wife. (Date uncertain.)

00533
THE COSTER AND HIS DONKEY (75)
Hepworth
D: Percy Stow
TRICK Donkey refuses to cross watersplash, and the film reverses. (Date uncertain.)

00534
WHEN DADDY COMES HOME (75)
Hepworth
D: Percy Stow
COMEDY Boys dress punchball as tax inspector and drunken father fights it. (Date uncertain.)

00535
THE FRUSTRATED ELOPEMENT (100)
Hepworth
D: Percy Stow
May Clark.....Girl
TRICK Father catches daughter eloping, and the film reverses.

00536
HOW TO STOP A MOTOR CAR (100)
Hepworth
D: Percy Stow
Cecil Hepworth.............Driver
T.C. Hepworth.............Inspector
Claude Whitten.............PC
TRICK Car drives over policeman and cuts him into pieces. (Date uncertain. Extract in THROUGH THREE REIGNS, 1922.)

00537
PEACE WITH HONOUR (100)
Hepworth
D: Cecil Hepworth, Percy Stow
Cecil Hepworth.............Briton
Norman Whitten...........Boer
May Clark....................Britannia
WAR Survey of Boer war with reconstructions and actualities.

00538
BIOGRAPH DRAMATISED SONGS (series)
Mutoscope & Biograph
D: SC: Hugh Moss
Miss E.H. Brooke   J.A. Cave
Nellie Wallace   W. Wyes
Annie Montilli   Tom Mowbray
Hilda Moss   Charles Cecil
Dorothea Moss   F.J. Reed
Edith Allen   Malcolm Dunn
Miss M. Barber   Herbert Stanley
Adeline Votieri   C.R. Bassett
Lillian Revel   Charles Stuart
Forbes Dawson   Eardley Turner

00539
1 – SIMON THE CELLARER
S: (SONG) Bellamy & Hatton

00540
2 – HERE'S HEALTH UNTO HIS MAJESTY
S: (SONG)

00541
3 – TOMORROW WILL BE FRIDAY
S: (SONG)

00542
4 – THE DIVER'S STORY
S: (SONG) Hugh Moss, Denham Harrison

00543
5 – THE KING
S: (SONG) Hugh Moss, Denham Harrison

MUSICAL Picturisation of popular songs, sung from the theatre stage by George Ridgwell.

00544
THE CORONATION CEREMONIES (320)
Gaumont
P: A.C. Bromhead
HISTORY Representation of Edward VII's coronation.

00545
SIGNING PEACE AT PRETORIA (165)
Gaumont
P: A.C. Bromhead
HISTORY Representation.

00546
THE TROUBLESOME COLLAR (90)
R.W. Paul
FACIAL Man's expressions as he tries to fasten shirt collar.

00547
HIS ONLY PAIR (75)
R.W. Paul
COMEDY Old woman sews patch on grandson's trousers while friends jeer.

00548
THE SWELLS (50)
R.W. Paul
COMEDY Men peep into girl's bathing machine and die of shock.

00549
THE ENCHANTED CUP (300)
R.W. Paul
D: W.R. Booth
FANTASY (7 scenes) Peasant uses magic cup and gorgon's head to save sweetheart from being burned by dwarfs.

00550
AT LAST! THAT AWFUL TOOTH (50) also: OH! THAT AWFUL TOOTH
G.A.S. Films (WTC)
D: G.A. Smith
COMEDY Man pulls out bad tooth which is then shown in closeup.

00551
THE MONK'S MACARONI FEAST (125)
G.A.S. Films (WTC)
D: G.A. Smith
D' Philippe.....Monk
TRICK Monk eats macaroni, then the film reverses.

00552
THE MONK'S RUSE FOR LUNCH (100)
G.A.S. Films (WTC)
D: G.A. Smith
D. Philippe.....Monk
COMEDY Monk shares tourist's lunch basket, and then reveals his contains dog.

00553
THE MONK IN THE STUDIO (100)
G.A.S. Films (WTC)
D: G.A. Smith
D. Philippe.....Monk
COMEDY

00554
HIS FIRST CIGAR, PROBABLY HIS LAST (100)
G.A.S. Films (WTC)
D: G.A. Smith
FACIAL Boy smokes cigar and feels sick.

00555
EPISODES IN THE LIFE OF A LODGER (110)
G.A.S. Films (WTC)
D: G.A. Smith
COMEDY

00556
THAT AWFUL CIGAR (100)
G.A.S. Films (WTC)
D: G.A. Smith
FACIAL Man is determined to smoke bad cigar.

00557
PA'S COMMENTS ON THE MORNING NEWS (75)
G.A.S. Films (WTC)
D: G.A. Smith
FACIAL Father's expression as he reads newspaper at breakfast.

00558
THE SOUTHERN BELLES AND CISSY HEATH IN A COON DANCE (60)
Warwick Trading Co
ACT

00559
THE AVRIGNY TROUPE OF JUGGLERS (60)
Warwick Trading Co
ACT

00560
THE SOUTHERN BELLES SPECIALTY DANCE (50)
Warwick Trading Co
ACT

00561
THE EVERHARDTS CLEVER HOOP MANIPULATION (75)
Warwick Trading Co
ACT

00562
THE SELBIN TROUPE OF MARVELLOUS CLEVER ACROBATS (150)
Warwick Trading Co
ACT

00563
ROBBINS, CHAMPION OF ALL CHAMPIONS (300)
Warwick Trading Co
A.D. Robbins
ACT Crystal Palace. American cowboy trick cyclist.

00564
AN EXTRA TURN (70) *also:* THE EXTREY TURN
Williamson
D: James Williamson
COMEDY Music Hall audience throws bad fruit at performer.

00565
THOSE TROUBLESOME BOYS (102)
Williamson
D: James Williamson
Alan Williamson.....Boy
Colin Williamson....Boy
COMEDY Boys play trick with road-rammer.

00566
A LADY'S FIRST LESSON ON THE BICYCLE (75)
Williamson
D: James Williamson
Nellie Wallace.....The Lady
John Cobbold.....The Instructor
COMEDY Clumsy woman tries to ride bicycle at gymkhana.

AUG

00567
A DAY IN CAMP WITH THE VOLUNTEERS (200)
Williamson
D: James Williamson
COMEDY (7 scenes) Episodic misadventures of volunteer soldier.

00568
CLOSE QUARTERS, WITH A NOTION OF THE MOTION OF THE OCEAN (115)
Williamson
D: James Williamson
COMEDY Couple try to dress in cabin of rolling ship.

00569
SAMBO (80)
Williamson
D: James Williamson
Sam Dalton.....Sambo
FACIAL Blackface comedian smokes cigar.

00570
THE ACROBATIC TRAMPS (104)
Williamson
D: James Williamson
John Cobbold.........Tramp
Charles Cobbold.....Tramp
TRICK Old carpenter chases tramps who can vanish, reappear, reverse.

00571
GOLDIN'S LITTLE JOKE
Mutoscope & Biograph
Horace Goldin
TRICK Conjurer demonstrates animated incubator and flighty fowl.

SEP

00572
THE PROFESSOR AND THE BUTTERFLY (100)
Gaumont
D: (Alf Collins)
COMEDY Naturalist chases butterfly and falls into lake.

00573
THE PIE-EATING COMPETITION (90)
Gaumont
COMEDY Two boys in white flannels eat blackcurrant pies for market quack's medal.

00574
THE TRAMP'S SURPRISE (100)
Gaumont
D: (Alf Collins)
COMEDY Man dresses as sweetheart to foil flirtatious tramp.

00575
THE DEAD CAT (40)
Gaumont
D: (Alf Collins)
COMEDY Dude frightens girl with dead cat.

00576
ABSENT WITHOUT LEAVE (145)
Gaumont
DRAMA (5 scenes) Plymouth. Sailors enter cottage; handcuff deserter; wife pleads to court martial; acquitted man walks home; reunion with wife.

00577
LITTLE JIM; OR, THE COTTAGE WAS A THATCHED ONE (170)
Harrison
D: SC: Dicky Winslow
S: (SONG)
PATHOS (2 scenes) Angel wafts spirit of collier's child to heaven. (Shown while song is sung.)

00578
FIGHT WITH SLEDGEHAMMERS (135)
Harrison
D: SC: Dicky Winslow
S: (SKETCH) Wilson Barrett (THE SLEDGEHAMMER)
A.W. Fitzgerald .... Blacksmith
Mrs Fitzgerald .... Girl
DRAMA Rival blacksmiths fight for girl.

00579
EAST LYNNE (500)
Harrison
D: SC: Dicky Winslow
S: *(SKETCH) (NOVEL)* Mrs Henry Wood
A.W. Fitzgerald.......Levison
Mrs Fitzgerald.........Lady Isobel
DRAMA (5 scenes) Elopement; Abandoned; Home Again; Little Willie; Death of Lady Isobel.

00580
THE MANIAC'S GUILLOTINE (125)
Haggar & Sons (WTC)
D: William Haggar
S: (PLAY)
CRIME Scene from play.

00581
DUEL SCENE FROM 'THE TWO ORPHANS' (100)
Haggar & Sons (WTC)
D: William Haggar
S: (PLAY) Adolphe Dennery
DRAMA Paris, period. Knife duel between cripple and Marquis.

00582
THE WILD MAN OF BORNEO (150)
Haggar & Sons (WTC)
D: William Haggar
S: (PLAY)
DRAMA Fight between Knight and forest hermit.

00583
TRUE AS STEEL (150)
Haggar & Sons (WTC)
D: William Haggar
S: (PLAY)
DRAMA 'Scenes from drama of the same title'.

OCT
00584
TOO LAZY TO WORK, TO HONEST TO STEAL (75)
Warwick Trading Co
COMEDY

00585
BREAKING UP THE HAPPY HOME (75)
Warwick Trading Co
COMEDY

00586
THE WEARY WILLIES AND THE POLICEMAN (100)
Warwick Trading Co
COMEDY Tramps trick policeman.

00587
MIDNIGHT INTERRUPTIONS (100)
Warwick Trading Co
COMEDY

00588
THE DEVIL OF THE DEEP AND THE SEA
URCHINS (50)
Warwick Trading Co
COMEDY

00589
THE CYCLIST'S MISHAP; OR, THE OLD
MAID'S REVENGE (75)
Warwick Trading Co
COMEDY

00590
THE LOST HAT AND THE PRICE OF ITS
RECOVERY (100)
Warwick Trading Co
COMEDY

00591
A PICNIC INTERRUPTED BY TRAMPS (100)
Warwick Trading Co
COMEDY Tramps.

00592
THE TRAMP'S UNEXPECTED BATH (50)
Warwick Trading Co
COMEDY Tramp.

00593
MR AND MRS HONEYSUCKLE AND THE
BEE (100)
Warwick Trading Co
COMEDY Kissing couple disturbed by bee.

00594
HOOLIGAN'S ATTACK ON THE HIGHWAY
(60)
Warwick Trading Co
COMEDY

00595
WEARY WILLIE AND HIS PAL ON THE
RAMPAGE (100)
COMEDY Two tramps steal things.

00596
EXCHANGE IS NO ROBBERY (100) also:
UNFAIR EXCHANGE IS ROBBERY
Warwick Trading Co
COMEDY

00597
COOL PROCEEDINGS (108)
Mitchell & Kenyon
COMEDY 'Very funny'.

00598
A SLIPPERY JOB (90)
Mitchell & Kenyon
COMEDY 'Good comic'.

00599
WHO STOLE THE BIKE? (151)
Mitchell & Kenyon
COMEDY 'Very laughable'.

00600
THE RIVAL SNOW SHOVELLERS (85)
Mitchell & Kenyon
COMEDY 'Most amusing'.

00601
NO BATHING ALLOWED (129)
Mitchell & Kenyon
COMEDY

00602
MARIA MARTIN; OR, THE MURDER AT THE
RED BARN (400)
Harrison
D: SC: Dicky Winslow

S: (PLAY) Unknown
A.W. Fitzgerald.......William Corder
Mrs Fitzgerald.........Maria Martin
CRIME (5 scenes) 1826. Maria's disguise; The
murder; The dream; The arrest; The condemned
cell.

NOV

00603
THE CORSICAN BROTHERS (300)
Harrison
D: SC: Dicky Winslow
S: *(PLAY) (NOVEL)* Alexandre Dumas
A.W. Fitzgerald.....Fabian & Louis de Franchi
DRAMA Period. Twin dies after his brother
dies in duel.

00604
A POLICEMAN'S DREAM (110)
Gaumont
D (Alf Collins)
COMEDY (3 scenes) PC dreams he flirts with
cook and maid and is awakened by fall of
snow.

00605
TRAINED DOGS (275)
Gaumont
D: (Alf Collins)
Miss Dundee
ACT Girl trainer's dogs perform funeral
and school lesson.

00606
SERPENTINE DANCER (82)
Gaumont
D: (Alf Collins)
Lina Eshrard
ACT Dancer.

00607
BOUDOIR SECRETS (82)
Gaumont
D: (Alf Collins)
COMEDY Girl at dressing table takes off wig
and removes false teeth

00608
A RESOURCEFUL DENTIST (82)
Gaumont
D. (Alf Collins)
COMEDY Dentist uses dog and weight to
extract stubborn tooth.

00609
AMERICAN KNOCKABOUTS (165)
Gaumont
D: (Alf Collins)
ACT Contortionists dressed as tramp and frog.

00610
BAKER AND BOY (170)
Gaumont
D: (Alf Collins)
COMEDY Boy hides in sack of flour and baker
sits on him.

00611
CLOWN, PANTALOON AND BOBBY (190)
Gaumont
D: (Alf Collins)
Lancy & Adams
COMEDY (2 scenes) Christmas harlequinade;
chase at grocer's; slapstick at barber's.

00612
FIGHTING HIS BATTLES OVER AGAIN
(145)
Williamson (Gau)
D: James Williamson

DRAMA Old pensioner describes war exploits
to cronies in pub.

00613
FATHER THAMES' TEMPERANCE CURE
(85)
R.W. Paul
D: W.R. Booth
TRICK Father Thames rises from river to
frighten drunkard.

00614
SOAP VERSUS BLACKING (110)
R.W. Paul
D: (W.R. Booth)
TRICK Drunkard changes friend's soap for
shoe blacking; then film reverses.

00615
AFTER DARK; OR, THE POLICEMAN AND
HIS LANTERN (225)
G.A.S. Films (WTC)
D: G.A. Smith
Tom Green
COMEDY (15 scenes) PC's lantern illumines
scenes of waif, drunkard, burglar, cook, beggar,
pie, etc.

00616
MOTHER GOOSE NURSERY RHYMES (600)
G.A.S. Films (WTC)
D: G.A. Smith
Tom Green
COMEDY (8 scenes) Sing a song of sixpence;
Old Mother Hubbard; Little Miss Muffet;
Goosey Gander; Jack and Jill; Old Woman in
a Shoe; Hey Diddle Diddle.

DEC

00617
THE EXTRAORDINARY WAITER (108)
also: THE MYSTERIOUS HEADS
R.W. Paul
D: (W.R. Booth)
TRICK Swiss tourist knocks head off negro
waiter.

00618
AN AMATEUR BILL SYKES (88)
Williamson (Gau)
D: James Williamson
'Mr D —'
COMEDY Bearded burglar comes towards
camera and doffs beard.

00619
THE LITTLE MATCH SELLER (210)
Williamson (Gau)
D: James Williamson
S: (STORY) Hans Andersen
PATHOS Waif strikes matches for warmth
until angel takes her spirit.

00620
A RESERVIST BEFORE AND AFTER THE
WAR (290)
Williamson (Gau)
D: James Williamson
PATHOS Ex-soldier arrested for stealing bread
but released when starving child begs mercy.

00621
THE AMAZONS' MARCH AND EVOLUTIONS
(75)
G.A.S. Films (WTC)
D: G.A. Smith
COMEDY Dance scene from pantomime
'Robinson Crusoe'.

00622
PANTOMIME GIRLS HAVING A LARK (50)
G.A.S. Films (WTC)
D: G.A. Smith
COMEDY Ballet girls and comedian leave
yacht in 'Robinson Crusoe'

00623
HILARITY ON BOARD SHIP (125)
G.A.S. Films (WTC)
D: G.A. Smith
COMEDY Mother Hubbard dances hoedown
and mutineers dance hornpipe in scene from
'Robinson Crusoe'.

00624
A FATHER'S VENGEANCE
New Century Pictures
DRAMA Coleshill. Squire strangles girl and
throws her in river and is shot by her father.
(Date uncertain.)

1903

JAN

00625
THE WASHERWOMAN, THE TRAMP AND
THE BIKE (125)
Warwick Trading Co
COMEDY 'very funny'.

00626
A STUDY IN FEET (100)
Warwick Trading Co
COMEDY Various feet pass area window.

00627
THE SQUIRE AND THE MAID (200)
Warwick Trading Co
ROMANCE (2 scenes) Proposal and rejection;
reconciliation.

00628
THE GREAT CITY FIRE (475)
USA: THE LIFE OF AN ENGLISH FIREMAN
Warwick Trading Co
DRAMA Firemen awakened by alarm, drive
through London and rescue fire victims.

00629
THE LADY THIEF AND THE BAFFLED
BOBBIES (200)
Hepworth
D: (Percy Stow)
COMEDY (3 scenes) Police chase woman
thief onto train, she removes skirt and escapes
as a man.

00630
GETTING UP MADE EASY (100)
Hepworth
D: (Percy Stow)
TRICK Man dresses without touching his
clothes.

FEB

00631
MARY JANE'S MISHAP; OR, DON'T FOOL
WITH THE PARAFFIN (250)
G A.S. Films (WTC)
D: G.A. Smith
TRICK Maid pours paraffin on fire and is
blown to pieces up chimney. (Cut in closeup.)

00632
NADJI THE HINDOO MARVEL (120)
R.W. Paul
ACT Princess walks on hands and revolves
in air from mouth-strap.

00633
WEARY WILLIE'S WILES (200)
R.W. Paul
COMEDY (2 scenes) Tramp locks PC in
larder and hides inside scarecrow.

00634
THE OLD LOVE AND THE NEW (100)
R.W. Paul
DRAMA Sailor promises to wed sweetheart;
later she appears at his wedding with baby.

MAR

00635
DAVID DEVANT, CONJURER
Mutoscope & Biograph
David Devant
TRICK Conjurer performs The Incubated
Head and The Fairy Dancer.

00636
POCKET BOXERS (80)
R.W. Paul

D: W.R. Booth
TRICK Sportsmen produce midget boxers
from pockets and wager on their fight.

00637
BLIND MAN'S BLUFF (80)
Alpha Trading Co (Paul)
D: Arthur Cooper
COMEDY Blind beggar sees coin false and
hits donor with wooden leg.

00638
THE DICE PLAYER'S LAST THROW (160)
R.W. Paul
D: W.R. Booth
TRICK Gambler loses, throws whiskey in fire,
sees cards become imps, and stabs himself.

00639
BILL SYKES UP TO DATE (100)
Alpha Trading Co (Paul)
D: Arthur Cooper
COMEDY Burglar traps PC in window sash,
and is chased.

00640
THE WASHERWOMEN AND THE SWEEP
(80)
R.W. Paul
TRICK Flirty sweep spoils maids' clothes;
they scrub and mangle him flat.

APR

00641
WEARY WILLIE AND TIRED TIM — THE
GUNPOWDER PLOT (125)
Warwick Trading Co
(Haggar?)
S: (CARTOON) Tom Browne
COMEDY Tramps stick hot poker in barrel
labelled beer but containing gunpowder.

00642
BURLESQUE NAVAL GUN DRILL (60)
Warwick Trading Co
Crew of HMS Excellent
COMEDY 'An amusing parody'.

00643
A DARING DAYLIGHT BURGLARY (275)
Sheffield Photo Co reissue: 1910 (Walt)
D: Frank Mottershaw
Sheffield Fire Brigade
CHASE (9 scenes) Burglar throws PC off roof,
is chased across country, river and cliffs to
train; police wire ahead and catch him at next
station

00644
THE MARVELLOUS SYRINGE (65)
Gaumont
D: (Alf Collins)
TRICK Boy squirts mud on couple's clothing,
and film reverses

00645
THE EFFECTS OF TOO MUCH SCOTCH (160)
Gaumont
D: (Alf Collins)
TRICK Drunken Scot undresses and his clothes
come alive.

00646
A PHOTOGRAPHIC EPISODE (65)
Gaumont
D: (Alf Collins)
TRICK Camera shoots inquisitive spinster
into wall.

00647
PAPA'S BATH (125)
Gaumont
D: (Alf Collins)
TRICK Drunk undresses and clothes reappear
on body, and he upsets bathtub.

00648
KING OF COINS (75)
Gaumont
D: (Alf Collins)
TRICK Conjurer's hand makes coins appear
from air.

MAY

00649
SPRING CLEANING (210)
Williamson
D: James Williamson
James Williamson....Father
COMEDY (5 scenes) Father has trouble with
whitewash and wallpaper.

00650
THE ABSENT-MINDED BOOTBLACK (50)
Hepworth
D: Cecil Hepworth
COMEDY Bootblack absorbed in client's
paper blackens white trousers.

00651
ALICE IN WONDERLAND (800)
Hepworth
D: Cecil Hepworth, Percy Stow
S: (NOVEL) Lewis Carroll
SC: Cecil Hepworth
May Clark.........................Alice
Cecil Hepworth.................Frog
Mrs Hepworth...................White Rabbit/Queen
Norman Whitten........... ...Fish/Mad Hatter
Stanley Faithfull...............Card
Geoffrey Faithfull.............Card
FANTASY (16 scenes) Period. Girl follows
rabbit down hole and has adventures in strange
world. (Extracts released as separate films.)

00652
ONLY A FACE AT THE WINDOW (50)
Hepworth
D: Percy Stow
May Clark
COMEDY Window cleaner kisses girl and
washes father's face.

JUN

00653
WELSHED — A DERBY DAY INCIDENT (195)
Gaumont
D: Alf Collins
Alf Collins
A.C. Bromhead
COMEDY The Derby is run and welshing
bookmaker is chased by angry crowd.

00654
MIND THE WET PAINT (100)
Gaumont
D: (Alf Collins)
COMEDY Boy hides sign so that courting
couple stick to newly-painted bench.

00655
THE SERVIAN TRAGEDY (54)
Gaumont
D: Dicky Winslow
HISTORY Representation of regicide at
Belgrade.

00656
THE ASSASSINATION OF THE KING AND
QUEEN OF SERVIA (110)
Harrison
D:(Dicky Winslow)
HISTORY (3 scenes) Attack on palace; murders;
throwing out the bodies.

00657
MIRTHFUL MARY, A CASE FOR THE
BLACK LIST (120)
Haggar & Sons (Gaumont)
D: William Haggar
Mog.....Mary
COMEDY Fat woman refused further drink
and fights with policemen.

00658
QUARRELSOME NEIGHBOURS (125)
Williamson
D: James Williamson
COMEDY Neighbours fight over fence with
black and white paint.

00659
REMORSE (450)
Williamson
D: James Williamson
S: (PLAY) D. Philippe
D. Philippe.....Blackmailer
CRIME (5 scenes) Killer plants knife on drunk,
is blackmailed, and confesses in court after
vision of injustice.

00660
BLOODHOUNDS TRACKING A CONVICT
(340) USA: TRAILED BY BLOODHOUNDS
R.W. Paul
CHASE (3 scenes) Convict escapes from
Portland Quarry and is caught in the woods by
bloodhounds from Radnage kennels. (Includes
extract from 'A Convict's Daring'.)

JUL

00661
A TRIP TO SOUTHEND OR BLACKPOOL
(168)
Williamson
D James Williamson
COMEDY Discomforts of crowded railway
compartment.

00662
THE WRONG POISON (160)
Williamson
D: James Williamson
FACAIL Suicide finds bottle labelled poison
contains gin, so he gets drunk instead.

00663
THE REVOLVING TABLE (100)
Hepworth
D: (Percy Stow)
COMEDY Diner revolves table and eats
neighbour's lunch.

00664
WEARY WILLIE AND TIRED TIM TURN
BARBERS (118)
Haggar & Sons (Gau)
D: William Haggar
S: (CARTOON) Tom Browne
James Haggar.... ......Weary Willie
Walter Haggar........Tired Tim
COMEDY Tramps take over shop of absent
barber.

00665
THE RIVALS (70)
Gaumont

D: (Alf Collins)
COMEDY Two women fight over man, tear
clothes off policeman and are arrested.

00666
THE OCTAROON (300)
Gaumont
D: (Dicky Winslow)
S: (PLAY) Dion Boucicault
CRIME America. Man kills boy for mailbag,
and is killed by Indian.

00667
A LOVER'S TROUBLES (92)
Gaumont
D: (Alf Collins)
COMEDY Girl's suitor spanks pea-shooting
boy, and is thrashed by his mother.

00668
NOTICE TO QUIT (135)
Gaumont
D: (Alf Collins)
COMEDY Three men receive landlord's bill,
wreck room, and fall through floor.

00669
THE MYSTERIOUS MECHANICAL TOY(120)
also: PHROSO THE MYSTERIOUS
MECHANICAL DOLL
Gaumont
D: (Alf Collins)
M. Trevallion.....Phroso
Mr. Webster.......Manager
Alf Collins.........Man from Audience
COMEDY Tivoli manager demonstrates
'mechanical man' who causes trouble for
audience.

00670
LITTLE NELL AND BURGLAR BILL (165)
Gaumont
D: Alf Collins
Alf Collins.....Bill
CRIME Burglar reforms when child mistakes
him for Santa Claus.

00671
MOSES IN THE BULLRUSHES (120)
Gaumont
RELIGION Egypt. Pharaoh's daughter finds
baby by river bank.

00672
THE GOOD SAMARITAN (190)
Gaumont
RELIGION (2 scenes) Traveller attacked by
thieves is helped by Samaritan.

00673
RIP VAN WINKLE (450)
Gaumont
D: Alf Collins
S: (STORY) Washington Irving
Alf Collins
William Carrington
FANTASY (5 scenes) Katskills. Ejected henpeck
returns home after twenty years' sleep.

00674
OUR NEW COOK (110)
Gaumont
D: (Alf Collins)
TRICK Scolded cook smashes dishes then
the film reverses.

00675
A ROW IN A LAUNDRY (85)
Gaumont
D: (Alf Collins)
COMEDY Policeman tries to stop washer-
women from fighting in laundry

00676
A PLEASANT BREAKFAST (72)
Gaumont
D: (Alf Collins)
COMEDY Husband and wife fight with bad
eggs coffee, etc.

00677
DESPERATE POACHING AFFRAY (220)
Haggar & Sons (Gau)
D: William Haggar
CHASE Police chase poachers and catch them
after gun battle in river.

00678
THE HARTLEY WONDERS (100)
Urban Trading Co
ACT Blindfold acrobats jump over water,
horse, and 16 chairs.

00679
THE MARVELLOUS HARTLEY BARREL
JUMPERS (75)
Urban Trading Co
ACT Blindfold acrobats with shackled feet
jump over barrels.

00680
SENORITA FILLIS, QUEEN OF THE
REVOLVING GLOBE (100)
Urban Trading Co
ACT

00681
LATELLES — AERIAL HIGH ROPE
CYCLISTS (100)
Urban Trading Co
ACT

00682
A GAME·OF LIVING WHIST (175)
Urban Trading Co
ACT 52 dancers dressed as playing cards.

AUG

00683
TWO PRETTY DANCES (110)
R W. Paul
Mlle Kaufmann
ACT Serpentine dance; Step dance.

00684
THE SWELL'S INTERRUPTED NAP (60)
R.W. Paul
COMEDY Boys cause fight between tramp and
toff.

00685
A CHESS DISPUTE (80)
R.W. Paul
COMEDY Chess players fight below screen,
throwing up pieces of body.

00686
HIGH DIVING AT HIGHGATE (60)
R.W. Paul
TRICK Swimmers dive into water; then film
reverses.

00687
THE WRONG CHIMNEY (150)
Williamson
D: James Williamson
COMEDY Men mistakenly put salt and water
down neighbours chimney.

00688
NO BATHING ALLOWED (140)
Williamson
D: James Williamson
Charles Cobbold.....Swimmer
COMEDY Undressed swimmer poses as
statue to fool old lady.

00689
THE NEGLECTED LOVER AND THE
STILE (75)
Hepworth
D: (Percy Stow)
May Clark..................Girl
Norman Whitten.........Boy
COMEDY Rival saws through stile so that
courting couple fall.

00690
THE ADVENTURES OF A BILL POSTER
(125)
Hepworth
D: (Percy Stow)
COMEDY Bill poster drops paste on
pedestrian, causing fight.

00691
THE KNOCKER AND THE NAUGHTY
BOYS (50)
Hepworth
D: (Percy Stow)
May Clark.....Maid
COMEDY Boys knock on door and hide so
maid throws water on mistress.

00692
FUN AT THE BARBER'S (75)
Hepworth
D: (Percy Stow)
COMEDY Barber uses paste instead of soap to
shave policeman.

SEP

00693
THE TRAGICAL TALE OF A BELATED
LETTER (200)
Hepworth
D: (Percy Stow)
Cecil Hepworth..........Husband
Mrs Hepworth...........Wife
DRAMA Wife brings belated remittance letter
in time to stop husband from drowning himself.

00694
A FREE RIDE (50)
Hepworth
D: Percy Stow
COMEDY Boys ride on water cart and get
soaked.

00695
THE UNCLEAN WORLD: THE SUBURBAN
-BUNKUM MICROBE-GUYOSCOPE (100)
Hepworth
D: Percy Stow
Cecil Hepworth..........Professor
COMEDY Professor looks through microscope
and sees clockwork fly, etc. (Burlesque of 'The
Unseen World: The Urban-Duncan Micro-
Bioscope'.)

00696
WAIT TILL JACK COMES HOME (430)
Williamson
D: James Williamson
DRAMA (7 scenes) Builder breaks leg and is
saved from eviction by return of sailor son.

00697
WEARY WILLIE AND TIRED TIM.— A DEAD
SHOT (150)
Warwick Trading Co
(Haggar?)
S: (CARTOON) Tom Browne
COMEDY 'A continuous farce from end to
end'.

00698
THE ANIMATED STATUE (200)
Warwick Trading Co
COMEDY Man poses as statue to fool life-
guard, baker, PC, and courters.

00699
HOME FROM THE CLUB (100)
Warwick Trading Co
COMEDY Drunkard returns home late and
dodges wife's missiles.

00700
THE CURATE'S ADVENTURE (75)
Warwick Trading Co
COMEDY Tramp robs curate and is himself
robbed.

00701
ROBBERY OF THE MAIL COACH (375)
also: A COACH HOLDUP IN DICK TURPIN'S
DAYS USA: JACK SHEPPARD
Sheffield Photo Co
D: Frank Mottershaw
CHASE (9 scenes) 1800. King's men chase two
highwaymen through inn, river, over wall,
through barn, into woods, and shoot them
down from treetop.

00702
DAVID DEVANT'S LAUGHABLE HAND
SHADOWS
Mutoscope & Biograph
David Devant
ACT Conjurer makes comic shadows with hands.

00703
INDIANS GAMBLING FOR FURS — IS IT
WAR OR PEACE? (60)
Urban Trading Co
D: Joe Rosenthal
DRAMA Canada. Indian cheats another of
furs; angry Indian smokes peace-pipe.

00704
HIAWATHA (800)
Urban Trading Co
D: Joe Rosenthal
S: (POEM) Henry Wadsworth Longfellow (THE
SONG OF HIAWATHA)
Ojibway Tribe
DRAMA Ontario. The birth, life, marriage and
death of Hiawatha. (20 scenes; made in Canada.)

00705
CHEESE MITES (150)
Urban Trading Co — Micro Bioscope
D: F. Martin Duncan
COMEDY Diner examines cheese through
magnifying glass and sees mites magnified
'30 diameters'.

OCT

00706
THE DESERTER (520)
Williamson
D: James Williamson
DRAMA (8 scenes) CO pardons private on
learning he deserted to see dying father.

00707
A SUBSTANTIAL GHOST (90)
Gaumont
D: (Alf Collins)
COMEDY PC poses as ghost to scare tramps
playing cards in cemetary.

00708
THE INSPECTOR'S BIRTHDAY (92)
Gaumont
D: (Alf Collins)
COMEDY Police present inspector with
birthday hamper containing children.

00709
THAT NAUGHTY GIRL (92)
Gaumont
D: (Alf Collins)
COMEDY Girl causes fight by putting
drawing pin on chair.

00710
THE DOUBLE-BEDDED ROOM (165)
Gaumont
D: (Alf Collins)
COMEDY Old spinster and man are let same
bedroom in inn; a struggle ensues.

00711
TOMMY ATKINS' DREAM (82)
Gaumont
D: (Alf Collins)
COMEDY Soldier dreams he flirts with
nursemaid.

00712
TWO LITTLE VAGABONDS; OR, THE
PUGILISTIC PARSON (84)
Gaumont
D: (Alf Collins)
Alf Collins..............................Parson
William Carrington.................Boy
DRAMA Gypsy whips boy for breaking jug
and is whipped by curate.

00713
MURPHY'S WAKE (190)
Gaumont
D: Alf Collins
S: (PLAY) Dion Bouicault (THE SHAUGRAUN)
Alf Collins
COMEDY Irishman pretends to die in fight and
revives at wake.

00714
THE CONVICT'S ESCAPE FROM PRISON
(206)
Sheffield Photo Co
D: Frank Mottershaw
CHASE Police chase convict in woman's garb,
fight in river, and throw him off cliff.

NOV

00715
A TRAGIC ELOPEMENT; OR, HER TERRIBLE
MISTAKE (320)
Mitchell & Kenyon
DRAMA (6 scenes) Mother lured from children;
flight in motor; husband chases on motor cycle;
pursuit, motor wins; motor explodes and wife
dies saving husband from bullet.

00716
THE ADVENTUROUS VOYAGE OF 'THE
ARCTIC' (600)
R.W. Paul
D: W.R Booth
Fred Farren............Captain Kettle
FANTASY (12 scenes) Cabin; deck; icebound;
icefield; baffled; Jack Frost; foot of pole;
compass; cave; foot of pole; top of pole.

00717
THE KIDDIES' CAKEWALK (62)
R.W. Paul
ACT Children aged four dance "Cakewalk".

00718
AN EXTRAORDINARY CAB ACCIDENT (50)
R.W. Paul
D: (W.R. Booth)
TRICK Horsedrawn four-wheeler runs over
man, who then revives.

00719
DIAVOLO'S DILEMMA (100)
R.W. Paul
Lilo, Lotto & Otto
ACT Bicyclist pedals on raised feet of partner.

00720
MARIONETTE PERFORMANCE (215)
R.W. Paul
ACT (3 scenes) Skeleton; chair; harlequinade.

00721
NIGGER COURTSHIP (80)
R.W. Paul
FACIAL Negro couple spoon and kiss.

00722
THE FINE FISHERMAN (60)
R.W. Paul
COMEDY Dude catches minnow, tramp
catches pike.

00723
A GOOD CATCH (60)
R.W. Paul
COMEDY Two tramps steal dude angler's
salmon.

00724
A PUNCH AND JUDY SHOW (150)
Warwick Trading Co
COMEDY Complete puppet performance.

00725
PUTTING HIM ON THE BLACK LIST (200)
Warwick Trading Co
COMEDY Prisoner objects to court photographer
and starts fight in dock.

00726
LETTIE LIMELIGHT IN HER LAIR (200)
G.A.S. Films (Urban)
D: G.A. Smith
COMEDY Pretty dancer enters dressing
room and takes off make-up and wig

00727
JOHN BULL'S HEARTH (185) also: JOHN
BULL'S FIRESIDE
G.A.S. Films (Urban)
D: G.A. Smith
DRAMA Symbolic scene of Britain crowded
out by foreign traders.

00728
THE FREE TRADE BENCH (50)
G.A.S. Films (Urban)
D: G.A. Smith
DRAMA 'The large and small loaf of Mr
Chamberlain's opponents.'

00729
THE BABY AND THE APE (150)
G.A.S. Films (Urban)
D: G.A. Smith
COMEDY Escaped monkey drinks baby's
bottle.

00730
WILL THE EXPRESS OVERTAKE THEM?
(75)
Urban Trading Co
D: Joe Rosenthal
CHASE Canada. Trackmen on hand trolley
escape from express train.

00731
FIREMEN TO THE RESCUE (321)
Hepworth
D: Cecil Hepworth
DRAMA (6 scenes) Child knocks clothes into
fire; alarm at station; engines emerge; engines
rush down street; arrival; fireman breaks through
wall and saves child.

00732
THE UNEXPECTED BATH (150)
Hepworth
D: Cecil Hepworth
COMEDY Lodger sleeps in bath and turns
tap on with foot.

00733
A POLITICAL DISCUSSION (90)
Gaumont
D: (Alf Collins)
COMEDY Two men and fight; tramps steal
their coats.

00734
DOTHEBOYS HALL; OR, NICHOLAS
NICKLEBY (225)
Gaumont
D: Alf Collins
S: (NOVEL) Charles Dickens (NICHOLAS
NICKLEBY)
William Carrington..........Pupil
COMEDY Period. Ignorant teacher beats pupil
and is caned by new assistant.

00735
THE SPORTIVE NAVVIES (100)
Gaumont
D: (Alf Collins)
COMEDY Workmen watch boys fighting;
join in, and fight with policemen.

00736
THE CHRISTMAS WAITS; OR, HIGH LIFE
BELOW STAIRS (186)
Gaumont
D: (Alf Collins)
COMEDY (2 scenes) Gouty man and servants
dance to waits' music.

00737
SUCH IS LIFE; OR, MIND YOUR OWN
BUSINESS (70)
Gaumont
D: (Alf Collins)
COMEDY Drunkard fights wife outside pub,
they both fight interfering passerby, who gets
arrested.

00738
THE SOMNAMBULIST (165) also: THE
SLEEPWALKER
Gaumont
D: (Alf Collins)
DRAMA (4 scenes) Sleeping girl walks onto
roof and falls to street.

00739
THE PICKPOCKET — A CHASE THROUGH
LONDON (300)
Gaumont
D: Alf Collins
CHASE (7 scenes) Piccadilly; escape by cycle;
struggle; through door; out back; chase; fight
in woodyard.

00740
THE RUNAWAY MATCH (290)
Gaumont
D: Alf Collins
CHASE (5 scenes) Mansion; father's car seen
from lover's car; vice versa; church; ring; father
arrives too late.

00741
THE TRAMP AND THE WASHERWOMAN
(100)
Haggar & Sons (Gaumont)
D: William Haggar
COMEDY Tramp steals clothes from washer-
woman and flees on bicycle.

00742
THE TRAMP AND THE BABY'S BOTTLE
(100)
Haggar & Sons (Gaumont)
D: William Haggar
COMEDY Tramp steals milk from baby in
park and is caught by soldier.

00743
A DASH FOR LIBERTY; OR, THE CONVICT'S
ESCAPE AND CAPTURE (300)
Haggar & Sons (Urban)
D: William Haggar
CHASE (5 scenes) Convict escapes from quarry,
steals cart, is wounded by warders and captured
after fight.

00744
AN EVIL-DOER'S SAD END (125)
Williamson
D: James Williamson
TRICK PC tears tramp to pieces and dustman
carts them away.

DEC

00745
THE DEAR BOYS HOME FOR THE
HOLIDAYS (290) also: BOYS WILL BE
BOYS
Williamson
D: James Williamson
James Williamson...............Father
Tom Williamson................Boy
Stuart Williamson..............Boy
COMEDY Boys play jokes on family and
are punished.

00746
JUGGIN'S MOTOR (125)
Williamson
D: James Williamson
COMEDY 'Why he now offers it for sale
cheap.'

00747
DIVING LUCY (100)
Mitchell & Kenyon
COMEDY (Animated title) Girl dives, gets
stuck in mud, and is saved by tramps.

00748
DOROTHY'S DREAM (600)
G.A.S. Films (Urban)
D: G.A. Smith
FANTASY (8 scenes) Girl dreams of Dick
Whittington, Robinson Crusoe, Forty Thieves,
Aladdin, Cinderella, Bluebeard and Red
Riding Hood.

00749
SATURDAY SHOPPING (150) USA:
SATURDAY'S SHOPPING
Hepworth
D: Cecil Hepworth
COMEDY Henpeck gets drunk while wife
does shopping.

00750
STOP THAT BUS! (175) USA: HOW THE
OLD WOMAN CAUGHT THE OMNIBUS
Hepworth
D: Percy Stow
TRICK Old woman trying to catch bus is run
over and pulls it backwards with umbrella.

00751
THE ALIEN CHICKEN AND THE SURREY
FOWL (75)
Warwick Trading Co
COMEDY Father tries to carve tough chicken;
it falls to floor, and dog spurns it.

00752
CAR RIDE
Alpha Trading Co
D: Arthur Cooper
TRICK Speeded car ride from St Albans to
London Colney ending in crash. (Date
uncertain.)

1904

JAN

00753
POLITICAL FAVOURITES (150)
R.W. Paul *Reissue:* 1906
ACT Cartoonist draws Chamberlain, Campbell-Bannerman, Lord Rosebery, etc.

00754
NO ROOM FOR FATHER (112)
Gaumont
D: (Alf Collins)
COMEDY Fat man tries to get into bed with six adult sons.

00755
THAT BUSY BEE (70)
Gaumont
D: Alf Collins
FACIAL Bee annoys man, who catches it in mouth and eats it.

00756
THE SILVER TENOR; OR, THE SONG THAT FAILED (104)
Gaumont
D: Alf Collins
COMEDY Theatre audience throws things at singer.

00757
FATHER'S BIRTHDAY PARTY (115)
Gaumont
D: (Alf Collins)
COMEDY Goose is too tough to carve and smashes table.

FEB

00758
MAN THE LIFEBOAT (750)
Gaumont
D: (Harold Hough)
DRAMA (8 scenes) Worthing. Lookout; lifeboat house; launching; floating body; in the rigging; return; resuscitation; death.

00759
WEARY WILLIE IN SEARCH OF HIDDEN TREASURE (280)
Mitchell & Kenyon
D: (CARTOON) Tom Browne
COMEDY (6 scenes) Tramps watch woman burying something, dig it up, and find it is a dead cat.

00760
THE SMUGGLERS (500)
Warwick Trading Co
D: (Will Barker)
CRIME (11 scenes) Cornwall. Look-out spots smugglers and fetches coastguard to their hide-out where fight ensues.

00761
LITTLE WILLIE AND THE APPLE (115)
Urban Trading Co
COMEDY Burlesque on 'William Tell'.

00762
AN UP-TO-DATE STUDIO (125)
Hepworth
D: Percy Stow
TRICK Operator takes scene of photographer flirting with dancer.

00763
THE ADVENTURES OF A WINDOW CLEANER (280)
R. W. Paul
COMEDY (6 scenes) Starting out; flower girls; villa; office; restaurant; the way home.

00764
AN ARTFUL YOUNG TRUANT (50)
R.W. Paul
COMEDY Boy hides in water butt from mother.

00765
AN AFFAIR OF OUTPOSTS (300)
R.W. Paul
WAR (4 scenes) Japanese soldiers ambush Russian sergeant, find plan of camp, and attack with success.

00766
A DASH WITH THE DESPATCHES (100)
Sheffield Photo Co
D: Frank Mottershaw
WAR Cossacks ambush Japanese despatch bearer but he escapes after fight.

00767
ATTACK ON A JAPANESE CONVOY (250)
Sheffield Photo Co
D: Frank Mottershaw
WAR Russians ambush Japanese convoy by but are defeated.

MAR

00768
JAP VERSUS RUSSIAN (100)
R.W. Paul
WAR Symbolic wrestling match.

00769
ALL FOR THE LOVE OF A GEISHA (540)
R.W. Paul
WAR (7 scenes) British naval officer helps Japanese soldiers save girl from burning hut.

00770
ATTACK ON A RUSSIAN OUTPOST (205)
Gaumont
WAR Yalu. Japanese kill Russian sentry, charge outpost and fight Cossacks.

00771
JACK'S RIVAL (250)
Gaumont
D: (Alf Collins)
COMEDY (3 scenes) Farmer's daughter loves sailor and causes trouble for mother's choice of suitor.

00772
THE APPLE WOMAN (120)
Gaumont
D: Alf Collins
William Carrington........Boy
COMEDY (3 scenes) Boys blame PC for stealing apples and he is arrested.

00773
ALL THROUGH THE PAGE BOY (190)
Gaumont
D: (Alf Collins)
COMEDY (2 scenes) Pageboy betrays cook's policeman lover to mistress.

00774
THE JOKE THAT FAILED (100)
Hepworth
D: Percy Stow
Cecil Hepworth..........Dr Jinks
May Clark..................Student
Norman Whitten........Student
COMEDY Boys alter sign, "Dr will receive his classes" by removing the 'c'; then girls remove the 'l'.

00775
TWO LEAP YEAR PROPOSALS (125)
Hepworth

D: Lewin Fitzhamon
Dolly Lupone
COMEDY Girls fight duel for man until bull chases them.

00776
A JOKE ON THE MOTORIST (75)
Warwick Trading Co
COMEDY Man ties yokels barrow to rear of motor car.

00777
EXCEEDING HIS LEGAL SPEED (125)
Warwick Trading Co
COMEDY PC stops motorist who fights him, strips him and drives off.

00778
LOVE'S LABOUR LOST (60)
Warwick Trading Co
COMEDY Dude awakens sleeping tramp and is thrown into pond.

00779
THE SERENADE (100)
Warwick Trading Co
COMEDY Lover climbs ladder to woo girl, and his rival takes it away.

00780
WHITEWASHING THE POLICEMAN (65)
Haggar & Sons (Gau)
D: William Haggar
COMEDY (2 scenes) Boys cause fight between tramp and gentleman in park.

00781
LURED FROM HOME (340)
Mutoscope & Biograph (Gau)
DRAMA (7 scenes) Farmer's daughter elopes with artist; he shoots gambler and she crawls home with baby.

00782
UP TO HIS TRICKS (185)
Mutoscope & Biograph (Gau)
John Warren
TRICK Conjuror plays tricks on friend.

00783
DAISY'S ADVENTURES IN THE LAND OF THE CHRYSANTHEMUMS (265)
Mutoscope & Biograph (Gau)
FANTASY Fairy takes girl to lands of flowers and distortion.

APR

00784
THE TRAMP'S DUCK HUNT (155)
Sheffield Photo Co
D: Frank Mottershaw
CHASE Two tramps chase duck and fall into river.

00785 •
BOYS WILL BE BOYS (200)
Sheffield Photo Co
D: Frank Mottershaw
COMEDY (7 scenes) Two town boys in the country play pranks.

00786
THE KIDNAPPED CHILD (300)
Autoscope (WTC)
D: Will Barker
Kenneth Barker........The Child
CRIME (10 scenes) Hag kidnaps rich woman's child and forces him to beg.

00787
THE STOLEN PUPPY (100)
Hepworth
D: Lewin Fitzhamon
COMEDY Boy takes girl's puppy and hides it in man's pocket.

00788
THE COSTER'S WEDDING (275)
Hepworth
D: Lewin Fitzhamon
COMEDY (5 scenes) Leaving church; wedding breakfast; Hampstead picnic; Spaniards' Inn; bridegroom's home.

00789
AFTER THE 'OLIDAY (150)
Hepworth
D: Lewin Fitzhamon
COMEDY Coster couple quarrel and are taken to court.

00790
THE COSTER'S WEDDING (250)
Gaumont
D: Alf Collins
COMEDY (4 scenes) Couple set out from Hoxton, marry at Bethnal Green, get drunk at Hampstead, and return home.

00791
THE PARSON'S COOKERY LESSON (100)
Hepworth
May Clark
COMEDY Girls smother parson with eggs, milk and flour.

00792
THE HAUNTED OAK (75)
Hepworth
D: Lewin Fitzhamon
COMEDY Boy hides in hollow tree to trick PC and girl.

00793
TWO'S COMPANY, THREE'S NONE (100)
Warwick Trading Co
COMEDY Cook's two admirers call on her at same time and fight.

00794
THE LADY TYPIST (125)
Warwick Trading Co
COMEDY Business man kisses typist as wife enters.

00795
A RUSSIAN SURPRISE (96)
R.W. Paul
COMEDY Chinese waiter serves Russian with bomb.

00796
THAT TERRIBLE SNEEZE (75)
R.W. Paul
COMEDY Old man sneezes, blowing up his wife's skirt.

00797
THE CAPTURE AND EXECUTION AS SPIES OF TWO JAPANESE OFFICERS (365)
R.W. Paul
WAR Japanese pose as coolies, blow up train, are caught and shot.

     MAY

00798
THE MUSIC HALL MANAGER'S DILEMMA (260)
R.W. Paul

00799
THE SNAPSHOT FIEND (145)
R.W. Paul
COMEDY Boy photographs lovers, and tries blackmail.

00800
THE CHAPPIE AT THE WELL (120)
R.W. Paul
COMEDY Flirtatious dude hides from yokel and is lowered into well.

00801
THE TALKING HEAD (80)
R.W. Paul
COMEDY Yokel exposes conjuror's talking head as fake.

00802
THE HAUNTED SCENE PAINTER (180)
R.W. Paul
D: (W.R. Booth)
TRICK Theatre properties (dragon, ghost, moon, etc) become animated.

00803
MODERN STAGE DANCES (75;60)
R.W. Paul
Margery Skelly
ACT Cakewalk dance; Acrobatic dance.

00804
CLEVER DANCES (100;50)
R.W. Paul
ACT Cakewalk dance by man in big boots.

00805
DRAT THAT BOY! (90)
R.W. Paul
COMEDY Boy causes his mother to be upset into water tub.

00806
FUNNY FACES (50)
R.W. Paul
FACIAL Man pulls faces.

00807
SMOKED OUT (150)
Warwick Trading Co
COMEDY Farmer drops match and sets fire to yokel hidden in straw.

00808
COURTING AND CAUGHT (180)
Warwick Trading Co
COMEDY (2 scenes) Before and after marriage.

00809
STAGE STRUCK (550)
Warwick Trading Co
DRAMA (9 scenes) Innkeeper's daughter elopes with acrobat who later cuts her tightrope out of jealousy.

00810
A ROUGH TIME FOR THE BROKER (100)
Hepworth
D: Lewin Fitzhamon
COMEDY Soldier returns and ejects bailiff from mother's cottage.

00811
THE GREAT SERVANT QUESTION (300)
Hepworth
D: Lewin Fitzhamon
May Clark....................The Maid

D: (W.R. Booth)
TRICK Unpaid artistes refuse to perform so posters come to life.

Cecil Hepworth............The Master
Mrs Hepworth.............The Mistress
COMEDY (6 scenes) PC helps sacked maid regain property.

00812
THE STORY OF A COLLIERY DISASTER (460)
Gaumont
D: Harold Hough
DRAMA West Bromwich. Miners fight over factory gil and upset lamp which causes the pit explosion.

00813
COOK'S LOVERS (128)
Gaumont
D: (Alf Collins)
COMEDY Cook's mistress lights copper in which PC is hiding, and swoons into chair which is disguised soldier.

00814
MILITARY TACTICS (200)
Gaumont
D: (Alf Collins)
COMEDY Dragoon outwits lieutenant by hiding girl in sentry box.

00815
A SMART CAPTURE (180)
Gaumont
D: (Alf Collins)
COMEDY Fat PC catches burglar in barrel and has him nailed in.

00816
TWO DECEIVED OLD MAIDS (200)
Gaumont[
D: (Alf Collins)
COMEDY Spinsters discover they love the same man, and fight for him.

00817
DR CUT'EMUP (190)
Gaumont
D: (Alf Collins)
TRICK Tramp sells 'dead' friend to doctor, whom they hit over head with mallets until explodes.

00818
THE OFFICE BOY'S REVENGE (165)
Gaumont
D: (Alf Collins)
COMEDY Office boy puts typist's hair on employer's shoulder.

00819
THE EVICTION (225)
Gaumont
D: Alf Collins
S: (SKETCH)
Morney Cash............The Slopper
Percy Heyes.............Corrigan
Arthur Carthy..........Grabbem
Jim McGrath............The Copper
J. Tray....................Pat
W. Frean................Mrs Pat
Bob King................Their Son
COMEDY Irish cottagers fight bailiffs.

00820
THE JEALOUS WIFE (120)
Gaumont
D: (Alf Collins)
COMEDY Wife discovers husband flirting with country maid.

00821
CHASED BY DOGS (84)
Gaumont
D: (Alf Collins)
CHASE Savage dogs chase crippled woman and
she belabours husband.

00822
THE BOMBARDMENT OF PORT ARTHUR
(300)
Gaumont
D: (Harold Hough)
Inventor: Lt L. Morgan
WAR Bradford Exhibition. Reconstruction in
fireworks of attack on Port Arthur on
February 8.

00823
ROBBERY OF A MAIL CONVOY BY
BANDITS (350)
Urban Trading Co
CRIME (10 scenes) Bushrangers rob mail van,
are chased by Colonial troopers, caught, court-
martialled and shot.

00824
DRIVEN FROM HOME (390)
Mitchell & Kenyon
PATHOS (7 scenes) Disowned girl's
husband dies in poverty and her father
repents to save her from eviction.

00825
VENGEANCE IS MINE
Autoscope
D: Will Barker
CRIME (9 scenes)

00826
THE GIDDY GIRL AND THE BUTTERFLY
(90)
Cricks & Sharp
COMEDY Footman tries to catch child's toy
butterfly and hits gouty master.

00827
A NAUGHTY BOY (85)
Cricks & Sharp
COMEDY Frenchman shows children
naughty magazine and is caught by mother.

00828
MRS STIGGINS' WASHING PARTY (85)
Cricks & Sharp
COMEDY Woman steals friend's beer and is
mangled.

00829
CAUGHT IN THE ACT (95)
Cricks & Sharp
COMEDY Man peeps through keyhole and
girl throws water on him.

JUN

00830
JAP THE GIANT KILLER (140)
Cricks & Sharp
TRICK (3 scenes) Japanese soldier dreams he
cuts head off Russian giant and wakes to find
the war is over.

00831
LIVELY LODGINGS (108)
Cricks & Sharp
COMEDY Old gent finds fleas in bed and sets
them afire.

00832
THE DRUNKARD'S HOME (90)
Cricks & Sharp

COMEDY Drunk throws baby through window
and is thrown out by wife.

00833
A DAY IN THE LIFE OF A THAMES
FIREMAN (520)
Cricks & Sharp
DRAMA (6 scenes) Alarm; turnout; rescue;
saving trapped suicide.

00834
THE MONKEY AND THE ICE CREAM (100)
Redfern (Urban)
D: Jasper Redfern
COMEDY Italian vendor's monkey eats girl's
ice cream.

00835
THE SLAVEY'S DREAM (100)
Hepworth
D: Lewin Fitzhamon
May Clark.......................The Slavey
Lewin Fitzhamon............The Villian
COMEDY Maid's dream of hero and villian
fighting.

00836
THE HONEYMOON: FIRST, SECOND AND
THIRD CLASS (125)
Hepworth
D: Lewin Fitzhamon
Cecil Hepworth .... Husband
Mrs Hepworth .... Wife
May Clark .... Wife
Norman Whitten .... Husband
COMEDY Three honeymoon couples in cross-
section of railway carriage.

00837
THE MARKET WOMAN'S MISHAP (75)
Sheffield Photo Co
D: Frank Mottershaw
COMEDY Boys pelt old woman and upset her
cart so she falls into stream.

00838
A CYCLE TEACHER'S EXPERIENCES (105)
Sheffield Photo Co
D: Frank Mottershaw
COMEDY Teacher tries to teach fat woman to
ride bicycle.

00839
ALL THE FUN OF THE FAIR (190)
R.W. Paul
COMEDY Peepsnow dancer douses farmer's
wife with whitewash.

00840
THE ENCHANTED TOYMAKER (190) also:
THE OLD TOYMAKER'S DREAM
Alpha Trading Co (Paul)
D: Arthur Cooper
TRICK Old man dreams fairy enlarges his
Noah's Ark and toy animals enter it.

00841
BUY YOUR OWN CHERRIES (300)
R.W. Paul
S: (SONG)
MUSICAL Drunkard beats wife and then
signs pledge.

00842
FAMOUS CONJURING TRICKS (250)
Urban Trading Co
Charles Bertram
ACT Balls and cup trick: wine glass trick.

00843
THE JAP STANDARD BEARER (150)
Urban Trading Co

WAR Japanese flag bearer dies after sword
fight with four Cossacks.

00844
TOMMY'S REVENGE (100)
Warwick Trading Co
COMEDY Boy ties firework to coat of
sister's beau.

00845
A WARM RECEPTION (100)
Warwick Trading Co
COMEDY Two waiters trick hotel
patron.

00846
THE ARTIST'S DILEMMA (60)
Warwick Trading Co
TRICK Artist's model vanishes and portrait
comes to life.

00847
FURNISHED ON EASY TERMS (133)
Warwick Trading Co
COMEDY Couple improvise furniture when
theirs is reclaimed by shop.

JUL

00848
DON'T BE GREEDY (125)
Warwick Trading Co
COMEDY

00849
THE LATEST NEWS (60)
Warwick Trading Co
TRICK Man reads newspaper whose moving
letters form "Bill Bailey has come home".

00850
HIS MASTER'S VOICE (75)
Warwick Trading Co
COMEDY Terrier looks for master in
phonograph.

00851
THE COINERS (280)
Sheffield Photo Co
D: Frank Mottershaw
CHASE Police raid den; coiners steal car;
police chase; car explodes.

00852
THE BOBBY'S DOWNFALL (150)
Sheffield Photo Co
D: Frank Mottershaw
COMEDY Tramp handcuffs sleeping policeman
to lamp post.

00853
LATE FOR WORK (165)
Sheffield Photo Co
D: Frank Mottershaw
COMEDY Landlady puts clock forward and
lodger rushes to work too soon.

00854
GARROTTING A MOTOR CAR (290)
Gaumont
D: (Harold Hough)
CRIME Crooks stop car by tying rope across
road. (Based on a crime in Surrey.)

00855
THE ELECTRIC SHOCK (120)
Gaumont
D: (Alf Collins)
COMEDY Boys fix 10,000 volt battery to bell
push

00856
THE STUDENT, THE SOOT AND THE SMOKE
(160)
R.W. Paul
COMEDY Student covers neighbour's chimney
and is sooted when sweep clears it.

00857
THAT TERRIBLE BARBER'S BOY (105)
R.W. Paul
COMEDY Barber's boy puts ink in bay rum.

00858
THE PLOUGHBOY'S DREAM (136)
R.W. Paul
COMEDY Ploughboy dreams he is pirate and
abducts farmer's daughter.

00859
LOOKING FOR TROUBLE (104)
R.W. Paul
COMEDY Man seeking gas leak strikes match.

00860
WHEN THE SLEEPER WAKES (50)
Hepworth
D: Lewin Fitzhamon
COMEDY Children devise seesaw trap for old
man in deck chair.

00861
THE PRESS ILLUSTRATED (200)
Hepworth
D: Lewin Fitzhamon
COMEDY Scenes illustrate magazine titles:
"Our Dogs", "Rapid Review", etc.

00862
THE GREAT SEA SERPENT (135)
Williamson
D: James Williamson
COMEDY Boy puts worm in seaside telescope.

00863
OH! WHAT A SURPRISE! (90)
Williamson
D: James Williamson
Tom Williamson .... Boy
Stuart Williamson .... Boy
COMEDY Boys fool suspicious wife with
bags of flour.

00864
THEY FORGOT THE GAMEKEEPER (65)
Williamson
D: James Williamson
COMEDY Tramp changes clothes with scare-
crow and is shot by keeper.

00865
THE CAPTURE OF A RUSSIAN SPY BY
THE JAPANESE (54)
Cricks & Sharp
WAR Japanese soldiers capture Russian spy.

00866
SHOOTING A RUSSIAN SPY (54)
Cricks & Sharp
WAR Japanese soldiers shoot Russian spy.

00867
SAVING THE DESPATCHES (150)
Cricks & Sharp
WAR Russian Cossack fights Japanese bearer
but escapes.

00868
OFF FOR THE HOLIDAYS (375)
Clarendon (Gau)
D: Percy Stow
COMEDY (5 scenes) Bedroom; outside house;
on the way; accident to cab; platform.

00869
ATTEMPTED MURDER IN A RAILWAY
TRAIN (225)
Clarendon (Gau)
D: Percy Stow
CRIME (7 scenes) The race special; inside
carriage; on footboard; tunnel entrance;
inside tunnel; end of tunnel; cardsharper
captured.

AUG
00870
THE BURGLAR AND THE GIRLS (300)
Clarendon (Gau)
D: Percy Stow
COMEDY (8 scenes) Burglar ties up girl, gets
drunk, and is thrown through window by
sisters.

00871
THE CONVICT AND THE CURATE (250)
USA: THE CONVICT'S ESCAPE
Clarendon (Gau)
D: Percy Stow
CHASE (6 scenes) Convict escapes quarries
and changes clothes with curate.

00872
THE SPOILT CHILD (100)
Hepworth
D: Lewin Fitzhamon
COMEDY Boy removes leaf from dining table
and replaces cloth.

00873
A CHEAP BOOT STORE (50)
Hepworth
D: Lewin Fitzhamon
COMEDY Dandy tries on tight boot and his
foot goes right through it.

00874
THE LOVER'S CRIME (300)
Hepworth
D: Lewin Fitzhamon
CHASE Man shoots girl, hides her in haystack,
is chased by police and caught after fight in
river.

00875
THE MISER AND HIS DAUGHTER (266)
Mitchell & Kenyon (WTC)
CRIME Girl hides lover from father, and he
saves him from thief.

00876
THE LOST SHUTTLECOCK (85)
Gaumont
D: (Alf Collins)
COMEDY Old man climbs on roof to retrieve
girl's shuttlecock; it collapses.

00877
THE FATAL WIG (118)
Gaumont
D: (Alf Collins)
COMEDY Boy's fishing line hooks woman's
wig.

00878
BEHIND THE SCENES; OR, ALGIE'S MISHAP
(125)
Gaumont
D: Alf Collins
COMEDY Lord flirts with dancer and causes
trouble backstage at "Camberwell Theatre".

00879
MR MOSENSTEIN (158)
Gaumont

D: (Alf Collins)
TRICK Vanishing boys play tricks on old jew.

00880
THE MASHER'S DILEMMA (70)
Gaumont
D: (Alf Collins)
COMEDY Flower woman gives dude baby as
he rings girl's doorbell.

00881
THE SWEEP (140)
Gaumont
D: (Alf Collins)
COMEDY Sweep kisses employer in mistake
for maid.

00882
ARTIST AND MUSICIAN (120)
Gaumont
D: (Alf Collins)
COMEDY Professional jealousy between
neighbours leads to fight.

00883
AN AFFAIR OF HONOUR (250)
Gaumont
D: Alf Collins
S: (PLAY) Percival H.T. Sykes
Percy Murray..........Lord Strathcoma
DRAMA 18thC. Gambler kills daughter's
suitor in duel, discovers he was his son and
takes poison.

00884
NIGHT DUTY (120)
Gaumont
D: (Alf Collins)
COMEDY Mistress thwarts amorous policeman
with red hot poker.

00885
FIXING THE SWING (130)
Gaumont
D: (Alf Collins)
COMEDY "A poor father screamer".

00886
STEWED MISSIONARY (165)
Gaumont
D: (Alf Collins)
COMEDY Cannibals cook cleric.

00887
THE SPITEFUL UMBRELLA MAKER (106)
R.W. Paul
COMEDY Shopkeeper cuts hole in sign and
douses shelterers.

00888
MR PECKSNIFF FETCHES THE DOCTOR
(145) *also:* OH, WHAT A SURPRISE!
R.W. Paul
COMEDY Husband rushes for doctor and wife
has triplets.

00889
THE SCULPTOR'S JEALOUS MODEL (183)
R.W. Paul
DRAMA Model smashes statue, stabs sculptor
and kills herself.

00890
LOVE LAUGHS AT LOCKSMITHS (150)
R.W. Paul
TRICK Lover climbs telegraph pole, falls and
smashes to pieces.

00891
WHY MARRIAGE IS A FAILURE (120)
R.W. Paul
COMEDY Girl rejects poor man but accepts
him when he becomes rich.

00892
THE CLOWN'S TELEGRAM (255)
Williamson
D: James Williamson
PATHOS Clown gives show despite death of
distant daughter.

00893
THE STUDENT AND THE HOUSEMAID (135)
Williamson
D: James Williamson
COMEDY Don discovers father's maid trying on
cap and gown.

00894
PROFESSOR RICHARD CODMAN'S PUNCH
AND JUDY SHOW
John Codman Enterprises
D: John Codman
S: Richard Codman
COMEDY Llandudno. Seaside puppet
performance.

00895
THE TRAMP AND THE BATHER (250)
Warwick Trading Co
COMEDY Eynsham Weir. Tramp steals
swimmer's clothes and is chased.

SEP

00896
ONCE TOO OFTEN (100)
Clarendon (Gau)
D: Percy Stow
CRIME "Exciting scene between thief and
shop girl".

00897
FIGHTING WASHERWOMEN (100)
Clarendon (Gau)
D: Percy Stow
COMEDY Washerwomen fight with soapy
water.

00898
FLY CATCHERS (65)
Sheffield Photo Co
D: Frank Mottershaw
COMEDY Toff gets stuck to vendor's
flypapers.

00899
THE DISAPPOINTED TOFFS (135)
Warwick Trading Co
COMEDY

00900
A TRIP TO THE PYRAMIDS (300)
Sheffield Photo Co
D: Frank Mottershaw
COMEDY (6 scenes) Mishaps of family on
holiday trip in Egypt.

00901
BERTIE'S COURTSHIP (100)
Sheffield Photo Co
D: Frank Mottershaw
CHASE (4 scenes) Girl's suitor chased by
father's dog.

00902
THE JONAH MAN; OR, THE TRAVELLER
BEWITCHED (250) USA: THE BEWITCHED
TRAVELLER
Hepworth
D: Lewin Fitzhamon, Cecil Hepworth
TRICK Man's coat, breakfast, bus and train
vanishes; so does he.

00903
THE NIGGER BOY'S REVENGE (100)
Hepworth
D: Lewin Fitzhamon
COMEDY Boy cuts hammock so that
courting couple fall.

00904
THE CONFIDENCE TRICK (175)
Hepworth
D: Lewin Fitzhamon
Lewin Fitzhamon
COMEDY Trickster and fake curate steal
countryman's wallet.

00905
RAGGING IN THE ARMY (130)
Warwick Trading Co
COMEDY "A good comic and most funny".

00906
SONGS ILLUSTRATED (325)
Warwick Trading Co
COMEDY (7 scenes) Scenes illustrate song titles:
"Just Like a Boy", "The Lost Chord", "Home
Sweet Home", etc.

00907
TWO BRAVE LITTLE JAPS (490)
Williamson (Urban)
D: James Williamson
WAR Nurse takes wounded father's despatch
to ship, is caught by Russians and saved by
sailors.

00908
THE STOWAWAY (550)
Williamson (Urban)
D: James Williamson
DRAMA (9 scenes) Boy stows away and on
return finds drunken mother reformed.

00909
FUN IN CAMP (75)
Urban Trading Co
COMEDY Soldiers playing "biff" interrupt
others polishing buttons.

00910
CRUELTY TO A HORSE (115) USA:
CRUELTY TO HORSES
Gaumont
CHASE Master and groom chase stable hand
and duck him in trough.

00911
REVENGE! (375)
Gaumont
D: Alf Collins
CRIME Mechanic avenges wronged wife by
strangling guilty officer.

00912
A RAILWAY TRAGEDY (325)
Gaumont
CRIME Thief robs girl in train and throws her
through window.

00913
A LITTLE BOY CALLED 'TAPS' (505)
Gaumont
CRIME Ex-convict jailed for stealing to
save starving boy.

OCT

00914
FATHER'S HAT; OR, GUY FAWKES' DAY
(150)
Clarendon (Gau)

D: Percy Stow
COMEDY (3 scenes) Father poses as guy and
children set him alight.

00915
THE ADVENTURES OF SANDY MACGREGOR
(300)
Clarendon (Gau)
D: Percy Stow
COMEDY Scotsman tries to undress on beach
without being seen.

00916
THE TRAMPS AND THE WASHERWOMAN
(140)
Sheffield Photo Co
D: Frank Mottershaw
COMEDY Tramp muddies woman's washing
and friend is blamed.

00917
CAUGHT ON THE HOP (50)
Cricks & Sharp
COMEDY Dude joins coster girls in dancing
to barrel organ.

00918
DUCKS ON SALE OR RETURN
Alpha Trading Co
D: Arthur Cooper
TRICK Farmer plucks duck and then film
reverses. (Date uncertain.)

00919
JAPANESE BRAVERY – AN INCIDENT
IN THE WAR (240)
Gaumont
WAR Russian scouts steal despatch from
sleeping Japanese, who wakes, snatches it
back and is chased.

00920
THE TRAMP'S TOILET (300)
Gaumont
D: (Alf Collins)
COMEDY Tramp breaks into house, has bath,
and jumps through window into slime.

00921
BROWN'S PUDDING (200) also: WHEN
FATHER MAKES A PUDDING
Gaumont
D: (Alf Collins)
COMEDY Trouble when father tries to make
Christmas pudding.

00922
THE AMOROUS MILITIAMAN (145)
Gaumont
D: (Alf Collins)
COMEDY Flirtatious soldier scrubbed by
washerwomen.

00923
FUTURE HACKENSCHMIDTS (108)
Gaumont
D: (Alf Collins)
COMEDY Old gent tries to stop urchins
from wrestling.

00924
BILL BAILEY'S RETURN (95)
Gaumont
D: (Alf Collins)
COMEDY Loafer loses racing bet and fights
newsboy and bypassers.

00925
THE FRUITS OF MATRIMONY (106)
Gaumont
D: (Alf Collins)
COMEDY (4 scenes) Clerk fathers four babies.

00926
BED AND BREAKFAST TWO SHILLINGS
(145)
Gaumont
D: (Alf Collins)
COMEDY A cheap boarding house.

00927
MY MOTHER-IN-LAW (115)
Gaumont
D: (Alf Collins)
COMEDY Mother-in-law catches husband
kissing maid and causes fight.

00928
REJECTED BY PA (85)
Gaumont
D: (Alf Collins)
COMEDY Girl's suitor kicked out by father.

00929
THE HAUNTED HOUSEBOAT (400)
Gaumont
D: Alf Collins
S: (SKETCH)
F. Mason......................Innkeeper
T. Costello....................Farmer
J. Harper......................Daughter
A. Murton ....Old Woman
J. Athlick.....................Fat Policeman
J. Morgan ....Tramp
W. Coe ....Constable
T. Harding..................Negro
W. Smith..................... Mischievous Man
J. Diamond.................. House Agent
COMEDY Fight in waterside inn.

00930
THE BLACKSMITH'S DAUGHTER (700)
Gaumont
DRAMA (6 scenes) Girl elopes, is deserted,
baby dies, and she walks home to father.

00931
MIXED BATHING (250)
Gaumont
D: Alf Collins
COMEDY Brighton. Fat husband flirts with
swimming girls.

00932
LOVERS ON THE SANDS (86) retitled:
A STROLL ON THE SANDS
Gaumont
D: Alf Collins
COMEDY Brighton. Boys make hole in sand and
trap young couple.

00933
ON BRIGHTON PIER (180)
Gaumont
D: Alf Collins
COMEDY Brighton. "The rendezvous of the
greatest comedians in the world".

00934
A DAY AT BRIGHTON (250)
Gaumont
D: Alf Collins
COMEDY Brighton. Family of eight spend
day by sea.

00935
LONDON IN A HURRY (425)
Mutoscope & Biograph (Gau)
TRICK Scenes of traffic in acceleration and
reverse.

00936
THE PIRATES (300) also: THE
BUCCANEERS

Warwick Trading Co
ADVENTURE Pirates abduct sailor; he
escapes and warns fleet.

00937
MIRTHFUL MARY IN THE DOCK (115)
Haggar & Sons (Gau)
D: William Haggar
Mog.........Mary
COMEDY Drunken woman causes fight in
police court.

00938
THE SIGN OF THE CROSS (700)
Haggar & Sons (Gau)
D: William Haggar
S: (PLAY) Wilson Barrett
Will Haggar Jr...............Marcus Superbus
Jenny Linden...............Mercia
James Haggar
Will Desmond
Kate Sylvester
DRAMA Rome, period. Prefect converted by
Christian maid and they die in arena.

00939
THE BATHERS' REVENGE (75)
Haggar & Sons (Urban)
D: William Haggar
COMEDY Boy swimmers upset bench and
throw lovers into stream.

00940
BRUTALITY REWARDED (75)
Haggar & Sons (Urban)
D: William Haggar
COMEDY Brutal man rebuffs beggar and is
chased into stream.

00941
THE MEDDLING POLICEMAN (125)
Haggar & Sons (Urban)
D: William Haggar
COMEDY Two tramps string PC with
sausages and pelt him with eggs.

00942
FLYNN'S BIRTHDAY CELEBRATIONS (125)
Haggar & Sons (Urban)
D: William Haggar
COMEDY Irishman gets drunk and throws
wife through window.

00943
THE BITER BITTEN (50)
Haggar & Sons (Urban)
D: William Haggar
COMEDY Two tramps attack cyclist who sets
dog on them.

00944
LADY PLUMPTON'S MOTOR (200)
Hepworth
D: Lewin Fitzhamon
Emily Custance................Lady Plumpton
Lewin Fitzhamon.............Chauffeur
W. Young........................Flunkey
Bob Bouchier....................Gardener
COMEDY Fat woman's car stalls in watersplash
and blows up chauffeur.

00945
A TRIP TO PARIS (500) USA: AN
ENGLISHMAN'S TRIP TO PARIS FROM
LONDON
Hepworth
D: (Lewin Fitzhamon)
COMEDY (15 scenes) Adventures of traveller
from London to Paris.

00946
DON'T INTERFERE WITH A COALHEAVER
(100)
Hepworth
D: Lewin Fitzhamon
COMEDY Navvies spoil man's white suit and
throw him into coal barge.

00947
A DEN OF THIEVES (425)
Hepworth
D: Lewin Fitzhamon
CRIME (12 scenes) Crook, acting on maid's tip,
poses as cleric to rob master on train; police
follow and shoot him in gun fight.

00948
HIS SUPERIOR OFFICER (125)
Hepworth
D: Lewin Fitzhamon
COMEDY Private's girl, stolen by sgt, is stolen
by lieut and col.

00949
WON BY STRATEGY (400)
Hepworth
D: Lewin Fitzhamon
Dolly Lupone
ROMANCE Girl elopes by pretending to take
poison and is taken to church by ambulance.

00950
A RACE FOR A KISS (225)
Hepworth
D: Lewin Fitzhamon
Lewin Fitzhamon............The Jockey
Dolly Lupone..................The Girl
CHASE Jockey races motorist who is arrested
for speeding

00951
AN INTERESTING STORY (235)
Williamson (Urban)
D: James Williamson
TRICK (6 scenes) Man absorbed in reading
is flattened by steamroller.

00952
ALL'S WELL THAT ENDS WELL
Williamson (Urban)
D: James Williamson
COMEDY

NOV

00953
GABRIEL GRUB THE SURLY SEXTON
(400)
Williamson (Urban)
D: James Williamson
S: (NOVEL) Charles Dickens (THE
PICKWICK PAPERS)
FANTASY Sexton reforms after dreaming
of abduction by goblins

00954
THE OLD CHORISTER (235)
Williamson (Urban)
D: James Williamson
S: (SONG)
DRAMA Old chorister returns to native
village. (Shown while song is sung.)

00955
A PICNIC DISTURBED (175)
Sheffield Photo Co
D: Frank Mottershaw
COMEDY Dude annoys picnickers; they tie
him behind cart.

00956
A WIFE'S REVENGE; OR, THE GAMBLER'S
END (240)
Cricks & Sharp
CRIME (2 scenes) Cardsharper kills victim in
duel and is killed in turn by the dead man's
disguised wife.

00957
THE STORY OF TWO CHRISTMASSES (200)
Hepworth
D: Lewin Fitzhamon
DRAMA Wife leaves poor man for rich lover
who is killed for cheating at cards.

00958
THE MISTLETOE BOUGH (500)
Clarendon (Gau)
D: Percy Stow
S: *(POEM)* E.T. Bayley
DRAMA (15 scenes) Bride hides in chest and
is found 15 years later.

00959
THE BROKEN BROOM (100) *USA: A KISS
AND A TUMBLE*
Clarendon (Gau)
D: Percy Stow
COMEDY Man climbs pole to kiss girl and
falls in mud cart.

DEC

00960
THE STOLEN PIG (290)
Clarendon (Gau)
D: Percy Stow
COMEDY Old woman steals pig and puts it in
sack; butcher substitutes his boy.

00961
THAT DREADFUL DONKEY (260)
Sheffield Photo Co
D: Frank Mottershaw
COMEDY Actors exchange farmer's donkey
for pantomime horse.

00962
A SOLDIER'S ROMANCE (280)
Sheffield Photo Co

D: Frank Mottershaw
DRAMA (10 scenes) Man enlists to escape
drunken wife, is disabled; and ten years later
son finds him begging.

00963
BLACK DIAMONDS (675)
Mitchell & Kenyon (Urban)
DRAMA (17 scenes) Collier saves friend when
explosion traps him.

00964
HANDS UP!; OR, CAPTURED BY
HIGHWAYMEN (500)
Gaumont
D: Alf Collins
S: (SKETCH) Bob Pender
Bob Pender's Troupe
COMEDY 18th C. Highwaymen on hobby
horses rob stage coach.

00965
HOW IT IS DONE (135)
Mutoscope & Biograph (Gau)
TRICK Conjuror demonstrates tricks.

00966
TOPICAL TRICKS (205)
Mutoscope & Biograph (Gau)
Walter R. Booth
TRICK Conjuror demonstrates tricks.

00967
SNOWBALLING (115)
Haggar & Sons (Gau)
D: William Haggar
'Mog'
COMEDY Fat woman wins snowball fight.

00968
FOR THE HAND OF A PRINCESS (125)
Hepworth
D: Lewin Fitzhamon
DRAMA Period. Knight fights baron to
rescue kidnapped princess.

00969
TRAMPS IN CLOVER
Warwick Trading Co

CHASE Tramp poses as PC to steal beef
from butcher.

00970
THE TRAMP'S REVENGE (210)
Williamson (Urban)
D: James Williamson
COMEDY Tramp steals PC's uniform, stops
motorists and accepts bribes

00971
AN AFFAIR OF HONOUR (215)
Williamson (Urban)
D: James Williamson
COMEDY Duelling Frenchmen shoot everyone
except themselves.

00972
THE CARELESS HOD CARRIER (50)
Urban Trading Co
COMEDY Builder drops brick on head of
passer-by. (Date uncertain.)

00973
A JUVENILE COMEDIAN (100)
Urban Trading Co
COMEDY Child dresses in father's clothes.
(Date uncertain.)

00974
THE PIERROT'S ROMANCE (550)
Urban Trading Co
S: (SKETCH) G.V. Rosi
G.V. Rosi............The Pierrot
DRAMA Jealous pierrot stabs unfaithful
milliner, and himself. (Date uncertain.)

00975
THE BICYCLE THIEF (200)
Urban Trading Co
CHASE Tramp steals bicycle and is chased
by PC and crowd.

00976
MR HUGHES AND HIS CHRISTMAS
TURKEY
John Codman Enterprises
D: John Codman
COMEDY (Date uncertain.)

1905

JAN

00977
BATHERS WILL BE PROSECUTED (150)
Hepworth
D: (Lewin Fitzhamon)
Cecil Hepworth..........Swimmer
Claude Whitten..........PC
TRICK PC tries to arrest swimmers; then film reverses.

00978
THE OTHER SIDE OF THE HEDGE (100)
USA: OVER THE HEDGE
Hepworth
D: Lewin Fitzhamon
COMEDY Couple put hats on hedge to allay a suspicious aunt.

FEB

00979
THE LOVE LETTERS (175)
Clarendon (Gau)
D: Percy Stow
COMEDY "Pleases the girls — enough said".

00980
THE GAMBLERS (260)
Clarendon (Gau)
D: Percy Stow
DRAMA 'Sensational sentiment cleverly handled".

00981
THE BURGLAR'S DILEMMA (190)
Cricks & Sharp
COMEDY (3 scenes) Maid and Lady trap burglar in window.

00982
THE LADY BARBER (120)
Cricks & Sharp
COMEDY Suffragette barber cuts flirtatious customer.

00983
LOST, STOLEN OR STRAYED (275)
Hepworth
D: Lewin Fitzhamon
Lewin Fitzhamon..........Ruffian
Doily Lupone................Girl
CRIME Lost girl, whipped by ruffian and forced to beg, is saved by gentleman who whips ruffian.

00984
THE TWO IMPS (50)
Hepworth
D: Lewin Fitzhamon
COMEDY Boys lower kitten onto man's head and pull off wig.

00985
THE SCENT SPRAY (230)
Gaumont
D: (Alf Collins)
COMEDY Girl puts ink in sister's atomiser.

00986
AS SPARROWS SEE US (165)
Gaumont
D: (Alf Collins)
COMEDY Parade of feet and ankles: city girl, errand boy, PC, etc.

00987
THE ALIEN QUESTION (350)
Gaumont
D: (Alf Collins)
DRAMA Jews, Russians, Poles and Germans come to London and force British artisans to emigrate to Canada.

00988
THE THREE TRAMPS (236)
Gaumont
D: (Alf Collins)
COMEDY Tramps steal food despite watchful policeman.

00989
A MOTOR MASQUERADE (260)
Gaumont
D: (Alf Collins)
COMEDY "A capital joke."

00990
THE ELECTRIC GOOSE (300)
Gaumont
D: (Alf Collins)
COMEDY Boy revives roast goose with father's shock machine.

00991
AUNTIE'S CYCLING LESSON (185)
Gaumont
D: (Alf Collins)
COMEDY Spinster falls off cycle, collides with gent, country woman, PC, etc.

00992
WIG AND BUTTONS (240)
Gaumont
D: (Alf Collins)
COMEDY "A double dose of delight."

00993
NOBBLER'S CARD PARTY (108)
Gaumont
D: (Alf Collins)
COMEDY "Captivating comic of sporting class."

00994
EYES RIGHT (68)
Gaumont
D: (Alf Collins)
COMEDY "Boys — dainty ankles in full sight."

00995
A MACARONI FEAST (72)
Gaumont
D: (Alf Collins)
COMEDY Couple chew length of macaroni, ending with kiss.

00996
A RAID ON A CANTEEN (145)
Gaumont
D: (Alf Collins)
COMEDY "Tipsy troopers try their thirst."

00997
COMIC CONJURING (130)
Mutoscope & Biograph (Gau)
Horace Goldin
TRICK Conjuror demonstrates tricks.

MAR

00998
AN INTERRUPTED HONEYMOON (375)
Hepworth
D: Lewin Fitzhamon
COMEDY PC chases jewel thief to train where he changes clothes with wife, catches PC, ties him up.

00999
POISON OR WHISKEY (175) *USA:* THE LOVER'S RUSE
Hepworth
D: Lewin Fitzhamon
COMEDY Man wins girl by pretending to take poison.

01000
THE AMATEUR ARCHITECT (100)
Hepworth
D: Lewin Fitzhamon
COMEDY Clumsy architect and builders fall into mortar.

01001
AN ECCENTRIC BURGLARY (400)
Sheffield Photo Co
D: Frank Mottershaw
TRICK Police try to catch acrobatic thieves who vanish at will.

01002
TWO YOUNG SCAMPS (240)
Sheffield Photo Co
D: Frank Mottershaw
COMEDY Boys play various tricks on people.

01003
THE YOUNG PHOTOGRAPHER (70)
Cricks & Sharp
COMEDY Children play with father's camera.

01004
THE CATCH OF THE SEASON (120)
Cricks & Sharp
COMEDY Fisherman has trouble trying to catch a salmon.

01005
A DIFFICULT SHAVE (60)
Urban Trading Co
D: (Tom Green)
FACIAL Man has trouble shaving with blunt razor.

01006
REVERSING A SHAVE (75)
Urban Trading Co
D: (Tom Green)
TRICK Reversed film of man shaving.

01007
NATURAL LAWS REVERSED (75)
Urban Trading Co
D: (Tom Green)
TRICK Log cabin dweller finds everything goes in reverse.

01008
JOVIAL EXPRESSIONS (50)
Urban Trading Co
D: (Tom Green)
FACIAL " A cheerful and soul-inspiring solace."

APR

01009
THE DEATH OF THE IRON HORSE (300)
Alpha Trading Co (WTC)
D: Arthur Cooper
DRAMA Porter fails to stop express and it crashes into train.

01010
THE MOTOR HIGHWAYMAN (600)
Alpha Trading Co (WTC)
D: Arthur Cooper
Basil Maclarty
CRIME Crook on motor-cycle holds up motorists and robs them.

01011
HIS WASHING DAY (75)
Alpha Trading Co (WTC)
D: Arthur Cooper
COMEDY

01012
THE DISAPPOINTED TOFFS (135)
Warwick Trading Co
COMEDY Toffs wait for surprise promised by shop sign; they are doused.

01013
THE JAILBIRD; OR, THE BISHOP AND THE CONVICT (475)
Warwick Trading Co
D: (Charles Raymond)
CHASE Convict changes clothes with swimming bishop, kills girl, steals boat, and is caught.

01014
PAPA HELPS THE PAINTERS (170)
R.W. Paul
COMEDY Father tries to help whitewash room.

01015
AUNTIE'S FIRST ATTEMPT AT CYCLING (200)
R.W. Paul
COMEDY Lady cyclist rides into trouble: a van drops boxes on her, etc.

01016
A VICTIM OF MISFORTUNE (250)
R.W. Paul
CHASE Painter pursued by PC, laundress, milkman, etc.

01017
THE FATAL NECKLACE (320)
R.W. Paul
D: (J.H. Martin)
CRIME Waif stops tramp from stealing rich child's necklace.

01018
A RACE FOR BED (200)
R.W. Paul
D: (J.H. Martin)
COMEDY Brothers race to undress and bed collapses on burglar.

01019
THE HANDCUFF MYSTERY SOLVED (492)
Walturdaw
The Two Cirnocs
ACT Escape from locked handcuffs.

01020
THE RIVAL SPORTSMEN (150)
Hepworth
D: Lewin Fitzhamon
COMEDY Foreign huntsman fooled by stuffed rabbit.

01021
PAINT AND PERFIDY (75)
Hepworth
D:(Lewin Fitzhamon)
COMEDY Man leans on wet post, threatens passer-by, and steals coat.

01022
CHARITY COVERS A MULTITUDE OF SINS (75)
Hepworth
D: (Lewin Fitzhamon)
COMEDY Fake beggar robs old man.

01023
ONLY HER BROTHER (275)
Hepworth
D: Lewin Fitzhamon
COMEDY Jealous husband finds wife's "lover" is her brother.

01024
DANGEROUS GOLFERS (350)
Clarendon (Gau)
D: Percy Stow
COMEDY Keen golfers destroy everything with swinging clubs.

01025
BLIND MAN'S BUFF (115)
Clarendon (Gau)
D: Percy Stow
COMEDY "A palpable hit."

01026
ABOVE AND BELOW STAIRS (100)
Clarendon (Gau)
D: Percy Stow
COMEDY "Every gesture and situation decidedly funny."

01027
SATURDAY'S WAGES (365)
Clarendon (Gau)
D: Percy Stow
CHASE Workman finds trousers containing wages have been sold.

01028
DARLING PUGGY (108)
Gaumont
D: (Alf Collins)
COMEDY Girl and pet dog.

01029
A MOTORBIKE ADVENTURE (195)
Gaumont
D: (Alf Collins)
COMEDY Motorbike explodes and owner comes home in cart.

01030
THE BIRTHDAY UMBRELLA (330) *also:*
THE UNLUCKY UMBRELLA
Gaumont
D: (Alf Collins)
COMEDY Mishaps ensue when father opens umbrella indoors.

01031
THE COSTER'S CHRISTENING (155)
Gaumont
D: (Alf Collins)
COMEDY Costers celebrate christening on Good Friday and are arrested.

MAY

01032
THE GARDENER'S NAP (95)
Gaumont
D: (Alf Collins)
COMEDY Gardener falls asleep and is hosed by boy.

01033
THE UPS AND DOWNS OF MURPHY (110)
Gaumont
D: (Alf Collins)
TRICK Worker is squashed flat by roller and brought back to normal size by hit on head.

01034
THE MOTOR HOOLIGANS (327)

R.W. Paul
CRIME

01035
TROUBLE BELOW STAIRS (120)
R.W. Paul
D: (J. H. Martin)
COMEDY Sweep and cook fight with flour and soot.

01036
THE KING OF CLUBS (175)
R.W. Paul
D: (J.H. Martin)
TRICK

01037
TABLE TURNING (100)
Hepworth
D: Lewin Fitzhamon
COMEDY Revolving table causes upset at spiritualist's seance.

01038
FALSELY ACCUSED (850)
Hepworth
D: Lewin Fitzhamon
CRIME (14 scenes) Framed bank clerk breaks jail and is sheltered by vicar until culprit is caught in Soho.

01039
A TERRIBLE FLIRT (225)
Hepworth
D: Lewin Fitzhamon
COMEDY Three men compete for girl; she elopes with fourth.

01040
WALTER GRAHAM THE HUMAN MARIONETTE (150)
Walturdaw
ACT Comic character studies.

01041
ATTEMPTED NOBBLING OF THE DERBY FAVOURITE (540)
Cricks & Sharp
D: (Tom Green)
SPORT (5 scenes) Crooks thwarted in attempt to dope racehorse.

01042
AN UNLUCKY DAY (330)
Clarendon (Gau)
D: Percy Stow
COMEDY

JUN

01043
MR BROWN'S BATHING TENT (205)
Clarendon (Gau)
D: Percy Stow
COMEDY Folkstone. Boy pins "Ladies" sign on man's bathing tent.

01044
THAT AWFUL BABY (500)
Gaumont
D: (Alf Collins)
COMEDY Woman feigns illness and gives unwanted baby to man, who then tries to get rid of it.

01045
THE ROOF GARDEN *also:* ROOFTOP GARDENS
Gaumont
COMEDY

01046
THE TALE OF A COAT (195)
Gaumont
D: (Alf Collins)
CHASE Tramp steals coat from dummy and
is chased by clothier and PC.

01047
MARRIED BLISS (65)
Gaumont
D: (Alf Collins)
COMEDY

01048
KEIRO'S CAT (150) also: PUSSY'S
BREAKFAST
Gaumont
D: (Alf Collins)
COMEDY Man's pet cat eats breakfast.

01049
THE HENPECKED HINDOO (100)
Gaumont
D: (Alf Collins)
COMEDY

01050
THE BURGLAR LOVER (155)
Gaumont
D: (Alf Collins)
COMEDY

01051
FATHER IN THE KITCHEN (204)
Gaumont
D: (Alf Collins)
COMEDY Father makes mess when he tries
to cook.

01052
THE YOUNG LADIES' DORMITORY (250)
Gaumont
D: (Alf Collins)
COMEDY Tramps hide under girls' beds, and
cause pillow fight.

01053
STUMP SPEECH
Gaumont
D: (Alf Collins)
FACIAL Man's expressions as he makes speech.

01054
JACK'S RETURN (465)
Gaumont
D: (Alf Collins)
COMEDY Sailor saves mother from eviction
by getting bailiffs drunk.

01055
GREEDY BILLY (145)
Gaumont
D: (Alf Collins)
COMEDY "A sleight of hand and mouth artist".

01056
A FUNNY STORY (80)
Redfern
D: Jasper Redfern
FACIAL Man's expressions as he tells story.

01057
KICK ME, I'M BILL BAILEY (80)
Redfern
D: Jasper Redfern
COMEDY Boy pins "kick me" label on man's
coat.

01058
UNCLE PODGER'S MISHAPS (350)
Redfern

01059
D: Jasper Redfern
COMEDY Misadventures of man and
mischievous nephews.

01059
WON'T YOU COME HOME? (120)
Warwick Trading Co
COMEDY

01060
A TALE OF JEALOUSY (120)
Warwick Trading Co
COMEDY

01061
WHAT HO! SHE BUMPS! (100)
Warwick Trading Co
COMEDY

01062
COME OUTSIDE (65)
Warwick Trading Co
COMEDY

01063
HOW JONES SAW THE DERBY
Warwick Trading Co
D: (Charles Raymond)
TRICK Drunk sees Derby race run backwards.

01064
THE MINER'S DAUGHTER
John Codman Enterprises
D: John Codman
DRAMA Wales. (Date uncertain.)

01065
LAZY WORKMEN (165)
Sheffield Photo Co
D: Frank Mottershaw
TRICK Workmen relax as work does itself.

01066
THE MASHER AND THE NURSEMAID (115)
Sheffield Photo Co
D: Frank Mottershaw
COMEDY Dude hides in pram, is tied in by
nurse, and pushed into river.

01067
THE TRAMP AND THE TYPEWRITER (650)
R.W. Paul
D: (J.H. Martin)
CHASE Tramp steals typewriter and is chased
by PC.

01068
THE PILFERED PORKER (220)
Cricks & Sharp
CHASE Tramp steals pig, is chased, caught
and ducked in river.

01069
SHE WOULD SING (285)
Cricks & Sharp reissue: 1910, SISTER MARY
JANE'S TOP NOTE (C & M)
COMEDY (5 scenes) Woman's persistent
singing causes trouble, and she is thrown in
river.

01070
THE SAILOR'S SWEETHEART (166)
Cricks & Sharp
COMEDY Photographer has trouble posing
sailor and girl.

01071
BERTIE AND THE TRAMP (110)
Cricks & Sharp
COMEDY Tramp sells stolen eggs to toff,
who puts them in hat.

01072
THE DUEL (175)
Hepworth
D: Lewin Fitzhamon
COMEDY Gambling Frenchmen fight duel
and shoot waiter.

01073
A BATTLE OF CAULIFLOWERS (100)
Hepworth
D: Lewin Fitzhamon
COMEDY Wagon driver and boy pelt angry
motorist with bad cauliflowers.

01074
REHEARSING A PLAY (150)
Hepworth
D: Lewin Fitzhamon
COMEDY PC thinks actors rehearsing play are
committing murder.

01075
FALSE MONEY (100)
Hepworth
D: Lewin Fitzhamon
COMEDY Man finds purse of counterfeit
money.

01076
THE RELUCTANT BRIDEGROOM (225)
Hepworth
D: Lewin Fitzhamon
COMEDY Weak man forced to wed strong
woman.

01077
UNIVERSAL PEACE (100)
Urban Trading Co
FANTASY Scene from the ballet Entente
Cordiale at the Alhambra.

01078
DON'T FLIRT NEAR A POND (150)
Urban Trading Co
COMEDY Wife catches husband flirting and
throws him into pond.

01079
BIRDS IN THEIR LITTLE NESTS (125)
Urban Trading Co
COMEDY Scenes of bird life disolve to scenes
of married couple.

01080
A GOOD JOKE (65)
Walturdaw
FACIAL "An amusing study in facial
expression".

01081
THE EIGHTEEN PENNY LUNCH (190)
Walturdaw
TRICK Scotsman's sausage changes into dog.

01082
ROUGH ON THE CONJURER (150)
Walturdaw
COMEDY

01083
IN THE GOOD OLD TIMES (165) also: POOR
OLD MR AND MRS BROWN IN THE STOCKS
Alpha Trading Co (Walturdaw)
D: Arthur Cooper
COMEDY Old couple confined to village stocks
and pelted.

01084
THE DUCKING STOOL (112)
Alpha Trading Co
D: Arthur Cooper
COMEDY Old woman ducked in village pond.

JUL

01085
W. WEARY AND T. TIRED (250)
Gaumont
D: (Alf Collins)
COMEDY Escapades of two tramps.

01086
THE BOBBY'S NIGHTMARE (200)
Gaumont
D: (Alf Collins)
COMEDY Policeman's dream.

01087
THE AWKWARD HORSEMAN (210)
Gaumont
D: (Alf Collins)
COMEDY Mishaps of novice horseman.

01088
THE GENTLEMAN BEGGAR (330)
Gaumont
D: (Alf Collins)
COMEDY "An event which happened some
time since".

01089
THE TERROR OF THE HOUSE (430)
Gaumont
D: (Alf Collins)
COMEDY Naughty child plays tricks on
household.

01090
WHO'S THAT A—CALLING? (100)
Gaumont
D: (Alf Collins)
COMEDY

01091
WILLIE AND TIM IN THE MOTOR CAR
(525)
Clarendon (Gau)
D: Percy Stow
CHASE Tramps steal lady's new car and are
chased by police.

01092
DRINK AND REPENTANCE (570)
Cricks & Sharp
D: (Tom Green)
CRIME (9 scenes) Drunkard jailed for theft,
escapes from quarry and is caught as wife
dies.

01093
A QUARTER DAY EPISODE (300)
Cricks & Sharp
D: (Tom Green)
COMEDY Family move house to dodge
rent collector.

01094
A MODERN DAY FAGIN (250)
Walturdaw
CRIME (4 scenes) Drunkard's son is trained as
pickpocket and adopted by rich victim.

01095
ACCIDENT TO TOMMY'S TROUSERS (140)
Walturdaw (Alpha?)
COMEDY Boy repairs friend's torn trousers with
paper patch.

01096
LIVING BEYOND YOUR MEANS (245)
R.W. Paul
COMEDY Broker removes hire-purchase
furniture during dinner party.

01097
BROWN'S HALF HOLIDAY (400)
Williamson (Urban)
D: James Williamson
COMEDY Henpeck forced to spring clean.

01098
SAUSAGES (275)
Williamson (Urban)
D: James Williamson
COMEDY Man changes pig into cat on
sandwich board advertisement.

01099
RIVAL BARBERS (125)
Williamson (Urban)
D: James Williamson
COMEDY Barber spoils sign of neighboring
rival.

01100
THE DOOM OF THE CRINOLINE (400)
Urban Trading Co
COMEDY (20 scenes) Woman's crinoline
causes so much trouble her husband burns it.

01101
WHEN FATHER LAID THE CARPET ON THE
STAIRS (200)
Sheffield Photo Co
D: Frank Mottershaw
S: (SONG)
COMEDY Father has trouble trying to lay
stair carpet.

01102
A FIREMAN'S STORY (490)
Sheffield Photo Co
D: Frank Mottershaw
DRAMA (9 scenes) Fireman hurt saving girl is
framed for theft by rival.

01103
THE INQUISITIVE BOOTS (300)
Hepworth
D: Lewin Fitzhamon
Sebastian Smith
COMEDY Hotel "boots" peeps through
keyholes.

01104
THE ANNUAL TRIP OF THE MOTHERS'
MEETING (300)
Hepworth
D: Lewin Fitzhamon
Sebastian Smith
Thurston Harris
Bertie Mainwaring
Mrs Smith
COMEDY Vicar has trouble escorting party
of women to Southend.

01105
CHILDREN V EARTHQUAKES —
EARTHQUAKES PREFERRED (425)
Hepworth
D: Lewin Fitzhamon
Hetty Potter
Gertie Potter
COMEDY Mischievous girl causes trouble.

01106
TWO SENTIMENTAL TOMMIES (300)
Hepworth
D: Lewin Fitzhamon
COMEDY Soldier fools sergeant by dressing
as girl.

01107
RESCUED BY ROVER (425)
Hepworth
D: Lewin Fitzhamon
S: Mrs Hepworth
Cecil Hepworth.................Father
Mrs Hepworth...................Mother
Barbara Hepworth.............Baby
May Clark.........................Nursemaid
Sebastian Smith................Soldier
Mrs Smith.........................Gipsy
Blair.................................Rover
ANIMAL Dog trails gipsy who stole baby and
returns home to fetch father.

AUG

01108
PREHISTORIC PEEPS (375)
Hepworth
D: S: Lewin Fitzhamon
Sebastian Smith.................Prof Chump
Mrs Smith.........................Martha Chump
Hetty Potter......................Bacteria
Lottie Martin.....................Scrofula
Rosina White.....................Germs
Harry Weekes....................Boko
W. Young..........................Giant
Wordsworth Harrison.........Apeman
Bob Boucher.....................Bucephalus
COMEDY Osteologist dreams of prehistoric
adventures.

01109
THE DEATH OF NELSON (275)
Hepworth
D: Lewin Fitzhamon
S: (SONG) Braham
Sebastian Smith
Tom Mowbray
MUSICAL (Shown while song is sung.)

01110
THE SHOPLIFTER (200)
Sheffield Photo Co
D: Frank Mottershaw
CAHSE Police chase shoplifter and fight in
quarry.

01111
A MAN ALTHOUGH A THIEF (184)
Sheffield Photo Co
D: Frank Mottershaw
CRIME Man steals bicycle and pawns it to feed
starving child.

01112
THE DEMON MOTORIST (115)
Sheffield Photo Co
D: Frank Mottershaw
TRICK Jew given lift by speedster who runs
over pedestrians.

01113
WHILE THE HOUSEHOLD SLEEPS (315)
R.W. Paul
D: (J.H. Martin)
COMEDY Boy and girl tie cat in bag and use
it to clog chimney.

01114
HE LEARNED JU-JITSU — SO DID THE
MISSUS (335)
R.W. Paul
D: (J.H. Martin)
COMEDY Drunkard and wife take same
ju-jitsu course.

01115
WHO'S TO BLAME? (340) *also:* WHY THE
TYPIST GOT THE SACK
Alpha Trading Co (Paul) *reissue:* 1906 (WTC)
D: Arthur Cooper
DRAMA Wife trails husband and secretary to
cafe, and fights her.

01116
THE ADVENTURES OF A £100 BANK NOTE
(600)
R.W. Paul
D: (J.H. Martin)
DRAMA Stolen bank note travels until it
returns to its owner

01117
THE PIERROT AND THE DEVIL'S DICE
(175) *also:* THE CONJURING CLOWN
R.W. Paul
D: (J.H. Martin)
TRICK Tiny Pierrot makes huge dice appear
and vanish, etc.

01118
TWO TRAMPS AND THE TAILOR'S
DUMMY (160)
Walturdaw
COMEDY Tailor catches thieves by posing
as dummy.

01119
CRICKET TERMS ILLUSTRATED (230)
Cricks & Sharp
COMEDY (7 scenes) Scenes burlesquing
terms used in cricket.

01120
FATHER'S PICNIC ON THE SANDS (256)
Cricks & Sharp
COMEDY Children's tricks spoil father's
picnic by sea.

01121
BEWARE OF THE RAFFLED TURKEY (375)
Urban Trading Co
D: (Tom Green)
COMEDY Drunkard helps wife cook turkey
which is too tough to carve.

01122
THE COSTER BURGLAR AND HIS DOG
(175)
Urban Trading Co
D: (Tom Green)
COMEDY Ventriloquial burglar fools
constable with stuffed dog.

01123
THE RIVAL PAINTERS (90)
Haggar & Sons (Gau)
D: William Haggar
COMEDY Painters fight with black and
white paint.

01124
A DAY WITH THE FRESH AIR FIEND (330)
Gaumont
D: (Alf Collins)
COMEDY

01125
JIMMY AND JOE AND THE WATER SPOUT
(115)
Clarendon (Gau)
D: Percy Stow
COMEDY

01126
THE PRODIGAL SON; OR, RUINED AT THE
RACES (585)

Williamson (Urban)
D: James Williamson
DRAMA (10 scenes) Disowned gambler finds
gold and returns in time to save blind father
from begging.

01127
OUR NEW ERRAND BOY (350)
Williamson (Urban)
D: James Williamson
Tom Williamson.........Boy
COMEDY Errand boy makes mistakes in his
deliveries and is chased.

SEP

01128
GOADED TO ANARCHY (480)
R.W. Paul
DRAMA Russia. Anarchist blows up general
who sent his wife to Siberia.

01129
THE DANCER'S DREAM (180)
R.W. Paul
D: (J.H. Martin)
TRICK Ballerina dreams of dancing under sea,
etc.

01130
WHEN THE WIFE'S AWAY (250)
R.W. Paul
D: (J.H. Martin)
COMEDY (5 scenes) Husband tries to boss
servants and ends up in dough.

01131
A CHARACTER RETRIEVED (770)
Gaumont
WAR Gambler is disowned but becomes
hero in Soudan.

01132
WHEN EXTREMES MEET (150)
Gaumont
D: Alf Collins
COMEDY Courting costers fight couple from
Belgravia.

01133
HOW THE POOR HELP THE POOR (390)
Gaumont
D: (Alf Collins)
PATHOS "Pathetic; telling".

01134
THE SQUIRE'S DAUGHTER (600)
Haggar & Sons (Gau)
D: William Haggar
S: *(PLAY)*
Fred Haggar
Lilian Haggar
John Freeman
DRAMA

01135
CHARLES PEACE (770)
Haggar & Sons (Gau)
D: William Haggar
Walter Haggar.........Charles Peace
Violet Haggar
Henry Haggar
Lilian Haggar
CRIME 1879. Fugitive burglar poses as parson,
is caught, tries to escape from train, is hanged.
(Extract in THE MARCH OF THE MOVIES
1938)

01136
WHEN FATHER LAID THE CARPET ON
THE STAIRS (165)

Clarendon (Gau)
D: Percy Stow
COMEDY Mishaps when father tries to lay
stair carpet.

01137
HOW THE TRAMPS TRICKED THE
MOTORIST (275)
Hepworth
D: Lewin Fitzhamon
COMEDY Three tramps use scarecrow to
fake man run over by car.

01138
ROVER TAKES A CALL (50)
Hepworth
D: Lewin Fitzhamon
Blair.........Rover
ANIMAL Curtain call to be shown after
RESCUED BY ROVER

01139
WHAT THE CURATE REALLY DID (250)
Hepworth
D: Lewin Fitzhamon
Claude Whitten.........Curate
Florence Nelson........Gossip
COMEDY Gossips exaggerate curate's gift to
small girl.

01140
THE ELEPHANT AT THE PICNIC (170)
Cricks & Sharp
COMEDY Two tramps in stolen elephant skin
scare picnickers.

01141
THE POLITE LUNATIC (100)
Williamson (Urban)
D: James Williamson
CHASE Workman flees from lunatic who
wishes to return putty knife.

01142
INQUISITIVE VISITORS AT THE DYE
WORKS (150)
Urban Trading Co
D: (Tom Green)
COMEDY Nosy pair thrown in dye vats.

01143
THE DISAPPOINTED SUITOR'S STRATEGY
AND REWARD (150)
Urban Trading Co
D: (Tom Green)
COMEDY Rejected suitor saves girl's father
from hired tramp.

01144
THE ADVENT OF THE MOTHER-IN-LAW
(150)
Urban Trading Co
D: (Tom Green)
COMEDY Henpeck plots to get rid of mother-
in-law.

01145
MISTAKEN FOR A BURGLAR IN HIS OWN
HOUSE (150)
Urban Trading Co
D: (Tom Green)
COMEDY Woman mistakes drunken husband
for burglar.

01146
MIXED BABIES (300)
Sheffield Photo Co
D: Frank Mottershaw
Mabel Strickland.........Mother
Lenore Fisher.............Girl
COMEDY Newsboy exchanges babies in prams.

01147
PHOTOGRAPHIC EXPRESSIONS
ILLUSTRATED (195)
Graphic (Gau)
D: (Harold Jeapes)
FACIAL "Refined comic".

01148
RACING SAYINGS ILLUSTRATED (260)
Graphic (Gau)
D: (Harold Jeapes)
COMEDY Scenes illustrating racing sayings.

OCT

01149
INCIDENTS IN THE LIFE OF LORD
NELSON (820)
Graphic (Gau) *Reissue:* 1907
D: (Harold Jeapes)
HISTORY (14 scenes) Actualities and staged
scenes.

01150
THE SAILOR'S WEDDING (525)
Clarendon (Gau)
D: Percy Stow
DRAMA (19 scenes) Sailor saved from burning
ship in time to save fiancee from villian.

01151
FATHER'S BIRTHDAY CHEESE (410)
Clarendon (Gau)
D: Percy Stow
COMEDY Boy hides cheese in father's pocket
and smell upsets railway passengers.

01152
THE KING'S SERVICE (series)
Gale & Polden
WAR Series of 'army life' films including
comic sequence of hag stealing baby from
nursemaid and soldier.

01153
DREAMY EYES (3) *sound*
Gaumont Chronophone
D: (Arthur Gilbert)
R.G. Knowles
MUSICAL Synchronised to gramophone
record.

01154
THE NEW WOMAN (530)
Gaumont
D: (Alf Collins)
COMEDY Suffragette makes husband do
housework while she goes to his office.

01155
THE RECORD SNEEZE (154)
Gaumont
D: (Alf Collins)
TRICK Man takes snuff and sneezes house
down.

01156
GRANDPA AND THE BUTTERFLY (375)
Gaumont
D: (Alf Collins)
CHASE "A novelty in chases".

01157
THE MILKMAID (138)
Gaumont
D: (Alf Collins)
COMEDY

01158
A FALSE ALARM; OR, THE MASHER'S
DUCKING (200)

Gaumont
D: (Alf Collins)
COMEDY Drunken swell summons fire
brigade and is hosed.

01159
HOW BROWN BROUGHT HOME THE
GOOSE (450)
Gaumont
D: (Alf Collins)
COMEDY Drunken father has trouble
bringing home Christmas goose.

01160
WHY THE LODGER LEFT (240)
Gaumont
D: (Alf Collins)
COMEDY Child cuts up lodger's trousers.

01161
THE PEASHOOTER; OR, A NEW WEAPON
FOR THE ARMY (135)
Gaumont
D: (Alf Collins)
COMEDY Boy blows peas at major, who
arrests sentry.

01162
AN ARTFUL DODGE (176)
Gaumont
D: (Alf Collins)
COMEDY Tramps makes fisherman fall in
river, then save him.

01163
THE GIPSY FORTUNE TELLER (190)
Gaumont
D: (Alf Collins)
DRAMA Sailor saves gipsy boy from being
thrashed.

01164
THE BURGLAR; OR, THE HUE AND CRY
(580)
Gaumont
D: (Alf Collins)
CHASE (5 scenes) Burglar changes clothes with
policeman he kills, and is caught by dog.

01165
D.T.s; OR, THE EFFECT OF DRINK (220)
Haggar & Sons (Gau)
D: William Haggar
TRICK Drunken clubman sees visions and
reforms.

01166
FUN AT THE WAXWORKS (225)
Haggar & Sons (Gau)
D: William Haggar
COMEDY Two men take place of wax dummies
and strike passers-by.

01167
BATHING NOT ALLOWED (145)
Haggar & Sons (Gau)
D: William Haggar
COMEDY Boys push PC and farmer into stream.

01168
A BOATING INCIDENT (130)
Haggar & Sons (Gau)
D: William Haggar
COMEDY Boating party ends up in river.

01169
TWO'S COMPANY, THREE'S NONE (75)
Haggar & Sons (Gau)
D: William Haggar
COMEDY Dude fights rival and they end up
in stream.

01170
THE SALMON POACHERS — A MIDNIGHT
MELEE (274)
Haggar & Sons (Gau)
D: William Haggar
Walter Haggar .... Poacher
CHASE Police chase poachers and fight them
in river but they escape by boat.

01171
MARY IS DRY (94)
Haggar & Sons (Gau)
D: William Haggar
Mog..........Mirthful Mary
COMEDY Fat woman steals drink and starts
fight.

01172
A MESSAGE FROM THE SEA (420)
Haggar & Sons (Gau)
D: William Haggar
Walter Haggar
Henry Haggar
DRAMA (5 scenes) Shipwrecked sailor sends
bottled message to wife and is saved by battle
ship.

01173
SHORT-SIGHTED SAMMY (235)
R.W. Paul
D: (J.H. Martin)
COMEDY Man robbed of spectacles mistakes
tramp for girl, etc.

01174
THE VISIONS OF AN OPIUM SMOKER (262)
R.W. Paul
D: (J.H. Martin)
TRICK Man smokes opium in Chinese den and
has weird dream.

01175
THE MISGUIDED BOBBY (120)
R.W. Paul
D: (J. H. Martin)
COMEDY PC mistakes fancy dress dancer for
real burglar.

01176
THE STOLEN GUY (150)
Hepworth
D: Lewin Fitzhamon
COMEDY Drunkard poses as guy until
children put him on bonfire.

01177
LODGINGS TO LET (250)
Hepworth
D: Lewin Fitzhamon
COMEDY Wife discovers husband signalling
neighbour's wife.

01178
THE ALIENS' INVASION (450)
Hepworth
D: Lewin Fitzhamon
DRAMA English workmen sacked and babies
die because Jews come to England and accept
low wages.

01179
TWO YOUNG SCAMPS (170) *also:* THE TWO
SCAMPS
Cricks & Sharp
COMEDY Naughty boys play various tricks.

01180
MCNAB'S VISIT TO LONDON (300)
Alpha Trading Co (WTC)
D: Arthur Cooper
Arthur Cooper..........McNab

Ruby Vivian
COMEDY Keen Scots golfer wrecks host's house.

01181
WHAT IS IT MASTER LIKES SO MUCH (100)
Alpha Trading Co (WTC)
D: Arthur Cooper
COMEDY "Excellent reproduction of wellknown poster."

01182
CATCHING A TARTAR (400)
Warwick Trading Co
D: (Charles Raymond)
Miss Nelson..........Cyclist
COMEDY Tramps attack cycling woman not knowing she is a professional boxer.

01183
THE TERROR OF THE NEIGHBOURHOOD (300)
Warwick Trading Co
D: (Charles Raymond)
Miss Nelson..........Nurse
DRAMA Ruffian beats wife but reforms after being beaten by nurse.

01184
THE ECCENTRICITIES OF TRAVELLING (375)
Warwick Trading Co
COMEDY

01185
IN THE GOOD OLD TIMES (55)
Williamson (Urban)
D: James Williamson
FACIAL Objects are thrown at man in stocks.

01186
THE TEMPEST (150)
Urban Trading Co
S: (PLAY) William Shakespeare
DRAMA Shipwreck scenes from "His Majesty's Theatre" production.

NOV

01187
THE LIFE OF CHARLES PEACE (870)
Sheffield Photo Co
D: Frank Mottershaw
CRIME (12 scenes) Burglar shoots mistress's husband and dons disguises to elude police.

01188
THE OLD HOMESTEAD; OR, SAVED FROM THE WORKHOUSE (240)
Cricks & Sharp
D: Tom Green
PATHOS (3 scenes) Sailor comes home in time to save blind mother from eviction.

01189
CARVING THE CHRISTMAS TURKEY (140)
Cricks & Sharp
D: (Tom Green)
COMEDY Father carves tough turkey which breaks table.

01190
THE ADVENTURES OF AN INSURANCE MAN (215)
Cricks & Sharp
D: Tom Green
COMEDY Householders throw out insurance collector, tear his clothes and whitewash him.

01191
THE HORSE STEALER; OR, A CASUAL ACQUAINTANCE (346)
Cricks & Sharp
D: Tom Green
Jennie Green..........Girl
CRIME Man makes love to girl, steals her horse, is chased and killed.

01192
PEEPING TOM (150)
Cricks & Sharp
D: (Tom Green)
COMEDY Hotel guest bores hole in wall and is caught by girl's husband.

01193
INTERNATIONAL EXCHANGE (275)
Hepworth
D: Lewin Fitzhamon
DRAMA John Bull unable to trade overseas, starts a tariff system.

01194
THE BABES IN THE WOOD (700)
Hepworth
D: Lewin Fitzhamon
DRAMA Wicked uncle hires robbers to kill orphan heirs.

01195
THE MOTOR COMPETITION (300)
Gaumont
D: (Alf Collins)
COMEDY Man tries to win prize contest.

01196
MIXED BATHING AT HOME (147)
Gaumont
D: (Alf Collins)
COMEDY Children get into bath wearing clothes.

01197
ROBBERY WITH VIOLENCE (235)
Gaumont
D: (Alf Collins)
CHASE Burglars beat old woman and are chased across railway by police.

01198
TOMMY'S EXPERIMENTS IN PHOTOGRAPHY (215)
Gaumont
D: (Alf Collins)
COMEDY Boy's trick camera fools sister's beau.

01199
SANTA CLAUS' MISTAKE (400)
Gaumont
D: (Alf Collins)
COMEDY Uncle goes down wrong chimney and is arrested.

01200
FATHER MAKES LOVE TO THE PUMP (200)
Gaumont
D: (Alf Collins)
COMEDY Drunkard mistakes pump for girl and gets wet.

01201
THE BLIND MAN'S CHILD (560)
Gaumont
D: (Alf Collins)
PATHOS "Seasonable pathetic."

01202
THE VILLAGE BLACKSMITH (240)
Clarendon (Gau)
D: Percy Stow
S: (POEM) Henry Longfellow
Roy Byford..........The Blacksmith
MUSICAL The life of a blacksmith. (Shown while song is sung.)

01203
BEAUTY AND THE BEAST (665)
Clarendon (Gau)
D: Percy Stow
FANTASY (15 scenes) 17thC. Beast reverts to prince after kiss from merchant's daughter.

01204
THE CITY MAN'S BUSY DAY (600)
Urban Trading Co
COMEDY (16 scenes) City man spends day at races, bars, theatres, etc.

01205
DOINGS IN DOLLY LAND (375)
Urban Trading Co (Alpha?)
TRICK Adventures of animated dolls.

01206
TWO LITTLE WAIFS (500)
Williamson (Urban)
D: James Williamson
DRAMA Gipsy steals boy; he flees with gipsy girl; she is caught but boy's father saves her from blazing caravan.

DEC

01207
A CHRISTMAS CARD; OR, THE STORY OF THREE HOMES (215)
R.W. Paul Reissue: 1906
D: (J.H. Martin)
FANTASY Rich girl helps poor orphan and fairy takes them to Santa Claus.

01208
A SHAVE BY INSTALMENTS ON THE UNEASY SYSTEM (267)
R.W. Paul
D: (J.H. Martin)
COMEDY Interruptions stop father shaving.

01209
THE FREAK BARBER (168)
R.W. Paul
D: (J.H. Martin)
TRICK Barber cuts heads off Negro and white customers, who then dismember him.

01210
THE VILLAIN'S WOOING (750)
Hepworth
D: Lewin Fitzhamon
Lewin Fitzhamon..........The Villian
May Clark..........The Girl
CRIME Simpleton frees framed man in time for him to save girl from being dropped over cliff.

01211
THE BURGLAR'S BOY (325)
Hepworth
D: Lewin Fitzhamon
CRIME Girl reforms boy when burglar forces him to rob house.

01212
THE STOLEN PURSE (315)
Clarendon (Gau)
D: Percy Stow
COMEDY (6 scenes) Girl frees old man wrongfully charged with theft.

01213
SHAMUS O'BRIEN; OR, SAVED FROM THE SCAFFOLD (300)
Cricks & Sharp
D: Tom Green
S: (SKETCH) (POEM) Sheridan le Fanu
CRIME (6 scenes) Man frames rival for stabbing rich uncle.

01214
THE SAME OLD TALE (145)
Cricks & Sharp
D: Tom Green
FACIAL (4 scenes) People tell funny joke
to one another.

01215
AN ECLIPSE OF THE MOON (170)
Williamson (Urban)
D: James Williamson
COMEDY Page peeps through end of
telescope to fool astrologer.

01216
LASSOED BY MOTOR (100)
Urban Trading Co
COMEDY Man stuck to painted seat is
tied to back of car.

01217
A RAID ON A CLUB (200)
Walturdaw
S: *(SKETCH)* Fred Karno
COMEDY (Date uncertain.)

01218
WHEN THE CAT'S AWAY THE MICE
PLAY (160)
Walturdaw
COMEDY (Date uncertain.)

01219
THE GOLDEN DUSTMAN'S WALK (150)
Walturdaw (Cinematophone?)
COMEDY (Date uncertain.)

01220
ROUGH ON THE POLICEMAN (50)
Walturdaw
COMEDY (Date uncertain.)

01221
TATCHO (100)
Walturdaw (Cinematophone?)
COMEDY (Date uncertain.) Man tries
remarkable hair restorer.

01222
AUGUST AND SEPTEMBER (120)
Walturdaw
ACT Circus clowns perform. (Date uncertain.)

01223
GRANDFATHER'S TORMENTORS (150)
Alpha Trading Co
D: Arthur Cooper
COMEDY Boys play tricks on grandfather.
(Date uncertain.)

1906

JAN

01224
THE VOTER'S GUIDE (325)
Hepworth
D: Lewin Fitzhamon
COMEDY Scenes illustrating phrases: Tariff Reform, Free Trade, Workman's Friend.

01225
THE TRAMP'S DREAM (450)
Hepworth
D: Lewin Fitzhamon
Sebastian Smith.........Tramp
Hetty Potter...............Fairy
COMEDY Tramp dreams fairy takes him to be Marquis' guest.

01226
THE MISSING LEGACY; OR, THE STORY OF A BROWN HAT (430)
Gaumont
D: (Alf Collins)
COMEDY Man gives away inherited hat, then finds it contains will.

01227
A COMIC DUEL (270)
Cricks & Sharp
D: (Tom Green)
COMEDY Old men fight with pistols, swords and boxing gloves, but lose the girl.

01228
PORTRAITS FOR NOTHING (150)
Cricks & Sharp
D: (Tom Green)
COMEDY Troubles of a street photographer.

01229
NIGHT DUTY; OR, A POLICEMAN'S EXPERIENCES (230)
Cricks & Sharp
D: (Tom Green)
CRIME (7 scenes) PC's varied duties ending in chase and capture at station of murderous pickpocket.

01230
WHEN FATHER GOT A HOLIDAY (355)
Clarendon (Gau) *Reissue:* 1913
D: Percy Stow
COMEDY Mother, Father and large family go for a cycle ride.

FEB

01231
HOW BABY CAUGHT COLD (165)
Clarendon (Gau)
D: Percy Stow
COMEDY Nurse flirts with soldier and neglects baby in bath.

01232
THE TRUANTS' CAPTURE (150)
Clarendon (Gau)
D: Percy Stow
CHASE PC chases three boy swimmers.

01233
THE RIVALS (175)
Hepworth
D: Lewin Fitzhamon
Lewin Fitzhamon..........Horseman
ROMANCE Girl agrees to wed whichever horseman finds glove.

01234
THE BEST LITTLE GIRL IN THE WORLD (250)
Hepworth
D: Lewin Fitzhamon
DRAMA Girl persuades rich father to help poor boy who robbed blind man.

01235
A TRAGEDY OF THE SAWMILLS (500)
Hepworth
D: Lewin Fitzhamon
Henry G. Shaw..........Foreman
Lewin Fitzhamon......Owner
Dolly Lupone............Girl
DRAMA Girl frees foreman from sawmill in time for him to save fiancee from lustful owner.

01236
MOTOR VERSUS MOKE (245)
Cricks & Sharp
COMEDY Costers put dead donkey in dude's motor car.

01237
HOAXING THE PROFESSOR (212)
Cricks & Sharp
Johnny Butt..........The Professor
CHASE Entymologist chases paper butterfly and ends in river.

01238
SWEETS TO THE SWEET (75)
Cricks & Sharp
COMEDY Coster helps cook by stirring pudding with poker.

01239
DOWN BY THE OLD BULL AND BUSH (200)
Cricks & Sharp
D: (Tom Green)
COMEDY Boys pose as girls to follow father into public house where he meets girl.

01240
A FISHERMAN'S LUCK (75)
Cricks & Sharp
COMEDY Fisherman catches dead cat.

01241
THE SWING AND THE SEESAW (75)
Cricks & Sharp
COMEDY "How the tomboy came to grief."

MAR

01242
A LUCKY PIG (400)
Warwick Trading Co
D: (Charles Raymond)
COMEDY (6 scenes) Two tramps hide stolen pig in picnicker's hamper.

01243
OH, THAT TOOTHACHE! (310)
Warwick Trading Co
COMEDY Family use clothesline to extract father's bad tooth.

01244
LOST IN THE SNOW (250)
Sheffield Photo Co
D: Frank Mottershaw
Lenore Fisher..........Child
ANIMAL Collie dog finds lost child in snow and brings her parents.

01245
OUR BOYHOOD DAYS (500)
Sheffield Photo Co
D: Frank Mottershaw

COMEDY Two old men recall tricks they played when boys.

01246
THE DOCTORED BEER (260)
R.W. Paul
D: (J.H. Martin)
COMEDY Burglar drugs policeman's beer.

01247
MISTAKEN IDENTITY (105)
R.W. Paul
D: (J.H. Martin)
COMEDY Maid tries on mistress's dress and is kissed by master.

01248
HE CANNOT GET A WORD IN EDGEWAYS (170)
R.W. Paul
D: (J.H. Martin)
COMEDY Wife nags tardy husband until he produces bracelet.

01249
THE OLD LIE AND THE NEW (100)
R.W. Paul
D: (J.H. Martin)
DRAMA Sailor promises to wed girl; later she appears at his wedding.

01250
THE FAKIR AND THE FOOTPADS (214)
R.W. Paul
D: (J.H. Martin)
TRICK Tramp steals food from picnicking professor and is blown up.

01251
A LIVELY QUARTER DAY (332)
R.W. Paul
D: (J.H. Martin)
TRICK Conjuror makes furniture return from bailiff's.

01252
A CURE FOR LUMBAGO (125)
Hepworth
D: Lewin Fitzhamon
COMEDY Old man's lumbago cured by violent friend.

01253
THE PEASANT GIRL'S REVENGE (300)
Hepworth
D: Lewin Fitzhamon
Lewin Fitzhamon .... Cossack
Dolly Lupone .... Peasant
DRAMA Russia. Cossacks kill peasant whose wife poisons their wine.

01254
THE DENTIST'S REVENGE (200)
Gaumont
D: Harold Hough
COMEDY "Harold Hough's latest sensation."

01255
THE HENPECKED HUSBAND (224)
Gaumont
D: (Alf Collins)
COMEDY Henpeck tries to escape wife by committing suicide.

01256
THIS SIDE UP (250)
Gaumont
D: (Alf Collins)
COMEDY Boys stick 'This side up' label on Jew's back.

01257
IT'S A HAVE (128)
Gaumont
D: (Alf Collins)
COMEDY Boys play trick with hare's ear in bag of flour.

01258
DINNER HOUR (130)
Gaumont
D: (Alf Collins)
COMEDY Boys trick workmen and cause fight.

01259
IN OUR ALLEY (88)
Gaumont
D: (Alf Collins)
COMEDY "Lively little comic taken from slum life."

01260
SAVED BY A LIE (395)
Clarendon (Gau)
D: Percy Stow
S: Langford Reed
Langford Reed
PATHOS Drunkard beats wife who dies after telling police he is innocent.

01261
WHO STOLE THE BEER? (210)
Clarendon (Gau)
D: Percy Stow
COMEDY

01262
MR HENPECK'S QUIET BANK HOLIDAY (854)
Warwick Trading Co
D: (Charles Raymond)
COMEDY Husband's troubles during spring cleaning.

01263
A LIFE FOR A LIFE (520)
Warwick Trading Co
D: (Charles Raymond)
DRAMA (8 scenes) Wife dies of shock when hire-purchase furniture is removed; husband bombs dealer and cleric helps him flee country.

01264
A PAIR OF DESPERATE SWINDLERS (465)
Warwick Trading Co
D: (Charles Raymond)
CRIME Thieves rob mails, forge cheque, escape police, pose as nuns and are caught after fight.

01265
ME AND MY TWO PALS (310)
Warwick Trading Co
D: (Charles Raymond)
ANIMAL Girl's pet dog trails man who stole pet cat.

01266
THE GAMBLER'S NIGHTMARE (255)
Warwick Trading Co
D: (Charles Raymond)
CRIME Drunken gambler reforms after dreaming of killing policeman.

01267
THE RETURN OF THE MISSUS (130)
Cricks & Sharp
D: (Tom Green)
COMEDY Mistress returns while cook is having party with PC and sailor.

01268
A BATHER'S DIFFICULTIES (215)
Cricks & Sharp
D: (Tom Green)
COMEDY "A pair of lovers, a maiden aunt, and a scarecrow."

01269
THE MASTER'S RAZOR (166)
Cricks & Sharp
D: (Tom Green)
COMEDY Maid uses master's razor to peel potatoes, scrape shoes, etc.

01270
THE TELL-TALE TELEPHONE (325)
Cricks & Sharp
D: (Tom Green)
COMEDY City man phones wife while flirting with secretary: his words, shown in captions above his head, have a double meaning.

APR
01271
THE ATTACK ON THE AGENT (540)
Cricks & Sharp
D: Tom Green
Jennie Green..........Wife
CRIME (8 scenes) Irish moonlighters tie eviction agent to railway tracks; he is saved by wife.

01272
DICK TURPIN'S LAST RIDE TO YORK (500)
Warwick Trading Co
D: (Charles Raymond)
S: (SKETCH) Fred Ginnett (TURPIN'S RIDE TO YORK)
Fred Ginnett..........Dick Turpin
Mrs Ginnett............Susan Truelove
ADVENTURE (10 scenes) 1737. Highwayman robs coach, is chased to York and caught when horse dies.

01273
ANYTHING FOR PEACE AND QUIETNESS (200)
Warwick Trading Co
COMEDY

01274
ALGY'S NEW SUIT (200)
Warwick Trading Co
COMEDY Girl is upset when she sees beau's new suit advertised cheaply.

01275
CUPID AND THE WIDOW (150)
Hepworth
D: Lewin Fitzhamon
ROMANCE Cupid shows young widow how love outweighs gold.

01276
A POET AND HIS BABIES (450)
Hepworth
D: Lewin Fitzhamon
CHASE Poet pursued by woman with babies.

01277
HOT PIE (100)
Gaumont
D: (Alf Collins)
COMEDY PC tries to steal cook's pie and is trapped in window.

01278
LOST! A LEG OF MUTTON (256)

Gaumont USA: THE LOST LEG OF MUTTON
D: (Alf Collins)
CHASE Tramp steals leg of mutton and is chased by butcher.

01279
SAVED BY A PILLAR BOX (240)
Gaumont
D: (Alf Collins)
CHASE Thieves chase bank messenger who hides cash in pillar box.

01280
THE COSTER'S REVENGE (150)
Clarendon (Gau)
D: Percy Stow
COMEDY "A film with a finish!"

01281
BEER TWOPENCE A GLASS (265)
Clarendon (Gau)
D: Percy Stow
COMEDY Partners in beer barrel sell each other drinks until they run out.

01282
A NAVAL ENGAGEMENT (225)
Norwood (Gau)
D: Harold Hough
COMEDY Sailor fights policeman for favours of maid.

01283
A GREAT TEMPTATION (450)
Norwood (Gau)
D: Harold Hough
DRAMA (7 scenes) Rich man lures a wife, abandons her, and is thrashed by husband.

01284
THE LUCKY HORSE-SHOE (230)
Sheffield Photo Co
D: Frank Mottershaw
COMEDY Boys heat horse-shoe and watch people pick it up.

01285
THE HUMOURS OF AMATEUR GOLF (400)
Urban Trading Co
COMEDY (16 scenes) Mishaps of fat golfer and small caddy.

01286
THE HAND OF THE ARTIST (200)
Urban Trading Co
D: W.R. Booth
TRICK Artist draws coster couple who come to life and dance cakewalk. (First British animated cartoon.)

MAY
01287
DICK TURPIN'S RIDE TO YORK (1000)
Hepworth
D: S: Lewin Fitzhamon
Lewin Fitzhamon..............Dick Turpin
Dorothy Lupone.............Innkeeper's Daughter
Louis Stanislaus..................Major Mowbray
Cliff Bing.........................Mr Tyrconnell
Claude Whitten.................Sir Luke Rookwood
Tom Mowbray...................Innkeeper
Willie Hartill.....................Mr Coates
Emily Custance.................Maid
Elco Mearson...................Mr Patterson
Frank Cousins.................Postillion
Nathaniel Menzies.............Ostler
George Curtiss.................Horse Boy
ADVENTURE (9 scenes) Pursuit of highwayman taking message to knight. (First British "one-reel" feature.)

01288
IN THE SUMMER TIME (175)
Hepworth
D: Lewin Fitzhamon
COMEDY Man ties tape to branch so that it tickles woman while he flirts with her daughter.

01289
THE KIDNAPPER AND THE CHILD (325)
Hepworth
D: Lewin Fitzhamon
CRIME Child foils kidnapper by placing doll in bed.

01290
THE MADMAN'S FATE (576)
R.W. Paul
D: (J.H. Martin)
Leah Marlborough..........The Wife
CRIME (11 scenes) Man kills escaped lunatic who tried to stab his wife and is pardoned when she tells story in court.

01291
SEASIDE LODGINGS (500)
R.W. Paul
D: (J.H. Martin)
COMEDY Crooks tie up landlord and rent room to several people.

01292
THE PRICE OF A DINNER (250)
Warwick Trading Co
CHASE (6 scenes) Tramp steals dinner and is chased up tree by dog.

01293
HER FIRST CAKE (300)
Williamson (Urban)
D: James Williamson
COMEDY Newlywed's first cake, too hard to eat, is used as brick.

01294
THE ANGLER'S DREAM (300)
Williamson (Urban)
D: James Williamson
COMEDY Angler lands big fish — and wakes up.

01295
FATHER, MOTHER WANTS YOU (200)
Urban Trading Co
COMEDY Henpeck's wife has triplets.

01296
ALL'S WELL THAT ENDS WELL (215)
Gaumont
D: (Alf Collins)
COMEDY Rejected lover catches thief and wins girl.

01297
MY WIFE'S A TEETOTALER (178)
Gaumont
D: (Alf Collins)
COMEDY Boy spoils burgundy which father is hiding from mother.

01298
INQUISITIVE BERTIE (290)
Norwood (Gau) *Reissue*: 1908, BERTIE AT THE GYMNASIUM
D: Harold Hough
COMEDY Dude snoops on lady gymnasts and is set upon.

01299
SLAVERY DAYS — THE NEW MASTER (285)
Norwood (Gau)
D: Harold Hough
DRAMA Planter abducts halfcaste, whips her, and shoots her Negro father.

01300
THOSE BOYS AGAIN (300)
Clarendon (Gau)
D: Percy Stow
COMEDY Naughty boys pin "kick me" label on man's coat.

01301
HOW FATHER KILLED THE CAT (425)
Clarendon (Gau)
D: Percy Stow
COMEDY Father fails to drown, mangle and mince cat, but kills it playing violin.

01302
A LITTLE BIT OF SUGAR FOR THE BIRDS (440) *also:* THE ADVENTURES OF MAUD
Graphic (Gau)
D: (Harold Jeapes)
COMEDY Holborn. Pursued girl given lift by curate.

01303
THE SAN FRANCISCO DISASTER (250)
Sheffield Photo Co
DRAMA (Staged topical) Earthquake; rescue of girl; faithful dog; Devil's exultation.

01304
SLIPPERY JIM THE BURGLAR (220)
Cricks & Sharp
D: (Tom Green)
CHASE Pursued burglar changes clothes with swell, coster, etc.

01305
THE ANIMATED DRESS STAND (266)
Cricks & Sharp
D: (Tom Green)
COMEDY Boys dress clothes on dummy and fool PC, etc.

01306
FATHER'S DERBY TRIP (385) *also:* FATHER AND THE BOOKMAKER
Cricks & Sharp
D: (Tom Green)
COMEDY Father backs winner but bookie welshes.

01307
THE MOTOR VALET (200) *also:* THE NEW MOTO VALET
Alpha Trading Co
D: Arthur Cooper
TRICK Robot servant smashes furniture and explodes. (Date uncertain.)

01308
THE HAPPY MAN (185)
Alpha Trading Co
D: Arthur Cooper
COMEDY (Date uncertain.)

01309
YOUTH REGAINED (270)
Alpha Trading Co
D: Arthur Cooper
COMEDY (Date uncertain.)

01310
ROBBING H.M. MAILS (350)
Alpha Trading Co
D: Arthur Cooper
CRIME Two crooks rob mail cart, are chased, and caught. (Date uncertain.)

JUN

01311
THE GUINEA ENTERTAINER (170)
Alpha Trading Co
D: Arthur Cooper
COMEDY Prof's trained mice escape at Lady's "At Home."

01312
WHEN THE CAT'S AWAY (110)
Alpha Trading Co (WTC)
D: Arthur Cooper
COMEDY Maid, cook and milkman dance while mistress is away.

01313
TICKET MANIA (325)
Warwick Trading Co
COMEDY Man collects bus tickets to win "Daily Mirror" lucky number contest

01314
AN EPISODE OF THE DERBY (300)
Hepworth
D: Lewin Fitzhamon
CRIME Parents save girl from being kidnapped.

01315
WHEN FATHER ELOPED WITH COOK (500)
Hepworth
D: Lewin Fitzhamon
COMEDY Son pursues eloping father.

01316
THE PIRATE SHIP (450)
Hepworth
D: Lewin Fitzhamon
Hetty Potter.................Girl
Lewin Fitzhamon..........Pirate
ADVENTURE Sailors save girl from pirates.

01317
THE VALET WHO STOLE THE TOBBACO (175)
Hepworth
D: Lewin Fitzhamon
COMEDY Man mixes concoction to foil thieving valet.

01318
BROWN'S FISHING (?) EXCURSION (320)
R.W. Paul
D: (J. H. Martin)
COMEDY Fisherman spends day with girl.

01319
THE CURATE'S DILEMMA (290)
R.W. Paul
D: (J. H. Martin)
COMEDY Curate sits on anthill at picnic.

01320
HOME WITHOUT MOTHER (220)
R.W. Paul
D: (J.H. Martin)
COMEDY Father's troubles with housework.

01321
THE ECCENTRIC THIEF (340)
Sheffield Photo Co
D: Frank Mottershaw
TRICK Fat policeman chases thin thief who vanishes at will.

01322
UNCLE GEORGE'S TRIP TO LONDON (510)
Gaumont
D: Alf Collins
COMEDY Farmer comes to city and is gulled by tricksters.

01323
NOSEY PARKER (300)
Gaumont
D: (Alf Collins)
COMEDY Crowd put snooper into barrel and roll him into water.

01324
NOT DETAINED AT THE OFFICE (160)
Gaumont
D: (Alf Collins)
COMEDY Wife catches husband kissing girl.

01325
THE CATCH OF THE SEASON (446)
Gaumont
D: (Alf Collins)
CHASE Plain spinster advertises in marriage paper and is chased by angry bachelors.

01326
THE UNDERGRADUATES (435)
Gaumont
D: (Alf Collins)
COMEDY "Real good scenes of college life."

01327
ATTACK IN THE REAR (250)
Norwood (Gau)
D: Harold Hough
COMEDY Boys put tintack on park bench.

01328
THE CHASER CHASED (285)
Norwood (Gau)
D: Harold Hough
CHASE Pursued persuades pursuers to pursue pursuer.

01329
SOME OF OUR RELATIONS (130)
Graphic
D: (Harold Jeapes)
COMEDY Man compared to animals.

01330
MOTOR MAD (300)
Urban Trading Co
CHASE Motorist makes chauffeur speed, shoots PC, is committed, and drives motorised bath chair.

01331
POOR PA; OR, MOTHER'S DAY OUT (300)
Cricks and Sharp
D: (Tom Green)
COMEDY Father must do housework while mother is away.

01332
THE MAD DOG (500)
Walturdaw
D: S: Dave Aylott
CHASE Boy tricks crowd into fleeing from puppy. (Date uncertain.)

01333
THE BOBBY AND THE BOB (470)
Walturdaw
COMEDY (8 scenes) PC tries to pass dud coin but it keeps returning. (Date uncertain.)

01334
THREE HALFPENNY WORTH OF LEEKS (400)
Walturdaw
COMEDY (Date uncertain.)

01335
MADAM'S TANTRUMS (248)
Walturdaw

COMEDY "All through a heavy supper."
(Date uncertain.)

01336
THE SUNDAY SCHOOL TREAT (500)
Walturdaw
COMEDY PC and soldier hide in hampers; picnickers put them in barrel and roll them into river. (Date uncertain.)

01337
THE LITTLE CONJURER (312)
Walturdaw
COMEDY Boy entertains friends with conjuring tricks. (Date uncertain.)

01338
THE PIRATES OF REGENTS CANAL
Walturdaw
D: Dave Aylott
Bill Haley.......Mother
COMEDY Children steal sheets to convert barge into pirate ship and are stopped by mother. (Date uncertain.)

JUL

01339
LADY AUDLEY'S SECRET
Walturdaw
S: (NOVEL) Dorothy Braddon
CRIME Bigamous lady drowns returned first husband and tries to burn second.

01340
THE VACUUM CLEANER NIGHTMARE (275)
Urban Trading Co
D: (W. R. Booth)
TRICK Salesman sucked into cleaner and turned into rubbish.

01341
BABY'S PERIL (150)
Urban Trading Co
DRAMA Parents try to get loaded revolver away from baby.

01342
THE EARLY ROUND WITH THE MILKMAN (350)
Urban
COMEDY Milkman delivers drunkard to angry wife.

01343
THE SHAM SWORD SWALLOWER (350)
Williamson (Urban)
D: James Williamson
COMEDY Two tramps put on fake show and are chased by PC and crowd.

01344
MRS BROWN GOES HOME TO HER MOTHER (350)
Williamson (Urban)
D: James Williamson
COMEDY Deserted husband makes such a mess of the housework that his wife returns.

01345
THE MEDIUM EXPOSED (385)
R.W. Paul
D: (J. H. Martin)
COMEDY Men expose fake medium's tricks and take revenge.

01346
HOUSE TO LET
R.W. Paul
D: (J. H. Martin)
COMEDY Crooks tie up caretaker of empty house and rob prospective tenants.

01347
JUST A LITTLE PIECE OF CLOTH (245)
R.W. Paul
D: (J. H. Martin)
COMEDY Man tears trousers, dons girl's skirt and is arrested.

01348
THE TWO ORPHANS (560)
Gaumont
D: (Alf Collins)
PATHOS (5 scenes) Girl poses as boy to get work but is too late to save dying brother.

01349
WILLIE AND TIM GET A SURPRISE (240)
Gaumont
D: (Alf Collins)
COMEDY "Highly amusing kid film."

01350
DOLLY VARDEN (740)
Gaumont
D: (Alf Collins)
S: (PLAY)
CHASE 17thC. Girl poses as boy to elope with highwayman who saves pursuing father from gang.

01351
WANTED — A HUSBAND (405)
Gaumont
D: (Alf Collins)
CHASE Bachelors answer marriage advert and find girl is a man!

CHRONOPHONE FILMS *Sound*
Gaumont
D: Arthur Gilbert

01352
THE COSTER'S SERENADE

01353
LET ME LIKE A SOLDIER FALL

01354
TICKLISH REUBEN

01355
THE WHISTLING COON (165)
Darktown Troupe
MUSICAL Synchronised to gramophone records.

01356
A LODGING HOUSE COMEDY (310)
Gaumont
D: (Alf Collins)
COMEDY Boots has revenge on drunken toff by changing room numbers.

01357
FLYPAPER (227)
Gaumont
D: (Alf Collins)
COMEDY Flypaper sticks to father, servants, guests etc.

01358
PONGO THE MAN MONKEY (535)
Gaumont (Haggar?)
COMEDY Family must mind wild monkey to please rich uncle.

01359
WORKHOUSE GRANNY AGE 93 (310)
Gaumont
FACIAL Old woman takes snuff, reads letter, flirts, etc.

01360
EARLY BIRDS (550)
Graphic
D: (Harold Jeapes)
COMEDY Drunks drink milk laced with
epsom salts as trap for thief.

01361
THE DOG DETECTIVE (730)
Norwood (Gau)
D: Harold Hough
ANIMAL Dog trails bank robbers and saves
master's life.

01362
RESCUED IN MID-AIR (605)
Clarendon (Gau)
D: Percy Stow
TRICK Car crash blows girl with parasol onto
steeple; she is saved by airship, which crashes.

01363
THE BURGLAR AND THE CAT (400)
Hepworth
D: Lewin Fitzhamon
Gertie Potter..........Girl
CRIME Girl saves cat when burglar sells it to
vivisectionist.

01364
HIS DAUGHTER AND HIS GOLD (250)
Hepworth
D: Lewin Fitzhamon
Dolly Lupone..........Daughter
DRAMA Miser repents when eloping daughter
steals gold.

01365
THE PILL MAKER'S MISTAKE (300)
Hepworth
D: Lewin Fitzhamon
COMEDY Cook knocks chemist's pills into
soup.

01366
THE SQUATTER'S DAUGHTER (600)
Hepworth
D: Lewin Fitzhamon
Dolly Lupone....................The Daughter
Lewin Fitzhamon..............The Squatter
Bertie Mainwaring..............The Indian Chief
WESTERN Indians capture girl; father saves
her from stake.

AUG

01367
A TOUCH OF HUMAN NATURE (225)
Walturdaw
DRAMA Widower's daughter elopes; later
baby brings reunion.

01368
MURPHY'S WAKE (335)
Walturdaw
S: (PLAY) Dion Boucicault (CONN THE
SHAUGRAUN)
COMEDY "Dead" Irishman revives and causes
fight at wake.

01369
HIS FIRST SILK HAT (320)
Sheffield Photo Co
D: Frank Mottershaw
COMEDY Man buys top hat and gets into fight.

01370
OUR SEASIDE HOLIDAY (330)
Sheffield Photo Co
D: Frank Mottershaw
COMEDY Family of six go to seaside by train.

01371
BLACK BEAUTY (475)
Hepworth
D: Lewin Fitzhamon
Lewin Fitzhamon .... Master
ANIMAL Horse fetches help when tramps attack
master.

01372
WHEN JENKINS WASHED UP (275)
Hepworth
D: Lewin Fitzhamon
COMEDY Clumsy husband smashes crockery.

01373
OH THAT HAT! (325)
Graphic (Gau)
D: (Harold Jeapes)
COMEDY Man buys white top hat which gets
him into fight.

01374
JANE ON THE WARPATH (190)
Gaumont
D: (Alf Collins)
COMEDY Amorous spinster tries to catch
constable.

01375
THE CONVICT'S DAUGHTER (530)
Gaumont
D: (Alf Collins)
CRIME Man jailed for stealing bread repents
after robbing house of cleric who adopted his
starving child.

01376
THE PUZZLE MANIAC (295)
Gaumont
D: (Alf Collins)
COMEDY Man buys puzzle and becomes so
absorbed that he ends up in asylum.

01377
THE WORLD'S WIZARD (350)
R. W. Paul
D: (J. H. Martin)
TRICK Wizard emerges from exploding Earth
and turns countries into girls.

01378
VARIOUS POPULAR LIQUORS
ILLUSTRATED (200)
R. W. Paul
D:(J. H. Martin)
COMEDY Scenes illustrating "Three of Irish
Hot" and other phrases.

01379
SPOONING (65)
R. W. Paul
D: (J. H. Martin)
FACIAL Couple's expressions as they kiss.

01380
THE POLICEMAN'S LOVE AFFAIR (125)
Alpha Trading Co (WTC)
D: Arthur Cooper
COMEDY Mistress throws water over cook and
PC lover.

01381
HELD TO RANSOM (560)
Alpha Trading Co (WTC)
D: Arthur Cooper
CRIME (9 scenes) Blackmailers kidnap girl who
sends carrier pigeon to fetch her fiance.

01382
A CATCHING STORY (55)
Alpha Trading Co (WTC)

D: Arthur Cooper
COMEDY Boy ties sister's skirt to maid's
washing.

01383
TARGET PRACTICE (70)
Alpha Trading Co (WTC)
D: Arthur Cooper
COMEDY Girl's beau misses target and shoots
washerwoman who sets dog on him.

01384
A SLIPPERY VISITOR (447)
Alpha Trading Co (WTC)
D: Arthur Cooper
CHASE Pursued burglar dresses as PC, old
woman, etc.

01385
A VISIT TO A SPIRITUALIST (120)
Alpha Trading Co (WTC)
D: Arthur Cooper
TRICK Man visits medium, sees ghost, and
finds he has innumerable overcoats.

CHRONOPHONE FILMS sound
Gaumont
D: Arthur Gilbert

01386
EXCELSIOR (215)
Ernie Mayne

01387
THE FIREMAN'S SONG (195)
Hamilton Hill

01388
THE WALTZ MUST CHANGE TO A MARCH
Hamilton Hill

01389
HOME TO OUR MOUNTAINS (IL
TROVATORE)
Edith Albord
Frank Rowe

01390
MISERERE (IL TROVATORE)
Edith Albord
Frank Rowe

01391
THE LORD HIGH EXECUTIONER

01392
TIT WILLOW

01393
THREE LITTLE MAIDS FROM SCHOOL

01394
HERE'S A HOW-D'YE-DO

01395
WERT THOU NOT TO KOKO PLIGHTED

01396
THE FLOWERS THAT BLOOM IN THE
SPRING
George Russell
Marie Grey
James Rouse
Albert Gater

01397
ANIMAL IMITATIONS
Gilbert Gerard

01398
WE ALL WALKED INTO THE SHOP
Thomas Graves

01399
THEY CAN'T DIDDLE ME
Dan Crawley

01400
CHORUS, GENTLEMEN!
Edwin Bryan

01401
THE HEART BOWED DOWN
Charles Moppett

01402
LITTLE NELL
Thomas Nye
MUSICAL Synchronised to gramophone records.

01403
THE MINER'S DAUGHTER (600)
Williamson (Urban)
D: James Williamson
ROMANCE (16 scenes) Girl elopes with artist
and is reunited with angry father by child.

01404
A DAY ON HIS OWN (330)
Williamson (Urban)
D: James Williamson
COMEDY Suspicious wife trails husband to fun
fair.

01405
LA MILO (300)
Urban Trading Co
ACT Poseuse seen at home, in dressing-room,
and on stage.

01406
THE MAGIC BOTTLE (200)
Urban Trading Co
D: (W. R. Booth)
TRICK Various magical effects involving bottle.

01407
THAT TERRIBLE DOG (150)
Sheffield Photo Co
D: Frank Mottershaw
COMEDY Man buys Great Dane which drags
him through streets.

01408
THE IMPOSSIBLE LOVERS (130)
Sheffield Photo Co
D: Frank Mottershaw
TRICK Cook's lovers change into dancing dolls.

01409
FOILED BY A WOMAN; OR, FALSELY
ACCUSED (480)
Cricks & Sharp
D:(Tom Green)
CRIME (7 scenes) Framed man breaks jail to
prove innocence.

01410
SWEET SUFFRAGETTES (160)
Cricks & Sharp
D: (Tom Green)
FACIAL Suffragette make speech and is pelted
with eggs.

01411
JONE'S PATENT MOTOR (215)
Cricks & Sharp
CHASE Man's fast car runs into whelk stall and
ends up in river.

01412
SEASIDE VIEWS (390)
Cricks & Sharp
D: (Tom Green)
COMEDY Tramps peep into bathing machine
and get caught.

01413
THE WORKHOUSE AS THE INMATES
EXPECT IT IN 1907 (405)

New Bioscope
COMEDY "Screamingly funny!"

01414
OUR NEW POLICEMAN (525)
Hepworth
D: Lewin Fitzhamon
Gertie Potter
Hettie Potter
COMEDY Village girls play tricks on police
recruit.

01415
THE BURGLAR AND THE JUDGE (450)
Hepworth
D: Lewin Fitzhamon
COMEDY Burglar breaks into judge's house and
lectures him.

01416
THE FATAL LEAP (250)
Hepworth
D:S: Lewin Fitzhamon
Lewin Fitzhamon .....Highwayman
CHASE Pursued highwayman's horse crashes
into five-barred gate.

CHRONOPHONE FILMS   sound
Gaumont
D: Arthur Gilbert

01417
YOU'LL REMEMBER ME
Gertrude Greenbank

01418
ONWARD, CHRISTIAN SOLDIERS
Male Choir

01419
CAPTAIN OF THE PINAFORE
Iago Lewis

01420
SWING SONG FROM "VERONIQUE"

01421
AVE MARIA (GOUNOD)

01422
STROLLING HOME WITH ANGELINA
Joe Mack

01423
THE LOVE SONG
Victoria Monks

MUSICAL Synchronised to gramophone records.

01424
CAUGHT BY THE TIDE (305)
Clarendon (Gau)
D: Percy Stow
ADVENTURE Couple, cut off by tide, are hauled
to cliff top.

01425
HE WASN'T ENGAGED AT THE OFFICE (160)
Graphic (Gau)
D: (Harold Jeapes)
COMEDY Wife catches flirtatious husband.

01426
WOMAN SUPREME
Graphic (Gau)
D: (Harold Jeapes)
COMEDY

01427
OH THAT DOCTOR'S BOY! (336)
R. W. Paul
D: (J.H. Martin)
Frank Miller .....The Boy
COMEDY Doctor's boy delivers wrong
medicines to patients.

01428
A WICKED BOUNDER (550)
Williamson (Urban)
D: James Williamson
DRAMA

01429
WHERE THERE'S A WILL THERE'S A WAY
(675)
Williamson (Urban)
D: James Williamson
COMEDY (18 scenes) Man elopes by posing as
gardener and fools her pursuing father by
putting dummies in car.

01430
AFTER THE CLUB (235)
Sheffield Photo Co
D: Frank Motershaw
COMEDY Drunkard comes home late and falls
in pond.

01431
THE TROUBLES OF THE TWINS (466)
Sheffield Photo Co
D; Frank Mottershaw
COMEDY Twin, mistaken for brother, weds
brother's fiancee.

01432
HOW A BRITISH BULLDOG SAVED THE
UNION JACK (575)
Walturdaw
ANIMAL Zulu captures soldier and sets fire to
flag; bulldog extinguishes fire and frees soldier,
who sets fire to kraal.

OCT

01433
THE TROUBLES OF A THEATRE FIREMAN
(265)
Walturdaw
COMEDY Peeps into stars' dressing-rooms leads
to mishaps with hose.

01434
THE TROUBLES OF A SEA-SIDE
PHOTOGRAPHER (320)
Walturdaw
COMEDY Mishaps of photographer at sea-side.

01435
THE HUMOURS OF A RIVER PICNIC (325)
Cricks & Sharp
D: (Tom Green)
COMEDY Tramp steals swimmer's clothes, etc.

01436
A WOMAN'S SACRIFICE (350)
Cricks & Sharp
D: (Tom Green)
DRAMA (6 scenes) Husband ejects wife when
she returns for child.

01437
THE NEW APPRENTICE: OR, FUN IN A
BAKEHOUSE (300)
Cricks & Sharp
D: Tom Green
Tom Green.....Baker
COMEDY Bakers pelt clumsy yokel with dough,
etc.

01438
THE "?" MOTORIST (190)
R.W. Paul
D: (Walter R Booth)
FANTASY Car drives to sun, around Saturn's
ring, and falls to Earth.

01439
WOMAN SUPREME (212)
R.W. Paul
D: (J.H. Martin)
COMEDY PC tries to stop boy's pranks and is
set upon by parents.

01440
WHY JONES SIGNED THE PLEDGE (530)
Warwick Trading Co
D: (Charles Raymond)
COMEDY Drunkard falls down drain and is
attacked by rats.

01441
THE CABBY'S DREAM (320)
Warwick Trading Co
D: (Charles Raymond)
FANTASY (7 scenes) Cabman dreams of weird
ride with magician.

01442
THE MODERN PIRATES (500)
Alpha Trading Co (Gau)
Reissue: 1911 (Cosmo)
THE RAID OF THE ARMOURED MOTOR
D: Arthur Cooper
CRIME Crooks in armoured car crash into police
car, speed downhill into river; the car explodes.

01443
STOLEN FRUIT (280)
Graphic (Gau)
D: (Harold Jeapes)
COMEDY

01444
THE END OF THE TROUBLE (140)
Graphic (Gau)
D: (Harold Jeapes)
COMEDY Man takes drink of whisky instead
of cutting throat.

01445
HOW ISAACS WON THE CUP (200)
Norwood (Gau)
D: Harold Hough
CHASE Jew wins motor race, is stripped and
flung into river.

01446
THE POSTMAN'S CHRISTMAS BOX (300)
Gaumont
D: (Alf Collins)
COMEDY "Full of fun, fancy, and frolic."

01447
THE FOUR HOOLIGANS (475)
Gaumont
D: (Alf Collins)
COMEDY Youths play tricks on old man,
street organist, ice-cream jack, etc.

01448
A SAILOR'S COURTSHIP (185)
Gaumont
D: (Alf Collins)
COMEDY Two sailors court two girls.

01449
WHEN CRIPPLES MEET (105)
Gaumont
D: Alf Collins
COMEDY Margate. Invalids fight when bath
chairs collide.

01450
HER MORNING DIP (330)
Gaumont
D: Alf Collins

COMEDY Margate. Peeping toms surprised
when comely girl is revealed by her costume
as bony.

01451
RESCUED BY LIFEBOAT (380)
Gaumont
D: Alf Collins
ADVENTURE Margate. Lifeboat launched
to rescue capsized trippers.

01452
JAM NOW IN SEASON (235)
Gaumont
D: (Alf Collins)
COMEDY Children steal jam when mother
isn't looking.

CHRONOPHONE FILMS   sound
Gaumont
D: Arthur Gilbert

01453
THERE IS A GREEN HILL FAR AWAY
Robert Allstone, Steadman's Choir

01454
GOODBYE SWEET MARIE
Charles Wingrove

01455
SERENADE FROM "FAUST"
Charles Wingrove, Gwendoline Burney

01456
IN MONTEZUMA FROM "THE BELLE OF
MAYFAIR"

01457
LAKME : LES STANCES

MUSICAL Synchronised to gramophone records.

01458
THE LUCKY NECKLACE (500)
Hepworth
D: Lewin Fitzhamon
ANIMAL Injured child sends for help by placing
necklace around pet dog's neck.

01459
WHO'S TAKEN MY PARCEL ? (323)
Mitchell & Kenyon (Walturdaw)
COMEDY Man loses parcel and forces shoppers
to untie theirs.

01460
THE INTERRUPTED PICNIC (125)
Mitchell & Kenyon (Walturdaw)
COMEDY Donkey frightens picnic party and
children eat remains.

01461
THE STOLEN BRIDE (650)
Clarendon (Gau)
D: Percy Stow
DRAMA Girl's lover saves her from enforced
marriage and father from sinking boat.

NOV

01462
A DOUBLE LIFE (580)
Clarendon (Gau)
D: Percy Stow
DRAMA Country girl elopes with city cad, is
abandoned, and threatens suicide at wedding.

01463
THE ARTFUL DODGER (346)
Clarendon (Gau)
D: Percy Stow
TRICK "A clever trick; natural surroundings;
extremely comic."

01464
THE HORSE THAT ATE THE BABY (275)
Clarendon (Gau)
D: Percy Stow
TRICK Horse eats baby and is cut open by vet
who finds baby alive.

01465
QUIT YE LIKE MEN (365)
Graphic (Gau)
D: (Harold Jeapes)
COMEDY "Be athletic - exercise!"

01466
THE AMOROUS POLICEMAN (115)
Norwood (Gau)
D: Harold Hough
COMEDY PC thwarts masher in park, flirts with
wife, and is caught by wife.

01467
JUST IN TIME (300)
Hepworth
D: Lewin Fitzhamon
COMEDY Fortune teller shows client a vision
of eloping husband.

01468
THE BRIGANDS (350)
Hepworth
D: Lewin Fitzhamon
CRIME Brigands capture tourist and free him
in exchange for police chief.

01469
AFTER THE MATINEE (325)
Hepworth
D: Lewin Fitzhamon
COMEDY Students take actresses into college
and hide them from dons.

01470
A GRANDCHILD'S DEVOTION (375)
Hepworth
D: Lewin Fitzhamon
DRAMA Grocer evicts drunken grandfather
whose granddaughter reforms him.

01471
INTRODUCTIONS EXTRAORDINARY (300)
R.W. Paul
D: (J.H. Martin)
TRICK Hotel guests get bags mixed and clothes
become alive.

01472
HOW TO MAKE TIME FLY (300)
R.W. Paul
D: (J.H. Martin)
TRICK Girl reverses clock's hands and life
speeds up.

01473
A WIFE'S FORGIVENESS (590)
Warwick Trading Co
D: (Charles Raymond)
CRIME (12 scenes) Gambler robs old man, is
jailed after fairground spree, and reunited with
wife by Salvation Army man.

01474
WITH A PIECE OF STRING (250)
Walturdaw
COMEDY Boys use string to upset milkman,
bootblack, etc.

01475
THE FAKE BLIND MAN (300)
Warwick Trading Co
D: (Charles Raymond)
COMEDY Blind beggar exposed as fraud.

01476
FATHER'S WASHING DAY (292)
Walturdaw
COMEDY Old man delivering washing bumps
into people.

01477
CAPTAIN KID AND HIS PIRATES (365)
Urban Trading Co
COMEDY Gang of children dress up as pirates
and play pranks.

01478
FOLLOWING IN FATHER'S FOOTSTEPS (475)
Urban Trading Co
D: (W.R. Booth)
COMEDY (16 scenes) Small boy takes father's
place for day at office, club, etc.

01479
THE LOAFER'S LUCKY DAY (400)
Urban Trading Co
COMEDY Tramp has luck with boat on river,
finds jewellry, etc.

01480
PUCK'S PRANKS ON A SUBURBANITE (400)
Urban Trading Co
D: (W.R. Booth)
TRICK Puck plays tricks on gardener.

01481
THE CONJURER'S PUPIL (300)
Urban Trading Co
D: (W.R. Booth)
TRICK Conjurer's son's tricks go wrong.

DEC

01482
PERCY'S HALF HOLIDAY (160)
Walturdaw
COMEDY Costers throw posh cyclist into pond.

01483
GRANDPAPA'S REVENGE (245)
Walturdaw
COMEDY Boy puts cheese into grandfather's
pipe, pepper in snuff, and vinegar in beer.

01484
THE COMING OF SANTA CLAUS (550)
Walturdaw
FANTASY Fairies help Santa Claus deliver
toys.

01485
A CHILD'S PRAYER (440)
Walturdaw
DRAMA Poor child's letter to Santa Claus
blows up chimney and down into rich house
next door.

01486
THE STOLEN BICYCLE (245)
Walturdaw
CHASE Man steals butcher's cart to chase man
who stole cycle.

01487
TURNING THE TABLES (290)
Norwood (Gau)
D: Harold Hough
COMEDY

01488
WHEN MOTHER FELL ILL AT CHRISTMAS
(450)
Clarendon (Gau)
D: Percy Stow
COMEDY Mishaps when family try to cook
Christmas dinner.

01489
THE RUNAWAY VAN (337)
Clarendon (Gau)
D: Percy Stow
CHASE Runaway two-horse dray chased
until it goes over cliff.

01490
JUST LIKE A GIRL (60)
Warwick Trading Co
COMEDY

01491
CURFEW SHALL NOT RING TONIGHT
(730)
Gaumont
D: Alf Collins
S: (POEM) Rose H. Thorpe
DRAMA (8 scenes) Girl ties herself to bell
clapper to save lover from execution.

01492
PUNCH AND JUDY (400)
Cricks & Sharp
D: (Tom Green)
PATHOS (10 scenes) Old showman evicted,
gives performance, and dies.

01493
THE FAIRY GODMOTHER (140)
Alpha (Cricks & Sharp)
D: Arthur Cooper
TRICK Child watches toy Noah's Ark come to
life while maid is asleep.

01494
THE TWO TOMBOYS (525)
Gaumont
D: (Alf Collins)
COMEDY Girls play tricks on carman, tramp,
PC, workman, etc.

01495
JIM THE SIGNALMAN (354)
R.W. Paul
D: (J.H. Martin)
CRIME Signalman's crippled son saves mother
when wreckers tie her to tracks.

01496
THE LOVER'S PREDICAMENT (245)
R.W. Paul
D: (J H. Martin)
COMEDY

01497
HARLEQUINADE (475)
Hepworth
Reissue : 1907
D: Lewin Fitzhamon
COMEDY Traditional harlequinade.

01498
THE DOLL MAKER'S DAUGHTER (600)
Hepworth
D: Lewin Fitzhamon
ROMANCE Poor girl takes place of Princess's
doll and flirts with Prince.

01499
LITTLE MEG AND THE WONDERFUL LAMP
(525)
Hepworth
D: Lewin Fitzhamon
Dolly Lupone
PATHOS Rich pair save orphan who steals
pantomime lamp

01500
THE JERRY-BUILT HOUSE (100)
Hepworth
D: Lewin Fitzhamon
COMEDY Roof and floors give way and family
falls into cellar.

01501
THE MAGIC RING (500)
Hepworth
D: Lewin Fitzhamon
Dolly Lupone
FANTASY Youth uses magic ring to save maiden
from witch's castle.

01502
THE JUVENILE BARBERS (160)
Warwick Trading Co
D: Will Barker
Kenneth Barker
COMEDY Two children take turns to cut
each other's hair.

1907

JAN

01503
CHEATING THE SWEEP
Williamson (Gau)
D: James Williamson
COMEDY "Where the soot went."

01504
THE VILLAGE FIRE BRIGADE (325)
Williamson (Gau)
D: James Williamson
DRAMA "A genuine and startling spectacle of a house in flames."

01505
OH THAT MOLAR! (215)
Alpha Trading Co (Gau)
D: Arthur Cooper
TRICK Man with toothache dreams of demon teeth dancing in head.

01506
DISTURBING HIS REST (386)
Clarendon (Gau)
D: Percy Stow
S: Langford Reed
COMEDY Father vainly tries to sleep.

01507
PAYING OFF OLD SCORES(192)
Clarendon (Gau)
D: Percy Stow
COMEDY "Short and strong appealing to young and old."

01508
JONES' BIRTHDAY (240)
Norwood (Gau)
D: Harold Hough
COMEDY

01509
TWO TRAMPS (160)
Walturdaw
COMEDY

01510
WHY JONES GOT THE SACK (245)
Walturdaw
CHASE Man late for work collides with bypassers and is chased.

01511
THE MAN MONKEY (170)
Walturdaw
CHASE India. Ape steals baby and is chased by soldiers.

01512
THE POETS'S BID FOR FAME (305)
Alpha Trading Co (Walturdaw)
D: Arthur Cooper
COMEDY Mad poet rejected by editor, thrown into jail, escapes, goes on stage, and is pelted.

01513
THE COOK'S DREAM (320)
R.W. Paul
D: (J.H. Martin)
TRICK Cook dreams of exploding pie, etc.

01514
A TRAGEDY OF THE ICE (95)
R.W. Paul
D: (J.H. Martin)
COMEDY "Full of startling incidents, laughs, and comical surprises."

01515
BURGLARS AT THE BALL (250)
Hepworth

D; Lewin Fitzhamon
COMEDY Disturbed burglars don fancy dress and join ballroom dancers.

01516
THE BUSY MAN (525)
Hepworth
D: Lewin Fitzhamon
TRICK Speeded scenes of day with business man.

01517
THE GREEN DRAGON (250)
Hepworth
D: Lewin Fitzhamon
COMEDY Drunkard chased by dragon.

01518
WILLIE GOODCHILD VISITS HIS AUNTIE (300)
Urban Trading Co
D: (W.R. Booth)
COMEDY Boy escapes punishment by changing clothes with urchin.

01519
SOAPY SOUP (320)
Alpha Trading Co
D: Arthur Cooper
COMEDY (Date uncertain)

01520
THE WOES OF A MARRIED MAN (400)
Alpha Trading Co
D: Arthur Cooper
COMEDY (Date uncertain)

01521
THE BAD SIXPENCE (260)
Alpha Trading Co (Walturdaw)
D: Arthur Cooper
COMEDY (Date uncertain)

01522
THE BOYS' HALF HOLIDAY (395)
Alpha Trading Co (Walturdaw)
Reissue: 1910,
THOSE BOYS AGAIN (Cosmo)
D: Arthur Cooper
COMEDY Two boys play tricks and save girl from a pond. (Date uncertain)

01523
BETWEEN ONE AND TWO A.M. (370)
Alpha Trading Co (Walturdaw)
D: Arthur Cooper
COMEDY (Date uncertain)

01524
SUNDAY'S DINNER
Alpha Trading Co
D: Dave Aylott
COMEDY (Date uncertain)

FEB

01525
PILLAGE BY PILLAR BOX (300)
Hepworth
D: Lewin Fitzhamon
COMEDY Crook hides inside dummy pillar box to steal letter.

01526
THE NUN (525)
Hepworth
D; Lewin Fitzhamon
ROMANCE Girl saved from convent by lover posing as abbot.

01527
AN OVERDOSE OF LOVE POTION (300)
Clarendon (Gau)
D: Percy Stow
S: Langford Reed
COMEDY Too much love potion makes man kiss everybody.

01528
A HUSBAND AND HOW TO TRAIN "IT" (405)
Norwood (Gau)
D: Harold Hough
COMEDY

01529
THE CHEF'S REVENGE (238)
R.W. Paul
D: (J.H. Martin)
TRICK Chef's rival for maid baked in oven and shrunk.

01530
SAVED BY A SAILOR (535)
R.W. Paul
D: (J.H. Martin)
DRAMA Sailor returns from sea in time to save wife from squire.

01531
PAPA'S LETTER (275)
Walturdaw
PATHOS Child writes letter to dead father, and is run over and killed on way to post.

01532
THERE IS ALWAYS ANOTHER (565)
Walturdaw
DRAMA 18th C. Man pursues eloping daughter and is later reconciled by their child.

01533
THE STORY OF A STRAY DOG (550)
Walturdaw
ANIMAL Dog traces lost girl and saves her from tramp.

01534
THE BORROWED LADDER (480)
Walturdaw
COMEDY Drunkard borrows ladder to rescue hat and is jailed.

01535
EASTER EGGS (300) retitled: EGGS!
Walturdaw
COMEDY Tramps steal eggs and pelt pursuing policemen.

01536
OUR NEW PILLAR BOX (325)
also: THE ANIMATED PILLAR BOX
Alpha Trading Co (Walturdaw)
D: Arthur Cooper
COMEDY Crooks hide inside dummy pillar box.

01537
LOTTIE'S PANCAKES (310)
also: HER FIRST PANCAKE
Alpha Trading Co (Walturdaw)
Reissue: 1910, HER FIRST ATTEMPT (Cosmo)
D: Arthur Cooper
COMEDY Maid helps newlywed cook pancake which makes husband sick.

01538
THEIR FIRST SNOWBALLS (250)
Urban Trading Co
COMEDY Children play tricks with snowballs.

MAR

01539
THE DOLL'S REVENGE (225)
Hepworth
D: Lewin Fitzhamon
Gertie Potter.....The Girl
Bertie Potter.....Her Brother
TRICK Boy breaks sister's doll and it mends, grows, tears him up and eats him.

01540
A SMART CAPTURE (225)
Hepworth
D: Lewin Fitzhamon
TRICK PC chases thieves to granary where they are chopped up .

01541
A FEATHER IN HIS CAP (275)
Hepworth
D: Lewin Fitzhamon
COMEDY Girl's suitor nailed inside hen house by her father catches a thief.

01542
THE SUNDAY SCHOOL TREAT (500)
Clarendon (Gau)
D: Percy Stow
COMEDY Troubles of cleric and children on picnic.

01543
HUSBANDS BEWARE (255)
Norwook (Gau)
D: Harold Hough
COMEDY "A racey little comedy."

01544
THE CHILD ACCUSER (250)
Norwood (Gau)
D: Harold Hough
DRAMA "Powerfully dramatic."

01545
RENT DAY (205)
Norwood (Gau)
D: Harold Hough
COMEDY "Screamingly funny."

01546
A MOTHER'S SIN (356)
R.W. Paul
D: (J. H. Martin)
DRAMA Ejected maid abandons baby and is later rejected by baby's adoptor when she recognises birthmark.

01547
A KNIGHT ERRANT (480)
R.W. Paul
D: J.H. Martin
S: Langford Reed
Langford Reed..........The Knight
FANTASY Fairy helps knight save princess from ogre, witch and dwarf.

01548
HIS FIRST TOP HAT (260)
R.W. Paul
D: (J.H. Martin)
COMEDY Eton boy's new silk hat causes trouble.

01549
THE WAIF AND THE STATUE (240)
Urban Trading Co
D: (W.R. Booth)
FANTASY Statue of Hope revives and finds home for waif.

01550
A MODERN GALATEA (305)
Urban Trading Co
D: (W.R. Booth)
COMEDY Girl breaks artist's statue and takes its place.

01551
SOLD AGAIN (230)
Sheffield Photo Co
D: Frank Mottershaw
COMEDY 'A clinking comic.'

01552
JOHNNY'S RIM (155)
Sheffield Photo Co
D: Frank Mottershaw
COMEDY Naughty boy gets in trouble with hoop.

01553
THE ROMANY'S REVENGE (155)
Sheffield Photo Co
D: Frank Mottershaw
DRAMA "Full of dramatic interest."

01554
THEIR FIRST CIGAR (210)
Cricks & Sharp
D: (Tom Green)
COMEDY Two boys smoke cigar which makes them sick.

CINEMATOPHONE SINGING PICTURES
sound
Walturdaw

01555
OCARINA SOLO

01556
XYLOPHONE SOLO

01557
LAUGHING SONG

01558
THE WHISTLING COON

01559
SWING SONG FROM "VERONIQUE"

01560
COSY CORNER GIRL

01561
MATTSCHICHE DANCE

01562
LOUBA DANCE

MUSICAL Synchronised to gramophone records.

APR

CHRONOPHONE FILMS *sound*
Gaumont
D: Arthur Gilbert

01563
PLEASE CONDUCTOR, DON'T PUT ME OFF THE TRAIN
Vesta Tilley

01564
THIS LITTLE GIRL AND THAT LITTLE GIRL
Alf Collins

01565
REGIMENT OF FROCKS AND FRILLS
Arthur Gilbert

01566
TWIN BROTHERS FROM "THE FRENCH MAID"

01567
THE LAUGHING NIGGER

01568
SONG FROM "THE BELLE OF MAYFAIR"

01569
I LOVE A LASSIE
Harry Lauder

01570
INVERARY
Harry Lauder

01571
SHE IS MY DAISY
Harry Lauder

01572
STOP YOUR TICKLING JOCK
Harry Lauder

01573
THE WEDDING OF SANDY MCNAB
Harry Lauder

01574
WE PARTED ON THE SHORE
Harry Lauder

01575
THE WRONG CHIMNEY (400)
Cricks & Sharp
D: (Tom Green)
COMEDY Old gent uses brick tied to brush to sweep wrong chimney.

01576
BERTIE'S LOVE LETTER (325)
Cricks & Sharp
D: (Tom Green)
COMEDY (10 scenes) Dude reading love letter unaware of where he walks.

01577
SHCOOLBOYS' PRANKS (265)
Cricks & Sharp
D: (Tom Green)
COMEDY Two boys play tricks on shopkeeper, old woman, PC, etc.

01578
DOLLY'S PAPA (385)
Walturdaw
DRAMA Drunkard reforms when lost child is brought into court.

01579
COMEDY CARTOONS (200)
Urban Trading Co
D: W.R. Booth
TRICK Artist's hand draws cartoons which come to life.

01780
THE MAGICAL PRESS (500)
Urban Trading Co
D; W.R. Booth
COMEDY Symbolic scenes illustrating titles of London newspapers.

01581
CATCH THE KID (270)
Gaumont
Reissue: 1912
D; Alf Collins
CHASE Escaped baby finds gun and chases pursuers.

01582
THE FATAL HAND (415)
R.W. Paul
D: (J. H. Martin)
CRIME Escaped lunatic kills woman, strangles railway passenger, climbs building, and is caught by sailor.

01583
NOT SUCH A FOOL AS HE LOOKS (325)
Hepworth
D: Lewin Fitzhamon
DRAMA Rejected suitor wins girl by fighting tramps.

01584
THE ARTIST'S MODEL (350)
Hepworth
D: Lewin Fitzhamon
ROMANCE Poor artist's rich patron lures model.

01585
A FATHER'S VENGEANCE (525)
Hepworth
D: Lewin Fitzhamon
DRAMA Foundry owner saves tramp from snow; tramp rapes his daughter and is thrown into furnace by workmen.

01586
THE FRAUDULENT SOLICITOR (350)
Hepworth
D: Lewin Fitzhamon
CRIME Solicitor robs and shoots client, is chased by police, and jumps off roof.

01587
I NEVER FORGET THE WIFE (385)
Warwick Trading Co
COMEDY Drunkard's mishaps taking bottle of wine to wife. (Date uncertain.)

01588
TRUE TILL DEATH (480)
Warwick Trading Co
ADVENTURE Period. Man frees fiancee from cavalier's dungeon; they are tracked by bloodhounds, caught, and shot. (Date uncertain)

01589
MY MOTHER-IN-LAW'S VISIT (275)
Warwick Trading Co
COMEDY Persecuted man blows up mother-in-law. (Date uncertain.)

01590
A BRAVE LAD'S REWARD (490)
Warwick Trading Co
CRIME Beggar boy and dog save widow's from kidnapping by spurned suitor. (Date uncertain.)

01591
UNCLE'S PRESENT RETURNED WITH THANKS (520)
Warwick Trading Co
COMEDY Uncle gives family pet monkey which wrecks their home. (Date uncertain)

MAY

01592
THE BET THAT DIDN'T COME OFF (285)
Norwood (Gau)
D: Harold Hough
COMEDY

01593
GETTING HIS CHANGE (305)
Norwood (Gau)
D: Harold Hough
COMEDY Customer takes barber's place while he is out seeking change.

01594
WILLIE'S DREAM (400)
Sheffield Photo Co
D: Frank Mottershaw

Mabel Strickland
Lenore Fisher
COMEDY Boy dreams of pranks he will play on the morrow.

01595
HIS CHEAP WATCH (250)
Sheffield Photo Co
D: Frank Mottershaw
COMEDY Cheap watch causes man to miss train.

01596
THE BLACKMAILER (585)
Sheffield Photo Co
D: Frank Mottershaw
CRIME Tec hides behind bush to catch blackmailer.

01597
THE WRECK OF THE MARY JANE (560)
Clarendon (Gau)
D: Percy Stow
S: Langford Reed
ADVENTURE Sailor, shipwrecked in storm, saved by lifeboat.

01598
CURING THE BLIND (215)
Clarendon (Gau)
D: Percy Stow
COMEDY "Blind" beggar watches pretty girl buttoning boot.

01599
LUCK OF LIFE (550)
Alpha Trading Co (Walturdaw)
D: Arthur Cooper
DRAMA Ruined banker's daughter climbs into neighbour's room to steal food.

01600
DUNCAN'S WIFE (300)
Walturdaw
COMEDY Father, family, and friends look after baby while mother away.

01601
SPRING CLEANING (300)
Walturdaw
TRICK Father papers walls; then film reverses.

01602
THE BOTHERED BATHERS (275)
R.W.Paul
D: (J.H. Martin)
COMEDY Swimmers try to get clothes without woman seeing them.

01603
ADVENTURES OF A BROKER'S MAN (305)
R.W. Paul
D: (J.H. Martin)
COMEDY Strong woman refuses to be evicted and throws bailiff in river.

01604
THE BOOKMAKER (140)
R.W. Paul
D: (J.H. Martin)
FACIAL Bookie watches race through field-glasses, then welshes.

01605
THE BURGLAR'S SURPRISE (140)
R.W. Paul
D: (J.H. Martin)
COMEDY Burglar threatens woman with unloaded revolver; husband loads it and captures him.

01606
HOW A BURGLAR FEELS (198)
R.W. Paul
D: (J.H.Martin)
FACIAL Burglar loots house and is caught by police.

01607
AN INHUMAN FATHER (420)
R.W. Paul
D: (J.H. Martin)
DRAMA Husband deserts wife and throws baby into lake; his mistress swims to save it.

01608
MY LADY'S REVENGE (520)
R.W. Paul
D: (J. H. Martin)
DRAMA Man kills rival in duel for girl, who then poses as man and kills him.

01609
THE FIDGETY FLY (248)
R.W. Paul
D: (J.H. Martin)
FACIAL Expressions of man bothered by fly.

01610
THE RIDE OF THE VALKYRIES
Graphic Cinematograph Co
D: (Harold Jeapes)
FANTASY (Made for use during Covent Garden opera production.)

01611
KIDNAPPED (275)
Hepworth
D: Lewin Fitzhamon
CHASE Crone steals nursemaid's baby and is thrown into horse trough.

01612
A LOVER'S QUARREL (375)
Hepworth
D: Lewin Fitzhamon
PATHOS Lovers reunited when go-between is run over.

01613
YOUNG SCAMPS (100)
Hepworth
D: Lewin Fitzhamon
COMEDY Old man birches boys and is pushed down coal hole.

01614
ORANGE PEEL (245)
Williamson (Gau)
D: James Williamson
Tom Williamson .... Boy
COMEDY Boy causes trouble by scattering orange peel.

JUN

01615
THE £1,000 SPOOK (155)
Urban Trading Co
D: W.R. Booth
TRICK Vapour from wizard materialises into ghost of woman.

01616
HANKY PANKY CARDS (225)
Urban Trading Co
D: W.R. Booth
TRICK Playing cards become animated.

01617
THE BAFFLED BURGLAR (360)
Urban Trading Co
D: (W.R. Booth)
CHASE Small dog hangs on to seat of
burglar's trousers.

01618
GOOD-NIGHT (20)
Gaumont
SCENE "An artistic and pleasing finish to a
picture show of any kind."

01619
THE STORY OF A MODERN MOTHER (375)
Clarendon (Gau)
D: Percy Stow
S: Langford Reed
COMEDY "New woman" neglects family.

01620
A WOODLAND TRAGEDY (470)
Graphic
D: (Harold Jeapes)
CHASE Two rabbit poachers chased by
keepers; one of each is shot.

01621
SONS OF MARTHA
Warwick Trading Co
D: (Charles Raymond)
S: (SERIAL) Arthur Applin
Arthur Applin
Mabel Russell
Henry Farmer
Edith Olive
Grace Noble
Loring Fernie
CRIME (3 scenes) Novelist dreams scenes of
a workman killing his boss in a fight to save
a shopgirl. (Advert "Evening News".)

01622
HAIR RESTORER (300)
Hepworth
D: Lewin Fitzhamon
COMEDY Man pushes wife into bath of
hair restorer and exhibits her as bear.

01623
THE BOASTER (200)
Hepworth
D: (Lewin Fitzhamon)
COMEDY Man saves girl from youths and
exaggerated story.

01624
SISTER MARY JANE'S TOP NOTE (100)
Hepworth
D: Lewin Fitzhamon
TRICK Singing pupil's voice wrecks room.

01625
THE MAN WHO COULD NOT COMMIT
SUICIDE (275)
Hepworth
D: Lewin Fitzhamon
COMEDY Rejected suitor's attempts to
commit suicide fail.

01626
THE MILKMAN'S WEDDING (425)
Hepworth
D: Lewin Fitzhamon
COMEDY Reluctant milkman fails to avoid
wedding

01627
THE NEW DRESS (475)
Hepworth
D: (Lewin Fitzhamon)
COMEDY

01628
THAT FATAL SNEEZE (350)
Hepworth
D: Lewin Fitzhamon
Thurston Harris...... Uncle
Gertie Potter .... Nephew
TRICK Boy shakes pepper on uncle whose
sneezes wreck house.

01629
HER FRIEND THE ENEMY (350)
Hepworth
D: (Lewin Fitzhamon)
COMEDY

01630
NEVER COMPLAIN TO YOUR LAUNDRESS
Hepworth
D: Lewin Fitzhamon
COMEDY Customer complains about washing
and is scrubbed, mangled and parcelled.

01631
THE ABSENT MINDED MAN (275)
Hepworth
D: (Lewin Fitzhamon)
COMEDY

01632
THE TALE OF A MOUSE (155)
R.W. Paul
D: (J.H. Martin)
COMEDY Man smashes furniture and water
pipe while trying to kill mouse.

01633
SEEN AT THE CHIROPODIST'S (310)
Alpha Trading Co (Walturdaw)
D: Arthur Cooper
COMEDY Barber tries to cut girl's toenails
while shaving man.

01634
WHEN THE MISTRESS TOOK HER HOLIDAY
(400)
Alpha Trading Co (Walturdaw)
D: Arthur Cooper
COMEDY Servants don absent employers'
clothes and have party.

01635
GOOD EVENING (36)
Walturdaw
SCENE To be shown at conclusion of film show.

CINEMATOPHONE SINGING PICTURES
sound
Walturdaw
D: John Morland

01636
THE LORD HIGH EXECUTIONER

01637
IF YOU WANT TO KNOW WHO WE ARE

01638
WERE YOU NOT TO KOKO PLIGHTED

01639
OUR GREAT MIKADO

01640
A WANDERING MINSTREL

01641
MIYA SAMA

01642
A MORE HUMAN MIKADO

01643
THREE LITTLE MAIDS

01644
THE FLOWERS THAT BLOOM IN THE
SPRING

01645
THE CRIMINAL CRIED

01646
HERE'S A FINE HOW D'YE DO

01647
TIT WILLOW
George Thorne .... Koko

01648
FOUR JOLLY SAILOR BOYS FROM
"THE PRINCESS OF KENSINGTON"

01649
CHURCH PARADE FROM "THE
CATCH OF THE SEASON"
MUSICAL Synchronised to gramophone
records.

01650
THE DRUNKEN MOTORCYCLIST (246)
Gaumont
D: (Alf Collins)
CHASE Wild ride of drunkard on motorcycle.

JUL

01651
THE MADMAN'S BRIDE (400)
Hepworth
D: (Lewin Fitzhamon)
CRIME Mad lord buys girl from father,
kills her during night, and is captured after
murderous struggle.

01652
A MODERN DON JUAN (350)
Hepworth
D: Lewin Fitzhamon
Dolly Lupone
Gertie Potter
CHASE Girls row after flirt in boat and duck
him in river.

01653
THE TRAMP'S REVENGE (150)
Hepworth
D: Lewin Fitzhamon
COMEDY Tramps cause fisherman to fall in
river.

01654
THE GHOSTS' HOLIDAY (550)
Hepworth
D: Lewin Fitzhamon
Gertie Potter
Thurston Harris
TRICK Ghosts rise from churchyard and hold
ball in hotel.

01655
A TOO DEVOTED WIFE (375)
Hepworth
D: Lewin Fitzhamon
COMEDY Henpeck tries to escape wife by
becoming railway stoker.

01656
DRINK (200)
Hepworth
D: Lewin Fitzhamon
COMEDY Drunkard dreams motorist in fur
coat is bear.

01657
THE BRIGAND'S DAUGHTER (806)
Williamson
D: (James Williamson)
Winnie Barton .... The Girl
DRAMA Girl helps artist escape from bandits;
they are chased onto bridge which is struck
by lightning.

CINEMATOPHONE SINGING PICTURES
sound
Walturdaw
D: John Morland

01658
DOWN BY THE OLD BULL AND BUSH

01659
ZUYDER ZEE

01660
HERE UPON WE'RE BOTH AGREED

01661
WERE I THY BRIDE

01662
GREAT FINALE TO ACT 1 ("THE YEOMAN
OF THE GUARD")

01663
WHAT D'YER WANT TO TALK ABOUT IT
FOR?

01664
IT'S A DIFFERENT GIRL AGAIN

01665
RIDING ON TOP OF A CAR

01666
WAITING FOR HIM TONIGHT

01667
WE ALL WALKED INTO THE SHOP

01668
THEY CAN'T DIDDLE ME

01669
THE OLD FOLKS AT HOME
MUSICAL Synchronised to gramophone
records

01670
THE HAUNTED BEDROOM (250)
Urban Trading Co
D: W.R. Booth
TRICK "Uncanny happenings follow each
other with bewildering rapidity"

01671
YOUTHFUL HACKENSCHMIDTS (190)
Urban Trading Co
COMEDY Old lady and policeman try to
separate wrestling urchins.

01672
AFTER THE FANCY DRESS BALL (345)
Williamson
D: (James Williamson)
COMEDY Dancer dressed as Satan has trouble
hailing cab.

01673
BOBBY'S BIRTHDAY (214)
Williamson
D: (James Williamson)
COMEDY Boy causes damage with new
football and is chased.

01674
SEYMOUR HICKS EDITS "THE TATLER"
(365)
Urban Trading Co

Seymour Hicks .... Himself
COMEDY Comedy scenes added to
"industrial"

01675
SAVED FROM THE SEA (455)
Cricks & Sharp
DRAMA (9 scenes) Fisherman goes to sea, is
wrecked, and saved by father in time to see
dying mother.

01676
ADVENTURES OF A BATH CHAIR (550)
Clarendon (Gau)
D: Percy Stow
S: Langford Reed
CHASE Pursuit of invalid in runaway bath
chair.

01677
THE CHEATERS CHEATED (510)
R.W. Paul
D: (J.H. Martin)
COMEDY Swindled man poses as PC to get
cash back from gamblers.

01678
MISCHIEVOUS GIRLS (250)
Hepworth
D: Lewin Fitzhamon
Gladys Godfrey .... Girl
Cossie Godfrey .... Girl
COMEDY Two girls play tricks with
householder's hat.

01679
A SOLDIER'S JEALOUSY (400)
Hepworth
D: Lewin Fitzhamon
Gertie Potter .... Girl
DRAMA Girl delivers despatch when jealous
officer delays soldier fiance.

01680
A SAILOR'S LASS
Hepworth
D: Lewin Fitzhamon
Dolly Lupone .... Girl
Lewin Fitzhamon .... Abductor
CHASE Bognor. Man tries to abduct girl and
is chased by sailors.

01681
SIMPKIN'S SATURDAY OFF (200)
Hepworth
D: Lewin Fitzhamon
Thurston Harris .... Simpkin
CHASE Bognor. Man rides carriage, donkey,
goat-cart, cycle, etc.

01682
A SEASIDE GIRL (325)
Hepworth
D: Lewin Fitzhamon
May Clark .... Girl
Frank Wilson ....Scotsman
Thurston Harris ..... Suitor
CHASE Bognor. Three suitors try to impress
girl; scotsman wins.

01683
PA TAKES UP PHYSICAL CULTURE (305)
Williamson
D: (James Williamson)
COMEDY Father tries to emulate circus
strong man and wrecks house.

01684
WHY THE WEDDING WAS PUT OFF (225)
Williamson
D: (James Williamson)

COMEDY Groom's rush to church causes him
to arrive in mess.

01685
JUST IN TIME (540)
Williamson
D: (James Williamson)
ADVENTURE Child sees Puritan plant papers
on Royalist, whose fiancee then rides for
Cromwell's pardon.

01686
IN QUEST OF HEALTH (475)
Alpha Trading Co (Walturdaw)
D: Arthur Cooper
COMEDY Man with backache seeks cure in
sanatorium vapour bath.

01687
WHO WINKED AT THE SOLDIER (560)
Graphic
D: (Harold Jeapes)
CHASE Scots soldier changes clothes with a
tramp to elude pursuing girls. ("Winking title.")

01688
TOMMY'S BOX OF TOOLS (460)
Norwood (Gau)
D: Harold Hough
COMEDY Naughty boy plays tricks with tools.

01689
PITY THE POOR BLIND (107)
R.W. Paul
D: (J.H. Martin)
FACIAL Expressions of a "blind" beggar given
a button.

01690
WILLIE'S MAGIC WAND (320)
Urban Trading Co
D: W.R. Booth
TRICK Magician's son plays tricks with father's
magic wand.

01691
DREAMLAND ADVENTURES (540)
Urban Trading Co
D: W.R. Booth
FANTASY Doll and gollywog take children to
Arctic in airship.

01692
ACCIDENTS WILL HAPPEN (440)
Urban Trading Co
D: (W.R. Booth)
COMEDY Employer bankrupted when employees
fake accidents and claim under new compensation
act.

01693
THE PAGE BOY AND THE BABY (550)
Warwick Trading Co
D: Jack Smith
COMEDY Family search for baby which page-
boy hides in rolltop desk.

01694
THE ABSENT-MINDED PROFESSOR (550)
Clarendon (Gau)
D: Percy Stow
S: Langford Reed
COMEDY Maths master chalks figures on
everything and has strange dream.

01695
A TRAMP'S DREAM OF WEALTH (425)
Hepworth
D: Lewin Fitzhamon
Thurston Harris .... Tramp
Gertie Potter .... Mermaid
COMEDY Bognor. Tramp dreams mermaid
takes him to ship full of money.

01696
DUMB SAGACITY (450)
Hepworth
D: Lewin Fitzhamon
Gertie Potter .... Girl
ANIMAL Bognor. Pet dog fetches horse to save
girl cut off by tide.

CHRONOPHONE FILMS sound
Gaumont
D: Arthur Gilbert

01697
FAUST
Complete opera: 22 songs

01698
CARMEN
Several songs

01699
NAVAHO
Gipsy Woolf

01700
THE FIREMAN
Hamilton Hill

01701
HOME AGAIN MY CHERRY BLOSSOM

01702
ARE YOU SINCERE?

01703
TALA - INDIAN LOVE SONG
Stanley & Bain

01704
WON'T YOU THROW ME A KISS
Alf Collins & Miss Horton

01705
THE BEDOUIN'S LOVE SONG
Peter Dawson

01706
THE BLIND VIOLINIST

01707
THE BROKEN MELODY
Auguste Van Biene

01708
EVERY LITTLE BIT HELPS

01709
CHRISTIANS AWAKE!

01710
HARRIGAN
Billy Murray

01711
CURFEW SHALL NOT RING TONIGHT

01712
WAIT TILL THE WORK COMES ROUND
Gus Elen

01713
CUPID
Ernie Mayne

01714
WILL EVANS: ON THE DOORSTEP;
NOVELETTE; THE JOCKEY
MUSICAL Synchronised to gramophone
records.

01715
THE WILY FIDDLER (345)
Alpha Trading Co
D: Arthur Cooper
COMEDY

01716
A SHILLING SHORT OF HIS WAGES (400)
Gaumont
D: (Alf Collins)
COMEDY Man hides in box to escape wife but
is delivered home.

01717
FALSELY ACCUSED (555)
Gaumont
CRIME Framed man breaks jail, poses as tinker
woman, is caught, and saved by dying confession.

01718
JU-JITSU (445)
Gaumont
D: Alf Collins
Madame Garrud
COMEDY Women pursue pickpockets from
Piccadilly to Hampstead and wrestle them.

01719
THE TALE OF THE TOOTH (378)
Walturdaw (Alpha?)
COMEDY Attempts to pull tooth fail.

01720
THE ADVENTURES OF A PERFORMING
FLEA (350)
Alpha Trading Co (Walturdaw)
D: Arthur Cooper
COMEDY Showman searches for escaped flea.

01721
THE MATINEE IDOL (480)
Walturdaw (Alpha?)
COMEDY Actor dons disguises to elude mob of
adoring women.

01722
AUNTY'S MOTOR BIKE (250)
Walturdaw
CHASE Old lady rides motor cycle into tar
barrel, cart, etc.

01723
THE 5-30 COLLECTION (250)
Graphic
D: (Arthur Cooper)
COMEDY "Full of surprising incidents and fun."

01724
THE LODGER HAD THE HADDOCK (295)
Graphic
D: (Arthur Cooper)
COMEDY Bad fish passed off on
unsuspecting lodger.

01725
THE LOVERS' CHARM (160)
Graphic
D: (Arthur Cooper)
TRICK "A picturesque trick film."

01726
THE TRICKY TWINS (330)
Graphic
D: (Arthur Cooper)
CHASE Boys tie pram behind horse cart; the
pram contains doll.

01727
THE SHOWMAN'S TREASURE (505)
Graphic
D: (Arthur Cooper)
CHASE Showman uses magnifying
glass to search for escaped flea.

01728
MY WORD IF YOU'RE NOT OFF (280)
Sheffield Photo Co

D: Frank Mottershaw
COMEDY "The popular saying of the day
humorously illustrated."

01729
THE DODGERS DODGED (276)
Sheffield Photo Co Reissue: 1911 (Walt)
D: Frank Mottershaw
TRICK Police chase vanishing robbers.

01730
OH THAT LIMERICK! (400)
Sheffield Photo Co
D: Frank Mottershaw
COMEDY "Clever skit on the competition
craze of the moment."

01731
THEY WOULD PLAY CARDS (685)
Warwick Trading Co
D: Jack Smith
COMEDY Couple get mania for playing cards.

01732
TRUTHFUL TELEGRAMS (220)
Warwick Trading Co
D: Jack Smith
COMEDY Telegrams of gambler, husband,
girl, thief, do not reflect truth.

01733
DESPERATE FOOTPADS (360)
Haggar & Sons (WTC)
D: William Haggar
CRIME

01734
CURING A JEALOUS WIFE (325)
Warwick Trading Co
D: Jack Smith
COMEDY Wife tracks husband to railway station
where he collects kitten.

01735
MOVING DAY (315)
Williamson
D: James Williamson
COMEDY Mean father's troubles moving
furniture in barrow.

01736
THE AMATEUR PAPER HANGER (282)
R.W. Paul
D: (J.H. Martin)
COMEDY Slapstick troubles of husband,
wife and maid.

01737
THE GAMEKEEPER'S DOG (460)
Norwood (Cinematograph Syndicate)
D: Harold Hough
ANIMAL Dog drives cart to save master
from gun duel with rival.

01738
SERVING A SUMMONS (190)
Cricks & Sharp
D:S: A.E. Coleby
A.E. Coleby ....Policeman
TRICK PC serves summons but furniture
disappears.

OCT

01739
LIFE ON AN ENGLISH REFORMATORY
SHIP (600)
Cricks & Sharp
DRAMA Purfleet. Poor urchin reformed after
serving term on "Cornwall"

01740
DAY DUTY (215)
Cricks & Sharp
D: (A.E. Coleby)
COMEDY Various happenings on
policeman's beat.

01741
DON'T GO TO THE LAW (250)
Cricks & Sharp
D: (A.E. Coleby)
COMEDY Farmers quarrel over cow and lose it
to lawyers.

01742
EVEN A WORM WILL TURN (275)
Cricks & Sharp
D: (A.E. Coleby)
COMEDY Henpeck tips nagging wife into bath.

01743
A DRINK CURE (395)
Cricks & Sharp
D: (A.E. Coleby)
COMEDY Actors cure drunkard by dressing up
as weird animals.

01744
FUN IN THE STUDIO (190)
Cricks & Sharp
D: (A.E. Coleby)
COMEDY Artist dresses drunkard as Cupid.

01745
MAY AND DECEMBER (245)
Cricks & Sharp
D: (A.E. Coleby)
COMEDY Old man lights stove in which
young wife has hidden lover.

01746
HIS ONLY PAIR OF TROUSERS (390)
Cricks & Sharp
D: (A.E. Coleby)
CHASE Plumber wraps himself in oilcloth
to chase tramp who stole his wet trousers.

01747
ONLY A LIMERICK (350)
Cricks & Sharp
D: (A.E. Coleby)
COMEDY Wife thinks husband's limerick
is love letter.

01748
THE ICE CREAM JACK (516)
Gaumont
D: Alf Collins
COMEDY Hampstead salesman jailed when
whitewash and cockroaches are found in ice
cream.

01749
ALL FOR NOTHING (265)
Gaumont
D: (Alf Collins)
CHASE Tramp steals watch and is chased
over cliff.

01750
SHORT-SIGHTED JANE (196)
Gaumont
D: (Alf Collins)
CHASE Myopic woman collides with people and
is chased into sea.

01751
THE BACHELOR'S PIECE OF WEDDING
CAKE (340)
Gaumont

01752
OH THAT CAT! (276)
Gaumont
D: (Alf Collins)
CHASE Tramps steal basket and find it holds
cat.

01753
CHEAP BEER (242)
Gaumont
D: (Alf Collins)
COMEDY Tramps siphon beer from
brewer's dray and sell it.

01754
FATHER BUYS A LAWN ROLLER (580)
Gaumont *Reissue* 1912
D: (Alf Collins)
COMEDY Father gets in trouble wheeling
lawn roller.

01755
REMEMBER REMEMBER THE FIFTH OF
NOVEMBER (535)
Gaumont
D: (Alf Collins)
COMEDY Children light confiscated fireworks
and set fire to house.

01756
TOMMY THE TINPOT HERO (436)
Gaumont
D: (Alf Collins)
COMEDY Boy gets saucepan stuck over
head.

01757
HER RIVAL'S NECKLACE (625)
Warwick Trading Co
CRIME Actress, suspected of stabbing rival
for necklace, escapes to cottage where she
sees real thief.

01758
MIND YOUR OWN BUSINESS (350)
Warwick Trading Co
D: (Jack Smith)
COMEDY Parents try to stop children's
quarrel and start fight.

01759
WHY JENKINS WEARS THE BLUE RIBBON
(378)
Warwick Trading Co
D: (Jack Smith)
CHASE Drunkard fails to catch hat and signs
pledge.

01760
SPOT, THE DOG THIEF (420)
Warwick Trading Co
ANIMAL Couple train dog to steal; police
trail it to den.

01761
THE SMOKER'S JOKE (390)
Graphic
D: (Arthur Cooper)
COMEDY Discarded box of explosive cigars
causes trouble for finders.

01762
A SACRIFICE FOR WORK (345)
Graphic
D: (Arthur Cooper)
TRICK Bearded labourer is shaved for job,
is unrecognised by wife, and has beard replaced.

01763
HIS SWEETHEART WHEN A BOY (550)
Graphic
D: (Arthur Cooper)
DRAMA Girl weds rich gambler who loses
everything and kills himself.

01764
A JUVENILE SCIENTIST (335)
Urban Trading Co
D: W.R. Booth
TRICK Scientist's son plays tricks with
father's chemicals.

01765
CATCH YOUR OWN FISH (320)
Urban Trading Co
D: W.R. Booth
COMEDY Boy photographs married angler
flirting with girl.

01766
THE SORCEROR'S SCISSORS (220)
Urban Trading Co
D: W.R. Booth
TRICK Scissors cut shapes which come to life.

01767
THE CURATE'S DOUBLE (435)
Urban Trading Co
D: W.R. Booth
COMEDY Husband eludes wife by posing as
clerical double.

01768
SAMMY'S SUCKER (295)
Urban Trading Co
D: W.R. Booth
COMEDY Boy plays tricks with sucker made
from soaked leather.

01769
HIS DAUGHTER'S VOICE (340)
Urban Trading Co
D: W.R. Booth
MUSICAL Girl dies saving blind father's life
and her spirit emerges from gramophone
horn. (Synchronises to record of "Daddy".)

01770
THE APPLE OF DISCORD (240)
Urban Trading Co
D: W.R. Booth
TRICK Wizard shows love scene acted
within slice of apple.

01771
WHEN THE DEVIL DRIVES (390)
Urban Trading Co *Reissue:* 1913
D: W.R. Booth
FANTASY Satan drives train over telegraph
wires, under sea, etc.

01772
DIABOLO NIGHTMARE (385)
Urban Trading Co
D: W.R. Booth
TRICK (22 scenes) Clerk, unable to stop
playing game of Diabolo, dreams of playing
under sea.

01773
GETTING RID OF HIS DOG (310)
Williamson
D: James Williamson
COMEDY Owner fails in every attempt to get
rid of pet dog.

01774
THE ANARCHIST AND HIS DOG (245)
Walturdaw
COMEDY Anarchist throws bomb at rival, dog
retrieves it, chases anarchist to hut, and it
explodes.

01775
THE FIFTH OF NOVEMBER (245)
Walturdaw
COMEDY Boys play tricks with fireworks until
police catch them.

01776
GUY FAWKES (355)
Walturdaw
HISTORY 1605. Catholic conspirator caught
before he can blow up Parliament.

01777
THE ELECTRIC FIRE GIRL
Walturdaw
Connie Edison
ACT "The Fire Queen".

01778
THE STICKY BICYCLE (100)
Hepworth
D: Lewin Fitzhamon
COMEDY Boys put poster paste on saddle of
old man's cycle.

01779
A LETTER IN THE SAND (200)
Hepworth
D: Lewin Fitzhamon
Dolly Lupone .... Girl
Thurston Harris .... Man
CHASE Bognor. Spinster mistakes youth and
chases him.

01780
REBELLIOUS SCHOOLGIRLS (100)
Hepworth
D: Lewin Fitzhamon
COMEDY Pupils birch mistress and pour ink
on her.

01781
THE ARTFUL LOVERS (300)
Hepworth
D: Lewin Fitzhamon
Thurston Harris .... Father
May Clark .... Girl
Dolly Lupone .... Girl
Frank Wilson .... Suitor
COMEDY Bognor. Suitors save girls' father from
drifting bathing-machine.

01782
THE BOY BANDITS (480)
R.W. Paul
COMEDY "Halfpenny blood" influences boys
to rob motorist.

01783
AN AWKWARD SITUATION (405)
Clarendon (Gaumont)
D: Percy Stow
S: Langford Reed
CHASE Naked man with bath on back pursues
man who has his trousers.

NOV

01784
DYING OF THIRST (175)
Hepworth
D: Lewin Fitzhamon
ADVENTURE Bognor. Sailors save parched man
and dog from wreck.

01785
THE VIKING'S BRIDE (400)
Hepworth
D: (Lewin Fitzhamon)
ADVENTURE Vikings help chief save bride
from rival tribe.

01786
THE HEAVENLY TWINS (350)
Hepworth
D: Lewin Fitzhamon
Thurston Harris .... Man
Gertie Potter .... Girl
COMEDY Bognor. Two girls play pranks at
seaside.

01787
PERSERVING EDWIN (400)
Hepworth
D: Lewin Fitzhamon
May Clark .... Girl
Thurston Harris .... Man
COMEDY Bognor. Suitor flirts with girl
despite tutor.

01788
THE ORPHANS (655)
Williamson
D: (James Williamson)
PATHOS Boy steals, is jailed, freed, and refused
work; he robs house where his sister has been
adopted.

01789
SAVED FROM THE BURNING WRECK (480)
Cricks & Sharp
D: (A.E. Coleby)
ADVENTURE Barque catches fire and explodes
so crew take to raft.

01790
AN ANXIOUS DAY FOR MOTHER (335)
Clarendon
D: Percy Stow
S: Langford Reed
COMEDY

01791
THAT'S NOT RIGHT - WATCH ME! (595)
Clarendon
D: Percy Stow
S: Langford Reed
COMEDY Mishaps of man who thinks he knows
everything.

01792
THE WATER BABIES; OR, THE LITTLE
CHIMNEY SWEEP (955)
Clarendon
D: Percy Stow
S: (NOVEL) Charles Kingsley
SC: Langford Reed
FANTASY Boysweep drowns while fleeing
master and is changed into water baby.

01793
THE PIED PIPER (755)
Clarendon
D: Percy Stow
S: (POEM) Robert Browning
SC: Langford Reed
FANTASY Piper lures children when payment
is refused for luring rats.

01794
A WET DAY (275)
Clarendon
D: Percy Stow
S: Langford Reed
CHASE Man with umbrella rushes to catch train
in rain.

01795
A SOLDIER'S WEDDING (675)
Clarendon
D: Percy Stow
S: Langford Reed
WAR Newly wed soldier sent to war and saved
from natives by wife who has become nurse.

01796
JOHNNY'S GUN (425)
Hepworth
D: Lewin Fitzhamon
COMEDY Boy plays tricks with toy pistol and
bow-and-arrow.

01797
CINDERELLA (1200)
Hepworth
D: Lewin Fitzhamon
Frank Wilson ...:........ Prince Charming
Dolly Lupone .... Cinderella
Gertie Potter .... Fairy
Thurston Harris .... Baron
FANTASY Fairy godmother helps drudge go to
royal ball.

01798
THE STOLEN BRIDLE (125)
Hepworth
D: Lewin Fitzhamon
ANIMAL Horse chases tramp who steals
bridle and bicycle.

01799
SERVING THE WRIT (600)
Hepworth
D: (Lewin Fitzhamon)
COMEDY Milliner serves writ on actress by
hiding it in bouquet.

01800
A PAINLESS EXTRACTION (250)
Hepworth
D: Lewin Fitzhamon
TRICK Dental patient's head swells with gas
and floats away.

01801
LOVE WILL FIND A WAY (700)
Warwick Trading Co
ROMANCE Girl changes place with maid on day
of her enforced marriage.

01802
BOBBY'S DREAM OF BATTLE (385)
Warwick Trading Co
COMEDY Boy dreams he is sentry shooting
bypassers.

01803
THE ADVENTURES OF A ROLL OF LINO
(335)
Gaumont *Reissue:* 1912, FATHER BUYS SOME
LINOLEUM
D: (Alf Collins)
COMEDY Father has trouble carrying roll of
linoleum.

01804
THE UNLUCKY HORSESHOE (480)
Norwood (Cinematograph Syndicate)
D: Harold Hough
COMEDY Horseshoe causes series of mishaps.

01805
THE GIDDY GOATS (235)
Walturdaw
D: (Dave Aylott)
COMEDY "Two knockabouts and a goat."

01806
UNDER THE MISTLETOE (300)
Walturdaw
D:Dave Aylott
COMEDY Boy attaches hose to mistletoe bunch
and soaks kissers.

CHRONOPHONE FILMS *sound*
Gaumont
D: Arthur Gilbert

01807
NELSON'S VICTORY
Max Darewski

01808
THE ROYAL STANDARD
Max Darewski

01809
MARCH OF THE LIGHT CAVALRY
Max Darewski

01810
MY INDIAN ANNA
Ellaline Terriss

01811
GLOW LITTLE GLOW WORM GLOW
Ellaline Terriss
MUSICAL Synchronised to gramophone records.

CINEMATOPHONE SINGING PICTURES
sound
Walturdaw
D: John Morland

01812
FLY ANN

01813
WHERE OH WHERE HAS MY LITTLE DOG
GONE?

01814
I WOULD LIKE TO MARRY YOU
MUSICAL Synchronised to gramophone
records.

1908

JAN

01815
THE LITTLE WAIF AND THE CAPTAIN'S
DAUGHTER (400)
Clarendon
D: Percy Stow
S: Langford Reed
ADVENTURE Stowaway saves captain's
daughter from abduction by mate.

01816
THE CAPTAIN'S WIVES (590)
Clarendon
D: Percy Stow
S: Langford Reed
COMEDY Captain's wife swims after his ship
and finds he has a wife in every port.

01817
THE DOWNFALL OF THE BURGLARS' TRUST
Clarendon (430)
D: Percy Stow
S: Langford Reed
CRIME Gang steal ruby from Clarendon studio
and chase traitor.

01818
MARCH WINDS (270)
Cricks & Martin
D: A E Coleby
CHASE Gent pursues windblown top hat.

01819
DIABOLO MAD (240)
Cricks & Martin
D: A.E. Coleby
COMEDY Man gets diabolo craze and wrecks
home.

01820
A RACE FOR A ROSE (577)
Gaumont
D: (Alf Collins)
SPORT Rivals race to win girl.

01821
HONOURS EVEN (256)
Gaumont
D: (Alf Collins)
COMEDY Maid hides soldier from sailor,
sailor from PC, and PC from master.

01822
THE HYPNOTIST'S JOKE (395)
Graphic Cinematograph Co
D: (Arthur Cooper)
COMEDY

01823
A FAITHLESS FRIEND (500)
Hepworth
D: Lewin Fitzhamon
CRIME Usurper repents after dreaming his
ancestor's portraits and a skeleton come to
life.

01824
THE CURATE'S COURTSHIP (140)
Hepworth
D: Lewin Fitzhamon
COMEDY Shy curate caught helping girl over
stile.

01825
THE STUBBORN MOKE (200)
Hepworth
D: Lewin Fitzhamon
ANIMAL PC finally moves stubborn donkey by
using traction engine.

01826
THE SKIRL OF THE PIBROCH (140)
Walturdaw
D: (Dave Aylott)
COMEDY Boy plays bagpipes and makes
everybody dance.

01827
THE OFFICE BOY'S DREAM (385)
Walturdaw
D: Dave Aylott
COMEDY Office boy dreams he is caught by
bandits and shot for treachery.

01828
MAZEPPA (500)
Walturdaw
D: Frank Dudley
S: (POEM) Lord Byron
DRAMA Poland, 1670. Nobleman ties wife's
lover to back of wild horse.

FEB

01829
TWIXT LOVE AND DUTY; OR, A WOMAN'S
HEROISM (455)
Cricks & Martin
D: A.E. Coleby
CRIME (10 scenes) Coastguard forced to betray
father-in-law as chief smuggler.

01830
FOR BABY'S SAKE (375)
Cricks & Martin
D: A.E. Coleby
A.E. Coleby .... Father
DRAMA (6 scenes) Child's letter reunites
parents after quarrel over amorous friend.

01831
THE GREEDY GIRL (250)
Hepworth
D: Lewin Fitzhamon
TRICK Sleepwalking girl dreams knights chop
her up.

01832
THE DOCTOR'S DODGE (250)
Hepworth
D: Lewin Fitzhamon
COMEDY Dr dresses as Santa Claus to give girl
medicine; burglar does same and is given
medicine.

01833
THE TELL-TALE KINEMATOGRAPH (400)
Hepworth
D: Lewin Fitzhamon
COMEDY Woman goes to
cinema and sees film of husband with girl.

01834
THE MAN AND HIS BOTTLE (350)
Hepworth
D: Lewin Fitzhamon
Thurston Harris .... Drunkard
TRICK Drunkard has vision of everything turning
into bottles.

01835
THE CARTER'S TERRIBLE TASK (419)
R.W. Paul
COMEDY Carter mistakes dummy in trunk for
dismembered corpse.

01836
BANANA SKINS (330)
Sheffield Photo Co
D: Frank Mottershaw
COMEDY Piano movers, PC, crook, etc, slip on
boy's banana skins.

01837
THAT NASTY STICKY STUFF (306)
Sheffield Photo Co
D: Frank Mottershaw
COMEDY Naughty boy plays pranks with
super glue.

01838
LAZY JIM'S LUCK (485)
Warwick Trading Co
D: (Charles Raymond)
TRICK Everything gets done for lazy man.

01839
PUT ME AMONG THE GIRLS (240)
Walturdaw
D: Dave Aylott
CHASE Tramp flirts and is chased.

01840
THE DOG'S DEVOTION (385)
Walturdaw
D: (Dave Aylott)
ANIMAL Man forces boy to kidnap girl and
they are traced by pet Newfoundland dog.

01841
DREAMS OF TOYLAND (350)
Alpha Trading Co (Walturdaw)
D:S: Arthur Cooper
TRICK Boy dreams toys come to life: a motor-
bus explodes.

01842
A DAY'S HOLIDAY (495)
Williamson
D: (James Williamson)
COMEDY Miseries of family forced to spend
holiday at home.

MAR

01843
THE SCANDALOUS BOYS AND THE FIRE
CHUTE (300)
Clarendon
D: Percy Stow
S: Langford Reed
CHASE Teacher follows pupils down fire chute
and lands in watertub.

01844
THE MEMORY OF HIS MOTHER (490)
Clarendon
D: Percy Stow
S: Langford Reed
DRAMA The memory of dead mother makes
man forgive friend.

01845
POOR AUNT MATILDA (275)
Clarendon
D: Percy Stow
S: Langford Reed
COMEDY Man attacks aunt in mistake for
disguised brother.

01846
SHE WOULD BE WED: OR, LEAP YEAR
PROPOSALS (345)
Cricks & Martin *Reissue:* 1912
D: A.E. Coleby
COMEDY Spinster's proposals rejected by all,
save blind beggar.

01847
FREDDY'S LITTLE LOVE AFFAIR (525)
Cricks & Martin
D: A.E. Coleby
COMEDY Dude hides in pram to flirt with maid
and she launders him.

CHRONOPHONE FILMS *sound*
Gaumont
D: Arthur Gilbert

01848
D'YE KEN JOHN PEEL

01849
ZUYDER ZEE

01850
WALTZ ME AROUND AGAIN WILLIE

01851
THE KEYS OF HEAVEN

01852
COME MY LAD AND BE A SOLDIER

01853
MONTEZUMA

01854
WE CLOSE AT TWO ON THURSDAY
Arthur Gilbert

01855
I GET DIZZY WHEN I DO THAT TWOSTEP
DANCE
Alf Collins

01856
GOODBYE LITTLE SISTER

01857
SHE'S PROUD AND SHE'S BEAUTIFUL

01858
HELLO LITTLE GIRL HELLO

01859
FOLLOWING IN FATHER'S FOOTSTEPS
Arthur Staples

01860
REDWING

01861
ALL COONS LOOK ALIKE TO ME (PARODY)

01862
MANY IS THE TIME
MUSICAL Synchronised with gramophone
records.

01863
CATCHING A BURGLAR (525)
Hepworth
D: Lewin Fitzhamon
CHASE Burglar steals car and is pursued by
police until tramp slashes tyres.

01864
THE TRAMPS AND THE PURSE (225)
Hepworth
D: Lewin Fitzhamon
COMEDY Tramp steals purse, hides it, and it is
stolen by another tramp.

01865
FATHER'S LESSON (500)
Hepworth
D: Lewin Fitzhamon
ANIMAL Angry father sells children's ponies;
dog leads them home.

01866
A DASH FOR LIBERTY (750)
Walturdaw
D: Dave Aylott
CHASE Warders chase escaped convicts and
shoot them in gun battle.

01867
ONLY A DOG BUT MORE THAN HUMAN
(366)
Urban Trading Co
ANIMAL Terrier's sagacity saves baby from
burning tower.

01868
A GRATEFUL DOG (655)
Warwick Trading Co
ANIMAL Boy bandages dog's leg; dog brings
help when boy is hurt.

01869
WON BY STRATEGY (260)
Warwick Trading Co
COMEDY Man loses girl to cunning rival.

01870
THE RIVAL CYCLISTS (360)
Williamson
D: (James Williamson)
CHASE Cyclist ties child in cart behind rival's
cycle.

APR
01871
THREE MAIDEN LADIES AND A BULL (348)
Clarendon *Reissue:* 1912, BEWARE OF THE
BULL
D: Percy Stow
S: Langford Reed
CHASE Picnicking spinsters chased by bull.

01872
AN INTERRUPTED BATH (345)
Cricks & Martin
D: A.E. Coleby
COMEDY Man's bath interrupted by
prospective tenants.

01873
THOSE FLIES (220)
Cricks & Martin *Reissue:* 1909 (THE FLIES)
D: A.E. Coleby
COMEDY Flies bother man who is trying to write
letter and he wrecks room.

01874
PROFESSOR BOUNDER'S PILLS (380)
Cricks & Martin
D: A.E. Coleby
COMEDY Tricksters sell pills made from earth
and are killed by mob.

01875
ONLY A PENNY A BOX (452)
Gaumont
D: (Alf Collins)
PATHOS Boy matchseller run over fetching
change; crippled brother takes change to
customer and is adopted.

01876
THE WOMAN WHO WASN'T (642)
Gaumont
D: (Alf Collins)
CHASE Suffragettes find one of their number
is a man in disguise.

01877
THE GAMBLER'S WIFE (535)
Graphic Cinematograph Co
CRIME Gambler steals wife's necklace and loses
it to crook.

01878
THE BURGLAR AND THE CLOCK (550)
Hepworth
D: Lewin Fitzhamon
Thurston Harris .... Burglar
TRICK Burglar steals wristwatch which turns
into pocket watch and then into alarm clock,
etc.

01879
THE ARTFUL DODGER (475)
Hepworth
D: Lewin Fitzhamon
CHASE Pursued thief escapes capture by donning
disguise.

01880
THE ELECTRIC TORCH (304)
Hepworth
D: (Lewin Fitzhamon)
TRICK Electric torch gives people shocks.

01881
OUR COUSIN FROM ABROAD (450)
Hepworth
D: (Lewin Fitzhamon)
COMEDY

01882
THE PNEUMATIC POLICEMAN
Hepworth
D: Frank Wilson
Frank Wilson .... Policeman
COMEDY Slight man pumps himself up to
become PC, chases crook and floats down river.

01883
BICYCLES REPAIRED (400)
Hepworth
D: (Lewin Fitzhamon)
COMEDY

01884
THE HIDDEN HOARD (600)
Hepworth
D: Lewin Fitzhamon
CHASE Miser hides fortune in picture which is
given to dustman.

01885
THE DOG OUTWITS THE KIDNAPPER (425)
Hepworth
D: Lewin Fitzhamon
Barbara Hepworth .... The Child
Blair .... Rover
ANIMAL Dog chases kidnapper's car and while
he is in pub, drives it home.

01886
THE MAGIC GARDEN
R.W. Paul
TRICK Drunken gardener sees giant frog, snake,
etc.

01887
IN THE LAND OF NOD (365)
Alpha Trading Co (Walturdaw) *Reissue:* 1910,
GRANDPA'S FORTY WINKS (Cosmo)
D:S: Arthur Cooper
TRICK Father dreams of toy fire engine saving
burning doll's house.

01888
TWO LITTLE MOTORISTS (300)
Urban Trading Co
D: (W.R. Booth)
CHASE (14 scenes) Children drive car pursued
by chauffeur on cycle.

01889
THE CRACKSMEN AND THE BLACK
DIAMONDS (345)
Wawick Trading Co
D: (Charles Raymond)
COMEDY Burglars find safe contains coal and
are caught by maid's policeman friend.

01890
£100 REWARD (400)
Williamson
D: (James Williamson)
ANIMAL Sacked man's dog finds hidden jewels
and tracks thieves.

01891
THE PROFESSOR'S GREAT DISCOVERY (350)
Williamson
D: (James Williamson)
COMEDY Professor's patent snuff makes
those who take it dance.

01892
SHE WOULD BE A SUFFRAGETTE (235)
Williamson
D: (James Williamson)
COMEDY Henpeck dons disguise and pets
suffragette wife at meeting.

01893
ANIMATED MATCHES (250)
Alpha Trading Co (Williamson)
D:S: Arthur Cooper
TRICK Matchsticks come to life and perform
tricks.

MAY

01894
THREE SUBURBAN SPORTSMEN AND A
HAT (380)
Clarendon
D: Percy Stow
S: Langford Reed
COMEDY "Smile-Preserving qualities."

01895
MR JONES HAS A TILE LOOSE (248)
Clarendon
D: Percy Stow
S: Langford Reed
COMEDY Dozens of people bring ladders to
rescue man from roof.

01896
IF WOMEN WERE POLICEMEN (400)
Clarendon
D: Percy Stow
S: Langford Reed
COMEDY Militant Suffragettes take over
police force.

01897
SAVED BY THE TELEGRAPH CODE (327)
Clarendon
D: Percy Stow
S: Langford Reed
CRIME Girl on train threatened by escaped
convict taps morse code message to postman.

01898
BILLY BORNTIRED (650)
Cricks & Martin
D: A.E. Coleby
COMEDY Nothing will arouse drowsy man -
except beer!

01899
THE MISSION OF A FLOWER (360)
Cricks & Martin
D: A.E. Coleby
DRAMA Small girl's flower reforms drunkard
father.

01900
FATHER BUYS A PICTURE (500)
Cricks & Martin *Reissue:* 1912
D: A.E. Coleby
COMEDY Father has trouble trying to carry
large painting.

01901
MUTINY IN THE KITCHEN (315)
Cricks & Martin
D: A.E. Coleby
COMEDY Rebellious maid causes fight and is
helped by PC fiance.

01902
THE FREEBOOTERS (395)
Cricks & Martin
D: A.E. Coleby
CHASE Tramps steal boots and are chased.

01903
BLACK-EYED SUSAN (880)
Gaumont
S: (PLAY) Douglas Jerrold
DRAMA Period. Smuggler's daughter loves
sailor courtmartialled for striking flirtatious
superior.

01904
THE THIEF AT THE CASINO (600)
Hepworth
D: Lewin Fitzhamon
CRIME Thief frames drunkard and is black-
mailed by witness until vision of victim's
maltreatment makes him confess.

01905
MY LITTLE LADY BOUNTIFUL (675)
Hepworth
D: Lewin Fitzhamon
DRAMA Child's appeal to rich father saves bank
from ruin.

01906
HI! STOP THOSE BARRELS (400)
Hepworth
D: Lewin Fitzhamon
CHASE Beer barrels roll off dray and are
chased

01907
CATCHING A TARTAR (475)
Hepworth
D: Lewin Fitzhamon
Gertie Potter
CHASE Gipsies chase girl on horse into
pantechnicon; she locks them in and
drives to police.

01908
THE TROUBLES OF A HOUSE AGENT (325)
Hepworth
D: Lewin Fitzhamon
COMEDY House, agent, and clients are
washed away by floods.

01909
PADDY'S WAY OF DOING IT (405)
Walturdaw
D: (Dave Aylott)
COMEDY Misadventures of clumsy Irish farm-
hand.

01910
OH THOSE BOYS! (395)
Alpha Trading Co (Walturdaw)
D: Arthur Cooper
CHASE Boys play tricks with paint and are
chased.

01911
A LITTLE STRANGER (350)
Alpha Trading Co (Walturdaw)
D: Arthur Cooper
Hilda Baron
COMEDY married man tries to get rid of
unwanted baby.

01912
THE CHAUFFEUR'S DREAM (420)
Urban Trading Co *Reissue:* 1915
D: W.R. Booth
TRICK Chauffeur dreams of driving under sea,
down volcano, etc.

01913
THE PRODIGAL SON
R.W. Paul
RELIGION Swineherd returns home when
disillusioned by false friends.

01914
UNCLE'S PICNIC (400)
Williamson
D: (James Williamson)
COMEDY Two naughty boys cause trouble
during country picnic.

01915
THE BULLY AND THE RECRUIT (336)
Williamson
D:S: Jack Chart
Jack Chart .... The Recruit
George V. Wibrough ...... The Bully
CRIME Bugler saves teetotal recruit from
drunken private's false charge of stealing belt.

01916
FATHER'S FIRST BABY (400)
Sheffield Photo Co
D: Frank Mottershaw
COMEDY Parent's problems with new baby.

01917
WHEN BOYS ARE FORBIDDEN TO SMOKE
(380)
Sheffield Photo Co
D: Frank Mottershaw
COMEDY PC confiscates cigarettes under new
bill and starts tobacconist's shop.

01918
THE FIGHTING CURATE (242) retitled: THE
LITTLE FLOWER GIRL
Sheffield Photo Co
D: Frank Mottershaw
Lenore Fisher
DRAMA Curate thrashes drunkard and adopts
stepdaughter.

JUN

01919
FOLLOW YOUR LEADER AND THE MASTER
FOLLOWS LAST (220)
Clarendon
D: Percy Stow
S: Langford Reed
CHASE Teacher chases pupil and is followed
by school, over roofs, etc.

01920
THE OLD COMPOSER AND THE PRIMA
DONNA (695)
Clarendon
D: Percy Stow
S: Langford Reed
DRAMA Child persuades opera star to help
old busker cheated by music publisher.

01921
ROMEO AND JULIET (1240)
Gaumont
S: (PLAY) William Shakespeare
Godfrey Tearle .... Romeo
Mary Malone .... Juliet
Gordon Bailey .... Mercutio
James Annand .... Tybalt
ROMANCE (25 scenes) Lyceum Theatre
production.

01922
THE MOTHERLY PRAM (350)
Hepworth
D: Lewin Fitzhamon
TRICK Coster ties pram to donkey and pram
goes home by itself.

01923
THE LOVE TOKEN (500)
Hepworth
D: Lewin Fitzhamon
Dolly Lupone .... Girl
WAR Girl saves wounded soldier left by rival
to die.

01924
THE MAN WHO LEARNED TO FLY (300)
Hepworth
D: Lewin Fitzhamon
TRICK Inventor dreams he is flattened by
roller and flown as kite.

01925
THE GENTLEMAN GYPSY (225) retitled: THE
TRIALS OF A GYPSY GENTLEMAN
Hepworth
D: Lewin Fitzhamon
Lewin Fitzhamon .... The Gypsy
May Clark .... A Girl
COMEDY Gypsy bathes in river and changes
clothes with PC.

01926
WHEN WOMEN RULE (600)
Hepworth
D: Lewin Fitzhamon
Dolly Lupone .... Girl
Gertie Potter .... Girl
COMEDY Suffragettes make men don skirts
and take over fire station.

01927
THE HARMLESS LUNATIC'S ESCAPE
Hepworth
D: (Lewin Fitzhamon)
CHASE Lunatic escapes in doctor's car and
crashes into wall.

01928
THE SERPENT'S TOOTH (600)
Hepworth
D: (Lewin Fitzhamon)
DRAMA Workman fights gentleman at society
ball to stop daughter's elopement.

01929
MONTY BUYS A MOTOR (500)
Urban Trading Co
COMEDY Man's new car ends up on scrap
heap.

01930
A BREACH OF PROMISE CASE (150)
B&C
D: (J.B. McDowell)
ANIMAL Bewigged child tries case between
two pet dogs.

01931
BILLIE'S BUGLE (235)
B&C (Walturdaw) Reissue: 1911 (B&C)
D: Dave Aylott
COMEDY Boy fills bugle with flour and soot
and blows it at people.

01932
DICK THE KISSER (355)
Walturdaw
D: (Dave Aylott)
CHASE Flirtatious man chased into pond, is
tarred and feathered.

01933
THE FIREMAN'S DAUGHTER
Warwick Trading Co
D: (Charles Raymond)
DRAMA Girl elopes with thief, upsets lamp, and
is saved by fireman father.

01934
A BIRD OF FREEDOM (568)
Warwick Trading Co
D: (Charles Raymond)
Will Barker .... The convict
CHASE Warders chase convict over telegraph
wires and into canal.

JUL

01935
GOT A PENNY STAMP? (370)
Clarendon
D: Percy Stow
S: Langford Reed
COMEDY Man asks passers-by for penny stamp.

01936
ROBIN HOOD AND HIS MERRY MEN (496)
Clarendon
D: Percy Stow
S: Langford Reed
ADVENTURE Outlaw saves captured man
from sheriff's gallows.

01937
TOMMY AND THE STICKTITE (430)
Cricks & Martin
D: A.E. Coleby
COMEDY Naughty boy plays tricks with tube
of strong glue.

01938
LOVE'S STRATEGY (255)
Cricks & Martin Reissue: 1912
D: A.E. Coleby
COMEDY Man hires tramp to scare girl and
throws him into river.

01939
HOW THE ARTFUL DODGER SECURED A
MEAL (320)
Cricks & Martin
D: A.E. Coleby
TRICK Tramp hypnotises farmer and food,
and is chased.

01940
THE DEVIL'S BARGAIN (530)
Cricks & Martin
D: A.E. Coleby
FANTASY Artist sells soul for month's wages;
girl in painting comes to life to save him from
Satan.

01941
NAPOLEON AND THE ENGLISH SAILOR
(530)
Gaumont Reissue: 1912
D: (Alf Collins)
S: (SKETCH) Herbert Darnley

Herbert Darnley .... Napoleon
Arthur Page .... The Sailor
WAR Emperor frees sailor who tries to float
home to mother in barrel.

01942
TOMMY AND THE POLICEMAN'S WHISTLE
(245)
Gaumont
D: (Alf Collins)
CHASE Boy steals policeman's whistle and
causes trouble.

01943
MECHANICAL LEGS (415)
Gaumont
D: (Alf Collins)
CHASE Legless man dons mechanical legs that
run away with him.

01944
MOVING IN (522)
Gaumont
D: (Alf Collins)
S: (SKETCH) Herbert Darnley
Herbert Darnley
Arthur Page
COMEDY Family have trouble moving into new
flat and blow it up searching for gas leak.

01945
HARRY LAUDER IN A HURRY (325)
Gaumont
D: (Alf Collins)
Harry Lauder
COMEDY Scots star takes time despite callboy,
commissionaire, and stage-manager.

01946
A STITCH IN TIME (170)
Gaumont
D: (Alf Collins)
COMEDY "A smart little comic."

01947
WEARY WILLIE STEALS A FISH (575)
Hepworth
D: Lewin Fitzhamon
TRICK Tramp dreams of adventures under sea
with submarine, mermaid, policeman, etc.

01948
AN ATTRACTIVE CATCH (450)
Hepworth
D: Lewin Fitzhamon
TRICK Tramp steals magnet and pulls it along,
attracting clocks, cycles, cars, and steamroller.

01949
BABY'S PLAYMATE (375)
Hepworth
D: Lewin Fitzhamon
ANIMAL Pony fetches fire brigade to save girl
from burning haystack.

01950
THE NE'ER-DO-WELL AND THE BABY (550)
Hepworth
D: (Lewin Fitzhamon)
DRAMA Window cleaner takes foundling to
hospital where mother, saved from suicide,
is a nurse.

01951
JACK IN THE LETTERBOX (300)
Hepworth
D: Lewin Fitzhamon
COMEDY Boy hides inside letter box and
plays pranks.

01952
DON QUIXOTE'S DREAM (250)
Hepworth
D: (Lewin Fitzhamon)
COMEDY Period. Don dreams of toughs
kidnapping girl.

01953
A FREE PARDON (525)
Hepworth
D: (Lewin Fitzhamon)
CRIME Starving man blamed when he joins
burglar who shoots householder.

01954
THE TRAMP
R.W. Paul
D: (Jack Smith)
TRICK Tramp cooks rabbit in hat, undresses
many times, etc.

01955
THE RED BARN CRIME: OR, MARIA
MARTIN (685)
Haggar & Sons (Tyler)
S: (PLAY) Unknown
Walter Haggar .... William Corder
Violet Haggar .... Maria Martin
CRIME 1826. Squire's murder of pregnant
mistress revealed by mother's dream.

01956
THE STOLEN DUCK (322)
Sheffield Photo Co
D: Frank Mottershaw
CHASE Old woman chases tramps chasing
duck.

01957
THE PIRATE SHIP (350)
Walturdaw
D: Dave Aylott
ADVENTURE Negro servant swims to fetch
sailors to save mistress from pirates.

01958
FOR HIS CHILD'S SAKE (460)
Walturdaw
D: Dave Aylott
S: Harry Gilbey
Harry Gilbey .... The Convict
PATHOS Bread thief escapes jail but finds wife
dead of starvation.

01959
THE LIGHTNING POSTCARD ARTIST (325)
Urban Trading Co
D: W.R. Booth
TRICK Pencil draws pictures which come to life.

01960
PAPER TEARING (400)
Urban Trading Co
D: W.R. Booth
TRICK Paper tears itself into shapes that
change into other shapes.

01961
UNCLE'S REJECTED PRESENT (500)
Warwick Trading Co
D: (Charles Raymond)
CHASE Couple throw away high duck, then
learn £50 was attached.

AUG

01962
JOHN GILPIN (495)
Clarendon
D: Percy Stow
S: (POEM) William Cowper
SC: Langford Reed
CHASE Period. Tradesman's wild ride on
horseback.

01963
WASHING DAY (290)
Gaumont
D: (Alf Collins)
COMEDY Fire engine called when boy hides
cigarette in mother's barrow of washing.

01964
THE BURGLAR'S JOKE WITH THE
AUTOMATIC DOLL (445)
Gaumont
D: (Alf Collins)
COMEDY Thief tries to rob house by taking
place of lifelike doll.

01965
THE DANCING GIRL (598)
Gaumont
D: (Alf Collins)
ROMANCE Slum girl becomes dancer and is
saved from impresario by sailor.

01966
THE DRUNKARD'S DREAM (312)
Gaumont
D: (Alf Collins)
DRAMA Drunkard reforms after dreaming of
killing wife and lover.

01967
THE CONVICT AND THE DOVE (180)
Gaumont
D: (Alf Collins)
CRIME Warder kills convict's pet dove; convict
kills warder and dies.

01968
JANE SHORE (695)
Gaumont
S: (PLAY) Nicholas Rowe
HISTORY 1480. Married woman becomes
King's mistress and is stoned.

01969
PUT PA AMONGST THE GIRLS (525)
Gaumont
D: (Alf Collins)
COMEDY Seaside. Man flirts with girls and is
caught by wife.

01970
SAVED FROM A TERRIBLE DEATH (550)
Hepworth
D: Lewin Fitzhamon
Gertie Potter .... The Girl
ANIMAL India. Colonel rides elephant to save
daughter from native sacrifice.

01971
CABBY'S SWEETHEART (300)
Hepworth
D: Lewin Fitzhamon
CRIME Jeweller abducts girl in cab but
driver takes them to police station.

01972
A HEARTLESS MOTHER (450)
Hepworth
D: (Lewin Fitzhamon)
DRAMA Woman's lover tries to abduct husband
but he escapes with their child.

01973
A CONVICT'S DASH FOR LIBERTY (225)
Hepworth
D: Lewin Fitzhamon
COMEDY Convict changes clothes with girl
and tries to escape down river.

01974
THE MAN AND THE LATCHKEY (200)
Hepworth
D: Lewin Fitzhamon
Thurston Harris .... Drunkard
TRICK Drunkard pursues an enlarged,
mobile keyhole.

01975
A TICKET FOR TWO (675)
Hepworth
D: (Lewin Fitzhamon)
COMEDY Couple take steamboat trip with six
children hidden in boxes.

01976
MARRYING UNDER DIFFICULTIES (475)
Hepworth
D: (Lewin Fitzhamon)
COMEDY Elopers escape from father and
curate by having them arrested.

01977
THE MAGIC BOX
R.W. Paul
D: (Jack Smith)
TRICK When man's magic box produces girl,
wife uses it to produce man.

01978
THE GREAT SALOME DANCE (300)
Walter Tyler
ACT Dancer kisses severed head and swoons.

01979
GREEN'S GOOSE (178)
Alpha Trading Co (Tyler)
D: Arthur Cooper
COMEDY Tough goose at dinner party defies
hatchet, saw, and pickaxe.

01980
IT'S JUST MY LUCK (350)
Alpha Trading Co (Tyler)
D: Arthur Cooper
COMEDY Husband is caught with typist and
thrown into pond.

01981
BATHING PROHIBITED (265)
Walter Tyler
COMEDY Tramps steal bathers' clothes; bathers'
steal girls' clothes; girls steal policemen's clothes.

01982
THE PLUMBER AND THE LUNATICS (325)
Walter Tyler Reissue: 1913
COMEDY Plumber chased by lunatic who merely
wishes to return his knife.

01983
GRANDPA'S PENSION DAY (398)
Alpha Trading Co (Tyler)
D: Arthur Cooper
DRAMA Old man gets drunk on pension,
is jailed, and bailed out by grand-daughter.

01984
HOW THE COSTER SOLD THE SEEDS (300)
Warwick Trading Co (B&C?)
COMEDY Coster sells dud seeds by planting
flowers at night.

01985
THE DIAMOND THIEVES (660)
Warwick Trading Co
D: (Charles Raymond)
CRIME Thieves rob jeweller and when their car
breaks down they hold up police and escape in
their car

01986
THE CHEEKIEST MAN ON EARTH (275)
B&C
D: (J.B. McDowell)
COMEDY Man is rude to everyone he meets and is thrown into river.

01987
LUCK OF A DIVER
John Codman Enterprises
D: John Codman
COMEDY (?) (Date uncertain)

01988
STILL WORTHY OF THE NAME (520)
Williamson
D:S: Jack Chart
Jack Chart
WAR (11 scenes) Cardsharp, saved from suicide by policeman, joins Lancers and wins VC.

01989
MY WIFE'S DOG (373)
Williamson
D: (James Williamson)
COMEDY Husband spends day trying to catch wrong dalmation.

SEP

01990
THE MISSIONARY'S DAUGHTER (672)
Clarendon
D: Percy Stow
S: Langford Reed
ADVENTURE Naval Lieut saves missionary's daughter from slave traders.

01991
A WILD GOOSE CHASE (370)
Clarendon
D: Percy Stow
S: Langford Reed
CHASE Old gent chased by savage goose.

01992
THE GUARDIAN OF THE BANK (570)
Cricks & Martin *Reissue:* 1912
D:S: A.E. Coleby

Hal Bert .... Thief
Regent Street Rajah .... Dog
ANIMAL Bulldog chases thief over roofs, down chimney, and into river, returns gold to bank and fetches police.

01993
GRANDFATHER'S BIRTHDAY; OR, THE LAST ROLL-CALL (440)
Cricks & Martin *Reissue:* 1912
D: A.E. Coleby
WAR Chelsea pensioner dreams of how he won VC, and dies.

01994
THE PHOTOGRAPHER'S FLIRTATION (350)
Hepworth
D: (Lewin Fitzhamon)
COMEDY Photographer kisses sitter and is doused by husband.

01995
A THOUGHTLESS BEAUTY (400) retitled: FORCED TO CONSENT (275)
Hepworth
D: Lewin Fitzhamon
Gertie Potter .... Girl
COMEDY Bognor. Couple tie girl's father to pier post and marry in boat.

01996
THE PETS' TEA PARTY (275)
Hepworth
D: Lewin Fitzhamon
Gertie Potter .... Girl
ANIMAL Children's horses and dogs invite each other to party.

01997
THE UNLUCKY THIEF (275)
Hepworth
D: (Lewin Fitzhamon)
COMEDY Burglar hides in dustbin which is eventually flung in river.

01998
A FASCINATING GAME (250)
Hepworth
D: Lewin Fitzhamon
Gertie Potter .... Girl
COMEDY Bognor. Girls continue to play bat and ball as tide comes in.

01999
AN UNFORTUNATE BATHE (275)
Hepworth
D: Lewin Fitzhamon
Gertie Potter
COMEDY Bognor. Girls trick old men by exchanging their clothing.

02000
THE DESERTER (425)
Hepworth
D: (Lewin Fitzhamon)
COMEDY Sailor hides in girl's copper, is chased to roof, and hosed by police.

02001
THE LUCKY PIE (400)
Hepworth
D: (Lewin Fitzhamon)
COMEDY Tramp steals pie in which cook has hidden stolen necklace.

02002
TOMKINS BUYS A DONKEY (325)
Hepworth
D: Lewin Fitzhamon
ANIMAL Countryman buys stubborn donkey and has trouble.

02003
THE LADY OR THE LIONS (400)
London Cinematograph Co
D: S. Wormald
COMEDY (18 scenes) Henpeck hides from wife in lions' cage.

02004
DADDY AS OF OLD (340)
R.W. Paul
D: (Jack Smith)
PATHOS Drunkard's child steals loaf and is saved from jail by lady.

02005
VENGEANCE IS MINE (530)
Walter Tyler
CRIME Blacksmith is about to blind wife's killer when lightning strikes him dead.

02006
THE GLADIATOR'S AFFIANCED BRIDE (410)
Walter Tyler
DRAMA Ancient Rome. Two gladiators fight for girl.

02007
THE SHEEP STEALER (520)
Walter Tyler
CHASE Starving workman steals sheep, is chased and caught in weir.

02008
THE CURATE'S HONEYMOON (420)
Alpha Trading Co (Tyler) Reissue: 1911 (Cosmo)
D: Arthur Cooper
COMEDY Curate's cab crashes and he has to pull it himself.

02009
WE ARE SO FOND OF ONIONS (268)
Walter Tyler
TRICK Old couple eat onions and dream of animated onions.

02010
A FLOWER GIRL'S LIFE STORY (670)
Walter Tyler
DRAMA Deserted wife with baby stops rich husband from marrying by killing herself in church.

02011
THE UNBELIEVER (315)
Walter Tyler
DRAMA Atheist's prayers cure dying child.

02012
WEARY WILLIE AND TIRED TIM ON THE MASH (318)
Walter Tyler
COMEDY Tramps steal swimmers' clothes and leave their own.

02013
THE KIND OLD LADY (395)
Walter Tyler
COMEDY Old lady is happy to return three adopted children to their father.

02014
MR HENPECK'S ADVENTURE WITH A BURGLAR (320)
Walter Tyler
COMEDY Henpeck catches burglar and forces him to do housework.

02015
WATERPROOF WILLIE (300)
Urban Trading Co
D: W.R. Booth
TRICK Water refuses to touch a man.

02016
A QUICK-CHANGE MESMERIST (315)
Urban Trading Co
D: W.R. Booth
TRICK Mesmerist changes costumes of victims, and vanishes.

02017
THE STAR GLOBE-TROTTER (320)
Urban Trading Co
D: W.R. Booth
TRICK Hypnotised gymnast walks round world.

02018
THE PREHISTORIC MAN (300)
Urban Trading Co
D: W.R. Booth
TRICK Artist draws prehistoric man who then comes alive.

02019
THE ADVENTURES OF A WATCH (385)
Urban Trading Co
D: W.R. Booth
TRICK Boy steals watch, ties it to dog's tail, and makes man swallow it.

02020
ONLY A DART (262)
Walturdaw
D: Dave Aylott
COMEDY Boy plays pranks with airgun and darts.

02021
THE INVISIBLE BUTTON (265)
Walturdaw
D: Dave Aylott
TRICK Man starts quarrels and vanishes by touching magic button.

02022
WHEN OTHER LIPS
Warwick Trading Co
D: (Charles Raymond)
DRAMA 18thC. General duels cavalier who eloped with his wife.

02023
HIS FIRST EXPERIMENT IN CHEMISTRY (510)
Warwick Trading Co
COMEDY

02024
OUR VILLAGE CLUB HOLDS A MARATHON RACE (422)
Warwick Trading Co
D: (Charles Raymond)
COMEDY Mishaps of cameraman trying to film cross-country race.

02025
ALL THAT TROUBLE FOR A DRINK (297)
Warwick Trading Co
COMEDY

02026
ARCHIE GOES SHOPPING WITH THE GIRLS (292)
Warwick Trading Co
COMEDY

CINEMATOPHONE SINGING PICTURES
sound
Walturdaw

02027
SHE'S A LASSIE FROM LANCASHIRE (175)

02028
BILLIE BROWN OF LONDON TOWN (185)

02029
IF THE MAN IN THE MOON WERE A COON (180)
MUSICAL Synchronised to gramophone records.

02030
A VISIT TO THE SEASIDE (517) kinema
Natural Colour Kinematograph Co
D:S: G.A. Smith
The White Coons
Cameron Highlanders' Band
COMEDY Brighton. Seaside scenes including girl falling in sea from boat and men peeping at bathing girls. (First British colour film.)

02031
THE AYAH'S REVENGE (660)
Williamson
D: (James Williamson)
Florence Williamson
CRIME India. Sacked nurse steals officer's child; mother rides to rescue and shoots nurse.

02032
THE LITTLE MOTHER (620)
Williamson
D: (James Williamson)
DRAMA Widowed sailor returns in time to save children from eviction.

02033
THE GREAT BARGAIN SALE (460)
Williamson
D: (James Williamson)
COMEDY Husband has trouble carrying wife's purchases.

02034
PHANTOM GAMES (265)
Wrench
TRICK "An excellent trick film and quite novel".

02035
STRATAGEM REWARDED (265)
Wrench
COMEDY "Good seaside comic, pithily portrayed."

02036
SUFFERING SUFFRAGETTES (305)
Wrench
COMEDY "Topical comic, screamingly funny throughout."

OCT

02037
THE CAVALIER'S WIFE (512)
Clarendon
D: Percy Stow
S: Langford Reed
ADVENTURE Friend takes place of captive Royalist while he rescues his wife.

02038
ALGY'S YACHTING PARTY (362)
Clarendon
D: Percy Stow
S: Langford Reed
COMEDY Dude takes fiancee's family for yachting trip.

02039
NANCY; OR, THE BURGLAR'S DAUGHTER (555)
Clarendon
D: Percy Stow
S: Langford Reed
CRIME Curate saves flowergirl from suicide, weds her, and is burgled by her father.

02040
LORD ALGY'S BEAUTY SHOW (385)
Cricks & Martin
D: A.E. Coleby
COMEDY Actors pose as girls and monkey to win beauty contest.

02041
A FIGHT FOR HONOUR (550)
Cricks & Martin
D:S: A.E. Coleby
A.E. Coleby .... Rancher
WESTERN Mexican boy fetches saloon keeper in time to save wife from lustful sheriff's gang.

02042
HIS WEDDING MORN (575)
Cricks & Martin
D: A.E. Coleby
A.E. Coleby .... Father
COMEDY Accidents make groom late for church on Friday 13th.

02043
THE AMOROUS NURSE (425)
Hepworth
D: (Lewin Fitzhamon)
COMEDY

02044
THE SAFETY SUIT FOR SKATERS (325)
Hepworth
D:(Lewin Fitzhamon)
COMEDY

02045
JOHN GILPIN'S RIDE (575)
Hepworth
D: SC: Lewin Fitzhamon
S: (POEM) William Cowper
CHASE Tradesman's wild ride on horseback.

02046
THE SCHOOLBOYS' REVOLT (250)
Hepworth
D: Lewin Fitzhamon
Bertie Potter .... Boy
Gertie Potter .... Boy
COMEDY Bognor. Two boys play pranks with bathing-machine, boat, etc.

02047
THE NURSEMAID'S DREAM (450)
Hepworth
D: Lewin Fitzhamon
Gertie Potter .... Fairy
TRICK Bognor. Nursemaid dreams fairies save her baby from giants.

02048
A COUNTRY GIRL (250)
Hepworth
D: (Lewin Fitzhamon)
COMEDY

02049
TWO TOUGH KIDS (315)
London Cinematograph Co
D: S. Wormald
COMEDY Boys steal swimmers' clothes while Negro servant sleeps.

02050
THERE'S LIFE IN THE OLD DOG YET (280)
London Cinematograph Co
D: S. Wormald
Jem Mace ....Himself
SPORT Aged boxer makes comeback.

02051
THE WEDDING THAT DIDN'T COME OFF (290)
Rosie Films
D: Joe Rosenthal
COMEDY "Hearty laugh from start to finish."

02052
NO GOOD FOR ANYTHING (550)
Rosie Films
D: Joe Rosenthal
COMEDY "A comic with real humour in it."

02053
WHAT WILLIAM DID (470)
Rosie Films
D: Joe Rosenthal
COMEDY Quarrelsome husband spends day with girl and comes home drunk.

02054
PERCY WANTED A MOUSTACHE (440)
Rosie Films
D: Joe Rosenthal
COMEDY Boy puts glue in brother's moustache lotion.

02055
THE ARTFUL TRAMPS (550)
Sheffield Photo Co
D: Frank Mottershaw
COMEDY Two tramps play tricks to obtain dinner without working.

02056
AN INDIAN'S ROMANCE (675)
Sheffield Photo Co
D: Frank Mottershaw
WESTERN Settler saves chief's daughter from canoe; she saves settler from attack and is shot by her father.

02057
WHAT WILLIE DID (560)
Sheffield Photo Co
D: Frank Mottershaw
Lenore Fisher
COMEDY Naughty boy plays tricks.

02058
THE ECCENTRIC BARBER (165)
Walter Tyler
COMEDY Barber shaves four Guardsmen by putting their heads through board.

02059
WANTED, A NICE YOUNG MAN (311)
Walturdaw
D: (Dave Aylott)
COMEDY Spinster rejected by all until gypsy gives her charm.

02060
THE TRAMP'S CYCLING MANIA (315)
Urban Trading Co
D: W.R. Booth
TRICK Tramp steals cycles and ends up squashed flat.

02061
SUNSHINE AFTER STORM (890)
Williamson
D: (James Williamson)
DRAMA Salvationist reforms suicidal drunkard, who is later wrecked while escorting emigrants, and saved from sea by ex-wife.

02060
THE RECONCILIATION (360)
Williamson
D: (James Williamson)
PATHOS Squire's disowned son shot while poaching to feed starving wife.

NOV

02063
A MODERN CINDERELLA (380)
Clarendon
D: Percy Stow
S: Langford Reed
ROMANCE Maid goes to servants' ball and falls for employer's son.

02064
THE PURITAN MAID AND THE ROYALIST REFUGEE (610)
Clarendon
D: Percy Stow
S: Langford Reed
Royalist saved by Roundhead's daughter, saves her in turn.

02065
THE TEMPEST (765)
Clarendon
D: Percy Stow
S: (PLAY) William Shakespeare

SC: Langford Reed
FANTASY Magician regains dukedom by bewitching shipwrecked usurper.

02066
A TRAITOR TO HIS KING (730)
Cricks & Martin
D: A.E. Coleby
A.E. Coleby .... Hero
ADVENTURE 1510. Girl frees framed man, who foils traitor and saves King.

02067
THE SOMNAMBULIST'S CRIME (1120)
Cricks & Martin
D: A.E. Coleby
CRIME Jailed cashier allowed to escape after saving warder and sees accuser dig up gold in sleep.

02068
POLLY'S EXCURSION (370)
Cricks & Martin Reissue: 1912
D: A.E. Coleby
CHASE Attempts to recapture escaped parrot.

02069
THE PHANTOM SHIP (490)
Cricks & Martin
D: J.H. Martin, A.E. Coleby
TRICK Strange happenings aboard phantom ship.

02070
THE VILLAGE BLACKSMITH (220)
Cricks & Martin
D: A.E. Coleby
S: (POEM) Henry Longfellow
George Roberts
MUSICAL (To be shown while song is sung.)

02071
HIGH GAME (560)
Cricks & Martin
D: A.E. Coleby
CHASE Couple throw away high goose and then learn uncle hid £50 in it.

02072
AN INGENIOUS REVENGE (265)
Cricks & Martin
D: A.E. Coleby
COMEDY Boys throw dummy into London Docks to fool PC.

02073
HOW JONES GOT A NEW SUIT (560)
Cricks & Martin
D: A.E. Coleby
ANIMAL When drunkard's wife hides suit, pet bulldog steals him a new one.

02074
BRAVE CHILDREN; OR, THE LITTLE THIEF CATCHERS (420)
Cricks & Martin
D: A.E. Coleby
CRIME Child holds burglar at bay while brother fetches police.

02075
LADY LETMERE'S JEWELLERY (1105)
Gaumont
D:S: George R. Sims
Masie Ellis .... Lady Letmere
CRIME Lady steals countess's pearls; burglar steals them; crooked lawyer returns them for reward.

02076
SAVED FROM THE SEA (815)
Gaumont
S: (PLAY) Arthur Shirley, Ben Landeck
DRAMA Fisherman is tied to mast of exploding ship, is saved by wife.

02077
SWEET LIBERTY (355)
Gaumont
D: (Alf Collins)
COMEDY Escaped convict has so much trouble he returns to jail.

02078
FOR THE LITTLE LADY'S SAKE (500)
Hepworth
D: Lewin Fitzhamon
Lewin Fitzhamon .... The Groom
Chrissie White .... The Girl
ANIMAL Drunken dream reforms sacked groom who sold child's horse to gypsies.

02079
THE DISHONEST BARBER (350)
Hepworth
D: (Lewin Fitzhamon)
COMEDY

02080
DANCES
Hepworth
Miss de Forest Leonard
MUSICAL

02081
THE ANARCHIST'S SWEETHEART (375)
Hepworth
D: (Theo Bouwmeester)
DRAMA Girl uses her arm to bar door against soldiers seeking lover.

02082
THE PROFESSOR'S ANTIGRAVITATIONAL FLUID (350)
Hepworth
D: Lewin Fitzhamon
Bertie Potter .... Boy
TRICK Youth steals prof's fluid and makes ball, bat, fish, and hat rise in the air.

02083
THE HOTTENTOT AND THE GRAMOPHONE (350)
Hepworth
D: (Lewin Fitzhamon)
COMEDY

02084
THE WRONG MEDICINE (325)
Hepworth
D: (Lewin Fitzhamon)
COMEDY

02085
THE DEVIL AND THE CORNET (250)
Hepworth
D: Lewin Fitzhamon
COMEDY Man's magic cornet forces girl's father to dance until he agrees to marriage.

02086
THE BEAUTY COMPETITION (450)
Hepworth
D: Lewin Fitzhamon
Gertie Potter .... Girl
COMEDY Girls canvass men for votes and end up in prison.

02087
THE DOG THIEF (325)
Hepworth
D: Lewin Fitzhamon
ANIMAL Stolen dogs escape and help to
capture thief.

02088
THE NEXT OF KIN (655)
London Cinematograph Co
D: S. Wormald
CRIME Miner kills cousin, takes place, and
strangles uncle; cousin survives, is framed,
and helps police shoot imposter.

02089
A MODERN GRACE DARLING (690)
Precision Films
D: (T.J. Gobbett)
DRAMA Lighthouse-keeper's daughter saves
fisherman from boat scuttled by rival.

02090
NAN'S SACRIFICE (585)
Walter Tyler
DRAMA Waif's savings save adopted parents
from broker's man.

02091
SKITS ON SONGS (250)
Walter Tyler
COMEDY Song titles satirised: "Sing Me to
Sleep"; "I Know a Bank"; "Come into the
Garden, Maud"; "Anchored".

02092
THE TRICKY CONVICT; OR, THE MAGIC
CAP (440)
Walter Tyler (B&C?)
D: (Dave Aylott)
TRICK Convict finds cap that makes wearer
disappear.

02093
TOMMY ON A VISIT TO HIS AUNT (380)
Alpha Trading Co (Tyler)
D: Arthur Cooper
COMEDY Schoolboy plays jokes on aunt, uncle,
cousin, cook.

02094
KNOCK ME (300)
Walter Tyler
COMEDY Clerk writes "Please knock" on boss's
bald head.

02095
THE LITTLE FLOWER GIRL AND THE
FIGHTING PARSON (300)
Walter Tyler
DRAMA Cleric thrashes drunkard and adopts
his stepdaughter.

02096
SKITS ON PLAYS (420)
Walter Tyler
COMEDY Play titles satirised: "What Happened
to Jones"; "The Worst Woman in London";
"The Lady Slavey"; "Under the Red Robe".

02097
MY SON THE CURATE (267)
Walturdaw
D: (Dave Aylott)
CHASE Angry mother chases flirty curate and
girls.

02098
FOR AN OLD LOVE'S SAKE (460)
Walturdaw

DRAMA Doctor kills himself so his insurance
will save daughter's husband from jail.

02099
A LITTLE HERO (650)
Walturdaw
PATHOS Drunkard kills his wife by drinking her
port and dies after robbing and setting fire to
house of cleric who adopted his son.

02100
THE WAIF'S CHRISTMAS (320)
Walturdaw
FANTASY Santa Claus gives orphans cracker
which produces fairy who conjures them
furniture.

02101
JESSICA'S FIRST PRAYER (490)
Walturdaw
D: (Dave Aylott)
S: (STORY) Hesba Stretton
DRAMA Coffee stall keeper adopts waif after
testing her honesty.

02102
RAISED FROM THE RANKS (360)
Williamson
D:S: Jack Chart
JAck Chart
DRAMA Commissioned private ragged by
officers until he saves flag from fire.

DEC

02103
FATHER'S HOLIDAY (570)
Wrench
COMEDY Misadventures of family man on
holiday.

02104
THE POSTER CHASE (340)
Urban Trading Co
CHASE Bill-poster chases children who stole
posters.

02105
THE GUARD'S ALARUM (430)
Urban Trading Co
D: W.R. Booth
TRICK Railway guard dreams of fantastic train
journey.

02106
WHEN THE MAN IN THE MOON SEEKS A
WIFE (970)
Clarendon
D: Percy Stow
S: Langford Reed
FANTASY Man in the moon comes to earth
in gas-balloon.

02107
THE MARTYDOM OF THOMAS A BECKET
(450)
Clarendon
D: Percy Stow
S: Langford Reed
HISTORY 1170. King has archbishop murdered,
then repents.

02108
IB AND LITTLE CHRISTINA (590)
Clarendon
D: Percy Stow
S: (STORY) Hans Christian Andersen
SC: Langford Reed
FANTASY

02109
THE OLD FAVOURITE AND THE UGLY
GOLLIWOG (250)
Clarendon
D: Percy Stow
S: Langford Reed
FANTASY Child's doll resents new favourite.

02110
THE SLOSHTON QUARTETTE (518)
Gaumont
D: (Alf Collins)
COMEDY Quartette jailed for singing and
bailed out by wives.

02111
A CHRISTMAS RAFFLE (435) retitled:
FATHER WINS A TURKEY
Gaumont
D: (Alf Collins)
CHASE Father wins live turkey in Christmas
draw; it gets away.

02112
MAJOR KIDSON'S POLICE BLOODHOUNDS
(526)
Gaumont
ANIMAL Tramp commits theft, is trailed and
caught by bloodhounds.

02113
AN ENEMY IN THE CAMP (175)
Hepworth
D: (Lewin Fitzhamon)
CRIME Child telephones soldiers to save
despatches from spy.

02114
THE FICKLE HUSBAND AND THE BOY (450)
Hepworth
D: Lewin Fitzhamon
COMEDY Boy stops sister's husband from
flirting with girl.

02115
THE UNLUCKY BRIDEGROOM (450)
Hepworth
D: Lewin Fitzhamon
CHASE Groom catches train after pursuing it
by cycle, car, cart.

02116
THE DETECTIVE'S RUSE (300)
Hepworth
D: Lewin Fitzhamon
COMEDY Tec catches burglars by posing as
old man in bathchair.

02117
TO THE CUSTODY OF THE FATHER (450)
Hepworth
D: (Theo Bouwmeester)
DRAMA Maid steals divorced father's child and
takes it to the mother.

02118
THE FAIRY'S SWORD (775)
Hepworth
D: Lewin Fitzhamon
FANTASY Prince uses magic sword to save
Princess from ogre.

02119
THE RUNAWAY KIDS (475)
Hepworth
D: Lewin Fitzhamon
DRAMA Parents search for runaway girls and
find them asleep in station.

02120
UNEMPLOYED AND UNEMPLOYABLE (225)
Hepworth
D: (Lewin Fitzhamon)
COMEDY Man, sacked for smashing crockery
and window, ends in jail.

02121
POVERTY AND COMPASSION (375)
Hepworth
D: (Theo Bouwmeester)
PATHOS Poor man jailed for stealing to help
starving family.

02122
THE ROBBER AND THE JEW (320)
R.W. Paul
D: (Jack Smith)
COMEDY (Date uncertain)

02123
THE LADY LUNA(TIC)'S HAT (185)
R.W. Paul
D: (Jack Smith)
TRICK Lady wearing large hat is blown to
moon.

02124
HARLEQUINADE (300)
Alpha Trading Co (Tyler)
D: Arthur Cooper
Harry Paula & Co
COMEDY Traditional harlequinade;
Drury Lane Theatre company.

02125
AN AMERICAN DOES LONDON IN TEN
MINUTES (580)
Walter Tyler
TRICK Speeded-up tour of sights of London.

02126
WHAT FARMER JONES SAW AT THE
PICTURE SHOW (225)
Alpha Trading Co (Tyler)
D: Arthur Cooper
COMEDY Henpecked countryman wrecks
arcade after seeing wife flirting in peepshow
machine.

02127
THE LOST HANDKERCHIEF (420)
Walter Tyler
COMEDY Man searching for stolen handkerchief
is boiled by laundress.

02128
POLKA ON THE BRAIN (435)
Urban Trading Co
D: W.R. Booth
COMEDY Man gets polka mania and cannot
stop dancing.

02129
THE HANDS OF A WIZARD (365)
Urban Trading Co
D: W.R. Booth
TRICK Conjuror's hands change eggs into
chickens, dice, cards.

02130
YOUR DOG ATE MY LUNCH MUM! (170)
Urban Trading Co
D: (W.R. Booth)
COMEDY House painter gives sandwich to dog
and claims free dinner.

02131
FOLLOWING IN MOTHER'S FOOTSTEPS
(465)
Urban Trading Co
D: W.R. Booth
COMEDY Boy age 6 and girl age 4 enact week
in parents lives.

02132
A JILTED WOMAN'S REVENGE (580)
Warwick Trading Co
D: (Charles Raymond)
DRAMA

02133
A NIGHT ALARM (415)
Warwick Trading Co
D: (Charles Raymond)
COMEDY

02134
THE LOVE OF A GYPSY
Warwick Trading Co
D: (Charles Raymond)
DRAMA

02135
A COUNTRYMAN'S DAY IN TOWN (350)
Williamson
D: (James Williamson)
COMEDY Yokel's misadventures with waxworks,
police and fire brigade.

02136
THE RENT COLLECTOR (360)
Williamson
D: (James Williamson)
COMEDY Rent collector paid with water, flour,
soot.

02137
THE DUMB MAN OF MANCHESTER
Haggar & Sons
D: William Haggar
S: (PLAY) Barnabus Rayner
Will Haggar jr
Jenny Linden
Will Desmond
CRIME Lawyer locates locket and witness to
save mute from murder charge.

02138
THE MAID OF CEFN YDFA
Haggar & Sons
D: William Haggar
S: (PLAY)
Will Haggar jr .... William Hopkins
Jenny Linden .... Ann Thomas
CRIME Wales. Lawyer tries to drown
thatcher to prevent marriage to heiress.

WARWICK CINEPHONE FILMS sound
Warwick Trading Co

02139
OH, OH, ANTONIO

02140
LOVE ME AND THE WORLD IS MINE
MUSICAL Synchronised with gramophone
records.

1909

JAN

02141
HIS WORK OR HIS WIFE (425)
Clarendon
D: Percy Stow
S: Langford Reed
DRAMA "Pathetic story of the present day."

02142
THE LOVE OF A NAUTCH GIRL (480)
Clarendon
D: Percy Stow
S: Langford Reed
ROMANCE Indian dancer saves tourist from lover, follows him to England, sees he is married and dies on doorstep.

02143
THE CRAFTY USURPER AND THE YOUNG KING (490)
Clarendon
D: Percy Stow
S: Langford Reed
DRAMA Ruritania. Princess loves miser's boy who is revealed as heir to throne when suicide rope opens cache.

02144
HARD TIMES (390)
Clarendon
D: Percy Stow
S: Langford Reed
DRAMA Doctor saves workless man from jail when he steals bread to save starving child.

02145
A FRIEND IN NEED (400)
Hepworth
D: Lewin Fitzhamon
WESTERN Miner tied to powder barrel by cardsharp, is saved by horse.

02146
A PRESENT FOR HER HUSBAND (300)
Hepworth
D: (Lewin Fitzhamon)
COMEDY

02147
IN THE SERVICE OF THE KING (500)
Hepworth
D: (Lewin Fitzhamon)
WAR New recruit fetches soldiers to save wounded officer.

02148
A PLUCKY LITTLE GIRL (500)
Hepworth
D: Lewin Fitzhamon
ANIMAL Bank messenger's daughter and pet dog tail bank robber.

02149
NO MORE HATS WANTED (425)
Hepworth
D: Lewin Fitzhamon
COMEDY Man pretends to drown himself to stop wife buying hats.

02150
THE DOG CAME BACK (325)
Hepworth
D: Lewin Fitzhamon
ANIMAL Every time beggar sells dog it returns.

02151
LAST YEARS TIMETABLE (425)
Hepworth
D: Lewin Fitzhamon
ROMANCE Girl dreams sailor is flirt but he returns to her.

02152
LOVE VERSUS SCIENCE (500)
R.W. Paul
D: (Jack Smith)
DRAMA Professor drugs wife's lover and ties him to time bomb.

02153
MY DOLLY (400)
R.W. Paul
D: (Jack Smith)
DRAMA Man disowns daughter on marriage but is reconciled by her child.

02154
THE DUPED OTHELLO (320) retitled: THE THEATRICAL CHIMNEY SWEEP
R.W. Paul
D: (Jack Smith)
COMEDY Sweep has revenge on actor by putting soot in makeup.

02155
THE PRICE OF BREAD (540)
Precision Film Co
D: (T.J. Gobbett)
DRAMA Unemployed man steals loaf and is jailed.

02156
ANARCHY IN ENGLAND (300)
Precision Film Co
D: (T.J. Gobbett)
CRIME Reconstruction of raid on Tottenham rubber factory with chase and gun battle.

02157
BABY'S REVENGE (220)
B&C (Tyler) Reissue: 1911
D: (J.B. McDowell)
COMEDY Neglected baby turns hose on sleeping gardener.

02158
WHAT THE ANGLER CAUGHT (480)
Walturdaw
D: (Dave Aylott)
COMEDY

02159
AN ABSORBING TALE (300)
Urban Trading Co
D: W.R. Booth
COMEDY Man absorbed in book is eventually blown up.

02160
THE ROYALIST'S WIFE (690)
Warwick Trading Co
D: (Charles Raymond)
DRAMA

WARWICK CINEPHONE FILMS sound
Warwick Trading Co
D: Frank Danvers Yates

02161
APACHE DANCE

02162
THE TAXIMETER CAB

02163
SNEEZING

02164
LAND OF HOPE AND GLORY
MUSICAL Synchronised with gramophone records.

02165
'ARRY AND 'ARRIET'S EVENING OUT (345)
D: (James Williamson)
COMEDY Coster couple cause trouble in music hall gallery.

FEB

02166
GETTING FATHER'S CONSENT (385)
Cricks & Martin
D: A.E. Coleby
COMEDY Butler poses as burglar to help elopement of master's daughter.

02167
THE MYSTERY OF EDWIN DROOD (1030)
Gaumont
D: Arthur Gilbert
S: (NOVEL) Charles Dickens
Cooper Willis .... Edwin Drood
Nancy Bevington .... Rosa Budd
James Annand .... Neville Landless
CRIME (13 scenes) Opium den; Jasper's study; River bank; Bow Street runner; Country church.

02168
ALL'S FAIR IN LOVE AND WAR (400)
Hepworth
D: (Lewin Fitzhamon)
COMEDY

02169
THE RIVAL MESMERIST (350)
Hepworth
D: (Lewin Fitzhamon)
COMEDY

02170
THE SPOILT CHILD (250)
Hepworth
D: (Lewin Fitzhamon)
COMEDY Child sets light to father's paper, and is taken for walk.

02171
MOTHER-IN-LAW HAS ALL THE LUCK (425)
Hepworth
D: Lewin Fitzhamon
COMEDY Man's tricks to drive away mother-in-law are thwarted by wife.

02172
THE LOST MEMORY (225)
Hepworth
D: Lewin Fitzhamon
COMEDY Old butcher has amnesia after pickpocket hits him on head.

02173
WHY FATHER LEARNED TO RIDE (375)
Hepworth
D: Lewin Fitzhamon
CHASE Old man rides cycle in pursuit of elopers.

02174
THE THREE ALPINISTS (380)
Urban Trading Co
COMEDY Misadventures during Alpine climb.

02175
COPPING THE COPPERS (265)
Walturdaw
D: (Dave Aylott)
COMEDY Tramps exchange clothes with those of swimming policeman.

02176
THE LIGHTHOUSE KEEPER (590)
Walturdaw
CRIME Coastguards catch robbers when
lighthouse keeper's daughter signals with
candlestick.

02177
BABY'S CHUM (340)
Warwick Trading Co
D: (Charles Raymond)
Hal Bert
ANIMAL Dog saves baby.

02178
THE IMMORTAL GOOSE
Warwick Trading Co
D: (Charles Raymond)
TRICK Goose survives attempts to kill it.

02179
SAVED BY A DREAM (485)
Williamson
D: (James Williamson)
DRAMA Gambler reforms after dreaming he
loses everything and is jailed.

02180
THE LETTER BOX THIEF (215)
Williamson
D: (James Williamson)
COMEDY Boys' fireworks blow PC onto tramp
who stole letters.

WARWICK CINEPHONE FILMS sound
Warwick Trading Co

02181
I FEAR NO FOE

02182
MY GIRL'S A YORKSHIRE GIRL

02183
FOR EVER AND FOR EVER

02184
SUE, SUE, SUE

02185
MY RAINBOW

02186
I'M AFRAID TO GO HOME IN THE DARK
Whit Cunliffe

02187
THE GALLOPING MAJOR

02188
THE RAIN CAME PITTER PATTER DOWN
MUSICAL Synchronised to gramophone records.

02189
NATURAL COLOUR PORTRAITURE (375)
kinema
Natural Colour Kinematograph Co
D:S: G.A. Smith
FACIAL Various scenes including remake of
SCANDAL OVER THE TEACUPS (GAS; 1900).

MAR
02190
THE CAT CAME BACK (500)
Hepworth
D: Lewin Fitzhamon
COMEDY Man tries various methods of getting
rid of cat.

02191
A WOMAN'S VANITY (450)
Hepworth

D: (Theo Bouwmeester)
DRAMA Gardener fetches man to save wife
from rich lover's drugged wine.

02192
THE SHEPHERD'S DOG (375)
Hepworth
D: Lewin Fitzhamon
ANIMAL Rover fetches sick shepherd to save
small daughter from snow.

02193
THAT MARVELLOUS GRAMOPHONE (500)
Hepworth
D: Lewin Fitzhamon
COMEDY Tramp hides in homemade
gramophone and sings through trumpet.

02194
THE CABMAN'S GOOD FAIRY (550)
Hepworth
D: Lewin Fitzhamon
Chrissie White
DRAMA Rich girl drives old cabman home and
brings food for starving family.

02195
THE POLITE PARSON (350)
R.W. Paul
D: (Jack Smith)
COMEDY Mild cleric's mishaps while
delivering tracts.

02196
WAS IT A SERPENT'S BITE? (300)
Walturdaw
D: (Dave Aylott)
COMEDY Boys prick passers-by with pin and
are chased.

02197
ENGLAND INVADED
Warwick Trading Co
S: Leo Stormont
WAR Leo Stormont narrates from stage.

02198
THE TOWER OF LONDON (1125)
Williamson
D: (James Williamson)
S: (NOVEL) Harrison Ainsworth
DRAMA 1553. Lord escapes from jealous
jailer to wed Lady's maid.

02199
WHY FATHER GREW A BEARD (300)
Urban Trading Co
D: W.R. Booth
COMEDY (9 scenes) Father's razor is used by
wife, servant, gardener.

02200
SAVED BY A BURGLAR (345)
Urban Trading Co
D: (W.R. Booth)
CRIME (13 scenes) Small girl gets locked in
safe and is freed by burglar.

WARWICK CINEPHONE FILMS sound
Warwick Trading Co

02201
BRAVO TERRITORIALS!

02202
THE VILLAIN OF THE PIECE

02203
HANNAH WON'T YOU OPEN THAT DOOR
Pete Hampton

02204
BECAUSE

02205
THE LAUGHING SONG

02206
EXCELSIOR

02207
I WANT YOU TO SEE MY GIRL

02208
SINCE DADDY WAS TAKEN AWAY
MUSICAL Synchronised with gramophone records

02209
TOREADOR sound
Animatophone Syndicate
MUSICAL Synchronised with a gramophone
record.

APR
02210
THE INVADERS (600)
Clarendon
D: Percy Stow
WAR Girl sends pigeons to fetch territorials
when foreign spies pose as Jewish tailors to
occupy her strategic house.

02211
A MAN HOUSEMAID (550)
Cricks & Martin
D: A.E. Coleby
COMEDY French manservant flirts with
employer's wife.

02212
MY WORD, IF I CATCH YOU SMOKING!
(490)
Cricks & Martin
D: A.E. Coleby
COMEDY Children foiled by new Act fool PC
with explosive cigar.

02213
THE DENTIST'S DAUGHTER (300)
Hepworth
D: Lewin Fitzhamon
COMEDY Beau elopes with dentist's daughter
by posing as patient.

02214
THE SPECIAL LICENSE (750)
Hepworth
D: (Theo Bouwmeester)
DRAMA Rival fells tree to make motor-cyclist
crash, dons his goggles, and takes his place at
wedding.

02215
THE GIPSY CHILD (400)
Hepworth
D: Lewin Fitzhamon
ANIMAL Horse fetches gipsies to save
child from snow.

02216
THE BALIFF AND THE DRESSMAKERS
Hepworth
D: (Theo Bouwmeester)
COMEDY Girls and beaux hide to fool landlord
and bailiffs.

02217
THE WRONG COAT (575)
Hepworth
D: (Theo Bouwmeester)
CRIME Diner takes wrong coat and leaves
behind one containing note that leads to
capture of burglars.

02218
THE MISER AND THE CHILD (675)
Hepworth
D: Lewin Fitzhamon
DRAMA Miser forces dead daughter's child to beg until she is found by soldier father.

02219
A PAIR OF TRUANTS (400)
Hepworth
D: Lewin Fitzhamon
COMEDY Ragamuffin leads boy into trouble and makes him scapegoat.

02220
WHEN THIEVES FALL OUT (450)
Hepworth
D: (Theo Bouwmeester)
CRIME Thief poses as policeman to rob jeweller and locks him in safe for burglars to find.

02221
CHICAGO MAY THE MODERN ADVENTURESS (985)
Anglo-American Films
CRIME (26 scenes) Girl leaves home, becomes cardshaper, joins gang, robs bank, kidnaps Lord's fiancee, breaks jail, and is caught.

02222
A BUSY NIGHT (140)
Anglo-American Films
COMEDY "A distinctly humorous film"

02223
MR HENPECK'S REVOLT (390)
Anglo-American Films
COMEDY Henpeck drinks vitaliser and revolts against wife.

WARWICK CINEPHONE FILMS *sound*
Warwick Trading Co

02224
MY LITTLE DEUTSCHER GIRL

02225
MY LITTLE YIDDISHER BOY

02226
ARE YOU SINCERE?

02227
IF I SHOULD PLANT A TINY SEED OF LOVE

02228
ORA PRO NOBIS

02229
SEAWEED

02230
LITTLE WILLIE'S WILD WOODBINES

02231
A WHITE MAN

02232
KISSING DUET FROM "THE GEISHA"

02233
THE SALOME DANCE MUSIC
MUSICAL Synchronised with gramophone records.

02234
THE MAGIC CARPET (350)
Urban Trading Co
D: W.R. Booth
TRICK (14 scenes) Tramp steals sorceror's flying carpet.

02235
A RUSTIC FLIRT (535)
Walturdaw
ROMANCE Harvester saves girl from flirtatious cyclists.

02236
A HOT TIME IN A COLD QUARTER (254)
Walturdaw
COMEDY Man is snowballed and dragged by sledge.

02237
THE CAPTAIN'S HONOUR (695)
Walter Tyler
ANIMAL Shipwrecked captain's dog swims ashore to fetch help.

MAY

02238
THE MORGANATIC MARRIAGE (490)
Clarendon
D: Percy Stow
ROMANCE Ruritania. Princess, forced to wed Prince, changes places with peasant to whom he is already wed.

02239
A LESSON IN ELECTRICITY (410)
Clarendon
D: Percy Stow
COMEDY

02240
BERTIE BUYS A BULLDOG (500)
Cricks & Martin *Reissue:* 1915
D: A.E. Coleby
CHASE Man buys bulldog and is dragged through streets.

02241
LITTLE JIM (375)
Cricks & Martin
D: A.E. Coleby
S: (SONG)
PATHOS Miner's son dies and angels waft his soul to Heaven.

02242
HE WOULD FISH (345)
Anglo-American Films
COMEDY Misadventures of determined fisherman.

02243
THE SPORTING MICE (300)
Armstrong (C&M)
D:S: Charles Armstrong
TRICK Silhouette film of acrobatic mice.

02244
CONVICT 99 (1060)
Gaumont
D: Arthur Gilbert
S: (PLAY) (NOVEL) Marie Connor, Robert Leighton
Frank Beresford .... Laurence Grey
CRIME Framed clerk, freed for saving bribed warder's daughter, is cleared by dying confession.

02245
A GAIETY DUET (610)
Gaumont
D: (Arthur Gilbert)
S: (PLAY) James Tanner, "Cryptos" (OUR MISS GIBBS)
George Grossmith .... Hon Hugh

Madge Melbourne .... Miss Gibbs
Edmund Payne .... Tim
COMEDY Scene from "Gaiety Theatre" production.

02246
THE VILLAIN'S DOWNFALL (725)
Hepworth
D: (Lewin Fitzhamon)
CRIME Rich man abducts girl, tricks pursuant motorcyclist into empty house, and sets it afire.

02247
THE DOG AND THE BONE (275)
Hepworth
D: Lewin Fitzhamon
CHASE Dog steals bone and is chased by butcher, people, and dogs.

02248
THE TREACHEROUS POLICEMAN (675)
Hepworth
D: (Theo Bouwmeester)
CRIME Crooked policeman runs over girl's father and blames his rival.

02249
THE FANCY DRESS BALL (350)
Hepworth
D: Lewin Fitzhamon
COMEDY Couple in fancy dress walk home and scare milkman.

02250
THE CURATE AT THE RACES (575)
Hepworth
D: Lewin Fitzhamon
Harry Buss .... The Curate
CHASE Bookie frames drunken curate for welshing and is chased.

02251
HIS ONLY FRIEND (350)
Hepworth
D: Lewin Fitzhamon
ANIMAL Dog tracks down thieves who robbed butcher's boy.

02252
TOO MUCH LOBSTER (275)
Hepworth
D: (Lewin Fitzhamon)
COMEDY Husband overeats and dreams of girls.

02253
INVISIBILITY (650)
Hepworth
D: Cecil Hepworth, Lewin Fitzhamon
Lewin Fitzhamon
TRICK Man buys magic powder which makes him invisible.

02254
THE ESCAPADES OF TEDDY BEAR
R.W. Paul
D: (Jack Smith)
Johnny Butt .... Taxidermist
COMEDY Friends dress sleeping taxidermist in bear's skin.

02255
THE BURNING HOME (485)
R.W. Paul
D: (Jack Smith)
DRAMA Man misses train, tram, and ferry but cycles home in time to see fireman save child.

02256
A TRAGEDY OF THE TRUTH (730)
Precision Films
D: (T.J. Gobbett)
CRIME Snubbed man robs Lady and frames rival.

02257
A BAD DAY FOR LEVINSKY (396)
Precision Films
D: (T.J. Gobbett)
CHASE Jew puts sovereign in slot machine by mistake.

02258
THE MAD MUSICIAN (245)
Sheffield Photo Co
D: Frank Mottershaw.
COMEDY "A poor fiddler in all sorts of ludicrous situations."

02259
THE WIZARD'S WALKING STICK (410)
Urban Trading Co
D: W.R. Booth
TRICK (15 scenes) Wizard uses magic wand to escape jail and elude pursuant police.

02260
CAPTURED BY BOY SCOUTS (440)
London Cinematograph Co
CRIME Boy scouts track tramp who stole money from farmer's wife.

02261
THE BELLE WHO TALKS (444)
London Cinematograph Co
D: (S. Wormald)
COMEDY Henpeck hires woman to out-nag wife.

02262
ALL SCOTCH (515)
London Cinematograph Co
D: (S. Wormald)
COMEDY Thief poses as stolen statue to rob passers-by.

02263
THE PATENT GLUE (550)
Walturdaw
COMEDY Naughty boy plays pranks with fast-drying glue.

02264
THE POACHER (630)
Walturdaw
CRIME Workless mechanic shoots policeman in struggle and is saved from murder charge by old women.

02265
THEY WOULD BE ACROBATS (390)
Warwick Trading Co
D: (Charles Raymond)
COMEDY Children try to emulate street enterainers.

02266
HOW THE BULLDOG PAID THE RENT (423)
Warwick Trading Co
D: (Charles Raymond)
ANIMAL Poor man's dog steals landlord's bag; man returns it for reward and pays rent.

02267
THE BOY AND THE CONVICT (750)
Williamson
D: (Dave Aylott)
CRIME (10 scenes) Convict freed by blacksmith's boy, makes fortune abroad, and is cleared by dying confession.

02268
HOW THEY MADE A MAN OF BILLY BROWN (575)
Williamson Reissue: 1912 (Kineto)
D: Jack Chart
Jack Chart
COMEDY Bumpkin makes good after service in territorials.

WARWICK CINEPHONE FILMS sound
Warwick Trading Co

02269
JOHN WILLIE, COME ON

02270
FOUR JOLLY SAILORMEN

02271
KATE, WON'T YOU ROLLER SKATE?

02272
WON'T YOU WALTZ THE MERRY WIDOW WALTZ WITH ME?

02273
ALL COONS LOOK ALIKE TO ME

02274
THE WALTZ MUST TURN TO A MARCH

02275
HOME AGAIN MY CHERRY BLOSSOM
Frank Barnes

02276
OH SALOME, OH, OH, OH!
MUSICAL Synchronised with gramophone records.

JUN

02277
JUGGINS' MOTOR SKATES (585)
Clarendon Reissue: 1912
D: Percy Stow
CHASE Pursuit of man wearing motorised rollerskates.

02278
WHEN JACK GOT HIS PAY (500)
Cricks & Martin
D: A.E. Coleby
CRIME Flower girl rides on back of cab to save drugged sailor from robbers.

02279
NAT'S CONVERSION (510)
Cricks & Martin
D: A.E. Coleby
DRAMA Fighting parson converts brutal drunkard.

02280
THE RECEIVER'S DOOM (480)
Cricks & Martin
D: A.E. Coleby
CRIME Receiver betrayed by wounded thief, chased over telephone wires by police.

02281
A COLD AND ITS CONSEQUENCES (500)
Cricks & Martin
D: A.E. Coleby
CHASE Sick man wraps himself in flannel and is pulled along by dogs.

02282
THE BUTCHER'S BOY AND THE PENNY DREADFUL (415)
Cricks & Martin
D: A.E. Coleby
CHASE Boy reading while cycling collides with people.

02283
FATHER, HOLD MY WOOL (345)
Cricks & Martin
D: A.E. Coleby
COMEDY Boy gets father entangled with knitting wool.

02284
VOTES FOR WOMEN - A CARICATURE (300)
Armstrong (C&M)
D:S: Charles Armstrong
TRICK Silhouette film of suffragette and policeman.

02285
A WELL-EARNED DRINK (290)
Anglo-American Films
CHASE Tramp runs after cart to return piece of scenery.

02286
TERRITORIAL ON THE BRAIN (485)
Anglo-American Films
COMEDY Keen volunteer soldier insists on drilling everybody.

02287
THE BACHELOR'S PUDDING (355)
Anglo-American Films
COMEDY Man tries to get rid of hard-boiled pudding.

02288
BIRDIE IN SEARCH OF A HUSBAND (440)
Anglo-American Films
COMEDY Trouble follows spinster's advertisement in marriage paper.

02289
WHAT WOMEN SUFFER (595)
Anglo-American Films
DRAMA Costers help family of jailed embezzler who rewards them after making fortune in Australia.

02290
THE RACE FOR THE FARMER'S CUP (725)
Hepworth
D: Lewin Fitzhamon
Lewin Fitzhamon
SPORT Farmer wins race and girl despite rival waving white flag.

02291
TWO BAD BOYS (550)
Hepworth
D: (Frank Wilson)
COMEDY Naughty boys play pranks fireworks.

02292
THE STORY OF A PICTURE (550)
Hepworth
D: (Lewin Fitzhamon)
Alma Taylor
DRAMA Man deserts wife and child but reforms on seeing painting in gallery.

02293
AN INEXPERIENCED ANGLER (475)
Hepworth
D:(Frank Wilson)
COMEDY Clumsy man's trouble with fishing tackle.

02294
ONLY A TRAMP (350)
Hepworth
D: (Theo Bouwmeester)
DRAMA Tramp returns stolen necklace and is jailed, but saved by magistrate's daughter.

02295
THE RIVALS (425)
Hepworth
D: (Lewin Fitzhamon)
COMEDY PC wins cook by hypnotising burglar.

02296
WITHIN AN ACE (350)
Hepworth
D: (Theo Bouwmeester)
WAR Sleeping sentry saved from courtmartial
when his wife saves his colonel from a spy's
dagger.

02297
BAITING THE BOBBY (400)
Hepworth
D: Lewin Fitzhamon
COMEDY Boys trick PC with fireworks, dummy
girl, glue.

02298
THE LUCK OF THE CARDS (475)
Hepworth
D: (Theo Bouwmeester)
DRAMA Busker becomes prima donna and
crowd saves her from jealous gambler's knive.

02299
THE BOY AND HIS KITE (350)
Hepworth
D: Lewin Fitzhamon
CHASE Boy's kite drags PC along street and
into pond.

02300
A MAN AND HIS BEES (300)
Hepworth
D: (Lewin Fitzhamon)
CHASE Railway passenger's bees escape and
chase people into haystack.

02301
ONE GOOD TURN DESERVES ANOTHER
(625)
Hepworth
D: (Theo Bouwmeester)
CRIME Waif sees girl kidnapped, saves her, and
takes her home.

02302
THE LOVE OF A HUNCHBACK (540)
Empire Films (Butcher)
DRAMA Period. Hunchback saves beloved
from Baron, and dies.

02303
THE WORK OF THE FIRST AID NURSING
YEOMANRY CORPS (500)
Empire Films (Butcher)
D: Frank E. Butcher
Capt. E.G. Baker
WAR Nurses aid wounded after Zulu attack.

02304
JAGGERS BREAKS ALL RECORDS (250)
Precision Films
D: (T.J. Gobbett)
CHASE Messenger wearing skates hangs on
back of car.

02305
SUSPECTED; OR, THE MYSTERIOUS
LODGER (300)
R.W. Paul
D: (Jack Smith)
COMEDY Landlady mistakes lodger's dummy
for dismembered corpse.

02306
THE LOVE OF A ROMANY LASS (767)
Rosie Films

D: Joe Rosenthal
CRIME Gipsy girl is ordered to stab lover when
he is cleared of killing squire, but kills herself.

02307
DISSOLVING THE GOVERNMENT (285)
Urban Trading Co
D: F. Percy Smith
TRICK Asquith's face dissolves into Balfour's,
etc.

02308
CHEMICAL PORTRAITURE (260)
Urban Trading Co
D: F.Percy Smith
TRICK Liquid screen changes Czar's face to
King Alfonso, etc.

02309
WHY TOMMY WAS LATE FOR SCHOOL (310)
Urban Trading Co
D: (W.R. Booth)
COMEDY Schoolboy plays pranks.

02310
MARIE LLOYD'S LITTLE JOKE (540)
Urban Trading Co
D: (W.R. Booth)
Marie Lloyd
COMEDY Star takes place of eloping girl to
fool pursuant parents, then drinks "Vinetrim".

02311
PROF PUDDENHEAD'S PATENTS - THE
AEROCAB AND VACUUM PROVIDER (385)
Urban Trading Co
D: W.R. Booth
FANTASY Children steal prof's plane, fly over
White City, and suck up food.

WARWICK CINEPHONE FILMS *sound*
Warwick Trading Co

02312
LITTLE WOODEN HUT
George Courtney

02313
THE LITTLE ROCKING CHAIR

02314
QUEEN OF THE EARTH

02315
I'M WEARING MY HEART AWAY FOR YOU

02316
LET'S HAVE A SONG ABOUT THE BOYS

02317
EILEEN ALLANAH

02318
ISN'T IT LOVELY TO BE IN LOVE
Walter Miller

02319
LOCH LOMOND
Madame Deering
MUSICAL Synchronised with gramophone
records.

02320
TURNING THE TABLES (528)
Walturdaw
TRICK Henpeck uses magic wand to avenge
himself on wife.

02321
DOMESTIC RIVALS (176)
B&C (Walturdaw) *Reissue:* 1911
D: (J.B. McDowell)
ANIMAL Dog and cat have boxing match; dog
wins and smokes pipe.

02322
SCOUTS TO THE RESCUE (550)
Williamson
D:S: Dave Aylott
Frank Sutherland .... The Gipsy
Mrs Sutherland .... Gipsy Woman
Dave Aylott .... Farmer Giles
Anita March .... Mrs Giles
CHASE Scouts track gipsies and save farmer's
kidnapped child.

02323
SQUARING THE ACCOUNT (370)
Williamson
D: (Dave Aylott)
COMEDY Sacked packer causes confusion by
mixing parcels.

02324
A DASH FOR HELP (515)
Williamson
D:S: Dave Aylott
WAR India. Messenger gets through native lines
to fetch Highlanders to save beseiged fort.

JUL

02325
THE TALE OF THE ARK (440)
Alpha Trading Co (Cosmo)
D:S: Arthur Cooper
TRICK Child dreams of Bible tale enacted
by toys.

02326
ZILLAH, A STORY OF GIPSY LIFE (275)
Anglo-American Films
DRAMA Gipsy girl tries to warn squire of
impending burglary and is killed by tribe.

02327
THE WAIF HEROINE (280)
Anglo-American Films
DRAMA Beggar dreams friend's house catches
fire, and it does; she saves his life and is adopted.

02328
AN AERIAL ELOPEMENT (540)
Clarendon
D: Percy Stow
CHASE Father pursues couple who elope in
aeroplane.

02329
SALOME MAD (500)
Cricks & Martin
D: A.E. Coleby
CHASE Man chases windblown poster of
"Salome" under sea.

02330
THE ROBBER'S RUSE: OR, FOILED BY
FIDO (425)
Cricks & Martin
D: A.E. Coleby
ANIMAL Thief poses as woman to steal
cashbox; terrier fetches police.

02331
DREADNOUGHT TO THE RESCUE (490)
Rosie Films
D: Joe Rosenthal
ANIMAL Child heir is saved from drowning
by pet dog.

02332
A CHEAP REMOVAL (550)
Hepworth
D: (Lewin Fitzhamon)
COMEDY Troubles of mean father pushing
furniture on barrow.

02333
THE SPY (350)
Hepworth
D: (Lewin Fitzhamon)
CRIME Spy drugs soldier, steals plans, is chased
by horsemen, and shot.

02334
SALOME MAD (600)
Hepworth
D: (Theo Bouwmeester)
COMEDY Man is obsessed by the "Salome"
dance.

02335
THE RANCH OWNER'S DAUGHTER (675)
retitled: THE REDSKIN'S OFFER
Hepworth
D: Lewin Fitzhamon
WESTERN Rejected man bribes Indian to
kidnap girl who is saved from stake by rival.

02336
MISTAKEN IDENTITY (400)
Hepworth
D: (Theo Bouwmeester)
COMEDY Strong girl saves man from being
framed for jewel theft.

02337
SAVED BY THE TELEGRAPH (400)
Hepworth
D: Lewin Fitzhamon
WESTERN Girl telegraphs for aid when
bushrangers beseige ranch.

02338
THE NEW SERVANT (475)
Hepworth
D: (Theo Bouwmeester)
COMEDY Man poses as maid to fool amorous
man and win his daughter.

02339
NECESSITY IS THE MOTHER OF
INVENTION (325)
Hepworth
D: Lewin Fitzhamon
COMEDY Man is forced to dress as woman
when son steals clothes.

02340
SIMPLE SIMON AT THE RACES (435)
London Cinematograph Co
D: (S. Wormald)
CHASE Dude stands in for bookie who welshes,
is chased and stripped.

02341
THE PERIL OF THE FLEET (535)
London Cinematograph Co
D: (S. Wormald)
CRIME Spithead. Spies throw tec over cliff
but he survives and stops them destroying fleet.

02342
PROFESSOR PUDDENHEAD'S PATENTS -
THE ELECTRIC ENLARGER (330)
Urban Trading Co
D: W.R. Booth
FANTASY Servant steals prof's invention and
enlarges dog, caterpillar, and himself.

02343
THE INCOMPETENT THIEF (512)
Walturdaw
COMEDY Shoemaker tries hand at burglary and
is caught by postman.

WARWICK CINEPHONE FILMS sound
Warwick Trading Co

02344
LOVE'S OLD SWEET SONG
Alan Turner

02345
ALWAYS

02346
A LITTLE BOY CALLED TAPS

02347
EVER OF THEE

02348
HEARD IN COURT

02349
CALLER HERRING

02350
JOLLY GOOD COMPANY

02351
COME INTO THE GARDEN, MAUD
MUSICAL Synchronised to gramophone
records.

02352
TWO NAUGHTY BOYS (375)
Williamson
D:S: Dave Aylott
Stuart Williamson .... Boy
Tom Williamson .... Boy
CHASE Boys play pranks on people and are
chased.

02353
THE UNWELCOME CHAPERONE (400)
Williamson
D:S: Dave Aylott
Bill Haley .... Auntie
Ernie Cornford .... The Beau
Anita March .... The Girl
COMEDY Courting couple strand aunt in boat
on river.

02354
FOR HER SAKE (590)
Williamson
D:S: Dave Aylott
Dave Aylott .... Officer
Anita March .... RSM's Wife
1th Royal Irish Dragoons
WAR Africa. Corporal shot while saving
wounded rival from Zulus.

AUG

02355
PUT A PENNY IN THE SLOT (535)
Clarendon
D: Percy Stow
COMEDY Children alter labels on slot machines.

02356
BOXING FEVER (600)
Cricks & Martin *Reissue:* 1912
D: A.E. Coleby
A.E. Coleby
COMEDY Man boxes everyone he meets until
wife knocks him out.

02357
WHEN JACK COMES HOME (380)
Cricks & Martin
D: A.E. Coleby
DRAMA Girl refuses to wed rent collector and
is saved from eviction by sailor lover.

02358
THE UNFORTUNATE CANVASSER (500)
Cricks & Martin

D: A.E. Coleby
CHASE Frenchman tries to sell "Art"
photographs to housewives and is thrown into
tar cauldron.

02359
THE SECRETARY'S CRIME (700)
Cricks & Martin
D: A.E. Coleby
CRIME Dying confession saves clerk from
robbery charge.

02360
FATHER BUYS A CHEAP GOOSE (315)
Anglo-American Films
COMEDY Father throws away high goose but
it keeps returning.

02361
THE MEANEST MAN ON EARTH (500)
Hepworth
D: Lewin Fitzhamon
COMEDY Period. Girl and suitor pose as
highwaymen to rob miserly father.

02362
TEACHING A HUSBAND A LESSON (600)
Hepworth
D: (Theo Bouwmeester)
COMEDY Man smashes wife's violin so she
pretends to elope with brother.

02363
THE JEWEL THIEVES (625)
Hepworth
D: Lewin Fitzhamon
Chrissie White .... Cyclist
CHASE Girl cyclist chases crooks posing police
and shoots their tyres.

02364
THE BOYS AND THE PURSE (250)
Hepworth
D: Lewin Fitzhamon
CHASE Boys hide purse in old man's bathchair.

02365
THE BURGLAR AND THE CHILD (450)
Hepworth
D: (Theo Bouwmeester)
CRIME Burglar kidnaps girl and frames father.

02366
THE LITTLE MILLINER AND THE THIEF
(325)
Hepworth
D: Lewin Fitzhamon
Alma Taylor
Chrissie White
CRIME Girl arrested for theft is freed when man
catches thief.

02367
FARMER GILES IN LONDON (550)
Hepworth
D: (Theo Bouwmeester)
COMEDY Visiting farmer gulled by coiners and
stripped by crooks.

02368
A GALLANT SCOUT (430)
Manufacturers' Film Agency
ANIMAL Gipsies kidnap girl whose dog fetches
scouts to rescue.

02369
HIS DAUGHTERS (420)
Manufacturers' Film Agency
DRAMA

02370
MONTY LEARNS TO SWIM (355)
Urban Trading Co
D: W.R. Booth
TRICK Amateur swimmer dreams of diving from moon, etc.

02371
GINGERBREAD (400)
Williamson
D:S: Dave Aylott
Stuart Williamson
COMEDY Ice cream man bribes boy to put pepper in baker's gingerbread.

02372
SORRY, CAN'T STOP! (235)
Williamson
D:S: Dave Aylott
Bill Haley .... Auntie
Stuart Williamson .... Boy
CHASE Boys fix roller-skates on sleeping aunt.

WARWICK CINEPHONE FILMS *sound*
Warwick Trading Co

02373
MONA

02374
IT'S A DIFFERENT GIRL AGAIN

02375
I'M OFF TO PHILADELPHIA

02376
FATHER O'FLYNN

02377
MARY

02378
WHEN WE'RE TOGETHER

02379
I DON'T CARE IF THERE'S A GIRL THERE
MUSICAL Synchronised to gramophone records.

SEP

02380
THE MISER'S FATE (460)
Anglo-American Films
CRIME Mother makes son strangle rich woman and then denounces him for reward.

02381
UNCLE'S DAY WITH THE CHILDREN (400)
Anglo-American Films
COMEDY Children play pranks on uncle.

02382
HER LOVER'S HONOUR (645)
B&C (Cosmo)
D:S: H.O. Martinek
H.O. Martinek ....The Messenger
Ivy Martinek .... Annette
ADVENTURE France. Girl saves King's Messenger from Richelieu's agent.

02383
SHIPMATES (440)
B&C (Cosmo)
D: (H.O. Martinek)
ADVENTURE Sailor saves girl from gipsies; she fetches sailors to save him.

02384
PATER'S PATENT PAINTER (350)
Clarendon *Reissue:* 1914
D: Percy Stow
COMEDY Father's automatic whitewash-pumper floods house.

02385
WHEN FATHER WEARS STAYS (355)
Clarendon
D: Percy Stow
COMEDY Fat man dons corsets and cannot pick up slippers.

02386
THE DEAR OLD DOG (460)
Clarendon
D: Percy Stow
ANIMAL Man tied to railway line is saved when dog pushes signal.

02387
A GLASS OF GOAT'S MILK (446)
Clarendon *Reissue:* 1913
D: Percy Stow
COMEDY Bearded man drinks goat's milk and butts people.

02388
THE CONVICT'S DREAM (650)
Cricks & Martin
D: A.E. Coleby
COMEDY Convict dreams of life of luxury.

02389
HOW POTTS BACKED THE WINNER (440)
Cricks & Martin
D: A.E. Coleby
COMEDY Punter finds horseshoe but it brings him bad luck.

02390
DANCING TABLOIDS (500)
Cricks & Martin
D: A.E. Coleby
COMEDY Boy gives dancing pills to PC, beggar, teacher, chickens.

02391
A SEASIDE EPISODE (440)
Cricks & Martin
D: A.E. Coleby
COMEDY Bexhill. Man flirts with girls and is caught by wife.

02392
THE PENALTY OF BEAUTY (450)
Hepworth
D: Lewin Fitzhamon
CHASE Enamoured men pursue girl in rowing boat.

02393
THE CURSE OF MONEY (525)
Hepworth
D: (Theo Bouwmeester)
DRAMA Heir wastes inheritance and is saved from suicide by Salvation Army.

02394
THE WRONG CAB (425)
Hepworth
D: Lewin Fitzhamon
COMEDY Father chases elopers' cab and finds it contains a lunatic.

02395
MARY JANE'S LOVES (250)
Hepworth
D: (Lewin Fitzhamon)
COMEDY Maid tries to drown herself after failing to woo a milkman and lunatic.

02396
THE SORROWS OF A CHAPERONE (325)
Hepworth
D: Lewin Fitzhamon
COMEDY Couple elude aunt forced to change clothes with convict.

02397
THE GYPSY LOVER (700)
Hepworth
D: Lewin Fitzhamon
DRAMA Father whips daughter for marrying gypsy; she sends pigeon for help.

02398
ROBBING THE WIDOWED AND FATHER-LESS (575)
Hepworth
D: (Theo Bouwmeester)
DRAMA Widow and child, evicted by usurpers, find true will in candlestick.

02399
THE KIDNAPPED KING (820)
Manufaturer's Film Agency
S: (PLAY) C. Douglas Carlile
Carlotta de Yonson .... Princess Thyra
C. Douglas Carlile .... Kit Karson
Lee Gilbert ....Patch
C.A. Carlile .... Prince Stephen
J. Duncan .... Clovis
J. Lowe .... Baron Votman
Fred Lewes .... King Otto of Merslen
CRIME Tec dons disguises to save boy King from kidnap.

02400
FATHER BUYS AN ARMCHAIR (390)
Rosie Films
D: Joe Rosenthal
COMEDY Antique chair's arms punch all who sit.

02401
ONE OF THE BULLDOG BREED (523)
Rosie Films
D: Joe Rosenthal
CRIME Wounded sailor saves girl from kidnap by robbers.

02402
ANGELINA'S BIRTHDAY PRESENT (297)
Rosie Films
D: Joe Rosenthal
COMEDY Maid preoccupied with bracelet.

02403
FROM WORKING HOUSE TO MANSION (600)
Urban Trading Co
D: (W.R. Booth)
DRAMA "A brave girl's courageous deeds reap a well-earned reward."

02404
A BOGUS MOTOR ELOPEMENT (335)
Urban Trading Co
D: W.R. Booth
CHASE Man pursues eloping wife and finds he has been tricked.

02405
ANIMATED COTTON (340)
Urban Trading Co *Reissue:* 1913
D: W.R. Booth
TRICK Stocking darns itself, etc.

02406
THE PROFESSOR'S DREAM (360)
Urban Trading Co
D: W.R. Booth
COMEDY Prof dreams he makes old friends young again, and they play pranks.

02407
HOW I COOK-ED PEARY'S RECORD (380)
Urban Trading Co
D: W.R. Booth
FANTASY Munchausen's fantastic conquest of the Pole.

02408
THE INVISIBLE DOG (355)
Urban Trading Co
D: W.R. Booth
TRICK Invisible dog steals sausages.

02409
THE ELECTRIC SERVANT (440)
Urban Trading Co
D: W.R. Booth
COMEDY "Prof Puddenhead's" electric servant
wreaks havoc.

02410
WILLIE SWAPPED PLACES WITH THE BOSS
(428)
Walturdaw
COMEDY Clerk puts on airs which lead to
downfall.

02411
SCRATCH AS SCRATCH CAN (410)
Williamson
D:S: Dave Aylott
COMEDY Boy sprinkles itching powder on
people.

02412
AND THEN HE WOKE UP (300)
Williamson
D:S: Dave Aylott
Ernie Cornford .... The Tramp
Margaret Scudamore .... The Girl
COMEDY Tramp dreams of saving rich girl's
life and marrying her.

02413
WHAT HAPPENED TO BROWN
R.W. Paul
D: (Jack Smith)
Johnny Butt .... Brown
COMEDY Punter steals "News of the World"
from bookie and is chased to factory, where
he is pressed and pulped. (Date uncertain)

02414
WHEN MAMA'S OUT (400)
Precision Films
D: (T.J. Gobbett)
COMEDY Girl's four young sisters wreak havoc
in house and garden while mother away.(Date
uncertain)

02415
CHOOSING THE WALLPAPER (215) *kinema*
Natural Colour Kinematograph Co
D:S: G.A. Smith
DRAMA Shopkeeper helps lady choose
patterned papers.

02416
KINEMACOLOUR PUZZLE (195) *kinema*
Natural Colour Kinematograph Co
D:S: G.A. Smith
TRICK Two coloured discs revolve in
kaleidoscopic fashion.

02417
MR TROUBLESOME
John Codman Enterprises
D: John Codman
COMEDY (Date uncertain)

   OCT

02418
THE EXPLOITS OF THREE-FINGERED
KATE (615)
B&C (Cosmo)
D: H.O. Martinek

Ivy Martinek .... Kate
Alice Moseley .... Mary
Charles Calvert ...... Daniel "Sheerluck" Finch
COMEDY Jewel thief eludes tec by changing
clothes with Negress at public baths.

02419
THREE SAILORMEN AND A GIRL (495)
Clarendon
D: Percy Stow
COMEDY Two rival sailors have clothes stolen
by third.

02420
BOBBY THE BOY SCOUT; OR, THE BOY
DETECTIVE (525)
Clarendon
D: Percy Stow
CHASE Scout trails burglars, locks them in,
and fetches police.

02421
NEVER LATE; OR, THE CONSCIENTIOUS
CLERK (470) *Reissue:* 1913
Clarendon
D: Percy Stow
COMEDY Clerks try to delay punctual
colleague.

02422
THE STOLEN FAVOURITE
Clarendon
D: Percy Stow
Actors from Drury Lane
SPORT Stableboy frees horse from crooks'
pantechnicon and rides to racetrack.

02423
ADOPTING A BABY (470)
Cricks & Martin
D: A.E. Coleby
CHASE Mothers chase advertiser who
refuses to adopt children.

02424
THE WANDERER'S RETURN: OR, MANY
YEARS AFTER (505)
Cricks & Martin
D: Dave Aylott
DRAMA Sailor returns from shipwreck as
wife remarries, and jumps off cliff.

02425
A YOUTHFUL HERO (620)
Cricks & Martin
D: A.E. Coleby
DRAMA Beggar boy, whipped by rich girl,
saves her from fire.

02426
THE YOUNG REDSKINS (415)
Cricks & Martin
D: Dave Aylott
COMEDY Boys dress as Red Indians and play
pranks.

02427
THE SUCCESS OF A CITY WAIF (380)
Empire Films (Butcher)
DRAMA Doctor adopts orphan who grows up
to wed his daughter.

02428
LITTLE NELL THE DRUNKARD'S CHILD
(380)
Empire Films (Butcher)
PATHOS Drunkard beats child, is jailed, and
signs pledge.

02429
THE AMOROUS SCOTCHMAN (133)
Empire Films (Butcher)
COMEDY Scotsman flirts with farmer's fat cook.

02430
THE ABSENT-MINDED BEGGAR (300)
Empire Films (Butcher)
COMEDY "In many cases the incidents are
ridiculous."

02431
ONLY A MOUSE (285)
Empire Films (Butcher)
COMEDY Boy catches mice and hides them in
dishes.

02432
THE TRIAL OF ABRAHAM'S FAITH (460)
Empire Films (Butcher)
RELIGION Father is ordered to sacrifice son.

02433
LOVE'S CURE FOR GOUT (253)
Empire Films (Butcher)
COMEDY Dude's apparatus fails to cure girl's
father of gout.

02434
A PRINCE OF KHYBER (600)
Empire Films (Butcher)
DRAMA India. Princess helps colonel and
family escape from Prince.

02435
A NARROW ESCAPE FROM LYNCHING
(375)
Hepworth
D: (Theo Bouwmeester)
CRIME Dumb witness saves miner when rival
frames him for shooting girl.

02436
A DRUNKARD'S SON (625)
Hepworth
D: Lewin Fitzhamon
CRIME Boy saves girl from runaway trap, is
given job in her father's bank, and is captured
by his father's gang.

02437
THE STOLEN CLOTHES (325)
Hepworth
D: (Lewin Fitzhamon)
COMEDY Tramp changes clothes with
swimming policeman.

02438
THE FATAL APPETISER (450)
Hepworth
D: Lewin Fitzhamon
Johnny Butt
COMEDY Hungry thin man eats everything
and grows fat.

02439
THE GYPSY'S BABY (575)
Hepworth
D: Lewin Fitzhamon
DRAMA Tramp saves doctor from gypsy and
doctor saves life of gypsy's baby.

02440
FELLOW CLERKS (975)
Hepworth
D: Theo Bouwmeester
CRIME Farmer's daughter saves bank clerk
from false charge of theft.

02441
A FATHER'S MISTAKE (625)
Hepworth
D: (Theo Bouwmeester)
CRIME Rich man rejects son's IOU and blames him when he is robbed.

02442
A PAIR OF DESPERADOES (450)
Hepworth
D: (Lewin Fitzhamon)
CRIME Escaped convicts steal car and rob post office.

02443
FATHER BUYS THE FIREWORKS (425)
Precision Films
D: T.J. Gobbett
COMEDY Trouble ensues when father buys fireworks.

02444
THE SWEEP'S THREEPENNY BATH (415)
Walturdaw
COMEDY

02445
SEXTON BLAKE (1280)
Gaumont
Melodrama Production Syndicate
D: C. Douglas Carlile
S: (PLAY) C. Douglas Carlile
C. Douglas Carlile .... Sexton Blake
Russell Barry .... Roger Blackburn
CRIME Tec poses as cleric to save squire's daughter from marrying murderer.

02446
SAVED BY THE BIOSCOPE (575)
Wrench Films
CRIME Buskers kidnap child and are filmed at carnival; parents see film at Empire, and rescue her.

02447
HIS LITTLE SISTER (310)
Wrench Films
DRAMA Alcoholic widow reforms when son hurt saving sister from fire.

02448
THE FOUR TOMBOYS (221)
Gaumont
D: (Alf Collins)
COMEDY Four girls play tricks.

02449
THE BOXING WAITER (315)
Gaumont
D: (Alf Collins)
COMEDY

02450
FROM SERVANT GIRL TO DUCHESS (366)
Gaumont
D: (Alf Collins)
COMEDY Maid dreams she is heroine of novelette and is wooed by Duke.

02451
CONSUL CROSSES THE ATLANTIC (810)
Urban Trading Co
COMEDY Adventures of performing ape aboard "SS George Washington".

02452
APPLES (335)
Urban Trading Co
COMEDY Boy and girl pick apples and are chased by tramp and PC.

02453
A TRUSTWORTHY SERVANT (430)
Urban Trading Co
COMEDY Couple's new maid turns out to be crook in disguise.

02454
THE TWELVE O'CLOCK EXPRESS (495)
Urban Trading Co
CRIME Signalman's daughter waves a lamp to save save train from wreckers.

02455
THE LASS WHO LOVES A SAILOR (445)
Urban Trading Co
ADVENTURE Girl posing as sailor fights bosun to save her sweetheart from burning ship.

02456
A CYCLING HONEYMOON (400)
Urban Trading Co
COMEDY Misadventures of newlyweds on bicycles.

02457
THE AIRSHIP DESTROYER (685)
USA: THE BATTLE IN THE CLOUDS
Urban Trading Co *reissue:* 1915, THE AERIAL TORPEDO
D: Walter R. Booth
FANTASY Inventor uses wireless-controlled flying torpedo to destroy enemy airships.

02458
BOBBY WIDEAWAKE (500)
Urban Trading Co
D: Walter R. Booth
TRICK Boy dreams motorised bed travels under sea to Arctica.

NOV

02459
THE PROFESSOR'S TWIRLY-WHIRLY CIGARETTES (425)
B&C (Cosmo)
D: (H.O. Martinek)
TRICK Prof mixes liver powder with tobacco, causing smokers to spin.

02460
ELECTRIC TRANSFORMATION (425)
Clarendon
D: Percy Stow
TRICK Professor's invention melts metal and people's faces.

02461
FATHER'S BABY BOY
Clarendon
D: Percy Stow
TRICK "Bovril" makes baby grow to enormous size.

02462
AN INGENIOUS SAFE DEPOSIT (460)
Clarendon
D: Percy Stow
COMEDY Tramp's search for boot containing money in sole.

02463
SAVED BY CARLO (510)
Cricks & Martin
D: A.E. Coleby
Dave Aylott
Anita March
ANIMAL Dog trails thieves who robbed rent collector, then fetches police.

02464
HYPNOTIC SUGGESTION (480)
Cricks & Martin
D: Dave Aylott
Bill Hewson
COMEDY Mesmerist makes man think he is horse.

02465
THE BITER BIT (340)
Cricks & Martin
D: A.E. Coleby
ANIMAL Dog chases bag snatcher.

02466
KATE'S REDEMPTION (580)
Empire Films (Butcher)
ROMANCE Farmer's daughter elopes with city cad and is saved by country sweetheart.

02467
THE BURGLARS AND THE OTTOMAN (470)
Empire Films (Butcher)
COMEDY Maid's policeman lover catches burglars hiding in sofa.

02468
A VETERAN'S STORY (320)
Empire Films (Butcher)
WAR Pensioner tells scouts how watch saved him from bullet.

02469
REWARD OF MERIT (308)
Empire Films (Butcher)
DRAMA Child's halfpenny reward eventually enables him to free mother from workhouse.

02470
A GAMIN'S GRATITUDE (400)
Hepworth
D: Lewin Fitzhamon
CRIME Urchin escapes ruffians by setting house afire and restores stolen purse.

02471
THE SLEEPWALKER (425)
Hepworth
D: (Theo Bouwmeester)
CRIME Girl sleepwalker captured by couple and saved by waif.

02472
A COWARD'S COURAGE (350)
Hepworth
D: (Theo Bouwmeester)
DRAMA Cowardly fireman wins girl by saving her from fire.

02473
A STREET ARAB (325)
Hepworth
D: Lewin Fitzhamon
DRAMA Urchin, freed from jail by dog, saves baby from drowning.

02474
A BRUTAL MASTER (800)
Hepworth
D: Lewin Fitzhamon
DRAMA Boss kidnaps foreman's daughter; dog leads strikers to her and they thrash the boss.

02475
THE BLIND MAN (650)
Hepworth
D: (Theo Bouwmeester)
CRIME Blind man saves policeman's daughter from kidnappers.

02476
SAVED FROM THE SEA (300)
Hepworth
D: (Lewin Fitzhamon)
DRAMA Sailor returns from shipwreck in time
to save family from eviction.

02477
THE FAITHFUL CLOCK (525)
Hepworth
D: Lewin Fitzhamon
Bob Boucher .... The Clock
COMEDY Thieves steal poor pair's grandfather
clock; it walks home.

02478
THAT AWFUL PIPE (370) *reissue:* 1915
Urban Trading Co
D: W.R. Booth
COMEDY Everyone overcome by fumes
from a smoker's pipe.

02479
SOOTY SKETCHES (395)
Urban Trading Co
D: W.R. Booth
TRICK Artist sketches silhouettes and they
come to life.

02480
THE MISADVENTURES OF A CYCLE
THIEF (330)
London Cinematograph Co
D: (S. Wormald)
CHASE Tramp steals bicycle and collides with
PC, bill-poster, ice-cream cart.

02481
A FATHER'S LOVE (445)
London Cinematograph Co
D: (Alf Wormald)
PATHOS Man shoots driver who killed child
and dies during trial.

02482
A WOULD-BE HERO (325)
Rosie Films
D: Joe Rosenthal
COMEDY

02483
GRETNA GREEN (685)
Walturdaw
CHASE Period. Parents pursue elopers to
Scotland, but arrive too late.

02484
TRACKED AND TRAPPED BY BOY SCOUTS
(585)
Walturdaw
CHASE Scouts trail burglars and trap them.

DEC

02485
THREE-FINGERED KATE — HER SECOND
VICTIM, THE ART DEALER (660)
B&C (Cosmo)
D: H.O. Martinek
Ivy Martinek .... Kate
Alice Moseley .... Mary
Charles Calvert ...... Sheerluck
COMEDY Girl helps sister rob Baron's art
gallery and escape over roof.

02486
DROWSY DICK'S DREAM (510)
B&C (Cosmo) *reissue:* 1912
D: H.O. Martinek
Nelson Keys .... Drowsy Dick
Ivy Martinek .... The Queen
COMEDY Tramp dreams he saves Queen
and is crowned King.

02487
IN LOVE WITH A PICTURE GIRL (380)
Clarendon
D: Percy Stow
CHASE Man pursues windblown cinema poster.

02488
THE PROFESSOR'S STRENGTH TABLETS
(450)
Clarendon
D: Percy Stow
TRICK Professor pots strong man and turns
him into explosive pills.

02489
UNDER THE MISTLETOE BOUGH (385)
Clarendon
D: Percy Stow
COMEDY "A comic you must have for
christmas"

02490
THE JEALOUS DOLL; OR, THE
FRUSTRATED ELOPEMENT (535)
Clarendon
D: Percy Stow
TRICK Doll fetches nurse when children elope.

02491
THE MARTYDOM OF ADOLF BECK (1630)
Gaumont
D:A: George R. Sims
Adolf Beck .... Himself
George R. Sims ... Himself
HISTORY True story of innocent man twice
jailed in mistake for swindler.

02492
QUICKSILVER PUDDING (430)
Gaumont
D: (Alf Collins)
COMEDY Boy puts quicksilver in Christmas
pudding and it rolls away.

02493
A SINNER'S REPENTANCE (650)
Hepworth
D: (Theo Bouwmeester)
DRAMA Drunkard reforms when cleric saves
starving child from being run over by bus.

02494
CUPID'S LOAF (775)
Hepworth
D: Lewin Fitzhamon
COMEDY Baker helps eloping couple elude
girl's father.

02495
THE GIRL WHO JOINED THE
BUSHRANGERS (925)
Hepworth
D: Lewin Fitzhamon
Chrissie White .... The Girl
WESTERN Girl joins outlaws and steals
father's cattle so that beloved sheriff may
recapture them.

02496
MR POORLUCK GETS MARRIED (675)
Hepworth
D: Lewin Fitzhamon
Harry Buss .... Mr Poorluck
COMEDY Boy causes groom to miss train so he
goes by coal cart.

02497
THE LITTLE FLOWER GIRL'S CHRISTMAS
(825)
Hepworth
D: Lewin Fitzhamon
CRIME Orphan flower girl saves rich benefactor
from tenement toughs

02498
AN ATTEMPT TO SMASH A BANK (625)
Hepworth
D: (Theo Bouwmeester)
DRAMA Banker's daughter rejects rich client
who then withdraws money to cause run on
bank.

02499
THE IDIOT OF THE MOUNTAINS (450)
Hepworth
D: (Theo Bouwmeester)
CRIME Idiot fetches police to save kidnapped
girl, and is cured.

02500
THE LAZY BOY (750)
Hepworth
D: Lewin Fitzhamon
COMEDY Stowaway on barge poses as girl
to avoid hard work.

02501
MUGGINS VC (485)
Cricks & Martin *reissues:* 1912; 1914; 1916
D:S: Dave Aylott
Arthur Charrington .... Muggins
Anita March .... His Girl
Dave Aylott .... Publican
4th Essex Regiment
WAR Bumpkin enlists and saves life of
bullying corporal. (Extract in THOSE WERE
THE DAYS (Butcher; 1946).)

02502
A MOTHERLESS WAIF (600)
Cricks & Martin
D: A.E. Coleby
PATHOS
Match girl beaten by drunken father, prays
for him, then dies.

02503
DIVER—SIONS (505)
Cricks & Martin *reissue:* 1916, DIVER'S
DIVERSIONS
D; Dave Aylott
Bill Hewson .... The Diver
COMEDY Man dresses in diving suit and
cannot remove it.

02504
THE COUNCIL OF THREE
London Cinematograph Co
S: (CHARACTER) Harry Blyth
CRIME "Sexton Blake" poses as gang's
messenger to save kidnapped girl.

02505
WHITE TO BLACK
London Cinematograph Co
D: (S. Wormald)
COMEDY Boy uses prof's liquid to cause
sister to turn black in her bath.

02506
THE OLD MAN'S PENSION DAY (400)
Rosie Films
D: Joe Rosenthal
CRIME Scouts trail and lasso man who robbed
pensioner.

02507
TOMMY LAD (560)
Walturdaw
DRAMA Boy soldier deserts on dreaming of
mother's death and is saved from courtmartial
by her pleas.

02508
ALMOST BY ACCIDENT: OR, SAVED BY
A SOCK (520)
Walturdaw
DRAMA Stranded steeplejack unravels sock
to pull up rescue rope.

02509
GILES' FIRST VISIT TO A HOTEL (380)
Wrench Films
COMEDY Farm labourer causes trouble in
posh city hotel.

02510
THE UNCONTROLLABLE MOTORCYCLE
(345)
Urban Trading Co
D: W.R. Booth
TRICK Boy fixes charge to brother's motor-
cycle, which then wrecks house.

1910

JAN

02511
THE CLERK'S DOWNFALL (690)
B&C (Cosmo)
D: Charles Raymond
Charles Raymond .... Clerk
CRIME Clerk steals for girl's sake and for-
given on saving life of boss's daughter.

02512
WHEN WE CALLED THE PLUMBER IN
(525)
Clarendon *reissue:* 1913
D: Percy Stow
COMEDY Clumsy plumber finds leak in
garret and floods house.

02513
THE TRUTH WILL OUT (680)
Clarendon
D: Percy Stow
CRIME Office boy witness saves clerk from
being framed for robbing safe.

02514
TEMPTATION AND FORGIVENESS (650)
Cricks & Martin
D: A.E. Coleby
CRIME Rich man disowns daughter but
forgives her when poor husband forges cheque.

02515
SCROGGINS PUTS UP FOR BLANKSHIRE
(500)
Cricks & Martin
D: A.E. Coleby
Charlie Bolton .... Scroggins
Dave Aylott .... Mrs Scroggins
COMEDY Suffragettes pelt candidate and he
wins but six votes.

02516
WHAT HAPPENED TO BROWN (630)
Cricks & Martin
D: Dave Aylott
COMEDY Man is mistakenly packed in box.

02517
THE SQUIRE'S ROMANCE (700)
Cricks & Martin
D: A.E. Coleby
Dave Aylott
DRAMA Squire saves gipsy girl from poacher,
and weds her.

02518
TARIFF REFORM (405)
Gaumont
DRAMA John Bull's home invaded by Italian,
Russian, and Frenchman.

02519
FREE TRADE (595)
Gaumont
DRAMA Rich British workman and clean
butcher contrasted with their French
counterparts.

02520
ALMOST (650)
Hepworth
D: (Theo Bouwmeester)
COMEDY Two brothers try to force unwilling
man to wed their sister.

02521
TEMPERED WITH MERCY (475)
Hepworth
D: (Lewin Fitzhamon)
PATHOS Starving flower girl steals loaf

and is prosecuted by baker.

02522
A WOMAN'S TREACHERY (600)
Hepworth
D: (Theo Bouwmeester)
CRIME Man takes blame for maid who steals
necklace, but denounces her when she weds
another.

02523
LOVE'S STRATEGY (800)
Hepworth
D: Lewin Fitzhamon
ROMANCE Girl elopes while maid takes
place at enforced wedding.

02524
HOT PICKLES (650)
Hepworth
D: Lewin Fitzhamon
Johnny Butt .... Colonel
COMEDY Colonel's home-made pickles make
diners belch flames.

02525
SAVED BY HIS SWEETHEART (450)
Hepworth
D: (Lewin Fitzhamon)
CRIME Framed clerk's fiancee trails thief
and locks him in.

02526
ARE YOU JOHN BROWN? (525)
Hepworth
D: (Lewin Fitzhamon)
COMEDY Lawyer advertises for ''John Brown''
and dozens reply.

02527
A FICKLE GIRL (475)
Hepworth
D: Lewin Fitzhamon
ROMANCE Gipsy girl jilts lover for squire but
he loves another.

02528
THE IRON HELMET (345)
Walturdaw
COMEDY Boy gets saucepan stuck over head.

02529
LOVE AND PROMOTION (565)
Walturdaw
CRIME Daughter of starving pedlar overhears
bankrobbers' plans.

02530
LADY CANDALE'S DIAMONDS (584)
London Cinematograph Co
D: (S. Wormald)
CRIME Jewel thieves steal Lady's car and are
trailed by tec.

02531
A MECHANICAL HUSBAND (415)
London Cinematograph Co
D: (S. Wormald)
COMEDY Girl objects to father's choice and
falls in love with automaton.

02532
PEDDLING PATRICK PINCHES POULTRY
(335)
Wrench Films
COMEDY Peddler steals chickens.

02533
THE FRESH AIR FIEND (445)
Wrench Films
COMEDY Man's mania for the open air.

FEB

02534
THE FIREMAN'S WEDDING (585)
B&C (Cosmo)
D: Charles Raymond
DRAMA Framed fireman cleared when he saves
life of rival's accomplice.

02535
MAGIC OF LOVE (465)
Clarendon
D: Percy Stow
TRICK Love helps suitor beat girl's father
at billiards.

02536
LIEUTENANT ROSE AND THE ROBBERS
OF FINGALL'S CREEK (960)
Clarendon
D: Percy Stow
CRIME Lieut ransoms millionaire's daughter
who fetches sailors to save him from sinking
yacht.

02537
ACCOMPANIED ON THE TOMTOM (540)
Cricks & Martin
D: A.E. Coleby
COMEDY Sultan gives rescuer a drummer
who follows him everywhere.

02538
'TWIXT RED MAN AND WHITE (590)
Cricks & Martin
D: Dave Aylott
A.E. Coleby .... Trapper
Johnny Butt .... Indian
Dave Aylott .... Cowboy
WESTERN Trapper surrenders to Indians to
save friends from attack.

02539
THE TERROR AND THE TERRIER (320)
Cricks & Martin *reissue:* 1915
D:S: A.E. Coleby
Frank Miller .... The Terror
CHASE Boy steals savage dog and sets it on
PC, sailor, blind man.

02540
THE TRAVELLING STILTWALKERS (510)
Gaumont
D: (Alf Collins)
Bob Pender and his Troupe
DRAMA Stiltwalking buskers save child from
burning house.

02541
THE BLUE BIRD (1380)
Gaumont
S: (PLAY) Maurice Maeterlinck
Pauline Gilmer .... Mytyl
Olive Walter .... Tytyl
Margaret Murray .... Mummy Tyl
E.A. Warburton .... Daddy Tyl
Ernest Hendrie .... Tylo
Norma Page .... Tylette
Carlotta Addison .... The Fairy
Edward Rigby .... Bread
H.R. Hignett .... Sugar
Doris Lytton .... Milk
Saba Raleigh .... Night
C.V. France .... Time
Roy Travers .... Cow
FANTASY Fairy helps selfish children find
bird of happiness. (Theatre Royal Production)

025
UNLUCKY BILL (300)
Hepworth
D: (Lewin Fitzhamon)
CHASE Pursued thief hides necklace in "blind" beggar's hat.

02543
IN THE HANDS OF THE ENEMY (550)
Hepworth
D: (Theo Bouwmeester)
WAR Nurse helps captured officer escape from old general.

02544
THE LITTLE HOUSEKEEPER (425)
Hepworth
D: Lewin Fitzhamon
CRIME Child hides money in doll while sister fetches father to catch burglars.

02545
WHO'S GOT MY HAT? (500)
Hepworth
D: Lewin Fitzhamon
CHASE Doctor chased when he takes wrong hat containing money.

02546
LET SLEEPING DOGS LIE (325)
Hepworth
D: (Lewin Fitzhamon)
CHASE Bulldog dragging policeman pursues old man.

02547
THE BURGLAR AND LITTLE PHYLLIS (750)
Hepworth
D: Lewin Fitzhamon
Alma Taylor .... Phyllis
CRIME Burglar reformed when he poses as conjuror at children's party.

02548
THE POSTMAN (575)
Hepworth
D: (Lewin Fitzhamon)
CRIME Sacked postman's son trails thief and locks him in.

02549
BLACK BEAUTY (441)
Hepworth remake: 1907
D:S: Lewin Fitzhamon
Lewin Fitzhamon
ANIMAL Horse fetches help when master attacked by tramps.

0255
DOROTHY'S MOTOR CAR (525)
Rosie Films
D: Joe Rosenthal
CHASE Girl in toy car leads cycling policemen to jewel thieves.

02551
POOR PA PAYS (475)
Rosie Films
D: Joe Rosenthal
COMEDY Miserly father fooled by disguised son and daughter.

02552
HOW I WON THE VC (388)
Walturdaw
WAR Grandfather tells children how he saved hospital and flag.

02553
BABY THE PEACEMAKER (470)
Walturdaw
DRAMA Miser forgives disowned daughter when he meets baby.

02554
THE TWO ARTISTS (455)
Wrench Films
DRAMA Poor artist saves academician's daughter from drowning.

02555
A DREAM OF PARADISE (320)
Wrench Films
COMEDY Tramp dreams girl motorist take him home for champagne.

02556
THE DUALITY OF MAN (580)
Wrench Films
S: (NOVEL) Robert Louis Stevenson (DR JEKYLL AND MR HYDE)
HORROR Dr's potion makes him steal banknotes and kill fiancee's father.

02557
THE JUVENILE FIREMEN (450)
Wrench Films
COMEDY Boys dress as firemen and set fire to house.

02558
THE SOUTH BEFORE THE WAR (535)
London Cinematograph Co
S: (SKETCH)
DRAMA Negro saves planter's daughter from sacked overseer.

02559
A LIVELY SKELETON (270)
London Cinematograph Co
D: (S. Wormald)
COMEDY Girl's suitor uses skeleton to scare away father's patients.

02560
A BIT OF OULDE IRELAND (725)
London Cinematograph Co
S: (PLAY)
DRAMA Betrayed Fenian sheltered by priest, escape jail, and poses as corpse at wake.

02561
THE DIVER'S WIFE (445)
London Cinematograph Co
S: (SKETCH)
DRAMA Woman dons diving suit to save husband from rival's minions.

02562
FOR THE LOVE OF A SHOWMAN (650)
London Cimematograph Co
S: (SKETCH)
DRAMA Dr's daughter elopes with clown, whose rival takes his place and shoots her.

02563
BABY BET (430)
Urban Trading Co
COMEDY Mischievous four-year old girl tricks tramp, policeman, doctor.

MAR
02564
THE BABY, THE BOY, AND THE TEDDY-BEAR (300)
B&C (Cosmo) reissue: 1912 (MP)
D: H.O. Martinek
Dorothy Foster .... The Nurse
COMEDY Boy puts baby's clothes on teddy-bear and throws it into river to fool PC.

02565
COCK-A-DOODLE-DOO (540)
Clarendon
D: Percy Stow
COMEDY Couple eat noisy cockerel and start crowing.

02566
THAT SKATING CARNIVAL (575)
Clarendon reissue: 1913
D: Percy Stow
COMEDY Family and maid learn to roller skate indoors.

02567
TOMMY'S LOCOMOTIVE (480)
Clarendon reissue: 1914
D: Percy Stow
CHASE Child in toy engine is chased through drainpipe and millstream.

02568
WANTED, A MUMMY (525)
Cricks & Martin
D: A.E. Coleby
COMEDY Tramp poses as mummy and his partner sells him to professor.

02569
A CLOWN'S CRIME (450)
Cricks & Martin
D: A.E. Coleby
ANIAML Terrier steals handbag to aid starving clown, and they are chased.

02570
VICE VERSA (465)
Cricks & Martin
D: Dave Aylott
A.E. Coleby
TRICK Boy uses magic wand to reverse policemen with sandwichmen, navvies with suffragettes.

02571
THE JEWEL THIEVES RUN TO EARTH BY SEXTON BLAKE (810)
Gaumont
S: (CHARACTERS) Harry Blyth
CRIME Tec saves clerk from gang who tie him to clock-operated gun.

02572
MISTAKEN INTENTION (285)
Gaumont
CHASE Father grinds knife, then chases his son.

02573
GRANDPA SEWS ON A BUTTON (205)
Gaumont
COMEDY Old man has trouble sewing button.

02574
MARY THE COSTER (650)
Hepworth
D: Lewin Fitzhamon
CRIME Coster couple save rich man's grandson from kidnappers.

02575
THE SARAMOUCHES (525)
Hepworth
D: Lewin Fitzhamon
Gertie Potter .... Girl
Bertie Potter .... Boy
COMEDY Four children steal car and eventually smash it.

02576
COCKSURE'S CLEVER RUSE (450) *also:*
TOO CLEVER FOR ONCE
Hepworth
D: (Lewin Fitzhamon)
COMEDY Man uses dead dog to extort money from motorists.

02577
THE SHARP-WITTED THIEF (500)
Hepworth
D: (Lewin Fitzhamon)
CHASE Barber chases thief who poses as woman.

02578
LORD BLEND'S LOVE STORY (1050)
Hepworth
D: (Theo Bouwmeester)
CRIME Rich woman has lord certified for rejecting her daughter; he is freed after saving doctor from madman.

02579
A WOMAN'S FOLLY (575)
Hepworth
D: (Theo Bouwmeester)
DRAMA Wife leaves home to live with husband's best friend, returns five years later, and dies.

02580
THE LITTLE BLUE CAP (600)
Hepworth
D: Lewin Fitzhamon
CRIME Boys save small girl from gipsy kidnappers.

02581
INVIGORATING ELECTRICITY (300)
Hepworth
D: (Lewin Fitzhamon)
COMEDY Electrified workman shocks spinster, cyclist, cook.

02582
THE CLOWN AND HIS DONKEY (265)
Armstrong (Urban)
D:S: Charles Armstrong
TRICK Animated paper silhouettes of clown and donkey.

02583
A ROMANCE OF HAYMAKING (600)
London Cinematograph Co
ROMANCE Ploughman wins farmer's daughter by proving rival framed him for poaching.

02584
THE LIFE OF A HIRED BIKE (385)
Warwick Trading Co
COMEDY Man's hired cycle used by maid, passerby, tramp.

02585
TWO BEAUTIFUL CRACKSMEN (417)
Warwick Trading Co
CRIME Crooks steal bag, rob safe, are chased and caught in cafe.

02586
A MARRIAGE OF CONVENIENCE (554)
Warwick Trading Co
ROMANCE Earl reconciled with enforced wife over deathbed of sweetheart.

02587
FATHER'S LEGACY — A GOAT (345)
Rosie Films
D: Joe Rosenthal
COMEDY Trouble ensues when family man inherits hungry goat.

02588
A LITTLE CHILD'S LETTER (635)
Walturdaw
DRAMA

APR

02589
MARY WAS A HOUSEMAID (465)
Clarendon
D: Percy Stow
COMEDY Clumsy housemaid wrecks home.

02590
THE LIGHT THAT FAILED (385)
Clarendon
D: Percy Stow
COMEDY Uncle tries to mend fuse and electrifies gas-bracket and bath.

02591
A HERO IN SPITE OF HIMSELF (465)
Clarendon
D: Percy Stow
COMEDY "Frightened Freddy" joins police and is promoted through mishaps.

02592
THE LAST OF THE DANDY (450)
Cricks & Martin
D: Dave Aylott
Fred Evans .... The Dandy
COMEDY Forgetful dude makes dates with girls, and they throw him in river.

02593
A MODERN PAUL PRY (410)
Cricks & Martin
D: A.E. Coleby
COMEDY Busybody interferes with maid, photographer, coster.

02594
TOO MANY ADMIRERS (320)
Cricks & Martin
D: A.E. Coleby
COMEDY Maid relaxes while three suitors do housework.

02595
A RACE FOR A BRIDE (460)
Cricks & Martin
D: Dave Aylott
Arthur Charrington .... Muggins
Margaret Hope .... The Girl
CHASE Rival rustics run race to win girl.

02596
ALGY TRIES FOR PHYSICAL CULTURE (610)
Gaumont
D: Alf Collins
COMEDY "Hon Algy Slacker" drinks potion that makes him very strong.

02597
THE COSTER'S PHANTOM FORTUNE (645)
Gaumont
D: Alf Collins
Alf Collins .... Alf
COMEDY Coster poses as namesake heir until lawyers learn truth.

02598
TOMMY ATKINS (1490)
Gaumont
S: (PLAY) Arthur Shirley, Ben Landeck
WAR Capt kills wife, frames mistress, and is killed trying to surrender.

02599
PERSUADING PAPA (425)
Hepworth
D: Lewin Fitzhamon
COMEDY Rejected suitor wins girl by saving father from faked attack by tramps.

02600
A BABY'S POWER (400)
Hepworth
D: (Lewin Fitzhamon)
DRAMA Workless man robs publican to feed starving wife and baby.

02601
THE MAN WHO THOUGHT HE WAS POISONED (375)
Hepworth
D: (Lewin Fitzhamon)
COMEDY Boys stick poison label on bottle stolen by tramp.

02602
DAVE CRAGGS, DETECTIVE (850)
Hepworth
D: Lewin Fitzhamon
CRIME Tec catches jewel thieves by wearing skates and hanging on their car.

02603
THE BROTHERS (775)
Hepworth
D: (Theo Bouwmeester)
CRIME PC catches robber brother who reforms and helps catch bank-robbers.

02604
MR POORLUCK'S LUCKY HORSESHOE (525)
Hepworth
D: Lewin Fitzhamon
Harry Buss .... Mr Poorluck
COMEDY Henpeck tries to get rid of horseshoe after it falls on rich aunt's head.

02605
MARRIED IN HASTE (475)
Hepworth
D: Lewin Fitzhamon
COMEDY Marriage agency supplies man with wife and large family.

02606
FROM STORM TO SUNSHINE (600)
Hepworth
D: (Theo Bouwmeester)
PATHOS Starving street organist finds work in time to save wife from suicide.

02607
OH THE CROCODILE! (295)
Rosie Films
D: Joe Rosenthal
COMEDY

02608
A GREAT MISTAKE (400)
Rosie Films
D: Joe Rosenthal
DRAMA

02609
THE BOOTMAKER'S TEN POUND NOTE (492)
Walturdaw
COMEDY Boot maker has difficulty in getting change for £10 banknote.

02610
ROGUES OF THE TURF (685)
Walturdaw
SPORT Stableboy foils bookie and tout who try to bribe jockey.

02611
WILFUL WILLIE (620)
Walturdaw
COMEDY Rich boy tries to live in woods like Indian squatter.

02612
THE HUNT FOR A COLLAR (350)
Urban Trading Co
D: W.R. Booth
COMEDY Man loses collar, cannot buy one, and dreams of collars.

MAY

02613
A DEAL IN BROKEN CHINA (345)
B&C (Cosmo) *Remake:* 1912
D: H.O. Martinek
Bill Haley .... Snorky
COMEDY Man poses as boy to sell broken china to Jews.

02614
THREE-FINGERED KATE — HER VICTIM THE BANKER (690)
B&C (Cosmo)
D: H.O. Martinek
Ivy Martinek .... Kate
Alice Moseley .... Mary
Edward Durrant .... Rickshaw
COMEDY Tec tracks girl through fingerprints on forged note.

02615
THE MAN WHO COULDN'T LAUGH (575)
Clarendon
D: Percy Stow
COMEDY People compete for miserable millionaire's £1,000 prize.

02616
FATHER AND SON (730)
Clarendon
D: Wilfred Noy
DRAMA Kent. Miner saves estranged father from pit explosion.

02617
FROM GIPSY HANDS (570)
Cricks & Martin
D: Dave Aylott
S: (STORY) (BOY'S FRIEND WEEKLY)
CHASE Scouts trail gipsy who stole pearl necklace from messenger.

02618
HOW SCROGGINS FOUND THE COMET (550)
Cricks & Martin *Reissue:* 1916
D: Dave Aylott
Charlie Bolton .... Scroggins
COMEDY Scroggins buys telescope and is fooled with boy's rockets.

02619
SUSAN'S REVENGE (570)
Acme Films (C&M)
D: Fred Rains
Fred Rains
COMEDY Sacked servant plants gorgonzola cheese in ex-boss's pocket.

02620
A NIGHT ATTACK (185)
Empire Films (Butcher)
COMEDY Seaside lodgers find fleas in bed.

02621
TWIXT LOVE AND GOLD (425)
Empire Films (Butcher)
ROMANCE Girl robs miserly father and elopes with cousin.

02622
A COPPER IN THE COPPER (330)
Empire Films (Butcher)
COMEDY Maid's PC lover hides from mistress and is boiled.

02623
A CAT'S NINE LIVES (285)
Empire Films (Butcher)
COMEDY Several attempts to kill cat.

02624
CISSY'S MONEY BOX (400)
Empire Films (Butcher)
DRAMA Child's savings save gambling father from ruin.

02625
UNCLE'S PRESENT (386)
Empire Films (Butcher)
COMEDY Couple give away high goose, then learn it contained banknote.

02626
FITS AND MISFITS (275)
Hepworth
D: (Lewin Fitzhamon)
TRICK Man chased by boots he has stolen.

02627
HIS ONLY DAUGHTER (850)
Hepworth
D: (Theo Bouwmeester)
Madge Campbell .... The Daughter
DRAMA Rich man steals disowned daughter's child when sailor husband drowned.

02628
A MOTHER'S GRATITUDE (275)
Hepworth
D: (Frank Wilson)
CRIME PC admonishes boy for stealing apple and is saved from robbers by mother.

02629
THE STOWAWAY (425)
Hepworth
D: Lewin Fitzhamon
Gertie Potter .... Captain's Daughter
ADVENTURE Poor youth stows away and is saved from lascar by captain's daughter.

02630
THE PICTURE THIEVES (675)
Hepworth
D: (Theo Bouwmeester)
CRIME Crooks pose as mad count and asylum warders to steal painting.

02631
A FUNNY STORY (400)
Hepworth
D: (Frank Wilson)
COMEDY Funny story in paper is passed to boys, PC, blind man.

02632
A PRESENT FOR HIS WIFE (450)
Hepworth
D: (Lewin Fitzhamon)
Madge Campbell .... The Wife
COMEDY Husband searches for blouse wife gave away by mistake.

02633
THE LITTLE ORPHAN (525)
Hepworth
D: (Theo Bouwmeester)
DRAMA Woman adopts dead man's children and they reunite with drunken husband.

02634
THE TELEPHONE CALL (425)
Hepworth
D: (Lewin Fitzhamon)
CRIME Wife holds burglar at pistol point while she telephones husband.

02635
THE NEW REPORTER (400)
Hepworth
D: (Lewin Fitzhamon)
COMEDY Society reporter breaks into dentist's home by mistake.

02636
THE STRICKEN HOME (725)
Hepworth
D: (Theo Bouwmeester)
PATHOS "Extremely pathetic story replete with dramatic interest."

02637
THE NEW RECRUIT (722)
Precision Films (Markt)
D: (T.J. Gobbett)
WAR Soldier escapes from cannibals by posing as one.

02638
THE EMIGRANT (820)
Precision Films (Markt)
D: (T.J. Gobbett)
DRAMA Sacked engineer makes good in Australia and returns to save wife who has lost sight sewing.

02639
A CHILD'S MESSAGE TO HEAVEN
Precision Films (Markt)
D: (T.J. Gobbett)
S: (PLAY) Percival H.T. Sykes
Dorothy StClair .... The Child
Mrs Percival Sykes .... Edith Smith
F.B. Conway .... Mr Smith
Julia Fuller .... Sister Catherine
J. Hill .... Dr Hawkins
PATHOS

02640
OUTWITTED BY A CHILD (585)
Walturdaw
CRIME Doctor's child drugs burglar's beer and exchanges loot for toys.

02641
HIDDEN UNDER CAMPFIRE (920)
Walturdaw
WESTERN Miner foils Indians by hiding gold under campfire.

02642
LIEUTENANT ROSE AND THE FOREIGN SPY (990)
Clarendon
D: Percy Stow
P.G. Norgate .... Lt Rose
ADVENTURE Lieut escapes capture, unmasks Moor posing as sailor, and shells town.

JUN

02643
WHAT HAPPENED TO THE DOG'S MEDICINE (380)
B&C (Cosmo)
D: H.O. Martinek
COMEDY Dog's medicine put into ice cream causes consumers to behave like dogs.

02644
LIEUTENANT ROSE AND THE GUN-RUNNERS (810)
Clarendon
D: Percy Stow
P.G. Norgate .... Lt Rose
ADVENTURE Lieut poses as woman to save Governor's daughter from rebel's cannon.

02645
THE HINDOO'S TREACHERY (780)
Cricks & Martin
D: Dave Aylott
WAR India. Troops save captain's daughter from abduction by sacked servant.

02646
PROFESSOR PIECAN'S DISCOVERY (580)
Cricks & Martin
D: A.E. Coleby
TRICK Boy squirts magic fluid onto weaklings, making them strong.

02647
MR TUBBY'S TRIUMPH (470)
Cricks & Martin
D: Dave Aylott
TRICK Meek fat man finds hat which causes persecutors to vanish.

02648
BILLY'S BULLDOG (500)
Cricks & Martin
D: A.E. Coleby
ANIMAL Bulldog leads police to gipsies who kidnapped owner.

02649
THE KIDNAPPED SERVANT (420)
Acme Films (C&M)
D: Fred Rains
Fred Rains
COMEDY Man puts native girl into box and sends sends her home to become family maid.

02650
THE FAKIR'S FLUTE (425)
Hepworth
D: (Lewin Fitzhamon)
COMEDY Fakir's magic flute makes everybody dance.

02651
THE OLD SOLDIER (625)
Hepworth
D: (Theo Bouwmeester)
CRIME Veteran suspected of stealing locket from colonel's daughter.

02652
SEVEN, SEVENTEEN, AND SEVENTY (250)
Hepworth
D: (Lewin Fitzhamon)
ROMANCE Boy and girl play as children, court later, and glide downstream as old couple.

02653
THE FARMER'S DAUGHTER (475)
Hepworth
D: (Lewin Fitzhamon)
ROMANCE Farmer's daughter elopes with city man, is deserted, and returns home.

02654
A NIGHT IN ARMOUR (450)
Hepworth
D: (Lewin Fitzhamon)
F. Oswell Jones .... The Knight
COMEDY Mishaps of man unable to remove suit of armour.

02655
A MAD INFATUATION (525)
Hepworth
D: (Theo Bouwmeester)
DRAMA Girl elopes with bigamist who forces her to work in tavern, and is saved by sailor.

02656
A NEW HAT FOR NOTHING (350)
Hepworth
D: Lewin Fitzhamon
Alma Taylor .... Girl
CHASE Girls chase large hatbox blown by wind.

02657
THE MERRY BEGGARS (450)
Hepworth
D: (Lewin Fitzhamon)
COMEDY "Blind" and "deaf" beggars betray themselves to police.

02658
THE CHILD AND THE FIDDLER (750)
Hepworth
D: (Theo Bouwmeester)
CRIME Amnesiac girl kidnapped and forced to dance to old busker's violin.

02659
EXTRACTING A CHEQUE FROM UNCLE (450)
Hepworth
D; (Lewin Fitzhamon)
COMEDY Cousins pretend empty house is theirs to impress rich uncle.

02660
MR MUGWUMP AND THE BABY (475)
Hepworth
D: (Frank Wilson)
COMEDY Man searches for nurse who left him baby to hold.

02661
THE TWO FATHERS (750)
Hepworth
D: (Theo Bouwmeester)
DRAMA Musician becomes busker when he is bankrupted by honouring brother-in-law's note.

02662
THE POORLUCK'S FIRST TIFF (575)
Hepworth
D: Lewin Fitzhamon
Harry Buss .... Mr Poorluck
Madge Cambell .... Mrs Poorluck
COMEDY Henpeck flirts at ball and tries to elude mother-in-law.

02663
MR MUGWUMP'S HIRED SUIT (650)
Hepworth
D: (Frank Wilson)
COMEDY Man goes to ball in hired dress suit and is mistaken for till-thief.

02664
A WORKER'S WIFE (575)
Hepworth
D: (Theo Bouwmeester)
DRAMA Rich man hires workman in order to seduce wife.

02665
RIGOLLO THE MAN OF MANY FACES (200)
Urban Trading Co
FACTAL Actor made up as suffragette.

02666
NEIL GOW MAD (300)

Urban Trading Co
TRICK Drunkard sees Derby run backward.

02667
JAILBIRD IN BORROWED FEATHERS (600)
Urban Trading Co
D: (Theo Bouwmeester)
CHASE Escaped convict changes clothes with police inspector.

02668
TOM HUXLEY'S HEAD (565)
Walturdaw
COMEDY Thief steals box containing model head and is accused of murder.

02669
WAIT AND SEE (172)
Gaumont
D: (Alf Collins)
COMEDY "An up-to-date English comic."

02670
FAUST sound
D: David Barnett
S: (OPERA) Gounod
MUSICAL Several songs synchronised to gramophone records.

JUL

02671
THE BUTLER'S REVENGE (375)
B&C (Cosmo) reissue: 1912
D: H.O. Martinek
Bill Haley .... Snorky
Ivy Martinek .... Alice
Jack Douglas .... PC Lookout
COMEDY Butler dons rival's police uniform and causes him trouble.

02672
PLAYING TRUANT (355)
B&C (Cosmo)
D: H.O. Martinek
COMEDY Truant schoolboy causes trouble for tramp and Negroes.

02673
WANTED A BATH CHAIR ATTENDANT (465)
B&C (Cosmo)
D: H.O. Martinek
CHASE Gouty old man in runaway bathchair.

02674
OFF FOR THE HOLIDAYS (685)
Clarendon remake: 1914
D: Percy Stow
COMEDY Large family has trouble setting out for seaside.

02675
HIS LITTLE SON WAS WITH HIM ALL THE TIME (565)
Clarendon
D: Percy Stow
COMEDY Father does not know small son is following him.

02676
HIS WEEK'S PAY (380)
Clarendon
D: Percy Stow
COMEDY Workman's pay is soon spent.

02677
PARTED TO MEET AGAIN (620)
Clarendon
D: Wilfred Noy
DRAMA Fisherman adopts shipwrecked child who turns out to be squire's lost daughter.

02678
MISTAKEN IDENTITY (375)
Cricks & Martin
D:(Dave Aylott)
CHASE Pursuit of man mistaken for crooked double.

02679
THE STOLEN HEIR (900)
Cricks & Martin
D: A.E. Coleby
Fred Paul
ANIMAL Gambler, disowned by squire, kidnaps child heir and is trailed by pet dog.

02680
A BOLT FROM THE BLUE (300)
Cricks & Martin
D: (Dave Aylott)
A.E. Coleby .... Sweep
CHASE PC chases pickpocket up chimney and gets stuck.

02681
COMPROMISED BY A KEY (480)
Cricks & Martin *reissue:* 1916
D: (A.E. Coleby)
COMEDY Girl puts key down nosebleeder's back and he is forced to undress before he can unlock door.

02682
THE NEW PARK-KEEPER (400)
Acme Films (C&M)
D: Fred Rains
Fred Rains
COMEDY Misadventures of new park-keeper.

02683
BECKWITH'S GUN (788)
Barker
P:Will Barker
CRIME Gamekeeper's torn trousers prove he shot squire with rival's gun.

02684
BLACK AND WHITE (473)
Barker
P: Will Barker
COMEDY Burlesque of Johnson-Jeffries fight.

02685
A CHANTICLER HAT (550)
Hepworth
D: (Lewin Fitzhamon)
COMEDY Man reads wrong side of newspaper cutting and thinks wife is meeting lover.

02686
A SAILOR'S SACRIFICE (725)
Hepworth
D: (Theo Bouwmeester)
DRAMA Sailor returns from shipwreck to find wife remarried.

02687
WITHOUT HER FATHER'S CONSENT (525)
Hepworth
D: (Lewin Fitzhamon)
COMEDY Elopers hide father's clothes and he pursues them dressed as woman.

02688
TRUE TO HIS DUTY (800)
Hepworth
D: (Theo Bouwmeester)
DRAMA Doctor is forced to operate on wife's lover.

02689
HIS NEW MAMA (650)
Hepworth
D: (Lewin Fitzhamon)
COMEDY Man mistakes flirtatious girl for father's new wife.

02690
THE DETECTIVE'S DOG (675)
Hepworth
D: (Lewin Fitzhamon)
ANIMAL Tec's dog trails crook who stole moneybag from train.

02691
MR MUGWUMP'S JEALOUSY (650)
Hepworth
D: (Frank Wilson)
COMEDY Suspicious husband thrashes wife's visitor — her brother!

02692
HIS WIFE'S BROTHER (775)
Hepworth
D: (Theo Bouwmeester)
DRAMA Jealous husband thinks wife's brother is her lover.

02693
NEVER SEND A MAN TO MATCH A RIBBON (450)
Hepworth
D: (Lewin Fitzhamon)
COMEDY Husband brings home ribbons from shops, stalls, hats, dogs.

02694
THE POORLUCKS TAKE PART IN A PAGEANT (475)
Hepworth
D: (Lewin Fitzhamon)
Harry Buss .... Mr Poorluck
Madge Campbell ....Mrs Poorluck
COMEDY Husband dressed as Roman causes ladies' dressing tent to collapse.

02695
JAKE'S DAUGHTER (650)
Hepworth
D: (Theo Bouwmeester)
DRAMA Striker robs millionaire whose "daughter" is his own abandoned child.

02696
THE MECHANICAL MARY ANNE (560)
Hepworth
D: (Lewin Fitzhamon)
COMEDY Clockwork maid wrecks house.

02697
THE TRAIL (635)
H.B. English Films (Walturdaw)
D:S: Ernest G. Batley
Dorothy Batley .... Child
CRIME Child leads police by hanging on thieves' car and laying trail of meal.

02698
THE GREAT FIGHT AT ALL-SERENO (350)
Kineto
D: (Theo Bouwmeester)
COMEDY Burlesque of Johnson-Jeffries match.

02699
THE PLANS OF THE FORTRESS (990)
Urban Trading Co
D: (Theo Bouwmeester)
WAR Officer steals plans in return for spy framing rival.

02700
THE LITTLE WIRE—WALKER (595)
Walturdaw
CRIME Girl walks over telephone wires to bring police when burglar stabs mother.

02701
THE GREAT BLACK VS WHITE PRIZE FIGHT (395)
Gaumont
COMEDY Burlesque of Johnson-Jeffries match, fought by cats.

02702
IL TROVATORE *sound*
Animatophone
D: David Barnett
S: (OPERA) Giuseppi Verdi
MUSICAL Several songs synchronised to gramophone records.

AUG

02703
A CHEAP REMOVAL (425)
B&C (Cosmo)
D: H.O. Martinek
COMEDY Mean father moves furniture in wheelbarrow.

02704
A PLUCKY LAD (695)
B&C (Cosmo)
D: H.O. Martinek
DRAMA Italian buskers kidnap girl and urchin saves her from burning house.

02705
THE KID'S KITE (264)
B&C (Cosmo)
D: H.O. Martinek
CHASE Child's kite causes trouble and pursuers end in river.

02706
FRIGHTENED FREDDY THE FEARFUL POLICEMAN (506)
Clarendon
D: Percy Stow
COMEDY PC has trouble with runaway horse, lunatic, and escaped convict.

02707
FRIGHTENED FREDDY — HOW FREDDY WON A HUNDRED POUNDS (545)
Clarendon
D: Percy Stow
COMEDY PC catches man who stole loaf and gets £100 reward.

02708
A WINDOW TO LET (556)
Clarendon *reissue:* 1914
D: Percy Stow
COMEDY Window overlooking regatta let to dozens of spectators.

02709
MISS SIMPKIN'S BOARDERS (495)
Clarendon
D: Percy Stow
COMEDY Curate mistaken for ghost while burglar steals silver.

02710
A MODERN GEORGE WASHINGTON (440)
Cricks & Martin
D: (Dave Aylott)
COMEDY Boy plays pranks and is rewarded when he confesses.

02711
A NOBLE OUTCAST (600)
Cricks & Martin
D: A.E. Coleby
CRIME Tramp overhears burglars' plans and fetches police.

02712
A COSTLY GIFT (380)
Cricks & Martin
D: (A.E. Coleby)
Fred Evans .... The Dandy
COMEDY Dandy causes trouble with swinging cane.

02713
THE MARRIAGE OF MUGGINS VC AND A FURTHER EXPLOIT (680)
Cricks & Martin reissue: 1914
D: Dave Aylott
Arthur Charrington .... Muggins
Fred Evans .... His Pal
Anita March .... Mrs Muggins
WAR Recalled soldier throws enemy cannon down ravine an is promoted by Kitchener.

02714
LOOKING FOR LODGINGS AT THE SEASIDE (480)
Acme Films (C&M)
D: Fred Rains
Fred Rains
COMEDY Family sleep in boat and drift out to sea.

02715
ONE WHO REMEMBERED (620)
Acme Films (C&M)
D: Fred Rains
Fred Rains
DRAMA Boy shows widowed father his new wife is thief.

02716
THE BURGLAR'S MISFORTUNE (525)
Acme Films (C&M)
D: Fred Rains
Fred Rains .... Burglar
CHASE Burglar mistaken for escaped lunatic.

02717
HIS MAJESTY'S GUESTS STEAL A HOLIDAY (645)
Barker
P: Will Barker
COMEDY Convicts overpower warders and have holiday in jail.

02718
A VILLAGE LOVE STORY (1000)
Hepworth
D: (Bert Haldane)
DRAMA Robbed father parted from girl whose father is killed in motor accident.

02719
MR MUGWUMP TAKES HOME THE WASHING (400)
Hepworth
D: (Frank Wilson)
COMEDY Mugwump makes mess of washing and wife pushes him in tub.

02720
TILLY THE TOMBOY PLAYS TRUANT (400)
Hepworth
D:S: Lewin Fitzhamon
Unity More .... Tilly
CHASE Girl escapes governess, and pushes pursuers in river.

02721
IN THE GOOD OLD DAYS (500)
Hepworth
D: Lewin Fitzhamon
ROMANCE Period. Girl poses as highwayman to force father's consent.

02722
TRIED AND FOUND TRUE (800)
Hepworth
D: (Bert Haldane)
CRIME Woman thinks husband is untrue but he is helping escaped convict.

02723
COALS OF FIRE (975)
Hepworth
D: (Bert Haldane)
DRAMA Squire repents after selling tenants' home for revenge.

02724
MR POORLUCK'S DREAM (300)
Hepworth
D: Lewin Fitzhamon
Harry Buss .... Mr Poorluck
TRICK Husband returns drunk and dreams of ride in bed.

02725
MR MUGWUMP'S BANKNOTES (475)
Hepworth
D; (Frank Wilson)
COMEDY Husband has trouble putting wife's savings in bank.

02726
CAST THY BREAD UPON THE WATERS (500)
Hepworth
D: (Bert Haldane)
DRAMA Tramps take blame for starving girl who steals meat.

02727
THE SHORT-SIGHTED ERRAND BOY (500)
Hepworth
D: (Lewin Fitzhamon)
COMEDY Myopic delivery boy causes trouble when he tries to hurry.

02728
THE CARDSHARPERS (600)
Hepworth
D: (Lewin Fitzhamon)
COMEDY Gamblers swindle yokel in village pub.

02729
BEHIND THE SCENES (325)
Hepworth
D: (Bert Haldane)
PATHOS Clown leaves dying wife to perform circus act.

02730
A DIFFICULT COURTSHIP (600)
Hepworth
D: (Lewin Fitzhamon)
COMEDY Girl's beau wins consent by hiring tramps to put her father in box.

02731
OVER THE GARDEN WALL (450)
Hepworth
D: (Lewin Fitzhamon)
Chrissie White
COMEDY Girls play tricks on neighbour.

02732
THE DRAWN BLIND (497)
H.B. English Films (Walturdaw)
D: Ernest G. Batley
Ernest G. Batley
DRAMA Boss's son tries to frame carpenter in order to seduce wife.

02733
THE SUFFRAGETTES AND THE HOBBLE SKIRT (550)
Kineto
D: (Theo Bouwmeester)
COMEDY Persecuted man gives women hobble skirts and they are jailed.

02734
IMPERSONATING THE POLICEMAN LODGER (675)
Kineto
D: (Theo Bouwmeester)
COMEDY Landlord dons lodger's police uniform and is forced to arrest lunatic.

SEP

02735
EVERY WRONG SHALL BE RIGHTED (755)
B&C (Cosmo)
D: Charles Raymond
DRAMA Rich man bribes actress to jilt son, who then turns thief and robs house of cleric who saved her from suicide.

02736
A CHILD'S PRAYER (470)
Clarendon
D: Percy Stow
DRAMA Rich man leaves wife and poses as burglar to visit child.

02737
LIEUTENANT ROSE AND THE STOLEN SUBMARINE (915)
Clarendon
D: Percy Stow
P.G. Norgate .... Lt Rose
Dorothy Bellew ..... The Girl
ADVENTURE Girl swims to fetch battleship crew to save kidnapped lieut.

02738
THE BURGLAR EXPECTED (750)
Clarendon
D: Percy Stow
COMEDY Wife's burglar trap traps her husband.

02739
THE JEALOUS CAVALIER (625)
Clarendon
D: (Wilfred Noy)
ROMANCE Cavalier mistakes wife's cousin for lover.

02740
BUNKER'S PATENT BELLOWS (400)
Cricks & Martin
D: (Dave Aylott)
TRICK Man's bellows blow wife up chimney and car backwards.

02741
A RAKE'S ROMANCE (800)
Cricks & Martin
D: A.E. Coleby
Edwin J. Collins
A.E. Coleby
Dave Aylott
WESTERN Miner stabs partner for goldmine and is killed by Indian.

02742
A RARE SPECIMEN (340)
Cricks & Martin
D: (Dave Aylott)
CHASE Boy attaches paper butterfly to
grandfather.

02743
SLEEPY SAM'S AWAKENING (485)
Cricks & Martin
D: (A.E. Coleby)
TRICK Tired man drinks energy restorer and
does everything fast.

02744
THE JEALOUS HUSBAND (485)
Acme Films (C&M)
D: Fred Rains
Fred Rains .... Husband
COMEDY Man suspects wife loves another.

02745
CAUGHT NAPPING (410)
Acme Films (C&M)
D: Fred Rains
Fred Rains
COMEDY Boys bundle sleeping policeman and
tramp steals him.

02746
UP-TO-DATE PICKPOCKETS (450)
Acme Films (C&M)
D: Fred Rains
S: Dave Aylott
Fred Rains
COMEDY Thieves hide in pillarbox and
steal from those using it.

02747
FATHER MINDS THE BABY (400)
Gaumont
D: (Alf Collins)
COMEDY Child plays pranks while father reads
racing news.

02748
THE THIEVES' DECOY (475)
Hepworth
D: (Bert Haldane)
CRIME Father forces child to beg and attacks
benefactor.

02749
TILLY THE TOMBOY GOES BOATING (425)
Hepworth
D:S: Lewin Fitzhamon
Alma Taylor .... Tilly
Chrissie White .... Sally
COMEDY Girls go boating and cause trouble
on river.

02750
ALL'S FAIR IN LOVE (600)
Hepworth
D: (Lewin Fitzhamon)
COMEDY Man wins girl by getting friend to
pose as his rival's wife.

02751
A MODERN LOVE POTION (475)
Hepworth
D: (Lewin Fitzhamon)
COMEDY Man gives love potion to girl.

02752
THE QUEEN OF THE MAY (750)
Hepworth
D: (Bert Haldane)
DRAMA Mad blacksmith fights rival brother
with red-hot irons.

02753
THE ADVENTURES OF A £5 NOTE (325)
Hepworth
D: (Lewin Fitzhamon)
COMEDY Thief steals banknote, has it stolen,
steals it back, and finds it false.

02754
THE PLUMBER (400)
Hepworth
D: (Frank Wilson)
COMEDY Drunken plumber causes gas leak and
explosion.

02755
TILLY THE TOMBOY VISITS THE POOR
(400)
Hepworth
D:S: Lewin Fitzhamon
Alma Taylor .... Tilly
COMEDY

02756
HER DEBT OF HONOUR (775)
Hepworth
D: (Bert Haldane)
ROMANCE Poor girl robs artist, is caught, and
becomes model.

02757
MR POORLUCK BUYS SOME FURNITURE
(350)
Hepworth
D: (Lewin Fitzhamon)
Harry Buss .... Mr Poorluck
COMEDY Man attends auction and obtains
goods after dispute.

02758
THE MISER'S LESSON (650)
Hepworth
D: (Bert Haldane)
PATHOS Gypsy child reforms miser.

02759
UNCLE JOE (450)
Hepworth
D: (Lewin Fitzhamon)
COMEDY Husband fakes note from sick uncle,
who then turns up.

02760
THE THREE INVENTIONS (310)
H.B. English Films (Walturdaw)
D: Ernest G. Batley
COMEDY Man's ruses extort £500 from rich
uncle.

02761
THE WEDDING THAT DIDN'T COME OFF
(590)
Kineto
D: (Theo Bouwmeester)
COMEDY Prizewinner tries to escape from
widow.

02762
THE BEWITCHED BOXING GLOVES (567)
Kineto reissue: 1913
D: (Theo Bouwmeester)
TRICK Man dons magic boxing gloves and
smashes motorcars.

02763
CHECKMATED (500) kinema
Natural Colour Kinematograph Co
D: Theo Bouwmeester
Theo Bouwmeester .... Napoleon
HISTORY Period. "A story of Napoleon."

02764
FROM FACTORY GIRL TO PRIMA DONNA
(545) kinema
Natural Colour Kinematograph Co
D: Theo Bouwmeester
DRAMA Country girl substitutes for sick singer
but forsakes success for sweetheart's sake.

02765
THE COSTERS' WEDDING (455) kinema
Natural Colour Kinematograph Co
D: Theo Bouwmeester
COMEDY Quarrelsome costers marry and hold
party in field.

02766
THE BULLY (375) kinema
Natural Colour Kinematograph Co
D: Theo Bouwmeester
DRAMA Bully repents when victim is injured
saving son. (Also released in monochrome by
Kineto.)

02767
JO THE CROSSING SWEEPER (450)
Walturdaw
S: (NOVEL) Charles Dickens (BLEAK HOUSE
CRIME Lawyer blackmails Lady over child by
previous marriage.

02768
FARMER JENKINS' VISIT TO WHITE CITY
(745)
Walturdaw
COMEDY Countryman's adventures at
exhibition.

OCT

02769
JONES BUYS CHINA (435)
Acme Films (C&M)
D: Fred Rains
Fred Rains .... Jones
COMEDY Father smashes every set of crockery
he buys.

02770
JONES DRESSES FOR THE PAGEANT (500)
Acme Films (C&M)
D: Fred Rains
Fred Rains .... Jones
COMEDY Man dressed as Red Indian tries to
hail cab.

02771
THE BOY AND THE PHYSIC (455)
Acme Films (C&M)
D: Fred Rains
Fred Rains
COMEDY Boy puts medicine in beer.

02772
THE TABLES TURNED (375)
B&C (Cosmo)
D: H.O. Martinek
COMEDY Dwarf poses as baby in order to beg
and is kidnapped by tramps.

02773
TRUST THOSE YOU LOVE (680)
B&C (Cosmo)
D: H.O. Martinek
DRAMA Man misunderstands letter and leaves
wife, taking their child, who then walks home
to mother.

02774
HIS MASTER'S VOICE (330)
B&C (Cosmo)
D: H.O. Martinek
COMEDY Tramps fake gramophone to beg
and are exposed by dog.

02775
MR BREAKNECK'S INVENTION (385)
Clarendon
)D: Percy Stow
COMEDY Inventor's fire-escape device fails to
function.

02776
WHAT THE PARROT SAW (510)
Clarendon
D: Percy Stow
COMEDY Parrot reunites parted lovers.

'02777
A WOMAN'S FOLLY (715)
Clarendon
D: (Wilfred Noy)
CRIME Wife forges cheque to pay gambling
debts and persuades her stepson to cash it.

02778
LIEUTENANT ROSE AND THE CHINESE
PIRATES (800)
Clarendon
D: Percy Stow
P.G. Norgate .... Lt Rose
WAR Laundryman ties lieut and girls in sea cave;
they are saved by sailors and shell town.

02779
THE £5 NOTE (430)
Cricks & Martin
D: A.E. Coleby
PATHOS Girl finds doctor's lost banknote and
buys food for sick father.

02780
ERRATIC POWER (405)
Cricks & Martin
D: Dave Aylott
TRICK Professor's electric wand reverses things
and people.

02781
PRISON REFORM (455)
Cricks & Martin
D:S: A.E. Coleby, Dave Aylott
Johnny Butt .... Convict
Fred Evans .... Convict
Bob Reed .... Convict
Fred Percy .... Convict
Dave Aylott .... Governor
COMEDY Life in prison when Winston
Churchill's Reform Bill passed.

02782
COMRADES: OR, TWO LADS AND A LASS
(475)
Cricks & Martin
D: Dave Aylott
WAR Sailor saves wounded rival from Dervishes.

02783
EMBROIDERY EXTRAORDINARY (225)
Hepworth
D: (Cecil Hepworth)
TRICK Designs embroider themselves and end
with "goodbye".

02784
THE WIDOW'S WOOERS (350)
Hepworth
D: (Lewin Fitzhamon)
COMEDY Tramp replies to widow's advertise-
ment for husband.

02785
ALL IS NOT GOLD THAT GLITTERS (825)
Hepworth
D: (Bert Haldane)

ROMANCE Girl elopes with rich man, is
abandoned, and found by sweetheart.

02786
DORA (575)
Hepworth
D: (Bert Haldane)
S: (POEM) Alfred Tennyson
ROMANCE Farmer disowns son for marrying
servant but repents on son's death.

02787
HE ELOPED WITH HER FATHER (400)
Hepworth
D: (Lewin Fitzhamon)
COMEDY Father dresses up as daughter to
thwart suitor.

02788
JOSEPHINE AND HER LOVERS (500)
Hepworth
D: (Lewin Fitzhamon)
COMEDY Child heals breach between sister and
suitor.

02789
THE DOG CHAPERONE (275)
Hepworth
D: Lewin Fitzhamon
COMEDY Suitor thwarts savage dog and wins
girl owner.

02790
A SAILOR'S LASS (425)
Hepworth
D: Lewin Fitzhamon
ROMANCE Lulworth. Sailor thwarts rival and
wins girl.

02791
A REAL LIVE TEDDY BEAR (375)
Hepworth
D: (Frank Wilson)
COMEDY Man takes a wild bear home and ends
in jail.

02792
CIRCUMSTANTIAL EVIDENCE (600)
Hepworth
D: (Bert Haldane)
CRIME Tramp witness proves girl stole
traveller's bag.

02793
HUNGER'S CURSE (550)
Hepworth
D: (Bert Haldane)
CRIME Sacked workman robs house and repents
after saving girl.

02794
LOVE ME LOVE MY DOG (500)
Hepworth
D: Lewin Fitzhamon
COMEDY Dandy tries to find girl's lost dog.

02795
EAST LYNNE (1500)
Precision Films
S: (NOVEL) Mrs Henry Wood
DRAMA Lady elopes with murderer, is
abandoned, and poses as nurse to dying son.

02796
THE MAN TO BEAT JACK JOHNSON (280)
Tyler Films
Willie Saunders .... Willie
Mr Saunders .... His Father
COMEDY Liverpudlian boy boxes father and
wins.

02797
THE TOYMAKER'S DREAM (420)
Alpha Trading Co (Tyler)
D:S: Arthur Cooper
TRICK Toymaker dreams of toy aeroplanes
crashing.

02798
THE UNFORTUNATE INVALID (680)
Walturdaw
COMEDY Tramp steals nurse's clothes and
takes sick man out in bathchair.

02799
THE SLEEP BREAKERS (450)
Gaumont
D: Alf Collins
COMEDY Railway guard tries to sleep after
night duty.

02800
WINNING A WIDOW (720)
Gaumont
D: Alf Collins
S: (SKETCH)
George Grossmith .... Mr Parsons Green
Jean Alwyn .... Mrs Fanny Fullabloom
Fred Raynham .... The Butler
Blanche Stocker .... Jane
COMEDY Shy man woos widow by acting out
play.

NOV

02801
JONES' LOTTERY PRIZE — A HUSBAND
(555)
Acme Films (C&M)
D: Fred Rains
Fred Rains .... Jones
COMEDY Bald bachelor dons wig and raffles
himself.

02802
THE NAVVY'S FORTUNE (530)
Acme Films (C&M)
D: Fred Rains
COMEDY Navvy loses fortune to rival, but
takes rival's coat.

02803
ABSENT-MINDED JONES (505)
Acme Films (C&M)
D: Fred Rains
Fred Rains .... Jones
COMEDY Father's search for baby he left on bus.

02804
JONES JUNIOR: OR, MONEY FOR NOTHING
(430)
Acme Films (C&M)
D: Fred Rains
Fred Rains .... Jones
COMEDY Father tries son's trick of crying
for lost money.

02805
WAIT TILL I CATCH YOU (420)
Clarendon
D: Percy Stow
CHASE Teacher pursues rebellious dunce.

02806
DR BRIAN PELLIE, THIEF AND COINER
(710)
Clarendon
D: Wilfred Noy
CRIME Crook hypnotises heiress on train and
waif fetches fiance and police.

02807
WHAT A PRETTY GIRL CAN DO (495)
Clarendon
D: Percy Stow
COMEDY Countrymen try to impress
visiting actress.

02808
ONLY ONE GIRL; OR, A BOOM IN
SAUSAGES (495)
Clarendon
D: Percy Stow
TRICK Bumpkin wins only girl in village by
making sausages out of rivals.

0280
DADDY'S LITTLE DIDUMS DID IT (575)
Clarendon
D: Wilfred Noy
COMEDY Boy causes trouble for father's
new wife.

02
MARIE'S JOKE WITH THE FLYPAPERS (330)
B&C (Cosmo)
D: H.O. Martinek
COMEDY Child uses flypapers to trick PC,
photographer, bootblack.

02811
THREE-FINGERED KATE — THE EPISODE
OF THE SACRED ELEPHANTS (890)
B&C (Cosmo)
D: H.O. Martinek
Ivy Martinek .... Kate
Alice Moseley .... Mary
Charles Calvert .... Sheerluck
Edward Durrant .... Rickshaw
COMEDY Girl robs colonel and eludes tec by
posing as curio dealer.

02812
WHEN WOMEN JOIN THE FORCE (375)
B&C (Cosmo)
D: H.O. Martinek
Ivy Martinek .... Policewoman
COMEDY Policewomen, scared of burglars,
arrest children.

02813
THE SCULPTOR'S DREAM (480)
Cricks & Martin
D: (A.E. Coleby)
TRICK Every time sculptor embraces model
she changes shape.

.02814
AT THE MERCY OF THE TIDE (555)
Cricks & Martin
D: (Dave Aylott)
ADVENTURE Girl swims to free sweetheart
tied to post in sea.

02815
BUMPKIN'S PATENT SPYOPTICON (450)
Cricks & Martin
D: (A.E. Coleby)
COMEDY Wife sees husband flirting through
periscope device.

02816
THE GAMEKEEPER'S DAUGHTER (500)
Cricks & Martin
D: (Dave Aylott)
CHASE Gamekeeper pursues poacher and dies
after fight is river.

02817
AS PRESCRIBED BY THE DOCTOR (800)
Cricks & Martin

D: (Dave Aylott)
S: Fred Evans
Fred Evans .... The Dude
COMEDY Dude is ordered to exercise and
fails at every sport.

02818
DUMB COMRADES (575)
Hepworth
D:S: Lewin Fitzhamon
ANIMAL Dog, pony, and pigeons saves girl
from kidnapper.

02819
TWO PERFECT GENTS (400)
Hepworth
D: (Frank Wilson)
CHASE Tramps change clothes with naval
officers.

02820
THE BLACK KITTEN (475)
Hepworth
D: Lewin Fitzhamon
DRAMA Man wins girl by saving life of
starving kitten.

02821
TILLY THE TOMBOY BUYS LINOLEUM
(450)
Hepworth
D:S: Lewin Fitzhamon
Alma Taylor .... Tilly
Chrissie White .... Sally
Bertie Potter .... Youth
Reggie Weller .... Sally
COMEDY Girl's misadventures carrying home
roll of linoleum.

02822
A WOMAN SCORNED (500)
Hepworth
D: (Lewin Fitzhamon)
ANIMAL Jealous woman tries to drown rival's
baby, which is saved by pet bulldog.

02823
THE SHERIFF'S DAUGHTER (850)
Hepworth
D: Lewin Fitzhamon
Chrissie White .... The Daughter
WESTERN Girl helps crook's double elude
sheriff father.

02824
A LUNATIC EXPECTED (400)
Hepworth
D: (Frank Wilson)
COMEDY Railwayman and yokels receive
telegram telling them to detain escaped
lunatic.

02825
THE MONEYLENDER'S MISTAKE (400)
Hepworth
D: (Lewin Fitzhamon)
CHASE Usurer abducts girl and his car is
pursued by lover on cycle.

02826
A FLOWERGIRL'S ROMANCE (650)
Hepworth
D: Bert Haldane
Flora Morris .... Flowergirl
CRIME Coster frames flowergirl for stealing
sailor's purse.

02827
LUST FOR GOLD (625)
Hepworth
D: (Bert Haldane)

CRIME Miner drugs partner and steals gold;
later his child stops their duel.

02828
HEART OF OAK (650)
Hepworth
D:S: Lewin Fitzhamon
Hay Plumb .... Jack
Claire Pridelle ...... The Girl
Jack Hulcup .... The Lieut
DRAMA Lulworth. Sailor charged with striking
superior saved from court-martial by girl's pleas.

02829
WHEN UNCLE TOOK CLARENCE FOR A
WALK (350)
Hepworth
D: (Frank Wilson)
COMEDY Small boy up to mischief.

02830
A SPOILT CHILD OF FORTUNE (600)
Hepworth
D: Lewin Fitzhamon
DRAMA Lulworth. Tramp swims to save spoilt
girl, cut off by tide.

02831
THE LAUNDRYMAN'S MISTAKE (300)
Hepworth
D: (Frank Wilson)
COMEDY Wife gets jealous when wrong
washing is delivered.

02832
THE CONQUERING CASK (300)
Hepworth
D:S: Lewin Fitzhamon
TRICK Lulworth. Adventures of runaway
barrel.

02833
THE FREEZING MIXTURE (600)
Kineto *reissue:* 1917, POTTED PLAYS No. 3
D: (Theo Bouwmeester)
COMEDY Henpeck's nephew freezes wife solid
for two hours.

02834
THE ELECTRICAL VITALIZER (550)
Kineto
D: (Theo Bouwmeester)
TRICK Man's invention revives waxworks
of Jem Mace, Queen Elizabeth, etc.

02835
THE MOVING PICTURE REHEARSAL (470)
Kineto
D: (Theo Bouwmeester)
COMEDY Misadventures of film company
producing "The Heroic Policeman."

02836
THE DISSOLVED GOVERNMENT (400)
Kineto
D: F. Percy Smith
TRICK Faces of MPs dissolve into one another.

02837
THE AERIAL SUBMARINE (750)
Kineto *reissue:* 1915
D: W.R, Booth
FANTASY Flying pirates torpedo liner then
travel under sea to salvage bullion.

02838
ALGY GOES ON THE STAGE (630)
Gaumont
D: Alf Collins
COMEDY "Hon Algy Slacker" acts as Romeo
in penny gaff.

02839
CHING-CHING'S REVENGE (665)
Walturdaw
CRIME Sacked Chinese servant poisons employer's sugar and ties his daughter to mill wheel.

02840
WINE OF COURAGE (465)
Walturdaw
COMEDY Henpeck drinks vintage wine which gives him courage to subdue his wife.

DEC

02841
THE ARTFUL BURGLAR (470)
Acme Films (C&M)
D: Fred Rains
Fred Rains
COMEDY Burglar tricks victims with strong glue.

02842
THE HARLEQUINADE (290)
Acme Films (C&M)
D: Fred Rains
Fred Rains .... Clown
TRICK Clown cuts off barber's head, fools suffragettes.

02843
A YULETIDE REFORMATION (485)
Acme Films (C&M)
D: Fred Rains
Fred Rains
CRIME Drunkard reforms after burgling home of rich man who adopted child.

02844
ONLY TWO LITTLE SHOES (780)
B&C (Cosmo)
D: H.O. Martinek
PATHOS Workless man, jailed for stealing bread, finds baby dead and wife living with lover.

02845
DROWSY DICK DREAMS HE'S A BURGLAR (675)
B&C (Cosmo)
D: H.O. Martinek
Nelson Keys .... Dick
COMEDY Tramp dreams rich man helps him burgle his house.

02846
LOST, A MONKEY (475)
B&C (Cosmo)
D: H.O. Martinek
COMEDY Tramp poses as monkey to claim reward.

02847
THE ARTIST'S RUSE (500)
B&C (Cosmo) reissue: 1913, THE ARTIST'S HOAX
D: H.O. Martinek
H.O. Martinek .... Conrad
Ivy Martinek .... His Sister
Fred Solo .... Algernon
COMEDY Artist scares neighbour by pretending to stab lay figure.

02848
WHEN FATHER BUYS THE BEER (460)
Clarendon reissue: 1914
D: Percy Stow
COMEDY Father orders too much beer and floods house.

02849
MARY HAD A LOVELY VOICE (510)
Clarendon
D: Percy Stow
COMEDY Spurned man wins girl by posing as music teacher.

02850
THE NERVOUS CURATE (535)
Clarendon
D: Percy Stow
COMEDY Shy cleric tries to evade determined spinster.

02851
THE CURATE'S NEW YEAR GIFTS (490)
Clarendon
D: Percy Stow
COMEDY Cleric's young brother changes labels on presents.

02852
THE AIRTIGHT SAFE (825)
Cricks & Martin
D: A.E. Coleby
CRIME Old man sees young wife's lover hide in safe and locks him in.

02853
THE DEVOTED APE (560)
Cricks & Martin
D: Dave Aylott
Jack Miller .... The Miner
Johnny Butt .... The Ape
ANIMAL China. Pet ape saves child kidnapped by sacked Chinaman.

02854
A THRILLING STORY (330)
Cricks & Martin
D: Dave Aylott
COMEDY Maid dreams she is Puritan who is saved by Cavalier.

02855
MARRIED FOR LOVE (800)
Cricks & Martin
D: A.E. Coleby
DRAMA Poor author becomes tramp thinking he has killed his wife.

02856
TILLY AT THE ELECTION (500)
Hepworth
D:S: Lewin Fitzhamon
Alma Taylor .... Tilly
COMEDY Girl disables candidate's car and uncovers bribery.

02857
CUPID'S MESSAGE GOES ASTRAY (350)
Hepworth
D: (Frank Wilson)
COMEDY Lover's note delivered to wrong girl.

02858
A CHUM'S TREACHERY (750)
Hepworth
D: (Bert Haldane)
ROMANCE Man saves room-mate's girl from cows and wins her despite jealous plot.

02859
A GOOD KICK-OFF (275)
Hepworth
D: (Lewin Fitzhamon)
TRICK Football leads pursuers into river.

02860
A PLUCKY KIDDIE (400)
Hepworth
D: (Bert Haldane)
CRIME Burglar traps butler but is caught by small girl.

02861
THE DETECTIVE IN PERIL (750)
Hepworth
D:S: Lewin Fitzhamon
Lewin Fitzhamon .... The Detective
CRIME Lulworth. Crooks capture tec and he is saved by dog.

02862
IN PURSUIT OF FASHION (325)
Hepworth
D:S: Lewin Fitzhamon
CHASE Lulworth. Stout woman chases wind-blown parasol into sea.

02863
JONES TESTS HIS WIFE'S COURAGE (425)
Hepworth
D: (Frank Wilson)
Harry Buss .... Jones
Madge Cambell .... Mrs Jones
COMEDY Husband dresses as burglar and breaks into own house.

02864
THE FARMER'S TWO SONS (850)
Hepworth
D: Bert Haldane
Flora Morris
DRAMA Scapegoat returns rich and saves farmer father from poverty.

02865
FATHER BUYS A SCREEN (400)
Hepworth
D: (Lewin Fitzhamon)
COMEDY Father's trouble carrying screen.

02866
THE HEART OF A FISHERGIRL (600)
Hepworth
D:S: Lewin Fitzhamon
Hay Plumb .... Fisherman
Claire Pridelle ...... Fishergirl
ADVENTURE Lulworth. Fishergirl saves sweetheart from drowning.

02867
TRACKING A TREACLE TIN (325)
Hepworth
D: (Frank Wilson)
COMEDY PC steals treacle tin containing valuable brooch.

02868
WOMAN VS WOMAN (525)
Hepworth
D: Bert Haldane
Flora Morris
ROMANCE Rejected woman tries to ruin niece's romance.

02869
HIS MOTHER'S NECKLACE (575)
Kineto
D: Theo Bouwmeester
CRIME Artist steals mother's necklace but his model returns it.

02870
SEEING LONDON IN ONE DAY (410)
Kineto
D: Theo Bouwmeester
TRICK American taken on speeded tour of London.

02871
JUGGLING ON THE BRAIN (565)
Kineto
D: Theo Bouwmeester
COMEDY Wife tries to emulate juggler.

02872
LITTLE WILLIE'S ADVENTURE WITH A
TRAMP (395)
Tyler
William Saunders .... Willie
COMEDY Liverpudlian boy boxer surprises
tramp.

02873
THE DOLL'S SECRET (615)
Walturdaw
CRIME Workman's child finds necklace hidden
in doll by burglar.

02874
THE WRONG PIG (595)
Walturdaw
COMEDY Girl wins suckling pig but man
brings old sow by mistake.

02875
MOVEITE, A NEW HUSTLING POWDER
(310)
Walturdaw
TRICK Prof's powder gyrates burglar, PC,
navvies, sheep.

02876
CAUGHT BY A CHILD (350)
Walturdaw
CRIME Small child traps tramp in cellar while
father fetches police.

02877
A HAPPY NEW YEAR (80)
Walturdaw
TRICK Clock dial of 1910 changes to 1911 and
girl toasts new year.

1911

JAN

02878
JOHNSON'S STRONG ALE (540)
Acme Films
D: Fred Rains
Fred Rains .... Tramp
CHASE Tramps steal beer and change clothes
with scarecrows.

02879
THE SUFFRAGETTES' DOWNFALL; OR,
WHO SAID "RATS"? (515)
Acme Films
D: Fred Rains
Fred Rains .... Husband
COMEDY Henpeck sets rats on golfing wife.

02880
THE PREHISTORIC MAN (370)
B&C (Cosmo)
D: H.O. Martinek
COMEDY Man dressed as cave man for pageant
is mistaken for real one.

02881
A TANGLE OF FATES (780)
B&C (Cosmo)
D: H.O. Martinek
DRAMA Man rigs affair between wife and
doctor to cause divorce and marry doctor's
wife.

02882
BILLY'S BOOK ON BOXING (400)
B&C (Cosmo)
D: H.O. Martinek
COMEDY Gent boxes everyone until he is
floored by fairground boxer.

02883
NAN, A COSTER GIRL'S ROMANCE (600)
Barker
D: (Charles Raymond)
DRAMA Orphan singer loses voice fighting
seducer in fire.

02884
LIEUTENANT ROSE AND THE STOLEN
CODE (915)
Clarendon
D: Percy Stow
P.G. Norgate .... Lt Rose
CRIME Foreigner poses as woman to steal
code, and his ship is blown up.

02885
A MIRACULOUS RECOVERY (750)
Clarendon
D: Wilfred Noy
DRAMA Incurable cured by shock of dam
bursting swims to save girl.

02886
THE POISON LABEL (560)
Cricks & Martin
D: Dave Aylott
COMEDY Tramp drinks whiskey and thinks
he is poisoned.

02887
TATTERS, A TALE OF THE SLUMS (785)
Cricks & Martin
D: A.E. Coleby
CRIME Crook kidnaps son of own son's
benefactor.

02888
WELL DONE, SCOUTS! (595)
Cricks & Martin
D: Dave Aylott
CRIME Scouts fetch coastguards to catch
saccharine smugglers.

02889
THE BRIGAND'S REVENGE (725)
Cricks & Martin
D: A.E. Coleby
CRIME Italy. Soldier saves girl from brigands
and fights leader on clifftop.

02890
BILLY'S BIBLE (475)
Cricks & Martin
D: Dave Aylott
4th Essex Volunteer Regiment
WAR Boy soldier's bible saves him from
native's bullet.

02891
STUDIES IN EXPRESSION (315)
Gaumont
James Blakeley
FACIAL "Rubber-faced" actor.

02892
PHAROS THE WONDER WORKER (340)
Tress Films
P: Henry Tress
TRICK Conjuror.

02893
FOLLOWING MOTHER'S FOOTSTEPS (555)
kinema
Natural Colour Kinematograph Co *reissue:* IN
MOTHER'S FOOTSTEPS (Kineto)
D: Theo Bouwmeester
COMEDY Girl and doll imitate mother's week.

02894
LADY BEAULAY'S NECKLACE (620) *kinema*
Natural Colour Kinematograph Co
D: Theo Bouwmeester
CRIME Tec poses as pedlar to recover necklace
stolen by flunkey.

02895
A TRAGEDY OF THE OLDEN TIMES (590)
kinema
Natural Colour Kinematograph Co
D: Theo Bouwmeester
CRIME 1830. Innkeeper tries to poison farmer
but kills highwayman son by mistake.

02896
THE LOST RING; OR, JOHNSON'S HONEY-
MOON (465) *kinema*
Natural Colour Kinematograph Co
D: Theo Bouwmeester
COMEDY Fisherman loses ring in sea and
finds it inside fish.

02897
STICKPHAST (375)
Hepworth
D: (Frank Wilson)
COMEDY Boy covers everything with super-
glue.

02898
THE THREE LOVERS (650)
Hepworth
D: (Lewin Fitzhamon)
Gladys Sylvani .... Girl
Hay Plumb .... Curate
ROMANCE Curate rescues girl from enforced
marriage to officer.

02899
A FOOL AND HIS MONEY (700)
Hepworth
D: Bert Haldane
Flora Morris .... The Girl
DRAMA Workman squanders legacy, reforms,
and weds poor girl.

02900
COLLEGE CHUMS (650)
Hepworth
D: (Lewin Fitzhamon)
DRAMA Poor man puts food in pocket at
reunion dinner and is thought to have stolen
curio.

02901
A PRESENT FROM INDIA (350)
Hepworth
D: (Frank Wilson)
TRICK Indian idol changes to magician when
touched by white man.

02902
A GIRL'S LOVE-LETTER (525)
Hepworth
D: Bert Haldane
Flora Morris .... The Girl
ROMANCE Man helps girl regain old love-
letter.

02903
FOR THE SAKE OF THE LITTLE ONES AT
HOME (275)
Hepworth
D: (Frank Wilson)
COMEDY Rogue tries to emulate pal's
trick, but is caught.

02904
RIGHT IS MIGHT (800)
Hepworth
D: (Bert Haldane)
CRIME Crook steals jewel and frames best
friend.

02905
THE DOUBLE ELOPEMENT (425)
Hepworth
D: (Lewin Fitzhamon)
COMEDY Elopers elude parents, who also
elope.

02906
THE DOG'S DEVOTION (400)
Hepworth
D: Lewin Fitzhamon
ANIMAL Pet dog reunites husband with
erring wife.

02907
NEIGHBOURING FLATS (425)
Hepworth
D: (Frank Wilson)
COMEDY Girl falls for neighbour after he
appropriates her lunch.

02908
N STANDS FOR NELLY (375)
Hepworth
D: (Lewin Fitzhamon)
COMEDY Infatuated youth carves 'N' every-
where; girl adds 'O'.

02909
THE PARSON'S WIFE (425)
Hepworth
D: (Lewin Fitzhamon)
COMEDY Wife spies on parson and catches him
in indiscretion.

02910
ANIMATED PUTTY (375)
Kineto *reissue:* 1913
D: W.R. Booth
TRICK Putty models itself into shapes.

02911
THE LOBSTER NIGHTMARE (495)
Walturdaw
TRICK Diner dreams of hell, Africa, and under
the sea.

02912
A PRIMITIVE MAN'S CAREER TO CIVILI-
ZATION (248)
Kearton (WTC)
D:S: Cherry Kearton
DRAMA Africa. Commissioner's influence
causes savage to buy European clothes and
go to church.

FEB

02913
JONE'S NIGHTMARE (435)
Acme Films (C&M)
D: Fred Rains
Fred Rains .... Jones
TRICK Jones dreams of big lobsters, demons,
and being blown to moon.

02914
HER FATHER'S PHOTOGRAPH (980)
B&C (Cosmo)
D: H.O. Martinek
DRAMA Woman accuses maid of theft and
later finds she is her own abandoned child.

02915
HENRY VIII (2000)
Barker (Globe)
P: Will Barker
D: Louis N. Parker
S: (PLAY) William Shakespeare
Herbert Tree .... Cardinal Wolsey
Arthur Bourchier .... Henry VIII
Violet Vanbrugh .... Queen Catherine
Laura Cowie .... Anne Boleyn
Edward O'Neill .... Duke of Suffolk
Basil Gill .... Duke of Buckingham
S.A. Cookson .... Cardinal
Charles Fuller .... Cranmer
A.E. George .... Duke of Norfolk
Gerald Lawrence .... Earl of Surrey
Edward Sass .... Lord Chamberlain
Reginald Owen .... Cromwell
Clifford Heatherley .... Garter King at Arms
Edmund Goulding ...... A Crier
Lila Barclay .... Patience
Mrs Charles Calvert ..... Old Lady
HISTORY (5 scenes). His Majesty's Theatre
production.
(First British '2-reel' feature).

02916
THE SERGEANT'S DAUGHTER (1035)
Clarendon
D: Wilfred Noy
WAR Sgt reduced for striking officer and wins
VC saving his life.

02917
A TICKET FOR THE THEATRE (345)
Clarendon
D: Percy Stow
COMEDY Maid sees juggler at music hall and
tries to juggle mistress' crockery.

02918
I'M SO SLEEPY (480)
Clarendon
D: Percy Stow
COMEDY Tired tramp interrupted every time
he tries to sleep.

02919
MAUD (710)
Clarendon
D: Wilfred Noy
S: (POEM) Alfred Tennyson
Dorothy Bellew .... Maud
Charles Calvert .... Her Brother
DRAMA Rich girl rejects poor lover when he
kills her brother in duel.

02920
THE DOLL'S REVENGE (410)
Clarendon
D: Percy Stow
TRICK Girl's doll tricks brother and tips him
into bath of water.

02921
DADDY'S LITTLE DIDUMS AND THE NEW
BABY (415)
Clarendon
D: Wilfred Noy
COMEDY Jealous boy objects to new baby, and
is chased.

02922
THE ADVENTURES OF PC SHARPE (830)
Cricks & Martin
D: A.E. Coleby
CRIME Disguised PC trails girl coiner and is
thrown down well.

02923
THE PIRATES OF 1920 (945)
Cricks & Martin reissue: 1915, PIRATES OF
19....
D: A.E. Coleby, Dave Aylott
FANTASY Pirates in airship bomb bullion ship
and kidnap girl.

02924
FATE AND THE WOMAN (740)
Cricks & Martin
D: A.E. Coleby
Edwin J. Collins
DRAMA Drunkard reforms when baby dies and
saves his wife from suicide.

02925
THE KING'S PARDON (780)
Cricks & Martin
D: Dave Aylott
ADVENTURE Charles I pardons cavalier after
Lady saves his life.

02926
MR MUGWUMP'S CLOCK (450)
Hepworth
D: (Frank Wilson)
COMEDY Man taking clock for repair is arrested
as anarchist.

02927
THE DETECTIVE AND THE JEWEL TRICK
(850)
Hepworth
D: Lewin Fitzhamon
CRIME Crook steals gems by posing as Lady,
and tec thwarts him by same trick.

02928
MR POORLUCK BUYS SOME CHINA (300)
Hepworth
D: (Lewin Fitzhamon)
Harry Buss .... Mr Poorluck
Madge Campbell .... Mrs Poorluck
COMEDY Henpeck smashes all the china he
buys.

02929
THE CONSTABLE'S CONFUSION (475)
Hepworth
D: (Frank Wilson)
COMEDY Sailor spoils policeman's flirtation.

02930
TILLY'S UNSYMPATHETIC UNCLE (500)
Hepworth
D:S: Lewin Fitzhamon
Alma Taylor .... Tilly
Frank Denton .... Uncle
COMEDY Girl with toothache gets revenge on
uncle.

02931
THE BAILIFF'S LITTLE WEAKNESS (450)
Hepworth
D: (Lewin Fitzhamon)
COMEDY Two baliffs get drunk and are jailed.

02932
THE FAITH HEALER (425)
Hepworth
D: (Bert Haldane)
DRAMA Faith healer cures sick child when
doctor gives up hope.

02933
NOW I HAVE TO CALL HIM FATHER (375)
Hepworth
D: (Lewin Fitzhamon)
COMEDY Girl's sweetheart stolen by her
mother.

02934
A HOPELESS PASSION (375)
Hepworth
D: (Frank Wilson)
DRAMA Servant fakes burglary to impress
master's daughter, but is arrested.

02935
POORLUCK'S EXCURSION TICKETS (450)
Hepworth
D: (Lewin Fitzhamon)
Harry Buss .... Poorluck
Marie de Solla .... Mother
COMEDY Man's search for mislaid tickets makes
him lose train.

02936
A JUVENILE HYPNOTIST (450)
Kineto reissue: 1918, JUVENILE PRANKS
D: W.R. Booth
TRICK Boy hypnotises photographer, dude,
constable.

02937
THROUGH FIRE TO FORTUNE (630)
Kineto
D: Theo Bouwmeester
ADVENTURE Shipwrecked elopers find treasure
cave and are rescued in time to save father from
poverty.

02938
TA-TA! COME AGAIN! (70)
New Agency
D: Charles Armstrong
TRICK Silhouettes of elephant and jackdaw
juggling letters.

02939
HIS DOUBLE (500)
Tress Films
P: Henry Tress
COMEDY 'A most amusing and original comic.'

02940
A CANINE DETECTIVE (650)
Walturdaw
ANIMAL India. Col's pet terrier saves child
when new wife bribes Hindu to throw it
into lake.

02941
SAHARY DJELI (150)
Warwick Trading Co
ACT Dancer from London Hippodrome.

02942
THE OLD HAT (435) kinema
Natural Colour Kinematograph Co
D: Theo Bouwmeester
COMEDY Henpeck hides winnings inside hat
and wife sells it.

02943
THE HIGHLANDER (600) *kinema*
Natural Colour Kinematograph Co
D: Theo Bouwmeester
ROMANCE Girl weds engineer while Scots
fiance is serving abroad.

02944
THE AMOROUS DOCTOR (500) *kinema*
Natural Colour Kinematograph Co
D: Theo Bouwmeester
COMEDY Married woman nails flirtatious
doctor inside box and has him delivered home.

02945
THE KING OF INDIGO (350) *kinema*
Natural Colour Kinematograph Co
D: Theo Bouwmeester
COMEDY Tramps drug native king and vizier
and take their places at reception.

MAR

02946
JIMSON JOINS THE PIECANS (615)
Acme Films (C&M)
D: Fred Rains
Fred Rains .... Jimson
COMEDY Man goes through strange initiation
ceremony to join secret society.

02947
JIMSON JOINS THE ANARCHISTS (625)
Acme Films (C&M)
D: Fred Rains
Fred Rains .... Jimson
COMEDY Anarchist recruit given bomb and
ordered to blow up prince.

02948
A VILLAGE SCANDAL (380)
Acme Films (C&M)
D: Fred Rains
Fred Rains
COMEDY The spread of gossip through village
with two actors playing all parts.

02949
ACCIDENTS WILL HAPPEN (300)
B&C (Cosmo)
D: H.O. Martinek
COMEDY Clumsy man smashes china, breaks
window, etc.

02950
THE MISADVENTURES OF BILL THE
PLUMBER (290)
B&C (Cosmo)
D: H.O. Martinek
COMEDY Farmer turns tables on tricksters by
catching escaped lunatics.

02951
GILES' FIRST VISIT TO LONDON (375)
B&C (Cosmo)
D: H.O. Martinek
COMEDY Farmer turns tables on tricksters by
catching escaped lunatics.

02952
DR BRIAN PELLIE AND THE BANK
ROBBERY (785)
Clarendon
D: Wilfred Noy
CRIME Crook captures bank manager, poses
as him, and robs safe.

02953
FRIGHTENED FREDDY AND THE DESPER-
ATE ALLEN (534)
Clarendon
D: Percy Stow

COMEDY Nervous PC eventually catches alien
when he goes to bed.

02954
LIEUTENANT ROSE AND THE BOXERS
(905)
Clarendon
D: Percy Stow
P.G. Norgate .... Lt Rose
CRIME Chinese rob Embassy and lieut poses as
Chinaman to row for help.

02955
THE SISTERS (670)
Clarendon
D: Wilfred Noy
DRAMA 'The sentiment of this picture will
make a direct appeal to all classes.'

02956
BERTIE'S BID FOR BLISS (630)
Cricks & Martin
D: Dave Aylott
COMEDY Barmaid's fiance poses as woman to
thwart married dude.

02957
A PAIR OF ANTIQUE VASES (500)
Cricks & Martin *reissue:* 1916
D: A.E. Coleby
COMEDY Man has trouble carrying two vases.

02958
SCROGGINS TAKES THE CENSUS (615)
Cricks & Martin *reissue:* 1916
D: Dave Aylott
COMEDY Census taker interviews spinster,
tough farmer, and suffragette.

02959
POLLY THE GIRL SCOUT (550)
Cricks & Martin
D: A.E. Coleby
CHASE Scouts trail gipsy who kidnapped baby.

02960
WHEN FATHER PUT UP THE BEDSTEAD
(350)
Hepworth
D: (Frank Wilson)
COMEDY Father has trouble erecting new bed.

02961
THE MAN WHO KEPT SILENT (725)
Hepworth
D: (Bert Haldane)
CRIME Clerk takes blame when girl robs safe to
help her gambling brother.

02962
THE LAWYER'S MESSAGE (400)
Hepworth
D: (Lewin Fitzhamon)
COMEDY Girl frightened of pursuing lawyer
bearing legacy.

02963
FITZNOODLE'S WOOING (375)
Hepworth
D: (Frank Wilson)
COMEDY Coward tries to be hero to impress
girl.

02964
UNCLE BUYS CLARENCE A BALLOON (275)
Hepworth
D: (Frank Wilson)
CHASE Man pursues nephew's escaped balloon.

02965
THE ROAD TO RUIN (775)
Hepworth

D: (Bert Haldane)
Hay Plumb
DRAMA

02966
CHILDREN MUSTN'T SMOKE (325)
Hepworth
D: Lewin Fitzhamon
Hay Plumb .... PC Hawkeye
COMEDY PC tries to enforce Act to stop chil-
dren from smoking.

02967
RIGHT OF WAY (375)
Hepworth
D: (Frank Wilson)
COMEDY Two swankers use balloon to settle
dispute.

02968
THE COURSE OF TRUE LOVE (475)
Hepworth
D: (Lewin Fitzhamon)
COMEDY Musician's cunning scheme to win
consent from girl's father.

02969
EVICTED (525)
Hepworth
D: Lewin Fitzhamon
Alma Taylor .... Squire's Daughter
Marie de Solla .... Old Woman
DRAMA Squire's child and pet dog save old
pair from eviction.

02970
MUGWUMP'S PAYING GUEST (450)
Hepworth
D: (Frank Wilson)
COMEDY Jealous man poses as woman to trap
wife, and sister poses as man.

02971
EXCEEDING HIS DUTY (500)
Hepworth
D: (Lewin Fitzhamon)
Johnny Butt .... Beggar
Harry Royston .... Policeman
DRAMA PC thrashes beggar for maltreating
child and is reprimanded.

02972
WHEN TILLY'S UNCLE FLIRTED (450)
Hepworth
D:S: Lewin Fitzhamon
Alma Taylor .... Tilly
Chrissie White .... Sally
Frank Denton .... Uncle
COMEDY Tomboys play tricks on uncle when
he flirts with maid.

02973
THE FAKIR'S FAN (575)
Kineto *reissue:* 1917, THE MAGIC FAN
D: W.R. Booth
TRICK When Indian waves fan it makes him fly.

02974
THE AUTOMATIC MOTORIST (610)
Kineto
D: W.R. Booth
FANTASY Robot chauffeur drives honey-
mooners to Saturn and under sea.

02975
HOW CHARLIE'S GAME WAS SPOILED (500)
Tress Film Co
P: Henry Tress
COMEDY 'Full of incidents which will cause
screams of laughter.'

02976
THE FACE ON THE ACE
Tress Film Co
P: Henry Tress
DRAMA 'A thrilling and dramatic story of club life.'

02977
A MODERN HERO (435) *kinema*
Natural Colour Kinematograph Co
D: Theo Bouwmeester
DRAMA Child steals bag and confesses when man who runs him over is accused of theft.

02978
THE TWO CHORUS GIRLS (425) *kinema*
Natural Colour Kinematograph Co
D: Theo Bouwmeester
ROMANCE Affianced dancer takes blame for sister's indiscretion.

02979
LOVE CONQUERS (520) *kinema*
Natural Colour Kinematograph Co
D: Theo Bouwmeester
ROMANCE Child repents after forcing widowed mother to reject widowed neighbour's proposal.

02980
HIS CONSCIENCE (635) *kinema*
Natural Colour Kinematograph Co
D: Theo Bouwmeester
CRIME Jealous officer frames rival for cheating at cards.

02981
PRINCESS CLEMENTINA (1800)
Barker
D: (Will Barker)
S: (PLAY) George Pleydell Bancroft, A.E.W. Mason
H.B. Irving .... Charles Wogan
Alice Young .... Princess Clementina
Dorothea Baird .... Jenny
Eille Norwood .... James Stuart
Nigel Playfair .... Prince of Baden
Arthu r Whitby .... Harry Whittington
Charles Allan .... Cardinal Origo
Henry Vibart .... Maj Richard Gaydon
Frederick Lloyd .... Capt John Missen
ADVENTURE King James' agent saves Dutch princess and marries her as king's proxy.

02982
JULIUS CAESAR (990)
Cooperative Cinematograph Co
S: (PLAY) William Shakespeare
Frank Benson .... Marc Antony
Constance Benson .... Portia
Murray Carrington .... Brutus
Guy Rathbone .... Julius Caesar
Eric Maxon .... Cassius
Nora Lancaster .... Calpurnia
HISTORY Rome. Senators conspire to assassinate ruler.

02983
A CHILD'S CHARITY (490)
Walturdaw
PATHOS Rich child gives necklace to poor child whose mother is jailed for theft when the rich child is run over.

02984
WILLIE'S BIRTHDAY PRESENT (205)
Walturdaw
COMEDY Boy uses penknife on potato sack and workman.

APR

02985
WEARY WILLIE AND TIRED TIM (series)
B&C (Cosmo)
D: H.O. Martinek
S: (CARTOON) Tom Browne
H.O. Martinek .... Weary Willie
Joe Archer .... Tired Tim

02986
1 — THE PLUM PUDDING STAKES (435)

02987
2 — THE SACRED (?) ELEPHANT (525)

02988
3 — WANTED, FIELD MARSHALS FOR THE GORGONZOLA ARMY (570)

02989
4 — THE WILD, WILD WESTERS (590)
COMEDY Adventures of two tramps based on comic strip in *Illustrated Chips.*

02990
THE ACTOR'S ARTIFICE (480)
Clarendon
D: Percy Stow
COMEDY Two broke actors steal landlady's plate and hoax jew.

02991
THE LURE OF LONDON (850)
Clarendon
D: Wilfred Noy
Charles Calvert
DRAMA Man kills count who feigned marriage to his sister, then wakes up!

02992
DADDY'S DIDUMS AND THE TALE OF THE TAILOR (475)
Clarendon
D: Wilfred Noy
COMEDY Child plants letter that makes father think wife loves tailor.

02993
OUR INTREPID CORRESPONDENT (445)
Clarendon
D: Percy Stow
COMEDY War correspondent's hairbreadth escapes.

02994
MACBETH (1360)
Cooperative Cinematograph Co
S: (PLAY) William Shakespeare
Frank Benson .... Macbeth
Constance Benson ... Lady Macbeth
DRAMA (Stratford Memorial Theatre production.)

02995
THE TAMING OF THE SHREW (1120)
Cooperative Cinematograph Co
S: (PLAY) William Shakespeare
Frank Benson .... Peruchio
Constance Benson ... Kathrine
COMEDY (Stratford Memorial Theatre production.)

02996
SPRING CLEANING IN THE HOUSE OF SCROGGINS (365)
Cricks & Martin
D: Dave Aylott
COMEDY Father seeking quiet, ordered from room to room, ends up on roof.

02997
ADVENTURES OF PC SHARPE — THE STOLEN CHILD (930)
Cricks & Martin
D: A.E. Coleby
CRIME PC trails cooked governess and is tied to railway line.

02998
SHE WOULD TALK (480)
Cricks & Martin
D: Dave Aylott
COMEDY Talkative woman's adventures at theatre and police court.

02999
MEPHISTO'S PLIGHT (460) USA: DIPPY'S PLIGHT
Cricks & Martin
D: A.E. Coleby
COMEDY Man dressed as Satan tries to get to fancy dress ball.

03000
HARRY THE FOOTBALLER (650)
Hepworth
D: Lewin Fitzhamon
Hay Plumb .... Harry
Gladys Sylvani .... Girl
Jack Hulcup .... Rival
Claire Pridelle ....Girl
SPORT Girl saves kidnapped footballer in time for him to win match.

03001
AN UNRULY CHARGE (375)
Hepworth
D: (Frank Wilson)
COMEDY Dog runs away from master and is made into sausages.

03002
TILLY'S PARTY (450)
Hepworth
D:S: Lewin Fitzhamon
Alma Taylor .... Tilly
Chrissie White .... Sally
COMEDY Midshipmen help unruly schoolgirls escape on cycles.

03003
TOO KEEN A SENSE OF HUMOUR (300)
Hepworth
D: (Frank Wilson)
COMEDY Troubles of man who cannot help laughing at everything.

03004
FOOZLE TAKES UP GOLF (450)
Hepworth
D: (Frank Wilson)
COMEDY Troubles of keen golfer.

03005
THE NEW COOK (550)
Hepworth
D: (Lewin Fitzhamon)
COMEDY Guest flirts with cook who is really his host's daughter.

03006
MOTHER'S BOY(900)
Hepworth
D: Lewin Fitzhamon
Gladys Sylvani .... The Girl
Hay Plumb .... Tom
Marie de Solla .... Mother
Frank Denton .... Employer
CRIME Clerk robs office safe to pay gambler and is saved from jail by mother's plea.

03007
A TOUCH OF HYDROPHOBIA (400)
Hepworth
D: (Frank Wilson)
Johnny Butt .... The Man
COMEDY Mad dog bites man, causing him to
act like dog.

03008
A SPRAINED ANKLE (850)
Hepworth
D:S: Lewin Fitzhamon
Arthur Holmes-Gore .... Brother
Gladys Sylvani .... Teacher
Chrissie White .... Girl
Marie de Solla .... Mother
CRIME Schoolteacher drugs wayward brother
and poses as him to catch masked robbers.

03009
LOTTERY TICKET NO. 66 (550)
Hepworth
D: (Bert Haldane)
COMEDY Lodger searches for lost ticket but it
is 99, not 66.

03010
FAUST (15) sound
Hepworth
D: Cecil M. Hepworth
S: (OPERA) Charles Gounod
Hay Plumb .... Faust
Claire Pridelle .... Marguerite
Jack Hulcup .... Mephistopheles
Frank Wilson .... Valentine
MUSICAL 'Vivaphone' film synchronised with
gramophone records.

03011
A VILLAGE TRAGEDY (780)
Tress Film Co
P: Henry Tress
CRIME 17th C. Innkeeper kills own son in
mistake for rich guest.

03012
THE HAREM SKIRT
Tress Film Co
P: Henry Tress
COMEDY Three Parisiennes in harem skirts see
sights of London.

03013
WANTED, A HUSBAND (685)
Urban Trading Co
George Bellamy
COMEDY Girl advertises for husband, chooses
one, and leaves dummy to fool remainder.

03014
THE TRAMPS' DAY OUT (475)
Walturdaw
COMEDY Two tramps beat carpet in return
for lunch, which is eaten by dog.

03015
LOVE'S STRATEGY (495) kinema
Natural Colour Kinematograph Co
D: Theo Bouwmeester
COMEDY Enamoured housekeeper repels
bachelor's fiancee by hiding bad cheese in
pocket.

03016
FATE (610) kinema
Natural Kinematograph Co
D: Theo Bouwmeester
WESTERN Texas. Spurned Englishman leads
renegade Indians and forces ex-sweetheart to
marry him.

03017
HIS LAST BURGLARY (500) kinema
Natural Colour Kinematograph Co
D: Theo Bouwmeester
CRIME Burglar is locked in safe and realeased by
another burglar.

03018
KITTY THE DRESSMAKER (530) kinema
Natural Colour Kinematograph Co
D: Theo Bouwmeester
ROMANCE Dressmaker dreams of marrying
rich client.

MAY

03019
A COMRADE'S TREACHERY (580)
B&C (Cosmo)
D: H.O. Martinek
Fred Paul
WAR India. Private shot in back by rival is
saved from death by Highlander.

03020
A PAIR OF NEW BOOTS (370)
Clarendon
D: Percy Stow
COMEDY 'The real owner informed by the
police he could not wear them.'

03021
GREAT SCOT ON WHEELS (450)
Clarendon
D: Percy Stow
CHASE Fat man on roller skates.

03022
THE STRIKE LEADER (525)
Clarendon
D: Wilfred Noy
DRAMA Strike leader's cut in electricity supply
causes his child to fall to death.

03023
THE FINGER OF FATE (655)
Clarendon
D: Wilfred Noy
DRAMA Fate parts married couple and brings
them together again.

03024
RICHARD III (1385)
Cooperative Cinematograph Co
S: (PLAY) William Shakespeare
Frank Benson .... Richard III
Constance Benson .... Lady Anne
Eric Maxon .... Earl of Richmond
Violet Farebrother .... Queen Elizabeth
Murray Carrington .... Clarence
Alfred Brydone .... Edward IV
Harry Caine .... Hastings
Moffat Johnston .... Buckingham
Marion Rathbone .... Queen Margaret
HISTORY Stratford Memorial Theatre
production.

03025
SCROGGINS GOES IN FOR CHEMISTRY
AND DISCOVERS A MARVELLOUS
POWDER (525)
Cricks & Martin
D: (A.E. Coleby)
TRICK Scroggins shrinks bride, constable,
lamp-post.

03026
CHARLEY SMILER JOINS THE BOY SCOUTS
(590)
Cricks & Martin reissue: 1915
D: Dave Aylott

Fred Evans .... Charley Smiler
COMEDY Man joins scouts and has trouble in
woods, bushes, trees, pond.

03027
SHE DREAMT OF ONIONS (415)
Cricks & Martin
D: (A.E. Coleby)
COMEDY Couple searching for treasure break
into neighbour's cupboard.

03028
SCROGGINS GETS THE SOCIALIST CRAZE
(600)
Cricks & Martin
D: (Dave Aylott)
COMEDY Scroggins demands half shares from
banker, Negro boxer, etc.

03029
TODDLES, SCOUT (400)
Hepworth
D: (Lewin Fitzhamon)
CRIME Boy scout tracks old man who robbed
yokel.

03030
THE AMATEUR BURGLAR (575)
Hepworth
D: (Lewin Fitzhamon)
COMEDY Suitor poses as burglar to impress
girl.

03031
A TOUCH OF NATURE (900)
Hepworth
D: (Bert Haldane)
Hay Plumb .... Frank Hardy
Madge Campbell .... Mrs Hardy
DRAMA Disowned man robs father for the sake
of starving child.

03032
THE SUBALTERN'S JOKE (475)
Hepworth
D: (Lewin Fitzhamon)
COMEDY Subaltern poses as aunt at dance
and colonel's daughter poses as chair.

03033
A STRUGGLING AUTHOR (425)
Hepworth
D: (Bert Haldane)
DRAMA Flowergirl saves poor author from
suicide and inherits fortune.

03034
TILLY AT THE SEASIDE (475)
Hepworth
D:S: Lewin Fitzhamon
Alma Taylor .... Tilly
Chrissie White .... Sally
COMEDY Girls in rowing boat cause trouble
with fishermen and yachtsmen.

03035
A HAPPY EVENT IN THE POORLUCK
FAMILY (350)
Hepworth
D: Lewin Fitzhamon
Harry Buss .... Mr Poorluck
Madge Campbell .... Mrs Poorluck
CHASE Husband fetches doctor by cycle,
butcher's carrier, horse.

03036
A NEPHEW'S ARTIFICE (500)
Hepworth
D: (Bert Haldane)
COMEDY Man poses as soldier to fool rich
uncle, who then poses as officer.

03037
THE BORROWED BABY (400)
Hepworth
D: (Frank Wilson)
COMEDY Couple borrow baby to impress
rich uncle.

03038
PC HAWKEYE'S BUSY DAY (375)
Hepworth
D: Lewin Fitzhamon
Hay Plumb .... PC Hawkeye
COMEDY PC's troubles with bookie, yokel,
and gamblers on a train.

03039
THE SILVER LINING (700)
Hepworth
D: Bert Haldane
Flora Morris .... Girl
Ruby Belasco .... Woman
Harry Royston .... Man
CRIME Couple force orphan to sell flowers and
kidnap her benefactor.

03040
WORKS LIKE MAGIC (450)
Tress Film Co
P: Harry Tress
COMEDY 'A most amusing travesty.'

03041
THE BULLDOG AND THE FLAG (560)
Walturdaw
WAR India. Bulldog rescues officer from
natives.

03042
FATHER GOES A-SAILING (385)
Walturdaw
CHASE Man attaches sail to invalid-chair and
is blown along.

03043
HAPPY HAROLD'S HOLIDAY (240)
Walturdaw
CHASE Tramp's victims chase him over cliff.

03044
SUPERSTITIOUS SAMMY (450)
Urban Trading Co
COMEDY Suitor's superstitions lead him into
difficulties.

03045
THE WOODCUTTER'S ROMANCE (540)
Kineto
D: Theo Bouwmeester
DRAMA 'Man's triumph over the strong
passions of jealousy and hate.'

03046
JOHNSON AT THE WEDDING (570) *kinema*
Natural Colour Kinematograph Co
D: Theo Bouwmeester
COMEDY Man's family alters outsize wedding
suit until it is too small.

03047
THE LITTLE DAUGHTER'S LETTER (535)
kinema
Natural Colour Kinematograph Co
D: Theo Bouwmeester
PATHOS Injured builder's child writes letter to
God and his benevolent employer finds it.

03048
THE BURGLAR AS FATHER CHRISTMAS
(465) *kinema*
Natural Colour Kinematograph Co

D: Theo Bouwmeester
DRAMA Burglar steals christmas tree for
widow's child.

03049
A NOBLE HEART (625) *kinema*
Natural Colour Kinematograph Co
D: Theo Bouwmeester
DRAMA Gold miner takes place of dead friend,
comes to England and falls in love with his
'sister'.

03050
KINEMACOLOR SONGS *kinema*
Natural Colour Kinematograph Co
D: Theo Bouwmeester
MUSICAL 'Simon the Cellarer'; 'Kitty of
Coleraine'.

JUN

03051
A NOBLE REVENGE (590)
B&C (Cosmo)
D: H.O. Martinek
Fred Paul .... The Man
DRAMA Workless man turns poacher and
saves squire's daughter from runaway horse.

03052
DADDY'S DIDUMS AND THE UMBRELLA
(430)
Clarendon
D: Wilfred Noy
COMEDY Boy uses father's umbrella as
parachute.

03053
A SOLDIER AND A MAN (895)
Clarendon
D: Wilfred Noy
WAR Wounded captain drugs private rival
to make him sleep on sentry.

03054
A FALSE FRIEND (855)
Clarendon
D: Wilfred Noy
DRAMA Doctor's friend poses as chauffeur to
abduct his wife and dies when he crashes car.

03055
BADEN-POWELL JUNIOR (730)
Clarendon
D: Percy Stow
CHASE Boy scouts track and catch burglars.

03056
DIDUMS AND THE HADDOCK (435)
Clarendon
D: Wilfred Noy
COMEDY Child nails bad haddock under-
neath dining table.

03057
CHARLEY SMILER TAKES BRAIN FOOD
(525)
Cricks & Martin
D: Dave Aylott
Fred Evans .... Charley Smiler
COMEDY Charley smashes every bag of eggs
he buys.

03058
SCROGGINS PLAYS GOLF (410)
Cricks & Martin
D: (A.E. Coleby)
COMEDY Golfer loses ball and uses coster's
fruit and eggs.

03059
THE LITTLE ARTISTS (325)
Cricks & Martin
TRICK Animated thread outlines Man in the
Moon, George V, etc.

03060
HOW PUNY PETER BECAME STRONG (705)
Cricks & Martin
D: A.E. Coleby
COMEDY Weakling becomes strong after eating
Standard Loaf.

03061
CHARLEY SMILER COMPETES IN A CYCLE
RACE (525)
Cricks & Martin
D: Dave Aylott
Fred Evans .... Charley Smiler
COMEDY Cyclist's mishaps with brick, dog,
clothes line, mud cart, etc.

03062
A DOUBLE DECEPTION (700)
Hepworth
D: (Lewin Fitzhamon)
Gladys Sylvani .... The Girl
Hay Plumb .... The Man
Madge Campbell ....
COMEDY Couple betrothed by parents fall
in love while posing as servants.

03063
AN UNROMANTIC WIFE (350)
Hepworth
D: (Frank Wilson)
COMEDY Man cures friend's jealous wife by
posing as husband.

03064
HILDA'S LOVERS (525)
Hepworth
D: (Bert Haldane)
COMEDY PC tries to win girl by arresting rival,
who then pretends to be dead.

03065
TILL DEATH DO US PART (900)
Hepworth
D: (Lewin Fitzhamon)
Gladys Sylvani Lil
Hay Plumb .... Jack
DRAMA Drunken wife leaves workman; he weds
dressmaker and brings sick ex-wife home to die.

03066
WHEN HUBBY WASN'T WELL (375)
Hepworth
D: (Frank Wilson)
COMEDY Gas leaks, ceiling falls, water over-
flows, etc.

03067
THE LITTLE BLACK POM (500)
Hepworth
D: (Lewin Fitzhamon)
COMEDY Man sells wife's dog and is thought
a thief when he tries to get it back.

03068
THE BABY AND THE BOMB (525)
Hepworth
D: (Bert Haldane)
CRIME Baby saves procession by carrying
anarchist's bomb to his hideout and blowing
it up.

03069
AN ENTHUSIASTIC PHOTOGRAPHER (325)
Hepworth
D: (Frank Wilson)
COMEDY Keen photographer tries to snap
yokel and cows.

03070
ROVER THE PEACEMAKER (500)
Hepworth
D: Lewin Fitzhamon
ANIMAL Dog reunites lovers who parted over
misunderstood letter.

03071
PC HAWKEYE LEAVES THE FORCE (425)
Hepworth
D: Lewin Fitzhamon
Hay Plumb .... Hawkeye
COMEDY PC has trouble with banker, burglars,
and lost luggage.

03072
KIDDIE (800)
Hepworth
D: Bert Haldane
Flora Morris .... Governess
DRAMA Man adopts sick child and hires
governess who is really the mother.

03073
THE CONVICT'S SISTER (625)
Hepworth
D: Bert Haldane
Flora Morris .... Mary Robbins
CRIME Policeman's wife shelters her brother, an
escaped convict.

03074
MR AND MRS POORLUCK SEPARATE (500)
Hepworth
D: Lewin Fitzhamon
Harry Buss .... Mr Poorluck
Madge Campbell ...... Mrs Poorluck
CHASE Husband and baby pursued by his wife
and friends.

03075
TILLY — MATCHMAKER (625)
Hepworth
D:S: Lewin Fitzhamon
Alma Taylor .... Tilly
Chrissie White .... Sally
Gertie Potter .... Gertie
Frank Denton .... Uncle
Reggie Weller .... Reggie
COMEDY Girl's help cousin elope on bicycles.

03076
SO LIKE A WOMAN (700)
Walturdaw
CRIME Spy persuades admiral's daughter to
steal plans, but she repents and returns them.

03077
HIS WIFE'S BIRTHDAY (453)
Urban Trading Co
COMEDY Drunkard smashes every present he
buys.

03078
FIFI (575)
Urban Trading Co
COMEDY Wife drinks 'poison' through
misunderstanding letter about dog.

03079
THE KINEMATOGRAPH FIEND (575)
Gaumont
COMEDY Persistent cameraman's attempts to
film cabinet council end in fight.

JUL

03080
QUITS (485)
B&C (Cosmo)
D: H.O. Martinek

Fred Paul .... The Crook
COMEDY Burglar robs house, is fooled by
swell crook, and robs him.

03081
THE COWARD (915)
Clarendon
D: Wilfred Noy
WAR Major's story of Zulu war causes recruit
to shoot foot, but later he saves Major's life.

03082
SARAH'S HERO (425)
Clarendon
D: Percy Stow
COMEDY Dude's plot to 'down' lady backfires.

03083
SILLY SAMMY (385)
Clarendon
D: Percy Stow
COMEDY Builder's labourer has trouble with
cistern, mortar, hose.

03084
SERVANTS SUPERCEDED (435)
Clarendon *reissue: 1914*
D: Percy Stow
TRICK Magician and assistants run household
by magic.

03085
FATHER'S SATURDAY AFTERNOON (610)
Cricks & Martin
D: (A.E. Coleby)
COMEDY Father searches for quiet and ends
up in kennel.

03086
CONSTABLE SMITH'S DREAM OF
PROMOTION (480)
Cricks & Martin *reissue: 1915*
D: (A.E. Coleby)
Kelly Storrie .... PC Smith
TRICK PC dreams boy changes to mop, cyclist
to donkey, etc.

03087
SCROGGINS AND THE WALTZ DREAM (435)
Cricks & Martin
D: (Dave Aylott)
COMEDY Dancer gets giddy at ball and waltzes
through streets.

03088
LOVE AND WAR (980)
Cricks & Martin
D: A.E. Coleby
WAR Gamekeeper, rejected in favour of
soldier, enlists and wins both medal and girl.

03089
ROYAL ENGLAND, A STORY OF AN
EMPIRE'S THRONE (650)
Cricks & Martin (Globe)
D: Leo Stormont, A.E. Coleby
S: Leo Stormont, J.E. McManus
Leo Stormont
Bransby Williams
Oscar Adye
Austin Melford
HISTORY From Alfred the Great to Edward
VII (Leo Stormont narrates from cinema stage.)

03090
CHARLEY SMILER TAKES UP JU-JITSU (405)
Cricks & Martin *reissue: 1915*
D: Dave Aylott
Fred Evans .... Charley Smiler
COMEDY Charley gets wrestling craze and
attacks passers-by.

03091
THE DEMON DOG (400)
Hepworth
D: (Lewin Fitzhamon)
Hay Plumb .... The Father
TRICK Father dreams of toy bulldog growing
bigger.

03092
THE VETERAN'S PENSION (550)
Hepworth
D: (Frank Wilson)
Alma Taylor .... The Girl
CRIME Sgt trails tramps who robbed old
pensioner.

03093
TWIN ROSES (550)
Hepworth
D: Lewin Fitzhamon
S: Hay Plumb
Hay Plumb .... The Boy
Gladys Sylvani .... The Girl
COMEDY Neighbours quarrel over rose trees
upsets childrens' love affair.

03094
GIPSY NAN (425)
Hepworth
D: (Lewin Fitzhamon)
Marie de Solla .... Gipsy
Chrissie White ,.......... Nan
DRAMA Farmer rides to save abducted gipsy
from being whipped.

03095
THE BABY SHOW (475)
Hepworth
D: (Frank Wilson)
COMEDY Naughty boys mix up babies and
prams.

03096
THE EARLY WORM (400)
Hepworth
D: (Lewin Fitzhamon)
CHASE Man rushes to keep appointment with
sweetheart.

03097
ELSIE THE GAMEKEEPER'S DAUGHTER
(875)
Hepworth
D: (Bert Haldane)
DRAMA Gamekeeper assumes daughter has
been seduced by squire and rejects her.

03098
THE WISDOM OF BROTHER AMBROSE
(575)
Hepworth
D: (Lewin Fitzhamon)
COMEDY Period. Monk tricks highwayman
into using his bullets.

03099
IN LOVE WITH AN ACTRESS (500)
Hepworth
D: (Frank Wilson)
COMEDY Man in bath fools dude into
believing he is an actress.

03100
FOR BETTER OR WORSE (875)
Hepworth
D: Bert Haldane
Flora Morris .... The Wife
DRAMA Married striker leaves country believing
he has killed foreman.

03101
TRACKED BY TIGER (575)
Hepworth
D:S: Lewin Fitzhamon
ANIMAL Dog follows tramp by train to rescue
stolen puppy.

03102
HER MOTHER'S IMAGE (975)
Urban Trading Co
George Bellamy .... Lord
DRAMA Artist adopted by Lord learns gipsy
is Lord's stolen daughter.

03103
THE NEW TWINS (540)
Urban Trading Co
COMEDY 'Will vastly amuse the light-hearted
of all ages.'

03104
SLOPER'S NEW HAT (560)
Crystal Films (Williams)
D: (Stuart Kinder)
COMEDY Misadventures of man with saucepan
stuck over head.

AUG

03105
RUN TO EARTH BY BOY SCOUTS (560)
B&C (Cosmo)
D: (Dave Aylott)
CHASE Scouts on bicycles chase crooks who
stole post office safe.

03106
LITTLE TOM'S LETTER (615)
Clarendon
D: Percy Stow
COMEDY Man's letter causes him to be
mistaken for rival in love.

03107
FIRST AID FLIRTATIONS (530)
Clarendon.
D: Percy Stow
COMEDY Three men win three girls by faking
car crash.

03108
THE LITTLE BOYS NEXT DOOR (445)
Clarendon
D: Percy Stow
COMEDY Neighbour's children play pranks
with hosepipe.

03109
CLEVER ILLUSIONS AND HOW TO DO
THEM (500)
Clarendon
D: Percy Stow
ACT Conjuror demonstrates tricks, then shows
how they are done.

03110
THAT TERRIBLE PEST (375)
Cricks & Martin
D: (Dave Aylott)
COMEDY City man tries to get rid of fleas
caught from tramp in tram.

03111
A RUINED LIFE (685)
Cricks & Martin
D: A.E. Coleby
CRIME Poacher wounds gamekeeper, escapes
jail and dies to save keeper from other poachers.

03112
CHARLEY SMILER IS ROBBED (225) USA:
CHARLEY SMILER LOSES HIS WATCH
Cricks & Martin
D: Dave Aylott
Fred Evans .... Charley Smiler
COMEDY Charley has watch stolen by
pickpocket.

03113
SCROGGINS AND THE FLY PEST (375)
Cricks & Martin
D: (Dave Aylott)
COMEDY Scroggins destroys room and upsets
butcher and navvies.

03114
THE HUNCHBACK (790)
Cricks & Martin
D: A.E. Coleby
Edwin J. Collins .... The Hunchback
CRIME Hunchback framed for theft sets fire
to farmhand's house.

03115
A SCOUT'S STRATEGY (635) USA: THE
RESOURCEFUL SCOUT
Cricks & Martin
D: A.E. Coleby
CRIME Scout slashes car tyre to save chum
from burglar.

03116
JACK'S SISTER (825)
Hepworth
D: Bert Haldane
Flora Morris .... The Girl
DRAMA Amnesiac girl, forced to beg by tramp,
is traced by sailor brother.

03117
TILLY AND THE MORMON MISSIONARY
(550)
Hepworth
D:S: Lewin Fitzhamon
Alma Taylor .... Tilly
Chrissie White .... Sally
Frank Denton .... Uncle
CHASE Girls posing as gipsies chased by uncle
amd Mormon.

03118
THE TRAIL OF SAND (450)
Hepworth
D: Bert Haldane
Flora Morris .... The Girl
CRIME Workman robs foreman, steals cart,
and is trailed by girl and scouts.

03119
AN ABSORBING GAME (350)
Hepworth
D: (Lewin Fitzhamon)
COMEDY 'Chess and what happened to its
participants.'

03120
A HORSE AND MRS GRUNDY (475)
Hepworth
D: Lewin Fitzhamon
Lewin Fitzhamon .... Mr Grundy
ANIMAL Henpeck buys horse which stops his
every attempt to elude his wife.

03121
PROUD CLARISSA (550)
Hepworth
D: (Bert Haldane)
CRIME Clerk takes blame when boss's daughter
robs safe.

03122
A VERY POWERFUL VOICE (400)
Hepworth
D: (Lewin Fitzhamon)
TRICK Singer's voice makes bus go backwards
and wrecks recording studio.

03123
AN' GOOD IN THE WORST OF US (550)
Hepworth
D: (Bert Haldane)
CRIME Ex-convict fights robbers while
daughter fetches police.

03124
PHYSICAL CULTURE (325)
Hepworth
D: (Frank Wilson)
COMEDY Two men start school to teach
gymnastics to girls.

03125
PC HAWKEYE TURNS DETECTIVE (475)
Hepworth
D: Lewin Fitzhamon
Hay Plumb .... Hawkeye
COMEDY Tec search for moustached man
who stole bather's watch.

03126
THE TORN LETTER (650)
Hepworth
D: (Bert Haldane)
Gladys Sylvani .... The Wife
COMEDY Woman hires tec to investigate
husband on evidence of half a letter.

03127
AN ACT OF KINDNESS (515)
Urban Trading Co
George Bellamy
COMEDY Man attempts to win editor's prize
for kindness to others.

03128
BURGLARS IN THE HOUSE (440)
Urban Trading Co
COMEDY Couple pose as burglars to scare
boastful neighbours.

03128
AN AERIAL ELOPEMENT (795)
Urban Trading Co
D: (W.R. Booth)
COMEDY Father pursues elopers in home-made
aeroplane.

03130
GILES HAS HIS FORTUNE TOLD (343)
Urban Trading Co
D: (W.R. Booth)
TRICK Yokel dreams Devil reduces him in size.

03131
A RUSTIC ROMANCE (770)
Urban Trading Co
CRIME Sacked ostler frames rival for robbing
squire.

03132
DELUDING THE DADS (660)
Urban Trading Co
COMEDY Lovers feign sickness to obtain
parents' consent.

03133
WET PAINT (385)
Urban Trading Co
COMEDY Dyer throws his daughter's suitor
into tank of dye.

03134
THE GENERAL'S ONLY SON (675) *kinema*
Natural Colour Kinematograph Co
D: Theo Bouwmeester
DRAMA General adopts grandchild when
disowned son dies in poverty.

03135
DANDY DICK OF BISHOPSGATE (645)
kinema
Natural Colour Kinematograph Co
D: Theo Bouwmeester
DRAMA 18thC. Insane man locks dead fiancee's
room for 40 years and dies after seeing vision
of her.

SEP

03136
A SOLDIER'S HONOUR (1000)
B&C
D: H.O. Martinek
S: Harold Brett
WAR Officer accused when spy persuades
colonel's daughter to steal plans.

03137
THE KING'S PERIL (795)
B&C (Cosmo)
D: H.O. Martinek
S: Harold Brett
CRIME King saved from anarchists who try
to blow him up during Coronation.

03138
THE ADVENTURES OF LIEUTENANT
DARING RN -- IN A SOUTH AMERICAN
PORT (760)
B&C (Cosmo)
D: Dave Aylott
S: Harold Brett
Clifford Marle .... Lt Daring
Fred Paul .... The Villain
Dorothy Foster .... The Girl
CRIME Lt saves kidnapped girl and is rescued
from torture.

03139
SPY FEVER (460)
B&C (Cosmo) *reissue:* 1912
D: (Dave Aylott)
S: Harold Brett
COMEDY Germany. British tourist with camera
mistaken for spy.

03140
FRIGHTENED FREDDY AND THE
MURDEROUS MARAUDER (520)
Clarendon
D: Percy Stow
COMEDY Nervous policeman gets credit when
girls catch burglar.

03141
A SAILOR'S BRIDE (760)
Clarendon
D: Wilfred Noy
Eva Rowland
DRAMA Sailor, two years away from bride,
is saved from burning ship.

03142
A TEST OF AFFECTION (695)
Clarendon
D: Percy Stow
COMEDY Two sailors test wives' love by
pretending to die.

03143
LIEUTENANT ROSE AND THE ROYAL
VISIT (1090)
Clarendon

D: Percy Stow
CRIME Lieut dives to fight anarchist diver
intent on blowing up King's ship.

03144
LADY LUCY RUNS AWAY (810)
Clarendon
D: Wilfred Noy
COMEDY Lady escapes enforced wedding by
posing as country maid.

03145
SCROGGINS HAS HIS FORTUNE TOLD
.(465) USA: SCROGGINS VISITS A PALMIST
Cricks & Martin
D: A.E. Coleby
COMEDY Palmist's prediction comes true

03146
A CASE FOR SHERLOCK HOLMES (410)
Cricks & Martin *Reissue:* 1915
D: A.E. Coleby
CHASE Bagsnatcher dons disguises to elude
pursuers.

03147
DUSTY DICK'S AWAKENING (425) USA:
DUSTY GETS A SHOCK
Cricks & Martin
D: A.E. Coleby
TRICK Sleepy tramp electrified.

03148
LEFT IN TRUST (565) USA: SAVED BY A
CHILD
Cricks & Martin
D: A.E. Coleby
CRIME Doctor's child holds nurse and jewel
thief at pistol-point until father returns.

03149
THE SCARECROW (350)
Hepworth
D: (Frank Wilson)
COMEDY Swimmer loses clothes in explosion
and dons those of a scarecrow.

03150
A FIGHT WITH FIRE (600)
Hepworth
D: (Lewin Fitzhamon)
Alma Taylor .... The Girl
DRAMA Girl rescues baby sister from burning
house.

03151
CIGARS OR NUTS (450)
Hepworth
D: (Frank Wilson)
COMEDY 'Mr Mugwump' wins cigar at fair
which makes him act drunkenly.

03152
A BURGLAR FOR A NIGHT (775)
Hepworth
D: Bert Haldane
Flora Morris .... Mary
John McAndrews .... The Man
CRIME Unemployed man robs house where
sweetheart is maid.

03153
THE HEAT WAVE (400)
Hepworth
D: (Frank Wilson)
Hay Plumb .... Smith
COMEDY Hot man tries to get cool and
explodes into vapour.

03154
JANET'S FLIRTATION (500)
Hepworth
D: (Lewin Fitzhamon).

Chrissie White .... The Neice
COMEDY Spinster flirts with neice's fiance.

03155
HIS SON (700)
Hepworth
D: (Bert Haldane)
Marie de Solla .... The Mother
CRIME Man shelters escaped convict who
turns out to be his son.

03156
THE SCOUTMASTER'S MOTTO (375)
Hepworth
D: (Frank Wilson)
COMEDY Scoutmaster gets into trouble trying
to do good deeds.

03157
WEALTHY BROTHER JOHN (650) USA:
OUR WEALTHY NEPHEW JOHN
Hepworth
D: (Bert Haldane)
Gladys Sylvani .... Nora
Chrissie White .... Mary
COMEDY Rich man tests relatives by feigning
bankruptcy, and weds their maid.

03158
TILLY AND THE FIRE ENGINES (525)
Hepworth *Reissue:* 1915
D:S: Lewin Fitzhamon
Alma Taylor .... Tilly
Chrissie White .... Sally
Frank Denton .... Uncle
COMEDY Tomboys drive fire engine through
fairground and hose firemen.

03159
JIM OF THE MOUNTED POLICE (650)
Hepworth
D: Lewin Fitzhamon
Gladys Sylvani .... Gipsy
CHASE Gipsy girl betrays horse thieves to
mounted police, who pursue and capture
them.

.03160
MY DEAR LOVE (375)
Hepworth
D: (Lewin Fitzhamon)
COMEDY Woman hires tec to investigate
husband after misunderstanding letter
about necklace.

03161
THE FOREIGN SPY (600)
Hepworth
D: Bert Haldane
Flora Morris .... Mabel
CRIME Girl escapes from French spies to
save sailor tied in sea.

03162
OH SCISSORS! (400)
Hepworth
D: (Frank Wilson)
COMEDY Small boy plays pranks with pair
of scissors.

03163
THE BARGEE'S DAUGHTER (500)
Crystal Films (Williams)
D: (Stuart Kinder)
ROMANCE River Wey. Bargee's daughter
flirts to annoy mate she loves.

03164
THE AERIAL ANARCHISTS (700)
Kineto
D: W.R. Booth
FANTASY Anarchists build super aircraft
and bomb railway, fort and St Paul's

03165
ROB ROY (2500)
United Films (Barker)
P: James Bowie
D: Arthur Vivian
S: (NOVEL) Sir Walter Scott; (PLAY)
John Clyde .... Rob Roy MacGregor

Theo Henries .... Helen MacGregor
Durward Lely .... Francis Osbaldistone
W.G. Robb .... The Baillie
George Hunter .... The Dougal Craitur
ADVENTURE Aberfoyle, 1715. Outlawed clan
leader rebels against George I. (First British
3-reel feature; made in Scotland.)

03166   (First British 3
THE BEAR SCARE (365)
Urban Trading Co
COMEDY Man dressed as bear for dance tries
to find taxi.

03167
GERALD'S BUTTERFLY (285) *kinema*
Natural Colour Kinematograph Co
D: Theo Bouwmeester
COMEDY Boy uses paper butterfly to fool
naturalist.

03168
BOYS WILL BE BOYS (425) *kinema*
Natural Colour Kinematograph Co
D: Theo Bouwmeester
COMEDY Boys dressed as Red Indians play
tricks on farmer.

03169
THE MODERN PYGMALION AND GALATEA
(335) *kinema*
Natural Colour Kinematograph Co
D: (W.R. Booth) Theo Bouwmeester
TRICK Artist's drawings of girl and children
come to life.

03170
MYSTIC MANIPULATIONS (495) *kinema*
Natural Colour Kinematograph Co
D: (W.R. Booth) Theo Bouwmeester
TRICK Conjuror's hands change milk into
claret.

03171
LITTLE LADY LAFAYETTE (485) *kinema*
Natural Colour Kinematograph Co *reissue:* 1914
(Kineto)
D: (W.R. Booth) Theo Bouwmeester
TRICK Girl changes flowers into flunkeys, boy
scouts, Mephistopheles.

03172
MISCHIEVOUS PUCK (425) *kinema*
Natural Colour Kinematograph Co
D: (W.R. Booth) Theo Bouwmeester
TRICK Puck plays tricks on haymaker, gardener,
motorcar.

03173
THE HYPNOTIST AND THE CONVICT (290)
kinema
Natural Colour Kinematograph Co
D: (W.R. Booth) Theo Bouwmeester
TRICK Hypnotist changes clothes with convict,
girl, cleric.

03174
THE WIZARD AND THE BRIGANDS (410)
kinema
Natural Colour Kinematograph Co
D: (W.R. Booth) Theo Bouwmeester
TRICK Wizard causes Spanish brigands to
disappear.

03175
SIMPKINS' DREAM OF A HOLIDAY (425)
kinema
Natural Colour Kinematograph Co
D: (W.R. Booth) Theo Bouwmeester
TRICK Clerk dreams of country holiday and
mysterious happenings to his clothes.

03176
UNCLE'S PICNIC (390) *kinema*
Natural Colour Kinematograph Co
D: (W.R. Booth) Theo Bouwmeester
TRICK Man tries to get to picnic by cycle,
car, trap, train and aeroplane, but all disappear.

03177
THE CAP OF INVISIBILITY (325) *kinema*
Natural Colour Kinematograph Co
D: (W.R. Booth) Theo Bouwmeester
TRICK Boy dreams conjuror gives him cap
that makes objects disappear.

OCT

03178
MEN WERE DECEIVERS EVER (340)
B&C (Cosmo)
D: (Dave Aylott)
Dorothy Foster .... The Wife
COMEDY Drunkard returns home late and has
friend pose as burglar.

03179
A SOLDIER'S SWEETHEART (740)
B&C (Cosmo)
D: (Dave Aylott)
S: Harold Brett
Dorothy Foster .... The Girl
WAR Girl poses as soldier to fetch Highlanders
to save wounded officer.

03180
AUNTIE'S PARROT (575)
B&C (Cosmo)
D' Dave Aylott
COMEDY Legatee's search for parrot he gave
away.

03181
GOOD NEWS FOR JONES (275)
B&C (Cosmo)
D: (Dave Aylott)
COMEDY Proud man shows newspaper report
to everyone he meets.

03182
A SPORTING OFFER (525)
Clarendon
D: Wilfred Noy
COMEDY Knight pays daughter's suitor £500
to wed first girl he meets.

03183
THE STAGE-STRUCK CARPENTER (460)
Clarendon
D: Percy Stow
COMEDY Stagehand dreams of acting in streets,
tram, etc.

03184
THE TWO BROTHERS (870)
Clarendon
D' Percy Stow
ADVENTURE Soldier saves brother from cliff
although they both love same girl.

03185
GETTING DAD'S CONSENT (615)
Clarendon
D: Percy Stow
COMEDY Girl's suitor forces father's consent
by holing his rowboat.

03186
THE DOCTOR'S DILEMMA (505)
Clarendon *reissue:* 1916, WHAT COULD THE
DOCTOR DO?
D: Percy Stow
COMEDY Shy doctor loses bashfulness when
he loses trousers.

03187
THE ADVANTAGES OF HYPNOTISM (445)
Cricks & Martin
D: A.E. Coleby
COMEDY Rejected suitor hypnotises his girl's
father.

03188
A BAG OF MONKEY NUTS (405) USA: THE
MAD MONKEY
Cricks & Martin
D: A.E. Coleby
COMEDY Eating peanuts causes workman to act
like monkey.

03189
BROWN BEWITCHED (440)
Cricks & Martin
D: A.E. Coleby
TRICK Man buys eggs, oranges, cheese, rabbit,
and sausages which come alive.

03190
CHARLEY SMILER IS STAGE STRUCK (560)
USA: SMILER HAS STAGE FEVER
Cricks & Martin
D: A.E. Coleby
Fred Evans .... Charley Smiler
COMEDY Dude emulates acrobats in tram and
on friend's chandelier.

03191
SCROGGINS WINS THE FIDDLE-FADDLE
PRIZE (460) USA: FOOL'S FANCY
Cricks & Martin
D: A.E. Coleby
COMEDY Scroggins wins £500, treats pals, and
finds it was mistake.

03192
WITHMASK AND PISTOL (860)
Urban Trading Co
CRIME Earl's disowned son turns highwayman
and forces brother to return father's jewels.

03193
KITTY IN DREAMLAND (570)
Urban Trading Co
D: (W.R. Booth)
FANTASY Girl dreams of witches, fairies, an
ogre.

03194
LITTLE EMILY (1254)
Britannia Films (Pathe)
D: Frank Powell
S: (NOVEL) Charles Dickens (DAVID
COPPERFIELD)
Florence Barker
DRAMA Fisherman searches for eloping neice.

03195
JANE SHORE (1238)
Britannia Films (Pathe)
D: Frank Powell
S: (PLAY) Nicholas Rowe
Florence Barker .... Jane Shore
HISTORY 1480. Goldsmith's wife becomes
King's mistress and is stoned for witchcraft.

03196
THE ELOPEMENT (806) *pathe [color system]*
Britannia Films (Pathe)
D: Frank Powell
S: (PAINTING) John Lomax
Florence Barker .... The Daughter
CHASE 18thC. Man chases eloping daughter
but is too late.

03197
THE PARSON PUTS HIS FOOT IN IT (230)
Crystal Films (Williams) *reissue:* 1913, WITH
THE BEST INTENTIONS (Gerrard)
D: (Stuart Kinder)
COMEDY Meek curate gets into awkward
situations.

03198
ALAS, POOR BUNNY (220)
Crystal Films (Cosmo)
D: (Stuart Kinder)
PATHOS Small boy buries dead rabbit.

03199
MUSIC HATH CHARMS (470) *kinema*
Natural Colour Kinematograph Co
D: Theo Bouwmeester
COMEDY Father seeks peace at home, on
beach, and aboard yacht.

03200
THE MILLIONAIRE'S NEPHEW (530) *kinema*
Natural Colour Kinematograph Co
D: Theo Bouwmeester
COMEDY Valet poses as householder while
employers away, to deceive rich uncle.

03201
NELL GWYNN THE ORANGE GIRL (640)
kinema
Natural Colour Kinematograph Co
D: Theo Bouwmeester
HISTORY King's mistress persuades him to
pardon her sailor sweetheart.

03202
THE MAGIC RING (525) *kinema*
Natural Colour Kinematograph Co
D: Theo Bouwmeester
COMEDY Archaeologist finds ring that causes
wearers to fall in love.

03203
LOVE AND A SEWING-MACHINE (675)
Hepworth
D: (Lewin Fitzhamon)
Gladys Sylvani .... The Girl
Hay Plumb .... The Salesman
ROMANCE Sewing-machine salesman falls for
drunkard's daughter.

03204
HAWKEYE LEARNS TO PUNT (400)
Hepworth
D: Lewin Fitzhamon
Hay Plumb .... Hawkeye
COMEDY Misadventures of amateur punter
following picnic party.

03205
A BID FOR FORTUNE (900)
Hepworth
D: (Bert Haldane)
CRIME Usurper poses as heir to fortune he
'killed' in Australia.

03206
THE LUNATIC AT LIBERTY (475)
Hepworth
D: (Frank Wilson)
COMEDY Escaped lunatic poses as policeman.

03207
THE SMUGGLER'S STEP-DAUGHTER (700)
Hepworth
D:S: Lewin Fitzhamon
Alma Taylor .... The Girl
Hay Plumb .... The Coastguard
Harry Gilbey .... The Step-Father
ADVENTURE Lulworth. Girl saves coastguard
from father's gang.

03208
KIND HEARTED PERCIVAL (375)
Hepworth
D: (Frank Wilson)
COMEDY Man tries to be kind but only gets
in trouble.

03209
THE IMPEDIMENT (500)
Hepworth
D: (Bert Haldane)
DRAMA Artist weds sacked milliner after
drunken husband dies in fire.

03210
A WILFUL MAID (675)
Hepworth
D: Lewin Fitzhamon
Alma Taylor .... The Girl
COMEDY Girl poses as boy to fool father's
choice.

03211
THE FLY'S REVENGE (400)
Hepworth
D: (Frank Wilson)
COMEDY Fly interferes with man's proposal
and entangles him in fly-paper.

03212
THE GAY LORD DUCIE (450)
Hepworth
D: (Lewin Fitzhamon)
COMEDY Flirtatious Lord ducked in pond by
angry girls.

03213
A SEASIDE INTRODUCTION (275)
Hepworth
D:S: Lewin Fitzhamon
Hay Plumb .... The Dude
Alma Taylor .... The Girl
COMEDY Brighton. Dude searches for girl's lost
shoes and stockings.

03214
THE FIREMAN'S DAUGHTER (700)
Hepworth
D: Lewin Fitzham on
Chrissie White .... Myrtle Chippen
DRAMA Sacked fireman's daughter drives
engine to save captain's children from fire.

03215
MANY A SLIP (700)
Hepworth
D: (Lewin Fitzhamon)
COMEDY Man's attempts to catch train.

03216
THE ADVENTURES OF CHILDLIKE
AND BLAND (520)
Sun Films (U)
COMEDY Tramps pose as Chinese conjurors
to rob villagers.

03217
SMITHSON BECOMES A COWBOY (450)
Urban Trading Co
COMEDY Youth tries to live like film cowboy.

03218
AN ADVENTURE OF ROB ROY (995)
Gaumont
ADVENTURE Argyll, period. Captain kills
own kidnapped son in mistake for outlaw's
child.

03219
MAJOR THE RED CROSS DOG (715)
Kineto
D: Theo Bouwmeester
ANIMAL Zulu war. Trained dog saves master's
life.

NOV

03220
THE PURITAN MAID (980)
B&C (Cosmo)
D: H.O. Martinek
Ivy Martinek
Dave Aylott
ADVENTURE Period. General's daughter
fights guards to let messenger escape.

03221
THE LIMIT FIRE BRIGADE (650)
B&C (Cosmo)
D: (Dave Aylott)
COMEDY Donkey-drawn fire engine arrives
too late.

03222
DIDUMS AND THE BATHING MACHINE (415).
Clarendon
D: Wilfred Noy
COMEDY Child exhibits father as Wild Man
from Borneo.

03223
DOLLY'S BIRTHDAY PRESENT (475)
Clarendon
D: Percy Stow
ANIMAL Girl saves old horse from brute and
later it saves her from drowning.

03224
SPEEDY THE TELEGRAPH BOY (365)
Clarendon *Reissue:* 1914
D: Percy Stow
COMEDY Slow telegraph boy causes man to
miss train.

03225
HER GUARDIAN (750)
Clarendon
D: Wilfred Noy
Dorothy Bellew .... Mabel Bentworthy
ROMANCE Girl realises she loves her guardian
when he saves child from train.

03226
AUNT TABITHA'S VISIT (395)
Cricks & Martin
D: A.E. Coleby
COMEDY Man poses as friend's rich aunt from
Australia.

03227
OUR VILLAGE HEROES (520)
Cricks & Martin
D: A.E. Coleby
COMEDY Village fire brigade go to wrong
cottage and arrive too late.

03228
HOW MARY DECIDED (440) USA: THE
RESULT OF A PICNIC
Cricks & Martin
D: A.E. Coleby
COMEDY Widow flirts with girl's two beaus to
help her decide between them.

03229
HAVE IT OUT, MY BOY, HAVE IT OUT!
(475)
Cricks & Martin
D: A.E. Coleby
TRICK Patient under gas dreams of imps
pulling teeth.

03230
THE PORTRAIT (740)
Cricks & Martin *Reissue:* 1912, ZILLAH, A
GIPSY ROMANCE
D: A.E. Coleby
DRAMA Gipsies adopt lost child whose parents
later recognise her portrait.

03231
THE MIGHTY ATOM (1090)
Cricks & Martin *Reissue:* 1914
D: A.E. Coleby
WAR Drummer boy fetches help when sergeant
father wounded.

03232
A HALFBREED'S GRATITUDE (875)
Hepworth
D: (Lewin Fitzhamon)
Jack Hulcup .... The Halfbreed
WESTERN Mexico. Halfbreed dies saving
daughter of man who saved him from cruelty.

03233
THE STOLEN PUPS (375)
Hepworth
D: (Frank Wilson)
ANIMAL Collie tracks man who stole her
puppies.

03234
THE GREATEST OF THESE (1000)
Hepworth
D: (Lewin Fitzhamon)
Hay Plumb .... The Artist
Gladys Sylvani .... Nancy
Chrissie White
DRAMA Girl elopes with artist, is abandoned,
and returns to her blind father.

03235
A CONTAGIOUS DIESEASE (400)
Hepworth
D: (Frank Wilson)
COMEDY Illiterate tramp steals swimmer's
clothes labelled 'leper'

03236
ENVY, HATRED AND MALICE (875)
Hepworth
D:S: Lewin Fitzhamon
Hay Plumb .... Artist
Alma Taylor .... Gypsy
ADVENTURE Lulworth. Artist saves gipsy
girl from being drowned by jealous fishergirl.

03237
THE RECLAMATION OF SNARKY (600)
Hepworth
D: (Bert Haldane)
Chrissie White .... Dressmaker
Harry Royston .... Snarky
DRAMA Dressmaker saves reformed burglar
by appeal to robbed man.

03238
THE PERSISTENT POET (350)
Hepworth
D: (Frank Wilson)
COMEDY Poet tries to capture editor.

03239
IN JEST AND EARNEST (650)
Hepworth

D: Lewin Fitzhamon
Chrissie White .... The Girl
Jack Hulcup .... The Dude
WESTERN Girl and cowboys pose as Indians
to scare dude, who later saves them from outlaws

03240
HIDDEN TREASURE (400)
Hepworth
D: (Frank Wilson)
COMEDY Burglar hides stolen silver in
neighbour's garden.

03241
RACHEL'S SIN (900)
Hepworth
D: (Lewin Fitzhamon)
Gladys Sylvani .... Rachel
Hay Plumb .... Jacob
Harry Royston .... Husband
CRIME Wife kills drunken husband and her
ex-fiance is blamed.

03242
THE DEJECTED LOVER (450)
Crystal Films (Cosmo)
D: (Stuart Kinder)
COMEDY Rejected suitor becomes tramp.

03243
THE LAST FAREWELL (815)
Kineto
D: (Theo Bouwmeester)
DRAMA Medical student seduces friend's wife
but makes reparation.

03244,
A LOVE STORY OF CHARLES II (670)
kinema
Natural Colour Kinematograph Co
D: Theo Bouwmeester
HISTORY Man marries lady to save her from
being king's mistress.

03245
TWO CHRISTMAS HAMPERS (685) *kinema*
Natural Colour Kinematograph Co
D: Theo Bouwmeester
COMEDY Boy exchanges labels so that mean
man's hamper goes to poor brother.

03246
A SEASIDE COMEDY (520) *kinema*
Natural Colour Kinematograph Co
D: Theo Bouwmeester
COMEDY Cardsharper pursued by policeman
changes clothes with swimming cleric.

03247
THE LITTLE WOODEN SOLDIER (965)
kinema
Natural Colour Kinematograph Co
D: Theo Bouwmeester
DRAMA Child's toy soldier contains grand-
father's will leaving everything to governess.
03248
THE FISHERMAN'S DAUGHTER (590) *kinema*
Natural Colour Kinematograph Co
D: Theo Bouwmeester
ADVENTURE Girl's father tests coastguard's
love by demanding he ignore smuggler's boat.

03249
OLIVER CROMWELL (615) *kinema*
Natural Colour Kinematograph Co
D: Theo Bouwmeester
HISTORY Royalist's son refuses to betray
his father and both are pardoned by Cromwell.

03250
THE INVENTOR'S SON (675) *kinema*
Natural Colour Kinematograph Co

D: Theo Bouwmeester
DRAMA Girl stands by blinded diamond-
maker despite mother's wish.

03251
A GAMBLER'S VILLAINY (390) *kinema*
Natural Colour Kinematograph Co
D: Theo Bouwmeester
CRIME Nurse prevents captain poisoning
sick father.

03252
THE TIDE OF FORTUNE (685) *kinema*
Natural Colour Kinematograph Co
D: Theo Bouwmeester
DRAMA Workless man becomes tramp on wife's
death and saves lost daughter from robber.

03253
AN ELIZABETHAN ROMANCE (565) *kinema*
Natural Colour Kinematograph Co
D: Theo Bouwmeester
HISTORY Countess intercepts condemned
man's ring to foil queen's pardon.

03254
THE GREAT FIGHT FOR THE CHAMPION-
SHIP IN OUR COURT (355)
Urban Trading Co
COMEDY Burlesque of Johnson-Wells fight:
cameraman films amateur boxers.

DEC

03255
THE TYPIST'S REVENGE (460)
B&C (Cosmo)
D: (Dave Aylott)
COMEDY Typist inserts 'wife wanted' advertise-
ment in boss's name.

03256
LIEUTENANT DARING RN AND THE
SECRET SERVICE AGENTS (770) also:
LIEUT DARING RN SAVES HMS MEDINA
B&C (Cosmo)
D: Dave Aylott
S: Harold Brett
Percy Moran .... Lt Daring
Edward Durrant .... Spy
CRIME Foreign agents kidnap lieut for plans of
secret gun trials.

03257
DR BRIAN PELLIE AND THE BARONET'S
BRIDE (680)
Clarendon
D: Wilfred Noy
CRIME Crook kidnaps millionaire's bride who
is saved after she sets yacht afire.

03258
DIDUMS AND THE CHRISTMAS PUDDING
(550)
Clarendon
D: Wilfred Noy
COMEDY Child changes christmas pudding for
cannon ball.

03259
IN COTTAGE AND CASTLE (880) USA: IN
CASTLE OR COTTAGE
Clarendon
D: Percy Stow
DRAMA Starving fisherman saves a bart's child-
ren and is invited for Christmas dinner.

03260
OH, IT'S YOU! (465)
Clarendon
D: Percy Stow
COMEDY Man and wife mistake each other
for burglars.

03261
SIGNOR POTTI'S LOVE AFFAIR (550)
Cricks & Martin
D: A.E. Coleby
COMEDY Jealous musician fails in attempts to commit suicide.

03262
LITTLE RED RIDING HOOD (460)
Cricks & Martin *reissue:* 1916
D: A.E. Coleby
Edwin J Collins .... Woodman
FANTASY Woodman saves girl from wolf posing as grandmother.

03263
TOPSY'S DREAM OF TOYLAND (1050)
Cricks & Martin
D:S: A.E. Coleby
Dorothy StJohn .... Topsy
Edwin J. Collins .... Rich Man
FANTASY Waif faints and dreams she weds Prince; on waking she is adopted by rich man.

03264
A WOMAN IN THE CASE (600)
Cricks & Martin
D: A.E. Coleby
COMEDY

03265
THE COURTSHIP OF MISS TWIGGLES (660)
Cricks & Martin
D: A.E. Coleby
COMEDY Girl helps old man propose to shy spinster.

03266
A RIDE FOR A BRIDE (995)
Barker
D: (Charles Raymond)
SPORT Jockey wins wife and Grand National despite crooks.

03267
TILLY AND THE SMUGGLERS (625)
Hepworth
D:S: Lewin Fitzhamon
Alma Taylor .... Tilly
Chrissie White .... Sally
Hay Plumb .... Smuggler
COMEDY Lulworth. Tomboys help smugglers, then fetch coastguards.

03268
TAKING UNCLE FOR A RIDE (425)
Hepworth
D: (Frank Wilson)
COMEDY Two boys take old man for wild ride in bathchair.

03269
TIGER THE 'TEC (675)
Hepworth
D:S: Lewin Fitzhamon
Lewin Fitzhamon
ANIMAL Tec poses as postman to catch burglar tracked by dog.

03270
ALL'S RIGHT WITH THE WORLD (825)
Heoworth
D: (Lewin Fitzhamon)
Gladys Sylvani .... Liz
Hay Plumb .... Pete
Marie de Solla .... Farmer's Wife
ROMANCE Unemployed man and girl find jobs with farmer and fall in love.

03271
HE DID ADMIRE HIS BOOTS (350)
Hepworth
D: (Frank Wilson)
COMEDY Yokel's new boots bring him trouble and are stolen by dog.

03272
THE BROAD ARROW (600)
Hepworth
D: Bert Haldane
Flora Morris .... The Girl
CRIME Escaped convict saves girl from tramps and father poses as highwayman to save him from recapture.

03273
THE STOLEN LETTERS (1000)
Hepworth
D: (Lewin Fitzhamon)
Gladys Sylvani .... The Wife
Hay Plumb .... The Husband
DRAMA Gold miner returns in time to save wife from suicide after jealous postman destroys his letters.

03274
A HUSTLED WEDDING (575)
Hepworth
D: (Frank Wilson)
COMEDY Man's rush to marry by three o'clock in order to inherit £1000.

03275
THREE BOYS AND A BABY (450)
Hepworth
D: (Frank Wilson)
CHASE Boys hide baby and tie pram behind car.

03276
NOT GUILTY (450)
Hepworth
D: (Lewin Fitzhamon)
DRAMA Framed coster saves girl from runaway pony and trap.

03277
FOR A BABY'S SAKE (675)
Hepworth
D:S: Lewin Fitzhamon
Alma Taylor .... The Girl
Hay Plumb ....The Doctor
ADVENTURE Lulworth. Island girl swims to fetch doctor to sick baby.

03278
STOP THE FIGHT (490)
Precision Films (MP)
D:S: Fred Evans
Fred Evans
COMEDY Pacifist tries to stop street fights and ends up in hospital.

03279
BUFFALO BILL ON THE BRAIN (445)
Kineto
D: Theo Bouwmeester
COMEDY Old man reading cowboy story dreams of fighting Indians.

03280
XMAS GREETING FILM (65)
Brighton & County Films
D: W.Harold Speer
TRICK Father Christmas magically produces Cinderella.

03281
A MERRY CHRISTMAS TO ALL OUR FRIENDS (90)
Crystal Films (Cosmo)
D: (Stuart Kinder)
TRICK Christmas greeting from exhibitor to patron.

03282
CAUGHT IN HER OWN TRAP (500)
Crystal Films (Cosmo)
D: (Stuart Kinder)
COMEDY Wife poses as nurse to catch husband flirting and finds it is gardener in husband's trousers.

03283
MRS JUGGINS (225)
Walturdaw
FACIAL Contortions of lady vocalist.

03284
LOVE OR RICHES (695) *kinema*
Natural Colour Kinematograph Co
D: Theo Bouwmeester
ROMANCE Fisherman's daughter adopted by rich couple returns to poor sweetheart.

03285
THE VICISSITUDES OF A TOP HAT (540) *kinema*
Natural Colour Kinematograph Co
D: Theo Bouwmeester
COMEDY Man throws away old top hat and tramp uses it to sole boots.

03286   D: Theo Bouwmeester
THE ADOPTED CHILD (685) *kinema*
Natural Colour Kinematograph Co
DRAMA Drunkard demands child from step-father and her pleas make him reform.

03287
A TRUE BRITON (650) *kinema*
Natural Colour Kinematograph Co
D: Theo Bouwmeester
Theo Bouwmeester .... Soldier
WAR Africa, 1900. Old schoolmaster shot by Boers for persuading pupils to wave Union Jack.

1912

JAN

03288
A MATRIMONIAL MUDDLE (490)
Clarendon
D: Percy Stow
COMEDY Man and wife hire detectives after mistaking each other's letters.

03289
LIEUTENANT ROSE AND THE STOLEN SHIP
Clarendon
D: Percy Stow
P.G. Norgate .... Lt Rose
WAR Spy poses as captured lieut and steals ship; lieut escapes and bombs ship from monoplane.

03290
PARTNERS (790)
Clarendon
D: Wilfred Noy
DRAMA Fisherman defeats crooked partner and wins girl.

03291
DR BRIAN PELLIE ESCAPES FROM PRISON (575)
Clarendon
D: Wilfred Noy
CHASE Crook poses as chaplain and escapes by car, chased by cycling warders.

03292
THE LONELY INN (880)
Cricks & Martin
D: A.E. Coleby
CRIME Period. Innkeeper dies of shock after killing jailbird son in mistake for rich guest.

03293
COMPULSORY INSURANCE (630)
Cricks & Martin
D: A.E. Coleby
COMEDY Man's problems when he has to insure.

03294
WHAT HAPPENED TO MARY (430)
Cricks & Martin
D: A.E. Coleby
COMEDY Girl weds sweep and discovers he is a Negro.

03295
CONSTABLE SMITH IN TROUBLE AGAIN (335)
Cricks & Martin
D: A.E. Coleby
Kelly Storrie .... PC Smith
TRICK PC has trouble with disappearing burglar.

03296
A TELEPHONE TANGLE (710)
Cricks & Martin
D: A.E. Coleby
COMEDY Jealous man mistakes telephone repairer for wife's lover.

03297
OVERCHARGED (350)
Hepworth
D: (Frank Wilson)
TRICK Weak man electrified becomes magnetic.

03298
THE BURGLAR'S DAUGHTER (475)
Hepworth
D: (Lewin Fitzhamon)
CRIME Policeman helps maid catch her burglar father.

03299
AN INDIAN VENDETTA (550)
Hepworth
D: Lewin Fitzhamon
WESTERN Girl rides for mounties to save settlers from Indians.

03300
THE GIRL AT THE LODGE (675)
Hepworth
D: (Bert Haldane)
ROMANCE Country girl elopes with city cad and is saved by her father and policeman sweetheart.

03301
HER ONLY PAL (850)
Hepworth
D: Lewin Fitzhamon
Chrissie White .... Flowergirl
Douglas Munro .... Tramp
DRAMA Tramp steals flowergirl's dog and sells it to research doctor.

03302
BILL'S TEMPTATION (400)
Hepworth
D: (Bert Haldane)
DRAMA Man who loves coster girl saves drunken husband from railway lines.

03303
BILLIARDS MAD (400)
Hepworth
D: (Frank Wilson)
COMEDY Man dreams he plays billiards in unlikely places.

03304
A CURATE'S LOVE STORY (750)
Hepworth
D: Lewin Fitzhamon
Hay Plumb .... Rev Harry Seaton
Chrissie White .... Eileen
Douglas Munro ...... Madman
Rachel de Solla ..... Mother
DRAMA Squire's daughter nurses madman and is saved by curate she rejected.

03305
HAROLD PREVENTS A CRIME (325)
Hepworth
D: (Frank Wilson)
COMEDY Eavesdropper fetches PC when men 'drown' gramophone.

03306
THE MERMAID (600)
Hepworth
D: Lewin Fitzhamon
Chrissie White .... The Mermaid
Hay Plumb .... The Man
DRAMA Lulworth. Man saves girl from being forced to pose as mermaid in show.

03307
A NIGHT OF PERIL (550)
Hepworth
D: Bert Haldane
Harry Royston .... The Man
Ruby Belasco .... The Woman
CRIME Couple's son fetches police when they kidnap sleepwalking girl.

03308
THE LOST WILL (700)
Hepworth
D: Lewin Fitzhamon
CRIME Dead earl's daughter and her pet dogs save father's will from disowned nephew.

03309
THE UMBRELLA THEY COULD NOT LOSE (350)
Hepworth
D: (Frank Wilson)
Violet Hopson .... Mildred
COMEDY People try to get rid of broken umbrella.

03310
WANTED A WIFE AND CHILD (670)
Precision Films (MP)
Fred Evans .... Bachelor
COMEDY Bachelor must find family to prove to his rich uncle he is married.

03311
PUPPETS OF FATE (626)
Britannia Films (Pathe)
D: Frank Powell
Florence Barker .... Mrs Shawnston
DRAMA Colonel gives pistol to lieut in love with his wife, but dies of heart failure.

03312
LEAVES FROM THE BOOKS OF CHARLES DICKENS (740)
Britannia Films (Pathe)
SC: Thomas Bentley
Thomas Bentley .... All Roles
DRAMA Character studies performed on sites of the novels.

03313
THE VICAR OF WAKEFIELD (923)
Britannia Films (Pathe)
D: Frank Powell
S:(NOVEL) Oliver Goldsmith
Florence Barker
DRAMA Squire jails vicar for debt and fakes marriage to daughter.

03314
THE JESTER'S JOKE (365) *reissue:* 1916
THE MERRY JESTER
Urban Trading Co
D: W.R. Booth
TRICK Jester causes pierrots to merge, fade, appear.

FEB

03315
A TRAGEDY OF THE CORNISH COAST (1050)
B&C (MP)
D: Sidney Northcote
S: Harold Brett
Wallett Waller .....,....... Tom Leigh
Dorothy Foster .... Mary Trelawney
O'Neil Farrell .... Villain
Sidney Northcote .... Villain
CRIME Cornwall. Artist and sailors save fishergirl from abduction.

03316
LIEUTENANT DARING AVENGES AN INSULT TO THE UNION JACK (625)
B&C (MP)
D: Dave Aylott
S: Harold Brett
Percy Moran .... Lt Daring
Fred Paul .... Paulo
CRIME Corsica. Lieut trails brigands and saves captured flag.

03317
DIDUMS AND A POLICEMAN (400)
Clarendon
D: Wilfred Noy
CHASE Child feigns theft to make PC pursue him into traps.

03318
BUSINESS IS BUSINESS (706)
Clarendon
D: Wilfred Noy
DRAMA Sacked man tries to drown him-
self but saves boss's daughter instead.

03319
LIEUTENANT ROSE AND THE MOORISH
RAIDERS (840)
Clarendon
D: Percy Stow
P.G. Ebbutt .... Lt Rose
WAR Africa. Lt poses as Moor to escape
besieged embassy and shells their hideout.

03320
HE WOULD SPEAK
Clarendon
D: Percy Stow
COMEDY 'A living cartoon of Loosetongue
Wurchill.'

03321
THE WIDOW'S MIGHT (655)
Clarendon
D: Percy Stow
COMEDY Tribulations of pretty widow.

03322
AT THE HOUR OF THREE (875)
Clarendon
D: Wilfred Noy
Dorothy Bellew ...... The Girl
CRIME Debtor's chance appearance in news-
reel proves he could not have shot father.

03323
OUT OF HIS ELEMENT (740)
Cricks & Martin
D: (A.E. Coleby)
Harry Granville .... Hawkins
COMEDY Coster saves Lord from tramps and
is invited to society ball.

03324
A PAIR OF TROUSERS (535)
Cricks & Martin
D: (A.E. Coleby)
CHASE Man's search for £100 hidden in
discarded trousers.

03325
HIS SECRET SIN (770)
Cricks & Martin
D: (A.E. Coleby)
DRAMA Woman poses as man to break gambling
husband.

03326
THE WIDOW'S LEGACY (550)
Cricks & Martin
D: A.E. Coleby
A.E. Coleby .... Artful Ernie
COMEDY Farmer thwarts rival by pretending
rich widow has lost fortune.

03327
WHILE THE COOK SLEPT (425)
Cricks & Martin
D: (A.E. Coleby)
TRICK Food prepares itself while cook sleeps.

03328
THE EDITOR AND THE MILLIONAIRE (875)
Hepworth
D: (Lewin Fitzhamon)
Gladys Sylvani .... Gladys Groves
ROMANCE Rich girl posing as poor writer loves
editor her father sacked.

03329
HER SACRIFICE (500)
Hepworth
D: (Bert Haldane)
ROMANCE Poor artist saved by sempstress's
legacy.

03330
PERCY LOSES A SHILLING (500)
Hepworth
D: (Frank Wilson)
COMEDY Man drops shilling down grating and
is mistaken for escaped lunatic.

03331
A FISHERMAN'S LOVE STORY (575)
Hepworth
D:S: Lewin Fitzhamon
Hay Plumb .... Jack
Gladys Sylvani .... Nellie
ADVENTURE Lulworth. Fisherman saves rival's
life and wins girl.

03332
A LITTLE GOLD MINE (575)
Hepworth
D: (Frank Wilson)
Harry Buss .... Tramp
COMEDY Tramps paint coal golden and sell
shares in fake mine.

03333
THE BLIND MAN'S DOG (600)
Hepworth
D:S: Lewin Fitzhamon
Lewin Fitzhamon .... The Tramp
ANIMAL Dog fetches doctor to blind man and
trails tramp who robbed him.

03334
A DISCIPLE OF DARWIN (350)
Hepworth
D: (Frank Wilson)
COMEDY Man poses as monkey to fool
sweetheart's father.

03335
THE LIEUTENANT'S BRIDE (600)
Hepworth
D: (Bert Haldane)
Chrissie White .... The Sempstress
Hay Plumb .... The Lieutenant
ROMANCE Lieut saves sacked sempstress from
starvation and attack by tramp.

03336
NEVER AGAIN, NEVER! (325)
Hepworth
D: (Lewin Fitzhamon)
TRICK Workman steals cask of beer and dreams
he is chased by it.

03337
DR RUSSELL'S LIE (890)
Britannia Films (Pathe)
D: (A.E. Coleby)
DRAMA Dr tries to win girl by telling rival he
has tuberculosis.

03338
A GIPSY GIRL'S HONOUR (548)
Britannia Films (Pathe)
D: (Lewin Fitzhamon)
ROMANCE Gipsy girl elopes in motor boat and
is chased by tribe.

03339
THE MUMMY (528)
Britannia Films (Pathe)
D: (A.E. Coleby)

COMEDY Man poses as revived mummy to
fool sweetheart's father.

03340
TO THEIR MUTUAL BENEFIT (676)
Britannia Films (Pathe)
D: (A.E. Coleby)
COMEDY Woman pays man £10 to wrestle
daughter's husband.

03341
FRED'S POLICE FORCE (630)
Precision Films (MP)
S: Fred Evans, Joe Evans
Fred Evans .... Fred
Joe Evans
COMEDY Rejected recruit starts own police
force.

03342
COWBOY MAD (520)
Precision Films (MP)
S: Fred Evans, Joe Evans
Fred Evans
Joe Evans
COMEDY Fan of cowboy films tries to
emulate idols.

03343
MR SWANKER GOES SHOOTING (595)
Heron Films (U)
P: Andrew Heron
COMEDY Braggart's misadventures during day's
grouse shooting.

MAR

03344
HAMLET (1525)
Barker
D: Charles Raymond
S: (PLAY) William Shakespeare
Charles Raymond .... Hamlet
Dorothy Foster .... Ophelia
Constance Backner .... Gertrude
DRAMA Ghost of prince's father spurs him to
wreak vengeance on king.

03345
THE FISHERGIRL OF CORNWALL (1150)
B&C (MP)
D: Sidney Northcote
S: Harold Brett
Dorothy Foster .... Mary Trelawney
Wallet Waller .... Tom Long
ROMANCE Cornwall. Fishergirl saves man's life
and he saves her from being abandoned by
seducer.

03346
WOMAN'S PRIVELEGE IN LEAP YEAR (410)
B&C (MP)
D: (Dave Aylott)
COMEDY Eligible male receives proposals from
every woman he meets.

03347
BROKEN FAITH (1160)
B&C (MP)
D: Dave Aylott
S: Harold Brett
Dorothy Foster .... Katie Liddell
Dave Aylott .... Jack Curtis
ROMANCE Country girl elopes, is abandoned,
and saved from drowning by blacksmith.

03348
A BRUTE'S REVENGE (626)
Britannia Films (Pathe)
D: (A.E. Coleby)
DRAMA District nurse saves doctor's child
kidnapped by vengeful coster.

03349
HUBBY'S LETTER (560)
Britannia Films (Pathe)
D: (Lewin Fitzhamon)
COMEDY Jealous wife misinterprets son's
letter and catches her husband flirting at
the seaside.

03350
THE OLD CURIOSITY SHOP (990)
Britannia Films (Pathe)
D: Frank Powell
S: (NOVEL) Charles Dickens
DRAMA Dwarf usurer persecutes gambler and
his sick grand-daughter.

03351
MIND THE BABY (410)
Cosmopolitan Films
COMEDY Coster couple's search for lost baby
left outside pub.

03352
DIDUMS ON HIS HOLIDAYS (500)
Clarendon
D: Wilfred Noy
COMEDY Child exchanges labels on ladies'
and gentlemen's bathrooms.

03353
DR BRIAN PELLIE AND THE SPANISH
GRANDEES (870)
Clarendon
D: Wilfred Noy
CRIME Gang captures duchess and party and
poses as them to rob ball.

03354
PERCY'S PERSISTENT PURSUIT (550)
Clarendon
D: Percy Stow
COMEDY Girl's suitor proposes to her and
loses trousers.

03355
THE STOLEN VIOLIN (520)
Cricks & Martin
D: (Edwin J. Collins)
DRAMA Starving busker, robbed of violin,
bu rgles home of impresario who purchased it.

03356
NOT SUCH A FOOL (390)
Cricks & Martin
D: (Edwin J. Collins)
COMEDY Clumsy maid catches burglar by
climbing onto back of his car.

03357
JONE'S MISTAKE (700)
Cricks & Martin
D: (Edwin J. Collins)
COMEDY Man mistakenly sends laundry
complaint to fiancee.

03358
A GIRL ALONE (1025)
Hepworth
D: (Bert Haldane)
Gladys Sylvani .... The Girl
Alec Worcester .... The PC
DRAMA Orphan tricked into mock marriage
and found by PC sweetheart.

03359
A PAIR OF BAGS (375)
Hepworth
D: (Frank Wilson)
COMEDY Train traveller forced to don hobble-
skirt when girls take bag by mistake.

03360
OUR BESSIE (1025)
Hepworth
D: (Bert Haldane)
Gladys Sylvani .... Bessie
Hay Plumb .... Jack Hard
DRAMA Village girl weds widower after saving
children from sea.

03361
TAKING FATHER'S DINNER (400)
Hepworth
D: (Frank Wilson)
COMEDY Girl delayed while carrying lunch
to father. .

03362
THE CHILD DETECTIVE (600)
Hepworth
D: (Bert Haldane)
CRIME Blind man's daughter chalks on walls
to lead police to burglars.

03363
TILLY AND THE DOGS (500)
Hepworth
D: Frank Wilson
Alma Taylor .... Tilly
Chrissie White .... Sally
COMEDY Girls, guarded by two dogs, cause
trouble for governess.

03364
WHEN JONES LOST HIS LATCHKEY (475)
Hepworth
D: (Frank Wilson)
COMEDY Drunkard tries to climb into room and
is arrested.

03365
PHOEBE OF THE INN (925)
Hepworth
D: (Bert Haldane)
ROMANCE Two men love one girl but one
prefers to inherit £300.

03366
A DETECTIVE FOR A DAY (475)
Hepworth
D: (Frank Wilson)
Jack Raymond .... Waiter
COMEDY Waiter mistakes policeman for
wanted crook.

03367
FROM BEHIND THE FLAG (295)
Urban Trading Co
D: W.R. Booth
TRICK Girl's Union Jack produces sailors,
Britannia, and King.

03368
ANIMATED TOYS (365)
Urban Trading Co reissue: 1915
D: W.R. Booth
TRICK Squares and circles dissolve into wooden
toys.

03369
THE ELUSIVE MISS PINKHURST (270)
Warwick Trading Co
TRICK Cabinet minister tries to catch
suffragette.

APR
03370
THROUGH DEATH'S VALLEY (1185)
B&C (MP)
D: Sidney Northcote
S: Harold Brett

Wallett Waller .... Waller
Fred Paul .... Paul
Anita Aylott .... Mrs Aylott
WESTERN Thirsty miners saved from Indians
by US Cavalry.

03371
SANDY'S NEW KILT (800)
B&C (MP)
D: (Dave Aylott)
William Gladstone Haley .... Sandy
COMEDY One by one, at night, family
shortens father's long kilt.

03372
LIEUTENANT DARING AND THE SHIP'S
MASCOT (1120)
B&C (MP)
D: Dave Aylott
S: Harold Brett
Percy Moran .... Lt Daring
Dorothy Foster ..... Margherita
Fred Rains .... Miguel
Sam Jones .... Jumbo
ADVENTURE Algiers. Brigands throw Lt over
cliff and sailors save him from flooding cave.

03373
A ROUGH DIAMOND (945)
Clarendon
D: Wilfred Noy
Dorothy Bellew ...... The Girl
WAR India. Drunkard's son enlists and saves
colonel's daughter from natives.

03374
A TALE OF TAILS (575)
Clarendon
D: Percy Stow
Dorothy Bellew .... Effie
COMEDY Sailors scheme to elope with
schoolgirls.

03375
ELECTRICAL HOUSE-BUILDING (495)
Clarendon
D: Percy Stow
TRICK House built by electrical invention.

03376
DIDUMS AND THE MONKEY (540)
Clarendon
D: Wilfred Noy
COMEDY Child changes a pet monkey for the
cook's baby.

03377
THE GAMEKEEPER'S REVENGE (940)
Clarendon
D: Wilfred Noy
Dorothy Bellew ...... The Wife
DRAMA Jealous bailiff tries to seduce farm
labourer's wife.

03378
SAVED BY FIRE (2500)
Clarendon (New Century)
D: Sidney W. Northcote
Dorothy Bellew .... Dora Stanmore
DRAMA Wife surprises husband in dancer's
boudoir unwittingly causing fire.

03379
THE MYSTIC RING (610)
Cricks & Martin
D: (Dave Aylott)
TRICK Tramp dreams Satan gives him ring
which makes him invisible.

03380
PURSUED BY PRISCILLA (650)
Cricks & Martin
D: (Edwin J. Collins)
COMEDY Office boy's plot causes seven girls
to rendezvous with clerk.

03381
BILLY BUNGLER THE SILENT BURGLAR
(590)
Cricks & Martin
D: (Dave Aylott)
COMEDY Child traps noisy burglar in
collapsible bed.

03382
TURNING THE TABLES (450)
Cricks & Martin reissue: 1916
D: (Edwin J. Collins)
COMEDY Woman thinks son's love-letter was
written by husband.

03383
THE HARVEST OF SIN (1250)
Cricks & Martin
D: (Edwin J. Collins)
CRIME Tec exposes bank cashier who framed
clerk for theft.

03384
A MOTHER AND SONS OF 1776 (857)
Britannia Films
D: (Lewin Fitzhamon)
DRAMA Widow avenges dead sons by poisoning
English soldiers.

03385
THE DECEPTION (975)
Hepworth
D: (Bert Haldane)
Gladys Sylvani .... Esme
Alec Worcester .... Hugh Mortimer
Chrissie White .... Fay
ROMANCE Girl takes sister's place when she
deserts blinded scientist.

03386
A PRESENT FOR HER HUSBAND (425)
Hepworth
D: Frank Wilson
CHASE Woman buys husband savage dog.

03387
HIS ACTRESS DAUGHTER (650)
Hepworth
D: (Bert Haldane)
DRAMA Disowned girl reunited with father
after running him over.

03388
PC HAWKEYE FALLS IN LOVE (500)
Hepworth
D:S: Hay Plumb
Hay Plumb .... PC Hawkeye
COMEDY PC trails girl, serenades her, and finds
she is married.

03389
THE TRAITRESS OF PARTON'S COURT
(1025) Reissue: 1915
Hepworth
D: Hay Plumb
Alec Worcester .... The Fireman
Gladys Sylvani .... Sally
Harry Royston .... Basher
CRIME Fireman saves coster girl from fire lit by
neighbours after she saves benefactor from
robbery.

03390
THE BLIND HEROINE (475)
Hepworth
D: (Bert Haldane)
CRIME Blind orphan discovers burglars and
summons police.

03391
THE COINER'S DEN (850)
Hepworth
D: Frank Wilson
Alec Worcester .... The Detective
Gladys Sylvani .... The Girl
Harry Royston .... The Cashier
CRIME Tec saved by dog poses as cabby to drive
coiners to police station.

03392
HE WANTED TO PROPOSE, BUT— (475)
Hepworth
D: (Frank Wilson)
COMEDY Lover's proposals constantly
interrupted.

03393
BILL'S REFORMATION (950)
Hepworth
D: (Bert Haldane)
Harry Royston .... Bill Brownlow
Alma Taylor .... Mary Brownlow
DRAMA Drunkard reforms when deserted wife
inherits and he saves baby from kidnapping by
nurse.

03394
THE LUNATIC AND THE BOMB (500)
Hepworth
D: (Frank Wilson)
COMEDY Escaped lunatic thinks tin can is bomb

03395
A MODERN MYSTERY (290)
Urban Trading Co
D:S: W.R. Booth
TRICK Animated clay models of conjuror,
skeleton, lady.

03396
THE JOKER'S MISTAKE (385)
Urban Trading Co reissue: 1916, GETTING HIS
OWN BACK
D:S: W.R. Booth
TRICK Conjuror's flowers blacken man's face in
revenge for explosive cigarette.

03397
AN ECCENTRIC SPORTSMAN (415)
Urban Trading Co
D:S: W.R. Booth
TRICK Magical sportsman's troubles with artist,
fish, and dog.

03398
A DAY WITH POACHERS (295)
Urban Trading Co
CRIME Poachers shoot rabbits, and use boat to
escape from keepers.

03399
BEWILDERING TRANSFORMATIONS (335)
Urban Trading Co
D:S: W.R. Booth
TRICK Lizard melts into boot; midget boxers
melt into grapes.

03400
PAPER CUTTINGS (325)
Kineto
D:S: W.R. Booth
TRICK Scissors cut paper shapes relevant to coal
strike.

03401
THE CRYSTAL GAZER (640)
Cosmopolitan
DRAMA Piccadilly clairvoyant leaves cruel
husband, is helped by officer, and saves him
from motor accident.

03402
UNCLE DUNN DONE (340)
Cosmolitan
COMEDY Spendthrifts pose as girl artist and
husband to blackmail rich uncle.

03403
THE LITTLE GENERAL (950)
Precision Films (MP)
D: Fred Evans
Fred Evans
COMEDY Clumsy maid redeems herself by
catching burglars.

03404
SEXTON BLAKE V BARON KETTLER (645)
Humanity Story Films
D: Hugh Moss
S: (STORY) (UNION JACK WEEKLY)
CRIME 'A story of the stolen plans.'

03405
JEWELS AND FINE CLOTHES (965)
Humanity Story Films
D: Hugh Moss
S: (STORY) (ANSWERS WEEKLY)
DRAMA 'A story which achieved great
popularity.'

MAY

03406
A CORNISH ROMANCE (1000)
B&C (MP)
D: Sidney Northcote
S: Harold Brett
Wallett Waller .... Sir Ralph Chetwynd
Dorothy Foster .... Sybilla Chetwynd
O'Neil Farrell .... Jules Marx
Ruth Sampson .... Miss Baston
Sidney Northcote .... Dark Davy
Fred Percy
CRIME Cornwall. Coastguards save knight's sis-
ter from abduction by usurer's pawn.

03407
THE BELLE OF BETTWS-Y-COED (1015)
USA: THE BELLE OF NORTH WALES
B&C (MP)
D: Sidney Northcote
S: Harold Brett
Dorothy Foster .... Gwladwys Williams
Percy Moran .... Hon Percy Morander
O'Neil Farrell .... Owen Davies
W. Gladstone Haley .... The Tramp
Miss C. Fisher
DRAMA Wales. Girl returns to sweetheart after
he thrashes tramps who attacked noble rival.

03408
THE OLD GARDENER (960)
B&C (MP)
D: H.O. Martinek
Harry Raneo .... John Collins
Ivy Clifford .... Mary Tayling
George Laundy .... Courtney Mayverne
Lillie Smead .... Beatrice Mayverne
S.P. Goodyer Kettle .... Sir John Tayling
CRIME Sacked gardner dies saving knight's
daughter from thief.

03409
THE BATALLION SHOT (890)
B&C (MP)
D: H.O.Martinek
S: Harold Brett
James Russell .... Cpl Farrell
Dorothy Foster .... Daisy Williams
Edward Durrant .... Sgt Delaney
Fred Rains
Alfred Wood
Harold Brett
CRIME Crackshot saves girl from abduction by
mad sgt.

03410
PEGGIE AND THE ROUNDHEADS (1006)
Britannia Films (Pathe) *reissue:* 1915
D: A. E. Coleby
Maude Derby .... Peggie
Claude King .... Father
DRAMA Girl unwittingly betrays hidden father.

03411
COSTER BILL (710)
Britannia Films (Pathe)
D: (A.E. Coleby)
Maude Derby .... The Child
DRAMA Coster adopts sailor's child to save her
from guardians.

03412
LIEUTENANT ROSE AND THE HIDDEN
TREASURE (1420)
Clarendon
D: Percy Stow
P.G. Norgate .... Lt Rose
ADVENTURE Lt finds treasure in underground
cave and signals with mirror for ship to shell
Portugese don.

03413
FOILED BY A GIRL (660)
Clarendon
D: Percy Stow
Dorothy Bellew
CRIME Typist catches thief and saves framed
clerk.

03414
A PAIR OF HANDCUFFS (530) *reissue:* 1916,
LINKS OF LOVE
Clarendon
D: Percy Stow
COMEDY Barrister handcuffs himself to girl
and loses key.

03415
A TAME CAT (560)
Clarendon
D: Percy Stow
COMEDY Disowned nephew poses as servant
saves aunt from burglar.

03416
MIND THE PAINT (475)
Clarendon
D: Percy Stow
COMEDY Man electrifies painted railings and
shocks rich aunt.

03417
HONOUR AMONG THIEVES (585)
Cricks & Martin *reissue:* 1916
D: (Dave Aylott)
COMEDY Two burglars bury swag, try to
cheat each other, and are caught.

03418
CONSTABLE SMITH AND THE MAGIC
BATON (600)
Cricks & Martin

D: (Edwin J. Collins)
Kelly Storrie .... PC Smith
TRICK Fairy gives PC magic truncheon which
produces magical policemen.

03419
OUT OF THE PAST (750)
Cricks & Martin
D: Edwin J. Collins
John Miller .... The Husband
CRIME Husband catches wife's blackmailer
and thrashes him.

03420
CHARLIE SMILER'S LOVE AFFAIR (645)
Cricks & Martin
D: Dave Aylott
COMEDY Bachelor thwarts spinster by faking
letter from his 'wife', then finds she has won
lottery.

03421
A CASE OF EXPLOSIVES (337)
Fitz Films (WI) *Reissue:* 1916, MUNITION
WORKERS (DFSA)
D:S: Lewin Fitzhamon
COMEDY Messenger tries to deliver leaking
parcel of explosive powder.

03422
CHILDREN OF THE FOREST (425)
Fitz Films (WI)
D:S: Lewin Fitzhamon
Roy Royston .... The Boy
Marie Royston .... The Girl
ANIMAL Boy and dog trail gipsy who
kidnapped sister.

03423
THE MISER AND THE MAID (750)
Hepworth
D: Warwick Buckland
Flora Morris .... Flora
Warwick Buckland .... The Miser
DRAMA Miser hides money in armchair and
wills it to flower-girl.

03424
MARY HAS HER WAY (725)
Hepworth
D: (Hay Plumb)
Gladys Sylvani .... Mary
Alec Worcester .... Fred
Harry Buss
COMEDY Girl objects to father's choice and
drives him distracted.

03425
TOMMY AND THE WHOOPING COUGH
(450)
Hepworth
D: (Frank Wilson)
CHASE Family think boy has whooping cough
and run round gasworks.

03426
THE LURE OF THE FOOTLIGHTS (1025)
Hepworth
D: (Warwick Buckland)
Madge Campbell .... Dorothy Trent
Alec Worcester .... Dr Trent
Harry Gilbey .... Halling
DRAMA Surgeon's wife leaves him to be singer
and is run over.

03427
TILLY WORKS FOR A LIVING (1000)
Hepworth
D: Frank Wilson
S: Victor Montefiore
Alma Taylor .... Tilly

Chrissie White .... Sally
Alec Worcester .... Jack Trent
COMEDY Typist's friend poses as office boy,
and then changes places.

03428
OUT OF EVIL COMETH GOOD (325)
Hepworth
D: (Warwick Buckland)
DRAMA Dying woman's daughter robs house
of mother's rich parents.

03429
WELCOME HOME (500)
Hepworth
D: (Hay Plumb)
Harry Buss
COMEDY Girl gets sweep to eject masher and
he ejects husband by mistake.

03430
A DOUBLE LIFE (800)
Hepworth
D: (Warwick Buckland)
Flora Morris .... Nellie Gray
Harry Royston .... Insp Gray
CRIME PC unmasks fiancee's father, inspector,
as chief crook.

03431
THE BURGLAR HELPED (400)
Hepworth
D: (Hay Plumb)
Madge Campbell .... Mary
COMEDY Girl's beau hides in cupboard and
saves father from burglar.

03432
LOST IN THE WOODS (500)
Hepworth
D: Frank Wilson
Blair .... Rover
ANIMAL Collie trails lost children and leads
them home.

03433
OH FOR A SMOKE! (425)
Hepworth
D: (Hay Plumb)
COMEDY Smoker keeps breaking clay pipes.

03434
FIFTY YEARS AFTER (324)
Precision Films (MP)
D: Fred Evans
Fred Evans
COMEDY Boy steals bicycle and is arrested
50 years later.

03435
A NOVEL BURGLARY (500)
Precision Films (MP)
D: Fred Evans
Fred Evans
COMEDY Cinematograph machine helps
cracksmen stage robbery.

03436
A NURSE'S DEVOTION (1017)
Brighton & County Films
D: Walter Speer
DRAMA Shoreham. Nurse adopts child she saves
from sea, and later inherits.

03437
THE MOTOR BANDITS (1370)
Brighton & County Films
D: Walter Speer
CRIME Pursued bank robbers kidnap cadets
who signal comrades to set fire to hideout.

03438
DREAM PAINTINGS (100)
Ivy Close Films (Butcher)
D:S: Elwin Neame
Ivy Close .... The Model
Austin Melford ...... The Artist
FANTASY Artist dreams model poses as
famous paintings.

03439
THE CONJURING TRAMPS (400)
Cosmopolitan
COMEDY Tramps steal conjuror's equipment
and rob blindfolded countryman.

03440
ALL THE COMFORTS OF HOME (1320)
Cosmopolitan
S: (SKETCH)
COMEDY Poor couple lose hire purchase
furniture and have to fake it for rich uncle's
visit.

03441
WHAT THE WINDOW CLEANER SAW (540)
Cosmopolitan
COMEDY Cleaner looks through windows of
hotel.

03442
THE FLYING DESPATCH (880)
Urban Trading Co
D: Stuart Kinder
WAR Girl poses as soldier to stow away in
fiance's plane and flies it while he fights spies.

03443
A FOOTBALL ABSURDITY (320)
Gaumont
CHASE Footballers play to coast and into sea.

JUN

03444
TWO BACHELOR GIRLS (900)
B&C (MP)
D: (H.O. Martinek)
Lillian Jeffries .... Leonora Leigh
Agnes Healy .... Nancy Sayers
Kenneth Ware .... Fred Haverley
Alfred Vetter .... M. Boulanger
COMEDY Girls pose as man and wife to share flat
with married pair.

03445
THE SMUGGLER'S DAUGHTER OF
ANGLESEA (1090)
B&C (MP)
D: Sidney Northcote
S: Harold Brett
Dorothy Foster .... Kate Price
Derek Powell .... David Price
Percy Moran .... Jack Morgan
Charles Seymour .... Richard Powys
CRIME Wales; Girl saves lighthouse keeper from
smuggler father.

03446
THE PEDLAR OF PENMAENMAWR (860)
B&C (MP)
D: Sidney Northcote
S: Harold Brett
Dorothy Foster .... Mfanwy Griffiths
Charles Seymour .... Llewellyn Rhys
George Trumpeter ... . Griffiths
O'Neil Farrell
Lady Geogina St George
Sidney Kearns
W. Gladstone Haley
DRAMA Wales. Pedlar saves girl from cliff
mishap.

03447
THE ADVENTURES OF DICK TURPIN —
THE KING OF HIGHWAYMEN (1132)
B&C (MP)
D: Charles Raymond
S: Harold Brett
Percy Moran .... Dick Turpin
Frank Pollard .... Tom King
Bert Murray .... Blueskin
Madge Thorpe .... Moonlight Nell
Ernest A. Trimingham .... Beetles
Raymond Cox .... O'Phelyn
Harry Missouri .... Peters
Herbert Trumper .... Ridgeway
Harold Houghton .... Hitchen
ADVENTURE Countryman steals cow, turns
highwayman, robs mail coach and is chased by
Bow Street Runners.

03448
THE GENTLEMAN RANKER (975)
B&C (MP)
D: (H.O. Martinek)
S: Harold Brett
Wallett Waller .... Herbert Coventry
Dorothy Foster .... Jocelyn Ferrers
Fred Paul .... Sir Thomas Coventry
Clifford Marle .... Rev Percival Ferrers
WAR Knight's disowned son joins cavalry,
fights Arabs, and weds vicar's daughter.

03449
SHARP PRACTICE (838)
Clarendon
D: Wilfred Noy
Dorothy Bellew ...... The Girl
CRIME Taxi-driver helps girl save miner from
being kidnapped by financier.

03450
MR DIDDLEM'S WILL (375)
Clarendon
D: Percy Stow
COMEDY Nephew inherits fortune if he weds
first woman to propose.

03451
SHEEPSKIN TROUSERS; OR, NOT IN
THESE (720)
Clarendon
D: Percy Stow
COMEDY Burlesque western; cowboy saves
girl from Indian's stake.

03452
DIDUMS AT SCHOOL (495)
Clarendon
D: Percy Stow
COMEDY Child sets trap for teacher and
hides in bed.

03453
DETECTIVE SHARP AND THE STOLEN
MINIATURES (1045)
Cricks & Martin
D: (Charles Calvert)
CRIME Tec catches burglar at garden party by
posing as partner.

03454
UNCLE'S PRESENT (535)
Cricks & Martin
D: (Dave Aylott)
COMEDY Man sells uncle's jacket before
learning it contains banknote.

03455
COLD STEEL (825)
Cricks & Martin reissue: 1916
D: Edwin J. Collins
Edwin J. Collins .... Terrance Astor
DRAMA Husband thinks wife loves artist
and faces him to fight with foils.

03456
HOW SMILER RAISED THE WIND (750)
Cricks & Martin reissue: 1916
D: Dave Aylott
COMEDY Smiler wrests rewards from uncle
by faking finding of lost purses.

03457
CONSTABLE SMITH IN COMMAND (440)
Cricks & Martin
D: (Edwin J. Collins)
Kelly Storrie .... PC Smith
TRICK PC's magic baton produces policemen
and poachers.

03458
THE FARMER'S DAUGHTER (975)
Cricks & Martin reissue: 1916
D: (Edwin J. Collins)
Una Tristram .... Rose Jones
John Miller .... Farmer Jones
DRAMA Squire saves girl from abduction by
jealous farmer.

03459
MUGGINS VC — THE DEFENCE OF KHUMA
HOSPITAL, INDIA (865)
Cricks & Martin reissue: 1916
D: Dave Aylott
Arthur Charrington .... Muggins
Anita Aylott .... Mrs Muggins
Sammy Jones .... Native
4th Essex Volunteer Regiment
WAR India. Sgt and nurse wife save beseiged
hospital.

03460
CHARLIE SMILER AT THE PICNIC (550)
Cricks & Martin
D: Dave Aylott
COMEDY Smiler falls in river at girl's picnic
and is forced to dress in leaves.

03461
THE PATCHED COAT (1040)
Cricks & Martin
D: (Edwin J. Collins)
CRIME Boy identifies tramp thief by patch
his grandmother sewed on his coat.

03462
ROBBERY AT OLD BURNSIDE BANK (750)
Hepworth
D: (Frank Wilson)
CRIME Police chase bank robbers and catch
them after gun battle on train.

03463
THE LAST OF THE BLACK HAND GANG
(450)
Hepworth
D: (Hay Plumb)
COMEDY Assassins mistake masher with hand-
print on coat for their victim.

03464
THE PASSING OF THE OLD FOUR-WHEELER
(875)
Hepworth
D: Warwick Buckland
Flora Morris .... The Daughter
Warwick Buckland .... The Cabby
DRAMA Cabby's dying daughter persuades him
to return lost £5.

03465
HER 'MAIL' PARENT (725)
Hepworth
D: (Hay Plumb)
Alec Worcester .... The Clerk
Chrissie White .... The Girl
COMEDY Clerk's letter to boss's daughter
misunderstood by her mother.

03466
IN WOLF'S CLOTHING (500)
Hepworth
D: (Frank Wilson)
S: Muriel Alleyne
CHASE Escaped convict dons swimmer's
clothes.

03467
THE BACHELOR'S WARD (875)
Hepworth
D: (Warwick Buckland)
Gladys Sylvani .... The Girl
Alec Worcester .... The Man
Harry Gilbey .... The Guardian
ROMANCE Old Guardian mistakenly thinks
ward loves younger man.

03468
THE INDIAN WOMAN'S PLUCK (950)
Hepworth
D: (Frank Wilson)
S: Muriel Alleyne
Ruby Belasco .... Ayah
DRAMA India. Ayah trails sacked workman to
save kidnapped baby.

03469
THE TRANSIT OF VENUS (400)
Hepworth
D: (Hay Plumb)
COMEDY Men follow shapely girl and find she
is Negress.

03470
THE CONVICT'S DAUGHTER (650)
Hepworth
D:S: Warwick Buckland
Flora Morris .... The Daughter
Warwick Buckland .... The Convict
CRIME Warder forces girl to betray escaped
father, who then dies.

03471
A MAN AND A SERVING MAID (775)
Hepworth
D: (Hay Plumb)
Alec Worcester .... Charles Waring
Chrissie White .... Elsie Waller
ROMANCE Girl poses as maidservant to test
beau's affection.

03472
WONKEY'S WAGER (550)
Hepworth
D: (Frank Wilson)
COMEDY Man poses as PC for bet and gets
into trouble.

03473
THE BROKEN MELODY (325)
Fitz Films (WI)
D:S: Lewin Fitzhamon
Constance Somers-Clarke ..... Girl
COMEDY Builders throw bricks at busker but
give chicken to girl singer.

03474
A DAY IN THE COUNTRY (500)
Fitz Films (WI)
D:S: Lewin Fitzhamon
Roy Royston .... The Boy
Marie Royston .... The Girl
COMEDY Children and dog chase farmer's •
chickens.

03475
THE STOLEN AIRSHIP PLANS (807)
Urban Trading Co *Reissue:* 1914, THE
REGIMENTAL PET

D:S: Stuart Kinder
Irene Vernon .... The Spy
Spot the Urbanora Dog
ANIMAL Inventor's partner and pet dog catch
girl spy.

03476
THE DANCER'S DREAM (355)
Urban Trading Co
D:S: Stuart Kinder
Irene Vernon .... The Dancer
TRICK Girl goes to ball as Swiss maid and
dreams of various dances.

03477
A COUNTRY HOLIDAY (745)
Urban Trading Co
D:S: Stuart Kinder
Irene Vernon .... The Actress
COMEDY Actress uses dummy to fool amorous
students.

03478
LOVE PATCHES (598)
Cosmopolitan
COMEDY Woman mends husband's coat with
professor's patent patch and he kisses everyone
he meets.

03479
THE ELECTRIC BELT (650)
Cosmopolitan
COMEDY Lazy maid's soldier suitor electrified
and shocks people with sword.

03480
THE ARTFUL WIDOW (480)
Cosmopolitian
COMEDY Girl's suitor, rejected by father, poses
as widow to force consent.

03481
A VAPOUR BATH (510)
Britannia Films (Pathe)
D: A.E. Coleby
COMEDY Burglar hides in vapour bath and
is caught by Lady's maid.

JUL

03482
YIDDLE AND HIS FIDDLE (500)
B&C (MP)
D: H.O. Martinek
S: Harold Brett
H.O. Martinek .... Yiddle
Gertrude le Sage .... Rachel Cohen
Marquenta Larralde .... Mrs Cohen
Harry Kingston .... Aaron Brettonsky
Harold Brett .... Mr Cohen
Vida Varrall .... Mrs Yiddle
COMEDY Jewess falls for violinist and finds he
has wife.

03483
THE UNDERGRADUATE'S VISITOR (602)
B&C (MP)
D: (Charles Raymond)
H.O. Martinek .... Jack
Ivy Martinek .... Anne
Hypatia Brand .... Mrs Baggs
Jack Stokes .... Simkins
COMEDY Students mistake wardrobe man
for friend's cousin.

03484
HER TEDDY BEAR (805)
B&C (MP)
D: (Charles Raymond)
Helen Beresford .... Nellie
Hubert Dare .... Jack
Cooie Miller .... Dora

H. Beecher .... Sir Humphrey
J. Buckland
DRAMA Knight reconciled to disowned son
when he runs over his child.

03485
THE WITCH OF THE WELSH MOUNTAINS
(990)
B&C (MP)
D: Sidney Northcote
S: Harold Brett
Dorothy Foster .... Catrin Morgan
Sidney Cairns .... Ewan ap Ewan
Beatrice de Burgh .... Yeda
Lady Georgina St George....... Widow Evans
DRAMA Wales. Wounded widow recovers in time
to save wrong girl from being burned at stake.

03486
THREE-FINGERED KATE — THE WEDDING
PRESENTS (940)
B&C (MP)
D: H.O. Martinek
S: Harold Brett
Ivy Martinek .... Kate
Alice Moseley .... Mary
Charles Calvert .... Sheerluck Finch
Fred Paul .... Sir Douglas Carrington
Olympia Sumner .... Evadne Carrington
Jack Stokes .... Chalmers
W. Gladstone Haley .... Tarvin
Bessie Booker .... Friend
COMEDY Crooks tunnel through fireplace to rob
house next door

03487
LIEUTENANT DARING DEFEATS THE
MIDDLEWEIGHT CHAMPION (1190)
B&C (MP)
D: Charles Raymond
S: Harold Brett
Percy Moran .... Lt Daring
Ivy Martinek .... Ivy Mountford
Charles Calvert .... Lt Derrick
Jack Stokes .... Jack Dent
Edward Durrant .... Martin Glover
J.W. Bremner .... Stumpy Dick
Harold Brett .... The Gent
Frank Bradley .... The Referee
Jack Mullins .... The Second
SPORT Lt saved from kidnappers in time to win
boxing match and colonel's daughter.

03488
THE MEXICAN'S LOVE AFFAIR (1090)
British Anglo-American (Tyler)
D: Fred Rains
Viola Hamilton .... The Girl
George Bellamy .... The Mexican
WESTERN Mexican landlord shoots miner,
kidnaps girl witness, and is shot by pursuant
police.

03489
LOVE CONQUERS CRIME (850)
British Anglo-American (Tyler)
D: Fred Rains
Viola Hamilton .... The Dancer
George Bellamy .... The Man
CRIME Ex-crook weds dancer, is framed by
his ex-partner, and cleared by witness.

03490
SAVING THE ROYAL MAIL (852)
Fitz Films (WI)
D:S: Lewin Fitzhamon
Constance Somers Clarke .... Cora
ANIMAL Pony fetches help for injured post-
man while dog tracks mail robbers.

03491
THE FLAPPER'S ELOPEMENT (575)
Fitz Films (WI)
D:S: Lewin Fitzhamon
Constance Somers-Clarke .... The Flapper
COMEDY Colonel's son poses as sweep to
elope with schoolgirl.

03492
GRANDMA'S SLEEPING DRAUGHT (680)
Clarendon
D: Percy Stow
COMEDY Child pours soporific into wine and
burglar drinks it.

03493
A PEPPERY AFFAIR (445)
Clarendon
D: Percy Stow
COMEDY Child puts pepper on sister's flower
to repel unwelcome squire.

03494
THE MINER'S MASCOT (1090)
Cricks & Martin
D: Dave Aylott
Sammy Jones .... Negro
ADVENTURE Australia. Miner saves Negro from
from thrashing and he tracks man who stole his
gold.

03496
CONSTABLE SMITH ON THE WARPATH
(560)
Cricks & Martin
D: (Edwin J. Collins)
Kelly Storrie .... PC Smith
TRICK PC uses magic baton to track down
Lord's stolen watch.

03495
A COUNTRY LASS (940)
Cricks & Martin reissue: 1916
D: (Edwin J. Collins)
Una Tristram .... Kitty Crouch
ROMANCE Girl spurns farmer for city artist
who is already married.

03497
CHARLIE SMILER CATCHES A TARTAR
(425)
Cricks & Martin Reissue: 1915
D: Dave Aylott
COMEDY Charlie follows tough woman who
turns out to be man.

03498
THE SIXTH COMMANDMENT (1125)
Cricks & Martin
D: (Edwin J. Collins)
Una Tristram .... The Girl
Fred Paul .... Jack Howard
CRIME Heir recovers from shot in time to stop
girl from marrying imposter.

03499
TWO BROTHERS AND A SPY (850)
Hepworth
D: (Hay Plumb)
Alec Worcester .... Lt Dick Fenton
Madge Campbell .... Col's Daughter
CRIME Lieut takes blame when he catches
brother stealing plans.

03500
A MAN OF MYSTERY (400)
Hepworth
D: (Frank Wilson)

TRICK Disappearing pierrot covers audience
with soot.

03501
POORLUCK'S PICNIC (450)
Hepworth
D: Hay Plumb
Harry Buss .... Poorluck
COMEDY Tramp steals man's picnic and he
loses pony.

03502
GRANDFATHER'S OLD BOOTS (475)
Hepworth
D: (Frank Wilson)
COMEDY Heir gives away old boots, then
learns each sole hid half a £1000 note.

03503
JIM ALL-ALONE (1000)
Hepworth
D: (Warwick Buckland)
Alec Worcester .... Jim Boyce
Flora Morris .... Lucy
ROMANCE Girl helps poor author and he weds
her upon inheriting fortune.

03504
SHE ASKED FOR TROUBLE (675)
Hepworth
D: (Hay Plumb)
COMEDY When wife fakes death her husband
fakes love affair.

03505
A GOOD TONIC (450)
Hepworth
D: (Frank Wilson)
TRICK Lazy bathchair attendant drinks tonic
and takes invalid for fast run.

03506
WHIST! HERE COMES THE PICTURE MAN
(500)
Hepworth
D: (Hay Plumb)
Harry Buss
COMEDY Tramps rig up camera and rob while
pretending to film.

03507
A PEASANT GIRL'S REVENGE (975)
Hepworth
D: (Warwick Buckland)
Flora Morris .... Aline
Alec Worcester .... Marquis de StGrise
DRAMA France, 1789. Peasant betrays seducer
to Tribunal.

03508
LIEUTENANT LILLY AND THE PLANS OF
THE DIVIDED SKIRT (600)
Hepworth
D: Hay Plumb
Harry Buss.................... Lt Lilly
COMEDY Lt and men save plans from spies.

03509
THE COURTIER CAUGHT (525)
Heron Films (U)
P: Andrew Heron
D:S: Mark Melford
Mark Melford .... Wolf Ribb
COMEDY Man and typist meet his wife and
manager at White City funfair.

03510
THE BIRTHDAY THAT MATTERED (900)
Barker
D: (Bert Haldane)

DRAMA Squire shoots disowned son when he
brings birthday gift.

03511
A DUMB MATCHMAKER (1000)
Barker
D: (Bert Haldane)
ROMANCE Girl adopts lost dog and becomes
engaged to its owner.

03512
WHEN GOLD IS DROSS (800)
Barker
D: (Bert Haldane)
DRAMA Usurer's son helps evicted banker's
wife and child.

03513
THE ROMANCE OF A ROYALIST MAID
(1000) Kinema also: FOR LOVE AND THE
KING
Natural Colour Kinematograph Co
D: F. Martin Thornton
ADVENTURE Royalist posing as Roundhead
saved by Cromwell's daughter.

AUG

03514
THE ADVENTURES OF DICK TURPIN —
THE GUNPOWDER PLOT (1133)
B&C (MP)
D: Charles Raymond
S: Harold Brett
Percy Moran .... Dick Turpin
Douglas Payne .... George II
George Foley .... Sir Robert Walpole
Jack Houghton .... Sir Hugh Melville
W. Gladstone Haley
Olympia Sumner
Harold Brett
Herbert Trumper
ADVENTURE Highwayman saves King from
assassination.

03515
THE GREAT ANARCHIST MYSTERY (2040)
B&C (MP)
D: Charles Raymond
S: Silas K. Hocking
Percy Moran .... Jack Logan
Dorothy Foster .... Betty Lyndhurst
Derek Powell .... Peter Nickoloff
Charles Seymour .... Insp Keen
CRIME Cornwall. Lighthouse keeper stops
foreign agent from sinking Duke's ship.

03516
THE BLIGGS FAMILY AT THE ZOO (650)
B&C (MP) Reissue: 1914
D: H. O. Martinek
W. Gladstone Haley .... Bliggs
Vida Varrell .... Mrs Bliggs
COMEDY Misadventures of couple at London
zoo.

03517
THREE-FINGERED KATE — THE CASE OF
THE CHEMICAL FUMES (1070)
B&C (MP)
D: H. O. Martinek
S: Harold Brett
Ivy Martinek .... Kate
Alice Moseley .... Mary
Charles Calvert .... Sheerluck Finch
Edward Durrant .... Baron Rochid
Harold Brett .... Carrick Carthew
COMEDY Broadstairs. Girls rob rich baron's
house party by pumping gas through secret panel.

03518
THE WINSOME WIDOW (697)
B&C (MP)
D: (Charles Raymond)
Ivy Martinek .... Mrs de Vere
H. O. Martinek .... Dick Wentworth
Mabel Clark .... Ophelia Drinkwater
Olympia Sumner
Bessie Booker
COMEDY Widow wins approval of beloved's
aunt.

03519
ETHEL'S DANGER (760)
Barker
D: (Bert Haldane)
CRIME Countryman saves girl from being
kidnapped by Soho crook.

03520
WAS HE JUSTIFIED? (1095)
Barker
D: (Bert Haldane)
CRIME Cleric hides evicted inventor who blew
up landlord to avenge wife's death.

03521
THE DISINHERITED NEPHEW (1010)
Barker
D: (Bert Haldane)
CRIME Rich man's disowned nephew kidnaps
child cousin.

03522
PEG WOFFINGTON (2145)
Britainnia Films (Pathe)
D: A. E. Coleby
S: (PLAY) Tom Taylor, Charles Reade
(MASKS AND FACES)
SC: George Pearson
Leslie Howard Gordon
COMEDY Period. Actress cures flirt by posing
as wife.

03523
HIS WIFE'S BROTHER (692)
Britannia Films (Pathe)
D: A. E. Coleby
DRAMA 1805. French prisoner sheltered by
sister while her husband leads pursuers astray.

03524
SOPPY GREEN LOSES A LEGACY (460)
Britannia Films (Pathe)
D: (A. E. Coleby)
COMEDY Rich woman tests nephew by letting
him run farm.

03525
THE LITTLE MOTHER (990)
Britannia Films (Pathe)
D: A. E. Coleby
DRAMA Orphan takes dead mother's place and
saves artist from blackmailing model.

03526
MARRIED IN HASTE (595)
British Anglo-American (Tyler)
D: Fred Rains
Fred Rains .... Bachelor
COMEDY Bachelor must marry to inherit
fortune.

03527
BACK AT THREE (695)
British Anglo-American (Tyler)
D: Fred Rains
Fred Rains .... Tramp
COMEDY Tramp poses as couple's rich uncle
and burgles house.

03528
HIS DUTY (650)
British Anglo-American (Tyler)
D: Fred Rains
George Bellamy .... Father
CRIME Tec discovers fiancee's father is crook.

03529
MY WIFE'S PET (520)
British Anglo-American (Tyler)
D: Fred Rains
Fred Rains .... Husband
COMEDY Woman's pet monkey wrecks house.

03530
THE NEW HOUSEKEEPER (965)
Clarendon *Reissue:* 1916, WANTED A
HOUSEKEEPER
D: Wilfred Noy
Dorothy Bellew .... The Housekeeper
COMEDY Men fall for new housekeeper who
turns out to be their father's new wife.

03531
DON'T TOUCH IT! (540)
Clarendon
D: Percy Stow
COMEDY Father throws whiskey into barrel,
cow drinks it, and father gets drunk on milk.

03532
HER RELATIONS (535)
Clarendon
D: Percy Stow
COMEDY Girl's lover poses as tramp to repel
rich suitor.

03533
WHICH OF THE TWO (485)
Clarendon
D: Percy Stow
Dorothy Bellew .... The Girl
COMEDY Squire poses as robber to test his
daughter's suitors.

03534
THE WOOING OF WIDOW WILKINS (750)
Cricks & Martin *Reissue:* 1916
D: (Dave Aylott)
COMEDY Village widow foils fortune-hunters
by marrying captain.

03535
THE VENGEANCE OF DANIEL WHIDDEN
(1000)
Cricks & Martin
D: Edwin J. Collins
Una Tristam .... Mary Whidden
Jack Leight .... Jan Stewer
CRIME Devon. Fisherman takes blame when
girl's father stabs rival.

03536
A MAN'S SHADOW (910)
Cricks & Martin
D: Edwin J. Collins
CRIME Ex-convict poses as double who
meanwhile has amnesia and joins gipsies.

03537
CHARLIE SMILER ASKS PAPA (850)
Cricks & Martin
D: Dave Aylott
COMEDY Shy man seeks to win girl by
tracing father's stolen tea service.

03538
AMOROUS ARTHUR (600)
Fitz Films (WI)
D:S: Lewin Fitzhamon
Constance Somers-Clarke .... Girl
Marie Royston .... Sister

COMEDY Girl's sister replies to suitor's
love-letter.

03539
REPAYING THE DEBT (600)
Fitz Films (WI)
D:S: Lewin Fitzhamon
Constance Somers-Clarke .... Girl
Roy Royston .... Boy
Marie Royston .... Girl
DRAMA Children save colonel's daughter
and later she saves them.

03540
UNLUCKY ANN (450)
Fitz Films (WI)
D:S: Lewin Fitzhamon
COMEDY Couple try to force man to marry
ugly daughter.

03541
LOVE WINS IN THE END (1000)
Hepworth
D: Warwick Buckland
Gladys Sylvani .... Esther Whedden
Alec Worcester .... Jack Foster
Harry Gilbey .... Employer
DRAMA Sacked manager turns tramp and saves
ex-fiance from lustful employer.

03542
THE APACHE (600)
Hepworth
D: Hay Plumb
Harry Buss .... Comte de Villeroche
COMEDY Comte dressed as apache forced to
help rob own house.

03543
RUTH (675)
Hepworth
D: (Frank Wilson)
ROMANCE Widow refuses to wed farmer
until mother-in-law dies.

03544
THE UNMASKING OF MAUD (650)
Hepworth
D: (Hay Plumb)
Chrissie White .... Christine
COMEDY Man proposes to wrong sister at
masked ball.

03545
ROSE O' THE RIVER (1000)
Hepworth
D: Warwick Buckland
ROMANCE Girl inherits £10,000 and rejects
fortune-hunter in favour of poor farmer.

03546
MR POORLUCK'S RIVER SUIT (300)
Hepworth,
D: (Hay Plumb)
Harry Buss .... Mr Poorluck
COMEDY Man's new boating outfit spoilt by
wet paint.

03547
PAID WITH INTEREST (450).
Hepworth
D: (Frank Wilson)
COMEDY Showman sends man in bear skin to
creditor.

03548
AT THE ELEVENTH HOUR (975)
Hepworth
D: Warwick Buckland
Gladys Sylvani .... Gladys Henderson
Alec Worcester .... Reggie Wells
CRIME Girl returns in time to prove lover did
not kill woman.

03549
CURFEW MUST NOT RING TONIGHT (1100)
Hepworth
D: Hay Plumb
S; (POEM) Rose Thorpe
Alec Worcester .... Basil Underwood
Alma Taylor .... Bessie
DRAMA Cromwell pardons cavalier after girl
hangs on bell to stay execution.

03550
A MAID OF THE ALPS (1330)
Terrier (Cooperative)
D: Alf Collins
S: (PLAY) George Moore Marriott
George Moore Marriott .... Mme Potard
CRIME Knight finds papers proving innkeeper's
daughter is stolen heiress and screws crone in
grape press.

03551
ALGIE'S EXPENSIVE STICK (335)
Terrier (Cooperative)
D:S: Alf Collins
Alf Collins .... Algie
COMEDY Dude's cheap walking stick causes
trouble.

03552
CARD MANIPULATIONS (500) *kinema*
Natural Colour Kinematograph Co *Reissue:*
1916 (Kineto)
D: W.R. Booth
TRICK Playing card characters come to life.

03553
A CHINAMAN'S FIRST DAY IN LONDON
(320)
Gaumont
COMEDY Chinaman thwarts boys by
electrifying pigtail.

03554
A DISASTROUS IMITATION (595)
Cosmopolitan
COMEDY Man tries to emulate street conjuror
and ruins man's watch.

03555
A CHILD'S STRATEGY (635)
HB Films (Cosmo)
D:S: Ernest G. Batley
Dorothy Batley .... The Girl
Ernest G. Batley .... The Father
CRIME Girl sits on back of robber's car and
drops trail of meal for father to follow.

03556
KLEPTOMANIA TABLETS (575)
HB Films (Cosmo)
D:S: Ernest G. Batley
Dorothy Batley .... The Girl
Bert Wynne .... The Policeman
COMEDY Girl gives grandfather's magic pills to
curate, soldier, policeman.

03557
THE HEAVENLY TWINS (585)
HB Films (Cosmo)
D:S: Ernest G. Batley
Dorothy Batley .... The Twins
Ernest G. Batley .... The Misogynist
COMEDY Girl poses as mischievous boy to
make misogynist alter will.

03558
THE SOUVENIR HUNTER (640)
Diamond Films (Cosmo)
COMEDY Man with pair of scissors cuts braces,
girl's harem skirt, etc.

03559
THE SURGEON'S CHILD (1000)
Eric Williams Speaking Pictures
P: SC: Eric Williams
D: Harry Thurston Harris
S: (POEM) Fred Weatherley
Eric Williams .... The Coachman
DRAMA Shown while Eric Williams recites
from cinema stage.

SEP
03560
LIEUTENANT DARING QUELLS A
REBELLION (1177)
B&C (MP)
D: (Charles Raymond)
S: Harold Brett
Percy Moran .... Lt Daring
Ivy Martinek .... Carmencita
H.O. Martinek .... Jose
A. Brian Plant .... Bianca
Jack Houghton ....Carlos
F. Barrington .... Garcia
WAR West Indies. Lt stops rebels from
extinguishing lighthouse beam as signal for
uprising.

03561
A DEAL IN CROCKERY (644)
B&C (MP) *Remake:* 1910
D: (H.O. Martinek)
W. Gladstone Haley .... Snorkey
Fred Rigby .... His Pal
T. Mackney .... Ikey
Tom Morriss .... Moses
COMEDY Man poses as child to sell broken
crockery to Jews.

03562
ROBIN HOOD OUTLAWED (1186)
B&C (MP)
D: Charles Raymond
S: Harold Brett
A. Brian Plant .... Robin Hood
Ivy Martinek .... Maid Marion
George Foley .... Friar Tuck
Edward Durrant .... Will Scarlet
Jack Houghton .... Sir Hubert de Boissy
J. Leonard .... Abbot of Ramsey
Harry Lorraine .... Little John
ADVENTURE Outlawed Earl forms robber
band saves girl from knight.

03563
THREE-FINGERED KATE — THE PSEUDO-
QUARTETTE (1010)
B&C (MP)
D: H.O. Martinek
S: Harold Brett
Ivy Martinek .... Kate
Alice Moseley .... Mary
Charles Calvert .... Sheerluck Finch
W. Gladstone Haley .... Snorkey
Edward Durrant .... Lord Malcolm
COMEDY Crooks kidnap musicians, take places,
and rob Lord's Ball.

03564
HER BETTER SELF
Barker
D: (Bert Haldane)
ROMANCE Spurned girl tries to spoil
ex-fiance's marriage.

03565
PETER PICKLES' WEDDING (790)
Barker
D: (Bert Haldane)
Peter Gale .... Peter Pickles
COMEDY Girl gets maid to take her place at
enforced wedding.

03566
PIPPIN UP TO HIS PRANKS
Barker
D: (Bert Haldane)
Kenneth Barker .... Pippin
COMEDY Small boy plays pranks on people.

03567
THE POACHERS FIGHT FOR LIBERTY
Barker
D: (Bert Haldane)
CHASE Gamekeepers pursue and capture
poachers after struggle.

03568
ONLY AN OUTCAST
Barker
D: (Bert Haldane)
CRIME Sacked stableboy shot erroneously
while warning squire of burglar.

03569
THE IRONY OF FATE
Barker
D: (Bert Haldane)
DRAMA 'Drowned' man returns to find
sweetheart married to cousin.

03570
THE LITTLE POACHER (895)
Barker
D: (Bert Haldane)
PATHOS Jealous gamekeeper ejects wife and
child and shoots child when he poaches to
save starving mother.

03571
BOB THE COSTER'S PONY (692)
Britannia Films (Pathe)
D: A.E. Coleby
DRAMA Sick pony wins prize and saves master
from debt.

03572
BOBBY'S LETTER (660)
Britannia Films (Pathe)
D: (A. E. Coleby)
DRAMA Poor child sends message on carrier
pigeon which is found by rich couple.

03573
DUPED BY DETERMINATION (510)
British Anglo- American (Tyler)
D: Fred Rains
Fred Rains .... Actor
COMEDY Actor poses as music teacher to
fool girl's father.

03574
LITTLE MISS DEMURE (455)
British Anglo-American (Tyler)
D: Fred Rains
Fred Rains .... Uncle
COMEDY Little girl plays tricks on uncle.

03575
SAMMY'S REVENGE (535)
British Anglo-American (Tyler)
D: Fred Rains
Fred Rains .... Sammy
COMEDY Clubman hires toughs to fight
tricksters.

03576
THE FORCED CONFESSION (1150)
Clarendon
D: Wilfred Noy
Dorothy Bellew .... Irene Mannering
CRIME French professor uses hypnosis and
filmed reconstruction to force confession from
servant.

03577
MOLLY LEARNS TO MOTE (470)
Clarendon
D: Percy Stow
COMEDY Girl learning to drive car crashes into house.

03578
THE SUIT THAT DIDN'T SUIT (450)
Clarendon
D: Percy Stow
COMEDY Dancer dressed as policeman mistaken for real one.

03579
LIEUTENANT ROSE AND THE TRAIN WRECKERS (955)
Clarendon
D: Percy Stow
Harry Lorraine .... Lt Rose
CRIME Lt fights train wreckers in tunnel, jumps from parapet on to another train, and rows to ship.

03580
THE LOST LOVE LETTER (515)
Clarendon
D: Percy Stow
Dorothy Bellew ...... The Girl
DRAMA Girl saves lover from drowning himself over mislaid letter.

03581
THE MASKED SMUGGLER (1000)
Cricks & Martin
D: Edwin J. Collins
Una Tristram .... The Girl
CRIME Devon, 1770. Lieut unmasks girl's father as chief smuggler.

03582
THE SPY MANIA (335)
Cricks & Martin Reissue: 1916
D: (Dave Aylott)
COMEDY British tourist arrested as spy.

03583
THE HEARTS OF MEN (982)
Cricks & Martin
D: Edwin J. Collins
DRAMA

03584
BAGGED (440)
Cricks & Martin Reissue: 1916
D: (Dave Aylott)
COMEDY Farmer stops daughter from eloping with squire.

03585
A SON OF MARS (1190)
Cricks & Martin
D: Dave Aylott
Wingold Lawrence .... Lt Winford
WAR Simla. Lieut poses as native to bring Highlanders to besieged fort.

03586
OH WHAT A PEACH! (960)
Cricks & Martin
D: Edwin J. Collins
COMEDY America. Manicurist feigns love for gold miner and absconds with wedding presents.

03587
JEMIMA AND THE EDITOR (500)
Fitz Films (Hepworth)
D:S: Lewin Fitzhamon
Constance Somers-Clarke .... Jemima
ROMANCE Maid rewrites author's story and editor accepts it.

03588
THE WRONG ENVELOPES (625)
Fitz Films (Hepworth)
D:S: Lewin Fitzhamon
Constance Somers-Clarke .... Flora
ROMANCE Man sends farewell letter to wrong girl.

03589
THE BAILIFF (590)
Cosmopolitan
COMEDY Muscular woman throws out persistant baliff.

03590
THE NEW BOARDER (500)
Cosmopolitan
COMEDY Widow's three sons play tricks on new lodger.

03591
A GOOD SELL (575)
Cosmopolitan
COMEDY Man fakes letter about hidden money and sells house to village wiseacre.

03592
SYDNEY'S SHARP POINTS (540)
Cosmopolitan
COMEDY Boy uses tacks to play tricks on maid, sister, beau, father, cook.

03593
FINDING FREDDY WORK (550)
Cosmopolitan
COMEDY Overgrown bo y jailed after trying hand as errand boy, waiter, etc.

03594
SPORTS IN MOGGYLAND (340)
Diamond Films (Cosmo)
TRICK Wooden toys hold sports gala.

03595
IN SPITE OF ALL (1450)
Diamond Films (Cosmo)
CRIME Heir tries to stop cousin from marrying in order to inherit fortune.

03596
PC HAWKEYE, SPORTSMAN (500)
Hepworth
D:S: Hay Plumb
Hay Plumb .... PC Hawkeye
COMEDY Policeman confiscates gun and shoots own foot.

03597
LOVE IN A LAUNDRY (725)
Hepworth
D: (Frank Wilson)
Alec Worcester
Gladys Sylvani
Flora Morris
Chrissie White
Violet Hopson
COMEDY Three laundresses refuse lovers' shirts when they are slighted in favour of three shopgirls.

03598
THE AVARICIOUS MONK (750)
Hepw orth
D: (Warwick Buckland)
ADVENTURE King pardons Robin Hood after girl pleads for him.

03599
TILLY IN A BOARDING HOUSE (525)
Hepworth

03600 (continued)
D: (Hay Plumb)
Alma Taylor ·.......... Tilly
Chrissie White .... Sally
COMEDY Girls dress in boys' clothes and trick boarders.

03600
BUNGLING BURGLARS (350)
Hepworth
D: (Frank Wilson)
COMEDY Burglars steal a bell rope.

03601
THE EMPEROR'S MESSENGER (950)
Hepworth
D: Hay Plumb
Jack Hulcup .... Lt Rentz
Claire Pridelle .... Bessie
Johnny Butt .... Napoleon
Harry Royston ...... Innkeeper
ADVENTURE 1812. Innkeeper's daughter saves Napoleon's messenger from Russian cavalry.

03602
OLIVER TWIST (3700)
Hepworth
D:SC: Thomas Bentley
S: (NOVEL) Charles Dickens
Ivy Millais .... Oliver Twist
John McMahon ...... Fagin
Harry Royston ...... Bill Sykes
Alma Taylor .... Nancy
Flora Morris .... Rose Maylie
E. Rivary .... Mr Brownlow
Willie West ...... Artful Dodger
CRIME Period. Workhouse orphan escapes from thieves' kitchen. (First British 4-reel feature.)

03603
A WIFE FOR A DAY (500)
Hepworth
D: (Frank Wilson)
COMEDY Married man gets girl to pose as wife to fool rich uncle.

03604
THEN HE DID LAUGH, BUT — (600)
Hepworth
D: (Frank Wilson)
Harry Buss
COMEDY Glum man offers £100 if friend makes him laugh.

03605
PAMELA'S PARTY (750)
Hepworth
D: Hay Plumb
Alec Worcester .... Father
Gladys Sylvani .... Mother
Barbara Hepworth .... Pamela
DRAMA Couple thought to have died in train crash while their child is at party.

03606
PC HAWKEYE GOES FISHING (475)
Hepworth
D:S: Hay Plumb
Hay Plumb .... Hawkeye
COMEDY PC gets into trouble punting in regatta.

03607
THE DEAR LITTLE TEACHER (750)
Hepworth
D: (Warwick Buckland)
Alec Worcester .... The New Teacher
Alma Taylor .... The Teacher
ROMANCE Schoolmistress falls for new teacher after he has accident.

03608
AN INDIAN'S RECOMPENSE (1200)
Kineto
D: F. Martin Thornton
WESTERN Foreman saves Indian who later
saves foreman.

03609
MEPHISTO (2000) *kinema*
Natural Colour Kinematograph Co
D: Alfred de Manby, F. Martin Thornton
S: Alfred de Manby, Leedham Bantock
Alfred de Manby .... Mephisto
FANTASY Sequences for stage production, later
used in the feature, The Tempter.

03610
CLEVER EGG CONJURING *kinema*
Natural Colour Kinematograph Co
D: W.R. Booth
TRICK Conjuror performs tricks with eggs.

03611
MISCHIEVOUS MARGERY (490)
Urban Trading Co
D:S: Stuart Kinder
COMEDY Girl tricks postman, PC, swans, etc.

OCT

03612
THE ADVENTURES OF DICK TURPIN – 200
GUINEAS REWARD, DEAD OR ALIVE (1147)
B&C (MP)
D: Charles Raymond
S: Harold Brett
Percy Moran   .... Dick Turpin
Harry Paulo   .... Constable Puffin
Tom Shelford .... Sir Mortimer Biggott
Mabel Clarke .... Lady Dennis
Dorothy Foster .... Her Daughter
Frank Pollard .... Tom King
Bert Murray .... Blueskin
Raymond Cox .... O'Phelyn
Ernest A. Trimingham ..... Beetles
Harry Missouri .... Peters
ADVENTURE Highwayman holds up stage and
dances with ladies, robs banker, and eludes
Runners by posing as old man.

03613
AUTUMN ROSES (913)
B&C (MP)
D: (H.O. Martinek)
Austin Milroy .... Jack Norton
Florence Winter ..... Julie Norton
Antonia Reith .... Lucy
Rollo Balmain .... Old Kendrew
Bessie Armitage ..... Mrs Kendrew
W. Maining .... Mr Kendrew
DRAMA Deserted wife has baby and returns to
live with farming parents. (Winner of £3.3.0
scenario contest.)

03614
DORA (960)
B&C (MP)
D: (H.O. Martinek)
S: (POEM) Alfred Tennyson
Hetty Johnson .... Dora
Miss L. Reeves .... Mary Morrison
E. Lugg .... William
Bernard Vaughan .... Allan
Ernest Jay .... Child
ROMANCE Farmer's daughter takes care of
widow and child of man she loved.

03615
THE BARGEE'S REVENGE (884)
B&C (MP)

D: (Frank R. Growcott)
S: Harold Brett
Percy Moran .... Joe Williams
Dorothy Foster ..... Hetty Silver
Harry Paulo .... Jack Silver
J.A. Bentham .... Bill Carlton
CRIME Rickmansworth. Bargee's daughter saves
lock-keeper from being drowned by sacked mate.

03616
HOW 'ARRY SOLD HIS SEEDS (343)
B&C (MP)
D: (Charles Raymond)
Bob Reed
Bert Berry
COMEDY Coster sells dud seeds by planting
flowers at night.

03617
HER BACHELOR GUARDIAN (1008)
B&C (MP)
D: H.O. Martinek
Ivy Martinek .... Diana Doone
Austin Milroy .... Mervyn Charters
Una Tristram .... Pauline
Jack Houghton .... Conrad Policastro
Ernest A. Trimingham ...... Negro
ROMANCE Guardian and ward duel slanderous
suitors and realise they love one another.

03618
A FATHER'S SACRIFICE (1134)
B&C (MP)
D: (Charles Raymond)
Capt H. Hargreaves ...... John Kilroy
Charles Alexander .... Jake Mathers
Miss L.M. Swift .... Mrs Kilroy
Bert Berry .... Sheriff
Maude Derby .... Child
Jack Houghton
Herbert Trumper
ADVENTURE Australia. Man saves starving
family by posing as outlaw for reward.

03619
THE REWARD OF PERSEVERANCE (410)
Barker
D: (Bert Haldane)
COMEDY Two tramps steal bag.

03620
HIS HONOUR AT STAKE (1070)
Barker
D: (Bert Haldane)
S: Rowland Talbot
CRIME Army surgeon blamed when burglar
kills doctor's wife.

03621
THE ECCENTRIC UNCLE'S WILL (980)
Barker
D: (Bert Haldane)
S: Rowland Talbot
CRIME Heiress finds codicil which cousin tries
to steal.

03622
THE POACHER'S REFORM (905)
Barker
D: (Bert Haldane)
S: Rowland Talbot
CRIME Gamekeeper catches fiancee's father
and lets him go.

03623
THE TRAIL OF THE FATAL RUBY (980)
Barker
D: (Bert Haldane)
S: Rowland Talbot
DRAMA Bad luck dogs those connected with
theft of ruby from mummy.

03624
THE PRODIGAL WIFE (1065)
Barker
D: (Bert Haldane)
S: Rowland Talbot
PATHOS Carpenter goes mad when wife leaves
him; she returns and dies of hunger.

03625
BIG BEN'S DREAM OF GREATNESS (660)
Britannia Films (Pathe)
D: A.E. Coleby
TRICK Tall man dreams he is Caesar and
awakens with power to change objects.

03626
BATTLING KELLY (1055)
Britannia Films (Pathe)
D: A.E. Coleby
SPORT Old ex-champion takes place of absent
boxer and wins match.

03627
THE NEW OWNER OF THE BUSINESS (795)
British Anglo-American (Tyler)
D: Fred Rains
Fred Rains .... Manager
DRAMA Manager tells typist his plan to raise
wages and is sacked — she is new owner.

03628
DAN NOLAN'S CROSS (550)
British Anglo-American (Gerrard)
D: Fred Rains
George Bellamy ..... Burglar
DRAMA Child reforms burglar who later saves
her from attack.

03629
LOVE AT ARMS (525)
British Anglo-American (Gerrard)
D: Fred Rains
Fred Rains .... Frenchman
COMEDY Frenchman duels Jew for girl and
finds she is married.

03630
THE STOLEN NECKLACE (555)
British Anglo-American (Gerrard)
D: Fred Rains
Fred Rains ..... Man/Sister/Burglar/Father/PC
COMEDY Man hires burglar to steal sister's
necklace.

03631
ALADDIN IN PEARLIES (795)
British Anglo-American (Gerrard)
D: Fred Rains
Fred Rains
TRICK Coster's lamp summons Mephistopheles
to grant wishes.

03632
THE ELECTRIC LEG (500)
Clarendon
D: Percy Stow
COMEDY Prof's electrified leg carries one-
legged man into girls' dormitory.

03633
MIDNIGHT MARAUDERS (625)
Clarendon
D: Percy Stow
COMEDY Henpeck persuades friend to pose
as burglar.

03634
THE FLOODED MINE (2160)
Clarendon
D: Wilfred Noy
Dorothy Bellew .... Lily Smith
CRIME Dancer learns her husband loves her
sister and tries to drown them in flooded mine.

03635
FOR HER MOTHER'S SAKE (1030)
Clarendon
D: Wilfred Noy
Dorothy Bellew .... Marjory StClair
DRAMA Australia. Girl forced to wed usurer to
save mother's life, is saved by bushrangers.

03636
WHEN JACK COMES HOME (505)
Clarendon
D: Percy Stow
DRAMA Sailor helps sick mother and falls for
girl next door.

03637
DIDUMS AS AN ARTIST (435)
Clarendon
D: Wilfred Noy
COMEDY Child puts mother's clothes on statue.

03638
THE DANCING GIRL (2000)
Cricks & Martin
D: (Edwin J. Collins)
Una Tristram .... The Girl
DRAMA Spain. Rejected lover becomes priest
and saves rival's life.

03639
BROWN'S DAY OFF (695)
Cricks & Martin Reissue: 1915
D: (Edwin J. Collins)
COMEDY Henpeck has day by sea where wife
takes his photograph.

03640
CAPTAIN DANDY, BUSHRANGER (975)
Cricks & Martin
D: (Dave Aylott)
ADVENTURE Australia. Outlaw saves captive
girl from own gang.

03641
ECONOMICAL PETER (350)
Cricks & Martin
D; (Edwin J. Collins)
COMEDY Mean man sends broken vase as
wedding present.

03642
THE RAJAH'S REVENGE (1170)
Cricks & Martin Reissue: 1916
D: Dave Aylott
Wingold Lawrence ...... The Officer
Cicely Gilbert .... The Wife
Jack Leigh .... The Rajah
DRAMA India, 1857. Rajah tortures officer to
force wife's submission and dies in own
crocodile pool.

03643
A SHOCK-ING COMPLAINT (375)
Cricks & Martin Reissue: 1915
D: Dave Aylott
COMEDY Electric Shock machine overcharges
man.

03644
AGAINST THE TIDE (1080)
Cricks & Martin
D: Edwin J. Collins
Una Tristram .... The Girl
DRAMA Devon. Fisherman weds girl to clear
father's debt, and falls off cliff.

03645
PETER'S RIVAL (325)
Cricks & Martin
D: (Edwin J. Collins)
COMEDY Two rivals vie for girl who loves
Scotsman.

03646
THE CATS' CUP FINAL (360)
Empire Films (MP)
D:S: Arthur Cooper
TRICK Toy cats play football match.

03647
THE UNJUST STEWARD (800)
Fitz Films (Hepworth)
D:S: Lewin Fitzhamon
Constance Somers-Clarke .... Bessie
DRAMA Earl returns from war in time to save
tenant and daughter from eviction.

03648
THE FLAPPER AND THE CURATES (750)
Fitz Films Reissue: 1916 (Regal)
D:S: Lewin Fitzhamon
Constance Somers-Clarke .... The Flapper
COMEDY Man poses as missionary to win Dean's
neice.

03649
THE SUBMARINE PLANS (675)
GS Films (Hepworth)
D: Gilbert Southwell
CRIME Lieut's sister stops adventuress from
stealing plans.

03650
JACK THE HANDY MAN (475)
GS Films (Hepworth)
D: Gilbert Southwell
COMEDY Adventures of strong sailor.

03651
FRUSTRATED (660)
GS Films (Hepworth)
D: Gilbert Southwell
CRIME Sacked Clerk reinstated after saving ex-
employer from robbery.

03652
FRENCH V ENGLISH (575)
GS Films (Hepworth)
D: Gilbert Southwell
COMEDY Neighbours' jealousy leads to duel
with ink pistols.

03653
HUBBY GOES TO THE RACES (600)
Hepworth
D: (Frank Wilson)
Harry Buss .... Hubby
COMEDY Henpeck goes to races and is mistaken
for welshing bookie.

03654
JIMMY LESTER, CONVICT AND
GENTLEMAN (1100)
Hepworth
D: (Warwick Buckland)
Alec Worcester .... Jimmy Lester
Gladys Sylvani .... Elsie Lincoln
Harry Royston .... Julian Ross
Harry Gilbey .... Mr Lincoln
CRIME Jailbird saves girl from tramp, becomes
gardener, and unmasks lover as ex-convict.

03655
GHOSTS (400)
Hepworth
D: (Hay Plumb)
Harry Buss .... The Man
COMEDY Men dress as ghosts to scare each other.

03656
THE BISHOP'S BATHE (500)
Hepworth
D:S: Hay Plumb
Hay Plumb .... Bishop
COMEDY Fisherman steals clothes of swimming
bishop who then takes those of scouts.

03657
BERTIE'S BOOK OF MAGIC (325)
Hepworth
D: (Frank Wilson)
TRICK Boarder turns landlady into black cat.

03658
THE COMING-BACK OF KIT DENVER (700)
Hepworth
D: (Warwick Buckland)
Alec Worcester .... Kit Denver
SPORT Workless coal miner becomes boxer for
sake of starving family.

03659
MARY'S POLICEMAN (475)
Hepworth
D: (Frank Wilson)
COMEDY Maid's policeman hides in basket and
is taken on back of motorcycle.

03660
CHURCH AND STAGE (775) Hepworth
D: (Warwick Buckland)
Alec Worcester .... Lionel Chance
Gladys Sylvani .... Poppy Hymes
Marie de Solla .... Gossip
ROMANCE Cleric's wife leaves him to become
dancer and they reunite at church fete.

03661
THE PRIMA DONNA'S DUPES (550)
Hepworth
D: (Frank Wilson)
COMEDY Tramps rig up dummy to steal gems
from prima donna.

03662
HER AWAKENING (1075)
Hepworth
D: (Hay Plumb)
DRAMA Fisherman's wife, deserted by sophisti-
cated lover, is saved from the sea by husband.

03663
HAWKEYE, COASTGUARD (475)
Hepworth
D:S: Hay Plumb
Hay Plumb .... Hawkeye
COMEDY Coastguard swims to France, but has
no passport so returns.

03664
JO, THE WANDERER'S BOY (1000)
Hepworth
D: (Warwick Buckland)
Harry Gilbey .... Poacher
Marie de Solla .... Mother
ROMANCE Artist saves poacher's 'son' from
river and finds 'he' is girl.

03665
THE LADY OF SHALLOT (800)
Ivy Close (Hepworth)
D:SC: Elwin Neame
S: (POEM) Alfred Tennyson
Ivy Close .... The Lady
FANTASY Lady looks in cursed mirror to see
knight, and dies.

03666
A DAY'S SPORT (407)
Heron Films (U)
P: Andrew Heron
D:S: Mark Melford
Mark Melford .... Fisherman
COMEDY Fisherman's day with inept boatman.

03667
A WHITE MAN'S WAY (1250)
Kineto
D: F. Martin Thornton
WESTERN Indian girl returns to tribe after
being seduced at white man's school.

03668
ALGY, DID HE DESERVE IT? (590)
Kineto
D: F. Martin Thornton
COMEDY Girls conspire to avenge themselves
upon flirt.

03669
PEGGY GETS RID OF THE BABY (760)
John Bull Films (Cosmo)
D: Ethyle Batley
S: Ernest G. Batley
Dorothy Batley .... Peggy
Ernest G. Batley .... Father
COMEDY Jealous girl changes new baby for
puppy.

03670
THE BLOOMSBURY BURGLARS (1770)
Cinema Productions
D: A.E. Coleby
S: (SKETCH) Lew Lake
Lew Lake .... Nobbler
Bob Morris .... Jerry
COMEDY Slapstick mishaps of clumsy burglars.

03671
THE POACHER'S PARDON (1000)
Kalem (MP)
D: Sidney Olcott
S: Gene Gauntier
Jack J. Clark .... Jim Warren
Alice Hollister .... Dora Wallace
J.P. McGowan .... Wallace
CRIME Derby. Gamekeeper's daughter shot
while warning poacher.

03672
PIMPLE DOES THE TURKEY TROT (295)
Ecko (Cosmo)
D: W.P. Kellino
Fred Evans .... Pimple
COMEDY Pimple emulates dancers, is arrested,
and slips out of coat.

03673
THE TAMING OF BIG BEN (430)
Ecko (Cosmo)
D: W.P. Kellino
Fred Evans
COMEDY Loafer fights everybody until he is
beaten by wife.

03674
DAVID GARRICK (1150)
London Films (Cosmo)
D: Percy Nash
S: (PLAY) T.W. Robertson
Gerald Lawrence .... David Garrick
Mary Dibley .... Ada Ingot
Charles Rock .... Simon Ingot
George Bellamy .... Squire Chiveley
Jean Cadell .... Araminta Brown
ROMANCE 1740. Actor feigns drunkeness to
repel girl, but falls in love with her.

03675
HIS DAUGHTER'S CHOICE (925)
Art Films (AFR)
DRAMA 'Strong drama showing the choice a
girl made.'

03676
MICKY THE MOOCHER (500)
Art Films (AFR)
COMEDY 'Ripping comic'

03677
A WIFE'S MISTAKE (595)
Art Films (AFR)
DRAMA 'The story of a woman's mistake and
its consequences.'

03678
A PERFECT ANGEL (316)
Cosmopolitan
COMEDY Rich admirer poses as gardener to
expose girl's ill temper.

03679
NOT IN THESE (510)
Cosmopolitan
TRICK Clairvoyant puts spell on Jew's trousers
so they return each time he sells them.

03680
HEADS OR TAILS (310)
Cosmopolitan
COMEDY Two soldiers toss up five shilling
reward, lose it, and fight.

03681
THERE'S NO FOOL LIKE AN OLD FOOL
(355)
P&B Films (Gerrard)
COMEDY Lovers deceive old uncle and
win his consent.

03682
THE PLOT THAT FAILED (390)
P&B Films (Gerrard)
COMEDY Old sailor's plot thwarted by pretty
widow.

03683
OTHER MEN'S GOLD (570)
P&B Films (Gerrard)
CRIME Works manager tempted to rob his
employer, meets with tragic end.

03684
THE TURKEY TROT: EVERYBODY'S
DOING IT (300)
Selsior Films (NC)
Joe Bissett & Enid Sellers
MUSICAL Dance to synchronise with cinema
orchestra.

03685
TO THE VICTOR THE SPOILS (503)
Vampire Films (MP)
Yukio Tani .... Tami
DRAMA Gambler demands girl in lieu of debt
but is defeated by fiance, a ju jitsu expert.

NOV

03686
WON BY A SNAPSHOT (430)
Barker
D: (Bert Haldane)
S: Rowland Talbot
COMEDY Misadventures of camera enthusiast.

03687
MURIEL'S DOUBLE (1225)
Barker
D: (Bert Haldane)
S: Rowland Talbot
CRIME 'Exciting drama featuring clever detec-
tive work .'

03688
A BROTHER'S SACRIFICE (985)
Barker
D: (Bert Haldane)
S: Rowland Talbot
DRAMA Gamekeeper gives up nurse for sake of
wounded brother.

03689
A FIGHT FOR LIFE (420)
Barker
D: (Bert Haldane)
S: Rowland Talbot
COMEDY Groom and gardener fight blindfold
duel for maid.

03690
THE TELL-TALE UMBRELLA (615)
Barker
D: (Bert Haldane)
S: Rowland Talbot
COMEDY Married man in trouble when
mistakenly takes girl's umbrella.

03691
NEIGHBOURS (700)
Barker
D: (Bert Haldane)
S: Rowland Talbot
Edward Viner .... The Son
Sybil Tracy .... The Daughter
Tom Coventry .... The Father
Rachel de Solla .... The Mother
COMEDY Neighbours end feud when children
elope.

03692
LIEUTENANT DARING AND THE PLANS OF
THE MINEFIELDS (1425) USA: THE INTER-
NATIONAL SPIES
B&C (MP)
D: H.O. Martinek
S: Harold Brett
Percy Moran .... Lt Daring
Charles Raymond .... Leon Scumwasser
Dickie Thorpe .... Marcella
Lt E.H. Hotchkiss .... Himself
Charles Austin .... Himself
CHASE Spy paints plan on girl's back and is
caught in Boulogne after chase by motorcycle,
horse, car, and monoplane.

03693
THE FAIRY DOLL (718)
B&C (MP)
D: Laurence Caird
Alice de Winton .... Mrs Drayton
Edward Durrant .... Will Drayton
Percy Dyer .... Little Will
Zola Woodruff .... Mary
Marjorie Manners .... Fairy
FANTASY Lady's gift doll saves poor girl's life.
(For 'Evening News Dress a Doll Fund'.)

03694
HIDDEN WEALTH (820)
B&C (MP)
D: Wallett Waller
Edward Durrant .... Edgar Manning
Clara Moore .... Lucy Stokes
Bernard Vaughan .... Farmer Stokes
Joseph Kirkwood .... Fernando Contie
ROMANCE Man wins girl by finding coal on
poor father's farm.

03695
A CHILD, A WAND AND A WISH (825)
B&C (MP)
D: (H.O. Martinek)
Helen Beresford ..... Molly Grey
Maudie Dagmar ..... Babs
Dick Tyrrell .... Shopkeeper
DRAMA Sick widow's daughter steals panto-
mime magic wand and is helped by rich neigh-
bours.

03696
THE MOUNTAINEER'S ROMANCE (1432)
B&C (MP)
D: Charles Raymond
S: Percy Moran
H.O. Martinek .... Ben Sayers
Ivy Martinek .... Nan Sayers
Percy Moran .... Jim Discombe
Dickie Thorpe .... Myrtle Madison
ADVENTURE Derby. Man fights sister's
fiance, thinking he loves American tourist.

03697
THE FIRST CHRONICLES OF DON Q – THE
DARK BROTHERS OF THE CIVIL GUARD
(1559)
B&C (MP)
D: H.O. Martinek
S: (STORY) Hesketh Pearson
SC: Harold Brett
Charles Raymond .... Don Q
Ivy Martinek .... Isabelillia
Percy Moran .... Manuelo
ADVENTURE Dead guard's colleagues pose as
bandits but are tricked by chief.

03698
THE ADVENTURES OF DICK TURPIN – A
DEADLY FOE, A PACK OF HOUNDS, AND
SOME MERRY MONKS (1198)
B&C (MP)
D: Charles Raymond
S: Harold Brett
Percy Moran .... Dick Turpin
Harry Missouri .... Peters
ADVENTURE Highwayman poses as monk and
is chased by Royal Surrey foxhounds.

03699
LILY OF LETCHWORTH LOCK (1115)
B&C (MP)
D: H.O. Martinek, Percy Moran
S: Harold Brett
Percy Moran .... Frank Mason
Dorothy Foster .... Lily
Ivy Martinek .... Zara Leigh
DRAMA Lock-keepers daughter saves fiance
from drifting barge set alight by jealous rival.

03700
A FISHERMAN'S INFATUATION (2012)
B&C (MP)
D: Wallett Waller
S: Harold Brett
Wallett Waller .... Dan
Dorothy Foster ...... Sybil
ROMANCE Polperro fisherman follows flighty
actress to London, then works way home.

03701
THE SMUGGLER'S REVENGE (990)
Union Films
ADVENTURE Cheated smuggler betrays
gang to disguised detective.

03702
FLO THE FLAPPER (428)
Britannia Films (Pathe)
D:S: Lewin Fitzhamon
Constance Somers-Clarke .... Flo
Marie Royston .... Girl
COMEDY Children play tricks on colonel and
spinster.

03703
HIS BURGLAR BROTHER (939)
Britannia Films (Pathe)
D: (A.E. Coleby)
CRIME Ex-convict takes blame when he catches
brother robbing house.

03704
LIGHT AFTER DARKNESS (2013)
Britannia Films (Pathe)
D: (A.E. Coleby)
DRAMA Reporter exposes fiancee's father as
rubber swindler but wins her back after losing
sight.

03705
THE WOLF AND THE WAIF (465)
British Anglo-American (Gerrard)
D: Fred Rains
ANIMAL Dog saves waif and catches ruffian.

03506
LIEUTENANT ROSE AND THE PATENT
AEROPLANE (1075)
Clarendon
D: Percy Stow
P.G. Norgate .... Lt Rose
Dorothy Bellew ...... Girl
CRIME Lieut escapes from spy's schooner and
wirelesses for help.

03707
WHERE'S BABY? (520)
Clarendon
D: Percy Stow
COMEDY Father bakes loaf of bread and finc
baby inside.

03708
DR BRIAN PELLIE AND THE SECRET
DESPATCH (745)
Clarendon
D: Percy Stow
CRIME Crook chased by tram and caught after
rooftop fight.

03709
NINA'S EVENING PRAYER (735)
Clarendon
D: Percy Stow
DRAMA Drunkard reforms on overhearing
child's prayer.

03710
A CHRISTMAS ADVENTURE (600)
Clarendon
D: Percy Stow
ADVENTURE Fisherfolk rescue children who
run away from lord's party.

03711
ALL'S FAIR IN LOVE (425)
Clarendon
D: Percy Stow
Dorothy Bellew .... Dorothy
COMEDY Girl's father mistakenly persecutes
suitor's rival.

03712
SHE MUST HAVE SWALLOWED IT (450)
Clarendon
D: Percy Stow
COMEDY Horse eats baby and is cut open by
vet.

03713
WILLIAM DRAKE, THIEF (1020)
Cricks & Martin
D: (Charles Calvert)
CRIME Suspected man proves maid stole jewels.

03714
WHEN FATHER FETCHED THE DOCTOR
(400)
Cricks & Martin Reissue: 1915
D: (Dave Aylott)
CHASE Father rides bicycle to fetch doctor.

03715
BLACKMAIL (1070)
Cricks & Martin
D: Edwin J. Collins
CRIME Knight saves daughter by forcing black-
mailer off cliff.

03716
HENPECK'S DOUBLE (420)
Cricks & Martin Reissue: 1916
D: (Dave Aylott)
COMEDY Actor poses as henpecked friend to
fool wife.

03717
THE BANDIT'S DAUGHTER (975)
Cricks & Martin

D: Edwin J. Collins
Una Tristram .... The Daughter
ADVENTURE Devon. Bandit's daughter fetches
troops to save captive lieut.

03718
WHAT'S THE JOKE? (335)
Cricks & Martin Reissue: 1916
D: (Dave Aylott)
CHASE Crowd pursues laughing man to read
joke in his paper.

03719
THE MISSING TIARA (840)
Cricks & Martin
D: (Charles Calvert)
CRIME Hypnotist forces man to steal
fiancee's tiara.

03720
CAPTAIN CUFF'S NEIGHBOURS (390)
Cricks & Martin
D: (Dave Aylott)
COMEDY Two spinsters mistake retired sailor
for bachelor.

03721
NAN IN FAIRYLAND (1250)
Cricks & Martin Reissue: 1916
D: Edwin J. Collins
Edwin J. Collins .... PC
FANTASY Orphan dreams Puck saves her from
ogre; she is adopted by PC.

03722
DIDDLED! (490)
Cricks & Martin
D: (Charles Calvert)
COMEDY Man poses as mummy to fool professor
and help daughter elope.

03723
PRIVATE HECTOR, GENTLEMAN (1345)
Cricks & Martin
D: Dave Aylott
WAR Private stops commissioned cousin from
selling plans to enemy.

03724
A SMOKY STORY (495)
Cricks & Martin
D: (Charles Calvert)
COMEDY Hookah smoker dreams he is in harem.

03725
A WOMAN'S WHIM (670)
Cosmopolitan
COMEDY Militant girl changes mind when
suitor treats her as he would a man.

03726
WHO DID IT? (610)
Cosmopolitan
COMEDY Burglar dons bear skin to rob party
and police, territorials and fire brigade are called.

03727
PIMPLE AND THE SNAKE (320)
Ecko (Cosmo)
D: W.P. Kellino
Fred Evans .... Pimple
CHASE Pimple pursues windblown feather boa
in mistake for snake.

03728
THE WHISTLING BET (490)
Ecko (Cosmo)
D: W.P. Kellino
Fred Evans .... Fred
Joe Evans .... Joe
COMEDY Man bets rival to dance whenever
whistle is played.

03729
GRAND HARLEQUINADE (890)
Ecko (Cosmo)
D: W.P. Kellino
Fred Evans .... Clown
Joe Evans
COMEDY Christmas harlequinade

03730
PIMPLE GETS A QUID (360)
Folly Films (Cosmo)
D:S: Fred Evans, Joe Evans
Fred Evans .... Pimple
Joe Evans .... Fare
COMEDY Cabman paid by his fare, and drives
away with his father.

03731
PIMPLE WINS A BET (350)
Folly Films (Cosmo)
D:S: Fred Evans, Joe Evans
Fred Evans .... Pimple
Joe Evans .... Victim
COMEDY Pimple bets sixpence to pick up a
cork and kicks his victims.

03732
A LETTER TO THE PRINCESS (1000)
Edison
D: Ashley Miller
S: Bannister Merwin
Mary Fuller .... Mary
Marc McDermott .... Lt Straker
Miriam Nesbitt .... Spy
Stewart Dyer .... Rev W. Cooper
CRIME Foreign spy poses as chauffeur to obtain
secret letter.
(Episode in series WHAT HAPPENED TO
MARY.)

03733
OLD MOTHER HUBBARD (410)
Empire Films (MP)
D:S: Arthur Cooper
TRICK Nursery rhyme enacted by toys.

03734
CINDERELLA (997)
Empire Films (MP)
D:S: Arthur Cooper
TRICK Fairy story enacted by toys.

03735
THE PONY WHO PAID THE RENT (700)
Fitz Films *Reissue:* 1916 (DFSA)
D:S: Lewin Fitzhamon
Constance Somers-Clarke .... Girl
Roy Royston .... Boy
ANIMAL Widow gives her child's pony for
rent; her dog frees it and saves landlord from
drowning.

03736
THE MISUNDERSTANDING (1000)
GS Films (Hepworth)
D: Gilbert Southwell
DRAMA Rejected suitor attempts suicide
but saves drowning girl.

03737
DETECTIVE FERRIS (925)
GS Films (Hepworth)
D: Gilbert Southwell
CRIME Tec poses as crone to save prince
from anarchists.

03738
THE HEART OF A MAN (625)
GS Films (Hepworth)
D: Gilbert Southwell
WESTERN Miner robs partner and causes wife's
death.

03739
A CHILD'S DREAM OF CHRISTMAS (750)
GS Films (Hepworth)
D: Gilbert Southwell
FANTASY Girl dreams of fairy-tale characters.

03740
FATHER'S COAT TO THE RESCUE (425)
GS Films (Hepworth)
D: Gilbert Southwell
CRIME Girl puts on father's police uniform
and arrests burglar.

03741
TOWN MOUSE AND COUNTRY MOUSE (875)
Hepworth
D: (Hay Plumb)
Alec Worcester .... Blacksmith
Marie de Solla .... Mother
ROMANCE Mother helps daughter win smith
and thwart farmer.

03742
WAS HE A GERMAN SPY? (525)
Hepworth
D: Hay Plumb
COMEDY Lulworth. Henpeck taking photo-
graphs mistaken for spy.

03743
JASMINE (900)
Hepworth
D: (Warwick Buckland)
Gladys Sylvani .... Jasmine Young
Alec Worcester .... The Man
ROMANCE Miller loves ward but lets her marry
man who saved her life.

03744
A CASE OF BURGLARS (550)
Hepworth
D: (Frank Wilson)
COMEDY Maid foils burglars who pose as
piano delivery men.

03745
HER ONLY SON (1100)
Hepworth
D: (Hay Plumb)
Alec Worcester .... Dick Meredith
Gladys Sylvani .... The Girl
Marie de Solla .... Mrs Meredith
DRAMA Man steals mother's gold, becomes
miller, marries, and is forgiven.

03746
COOK'S BID FOR FAME (550)
Hepworth
D: (Frank Wilson)
COMEDY Filmstruck cook takes part in
cowboy film.

03747
LADY ANGELA AND THE BOY (925)
Hepworth
D: (Warwick Buckland)
DRAMA Rich child feigns blindness to collect
money for sick newsboy.

03748
THE STOLEN PICTURE (625)
Hepworth
D: (Frank Wilson)
COMEDY Curate returning corsets to shop is
mistaken for picture thief.

03749
A BOLD VENTURE (1050)
Hepworth
D: (Warwick Buckland)

S: Muriel Alleyne
CRIME Bank robbers pose as rag pickers and
frame clerk for theft.

03750
KING ROBERT OF SICILY (1100)
Hepworth
D: Hay Plumb
S: (POEM) Henry Longfellow
Alec Worcester .... King Robert/Jester
Alma Taylor .... Princess
FANTASY Jester changes places with arrogant
King, and is revealed as angel.

03751
THE CODICIL (1050)
Hepworth
D: (Warwick Buckland)
Harry Royston
CRIME Grandfather foils grasping couple by
posting will before he dies.

03752
PYGMALION AND GALATEA (625)
Ivy Close Films (Hepworth)
D:S: Elwin Neame
Ivy Close .... Galatea
FANTASY Sculptor's statue comes to life.

03753
A DAY IN LONDON (680)
Gaumont
D: (Lewin Fitzhamon)
COMEDY Man poses as maid to save girl from
flirtatious uncle.

03754
PEGGY BECOMES A BOY SCOUT (470)
John Bull Films (Cosmo)
D: Ethyle Batley
S: Ernest G. Batley
Dorothy Batley .... Peggy
COMEDY Girl dons brother's uniform and tries
to do good deeds.

03755
AN OUTLAW YET A MAN (1250)
Kineto
D: F.Martin Thornton
WESTERN Outlaw pardoned after saving
sheriff's child from Indians.

03756
TIT FOR TAT (645)
Kineto
D: F. Martin Thornton
COMEDY Algy poses as PC to wrest cheque
from flirtatious uncle.

03757
JACK SHEPPARD (3200)
London Films (Cosmo)
D: Percy Nash
S: (PLAY) John Buckstone
CRIME 1720. Capture and escape of notorious
highwayman.

03758
IN FAIRYLAND (-) *kinema*
Natural Colour Kinematograph Co
D: (Walter Booth)
TRICK Child dreams of fairies, Mephistopheles,
etc.

03759
THE CONJUROR AS A GOOD SAMARITAN
(-) *kinema*
Natural Colour Kinematograph Co
D: (Walter Booth)
TRICK Conjuror hypnotises baliffs and saves
widow's children.

03760
SANTA CLAUS (2000) *kinema*
Natural Colour Kinematograph Co *Reissue:*
1913
D: F. Martin Thornton, R.H. Callum,
W.R. Booth
S: Alfred de Manby, Leedham Bantock,
Harold Simpson
Leedham Bantock .... Santa Claus
Margaret Favronova .... Ting-a-ling
FANTASY Girl dreams she visits toyland
and helps Santa Claus.

03761
IN GOLLYWOG LAND (590) *kinema* USA:
GOLLYWOG'S MOTOR ACCIDENT
Natural Colour Kinematograph Co *Reissue:*
1916 (Kineto)
D: F. Martin Thornton, W.R. Booth
TRICK Gollywog and apple; Gollywog's motor
mishap.

03762
THE PURITAN (850)
Art Films (AFR)
COMEDY 'A ripping comic'

03763
THE ARAB GIRL'S LOVE (1000)
Art Films (AFR)
DRAMA 'A story full of interesting dramatic
situations."

03764
RAGTIME TEXAS TOMMY (350)
Selsior Films
Harry Perry & Millicent Ray
MUSICAL Dance to synchronise with cinema
orchestras.

03765
SHERLOCK HOLMES (series)
Franco-British Film Co -Eclair (Fenning)
D: Georges Treville
S: (STORIES) Arthur Conan Doyle
Georges Treville .... Sherlock Holmes
Mr Moyse .... Dr Watson

03766
1—THE SPECKLED BAND (1700) (A)

03767
2—SILVER BLAZE (1300) (U)

03768
3—THE BERYL CORONET (2300) (U)

03769
4—THE MUSGRAVE RITUAL (1290) (U)

03770
5—THE REIGATE SQUIRES (1800) (U)

03771
6—THE STOLEN PAPERS (1400) (U)

03772
7—THE MYSTERY OF BOSCOMBE VALE
(1700) (U)

03773
8—THE COPPER BEECHES (1700) (U)
CRIMES Private detective solves various crimes.

03774
THE CHAPERONE (590)
Urban Trading Co
D: (Stuart Kinder)
COMEDY Student fools friends and girls by
posing as woman.

03775
MAKING A MAN OF HIM (550)
Urban Trading Co

D: (F. Martin Thornton)·
WESTERN Stockbroker sends son to brother's
ranch.'

03776
SPOT AS CUPID (635)
Urban Trading Co Reissue: 1915
D:S: Stuart Kinder
Irene Vernon .... Gladys
Spot the Urbanora Dog
ANIMAL Dog patches quarrel by posting
discarded love-letters.

03777
NETTIE'S RIDE
Sydney Carter (New Century)
Mr Bulmer
Mrs Bulmer
Mr Canon Dalby
DRAMA Yorkshire.

DEC
03778
THE FIGHTING PARSON (3000)
Barker (Jury)
D: George Gray, Bert Haldane
S: (PLAY) George Gray, Chris Davis
George Gray .... George Gordon
DRAMA Disowned heir takes blame for brother's
bastard, joins church and fights slum bully.

03779
HOW VANDYCK WON HIS WIFE (930)
Barker
D: (Bert Haldane)
S: Rowland Talbot
Edward Viner .... Vandyck
Sybil Tracy .... Millie Marlow
Peter Gale .... Jimmy
Tom Coventry .... Mr Marlow
Rachel de Solla .... Mrs Marlow
Blanche Forsythe .... The Model
COMEDY Poor artist sells girl's portrait to
advertise face-cream.

03780
FOR BABY'S SAKE (690)
Barker
D: (Bert Haldane)
S: Rowland Talbot
Blanche Forsythe .... Millie.
Tom Coventry ....PC Robert
Rachel de Solla .... Mrs Brooks
DRAMA Widow steals milk for baby and is
adopted by victims.

03781
THE STAB OF DISGRACE (940)
Barker
D: (Bert Haldane)
S: Rowland Talbot
Roy Travers .... Ted
May Morton .... Mary
Peter Gale .... Peter
J. Hastings Batson .... Old Jim
DRAMA Gamekeeper dies of shock when
drunkard son is jailed for poaching.

03782
ROBERT'S LOST SUPPER (470)
Barker
D: (Bert Haldane)
S: Rowland Talbot
Peter Gale .... Nobby
Tom Coventry .... PC Robert
Rachel de Solla ...... The Mistress
COMEDY Burglar thwarts PC by finding cook's
love-letter.

03783
JEFF'S DOWNFALL (995)
Barker

D: (Bert Haldane)
S: Rowland Talbot
Edward Viner .... Jeff
Sybil Tracy ....Ruby
Edward Burnham .... Charley
CRIME Thief repents after breaking into house
of man who helped him escape.

03784
HOW MOLLY AND POLLY GOT PA'S
CONSENT (575)
Barker
D: (Bert Haldane)
S: Rowland Talbot
Doreen O'Connor .... Molly Perkins
May Morton .... Polly Perkins
Edward Viner .... Frank
Edward Burnham .... George
Tom Coventry .... Pa Perkins
COMEDY Girls persuade father to let them visit
theatre.

03785
THE DRAUGHTSMAN'S REVENGE (1115)
Barker
D: (Bert Haldane)
S: Rowland Talbot
Edward Viner .... Sidney Lang
Sybil Tracy .... Mary Hardacre
Fred Paul .... James Goff
Doreen O'Connor .... Alice Goff
Tom Coventry .... Mr Hardacre
PATHOS Artist jailed for stealing bread finds
wife dead and dies trying to kill betrayer.

03786
LIEUTENANT DARING AND THE PHOTO-
GRAPHING PIGEON (1245)
B&C (MP)
D: (Charles Raymond)
S: Harold Brett
Percy Moran ...._ Lt Daring
Ivy Martinek .... Girl
W. Gladstone Haley .... Spy
CRIME Lt saves spy's daughter from fire and
she saves him from sewer.

03787
A FACTORY GIRL'S HONOUR (1000)
B&C (MP)
D:S: Harold Brett
Dorothy Foster .... Kitty Burnett
Violet Graham .... Daphne
S.P. Goodyear Kettley ..... Caleb Standish
DRAMA Owner's daughter poses as worker to
expose rapacious foreman.

03788
FROM COWARDICE TO HONOUR (1377)
B&C (MP)
D: Charles Raymond
S: Harold Brett
H.O. Martinek .... Neville Murray
Dorothy Foster .... Miss Murray
W. Gladstone Haley .... Negro Servant
WAR America, period. Deserter's sister poses
as confederate soldier to deliver despatches.

03789
DON Q — HOW HE OUTWITTED DON LUIS
(1113)
B&C (MP)
D: H.O. Martinek
S: (STORY) Hesketh Pearson
SC: Harold Brett
Charles Raymond .... Don Q
Ivy Martinek .... Isabelilla
Percy Moran .... Don Luis
W. Gladstone Haley .... Felipe
ADVENTURE Girl's warning causes bandit
chief to exchange glasses with hired assassin.

03790
DON Q AND THE ARTIST (1170)
B&C (MP)
D: H.O. Martinek
S:(STORY) Hesketh Pearson
SC: Harold Brett
Charles Raymond .... Don Q
H.O. Martinek .... Gevil Hay
ADVENTURE Bandit chief tests British captive
by arranging his escape.

03791
DON Q — HOW HE TREATED THE PAROLE OF
GEVIL HAY (958)
B & C (MP)
D: H.O. Martinek
S: (STORY) Hesketh Pearson
SC: Harold Brett
Charles Raymond ..... Don Q
H.O. Martinek .... Gevil Hay
ADVENTURE Bandit chief tests British capture by
arranging his escape.

03792
FROM COUNTRY TO TOWN (2112)
Britannia Films
D: (A.E. Coleby)
ROMANCE Countryman falls in love with Lady,
is shamed by rustic parents, and returns to
village sweetheart.

03793
HER SISTER'S SILENCE (1287)
Britannia Films
D: (A.E. Coleby)
DRAMA Girl takes blame for married sister's
lapse, and is cleared by dying confession.

03794
THE OLD COLONEL'S GRATITUDE (1863)
Britannia Films (Pathe)
D: (A.E. Coleby)
ROMANCE Sgt appeals to colonel to win
approval for children's marriage.

03795
THE ORPHAN (1966)
Britannia Films (Pathe) *Reissue:* 1915
D: (A.E. Coleby)
ROMANCE Bully adopts orphan who falls
in love with artist who paints her portrait.

03796
AN AFRIKANDER GIRL (1005)
Clarendon
D: Wilfred Noy
Dorothy Bellew .... Jess
WAR Africa. Boer captures British officer but
frees him for his sister's sake.

03797
A BREACH IN BREECHES (635)
Clarendon
D: Percy Stow
COMEDY Military student loses trouserleg in
headmistress's mantrap.

03798
LIEUTENANT ROSE IN CHINA SEAS (1215)
Clarendon
D: Percy Stow
P.G. Norgate .... Lt Rose
WAR China. Lieut escapes from Boxers' torture
and shells them.

03799
NORAH'S DEBT OF HONOUR (1100)
Clarendon
D: Wilfred Noy
Norah Chaplin .... Norah
CRIME Gambler forces girl to steal but her
brother intervenes.

03800
A BALD STORY (600)
Clarendon
D: Percy Stow
Norah Chaplin
COMEDY Bald man uses vegetable fertilizer to
grow hair.

03801
AN ADVENTURESS OUTWITTED (715)
Clarendon
D: Percy Stow
CRIME Army officer's young brother foils
woman spy.

03802
THE EYE OF THE IDOL (1285)
Clarendon
D: Wilfred Noy
CRIME Explorer steals jewel from god and is
tracked by high priest.

03803
LORNA DOONE (4300)
Clarendon (Gaumont)
D: Wilfred Noy
S:(NOVEL) R.D. Blackmore
Dorothy Bellew .... Lorna Doone
ADVENTURE Exmoor, 1625. Yeoman loves
outlaw's daughter who is stolen heiress. (First
British 5-reel feature.)

03804
MOTHER'S DAY OUT (390)
Clarendon
D: Percy Stow
COMEDY Father tries to cope with children
and escaped parrot.

03805
CAUGHT IN HIS OWN NET (990)
Cricks & Martin
D: (Edwin J. Collins)
Charles Vane .... Squire
CRIME Tec posing as tramp catches crook who
kidnapped own fiancee.

03806
THE TRIALS OF A MERRY WIDOW (710)
Cricks & Martin
D: (Charles Calvert)
Una Tristram .... Mary
Leah Marlborough ...... Woman
Charles Vane .... Employer
COMEDY Widow is too pretty to retain any job.

03807
HER BROTHER'S TUTOR (930)
Cricks & Martin
D: (Edwin J. Collins)
Una Tristram .... Mary Ewell
John Miller .... Sir George Ewell
DRAMA Jealous tutor cripples pupil but later
saves him from fire.

03808
CAUGHT (430)
Cricks & Martin
D: (Dave Aylott)
COMEDY Crook's policeman lover hides in
cupboard and catches burglar.

03809
A WORKMAN'S HONOUR (990)
Cricks & Martin
D: (Charles Calvert)
CRIME Crooked manager frames workman who
later saves him from fire.

03810
MUCH ADO ABOUT — !! (460)
Cricks & Martin

D: (Dave Aylott)
COMEDY Jealous man hires tec to investigate
wife's locked box.

03811
WHAT MATTER THE PRICE (645)
Cricks & Martin
D: (Edwin J. Collins)
Charles Vane .... Doctor
DRAMA Suffragette destroys pillar-box with
letter that would have saved child's life.

03812
TOOTLES BUYS A GUN (435)
Cricks & Martin
D: (Dave Aylott)
COMEDY Amateur sportsman joins shooting
party and kills rook.

03813
PAUL SLEUTH CRIME INVESTIGATOR:
THE BURGLARY SYNDICATE (1140)
Cricks & Martin
D: Dave Aylott
Charles Vane .... Paul Sleuth
Minna Grey .... The Girl
CRIME Tec captures killer, poses as him, and
captures gang.

03814
SOLD, A 'BEAR' FACT (430)
Cricks & Martin
D: (Dave Aylott)
COMEDY Newlywed dons bear-skin to
escape landlord.

03815
THE GREAT TIGER RUBY (1090)
Cricks & Martin
D: (Charles Calvert)
CRIME Tec poses as old woman to catch gem
thief posing as sailor.

03816
ADHESION (410)
Cricks & Martin
D: (Dave Aylott)
COMEDY Boy uses strong glue to play tricks
on cook, sister and lover.

03817
THE THIEF (720)
Cricks & Martin
D: (Edwin J. Collins)
Una Tristram .... Cissie Dalmaine
Jack Jarman .... Jack Spicer
Leah Marlborough ...... Mrs Spicer
CRIME Sailor blamed when sweetheart's brother
steals wages to pay gambling.

03818
WHEN IT COMES OFF (485)
Cricks & Martin
D: (Dave Aylott)
COMEDY Suffragettes take over police force.

03819
PAUL SLEUTH — THE MYSTERY OF THE
ASTORIAN CROWN PRINCE (765)
Cricks & Martin
D: Dave Aylott
Charles Vane .... Paul Sleuth
CRIME Tec poses as King to save Prince from
kidnappers.

03820
GRANDAD'S EXILE (910)
Cricks & Martin
D: (Charles Calvert)
PATHOS Sailor's wife puts father in workhouse
and his daughter is run over while following him.

03821
THE COSTER'S HONEYMOON (405)
Ecko (Cosmo)
D: W.P. Kellino
Brothers Egbert
COMEDY Coster arrested at railway station
over mixup of baggage.

03822
PIMPLE'S FIRE BRIGADE (415)
Folly Films (Cosmo)
D:S: Fred Evans, Joe Evans
Fred Evans .... Pimple
Joe Evans .... Fireman
COMEDY Slow engine arrives too late so fire-
men play football.

03823
PIMPLE BECOMES AN ACROBAT (295)
Folly Films (Cosmo)
D:S: Fred Evans, Joe Evans
Fred Evans .... Pimple
COMEDY Pimple tries to emulate street
acrobat.

03824
PIMPLE'S EGGS-TRAORDINARY STORY
(295)
Folly Films (Cosmo)
D:S: Fred Evans, Joe Evans
Fred Evans .... Pimple
COMEDY Grocery boy pretends he fought
thieves to explain broken eggs

03825
YIDDLE ON MY FIDDLE (390)
Ecko (Cosmo)
D: W.P. Kellino
Brothers Egbert
COMEDY Man fools rich aunt by miming to
concealed violinist.

03826
THE FOUNDLING (1000)
Edison
D: Ashley Miller
S: Harry Furniss
Harry Furniss .... The Artist
Marc McDermott ... Frank
Miriam Nesbitt ...... The Girl
ROMANCE Dorking. Club candidate proves
parentage to win vicar's daughter.

03827
A SUFFRAGETTE IN SPITE OF HIMSELF
(600)
Edison
D: Ashley Miller
S: Bannister Merwin
Marc McDermott .... The Gentleman
Miriam Nesbitt .... His Wife
Ethel Browning .... The Maid
COMEDY Man arrested while posing as woman
and is saved by suffragettes.

03828
PIMPLE AS A CINEMA ACTOR (495)
Folly Films (Cosmo)
D:S: Fred Evans, Joe Evans
Fred Evans .... Pimple
COMEDY Film aspirant must cycle, juggle
and wrestle.

03829
PIMPLE AS A BALLET DANCER (240)
Folly Films (Cosmo)
D:S: Fred Evans, Joe Evans
Fred Evans .... Pimple
COMEDY Pimple tries to emulate ballerina.

03830
PIMPLE AS A RENT COLLECTOR (405)
Folly Films (Cosmo)

D:S: Fred Evans, Joe Evans
Fred Evans .... Pimple
COMEDY Pimple has trouble trying to collect
rents.

03831
TEN LITTLE NIGGER BOYS (380)
Empire Films (MP)
D:S: Arthur Cooper
TRICK Nursery rhyme enacted by toys.

03832
A VILLAGE SCANDAL (800)
Gaumont
D: (Lewin Fitzhamon)
COMEDY Wiltshire. Villagers mistake
rehearsal by London actors for real crime.

03833
THE COPPER'S REVENGE (880)
Gaumont
D: (Lewin Fitzhamon)
COMEDY PC changes places with dummy
policeman which a rough couple use as
punching-bag.

03834
A HARLEQUINADE LET LOOSE (550)
Hepworth
D: (Hay Plumb)
Chrissie White
COMEDY Drunken property-man dreams of
harlequinade in streets.

03835
A WOMAN'S WIT (625)
Hepworth
D: (Warwick Buckland)
Alec Worcester .... Jack Dale
Gladys Sylvani .... Lucy Price
John MacAndrews ..... Sir William Drainger
CRIME Devon. Engineer's fiance steals aero-
plane plans to save him from ambush by rivals.

03836
A NEW ALADDIN (500)
Hepworth
D: (Frank Wilson)
TRICK Tramp finds lamp and dreams it is
Aladdin's.

03837
FOR LOVE AND LIFE (925)
Hepworth
D: Hay Plumb
Alma Taylor .... Jean
ADVENTURE Lulworth. Girl swims to save
lover from post in sea.

03838
THE GENEROSITY OF MR SMITH (675)
Hepworth
D: (Warwick Buckland)
COMEDY Girl thwarts married flirt by buying
gifts and sending them to wife.

03839
HAWKEYE, SHOWMAN (600)
Hepworth
D:S: Hay Plumb
Hay Plumb .... Hawkeye
COMEDY Showman offers money to whoever
ties him in knot, but his hidden confederate
decamps.

03840
MR POORLUCK AS AN AMATEUR
DETECTIVE (475)
Hepworth
D: (Frank Wilson)
Harry Buss .... Poorluck
COMEDY Rejected policeman mistaken for
burglar.

03841
THE HEART OF A WOMAN (625)
Hepworth
D: (Warwick Buckland)
Flora Morris .... The Spy
CRIME Woman spy falls for victim and returns
stolen treaty.

03842
THE LUCK OF THE RED LION (750)
Hepworth
D: (Hay Plumb)
COMEDY Innkeeper mistakes poor actor for
rich prince.

03843
PLOT AND PASH (750)
Hepworth
D: Hay Plumb
Madge Campbell
Jack Raymond
Chrissie White
Johnny Butt
COMEDY Villain frames hero for killing
heroine's old father.

03844
THE SLEEPING BEAUTY (1000)
Ivy Close Films (Hepworth)
D:S: Elwin Neame
Ivy Close .... Sleeping Beauty
FANTASY Cursed princess awakened by prince's
kiss.

03845
THE HERNCRAKE WITCH (710)
Heron Films (U)
P: Andrew Heron
D:S: Mark Melford
Jakidawdra Melford .... Jakidawdra
Mark Melford .... The Father
FANTASY Witch helps grandchild's romance
by changing lover's father into woman.

03846
THE LAND OF THE NURSERY RHYMES
(436)
Heron Films (U) *Reissue:* 1914
P: Andrew Heron
D:S: Mark Melford
Mark Melford
Jakidawdra Melford
FANTASY Girl dreams of nursery rhyme
characters.

03847
THE LEGEND OF KING COPHETUA (625)
Ivy Close Films-Hepworth
D:S: Elwin Neame
Ivy Close .... The Beggarmaid
Alec Worcester .... King Cophetua
ROMANCE Period. King weds beggarmaid.

03848
MICHAEL DWYER (850)
Irish Films (Cosmo)
CRIME Ireland. Outlaw thwarts informer and
escapes capture.

03849
LOVE IN A FIX (965)
Irish Films (Cosmo)
COMEDY Ireland. Rivals duel for girl; she
accepts loser.

03850
GRETNA GREEN (700)
Heron Films (U)
P: Andrew Heron
D: Mark Melford
S:(SKETCH) Mark Melford
Mark Melford .... Father
CHASE Period. Father chases elopers but
arrives at smithy too late.

03851
HIS FIRST SOVEREIGN (484)
Heron Films (U)
P: Andrew Heron
D:S: Mark Melford
Mark Melford
COMEDY Soldier hides sovereign in scabbard.

03852
THROUGH THE FLAMES (1250)
John Bull Films (Cosmo)
D: Ethyle Batley
S: Ernest G. Batley
Dorothy Batley .... Peggy
Ernest G. Batley
CRIME Child crosses telephone wire when
murderous cousin sets fire to house.

03853
WHERE THERE'S A WILL THERE'S A WAY
(695)
Kineto
D: F. Martin Thornton
COMEDY Algy hires men to kidnap girl's
father, then rescues him.

03854
ILLUSTRATED PROVERBS (355)
Kineto
D: (F. Martin Thornton)
COMEDY Scenes illustrating familiar proverbs.

03855
CHILDREN'S THOUGHTS FOR THE
FUTURE (295)
Kineto Reissue: 1918, AMBITIOUS CHILDREN
D: (F. Martin Thornton)
COMEDY Children dress according to ambition:
artist, peeress, etc.

03856
THE SOCIETY PLAYWRIGHT (1410)
Kineto Reissue: 1917, POTTED PLAYS No 1
D: F. Martin Thornton
COMEDY Amateur actors perform play and
burn down theatre.

03857
THE KNOCKOUT BLOW (575)
Kineto

D: (F. Martin Thornton)
SPORT 'A famous hard-fought encounter in
the boxing ring.'

03858
IN THE SHADOW OF THE ROPE (1000)
London (Cosmo)
D: Percy Nash
S: (SKETCH)
CRIME Period. Judge frees highwayman in
exchange for rival's murder.

03859
MODELLING EXTRAORDINARY (1000)
kinema
Natural Colour Film Co Reissue: 1914 (Kineto)
D: W.R. Booth
TRICK Animated putty forms shapes.

03860
JACK AND THE FAIRIES (895)
Urban Trading Co
D: Stuart Kinder
FANTASY Boy sweep escapes rough mother and
is taken to fairyland.

03861
THE PALACE OF MYSTERY (590)
Urban Trading Co
D: Stuart Kinder
TRICK Devil's tricks reform ill-tempered king.

03862
A CANINE SHERLOCK HOLMES (1040)
Urban Trading Co
D:S: Stuart Kinder
Spot the Urbanora Dog
ANIMAL Dog leads tec to robber's hideout
and fetches police.

03863
JAPANESE MAGIC (465)
Urban Trading Co
D:S: Stuart Kinder
TRICK Mandarin and geisha girl perform
tricks with magic fan.

03864
MIRTH AND MYSTERY (445)
Urban Trading Co

D:S: Stuart Kinder
TRICK Conjuror and assistant enlarge and
reduce their heads.

03865
BUNNY AT THE DERBY (577)
Vitagraph
D:S: Larry Trimble
John Bunny .... The Coster
Bertina Smith .... Anne
COMEDY Coster takes girl to Epsom and
saves pony trap from theft.

03866
MICHAEL McSHANE, MATCHMAKER (695)
Vitagraph
D:S: Larry Trimble
John Bunny .... Michael McShane
Mabelle Lumley .... Colleen O'Brian
Charles Cox .... Danny O'Toole
Beatrice Grovenor ...... Mrs O'Brian
James Pryor .... Mr O'Brian
COMEDY Cork. Old pedlar helps middle-aged
man elope with young girl.

03867
PERSEVERING PEGGY (660)
Cosmopolitan
COMEDY Girl helps rejected suitor pose as
maid to win father's consent.

03868
A WORM WILL SQUIRM (470)
Cosmopolitan
COMEDY Henpeck puts glue on park bench to
catch wife with lodger.

03869
THE BURGLAR BURGLED (660)
Cosmopolitan
COMEDY Burglar robs man and is himself
robbed.

03870
BOBBY THE TAMAR (575)
Cosmopolitan
COMEDY Henpeck learns lion-taming and tries
it on sheep, cook, wife.

1913

JAN

03871
MARY OF BRIARWOOD DELL (1165) (U)
Barker
D: (Bert Haldane)
S: Rowland Talbot
Aithna Gover .... Mary
Roy Travers .... Joe
Edward Viner .... Stranger
ROMANCE Village smith's sweetheart attracted
to stranger from London. (First British film to
receive a Censor's certificate.)

03872
THE INTERRUPTED HONEYMOON (635) (U)
Barker
D: (Bert Haldane)
S: Rowland Talbot
Peter Gale .... The Groom
Doreen O'Connor .... The Bride
Blanche Forsythe .... The Nurse
COMEDY Nurse mistakenly leaves baby in
honeymoon couple's room.

03873
SUSPICIOUS MR BROWN (714) (U)
Barker
D: (Bert Haldane)
S: Rowland Talbot
Tom Coventry .... John Brown
Blanche Forsythe .... Mrs Brown
Rolf Leslie .... John Brown
Doreen O'Connor ...... Mrs Brown
COMEDY Wife ejects husband but welcomes
him back to fight burglar.

03874
THE PRICE OF DECEPTION (1070) (U)
Barker
D: (Bert Haldane)
S: Rowland Talbot
Fred Paul .... Lord Neston
Blanche Forsythe .... Lady Neston
Roy Travers .... The Thief
Tom Coventry .... Aaron
CRIME Lord replaces wife's pearls with paste
copy, which is stolen.

03875
ALFRED HARDING'S WOOING (740) (U)
Barker
D: (Bert Haldane)
S: Rowland Talbot
Peter Gale .... Alfred Harding
Aithna Gover ... Rosie
COMEDY Advertiser flirts with wrong girl at
rendezvous.

03876
A LITTLE GIRL SHALL LEAD THEM (2085)
(U)
Barker
D: (Alexander Butler)
S: Rowland Talbot
Fred Paul .... Frank Russell
Blanche Forsythe .... Doris Russell
Roy Travers .... Louis Russell
Pippin Barker .... Cecil Russell
DRAMA Banker buys child of his disowned
son, whose wife then poses as governess.

03877
THAT AWFUL PIPE (450) (U)
Barker
D: (Bert Haldane)
S: Rowland Talbot
COMEDY Smoker's pipe fumes cause trouble.

03878
WAS HE A COWARD? (670) (U)
Barker
D: (Bert Haldane)

S: Rowland Talbot
DRAMA

03879
AN APE'S DEVOTION (870) (U)
Clarendon
D: Percy Stow
CRIME Jealous Spaniard wounds pet ape in
mistake for camper.

03880
FREDA'S PHOTO (1025) (U)
Clarendon
D: Wilfred Noy
Dorothy Bellew .... Freda
CRIME Manager frames clerk for theft and is
thwarted by girl.

03881
BUSINESS AS USUAL DURING
ALTERATIONS (455) (U)
Clarendon *Reissue:* 1916, OPEN DURING
ALTERATIONS
D: Percy Stow
COMEDY Trouble in restaurant when builders
are in.

03882
LOVE VERSUS PRIDE (885) (U)
Clarendon
D: Percy Stow
Dorothy Bellew .... Nettie
ROMANCE Heiress to £60,000 feigns illness to
win back poor lover.

03883
A STRONG MAN'S LOVE (2095) (A)
Clarendon
D: Wilfred Noy
S: Marchioness of Townshend
Dorothy Bellew .... Elizabeth
CRIME Vicar's daughter elopes with actor who
kills manager and is acquitted by barrister who
loves her.

03884
OH! MY AUNT (720) (U)
Cricks & Martin
D: Edwin J. Collins
Edwin J. Collins .... Mr Collins
COMEDY Man dresses as aunt to woo schoolgirl.

03885
THE CRACKSMAN'S DAUGHTER (1640) (U)
Cricks & Martin
D: (Charls Calvert)
CRIME Girl thief weds Lord and her ex-partner
dies trying to bomb her.

03886
ISAACS AS A BROKER'S MAN (610) (U)
Cricks & Martin
D: (Charles Calvert)
COMEDY Man and daughter fool bailiff and
remove their furniture.

03887
FROM THE DEPTHS (1145) (U)
Cricks & Martin
D: (Edwin J. Collins)
CRIME Man saved from suicide steals bene-
factor's plans but is betrayed by blackmailing
maid.

03888
THE SURPRISE PACKET (535) (U)
Cricks & Martin
D: (Charles Calvert)
COMEDY Man's marriage advertisement
answered by spinster sister.

03889
WON BY A CHILD (730) (U)
Cricks & Martin

D: (Edwin J. Collins)
CRIME Sick child reforms burglar who
returns her teddy-bears.

03890
THE MYSTIC MOONSTONE (325) (U)
Cricks & Martin *Reissue:* 1916
D: (Dave Aylott)
TRICK Farmer finds magic ring that causes
objects to vanish.

03891
FOG (1000) (U)
Edison
D: Ashley Miller
S: Bannister Merwin
Mary Fuller .... Liz
Marc McDermott .... Hon Jack Penderberry
Miriam Nesbitt .... Lady Cecily
Robert Brower .... Lord Malvern
Harry Eytinge .... Slogger Bill
John Sturgeon .... The Rat
DRAMA Toff is attacked, has amnesia, is cared
for by coster girl, and recovers when fiancee
visits East End.

03892
THE NEW SQIURE (1000) (U)
Edison
D: Ashley Miller
S: Bannister Merwin
Marc McDermott .... The Squire
Miriam Nesbitt .... The Neice
Edward Durrant .... The Suitor
John le Fre .... The Farmer
ROMANCE Wallingford. Squire poses as farm-
hand to woo girl and is framed for breaking
machine.

03893
PIMPLE'S MOTOR BIKE (275) (U)
Folly Films (Cosmo)
D:S: Fred Evans, Joe Evans
Fred Evans .... Pimple
COMEDY Pimple find s money and buys
motor-bicycle.

03894
INKEY AND CO (320) (U)
HD Films (Cosmo)
D: Ernest Lepard
S: Brothers Egbert
Albert Egbert .... Inkey
Seth Egbert .... Co
COMEDY Workman feigns illness to obtain
brandy from publican.

03895
THE JEWEL THIEVES OUTWITTED (850) (U)
Hepworth
D: (Frank Wilson)
Jack Hulcup .... Thief
Violet Hopson .... Maid
Rachel de Solla ...... Lady
CHASE Police pursue jewel thieves by motor-
car and aeroplane.

03896
THE TOUCH OF A BABE (750) (A)
Hepworth
D: (Warwick Buckland)
Flora Morris .... Jenny
Harry Royston ...... Bill
CRIME Child stops ex-convict from killing wife.

03897
THE BADNESS OF BURGLAR BILL (475) (U)
Hepworth
D: (Frank Wilson)
COMEDY PC poses as tramp to catch burglar
posing as woman.

03898
THE CURATE'S BRIDE (750) (U)
Hepworth
D: (Hay Plumb)
Alec Worcester ...... Jack
Chrissie White .... Kitty
Harry Gilbey .... Father
Ruby Belasco .... Mother
Alma Taylor ....Girl
COMEDY Curate weds actress who poses as
coster to shock his parents.

03899
OVER THE FERRY (750) (U)
Hepworth
D: Warwick Buckland
Flora Morris .... Alice
Alec Worcester ...... Jack
ROMANCE Girl loves poacher who dies; she
weds ferryman.

03900
THREE OF THEM (425) (U)
Hepworth
D: (Frank Wilson)
COMEDY Three boys play tricks on park-keeper,
who chases them.

03901
THE REAL THING (550) (U)
Hepworth
D: (Hay Plumb)
Harry Buss .... Jack
Chrissie White .... Phyllis
Alma Taylor .... Miss Merriman
COMEDY Girl's fiance falls for girl with long
hair — until her brother unpins it.

03902
THE BURGLAR AT THE BALL (575) (U)
Hepworth
D: (Hay Plumb)
Harry Buss .... Doctor
Johnny Butt .... Burglar
Madge Campbell ... Fiancee
COMEDY Burglar changes clothes with doctor
and robs fancy-dress ball.

03903
AT THE FOOT OF THE SCAFFOLD (1925) (A)
Hepworth
D: (Warwick Buckland)
Alec Worcester ...... John West
Chrissie White .... Emily West
Harry Royston ...... The Convict
Harry Gilbey .... The Banker
Ruby Belasco .... The Banker's Wife
CR IME Escaped convict's dying confession
clears clerk convicted for stabbing banker.

03904
A STICKY AFFAIR (475) (U)
Hepworth
D: (Frank Wilson)
COMEDY Birdlime causes fence to adhere to
tramp's back.

03905
HAWKEYE HAS TO HURRY (528) (U)
Hepworth
D:S: Hay Plumb
Hay Plumb .... Hawkeye
CHASE Hawkeye dons roller-skates to meet
sister's train.

03906
WINNING HIS STRIPES (875) (U)
Hepworth
D: (Frank Wilson)
Cyril Morton .... Jack Harris

Alma Taylor .... Mrs Harris
Harry Royston ...... PC Warner
CRIME Policeman helps escaped convict, who
helps him catch bank-robbers.

03907
LOVE AND A BURGLAR (650) (U)
Hepworth
D: (Hay Plumb)
Johnny Butt .... Percy
Chrissie White .... Winnie
COMEDY Girl's father mistakes beau for burglar,
and vice versa.

03908
SALLY IN OUR ALLEY (900) (U)
Hepworth
D: (Hay Plumb)
Flora Morris .... Sally
Alec Worcester .... The Curate
Cecil Manning .... Jack
ROMANCE Curate lets his beloved coster wed
one of her own class.

03909
THE PRODIGAL'S RETURN (875) (U)
Hepworth
D: (Frank Wilson)
Alec Worcester .... Arthur Blanchard
CRIME Banker disowns son for forgery and
shoots him in mistake for burglar.

03910
PASS IT ON (550) (U)
Hepworth
D: (Frank Wilson)
COMEDY Man pins £100 to abandoned baby
which is eventually returned to him without
money.

03911
THE TAILOR'S REVENGE (450) (U)
Hepworth
D: (Hay Plumb)
Harry Buss .... Algy
Alma Taylor .... The Girl
Jack Hulcup .... The Tailor
COMEDY Tailor makes debtor suit that shrinks
in rain.

03912
THE BOOK (1200) (U)
Hepworth
D: (Warwick Bucland)
Alec Worcester .... Jack Arkwright
Marie de Solla .... Mrs Arkwright
CRIME Cashier gambles and robs bank, but
returns money for mother's sake.

03913
MIFANWY — A TRAGEDY (675) (U)
Ivy Close Films (Hepworth)
D:S: Elwin Neame
Ivy Close .... Mifanwy
ROMANCE Wales. Girl dreams dead fisherman
calls her, and dies.

03914
PAT'S IDEA (316) (U)
Heron Films (U)
P: Andrew Heron
D: (Mark Melford)
COMEDY Irishman fails to kill himself and
revives at wake.

03915
BOTTLED COURAGE (408) (U)
Heron Films (U)
P: Andrew Heron
D: (Mark Melford)
COMEDY Friends make henpeck drunk and he
has revenge on his wife.

03916
BLACK-EYED SUSAN (1480) (U)
London Films (Cosmo)
D: Percy Nash
S: (PLAY) Douglas Jerrold
DRAMA 1825. His discharge saves sailor from
court-martial for striking officer.

03917
MONTY'S PROPOSAL (990) (U)
London Films (Cosmo)
D: Percy Nash
COMEDY Shy lover's recorded proposal
played by girl's cook.

03918
THE GOLDEN CHANCE (1100) (U)
London Films (Cosmo)
D: Percy Nash
S:(PLAY) StAubin Miller
ROMANCE Gretna Green, period. Eloping
couple 'change partners' with a squire and
his ward.

03919
THE FISHMONGER'S APPRENTICE (405)
Kineto
D: (F. Martin Thornton)
COMEDY Slapstick misadventures of apprentice
fishmonger.

03920
BILLY'S FIRST COURTSHIP (500)
Gerrard Films
COMEDY Girl's suitor innocently offends
family and is ejected.

03921
THE OPAL STEALERS (660)
Britannia Films (Pathe)
D: A.E. Coleby
WESTERN Girl fetches boy scouts to save
prospectors from bushrangers.

03922
FRA GIACONE:
Eric Williams Speaking Pictures-Searchlight
S: (POEM) Robert Buchanan
Eric Williams .... The Count
DRAMA Shown whilst Eric Williams recites
from stage.

03923
RAGTIME A LA CARTE
Selsior Films
Mercy Manners
MUSICAL Dance synchronises with cinema
orchestras.

03924
BUNNY BLARNEYED; OR, THE BLARNEY
STONE (839)
Vitagraph
D:S: Larry Trimble
John Bunny .... John Bull
COMEDY Cork. Girl's suitor forces her father's
consent by hanging him over the Blarney Stone.

FEB

03925
ALLAN FIELD'S WARNING (667) (U)
Barker
D: (Bert Haldane)
S: Rowland Talbot
Fred Paul .... Allan Field
Blanche Forsythe .... Mrs Field
Pippin Barker .... Master Field
CRIME Gambler dreams loses his all and turns
to crime.

03926
A VILLAGE SCANDAL (595) (U)
Barker
D: (Bert Haldane)
S: Rowland Talbot
Rolf Leslie .... Mr Bolt
Blanche Forsythe .... Mrs Bolt
Tom Coventry .... Skipper
COMEDY Jealous man tests wife by posing as
old skipper.

03927
THE DEBT OF GAMBLING (780) (U)
Barker
D: (Bert Haldane)
S: Rowland Talbot
Thos H. MacDonald .... Jack Argyll
Doreen O'Connor .... Bertha Argyll
Tom Coventry .... Mr Marks
Rachel de Solla .... Mrs Marks
May Morton .... French Maid
CRIME Man's gambling wife steals bracelet
and kills herself.

03928
JUST LIKE A MOTHER (724) (U)
Barker
D: (Bert Haldane)
S: Rowland Talbot
Thos H. MacDonald .... Arthur Rose
May Morton .... Betty Ware
Rachel de Solla .... Mrs Rose
Tom Coventry .... Mr Ware
ROMANCE Widow makes son promise to stay
single but he falls for her nurse.

03929
IN THE TOILS OF THE BLACKMAILER
(1170) (U)
Barker
D: (Alexander Butler)
S: Rowland Talbot
Peter Gale .... Dick
Blanche Forsythe .... Lydia
Rolf Leslie .... Mr Morton
May Morton .... Miss Morton
Rachel de Solla .... Mrs Morton
Edward Burnham .... Harry
CRIME Reformed crook saves rich man from
woman's blackmail.

03930
PETER TRIES SUICIDE (455) (U)
Barker
D: (Bert Haldane)
S: Rowland Talbot
Peter Gale .... Peter
COMEDY Rejected suitor tries suicide and fails
at every attempt.

03931
POLLY THE GIRL SCOUT AND
GRANDPA'S MEDALS (460) (U)
Barker
D: (Bert Haldane)
S: Rowland Talbot
May Morton .... Polly
J. Hastings Batson .... Grandpa
Pippin Barker.................. Newsboy
PATHOS Bully's newsboy son steals pensioner's
medals, is run over, and dies.

03932
THE TEST (855) (A)
Barker
D: (Bert Haldane)
S: Rowland Talbot
Fred Paul .... Jim Wade
Blanche Forsythe .... Madge Wade

Rolf Leslie .... Mr Thorne
Rachel de Solla .... Mrs Thorne
DRAMA Spiteful policeman tells diamond
merchant his employee is an ex-convict.

03933
SAGACITY VERSUS CRIME (1254) (A)
B&C (MP)
D: H.O. Martinek
H.O. Martinek .... Arthur Wellesley
Pearl Brooke .... Banker's Daughter
Hal Charlton .... Robert Hartley
Thomas Brooklyn ..:... Crook
ANIMAL Bank clerk uses bulldog to catch
robbing rival.

03934
BLIGGS ON THE BRINY (400) (U)
B&C (MP)
D: Charles Raymond
W. Gladstone Haley .... Bliggs
Percy Moran .... Pirate
COMEDY Seasick traveller dreams of pirates
and is thrown in sea.

03935
A FLASH OF LIGHTNING (760) (U)
B&C (MP)
D: Charles Raymond
Percy Moran .... Cyril Lindsay
Gladys Barnett ...... Isabel
John B. Glover ..... Ranleigh
George Melville ...... Childs
CRIME Shipboard gambler accidentally
photographed while framing loser for theft.

03936
IN THE GRIP OF DEATH (1070) (A)
B&C (MP)
D: (H.O. Martinek)
Norman Yates .... Dennis McLeod
Marie d'Albert .... Kitty
M. Gray Murray .... Lord Verula
S.P. Goodyer Kettley ...... Garston
Wilfred Ellis .... Officer
ADVENTURE Period. Lord's daughter elopes
with man who is arrested when he dons dying
highwayman's coat.

03937
THE ANTIQUE VASE (590) (U)
B&C (MP)
D: H.O. Martinek
S: Harold Brett
H.O. Martinek .... Martin
Sadie Strande .... Stella
Harold Brett .... Isaacs
COMEDY Girl artist helps old man swindle
Jewish dealer.

03938
JOBSON'S LUCK (940) (U)
B&C (MP)
D: H.O. Martinek
George Foley .... Jobson
Hal Charlton .... Gilbert Fanshawe
M. Gray Murray .... Mr Fanshawe
Violet Graham .... Girl
Letty Paxton .... Girl
COMEDY Disowned gambler becomes valet's
valet when valet inherits fortune.

03939
A DREAM OF GLORY (589) (U)
Britannia Films (Pathe)
D: (A.E. Coleby)
ROMANCE Actress dreams of future fame
but weds poor artist.

03940
LOVE AND THE VARSITY (660) (U)
Clarendon
D: Percy Stow
Dorothy Bellew
COMEDY Students pose as girls to get inside
girl's school.

03941
MAUDIE'S ADVENTURE (400) (U)
Clarendon
D: Percy Stow
Maude Derby .... Maudie
Dorothy Bellew ...... Her Sister
COMEDY Girl pins 'Kiss Me' notice to sister's
blouse.

03942
THE COSTER'S WEDDING (745) (U)
retitled: COSTER JOE
Clarendon
D: Percy Stow
DRAMA Greengrocer has to sell donkey to rival
but saves his daughter when donkey bolts.

03943
A MODERN DICK WHITTINGTON (655) (U)
Clarendon
D: Percy Stow
S: H.S. Middleton
CRIME Boy hangs to back of thieves' car and
fetches police to their hideout.

03944
KINDLY REMOVE YOUR HAT; OR, SHE
DIDN'T MIND (43)
Clarendon
D: Percy Stow
COMEDY 'Telling our dear friends the ladies,
courteously and so gently, the advisability of
removing their hats.'

03945
THE CROWD OUTSIDE; OR, WAITING FOR
YOU (70)
Clarendon
D: Percy Stow
COMEDY 'Quite without offence, most court-
eous, but what a long felt want.'

03946
A BROKEN LIFE (1050) (U)
Cricks & Martin
D: (Edwin J. Collins)
CRIME Spurned man shot by ex-fiancee when
he robs her husband.

03947
THE FAIRY BOTTLE (790) (U)
Cricks & Martin *Reissue:* 1916
D: (Dave Aylott)
Una Tristram .... The Fairy
Bill Haley .... Pat Murphy
TRICK Irishman's magic bottle contains evil
spirit.

03948
SECRET SERVICE (1335) (A)
Cricks & Martin
D: (Charles Calvert)
CRIME Chinaman captures captain, poses as
him, and is caught by tec posing as lascar.

03949
BELINDA'S ELOPEMENT (495) (U)
Cricks & Martin
D: (Dave Aylott)
COMEDY Man helps friend elope to save girl
from forced marriage.

03950
THE SPORT OF FATE (1095) (U)
Cricks & Martin
D: (Edwin J. Collins)
CRIME Ruined farmer, framed for killing miser, breaks jail and is saved by confession.

03951
BILLIKEN REVOLTS (355) (U)
Cricks &Martin
D: (Dave Aylott)
COMEDY Rebellious henpeck thwarted by his mother-in-law.

03952
THE MURDER OF SQUIRE JEFFREY (950) (A)
Cricks & Martin
D: Dave Aylott
Charles Vane .... Paul Sleuth
CRIME Tec poses as murdered squire to trap burglar.

03953
ALL'S WELL THAT ENDS WELL (830) (U)
Cricks & Martin
D: (Edwin J. Collins)
Una Tristram .... The Girl
COMEDY Girl poses as maid to escape wedding.

03954
PROVING HIS WORTH (970)
Cricks & Martin
D: (Charles Calvert)
WAR Disowned wastrel enlists, is wounded, and reunited with his father.

03955
SOCIAL ASPIRATIONS (435) (U)
Cricks & Martin
D: (Edwin J. Collins)
S: Ernest A. Dench
COMEDY Butcher tries to woo wealthy widow.

03956
AN OLD APPOINTMENT (500) (U)
Edison
D: Ashley Miller
S: Harry Furniss
Marc McDermott .... The Millionaire
John le Fre .... His Friend
DRAMA Millionaire finds friend after searching Chelsea Hospital, Charterhouse, etc.

03957
THE LADY CLARE (700) (U)
Edison
D: Ashley Miller
S: (POEM) Alfred Tennyson
SC: Bannister Merwin
Marc McDermott .... Lord Ronald
Miriam Nesbitt .... Lady Clare
Mae Wells .... Alice
ROMANCE Arundel. Lord weds Lady despite knowledge of lowly birth.

03958
PIMPLE GOES A-BUSKING (210) (U)
Folly Films (Cosmo)
D:S: Fred Evans, Joe Evans
Fred Evans .... Pimple
COMEDY Pimple plays 'Glorious Beer' on flute and is given some.

03959
THE TEMPERANCE LECTURE (630) (U)
HD Films (Cosmo)
D: Ernest Lepard
S: Brothers Egbert
Albert Egbert .... Lecturer
Seth Egbert .... Assistant
COMEDY Reformed drunkard causes lecturer to get drunk during his address.

03960
EVERYBODY'S DOING IT (405) (U)
EcKo (Cosmo)
D: W.P. Kellino
COMEDY Buskers play popular tune and everybody dances.

03961
GEORGE BARNWELL THE LONDON APPRENTICE (2500) (U) USA: IN THE TOILS OF THE TEMPTRESS
Hepworth
D: Hay Plumb
S: (PLAY) George Lillo
SC: Ivan Patrick Gore
Alec Worcester .... George Barnwell
Flora Morris .... Sarah Millwood
CRIME Period. Woman persuades workman to kill her rich uncle.

03962
THE DEFECTIVE DETECTIVE (575) (U)
Hepworth
D: (Hay Plumb)
Harry Buss .... Roland
Chrissie White........ Rachel
COMEDY Detective mistakes girl's rich uncle for burglar.

03963
WE ARE BUT LITTLE CHILDREN WEAK (925) (925) (U)
Hepworth
D: (Warwick Buckland)
Flora Morris .... Daisy Goodheart
Harry Royston ...... David Marr
DRAMA Lame girl saves drunken father from railway line.

03964
RAGTIME MAD (500) (U)
Hepworth
D: (Hay Plumb)
Flora Morris .... The Girl
Hay Plumb .... A Second
COMEDY Girl dances ragtime and everyone joins in.

03965
THE LAW IN THEIR OWN HANDS (550) (U)
Hepworth
D: (Frank Wilson)
Johnny Butt .... Tramp
Harry Gilbey .... Tramp
COMEDY Tramps pose as policemen and stop Town Hall whist drive.

03966
THE ARGENTINE TANGO AND OTHER DANCES (500)
Hepworth (KTC) *Reissue:* 1915
George Grossmith
Phyllis Dare
Empire Theatre chorus
MUSICAL Two drawing-room dances: Bunny Hug; Spanish tango.

03967
TWO LITTLE PALS (1050) (U)
Hepworth
D: (Warwick Buckland)
Alec Worcester .... Squire Wilmott
Flora Morris .... Edna Wilmott
Harry Royston .... Slogger Pete
Violet Hopson .... Mrs Pete
DRAMA Squire saves orphan whose locket proves she is his wife's sister.

03968
LITTLE BILLIE AND THE BELLOWS (475) (U)
Hepworth

D: (Frank Wilson)
COMEDY Boy puts flour and soot in bellows.

03969
FATHER'S LITTLE FLUTTER (600) (U)
Hepworth
D: (Frank Wilson)
Harry Buss .... Father
Johnny Butt ..... Tailor
COMEDY Family bribe tailor to sell jacket cheaply and father sells it at profit.

03970
THE SILENCE OF RICHARD WILTON (725) (U)
Hepworth
D: (Warwick Buckland)
Alec Worcester .... Richard Wilton
Flora Morris .... Mrs Porson
Harry Royston .... Tommy Porson
CRIME Wife's ex-lover is accused when he saves her necklace from theft.

03971
BLOOD AND BOSH (650) (U)
Hepworth
D: Hay Plumb
Jack Hulcup .... The Hero
Chrissie White .... The Heroine
Ruby Belasco .... The Villainess
COMEDY Couple kidnap baby and are killed by exploding gas-meter.

03972
DRAKE'S LOVE STORY (2325) (U) USA: THE LOVE ROMANCE OF ADMIRAL SIR FRANCIS DRAKE
Hepworth
D: Hay Plumb
Hay Plumb .... Francis Drake
Chrissie White .... Elizabeth Sydenham
Violet Hopson ...... Queen Elizabeth
HISTORY 1588. Admiral defeats Spanish Armada.

03973
MONTY'S MISTAKE (425) (U)
Hepworth
D: (Frank Wilson)
COMEDY Jealous man tries to commit suicide after mistaking girl's grandfather for lover.

03974
DECEIVERS BOTH (900) (U)
Hepworth
D: (Hay Plumb)
Alec Worcester .... Lord Lyndford
Chrissie White .... Alice Debenham
Harry Gilbey .... George Debenham
COMEDY Peer posing as chauffeur loves employer's daughter posing as maid.

03975
THE MILL GIRL (845) (U)
Hepworth
D: (Warwick Buckland)
Alma Taylor .... Lizzie
Harry Royston ...... Foreman
Jack Hulcup .... Softy
CRIME Lancs. Foreman frames millgirl for theft and is forced to police station by workmates.

03976
LIEUTENANT LILLY AND THE SPLODGE OF OPIUM (725) (U)
Hepworth
D: Hay Plumb
Harry Buss .... Lt Lilly
COMEDY Lt and men quell Boxer uprising and save girl from opium den.

03977
DECEIVING UNCLE (550) (U)
John Bull Films (Cosmo)
D: Ethyle Batley
S: Ernest G. Batley
COMEDY Couple borrow baby to impress their
uncle.

03978
THE PICKWICK PAPERS (series) (U)
Vitagraph Co
D:SC: Larry Trimble
S: (NOVEL) Charles Dickens
John Bunny .... Samuel Pickwick
James Pryor .... Mr Tupman
Sidney Hunt .... Mr Snodgrass
Fred Hornby .... Mr Winkle
Arthur Ricketts .... Mr Jingle
H.P. Owen .... Sam Weller
George Temple .... The Fat Boy
Minnie Rayner .... Mrs Budger
Arthur White .... Dr Slammer

03979
1 – THE HONOURABLE EVENT (1000)

03980
2 – THE ADVENTURE OF WESTGATE
SEMINARY (1000)

03981
3 – THE ADVENTURE OF THE SHOOTING
PARTY (675)
COMEDIES Period. Misadventures of elderly
gentleman and his companions. (First two parts
released in Britain as one film.)

03982
THE BABY (505) kinema
Natural Colour Kinematograph Co Reissue:
1917, POTTED PLAYS No 2 (Kineto)
D: (F. Martin Thornton)
COMEDY Married man tries to convince father
he is single by sending baby to his brother.

03983
A BALLAD OF SPLENDID SILENCE
Eric Williams Speaking Pictures-Barker
S:(POEM) E. Nesbitt
Eric Williams .... Renyi
DRAMA Shown while Eric Williams recites
from stage.

MAR
03984
A DOUBLE LIFE (880) (A)
Barker
D: (Bert Haldane)
S: Rowland Talbot
Fred Paul .... Walter Clare
Blanche Forsythe .... Madge Clare
Thos H. MacDonald .... Frank Norman
Rachel de Solla .... Mrs Norman
Roy Travers .... Logan
CRIME Husband jailed for theft and partner
killed while wearing his suit.

03985
BINKS' WIFE'S UNCLE (780) (U)
Barker
D: (Bert Haldane)
S: Rowland Talbot
Rolf Leslie .... Binks
Doreen O'Connor........ Mrs Binks
Tom Coventry .... Deaf Joe
J. Hastings Batson .... Uncle
COMEDY Man mistakes deaf man for wife's
rich uncle.

03986
UNCLE AS CUPID (865) (U)
Barker
D: Bert Haldane
S: Rowland Talbot
Edward Viner .... Jack Graham
Irene Vernon .... Nellie Miles
Fred Paul .... Selwyn
Rachel de Solla .... Mrs Miles
ROMANCE Man neglects sweetheart when he is
adopted by rich uncle.

03987
NEVER FORGET THE RING (630) (U)
Barker
D: Bert Haldane
S: Rowland Talbot
Thos H. MacDonald......... Percy Goldboy
Irene Vernon .... Connie Bliss
Fred Paul .... Jack Goldboy
COMEDY Rich man woos son's fiancee.

03988
IN LONDON'S TOILS (2395) (A)
Barker
D: (Alexander Butler)
S: Rowland Talbot
Thos H. MacDonald .... Gilbert Mowbray
Maud Yates .... Stella
Fred Paul .... John Eames
Roy Travers .... Spider
CRIME Farmer's son robs uncle to pay
gambler and is framed for murder.

03989
NOW SHE LETS HIM GO OUT (400) (U)
Barker
D: (Bert Haldane)
S: Rowland Talbot
Roy Travers .... Tomkins
Blanche Forsythe .... Mrs Tomkins
COMEDY Henpeck's friend poses as woman to
fool wife.

03990
THE SANCTIMONIOUS SPINSTERS' SOCIETY
(587) (U)
B&C (MP)
D: (H.O. Martinek)
Letty Paxton .... Spinster
Bessie Booker .... Spinster
Florence Miller .... Spinster
Hal Charlton .... Bachelor
Thomas Brooklyn ... Bachelor
Henry Wright .... Bachelor
COMEDY Men pose as women to join spinsters'
club.

03991
THE FAVOURITE FOR THE JAMAICA CUP
(948) (U)
B&C (MP)
D: Charles Raymond
Dorothy Foster .... Doris
Percy Moran .... Her Brother
John Glover
George Melville
Harry Lorraine
CRIME Jamaica. Gambler wrecks train to kill
racehorse.

03992
STOCK IS AS GOOD AS MONEY (372) (U)
B&C (MP)
D: (H.O. Martinek)
Harry Lorraine .... Husband
May Hamerton .... Wife
Herbert Trumper .... Friend
COMEDY Expectant father dreams he is
Sultan of Turkey.

03993
LIEUTENANT DARING AND THE LABOUR
RIOTS (1242) (A)
B&C (MP)
D: Charles Raymond
Percy Moran .... Lt Daring
Dorothy Foster .... Edith Carr
J. O'Neil Farrell .... Oswald Carr
Charles Raymond .... Agitator
CRIME Jamaica. Girl signals Lt's ship for help
when rioting workmen set fire to father's
plantation.

03994
FREDDY'S DUMB PLAYMATES (487) (U)
B&C (MP)
D:S: Lewin Fitzhamon
Roy Royston .... Freddy
Marie Royston .... His Sister
ANIMAL Boy's dog releases pony to fetch
sister to save him from well.

03995
A WHIFF OF ONION (754) (U)
Britannia Films (Pathe)
D: (A.E. Coleby)
COMEDY Landlady advertises for husband
and her lodger replies.

03996
MARY THE FLOWER GIRL (1281)
Britannia Films (Pathe)
D: (A.E. Coleby)
DRAMA Woman saves rich man's daughter from
acid thrown by gardener, and finds she is her
own child.

03997
WHAT COULD THE POOR MAN DO? (575)
(U)
Clarendon
D: Percy Stow
COMEDY Groom's wet trousers blow out of
train window, forcing him to wrap legs in
paper.

03998
DR BRIAN PELLIE AND THE WEDDING
GIFTS (935) (A)
Clarendon
D: Percy Stow
CRIME Crook poses as PC to rob sugar king,
whose daughter sends pigeon message to her
fiance.

03999
SWEEP! SWEEP! SWEEP! (465) (U)
Clarendon
D: Percy Stow
COMEDY Three children play tricks on
chimney-sweep .

04000
BE SURE AND INSURE (520) (U)
Clarendon
D: Percy Stow
S: H.S. Middleton
COMEDY Man fakes illness to fool insurance
company's doctor.

04001
BEHIND THE SCENES (2390) (A)
Clarendon
D: Wilfred Noy
S: Marchioness of Townshend
Dorothy Bellew .... Flo
CRIME Cowboy film actor mistakenly uses
real bullets and kills a faithless actress.

04002
A SPORTING CHANCE (1955) (A)
Cricks & Martin *Reissue:* 1915
D: Edwin J. Collins
S: Joseph Caldwell
Una Tristram .... Dorothy Hampden
Lionel d'Aragon .... Capt Panton
Rex Davis .... Cecil Ormonde
Jack Miller .... Sir John Hampden
SPORT Capt tries to win squire's daughter by
kidnapping his champion.

04003
LARRY'S REVENGE (545) (U)
Cricks & Martin
D: (Charles Calvert)
COMEDY Lovelorn yokel uses widow's pig
to avenge himself on villager.

04004
THE MILL ON THE HEATH (740) (U)
Cricks & Martin
D: (Charles Calvert)
S: Frederick H-U Bowman
ROMANCE Rich man lets son wed miller's
daughter when she refuses chance to destroy
their mortgage.

04005
ONE OF THE NUTS (440) (U)
Cricks & Martin
D: (Charles Calvert)
COMEDY Man tries to crack coconut.

04006
THE DIAMOND STAR (1280) (U)
Cricks & Martin
D: Edwin J. Collins
CRIME Gipsy poacher joins gang but
repents to clear framed gamekeeper.

04007
WOOING AUNTIE (497) (U)
Cricks & Martin
D: (Edwin J. Collins)
S: Rady & Matthews
COMEDY Boy fools sister's beau by pretending
her aunt has legacy.

04008
HIS YOUNGER BROTHER (910) (U)
Cricks & Martin
D: Charles Calvert
WAR Wounded soldier secures Russian plans
and saves brother from court-martial.

04009
STOP THIEF! (302) (U)
Cricks & Martin
D: (Charles Calvert)
CHASE Tramp steals watch, swallows it, and
sucks it out with vacuum cleaner.

04010
HOW THEY GOT THE VOTE (625) (U)
Edison
D:S: Ashley Miller
Barry O'Moore .... The Lover
Bessie Learn .... The Girl
William Wadsworth .... The Prime Minister
Elizabeth Miller .... The Suffragette
Herbert Prior .... The Magician
TRICK Suffragette's suitor forces prime
minister to accept suffrage by causing chaos
in London. (Completed in America.)

04011
PROP'S ANGEL (675) (U)
Hepworth
D:S: Hay Plumb
Warwick Buckland .... Props

Madge Dolphin .... Child
DRAMA Actor's disowned wife befriends girl
who is her own child.

04012
TRIED IN THE FIRE (1215) (U)
Hepworth
D: (Warwick Buckland)
Alec Worcester .... Rev Paul Brayton
Alma Taylor .... Thelma
Harry Royston .... Denzil
CRIME Cleric saves spoilt rich girl from
kidnappers.

04013
THE HOUSE THAT JERRY BUILT (675) (U)
Hepworth
D: (Frank Wilson)
TRICK Man builds house during strike and
demolishes it when refused payment.

04014
HIS EVIL GENIUS (2025) (U) retitled: AT
THE PROMPTING OF THE DEVIL
Hepworth
D: (Frank Wilson)
Alec Worcester .... Jim Dowling
Flora Morris .... Alice
Harry Royston .... Harry Beecham
Frank Wilson .... The Baker
CRIME Drunkard robs house and is confronted
by maid — his wife whom he thought he killed.

04015
THE LOVER WHO TOOK THE CAKE (600) (U)
Hepworth
D: (Hay Plumb)
Cyril Morton .... The Lodger
Alma Taylor .... The Girl
COMEDY Lodger flatters landlady's cooking but
throws it away.

04016
A POLICY OF PINPRICKS (450) (U)
Hepworth
D: (Hay Plumb)
COMEDY Boy uses hatpin to burst balloons,
tyres, etc.

04017
A MIST OF ERRORS (A)
Hepworth
D: (Warwick Buckland)
Flora Morris .... Mary Gordon
Harry Gilbey .... Richard Gordon
Harry Royston ...... Frank
DRAMA Jealous man mistakes wife's scapegrace
brother for her lover.

04018
MR POORLUCK REPAIRS HIS HOUSE (650)
(U)
Hepworth
D: (Frank Wilson)
Harry Buss .... Mr Poorluck
COMEDY Man makes mess when he tries to
repair house.

04019
THE CAT AND THE CHESTNUTS (800) (U)
Hepworth
D: (Warwick Buckland)
Flora Morris .... The Girl
Cyril Morton .... Gerald
CRIME Girl crook thwarts debtor who steals
uncle's necklace.

04020
HELD FOR RANSOM (1025) (U)•
Hepworth
D: (Frank Wilson)

Chrissie White .... The Daughter
Harry Royston .... The Tramp
CRIME Tramp's daughter adopted after returning
farmer's kidnapped child.

04021
HAWKEYE RIDES IN A POINT-TO-POINT
(525) (U)
Hepworth
D:S: Hay Plumb
Hay Plumb .... Hawkeye
COMEDY Latecomer wins race by setting fire to
haystack.

04022
THE INCORRIGIBLES (526) (U)
Heron Films (Cosmo)
P: Andrew Heron
COMEDY Children use pet bulldog to trick
grandfather.

04023
THE ADVENTURES OF PIMPLE — PIMPLE
PC (350) (U)
Folly Films (Cosmo) *Reissue:* 1917, PIMPLE
JOINS THE POLICE FORCE (H&S)
D:S: Fred Evans .... Pimple
COMEDY Dutiful policeman meets with trouble
and beatings.

04024
PIMPLE, DETECTIVE (460) (U)
Folly Films (Cosmo)
D:S: Fred Evans, Joe Evans
Fred Evans .... Pimple
COMEDY Tec searches for stolen baby and finds
it in kennel.

04025
ALL ON ACCOUNT OF A LITTLE BIT OF
STRING (295)
Gerrard Film Co
COMEDY Girl ties cotton reel to father's leg
and he calls police to investigate noise.

04026
THE FIRST STEEPLECHASE (600) (U)
Urban Trading Co
D:S: Lewin Fitzhamon
Lewin Fitzhamon .... The Major
CHASE Period. Army major loses race when he
is robbed by highwayman.

04027
FIVE POUNDS REWARD (615) (U)
Urban Trading Co
D:S: Stuart Kinder
Spot the Urbanora Dog
ANIMAL Lost dog adopts workless man and
wins reward saving baby.

APR

04028
POLLY THE GIRL SCOUT AND THE JEWEL
THIEVES (780) (U)
Barker
D: (Bert Haldane)
S: Rowland Talbot
May Morton .... Polly
CRIME Girl chases thieves, captures van and
drives for police.

04029
PETER PENS POETRY (585) (U)
Barker
D: (Bert Haldane)
S: Rowland Talbot
Peter Gale .... Peter
COMEDY Poet cannot complete poem for
family interruptions.

04030
WHEN PATHS DIVERGE (1295) (A)
Barker
D: Bert Haldane
S: Rowland Talbot
Thos H. MacDonald .... Jack Cotterell
Irene Vernon .... Mary Milton
Fred Paul .... Squire Milton
Edward Viner .... The Hunchback
Roy Travers .... Jim
Rachel de Solla .... Mrs Cotterell
CRIME Crooks steal squire's keys and frame
his ex-convict secretary.

04031
LUGGAGE IN ADVANCE (876) (U)
Barker
D: (Bert Haldane)
S: Rowland Talbot
Peter Gale .... Peter
Doreen O'Connor .... Flossie
COMEDY Eloper hides in basket and is
delivered to girl's school.

04032
O.H.M.S. (1450) (U)
Barker
D: (Alexander Butler)
S: Rowland Talbot
Harry W. Scaddan .... Cdr Scott-Neville
Blanche Forsythe .... Mrs Scott-Neville
Fred Paul .... Col von Harlan
Doreen O'Connor .... Mary
CRIME Spy blackmails com mander's wife into
stealing treaty. (Gold medal in National Kine-
matograph Exhibition scenario contest.)

04033
ZAZA THE DANCER (1195) (A)
Barker
D: Bert Haldane
S: Rowland Talbot
Blanche Forsythe .... Zaza Railton
Fred Paul .... Jack Horton
Irene Vernon .... Mrs Horton
Roy Travers .... Jim Railton
CRIME Crook shoots wife with his lover's
wife's pistol.

04034
POLLY THE GIRL SCOUT'S TIMELY AID
(855) (U)
Barker
D: (Bert Haldane)
S: Rowland Talbot
May Morton .... Polly
DRAMA Workman turns thirf and is jailed by
girl scout, who then helps starving wife.

04035
A LUCKY ESCAPE FOR DAD (890) (U)
Barker
D: (Bert Haldane)
S: Rowland Talbot
COMEDY Youth takes blame for father's nigh t
out — for a price.

04036
HIS MAIDEN AUNT (880) (U)
B&C (MP)
D: (H.O. Martinek)
COMEDY Man fools greedy couple by posing
as rich aunt.

04037
THE OLD COLLEGE BADGE (1256) (U)
B&C (MP)
D: Charles Raymond
Percy Moran .... Ronald Long

Dorothy Foster .... Violet Onslow
Jack Melville
John B. Glover
J. O'Neil Farrell
DRAMA Jamaica. Girl fetches cricket team to
save captain when rival blows up sugar factory.

04038
A FLIRTATION AT SEA (442) (U)
B&C (MP)
D: Charles Raymond
J. O'Neil Farrell .... Tom
John B. Glover .... Dick
Jack Melville .... Harry
Elsie Barone .... Elsie
Gladys Barnett .... Gladys
Peggy Moxey .... Peggy
COMEDY Boastful trio's flirtations spoiled
by seasickness.

04039
WITH HUMAN INSTINCT (845) (A)
B&C (MP)
D: (H.O. Martinek)
George Foley .... Mr West
Alice Moseley .... Janet
Henry Harrison .... Crooky
Minnie Levine .... Mrs West
Ida Strathan .... Baby West
Francis Everard .... Ginger
ANIMAL Maid and burglar kidnap baby; it is
saved by pet bulldog.

04040
TOM CRINGLE IN JAMAICA (992) (U)
B&C (MP)
D: Charles Raymond
S: (NOVEL) Michael Scott
Harry Lorraine .... Tom Cringle
George Melville .... Lt Splinter
Percy Moran .... Spaniard
Elsie Barone .... Senora
John B. Glover .... Admiral
ADVENTURE Jamaica. Soldiers save ship-
wreckes sailors from Spaniards.

04041
SIGNALS IN THE NIGH T (730) (U)
B&C (MP)
D: (H.O. Martinek)
Harry Lorraine .... Jack Dennison
May Hamerton .... Winnie Dennison
James Russell .... Bill
Nancy Roberts .... Sarah
M. Gray Murray .... Mr Dennison
E. Romney .... Mrs Dennison
CRIME Girl flashes morse message to scout-
master brother when maid admits a burglar.

04042
SUFFRAGETTES IN THE BUD (375) (U)
Clarendon
D: Percy Stow
Maude Derby .... Schoolgirl
COMEDY Schoolgirls play tricks on mistress.

04043
A CUNNING CANINE (395) (U) *Reissue:* 1916,
A LITTLE DOGGEREL
Clarendon
D: Percy Stow
ANIMAL Dog collects money to pay license.

04044
MILLING THE MILITANTS (500) (U)
Clarendon
D: Percy Stow
COMEDY Suffragette's henpecked husband
dreams he is Prime Minister.

04045
THE HOUSE OF MYSTERY (209) (A)
Clarendon
D: Wilfred Noy
S: Marchioness of Townshend
Dorothy Bellew .... The Girl
CRIME Fake ghost, gas chamber, and raid on
den of 50 coiners by 100 policemen.

04046
KIND HEARTS ARE MORE THAN CORONETS
(725) (U)
Clarendon
D: Percy Stow
S: W . Saville
CRIME Old soldier's daughter helps policeman
battle burglars.

04047
THE BOATSWAIN'S DAUGHTER (745) (U)
Britannia Films (Pathe)
D: (A.E. Coleby)
ROMANCE Fisherman suspects wife of
infidelity but is mistaken.

04048
THE FALSE CLUE (2158) (U)
Britannia Films (Pathe)
D: (A.E. Coleby)
CRIME Girl's father borrows £25,000 to replace
money stolen by butler.

04049
THE FATE OF A KING (1926) (U)
Britannia Films (Pathe)
D: A.E. Coleby
HISTORY Perth. James I ignores witch's
warning and is murdered.

04050
THE SMUGGLER'S DAUGHTER (895) (U)
Cricks & Martin
D: Edwin J. Collins
ADVENTURE Smuggler's daughter saves excise
man from stake in sea.

04051
WHERE THERE'S A SWILL THERE'S A
SPRAY (435) (U)
Cricks & Martin
D: (Charles Calvert)
COMEDY Film company tries to photograph
new fire hose.

04052
THE POSTMAN (820) (U)
Cricks & Martin
D: (Edwin J. Collins)
DRAM A Daily round of rural postman.

04053
GETTING HIS OWN BACK (485) (U)
Cricks & Martin
D: (Charles Calvert)
COMEDY Clerk wins contest, buys
partnership in office, and avenges himself
on his persecutors.

04054
THE FOREIGN SPY (940) (U)
Cricks & Martin
D: (Charles Calvert)
Jack Leigh .... Henkel
CRIME Spy poses as artist to steal gun
plans and is caught by thumb-print.

04055
DAYDREAMS (425) (U)
Cricks (C&M)
D: (Edwin J. Collins)
TRICK Tramp dreams he is dude with magic
cane.

04056
THE JAILBIRD (875) (U)
Cricks (C&M)
D: (Edwin J. Collins)
Jack Leigh .... Jam rs Duke
Jack Miller .... Mr Forrester
CRIME Ex-convict saves wife from horse and
kills blackmailer.

04057
SMUDGE THE GREAT DETECTIVE (495) (U)
Cricks (C&M)
D: (Charles Calvert)
COMEDY Amateur tec tries to trail lost child.

04058
HOW ARCHIBALD CAUG HT THE LION (463)
(U)
Diamond Films
COME DY Man poses as lion to fool rival in
love.

04059
AN OLD TOYMAKER'S DREAM (311) (U)
Empire Films (MP)
D:S: Arthur Cooper
TRICK Old toymaker dreams toys come to life.

04060
PIMPLE WRITES A CINEMA PLOT (395) (U)
Folly Films (Cosm o)
D:S: Fred Evans
Fred Evans .... Pimple
COMEDY Everybody laughs at Pimple's script,
except the film manager.

04061
PIMPLE A ND THE GORILLA (498) (U)
Folly Films (Phoenix)
D:S: Fred Evans, Joe Evans
Fred Evans .... Pimple
COMEDY Pimple takes place of sick circus
gorilla, escapes and is put in zoo.

04062
MISS PIMPLE, SUFFRAGETTE (550) (U)
Folly Films (Phoenix)
D:S: Fred Evans, Joe Evans
Fred Evans .... Pimple
COMEDY Pimple poses as suffragette to blow
up boat race.

04063
DODGING THE LANDLORD (405) (U)
HD Films (Cosmo)
D: Ernest Lepard
S: Broth ers Egbert
Albert Egbert .... Landlord
Seth Egbert .... Householder
COMEDY Householder tries to hide from
landlord and is chased.

04064
INKEY AND CO IN BUSINESS (335) (U)
HD Films (Cosmo)
D: Ernest Lepard
S: Brothers Egbert
Albert Egbert .... Inkey
Seth Egbert .... Co
COMEDY Pickpockets try to sell hot potatoes,
chestnuts and ice-cream.

04065
AND HE HAD A LITTLE GUN (400) (U)
Hepworth
D: (Frank Wilson)
COMEDY Boy plays tricks with uncle's airgun.

04066
THE LESSON (975) (U)
Hepworth
D: (Warwick Buckland)

Flora Morris .... Violet
Cyril Morton .... Husband
DRAMA Actress cures husband's alcoholism
by feigning drunkeness.

04067
MR POORLUCK, JOURNA LIST (550) (U)
Hepworth
D: (Frank Wilson)
Harry Buss .... Mr Poorluck
COMEDY Children stop uncle from writing in
peace.

04068
THE MYSTERIOUS PHILANTHROPIST
(1200) (U)
Hepworth
D: (Warwick Buckland)
Harry Gilbey .... Martin Hazlitt
Chrissie White .... Maud Hazlitt
Harry Royston ...... Millson
DRAMA Miser saves daughter from cad and is
revealed as local benefactor.

04069
HAUNTED BY HAWKEYE (740) (U)
Hepworth
D:S: Hay Plum b
Hay Plumb .... Hawkeye
COMEDY Hawkeye fakes own death for
insurance money.

04070
PAYING THE PENALTY (2000) (A)
Hepworth
D: (Warwick Buckland)
Alec Worcester .... Alf Smollett
Alma Taylor .... Ruby Jenkins
Harry Royston .... Mark Jones
Harry Gilbey .... The Master
CRIME Sawmill owner abducts workman's
daughter and locks her lover in safe.

04071
PUZZLED (525) (U)
Hepworth
D: (Frank Wilson)
Harry Buss .... Mr Knowall
Flora Morris .... Mrs Knowall
Johnny Butt .... Burglar
COMEDY A puzzle absorbs man, wife, burglar
and PC.

04072
ALL'S FAIR (650) (U)
Hepworth
D: (Hay Plumb)
Chrissie White .... Mary
Jack Raymond .... Micky
Percy Manton .... Sgt Tim
COMEDY Clerk enlists to impress girl but
she weds soldier who takes his job.

04073
IN THE HOUR OF HIS NEED (825) (U)
Hepworth
D: (Warwick Buckland)
S: H.S. Middleton
Alec Worcester .... David
Flora Morris .... The Wife
Harry Gilbey .... Mr Grant
Claire Pridelle .... Mrs Grant
DRAMA Poor artist breaks into rich one's house
and completes mosaic design.

04074
PROFESSOR LONGHEAD'S BURGLAR
TRAP (650) (U)
Hepworth
D: (Frank Wilson)
Johnny Butt .... Prof Longhead
COMEDY Prof and police are caught in
burglar trap.

04075
MANY HAPPY RETURNS (800) (U)
Hepworth
D: (Hay Plumb)
Harry Buss .... Father
COMEDY Man given bad cigars and high
pheasant on birthday.

04076
HAUNTED BY HIS MOTHER-IN-LAW (550)
(U)
Hepworth
D: (Frank Wilson)
TRICK Henpeck thinks he sees mother-in-law
everywhere.

04077
POOR PA PAYS (670) (U)
Martin Films (C&M)
D: (Dave Aylott)
COMEDY Rich man's son fakes own kidnapp-
ing and sends pieces of 'body' to his father.

04078
THE MYSTIC MAT (430) (U)
Martin Films (C&M)
D: (Dave Aylott)
S: W. Saville
TRICK Magician's carpet makes people
disappear.

04079
THE CHILD OF A SUFFRAGETTE (990) (U)
Kineto
D: (F. Martin Thornton)
DRAMA Child trails suffragette mother and
extinguishes her bomb.

04080
THE NIGHTMARE OF THE GLAD-EYE
TWINS (770) (U)
Kineto *Reissue:* 1916, ELSIE'S NIGHTMARE
D: Edgar Rogers
TRICK Girl dreams two dolls come alive and
play tricks.

04081
BILLY BUNGLE'S LUCK (450) (U)
Sun Film Co (Cosmo)
COMEDY Victim of blindfold trick fails to
trick others.

04082
THE STORY OF HYAM TOUCHED (580) (U)
Phoenix Film Agency
D: (Fred Evans)
COMEDY 'Or the triumph of Lady Bird.'

04083
HIS FATHER'S VOICE: MRS KELLY *sound*
UK Kinoplastikon
D: (W.R. Booth)
Dan Leno Jr
MUSICAL Comic song synchronising with a
gramophone record.

04084
GOOD QUEEN BESS *sound*
UK Kinoplastikon
D; (W.R. Booth)
George Robey
MUSICAL Comic song synchronising with
gram ophone record.

04085
AND VERY NICE TOO *sound*
UK Kinoplastikon
D: (W.R. Booth)
George Robey
MUSICAL Comic song synchronising with
gramophone record.

04086
PERSIAN DANCE: EIGHTPENCE A MILE
sound
UK Kinoplastikon
D: (W.R. Booth)
Phyllis Monkman
MUSCAL Synchronises with gramophne
record.

04087
MY WIFE WON'T LET ME (623) (U)
Tyler
S: (SKETCH)
COMEDY Parson thinks his verger is flirting
with a music hall artiste whose car has broken
down.

04088
HE WAS SO FOND OF ANIMALS (610) (U)
Urban Trading Co
D:S: Lewin Fitzhamon
Constance Somers-Clarke ..... Girl
Lewin Fitzhamon .... Man
ANIMAL Man saves girl from runaway pony.

04089
BY THE SEA
Selsior
Mercy Manners
MUSICAL Dance to synchronise with cinema
orchestras: bathing girls interrupted by masher.

04090
HAPPY FANNY FIELDS AND THE FOUR
LITTLE DUTCHMEN (450)
Selsior
Fanny Fields
MUSICAL Dance to synchronise with cinema
orchestras.

MAY

04091
FOR £50,000 (1680)
Barker
D: (Alexander Butler)
S: Rowland Talbot
Fred Paul .... Fred Burton
Sybil Tracy .... Ida Burton
Blanche Forsythe .... Lucille Grey
Rolf Leslie .... Mr Willis
Rachel de Solla .... Mrs Burton
CRIME Wastrel abandons wife and has mistress
forge her signature on learning she is an heiress.

04092
A PAIR OF FRAUDS (650)
Barker
S: Rowland Talbot
Peter Gale .... Milligam
Rolf Leslie .... Mulligan
COMEDY Tramps steal posh clothes and get
free meal.

04093
THE PASSIONS OF MEN (2520) (U)
Barker
D: (Alexander Butler)
S: Rowland Talbot
DRAMA Jealous chemist poisons wife, learns she
is innocent, and poisons himself just as she
recovers.

04094
THE RECLAMATION OF JIM THE LOAFER
(600) (U)
Barker
S: Rowland Talbot
Edward Durrant .... Jim
Mary Jose .... Mary Wilson

Harry Softley .... Crabb
DRAMA Loafer reforms after saving girl from
pugilist.

04095
JOHN COLEMAN'S KID (530) (U)
Barker
S: Rowland Talbot
Rolf Leslie .... John Coleman
Rachel de Solla ...... Mrs Coleman
COMEDY Wife mistakes husband's kid for his
child.

04096
EAST LYNNE (6200) (U)
Barker (Walturdaw)
D: Bert Haldane
S:(NOVEL) Mrs Henry Wood
SC: Harry Engholm
Blanche Forsythe .... Lady Isobel
Fred Paul .... Archibald Carlyle
Fred Morgan .... Capt Levison
Rachel de Solla .... Cornelia Carlyle
May Morton .... Joyce
Pippin .... Little Willie
Doreen O'Connor .... Afy Hallijohn
Roy Travers
Rolf Leslie
DRAMA 1840. Lady elopes with murderer and
poses as nurse to be with her dying child. (First
British 6-reel feature.)

04097
A CREOLE'S LOVE STORY (991) (U)
B&C (MP)
D: Charles Raymond
Percy Moran .... Harry Dean
Dorothy Foster .... Cora
Sho'gun Charlie .... Jose
Trixie Trimmingham .... Melinda
ADVENTURE Jamaica. Girl saves lover when
jealous native throws him into sea.

04098
RICHES AND ROGUES (1245) (A)
B&C (MP)
D: (Charles Weston)
Mae Hamilton .... Portia Fielding
E. Trelawney .... Mr Whittingham
Margot Kelly .... Mrs Whittingham
Harold Holland .... Dr Rogers
R. Peyton .... Ernest Holt
Cedric Hardwicke .... 6 Characters
CRIME Girl poses as accident victim and robs
her ben efactor.

04099
THE WAGER (1061) (U)
B&C (MP)
D:S: Harold Brett
George Foley .... Bill McCann
Harold Brett .... Cavendish
CRIME Rich man bets he can reform theif, is
robbed, and proves thief was framed.

04100
JUST A GIRL (1830) (U) retitled: ONLY A
GIRL
B&C (MP))
D: (Charles Weston)
Marie Pickering .... Mary
George Foley .... Harry Trevor
Alice Inward .... The Other Woman
ROMANCE Country girl weds socialite and
leaves him to return to her own class.

04101
THE FOOL (3343) (U)
Big Ben Films-Union (Pathe)
D:SC: George Pearson
S: (POEM) Rudyard Kipling (A FOOL THERE
WAS)

Godfrey Tearle .... Sterndale
Mary Malone .... Mrs Brockwood
James Carew .... Arthur Warde
Rex Davis
CRIME Man takes blame for girl cardsharper
and she saves him from blackmailer.

04102
TRACKING THE BABY (1078) (U)
Brightonia (MP)
D: Arthur Charrington
COMEDY Couple adopt baby and its parents
steal it back.

04103
COMING TO THE POINT (465) (U)
Clarendon
D: Percy Stow
Maud Derby .... Maudie
Dorothy Bellew ..... Sister
COMEDY Girl saves sister from persistent old
gentleman.

04104
BILL BUMPER'S BOY (455) (U)
Clarendon
D: Percy Stow
COMEDY Boxer chases son's teacher — to
thank him for spanking.

04105
FACE TO FACE (1877) (U)
Clarendon
D: Wilfred Noy
Dorothy Bellew .... The Girl
DRAMA Lord deserts woman and child and her
ex-fiance saves them from fire.

04106
DADDY'S DIDUMS AND THE BOX TRICK
(560) (U)
Clarendon
D: Wilfred Noy
COMEDY Child hides father's clothes in box
which is auctioned to married woman.

04107
A PRESENT FROM FATHER (370) (U)
Clarendon
D: Percy Stow
COMEDY Boy plays tricks with new fountain-
pen.

04108
DAD CAUGHT NAPPING (970) (U)
Clarendon
D: Percy Stow
Dorothy Bellew ...... The Girl
COMEDY Student poses as girl to flirt with
beloved's father.

04109
A TRUE SCOUT (915) (U)
Cricks (C&M)
D: (Charles Calvert)
CRIME Office boy refuses to reveal hidden
money despite torture.

04110
HITCHY-KOO (394) (U)
Cricks (C&M)
D: (Edwin J. Collins)
COMEDY Boy plays ragtime music on mouth
organ, causing everyone to dance.

04111
THE SCAPEGRACE (1885) (U)
Cricks (C&M)
D: Edwin J. Collins
S: Frank Dilnotte
ADVENTURE Yukon. Coward chases girl and
falls from bridge.

04112
THE VILLAIN STILL PURSUED HER (300)
(U)
Cricks (C&M)
D: (Charles Calvert)
COMEDY Dude saves girl from tramp.

04113
SPUD MURPHY'S REDEMPTION (795) (U)
Cricks (C&M)
D: (Charles Calvert)
WAR China. Irish private scouts without
orders and saves regiment.

04114
THE ADVENTURES OF A BAD SHILLING
(350) (U)
Cricks (C&M)
D: (Edwin J. Collins)
COMEDY Dud shilling travels from boys to PC,
beggar, dude, etc.

04115
THE HEADMAN'S VENGEANCE (1050) (U)
Cricks (C&M)
D: (Edwin J. Collins)
ADVENTURE Africa. Botanist saves native who
later saves daughter.

04116
THE ELECTRIC SNUFF (285) (U)
Cricks (C&M)
D: (Charles Calvert)
COMEDY Boy gives powerful snuff to father,
workmen, etc.

04117
PONKY'S BURGLAR (450) (U)
Dart Films (Anderson)
D: Stuart Kinder
Joe Omar .... Ponky
COMEDY Henpeck tries to thwart wife by
having friend pose as burglar.

04118
CIRCUMSTANCES ALTER FACES (680) (U)
Bull's Eye (Anderson)
COMEDY Suitor circumvents sweetheart's father.

04119
PIMPLE MEETS CAPTAIN SCUTTLE (590)
(U)
Folly Films (Phoenix)
D:S: Fred Evans, Joe Evans
Fred Evans .... Pimple
Joe Evans .... Capt Scuttle
COMEDY Capt saves Pimple from suicide and
they charge 6d to see a 'what-is-it' swindle.

04120
ADVENTURES OF PIMPLE — THE INDIAN
MASSACRE (450) (U)
Folly Films (Phoenix)
D:S: Fred Evans, Joe Evans
Fred Evans .... Pimple
COMEDY Burlesque western.

04121
MOTHERHOOD OR POLITICS (1300) (U)
retitled: A CASE FOR SOLOMON
Hepworth
D: (Warwick Buckland)
Flora Morris .... Mrs Jones
Harry Royston ...... Mr Pearce
Rub y Belasco .... Mrs Pearce
DRAMA Mother steals baby from adopters
and later hires them as servants.

04122
PETTICOAT PERFIDY (1000) (U)
Hepworth

D: (Hay Plumb)
Alma Taylor .... Jane
COMEDY Man fools friend by posing as girl;
she poses as him.

04123
MR POORLUCK'S IOUS (500) (U)
Hepworth
D: (Frank Wilson)
Harry Buss .... Mr Poorluck
COMEDY Bankrupt forges lawyer's letter
and poses as heir.

04124
THE MAN OR HIS MONEY (1100) (U)
Hepworth
D: (Warwick Buckland)
Chrissie White .... Freda Haywell
CRIME Man feigns wealth to test son's fiancee
who then saves him from burglars.

04125
TRUE LOVE AND A TRAILER (525) (U)
Hepworth
Claire Pridelle .... Elsie
COMEDY Eloper poses as highwayman to fool
sweetheart's father.

04126
AS THE SPARKS FLY UPWARD (2800) (U)
Hepworth Reissue: 1914
D: Hay Plumb
Alec Worcester .... Frank Emery
Claire Pridelle .... Gladys Mayne
Harry Gilbey .... George Mayne
Harry Royston .... PC Winter
DRAMA Wounded man returns from
Australia in time to save starving family.

04127
HER CROWNING GLORY (925) (U)
Hepworth
D: (Warwick Buckland)
Chrissie White .... Janet
Cecil Mannering .... Doctor
Harry Royston .... Blinkinstow
DRAMA Doctor thrashes barber who swindled
girl out of her long hair.

04128
TILLY'S BREAKING-UP PARTY (950) (U)
Hepworth
D: (Frank Wilson)
Alma Taylor .... Tilly
Chrissie White .... Sally
COMEDY Girl poses as friend's cousin to go to
party.

04129
THE OF-COURSE-I-CAN BROTHERS (575)
(U)
Hepworth
D: Hay Plumb
Harry Buss .... The Brothers
COMEDY Man caught in fight causes pain to
sympathetic twin.

04130
CAPTAIN JACK VC (2125) (U)
Hepworth
D: Hay Plumb
Alec Worcester .... Hon Jack Delton
Chrissie White .... Lady Helen Mavering
Hay Plumb .... Mullah Chief
WAR India. Explorer enlists after duelling man
and wins VC saving his life.

04131
A HERRING ON THE TRAIL (525) (U)
Hepworth

D: (Frank Wilson)
Harry Buss .... Bill
COMEDY Poacher decoys farmer while
partner poaches.

04132
WILL EVANS HARNESSING A HORSE
(1175) (U)
Hepworth (KTC)
D: (Frank Wilson)
S:(SKETCH) Will Evans
Will Evans
Arthur Conquest
COMEDY Man's mishaps while harnessing
horse.

04133
INKEY AND CO — GLAD EYE (380) (U)
HD Films (Cosmo)
D: Ernest Lepard
S: Brothers Egbert
Albert Egbert .... Inkey
Seth Egbert .... Co
COMEDY Man poses as girl to thwart rival.

04134
PEGGY AS PEACEMAKER (650) (U)
John Bull Films (Cosmo)
D: Ethyle Batley
S: Ernest G. Batley
Dorothy Batley .... Peggy
Ernest G. Batley .... Father
COMEDY Girl reunites parted parents.

04135
THE BURGLAR'S CHILD (605) (U)
London Films (Cosmo)
D: Percy Nash
CRIME Widowed ex-convict shoots man who
convicted him before learning he adopted his
starving child.

04136
THE WARTY WOOING (435) (U)
Martin (C&M)
D: (Dave Aylott)
COMEDY Man tries to cure nasal wart and is
mistaken for burglar.

04137
FURNISHING EXTRAORDINARY (280) (U)
Martin (C&M)
D: (Dave Aylott)
TRICK Wife moves furniture by throwing it up
through window.

04138
PC PLATT'S PROMOTION (485) (U)
Martin (C&M)
D: (Dave Aylott)
COMEDY Maid's policeman friend finds
burglars hiding in ottoman.

04139
BILLY'S BOXING GLOVES (430) (U)
Martin (C&M)
D: (Dave Aylott))
TRICK Boy with magic boxing gloves dreams
of Ancient Rome.

04140
A RACE FOR LOVE (1050) (U)
Martin (C&M)
D: Lewin Fitzhamon
S: Frank C. Barnaby
Constance Somers-Clarke ..... Girl
Frank Duller .... Lieutenant
SPORT Lieut wins horse race and girl despite
being shot in arm by rival

04141
ARCHIBALD APPLIES FOR A SITUATION
AS CHAUFFEUR-GARDENER (420) (U)
Summit (Cosmo)
COMEDY Man makes mess of new job.

04142
THE WOULD-BE DETECTIVES (365) (U)
Sun (Cosmo)
COMEDY 'Bexton Slake' searches for kidnapped
baby.

04143
TRIO: EVERYBODY'S DOING IT sound
UK Kinoplastikon
D: (W.R. Booth)
MUSICAL Synchronises to gramophone record.

04144
THE PICNIC ON THE ISLAND (510) (U)
Urban Trading Co
D:S: Lewin Fitzhamon
Constance Somers-Clarke .... Edith
COMEDY Flapper's suitors save father from
drifting rowboat.

04145
SEYMOUR HICKS AND ELLALINE TERRISS
(800)
Zenith Films
D: Leedham Bantock
Seymour Hicks
Ellaline Terriss
COMEDY 'Bumble-bee Sting'; 'Alexander's
Ragtime Band'; 'If I Were a Boy.'

04146
ALWAYS GAY (250)
Hepworth (KTC)
D: (Frank Wilson)
Vera Maxwell & Jack Jarrott
MUSICAL Dance: 'The Evening News'
Waltz No 3.

JUN

04147
THE TUBE OF DEATH (2790) (A) retitled:
THE ANARCHIST'S DOOM
Barker (Royal)
D: (Alexander Butler)
S: Rowland Talbot
Fred Paul .... M. Sardies
Blanche Forsythe .... Mary Dacre
Rolf Leslie .... John Dacre
CRIME Inventor's wife avenges death by posing
as anarchist and exploding their den.

04148
THE DASHING HUSSAR (675) (U)
Barker
S: Rowland Talbot
COMEDY Village girls fall for hussar who
turns out to be bigamist.

04149
PETER'S PERIL (515) (U)
Barker
S: Rowland Talbot
Peter Gale .... Peter
COMEDY Bankrupt takes 'poison' and then
learns he is an heir.

04150
LITTLE ELSIE (1350) (U)
Barker
D: (Bert Haldane)
S: Rowland Talbot
Eileen Daybell .... Elsie
Roy Travers ....Convict 87
CRIME Escaped convict wounded while
saving governor's child from gipsies.

04151
A FISHING STORY (718) (U)
Barker
S: Rowland Talbot
COMEDY Fisherman photographed with girl
and blackmailed.

04152
OUTWITTING MAMA (835) (U)
B&C (MP)
D: (Charles Weston)
ROMANCE Old man bribes nephew to wed
girl without realising they love each other.

04153
LIEUTENANT DARING AND THE DANCING
GIRL (1742) (U)
B&C (MP)
D: Charles Raymond
Percy Moran .... Lt Daring
Dorothy Foster ..... The Dancing Girl
CRIME Jamaica. Lt saves dancer from jealous
lover's mob.

04154
EAST LYNNE (2200)
Brightonia (MP)
D: Arthur Charrington
S: (NOVEL) Mrs Henry Wood
Nell Emerald .... Lady Isabel
H. Agar Lyons .... Capt Levison
Frank Petley .... Archibald Carlyle
Monnie Mine .... Barbara Hare
C.S. McConnell ...... Earl
DRAMA Lady elopes with murderer and poses
as nurse to be near her dying child.

04155
MERCIA THE FLOWER GIRL (1560) (A)
Brightonia (MP)
D: Arthur Charrington
S: (PLAY)
Nell Emerald .... Mercia
H. Agar Lyons .... Capt Jack
Frank Petley .... Sir Harry Fielding
Eily Adair
Monnie Mine
CRIME Lord weds flower girl and saves her
from blackmailing nephew.

04156
HIS SECOND CHANCE (1888) (A)
Britannia Films (Pathe)
DRAMA Actor deserted by mistress and saved
from suicide by his destitute wife and child.

04157
THE NEW HAT (305) (U)
Clarendon
D: Percy Stow
COMEDY Husband's birthday hat gets tarred
and feathered .

04158
IT'S BEST TO BE NATURAL (740) (U)
Clarendon
D: Percy Stow
COMEDY Southend. Childhood sweethearts
meet again and pretend to be still youthful.

04159
NOT WANTED (525) (U)
Clarendon
D: Percy Stow
S: Ernest Dangerfield
Mrs Dangerfield .... Widow
Winnie Dangerfield .... Child
DRAMA Widow must get rid of her three
children before she can marry.

04160
THE NEW LETTER BOX (495) (U)
Clarendon
D: Percy Stow
COMEDY Man uses fake letter-box to thwart
daughter's elopement.

04161
A VIOLENT FANCY (425) (U)
Clarendon
D: Percy Stow
COMEDY Man is kind to dog and it follows
him everywhere.

04162
GOOD FOR EVIL (1600) (U)
Cricks (C&M)
D: (Charles Calvert)
S: Frederick H-U. Bowman
DRAMA Drunkard sets fire to house of cleric,
not knowing his wife and child are there.

04163
WILL HE DO IT? (310) (U)
Cricks (C&M)
D: (Edwin J. Collins)
CHASE Butcher running with knife is actually
seeking grinder.

04164
MISS AUSTEN'S ADVENTURE (365) (U)
Cricks (C&M)
D: (Charles Calvert)
COMEDY Old spinster mistaken for militant
suffragette.

04165
AN ISLAND ROMANCE (1125) (U)
Cricks (C&M)
D: (Edwin J. Collins)
ADVENTURE Girl rows to escape marriage
and saves drowning lover.

04166
HAVE YOU A MATCH? (305) (U)
Cricks (C&M)
D: Charles Calvert)
COMEDY Man seeks match for cigar; it explodes.

04167
THE WHIRLIGIG OF TIME (1820) (U)
Cricks (C&M)
D: (Edwin J. Collins)
ROMANCE Artist buys poor squire's mortgage
to force daughter's consent.

04168
ALGY AND THE PIERRETTE (285) (U)
Cricks (C&M)
D: (Edwin J. Collins)
COMEDY Dude carries girl's luggage and then
finds she is married.

04169
A KNIFE TO GRIND (233) (U)
EcKo (U)
D: W.P. Kellino
Sam T. Poluski ...... The Man
CHASE Man running with knife is actually
seeking grinder.

04170
BUMBLES' WALK TO BRIGHTON (488) (U)
EcKo (U)
D: W.P. Kellino
Phillipi .... Bumble
COMEDY Bumbles bets he can walk to Brighton
and his opponents change signposts.

04171
MRS LeTARE LETS APARTMENTS (300) (U)
EcKo (U)
D: W.P. Kellino
Sam T. Poluski
Will Poluski
The Famous Kellinos
COMEDY Landlady lets rooms to tragedian, acrobats, dogs.

04172
THE FLIGHT OF WEALTH (413) (U)
EcKo (U)
D: W.P. Kellino
Sam T. Poluski .... The Man
CHASE Man pursues windblown £5 note.

04173
HE DID IT FOR THE BEST (494) (U)
EcKb (U)
D: W.P. Kellino
Sam T. Poluski .... The Man
COMEDY Man mistakes tramp for eccentric rich uncle.

04174
THE JOVIAL FLUID (432) (U)
EcKo (U)
D: W.P. Kellino
Sam T. Poluski .... The Boy
COMEDY Boy fills scent-spray with professor's 'laughter liquid'.

04175
JUGGLING MAD (494) (U)
EcKo (U)
D: W.P. Kellino
Sam T. Poluski .... The Man
COMEDY Drunk tries to emulate juggler.

04176
BUMBLES' DIMINISHER (500) (U)
EcKo (U)
D: W.P. Kellino
Phillipi .... Bumbles
TRICK Magic powder shrinks beer and fat circus child.

04177
PIMPLE'S COMPLAINT (450) (U)
Folly Films (Phoenix)
D:S: Fred Evans, Joe Evans
Fred Evans .... Pimple
COMEDY Boys pin smallpox notice on Pimple's back.

04178
TWO TO ONE ON PIMPLE (370) (U)
Folly Films (Phoenix)
D:S: Fred Evans, Joe Evans
Fred Evans .... Pimple
COMEDY Horse race burlesque.

04179
THE DOGS AND THE DESPERADO (450) (U)
Hepworth
D: Frank Wilson
Chrissie White .... The Girl
ANIMAL Policeman follows two dogs who pursue bag-snatcher.

04180
ON THE BRINK OF THE PRECIPICE (1800) (U)
Hepworth
D: (Warwick Buckland)
Harry Gilbey .... Stephen Veriker
Harry Royston .... Groom
John McAndrews .... Detective
Jack Raymond
Johnny Butt
CRIME Acrobats save kidnapped child of nobleman's widow.

04181
BOUNDING BERTIE'S BUNGALOW (500) (U)
Hepworth
D: (Hay Plumb)
COMEDY Tramp lets riverside bungalow while owner away.

04182
THE INEVITABLE (900) (U)
Hepworth
D: (Frank Wilson)
Chrissie White .... Kathleen
Jack Raymond .... Nephew
Harry Gilbey .... Recluse
ROMANCE Recluse loves old sweetheart's neice, but she loves his nephew.

04183
THE PROMISE (1450) (U)
Hepworth
D: (Warwick Buckland)
Alec Worcester .... Jack
Chrissie White .... Ivy Morton
Harry Royston .... Tom Parker
CRIME Vicar's son saves squire from burglars and weds son's fiancee.

04184
PETER'S LITTLE PICNIC (525) (U)
Hepworth
D: (Hay Plumb)
Chrissie White .... Gertie
COMEDY Tramps steal boat of picnicking couple.

04185
PARTNERS IN CRIME (2275) (U)
Hepworth
D: (Warwick Buckland)
Alma Taylor .... Ruth Merideth
Harry Royston ...... Sam Surridge
Flora Morris .... Innkeeper's Daughter
Harry Gilbey .... Mr Merideth
CRIME Sailor is blamed when smuggler stabs fiancee's father.

04186
HER LITTLE PET (450) (U)
Hepworth
D: Frank Wilson
Alma Taylor .... Flossie
ANIMAL Man's sheepdog tracks his ex-fiancee's lost terrier.

04187
LITTLE WILLIE'S APPRENTICESHIPS (440) (U)
Martin (C&M) *Reissue:* 1915
D:S: Lewin Fitzhamon
Roy Royston .... Willie
COMEDY Boy fails several jobs: as gardener, china salesman, etc.

04188
THREE LITTLE VAGABONDS (475) (U)
Martin (C&M) *Reissue:* 1915, HOME FOR THE HOLIDAYS
D:S: Lewin Fitzhamon
Constance Somers-Clarke ..... Girl
Roy Royston .... Boy
Marie Royston .... Girl
COMEDY Three children drive car and cause trouble in farm-yard.

04189
THE CLOISTER AND THE WOMAN (1995) (U)
Searchlight (MP)
Eva Stuart .... Adele
Wallace Aldridge .... Andre
Bernard Vaughan .... Abbe
George Ashley ....; Michael
Rosamund Tatton ...... Rose
DRAMA Jealous abbe chains up monk, who dies in fire while abbe is struck by lightning.

04190
A CHILD'S HAND (730) (U)
Searchlight (MP)
Wallace Aldridge .... Jack
ROMANCE Man returns after 20 years to find fiancee apparently married.

04191
A USELESS DECEP TION (588) (U)
Searchlight (MP)
Wallace Aldridge .... The Man
DRAMA Girl blinded in car crash which killed her fiance; his friend poses as him until she recovers.

04192
A LIGHTER BURDEN (1900)
Big Ben Films (Siemens)
D: George Pearson
TRICK City man who cannot pay electric bill dreams advertisements come to life.

04193
HE THAT LAUGHS LAST (365) (U)
Sun Films (Cosmo)
COMEDY Boy cyclist rides into people and is pelted with eggs.

04194
BILLY BUNGLE'S FIRST DAY ON THE FORCE (455) (U)
Sun Films (Cosmo)
COMEDY Misadventures of officious policeman.

04195
AND THEN SHE WOKE UP (490)
Summit Films (Tyler)
COMEDY Maid dreams master loves her, enabling her to bully mistress.

04196
THE NEW TRIUMPH (615)
Su mmit Films (Tyler)
CHASE Doctor rides new 'Triumph' motor-cycle to catch elopers.

04197
THE APACHE DANCE (200)
Motograph
D: J.J. Bam berger
Fred Farren
Beatrice Collier
MUSICAL Empire Theatre dancers synchronised to music score.

JUL

04198
IN THE SHADOW OF DARKNESS (2142) (A)
Barker
D: (Bert Haldane)
S: Rowland Talbot
Harry W. Scaddan .... Cdr Ronald Arnesby
Blanche Forsythe .... Nora Arnesby
Roy Travers .... Curtis Rule
Rachel de Solla .... Mrs Arnesby
DRAMA Blinded officer fights duel in dark with squire who abandoned his sweetheart.

04199
MOLLY'S BURGLAR (840) (U)
Barker
D: (Bert Haldane)
S: Rowland Talbot
Doreen O'Connor .... Molly
Peter Gale .... Suitor
Tom Coventry .... Pa
COMEDY Girl's father mistakes suitor for burglar

04200
ROBERT'S CAPTURE (450) (U)
Barker
S: Rowland Talbot
Tom Coventry .... PC Robert
Rachel de Solla .... The Mistress
COMEDY PC hides from vengeful mistress and
catches burglar.

04201
THE GREAT BULLION ROBBERY (2110) (U)
Barker (Bendon)
D: (Alexander Butler)
S: Rowland Talbot
Fred Paul .... Stephen Crasp
Will Asher .... Chauffeur
CRIME Gang use shop to break into vault and
are chased by Thames police.

04202
FISHERMAN'S LUCK (775) (U)
Barker
D: (Bert Haldane)
S: Rowland Talbot
Gladys Sylvani .... Winnie
Thos H. MacDonald .... Tom
Edward Viner .... George
Roy Travers .... Tramp
COMEDY Tramp leaves winkles in exchange
for rich man's picnic.

04203
THE PLANTER'S DAUGHTER (1100) (U)
B&C (MP)
D: Charles Raymond
Percy Moran .... Jack Armstrong
Dorothy Foster ..... Mary Etheridge
CRIME Jamaica. Overseer ties employer's
daughter to railway line.

04204
THE BATTLE OF WATERLOO (4500) (U)
B&C (Ruffells)
D: Charles Weston
Ernest G. Batley .... Napoleon
George Foley .... Blucher
Vivian Ross .... Marshal Ney
HISTORY 1815. Wellington defeats Napoleon.

04205
THE HUNGER STRIKE (495) (U) retitled:
'TWAS ONLY A DREAM
B&C (MP)
COMEDY Hungry convict dreams of feast.

04206
DICK TURPIN'S RIDE TO YORK (1737) (U)
B&C (Walturdaw)
D: Charles Raymond
Percy Moran .... Dick Turpin
ADVENTURE Period. Highwayman betrayed
by jealous wife and chased by Bow Street
Runners.

04207
WANTED A HUSBAND (618) (U)
Brightonia (MP)
D: Arthur Charrington
S: (SKETCH) Mark Melford
Mark Melford ....Husband
COMEDY Henpeck persuades plumber to
pose as doctor.

04208
THE GRIP OF IRON (3250) (U)
Brightonia (Andrews)
D: Arthur Charrington
S: (PLAY) Arthur Shirley
Fred Powell .... Jagon/Simmonet
Nell Emerald .... Cora Jagon
H. Agar Lyons .... Lorenz de Rifas

Frank E. Petley .... Smiler
Gertrude Price
Stanley Bedwell
CRIME Paris. Lawyer's clerk strangles and
robs for daughter's sake.

04209
FLYING FROM JUSTICE (2000) (U)
Brightonia (Popular)
D: Arthur Charrington
S: (PLAY) Mark Melford
Mark Melford .... Gully
Nell Emerald .... Mildred Parkes
H. Agar Lyons .... Charles Baring
Frank E. Petley .... James Woodruff
CRIME Counterfeiting gang ensnare cleric's
pupil.

04210
A MASTER OF MEN (1070) (U)
Britannia Films (Pathe)
D: (A.E. Coleby)
DRAMA Strikers won over after failing to
blow up their employer.

04211
KIDNAPPED FOR REVENGE (795) (U)
All-British Films (Cosmo)
ANIMAL Dog saves farmer's baby from kidnap
by gipsy.

04212
THE WOODCUTTER'S DAUGHTER (1235)
(U)
All-British Films (Cosmo)
DRAMA Tourist saves girl from forced marriage
to landlord.

04213
A WOMAN'S HATE (760) (U)
All-British Films (Cosmo)
CRIME Jealous girl promises to marry man if
he kills her ex-fiance.

04214
MISS GLADEYE SLIP'S VACATION (525) (U)
Clarendon
D: Percy Stow
COMEDY Berkshire villagers and their vicar fall
for visiting actress.

04215
HAY HO! (375) (U)
Clarendon
D: Percy Stow
COMEDY Search for baby lost in haystack.

04216
A SURPRISING ENCOUNTER (485) (U)
Reissue: 1916, THE MISFITS
Clarendon
D: Percy Stow
COMEDY Boys change girl swimmer's clothes
with those of swimming cleric.

04217
LIEUTENANT ROSE AND THE STOLEN
BULLION (1950) (U)
Clarendon
D: Percy Stow
P.G. Norgate .... Lt Rose
ADVENTURE Lt chases gang across sea and
ice-floes.

04218
INCOMPATIBILITY OF TEMPER (470) (U)
Clarendon
D: Percy Stow
COMEDY 1874-1913. Couple fight their way
through the years.

04219
DAYLIGHT ROBBERY (350) (U)
Cricks (C&M)
D: (Charles Calvert)
CHASE Tramps steal basket which contains —
dogs.

04220
EXPRESS DELIVERY (485) (U)
Cricks (C&M)
D: (Edwin J. Collins)
COMEDY Lazy postman puts his letters in
pillar-box which is then set afire by suffragette.

04221
REVENGE IS SWEET (480) (U)
Cricks (C&M)
D: (Edwin J. Collins)
COMEDY Tramp exchanges clothes of swim-
ming cleric and policeman.

04222
MOTHER GETS THE WRONG TONIC (431)
(U)
Cricks (C&M)
D: (Charles Calvert)
COMEDY Neuralgic woman drinks horse tonic
and acts like one.

04223
IN THE DEAD MAN'S ROOM (1860) (A)
Cricks (C&M)
D: (Charles Calvert)
CRIME 'Dead' heir returns to prove crook
posed as his dying father to alter will.

04224
A FISHY STORY (270) (U)
Cricks (C&M)
D: (Edwin J. Collins)
CHASE Man with fish is mistaken for thief.

04225
A BRIGAND'S WOOING (1728) (U)
Cricks (C&M)
D: (Edwin J. Collins)
CRIME Soldiers save innkeeper's daughter
from brigand.

04226
WHAT A HOLIDAY! (520) (U)
Cricks (C&M)
D: (Charles Calvert)
COMEDY Misadventures of three men on
river camping holiday.

04227
PONKY'S HOUSEBOAT (810) (U)
Dart Films (Anderson)
D: Stuart Kinder
Joe Omar .... Ponky
COMEDY Thames Ditton. Married man caught
flirting with swimming girls.

04228
OH THAT WOOLLEN UNDERVEST! (488)
(U)
EcKo (U)
D: W.P. Kellino
Sam T. Poluski .... The Man
COMEDY New undervest causes man to itch.

04229
ON THE HOP (370)
EcKo (U)
D: W.P. Kellino
Sam T. Poluski .... The Man
COMEDY Man tears boot and must hop to
cobblers.

04230
PARCELS OR THE BABY (378)
EcKo (U)
D: W.P. Kellino
Sam T. Poluski .... The Man
COMEDY Man carries wife's shopping and loses
most of it.

04231
BUMBLES' GOOSE (458) (U)
EcKo (U)
D: W.P. Kellino
Phillipi .... Bumbles
COMEDY Bumbles gives away high goose before
learning it contained £20.

04232
BUMBLES' RADIUM MINSTRELS (513)
EcKo (U)
D: W.P. Kellino
Phillipi .... Bumbles
COMEDY Minstrel shows manager absconds
with proceeds.

04233
HOW WILLY JOINED BARNUM BILL
(529) (U)
EcKo (U)
D: W.P. Kellino
Will Kellino .... Willy
COMEDY Clown becomes partner in small
circus.

04234
PIMPLE'S MOTOR TRAP (410) (U)
Folly Films (Phoenix)
D:S: Fred Evans, Joe Evans
Fred Evans .... Pimple
Joe Evans .... Capt Scuttle
COMEDY Crooks pose as policemen, stop
motorists, and take bribes.

04235
PIMPLE'S SPORTING CHANCE (495) (U)
Folly Films (Phoenix)
D:S: Fred Evans, Joe Evans
Fred Evans .... Pimple
Joe Evans .... Capt Scuttle
COMEDY Pimple wins £10 boxing prize and
saves widow from eviction.

04236
PIMPLE TAKES A PICTURE (360) (U)
Folly Films (Phoenix)
D:S: Fred Evans, Joe Evans
Fred Evans .... Pimple
COMEDY Misadventures of film
cameraman.

04237
PIMPLE GETS THE SACK (375)
Folly Films (Phoenix)
D:S: Fred Evans, Joe Evans
Fred Evans .... Pimple
COMEDY Pimple robs house, hides in burglar's
sack, and is thrown in river.

04238
ADVENTURES OF PIMPLE — THE BATTLE
OF WATERLOO (587) (U)
Folly Films (Phoenix)
D:S: Fred Evans, Joe Evans
Fred Evans .... Napoleon
Joe Evans .... Wellington
COMEDY Burlesque of 'Battle of Waterloo'
(B&C).

04239
A HELPING HAND (1100) (U)
Hepworth
D: (Warwick Buckland)
Alec Worcester .... Busker

Jamie Darling .... Cobbler
DRAMA Old cobbler helps busker and his child;
later they repay him.

04240
THE OLD NUISANCE (700) (U)
Hepworth
D: (Hay Plumb)
Chrissie White .... The Wife
Claire Pridelle .... The Friend
COMEDY Couple persuade friend to flirt with
unwanted mother-in-law.

04241
WHISTLING WILLIAM (400) (U)
Hepworth
D: (Frank Wilson)
COMEDY Busker forced to swallow whistle.

04243
DR TRIMBALL'S VERDICT (1100) (A)
Hepworth
D: (Frank Wilson)
Alec Worcester .... Dr Trimball
Chrissie White .... Alice
FANTASY Dr kills rival and dies of shock on
seeing him materialise on purchased skeleton.

04243
ADRIFT ON LIFE'S TIDE (1750) (U)
Hepworth
D: (Warwick Buckland)
Alma Taylor .... Edna Wilson
Flora Morris .... Mrs Wilson
Harry Royston ...... Mr Wilson
Harry Gilbey .... The Rich Man
DRAMA Drunkard's daughter is adopted,
rejected, becomes a dancer, and spurns wealth
for love.

04244
FATHER TAKES THE BABY OUT (650) (U)
Hepworth
D: (Frank Wilson)
COMEDY Children hide pram while henpeck
is asleep.

04245
THEN HE JUGGLED (525) (U)
Hepworth
D: (Frank Wilson)
COMEDY Man emulates street juggler and
smashes shopman's wares.

04246
THE RED LIGHT (1050) (U)
Hepworth
D: Warwick Buckland
Alec Worcester .... Joe
Chrissie White .... Mrs Joe
CRIME Wounded signalman drapes bloody
bandage over signal and saves a train from
wreckers.

04247
LIEUTENANT PIE'S LOVE STORY (775) (U)
Hepworth
D: Hay Plumb
Harry Buss .... Lt Pie
Chrissie White .... The Girl
Claire Pridelle
Reggie Sheffield
COMEDY Lt and his men save girl from
kidnappers.

04248
THE ADVENTURES OF JOE SLUDGE AB
(445) (U)
Searchlight Films (Phoenix)
COMEDY Sailor's tale of storm rocks room
and makes his audience seasick.

04249
BUTTERCUP PC (475) (U)
H&W Films (Prieur)
D: (Stuart Kinder)
COMEDY Misadventures of flirtatious police-
man.

04250
HER PONY'S LOVE (1070) (U)
Gaumont
D:S: Lewin Fitzhamon
Constance Somers-Clarke .... Cora
ANIMAL Bognor. Girl's pony fetches fiance to
save her from sea.

04251
IVANHOE (3300) (U)
Independent Moving Pictures
D:SC: Herbert Brenon
S: (NOVEL) Sir Walter Scott
King Baggot .... Ivanhoe
Leah Baird .... Rebecca
Evelyn Hope .... Lady Rowena
Herbert Brenon .... Isaac
Wallace Widdecombe ...... Sir Brian
Jack Bates .... Sir Reginald
Wallace Bosco .... Cedric
George Courtney .... Prince John
Arthur Scott-Craven ...... King Richard
W. Thomas .... Robin Hood
H. Holles .... Friar Tuck
W. Calvert .... Gurth
A.J. Charlwood .... Athelstane
ADVENTURE Period. Disowned knight
rescues heiress and Jewess from charge of
sorcery.

04252
IVANHOE (6000) USA: "REBECCA THE
JEWESS
Zenith Films (Big A)
D:SC: Leedham Bantock
S: (PLAY) Walter & Frederick Melville
Lauderdale Maitland .... Ivanhoe
Edith Bracewell .... Rebecca
Nancy Bevington .... Lady Rowena
Hubert Carter .... Isaac
Henry Lonsdale .... Sir Brian
Austin Milroy .... Front de Boeuf
ADVENTURE Period. Disowned knight rescues
heiress and Jewess from charge of sorcery.

04253
A MESSAGE FROM MARS (4000)
United Kingdom Films
P: Nicholson Ormsby-Scott
D:SC: J. Wallett Waller
S: (PLAY) Richard Ganthony
Charles Hawtrey .... Horace Parker
E. Holman Clark .... Ramiel
Crissie Bell .... Minnie
Frank Hector .... Arthur Dicey
Hubert Willis .... Tramp
Kate Tyndale .... Aunt Martha
Evelyn Beaumont ...... Bella
Eileen Temple .... Mrs Clarence
R. Crompton .... God of Mars
B. Stanmore .... Wounded Man
Tonie Reith .... His Wife
FANTASY Martian sentenced to visit earth to
cure selfish man.

04254
WAY DOWN THE MISSISSIPPI
Selsior Films
John Raker & Nat Lewis
MUSICAL Dance to synchronise with cinema
orchestras.

04255
THE EMPIRE GLIDE
Selsior Films
The Empire Theatre girls
MUSICAL Dance to synchronise with cinema orchestras.

04256
THE TANGO WALTZ (550)
Selsior Films
Ernest Belcher & Norah Walker
MUSICAL Dance to synchronise with cinema orchestras.

AUG

04257
HIS GRANDSON (1200) (U)
All-British Films (Cosmo)
DRAMA Disowned man dies and father finds family in time to save them from starvation.

04258
ASHAMED OF HIS WIFE (835) (U)
All-British Films (Cosmo)
ROMANCE Londoner's country wife leaves him to become singer but returns when he saves her from cad.

04259
THE FOUNDLING (775) (U)
All-British Films (Cosmo)
CRIME Period. Usurper hires poachers to kill squire step-brother.

04260
LOVE DARES ALL (825) (U) retitled: A SAILOR'S SWEETHEART
Anderson
ADVENTURE Girl dives from cliff to save drowning sailor.

04261
LONDON BY NIGHT (3250) (A)
Barker (Walturdaw)
D: (Alexander Butler)
S: (PLAY) Charles Selby
SC: Harry Engholm, Rowland Talbot
Thos H. MacDonald .... Dick Ralston
Doreen O'Connor .... Mary Lucas
Roy Travers .... Sly Ned
Joan Scaddan .... Estelle
J. Hastings Batson .... Sir John Ralston
CRIME Disowned lawyer cleared of killing girl crook when he saves tramp from burning dosshouse.

04262
THROUGH THE CLOUDS (3158) (U)
B&C (Ruffells)
D:S: Charles Weston
Ernest G. Batley .... Halifax Hilliard
Marie Pickering .... Kitty Hilliard
George Foley .... Lord Denison
Harry Lorraine .... Silk Hat Harry
Jack Jarman .... Rudolf Berkman
ADVENTURE Girl flies aeroplane to save detective father from jewel thief's balloon.

04263
REUB'S LITTLE GIRL (1960) (U)
Big Ben Films-Union (Pathe)
Reissue: 1915, THE COASTGUARD'S HAUL
D: H.O. Martinek
H.O. Martinek .... Coastguard
Ivy Martinek .... The Girl
CRIME Jersey. Girl saves smuggler father from coastguard.

04264
MR HENPECK'S DILEMMA (700) (U)
Big Ben Films-Union (Pathe)

04265
THE CHAPLET OF PEARLS (1135) (U)
Britannia Films (Pathe)
D: H.O. Martinek
ROMANCE Officer sends necklace to his fiancee, who loses it.

04266
THE SENTENCE OF DEATH (2370) (A)
Britannia Films (Pathe)
D:S: George Pearson
DRAMA Doctor learns he has weak heart, leaves his fiancee, and dies.

04267
THERE ARE GIRLS WANTED HERE (479) (U)
Clarendon
D: Percy Stow
COMEDY Military students advertise for girl pupils.

04268
THE HOME BEAUTIFUL (385) (U)
Clarendon
D: Percy Stow
COMEDY Couple's house wrecked by builders.

04269
THE DRAMATIC STORY OF THE VOTE (845) (U)
Clarendon
D: Percy Stow
DRAMA 'Pity', refused vote by 'John Bull', takes baby instead.

04270
UNSKILLED LABOUR (395) (U)
Clarendon
D: Percy Stow
COMEDY Music Hall manager has trouble substituting for striking staff.

04271
PERSEVERING PETER (399) (U)
Cricks (C&M)
D: (Charles Calvert)
S: F. Moores
COMEDY Debtor dreams of persistent clerk.

04272
MONEY FOR NOTHING (450) (U)
Cricks (C&M)
D: Edwin J. Collins)
CHASE Man in fancy dress mistaken for escaped lunatic.

04273
A LIFE FOR A LIFE (964) (A)
Cricks (C&M)
D: (Charles Calvert)
CRIME Escaped convict strangles doctor who let wife die.

04274
WHEN FATHER LEARNT TO BIKE (532) (U)
Cricks (C&M) *Reissue:* 1915
D: (Edwin J. Collins)
COMEDY Father's mishaps trying to ride bicycle.

04275
THE HEART OF A GYPSY MAID (835) (U)
Cricks (C&M)
D: (Edwin J. Collins)
DRAMA Squire saves gipsy from snakebite and she dies saving him from lover's bullet.

04276
BUMBLES, PHOTOGRAPHER (500)
EcKo (U)
D: W.P. Kellino
Phillipi .... Bumbles
Famous Kellinos .... Acrobats
COMEDY Bumbles photographs various people and ends in river.

04277
BUMBLES BECOMES A CROOK (479) (U)
EcKo (U)
D: W.P. Kellino
Phillipi .... Bumbles
COMEDY Bumbles joins cardsharping gang, cracks safe, and is chased.

04278
PIMPLE'S WONDERFUL GRAMOPHONE (495) (U)
Folly Films (Phoenix)
D:S: Fred Evans, Joe Evans
Fred Evans .... Pimple
COMEDY Pimple builds a gramophone and hides inside it.

04279
PIMPLE'S REST CURE (550) (U)
Folly Films (U)
D:S: Fred Evans, Joe Evans
Fred Evans .... Pimple
COMEDY Pimple searches for peace beside sea and ends in pigsty.

04280
A FIVER FOR A PENNY (930) (U)
Gaumont
COMEDY Man bets he can sell £5 note for penny.

04281
A PRECIOUS CARGO (1125) (U)
Hepworth
D: Hay Plumb
Hay Plumb .... Lt Troon
Claire Pridelle .... Jennifer
Harry Royston ...... Black Coffinger
ADVENTURE Cornwall. Customs officer loves smuggler's daughter.

04282
THE GIRL AT LANCING MILL (1125) (U)
Hepworth
D: Warwick Buckland
Alec Worcester .... Bob Francis
Alma Taylor .... Esther Alloway
Harry Royston .... Stephen Barling
Harry Gilbey .... Mr Francis
DRAMA New mill-owner poses as worker to save girl from manager.

04283
THE MISSIONER'S PLIGHT (500) (U)
Hepworth
D: (Frank Wilson)
Jack Hulcup .... The Son
Jack Raymond .... Friend
COMEDY Religious man seeks his son and is caught in club raid.

04284
A LITTLE WIDOW IS A DANGEROUS THING (600) (U)
Hepworth
D: (Frank Wilson)
Alma Taylor .... Maudie
Jack Raymond
Jamie Darling
Violet Hopson
COMEDY Girl poses as widow to win marriage proposal.

04285
DAVID COPPERFIELD (7500) (U)
Hepworth (Walturdaw)
D:SC: Thomas Bentley
S: (NOVEL) Charles Dickens
Kenneth Ware .... David Copperfield
Eric Desmond .... David (child)
Len Bethel .... David (youth)
Alma Taylor .... Dora Spenlow
H. Collins .... Wilkins Micawber
Jack Hulcup .... Uriah Heep
Jamie Darling .... Daniel Peggorty
Edna May .... Little Emily (child)
Amy Verity .... Little Emily
Cecil Mannering .... Steerforth
Ella Fineberg .... Agnes Wickfield
Miss Harcourt .... Betsy Trotwood
Johnny Butt .... Mr Murdstone
Miss West .... Mrs Micawber
Shiel Porter .... Mr Wickfield
Tom Arnold .... Ham
Harry Royston .... Mr Creakle
Marie de Solla .... Mrs Gummidge
DRAMA Runaway orphan adopted by aunt
eventually finds love. (First British 8-reel
feature)

04286
THE GIFT (3500) (U) Retitled: KISSING CUP
Hepworth (KTC)
D: Jack Hulcup
S: Percy Manton
Alec Worcester .... Richard Cardew
Chrissie White .... Chrissie Heatherington
Cecil Mannering .... Jack Heatherington
Flora Morris .... Daisy Ingham
John McAndrews .... R. Ingham
Harry Gilbey .... Squire Heatherington
SPORT Squire's jockey escapes kidnappers and
flies to Sandown in time to win race.

04287
ROSE OF SURREY (2000) (U)
Turner Films (Hepworth)
D: Larry Trimble
Florence Turner .... Rose Moore
Frank Powell .... Edmund Grey
Shirley Lea .... John Grey
Millicent Vernon .... Vivienne Hunter
Arthur Rodney .... The Solicitor
Leal Douglas .... Mrs Moore
ROMANCE Widow tries to lure rich man's son
from partner's daughter.

04288
JEAN'S EVIDENCE (1800) (U)
Turner Films (Hepworth)
D:S: Larry Trimble
Florence Turner .... Rose Moore
Shirley Lea .... Edward Harvey
Jean the Vitagraph Dog
ANIMAL Dog proves inventor's daughter stole
diamond in her sleep.

04289
BLACK AND WHITE (350) (U)
H&W Films (Prieur)
D: (Stuart Kinder)
TRICK Boy's magic powder makes black
objects turn white.

04290
LA CIGALE (2600) (U)
Ivy Close Films (Walturdaw)
D:SC: Elwin Neame
S: (STORY) La Fontaine
Ivy Close .... La Cigale
PATHOS Girl dreams she is strolling player
who rejects love and dies.

04291
BEAUTY AND THE BOAT (593) (U)
Martin Films (C&M)
D: (Lewin Fitzhamon)
S: A.R. Lewis
DRAMA Man wins boatman's daughter by saving
father from tramps.

04292
LIQUID LOVE (425) (U)
Martin Films (C&M) *Reissue*: 1915, LITTLE
GRAINS OF LOVE
COMEDY Prof's son squirts people with love-
inducing liquid.

04293
A SHOCKING JOB (535) (U)
Martin Films (C&M) *Reissue*: 1915, SHOCKS
AND SHORTS
D: (Dave Aylott)
S: F. Moores
COMEDY Man and son have trouble wiring
house for electricity.

04294
THE STAR AND CRESCENT (1700) (U)
Searchlight Films (Phoenix)
CRIME Solicitor's typist tries to kill heir.

04295
THE GOOD SAMARITAN (700)
Searchlight Films (Phoenix)
CRIME Small child reforms thief.

04296
THE ELEVENTH COMMANDMENT (2505)
Kisch-Barker Films (Gerrard)
S: Samuel M. Gluckstein
James Welch .... Marmaduke Wright
Gladys Cooper .... Edith
Vincent Clive .... Capt Henry Vane
Ronald Notcutt .... Claude Bilderton
Helena Callen .... Bimbo
DRAMA Guardian spends ward's inheritance
and tries to make her marry rich cad.

04297
THE FLAPPERS AND THE COLONEL
(580) (U)
Gaumont
D:S: Lewin Fitzhamon
Constance Somers-Clarke ..... Flapper
Peggy Manning .... Flapper
COMEDY Bognor. Flappers fool governess and
maroon colonel in leaking boat.

SEP

04298
GREATER LOVE HATH NO MAN (3500) (U)
Barker (World)
D: (Alexander Butler)
S: Rowland Talbot
Thos H. McDonald .... Herbert Crawley
Blanche Forsythe .... Mary
Fred Paul .... Tom Jameson
Rolf Leslie .... Vicar
DRAMA Society doctor leaves ill Princess to
suck growth from poor girl's throat.

04299
HUMANITY; OR, ONLY A JEW (3000) (A)
Barker (Magnet)
D: John Lawson, Bert Haldane
S:(PLAY) John Lawson
John Lawson .... Silvani
Lucille Sidney .... Adele Silvani
Charles Stafford .... Jacob Cuthbert
Rollo Balmain .... Gabriel
Frank Seddon .... Moses Silvani
Henry Ludlow .... Capt Grey
Jessica Elvin .... Mrs Grey

CRIME Jewish gambler saves man from suicide
and kills him after he shoots his friend and
seduces wife.

04300
YOUNITA — FROM GUTTER TO FOOT-
LIGHTS (4000) (A)
Barker (Arton)
D: (Bert Haldane)
S: Rowland Talbot
Fred Paul .... Giovanni
DRAMA Italian street-dancer rises to stardom
and is shot by her jealous lover.

04301
BIFFY VISITS THE THEATRE (580)
Barker (Royal)
S: Rowland Talbot
COMEDY 'The first exclusive comic.'

04302
A TRAGEDY IN THE ALPS (3000)
B&C (Apex)
D:S: Charles Weston
Ernest G. Batley .... Ted Matthews
Marie Pickering .... Phyllis
Claudia Guillot .... Maisie Carlton
George Foley .... George Tristy
Harry Lorraine .... Banker
ADVENTURE Clerk takes blame for gambler's
theft and later saves his daughter on Mont Blanc.

04303
LIEUTENANT DARING AND THE MYSTERY
OF ROOM 41 (2270) (U) USA: LIEUTENANT
DARING AND THE INTERNATIONAL
JEWEL THIEVES
B&C (DFSA)
D: Charles Weston
Harry Lorraine .... Lt Daring
George Foley .... Thief
CRIME Lieut trailing American hotel-robber is
thrown from Walton Bridge and saved by bargee's
daughter. (Extract in ALL GOOD FUN (Butcher,
1956).)

04304
THE BROKEN CHISEL (2986) (U) USA:
ESCAPE FROM BROADMOOR
B&C (DFSA)
D: Charles Weston
S: Ernest G. Batley
Ernest G. Batley .... Jack Hinton
Dorothy Batley .... Eva Barker
Marie Pickering .... May Caversham
CRIME Man escapes jail by balloon and saves
daughter of thief who framed him.

04305
THE NEST ON THE BLACK CLIFF (900) (U)
Big Ben Films-Union (Pathe)
D: H.O. Martinek
H.O. Martinek .... The Man
Ivy Montford ....The Girl
ADVENTURE Cornwall. Girl saves sweetheart
when rival knocks him over cliff.

04306
AUNTIE'S SECRET SORROW (975) (U)
Clarendon
D: Percy Stow
Dorothy Bellew .... Betty
COMEDY Girl thinks spinster aunt is secretly
wed but finds she is in wrong house.

04307
A HORSE! A HORSE! (355) (U0
Clarendon
D: Percy Stow
COMEDY Charwoman searches for horse for
actor playing King Richard; and brings donkey.

04308
KING CHARLES (4120) (U)
Clarendon
D: Wilfred Noy
S: (NOVEL) Harrison Ainsworth
SC: Low Warren
P.G. Ebbutt .... King Charles II
Dorothy Bellew ..... Dulcia Beard
HISTORY King escapes to France after battle
of Worcester.

04309
RINGING THE CHANGES (410) (U)
Clarendon
D: Percy Stow
COMEDY Man dresses as aunt to fool brother.

04310
THE CONVENT GATE (2175) (U)
Clarend on
D: Wilfred Noy
S: Marchioness of Townshend
Dorothy Bellew .... Marie StClair
DRAMA Jilted bride recovers sanity after being
saved from fire.

04311
HE WHO TAKES WHAT ISN'T HIS'N (230) (U)
Clarendon
D: Percy Stow
COMEDY Cyclist breaks umbrella and snatches
one from by-passer.

04312
A FISHERGIRL'S LOVE (970) (U)
Cricks (C&M)
D: (Edwin J. Collins)
ADVENTURE Fisherman swims to save sweet-
heart and artist from wrecked boat.

04313
TIME FLIES (276) (U)
Cricks (C&M)
D: (Edwin J. Collins)
Edwin J. Collins .... Prof Collins
TRICK Policeman pursues vanishing tramp.

04314
CAUGHT NAPPING (46 5) (U)
Cricks (C&M)
D: (Charles Calvert)
COMEDY Tramp poses as rich man and steals
spoons.

04315
OLD FLYNN'S FIDDLE (1020) (U)
Cricks (C&M)
D: (Charles Calvert)
DRAMA Irish villager's violin saves family
from poverty.

04316
NABBEM JOINS THE FORCE (400) (U)
Cricks (C&M)
D: (Edwin J. Collins)
S: F. Moores
COMEDY Police recruit arrests gambling boys,
suffragettes, navvies.

04317
NOSEY PARKER (477) (U)
EcKo (U)
D: W.P. Kellino
Sam T. Poluski .... Nosey Parker
COMEDY Snooper mistakes clock for bomb
and spoils film scene.

04318
PIMPLE JOINS THE ARMY (590) (U)
Folly Films (Phoenix)
D:S: Fred Evans, Joe Evans
Fred Evans .... Pimple
COMEDY Recruit borrows medals to impress
girl and is court-martialled.

04319
A BATHROOM PROBLEM (210) (U)
Folly Films (Phoenix)
D:S: Fred Evans, Joe Evans
Fred Evans .... Pimple
COMEDY Lodgers fail to open bathroom door:
it slides.

04320
A TRAGEDY IN PIMPLE'S LIFE (300) (U)
Folly Films (Phoenix)
D:S: Fred Evans, Joe Evans
Fred Evans .... Pimple
COMEDY

04321
DICKE TURPIN'S RIDE TO YORKE (695) (U)
Folly Films (Phoenix)
D:S: Fred Evans, Joe Evans
Fred Evans .... Dicke Turpin
COMEDY Burlesque pf 'Dick Turpin's Ride to
York' (B&C).

04322
THE CAMERA FIEND (550) (U)
Hepworth
D: (Frank Wilson)
Eric Desmond .... Eric
COMEDY Boy takes photographs of people in
compromising situations.

04323
THE FORSAKEN (1800) (U)
Hepworth
D: Warwick Buckland
S: Muriel Alleyne
Flora Morris .... Mrs Roberts
Harry Royston ...... Bill Roberts
Harry Gilbey .... Mr Gilbey
Ruby Belasco .... Mrs Gilbey
Eric Desmond .... Jack
CRIME Ex-convict robs house of man who
adopted his son.

04324
A MIDNIGHT ADVENTURE (1300) (U)
Hepworth
D: (Frank Wilson)
Alma Taylor .... Mary
Jack Raymond ...... Her Lover
Harry Royston ...... Joe Barker
Ruby Belasco .... Mrs Barker
Jamie Darling .... Father
Marie de Solla .... Mother
DRAMA Coachman, robbing his ex-employer,
poses as dummy Santa Claus and thwarts
elopement.

04325
A STORM IN A TEACUP (725) (U)
Hepworth
D: (Warwick Buckland)
Flora Morris .... Phoebe Dennison
Claire Pridelle
Ruby Belasco
CRIME Man posing as odd-jobber saves
ex-fiancee from burglars.

04326
THE VICAR OF WAKEFIELD (3275) (U)
Hepworth (KTC)
D: Frank Wilson
S: (NOVEL) Oliver Goldsmith
SC: Blanche McIn tosh
Violet Hopson .... Olivia Primrose
Harry Royston .... Richard Thornhill
Warwick Buckland ...... Dr Charles Primrose
Chrissie White .... Sophia Primrose
Harry Gilbey .... Sir William Thornhill
Marie de Solla .... Mrs Primrose
Jack Raymond .... Moses Primrose
Harry Buss .... Jenkinson
John McAndrews .... Minister

Jamie Darling .... Innkeeper
Claire Pridelle .... Lady
DRAMA Squire has poor vicar jailed for debt
and fakes marriage to his daughter.

04327
FOR THE HONOUR OF THE HOUSE (1150)
(U)
Hepworth
D: (Warwick Buckland)
Chrissie White .... Mary
Jamie Darling .... Richard Markham
Harry Gilbey .... Uncle
CRIME Girl's lover takes blame when drunken
brother robs rich uncle.

04328
AN EGGS-TRAOR DINARY AFFAIR (425) (U)
Hepworth
D: (Hay Plumb)
Jack Raymond .... The Man
Claire Pridelle .... The Girl
COMEDY Grocer casts doubts on rival's eggs
by exchanging hens for cockerels.

04329
ONE FAIR DAUGHTER (1625) (U)
Hepworth
D: (Warwick Buckland)
S: Alice de Winton
Alice de Winton .... Hester
Chrissie White .... Dolly
Jamie Darling .... Father
Harry Gilbey .... Cad
DRAMA Girl's companion takes blame to stop
her eloping with cad.

04330
A DAMP DEED (425) Retitled: LOOK BEFORE
YOU LEAP
Hepworth
D: (Hay Plumb)
Jack Raymond .... Percy
Chrissie White .... Kitty
COMEDY Suitor frames river rescue of girl to
win father.

04331
A CIGARETTE-MAKER'S ROMANCE (4000)
Hepworth (Gaumont)
D: Frank Wilson
S: (PLAY) Charles Hannan (NOVEL) Marion
Crawford
Martin Harvey .... Count Skariartine
Nellde Silva .... Viera
Margaret Yarde .... Woman
DRAMA Munich. Amnesiac Russian count
working in factory regains his memory in time
to thwart cousin.

04332
THE HOUSE OF TEMPERLEY (4500) (U)
London (Jury) Reissue: 1918
D: Harold M. Shaw
S:(NOVEL) Arthur Conan Doyle (RODNEY
STONE)
Charles Maude .... Capt Jack Temperley
Ben Webster .... Sir Charles Temperley
Lillian Logan .... Ethel Morley
Charles Rock .... Sir John Hawker
Edward O'N eill .... Jakes
Wyndham Guise .... Ginger Stubbs
Cecil Morton York .... Gentleman Jackson
Claire Pauncefoot .... Lady Temperly
Rex Davis .... Gloster Dick
John M. East .... Tom Cribb
Hubert Willis .... Shelton
F. Bennington .... Joe Berks
Yolande May .... Lucy
DRAMA 1770. Blacksmith's adopted son accused
of killing cardsharping brother.

04333
THE MISADVENTURES OF MIKE MURPHY
(530) (U)
Martin Films (C&M) *Reissue:* 1914, MURPHY
AND THE MAGIC CAP
D: Dave Aylott
Ernie Westo .... Mike Murphy
TRICK Irish labourer finds cap that makes
people and objects vanish.

04334
TIM THE MESSENGER (690)
Phoenix Film Agency
CRIME Messenger boy saves girl from kidnappers.

04335
THE VAMPIRE (1020)
Searchlight Films (Phoenix)
HORROR India. Explorer shoots vampire woman
who killed friend; she becomes snake and kills
him.

04336
THE FALLEN IDOL (1000) (U)
Motograph (U)
P: Joseph Bamberger
D: Maurice Elvey
S: (PAINTING) John Lomax
SC: Albert Ward
Douglas Payne .... Dr Douglas Ewart
Babs Neville .... Mrs Ewart
Maurice Elvey .... The Lover
ROMANCE Dr's wife returns to him after
flirtation in Richmond Park.

04337
DAVID GARRICK (2500)
Zenith Films
D: Leedham Bantock
S:(PLAY) T.W. Robertson
SC: Max Pemberton
Seymour Hicks .... David Garrick
Ellaline Terriss .... Ada Ingot
William Lugg .... Simon Ingot
Nellie Dade .... Arminta Brown
Henry Kitts .... Mr Brown
J.C. Buckstone .... Mr Smith
Lawrence Caird .... Mr Jones
Vincent Sternroyd ...... Lord Fareleigh
ROMANCE 1741. Actor poses as drunkard to
repel girl but falls in love with her.

04338
SCROOGE (2500)
Zenith Films
D: Leedham Bantock
S: (NOVEL) Charles Dickens (A CHRISTMAS
CAROL)
SC: Seymour Hicks
Seymour Hicks .... Ebenezer Scrooge
William Lugg
Leedham Bantock
J.C. Buckstone
Dorothy Buckstone
Leonard Calvert
Osborne Adair
Adela Measor
FANTASY Period. Old miser reformed by
ghosts of past, present and future.

04339
THE VICAR OF WAKEFIELD (3000)
Planet Films (DFSA)
D: John Douglas
S: (NOVEL) Oliver Goldsmith
Christine Rayner .... Olivia Primrose
Alys Collier .... Sophia Primrose
DRAMA Period. Squire jails poor vicar for debt
and tricks his daughter into mock marriage.

04340
A TERRIBLE PLANT (420) (U)
Urban Trading Co
D: (Lewin Fitzhamon)
COMEDY Wife throws away flower-pot
containing husband's wages and daughter's ring.

04341
LOVE IN A BOARDING HOUSE (1090) (U)
Urban Trading Co
D:S: Lewin Fitzhamon
Constance Somers-Clarke .... Edith Jackson
COMEDY Folkestone. Girl has rejected suitor
pose as chauffeur.

04342
THE FLAPPERS AND THE NUTS (1235) (U)
Urban Trading Co
D:S: Lewin Fitzhamon
Constance Somers-Clarke .... Enid
COMEDY Folkestone. Runaway schoolgirls
placate parents by faking an attack by bull.

04343
THE TRAMP'S DREAM
Selsior Films
MUSICAL Tramp dreams of dancing elfins;
synchronises to cinema orchestras.

OCT

04344
SCALLYWAG FOOLS THE MISSUS (698) (U)
A.R. Films (A&C)
COMEDY Henpeck poses as monkey and
wrecks house.

04345
GUSSY RIDES A PONY (500) (U)
B&C (DFSA)
COMEDY Man's love-letter exchanged for
letter about pony.

04346
THE LITTLE MOTHER (1629) (U) retitled:
THE CHILD MOTHER
B&C (DFSA)
D: Ethyle Batley
S: Ernest G. Batley
Ernest G. Batley .... Jack Andrews
Dorothy Batley .... Mary Andrews
DRAMA Mother's amnesia from crane accident
is cured by visit to cinema.

04347
THE TROUBLE A STOCKING CAUSED (870)
(U)
B&C (DFSA)
COMEDY Honeymoon wife suspicious when
stocking blows in the window.

04348
GUY FAWKES AND THE GUNPOWDER
PLOT (2000)
B&C (Royal)
D: Ernest G. Batley
Caleb Porter .... Guy Fawkes
Ernest G. Batley ..... The Traitor
HISTORY 1605. Catholic conspirator foiled in
attempt to explode parliament.

04349
HEROES OF THE MINE (3375) (U) USA:
THE GREAT MINE DISASTER
Big Ben Films-Union (Pathe)
D: George Pearson
S: George Pearson, L.C. MacBean
Percy Moran .... Frank Conway
Lionel d' Aragon .... Dudley Hamilton
DRAMA Midlands. Enemies become friends
after coal mine disaster.

04350
ALGY'S TORMENTOR (575) (U)
Britannia Films (Pathe)
D:S: Lewin Fitzhamon
Constance Somers-Clarke .... Kitty
Roy Royston .... Bob
COMEDY Margate. Girl's brother fools beau
by pretending to float out to sea in drum.

04351
THE GRIP (4000)
Britannic Film Producing Syndicate (Martin's)
D:SC: A.E. Coleby
S:(PLAY) Jean Sartene (LA GRIFFE)
Louis Bouwmeester .... John Strong
Annesley Healy
CRIME Paralised farmer regains voice in time
to stop second wife from killing son.

04352
THE MYSTERY OF THE £500,000 PEARL
NECKLACE (3000) USA: $1,000,000 PEARL
MYSTERY
ACL Feature Films (Henderson)
D:S: Harold Heath
Harold Heath .... Jack Dacre
CRIME Based on the £150,000 pearl necklace
robbery of July, 1913.

04353
IT'S LOVE THAT MAKES THE WORLD GO
ROUND (520) (U)
Clarendon
D: Percy Stow
COMEDY Cupid uses magic arrows to stop
quarrel.

04354
THE RENT IN A-REAR (460) (U)
Clarendon
D: Percy Stow
COMEDY Matron sets trap for cadets secretly
visiting nurses.

04355
SOLD! (565) (U)
Clarendon
D: Percy Stow
COMEDY Ejected terrier returns home and
is mistaken for burglar.

04356
SNATCHED FROM DEATH (2400) (U)
Cricks (Gaumont)
D: Charles Calvert
CRIME Tec catches crooks after escaping
from canal lock.

04357
LAND AND SEA (1865) (U)
Cricks (C&M)
D: Edwin J. Collins
ADVENTURE Trawlerman thrown in the sea by
rival and washed ashore.

04358
PC NABBEM AND THE ANARCHISTS (400)
(U)
Cricks (C&M)
D: (Edwin J. Collins)
S: F. Moores
COMEDY Anarchists use dummy bomb to
fool policeman.

04359
PISTOLS FOR TWO (485) (U)
Cricks (C&M)
D: (Charles Calvert)
COMEDY Rivals duel for girl.

04360
A NEWSBOY'S CHRISTMAS DREAM (1940)
(U)
Cricks (C&M) *Reissue:* 1916
D: Edwin J. Collins
Eileen Daybell
Leo Cauty
R. Howard Cricks
FANTASY Orphan newsboy adopted after
dreaming of wizards and dragons.

04361
HOW CECIL PLAYED THE GAME (984) (U)
Cricks (C&M)
D: (Edwin J. Collins)
ADVENTURE Poor man wins rich girl by saving
rival from cliff.

04362
HIS WONDERFUL LAMP (463) (U)
Cricks (C&M)
D: (Edwin J. Collins)
Jack Leigh .... Prof Leigh
TRICK Tramp steals lamp which emits rays
that cause objects to vanish.

04363
WILLY WOULD A-WOOING GO (348) (U)
Cricks (C&M)
D: Charles Calvert)
COMEDY Man buys ladle of love potion for
landlady's daughter.

04364
HERE WE ARE AGAIN (495) (U)
Cricks (C&M) *Reissue:* 1916, THE HARLE-
QUINADE
D: (Edwin J. Collins)
COMEDY Policeman dreams tramps and lovers
turn into harlequinade.

04365
FOR EAST IS EAST (3300) USA: IN THE
PYTHON'S DEN
Martin Films (Winik)
D: Dave Aylott
Wingold Lawrence .... Captain
DRAMA India. Prince captures soldier's wife
and throws husband into python pit.

04366
IN THE SMUGGLER'S GRIP (1990) (U)
Cricks (C&M)
D: Edwin J. Collins
ADVENTURE Girl fetches coastguards to
save lover from smugglers.

04367
CRIME AT THE MILL (1800) (U)
Dart Films (Anderson)
D: Stuart Kinder
CRIME Rich miller abducts girl in car and is
caught after chase.

04368
THE RIVAL MUSICIANS (475) (U)
EcKo (U)
D: W.P. Kellino
Sam T. Poluski .... Musician
COMEDY Musical neighbours try to outdo
each other with noise.

04369
NOBBY THE NEW WAITER (593) (U)
EcKo (U)
D: W.P. Kellino
Sam T. Poluski .... Nobby
COMEDY Waiter is blindfolded and wears
skates to catch diner who will pay bill.

04370
THE COASTGUARD'S SISTER (1000) (U)
Edison

D: Charles Brabin
S: Bannister Merwin
Marc McDermott .... George Rowe
Miriam Nesbitt .... Fay Trevenna
J. Warren Foster .... Mr Trevenna
ADVENTURE Cornwall. Girl poses as man to
save fisherman from tobacco smugglers.

04371
THE FLOODTIDE (1000) (U)
Edison
D: Charles Brabin
S: Goring Cholmers
Marc McDermott .... Sidney Brandon
Miriam Nesbitt .... Connie Lee
Frederick Annerley .... Joe Muzzey
Alice Mansfield .... Mr Lee
ADVENTURE Cornwall. Girl climbs cliff to
save injured artist from tide.

04372
PIMPLE DOES THE HAT TRICK (225)
Folly Films (Phoenix)
D:S: Fred Evans, Joe Evans
Fred Evans .... Pimple
COMEDY Pimple in trouble for refusing to
remove hat in restaurant.

04373
PIMPLE'S WIFE (280)
Folly Films (Phoenix)
D:S: Fred Evans, Joe Evans
Fred Evans .... Pimple
COMEDY Pimple buys wife from Jew's machine;
she is Negress.

04374
PIMPLE'S INFERNO (720)
Folly Films (Phoenix)
D:S: Fred Evans, Joe Evans
Fred Evans .... Pimple
COMEDY Pimple reads Dante and dreams hell
is full of suffragettes and film comedians.

04375
BUTTERCUP PC, DETECTIVE (385)
H&W Films (Prieur)
D: (Stuart Kinder)
COMEDY Constable dons disguises to trail
noisy beetle.

04376
A RIVERSIDE ROMANCE (490)
H&W Films (Prieur)
D: Stuart Kinder
'Spot' the Dog
ANIMAL Dog fetches man to save stranded girl.

04377
DAN BACKS A WINNER (395)
H&W Films (Prieur)
D: (Stuart Kinder)
COMEDY Punter tries to reach bookmaker in
time to place bet.

04378
HAMLET (5800) (U)
Hepworth (Gaumont)
D: Hay Plumb
S:(PLAY) William Shakespeare
Johnston Forbes-Robertson ... Hamlet
Gertrude Elliot .... Ophelia
Walter Ringham .... Claudius
Adeleine Bourne .... Gertrude
J.H. Barnes .... Polonius
S.A. Cookson .... Horatio
Alex Scott-Gatty .... Laertes
Grendon Bentley .... Fortinbras
Montagu Rutherford .... Rosencrantz
J.H. Ryley .... Gravedigger

Percy Rhodes .... Ghost
Robert Atkins .... First Player
DRAMA Denmark. Prince avenges his father's
murder.

04379
MORE THAN HE BARGAINED FOR (625) (U)
Hepworth
D: Frank Wilson
'Sandow' the Pony
ANIMAL Man steals girl's pony and ends up
in jail.

04380
FOR MARION'S SAKE (1150)
Hepworth
D: (Warwick Buckland)
Alec Worcester .... Bob Carton
Chrissie White .... Marion
Harry Gilbey .... Squire
CRIME Man takes blame when beloved's hus-
band robs her father.

04381
THE LADY OF LYONS (3900) (A)
Hepworth (Co-operative)
D: Leon Bary
S: (PLAY) Lord Lytton
Cecil Mannering .... Claude Meliotte
DRAMA France, 1795. Man returns from
war in time to stop wife from marrying
scoundrel.

04382
RETRIBUTION (1125) (A)
Hepworth
D: (Frank Wilson)
Jack Raymond .... Clerk
Harry Royston .... Robber
John McAndrews ... Robber
CRIME Police pursue bank robbers and set
fire to hideout.

04383
HOW IS IT DONE? (575) (U)
Hepworth
D: (Frank Wilson)
Lionel Cardac
TRICK Conjuror's tricks with playing cards,
billiard balls, etc.

04384
HAWKEYE MEETS HIS MATCH (650) (U)
Hepworth
D:S: Hay Plumb
Hay Plumb .... Hawkeye/Seedy Samuel
COMEDY Crook poses as lecturer and steals
collection.

04385
THE YOUNGER SISTER (1100) (U)
Turner Films (Hepworth)
D: Larry Trimble
S: Florence Turner
Florence Turner .... Peggy Wright
Rex Davis .... John Wright
Arthur Ricketts .... Prof Dinglefritz
Charles Fleming .... Algy Dinglefritz
Shirley Lea .... Mr Wright
COMEDY Tomboy posing as her sister is loved
by professor and his son.

04386
THE OLD WOOD CARVER (3000)
Herkomer (Tyler)
P:D:S: Hubert von Herkomer
Hubert von Herkomer ...... The Wood Carver
Maud Milton .... His Wife
May Blaney .... His Daughter
DRAMA Wood carver reconciled to his daughter's
elopement on the birth of her baby.

04387
LOVE IN A TEASHOP (980) (U)
Herkomer (Tyler)
P:D:S: Hubert von Herkomer
Hubert von Herkomer .... The Father
COMEDY Couple obtain widowed parents'
consent by causing them to fall in love with
each other.

04388
THE WHITE WITCH (1690) (U)
Herkomer (Tyler)
P:D:S: Hubert von Herkomer
Hubert von Herkomer .... The Witch
FANTASY 14th C. Witch's magic saves
woodman's daughter from wicked baron.

04389
LITTLE MICKY THE MESMERIST (525)
Kineto
D: (W.R. Booth)
COMEDY Precocious child hypnotises
people.

04390
THE COWBOY TWIST
Selsior Films
Rosie Sloman
MUSICAL Dance to synchronise with cinema
orchestras.

04391
THE SPANISH-AMERICAN QUICKSTEP
Selsior Films
Harry Perry & Rosie Sloman
MUSICAL Dance to synchronise with cinema
orchestras.

04392
TWO BROWN BAGS (545) (U)
Martin Films (C&M)
D: (Dave Aylott)
COMEDY Messenger mistakenly takes bag
containing coronet.

04393
UNCLE'S PRESENT (430) (U)
Martin Films (C&M) Reissue: 1915, A
PRESENT FROM UNCLE
D: Dave Aylott
COMEDY Boy plays tricks with toy bow and
arrow.

04394
SPIRITUALISM EXPOSED (2840) (U) retitled:
FRAUDULENT SPIRITUALISM EXPOSED
USA: THE SEER OF BOND STREET
Motograph
D:S: Charles Raymond
Louis Nikola .... The Chief
Violet Stacey .... Norah
Douglas Payne .... Clipper Burke
Harry Gower .... Jules
Nessie Blackford ... Mrs Hearn
Luna Lindon .... Palmist
CRIME Fake medium persuades heiress to
invest in crook's shares.

04395
IN THE DAYS OF ROBIN HOOD (1950) (U)
kinema
Natural Colour Kinematograph Co
D: F. Martin Thornton
H. Agar Lyons .... Robin Hood
Mercy Hatton .... Lady Christobel
John M. East .... Little John
Cecil Dereham .... Will Scarlet
Harry Ashton .... Friar Tuck
ADVENTURE Period. Outlaw poses as monk
to save one of his men from sheriff.

04396
THE FISH AND THE RING (2135) (U)
kinema
Natural Colour Kinematograph Co
D: F. Martin Thornton, R.H. Callum
Nancy Barrett .... Joan
Gerald Royston .... Nicholas
H. Agar Lyons .... Baron Humphrey
Harold Barrett
Percy Dyer
FANTASY Fairies, swans and fish save poor
girl from magical baron.

04397
DADDY'S DARLINGS (795) (U)
Urban Trading Co
D:S: Lewin Fitzhamon
Roy Royston .... Boy
Marie Royston .... Girl
ANIMAL Folkestone. Dog saves children from
tide and reconciles parted parents.

04398
GIPSY HATE (1050) (U)
Urban Trading Co
D:S: Lewin Fitzhamon
Constance Somers-Clarke .... Norma
DRAMA Folkestone. Gipsy loves fisherman
and tries to drown her rival.

04399
FANTASIE: DRESDEN CHINA sound
UK Kineplastikon Co
D: (W.R. Booth)
E. Baker
MUSICAL Dance synchronising with gramo-
phone record.

04400
THE COLLAR STUD (1000)
GCA
S:(SKETCH)
COMEDY Search for lost collar stud.

NOV

04401
QUITS (562)
A.R. Films (A&C)
COMEDY Girl dons disguises to fool fickle
fiance.

04402
SIXTY YEARS A QUEEN (750)
Barker (Royal)
P: Will Barker, G.B. Samuelson
D: Bert Haldane
S: (BOOK) Sir Herbert Maxwell
SC: G.B. Samuelson, Arthur Shirley, Harry
Engholm
Blanche Forsythe .... Queen Victoria (2)
Mrs Lytton .... Queen Victoria (3)
Fred Paul .... Archbishop of
                                          Canterbury (etc)
Roy Travers .... Prince Albert
Gilbert Esmond .... Duke of Wellington
E. Story Gofton .... W.E. Gladstone
Rolf Leslie .... 27 Characters
J. Hastings Batson
Jack Brunswick
HISTORY 1837-1901. Main events during Queen
Victoria's reign.

04403
TWO SIDES TO A BOAT (419) (U)
B&C (DFSA)
COMEDY Pursued suffragette hides and thinks
sailors intend to tar her.

04404
IN FATE'S GRIP (2670)
B&C (DFSA)
D: Charles Weston
Ernest G. Batley .... John Brown
Marie Pickering .... Ruth Finch
Harry Lorraine .... Harry
Jack Jarman .... Finch
Henri Farman .... Pilot
ADVENTURE Ship's doctor, forced to operate
on beloved's husband, is saved by hydroplane
when ship explodes.

04405
THE LITTLE SNOW WAIF (1658) (U)
B&C (DFSA)
D: Charles Weston
Marie Pickering .... Fairy Goodheart
Eileen Daybell .... Etta Brown
Harry Lorraine .... Millionaire
PATHOS Millionaire adopts waif when mother
dies of starvation.

04406
THE TWO FATHER CHRISTMASSES (1620)
(U)
B&C (DFSA)
D: Ethyle Batley
S: Ernest G. Batley
Ernest G. Batley .... Burglar
Dorothy Batley .... Child
CRIME Burglar dresses as Santa Claus and is
reformed by child.

04407
THE ARTIST AND HIS MODEL (1342) (A)
B&C (DFSA)
D: (Ethyle Batley)
ROMANCE Artist returns to model after
drunken dream of living with a coquette.

04408
THE MASTER CROOK (3169) (U)
B&C (DFSA)
D: Charles Weston
Arthur Finn .... The Master Crook
Marie Pickering ...... The Blind Girl
Harry Lorraine .... Crook
Bert Berry .... Crook
Jack Jarman .... Crook
CRIME Crook returns stolen gems after blind
girl frees him when gang tie him upside-down
in sewer.

04409
WHILE SHEPHERDS WATCHED (1075) (U)
Britannia Films (Pathe)
D:S: Lewin Fitzhamon
Constance Somers-Clarke ...... Stella Green
Ernest A. Douglas .... John Green
Amy Coleman .... Mrs Green
CRIME Owner of touring cinema kidnaps
farmer's daughter as violinist.

04410
WHAT HAPPENED TO LIZZIE (315) (U)
Clarendon
D: Percy Stow
COMEDY Woman falls into barrel near
bulldog's kennel.

04411
TWO FLATS AND A SHARP (795) (U)
Clarendon
D: Percy Stow
Dorothy Bellew .... The Girl
Evan Thomas .... The Man
COMEDY Girl learns man is feigning sickness
to win bet.

04412
CLARENDON SPEAKING PICTURES (series)
Clarendon
D: Wilfred Noy

04413
1 – PICKWICK VERSUS BARDELL (1000)
S: (NOVEL) Charles Dickens

04414
2 – THE LITTLE VULGAR BOY (1000)
S: (POEM) Thomas Ingoldsby

04415
3 – DAGOBERT THE JESTER (1000)
S: (POEM) Anon

04416
4 – PHIL BLOOD'S LEAP (1000)
S: (POEM) Robert Buchanan

04417
5 – THE GARDENER'S DAUGHTER (1000)
S: (POEM) Alfred Tennyson

04418
6 – COMING HOME (1000)
S: (POEM) Alfred Berlyn

04419
7 – THE HAND OF A CHILD (1000)
S: (POEM) Alfred Berlyn

04420
8 – MR PICKWICK IN A DOUBLE BEDDED
ROOM (1000)
S: (NOVEL) Charles Dickens

04421
9 – MRS CORNEY MAKES TEA (1000)
S: (NOVEL) Charles Dickens

04422
10 – HERE SHE GOES AND THERE SHE
GOES (1000)
S: (SONG)

04423
11 – THE PRIDE OF BATTERY B (1000)
S: (POEM) Anon
DRAMAS Dramatisations of stories and
monologues to accompany stage reciters.

04424
GOOD FOR THE GOUT (500)
Cricks (Hibbert)
D: (Edwin J. Collins)
COMEDY Tribulations of a gent with gout.

04425
FOR HER MOTHER'S SAKE (1120) (U)
retitled: A TYPIST'S LOVE AFFAIR
Cricks (C&M)
D: (Edwin J. Collins)
DRAMA Girl's sick mother dies in time to
save her from marring rich employer.

04426
THROUGH THE KEYHOLE (524) (U)
Cricks (C&M)
D: (Charles Calvert)
COMEDY Girl's father sees nose-bleeding beau
removing trousers to find key.

04427
GOT 'EM AGAIN! (373) (U)
Cricks (Walturdaw)
D: (Charles Calvert)
COMEDY

04428
BUMBLES AND THE BASS (560) (U)
EcKo (U)
D: W.P. Kellino
Phillipi .... Bumbles
COMEDY Bumbles steals band's bass, is chased,
and floats down river.

04429
BUMBLE'S HOLIDAY (605) (U)
EcKo (U)
D: W.P. Kellino
Phillipi .... Bumbles
COMEDY Family on holiday lose baby, train,
and end in river.

04430
NOBBY AND THE PEARL MYSTERY (552)
(U)
EcKo (U)
D: W.P. Kellino
Sam T Poluski .... Nobby
COMEDY Jewel thief turns up in unlikely places.

04431
MONEY-MAKING COATS (387) (U)
EcKo (U)
D: W.P. Kellino
COMEDY Petticoat Lane. Coster plays trick
with coats and bank-notes.

04432
KEEPERS OF THE FLOCK (1030) (U)
Edison
D: Charles Brabin
S: (PAINTING) Luke Fildes (A VILLAGE
WOOING)
SC: Bannister Merwin
Marc McDermott .... Old Luke
Miriam Nesbitt .... Ellen
Charles Vernon .... Tom Drake
James Le Fre .... Farmer
Phyllis Stuckley .... Bess
DRAMA 1850. Shepherd returns to work when
son-in-law drinks daughter's dowry.

04433
THE STROKE OF PHOEBUS EIGHT (1000) (U)
Edison
D: Charles Brabin
S: Anne & Bannister Merwin
Marc McDermott .... Eric Barclay
Miriam Nesbitt .... Violet Lanby
Charles Vernon .... Dick Moreton
Douglas Munro .... Bill Whittle
Frederick Annerley .... Guy Strong
Phyllis Stuckley .... Barbara Lanby
SPORT Henley. Stroke kidnaps his replacement,
who escapes in time to win race.

04434
PIMPLE GOES FISHING (420) (U)
Folly Films (Phoenix)
D:S: Fred Evans, Joe Evans
Fred Evans .... Pimple
COMEDY Pimple hires punt, catches dead cat,
and buys cod.

04435
WHEN PIMPLE WAS YOUNG (480) (U)
Folly Films (Phoenix)
D:S: Fred Evans, Joe Evans
Fred Evans .... Pimple
COMEDY Schoolboy plays truant and tricks
policeman.

04436
PIMPLE THE SPORT (580) (U)
Folly Films (Phoenix)
D:S: Fred Evans, Joe Evans
Fred Evans .... Pimple
COMEDY Pimple enters Olympics trials and
upsets mayor.

04437
PIMPLE GETS THE JUMPS (350) (U)
Folly Films (Phoenix)
D:S: Fred Evans, Joe Evans
Fred Evans .... Pimple
COMEDY

04438
PIMPLE'S IVANHOE (950) (U)
Folly Films (Phoenix) Reissue: 1915 (H&S)
D:S: Fred Evans, Joe Evans
Fred Evans .... Pimple
COMEDY Crusader poses as palmer to save
American Jew's daughter from knight.

04439
FOR SUCH IS THE KINGDOM OF HEAVEN
(1300) (U) retitled: THE CHRISTMAS STRIKE
Hepworth
D: (Warwick Buckland)
Jack Raymond .... The Owner
Harry Royston .... The Striker
Eric Desmond .... The Child
DRAMA Owner stops strikers from destroying
steelworks.

04440
THE FAIRIES' REVENGE (750) (U)
Hepworth
D: (Hay Plumb)
Percy Manton .... Uncle Alfred
TRICK Fairies change scoffer's clothes into
ballet dress.

04441
SHADOWS OF A GREAT CITY (3700)
Hepworth
D: Frank Wilson
S: (PLAY) Herbert Blache, Aaron Hoffman
Alec Worcester .... Tom Cooper
Chrissie White .... Nellie Standish
Harry Royston .... Jim Malone
William Felton .... Abe Nathan
Harry Gilbey .... George Benson
John McAndrews .... Insp Arkwright
Ruby Belasco .... Biddy Malone
CRIME Ex-convict sailor saves disowned
gambler's ward from abduction by escaped
convict.

04442
FOR LOVE OF HIM (1400) (U)
Hepworth
D: (Warwick Buckland)
Alec Worcester .... Dick Hermen
Chrissie White .... Ethel Allinsen
Cecil Mannering .... Fred Allinsen
Harry Gilbey .... Mr Allinsen
Ruby Belasco .... Mrs Allinsen
Harry Royston
Rachel de Solla
CRIME Man catches burglar and finds he is his
wife's brother.

04443
POORLUCK AS A MESSENGER BOY (500) (U)
Hepworth
D: (Frank Wilson)
Harry Buss .... Poorluck
COMEDY Messenger loses youthful charge, so
takes place in school.

04444
THE CLOISTER AND THE HEARTH (4725)
(U)
Hepworth
D: Hay Plumb
S: (NOVEL) Charles Reade
Alec Worcester .... Gerard Eliasson
Alma Taylor .... Margaret
Hay Plumb .... Denys
Jamie Darling .... Elias Eliasson
Ruby Belasco .... Mrs Eliasson
Harry Buss .... Hans
DRAMA Holland, 15th C. Artist turns priest and
saves heiress from usurping burgomaster.

04445
THE LUCKY STONE (875)
Turner Films (Hepworth)
D: Larry Trimble
S: Norman Endell
Florence Turner .... Alice Scott
Frank Powell .... Harry Hopper
COMEDY Rochester. Shy wooer feigns head
injury to gain sympathy.

04446
MARIE LLOYD AT HOME, AND BUNKERED
(300)
Magnet Producing Co
Marie Lloyd
COMEDY 'Short, but with a name to conjure
with.'

04447
HOW A HOUSEKEEPER LOST HER CHARAC-
TER (1000)
Magnet Producing Co
D: Fred Rains
S: (SKETCH) Malcolm Scott
Malcolm Scott
COMEDY 'A scream from end to end.'

04448
DAPHNE AND THE DEAN (2000)
Magnet Producing Co
D: Fred Rains
S: (SKETCH) Arthur Chesney
Arthur Chesney .... The Dean
Miss le Hay .... Daphne
COMEDY 'The well-known side-splitting comedy'

04449
LANDLADIES BEWARE (570) (U)
Martin Films (C&M)
D: (Dave Aylott)
COMEDY Seaside landlady forced to board
tramp for week.

04450
A DAY ON ROLLERS (524) (U)
Martin Films (Imperial)
D: Lewin Fitzhamon
Roy Royston .... Roy
Marie Royston .... Marie
COMEDY Family learn to roller-skate, then do
everything on skates.

04451
THE GENTLEMAN RANKER (2930) (U)
retitled: RAISED FROM THE RANKS
USA: NOT GUILTY
D: Dave Aylott
WAR Broke gentleman enlists, wins VC in India,
and is framed for stealing secret plans.

04452
JOHN WILLIE AT BLACKPOOL (570) (U)
Sphinx Films (DFSA) Reissue: 1916, SMIFFY
AT BLACKPOOL
COMEDY Thin man and girl spend day by sea.

04453
HENPECK'S HOLIDAY (500) (U)
Sphinx Films (DFSA)
COMEDY Blackpool. Henpeck and family
spend day by sea.

04454
THE GREAT GOLD ROBBERY (2150) (U)
Motograph
P: Joseph Bamberger
D: Maurice Elvey
Douglas Payne .... Walter Hyde
Babs Neville .... Dot
Sydney Smith .... The Diver
CRIME Tec dives from Westminster Bridge to
catch gold thieves in barge.

04455
JU-JITSU TO THE RESCUE (1882) (U)
Motograph Reissue: 1915, SELF DEFENCE
(Tress)
D: Charles Raymond
Yukio Tani .... Himself
Babs Neville .... Mrs Rose
Douglas Payne ....,... Big Jake
CRIME Girl learns ju-jitsu and uses it to thwart
criminal.

04456
BRIDEGROOMS BEWARE (628) (U)
Motograph
D: Maurice Elvey
Elizabeth Risdon .... The Bride
Fred Groves .... The Bridegroom
COMEDY Seaside. Groom's lunatic double
returns to asylum rather than stay married.

04457
THE TEMPTER (2483) (A) kinema
Natural Colour Kinematograph Co
D: F. Martin Thornton, R.H. Callum
S: Leedham Bantock, Alfred de Manby
H. Agar Lyons .... The Husband
Alfred de Manby .... The Devil
F. Martin Thornton ..... The Drunkard
Leedham Bantock .... The Gambler
FANTASY Satan tells stories illustrating drink,
deceit and greed.

04458
THE STAFF DINNER (625) (A)
Urban Trading Co
S: (SKETCH) A.W. Baskcomb
A.W. Baskcomb .... Jones
Ninon Dudley .... Mrs Jones
COMEDY Clerk gets drunk at annual dinner
and comes home late.

04459
WHEN COUNTRY COUSINS COME TO TOWN
(558) (U)
Heron Films (U) Reissue: 1916 (Browne)
P: Andrew Heron
COMEDY Lancashire couple visit Earls Court
Exhibition.

04460
KELLY TAKES HIS MISSUS TO SOUTHEND
(700)
Martin's
COMEDY Couple have day's holiday in Southend.

04461
THE REJUVENATION OF DAN (465)
H&W Films (Prieur)
D: (Stuart Kinder)
COMEDY Old man is rejuvenated.

DEC

04462
TALKING TO THE PICTURE (1000)
Barker (Hemsley)
S: Harry May Hemsley
Harry May Hemsley .... Father
Norman Hemsley .... Johnny
Edna Maude .... Elsie
COMEDY Ventriloquist on stage talks to
children in film.

04463
IN THE HANDS OF THE LONDON CROOKS
(4896) (A)
Barker (City)
D: (Alexander Butler)
S: Rowland Talbot
Thos. H. MacDonald .... Frank Linley
Blanche Forsythe ....Hilda Linley

Fred Paul .... Capt Bland
Roy Travers .... Harry Norman
Dora de Winton .... Delilah
J. Hastings Batson ....Sir James Linley
CRIME Disowned gambler, framed for forgery,
becomes hero in Afghanistan and wins at
Goodwood.

04464
THE ROAD TO RUIN (4000) (U)
Barker (New Era)
D: (George Gray, Bert Haldane)
S: (PLAY) George Gray
George Gray .... George Wyndham
G. Somerset .... Lucy Probyn
Harry W. Scadden .... Jack Probyn
Thos H. MacDonald .... Lord Layton
Val Gurney .... Dick Hinton
E. Vaudray .... Mrs Wyndham
Mary Smithers .... Katy Probyn
DRAMA Drunken gambler reforms after dream-
ing of ruination.

04465
A SON OF JAPAN (950) (A)
B&C (DFSA)
D: Charles Weston
Arthur Finn .... Cantoo
ROMANCE Ambassador forces girl to renounce
Japanese student who loves her.

04466
WHEN THE HURRICANES VISITED THE
DOUGHNUTS (544) (U)
B&C (DFSA)
D:S: Lewin Fitzhamon
Constance Somers-Clarke ...... Bella
Marie Royston .... Beano
Roy Royston .... Buster
COMEDY Children visit bakery and cause fight
with flour and eggs.

04467
WHAT HE DID WITH HIS £5 (657) (U)
B&C (DFSA)
COMEDY 'Set amid the beauties of old and
modern Paris.'

04468
THE RAGGED PRINCE (1020) (U)
B&C (DFSA)
D: Charles Weston
Arthur Finn .... The Prince
Marie Pickering ...... Marguerite
ADVENTURE Cavalier saves girl from rich
cad's burning mansion.

04469
MARRIED AT LAST (1147) (A)
B&C (DFSA)
COMEDY Groom's wedding delayed by
wrongful arrest as burglar.

04470
THERE'S GOOD IN THE WORST OF US
(882) (U)
B&C (DFSA)
D: Ethyle Batley
Ernest G. Batley .... William Stuart
DRAMA Ex-convict has himself arrested so
wife may continue to receive charity allowance.

04471
TO SAVE HER DAD (2140) retitled: BESS THE
DETECTIVE'S DAUGHTER
B&C (Prince)
D: Charles Weston
Ernest G. Batley .... The Detective
Dorothy Batley .... Bess
CRIME Ex-detective's daughter poses as boy to
prove lord was killed by secretary.

04472
THE SUFFRAGETTE (1875) (U)
Britannia Films (Pathe)
Agnès Glynne .... Agnes Jackson
James Carew .... Arthur Jackson
Evangeline Hilliard
CRIME Disowned schoolmistress's uncle
destroys father's amended will.

04473
A BORE OF A BOY (625) (U)
Britannia Films (Pathe)
D:S: Lewin Fitzhamon
Constance Somers-Clarke .... Kitty
Roy Royston .... Bob
COMEDY Boy torments sister's fiance and is
thrown in river.

04474
THE GIRL NEXT DOOR (425) (U)
Britannia Films (Pathe)
D:S: Lewin Fitzhamon
Constance Somers-Clarke ...... Marjorie Ivy
Lewin Fitzhamon .... William Fitznoodle
Roy Royston .... Bobby
COMEDY Girl wins father's consent by catch-
ing him flirting.

04475
A CASE OF ARSON (4000)
Britannic Film Producing Syndicate (Big A)
D:SC: A.E. Coleby
S:(PLAY) Herman Heijermans (IN DE JONGE
JAN)
Henri de Vries .... 7 roles
CRIME Trial of arsonist whose child died in
one of his fires.

04476
A GLUE-MY AFFAIR (450)
Borup Bioscope (Premier)
D: C. Borup
COMEDY Drunkard mistakenly drinks glue
and his mouth is sealed.

04477
£1,000 REWARD (3800) (U)
Anchor Films
D: Harold Heath
Harold Heath .... Jack Strong
CRIME Portland escapee joins countess's coining
gang and is caught by tec and flower-girl.

04478
NOBODY'S CHILD (1000)
Anchor Films
D: Harold Heath
DRAMA 7 year old girl dives into Thames and
is adopted by her rescuer.

04479
MRS RABBIT'S HUSBAND TAKES THE
SHILLING (570) (U)
Clarendon
D: Percy Stow
COMEDY Woman poses as soldier to recapture
enlisted husband.

04480
WHEN MOTHER IS ILL (540) (U)
Clarendon
D: Percy Stow
COMEDY Mishaps ensue when family tries to
cope with housework.

04481
GIGANTIC MARIONETTES (370)
Clarendon
D: (Wilfred Noy)
ACT Performance by monstrous marionettes.

04482
A TALE OF TWO TABLES (495) (U)
Cricks (C&M)
D: (Edwin J. Collins)
COMEDY Father has trouble trying to
carry a new table.

04483
PC NABBEM'S SMART CAPTURE (530) (U)
Cricks (DFSA)
D: (Edwin J. Collins)
COMEDY PC ambushes fugitive.

04484
HE ATTENDED THE MEETING (405) (U)
Cricks (DFSA)
D: (Edwin J. Collins)
COMEDY Tramp steals carpenter's trousers.

04485
BABY'S PHOTOGRAPH (413) (U)
EcKo (U)
D: W.P. Kellino
COMEDY Parents try to keep child clean for
photographer.

04486
THE HAPPY DUSTMEN (593) (U)
EcKo (U)
D: W.P. Kellino
S: Brothers Egbert
Albert Egbert .... Bill
Seth Egbert .... Walter
COMEDY 'Elaborated version of the famous act.'

04487
THE DUSTMEN'S HOLIDAY (433) (U)
EcKo (U)
D: W.P. Kellino
Albert Egbert .... Bill
Seth Egbert .... Walter
COMEDY Swansea. Tourists take swimmer's
clothes.

04488
STOGGLES' CHRISTMAS DINNER (663) (U)
EcKo (U)
D: W.P. Kellino
COMEDY Father cannot kill pet rooster so he
buys bird, which is tough.

04489
BUMBLE'S ELECTRIC BELT (418) (U)
EcKo (U)
D: W.P. Kellino
Phillipi .... Bumbles
COMEDY Sciatica sufferer dons electrified
belt which gives shocks.

04490
THE DAUGHTER OF ROMANY (1000)
Edison
D: Charles Brabin
S: Anne & Bannister Merwin
Marc McDermott .... Capt Courtney
Miriam Nesbitt .... Mona
Winifred Albion .... Their Daughter
ROMANCE Knole. Nobleman deserts secret
gipsy wife; later their child weds gipsy.

04491
LARKS IN TOYLAND (496) (U)
Empire Films (DFSA)
D:S: Arthur Cooper
TRICK Animated toys.

04492
ONCE UPON A TIME (700) (U)
Folly Films (Phoenix)
D:S: Fred Evans, Joe Evans
Fred Evans .... Yokel
Joe Evans ....Tramp
COMEDY Fairy changes yokel; tramp, farmer
and daughter into first harlequinade.

04493
SLIPPERY PIMPLE (350) (U)
Folly Films (Phoenix)
D:S: Fred Evans, Joe Evans
Fred Evans .... Pimple
CHASE Pimple steals meat and disguises himself
to avoid pursuers.

04494
LIEUTENANT PIMPLE ON SECRET SERVICE
(695) (U)
Folly Films (Phoenix)
D:S: Fred Evans, Joe Evans
Fred Evans .... Pimple
COMEDY Lt thwarts spies and delivers treaty
to King of Montynigger.

04495
HOW PIMPLE SAVED KISSING CUP (595) (U)
Folly Films (Phoenix) *Reissue:* 1916 (H&S)
D:S: Fred Evans, Joe Evans
Fred Evans .... Pimple
COMEDY Stable-boy saves Lord's horse from
baron and wins race.

04496
PIMPLE'S GREAT BULL FIGHT (570) (U)
Folly Films (Phoenix) *Reissue:* 1916 (H&S)
D:S: Fred Evans, Joe Evans
Fred Evans .... Pimple
COMEDY Spain. Tourist substitutes for sick
toreador.

04497
PIMPLE'S MIDNIGHT RAMBLE (350) (U)
Folly Films (Phoenix)
D:S: Fred Evans, Joe Evans
Fred Evans .... Pimple
COMEDY Sleepwalker catches burglars.

04498
WHAT HAPPENED TO PIMPLE — THE
SUICIDE (698) (U)
Folly Films (Phoenix)
D:S: Fred Evans, Joe Evans
Fred Evans .... Pimple
COMEDY 'Brimful of comedy and genuine
mirth.'

04499
PIMPLE'S NEW JOB (400) (U)
Folly Films (Phoenix)
D:S: Fred Evans, Joe Evans
Fred Evans .... Pimple
COMEDY Pimple tries bill-posting and gets
pasted.

04500
CINDERELLA (8) *sound*
Hepworth
D: Harry Buss
S: (SKETCH) Herbert C. Rideout
Gertie Potter .... Cinderella
FANTASY 'Vivaphone' film, synchronised to
'Columbia' record.

04501
THE BROKEN SIXPENCE (1125) (U)
Hepworth
D: (Frank Wilson)
Alec Worcester .... Dick Sutor
WAR Wounded officer nursed by fiancee.

04502
THE OLD CURIOSITY SHOP (5300)
Hepworth (Renters)
D: SC: Thomas Bentley
S: (NOVEL) Charles Dickens
Mai Deacon .... Little Nell
Warwick Buckland ...... Grandfather Trent
E. Felton .... Quilp
Alma Taylor .... Mrs Quilp
Jamie Darling .... The Single Gentleman
Willie West .... Dick Swiveller
Billy Rex .... Tom Codlin
S. May .... Sampson Brass
Bert Stowe .... Short
Sydney Locklynne ..... Jerry
Moya Nigent .... Marchioness
R. Phillips .... Mrs Jarley
DRAMA Period. Dwarf usurer stops rich man
from tracking po or brother and grand-daughter.

04503
WHERE THERE'S A SWILL THERE'S A SWAY
(780) (U)
Hepworth
D: Frank Wilson
Sandow the Pony
ANIMAL Pony jailed for drunkenness, goes on
hunger strike.

04504
DAVID GARRICK (4000)
Hepworth (Ruffell)
D: Hay Plumb
S: (PLAY) T.W. Robertson
Charles Wyndham .... David Garrick
Mary Moore .... Ada Ingot
Louis Calvert .... Simon Ingot
Chrissie White
James Blakeley
Bertram Steer
T.N. Walter
Hay Plumb .... Billy Banter
ROMANCE Period . Actor poses as drunkard
to repel girl, but falls in love with her.

04505
NO FLIES ON CIS (650) (U)
Hepworth
D: (Frank Wilson)
COMEDY Broke husband borrows friend's
house to fool rich uncle.

04506
THE BROKEN OATH (1650) (U)
Hepworth
D: Warwick Buckland
Alec Worcester .... Peter Holden
Alma Taylor .... Mary Martin
Harry Royston .... Dan Williams
Flora Morris
Harry Gilbey .... Father
DRAMA Rottingdean. Jealous husband
fights wrong man on clifftop.

04507
NOT AS REHEARSED (675) (U)
Hepworth
D: (Frank Wilson)
COMEDY Rejected suitor weds actress by
substituting real parson in play.

04508
A QUESTION OF IDENTITY (1150) (U)
Hepworth
D: (Warwick Buckland)
Flora Morris .... The Girl
COMEDY Girl thwarts father's choice by
exchanging photograph with cook's.

04509
A SILENT WITNESS (1000) (U)
Hepworth
D: (Frank Wilson)
Eric Desmond .... The Boy
CRIME Boy's use of film company's camera
clears convicted man of killing fiancee's father.

04510
A LITTLE KNOWLEDGE (1025) (U)
Hepworth
D: (Warwick Buckland)
CRIME Lawyer's clerk outwits captain's attempt
to kidnap heiress.

04511
A THROW OF THE DICE (1975) (U)
Hepworth
D: (Frank Wilson)
S: Alice de Winton
Alice de Winton ...... Mrs Evans
Harry Royston .... Buck Evans
Stewart Rome .... Mark Grimsby
John McAndrews
DRAMA Agitator's wife kidnaps mine-
owner's baby when her own dies during strike.

04512
HIGHWAYMAN HAL (1000) (U)
Hepworth
D: (Hay Plumb)
Harry Buss .... Hal Harkaway
COMEDY Girl brings pardon from King in time
to save highwayman from hanging.

04513
THE PRINCES IN THE TOWER
Hepworth
D: Hay Plumb
Eric Desmond
Ruby Belasco
HISTORY

04514
THE TANGO (500)
Hepworth
D: (Frank Wilson)
Pete & Petita
MUSICAL Dancers demonstrate common
mistakes, Parisian Tango, and ballroom version.

04515
CONEY AS PEACEMAKER (1200)
Hepworth (KTC)
D:S: George Mozart
George Mozart .... Coney
COMEDY

04516
CONEY GETS THE GLAD EYE (1200)
Hepworth
D:S: George Mozart
George Mozart .... Coney
COMEDY 'The mock serious character of the
story accentuates the humour.'

04517
CONEY, RAGTIMER (1200)
Hepworth (KTC)
D:S: George Mozart
George Mozart .... Coney
COMEDY

04518
THE HARPER MYSTERY (3100)
Turner Films (Gaumont)
D:S: Larry Trimble
Florence Turner .... Margaret Kent
Coley Goodman .... Joe Miller
Frank Tennant .... Steve Bright
Mr Sefton .... Inspector

Mr Lewellyn
Mr Wrighton
Miss Sibley
CRIME Girl detective poses as ex-convict to
save old woman from kidnappers.

04519
BELINDA'S DREAM (400)
H&W Films (Prieur)
D: (Stuart Kinder)
COMEDY Maid dreams she changes places with
her mistress.

04520
ONLY A WEDDING (505)
H&W Films (Prieur)
D: (Stuart Kinder)
S: (SKETCH) Mark Melford
Mark Melford
COMEDY 'A most diverting item.'

04521
HIS CHOICE (2275)
Herkomer (Tyler)
P:D: Hubert von Herkomer
S: Marie Corelli
SC: Siegfried von Herkomer
Hubert von Herkomer ....The Miller
Clarissa Selwyn .... Mary
Owen Nares .... Hugh West
May Blaney .... Helen
ROMANCE City girl's artist fiance loves miller's
daughter he saves from fire.

04522
GOLFING (900) (U) also: COMIC GOLF
Hewitt Films (Barn et)
D: G. Fletcher Hewitt
Harry Lauder
Neil Kenyon
COMEDY Music Hall stars' impromptu antics
on golf-course.

04523
WILLIE'S DREAM OF MICK SQUINTER
(674) (U)
Martin (Thanhouser)
D: (Dave Aylott)
COMEDY Boy reads penny 'blood' dreams
he is captured by gang.

04524
PROFESSOR HOSKIN'S PATENT HUSTLER
(434) (U)
Martin (Thanhouser)
D: (Dave Aylott)
TRICK Professor's invention makes things
accelerate.

04525
WILY WILLIAM'S WASHING (592) (U)
Martin (Thanhouser)
D:(Dave Aylott)
COMEDY Tramp steals clothes and poses as
laundress.

04526
MARIA MARTEN; OR, THE MURDER IN
THE RED BARN (2850) (A)
Motograph
D: SC: Maurice Elvey
S: (PLAY)
Elizabeth Risdon .... Maria Marten
Fred Groves .... William Corder
Douglas Payne .... Roger Deaves
Nessie Blackford .... Mary Marten
A.G. Ogden .... Tom Marten
Mary Mackenzie .... Mary Moore
Maurice Elvey .... Capt Matthews
CRIME Polstead, 1826. Squire kills pregnant
mistress and is exposed by her mother's dream.

04527
POPSY WOPSY (478) (U)
Motograph (U)
D: Maurice Elvey
Fred Groves . . . . The Composer
TRICK Composer gets drunk on proceeds of
song and sees furniture dance.

04528
LOVE AND WAR IN TOYLAND (3000) *Kinema*
Natural Colour Kinematograph Co
D: F. Martin Thornton, Edgar Rodgers
TRICK Animated toys: the Lovelanders versus
the No-goods.

04529
THE SOCIETY TANGO
Selsior Films
R.L. Leonard and Amelie de S-
MUSICAL Dance to synchronise with cinema
orchestras.

04530
THE MAXIXE BRASILIENNE
Selsior Films
R.L. Leonard and Amelie De S-
MUSICAL Dance to synchronise with cinema
orchestras.

04531
A SISTER TO ASSIST 'ER *sound*
UK Kineplastikon
D: (W.R. Booth)
George Graves
MUSICAL Comic song sychronising with a
gramophone record.

04532
RECITATION BY JAMES WELCH *sound*
UK Kineplastikon
D: (W.R. Booth)
James Welch
ACT Comedian recites; synchronises with a
gramophone record.

04533
SAILOR'S SONG *sound*
UK Kineplastikon
D: (W.R. Booth)
MUSICAL Synchronises with a gramophone
record.

04534
ARTFUL ATHLETICS *sound*
UK Kineplastikon
D: S: W.R. Booth
Walter R. Booth
TRICK Impossible athletics synchronising to a
gramophone record.

1914

JAN

04535
ISN'T IT WONDERFUL! (430) (U)
Armstrong (Anderson)
D:S: Charles Armstrong
TRICK Silhouettes of circus performers.

04536
A BROTHER'S ATONEMENT (2000) (U)
Barker (Walturdaw)
D: (Bert Haldane)
S: Rowland Talbot
Roy Travers . . . . George Harding
CRIME Framed gamekeeper breaks jail to kill witness when his brother admits to killing lord.

04537
SAWNEY SAM'S DILEMMA (530) (U)
Barker (Walturdaw)
S: Rowland Talbot
COMEDY "Exclusive comic."

04538
WHAT MEN WILL DO (1972) (A)
B & C (DFSA)
D: Charles Weston
Arthur Finn
Marie Pickering
CRIME Man robs remarried wife's house and she shuts him in safe.

04539
POTTS IN A PICKLE (590) (U)
B & C (DFSA)
Charles Calvert . . . . Septimus Calvert
COMEDY Actor poses as rival to woo JP's daughter.

04540
THREE LITTLE ORPHANS (2127) (U)
B & C (DFSA)
D: Ethyle Batley
Dorothy Batley . . . . Peggy
Gladys Johnson . . . . Child
Iris O'Gorman . . . . Child
PATHOS Rich woman finds three orphans are her dead sister's children.

04541
MARY'S NEW BLOUSE (631) (U)
B & C (DFSA)
D: (Ethyle Batley)
ROMANCE Child sends telegrams to reconcile her sister with fiance.

04542
SAVED BY A DREAM (1097) (A)
B & C (DFSA)
D: (Ethyle Batley)
FANTASY Rich man stops flirting with blacksmith's wife after dreaming he is Satan.

04543
WHEN THE HURRICANES BOUGHT THE LINO (447) (U)
B & C (DFSA)
D:S: Lewin Fitzhamon
Constance Somers-Clarke. . . . . .Bella
Marie Royston . . . . Beano
Roy Royston . . . . Buster
COMEDY Children's adventures bringing home a roll of lino.

04544
LIEUTENANT DARING, AERIAL SCOUT (1760) (U)
B & C (DFSA)
D: (Ernest Batley)
Harry Lorraine . . . . Lt. Daring
CRIME Spy wrecks lieut's airplane and hangs him upside down in straightjacket.

04545
MEDDLESOME MIKE (485) (U)
Cricks (Walturdaw)
D: (Edwin J. Collins)
COMEDY Misadventures of a man bent on interfering.

04546
PC NABBEM AND THE COINERS (495) (U)
Cricks (DFSA)
D: (Edwin J. Collins)
COMEDY PC arrests coiners and finds they are makers of Sunday School medals.

04547
SELINA'S FLIGHT FOR FREEDOM (481) (U)
Cricks (DFSA)
D: (Edwin J. Collins)
COMEDY Suffragette forces husband to do housework.

04548
BERTIE BUY$ A CARETAKER (425) (U)
Cricks (DFSA)
D: (Edwin J. Collins)
COMEDY Burglar poses as dress-dummy to rob drunkard.

04549
PERCY ATTENDS A MASQUERADE (485)(U)
Cricks (DFSA)
D: (Edwin J. Collins)
COMEDY Dancer dressed as policeman catches burglar.

04550
A DAUGHTER OF SATAN (2895) (A)
Cricks (Ruffells)
D: Edwin J. Collins
Jack Leigh . . . . .Jack Fortescue
Una Tristram . . . . Alicia Fortescue
Lionel d'Aragon . . . . . Ralph Mervale
CRIME Divers fight beneath sea for plans stolen by French spy.

04551
A DOUBLE EXPOSURE (545) (U)
Cricks (DFSA)
D: (Edwin J. Collins)
COMEDY Man hides winnings in insured trousers, which his wife scorches.

04552
THE DOMESTIC GAME HUNT (380) (U)
EcKo (U)
D: W.P. Kellino
COMEDY Father tries to track a mouse.

04553
THE STUDENTS' NIGHT OUT (493) (U)
EcKo (U)
D: W.P. Kellino
COMEDY Three tipsy students cause trouble at Music Hall.

04554
NOBBY THE KNUT (605) (U)
D: W.P. Kellino
Sam T. Poluski . . . . . .Nobby
COMEDY Man in pub plays funnel trick and is tricked in return.

04555
BUMBLES GOES BUTTERFLYING (430) (U)
EcKo (U)
D: W.P. Kellino
Phillipi . . . . .Bumbles
CHASE Bumbles chases butterfly through picnic, river, stable.

04556
BETTY'S BIRTHDAY (575) (U)
EcKo (U)
D: W.P. Kellino
Sam T. Poluski . . . . The Bear
Lottie Bellman . . . . Betty
COMEDY Uncle gives girl pet bear for birthday.

04557
THE WHITE STOCKING (404)
EcKo (U)
D: W.P. Kellino
COMEDY

04558
PIMPLE'S HUMANITY (690) (U)
Folly Films (Phoenix)
D:S: Fred Evans, Joe Evans
Fred Evans . . . . Johnny Walker
COMEDY Scots Jew fights faithless friend.

04559
LIEUTENANT PIMPLE AND THE STOLEN SUBMARINE (950) (U)
Folly Films (Phoenix)
D:S: Fred Evans, Joe Evans
Fred Evans . . . . Pimple
COMEDY Lt poses as diver to save submarine from Soho spies.

04560
WHAT HAPPENED TO PIMPLE — THE GENTLEMAN BURGLAR (745) (U)
Folly Films (Phoenix)
D:S: Fred Evans, Joe Evans
Fred Evans . . . . Pimple
Joe Evans . . . . Raffles
COMEDY Pimple joins forces with gentleman burglar but his clumsiness almost causes their arrest.

04561
BLIND FATE (2000) (U)
Hepworth
D: Cecil M. Hepworth
S: Blanche McIntosh
Alma Taylor. . . . . Molly
Alec Worcester
Jamie Darling . . . . Father
CRIME Blind girl feels broken finger of father's killer and, cured, gains confession by dramatising crime.

04562
A PRICE ON HIS HEAD (1900) (U)
Hepworth
D: (Warwick Buckland)
Eric Desmond . . . . Eric
CRIME Kidnappers capture tec, who flashes for help by heliograph.

04563
ON A FALSE SCENT (650) (U)
Hepworth
D: (Hay Plumb)
COMEDY Newlyweds are suspicious when they smell scent and smoke on one another.

04564
JUSTICE (3400) (A)
Hepworth (Renters)
D: Frank Wilson
Alec Worcester . . . . Jack Raynor
Alma Taylor . . . . Nan Prescott
Stewart Rome . . . . Paul Meredith
Harry Royston . . . . Joe Prescott
Ruby Belasco . . . . Mrs. Prescott
Jamie Darling . . . . John Meredith
Marie de Solla . . . . .Mrs. Meredith
CRIME Man hires crook to kill his father, then betrays him and abducts crook's daughter.

04565
HAWKEYE, HALL PORTER (525) (U)
Hepworth
D:S: Hay Plumb
Hay Plumb . . . . Hawkeye
COMEDY Hotel porter doubles as waiter and
falls asleep on night duty.

04566
BRIEF AUTHORITY (950) (U)
Hepworth
D: (Warwick Buckland)
Alec Worcester . . . . Squire
DRAMA Farmer and daughter saved from
eviction by new squire posing as fisherman.

04567
TANGO MAD (725) (U)
Hepworth
D: (Hay Plumb)
COMEDY Girl promises to marry whichever
suitor learns to tango best.

04568
THE IMPORTANCE OF BEING ANOTHER
MAN'S WIFE (2000)
Hepworth (KTC)
D: (Frank Wilson)
S: (PLAY) Harry Pleon
Arthur Roberts . . . . Arthur Fitzawful-Smith
COMEDY Man poses as girl to woo married
woman.

04569
OUT OF THE FRYING PAN (550) (U)
Hepworth
D: (Hay Plumb)
COMEDY Deserter hired to pose as wild man
weds showman's daughter.

04570
THE WHIRR OF THE SPINNING WHEEL
(1975) (U)
Hepworth
D: Frank Wilson
Alma Taylor . . . . Nan
Stewart Rome . . . . Jasper
Alice de Winton . . . . Black Meg
Marie de Solla . . . . Mother
Ruby Belasco . . . . Lady Betty
ROMANCE Villager elopes with rich cad but
returns to blacksmith.

04571
THE PRICE OF FAME (800) (U)
Hepworth
D: (Warwick Buckland)
Alma Taylor . . . . Mary
Stewart Rome . . . . Julian
ROMANCE Jealous model slashes artist's portrait
of connoisseur's daughter and kills herself.

04572
POORLUCK MINDS THE SHOP (350) (U)
Hepworth
D: (Frank Wilson)
Harry Buss . . . . Poorluck
COMEDY Drunk looking after shop is tormented
by children.

04573
BILLY'S BIOSCOPE (450) (U)
Captain Kettle Films (Walturdaw)
S: C.J. Cutcliffe-Hyne
COMEDY Adventures of a boy and his moving
picture camera.

04574
THE ADVENTURES OF A FOOTBALL (250)(U
Urban Trading Co
D: (Stuart Kinder)
TRICK Crowd chase football which runs up tree.

04575
MARJORY'S GOLDFISH (490) (U)
Urban Trading Co.
D: S: Stuart Kinder
FANTASY Magic goldfish takes small girl for
voyage under sea.

04576
THE GRIT OF A DANDY (2520) (U)
Herkomer Films (Tyler)
D: Hubert von Herkomer
S: Siegfried von Herkomer
Sybil Sparkes . . . . Gladys
Leonard Ceily . . . . Clifford Maythorne
Clarissa Selwyn . . . . . .
Archibald Forbes . . . . . .
CRIME Rejected dandy saves doctor's daughter
from being abducted by burglars.

04577
THE FOREMAN'S TREACHERY (2) (U)
Edison
D: Charles Brabin
S: Anne & Bannister Merwin
Marc McDermott . . . . David Llewellyn
Miriam Nesbitt . . . . Anna Lloyd
Charles Vernon . . . . Griffith
Douglas Munro . . . . Mr. Lloyd
CRIME Wales. Halfwit sees foreman kill owner
of copper-mine.

04578
TO SAVE THE KING (955) (U)
Martin Films (Thanhouser)
reissue: 1915, THE ENEMY WITHIN (DFSA)
D: (Dave Aylott)
Harry Granville
CRIME Tec saves Ruritanian King from
anarchists.

04579
MIKE MURPHY AS A PICTURE ACTOR
(531) (U)
Martin Films (Imperial)
D: Dave Aylott
Ernie Westo . . . . Mike Murphy
COMEDY Tramp causes trouble in studio
while acting as cavalier.

04580
THE LOST COLLAR STUD (1140) *Kinema*
Natural Colour Kinematograph Co
D: (F. Martin Thornton)
TRICK Animated collar-stud causes government
official to lose his job.

04581
THE SEVENTH DAY (1638)
Regent Films (MP)
P: Charles Weston, Arthur Finn
D:S: Charles Weston
Arthur Finn . . . . James Inward
Alice Inward . . . . Mrs. Inward
DRAMA Northumberland. Steelworker takes to
drink and dies in brawl after council closes
cinemas on Sundays.

04582
THE BRASS BOTTLE (3600)
Theatre & General
P: Nicholson Ormsby-Scott
D:SC: Sidney Morgan
S: (PLAY) F. Anstey
Holman Clark . . . . Fakrash-al-Amash
Alfred Bishop . . . . Prof Futvoye
Doris Lytton . . . . Sylvia Futvoye
Lawrence Grossmith . . Horace Ventmire
Tom Mowbray . . . . . . Samuel Wackerbath
J.R. Tozer . . . . King Solomon
Mary Brough . . . . Mrs Futvoye
Vane Featherstone . . . . .
Rudge Harding . . . .

Molly Farrell . . . .
FANTASY Jinn's magic helps a poor architect
win a professor's daughter.

04583
THE BROTHER'S MISTAKE (1240)
Gaumont
DRAMA Yorkshire. Mean man in love with
widowed housekeeper tells his brother that her
child is a bastard.

FEB

04584
JUST IN TIME (1179) (U)
B & C (DFSA)
CRIME Kidnapped groom escapes in time for
wedding.

04585
THE TATTOOED WILL (2525) (U)
B & C (DFSA)
D: Ernest G. Batley
Ernest G. Batley . . . . The Millionaire
Dorothy Batley . . . . Pat
Jack Mullins . . . . Sailor
Gladys Johnson . . . . Child
DRAMA Crossing-sweeper inherits when
millionaire tattoos will on shipwrecked sailor's
back.

04586
A LITTLE CHILD SHALL LEAD THEM
(2359) (U)
B & C (DFSA)
D: Ethyle Batley
Dororthy Batley . . . . Peggy
Little Frances . . . . Child
ROMANCE Eldest child heals breach between
parted parents.

04587
WHEN THE HURRICANES TOOK UP
FARMING (572) (U)
B & C (DFSA) *reissue:* 1917
D:S: Lewin Fitzhamon
Constance Somers-Clarke. . Bella
Marie Royston . . . . Beano
Roy Royston . . . . Buster
COMEDY Children on holiday annoy sweep and
farmer, and are chased.

04588
THE LIFE OF SHAKESPEARE (5) USA: LOVE
AND ADVENTURES IN THE LIFE OF
SHAKESPEARE
B & C (MP)
D: J.B. McDowell, Frank R. Growcott
S: Frank R. Growcott, Sidney Low
Albert Ward , ... William Shakespeare
Sybil Hare . . . . Ann Hathaway
Aimee Martinek . . . . Queen Elizabeth
George Foley . . . . Sir Thomas Lucy
M. Gray Murray . . . . Sir Hugh Clopton
Eva Bayley . . . . Mrs. Shakespeare
Miss Bennett . . . . Charlotte Clopton
HISTORY Biography of Stratford playwright.

04589
THE LAST ENCAMPMENT (2025) (U)
Barker
D: (Bert Haldane)
S: Rowland Talbot
DRAMA

04590
THE THREE MILE LIMIT (1050) *pathe*
Britannia Films (Pathe)
ROMANCE Elopers in fishing boat elude
pursuers and marry outside 3-mile limit.

04591
OLD ST PAUL'S (3077) (U) USA:
WHEN LONDON BURNED
Clarendon *reissue:* 1915
D: Wilfred Noy
S: (NOVEL) Harrison Ainsworth
SC: Low Warren
Lionelle Howard . . . . Leonard Holt
R. Juden . . . . Annabel
P.G. Ebbutt . . . . King Charles
Ivan Cleveland . . . . Earl of Rochester
J. Cooper . . . . Solomon Eagle
M. Sinclair . . . . Nurse Malmayne
F.J.J. Hunt . . . . Chowles
Cyril Smith . . . . Boy
HISTORY 1665. Couple's adventures during Great
Fire and Plague.

04592
WHEN PIMPLE WAS YOUNG — HIS FIRST
SWEETHEART (950) (U)
Folly Films (Phoenix)
D:S: Fred Evans, Joe Evans
Fred Evans . . . . Pimple
Tommy Collet . . . . Young Pimple
COMEDY Youthful Pimple elopes and gets friend
to pose as parson.

04593
PIMPLE ELOPES (545) (U)
Folly Films (Phoenix)
D:S: Fred Evans, Joe Evans
Fred Evans . . . . Pimple
COMEDY Pimple helps friend elope to registry
office.

04594
WHO WILL MARY MARTHA? (745) (U)
Phoenix Film Agency
D:S: Joe Evans
Joe Evans . . . . Martha
COMEDY Girl advertises for suitors and landlady
blackmails them by posing as her husband

04595
LIEUTENANT PIMPLE'S DASH FOR THE
POLE (950) (U)
Folly Films (Phoenix)
D:S: Fred Evans, Joe Evans
Fred Evans . . . . Lt Pimple
Joe Evans . . . .
COMEDY Naval lieut discovers the pole.

04596
WHEN PIMPLE WAS YOUNG — YOUNG
PIMPLE'S SCHOOLDAYS (560) (U)
Folly Films (Phoenix)
D:S: Fred Evans, Joe Evans
Fred Evans . . . . Pimple
Tommy Collet . . . . Young Pimple
COMEDY Schoolboy plays various pranks.

04597
THE MAN BEHIND THE MASK (1075) (U)
Hepworth
D: (Warwick Buckland)
Flora Morris . . . . Dorothy Oliver
Alec Worcester . . . . Harry Lowremer
ADVENTURE 18th C. Girl hides highwayman
from Bow Street Runners.

04598
ONCE ABOARD THE LUGGER (550) (U)
Hepworth
D: Hay Plumb
Johnny Butt . . . . Count Verdigris
Harry Buss . . . . Harold
COMEDY Framed hero breaks jail in time to
save sweetheart from count.

04599
THE NIGHT BELL (1075) (U)
Hepworth
D: (Frank Wilson)
Jamie Darling . . . . Bill Woodford
CRIME Burglar robs doctor almost causing wife's
death.

04600
A FRIEND IN NEED (550) (U)
Hepworth
D: Frank Wilson
Sandow the pony
HayPlumb . . . . Gamekeeper
Frank Wilson . . . . Doctor
ANIMAL Pony tracks poacher who injured
gamekeeper, and fetches police.

04601
DIAMOND CUT DIAMOND (1075) (U)
Hepworth
D: (Warwick Buckland)
Claire Pridelle . . . . Grace Lewin
CRIME Inventor kidnaps daughter of capitalist
who stole his plans.

04602
HOW BILLY KEPT HIS WORD (1125) (U)
Hepworth
D: (Frank Wilson)
Eric Desmond . . . . Billy
CRIME Boy sets bees onto stepfather for making
him rob his uncle.

04603
A DOUBTFUL DEAL IN DOGS (600) (U)
Hepworth
D: (Hay Plumb)
COMEDY Owner of heroic dog sells similar dogs
to hopeful purchasers.

04604
THE GIRL FROM THE SKY (1200) (U)
Ivy Close Films (Hepworth)
D: Elwin Neame
Ivy Close . . . . Muriel King
F. Pope-Stamper . . . . Harold Teale
COMEDY Aviatrix lands in misogynist's garden.

04605
CREATURES OF HABIT (765) (U)
Turner Films (Hepworth)
D:S: Larry Trimble
Florence Turner . . . . Flo
Tom Powers . . . . Tom
COMEDY Fussy couple's nervous habits
imitated by their children.

04606
THOU SHALT NOT STEAL(1025) (U)
Hepworth
D: (Warwick Buckland)
Stewart Rome . . . . Frank Armstrong
Ruby Belasco . . . . Mrs. Armstrong
DRAMA Man robs neighbour to feed sick mother,
who turns out to be neighbour's ex-wife.

04607
WHAT THE FIRELIGHT SHOWED (700) (U)
Hepworth
D: (Frank Wilson)
Stewart Rome . . . . The Man
Eric Desmond . . . . Bobby
COMEDY Girl mistakes beau in fancy dress for
escaped gorilla.

04608
THE "SIMPLE LIFE" CURE (725) (U)
Hepworth
D: (Hay Plumb)
Harry Buss . . . . The Gent

Ruby Belasco . . . . His Wife
COMEDY City man tries life on farm but soon
returns home.

04609
GOLIGHTLY PUNISHED (535)
Gaumont
COMEDY Salop, 1745. Squire returns from
Edinburgh to avoid rebellion and catches his
wife flirting.

04610
THE LURE OF LONDON (5250) (U)
Barker (Co-operative)
D: (Bert Haldane)
S: (PLAY) Arthur Applin
SC: Rowland Talbot
Ivy Close . . . . Daisy Westbury
Edward Viner . . . . William Anderson
M. Gray Murray . . . . . . Charlie Brooks
William Harbord . . . . . . Sir John Westbury
Leal Douglas . . . . Lady Westbury
Gwenda Wren . . . . Olga Westbury
H.L. Pringle . . . . George Stamford
DRAMA Surgeon's lost daughter is adopted by
cockney drunkard, becomes a dancer, is run
over, and operated upon by her father.

04611
BETTER LATE THAN NEVER (530)
H. & W. Films (Prieur)
D: (Stuart Kinder)
COMEDY Wife gets her lazy husband job, but
he arrives drunk.

04612
CAPTURED BY CONSENT (550) (U)
Dart Films (Cosmo)
D: (Stuart Kinder)
S: (SKETCH)
COMEDY Man poses as burglar to scare boastful
friend.

04613
BY THE SAD SEA WAVES (530)
Dart Films (Cosmo)
D: (Stuart Kinder)
COMEDY Henpeck has day out while wife is
away.

04614
NOBBY WINS THE CUP (505)
EcKo (U)
D: W.P. Kellino
Sam T. Poluski . . . . Nobby
COMEDY Nobby trains to be boxer but loses
match.

04615
NOBBY'S TANGO TEAS (560)
EcKo (U)
D: W.P. Kellino
Sam T. Poluski . . . . Nobby
COMEDY Nobby runs tango tea for costers and
stages fashion parade.

04616
SILAS Q. PINCH, SENSATIONALIST (1462)
Solograph (U)
S: (STORY) Pearson Choate
COMEDY American cures bored lord by
persuading him to take up burglary.

04617
TANGO MAD (403) retitled: THE CRAZE
Planet (DFSA)
COMEDY Dance enthusiast visits tea-garden and
dreams of tangoing.

04618
THE ELECTRIC DOLL (485) (U)
Cricks (DFSA)
D: Edwin J. Collins
COMEDY Prof's electric doll causes trouble and
is mistaken for a corpse.

04619
A SOLDIER'S HONOUR (3000)
USA: BROTHER OFFICERS
Cricks (Fenning)
D: Charles Calvert
S: Leo Trevor
Harry Hargreaves . . . . Lt. Harry Graham
WAR India. Colonel's son confesses to cardsharp-
ing after the lieut he framed saves his life.

04620
THEY ALL WANT A GIRL (845) (U)
Cricks (DFSA)
D: (Edwin J. Collins)
S: Ernest Dangerfield
COMEDY Woman doctor changes clothes with a
girl to foil persistent suitors.

04621
THE WORLD, THE FLESH AND THE DEVIL
(5125) (A) *Kinema*
Natural Colour Kinematograph *Co*-Union Jack
Photoplays
D: F. Martin Thornton
S: (PLAY) Laurence Cowan
SC: Laurence Cowan
Frank Esmond . . . . Nicholas Brophy
Stella St. Audrie . . . . Caroline Stanger
Warwick Wellington . . . . . . Sir James Hall
Charles Carter . . . . Rupert Stanger/
Dyke
Rupert Harvey . . . . Robert Hall
Jack Denton . . . . George Grigg
Gladys Cunningham . . . . . Mrs Brophy
Frances Midgeley . . . . Gertrude Grant
Mercy Hatton . . . . Lady Hall
H. Agar Lyons . . . . The Devil
Nell Carter . . . . Beatrice Cuthbert
Frank Stather . . . . Insp Toplin
Roger Hamilton . . . . Wylde
CRIME Crooked lawyer's scheme to dispossess
heir to baronetcy.

04622
RIP VAN WINKLE (3000)
retitled: FORGOTTEN
Climax
D: Stuart Kinder
S: (PLAY) Fred Storey
(NOVEL) Washington Irving
Fred Storey . . . . Rip Van Winkle
Ella Brandon . . . . Gretchen
Martin Stuart . . . . Nick Vedder
Maitland Stapley . . . . . . Derrick Beekman
FANTASY Catskills. Husband returns home
after sleeping twenty years.

04623
BEAUTY AND THE BARGE (1242) (U)
London (Fenning)
D: Harold Shaw
S: (STORY) W.W. Jacobs
Cyril Maude . . . . Capt Barley
Lillian Logan . . . . Ethel Smedley
Gregory Scott . . . . Lt Seton Boyne
Mary Brough . . . . Mrs Baldwin
Judd Green . . . . Dibbs
COMEDY Bargee adopts mayor's runaway
daughter and she falls in love with his mate.

04624
LAWYER QUINCE (1078) (U)
London (Fenning)

D: Harold Shaw
S: (STORY) W.W. Jacobs
Charles Rock . . . . Lawyer Quince
Lillian Logan . . . . Celia Rose
Gregory Scott . . . . Ned Quince
Mary Brough . . . . Mrs Quince
Judd Green . . . . Farmer Rose
COMEDY Cobbler learns son is wooing a farmer's
daughter.

04625
THE BOSUN'S MATE (1130) (U)
London (Fenning)
D; Harold Shaw
S: (STORY) W.W. Jacobs
W.H. Berry . . . . George Benn
Mary Brough . . . . Mrs Walters
Wyndham Guise . . . . Ned Travers
Charles Rock . . . .
George Bellamy . . . .
Judd Green . . . .
John East . . . .
Brian Daly . . . .
COMEDY Retired boatswain hires ex-soldier to
burgle widow's inn.

04626
THE THIRD STRING (1990) (U)
London (Fenning)
D: George Loane Tucker
S: (STORY) W.W. Jacobs
Jane Gail . . . . Julia
Frank Stanmore . . . . Ginger Dick
George Bellamy . . . . Peter Russett
Judd Green . . . . Sam Small
Charles Rock . . . . Landlord
Charles Vernon . . . . Bill Lumm
COMEDY Man poses as boxer to impress barmaid
and is forced to fight champion.

04627
THE STOLEN PLANS (1040) (U)
Edison
D: Charles Brabin
S: Goring Chalmers
Marc McDermott . . . . Capt West
Miriam Nesbitt . . . . Miss Ashmay
Charles Vernon . . . . Capt Ashmay
William Luft . . . . Burgovitch
Winifred Albion . . . . Mary
CRIME Spy blackmails captain into stealing
plans of new biplane.

04628
GETTING EVEN (467) (U)
A.R. Films (Brockliss)
COMEDY Sacked maid sends mistress monkey
that wrecks house.

04629
WHITEWASHING THE CEILING (1500)
Will Day Kinutilities
D: Will Day
S: (PLAY) Will Evans
Will Evans
Arthur Conquest
COMEDY Slapstick mishaps of decorators who
whitewash wrong house.

04630
KINEMAPOEMS (series)
Cinema film & Theatrical Exclusives
D: Donald Cornwallis

04631
1: PAPA'S LETTER (1000)

04632
2: THE CONVICT'S DREAM (1000)

04633
3: THE NEWSBOY'S DEBT (1000)
DRAMA Picturisations of poems which are
recited from cinema stage.

04634
THE OPIUM CIGARETTES (1000)
Climax
D:S: Stuart Kinder
TRICK Man smokes drugged cigarette and sees
weird visions.

MAR

04635
RETRIBUTION (483) (U)
B & C (DFSA)
D: Ethyle Batley
Ernest Batley . . . . Husband
Ethel Bracewell . . . . Wife
Dorothy Batley . . . . Child
PATHOS Unemployed man steals doctor's
watch, causing own child's death.

04636
A SUBURBAN PAL (1071) (A)
B & C (DFSA)
COMEDY Drunkard wakes to find he is
without trousers at suffragette meeting.

04637
THE MASTER CROOK OUTWITTED BY
A CHILD (2489) (U)
B & C (DFSA)
D: Ernest G. Batley
Ernest G. Batley . . . . The Master Crook
Dorothy Batley. . . . . The Child
Ethel Bracewell . . . . The Girl
CRIME Crook plants stolen diamond on orphan
fruit-seller.

04638
THE CROSSED FLAGS (2182) (U)
B & C (DFSA)
WAR Balkans. Scapegrace becomes spy for
Turkey and is saved from death by sister,
who has become nurse.

04639
THE TROUBLES OF AN HEIRESS (1095) (U)
B & C (DFSA)
D: (Sidney Northcote)
Miss Normand . . . . Diana Coney
M. Gray Murray . . . . Lord Painkurst
Vera Northcote. . . . . The Kandy Kid
Mr. Billington . . . . Mark Coney
COMEDY Disowned girl wins uncle's fortune
by marrying favourite nephew.

04640
A PLEASANT WAY OF GETTING THIN (450)(
B & C (DFSA)
COMEDY Fat man joins girls' ballet class.

04641
THE HIDDEN WITNESS (2790)
Big Ben Films-Union (Pathe)
D: H.O. Martinek
S: L.C. MacBean
H.O. Martinek
Ivy Montford
CRIME Girl's photograph proves secretary killed
her uncle and framed cousin.

04642
A WARM RECEPTION (600)
Big Ben Films-Union (Pathe)
D: H.O. Martinek
COMEDY Spinster mistakes escaped lunatic for
rich American uncle.

04643
THE FRIEND IN BLUE (1275)
Big Ben Films-Union (Pathe)
D: H.O. Martinek
S: L.C. MacBean
H.O. Martinek
CRIME PC captures burglar and adopts his
starving children.

04644
THE MYSTERY OF THE OLD MILL (3000)
Big Ben Films-Union (Pathe)
D: H.O. Martinek
S: L.C. MacBean
H.O. Martinek . . . . Dick Steele
Ivy Montford . . . . Kate Halifax
Irene Vernon . . . . Daphne Morrison
CRIME Detectives unmask blackmailer.

04645
LIEUTENANT ROSE AND THE SEALED
ORDERS (2335) (U)
Clarendon
D: Percy Stow
S: Jack W. Bobin
Harry Lorraine . . . . Lt Rose
CRIME Lieut in car chases count in train and is
scooped aboard with mailbag.

04646
WHEN EVERY MAN'S A SOLDIER (515) (U)
Clarendon
D: Percy Stow
COMEDY Army service brings success to
grocer's son.

04647
AUNT SUSAN'S WAY (538) (U)
Clarendon
D: Percy Stow
COMEDY Aunt tests niece and nephew by
pretending to lose fortune.

04648
GRANDPA'S WILL (520) (U)
Clarendon
D: Percy Stow
COMEDY Heir is forced to wear grandfather's
claret suit to the office.

04649
LOVE THY NEIGHBOUR (430) (U)
Clarendon
D: (Toby Cooper)
COMEDY Man connects garden hose to
neighbour's airpipe.

04650
NON-SUITED (347) (U)
Cricks
D: (Edwin J. Collins)
COMEDY Two tramps fake fight to steal
victim's clothes.

04651
THE WRECKER OF LIVES (3000)
Cricks (Ruffells)
D: Charles Calvert
Jack Leigh . . . . Vivian Raymond
Una Tristram . . . . Alice Graham
Lionel D'Aragon . . . . Bill Blake
Edward Sydney . . . . .Jack Courtney
Fred Morgan. . . . . Gen Graham
CRIME Spy poses as secretary to kill general
and frame his daughter's fiance.

04652
A GRAVE AFFAIR (1030)
Gaumont
COMEDY Staines. Rich widow learns of
man's plot to impress her by having friend
pose as burglar.

04653
AN ENGAGEMENT OF CONVENIENCE
(1075) (U)
Hepworth
D: (Hay Plumb)
Alma Taylor . . . . The Typist
Cyril Morton . . . . The Nephew
Harry Royston . . . . The Boss
Marie de Solla . . . . The Aunt
COMEDY Man fakes engagement to typist to
please rich aunt.

04654
THE QUALITY OF MERCY (1000) (U)
Hepworth
D: (Warwick Buckland)
Alma Taylor . . . . The Mother
Harry Royston . . . . The Policeman
John MacAndrews . . . . . . The Tramp
PATHOS Magistrate adops girl who steals bread
for starving mother.

04655
THE GARDENER'S HOSE (550) (U)
Hepworth reissue: 1916
D: (Frank Wilson)
COMEDY Spinster mistakes gardener's letter
for proposal.

04656
FAIR GAME (625) (U)
Hepworth
D: (Frank Wilson)
John MacAndrews . . . . . Squire Goodfellow
COMEDY Farmer sells rabbits at shilling,
brother buys them back for sixpence, and
farmer sells them again.

04657
A MISLEADING MISS (650) (U)
Hepworth
D: (Hay Plumb)
Chrissie White . . . . Kate Matthews
Cyril Morton . . . . Gerald Young
Claire Pridelle . . . . Nellie Prince
COMEDY Estranged couple reunite after they
each fall for actor and wife.

04658
THE MURDOCK TRIAL (3425) (A)
Turner Films (Hepworth)
D: Larry Trimble
Florence Turner . . . . Helen Story
Frank Tennant . . . . Lionel Mann
Richard Norton . . . . Henry Murdock
William Felton . . . . The Butler
G.C. Colonna. . . . . The Nephew
Eric Forbes-Robertson . . . . The Prosecution
Alfred Phillips . . . . The Defence
Lucy Sibley . . . . The Housekeeper
Larry Trimble . . . . A Butler
CRIME Heiress takes blame for stabbing her
uncle, thinking her lover guilty.

04659
PIMPLE AND GALATEA (575) (U)
Folly Films (Phoenix)
D:S: Fred Evans, Joe Evans
Fred Evans . . . . Pimple
COMEDY Sculptor has trouble with wife when
statue comes to life.

04660
PIMPLE IN THE GRIP OF THE LAW (465) (U)
Folly Films (Phoenix)
D:S: Fred Evans, Joe Evans
Fred Evans . . . . Pimple
COMEDY "How he got in the grip of the law and
how he got out of it."

04661
WHAT HAPPENED TO PIMPLE — IN THE
HANDS OF THE LONDON CROOK (280) (U)
Folly Films (Phoenix)
D:S: Fred Evans, Joe Evans
Fred Evans . . . . Pimple
COMEDY Pimple blackmailed into stealing gems.

04662
THE HOUSE OF DISTEMPERLEY (990) (U)
Folly Films (Phoenix) reissue: 1916 (H & S)
D:S: Fred Evans, Joe Evans
Fred Evans . . . . Pimple
COMEDY Knight loses home to gambler and
weds rich Lady.

04663
THE BOBBY'S BOB (400) (U)
Phoenix Film Agency
COMEDY

04664
THE TEST OF LOVE (1237) (U)
DD Films
ROMANCE Squire's daughter rejects disfigured
dairy engineer who then returns to milkmaid

04665
AFTER THE BALL WAS OVER (605) (U)
EcKo (U)
D: W.P. Kellino
Sam Poluski . . . . Mephistopheles
COMEDY Dancer dressed as Mephistopheles
scares burglar.

04666
THE POSTMAN'S DILEMMA (625) (U)
EcKo (U)
D: W.P. Kellino
Sam Poluski . . . . Postman
COMEDY Postman's moveable pillar-box foils
militant suffragettes.

04667
THE TANGRAM (370)
Kineto
D: (W.R. Booth)
TRICK Pieces of Chinese puzzle form Henry
VIII, Lloyd George, and Chinese love drama.

04668
ALL'S FAIR IN LOVE (700)
Kineto
COMEDY Bookworms' feud healed by love of
their children.

04669
THE RING AND THE RAJAH (1170) (U)
London
D: Harold Shaw
S: Anne Merwin
Edna Flugrath . . . . Edith Blayne
Arthur Holmes-Gore . . . . The Rajah
Vincent Clive . . . . Capt Blayne
Edward O'Neill . . . . Ferak
CRIME Rajah dies saving captain's wife when
plan to poison her husband goes wrong.

04670
BRANSCOMBE'S PAL (2042) (U)
London
D: Harold Shaw
S: BannisterMerwin
Lillian Logan . . . . Helen Caerlyon
Arthur Holmes-Gore . . . . Jack Branscombe
Gregory Scott . . . . Bob Caerlyon
DRAMA Man takes blame for girl's cardsharping
brother.

04671
HER CHILDREN (1071) (U)
London
D: Harold Shaw
S: Bannister Merwin
Lillian Logan . . . . Mrs Clode
Arthur Holmes-Gore . . . . Vicar
George Bellamy . . . .
DRAMA Vicar reforms widow after finding her
neglected children locked in church.

04672
DUTY (1150) (U)
London
D: Harold Shaw
S: Bannister Merwin
Edna Flugrath . . . . Molly Brown
Gregory Scott . . . . PC Fred Allen
George Bellamy . . . . Mr. Allen
CRIME East End policeman forced to arrest
dissolute father.

04673
SHE STOOPS TO CONQUER (3060) (U)
London (Gaumont)
D: George Loane Tucker
S: (PLAY) Oliver Goldsmith
SC: Bannister Merwin
Henry Ainley . . . . Marlow
Jane Gail . . . . Kate Hardcastle
Gregory Scott . . . . Jeremy
Charles Rock . . . . Hardcastle
Wyndham Guise . . . . Tony Lumpkin
Christine Rayner . . . . Constance Neville
Gerald Ames . . . . Hastings
Lewis Gilbert . . . . Sir Charles Marlow
Stella St Audrie . . . . Mrs. Hardcastle
Nelson Ramsey . . . . Landlord
Fay Compton . . . . Barmaid
COMEDY 1770. Suitor tricked into thinking
rich man's house is inn.

04674
THE CUP FINAL MYSTERY (2600) (U)
Motograph
D: Maurice Elvey
Elizabeth Risdon . . . . Lizzie Keen
Fred Groves . . . . Joe Archer
Douglas Payne . . . . Charles West
Joan Morgan . . . . Delia Keen
Maurice Elvey . . . .
SPORT Girl saves kidnapped goalkeeper in time for
him to win Cup Final at Crystal Palace.

04675
THE FINGER OF DESTINY (2100) (U)
Motograph
D: Charles Raymond
Elizabeth Risdon . . . . .Doris
Babs Neville . . . . Irene
Douglas Payne . . . . Manadarin
Austin Camp . . . . Harry
Norman Yates . . . . Fred
WAR Man destroys father's foundry and
blames brother, who later helps sailor save
father from Boxer rebellion.

04676
INQUISITIVE IKE (250) (U)
Motograph (U)
D: (Maurice Elvey)
Elizabeth Risdon . . . . Dora
Fred Groves . . . . Fred
COMEDY Seaside. Man poses as girl to fool
peeping-tom.

04677
THE GLOVES OF PTAMES (568) (U)
Martin Films (DFSA)

D: Dave Aylott
TRICK Tramp dons Egyptian gloves which
cause objects to disappear.

04678
MIKE MURPHY'S DREAM OF LOVE AND
RICHES (593) (U)
Martin Films (DFSA) *reissue:* 1915,
MURPHY'S MILLIONS
D: Dave Aylott
Ernie Westo . . . . Mike Murphy
COMEDY Tramp dreams he is duke and saves
rich girl from ruffians.

04679
PANIC! (350) (U)
Martin Films (DFSA) reissue: 1915.
D: Dave Aylott
COMEDY Tramp mistakes film actors for
Germans and brings police.

04680
THE SORROWS OF SELINA (595) (U)
Martin Films (DFSA)
D: Dave Aylott
TRICK Maid dreams she uses magic lamp to
save suffragette from sultan.

04681
NO FOOL LIKE AN OLD FOOL (1200) (U)
GCA Films
George Formby . . . . John Willie
COMEDY "We have filmed that well-known
music hall star in a new cinema scream."

04682
DETECTIVE DARING AND THE THAMES
COINERS (2450) (U)
Daring Films (Cosmo)
P: Harry Lorraine
D: Sidney Northcote
S: B. Harold Brett
Harry Lorraine . . . . .Daring
Arthur Mavity . . . . . . .Barney
Bert Berry . . . . Spider
Claude Winn . . . . Flash Harry
Eileen Daybell . . . . Eileen
Will Discombe . . . . Grandfather
CRIME Tec catches counterfeiters to prove
girl's grandfather innocent.

04683
DETECTIVE FINN, OR, IN THE HEART OF
LONDON (2800) (U) USA: SOCIETY
DETECTIVE
Regent Films (Gaumont)
P: Charles Weston, Arthur Finn
D:S: Charles Weston
Arthur Finn . . . . Det Finn
Alice Inward . . . . Slippery Kate
Charles Weston . . . . Silk Hat Harry
CRIME Tec chases crooks who posed as maid
and inspector to steal lord's diamond.

04684
THE ANTIQUE BROOCH (2060) (U)
Edison
D: Charles J. Brabin
S: Bannister Merwin
Marc McDermott . . . . Jack Morley
Miriam Nesbitt . . . . Veronica
Kathleen Russell . . . . Lady Stanley
CRIME Lord's disowned nephew takes blame
when cousin steals brooch.

04685
BY HIS FATHER'S ORDERS (1455) (U)
Barker
D: (Bert Haldane)

S: Rowland Talbot
CRIME Man shot robbing father's office to pay
actress's fake IOU.

04686
THE DANCER IN DARKNESS (1100) (U)
Solograph (U)
S: (STORY)
DRAMA Wire-walker's rival switches off light
to cause death, not realising she is blind.

04687
FEAR OF THE HANGMAN (1462)
Solograph (U)
S: (STORY)
CRIME

APR

04688
AN UNWELCOME LODGER (557) (A)
B & C (DFSA)
COMEDY Landlady lets same room to Frenchma
and python trainer.

04689
THE MIDNIGHT WEDDING (3336) (U)
B & C (Moss)
D: Ernest G. Batley
S: (PLAY) Walter Howard
Ernest G. Batley . . . . Paul Valmar
Ethel Bracewell . . . . Princess Astrea
von Strelsburg
George Foley . . . . Crown Prince
Leopold
Joseph Del Lungo . . . . Capt. Rudolph
von Scarsbruck
Ethyle Batley . . . . Satanella
Alfred Lindsay . . . . .Prince Eugene
von Strelsburg
Winifred Dalby . . . . Stephanie
heir to throne.

04690
OUT OF EVIL COMETH GOOD (919) (U)
B & C (DFSA)
D: Ethyle Batley
Dorothy Batley . . . . Child
PATHOS Drunkard cripples his child and
repents in prison.

04691
I DON'T THINK! (494) (U)
B & C (DFSA)
COMEDY Disowned son returns home and
saves father from eviction.

04692
WHAT HO! THE JUNGLE (532) (U)
B & C (DFSA)
COMEDY Hero goes to Africa to save girl from
forger.

04693
PEGGY'S NEW PAPA (545) (U)
B & C (DFSA)
D: Ethyle Batley
Dorothy Batley . . . . Peggy
COMEDY Girl feigns madness to frighten
mother's suitor.

04694
LIEUTENANT DARING AND THE STOLEN
INVENTION (1864) (U)
B & C (DFSA)
D: Ernest G. Batley
James Russell . . . . Lt. Daring
George Foley . . . . Officer
CRIME Lt escapes from spies and swims to
recover model submarine.

04695
BLACK RODERICK THE POACHER (2025)
Big Ben Films-Union (Pathe)
D: H.O. Martinek
H.O. Martinek . . . . Lord Dane
Ivy Montford . . . . Mary Donald
CRIME Scotland. Shot gamekeeper recovers in
time to clear framed Lord.

04696
A HATEFUL BONDAGE (2300)
Britannia Films (Pathe)
D: (Lewin Fitzhamon)
Enid Groome . . . . Margaret Spencer
CRIME Children's entertainer stops sister from
robbing their host.

04697
A BET WITH A VENGEANCE (850)
Britannia Films (Pathe)
COMEDY Man drives cab for bet and picks up
wife and lover.

04698
A TANGO TANGLE (725)
Britannia Films (Pathe)
COMEDY Tango-crazy wife goes to dance with
another man.

04699
A FOOTBALLER'S HONOUR (2600)
Britannia Films (Pathe)
D: (Lewin Fitzhamon)
SPORT Footballer escapes from kidnappers in
time to win match.

04700
THE KINEMA GIRL (590) (U)
Clarendon
D: Percy Stow
Dorothy Bellew . . . . Herself
COMEDY Man's infatuation with film actress
causes trouble in studio.

04701
GEORGE'S JOY RIDE (630) (U)
Clarendon
D: Percy Stow
CHASE Doctor ties malingerer's bed behind
motorcycle.

04702
THE PUDDLETON POLICE (560) (U)
Clarendon
D: Percy Stow
COMEDY Misadventures of village police force.

04703
THAT'S TORN IT! (500) (U)
Clarendon
D: Percy Stow
COMEDY Naval cadets cause nurses' skirts to
tear, so all nurses tear skirts to fool matron.

04704
A SECRET LIFE (2730) (A)
Clarendon
D: Wilfred Noy
Lionelle Howard
Dorothy Bellew
CRIME Squire kills captain and fakes suicide by
posing as him and driving car over cliff.

04705
NO CURE LIKE FATHER'S (540) (U)
Cricks (DFSA)
D: (Edwin J. Collins)
S: Ernest Dangerfield

COMEDY Boy fakes St. Vitus Dance in order to
visit country.

04706
WHEN THE INK RAN OUT (595) (U)
Cricks (DFSA)
D: (Edwin J. Collins)
S: Ernest Dangerfield
COMEDY Wife mistakes husband's unfinished
letter as sign of foul play.

04707
ASKING FOR TROUBLE (640) (U)
Cricks (DFSA)
D: (Edwin J. Collins)
COMEDY Dude puts lead in boxing gloves to
win £50 prize.

04708
THE CURTAIN (1150) (U)
Hepworth
D: (Warwick Buckland)
Chrissie White . . . . Mary
Cyril Morton . . . . Philip
CRIME Amnesiac robs fiancee's house and
saves her from attack.

04709
CAUGHT BENDING (775) (U)
Hepworth

04710
THE SNEEZE (825) (U)
Hepworth
D: (Hay Plumb)
Chrissie White . . . . Enid
Jack Raymond . . . . Tom
COMEDY Girl's sneezing suitor mistaken for
burglar's associate.

04711
THE HEART OF MIDLOTHIAN (4275) (A)
Hepworth (Renters)
D: Frank Wilson
S: (NOVEL) Sir Walter Scott
SC: Blanche McIntosh
Flora Morris . . . . Effie Deans
Violet Hopson . . . . Jeanie Deans
Alma Taylor . . . . Madge Wildfire
Stewart Rome . . . . Ratcliffe
Cecil Mannering . . . . George Staunton
Cyril Morton. . . . . Reuben Butler
Harry Gilbey . . . . Duke of Argyll
Warwick Buckland . . . . Davie Deans
Marie de Solla . . . . Old Margery
Harry Royston . . . . Saddletree
John MacAndrews . . . . . Gaoler
Harry Buss . . . . Captain Lorrimer
Hay Plumb . . . . Fiscal Sharpitlaw
DRAMA Edinburgh, 1736. Crofter's daughter
has child by outlaw and is condemned to death
when it is stolen by midwife's mad daughter.

04712
THE ANGEL OF DELIVERANCE (1100)
Hepworth
D: (Warwick Buckland)
Jack Raymond . . . . Joe Brown
John MacAndrews . . . . Seth
Cyril Morton . . . . Dr. Lenton
DRAMA Chauffeur heals breach between doctor
and gypsy when her child falls ill.

04713
JUDGED BY APPEARANCES (800) (U)
Hepworth
D: (Hay Plumb)
Tom Powers . . . . Ralph Bellamy
Violet Hopson . . . . Countess Vezin
Johnny Butt. . . . . Count Vezin

D: (Hay Plumb)
COMEDY Prospective town councillor caught
raiding opponent's henroost.
Chrissie White . . . . Mamie
Harry Buss . . . . Borkins
COMEDY Jealous Count sees artist put key
down his wife's back to cure nosebleed.

04714
GHOSTS (1125) (U)
Ivy Close Films (Hepworth)
D: Elwin Neame)
Ivy Close . . . . The Girl
Pope Stamper . . . . The Man
COMEDY Girl investigates haunted house and
finds ghost is another investigator.

04715
THE HON. WILLIAM'S DONAH (900) (U)
Ivy Close Films (Hepworth)
D: Elwin Neame
Ivy Close . . . . Miss Ashley
COMEDY Girl poses as coster to shock nobleman

04716
THE TERRIBLE TWINS (1100) (U)
Ivy Close Films (Hepworth)
D: Elwin Neame
Ivy Close . . . . Ivy Brown
Austin Melford . . . . Austin Brown
COMEDY Girl and sailor brother swap
identities to shock Count.

04717
FLOTILLA THE FLIRT (575) (U)
Turner Films (Hepworth)
D:S: Larry Trimble
Florence Turner . . . . Flotilla
Tom Powers . . . . Tompasso
Jack Raymond . . . . Raymondo
James Pryor . . . . Gympryo
COMEDY Spain. Three rivals for girl fight it out
with pistols.

04718
DAISY DOODAD'S DIAL (580) (U)
Turner Films (Hepworth)
D: Larry Trimble
S: Florence Turner
Florence Turner . . . . Daisy Doodad
COMEDY Wife enters face-pulling contest and
dreams of her own face.

04719
THE BLACK SPOT (2417) (A)
London
D: George Loane Tucker
S: John Alwin
SC: Bannister Merwin
Jane Gail . . . . Olga Scerloff
Arthur Holmes-Gore . . . . Duke Paul
Charles Rock . . . . Prof Scerloff
Gerald Ames . . . . Serge Malkow
CRIME Soho. Duke dons disguises to save
Russian professor's daughter from assassination

04720
THE CAGE (2010) (U)
London
D: George Loane Tucker
S: (STORY) Hesketh Pearson
SC: Bannister Merwin
Lillian Logan . . . . Adrienne
Gerald Ames . . . . Comte de Lavalle
Charles Rock . . . . Baron de Tartas
George Bellamy . . . . The Monk
ADVENTURE. Mediaeval. Knight thwarts
wicked baron and wins lady.

04721
AN EGGS—TRAORDINARY COMPLAINT
(465) (U)
Martin Films (DFSA)
D; Dave Aylott
Bob Reed
COMEDY Greedy man eats so many eggs he thinks he is a chicken.

04722
JOLLYBOY'S DREAM (569) (U)
Martin (DFSA)
D: Dave Aylott
TRICK Drunkard dreams of riding in bed to savage island.

04723
THE NEW BOY (450) (U)
Martin (DFSA)
D: Dave Aylott
COMEDY Schoolboy tricks tormentors by causing them to trick headmaster's sister.

04724
THROUGH THE AGES (965) (U)
Martin (DFSA)
D: Dave Aylott
Ernie Westo . . . .
Bob Reed . . . .
Sid Butler . . . .
COMEDY Knocked-out boxer dreams of fighting in stone age.

04725
LIEUTENANT GERANIUM AND THE
STEALED ORDERS (934) (U)
Martin (DFSA)
D: Dave Aylott
COMEDY Lieut saves stolen orders from spies.

04726
YOUNG PIMPLE AND HIS LITTLE SISTER
(465) (U)
Folly Films (Phoenix)
D:S: Fred Evans, Joe Evans
Fred Evans . . . . Pimple
Tommy Collet . . . . Young Pimple
COMEDY Misadventures of Pimple as a small boy.

04727
PIMPLE GOES TO PARIS (685) (U)
Folly Films (Phoenix)
D:S: Fred Evans, Joe Evans
Fred Evans . . . . Pimple
COMEDY Pimple visits Paris and has trouble with gendarmes.

04728
THE BATTLE OF GETTYSOWNBACK (820) (U)
Folly Films (Phoenix)
D:S: Fred Evans, Joe Evans
Fred Evans . . . . Pimple
COMEDY Tramp tells how he joins Scots Guards and rises to command.

04729
LIEUTENANT PIMPLE'S SEALED ORDERS
(940) (U)
Folly Films (Phoenix) *Reissue:* 1917 (H & S)
D:S: Fred Evans, Joe Evans
Fred Evans . . . . Lt Pimple
COMEDY Lieut goes to ball as pierrot, is drugged by foreign girl spy, but delivers orders to Downing Street.

04730
THE FLIGHT OF DEATH (1250) (U)
Solograph (U)
S:(STORY)

James Carew
Reginald Owen
Lyston Lyle
WAR Footballer enlists and flies monoplane into enemy biplane.

04731
NOBBY'S STUD (446) (U)
EcKo (U)
D: W.P. Kellino
Sam Poluski . . . . Nobby
COMEDY Nobby damages furniture looking for collar stud.

04732
SNOOKS AS A FIREMAN (576)
EcKo (U)
D: W.P. Kellino
COMEDY Misadventures of clumsy fireman.

04733
A MAN'S CROSSROADS (573)
Heron Films (U)
P: Andrew Heron
COMEDY Burlesque of transpontine melodrama.

04734
LITTLE LORD FAUNTLEROY (5280) (U)
kinemacolor
Natural Colour Kinematograph Co.
D: F. Martin Thornton
S: (NOVEL) Frances Hodgson Burnett
Gerald Royston . . . . Cedric Erroll
Jane Wells . . . . "Dearest" Erroll
H. Agar Lyons . . . . Earl of Dorincourt
Bernard Vaughan . . . . . . Havisham
V. Osmond . . . . Minna Tipton
Frank Stather . . . . Ben Tipton
D. Callan . . . . Tommy Tipton
Harry Edwards . . . . Dick Tipton
Edward Viner . . . . Cedric
John M. East . . . . Thomas
Stella St Audrie . . . . Bridget
F. Tomkins . . . . Silas Hobbs
Fred Eustace . . . . Bliss
DRAMA American heir to Earldom reconciles grandfather to widowed mother.

04735
THE LITTLE PICTURE PRODUCER (950)
kinemacolor
Natural Colour Kinematograph Co.
D: F. Martin Thornton, Edgar Rogers
TRICK Three children use toys to make a cowboy film.

04736
THE LITTLE GOD (930) (U) *kinemacolor*
Natural Colour Kinematograph Co.
D:S: Langford Reed
COMEDY Adventurer steals sacred idol and uses fakes to outwit woman thief.

04737
THE TEMPTATION OF JOSEPH (1265) (A)
Kineto
D:S: Langford Reed
COMEDY Amorous mummy revives and embarrasses antiquarian.

04738
THE RIVAL ANARCHISTS (715) (U)
Kineto
D:S: Langford Reed
Bert Grahame
COMEDY Leaders of two secret societies duel for love of suffragette.

04739
THE CATCH OF THE SEASON (737) (U)
Kineto

D:S: Langford Reed
William Allinson . . . . Izaak Walton-Smith
Mrs Edmund Tearle . . . . . Mrs Walton-Smith
COMEDY Husband buys large fish and boasts that he caught it.

04740
THE LIFEBOAT
Eric Williams Speaking Pictures
S: (POEM) George R. Sims
SC: Eric Williams
Eric Williams . . . . The Lifeboatman
DRAMA (Shown while Eric Williams recites from stage).

04741
HENPECK'S NIGHTMARE (440)
Waterwheel (Tyler)
TRICK Drunkard dreams he is pursued by apparitions.

04742
JIM THE FIREMAN (2200) (A)
Barker (London Exclusives)
D: (Bert Haldane)
S: Rowland Talbot,
Roy Travers . . . . Jim
Blanche Forsythe . . . . Kate
Fred Paul . . . . Flash Ted
Hedda Kostner . . . . Mary
DRAMA Fireman rescues wife after she elopes with criminal.

04743
THE LIGHTS O' LONDON (4000)
Barker (Magnet)
D: (Bert Haldane)
S: (PLAY) George R. Sims
SC: Harry Engholm
Arthur Chesney . . . . Harold Armytage
Phyllis Relph . . . . Hetty Preene
Fred Paul . . . . Clifford Armytage
Tom H. MacDonald . . . .
J. Hastings Batson . . . .
Roy Travers . . . .
Rolf Leslie . . . .
CRIME Framed man breaks jail in time to save sweetheart's ruined father from being drowned by cousin.

04744
MONEY FOR NOTHING (495) (U)
Sphinx Films (DFSA) *Reissue:* 1916 (YCC)
COMEDY Tramps pose as showmen to extort money.

04745
ALMOST A CRIME (1292) (U)
Sphinx Films (DFSA)
CRIME Workless man robs doctor for starving child but repents when doctor treats child for nothing.

04746
WHAT A BIRTHDAY (433) (U)
Planet Films (DFSA)
COMEDY Suitor meets with mishaps on way to meet girl.

04747
LOVE SPOTS (557) (U)
Planet Films (DFSA)
COMEDY Magic tonic causes love at first sight.

04748
WHY MEN LEAVE HOME (358) (U)
Planet Films (DFSA)
COMEDY Wife's pursuit of henpecked husband.

04749
THE WHIRLWIND KIDS (497) (U)
Fitz Films (DFSA)
D:S: Lewin Fitzhamon
Roy Royston .... The Boy
Marie Royston .... The Girl
COMEDY Children kidnap baby and pet dog restores it.

04750
THE KING OF SEVEN DIALS (2800) (U)
Regent (Gaumont)
P: Charles Weston, Arthur Finn
D: Charles Weston
Arthur Finn .... Jim
Alice Inward .... Mary Fuller
Charles Weston .... Bill
CRIME Jealous crook tries to depose boss by framing him.

04751
THE GREAT PYTHON ROBBERY (2800) (U)
Regent (Gaumont)
P: Charles Weston, Arthur Finn
D: Arthur Finn
Arthur Finn .... Detective Finn
CRIME Crooks use airship to rob train and are caught by tec whom boy saves from snakepit.

04752
KINEQUIPS (series)
Cherry Kearton Films
D: (Rex Wilson)
COMEDIES "The kinematograph Punch." (bi-weekly issues.)

MAY

04753
THE LOOSENED PLANK (795) (U)
B & C (DFSA)
D:S; Lewin Fitzhamon
Roy Royston .... The Boy
Marie Royston .... The Girl
DRAMA Pedlar saves children when jealous gypsy loosens bridge plank.

04754
UNCLE MAXIM'S WILL (690) (U)
B & C (DFSA)
D: (Ethyle Batley)
COMEDY Legatee must marry shrew if he is to inherit fortune.

04755
THE DRAWN BLIND (1477) (U)
B & C (DFSA)
D: Ethyle Batley
Ernest G. Batley .... Bill
Dorothy Batley .... Lucy
Ethel Bracewell .... Bessie
DRAMA Blind girl refuses cure that entails sister becoming lord's mistress.

04756
CHARLES PEACE, KING OF CRIMINALS (2000) (A)
B & C (Clarion)
D: Ernest G. Batley
Jeff Barlow .... Charles Peace
HISTORY 1875. Burglar dons disguises but is unable to elude police.

04757
BLACK-EYED SUSAN (2864) (U)
retitled: IN THE DAYS OF TRAFALGAR
USA: THE BATTLING BRITISH
B & C (KTC)
D: Maurice Elvey
S: (PLAY) Douglas Jerrold
Elizabeth Risdon .... Black-eyed Susan
Fred Groves .... William Lorman

A.V. Bramble .... Hatchett
M. Gray Murray .... Capt Crosstree
Henry Kitts .... Doggrass
J. De Lungo .... Raker
DRAMA 1830. Sailor court-martialled for striking officer who tried to seduce smuggler's daughter.

04758
BEER AND PYJAMAS (610) (U)
Clarendon
D: (Toby Cooper)
COMEDY Drunkard mistakes pyjama-clad girl for wife's lover.

04759
THE LITTLE DARLINGS (540) (U)
Clarendon
D: (Toby Cooper)
COMEDY Neighbours' children cause fight.

04760
A BEAUTIFUL GARDEN OF ROSES (575) (U)
Clarendon
D: (Toby Cooper)
COMEDY Drunkard mistakes neighbour's bedroom for his own.

04761
SNUFFY STUFF, SNUFF (540) (U)
Cricks (DFSA)
D: (Edwin J. Collins)
COMEDY Small boy plays pranks with powerful snuff.

04762
TEMPTATION (3000)
Cricks (KTC)
D: Charles Calvert
Jack Leigh .... Jack Newton
CRIME Girl saves inventor of wireless-controlled torpedo from spy's bomb.

04763
A KISS, NEARLY (590) (U)
Cricks (DFSA)
D: (Edwin J. Collins)
COMEDY Man posing as painter stages fire to rescue builder's daughter.

04764
SNIFFKINS DETECTIVE AND THE MISSING CIGARETTE CARDS (658) (U)
Cricks (DFSA)
D: (Edwin J. Collins)
COMEDY Tec tracks cigarette card thieves.

04765
SAVED BY THE SUN (1615) (U)
Cricks (DFSA)
D: (Charles Calvert)
ADVENTURE Africa. Girl's signals with mirror bring help to save captured father from native Chief.

04766
THE KITCHEN COUNTESS (736) (U)
London
D: Ralph Dewsbury
Lillian Logan .... Eliza
Gerald Ames .... The Hero
COMEDY Maid dreams she is Countess and saves captured lover.

04767
LUNCHEON FOR THREE (720) (U)
London
D: Ralph Dewsbury
Lillian Logan .... Dot
Judd Green .... Charlie
Gregory Scott .... Tom

Walter Gay ....
Arthur Cullin ....
COMEDY Penniless rivals find their beloved has paid luncheon bill.

04768
CLANCARTY (1760) (U)
London
D: Harold Shaw
S: (PLAY) Tom Taylor
Lillian Logan .... Lady Mary Spencer
Walter Gay .... Lord Clancarty
Charles Rock .... Goodman
Edward O'Neill .... William III
George Bellamy ....
Eva Westlake ....
Henry Edwards ....
Tom Hesslewood ....
ADVENTURE Scotland, period. Banished Lord saves King from Jacobites.

04769
THE VENGEANCE OF THE AIR (2450)
Martin (Pathe)
D: Dave Aylott
Ivan Cleveland .... Lt Douglas Blake
Constance Little .... Dora Frazer
Lionel d'Aragon .... Capt Kesdale
Margaret Scudamore ...... Enid Mortimer
Donald Bruce .... Col Frazer
CRIME Framed lieut flies to save col's daughter from being kidnapped by rival.

04770
MIKE JOINS THE FORCE (618) (U)
Martin (DFSA)
D: Dave Aylott
Ernie Westo .... Mike Murphy
COMEDY Tramp becomes PC and has trouble with unwanted baby.

04771
THE DAUGHTER OF GARCIA, BRIGAND (1329) (U)
Martin (DFSA)
D: Dave Aylott
CRIME Spain. Brigand's daughter dies saving disgraced soldier from rival's bullet.

04772
TELLING THE TALE (443) (U)
Martin (DFSA)
D: Dave Aylott
COMEDY Married man loses trouser button while visiting spinster.

04773
THE TRAGEDY OF BASIL GRIEVE (3250) (A)
retitled: THE GREAT POISON MYSTERY
Hepworth (Feature)
D: Frank Wilson
Violet Hopson .... Vera Duncan
Stewart Rome .... Basil Grieve
Cyril Morton .... Roland Nashley
Harry Gilbey .... Fothergill
Marie de Solla .... Brenda Welham
John MacAndrews .... Detective
CRIME Woman poisons husband and is killed fleeing to lover.

04774
THE GIRL WHO PLAYED THE GAME (1150) (U)
Hepworth
D: (Warwick Buckland)
Stewart Rome .... Paul Warrener
Violet Hopson .... Julia Stevens
Chrissie White .... Elsie Stevens
ROMANCE Girl poses as thief so artist she loves may succeed.

04775
CREATURES OF CLAY (2350) (U)
Hepworth
D: (Frank Wilson)
Alice de Winton . . . . Vasca de Lisle
Stewart Rome . . . . Stuart Finlay
Jack Raymond . . . . Michael Trevis
Harry Gilbey . . . . Mr. Trevis
Rachel de Solla . . . . Mrs Trevis
Henry Vibart . . . . Hilary Sinclair
CRIME Actress's ex-lover takes blame when
she steals mother's gems.

04776
TWO OF A KIND (1125) (U)
Hepworth
D: (Hay Plumb)
Jack Raymond . . . . Hal
Violet Hopson . . . . Delia Highspite
Chrissie White . . . . Chrissie
Harry Buss . . . . Cyrus Hanks
COMEDY Man poses as millionaire to win
vicar's daughter.

04777
THE MYSTERY OF MR MARKS (2275) (A)
retitled: BY WHOSE HAND?
Hepworth
D: (Warwick Buckland)
Alma Taylor . . . . Isobel Denton
Lionelle Howard . . . . . . Gerald Lee
CRIME Socialite proves father killed usurer
while sleepwalking.

04778
A NOBLE DECEPTION (1000) (U)
Hepworth
D: (Warwick Buckland)
Violet Hopson . . . . Wife
DRAMA Man poses as drunkard to repel wife of
clerical brother.

04779
THE CRY OF THE CAPTIVE (2075) (A)
Hepworth
D: Frank Wilson
S: Percy Manton
Stewart Rome . . . . Thornley Vibart
Violet Hopson . . . . Zorah Vibart
Edward Lingard . . . . Cardsharper
James Lindsay . . . . Charles Glenney
CRIME Cardsharper uses man's cowardice to
force sister to act as his decoy.

04780
THE CHICK THAT WAS NOT EGGS-TINCT
(600) (U)
Hepworth
D: (Hay Plumb)
COMEDY Man sells nephew bad eggs for
broody hen.

04781
OVER THE GARDEN WALL (1000)
Hepworth
D: (Hay Plumb)
Tom Powers . . . . Billy Birch
Alma Taylor . . . . Julia Barlow
COMEDY Suitor foils sweetheart's father and
elopes.

04782
THE GIRL WHO LIVED IN STRAIGHT STREET
(1850) (U)
Hepworth
D: (WarwickBuckland)
Stewart Rome . . . . Hilary Farles
Alma Taylor . . . . Effie
Chrissie White . . . . Stella Leighton
Cyril Morton . . . . Michael Farles
Claire Pridelle . . . . Phoebe Farles

Warwick Buckland . . . . Father
CRIME Chorus girl saves starving wife of man
jailed for brother's crime.

04783
THE GUEST OF THE EVENING (1100) (U)
Hepworth
D: (Frank Wilson)
Stewart Rome . . . . Harry Vane
Alice de Winton. . . . . Mrs Vane
Cyril Morton . . . . Philip Orgill
CRIME Earl poses as bankrupt to expose friend
as thief.

04784
OH WHAT A DAY! (475) (U)
Hepworth
D: (Hay Plumb)
COMEDY Holiday husband loses ticket and
hides in trunk.

04785
THE PRICE OF A GIFT (1125) (U)
Hepworth
D: (Warwick Buckland)
Ruby Belasco . . . . Mrs Martin
CRIME Drunken woman's husband robs office
to feed starving child.

04786
HOW THINGS DO DEVELOP (525) (U)
Hepworth
D: (Hay Plumb)
COMEDY Professor takes daughter's suitor's
camera by mistake.

04787
THE BREAKING POINT (1275) (U)
Hepworth
D: Frank Wilson
Stewart Rome . . . . Howard Esmond
Chrissie White . . . . Clarice Armitage
Lionelle Howard . . . . . . Croyle
CRIME Framed man's fiancee gains confession
by filming reconstruction of murder.

04788
THE STRESS OF CIRCUMSTANCE (1100) (U)
Hepworth
D: (Warwick Buckland)
Stewart Rome . . . . Ralph Densmore
Violet Hopson . . . . Roma Barton
Lionelle Howard . . . . Lawrence Steynor
Henry Vibart . . . . Mr Barton
CRIME Ex-tramp becomes magistrate's secretary
and take blame for theft.

04789
FOLLOW YOUR LEADER (400) (U)
Hepworth
D: (Hay Plumb)
Eric Desmond . . . . Tommy
Percy Manton . . . . Uncle
Johnny Butt . . . . Policeman
CHASE Uncle follows boy in game and is led
into trouble..

04790
THE WHITEWASHERS (765) (U)
Folly Films (Phoenix)
D:S: Fred Evans, Joe Evans
Fred Evans . . . . Pimple
Joe Evans . . . . Raffles
COMEDY Crooks pose as house decorators.

04791
HOW PIMPLE WON THE DERBY (660) (U)
Folly Films (Phoenix)
D:S: Fred Evans, Joe Evans
Fred Evans . . . . Pimple
COMEDY Pimple and pantomime horse win
Derby in taxi.

04792
PIMPLE'S BURGLAR SCARE (530) (U)
Folly Films (Phoenix)
D:S: Fred Evans, Joe Evans
Fred Evans . . . . Pimple
COMEDY Pimple poses as burglar to scare wife,
and she fights him.

04793
LIEUTENANT PIMPLE GOES TO MEXICO
(865) (U)
Folly Films (Phoenix)
D:S: Fred Evans, Joe Evans
Fred Evans . . . . Lt Pimple
Joe Evans . . . . Gen Hurtyer
COMEDY Mexico. Secret agent feigns death to
escape general's firing squad.

04794
PIMPLE 'MIDST RAGING BEASTS (655) (U)
Folly Films (Phoenix)
D:S: Fred Evans, Joe Evans
Fred Evans . . . . Pimple
COMEDY Pimple goes on jungle safari and is
attacked by gorillas.

04795
STOLEN HONOURS (3000)
Phoenix Film Agency
D:S: Joe Evans
Joe Evans. . . . . John Weston
Fred Evans . . . . James Weston
Geraldine Maxwell. . . . . Isobel Drummond
WAR Africa. Amnesiac lieutenant cashiered while
his brother steals his honours and colonel's
daughter.

04796
PEARLS OF DEATH (3000)
Phoenix Film Agency
D:S: Joe Evans
Joe Evans . . . . Lockwood Beck
Geraldine Maxwell . . . .
CRIME Tec foils anarchists who put explosive in
necklace of earl's wife.

04797
BILL'S RETURN TO PICTURES (553) (U)
Alpha Films (Prieur)
Paul Bertho . . . . Bill
COMEDY "Lux Films" comedian comes to
London to make a film.

04798
BILL WANTS BRITISH WASHING (430) (U)
Alpha Films (Prieur)
Paul Bertho . . . . Bill
COMEDY "Lux Films" comedian brings dirty
laundry to London.

04799
THE LAST ROUND (2650) (U)
Barker (Moss)
D: (Bert Haldane)
S: Rowland Talbot
Thos H. MacDonald . . . . Jack Fordyce
Blanche Forsythe . . . . Mary Mollett
Fred Paul . . . . Ralph Morton
J. Hastings Batson . . . . Col Mollett
SPORT Captain wins boxing match despite
usurer's grip on fiancee's father.

04800
WONDERFUL NIGHTS WITH PETER KINEMA
(series)
Big Ben Films-Union (Pathe)
D: George Pearson
Gerald Royston . . . . Peter Kinema
ADVENTURE Travel and instructional films
linked by dream sequences.

04801
THE LIVE WIRE (2542) (U)
Big Ben Films-Union (Pathe)
D: George Pearson
S: L.C. MacBean
Percy Moran . . . . Blake
Jack Clair . . . . His Rival
CRIME Devon. Jealous engineer tries to
electrocute rival.

04802
MADCAP MARY (596) (U)
Eagle Films (U)
COMEDY Tomboy's exploits cause trouble
for victims.

04803
HOW TO MAKE £2,000 (794) (U)
Heron Films (U)
P: Andrew Heron
COMEDY Man schemes to get rich quick.

04804
DEAD MEN TELL NO TALES (1240) (A)
Kineto
D: (F. Martin Thornton)
WESTERN Girl escapes from leaking boat to
save sheriff from outlaws.

04805
BUYING A HORSE (582) (U)
Lucrative Films (U)
S: (SKETCH) Freddie Rigby
Freddie Rigby . . . . The Owner
Nat Lewis . . . . The Customer
Brothers Shanks . . . . The Horse
COMEDY Customer's mishaps in purchasing
pantomime horse.

04806
BILL-POSTING (438) (U)
Lucrative Films (U)
S: (SKETCH) Freddie Rigby
Freddie Rigby . . . . The Bill-Poster
Nat Lewis
Edgar Max
COMEDY Slapstick troubles of Welsh bill-poster

04807
THE SECOND PENALTY (1900)
Kineto
D: (F. Martin Thornton)
CRIME Man's vengeance on convict who
swindled his mother and caused her death.

04808
WINKY LEARNS A LESSON IN HONESTY
(820) (U)
Bamforth (YSA)
D: Cecil Birch
Reggie Switz . . . . Winky
COMEDY Landlord fools handyman by
sticking 'poison' labels on whisky bottles.

04809
KILL THAT FLY (460)
Bamforth (YSA)
D: Cecil Birch
Reggie Switz . . . . Winky
COMEDY Winky's mishaps in trying to swat fly.

04810
WINKY AND THE GORGONZOLA CHEESE
(420) (U)
Bamforth (YSA)
D: Cecil Birch
Reggie Switz . . . . Winky
COMEDY Spurned hawker puts smelly cheese in
theatregoer's back pocket.

04811
WINKY AND THE LEOPARD (755)
Bamforth (YSA)
D: Cecil Birch
Reggie Switz . . . . Winky
COMEDY Winky uses stuffed leopard to fool
party searching for escaped leopard.

04812
A HIGHWAYMAN'S HONOUR (2000)
Herkomer Films (ACL)
P: Hubert von Herkomer
D: Siegfried von Herkomer
S: Arthur Eckersley
Hubert von Herkomer
Winsome Russell
A.E. Matthews
Gerald Ames
Leonard Ceily
D.J. Williams
Lady von Herkomer
ADVENTURE Period. Squire's daughter elopes
with steward who kills her brother in duel.

04813
ALWAYS TELL YOUR WIFE (2000)
Zenith
D: Leedham Bantock
S: (PLAY) E. Temple Thurston
Seymour Hicks . . . . The Husband
Ellaline Terriss . . . . The Wife
COMEDY Husband fakes cold to meet
blackmailing girl.

04814
A MOTORCYCLE ELOPEMENT (670)
Zenith
D: (Leedham Bantock)
CHASE Couple elope on motorcycle.

04815
THOSE WHO DWELL IN DARKNESS (500)
Motograph
D: (Charles Raymond)
DRAMA Appeal for National Institute of the
Blind.

JUN

04816
THE WATER RATS OF LONDON (1846) (U)
B & C (DFSA)
D:S: James Youngdeer
Lillian Wiggins . . . . May
Fred Morgan . . . . Dr Chatlet
Gladys Johnson . . . . His Daughter
CRIME Black Cross Gang woman returns dr's
kidnapped daughter when he saves her own
child from fire.

04817
HER FAITHFUL COMPANIONS (1176) (U)
B & C (DFSA)
D:S: Lewin Fitzhamon
Constance Somers-Clarke . Cora
ANIMAL Girl's pet dog and pony fetch doctor
when she is stabbed by jealous gypsy.

04818
THE MASTER CROOK TURNS DETECTIVE
(2864) (U)
B & C (DFSA)
D: Ernest G. Batley
Ernest G. Batley . . . . The Master Crook
Ethel Bracewell . . . . The Girl
CRIME Crook framed for stealing necklace wins
it back at roulette.

04819
WINKY CAUSES A SMALLPOX PANIC (500)
Bamforth (YSA)
D: Cecil Birch
Reggie Switz . . . . Winky
COMEDY Tramps get free meal by posing as
doctor and pox victim.

04820
WINKY DONS THE PETTICOATS (541)
Bamforth (YSA)
D: Cecil Birch
Reggie Switz . . . . Winky
COMEDY When husband does housework he
sets house on fire.

04821
THE MUDDLETON FIRE BRIGADE (650)
Bamforth (YSA)
D: Cecil Birch
Reggie Switz . . . . Winky
COMEDY Fireman extinguishes town council's
smoking concert.

04822
UNLUCKY THIRTEEN (585) (U)
Cricks
D: (Charles Calvert)
COMEDY Cleric and girl have trouble punting
on river.

04823
HIS SECOND CHILDHOOD (595) (U)
Cricks
D: (Charles Calvert)
COMEDY Pills make old bachelor act like boy.

04824
FITZNOODLE'S HUNT FOR WEALTH (636(U)
Cricks
D: Charles Calvert)
COMEDY Man finds map and digs for hidden
treasure.

04825
EUGENE ARAM (4300) (U)
Cricks
D: SC: Edwin J. Collins
S: (NOVEL) Edward Bulwer Lytton
Jack Leigh . . . . Eugene Aram
Mary Manners . . . . Madeleine Lester
John Sargent . . . . Richard Houseman
Stewart Patterson . . . . Walter Lester
Wingold Lawrence . . . . Geoffrey Lester
Antonia Reith . . . . Elinor Lester
Frank Melrose . . . . Rowland Lester
Lionel d'Aragon . . . . The Judge
Henry Foster . . . . Cpl Bunting
Harold Snell . . . . Mr Courtland
Fred Southern . . . . Peter Dealtry
CRIME (75 scenes) 1757. Respected scholar
blackmailed by ex-partner in robbery and
executed for crime he did not commit.

04826
PAUL SLEUTH AND THE MYSTIC SEVEN
(3500) USA: THE SECRET SEVEN
Cricks
D: Charles Calvert
Charles Vane . . . . Paul Sleuth
Lionel d'Aragon . . . . The Crook
CRIME Tec saves kidnapped heiress by hiding
film camera in headlamp of ransom car.

04827
DIP 'EM AND DO 'EM LTD (396) (U)
EcKo (U)
D: W.P. Kellino
COMEDY Tramps devise wash-and-brush-up
machine to rob customers.

04828
BUMBLES' APPETITE (442) (U)
EcKo (U)
D: W.P. Kellino
Phillipi . . . . Bumbles
COMEDY Bumbles eats everything.

04829
THE TERROR OF THE AIR (2300) (U)
Hepworth
D: Frank Wilson
Tom Powers . . . . Roger Doubleday
Stewart Rome . . . . Philip Townsend
Violet Hopson . . . . Gabrielle Townsend
Harry Royston . . . . The Spy
Henry Vibart . . . . Prof Doubleday
FANTASY Spy steals secret ray and destroys
liner by using it to fire explosives from distance.

04830
ONLY A FLOWER GIRL (750) (U)
Hepworth
D: (Warwick Buckland)
Stewart Rome . . . . Victor Elmore
Chrissie White . . . . Jessie
CRIME Girl saves rescuer from railway line to
which cousin ties him.

04831
LITTLE BOY BOUNTIFUL (850) (U)
Hepworth
D: (Warwick Buckland)
Eric Desmond . . . . Reggie
DRAMA Rich boy takes supper to poor boy
who stole his lunch.

04832
THE MAGIC GLASS (825) (U)
Hepworth
D: (Hay Plumb)
S: S.A. Screech
Eric Desmond . . . . Tommy
TRICK Boy uses professor's liquid to make
objects transparent.

04833
DR FENTON'S ORDEAL (2100) (U)
Hepworth
D: (Frank Wilson)
Tom Powers . . . . Rupert Harding
Stewart Rome . . . . Guy Fenton
Chrissie White . . . . Sybil Harding
Henry Vibart . . . . Mr. Harding
CRIME Thief becomes oculist and cures blind
girl witness.

04834
WE DON'T THINK! (625) (U)
Hepworth
D: (Hay Plumb)
COMEDY Henpecked husband vamped while
wife is at work.

04835
THE GRIP OF AMBITION (2025) (U)
Hepworth
D: Frank Wilson
Stewart Rome . . . . Rev Basil Hunt
Lionelle Howard . . . . John Bannister
CRIME Author's ejected wife becomes slum
worker and saves him from political poisoning.

04836
ENTERTAINING UNCLE (550) (U)
Hepworth
D: (Hay Plumb)
Eric Desmond . . . . The Boy
COMEDY Children mistake burglar for visiting
uncle.

04837
IVY'S ELOPEMENT (1100) (U)
Ivy Close Films (Hepworth)
D: Elwin Neame
Ivy Close . . . . Ivy Trevyse
Cecil Mannering . . . . Farley
Richard Boscoe . . . . Arthur Penwarden
Harry Horsecroft . . . . Mr. Trevyse
COMEDY Man saves girl from cad and is mis-
understood by her father.

04838
CHILD O' MY HEART (1920) (U)
London
D: Harold Shaw
S: Bannister Merwin
Edna Flugrath . . . . Kate Landers
Chappell Dossett . . . . Young Varney
Edward O'Neill . . . . Lord Varney
Douglas Munro . . . . Mr. Landers
ROMANCE Country girl weds Lord's son but
returns to care for widowed father.

04839
A BACHELOR'S LOVE STORY (1140) (U)
London
D: George Loane Tucker
S: Bannister Merwin
Henry Ainley . . . . Henry Norman
Lillian Logan . . . . Mabel Howard
Joan Ritz . . . .
Henry Edwards . . . .
Charles Kitts
ROMANCE Bachelor agrees to niece's wedding
after she finds his old love tokens.

04840
ENGLAND'S MENACE (2230) (U)
London (Gaumont)
D: Harold Shaw
S: Bannister Merwin
Edna Flugrath . . . . Lady Betty Talbot
Arthur Holmes-Gore . . . . . . Lord Talbot
Vincent Clive . . . . Chief Spy
Gerald Ames . . . . Ambassador
Charles Rock . . . . Prime Minister
Lewis Gilbert . . . . Emperor
Douglas Munro . . . . Chancellor
George Bellamy . . . . Chancellor
Arthur Cullin . . . .
Horace Furley . . . .
WAR Daughter of PM's secretary unmasks
butler as spy and foils foreign invasion.

04841
NAN GOOD-FOR-NOTHING (1140) (U)
London
D: Arthur Holmes-Gore
Edna Flugrath . . . . Nan
Frank Stanmore . . . . Tom Dibbles
DRAMA Men adopt poor girl who later saves
them with her savings.

04842
PIMPLE IN SOCIETY (950) (U)
Folly Films (Phoenix)
D:S: Fred Evans, Joe Evans
Fred Evans . . . . Pimple
Joe Evans . . . . Raffles
COMEDY Pimple crashes society and is
blackmailed into stealing jewels.

04843
PIMPLE'S ADVICE (770) (U)
Folly Films (Phoenix)
D:S: Fred Evans, Joe Evans
Fred Evans . . . . Pimple
COMEDY "Pimple's advice to husbands and
what became of it."

04844
PIMPLE'S TROUSERS (710) (U)
Folly Films (Phoenix)
D:S: Fred Evans, Joe Evans
Fred Evans . . . . Pimple
COMEDY Pimple speaks at public meeting
and is thrown out.

04845
BIG CHIEF LITTLE PIMPLE (680)
Folly Films (Phoenix)
D:S: Fred Evans, Joe Evans
Tommy Collet . . . . Young Pimple
COMEDY Boys dress up as Red Indians and hunt
for scalps.

04846
THE RING THAT WASN'T (537) (U)
Martin Films (DFSA)
D. Dave Aylott
TRICK Convict dreams fairy gives him ring
that makes things vanish.

04847
MIKE MURPHY, BROKER'S MAN (524) (U)
Martin Films (DFSA)
D: Dave Aylott
Ernie Westo . . . . Mike Murphy
COMEDY While girl flirts with bailiff, her
parents sneak furniture away.

04848
TWO LITTLE ANGELS (650) (U)
Martin Films (DFSA)
D: (Lewin Fitzhamon)
COMEDY Twins play tricks on maid, and PC
while their father is away.

04849
AND VERY NICE TOO (692) (U)
Piccadilly (MP) *Reissue:* 1916 (Wardour)
D: (Charles Weston)
COMEDY Chorus girl wearing pyjamas is
found in cleric's room.

04850
THE SEVEN AGES OF MAN (1000)
Planet Films (Hibbert)
D: Charles Vernon
S: (POEM) William Shakespeare
Bransby Williams
DRAMA Character studies of man from infancy
to old age.

04851
BERNARDO'S CONFESSION (1000)
Planet Films (Hibbert)
D: Charles Vernon
S: (SKETCH) Bransby Williams
Bransby Williams . . . . Count Bernardo
Sidney Kearns . . . .
CRIME Italy. Count, framed for anarchy, kills
wife and lover.

04852
THE STREET WATCHMAN'S STORY (1000)
Planet Films (Hibbert)
D: Charles Vernon
S: (SKETCH) Bransby Williams
Bransby Williams . . . . The Watchman
COMEDY Watchman dreams he is invited to
society party.

04853
GRIMALDI (1000)
Planet Films (Hibbert)
D: Charles Vernon
S: (PLAY) Dion Boucicault
Bransby Williams . . . . Joseph Grimaldi
Sidney Kearns . . . .
DRAMA Italy. Count becomes clown and helps
Lord save his beloved from captain.

04854
DETECTIVE FINN AND THE FOREIGN SPIES
(3000) USA: THE FOREIGN SPIES
Regent (MP)
P: Charles Weston, Arthur Finn
D: Arthur Finn
Arthur Finn . . . . Detective Finn
Alice Inward . . . .
CRIME Tec poses as crook to catch butler who
stole inventor's gun plans.

04855
A FISHERGIRL'S FOLLY (1465) (U)
Big Ben Films-Union (Pathe) *Reissue:* 1915
D: George Pearson
S: L.C. MacBean
Percy Moran
Jack Clair
ROMANCE Devon. Londoner tries to woo
fishergirl away from her sweetheart.

04856
THE SECRET OF THE AIR (2567) (U)
USA: ACROSS THE ATLANTIC
Imp Films (Transatlantic)
D: Herbert Brenon
King Baggott . . . . Wilbur Norton
Leah Baird . . . . Mrs. Norton
Herbert Brenon . . . . Turkish Spy
Claude Grahame-White . . Pilot
Gustav Hamel . . . . Pilot
CRIME Framed inventor flees to England and
catches spy at Epsom.

JUL

04857
THE SUICIDE CLUB (3386) (A)
B & C (Renters)
D: Maurice Elvey
S: (STORIES) Robert Louis Stevenson
Montagu Love . . . . Prince Florizel
Elizabeth Risdon . . . . Zephyrine
Fred Groves . . . . The President
M. Gray Murray . . . . Col Geraldine
A.V. Bramble . . . .
CRIME Colonel saves prince's life when he joins
club of men who draw lots to kill one another.

04858
THE HAIRPIN TRAIL (625) (U)
B & C (DFSA)
D: (Ethyle Batley)
COMEDY Kidnapped heiress saved by leaving
trail of hairpins.

04859
WHEN THE HURRICANES VISITED THE
SAWMILLS (558) (U)
B & C (DFSA) *Reissue:* 1917
D:S: Lewin Fitshamon
Constance Somers-Clarke . . . . Bella
Marie Royston . . . . Beano
Roy Royston . . . . Buster
COMEDY Children use strong cement to trick
billposter, PC, etc.

04860
THE LOSS OF THE BIRKENHEAD (3499) (U)
B & C (Ruffells)
D: Maurice Elvey
Elizabeth Risdon . . . . Deborah
Fred Groves . . . . Seth
A.V. Bramble . . . .
M. Gray Murray . . . .
Joyce Templeton . . . .
Beatrix Templeton . . . .
DRAMA 1852. Squire's disowned son dies to
save wife and soldier lover from shipwreck.

04861
QUEEN OF THE LONDON COUNTERFEITERS
(2746) (A) USA: QUEEN OF THE
COUNTERFEITERS
B & C (L & Y)
D. James Youngdeer
Lillian Wiggins . . . . Lillian Howard
Fred Morgan . . . . Dick Garter
CRIME Tec trailing girl coiner is thrown into
Thames in sack.

04862
THE OLD OLD STORY (462) (U)
B & C (DFSA)
D: Ethyle Batley
Dorothy Batley . . . . The Girl
COMEDY Girl poses as boy to lure away rival.

04863
THE KING'S ROMANCE (4074) (U)
retitled: REVOLUTION
USA: THE REVOLUTIONIST
B & C (KTC)
D: Ernest G. Batley
S: (PLAY) May Austin, E.V. Edmonds
Fred Morgan . . . . The Baron
Ethel Bracewell . . . . Vera
Henry Victor . . . . Prince Andreas
George Foley . . . . The Anarchist
Dick Webb . . . . Dick
Ethyle Batley . . . . The Queen
CRIME Ruritania. Baron poses as prince to elope
with anarchist's sister.

04864
THE PROFESSOR'S FALSE TEETH (594) (U)
B & C (DFSA)
COMEDY Student posing as tutor hides prof's
daughter under bed.

04865
THE CORNER HOUSE BURGLARY (2385)(U)
Big Ben Films-Union (Pathe)
D: H.O. Martinek
S: L.C. MacBean
James Carew . . . . Henry Arnold
Ivy Montford . . . . Dolores
Mr. Jackson . . . . Fred Creston
H. Maligny . . . . James Heron
H. Nicholson . . . . Dr. Nash
CRIME "Gang of the Pointing Finger" rob
doctor by planting maid and using poison gas.

04866
THE POWER TO KILL (1979) (U)
Big Ben Films-Union (Pathe)
D: H.O. Martinek
S: L.C. MacBean
DRAMA Doctor thinks patient is wife's lover
and is tempted to let him die.

04867
THE RAJAH'S TIARA (2275) (U)
Big Ben Films-Union (Pathe)
D: H.O. Martinek
S: L.C. MacBean
James Carew . . . . Henry Arnold
Ivy Montford . . . . Dolores
Mr. Jackson . . . . Fred Creston
CRIME "Gang of the Pointing Finger" steal
gems by using X-ray device to see through walls.

04868
THE SILENT MESSENGER (2250)
Britannia (Pathe)
Alison Hunter . . . . Peggy Eyre
DRAMA Bank manager loses everything to
usurer and is helped by poor couple.

04869
THE OPEN DOOR (345) (U)
Clarendon
D: (Toby Cooper)
CHASE Irish farmer tries to catch escaped
horse to visit sick aunt.

04870
DIVERGENT VIEWS; NOS 41 AND 42
JOHN STREET (595) (U)
Clarendon
D: (Toby Cooper)
COMEDY Feuding neighbours end up in jail.

04871
TWENTY YEARS AFTER (495) (U)
Clarendon
D: (Toby Cooper)
COMEDY Bachelor finds childhood sweetheart
has grown fat.

04872
SOUTHERN BLOOD (3045) (U)
Clarendon (Gaumont)
D: Wilfred Noy
Dorothy Bellew . . . . Juanita Derosa
Lionelle Howard . . . . Edwin Ashby
DRAMA Corsica. Nurse mistakes wounded
soldier for man she has sworn to kill for killing
brother in duel.

04873
A HAIR-RAISING EPISODE IN ONE SPLASH
(540) (U)
Cricks
D: (Edwin J. Collins)
COMEDY Prof's hair restorer causes Frenchman
to be mistaken for ape.

04874
WHOSE BABY? (725) (U)
Cricks
D: (Edwin J. Collins)
COMEDY Butler posing as bachelor is forced to
mind his own baby.

04875
AUNTIE'S DILEMMA (585) (U)
Cricks
D. (Edwin J. Collins)
COMEDY Convict changes clothes with
spinster.

04876
A NOVEL WOOING (935) (U)
Cricks
D: (Edwin J. Collins)
Norman Howard
COMEDY Man dressed as girl forced to share
bedroom with girl dressed as man.

04877
WINKY'S GUILTY CONSCIENCE (540)
Bamforth (YSA)
D: Cecil Birch
Reggie Switz . . . . Winky
COMEDY Winky thinks wife has found typist's
note and buys her presents.

04878
WINKY'S RUSE (426) (U)
Bamforth (YSA)
D: Cecil Birch
Reggie Switz . . . . Winky
COMEDY Tramp tricks wine from publican,
who then puts laudanum in wine bottle.

04879
WINKY THE TALLYMAN (574) (U)
Bamforth (YSA)
D: Cecil Birch
Reggie Switz . . . . Winky
COMEDY Misadventures of Winky as a collector

04880
LOVE AND THE BOXING GLOVES (620) (U)
Bamforth (YSA)
D: Cecil Birch
COMEDY

04881
THE WANDERER RETURNS (400) (U)
Bamforth (YSA)
D: Cecil Birch
COMEDY

04882
DONALD'S BIRTHDAY GIFT (860) (U)
Captain Kettle Films
S: C.J. Cutcliffe-Hyne
DRAMA Boy is given sovereign and he gives it
to tramp.

04883
OH THAT RAZOR! (240) (U)
Captain Kettle Films
S: C.J. Cutcliffe-Hyne
CHASE Man running to barber with blunt
razor mistaken for mad killer.

04884
THE KLEPTOMANIAC (1075) (U)
Hepworth
D: (Warwick Buckland)
Alma Taylor . . . .   Helen
Violet Hopson . . . .   Lady Cynthia
CRIME When lady robs shop, her companion is
blamed.

04885
THE CORPORAL'S KIDDIES (675) (U)
Hepworth
D: (Warwick Buckland)
DRAMA Colonel helps crippled corporal after
daughter learns he served in his regiment.

04886
OUTLINED AND OUTWITTED (675) (U)
Hepworth
D: (Hay Plumb)
COMEDY Rejected suitor has cousin cut
compromising silhouettes.

04887
THE SCHEMERS: OR, THE JEWELS OF
HATE (1800) (U)
Hepworth
D: (Frank Wilson)
Tom Powers . . . .   James Mortimer
Stewart Rome . . . .   George Kingsley
Alma Taylor . . . .   Doreen Milford
Violet Hopson . . . .   Vera Mortimer
Henry Vibart . . . .   Mr Milford
Ruby Belasco . . . .   Mrs Milford
CRIME Man proves fiancee framed for gem
theft.

04888
THE ALSO-RANS (750) (U)
Hepworth
D: (Hay Plumb)
COMEDY Broke nephews answer sick aunt's
summons and find her marrying the doctor.

04889
A KNIGHT OF THE ROAD (1200) (U)
Hepworth
D: (Warwick Buckland)
Chrissie White . . . .   Marion
Jamie Darling . . . .   The Squire
ROMANCE Period. Highwayman saves girl
from enforced elopement.

04890
RHUBARB AND RASCALS (700) (U)
Hepworth

D: Hay Plumb
Jack Raymond . . . .   Hero
Chrissie White . . . .   Heroine
COMEDY Hero thwarts villain and saves widow's
home.

04891
WHAT A SELL! (600) (U)
Hepworth
D: (Hay Plumb)
COMEDY Tramp forces rooster to swallow
stolen pendant and later finds it a fake.

04892
THE HUNCHBACK (2075) (U)
Hepworth
D: (Frank Wilson)
Tom Powers . . . .   Tom
Violet Hopson . . . .   Girl
Harry Royston . . . .   Badger
Ruby Belasco . . . .   Mother
Eric Desmond . . . .   Child
CRIME Cripple boy brought up in thieves'
kitchen reforms for love.

04893
ALL IN A DAY'S WORK (400) (U)
Hepworth
D: (Hay Plumb)
Eric Desmond . . . .   Freddie
COMEDY Boy makes trouble for maid and
policeman.

04894
THE CLEANSING OF A DIRTY DOG (1030)
(U)
Kineto
D: (Langford Reed)
COMEDY Rich uncle catches wastrel nephew
after gay night out.

04895
WHAT HAPPENED AT THE WAXWORKS (306)
Motograph (U)
COMEDY "Meddlesome pranks at dime museum."

04896
TRILBY (3400) (U)
London (Jury)
D: Harold Shaw
S: (NOVEL) George du Maurier
SC: Bannister Merwin
Sir Herbert Tree . . . .   Svengali
Viva Birkett . . . .   Trilby O'Ferrall
Ion Swinley . . . .   Little Billee
Charles Rock . . . .   Sandy McAllister
Phillip Merivale . . . .   Taffy Wynne
Wyndham Guise . . . .   Mr. O'Ferrall
Cicely Richards . . . .   Mme Vinard
Douglas Munro . . . .   Rev Bagot
ROMANCE Paris, 1890. Hypnotist makes
artist's model sing, but cannot force her love.

04897
HIS REFORMATION (1270) (A)
London
D: Arthur Holmes-Gore
S: William J. Elliott
Edna Flugrath . . . .   Ruth Sumner
Gregory Scott . . . .   Hubert Morton
Frank Stanmore . . . .   Jim Bowkett
Arthur Cullin . . . .
CRIME Disowned man weds cleric's daughter and
takes blame for theft.

04898
TURTLE DOVES (815) (U)
London
D: Arthur Holmes-Gore
S: John Penstowe

Edna Flugrath . . . .   Maisie
Langhorne Burton . . . .   Jack
Douglas Munro . . . .   Father
COMEDY Man returns to sweetheart and finds
her married.

04899
THE DIFFICULT WAY (2166) (U)
London
D: George L. Tucker
Jane Gail . . . .   Nan
Gerald Ames . . . .   Roger Wentwort
Langhorne Burton . . . .   Rev. John Pilgrim
ROMANCE Jealous socialite makes curate
believe his wife is in love with artist.

04900
YOU'RE WANTED ON THE PHONE, SIR (488)
EcKo (U)
D: W.P. Kellino
COMEDY City man's wife suspicious when he
refuses to answer phone.

04901
LOVE AND A TUB (514)
EcKo (U)
D: W.P. Kellino
COMEDY Father advertises dowry for daughter's
chosen suitor.

04902
PIMPLE TURNS HONEST (586) (U)
Folly Films (Phoenix)
D:S: Fred Evans, Joe Evans
Fred Evans . . . .   Pimple
COMEDY Pimple's trouble trying to be honest.

04903
PIMPLE, ANARCHIST (950) (U)
Folly Films (Phoenix)
D:S: Fred Evans, Joe Evans
Fred Evans . . . .   Pimple
COMEDY Pimple tries to blow up the King of
Whitechapel.

04904
BRONCHO PIMPLE (575) (U)
Folly Films (Phoenix)
D:S: Fred Evans, Joe Evans
Fred Evans . . . .   Pimple
COMEDY Pimple tries to be a cowboy

04905
PIMPLE, COUNTER JUMPER (920) (U)
Folly Films (Phoenix)
D:S: Fred Evans, Joe Evans
Fred Evans . . . .   Pimple
COMEDY Pimple causes chaos working in a
shop.

04906
PIMPLE'S VENGEANCE (655) (U)
Folly Films (Phoenix)
D:S: Fred Evans, Joe Evans
Fred Evans . . . .   Pimple
COMEDY

04907
PIMPLE PINCHED (900) (U)
Folly Films (Phoenix)
D:S: Fred Evans, Joe Evans
Fred Evans . . . .   Pimple
Joe Evans . . . .   Raffles
COMEDY Pimple becomes a thief and is arrested.

04908
SHOCKING BAD FORM (443) (U)
Martin Films (DFSA)
D: Dave Aylott
TRICK Toff unable to doff electric belt which
goes wrong.

04909
A MERRY NIGHT (680) (U)
Martin Films (DFSA) *Reissue:* 1915: SOME
EVENING
D: Dave Aylott
TRICK Drunkard beset by animated objects
takes flight in his bed.

04910
THE STRENGTH THAT FAILED (714) (U)
Martin Films (DFSA)
D: Dave Aylott
Ernie Westo
TRICK Tired man becomes super-strong after
taking doctor's pills.

04911
GEORGE ROBEY TURNS ANARCHIST (1375)
(U)
Burns Films
S: George Robey
George Robey . . . . . . Himself
COMEDY Comic ordered to blow up Parliament
tries to dispose of bomb.

04912
BERTIE AT THE LADIES' COLLEGE (832)(U)
Eclair
"Bertie"
COMEDY Brixton. French comedian lectures
at girls' school and wins girl despite her mother.

04913
THE MYSTERY OF THE DIAMOND BELT
(3500)
I.B. Davidson (KTC)
D:SC: Charles Raymond
S: (CHARACTERS) Harry Blyth
Philip Kay . . . . Sexton Blake
Lewis Carlton . . . . Tinker
Douglas Payne . . . . George Marsden
                                   Plummer
Eve Balfour . . . . Kitty the Moth
Percy Morran . . . . Flash Harry
Austin Camp . . . . Jack Braham
Lily Maxwell . . . . Nora Plummer
Harry Graham . . . . Maurice Braham
CRIME Crook poses as Lord to rob merchant
and holds tec captive in cellar.

04914
A MOTHER IN EXILE (1088)
Piccadilly (MP) *Reissue:* 1916 (Wardour)
D: Charles Weston
DRAMA Woman, divorced for having a convict
brother, becomes morphia addict and dies.

04915
GET IN AND GET OUT (404)
Piccadilly (MP) *Reissue:* 1916 (Wardour)
D: Charles Weston
COMEDY Drunken dancer dressed as devil
enters newlyweds' room.

04916
FREDDY'S NIGHTMARE: OR. TOO MUCH
MONEY (1800)
Premier Film Agency
P:D: Mr. Doff
S: Mr. Doff, "WHST"
Fred Kitchen . . . . Freddy
Aggie Norris . . . . Mrs Muchmoney
Henry Piddock . . . . Pal
Dudley Powell . . . . Mr Muchmoney
Mrs Fred Kitchen . . . . Lady
Nora Shaw . . . . Sister/Nurse
COMEDY Legatee to £10,000 dreams he robs
hotel posing as rich man who is wife deserter.

04917
THE PASSIONS OF MEN (3050) (A)
Clarendon (Moss)

D: Wilfred Noy
Norah Chaplin . . . . Enid Holt
DRAMA Girl's fiance charged with killing
general whose heart failed while attempting to
seduce her.

04918
THE LIFE OF A LONDON SHOPGIRL(2385)
(A)
Motograph
P: Joseph Bamberger
D: Charles Raymond
Babs Neville . . . . .Peggy Pink
H.J. Lord . . . . .Hon Billy Drysden
Edmund Goulding . . . .Walter Brand
Sybil de Bray . . . . . . .Lady Edith Drysden
Cecil Morton York . . . .Earl Drysden
CRIME Earl's disowned son becomes greengrocer
and finds father's stolen diamond in an orange.

04919
A STARTLING ANNOUNCEMENT (510)(U)
Stather-Brown Films (U)
D: Frank Stather
COMEDY "Complex situations evolve in con-
sequence of a misconception."

04920
AS A MAN SOWS; OR, AN ANGEL OF THE
SLUMS (3400)
Barker (Ideal)
D: (Bert Haldane)
S: H. Grenville-Taylor
Thos H. MacDonald
Fred Paul
Edna Maude
Eva Westlake
DRAMA Reformed slum landlord thrashes cruel
rent collector and adopts evicted orphans.

04921
THE FAKIR'S SPELL (2500) (U)
Dreadnought (Day)
D: Frank Newman
Ildeton Newman . . . . Child
HORROR India. Girl's British lover, changed
into gorilla by her father, is captured by circus.

AUG

04922
WHEN LONDON SLEEPS (3357) (U)
B & C (Ideal)
D: Ernest G. Batley
S: (PLAY) Charles Darrell
Lillian Wiggins . . . . Queenie Carruthers
Douglas Mars . . . . David Engelhardt
George Foley . . . . Captain
CRIME Captain tries to kill heiress by fire but
she escapes across telephone wires.

04923
THE STORY OF A CROSS (1165) (U)
B & C (DFSA)
CRIME "Dead" miner returns to kill partner
who has married his ex-fiancee and caused her
death.

04924
A GAME OF BLUFF (483) (U)
Bamforth (YSA)
D: Cecil Birch
COMEDY

04925
WINKY, PARK POLICEMAN (345)
Bamforth (YSA)
D: Cecil Birch
Reggie Switz . . . . Winky
COMEDY Winky's misadventures patrolling
park.

04926
WINKY GOES CAMPING (533)
Bamforth (YSA)
D: Cecil Birch
Reggie Switz . . . . Winky
COMEDY Winky and rival fight over milkmaid
who loves another.

04927
WINKY DIDDLES THE HAWKER (436)
Bamforth (YSA)
D: Cecil Birch
Reggie Switz . . . . Winky
COMEDY Winky changes hawker's strawberries
for bad ones.

04928
WINKY'S WEEKEND (489)
Bamforth (YSA)
D: Cecil Birch
Reggie Switz . . . . Winky
COMEDY In the absence of his wife Winky
sweeps chimney with hens.

04929
WINKY AND THE ANTS (374) (U)
Bamforth (YSA)
D: Cecil Birch
Reggie Switz . . . . Winky
COMEDY Winky's misadventures with ants.

04930
WINKY'S NEXT—DOOR NEIGHBOUR (395)
(U)
Bamforth (YSA)
D: Cecil Birch
Reggie Switz . . . . Winky
COMEDY Winky and neighbour fight over
bonfire.

04931
HOW WINKY WHACKED THE GERMANS
(677) (U)
Bamforth (YSA) *Reissue:* 1917
D: Cecil Birch
Reggie Switz . . . . Winky
Lily Ward . . . . Lily
COMEDY Winky causes trouble for German
band.

04932
JACK SPRATT AS A DUDE (517)(U)
Clarendon
D: Toby Cooper
COMEDY Sailor breaks ship and dons dude's
clothes.

04933
JACK SPRATT AS A GARDENER(500)(U)
Clarendon
D: Toby Cooper
COMEDY Sailor breaks ship and takes job as
gardener.

04934
JACK SPRATT AS A BLACKLEG WAITER (506
(U)
Clarendon
D. Toby Cooper
COMEDY Sailor breaks ship and dons waiter's
uniform during strike.

04935
JACK SPRATT AS A POLICEMAN (405) (U)
Clarendon
D: Toby Cooper
COMEDY Sailor breaks ship and dons policeman's
uniform.

04936
JACK SPRATT AS A BUS CONDUCTOR (511)
(U)
Clarendon
D: Toby Cooper
COMEDY Sailor breaks ship and dons
conductor's uniform.

04937
JACK SPRATT AS A BRICKLAYER (445) (U)
Clarendon
D: Toby Cooper
COMEDY Sailor breaks ship and dons bricklayer's
coat.

04938
THE LOVE OF AN ACTRESS (3000) (U)
Clarendon
D: Wilfrey Noy
S: Marchioness of Townshend
Dorothy Bellew . . . . Actress
Evan Thomas . . . . Peer
DRAMA Film actress feigns drunkenness to
repel peer but saves him from suicide after he
takes to drink.

04939
WRECK AND RUIN (2755) (U)
Clarendon
D: Wilfred Noy
S: Marchioness of Townshend
Dorothy Bellew
DRAMA Foreman saves mill owner from flood
caused by striking workmen.

04940
HIS COUNTRY'S HONOUR (3000)
USA: THE AVIATOR SPY
Cricks (Gaumont)
D: Charles Calvert
Douglas Payne . . . . Paul Koffman
Norman Howard . . . .
CRIME Spy saves foreign secretary's daughter
from drowning, photographs secret treaty, and
is shot down by pilot fiancee.

04941
SWANKER MEETS HIS GIRL (460) (U)
Cricks
D: (Edwin J. Collins)
TRICK Girl's father chases her magical suitor.

04942
JAWLOCK JONES (625)
Captain Kettle Films
S: C.J. Cutcliffe-Hyne
COMEDY Detective searches for nurse's lost
baby.

04943
A GOOD HOUSE DOG (770)
Captain Kettle Films
S: C.J. Cutcliffe-Hyne
COMEDY Troublesome escapades of captain's
pet dog.

04944
IN PAWN (960)
Captain Kettle Films
D: Dalton Somers
S: C.J. Cutliffe-Hyne
Connie Somers . . . . The Girl
COMEDY Father pawns girl's clothes to thwart
elopement, but she wears his.

04945
THE SENTENCE IS DEATH (1640) (U)
Captain Kettle Films
D: Dalton Somers
S: C.J. Cutcliffe-Hyne

Connie Somers . . . . The Girl
WAR Africa. Boer girl saves captain's despatches
from father.

04946
EGGS IS EGGS (585) (U)
Captain Kettle Films
D: Dalton Somers
S: C.J. Cutcliffe-Hyne
Connie Somers . . . . The Girl
COMEDY Farmer forms hens' union and they
go on strike.

04947
A POINTED JOKE (545)
EcKo (U)
D: W.P. Kellino
COMEDY

04948
LUCKY JIM (850) (U)
Hepworth
D: (Frank Wilson)
Tom Powers . . . . Jim Brown
Chrissie White . . . . Lady Winnie
COMEDY Doctor's disowned son uses castor
oil to save lady's sister.

04949
THE DEAD HEART (3225)
Hepworth (Walturdaw)
D: Hay Plumb
S: (PLAY) Watts Phillips
SC: Muriel Alleyne, Reginald Hargreaves
Alice de Winton . . . . Catherine
Lionelle Howard . . . . St Valery
Harry Gilbey . . . . Robert Landy
Edward Lingard . . . . Count St Valery
William Felton . . . . Abbe Latour
Claire Pridelle . . . . Cerisette
John MacAndrews . . . . Jocrisse
James Lindsay
ADVENTURE France, 1795. Framed man
avenges himself on count's son.

04950
TWO ELDERLY CUPIDS (1200) (U)
Ivy Close Films (Hepworth)
D: Elwin Neame
S: John Penstone
Ivy Close . . . . Girl
Austin Melford . . . . Boy
H. Gomer May . . . . Knight
D. Pringle . . . . Squire
COMEDY Period. Knight and squire try to
thwart their children's romance.

04951
FOR HER PEOPLE (3000)
Turner Films (Walturdaw)
D:S: Larry Trimble
Florence Turner . . . . Joan
Clifford Pembroke . . . . Leslie Calder
Rex Davis . . . . Tom
Franklyn Bellamy . . . . Henry Calder
Herbert Dansey . . . . William Arnold
John MacAndrews . . . . Greengrocer
DRAMA Lancs. Millgirl loved by owner's son
and socialist foreman who incites strike and
burns mill.

04952
THE CHIMES (2500)
Hepworth (Renters)
D:SC: Thomas Bentley
S: (STORY) Charles Dickens
Stewart Rome . . . . Richard
Violet Hopson . . . . Meg Veck
Warwick Buckland . . . . Trotty Veck
Harry Gilbey . . . . Sir Richard Bowley
Johnny Butt . . . . Alderman Cute

John MacAndrews . . . . Will Fern
Muriel Smith . . . . Lilian
FANTASY Father Time shows old messenger
tragic future of his child and her fiance.

04953
THE TRICKY STICK (465) (U)
Martin Films (DFSA)
D: Dave Aylott
TRICK Boy finds Egyptian wand that reverses
people and things.

04954
NOT LIKELY! (480) (U)
Martin Films (DFSA)
D: Dave Aylott
COMEDY Odd job man dreams of wooing
princess.

04955
MIKE WINS THE CHAMPIONSHIP (595) (U)
Martin Films (DFSA)
D: Dave Aylott
Ernie Westo . . . . Mike Murphy
COMEDY Mike defeats champion and every one
else, except his wife.

04956
PIMPLE'S LAST RESOURCE (635) (U)
Folly Films (Phoenix)
D:S: Fred Evans, Joe Evans
Fred Evans . . . . Pimple
COMEDY

04957
PIMPLE BEATS JACK JOHNSON (790) (U)
Folly Films (Phoenix) *Reissue:* 1916 (H & S)
D:S: Fred Evans, Joe Evans
Fred Evans . . . . Pimple
COMEDY Pimple dreams he beats Negro boxer.

04958
PIMPLE'S ESCAPE FROM PORTLAND (745) (U
Folly Films (Phoenix)
D:S' Fred Evans, Joe Evans
Fred Evans . . . . Pimple
COMEDY Pimple escapes from convict quarries
and is chased.

04959
A CHINESE VENGEANCE (3000)
Phoenix Film Agency
CRIME Chinese priest kidnaps daughter of
collector who bought stolen idol.

04960
BOOTLE'S BABY (3794) (U)
London (Fenning) *Reissue:* 1918
D: Harold Shaw
S: (NOVEL) John Strange Winter
SC: Bannister Merwin
Ben Webster . . . . Bootles
Edna Flugrath . . . . Helen Grace
Langhorne Burton . . . . Capt Lucy
Lewis Gilbert . . . . The Colonel
Menisse Johnson . . . . Capt Gilchrist
Hubert Willis . . . . The Adjutant
Brenda Patrick . . . . The Baby
DRAMA Captain's secret wife plants baby on
friend and he weds her when captain is killed.

04961
THE KING OF CRIME (3600)
Magnet
D: Sidney Northcote
S: (PLAY) Arthur Shirley
John Lawson . . . . Roujarre
Claudia Guillot . . . .
CRIME Paris, 1800. Stolen heiress secretly wed
to man framed for killing her miserly guardian.

04962
THE BELLE OF CRYSTAL PALACE (1886)
Motograph
P: Joseph Bamberger
D:S: James Youngdeer
Babs Neville
Harry Lorraine
DRAMA "Romance and revenge."

04963
THE BLOODSTAINED SHOE (2200) (U)
Urban Trading Co
Henri Houry . . . . Barnet-Parker
CRIME French tec, blamed for killing
blackmailer, poses as woman to find missing
witness.

04964
A DESPERATE STRATAGEM (1125) (U)
Big Ben Films-Union (Pathe)
D: H.O. Martinek
S: L.C. MacBean
H.O. Martinek
Ivy Montford
CRIME Engineer unmasks coiners behind
mystery of apparently insane girl.

04965
THE MAID OF CEFN YDFA (3000)
Haggar
D:SC: William Haggar jr.
S: (PLAY) James Haggar
William Haggar jr . . . . Will Hopkins
Jenny Haggar . . . . Ann Thomas
CRIME Wales. Lawyer tries to drown thatcher
to prevent his marriage to heiress.

04966
ENGLAND EXPECTS (2360)(U)
London (Fenning)
D:S: George Loane Tucker
Jane Gail . . . . Mary Browne
Charles Rock . . . . Grandfather
George Bellamy . . . . Mr Browne
Arthur Cullin . . . .
WAR Cowardly son of military family cured by
wife's faith.

04967
PICTURE PALACE PIECANS (595) (U)
Vaudefilms (A & C)
D: W.P. Kellino
Sam T. Poluski
Will Poluski
Hanvair & Lee
COMEDY Tramps break into old cinema and
put on show.

04968
THE HAPPY DUSTMEN PLAY GOLF (413)(U)
Vaudefilms (A & C)
D: W.P. Kellino
Albert Egbert . . . . Bill
Seth Egbert . . . . Walter
COMEDY Dustmen's misadventures on golf
course.

04969
HOW SPOTTED DUFF SAVED THE SQUIRE
(550) (U)
Vaudefilms (A & C)
D: W.P. Kellino
Goodfellow & Gregson
COMEDY Welsher foiled in attempt to dope
squire's racehorse.

04970
BERTIE'S BABY (565) (U)
Vaudefilms (Imperial)
D: W.P. Kellino
COMEDY Father has shock when friend changes
baby for Negro's.

04971
WHAT A NIGHT! (491)
Piccadilly (MP) *Reissue:* 1916 (Wardour)
D: Charles Weston
COMEDY Esher. Uncle returns unexpectedly and
is mistaken for burglar.

04972
JUST A NUT (503)
Piccadilly (MP) *Reissue:* 1916 (Wardour)
D: Charles Weston
COMEDY Masher pursues girl and is beaten by
boxer brother.

04973
THE HOUSEBOAT MYSTERY (2450)
Cygnet Films (Wynne, Taylor)
P: Henry P. Smither
D:S: B. Harold Brett
Percy Moran
Arola Brereton
Douglas Payne
Eddie Willey
CRIME

04974
THE CHASE OF DEATH (1) (U)
Cygnet Films (Wynne, Taylor)
P: Henry P. Smither
DS: B. Harold Brett
Percy Moran . . . . . . Fisherman
CHASE Fisherman on motorcycle pursues
kidnapper's car.

04975
THROUGH STORMY SEAS (2100)
Cygnet Films (Bio)
P: Henry P. Smither
D:S: B. Harold Brett
Dorothy Keen . . . . Nell Jago
Conway Ross . . . . Arnold Mackenzie
Arthur D. Mavity . . . . Wilfred Trethenny
May Hammerton . . . . Ruth Jago
ADVENTURE Polperro. Girl poses as saccharine
smuggler to save captive artist from cave.

04976
THE CAUSE OF THE GREAT EUROPEAN
WAR (1850) (U)
Samuelson (Imperial)
D:S: George Pearson
Fred Paul . . . . Kitchener/Kaiser/
Serb
Norman Stuart . . . . Winston Churchill
M. Bernasconi . . . . Franz-Josef
WAR Reconstruction of events leading to
declaration of war.

04977
CALLED TO THE FRONT (2200) (U)
Regent Films (MP)
P: Charles Weston, Arthur Finn
D: Charles Weston
Arthur Finn . . . . Jim Warrington
Rowland Moore . . . .
WAR Agent escapes from German invasion
ship and gets news to war office.

04978
THE THIRD GOD (1700)
Climax Films (KTC)
D:SC: Stuart Kinder
S: (STORY) R.S. Warren Bell
DRAMA "Powerful drama of the far east."

SEP

04979
BEAUTIFUL JIM (3253) (U) USA: THE PRICE
OF JUSTICE
B & C (Renters)

D: Maurice Elvey
S: (NOVEL) John Strange Winter
SC: Eliot Stannard
Elizabeth Risdon . . . . Nancy Earle
Fred Groves . . . . Lt Jim Beresford
Bootles Winter . . . . Capt Owen
A.V. Bramble . . . . Lieut Tommy Earle
M. Gray Murray . . . . Col Earle
CRIME Col's son kills sister's fiance with
lieut's golf club.

04980
LEST WE FORGET (1171) (U)
B & C (DFSA)
D: Maurice Elvey
Beatrix Templeton . . . . . The Girl
WAR British girl caught on Franco-German
frontier by war.

04981
MAGIC SQUARES (498) (U)
B & C (DFSA)
D:S: Louis Nikola
TRICK Paper squares animate into people,
monsters, etc.

04982
THE PRICE OF HER SILENCE (1964) (U)
B & C (DFSA)
D:(Ernest G. Batley)
CRIME Married woman's ex-lover drives black-
mailer over cliff in his car.

04983
THE GIRL BOY SCOUT (498) (U)
B & C (DFSA)
D: Ethyle Batley
Dorothy Batley . . . . The Girl
COMEDY Girl dons brother's scout uniform and
catches German ice cream salesman.

04984
THE BLACK CROSS GANG (1828) (A)
B & C (DFSA)
D:S: James Youngdeer
Lillian Wiggins . . . . Gypsy
Fred Morgan . . . . Dr Kish
CRIME Gang kidnap doctor for safe's
combination and he is saved by gypsy girl.

04985
AN ENGLISHMAN'S HOME (2200) (U)
B & C (DFSA)
D: Ernest G. Batley
S: (PLAY) Guy du Maurier
George Foley
Ernest G. Batley
Dorothy Batley
WAR Pacifist reforms after foreign invaders
occupy his house and kill his son.

04986
CHAINED TO THE ENEMY (2232) (U)
Barker (Moss)
D: F. Martin Thornton
S: Rowland Talbot
Blanche Forsythe . . . . Evelyn von Alton
Thos. H. McDonald . . . . Correspondent
WAR German officer's British wife forced to
nurse both him and wounded war correspondent
she loves.

04987
THE GERMAN SPY PERIL (1160) (U)
Barker (Award)
D: (Bert Haldane)
S: Rowland Talbot
J. Hastings Batson
CRIME Unfit carpenter trails spies through
secret tunnel and blows them up.

04988
THE LOOTERS OF LIEGE (985) (U)
Barker (Dominion)
D: F. Martin Thornton
S: Rowland Talbot
Tom Coventry
WAR Belgium. War correspondent fetches
soldiers to save village.

04989
YOUR COUNTRY NEEDS YOU (1200) (U)
Barker (Renters)
D: (Bert Haldane)
S: Rowland Talbot
J. Hastings Batson
WAR Scapegrace enlists and dies saving
wounded brother.

04990
YOUNG BRITON FOILS THE ENEMY (1255)
(U)
Barker (Moss)
D: F. Martin Thornton
S: Rowland Talbot
WAR Scout brings help when German count
tries to blow up cable house.

04991
WINKY'S INSURANCE POLICY (540) (U)
Bamforth (YSA)
D: Cecil Birch
Reggie Switz . . . . Winky
COMEDY Trouble ensues when Winky insures.

04992
WINKY TAKES TO FARMING (438) (U)
Bamforth (YSA)
D: Cecil Birch
Reggie Switz . . . . Winky
COMEDY Winky mistakes jackass for cow and
picks worker's pocket.

04993
WINKY AS A SUFFRAGETTE (686) (U)
Bamforth (YSA)
D: Cecil Birch
Reggie Switz . . . . Winky
COMEDY Winky poses as suffragette lecturer
and collects money.

04994
WINKY GETS SPOTTED (615) (U)
Bamforth (YSA)
D: Cecil Birch
Reggie Switz . . . . Winky
COMEDY Winky's friend feigns illness to pick
doctor's pocket.

04995
WINKY GETS PUFFED UP (479) (U)
Bamforth (YSA)
D: Cecil Birch
Reggie Switz . . . . Winky
COMEDY Winky eats self-raising flour that
blows him up like balloon.

04996
WINKY WAGGLES THE WICKED WIDOW
(642)
Bamforth (YSA)
D: Cecil Birch
Reggie Switz . . . . Winky
COMEDY Winky and lawyer conspire to obtain
landlady's legacy.

04997
WINKY'S LIFEBOAT (442) (U)
Bamforth (YSA)
D: Cecil Birch
Reggie Switz . . . . Winky
COMEDY Winky rescues girl in patent lifeboat.

04998
THE STOLEN MASTERPIECE (3245) (U)
Big Ben Films-Union (Pathe)
D: H.O. Martinek
S: L.C. MacBean
H.O. Martinek . . . . Dick Steele
Ivy Montford . . . . Kate Halifax
Douglas Payne . . . . The Thief
CRIME "The Sleuth Hounds" catch clubman
after rescue from snakepit and fight in morass.

04999
THE SINS OF HARVEY CLARE (2166) (U)
retitled: VICTIMS OF BLACKMAIL
Britannia Films (Pathe)
CRIME Man frames cousin and drowns after
fighting mad witness on railway bridge.

05000
THE TRAMP AND THE LADY (780)
Captain Kettle Films
D: Dalton Somers
S: C.J. Cutcliffe-Hyne
Connie Somers
COMEDY Tramp steals clothes of swimming
girl.

05001
THE COSTERS' HOLIDAY (635) (U)
Captain Kettle Films *Reissue:* 1915 (YCC)
S: C.J. Cutcliffe-Hyne
COMEDY Costers cause fight at Hampstead
Heath fair.

05002
A MODERN DON JUAN (945) (U)
Captain Kettle Films
D: Dalton Somers
S: C.J. Cutcliffe-Hyne
Connie Somers . . . . The Girl
COMEDY Man becomes engaged to several
girls, and turns Mormon.

05003
THE SCALES OF JUSTICE (2100) retitled:
A BRITISH BULLDOG CONQUERS
Captain Kettle Films
D: Alfred Lord
S: C.J. Cutcliffe-Hyne
Alf Collingham
ANIMAL Shipley. Jealous suitor's revenge on
rival thwarted by pet bulldog.

05004
CAPTAIN 'POSTMAN' BLAKE, VC (1380)
Captain Kettle Films
S: C.J. Cutcliffe-Hyne
WAR Wounded captain delivers message by
bandaging it to his head.

05005
THE ENEMY IN OUR MIDST (2360) (U)
Clarendon (Argus)
D: Percy Stow
CRIME "Dr Brian Pellie" bombs bullion cars
and is betrayed to Navy.

05006
THE MID-NIGHTLY WEDDING (560) (U)
Clarendon
D: (Toby Cooper)
COMEDY

05007
THE FAMILY SOLICITOR (2772) (U)
Clarendon
D: Wilfred Noy
S: Marchioness of Townshend
Dorothy Bellew . . . . The Girl
CRIME Lawyer forges earl's will so that his
indebted son may inherit.

05008
GUARDING BRITAIN'S SECRETS (3300)
USA: THE FIENDS OF HELL
Cricks (Walturdaw)
D: Charles Calvert
S: Dr Nikola Hamilton
Douglas Payne . . . . Rex Omar
Dr Nikola Hamilton . . . .
Norman Howard . . . .
CRIME Tec and hypnotised girl save inventor's
plans from Chinese secret society.

05009
THE GRIP OF THE PAST (3000)
Cricks (KTC)
D: Edwin J. Collins
DRAMA

05010
THELMA; OR, SAVED FROM THE SEA (2500)
Cygnet (Bio)
D:S: Harold Brett
Dorothy Keen . . . . Esme Villiers
Arthur D. Mavity . . . . David Trelawney
Arthur Charrington . . . . Derek Villiers
CRIME Polperro. Fisherman saves amnesiac
heiress from being drowned by her cousin.

05011
POPPIES (1250) (U)
Climax Films (Browne)
D: Stuart Kinder
S: (POEMS) Clement Scott (POPPYLAND)
De Lana (GARDEN OF SLEEP)
ROMANCE Norfolk. Wife led astray but
returns to husband.

05012
THE BOY SCOUT DETECTIVE (714)
Conqueror Films (Bio)
CRIME Girl's boy scout brother tracks coiners.

05013
MARY THE FISHERGIRL (1100)
Daring Films (Cosmo)
P: Harry Lorraine
D: Sidney Northcote
S: Harold Brett
Harry Lorraine . . . . Vicar
ADVENTURE Vicar saves fiancee from
drowning after fight with jealous girl.

05014
FOR LOVE AND THE CROWN (2674) (U)
Anchor Films
Lillian Hallows . . . . Queen Irene
ADVENTURE Ruritania. Prince saves queen and
crown jewels from rival prince.

05015
THE MYSTERY OF THE LANDLADY'S CAT
(629)
EcKo (U)
D: W.P. Kellino
COMEDY Tec dons disguises to discover which
lodger killed cat.

05016
CONSPICUOUS BRAVERY (365)
EcKo (U)
D: W.P. Kellino
COMEDY

05017
DR DOSEM'S DEPUTY (456)
EcKo (U)
D: W.P. Kellino
Sam T. Poluski . . . . Nobby
COMEDY Doctor's clumsy deputy makes
mistakes in hospital.

05018
DOMESTIC ECONOMY (687)
Favourite Films (U)
S: (SKETCH)
COMEDY Farmer does housework while wife
works the farm.

05019
THE BRONZE IDOL (1300) (U)
Hepworth
D: Frank Wilson
Stewart Rome . . . . The Secretary
Harry Royston . . . . The Burglar
CRIME Rich man's secretary catches burglar
who exposes him as an ex-convict.

05020
ALGY'S LITTLE ERROR (725) (U)
Hepworth
D: (Hay Plumb)
COMEDY Wastrel becomes detective and
mistakes police inspector for thief.

05021
CINDER-ELFRED (950) (U)
Hepworth
D: (Hay Plumb)
S: Percy Darmstatter
Tom Powers . . . . Elfred
COMEDY Poor artist dreams fairy gives him
dress suit to wear to American girl's ball.

05022
MEMORY (1725) (U)
Hepworth
D: (Warwick Buckland)
Tom Powers . . . . Paulo
Violet Hopson . . . . Marita
Eric Desmond . . . . Noel Stevens
DRAMA Amnesiac child recalls father died
accidentally in time to save gipsy from jail.

05023
SIMPKINS' SUNDAY DINNER (750) (U)
Hepworth
D: (Hay Plumb)
Johnny Butt . . . . Simpkins
COMEDY Henpeck's dinner stolen so he fishes
for his neighbour's.

05024
UNFIT; OR, THE STRENGTH OF THE WEAK
(1175) (U)
Hepworth
D: Cecil M. Hepworth
Tom Powers . . , ... Ned Osborne
Stewart Rome . . . . Jack Osborne
Violet Hopson . . . . Margaret Adams
Eric Desmond . . . . The Boy
Marie de Solla . . . . Mrs Osborne
WAR Army reject becomes war correspondent
and saves life of his healthy brother.

05025
SO MUCH GOOD IN THE WORST OF US
(925) (U)
Hepworth
D: (Frank Wilson)
S: William J. Elliott
Stewart Rome . . . . .Doctor
Harry Royston. . . . . .Burglar
PATHOS Burglar finds dying child and reforms,
fetching doctor.

05026
HER SUITOR'S SUIT (850) (U)
Hepworth
D: (Warwick Buckland)
DRAMA Man saves child from drowning and dons
suit secreting valuable letter.

05027
A GHOSTLY AFFAIR (575) (U)
Hepworth
D: (Hay Plumb)
TRICK Burglar robs old castle where paintings
come alive.

05028
THE HILLS ARE CALLING (1150) (U)
Hepworth
D: Cecil M. Hepworth
S: Reginald Hargreaves
Tom Powers . . . . Donald
Alma Taylor . . . . Sheila
Henry Vibart . . . . Thomas Stacey
ROMANCE Scots violinist discarded by London
socialite returns home.

05029
THE MAID AND THE MONEY (875) (U)
Hepworth
D: (Hay Plumb)
COMEDY Suitor robs girl's mean father to
enforce consent.

05030
SIMPKINS GETS THE WAR SCARE (525) (U)
Hepworth
D: (Frank Wilson)
Johnny Butt . . . . Simpkins
Chrissie White . . . . Mary Jane
COMEDY Henpeck poses as PC and is mistaken
for spy.

05031
THE BASILISK (2500) (A)
Hepworth
D:S: Cecil M. Hepworth
Tom Powers . . . . Eric Larne
Alma Taylor . . . . Freda Hampton
William Felton . . . . Basil Reska
Chrissie White . . . .
Cyril Morton . . . .
CRIME Snake kills hypnotist in time to save
victim from stabbing her fiance.

05032
THE WHITE HOPE ON CHAMPIONSHIP(710)
Heron (U)
P: Andrew Heron
COMEDY Burlesque boxing match between tall
and short contestants.

05033
ALONE I DID IT (545) (U)
Heron (U)
P: Andrew Heron
Nelson Keys
COMEDY Misadventures of novice grouse-
shooter.

05034
ONE UP ON FATHER (518)
Heron (U)
P: Andrew Heron
COMEDY Film actor changes convict suit for
that of swimmer and elopes with swimmer's
daughter.

05035
WAS IT HE? (2020)
Hewitt Films (Kimberley)
D:S: G. Fletcher Hewitt
John Starchfield . . . . Himself
Horatio Bottomley . . . . Himself
CRIME Newsvendor wounded while stopping
killer, becomes gardener and save employer's
child from kidnap.

05036
LOVE AND MAGIC (470)
Kineto

D: (W.R. Booth)
TRICK Girl's suitor conjures imp to annoy her
father.

05037
MAGICAL MYSTERIES (500)
Kineto
D: (W.R. Booth)
TRICK

05038
THE SCOUT'S MOTTO (827) (U)
Martin (DFSA)
D: Dave Aylott
CRIME Scout trails burglar, is caught, and
saved by his troop.

05039
MIKE MURPHY, MOUNTAINEER (491) (U)
Martin (DFSA)
D: Dave Aylott
Ernie Westo . . . . Mike Murphy
COMEDY Mike climbs mountain, disturbs
picnickers, and eats their food.

05040
ENGLAND'S CALL (652) (U)
Martin (DFSA) Reissue: 1916
D:S: Dave Aylott
WAR Slacker enlists after dreaming heroes'
portraits come to life.

05041
A BOX OF REAL TURKISH (533) (U)
Martin (DFSA)
D: Dave Aylott
TRICK "Introducing many novel trick
effects."

05042
WAR'S GRIM REALITY (1112) (U)
Martin (DFSA)
D:S: Dave Aylott
Ashmore Vincent
Tom Morriss
Johnny Butt
Bob Reed
WAR France. Villagers avenge dead despatch-
rider's wife after she is raped by Uhlan officer.

05043
LIEUTENANT PIMPLE, GUNRUNNER
(795) (U)
Folly Films (Phoenix)
D:S: Fred Evans, Joe Evans
Fred Evans . . . . Lt Pimple
COMEDY Lieut runs guns.

05044
PIMPLE, MP (585) (U)
Folly Films (Phoenix)
D:S: Fred Evans, Joe Evans
Fred Evans . . . . Pimple
COMEDY Pimple is elected MP and holds
meetings.

05045
PIMPLE'S PROPOSAL (535) (U)
Folly Films (Phoenix)
D:S: Fred Evans, Joe Evans
Fred Evans . . . . Pimple
COMEDY "Extravaganza upon the lines of the
domestic love drama."

05046
PIMPLE'S CHARGE OF THE LIGHT BRIGADE
(710)
Folly Films (Phoenix)
D:S: Fred Evans, Joes Evans
Fred Evans . . . . Pimple
COMEDY

05047
MY SON (1151)
Piccadilly (MP)
D: Charles Weston
CRIME Bank manager shoots drunken son in mistake for new wife's lover.

05048
SAVING THE COLOURS (3000)
Regent (MP)
P: Charles Weston, Arthur Finn
D: Charles Weston
Rowland Moore
WAR Squire's cowardly son enlists and is wounded at Mons while saving the flag.

05049
MARRIED LIFE, THE SECOND YEAR (1455)
Regent (MP)
P: Charles Weston, Arthur Finn
D: Charles Weston
DRAMA Drunken gambler returns to wife after her lover thwarts his elopement with vicar's daughter.

05050
WHAT A WOMAN WILL DO (3000)
Regent (MP)
P: Charles Weston, Arthur Finn
D: Charles Weston
CRIME Girl tries to kill judge's son to avenge innocent father's conviction.

05051
WIFE OF A THIEF (2000)
Regent (MP)
P: Charles Weston, Arthur Finn
D: Charles Weston
Gordon Begg
CRIME Thief uses corpse to fake own drowning and saves his remarried wife from gambler.

05052
FOR THE EMPIRE (2100) (U) USA: FOR HOME AND COUNTRY
London (Gaumont)
D: Harold Shaw
Douglas Munro . . . . Rev Pendleton
George Bellamy . . . . The German
Charles Rock . . . . The Minister
Christine Rayner . . . . Ruth Pendleton
Wyndham Guise . . . . The Shopkeeper
Frank Stanmore . . . . The Spy
WAR Pacifist vicar fights back after Germans occupy his house.

05053
ON HIS MAJESTY'S SERVICE (3300) (U)
USA: 0–18 OR A MESSAGE FROM THE SKY
London (Globe)
D: George L. Tucker
S: Frank Fowell
Jane Gail 0–18
Douglas Munro . . . . Otto Bergmann
Gerald Ames . . . . Secret Agent
Edward O'Neill . . . . Spy
Wyndham Guise . . . . William Bergmann
Lewis Gilbert . . . . Porter
CRIME Typist exposes businessmen as spies plotting to blow up bridge.

05054
OHMS – OUR HELPLESS MILLIONS SAVED (2000) (U)
George A. Cooper
D:S: Percy Moran
Percy Moran . . . . Lt Jack Moran
CRIME Lt stops spies from using liquid explosive to blow up water reservoir.

05055
THE GREAT SPY RAID (2300)
P & M Films (Feature Supply)
P: John M. Payne
D:S: Sidney Morgan
Harry Lorraine . . . . George England
Eva Norman . . . . Mrs England
Joan Morgan . . . . Joan England
CRIME Spies fail to blow up railway line and are caught in Soho.

05056
HOW I WON THE BELT (1000)
Stather-Brown
D:S: Frank Stather
Jack Collinson . . . . Tom Sayers
Billy Ross . . . . Heenan
SPORT Old boxer recalls match fought in 1860 and dies to save his drowning grand-daughter.

05057
FOR MOTHER'S SAKE (1500)
St George and Dragon (Anglo-Spanish)
D: A. Ray
Harry Moss . . . . The Convict
Evandne Moore . . . . . . The Mother
CRIME Escaped convict.

05058
MEN OF THE MOMENT (300)
Tressograph
P: Henry Tress
Charles Goff . . . . Himself
ACT Actor makes up as Sir Edward Grey, Mr. Asquith, Kitchener, King George, etc.

05059
NOBBY'S JU-JITSU EXPERIMENTS (435) (U)
Vaudefilms (Imperial)
D: W.P. Kellino
Sam T. Poluski . . . . Nobby
Brothers Egbert
COMEDY Nobby buys ju-jitsu book and wrestles fairground crowd.

05060
FIDGETT'S SUPERSTITIONS (440) (U)
Vaudefilms (Imperial)
D: W.P. Kellino
COMEDY Nervous man's superstitions backfire.

05061
THE GYPSY'S CURSE (412)
Vaudefilms (A & C)
D: W.P. Kellino
COMEDY Gypsy's curse causes misfortune to gambler.

05062
CHUMS (1057)
Vaudefilms (A & C)
D: W.P. Kellino
ANIMAL Poor old man forced to sell grand-child's terrier, but it returns.

05063
THE RIVALS (DUEL SCENE)
Eric Williams Speaking Pictures
S: (PLAY) Richard Sheridan
Eric Williams . . . . Sir Lucius O'Trigger
COMEDY Shown while Eric Williams recites from stage.

05064
HUBERT AND ARTHUR
Eric Williams Speaking Pictures - Gaumont
S:(PLAY) William Shakespeare (KING JOHN)
Eric Williams . . . . Hubert
DRAMA Shown while Eric Williams recites from stage.

05065
THE CHARGE OF THE LIGHT BRIGADE
Eric Williams Speaking Pictures
S:(POEM) Alfred Tennyson
Eric Williams
WAR Shown while Eric Williams recites from stage.

05066
HAMLET
Eric Williams Speaking Pictures
S:(PLAY) William Shakespeare
Eric Williams . . . . Hamlet
DRAMA Shown while Eric Williams recites from stage.

05067
THE HARBOUR LIGHTS (3275) (U)
Neptune (Globe)
D: Percy Nash
S: (PLAY) George R. Sims, Henry Pettitt
SC: John M. East, Brian Daly
Gerald Lawrence . . . . Lt David Kingsley
Mercy Hatton . . . . Dora Vane
Daisy Cordell . . . . : . . Lina Nelson
Fred Morgan . . . . Nicholas Morland
Gregory Scott . . . . Frank Morland
Douglas Payne . . . . Mark Helstone
Joan Ritz . . . . Peggy Chudleigh
John East . . . . Capt Nelson
May Lynn . . . . Mrs Helstone
Brian Daly . . . . Tom Dossiter
Bryan Powley . . . . Capt Hardy
Helen Lainsbury . . . . Polly
CRIME Lieut accused of shooting squire to save heiress is cleared by dying confession.

OCT

05068
A LONDON MYSTERY (2993) (U)
B & C (Century)
D: Charles Calvert
CRIME "A mysterious plot is unravelled with extraordinary skill."

05069
ANSWERING THE CALL (590) (U)
B & C (DFSA)
D: Ethyle Batley
WAR "Dramatised call to arms."

05070
HEADS OR TAILS (496) (U)
B & C (DFSA)
COMEDY Jews buy cow and try to share it exactly.

05071
THE BELLS OF RHEIMS (2088) (U)
B & C (Kin-Ex)
D: Maurice Elvey
S: Eliot Stannard
Elizabeth Risdon . . . . Nurse
A.V. Bramble . . . . Uhlan
Joyce Templeton . . . . Child
WAR Uhlan tries to shoot nurse as spy when she thwarts his rape.

05072
WINKY ACCUSED OF AN 'ORRIBLE CRIME (674)
Bamforth (YSA)
D: Cecil Birch
Reggie Switz . . . . Winky
COMEDY Red ink makes police suspect builder of killing his wife.

05073
WINKY AND THE CANNIBAL CHIEF (554) (U)
Bamforth (YCC)
D: Cecil Birch
Reggie Switz . . . . Winky
COMEDY Winky poses as a savage to scare
picnickers and catches a real one.

05074
WINKY BECOMES A FAMILY MAN (526) (U)
Bamforth (YCC)
D: Cecil Birch
Reggie Switz . . . . Winky
COMEDY Father conspires with nurse to obtain
bounty for triplets.

05075
WINKY GOES SPY CATCHING (529) (U)
Bamforth (YCC)
D: Cecil Birch
Reggie Switz . . . . Winky
COMEDY Winky mistakes film actors for spies
and is doused.

05076
WINKY'S MOTHER-IN-LAW (480)
Bamforth (YCC)
D: Cecil Birch
Reggie Switz . . . . Winky
COMEDY Winky plots with yokel to get rid of
picnicking mother-in-law.

05077
WINKY WINS (660)
Bamforth (YCC)
D: Cecil Birch
Reggie Switz . . . . Winky
COMEDY Tramp steals boarder's clothes and
poses as visitor.

05078
WINKY TRIES CHICKEN RAISING (512)
Bamforth (YCC) Reissue: 1917
D: Cecil Birch
Reggie Switz . . . . Winky
COMEDY Neighbour steals Winky's eggs and
leaves bad ones.

05079
THE TRAMP AND THE TENNER (660)
H.A. Browne
COMEDY Tramp's trouble changing £10 note
reward.

05080
THE HATTER AND HIS DOG (242) (U)
Captain Kettle
S: C.J. Cutcliffe-Hyne
ANIMAL Hatter drums up trade with help of
retriever.

05081
MAKING A MAN OF HIM (990) (U)
Captain Kettle
S: C.J. Cutcliffe-Hyne
WAR Disowned drunkard turns tramp, enlists,
and is reformed.

05082
THE GIRL AND THE GOLD MINE (940)
Captain Kettle
D: Dalton Somers
S: C.J. Cutcliffe-Hyne
Connie Somers . . . . The Girl
DRAMA Man wins girl by promoting father's
gold mine shares.

05083
PINCHER'S LUCKY DAY (387)
Captain Kettle
S: C.J. Cutcliffe-Hyne
COMEDY Tramp steals food and is arrested.

05084
THE PEOPLE OF THE ROCKS (1200)
Captain Kettle Reissue: 1917 (DFSA)
D: Dalton Somers
S: C.J. Cutcliffe-Hyne
Connie Somers . . . . The Girl
FANTASY Wales. Family on tour dream druids.

05085
THE KAISER'S DREAM (300) (U)
Captain Kettle (Imperial)
S: C.J. Cutcliffe-Hyne
TRICK "Clever satire on recent events."

05086
THE DANCING GIRL (410)
Captain Kettle
S: C.J. Cutcliffe-Hyne
COMEDY

05087
A MODERN HIGHWAYMAN (843)
Captain Kettle
D: Dalton Somers
S: C.J. Cutcliffe-Hyne
Connie Somers . . . . The Girl
DRAMA Man wins girl by unmasking
cardsharper.

05088
A CO'D IN HIS HEAD (735) (U)
Clarendon
D: (Toby Cooper)
CHASE Girl chases naked man bearing bath on
his back.

05089
THE HEROINE OF MONS (1670) (U)
Clarendon (Gaumont)
D: Wilfred Noy
Dorothy Bellew . . . . The Girl
Bert Wynne
Leslie Howard
WAR France. Girl hides officer and poses as
German soldier to summon help.

05090
THE CALL (1750) (U) retitled: HIS COUNTRY'S
BIDDING
Hepworth
D: Cecil M. Hepworth
Stewart Rome . . . . The Squire
Alma Taylor . . . . Mary Brown
Harry Royston . . . . John Brown
DRAMA Drunken gamekeeper wounds squire
and returns from sea to find squire loves his wife.

05091
THE UNSEEN WITNESS (1750) (U)
Hepworth
D: (Frank Wilson)
Tom Powers . . . . Brian Foster
Chrissie White . . . . Anne
Violet Hopson . . . . Ethel
William Felton . . . . Footman
Ruby Belasco . . . . Mrs Foster
CRIME Companion blamed when employer's
necklace stolen by son's fiancee.

05092
THAT MYSTERIOUS FEZ (450) (U)
Hepworth
D: (Hay Plumb)
TRICK Magic fez grants any wish, save wish for
money.

05093
TOPPER TRIUMPHANT (525) (U)
Hepworth
D: (Hay Plumb)
COMEDY Dandy embarrasses friends by
joining army.

05094
MR MEEK'S MISSUS (575) (U)
Hepworth
D: (Hay Plumb)
Arthur Staples . . . . Mr Meek
Ruby Belasco . . . . Mrs Meek
COMEDY Suffragette catches husband returning
stolen bag.

05095
IN THE SHADOW OF BIG BEN (3000)
Hepworth
D: Frank Wilson
S: Frank Howel Evans
Tom Powers . . . . Harry Forrest
Alma Taylor . . . . Clara Maitland
Jack Raymond . . . . Richard Nash
Henry Vibart . . . . Mr Hamel
Ruby Belasco . . . . Mrs Hamel
CRIME Crook seeks to marry girl by framing
her for forgery and smashing her benefactor's
bank.

05096
THE HUMPTY DUMPTY CIRCUS (448)
Humpty Dumpty (Prieur)
TRICK Animated dolls perform in circus.

05097
TRICKED BY HIS PAL (824)
Heron (U)
P: Andrew Heron
COMEDY Flirt's friend wins widow.

05098
DREAMY JIMMY DREAMS AGAIN (495) (U)
Martin (DFSA)
D: Dave Aylott
COMEDY Boy dreams he is caught by brigands
and made to walk plank.

05099
I SHOULD SAY SO! (680) (U)
Martin (DFSA)
D: Dave Aylott
COMEDY Boy dreams he is caught by Indians
and rescued by boy scouts.

05100
THE MAT THAT MATTERED (429) (U)
Martin (DFSA)
D: Dave Aylott
TRICK Man uses fakir's magic mat to make
mother-in-law vanish.

05101
LOVE, POETRY AND PAINT (661)
Martin (DFSA) Reissue: 1915, LOVE AND
BULLETS
D: Dave Aylott
COMEDY Poet and artist duel for girl who loves
another.

05102
MIKE MURPHY'S DREAM OF THE WILD
WEST (539) (U)
Martin Films (DFSA)
D: Dave Aylott
Ernie Westo . . . . Mike Murphy
COMEDY Tramp dreams he rescues girl from
Indians.

05103
FATHER'S FIGHTING FEVER (667) (A)
Martin Films (DFSA) Reissue: 1916
D: Dave Aylott
Ernie Westo . . . . Father
COMEDY Enthusiastic man trains family as
Home Guards.

05104
LIEUTENANT PIMPLE AND THE STOLEN
INVENTION (612) (U)
Folly Films (Phoenix)
D:S: Fred Evans, Joe Evans
Fred Evans .... Lt Pimple
COMEDY Lt and men save invention from spies.

05105
PIMPLE ENLISTS (850)(U)
Folly Films (Phoenix) *Reissue:* 1916 (H & S)
D:S: Fred Evans, Joe Evans
Fred Evans .... Pimple
COMEDY Territorial on sentry dreams he is
caught by Huns and stones.

05106
PIMPLE'S GREAT FIRE (825) (U)
Folly Films (Phoenix)
D:S: Fred Evans, Joe Evans
Fred Evans .... Pimple
COMEDY Fireman fakes fire to rob reception.

05107
PIMPLE, SPECIAL CONSTABLE (795) (U)
Folly Films (Phoenix)
D:S: Fred Evans, Joe Evans
Fred Evans .... Pimple
COMEDY Constable guards pillar box from
spies.

05108
PIMPLE'S PRISON (675) (U)
D:S: Fred Evans, Joe Evans
Fred Evans .... Pimple
COMEDY Benevolent governor takes
prisoners to seaside.

05109
LIEUTENANT PIMPLE, KING OF THE
CANNIBAL ISLANDS (1000) (U)
Folly Films (Phoenix)
D:S: Fred Evans, Joe Evans
Fred Evans .... Pimple
COMEDY Lt's adventures with cannibals.

05110
THE TERRIBLE TWO (675) (U)
Phoenix
D:S: Joe Evans
Joe Evans .... Lemon
James Read .... Dash
COMEDY "Some capital knockabout business."

05111
THE TERRIBLE TWO ON THE MASH (570) (U)
Phoenix
D:S: Joe Evans
Joe Evans .... Lemon
James Read .... Dash
COMEDY Rivals serenade girl and box each
other.

05112
THE FIERY DEEDS OF THE TERRIBLE TWO
(835) (U)
Phoenix
D:S: Joe Evans
Joe Evans .... Lemon
James Read .... Dash
COMEDY Fire brigade captain turns out to
false alarms.

05113
ARCHIBALD'S EGG DIET (750) (U)
Phoenix
D: (Joe Evans)
COMEDY Man tries to comply with doctor's
egg diet.

05114
WHO WAS TO BLAME? (640)
Vaudefilms (A & C)
D: W.P. Kellino
COMEDY Husband follows wife and finds she is
the maid in his wife's clothes.

05115
GINGER SEEKS A SITUATION (550)
Vaudefilms (A & C)
D: W.P. Kellino
COMEDY Clumsy manservant upsets boarders.

05116
SPY CATCHERS (760) (U)
Vaudefilms (Imperial)
D: W.P. Kellino
Sam T. Poluski
The Brothers Egbert
COMEDY Rejected police recruit starts own
force and catches spies.

05117
THE TROMBONER'S STRONG NOTE (607)
Vaudefilms (A & C)
D: W.P. Kellino
COMEDY Trombonist's loud playing brings down
house.

05118
'TWIXT TIME AND TIDE (804)
Cable Films (U)
DRAMA Mate tied in sea by rival for captain's
daughter.

05119
HER OWN RIVAL (1250)
English Films (Browne)
ROMANCE Artist falls for veiled dancer who is
his own country sweetheart.

05120
THE MAY QUEEN (2300) (U)
Favourite Films (U)
S: (POEM) Alfred Tennyson
DRAMA Period. Village girl dies after being
crowned Queen of the May.

05121
BILLY'S BABIES (714) (U)
Favourite Films (U)
COMEDY Bachelor must find family to comply
with inheritance.

05122
WHEN EMPIRE CALLS (804) (U)
Favourite Films (U)
DRAMA Foreign furniture dealers pose as
Britons.

05123
THE CLEVER ONE (1540) (U)
Piccadilly (MP)
D: Charles Weston
Arthur Finn .... Burglar
DRAMA Man saves burglar from arrest and he
saves man from suicide.

05124
THROUGH THE FIRING LINE (3000)
Regent (MP)
P: Charles Weston, Arthur Finn
D: Charles Weston
Rowland Moore
WAR Mons. Englishman helps farmer hold
enemy while daughter fetches troops

05125
THE BISHOP'S SILENCE (3000)
Regent (MP)
P: Charles Weston, Arthur Finn
D: Charles Weston
Arthur Finn .... Bishop Lawrence
Rowland Moore ....
Gordon Begg ....
Cissie Elen ....
CRIME Bishop dies after confessing he framed
an actor for murder of seduced girl's father.

05126
THE MASTER SPY (3000)
Regent (MP)
P: Charles Weston, Arthur Finn
D: Charles Weston
Rowland Moore
Gordon Begg
CRIME Detective foils clever German spy.

05127
FOR KING AND COUNTRY (2800) (U)
Regent (LIFT)
P: Charles Weston, Arthur Finn
D: Arthur Finn
Arthur Finn .... The Lonely Man
Gordon Begg ....
WAR Lonely man converts boarding-house
slackers and they enlist.

05128
THE PHANTOM OF THE BRAIN (1120)
Searchlight (Prieur)
CRIME Jealous man kills wife's lover and finds
it was a dream.

05129
OH! WHAT A NIGHT (2000)
XL Films
COMEDY "A farce upon the lines of certain
Continental productions."

05130
ONE SHALL BE TAKEN (1000) (U)
Burlingham Standard (NA)
D: Ethyle Batley
Dorothy Batley
WAR Private adopts sister's family when her
shirker husband dies.

05131
JACK'S AWAKENING (500)
Barker (Powers)
S: Rowland Talbot
WAR Clerk inspired to enlist saves wounded
friend.

05132
INCIDENTS OF THE GREAT EUROPEAN
WAR (2000)
Samuelson (Royal)
D:S: George Pearson
Fred Paul
Gilbert Esmond
WAR Reconstruction of events following
declaration of war.

05133
A STUDY IN SCARLET (5749) (U)
G.B. Samuelson (Moss)
D: George Pearson
S: (NOVEL) Arthur Conan Doyle
SC: Harry Engholm
Fred Paul .... Jefferson Hope
Agnes Glynne .... Lucy Ferrier
Harry Paulo .... John Ferrier
James Braginton .... Sherlock Holmes
James Le Fre .... Father
Winifred Pearson .... Lucy (child)
CRIME Detective solves murder rooted in the
Mormon trek of 1850.

05134
THE RAID OF 1915 (2268) (U) retitled:
IF ENGLAND WERE INVADED
Gaumont
D: Fred W. Durrant
S: (NOVEL) William le Queux (THE
INVASION OF 1910)
Leo Lilley . . . . Lt Dick Pontifex
Diana Shaw . . . . Elsie Ashcroft
Mr Dunn . . . . Karl Kruse
WAR Norfolk. Officer and Girl fetch troops when
invaders occupy village.

05135
HER HOUR OF RETRIBUTION (2000)
Cygnet
P: Henry P. Smither
D:S: Harold Brett
Dorothy Keen . . . . Jean Armstrong
Conway Ross . . . . Paul Redfern
Arthur D. Mavity . . . . Steve
Arthur Hutchings . . . . David Armstrong
Henry P. Smither . . . . Dr Thorn
DRAMA Polperro. Fishergirl elopes to London,
is abandoned, and returns as her sweetheart dies
in fire.

05136
THE INN ON THE HEATH (1300)
Jackdaw Films (Prieur)
D:S: Jakidawdra Melford
Jakidawdra Melford . . . . Girl
Mark Melford . . . . Stepfather
ADVENTURE 1746. Girl saves highwayman
from murderous stepfather.

05137
POLLY'S PROGRESS (1000)
Turner Films (Hepworth)
D: Larry Trimble
S: Hector Dion
Florence Turner . . . . Polly
Rex Davis . . . . The Youth
Hector Dion . . . . The Man
Dorothy Rowan . . . . The Woman
COMEDY Old and young couples get their love
affairs in a tangle.

05138
THROUGH THE VALLEY OF SHADOWS (3700)
Turner Films (KTC)
D: Larry Trimble
S: Florence Turner, Larry Trimble
Florence Turner . . . . Alice Cross
Edward Lingard . . . . Oscar Mailing
James Lindsay . . . . Foreman
Clifford Pembroke . . . . Dr Cross
Jean the Dog
DRAMA Doctor cures wife of brain fever after
she stabs her film star lover.

05139
THE SHEPHERD LASSIE OF ARGYLE (3000)
Turner Films (KTC)
D: Larry Trimble
S: Hector Dion
Florence Turner . . . . Mary Lachan
Rex Davis . . . . Alan MacPherson
Hector Dion . . . . The MacPherson
Clifford Pembroke . . . . Lachlan
Isobel Carma . . . . Isobel
Arnold Rayner . . . . The Maniac
Jean the Dog
DRAMA Scotland. Shepherd's daughter struck
dumb when her dog frustrates attack on her
by laird's mad brother.

05140
HER ONLY SON (1130) (U) retitled: A
WIDOW'S SON
Neptune (Browne)

D:S: Gerald Lawrence
Gregory Scott . . . . The Son
Fay Davis . . . . The Girl
Joan Ritz . . . . The Widow
WAR Widow's only son joins army and wins VC.

05141
TWIN TRUNKS (885) (U)
Neptune (Browne)
D: (Percy Nash)
Gregory Scott . . . . The Man
Joan Ritz . . . . The Woman
COMEDY Strangers take wrong trunks at
railway station, and fall in love.

05142
A DAUGHTER OF BELGIUM (1350) (U)
Barker
D: (F. Martin Thornton)
S: Rowland Talbot
WAR Girl avenges deaths of father and lover and
is saved by Highlanders.

05143
IN THE GRIP OF SPIES (3480) (U)
Big Ben Union (Pathe)
D: H.O. Martinek
S: L.C. MacBean
H.O. Martinek . . . . Dick Steele
Ivy Montford . . . . Kate Halifax
WAR Tec poses as lascar to save naval code
from Chinese crook.

05144
THE FALSE WIRELESS (3267) (U)
Big Ben Union (Pathe)
D: H.O. Martinek
S: L.C. MacBean
H.O. Martinek . . . . Officer
Ivy Montford . . . . His Sister
CRIME Ship's officer foils girl jewel thief while
sister holds gang at bay.

05145
THE GREAT GERMAN NORTH SEA TUNNEL
(3000)
Dreadnought
D: Frank Newman
FANTASY Germans build tunnel beneath North
Sea and invade England.

05146
CALLED BACK (3536) (U)
London (Fenning) Reissue: 1918
D: George L. Tucker
S: (NOVEL) Hugh Conway (PLAY) Comyns
Carr
Henry Ainley . . . . Gilbert Vaughan
Jane Gail . . . . Pauline March
Charles Rock . . . . Macari
George Bellamy . . . . Dr Manuel Ceneri
Vincent Clive . . . . Anthony March
Ackerman May . . . . Petroff
Judd Green . . . . Drunk
CRIME Blind husband of Italian doctor's mad
ward "sees" her brother murdered during a
trance.

05147
THE KING'S MINISTER (2922) (U)
London (Globe)
D: Harold Shaw
S: (PLAY) Cecil Raleigh
SC: Bannister Merwin
Edna Flugrath . . . . Lady Muriel Delissa
Arthur Holmes-Gore . . . . . . Braun
Langhorne Burton . . . . Lord Lincoln
Charles Rock . . . . Lord Draconsmere
George Bellamy . . . . Carl Wagner
Gerald Ames . . . . Aubrey Tremayne
CRIME German frames Prime Minister for
murder to force his daughter to steal treaty.

05148
TWO LITTLE BRITONS (3100) (U)
London (Gaumont)
D:S: Harold Shaw
Edna Flugrath
Charles Rock
George Bellamy
WAR Brussels. Foreign Secretary's children
unmask teacher as spy.

05149
HUNS OF THE NORTH SEA (2000)
P & M Films (Feature)
P: John M. Payne
D:S: Sidney Morgan
Harry Lorraine . . . . Norman Royce
Eva Norman . . . . Nora Wolfe
WAR Ramsgate. Spy's English wife stops him
from laying mines from fishing smack.

05150
THE WORLD AT WAR (2170) (U)
Motograph
P: Joseph Bamberger
D:S: James Youngdeer
Harry Lorraine . . . . Lt Daring
Lillian Wiggins . . . . Meg Dauntless
WAR Pilot catches spies and shoots Zeppelins
with new skyguns.

05151
SAVED BY THE UNION JACK (1950) (U)
Motograph
P: Joseph Bamberger
WAR

05152
THEIR ONLY SON (2583) (U)
Barker (Moss)
D: (Bert Haldane)
S: Rowland Talbot
Thos H. MacDonald . . . . . . Dick Cranston
Blanche Forsythe . . . . Mrs Cranston
Rolf Leslie . . . . Dr Cranston
WAR Doctor's disowned son becomes despatch
rider and when wounded is nursed by ex-wife.

05153
BY THE KAISER'S ORDERS (2880) (U)
Barker
D: F. Martin Thornton
S: Rowland Talbot
CRIME Unemployed man stops chemist spy
from using stolen F-ray to ignite explosives.

05154
THE KISS OF CLAY (1078)
Climax (ACL)
D: Stuart Kinder
DRAMA Paris. Sculptor's wife goes mad when
he stuffs her lover's mouth with clay.

05155
WAKE UP! OR, A DREAM OF TOMORROW
(3500)
Union Jack Photoplays (Eclair)
D:S: Lawrence Cowen
Bertram Burleigh
WAR Pacifist secretary of war converted after
dreaming England is invaded by 'Valvictians'.

05156
A PATRIOTIC ENGLISH GIRL (1000)
Zenith
D: Leedham Bantock
Agnes Glynne . . . . The Girl
WAR

NOV

05157
THE WHITE FEATHER (1063) (U)
B & C (DFSA)
D: Maurice Elvey
Douglas Payne
WAR Cowardly coster wounded saving officer's life.

05158
THE SPECIAL CONSTABLE (442) (U)
B & C (DFSA)
D: Ernest Batley
COMEDY Children put constable's arm-band on old man.

05159
CHRISTMAS WITHOUT DADDY (1192) (U)
B & C (DFSA)
D: Ernest Batley
Dorothy Batley . . . . Dolly
DRAMA Soldier's child dreams how her toys, once made in Germany, are now made in Britain.

05160
IT'S A LONG, LONG WAY TO TIPPERARY (2575) (U)
B & C (Apex)
D: Maurice Elvey
S: Eliot Stannard
Elizabeth Risdon . . . . Molly Molloy
James Russell . . . . Paddy
A.V. Bramble . . . . Mike Maloney
M. Gray Murray . . . . Sir Charles M'Hoy
Ernest Cox . . . . His Son
A.C. Ogan . . . . Mr. Molloy
WAR Irish Nationalist gives life to save rival, an Ulster Volunteer.

05161
HER LUCK IN LONDON (3900) (A)
B & C (Ashley)
D: Maurice Elvey
S: (PLAY) Charles Darrell
SC: Eliot Stannard
Elizabeth Risdon . . . . Nellie Harbourne
Fred Groves . . . . Richard Lenowen
A.V. Bramble . . . . Hon Gerald O'Connor
M. Gray Murray . . . . Stephen Harbourne
CRIME Gambler blackmails Lord's wife upon discovering his mistress is her mother.

05162
WINKY'S FIREWORKS (480) (U)
Bamforth (YSA)
D: Cecil Birch
Reggie Switz . . . . Winky
COMEDY Winky scares policemen by pretending fireworks are bombs.

05163
WINKY'S STRATAGEM (693) (U)
Bamforth (YSA)
D: Cecil Birch
Reggie Switz . . . . Winky
COMEDY Rejected suitor fakes the rescue of sweetheart's father.

05164
WINKY AT THE FRONT (660) (U)
Bamforth (YCC)
D: Cecil Birch
Reggie Switz . . . . Winky
COMEDY Winky joins army and is sent to France.

05165
WINKY'S JEALOUSY (898) (U)
Bamforth (YCC)

D: Cecil Birch
Reggie Switz . . . . Winky
COMEDY Winky misunderstands wife's letter to butcher and hires female detective.

05166
WINKY, BIGAMIST (650) (U)
Bamforth (YCC)
D: Cecil Birch
Reggie Switz . . . . Winky
COMEDY Winky's wife learns he spent evening at pantomime.

05167
HOW WINKY FOUGHT FOR A BRIDE (990) (U)
Bamforth (YCC)
D: Cecil Birch
Reggie Switz . . . . Winky
COMEDY Winky gets boxer to fight rival.

05168
ALGY GOES IN FOR PHYSICAL CULTURE (1016)
Bamforth (YCC)
D: Cecil Birch
COMEDY Weak dude takes up exercise.

05169
THE SCALLAWAG (2805) (A)
Big Ben Union (Pathe)
D:S: Lewin Fitzhamon
Constance Somers-Clarke . . . . Viola
CRIME PC catches son stealing jewels; son escapes jail, reforms, and leads dock strike.

05170
MEN WILL DECEIVE (775) (U)
Big Ben Union (Pathe)
D: (Lewin Fitzhamon)
COMEDY Drunk returns late from club and schemes to fool wife.

05171
S.O.S. (500) (U)
Burlingham Standard (NA)
D: Ethyle Batley
COMEDY German general frees lions and they turn on him.

05172
THE FULFILMENT OF THE LAW (98) (U)
Burlingham Standard (NA)
D: Ethyle Batley
DRAMA Rich man stabbed after wife leaves him for poor artist.

05173
BLACK MONDAY (560)
Captain Kettle (A & C)
S: C.J. Cutcliffe-Hyne
COMEDY Superstitious man's trouble caused by "lucky" horseshoe.

05174
THE MAN WITH A SCAR (1135)
Captain Kettle
S: C.J. Cutcliffe-Hyne
CRIME Roue stabs himself trying to kill rival.

05175
AN INNOCENT THIEF (880)
Captain Kettle (A & C)
S: C.J. Cutcliffe-Hyne
DRAMA Governess accused of theft when her charge hides necklace.

05176
THE DESERT ISLAND (1340)
Captain Kettle (A & C)

S: C.J. Cutcliffe-Hyne
ADVENTURE Child dreams he is shipwrecked and natives help him fight pirates.

05177
A HUSBAND'S LOVE (345) (U)
Clarendon
D: Toby Cooper
COMEDY "The final subtitle will greatly amuse those not in the joke."

05178
THE KANGO FIRE BRIGADE (530) (U)
Clarendon
D: Toby Cooper
COMEDY Misadventures of private fire brigade with old engine.

05179
THE PROOF OF THE PUDDING (580) (U)
Clarendon
D: Toby Cooper
S: Ernest Dangerfield
Winnie Dangerfield . . . . Winnie
Mrs Dangerfield . . . . Mother
COMEDY Children spoil mother's Xmas pudding and make one from coal.

05180
FOLLOWING THE TRAIL (440) (U)
Clarendon
D: Toby Cooper
COMEDY Policemen trail female spies.

05181
A KNIGHT IN ARMOUR (530) (U)
Clarendon
D: Toby Cooper
COMEDY Man steals girl's clothes and is foiled by dancer dressed as knight.

05182
A WARM RECEPTION (445) (U)
Clarendon
D: Toby Cooper
COMEDY Porter fights girl's pursuer, but picks wrong man.

05183
SWANKER AND THE WITCH'S CURSE (510) (U)
Cricks (DFSA)
D: (Edwin J. Collins)
TRICK Beggar woman's curse makes man's shopping come to life.

05184
THE PURSUIT OF VENUS (426) (U)
Cricks (DFSA)
D: (Edwin J. Collins)
TRICK Artist dreams statue of Venus comes to life.

05185
THE DEAD PAST RECALLED (1350) (U)
Barker
D: (F. Martin Thornton)
S: Rowland Talbot
WAR Colonel's disowned son gets amnesia saving nurse from fire and recovers saving wounded father.

05186
BRAVO KILTIES! (1066) (U)
Barker
D: (F. Martin Thornton)
S: Rowland Talbot
WAR Belgium. Soldier defends post office until Highlanders arrive.

05187
HIS SISTER'S HONOUR (1250) (U)
Barker (Walturdaw)
D: Bert Haldane
S: Rowland Talbot
Blanche Forsythe . . . . Beatrice
Moore Marriott . . . .
CRIME Nurse's dying confession clears soldier
brother of stealing necklace.

05188
THE SHIRKER'S NIGHTMARE (650)
Cherry Kearton
D:S: W.R. Booth
TRICK Dude's dream of Prussians and
Zeppelins makes him join Guards.

05189
A DAUGHTER OF FRANCE (2000)
Crusade (LIFT)
WAR Wounded soldier gives life to save French
girl, who then fetches Highlanders to save village.

05190
THE EARL OF CAMELOT (1250) *colour*
Aurora
P: William Friese-Greene
D:S: Henry Wilson
DRAMA 14th C. Earl's baby, adopted by
servant, grows up to become king's jester.

05191
SPORTS IN TOYLAND (310)
Excel
D: (Stuart Kinder)
TRICK Toys hold sports day and spell out
"Good Night".

05192
MRS SCRUBBS' DISCOVERY (600)
Harry Furniss (DFSA)
D:S: Harry Furniss
Mary Brough . . . . Mrs Scrubbs
COMEDY Washerwoman causes trouble by
finding note written on cuff.

05193
RIVAL REFLECTIONS (945)
Harry Furniss (DFSA) *Reissue:* 1916
D:S: Harry Furniss
Harry Furniss . . . . Artist
COMEDY Twins pose for rival artists who then
find themselves exhibiting identical portraits.

05194
WILDFLOWER (1050) (U)
Hepworth
D: (Warwick Buckland)
Chrissie White . . . . Priscilla Angelina
CRIME Gipsies adopt orphan girl who later warns
rich man of impending robbery.

05195
THE PET OF THE REGIMENT (725) (U)
Hepworth
D: (Frank Wilson)
Tom Powers . . . . Tommy Atkins
ANIMAL Soldier saves dog's life and it save his.

05196
SIMPKINS' LITTLE SWINDLE (500) (U)
Hepworth
D: (Hay Plumb)
Johnny Butt . . . . Simpkins
COMEDY Publican puts sponges in bottom of
mugs and jugs.

05197
THE BROTHERS (2100) (U)
Hepworth
D: (Frank Wilson)

Stewart Rome . . . . The Man
ROMANCE Man attempts suicide to win
sweetheart from cunning brother.

05198
THE AWAKENING OF NORA (1850) (U)
Hepworth
D: Larry Trimble
Alma Taylor . . . . Nora
Stewart Rome . . . . Her Husband
DRAMA Wife learns husband killed father in
brawl.

05199
THE BRIDGE DESTROYER (1075) (U)
Hepworth
D: (Frank Wilson)
Violet Hopson . . . . The Girl
Lionelle Howard . . . . The Spy
William Felton . . . . The Vicar
Eric Desmond . . . . The Scout
Johnny Butt . . . .
CRIME Vicar's daughter and scout stop spy
from blowing up bridge.

05200
ALADDIN; OR, A LAD OUT (925) (U)
Hepworth
D: (Hay Plumb)
S: Tom Powers
Tom Powers . . . . The Lad
Alma Taylor . . . . The Girl
FANTASY Art student dreams uncle's present
is Aladdin's magic lamp.

05201
PALS (1025) (U)
Hepworth
D: Frank Wilson
Chrissie White . . . . Flower Girl
CRIME Flower girl catches crook who framed
poor artist for theft.

05202
THE TERRIBLE TWO (850) (U)
Hepworth
D: (Hay Plumb)
COMEDY Tourists discover America.

05203
MR MEEK'S NIGHTMARE (450) (U)
Hepworth
D: (Hay Plumb)
Arthur Staples . . . . Mr Meek
Ruby Belasco . . . . Mrs Meek
TRICK Henpeck dreams he is everybody.

05204
THE QUARRY MYSTERY (1800) (U)
Hepworth
D: Cecil M. Hepworth
Stewart Rome
Violet Hopson
John MacAndrews
CRIME Detective proves blacksmith did not kill
debtor.

05205
TIME THE GREAT HEALER (2875) (U)
Hepworth
D: Cecil M. Hepworth
S: Blanche McIntosh
Tom Powers . . . . Dick/Harry
Alma Taylor . . . . Mary
Stewart Rome . . . . Peter
Chrissie White . . . . Alice
Violet Hopson . . . . Kate
DRAMA Jealous woman causes groom to desert
bride, causing her to suffer 25-year trance.

05206
MORPHIA THE DEATH DRUG (1950) (A)
Hepworth
D: Cecil M. Hepworth
S: Tom Powers
SC: Blanche McIntosh
Tom Powers . . . . The Boy
Alma Taylor . . . . The Girl
William Felton . . . . The Doctor
DRAMA Doctor forces secretary to become
morphia addict.

05207
HELD BY A CHILD (996) (U)
Martin Films (DFSA)
D: (Dave Aylott)
S: Ernest Dangerfield
Winnie Dangerfield . . . . Child
WAR France. Small girl holds Uhlans at bay
until troops arrive.

05208
ONE WINTER'S NIGHT (830) (U)
Martin (DFSA) *Reissue:* 1915, ONE CHRISTMAS
EVE
D: (Edwin J. Collins)
CRIME Man posing as Santa Claus catches burglar
and wins squire's daughter.

05209
SOME FISH! (662) (U)
Martin (DFSA)
D: Dave Aylott
TRICK Angler dreams of visit to Father
Neptune, who grills him.

05210
FOR THE HONOUR OF BELGIUM (985) (U)
Martin (DFSA)
D: (Edwin J. Collins)
WAR Belgium. British tourists help household
keep Uhlans at bay until troops arrive.

05211
THUMBS UP! (578) (U)
Martin (DFSA)
D: (Dave Aylott)
COMEDY Poet tries to get rid of sailor rival,
who is really his sweetheart's brother.

05212
PIMPLE'S LEAP TO FORTUNE (760) (U)
Folly Films (Phoenix)
D:S: Fred Evans, Joe Evans
Fred Evans . . . . Pimple
COMEDY Pimple dreams fairy gives him
unlimited wealth.

05213
THE CLOWNS OF EUROPE (795) (U)
Phoenix
D:S: Fred Evans, Joe Evans
Fred Evans
Joe Evans
COMEDY Harlequinade featuring Kaiser, Crown
Prince, and Prime Minister.

05214
INSPECTOR PIMPLE (355) (U)
Folly Films (Phoenix)
D:S: Fred Evans, Joe Evans
Fred Evans . . . . Pimple
COMEDY Police inspector saves sleepwalking
girl.

05215
HOW LIEUTENANT PIMPLE CAPTURED
THE KAISER (955) (U)
Folly Films (Phoenix) *Reissue:* 1916 (H & S)
D:S: Fred Evans, Joe Evans
Fred Evans . . . . Lt Pimple
COMEDY Lieut poses as porter and catches
Kaiser by balloon.

05216
THE TERRIBLE TWO ON THE WARPATH
(680) (U)
Phoenix
D:S: Joe Evans
Joe Evans . . . . Lemon
James Read . . . . Dash
COMEDY Flirty girl's suitor fights foreigner
with garden roller.

05217
THE TERRIBLE TWO ON THE TWIST
(795) (U)
Phoenix
D:S: Joe Evans
Joe Evans . . . . Lemon
James Read . . . . Dash
COMEDY Tramps find banknotes and pose as
foreigners to crash society.

05218
THE TERRIBLE TWO ON THE STAGE (780)
(U)
Phoenix
D:S: Joe Evans
Joe Evans . . . . Lemon
James Read . . . . Dash
COMEDY Bad actors retaliate upon unapprecia-
tive audience.

05219
SOME LITTLE THINGS OUR TOMMIES
LEAVE BEHIND THEM (320) (U)
New Agency
D: Arrigo Bocchi
TRICK Montage of children, flowers, and
Union Jack.

05220
ONE — THING AFTER ANOTHER (1000)
Turner Films (Hepworth)
D:S: Larry Trimble
Florence Turner . . . . Fleurette
COMEDY French maid tries to inject policeman
with love potion.

05221
FILM FAVOURITES (975) (U) USA:
FLORENCE TURNER IMPERSONATES FILM
FAVORITES
Turner Films (Hepworth) *Reissue:* 1916
D: Larry Trimble
S: Florence Turner
Florence Turner . . . . Lola
Larry Trimble . . . . Himself
COMEDY Maid dreams she is 'Pathe' heroine,
'Biograph' blonde, Ford Sterling, Sarah
Bernhardt, Mabel Normand, and Wild West
Billy.

05222
THE GIRL NEXT DOOR (926) (U)
Piccadilly-Pussyfoot (MP) *Reissue:* 1916
(Wardour)
D: Arthur Finn
Arthur Finn . . . . Harry
Winifred Fitch . . . . Doris
COMEDY Jealous girl fakes love scene with lay
figure.

05223
WAS HE A GENTLEMAN? (1030)
Piccadilly (MP) *Reissue:* 1916 (Wardour)
D: Arthur Finn
Arthur Finn . . . . The Lover
DRAMA Woman's lover poses as burglar to save
her from husband.

05224
ON THE RUSSIAN FRONTIER (3000)
Regent (MP)
P: Charles Weston, Arthur Finn
D: Charles Weston
Gordon Begg
WAR "Stirring European war drama"

05225
FACING THE ENEMY (3000)
Regent (MP)
P: Charles Weston, Arthur Finn
D: Charles Weston
Rowland Moore
Gordon Begg
WAR Soldier unknowingly kills his own
brother.

05226
NONE BUT THE BRAVE (3000)
Regent (Henderson)
P: Charles Weston, Arthur Finn
D: Charles Weston
WAR

05227
THE WAR BABY (2000)
Regent (MP)
P: Charles Weston, Arthur Finn
D: Charles Weston
WAR

05228
THE FAITHFUL BUTLER (2320)
Kineto
DRAMA Butler finds master's message in bottle
and saves him from shipwreck.

05229
SHIRTS (439) (U)
Tressograph (DFSA)
P: Henry Tress
D:S: Kelly Storrie
Kelly Storrie . . . . The Man
COMEDY Would-be victim turns tables on
practical jokers.

05230
HUBBY'S BEANO (359) (U)
Tressograph (DFSA)
P: Henry Tress
D:S: Kelly Storrie
Kelly Storrie . . . . Hubby
COMEDY Henpeck spends afternoon at
Brighton.

05231
THE HAPPY DUSTMEN'S CHRISTMAS (860)
Vaudefilms (A & C)
D: W.P. Kellino
S: Reuben Gillmer
Albert Egbert . . . . Bill
Seth Egbert . . . . Walter
COMEDY Dustmen win Christmas hamper and
have trouble cooking goose.

05232
GRAND CHRISTMAS HARLEQUINADE (850)
Vaudefilms (A & C)
D: W.P. Kellino
Sam T. Poluski
The Brothers Egbert
Will Kellino
COMEDY Traditional pantomime harlequinade.

05233
THE PET HEN (600)
Vaudefilms (A & C)
D: W.P. Kellino

S: Reuben Gillmer
COMEDY

05234
CAPTAIN NIGHTHAWK (1668) (U)
Neptune (Browne)
D:S: Gerald Lawrence
Gerald Lawrence . . . . Capt Nighthawk
Douglas Payne . . . . Charles Darrell
John East . . . . Squire
ADVENTURE. Man framed for poaching unmask
highwayman as squire's son.

05235
ALMOST HUMAN (620) (U)
Neptune (Browne)
D: (Percy Nash)
DRAMA Gorilla saves child from burning
house.

05236
HIS JUST DESERTS (1160) (U)
Neptune (Browne)
D:S: Gerald Lawrence
Frank Collins . . . . The Spy
Daisy Cordell . . . . His Wife
Gregory Scott . . . . The Manager
CRIME Spy fakes own death and poses as his
barber brother-in-law.

05237
ENOCH ARDEN (3450) (U)
Neptune (Renters)
D: Percy Nash
S: (POEM) Alfred Tennyson
SC: Gerald Lawrence
Gerald Lawrence . . . . Enoch Arden
Fay Davis . . . . Annie Lee
Ben Webster . . . . Philip Ray
May Whitty . . . . Miriam Lane
Gregory Scott . . . . Charles
John East . . . . John Lane
Douglas Payne . . . . The Priest
Joan Ritz . . . .
Douglas Cox . . . .
DRAMA Cornwall. Shipwrecked man returns to
find his wife has married her first love.

05238
CHRISTMAS DAY IN THE WORKHOUSE
(1000)
G.B. Samuelson (Imperial)
D: George Pearson
S: (POEM) George R. Sims
SC: Harry Engholm
Fred Paul . . . . The Pauper
DRAMA Pauper tells workhouse visitors of his
wife's death from starvation.

05239
A SON OF FRANCE (2000)
G.B. Samuelson (Royal)
D: George Pearson
S: Harry Engholm
Gerald Royston . . . . The Boy
Fred Paul . . . . The Father
WAR France. Boy fetches Highlanders in
time to save captured father.

05240
THE SMUGGLERS' CAVE (2100)
Cunard (George)
D: Wallett Waller
S: Harold Weston
Harold Weston . . . . Arthur Morris
Mary Manners . . . . Nell
Charles Cantley . . . . Ben Lee
CRIME Cornwall. Fishergirl poses as man to
save captured artist from smugglers.

05241
DANDY DONOVAN, THE GENTLEMAN
CRACKSMAN (2000)
Cunard (Jury)
D: Wallett Waller
Thomas Meigham . . . .   Dandy Donovan
Gladys Cooper . . . .   Mrs Ashworth
Owen Nares . . . .   Frank Ashworth
CRIME Woman kisses gem thief in error and he
gives himself up to placate her husband's
jealousy.

05242
THE CALL OF THE DRUM (2550)
Cunard (George)
D:S: Harold Weston
J.R. Tozer . . . .   Jimmy Leonard
Mary Manners . . . .   Muriel Walters
Henry G. Shaw . . . .   Harry Leonard
Slaine Mills . . . .   Carden
Gladys Ascot . . . .   Stella Crane
CRIME War hero learns borther is thief and
their mother repays stolen money.

05243
A CHRISTMAS CAROL (1340) (U)
London (Fenning)
D:SC: Harold Shaw
S: (NOVEL) Charles Dickens
Charles Rock . . . .   Ebenezer Scrooge
Edna Flugrath . . . .   Belle
George Bellamy . . . .   Bob Cratchit
Mary Brough . . . .   Mrs Cratchit
Franklyn Bellamy . . . .   Fred
Edward O'Neill . . . .   Jacob Marley
Arthur Cullin . . . .   Christmas Past
Windham Guise . . . .   Christmas Present
Assheton Tonge . . . .   Christmas Future
FANTASY Miser reformed by visions of past,
present, and future.

05244
THE TWO COLUMBINES (2036) (U)
London (Fenning)
D: Harold Shaw
S: Harold Shaw, George L. Tucker
Edna Flugrath . . . .   Columbine
Christine Rayner . . . .   Columbine
Charles Rock . . . .   Stage Doorman
Hubert Willis . . . .   Harlequin
George Bellamy . . . .   Pantaloon
John East . . . .   Policeman
Judd Green . . . .   Actor
Percy Nash . . . .   Stage Manager
DRAMA Dancer has accident, becomes cleaner,
and dies after dancing for child.

05245
V.C. (2942) (U) USA: THE VICTORIA CROSS
London (Jury) *Reissue:* 1918
D: Harold Shaw
S: Anne & Bannister Merwin
Ben Webster . . . .   Charles Oldwood
Edna Flugrath . . . .   Alice Bilson
Charles Rock . . . .   Col Oldwood
Douglas Munro . . . .   John Bilson
Gwynne Herbert . . . .   Mrs Oldwood
WAR Col's son dies a hero after learning father's
VC was an error.

05246
LONDON'S UNDERWORLD (3800)
Daring (Anderson)
Harry Lorraine . . . .   Detective Daring
CRIME Tec chases pearl thieves to Newhaven
and saves girl from warehouse fire.

05247
THE FRINGE OF WAR (3276) (U)
London (Globe)
D: George L. Tucket

S: Anne & Bannister Merwin
Jane Gail . . . .   Amy Marlow
Gerald Ames . . . .   Capt Gerald Anstey
Lewis Gilbert . . . .   Capt von Endig
WAR German captain blackmails general's wife
into stealing gun plans.

05248
BRITAIN'S SECRET TREATY (3000)
I.B. Davidson (KTC)
D:S: C: Charles Raymond
S: (Characters) Harry Blyth
Philip Kay . . . .   Sexton Blake
Lewis Carlton . . . .   Tinker
Thomas Canning . . . .   The Count
CRIME Count catches tec posing as foreign war
minister and hangs him over Beachy Head with
a fuse.

05249
THE KAISER'S SPIES (3000)
I.B. Davidson (KTC)
D:SC: Charles Raymond
S: (Characters) Harry Blyth
Philip Kay . . . .   Sexton Blake
Lewis Carlton . . . .   Tinker
CRIME Entymologist runs spy ring of bus
drivers from tower in Epping Forest.

05250
QUEENIE OF THE CIRCUS (2850)
Motograph
P: Joseph Bamberger
D: Charles Raymond
Lieut Pommerol . . . .   Julian
Joan Morgan . . . .   Queenie
Harry Lorraine . . . .   The Secretary
Joan Legge . . . .   The Maid
Martin Valmour . . . .   The Valet
Scott Clarke . . . .   Sir Edward Ware
Hazel Hastings . . . .   The Girl
Hen Pearce . . . .   The Gypsy
CRIME Usurper kidnaps child heiress and sells
her to travelling circus.

DEC

05251
TWO OF SCOTCH HOT (473)
A.R. Films (Prieur)
COMEDY Frenchmen pose as Scotsmen to
impress London girls.

05252
THE COURAGE OF A COWARD (911) (U)
B & C (DFSA)
D:S: Eliot Stannard
Elizabeth Risdon . . . .   The Wife
A.V. Bramble . . . .   The Burglar
Ernest Cox . . . .   The Husband
M. Gray Murray . . . .   The Doctor
CRIME Frightened woman stabs burglar while
husband ill in bed.

05253
THE BOY AND THE CHEESE (652) (U)
B & C (DFSA)
D: A.V. Bramble
COMEDY Church disturbed when boy puts
limburger in mother's muff.

05254
MADE IN GERMANY (483) (U)
B & C (DFSA)
D: (Ernest G. Batley)
COMEDY Children write "I am a German" on
father's back.

05255
THE SOUND OF HER VOICE (1065) (U)
B & C (DFSA)
D: Maurice Elvey

S: Eliot Stannard
Elizabeth Risdon . . . .   Violet Morne
A.V. Bramble . . . .   Henry Morne
ROMANCE Blind man learns wife is music hall
singer when he hears her voice on electrophone.

05256
THE IDOL OF PARIS (3400)
B & C (Ideal)
D: Maurice Elvey
S: (PLAY) Charles Darrell
SC: Eliot Stannard
Elizabeth Risdon . . . .   Flare-Flare
Fred Groves . . . .   Philippe Castelle
A.V. Bramble . . . .   Prince Serbius
Gordon Dennis . . . .   Victor Sancterre
Constance Walton . . . .   Madame
CRIME France. Crook demands his Princess
cousin in return for clearing Prince of theft
charge.

05257
MONEY WORKS WONDERS (598) (U)
B & C (DFSA)
D: (Ernest G. Batley)
COMEDY Nothing disturbs sleeping Jew save
the jingling of coins.

05258
A PLACE IN THE SUN (619) (U)
B & C (DFSA)
D: (Ethyle G. Batley)
WAR Allergory of cause of war and Germany's
ultimate defeat.

05259
WINKY'S CAT (650) (U)
Bamforth (YCC)
D: Cecil Birch
Reggie Switz . . . .   Winky
COMEDY Men pose as sailor and cat to sell cat
to widow.

05260
WINKY'S INVISIBLE INK (760) (U)
Bamforth (YCC)
D: Cecil Birch
Reggie Switz . . . .   Winky
COMEDY Girl's father will give his consent if
her suitor can contrive to get a letter to her.

05261
WINKY'S CARVING KNIFE (497) IU)
Bamforth (YCC)
D: Cecil Birch
Reggie Switz . . . .   Winky
COMEDY Winky describes to his drinking
friends how he fought Germans.

05262
BIRDS OF A FEATHER PLOT TOGETHER
(695) (U)
Bamforth (YCC)
D: Cecil Birch
Reggie Switz . . . .   Winky
COMEDY Baker, doctor, and publican conspire
to put thirst powder in bread.

05263
PAPA'S LITTLE WEAKNESS (667) (U)
Bamforth (YCC)
D: Cecil Birch
COMEDY Elopers scare girl's father by faking
thunderstorm.

05264
PEPPERING HIS OWN PORRIDGE (630) (U)
Bamforth (YCC)
D: Cecil Birch
Reggie Switz . . . .   Winky
COMEDY Husband bribes poor man to pose as
wife's rich uncle.

05265
WHO'S WHICH? (630) (U)
Bamforth (YCC)
D: Cecil Birch
COMEDY Henpeck mistaken for army deserter.

05266
JACK SPRATT AS A WOUNDED PRUSSIAN
(900) (U)
Clarendon
D: Toby Cooper
COMEDY Surgeon pretends to amputate
sailor's leg.

05267
JACK SPRATT AS A SPECIAL CONSTABLE
(865) (U)
Clarendon
D: Toby Cooper
COMEDY Sailor catches burglar in drunkard's
house.

05268
BRINGING IT HOME TO HIM (904) (U)
Clarendon
D: Toby Cooper
COMEDY Friends fake German invasion to
make slacker enlist.

05269
THE GARDENER'S DAUGHTER (1460) (U)
Clarendon
D: Wilfred Noy
S: (POEM) Alfred Tennyson
Norah Chaplin . . . . Rose
ROMANCE Girl drowns and artist paints her
portrait from memory.

05270
JACK SPRATT AS A WAR LORD (880) (U)
Clarendon
D: Toby Cooper
COMEDY Sailor dons Prussian uniform and
sends messages in shells.

05271
IN PEACE AND WAR (2365) (U)
Clarendon
D: Wilfred Noy
Dorothy Bellew . . . . The Girl
Evan Thomas . . . . The Man
WAR Captured midshipman freed by his German
half-brother in return for relinquishing girl they
love.

05272
HAVE A CIGAR (493) (U)
Cricks
D: (Charles Calvert)
COMEDY Explosive cigars almost ruin man's
chances with girl's father.

05273
THE COWARD (1093) (U)
Cricks
D: (Charles Calvert)
WAR Poacher attacks lieut, enlists to escape
justice, and saves lieut's life.

05274
PICKLED HISTORY (400)
Captain Kettle (A & C)
S: C.J. Cutcliffe-Hyne
COMEDY Burlesque of various historical
events.

05275
SAVED FROM THE SPY (1090)
Captain Kettle (A & C)
S: C.J. Cutcliffe-Hyne
CRIME Boy scout stops spy from blowing up
troop train.

05276
THE NATION'S PERIL (1280)
Excel (Prieur)
D: (Stuart Kinder)
WAR Spy persuades girl to drug fiance and steal
chart of East Coast minefields.

05277
THE FLAPPER AND THE FAN (450)
Crusade (U)
TRICK Girl finds magic fan which grants wishes.

05278
THE BITER BIT (583)
Crusade (Tyler)
COMEDY Girl overhears her rejected suitor's
plot for revenge.

05279
FUN ON THE SANDS AT BLACKPOOL
(1500) also: FUN AT THE SEASIDE
Blackpool Town Hall (KTC)
August . . . . Nephew
September . . . . Nephew
E. Hannaford . . . . Uncle
E. Alrag . . . . Aunt
COMEDY Family's misadventures at
Blackpool beach and funfair.

05280
A BOX OF MATCHES (396)
Humpty Dumpty Films (Prieur)
TRICK Animated match sticks.

05281
TOMMY'S MONEY SCHEME (900) (U)
Hepworth
D: (Frank Wilson)
Eric Desmond . . . . Tommy
Stewart Rome . . . . Father
PATHOS Sacked thief's son raises money for
dying sister.

05282
SNOBS (1000)
Turner Films (Hepworth)
D:S: Larry Trimble
Florence Turner . . . . Gertie Childs
COMEDY Waitress poses as countess and weds
millionaire who loses his money.

05283
SHOPGIRLS; OR, THE GREAT QUESTION
(3575) (A)
Turner Films (Ideal)
D: Larry Trimble
S: Hector Dion
Florence Turner . . . . Judith
Sidney Sinclair . . . . Archer
Richard Steele . . . . James Walker
Hector Dion . . . . John Carter
Rhoda Grey . . . . Grace
DRAMA Drapery assistant tries to sell herself to
employer to save her sister from shame.

05284
GETTING HIS OWN BACK (550) (U)
Hepworth
D: (Hay Plumb)
Chrissie White . . . . Flossie
COMEDY Suitor breaks professor's vase and has
it repaired.

05285
HIS GREAT OPPORTUNITY (1600) (U)
Hepworth
D: (Warwick Buckland)
Tom Powers . . . . The Understudy
Alma Taylor . . . . The Actress
Edward Lingard . . . . The Actor
CRIME Sacked actor tries to kill understudy
by putting real bullet in property gun.

05286
SIMPKINS, SPECIAL CONSTABLE (500) (U)
Hepworth
D: (Hay Plumb)
Johnny Butt . . . . Simpkins
COMEDY Constable helps professor guard post
office against spy.

05287
DESPISED AND REJECTED (2075) (U)
Hepworth
D: (Frank Wilson)
Stewart Rome . . . . Artist
Chrissie White . . . . Model
Lionelle Howard . . . . Man
ROMANCE Spurned model brings fame to
poor drunkard who paints her.

05288
THE TERRIBLE TWO JOIN THE POLICE
FORCE (775) (U)
Hepworth
D: (Hay Plumb)
COMEDY Policemen guard Rajah's jewels and
catch thieves.

05289
THE DOUBLE EVENT (900) (U)
Hepworth
D: (Warwick Buckland)
Stewart Rome . . . . Suitor
Alma Taylor . . . . Ward
SPORT Usurper bets ward's suitor he will not
win air race and steeplechase.

05290
OH MY AUNT! (1525) (U)
Hepworth
D: Cecil M. Hepworth
Tom Powers . . . . Suitor
Alma Taylor . . . . Girl
Ruby Belasco . . . . Mother
Dorothy Rowan . . . . Aunt
COMEDY Aunt drinks rejuvenating elixir and
falls for niece's fiance.

05291
THE MAN FROM INDIA (1925) (U)
Hepworth
D: Frank Wilson
S: Wernham Ryott (Stewart Rome)
Stewart Rome . . . . Rajah
Violet Hopson . . . . Girl
Lionelle Howard . . . . Spy
Warwick Buckland . . . . Father
Ruby Belasco . . . . Mother
William Felton . . . . Footman
WAR Rajah exposes club owner as spy and kills
him in battle.

05292
THEY SAY — LET THEM SAY (800) (U)
Hepworth
D: (Warwick Buckland)
Stewart Rome . . . . The Soldier
Violet Hopson . . . . The Sister
Lionelle Howard
DRAMA Gossips suspect soldier's sister of being
mother of baby left on step.

05293
JOHN LINWORTH'S ATONEMENT (625) (U)
Hepworth
D: (Frank Wilson)
Stewart Rome . . . . John Linworth
Chrissie White . . . . Mary Linworth
Warwick Buckland . . . . Mr. Merton
Ruby Belasco . . . . Mrs Merton
John MacAndrews . . . . The Beggar
DRAMA Clerk robs boss's safe for sick sister's
sake and saves him from beggar's attack.

05294
A BOTHER ABOUT A BOMB (550) (U)
Hepworth
D: (Hay Plumb)
COMEDY Spies try to blow up London Bridge.

05295
THE LIE (1000) (U)
Hepworth
D: Frank Wilson
S: Lionelle Howard
Stewart Rome . . . . Dr Hume
Chrissie White . . . . Doris Sloane
Lionelle Howard . . . . Frank Forrester
DRAMA Jealous doctor dies after telling rival
he will die.

05296
LIFE'S DARK ROAD (2175) (U)
Hepworth
D: (Frank Wilson)
S: J. Clay Powers
Stewart Rome . . . . George Winton
Tom Powers . . . . The Lover
Violet Hopson . . . . Helen Winton
DRAMA Ex-convict becomes butler to couple
who adopted his daughter, and saves her from
cad.

05297
TILLY AT THE FOOTBALL MATCH (600)
(U)
Hepworth
D: (Hay Plumb)
Alma Taylor . . . . Tilly
Chrissie White . . . . Sally
COMEDY Tramp blamed when girls take
football shield and prize cake.

05298
THE FIGHTING STRAIN OF OLD ENGLAND
(2858) (U)
Martin (Standard)
D:S: Dave Aylott
George Wynn . . . . Jack Aliston
Joan West . . . . Molly Warde
R. Harley West . . . . Sgt Warde
Ashmore J. Vincent . . . . Col Aliston
Winifred Dangerfield . . . . . . Jack (child)
WAR Colonel's son stolen by gipsy later meets
his father in war.

05299
BIFF! BANG!! WALLOP!!! (839)
Martin (DFSA)
D: (Dave Aylott)
TRICK Firework maker blown to Barbary and
sold as slave.

05300
AUBREY'S BIRTHDAY (451) (U)
Martin (DFSA)
D: (Edwin J. Collins)
TRICK "An ingenious trick comic."

05301
CONSTABLE COPPEM AND THE SPY PERIL
(526) (U)
Martin (DFSA)
D: (Edwin J. Collins)
COMEDY Zealous policeman tracks spies.

05302
SHA (W) LY NOT (600) (U)
Martin (DFSA)
D: (Dave Aylott)
TRICK Stagehand uses magician's shawl to make
objects disappear.

05303
MIKE MURPHY VC (592) (U)
Martin (DFSA)
D: Dave Aylott
Fred Percy . . . . Mike Murphy
COMEDY Mike dreams of German invasion
and captures the Kaiser.

05304
AH! AHH!!TISHOO!!! (478) (U)
Martin (DFSA) *Reissue:* 1916, SOME SNUFF
D: (Edwin J. Collins)
TRICK Boy's magic snuff causes father to
sneeze house to pieces.

05305
A JOKE IN JERKS (524) (U)
Martin (DFSA)
D: (Dave Aylott)
COMEDY Boys apply electric battery to gas
and water pipes.

05306
THE NEW DENTIST (684) (U)
Martin (DFSA)
D: (Edwin J. Collins)
COMEDY Dentist quarrels with chemist over
his sister.

05307
LOVE AT THE CIRCUS (570) (U)
Burlingham Standard (NA)
D: Ethyle Batley
COMEDY Rejected clown causes trouble for
ringmaster.

05308
FRIENDS V. FOES (220) (U)
New Agency
D: Arrigo Bocchi
TRICK Montage of warring nations, bulldog and
Union Jack.

05309
OUR BABY (490) (U)
Piccadilly-Pussyfoot (MP) *Reissue:* 1916 (Wardour)
D: Arthur Finn
Gordon Begg . . . . Mr Brown
COMEDY Father and bachelor friends try to
quieten baby.

05310
YOUR NAME BROWN? (1080) (U)
Piccadilly-Pussyfoot (MP) *Reissue:* 1916
(Wardour)
D: Arthur Finn
Gordon Begg . . . . Major Brown
COMEDY Tec mistakes major for faithless hus-
band with same name.

05311
WHAT A KISS WILL DO (663)
Piccadilly-Pussyfoot (MP) *Reissue:* 1916
(Wardour)
D: Arthur Finn
Arthur Finn . . . . Dick Spend
Gordon Begg . . . . Father
COMEDY Spendthrift's sweetheart foils
bailiff.

05312
SANTA CLAUS VC (941)
Pennant Films (YCC)
DRAMA "Dead" soldier returns and traces
evicted family through pet dog.

05313
THE BUGLE BOY OF LANCASHIRE (3000)
Regent (MP)
P: Charles Weston, Arthur Finn
D: Charles Weston
WAR Namur. Bank manager framed for
robbery enlists with fiancee's brother.

05314
THE DOCTOR'S CRIME (3000)
Regent (MP)
P: Charles Weston, Arthur Finn
Charles Weston
CRIME

05315
THE ROAD TO CALAIS (3000)
Regent (MP)
P: Charles Weston, Arthur Finn
D: Charles Weston
Rowland Moore
Guy Rupert Lane
Winifred Fitch
Frank R. Growcott
E. Scott Arundell
WAR Captured despatch rider escapes and saves
French dancer from Uhlans.

05316
SELF-ACCUSED (3000)
Regent (MP)
P: Charles Weston, Arthur Finn
D:S: Charles Weston
Arthur Finn
Charles Weston
CRIME Burglar clears man accused of
shooting count's rival.

05317
BATTLING BROWN OF BIRMINGHAM (3000)
Regent (MP)
P: Charles Weston, Arthur Finn
D: Charles Weston
Rowland Moore
Alesia Leon
SPORT Girl poses as man to enter ring and
persuade boxer lover to win.

05318
THE YOUNG SAMARITAN (700)
Searchlight (U)
CRIME Small child reforms thief.

05319
THE REFORMATION OF CHRISTOPHER
WINKLE (843)
Searchlight (U)
COMEDY

05320
THE SPY (985)
Searchlight (U)
CRIME Woman tends wounded spy and lets
him go after learning he killed her son.

05321
ARCHIBALD IN A TANGLE (764)
Phoenix Film Agency
D: (Joe Evans)
COMEDY Clumsy man tries to dance at Tango
Tea.

05322
PIMPLE AND THE STOLEN PLANS (975) (U)
Folly Films (Phoenix)
D:S: Fred Evans, Joe Evans
Fred Evans . . . . Pimple
Joe Evans . . . . Raffles
COMEDY Crooks pardoned by PM when they
save plans from spies.

05323
PIMPLE ON FOOTBALL (640) (U)
Folly Films (Phoenix)
D:S: Fred Evans, Joe Evans
Fred Evans . . . . Pimple
COMEDY Football enthusiast tries to emulate
local champion.

05324
YOUNG PIMPLE'S FROLICS (460) (U)
Folly Films (Phoenix)
D:S: Fred Evans, Joe Evans
Tommy Collet . . . . Young Pimple
COMEDY Boy poses as escaped gorilla.

05325
THE ADVENTURES OF PIMPLE — THE
SPIRITUALIST (810) (U)
Folly Films (Phoenix) *Reissue:* 1916 (H & S)
D:S: Fred Evans, Joe Evans
Fred Evans . . . . Pimple
Joe Evans . . . . Raffles
COMEDY Crooks pose as a medium and a
spirit to fool an old woman.

05326
THE ADVENTURES OF PIMPLE — TRIBLY
(1245) (U) also: TRILBY BY PIMPLE AND CO.

Folly Films (Phoenix)
D:S: Fred Evans, Joe Evans
Fred Evans . . . . Trilby
Joe Evans . . . . Svengali
COMEDY Hypnotist makes girl singer star of
Covent Garden.

05327
THE TERRIBLE TWO ON THE WAIT (790)
Phoenix
D:S: James Read
Joe Evans . . . . Lemon
James Read . . . . Dash
COMEDY Couple get work as footmen and wait
on family for dinner.

05328
THE TERRIBLE TWO ON THE WANGLE (705)
Phoenix
D:S: James Read
Joe Evans . . . . Lemon
James Read . . . . Dash
COMEDY Broke lodgers stage burglary and
thwart real one.

05329
THE TERRIBLE TWO IN LUCK (790)
Phoenix
D:S: James Read
Joe Evans . . . . Lemon
James Read . . . . Dash
COMEDY Couple pose as ghosts to scare
each other and find treasure.

05330
THE TERRIBLE TWO, KIDNAPPERS (850)(U)
Phoenix
D:S: James Read
Joe Evans . . . . Lemon
James Read . . . . Dash
COMEDY Villain hires two crooks to kidnap
girl.

05331
POTTED PANTOMIMES (2000)
Vaudefilms (Gaumont) *Reissue:* 1915
D: W.P. Kellino
The Brothers Egbert
The Famous Kellinos
Lillian Russell
Daisy Dormer
COMEDY Child visualises Goody Twoshoes,
Sinbad, Cinderella.

05332
THE LITTLE MATCH GIRL (500) (U)
Neptune (Browne)
D: (Percy Nash)
S: (STORY) Hans Anderson
John East . . . . Warder
PATHOS Poor child strikes matches for
warmth and dies in snow.

05333
THE YULE LOG (860) (U)
Neptune (Browne)
D: Jack Denton
S: John East, Brian Daly
John East . . . . Father
ROMANCE Names carved on yule log reunite
elopers with parents.

05334
THE STEEPLEJACKS (840) (U)
Neptune (Browne)
D: (Percy Nash)
DRAMA Steeplejack fights foreman over
daughter and falls to death.

05335
BILL'S RISE IN THE WORLD (600) (U)
Neptune (Browne)
D: (Percy Nash)
COMEDY Workman's cigarette causes explosion
and he feigns death to collect whipround.

05336
OVER THE GARDEN WALL (780)(U)
Neptune (Browne)
D: (Percy Nash)
John East . . . . Farmer
COMEDY Farmers heal quarrel when their
children elope.

05337
IN THE RANKS (3945) (U)
Neptune (Jury)
D: Percy Nash
S: (PLAY) George R. Sims, Henry Pettitt
SC: John East, Brian Daly
Gregory Scott . . . . Ned/John Drayton
Daisy Cordell . . . . Jocelyn Hare
James Lindsay . . . . Capt Holcroft
Peggy Hyland . . . . Barbara Herrick
Douglas Payne . . . . Richard Belton
Frank Tennant . . . . Capt Wynter
Joan Ritz . . . . Ruth Herrick
Edward Sass . . . . Gidgeon Blake
Jack Denton . . . . Joe Buzzard
John East . . . . Farmer Herrick
Douglas Cox . . . . Sgt Searle
Ruby Wyndham . . . . Mrs Buzzard
CRIME Steward frames captain's adopted son
for shooting his colonel.

05338
KISMET (4000) (U)
Zenith
D: Leedham Bantock
S: (PLAY) Edward Knoblock
Oscar Asche . . . . Hajj
Lily Brayton . . . . Marsinah
Herbert Grimwood . . . . Wasir Mansur
Frederick Worlock . . . . Caliph
Caleb Porter . . . . White Sheik
Suzanne Sheldon . . . . Kut-al-Kulub
Bessie Major . . . . Nurse
ROMANCE Baghdad. Daughter of beggar posing
as prince loves caliph posing as gardener.

05339
THE INCOMPARABLE BELLAIRS (3400) (U)
USA: THE INCOMPARABLE MISTRESS
BELLAIRS
London (Renters)
D: Harold Shaw
S: (PLAY) Agnes & Egerton Castle (THE BATH
COMEDY)
SC: Bannister Merwin
Edna Flugrath . . . . Kitty Bellairs
Gregory Scott . . . . Jernigan
Mercy Hatton . . . . Rachael Page
Wyndham Guise . . . . Dennis O'Hara
Lewis Gilbert . . . . Stafford

Christine Rayner . . . . Lydia
Wallace Bosco . . . . Lord Mandeville
Hubert Willis . . . . Capt Spencer
Florence Wood . . . . Lady Dare-Stanme
ROMANCE Period. Maid plots to wed mistress to
poor Irishman instead of rich Lord.

05340
LIL O' LONDON (2100) (U)
London (Jury)
D: Harold Shaw
S: Bannister Merwin
Ben Webster . . . . Tommy Mordaunt
Edna Flugrath Lil
Douglas Munro . . . . The Bull
Helen Green . . . . Diana Carruthers
Wyndham Guise . . . . Wilson
Gwynne Herbert . . . . Mrs Mordaunt
Brenda Patrick . . . . Baby
CRIME Affianced socialite falls for cockney he
shelters in return for saving him from burglar
father.

05341
LIBERTY HALL (3600) (U)
London (Jury)
D: Harold Shaw
S: (PLAY) R.C. Carton
SC: Bannister Merwin
Ben Webster . . . . Sir Hartley Chilworth
Edna Flugrath . . . . . . Ann Chilworth
O.B. Clarence . . . . . . Todman Crafer
Ranee Brooks . . . . . . Blanche Chilworth
Douglas Munro. . . . . . Briginshaw
Langhorne Burton . . . Gerald Haringay
Gwynne Herbert . . . . . Mrs Crafer
Hubert Willis . . . . Pedrick
COMEDY Rich heir poses as bookseller's
lodger to save cousins from lustful tradesman.

05342
THE REVENGE OF MR THOMAS ATKINS
(2000) (U)
London (Globe)
D: George Loane Tucker
S: Anne & Bannister Merwin
Frank Stanmore . . . . Tommy Atkins
Gerald Ames . . . . The Spy
Judd Green . . . . Gen von Gutz
Hubert Willis . . . . Colonel
George Bellamy . . . . Manservant
COMEDY Spies mistake colonel's golf score for
secret code message.

05343
TRANSFORMATIONS (470)
Kineto
D: (F. Percy Smith)
TRICK Pictures of famous person transform
into related objects.

05344
THE ARTIST AND THE GIRL (1000)
Kineto
ADVENTURE Brighton. Villager wins girl after
saving artist rival from cliff.

05345
THE LAST OF THE SMUGGLERS (2005)
Kineto
ADVENTURE Brighton. Tec saves girl from
snake and she saves him from smugglers.

05346
THE LIFE OF LORD ROBERTS VC (3000)
G.B. Samuelson (Imperial)
D: George Pearson
S: George Person, Harry Engholm
Hugh Nicholson . . . . Lord Roberts
Agnes Glynne
Fred Paul
HISTORY Biography of professional soldier
(1832-1914).

05347
BUILDING A CHICKEN HOUSE (1150)
Sunny South (Walturdaw)
D: F.L. Lyndhurst
S: (SKETCH) Will Evans
Will Evans . . . . The Man
Arthur Conquest . . . . The Neighbour
COMEDY Man tries to build chicken house
despite interfering neighbour.

05348
THE JOCKEY (1150)
Sunny South (Walturdaw)
D: F.L. Lyndhurst
S: (SKETCH) Will Evans
Will Evans . . . . The Jockey
Arthur Conquest
George Graves
COMEDY Jockey starts in 2.30 race, leaves
track, and wins 4.30.

05349
MOVING A PIANO (1150)
Sunny South (Walturdaw)
D: F.L. Lyndhurst
S: (SKETCH) Will Evans
Will Evans . . . . The Man
Arthur Conquest . . . . . The Helper
COMEDY Slapstick misadventures while men
try to move piano.

05350
THE SHOWMAN'S DREAM (1150)
Sunny South (Walturdaw)
D: F.L. Lyndhurst
.S: (SKETCH) Will Evans
Will Evans . . . . The Showman
Arthur Conquest . . . . . The Artiste
COMEDY Showman let down by artistes dreams
he stages show.

05351
TINCTURE OF IRON (1150)
Sunny South (Walturdaw)
D: F.L. Lyndhurst
S: (SKETCH) Will Evans
Will Evans
Arthur Conquest
COMEDY

05352
MERMAIDS OF THE THAMES (357) (U)
Tressograph (DFSA)
P: Henry Tress
D: Kelly Storrie
Kelly Storrie . . . . The Old Man
Pansy Seaby . . . . The Swimmer
COMEDY Girl swimming champion foils aged
flirt.

05353
COME BACK TO HEARING (468) (U)
Tressograph (DFSA)
P: Henry Tress
D: Kelly Storrie
Kelly Storrie . . . . The Deaf Man
COMEDY Deaf man buys hearing aid but finds
he prefers to be deaf.

05354
THE BUSKER'S REVENGE (500)
Tressograph
P: Henry Tress
D: Kelly Storrie
Kelly Storrie . . . . The Busker
COMEDY "Not a bit like the old English style
of comics."

05355
24 CARAT (1300)
Barker (KTC)
D: (F. Martin Thornton)
S: Rowland Talbot
WAR Adventures of Scottish Highlander in
France.

05356
THE GURKA'S REVENGE (1280) (A)
Barker (Dominion)
D: A.E. Coleby
S: Rowland Talbot
WAR India. Gurka saves life of German trader
who then strangles Ghurka's wife while trying
to rape her.

05357
RED CROSS PLUCK (1195) (U)
Burlingham Standard (New Agency)
D: Ethyle Batley
Martin Valmour . . . . Lt Jack Gordon
WAR France. Nurse swims to warn troops of
impending attack.

05358
ISLAND JESS (1600)
GTG Film Co (YCC)
D: F.C. Tudor
Alesia Leon . . . . Jess
Marsh Allen . . . . Henry Ackland
Joyce Templeton . . . .
ADVENTURE Artist's jealous wife drowns
while trying to kill island girl.

05359
DR PAXTON'S LAST CRIME (2170) (U)
P & M Films
P: John M. Payne
D:S: Sidney Morgan
CRIME

05360
FULL UP (580)
Broadwest (Tyler)
P:D: Walter West
COMEDY

05361
THE THICK AND THIN OF IT (580)
Broadwest (Tyler)
P:D. Walter West
COMEDY

1915

JAN

05362
AMUSING THE KIDS (667) (U)
B & C (DFSA)
D: (Ernest Batley)
S: Ernest Dangerfield
Winnie Dangerfield . . . . . . The Child
COMEDY Old men are upset by childrens'
party.

05363
THERE'S GOOD IN EVERYONE (895) (A)
B & C (DFSA)
D: Maurice Elvey
S: Eliot Stannard
Elizabeth Risdon . . . . Beatrice Maybrook
Fred Groves . . . . Hon Reginald
A.V. Bramble . . . . Marquis
M. Gray Murray . . . . Mr Maybrook
ROMANCE Nobleman foils marquis's compro-
mise plot by secretly marrying manicurist.

05364
A HONEYMOON FOR THREE (3960) (U)
B & C (KTC)
D: Maurice Elvey
S: Dr Charles
SC: Eliot Stannard
Charles Hawtrey . . . . . Prince Ferdinand
Elizabeth Risdon . . . . . Molly Van Dam
Fred Groves . . . . Cornelius P. Van Dam
A.V. Bramble . . . . Duke of Monte Casa
Ruth Mackay . . . . Mme Alova
Compton Coutts . . . . . Detective
M. Gray Murray . . . . .
Edith Evans . . . .
M. Gray Murray . . . .
Edith Evans . . . .
COMEDY Incognito prince foils detectives by
switching identities with newlywed American
millionaire.

05365
A HAIR-RAISING EPISODE (558) (U)
B & C (DFSA)
D: (Ernest Batley)
COMEDY Bald man tries fertilizer on his head
and finds fiancee is bald.

05366
A DAY OF REST (540) (U)
Clarendon
D: (Toby Cooper)
COMEDY Boy ties grandfather's leg to
boarhound.

05367
SENTIMENTAL TOMMY 9675) (U)
Clarendon
D: (Toby Cooper)
COMEDY Territorials dress up as girls and are
mistaken for spies.

05368
THE UNMENTIONABLES (465) (U)
Clarendon
D: (Toby Cooper)
Dorothy Bellew . . . . Understudy
COMEDY Poor understudy makes her room
look smart to impress manager.

05369
SOME ACTORS (535) (U)
Cricks (DFSA)
D:S: W.P. Kellino
COMEDY Stage producer has trouble with
aspiring actors.

05370
EXTRAVAGANT MOLLY (624) (U)
Cricks (DFSA)
D:S: W.P. Kellino
COMEDY Poor couple fake furniture to impress
rich uncle.

05371
POTE'S POEM (427) (U)
Cricks (DFSA)
D:S: W.P. Kellino
COMEDY Poet uses heated penny to get rid of
noisy organ-grinder.

05372
THE WRONG HOUSE (638) (U)
Cricks (DFSA)
D:S: W.P. Kellino
Sam T. Poluski
The Kellinos
COMEDY "Introducing some clever acrobats
and dancers."

05373
THE LURE OF THE WORLD (1200)
Cricks (DFSA)
D: (Charles Calvert)
DRAMA Author robs house of his wife's lover
and saves her child from fire.

05374
BE SURE YOUR SINS retitled: THE CANKER
OF JEALOUSY (2900) (A)
Hepworth (KTC)
D: Cecil M. Hepworth
S: Blanche McIntosh
Alma Taylor . . . . Maggie White
Stewart Rome . . . . Dr Wynne
Tom Powers . . . . Leo Garth
Violet Hopson . . . . Mrs Wynne
Eric Desmond . . . . Reggie Wynne
Ruby Belasco . . . . Mrs White
CRIME Doctor strangles his wife's lover, then
gives his life to save diseased baby.

05375
THE PAINTED LADY BETTY (1025) (U)
Hepworth
D: Frank Wilson
S: C.C.G. Bennett
Tom Powers . . . . The Man
Alma Taylor . . . . The Girl
Chrissie White . . . . Lady Betty
ROMANCE Lyme Regis. Man falls for visiting
Londoner but returns to sweetheart.

05376
A LOSING GAME (500) (U)
Hepworth
D: (HayPlumb)
Violet Hopson . . . . The Girl
Chrissie White . . . . The Friend
COMEDY Girls try to lose smelly gorgonzola
cheese.

05377
THE MAN WHO WASN'T (550) (U)
Hepworth
D: (Hay Plumb)
S: Lionelle Howard
Lionelle Howard . . . . The Husband
TRICK Drunk dreams he becomes invisible.

05378
THE HAUNTING OF SILAS P. GOULD (1000)
Ivy Close Films (Hepworth)
D: Elwin Neame
Ivy Close . . . . Heiress
COMEDY Heiress sells home to American
millionaire and poses as ghost to frighten him
away.

05379
THE SHEPHERD OF SOULS (1525) (U)
Hepworth
D: Frank Wilson
S: Wernham Ryott (Stewart Rome)
Stewart Rome . . . . Minister
Violet Hopson . . . . Girl
Henry Vibart . . . . Magistrate
Ruby Belasco . . . . Wife
CRIME Magistrate's second wife robs him and
frames maid, who turns out to be his daughter.

05380
BARNABY RUDGE (5325) (U)
Hepworth (KTC)
D: SC: Thomas Bentley
S: (NOVEL) Charles Dickens
Tom Powers . . . . Barnaby Rudge
Violet Hopson . . . . Emma Haredale
Stewart Rome . . . . Maypole Hugh
Chrissie White . . . . Dolly Varden
Lionelle Howard . . . . Edward Chester
John MacAndrews . . . . Geoffrey Haredale
Henry Vibart . . . . Sir John Chester
Harry Gilbey . . . . Lord George Gordon
Harry Royston . . . . Dennis
Harry Buss . . . . Simon Tappertit
William Felton . . . . Mr. Rudge
William Langley . . . . Gabriel Varden
DRAMA 1780. Murderer's idiot son, jailed as an
anti-Catholic rioter, is pardoned on the scaffold.

05381
THE LITTLE MOTHER (1025) (U)
Hepworth
D: (Warwick Buckland)
Chrissie White . . . . The Orphan
DRAMA Orphan works to send her brother to
university and marries to save him from prison.

05382
THE MIDNIGHT MAIL (825) (U)
Hepworth
D: (Warwick Buckland)
CRIME Maid signals to engine-driver sweetheart
to fetch police and catch burglars.

05383
THE MAN WITH THE SCAR (1575) (U)
Hepworth
D: Frank Wilson
Stewart Rome . . . . The Doctor
Chrissie White . . . . The Girl
Lionelle Howard . . . . The Crook
Harry Gilbey . . . . The Father
CRIME Girl proves scarred crook framed doctor
for her father's murder.

05384
THINGS WE WANT TO KNOW (650) (U)
Hepworth
D: (Hay Plumb)
S: Lionelle Howard
Lionelle Howard . . . . Husband
DRAMA Husband dreams he murders his wife's
lover and goes to prison.

05385
COWARD! (1525) (U) retitled: THEY CALLED
HIM COWARD
Hepworth
D: Frank Wilson
S: Stewart Rome
Stewart Rome . . . . Jack Harston
Chrissie White . . . . Mrs Harston
Lionelle Howard . . . . Lord Linton
Nichol Simpson . . . . Himself
SPORT Boxer's baby has eye operation during
important match.

05386
HAWKEYE, KING OF THE CASTLE (375) (U)
Hepworth
D:S: Hay Plumb
Hay Plumb . . . . Hawkeye
COMEDY Castle caretaker dreams he fights
knight for maiden.

05387
A LANCASHIRE LASS (3000)
Hepworth (Palatine)
D: Frank Wilson
S: H. Grenville-Taylor
Stewart Rome . . . . Joe
Alma Taylor . . . . Mary
Tom Powers . . . . Howard
William Felton . . . . Manager
Warwick Buckland . . . . Father
Ruby Belasco . . . . Mother
John MacAndrews . . . . Workman
CRIME Blackburn. Foreman framed for
stealing holiday fund breaks jail and frees his
crooked manager from flywheel.

05388
FIGHTING SELINA (445) (U)
Martin (DFSA)
D: Dave Aylott
COMEDY Maid dreams she is a Red Cross
nurse at the war.

05389
ODD MAN OUT (530) (U)
Martin (DFSA)
D: (Edwin J. Collins)
COMEDY Clumsy man loses jobs in china
shop, as gardener, etc.

05390
THE CAKES OF KHANDIPORE (500) (U)
Martin (DFSA)
D: Dave Aylott
COMEDY Boy gives away Indian cakes that
cause eater's mouths to stick.

05391
JOHN PAWKSON'S BRUTALITY (543) (U)
Martin Films (DFSA)
D: (Edwin J. Collins)
COMEDY Man comes home to find his wife
flirting with decorator.

05392
THE AIRMAN'S CHILDREN (1400) (U)
Neptune (Browne)
D: Jack Denton
Douglas Payne . . . . Pilot
CRIME Pursuit of a sacked German pilot who
kidnaps detective's children.

05393
A STRONG ARGUMENT (410) (U)
Neptune (Browne)
D: (Percy Nash)
S: Brian Daly
Brian Daly
COMEDY Political rivals fall for girl who loves
sailor.

05394
THE WAIFS (450) (U)
Neptune (Browne)
D: (Percy Nash)
DRAMA Waif saves child stolen from his nurse
by beggar.

05395
THE LOVE OF THEIR LIVES (530) (U)
Neptune (Browne)
D: (Percy Nash)

John East . . . . John Trusty
Harry Ashton . . . . William Trusty
COMEDY Bachelor brothers conspire to get rid
of their former sweetheart.

05396
THE MESMERIST (1250) (U)
Neptune (Browne)
D: (Percy Nash)
Douglas Payne . . . . Mesmerist
CRIME Hypnotist forces his victims to steal.

05397
CHICKEN HEARTED (530) (U)
Neptune (Browne)
D: (Percey Nash)
John Collins . . . . Tramp
John East . . . . Tramp
Frank Tennant . . . . Tramp
COMEDY Three tramps steal farmer's
chickens and are caught by police.

05398
THE ADVENTURES OF WILLIE WOODBINE
AND LIGHTNING LARRY — A JOYRIDE TO
THE CANNIBAL ISLANDS (700) (U)
New Agency
D:S: Sidney Aldridge
TRICK Tramps use magic wand and amulet to
visit cannibal islands in balloon.

05399
MRS RAFFLES NEE PIMPLE (892) (U)
Folly Films (Phoenix)
D:S: Joe & Fred Evans
Fred Evans . . . . Pimple
Joe Evans . . . . Raffles
COMEDY Pimple poses as crook's wife and
borrows children to extort cheque from his
rich relations.

05400
PIMPLE IN THE KILTIES (900) (U)
Folly Films (Phoenix)
D:S: Joe & Fred Evans
Fred Evans . . . . Pimple
COMEDY Pimple joins Scottish regiment and
becomes war hero.

05401
JUDGE PIMPLE (756) (U)
Folly Films (Phoenix)
D:S: Joe & Fred Evans
Fred Evans . . . . Pimple
Joe Evans . . . . Raffles
COMEDY Pimple poses as judge and lets criminals
go free.

05402
SEXTON PIMPLE (966) (U)
Folly Films (Phoenix)
D:S: Joe & Fred Evans
Fred Evans . . . . Sexton Pimple
COMEDY Tec takes over train to save King of
Cork from spies.

05403
THE TERRIBLE TWO ABROAD (715) (U)
Phoenix
D:S: James Read
Joe Evans . . . . Lemon
James Read . . . . Dash
COMEDY Couple mistake harem for workhouse
pose as slaves and kill the Sultan.

05404
THE TERRIBLE TWO — A.B.S. (720) (U)
Phoenix
D:S: James Read
Joe Evans . . . . Lemon

James Read . . . . Dash
COMEDY Sailors in submarine capture
prisoners.

05405
MR AND MRS PIECAN — THE GIDDY
HUSBAND (650) (U)
Phoenix
D:S: Joe Evans
Joe Evans . . . . Mr Piecan
Geraldine Evans . . . . Mrs Piecan
COMEDY Wife fools flirty husband by having
man pose as their maid.

05406
PIECAN'S TONIC (575) (U)
Phoenix
D:S: Joe Evans
Joe Evans . . . . Mr Piecan
Geraldine Evans . . . . Mrs Piecan
COMEDY Wife arouses sleepy husband by
having their lodger pose as Demon King.

05407
DODGING THE BEER TAX (315)
Excel Films (Prieur)
COMEDY Two tramps steal barrel of beer and
are arrested.

05408
HUMPTY DUMPTY R.A. (525)
Humpty Dumpty Films (Prieur)
TRICK Doll sketches Jellicoe, French,
Churchill, Kitchener.

05409
BRITAIN'S NAVAL SECRET (1197) (U)
Lieut Moran Films (DFSA)
D: Percy Moran
Percy Moran . . . . Lt Jack Moran
Noel Grahame . . . .
WAR Naval lieut saves secret plans from spy
gang.

05410
WINKY, PHOTOGRAPHER (474) (U)
Bamforth (YCC)
Reggie Switz . . . . Winky
COMEDY Winky poses as mad photographer
and his friend as asylum warden.

05411
WINKY'S BLUE DIAMOND (540) (U)
Bamforth (YCC)
D: Cecil Birch
Reggie Switz . . . . Winky
COMEDY Winky poses as rajah to catch
diamond thieves with flypaper.

05412
OH MY! (480) (U)
Bamforth (YCC)
D: Cecil Birch
Reggie Switz . . . . Winky
COMEDY Hotel porter causes confusion by
exchanging room numbers.

05413
THE TROUBLES OF A HYPOCHONDRIAC
(431) (U)
Bamforth (YCC)
D: Cecil Birch
Reggie Switz . . . . Winky
COMEDY Liquid electricity cures old man.

05414
AN UNLUCKY NIGHT AT THE BROWNS
(359) (U)
Horseshoe (YCC)
COMEDY Wife mistakes drunken husband for
burglar.

05415
TOMMY ATKINS (3800) (U)
Barker (ICC)
D: Bert Haldane
S: (PLAY) Arthur Shirley, Ben Landeck
SC: Rowland Talbot
Blanche Forsythe . . . . Ruth Raymond
Jack Tessier . . . . The Curate
Roy Travers . : . . . . Capt Richard Maitland
Maud Yates . . . . Rose Selwyn
Barbara Rutland . . . .
WAR Germon-born captain kills his wife and
frames her fiancee, who loves curate.

05416
1914 (3500) (U)
London (Jury)
D: George Loane Tucker
S: "Rita" (Mrs Humphreys)
Jane Gail . . . . Jeanne Lemont
Hayford Hobbs . . . . Pierre Lemont
Gerald Ames . . . . Capt von Hindburg
Sydney Vautier . . . . Donald MacPherson
Gwynne Herbert . . . . Grandmother
WAR German captain demands woman in return
for her husband's liberty.

05417
FROM FLOWER GIRL TO RED CROSS NURSE
(2600)
Zenith
D: Leedham Bantock
Mlle Karina . . . . '. Nelly
WAR Girl saved from suicide becomes a dancer
and a nurse in France.

05418
A PREHISTORIC LOVE STORY (2000)
Zenith
D: Leedham Bantock
S: (SKETCH) Seymour Hicks
Seymour Hicks . . . . The Man
Isobel Elsom . . . . The Girl
Franklyn Bellamy
Violet Russell
COMEDY Burlesque romance set in cave-man
days.

05419
HANGING A PICTURE
Eric Williams Speaking Pictures
S: (NOVEL) Jerome K. Jerome
(THREE MEN IN A BOAT)
Eric Williams . . . . Uncle Podger
COMEDY Shown while Eric Williams recites
from the stage.

05420
THE HAND AT THE WINDOW (4000)
Regent (MP)
P: Charles Weston, Arthur Finn
D: Charles Weston
CRIME "Features a despicable hero, drugs, the
eternal triangle, revolvers and a murderess."

FEB

05421
THE SOCIETY VISIT (622) (U)
B & C (DFSA)
S: Ernest Dangerfield
Winnie Dangerfield . . . . . . The Child
COMEDY Child sends mother's party
invitations to sweep, dustman, etc.

05422
GILBERT GETS TIGER-ITIS (571) (U)
B & C (DFSA)
D: (Maurice Elvey)
Fred Groves . . . . Gilbert

Elizabeth Risdon . . . . Mrs Gilbert
COMEDY Drunkard's wife and family fool him
with tiger skin.

05423
GILBERT DYING TO DIE (524) (U)
B & C (DFSA)
D: (Maurice Elvey)
Fred Groves . . . . Gilbert
COMEDY Dude tries to commit suicide, fails,
and inherits fortune.

05424
MIDSHIPMAN EASY (2700)
B & C (Ideal)
D: Maurice Elvey
S: (NOVEL) Frederick Marryatt
SC: Eliot Stannard
Elizabeth Risdon . . . . Don's Daughter
Fred Groves . . . . Don Sylvio
A.V. Bramble . . . . Mesty
Compton Coutts . . . . Easy
ADVENTURE Period. Midshipman's
adventures fighting Spanish privateers.

05425
HIS FATHER'S SIN (1234) (U)
Cricks (DFSA)
D: W.P. Kellino
S: Reuben Gillmer
Norman Howard . . . . Jack Harker
DRAMA Drunkard reforms after saving
sleepwalking daughter from roof.

05426
THE ORDER OF THE BATH (382) (U)
Cricks (DFSA)
D: W.P. Kellino
COMEDY Bag thief changes clothes with man
in Turkish bath.

05427
PLAYING THE DEUCE (536) (U)
Cricks (DFSA)
D: W.P. Kellino
Will Kellino . . . .'. . . . . The Man
Sam Poluski. . . . . Neighbour
COMEDY Neighbours' duel with musical
instruments end in fight.

05428
UNDER THE GERMAN YOKE (2430) (A)
Clarendon
D: Wilfred Noy
Dorothy Bellew . . . . The Girl
George Keene. . . . . The Man
Elizabeth Grayson . . . . The Nurse
WAR France. Mayor's daughter shoots Prussian
captain and her old nurse brings the British to
save mayor from execution.

05429
HOW LIEUTENANT ROSE RN SPIKED THE
ENEMY'S GUNS (1950) (U)
Clarendon
D: Percy Stow
P.G. Norgate . . . . Lt Rose
WAR Belgium. Lieut signals flagship to destroy
enemy chateau.

05430
NIGHT AND MORNING (2995) (U)
Clarendon (Westminster)
D: Wilfred Noy
S: (NOVEL) Lord Lytton
Dorothy Bellew . . . . The Girl
CRIME Son of rich man's secret wife is adopted
by coiner and saves his sister from forced marriage
to crooked cousin.

05431
WHEN EAST MEETS WEST (3000) (U)
Clarendon
D: Wilfred Noy
S: Marchioness of Townshend
Dorothy Bellew . . . . The Girl
CRIME Indian fakir hypnotises officer's daughter
and explodes gas bulbs from afar with electric
rays.

05432
SCHOOLGIRL REBELS (850) (U)
Hepworth
D: (Frank Wilson)
Chrissie White . . . . Phyllis
Stewart Rome . . . . Inspector
Violet Hopson . . . . Teacher
COMEDY Schoolgirl annoys the new teacher by
getting her friends to answer an inspector
incorrectly.

05433
COCK O' THE WALK (575) (U)
Hepworth
D: (Hay Plumb)
Jamie Darling . . . . Farmer
COMEDY Ill-tempered farmer cured after
tramps attack him.

05434
THE CONFESSION (1000) (U)
Hepworth
D: Frank Wilson
Stewart Rome . . . . Edward Clavering
Chrissie White . . . . Pauline Allington
Lionelle Howard . . . . Rupert Hartley
Harry Gilbey . . . . Mr Allington
CRIME Girl extracts confession on from gambler
who framed her fiance for murder.

05435
WHAT'LL THE WEATHER BE? (400) (U)
Hepworth
D: (Hay Plumb)
COMEDY New barometer's prediction of wet
weather comes true when the owner upsets his
bath.

05436
SPIES (1000) (U)
Hepworth
D: Frank Wilson
S: Edith Banks
Alma Taylor . . . . Penelope
Lionelle Howard . . . . The Poet
Stewart Rome . . . . The Suitor
Henry Vibart . . . . The Father
COMEDY Girl elopes with poet and they are
mistaken for spies.

05437
ALMA TAYLOR (575) (U)
Hepworth
Alma Taylor . . . . Herself
COMPILATION Extracts from Alma Taylor's
films from 1907 to date.

05438
AS YE REPENT (3600) (A) USA:
REDEEMED
Turner Films (Moss)
D:SC: Larry Trimble
S: Florence Turner
Florence Turner . . . . Marea
Tom Powers . . . . Jim Somers
Maud Stewart . . . . Roma Sarno
Anthony Keith . . . . John Gordon
Edward Lingard . . . . Howard Grimshaw
Clifford Pembroke . . . . . . Dr Holmes
Henry Vibart . . . . Father Anselm
DRAMA Selfish actress weds her cousin's lover
and dies saving her jewels from fire.

05439
A FLUKE IN THE 'FLUENCE (595) (U)
Martin (DFSA)
D: (Edwin J. Collins)
COMEDY Mesmerist makes his victim act like
goat and monkey.

05440
THE CLUB OF PHAROS (565) (U)
Martin (DFSA)
D: Dave Aylott
TRICK Burglar steals Egyptian club that makes
objects disappear.

05441
P'RAPS, P'RAPS NOT (589) (U)
Martin (DFSA)
D: (Edwin J. Collins)
COMEDY Girl tries to hid her sweetheart from
her father and his choice.

05442
SELINA OF THE WEEKLIES (614) (U)
Martin (DFSA)
D: Dave Aylott
COMEDY Girl reporter tracks down spies at
Highgate Ponds.

05443
DISCORD IN THREE FLATS (471) (U)
Martin (DFSA)
D: (Edwin J. Collins)
COMEDY Girl's musical evening annoys
neighbours who call the police.

05444
DIAMOND CUT DIAMOND (598) (U)
Martin (DFSA)
D: (Dave Aylott)
COMEDY Burglar watches gentleman cracksman
at work, then robs him.

05445
SISTERS (1255) (U)
Neptune (Browne)
D: (Percy Nash)
ROMANCE Widower marries orphan and then
falls in love with her sister.

05446
DID HE? THE BRUTE! (700) (U)
Neptune (Browne)
D: (Percy Nash)
John East
Brian Daly
Douglas Cox
COMEDY Professor's pet chimpanzee frightens
burglars.

05447
BUNTING'S BLINK (536) (U)
Neptune (Browne)
D: (Percy Nash)
John East
COMEDY Cleric afflicted with a winking eye
ends up in jail.

05448
TAKING A FILM (615) (U)
Neptune (Browne)
D: (Percy Nash)
John East
COMEDY Film company on location for
western drama have lunch basket stolen by
tramps.

05449
HER FIRST HUSBAND (950) (A)
Neptune (Browne)
D: (Percy Nash)
DRAMA

05450
JUST IN TIME (825) (U)
Neptune (Browne)
D: (Percy Nash)
COMEDY

05451
THE LITTLE MINISTER (3920) (U)
Neptune (Jury)
D: Percy Nash
S: (PLAY) J.M. Barrie
SC: J.M. Barrie
Joan Ritz . . . . Babbie
Gregory Scott . . . . Gavin Dishart
Henry Vibart . . . . Rob Dow
Fay Davis . . . . Margaret Dishart
May Whitty . . . . Nanny Webster
Douglas Payne . . . . Lord Rintoul
Frank Tennant . . . . Capt Halliwell
John East . . . . Thomas Whamond
Brian Daly . . . . Snecky Hobart
Douglas Cox . . . . Silva Tosh
Alfred Wilmore . . . . Micah Dow
ROMANCE Scotland, period. Lord's fiancee
poses as gipsy and falls in love with new minister.

05452
INSTRUMENTS OF FATE (950(U)
Burlingham Standard (NA)
D: Ethyle Batley
Ernest G. Batley . . . . The Man
DRAMA Workless man steals doctor's
instruments to pawn them, but repents in time
to save a life.

05453
HONOUR AMONG THIEVES (1270) (U)
Burlingham Standard (NA)
D: Ernest G. Batley
Ernest G. Batley . . . . The Man
CRIME Ex-crook becomes butler and adopts
his ex-partner's son, who becomes thief.

05454
YE OLDE WAXWORKS BY THE TERRIBLE
TWO (575) (U)
Phoenix
D:S: James Read
Joe Evans . . . . Lemon
James Read . . . . Dash
COMEDY Tramp poses as models of Napoleon
and Kitchener but is exposed by boy's
peashooter.

05455
THE TERRIBLE TWO HAD (595) (U)
Phoenix
D:S: James Read
Joe Evans . . . . Lemon
James Read . . . . Dash
COMEDY Scapegraces learn to play bass and
trombone to please rich aunt.

05456
FLASH PIMPLE THE MASTER CROOK (745)
(U)
Folly Films (Phoenix)
D:S: Fred Evans, Joe Evans
Fred Evans . . . . Flash Pimple
Joe Evans . . . . PC
COMEDY Confidence trickster caught by
constable.

05457
PIMPLE'S STORYETTE (730) (U)
Folly Films (Phoenix)
D:S: Fred Evans, Joe Evans
Fred Evans . . . . Pimple
COMEDY Pimple writes story and reads it to
friends.

05458
PIMPLE'S DREAM OF VICTORY (964) (U)
Folly Films (Phoenix)
D:S: Fred Evans, Joe Evans
Fred Evans . . . . Pimple
COMEDY Sailor dreams of adventures under the
sea with torpedoes, etc.

05459
PIMPLE, THE BAD GIRL OF THE FAMILY
(810) (U)
Folly Films (Phoenix)
D:S: Fred Evans, Joe Evans
Fred Evans . . . . Pimple
Joe Evans . . . . The Squire
COMEDY Blacksmith saves his sweetheart from
sporting squire.

05460
POOR OLD PIECAN (370) (U)
Phoenix
D:S: Joe Evans
Joe Evans . . . . Mr Piecan
Geraldine Evans . . . . Mrs Piecan
COMEDY Landlady's boarders tackle burglar.

05461
WHEN THE GERMANS CAME (565) (U)
Phoenix
D:S: Joe Evans
Joe Evans . . . . Mr Piecan
Geraldine Evans . . . . Mrs Piecan
COMEDY German soldiers invade England.

05462
GOLF MAD (387) (U)
Horseshoe (YCC)
"Gussy"
COMEDY Dude gets golfing craze and wreaks
havoc with clubs.

05463
CINEMA STRUCK (367)
Horseshoe (YCC)
"Gussy"
COMEDY Dude gets job at a film studio and
causes trouble.

05464
THE LION TAMER (534) (U)
Horseshoe (YCC)
COMEDY Henpeck escapes wife by changing
places with lion tamer.

05465
THE ORDER OF THE BATH (382)(U)
Horseshoe (YCC)
COMEDY Bath attendant gets bathers mixed
and is forced into duel.

05466
THE CONJURER'S NEW ASSISTANT (343)
(U)
Horseshoe (YCC)
"Gussy"
COMEDY Conjurer plants foolish helper behind
curtain at an "At Home".

05467
NEXT PLEASE (308) (U)
Horseshoe (YCC)
"Gussy"
COMEDY Mishaps of amateur barber.

05468
BILL'S MONICKER (470) (U)
Ec-Ko (YCC)
D: W.P. Kellino
Albert Egbert . . . . Bill
Seth Egbert . . . . Walter
COMEDY Dustman uses friend's name to
obtain credit at pub.

05469
THE ARAB'S CURSE (399) (U)
Planet (YCC)
D: (A. Kiralfy)
COMEDY Mishaps pursue man who insulted
Arab.

05470
A NIGHT OUT (660)
Searchlight (YCC)
COMEDY Drunkard returning from club meets
girl.

05471
A CINEMA GIRL'S ROMANCE (3500)
G.B. Samuelson (Royal)
D: George Pearson
S: (NOVEL) Ladbrooke Black
SC: Harry Engholm
Agnes Glynne . . . . Hazel Wilmot
Fred Paul . . . . .Sir Robert Loftus
Alice de Winton . . . . Ruth Roland
Bernard Vaughan . . . .
Donald Young . . . .
DRAMA Actress's lover returns from aborad in
time to kill seducer.

05472
THE MIDDLEMAN (4900) (A)
London (Jury) *Reissue:* 1918
D: George Loane Tucker
S: (PLAY) Henry Arthur Jones
SC: Bannister Merwin
Albert Chevalier . . . . Cyrus Blenkarn
Jane Gail . . . . Mary Blenkarn
Gerald Ames . . . . Julian Chandler
Douglas Munro . . . . Joseph Chandler
George Bellamy . . . . Sir Seaton Umfraville
Frank Stanmore . . . . Jesse Pegg
Minna Grey . . . . Maud Chandler
Christine Rayner . . . . Nancy
Hubert Willis . . . . Batty Todd
Gwynne Herbert . . . . Mrs Chandler
DRAMA Pottery owner's son weds workman's
daughter and their baby dies, so her father ruins
his.

05473
BROTHER OFFICERS (3975) (U)
London (Jury) *Reissue:* 1918
D: Harold Shaw
S: (PLAY) Leo Trevor
SC: Bannister Merwin
Henry Ainley . . . . John Hinds
Lettice Fairfax . . . . . Baroness Honour Royden
Gerald Ames . . . . Lt Lancelot Pleydell
Charles Rock . . . . Jim Stanton
George Bellamy . . . . Col Stapleton
Frank Stanmore . . . . Dean
Wyndham Guise . . . . Bookmaker
Gwynne Herbert . . . . Lady Pleydell
WAR Private wins sweepstake and VC, lets his girl
wed his friend, and saves him from the cardsharp
who killed his father.

05474
THE KING'S OUTCAST (3500) (U) USA: HIS
VINDICATION
London (Jury)
D: Ralph Dewsbury
S: (PLAY) W. Gayer Mackay, Robert Ord
SC: Bannister Merwin
Gerald Ames . . . . Edward Farley
Blanche Bryan . . . . Marjorie
Charles Rock . . . . Squire
Philip Hewland . . . . Capt Hatherley
W. Kershaw . . . . Farley
Douglas Munro . . . . Innkeeper

Chappel Dossett . . . .
CRIME Framed man poses as old violinist to
save son from gambler who killed his brother.

05475
BENEATH THE MASK (2246) (A)
Barker (Award)
D: (Bert Haldane)
S: Rowland Talbot
CRIME Chemist regains his sight in time to see
his assistant poisoning his drink.

05476
THE UNDER-SECRETARY'S HONOUR (1935)
(U)
Barker
D: (A.E. Coleby)
S: Rowland Talbot
DRAMA

05477
SATAN'S AMAZON (2960) (A)
Barker (Award)
D: (A.E. Coleby)
S: Rowland Talbot
CRIME Female criminal brought to ultimate
justice.

05478
THE CALL OF THE MOTHERLAND (2235)
(A)
Barker (Palmer)
D: F. Martin Thornton
S: Rowland Talbot
Roy Travers
WAR Canadian soldier saves French
ex-sweetheart from attack by Uhlans.

05479
HARRY THE SWELL (2325) (U)
Big Ben Union (Pathe)
D: H.O. Martinek
S: L.C. MacBean
H.O. Martinek . . . . Jim the Scorpion
Ivy Montford . . . . Ruth Renton
Wallace Bosco . . . . Harry Ray
CRIME Crook saves girl from drowning, robs her
father, and frames his partner.

05480
THE BOAT RACE MYSTERY (2375) (U)
Britannia (Pathe)
SPORT Bargee tampers with rival's boat to
make him lose race.

05481
THE SUNSHINE AND CLOUDS OF PARADISE
ALLEY (2200)
Kineto
D: Frank Stather
Claudine Guilliot . . . . Big Amy
Vera Carlisle . . . . Molly Laver
Harry Dunn . . . . Fred
Madge Tree . . . . Mrs Laver
Kitty Vane . . . . Sister of Mercy
ROMANCE Coster girl weds lady's nephew but
returns to slums.

05482
THE CONFESSIONS OF PONGO (515)
Kineto
ANIMAL "Above the ordinary animal film."

05483
THE MONKEY'S PAW (2800)
Magnet
D: Sidney Northcote
S: (PLAY) W.W. Jacobs
John Lawson . . . . John White
FANTASY Paw grants owner three wishes, causing
his son to die and return from the grave.

05484
FOR ENGLAND'S SAKE (880) (U)
Urban
CRIME Cornwall. Girl sees fiance release carrier
pigeon and exposes him as spy.

MAR
05485
ROUGH ON UNCLE (524) (U)
B & C (DFSA)
S: Ernest Dangerfield
Winnie Dangerfield . . . . .The Child
COMEDY Child pins 'Husband wanted' notice
on uncle's gate.

05486
LONDON'S YELLOW PERIL (2172) (U)
B & C (Standard)
D: Maurice Elvey
SC: Eliot Stannard
Elizabeth Risdon . . . . Ruth Graham
Fred Groves . . . . Gilbert
A.V. Bramble . . . . Negro
M. Gray Murray . . . . Rev Graham
CRIME Dude saves missionary's daughter from
Chinese opium den.

05487
FLORENCE NIGHTINGALE (3570) (U)
B & C (Ideal)
D: Maurice Elvey
S: (BOOK) Edward Cook (THE LIFE OF
FLORENCE NIGHTINGALE)
SC: Eliot Stannard
Elizabeth Risdon . . . . Florence Nightingale
Fred Groves . . . . Doctor
A.V. Bramble . . . . Sydney Herbert
M. Gray Murray . . . .
Beatrix Templeton . . . .
Pauline Peters . . . .
HISTORY Biography of nurse to award of the
OM in 1908.

05488
THE LORD GAVE retitled: THE WORLD'S
DESIRE (3259) (U)
B & C (Ideal)
D:S: Sidney Morgan
Lilian Braithwaite . . . . Claire Bennett
Fred Groves . . . . Sir Richard Bennett
A.V. Bramble . . . . George Cleaver
Joan Morgan . . . . Betty
M. Gray Murray . . . . Dr Frank Saxon
Kathleen Warwick . . . . Mrs Cleaver
DRAMA Doctor exchanges unwanted child for
stillborn baby who is later suspected of being
bastard.

05489
WHEN THE PIE WAS OPENED (633) (U)
B & C (DFSA)
S: Ernest Dangerfield
Winnie Dangerfield . . . . The Child
COMEDY Father find sack of flour and makes
huge pie.

05490
FIGHTING BILLY (521) (U)
Cricks (DFSA)
D:S: W.P. Kellino
Sam T. Poluski . . . . .The Man
COMEDY Bully is worsted by goat with boxing
gloves on horns.

05491
SPOOF! (544) (U)
Cricks (DFSA)
D: W.P. Kellino
S: Reuben Gillmer
Sam T. Poluski . . . . The Dude
COMEDY Dude plays a practical joke with funnel
on soldiers.

05492
HE WOULD ACT (527) (U)
Cricks (DFSA)
D: W.P. Kellino
S: Reuben Gillmer
COMEDY Man tries to become film actor and
gets blown up.

05493
WHO KISSED HER?
Cricks (DFSA)
D: W.P. Kellino
S: Reuben Gillmer
Fred Hyde . . . . Husband
Miss Bella . . . . Wife
Miss Bijou . . . . Secretary
COMEDY Wife puts soot on husband's mustache
to see if he kisses secretary.

05494
A MOMENT OF DARKNESS (1625) (A)
Hepworth
D: Cecil M. Hepworth
Alma Taylor . . . . The Girl
Violet Hopson . . . . The Woman
Stewart Rome
Lionelle Howard
CRIME Girl, trained by father to steal jewels,
after release from jail becomes companion to
woman she robbed.

05495
MARMADUKE AND HIS ANGEL (825) (U)
Hepworth
D: (Frank Wilson)
Chrissie White . . . . Angela
Lionelle Howard . . . . Marmaduke
Violet Hopson . . . . .Fleurette de Lys
ROMANCE Dancer helps girl win back
infatuated grocery clerk.

05496
ALL THE WORLD'S A STAGE (700) (U)
Hepworth
D: (Frank Wilson)
John MacAndrews . . . . Alexander Aitchbee
COMEDY Tragedian's magic potion renders
pupils stage-struck.

05497
ONE GOOD TURN (500) (U)
Hepworth
D: Frank Wilson
Stewart Rome . . . . The Artist
Chrissie White . . . . The Girl
John MacAndrews . . . . The Robber
CRIME Artist saves girl from purse snatcher; and
she saves him from robbery.

05498
JILL AND THE OLD FIDDLE (975) (U)
Hepworth
D: Hay Plumb
S: Reginald Hargreaves, Alice de Winton
Alma Taylor . . . . Jill
Stewart Rome . . . . The Man
Thomas Andrews . . . . Grandfather
DRAMA Girl hears her dead grandfather's
violin and follows it to her death.

05499
THEY'RE ALL AFTER FLO (825) (U)
Hepworth
D: (Frank Wilson)
COMEDY Rivals take up boxing to win a girl.

05500
TILLY AND THE NUT (725) IU)
Hepworth
D: Frank Wilson
S: Cecil Hepworth
Alma Taylor . . . . Tilly
Chrissie White . . . . Sally
Henry Vibart . . . . Father
COMEDY Girl's exploits with water drive away
visiting dude.

05501
WHO STOLE PA'S PURSE? (975) (U)
Hepworth
D: (Frank Wilson)
Johnny Butt . . . . Willie Watrot
COMEDY Girl's suitors search for her father's
lost speech.

05502
THE SMALLEST WORM (700) (U)
Hepworth
D: (Frank Wilson)
Arthur Staples . . . . The Worm
Ruby Belasco . . . . Mother-in-law
COMEDY Henpeck is able to rout his mother-in-
law after joining the army.

05503
A CALL FROM THE PAST (725) (U)
Hepworth
D: (Frank Wilson)
Eric Desmond . . . . The Boy
DRAMA Poor boy saves bookseller's daughter
from fire and finds lost parents busking.

05504
SISTER SUSIE'S SEWING SHIRTS FOR
SOLDIERS (625) (U)
Hepworth
D: Harry Buss
Chrissie White . . . . Susie
Johnny Butt
Ruby Belasco
ROMANCE Sempstress unites unemployed
dressmaker with soldier.

05505
MALOOLA FROM PALOONA (555) (U)
Martin (DFSA)
D: (Dave Aylott)
COMEDY Family attempts to keep a native
servant maid.

05506
THE DEVIL TO PAY (585) (U)
Martin (DFSA)
D: (Edwin J. Collins)
Jack Jarman . . . . .The Man
TRICK Old alchemist summons Mephistopheles
and is given youth.

05507
MIKE MURPHY'S MARATHON (541) (U)
Martin (DFSA)
D: Dave Aylott
Fred Percy . . . . Mike Murphy
CHASE Workshy, ejected by wife, is pursued by
police.

05508
NABBED! (525) (U)
Martin (DFSA)
D: (Edwin J. Collins)
COMEDY Maid's policeman friend, locked in
by mistress, catches burglar.

05509
THE CONJURING COOK (410)
H.A. Browne
TRICK Two white cooks against black background

05510
DEWDROP BRAVES THE FLOODS OF
MAIDENHEAD (590) (U)
Burlingham Standard (NA)
D:S: Ernest G. Batley
Ernest G. Batley . . . . Dewdrop
COMEDY Man's ingenious methods of crossing
flooded streets.

05511
WAR IS HELL (2300) (A)
Burlingham Standard (Walturdaw) Reissue: 1917
D: Ethyle Batley
Martin Valmour . . . . Francois
Nancy Bevington . . . . Marthe
Dorothy Batley . . . . Pierre
James Russell . . . . Maj Reitz
Schach Johnson . . . . Maj Schlitz
WAR Belgium. Boy is ordered to shoot father
and shoots German major.

05512
PIMPLE, CHILD STEALER (607) (U)
Folly Films (Phoenix)
D:S: Fred Evans, Joe Evans
Fred Evans . . . . Pimple
COMEDY Bachelor tries to get rid of unwanted
baby.

05513
PIMPLE COPPED (745) (U)
Folly Films (Phoenix)
D:S: Fred Evans, Joe Evans
Fred Evans . . . . Pimple
Joe Evans . . . . Raffles
COMEDY Burglar's unwilling assistant gets lost
carrying safe.

05514
MACDOUGAL'S AEROPLANE (530) (U)
Phoenix
D:S: James Read
James Read . . . . MacDougal
COMEDY Scotsman builds aeroplane but it
explodes.

05515
THE TRAMP'S PARADISE (695) (U)
Phoenix
D:S: James Read
James Read . . . . The Tramp
COMEDY Man mistakes tramp for his eccentric
uncle.

05516
PUGILISTIC POTTS (570) (U)
Phoenix
D:S: James Read
James Read . . . . Potts
COMEDY Henpeck is mistaken for champion
boxer.

05517
THE NEW GOVERNESS (471) retitled:
THE GOVERNESS'S LOVE AFFAIR
Horseshoe (YCC)
COMEDY Professor's love powder causes
trouble with wife and governess.

05518
A FRUITLESS ERRAND (287)
Horseshoe (YCC)
"Gussy"
COMEDY Clumsy man smashes eggs.

05519
BEWARE OF ZEPPELINS (485)
Horseshoe (YCC)
COMEDY Tramps frighten couple into air raid
shelter and rob their house.

05520
A GOOD LITTLE PAL (576)
Bamforth (YCC)
D: Cecil Birch
Baby Langley . . . . Hilda
COMEDY Child plays pranks on sister's
unwanted suitor.

05521
ALWAYS TELL YOUR HUSBAND (338) (U)
Bamforth (YCC)
D: Cecil Birch
Lily Ward . . . . Mrs Graball
COMEDY Jealous husband mistakes insurance
salesman and landlord for wife's lover.

05522
WINKY IS THE LONG AND SHORT OF IT
(612)
Bamforth (YCC)
D: Cecil Birch
Reggie Switz . . . . Winky
COMEDY Winky swindles two showmen by
posing as dwarf and giant.

05523
AND THAT'S HOW THE ROW BEGAN (578)
Bamforth (YCC)
D: Cecil Birch
Reggie Switz . . . . PC
Lily Ward . . . . Florrie Catchem
Alf Scotty . . . . Alf
COMEDY PC wins girl by writing best sonnet.

05524
LOVE AND A LEGACY (679)
Bamforth (YCC)
D: Cecil Birch
Lily Ward . . . . Widow Dunn
COMEDY Yokels compete to woo wealthy
widow.

05525
A CHIP OFF THE OLD BLOCK (595)
Bamforth (YCC)
D: Cecil Birch
COMEDY

05526
ARTFUL, NOT 'ALF (668) (U)
Bamforth (YCC)
D: Cecil Birch
Alf Scotty . . . . Alf Sloppy
COMEDY Man pretends to enlist but becomes
waiter in next town.

05527
WHAT THE? (411) (U)
Bamforth (YCC)
D: Cecil Birch
Alf Scotty . . . . Alf
TRICK Butcher's nightmare.

05528
VENUS AND THE KNUTS (595) (U)
Bamforth (YCC)
D: Cecil Birch
Lily Ward . . . . Miss Merryheart
Reggie Switz . . . . Winky
COMEDY Yokels bribe thugs to attack doctor's
daughter and then stage a rescue.

05529
THAT'S DONE IT (623) (U)
Bamforth (YCC)
D: Cecil Birch
Lily Ward . . . . Gertie Getout
Alf Scotty . . . . Alf
Bertie Wright . . . . Bertie Fopnoodle
COMEDY Suitor poses as girl and has to fight off
her father.

05530
LOVE AND CAMERAS (535)
Bamforth (YCC)
D: Cecil Birch
Lily Ward . . . . The Girl
Alf Scotty . . . . The Photographer
Reggie Switz . . . . The Rival
COMEDY Photographer compromises his rival.

05531
HUSHABYE BABY (509)
Coronet (YCC)
The Brothers Egbert
COMEDY Children hide father's spectacles.

05532
POTTY'S WEDDING DAY (508)
Coronet (YCC)
The Brothers Egbert
COMEDY Rich uncle insists that groom remains
bachelor.

05533
AERIAL INVASION FRUSTRATED (1)
Cherry Kearton
D: (Rex Wilson)
WAR "A wartime drama."

05534
HIS UNKNOWN RIVAL (650)
Mascot (Prieur)
D:S: Frederick J. Allen
COMEDY "Brisk Humorous comedy of
amorous and knockabout sentiment."

05535
FROM SHOPGIRL TO DUCHESS (3600)
B & C (Ideal)
D: Maurice Elvey
S: (PLAY) Charles Darrell
SC: Eliot Stannard
Elizabeth Risdon . . . . Sylvia Gray
Fred Groves . . . . Duke of St. Baynum
A.V. Bramble . . . . Gilbert Spate
Hilda Sims . . . . Gertrude Haynes
M. Gray Murray . . . . Lord Camperdown
Gertrude Evans . . . . Lady Delamere
Jack Webster . . . . Tommy Tinkler
Dolly Tree . . . . Tilly
Pauline Peters . . . . Girl
DRAMA Duke deserts wife on learning she was
shopgirl and is blinded in train crash.

05536
THE PRISONER OF ZENDA(5500) (U)
London (Jury) *Reissue:* 1918
D: George Loane Tucker
S: (NOVEL)Anthony Hope (PLAY) Edward
Rose
SC: William Courtenay Rowden
Henry Ainley . . . . Rudolph Rassendyl
Jane Gail . . . . Princess Flavia
Gerald Ames . . . . Rupert
Arthur Holmes-Gore . . . . . . Duke Michael
Charles Rock . . . . Col Sapt
George Bellamy . . . . Capt Reichenheim
Norman Yates . . . . Fritz von Tarlenheim
Marie Anita Bozzi . . . . Antoinette
ADVENTURE Ruritania. English tourist poses
as royal double to foil revolutionary kidnappers.

05537
RUPERT OF HENTZAU (5500) (U)
London (Jury)   *Reissue:* 1918
D: George Loane Tucker
S: (NOVEL) Anthony Hope
SC: William Courtenay Rowden
Henry Ainley . . . . Rudolph Rassendyl
Jane Gail . . . . Queen Flavia
Gerald Ames . . . . Rupert
Charles Rock . . . . Col Sapt
George Bellamy . . . . Count Reichenheim
Warwick Wellington . . . . Lt Berenstein
Douglas Munro . . . . Bauer
Stella St Audrie . . . . Chancellor's Wife
Jeff Barlow . . . .
Eva Westlake . . . .
ADVENTURE Ruritania. When king is killed by
rival, English double takes place and is shot.

05538
JANE SHORE (6300) (U) USA: THE
STRIFE ETERNAL
Barker (Walturdaw)
D: Bert Haldane, F. Martin Thornton
S: (PLAY) Nicholas Rowe, W.G. Wills
SC: Rowland Talbot
Blanche Forsythe . . . . Jane Winstead
Roy Travers . . . . Edward IV
Robert Purdie . . . . Matthew Shore
Thos H. MacDonald . . . . Lord Hastings
Dora de Winton . . . . Margaret
Maud Yates . . . . Queen Elizabeth
Nelson Phillips . . . . William Shore
Rolfe Leslie . . . . Duke of Gloucester
Tom Coventry . . . . Master Winstead
Rachel de Solla . . . . Dame Winstead
Frank Melrose . . . . Garth the Bard
Fred Pitt . . . . Warwick
HISTORY 1480. Goldsmith's wife becomes king's
mistress to save husband's life.

05539
THE MYSTERIES OF LONDON (4000)(A)
Martin's Exclusives *Reissue:* 1917 (Albion)
D:S: A.E. Coleby
Wingold Lawrence . . . . Bob Willis
Flora Morris . . . . Louise Willis
CRIME Framed clerk is freed in time to save
daughter from being murdered for inheritance.

05540
DARKEST LONDON: OR, THE DANCER'S
ROMANCE (4000)
Barker (Renters)
D: (Bert Haldane)
Ivy Close . . . . Mabel Carstairs
CRIME Abducted heiress leaves crooked husband,
becomes dancer, and loves blackmailed earl.

05541
THE MASTER OF MERRIPIT (3445) (U)
Clarendon (Renters)
D: Wilfred Noy
S: (NOVEL) E. Phillips Oppenheim
Dorothy Bellew . . . . Sarah Dennis
ADVENTURE 18thC. Squire must capture
highwayman to win girl.

05542
THE GUEST OF THE REGIMENT (2715) (U)
Clarendon
D: Wilfre Noy
Dorothy Bellew . . . . The Girl
WAR Colonel's daughter drugs German officer
and poses as him to deliver despatch.

05543
THE GREAT BANK SENSATION (2890) (A)
Clarendon (Argus)
D: Wilfred Noy
CRIME Fence frames bank clerk by forging
cheque with invisible ink.

05544
ROSY RAPTURE (SCENE SIX)
Neptune
D: Percy Nash
S: J.M. Barrie
Gaby Deslys . . . . Rosy Rapture
Biddy de Burgh . . . . Hon Babette
John East . . . .
COMEDY (Film sequence for revue at Duke of
York's Theatre) Showgirl's baby has adventure
with brigands.

05545
THE CALL OF THE SEA (3700)
Cunard (BEF)
D: Wallett Waller
Tonie Reith . . . . The Girl
Bobbie Roberts
CRIME Fisherman saves amnesiac heiress from
being drowned by cousin.

05546
A FISHERMAN'S INFATUATION (2650)
Cunard (King)
D: Wallett Waller
DRAMA Cornwall. Fisherman follows actresss
to London, is disillusioned and works way home
to sweetheart.

05547
THE WAR CLOUD (2500)
Cunare (King)
D:S: Harold Weston
George Keene . . . . The Man
DRAMA Tin box maker enlists and saves wife
from rape by German-born foreman.

05548
IN THE CLUTCHES OF THE HUN (1800) (U)
Phoenix
D: (Joe Evans)
Kenneth Maxwell (Joe Evans) .Norton
Irene McLaren . . . . Clare St Denis
WAR France. Dispatch rider is helped by girl
and later helps her to escape Germans.

05549
THE MAN IN THE ATTIC (3478) (A)
London (Jury)
D: Ralph Dewsbury
S: (PLAY) Charles McEvoy
Blanche Bryan . . . . Maggie Holmes
Charles Rock . . . . Jacob Clay
Philip Hewland . . . . Paul Prior
Hubert Willis . . . . Jarvis
Gwynne Herbert . . . . Mrs Holmes
CRIME Reporter proves girl's drunken mother
did not strangle her miserly benefactor.

05550
THE ROMANY RYE (3030) (U)
Neptune (Bishop, Pessers)
D: Percy Nash
S: (PLAY) George R. Sims
SC: John East, Brian Daly
Gerald Lawrence . . . . Paul Royston
Gregory Scott . . . . Philip Royston
Daisy Cordell . . . . Lora Lee
Frank Tennant . . . . Ralph Endicott
Joan Ritz . . . . Gertie Heckett
Mercy Hatton . . . . Gertie Heckett
Douglas Payne . . . . Edward Marsden
Frank Arlton . . . . Goliath Lee
Lindsay Fincham . . . . Sinfi Lovell
Douglas Cox . . . . Boss Knivett
John East . . . . Black Nathan
Brian Daly . . . . Joe Heckett
Evelyn Maude . . . . Ivy Adrian
ADVENTURE Heir turns gipsy and eludes his
usurping half-brother.

05551
A BOLD ADVENTURESS (3466) (A)
Broadwest (Award)
D:S: Walter West
Nell Emerald . . . . Clara Blythe
Walter West . . . . James Ridgeway
CRIME Earl's fiancee hires burglar to steal letters
from blackmailer.

APR
05552
ARMSTRONG'S TRICK WAR INCIDENTS (360)
Armstrong (Serra)
D:S: Charles Armstrong
TRICK Silhouettes of sergeant, bulldog, donkey,
zeppelin.

05553
THE LIGHTNING BILL-POSTER (661) (U)
B & C (DFSA)
COMEDY Bill-poster's mishaps lead to chase.

05554
THE DISORDER OF THE BATH (454) (U)
B & C (DFSA)
Dolly Tree . . . . Girl
Enid Heather . . . . Girl
COMEDY Plumbers try to mend bath whilst
householders try to use it.

05555
A HERO OF THE TRENCHES (1300)
Barker (KTC)
D: (F. Martin Thornton)
S: Rowland Talbot
WAR "By far the best war film I have screened-
An exhibitor."

05556
THE ANGEL OF THE WARD (3000)
Barker (Gerrard)
D: Tom Watts
S: (NOVEL) Murray Herbert
SC: Langford Reed
Evelyn Cecil . . . . Barbara
Arthur Chisholm . . . . Gentleman Jack
Herbert Trumper . . . . ` Philip
CRIME Surgeon's son tries to kill amnesiac heir.

05557
WHERE THEIR CARAVAN WAS WRESTED
(775) (U)
Britannia (Pathe)
COMEDY Misadventures of couple in horse-
drawn caravan.

05558
THE LIVE MUMMY (924) (U)
Britannia (Pathe)
COMEDY Man poses as Egyptian mummy to
fool scientist.

05559
PEGGY'S PRESENT (1022) (U)
Britannia (Pathe)
COMEDY Wife mistakes husband's hat order for
love letter.

05560
BULLDOG GRIT (1230) (U)
Burlingham Standard (NA)
D: Ethyle Batley
Ernest G. Batley . . . . Gerald Openshaw
Dorothy Batley . . . . Girl
Eily O'Donohue . . . . Mrs Arbuthnot
Ruby Belasco . . . . Gipsy Woman
Henry Harrison . . . . Gipsey Man
Martin Valmour . . . . Lawyer
ANIMAL Girl's pet bulldog saves her from
burning caravan.

05561
DELIVER THE GOODS (1170) (U)
`Burlingham Standard (NA)
D: Ethyle Batley
James Russell . . . . .The Man
WAR German secret agent causes strike in
munitions factory.

05562
WHAT A BOUNDER (434) (U)
Cricks (DFSA)
D: W.P. Kellino
S: Reuben Gillmer
COMEDY Man takes actress to see her film and
fights with villain on screen.

05563
HAMLET (882) (U)
Cricks (DFSA)
D: W.P. Kellino
S: Reuben Gillmer
COMEDY "Mudford Amateur Dramatic Society"
stages Hamlet.

05564
A CHILD OF THE SEA (500) (U)
Hepworth
D: (Frank Wilson)
DRAMA Fisherman saves adopted daughter
when she is abandoned by cad from London.

05565
LOVE ME LITTLE, LOVE ME LONG (850) (U)
Hepworth
D: (Frank Wilson)
COMEDY Broke bachelor weds poor spinster
by mistake.

05566
PHYLLIS AND THE FOREIGNER (700) (U)
Hepworth
D: (Frank Wilson)
Chrissie White . . . . Phyllis
Johnny Butt . . . . Foreigner
COMEDY Schoolgirl suspects new French
master of being German spy.

05567
OH, WIFEY WILL BE PLEASED! (375) (U)
Hepworth
D: (Frank Wilson)
Arthur Staples . . . . Hubby
Ruby Belasco . . . . Wifey
COMEDY Wife mistakenly gives blouse to
ragman.

05568
SPOOF FOR OOF (478) (U)
Martin (DFSA)
D: (Edwin J. Collins)
TRICK Hypnotised man dreams he is a
hypnotist.

05569
JEWELS AND JIMJAMS (610) (U)
Martin (DFSA)
Reissue: 1916, THE DEFECTIVE DETECTIVE
D: (Dave Aylott)
TRICK Detective tracks down burglar with
removable legs and finds it is a cat.

05570
THE KAISER'S PRESENT (615) (U)
Martin (DFSA)
D: Dave Aylott
COMEDY Trouble ensues when Kaiser gives
fat fraulein to Sultan.

05571
A CHIP OFF THE OLD BLOCK (1190) (U)
Martin (DFSA)
D: (Dave Aylott)
WAR Boy Scout stows away to France,
carries despatches, and is saved from capture.

05572
ARABELLA OUT OF A JOB (660) (U)
Phoenix—Comedio
D:S: James Read
Little Chrysia . . . . Arabella
COMEDY Clumsy costumier is sacked from
several jobs.

05573
ARABELLA THE LADY SLAVEY (695) (U)
Phoenix Comedio
D:S: James Read
Little Chrysia . . . . Arabella
COMEDY Maid ruins furniture whilst spring
cleaning but catches burglar.

05574
ARABELLA'S ANTICS (420) (U)
Phoenix-Comedio
Little Chrysia .. . . Arabella
COMEDY Maid's pranks on people upset the
police.

05575
ARABELLA'S FRIGHTFULNESS (690) (U)
Phoenix-Comedio
D:S: James Read
Little Chrysia . . . . Arabella
COMEDY Reading novels makes maid
absent minded

05576
THERE'S HAIR (625)
Bamforth (YCC)
D: Cecil Birch
Baby Langley . . . . Hilda
COMEDY Girl thwarts governess who tries to
wed her widowed father.

05577
MOONSTRUCK (635)
Bamforth (YCC)
D: Cecil Birch
Lily Ward . . . . Lily Orbit
Bertie Wright . . . . Bertie Fitznoodle
COMEDY Astronomer's wife mistakes fop for
her husband.

05578
NEVER AGAIN (599) (U)
Bamforth (YCC)
D: Cecil Birch
Lily Ward . . . . Tiny
Alf Scotty . . . . Alf
COMEDY Tramp tries to steal widow's savings.

05579
FOUL PLAY (633) (U)
Bamforth (YCC)
D: Cecil Birch
Lily Ward . . . . Maggie
Alf Scotty . . . . Giles
COMEDY Tramp exchanges yokel's picnic
chicken for sparrow.

05580
ALWAYS LOVE YOUR NEIGHBOURS (460)
(U)
Bamforth (YCC)
D: Cecil Birch
COMEDY Neighbours fight when one hangs out
washing and the other lights fire.

05581
HILDA ROUTS THE ENEMY (655)
Bamforth (YCC)
D: Cecil Birch
Baby Langley . . . . Hilda
COMEDY Child poses as ghost to scare
grandmother.

05582
JACK THE HANDYMAN (597)
Horseshoe (YCC)
COMEDY Sailor saves girl from unwanted
admirer.

05583
NOTHING BUT WIND (485)
Horseshoe (YCC)
"Gussy"
COMEDY Dude tries to get job as trombonist.

05584
THE DUSTMAN'S NIGHTMARE (541)
EcKo (YCC)
D: W.P. Kellino
S: Brothers Egbert
Albert Egbert . . . . Bill
Seth Egbert . . . . Walter
COMEDY Dustman buys rubber face and dreams
about it.

05585
THE ADVENTURES OF BIG AND LITTLE
WILLIE (355)
Hazelden Mario-Toons (YCC)
S: W.K. Hazelden
TRICK Marionette film based on cartoon characters
in Daily Mirror.

05586
THE CRIPPLE OF YPRES (1921) (U)
GTG Films (YCC)
D: F.C.S. Tudor
WAR Germans force French cripple to guide
them and he leads them into ambush.

05587
OUR BOYS (2450)
Cherry Kearton (Standard)
P: Sidney Morgan, John M. Payne
D:SC: Sidney Morgan
S: (PLAY) H.J. Byron
Maitland Marler . . . . Perkyn Middlewick
W. Compton Coutts . . . . Talbot Chapneys
Kathleen Harrison . . . . Belinda
COMEDY 1875. Sons of bart and butterman
take lodgings when they are disowned for
loving each other's sisters.

05588
A DEVIL OF A HONEYMOON (550)
Cherry Kearton
D:S: W.R. Booth
TRICK Satan drives honeymooner's car via
volcano to North Pole.

05589
THE STOLEN HEIRLOOMS (3000)
I.B. Davidson (Walturdaw)
D: Charles Raymond
S: (CHARACTERS) Harry Blyth
Harry Lorraine . . . . Sexton Blake
Bert Rex . . . . Tinker
CRIME Detective is drugged with flowers and
tied to sawmill while saving ex-gambler from
jewel theft charge.

05590
THE ROGUES OF LONDON (4450) (A)
Barker (Ashley)
D: (Bert Haldane)
S: Rowland Talbot
Blanche Forsythe . . . . Ruth Davies
Fred Paul . . . . Ralph Munt
Maud Yates . . . . Vera Verez
Roy Travers . . . .
CRIME Cleric's son saves maid from suicide and
she saves him when he is framed for killing
crook's mistress.

05591
THE LURE OF DRINK (2700) (A)
Barker (Sherwood)
D: A.E. Coleby
S: Rowland Talbot
Blanche Forsythe . . . . Peggy
Roy Travers . . . . Ned
A.E. Coleby . . . .
DRAMA Married man's mistress has revenge by
making him an insane dipsomaniac.

05592
THE CLUE OF THE CIGAR BAND (3453) (U)
Big Ben (Pathe)
D: H.O. Martinek
S: L.C. MacBean
H.O. Martinek . . . . The Officer
Ivy Montford . . . . The Girl
CRIME Customs officer poses as blind skipper
to save girl from cigar smugglers.

05593
IN THE BLOOD (3540) (A)
Clarendon
D: Wilfred Noy
S: Benedict James
Ben Webster . . . . The Husband
Dorothy Bellew . . . . The Wife
Elizabeth Grayson . . . . The Mother
DRAMA Hereditary drunkard reforms when he
discovers wife refused to elope with lover.

05594
THE MOTORIST'S DREAM (516)
Neptune (Browne)
D: (Percy Nash)
COMEDY Motorist dreams he avenges himself
upon policeman.

05595
A TOUCH OF NATURE (610)
Neptune (Browne)
D: (Percy Nash)
COMEDY Husband's mishaps in the kitchen
make him appreciate his wife.

05596
THE TRUMPET CALL (4480) (U)
Neptune (Gaumont)
D: Percy Nash
S: (PLAY) George R. Sims, Robert Buchanan
SC: John East, Brian Daly
Gregory Scott . . . . Cuthbert Cuthbertson
Joan Ritz . . . . Constance Barton
Douglas Payne . . . . James Redruth
Daisy Cordell . . . . Paula Redruth
Frank Tennant . . . . Richard Featherstone
Cecil Morton York . . . . Sir William Barton
John East . . . . Prof Ginnifer
Agnes Paulton . . . . Lavinia Ginnifer
Douglas Cox . . . . Sgt-Maj Milligan
Jack Denton . . . . Tommy Wicklow
Stella St Audrie . . . . Mrs Wicklow
Brian Daly . . . . Stage Manager
Biddy de Burgh . . . . Cuthbert
DRAMA Rich man's wife elopes with squire who
deserts her, and dies in church as he weds another.

05597
BUTTONS (2000)
G.B. Samuelson (Moss)
D: George Pearson
S: G.B. Samuelson
SC: Harry Engholm
Gerald Royston . . . . Crummings
Fred Paul . . . . Mr Alendale
CRIME Page trails burglars and is saved by dog.

05598
THE TRUE STORY OF THE LYONS MAIL
(2000)
G.B. Samuelson (Moss)
D: George Pearson
S: (PLAY) Charles Reade
SC: Harry Engholm
Fred Paul .... Lesurques
CRIME France, period. Rich man mistaken for
double, a murderous highwayman.

05599
VICE AND VIRTUE; OR, THE TEMPTERS OF
LONDON (3200)
Weston Feature Films (Standard)
D:S: Charles Weston
Rowland Moore .... Jack
Alice Inward .... Alice Brown
Lily Saxby .... Bella Brown
Charles Weston .... Bob the Dip
Harry Webb .... Detective
Gordon Begg .... Father
CRIME Disowned man framed for shooting his
rich father by partner of his wife's criminal
sister.

05600
SLAVERS OF THE THAMES (2450)
H. Ambrose
D:S: Percy Moran
Percy Moran .... Hon Jack Courtney
CRIME Lord's disowned son saves boatman's
daughter from white slaver's houseboat.

MAY

05601
WAR IN CHINA (475) (U)
B & C (DFSA)
Enid Heather .... The Girl
COMEDY Lady kleptomaniac causes trouble
in china shop.

05602
THE LOST SATCHEL (542)
B & C (DFSA)
COMEDY New York. Mixup of satchels in
hotel causes fight.

05603
FITS (418)
B & C (DFSA)
COMEDY Thirsty man fakes fits to obtain free
brandy.

05604
ANOTHER MAN'S WIFE (3000)
B & C (Renters)
D:SC: Harold Weston
S: (PLAY) Miles Wallerton
Elizabeth Risdon .... The Wife
Fred Groves .... The Man
A.V. Bramble .... The Husband
DRAMA

05605
HER NAMELESS (?) CHILD (3450) (U)
B & C (Ideal)
D: Maurice Elvey
S: (PLAY) Madge Duckworth
SC: Eliot Stannard
Elizabeth Risdon .... Phyllis/Alice Ford
Fred Groves .... Arthur Ford
A.V. Bramble .... Lord Harry Woodville
M. Gray Murray .... Earl of Richborough
drama Smith's daughter secretly weds earl and has
baby while posing as spinster to secure inheritance
for her weak brother.

05606
FIVE NIGHTS (5718) (A)
Barker (Imperial)
D: (Bert Haldane)
S: (NOVEL) Victoria Cross
SC: Rowland Talbot
Eve Balfour .... Viola
Thos H. MacDonald .... Trevor Lonsdale*
Sybil de Bray .... Suzee
Tom Coventry .... Hop Lee
ROMANCE (Banned by many local authorities.)

05607
THE LITTLE HOME IN THE WEST (3000)
Barker (Westminster)
D: Tom Watts
S: H. Grenville-Taylor
DRAMA

05608
THE LOSER WINS (993) (U)
Burlingham Standard (NA)
D: Ernest G. Batley
SPORT Rivals box for Red Cross Fund and girl
marries loser.

05609
LOVE ON A YACHT (1475) (U)
Britannia (Pathe)
ROMANCE Poor doctor wins rich girl by saving
her from sea.

05610
EGGS! (526) (U)
Cricks (DFSA)
D: W.P. Kellino
S: Reuben Gillmer
COMEDY Brothers search for eggs to please rich
uncle.

05611
OH THAT FACE! (442) (U)
Cricks (DFSA)
D: W.P. Kellino
S: Reuben Gillmer
COMEDY Groom forgets bride's address and
goes to wrong church.

05612
A FIGHT FOR LIFE (921) (A)
Cricks (DFSA)
D: W.P. Kellino
S: Reuben Gillmer
Edward Sydney .... Jack
CRIME Sailor saves ex-fiancee from husband
who runs coining den in his cellar.

05613
CAUGHT IN A KILT (998) (U)
Cricks (DFSA)
D: W.P. Kellino
S: Reuben Gillmer
COMEDY Jealous man tries to catch wife
flirting with neighbour.

05614
BEHIND THE CURTAIN (2750) retitled: THE
CURTAIN'S SECRET (U)
Hepworth (Renters)
D: Frank Wilson
S: Kate Murray)
Stewart Rome .... Sir Geoffrey Atherton
Chrissie White ....
Lionelle Howard ....
Violet Hopson ....
Henry Vibart ....
CRIME Cousin tries to kill heir through the
family tradition of cursed curtain.

05615
THE INCORRUPTIBLE CROWN (3075) (U)
Hepworth
D: Frank Wilson
Stewart Rome .... Philip
Chrissie White .... Mary
Lionelle Howard .... Bruce
Henry Vibart .... John Milton
Harry Gilbey .... Minister
CRIME Escaped convict hides aboard liner, which
sinks.

05616
THE TRAITOR (2925) (U) retitled: COURT-
MARTIALLED
Hepworth (Gau)
D:S: Cecil M. Hepworth
Stewart Rome .... Maj Carruthers
Tom Powers .... Lt Shaw
Alma Taylor .... Dora Mavis
Lionelle Howard .... Lt Green
William Felton .... von Kaiserstein
Henry Vibart .... Rev James Mavis
WAR Spy has Lt cashiered for signalling to enemy
when actually he was arranging elopement with
CO's wife.

05617
THE PASSING OF A SOUL (1775) (U)
Hepworth
D:S: Cecil Hepworth
Tom Powers .... The Son
Alma Taylor .... The Girl
Henry Vibart .... The Father
DRAMA Man saves girl from suicide and has
her pose as double whom his sick son killed.

05618
SOMETHING LIKE A BAG (450) (U)
Hepworth
D: (Frank Wilson)
TRICK Dunken burglar's swag bag increases and
decreases in size.

05619
WHAT'S YOURS IS MINE (800) (U)
Hepworth
D: (Frank Wilson)
COMEDY Amateur reciter borrows umbrella
and finds it full of eggs.

05620
THE BOTTLE (3175) (A)
Hepworth (Ideal)
D: Cecil M. Hepworth
S: (CARTOONS) George Cruickshank
SC: Arthur Shirley
Albert Chevalier .... Harry Ashford
Ivy Millais .... Mary Ashford
Harry Brett .... Jim Brewster
Stewart Rome .... Barman
John MacAndrews ....
DRAMA Dipsomaniac carpenter loses job and
dies after child steals to save starving wife.

05621
A KWEER KUSS (555) (U)
Martin (DFSA)
D: (Dave Aylott)
TRICK Odd things happen to man who is
cursed by beggar.

05622
BOSH! (559) (U)
Martin (DFSA)
D: (Edwin J. Collins)
COMEDY Farmer thwarts villain and weds
heiress.

05623
MIKE AND THE ZEPPELIN RAID (593)(U)
Martin (DFSA)
D: Dave Aylott
TRICK Tramp dreams of destroying fleet of
airships.

05624
WATCH YOUR WATCH (528) (U)
Martin (DFSA)
D: (Edwin J. Collins)
COMEDY Tramps steal man's large watch.

05625
ARABELLA MEETS RAFFLES (695) (U)
Phoenix-Comedio
D:S: James Read
Little Chrysia . . . .   Arabella
Joe Evans . . . .   Raffles
COMEDY Girl joins forces with a crook and
thwarts police.

05626
ARABELLA IN SOCIETY (745)
Phoenix-Comedio Reissue: 1917(Aero)
D:S: James Read
Little Chrysia . . . . - Arabella
COMEDY Solicitor mistakes maid for heiress
and she goes to ball.

05627
ARABELLA V. LYNXEYE (585) (U)
Phoenix-Comedio
D:S: James Read
Little Chrysia . . . .   Arabella
James Read . . . .   Lynxeye
COMEDY Crooks elude detectives.

05628
ARABELLA AND THE SOFT SOAP (429) (U)
Phoenix-Comedio Reissue: 1917, ARABELLA
SELLS SOFT SOAP (Aero)
D:S: James Read
Little Chrysia . . . .   Arabella
COMEDY Saleswoman plays jokes with soft
soap.

05629
PIMPLE'S MILLION DOLLAR MYSTERY
(1025) (U) USA: FLIVVER'S FAMOUS
CHEESE HOUND
Piccadilly (Browne)
D: Charles Weston
Fred Evans . . . .   Sherlock Pimple
COMEDY Tec tracks down bank robber and fights
him on roof of train.

05630
PIMPLE'S THE MAN WHO STAYED AT
HOME (975) (U)
Piccadilly (Browne)
D: Charles Weston
Fred Evans . . . .   Lt Pimple
COMEDY Lt feigns death by poison to catch
girl spy.

05631
PIMPLE'S PAST (928) (U) USA: FLIVVER'S
TERRIBLE PAST
Piccadilly (Browne)
D: Charles Weston
Fred Evans . . . .   Pimple
COMEDY Escaped convict tells how as engine
driver he saved wife from railway lines.

05632
PIMPLE'S THE CASE OF JOHNNY WALKER
(822) (U)
Piccadilly (Browne)
D: Charles Weston
Fred Evans . . . .   Sherlock Pimple
COMEDY Tec pose as statues, cabby and pillar
box, to trail whisky thieves.

05633
THE UNDERWORLD OF LONDON (3511) (A)
Weston Feature Film (Powers)
D: Charles Weston
Arthur Finn . . . .   Dan
Lily Saxby . . . .
Winnie Fitch . . . .
Harry Webb . . . .
Thomas Brooklyn . . . .
Guy Rupert Lane . . . .
Gordon Begg . . . .
Frank R. Growcott . . . .
CRIME Lord gives unwanted girl to Jewish
crook who trains her to beg.

05634
THE DUNGEON OF DEATH (3100)
Weston Feature Film (Gau)
D: Charles Weston
George Keen
Alice Inward
Lily Saxby
James Lindsay
Gordon Begg
CRIME Mad actor captures blackmailing
producer who framed him for theft to steal his
play.

05635
PIMPLE'S THREE WEEKS (WITHOUT THE
OPTION) (3200)
Piccadilly (Browne)
D: Charles Weston
Fred Evans . . . .   Princess Pimpelian
COMEDY Burlesque of Elinor Glyn's "Three
Weeks".

05636
PIMPLE'S ROYAL DIVORCE (2150)
Piccadilly (Victory)
D: Charles Weston
Fred Evans . . . .   Napoleon Bonypart
Joe Evans . . . .   Josephine
COMEDY Emperor sues for divorce when his wife
refuses to have baby.

05637
THE LIFE OF AN ACTRESS (3300)
Weston Feature Film (Star)
D: Charles Weston
Alice Inward
George Keene
Lily Saxby
George Foley
Gordon Begg
James Lindsay
Clarissa Selwyn
Rowland Moore
Alesia Leon
Mabel Bunyea
DRAMA "Enthralling drama of stage life."

05638
THE PORT OF MISSING WOMEN (3000)
Weston Feature Film (Clarion)
D: Charles Weston
Alice Inward
James Lindsay
Lily Saxby
Gordon Begg
CRIME White slavers run fashion model agency
in Piccadilly.

05639
THE VENGEANCE OF NANA (3250)
Weston Feature Film
D: Charles Weston
Elizabeth Grayson . . . .   Nana
DRAMA "Powerful Eastern drama."

05640
THE WOMAN WITHOUT A SOUL (3436)(A)
Weston Feature Film (Browne)
D: Charles Weston
George Keene
Lily Saxby
Gordon Begg
DRAMA "Great modern drama of intense
human interest."

05641
THE SEVENTH WORD (2835) (U)
Clarendon
D: Wilfred Noy
Dorothy Bellew . . . .   The Girl
CRIME France. Girl and Prussian count hold
halves of locket which are clues to hidden
fortune.

05642
THE POLO CHAMPION (2550)
Britannia (Pathe)
D: M. Hugon
James Carew. . . . .   Harry Melrose
SPORT American heiress must marry so she
promises to wed winner of polo match.

05643
MAMA'S D–E–A–R (599)
Bamforth (YCC)   •
D: Cecil Birch
Baby Langley . . . .   Hilda
COMEDY Child plays tricks on rich aunt.

05644
DR VIOLET DEARING (800) (U)
Bamforth (YCC)
D: Cecil Birch
Lily Ward . . . .   Violet Dearing
Alf Scotty . . . .   Rival
Reggie Switz . . . .   Rival
COMEDY Men feign sickness to impress new
lady doctor.

05645
SCOTTIE TURNS THE HANDLE (486) (U)
Bamforth (YCC)
D: Cecil Birch
Alf Scotty . . . .   Scottie
COMEDY Girl distracts cameraman so that he
unwinds film.

05646
PAPA SCORES (766)
Bamforth (YCC)
D: Cecil Birch
Lily Ward . . . .   Lilian Mascot
COMEDY Man's secret wife poses as boy to
deceive rich uncle.

05647
A PAIR OF STARS (450) (U)
Bamforth (YCC)
D: Cecil Birch
Lily Ward . . . .   Mrs Pippit
COMEDY Couple emulate Chinese jugglers.

05648
THE MAN IN POSSESSION (621)
Bamforth (YCC)
D: Cecil Birch
Lily Ward . . . .   Mrs Neverpay
COMEDY Wily couple fool bailiff.

05649
WHAT SCOTTIE HEARD (422)
Bamforth (YCC)
D: Cecil Birch
Alf Scotty . . . .   Scottie
COMEDY Man makes mistake when he overhears
naturalists planning to kill ants.

05650
TOMMY'S FREEZING SPRAY (693)
Bamforth (YCC)
D: Cecil Birch
Baby Langley . . . . Tommy
Lily Ward . . . . Mother
Reggie Switz . . . . Father
COMEDY Child freezes household with
professor's mixture.

05651
THE FALSE CLUE (484)
Horseshoe (YCC)
COMEDY Lost handbag containing bad venison
is mistaken for murder victim.

05652
A MUDDLED AFFAIR (626)
Horseshoe (YCC)
COMEDY Neighbours suspicions lead to duel.

05653
MIZPAH; OR, LOVE'S SACRIFICE (4000)
Magnet
D: Stuart Kinder
S: (PLAY) Wood Lawrence
Kahli Ru . . . . Princess Zaga
ADVENTURE Egypt. Princess loves soldier who
beats prince in combat.

05654
THE PRIDE OF NATIONS (661) color
Aurora British Natural Colour Films
(DFSA)
D: Claude Friese-Greene
WAR Flags of the Allies, John Bull, etc.

05655
TIME AND THE HOUR (2000)
Michaelson-Lloyd British-Venus
D: Warwick Buckland
S: Muriel Alleyne
Flora Morris . . . . The Woman
J.R. Tozer
Warwick Buckland
CRIME Innocent man cleared when knight
confesses in trance at New Year Ball that he is
gang leader.

05656
THE STORY OF A PUNCH AND JUDY SHOW
(1882)
Michaelson-Lloyd British-Venus (DFSA)
D: Warwick Buckland
S: Mrs K Beck
Warwick Buckland . . . . . . The Showman
DRAMA Boy helps sick father give puppet
show for invalid girl.

05657
HIS BROTHER'S WIFE (1867) (U)
Michaelson-Lloyd British-Venus (DFSA)
D: Warwick Buckland
S: Hamilton Page
Flora Morris . . . . Violet Elmere
J.R. Tozer . . . . John Elmere
Hamilton Page . . . . Philip Elmere
Warwick Buckland
CRIME Woman's brother-in-law takes blame
when she forges husband's signature to pay
gambling debt.

05658
A DAUGHTER OF ENGLAND (3500) (A)
British Empire
D: Leedham Bantock
S: (PLAY) Jose G. Levy, E.V. Miller,
Percy Barrow
Marga Rubia Levy . . . . Sylvia Chetwynd

Frank Randall . . . . Capt Verbois
Frank H. Dane . . . . Lt von Firstner
George Barran . . . . Col Baron von Reiter
Mme d'Esterre . . . . Baroness von Reiter
WAR French captain helps English girl escape
false charge of code theft.

05659
MASTER AND MAN (3612) (A)
Neptune (Walturdaw)
D: Percy Nash
S: (PLAY) George R. Sims, Henry Pettitt
SC: John M. East, Brian Daly
Gregory Scott . . . . Jack Walton
Joan. Ritz . . . . Hester Thornbury
Douglas Payne . . . . Jim Burleigh
Daisy Cordell . . . . Ruth Burleigh
Frank Tennant . . . . Robert Carlton
Brian Daly . . . . Humpy Logan
Jack Denton . . . . Tom Honeywood
Stella St Audrie . . . . Keziah Honeywood
Biddy de Burgh . . . . Little John Walton
DRAMA Ironmaster lures engineer's wife and when
she dies has husband convicted for attempted
murder.'

05660
THE DEVIL'S PROFESSION (3300) (A)
Arrow (YCC)
D:SC: F.C.S. Tudor
S: (NOVEL) Gertie de S. Wentworth James
Rohan Clensy . . . . Dr Felix Emerson
Alesia Leon . . . . Lionne
Sidney Strong . . . . Clifford Carton
May Lynn . . . .
Nancy Roberts . . . .
CRIME Doctor is paid to inject rich people with
madness simulant.

05661
LONDON NIGHTHAWKS (3000)
H. Ambrose
D: Percy Moran
Percy Moran . . . . The Man
CRIME Artist's brother is drug-addicted
criminal.

05662
THE DEADLY MODEL (2575) (U)
Big Ben Union (Pathe)
D: H.O. Martinek
S: L.C. MacBean
H.O. Martinek
Ivy Montford
CRIME German spies try to steal inventor's
model gun.

05663
THE LION'S CUBS (2890) (U)
London (Jury)
D: Ralph Dewsbury
Hubert Willis . . . . Karl Kampf
Wally Bosco . . . . Jules Schoenberg
CRIME German spies gas French generals for
their plans and are caught by scouts.

05664
THE ASHES OF REVENGE (3600) (U)
London (Jury)
D: Harold Shaw
S: (NOVEL) R.C. Carton
SC: Bannister Merwin
Edna Flugrath . . . . Bess
Philip Hewland . . . . Hugh Graydon
Gwynne Herbert . . . . Lady Graydon
DRAMA Widowed lady rejects business man so
he buys gipsy girl and contrives to have her
marry the lady's son.

JUN

05665
WILD OATS (3147) (U)
B & C (Monopol)
D: Harold Weston
S: Eliot Stannard
Arthur Finn . . . . The Man
Fay Temple . . . . The Girl
A.V. Bramble
M. Gray Murray
ROMANCE Girl makes artist jealous to make
him give up dancer.

05666
ALL FOR LOVE (575)
B & C (DFSA)
Enid Heather . . . . Girl
COMEDY "This film is made by the actors
themselves as they go along."

05667
SHADOWS (3840) (A)
B & C (KTC)
D:S: Harold Weston
Fay Temple . . . . Creda
Henry Hargreaves . . . . Vivian Rodney
Ivy Clemow . . . . Millicent
A.V. Bramble . . . . Sir William Morris
Una Venning . . . . Sally
M. Gray Murray . . . . Lord Anthony
Evelyn Shelley . . . . Lady Rodney
DRAMA Sacked modiste becomes rich student's
mistress but leaves him so he may marry
suitably.

05668
THE TAMING OF THE SHREW (2000)
B & C — Voxograph
D:SC: Arthur Backner
S: (PLAY) William Shakespeare
Arthur Backner . . . . Petruchio
Constance Backner . . . . Katherine
COMEDY Scenes synchronised to offstage
reciters.

05669
BLUFF (2000)
B & C — Voxograph
D:SC: Arthur Backner
Arthur Backner . . . . The Man
Constance Backner . . . . . . The Woman
COMEDY Synchronised to offstage reciters.

05670
INVENTING TROUBLE (589) (U)
Cricks (DFSA)
D: W.P. Kellino
S: Reuben Gillmer
COMEDY Inventor demonstrates labour-saving
devices, until prehistoric monster eats him.

05671
PAYING HIM OUT (772) (U)
Cricks (DFSA)
D: W.P. Kellino
S: Reuben Gillmer
Blanche Bella . . . . The Wife
COMEDY Woman changes places with twin to
pay out bullying husband.

05672
MISS DECEIT (575) (U)
Hepworth
D: Frank Wilson
COMEDY Clerk enlists and finds himself superior
to his ex-employer.

05673
THE BABY ON THE BARGE (2825) (U)
Hepworth
D: Cecil M. Hepworth
S: Blanche McIntosh
Stewart Rome . . . . Bob Jennis
Alma Taylor . . . . Nellie Jennis
Lionelle Howard . . . . Jack Storm
Violet Hopson . . . . Lady Lafene
Edward Lingard . . . . Lord Lafene
Henry Vibart . . . . Doctor
William Felton . . . . Thief
CRIME Bargee's ejected wife helps brother
escape murder charge.

05674
CONSCRIPTION (566) (U)
Martin (DFSA)
D: (Dave Aylott)
COMEDY Sgt eventually catches conscription
dodgers.

05675
AWKWARD ANARCHISTS (497) (U)
Martin (DFSA)
D: (Dave Aylott)
TRICK Policeman tracks down anarchist.

05676
SURELY YOU'LL INSURE (472) (U)
Martin (DFSA)
D: (Dave Aylott)
TRICK Business man dreams everybody turns
into a persistent salesman.

05677
PATRIOTIC ARABELLA (546)
Phoenix-Comedio *Reissue:* 1917, ARABELLA
SPIES SPIES (Aero)
D:S: James Read
Little Chrysia . . . . Arabella
COMEDY Sacked maid discovers her employers
are spies.

05678
LYNXEYE'S NIGHT OUT (450)
Phoenix-Comedio
D:S: James Read
James Read . . . . Lynxeye
Little Chrysia . . . . Arabella
COMEDY Tec finds masked dancer is girl
crook.

05679
ARABELLA'S MOTOR (520) (U)
Phoenix-Comedio *Reissue:* 1917 (Aero)
D:S: James Read
Little Chrysia . . . . Arabella
James Read . . . . Lynxeye
COMEDY Girl crook fools tec with moveable
numberplates.

05680
A WATERY ROMANCE (696) (U)
Phoenix-Comedio
D:S: James Read
James Read . . . . Man
Little Chrysia . . . . Girl
COMEDY Man saves girl from abduction by
houseboat owner.

05681
SERGEANT LIGHTNING AND THE
GORGONZOLA GANG (1000)
Phoenix-Comedio
D:S: James Read
James Read . . . . Sgt Lightning
Little Chrysia . . . . Arabella
COMEDY Tec catches houseboat thieves who
use poison gas.

05682
PIMPLE'S PERIL (500) (U)
Piccadilly (Browne)
D: Charles Weston
Fred Evans . . . . Pimple
COMEDY Pimple is scared to duel his
beloved's husband until he finds he is a dwarf.

05683
BAD BOY BILLY (580)
Piccadilly (Browne)
D: Charles Weston
COMEDY Tricks of naughty boy and
intelligent dog.

05684
PIMPLE'S ART OF MYSTERY (925) (U)
USA: FLIVVER'S ART OF MYSTERY
Piccadilly (Browne)
D: Fred Evans, Joe Evans
Fred Evans . . . . Pimple
COMEDY Pimple ruins party when he tries to
emulate conjurer.

05685
PIMPLE'S RIVAL (846) (U)
Piccadilly (Browne)
D:S: Fred Evans, Joe Evans
Fred Evans . . . . Pimple
COMEDY Dwarf dons tiger skin to scare
boastful boarder.

05686
PIMPLE'S DILEMMA (937) (U) USA:
FLIVVER'S DILEMMA
Piccadilly (Browne)
D:S: Fred Evans, Joe Evans
Fred Evans . . . . Pimple
COMEDY Cleric's son has six girls pose as
furniture when father and curate visit.

05687
UNCLE'S VISIT (566)
H.A. Browne
COMEDY Man mistakes tramp for rich
American uncle.

05688
THE LADY DETECTIVE (726) (U)
Piccadilly (Browne)
D: Joe Evans
Geraldine Maxwell . . . . Sally
COMEDY Girl tec tracks down gang of
crooks.

05689
CAUGHT BY THE LEG (537)
Horseshoe (YCC)
COMEDY Tramp fakes injury to fool doctor.

05690
SPIRITS FREE OF DUTY (876)
Horseshoe (YCC)
COMEDY Suitor poses as ghost to scare farmer
into giving his consent.

05691
A COMEDY OF ERRORS (630)
Bamforth (YCC)
D: Cecil Birch
Lily Ward . . . . Angelina
Reggie Switz . . . . The Poet
COMEDY Slavey assumes that poet's
declarations of love are for her.

05692
LILY, TOMBOY (654) (U)
Bamforth (YCC)
D: Cecil Birch
Lily Ward . . . . Lily
Alf Scotty . . . . Caddie
COMEDY Fogeys force wilful girl to wear
golfing clothes.

05693
HILDA'S BUSY DAY (486) (U)
Bamforth (YCC)
D: Cecil Birch
Baby Langley . . . . Hilda
COMEDY Child puts blacklead on sleeping
father's face.

05694
DON'T JUMP TO CONCLUSIONS (490)
Bamforth (YCC)
D: Cecil Birch
Lily Ward . . . . Lily
COMEDY Girl flirts with three dudes, then
reveals she is married.

05695
SCOTTIE AND THE FROGS (486) (U)
Bamforth (YCC)
D: Cecil Birch
Alf Scotty . . . . Scottie
COMEDY Boy's frogs upset visiting explorer.

05696
SHARPS AND FLATS (800) (A)
Bamforth (YCC)
D: Cecil Birch
COMEDY Husbands go on holiday and pretend
they are at VT Corps camp.

05697
THE BOSUN'S YARN (525)
Excel (YCC)
COMEDY Sailor's dramatic story causes pub to
rock.

05698
HOW BILL 'ARRIS TOOK THE
DARDANELES (477)
Excel (YCC)
COMEDY Soldier's dramatic story causes
pub to rock.

05699
THE BOOT BUSINESS (645)
Moonshine (YCC)
Bertie Wright . . . . Bertie Bungle
COMEDY Dude gets job in boot shop and flirts
with owner's wife.

05700
ALONE IN LONDON (4525) (U)
Turner Films (Ideal)
D: Larry Trimble
S: (PLAY) Robert Buchanan, Harriet Jay
Florence Turner . . . . Nan Meadows
Henry Edwards . . . . John Biddlecombe
Edward Lingard . . . . Redcliffe
James Lindsay . . . . Chick
Amy Lorraine . . . . Mrs Burnaby
CRIME Crook tries to make thief of boss's son
and ties flower girl to lock gates of canal.

05701
MY OLD DUTCH (5450) (U)
Turner Films (Ideal) *Reissue:* 1918
D: Larry Trimble
S: Albert Chevalier, Arthur Shirley
Albert Chevalier . . . . Joe Brown
Florence Turner . . . . Sal Gray
Henry Edwards . . . . Herbert Brown
Harry Brett . . . . Erb Uggins
Arthur Shirley . . . . Doctor
Richard Cotter . . . . Nipper
Amy Lorraine . . . .
Minnie Rayner
DRAMA Man returns from colonies in time to
save cockney parents (Extract in 1934 version).

05702
THE BEGGAR GIRL'S WEDDING (4500)(A)
British Empire
D: Leedham Bantock
S: (PLAY) Walter Melville
Henry Lonsdale . . . . Gilbert Lindsay
Ethel Bracewell . . . . Bessie Webster
Lauderdale Maitland . . . . . .Jack Cunningham
Nina Lynn . . . . Maud Villiers
Cecil du Gue . . . . Dr Millbank
George Mitchell . . . . Robert Grimshaw
Wilfred Payne . . . . Norman Marsh
J.C. MacMillian . . . . Joe Webster
Fred Ingram . . . . Dicky Storm
Bernice Walters. . . . . Tina
Harry Hartley . . . . Dodger
CRIME Wastrel heir forced to wed thief's
daughter is put in mad dr's asylum by cousin.

05703
THE NEW ADVENTURES OF BARON
MUNCHAUSEN (995)
Kent Films
D: F. Martin Thornton
TRICK Liar's unlikely war exploits.

05704
THE FAITH OF A CHILD (3500)
Lotus (Serra)
D: F. Martin Thornton
S: Niranjan Pal
Evelyn Boucher . . . . Mother
Rolfe Leslie . . . . Landlord
Bert Grahame . . . .
WAR India. Child's prayers bring soldier father
to save mother from lustful landlord.

05705
IRON JUSTICE (4000) (A)
Renaissance (KTC)
P: John M. Payne
D:S: Sidney Morgan
Fanny Tittell-Brune . . . . Margaret Brand
Sydney Fairbrother . . . . Mrs O'Connor
Julian Royce . . . . Martin Brand
Alfred Drayton . . . . Frank Deakin
Cecil Fletcher . . . . Ronald O'Connor
Marguerita Jesson . . . . Phyllis Brand
A. Harding Steerman . . . . . . Jabez Cole
Joan Morgan . . . . Phyllis (child)
John M. Payne . . . . Footman
CRIME Clerk is jailed for fraud and his employer's
wife make his daughter a whore.

05706
FLYING FROM JUSTICE (4010) (U)
Neptune
D: Percy Nash
S: (PLAY) Mark Melford
Gregory Scott . . . . Charles Baring
Joan Ritz . . . . Winnie
Douglas Payne . . . . John Gully
Alice Moseley . . . . Mildred Parkes
Fred Morgan . . . . James Woodruffe
Cecil Morton York . . . . Rev Lacarsey
Frank Tennant . . . . John Lacarsey
Jack Denton . . . . Pearly Tanner
Maud Williams . . . . Mrs Baring
Brian Daly . . . . Maj Parkes
CRIME Counterfeit gang ensnare cleric's pupil.

05707
JOHN HALIFAX, GENTLEMAN (5350) (U)
G.B. Samuelson (Moss)
D: George Pearson
S: (NOVEL) Elizabeth Craik
SC: James L. Pollitt
Fred Paul . . . . John Halifax
Peggy Hyland . . . . Ursula March
Harry Paulo . . . . Abel Fletcher
Lafayette Ranney . . . . Phineas Fletcher
Charles Bennett . . . . John (child)
Edna Maude . . . . Ursula (child)
Bertram Burleigh . . . .
DRAMA Tewkesbury, 1800. Apprentice inherits
master's mill, weds disowned heiress, and remains
true to his class.

05708
THE LOCKET (2647) (U)
Clarendon (Pathe)
D: Wilfred Noy
Dorothy Bellew . . . . Hilda Noel
DRAMA Locket reunites man with daughter he
thought dead.

05709
THE SONS OF SATAN (4730) (U)
London (Jury)
D: George Loane Tucker
S: (NOVEL) William le Qeuex
Gerald Ames . . . . Henry Normand
Blanche Bryan . . . . Winifred West
Hayford Hobbs . . . . Dick Fenton
Charles Rock . . . . Lord Desford
Windham Guise . . . . .Earl of Littleborough
Lewis Gilbert . . . . William Freshley
Arthur Cullin . . . . Felix Sawyer
Douglas Munro . . . . Insp Ransom
George Bellamy . . . . Editor
CRIME Detective who secretly heads gang of
jewel thieves loves actress engaged to earl's son.

05710
A GARRET IN BOHEMIA (2795) (U)
London (Jury)
D: Harold Shaw
S: (NOVEL) G.E.R. Mayne
Edna Flugrath . . . . Sarah
Ben Webster . . . . Kenneth Douglas
Christine Rayner . . . . Miriam West
Gwynne Herbert . . . . Landlady
Jeff Barlow . . . . Blind Fiddler
ROMANCE Ghost of blind fiddler inspires poor
composer and enables him to marry art teacher.

05711
THE MYSTERY OF A LONDON FLAT (3000)
(U) retitled: A LONDON FLAT MYSTERY
Broadwest (Gerrard)
P:D: Walter West
Vera Cornish . . . . Margaret Foster
George Foley . . . . Bentley
Reginald Stevens . . . . Bob Pritchard
Constance Backner . . . . Mrs Hooper
Richard Norton . . . . Will Hooper
Andrew Jackson . . . . Leo Scott
Hugh Croise . . . . Inspector
CRIME Shot girl recovers in time to save
framed fiance.

05712
BY THE HAND OF A BROTHER (2000)
(U) retitled: BY A BROTHER'S HAND
Broadwest (Gerrard)
P:D: Walter West
Jack Jarman . . . . The Man
Pauline Peters . . . . The Girl
CRIME Ruined man shoots burglar and finds he
is brother who has secretly helped him.

95713
CAN YOU DO THIS? (600) (U)
Urban
D: (W.R. Booth)
TRICK Girl models clay portraits of notable
Allies.

05714
ROMEO AND JULIET (970) (U)
Cricks (DFSA)
D: W.P. Kellino
S: Reuben Gillmer
Willy Clarkson . . . . Himself
COMEDY "Mudford Amateur Dramatic Society"
stages "Romeo and Juliet."

05715
NONE BUT THE BRAVE (1594) (U)
Cricks (DFSA)
D: W.P. Kellino
S: Reuben Gillmer
WAR Slacker enlists and catches spies.

05716
DOWELL'S DUELS (522) (U)
Martin (DFSA)
D: (Edwin J. Collins)
COMEDY Dueller's duels end with bomb battle.

05717
WHEN CLUBS WERE CLUBS (700) (U)
Martin (DFSA)
D: Dave Aylott
Ernie Westo . . . . .Caveman
Bob Reed . . . . .Caveman
Johnny Butt . . . . .Caveman
COMEDY Prehistoric caveman saves girl from
rival's ruffians.

05718
LEFT IN THE LURCH (480) (U)
Martin (DFSA)
D: (Edwin J. Collins)
COMEDY Three men vie for girl.

05719
PODGY PORKINS' PLOT (625) (U)
Martin (DFSA)
D: Dave Aylott
Ernie Westo . . . . .Schoolboy
Gladys Nolan . . . . .Schoolgirl
COMEDY Fat schoolboy's revenge on Girls'
School next door.

05720
GOING! GOING !! GONE!!! (581) (U)
Martin (DFSA)
D: (Edwin J. Collins)
TRICK "Comedy that will convulse your
audience."

05721
LYNXEYE ON THE PROWL (470)
Phoenix-Comedio
D:S: James Read
James Read . . . . Lynxeye
Little Chrysia . . . . Arabella
COMEDY Tec's pursuit of female crook who
stole tiara.

05722
LYNXEYE TRAPPED (612)
Phoenix-Comedio
D:S: James Read
James Read . . . . Lynxeye
Little Chrysia . . . . Arabella
Joe Evans . . . . Raffles
COMEDY Girl crook and her partner foil tec.

05723
THE KIDNAPPED KING (723) (U)
Piccadilly (Browne)
D: Joe Evans
Geraldine Maxwell . . . . Sally
COMEDY Girl detective saves King of Carlisle
from kidnappers.

05724
LIZA'S LEGACY (950) (U)
Piccadilly (Browne)
D:S: Joe Evans
Geraldine Maxwell . . . . Liza
Fred Evans . . . . Bill
COMEDY Coster girl inherits fortune.

05725
PIMPLE'S HOLIDAY (482) (U)
Piccadilly (Browne)
D:S: Fred Evans, Joe Evans
Fred Evans . . . . Pimple
COMEDY Two men meet their wives on
holiday at the Karsino.

05726
TALLY HO! PIMPLE (845) (U)
Piccadilly (Browne)
D:S: Fred Evans, Joe Evans
Fred Evans . . . . Pimple
COMEDY Drunkard's donkey is changed for
dog, cat, wooden horse, etc.

05727
PIMPLE'S SCRAP OF PAPER (533) (U)
Piccadilly (Browne)
D:S: Fred Evans, Joe Evans
Fred Evans . . . . Pimple
COMEDY Pimple mistakes removal man for
bailiff.

05728
THE KAISER CAPTURES PIMPLE (998) (U)
Piccadilly (Browne)
D:S: Fred Evans, Joe Evans
Fred Evans . . . . Pimple
COMEDY Pimple dreams he is captured by
Kaiser.

05729
THE SMUGGLERS (1293)
R. Prieur
D: Fred Evans
Fred Evans . . . . Dan
CRIME Beachy Head. Smuggler, betrayed by
jealous girl saves tec from cliff.

05730
FOR HER BROTHER'S SAKE (1095)
R. Prieur
D: Fred Evans
Fred Evans . . . . The Man
DRAMA

05731
DRIVEN BY HUNGER (978)
R. Prieur
D: Fred Evans
Fred Evans . . . . Bill Watson
CRIME Starving man jailed for stealing bread
finds PC has adopted his child.

05732
LILY'S BIRTHDAY (438)
Bamforth (YCC)
D: Cecil Birch
Lily Ward . . . . Lily
Alf Scottie . . . . Alfie
COMEDY Wilful girl and her beau wreck
parents' garden party.

05733
SCOTTIE LOVES ICE CREAM (527)
Bamforth (YCC)
D: Cecil Birch
Alf Scotty . . . . Scottie
COMEDY Youth tricks ice cream salesman
and fools customers.

05734
'IGH ART (641)
Bamforth (YCC)
D: Cecil Birch
COMEDY Poor pair extort beer from publican.

05735
ONE ON IKEY (423)
Bamforth (YCC)
D: Cecil Birch
Alf Scotty . . . . Alf
COMEDY Sacked clerk and friend fake robbery
and fram usurer.

05736
PIN PRICKS (882)
Bamforth (YCC)
D: Cecil Birch
Lily Ward . . . . Lily
COMEDY Man wins girl by posing as mystic.

05737
WHAT'S IN A NAME? (733)
Bamforth (YCC)
D: Cecil Birch
Lily Ward . . . . Mrs Smith
COMEDY Jealous wife throws away husband's
jewels, and then finds they were for her.

05738
A PAIR OF DUMMIES (655)
Bamforth (YCC)
D: Cecil Birch
Alf Scotty . . . . Alf
COMEDY Tramp's revenge on PC by faking
drowning with dummy.

05739
BERTIE'S HOLIDAY (607)
Moonshine (YCC)
Bertie Wright . . . . Bertie
COMEDY Yokel dons clothes of his dude double.

05740
ONE HONEST MAN (1090) (U)
New Agency
D: Ethyle Batley
DRAMA Three tramps each given £5; one repays
after making profit.

05741
HIS MOTHER'S SACRIFICE (1080) (U)
New Agency
D: Ethyle Batley
DRAMA Mother mortgages cottage to pay son's
gambling debts.

05742
A SON OF THE SEA (996) (U)
New Agency
D: Ernest G. Batley
CRIME Sailor kills rapist launderer, breaks jail
and catches spy.

05743
A CRY IN THE NIGHT (1200) (A)
New Agency
D: Ernest G. Batley
James Russell . . . . The Thing
HORROR Tec proves girl's father was killed
by mad scientist's winged gorilla.

05744
THE PRESSURE OF THE POSTER (800) (U)
New Agency
D: Ethyle Batley
WAR War posters cause shirker to enlist.

05745
ON THE BRINK (1038) (A)
Michaelson-Lloyd British-Venus (DFSA)
D: Warwick Buckland

Flora Morris . . . . Claire Brandon
J.R. Tozer . . . . Charles Dalton
DRAMA Novelist's neglected wife plans to elope
but is topped by child.

05746
HER ONE REDEEMING FEATURE (785) (A)
Michaelson-Lloyd British-Venus (DFSA)
D: Warwick Buckland
Flora Morris . . . . Sybil Norton
J.R. Tozer . . . . Jack Murgatroyd
CRIME Girl thief drugs rich man but repents on
learning his mother is dying.

05747
THE WORLD'S WORST WIZARD (440)
Kineto
D: W.R. Booth
TRICK Mechanical goose spoils conjurer's tricks.

05748
KINETO'S SIDE-SPLITTERS No. 1 (490)
Kineto
D: W.R. Booth
TRICK Dove of peace; first battleship through
the Panama canal; ride on a wild torpedo.

05749
ENGLAND'S WARRIOR KING
Eric Williams Speaking Pictures (YCC)
D:SC: Eric Williams
S: (PLAY) William Shakespeare (HENRY V)
Eric Williams . . . . Henry V
Men of the Royal Scots Greys
HISTORY (Film accompanies reciter on cinema
stage).

05750
THE HEART OF A CHILD (4590) (U)
London (Jury)
D: Harold Shaw
S: (NOVEL) Frank Danby
Edna Flugrath . . . . Sally Snape
Edward Sass . . . . Lord Kidderminster
Hayford Hobbs . . . . Lord Gilbert
Mary Dibley . . . . Lady Dorothea Lytham
George Bellamy . . . . Mr Peastone
Douglas Munro . . . . Joe Aarons
Frank Stanmore . . . . Johnny Doone
Christine Rayner . . . . Mary
ROMANCE Slum orphan, injured by lady's car,
becomes dancer and marries lady's brother.

05751
WHOSO DIGGETH A PIT (3660) (U)
London (Jury)
D: Ralph Dewsbury
S: Frank Fowell
Gerald Ames . . . . Dr Hartley
Charles Rock . . . . Frank Edwards
Gwynne Herbert . . . . Mrs Warde
Mary Dibley . . . . Grace Warde
CRIME Financier kills tramp in mistake for his
partner and is exposed by doctor's injection of
death simulant.

05752
THE SHULAMITE (4805) (A)
London (Jury)
D: George Loane Tucker
S: (PLAY) Edward Knoblauch
(NOVEL) Claude & Alice Askew
SC: Kenelm Foss
Norman McKinnel . . . . Simeon Knollett
Manora Thew . . . . Deborah
Gerald Ames . . . . Robert Waring
Mary Dibley . . . . Joan Waring
Gwynne Herbert . . . . Mrs Waring
Minna Grey . . . . Tanta Anna
Bert Wynne . . . . Jan Van Kennel
DRAMA Africa. Fanatical Boer farmer
mistreats young wife.

05753
THE DERBY WINNER (4900) (U)
London (Jury)
D: Harold Shaw
S: (PLAY) Cecil Raleigh, Henry Hamilton,
Augustus Harris
Edna Flugrath . . . . May Aylmer
Gerald Ames . . . . .Capt Douglas Desburn
Mary Dibley . . . . Lady Muriel Fortescue
Lewis Gilbert . . . . Col Donnelly
Christine Rayner . . . . Annette Donnelly
Wyndham Guise . . . . Joe Aylmer
Gwynne Herbert . . . . Duchess
J.L. Mackay . . . . Capt Geoffrey Mostyn
George Bellamy . . . . Rupert Leigh
Winifred Dennis . . . . Mrs Donnelly
H. Hargreaves . . . . Dr Cyprian Streatfield
Will Asher . . . . Dick Hand
SPORT Man in love with lady frames her
husband for seducing girl.

05754
THE SWEATER (2700) (U)
Hepworth (Globe)
D: Frank Wilson
S: William J. Elliott
Stewart Rome . . . . Septimus Storke
Chrissie White . . . . Enid Miller
Lionelle Howard . . . . Rev Hugh Foster
Ivy Millais . . . . The Cripple
John McAndrews . . . . Manager
Frank Wilson . . . . Foreman
DRAMA Girl weds East End clothier in return
for better conditions and organises revolt when he
reneges.

05755
THE SECOND STRING (2675) (U)
Hepworth
D:S: Frank Wilson
Stewart Rome . . . . Alec Dale
Violet Hopson . . . . Diana Nugent
Lionelle Howard . . . . Rupert Dale
William Felton . . . . Maurice Lefevre
Chrissie White . . . . Girl
SPORT Suicide's brother wins race to break
woman responsible.

05756
THE MAN WHO STAYED AT HOME (3575) U)
Hepworth (Central)
D: Cecil M. Hepworth
S: (PLAY) Letchmere Worrall, Harold Grey
Dennis Eadie . . . . Christopher Brent
Violet Hopson . . . . Miriam Leigh
Alma Taylor . . . . Molly Preston
Lionelle Howard . . . . Carl Sanderson
Chrissie White . . . . Daphne Kidlington
Henry Edwards . . . . Fritz
Dorothy Rowan . . . . Mrs Sanderson
William G. Saunders . . . . Col Preston
Jean Cadell . . . . Miss Myrtle
CRIME Tec poses as shirker to unmask spies at
East Coast boarding house.

05757
THE GREAT CHEQUE FRAUD (3000)
I.B. Davidson (Walturdaw)
D:SC: Charles Raymond
S: (CHARACTERS) Harry Blyth
Harry Lorraine . . . . Sexton Blake
Douglas Payne . . . . George Marsden Plummer
Bert Rex . . . . Tinker
CRIME Tec saves boy assistant from bank
swindler after escaping fire by overhead cable.

05758
THE GREAT MOTOR BUS OUTRAGE (1975) (U)
Clarendon

D: Wilfred Noy
CRIME Sacked chauffeur poses as bus driver to
rob bookies' outing.

05759
THE TIFF AND WHAT BECAME OF IT (541)
(U)
Clarendon
D: (Toby Cooper)
COMEDY Man poses as waiter and annoys love
rival.

05760
SHE DIDN'T WANT TO DO IT (516) (U)
Clarendon
D: (Toby Cooper)
COMEDY "The comical story of a love affair."

05761
THE IVORY HAND (3106) (U)
Clarendon
D: Wilfred Noy
CRIME Chinese priest's vengeance on man who
stole jewelled hand of sacred idol.

05762
SOMEWHERE IN FRANCE (3000)
Regal (YCC)
D: Tom Watts
S: (NOVEL) Ruby M. Ayres (NONE BUT
THE BRAVE)
Vera Cornish . . . . Marie
WAR France. Soldier poses as priest to save
wife from Uhlan.

05763
HIS LITTLE LORDSHIP (3000)
Regal (YCC)
D: Tom Watts
Little Rex . . . . His Lordship
CRIME Poacher steals earl's son and trains him
to be circus performer and thief.

05764
THE GIRL OF MY HEART (4500)
British Empire
D: Leedham Bantock
S: (PLAY) Herbert Leonard
Herbert Leonard . . . . Will Stewart
Mary Linley . . . . Mary Graham
J. Graeme Campbell . . . . . . Maj Fulton
Leal Douglas . . . . Jennie Warden
Frank Dane . . . . Dr Peter Scragg
Ray Raymond . . . . Gnr Phillips
CRIME Cardsharp bribes doctor to certify wife,
but her shipwrecked lover returns in time.

05765
DO UNTO OTHERS (3500)
Barker
D: (Bert Haldane)
S: H. Grenville—Taylor
Tom H. MacDonald . . . . Curley
Peggy Richards . . . . Renee
Patrick J. Noonan . . . . Steve
Pippin Barker . . . . Curley (child)
Connie Barnes . . . . Renee(child)
Willie Harris . . . . Steve(child)
CRIME Childhood friend elopes with Sgt's
wife, kills her, and later dies saving sgt's life.

05766
GRIP (3000)
B & C (Renters)
D: Maurice Elvey
S: (NOVEL) John Strange Winter
SC: Eliot Stannard
Leon M. Lion . . . . Count de Lacy
Elizabeth Risdon . . . . Margaret Eden

Fred Groves . . . . George Somers
A.V. Bramble . . . . Anton le Rocque
E. Compton Coutts . . . . Leroy
M. Gray Murray . . . . Mr Eden
Eliot Stannard . . . . Charles X
James Nott . . . . Interpreter
CRIME France 1820. Convict discovers the man
chained to him is the count who framed him.

05767
ADMIRAL'S ORDERS (2760)
Cunard (King)
D: Harold Weston
WAR

05768
REMEMBER BELGIUM (2010) (U)
Burlingham Standard (Walturdaw)
D: Ethyle Batley
Dorothy Batley . . . . The Child
Ernest Batley
Martin Valmour
James Russell
WAR Belgium.

05769
AN ENGLISHMAN'S HONOUR (3000)
English Films (MP)
DRAMA "How he protects his wife's good
name."

05770
ANSWER THE CALL (3000)
Big Ben Union (L & P)
D:S: L.C. MacBean
Herbert Sydney . . . . The Man
R.D. Nicholson
WAR

05771
THE WAYS OF THE WORLD (4000)
Big Ben Union (L & P)
D:S: L.C. MacBean
DRAMA

AUG

05772
WELL I'M — (456) (U)
Martin (DFSA)
D: Edwin J. Collins
TRICK Professor hypnotises man who dreams
he is hypnotist.

05773
SLIPS AND SLOPS (497) (A)
Martin (DFSA)
D: Dave Aylott
Bob Reed . . . . Policem.
Sid Butler
Johnny Butt
Bert Ford
TRICK Inept policemen try to catch elusive
burglar.

05774
HER FATAL HAND (543) (U)
Martin (DFSA)
D: (Dave Aylott)
TRICK Poet's rival blows girl's father to Milky
Way.

05775
LOVE AND SPANISH ONIONS (568) (U)
Martin (DFSA)
D: (Edwin J. Collins)
COMEDY Man dreams that he, girl, and rival,
are in Spain.

05776
THE SECOND LIEUTENANT (2791) (U)
Martin (Kin-Ex)
D: Dave Aylott
Jack Jarman
Bert Grahame
WAR

05777
THE WOMAN PAYS (1120)(U)
New Agency
D: Ethyle Batley
DRAMA "Dead" child recovers in time for
father to save mother from river.

05778
A JUSTIFIABLE DECEPTION (1058) (U)
New Agency
D: Ethyle Batley
Dorothy Batley . . . . The Girl
DRAMA Girl stops father from marrying
governess by proving that she is a secret drinker.

05779
TO SAVE HER LIFE (1076) (U)
New Agency
D: Ethyle Batley
DRAMA Actor poses as dead soldier to save
sick mother's life.

05780
NOBODY'S CHILD (1000) (U)
New Agency
D: Ethyle Batley
Thomas Canning . . . . The Man
CRIME Waif's dog saves widow from being
kidnapped by stepfather.

05781
THE LIE THAT BECAME THE TRUTH (1033)
(U)
New Agency
D: Ethyle Batley
DRAMA Girl fakes fatal illness to win man and
is shot by mistake.

05782
PIMPLE'S BOY SCOUT (740) (U)
Piccadilly (Browne)
D:S: Fred Evans, Joe Evans
Fred Evans . . . . Sherlock Pimple
COMEDY Two tecs pose as boy scouts to track
kidnapper.

05783
MADEMOISELLE PIMPLE (720)(U)
Piccadilly (Browne)
D:S: Fred Evans, Joe Evans
Fred Evans . . . . Pimple
COMEDY Pimple poses as Russian ballerina.

05784
PIMPLE'S BURLESQUE OF THE STILL
ALARM (1775) (U) USA: FLIVVER'S
STILL ALARM
Piccadilly (Browne)
D:S: Fred Evans, Joe Evans
Fred Evans . . . . Pimple
COMEDY Fireman saves kidnapped girlfriend
from burning barn.

05785
PIMPLE HAS ONE (526) (A)
Piccadilly (Browne)
D:S: Fred Evans, Joe Evans
Fred Evans . . . . Pimple
COMEDY Servant fetching wine gets drunk and
has trouble with police.

05786
PIMPLE'S GOOD TURN (787) (U)
USA: FLIVVER'S GOOD TURN
Piccadilly (Browne)
D:S: Fred Evans, Joe Evans
Fred Evans . . . . Pimple
Joe Evans . . . . Archibald
COMEDY Pimple poses as burglar to help friend
impress girl.

05787
SCOTTIE'S DAY OUT (550)
Bamforth (YCC)
D: Cecil Birch
Alf Scotty . . . . Scottie
Lily Ward . . . . Lily
COMEDY Youth plays practical jokes on man
and girl.

05788
NEVER DESPAIR (390)(U)
Bamforth (YCC)
D: Cecil Birch
COMEDY Anti-gambling woman mistakes
bookie's tout for beggar.

05789
WHAT A PICNIC (522)
Bamforth (YCC)
D: Cecil Birch
Alf Scotty . . . . Scottie
COMEDY Snubbed youth sets ants onto
picnicking children.

05790
A BACHELOR'S BABIES (797)
Bamforth (YCC)
D: Cecil Birch
COMEDY Bachelor borrows babies to fool rich
uncle.

05791
HAVE SOME MORE MEAT (512)
Bamforth (YCC)
D: Cecil Birch
Lily Ward . . . . Hostess
COMEDY Guest thinks married hostess is
flirting with him.

05792
CODFISH AND ALOES (775)
Bamforth (YCC)
D: Cecil Birch
Lily Ward . . . . Lily
Alf Scotty . . . . Alf
COMEDY Girl will wed suitor if he cures
alcoholic father.

05793
NO FOOL LIKE AN OLD FOOL (889)
Bamforth (YCC)
D: Cecil Birch
COMEDY Old man flirts to make wife jealous.

05794
HEBA THE SNAKE WOMAN (1000)
Excel (YCC)
HORROR Aztec Princess changes into snake
and kills doctor.

05795
MUDDLED MILLINERY (870)
Moonshine (YCC)
Bertie Wright . . . . Bertie
COMEDY Army reject becomes milliner's
assistant.

05796
TEDDY, THE ACTOR'S SINGING DOG (995)
Kineto
DRAMA "Many touching scenes and sensational
incidents."

05797
BILLY'S SPANISH LOVE SPASM (3000)
Homeland (Globe)
D: W.P. Kellino
S: (SKETCH) Billy Merson (SERENTATA)
SC: Reuben Gillmer
Billy Merson . . . . Billy
Teddie Gerrard . . . . Dolores
Blanche Bella . . . . The Fiancee
F. Fullbrook . . . .
COMEDY Spain. Englishman wins holiday and
fights bull.

05798
MARRIED FOR MONEY (3500)
Neptune (Walturdaw)
P: Percy Nash
D: Leon Bary
S: Louise Maclean
Gregory Scott . . . . Harry Johnson
Daisy Cordell . . . . Grace Meredith
Constance Backner . . . . Cynthia Harrison
Frank Tennant . . . . Jack Harrison
Fred Morgan . . . . Boris Balinsky
Douglas Payne . . . . Robert Sims
Cecil Morton York . . . . Rev William Sims
Laurence Phillips . . . . Gerald Sims
Douglas Cox . . . . Sir Gordon Smith
Louise MacLean . . . . Mrs Meredith
CRIME Blinded man shoots mistress's rich
husband and later poses as gardener to save
daughter from her influence.

05799
THE COAL KING (3600)
Neptune (KTC)
D: Percy Nash
S: (PLAY) Ernest Martin, Fewlass Llewellyn
Douglas Cox . . . . Sir Reginald Harford
May Lynn . . . . Ann Roberts
Frank Tennant . . . . Walter Harford
Daisy Cordell . . . . Grace Shirley
Gregory Scott . . . . Tom Roberts
Douglas Payne . . . . James Hawker
Jack Denton . . . . Jim Matthews
Joan Ritz . . . . Araminta
John East . . . . William Shirley
Helen Lainsbury . . . . Mrs Shirley
DRAMA Nurse changes baby with employer's:
her son becomes wastrel, his an heroic mine
manager.

05800
STRATEGY (2330) retitled :SOCIETY CROOKS
B & C (Pioneer)
D:S: Harold Weston
Fay Temple . . . . Woman
A.V. Bramble . . . . Detective
Marjorie Unett . . . . Crook
M. Gray Murray . . . . Crook
James Dale . . . . Crook
CRIME Disuised crooks use mechanical devices
to steal pearls from hotel room.

05801
HEARTS THAT ARE HUMAN (3565) (U)
B & C (KTC)
D: A.V. Bramble
S: John Jackson
Fay Temple . . . . Lucy Laybourne
Roy Beard . . . . Bertram Squire
Somers Bellamy . . . . David Laybourne
Kathleen Warwick . . . . Mary Laybourne
J. del Lungo . . . . Gerald Bennett
M. Gray Murray . . . . John Scudamore
Beatric Grosvenor . . . . Mrs Squire
ROMANCE Buskers give home to maid
abandoned by married seducer.

05802
BY THE SHORTEST OF HEADS (3500) (U)
Barker (LIFT) *Reissue:* 1918
D: Bert Haldane
S: Jack Hulcup, Percy Manton
George Formby jr . . . . Tony Dawson
Jack Tessier . . . . Eric Dawson
Moore Marriott . . . . Capt Fields
Jack Hulcup . . . . Geoffrey Warrington
Percy Manton . . . . Squire Markham
SPORT Squire's nephew's bastard is adopted by
trainer and rides race to win squire's bequest.

05803
LADY JENNIFER (3500) (U)
International Cine Corp
D: James Warry Vickers
S: (NOVEL) John Strange Winter
Barbara Rutland . . . . Nancy Trevor
Harry Royston . . . . Reeves
DRAMA

05804
ODDS AGINST (4000) retitled: LOST AND WON
Turner Films (Ideal)
D: Larry Trimble
S: Henry Edwards
Florence Turner . . . . Barbar Weston
Henry Edwards . . . . Dick Barry
Edward Lingard . . . . Howard Lyston
Herbert Dansey . . . . Mr Weston
James Lindsay . . . .
Minnie Rayner . . . .
DRAMA Ruined man turns thief but reforms to
save beloved from marrying crooked lawyer.

05805
THE THIRD GENERATION (4650) (U)
London (Jury)
D: Harold Shaw
S: (NOVEL) Charles McEvoy
Edna Flugrath . . . . Irma Sherston
Sydney Vautier . . . . Mark Sherston
Charles Rock . . . . Farmer Hayes
Hayford Hobbs . . . . Lord Sherston
Mary Dibley . . . . Lady Sherston
Dorothy Holmes-Gore . . . . . Rhoda Hayes
Douglas Munro . . . . Earl Sherston
Hubert Willis . . . . Onslow Flail
George Bellamy . . . . Earl Sherston (1865)
Minna Grey . . . . Mrs Hayes
ROMANCE Lord's daughter elopes with
bastard who is rightful heir.

05806
A PARK LANE SCANDAL (2000)
Michaelson-Lloyd British-Venus (Gerrard)
D:SC: Warwick Buckland
S: (NOVEL) "Rita"
Flora Morris . . . . The Woman
J.R. Tozer . . . . The Man
Austin Camp
Harry Gilbey
Sybil Wollaston
James Lewis
DRAMA Wife leaves debauched man for actor;
he is killed in duel, she kills herself.

05807
LOCHINVAR (2100)
Gaumont
D:SC: Leslie Seldon-Truss
S: (POEM) Walter Scott
Godfrey Tearle . . . . Lochinvar
Peggy Hyland . . . . Ellen
ROMANCE Scotland, period. Laird abducts
beloved on eve of enforced marriage.

05808
THE VERDICT OF THE HEART (3200) (U)
Clarendon (Moss)
D: Wilfred Noy
S: (NOVEL) Charles Garvice
Harry Welchman
Barbara Conrad
Frank Royde
CRIME Lord's nephew learns gamekeeper is
true heir and frames him for stabbing blackmailer.

05809
JACK SPRATT'S PARROT (960) (U)
Clarendon (Browne)
D: (Toby Cooper)
COMEDY "A clever parrot appears as star
artiste."

05810
THE OUTPOST (950)
Clarendon
D: Wilfred Noy
WAR France. Soldiers escape through underground
passage when spy fetches enemy troops.

05811
THE GOLDEN CHANCE (3000)
Frank Stather (Browne)
D: Frank Stather
DRAMA "Several good sea pictures and
dramatic compositions."
SEP

05812
SH! NOT A WORD (787) (U)
Cricks (DFSA)
D: Toby Cooper
COMEDY Colonel, wife, daughter, lover and
burglar hide from each other behind screen.

05813
BOOTS? NOT 'ARF! (610) (U)
Martin (DFSA)
D: Edwin J. Collins
Edourd Musto . . . . Boots
COMEDY Unemployed music hall artiste with
big feet becomes waiter.

05814
THE CHARM THAT CHARMED (680) (U)
Martin (DFSA)
D: Dave Aylott
TRICK Man dreams he finds magic charm.

05815
YOUNG NICK AT THE PICNIC (569) (U)
Martin (DFSA)
D: (Edwin J. Collins)
TRICK Magic sprite plays tricks on
picnickers and tramps.

05816
NOBBLING THE BRIDGE (578) (U)
Martin (DFSA)
D: (Edwin J. Collins)
COMEDY Man's search for kidnapped bridge.

05817
COPPERS AND CUTUPS (557) (U)
Martin (DFSA)
D: Dave Aylott
TRICK Rejected suitor drinks fluid that gives
him strength.

05818
THE CRIMSON TRIANGLE (4000)
Martin (Ogden)
D: Dave Aylott
R. Harley West . . . . Marcus Plane
Jack Jarman . . . .
CRIME Embassy attache forced to join secret
society thwarts assassination plot.

05819
THE VULTURES OF LONDON (3000)
Martin (KTC)
D: R. Harley West
H. St Barbe West . . . . The Artist
Dora de Winton . . . . Cora l'Estrange
Mollie Vaughan . . . . The Girl
Alfred Brandon . . . . The Crook
Edwin Beach . . . . The Accomplice
CRIME Girl crook acts as model to help her gang
rob artist who loves leader's sister.

05820
RAGTIME COWBOY PIMPLE (639) (U)
Piccadilly (Browne)
D:S: Fred Evans, Joe Evans
Fred Evans . . . . Pimple
COMEDY Pimple tells girl how as sheriff he
caught bank robber.

05821
PIMPLE'S WILLIT-WASIT-ISIT (794) (U)
Piccadilly (Browne)
D:S: Fred Evans, Joe Evans
Fred Evans . . . . Pimple
COMEDY Hastings. Pimple's pals pose as
brigands and threaten to kill him.

05822
PIMPLE'S SOME BURGLAR (665) (U)
Piccadilly (Browne)
D:S: Fred Evans, Joe Evans
Fred Evans . . . . Pimple
COMEDY Crooks try to rob iron foundry.

05823
PIMPLE'S MOTOR TOUR (827) (U)
Piccadilly (Browne)
D:S: Fred Evans, Joe Evans
Fred Evans . . . . Pimple
COMEDY Hastings. Father takes family to sea
and drives over cliff.

05824
PIMPLE'S THREE O'CLOCK RACE (525) (U)
Piccadilly (Browne)
D:S: Fred Evans, Joe Evans
Fred Evans . . . . Pimple
COMEDY Broke friends get into races by
posing as owner, and jockey.

05825
SILAS SIMPLE'S LOVE AFFAIR (679) (U)
Piccadilly (Browne)
COMEDY Simpleton, rejected by boss's
daughter, tries to shoot rival.

06826
THE CALL OF A SONG (730)
H.A. Browne
DRAMA Man leaves his wife, mistaking her
father's letter for one from a lover.

05827
WHO WERE YOU WITH LAST NIGHT? (792)
Bamforth (YCC)
D: Cecil Birch
COMEDY Man uses dummy to compromise
daughter's mean husband.

05828
ONCE UPON A TIME (699)
Bamforth (YCC)
D: Cecil Birch
COMEDY Doctor puts sleeping draught in wine
to catch butler.

05829
PUTTING ON THE 'FLUENCE (861)
Bamforth (YCC)
D: Cecil Birch
COMEDY Son extorts money by fooling
father's hypnotist.

05830
THE TELL-TALE GLOBE (956)
Bamforth (YCC)
D: Cecil Birch
COMEDY Magic globe reveals husband's
flirtations.

05831
A BID FOR BOUNTY (493)(U)
Bamforth (YCC)
D: Cecil Birch
Reggie Switz . . . . The Husband
COMEDY Man fakes triplets to obtain state
bounty.

05832
THE COUNTERFEIT COWBOY (999) ·
Bamforth (YCC)
D: Cecil Birch
COMEDY Man poses as cowboy to win girl.

05833
WON BY A FLUKE (1088)
Bamforth (YCC)
D: Cecil Birch
COMEDY Suitor poses as doctor to take girl to
seaside.

05834
BUNGLED BURGLARY (840)
Horseshoe (YCC)
Berties Wright . . . . Bertie
COMEDY Small man becomes burglar's
assistant.

05835
THE WOOING OF LOUIE (845)
Horseshoe (YCC)
Bertie Wright . . . . Louie
COMEDY Man thwarts rival and weds girl.

05836
CURING UNCLE (972)
Moonshine (YCC)
Bertie Wright . . . . Uncle
COMEDY Old drunkard cured by relatives.

05837
CRAZED ON CHARLIE (370)(U)
Tower Films (YCC)
Lily Ward . . . . The Girl
COMEDY Film fan dreams everybody looks
like Charlie Chaplin.

05838
HIS COOLING COURTSHIP (1181)(U)
John Bull (DFSA) *Reissue:* 1919 (Globe)
Lupino Lane . . . . Lord Clarence
COMEDY Rescuer saves girl from persistent Count.

05839
THE DUMB MAN'S EVIDENCE (1150) (U)
New Agency
D: Ernest G. Batley
James Russell . . . . The Man
CRIME Mute mimes in court to prove jealous
man killed his boss by accident.

05840
ACROSS THE WIRES (1227) (U)
New Agency
D: Ernest G. Batley
Ernest G. Batley . . . . The Man
Dorothy Batley . . . . The Child
James Russell
CRIME Gem thieves pose as firemen; tec saves
a girl from fire by carrying her across wires.

05841
RESPIRATORS (450)(U)
New Agency
D: (Ernest G. Batley)
COMEDY Man shoots at cats and is mistaken
for burglar.

05842
THE MAN WHO WENT (950)(U)
New Agency
D: Ethyle Batley
James Russell . . . . The Man
WAR Wounded soldier returns to win girl away
from slacker.

05843
BELINDA AND THE EGGS (540)(U)
New Agency
D: (Ethyle Batley)
COMEDY Maid contributes bad eggs to
campaign for convalescent soldiers.

05844
A CHILD OF THE STREETS (1070)(U)
New Agency
D:S: Ernest G. Batley
Dorothy Batley . . . . The Child
CRIME Newsboy and Women's Emergency
Corps foil jewel robbers.

05845
HIS BITTER LESSON (1115)(U)
New Agency
D:S: Ethyle Batley
DRAMA Man is reconciled to wife after death
report proves false.

05846
HARD TIMES (4000) (U)
Transatlantic
D:SC: Thomas Bentley
S: (NOVAL)Charles Dickens
Bransby Williams . . . . Gradgrind
Leon M. Lion . . . . Tom Gradgrind
Dorothy Bellew . . . . Louisa
Madge Tree . . . . Rachael
Mr Forrest . . . . Stephen Blackpool
F Lymons . . . . Josiah Bounderby
Will Corrie . . . . Sleary
Clara Cooper . . . . Cissie Jupe
J. Wynn Slater . . . . James Harthouse
DRAMA Period. Man robs mill-owning brother-in-
law and frames weaver.

05847
THE MYSTERY OF A HANSOM CAB (5500) (A)
B & C (Ideal)
D: Harold Weston
S:(NOVEL) Fergus Hume
SC: Eliot Stannard
Milton Rosmer . . . . Mark Frettleby
Fay Temple . . . . Madge Frettleby
A.V. Bramble . . . . Moreland
Arthur Walcott . . . . Oliver White
James Dale . . . . Brian Fitzgerald
CRIME Heiress helps counsel prove fiance did not
kill cabby's passenger.

05848
HOME (4000)
B & C (Ashley)
D: Maurice Elvey
S: (PLAY) Frank Lindo (HOME SWEET HOME)
SC: Eliot Stannard
Elizabeth Risdon . . . . Joan Bicester
Fred Groves . . . . Steven Armitage
A.V. Bramble . . . . Dan
M. Gray Murray . . . . Duke
E. Compton Coutts . . . .
Clarence Derwent . . . .
Joyce Templeton . . . .
Pauline Peters . . . .
ROMANCE Fishergirl learns she is duke's lost
daughter but returns to humble family.

05849
A VAGABOND'S REVENGE (4770)
Cunard (King)
D: Wallett Waller

S: Florence Britton
Agnes Glynne . . . . Enid
Jack Morrison . . . . Clive Emmett
Lyston Lyle . . . . Lord Hayhurst
Alice de Winton . . . . Sarah
Sydney Paxton . . . . Doctor
DRAMA Lord's blind daughter kidnapped by
gipsy but later her protrait is recognised by
father.

05850
ESTHER REDEEMED (3000)
Renaissance (Standard)
D:SC: Sidney Morgan
S: (PLAY) Arthur Bertram (THE WOLF WIFE)
Fanny Tittell-Brune . . . . Esther
Julian Royce . . . . .Sir Richard Franklyn
Cecil Fletcher . . . . Roland
William Brandon . . . .
A. Harding Steerman . . . . . .
Mona K. Harrison . . . .
CRIME Girl crook, cured by operation, weds
surgeon's nephew but relapses on meeting
ex-partner.

05851
THE COUNTERFEITERS (2600)(A)
I.B. Davidson-St. George (KTC)
D:SC: Charles Raymond
S: (CHARACTERS) Harry Blyth
Harry Lorraine . . . . Sexton Blake
Bert Rex . . . . Tinker
Jack Jarman . . . .
N. Watts-Phillips . . . .
CRIME Counterfeiters using old mill tie
detective to the waterwheel and boy assistant
to lock gates.

05852
THE MAN IN POSSESSION (3000)
Homeland (Globe)
D: W.P. Kellino
S: Reuben Gillmer
Billy Merson . . . . Mr. Bunce
Lupino Lane . . . . Freddy
Winifred Delevanti . . . . Mollie Topping
Blanche Bella . . . . Mrs Topping
COMEDY Bankrupt persuades bailiff to pose as
millionaire at daughter's party.

05853
THE GIRL WHO TOOK THE WRONG
TURNING (5000)
British Empire
D: Leedham Bantock
S: (PLAY) Walter Melville
Henry Lonsdale . . . . James Harcourt
Alice Belmore . . . . Sophie Coventry
Nina Lynn . . . . Vesta le Clere
Ronald Adair . . . . Willie Mason
Mercy Hatton . . . . Lucy Coventry
Wingold Lawrence . . . . Jack Fenton
Andrew Emm . . . . Johnny Walker
Sidney Sarl . . . . Bill Slater
Eva Dare . . . . Poppy Slater
C.F. Collings . . . . Richard Fenton
CRIME Squire's nephew frames disowned cousin
for murder and lures his wife's sister into vice.

05854
HER BOY (5000)
Hepworth (Thanhouser)
D: Frank Wilson
S: Gertrude Allen
Stewart Rome . . . . Hugh Vane
Violet Hopson . . . . Nance
Lionelle Howard . . . . Eric
Chrissie White . . . . Isabelle
DRAMA Gambler spends mother's savings,
bankrupts rich wife, and dies repentant.

05855
BRIGADIER GERARD (5260)(U)
Barker (Walturdaw)
D: Bert Haldane
S: (NOVEL/PLAY) Arthur Conan Doyle
(THE EXPLOITS OF BRIGADIER GERARD)
SC: Rowland Talbot
Lewis Waller . . . . Brigadier Gerard
Madge Titheradge . . Countess de Rochequelaune
A.E. George . . . . Napoleon
Blanche Forsythe . . . . Agnes
Austin Leigh . . . . Gen Coulaincourt
Frank Cochrane . . . . Pierre
Fernand Mailly . . . . Talleyrand
R.F. Symons . . . . Maj Olivier
Philip Renouf . . . . Jacques
ADVENTURE France, period. Captain and
countess save emperor's secret papers.

05856
JACK TAR (4500)(U)
Barker (ICC) Reissue: 1918
D: Bert Haldane
S: (PLAY) Arthur Shirley, Ben Landeck
SC: Rowland Talbot
Jack Tessier . . . . Lt Jack Atherley
Edith Yates . . . . Mary Westwood
Eve Balfour . . . . Margherita
Thos H. MacDonald . . . . Max Schultz
Harry Royston . . . . Dick Starling
J. Hastings Batson . . . . . Sir Michael Westwood
Blanche Forsythe . . . . Maid
WAR Admiral's daughter poses as Turk to fetch
framed lieut to save Smyrna consulate from
German spy's mob.

05857
THE ANGELS OF MONS (2000)
G.B. Samuelson (Midland)
D: Fred Paul, L.C. MacBean
S: Harry Engholm
Peggy Hyland . . . . The Girl
Bertram Burleigh . . . . The Man
WAR Drama based on popular topical myth.

05858
THE FACE AT THE TELEPHONE (2000)
G.B. Samuelson (John Bull)
D: Fred Paul, L.C. MacBean
S: Harry Engholm
Agnes Glynne . . . . The Girl
Gerald Royston . . . . The Boy
DRAMA

05859
INFELICE (6000)
G.B. Samuelson (Moss)
D: Fred Paul, L.C. MacBean
S: (NOVEL) Augusta J. Evans-Wilson
SC: Harry Engholm
Peggy Hyland . . . . Minnie Merle
Fred Paul . . . . Peleg Peterson
Bertram Burleigh . . . . Cuthbert Lawrence
Queenie Thomas . . . . Regina
Richard Vaughan . . . . General Lawrence
Rowland Moore . . . . Lawyer
Harry Lofting . . . . Vicar
DRAMA General forces married son to wed
heiress, but he returns to true wife when she acts
in play of her life.

05860
THE WRAITH OF THE TOMB (3000) retitled:
THE AVENGING HAND
Cricks (Ogden)
D: Charles Calvert
S: William J. Elliott
Dorothy Bellew . . . . Natalie Vaughan
Sydney Vautier . . . . Harry Newby
Douglas Payne . . . .
FANTASY Ghost of Egyptian Princess curses
archaeologist who stole her mummified hand.

OCT
05861
KEEP IT DARK (830) (U)
Cricks (DFSA)
D: Toby Cooper
COMEDY Man must wed Negress to inherit
£75,000.

05862
A WILD NIGHT (814) (U)
Cricks (DFSA)
D: Toby Cooper
COMEDY Suspected burglary upsets boarding
house.

05863
WHICH IS WITCH? (533)(U)
Martin (DFSA)
D: (Edwin J. Collins)
TRICK Rich landowner's troubes when he is
cursed by old hag.

05864
TOUGH NUTS AND ROUGHS (500) (U)
Martin (DFSA)
D: (Edwin J. Collins)
COMEDY Attempts to crack tough cocoanut.

05865
PUSS AND BOOTS (546)(U)
Martin (DFSA)
D: Edwin J. Collins
Edourd Musto . . . . Boots
COMEDY Big-footed suitor elopes in small car.

05866
HIS PHANTOM BURGLAR (517) (U)
Martin (DFSA)
D: (Dave Aylott)
TRICK Police recruit chases magical burglar.

05867
SELINA-ELLA (734) (U)
Martin (DFSA)
D: Dave Aylott
TRICK Maid dreams she is Cinderella and
Kaiser is Demon King.

05868
THE JADE HEART (3215) (A)
Martin
D: Dave Aylott
Jack Jarman . . . . Jim Neville
Bunty Stewart . . . . Marjorie
Fred Rains . . . . Slippery Sam
Joyce Templeton . . . . Child
CRIME Framed convict saves warder's child and
is allowed to escape with man who killed his
father.

05869
NIPPER'S BUSY HOLIDAY (1053)(U)
John Bull (DFSA) Reissue: 1919, HIS BUSY
HOLIDAY (Globe)
S: Reginald Crompton
Lupino Lane . . . . Nipper
COMEDY Youth poses as aunt to thwart
persistant professor.

05870
MAX HAS A BIRTHDAY (690)(U)
New Agency
D: (Ernest G. Batley)
COMEDY Man takes wrong coat from
restaurant.

05871
A TRAGIC MISTAKE (970)(U)
New Agency
D: Ethyle Batley
DRAMA Tramp saves benefactor's wife from
burning house.

05872
THE TICHTOWN TUMBLERS (490)
New Agency
D: (Ernest G. Batley)
COMEDY Two boys emulate street acrobats.

05873
FALSELY ACCUSED (990)(U)
British Oak (NA)
D: Ethyle Batley
Dorothy Batley . . . . The Child
DRAMA Widow's child gives necklace to poor
woman who is accused of stealing it.

05874
BELINDA MAKES A BLOOMER (450)(U)
New Agency
D: (Ernest G. Batley)
COMEDY Maid beats rugs and causes trouble
with tramps and neighbours.

05875
THE BARGEE'S DAUGHTER (870)
New Agency
D: Ethyle Batley
DRAMA Jealous woman tries to drown mate,
who is saved by her daughter.

05876
THE EAR-RING (1045)(U)
British Oak (NA)
D: Ethyle Batley
Martin Valmour . . . . Mr Bowman
Nancy Bevington . . . . Mrs Bowman
Nell Emerald . . . . Mrs Trevor
DRAMA Spurned widow plants ear-ring on man
to ruin his marriage.

05877
LIZA ON THE STAGE (812)(U)
Piccadilly (Browne)
D:S: Joe Evans
Geraldine Maxwell . . . . Liza
COMEDY Coster girl acts in "Romeo and Juliet."

05878
SHELLS, MORE SHELLS (1160)
Piccadilly (Browne)
D:S: Joe Evans
Joe Evans . . . . The Man
DRAMA Wounded son of munitions factory
foreman persuades strikers to return to work.

05879
WHEN WOMEN RULE (530)
Piccadilly (Browne)
D:S: Joe Evans
Geraldine Maxwell . . . . The Woman
COMEDY Woman take over jobs of men at war.

05880
PIMPLE UP THE POLE (907) (U)
Piccadilly (Browne)
D:S: Fred Evans, Joe Evans
Fred Evans . . . . Pimple
COMEDY Pimple gets own back on friends by
posing as lunatic.

05881
PIMPLE'S THREE (433)(U)
Piccadilly (Browne)
D:S: Fred Evans, Joe Evans
Fred Evans . . . . Pimple
COMEDY Pimple's friends think he has triplets
when he has three teeth removed.

05882
PIMPLE'S ROAD TO RUIN (815) (U)
Piccadilly (Browne)
D:S: Fred Evans, Joe Evans
Fred Evans . . . . Pimple
COMEDY Burglar tells PC story of his downfall.

05883
PIMPLE EXPLAINS (950)(A)
Piccadilly (Browne)
D:S: Fred Evans, Joe Evans
Fred Evans . . . . Pimple
COMEDY Special constable gets a night out
by telling wife an air rad is expected.

05884
GETTING ON HIS NERVES (850)
Bamforth (YCC)
D: Cecil Birch
COMEDY Indian helps girl frighten her father
with bees.

05885
MISS MADCAP MAY (1088)
Bamforth (YCC)
D: Cecil Birch
COMEDY Girl poses as boy to fool admirer.

05886
MONTY'S MONOCLE (755)
Bamforth (YCC)
D: Cecil Birch
COMEDY Dude's eyeglass reveals things that
are invisible to others.

05887
WHAT A FIND (737)
Bamforth (YCC)
D: Cecil Birch
COMEDY Girl helps beau extort money from
Egyptologist father.

05888
THE COWBOY VILLAGE (607)(U)
Gaumont
D: J.L.V. Leigh
COMEDY Village boys emulate film cowboys.

05889
POOR CLEM (925) (U)
Transatlantic
D: Bert Haldane
Will Page . . . . Clem
Ruby Belasco . . . . Widow
Harry Royston . . . . Nephew
COMEDY Musician turns busker and poses as
widow's maid.

05890
COWBOY CLEM (744) (U)
Transatlantic
D: Bert Haldane
Will Page . . . . Clem
Clara Cooper . . . . Mary Brown
Harry Daniels . . . . Her Lover
COMEDY Cowboy will inherit fortune if he weds
girl named Mary Brown.

05891
ROYAL LOVE (3949) (A)
Transatlantic
D: Percy Nash
S: Rowland Talbot
Joan Ritz . . . . Grand Duchess Thora
Eve Balfour . . . . Anita
Gregory Scott . . . . Prince
Frank Tennant . . . . Alexis
Daisy Cordell . . . . The Queen
Patrick Noonan . . . . Capt Moran
J. Hastings Batson . . . . King
Charles Vane . . . .
Douglas Payne . . . .
ADVENTURE Ruritania. King's son grows up
and avenges father's murder.

05892
JELF'S (5376) (U) USA: A MAN OF HIS WORD
London (Jury)

D:SC: George Loane Tucker
S: (PLAY) Horace Annesley Vachell
Henry Ainley . . . . Richard Jelf
Mary Dibley . . . . Lady Fenella Maull
Gerald Ames . . . . Jim Palliser
Charles Rock . . . . Thomas Jelf
Hayford Hobbs . . . . Hon Archibald Maull
George Bellamy . . . . Perkins
Douglas Munro . . . . Tom Harkaway
Lewis Gilbert . . . . Bad Bill
Philip Hewland . . . . Sir Julian Dunne
Gwynne Herbert . . . . Countess of Skene
Hubert Willis . . . . Adam Winslow
Christine Rayner . . . . Dorothy
DRAMA Banker helps broke friend who later
causes a run on his bank.

05893
UNDER THE RED ROBE (3747) (U)
Clarendon (Gau)
D: Wilfred Noy
S: (PLAY) Edward Rose (NOVEL) Stanley Weyman
Owen Roughwood . . . . Gil de Berault
Dorothy Drake . . . . Renee de Cochefort
Jackson Wilcox . . . . Cardinal Richelieu
Sydney Bland . . . . M. de Cochefort
ADVENTURE France, 1630. Cardinal's emissary
must capture beloved's brother or die.

05894
A SOLDIER'S GIRL (2000) (A)
Barker (G & H)
WAR

05895
SWEET LAVENDER (5000) (U)
Hepworth (LIFT) *Reissue:* 1918
D: Cecil M. Hepworth
S: (PLAY) Arthur Wing Pinero
Henry Ainley . . . . Dick Phenyl
Chrissie White . . . . Lavender
Alma Taylor . . . . Ruth Rolfe
Stewart Rome . . . . Geoffrey Wedderburn
J.V. Bryant . . . . Clement Hale
ROMANCE Housekeeper's daughter loves toper's
affianced friend.

05896
WIFE THE WEAKER VESSEL (625) (U)
Hepworth
D: Frank Wilson
Chrissie White . . . . The Wife
COMEDY Women rebel against husbands.

05897
THE GOLDEN PAVEMENT (3900)(A)
Hepworth
D: Cecil M. Hepworth
S: Percy Manton
Alma Taylor . . . . Brenda Crayle
Stewart Rome . . . . Dennis
Lionelle Howard . . . . Martin Lestrange
William Felton . . . . The Crook
Henry Vibart . . . . The Nobleman
DRAMA Devon girl weds nobleman's son and is
ejected after being blackmailed by father of her
child.

05898
CASTLE (4500)(U)
Turner Films (Ideal) *Reissue:* 1918
D: Larry Trimble
S: (PLAY) T.W. Robertson
SC: Benedict James
Sir John Hare . . . . Eccles
Peggy Hyland . . . . Esther Eccles
Esme Hubbard . . . . Polly Eccles
Dawson Millward . . . . Capt Hawtree
Roland Pertwee . . . . Hon George D'Alroy
Campbell Gullan . . . . Sam Gerridge
Mary Rorke . . . . Marquise

COMEDY Marquise objects to son marrying
cockney, but they reunite on his return from
war.

05899
THE FATAL FORMULA (2000)
Kineto
D:S: Frank Stather
CRIME Inventor's daughter uses new
explosive to destroy spies.

05900
NELLY (1150)
Britannia (Pathe)
S: (NOVEL) Richard Marsh
ROMANCE Artist's model wins man by
posing as childhood sweetheart.

05901
FROM THE DEPTHS OF DESPAIR (3500)
Regal
D: Tom Watts
DRAMA PC saves drunkard's wife from suicide
and later arrests her for killing husband.

05902
WIRELESS (4000)
Famous British
D:S: Harry Lorraine
Harry Lorraine . . . . Cdr Daring
Violet Graham . . . . The Spy
Jack Wayho . . . . Cdr Metz
Bert Rex . . . . Billy
WAR Naval commander sinks spies' U-boat.

05903
THE ADVENTURES OF DEADWOOD DICK
(series) (A)
G.B. Samuelson (Ideal)
D: Fred Paul, L.C. MacBean
S: (STORIES)
Fred Paul . . . . Dick Harris
Joan Ferry . . . . Girl

05904
1-HOW RICHARD HARRIS BECAME KNOWN
AS DEADWOOD DICK (2000)

05905
2-DEADWOOD DICK'S VENGEANCE (2000)

05906
3-DEADWOOD DICK AND THE MORMONS
(2000)

05907
4-DEADWOOD DICK SPOILS BRIGHAM
YOUNG (2000)

05908
5-DEADWOOD DICK'S RED ALLY (2000)

05909
6-DEADWOOD DICK'S DETECTIVE PARD
(2000)
WESTERN America, period. Adventures of an
Englishman in the Wild West.

05910
THE WOMAN WHO DID (6000) (A)
Broadwest (Gerrard)
P:D: Walter West
S: (NOVEL) Grant Allen
SC: Aubrey Fitzmaurice
Eve Balfour . . . . Hermina Barton
Thos. H. MacDonald . . . . . . Allen Merrick
George Foley . . . . Sir Anthony Merrick
Lily Saxby . . . . Mrs Denby
Thelma Giddens . . . . Dolores Barton
Joan Morgan . . . . Dolores (child)
William Brandon . . . . The Dean
ROMANCE Italy. Suffragette protests against
marriage by openly living with lover.

NOV

05911
ORPHEUS SONG FILMS (series)
Orpheus Song Films
D: Geoffrey H. Malins

05912
1-HEARTS OF GOLD

05913
2-THE CASTAWAYS

05914
3-ABIDE WITH ME

05915
4-ON THE BANKS OF ALLAN WATER
Amy Sissons
MUSICAL Synchronised for accompanying
singers.

05916
DOUBLE AND QUITS (445) (U)
Cricks (DFSA)
D: Toby Cooper
COMEDY Injured old gent is mistaken for
escaped lunatic and chased.

05917
MIKE ALONE IN THE JUNGLE (848) (U)
Martin (DFSA)
D: Dave Aylott
Ernie Westo . . . . Mike Murphy
COMEDY Mike dreams he is in jungle and saves
girl's life.

05918
MIKE'S GOLD MINE (553) (U)
Martin (DFSA)
D: Dave Aylott
Ernie Westo . . . . Mike Murphy
COMEDY Mike dreams he finds gold at
Peckham Rye.

05919
DREAM BAD, LUCK DITTO (538) (U)
Martin (DFSA)
D: (Edwin J. Collins)
TRICK Man has nightmares and later his watch
is stolen.

05920
CHRISTMAS EVE (1166) (U)
Neptune (Browne)
D: Alfonse Frenguelli
Gregory Scott . . . . Charles
DRAMA Child stops sacked thief from shooting
father.

05921
THREE CHRISTMASSES (916) (U)
Neptune (Browne)
D: Alfonse Frenguelli
ROMANCE Squire eventually forgives artist
for eloping with daughter.

05922
COSTER JOE (1114) (U)
Neptune (Browne)
D: Alfonse Frenguelli
COMEDY Cockney woos and wins amateur
comedienne.

05923
THE BROTHERS (950) (U)
New Agency
D: Ethyle Batley
James Russell . . . . The Man
WAR Blind widow's son tries to get scapegrace
brother to enlist.

05924
NURSERY RHYMES (920)
British Oak (NA)
D: Ethyle Batley
Dorothy Batley . . . . The Child
COMEDY Cat and the fiddle; Mother Hubbard;
Old woman in the shoe; etc.

05925
THE AFFAIR AT NO. 26 (1070)(U)
British Oak (NA)
D: Ernest G. Batley
CRIME Man kills woman in mistake for wife
and frames his brother.

05926
THE HATTON GARDEN ROBBERY (1130) (A)
British Oak (NA)
D: Ethyle Batley
James Russell . . . . The Man
CRIME Coster buys coat in which is hidden
stolen diamond.

05927
ALADDIN (1280)
Piccadilly (Browne)
D:S: Fred Evans, Joe Evans
Fred Evans
FANTASY Chinese boy's magic lamp helps him
foil uncle and win Princess.

05928
WAR PIMPLE (W) RIGHT? (1025) (U)
Piccadilly (Browne)
D:S: Fred Evans, Joe Evans
Fred Evans . . . . Pimple
COMEDY Two men pose as landlady's longlost
husband.

05929
PIMPLE'S UNCLE (1012) (U)
Piccadilly (Browne)
D:S: Fred Evans, Joe Evans
Fred Evans . . . . Pimple
COMEDY Rich man wills fortune to most
deserving of nephews.

05930
PIMPLE SEES GHOSTS (1013) (U)
Piccadilly (Browne)
D:S: Fred Evans, Joe Evans
Fred Evans . . . . Pimple
COMEDY Pimple's pals pose as ghosts.

05931
BUMBLE'S BLUNDER (668) (U)
Bamforth (YCC)
D: Cecil Birch
COMEDY Cleric mistakes woman's hot
hair-curler for smoking pipe.

05932
MUSHROOM STEW (540) (U)
Bamforth (YCC)
D: Cecil Birch
Reggie Switz . . . . The Husband
COMEDY Henpeck tries to poison mother-in-law
with toadstools.

05933
A WIFE ON LOAN (852)
Bamforth (YCC)
D: Cecil Birch
COMEDY Married man borrows friend's wife
to deceive rich uncle.

05934
EVER BEEN HAD? (629)
Bamforth (YCC)
D: Cecil Birch
COMEDY Shoppers mistake meaning of sign
in shop window.

05935
PEACE AT ANY PRICE (984)
Bamforth (YCC)
D: Cecil Birch
Alf Foy . . . . Old Foy
COMEDY Man fakes burglary to win policeman's
daughter.

05936
THE GREEN-EYED MONSTER (876)
Bamforth (YCC)
D: Cecil Birch
COMEDY Jealous woman's plan to trap
husband backfires.

05937
DREAMING OF ROBINSON CRUSOE (899)
Fay Films (YCC)
COMEDY Man dreams he is Robinson Crusoe.

05938
LILY'S FIRST AID TRAGEDY (367)
Pyramid (YCC)
Lily Ward . . . . Lily
COMEDY Girl's first aid cures lazy father.

05939
CAPTAIN JOLLY'S CHRISTMAS (636)
Pyramid (YCC)
"Jolly" . . . . Capt Jolly
Leslie Hatton . . . . Soldier
Mme Pareva . . . .
ROMANCE Captain loves adopted waif but lets
her marry soldier.

05940
CHAPLIE CHARLIN SPECIAL CONSTABLE
(592)
Pyramid (YCC)
Leslie Hatton . . . . Chaplie Charlin
COMEDY Charlie Chaplin's double becomes
special constable.

05941
TAMING A SHREW (355)
Pyramid (YCC)
Lily Ward . . . . Lily
Leslie Hatton . . . . Leslie
COMEDY Nagging wife tries to get rid of
husband.

05942
A NICE LITTLE GIRL (576)
Pyramid (YCC)
Lily Ward . . . . Lily
Leslie Hatton . . . . Leslie
COMEDY Girl tests affections of short-sighted
admirer.

05943
A VILLAGE INTERLUDE (733)
Pyramid (YCC)
"Jolly"
Leslie Hatton
Mme Pareva
COMEDY "Bright and brisk."

05944
A CHRISTMAS REFORMATION (935) (U)
Vanguard (DFSA) *Reissue:* 1916
DRAMA Burglar's child reforms rake who then
reforms burglar.

05945
BILLIE "BOW-WOW" (981) (U)
Touchstone (DFSA)
D: Rowland Moore
Bille Boreham . . . . Billie
Alesia Leon . . . . The Girl
COMEDY Suitor smears himself with dog food
to win dog-loving girl.

05946
WHEN PASSIONS RISE (2855) (U)
Clarendon (Walturdaw)
D: Wilfred Noy
CRIME Villain abducts rival's fiancee.

05947
IN SEARCH OF A HUSBAND (3000)
Clarendon (BCT)
D: Wilfred Noy
S: (NOVEL Max Permberton (BEHIND THE
CURTAIN)
Barbara Conrad . . . . Violet Cordai
Murray Carrington . . . . Jack Heather
Frank Hilton . . . . John Delamere
DRAMA Opera star's husband returns from
abroad after five years of amnesia.

05948
THE WOMAN WHO DARED (3503) (A) USA:
A SOUL FOR SALE
Transatlantic
D: Thomas Bentley
S: Rowland Talbot
Austen Camp . . . . The Lord
CRIME Artist blamed when drunkard
father shoots brutal husband.

05949
THE DEVIL'S BONDMAN (3892) (A) USA:
THE SCORPION'S STING
Transatlantic
D: Percy Nash
S: Rowland Talbot
George Bellamy . . . . Morton Masters
Fay Temple . . . . Peggy Lofting
Gregory Scott . . . . .Gerald Carstairs
Douglas Payne . . . . Satan
Daisy Cordell . . . . Myra
J. Hastings Batson . . . . Bishop of Lowden
Arthur M. Cullin . . . . Rev Hughes
FANTASY Ex-convict sells soul to devil for
riches and kills his mistress at engagement
party.

05950
THE KNUT AND THE KERNEL (1005) (A)
Transatlantic
D: Bert Haldane
Whimsical Walker . . . . The Kernel
Al Brown . . . . The Knut
Will Page . . . . Mrs Nagger
COMEDY Anti-vice league president's husband
has night out with nephew.

05951
THE THORNTON JEWEL MYSTERY (2600) (A)
(A)
I.B. Davidson-St George (Serra)
D: Charles Raymond
S: (CHARACTERS) Harry Blyth
Harry Lorraine . . . . Sexton Blake
Bert Rex . . . . Tinker
Miss Vere . . . . Flash Kate
CRIME Girl frames drunkard for gem theft and
tec is saved from crook's launch by boy's 60ft.
dive.

05952
THE WHITE HOPE (3650) (U)
Hepworth (Moss)
D: Frank Wilson
S: (NOVEL) W.H.R. Trowbridge
SC: Victor Montefoire
Stewart Rome . . . . Jack Delane
Violet Hopson . . . . Claudia Carisbrooke
Lionelle Howard . . . . Durward Carisbrooke
John MacAndrews . . . . Shannon
Frank Wilson . . . . Royce

George Gunther . . . . Sam Crowfoot
SPORT Earl's sister returns to boxer in time to
help him win.

05953
THE OUTRAGE (2700) (A)
Hepworth (Thompson)
D: Cecil M. Hepworth
S: Albert Chevalier
Henry Ainley . . . . The French Officer
Alma Taylor . . . . The Girl
Lionelle Howard . . . . Lt Arlstein (1870)
Violet Hopson . . . . The Wife
John MacAndrews . . . . Gen Arlstein(1914)
Mamie Murray . . . . The Nurse
WAR France. Prussian Lt rapes girl in 1870 and
is killed by their son in 1914.

05954
THE ONLY MAN (3000)
Homeland (Globe)
D: W.P. Kellino
S: Reuben Gillmer
Billy Merson . . . . Billy Whattle
Winifred Delevanti . . . . Tiny
Fred Dunning . . . . Bassett
Blanche Bella . . . . Landlady
COMEDY Shopwalker's holiday at seaside village
where all men have enlisted.

05955
TRAFFIC (3000) (A)
I.B. Davidson-St. George (Anima)
D:SC: Charles Raymond
S: (NOVEL) E. Temple Thurston
Marjorie Villis . . . . Nanno
Charles Vane . . . . Jamesy Ryan
Alden Lovett . . . . .Philip Jerningham
Lily Saxby . . . . Miss Shad
Arthur H. Rooke . . . .
DRAMA Ireland. Catholic peasant refuses to
divorce brutal farmer and turns whore until his
death.

05956
AT THE TORRENT'S MERCY (3500) (U)
B & C (KTC)
D: H.O. Martinek
Percy Moran . . . . Ronald
Ivy Montford . . . . Mary
A.V. Bramble . . . .
Jack Jarman . . . .
M. Gray Murray . . . .
James Dale . . . .
Margaret Adamson . . . .
DRAMA Scotland. Gamekeeper's daughter
saves lover when poacher throws him into
river.

05957
FOR THE ALLIES (3000)
B & C (DFSA)
WAR "A terrific money-maker."

05958
THE NIGHTBIRDS OF LONDON (4150) (U)
Hepworth
D: Frank Wilson
S: (PLAY) George R. Sims
SC: Blanche McIntosh
Stewart Rome
Chrissie White
Violet Hopson
Lionelle Howard
William Felton
John MacAndrews
Henry Vibart
Arthur Staples
CRIME

05959
THE RECALLING OF JOHN GREY (1625) (U)
Hepworth (Moss)
D: Frank Wilson
S: L.J. Williams
Stewart Rome . . . . Rev John Grey
Violet Hopson . . . . Mary Loder
Chrissie White . . . . Helen Fane
John MacAndrews . . . . Jim Loder
Ivy Millais . . . . Ethel Loder
DRAMA Boxing curate leaves socialite to save
wife of murderous ex-convict.

05960
AS THE SUN WENT DOWN (3075) (U)
Hepworth (UK)
D: Frank Wilson
S: Wernham Ryott
Stewart Rome . . . . David Grant
Chrissie White . . . . Mildred Blair
Lionelle Howard . . . . Wilbur Leon
Gwynne Herbert . . . . Mrs Blair
Frank Wilson . . . . Captain
DRAMA Girl rejects poor man to marry rich
man and they are all shipwrecked on island.
island.

05961
IRIS (5500) (U)
Hepworth (Ideal)
D: Cecil M. Hepworth
S: (PLAY) Arthur Wing Pinero
Henry Ainley . . . . Maldonado
Alma Taylor . . . . Iris
Stewart Rome . . . . Laurence Trenwith
ROMANCE Widowed heiress, forbidden to
re-marry, takes lover.

05962
FAR FROM THE MADDING CROWD (4580) (U)
(U)
Turner Films (Ideal)
D:SC: Larry Trimble
S: (NOVEL) Thomas Hardy
Florence Turner . . . . Bathsheba Everdene
Henry Edwards . . . . Gabriel Oak
Malcolm Cherry . . . . Farmer Boldwood
Campbell Gullan . . . . Sgt Troy
Marion Grey . . . . Fanny Robin
Dorothy Rowan . . . . Lyddie
John MacAndrews . . . . Farmhand
Johnny Butt . . . . Farmhand
ROMANCE Dorset. Girl farmer weds faithless
sergeant who is killed by suitor, and realises she
loves baliff.

05963
THE VENGEANCE OF ALLAH (2800) (U)
Windsor (LIFT)
D: F. Martin Thornton
S: Niranjan Pal
Queenie Thomas . . . . The Girl
Roy Travers . . . . The Usurer
DRAMA India. Usurer's son has debtor jailed and
abducts his daughter.

05964
THE SHOPSOILED GIRL (4050) (A)
British Empire
D: Leedham Bantock
S: (PLAY) Walter Melville
Henry Lonsdale . . . . Mark Faulkner
Alice Belmore . . . . Jessie Brown
Nina Lynn . . . . Flossie de Vigne
Frank Randall . . . . Joe Kelly
Gladys Williams . . . . Vera Thurston
CRIME Man helps mistress murder husband and
frame husband of her step-daughter.

05965
THE DOP DOCTOR (5766) (A) USA: THE
LOVE TRAIL
G.B. Samuelson (Pathe) *Reissue:* 1917, THE
TERRIER AND THE CHILD (Shaftesbury)
D: Fred Paul, L.C. MacBean
S: (NOVEL) Richard Dehan
SC: Harry Engholm
Fred Paul . . . . Dr Owen Saxham
Agnes Glynne . . . . Lynette Mildare
Bertram Burleigh . . . . Lord Beauvais
Booth Conway . . . . Abraham Bough
Minna Grey . . . . Mother Superior
DRAMA Africa, 1900. Orphan girl loves married
soldier but weds exiled doctor. (Banned under
DORA).

05966
PAULA (6000) (A)
Holmfirth (Initial)
D: Cecil Birch
S: (NOVEL) Victoria Cross
Hettie Payne . . . . Paula
Frank McClellan . . . . Vincent Hallam
DRAMA Widow follows sick lover to Italy and
dies after donating blood.

05967
HOW MEN LOVE WOMEN (3000)
Phoenix-Couragio
D: Percy Moran
Percy Moran . . . . The Man
Marietta de Leyse . . . . The Woman
DRAMA Dr fakes marriage to gipsy and leaves
her when baby dies.

05968
PARTED BY THE SWORD (3000) (A)
Phoenix-Couragio
D: Percy Moran
Percy Moran . . . . Jack Moran
Marietta de Leyse . . . . Countess
WAR Tourist saves German countess from
runaway coach; later she saves him when war is
declared.

05969
NURSE AND MARTYR (3000) (U)
Phoenix (Midland) *Reissue:* 1928
D: Percy Moran
S: Edgar Wallace
Percy Moran
Cora Lee
WAR Belgium. German betrays Edith Cavell
for helping wounded soldiers escape.

05970
THE CHRISTIAN (9170)(A)
London (Jury)
D: George Loane Tucker
S: (NOVEL) Hall Caine
Derwent Hall Caine . . . . John Stone
Elizabeth Risdon . . . . Glory Quayle
Gerald Ames . . . . Francis Drake
Mary Dibley . . . . Mercy McRae
Charles Rock . . . . Parson Quayle
Bert Wynne . . . . Lord Robert Ure
Philip Hewland . . . . Lord Storm
Christine Rayner . . . . Polly Love
George Bellamy . . . . Father Lampleigh
Douglas Munro . . . . Canon Wealthy
Frank Stanmore . . . . Rev Golightly
Gwynne Herbert . . . . Mrs McRae
DRAMA Lord's mob kills cleric who sought to
save soul of beloved actress.

05971
MR LYNDON AT LIBERTY (5130) (A)
London (Jury)

D: Harold Shaw
S: (NOVEL) Victor Bridges
Edna Flugrath . . . . Joyce Aylmer
Fred Groves . . . . Tom Morrison
Harry Welchman . . . . Neil Lyndon
Manora Thew . . . . Sonia Savaroff
Charles Rock . . . . Dr McMurtie
S. Jensen . . . . George Marwood
CRIME Agent helps escaped convict prove doctor
is spy.

05972
A WILL OF HER OWN (3370)(U)
London-Diploma (Jury)
D:S: Maurice Elvey
Elizabeth Risdon . . . . Isabel Stanton
Fred Groves . . . . Dr Blake
Hilda Sims . . . .
Ernest Cox . . . .
Dolly Tree . . . .
DRAMA Actress weds poor doctor, leaves him
for stage, and reunites with him at baby show.

05973
CHARITY ANN (3710) (A)
London-Diploma (Jury)
D: Maurice Elvey
S: Chappell Dossett
Elizabeth Risdon . . . . Ann Charity
Fred Groves . . . . Graham Trevor
Chappell Dossett . . . . Prof Woolsey
Winifred Sadler . . . .
DRAMA Blind beggar's violinist daughter shoots
and blinds man who wronged her as child.

05974
FINE FEATHERS (3610) (A)
London-Diploma (Jury)
D:S: Maurice Elvey
Elizabeth Risdon . . . . Meg Roberts
Fred Groves . . . . Richard Dean
Douglas Payne . . . . Dr Beverley
Daisy Cordell . . . . Mrs Beverley
Dolly Tree . . . .
Kenelm Foss . . . . Caxton
ROMANCE When blind man is cured his plain
wife tries to make herself pretty, but causes
divorce.

05975
LOVE IN A WOOD (4189) (U)
London-Diploma (Jury)
D: Maurice Elvey
S: (PLAY) William Shakespeare (AS YOU
LIKE IT)
SC: Kenelm Foss
Elizabeth Risdon . . . . Rosalind
Gerald Ames . . . . Orlando
Vera Cunningham . . . . Celia
Frank Stanmore . . . . Touchstone
Kenelm Foss . . . . Oliver
Cyril Percival . . . .
Dolly Tree . . . .
COMEDY Modern dress version of "As You
Like It."

05976
LIGHT (3000)
Renaissance (DFSA)
D:S: Sidney Morgan
Julian Royce . . . . The Husband
Mona K. Harrison . . . . The Wife
Joan Morgan . . . . The Child
A. Harding Steerman . . . . . The Brother
DRAMA Angelic child heals breach between rich
man, wife, and estranged brother.

05977
FARMER SPUDD AND HIS MISSUS TAKE A
TRIP TO TOWN (676) (U)
Gaumont
D: J.L.V. Leigh

COMEDY Country couple visit Madame
Tussaud's exhibition and dream Chamber of
Horrors comes to life.

05978
FETTERS OF FEAR (1214) (U)
Gaumont
D:S: Leslie Seldon-Truss
Peggy Hyland . . . . Mavis Sinclair
J.L.V. Leigh . . . . Roland Stuart
Clarence Derwent . . . . Jasper Haynes
ROMANCE Scotland. Hypnotised girl's lover
poses as servant to prevent her marriage to
guardian.

05979
A ROGUE'S WIFE (3500)
Neptune (Walturdaw)
D: Percy Nash
Gregory Scott
Daisy Cordell
Joan Ritz
Frank Tennant
Douglas Payne
CRIME Scotland. Thief steals laird's diamond,
weds vicar's daughter, and is betrayed by former
mistress.

05980
THE STRIPED STOCKING GANG (3527) (A)
retitled: MRS CASSELL'S PROFESSION
Barker-Neptune (Anima)
D: Fred W. Durrant
S: (NOVEL) Irene Miller
SC: Irene Miller
Margaret Belona . . . . Viola Cassell
Miriam Ferris . . . . Mrs Cassell
CRIME Girl posing as maid takes blame when
milliner mother's gang steals Lady's pearls.

05981
A BELGIAN GIRL'S HONOUR (1355)(A)
Barker (G & H)
S: Rowland Talbot
Olive Gordon . . . . Girl
Phyllis Gordon . . . . Girl
WAR

05982
MOTHERHOOD retitled: THE CLIMAX (4875)
(A)
B & C Pall Mall (Gaumont)
D:S: Harold Weston
Lilian Braithwaite . . . . Lady Cadby
Fay Temple . . . . Gwen
A.V. Bramble . . . . Sir Thomas Cadby
A. Caton Woodville . . . . . . Hal Carruthers
Laura Leycester . . . . Mrs Preece
Victor Boggetti . . . . Agent
DRAMA Tory magnate rejects ward's
socialistic suitor until dying sempstress revals
he is bastard son.

05983
QUICKSANDS OF LIFE (4000)
Gaumont-Victory
P: George Pearson
D: J.L.V. Leigh
Malcolm Mortimer . . . . The Man
CRIME

DEC

05984
YVONNE (1065) (A)
B & C (DFSA)
D: Dave Aylott
Fred Groves . . . . The Artist
A.V. Bramble . . . . The Count
Lettie Paxton . . . . Yvonne
ROMANCE Paris. Artist duels rich patron for
love of model.

05985
THE WINNER (1114) (U)
Cricks (DFSA)
D: Charles Calvert
S: Reuben Gillmer
J. Palmer . . . . Referee
SPORT Girl promises to marry boxer who loses match.

05986
THE SILENCE OF JASPER HOLT (1954)(U)
Martin (DFSA)
D: (Edwin J. Collins)
George Keene . . . . Jasper Holt
DRAMA Crippled orphan releases brother from promise so he may join army.

05987
MAD MOKES AND MOTORS (589) (U)
Martin (DFSA)
D: (Edwin J. Collins)
COMEDY Motorists rebel against conscientious policeman.

05988
FICKLE FLO'S FLIRTATION (571) (U)
Martin (DFSA)
D: (Edwin J. Collins)
TRICK Two rivals fight for girl who loves tennis player.

05989
TWO OF A SUIT (642) (U)
Martin (DFSA)
D: (Edwin J. Collins)
COMEDY Clerk mistaken for crooked double.

05990
THE HARLEQUINADE (518) (U)
Union Jack (DFSA)
COMEDY Traditional harlequinade.

05991
THE WIFE WHO DARED (2312) (U)
A.A.A. (DFSA)
DRAMA Liberia. Starving man tells professor how he stole for woman he loved, who turns out to be the professor's wife.

05992
SAVED FROM HERSELF (1200) (A)
A.A.A. (DFSA)
DRAMA Major's young wife decides not to elope after dreaming of divorce and suicide.

05993
LARRY AND 'ERB GET A JOB (902)(U)
A.A.A. (DFSA)
COMEDY Film studio hands play cards, fight and cause riot.

05994
COMMISSIONAIRE (1182) (U)
A.A.A. (DFSA)
CRIME Commissionaire foils blackmailed clerk who steals plans of loom for foreign spies.

05995
THE WOMAN BETWEEN (1755) (A)
A.A.A. (DFSA)
DRAMA Sick woman shoots companion for flirting with husband and son.

05996
PIMPLE ACTS (720) (U)
Piccadilly (Browne)
D:S: Fred Evans, Joe Evans
Fred Evans . . . . Pimple
COMEDY Pimple has trouble when he plays a detective in a film.

05997
PIMPLE WILL TREAT (683) (U)
Piccadilly (Browne)
D:S: Fred Evans, Joe Evans
Fred Evans . . . . Pimple
COMEDY Pimple and drinking companions find way round "no treating" law.

05998
PIMPLE'S ARTFUL DODGE (834) (U)
Piccadilly (Browne)
D:S: Fred Evans, Joe Evans
Fred Evans . . . . Pimple
COMEDY Pimple and friends use dummy to cheat publican.

05999
PIMPLE GETS THE HUMP (699) (U)
Piccadilly (Browne)
D:S: Fred Evans, Joe Evans
Fred Evans . . . . Pimple
COMEDY Pimple dreams his nagging wife changes into camel.

06000
JOEY'S 21ST BIRTHDAY (1010)
Piccadilly (Browne)
D:S: Joe Evans
Joe Evans . . . . Joey
Geraldine Maxwell . . . . Mrs Joey
COMEDY Joey's drunken party ends in lecture from wife and cold bath.

06001
THE WHITE HAND (765)
Bamforth (YCC)
D: Cecil Birch
COMEDY Tec follows trail of white hand-prints and catches another tec.

06002
JOLLY MAKES A HASH OF THINGS (944)
Pyramid (YCC)
"Jolly"
Lily Ward
COMEDY "Mildly amusing."

06003
JOLLY'S LITTLE BIT (765)
Pyramid (YCC)
"Jolly" . . . . Captain Jolly
COMEDY Naval captain, too old to enlist, becomes special constable.

06004
THOSE CHILDREN! (970)
British Oak (NA)
D: Ethyle Batley
Dorothy Batley . . . . The Child
Joy Buglear . . . . The Baby
COMEDY Widow adopts homeless waif whom her own child followed.

06005
THE BARNSTORMERS (620)(U)
Transatlantic
D: Bert Haldane
Will Page . . . . Manager
Clara Cooper . . . . Maria Marten
COMEDY Travelling players stage "Maria Marten" in village barn.

06006
BRITONS AWAKE! (3500)
Magnet
D: (Stuart Kinder)
WAR "Stirring drama depicting love and war, showing Zeppelin raids."

06007
SOME FUN (2000)
Comedy Combine - Sunny South
D:S: Fred Evans, Will Evans
Fred Evans . . . . Pantaloon
Will Evans . . . . Clown
COMEDY Christmas harlequinade.

06008
A STUDY IN SKARLIT (2000)
Comedy Combine-Sunny South (Pioneer)
D:S: Fred Evans, Will Evans
Fred Evans . . . . Sherlokz Homz
Will Evans . . . . Prof Moratorium
COMEDY Private detective versus master criminal.

06009
YOUNG CHARLIE'S HALF DAY (1000)
G & Y Films
Little Leslie . . . . Young Charlie
COMEDY Naughty schoolboy plays pranks on half holiday.

06010
THE MAN IN THE SHADOWS (3000)
Charles McEvoy (YCC)
D:SC: Charles McEvoy
S: (PLAY) Charles McEvoy (VILLAGE WEDDING)
Aldbourne Village Players
DRAMA Wiltshire. "Simple but effective story of the English countryside."

06011
THE YOKE (4468) (A) retitled: LOVE'S LEGACY
International Cine Corp
D: James Warry Vickers
S: (NOVEL) Hubert Wales
SC: Arthur Shirley, Miss Shirley
Barbara Rutland . . . . Angelica
Leon Belcher . . . . Maurice
Jack Hobbs . . . . Christopher Grahame
Molly Terraine . . . . The Girl
DRAMA Girl adopts dying lover's son, falls in love with him, saves him from drugs, and gives him up to younger girl.

06012
THE COBBLER (3000) retitled: THE FIGHTING COBBLER
I.B. Davidson-St George (XL)
D:S: A.E. Coleby
A.E. Coleby . . . . John Strong
Marjorie Villis . . . . Mary Strong
Arthur Rooke . . . . Bill Smith
N. Watts-Phillips . . . . Ralph Ingram
Mrs. Watts-Phillips . . . . Mrs Strong
ROMANCE Artist lures Mrs Strong cobbler's daughter to London whilst fiance is abroad in army.

06013
AND THEN HE WOKE UP (1025)
I.B. Davidson-St. George (Browne)
D: A.E. Coleby
TRICK Small man, rejected by the army, dreams he flies to France in bed.

06014
THE BLACKMAILERS (3000) (A)
I.B. Davidson-St. George (LIFT)
D: A.E. Coleby
Arthur Rooke . . . . John Drew
Joan Legge . . . . Pickles
CRIME Detective escapes from drowning in water tank, fire, and being tied to windmill sails.

06015
A WORLD OF SIN (4400) (A)
British Empire
S: (PLAY) Walter Melville
CRIME Socialite betrays gang to police, kills lord, abducts heiress, and is killed by minion.

06016
AFTER DARK (3000)
Buckland Films (A1)
P:D: Warwick Buckland
S: (PLAY) Dion Boucicault
Flora Morris . . . . Eliza Medhurst
Harry Royston . . . . Charles Dalton
Harry Gilbey . . . . Gordon Chumley
Beatrice Read . . . . Rose Egerton
B.C. Robinson . . . . Chandos Bellingham
CRIME Bart's scapegrace son weds barmaid to fulfil terms of will.

06017
THE WHITE STAR (4893) (U)
Holmfirth (Harma)
D: Bertram Phillips
Queenie Thomas . . . . Iris Ballard
Norman Howard . . . . David Marks
Rowland Moore . . . . Lord Hawksett
Arthur Walcott . . . . Julian Marks
W. Willets . . . . Wilson Harley
L. Ashwell . . . . Frank Ballard
Alf Foy . . . . Stagedoor Keeper
Syd Baker . . . . Tramp
Billy Asher . . . . Jack Higgs
SPORT Financier's son drops bomb on girl's racehorse but hack has been substituted.

06018
HER LIFE IN LONDON (4100) (A)
Martin (DFSA)
D: R. Harley West
S: (PLAY) Arthur Shirley
Alesia Leon . . . . The Girl
Fred Morgan . . . . The Man
Nina Lynn
CRIME Detective's daughter poses as soldier to help cleric save vicar's daughter from blind crook's gang.

06019
A WELSH SINGER (4640) (U)
Turner Films (Butcher) *Reissue:* 1918
D: Henry Edwards
S: (NOVEL) Allen Raine
SC: Henry Edwards, Larry Trimble
Florence Turner . . . . Mifanwy
Henry Edwards . . . . Leuan
Campbell Gullan . . . . Tom Pomfrey
Malcolm Cherry . . . . John Powys
Una Venning . . . . Laissabeth Powys
Fred Rains . . . . Music Master
Edith Evans . . . . Mrs Pomfrey
ROMANCE Wales. Shepherdess becomes opera star, shepherd becomes a sculptor.

06020
THE GREAT ADVENTURE (5500) (U)
Turner Films (Ideal)
D; Larry Trimble
S: (PLAY) Arnold Bennett
SC: Benedict James
Henry Ainley . . . . Ilam Carve
Esme Hubbard . . . . Janet Cannott
Rutland Barrington . . . . Mr Texel
E.H. Brooke . . . . Sampson Ebag

Amy Lorraine . . . . Mrs Shawn
Arthur M. Cullin . . . . Albert Shawn
Hubert Harben . . . . Cyrus Carve
Dorothy Rowan . . . . Lady Alice Rowfant
Fred Rains . . . . Courier
Campbell Gullan . . . . Reporter
COMEDY Rich artist changes places with dead valet and weds poor woman, only to find his valet had wife and sons.

06021
ULTUS, THE MAN FROM THE DEAD (6147) (U) USA: ULTUS 1:THE TOWNSEND MYSTERY; ULTUS 2: THE AMBASSADOR'S DIAMOND
Gaumont—Victory
D: George Pearson
S: George Pearson, Thomas Welsh
Aurele Sydney . . . . Dick Morgan
J.L.V. Leigh . . . . Conway Bass
Marjorie Dunbar . . . . Lady Townsend
A. Caton Woodville . . . . . . .Sir Gilbert Townsend
M. Gouget . . . . Eugene Lester
CRIME Diamond miner survives attack and dons disguises to kill partner.

06022
'TWIXT CUP AND LIP (1017) (U)
Gaumont
D: J.L.V. Leigh
Peggy Hyland . . . . Doris
COMEDY Man dressed as tramp is confused with real one at fancy dress ball.

06023
IN THE GRIP OF THE SULTAN (4000)
Barker-Neptune (Renters)
D: Leon Bary
Miriam Ferris . . . . Girl
ADVENTURE Christian slave fetches British sailors to save imprisoned missionary and girl from Sultan.

06024
HIS LORDSHIP (2065) (U)
London (Jury)
D: George Loane Tucker
S: (STORY) W.W. Jacobs
Frank Stanmore . . . . Lord Fairmont
Judd Green . . . . Farmer Rose
Mary Brough . . . . Mrs Rose
COMEDY Man poses as lord to fool farmer's daughter.

06025
HER UNCLE (1350) (U)
London (Jury)
D: George Loane Tucker
S: (STORY) W.W. Jacobs
Charles Rock . . . . Mr Wragg
Edward Silwood . . . . George Gale
Judd Green . . . . Sailor
COMEDY Man feigns illness to woo old man's niece and saves him from escaped ape.

06026
THE FIRM OF GIRDLESTONE (5100) (U)
London (Jury)
D: Harold Shaw
S: (NOVEL) Arthur Conan Doyle
SC: Bannister Merwin
Edna Flugrath . . . . Kate Horston
Fred Groves . . . . Ezra Girdlestone
Charles Rock . . . . John Girdlestone
Windham Guise . . . . Maj Clutterbuck

Hayford Hobbs . . . . Tom Dimsdale
Gwynne Herbert . . . . Mrs Scully
Molly Terraine . . . . Rebecca
CRIME Old merchant tries to save firm by attempting to kill his ward.

06027
THE HEART OF SISTER ANN (3945) (A)
London (Jury)
D: Harold Shaw
S: (NOVEL) G.E.R. Mayne
Edna Flugrath . . . . Ann Milton
Hayford Hobbs . . . . Serge Laoloff
Guy Newall . . . . John Blaine
Micheline Potous . . . . Mary Milton
Winifred Sadler . . . .
DRAMA Orphan dancer repays sister's sacrifice by becoming pregant by rich Russian and marryin novelist her sister loves.

06028
THE TWO ROADS (4070) (U)
London (Jury)
D: Harold Shaw
S: (PLAY) Ben Landeck
Edna Flugrath . . . . Linda Murdoch
Ben Webster . . . . .Sir Cuthbert Maclaine
Fred Groves . . . . Rev Basil Egerton
Douglas Munro . . . . Toby Murdoch
Wallace Bosco . . . . Taplow
Florence Nelson . . . . Lady Maclaine
CRIME Counterfeiter's daughter blackmailed by father's partner to steal secret formula.

06029
G.P. AS BASIL THE BRAINLESS (2000)
G.P. Huntley
D:S: G.P. Huntley
G.P. Huntley . . . . Basil
COMEDY Drunkard poses as poultryman on lady's estate. (Date uncertain).

06030
LITTLE PIPPIN (2000)
G.P. Huntley
D:S: G.P. Huntley
DRAMA Little girl living with old grocer is lady's lost child.

06031
FROM SCOTLAND YARD
Vernon Films (YCC)
D: Charles Vernon
Harold A. Crawford . . . . The Man
CRIME

06032
THE INGRATE (3000)
Big Ben Union (L & P)
D: H.O. Martinek
DRAMA.

06033
JIM THE SCORPION (3000)
Big Ben Union (L & P)
D: H.O. Martinek
Ivy Martinek . . . . The Girl
CRIME

06034
THE OCTOPUS GANG (4000)
Big Ben Union (L & P)
D: H.O. Martinek
Ivy Martinek . . . . The Girl
CRIME

1916

JAN

06035
WHEN A MAN'S SINGLE (699)(U)
British Photoplay Productions (YCC)
P: Edward Godal
D: Kelly Storrie
COMEDY Drunken bachelor reformed by friend.

06036
MATRIMONIAL BLISS (670)(U)
British Photoplay Productions (YCC)
P: Edward Godal
D: Kelly Storrie
COMEDY Man, angered by mother-in-law,
takes girl out.

06037
THE FORGERY OF THE £1 NOTES (1040)(U)
British Oak (NA)
D: Ethyle Batley
CRIME Detective catches forgers.

06038
THE GREAT RED WAR (2900) (A)
British Oak (NA)
D: Ethyle Batley
Dorothy Batley . . . . The Child
WAR

06039
MIKE BACKS THE WINNER (581) (U)
Martin (DFSA)
D: Dave Aylott
Ernie Westo . . . . Mike Murphy
COMEDY Tramp dreams he backs outsider and
buys piebald horse.

06040
OH AUNTIE! (965) (U)
Martin (DFSA)
D: (Dave Aylott)
COMEDY Girl's beau wins parents' consent by
posing as aunt.

06041
WEST END PALS (956) (U)
Piccadilly (Browne)
D:S: Joe Evans
Joe Evans . . . . The Husband
COMEDY Henpecked husband dreams he attends
bachelors' reunion.

06042
JOEY'S AUNT (972) (A)
Piccadilly (Browne)
D:S: Joe Evans
Joe Evans . . . . Joey
Geraldine Maxwell . . . . Mrs Joey
COMEDY Joey hides girls in an ottoman and
poses as his aunt.

06043
JOEY'S PERMIT (891)(U)
Piccadilly (Browne)
D:S: Joe Evans
Joe Evans . . . . Joey
Geraldine Maxwell . . . . Mrs Joey
COMEDY Joey dreams he is Prime Minister and
can kill useless people.

06044
JOEY'S HIGH JINKS (960)(A)
Piccadilly (Browne)
D:S: Joe Evans
Joe Evans . . . . Joey
Geraldine Maxwell . . . . Mrs Joey
COMEDY Joey poses as waiter to escape wrathful
wife and is forced to serve her.

06045
PIMPLE'S GREAT ADVENTURE (1030)(U)
Piccadilly (Browne)
D:S: Fred Evans, Joe Evans
Fred Evans . . . . Pimple
COMEDY Pimple loves British wife of German
spy, whom he captures.

06046
PIMPLE'S CRIME (832)(U)
Piccadilly (Browne)
D:S: Fred Evans, Joe Evans
Fred Evans . . . . Pimple
COMEDY Pimple's friends pose as detectives
when he thinks he has killed man.

06047
PIMPLE'S PART (781)(U)
Piccadilly (Browne)
D:S: Fred Evans, Joe Evans
Fred Evans . . . . Pimple
COMEDY Pimple tries to be an actor.

06048
TIT FOR TAT (663) retitled: VICE VERSA;
OR, THE TABLES TURNED (U)
Union Jack (DFSA)
COMEDY Henpeck does housework whilst wife
goes to his office.

06049
NIPPER AND THE CURATE (1036)(U)
John Bull (DFSA) Reissue: 1919, THE
CURATE (Globe)
S: Reginald Crompton
Lupino Lane . . . . Nipper
COMEDY Youth poses as heiress to save sister
from infatuated curate.

06050
HIS DAUGHTER'S DILEMMA (5070)(U)
London (Jury)
D: Ralph Dewsbury
S: Frank Fowell
Ben Webster . . . . Bernard Venn
Manora Thew . . . . Madeleine Kingsley
Philip Hewland . . . . Dr Mackenzie
Gwynne Herbert . . . . Lady Kingsley
Hubert Willis . . . . Sharp
Christine Rayner . . . . Rose Twining
DRAMA Aspiring MP blackmails philanthropist's
ward to save her father from jail.

06051
YOU (1330)(U)
London (PCT)
D: Harold Shaw
S: Bannister Merwin
Edna Flugrath . . . . The Girl
Gerald Ames . . . . The Man
Charles Rock . . . . The Veteran
Douglas Munro . . . .
WAR Note asking "what are you doing for your
country?" is passed from hand to hand. (Profits
to the Cinema Ambulance Fund.)

06052
THE GAME OF LIBERTY (5725)(U) USA:
UNDER SUSPICION
London (Jury)
D: George Loane Tucker
S: (NOVEL) E. Phillips Oppenheim
Gerald Ames . . . . Hon Paul Walmsley
Douglas Munro . . . . Joseph H. Parker.
Laura Cowie . . . . Eve Parker
Bert Wynne . . . . Insp Cullen
Sydney Fairbrother . . . . Mrs Bundercombe
Hugh Croise . . . . Bert Johnson
CRIME Lord's son loves daughter of counter-
feiter who steals necklace.

06053
MEG THE LADY (4740)(U)
London-Diploma (Jury)
D: Maurice Elvey
S: (NOVEL) Tom Gallon
Elizabeth Risdon . . . . Lady Brisby
Fred Groves . . . . Giles Curwen
Eric Stuart . . . . Teddy
CRIME Lord's faithless wife kills robber and is
blackmailed by her lover.

06054
PASTE (5700)(A)
London (Jury)
D: Ralph Dewsbury
S: Bannister Merwin
Henri de Vries . . . . Richard Waite
Gerald Ames . . . . Prince Maletta
CRIME Jewel setter's partner blackmails him
over his kleptomaniac wife and makes him use
daughter in plan to defraud Prince.

06055
ESTHER (3900)(U)
London-Diploma (Jury)
D:SC: Maurice Elvey
S: (BOOK) Anon (THE BOOK OF ESTHER)
Elizabeth Risdon . . . . Esther
Fred Groves . . . . Haman
Charles Rock . . . . Mordecai
Ruth Mackay . . . . Vashti
Franklin Dyall . . . .
Guy Newall . . . .
James Dale . . . .
Beatrix Templeton . . . .
HISTORY 500 BC. Persian queen frustrates
vizier's plot against Jews.

06056
AN ODD FREAK (1360)(U)
London (Jury)
D:SC: George Loane Tucker
S: (STORY) W.W. Jacobs
Frank Stanmore . . . . Sam Small
Judd Green . . . . Mr Reddish
COMEDY Sailor sells nephew to showman as
wild man from Borneo.

06057
MIXED RELATIONS (1828)(U)
London(Jury)
D:SC: George Loane Tucker
S: (STORY) W.W. Jacobs
Frank Stanmore . . . . Bert
COMEDY Cook poses as girl's brother to fool
infatuated captain.

06058
DRIVEN (5239) (A) USA: DESPERATION
London-Diploma (Jury)
D:SC: Maurice Elvey
S: (PLAY) E. Temple Thurston (THE
EVOLUTION OF KATHERINE)
Elizabeth Risdon . . . . Katherine Crichton
Fred Groves . . . . John Stafforth
Guy Newall . . . . Richard Furness
Henrietta Watson . . . . Lady Crichton
Hugh Croise . . . . Mr Crichton
DRAMA Scientist's wife learns she has two years
to live and tries affair with friend.

06059
SIR JAMES MORTIMER'S WAGER (938)(U)
Gaumont
P: George Pearson
D:S: Leslie Seldon-Truss
Godfrey Tearle . . . . Sir James Mortimer
Peggy Hyland . . . . Lady Betty
Clarence Derwent . . . . Lord Fopleigh
ROMANCE Period. Lord wagers he can win lady
and almost loses when she learns of it.

06060
A MAN AND A WOMAN (3770)(A)
Sealight
D: F.L. Lyndhurst
DRAMA

06061
WHOSO IS WITHOUT SIN (4700)(A)
Ideal *Reissue:* 1918
D: Fred Paul
S: May Sherman
SC: Fred Paul, Benedict James
Hilda Moore . . . . Mary Linton
Milton Rosmer . . . . The Vicar
Flora Morris . . . . Alice Repton
Ronald Squire . . . . Roger Markham
Arthur M. Cullin . . . . John Linton
Lawrence Leyton . . . . James
DRAMA Clerk's suicide reforms extravagant
wife who then saves whore and stops mob
from killing sweater. (Winner of £25 scenario
contest).

06062
HONOUR AMONG THIEVES (2915)(U)
Clarendon
D: Wilfred Noy
CRIME

06063
A PRINCESS OF THE BLOOD (3855)(U)
Clarendon
D: Wilfred Noy
Harry Welchman
Barbara Conrad
DRAMA

06064
STILL WATERS RUN DEEP (4500)(U)
Ideal
D: Fred Paul
S: (PLAY) Tom Taylor
SC: Dane Stanton
Lady Tree . . . . Mrs Sternhold
Milton Rosmer . . . . John Mildmay
Rutland Barrington . . . . Mr Potter
Sydney Lewis Ransome . . . . Capt Hawksley
Hilda Bruce-Potter . . . . Mrs Mildmay
E.H. Brooke . . . .
CRIME Captain instals himself in wealthy home
and uses letters for blackmail.

06065
BURNT WINGS (3640)(A)
Broadwest (Monopol)
P:D: Walter West
S: (NOVEL) Mrs Stanley Wrench
SC: R. Byron-Webber
Eve Balfour . . . . Margaret Dennis
J.R. Tozer . . . . Paul Westlake
Tom H. MacDonald . . . . . . Frank Vane
Lily Saxby . . . . Lila Stebbing
DRAMA Wife adopts husband's bastard because
she has been unfaithful in thought.

06066
THE LITTLE MAYORESS (3000) retitled:
THE MILL-OWNER'S DAUGHTER
Neptune (Globe)
D: Fred W. Durrant
Nancy Lewis Waller . . . . . . Little Mayoress
Cecil Mannering . . . . Harry Wright
Cecil Morton Yorke . . . . . . Martin Thorndike
Blanche Forsythe . . . . Miss Snagg
Brian Daly . . . . Snagg
DRAMA Northern mayor cuts mill-workers'
wages but daughter weds wounded strike leader.

06067
THE TERRIBLE 'TEC (3000)

Homeland (Globe)
D: W.P. Kellino
S: Reuben Gillmer
Billy Merson . . . . Sherlock Blake
Winifred Delevanti . . . . Secretary
Blanche Bella . . . . Mother
Fred Dunning . . . . Crook
COMEDY Tec dons disguises to catch diamond
thieves.

06068
THE MAN WHO BOUGHT LONDON (5000)(A)
Windsor (Int-Ex)
P: Guido Serra
D: F. Martin Thornton
S: (NOVEL) Edgar Wallace
E.J. Arundel . . . . King Kerry
Evelyn Boucher . . . . Elsie Marion
Roy Travers . . . . .Hermon Zeberlieff
Nina Leonise . . . . .Vera Zeberlieff
Reginald Fox . . . . Gordon Bray
Rolfe Leslie . . . . Horace Baggin
Jeff Barlow . . . . James Leete
Harold Snell . . . . Micheloff
James Davis . . . . Tack
A.G. Gardner . . . . Gillette
Helen Stewart . . . . Mrs Gritter
CRIME Millionaire buys City and his half-
brother tries to kill sister to inherit share.

06069
THE WEB OF FATE
Everyman
P: W.D. Henderson
D: Lewis Gilbert
Manora Thew
George Keene
Lily Saxby
Charles Ashwell
Judd Green
Sara de Groot
DRAMA

06070
THE LADY SLAVEY (1905) (U) retitled:
THE SLAVEY'S LEGACY
Transatlantic
D: Bert Haldane
Louie Freear . . . . The Slavey
Will Page . . . . The Footman
COMEDY Clumsy maid entertains
ex-employers on her legacy.

06071
SOME DETECTIVES (950)(U)
Transatlantic
D: Bert Haldane
Will Page . . . . Clem
COMEDY Tecs try to trail counterfeiters
and are arrested by mistake.

06072
THE STRONGER WILL (2000)
Henry Howse (Ogden)
S: Helena Millais
Helena Millais . . . . Marigold
Douglas Payne . . . . Mark Birch
Constance Elgin . . . . Lady Nelson
ROMANCE Canadian millionaire weds lady's
daughter and feigns poverty to test her.

06073
MEG OF THE SLUMS (3000)
Henry Howse (Ogden)
S: Helena Millais
Helena Millais . . . . Meg
Bertram Burleigh . . . . Harry Newman
DRAMA Coster forsakes crime to enlist and
saves drudge from white slavery.

FEB

06074
THE ENEMY AMONGST US (1120)(U)
British Oak (NA)
D: Ernest G. Batley
CRIME Detectives unmask spies.

06075
INTO THE LIGHT (1060) (U)
British Oak (NA)
D: Ethyle Batley
CRIME Lieut's wife has amnesia when she is
attacked whilst returning jewels stolen by her
brother.

06076
KEEP THE HOME FIRES BURNING (1120)
(A) retitled: KEEP OUR LAD'S HOME GOING
British Oak (NA)
D: Ethyle Batley
ROMANCE Soldier returns home and wrongly
suspects wife of infidelity.

06077
THE ELEVENTH HOUR (1195) (U)
British Oak (NA)
D: Ernest G. Batley
James Russell
CRIME Cinematographer proves gambler
framed cousin for murdering their stepfather.

06078
WAND-ERFUL WILL (663)(U)
Cricks (DFSA)
D: Toby Cooper
Jack Jarman . . . . The Man
TRICK Penniless man shares lodgings with
professor whose magic wand makes furniture
move.

06079
HOW LOVE CAME (990)(A)
Cricks (DFSA)
D: (Charles Calvert)
DRAMA Man loses wife to lover in draw of
cards but she repents in time to stop him from
driving over cliff.

06080
JACK SPRATT'S PARROT AS THE ARTFUL
DODGER (975) (U)
Clarendon
D: (Toby Cooper)
COMEDY Sailor's parrot causes trouble with
sweetheart.

06081
ONLY ONE PAIR (990)(U)
Clarendon
D: (Percy Stow)
COMEDY Two playwrights with one dress
suit are invited to lady's dance.

06082
PATRIOTIC MRS BROWN (1070)
Homeland (Browne)
D: W.P. Kellino
S: Reuben Gillmer
Fred Leslie . . . . Mr Brown
Blanche Bella . . . . Mrs Brown
COMEDY Henpeck's wife causes trouble
trying to do wartime duty.

06083
MANY HAPPY RETURNS (734)(U)
Martin (DFSA)
D: (Edwin J. Collins)
TRICK Husband dreams of flirting with girls
at party.

06084
A DEUCE OF A GIRL (760)(U)
Martin (DFSA)
D: (Edwin J. Collins)
TRICK Employer dreams that girl typist changes into devil.

06085
PIMPLE ENDS IT (867)(U)
Piccadilly (Browne)
D:S.: Fred Evans, Joe Evans
Fred Evans . . . . Pimple
COMEDY Rejected by rich girl, Pimple drinks poison — but it is whisky.

06086
PIMPLE'S ZEPPELIN SCARE (1598)(U)
Piccadilly (Browne)
D:S: Fred Evans, Joe Evans
Fred Evans . . . . Pimple
COMEDY Couple mistake musician for air raid alert and move to basement until war ends.

06087
JOEY'S NIGHT ESCAPADE (970)(U)
Piccadilly (Browne)
D:S: Joe Evans
Joe Evans . . . . Joey
Geraldine Maxwell . . . . Mrs Joey
COMEDY Joey, kept late at office, has night out.

06088
JOEY'S APACHE MANIA (877)(U)
Piccadilly (Browne)
D:S: Joe Evans
Joe Evans . . . . Joey
COMEDY Joey tries to emulate apache dancer.

06089
LOVE IN A MIST (1250)(U)
Hepworth
D: Cecil M. Hepworth
S: Blanche McIntosh
Stewart Rome . . . . The Woodman
Alma Taylor . . . . The Girl
Tom Powers . . . . The Fiance
Ruby Belasco . . . . The Mother
ROMANCE Bored rich girl loses fortune and fiance and marries poor woodsman.

06090
A DEAL WITH THE DEVIL (1025)(U)
Hepworth
D: Frank Wilson
FANTASY Old chemist sells soul to the devil for youth and wins girl from policeman.

06091
THE MAN AT THE WHEEL (1000) (U)
Hepworth
D: Frank Wilson
Alma Taylor . . . . The Girl
Lionelle Howard . . . . The Man
COMEDY Girl poses as chauffeur to win affianced man.

06092
I DO LIKE A JOKE (625)(U)
Hepworth
D: Frank Wilson
Johnny Butt . . . . The Man
COMEDY Village idiot plays tricks.

06093
SALLY IN OUR ALLEY (4500)(U)
Turner Films (Ideal)
D: Larry Trimble
S: Benedict James
Hilda Trevelyan . . . . Sally
Reginald Owen . . . . Harry
Mary Dibley . . . . Belle Cavendish

Edward O'Neill . . . . Beauvais
Windham Guise . . . . Squire
Fred Rains . . . . Steward
ROMANCE Period. Blacksmith's apprentice wastes inheritance on socialite and walks home to true love.

06094
ME AND ME MOKE (4138) (U) USA: ME AND M'PAL
London (Jury)
D: Harold Shaw
S: Richard Ganthony
Edna Flugrath . . . . Kitty Kingsland
Gerald Ames . . . . Harry Masterman
Hubert Willis . . . . Labby
Sydney Fairbrother . . . . . . Mammy
Lewis Gilbert . . . . Flash Hawkins
Douglas Munro . . . . James Hilliard
Gwynne Herbert . . . . Mrs Kingsland
DRAMA Rich man's nephew becomes Covent Garden porter and wins fame by painting friendly coster.

06095
TOO MUCH SAUSAGE (475)
Kineto
D: (W.R. Booth)
TRICK Animated clay modelling.

06096
THE HARD WAY (4800) (A)
Broadwest (Walturdaw)
P:D: Walter West
S: (NOVEL) "A Peer"
Muriel Martin Harvey . . . . . Lilah Chertsey
J.R. Tozer . . . . Noel Creighton
Thos H. MacDonald . . . . Arnold Graves
Lily Saxby . . . . Clarice Creighton
George Bellamy . . . . Lepine
Owen Francis . . . . Martin Graves
DRAMA Paris. Artist's wife commits bigamy and is blackmailed until she learns of artist's death.

06097
LOOKING FOR THE DERBY RESULT (325) (U)
Urban Trading Co
COMEDY Man reading Lord Derby's scheme doesn't look where he's going.

06098
SHE (5400)(U)
Barker (Lucoque)
D: Will Barker, H. Lisle Locoque
S: (NOVEL) H. Rider Haggard
SC: Nellie E. Lucoque
Alice Delysia . . . . Ayesha
Henry Victor . . . . Leo Vincey
Sydney Bland . . . . Horace Holley
Blanche Forsythe . . . . Ustane
Jack Denton . . . . Job
J. Hastings Batson . . . . Bilali
FANTASY Africa. Explorer is reincarnated lover of 2000-year old queen.

06099
THE CHARLATAN (4363)(U)
Famous Authors (Crown)
D: Sidney Morgan
S: (PLAY) Robert Buchanan
SC: Austin Fryers
Eille Norwood . . . . Dr O'Kama
Violet Graham . . . . Isobel Arlington
Anna Mather . . . . Mme Obnowsky
Frederick de Lara . . . . . Earl of Wansborough
Ernest A. Dagnall . . . . Col Arlington
R. Courtland . . . . Lord Dewsbury
DRAMA Fake occultist, reformed by col's daughter, saves earl from his ex-partner.

06100
IN THE HANDS OF THE SPOILERS (4000)
Barker-Neptune (Renters)
D: Leon Bary
S: (NOVEL) Sydney Paternoster
CRIME Gambling Lieut fakes suicide, kidnaps rival's child, and trains him to steal father's secrets.

06101
ON THE STEPS OF THE ALTAR (4000)
Martin (Paragon)
D: R. Harley West
Harry Lofting
Jack Jarman
Bunty Stewart
DRAMA "Love, sport and adventure in rural England and California."

06102
ABIDE WITH ME (4200)
Grenville-Taylor (Kin-Ex)
D: Tom Watts
S: H. Grenville-Taylor
SC: Ashmore Russan
Austin Camp . . . . Ralph Stoneham
George Foley . . . . Father Eustace
Vera Cornish . . . . Amy
N. Watts-Phillips . . . . Denham Thorpe
Jack Berry . . . . Hubert Stoneham
Mme d'Esterre . . . . Miss Stoneham
CRIME Hastings. Rich man kills brother, confesses, and dares monk to tell the truth.

06103
A SOLDIER AND A MAN (4191)(U)
B & C (Kin-Ex)
D: Dave Aylott
S: (PLAY) Ben Landeck
SC: Eliot Stannard
George Keene . . . . Harold Sinclair
Minna Grey . . . . Rose Melbury
A.V. Bramble . . . . Hubert Walpole
Charles Vane . . . . Gen Sinclair
M. Gray Murray . . . . David Melbury
Arthur Walcott . . . .
WAR General's son, framed by spy for cardsharping, enlists as private and saves father and fiancee from capture.

06104
THE TAILOR OF BOND STREET (4780) (U)
Barker (Gerrard)
Augustus Yorke . . . . Marcovitch Einstein
Robert Leonard . . . . Lew Mendel
Thos H. MacDonald . . . . Reggie Einstein
Peggy Richards . . . . Esther
Kenneth Barker . . . . Reggie (child)
DRAMA Jewish student changes name and denies father until he is dying.

06105
WANTED A WIDOW (3000)
British Actors
S: Arthur Shirley, Walter Howard
Donald Calthrop
Leslie Henson
Alfred Bishop
A.E. Matthews
Frederick Norton
Walter Howard
Alfred Paumier
COMEDY

MAR
06106
THE RIVAL CAPTAINS (970)(U)
British Oak (NA)
D: Ethyle Batley
ANIMAL Football captain kidnapped by rival and rescued by sweetheart's dog.

06107
THE MAN WHO FORGOT (1095)(U)
British Oak (NA)
D: Ernest G. Batley
James Russell
CRIME Girl crook saves millionaire's son
from kidnapper's bullet.

06108
WHEN THE GERMANS ENTERED LOOS
(1020)(A)
British Oak (NA)
D: Ernest Batley
James Russell
WAR France German officer kills French
soldier's child.

06109
RAYS THAT ERASE (567)(U)
Martin (DFSA)
D: (Edwin J. Collins)
TRICK Rays from professor's lamp make
objects disappear.

06110
ON THE CARPET (1048) (U)
Martin (DFSA)
D: (Edwin J. Collins)
TRICK Drunken groom dreams he and
landlady fly by carpet to sultan's harem.

06111
THE TEST (1018) (U)
Cricks (DFSA)
D: (Charles Calvert)
Alexandra Hastings . . . . The Girl
Farmer Skein . . . . The Man
DRAMA Rich girl test husband by burning
down house and pretending to be scarred.

06112
ONLY A ROOM-ER (663)(U)
Cricks (DFSA)
D: Toby Cooper
S: Ernest Dangerfield
Jack Jarman . . . . The Roomer
Mrs Dangerfield . . . . The Landlady
COMEDY Men persuade friend to sleep in
haunted room and play tricks on him.

06113
FLAPPER GOES TO SCHOOL (889)(U)
Special (DFSA)
Nettie Wheeler . . . . The Flapper
COMEDY Tomboy tricks her way to the top
of the class.

06114
WHO'S YOUR FRIEND? (1025) (U)
Hepworth
D: Frank Wilson
Chrissie White . . . . The Wife
Lionelle Howard . . . . The Husband
Johnny Butt . . . . The Bailiff
COMEDY Broke gambler makes bailiff pose as
old school friend.

06115
MIGGLES' MAID (650)(U)
Hepworth
D: Frank Wilson
Chrissie White . . . . The Maid
Lionelle Howard . . . . The Man
Johnny Butt . . . . Miggles
COMEDY Clubman becomes popular when he
hires pretty maid.

06116
SILAS AT THE SEASIDE (430)(U)
Piccadilly (Browne)

D:S: Joe Evans
Joe Evans . . . . Silas
COMEDY Bumpkin is robbed and takes job
as bathchair attendant.

06117
TAMING LIZA (1188) (U)
Piccadilly (Browne)
D:S: Joe Evans
Geraldine Maxwell . . . . Liza
COMEDY Lord weds coster girl and tries to
make her a lady.

06118
PIMPLE'S DOUBLE (946)(U)
Piccadilly (Browne)
D:S: Fred Evans, Joe Evans
Fred Evans . . . . Pimple
Joe Evans . . . . The Double
COMEDY Pimple poses as rival and catches
burglar, for which his rival takes credit.

06119
PIMPLE'S PINK FORMS (852)(U)
Piccadilly (Browne)
D:S: Fred Evans, Joe Evans
Fred Evans . . . . Pimple
COMEDY Pimple is rejected by army, takes job
delivering official forms.

06120
PIMPLE SPLITS THE DIFFERENCE (809)(U)
Piccadilly (Browne)
D:S: Fred Evans, Joe Evans
Fred Evans . . . . Pimple
COMEDY "Pimple does his best with somewhat
poor material."

06121
PIMPLE'S ARM OF THE LAW (946)(U)
Piccadilly (Browne)
D:S: Fred Evans, Joe Evans
Fred Evans . . . . Insp Pimple
COMEDY Inspector tries to save boy from
prison until he learns boy broke his window.

06122
PIMPLE – HIMSELF AND OTHERS (940) (U)
Piccadilly (Browne)
D:S: Fred Evans, Joe Evans
Fred Evans . . . . Himself
COMEDY Soldier on leave makes up as Ford
Sterling, Max Linder, Charlie Chaplin and
Pimple.

06123
FATE AND THE WOMAN
Neptune-Barker
D: Fred W. Durrant
S: Rowland Talbot
DRAMA.

06124
EVE'S DAUGHTER (4100) retitled:
LOVE (A)
Eve Balfour Films (JTR)
D: L.C. MacBean
S: (NOVEL) Rathmell Wilson
(WHEN LOVE DIES)
SC: Rowland Talbot
Eve Balfour . . . . Veronica Leigh
Frank Tennant . . . . Hubert Price
Agnes de Winton . . . . Lil Trancing
Arthur M. Cullin . . . . Roger Hoskin
Dora de Winton . . . . la Belle Lola
J. Hastings Batson . . . .
DRAMA Man dies saving remarried wife from
ex-mistress's bullet.

06125
THE HYPOCRITES (5600) (A) retitled:
THE MORALS OF WEYBURY
London(Jury)
D: George Loane Tucker
S: (PLAY) Henry Arthur Jones
SC: Kenelm Foss
Elizabeth Risdon . . . . Rachel Neve
Charles Rock . . . . SquireWilmore
Cyril Raymond . . . . Leonard Wilmore
Douglas Munro . . . . Sir John Plugenet
Hayford Hobbs . . . . Rev Edgar Linnell
Barbara Everest . . . . Helen Plugenet
Gerald Ames . . . . Aubrey Viveash
DRAMA Squire tries to make son deny he
fathered villager's child, and wed heiress.

06126
THE LAST CHALLENGE (3200)(U)
London (Jury)
D: Harold Shaw
S: Bannister Merwin
Chesterfield 'Billy' Goode . . . . . . Boxer
Jem Smith . . . . Boxer
G.T. Dunning . . . . Boxer
Toff Wall . . . . Boxer
Sam Howard . . . . Boxer
Eugene Corri . . . . Referee
SPORT Innkeeping ex-champion boxes rival of
his daughter's fiance.

06127
MONEY FOR NOTHING (2800) (U)
London (Jury)
D: Maurice Elvey
S: (PLAY) Arthur Eckersley, Guy Newall
Guy Newall . . . . .Rev Cuthbert Cheese
Manora Thew . . . . Mrs Boulderwood
Hayford Hobbs . . . . Paul Norwood
COMEDY Ostend. Gem thieves mistake curate on
holiday for detective.

06128
PARTNERS AT LAST (4068)(U)
London (Jury)
D: Ralph Dewsbury
S: Frank Fowell
Amy Brandon-Thomas . . . . . .Muriel Wright
Charles Rock . . . . Edward Bradston
Chappel Dossett . . . . William Wright
Hubert Willis . . . . Joseph Trood
CRIME Manager and cousin plot to blackmail
business heir.

06129
VICE VERSA (3900)(U)
London (Jury)
D: Maurice Elvey
S: (NOVEL) F. Anstey
Charles Rock . . . . Paul Bultitude
Douglas Munro . . . . Marmaduke Paradine
Edward O'Neill . . . . Dr Grimstone
Guy Newall . . . . Dick Bultitude
FANTASY Pompous father magically changes
places with schoolboy son.

06130
MOTHERLOVE (4750) (A)
London (Jury)
D: Maurice Elvey
S: Kenelm Foss
Elizabeth Risdon . . . . Mary
Fred Groves . . . . Alfie
Frank Stanmore . . . .
Guy Newall . . . .
Dolly Tree . . . .
DRAMA Servant maid ends her life as a char-
woman.

06131
DOORSTEPS (4415) (U)
Turner Films (Hepworth)
D: Henry Edwards
S: (PLAY) Henry Edwards
SC: Larry Trimble
Florence Turner . . . . Doorsteps
Henry Edwards . . . . George Newlands
Campbell Gullan . . . . Tozer
Amy Lorraine . . . . Mrs Skipps
Fred Rains . . . . Stage-manager
DRAMA Boarding house skivvy helps poor
playwright, becomes actress and save him from
insane convict.

06132
FACE TO FACE (2725) (U)
Hepworth (Butcher)
D: Frank Wilson
S: Marion Carr
Stewart Rome . . . . Geoffrey Cunliffe/
Richard Waine
Chrissie White . . . . Kathleen Dare
Lionelle Howard . . . . Bernard Cunliffe
William Felton . . . . Stephen Morel
Charles Vane . . . . John Cunliffe
Frank Wilson . . . . Henry Dare
CRIME Millionaire's nephew accused of
burglary committed by double.

06133
TRELAWNEY OF THE WELLS (4875) (U)
Hepworth (Butcher)
D: Cecil M. Hepworth
S: (PLAY) Arthur Wing Pinero
SC: Blanche McIntosh
Alma Taylor . . . . Rose Trelawney
Stewart Rome . . . . Tom Wrench
Violet Hopson . . . . Imogen Parrott
Lionelle Howard . . . . Arthur Gower
John MacAndrews . . . . James Telfer
Warwick Buckland . . . . Sir William Gower
Gwynne Herbert . . . . Trafalgar Gower
Margaret Blanche . . . . Claire de Foenix
Percy Manton . . . . Capt de Foenix
William Felton . . . . Ablett
Ivy Millais . . . . Sarah
Amy Lorraine . . . . Mrs Telfer
Johnny Butt . . . . Augustus Colpoys
Sybil Coventry . . . . Mrs Mossup
Bob Bouchier . . . . Hall Keeper
ROMANCE Period. Actress marries chancellor's
son but returns to stage.

06134
'ORACE'S ORDEAL (950) (U)
Hepworth
D: Frank Wilson
S: Percy Manton
Johnny Butt . . . . 'Orace
Percy Manton . . . . Kelly
COMEDY Actor pays landlady by borrowing
from her husband.

06135
A FALLEN STAR (4500) (U)
Hepworth (Ideal)
D: Cecil M. Hepworth
S: (SKETCH) Albert Chevalier
Albert Chevalier . . . . Barry Belvedere
Harry Brett . . . . Richard Tubb
Janet Alexander . . . . Mrs Belvedere
DRAMA Actor takes to drink when wife elopes;
she is killed by car and driver adopts her child.

06136
THE SECOND MRS TANQUERAY (6000) (A)
Ideal *Reissue*: 1918

D: Fred Paul
S: (PLAY) Arthur Wing Pinero
SC: Benedict James
Sir George Alexander . . . . . . Aubrey Tanqueray
Hilda Moore . . . . Paula
Norman Forbes . . . . Cayley Drumble
Marie Hemingway . . . . Ellean Tanqueray
James Lindsay . . . . Sir George Orreyd
May Leslie Stuart . . . . Lady Orreyd
Nelson Ramsey . . . . Misquith
Mary Rorke . . . . Mrs Cortellion
Roland Pertwee . . . . Capt Hugh Ardale
Minna Grey . . . . Mrs Tanqueray
Bernard Vaughan . . . . Gordon Jayne
DRAMA Rich man's second wife finds
stepdaughter loves ex-lover.

06137
LONDON'S ENEMIES (4500) (U)
Phoenix-Couragio (Phillips)
D: Percy Moran
Percy Moran . . . . Lt Jack Moran
Marietta de Leyse . . . . Zareda
Lionel d'Aragon . . . . Butler
CRIME Lieut saves sister from spies and destroys
U-Boat.

06138
A SUCCESSFUL OPERATION (2000) (U)
Regal Films
D:S: Aubrey Fitzmaurice
Billie Boreham . . . . The Man
COMEDY Mixup of patients almost causes
operation on wrong man.

06139
THE PRICE HE PAID (2920) (U)
Regal Films
D:S: Dave Aylott
George Keene . . . . John Clive
Letty Paxton . . . . Irene Clive
George Foley . . . . Insp Brill
Wingold Lawrence . . . . Capt Lanson
Lionel d'Aragon . . . . Blakeson
Charles Ashwell . . . . Priest
CRIME Tibetan priest kills blackmailer for
stealing jewel from idol.

06140
TOM BROWN'S SCHOOLDAYS (5700) (U)
Windsor (Int Ex)
D:SC: Rex Wilson
S: (NOVEL) Thomas Hughes
Joyce Templeton . . . . Tom Brown (1)
Jack Coleman . . . . Tom Brown (2)
Jack Hobbs . . . . Tom Brown (3)
Evelyn Boucher . . . . Cynthia Brown
Wilfred Benson . . . . Dr Arnold
Mr Daniels . . . . Squire Brown
Mr Johnson . . . . Harry East
Laurie Leslie . . . . Flashman
C. Arundell . . . . Wheelwright
Mona Damt . . . . Dame Brown
Eric Barker . . . . Arthur
Rolf Leslie . . . . Jacob Doodlecalf
Miss Marley . . . . Mrs Arnold
H. Dobell . . . . Benjy
Mr. Morley . . . . Tadpole
Mr. Canieli . . . . Slogger Williams
DRAMA 1834. Squire's mischievous son becomes
boarder at Rughy. (Royal Command Performance,
Feb 24 1917).

06141
JIMMY (4080) (U)
B & C (Gau)
D: A.V. Bramble, Eliot Stannard
S: (NOVEL) John Strange Winter
SC: Eliot Stannard

John Astley . . . . Jimmy St Quinton
George Tully . . . . Sir Phillip St Quinton
Letty Paxton . . . . Marion Denbeigh
A.V. Bramble . . . . John Denbeigh
Phyllis Thatcher . . . . Ruth Denbeigh
M. Gray Murray . . . . Ferguson
Malcolm Keen . . . . Dr Stoneham
Betty O'Neill . . . . Nurse Vivian
Bett Strange Winter . . . . Cook
WAR Banker's thieving son enlists, is wounded,
and wins DSO.

06142
FRILLS (2000)
Holmfirth (YCC)
D: Bertram Phillips
Queenie Thomas . . . . Queenie
Ruby Miller . . . . Ruby
Gregory Scott . . . . Hon Gregory
Bernard Vaughan . . . . Lord Vaughan
COMEDY Pierrette flees from forced marriage
and falls for Lord's nephew.

06143
WON BY LOSING (3000)
Holmfirth (Initial)
D: Bertram Phillips
Queenie Thomas . . . . Polly/Daphne
Frank McClellan . . . .
DRAMA Cleric weds woman to reform her but
she takes to drink and dies.

06144
THE REAL THING AT LAST (2000)
British Actors
D: L.C. MacBean
S: James Barrie
Edmund Gwenn . . . . Rupert K. Thunder
Nelson Keys . . . . Lady Macbeth
Godfrey Tearle . . . . Macduff
Owen Nares . . . . General Banquo
Norman Forbes . . . . Duncan
Caleb Porter . . . . Witch
George Kelly . . . . Witch
Ernest Thesiger . . . . Witch
Gladys Cooper . . . . American Witch
Teddie Gerard . . . . American Witch
Pauline Chase . . . . American Witch
Fred Volpe . . . . Murderer
Moya Mannering . . . . Messenger
A.E. Matthews . . . . Murdered
Marie Lohr . . . . Murdered
Fred Kerr . . . . Murdered
Irene Vanbrugh . . . . Lady
Eva Rowland . . . . Lady
Arthur Shirley . . . . Courtier
Leslie Henson . . . . Charlie Chaplin
COMEDY American producer modernises
"Macbeth".

06145
TRUTH AND JUSTICE (3000)
Birmingham Film Producing Co (Brum)
D: Bert Haldene
S: G. Fletcher Hewitt, Horatio Bottomley
Horatio Bottomley . . . . Himself
Florence Aliston . . . . Child
DRAMA Six episodes in which editor of "John
Bull" criticises social injustices.

06146
A STRING OF PEARLS (630) (U)
Transatlantic
D:S: Will Page
Will Page . . . . The Husband
Betty O'Neill . . . . The Wife
COMEDY Man steals wife's pearls to buy kiss
from pierrette.

06147
SANDY'S SUSPICION (600)(U)
Transatlantic
D:S: Will Page
Will Page . . . . Sandy McKie
Betty O'Neill . . . . Mrs Mc Kie
Eddy Stanley . . . . The Man
COMEDY Jealous Scot trails wife to cafe.

06148
SANDY AT HOME (605) (U)
Transatlantic
D:S: Will Page
Will Page . . . . Sandy McKie
Betty O'Neill . . . . Mrs McKie
Eddy Stanley . . . .
Laurie Wynne . . . .
Dan Hendy-Clarke . . . .
Teddy Sheppard . . . .
COMEDY Scot left in charge of wife's and
sister's babies.

06149
THE BLACK TRIANGLES (695)(U)
Clarendon
D: (Percy Stow)
COMEDY Bachelor joins secret society and
falls in love.

06150
THE QUEEN MOTHER (4500)(U)
Clarendon
D: Wilfred Noy
S: (PLAY) J.A. Campbell
Owen Roughwood . . . . The Duke
Gladys Mason . . . . Princess of Saxonia
Barbara Rutland . . . . Duchess Miramar
Sydney Lewis Ransome . . . . Prince Ludwig
Ronald Hammond . . . . Osric
M. Mills . . . . King of Montania
DRAMA Ruritania. Queen's ex-lover saves her
from prince who killed her father.

06151
HIS HIGHNESS (2000)
Club Comedies (Green)
P: George Green
D: Mr. Foote
COMEDY Glasgow.

APR

06152
PERKIN'S PHEASANTS (1050)(U)
British Oak (NA)
D: Ethyle Batley
COMEDY Henpeck uses wife's shopping
money to back loser.

06153
THE BLACK CIRCLE GANG (1090) (U)
British Oak (NA)
D: Ernest G. Batley
CRIME Detective thwarts Chinaman's plans to
rob solicitor.

06154
A HIGHER POWER (1050)(U)
D: Ethyle Batley
DRAMA Doctor allows girl's incurable father
to die.

06155
ENGLAND'S FUTURE SAFEGUARD
(1080)(U)
British Oak (NA)
D: Ethyle Batley
WAR Bus driver and conductress save anti-
zeppelin gun from spies.

06156
LEAVES FROM A MOTHER'S ALBUM
(985)(U)
Clarendon
D: Percy Stow
Mary Ford . . . . Mother
WAR Mother recalls son's boyhood and he
returns from war.

06157
A QUESTION OF HAIRS (1065)(U)
Clarendon
D: Percy Stow
Dorothy Bellew . . . . Maisie
Robert Nainby . . . . Mr Holder
COMEDY Youthful father falls for son's
fiancee.

06158
BOOTS FROM BOOTLE (718)(U)
Martin (DFSA)
D: (Edwin J. Collins)
TRICK Man buys sailor's boots that kick
people and make them vanish.

06159
CRIME AND THE PENALTY (3400)(A)
Martin (DFSA)
D: R. Harley West
Alesia Leon . . . . Mildred
Jack Lovatt . . . . Jack
Louis Nanten . . . . Jabez Burke
CRIME Crook hires scientist to kidnap
cousin's wife with aid of chimpanzee that
strangles when hypnotised.

06160
PIMPLE'S MIDSUMMER NIGHT'S DREAM
(805)(U)
Piccadilly (Browne) *reissue:* 1917 (Walt)
D:S: Fred Evans, Joe Evans
Fred Evans . . . . Pimple
COMEDY Pimple eats lobster and has
nightmare about cannibals.

06161
PIMPLE POOR BUT DISHONEST (988) (U)
Piccadilly (Browne)
D:S: Fred Evans, Joe Evans
Fred Evans . . . . Pimple
COMEDY Pimple swindles barman into
buying old violin as a Stradivarius.

06162
PIMPLE AS HAMLET (2000)
Piccadilly (Browne)
D:S: Fred Evans, Joe Evans
Fred Evans . . . . Pimple
COMEDY "Two reels of unmitigated humour."

06163
JOEY'S AUTOMATIC FURNITURE (580)(U)
Piccadilly (Browne)
D:S: Joe Evans
Joe Evans . . . . Joey
Geraldine Maxwell . . . . Mrs Joey
COMEDY When bailiffs take his furniture,
Joey obtains automatic furniture to impress
rich uncle.

06164
JOEY'S DREAM (570)(U)
Piccadilly (Browne)
D:S: Joe Evans
Joe Evans . . . . Joey
COMEDY Joey repulses tramp and dreams
Devil turns him into tramp.

06165
JOEY'S LIAR METER (620)(U)
Piccadilly (Browne)
D:S: Joe Evans
Joe Evans . . . . Joey
Geraldine Maxwell . . . . Mrs Joey
COMEDY Joey's wife buys meter to test his
veracity.

06166
A BOARDING HOUSE SCANDAL (891)(U)
Piccadilly (Browne)
D:S: Joe Evans
Joe Evans . . . . Boarder
COMEDY Fat and thin boarders rivals for
landlady's love.

06167
WHEN FLIRTING DIDN'T PAY (598)(U)
Transatlantic
D:S: Will Page
Will Page . . . . Mr Jollyboy
COMEDY Flirtations old gent gets pushed into
Thames.

06168
THE GENTLE ART OF FISHING (660)(U)
Transatlantic
D:S: Will Page
Will Page . . . . Percy Split-Lemon
COMEDY Two fishermen's misadventures
punting on Thames.

06169
SCHMIDT THE SPY (950) (U)
Phoenix (Phillips)
S: (CARTOONS) Alfred Leete
Lewis Sydney . . . . Schmidt
COMEDY Misadventures of incompetent
German spy.

06170
A.W.S. (1890) (U)
Lucoque (KTC)
D: Harry Buss
Mercy Hatton . . . . The Girl
Harry Buss . . . . The Man
Blanche Bella . . . . The Woman
COMEDY Girl promises to marry winner of
skating carnival.

06171
BORED (1000)(U)
Lucoque
Dorothy Minto . . . . The Girl
Harry Buss . . . . The Man
Harry Buss
COMEDY Consequences of halfpenny stamp
stuck on pavement.

06172
THE MODEL (1000)(A)
Lucoque
D: Harry Buss
Harry Buss . . . . The Man
COMEDY "A Roman warrior, love, and an
unrelenting mother."

06173
SALLY BISHOP (3752)(A)
Gaumont
D:SC: George Pearson
S: (NOVEL) E. Temple Thurston
Aurele Sydney . . . . John Traill
Marjorie Villis . . . . Sally Bishop
Peggy Hyland . . . . Janet Hallard
Alice de Winton . . . . Mrs Durlacher
Jack Leigh . . . . Arthur
Christine Rayner . . . . Miss Standish Rowe
Hugh Croise . . . . Charles Devenish
Fred Rains . . . . Rev Bishop
DRAMA Barrister abandons mistress for
socialite but returns in time to save her from
suicide.

06174
A BUNCH OF VIOLETS (3725)(A)
Hepworth (Ward)
D: Frank Wilson
S: (PLAY) Sidney Grundy
SC: Victor Montefiore
Chrissie White . . . . Violet Marchant
Gerald Lawrence . . . . . . Sir Philip Marchant
Violet Hopson . . . . Mrs Murgatroyd
Lionelle Howard . . . . Harold Inglis
Margaret Halstan . . . . Lady Marchant
Charles Vane . . . . Harker
Tom Mowbray . . . . Mark Murgatroyd
DRAMA Banker loses election, bank fails, wife
learns he is bigamist, secretary robs him, but his
daughter loves him.

06175
WHAT'S BRED . . . COMES OUT IN THE
FLESH (3374)(A)
Master (Kino Exclusives)
D:SC: Sidney Morgan
S: (NOVEL) Grant Allen (WHAT'S BRED IN
THE BONE)
Janet Alexander . . . . Elma
Lauderdale Maitland . . . . . . Judge Gildersleve
Frank Tennant . . . . Kelvin Scott
Richard Norton . . . . Nevitt
H.J. Lord . . . . Guy
Rupert Stutfield . . . . Cyril
CRIME Judge tries man for his own crime but
confesses in court when gipsy makes him 'see'
event.

06176
A PAIR OF SPECTACLES (3000)
G.B. Samuelson (Moss)
D: Alexander Butler
S: (PLAY) Sidney Grundy
SC: Harry Engholm
Sir John Hare . . . . .Benjamin Goldfinch
Peggy Hyland . . . . Mrs Goldfinch
Booth Conway . . . . Uncle Gregory
James le Fane . . . . Ben Goldfinch
COMEDY Disillusioned rich man turns mean
when he wears miserly brother's spectacles.

06177
THE STOLEN SACRIFICE (4000)
Renaissance (Gerrard)
D:S: Sidney Morgan
Peggy Richards . . . . Nancy Wilford
CRIME Tec saves girl who attempted suicide
from being sacrificed by priest of Indian sect.

MAY

06178
THE INITIAL BROOCH (1115)(A)
British Oak (NA)
D: Ethyle Batley
CRIME Wounded soldier and post-girl thwart
thieves.

06179
RETRIBUTION (1180)(A)
British Oak (NA)
D: Ernest G. Batley
CRIME Disowned gambler tries to kill
cousin's doctor fiance.

06180
JUDGEMENT (1090)(A)
British Oak (NA)
D: Ernest G. Batley
CRIME Gambling clerk frames employer's
nephew for forgery,

06181
FOLKS OF THE FAIR (1080) (U)
British Oak (NA)

D; Ethyle Batley
ROMANCE Doctor gives up circus girl so she
may wed colleague.

06182
ZEPPELINS OF LONDON (660)
Bamforth (YCC)
D: Cecil Birch
COMEDY Family's consternation during air
raid.

06183
THE BETTER BET (660)
Bamforth (YCC)
D: Cecil Birch
COMEDY Youth wins bet against aunt and
suitor.

06184
TELLING THE TALE (800)
Bamforth (YCC)
D: Cecil Birch
COMEDY Lovers trick girl's father.

06185
THE SCARECROW (650)
Bamforth (YCC)
D: Cecil Birch
COMEDY Scarecrow comes to life and is
mistaken for eccentric Lord.

06186
STORMY IS MISUNDERSTOOD (600)
Bamforth (YCC)
D: Cecil Birch
Alf Foy . . . . Stormy
COMEDY Bargee's tattooed arm causes
misunderstanding with wife.

06187
STARVE A FEVER (660)
Bamforth (YCC)
D: Cecil Birch
COMEDY Doctor starves sweetheart's father
into consenting.

06188
MY WIFE'S HUSBAND (740)
Bamforth (YCC)
D: Cecil Birch
COMEDY "The plot is somewhat obscure."

06189
LOVE AND 'FLUENCE (1090)
Bamforth (YCC)
D: Cecil Birch
COMEDY Hypnotist foils daughter's unwanted
suitors by hiring them as assistants.

06190
SOMETHING IN THE WIND (940)
Holmfirth (YCC)
D: Bertram Phillips
Queenie Thomas . . . . Queenie
COMEDY Ostler fights swanker for storekeeper's
daughter.

06191
JACK SPRATT'S PARROT GETTING HIS
OWN BACK (1000)(U)
Clarendon
D: (Toby Cooper)
COMEDY Sailor's parrot gets soot on maid's
pillow and she is accused of flirting with sweep.

06192
THE FIVE WISHES (1035)(U)
Clarendon
D: (Wilfred Noy)
S: (PLAY) Laura Leycester
FANTASY Couple given magic idol that grants
wishes literally.

06193
FUN AT A FINGLAS FAIR (1000)
Film Co of Ireland
D: F.J. McCormick
S: Cathal McGarvey
COMEDY (Not shown in England)

06194
FOR THE EMPIRE (600)
Gaumont
D:S: George Pearson
WAR Patriotic appeal for war savings on
behalf of the Treasury.

06195
THE COURSE OF TRUE LOVE (855)(U)
Transatlantic
D:S: Will Page
Will Page . . . . Husband
COMEDY Newlywed wife mistakes her glove
for another woman's.

06196
JOEY THE SHOWMAN (505)(A)
Piccadilly (Browne)
D:S: Joe Evans
Joe Evans . . . . Joey
COMEDY Punch and Judy showman picks
pockets and is arrested.

06197
JOEY'S PLUCK (618) (U)
Piccadilly (Browne)
D: Joe Evans
S: (SKETCH) Joe Evans (HER BURGLAR)
Joe Evans . . . . Joey
Geraldine Maxwell . . . . Mrs Joey
COMEDY Joey's wife poses as burglar to stop
his boasting.

06198
JOEY'S BLACK DEFEAT (590)(U)
Piccadilly (Browne)
D:S: Joe Evans
Joe Evans . . . . Joey
COMEDY Love rivals trick each other into
having black faces.

06199
JOEY WALKS IN HIS SLEEP (720)(A)
Piccadilly (Browne)
D:S: Joe Evans
Joe Evans . . . . Joey
COMEDY Joey's misadventures while walking
in his sleep.

06200
PIMPLE'S A WOMAN IN THE CASE (1090)
(U)
Piccadilly (Browne)
D:S: Fred Evans, Joe Evans
Fred Evans . . . . Pimple
Joe Evans . . . . Raffles
COMEDY Burglar poses as woman to save
partner from arrest.

06201
DIAMOND CUT DIAMOND (980)(U)
Piccadilly (Browne) *reissue*: 1917 (Walturdaw)
D:S: Fred Evans, Joe Evans
Fred Evans . . . . Pimple
COMEDY Pimple cheated when he joins secret
society and pays £25 for diamonds.

06202
PIMPLE'S TENTH COMMANDMENT (548)(U)
Piccadilly (Browne)
D:S: Fred Evans, Joe Evans
Fred Evans . . . . Pimple
COMEDY Pimple suspects wife's fidelity and
finds he is in wrong house.

06203
PIMPLE'S SILVER LAGOON (1800)(U)
Piccadilly (Browne)
D:S: Fred Evans, Joe Evans
Fred Evans . . . . Pimple
COMEDY

06204
PIMPLE'S MONKEY BUSINESS (860) (A)
retitled: SOME MONKEY BUSINESS
Piccadilly (Browne)
D:S: Fred Evans, Joe Evans
Fred Evans . . . . Pimple
Joe Evans . . . . Raffles
COMEDY Crook's pal poses as gorilla and is
sold to circus.

06205
PIMPLE'S CLUTCHING HAND (769)(U)
Piccadilly (Browne)
D:S: Fred Evans, Joe Evans
Fred Evans . . . . Pimple
COMEDY Pimple bets he can catch crook so
his six friends pose as the crook.

06206
PIMPLE'S MERRY WIVES (1070) (A) retitled:
THE MERRY WIVES OF PIMPLE
Piccadilly (Browne)
D:S: Fred Evans, Joe Evans
Fred Evans . . . . Pimple
COMEDY Parliament passes bill allowing every
man to have six wives chosen by his first wife.

06207
THE WHITE BOYS (3650)(U)
Hepworth
D: Frank Wilson
Stewart Rome . . . .
Chrissie White . . . .
Lionelle Howard . . . .
DRAMA Ireland.

06208
SOWING THE WIND (5100)(A)
Hepworth
D: Cecil M. Hepworth
S: (PLAY) Sidney Grundy
SC: Blanche McIntosh
Henry Ainley . . . . Tom Brabazon
Alma Taylor . . . . Rosamond
Stewart Rome . . . . Ned Annersley
Violet Hopson . . . . Helen Gray
Chrissie White . . . . Maude Fretwell
Lionelle Howard . . . . Bob Watkin
Charles Vane . . . . Lord Petworth
Percy Manton . . . . Sir Richard Cursitor
ROMANCE Man demands proof that adopted
son's fiancee is highborn and discovers she is his
own daughter.

06209
FATAL FINGERS (6423) (A)
B & C (DFSA)
D: A.V. Bramble, Eliot Stannard
SC: Eliot Stannard
George Bellamy . . . . Earl of Ellersdale
Mary Merrall . . . . Irene Lambton
A.V. Bramble . . . . Rollo Lambton, MP
Harry Latimer . . . . Don Mario
Farmer Skein . . . . Home Secretary
Icilma Rae . . . . Irene (child)
CRIME Earl fakes suicide to prove Italian don
poisoned MP to thwart bill against aliens.

06210
THE TALE OF A SHIRT (3000)(U)
Homeland (Globe)
D: W.P. Kellino
S: Reuben Gillmer
Billy Merson . . . . Billy Jones
Miss Bijou . . . . Angeline
COMEDY Baker poses as marquis to win
laundress posing as duke's daughter.

06211
THE VALLEY OF FEAR (6500)(U)
G.B. Samuelson (Moss)
D: Alexander Butler
S: (NOVEL) Arthur Conan Doyle
SC: Harry Engholm
H.A. Saintsbury . . . . Sherlock Holmes
Daisy Burrell . . . . Ettie Douglas
Booth Conway . . . . Prof Moriarty
Jack Macaulay . . . . McGinty
Cecil Mannering . . . . John McMurdo
Arthur M. Cullin . . . . Dr Watson
Lionel D'Aragon . . . . Capt Marvin
Bernard Vaughan . . . . Shafter
Jack Clair . . . . Ted Baldwin
CRIME Exconvict tries to kill detective who
once posed as member of American hooded
clan.

06212
THE ANSWER (4604)(A)
Broadwest (Browne)
D: Walter West
S: (NOVEL) Newman Flower (IS GOD DEAD?)
SC: Dane Stanton
Muriel Martin-Harvey . . . . . The Lonely Woman
George Foley . . . . Justin Siddeley
Dora Barton . . . . The Lost Magdalene
George Bellamy . . . . The Clerk
J.R. Tozer . . . .
Gregory Scott . . . .
Arthur M. Cullin . . . .
DRAMA Spirit shows bankrupt three stories of
faith overcoming distress.

06213
WHEN KNIGHTS WERE BOLD (4800)(U)
London (Jury)
D: Maurice Elvey
S: (PLAY) Charles Marlowe
SC: Frank Miller
James Welch . . . . Sir Guy de Vere
Janet Ross . . . . Lady Rowena
Gerald Ames . . . . Sir Brian Ballymote
Hayford Hobbs . . . . Widdicombe
Gwynne Herbert . . . . .Isaacson
Philip Hewland . . . . Barker
Bert Wynne . . . . Whittle
Edna Maude . . . . Aunt Thornridge
Marjorie Day . . . . The Maid
COMEDY Commoner inherits title and wins Lady
after dreaming of medieval days.

JUN

06214
TRAGEDY AT HOLLY COTTAGE (1070)(A)
British Oak (NA)
D: Ernest G. Batley
CRIME Rich man is strangled by disowned son
whilst living with nephew.

06215
THE FINGER OF SUSPICION (935)(U)
British Oak (NA)
D: Ethyle Batley
DRAMA Rich widower's new wife accuses his
daughter of poisoning her son.

06216
A LITTLE BOOTBLACK (1095)(U)
British Oak (NA)
D: Ethyle Batley
CRIME Crook kidnaps judge's son and poses
as him to rob judge's safe.

06217
THE LITTLE BREADWINNER (4875)(A)
Clarendon
D: Wilfred Noy
S: (PLAY) James A. Campbell
Kitty Atfield . . . . Meg
Maureen O'Hara . . . . Margaret
CRIME Quaker peer's disowned son kidnapped
by usurping secretary.

06218
MORE TO HIM THAN LIFE (1690)(A)
Clarendon
D: Wilfred Noy
CRIME Steward frames colleague for murder
so as to woo his wife.

06219
RUBBERFACE AS A SPECIAL CONSTABLE
(2000)(U)
Cricks (XL)
Mr. Bevan . . . . Rubberface
P.R. Bennett . . . .
COMEDY Ugly policeman has misadventures
with cook, small boys, and robber.

06220
PIMPLE'S NAUTICAL STORY (2000)(U)
Piccadilly (Kin-Ex)
D:S: Fred Evans, Joe Evans
Fred Evans . . . . Pimple
COMEDY Sailor tells how he escaped from whale
and defeated shark.

06221
A PLACE IN THE SUN (4600)(A)
Turner Films (Butcher)
D:SC: Larry Trimble
S: (PLAY) Cyril Harcourt
Reginald Owen . . . . Stuart Capel
Margaret Blanche . . . . Rosie Blair
Malcolm Cherry . . . . Dick Blair
Lydia Bilbrooke . . . . Marjorie Capel
Campbell Gullan . . . . Arthur Blagden
Lyston Lyle . . . . Sir John Capel
Frances Wetherall . . . . Mrs Moultrie
John MacAndrews . . . . Ben Goodge
DRAMA Knight refuses to let son wed pregnant
peasant so his daughter compromises herself with
girl's brother.

06222
ANNIE LAURIE (3800)(U)
Hepworth (Harma)
D: Cecil M. Hepworth
S: Alma Taylor
Alma Taylor . . . . Annie Laurie
Stewart Rome . . . . Sir John Mc Dougal
Lionelle Howard . . . . Alfred English
Gwynne Herbert . . . . Hannah Black
Henry Vibart . . . . Doctor
ROMANCE Scotland. Laird weds peasant's
neice who falls in love with his nephew.

06223
PARTNERS (2175)(A)
Hepworth (Wards)
D: Frank Wilson
Stewart Rome . . . . Jack Brent
Chrissie White . . . . Mary
Lionelle Howard . . . . Ned
William Felton . . . . Silas Milton
Henry Vibart . . . . Father
John MacAndrews . . . . Sheriff
WESTERN Miner blamed for stabbing ex-partner who fathered girl's baby.

06224
CYNTHIA IN THE WILDERNESS (4025)(A)
Pioneer Films Agency
D:SC: Harold Weston
S: (NOVEL) Hubert Wales
Eve Balfour . . . . Cynthia Elwes
Ben Webster . . . . Laurence Cheyne
Milton Rosmer . . . . Harvey Elwes
Odette Goimbault . . . . Erica
Barbara Hannay . . . .
DRAMA Drunkard's wife lives with her lover
and poisons him when he goes mad.

06225
THE BLIND MAN OF VERDUN (2550)(A)
B&C (DFSA)
D: A. V. Bramble
S: Eliot Stannard
A.V. Bramble . . . .
WAR French officer poses as peasant and is
caught, but bomb saves him from firing squad.

06226
TRAPPED BY THE LONDON SHARKS (4464) (A)
Barker (Magnet)
D: L.C. MacBean
Blanche Forsythe . . . . Hilda Manton
Bertram Burleigh . . . . Insp James Graham
Maud Yates . . . . Countess Zena
Humberston Wright . . . . . . John Manton
High Nicholson . . . . Baron Slomann
CRIME Cardsharpers gas drunkard and make
him think he has killed his wife, so that he
helps them plan bank raid.

06227
THE PICTURE OF DORIAN GRAY (5752)(A)
Barker-Neptune (Browne)
D: Fred W. Durrant
S: (NOVEL) Oscar Wilde
SC: Rowland Talbot
Henry Victor . . . . Dorian Gray
Pat O'Malley . . . . Sybil Vane
Jack Jordan . . . . .Lord Henry Wootton
Sydney Bland . . . . Basil Hallward
A.B. Imeson . . . . Satan
Douglas Cox . . . . James Vane
Dorothy Fane . . . . Lady Marchmont
Miriam Ferris . . . .
FANTASY Period. Rake remains young while his
portrait grows old.

06228
THE STRANGE CASE OF PHILIP KENT (3500)
Barker-Neptune (KTC)
D: Fred W. Durrant
S: Rowland Talbot
Cyril Morton . . . . Dr Cecil Mortimer
J. Hastings Batson . . . . Sir George Terry
CRIME Man persuades dying friend to insure,
marries his widow, and murders her.

06229
ARSENE LUPIN (6400)(U)
London (Jury)
D: George L. Tucker

S: (PLAY) Maurice le Blanc, Francois de Crosset
SC: Kenelm Foss
Gerald Ames . . . . Arsene Lupin
Manora Thew . . . . Savia
Kenelm Foss . . . . Insp Guerchard
Douglas Munro . . . . Gournay-Martin
Marga la Rubia . . . .
Philip Hewland . . . .
CRIME Paris. Inspector tries to catch gentleman
thief.

06230
THE GAY DECEIVERS (1263)(U)
Regal
D:S: Dave Aylott
Ernie Westo
Nettie Grossman
Bob Reed
Letty Paxton
COMEDY

06231
ULTUS AND THE GREY LADY (4488) (U)
USA: ULTUS 3: THE GREY LADY,
ULTUS 4: THE TRAITOR'S FATE
Gaumont-Victory
D:S: George Pearson
Aurele Sydney . . . . Ultus
Mary Dibley . . . . Mary Ferris
Jack Leigh . . . . Conway Bass
Frank Dane . . . . Dick
M. Gouget . . . . Eugene Lester
CRIME Girl helps "Avenger" trace betrayer,
the man who killed her father.

06232
TEMPTATION'S HOUR (4000) retitled:
FRAILTY
Renaissance
P: John M. Payne
D:S: Sidney Morgan
Fanny Tittell-Brune
Eille Norwood
Sydney Fairbrother
Julian Royce
Arthur Wontner
Joan Morgan
ROMANCE Girl's ex-fiance takes her family
maid to lady's fete.

06233
BEAU BROCADE (5400)(U)
Lucoque reissue: 1919 (Artistic)
P: H. Lisle Lucoque
D: Thomas Bentley
S: (NOVEL) Baroness Orczy
SC: Nellie E. Lucoque
Mercy Hatton . . . . Lady Patience
Charles Rock . . . . . . Sir Humphrey Challoner
Austin Leigh . . . . Jack Bathurst
Cecil Mannering . . . . Lord Stretton
George Foley . . . . John Stitch
Cecil Morton York . . . . Matterchip
Frank Harris . . . . Jock Miggs
Harry Brayne . . . . Duffy
Kitty Arlington . . . . Betty
ADVENTURE 1746. Cashiered cardsharper turns
highwayman and proves lord posing as
apprentice was framed by cousin.

06234
THE NEW CLOWN (4500)(U)
Ideal
D: Fred Paul
S: (PLAY) H.M. Paull
SC: Benedict James
James Welch . . . . .Lord Cyril Garston
Manora Thew . . . . Rosie Dixon

Richard Lindsay . . . . Capt Trent
Tom Coventry . . . . Tom Baker
Brian Daly . . . . Pennyquick
E.C. Arundell . . . . Strong Man
Kathleen Blake . . . . Maud Chesterton
Marjory Day .. . . Winnie Chesterton
Edward Sass . . . . Showman
Arthur Milton . . . . Innkeeper
COMEDY Lord thinks he kills man so becomes
clown in touring circus.

JUL

06235
THE MAN IN HIS PLACE (1190)(U)
British Oak (NA)
D: Ernest G. Batley
DRAMA Engineer takes place of rich double
injured in car crash.

06236
THE DAYLIGHT SAVING BILL (600)(U)
British Oak (NA)
D: Ethyle Batley
COMEDY Man rushes to work not knowing
wife has put clock forward against his wishes.

06237
A GOOD HOUSE DOG (669)
Pyramid (YCC)
COMEDY Captain buys bulldog from burglar
and is robbed.

06238
MAGGIE THE MILL GIRL (680)
Pyramid (YCC)
DRAMA Owner sets mill on fire to kill
workman rival, who climbs chimney and is
saved by sweetheart's rope.

06239
JACK SPRATT'S PARROT IN PUTTING THE
LID ON IT (1000)(U)
Clarendon
D: (Toby Cooper)
COMEDY Naval deserter loses parrot and finds
girl married to butcher.

06240
THE WOMAN WHO DID 'EM (1800)(U)
New Agency (Harma)
COMEDY Burlesque of "The Woman Who
Did."

06241
O'NEIL OF THE GLEN (2572) (A)
Film Co. of Ireland (DFSA)
D: J.M. Kerrigan
S: (PLAY) M.T. Pender
SC: W.J. Lysaght
J.M. Kerrigan . . . . Don O'Neil
Nora Clancy . . . . Nola Tremaine
Fred O'Donovan . . . . Graves
Brian Magowan . . . . Tremaine
J. Smith . . . .
J.M. Carre . . . .
R.V. Justice . . . .
CRIME Ireland. Man's rival tries to win girl by
blackmailing her father.

06242
IF— (4800)(U)
London (Fenning) reissue: 1918
D: Stuart Kinder
Iris Delaney . . . . Mme X
Ernest Leicester . . . . Armstrong
Judd Green . . . . Count Hoffman
WAR Girl thief helps detective foil Count's plan
to divert defences with fake airships while
hidden guns destroy London.

06243
A ROGUE IN LOVE (3800)(A)
London (Jury)
D:SC: Bannister Merwin
S: (NOVEL) Tom Gallon
James Reardon
DRAMA Ex-convict tries to tell friend his
legacy does not exist.

06244
ODD CHARGES (2300)(A)
London (Jury)
D:SC: Frank Miller
S: (STORY) W.W. Jacobs
Frank Stanmore . . . . Bob Pretty
James Reardon . . . . Dicky Weed
Kenelm Foss . . . . Conjuror
Vivien Gibson . . . . Landlord's Daughter
Judd Green . . . . Landlord
COMEDY Conjuror flirts with landlord's
daughter.

06245
THE MAN WITHOUT A SOUL (7200) (A)
USA: I BELIEVE
London (Jury)
D:SC: George L. Tucker
S: Kenelm Foss
Milton Rosmer . . . . Stephen Ferrier
Edna Flugrath . . . . Lucy
Barbara Everest . . . .
Edward O'Neill . . . . The Atheist
Charles Rock . . . . Rev John Ferrier
Frank Stanmore . . . .
Kitty Cavendish . . . . :.
Hubert Willis . . . .
FANTASY Church student loses soul after
scientist revives his dead body.

06246
THE MARRIAGE OF WILLIAM ASHE (5175)
(A)
Hepworth (Harma)
D: Cecil M. Hepworth
S: (NOVEL) Mrs Humphry Ward
Henry Ainley . . . . William Ashe
Alma Taylor . . . . .Lady Kitty Bristol
Stewart Rome . . . . Geoffrey Cliffe
Violet Hopson . . . . Mary Lyster
Lionelle Howard . . . . .Eddie Helston
Alice de Winton . . . . Mme d'Estrees
Mary Rorke . . . . Lady Tranmere
Henry Vibart . . . . Lord Parham
Amy Lorraine . . . . Lady Parham
Fred Rains . . . . Dean Maitland
DRAMA MP weds Lady but leaves her when she
writes book about him.

06247
LADY WINDERMERE'S FAN (4500)(U)
Ideal
D: Fred Paul
S: (PLAY) Oscar Wilde
SC: Benedict James
Milton Rosmer . . . . Lord Windermere
Netta Westcott . . . . Lady Windermere
Nigel Playfair . . . . . Lord Augustus Lorton
Irene Rooke . . . . Mrs Erlynne
Arthur Wontner . . . . Lord Darlington
Alice de Winton . . . .' Duchess of Berwick
Vivian Reynolds . . . . Mr Dumby
Joyce Kerr . . . . Agatha
Evan Thomas . . . . Cecil Graham
Sidney Vautier . . . . Hooper
COMEDY Lady mistakes husband's mother for
mistress and takes lover.

06248
JUST A GIRL (6300)(U)
G.B. Samuelson (Moss)

D: Alexander Butler
S: (NOVEL) Charles Garvice
SC: Harry Engholm
Owen Nares . . . . Lord Trafford
Daisy Burrell . . . . Esmeralda
J. Hastings Batson . . . . The Duke
Minna Grey . . . . The Duchess
Paul England . . . . The Miner
ROMANCE Australian heiress gives up poor
lord to marry miner.

06249
KENT THE FIGHTING MAN (5500) (A)
I.B. Davidson-Tiger (Gaumount)
D: A.E. Coleby
S: (NOVEL) George Edgar
SC: Rowland Talbot
Bdr Billy Wells . . . . John Westerley
Hetty Payne . . . . Constance
A.E. Coleby . . . . Adams
Arthur Rooke . . . . Hon Jimmy Greenback
Charles Vane . . . .
Sidney Bland . . . .
Frank Dane . . . . Brother
Nelson Phillips . . . . Col Rapton
Harry Lofting . . . . Jim Dace
Fred Drummond . . . . Button
Tom Coventry . . . . Clown
Dick Webb . . . .
Judd Green . . . .
N. Watts-Phillips . . . .
Ernie Collins . . . .
SPORT Disowned gambler turns boxer and
ruins cardsharpers by getting them to bet on
opponent.

06250
THE GREEN ORCHARD (5000)(U)
Broadwest
P: Walter West
D.SC: Harold Weston
S: (NOVEL) Andrew Soutar
Gregory Scott . . . . .Martin Wilderspin
Dora Barton . . . . Fauvette Hyne
E. Vassal-Vaughan . . . . Tony Rye
Ernie Collins . . . .
DRAMA Barrister's parents cause wife to leave
him and she becomes novelist.

06251
THE MERCHANT OF VENICE (6000)(U)
Broadwest
P:D: Walter West
S: (PLAY) William Shakespeare
Matheson Lang . . . . Shylock
Nellie Hutin Britton . . . . Portia
J.R. Tozer . . . . Bassanio
George Skillan . . . . Antonio
Kathleen Hazel Jones . . . . . Jessica
Ernest Caselli . . . . Lorenzo
Marguerite Westlake . . . . . . .Nerissa
Terence O'Brien . . . . Tubal
George Morgan . . . . Lancelot
DRAMA Venice. Girl advocate foils Jewish
usurer's claim for pound of debtor's flesh.

06252
THE BROKEN MELODY(5200)(U)
Ideal *reissue*: 1918
D: Cavendish Morton
S: (SKETCH) August Van Biene
SC: Benedict James
Martin Harvey . . . . Paul
Hilda Moore . . . . Duchess
Manora Thew . . . . Mabel
Courtice Pounds . . . . ·
Edward Sass . . . .
Barbara Hannay . . . .

Nelson Ramsey . . . . ,
Fred Rains . . . .
ROMANCE Duchess persuades wife to leave
Polish violinist but she returns when he is
wounded in duel.

06253
THE GIRL WHO DIDN'T CARE (3900)(A)
Barker-Neptune (Cross)
D: Fred W. Durrant
S: Rowland Talbot
Agnes Paulton . . . . Eve Latimer
Mercy Hatton . . . . Kitty
Tom Coventry . . . .
Jerrold Robertshaw . . . .
CRIME Sacked girl robs father to pay for
wedding and becomes morphia maniac's
mistress.

06254
THE CHANCE OF A LIFETIME (5250)(U)
Holmfirth (Pathe)
D: Bertram Phillips
S: (NOVEL) Nat Gould
Queenie Thomas . . . . Mrs Edgar
Austin Camp . . . . Dick Douglas
Fay Temple . . . . . :. . . . . . Diana Lawson
H. Agar Lyons . . . . Capt Clinch
Frank E. Petley . . . .
Rohan Clensy . . . .
Ernest Collins . . . .
Will Asher . . . .·. Jockey
SPORT Captain steals owner's cup and trainer's
daughter steals it back.

06255
GOLD AND THE DROSS (3000) *
Enterprise
D: B.C. Gibbs
Mary Leigh
Frank L. Cooper
J. Newton Byerley
DRAMA

AUG

06256
GRIM JUSTICE (4250)(U)
Turner Films (Butcher)
D:SC: Larry Trimble
S: (NOVEL) "Rita"
Florence Turner . . . . Crystal Transom
Henry Edwards . . . . Gideon Midhurst
Malcolm Cherry . . . . James Midhurst
Winnington Barnes . . . . Jude Midhurst
Una Venning . . . . Drusilla Midhurst
Dorothy Rowan . . . . Hester Midhurst
George Moore . . . . Grandfather Trans
Maud Williamson . . . . Stepmother
DRAMA Rich man pretends injured son's marriag
illegal and makes his wife marry drunken wastrel

06257
THE GRAND BABYLON HOTEL (5275)(A)
Hepworth (Shaftesbury)
D: Frank Wilson
S: (NOVEL) Arnold Bennett
Fred Wright . . . . Theodore Rackso
Margaret Blanche . . . . Nella Racksole
Gerald Lawrence . . . . Jules
Lionelle Howard . . . . Prince Eugen
Stewart Rome . . . . Prince Aribert
Violet Hopson . . . . Miss Spencer
Alma Taylor . . . . Princess Anna
Charles Vane . . . . Rocco
Henry Vibart . . . . King of Ragatz
Johnny Butt . . . . Sampson Levi
CRIME American millionaire's daughter saves
Ruritanian prince from kidnappers.

06258
THE GREATER NEED (4700)(A)
London (Jury)
D: Ralph Dewsbury
S: Frank Fowell
Milton Rosmer . . . . Bob Leroy
Gerald Ames . . . . Jack Leroy
Amy Brandon-Thomas . . . . . Mary Firth
Philip Hewland . . . . Inspector
Gwynne Herbert . . . .
Mary Dibley . . . .
Hubert Willis . . . .
DRAMA Wastrel enlists after soldier brother
loses arm.

06259
THE SKIPPER OF THE OSPREY (1320)(U)
London (Jury)
D:SC: Frank Miller
S: (STORY) W.W. Jacobs
Hayford Hobbs . . . . Charlie Lee
Renee Wakefield . . . . Maggie Cringle
Frank Stanmore . . . . Skipper Cringle
Kenelm Foss . . . .
Judd Green . . . .
COMEDY Sacked mate saves girl skipper from
lustful replacement.

06260
THE PERSECUTION OF BOB PRETTY
(1100)(U)
London (Jury)
D:SC: Frank Miller
S: (STORY) W.W. Jacobs
Frank Stanmore . . . . Bob Pretty
Vivian Gibson . . . . The Girl
James Reardon . . . . Dicky Weed
Philip Hewland . . . . Squire
Douglas Munro . . . . Cutts
Judd Green . . . . Wick
Kenelm Foss . . . . Lewis
Pollie Emery . . . . Widow
COMEDY Village squire's keeper feigns illness
to trap poacher.

06261
A MARKED MAN (1795)(U)
London (Jury)
D:SC: Frank Miller
S: (STORY) W.W. Jacobs
Frank Stanmore . . . . Sam Small
Judd Green . . . . Peter Russett
James Reardon . . . . Ginger Dick
Kenelm Foss . . . .
COMEDY Sailors tattoo their mate so he can
pose as widow's lost son.

06262
TROUBLE FOR NOTHING (2300)(A)
London (Jury)
D: Maurice Elvey
S: (PLAY) Arthur Eckersley, Guy Newall
Guy Newall . . . . .Rev Cuthbert Cheese
Hayford Hobbs . . . .
Jeff Barlow . . . .
Winifred Sadler . . . .
COMEDY

06263
IT'S ALWAYS THE WOMAN (5050)(A)
Clarendon
D: Wilfred Noy
S: (PLAY) Bryant Adair
Hayden Coffin . . . . Maj Sterrington
Barbara Conrad . . . . Esmeralda Chetwynde
Daisy Burrell . . . . Mrs Sterrington
DRAMA Vamp breaks major's marriage, weds
him, and sends his daughter to convent where
her 'dead' mother is nun.

06264
THE ACE OF HEARTS (3600)(A)
Clarendon
D: Charles Calvert
S: (PLAY) James Willard
James Willard . . . . James Fairburn
Dolly Bishop . . . . Lola Vane
Frank Sargent . . . . Dick Rayston
DRAMA Editor gambles life on draw of cards
with wife's lover.

06265
WHEN WOMAN HATES (5500)(A)
British Empire Films
D:SC: Albert Ward
S: (PLAY) Fred Bulmer
Henry Lonsdale
Mercy Hatton
Jose Brooks
CRIME Gamblers force girl to rob father and
frame her brother for murder.

06266
THE MAN WITH THE GLASS EYE (3500) (A)
British Empire Films
S: (PLAY)
Henry Lonsdale . . . . Victor St Aubyn
Mercy Hatton . . . .
CRIME Society cracksman caught when dying
victim pulls out glass eye.

06267
THE PHANTOM PICTURE (5500)(A)
British Empire Films
D:SC: Albert Ward
S: (PLAY) Harold Simpson
Henry Lonsdale . . . . John Gordon
Violet Campbell . . . . Pauline Mainwaring
Arthur Poole . . . . Lionel Carruthers
Ivan Berlyn . . . . Isaac Bernstein
CRIME Artist's model poses as painting to shock
Jew into confessing that he stabbed connoisseur.

06268
QUEEN OF THE WICKED (5500)(A)
British Empire Films
D:SC: Albert Ward
S: (PLAY) Ronald Grahame
Henry Lonsdale . . . . Lucien la Verne
Nina Lynn . . . . Ligeah Dupont
Janet Alexander . . . . . . Lady Doris Manners
CRIME Dancer drugs husband, robs safe, strangles
him and frames lord for murder.

06269
THE GIRL WHO WRECKED HIS HOME (5000)
British Empire Films
D:SC: Albert Ward
S: (PLAY) Walter Melville
Henry Lonsdale . . . . Lord Lynton
Alice Belmore . . . . Bertha Marshall
Arthur Poole . . . . Leonard Kenyon
Maud Olmar . . . . Winnie
Andrew Emm . . . . Josh
Cyril Bennell . . . . William (child)
Frances Davies . . . . Winnie (child)
CRIME Cardsharp frames neglected wife for
murder and elopes with her.

06270
RESCUING AN HEIRESS (1000)
Lucoque Pip-Cure
D: Harry Buss
Mercy Hatton . . . .
Charles Rock . . . .
COMEDY

06271
SOME FISH! (1000)
Lucoque Pip-Cure
D: Harry Buss
Mercy Hatton . . . .
Charles Rock . . . .
COMEDY

06272
BOB DOWNE'S SCHOOLDAYS (1040)(A)
Union Jack (DFSA)
D: Dave Aylott
Bob Reed . . . . Bob Downe
Ernie Westo . . . . The Hero
Gladys Dolan . . . . The Girl
COMEDY Schoolboy's misadventures with
chemicals and a girls' school.

06273
NIPPER'S BUSY BEE TIME (824)(U)
Little Nipper (DFSA)
Lupino Lane . . . . Nipper
COMEDY Suitor poses as girl to divert man
from beekeeper's daughter.

06274
SOME WAITER! (3000)
George Carney
D:S: George Carney
George Carney
George Hughes
Robert Chester
Vesta Leonard
Robert Leonard
George Reed
COMEDY

06275
THE LIFEGUARDSMAN (4279)(U)
British Actors (Int-Ex)
D: Frank G. Bayly
S: (PLAY) Walter Howard
SC: Arthur Shirley, William Deveraux
Annie Saker . . . . Princess Dorine
Alfred Paumier . . . . Prince Max
Leslie Carter . . . . Prince Hugo
Alfred Bishop . . . . Gen Rosenburg
Cecil Ward . . . . Baron Strelzer
Frederick Volpe . . . . .Lord Chamberlain
Sam Livesey . . . . Capt Salzburg
Fred Kerr . . . . Premier
A.E. Matthews . . . . Lt Tosh
Spencer Trevor . . . . Lt Dinkie
Leslie Henson . . . . Lt Spiff
Cecil Humphreys . . . . Valet
Eva Rowland . . . . Sylva
Ninon Dudley . . . . Nora
ADVENTURE Ruritania. Idiot heir helps
wounded prince save princess from forced
marriage to usurper.

06276
HER GREATEST PERFORMANCE (6000)(U)
Ideal reissue: 1918
D: Fred Paul
S: Enid Lorimer
SC: Benedict James
Ellen Terry . . . . Julia Lovelace
Dennis Neilson-Terry . . . . . . Gerald Lovelace
Joan Morgan . . . . Barbara Lovelace
James Lindsay . . . . Jim Douglas
Gladys Mason . . . . Mary Scott
Edith Craig . . . . The Dresser
Nelson Ramsay . . . .
Barbara Hannay . . . .
E. Vivian Reynolds . . . .
Fred Rains . . . .
Harry Lofting . . . .
CRIME Retired actress poses as dresser to scare
murderer into confessing and clearing her son.

06277
LEAD' KINDLY LIGHT (4000) (A) retitled:
THE PRODIGAL DAUGHTER
Surrey (Renters)
S: J. Hamilton Page
Derra de Moroda . . . . Sybil Frane
Harry Gilbey . . . . Philip Chester
DRAMA Vicar's daughter reforms after becoming
dancer, gambler, home-wrecker, and blackmailer.

SEP

06278
THE ECONOMISTS (2040) (U)
Renaissance (Gaumont)
D:S: John M. Payne
Fanny Tittell-Brune . . . . . . Sylvia
John Castle (Payne) . . . . . . Archie
Florence Nelson . . . . Mother
COMEDY Extravagant wife causes trouble
when she tries to economise.

06279
THE MAN IN MOTLEY (4757) (A)
London (Jury)
D: Ralph Dewsbury
S: (NOVEL) Tom Gallon
Fred Morgan
Hayford Hobbs
Winifred Sadler
Phillip Hewland
Hubert Willis
Jeff Barlow
Judd Green
John East
CRIME Framed juggler breaks jail and poses as
ghost to force killer to confess.

06280
THE PRINCESS OF HAPPY CHANCE (4885) (U)
(U)
London (Jury)
D: Maurice Elvey
S: (NOVEL) Tom Gallon
Elizabeth Risdon . . . . . .Princess Felicia/
                            Lucidora Eden
Gerald Ames . . . . Prince Jocelyn
Hayford Hobbs . . . . Harvey Royle
Dallas Cairns . . . . Prince
Douglas Munro . . . .
Gwynne Herbert . . . .
Edna Maude . . . .
Cyril Percival . . . .
Janet Ross . . . .
Beatrix Templeton . . . .
ROMANCE Ruritania. Princess avoids forced
marriage by changing places with her double.

06281
THE NEW GIRL (1020) (U)
Clarendon
D: (Wilfred Noy)
Betty the Chimpanzee
COMEDY Schoolgirl dresses chimpanzee pet
as King's daughter.

06282
THE INTERRUPTED HONEYMOON (1000) (U)
Clarendon
D: (Wilfred Noy)
Betty the Chimpanzee
COMEDY Chimpanzee acts as maidservant to
honeymooners.

06283
THE LITTLE DAMOZEL (5050) (U)
Clarendon (Harma)
D: Wilfred Noy
S: (PLAY) Monckton Hoffe
Barbara Conrad . . . . Julie Alardy
Geoffrey Wilmer . . . . Recklaw Poole

Nora Chaplin . . . . Sybil Craven
Richard Lindsay . . . . Capt Partington
J. Hastings Batson . . . . Admiral Craven
Roy Byford . . . . Beppo
W.D. Fazan . . . . Angel
ROMANCE Monte Carlo. Singer learns to love
gambler bribed to marry her.

06284
THE EXPLOITS OF TUBBY (series)
Hepworth (Thanhouser)
D: Frank Wilson
S: Percy Manton
Johnny Butt . . . . Tubby
Violet Hopson . . . . Mrs Tubby

06285
1—TUBBY'S UNCLE (650) (U)
Frank Wilson . . . . Uncle

06286
2 — TUBBY'S TYPEWRITER (725) (U)

06287
3—TUBBY AND THE CLUTCHING HAND
(675) (U)

06288
4—TUBBY'S SPANISH GIRLS (800) (U)
Chrissie White . . . . Senorita

06289
5—TUBBY'S BUNGLE-OH! (875) (U)
Chrissie White . . . . Helen Smith
Lionelle Howard . . . . Jack Smith

06290
6—TUBBY'S GOOD WORK (875) (U)
Chrissie White . . . . The Tramp

06291
7—TUBBY'S REST CURE (875) (U)

06292
8—TUBBY'S TIP (900) (U)
Lionelle Howard . . . . Tony

06293
9—TUBBY'S RIVER TRIP (800) (U)

06294
10—TUBBY'S DUGOUT (1050) (A)
COMEDIES

06295
EAST IS EAST (4895) (U)
Turner Films (Butcher) *reissue:* 1919
D:SC: Henry Edwards
S: (PLAY) Philip Hubbard, Gwendolen Logan
Florence Turner . . . . Victoria Vickers
Henry Edwards . . . . Bert Grummett
Ruth Mackay . . . . Mrs Carrington
W.G. Saunders . . . . Dawson
Edith Evans . . . . Aunt
ROMANCE Cockney hop-picker inherits
£250,000 but returns to fishmonger sweetheart.

06296
HELLO EXCHANGE (1064)
British Photoplay Productions (DFSA)
P: Edward Godal
D: Kelly Storrie
COMEDY Man poses as burglar to reform gay
wife.

06297
HOME COMFORTS (674)
British Photoplay Productions (DFSA)
P: Edward Godal
D: Kelly Storrie
COMEDY Mother finds note incriminating
daughter's husband.

06298
£66.13.9¾ FOR EVERY MAN, WOMAN AND
CHILD (1500) (U)
Ideal
D: Edwin J. Collins
S: George Robey
Geroge Robey . . . . The Man
COMEDY Cobbler dreams of being given his
exact share of the world's wealth.

06299
BLOOD TELLS; OR, THE ANTI-FRIVOLITY
LEAGUE (1900) (U)
Ideal
D: Edwin J. Collins
S: George Robey
George Robey . . . . Timothy Bing
Harry Lofting . . . . Vicar
Florence Nelson . . . .
Fred Rains .. . .
COMEDY Purity league chairman has blood
transfusion from burglar and becomes rake.

06300
NURSIE! NURSIE! (2000) (U)
G.B. Samuelson (Moss)
D: Alexander Butler
S: Reuben Gillmer
Clarice Mayne . . . . Nursie
James W. Tate . . . . Patient
Bernard Vaughan . . . . Doctor
Percy C. Johnson . . . . Pageboy
COMEDY Man feigns illness to woo nurse.

06301
THE GIRL WHO LOVES A SOLDIER (4300) (U)
G.B. Samuelson (Moss)
D: Alexander Butler
Vesta Tilley . . . . Vesta Beaumont
Sydney Folker . . . . Chris Barker
James Lindsay . . . . Lord Strathmore
Norman Cheyne . . . . Billy Williams
Rutland Barrington . . . . Mr Beaumont
WAR Tomboy becomes nurse and poses as man to
deliver wounded fiance's despatches.

06302
THE DUSTMAN'S WEDDING (2900) (U)
Homeland (Globe)
D: W.P. Kelljno
S: Reuben Gillmer
Albert Egbert . . . . Bill
Seth Egbert . . . . Walter
COMEDY Foreman tries to make dustman
work on wedding day.

06303
THE PERILS OF PORK PIE (3000) (U)
Homeland (Globe)
D: W.P. Kellino
S: Reuben Gillmer
Billy Merson . . . . Billy Muggins
Charles Cohen . . . .
COMEDY Man dreams he buys British
Museum where mummy revives and makes
him pharoah.

06304
MIKE AND THE MISER (569) (U)
Martin (DFSA)
D: Dave Aylott
Tom Morriss . . . . Mike Murphy
TRICK Tramp robs miser and is chased by barrel,
fairy, policeman, etc.

06305
BOBBIKINS AND THE BATHING BELLES
(664) (U)
AEM Films - Union Jack (DFSA)
P: A.E. Martin
D: (Dave Aylott)
COMEDY Woman catches husband flirting at
swimming bath.

06306
HITCHY-COO (595)(U)
AEM Films-Union Jack (DFSA)
P: A.E. Martin
D: (Dave Aylott)
COMEDY Pageboy squirts professor's itching fluid on policeman, costers, woman, etc.

06307
THE TRIALS OF A MILKMAN (860)(A)
retitled: MILKO!
C. Goodman (Pathe)
COMEDY Milkman's adventures with angry wife, drunkard, policeman, etc.

OCT

06308
THE ANTAGONISTS (1965)(U)
Renaissance (Gaumont)
D:S: John M. Payne
Fanny Tittell-Brune . . . . Sylvia
John Castle (Payne) . . . . Archie
COMEDY Girl leaves husband, poses as housekeeper, and catches burglar.

06309
COMIN' THRO' THE RYE (5600)(U)
Hepworth (Harma) *reissue: 1919*
D: Cecil M. Hepworth
S: (NOVEL) Helen Mathers
SC: Blanche McIntosh
Alma Taylor . . . . Helen Adair
Stewart Rome . . . . Paul Vasher
Margaret Blanche . . . . Sylvia Fleming
Campbell Gullan . . . . George Tempest
Lionelle Howard . . . . Dick Fellows
Charles Vane . . . . Col Adair
Ivy Millais . . . . Jane Peach
Chrissie White . . . . Alice Adair
Violet Hopson . . . .
ROMANCE Girl wins rival's fiance with fake marriage announcement. (Royal Command Performance).

06310
THE MOTHER OF DARTMOOR (5500)(U)
London (Jury)
D: George L. Tucker
S: (NOVEL) Eden Philpotts
SC: Kenelm Foss
Elizabeth Risdon . . . . Avesa Pomeroy
Bertram Burleigh . . . . Ives Pomeroy
Enid Bell . . . . Jill Bell
George Bellamy . . . . Matthew Northmore
Sydney Fairbrother . . . . . . Mrs Bolt
Frank Stanmore . . . . Sammy Bolt
Hubert Willis . . . . Moleskin
DRAMA Dartmoor. Man turns poacher for love of married woman and is jailed by his widowed mother's evidence.

06311
A MOTHER'S INFLUENCE (2500)(U)
London (Jury)
D: George L. Tucker
S: (NOVEL) Eden Philpotts (THE MOTHER)
SC: Kenelm Foss
Elizabeth Risdon . . . . Avesa Pomeroy
Bertram Burleigh . . . . Ives Pomeroy
Enid Bell . . . . Jill Wicket
George Bellamy . . . . Matthew Northmore
Sydney Fairbrother . . . . . . Mrs Bolt
Frank Stanmore . . . . Sammy Bolt
DRAMA Dartmoor. Widow's strong personality influences son after death.

06312
ALTAR CHAINS (4600)(U)
London (Jury)
D:S: Bannister Merwin
Dawson Millward . . . . Capt Kerr

Heather Thatcher . . . . Alice Vaughan
Philip Hewland . . . . Harry Avery
Edward O'Neill . . . . Philip Anson
Minna Grey . . . . Mrs Anson
Fred Volpe . . . . Harky
Hubert Willis . . . . Charles Vaughan
Donald Calthrop . . . .
CRIME Captain with month to live forces usurer to join him in drinking poison.

06313
DIANA AND DESTINY (5000)(U)
Windsor (Gaumont)
D: F. Martin Thornton
S: (NOVEL) Charles Garvice
Evelyn Boucher . . . . Diana
Wyndham Guise . . . . William Bourne
Roy Travers . . . .
Frank E. Petley . . . .
Harry Royston . . . .
H. Agar Lyons . . . .
Ernie Collins . . . .
Greta Wood . . . .
CRIME Ex-burglar millionaire, blackmailed by Earl's nephew, steals gems from Earl who adopted his lost daughter.

06314
A WIFE IN A HURRY (2700)(U)
Homeland (Butcher)
D: W.P. Kellino
S: Reuben Gillmer
Lupino Lane . . . . Tony Melton
Winifred Delevanti . . . .
Blanche Kellino . . . .
Will Kellino . . . .
Fred Toose . . . .
COMEDY Prospective heir must marry within 24 hours.

06315
TATTERLY (5400)(U)
Lucoque *reissue: 1919 (Artistic)*
D: H. Lisle Lucoque
S: (NOVEL) Tom Gallon
SC: Nellie E. Lucoque
Cecil Mannering . . . . Donald Brett
Mercy Hatton . . . . Ellen Tarrant
Charles Rock . . . . Caleb Fry
George Foley . . . . Hector Kindon
Harry Lofting . . . . Morton Tarrant
Madge Tree . . . .
DRAMA Miser takes place of dead servant and helps couple he had ruined.

06316
FAIRYLAND (1959)(U)
Lucoque *reissue: 1925 (Standard)*
D: H. Lisle Lucoque
S: Pauline Lewis
Phyllis Bedells . . . . Fairy Queen
Little Alan . . . . Boykins
Babs Farren . . . .
Wynne St Clair . . . .
Daphne Wynne . . . .
FANTASY Small boy's dream of fairyland.

06317
HONOUR IN PAWN (4800)(A)
Broadwest
P: Walter West
D:SC: Harold Weston
S: (NOVEL) W.B. Maxwell
Manora Thew . . . . Nancy Raeburn
Julian Royce . . . . Sir Roger Singleton
George Bellamy . . . . Harvey Denman
Ivan Berlyn . . . . Giovanni Leracca
Helen Haye . . . . Mrs Fortescue
Hetta Bartlett . . . .
Marjorie Compton . . . .
CRIME Crooked dealer adopts girl thief and forces her to steal knight's plate.

06318
ULTUS AND THE SECRET OF THE NIGHT (4000)(A) USA: ULTUS 5: THE SECRET OF THE NIGHT.
Gaumont-Victory
D:S: George Pearson
Aurele Sydney . . . . Ultus
Mary Dibley . . . . Mary Ferris
J.L.V. Leigh . . . . Conway Bass
Lionel d'Aragon . . . . Banks
Mary Forbes . . . . Lady Fleet
Leonard Shepherd . . . . Sir Miles Fleet
Frank Dane . . . .
CRIME Devon. Girl helps "Avenger" save child heiress from couple hired to kill her.

06319
DR WAKE'S PATIENT (4300)(U)
G.B. Samuelson (Moss)
D: Fred Paul
S: (PLAY) W. Gayer Mackey, Robert Ord
SC: Harry Engholm
Phyllis Dare . . . . Lady Gerania
Gerald McCarthy . . . . Dr Wake
James Lindsay . . . . The Earl
Mary Rorke . . . . Mrs Wake
Wyndham Guise . . . . Farmer Wake
Dora Barton . . . . The Countess
ROMANCE Farmer's doctor son loves titled patient who loves nobleman.

06320
THE VICAR OF WAKEFIELD (6000)(U)
Ideal
D: Fred Paul
S: (NOVEL) Oliver Goldsmith
SC: Benedict James
Sir John Hare . . . . Dr. Charles Primrose
Laura Cowie . . . . Olivia Primrose
Ben Webster . . . . Sir William
Marie Illington . . . . Mrs Primrose
A.E. George . . . . Jenkinson
Margaret Shelley . . . . Sophia Primrose
Frank Woolfe . . . . Mr Burchell
Martin Lewis . . . . George Primrose
Lambert Terry . . . . Moses Primrose
Mabel Twemlow . . . . Hon Miss Skeggs
Jess Dorynne . . . . Lady Blarney
DRAMA Squire jails vicar for debt and fakes marriage to his daughter.

06321
THE FEMALE SWINDLER (5500)(A)
British Empire
D: Albert Ward
S: (PLAY) Walter Melville
Henry Lonsdale . . . . Jack Coulson
Alice Belmore . . . . Lu Valroy
Arthur Poole . . . . Geoffrey Warden
Maud Olmar . . . . May Oliver
Ralph Forster . . . . Sir James Oliver
Andrew Emm . . . . Billy Binks
Newman Maurice . . . . Mikestein
Bessie Walters . . . . Mary
Charles Grenville . . . . Harold Travers
Ninette de Valois . . . . Dancer
CRIME Tec loves jewel thief who drugs victims with Indian flower.

06322
THE PLEYDELL MYSTERY (5000)(U)
British Empire
D:SC: Albert Ward
S: (NOVEL) Claude & Alice Askew (POISON)
Cecil Humphreys . . . . John Pleydell
Christine Silver . . . . Felicity Harwood
Richard Lindsay . . . . Tony Masters
Mrs Bennett . . . . Rosa Latimer
Frank Randall . . . .
CRIME Man abandons wife and when she inherits frames her for poisoning his mistress.

06323
THE PORTRAIT OF DOLLY GREY (1960)(U)
Kineto
D:S: W.R. Booth
TRICK Lord hypnotises model into becoming
revue star and is thwarted when poster of Satan
comes to life.

06324
THE FOOD OF LOVE (1080) (U)
Film Company of Ireland (DFSA)
D: J.M. Kerrigan
J.M. Kerrigan
Kathleen Murphy
Fred O'Donovan
COMEDY

06325
THE MISER'S GIFT (1945)(U)
Film Company of Ireland (DFSA)
D: J.M. Kerrigan
J.M. Kerrigan . . . . Ned McGrath
Kathleen Murphy . . . . Eileen Dolan
Fred O'Donovan . . . . Dolan
COMEDY Killaloe. Girl and lover get mean
father drunk to dream of leprechaun's gold.

06326
AN UNFAIR LOVE AFFAIR (1782)(U)
Film Company of Ireland (DFSA)
D: J.M. Kerrigan
J.M. Kerrigan . . . . Joe
Nora Clancy . . . . Nora
Fred O'Donovan . . . . Fred
COMEDY Man wins girl by foiling his rival's
plot with tinker.

06327
WOMAN'S WIT (1670)(U)
Film Company of Ireland (DFSA)
D: J.M. Kerrigan
J.M. Kerrigan
Kathleen Murphy
Fred O'Donovan
COMEDY

06328
TWO LANCASHIRE LASSES IN LONDON
(5100)(U)
Martin's Cinematograph (Walturdaw)
P: A.E. Martin
D:SC: Dave Aylott
S: (PLAY) Arthur Shirley, Sutton Vane
Lettie Paxton . . . . Nell Hallett
Dolly Tree . . . . Constance Hallett
Wingold Lawrence . . . . John Edwards
Dave Aylott . . . . Jim Price
Frank Dane . . . . Rev Frank Selby
CRIME Girl weds crook who kills her sister; mill
owner tries to swindle an inventor.

06329
TRACKING THE ZEPPELIN RAIDERS
(3500)(U)
J. Bartlett (Criterion)
WAR Spies send information by wireless and
pigeons, and are bombed.

06330
THE HUNGER STRIKE (1500)
Barker (Magnet)
S: (PLAY)
Edmund Payne . . . . The Man
COMEDY

06331
FROM HEN TO HOSPITAL (2000)
British Oak (General)

D: Hugh Croise
S: Frederick Fenn
Joyce Templeton . . . . Faith Godsell
J. Hastings Batson . . . . Old Godsell
Tom Hanley . . . . Jerry
ROMANCE Wounded Australian traces
country girl through message on eggshell.

06332
MY YORKSHIRE LASS (4000)
Pyramid (YCC)
S: Max Pemberton
ROMANCE

06333
HER AWAKENING (1180)
Speed (DFSA)
DRAMA Neglected wife dreams she elopes and
her lover is killed by her husband.

06334
POPULAR SONG FAVOURITES (series)
Henry Tress
Donna Haydon   Austin Camp
Maud Williamson   Charles Goff
Dolly Tree   Tatten Hall
Dorothy Mertle   Harry Lorraine
Marjory Russell   Alfred Woods
Violet Blythe   George Lenord

06335
1—I WAS A GOOD LITTLE GIRL UNTIL I
MET YOU

06336
2—IF I WERE THE ONLY GIRL

06337
3—WHEN YOU'RE A LONG WAY FROM
HOME

06338
4—ON HIS FIRST DAY HOME ON LEAVE

06339
5—THERE'S A GOOD TIME COMING FOR
THE LADIES

06340
6—FATHER'S GOT THE SACK FROM THE
WATERWORKS

06341
7—DOWN HOME IN TENNESSEE

06342
8—LITTLE BIT OF HEAVEN

06343
9—WHEN I LEAVE THE WORLD BEHIND

06344
10—FARE THEE WELL MOLLY DARLING
MUSICAL Dramatisations of songs synchronising
with singer on cinema stage.

NOV

06345
ALL STARS (1008)(U)
Martin (DFSA)
D: (Edwin J. Collins)
Edourd Musto . . . . Wonwiff
COMEDY Backstage misadventures at Music
Hall cause it to catch fire.

06346
THE HOUSE OF FORTESCUE (4025)(U)
Hepworth (Harma)
D: Frank Wilson
S: Percy Gordon Holmes

Stewart Rome . . . . Fortescue
Violet Hopson . . . . Cecile Harding
Lionelle Howard . . . . Gerald Mason
Harry Gilbey . . . . Charles Harding
Charles Vane . . . . Jasper Mason
DRAMA Australian millionaire weds girl to
save her father's firm.

06347
BETTY'S NIGHT OUT (1000)(U)
Clarendon
D: (Wilfred Noy)
Betty the Chimpanzee
COMEDY Chimpanzee causes lodgers to
mistake one another for burglars.

06348
ALL THROUGH BETTY (950)(U)
Clarendon
D: (Wilfred Noy)
Betty the Chimpanzee
COMEDY Suspicious wife discovers 'girl' her
husband is hiding is chimpanzee.

06349
CHAINS OF BONDAGE (4000)(A)
I.B. Davidson-Tiger (XL)
D: A.E. Coleby
S: (NOVEL) Paul Howard
SC: Rowland Talbot
Basil Gill . . . . John Malcolm
Eveyln Millard . . . . Margaret Cornish
Arthur Rooke . . . . Reuben Joyce
Dora de Winton . . . . Mrs Malcolm
Winnie Shepherd . . . . Peggy
DRAMA Rich bigamist's wife becomes
secretary to inventor and foils strike.

06350
THE WHEEL OF DEATH (3000)(A)
I.B. Davidson (XL)
D: A.E. Coleby
Arthur Rooke . . . . John Drew
Joan Legge . . . . Pickles
Frank Rosbert Cheroka . . . . Hastings
Charles Vane . . . . Professor
Peggy Richards . . . . Mrs Merton
CRIME Blackmailer kidnaps clubman's wife
and traps tec in mad professor's torture
chamber.

06351
IT IS FOR ENGLAND (10000)
Union Jack (P & C) *reissue*: 1918
THE HIDDEN HAND (Gau; 5 rls cut)
P:D:S: Lawrence Cowen
Helene Gingold . . . . . . .Rev Christian St George
Percy Moran . . . . Lt Stephen English
Marguerite Shelley . . . . Mary Marshall
Gilbert Esmond . . . .
Sir Gilbert Parker . . . .
Sir William Bull . . . .
Sir Kinloch-Cooke . . . .
Arthur Collins . . . .
Willie Clarkson . . . .
WAR Reincarnated Saint unmasks baronet as
German spy.

06352
SANCTUARY (4000)
Claude Harris (DFSA)
P:D: Claude Harris
S: (PLAY) Malcolm Watson
SC: Sylvia Cavalho
Sylvia Cavalho . . . . Mrs Carlton
Clifford Pembroke . . . . Ned Ferrers
CRIME Artist aids wife of MP who shot her
blackmailer.

06353
DISRAELI (6500)(U)
NB Films
P: Arrigo Bocchi
D: Percy Nash, Charles Calvert
S: (PLAY) Louis N. Parker
SC: Louis N. Parker
Dennis Eadie . . . . Benjamin Disraeli
Mary Jerrold . . . . Lady Beaconsfield
Cyril Raymond . . . . Lord Deeford
Dorothy Bellew . . . . Clarissa
Fred Morgan . . . . Nigel Foljambe
Daisy Cordell . . . . Mrs Travers
Cecil Morton York . . . . Duke of Glastonbury
Evelyn Harding . . . . Duchess of Glastonbury
Arthur Cullin . . . . Sir Michael Probert
A.B. Imeson . . . . Meyers
Mrs. Lytton . . . . Queen Victoria
HISTORY Prime Minister's wife helps acquire
shares in Suez Canal.

06354
THE BLACK NIGHT (4124)(A)
Broadwest
P: Walter West
D:SC: Harold Weston
S: (NOVEL) Andrew Soutar
Gregory Scott . . . . Lord Dupois
J.R. Tozer . . . . Lord Somerdans
CRIME Lord changes places with dead jewel thief
to steal wife's letters back from blackmailer.

06355
BILLY'S STORMY COURTSHIP (2200)
Homeland (Globe)
D: W.P. Kellino
S: Reuben Gillmer
Billy Merson . . . . Billy Thorpe
Winifred Delevanti . . . . . . Nellie Short
Albert Rebla . . . . Mr Short
COMEDY Deaf man thinks agent who loves his
daughter loves his sister.

06356
A SHATTERED IDYLL (5000)
British Photoplay Productions
P: Edward Godal
D: Dave Aylott
Peggy Mills
Peter Lewis
Dorothy Dare
Martin Herbert
DRAMA "Love, hate and jealousy among
gypsy caravans."

06357
THE BIGAMIST (4000)
L & P Exclusives
Arthur Wontner . . . . Tony Henderson
Ethel Warwick . . . . Grace Henderson
Dorothy Fayne . . . . Iris Cooper
Hayden Coffin . . . . Arthur Greville
CRIME Drunkard abandons wife, weds rich
girl, takes mistress, steals legacy and kills his
first wife.

06358
HE DIDN'T WANT TO DO IT (2000)
Gaumont-Brimstone
D: J.L.V. Leigh
Jock Preston . . . . Geordie
Miss Myers . . . . Girl
COMEDY Groom elopes with shoe salesgirl on
his wedding day.

06359
THE CELLAR OF DEATH (2500)(A)
Cricks (Apex)
D: Charles Calvert
CRIME

06360
A ROMANCE OF PUCK FAIR (897)(U)
Film Company of Ireland (DFSA)
D: J.M. Kerrigan
J.M. Kerrigan . . . . Jack Manning
Kathleen Murphy . . . . Maureen
ROMANCE Traveller and artist fall in love,
each thinking the other owns a farm.

06361
WIDOW MALONE (1235)
Film Company of Ireland (DFSA)
D: J.M. Kerrigan
COMEDY Rich widow feigns poverty to
thwart councillor and schoolmaster.

DEC

06362
THE BOYS OF THE OLD BRIGADE (5000) (U)
(U)
British Oak (NA)
D: Ernest G. Batley
S: (SKETCH) R.P. Weston, Frank Carter (BOYS
OF THE CHELSEA SCHOOL)
SC: Ethyle & Ernest G. Batley
George Leyton . . . . John Seymour
Lettie Paxton . . . . Betty Matthews
Stella Brereton . . . . Lydia Matthews
Charles Vane . . . . Uncle John
Dorothy Batley . . . . Joan
WAR Exempted singer enlists, loses arm, and
wins VC as his uncle did in Crimea.

06363
THE MANXMAN (9000)(A)
London (Jury)
D: George L. Tucker
S: (NOVEL) Hall Caine
SC: Kenelm Foss
Henry Ainley . . . . Philip Christian
Elizabeth Risdon . . . . Kate Cregeen
Fred Groves . . . . Pete Quilliam
Edward O'Neill . . . . Iron Christian
Bert Wynne . . . . Peter Christian
Kenelm Foss . . . . Ross Christian
Lewis Gilbert . . . . Black Tom
John East . . . . Caesar Cregeen
Gwynne Herbert . . . . Aunt Nan
Hubert Willis . . . . Clerk
Frank Stanmore . . . . Kelley
Minna Grey . . . . Mona
Philip Hewland . . . . Governor
Adeline Hayden Coffin . . . . . His Wife
Guy Newall . . . . Secretary
Mary Merrall . . . . Tom's Girl
John Milton . . . . Quiggan
Will Corri . . . . Fisherman
DRAMA Isle of Man. Fisherman's wife has
baby by lawyer who weds her after her father
denounces him in court.

06364
ON THE BANKS OF ALLAN WATER (4125) (A)
(A)
Clarendon (Lucoque)
D: Wilfred Noy
S: Reuben Gillmer
Basil Gill . . . . Richard Warden
Violet Leicester . . . . Elsie
J. Hastings Batson . . . .
F.G. Clifton . . . .
Roy Byford . . . .
Grania Gray . . . .
ROMANCE Scotland. Bart's son weds miller's
daughter and their class disparity almost causes
her suicide.

06365
THE KING'S DAUGHTER (4414)(U)
London (Jury)
D: Maurice Elvey
S: (NOVEL) Alexandre Dumas (UNE FILLE
DE REGENT)
Gerald Ames . . . . Montrose
Janet Ross . . . . Helene
Edward O'Neill . . . . The King
Hayford Hobbs . . . . Dubois
Hubert Willis . . . . Chief of Police
CRIME Assassin's daughter learns she is King's
bastard and dies to save his life.

06366
MOLLY BAWN (4510)(U)
Hepworth
D: Cecil M. Hepworth
S: (NOVEL) Mrs Hungerford
SC: Blanche McIntosh
Alma Taylor . . . . Eleanor Massareene
Stewart Rome . . . . Tedcastle Luttrell
Violet Hopson . . . . Marcia Amherst
Lionelle Howard . . . . Philip Shadwell
Fred Wright . . . . Mr Amherst
Chrissie White . . . . Lady Cecil Stafford
John MacAndrews . . . . John Massareene
Henry Vibart . . . . Marigny
Valerie McLintock . . . . Letitia Massereene
Percy Manton . . . . Plantaganet Potts
ROMANCE Ireland, 1850. Couple try to regain
grandfather's favour.

06367
A FAIR IMPOSTER (5000)
G.B. Samuelson (Moss)
D: Alexander Butler
S: (NOVEL) Charles Garvice
SC: Harry Engholm
Madge Titheradge . . . . Lady Irene
Gerald McCarthy . . . . Terence Castleford
Charles Rock . . . . Lord Mercia
Alice de Winton . . . . Elsa Graham
Edward O'Neill . . . . Mayne Redmayne
Lionel d'Aragon . . . .
Florence Nelson . . . .
Harry Lofting . . . . Vicar
DRAMA Lord's daughter learns maid is her sister
and poses as her to usurp inheritance.

06368
MILESTONES (8640)(U)
G.B. Samuelson (Moss)
D: Thomas Bentley
S: (PLAY) Arnold Bennett, Edward Knoblauch
SC: Harry Engholm
Isobel Elsom . . . . Lady Monkhurst
Owen Nares . . . . Lord Monkhurst
Campbell Gullan . . . . Sir John Rhead
Minna Grey . . . . Gertrude Rhead
Mary Lincoln . . . . Rose Sibley
Hubert Harben . . . . Sam Sibley
Esme Hubbard . . . . Nancy Sibley
Cecil Morton York . . . . Joseph Sibley
Roy Travers . . . . Arthur Preece
Lionel d'Aragon . . . . Andrew Maclean
Herbert Daniel . . . . Richard Sibley
Ernest A. Graham . . . . Ned Pym
Winifred Delevanti . . . . . . Hon Muriel Pym
Molly Hamley Clifford . . . . . Mrs Rhead
DRAMA Radical shipbuilder revolts against his
father in 1860, yet seems reactionary to his son
in 1912.

06369
PARKER'S WEEKEND (2300)(A)
Homeland (Globe)
D: W.P. Kellino
S: Charles Austin
SC: Reuben Gillmer
Charles Austin . . . . Parker
Winifred Delevanti . . . . . . Chorus Girl
COMEDY Man takes dancers to uncle's
riverside bungalow.

06370
THE DUMMY (2000)
Homeland (Globe)
D: W.P. Kellino
S: Reuben Gillmer
Lupino Lane . . . . Nipper
Winifred Delevanti . . . . The Girl
COMEDY Men have race to win girl and get involved with crooks posing as a beautifying machine.

06371
THE DUSTMEN'S OUTING (2136)(U)
Homeland (Globe)
D: W.P. Kellino
S: Albert & Seth Egnert
SC: Reuben Gillmer
Albert Egbert . . . . Bill
Seth Egbert . . . . Walter
COMEDY Misadventures of dustmen on a day's outing.

06372
DOING HER BIT (2000)(U)
Renaissance (Gaumont)
D:S: John M. Payne
Fanny Tittell-Brune . . . . Sylvia
John Castle (Payne) . . . . Archie
COMEDY Wife tries to knit socks and stage troop concert.

06373
THE TREASURE OF HEAVEN (5000)
I.B. Davidson-Tiger (Gaumont)
D: A.E. Coleby
S: (NOVEL) Marie Corelli
SC: Rowland Talbot
Janet Alexander . . . . Mary Deane
A.E. Coleby . . . . David Helmsley
Langhorne Burton . . . . Angus Reay
Arthur Rooke . . . . Tom o'the Gleam
Dorothy Bellew . . . . Lucy Sorrell
Annesley Healy . . . . Sir Frances Veasey
Judd Green . . . . Abel Twitt
Olive Colin Bell . . . . Mrs Twitt
N. Watts-Phillips . . . . Dr Bunce
ROMANCE Devon. Disillusioned millionaire poses as tramp and helps reporter's romance.

06374
JUDGED BY APPEARANCES (4000)
British Oak (NA)
D: Hugh Croise
S: (PLAY) Frederick Fenn
Nelson Keys
Arthur Playfair
COMEDY

06375
THE LYONS MAIL (5200) (A)
Ideal
D: Fred Paul
S: (PLAY) Charles Reade
SC: Benedict James
H.B. Irving . . . . Lesurques/Dubosc
Nancy Price . . . . Janette
Harry Welchman . . . . Andre
James Lindsay . . . . Courriol
Tom Reynolds . . . . Founiard
Windham Guise . . . . Choppard
Nelson Ramsey . . . . Durochat
Violet Campbell . . . . Julie
Alfred Brydone . . . . .Jerome Lesurques
Charles Vane . . . .
Edward Arundell . . . .
CRIME France, period. Rich man mistaken for highwayman double.

06376
EVERYMAN CAMEOS (series)
Everyman Films
D: Lewis Gilbert, Alfonse Frenguelli
SC: Kate Gurney
Kinsey Peile
Lily Saxby
Kathleen Vincent
Kate Gurney
Lewis Gilbert

06377
1—BURGLAR BILL (1)

06378
2—SOLOMON'S TWINS (1)
S: (PLAY) Kinsey Peile
COMEDY

1917

JAN

06379
DOING HIS BIT (2200)(A)
Ideal
D: Edwin J. Collins
S: George Robey
George Robey . . . .   The Man
Marjorie Hume . . . .   The Girl
Howard Boddey . . . .
COMEDY Army reject poses as woman and
becomes nurse.

06380
PROFIT AND THE LOSS (5300)(A)
Ideal
D: A.V. Bramble, Eliot Stannard
S: (PLAY) H.F. Maltby
SC: Eliot Stannard
James Carew . . . .   Dicky Bransome
Randle Ayrton . . . .   Jenkins
Margaret Halstan. . . . .
Saba Raleigh . . . .
DRAMA When friends fail him, tenant farmer
turns to making money.

06381
HER MARRIAGE LINES (3450)(A)
Hepworth (Harma)
D: Frank Wilson
S: Edith Banks
Stewart Rome . . . .   Godfrey
Chrissie White . . . .   Jean Neville
Violet Hopson . . . .   Sybil Ransley
Lionelle Howard . . . .   Stephen Maybridge
Henry Vibart . . . .   Lord Ransley
Florence Nelson . . . .   Lady Ransley
Frank Wilson . . . .   Rev Neville
DRAMA Cousin forges marriage certificate to
force Lord's heir to marry his sister.

06382
THE COBWEB (5700)(A)
Hepworth (Harma)
D: Cecil M. Hepworth
S: (PLAY) Leon M. Lion, Naunton Davies
SC: Blanche McIntosh
Henry Edwards . . . .   Stephen Mallard
Alma Taylor . . . .   Irma Brian
Stewart Rome . . . .   Merton Forsdyke
Violet Hopson . . . .   Dolorosa
Margaret Blanche . . . .   Miss Debb
Lionelle Howard . . . .   Poacher
John MacAndrews . . . .   Insp Beall
Charles Vane . . . .   Sir George Gillingham
Molly Hamley-Clifford . . . . .   Mrs Brian
CRIME Millionaire thinks he strangled his
blackmailing Mexican wife who actually died of
shock.

06383
THE LOST CHORD (5000)(U)
Clarendon
D: Wilfred Noy
S: Reuben Gillmer
Barbara Conrad . . . .   Madeleine
Malcolm Keen . . . .   David
Concordia Merrill . . . .   Joan
Dorothy Bellew . . . .
Mary Ford . . . .
Manning Haynes . . . .
ROMANCE Musician loves married woman
who becomes nun and dies; later he loves her
daughter.

06384
ORA PRO NOBIS (4400)(A)
Windsor (Walturdaw)
P: Arrigo Bocchi
D: Rex Wilson

S: Rowland Talbot
Henry Victor . . . .   Lord Osborne
Harding Thomas . . . .   The Organist
DRAMA Organist dreams he kills lord who
eloped with his adopted daughter.

FEB

06385
A KING OF THE PEOPLE (5000)(U)
NB Films
P: Arrigo Bocchi
D: Percy Nash
DRAMA

06386
THE SORROWS OF SATAN (5000)(A)
G.B. Samuelson (Walker)
D: Alexander Butler
S: (NOVEL) Marie Corelli
SC: Harry Engholm
Gladys Cooper . . . .   Lady Sybil Elton
Owen Nares . . . .   Geoffrey Tempest
Cecil Humphreys . . . .   Prince Ramirez
Lionel d'Aragon . . . .   Earl Elton
Winifred Delevanti . . . .   Diana Chesney
Alice de Winton . . . .
Minna Grey . . . .
FANTASY Girl loves prince who is really Satan
but sells herself to highest bidder.

06387
THE VEILED WOMAN (4450)(A)
British Empire Films
D: Leedham Bantock
S: (PLAY) Harold Simpson
Cecil Humphreys . . . .   Gascoigne Devine
Gladys Mason . . . .   Coralie Travers
Frank Randell . . . .   Robert Travers
Marjorie Chard . . . .   Naomi Sinclair
DRAMA Gambler's mistress changes places with
married woman he blackmails into becoming
mistress.

06388
THE AMERICAN HEIRESS (2800)(A)
Hepworth (Harma)
D: Cecil M. Hepworth
S: Blanche McIntosh
Alma Taylor . . . .   Bessie
Violet Hopson . . . .   Cynthia Hunks
Stewart Rome . . . .   Parker
Lionelle Howard . . . .   Bob Summers
John MacAndrews . . . .   Viper Smith
Johnny Butt . . . .   Sir John Higgins
CRIME Maid posing as heiress kidnapped by
thieves and saved by butler.

06389
THE MAN BEHIND "THE TIMES" (3725)(A)
Hepworth (Harma)
D: Frank Wilson
S: Percy Manton
Stewart Rome . . . .   Aaron Moss
Chrissie White . . . .   Jet Overbury
Lionelle Howard . . . .   Allan Garth
Harry Gilbey . . . .   John Overbury
Charles Vane . . . .   John Walcott
Mrs Bedells . . . .   Mrs Overbury
John MacAndrews . . . .   Doctor
Johnny Butt . . . .   Clerk
CRIME Usurer weds girl whose lover is blamed
when her father is killed by butler.

06390
DAWN (5500)(A)
Lucoque
D: H. Lisle Lucoque
S: (NOVEL) H. Rider Haggard
SC: Pauline Lewis

Karina . . . .   Mildred Carr
Hubert Carter . . . .   Devil Caresfoot
Madeleine Seymour . . . .   Mildred Caresfoot
Edward Combermere . . . . . .   George Caresfoot
R. Heaton Grey . . . .   Philip Caresfoot
Annie Esmond . . . .   Mrs Bellamy
Frank Harris . . . .   Mr Bellamy
George Snazelle . . . .   Arthur Heigham
DRAMA Woman helps lover marry heiress and
kills him when he refuses to share spoils.

06391
SMITH (3440)(A)
London (Jury)
D: Maurice Elvey
S: (PLAY) W. Somerset Maugham
Elizabeth Risdon . . . .   Smith
Fred Groves . . . .   Tom Freeman
Manora Thew . . . .   Rose Baker
Guy Newall . . . .   Algy Peppercorn
Douglas Munro . . . .   Otto Rosenburg
Lydia Bilbrooke . . . .   Mrs Rosenburg
ROMANCE Rich man weds housekeeper and
eventually falls in love with her.

06392
PIMPLE'S THE WHIP (2000)
Piccadilly (Walturdaw) *reissue:* 1919 (Royal)
D:S: Fred Evans, Joe Evans
Fred Evans . . . .   Lord Elpus
COMEDY Lord foils plot to kill favourite and
rides it to win.

06393
THE COST OF A KISS (4200)
Mirror Films
D: Adrian Brunel
S: H. Fowler Mear
Bertram Wallis . . . .   Lord Darlington
Marjorie Day
Edward Cooper
Thomas Canning
R. Van Cortlandt
Joan Marshall
Pino Conti
Ethel Griffies
Noel Grahame
Gordon Begg
Babs Brunel
DRAMA Madrid. Lord atones for misdeeds of
dissolute father.

06394
WHEN PARIS SLEEPS (4652)(A)
B & C (Kineto)
D: A.V. Bramble
S: (PLAY) Charles Darrell
SC: Eliot Stannard
A.V. Bramble
Ivy Martinek
Pauline Peters
Ernie Collins
Jose Brookes
CRIME Paris. Apache's mistress reforms and
helps police trick him into confession.

06395
THE GENTLEMAN IN BLUE (4000)
Kinematograph Concessions (Monopol)
S: (NOVEL) Mark Allerton (JOHN HINTE,
GENTLEMAN IN BLUE)
CRIME Story of a policeman.

06396
BEDS, BATHS AND BEDLAM (2000)
Gaumont—Brimstone
D: J.L.V. Leigh
Jock Preston . . . .   Geordie
COMEDY

MAR

06397
MASKS AND FACES (6200)(U)
Ideal
D: Fred Paul
S: (PLAY) Tom Taylor, Charles Reade
SC: Bendict James
Sir Johnstone Forbes-Robertson . . . Triplet
Irene Vanbrugh . . . . Peg Woffington
H.B. Irving . . . . Colander
Gerald du Maurier . . . . Hunsdon
Dennis Neilson-Terry . . . . . . Ernest Vane
Gladys Cooper . . . . Mabel Vane
Ben Webster . . . . Sir Charles Pomander
C.M. Lowne . . . . Quinn
Nigel Playfair . . . . Rich
Lillah McCarthy . . . . Kitty Clive
Dion Boucicault . . . . Colley Cibber
Henry Vibart . . . . Burdock
Donald Calthrop . . . . Lovell
J. Fisher White . . . . Snarl
Lyall Swete . . . . Soper
Helen Haye . . . . Dame Best
Matheson Lang . . . . Coachman
Weedon Grossmith . . . . Fiddler
Gerald Ames . . . . Fencing Master
Mary Brough . . . . Landlady
Gertrude Elliott . . . . Actress
Lilian Braithwaite . . . . Actress
Ellaline Terriss . . . . Actress
Fabia Drake . . . . Child
Charles Hawtrey; Sir George Alexander;
J.M. Barrie; George Bernard Shaw.
COMEDY 1740. Actress cures aged flirt by
posing as wife.

06398
THE THIRD WITNESS (2830)(A)
I.B. Davidson (LIFT)
D: A.E. Coleby
Arthur Rooke . . . . John Drew
Joan Legge . . . . Pickles
CRIME Tec uses photograph to trace crook, who
tries to kill him in fire.

06399
A PIT-BOY'S ROMANCE (4000)(A)
I.B. Davidson-Tiger (Film Bureau)
D:S: A.E. Coleby, Arthur Rooke
Jimmy Wilde . . . . Jimmy Davis
Tommy Noble . . . .
A.E. Coleby . . . .
Arthur Rooke . . . .
J. Hastings Batson . . . .
SPORT Wales. Boxing collier ruins actor who
abandoned former sweetheart.

06400
THE WARE CASE (6191)(A)
Broadwest (FBO) *reissue:* 1919
reissue: 1919
P:D: Walter West
S: (PLAY) George Pleydell Bancroft
SC: J. Bertram Brown
Matheson Lang . . . . Sir Hubert Ware
Violet Hopson . . . . Lady Magdalen Ware
Ivy Close . . . . Marian Scales
Gregory Scott . . . . Michael Ayde
George Foley . . . . Sir Henry Egerton
CRIME Acquitted knight admits to drowning
wife's rich brother, and takes poison.

06401
THE HOUSE OPPOSITE (4072)(A)
Broadwest
P: Walter West
D: Frank Wilson
S: (PLAY) Percival Landon

SC: Reuben·Gillmer, Enid Lorimer
Matheson Lang . . . . Henry Rivers MP
Violet Hopson . . . . Mrs Anstruther
Ivy Close . . . . Mrs Rivers
Gregory Scott . . . . Richard Cardyne
Dora de Winton . . . .
J. Hastings Batson . . . .
Terence O'Brien . . . . The Thief
Dora Barton . . . .
CRIME Agent's jealous wife witnesses murder
whilst visiting lover.

06402
CARROTS (3775)(A)
Hepworth (Pioneer)
D: Frank Wilson
S: Percy Gordon Holmes
Chrissie White . . . . Carrots
Lionelle Howard . . . . Mike
Gerald Lawrence . . . . PC Park
W.G. Saunders . . . . Old 'Un
Johnny Butt . . . .
Gordon Begg . . . . Nobby
Harry Gilbey . . . .
CRIME Coster girl saves policeman sweetheart
from convict brother's gang.

06403
THE ETERNAL TRIANGLE (5100)(A)
Hepworth (Pioneer)
D: Frank Wilson
S: Percy Gordon Holmes
Chrissie White . . . . Margaret Clive
Stewart Rome . . . . Frank Waring
Violet Hopson . . . . Audrey
Lionelle Howard . . . . Sackville Horton
W.G. Saunders . . . . Squire Waring
Harry Gilbey . . . .
Mrs Bedells . . . .
ROMANCE Girl loves poor squire's son but weds
rich playwright who is killed in car crash.

06404
A GRAIN OF SAND (2900)(A)
Hepworth (UK)
D: Frank Wilson
S: Victor Montefiore
Stewart Rome . . . . Dennis Grayle
Chrissie White . . . . Doris Kestevan
Lionelle Howard . . . . Howard Langton
Ivy Millais . . . . Liza
William Felton . . . . James Fordyce
John MacAndrews . . . . Liza's Father
CRIME Kitchen maid clears Lady's gambling son
when he is framed for forgery.

06405
THE COUNTESS OF SUMMACOUNT (1075)(U)
Hepworth
D: Frank Wilson
S: Percy Manton
Chrissie White . . . . The Girl
COMEDY

06406
LOLLIPOPS AND POSIES (950) (U)
Hepworth
D: Frank Wilson
S: Percy Manton
Chrissie White . . . . The Girl
COMEDY

06407
NEIGHBOURS (1525)(U)
Hepworth (Butcher)
D: Frank Wilson
S: Percy Manton
Chrissie White . . . . The Girl
Lionelle Howard . . . . The Boy
Johnny Butt . . . . The Man
Ruby Belasco . . . . The Woman
COMEDY

06408
DRINK (6040)(A)
British Pictures (Gau)
P: Harry T. Roberts
D:SC: Sidney Morgan
S: (PLAY) Charles Reade (NOVEL) Emile Zola
(L'ASSOMOIR)
Fred Groves . . . . Coupeau
Irene Browne . . . . Gervaise
Alice O'Brien . . . . Virginie
George Foley . . . . Gouget
Lionel d'Aragon . . . . Auguste Lautier
Arthur Walcott . . . . Chabot
Joan Morgan . . . . Gervaise (child)
Stanley Arthur . . . . Bibi
William Brandon . . . . Mes-Bottes
DRAMA Paris, 1877. Laundress takes to drink
and dies after alcoholic husband goes mad.

06409
A JUST DECEPTION (5635) (A)
I.B. Davidson-Tiger (Walturdaw)
D: A.E. Coleby
S: (NOVEL) B.L. Farjeon (AARON THE JEW)
Augustus Yorke . . . . Aaron Cohen
Robert Leonard . . . . Moses Moss
Blanche Forsythe . . . . Mary Turner
Maud Yates . . . . Rachel
DRAMA Jew bribed to exchange Christian's
bastard girl for his blind wife's dead baby, and
is later ruined by girl's father.

06410
HOME SWEET HOME (3965)(U)
Clarendon (Harma)
D: Wilfred Noy
S: Reuben Gillmer
Rita Otway
Manning Haynes
Thomas Canning
DRAMA Farmer returns to former city life and
unwittingly ruins son.

06411
ULTUS AND THE THREE-BUTTON MYSTERY
(4650)(U) USA: ULTUS 6: THE THREE
BUTTON MYSTERY; ULTUS 7.
Gaumont-Victory
D:S: George Pearson
Aurele Sydney . . . . Ultus
Manora Thew . . . . Elsie Meredith
Charles Rock . . . . Derwent
Alice de Winton . . . .
Fred Morgan . . . .
Frank Dane . . . .
CRIME Hotelier's daughter helps "Avenger"
rescue kidnapped statesman.

06412
IN ANOTHER GIRL'S SHOES (5000)
G.B. Samuelson
D: G.B. Samuelson, Alexander Butler
S: (NOVEL) Berta Ruck
Mabel Love . . . . Rose Whitelands
Ruby Miller . . . . Vera Vayne
Leo Belcher . . . . Capt George Meredith
Lionel d'Aragon . . . . Sir Richard Meredith
Olive Lovelle . . . . Phillippa Tracy
Esme Hubbard . . . . Mrs Smythe
Mrs. John Douglas . . . . Lady Meredith
Ronald Power . . . . Drake
ROMANCE Parents assume girl with amnesia is
married to their soldier son.

06413
ECONOMY (2080)(U)
Homeland (Globe)
D: W.P. Kellino
S: Reuben Gillmer
Blanche Bella . . . . Mother
COMEDY Family attempts to economise.

06414
DERELICTS (5000) (A)
Unity-Super (Olympic)
D:SC: Sidney Morgan
S: (NOVEL) W.J. Locke
Violet Graham . . . . Yvonne Latour
Sydney Vautier . . . . Stephen Chiseley
Julian Royce . . . . Canon Chiseley
Mona K. Harrison . . . . Annie Bevan
F. Yensen . . . . Amedee Bazauge
DRAMA Ex-embezzler makes good in Africa and
marries singer abandoned by canon.

06415
DIANA OF DOBSON'S (5000) (A)
Barker (Ideal)
S: (PLAY) Cicely Hamilton
Cecilia Loftus . . . . Diana
A.B. Imeson . . . .
Rachel de Solla . . . .
ROMANCE Shopgirl poses as lady and is
proved innocent of theft by reformed fortune-
hunter.

APR

06416
BILLY THE TRUTHFUL (2351) (U)
Homeland (Globe)
D: W.P. Kellino
S: Reuben Gillmer
Billy Merson . . . . Billy Washington
Winifred Delevanti . . . . The Girl
Blanche Bella . . . . Mrs Slick
J. Phillipi . . . : . . . . Cyrus Q. Slick
COMEDY Problems beset man who is compelled
to tell truth.

06417
HULLO! WHO'S YOUR LADY FRIEND?
(2259) (U)
Homeland (Globe)
D: W.P. Kellino
S: Reuben Gillmer
Lupino Lane . . . . Mr Pink
Violet Blythe . . . . Mrs Pink
Winifred Delevanti . . . . Josie Clifton
Blanche Bella . . . . Mother
COMEDY Man poses as twin brother to deceive
jealous wife.

06418
CHASE ME CHARLIE (4500) (U)
Essanay (FBO)
D:S: Langford Reed
Ed: H.G. Doncaster
Graham Douglas . . . . Charlie Chaplin
COMPILATION Tramp makes good in London
and weds a millionaire's daughter. (Includes
extracts from USA films).

06419
A BID FOR FORTUNE (4000)
Unity-Super
D:SC: Sidney Morgan
S: (NOVEL) Guy Boothby
A. Harding Steerman . . . . . . Dr Nikola
Violet Graham . . . . Phyllis Wetherall
Sydney Vautier . . . . Dick Hattaras
CRIME Occult scientist tries to steal collector's
Chinese staff.

06420
THE PROFLIGATE (4000) (A)
Milton (Walturdaw)
D:SC: Meyrick Milton
S: (PLAY) Arthur Wing Pinero
Ben Webster . . . . Dunstan Renshaw
Dorothy Bellew . . . . Leslie Brundenall
Langhorne Burton . . . . Hugh Murray
Cecil Humphreys . . . . Lord Danvers
Amy Brandon Thomas . . . . . Irene Stonehay

Geoffrey Kerr . . . . Wilfred
Isabel Jeans . . . . Janet Preece
Fred Volpe . . . . Mr Cheal
Edith Mellor . . . . Mrs Stonehay
Isobel Foster . . . . Miss Grieves
DRAMA Italy. Lord weds schoolgirl while girl
he seduced becomes servant beloved by his
brother.

06421
PIMPLE'S SENSELESS CENSORING (1092) (U)
Piccadilly (Walturdaw)
D:S: Fred Evans, Joe Evans
Fred Evans . . . . Pimple
COMEDY

06422
PIMPLE'S MOTOR TOUR (2150) (U)
Piccadilly (Walturdaw)
D:S: Fred Evans, Joe Evans
Fred Evans . . . . Pimple
COMEDY

06423
PIMPLE'S MYSTERY OF THE CLOSED
DOOR (734) (U)
Piccadilly (Walturdaw)
D:S: Fred Evans, Joe Evans
Fred Evans . . . . Pimple
COMEDY

06424
SOME DANCER (1085) (U)
Piccadilly (Walturdaw)
D:S: Fred Evans, Joe Evans
Fred Evans . . . . Pimple
COMEDY

06425
SAVING RAFFLES (940) (U)
Piccadilly (Walturdaw)
D:S: Fred Evans, Joe Evans
Fred Evans . . . . Pimple
Joe Evans . . . . Raffles
COMEDY

06426
PIMPLE'S TABLEAUX VIVANTS (1075) (U)
Piccadilly (Walturdaw)
D:S: Fred Evans, Joe Evans
Fred Evans . . . . Pimple
COMEDY

06427
OLIVER TWISTED (2360) (A)
Piccadilly (Walturdaw)
D:S: Fred Evans, Joe Evans
Fred Evans . . . . Pimple
COMEDY

06428
PIMPLE — HIS VOLUNTARY CORPS
(1730) (U)
Piccadilly (Walturdaw)
D:S: Fred Evans, Joe Evans
Fred Evans . . . . Pimple
COMEDY

06429
DAUGHTER OF THE WILDS (3575) (A)
Hepworth
D: Frank Wilson
Chrissie White . . . . The Girl
DRAMA

06430
ALL THE WORLD'S A STAGE (5000)
Hagen & Double
P: Julius Hagen, Harold Double
D: Harold Weston
S: (NOVEL) Herbert Everett
SC: Leslie Howard Gordon

Eve Balfour . . . . Lavender Lawn
Esme Beringer . . . . Delia Rackham
James Lindsay . . . . Geoffrey Daunton
Leslie Howard Gordon . . . . . David Hart
Judd Green . . . . Capt Offley
CRIME Jealous actress shoots producer and frames
protege, who weds fisherman who is really
squire's son.

06431
THE MAN WHO MADE GOOD (5000)
Zeitlin & Dewhurst
P: Leon Zeitlin, George Dewhurst
D: Dave Aylott
S: George Leyton
George Leyton . . . . The Man
Lettie Paxton . . . . The Girl
George Dewhurst . . . .
Daisy Cordell . . . .
Charles Vane . . . .
Phyllis Titmuss . . . .
Marie Lloyd . . . . Herself
WAR

MAY

06432
A BOY SCOUT'S DREAM; OR, HOW BILLIE
CAPTURED THE KAISER (2000)
Brum Films
COMEDY Boy scout dreams he captures the
Kaiser.

06433
A BIRMINGHAM GIRL'S LAST HOPE (2000)
also: THE LAST HOPE
Brum Films
D: Bert Haldane
G. Daniels . . . . Billy Jones
COMEDY Idler refuses to enlist and becomes
last man in the city.

06434
MEN WERE DECEIVERS EVER (2000)
Brum Films
D: Bert Haldane
S: A.J. Waldron
A.J. Waldron . . . . Tommy
Irene Selwyn . . . . The Girl
DRAMA Warwick.

06435
THE GRIT OF A JEW (4600) (U)
Butcher's Film Service
P: F.W. Baker
D: Maurice Elvey
S: Kenelm Foss
Augustus Yorke . . . . Moses Levi
Manora Thew . . . . Leah
Fred Groves . . . . Russell
Hayford Hobbs . . . . Ben Levi
Margaret Blanche . . . . Elsie Maudsley
Rachel de Solla . . . . Mrs Levi
Cecil Mannering . . . .
Frank Stanmore . . . .
Fred Morgan . . . .
Will Asher . . . .
Inez Bensusan . . . .
DRAMA Jew finds loophole in marriage
contract with usurer that allows son to wed
Jewess.

06436
YE WOOING OF PEGGY (2000)
Holmfirth (Pathe)
D:S: Bertram Phillips
Queenie Thomas . . . . Peggy
Jack Grey . . . . Noel
Frank Petley . . . . Sir John
COMEDY 28th C. Girl poses as ghost to frighten
her father's choice.

06437
PIMPLE'S ROMANCE (1185) (U)
Piccadilly (Walturdaw)
D:S: Fred Evans, Joe Evans
Fred Evans . . . . Pimple
COMEDY

06438
PIMPLE'S PITTER-PATTER (960) (U)
Piccadilly (Walturdaw)
D:S: Fred Evans, Joe Evans
Fred Evans . . . . Pimple
COMEDY

06439
PIMPLE'S LADY GODIVA (2327) (A)
Piccadilly (Walturdaw)
D:S: Fred Evans, Joe Evans
Fred Evans . . . . Pimple
COMEDY

06440
PIMPLE'S THE WOMAN WHO DID (1925) (U)
Piccadilly (Walturdaw)
D:S: Fred Evans, Joe Evans
Fred Evans . . . . Pimple
COMEDY

06441
SISTER SUSIE'S SEWING SHIRTS FOR SOLDIERS (1805) (U)
Clarendon
D: Wilfred Noy
S: Hetty Langford Reed
COMEDY

06442
THE MISSING LINK (2450) (U)
Homeland (Globe)
D: W.P. Kellino
S: Reuben Gillmer
Lupino Lane . . . . Nipper
Winifred Delevanti . . . . Kitty
Blanche Bella . . . . Mother
Will Kellino . . . . Monkey
COMEDY Widow makes son pose as boy to appear younger to professor, but he is wed to professor's daughter.

06443
HOW'S YOUR POOR WIFE? (2000)
Homeland (Globe)
D: W.P. Kellino
S: Reuben Gillmer
Jack Edge . . . . Mr Snow
Winifred Delevanti . . . . Nurse
Blanche Bella . . . . Mrs Snow
Marjorie Sousa . . . . Miss Snow
Fred Tooze . . . . Doctor
Arabella . . . . Cook
COMEDY

06444
THE JOKE THAT FAILED (850) (U)
Hepworth (Butcher)
D: Frank Wilson
S: Percy Manton
Chrissie White . . . . Betty Finch
Lionelle Howard . . . . Frank
Johnny Butt . . . . Jack Finch
Miss Picard . . . . Sybil Finch
COMEDY Girl's beau poses as burglar to fool boastful father.

06445
MOTHERHOOD (2000)
Transatlantic
D: Percy Nash
S: Dorothea Baird
Lettie Paxton . . . . Mary
Jack Denton . . . . Jack
Dorothea Baird . . . . The Helper
Lady Rhondda; Mrs Lloyd George; Duchess of Marlborough
DRAMA Factory girl makes use of National Baby Week Council while slut's baby dies.

JUN

06446
A MUNITION GIRL'S ROMANCE (4500) (U)
Broadwest
P: Walter West
D: Frank Wilson
S: Charles Barnett
Violet Hopson . . . . Jenny Jones
Gregory Scott . . . . George Brandon
George Foley . . . . Sir Harrison
Tom Beaumont . . . . Heckman
H. Sykes . . . . Pilot
CRIME Bart's daughter working as munitionette helps designer save plans from spying foreman.

06447
EVERYBODY'S BUSINESS (2000)
Western Import
D: Ralph Dewsbury
S: Frank Fowell
Norman McKinnel . . . . John Briton
Gerald du Maurier . . . . Tom Briton
Matheson Lang . . . . Lt Jack Goudron
Renee Kelly . . . . Mabel Briton
Kate Rorke . . . . Mrs Briton
Gwynne Herbert . . . . Cook
Edward O'Neill . . . . Mr Keen
DRAMA Soldier's father dreams food economy helps win war.

06448
THE KNOCKOUT BLOW (500)
Broadwest
P:D: Walter West
WAR "Animated poster for National Service."

06449
IT'S NEVER TOO LATE TO MEND (5492) (U)
Martin's Cinematograph
P: A.E. Martin
D:SC: Dave Aylott
S: (PLAY) Charles Reade, Arthur Shirley
George Leyton . . . . Tom Robertson
Margaret Hope . . . . Susan Merton
George Dewhurst . . . . Peter Crawley
Charles Vane . . . . Isaac Levi
Frank Robertson . . . . George Fielding
Maurice Gerrard . . . . John Meadows
Sammy Jones . . . . Jack
CRIME Jew repents and frees jailed farmer in time to save fiancee from villain.

06450
BROKEN BARRIER (5612) (U) retitled: QUICKSANDS
Zeitlin & Dewhurst (Int Ex)
P: Leon Zeitlin, George Dewhurst
D: George Bellamy
S: (PLAY) Ben Landeck (A GUILTY MOTHER)
SC: George Dewhurst
George Dewhurst . . . . Dick Ransom
Vera Cornish . . . . Mary Barton
George Bellamy . . . . Sir Gilbert Foster
Mercy Hatton . . . . Flossie
Douglas Munro . . . . George Parsons
Minna Grey . . . . Mrs Dowling
J. Hastings Batson . . . . Rev Barton
Hayford Hobbs . . . .
Windham Guise . . . .
Nelson Ramsey . . . .
Mrs Sterling McKinlay . . . . .
CRIME Forger blackmails wife when she weds aged knight.

06451
ONE SUMMER'S DAY (4000)
British Actors (Int Ex)
D: Frank G. Bayley
S: (PLAY) H.V. Esmond
SC: H.V. Esmond
Fay Compton . . . . Maisie
Owen Nares . . . . Capt Dick Rudyard
Sam Livesey . . . . Philip Marsden
Eva Westlake . . . . Chiara
A.G. Poulton . . . .
Caleb Porter . . . .
Roy Royston . . . .
Gwendoline Jesson . . . .
ROMANCE Captain adopts friend's son who is later blackmailed by gipsy mother.

06452
BILLY STRIKES OIL (2000)
Homeland (Globe)
D: W.P. Kellino
S: Reuben Gillmer
Billy Merson . . . . Billy
Winifred Delevanti . . . .
COMEDY

06453
THE LABOUR LEADER (5888) (A)
British Actors (Int Ex)
D: Thomas Bentley
S: Kenelm Foss
Fred Groves . . . . John Webster
Fay Compton . . . . Diana Hazlitt
Owen Nares . . . . Gilbert Hazlitt
Christine Silver . . . . Nell Slade
Lauri De Frece . . . . Bert Slade
Fred Volpe . . . . Sir George Hazlitt
Mrs Charles Macdona . . . . . Mrs Slade
DRAMA Socialist weds pregnant laundress and becomes first Labour MP.

06454
THE WOMAN WHO WAS NOTHING (5390) (A)
Butcher's Film Service
P: F.W. Baker
D: Maurice Elvey
S: (NOVEL) Tom Gallon
SC: Eliot Stannard
Lilian Braithwaite . . . . The Wife
Madge Titheradge . . . . Brenda
George Tully . . . . Richard Marsden
Leon M. Lion . . . . Ferret
Lyston Lyle . . . . Financier
Ruth Mackay . . . . Duchess
Douglas Munro . . . . Chairman
Marjorie Day . . . . Hope Dacre
CRIME Ex-convict takes identity of dying heiress and is loved by fortune hunter, who reforms and thwarts blackmailer.

06455
LOVE'S OLD SWEET SONG (4120) (A)
Clarendon (New Bio)
D: F. Martin Thornton
S: Reuben Gillmer
Evelyn Boucher . . . . Ruth Mereton
Leo Belcher . . . . Dan Ash
Clifford Pembroke . . . . Robert Ash
Rita Otway . . . . Muriel Mereton
Jeff Barlow . . . . Farmer Mereton
ROMANCE Musician's wife shoots lover and becomes nun; later her daughter loves lover's son.

06456
ASTHORE (4745) (U)
Clarendon (Ideal)
D: Wilfred Noy
S: Kenelm Foss
Hayford Hobbs . . . . . . Lord Frederick Armitage
Violet Marriott . . . . Elsa
CRIME Ireland. Lady promises to marry man if he disfigures her ex fiance, but he attacks her stepfather by mistake.

JUL

06457
MERELY MRS STUBBS (4653)(U)
Hepworth (Butcher)
D:S: Henry Edwards
Henry Edwards . . . . Joe Stubbs
Alma Taylor . . . . Edith Dudley
Lionelle Howard . . . . Sidney Dudley
Mary Rorke . . . . Mrs Stubbs
Ruth Mackay . . . . Mrs Quiltock
Charles Vane . . . . Grandfather
Fred Johnson . . . . Ingram
W.G. Saunders . . . . Solicitor
Molly Hamley-Clifford . . . . . Woman
ROMANCE Heiress marries newsboy to obey
will and they are reconciled by his blind
mother's death.

06458
THE LAUGHING CAVALIER (5509)(U)
Dreadnought (Jury)
P:D: A.V. Bramble, Eliot Stannard
S: (NOVEL) Baroness Orczy
SC: Eliot Stannard
A.V. Bramble . . . . Diogenes
Mercy Hatton . . . . Gilda Beresteyn
George Bellamy . . . . Lord Stoutenberg
Edward O'Neill . . . . Governor Beresteyn
Frederick Sargent . . . . Nicholas Beresteyn
Eva Westlake . . . . Lady Stoutenberg
Will Corri . . . .
Judd Green . . . .
ADVENTURE Holland, period. Cavaliers rescue
governor and daughter from Spanish spies.

06459
THE VILLAGE BLACKSMITH (3970)(A)
I.B. Davidson-Tiger (Walturdaw)
D: A.E. Coleby, Arthur H. Rooke
S: (POEM) Wadsworth Longfellow
SC: A.E. Coleby
Janet Alexander . . . . Mary Rivers
A.E. Coleby . . . . Dan Thorne
Arthur Rooke . . . . Arthur Thorne
C. Arundale . . . . David Thorne
Joyce Templeton . . . . Child
N. Watts-Phillips . . . .
DRAMA Old blacksmith dies: one son takes over
smithy, other is hunchbacked cellist.

06460
SPLASH ME NICELY (2050)(U)
Homel and (Globe)
D: W.P. Kellino
S: Reuben Gillmer
Lupino Lane . . . . Nipper
Winifred Delevanti . . . .
Viola Marriott . . . .
COMEDY

06461
WHEN THE HEART IS YOUNG (2000)
Gaiety (L & P)
D: Dave Aylott
Bob Reed . . . . Bob Downe
COMEDY Misadventures of an old "new boy"
at school.

06462
THE WALRUS GANG (1774)(U)
Gaiety (L & P)
D: Dave Aylott
Bob Reed . . . . Prof Ollio
COMEDY

06463
HIS UNCLE'S HEIR (2000)
Gaiety (L & P)
D: Dave Aylott
Bob Reed . . . . Reggie
COMEDY

06464
LITTLE WOMEN (5000)
G.B. Samuelson (Moss)
D: G.B. Samuelson, Alexander Butler
S: (NOVEL) Louisa May Alcott
Daisy Burrell . . . . Amy March
Mary Lincoln . . . . Meg March
Minna Grey . . . . Marmie March
Ruby Miller . . . . Jo March
Milton Rosmer . . . . Theodore Laurence
Muriel Myers . . . . Beth March
Windham Guise . . . . The Professor
Roy Travers . . . . John Brooke
Lionel d'Aragon . . . . Mr Laurence
Florence Nelson . . . . Aunt March
Bert Darley . . . . Pastor March
Molly Vaughan . . . . Sally Moffatt
Vivian Tremaine . . . . Belle Moffatt
Sylvia Cavalho . . . . Anne Moffatt
ROMANCE America, 1864. Lives and loves of
four sisters during pastor father's absence.

06465
JUSTICE (5780)(A)
Ideal
D: Maurice Elvey
S: (PLAY) John Galsworthy
SC: Eliot Stannard
Gerald du Maurier . . . . Falder
Hilda Moore . . . . Ruth Honeywell
Lilian Braithwaite . . . . Falder's Sister
James Carew . . . . Wister
E. Vivian Reynolds . . . . . . James How
Douglas Munro . . . . Cokeson
Hayford Hobbs . . . . Walter How
Margaret Bannerman . . . . . . Miss Cokeson
Teddy Arundell . . . . Honeywell
Bert Wynne . . . . Davis
Hubert Willis . . . . Brother-in-law
Frank Dane . . . . Frome
Edward O'Neill . . . . Governor
CRIME Clerk jailed for forging cheque to help
drunkard's wife.

06466
DADDY (4978) (U)
British Actors (Int Ex)
D: Thomas Bentley
S: H. Hurlock, Reuben Gillmer
SC: Kenelm Foss
Langhorne Burton . . . . John Melsher
Peggy Kurton . . . . Elsie Vernon
William Lugg . . . . Andrew Vernon
M.R. Morand . . . . John Melsher
Charles T. Macdona . . . . . . Farmer Bruff
Eric Barker . . . . John (child)
Audrey Hughes . . . . Elsie (child)
ROMANCE Dying musician's son turns beggar,
is adopted by violin maker, and marries his
daughter.

AUG

06467
A GAMBLE FOR LOVE (5609) (U)
Broadwest
P: Walter West
D: Frank Wilson
S: (NOVEL) Nat Gould
SC: Benedict James
Violet Hopson . . . . Fay de Launey
Gerald Ames . . . . Dennis Laurenny
James Lindsay . . . . Lord Ingleby
George Foley . . . .
Arthur Walcott . . . . Joe Rothery
Hubert Willis . . . . Brynyng
John McAndrews . . . .
J. Hastings Batson . . . .
Elijah Wheatley . . . . Jockey
SPORT Lord tries to nobble rich widow's horse
which he wagers against lover's.

06468
MY LADY'S DRESS (8516) (A)
G.B. Samuelson (Moss) reissue: 1922
D: Alexander Butler
S: (PLAY) Edward Knoblauch
Gladys Cooper . . . . The Wife
Malcolm Cherry . . . . The Husband
Andre Beaulieu . . . .
Alice de Winton . . . .
Olive Richardson . . . .
Leal Douglas . . . .
DRAME Stories 'dreamed' around dress, set in
Italy, France, Holland, Russia, and East and
West of London.

06469
THE HAPPY WARRIOR (3468) (U)
Harma
D: F. Martin Thornton
S: (NOVEL) A.S.M. Hutchinson
James Knight . . . . The Happy Warrior
Evelyn Boucher . . . . Dora
Joan Legge . . . . Audrey Oxford
Minna Grey . . . . Maggie Oxford
Harry Lorraine . . . . Foxy
Sydney Lewis Ransome . . . . Jaffra
H. Agar Lyons . . . . Lord Burdon
Leslie Howard . . . . Rollo
Roy Byford . . . . Latham
Jeff Barlow . . . . Amber
Winifred Evans . . . . Lady Burdon
SPORT Postmistress adopts heir who becomes
boxer and rejects title when he finds friend is
usurper.

06470
HOLY ORDERS (4744) (A)
I.B. Davidson (Ruffells)
D: A.E. Coleby, Arthur Rooke
S: (NOVEL) Marie Corelli
SC: Rowland Talbot
Malvina Longfellow . . . . . . Jacynth
A.E. Coleby . . . . Dan Kiernan
Arthur Rooke . . . . Rev Richard Everton
Dorna Leigh . . . . Azalea Everton
Maud Yates . . . . Jenny Kiernan
Terence Boddy . . . . Lawrence
N. Watts-Phillips . . . .
Olive Bell . . . .
DRAMA Drunkard's mistress causes death of his
wife, runs him over, marries millionaire, and falls
out of balloon.

06471
THE FAILURE (4275) (A) Retitled: DICK
CARSON WINS THROUGH
Hepworth (Butcher)
D:S: Henry Edwards
SC: Blanche McIntosh
Henry Edwards . . . . Dick Carson
Chrissie White . . . . Margaret Gilder
Lionelle Howard . . . . Sidney Carson
Fred Johnson . . . . Gustave le Sage
Charles Vane . . . . Police Chief
W.G. Saunders . . . . Mr Gilder
CRIME Frenchman causes man to drink
brother's poison and charges brother with
murder.

06472
THE GAY LORD QUEX (5670)(A)
Ideal
D: Maurice Elvey
S: (PLAY) Arthur Wing Pinero
SC: Eliot Stannard
Ben Webster . . . . Lord Quex
Irene Vanbrugh . . . . Sophie Fullgarney
Lilian Braithwaite . . . . Duchess of Strood
Hayford Hobbs . . . . Capt Bartling
Margaret Bannerman . . . . . Muriel Eden

Donald Calthrop . . . . Valma
Claire Pauncefort . . . . Lady Owbridge
Lyston Lyle . . . .
ROMANCE Affianced Lord tries to compromise maid, witness to his affair with Duchess.

06473
WHAT EVERY WOMAN KNOWS (5100)
Barker-Neptune (Lucoque)
D: Fred W. Durrant
S: (PLAY) J.M. Barrie
Hilda Trevelyan . . . . Maggie Wylie
A.B. Imeson . . . .
Maud Yates . . . . The Comtesse
ROMANCE Porter, educated in return for marrying rich man's daughter, learns love after entering parliament.

06474
BOY SCOUTS BE PREPARED (serial) (U) USA:
BOY SCOUTS TO THE RESCUE
Transatlantic
D: Percy Nash
S: Bannister Merwin
Eric Stuart . . . . Eric Grey
Derek Boddey . . . . Jack Blake
Edward O'Neill . . . . The Gypsy
Madge Tree . . . . Mother
Sir Robert Baden-Powell . . . Himself

06475
1—THE SCOUT INSTINCT (819)

06476
2—THE CHIEF'S PROPHECY (1093)

06477
3—AT BAY (800)

06478
4—FRIENDS IN NEED (909)

06479
5—THEIR ENEMY (1167)

06480
6—A DESPERATE REVENGE (1072)

06481
7—THE ADMIRALTY'S CALL (1253)

06482
8—THE TRAITOR'S REWARD (1067)

USA titles for above:

1—AIDS OF THE NATION (2000)

2—ON THE TRAIL (2000)

3—THE GREAT MINE DISASTER (2000)

4—THE SPIES' NEST (2000)

5—TREACHERY AT SEA (2000)
ADVENTURE Squire's son and miner's son join Scouts and foil gipsy spy supplying petrol to U-boats.

06483
THE LIFE OF LORD KITCHENER (6240)(U)
Windsor (LIFT)
D: Rex Wilson, W. Dane Stanton
S: Rex Wilson
HISTORY Biography of Lord Kitchener (1850-1916).

SEP

06484
FLAMES (5200)(A)
Butcher's Film Service
D: Maurice Elvey

P: F.W. Baker
S: (NOVEL) Robert Hichens
SC: Eliot Stannard
Margaret Bannerman . . . . . . Cuckoo
Owen Nares . . . . Valentine Cresswell
Edward O'Neill . . . . Richard Marr
Douglas Munro . . . . Dr Levetier
Clifford Cobbe . . . . Julian Addison
FANTASY Old occultist exchanges souls with a young man, whose friends force the souls to change back.

06485
THE RAGGED MESSENGER (5025) (A)
Broadwest
P: Walter West
D: Frank Wilson
S: (NOVEL) W.B. Maxwell
Violet Hopson . . . . Mary Ainslee
Gerald Ames . . . . Walter Bowman
Basil Gill . . . . Rev John Morton
George Foley . . . . Henry Vavasour
Harry Gilbey . . . .
Ruby Belasco . . . .
John McAndrews . . . .
Marjorie West . . . .
DRAMA Paralysed millionaire's son gets brain fever on learning he married his father's mistress.

06486
QUEEN OF MY HEART (5000)
Clarendon (Globe)
D: Albert Ward
S: Hetty Langford Reed
SC: Reuben Gillmer
Hayden Coffin . . . . The Singer
Christine Rayner . . . . Dorothy Lethridge
Charles Vane . . . . Joseph Hawks
Alfred Lugg . . . . Jack Lethridge
Jack Wilcocks . . . . Mr Lethridge
CRIME Crook frames cousin for forgery and lures away his wife.

06487
THE CALL OF THE PIPES (5000)(U)
Regal Films
D: Tom Watts
S: H. Grenville-Taylor
Ernest A. Douglas . . . . The Father
WAR Scot wins VC saving rival and returns home in time to save blind father from eviction.

06488
GIDDY GOLIGHTLY (2700)(U)
Regal Films
D: Cecil Mannering
COMEDY

OCT

06489
DOMBEY AND SON (6800)(U)
Ideal
D: Maurice Elvey
S: (NOVEL) Charles Dickens
SC: Eliot Stannard
Norman McKinnel . . . . Paul Dombey
Lilian Braithwaite . . . . Edith Dombey
Hayford Hobbs . . . . Walter Dombey
Odette Goimbault . . . . Florence Dombey
Douglas Munro . . . . Solomon Gillis
Jerrold Robertshaw . . . . Carker
Fewlass Llewellyn . . . . Bagstock
Will Corrie . . . . Captain Scuttle
Evelyn Walsh Hall . . . . Mrs Skewton
DRAMA Magnate's wife and son die, his second wife elopes, he goes bankrupt, and reforms on meeting grandson.

06490
A MASTER OF MEN (5040)(U)
Harma Photoplays
D: Wilfred Noy
S: (NOVEL) E. Phillips Oppenheim
Malcolm Keen . . . . Enoch Strone
Dorothy Bellew . . . . Milly Wilson
Marie Hemingway . . . . Lady Malingcourt
Sydney Lewis Ransome . . . . Rev Martinhoe
Jeff Barlow . . . . Dobell
DRAMA Lady helps workman become Labour MP, but he resigns for the sake of working class wife.

06491
A MAN THE ARMY MADE (4089) (U)
Holmfirth
D: Bertram Phillips
S: Capt Cecil Shaw
SC: F. Martin Thornton
Queenie Thomas . . . . Queenie Clarke
Cpl Paul R. Hall . . . . Dick Clarke
H. Agar Lyons . . . . Irwin Lockwood
Micky Brantford . . . . Derry Clarke
WAR Drunkard enlists and returns home a hero in time to save wife from cad.

06492
LES CLOCHES DE CORNEVILLE (6000)(U)
British Actors (Int Ex)
D: Thomas Bentley
S: (OPERA) Robert Planquette
SC: Bannister Merwin
Elsie Craven . . . . Germaine
Moya Mannering . . . . Serpolette
M.R. Morand . . . . Gaspard
Leslie Stiles . . . . Grenicheaux
Fred Volpe . . . . Baillie
Ben Field . . . . Iolo
COMEDY Normandy. Miser tries to make his adopted daughter wed Marquis.

06493
AULD LANG SYNE (4400)
B & C (Unicorn)
D:S: Sidney Morgan
Violet Graham . . . . Beatrice Potter
Henry Baynton . . . . Wilton Daneford
Sydney Fairbrother . . . . Mrs Potter
George Bellamy . . . . Luke Potter
Roy Travers . . . . Ned Potter
Jack Buchanan . . . . Vane
DRAMA Hoxton shopgirl weds Lord and takes blame when her brother steals necklace.

06494
THE GIRLS OF THE VILLAGE (2000)
Gaiety
P:D: Maurice Sandground
Bob Reed . . . . Bud Hambone
COMEDY Agent forms phoney film company to dupe clients.

06495
CAST ADRIFT (2000)
Gaiety
P:D: Maurice Sandground
Bob Reed . . . . The Man
COMEDY

06496
AS IN DAYS OF YORE (2000)
Gaiety
D: Maurice Sandground
Bob Reed . . . . Caveman
COMEDY "Prehistoric fantasy."

06497
CURLY'S HOLIDAY (2000)
Tower Films
P:D:S: J.F. Carr
J.F. Carr . . . . Curly
COMEDY Blackpool. (In conjunction with £5
prize for discovering "Curly" in audience).

NOV

06498
NEARER MY GOD TO THEE (5275)(U)
Hepworth (Moss)
D: Cecil M. Hepworth
S: Herbert Pemberton
Henry Edwards . . . . John Drayton
Alma Taylor . . . . Joan
A.V. Bramble . . . . Jim Boden
Teddy Taylor . . . . Alec
Beryl Rhodes . . . . Littlest Girl
John McAndrews . . . .
ROMANCE 1894-1914. Crippled teacher adopts
child of beloved assistant, who married criminal.

06499
THE WILL OF THE PEOPLE (3760)(A) retitled:
A STRONG MAN'S WEAKNESS
I.B. Davidson-Tiger (LIFT)
D: A.E. Coleby
Malvina Longellow
A.E. Coleby
Arthur Rooke
Janet Alexander
Thomas Canning
DRAMA MP, ruined because he traded with
Germany, returns to wife after affair with a
socialite.

06500
FOR ALL ETERNITY (4500)
I.B. Davidson (Ruffells)
D: A.E. Coleby, Arthur Rooke
S: Rowland Talbot
SC: A.E. Coleby
Malvine Longellow . . . . Ella Morgan
A.E. Coleby . . . . Clifford Morgan
Arthur Rooke . . . . Desmond Leach
Janet Alexander . . . . Nurse Hillyer
Richard Buttery . . . .
Joyce Templeton . . . .
N. Watts-Phillips . . . .
CRIME Framed man saved when nurse
confesses to killing her bastard child's father.

06501
THE CHILD AND THE FIDDLER (2000)
Brum Films
D: Bert Haldane
Edna Maude . . . . Graham
DRAMA Circus fiddler adopts amnesiac child
and they become buskers.

DEC

06502
TOM JONES (6700)
Ideal
D: Edwin J. Collins
S: (NOVEL) Henry Fielding
SC: Eliot Stannard
Langhorne Burton . . . . Tom Jones
Miss June . . . . Sophie Western
Sybil Arundale . . . . Molly Seagrim
Will Corrie . . . . Squire Western
Wyndham Guise . . . . Squire Allworthy

Bert Wynne . . . . William Blifil
Nelson Ramsey . . . . Thwackum
Dora de Winton . . . . Miss Western
Jeff Barlow . . . . Lt Waters
COMEDY 18th C. Adventures of squire's
disowned son who proves to be his bastard heir.

06503
ALL CLEAR: NO NEED TO TAKE COVER
(1000)
Denvirose Films
P:D: Jane Denison
Jane Denison . . . . Fairy
Anne Bolt . . . . Child
FANTASY Fairy tale including impersonations
of Doris Keane and Charles Chaplin.

06504
THE BLINDNESS OF FORTUNE (3375)(U)
Hepworth (UK)
D:SC: Frank Wilson
Chrissie White . . . . Rose Jordan
Lionelle Howard . . . . Sir Hector Gray
Violet Hopson . . . . Grace Hardfeldt
William Felton . . . . Basil Hardfeldt
John MacAndrews . . . . Joe Greenwell
Henry Vibart . . . . Dr Lindley
DRAMA Farmer's son inherits £50,000 and goes
blind on learning his wife is married to convict.

06505
BROKEN THREADS (4575)(U)
Hepworth (Butcher)
D: Henry Edwards
S: Harold Bartholomew
Henry Edwards . . . . Jack Desmond
Chrissie White . . . . Helen Desmond
A.V. Bramble . . . . Pierre
Harry Gilbey . . . . Murray
Gwynne Herbert . . . . Housekeeper
W.G. Saunders . . . . Boniface
Fred Johnson . . . . Stepfather
John MacAndrews . . . . Confederate
DRAMA Devon. Girl presumed drowned escapes
from lighthouse keeper to find her husband insane
and framed for murder.

06506
IF THOU WERT BLIND (5000)(A)
Clarendon (New Bio)
D: F. Martin Thornton
S: Kenelm Foss
Ben Webster . . . . Hayden Strong
Evelyn Boucher . . . . Christine Leslie
Joan Legge . . . . Mary Barton
Minna Grey . . . .
Clifford Pembroke . . . .
Sydney Lewis Ransome . . . .
Harry Lorraine . . . .
DRAMA Blind sculptor's sweetheart returns to
him after dreaming of his future helplessness.

06507
THE BLIND BOY (4130)(U)
British Photoplay Productions (Ruffells)
P: Edward Godal
D: Edwin J. Collins, Jack Clare
S: (PLAY) George H. Chirgwin
G.H. Chirgwin . . . . Hubert
Ivy Montford . . . . Inez
Evelyn Sydney . . . . Mary
Frank Dane . . . . Claude

Jack Clare . . . . Harry
Victoria Cinema College students
DRAMA Violinist adopts blind boy busker and
dreams a cousin tries to kill him for inheritance.

06508
MARY GIRL (4730)(U)
Butcher
P: F.W. Baker
D: Maurice Elvey
S: (PLAY) Hope Merrick
SC: Eliot Stannard
Norman McKinnel . . . . Ezra
Jessie Winter . . . . Mary
Margaret Bannerman . . . . .Countess Folkington
Edward O'Neill . . . . George Latimer
Marsh Allen . . . .
ROMANCE Poor gardener's wife nurses
countess's weak baby, gets taste for wealth and
takes rich lover.

06509
THE ADVENTURES OF DICK DOLAN (2000)
Broadwest
P: Walter West
D: Frank Wilson
Basil Gill . . . . Dick Dolan
Violet Hopson . . . . Mrs Cambray
Ivy Close . . . . Her Niece
John McMahon . . . . George Cambray
Tom Beaumont . . . . Charles Morrison
Delia Bottomley . . . . Delia
Frank Wilson . . . . Doctor
Walter West . . . . Bystander
DRAMA Tramp reforms and saves soldier's wife
from gambler. (War Bonds appeal).

06510
AULD ROBIN GRAY (4500)(U)
Ideal
D: Meyrick Milton
S: Kenelm Foss
Langhorne Burton . . . . Jamie
Miss June . . . . Jenny
R.A. Roberts . . . . Robin Gray
ROMANCE Scotland. Sailor returns from
shipwreck in time to save fiancee from
marrying farmer.

06511
BLARNEY
Film Co of Ireland
D: J.M. Kerrigan
Fred O'Donovan
COMEDY

06512
THE UPSTART
Film Co of Ireland
D: J.M. Kerrigan
COMEDY

06513
THE BYEWAYS OF FATE
Film Co of Ireland
D: J.M. Kerrigan
DRAMA

06514
THE IRISH GIRL
Film Co of Ireland
D: J.M. Kerrigan
DRAMA

1918

JAN

06515
MISSING THE TIDE (5063)(A)
Broadwest
D: Walter West
S: (NOVEL) Alfred Turner
SC: R. Byron-Webber
Violet Hopson . . . .   Margaret Carson
Basil Gill . . . .   Sir Felix Faber
Ivy Close . . . .   Letty Fairfax
Gerald Ames . . . . Capt Harry Wyndham
James Lindsay . . . .   Carson
Nicholas Hopson Worcester . . The Child
ROMANCE Wife leaves cruel husband too late,
her lover has wed nurse.

06516
THE EXPLOITS OF PARKER (2343)(U)
(Ruffell's)
S: (SKETCH) Charles Austin, Charles
Ridgwell (PARKER PC)
Charles Austin . . . .   PC Parker
COMEDY Discharged constable sets up private
police station.

FEB

06517
THE GREATEST WISH IN THE WORLD
(5800)(U)
International Exclusives
D: Maurice Elvey
S: (NOVEL) E. Temple Thurston
SC: Bannister Merwin
Bransby Williams . . . .   Father O'Leary
Odette Goimbault . . . .   Peggy
Edward Combermere . . . . . .   Stephen Gale
Ada King . . . .   Mrs Parfitt
Douglas Munro . . . .   Pinches
Gwynne Herbert . . . .   Mrs Gooseberry
Edward Arundell . . . .
Jean Alwyn . . . .   Mother Superior
Will Corri . . . .
ROMANCE Waif adopted by priest is seduced,
has baby, and becomes nun.

06518
MEG O' THE WOODS (5464)(A)
Holmfirth (Butcher)
D: Bertram Phillips
S: Irene Miller
Queenie Thomas . . . .   Meg
Harry Drummond . . . .   Harry
Alice de Winton . . . .   Cecilia
Cameron Carr . . . .   Gerald
Minna Grey . . . .
Frank Randell . . . .
ROMANCE Lord destroys the evidence of
son's marriage to gipsy, but their grand-daughter
weds his heir.

06519
THE ADMIRABLE CRICHTON (7817)(U)
G.B. Samuelson (Jury)
D: G.B. Samuelson
S: (PLAY) J.M. Barrie
SC: Kenelm Foss
Basil Gill . . . .   Crichton
Mary Dibley . . . .   Lady Mary
James Lindsay . . . .   Woolley
Lennox Pawle . . . .   Lord Loam
Lilian Hall-Davis . . . .   Agatha
COMEDY When Lord and family shipwrecked
on island their butler becomes king.

06520
THE SPLENDID COWARD (5835)(U)
Harma
D: F. Martin Thornton
S: (NOVEL) Houghton Townley

James Knight . . . .   Dick Swinton
Joan Legge . . . .   Dora Dundas
Roy Travers . . . .   Vivian Ormsby
Winifred Evans . . . . Lady Mary Swinton
Clifford Pembroke . . . . .Rev Swinton
Sydney Lewis Ransome . . . .   Trimmer
Jeff Barlow . . . .   Earl of Heresford
Thomas Canning . . . .   Col Dundas
Edward Arundell . . . .   Jack Lorrimer
CRIME Lady's son takes blame for her forgery
but she confesses in time to save heiress from
marrying blackmailer.

06521
HINDLE WAKES (5250)(A)
Diamond-Super (Royal)
P: William Baker
D: Maurice Elvey
S: (PLAY) Stanley Houghton
SC: Eliot Stannard
Norman McKinnel . . . .   Nat Jeffcoate
Colette O'Neil . . . .   Fanny Hawthorne
Hayford Hobbs . . . .   Alan Jeffcoate
Ada King . . . .   Mrs Hawthorne
Edward O'Neill . . . .   Chris Hawthorne
Margaret Bannerman . . . . . .   Beatrice Farrar
Frank Dane . . . .   Sir Timothy
Dolly Tree . . . .   Mary Hollins
ROMANCE Lancs. Millgirl leaves home rather
than marry owner's son, with whom she spent
holiday.

06522
AVE MARIA (5000)(A)
Clarendon (Harma)
D: Wilfred Noy
S: Reuben Gillmer
Concordia Merrill . . . .   Margaret
Rita Jonson . . . .   Helen Grey
Roy Travers . . . .   Jim Masters
H. Manning Haynes . . . .   Jack Haviland
A.B. Imeson . . . .   Guy Fernandez
Sydney L. Ransome . . . .   Providence
William Lugg . . . .   Sir John Haviland
DRAMA Knight's heir weds girl while doctor
sweetheart has amnesia not knowing she is
knight's grand-daughter.

MAR

06523
THE TOUCH OF A CHILD (4750)(U)
Hepworth (Moss)
D: Cecil M. Hepworth
S: (PLAY) Leon M. Lion (STORY) Tom Gallon
SC: Blanche McIntosh
Alma Taylor . . . .   Barbara Dell
Henry Edwards . . . .   Godfrey Steen
Stewart Rome . . . .   Capt James Fullard
A. Trevor Addinsell . . . .   Sidney Fullard
Valerie McClintock . . . .   Nancy Fullard
Amy Lorraine . . . .   Duchess
Betty Russon . . . .   Child
DRAMA Captain swears to kill man who killed
his brother in duel, but is stopped by his child.

06524
THE SLAVE (4707)
Windsor (LIFT)
D: Arrigo Bocchi
S: (NOVEL) Robert Hichens
SC: Kenelm Foss
Marie de Lisle . . . .   Lady Caryll Knox
Hayford Hobbs . . . .   Aubrey Herrick
Charles Vane . . . .   Sir Reuben Allabruth
Hettie Grossman . . . .   Diamond Manners
Ernest Wallace . . . .
Paul Courtenay . . . .
DRAMA Lady weds old man for emerald, which
her ex-lover steals to lure her back.

06525
HERSELF (1080)(U)
Transatlantic
D: Percy Nash
Ella Shields . . .*. . . . .   Cecil Bonfield
Leslie Stiles . . . .   Artist
Henry Vibart . . . . Sir John Bonfield
ROMANCE Widower's daughter raised as boy falls
in love with artist, and poses as her grandmother's
portrait.

06526
THELMA (5794)(U)
I.B. Davidson (Russells) *reissue:* 1920 (BEF)
D: A.E. Coleby, Arthur Rooke
S: (NOVEL) Marie Corelli
SC: Rowland Talbot
Malvina Longfellow . . . .   Thelma
Arthur Rooke . . . .   Sir Phillip Errington
Maud Yates . . . .   Violet Vere
Marsh Allen . . . .   Sir Francis Lennox
Leal Douglas . . . .   The Bonde
Humberston Wright . . . .   George Lorimer
Judd Green . . . .   Olaf Olsen
ROMANCE Norwegian girl weds English
nobleman and suspects his fidelity.

06527
MATT (5128)(U)
I.B. Davidson-Tiger (Ruffells)
D: A.E. Coleby
S: (NOVEL) Robert Buchanan
SC: Rowland Talbot
Greta MacDonald . . . .   Matt
A.E. Coleby . . . .   Charles Brinkley
Ernest A. Douglas . . . .   Squire Monk
ROMANCE Devon. Artist proves wrecker's
adopted child is heiress in time to prevent
marriage to crooked squire.

06528
GOODBYE (4685)(A)
Butcher's Film Service
P: F.W. Baker
D: Maurice Elvey
S: (NOVEL) John Strange Winter
SC: Eliot Stannard
Margaret Bannerman . . . .   Florence Tempest
Jessie Winter . . . .   Hope Adair
Donald Calthrop . . . .   Capt Richard Adair
Douglas Munro . . . .   Bates
Ruth Mackay . . . .   Rosalie
Edward O'Neill . . . .   Frith
Frank Dane . . . .   Doctor
Fewlass Lewellyn . . . .   Lawyer
ROMANCE Girl frames woman to cause divorce
and marries her husband.

06529
LIVING BY THEIR WITS (2000)
Gaiety
P:D: Maurice Sandground
Bob Reed . . . .   Lord
Fanny Wright . . . .   Soubrette
COMEDY Soubrette poses as actress to get lord
to back revue.

06530
THE BASE DECEIVERS (2000)
Gaiety
P:D: Maurice Sandground
Bob Reed . . . .   Husband
Fanny Wright . . . .   Wife
COMEDY Husbands take trip to Paris and go
fishing with land army girls.

06531
THE MAGISTRATE'S DAUGHTER (2000)
Gaiety
P:D: Maurice Sandground

Bob Reed . . . . Magistrate
Fanny Wright . . . . Daughter
COMEDY Magistrate flirts with daughter after visit to beautician.

06532
RATIONS (2270) (U)
Ideal
D: (Edwin J. Collins)
S: Fred Evans
Fred Evans . . . . Pimple
COMEDY Pimple finds he needs ration card for kissing, coughing, and even hanging.

APR

06533
THE SNARE (5500) (U)
Broadwest
P: Walter West
D: Frank Wilson
Violet Hopson . . . . Diana
George Foley . . . . Lord Marston
Trevor Bland . . . . Hugh
James Lindsay . . . . Carlton Flint
ROMANCE Socialite weds poaching millionaire and learns to love him.

06534
ADAM BEDE (5400) (U)
International Exclusives
D: Maurice Elvey
S: (NOVEL) George Eliot
SC: Kenelm Foss
Bransby Williams . . . . Adam Bede
Ivy Close . . . . Hetty Sorrel
Malvina Longfellow . . . . Dinah Morris
Gerald Ames . . . . Arthur Donnithorne
Claire Pauncefort . . . . Aunt Lydia
Inez Bensusan . . . . Sarah Thorne
Will Corrie . . . . Farmer Poyser
Charles Stanley . . . . Seth Bede
Ralph Forster . . . . Squire
DRAMA 1850. Squire's grandson saves farmer's niece from charge of murdering bastard baby.

06535
MY SWEETHEART (4435) (U)
Ideal
D: Meyrick Milton
S: (PLAY) Minnie Palmer
SC: Kenelm Foss
Margaret Blanche . . . . Tina Hatzell
Concordia Merrill . . . . Mrs Fleeter
Randle Ayrton . . . . Joe Shotwell
Bert Wynne . . . . Tony
E.H. Kelly . . . . Dudley Harcourt
COMEDY Holland. Flighty wife pursues myopic artist.

06536
GOD AND THE MAN (6935) (A)
Ideal
D: Edwin J. Collins
S: (NOVEL) Robert Buchanan
SC: Eliot Stannard
Langhorne Burton . . . . Christiansen
Joyce Carey . . . . Priscilla Sefton
Bert Wynne . . . . Richard Christiansen
Edith Craig . . . . Dame Christiansen
Sybil Arundale . . . . Kate Orchardson
Henry Vibart . . . . Mr Sefton
Nelson Ramsey . . . . Squire Christiansen
E. Vivian Reynolds . . . . John Wesley
ADVENTURE 1745. Squire's son pursues sister's seducer to Labrador.

06537
THE BETTER 'OLE; OR, THE ROMANCE OF OLD BILL (6600) (A) US: CARRY ON
Welsh-Pearson (Jury)
D: George Pearson

S: (PLAY) Bruce Bairnsfather, Arthur Elliot
SC: George Pearson, T.A. Welsh
Charles Rock . . . . Old Bill
Arthur Cleave . . . . Bert
Hugh E. Wright . . . . Alf
Mary Dibley . . . . Maggie Busby
Hayford Hobbs . . . . Jim
Lilian Hall Davis Lil
Alfred Phillips . . . . Spy
Michelin Potous . . . . Suzette
Marguerite Blanche . . . . Victoire
J.M. Wright . . . . Singer
Sid Jay . . . . Juggler
Mansell Fane . . . . Grouser
Frank Adair . . . . Colonel
Meggie Albanesi . . . . Waitress
Mercy Hatton . . . .
WAR 1914. Cockney enlists, catches spy, saves French batallion, and is decorated.

06538
BECAUSE (5000)
Progress (Butcher)
P: Frank E. Spring
D:S: Sidney Morgan
Lilian Braithwaite
Ben Webster
George Foley
Joyce Carey
Joan Morgan
J. Hastings Batson
ROMANCE Girl rejects father's choice of husband and he locks her up.

06539
RAFFERTY'S RISE (2535) (U)
Film Company of Ireland
D: J.M. Kerrigan
S: (PLAY) Nicholas Hayes (THE RISE OF CONSTABLE RAFFERTY)
Fred O'Donovan . . . . Rafferty
Kathleen Murphy . . . . Kitty Hogan
Brian Magowan . . . .
Arthur Shields . . . .
COMEDY Ireland.

MAY

06540
ONCE UPON A TIME (6413) (U)
British Actors (Stoll)
D: Thomas Bentley
S: Kenelm Foss
Lauri de Frece . . . . Sam Dunn
Manora Thew . . . . Sally Drury
Dorothy Minto . . . . Lottie Price
Nelson Keys . . . . Harry Gwynne
Joan Legge . . . . Mary Gwynne
A.E. Matthews . . . . Guy Travers
Noel Fisher . . . . Eustace Travers
Fred Volpe . . . . Mr Goodheart
Charles Macdona . . . . Dr Brown
Adelaide Grace . . . . Mrs Gwynne
Jeff Barlow . . . . Ned Drury
Kenelm Foss . . . . Charles Dickens
ROMANCE 1875-1884-1915. Clown's daughter refuses to marry comedian to please her adoptive parents.

06541
THE GREAT IMPOSTER (4682) (A)
Harma Photoplays
D: F. Martin Thornton
S: Reuben Gillmer
Marie Blanche . . . . Enid Linden
Bernard Dudley . . . . Roger Garnett
Edward O'Neill . . . . Lord Sellington
Lionel d'Aragon . . . . Dolan
Harry Lorraine . . . . Hixton
Rupert Stutfield . . . .
James Prior . . . .

Cecil Stokes . . . .
Gladys Foyle . . . .
DRAMA Sailor poses as Lord's lost son and then finds he really is.

06542
THE WAY OF AN EAGLE (6300) (A)
G.B. Samuelson (Sun)
D: G.B. Samuelson
S: (NOVEL) Ethel M. Dell
Isobel Elsom . . . . Muriel Roscoe
Andre Beaulieu . . . . Nick Ratcliffe
Odette Goimbault . . . . Olga
Mary Dibley . . . . Daisy Musgrave
Annie Esmond . . . . Lady Barrett
WAR India. Colonel's daughter weds soldier who saves legation from siege.

06543
WHAT WOULD A GENTLEMAN DO? (5220) (
Butcher's Film Service
P: F.W. Baker
D: Wilfred Noy
S: (PLAY) Gilbert Daylis
Stanley Logan . . . . Dickie Hook
Queenie Thomas . . . . Madge Kenderby
A.B. Imeson . . . .
Dora de Winton . . . .
Jean Cavendish . . . .
Will Corrie . . . .
Harry Drummond . . . .
Jeff Barlow . . . .
Rupert Stutfield . . . . Sir Bruce Kenderby
Mabel Bunyea . . . .
COMEDY Australian miner inherits fortune but returns home on learning colonel's daughter loves another.

06544
HEROES OF THE SEA (300)
Wonder Plays
P: Roscoe C. Spurin
S: Lt. Col Drury
Kitty Darling . . . . Britannia
WAR Pictorial foreword to an unmade patriotic film.

06545
KNOCKNAGOW (7910) (U)
Film Co of Ireland
D: Fred O'Donovan
S: (PLAY) Charles Kickham (THE HOMES OF TIPPERARY)
SC: N.F. Patton
Fred O'Donovan . . . . Arthur O'Connor
Kathleen Murphy . . . . Norah Laby
Brian Magowan . . . . Mat Donovan
Nora Clancy . . . . Mary Karney
Brenda Burke . . . . Honor Laby
Valentine Roberts . . . . Father O'Donnell
Moira Breggni . . . . Peg
Cyril Cusack . . . . Child
CRIME Ireland. 1850. Absentee landlord's agent frames rival for burglary.

06546
WHEN LOVE CAME TO GAVIN BURKE (3670) (U)
Film Co of Ireland
D: Fred O'Donovan
Brian Magowan . . . .
Kathleen Murphy . . . .
DRAMA

06547
TOMMY'S INITIATION (495)
Kineto
D: Walter Booth
COMEDY France. Soldiers use trench periscope for various purposes.

06548
HOW COULD YOU UNCLE? (5000)
Gaiety
P:D: Maurice Sandground
Bob Reed . . . . Jerry
Rowland Hill . . . . Uncle Joe
COMEDY

06549
KINEKATURE COMEDIES (series)
Hagen & Double
P: Julius Hagen
D: Fred Rains

06550
1—THE BLUNDERS OF MR BUTTERBUN:
UNEXPECTED TREASURE (2070)(U)
Lupino Lane . . . . Mr Butterbun
Wallace Lupino . . . .

06551
2—THE BLUNDERS OF MR BUTTERBUN:
TRIPS AND TRIBUNALS (2000)(A)
Lupino Lane . . . . Mr Butterbun
Judd Green . . . . Slopson

06552
3—THE HAUNTED HOTEL (1000) (A)
Will Asher . . . . Buttons
Marion Peake . . . . Miss Falloffski

06553
4—HIS BUSY DAY (1630)(U)
Lupino Lane . . . . Mr Butterbun

06554
5—HIS SALAD DAYS (2130)(U)
Lupino Lane . . . . Mr. Butterbun

06555
6—LOVE AND LOBSTER (1960)(U)
Lupino Lane . . . . Mr Butterbun

06556
7—DIAMONDS AND DIMPLES (1000)(U)
Will Asher . . . .

06557
8—A CASE OF COMFORT (1190)(U)
Will Asher . . . .

06558
9—PAINT AND PASSION (1190)(U)
Will Asher . . . .
COMEDIES Each film features sequence of
distorted images.

JUN

06559
THE SECRET WOMAN (6297) (A)
I.B. Davidson-Tiger (Gaumont)
D: A.E. Coleby
S: (NOVEL) Eden Philpotts
SC: Rowland Talbot
Maud Yates . . . . Ann Redvers
Janet Alexander . . . . Salome Westaway
Henry Victor . . . . Jesse Redvers
A.E. Coleby . . . . Anthony Redvers
Olive Noble . . . . Barbara Westaway
H. Nicholls-Bates . . . . Michael Redvers
Humberston Wright . . . . . . William Arscott
Olive Bell . . . . Sarah Tapp
W.S. Manning . . . . Flockmaster Westaway
DRAMA Devon. Woman kills husband on dis-
covering that their son loves husband's mistress.

06560
JO THE CROSSING SWEEPER (5000)
Barker (Bolton)
D: Alexander Butler
S: (NOVEL) Charles Dickens (BLEAK HOUSE)
SC: Irene Miller
Unity More . . . . Jo
Dora de Winton . . . . Lady Dedlock
Andre Beaulieu . . . . Tulkinghorne
Connie Lever . . . . Esther
Rolf Leslie . . . . Bucket
DRAMA Lady dies of grief after being
suspected of killing lawyer who learned of
child by previous marriage.

06561
ON LEAVE (5000)
Barker (Anglo)
D: Alexander Butler
S: Irene Miller
Daphne Glenne . . . . Claude Carewe
George Foley . . . . Col Carewe
Aubrey Fitzmaurice . . . . . . Lt Jack Fordyce
Rolf Leslie . . . . Burglar
Judd Green . . . .
Nita Russell . . . .
DRAMA Lieut takes blame for shopgirl's theft
and finds her married to his colonel.

06562
THEN YOU'LL REMEMBER ME (4000)
Anglo Film Agency
D: Edward Waltyre
S: Edward Waltyre, Edith Mellor
Lionel D'Aragon . . . . Squire Trelawney
Mabel Hirst . . . . Gilda
Babby Reynolds . . . . Gilda (Child)
ROMANCE Fisherman adopts baby who becomes
opera star with amnesia.

06563
SPINNER O' DREAMS (5340)(U)
Butcher's Films Service
D:SC: Wilfred Noy
P: F.W. Baker
S: (PLAY) Leon M. Lion, W. Strange Hall
Basil Gill . . . . Adam Hundred
Odette Goimbault . . . . Sue Fawthorpe
James Carew . . . . Richard Strome
Stella Mervyn Campbell . . . . Hester Hundred
Sam Livesey . . . . Reuben Hundred
Jeff Barlow . . . . Andrew Fawthorpe
Seth Taylor . . . . Joseph Boddy
Molly Hamley-Clifford . . . . . Martha Hundred
Arthur Walcott . . . . Lawyer Quint
Gladys Foyle . . . . Ruth
DRAMA Lancs, 1786. Farmer tries to ruin rival,
who invents power loom.

06564
RED POTTAGE (4825)(A)
Ideal
D: Meyrick Milton
S: (NOVEL) Mary Cholmondeley
SC: Eliot Stannard
C. Aubrey Smith . . . . Lord Newhaven
Mary Dibley . . . . Lady Newhaven
Gerald Ames . . . . Hugh Scarlett
E. Holman Clark . . . . The Bishop
Marjorie Hume . . . . Rachel West
DRAMA Lady's lover draws spills with husband
to decide who shall commit suicide.

06565
A FORTUNE AT STAKE (6500)(A)
Broadwest (Royal)
P:D: Walter West
S: (NOVEL) Nat Gould
Violet Hopson . . . . Lady Launcelot
Gerald Ames . . . . Will Martindale
Edward O'Neill . . . . Lord Launcelot
James Lindsay . . . .
Gwynne Herbert . . . .
Windham Guise . . . .
Tom Coventry . . . .
SPORT Lord shot after trying to raise loan from
jockey who loves his wife.

06566
THE HANGING JUDGE (5300)(A)
Hepworth (Moss)
D:SC: Henry Edwards
S: (PLAY) Leon M. Lion (STORY) Tom Gallon
Henry Edwards . . . . Dick Veasey
Chrissie White . . . . Molly
Hamilton Stewart . . . . Sir John Veasey
Randle Ayrton . . . . Reginald Tamlyn
Gwynne Herbert . . . . Lady Veasey
A.V. Bramble . . . . Prosecution
John McAndrews . . . . Ned Blake
DRAMA Judge's disowned son becomes
reporter and marries condemned man's
daughter.

06567
HEARTS OF THE WORLD (13000)
D.W. Griffith Inc-War Office Committee
reissue: 1926(cut)
P:D:S: David Wark Griffith
Lilian Gish . . . . Marie Stephenson
Robert Harron . . . . Douglas Hamilton
Dorothy Gish . . . . The Little Disturber
Geroge A. Siegmann . . . . . Von Strohm
Robert Anderson . . . . M. Cuckoo
Jack Cosgrove . . . . Mr. Hamilton
Kate Bruce . . . . Mrs Hamilton
Josephine Crowell . . . . . . Mrs Stephenson
Adolphe Lestina . . . . Grandfather
Ben Alexander . . . . .The Littlest Brother
Fay Holderness . . . . Innkeeper
Erich von Stroheim . . . . . Officer
Noel Coward . . . . Villager
WAR France. Maddened girl reunited with
wounded lover behind German lines.

06568
LEAD, KINDLY LIGHT (4000)
H.B. Parkinson (White)
D: Rex Wilson
S: H. Hurlock
SC: H.B. Parkinson
Dorothy Bellew
Manning Haynes
Gwen Williams
ROMANCE Flower girl becomes actress and
finds poor parson she loved is now street
organist.

06569
THE GIRL FROM DOWNING STREET
(4832)(U)
International Exclusives (Butcher)
D: SC: Geoffrey H. Malins
S: Garth Grayson
Ena Beaumont . . . . Peggy Marsden
Sydney Paxton . . . . Capt Paul Muller
William Stack . . . . Cyril Godfrey
WAR Girl spy steals plans of Hindenburg Line
and is chased by German spy, who is really
British.

JUL

06570
FILM TAGS (series)(U)
Hepworth (Ministry of Information)

06571
1—A NEW VERSION (150)
D: Cecil Hepworth
Alma Taylor . . . . The Woman
Henry Edwards . . . . The Man

06572
2—THE W.L.A. GIRL (150)
D: Cecil Hepworth
Alma Taylor . . . . The Girl

06573
3—THE LEOPARD'S SPOTS (150)
D: Cecil Hepworth
Alma Taylor . . . .   The Woman
John McAndrews . . . .   The Man

06574
4—THE MESSAGE (150)
D: Henry Edwards
Henry Edwards . . . .   The Man
Chrissie White . . . .   The Woman
A.V. Bramble . . . .
John McAndrews . . . .

06575
5—AGAINST THE GRAIN (150)
D: Henry Edwards
Henry Edwards . . . .   The Man
Chrissie White . . . .   The Woman

06576
6—OLD MOTHER HUBBARD (150)
D: Henry Edwards
Mac the Collie . . . .   The Dog

06577
7—ANNA (150)
D: Henry Edwards
Henry Edwards . . . .   The Man
Chrissie White . . . .   Anna

06578
8—HER SAVINGS SAVED (150)
D: Henry Edwards
Henry Edwards . . . .   The Man
Chrissie White . . . .   The Woman
John McAndrews . . . .

06579
9—THE POET'S WINDFALL (150)
D: Henry Edwards
Henry Edwards . . . .   The Poet
Chrissie White . . . .   The Girl
John McAndrews . . . .   The Man

06580
10—THE INEVITABLE (150)
D: Henry Edwards
Chrissie White . . . .   The Girl
Bob Russell . . . .   The Man

06581
11—WHAT'S THE USE OF GRUMBLING (150)
D: Henry Edwards
Basil Gill . . . .   The Man
Chrissie White . . . .   The Girl
Gwynne Herbert . . . .   The Woman

06582
12—THE SECRET (150)
D: Henry Edwards
Henry Edwards . . . .   The Husband
Chrissie White . . . .   The Wife
DRAMAS Patriotic stories.

06583
THE MAN AND THE MOMENT (5850)(A)
Windsor (Walturdaw)
D: Arrigo Bocchi
S: (NOVEL) Elinor Glyn
SC: Kenelm Foss
Manora Thew . . . .   Sabine Delburg
Hayford Hobbs . . . . .Lord Michael Arranstoun
Charles Vane . . . . .Lord Henry Fordyce
Maud Cressall . . . .   Princess Moravia
Peggy Carlisle . . . . .Miss Van Der Water
Jeff Barlow . . . .   Armstrong
Kenelm Foss . . . . .Prince Torniloni
ROMANCE American heiress weds Scots lord
to fulfil will, leaves him for Italy, but returns
after baby's death.

06584
BIG MONEY (5320)(U)
Harma Photoplays
D: Harry Lorraine
S: (NOVEL) May Wynne (A RUN FOR HIS
MONEY)
SC: Reuben Gillmer
Rose Manners . . . .   Noreen O'Mara
James Knight . . . .   Tom Carbyn
Charles Rock . . . .   Father O'Mara
Edward O'Neill . . . .   Sir Hugh Marrimore
Lionel d'Aragon . . . .   Larry O'Callaghan
DRAMA Rich man pays nephew to pose as his
murderer and elude capture for three months.

06585
ALL THE SAD WORLD NEEDS (4854)(U)
British Actors (Stoll)
D: Hubert Herrick
S: Kenelm Foss
Lauri de Freece . . . .   Peep O'Day
Joan Legge . . . .   Rhoda Grover
Lennox Pawle . . . .   George Grover
Adelaide Grace . . . .   Miss Flint
Cyprian Hyde . . . .   Ernest Hanbury
DRAMA Concertina player's rise to fame on
poor violinist's music.

06586
CONSEQUENCES (2000)
New Agency (Lucoque)
D: Arthur Rooke
S: Kenelm Foss
Gordon Craig . . . .   Bobbie
Joyce Templeton . . . .   Joyce
J. Hastings Batson . . . .   Guardian
COMEDY Children dream they elope and are
chased by guardians.

06587
THE RUGGED PATH (5000)(A)
New Agency (Lucoque)
SC: Arthur Rooke
S: (NOVEL) Charles Garvice
Marjorie Villis . . . .   Clytie Bromley
Hayford Hobbs . . . .   Wilfred Carlton
Cameron Carr . . . .   Herbert Carlton
Ivy Stanborough . . . .   Mary Seaton
Michelin Poteous . . . .   Sir Wilfred Mally
J. Hastings Batson
DRAMA Poor bart's son tramps Australia and
saves girl from poison.

AUG

06588
ROCK OF AGES (5300)(U)
Screen Plays (Walturdaw)
P: H.B. Parkinson
D: Bertram Phillips
S: Kenelm Foss
Queenie Thomas . . . .   Biddy Kinsella
Leslie George . . . .   Austin Summers
Ronald Power . . . .   The Master
Bernard Vaughan . . . .   Father O'Flynn
Charles Garry . . . .   Pat Reilly
Lottie Blackford . . . .   Widdy Kinsella
Ernest A. Douglas . . . .   Priest
ROMANCE Irish model converts atheist by
posing for church mural.

06589
A POTTERY GIRL'S ROMANCE (4000)
Hewitt Films
D:S: G. Fletcher Hewitt
Madeleine Tighe . . . .   The Girl
ROMANCE "Among other stirring incidents
contains realistic fire scenes."

06590
THE FIREMAN'S WEDDING
Eric Williams Speaking Pictures-Barker
S: (POEM) W.A. Eaton
Eric Williams . . . .   Artizan
DRAMA Shown while Eric Williams recites
from the stage. (Date uncertain).

06591
BRUTUS AND CASSIUS
Eric Williams Speaking Pictures
S: (PLAY) William Shakespeare (Julius Caesar)
D: Marshall Moore
Eric Williams . . . .   Brutus
DRAMA Shown while Eric Williams recites
from the stage (Date uncertain).

06592
THE REDEMPTION OF HIS NAME (5000)
All-British (Albion)
D: Percy Moran
Aldon Neilson . . . .   Wake
Jock Hood . . . .   Robert
Farmer Skein . . . .   Baronet
CRIME Gambler blackmailed for thinking he
killed cardsharp.

06593
PIMPLE'S BETTER 'OLE (2000)
Fred Evans
D:S: Fred Evans, Joe Evans
Fred Evans . . . .   Pimple
Joe Evans . . . .
COMEDY

06594
BOYS OF THE OTTER PATROL (5000)
Transatlantic
D: Percy Nash
S: (NOVEL) E. LeBreton Martin
SC: Bannister Merwin
Alfred Harding . . . .   The Scout
Dorothy Mason . . . .   The Girl
Edward Dryhurst Roberts . .   A Scout
Sir Robert Baden-Powell . . .   Himself
ADVENTURE "Fine drama of boyhood's
adventures."

06595
TINKER, TAILOR, SOLDIER, SAILOR (7000)
G.B. Samuelson (Granger)
D: Rex Wilson
S: G.B. Samuelson
SC: Kenelm Foss
Isobel Elsom . . . .   Isobel Bunter
Owen Nares . . . .   John Tinker
James Lindsay . . . . .Sir William Taylor
Tom Reynolds . . . .   Herbert Bunter
Minna Grey . . . .   Mrs Tinker
Mary Rorke . . . .   Jemima Bunter
ROMANCE 1860-1910. Life of a mayor's daugh
if she married (a) a rich baronet; (b) a poor
shopkeeper; (c) nobody.

06596
A ROMANY LASS (6738) (U)
Harma Photoplays
reissue: 1927, RILKA; OR, THE GYPSY
QUEEN (N. of E.)
D: F. Martin Thornton
S: Reuben Gillmer
James Knight . . . .   Donald MacLean
Marjorie Villis . . . .   Rilka
Bernard Dudley . . . .   Wolf
Charles Rock . . . .   Col MacLean
Arthur Cullin . . . .   Dr Harris
F.G. Thurstans . . . .   Rev Angus MacTi?
Adeline Hayden Coffin . . . . .
James Reardon . . . .
ROMANCE Scotland. Colonel's son conquers
cowardice by fighting rival for gipsy.

06597
WHERE'S WATLING? (2000)
Harma Photoplays
D: F. Martin Thornton
S: Reuben Gillmer
Lawrence Leyton . . . . Mr Watling
Mrs Lawrence Leyton . . . . . . Mrs Watling
F.G. Thurstans . . . .
Maud Yates . . . .
COMEDY

06598
THE TICKET-OF-LEAVE MAN (5800)
Barker (Moss)
D: Bert Haldane
S: (PLAY) Tom Taylor
Daphne Glenne . . . . May Edwards
George Foley . . . . Bob Brierley
Aubrey Fitzmaurice . . . . . . Hawkshaw
Wilfred Benson . . . . James Tiger Dalton
Rolf Leslie . . . . Melter Moss
Rachel de Solla . . . . Mrs Willoughby
George Harrington . . . . Eliza
CRIME Framed man released from prison
uncovers burglary plot.

06599
THE DIVINE GIFT (5300)(U)
British Actors (Phillips)
D: Thomas Bentley
S: Kenelm Foss
Joyce Dearsley . . . . The Shopgirl
Jack Livesey . . . . The Bank Clerk
George Tully . . . . The Host
Henrietta Watson . . . . The Hostess
Ernest Hendrie . . . . The Professor
Sydney Paxton . . . . The Butler
Madge Saunders . . . . The Mother
Muriel Dole . . . . Katharine
F. Pope-Stamper . . . . Tristan
Wanda Redford . . . . Iseult
Micheline Poteous . . . . . . Prehistoric Woman
DRAMA Stories illustrate discussion on
whether God's greatest gift is humanity, piety,
love, intellect, or self-sacrifice.

06600
THE REFUGEE (2400)(U)
Hepworth (Moss)
D: Cecil M. Hepworth
S: E. Temple Thurston
Henry Edwards . . . . Capt Galloway
Alma Taylor . . . . Phyllis Galloway
Chrissie White . . . . Peasant
WAR "Dead" soldier poses as Belgian refugee
and returns home in time for Christmas.

06601
TARES (1625) (A)
Hepworth (Moss)
D: Cecil M. Hepworth
S: E. Temple Thurston
Henry Edwards . . . . M Colin
Alma Taylor . . . . Mme Colin
WAR Belgium. Baker shot for refusing to
supply Germans, and his wife is raped and kills
herself.

SEP

06602
WHERE'S THE KEY? (2158)(U)
Harma Photoplays
D: James Reardon
S: Reuben Gillmer
James Reardon . . . . Perks
Peggy Patterson . . . . Mrs O'Grady
COMEDY Lawyer poses as girl to retrieve safe
key from girl's dress.

06603
THE ELEVENTH HOUR (2185)(A)
Film Company of Ireland
D: Fred O'Donovan
Brian Magowan . . . . The Man
Kathleen Murphy . . . . The Girl
DRAMA

06604
THE ADVENTURES OF EVE (series)IU)
Gaumont
D: J.L.V. Leigh
S: (CARTOONS) Miss Fish (THE TATLER)
Eileen Molyneux . . . . Eve
Pat Somerset . . . . Adam
Cecil Morton York . . . . Uncle Fred

06605
ADAM AS A SPECIAL CONSTABLE (667)

06606
EVE ADOPTS A LONELY SOLDIER (686)

06607
EVE AND THE INTERNEMENT QUESTION
(588)

06608
EVE AND THE NERVOUS CURATE (588)

06609
EVE AS MRS ADAM (850)

06610
EVE ASSISTS THE CENSOR (605)

06611
EVE OUTWITS ARTFUL ADAM (767)

06612
EVE RESOLVES TO DO WAR WORK (730)

06613
EVE GOES TO THE EAST COAST (795)

06614
EVE'S BURGLAR (500)

06615
HOW EVE HELPED THE WAR FUND (665)

06616
EVE IN THE COUNTRY (456)
COMEDIES

06617
THE ELDER MISS BLOSSOM (5000) USA:
WANTED A WIFE
G.B. Samuelson (Sun)
D: Percy Nash
S: (PLAY) Ernest Hendrie, Metcalfe Wood
Isobel Elsom . . . . Sophie Blossom
Owen Nares . . . . Curate
C.M. Hallard . . . . Andrew Quick
Minna Grey . . . . Dolly Blossom
Tom Reynolds . . . .
ROMANCE Aunt disillusioned when she learns
explorer's loveletter was meant for niece.

06618
THE MASTER OF GRAY (5000)
Monarch
D:S: Tom Watts
Athalie Davis . . . . Jenny
Harry Clifford . . . . Master of Gray
Ethel Douglas Ross . . . . Mountain Girl
Ernest A. Douglas . . . . Auld Robin Gray
Little Rex . . . . Shadow
ROMANCE Scotland, 1860. Wild girl seduced
by laird weds old man who drowns himself on
learning she loves another.

06619
A TURF CONSPIRACY (5600)(U)
Broadwest (Granger)
P: Walter West
D: Frank Wilson
S: (NOVEL) Nat Gould
SC: Bannister Merwin
Violet Hopson . . . . Madge Iman
Gerald Ames . . . . Gordon Chorley
Joan Legge . . . . Olga Bell
Cameron Carr . . . . Supt Ladson
Arthur Walcott . . . . Jack Rook
Windham Guise . . . . Tilston
Tom Coventry . . . . Abe Wrench
Frank Wilson . . . . Dick Bell
W.R. Harrison . . . . Det Thawton
SPORT Betting ring hires widow to keep stable
under their control.

06620
THE TOP DOG (6250)
Windsor (Walturdaw)
D: Arrigo Bocchi
S: (NOVEL) Fergus Hume
SC: Kenelm Foss
Kenelm Foss . . . . Jerry Perris
Odette Goimbault . . . . Margaret Drum
Hayford Hobbs . . . . Dick Drum
Evelyn Harding . . . . Mlle Cibot
Charles Vane . . . . Sir Gregory Horne
Edward O'Neill . . . . The Octopus
Douglas Munro . . . . Mr Margin
Bert Wynne . . . . Pedro Medina
Clive Currie . . . . Giles
CRIME Novelist becomes secretary to knight
who is framed by governess for killing Spaniard.

06621
KILTIES THREE (5819) (U)
Gaiety (Gau)
P:D: Maurice Sandground
S: Bernard Merivale
Bob Reed . . . . Kiltie
Rowland Hill . . . . Kiltie
Robert Vallis . . . . Kiltie
Ernest Esdaile . . . . Otto Klein
Gladys Foyle . . . . Mary Strong
Scott Layton . . . . Silas Strong
Phyllis Beadon . . . . Mrs Strong
WAR Edinburgh foundry owner weds German
spy's widow who becomes nurse.

06622
DECEPTION (5544)(U)
Harma Photoplays
D: A.C. Hunter
S: Reuben Gillmer
James Knight . . . . Jeffrey North
Rose Manners . . . . Tuesday North
Charles Rock . . . . Jeffrey North
Frank Gerrard . . . . Capt Hawkes
Maud Yates . . . . Mrs North
Leal Douglas . . . .
Arthur Cullin . . . .
Maxine Hunter . . . .
CRIME Capt persuades rich man's niece to run
gambling game and then involves her in
murder.

06623
HEAR THE PIPERS CALLING (5000)
Grenville-Taylor
D: Tom Watts
S: H. Grenville-Taylor
Hilda Oldfield . . . .
ROMANCE Scotland.

OCT

06624
TOWARDS THE LIGHT (5950)(U)
Hepworth (Moss)
D:S: Henry Edwards

Henry Edwards	Surly
Chrissie White	Annie Wilton
A.V. Bramble	Convict 65
Marsh Allen	Rex Richards
Henry Vibart	Rev Thorne
George Traill	Neighbour
John MacAndrews	Villager

DRAMA Hunchbacked atheist weds girl whose father breaks jail to prove innocence.

06625
THE KEY OF THE WORLD (6202)(U)
Gaumont
D: J.L.V. Leigh
S: (NOVEL) Dorin Craig
SC: Helen Blizzard

Eileen Molyneux	Honesty Vethick
Heather Thatcher	Drina Destin
Eric Harrison	Garth Berry
Pat Somerset	Evelyn Carew
Lionel D'Aragon	Liston Crawley
Cecil Morton York	Adam
H. Hamilton Stewart	Earl of Carne
Florence Nelson	Lady Boddy
Frank Harris	Farmer Berry

ROMANCE Devon. Solicitor pretends farmer is heir to earldom.

06626
IT'S HAPPINESS THAT COUNTS (4531)(U)
BP Films (Butcher)
P:D: Bertram Phillips

Queenie Thomas	Prudence
Harry Drummond	Richard Blair
Ralph Hollis	Galahad Sanctuary

ROMANCE Man forsakes wealth to wed tomboy whose father was ruined by riches.

06627
A GIRL OF GLENBEIGH (2195)(U)
Film Co of Ireland
D: J.M. Kerrigan

Fred O'Donovan	Maurice Blake
Kathleen Murphy	Kathleen O'Connor
Irene Murphy	Nora Ashe

ROMANCE

06628
DEMOCRACY (6000)
Progress (Butcher)
P: Frank E. Spring
D:S: Sidney Morgan

Bruce Gordon	George Greig
Alice O'Brien	Diana Tudworth
Frank Dane	Gerald Tudworth
Alice Russon	Rose Greig
Alice de Winton	Lady Tudworth
Wyndham Guise	Sutton Tudworth
Jack Andrews	Daniel Greig
Mrs Hubert Willis	Mary Greig

WAR Labourer's son enlists and save life of squire's son who seduced his sister.

06629
WHAT A LIFE! (2400)(U)
Harma *reissue:* 1921 (Sherwood)
D: James Reardon
S: Reuben Gillmer

James Reardon	Mr Box
Leal Douglas	Mrs Box
Maxine Hunter	Anita
Peggy Patterson	
Nellie Jackson	
Maude Harris	
Trevor Eaton	

COMEDY Newlywed persuades golfing friend to take blame for his past.

06630
KISS ME (2582)(U)
Harma *reissue:* 1921 (Sherwood)
D: James Reardon
S: Reuben Gillmer

James Reardon	Mr Wick
Leal Douglas	Mrs Wick
Peggy Patterson	
Trevor Eaton	
Dora Henwood	

COMEDY Seaside girls mistake married man for representative giving prizes for kisses.

06631
ROSES OF PICARDY (4000)
Union Photoplays
P: David Rosenfeld
CRIME Actress loves an engineer whose hydroplane is stolen by spies.

06632
MRS JOHN BULL PREPARED (500)
MOI Cinematograph Dept
DRAMA Business man sleeps 4 years and the Spirit of Womanhood shows him how women now work.

06633
INNS AND OUTS (1000)
Fred Evans (Horder)
D:S: Fred Evans, Joe Evans

Fred Evans	Pimple
Joe Evans	

COMEDY

NOV

06634
A SHEFFIELD BLADE (5000)
British Pictures
D: Harry Roberts, Joseph Jay Bamberger
S: A.G. Hales
SC: Joseph Jay Bamberger

George Foley	Billy Baxter
Jill Willis	Ruth Roland

DRAMA Factory owner's son poses as workman and invents rustless knife.

06635
THE WOMAN WINS (5500)(U)
Broadwest (Granger)
P: Walter West
D: Frank Wilson
S: (NOVEL) Cecil H. Bullivant
SC: R. Byron-Webber, Kenelm Foss

Violet Hopson	Brenda Marsh
Trevor Bland	Hugh Fraser
Cameron Carr	Raymond Vascour
George Dewhurst	Hadley Barfield
Arthur Walcott	John Farley
S. Creagh Henry	Justin Marsh
J. Hastings Batson	Admiral Fraser
Vera Cornish	Mrs Fane

CRIME Man usurps his bastard's legacy by exchanging her for dead baby and later framing her lover for forgery.

06636
GOD BLESS OUR RED, WHITE AND BLUE (5000)
G.B. Samuelson (Jury)
D: Rex Wilson
S: G.B. Samuelson

Isobel Elsom	The Wife
Owen Nares	Thomas Atkinson
Madge Titheridge	The Nurse
J. Fisher White	John Hargreaves
G.H. Mulcaster	The Fianceee
Marie Wright	The Woman
Martin Lewis	The Son

WAR Pensioner visits neglectful son; nurse meets soldier fiance in France; duke enlists as private.

06637
THE KIDDIES IN THE RUINS (2600)(U)
Welsh-Pearson (Jury)
P:D:SC: George Pearson
S: (PLAY) Paul Grex, M. Poulbot (LES GOSSES DANS LES RUINES)

Emmy Lynn	Francoise Regnard
Hugh E. Wright	Tommy
Georges Colin	Maurice Regnard
Simone Prevost	Nini
Georges Merouze	Jeannot
Mme Jalabert	Grandma

WAR France. Orphaned children help lost British private. (Made at Epinay).

06638
NATURE'S GENTLEMAN (5085)(U)
Harma Photoplays
D: F. Martin Thornton
S: Reuben Gillmer

James Knight	James Davis
Madge Stuart	Lady Harcourt
Arthur Cullin	Sir Herbert Waring
Cameron Carr	
Frank E. Petley	
Edna Moore	
Frank Gerrard	
Diana Moncrieff	

ROMANCE Millionaire's valet will inherit fortune if he weds lord's niece.

06639
SISTERS IN ARMS (1000)
Broadwest
P.D: Walter West

Violet Hopson	WRAF Girl
Hazel Jones	WRNS Girl
Hilda Bayley	WAAC Girl

WAR Recruiting film.

06640
A CHRISTMAS STORY (1000)
Eric Williams Speaking Pictures
S: (POEM) Fred Weatherley

Eric Williams	

DRAMA Shown while Eric Williams recites from cinema stage.

06641
GOODBYE 1918 (250)
Cinema Supply Service

Mona Moore	1919

DRAMA Christmas greeting from exhibitors to patrons.

06642
THE WAGES OF SIN (5190) (A)
Windsor (Walturdaw)
D: Arrigo Bocchi
S: (NOVEL) Lucas Malet
SC: Kenelm Foss

Kenelm Foss	James Colthurst
Odette Goimbault	Mary Crookender
Mary Marsh Allen	Jenny Parris
Hayford Hobbs	Lance Crookende
Charles Vane	Cyprian Aldham
Edward O'Neill	Bill Parris
Bert Wynne	Steve Kingdom
Arthur Walcott	Isaacstein
Judd Green	Wilmot
Harry Lofting	Capt Prust

ROMANCE Devon. Fishergirl's father pushes philandering artist over cliff.

06643
ONWARD CHRISTIAN SOLDIERS (5000)
G.B. Samuelson
D: Rex Wilson

Isobel Elsom	The Girl
Owen Nares	The Soldier
Minna Grey	The Sister
Tom Reynolds	The Man

ROMANCE Plain girl sends sister's picture to soldier penpal and weds him when he is blinded.

DEC

06644
BOUNDARY HOUSE (5250)(U)
Hepworth (Moss)
D: Cecil M. Hepworth
S: (NOVEL) Peggy Webling
Alma Taylor . . . . Jenny Gay
Gerald Ames . . . . Cherry Ricardo
William Felton . . . . Old Fob
Victor Prout . . . . Henry Gay
John Mc Andrews . . . . Ricardo
Gwynne Herbert . . . . Miss Gay
DRAMA Miser forces girl to marry him and
pose as his dead wife who was her double.

06645
PEACE, PERFECT PEACE (2000)
Windsor (Walturdaw)
D: Arrigo Bocchi
S: Kenelm Foss
Hayford Hobbs . . . . Poilu
Odette Goimbault . . . . Marie Odette
Mary Marsh Allen . . . . Mrs Atkins
Charles Vane . . . . Pensioner
Bert Wynne . . . . Tommy Atkins
Evelyn Harding . . . . Mother
Mme Goimbault . . . . Mme Odette
Chubby Hobbs . . . . Child
WAR Armistice permits British and French
soldiers to return home in time to solve
problems.

06646
NOT NEGOTIABLE (3500)(A)
Broadwest
D: Walter West
S: Kenelm Foss
Julian Royce . . . . John Carslake
Manora Thew . . . . Dorothy Saville
Gregory Scott . . . . Claude Saville
Hubert Woodward . . . . James Coglan
Arthur Walcott . . . .
Helen Haye . . . .
CRIME Man forges guardian's cheque to swindle
financier who turns out to be his father.

06647
THE GREAT GAME (6000)(A)
I.B. Davidson (Ruffells)
D:SC: A.E. Coleby
S: (NOVEL) Andrew Soutar (THE
STRAIGHT GAME)
Bdr Billy Wells . . . . John Cranston
A.E. Coleby . . . .
Ernest A. Douglas . . . .
Judd Green . . . .
H. Nicholls-Bates . . . .
Eve Marchew . . . .
SPORT Squire's son must win turf Blue Riband
to inherit fortune.

06648
BONNIE MARY (5000)
Master Films (Int Ex)
P: Low Warren
D: A.V. Bramble
S: Herbert Pemberton
SC: Eliot Stannard
Miriam Ferris . . . . Mary Douglas
Leon Belcher . . . . Rob McAllister
Arthur Cullin . . . . Andrew Douglas
Jeff Barlow . . . . James McAllister
Elaine Madison . . . . Jeannie Douglas
ROMANCE Scotland. Feud between laird and
farmer ends when children marry.

06649
A PEEP BEHIND THE SCENES (5000)
Master Films (New Bio)
P: Low Warren
D: Geoffrey H. Malins, Kenelm Foss
S: (NOVEL) Mrs. O.F. Walton
SC: Kenelm Foss
Ivy Close . . . . Norah Joyce
Gerald Ames . . . . Augustus Joyce
Gertrude Bain . . . . Lucy Leslie
Vera Bryer . . . . Rosalie Joyce
Kenneth Gore . . . . Toby Charlton
E. Blackton . . . . Mother Manikin
DRAMA Girl elopes with actor, dies when he
deserts her, and their child walks home to her
aunt.

06650
NELSON (7000)
Master-International Exclusives (Apex)
P: Low Warren
D: Maurice Elvey
S: (BOOK) Robert Southey (THE LIFE OF
NELSON)
SC: Eliot Stannard
Donald Calthrop . . . . Horatio Nelson
Malvina Longfellow . . . . Lady Hamilton
Ivy Close . . . . Mrs Nesbit
Ernest Thesiger . . . . William Pitt
Allan Jeayes . . . . Sir William Hamilton
Edward O'Neill . . . . King of Naples
Teddy Arundell . . . . Capt Berry
Eric Barker . . . . Nelson (child)
Judd Green . . . .
Sir Edmund Freemantle . . . .
HISTORY 1794-1805. Lord Nelson's life, loves,
and death.

06651
THE MAN WHO WON (6000)
G.B. Samuelson (Granger)
D: Rex Wilson
S: (NOVEL) Mrs. Baillie Reynolds
Isobel Elsom . . . . Milly Cooper
Owen Nares . . . . Capt Bert Brook
John Kelt . . . . Rev Chetwood Cooper
Annie Esmond . . . . Mrs Cooper
ROMANCE Proud architect learns vicar's
daughter is adopted, so she weds workman who
inherits fortune.

06652
GEORGE ROBEY'S DAY OFF (2000)
Kinsella and Morgan (Stoll)
D:S: E.P. Kinsella, Horace Morgan
George Robey . . . . Himself
Norman Howard
Dora Gregory
Hargrave Mansell
Nina Oldfield
Basil Griffen
Beryl Maude
Countess Tolstoi
COMEDY Day in the life of a comedian.

06653
BETTA THE GYPSY (4100)(A)
Famous Productions (Butcher)
D: Charles Raymond
S: (OPERA) Edward Waltyre
SC: Edith Mellor
Marga la Rubia . . . . Betta
Malvina Longfellow . . . . Alesky
George Foley . . . . Tempestro
Edward Combermere . . . . . . Hubert
Frank Dane . . . .
Barbara Gott . . . .
ROMANCE Wales. Gipsy queen changes sister's
dead baby for one by same father; child grows
up to marry her daughter.

06654
THE FOUNDATIONS OF FREEDOM (6000)
Birmingham Film Producing Co.
D:S: Arthur Branscombe
Maud Yates . . . . Jane Butler
Cecil Morton York . . . . . . Col Washington Butler
HISTORY Romance between English and
American families connected with Washington
and Franklin.

06655
CHEATED VENGEANCE
Britamer
D: Maurice Earle Balk
S: Maurice Earle Balk, H.V. Emery
Maurice Earle Balk
Connie Sweet
Doris Vivian Earle
E. James Morrison
CRIME

06656
WILLY REILLY AND HIS COLLEEN
BAWN (5000)
Film Co of Ireland
D: Fred O'Donovan
S: (PLAY Charles Kickham (THE HOMES OF
TIPPERARY)
Brian Magowan . . . . Willy Reilly
Kathleen Murphy . . . . The Colleen
DRAMA (Not shown in Britain)

06657
THE LIFE STORY OF DAVID LLOYD
GEORGE (6000)
Ideal
D: Maurice Elvey
S: Sir Sydney Low
Norman Page . . . . David Lloyd George
Alma Reville . . . . Megan Lloyd George
Ernest Thesiger . . . . Joseph Chamberlain
Douglas Munro . . . . Benjamin Disraeli
Thomas Canning . . . .
Judd Green . . . .
Winifred Sadler . . . .
Miriam Stuart . . . .
Eric Stuart . . . .
Leonard Tugwell . . . .
HISTORY Biography of Welsh politician. (Not
shown).

06658
VICTORY AND PEACE (8000)
National War Aims Committee
D: Herbert Brenon
S: Hall Caine
Matheson Lang . . . . Edward Arkwright
Marie Lohr . . . . Barbara Rowntree
James Carew . . . . Karl Hoffman
Ellen Terry . . . . Widow Weaver
Renee Mayer . . . . Jenny Banks
Hayford Hobbs . . . . Charlie Caine
Fred Kerr . . . . Sir Richard Arkwright
Jose Collins . . . . Madge Brierley
Sam Livesey . . . . Capt Schiff
Edith Craig . . . . Mary Rowntree
Bertram Wallis . . . . Bob Brierley
Ben Greet . . . . Mayor of Castleton
Harding Thomas . . . . Jim Banks
Arthur Applin . . . . Capt von Lindheimer
Henry Vibart . . . . Bishop
Sydney Lewis Ransome . . . . Sgt Schiff
Joyce Templeton . . . . Joyce Brierley
Helena Millais . . . . Liz Lowery
Rolf Leslie . . . . Abraham Lincoln
WAR Nurse saves captain from invading Germans
and is saved herself when he leads counter-
attack (Not shown).

1919

JAN

06659
BROKEN IN THE WARS (400)
Hepworth
D: Cecil M. Hepworth
Henry Edwards . . . . Joe
Chrissie White . . . . Mrs Joe
Alma Taylor . . . . Lady Dorothea
John Hodge MP . . . . Himself
DRAMA Lady introduces wounded cobbler to
Minister of Pensions, who makes him gift from
King's Fund.

06660
HIS DEAREST POSSESSION (5150)(A)
Hepworth
D: Henry Edwards
S: E. Temple Thurston
Henry Edwards . . . . Stephen Ayliff
Chrissie White . . . . Red Emma Lobb
John McAndrews . . . . Herbert Lobb
Esme Hubbard . . . . Mrs Lobb
Gwynne Herbert . . . . The Cottager
Eric Barker . . . . Charlie Lobb
DRAMA Poor artist weds socialist's daughter and
becomes sandwich-board man to provide for
their baby.

06661
AS HE WAS BORN (4865)
Butcher's Film Service
D: SC: Wilfred Noy
P: F.W. Baker
S: (PLAY) Tom Gallon, Leon M. Lion
(FELIX GETS A MONTH)
Stanley Logan . . . . Felix Delaney
Odette Goimbault . . . . Ninette Monday
Mary Dibley . . . . Evelyn Garland
Will Corrie . . . . Soper
Athol Ford . . . . Dr Twentyman
Nellie Dangerfield . . . . Mrs Twentyman
Stanley Turnbull . . . . The Mayor
Jeff Barlow . . . . The Solicitor
COMEDY Mayor's son inherits if he lives a
month without help.

06662
PALLARD THE PUNTER (6600)(A)
Gaumont
D: J.L.V. Leigh
S: (NOVEL) Edgar Wallace (GREY TIMOTHY)
SC: George Pearson
Jack Leigh . . . . Brian Pallard
Heather Thatcher . . . . Gladys Callender
Lionel d'Aragon . . . . Lord Pinlow
Cecil Morton York . . . . Peter Callender
Cyril Smith . . . . Horace Callender
SPORT Sportsman prevents Lord from killing
favourite with tsetse fly.

06663
AFTER MANY DAYS (6000)
Progress (Butcher)
P: Frank E. Spring
D:S: Sidney Morgan
Bruce Gordon . . . . Paul Irving
Alice Russon . . . . Marion Bramleyn
Irene Brown . . . . Connie
Adeline Hayden Coffin . . . . Mrs Irving
DRAMA Girl thinks artist fathered model's
baby, but learns it is child of his burglar
brother.

06664
ALL MEN ARE LIARS (4800)
Progress (Butcher)
P: Frank E. Spring

D:SC: Sidney Morgan
S: (NOVEL) Joseph Hocking
Alice Russon . . . . Hope
Bruce Gordon . . . . Stephen
Jessie Earle . . . .: . . . . Isobel
George Harrington . . . . Luke
DRAMA Uncle makes son of East End
missionary marry vain woman.

06665
THE SOUL OF GUILDA LOIS (5500) (A)
retitled : A SOUL'S CRUCIFIXION
Broadwest (Granger)
P: Walter West
D: Frank Wilson
S: (NOVEL) Newman Flower (CRUCIFIXION)
SC: Kenelm Foss
Violet Hopson . . . . Guilda Lois
Basil Gill . . . . Julian Neave
Cameron Carr . . . . Paul Brian
Richard Buttery . . . . Dicky Tremayne
Clifford Pembroke . . . . Major Hardene
J. Hastings Batson . . . . Gregoire
Hilda Bayley . . . .
DRAMA Brittany. Surgeon leaves mistress and
baby after learning she has caused couple to
commit suicide.

06666
THE HOMEMAKER (5000)
Dewhurst Productions *reissue*: 1920
(Equitable)
D: George Dewhurst
S: Donovan Bayley
Manora Thew . . . . Lysbeth
Basil Gill . . . . Wilbur Benson
Gwynne Herbert . . . ʱ. . . . Lady Sturdy
Peggy Patterson . . . . Esther
Jeff Barlow . . . .
Lottie Blackford . . . .
Nessie Blackford . . . .
ROMANCE Rich husband deserts socialite and
becomes village blacksmith.

06667
THE SILVER GREYHOUND (4775) (U)
Harma Photoplays
P: Harry Maze Jenks
D: S: Bannister Merwin
James Knight . . . . John Vane
Marjorie Villis . . . . Nance Lisle
Mary Dibley . . . . Lady Chalmore
Frank E. Petley . . . . The Master
Jeff Barlow. . . . .
Clifford Pembroke . . . .
Charles Ashley . . . . Lord Chalmore
Dallas Cairns . . . .
Hamilton Stewart . . . .
Frank Gerrard . . . .
CRIME Girl helps King's Messenger regain secret
plans from spy who is her father.

06668
COMRADESHIP (6000)
Stoll
D: Maurice Elvey
S: Louis N. Parker
SC: Jeffrey Bernerd
Lily Elsie . . . . Betty Mortimore
Gerald Ames . . . . Bob Armstrong
Guy Newall . . . . .Lt. Baring
Dallas Cairns . . . . Leibmann
Peggy Carlisle . . . . Peggy
Teddy Arundell . . . . Ginger Dickens
Kate Gurney . . . . Housekeeper
WAR Pacifist enlists and is blinded while his friend
weds shopgirl who was seduced by German spy.

06669
THE LACKEY AND THE LADY (5000)
British Actors (Phillips)
D: SC: Thomas Bentley
S: (NOVEL) Tom Gallon
Odette Goimbault . . . .
Roy Travers . . . .
Leslie Howard . . . . Tony Dunciman
Alban Attwood . . . . Mr. Dunciman
A.E. Matthews . . . .
Violet Graham . . . .
Pope Stamper . . . . Garrett Woodruffe
Adelaide Grace . . . .
Jeff Barlow . . . .
Gladys Foyle . . . .
DRAMA Rich banker's eldest daughter marries
servant.

FEB

06670
WHOSOEVER SHALL OFFEND (5900) (A)
Windsor (Walturdaw)
D: Arrigo Bocchi
S: (NOVEL) Marion Crawford
SC: Kenelm Foss
Kenelm Foss . . . . Guido folco
Odette Goimbault . . . . Aurora
Mary Marsh Allen . . . . Regina
Hayford Hobbs . . . . Marcello Consalvi
Evelyn Harding . . . . Signora Consalvi
Charles Vane . . . . Ercole
Maud Cressall . . . . Countess Del Armi
Barbara Everest . . . . Maddalena
Philip Hewland . . . . Prof. Kalmon
Joyce Templeton . . . . Regina (child)
CRIME Italy. Wife-murderer weds rich widow
and tries to kill her.

06671
THE IRRESISTIBLE FLAPPER (3800) (A)
Broadwest (Granger)
P: Walter West
D: Frank Wilson
S: Percy Gordon Holmes
Violet Hopson . . . . Gladys Standish
Ivy Close . . . . Audrey Tremayne
Gerald Ames . . . . Victor Standish
Basil Gill . . . . Ormande Yorke
Charles Vane . . . . Sir Neville Tremayne
Ruby Belasco . . . . Miss Frewin
Iveah Stanley . . . . Camille
Mme d'Esterre . . . . Lady Tremayne
Frank Wilson . . . . Vicar
COMEDY Girl takes blame for married sister when
her earing is found in actor's room.

06672
HER LONELY SOLDIER (5000)
Barker (New Bio)
P: Jack W. Smith
D: Percy Nash
S: Irene Miller
Daphne Glenne . . . . Veronica
Dulcie Parsons . . . . Kitterkins de Vere
Eva Brooke . . . .
Suzanne Morris . . . .
ROMANCE Spinster sends sister's photograph to
soldier, whose friend poses as him.

06673
THE CASE OF A DOPED ACTRESS (2000)
Life Dramas (National)
D: Wilfred Carlton
Clare Barrington . . . . Bobbie Barton
Walter Drake . . . . Dr. Edwards
F.E. Harrison . . . . Hubert Van Dorl
Ella Dore . . . . Mrs. Van Dorl
CRIME Agent causes actress's death by inducing
her to take opium.

06674
RUSSIA - LAND OF TOMORROW (5000)
Gaiety
P:D: Maurice Sandground
S: Bernard Merivale
Eve Balfour . . . . Anna Cargill
A.B. Imeson . . . . The Baron
Clifford Cobbe . . . . Lord Cargill
Bob Reed . . . .
Mr. Bayton
DRAMA Lord's Russian wife returns home for
revolution and is used by German baron.

06675
YE BANKS AND BRAES (5000)
Regal
D: Tom Watts
Ethel Douglas Ross . . . . Jean
John Jenson . . . . Angus MacDonald
Daisy Jackson . . . . The Wife
ROMANCE Scots girl follows nobleman to
London and returns after discovering he is already
married.

MAR

06676
A NON-CONFORMIST PARSON (6500) (A)
retitled: HEART AND SOUL
British Lion (Moss)
P: David Falcke
D: A.V. Bramble
S: (Novel) Roy Horniman
SC: Eliot Stannard
Gwen Williams . . . . Mary Hackett
George Keene . . . . Joshua Reed
Constance Worth . . . . Jessie Hackett
Evan Thomas . . . . Harry Yule
Arthur Cullin . . . . Mr. Hackett
E. Story Gofton . . . . Dr. Bright
CRIME Artist frames parson for poisoning his
wife.

06677
SO LIKE HIM (2370) (A)
Harma Photoplays
D: James Reardon
S: Reuben Gillmer
James Reardon . . . . Husband
Peggy Patterson . . . . Wife
COMEDY Husband poses as his double to take
girl out to dine.

06678
HER HERITAGE (5000)
Ward's Films
D: Bannister Merwin
S: Arthur Weigell
Jack Buchanan . . . . Bob Hales
Phyllis Monkman . . . . Lady Mary Strode
E. Holman Clark . . . . Gerald Pridling
Edward O'Neill . . . . Lord Heston
Winifred Dennis . . . . Mrs. Wilter
CRIME Artist helps lady posing as maid to steal
her letters from blackmailing cousin.

06679
NOT GUILTY (5429) (A)
Windsor (Walturdaw)
D: Arrigo Bocchi
S: Kenelm Foss
Kenelm Foss . . . . Sir Graham Carfax
Charles Vane . . . . Andrew McTaggart
Hayford Hobbs . . . . Donald McTaggart
Olive Atkinson . . . . Minnie Day
Barbara Everest . . . . Hetty Challis
Bert Wynne . . . . Tom Dent
Evelyn Harding . . . . Matron
Philip Hewland . . . . Dillingham
COMEDY Barrister defends himself when caught
tricking mean millionaire into donating for charity.

06680
TO LET (1788) (U)
Harma Photoplays
D: James Reardon
S: Reuben Gillmer
James Reardon . . . . Mr. Briggs
Peggy Patterson . . . . Mrs. Briggs
James Prior . . . . Husband
Ida Fane . . . . Wife
COMEDY Retired conjuror tries to scare couple
from his house.

06681
HER CROSS (5000)
Master Films (Screen Plays)
P: H.B. Parkinson
D: A.V. Bramble
S: Eliot Stannard
Ivy Close . . . . Bess
Lionel Belcher . . . . Gould
C. Hargreave Mansell . . . . . Tom Gould
Alice de Winton . . . . Lavender Hathaway
Vivian Harboard . . . . Parson
DRAMA Blind carpenter adopts waif who weds
his cruel son but loves parson;

06682
THE ROMANCE OF LADY HAMILTON
(7000) (A)
Famous Pictures (Phillips)
D: Bert Haldane
S: Kenelm Foss
Malvina Longfellow . . . . . . Emma Cadogan
Humberston Wright . . . . . . Horatio Nelson
Cecil Humphreys . . . . Charles Greville
Jane Powell . . . . Irene Greville
Teddy Arundell . . . . Prince Of Wales
Barbara Gott . . . . Mrs Kelly
Frank Dane . . . . King of Naples
Maud Yates . . . . Queen of Naples
Will Corri . . . . Featherstonehaugh
Irene Tripod . . . . Mrs. Budd
HISTORY Aged ambassador's wife loves admiral
but is rejected by society after his death.

06683
THE POWER OF RIGHT (4340) (U)
Harma Photoplays
D: F. Martin Thornton
S: Reuben Gillmer
James Knight . . . . Gerald Stafford
Evelyn Boucher . . . . Elsie Vigor
Frank E. Petley . . . . Danvers
Leslie Reardon . . . . Leslie Stafford
Marjorie Villis . . . .
Adeline Hayden Coffin . . . .
Sidney Grant . . . .
Clifford Pembroke . . . .
John Gliddon . . . .
Prince of Wales . . . . Himself
WAR Interned German escapes and is killed by
colonel's cadet son.

06684
THE WARRIOR STRAIN (3393) (U)
Harma Photoplays
D:S: F. Martin Thornton
Sydney Wood . . . . Lord Billy
H. Agar Lyons . . . . Sir William Halsford
Evelyn Boucher . . . . Mother
James Edwards Barber . . . . Baron Housen
William Parry . . . . Stocker
Mrs. Frank Petley . . . . Governess
Prince of Wales . . . . Himself
WAR Earl's cadet son stops German baron from
planting wireless-controlled signals at Brighton.

06685
CONVICT 99 (6075) (U)
G.B. Samuelson (Granger)
D: G.B. Samuelson

S: (NOVEL) Marie Connor, Robert Leighton
C.M. Hallard . . . . Ralph Vickers
Daisy Burrell . . . . Geraldine Lucas
Wee Georgie Wood . . . . . . James
Ernest A. Graham . . . . Laurence Gray
Wyndham Guise . . . . Mr. Lucas
Tom Coventry . . . . Hewett
Arnold Bell . . . . Warder Gannaway
CRIME Framed clerk freed after saving cruel
warder's daughter.

06686
QUINNEYS (6000)
G.B. Samuelson (Granger)
D: Rex Wilson
S: (PLAY) Horace Annesley Vachell
SC: Roland Pertwee
Henry Ainley . . . . Joe Quinney
Isobel Elsom . . . . Posy Quinney
Eric Harrison . . . . James Miggott
Tom Reynolds . . . . Sam Tomlin
Marie Wright . . . . Mabel Dredge
Roland Pertwee . . . . Cyrus Hunsacker
ROMANCE Antique dealer's daughter loves
foreman who sells fakes to ex-partner

06687
KEEPER OF THE DOOR (5466)
Stoll
D: Maurice Elvey
S: (NOVEL) Ethel M. Dell
SC: R. Byron-Webber
Basil Gill . . . . Max Wyndham
Peggy Carlisle . . . . Olga Ratsliffe
Hamilton Stewart . . . . Nick Ratcliffe
Marjorie Hume . . . . Violet Campion
George Harrington . . . . . . Dr. Ratcliffe
Ivo Dawson . . . . J. Hunt Goring
DRAMA Dr's daughter has amnesia after poisoning
mad friend and recovers on meeting her ex-lover
who saved her brother's sight.

06688
12-10 (4894) (A)
B & C (World)
P: Edward Godal
D: Herbert Brenon
S: Earle Carroll
SC: George Edwardes Hall
Marie Doro . . . . Marie Fernando
Ben Webster . . . . Lord Chatterton
Geoffrey Kerr . . . . Geoffrey Brooke
James Carew . . . . Arthur Newton
Fred Kerr . . . . Dr. Wrightman
CRIME Lord fakes death with life-suspending drug
to stop secretary from killing adopted orphan.

06689
WOMEN WHO WIN (6000)
T.H. Davison
D: Percy Nash, Fred W. Durrant
S: (NOVEL) Mrs. E. Almaz Stout
SC: Percy Nash
Unity More . . . . Betty Graham
Mary Dibley . . . . Margaret Graham
Mary Forbes . . . . Ella Graham
Minna Grey . . . . Mrs Graham
Stanley T. Barrie . . . . Dr Richard Seaton
Lloyd Morgan . . . . Harry Travers
Phyllis Villiers . . . . Miss Wilson
Alice de Winton . . . .
Rachel de Solla . . . .
Frank Adair . . . .
Frank G. Richardson . . . . . .
Queen Mary; Queen Alexandra; Princess Victoria;
Princess Patricia; The Crown Princess of Sweden.
DRAMA Widow and daughters join Women's
Service Training Bureau and become nurse,
journalist, and landscape gardener.

06690 *
THE TOILERS (5000)
Diamond Super Neville Bruce)
D: Tom W. Watts
S: Eliot Stannard
Manora Thew . . . . Rose
George Dewhurst . . . . Jack
Gwynne Herbert . . . . Mother
Ronald Colman . . . . Bob
Eric Barker . . . . Jack (child)
John Corrie . . . . Lighthouse-keeper
Mollie Terraine . . . . Merchant's Daughter
ROMANCE Fisherman's widow adopts bastard
who leaves her for flighty socialite.

06691
THE LAUNDRY GIRL (4570) (U)
Hooper-Mellor *reissue:* 1921, BECAUSE
(Renters)
D: Albert G. Frenguelli, Edith Mellor
S: (OPERETTA) Edward Waltyre
SC: Edith Mellor
Margaret Campbell . . . . . Lady Winifred Stockholm
Geoffrey Wilmer . . . . Lord Cecil Brabazon
Ida Fane . . . . Moggy Pailings
John Glidden . . . . Lord Sefton
ROMANCE Runaway schoolgirl poses as laundress,
leaves Lord she marries, has baby and returns to
school.

06692
THE GREATER LOVE (5700)
Garrick (Pioneer)
D: Geoffrey H. Malins
S. Esmond O'Donnell
Ena Beaumont . . . . Joyce Henderson
Victor Robson . . . . Lionel Dale
Leslie Barrie . . . . Bob Henderson
Charles Rock . . . . Mr Lakey
Arthur Cullin . . . . Sir Reynold Henderson
Adeline Hayden Coffin . . . Lady Henderson
CRIME Bart's son uses forged fingerprints to
frame sister's fiance.

MAY
06693
A LITTLE BIT OF FLUFF (5000)
Q Films (Ruffells)
P: Jack Clair, Leonide Zarine
D: SC: Kenelm Foss
S: (PLAY) Walter Ellis
Ernest Thesiger . . . . Bertram Tully
Dorothy Minto . . . . Mamie Scott
Bertie Wright . . . . John Ayers
Kitty Barlow . . . . Pamela Ayers
James Lindsay . . . . Aunt Agnes
Alfred Drayton . . . . Dr Bigland
Stanley Lathbury . . . . Nixon Trippett
COMEDY Flirt's troubles with dancer's necklace
and suspicious wife.

06694
DAMAGES FOR BREACH (2000)
Windsor (Walturdaw)
D: Arrigo Bocchi
S: Kenelm Foss
Kenelm Foss . . . . Freddie
Manora Thew . . . .
Hayford Hobbs . . . .
Evelyn Harding . . . .
COMEDY Bachelor, sued by numerous fiancees,
marries cook;

06695
THE LIFE OF A LONDON ACTRESS (5000)
Barker (Urban)
P: Jack W. Smith
D: Alexander Butler
S: Irene Miller
Daphne Glenne . . . . Daphne Darling
James Lindsay . . . . Slade
Daisy Cordell . . . . Mill Talbot
Judd Green . . . . Mr Darling
Rolf Leslie . . . .
ROMANCE Financier's secret wife saves dancer
from bigamy.

06696
THE THUNDERCLOUD (4780) (U)
Barker (Urban)
P: Jack W. Smith
D: Alexander Butler
S: (PLAY) Tom Taylor (STILL WATERS RUN
DEEP)
Unity More . . . . Emily Potter
James Lindsay . . . . Capt Hawksley
Mary Dibley . . . . Mrs Sternhold
Daisy Cordell . . . . Mrs Mildmay
CRIME Man weds family drudge and saves her
father from swindler.

06697
THE LAMP OF DESTINY (4600) (A)
Barker
P: Jack W. Smith
D: Alexander Butler
S: Irene Miller
Daphne Glenne . . . .
Leal Douglas . . . .
Judd Green . . . .
Florence Nelson . . . .
Laura Smithson . . . .
DRAMA

06698
IN THE GLOAMING (5000)
Broadwest
P: Walter West
D: Edwin J. Collins
S: J. Bertram Brown
Violet Hopson . . . . Adrienne Morland
Jack Jarman . . . . Jack Martin
Cameron Carr . . . . Charles Woburn
Nicholas Hopson . . . . Jack (child)
Vesta Sylva . . . . Adrienne (child)
Ray Dore . . . . Dancer
DRAMA Speculator escapes jail, makes good
abroad, and returns to find wife wed to former
lover.

06699
UNDER SUSPICION (5000) (U)
Broadwest (Moss)
P:D: Walter West
S: (PLAY) Horace Hunter
SC: Kenelm Foss, Benedict James
Horace Hunter . . . . Maj Paul Holt
Hilda Bayley . . . . Countess Nadia
Jack Jarman . . . . Her Brother
Cameron Carr . . . . Count Vasiloff
Arthur Walcott . . . . Peter Kharolff
Dorothy Warren . . . . Marie Petrovsky
Henry Latimer . . . . Gen Noivard
DRAMA Russia. American major duels police
chief to save countess's brother and husband.

06700
I HEAR YOU CALLING ME (5000)
I.B. Davidson (Ruffells)
D: A.E. Coleby
S: Andrew Soutar
Janet Alexander . . . . Jean
Richard Buttery . . . . John Maskman
Baby Shepherd . . . . Paul
Eve Marchew . . . .
CRIME Employer frames clerk, steals invention,
and seduces his wife.

06701
A SMART SET (5000) (A)
British Lion
P: David Falcke
D: A. V. Bramble
S: Neville Percy
SC: Eliot Stannard
Concordia Merrill . . . . Pauline
Neville Percy . . . . Neville Temple
S. J. Warmington . . . . Herbert Sterne
Doriel Paget . . . . Fay Trevor
Arthur Cullin . . . . Sir Philip Trevor
Gwen Williams . . . .
Iris Mackie . . . .
Judd Green . . . . Parson
Gordon McLeod . . . .
Rex Harold . . . .
CRIME Detective poses as opium fiend to save
addicted knight and daughter from abduction
by jeweller.

06702
THE ARTISTIC TEMPERAMENT (4800) (U)
British Lion *reissue:* 1921, HER GREATER
GIFT (Globe)
P: David Falcke
D: Fred Goodwins
S: Eliot Stannard
Lewis Willoughby . . . . John Trevor
Margot Kelly . . . . Helen Faversham
Frank Adair . . . . Edward Faversham
Daisy Burrell . . . .
Patrick Turnbull . . . .
ROMANCE Clovelly. Girl rejects rich nobleman
takes to violin when sister dies, and marries
poor artist.

06703
WHERE AMBITION LEADS (5000)
Beacon Films
D:SC: Billy Asher
S: Dora Savi
Donalda Campbell . . . . Beauty
Gerald Ivas . . . . Ambition
Ernie Collins . . . . Youth
Sha Lebosi . . . . Trouble
Dora Savi . . . . Fortune
Wallace Bosco . . . . Time
ROMANCE Fortune lures Youth to city, but
he returns to Beauty.

06704
TOWER OF STRENGTH (4550) (U)
retitled: GATES OF DUTY
Harma Photoplays
D: Randle Ayrton
S: Reuben Gillmer
James Knight . . . . Lt Jack Ferrars
Mary Mayfren . . . . Agnes Hallows
Bertram Burleigh . . . . David Shannon
Evelyn Trevor . . . . Hilda Bishop
Madge McIntosh . . . . Mrs Shannon
Charles Groves . . . . Jannock
Frederick Victor . . . . Haley
ROMANCE Lieut. loves nurse in Greece but
returns to wife and becomes Labour MP.

06705
THE FIRST MEN IN THE MOON (5175) (U)
Gaumont
D: J. L. V. Leigh
S: (NOVEL) H. G. Wells
SC: R. Byron-Webber
Bruce Gordon . . . . Hogben
Heather Thatcher . . . . Susan
Hector Abbas . . . . Samson Cavor
Lionel d'Aragon . . . . Rupert Bedford
Cecil Morton York . . . . Grand Lunar
FANTASY Space sphere inventor flies to moon
and is marooned by crooked financier.

06706
FORGIVE US OUR TRESPASSES (6000)
Mary Marsh Allen (Walturdaw)
D: L. C. MacBean
S: Alice Bird
Mary Marsh Allen . . . . Mary Gordon
Marsh Allen . . . . Jim
George Bellamy . . . . Bryant
H.R.Hignett . . . . Gerald Guy
Booth Conway . . . . Robert Gordon
Annesley Healy . . . . Producer
Joyce Templeton . . . . Jenny Gordon
DRAMA Girl's marriages to cruel man, squire,
and surgeon in Africa.

JUN

06707
THE STARTING POINT (5250)
British Lion (Butcher)
P: David Falcke
D: Edwin J. Collins
S: Eliot Stannard
Constance Worth . . . . Nancy
Evan Thomas . . . . Lawrence Murray
Marjorie Villis . . . . Camille
Henry Thompson . . . . Mayne
Whimsical Walker . . . . Mr. Murray
ROMANCE Devon. Clerk wins fortune, feigns
bankruptcy to test socialite, and weds fishergirl.

06708
THE NATURE OF THE BEAST (5350) (A)
Hepworth (Butcher)
D: Cecil M. Hepworth
S: E. Temple Thurston
Alma Taylor . . . . Anna de Berghem
Gerald Ames . . . . John Ingledew
James Carew . . . . Kleinenberger
Gwynne Herbert . . . . Mrs de Berghem
Stephen Ewart . . . . Sir James Standish
Mary Dibley . . . . Lady Standish
Victor Prout . . . . Mr de Berghem
Christine Rayner . . . . Guest
John McAndrews . . . . Friend
DRAMA Belgian refugee weds aircraft
manufacturer and is blackmailed by German
who raped her.

06709
HUGHIE AT THE VICTORY DERBY (1000)
Welsh-Pearson (Jury)
D: George Pearson
S: George Pearson, Hugh E. Wright
Hugh E. Wright . . . . Hughie
COMEDY Epsom. Punter loses when he backs
gypsy's tip.

06710
TILL OUR SHIP COMES IN (SERIES) (U)
Q Film Productions (Ideal)
reissue: MARRIED BLISS (Crest)
P: Jack Clair, Leon Comnen
D: Frank Miller
S: (NOVEL) Kenelm Foss
SC: Kenelm Foss
Kenelm Foss . . . . Dr Herbert Foster
Barbara Everest . . . . Mary Foster
Jack Miller . . . . Dr Foster, Sr.
Charlie Rose . . . . Kiffer Foster

06711
1: THE AUCTION (1000)

06712
2. EENA DEENA DINAH DO (1000)

06713
3: THE LODGER WHO WASN'T EXACTLY A
PAYING GUEST (1000)

06714
4: THE DREAM THAT CAME TRUE (1000)

06715
5: KIFFER'S HIGH FINANCE (1000)

06716
6: ARCADIA REVISITED (1000)
COMEDIES Struggles of poor doctor, wife,
and five children.

06717
THE AUTOCRAT (6000)
Regal Films
D:S: Tom Watts
Ethel Douglas Ross . . . . . . Elsie
Reginald Fox . . . . Jack Blake
Ralph Foster . . . . Admiral Blake
Eileen Moore . . . .
William Brandon . . . . Philip
Myra Aberg . . . .
Tom Coventry . . . .
DRAMA Admiral's disowned son returns from
shipwreck and saves sister from abduction by
cousin.

06718
CASTLE OF DREAMS (5000)
British Actors (Phillips)
D: Wilfred Noy
S: Audrey Oliver
Mary Odette . . . . Lorelei Redfern
Fred Groves . . . . John Morton
Gertrude McCoy . . . . Irene Redfern
A. E. Matthews . . . . Gerald Sumner
Henry Vibart . . . . David Redfern
Mrs. Charles Macdona . . . . Mrs Trundle
ROMANCE Guest's discovery saves rich girl
from eloping with her own father.

06719
THE ROCKS OF VALPRE (6272) (A)
Stoll
D: Maurice Elvey
S: (NOVEL) Ethel M. Dell
SC: R. Byron-Webber
Basil Gill . . . . Trevor Mordaunt
Peggy Carlisle . . . . Christine Wyndham
Cowley Wright . . . . . . Bertrand de Montville
Humberston Wright . . . . . . Capt Rodolphe
Barry Bernard . . . . Noel Wyndham
Hugh Dabernon-Stoke . . . . Rupert Wyndham
William Saville . . . . Jack Forrest
Winifred Sadler . . . . Aunt
CRIME France, 1860. Framed captain breaks
jail and saves ex-fiancee from blackmail.

06720
THE BRIDAL CHAIR (6000)
G.B. Samuelson (FBO)
D: G. B. Samuelson
S: G. B. Samuelson, Roland Pertwee
Miriam J. Sabbage . . . . Sylvane Sheridan
C. M. Hallard . . . . Lord Louis Lewis
Daisy Burrell . . . . Jill Hargreaves
Mary Rorke . . . . Mrs Sheridan
John Kelt . . . . Butler
ROMANCE Lord vows not to marry while
crippled fiancee lives.

06721
THE KINSMAN (5350) (U)
Hepworth (Butcher)
D:SC: Henry Edwards
S: (NOVEL) Mrs. Alfred Sedgwick
Henry Edwards . . . . . . Bert Gammidge/
. . . . Roger Blois
Chrissie White . . . . Pamela Blois
James Carew . . . . Col. Blois

Christine Rayner . . . . Julia
Gwynne Herbert . . . . Mrs Blois
Victor Prout . . . . Col Lorraine
John MacAndrews . . . . Dobbs
Marie Wright . . . . Duchess
Judd Green . . . . Dr Spott
Bob Russell . . . . Footman
COMEDY Cockney poses as drowned double,
who is saved and poses as chauffeur.

06722
THE SINS OF YOUTH (5000)
Central Films
P: Will Gadsby
D:S: Ernest G. Batley
Ernest G. Batley
Dorothy Batley
Sam Livesey
Nancy Bevington
Lewis Gilbert
Martin Valmour
Harry Royston
Ruby Belasco
Arthur Gadsby
Zoe Gordon
Bert Berry
Jack Mullins
DRAMA "Domestic drama centreing round an
old farm."

06723
MISS MISCHIEF (1000)
Midland Actors
D: Max Leder
S: Mr Benson
Phyllis Lea
Dorothy Brame
Bruce Channing
COMEDY Blackpool.

06724
THE HEART OF A ROSE (5600)
Grenville-Taylor (Union Photoplays)
P: H. Grenville-Taylor
D: Jack Denton
S: Langford Reed
Stella Muir . . . . Rose Fairlie
Henry Victor . . . . Dick Darrell
Douglas Payne . . . . Stephen Carnforth
Edward Thilby . . . . . . Father Gregory
Joan Langford Reed . . . . . . Baby
DRAMA Iron founder's adopted child loves
rival's manager who is really the founder's
son, sworn to avenge dead mother.

06725
THE KNAVE OF HEARTS (5418) (A)
Harma Photoplays
D: F. Martin Thornton
S: Reuben Gillmer
James Knight . . . . Lord Hillsdown
Evelyn Boucher . . . . Peggy Malvern
H. Agar Lyons . . . . Earl of Brinmore
J. Edwards Barber . . . . Oliver Slade
Lottie Blackford . . . .
Nessie Blackford . . . .
Arthur J. Mayne . . . . Sir Guy
Adeline Hayden Coffin . . .
ROMANCE Lord and discharged worker's
niece are tricked into marriage and later fall
in love without recognising each other.

06726
A LITTLE CHILD SHALL LEAD THEM (5000)
Screen Plays — B P Films (Moss)
P: H. B. Parkinson
D: Bertram Phillips
S: Bay Rothe
Queenie Thomas . . . . Marjorie Hardy

Bruce Gordon . . . . Bruce Hardy
Walter Timms . . . . Octavius Purcell/
Frank Lalor
Alice de Winton . . . .
ROMANCE Husband stops wife from eloping
with artist and adopts gypsy child.

06727
THE CALL OF THE SEA (5000)
Grenville-Taylor (Union)
S: H. Grenville-Taylor
Stella Muir . . . .
Henry Victor . . . .
Booth Conway . . . .
DRAMA

06728
THE ADVENTURES OF DORCAS DENE,
DETECTIVE (SERIES)
Life Dramas
D: Frank Carlton
S: (STORIES) George R. Sims
Winifred Rose . . . . Dorcas Dene
Tom A. Radford . . . . Paul Dene

06729
1: THE BLACKMAILER (2000)

06730
2: A WELL-PLANNED WEST END JEWEL
ROBBERY (2000)

06731
3: AN INSURANCE FRAUD (2000)

06732
4. A MURDER IN LIMEHOUSE (2000)
CRIME Wife of blinded lieutenant takes over
detective agency.

06733
BAMBOOZLED (2000)
Swastika Films
D: SC: Fred Rains
S: S. W. Clark
Fred Rains . . . . Shingles
Stan Paskin . . . . Priceless Percy
Agnes Healy . . . . Gladys
COMEDY Old gent fools flirt by posing as
automatic doll.

06734
GAIETY COMEDIES (SERIES)
Gaiety
P: D: Maurice Sandground

06735
1: GRIFF'S LOST LOVE

06736
2: GRIFF SWIMS THE CHANNEL

06737
3: THE NE'ER DO WELL

06738
4: THE SLOCUM HARRIERS

06739
5: PUSSYFOOT
COMEDY

06740
A DREAMLAND FROLIC (2000)
Globe
Lupino Lane . . . . Nipper
COMEDY Schoolboy dreams he dons
father's clothes and has night out on town.

06741
EVERYBODY'S DOING IT (1000)
Garrick Scenic Comedies

D: S: Geoffrey H. Malins
Ena Beaumont . . . . Mrs Newlywed
Victor Robson . . . . Mr Newlywed
COMEDY Couple house-hunt along the Thames

06742
I WILL (5000)
Lucky Cat (Ideal)
P: George Clark
D: Hubert Herrick, Kenelm Foss
S: Kenelm Foss
Guy Newall . . . . . Lord Eustace Dorsingham
Ivy Duke . . . . Ida Sturge
Dorothy Minto . . . . Mrs Giles
Cyril Raymond . . . . Harry Giles
Ronald Power . . . . Bart Sturge
Will Corrie . . . . Kiffin
Wally Bosco . . . . Sherlock Blake
Percy Crawford . . . . Boosey
Lyell Johnston . . . . Prof Biggs
Philip Hewland . . . . Landlord
COMEDY Fop wins socialist's daughter by
earning living as farm-hand.

06743
FATHER O'FLYNN (6000)
Regal Films
D: S: Tom Watts
Ethel Douglas . . . . Molly O'Brien
Reginald Fox . . . Terence O'Connor
Ralph Foster . . . . Father O'Flynn
Eileen Bellamy . . . . Eileen O'Brien
Little Rex . . . . Jim
Tom Coventry . . . . John O'Sullivan
CRIME Killarney. Peasant blamed when tenant
shoots landlord who seduced his daughter.

06744
PATRICIA BRENT, SPINSTER (5480) (U)
Garrick Films
D: Geoffrey H. Malins
S: (NOVEL) Herbert Jenkins
SC: Eliot Stannard
Ena Beaumont . . . . Patricia Brent
Laurence Leyton . . . . Lord Peter Bowen
Victor Robson . . . . The MP
Nessie Blackford . . . . Miss Wangle
Bruce Winston . . . . Bolton
Pollie Emery . . . . Lodger
COMEDY Secretary persuades man to pose as
her fiancee.

06745
THE GREEN TERROR (6524) (U)
Gaumont
D: W. P. Kellino
S: (NOVEL) Edgar Wallace
SC: G. W. Clifford
Aurele Sydney . . . . Beale
Heather Thatcher . . . . Oliva Cresswell
W. T. Ellwanger . . . . Dr Harden
Cecil du Gue . . . . Punsunby
Maud Yates . . . . Hilda Glaum
Arthur Poole . . . . Kitson
CRIME American tec saves heiress from doctor
who plans to destroy world's wheat.

06746
THE DOUBLE LIFE OF MR ALFRED BURTON
(5000)
Lucky Cat (Ideal)
P: George Clark
D: Arthur Rooke
S: (NOVEL) E. Phillips Oppenheim
SC: Kenelm Foss
Kenelm Foss . . . . Alfred Burton
Ivy Duke . . . . Edith Cowper
Elaine Madison . . . . Mrs Burton
Joe Peterman . . . . Mr Waddington

James Lindsay . . . . Mr Bomford
Philip Hewland . . . . Lord Idlemay
H. Humberston Wright . . . . . Kamar Shri
Ronald Power . . . . Cowper
Gordon Craig . . . . Alfie Burton
COMEDY Cockney clerk eats bean from tree
of knowledge and becomes poet.

06747
THE CRY FOR JUSTICE (5000)
Vanity (J&S)
D: A. G. Frenguelli
Amy Brandon Thomas . . . . . Myra Stuart
Norman Page . . . . Bruce Stuart
Mary Glynne . . . . Jeannette
Geoffrey Wilmer . . . . Beveridge
Charles Childerstone . . . . . . Jim
Victor Lusk . . . . Mr. Stuart
CRIME Inventor jailed when assistant fakes his
own murder to steal plans and wife.

06748
THE LADS OF THE VILLAGE (3000)
Atlantic (IVTA)
D: Harry Lorraine
S: (PLAY)
Joe Peterman
Jimmy Learmonth
Maudie Dunham
Bernard Dudley
COMEDY "Film of the patriotic musical
comedy-drama."

AUG

06749
GOD'S GOOD MAN (5777) (U)
Stoll
D: Maurice Elvey
S: (NOVEL) Marie Corelli
SC: Kate Gurney
Basil Gill . . . . Rev John Walden
Peggy Carlisle . . . . Maryilla Vancourt
Barry Bernard . . . . Julian Adderley
Hugh Dabernon-Stoke . . . . . Oliver Leach
Teddy Arundell . . . . Bainton
Julian Henry . . . . Lord Roxmouth
Temple Bell . . . . Cicely Bourne
Kate Gurney . . . . Mrs Spice
ROMANCE Heiress weds poor parson after
discharged agent hurts her during hunt.

06750
A SINLESS SINNER (6000) U.S.A:
MIDNIGHT GAMBOLS
B&C (World)
P: Edward Godal
D: James McKay
S: George Edwardes Hall
Marie Doro . . . . Irene Hendon
Godfrey Tearle . . . . Tom Harvey
Sam Livesey . . . . Sam Stevens
Mary Jerrold . . . . Mary Hendon
Christine Maitland . . . . Helen Legrande
Gladys Ffolliott . . . . Martha McBain
Gordon Begg . . . . Dr Norton
DRAMA Forger's arrest shocks his pregnant
wife causing their daughter to suffer strange
trances.

06751
FAITH (5300) (U) retitled: IN BONDAGE
G.B. Samuelson (Granger)
D: Rex Wilson
S: Roland Pertwee, G.B. Samuelson
Sydney Fairbrother . . . . . . Lavinia Brooker
Haidee Wright . . . . Miss Bryany
C. M. Hallard . . . . Lord Louis Lewis
DRAMA Persecuted servant steals crucifix not
knowing her late mistress had bequeathed it to
her.

06752
HOPE (5334) (U) retitled: SWEETHEARTS
G.B. Samuelson (Granger)
D: Rex Wilson
S: (STORY) William Schwenk Gilbert
SC: Roland Pertwee
Isobel Elsom . . . . Jenny Northcote
Malcolm Cherry . . . . Harry Thurston
Windham Guise . . . . . Sir Wallace Northcote
ROMANCE Girl waits 50 years for doctor's
son to return from India, but when he does so
he is married.

06753
CHARITY (4981) (A) retitled: SOME ARTIST
G.B. Samuelson (Granger)
D: Rex Wilson
S: Roland Pertwee, G.B. Samuelson
Campbell Gullan . . . . Samuel Pester
Eric Harrison . . . . George Turner
Cecily Debenham . . . . Elsie Pester
COMEDY Detective poses as beggar to save
fake pavement artist from arrest.

06754
LINKED BY FATE (5000)
G.B. Samuelson (General)
D:SC: Albert Ward
S: (NOVEL) Charles Garvice
Isobel Elsom . . . . Nina Vernon
Malcolm Cherry . . . . Vane Mannering
Clayton Green . . . . Julian
Esme Hubbard . . . . Polly Bamford
H.Manning Haynes . . . . Lord Sutcombe
Elaine Innescourt . . . . Juliet Orme
Bernard Vaughan . . . . Dr Vernon
Barbara Gott . . . . Deborah
Ernest A. Douglas . . . . . . Rev Fleming
ROMANCE Dying cleric weds shipwrecked
couple, who are saved separately and meet
again on same island.

06755
A DAUGHTER OF EVE (5000) (A)
Broadwest (Walturdaw)
P:D: Walter West
Violet Hopson . . . . Jessica Bond
Stewart Rome . . . . Sidney Strangeways
Cameron Carr . . . . . . Charles Strangeways
Ralph Forster . . . . John Bond
Edward Banfield . . . . . Sir Hugh Strangeways
Vesta Sylva . . . . Jessica (child)
Ronald Colman . . . .
CRIME Lord's wife lends money to ex-lover,
who is framed for killing husband - but it is all
a dream.

06756
THE FURTHER EXPLOITS OF SEXTON
BLAKE — THE MYSTERY OF THE
S.S. OLYMPIC (4529) (A)
Atlantic Films (Gaumont)
P:D: Harry Lorraine
S: (CHARACTERS) Harry Blyth
Douglas Payne . . . . Sexton Blake
Marjorie Villis . . . . Gwenda Howard
Jeff Barlow . . . . Mr Reece
Frank Dane . . . . Hamilton
Neil Warrington . . . . Tinker
William Brandon . . . .
CRIME Tec saves kidnapped daughter of
inventor murdered for his formula.

06757
THE SANDS OF TIME (5899) (A)
Harma Photoplays
D: Randle Ayrton
S: Reuben Gillmer
Mercy Hatton . . . . Esther Conway

Bertram Burleigh . . . . Allan Ross
Charles Groves . . . .
John Gliddon . . . . Kenneth Wayne
Kate Phillips . . . . Miss Wayne
Adeline Hayden Coffin . . . . Mrs Ross
Jeff Barlow . . . .
J. Edwards Barber . . . .
DRAMA Squire's son and blacksmith rival
seek rare orchid in Tibet

06758
WISP O' THE WOODS (5360) (U)
British Lion (Granger)
P: David Falcke
D: Lewis Willoughby
S: Norman Macdonald
Constance Worth . . . . Echo
Evan Thomas . . . . Richard Blake
S.J. Warmington . . . . James Whitmore
Eric Maturin . . . . Capt Arthur Mason
Arthur Cullin . . . . Sir Phillips Blake
Maude Zimbla . . . . Madge Collins
Micheline Colleen . . . . Juanita
ROMANCE Rich man's son loves nature girl
loved by gipsy who is really her half-brother.

06759
SUNKEN ROCKS (5200) (A)
Hepworth (Butcher)
D: Cecil M. Hepworth
S: E. Temple Thurston
Alma Taylor . . . . Evelyn Farrar
Gerald Ames . . . . Dr Purnell
James Carew . . . . J.H.Farrar
Nigel Playfair . . . . Mr Gurney
John McAndrews . . . . Tramp
Minnie Rayner . . . . Cook
DRAMA Dr makes drunkard's death look like
murder so he may marry his widow.

06760
THE MARCH HARE (5600)
Lucky Cat (Ideal)
P: George Clark
D:SC: Frank Miller
S: Guy Newall
Godfrey Tearle . . . . Guy
Ivy Duke . . . . Ivy
Will Corrie . . . .
Philip Hewland . . . .
Lewis Gilbert . . . .
Douglas Heathcote . . . .
Percy Crawford . . . .
Peggy Maurice . . . .
John Miller . . . .
COMEDY New Forest. Man helps gambler by
posing as escaped lunatic to rob his father.

06761
FETTERED (5000)
Windsor (Walturdaw)
D: Arrigo Bocchi
S: (NOVEL) Joan Sutherland
SC: Kenelm Foss
Manora Thew . . . . Sheila Clavering
Hayford Hobbs . . . . Lucien de Guise
Fred Morgan . . . . Rocci
Charles Vane . . . . General Clavering
Evelyn Harding . . . . Lady Clavering
Bert Wynne . . . . Harry Logan
Peggy Patterson . . . . . . Monica Hewlett
George Butler . . . . Capt Galveston
Ethel Royale . . . . Lady Mortimer
DRAMA Italy.

SEP

06762
POSSESSION (5275) (A)
Hepworth (Butcher)

D: Henry Edwards
S: (NOVEL) Olive Wadsley
Henry Edwards . . . . Blaise Barewsky
Chrissie White . . . . Valerie Sarton
Gerald Ames . . . . Richard Staire
Gwynne Herbert . . . . Tante
Stephen Ewart . . . . John Sarton
Annie Esmond . . . . Marquise
Bubbles Brown . . . . Valerie (child)
ROMANCE Russian's secret wife marries cousin
to give baby a name.

06763
FANCY DRESS (5000)
Lucky Cat (Ideal)
P: George Clark, Guy Newall
D:S: Kenelm Foss
Godfrey Tearle . . . . Tony Broke
Ivy Duke . . . . Hebe
Guy Newall . . . . Earl of Richborne
Will Corrie . . . . The Guv
Frank Miller . . . . Dick Scribe
Elaine Madison . . . . Eighth Wonder
George Tawde . . . . Mike
Kitty Barlow . . . . Ma
Patricia Stannard . . . . Mrs Van Graft
Bryan Powley . . . . Mr Rong
James English . . . . Mr Wright
COMEDY Lawyer bribes touring actor to pose
as heir to earldom.

06764
THE DISAPPEARANCE OF THE JUDGE (5000)
Barker (Globe)
P: Jack W. Smith
D: Alexander Butler
S: (NOVEL) Guy Thorne
James Lindsay . . . . Judge Moultrie/
Augustus
Florence Nelson . . . . Mme Julia
Mark Melford . . . . Capt Hayter
Joan Lockton . . . . Miss Moultrie
Wilfred Benson . . . .
Daisy Cordell . . . .
CRIME Cornwall. German gang kidnap judge to
obtain aero-engine plans; his twin takes his place.

06765
THE FLAG LIEUTENANT (5200) (U)
Barker (Jury)
P: Jack W.Smith
D: Percy Nash
S: (PLAY) W. P. Drury, Leo Tover
Ivy Close . . . . Lady Hermione Wynne
George Wynn . . . . . Lt Dicky Lascelles
Dorothy Fane . . . . Mrs Cameron
Ernest Wallace . . . . Maj Thesiger
Frank Adair . . . . Admiral Wynne
Wallace Bosco . . . . Villain
WAR Lieut branded coward after saving fort
from Bashi Bazouks and letting amnesiac major
take credit.

06766
THE SECRET OF THE MOOR (5095) (U)
British Lion (Granger)
P: David Falcke
D: Lewis Willoughby
S: (NOVEL) Maurice Gerard
Gwen Williams . . . . Margaret Marson
Philip Hewland . . . . George Marson
Henry Thompson . . . . Adam Ducros
Edgar W. Hylton . . . . Jack Myddleton
Hazel Jones . . . . Mildred Morpeth
George Goodwin . . . . Dr Morpeth
CRIME Boatman smuggles gold for mining
expert but reforms when his child falls ill.

06767
THE USURPER (4782) (A)
British Actors (Phillips)
P: Gerald Malvern
D: Duncan Macrae
S: (NOVEL) W.J. Locke
SC: Adrian Brunel
Gertrude McCoy . . . . . .   Lady Alice Holden
Cecil Ward . . . .   Burke
Stephen T. Ewart . . . . .   Jasper Vellacott
Geoffrey Kerr . . . .   Bonamy Tredgold
Pauline Peters . . . .   Vittoria
Murray Moncrieff . . . . . .   Antonelli
Ivan Berlyn . . . .   Giuseppe
Frederick Volpe . . . .
Athol Forde . . . .
Sir Simeon Stuart . . . . . .
Spencer Trevor . . . .
CRIME Amnesiac tramp denounces head of
benevolent institute as false heir to Australian
tin mine.

06768
THE IMPOSSIBLE WOMAN (5000)
Ideal
D: Meyrick Milton
S: (PLAY) Haddon Chambers
(NOVEL) Anne Sedgwick (TANTE)
Constance Collier . . . .   Mme Kraska
Langhorne Burton . . . . . .   Gregory Jardine
Christine Rayner . . . .   Karen
Alan Byrne . . . .   Edwin Drew
Edith Craig . . . .   Mrs. Talcotte
COMEDY Arty aunt and poet lover cause trou-
ble when her ward weds barrister.

OCT

06769
THE MAN WHO FORGOT (6229) (U)
Harma Photoplays
D: F. Martin Thornton
S: Rev A. J. Waldron
SC: Reuben Gillmer
James Knight . . . .   Seth Nalden
Marjorie Villis . . . .   Mona Jennifer
Bernard Dudley . . . .   Jim Hallibar
Evelyn Boucher . . . .   Violet Selwyn
H. Agar Lyons . . . .   Tarpaulin Jack
Mowbray Macks . . . .   Salty Felton
ROMANCE Cornwall. Amnesiac skipper
returns from shipwreck to find his sweetheart
wed to sailor.

06770
THE RAINBOW CHASERS (2000)
Garrick (Educational Film Supply)
D: Geoffrey H. Malins
S: "Magister"
Ena Beaumont . . . .   The Girl
DRAMA "The vital need for more production
if we are to survive as a nation."

06771
THE CHINESE PUZZLE (5000)
Ideal
D: SC: Fred Goodwins
S: (PLAY) Leon M. Lion, Marion Bower
Leon M. Lion . . . . .   Marquis Li Chung
Lilian Braithwaite . .   Lady de la Haye
Milton Rosmer . . . .   Sir Roger de la Haye
Sybil Arundale . . . . .   Naomi Melsham
Dora de Winton . . . .   Mrs Melsham
Charles Rock . . . .   Sir Aylmer Brent
Reginald Bach . . . .   Henrik Stroom
Sam Livesey . . . .   Paul Markatel
Alexander Sarner . . . .   Raoul d'Armand
CRIME Mandarin takes blame when wife of
friend's son steals secret papers.

06772
WHEN IT WAS DARK (6700)
Windsor (Walturdaw)
D: Arrigo Bocchi
S: (NOVEL) Guy Thorne
SC: Kenelm Foss
Manora Thew . . . .   Gertrude Hunt
Hayford Hobbs . . . .   Rev Basil Gortrie
George Butler . . . .   Constantin Sharke
Charles Vane . . . .   Prof Llewellyn
Evelyn Harding . . . .   Princess Lontaine
Bert Wynne . . . .   Harold Spence
Peggy Patterson . . . .   Helena Byars
Judd Green . . . .`. . . .   Father Riposi
Arthur Walcott . . . .   Governor
DRAMA Palestine. Atheist millionaire forces
professor to destroy Christianity by discovering
fake sepulchre.

06773
DARBY AND JOAN (6500)
Master Films (BEF)
P: H. B. Parkinson
D: Percy Nash
S: Hall Caine
Derwent Hall Caine . . . . . .   Patrick Garry
Ivy Close . . . .   Sheila Moore
Meggie Albanesi . . . .   Elin Garry
George Wynne . . . .   Reginald Stevenson
Joan Ritz . . . .   Lizzie
Leal Douglas . . . .   Mrs Garry
Edward O'Neill . . . .   Sayle Moore
Douglas Munro . . . .   Malatesta
Ernest A. Douglas . . . .   Joseph Montagu
DRAMA Isle of Man. Rich man diverts widow's
millstream to make pond.

06774
THE SINGLE MAN (5000)
British Lion (Ideal)
P: David Falcke
D: A.V. Bramble
S: (PLAY) Hubert H. Davies
Cecil Mannering . . . .   Maj Henry Worthington
Doris Lytton . . . . .   Mrs Worthington
George Mallett . . . . .   Robert Worthington
Alice de Winton . . . .   Louise Parker
Irene Drew . . . .   Miss Hesletine
COMEDY Old author weds secretary after
flirting with flapper and determined spinster.

06775
SHEBA (5475) (U)
Hepworth (Butcher)
D: Cecil M. Hepworth
S: (NOVEL) "Rita"
SC: Blanche McIntosh
Alma Taylor . . . .   Sheba Ormatroyd
Gerald Ames . . . .   Paul Meredith
James Carew . . . .   Levison
Lionelle Howard . . . . . .   Count Pharamond
Eileen Dennes . . . .   Bessie Saxton
Mary Dibley . . . .   Rhoda Meredith
Diana Carey . . . .   Mrs Ormatroyd
Eric Barker . . . .   Rex Ormatroyd
ROMANCE Rich Jew's stepdaughter weds
opera singer's son and learns he is already
married.

06776
MR WU (5170) (A)
Stoll *reissue:* 1922
D: Maurice Elvey
S: (PLAY) Harry Vernon, Harold Owen
SC: Frederick Blatchford
Matheson Lang . . . .   Mr Wu
Lillah McCarthy . . . .   Mrs Gregory
Meggie Albanesi . . . .   Nang Ping
Roy Royston . . . .   Basil Gregory

Teddy Arundell . . . .   Mr Gregory
CRIME Chinese merchant kills daughter,
kidnaps seducer, and demands his mother in exchange.

06777
A MEMBER OF TATTERSALL'S (6000) (U)
G.B. Samuelson (Granger)
D: Albert Ward
S: (PAY) H.V. Browning
Isobel Elsom . . . .   Mary Wilmott
Malcolm Cherry . . . .   Capt Brookes Greville
Campbell Gullan . . . .   Foxey
Tom Reynolds . . . .   Peter Perks
James Lindsay . . . .   Lord Winthrop
SPORT Bookmaker's daughter is adopted by
widow and loves captain whose winner is
disqualified by crooked lord.

06778
EDGE O'BEYOND (6000)
G.B. Samuelson (General)
D: Fred W. Durrant
S: (NOVEL) Gertrude Page
SC: Irene Miller
Ruby Miller . . . .   Dinah Webberley
Owen Nares . . . .   Dr Cecil Lawson
Isobel Elsom . . . .   Joyce Grey
C.M. Hallard . . . .   Capt Burnett
Minna Grey . . . .   Dulcie Maitland
Fred Raynham . . . .   Oswald Grant
James Lindsay . . . .   Maj Egerton
DRAMA Rhodesia. Woman leaves cruel husband
when their baby dies.

06779
GAMBLERS ALL (5500) (A)
G. B. Samuelson (Granger)
D: SC: Dave Aylott
S: (PLAY) May Martindale
Madge Titheradge .   Doris Longworthy
Owen Nares . . . . . .   Harold Tempest
Ruby Miller . . . .   Millicent Hope
C. M. Hallard . . . . . .   John Leighton
Henry Vibart . . . . . .   Sir George Longworthy
James Lindsay . . . .   Maj Stocks
Madge Stuart . . . . . .   Ruth Longworthy
CRIME Lady gambler takes blame for
brother's forgery.

06780
NOBODY'S CHILD (5200) (A)
B & C (Butcher)
P: Edward Godal
D: George Edwardes Hall
S: (PLAY) George Edwardes Hall (THE
WHIRLPOOL)
Jose Collins . . . . . .   Francesca Samarjo
Godfrey Tearle . . . .   Ernest d'Alvard
Ben Webster . . . . .   Joseph Samarjo
Christine Maitland . . . . . .   Countess Althea
J. Fisher White . . . .   Baron Troeffer
Saba Raleigh . . . . . .   Baroness d'Alvard
Pardoe Woodman . . . .   Antoine
Frances Wetherall . . . .   Nita Samarjo
ROMANCE Corsica. Wife becomes opera star
when husband leaves her to succour his sick
mother.

06781
THE GENTLEMAN RIDER (5000) (U)
USA: HEARTS AND SADDLES
Violet Hopson (Walturdaw)
D: Walter West
Violet Hopson . . . .   Marjorie Denton
Stewart Rome . . . .   Frank Cunningham
Gregory Scott . . . .   Sir Reginald Buckley
Cameron Carr . . . .   Billbrook
Violet Elliott . . . . .   Aunt Cynthia
SPORT Gentleman jockey wins on girl's horse
despite crooked agent.

06782
THE CITY OF BEAUTIFUL NONSENSE
(5725) (U)
Hepworth (Butcher)
D: Henry Edwards
S: (NOVEL) E. Temple Thurston
Henry Edwards . . . . John Grey
Chrissie White . . . . Jill Dealtry
James Lindsay . . . . Skipworth
Henry Vibart . . . . Thomas Grey
Gwynne Herbert . . . . Mrs Grey
Douglas Munro . . . . Chesterton
Stephen Ewart . . . . Mr Dealtry
Teddy Taylor . . . . Tommy Dealtry
ROMANCE Poor author feigns marriage to
please dying father.

06783
ANGEL ESQUIRE (6741) (A)
Gaumont
D: W. P. Kellino
S: (NOVEL) Edgar Wallace
SC: George Pearson
Aurele Sydney . . . . Jimmy
Gertrude McCoy . . . . Kathleen Kent
Dick Webb . . . . Angel
W.T.Ellwanger . . . . Spedding
George Traill . . . . Connor
Cecil del Gue . . . . Reale
Florence Nelson . . . . Mrs Reale
CRIME Millionaire gambler leaves fortune to
whoever discovers the combination of his safe.

06784
THE ODDS AGAINST HER (5500) (A)
Barker (Jury)
P: Jack W. Smith
D: Alexander Butler
Milton Rosmer . . . . Leo Strathmore
Edmee Dormeuil . . . . Nanette
Lorna Della . . . . Lolita Rios
George Foley . . . . The Baron
Thos. H. MacDonald . . . . .
Nancy Benyon . . . .
Vernon Davidson . . . .
Andre Randall . . . .
CRIME Orphan dancer saves guardian from
German baron and Spanish adventuress.

06785
THE BEETLE (5600) (A)
Barker (Urban)
P: Jack W. Smith
D: Alexander Butler
SC: Helen Blizzard
Maudie Dunham . . . . . . Dora Greyling
Hebden Foster . . . . Paul Lessingham
Fred Morgan . . . . Neces
Nancy Benyon . . . . Marjorie Linden
Frank Reade . . . . Sidney Atherton
Leal Douglas . . . . High Priestess
Rolf Leslie . . . . Holt
HORROR Egyptian priest tries to burn MP's
fiancee to avenge priestess whose soul inhabits
monstrous beetle.

06786
GOD'S CLAY (4500) (A)
Arthur Rooke
D: SC: Arthur Rooke
S: (NOVEL) Claude & Alice Askew
Janet Alexander . . . . Angela Clifford
Humberston Wright . . . . . . Geoffrey Vance
Arthur Rooke . . . . Horace Newton
Maud Yates . . . . Poppy Stone
Adeline Hayden Coffin . . . .
John Hastings Batson . . . .
CRIME Cornwall. Man's paralysed wife kills
her seducer and frames his mistress.

06787
SPLENDID FOLLY (5000)
Windsor (Walturdaw)
D: Arrigo Bocchi
S: (NOVEL) Margaret Pedlar
SC: Hedley Sedgwick
Manora Thew . . . . Diana Quentin
Hayford Hobbs . . . . Max Errington
Evelyn Harding . . . . Adrienne de Gervais
Charles Vane . . . . Barohi
Bert Wynne . . . .
Peggy Patterson . . . .
ROMANCE Naples. Playwright's wife leaves
him to become opera star, thinking exiled
heiress is his mistress.

06788
HIS LAST DEFENCE (5000)
Vanity Films (Walker)
D: Geoffrey Wilmer
S: (PLAY) Dion Titherage (THE KC)
SC: Ronald Byron-Webber
Dennis Neilson-Terry . . . . . Arthur Dawson
Mary Glynne . . . . . . Dorothea Oddington
Alfred Bishop . . . . . Sir Benjamin Oddington
Cyril Raymond . . . . David Hislop
Helen Haye . . . . Hesper Oddington
Peggy Surtees . . . . Lilian Alvin
Alfred T. Jones . . . . Beagle
Harold Anstruther . . . . . .
Howard Cochran . . . . Detective
CRIME Retired KC acquits daughter's fiance,
then discovers he stole to pay blackmailing
mistress.

06789
THE LADY CLARE (6000)
British Actors (Phillips)
S: (POEM) Alfred Tennyson
SC: Dale Laurence Brunel
Mary Odette . . . . Lady Clare
Jack Hobbs . . . . Lord Ronald Medwin
Charles Quartermaine . . . Marquis of Hartlepool
Sir Simeon Stuart . . . Earl of Robhurst
Gladys Jennings . . . . Ann Sheldrake
Mary Forbes . . . . Lady Julia Medwin
Barbara Everest . . . . Alice
Fewlass Llewellyn . . . . . . Dr Jenner
Arthur Cleave . . . . Charles Boulton
Gilbert Esmond . . . . Duke
Winifred Evans . . . . Clare Hampden
Nancy O'Hara . . . . Ursula Hampden
ROMANCE Period. Lord weds lady despite
discovering that she is a substituted village child.

06790
SWEET AND TWENTY (4800) (U)
Progress (Butcher)
P: Frank E. Spring
D:SC: Sidney Morgan
S: (PLAY) Basil Hood
Marguerite Blanche . . . . Jean Trevellyan
Langhorne Burton . . . . Douglas Floyd
George Keene . . . . Eustace Floyd
Arthur Lennard . . . . Rev James Floyd
George Bellamy . . . . Prynne
Nell Emerald . . . . Ellen
ROMANCE Cleric's son is court-martialled ,
makes good in Australia, and marries his
brother's sweetheart.

06791
HER SECRET (5000)
Barker (Urban)
P: Jack W. Smith
D:S: Frederick S.Jensen
Margaret Bannerman . . Margaret Henderson
Frederick Jensen . . . . . Dr Paul Henderson
DRAMA Jealous Dr. leaves wife but returns in
time to save her life.

06792
WESTWARD HO! (6000)
Master Films (BEF)
P: H. B. Parkinson
D: Percy Nash
S: (NOVEL) Charles Kingsley
SC: Walter Courtenay Rowden
Renee Kelly . . . . Rose Salterne
Charles Quartermaine . . . . . Don Guzman
Eric Harrison . . . . Amyas Leigh
Booth Conway . . . . Salvation Yeo
Irene Rooke . . . . Mistress Leigh
Ernest Wallace . . . . John Oxenham
Dolly Robbins . . . . Aya Canova
Hilton Allen . . . . Frank Leigh
J.H. Barnes . . . . Master Salterne
ADVENTURE 1588. Sailor saves fiancee
from Spanish don and is blinded whilst fighting
Armada.

06793
JACK, SAM AND PETE (5000)
Pollock-Daring Productions
P: Leon Pollock
D: Jack Daring (Percy Moran)
S: (STORIES) S. Clarke-Hook
Percy Moran . . . . Jack
Eddie Willey . . . . Sam
Ernest A. Trimingham . . . . Pete
Manning Haynes . . . . Cyril Danvers
Enid Heather . . . . Violet Danvers
Capt Jack Kelly . . . . The Scorpion
Garrick Aitken . . . . The Boy
Jack Harding . . . . The Ferret
ADVENTURE Cowboys save kidnapped child
from gang seeking hidden jewels.

06794
A LASS O' THE LOOMS (4500) (U)
Grenville-Taylor—Union Photoplays (Kilner)
P: H. Grenville-Taylor
D: Jack Denton
S: Langford Reed
Stella Muir . . . . Nellie Hesketh
Henry Victor . . . . Jack Brown
Douglas Payne . . . . Foreman
Betty Hall . . . . Girl
CRIME Lancs. Mill owner's son poses as
workman to unmask foreman as stealer of cloth.

06795
THE SILVER LINING (6458) (U)
I. B. Davidson (Gaumont)
D: A. E. Coleby
Bdr Billy Wells . . . . . Jerrold O'Farrell
Ella Milne . . . . Pamela Hillsbury
Richard Buttery . . . . Jack Hillsbury
Warwick Ward . . . . . Mark Cathcart
Ralph Forster . . . . . Sir Thomas Hillsbury
George Harrington . . . . Mr Hamilton
Doris Paxman . . . . . Sybil Harrington
H. Nicholls-Bates . . . . Mr Spagnoli
Olive Colin Bell . . . . Mrs Spagnoli
SPORT Pilot foils racehorse dopers and
marries girl whom gambler seduced.

06796
THE FOREST ON THE HILL (6298) (A)
Hepworth (Butcher)
D: Cecil M. Hepworth
S: (NOVEL) Eden Philpotts
SC: Blanche McIntosh
Alma Taylor . . . . Drusilla Whyddon
James Carew . . . . Timothy Snow
Gerald Ames . . . . John Redstone
Lionelle Howard . . . . Frederick Moyle
Eileen Dennes . . . . Audrey Leaman
Gwynne Herbert . . . . Mrs. Snow
Stephen Ewart . . . . Lord Champernowne
John McAndrews . . . . Mr Leaman
Judd Green . . . . Lot Snow
DRAMA Devon. Farmer killed by ex-game-
keeper and his nephew is blamed.

DEC

06797
QUEEN'S EVIDENCE (5000)
B & C (Moss)
P: Edward Godal
D: James McKay
S: (PLAY) Louisa Parr, C. E. Munro
(ADAM AND EVE)
SC: George Edwardes Hall

Godfrey Tearle	Adam Pascall
Unity More	Eve Pascall
Janet Alexander	Joan Hocking
Lauderdale Maitland	Jerrem
Edward Sorley	Jonathan
Bruce Winston	Job
Ada King	
Pardoe Woodman	Reuben May

ADVENTURE Polperro. Smuggler blames brother when rival betrays him to coastguards.

06798
BLADYS OF THE STEWPONY (5000)
Ben Priest Films
D: SC: L. C. MacBean
S: (NOVEL) Sabine Baring Gould

Marguerite Fox	Bladys Rhea
Arthur Chisholm	Crispin Ravenhill
Windham Guise	Holy Austin
Harry J. Worth	William Onions
E. J. Caldwell	Luke Francis
James Broadhurst	Parson Toogood
Noel Grahame	Noel
Nan Carroll	Nan
H. R. Plummer	Highwayman

ADVENTURE 1790. Innkeeper's daughter is won by hangman, who falls off cliff after she is rescued by highwayman's mistress.

06799
THE GARDEN OF RESURRECTION (6470) (A)
George Clark Productions (Stoll)
D: Arthur Rooke
S: (NOVEL) E. Temple Thurston
SC: Guy Newall

Guy Newall	Bellairs
Ivy Duke	Clarissa
Franklin Dyall	Cruickshank
Mary Dibley	Belwottle
Douglas Munro	Moxon
Lawford Davidson	Fennell
Hugh C. Buckler	Dr Perowne
Humberston Wright	Gen French
Madge Tree	Aunt

ROMANCE Rich halfcaste abandoned after mock marriage, has stillborn baby, and weds man who helps her.

06800
SNOW IN THE DESERT (7000) (U)
Broadwest (Walturdaw)
D: Walter West
S: (NOVEL) Andrew Soutar
SC: Benedict James

Violet Hopson	Felice Beste
Stewart Rome	William B. Jackson
Poppy Wyndham	
Sir Simeon Stuart	Sir Michael Beste
Ronald Colman	Rupert Sylvester
Mary Masters	
A. B. Caldwell	

ROMANCE Colombo. Magnate's wife elopes with poet but returns to run business when he falls ill.

06801
A GREAT COUP (4400) (U)
Broadwest (Walturdaw)
P: Walter West
D: George Dewhurst

S: (NOVEL) Nat Gould
SC: J. Bertram Brown

Stewart Rome	Squire Hampton
Poppy Wyndham	Kate Hampton
Gregory Scott	Reid Gordon
Cameron Carr	Richard Foxton

SPORT Squire's adopted daughter rides beloved's horse when her mother bribes his jockey to lose.

06802
THE SWINDLER (5436) (A)
Stoll
D: Maurice Elvey
S: (NOVEL) Ethel M. Dell
SC: Kate Gurney

Cecil Humphreys	Nat Verney
Marjorie Hume	Cynthia Mortimer
Neville Percy	Archie Mortimer
Teddy Arundell	Insp West
Allan Hunter	Lord Babbacombe

DRAMA Man takes blame for girl's crooked brother and weds her when her hand is amputated.

06803
THE ELUSIVE PIMPERNEL (5143) (U)
Stoll
D: Maurice Elvey
S: (NOVEL) Baroness Orczy
SC: Frederick Blatchford

Cecil Humphreys	Sir Percy Blakeney
Marie Blanche	Lady Marguerite
Norman Page	Chauvelin
Fotheringham Lysons	Robespierre
Teddy Arundell	Colet d'Herbois
Madge Stuart	Juliette Marny
A. Harding Steerman	Abbe Jouquet
Dorothy Hanson	Mlle Cardeille

ADVENTURE France, 1792. Fop forced to confess to spying to save wife from guillotine.

06804
ONLY A MILL GIRL (5000)
Foxwell (Ideal)
P: Harry Foxwell
D: Lewis Willoughby
S: (PLAY) Sheila Walsh

Harry Foxwell	John Raymond
Betty Farquhar	Mary
Arthur Condy	Jack Ainsleigh
Ida Lambert	Constance Darville
Frank Lovett	George Thornton

DRAMA Lancs. Foreman's daughter stops rich woman from stealing inventor's plans.

06805
MRS THOMPSON (5000)
G. B. Samuelson (General)
D: Rex Wilson
S: (NOVEL) W. B. Maxwell

Minna Grey	Mrs Thompson
C.M.Hallard	Prentice
Isobel Elsom	Enid Thompson
Bertram Burleigh	Dicky Marsden
Tom Reynolds	Archibald Bence
James Lindsay	Charles Kennion
Marie Wright	Yates
Wyndham Guise	Mears

DRAMA Shopkeeper's daughter marries cad who ruins business.

06806
DAMAGED GOODS (5000)
G.B. Samuelson (W & F)
D: Alexander Butler
S: (PLAY) Eugene Brieux (LES AVARIES)

Campbell Gullan	George Dupont
Marjorie Day	Henriette Louches

J Fisher White	Doctor
James Lindsay	Rouvenal
Joan Vivian Reese	Edith Wray
Bassett Roe	Henry Louches
Annie Esmond	Marie Dupont
Winifred Dennis	The Wife

DRAMA Quack doctor 'cures' victim of venereal disease, whose baby is later born infected.

06807
THE RIGHT ELEMENT (5869) (U)
G .B. Samuelson (Granger)
D: Rex Wilson
S:(STORY) Roland Pertwee
SC: Roland Pertwee

Campbell Gullan	Frank Kemble
Miriam Ferris	Madeleine Wade
Tom Reynolds	Mr Wade
Mary Rorke	Aunt Harriet
Annie Esmond	Mrs Wade
John Kelt	Pender
George Gee	Pender jr.

DRAMA Clerk gambles to pay for wife's operation, loses, goes mad, and finds It was a dream.

06808
THE POLAR STAR (5000)
Windsor (Walturdaw)
D: Arrigo Bocchi
S: Leslie Stiles
Manora Thew
Hayford Hobbs
Peggy Patterson
Bert Wynne
Charles Vane
CRIME Italy. Mystery of a London solicitor's death and dishonour.

06809
BARNABY (5000)
Barker
P: Jack Smith
D: Jack Denton
S: (NOVEL) Rina Ramsey
SC: Gerald de Beaurepaire

Dick Webb	Barnaby
Cyril Vaughan	Doctor
Athalie Davis	
Dorothy Fane	
Reginald Fox	
Terence Cavanagh	Lord Rackham
Dora de Winton	
Eileen Moore	

SPORT "Love and adventures of a dashing young squire."

06810
KIDS TOGETHER (1000)
Blue Star Photoplay
D:S: Will Scott

Garrick Aitken	The Boy
Enid Heather	The Girl
James Bonner	The Showman

COMEDY Boy tramp saves rich girl from bad man, but returns to gutter.

06811
SALVAGE (1000)
Associated Film Exclusives
P:D:S: E. R. Bashame

Garrick Aitken	The Boy
Booth Conway	Sir Jermyn Broadhurst
Elaine Madison	
Ernest Montefiore	

DRAMA Adventures of six-year old guttersnipe who ends up in Dr. Barnado's Home.

06812
THE GATES OF DOOM (7000)
Posner Films
P: William Posner
D: Sidney M. Goldin
S: (NOVEL) Rafael Sabatini
Marie Zola
DRAMA (Not shown.)

06813
CLARENCE, CROOKS AND CHIVALRY
Lupino Lane (Ideal)   (2000)
Lupino Lane . . . . Clarence
COMEDY Dude tramp becomes builder, is
robbed by foreman, and meets bathing girls.

06814
A DEAD CERT (2000)
Assurance Films (Redthorpe)
D:S: Rowland Whiting
Hugh Maynard . . . . Jim
Patricia Webster . . . . The Girl
COMEDY

06815
HORACE COMEDIES (series)
New Agency (Artistic)
D: Arthur Rooke
S: Kenelm Foss
Bertie Wright . . . . Horace

06816
1. MORE THAN HE BARGAINED FOR (1000)
Mrs Phillips . . . . The Widow
Ivy Stanborough . . . . The Slavey
Tiny Fairlie . . . . The Child
Olive Colin Bell . . . . The Mother

06817
2: EXCEEDING THE LIMIT (1000)

06818
3: HORACE EARNS A HALO (1000)

06819
4: HORACE'S TRIUMPH (1000)
COMEDY Misadventures of bachelor.

1920

JAN

06820
A TEMPORARY VAGABOND (5050) (U)
Hepworth (Butcher)
D:SC: Henry Edwards
S: Stuart Woodley

Henry Edwards	Dick Derelict
Chrissie White	Peggie Hurst
Stephen Ewart	James Hurst
Gwynne Herbert	Emma
Douglas Munro	Mike
John McAndrews	Davis

COMEDY Mean squire's novelist son becomes village benefactor.

06821
THE PRIDE OF THE NORTH (5165) (U)
I. B. Davidson (Ruffells)
D:S: A. E. Coleby

Cecil Humphreys	John Hargreaves
Nora Roylance	Rose Eva
Richard Buttery	Jack Hargreaves
James English	Bill Webster
Blanche Kellino	Mother
H. Nicholls-Bates	Father
Eva Llewellyn	
Eve Marchew	

SPORT Mine owner reunited with son after greyhound wins Waterloo Cup.

06822
WITH ALL HER HEART (4845) (U)
I. B. Davidson (Ruffells)
D: Frank Wilson
S: (NOVEL) Charles Garvice

Milton Rosmer	Geoffrey Bell
Mary Odette	Cottie
Jack Vincent	Sidney Bassington
J. Hastings Batson	Earl of Stanborough
Harry Gilbey	Solicitor

DRAMA Australian miner adopts orphan, sends her to England, and finds they are both an Earl's heirs.

06823
THE HOUR OF TRIAL (5000)
I. B. Davidson (Ruffells)
D: A. E. Coleby

Cecil Humphreys	John Graham
Janet Alexander	Margaret Graham
Maud Yates	Alice Howell
Percy Rhodes	Doctor

CRIME Barrister forced to prosecute neglected wife who has become shoplifter.

06824
THE HUSBAND HUNTER (6000) (U)
G. B. Samuelson (Granger)
D: Fred W. Durrant
S: (NOVEL) Olivia Roy

C.M. Hallard	Sir Robert Chester
Madge Titheradge	Lalage Penrose
Tom Reynolds	James Ogilvy
Minna Grey	Joanna Marsh
Reginald Dane	Lord Bayard

DRAMA "Dead" explorer poses as butler to test wife's fidelity.

06825
LADY NOGGS - PEERESS (5000) (A)
Progress (Butcher)
P: Frank Spring
D: SC: Sidney Morgan
S: (PLAY) Cicely Harrington (NOVEL)
(NOVEL) Selwyn Jepson

Joan Morgan	Lady Noggs
George Bellamy	Lord Errington
Yvonne Duquette	Mme Karsovitch
Arthur Lennard	Rev Greig

James Prior	Caldicott Beresford
Jenny Earle	Miss Stetson

DRAMA Adopted orphan saves MP's grandson from foreign adventuress.

06826
HER BENNY (5900) (U)
Diamond Super (Granger)
P: W. H. Baker
D: A. V. Bramble
S: (NOVEL) Silas K. Hocking
SC: George Dewhurst

Sydney Wood	Benny (child)
Babs Reynolds	Nellie Bates
Charles Buckmaster	Benny Bates
Peggy Patterson	Eva Lawrence
C. Hargrave Mansell	Joe Wragg
Lottie Blackford	Mrs Wragg
Robert Vallis	Dick Bates
Anthony StJohn	Perks

ROMANCE Liverpool slum boy, blamed for theft, becomes farmer in Wales and saves life of childhood sweetheart.

06827
THE DUCHESS OF SEVEN DIALS (5474) (A)
London (Jury)
D: Fred Paul
S: Harry Engholm

Cecil Mannering	Rev Noel Fortescue
Marjorie Hume	Lady Irene Worth
Adelaide Grace	Grace Milton
Daisy Elliston	Grace Milton
Daphne Grey	Melia
Teddy Arundell	Joe Murden
Harry Paulo	Duke of Fivepence
George Turner	Spivy
Hubert Willis	Lord Sloane
Cyril Percival	Lord Marcus

ROMANCE Ex-Music Hall star learns friend's lies caused Duke to jilt her in 1870.

06828
THE PURSUIT OF PAMELA (5241) (U)
London (Jury)
D: Harold Shaw
S: (PLAY) C.B.Fernald
SC: Bannister Merwin

Edna Flugrath	Pamela Dodder
Templar Powell	Alan Graeme
Douglas Munro	John Dodder
Ada Palmer	Miss Astley
Hubert Willis	Peter Dodder
Windham Guise	Scot McVelie
Ma Fue	Fah Nin

DRAMA China. Runaway heiress poses as widow and weds her lover after servant infects her pursuing husband.

06829
LONDON PRIDE (5200) (U)
London (Jury)
D: Harold Shaw
S: (PLAY) Arthur Lyons, Gladys Unger
SC: Bannister Merwin

Edna Flugrath	Cherry
Fred Groves	Cuthbert Tunks
O.B.Clarence	Mr Tunks
Mary Brough	Mrs Tunks
Constance Backner	Maud Murphy
Frank Stanmore	Mooney
Douglas Munro	Garlic
Mary Dibley	Mrs Topleigh-Trevor
Edward Arundell	Bill Guppy
Cyril Percival	Menzies

COMEDY 1914. Cockney greengrocer fakes amnesia to be sent home from the war, and is ultimately awarded the VC.

06830
TRUE TILDA (4654) (U)
London (Jury)
D: Harold Shaw
S: (NOVEL) Arthur Quiller-Couch
SC: Bannister Merwin

Edna Flugrath	Tilda
Teddy Gordon Craig	Arthur
Edward O'Neill	Dr Purdie J. Gasson
Sir Simeon Stuart	
Douglas Munro	
George Bellamy	

DRAMA Injured circus girl helps boy escape from orphanage and finds he is lord's lost son.

06831
THE LITTLE WELSH GIRL (5240) (A)
London (Jury)
D: Fred Paul

Christine Silver	Ellen Lloyd
Humberston Wright	Cedri Lloyd
Booth Conway	Peter the Fiddler
Adelaide Grace	Mrs Lloyd
Daphne Grey	Dylis Moran
Robert Michaelis	Rhys Bowen
Dorothy Ardley	Tessie Dunbar

DRAMA Wales. Expelled priest accused of killing servant girl who fled from his attack.

06832
LADY TETLEY'S DECREE (4797) (A)
London (Jury)
D:SC: Fred Paul
S: (PLAY) W.F. & Sybil Downing

Marjorie Hume	Lady Rachel Tetley
Hamilton Stewart	Sir Oliver Tetley
Philip Hewland	Robert Trentham
Basil Langford	Ronald Tetley
Sydney Lewis Ransome	Lionel Crier
Bernard Vaughan	Lord Herondale

DRAMA Foreign Office man hires bohemian to compromise rival's separated wife.

06833
THE GRIP OF IRON (5000)
Famous Pictures (General)
D: Bert Haldane
S: (PLAY) Arthur Shirley (NOVEL) Belot
(LES ETRANGLEURS DE PARIS)
SC: Arthur Shirley, Bert Haldane

George Foley	Jagon/Simonnet
Malvina Longfellow	Cora Jagon
James Lindsay	Lorenz de Rifas
Laurence Tessier	Paul Blanchard
Ronald Power	Capt Guerin
Ivy King	Marie Guerin
Warwick Buckland	Rolf de Belfort
John Power	Coucou
Moore Marriott	Smiler

CRIME Paris, period. Lawyer's clerk is secret strangler who robs for extravagant daughter's sake.

06834
THE LURE OF CROONING WATER (6323) (A)
George Clark (Stoll)
D: Arthur Rooke
S:(NOVEL) Marion Hill
SC: Guy Newall

Guy Newall	Horace Dornblazer
Ivy Duke	Georgette
Hugh C. Buckler	Dr John Longden
Douglas Munro	Yes Smith
Mary Dibley	Rachel Dornblazer
Lawford Davidson	Frank Howard
Arthur Chesney	Gerald Pinkerton

Winifred Sadler . . . . Mrs Dusenberry
The Hood Children . . . . . . The Children
ROMANCE Convalescent actress ruins farmer's
marriage, then mends it.

06835
BLEAK HOUSE (6400) (A)
Ideal
D: Maurice Elvey
S: (NOVEL) Charles Dickens
SC: William J. Elliott
Constance Collier . . . . Lady Dedlock
Berta Gellardi . . . . Esther Summerson
E.Vivian Reynolds . . . . Tulkinghorne
Norman Page . . . . Guppy
Clifford Heatherley . . . . . . Bucket
Ion Swinley . . . . Capt Hawdon
A.Harding Steerman . . Sir Leicester Dedlock
Anthony StJohn . . . . Jo
Helen Haye . . . . Miss Barbay
Teddy Arundell . . . . George
Beatrix Templeton . . . . . . Rachel
CRIME Lady suspected of killing black-
mailing lawyer who learned of her child by
earlier marriage to criminal.

06836
DESIRE (4460) (U) retitled: THE MAGIC SKIN
B & C (Butcher)
P: Edward Godal
D:SC: George Edwardes Hall
S: (STORY) Honore de Balzac
(LE PEAU DE CHAGRIN)
Dennis Neilson-Terry. . . Raphael Valentin
Yvonne Arnaud . . . . Pauline
Christine Maitland . . . . Fedora
G. W. Anson . . . . Duval
Chris Walker . . . . Jonathon
Pardoe Woodman . . . . Emile
Austin Leigh . . . . Andre Valentin
Saba Raleigh . . . . Mother
FANTASY Ass's skin grants author's
wishes and makes him rich, but it is a dream.

06837
THE STORY OF THE ROSARY (5000)(U)
Master Films (BEF)
P: H.B. Parkinson
D: Percy Nash
S: (PLAY) Walter Howard
SC: W: Courtenay Rowden
Malvina Longfellow . . . . . Venetia
Dick Webb . . . . Paul Romaine
Charles Vane . . . . Prince Sabran
Frank Tennant . . . . Philip Romaine
Cameron Carr . . . . Venetia's Lover
Marjorie Day . . . . Princess Venetia
Irene Rooke . . . . Mother Superior
Victor Lusk . . . . Father Theodore
E.F. Wallace . . . . Colonel
DRAMA Ruritania. Man escapes from
revolution and saves beloved princess from
crooked brother.

06838
A SON OF DAVID (4700) (A)
Broadwest (Walturdaw)
P: Walter West
D: Hay Plumb
S: Charles Barnett
SC: Benedict James
Poppy Wyndham . . . . Esther Raphael
Ronald Colman . . . . Maurice Phillips
Arthur Walcott . . . . Louis Raphael
Constance Backner . . . . Miriam Myers
Robert Vallis . . . . Sam Myers
Joseph Pacey . . . . Maurice (child)
Vesta Sylva . . . . Esther (child)
SPORT Rabbi adopts orphan who becomes
boxer and fights man he thinks killed his
father.

06839
GARRYOWEN (5900) (U)
Welsh-Pearson
D:SC: George Pearson
S: (NOVEL) H. DeVere Stacpoole
Fred Groves . . . . Michael French
Hugh E. Wright . . . . Moriarty
Moyna McGill . . . . Violet Grimshaw
Bertram Burleigh . . . . . . Robert Dashwood
Arthur Cleave . . . . Giveean
Alec Thompson . . . . Andy
Little Zillah . . . . Effy French
Stella Brereton . . . . Mrs Moriarty
Mrs Braithwaite . . . . Mrs Driscoll
Marjorie Gaffney . . . . Biddy
Betty Cameron . . . . Susie
SPORT Ireland. Widower wins Derby and
daughter's American governess.

06840
THE HARP KING (5000)
Ace Films
Nan Wilkie . . . . Cynthia
W. R. Bell . . . . John Davenport
Jack Baker . . . . Stephen Graham
David Watt . . . . Leo Gordon
Miss Renny . . . . Cook
DRAMA Scotland. "The story is rather
slender and somewhat disconnected."

06841
THE ROMANCE OF ANNIE LAURIE (5000)
Lancashire Film Studios
D: Gerald Somers
S: (PLAY) Alfred Denville
Joan Gray . . . . Annie Laurie
Allan McKelvin . . . . Tammas Laurie
ROMANCE Scotland, period. Laird's bastard
child elopes with laird who is wed to mad
woman.

06842
STOP PRESS COMEDIES (series)
International Cine Corp
D:SC: Frank Miller
S: (CARTOONS) "Poy" (Percy Fearon)
Frank Stanmore . . . . John Citizen
Pauline Peters . . . . Mrs Citizen
Irene Tripod . . . . Mother
Lydia Sharpe . . . . Maid

06843
1: THE COAL SHORTAGE (1000)

06844
2: THE GOLDEN BALLOT (1000)

06845
3: STRIKE FEVER (1000)

06846
4: HOUSING (1000) reissue: 1922

06847
5: CONTROL (1000)
COMEDY Henpecked suburbanite in topical
situations.

06848
WILL O' WISP COMEDIES (series)
Gaumont
D: Cecil Mannering
S: William J. Elliott

06849
1: HORATIO'S DECEPTION (1000)
Arthur Riscoe . . . . Horatio
Nita Russell . . . . His Wife

06850
2: A COMPLETE CHANGE (1000)
William Burr . . . . The Bachelor
Daphne Hope . . . . The Girl

06851
3: THE OTHER DOG'S DAY (1000)
Arthur Riscoe . . . . The Husband
Nita Russell . . . . The Wife

06852
4: A LITTLE BET (1000)
Heather Thatcher . . . . The Daughter
Cyril Smith . . . . The Lover

06853
5: OH! JEMIMAH! (1000)
Arthur Riscoe . . . . The Master
Nita Russell . . . . The Mistress

06854
6: A PAIR OF GLOVES (1000)
Heather Thatcher . . . . The Girl
Cyril Smith . . . . The Man

06855
7: THE BITTEN BITER (1000)
Arthur Riscoe . . . . The Husband
Nita Russell . . . . The Wife

06856
8: HOME INFLUENCE (1000)
Heather Thatcher . . . . The Daughter
Cyril Smith . . . . The Lover
COMEDIES

06857
ONLY A MILL GIRL (5000)
Foxwell Films (Ideal)
P: Harry Foxwell
D: Lewis Willoughby
S: (PLAY) Sheila Walsh
Harry Foxwell . . . . John Raymond
Betty Farquhar . . . . Mary
Arthur Condy . . . . Jack Ainsleigh
Ida Lambert . . . . Constance Darville
Frank Lovett . . . . George Thornton
DRAMA Lancs. Mill foreman's daughter stops
rich woman from stealing inventor's plans.

06858
THE DEPARTMENT STORE (2000)
Martin's Photoplays
D:S: Fred Goodwins
Fred Goodwins . . . . Freddie
Gerald Thornton . . . . Shopwalker
Andy Hagen . . . . Detective
COMEDY Slapstick pursuit through large
department store.

06859
THE IMPOSSIBLE MAN (2000)
Martin's Photoplays
D:S: Fred Goodwins
Fred Goodwins . . . . Freddie
COMEDY

06860
THE NOBLE ART (2000)
Martin's Photoplays (ICC)
D:S: Fred Goodwins
Fred Goodwins . . . . Freddie
COMEDY Girl's weak suitor takes up boxing
and beats champion by mistake.

06861
THE SCARLET KISS (5000)
Martin's Photoplays (Faulkner)
D: SC: Fred Goodwins
S: (NOVEL) Gertrude deS. Wentworth James
Marjorie Hume
Cyril Raymond
Maud Cressall
Philip Hewland
SPORT

FEB

06862
ANNA THE ADVENTURESS (6280) (A)
Hepworth (National)
D: Cecil M. Hepworth
S: (NOVEL) E. Phillips Oppenheim
SC: Blanche McIntosh
Alma Taylor . . . . . . Anna/Annabel Pelissier
James Carew . . . . .Montagu Hill
Gerald Ames . . . . Nigel Ennison
Gwynne Herbert . . . . .Aunt
Christine Rayner . . . . Mrs Ellicote
Ronald Colman . . . . Brendan
James Annand . . . . Sir John Ferringhall
Jean Cadell . . . . Mrs White
CRIME Paris. Dancer poses as twin to shoot
crooked husband.

06863
THE AUCTION MART (5684) (A)
British Actors (Phillips)
D: Duncan Macrae
S: (NOVEL) Sydney Tremaine
SC: Adrian Brunel
Gertrude McCoy . . . . Jacqueline
Charles Quartermaine . . . . Her Father
Gerald Moore . . . . Basil Stair
Basil Foster . . . . Carver
Sir Simeon Stuart . . . . Peer
Moya Nugent . . . .
Henry Doughty . . . .
Minnie Rayner . . . .
DRAMA Paris. Cynical widower makes daughter
become crooked dancer, but she is reformed by
love.

06864
THE FALL OF A SAINT (6400) (A)
Gaumont-British Screencraft
D: W.P.Kellino
S: (NOVEL) Eric Clement Scott
Josephine Earle . . . . Countess de la Merthe
Gerald Lawrence . . . . . . Claude Maitland
W. T. Ellwanger . . . . Elkin Smith
Dallas Anderson . . . . . . Count de la Merthe
R. Heaton Grey . . . . Lord Norten
Thea Godfrey . . . . Katie Thimm
Reginald Culhane . . . . Sport Kennison
CRIME Tec blackmails lord who is lured from
East End mission by countess who killed
his brother.

06865
THE BARTON MYSTERY (6158) (A)
Stoll
D: Harry Roberts
S: (PLAY) Walter Hackett
SC: R. Byron -Webber
Lyn Harding . . . . Beverley
Hilda Bayley . . . . Ethel Standish
Vernon Jones . . . . Phyllis Grey
Maud Cressall . . . . Mrs Barton
Edward O'Neill . . . . Richard Standish
Arthur Pusey . . . . Harry Maitland
Ernest A. Cox . . . . Sir Everard Marshall
Eva Westlake . . . . Lady Marshall
Austen Camp . . . . Gerald Barton
CRIME Fake medium's inspiration proves man
did not kill blackmailer.

06866
THE WORLDLINGS (6000) (U)
General Attractions (Globe)
D:SC: Eric Harrison
S: (NOVEL) Leonard Merrick
Basil Gill . . . . . . Maurice Blake/Philip Jardine
Ivy Close . . . . Lady Helen Cleve
Margaret Halstan . . . . . . Rosa Fleming

Edward O'Neill . . . . Sir Noel Jardine
DRAMA Lady stands by husband when his
ex-mistress proves he is impostor.

06867
LORNA DOONE (5150) (A)
Butcher
D: H. Lisle Lucoque
S: (NOVEL) R. D. Blackmore
SC: Nellie E. Lucoque
Dennis Wyndham . . . . Jan Ridd
Bertie Gordon . . . . Lorna Doone
Roy Raymond . . . . Carver Doone
George Bellamy . . . . John Fry
Cecil Morton York . . . . Sir Ensor Doone
Frank Dane . . . . Tom Faggus
Tom Ronald . . . . Jeremy Stickles
Joan Cockram . . . . Annie Ridd
Gertrude Sterroll . . . . Mistress Ridd
Bessie Herbert . . . . Betty Muxworthy
ADVENTURE Exmoor, 1625. Yeoman loves
outlaw's daughter who is really stolen
heiress.

06868
CALVARY (5200) (A)
Master Films (BEF)
P: H. B. Parkinson
D: Edwin J. Collins
S: (NOVEL) Rita
SC: William Courtenay Rowden
Malvina Longfellow . . Lady Pamela Stevenage
Henry Victor . . . . David Penryn
Charles Vane . . . . Lord Stevenage
Dorothy Moody . . . . Ruth Penryn
Wallace Bosco . . . . Reuben Leaffe
J ames F. Henry . . . . Stephen Ormiston
Barbara Everest . . . . Rachel Penryn
E. F. Wallace . . . . Mr Penryn
George Goodwin . . . . . Squire Craddock
ROMANCE Cornwall. Shipwrecked boy becomes
priest and loves slum landlord's wife.

06869
THE LAST ROSE OF SUMMER (6500) (U)
G.B. Samuelson (Granger)
D: Albert Ward
S: (NOVEL) Hugh Conway
SC: Roland Pertwee
Daisy Burrell . . . . Lotus Devine
Owen Nares . . . . Oliver Selwyn
Minna Grey . . . . Amy Palliser
Tom Reynolds . . . . Mr Palliser
Richard Barry . . . . Alf Purvis
John Phelps . . . . Percy Melville
ROMANCE Collector feigns love for
spinster to obtain her father's tea service.

06870
ROSALEEN DHU (4000)
Celtic Producing Co
D: William Powers
S: (PLAY) Joseph Denver
William Powers . . . . Ned Malone
ADVENTURE Irish heir framed for murder
joins Legion and weds Algerian who is
really stolen heiress.

06871
THE SHOEBLACK OF PICCADILLY (5000)
Academy Photoplays
D: L. Stuart Greening
Eileen Magrath . . . . Cherry
Daisy Cordell . . . .
Victor Humfrey . . . .
Ernest A. Douglas . . . .
Eric Gray . . . .
DRAMA Slum girl saves benefactor's son
from tricksters.

MAR

06872
GENERAL POST (5000)
Ideal reissue: 1922 (3 rls cut)
D: Thomas Bentley
S: (PLAY) J. E. Howard Terry
SC: Eliot Stannard
Lilian Braithwaite . . . . Lady Broughton
Henderson Bland . . . . Edward Smith
Joyce Dearsley . . . . Betty Broughton
Dawson Millward . . . . Sir Denys Broughton
Douglas Munro . . . . Albert Smith
Colstan Mansell . . . . . . Alec Broughton
Teddy Arundell . . . . Jobson
Sara de Groot . . . . Miss Prendergast
Adelaide Grace . . . . Lady Wareing
Thomas Canning . . . . Lord Wareing
Irene Drew . . . . Mary Wareing
WAR 1914. Aristocrat allows daughter to
marry tailor after he wins VC saving son's life.

06873
THE HOUSE ON THE MARSH (5250) (A)
London (Jury)
D: Fred Paul
S: (NOVEL) Florence Warden
Cecil Humphreys . . . . Gervas Rayner
Peggy Patterson . . . . Violet Christie
Harry Welchman . . . . Laurence Reed
Frank Stanmore . . . . Rev Golightly
Madge Tree . . . . Sarah Gooch
Mary Godfrey . . . . Miss Rayner
CRIME Norfolk. Governess unmasks employer
as leader of gang of thieves.

06874
THE JOYOUS ADVENTURES OF ARISTIDE
PUJOL (5000)
Foss (Phillips)
P: Kenelm Foss
D: SC: Frank Miller
S: (NOVEL) W.J. Locke
Kenelm Foss . . . . Aristide Pujol
Pauline Peters . . . . Arlesienne/Euphemie
Barbara Everest . . . . Anne Honeywood
George Tawde . . . . Bondon
Irene Tripod . . . . Mme Gougasse
Arthur Helmore . . . . . . Smith
Bryan Powley . . . . Bocardon
Douglas Heathcote . . . . Hon Harry Ralston
Blanche Churms . . . . . . Christabel Smith
COMEDY France. Man poses as baron,
reconciles couple, sells corn cure, adopts child,
and marries spinster.

06875
LET'S PRETEND (2000)
Reardon-British
D: James Reardon
S: Frank Miller
James Reardon . . . . Clerk
Pauline Peters . . . . Girl
Dennis Cooper . . . . Man
Donald Lush . . . . Boss
James Chilcott . . . . Manager
COMEDY Sacked clerk poses as his boss to
deceive job hunter.

06876
THE AMATEUR GENTLEMAN (7435) (A)
Stoll
D: Maurice Elvey
S: (NOVEL) Jeffrey Farnol
Langhorne Burton . . . . Barnabas Barty
Madge Stuart . . . . . Lady Cleone Meredith
Cecil Humphreys . . . . . Wilfred Chichester
Herbert Synott . . . . John Barty
Pardoe Woodman . . . . , Ronald Barrymaine

Alfred Paumier . . . . Prince Regent
Gerald McCarthy . . . Vis Horatio Debenham
Geoffrey Wilmer . . . . . . Capt Slingsby
Sydney Seaward . . . . Sir Mortimer Carnaby
Vivian Reynolds . . . . Jasper Gaunt
Dalton Somers . . . . Natty Bell
Teddy Arundell . . . . Digby Smivvle
Will Corri . . . . Capt Chumley
Judd Green . . . . Jerry the Bosun
A.C.Fotheringham-Lysons . . Peterby
Sinclair Hill . . . . Jerningham
ADVENTURE 1820. Innkeeper's son poses as
gentleman and saves Lady's brother from
creditors.

06877
HOBSON'S CHOICE (5547) (U)
Master (BEF)
D: Percy Nash
S: (PLAY) Harold Brighouse
SC: W. C. Rowden
Joe Nightingale . . . . Will Mossup
Joan Ritz . . . . Maggie Hobson
Arthur Pitt . . . . Henry Hobson
Joan Cockram . . . . Vickey Hobson
George Wynn . . . . Albert Prosser
Phyllis Birkett . . . . Alice Hobson
Charles Heslop . . . . Fred Beenstock
Ada King . . . . Mrs Hepworth
Mary Byron . . . . Ada Figgins
Louis Rihll . . . . Jim Heeler
Charles Stone . . . . Tubby Wadlow
Judd Green . . . . Landlord
COMEDY Lancs, 1885. Tyrannical boot-
maker's daughter weds meek assistant.

06878
IN THE DAYS OF SAINT PATRICK (4200)(U)
General Film Supply (Janion)
P: D: Norman Whitten
S: Mr McGuinness
Ira Allen . . . . St Patrick
Vernon Whitten . . . . St Patrick (child)
Alice Cardinall . . . . Conchessa
Dermot McCarthy . . . . Calpurnius
J. B. Carrickford . . . . St. Martin
George Brame . . . . Pope Celestin
Ernest Matthewson . . . . Bishop Tassach
George Griffin . . . . King Laoghaire
Maude Hume . . . . Queen
Mary Murnane . . . . Foster Mother
Herbert Mayne . . . . Gornias
Eddie Lawless . . . . Milcho
O'Carroll Reynolds . . . . . . Niall
Jack McDermott . . . . Victor
HISTORY Ireland, 400. Bishop establishes
missionary settlements.

06879
WATCH YOUR STEP (2000)
Peacock Dance Comedies
D: S: Geoffrey H. Malins
Ena Beaumont . . . . The Girl
Victor Robson . . . . The Man
Polly Emery . . . . The Wife
COMEDY

06880
OUR GIRLS AND THEIR PHYSIQUE (series)
Physical Film Agency (Neville Bruce)
D:S: Geoffrey H. Malins
Ena Beaumont . . . . Peggy O'Connor
Wyn Weaver . . . . Mr Brown
Victor Robson . . . . Victor

06881
No. 1 (784) (U)

06882
No. 2 (756) (U)

06883
No. 3 (632) (U)

06884
No. 4 (760) (U)

06885
No. 5 (892) (U)

06886
No. 6 (1000) (U)
COMEDIES Rich man's athletic niece reforms
lazy daughters.

06887
THE BLACK SHEEP (5000) (A)
Progress (Butcher)
P: Frank E. Spring
D:SC: Sidney Morgan
S: (NOVEL) Ruby M. Ayres
Marguerite Blanche . . . . Nora Ackroyd
George Keene . . . . George Laxton
Eve Balfour . . . . Laurie Fenton
George Bellamy . . . . Mr Ackroyd
Arthur Lennard . . . . Mr Fenton
ROMANCE Vamp tries to lure penniless heir
away from financier's daughter.

06888
THE SCARLET WOOING (5000) (A)
Progress (Butcher)
P: Frank E. Spring
D: S: Sidney Morgan
Eve Balfour . . . . Mrs Raeburn
George Keene . . . . Paul Raeburn
Marguerite Blanche . . . . Nancy
Joan Morgan . . . . May Raeburn
George Bellamy . . . . Dr Andrew Hooper
Harry Newman . . . . Roland Standish
Arthur Walcott . . . . John Pollock
Edward Godal . . . . Clubman
Nigel d'A. Black-Hawkins . . . Clubman
DRAMA Author's sensational novel pays for
daughter's operation but leads sister-in-law
astray.

06889
MR GILFIL'S LOVE STORY (5400) (U)
Ideal
D: A. V. Bramble
S: (NOVEL) George Eliot
(SCENES OF CLERICAL LIFE)
SC: Eliot Stannard
R. Henderson Bland . . . . . . Maynard Gilfil
Mary Odette . . . . Caterina
Peter Upcher . . . . Anthony Wybrow
Dora de Winton . . . . Lady Cheverel
A. Harding Steerman . . . Sir Christopher Chevere
Aileen Bagot . . . . Beatrice Assher
Norma Whalley . . . . .Lady Assher
John Boella . . . . Signor Sarti
Irene Drew . . . . Dorcas
Bobbie Clifton . . . . Knott
DRAMA Lord adopts Italian girl who falls
in love with his son, and stabs him when he
marries heiress.

06890
WALLS OF PREJUDICE (5200)
Gaumont-British Screencraft
D: C.C. Calvert
S: (PLAY) Mrs Alexander Grossman
(BREAK DOWN THE WALLS)
Josephine Earle . . . . Margaret Benson
Dallas Anderson . . . . Patrick Benson
Pat Somerset . . . . Townsend
Zoe Palmer . . . . Madge Benson
Humberston Wright . . . . . . Bigton
Cyril Smith . . . . Karpat
DRAMA Woman who secretly owns dress shop
saves her bankrupt husband from crooked
wholesaler.

06891
A DEAD CERTAINTY (4494)(U)
Broadwest (Walturdaw)
P: Walter West
D: George Dewhurst
S: (NOVEL) Nat Gould
SC: P.L. Mannock
Gregory Scott . . . . Arthur Dunbar
Poppy Wyndham . . . . Pat Stone
Cameron Carr . . . . Henry Stone
Harry Royston . . . . Martin Mills
Mary Masters . . . . Mrs Woodruff
Wallace Bosco
SPORT Usurper tries to force niece's suitor to
lose horse race.

06892
YOUNG EVE AND OLD ADAM
Union Photoplays
S: (NOVEL) Tom Gallon
DRAMA

APR

06893
WILL O'WISP COMEDIES (series)
Gaumont
D: W.P. Kellino

06894
9—SWEEP (1000)
Cyril Smith . . . . Horace Smith
Nita Russell . . . . Dolly

06895
10—ON THE RESERVE (1309)(U)
Cyril Smith . . . . Lightning
Nita Russell . . . . Dolly
Zoe Palmer . . . . Clara
Dick Webb . . . . Horace
Iris Rowe . . . . Sarah

06896
11—CUPID'S CARNIVAL (1485)(U)
Cyril Smith . . . . Horace
Nita Russell . . . . Achille

06897
12—RUN! RUN! (1000)
Cyril Smith . . . . Horace Bruce
Nita Russell . . . . Dolly Bruce

06898
13—A BROKEN CONTRACT (1116)(A)
Cyril Smith . . . . Horace
Nita Russell . . . . Dolly
Zoe Palmer . . . . The Girl

06899
14—COUSIN EBENEZER (1000)
Cyril Smith . . . . Mr Doolittle
Nita Russell . . . . The Wife
Dick Webb . . . . The Husband

06900
15—SOUVENIRS (1000)
Cyril Smith . . . . Hubby
Nita Russell . . . . Wifie

06901
16—THE LIGHTNING LIVER CURE (1000)
Cyril Smith . . . . Horace
Nita Russell . . . . Dolly
COMEDIES

06902
SILVER BADGE COMEDIES (series)
Silver Badge
D:S: Jack Ross
Jack Eaton
Frank Howard
Harold Vesta
Minnie Connolly

06903
1. — WHAT MIGHT HAVE BEEN (2000)

06904
2—BOOKS AND CROOKS (2000)

06905
3—IT MAY COME TO THIS (2000)
COMEDIES Made and acted by
ex-servicemen.

06906
MARY LATIMER, NUN (5000)
Famous Pictures
D: Bert Haldane
S: (NOVEL) Eva Elwen, (PLAY) Will H. Glaze
SC: R. Byron-Webber
Malvina Longfellow ..... Mary Latimer
Warwick Ward .... Hon Alfred Pierpoint
Ethel Fisher .... Clarice Pierpoint
George Foley .... Sam Stubbs
H. Agar Lyons .... Lord Pierpoint
Moore Marriott .... Dicky Stubbs
Laurence Tessier ....
Minnie Rayner ....
DRAMA Peer's son weds slum girl, deserts her,
and she becomes music hall singer.

06907
UNMARRIED (6000)(A)
Granger's Exclusives
P: A.G. Granger
D: Rex Wilson
S: Dr. C.H. Charles, Arthur Backner
Gerald du Maurier ..... Rev Roland Allington
Malvina Longfellow ..... Jenny Allington
Edmund Gwenn .... Simon Vandeleur
Mary Glynne .... Vivien Allington
Hayford Hobbs .... Cyril Myles
Mary Rorke .... Prudence
Arthur Walcott .... Sir John Allington
Constance Backner .... Mary Myles
Annie Esmond .... Miss Pringle
Vivian Palmer .... Cyril Morley
Ralph Forster .... Harker
Gladys Cooper
Dennis Eadie
Viola Tree
Lady Diana Cooper
Lord Bentinck
Earl of Craven
Lady Greenwood
Lady Trevor
Dr Saleeby
DRAMA Squire's daughter weds landlord
who later falls for her grown-up bastard
daughter.

06908
ENCHANTMENT (6000)(A)
London (Jury)
D: Einar J. Bruun
S: (NOVEL) E. Temple Thurston
SC: Frank Fowell
Henry Krauss .... John Desmond
Mary Odette .... Pat Desmond
Eric Barclay .... Charles Stuart
Edward O'Neill .... Sandy Stuart
Henry Vibart .... Father Casey
Mary Brough .... Mrs Slattery
George Bellamy .... Tim Cassidy
Joyce Barbour .... Sophie Desmond
Hargreave Mansell ..... Dr O'Connor
Caleb Porter .... Sailor
DRAMA Ireland. Smuggler's son saves
drunkard's daughter from convent.

06909
UNREST (6000)
Cairns Torquay Films (Allied Exporters)
P:D: Dallas Cairns
S: (NOVEL) Warwick Deeping
SC: R. Byron-Webber
Dallas Cairns .... Martin Frensham
Mary Dibley .... Nella Frensham
Maud Yates .... Judith Ruddinger
Edward O'Neill ....
George Harrington ....
Marjorie Hoare ....
ROMANCE Playwright deserts wife for globe-
trotting widow but returns on learning she
has borne him son.

06910
TROUSERS (5000)
BP Productions (Lionel Phillips)
P:D: Bertram Phillips
S: Harry Engholm
Queenie Thomas .... Trousers
Jack Leigh .... Martin Chester
Fred Morgan .... Prof Dewbiggin
Bernard Vaughan .... Peter Salt
Barbara Leigh .... Trousers (child)
Elizabeth Herbert ....
ROMANCE Orphan girl, raised as boy, loves
man who does not know his wife is dead.

06911
THE FACE AT THE WINDOW (5650)(A)
British Actors (Phillips)
P: Gerald Malvern
D: Wilfred Noy
S: (PLAY) F. Brooke Warren
SC: Adrian Brunel
C. Aubrey Smith .... Bentick
Gladys Jennings .... Marie de Brisson
Jack Hobbs .... Lucien Cartwrigh
Charles Quartermaine .... Lucien Degradoff
Ben Field .... Peter Pottlebury
Sir Simeon Stuart ..... Henri de Brisson
Kathleen Vaughan ...... Babette
Kinsey Peile .... Dr le Blanc
CRIME Paris. Dead detective electrically
revived to expose chevalier as bank robber.

06912
AT THE VILLA ROSE (7038)(A)
Stoll
D: Maurice Elvey
S: (NOVEL) A.E.W. Mason
SC: Sinclair Hill
Manora Thew .... Celia Harland
Langhorne Burton ..... Harry Weathermill
Teddy Arundell .... Insp Hanaud
Norman Page .... Julius Ricardo
Joan Beverley .... Adele Rossignol
Eva Westlake .... Mme Dauvray
Kate Gurney .... Helene
J.L. Boston .... Besnard
Armand Lenders .... Perichet
CRIME Monaco. Jewel thieves kidnap
fraudulent medium and frame her for
strangling widow.

MAY
06913
BROKEN BOTTLES (2000)
Gaumont-Around The Town
D:S: Leslie Henson
Leslie Henson .... Bottling Barrows
Nora Howard .... Lillian Swish
Stanley Brightman ..... The Chink
Peggy Carlisle .... Girl
COMEDY Boxer beaten by his drunken
daughter and killed by his opponent.

06914
ALF'S BUTTON (7050) (U)
Hepworth *reissue*: 1921
D: Cecil M. Hepworth
S: (PLAY) W.A. Darlington
SC: Blanche McIntosh
Leslie Henson .... Alf Higgins
Alma Taylor .... Liz
Gerald Ames .... Lt Denis Allen
James Carew .... Eustace the Genie
Eileen Dennes .... Lady Isobel Fitzpeter
John McAndrews .... Bill Grant
Gwynne Herbert .... Lady Fitzpeter
Jean Cadell .... Vicar's Wife
COMEDY 1917. Soldier's tunic button made
from Aladdin's lamp, grants his wishes.

06915
SOME PICNIC (1000)
Victor Washington Films
D:S: Frederick H. Washer
Mabel Holland .... The Girl
Archie Decoy .... Man
Herbert Jameson .... Man
COMEDY Warwick.

06916
THE DEFINITE OBJECT (4200)(A)
Eros Films
P: Countess Bubna
D:SC: Edgar J. Camiller
S: (NOVEL) Jeffrey Farnol
Ann Elliott .... Hermione Chesterton
Peter Upcher .... Geoffrey Ravenslee
Lionel Scott .... Joe Shaddon
Charles Stafford-Dickens ...
Eric Lugg ....
J. Cleak-Morton ....
CRIME New York. Slum girl reforms gangster.

06917
THE BLACK SPIDER (5800)(A)
B & C (Butcher)
P: Edward Godal
D:SC: William J. Humphrey
S: (NOVEL) Carlton Dawe
Lydia Kyasht .... Angela Carfour
Bertram Burleigh .... Archie Lowndes
Sam Livesey .... Reginald Conway
Ronald Colman ...... Vicomte de Beauvais
Hayden Coffin .... Lord Carfour
Adeline Hayden Coffin .... Lady Carfour
Mary Clare .... Coralie Mount
Dorothy Cecil .... Marjorie West
CRIME Monte Carlo. Girl poses as masked
thief to fool detective and is saved from
crooked vicomte.

06918
AT THE MERCY OF TIBERIUS (6000) USA:
THE PRICE OF SILENCE
G.B. Samuelson (General)
D: Fred Leroy Granville
S: (NOVEL) Augusta Wilson
Peggy Hyland .... Beryl Brentano
Campbell Gullan .... Col Luke Darrington
Tom Chatterton .... Lennox Dunbar
Van Dycke .... Frank Darrington
Dorothy Gordon .... Mrs Brentano
CRIME Accused girl saved when lightning
imprints her grandfather's murder upon
window. (Made in Hollywood)

06919
LOVE IN THE WILDERNESS (6000)(A)
G.B. Samuelson (General)
D: Alexander Butler
S: (NOVEL) Gertrude Page
Madge Titheradge .... Enid Davenport

C.M. Hallard	Keith Meredith
Campbell Gullan	Hon Dicky Byrd
Maudie Dunham	Nancy Johnson
Hubert Davies	George Whiting
Frances Griffiths	Marion Davenport
Lynore Linard	Mrs Meredith

DRAMA Rhodesia. Girl's married lover kills her cruel husband. (Made in Hollywood)

06920
THE IRON STAIR (5972)(A) USA: THE BRANDED SOUL
Stoll
D:SC: F. Martin Thornton
S: (NOVEL) "Rita"

Reginald Fox	Geoffrey/George Gale
Madge Stuart	Renee Jessup
Frank Petley	Andrew Jessup
H. Agar Lyons	Mortimer Peacham
J. Edwards Barber	Warder Donkin

CRIME Man poses as clerical twin to cash forged cheque but later takes cleric's place when he breaks jail.

06921
FATE'S PLAYTHING (5500)(U)
Anglo-Hollandia (Butcher)
P: Maurits Binger
D: B.E. Doxat-Pratt
S: (NOVEL) C.F. Harding (ORANGES AND LEMONS)
SC: Reginald Lawson

Constance Worth	Dolores Blackett
Bruce Gordon	Dr Lucas Murray
Adelqui Migliar	Hugo Amadis
Frank Dane	Charles Blackett
Hector Abbas	Sylvester
Henry Scofield	Blackett

ROMANCE Man abandons wife and sick baby, and she is saved by her ex-fiancee. (Made in Holland).

06922
AS GOD MADE HER(5000)
Anglo-Hollandia (National)
P: Maurits Binger
D:SC: B.E. Doxat-Pratt
S: (NOVEL) Helen Prothero-Lewis

Mary Odette	Rachel Higgins
Henry Victor	Seward Pendyne
Adelqui Migliar	Sir Richard Pendyne
Lola Cornero	Lady Muriel Pendyne

ROMANCE Cornwall. Lady persuades son's lowly wife to desert him. (Made in Holland).

06923
JUDGE NOT (4100)(A)
London (Jury)
D: Einar J. Bruun
S: Holger Madsen

Fay Compton	Nelly
Fred Groves	Burke
Chappell Dossett	Frank Raymond
Eric Barclay	Billy
Frank Stanmore	
Mary Brough	
Henry Vibart	
George Bellamy	
Wallace Bosco	
Christine Silver	

DRAMA Street missionary seeks lost daughter after shooting wife on suspicion of adultery.

06924
TROTTER ON THE TROT (2000)
Southend Films
P: Lucy Heys Thomson
D:S: Tom Aitken

Arthur Lenville	Trotter
Irene Tripod	Mrs Trotter
Molly Desmond	

Fred Cunninghame ....
COMEDY Southend. Henpeck tries to elude wife at seaside.

06925
THE DAWN OF TRUTH (5000)
L.C. MacBean (Equitable)
D:S: L.C. MacBean

John Gliddon	Frank Bathurst
Helga Jerome	Enid Bathurst
Frederick Sargent	Neil Claverton
Bernard Vaughan	Uncle John
H.R. Hignett	Robert Bathurst
Sydney Wood	Frank (child)
Babs Ronald	Enid (child)
Ida Handley	Clara Bathurst
Lottie Blackford	Neighbour
Nessie Blackford	Landlady
Tom Ronald	Groom

DRAMA Financier's daughter loves adopted brother, who is saved from explosion by inventor who is really her father.

06926
THE GLAD EYE (6000)
Reardon British Films (IFT)
P: James Reardon
D:SC: Kenelm Foss
S: (PLAY) Paul Armont, Nicholas Nancy (LE ZEBRE)

James Reardon	Gaston Bocard
Dorothy Minto	Kiki
Hayford Hobbs	Maurice Polignac
Pauline Peters	Lucienne Bocard
Peggy Marsh	Suzanne Polignac
Will Corrie	Gallipot
Lyell Johnstone	Tricassin
William Armstrong	Sox
Blanche Churms	Juliette
Douglas Munro	Gendarme
Joe Peterman	Manager
George Bellamy	Spiritualist

COMEDY France. Spiritualist's son forced to feign death when airship he is supposed to be on crashes.

JUN

06927
THE HUNDREDTH CHANCE (6585)(A)
Stoll
D: Maurice Elvey
S: (NOVEL) Ethel M. Dell
SC: Sinclair Hill

Dennis Neilson-Terry	Lord Saltash
Mary Glynne	Lady Maud Brian
Eille Norwood	Dr Jonathon Capper
Sydney Seaward	Jack Bolton
Teddy Arundell	Giles Sheppard
Patrick Key	Bunny Brian
Carmita Lascelles	Mrs Sheppard

ROMANCE Lady marries horse trainer but withholds herself until crippled brother is cured.

06928
HER SON (6023)(A)
Broadwest (Walturdaw)
D: Walter West
S: (PLAY) Horace Annesley Vachell
SC: Bertram Brown

Violet Hopson	Dorothy Fairfax
Stewart Rome	Dick Gascoyne
Mercy Hatton	Crystal Wride
Cameron Carr	David Hesseltine
John Stuart	Min Gascoyne
Mary Masters	Susan
Nicholas Hopson Worcester	Min (child)

ROMANCE Explorer's return from 'death' kills his French wife and he marries girl who adopted his son.

06929
A TEMPORARY GENTLEMAN (6000)(U)
G.B. Samuelson (Granger)
D: Fred W. Durrant
S: (PLAY) H.F. Maltby

Owen Nares	Walter Hope
Madge Titheradge	Miss Hudson
Tom Reynolds	Mr. Jack
Maudie Dunham	Alice Hope
Sydney Fairbrother	Mrs Hope
Alfred Drayton	Sir Herbert Hudson

COMEDY Clerk's service as subaltern spoils him for menial work.

06930
HER STORY (5000)
G.B. Samuelson (General)
D: Alexander Butler
S: Dion Titheradge
SC:William B. Laub

Madge Titheradge	Betty Thorpe
Campbell Gullan	Oscar Koplan
C.M. Hallard	Ashelyn

DRAMA Russian gambler breaks jail to attack wife who married her employer. (Made in Hollywood).

06931
FOUL PLAY (4594)(A)
Master (BEF)
S: (NOVEL) Charles Reade
SC: W.C. Rowden

Renee Kelly	Helen Rollaston
Henry Hallett	Penfold
Randolph McLeod	Wardlow
Cecil Morton York	Mr Wardlow
C. Hargrave Mansell	Rev Penfold
Charles Vane	Gen Rollaston
N. Watts-Phillips	Joseph Wylie

CRIME 1870. Owner's son mistakenly scuttles ship aboard which are framed tutor and Australian Governor's daughter.

06932
THE SHADOW BETWEEN (5000)(A)
Seal (Granger)
D:SC: George Dewhurst
S: (NOVEL) Silas K. Hocking

Doris Lloyd	Marion West
Lewis Dayton	Clement Mawgan
Sir Simeon Stuart	Lord Grovely
Cherry Winter	Esther Mawgan
Gertrude Sterroll	Mrs Mawgan
Wally Bosco	Dick West
Billie Berkeley	Julia Treven
Horace Corbyn	Mr Jackson
H. Lane Bayliff	Mr Evans

CRIME Cornwall. Lord steals servant's papers proving she is his dead brother's child.

06933
CASTLES IN SPAIN (5000)
Lucoque-Taylor (Gau)
D: H. Lisle Lucoque
S: (NOVEL) Ruby M. Ayres
SC: Nellie E. Lucoque

C. Aubrey Smith	The Builder
Lilian Braithwaite	Elizabeth Cherry
Bertie Gordon	Rachael
Hayford Hobbs	Roger Welchman
Maud Yates	Gwendolen Welchman
Charles Vane	The Lame Man
R. Heaton Grey	George Henson
Jeff Barlow	The Lavender Man
May Lind	Diana Wynne

ROMANCE Author's nephew loves mother's companion, who turns out to be author's bastard.

06934
DUKE'S SON (6000)(USA: SQUANDERED LIVES)
George Clark (Stoll)
D: Franklin Dyall
S: (NOVEL) Cosmo Hamilton
SC: Guy Newall
Guy Newall . . . . Lord Francis Delamere
Ivy Duke . . . . Loan Lambourne
Hugh C. Buckler . . . . Sir Robert Sheen
C. Lawford Davidson . . . .Charles Denbeigh-Smith
Ruth Mackay . . . . Mrs Denbeigh-Smith
Edward O'Neill . . . . Duke of Cheshire
Mary Merrall . . . . Billy Honour
Philip Hewland . . . . Lord Tarporley
Toni Edgar Bruce . . . . Mary Delamere
Douglas Munro . . . . Burberry
Winifred Sadler . . . . Mrs Burberry
DRAMA Duke's heir, exposed as cardsharp by millionaire who covets his wife, plans their mutual gassing but goes blind.

06935
THE WAY OF THE WORLD (5000)(A)
I.B. Davidson (Granger)
D:S: A.E. Coleby
A.E. Coleby . . . . Seth Langton
Capt Gordon Coghill . . . . . . Dick Jefferson
Charles Vane . . . . Marshall
Babs Ronald . . . . Angela (child)
Cherry Hardy . . . . Angela Burton
Sgt Stanley . . . . Bill Swayne
Olive Bell . . . . Landlady
H. Nicholls-Bates . . . . Landlord
Humberston Wright . . . . Manager
SPORT Carter adopts sick child and beats her father in boxing match.

06936
SEEING DOUBLE (2000)
Reardon-British
D: James Reardon
S: Bertram Fryer
James Reardon . . . . Husband
Irene Tripod . . . . Wife
Eileen Carol . . . . Maid
Heather Carol . . . . Maid
COMEDY Wife discovers husband's intrigue with twin maids.

JUL

06937
THE EVER-OPEN DOOR (4850)(U)
Ideal
D: Fred Goodwins
S: (PLAY) George R. Sims, H.H. Herbert
SC: William J. Elliott
Hayford Hobbs . . . . Dick
Daphne Glenne . . . . Miriam
Margaret Hope . . . . Janet
Sydney Wood . . . . Robbie
Terence Cavanagh . . . . . . Hon John Halstead
Ralph Forster . . . . Father Clement
CRIME Crooked Lord's ex-mistress discloses shot boy is stolen heir.

06938
COLONEL NEWCOME THE PERFECT GENTLEMAN (5500)(U)
Ideal
D: Fred Goodwins
S: (NOVEL) William Thackeray (THE NEWCOMES)
SC: William J. Elliott
Milton Rosmer . . . . Barnes Newcome
Joyce Carey . . . . Rose
Temple Bell . . . . Ethel Newcome
Lewis Willoughby . . . . Col Newcome
Dame May Whitty . . . . Mrs MacKenzie

Fred Morgan . . . . Baynham
Haidee Wright . . . . Lady Newcome
Bobby Andrews . . . . Clive Newcome
Norma Whalley . . . . Lady Clare
DRAMA Col's son loves girl compromised by widow's son in scheme to enforce rich marriage.

06939
DAVID AND JONATHAN (6000)(A)
G.B. Samuelson (General)
D: Alexander Butler
S: (NOVEL) E. Temple Thurston
Madge Titheradge . . . . Joan Meredith
Geoffrey Webb . . . . David Mortlake
Richard Ryan . . . . Jonathan Hawksley
Sidney Wood . . . . David (child)
Jack Perks . . . . Jonathan (child)
ADVENTURE Africa. Shipwrecked friends love same girl. (Made in Hollywood)

06940
THE NIGHT RIDERS (6000)
G.B. Samuelson (General)
D: Alexander Butler
S: (NOVEL) Ridgwell Cullum
SC: Irene Miller
Albert Ray . . . . John Tresler
Maudie Dunham . . . . Diana Marbolt
Andre Beaulieu . . . . Jake Marbolt
WESTERN Alberta. Cornish emigrant unmasks chief rustler as girl's "blind" father. (Made in Hollywood).

06941
THE UGLY DUCKLING (6000)
G.B. Samuelson (General)
D: Alexander Butler
Albert Ray . . . . Owen Wilshire
Florence Turner . . . . Charmis Graham
Maudie Dunham . . . . Sally Lee
William Merrick . . . . John Wilshire
COMEDY Telephone supervisor saves banker's son from theft charge. (Made in Hollywood).

06942
NANCE (5500)(U)
G.B. Samuelson (General)
D:SC: Albert Ward
S: (NOVEL) Charles Garvice
Isobel Elsom . . . . Nance Gray
James Lindsay . . . . Lord Stoyle
Ivan Samson . . . . Bernard Yorke
Mary Forbes . . . . Felicia Damarche
J.R. Crawford . . . .
Percival Clarke . . . .
Bassett Roe . . . .
Howard Sturge . . . .
Mme d'Esterre . . . .
DRAMA Gambling squire's mistress inherits mortgage from unknown father, and is blackmailed.

06943
AUNT RACHEL (5500)(U)
G.B. Samuelson (Granger)
D: Albert Ward
S: (NOVEL) David C. Murray
SC: Roland Pertwee, Hugh Conway
Isobel Elsom . . . . Ruth
Haidee Wright . . . . Aunt Rachel
James Lindsay . . . . .Ferdinand de Blacquaire
Lionelle Howard . . . . Reuben
Tom Reynolds . . . . Eld
Dalton Somers . . . . Fuller
Leonard Pagden . . . . Ezra Gold
Hubert Willis . . . . Earl
Dan Godfrey . . . . Isiah
ROMANCE Stafford, 1850. Jilted aunt refuses to let niece marry violinist's nephew.

06944
THE LAND OF MYSTERY (7220)(A)
Harold Shaw (Laurillard & Grossmith)
P:D: Harold Shaw
S: Basil Thompson
SC: Bannister Merwin
Edna Flugrath . . . . Masikowa
Norman Tharp . . . . Lenoff
Fred Morgan . . . . Prince
Christine Rayner . . . .
Harold French . . . .
M.R. Morand . . . .
Lewis Gilbert . . . .
John East . . . .
Phyllis Bedells . . . .
Laurent Nordikoff . . . .
DRAMA Russia. Thief, saved by prince, becomes revolutionary and lets prince escape with dancer.

06945
WON BY A HEAD (4198)(A)
Sterling (BEF)
D: Percy Nash
S: (NOVEL) John Gabriel
Rex Davis . . . . Chester Lawton
Frank Tennant . . . . Milton Bell
Vera Cornish . . . . Phyllis Reid
Wallace Bosco . . . . Jim Kort
Douglas Payne . . . .
J. Edwards Barber . . . .
Madge Tree . . . .
SPORT Boxer breaks jail to win race and prove he did not kill father.

06946
A CIGARETTE MAKER'S ROMANCE (5000)
International Producers Federation
D: Tom Watts
S: (PLAY) Charles Hannan (NOVEL) Marion Crawford
SC: E. Ross
Henderson Bland . . . . Count Skariatine
Dorothy Vernon . . . . Vjera
William Parry . . . . Shopkeeper
Tom Conventry . . . .
Margaret Phillips . . . .
DRAMA France. Amnesiac Russian Count goes mad every Wednesday; girl sells her hair to pay for doll he breaks.

06947
JOHN HERIOT'S WIFE (5600)
Anglo-Hollandia (National)
P: Maurits Binger
D:SC: B.E. Doxat-Pratt
S: (NOVEL) Claude & Alice Askew
Mary Odette . . . . Camilla Heriot
Henry Victor . . . . John Heriot
Adelqui Migliar . . . . Eric Ashlynne
Anna Bosilova . . . . Sara Headcombe
CRIME Usurer cancels woman's debt in return for wresting financial secret from minister's wife.

06948
AYLWIN (5485) (U)
Hepworth
D: Henry Edwards
S: (NOVEL) Theodore Watts-Dunton
Henry Edwards . . . . Hal Aylwin
Chrissie White . . . . Winifred Wynne
Gerald Ames . . . . Wilderspin
Mary Dibley . . . . Sinfi Lovell
Henry Vibart . . . . Philip Aylwin
Gwynne Herbert . . . . Mrs Aylwin
Valentine Grace . . . . Tom Wynne
E.C. Matthews . . . . Shales
Amy Lorraine . . . . Meg Gudgeon
DRAMA Wales. Woman disapproves of stepson's love for girl who goes mad when her drunken father dies in landslide.

06949
THE EDGE OF YOUTH (6260)(A)
Gaumont-British Screencraft
D: C.C. Calvert
S: Paul Rooff
Josephine Earle . . . . Joan Barbour
Dallas Anderson . . . . John Steel
Dick Webb . . . . Dick Jerningham
Violet Elliott . . . . Hon Mrs Allinson
George Bellamy . . . . Mr Jenningham
Cecil del Gue . . . . Sir Henry Hargreave
ROMANCE Girl weds for money when her
engagement to bankrupt heir is broken by
scheming aunt.

06950
BURNT IN (4994)(A)
British Actors (Phillips)
D: Duncan MacRae
S: (NOVEL) S.B. Hill
SC: S.H. Herkomer
Gertrude McCoy . . . . Nancy Risdon
Bertram Burleigh . . . . Mark Heron
Sam Livesey . . . . Joseph Heron
Henry Vibart . . . . Mr Heron
Oswald Marshall . . . . .Richard Heron
Jean Miller . . . . Stella Mannering
Adelaide Grace . . . . Housekeeper
Bert Darley . . . . Josh
Lord Lyvenden . . . .
CRIME Sussex. Potter's confession to killing
brother gets burned into vase beneath which it
was hidden.

06951
NOTHING ELSE MATTERS (6400)(U)
Welsh-Pearson (Jury)
D:SC: George Pearson
S: Hugh E. Wright
Hugh E. Wright . . . . Jimmy Daw
Moyna McGill . . . . Margery Rose
Betty Balfour . . . . Sally
George Keene . . . . Mark Rose
Mabel Poulton . . . . Doris Rose
Arthur Cleave . . . . Dick Lane
Alec Thompson . . . . Alf Higgs
Leal Douglas . . . . Tiny Higgs
Pollie Emery . . . . Auntie Rose
Reginald Denham . . . . Flash Harry
Steadman Dancers
DRAMA Music hall comedian fails to make
comeback and suspects his wife of loving
playwright.

06952
FORTY WINKS (2000)
Thespian Productions
D: Arthur Finn
S: Robert Hargreaves
Albert Rebla . . . . The Tramp
Maud Lofting . . . . The Girl
J. Edwards Barber . . . . Policeman
Fred Read . . . . Chinaman
Charles Leoville . . . . Chinaman
Pip Powell . . . .
COMEDY Tramp has strange dream and
saves girl from drowning.

06953
WHO LAUGHS LAST (2000)
Thespian Productions
D: James Youngdeer
S: Kenneth Easton
Albert Rebla
Pip Powell
Elsie Harrison
G.H. Miles
Judy Lofting
COMEDY

06954
THE FLAME (6358) (U)
Stoll
D:SC: F. Martin Thornton
S: (NOVEL) Olive Wadsley
Evelyn Boucher . . . . Toni Saumarez
Reginald Fox . . . . Lord Robert Wyke
Dora de Winton . . . . Lady Henrietta
Fred Thatcher . . . . Fane
Roland Myles . . . . Boris Ritsky
Ernest Maupain . . . . Sparakoff
Arthur Cullin . . . . Sir Charles Saumarez
Clifford Pembroke . . . . . . Capt Wynford Saumare;
Frank E. Petley . . . . Miskoff
J. Edwards Barber . . . . Dr Lindsay
Sydney Wood . . . . Fane (child)
ROMANCE Paris. Orphan cartoonist loves man
with mad wife, who dies in time to prevent
marriage to jilted Comte.

06955
THE ISLAND OF WISDOM (5000)
Cairo Films (Shadow Plays)
D:S: Anthony Keith
Margaret Hope . . . . Helen Fairfax
Percy Standing . . . . Darrell Blake
Anthony Keith . . . . Ronald Keith
Eva Westlake . . . . Mrs Fairfax
James English . . . . John Fairfax
James Prior . . . . Bill Hardy
Jean Lomond . . . . Nurse
Cyril Rawden . . . . Valet
Stacey Gaunt . . . . Lawyer
Nelson Barry . . . . Yokel
ADVENTURE Rich hunter weds heiress,kidnaps
her with lover, and forces them to work on
desert island.

06956
WUTHERING HEIGHTS (6230)(A)
Ideal reissue: 1922 (4 rls cut)
D: A.V. Bramble
S: (NOVEL) Emily Bronte
SC: Eliot Stannard
Milton Rosmer . . . . Heathcliff
Colette Brettel . . . . Catherine Hareton
Warwick Ward . . . . Hindley Earnshaw
Anne Trevor . . . . Cathy
John L. Anderson . . . . Edgar Linton
Cecil Morton York . . . . Earnshaw
Cyril Raymond . . . . Hareton
Dora de Winton . . . . Mrs Linton
Aileen Bagot . . . . Frances Earnshaw
Mrs Templeton . . . . Nelly Dean
George Traill . . . . Joseph
Alfred Bennett . . . . Rev Shields
Albert Brantford . . . . Heathcliff (child)
Lewis Barber . . . . Hareton (child)
DRAMA Period. Gipsy wins squire's estate,
brutalises adopted son, and makes him wed
dead step-sister's daughter.

06957
FANTEE
Anglo-Indian Films
D: Lewis Willoughby
S: (NOVEL) Joan Sutherland (WYNGATE SAHIB)
Lewis Willoughby . . . . Joan Carruthers
Olive Valerie . . . . Zira
Philip Anthony . . . . Reginald Ordeyne
Edna Monti . . . . Sybil Carruthers
Dorothy Radcliffe . . . . Miranda Anstruther
Constantin Nicoletto . . . . . . The Potter
DRAMA India.

06958
DOWN ON THE FARM (2000)
Empire Comedies (Film Sales)
D: Maurice Sandground

Charles Stevens . . . . Peter
Muriel Sothern . . . . Girl
COMEDY Man and chorus girls spend holiday
on health farm.

06959
THE LAMBS OF DOVE COURT (2000)(A)
Empire Comedies (Film Sales)
D: Maurice Sandground
Charles Stevens . . . . Doorman
Muriel Sothern . . . . Liza Lamb
Vic Derham . . . . Pa Lamb
COMEDY Slum dweller thinks he inherits
fortune and tries to be toff.

06960
THE BOY MESSENGER (2000)(U)
Empire Comedies (Film Sales)
D: Maurice Sandground
Charles Stevens . . . . Messenger
Muriel Sothern . . . . Schoolgirl
Vic Derham . . . . Tramp
COMEDY Tall messenger saves schoolgirl from
tramp.

06961
THE HYDRO (1000)
Empire Comedies (Film Sales)
D: Maurice Sandground
Charles Stevens . . . . Patient
Vic Derham . . Attendant
COMEDY Droitwich Spa. Patient and
attendant fight after drinking alcholol
secreted in a medicine bottle.

06962
IN BORROWED PLUMES (1000)
Empire Comedies (Film Sales)
D: Maurice Sandground
Charles Stevens . . . . Gent
Muriel Sothern . . . . Maid
COMEDY Maid dons mistress's clothes and
flirts with pseudo gent.

06963
TRUANTS (1000)
Empire Comedies (Film Sales)
D: Maurice Sandground
COMEDY Warwick. Boy and girl steal motor
car and view Kenilworth Castle.

06964
THE LITTLE POACHER (1000)
Empire Comedies (Film Sales)
D: Maurice Sandground
Muriel Sothern . . . . Gipsy
George Queen . . . . Gamekeeper
COMEDY Gipsy girl thwarts gamekeepers
and huntsmen.

06965
MANY A SLIP (2000)
Aerofilms
D:S: Eric Harrison
Poppy Wyndham . . . . The Girl
Eric Lyons . . . . The Boy
Harry Worth . . . . The Crook
COMEDY Hendon.

06966
THE ROMANCE OF A MOVIE STAR
Broadwest (Walturdaw)
P: Walter West
D: Richard Garrick
S: (NOVEL) Coralie Stanton, E. Hoskin
(THE WORLD'S BEST GIRL)
SC: J. Bertram Brown
Violet Hopson . . . . Vanna George
Stewart Rome . . . . Garry Slade
Gregory Scott . . . . Robert Arkwright

Mercy Hatton . . . . Cynthia Justice
Cameron Carr . . . . Philip Justice
Violet Elliott . . . . Mrs Slade
ROMANCE Film star risks reputation to save
beloved scenarist's married sister from infidelity.

AUG

06967
BEYOND THE DREAMS OF AVARICE
(5900)(A)
Ideal
D: Thomas Bentley
S: (NOVEL) Sir Walter Besant
SC: William J. Elliott
Henry Victor . . . . Dr Lucien Calvert
Joyce Dearsley . . . . Margaret Calvert
Alban Atwood . . . . Sir Joseph Burnley
Frank Stanmore . . . . Alf Burnley
Lionel d'Aragon . . . . Bill Burnley
Adelaide Grace . . . . Old Lucy
Jeff Barlow . . . . John Burnley
Howard Cochran . . . . . . James Calvert
A. Harding Steerman . . . . . . Nicholson
DRAMA Doctor inherits fortune, his wife
leaves him and he becomes miser.

06968
THE SWORD OF DAMOCLES (4920)(A)
B & C (Butcher)
P: Edward Godal
D:SC: George Ridgwell
S: (PLAY) H.V. Esmond(LEONIE)
Jose Collins . . . . Leonie Paoli
H.V. Esmond . . . . Hugh Maltravers
Claude Fleming . . . . Geoffrey Moray
Bobbie Andrews . . . . Jack Moray
Thomas Nesbitt . . . . Bruce Leslie
Chiquita de Lorenzo . . . . . Una Paoli
Edward Sorley . . . . Raikes
CRIME Barrister's letter proves bride shot
aged husband on learning he was already
married.

06969
A QUESTION OF TRUST (4549)(A)
Stoll
D: Maurice Elvey
S: (NOVEL) Ethel M. Dell
SC: Sinclair Hill
Madge Stuart . . . . Stephanie
Harvey Braban . . . . Pierre Dumaresque
Teddy Arundell . . . . Jouvain
C.H. Croker-King . . . . . . Governor of Maritas
Kitty Fielder . . . . Anita
ADVENTURE Ruritania. Patrician rebel saves
cruel governor's daughter from revolution and
tames her aboard his yacht.

06970
THE VANISHING DAGGER (Serial)
Universal
D: Edward Kull, Eddie Polo, John F. Magowan
S: Hope Loring, Jacques Jaccard, Milton Moore
SC: Hope Loring, George W. Pyper
Eddie Polo . . . . John Grant
Ray Ripley . . . . Prince Narr
Thelma Perry . . . . Beth Latimer
John F. Magowan . . . .
Bert Darley . . . .

06971
11: WHEN LONDON SLEEPS (2000)

06972
12: A RACE TO SCOTLAND (2000)
CRIME (Two episodes of American serial,
filmed in London, Liverpool and Glasgow.)

06973
LA POUPEE (5200) (U)
Meyrick Milton (Ward)
D: SC: Meyrick Milton
S: (PLAY) Edmond Audran
Fred Wright . . . . Hilarius
Flora le Breton . . . . Alesia
Richard Scott . . . . Launcelot Chantrelle
William Farren . . . . Father Maxim
Gladys Vicat . . . . Mme Hilarius
COMEDY France. Monk fulfills will by marrying
doll, not knowing the maker's daughter has taken
its place.

06974
THE AMAZING QUEST OF MR ERNEST
BLISS (Serial) (11,214) (A)
Hepworth (Imperial)
D: Henry Edwards
S:(NOVEL) E. Phillips Oppenheim
Henry Edwards . . . . Ernest Bliss
Chrissie White . . . . Frances Clayton
Gerald Ames . . . . Dorrington
Mary Dibley . . . . Kate Brent
Reginald Bach . . . . Jack Brent
Henry Vibart . . . . Sir James Alroyd
Douglas Munro . . . . John Masters
Mary Brough . . . . Gloria Mott
Stanley Turnbull . . . . Willie Mott
Gerald Hillier . . . . Dick Honerton
James Annand . . . . Crawley
Esme Hubbard . . . . Mrs Heath
James MacWilliams . . . . . . Clowes
Ernest Milton . . . . Mr Montague
John R. Allan . . . . Sam Brownley

06975
1 ; THE AMAZING QUEST

06976
2: THE RETURN OF ULYSSES

06977
3: A RACING EPISODE

06978
4: THE OTHER MR BLISS

06979
5: SIR JAMES PAYS
COMEDY Millionaire bets £25,000 that he can
earn his own living for six months.(Also released
as a 5-reel feature.)

06980
THE WINNING GOAL (5000) (U)
G.B. Samuelson (General)
D: G.B. Samuelson
S:(PLAY) Harold Brighouse
Harold Walden . . . . Jack Metherill
Maudie Dunham . . . . Elsie Whitworth
Tom Reynolds . . . . Uncle Edmund
Haidee Wright . . . . Mrs Whitworth
Jack Cock and other footballers
SPORT Footballer sold to rival club, wins match
despite broken arm.

06981
THROUGH STORMY WATERS (6000)
Goddard Films (Cinematography)
D:S: Frederick Goddard
Eileen Bellamy . . . . Eileen Donovan
George Keene . . . . Frank Evans
Harry J. Worth . . . . Employer
Fred Morgan . . . . Manager
CRIME Suspected amnesia victim cleared when
hypnotist reveals real thief. (Winner of ''Sunday
Express'' scenario prize of £200.)

06982
THE FORDINGTON TWINS (6570) (U)
Gaumont-Westminster
D: W.P. Kellino
S: (NOVEL) E. Newton-Bungey
SC: Paul Rooff
The Terry Twins . . . . James & John
Dallas Anderson . . . . Basil Markham
Mary Brough . . . . Mrs Margetson
Nita Russell . . . . Pat Wentworth
Cyril Smith . . . . Cyril Rayleigh
Whimsical Walker . . . . Snagsby
Cecil du Gue . . . . Mr Wentworth
COMEDY Fishmongers inherit and are blackmailed
by their tutor who pretends their uncle is still
alive.

06983
THE CASE OF LADY CAMBER (6000) (A)
Broadwest (Walturdaw)
D: Walter West
S: (PLAY) H.A. Vachell
SC: Benedict James
Violet Hopson . . . . Esther Yorke
Stewart Rome . . . . Dr Harley Napier
Gregory Scott . . . . Lord Camber
Mercy Hatton . . . . Lady Camber
C.M. Hallard . . . . Sir Bedford Slufter
Pollie Emery . . . . Peach
CRIME Dr proves nurse did not give strychnine
to invalid wife of philandering Lord.

06984
THE LITTLE HOUR OF PETER WELLS (5000)
(U)
Granger-Binger
D: B.E. Doxat-Pratt
S:(NOVEL) David Whitelaw
SC: Eliot Stannard
O.B. Clarence . . . . Peter Wells
Heather Thatcher . . . . Camille Pablo
Hebden Foster . . . . Carlos Faroa
Adelqui Migliar . . . . Pranco
William Huncher . . . . King Enrico
Nico de Jong . . . . Raoul Pablo
ADVENTURE Ruritania. Cockney greengrocer
helps revolutionary win reactionary's daughter.

06985
RODNEY STONE /195) (A)
Screen Plays (BEF)
D: Percy Nash
S: (NOVEL) Arthur Cocan Doyle
SC: W. Courtenay Rowden
Rex Davis . . . . Boy Jim
Lionel d'Aragon . . . . Sir Charles Tregellis
Cecil Morton York . . . . Sir Lothian Hume
Ethel Newman . . . . Polly Hinton
Robertson Braine . . . . Rodney Stone
Douglas Payne . . . . James Harrison
Fred Morgan . . . . Ambrose
Frank Adair . . . . Lord Avon
Joan Ritz . . . . Mary Stone
Frank Tennant . . . . Capt Barrington
Ernest Wallace . . . . Lt Anson Stone
SPORT 1796. Blacksmith's boy becomes boxer
and is revealed as son of peer blamed for killing
cardsharper.

06986
LITTLE DORRIT (6858) (U)
Progress (Butcher)
P: Frank Spring
D: SC: Sidney Morgan
S: (NOVEL) Charles Dickens
Lady Tree . . . . Mrs Clenman
Langhorne Burton . . . . Arthur Clenman

Joan Morgan . . . . Amy Dorrit
Compton Coutts . . . . Pancks
Arthur Lennard . . . . William Dorrit
J. Denton-Thompson . . . . . John Chivers
George Foley . . . . Merdle
George Bellamy . . . . Fred Dorrit
Arthur Walcott . . . . Flintwick
Judd Green . . . . Old Bob
Betty Doyle . . . . Fanny Dorrit
Mary Lyle . . . . Mrs Merdle
DRAMA 1850. Jailed debtor refuses to marry heiress until she loses fortune and he gains another.

06987
ALL THE WINNERS (6000)
G.B. Samuelson (General)
D: Geoffrey H. Malins
S: (NOVEL) Arthur Applin (WICKED)
Owen Nares . . . . Tim Hawker
Maudie Dunham . . . . Dora Dalton
Sam Livesey . . . . Pedro Darondarez
Maidie Hope . . . . Picco
Ena Beaumont . . . . Daphne Dression
CRIME Woman tries to blackmail rich trainer into forcing daughter to marry thief.

06988
NEW DANCE SERIES (Series)
Debenham & Co (Famous)
MUSICAL Eleven one-reel films of different dances to synchronise with cinema orchestras.

06989
THE HANDY MAN (2000)
Castle
D:S: Walter Forde
Walter Forde . . . .
COMEDY

06990
FISHING FOR TROUBLE (2000)
Castle
D:S: Walter Forde
Walter Forde . . . .
COMEDY Fisherman saves picknicker's mother from drowning and is framed for theft.

06991
NEVER SAY DIE (2000)
Castle
D:S: Walter Forde
Walter Forde . . . .
COMEDY

06992
HORSESHOE COMEDIES (Series)
Monarch (L&P)
P: Sidney Goldin, J.F. Lloyd
D: Sidney Goldin
S: Langford Reed
Sidney Goldin . . . . Sidney
Eileen Moore . . . .
George Bishop . . . .

06993
1— THE BIRD FANCIER (1000)

06994
2— THE WOMAN HATER (1200)
COMEDY

06995
THE TIDAL WAVE (6226) (U)
Stoll
D: SC: Sinclair Hill
S: (NOVEL) Ethel M. Dell
Poppy Wyndham . . . . Columbine
Sydney Seaward . . . . Matt Brewster
Pardoe Woodman . . . . Frank Knight

Annie Esmond . . . . Aunt Liza
Judd Green . . . . Adam Brewster
ROMANCE Cornwall. Fisherman saves girl artist from sea and falls in love with her.

SEP

06996
THE WOMAN OF THE IRON BRACELETS (5376) (A)
Progress (Butcher)
P: Frank E. Spring
D: SC: Sidney Morgan
S: (NOVEL) Frank Barrett
Eve Balfour . . . . Norah Berwell
George Keene . . . . Harry St John
Margaret Blanche . . . . Olive St John
George Bellamy . . . . Dr Harvey
Arthur Walcott . . . . Mr Lawson
Alice de Winton . . . . Mrs Lawson
CRIME Girl fleeing from murder charge helps disowned heir prove his stepfather is criminal hypnotist.

06997
THE SILVER BRIDGE (5000)
Cairns Torquay Films
P: D: Dallas Cairns
S: (NOVEL) Helen Prothero Lewis
SC: Eliot Stannard
Dallas Cairns . . . . Mordred Baskerville
Betty Farquhar . . . . Mystery Destin
Madeleine Meredith . . . . . . Mrs Baskerville
Madge Tree . . . . Eillean Destin
J. Hastings Batson . . . . Shepherd
Stella Wood-Sims . . . . Child
Alan Michaels . . . . Child
CRIME Squire's new wife tries to poison his son and frame witch's adopted daughter.

06998
THE TAVERN KNIGHT (6735) (A)
Stoll
D: Maurice Elvey
S: (NOVEL) Rafael Sabatini
SC: Sinclair Hill
Eille Norwood . . . . The Tavern Knight
Madge Stuart . . . . Cynthia Ashburn
Cecil Humphreys . . . . Joseph Ashburn
Teddy Arundell . . . . Capt Hogan
Lawrence Anderson . . . . . . Kenneth
C.H. Croker-King . . . . Gregory Ashburn
Clifford Heatherley . . . . . . Col. Pride
Booth Conway . . . . Oliver Cromwell
J.E. Wickers . . . . Charles Stuart
ADVENTURE 1651. Royalist and unknown son seek vengeance on his murdered wife's brothers.

06999
THE BREED OF THE TRESHAMS (6000) (A)
Astra Films
P: H.W. Thompson
D: SC: Kenelm Foss
S: (PLAY) Beulah Marie Dix, E.G. Sutherland
Martin Harvey . . . . Lt."Rat" Reresby
Mary Odette . . . . Margaret Hungerford
Hayford Hobbs . . . . Hon Francis Tresham
A.B.Imeson . . . . Hon Clement Hungerford
Charles Vane . . . . Vis Dorsington
Margot Drake . . . . Margaret
Fred Morgan . . . . Capt Rashleigh
Gordon Craig . . . . Batty
Will Corrie . . . . Cpl Lumsford
Philip Hewland . . . . Col Henry Curwen
Nelson Ramsey . . . . Col Bagshawe
Norman Tharp . . . . Capt Stanhope
Gwen Williams . . . . Mrs Bagshawe
Farmer Skein . . . . Lord Tresham
ADVENTURE 1642. Royalist unmasks Viscountess's halfbrother as Roundhead spy.

07000
THE TWELVE POUND LOOK (5100) (U)
Ideal
D: Jack Denton
S: (PLAY) J.M. Barrie
SC: Eliot Stannard
Milton Rosmer . . . . Harry Sims
Jessie Winter . . . . Kate Sims
Ann Elliott . . . . Mrs Sims
Nelson Ramsey . . . .
Athalie Davis . . . .
Gwen Williams . . . .
Alfred Wellesley . . . .
Aileen Bagot . . . .
E. Story Gofton . . . .
Roy Byford . . . .
Leonard Robson . . . .
DRAMA Selfmade man divorces wife who becomes typist and warns him his second wife may leave him too.

07001
LADDIE (5000) (U)
Master (Butcher) reissue: 1926 (2 rls)
D: SC: Bannister Merwin
S: (NOVEL) "Author of Tipcat"
Sydney Fairbrother . . . . . . Mrs Carter
C. Jervis Walter . . . . Dr Carter
Dorothy Moody . . . . Violet Meredith
Charles Vane . . . . Sir John Meredith
Leslie Steward . . . . Harry Joyce
Laverick Brown . . . . Dr Saville
DRAMA Society doctor makes widowed mother pose as old nurse.

07002
THE WINDING ROAD (6966) (A)
Famous Pictures (Ashley)
D: Bert Haldane, Frank Wilson
Cecil Humphreys . . . . Maj Gawthorne
Edith Pearson . . . . Ruth Gledhill
Annesley Hely . . . . Jack Gledhill
Jack Jarman . . . . Lt Chatterton
Dorothy Cecil . . . . Hon Mrs Dunoyne
Moore Marriott . . . . Jed Skerrett
CRIME Cashiered major is jailed for forgery and freed when he saves brutal warder from rioting convicts.

07003
HELEN OF FOUR GATES (5800) (A)
Hepworth
D: Cecil M. Hepworth
S: (NOVEL) Mrs E. Holdsworth
SC: Blanche McIntosh
Alma Taylor . . . . Helen/Helen
James Carew . . . . Abel Mason
Gerald Ames . . . . Hinson
George Dewhurst . . . . Martin Scott
Gwynne Herbert . . . . Mrs Trip
John McAndrews . . . . Fielding Day
DRAMA Madman adopts daughter of dead woman who rejected him and forces her to marry crook.

07004
BRANDED (5835) (A)
Gaumont-British Screencraft
D: C.C. Calvert
S: (NOVEL) Gerald Biss
SC: Paul Rooff
Josephine Earle . . . Phyllis/Helen Jerningham
Dallas Anderson . . . . Caton Brember
Nora Swinburne . . . . Doris Jerningham
Francis Lister . . . . Ralph Shopwyke
Maud Yates . . . . Lady Margaret Maitland
Terence Cavanagh . . . . . . Sir Lionel Erskine
Morton Selton . . . . Marquis of Shelford
Emilie Nichol . . . . Mrs Chichele
CRIME Girl rejects mother after she is jailed for poisoning father.

07005
THE GOLDEN WEB (5000)
Garrick (Anchor)
D: Geoffrey H. Malins
S: (NOVEL) E. Phillips Oppenheim
SC: Milton Rosmer

Milton Rosmer	Sterling Deans
Ena Beaumont	Winifred Rowan
Victor Robson	Sinclair
Nina Munro	Rosalie

CRIME Dead crook's sister weds heir to gold mine but leaves him when he gives it to neice of brother's partner.

07006
PILLARS OF SOCIETY (5000) (U)
R.W. Syndicate (Moss)
P: D: Rex Wilson
S: (PLAY) Henrik Ibsen
SC: Walter Courtenay Rowden

Ellen Terry	Widow Bernick
Norman McKinnel	John Halligan
Mary Rorke	Mrs Halligan
Irene Rooke	Martha Karsten
Joan Lockton	Dina Dorf
Lydia Hayward	Lena Hessel
Charles Ashton	Dick Alward
John Kelt	Parson Rogers
Pamela Neville	Florence

DRAMA Norway. Shipping magate frames absent brother-in-law for theft and betrayal of his mistress.

07007
TWO LITTLE WOODEN SHOES (5325) (U)
Progress (Butcher)
P: Frank Spring
D: SC: Sidney Morgan
S: (NOVEL) Ouida

Joan Morgan	Dedee
Langhorne Burton	Victor Flamen
J. Denton-Thompson	Jeannot
Constance Backner	Liza
Faith Bevan	The Model
Ronald Power	The Master
Maude Cressall	Mme Vallier

ROMANCE France. Orphan walks to Paris to visit sick artist and finds him carousing with model.

07008
THE WOMAN AND OFFICER 26 (5000)
Atlantic Films
P:S: Harry Lorraine
D: Harry Lorraine, Bert Haldane

Marguerite de Belabre	Denver May
Jeffrey Julian	Officer 26
Harry Lorraine	Leggatt
Jack Mullins	Milwaukee Joe
George Foley	
Wingold Lawrence	
J. A. Bentham	

CRIME America. Girl novelist becomes involved with Barbary Coast gang.

07009
THE CONTROLLERS (2000)
West London Variety Agency
P:J: C. Harold
D:Harold A. Crawford

Joe Cohan	Coster
Anna Dorothy	Spinster

COMEDY Costers pose as widow and children to take over spinster's villa.

07010
JENNY OMROYD OF OLDHAM (5000)
Success Films
P: D: Frank Etherridge
S: (PLAY)T. G. Bailey

SC: Frank Etheridge, Noreen Hill, Lester Bidston

Nelly Freeland	Jenny Omroyd

ROMANCE Lancs

OCT
07011
INHERITANCE (4850)(A)
British Actors (Phillips)
D: Wilfred Noy
S: H. Pullein-Thompson
SC: S. H. Herkomer

Mary Odette	Rachel
Jack Hobbs	David StMaur
Ursula Hughes	Peggy Falconer
Sir Simeon Stuart	Sir Henry StMaur
D: J. Williams	Tulliver
Pope Stamper	Walter Clifford
Mary Forbes	Lady Isabel
Harry Frankiss	Aaron Palk
Charles W. Somerset	The Old Squire
Thelma Murray	Maid

DRAMA Squire's son weds fishergirl who saved his life, becomes dockers' leader, and weds Lady he loves on wife's death.

07012
THE CALL OF THE ROAD (6000)(A)
I.B.Davidson (Granger) reissue: 1925
D:S: A. E. Coleby

Victor McLaglen	Alf Truscott
Phyllis Shannaw	Lady Rowena
Warwick Ward	Lord Delavel
Philip Williams	Sir Martin Trevor
A. E. Coleby	Punch Murphy
Adeline Hayden Coffin	Lady Ullswater
Ernest A. Douglas	Silas
H. Nicholls-Bates	Paganini Primus
Barry Furness	Paganini Secundus
Fred Drummond	Hammer John
Olive Bell	Miller's Wife

ADVENTURE 1820. Disowned gambler becomes boxer and saves noble uncle from a highway man

07013
THE GREAT GAY ROAD (5300)(U)
Broadwest (Walturdaw)
D: SC: Norman MacDonald
P: Walter West
S: (NOVEL) Tom Gallon

Stewart Rome	Hilary Kite
Pauline Johnson	Nancy
John Stuart	Rodney Foster
Ernest Spaulding	Crook Perkins
A. Bromley Davenport	Sir Crispin Vickrey
Ralph Forster	Backus
Helena Lessington	Mother Grogan

ROMANCE Knight hires tramp to pose as lost son and wed his niece, who loves younger man.

07014
TRENT'S LAST CASE (5500)(A)
Broadwest (Walturdaw)
D: Richard Garrick
S:(NOVEL) E. C. Bentley
SC: P. L. Mannock

Gregory Scott	Philip Trent
Pauline Peters	Mabel Manderson
Clive Brook	John Marlow
George Foley	Sigsbee Manderson
Cameron Carr	Insp Murch
P. E. Hubbard	Nathaniel Cupples
Richard Norton	Martin

CRIME Millionaire commits suicide and frames secretary for murder.

07015
ONCE ABOARD THE LUGGER (5250)
Hepworth (Imperial)
D: Gerald Ames, Gaston Quiribet
S: (NOVEL) A. S. M. Hutchinson
SC: Blanche McIntosh

E. Holman Clarke	Mr Marrapit
Eileen Dennes	Mary Humfray

Evan Thomas	George
Denis Cowles	Bill Wyvern
Reginald Bach	Bob Chater
Gwynne Herbert	Mrs Major
John MacAndrews	Fletcher
Winifred Sadler	Mrs Chater
Fred Lewis	Vyvian Howard

COMEDY Student kidnaps rich uncle's cat and holds it to ransom.

07016
TESTIMONY (7189)(U)
George Clark (Stoll)
D: SC: Guy Newall
S: (NOVEL) Claude & Alice Askew

Ivy Duke	Althea May
David Hawthorne	Gilian Lyons
Lawford Davidson	Cecil Coram
Mary Rorke	Rachel Lyons
Douglas Munro	Reuben Curtis
Marie Wright	Lizzie Emmett
Barbara Everest	Lucinda
Ruth MacKay	Lady Yetty

DRAMA Farmer's runaway wife returns but is ejected by his mother.

07017
BUILD THY HOUSE (5230) (U)
Ideal
D: Fred Goodwins
S: S. Trevor Jones
SC: Eliot Stannard

Henry Ainley	Arthur Burnaby
Ann Trevor	Helen Dawson
Reginald Bach	Jim Medway
Warwick Ward	Burnaby
Jerrold Robertshaw	John Dawson
Adelaide Grace	Mrs Medway
Howard Cochran	Marshall
Claude Rains	Clarkis
R. Van Courtlandt	Mr Cramer
Mrs Ainley	Miss Brown
V. Vivian-Vivian	Florence Burnaby

DRAMA Padre, acting for dying soldier, poses as heir to slum property and becomes Labour MP. (Winner of £200 scenario contest).

07018
TORN SAILS (5000) (U)
Ideal
D: A.V. Bramble
S: (NOVEL) Allen Raine
SC: Eliot Stannard

Milton Rosmer	Hugh Morgan
Mary Odette	Gwladys Price
Geoffrey Kerr	Ivor Parry
Jose Shannon	Maud Owen
Leo Gordon	Josh Howells
Beatrix Templeton	Mrs Price

DRAMA Wales. Girl loves manager but weds employer who dies in fire lit by jealous madwoman.

07019
THE MANCHESTER MAN (5000)
Ideal
D: Bert Wynne
S: (NOVEL) Mrs Linnaeus Banks
SC: Eliot Stannard

Hayford Hobbs	Jabez Clegg
Aileen Bagot	Augusta Ashton
Warwick Ward	Capt Aspinall
A. Harding Steerman	Mr Ashton
Dora de Winton	Mrs Ashton
Hubert Willis	Simon Clegg
Joan Hestor	Bess Clegg
William Burchill	Rev Jotty Brooks
Charles Pelly	Kit
Cecil Calvert	Man of Affairs

ROMANCE Lancs, 1800. Clerk loves merchant's daughter who elopes with crook.

07020
LADY AUDLEY'S SECRET (5150) (A)
Ideal
D: Jack Denton
S: (NOVEL) Dorothy Braddon
SC: Eliot Stannard
Margaret Bannerman . . . . . . Lady Audley
H. Manning Haynes . . . . . . Robert Audley
Betty Farquhar . . . . Alysia Audley
Randolph McLeod . . . . . . Capt George Talboys
Wallace Bosco . . . . Luke Marks
Berenice Melford . . . . Phoebe
Hubert Willis . . . . Sir Michael Audley
William Burchill . . . . Captain Malden
Ida Millais . . . . Mrs Plowson
CRIME Old knight's new wife throws first husband
down well and tries to burn blackmailing gardener.

07021
THREE MEN IN A BOAT (5000) (U)
Artistic
P: George Redman
D: Challis Sanderson
S: (NOVEL) Jerome K. Jerome
SC: Manning Haynes,Lydia Hayward
Lionelle Howard . . . . J.
Manning Haynes . . . . Harris
Johnny Butt . . . . George
Eva Westlake
Edward C. Bright
COMEDY Misadventures of three friends on
Thames boating holiday.

07022
THE BUMP (2000)
Minerva
D: Adrian Brunel
S: A.A. Milne
C. Aubrey Smith . . . . John Brice
Faith Celli . . . . Lillian Montrevor
Douglas Marshall . . . . Freddy
Nellie Cooper . . . . Mrs Montrevor
F.W. Grant . . . . Mr Montrevor
COMEDY Famous explorer unable to find his
way across London.

07023
FIVE POUNDS REWARD (2000)
Minerva
D: Adrian Brunel
S: A.A. Milne
Leslie Howard . . . . Tony Marchmont
Barbara Hoffe . . . . Audrey Giles
Lewis Ransome . . . . Framer Giles
COMEDY Farmer witholds consent until earl earns
himself £5.

07024
BOOKWORMS (2000)
Minerva
D: Adrian Brunel
S: A.A. Milne
Leslie Howard . . . . Richard
Pauline Johnson . . . . Miranda
Henrietta Watson . . . . Aunt Priscilla
Jeff Barlow . . . . Uncle Josiah
Ivan Berlyn . . . . Ernest
Mrs R. Podevin . . . . The Dragon
COMEDY Suitor dons disguises to woo
chaperoned girl.

07025
TWICE TWO (2000)
Minerva
D: Adrian Brunel
S: A.A. Milne
Ivan Samson . . . . Jack Romer
Barbara McFarlane . . . . Jill Medway
Sir Simeon Stuart . . . . Col Medway

Adeline Hayden Coffin . . . . Mrs Romer
COMEDY Couple in love contrive to marry off
widowed parents.

07026
THE HONEYPOT (6000) (A)
G.B. Samuelson (Granger)
D: Fred Leroy Granville
S: (NOVEL) Countess Barcynska
Peggy Hyland . . . . Maggie Delamere
Campbell Gullan . . . . Lord Chalfont
James Lindsay . . . . Fred Woolf
Lilian Hall Davis . . . . Alexandra Hersey
Alfred Drayton . . . . De Preyne
Maidie Hope . . . . Lady Susan Woolf
Grace Lane . . . . Mrs Lambert
Lillian La Verne . . . . Mrs Bell
ROMANCE Lord weds playboy's mistress after
saving her from suicide.

07027
FILM PIE (series)
Neville Bruce Film Service
D: Geoffrey H. Malins, Neville Bruce
George McNaughton . . . . . .
Stella Muir . . . .
Arthur Reynolds . . . .
April Harmon . . . .
Dora Henwood . . . .

07028
No. 1 (750) (A)

07029
No. 2 (750) (A)

07030
No. 3 (750) (A)

07031
No. 4 (750) (A)

07032
No. 5 (750) (A)

07033
No. 6 (750) (A)

07034
No. 7 (750) (A)

07035
No. 8 (750) (U)

07036
No. 9 (750) (U)

07037
No.10 (733) (A)

07038
No.11 (770) (U)

07039
No.12 (768) (U)
COMEDIES Each episode composed of several
items.

07040
SAVED FROM THE SEA (5960) (A)
Gaumont-Westminster
D: W.P. Kellino
S:(PLAY) Arthur Shirley, Ben Landeck
SC: Paul Rooff
Nora Swinburne . . . . Nancy Brooks
Philip Anthony . . . . Dan Ellington
Cecil Calvert . . . . Jim Weaver
Wallace Bosco . . . . Peter Scalcher
Terence Cavanagh . . . . Dick Fenton
Mary Saville . . . . Mrs Ellington
CRIME Cornwall. Cardsharper and heir frame
fisherman for death of jealous partner.

07041
JOHN FORREST FINDS HIMSELF (4860) (A)
Hepworth
D: Henry Edwards
S: (STORY) Donovan Bayley
SC: H. Fowler Mear
Henry Edwards . . . . John Forrest
Chrissie White . . . . Joan Grey
Gerald Ames . . . . Ezra Blott
Hugh Clifton . . . . O'Reilly
Gwynne Herbert . . . . Mrs Forrest
Henry Vibart . . . . Mr Forrest
Mary Brough . . . . Biddy
Eileen Dennes . . . . The Pet
John McAndrews . . . . Carter Joe
Victor Prout . . . . Stephen Grey
John Deverell . . . . Hon Vere Blair
Marion Dyer . . . . Sylvia Grey
ROMANCE Devon. Amnesiac loves poor squire's
daughter who is engaged to rich man he thought
he killed.

07042
A BACHELOR HUSBAND (5000) (A)
Astra Films
P: H.W. Thompson
D: SC: Kenelm Foss
S: (NOVE) Ruby M. Ayres
Lyn Harding . . . . Feathers Dakers
Renee Mayer . . . . Marie Celeste
Hayford Hobbs . . . . Chris Lawless
Irene Rooke . . . . Aunt Madge
Lionelle Howard . . . . Atkins
Gordon Craig. . . . . Chris (child)
Margot Drake . . . . Mrs Chester
Will Corri . . . . George Chester
R. Heaton Grey . . . . Aston Knight
Phyllis Joyce . . . . Mrs Heriot
ROMANCE Inheritor weds stepsister who elopes
with cad.

NOV

07043
BARS OF IRON (6053) (A)
Stoll
D: SC: F. Martin Thornton
S: (NOVEL) Ethel M. Dell
Madge White . . . . Avery Denys
Roland Myles . . . . Piers Evesham
J.R. Tozer . . . . Dr Lennox Tudor
Leopold McLaglen . . . . Eric Denys
Olga Conway . . . . Ina Rose
Eric Lankester . . . . Sir Beverley Evesh
Lewis Ransome . . . . Rev Lorimer
Gertrude Sterroll . . . . Mrs Lorimer
Gordon Webster . . . . .Dick Guyes
J. Edwards Barber . . . . .Crowther
ROMANCE Man kills drunkard in Australia, flees
to England, and unknowingly weds man's wife.

07044
BY BERWIN BANKS (4900) (U)
Progress (Butcher)
P: Frank Spring
D: Sidney Morgan
S: (NOVEL) Allen Raine
SC: Hugh Croise
Langhorne Burton . . . . Cardo Wynne
Eileen Magrath . . . . Valmai Powell
J. Denton-Thompson . . . . . Owen Davies
C.W. Somerset . . . . Essec Powell
Arthur Lennard . . . . Rev Menrig Wynn
Judd Green . . . . Joe Powell
Charles Levy . . . . Rev Gwynne Ellis
ROMANCE Wales. Anglican vicar's son secretly
weds dissenter's daughter and recovers from
amnesia in time to save her from shame.

07045
THE SHUTTLE OF LIFE (4256) (A)
British Actors (Phillips)
D: D.J. Williams
S: (NOVEL) Isobel Bray
SC: S.H. Herkomer
C. Aubrey Smith . . . .   Rev John Stone
Evelyn Brent . . . .   Miriam Grey
Jack Hobbs . . . .   Ray Sinclair
Gladys Jennings . . . .   Audrey Bland
Bert Darley . . . .   Tom
Cecil Ward . . . .   Meeson
Rachel de Solla . . . .   Mrs Bland
CRIME Actress poses as heiress who died, and
dies fighting blackmailing detective in burning
house.

07046
THE CHILDREN OF GIBEON (5000) (A)
Progress (Butcher)
P: Frank Spring
D: Sidney Morgan
S: (NOVEL) Sir Walter Besant
SC: Irene Miller
Joan Morgan . . . .   Violet
Langhorne Burton . . . .   Clive
Eileen Magrath . . . .   Valentine
Sydney Fairbrother . . . . . .   Mrs Gibeon
Alice de Winton . . . .   Lady Eldridge
Arthur Lennard . . . .   Mr Gibeon
Charles Cullum . . . .   Jack Conyers
Barbara MacFarlane . . . . . .   Violet
DRAMA Lady adopts crook's daughter and raises
her with her own without revealing which is which.

07047
THE GREAT LONDON MYSTERY (serial) (A)
Torquay & Paignton Photoplay Productions
(Shaftesbury)
P: R. Reubenson
D: Charles Raymond
S: Hope Loring, Charles Raymond
David Devant . . . .   The Master Magican
Lady Doris Stapleton . . . . .   Audrey Malvern
Charles Raymond . . . .   Ching Fu
Robert Clifton . . . .   Bob Sefton
Kenneth Duffy . . . .   Edward Selwyn
Martin Valmour . . . .   Webb
Lester Gard . . . .   The Man Monkey
Sadie Bennett . . . .   Curley
Lola de Liane . . . .   Froggie the Vampire

07048
1: THE SACRED SNAKE WORSHIPPERS (1900)
07049
2: THE VENGEANCE OF CHING FU (1205)
07050
3: THE SEARCH FOR THE WILL (1790)
07051
4: THE DAYLIGHT GOLD ROBBERY (2111)
07052
5: THE HOUSE OF MYSTERY (1615)
07053
6: ECHOES OF THE PAST (1467)
07054
7: THE ROGUE UNMASKED (1714)
07055
8: THE FRAUDULENT SPIRITUALISTIC
SEANCE (1714)
07056
9: THE LIVING DEAD (1690)
07057
10: HER FORTUNE AT STAKE (1462)

07058
11: CHECKMATED (1464)

07059
12: EAST AND WEST (1392)
CRIME Magician helps outwit chinaman's gang.

07060
THE OLD ARM CHAIR (5400) (A)
Screen Plays (BEF)
D: Percy Nash
S: (NOVEL) Mrs O. F. Walton
SC: George Pickett
Manora Thew . . . .   Mrs Soper
Cecil Mannering . . . .   Arthur Bentley
Joan Ritz . . . .   Kate
Frank Tennant . . . .   Samuel Soper
Cecil Morton York . . . .   Richard Pringle
Ida Fane . . . .   Miss Soper
Pat Royale . . . .   Sammy Soper
CRIME 1840. Blackmailing usurer frames clerk
who later adopts thief's son.

07061
THE CHANNINGS (4500) (U)
Master (Butcher) reissue: 1926 (2 rls)
P: H.B. Parkinson
D: Edwin J. Collins
S: (NOVEL) Mrs Henry Wood
SC: William J. Elliott
Lionelle Howard . . . .   Arthur Channing
Dick Webb . . . .   Hamish Channing
Dorothy Moody . . . .   Constance Channing
Cowley Wright . . . .   Roland Yorke
Charles Vane . . . .   Huntley
Frank Arlton . . . .   Galloway
CRIME Clerk takes blame for brother's theft but
finds his sister's fiancee is culprit.

07062
THE LAW DIVINE (4700) (A)
Master (Butcher)
P: H.B. Parkinson
D: Challis Sanderson, H.B. Parkinson
S: (PLAY) H.V. Esmond
SC: Frank Miller
H.V. Esmond . . . .   Capt Jack le Bas
Eva Moore . . . .   Edie le Bas
Evelyn Brent . . . .   Daphne Grey
Mary Brough . . . .   Cook
Leonard Upton . . . .   Ted le Bas
John Reid . . . .   Bill le Bas
Dorothy Wordsworth . . . . .   Claudia Merton
Florence Wood . . . .   Mrs Gaythorne
Margaret Watson . . . .   Kate
ROMANCE 1915. War worker wins back
wounded husband with recollections of
honeymoon.

07063
A GAMBLE IN LIVES (5242) (U)
B & C (Pathe)
P: Edward Godal
D: SC: George Ridgwell
S: (PLAY) Frank Stayton (THE JOAN
DANVERS)
Malvina Longfellow . . . . . .   Joan Danvers
Norman McKinnel . . . .   James Danvers
Alec Fraser . . . .   Capt Ross
John Reed . . . .   Jimmie Danvers
Mollie Adair . . . .   Gladys Danvers
Frances Ivor . . . .   Mrs Danvers
Bobbie Andrews . . . .   Harry Riggs
Alec Wynn-Thomas . . . . . .   Sims
CRIME Insurance agent demands shipowner's
daughter in return for silence regarding
scuttling plans.

07064
THE TEMPTRESS (4585) (A)
B & C (Pathe)
P: Edward Godal
D: SC: George Edwardes Hall
S: (PLAYS) Tom Robertson (HOME) Emile
Augier (L'AVENTURIERE)
Yvonne Arnaud . . . .   Amy Howard
Langhorne Burton . . . .   Allan Ashton
John Gliddon . . . .   Paul Howard
Christine Maitland . . . .   Ruth Tredgett
Austin Leigh . . . .   John Howard
Edward Sorley . . . .   Arthur Stanley
Bruce Winston . . . .   Reggie Featherstone
Lennox Pawle . . . .   Perkins
Saba Raleigh . . . .   Mrs Tredgett
ROMANCE Widow schemes to wed rich squire
by persuading his son to woo governess.

07065
THE GREAT DAY (3700) (U)
Famous Players-Lasky (Par)
D: Hugh Ford
S: (PLAY) Louis N. Parker, George R. Sims
SC: Eve Unsell
Arthur Bourchier . . . .   Sir Jonathon Borstwick
Mary Palfrey . . . .   Susan Borstwick
Bertram Burleigh . . . .   Frank Beresford
Marjorie Hume . . . .   Clara Beresford
Parcy Standing . . . .   Paul Nikola
Geoffrey Kerr . . . .   Dave Leeson
Meggie Albanesi . . . .   Lilla Leeson
Lewis Dayton . . . .   Lord Medway
DRAMA "Dead" wife of steel process
inventor returns, as does her "dead" husband,
a war amnesiac.

07066
THE CALL OF YOUTH (3900) (U)
Famous Players-Lasky (Par)
D: Hugh Ford
S: (PLAY) Henry Arthur Jones (JAMES THE
FOGEY)
SC: Eve Unsell
Mary Glynne . . . .   Betty Overton
Ben Webster . . . .   Mark Lanton
Jack Hobbs . . . .   Hubert Richmond
Marjorie Hume . . . .   Joan Lanton
Malcolm Cherry . . . .   James Agar
Gertrude Sterroll . . . .   Mrs Lanton
ROMANCE Poor girl refuses to wed millionaire
when he sends her sick sweetheart to Africa.

07067
ERNEST MALTRAVERS (5000)
Ideal
D: Jack Denton
S: (NOVEL) Lord Lytton
SC: Eliot Stannard
Cowley Wright . . . .   Ernest Maltravers
Lilian Hall Davis . . . .   Alice Darvil
Hubert Gordon Hopkirk . . .   George Legard
Norman Partridge . . . .   Luke Darvil
George Bellamy . . . .   Mr Merton
Florence Nelson . . . .   Mrs Merton
Ernest A. Douglas . . . .   Lord Vargrave
Stella Wood-Sims . . . .   Evelyn
N. Watts-Phillips . . . .   Waters
DRAMA Period. Girl saves rich man from
murderous father and meets him again after
escaping forced marriage and having baby.

07068
A LOT ABOUT LOTTERY (2000)
Ideal
Lupino Lane . . . .
COMEDY

07069
A NIGHT OUT AND A DAY IN (2000)
Ideal
Lupino Lane . . . .
Eric Blore . . . .
Florence Vie . . . .
Jo Monkhouse . . . .
Dmitri Vetter . . . .
COMEDY Drunk pays for night out by having
to do housework.

DEC

07070
MRS ERRICKER'S REPUTATION (5780) (U)
Hepworth
D: Cecil M. Hepworth
S: (NOVEL) Thomas Cobb
SC: Blanche McIntosh
Alma Taylor . . . . Georgiana Erricker
Gerald Ames . . . . Vincent Dampier
James Carew . . . . .Sir Richard Erricker
Eileen Dennes . . . . Lady Lettice Erricker
Gwynne Herbert . . . . Lady Erricker
DRAMA Widow compromises herself to
protect sister-in-law.

07071
A MAN'S SHADOW (5500) (A)
Progress (Butcher)
P: Frank E. Spring
D: SC: Sidney Morgan
S: (PLAY) Robert Buchanan
Langhorne Burton . .Peter Beresford/Julian Grey
Violet Graham . . . . .Vivian Beresford
Gladys Mason . . . . Yolande Hampden
Arthur Lennard . . . . Robert Hampden
J. Denton-Thompson . . . . . Williams
Sydney Paxton . . . . Billings
Babs Ronald . . . . Helen Beresford
Warris Linden . . . . Simon Oppenheim
CRIME Poor Man's double murders Jewish
usurer and is betrayed by ex-mistress.

07072
PIMPLE'S TOPICAL GAZETTE (500)
Fred Evans (Anchor)
D: S: Fred Evans, Joe Evans
Fred Evans . . . . Pimple
Joe Evans . . . .
Ernie Mayne . . . .
COMEDY Burlesque newsreel.

07073
BRENDA OF THE BARGE (4727) (U)
Harma-Associated Exhibitors (Walturdaw)
D: S: Arthur Rooke
Marjorie Villis . . . . Brenda
James Knight . . . . Jim Walden
Bernard Dudley . . . . Harry
Blanche Stanley . . . . Mary Brown
Tom Coventry . . . . Judd Brown
Rose Sharp . . . . Mrs Walden
ROMANCE Farmer's son loves bargee's
daughter who is really his kidnapped stepsister

07074
THE SKIN GAME (6000) (U)
Granger-Binger
D: SC: B.E. Doxat-Pratt
S: (PLAY) John Galsworthy
Edmund Gwenn . . . . Hornblower
Mary Clare . . . . Chloe Hornblower
Helen Haye . . . . Mrs Hillcrist
Dawson Millward . . . . Mr Hillcrist
Malcolm Keen . . . . Charles Hillcrest
Meggie Albanesi . . . . Jill Hillcrest
Frederick Cooper . . . . Rolf Hornblower

Ivor Barnard . . . . Dawker
Muriel Alexander . . . . Anna
James Dodd . . . . Jackman
Blanche Stanley . . . . Mrs Jackman
John H. Roberts . . . . Auctioneer
DRAMA Rich woman thwarts pottery
manufacturer's plans by exposing his daughter-in
law's past.

07075
IN THE NIGHT (5000) (A)
Granger-Binger
D: Frankland A. Richardson
S: (PLAY) Cyril Harcourt
SC: Frank Fowell
C.M. Hallard . . . . The Stranger
Dorothy Fane . . . . Estelle
Hayford Hobbs . . . . George Stanton
Adelqui Migliar . . . . James Marston
Gladys Jennings . . . . Anne Marston
Frank Dane . . . . Inspector
CRIME Faithless man's young wife loves poor
man framed for theft.

07076
KISSING CUP'S RACE (6337) (U)
Hopson Productions (Butcher) *reissue:* 1926
(4 rls cut)
D: Walter West
S: POEM) Campbell Rae Brown
SC: J. Bertram Brown, Benedict James
Violet Hopson . . . . Constance Medley
Gregory Scott . . . . Lord Hilhoxton
Clive Brook . . . . Lord Rattlington
Arthur Walcott . . . . John Wood
Philip Hewland . . . . Vereker
Adeline Hayden Coffin . . . . Lady Corrington
Joe Plant . . . . Bob Doon
SPORT Lord's horse wins big race despite
schemes of rival.

07077
THE YELLOW CLAW (6029) (A)
Stoll
D: Rene Plaissetty
S: (NOVEL) Sax Rohmer
SC: Gerard Fort Buckle
Kitty Fielder . . . . .Lady of the Poppies
Norman Page . . . . Soames
Harvey Braban . . . . Gaston Max
Sydney Seaward . . . . Insp Dunbar
Kiyoshi Takase . . . . Ho-Pin
Fothringham Lysons . . . . . Henry Leroux
Mary Massart . . . . Helen Cumberley
Cyril Percival . . . . John Howard Exel
Arthur Cullin . . . . Dr Cumberley
Ivy King . . . . Mrs Leroux
Annie Esmond . . . . Denise Ryland
June . . . . Mrs Vernon
Eric Albury . . . . Gianopolis
Geoffrey Benstead . . . . Sowerby
CRIME French and English tecs catch opium
smugglers who killed novelist's wife.

07078
THE TOWN OF CROOKED WAYS (5120) (A)
A.R.T. Films (Stoll)
P: A. Randall Terraneau
D: SC: Bert Wynne
S: (NOVEL) J.S. Fletcher
Edward O'Neill . . . . .Solomon Quamperdene
Poppy Wyndham . . . . Queenie Clay
Denis Cowles . . . . Bevis Coleman
Cyril Percival . . . . .Clarence Quamperdene
Eileen Magrath . . . . Millie Earnshaw
George Bellamy . . . . James Winter
Joan Ferry . . . . .Beatrice Quamperdene
Bert Wynne . . . . Winterton Loring

Charles Vane . . . . Alderman Tanqueray
Arthur Cullin . . . . Partisan
Arthur Walcott . . . . Jack Ricketts
Judd Green . . . . Chancellor Slee
Lyell Johnstone . . . . Ben Claybourne
Ida Fane . . . . Miss Grampayne
Wallace Bosco . . . . Mallowes
Fred Rains . . . . Chyver
DRAMA Yorks, period. Corn factor forces
farmers to boycott rival and dies of shock on
shooting nephew as thief.

07079
THE LIGHTS OF HOME (5500) (A)
Screen Plays (BEF)
D: Fred Paul
S: (PLAY) George R.Sims, Robert Buchanan
SC: J. Bertram Brown, Charles Barnett
George Foley . . . . Dave Purvis
Nora Hayden . . . . Tress Purvis
Jack Raymond . . . . Mark
Moya Nugent . . . . Sybil Garfield
John Stuart . . . . Philip Compton
Cecil Morton York . . . . . . Squire Garfield
Frank Tennant . . . . Arthur Tredgold
DRAMA Cornwall. Seduced girl's sailor fiance
saves artist flung over cliff by her father.

07080
THE PRIDE OF THE FANCY (6000) (A)
G.B. Samuelson (General)
D: Albert Ward
S: (NOVEL) George Edgar
Rex Davis . . . . Phil Moran
Daisy Burrell . . . . Kitty Ruston
Tom Reynolds . . . . Prof Ruston
Fred Morgan . . . . Ireton
Dorothy Fane . . . . Hilda Douglas
Wyndham Guise . . . . .Sir Rufus Douglas
Pope Stamper . . . . Oswald Gordon
Kid Gordon . . . . James Croon
SPORT Boxer wins match and showman's
daughter despite lustfulcrook's hold on knight.

07081
A RANK OUTSIDER (4236) (U)
Broadwest (Walturdaw) *reissue:* 1926
(Butcher; 2 rls)
P: Walter West
D: Richard Garrick
S: (NOVEL) Nat Gould
SC: Patrick L. Mannock
Gwen Stratford . . . . .Myra Wynchmore
Cameron Stratford . . . . Capt Ferndale
Lewis Dayton . . . . Guy Selby
John Gliddon . . . . Ralph Wynchmore
Luther Miles . . . .
Martita Hunt . . . .
SPORT Man framed for murder returns from
Australia to trace sister's stolen racehorse.

07082
THE MIRAGE (5500) (U)
George Clark (Stoll)
D: Arhur Rooke
S: (NOVEL) E. Temple Thurston
SC: Guy Newall
Edward O'Neill . . . . .Viscount Guescin
Dorothy Holmes-Gore . . . . Rozanne
Douglas Munro . . . . Courtot
Geoffrey Kerr . . . . .Richard Dalziell
William Parry . . . . Somerset
Blanche Stanley . . . . Mrs Bulpitt
ROMANCE Poor viscount leaves farmer's
daughter to younger man when legacy falls
through.

07083
THE BITER BIT (2000)
British & American Syndicate
P: Gus Elen jr
D: S. Vanderlyn
George Turner . . . .
Bob Reed . . . .
COMEDY

07084
A WATERY ROMANCE (2000)
British & American Syndicate
P: Gus Elen jr
D: S. Vanderlyn
Ray Forrest . . . . . : . . . . .
Eileen More . . . .
COMEDY

07085
SETTLED IN FULL
P.M. Productions
P: G.P. Powles
D: Geoffrey H. Malins
S: Colden Lore
Hayford Hobbs . . . .
Ena Beaumont . . . .
Margaret Hope . . . .
Ray Raymond . . . .
Johnny Butt . . . .
Pablo Ramos
WESTERN

07086
UNCLE DICK'S DARLING (4890) (U)
British Standard (Anchor)
P: John Robyns
D: Fred Paul
S: (PLAY) H.J. Byron
SC: R. Byron-Webber
George Bellamy . . . .   Uncle Dick
Athalie Davis . . . .   Mary
Humberston Wright . . . . . .   Chevenix
Ronald Power . . . .   Mr Lorimer
Sydney Folker . . . .
Frank Dane . . . .
Gordon Craig . . . .

Adelaide grace . . . .
ROMANCE Caravanner dreams adopted
daughter weds MP instead of pilot she loves.

07087
THE ENGLISH ROSE (4890) (U)
British Standard (Whincup)
P: John Robyns
D: Fred Paul
S: (PLAY) George R. Sims, Robert Buchanan
SC: Paul Rooff
Fred Paul . . . .   Father Michael
Humberston Wright . . . . . .   Capt MacDonnell
Sydney Folker . . . .   Harry O'Malley
Mary Morton . . . .
Jack Raymond . . . .
Amy Brandon Thomas . . . . .
George Turner . . . .
Clifford Desborough . . . . . .
CRIME Ireland. Priest learns truth of murder
but is unable to save framed man.

07088
THE WIFE WHOM GOD FORGOT (5500) (A)
retitled: TANGLED HEARTS
Alliance Film Corp (Anchor)
D: William J. Humphrey
S: (NOVEL) Cecil H. Bullivant
SC: Adrian Johnstone
Gertrude McCoy . . . .   Sylvia Fairfax
G.H. Mulcaster . . . .   Fairfax
R. Henderson-Bland . . . . . .   Maurice Rainham
Peter Upcher . . . .   Brian Dainsford
Maresco Marescini . . . .
Joan Hestor . . . .
DRAMA Explorer divorces wife on word of her
lover, then shoots him on learning he lied.

07089
THE MONEY MOON
Alliance Film Corp
D: Fred Paul
S: (NOVEL) Jeffrey Farnol
SC: Adrian Johnstone
Stella Patrick Campbell . . . .
Gordon Craig . . . .
DRAMA "Charming British story in a typical
British setting."

07090
THE HOLIDAY HUSBAND (5407) (U)
Alliance Film Corp (Shaftesbury)
D: A.C. Hunter
S: (NOVEL) Dolf Wyllarde
Harry Welchman . . . .
Irma Royce . . . .
Adeline Hayden Coffin . . . .
Amy Verity . . . .
Eric Barclay . . . .
DRAMA "The dream that cometh through a
multitude of business."

07091
THE GOLDEN PIPPIN GIRL (5000) (A)
retitled: WHY MEN LEAVE HOME
Alliance Film Corp (Anchor)
D: A.C. Hunter
Nellie Wallace . . . .
Ray Forrest . . . .
Irene Tripod . . . .
COMEDY Servant wins beauty contest but
fails screen test.

07092
MARZIPAN OF THE SHAPES
Alliance Film Corp
D: A.C. Hunter
Ray Forrest . . . .
Irene Tripod . . . .
Frank Stanmore . . . .
COMEDY Burlesque of "Tarzan of the Apes".

07093
GREAT SNAKES
Hepworth
D: Gerald Ames, Gaston Quiribet
S: (NOVEL) William Caine
Eileen Dennes . . . .
Frank Stanmore . . . .
Hugh Clifton . . . .
Gladys Humphries . . . .
John McAndrews . . . .
John Beresford . . . .
COMEDY

1921

JAN

07094
KIPPS (6194) (A)
Stoll
D: Harold Shaw
S: (NOVEL) H.G. Wells
SC: Frank Miller
George K. Arthur . . . . Arthur Kipps
Edna Flugrath . . . . Ann Pornick
Christine Rayner . . . . Helen Walsingham
Teddy Arundell . . . . Chitterlow
Norman Thorpe . . . . Chester Coote
Arthur Helmore . . . . Shalford
John M. East . . . . Old Kipps
Miss Atterbury . . . . Mrs Walsingham
Mr Gerard . . . . Young Walsingham
Mr Barbour . . . . Old Pornick
Judd Green . . . . Old Gentleman
COMEDY Sacked clerk inherits £3,000 a year,
tries society, and returns to working-class
sweetheart.

07095
THE LIKENESS OF THE NIGHT (5434) (A)
Screen Plays (BEF)
D: Percy Nash
S: (PLAY) Mrs W.K. Clifford
Renee Kelly . . . . Mary
Minna Grey . . . . Mildred
Harold Deacon . . . . Bernard Archerson
Florence Shee . . . . Lady Carruthers
ROMANCE Faithless barrister's wife enters
convent and fakes drowning so he may marry
his mistress.

07096
THE SWORD OF FATE (5200) (A)
Screen Plays (BEF)
D: Frances E. Grant
S: (NOVEL) Henry Herman
SC: Frances E. Grant, Kate Gurney
David Hawthorne . . . . Frank Usselby
Lionel d'Aragon . . . . Daniel Uncoat
Dorothy Moody . . . . Grace Repton
Sir Simeon Stuart . . . . Ralph Usselby
Mabel Archdale . . . . Mary Mortimer
Charles Vane
Norma Beryl . . . . Marion Grey
Kate Gurney . . . . Mrs Mottram
CRIME Girl proves mine manager rigged death
of mad owner's wife and framed his son, her
fiance.

07097
LOVE MAGGY (6000) (A)
Samuelson (Granger)
D: Fred Leroy Granville
S: (NOVEL) Countess Barcynska
SC: Colden Lore
Peggy Hyland . . . . Maggy Chalfont
Campbell Gullan . . . . Lord Chalfont
James Lindsay . . . . Fred Woolf
Maudie Dunham . . . . Joan
Maidie Hope . . . . Lady Susan
Lilian Hall Davis . . . . Alexandra Hersey
Alfred Drayton . . . . De Preyne
Fred Thatcher . . . . Lord Lancing
Mabel Terry-Lewis . . . . . . Lady Shelford
Afred Wood . . . . Raymond Spellman
Saba Raleigh . . . . Mrs Simmons
DRAMA Crook uses ex-mistress to force
introduction to titled husband.

07098
THE WHITE HEN (5000) (U)
Zodiac (Walker)
P: Jospeh J. Bamberger
D: Frank Richardson

S: (NOVEL) Phyllis Campbell
Mary Glynne . . . . Celeste de Crequy
Leslie Faber . . . . Duc de Crequy
Pat Somerset . . . . Beaufort Lynn
Cecil Humphreys . . . . Louis St Romney
COMEDY France. Man poses as tec to woo poor
Duc's daughter whose dowry diamond is
swallowed by pet hen.

07099
HER PENALTY (4400) (A)
Broadwest (Walturdaw)
P: Walter West
D: Einar J. Bruun
S: Benedict James
SC: Eliot Stannard
Stewart Rome . . . . James Fenwick
Pauline Peters . . . . Vera Trenchard
Clive Brook . . . . Robert Trenchard
Philip Hewland . . . . Arthur Winterby
DRAMA Man marries secretary and her 'dead'
husband returns.

07100
THE DIAMOND NECKLACE (5900) (A)
Ideal
D:SC: Denison Clift
S: (STORY) Guy de Maupassant (LA PARURE)
Milton Rosmer . . . . Charles Furness
Jessie Winter . . . . Lily Faraday
Sara Sample . . . . Margaret Bayliss
Warwick Ward . . . . Ford
Mary Brough . . . . Mrs Tudsberry
Johnny Butt . . . . Maurice Pollard
F.E. Montague-Thacker . . . . Basil Mortimer
John Peachey . . . . Mr Bainbridge
Miss Fordyce . . . . Mrs Faraday
DRAMA Cashier and wife suffer ten years'
poverty to replace lost necklace before
learning it was fake.

07101
THE WILL (5000)
Ideal
D: A.V. Bramble
S: (PLAY) J.M. Barrie
SC: Eliot Stannard
Milton Rosmer . . . . Philip Ross
Evangeline Hilliard . . . . . . Emily Ross
J. Fisher White . . . . Mr Devises
Alec Fraser . . . . Robert Devises
Reginald Bach . . . . Lord Chelsea
Mary Brough . . . . Bessie
Antony Holles . . . . Charles Ross
DRAMA Rich man's mean wife dies, his
wastrel, and his daughter elopes with chauffeur.

07102
THE WAY OF A MAN (6500)
Gaumont-British Screencraft
D: C.C. Calvert
S: H.V. Bailey
Josephine Earle . . . . Lady Ethel Elsford
Philip Anthony . . . . Roger Garson
Lewis Dayton . . . . Maj Darlow
Cecil du Gue . . . . Warren Garson
George Bellamy . . . . Lord Elsford
Cyril Smith . . . . Hon Guy Elsford
Gertrude Walton . . . . Lady Elsford
R. Van Courtlandt . . . . Capt Grey
ROMANCE Lady loves major but weds usurer's
nephew to save father.

07103
THE HEADMASTER (5500)
Astra Films
P: H.W. Thompson
D:SC: Kenelm Foss
S: (PLAY) Edward Knoblock, Wilfred Coleby
Cyril Maude . . . . Rev Cuthbert Sanctuary

Margot Drake . . . . Portia Sanctuary
Miles Malleson . . . . Palliser Grantley
Marie Illington . . . . Cornelia Grantley
Lionelle Howard . . . . Jack Strahan
Sir Simeon Stuart . . . . Dean of Carchester
Ann Trevor . . . . Antigone Sanctuary
Louie Freear . . . . Bella
Will Corrie . . . . Sgt Munton
Alan Selby . . . . Richards
Gordon Craig . . . . Stuart Minor
DRAMA Headmaster seeks bishopric by forcing
daughter to marry rich woman's vapid son.

FEB

07104
MY LORD CONCEIT (6034) (A)
Stoll
D:SC: F. Martin Thornton
S: (NOVEL) 'Rita'
Evelyn Boucher . . . . Beryl Foster
Maresco Marisini . . . . Count Savona
Rowland Myles . . . . Ivor Grant
E.L. Frewen . . . . Sir Hector Grant
Frank E. Petley . . . . John Marsden
J. Edwards Barber . . . . Dr Clark
Emilie Nichol . . . . Mrs Grant
Eric George . . . . Cyril
Edward Thornton . . . . Jackie
Coomarie Gawthorne . . . . . Matabia
CRIME India. Count frames runaway wife for
killing husband over daughter of blackmailing
rajah.

07105
HANDY ANDY (5000)
Ideal
D: Bert Wynne
S: (NOVEL) Samuel Lover
SC: Eliot Stannard
Peter Coleman . . . . Handy Andy
Kathleen Vaughan . . . . Una O'Reilly
Warwick Ward . . . . Squire O'Grady
John Wyndham . . . . Michael Dwyer
Wally Bosco . . . . Murphy
Fred Morgan . . . . Squire O'Grady
May Price . . . . Ragged Nan
Hessel Crayne . . . . Dr Browling
COMEDY Ireland, 1840. Stableboy poses as
cousin to foil kidnapper and is forced to wed
his sister.

07106
THE RIVER OF LIGHT (4949) (A)
Brilliant Photoplays (Globe)
D:S: Dave Aylott
Jack Jarman . . . . Jimmy Harcourt
Blanche Walker . . . . Betty Webster
Phyllis Shannaw . . . . Sybil
Dave Aylott . . . . David Webster
Vivian Palmer . . . . Capt Melville
Noel W. Moses . . . . Native Chief
ADVENTURE Africa. Bankrupt finds diamonds
and is saved from crooks by halfcaste hottentot.

07107
BLOOD MONEY (4722) (A)
Granger-Binger
D: Fred Goodwins
S: (NOVEL) Cecil Bullivant
Adelqui Migliar . . . . Le Grand
Dorothy Fane . . . . :. Felice Deschanel
Frank Dane . . . . ,. . . Sarne
Arthur Cullin . . . . Matthew Harper
Colette Brettel . . . . Marguerite Deschanel
Harry Ham . . . . Insp Bell
Fred Goodwins . . . . Bruce Harper
CRIME Gambler kidnaps mistress's husband and
fakes death by using corpse of his brother, a
suicide.

07108
THE LOUDWATER MYSTERY (4800)(A)
Braodwest (Walturdaw)
D:SC: Norman Macdonald
P: Walter West
S: (NOVEL) Edgar Jepson
Gregory Scott . . . . Hubert Manley
Pauline Peters . . . . Lady Loudwater
Clive Brook . . . . Lord Loudwater
Cameron Carr . . . . Insp Flexen
C. Tilson-Chowne . . . . Col Grey
Arthur Walcott . . . . Carrington
Nan Heriot . . . . Miss Truslove
Charles Poulton . . . . Roper
CRIME Tec proves Lord was stabbed by secretary

07109
HARD CASH (5150)(U)
Master Films (Butcher)
P: H.B. Parkinson
D: Edwin J. Collins
S: (NOVEL) Charles Reade
SC: Walter Courtenay Rowden
Dick Webb . . . . Alfred Hardie
Alma Green . . . . Julia Dodd
Frank Arlton . . . . Capt Dodd
Cecil Morton York . . . . Richard Hardie
Ethel Griffies . . . . Mrs Hardie
A.F. Bassett . . . . Skinner
CRIME 1850. Rich banker has son certified
insane and is shot by maddened depositor.

MAR

07110
INNOCENT (5933)(U)
Stoll
D; Maurice Elvey
S: (NOVEL) Marie Corelli
SC: William J. Elliott
Madge Stuart . . . . Innocence
Basil Rathbone . . . . Amadis de Jocelyn
Lawrence Anderson . . . . . Robin
Edward O'Neill . . . . Hugo de Jocelyn
Frank Dane . . . . Ned Landon
W. Cronin Wilson . . . . Armitage
Ruth Mackay . . . . Lady Maude
Mme d'Esterre . . . . Miss Leigh
Annie Esmond . . . . Housekepper
ROMANCE Orphan learns artist's love is false,
returns to farm, and dies in a storm.

07111
THE LUNATIC AT LARGE (5120)(U)
Hepworth
D: Henry Edwards
S: (NOVEL) J. Storer Clouston
SC: George W. Dewhurst
Henry Edwards . . . . Mandell Essington
Chrissie White . . . . Lady Irene
Lyell Johnston . . . . Baron Gauche
Gwynne Herbert . . . . Countess Coyley
George Dewhurst . . . . Dr Welsh
Hugh Clifton . . . . Dr Twiddell
James Annand . . . . Dr Congleton
P. K. Esdaile . . . . Dr Watson
Beuna Bent . . . . Lady Alicia a Fyre
John MacAndrews . . . . Attendant
COMEDY Rich madman escapes from asylum
and saves lady from Danish baron.

07112
THE SCALLYWAG (4400)(U)
Master (Butcher)
P: H. B. Parkinson
D: Challis Sanderson
S: (NOVEL) Grant Allen
SC: Walter Courtenay Rowden
Fred Thatcher . . . . Paul Gascoyne

Muriel Alexander . . . . Nea Blair
Ann Elliott . . . . Isobel Boynton
Hubert Carter . . . . Judah Solomon
Cecil Morton York . . . . Emery Gascoyne
Yolande Duquette . . . . Mme Cerrolo
ROMENCE Jewish usurer educates poor heir on
condition he forsakes poor sweetheart to wed
American heiress.

07113
IN FULL CRY (5700)(A)
Broadwest (Walturdaw)
P: Walter West
D: Einer J. Bruun
S: (NOVEL) Richard Marsh
SC: Benedict James, Frank Fowell
Gregory Scott . . . . Blaise Palhurston
Pauline Peters . . . . Pollie Hills
Cecil Mannering . . . . Bob Foster
Philip Hewland . . . . Frank C. Baynes
Charles Tilson-Chowne . . . . John Shapcott
CRIME Slum laundress blamed when man kills
wife's rich lover.

07114
MARY-FIND-THE-GOLD (5400)(U)
Welsh-Pearson (Jury)
D: S: George Pearson
Betty Balfour . . . . Mary Smith
Hugh E. Wright . . . . Alfred Smith
Colin Craig . . . . Jack Bryant
Mabel Poulton . . . . Bessie Bryant
Arthur Cleave . . . . Arthur Drew
Mary Dibley . . . . Miss Reeve
Madge Tree . . . . Miss Stagg
Betty Farquhar . . . . Miss Payne
Mrs Braithwaite . . . . .Widow Mather
Thomas Weguelin . . . . Wurzel Blake
Gladys Hamer . . . . Higgs
Tom Coventry . . . . Tom
DRAMA Sacked clerk's daughter turns
dressmaker and is saved   from false charge
of theft by country sweetheart.

07115
GRAND GUIGNOL (Series)
Screen Plays (BEF)
D: Fred Paul

07116
1—THE OATH (1080) (A)
S: Fred Paul
Lewis Gilbert . . . . The Priest
Margot Drake . . . . Lizette

07117
2—THE FLAT (623)(A)
S: Fred Paul
Jack Raymond . . . . John Timkins
George Foley . . . . The Stranger

07118
3—THE LAST APPEAL (920)(A)
S: George Saxon
Jack Raymond . . . . John Martin
Jeanne di Ramo . . . . Lillian
Henry Doughty . . . . The Judge

07119
4—THE WOMAN UPSTAIRS (810)(A)
S: Percy Nash
Joan Beverley . . . . Rose
Frank Hill . . . . Fred Ellsworthy

07120
5—THE GENTLE DOCTOR (884)(A)
S: George Saxon
Fred Paul . . . . The Doctor
Olive Eltone . . . . Anna
DRAMAS Macabre short stories.

07121
CARNIVAL (7400)(A)
Alliance Film Corp reissue: 1922 (Cosmo)
D: Harley Knoles
S: (PLAY) Matheson Lang, C. M. Hardinge
SC: Adrian Johnson, Rosina Henley
Matheson Lang . . . . Silvio Steno
Hilda Bayley . . . . Simonetta Steno
Ivor Novello . . . . Count Andrea Scipione
Clifford Grey . . . . Celio
Victor McLaglan . . . . Baron
Florence Hunter . . . . Nino
DRAMA Venice. Jealous actor tries to strangle
wife during "Othello"

07122
THE DOOR THAT HAS NO KEY (5400)(A)
Alliance Film Corp
P: Harley Knoles
D: Frank H. Crane
S: (NOVEL) Cosmo Hamilton
SC: Adrian Johnstone
George Relph . . . . Jack Scorrier
Betty Faire . . . . Margaret Hubbard
Evelyn Brent . . . . Violet Melton
Wilfred Seagram . . . . Pat Malloy
Olive Sloane . . . . Blossy Waveney
W. Cronin Wilson . . . . Yearsley Morrow
Alice de Winton . . . . Lady Emily Scorrie
A. Harding Steerman . . . . Hon Claude Scorrie
Gorden Craig . . . . Clive
DRAMA Barrister's faithless wife returns after
he has had child by secretary.

07123
MR PIM PASSES BY (6077)(U)
G. B. Samuelson (General)
D: SC: Albert Ward
S: (PLAY) A. A. Milne
Peggy Hyland . . . . Olivia Marsden
Campbell Gullan . . . . Carraway Pim
Maudie Dunham . . . . Dinah Marsden
Tom Reynolds . . . . James Brymer
Henry Kendall . . . . Brian Strange
Hubert Harben . . . . George Marsden
Annie Esmond . . . . Lady Marsden
Wyndham Guise . . . . Mr Fanshawe
COMEDY When woman's 'dead' husband
returns she refuses to remarry her second
until he consents to niece's wedding.

APR

07124
THE EDUCATION OF NICKY (4200)
Harma-Associated Exhibitors (Walturdaw)
D: SC: Arthur Rooke
S: (NOVEL) May Wynn
James Knight . . . . Nicky Malvesty
Marjorie Villis . . . . Trixie Happinleigh
Constance Worth . . . . Chloe
Mary Rorke . . . . Lady Aberleigh
Keith Weatherley . . . . Col Trouville
Dolores Courtenay . . . . Virginia
George Williams . . . . Mr Malvesty
Winifred Sadler . . . . Mrs Malvesty
ROMANCE Rich cousins marry after they are
both bankrupted.

07125
THE TINTED VENUS (5200)(U)
Hepworth
D: Cecil M. Hepworth
S: (NOVEL) F. Anstey
SC: Blanche McIntosh
Alma Taylor . . . . Matilda Collum
George Dewhurst . . . . Leander Tweddle
Maud Cressall . . . . Venus
Eileen Dennes . . . . Bella Parkinson
Hugh Clifton . . . . Jauncey

Gwynne Herbert . . . . Mrs Collum
Mary Brough . . . . Landlady
FANTASY Statue of Venus comes to life and
tries to lure affianced barber to Cytherian Groves.

07126
BELPHEGOR THE MOUNTEBANK (5500)
Ideal
D: Bert Wynne
S: (NOVEL) Charles Webb
SC: Eliot Stannard
Milton Rosmer . . . . Belphegor
Kathleen Vaughan . . . . Pauline de Blangy
Warwick Ward . . . . Laverennes
Nancy Price . . . . Countess de Blangy
Margaret Dean . . . . Madeleine
Peter Coleman . . . . Fanfaronade
Leal Douglas . . . . Catherine
R. Heaton Grey . . . . Comte de Blangy
A. Harding Steerman . . . . Duc de Sarola
DRAMA Ruritania. Rogue poses as Comte he
killed and weds Princess, but heir to throne
steals their child.

07127
DEMOS (5700) (A) USA: WHY MEN FORGET
Ideal
D: SC: Denison Clift
S: (NOVEL) George Gissing
Milton Rosmer . . . . Richard Mortimer
Evelyn Brent . . . . Emma Vine
Warwick Ward . . . . Willis Rodman
Bettina Campbell . . . . Adela Waltham
Olaf Hytten . . . . Daniel Dabbs
Gerald McCarthy . . . . Hubert Eldon
Mary Brough . . . . Mrs Mortimer
Haidee Wright . . . . Mrs Eldon
Vivian Gibson . . . . Alice Mortimer
Daisy Campbell . . . . Mrs Waltham
James G. Butt . . . . Jim Cullen
Leonard Robson . . . . Longwood
DRAMA Sacked agitator inherits ironworks,
loses it by another will, and leaves rich wife
for poor girl.

07128
THE OLD COUNTRY (5000)
Ideal
D: A. V, Bramble
S:(PLAY) Dion Clayton Calthrop
SC: Eliot Stannard
Gerald McCarthy . . . . James Fountain
Kathleen Vaughan . . . . Mary Lorimer
Haidee Wright . . . . Mrs Fountain
George Bellamy . . . . Squire
Ethel Newman . . . . Annette Alborough
Stanley Roberts . . . . Austin Wells
Sydney Paxton . . . . Steward
DRAMA Yankee planter buys squire's hall,
instals exiled mother, and learns his is squire's son.

07129
THE OTHER PERSON (5319)(A)
Granger-Binger
D: B. E. Doxat-Pratt
S: (NOVEL) Fergus Hume
SC: Benedict James
Zoe Palmer . . . . Alice Dene
Adelqui Migliar . . . . Andrew Grain
Arthur Pusey . . . . Chris Larcher
E. Story-Gofton . . . . Dr Pess
William Huntre . . . . Amos Larcher
Ivo Dawson . . . . Squire Grain
Nora Hayden . . . . Dolly Banks
Arthur Walcott . . . . Rev Augustus Dene
FANTASY Seance proves ghost impelled
spiritualist to kill rich father.

07130
KITTY TAILLEUR (4900)(A)
Granger-Binger
D: Frankland A. Richardson
S: (NOVEL) Mary Sinclair
SC: Frank Fowell
Marjorie Hume . . . . Kitty Tailleur
Lewis Dayton . . . . Robert
Ivo Dawson . . . . Wilfred Marson
Nora Hayden . . . . Janette Lucy
William Hunter . . . . Col Hankin
Constance Dawson . . . . Mrs Hankin
ROMANCE Girl refuses to marry either her
illegal husband or widower with family.

07131
STELLA (5500)(U)
Master (Butcher)
D:SC: Edwin J. Collins
S: (NOVEL) H. Rider Haggard (STELLA
FREGELIUS)
Molly Adair . . . . Stella Fregelius
Manning Haynes . . . . Maurice Cook
Charles Vane . . . . Col Monk
Betty Farquhar . . . . Mary Porson
Wilfred Fletcher . . . . Stephen Lanyard
Mildred Evelyn . . . . Eliza Lanyard
ROMANCE Poor colonel's son, engaged to
heiress, loves daughter of shipwrecked vicar.

07132
BINGLE AT THE PAPER CHASE (2000)
Debenham & Co
Gilbert Payne . . . . Bingle
COMEDY

07133
THE FORTUNE OF CHRISTINA MCNAB
(6200)
Gaumont-Westminister
D: W.P. Kellino
S: (NOVEL) Sarah McNaughton
SC: Paul Rooff
Nora Swinburne . . . . Christina McNab
David Hawthorne . . . . Colin McCrae
Francis Lister . . . . Duke of Sothwark
Sara Sample . . . . Muriel Stonor
Marjorie Chard . . . . Lady Anne Drummond
Chick Farr . . . . Archie Anstruthers
Norman Tharp . . . . Mr Drummond
Gena Ray . . . . Joan Drummond
Eva Westlake . . . . Lady Tarbutt
Dora Levis . . . . Jessie
COMEDY Affianced duke causes infatuated
heiress to return to soldier sweetheart.

07134
THE OLD CURIOSITY SHOP (6587)(U)
Welsh-Pearson (Jury)
P: George Pearson
D: Thomas Bentley
S: (NOVEL) Charles Dickens
SC: J.A. Atkinson
Mabel Poulton . . . . Little Nell
William Lugg . . . . Grandfather
Hugh E. Wright . . . . Tom Codlin
Pino Conti . . . . Daniel Quilp
Bryan Powley . . . . Single Gentleman
Barry Livesey . . . . Tom Scott
Cecil Bevan . . . . Sampson Brass
Beatie Olna Travers . . . . . . Sally Brass
Minnie Rayner . . . . Mrs Jarley
Dennis Harvey . . . . Short Trotters
Dezma du May . . . . Mrs Quilp
Colin Craig . . . . Dick Swiveller
Fairy Emlyn . . . . Marchioness
A. Harding Steerman . . . . Mr Marton
DRAMA Period. Dwarf usurer prevents rich man
from finding evicted gambler and his granddaughter.

07135
WATCHING EYES (5558) (series)(A)
Fraser Productions (Regent)
D: Geoffrey H. Malins
S: John Wickens
Ena Beaumont . . . . Eve Selby
Geoffrey H. Malins . . . . Adam Selby
John Wickens . . . . Clifton Miles
Episodes 1 — 6
COMEDY Wife's pekinese dog saves stolen
banknotes, foils horsedopers, etc.

07136
THE ADVENTURES OF SHERLOCK HOLMES
(series)
Stoll
D: Maurice Elvey
S: (STORIES) Arthur Conan Doyle
SC: William J. Elliott
Eille Norwood . . . . Sherlock Holmes
Hubert Willis . . . . Dr John Watson

07137
1—THE DYING DETECTIVE (2273)(A)
Cecil Humphreys . . . . Culverton Smith
Mme d'Esterre . . . . Mrs Hudson

07138
2—THE DEVIL'S FOOT (2514)(A)
Harvey Braban . . . . Mortimer Tregennis
Hugh Buckler . . . . Dr Sterndale

07139
3—A CASE OF IDENTITY (2610)(U)
Edna Flugrath . . . . Mary Sutherland
Nelson Ramsey . . . . Hosmer Angel

07140
4—YELLOW FACE (2020)(A)
Clifford Heatherley . . . . Grant Munro
Norman Whalley . . . . Effie Munro

07141
5—THE RED-HEADED LEAGUE (2140)(U)
Edward Arundell . . . . Jabez Wilson
H. Townsend . . . . Spalding

07142
6—THE RESIDENT PATIENT (2404)(A)
Arthur Bell . . . . Insp Lestrade
C. Pitt-Chatham . . . . Dr Percy Trevelyan
Judd Green . . . . Blessington
Wally Bosco . . . . Moffatt

07143
7—A SCANDAL IN BOHEMIA (2100)(U)
Joan Beverley . . . . Irene Adler
Alfred Drayton . . . . King of Bohemia

07144
8—THE MAN WITH THE TWISTED LIP (2412)
(A)
Robert Vallis . . . . Neville St Clair
Paulette del Baye . . . . Mrs St Clair
Mme d'Esterre . . . . Mrs Hudson

07145
9—THE BERYL CORONET (2340)(A)
SC: Charles Barnett
Henry Vibart . . . . Alexander Holder
Molly Adair . . . . Mary
Lawrence Anderson . . . . Arthur
Jack Selfridge . . . . Sir George Burnwell
Mme d'Esterre . . . . Mrs Hudson

07146
10—THE NOBLE BACHELOR (2100)(U)
Arthur Bell . . . . Insp Lestrade
Cyril Percival . . . . Simon
Temple Bell . . . . Hetty Doran
Fred Earle . . . . Moulton
Mme d'Esterre . . . . Mrs Hudson

07147
11—THE COPPER BEECHES (2193)(A)
Madge White . . . . Violet Hunter/Ada
Lyell Johnson . . . . Jephro Rucastle
Fred Raynham . . . . Toller
Eve McCarthy . . . . Mrs Toller
Lottie Blackford . . . . Mrs Rucastle
Bobbie Harwood . . . . Roger Wilson
William J. Elliott Jr . . . . Japhat

07148
12 —THE EMPTY HOUSE (1800)(A)
Austin Fairman . . . . Ronald Adair
Cecil Kerr . . . . Sir Charles Ridge
Arthur Bell . . . . Insp Lestrade
Mme d'Esterre . . . . Mrs Hudson

07149
13—THE TIGER OF SAN PEDRO (2080)(A)
Lewis Gilbert . . . . Murillo
George Harrington . . . . Scott Eccles
Arthur Walcott . . . . Garcia
Arthur Bell . . . . Insp Lestrade
Mme d'Esterre . . . . Mrs Hudson

07150
14—THE PRIORY SCHOOL (2100)(U)
SC: Charles Barnett
Leslie English . . . . Dr Huxtable
C.H. Croker-King . . . . . . Duke of Holderness
Irene Rooke . . . . Duchess
Tom Ronald . . . . Reuben Hayes
Patrick Kay . . . . Lord Saltire
Cecil Kerr . . . . Wilder
Mme d'Esterre . . . . Mrs Hudson

07151
15—THE SOLITARY CYCLIST (2140)(A)
R.D. Sylvester . . . . Carruthers
Violet Hewitt . . . . Violet Relph
Allan Jeayes . . . . Woodley
CRIME Private detective solves various crimes.

07152
LEAVES FROM MY LIFE (series)
Master Films (White)
P: H.B. Parkinson
D: Edward R. Gordon
S: (STORIES) Ernest Haigh (SECRETS OF
SCOTLAND YARD)
SC: Frank Miller
Ernest Haigh . . . . Insp Haigh
Geoffrey Benstead . . . . His Friend
Suzanne Morris . . . . Mrs Haigh

07153
1—THE GIRL WHO CAME BACK (2000)
Joan Lockton . . . . Jessie Blane
Olaf Hytten . . . . Lt Blane
Jack Selfridge . . . . The Betrayer

07154
2—THE LADY IN BLACK (2000)
Kitty Fielder . . . . The Lady

07155
3—FIGHT IN A THIEVES' KITCHEN (2000)
Charles Danvers . . . . The Publican

07156
4—LOST, STOLEN OR STRAYED (2000)

07157
5—MOTHER'S DARLING (2000)

07158
6—THE PRODIGAL SON (2000)
CRIMES Ex-Chief inspector narrates cases he
has solved.

MAY
07159
FOR HER FATHER'S SAKE (4983)
G.B. Samuelson (General)
D: Alexander Butler
S: (PLAY) Alfred Sutro (THE PERFECT
LOVER)
Owen Nares . . . . Walter Cardew
Isobel Elsom . . . . Lilian Armitage
James Lindsay . . . . William Tremblett
Tom Reynolds . . . .
Renee Davies . . . . May Tremblett
Norman Partridge . . . . Joseph Tremblett
Cicely Reid . . . . Martha Tremblett
Wyndham Guise . . . . Mr Armitage
ROMANCE Girl weds rich man for father's sake
and then her true love inherits fortune.

07160
THE MAGISTRATE (5400)(U)
Samuelson (General)
D:SC: Bannister Merwin
S: (PLAY) Arthur W. Pinero
Tom Reynolds . . . . Mr Poskett
Maudie Dunham . . . . Beattie Tomlinson
Ethel Warwick . . . . Agatha Poskett
Roy Royston . . . . Cis Farringdon
Cyril Percival . . . . Capt Horace Vale
Dawson Millward . . . . Col Lukyn
Nell Graham . . . . Charlotte Poskett
COMEDY Widow weds a magistrate and makes
her 19-year old son act as a boy.

07161
THE PRINCE AND THE BEGGARMAID
(4960) (U)
Ideal
D: A.V. Bramble
S: (PLAY) Walter Howard
SC: Eliot Stannard
Henry Ainley . . . . Prince Olaf
Kathleen Vaughan . . . . Princess Monika
Harvey Braban . . . . King Hildred
Sam Wilkinson . . . . Prince Michael
Sydney Paxton . . . . Chief of State
John Wyndham . . . . Capt Karsburg
Laurence Forster . . . . Gen Erlenberg
Francis Duguid . . . . Capt Schwartz
Frank Woolf . . . . Capt Hector
DRAMA Ruritania. King declares war to force
Princess to wed his hunch-backed brother.

07162
THE FOUR FEATHERS (6290(U)
Stoll
D: Rene Plaissetty
S: (NOVEL) A.E.W. Mason
SC: Daisy Martin
Harry Ham . . . . Harry Faversham
Mary Massart . . . . Ethne Eustace
Cyril Percival . . . . Jack Durrance
Henry Vibart . . . . Gen Faversham
Tony Fraser . . . . Abou Fatma
Robert English . . . . Lt Sutch
Harry J. Worth . . . . Maj Willoughby
Gwen Williams . . . . Mrs Adair
M. Gray Murray . . . . Dermod Eustace
C.W. Cundell . . . . Lt Trench
Roger Livesey . . . . Harry (child)
WAR Egypt. "Coward" resigns commission and
poses as Arab to save former comrades.

07163
THE FOUR JUST MEN (4980) (U)
Stoll
D:SC: George Ridgwell
S: (NOVEL) Edgar Wallace
Cecil Humphreys . . . . Manfred
Teddy Arundell . . . . Insp Falmouth
C.H. Croker-King . . . . Thery
C. Tilson-Chowne . . . . Sir Philip Ramon
Owen Roughwood . . . . Poiccart
George Bellamy . . . . Gonsalez
Robert Vallis . . . . Billy Marks
CRIME Gang force rich man to donate to
charity and are betrayed by Spanish member.

07164
DANIEL DERONDA (5600)(A)
Master (Butcher) *reissue:* 1926 (2 rls)
P: H.B. Parkinson
D: W.C. Rowden
S: (NOVEL) George Eliot
SC: Frank Miller
Reginald Fox . . . . Daniel Deronda
Ann Trevor . . . . Mirah Lapidoth
Clive Brook . . . . Mallinger Grandcourt
Dorothy Fane . . . . Gwendolyn Harlet
Yolande Duquette . . . . Mrs Glasher
ROMANCE 1860. Jewess refuses to wed man
who saved her from suicide until he discovers
his mother is Jewish.

07165
SHADOW OF EVIL (5694)(A)
British Art (Regent)
P: Arrigo Bocchi
D: James Readon
S: (NOVEL Carlton Dawe
SC: Harry Hughes
Cecil Humphreys
Mary Dibley
Reginald Fox
Gladys Mason
CRIME Burglar blackmails actress who thinks
she killed husband.

JUN
07166
GRAND GUIGNOL (series)
Screen Plays (BEF)
D: Fred Paul

07167
6—DELILAH (930)(A)
S: C.E. Dering

07168
7—A VOICE FROM THE DEAD (775)(A)
S: Fred Paul

07169
8—THE GUARDIAN OF HONOUR (935)(A)
S: Eric Clare

07170
9—THE HAPPY PAIR (1320) (A)
S: George Saxon

07171
10—THE RETURN (1050)(A)
S: Norman Ramsay
George Foley
Ethel Oliver

07172
11—THE STING OF DEATH (1200)(A)
S: Norman Ramsay
Fred Paul
Lionel D'Aragon

07173
12—THE NURSE (925)(A)
S: George Saxon
Fred Morgan
Reginald Fox

07174
13—POLLY (1160)(U)
DRAMAS Macabre Short Stories.

07175
SENORITA (2000)
Gliddon-d'Eyncourt Productions
P: Tennyson d'Eyncourt
D:S: John Gliddon
Francis Innys . . . . The Man
Elizabeth Brandt . . . . The Girl
COMEDY Spain. Poor man hired to save
British girl from brigands.

07176
PINS AND NEEDLES (2000)
Gliddon-d'Eyncourt Productions
P: Tennyson d'Eyncourt
D:S: John Gliddon
Francis Innys . . . . The Man
Elizabeth Brandt . . . . The Girl
COMEDY Margate. Man on motor scooter
follows girl and saves her from cad.

07177
MONTY WORKS THE WIRES (4600)(U)
Artistic
P: George Redman
D: Challis Sanderson, Manning Haynes
S: Lydia Hayward, Manning Haynes
Manning Haynes . . . . The Man
Mildred Evelyn . . . . The Girl
Eva Westlake . . . . The Auntie
Charles Ashton . . . . The Brother-in-law
Gladys Hamer . . . . The Maid
Thomas Canning . . . . The Doctor
COMEDY Dog tells puppy how master wed
owner of pekinese.

07178
SYBIL (5300)(U)
Ideal
D: Jack Denton
S: (NOVEL) Benjamin Disraeli
SC: Colden Lore
Evelyn Brent . . . . Sybil Gerard
F. Cowley Wright . . . . . . Hon Charles Egremont
Hubert Gordon Hopkirk . . . . Stephen Hatton
Harry Gilbey . . . . James Hatton
Philip D. Williams . . . . James Marney
William Burchill . . . . Father
DRAMA Labour leader inherits MP's estate and
gives it to daughter who later marries the MP.

07179
MONEY (4500)(U)
Ideal
D: Duncan Macrae
S: (PLAY) Lord Lytton
SC: Eliot Stannard
Henry Ainley . . . . Alfred Evelyn
Faith Bevan . . . . Georgina Vesey
Margot Drake . . . . Clara Douglas
Sam Wilkinson . . . . Sir Frederick Blount
James Lindsay . . . . Capt Smooth
Olaf Hytten . . . . Henry Graves
Sydney Paxton . . . . Sir John Vesey
Adelaide Grace . . . . Nanny
Ethel Newman . . . . Lady Franklyn
DRAMA Poor bart's daughter weds rich
secretary but leaves him when he pretends to
lose money on horses.

07180
THE BACHELORS' CLUB (5500)(A)
Ideal
D: A.V. Bramble
S: (NOVEL) Israel Zangwill
SC: Eliot Stannard
Ben Field . . . . Peter Parker

Ernest Thesiger . . . . Israfel Mondego
Mary Brough . . . . Mrs Parker
Sydney Fairbrother . . . . Tabitha
Arthur Pusey . . . . Paul Dickray
Margot Drake . . . . Jenny Halby
James Lindsay . . . . Eliot Dickray
Sydney Paxton . . . . Caleb Twinkletop
A.G. Poulton . . . . Edward Halby
Arthur Cleave . . . . Warlock Combs
Dora Lennox . . . . Israfel's Sweetheart
Jack Denton . . . . Mandeville Brown
Alice de Winton . . . . Dowager
COMEDY Henpeck inherits fortune and starts
club for women-haters.

07181
THE NARROW VALLEY (5400)(U)
Hepworth
D: Cecil M. Hepworth
S: George W. Dewhurst
Alma Taylor . . . . Victoria
George Dewhurst . . . . Jerry Hawkins
James Carew . . . . Eli Jones
Hugh Clifton . . . . Richard Jones
Gwynne Herbert . . . . Ursula Jones
Lottie Blackford . . . . Miss Pine
Nessie Blackford . . . . Miss Pine
Gordon Holloway . . . . Mr Pine
ROMANCE Draper's maid weds poacher's son
when village watch committee tries to expel her.

07182
A GENTLEMAN OF FRANCE (5951)(U)
Stoll
D: Maurice Elvey
S: (NOVEL) Stanley J. Weyman
SC: William J. Elliott
Eille Norwood . . . . Gaston de Marsac
Madge Stuart . . . . Mlle de la Vere
Hugh Buckler . . . . Vicomte de Turennes
Sydney Seaward . . . . de Bruhl
Pardoe Woodman . . . . Henry III
Allan Jeayes . . . . Henry of Navarre
Harvey Braban . . . . Baron de Rosny
Faith Bevan . . . . Mme de Bruhl
Teddy Arundell . . . . Fresnay
William Lenders . . . . Simon Fleix
Robert Vallis . . . . Jester
Mme d'Esterre . . . . Mme de Marsac
ADVENTURE France, 1589. Guardian imprisons
ward when she uncovers his plot against king.

07183
GREATHEART (5551)(A)
Stoll
D: George Ridgwell
S: (NOVEL) Ethel M. Dell
SC: Sidney Broome
Cecil Humphreys . . . . Eustace Studley
Madge Stuart . . . . Diana Bathurst
Ernest Benham . . . . Sir Scott Studley
Olive Sloane . . . . Rose de Vigne
William Ferris . . . . Guy Bathurst
Norma Whalley . . . . Isobel Evrard
Winifred Evans . . . . Lady Grace deVigne
Paulette del Baye . . . . Mrs Bathurst
Teddy Arundell . . . . Col de Vigne
ROMANCE Switzerland. Invalid saves girl from
suicide after she has broken engagement to rich
brother.

07184
THE BROKEN ROAD (5224) (U)
Stoll
D: Rene Plaissetty
S: (NOVEL) A.E.W. Mason
SC: Daisy Martin
Harry Ham . . . . Dick Linforth/Harry
Mary Massart . . . . Violet Oliver
Tony Fraser . . . . Shere Ali

June Putnam . . . . Phyllis Casson
Robert English . . . . Luffe
Cyril Percival . . . . Sir John
William Crundall . . . . Maj Dawes
Hugh Westlake . . . . Dr Bodley
Charles Wemyss . . . . Capt Phillips
DRAMA India. Three generations of British
family try to build road despite educated Prince.

07185
THE AMAZING PARTNERSHIP (5153)(A)
Stoll
D: George Ridgwell
S: (NOVEL) E. Phillips Oppenheim
SC: Charles Barnett
Milton Rosmer . . . . Pryde
Gladys Mason . . . . Grace Burton
Arthur Walcott . . . . Julius Hatten
Temple Bell . . . . Stella
Teddy Arundell . . . . Baron Feldemay
Robert Vallis . . . . His Confederate
Harry J. Worth . . . . Jean Marchand
Charles Barnett . . . . M. Dupay
CRIME Girl tec and reporter recover stolen
gems hidden in Chinese idol.

07186
THE RIGHT TO LIVE (5750)(U)
I.B. Davidson (Granger)
D:S: A.E. Coleby
A.E. Coleby . . . . Bill Rivers
Phyllis Shannaw . . . . Marjorie Dessalar
Peter Upcher . . . . .Sir Robert Martindale
Marguerite Hare . . . . Mrs Rivers
H. Nicholls-Bates . . . . Grandpa Rivers
Agnes Paulton . . . . Cousin Amelia
Sam Austin . . . . Uncle
SPORT Cockney fishmonger's daughter weds
bart who loses his all on trotting race.

07187
A SPORTSMAN'S WIFE (7025)(A)
Broadwest (Walturdaw)
D: Walter West
S: J. Bertram Brown
Violet Hopson . . . . Jessica Dundas
Greogry Scott . . . . Harry Kerr
Clive Brook . . . . Dick Anderson
Mercy Hatton . . . . Kitty Vickers
Arthur Walcott . . . . The Agent
Adeline Hayden Coffin . . . . . Mrs Dundas
SPORT Crooked rider gets wife's lover to back
horse fixed to lose.

07188
CANDYTUFT, I MEAN VERONICA (5000)
Zodiac (Cosmograph)
P: Joseph J. Bamberger
D: Frank Richardson
S: (NOVEL) Mabel Barnes Grundy
Mary Glynne . . . . .Veronica Anstruther
Leslie Faber . . . . Tony Westlake
George Relph . . . . George Anstruther
Ena Grossmith . . . . Aurora Twinkles
Daisy Markham . . . . Gwynne
Mary Jerrold . . . . Mrs Anstruther
COMEDY Man cures ambitious wife by faking
affair with friend's wife.

07189
THE PLACE OF HONOUR (5060)
Stoll
D: Sinclair Hill
S: (NOVEL) Ethel M. Dell
SC: William J. Elliott
Hugh Buckler . . . . Maj Eustace Tudor
Madge White . . . . Mrs Tudor
Pardoe Woodman . . . . Lt Philip Trevor
Luther Miles . . . . Lt Devereaux
M. Gray Murray . . . . Capt Raleigh

Ruth Mackay . . . . Mrs Raleigh
Bob Vallis . . . . Pte Archie Smith
ADVENTURE India. Major saves wife's lover from
capture by taking place.

07190
IN HIS GRIP (5945)(U)
Gaumont-British Screencraft
D: C.C. Calvert
S: (NOVEL) David Christie Murray
SC: Paul Rooff
Cecil Morton York . . . . . . Sir Donald McVeigh
David Hawthorne . . . . James Rutledge
Netta Westcott . . . . Jessie Vicars
Cecil du Gue . . . . Benjamin Hart
George Bellamy . . . . Norman Vicars
Hugh Miller . . . . Alec Vicars
W.T. Ellwanger . . . . Izzy
DRAMA Glasgow. Bankrupt contractor tries to
steal ward's rough diamonds, as does her 'dead'
brother.

07191
THE PRINCESS OF NEW YORK (6400)(U)
Famous Players-Lasky (Par)
D: Donald Crisp
S: (NOVEL) Cosmo Hamilton
SC: Margaret Turnbull
David Powell . . . . Geoffrey Kingswood
Mary Glynne . . . . Helen Stanton
Ivo Dawson . . . . Alan Merstham
Dorothy Fane . . . . Violet Merstham
Wyndham Guise . . . . .Eardley Smith
George Bellamy . . . . Sir George Merstham
R. Heaton Grey . . . . Mr Greet
Philip Hewland . . . . Mr Kingswood
Saba Raleigh . . . . Mrs Raffan
CRIME US Steel King pawns gems of daughter
who is loved by student and crook.

07192
APPEARANCES (5374) (A)
Famous Players-Lasky (Par)
D: Donald Crisp
S: (PLAY) Edward Knoblock
SC: Margaret Turnbull
David Powell . . . . Herbert Seaton
Mary Glynne . . . . Kitty Marshall
Langhorne Burton . . . . Lord Thornton
Marjorie Hume . . . . Agnes
Percy Standing . . . . Percy Dawkins
Mary Dibley . . . . Lady Rutherford
DRAMA Lord gives beloved blank cheque and
her husband fills it in for £500.

07193
CORINTHIAN JACK (5000)(A)
Master Films (Butcher) *reissue:* 1926,
FIGHTING JACK (3 rls cut)
P: H.B. Parkinson
D:SC: Walter Courtenay Rowden
S: (NOVEL) Charles E. Pearce
Victor McLaglen . . . . Jack Halstead
Kathleen Vaughan . . . . Nyra Seaton
Warwick Ward . . . . Sir Philip Tenbury
Dorothy Fane . . . . Lady Barbara
Malcolm Tod . . . . Lord Walsham
Conway Dixon . . . . Col Dane
William Lenders . . . . Weare
Roy Raymond . . . . Mike
ADVENTURE Regency. Boxer saves girl from
noble kidnapper.

07194
FLOTSAM (5000)
Isle of Man Films
D: Edmund Blake
Marjorie Battress

Jack Warboys
Dorothy Warboys
DRAMA

07195
GRASS WIDOWERS (1000)
Union Films
D: William Drury
S: George Roberts
Billie Bird
Paul Square
COMEDY Liverpool.

JUL

07196
THE DOUBLE EVENT (5000)
Astra Films
P: H.W. Thompson
D:SC: Kenelm Foss
S: (PLAY) Sidney Blow, Douglas Hoare
Mary Odette . . . . Dot Martingale
Roy Travers . . . . Capt Dennison
Lionelle Howard . . . . Charles Martingale
Tom Coventry . . . . Angus McWeir
Roy Byford . . . . James Bennington
Beatie Olna . . . . Laura Bennington
James McWilliams . . . . . . Rev Hubert Martingale
Louie Freear . . . . Susannah
Sidney Wood . . . . Dick Martingale
Julie Kean . . . . Harriet Martingale
COMEDY Country cleric's daughter becomes
bookie's partner and makes good father's losses.

07197
GRAND GUIGNOL (series)
Screen Plays (BEF)
D.: Fred Paul

07198
14—THE SECRET OF THE SAFE (900)(A)
S: George Saxon

07199
15 — THE JEST (950) (A)
S: Norman Ramsay

07200
16—A BIT OF BLACK STUFF (1060)(A)
S: George Saxon

07201
17—SIX AND HALF A DOZEN (1200)(A)
S: Frank King Jr

07202
18—HER ROMANCE (700)(A)

07203
19—THAT LOVE MIGHT LAST (1030)(A)

07204
20—LETTERS OF CREDIT (1280)(A)
S: Laurence Therval
DRAMAS Macabre short stories.

07205
VI OF SMITH'S ALLEY (5584)(U)
Broadwest (Walturdaw)
P:D: Walter West
S: Charles Barnett
Violet Hopson . . . . Vi Jeffries
Cameron Carr . . . . Sydney Baxter
George Foley . . . . Nathaniel Baxter
Sydney Folker . . . . Bill Saunders
Amy Verity . . . . Eileen Boston
Peter Upcher . . . . Reggie Drew
Sydney Frayne . . . . Teddy
DRAMA Jam manufacturer's cockney maid saves
him from being shot by manager.

07206
TOO MANY COOKS (2000)
Minerva Films
D:SC: Adrian Brunel
S: Mrs. J.E. Wheelwright
Phyllis Joyce
Arthur Booth . . . .
Nan Patterson . . . .
Bert Darley . . . .
COMEDY

07207
ALL SORTS AND CONDITIONS OF MEN
(4880)(U)
Ideal
D: Georges Treville
S: (NOVEL) Sir Walter Besant
SC: Colden Lore
Renee Kelly . . . . Angela Messenger
Rex Davis . . . . Harry le Briton
James Lindsay . . . . Lord Jocelyn
Mary Brough . . . . Landlady
DRAMA Brewery heiress and Lord's nephew
open shops in East End and build People's Palace.

07208
A WOMAN OF NO IMPORTANCE (5250)(A)
Ideal
D: Denison Clift
S: (PLAY) Oscar Wilde
SC: Arthur Q. Walton
Fay Compton . . . . Rachel Arbuthnot
Milton Rosmer . . . . Lord Illingworth
Ward McAllister . . . . Gerald Arbuthnot
Lilian Walker . . . . Hester Worsley
Henry Vibart . . . . Farquhar
Gwen Carton . . . . Elsie Farquhar
M. Gray Murray . . . . Sir Thomas
Hetta Bartlett . . . . Lady Cecilia
Daisy Campbell . . . . Lady Hunstanton
Julie Hartley-Milburn . . . . . . Lady Rofford
DRAMA Widow's son refuses to be adopted by
Lord when he learns Lord is his father.

07209
THE AUTUMN OF PRIDE (6300)(A)
Gaumont-Westminster
D: W.P. Kellino
S: (NOVEL) E. Newton Bungey
SC: Paul Rooff
Nora Swinburne . . . . Peggy Naylor
David Hawthorne . . . . .John Stone
Mary Dibley . . . . Helen Stone
Cecil Morton York . . . . Abel Lytton
Cecil du Gue . . . . Mr Naylor
Clifford Heatherley . . . . George Pentecost
Donald Castle . . . . Willoughby
Hargrave Mansell . . . . Handley
ROMANCE Man buys farm to stop rich father
from evicting farmer's daughter.

07210
THE KNAVE OF DIAMONDS (5569)(A)
Stoll
D: Rene Plaissetty
S: (NOVEL) Ethel M. Dell
SC: Frank Miller, Leslie Howard Gordon
Mary Massart . . . . Lady Anne Carfax
Alec Fraser . . . . Nap Errol
Cyril Percival . . . . Lucas Errol
Olaf Hytten . . . . Sir Giles Carfax
Annie Esmond . . . . Mrs Errol
George Calliga . . . . Tommy Hudson
Stephen Wentworth . . . . . . Dr Capper
ROMANCE Drunken bart's widow agrees to
marry lover's sick brother in order to save his
life.

07211
A DEAR FOOL (6454) (U)
Stoll
D: Harold Shaw
S: (NOVEL) "Artemas" (Arthur T. Mason)
SC: Frank Miller
George K. Arthur . . . . John Denison
Edna Flugrath . . . . Viva Hamilton
Edward O'Neill . . . . Stephen Blair
Bertie Wright . . . . Sir John Boscatel
Vere Tyndale . . . . Lady Boscatel
C. Tilson-Chowne . . . . Oliver Chambers
Mabel Archdale . . . . Sylvia Polesworthy
COMEDY Girl reporter ordered to expose anony-
mous playwright discovers he is her beloved
rival.

07212
THE WOMAN OF HIS DREAM (4320)(A)
Stoll
D: Harold Shaw
S: (NOVEL) Ethel M. Dell
SC: Leslie Howard Gordon
Mary Dibley . . . . Naomi
Alec Fraser . . . . Reginald Carey
Sydney Seaward . . . . Jeffrey Coningsby
Fred Thatcher . . . . Charles Rivers
Teddy Arundell . . . . Admiral Rivers
Winifred Harris . . . . Lady Emberdale
Betty Howes . . . . Gwen Emberdale
John East . . . . Fisherman
DRAMA Drunkard's wife leaves him and is
saved from shipwreck by friend.

07213
THE WOMAN WITH THE FAN (4998(A)
Stoll
D: Rene Plaissetty
S: (NOVEL) Robert Hichens
SC: Leslie Howard Gordon
Mary Massart . . . . . Lady Violet/Pimpernel Schley
Alec Fraser . . . . Lord Fritz Holme
Cyril Percival . . . . Rupert Carey
Paulette del Baye . . . . Mrs Wolfstein
Harold Deacon . . . . Robin Pearce
George Calliga . . . . Leo Ullford
DRAMA Lord leaves disfigured wife for her
double.

07214
FRAILTY (5966)(A)
Stoll
D: F. Martin Thornton
S: (NOVEL) Olive Wadsley
SC: Leslie Howard Gordon
Madge Stuart . . . . Diana
Rowland Myles . . . . Charles Ley
Sydney Lewis Ransome . . . . Beverley Dacre
Paulette del Baye . . . . Felice Ley
H. Agar Lyons . . . . Harman
J. Edwards Barber . . . . Partner
Mrs Gerald . . . . Marie Ley
DRAMA Orphaned bastard marries reformed
drunkard and is made drug addict by mother's
lover.

07215
THE COUNT OF NO-ACCOUNT (970)(U)
Franco-British Films
D: George Dunstall
Alec McKee . . . . The Count
COMEDY Clerk poses as count to disgust
ambitious woman and win her daughter.

07216
THE COLONEL'S LITTLE LOVE AFFAIR
(2054)(U)
Hartwood (Sherwood)
Harry Hearty . . . . The Colonel
COMEDY "The English Fatty Arbuckle."

07217
OH THOSE SHOES! (1525)(A)
Hartwood (Sherwood)
Harry Hearty . . . . The Man
COMEDY "The English Fatty Arbuckle."

07218
THE TRAGEDY OF A COMIC SONG (1050)
(U)
Stoll
D: Maurice Elvey
S: (STORY) Leonard Merrick
SC: Leslie Howard Gordon
Valia . . . . Paulette
Robert Vallis . . . . Tricotorin
Teddy Arundell . . . . Pictou
COMEDY Paris. Composer and poet recall how
they wrote song for cafe girl who loved another.

AUG

07219
GRAND GUIGNOL (series)
Screen Plays (BEF)
D: Fred Paul, Jack Raymond

07220
21—THE UPPER HAND (1080)(A)
Frank Stanmore . . . . The Man
Muriel Minty . . . . The Woman

07221
22—A GAME FOR TWO (1130)(A)
S: Laurence Therval
Charles Tilson-Chowne . . . The Man
Enid Sass . . . . The Girl

07222
23—THE FLIRTATIONS OF PHYLLIS (1143)
(A)
S: Margaret Strickland

07223
24—MARY'S WORK (1000)
S: Laurence Therval
DRAMAS

07224
THE SPIRIT OF THE HEATH (1000)
Zodiac
P: Joseph Bamberger
FANTASY Puck shows the beauty of the world
to foolish young wife.

07225
THE HOUND OF THE BASKERVILLES
(5500)(A)
Stoll
D: Maurice Elvey
S: (NOVEL) A. Conan Doyle
SC: William J. Elliott, Dorothy Westlake
Eille Norwood . . . . Sherlock Holmes
Catina Campbell . . . . Beryl Stapleton
Rex McDougall . . . . . . .Sir Henry Baskerville
Lewis Gilbert . . . . James Barrymore
Hubert Willis . . . . Dr Watson
Robert English . . . . Dr Mortimer
Fred Raynham . . . . Barrymore
Miss Walker . . . . Mrs Barrymore
Mme d' Esterre . . . . Mrs Hudson
Robert Vallis . . . . The Convict
CRIME Dartmoor. Cousin poses as farmer and
tries to kill heir with 'ghost' dog.

07226
THE BIGAMIST (10,000) (A)
George Clark (Stoll)
D:SC: Guy Newall
S: (NOVEL) F.E. Mills Young
Guy Newall . . . . George Dane
Ivy Duke . . . . Pamela Arnott
Julian Royce . . . . Herbert Arnott
A. Bromley Davenport . . . . . Richard Carruthers
Barbara Everest . . . . Blanche Maitland
Dorothy Scott . . . . Mrs Carruthers
Douglas Munro . . . . Proprietor
ROMANCE Nice. Wife learns husband has
another wife but stays with him for children's
sake.

07227
THE RIVER OF STARS (4625)(A)
Stoll
D: F. Martin Thornton
S: (NOVEL) Edgar Wallace
SC: Leslie Howard Gordon
Philip Anthony . . . . John Amber
Faith Bevan . . . . Cynthia Sutton
Teddy Arundell . . . . Augustus Lambaire
W. Dalton Somers . . . . Cornelius J. Whitney
Fred Thatcher . . . . Francis Sutton
H. Agar Lyons . . . . . . Commissioner Sanders
J. Edwards Barber . . . . Insp Fells
Ronald Power . . . . Mr Sutton
ADVENTURE Africa. Crooked financier tries
to wrest diamond mine from heirs.

07228
CHERRY RIPE (5000)
Astra Films
P: H.W. Thompson
D:SC: Kenelm Foss
S: (NOVEL) Helen Mathers
Mary Odette . . . . Mignon
Lionelle Howard . . . . Adam Montrose
Roy Travers . . . . Philip Lamert
Peggy Bayfield . . . . Muriel
Gwen Williams . . . . Miss Sorel
Will Corrie . . . . Silas Sorel
Julie Kean . . . . Puck
Beatie Olna . . . . Prue
ROMANCE 1885. Lawyer evicts gipsy orphan,
weds her stepsister, and reforms after killing
squire who attacks her.

07229
THE STREET OF ADVENTURE (5000)
Astra Films
P: H.W. Thompson
D:SC: Kenelm Foss
S: (NOVEL) Sir Philip Gibbs
Lionelle Howard . . . . Frank Luttrell
Margot Drake . . . . Katherine Halstead
H.V. Tollemach . . . . Christopher Codrington
Irene Rooke . . . . Margaret Hubbard
Peggy Bayfield . . . . Peg
Roy Travers . . . . Will Brandon
Will Corrie . . . . Edmund Grattan
DRAMA Reporter almost loses fiance to critic
when he saves girl from prostitution.

07230
THE PUPPET MAN (5818) (U) *reissue:* 1930,
PUPPETS OF FATE (B & FF)
B & C (FBO)
P: Edward Godal
D: Frank H. Crane
S: (NOVEL) Cosmo Gordon Lennox
Hugh Miller . . . . Alcide le Beau
Molly Adair . . . . Jenny Rose
Hilda Anthony . . . . Lilla Lotti
Marie Belocci . . . . Little Bimbo
Harry Paulo . . . . Joe
Leo Fisher . . . . Bimbo
Johnny Reid . . . . Bobby
DRAMA Austria. Disfigured man becomes circus
puppeteer and tries to destroy waif's love.

07231
THE ROTTERS (5000)
Ideal
D: A.V. Bramble
S: (PLAY) H.F. Maltby
SC: Arthur Q. Walton

Joe Nightingale . . . . Joe Barnes
Sydney Fairbrother . . . . Jemima Nivet
Sydney Paxton . . . . John Clugson MP
Margery Meadows . . . . Estelle Clugson
Roger Treville . . . . Percy Clugson
Ernest English . . . . John Wait
Cynthia Murtagh . . . . Margaret Barnes
Clare Greet . . . . Mrs Clugson
Stanley Holloway . . . . Arthur Wait
Margaret Shelley . . . . . . Winnie Clugson
COMEDY Headmistress recognises married JP
as ex-lover and stops him from sentencing
Mayor's son.

07232
THE BLACK TULIP (5269)(U)
Granger-Binger
D: Frankland A. Richardson
S: (NOVEL) Alexandre Dumas
SC: Marjorie Bowen
Zoe Palmer . . . . Rosa
Gerald McCarthy . . . . . . Cornelius van Baerle
Frank Dane . . . . Prince William
Harry Walter . . . . Isaac Boxtel
Edward Verkade . . . . Cornelius de Witt
Dio Huysmans . . . . John de Witt
Coen Hissink . . . . Gryphus
ADVENTURE Holland, 1672. Royalist jails
ruler's son to obtain secret of black tulips.

07233
LAUGHTER AND TEARS (5947) (A)
Granger-Binger
D: B.E. Doxat-Pratt
S: Adelqui Millar
Evelyn Brent . . . . Pierrette
Adelqui Migliar . . . . Mario Mari
Dorothy Fane . . . .'. Countess Maltakoff
E. Story Gofton . . . . Adolpho
Maudie Dunham . . . . Zizi
Bert Darley . . . . Ferrado
ROMANCE Venice. Artist has affair with
Countess but returns to his model.

07234
MISS CHARITY (5000)(U)
Master (Butcher)
P: H.B. Parkinson
D:SC: Edwin J. Collins
S: (NOVEL) Keble Howard
Margery Meadows . . . . Charity Couchman
Dick Webb . . . . John Coghill
Joan Lockton . . . . Philippa
Ralph Forster . . . . Rev Couchman
James Read . . . . Crazy Jim
ROMANCE City cousin of village vicar's
daughter flirts with farmer fiance.

07235
SQUIBS (5527)(U)
Welsh-Pearson (Jury)
D: George Pearson
S: (SKETCH) Clifford Seyler
SC: George Pearson, Eliot Stannard
Betty Balfour . . . . Squibs Hopkins
Hugh E. Wright . . . . Sam Hopkins
Fred Groves . . . . PC Charlie Lee
Mary Brough . . . . Mrs Lee
Cronin Wilson . . . . Bully Dawson
Annette Benson . . . . Ivy Hopkins
Ambrose Manning . . . . Insp Robert Lee
Tom Morriss . . . . Gus Holly
William Matthews . . . . Peters
COMEDY Cockney flowergirl loves PC although
father is bookie and sister loves crook.

07236
WILD HEATHER (5735)(U)
Hepworth

D: Cecil M. Hepworth
S: (PLAY) Dorothy Brandon
SC: George W. Dewhurst
Chrissie White . . . . Heather Bond
Gerald Ames . . . . Bevan Hutchinson
G.H. Mulcaster . . . . John O'Rourke
George Dewhurst . . . . George O'Rourke
James Carew . . . . Senator O'Rourke
Hugh Clifton . . . . Edward O'Rourke
Gwynne Herbert . . . . Mrs Boyd
Eileen Dennes. . . . . Dolly
James Annand . . . . Prof Boyd
Marion Dyer . . . . Trixie
ROMANCE Dying senator weds girl reporter
to make her guardian of his three sons.

07237
DOLLARS IN SURREY (5000)
Hepworth
D: George Dewhurst, Anson Dyer
S: George Dewhurst
Alma Taylor . . . .
James Carew . . . .
High Clifton . . . .
Gwynne Herbert . . . .
Esme Hubbard . . . .
Victor Prout . . . .
Rolf Leslie . . . .
Wallace Bosco . . . .
COMEDY

SEP
07238
THE CROXLEY MASTER (3900)(A)
Screen Plays (BEF)
D: Percy Nash
S: (NOVEL) Arthur Conan Doyle
SC: Harry Engholm, Gerald de Beaurepaire
Dick Webb . . . . Robert Mongomery
Dora Lennox . . . . Dorothy Oldacre
Jack Stanley . . . . Silas Craggs
Joan Ritz . . . . Anastasia Craggs
Cecil Morton York . . . . Dr Oldacre
Louis Rihll . . . . Mr Grain
Mabel Penn . . . . Mrs Oldacre
J.T. MacMillan . . . . Mr Purvis
Ernest Wallace . . . . Mr Wilson
George Turner . . . . Mr Fawcett
SPORT Wales. Doctor's assistant boxes local
champion to buy practise and win doctor's
daughter.

07239
SHIPS THAT PASS IN THE NIGHT (54)))(U)
Screen Plays (BEF)
D:SC: Percy Nash
S: (NOVEL) Beatrice Marraden
Filippi Dowson . . . . Bernardine Holme
Francis Roberts . . . . Robert Allitsen
Daisy Markham . . . . Winifred Reffold
Arthur Vezin . . . . Mr Reffold
Irene Rookee . . . . Esther Allitsen
ROMANCE Switzerland. Architect and
suffragist schoolteacher fall in love at TB
sanatorium.

07240
HIS OTHER WIFE (4800)(A)
Screen Plays (BEF)
D:SC: Percy Nash
S: (PLAY) George R. Sims
Eileen Magrath . . . . Dorothy Ashton
Jack Raymond . . . . Dick Riviere
Maria Minetti . . . . Minna Ashton
Dennis Cowles . . . .
Frances Cadman . . . .
DRAMA Child of captain's faithless wife is
eventually adopted by his second wife.

07241
LAND OF MY FATHERS (5000)(U)
Glen Films
P: George Leyton
D: Fred Rains
S: Diana Torr
John Stuart . . . . David Morgan
Edith Pearson . . . . Lady Gwenneth Beaulah
Yvonne Thomas . . . . Dilwys Colwyn
George Leyton . . . . Lord Beaulah
Fred Rains . . . . Bad Bill
Ernest Moore . . . . Owen Morgan
Florence Lynn . . . . Mrs Colwyn
David Teriotdale . . . . Agent
ROMANCE Aberwystwyth. Lady weds amnesiac
earl and drowns herself when he is cured by
meeting ex-fiancee.

07242
THE WONDERFUL YEAR (6000)
Astra Films
P: H.W. Thompson
D:SC: Kenelm Foss
S: (NOVEL) W.J. Locke
Mary Odette . . . . Felise
Lionelle Howard . . . . Martin Openshaw
Randle Ayrton . . . . The Happiness Dispenser
Margot Drake . . . . Corinna Hastings
Hubert Carter . . . . Bigourdin
Frank Stanmore . . . . Polydor
Gwen Williams . . . . Lucilla
ROMANCE Switzerland. War wounds change
poor artist from dreamer to man.

07243
THE PENNILESS MILLIONAIRE (4900)(A)
Broadwest (Walturdaw)
P: Walter West
D: Einar J. Bruun
S: (NOVEL) David Christie Murray
SC: Frank Fowell
Stewart Rome . . . . Bernard Jarrold
Fabienne Fabreges . . . . Angela Jarrold
Gregory Scott . . . . Belthorp
Cameron Carr . . . . Tim Dolan
George Foley . . . . Martin Stornaway
ADVENTURE Shanghai. Banker's disowned son
escapes from bandits and proves marriage to
usurper is false.

07244
TILLY OF BLOOMSBURY (5200)(U)
G.B. Samuelson (Moss)
D: Rex Wilson
S: (PLAY) Ian Hay
Edna Best . . . . Tilly Welwyn
Tom Reynolds . . . . Samuel Stillbottle
Campbell Gullan . . . . Percy Welwyn
Henry Kendall . . . . Dick Mainwaring
Helen Haye . . . . Lady Adela Mainwaring
Fred Lewis . . . . Abel Mainwaring
Georgette Esmond . . . . Martha Welwyn
Leonard Pagden . . . . Lucius Welwyn
Isobel Jeans . . . . Sylvia Mainwaring
Vera Lennox . . . . Amelia Mainwaring
Lottie Blackford . . . . Mrs Banks
COMEDY Lady objects to son's love for
boarding-house keeper's daughter.

07245
THE GOLDEN DAWN (5910) (A)
Ralph Dewsbury (Pathe)
D: Ralph Dewsbury
S: Bannister Merwin
Gertrude McCoy . . . . Nancy Brett
Warwick Ward . . . . Dick Landon
Frank Petley . . . . Henry Warville
Sydney Fairbrother . . . . Mrs Briggs
Charles Vane . . . . Jim Briggs

Mary Brough . . . . Mrs Powers
Philip Hewland . . . . Insp Martin
Charles Pelly . . . . Charles Proctor
CRIME Actress accused of shooting ex-husband when he appears on eve of her marriage to blind man.

07246
SONIA (6060)(A)
Ideal
DSC: Denison Clift
S: (NOVEL) Stephen McKenna
Evelyn Brent . . . . Sonia Dainton
Clive Brook . . . . David O'Raine
Cyril Raymond . . . . Tom Dainton
Olaf Hytten . . . . Fatty Webster
Henry Vibart . . . . Rev Burgess
M. Gray Murray . . . . Sir Roger Dainton
Hetta Bartlett . . . . Lady Dainton
Leo Stormont . . . . Sir Adolph Erckmann
Gladys Hamilton . . . . Lady Erckmann
George Travers . . . . Lord Loring
Julie Hartley-Milburn . . . . . Lady Loring
DRAMA Student makes fortune in Mexico, is blinded in war, becomes teacher, and weds reformed flirt.

07247
DANGEROUS LIES (6600)(A)
Famous Players-Lasky British Producers (Par)
D: Paul Powell
S: (NOVEL) E. Phillips Oppenheim
SC: Mary O'Connor
David Powell . . . . Sir Henry Bond
Mary Glynne . . . . Joan Farrant
Minna Gray . . . . Olive Farrant
Warburton Gamble . . . . Leonard Pearce
Clifford Grey . . . . Franklin Bond
Arthur Cullin . . . . Eli Hodges
Harry Ham . . . . Phelps Westcott
Ernest A. Douglas . . . . Rev Farrant
Daisy Sloane . . . . Nanette
Philip Hewland . . . . Doctor
DRAMA Widow's husband returns after her second marriage, and dies while assaulting her.

07248
LOVE AT THE WHEEL (5500)(U)
Master Films (Butcher)
P:S: H.B. Parkinson
D: Bannister Merwin
SC: Frank Miller
Victor Humfries . . . . Eric Gordon
Pauline Johnson . . . . Ruth Emerson
Leslie Steward . . . . Ned Wright
Annette Benson . . . . Helen Warwick
Arthur Claremont . . . . Enoch Emerson
Clare Greet . . . . Martha
A. Harding Steerman . . . . . . John Gordon
May Price . . . . Mrs Gordon
SPORT Sacked foreman sets up own car business and wins race.

07249
THE FRUITFUL VINE (7100)(A)
Stoll
D: Maurice Elvey
S: (NOVEL) Robert Hichens
SC: Leslie Howard Gordon
Basil Rathbone . . . . Don Cesare Carelli
Valia . . . . Dolores Cannynge
Robert English . . . . Sir Theodore Cannynge
Mary Dibley . . . . Edna Denzil
Teddy Arundell . . . . Francis Denzil
Fred Raynham . . . . Dr Mervynn Ides
Irene Rooke . . . . Lady Sarah Ides
Paulette del Baye . . . . Princess Mancelli
Peter Dear . . . . Theo Denzil
DRAMA Old knight weds dead friend's daughter and she gives herself to Italian Don to bear heir.

07250
THE NIGHT HAWK (5000)
International Artists (Anchor)
P: Alan Butler, Martin Sabine
D: John Gliddon
S: Eden Philpotts (THE HAVEN)
SC: Gerard Fort Buckle
Henri de Vries . . . . John Major
Malvina Longfellow . . . . Lydia Major
Sydney Seaward . . . . Sam Brokenshire
Nadja Ostreovska . . . . Deborah Honeywill
Mary Brough . . . . Aunt Emma
Francis Innys . . . . Ned Major
Caleb Porter . . . . William Gilberd
Edward Sorley . . . . Tumbledown Dick
Roy Byford . . . . Mr Mundy
DRAMA Torquay.

07251
THE TEMPORARY LADY (2000)
Minerva Films
D: Adrian Brunel
S: Adrian Brunel, Mill Wadham
Annette Benson . . . . Mary Lamb
Miles Mander . . . . Monckton
Arthur Claremont . . . . Glenville
Eileen Munro . . . .
COMEDY Maid poses as boy to befriend rich man who is really salesman.

07252
TEDDY LAUGHS LAST (2000)
Regulus Films
D: Milton Elmore
S: James Dicks
Teddy Hayes . . . . Teddy
Audrey Edwardes . . . . The Girl
COMEDY

07253
THE FIFTH FORM AT ST DOMINIC'S (6886)
(U)
I.B. Davidson (Granger) reissue: 1923
D: A.E. Coleby
S: (NOVEL) Talbot Baines Reed
SC: A.E. Coleby, Dave Aylott
Ralph Forbes . . . . Oliver Greenfield
Maurice Thompson . . . . Stephen Greenfield
Humberston Wright . . . . Dr Senior
Phyllis Shannaw . . . . Nancy Senior
William Freshman . . . . Loman
Percy Field . . . . Horace Wrayford
Clifford Cobbe . . . . Mr Rastle
Sam Austin . . . . Ben Cripps
Douglas Phair . . . . Tony Pembury
Cecil Susands . . . . Bullinger
Royce Milton . . . . Mr Jellicot
DRAMA School prefect's brother blamed for stealing examination papers taken by senior in publican's grip.

07254
THE PREY OF THE DRAGON (5305)(A)
Stoll
D: F. Martin Thornton
S: (NOVEL) Ethel M. Dell
SC: Leslie Howard Gordon
Victor McLaglen . . . . . . Brett "Dragon"Mercer
Gladys Jennings . . . . Sybil Dehan
Harvey Braban . . . . Robin Wentworth
Hal Martin . . . . Jim Curtis
ADVENTURE Australia. Drunkard hires gang to kill ex-fiancee's husband.

07255
TANSY (5570) (U)
Hepworth
D: Cecil M. Hepworth
S: (NOVEL) Tickner Edwards
SC: George W. Dewhurst
Alma Taylor . . . . Tansy Firle
Gerald Ames . . . . Clem Fordrough
James Carew . . . . Joad Wilverley
Hugh Clifton . . . . Will Wilverley
George Dewhurst . . . . George Baston
Eileen Dennes . . . . Vicar's Daughter
Rolf Leslie . . . . George Firle
Teddy Royce . . . . Mark Wilverley
ROMANCE Devon. Farming brothers give home to orphan shepherdess evicted for suspected immorality.

07256
WALTER'S WINNING WAYS (2000)
Zodiac
D: William Bowman
S: Walter Forde
Walter Forde . . . . Walter
Marjorie Russell . . . . Rose Weeps
Billy le Fre . . . .
COMEDY Removal man saves school by foiling crook seeking idol.

07257
WALTER FINDS A FATHER (2000)
Zodiac
D: Joe Bamberger
S: Walter Forde
Walter Forde . . . . Walter
Marjorie Russell . . . . Rose Fish
Lyell Johnston . . . . Count
Billy le Fre . . . . Bill
COMEDY Builder mistaken for lord's lost heir duels count.

07258
ALLY SLOPER'S ADVENTURES (series)
Kinema Expansions (Phillips)
D: Geoffrey H. Malins
S: (CARTOONS) Charles Ross
SC: R. Byron-Webber
Max Gionti . . . . Ally Sloper
Ena Beaumont . . . . Tootsie Sloper
Bob Reed . . . . The Hon Billy
Margaret Hope . . . . Araminta

07259
1—ALLY SLOPER GOES YACHTING (2000)

07260
2—ALLY SLOPER RUNS A REVUE (2000)

07261
3—ALLY SLOPER'S HAUNTED HOUSE (2000)

07262
4—ALLY SLOPER'S TEETOTAL ISLAND (2000)

07263
5—ALLY SLOPER'S LOAN OFFICE (2000)

07264
6—ALLY SLOPER GOES BATHING (2000)
COMEDIES Based on cartoons appearing in the weekly paper, Ally Sloper's Half-holiday.

07265
GRAND GUIGNOL (series)
Screen Plays (BEF)
D: Fred Paul, Jack Raymond

07266
25—THE CURSE OF WESTACOTT (1122)(A)
S: (STORY) G.B. Stern
Annette Benson . . . . The Woman
Bertram Burleigh . . . . The Man

07267
26—A WOMAN MISUNDERSTOOD (842)(A)
S: Norman Ramsay

07268
27—THE JOKE THAT FAILED (1000)
S: Norman Ramsay
Leo Carelli . . . . Dan
Margaret Denniston . . . . Mary

07269
28—BARBARA ELOPES (1000)
S: Norman Ramsay
Vivian Gibson . . . . Barbara
Harry Paulo . . . .
DRAMAS

07270
A LIVELY DAY (1000)
Golden West Productions
D:S: Harry Granville
Paddy Burke . . . . The Man
COMEDY Southend

07271
'ORACE (3000)
Temple
D:S: Bannister Merwin
A. Bromley Davenport . . . . . Horace
Phyllis le Grand . . . .
A.G. Poulton . . . .
Nadine March . . . .
Florence Nelson . . . .
COMEDY

07272
THE BATTLE OF JUTLAND (3000)(U)
British Instructional
D: H. Bruce Woolfe
S: Sir George Aston
WAR 1916. Reconstruction of how Admiral
Beatty lured the German fleet into a trap.

07273
MR JUSTICE RAFFLES (5810)(U)
Hepworth
D: Gerald Ames, Gaston Quiribet
S: (NOVEL) E.W. Hornung
SC: Blanche McIntosh
Gerald Ames . . . . A.J. Raffles
Eileen Dennes . . . . Camilla Belsize
James Carew . . . . Dan Levy
Hugh Clifton . . . . Teddy Garland
Lyonel Watts . . . . Bunny
Gwynne Herbert . . . . Lady Laura Belsize
Henry Vibart . . . . Mr Garland
Peggy Patterson . . . . Dolly Fairfield
Pino Conti . . . . Foreigner
Townsend Whitling . . . . Tough
CRIME Gentleman thief helps friend's fiancee
foil Jewish usurer.

OCT

07274
THE FILM STAR'S PERFECT DAY (2000)
Perfect Day Productions (Globe)
D: Neville Bruce
Harry Hearty . . . . Producer
Dora Henwood . . . . Marion Pickwick
COMEDY Village shopkeeper plays lead in serial.

07275
CHRISTIE JOHNSTONE (5161)(U)
Broadwest (Walturdaw)
P: Walter West
D: Norman Macdonald
S: (NOVEL) Charles Reade
SC: W.G. Clifford
Gertrude McCoy . . . . Christie Johnstone
Stewart Rome . . . . Viscount Ipsden
Clive Brook . . . . Astral Hither
Mercy Hatton . . . . Lady Barbara Sinclair
J. Denton-Thompson . . . . . . Wully

Peggy Hathaway . . . . Jean
Adeline Hayden Coffin . . . . Mrs Gatty
R. Gordon Craig . . . . Charles Gatty
Dorothy Vernon . . . . Window McKay
Tom Beaumont . . . . Saunders
ROMANCE Scotland, 1850. Bored lord saves
fishergirl's lover from drowning.

07276
ROSES IN THE DUST (6133)(A)
Gaumont-British Screencraft
D: C.C. Calvert
S: H. Morgan
SC: Rudolph de Cordova
Iris Rowe . . . . Rose Trevelyan
David Hawthorne . . . . William Temple
Gordon Craig . . . . Gerald Mortimer
Gladys Mason . . . . , Nina Ray
Robert Field . . . . Harold Smithson
Bert Tooze . . . . Valentine Harvey
May Price . . . . Hester Trevelyan
Winifred Nelson . . . . Rose Trevelyan
DRAMA Cornwall. Surgeon forced to operate on
crooked gambler who eloped with wife.

07277
SINGLE LIFE (4750)(U)
Ideal
D: Edwin J. Collins
S: (PLAY) J.B. Buckstone
SC: Adrian Johnston
Campbell Gullan . . . . Gerald Hunter
Kathleen Vaughan . . . . Hester
Sydney Paxton . . . . John Pierce
Evelyn Hope . . . . Mme Roland
Cyril Raymond . . . . John Henty
COMEDY Two sworn bachelors, jilted by same
girl, remain single against will.

07278
MARRIED LIFE (5000)
Ideal
D: Georges Tréville
S: (PLAY) J.B. Buckstone
SC: Adrian Johnston
Gerald McCarthy . . . . Arthur Winchester
Peggy Hathaway . . . . Margaret
Roger Treville . . . . Charles Dawson
Hilda Anthony . . . . Mrs Winchester
M. Gray Murray . . . . Mr Dawson
Hugh Higson . . . .
Dorothy Fane . . . .
Beatrix Templeton . . . .
Gordon Begg . . . .
Leonard Robson . . . .
DRAMA MP'S adopted daughter loves son of
blackmailing financier who turns out to be her
father.

07279
THE GOD IN THE GARDEN (5510)(U)
Master (Butcher)
P: H.B. Parkinson
D:SC: Edwin J. Collins
S: (NOVEL) Keble Howard
Edith Craig . . . . Miss Carroway
Arthur Pusey . . . . Rev Mr Hatch
Mabel Poulton . . . . Stella
Mabel Archdale . . . . Alicia Snitterfield
James English . . . . Mr Snitterfield
Cecil Morton York . . . .
Beatrice Grosvenor . . . . Jane Box
A. Harding Steerman . . . . . .
COMEDY Cupid brings love to those who enter
spinster's garden.

07280
DICK'S FAIRY (5000)
Seal (Curry)
D: Bert Wynne

S: (NOVEL) Silas K. Hocking
SC: Eliot Stannard
Joan Griffiths . . . . Fairy
Hargrave Mansell . . . . Luther Cobb
Albert Brantford . . . . Dick
Eva Westlake . . . . Mrs Limber
Bernard Vaughan . . . .
Gordon Craig . . . .
Ernest Spalding . . . .
Peter Coleman . . . .
Mme d'Esterre . . . .
DRAMA Isle of Man. Blind circus girl, cured
after cliff fall, finds crippled friend is lost
brother.

07281
GENERAL JOHN REGAN (6300)(U)
Stoll
D: Harold Shaw
S: (PLAY) George A. Birmingham
SC: William J. Elliott
Milton Rosmer . . . . Dr O'Grady
Madge Stuart . . . . Mary Ellen Doyle
Edward O'Neill . . . . Tim Doyle
Ward McAllister . . . . Horace P. Billings
Bertie Wright . . . . Thady Gallagher
Teddy Arundell . . . . PC Moriarty
Robert Vallis . . . . Sgt Colgan
Judd Green . . . . Kerrigan
Gordon Parker . . . . Maj Kent
Windham Guise . . . . Father McCormac
COMEDY Ireland. Village doctor and rich
American pretend Bolivia was liberated by a local

07282
THE IMPERFECT LOVER (6700)(A)
Broadwest (Walturdaw)
D: Walter West
S: Andrew Soutar
SC: Patrick L. Mannock
Violet Hopson . . . . Noreen Grene
Stewart Rome . . . . Robert Lawne
Cameron Carr . . . . Capt Sterne
Sir Simeon Stuart . . . . Mr Grene
Pauline Johnson . . . . Barbara Grene
Dennis Esmond . . . . Conrad Grene
DRAMA Newlyrich man saves neighbouring
family from debt, gamblers, and seduction.

NOV

07283
THE MYSTERY ROAD (6800)(A)
Famous Players-Lasky British Producers (Par)
D: Paul Powell
S: (NOVEL) E. Phillips Oppenheim
SC: Mary O'Connor, Margaret Turnbull
David Powell . . . . Hon Gerald Dombe
Mary Glynne . . . . Lady Susan Farrington
Ruby Miller . . . . Vera Lypasht
Nadja Ostrovska . . . . Myrtle Sargot
Percy Standing . . . . Luigi
Pardoe Woodman . . . . Christopher West
Lewis Gilbert . . . . Jean Sargot
Arthur Cullin . . . . .Lord Farrington
Lionel d'Aragon . . . . Pierre Naval
Judd Green . . . . Vagabond
DRAMA Nice. Lord's affianced son has affairs
with a French peasant and English girl who kills
herself.

07284
THE BARGAIN (5800)(U)
Hepworth
D:SC: Henry Edwards
S: (PLAY) Henry Edwards, Edward Irwin
Henry Edwards . . . . Dennis Trevor
Chrissie White . . . . Mary
Rex McDougall . . . . Dick Wentworth

Mary Dibley . . . . Bella Wentworth
Henry Vibart . . . . Grosvenor Wentworth
James Annand . . . . Tamplin
John McAndrews . . . . Murphy
John East . . . . Longhurst
CRIME Rescued man takes place of convicted heir, who later blackmails him.

07285
WHERE THE RAINBOW ENDS (5000)
British Photoplay Productions (Pioneer)
P: Edward Godal
D: H. Lisle Lucoque
S: (PLAY) Clifford Mills, John Ramsey
Babs Farren . . . . Rosamund Carey
B. Cave Chinn . . . . Crispian Carey
Muriel Pointer . . . . Betty Blunders
Eric Gray . . . . Jim Blunders
Roger Livesey . . . . Cubby the Lion
Harold Deacon . . . . Saint George
George Bishop . . . . Dragon King
Vesta Sylva . . . . Will o'the Wisp
Walter Gay . . . . Capt Carey
Ruth Maitland . . . . Mrs Carey
Fred Glover . . . . Joseph Flint
Ernest A. Trimingham . . . . . Genie
FANTASY Orphans find magic carpet and save shipwrecked parents from dragon.

07286
GWYNETH OF THE WELSH HILLS(6470)(A)
Stoll
D: F. Martin Thornton
S: (NOVEL) Edith Nepean
SC: Leslie Howard Gordon
Madge Stuart . . . . Gwyneth
Eille Norwood . . . . Lord Pryse
Lewis Gilbert . . . . Davydd Owen
R. Henderson Bland . . . . . . Shadrack Morgan
J.R. Tozer . . . . Evan Pryse
Gladys Jennings . . . . Blodwen
Harvey Braban . . . . Gwylim Rhys
W. Dalton Somers . . . . Denis
Elizabeth Herbert . . . . Megan Powys
Robert Vallis . . . . But Lloyd
Mrs. Hubert Willis . . . . Jan Rhys
Sam Wilkinson . . . . Shores
ROMANCE Wales. Girl learns marriage was faked and weds cleric.

07287
A ROMANCE OF WASTDALE (6060)(A)
Stoll
D: Maurice Elvey
S: (NOVEL) A.E.W. Mason
SC: Leslie Howard Gordon
Milton Rosmer . . . . David Gordon
Valia Venitskaya . . . . Kate Nugent
Fred Raynham . . . . Austin Hawke
Irene Rooke . . . . Mrs Jackson
ADVENTURE Lancs. Climber throws fiancee's blackmailer over cliff and finds all was a dream.

07288
THE ADVENTURES OF MR PICKWICK (6000)
Ideal
D: Thomas Bentley
S: (NOVEL) Charles Dickens (THE PICKWICK PAPERS)
SC: Eliot Stannard, E.A. Baughan
Fred Volpe . . . . Samuel Pickwick
Mary Brough . . . . Mrs Bardell
Bransby Williams . . . . Sgt Buzfuz
Ernest Thesiger . . . . Mr Jingle
Kathleen Vaughan . . . . Arabella Allen
Joyce Dearsley . . . . Isabella Wardle
Arthur Cleave . . . . Mr Winkle
Athene Seyler . . . . Rachel Wardle
John Kelt . . . . Mr Snodgrass

Hubert Woodward . . . . Sam Weller
Norman Page . . . . Justice Stoneleigh
Thomas Weguelin . . . . Mr Wardle
Townsend Whitley . . . . Dodson
Harry Gilbey . . . . Fogg
John E. Zecchini . . . . Fat Boy
COMEDY Period. Clubman's country jaunt with friends leads to breach of promise suit by landlady.

07289
THE MARRIAGE LINES (5880)(A)
Master Films (Butcher)
P: H.B. Parkinson
D:SC: Wilfred Noy
S: (NOVEL) J.S. Fletcher
Barbara Hoffe . . . . Judith
Lewis Dayton . . . . Michael Muscroft
Sam Livesey . . . . Martin Muscroft
Charles Tilson-Chowne . . . . Parkhill
Arthur Walcott . . . . Stephen
Enid Sass . . . . Sherratt
DRAMA Girl weds bastard heir who inherits when their baby finds hidden will.

07290
THE FISHERMAN'S PERFECT DAY (1000)
Perfect Day Productions (Globe)
D: Neville Bruce
Stanley McNaughton . . . . . The Fisherman
COMEDY Fisherman catches almost everything except fish.

07291
HOW KITCHENER WAS BETRAYED (6000)
Screen Plays (BEF)
D: Percy Nash
S: Norman Ramsey
Fred Paul . . . . Lord Kitchener
Peggy Hathaway . . . . Mrs Mack
Bertram Burleigh . . . . Lt Mack
Ion Swinley . . . . The Spy
Frank Goldsmith . . . .
Wallace Bosco . . . .
Winifred Evans . . . .
WAR Dead officer's German wife betrays "Hampshire's" secret route.

07292
THE ROAD TO LONDON (4574)(U)
Screen Plays (Phillips)
P: Bryant Washburn
D: Eugene Mullen
S: (NOVEL) David Skaats Foster
SC: Dwight Cleveland
Bryant Washburn . . . . Rex Rowland
Joan Morgan . . . . Lady Emily
George Foley . . . . Mr Rowland
Gibb McLaughlin . . . . Viscount
Saba Raleigh . . . . Duchess
Rev Dr Batchelor . . . . Vicar
Mabel Washburn . . . . Maid
COMEDY Yankee and duchess's runaway niece pose as society couple.

07293
BLUFF (6240)(U)
Hardy (Gaul) reissue: 1930 (Benstead)
P: Sam Hardy
D: Geoffrey H. Malins
S: (NOVEL) Rafael Sabatini
SC: Rafael Sabatini
Lewis Willoughby . . . . Courtenay Boscawen
Marjorie Hume . . . . Dorothy Channing
Lawrence Anderson . . . . . . James Legge
Sydney Paxton . . . . Everard Wade
A. Harding Steerman . . . . . Geoffrey Channing
Guy Graham . . . . Lord Landassyl
Mme d'Esterre . . . . Mrs Channing
CRIME Ex-embezzler bluffs blackmailer into thinking he can be murdered without detection.

07294
MOTH AND RUST (4796)(U)
Progress (Butcher)
P: Frank E. Spring
D:SC: Sidney Morgan
S: (NOVEL) Mary Cholmondeley
Sybil Thorndike . . . . Mrs Brand
Malvina Longfellow . . . . Janet Black
Langhorne Burton . . . . Ray Meredith
Cyril Raymond . . . . Fred Black
George Bellamy . . . . MacAlpine Brand
Malcolm Tod . . . . Sir George Trefusis
Ellen Nicholls . . . . Lady Trefusis
Phyllis le Grand . . . . Lady Anne Varney
DRAMA Girl burns brothers letters to usurer's dead wife and is accused of burning his IOUs.

07295
THE MAYOR OF CASTERBRIDGE (5500)(A)
Progress (Butcher) reissue: 1926 (2 rls)
P: Frank Spring
D:SC: Sidney Morgan
S: (NOVEL) Thomas Hardy
Fred Groves . . . . Michael Henchard
Pauline Peters . . . . Susan Henchard
Warwick Ward . . . . Donald Farfrae
Nell Emerald . . . . The Fermity Woman
Mavis Clare . . . . Elizabeth Jane
DRAMA Man sells wife and child to sailor, remarries on becoming mayor, and learns his daughter is actually the sailor's.

07296
BESIDE THE BONNIE BRIER BUSH (4500)
(U) USA: THE BONNIE BRIAR BUSH
Famous Players-Lasky (Par)
D: Donald Crisp
S: (PLAY) James MacArthur, Augustus Thorne
SC: Margaret Turnbull
Donald Crisp . . . . Lachlan Campbell
Mary Glynne . . . . Flora Campbell
Langhorne Burton . . . . John Carmichael
Alec Fraser . . . . Lord Donald Hay
Dorothy Fane . . . . Kate Carnegie
Humbertson Wright . . . . . . Dr MacClure
Jerrold Robertshaw . . . . . . Earl of Kilspindie
Adeline Hayden Coffin . . . . . Margaret Hare
John M. East . . . . Postie
ROMANCE Scotland. Lord's son engaged to rich ward prefers peasant.

07297
THE LONELY ROAD
North British Productions
D: Alfred Vanderbosch
S: Paul du Bois
Robert Fenemore . . . . . Hon Maurice/Franz
Gwyneth Roden . . . . The Girl
ADVENTURE 15th C. Secret agent catches his double's gang.

07298
FOOTBALL DAFT (2000)
Broadway Cinema Productions (Walker)
reissue: 1923 (Waverley)
D: Victor W. Rowe
S: (SKETCH) James Milligan (2-0)
Jimmy Brough . . . . Jock
COMEDY Scotland. Toper hides whiskey in vinegar bottle and makes temperance advocate drunk.

07299
CLASS AND NO CLASS (6207)(U)
Gaumont-Westminster
D: W.P. Kellino
S: (NOVEL) E. Newton Bungey
SC: Paul Rooff
Judd Green . . . . Jeremy Russell
Pauline Johnson . . . . Nancy Russell

David Hawthorne . . . . Dick Foster
Marie Ault . . . . Lizer Ann
Tom Coventry . . . . Sam West
Cecil du Gue . . . . Sir John Gatfield
Cyril Smith . . . . Lord Daventry
CRIME Rich coster's daughter loves steward
who is blamed for killing blackmailing tramp.

07300
FILM SONG ALBUM (series) (U)
Master Films (BEF)
P: H.B. Parkinson
D: W.C. Rowden, H.B. Parkinson, George Wynn
S: W.C. Rowden

07301
1: THE CHILDREN'S HOME (800)
D: W.C. Rowden
Reginal Fox . . . . The Man
Evelyn Hope . . . . The Girl

07302
2: SWEET GENEVIEVE (960)
Evelyn Hope . . . . Genevieve

07303
3: THE VILLAGE BLACKSMITH (655)
George Wynn . . . . Labourer
Muriel Gregory . . . . Wife

07304
4: EILEEN ALANNAH (1038)
D: W.C. Rowden
John Stuart . . . . The Man
Muriel Gregory . . . . Eileen
Reginald Fox . . . .

07305
5: SALLY IN OUR ALLEY (915)
D: W.C. Rowden
Zoe Palmer . . . . Sally
John Stuart . . . . The Man
Bert Wynne . . . .

07306
6: HOME SWEET HOME (1215)
D: H.B. Parkinson
John Stuart . . . . Husband
Joan Lockton . . . . Wife
George Wynn . . . . Villain

07307
7: THE BONNIE BANKS OF LOCH
LOMOND (930)

07308
8: WON'T YOU BUY MY PRETTY
FLOWERS? (1140)
Joan Lockton . . . . Flower Girl

07309
9: COMRADES (1020)
D: George Wynn
Dick Webb . . . . The Man

07310
10: SILVER THREADS AMONG THE GOLD
(985)
D: W.C. Rowden

07311
11: AFTER THE BALL (1080)
D: H.B. Parkinson

07312
12: QUEEN OF THE EARTH (980)
D: George Wynn
MUSICAL Dramatisations of popular songs.

07313
THE MYSTERY OF MR BERNARD BROWN
(5558) (A)

Stoll
D: Sinclair Hill
S: (NOVEL) E. Phillips Oppenheim
SC: Mrs Sydney Groome
Ruby Miller . . . . Helen Thirwell
Pardoe Woodman . . . . Bernard Brown
Clifford Heatherley . . . . . Sir Alan Beaumerville
Annie Esmond . . . . Lady Thirwell
Ivy King . . . . Rachel Kynaston
Lewis Dayton . . . . Sir Geoffrey Kynaston
Frank E. Petley . . . . Benjamin Levy
Teddy Arundell . . . . Guy Thirwell
Norma Whalley . . . . Mrs Martival
CRIME Novelist is blamed for stabbing squire's
daughter's fiance.

07314
CIRCUS JIM (5000) (A)
Granger-Binger
D: B.E. Doxat-Pratt
S: Adelqui Migliar
Adelqui Migliar . . . . Jim
Evelyn Brent . . . . Iris Belmore
Norman Doxat-Pratt . . . . . . Billy Belmore
DRAMA Jealous circus owner causes sharpshooter
to wound partner.

07315
WHO IS THE BOSS? (2170) (U)
Brouett Productions (BEF)
P:D:S: Albert Brouett
Albert Brouett . . . . Mr Pip
Amy Verity . . . . Mrs Pip
COMEDY Newlyweds' quarrel mended by
parents.

07316
PARKSTONE COMEDIES (series)
Parkstone Films
D: Dave Aylott
S: A.A. Thompson
Dawn Meredith . . . .
Harry Low . . . .
Jack Mitchell . . . .
Beryl Kendrick . . . .
Joan Merle . . . .
Molly Mitchell . . . .
COMEDY Six untitled comedy two-reelers.

DEC

07317
THE SPORT OF KINGS (5100) (A)
I.B. Davidson (Granger)
D:S: Arthur Rooke
Victor McLaglen . . . . Frank Rosedale
Phyllis Shannaw . . . . Elaine Winter
Cyril Percival . . . . Harry Lawson
Douglas Munro . . . . James Winter
SPORT Man helps rich girl's slum work and wins
race on ex-fiance's horse.

07318
LEAVES FROM MY LIFE (series)
Master Films (White)
P: H.B. Parkinson
D: H.B. Parkinson, Edward R. Gordon
S: (BOOK) Ernest Haigh
SC: Frank Miller
Ernest Haigh . . . . Himself
Geoffrey Benstead . . . . His Friend
John Stuart . . . .
Colette Brettell . . . .
Malcom Tod . . . .

07319
7: SOMETHING IN THE CITY (2000)
D: Edward R. Gordon

07320
8: THE STOLEN JEWELS (2000)
D; Edward R. Gordon

07321
9: BELLE OF THE GAMBLING DEN (2000)
D: H.B. Parkinson

07322
10: THE NOTORIOUS MRS FAGIN (2000)
D: Edward R. Gordon

07323
11: THE CASE OF A PACKING CASE (2000)
D: Edward R. Gordon

07324
12: THE MAN WHO CAME BACK (2000)
D: H.B. Parkinson
CRIME Ex-chief inspector tells friend how he
solved various crimes.

07325
FOUR MEN IN A VAN (7000)
Direct Film Traders-Titan *reissue*: 1925
(United; cut)
D:SC: Hugh Croisé
S: (NOVEL) "R. Andom" (WE THREE AND
TRODDLES)
Manning Haynes . . . . Wilkes
Donald Searle . . . . Buggins
Johnny Butt . . . . Troddles
Gordon Hopkirk . . . . Murray
Moore Marriott . . . . Mudley
COMEDY Episodic misadventures of friends
on caravan holiday.

07326
THE OLD WIVES' TALE (5000)
Ideal
D:SC: Denison Clift
S: (NOVEL) Arnold Bennett
Fay Compton . . . . Sophie Barnes
Florence Turner . . . . Constance Barnes
Henry Victor . . . . Gerald Scales
Francis Lister . . . . Cyril Povey
Mary Brough . . . . Mrs Barnes
J.R. Tozer . . . . Chirac
Norman Page . . . . Samuel Povey
Drusilla Wills . . . . Maggie
Tamara Karsavina . . . . Dancer
DRAMA 1913. Woman leaves husband to run
Paris boarding house, and reunites with sister
after the war.

07327
SHEER BLUFF (5300) (A)
Granger-Binger
P: Maurits Binger
D: Frankland A. Richardson
S: Benedict James
Henry Victor . . . . Maurice Hardacre
Maudie Dunham . . . . Esther
Percy Standing . . . . Jasper Hardacre
Nico de Jong . . . . Stokes
William Hunter . . . .
Julie Ruston . . . .
Lilian Ruston . . . .
DRAMA Rich man bankrupts rival nephew
before allowing him to marry his daughter.

07328
NO. 5 JOHN STREET (5300)
Astra Films
P: H.W. Thompson
D:SC: Kenelm Foss
S: (NOVEL) Richard Whiteing
Zena Dare . . . . Tilda
Mary Odette . . . . Celia Ridler
Lionelle Howard . . . . Seton Ridler
Randle Ayrton . . . . I. Azreal
Roy Travers . . . . Sir Charles Pounds
Charles Danvers . . . . Sir Marmaduke Ridler
James McWilliams . . . . Stubbs
Peggy Bayfield . . . . Nance

DRAMA Soap factory heir poses as worker to reform conditions, and is saved from anarchist by flower-girl.

07329
ALL ROADS LEAD TO CALVARY (5000)
Astra Films
P: H.W. Thompson
D:SC: Kenelm Foss
S:(NOVEL) Jerome K. Jerome
Minna Grey . . . . Nan Phillips
Bertram Burleigh . . . . Bob Phillips
Mary Odette . . . . Joan Allway
Roy Travers . . . . Preacher
Julie Kean . . . . Hilda Phillips
J. Nelson Ramsay . . . . Mr Allway
David Hallett . . . . Arthur Allway
George Travers . . . . Editor
Lorna Rathbone . . . . Editor's Wife
Kate Gurney . . . . Landlady
DRAMA Hastings, 1909. Fisherman MP gives up career and mistress when lowly wife takes poison.

07330
A LOWLAND CINDERELLA (5300)(U)
Progress (Butcher)
P: Frank Spring
D:SC: Sidney Morgan
S: (NOVEL) S.R. Crockett
Joan Morgan . . . . Hester Stirling
George Foley . . . . David Stirling
Ralph Forbes . . . . Master of Durrock
Mavis Clare . . . . Ethel Torpichan
Charles Levey . . . . Dr Silvanus Torpichan
Frances Wetherell . . . . . . Duchess of Middlesdale
Kate Phillips . . . . Mrs Stirling
Mary Carnegy . . . . Mrs Torpichan
Nell Emerald . . . . Meggsy
Eileen Grace . . . . Claudia Torpichan
Cecil Susands . . . . Tom Torpichan
DRAMA Girl flees when uncle steals rubies and accuses her.

07331
AN EPISODE OF LIFE IN GREATER LONDON (2000)
Kelstor Productions
D:S: Kelly Storrie
Kelly Storrie . . . . The Man
Lily Ford . . . . The Woman
COMEDY

07332
OUR AGGIE (2000)
Milo Films
D:S: Jack Denton

Mary Patterson . . . . Aggie
Jack Jarman . . . . Sailor
Bart Darley . . . . Author
Arthur Walcott . . . . Manager
COMEDY Boarding house maid becomes music hall star and is reunited with sailor, thought drowned.

07333
STORMFLOWER (2205)
A.R.T.
P: A. Randall Terraneau
D: Bert Wynne
S: Anne Merwin
Hayford Hobbs . . . . Peter
Joan Ferry . . . . Stormflower
Philip Hewland . . . . John Fulton
Beatrix Templeton . . . . Cicely Fulton
Arthur Walcott . . . . Banks
Toby Cooper . . . . Tim Blake
DRAMA Man ejects dying wife, unknowingly adopts daughter, and ejects her when she weds officer who dies in war.

07334
LOVE IN THE WELSH HILLS (6057)(A)
Harma-Associated Exhibitors (Regent)
D: Bernard Dudley
James Knight . . . . Bob Lloyd
Marjorie Villis . . . . Nan Price
Constance Worth . . . .
R. Heaton-Grey . . . . Owen Hughes
Roy Raymond . . . . Morgan Briggs
Florence Nelson . . . .
J. Edwards Barber . . . .
Ernest Spalding . . . .
CRIME Wales. Farmer frames petty officer for theft and confesses after falling over cliff.

07335
THE CORNER MAN (5123) (U)
Harma-Associated Exhibitors (NE)
D: Einar J. Bruun
S: Frank Fowell, Helen Blizzard
Hugh E. Wright . . . . Bob Warner
Ida Lambert . . . . His Daughter
Eric Barclay . . . . Hugh Morland
Sidney Folker . . . . John West
A. Harding Steerman . . . . . .
DRAMA Minstrel becomes busker while his daughter is adopted by rich aunt.

07336
LITTLE MEG'S CHILDREN (5000)
Seal (Lester)
D: Bert Wynne
S: (NOVEL) Hesba Stretton

Joan Griffiths . . . . Meg
Warwick Ward . . . .
Hargrave Mansell . . . .
DRAMA Isle of Man.

07337
JESSICA'S FIRST PRAYER
Seal
D: Berty Wynne
S: (STORY) Hesba Stretton
Joan Griffiths . . . . Jessica
Peter Coleman . . . .
Hargrave Mansell . . . .
Beatrix Templeton . . . .
DRAMA

07338
ONE WEEK TO LIVE (2000)
Sinclair Hill Productions
D: Sinclair Hill
S: Frank Miller
Campbell Gullan . . . .
Dorothy Fane . . . .
COMEDY Man who thinks he has week to live goes on a spree at the Karsino.

07339
ROMANCE AND REALITY
Lambart Films
D: Harry Lambart
S: (BOOK) Arthur Branscombe (THE CRADLE OF THE WASHINGTONS)
Cora Goffin . . . .
Isobel Jeans . . . .
DRAMA Period.

07340
FROGGY'S LITTLE BROTHER (5250)(U)
Stoll *reissue*: 1930, CHILDREN OF COURAGE (EB)
D:SC: A.E. Coleby
S: (NOVEL) "Brenda"
Maurice Thompson . . . . Froggy
Stephen Frayne . . . . Benny
Henry Doyle . . . . Mac Ragbon
Mrs. Watts-Phillips . . . . Mrs Ragbon
Harry Gilbey . . . . Harry
Agnes Poulton . . . . Jenny
James English . . . . Dr Brown
Laura Walker . . . . Mrs Blunt
Violet Ambert . . . . Debby Blunt
Alec Flood . . . . Rev Wallace
DRAMA Boy and sick brother adopted by orphanage official who accidentally killed their showman father.

1922

JAN

07341
THE GLORIOUS ADVENTURE (8000) (U)
Prizma (color)
J. Stuart Blackton (Stoll))
D: J.Stuart Blackton
S: Felix Orman
Lady Diana Manners . . . . . Lady Beatrice Fair
Gerald Lawrence . . . . Hugh Argyle
Cecil Humphreys . . . . Walter Roderick
Victor McLaglen . . . . Bullfinch
Alice Crawford . . . . Stephanie
Hon Lois Sturt . . . . Nell Gwyn
William Luff . . . . Charles II
Fred Wright . . . . Humpty
Flora le Breton . . . . Rosemary
Lennox Pawle . . . . Samuel Pepys
Haidee Wright . . . . Mrs Bullfinch
Rudolf de Cordova . . . . . . Thomas Unwin
Lawford Davidson . . . . Lord Fitzroy
Rosalie Heath . . . . Queen Catherine
Gertrude Sterroll . . . . Duchess of Morland
Tom Heslewood . . . . Solomon Eagle
Marjorie Day . . . . Olivia
Geoffrey Clinton . . . . Charles Hart
Tom Coventry . . . . Leclerc
Jeff Barlow . . . . Valet
John East . . . . Major Domo
Violet Blackton . . . . Rosalie
ADVENTURE 1666. Earl's cousin survives
drowning and saves lady from great fire of
London (First British feature in colour.)

07342
LAMP IN THE DESERT (5820) (A)
Stoll
D: F. Martin Thornton
S: (NOVEL) Ethel M. Dell
SC: Leslie Howard Gordon
Gladys Jennings . . . . Stella Denvers
Lewis Willoughby . . . . . . Capt Everard Monck
George K. Arthur . . . . Tony Denvers
J.R. Tozer . . . . Capt Raleigh Dacres
Teddy Arundell . . . . Maj Ralston
Lewis Gilbert . . . . Col Mansfield
Gladys Mason . . . . Mrs Ralston
Tony Fraser . . . . Waziri Spy
DRAMA India. Capt forces bigamist to feign
death so he can marry his widow.

07343
THE PASSIONATE FRIENDS (7231) (A)
Stoll
D: Maurice Elvey
S: (NOVEL) H.G. Wells
SC: Leslie Howard Gordon
Milton Rosmer . . . . Steven Stratton
Valia . . . . Lady Mary Christian
Fred Raynham . . . . Harrison Justin
Madge Stuart . . . . Rachel Moore
Lawford Davidson . . . . . . Guy Ladislaw
Ralph Forster . . . . Philip Evesham
Teddy Arundell . . . . Edward Stratton
Annie Esmond . . . . Maid
ROMANCE Armaments king's wife kills herself
to save MP lover from divorce scandal.

07344
SINISTER STREET (4495) (A)
Ideal
D: George Andre Beranger
S: (NOVEL) Compton Mackenzie
SC: Arthur Q. Walton
John Stuart . . . . Michael Farr
Amy Verity . . . . Stella Vane
Maudie Dunham . . . . Lily Haden
Molly Adair . . . . Sylvia Scarlett
Roger Treville . . . . George Ayliff
C. Tilson-Chowne . . . . Lord Saxby

Kate Carew . . . . Mrs Fane
A.G. Poulton . . . .
Wilfrid Fletcher . . . .
John Reid . . . .
Kathleen Blake . . . .
Marjorie Day . . . .
DRAMA Bastard idealist saves girl from shame
and sets her up for trial period, but she slips
again.

07345
MORD EM'LY (6000) (U) USA: ME AND MY
GIRL
Welsh-Pearson (Jury)
P:D: George Pearson
S: (NOVEL) W. Pett Ridge
SC: Eliot Stannard
Betty Balfour . . . . Maud Emily
Rex Davis . . . . Barden
Elsie Craven . . . . Gilliken
Edward Sorley . . . . Father
Mrs Hubert Willis . . . . Mother
DRAMA Cockney thief reforms, ex-convict
father kills mother, and she weds boxer.

07346
TENSE MOMENTS WITH GREAT AUTHORS
(series)
Master Films (BEF)
P: H.B. Parkinson
D: H.B. Parkinson, George Wynn, W.C. Rowden
SC: W.C. Rowden

07347
1—TRILBY (1300) (A)
S: (NOVEL) George du Maurier
Phyllis Neilson-Terry . . . . . . Trilby
Charles Garry . . . . Svengali

07348
2—LES MISERABLES (1195) (A)
S: (NOVEL) Victor Hugo
Lyn Harding . . . . Jean Valjean

07349
3—SAPPHO (1216) (A)
S: (NOVEL) Alphonse Daudet
Hilda Moore . . . . Sappho

07350
4—NANCY (1578) (A)
D: H.B. Parkinson
S: (NOVEL) Charles Dickens (OLIVER
TWIST)
Sybil Thorndike . . . . Nancy
Ivan Berlyn . . . . Fagin

07351
5—FAGIN (1260) (A)
D: H.B. Parkinson
S: (NOVEL) Charles Dickens (OLIVER
TWIST)
Ivan Berlyn . . . . Fagin

07352
6—LA TOSCA (1320) (A)
S: (OPERA) Giacomo Puccini
Ethel Irving . . . . La Tosca

07353
7—SCROOGE (1280) (U)
D: George Wynn
S: (NOVEL) Charles Dickens (A CHRISTMAS
CAROL)
H.V. Esmond . . . . Scrooge

07354
8—VANITY FAIR (1198) (A)
D: W.C. Rowden
S: (NOVEL) William Thackeray
Kyrle Bellew . . . . Becky Sharp

Clive Brook . . . . Rawdon Crawley
Douglas Munro . . . . Marquis of Staines
Henry Doughty . . . . Mr Wenham

07355
9—EAST LYNNE (1240) (U)
S: (NOVEL) Mrs Henry Wood
Iris Hoey . . . . Isabel Carlyle

07356
10—A TALE OF TWO CITIES (1174) (U)
D: W.C. Rowden
S: (NOVEL) Charles Dickens
J. Fisher White . . . . Dr Manette
Clive Brook . . . . Sidney Carton
Ann Trevor . . . . Lucie Manette

07357
11—MOTHS (1129) (U)
S: (NOVEL) Ouida
Cameron Carr . . . .

07358
12—DAVID GARRICK (1300) (U)
S: (PLAY) T.W. Robertson
Milton Rosmer . . . . David Garrick
DRAMAS Picturised highlights from famous plays
and novels.

07359
MASTER SONG SCENAS (Series)
Retitled;CAPITOL SONG CYCLE
Master Films (Capitol)
P: H. B. Parkinson
D:H. B. Parkinson, George Wynn, W. C. Rowden
S: W. C. Rowden

07360
1: OLD PAL WHY DON'T YOU ANSWER ME?
(1000)

07361
2: MAKE BELIEVE (1000)

07362
3: SMILIN' THRO' (1000)

07363
4: I'D LOVE TO FALL ASLEEP AND WAKE
UP IN MY MAMMY'S ARMS (1000)

07364
5: THERE'S A VACANT CHAIR AT HOME
SWEET HOME (1000)

07365
6: I THOUGHT YOU LOVED ME AS I LOVED
YOU (1000)

07366
7: WHISPERING (1000)
Clive Brook . . . . The Man
Joan Lockton . . . . The Girl

07367
8: ANGELS, WE CALL THEM MOTHERS
DOWN HERE (1000)

07368
9: JUST KEEP A THOUGHT FOR ME (1000)

07369
10: IN MY HEART, ON MY MIND, ALL DAY
LONG (1000)

07370
11: WHEN SHALL WE MEET AGAIN ? (1000)

07371
12: THE SHEIK (1000)
D: George Wynn
Clive Brook . . . . The Sheik
Ward McAllister . . . .
MUSICAL Dramatisations of popular songs

07372
THE ADVENTURES OF MR PUSHER LONG
(series)
Kenneth Graeme Film Syndicate (Anchor)
P: D: SC: Kenneth Graeme
S: (STORIES) Derwent Nicol
Kenneth Graeme .... Mr Pusher Long

07373
1: THE HYPNOTIC PORTRAIT (2000)

07374
2: THE WAR AT WALLAROO MANSIONS
(2000)

07375
3: THE GREAT HUNGER DUEL (2000)
Sydney N. Folker .... The Lover
Clive Tristi .... The Rival
Dawn Meredith .... The Girl
COMEDY American press agent stages publicity
stunts.

07376
THE ISLAND OF ROMANCE (5000)
Raleigh King Films
D: Humberston Wright
S: Raleigh King
Leonard Tremayne .... The Man
Dora Henwood .... The Girl
Raleigh King ....
ROMANCE

07377
BEAUTY AND THE BEAST (2000)
George Clark (Stoll)
D: S: Guy Newall
Guy Newall .... The Beast
Ivy Duke .... Beauty
Douglas Munro .... Father
Winifred Sadler .... Mother
COMEDY Theatre patron unravels girl's woollen
vest.

07378
DUTCH COURAGE (2000)
Sterling Photoplays
D: George Dunstall
S: Alec McKee
Jock Cameron .... The Man
Dorothy Peters .... The Wife
COMEDY

07379
THE EXCLUSIVE MODEL (2000)
Sterling Photoplays
D: George Dunstall
S: Cyril Murrell
Molly Adair .... The Girl
COMEDY

07380
SIMPLE SIMON (5400)(U)
Hepworth
D: Henry Edwards
S: Henry Edwards, Walter Courtenay Rowden
Henry Edwards .... Simon
Chrissie White .... Rosemary/Ruth
Mary Dibley .... Sylvia Royal
Hugh Clifton .... Mark
Henry Vibart .... Abbot
Esme Hubbard .... Minty Weir
E.C. Matthews .... Adam Spice
ROMANCE Falsely accused monk flirts with
authoress but realises he loves islander.

FEB

07381
THE HOUSE OF PERIL (5000)
Astra Films
P: H.W. Thompson

D:SC: Kenelm Foss
S: (NOVEL) Mrs Belloc Lowndes (CHINK IN
THE ARMOUR)
(PLAY) Horace Annesley Vachell
Fay Compton .... Sylvia Bailey
Roy Travers .... Bill Chester
A.B. Imeson .... Comte de Virieu
Madeleine Seymour .... Anna Wolsky
J. Nelson Ramsey .... Herr Wachner
Irene Tripod .... Frau Wachner
Wallace Bosco .... Polperro
Flora le Breton .... French Maid
Blanche Walker .... Maid
George Bellamy .... Gambler
Hubert Carter .... Gambler
Jeff Barlow .... Gambler
Lewis Gilbert .... Gambler
Tom Coventry .... Gambler
Madge Tree .... Gambler
CRIME Deauville German Couple lure girl
gamblers to 'haunted' house and kill them for
jewels.

07382
DICKY MONTEITH (5000)
Astra Films
P: H.W. Thompson
D:SC: Kenelm Foss
S: (PLAY) Tom Gallon, Leon M. Lion,
Stewart Rome .... Dicky Monteith
Joan Morgan .... Sally/Dorothy Weston
Jack Minister .... Vincent Hepburn
Douglas Munro .... Mayor
J. Nelson Ramsey .... Barty
Jack Frost .... Ginger
Gertrude Sterroll .... Miss Tillotson
David Hallett .... Gilbert Collingwood
James English .... Sydney Carton
Fay Segel .... Lucie Manette
A.B. Imeson .... Charles Darnay
Lewis Gilbert .... Defarge
Irene Tripod .... Mme Defarge
Kenelm Foss .... Charles Dickens
CRIME Crooked lawyer convinces drunkard that
he has spent stepbrother's fortune.

07383
BENTLEY'S CONSCIENCE (4120)(U)
Ideal
D:SC: Denison Clift
S: (NOVEL) Paul Trent
Robert Loraine .... Clive Bentley
Betty Faire .... Diane Carson
Henry Victor .... Fletcher
Harvey Braban .... Richard Glyn
Ivo Dawson .... Murdoch
J. Fisher White .... John Carson
DRAMA Secretary takes blame when fiancee's
father ruins oil company.

07384
THE KNIGHT ERRANT (5290)(U)
Stoll
D: George Ridgwell
S: (NOVEL) Ethel M. Dell
SC: Leslie Howard Gordon, Mrs Sydney Groome
Madge Stuart .... Ernestine
Rex McDougall .... Cecil Mordaunt Rivington
Olaf Hytten .... Hernando Parez
Norma Whalley .... Lady Cardwell
Judd Green .... Mr Perkiss
Eva Westlake .... Mrs Perkiss
ROMANCE Caravanner saves lady's stepdaughter
from enforced marriage to rich Brazilian.

07385
FILM SONG ALBUM (series)(U)
Master Films (BEF)
P: H.B. Parkinson
S: Walter Courtenay Rowden

07386
1—AT TRINITY CHURCH I MET MY DOOM
(1150)

07387
2—LONDON'S BURNING (763)

07388
3—TA-RA-RA-BOOM-DE-RE (1100)
Flora le Breton .... The Girl

07389
4—WE ALL WALKED INTO THE SHOP (1100)
MUSICAL Picturisations of popular songs.

07390
SAM'S BOY (4300)(U)
Artistic
P: George Redman
D: Manning Haynes
S: (NOVEL) W.W. Jacobs
SC: Lydia Hayward
Johnny Butt .... Captain Hunt
Tom Coventry .... Sam Brown
Bobbie Rudd .... Billy Jones
Charles Ashton .... Harry Green
Toby Cooper .... Charlie Legge
Mary Braithwaite .... Mrs Hunt
Kate Gurney .... Mrs Brown
Harry Newman .... Mate
COMEDY Poor orphan pretends married sailor
is his father.

07391
A WILL AND A WAY (3570)(U)
Artistic
P: George Redman
D: Manning Haynes
S: (NOVEL) W.W. Jacobs
SC: Lydia Hayward
Ernest Hendrie .... Foxey Green
Pollie Emery .... Mrs Pottle
Johnny Butt .... Joe Chambers
Cynthia Murtagh .... Flora Pottle
Charles Ashton .... George Smith
Ada Palmer .... Eliza Collins
Agnes Brantford .... Mrs Walker
Peggie Beans .... Jenny Pottle
Maisie Beans .... Lertie Pottle
COMEDY Old bachelor inherits if he weds the
first woman to propose.

MAR

07392
THE LITTLE MOTHER (5000)
Ideal
D: A.V. Bramble
S: (NOVEL) May Wynn
SC: Audrey Oliver
Florence Turner .... The Mother
John Stuart .... Jack
Lilian Douglas .... Jessie Moore
Harvey Braban .... John Moore
Evan Thomas .... Robert Endale
Hal Martin .... Jimmy Wentworth
Richard Atwood .... Arthur Merle
Charles Thursby .... Fenlake
DRAMA Framed clerk uses widowed mother's
savings to flee to Canada where he saves
culprit's life.

07393
THE LONELY LADY OF GROSVENOR
SQUARE (4600)(U)
Ideal
D: Sinclair Hill
S: (NOVEL) Mrs. Henry de la Pasture
SC: Arthur Q. Walton, Sinclair Hill
Betty Faire .... Jeanne Marney
Jack Hobbs .... Duke of Monagha

Eileen Magrath . . . . Cissie
Dorothy Fane . . . . Anne-Marie Marney
Arthur Pusey . . . . Louis Marney
Gertrude Sterroll . . . . Miss Marney
Ralph Forster . . . . Butler
MrsHubert Willis . . . . Durham
Daisy Campbell . . . . Duchess
Emilie Nichol . . . . Mrs Wheeler
ROMANCE Country girl inherits, weds Duke, and meets dead brother's family.

07394
POTTER'S CLAY (5858) (U)
Big Four Famous (Anchor)
D: H. Grenville-Taylor, Douglas Payne
S: Langford Reed, Hetty Spiers
Ellen Terry . . . . Lady Merrall
Dick Webb . . . . Clifford Merrall
Peggy Hathaway . . . . Hypatia Dalroy
Douglas Payne . . . . Henry J. Smith
Wally Bosco . . . . Louis
Henry Doughty . . . . Mr Dalroy
DRAMA Doulton. Crook hires actress to wrest pottery secret from owner's son.

07395
THE SCARLET LADY (6100)(U)
Violet Hopson Productions *reissue:* 1926 (2rls)
D: Walter West
S: J. Bertram Brown
Violet Hopson . . . . Gwendoline Gordon
Lewis Willoughby . . . . Martin Strong
Cameron Carr . . . . Henry Wingate
Arthur Walcott . . . . Mark Worth
Gertrude Sterroll . . . . Felicity
Adeline Hayden Coffin . . . . . . Aunt Priscilla
SPORT Widow's crooked trustee tries to nobble bachelor's racehorses.

07396
THREE LIVE GHOSTS (6600)
Famous Players-Lasky (Par)
D:George Fitzmaurice
S: (PLAY) Max Marcin, Frederick Isham
SC: Margaret Turnbull, Ouida Bergere
Norman Kerry . . . . Billy Foster
Anna Q. Nillson . . . . Ivis
Edmund Goulding . . . . Jimmy Gubbins
John Milterne . . . . Jimmy Larne
Cyril Chadwick . . . . Spoofy
Clare Greet . . . . Mrs Gubbins
Dorothy Fane . . . . Duchess
Annette Benson . . . . Mrs Woofers
Windham Guise . . . . Briggs
COMEDY Three 'dead' POWs return: one with amnesia, one framed for murder and one forced to stay dead for insurance.

07397
TRAPPED BY THE MORMONS (6200)(A)
Master (White) *reissue:* 1928, THE MORMON PERIL
P:D: H.B. Parkinson
S: (NOVEL) Winifred Graham (THE LOVE STORY OF A MORMON)
SC: Frank Miller
Evelyn Brent . . . . Nora Prescott
Lewis Willoughby . . . . Isoldi Keene
Ward McAllister . . . . Elder Kuyler
Olaf Hytten . . . . Elder Marz
Olive Sloane . . . . Sadie Keene
George Wynn . . . . Jim Foster
Cecil Morton York . . . . Mr Prescott
CRIME Manchester girl, forced to join secret society, is freed by police.

07398
FALSE EVIDENCE (6050) (U)
Stoll
D: Harold Shaw

S: (NOVEL) E. Phillips Oppenheim
SC: Frank Miller
Edna Flugrath . . . . Maud Deveraux
Cecil Humphreys . . . . Rupert Deveraux
E. Holman Clark . . . . . . Sir Francis Arbuthnot
Frank Petley . . . . Herbert Arbuthnot
Eric Lugg . . . . Hugh Arbuthnot
Constance Rayner . . . . Marian Arbuthnot
Teddy Arundell . . . . Hilton
Miss Costello . . . . Marian Arbuthnot
DRAMA Man proves disinherited father took blame for cousin's cowardice in Zulu war.

07399
THE FURTHER ADVENTURES OF SHERLOCK HOLMES (series)
Stoll
D: George Ridgwell
S: (STORIES) Arthur Conan Doyle
SC: Patrick L. Mannock, Geoffrey H. Malins
Eille Norwood . . . . Sherlock Holmes
Hubert Willis . . . . Dr John Watson

07400
1—CHARLES AUGUSTUS MILVERTON (1900)(A)
Teddy Arundell . . . . Insp Hopkins
George Foley . . . . Milverton
Harry J. Worth . . . . Butler
Tonie Edgar Bruce . . . . . Lady Eva Bracknell
Mme d'Esterre . . . . Mrs Hudson
Edith Bishop . . . . Maid

07401
2—THE ABBEY GRANGE (2200)(A)
Teddy Arundell . . . . Insp Hopkins
Madeleine Seymour . . . . . . Lady Brackenstall
Lawford Davidson . . . . . Sir Eustace Brackenstall
Leslie Stiles . . . . Capt Croker
Madge Tree . . . . Theresa
Mme d' Esterre . . . . Mrs Hudson

07402
3—THE NORWOOD BUILDER (2100)(U)
Teddy Arundell . . . . Insp Hopkins
Fred Wright . . . . James Oldacre
Cyril Raymond . . . . John McFarlane
Laura Walker . . . . Miss McFarlane
Mme d'Esterre . . . . Mrs Hudson

07403
4—THE REIGATE SQUIRES (1900)(A)
Teddy Arundell . . . . Insp Hopkins
Richard Atwood . . . . Alec Cunningham
Edward O'Neill . . . . Squire Cunningham
Arthur Lumley . . . . Col Hayter
Mme d'Esterre . . . . Mrs Hudson

07404
5—THE NAVAL TREATY (1600)(U)
Jack Hobbs . . . . Percy Phelps
Francis Duguid . . . . Joseph Harrison
Nancy May . . . . Miss Harrison

07405
6—THE SECOND STAIN (2200)(A)
Teddy Arundell . . . . Insp Hopkins
Cecil Ward . . . . Lord Bellinger
Dorothy Fane . . . . Miss Hope
Maria Minetti . . . . Mrs Lucas
Mme d'Esterre . . . . Mrs Hudson

07406
7—THE RED CIRCLE (1780)(A)
Teddy Arundell . . . . Insp Hopkins
Bertram Burleigh . . . . Gennaro Lucca
Maresco Marescini . . . . Gorgiano
Sybil Archdale . . . . Amelia Luuca
Tom Beaumont . . . . Leverton
Mme d'Esterre . . . . Mrs Hudson
Esme Hubbard . . . . Mrs Warren

07407
8—THE SIX NAPOLEONS (1790)(A)
Teddy Arundell . . . . Insp Hopkins
George Bellamy . . . . Beppo
Jack Raymond . . . . Pietro Venucci
Alice Moffatt . . . . Lucretia
Mme d'Esterre . . . . Mrs Hudson

07408
9—BLACK PETER (1800)(A)
Teddy Arundell . . . . Insp Hopkins
Fred Paul . . . . PeterCarey
Hugh Buckler . . . . Pat Cairns
Jack Jarman . . . . John Neligan
Fred Rains . . . . Neligan Sr
Mrs Willis . . . . Mrs Carey
Miss Willis . . . . Miss Carey
Mme d'Esterre . . . . Mrs Hudson

07409
10—THE BRUCE PARTINGTON PLANS (2196)(A)
Teddy Arundell . . . . Insp Hopkins
Malcolm Tod . . . . Cadogan West
Lewis Gilbert . . . . Mycroft Holmes
Ronald Power . . . . Col Valentine Walter
Edward Sorley . . . . Hugh Oberstein
Leslie Brittain . . . . Sidney Johnson

07410
11—THE STOCKBROKER'S CLERK (1830)(A)
Olaf Hytten . . . . Hall Pycroft
Aubrey Fitzgerald . . . . Pinner
George Ridgwell . . . . Beddington

07411
12—THE BOSCOMBE VALLEY MYSTERY (2450)(A)
Hal Martin . . . . Charles McCarthy
Roy Raymond . . . . James McCarthy
Fred Raynham . . . . John Turner
Thelma Murray . . . . Miss Turner

07412
13—THE MUSGRAVE RITUAL (1750)(U)
Geoffrey Wilmer . . . . Musgrave
Clifton Boyne . . . . Brunton
Betty Chester . . . . Rachel Howells

07413
14—THE GOLDEN PINCE—NEZ (1675)(A)
Teddy Arundell . . . . Insp Hopkins
Norma Whalley . . . . Anna Coram
Cecil Morton York . . . . Prof Coram

07414
15—THE GREEK INTERPRETER (1862)(U)
J. R. Tozer . . . . Latimer
Robert Vallis . . . . Wilson Kemp
Cecil Dane . . . . Melas
Edith Saville . . . . Sophy Katrides
H. Wheeler . . . . Insp Hopkins
Mme d'Esterre . . . . Mrs Hudson
CRIMES Private detective solves various crimes.

07415
BELONGING (5253)
Stoll
D: F. Martin Thornton
S: (NOVEL) Olive Wadsley
SC: Leslie Howard Gordon
Barbara Hoffe . . . . Sara Lansdale
Hugh Buckler . . . . Charles Carton
William Lenders . . . . Count Desanges
Cecil A. Barry . . . . Julian Guise
George Garvey . . . . Dominique Guise
Winifred Harris . . . . Lady Diana
Leo Pinto . . . . Anatole Colin
CRIME Paris. Count's Enforced wife takes blame when her ex-lover is killed by diplomat she loves.

07416
THE PEACEMAKER (4100)(U)
Stoll
D: S: A. E. Coleby
A. E. Coleby . . . . Big Ben Buckle
H. Nicholls-Bates . . . . Ted Staples
Bob Vallis . . . . Jim Blakeley
Sam Austin . . . . Fred Smith
Maud Yates . . . . Miss Brown
Minna Leslie . . . . Widow Smith
Frank Wilson . . . . Charles Wilkes
Humberston Wright . . . . . . George Brownlow
DRAMA Carpenter stops threatened strike when friend refuses to join union.

07417
A ROMANCE OF OLD BAGDAD (6300)(A)
Astra Films
P: H. W. Thompson
D: SC: Kenelm Foss
S: (NOVEL) Jessie Douglas Kerruish
(MISS HAROUN AL RASCHID)
Matheson Lang . . . . Prince Omar
Manora Thew . . . . Sourna
Henry Victor . . . . Horne Jerningham
Roy Travers . . . . Harvey P. Wilbur
Jack Minster . . . . Piers Blessington
Victor McLaglen . . . . Miski
Lorna Rathbone . . . . Evelyn Jerningham
George Foley . . . . The Kadi
Douglas Munro . . . . Abdul Bey
Clyne Dacia . . . . Rathia
George Bellamy . . . . Gen Walters
A. Harding Steerman . . . . . . Mr Jocelyn
Barbara Everest . . . . Mrs Jocelyn
Rolf Leslie . . . . Haji
Beatie Olna . . . . Sulti
ROMANCE Baghdad. Governor's disowned daughter ejected by English husband and loved by Persian Prince

07418
THE RECOIL (5000)(A)
Hardy (Stoll)
P: Sam Hardy
D: Geoffrey H. Malins
S:(NOVEL) Rafael Sabatini (THE DREAM)
SC: Rafael Sabatini
Eille Norwood . . . . Francis
Phyllis Titmuss . . . . Adelaide Wallace
Lawrence Anderson . . . . Digby Raikes
Dawson Millward . . . . Anthony Orpington
Annie Esmond . . . . Miss Orpington
CRIME Psychic expert hypnotises cousin to shoot rich uncle.

07419
LEVITY AND LAITY (2000)
Union Films
D: William Drury
S: George Roberts
Alan Dudley . . . . The Man
COMEDY

APR
07420
THE PERSISTENT LOVERS (6420)(U)
George Clark Productions (Stoll)
D: SC: Guy Newall
S: (NOVEL) Hamilton Gibbs
Guy Newall . . . . Richard Ardley-Manners
Ivy Duke . . . . Lady Audrey Beaumont
A. Bromley Davenport . . Duke of Harborough
Julian Royce . . . . Anthony Waring
Lawford Davidson . . . . . . Hon Ivor Jocelyn
Douglas Munro . . . . John
Barbara Everest . . . . Joyce
Ernest A. Douglas . . . . . . Rev Ardley-Manners

Emilie Nichol . . . . Duchess
ROMANCE Norfolk. Duke's daughter loves author and follows him to France, discovering father withheld letters.

07421
LITTLE BROTHER OF GOD (6560)(A)
Stoll
D: F. Martin Thornton
S: Leslie Howard Gordon
SC: Leslie Howard Gordon
Victor McLaglen . . . . King Kennidy
Valia . . . . Helen McFee
Alec Fraser . . . . Donald Wainwright
Fred Raynham . . . . Bliss
Bertie Wright . . . . Etienne Parouche
Lionelle Howard . . . . Douglas Wainwright
Bob Vallis . . . . Johnny Jackpine
Varies Nickawa . . . . Jean Marie
Fred Rains . . . . Father Joseph
WESTERN Canada. Man investigates brother's death and saves suspected girl from kidnap.

07422
SHIRLEY (5584)(U)
Ideal
D: A. V. Bramble
S: (NOVEL) Charlotte Bronte
SC: Arthur Q. Walton
Carlotta Breese . . . . Shirley
Clive Brook . . . . Robert Moore
Harvey Braban . . . . Nunnally
Joe Nightingale . . . .
David Miller . . . . Joe Scott
Elizabeth Irving . . . . Caroline Helston
Mabel Terry-Lewis . . . . . . Mrs Prior
DRAMA Period. Workmen wound mill-owner when he instals machinery.

07423
A MASTER OF CRAFT (4937)(U)
Ideal
D: Thomas Bentley
S: (STORY) W. W. Jacobs
SC: Eliot Stannard
Fred Groves . . . . Capt Flower
Mercy Hatton . . . . Matilda Tapping
Judd Green . . . . George
Arthur Cleave . . . . Joe
John Kelt . . . . Green
Roy Byford . . . . Pat
Pope Stamper . . . . Mate
Lilian Douglas . . . .
Jerrold Robertshaw . . . .
Eva Westlake . . . .
Ian Wilson . . . . Tim
COMEDY Captain fakes own drowning to escape marriage clause in uncle's will.

07424
THE CARD (5080)(U)
Ideal
D: A. V. Bramble
S: (NOVEL) Arnold Bennett
SC: Eliot Stannard
Laddie Cliff . . . . Denry Machin
Hilda Cowley . . . . Ruth Earp
Joan Barry . . . . Nellie Cotterill
Mary Dibley . . . . Countess of Chell
Sydney Paxton . . . . Councillor Cotterill
Dora Gregory . . . . Mrs Machin
Norman Page . . . . Mr Duncalf
Arthur Cleave . . . . Mr Shillitoe
Jack Denton . . . . Barlow
Frank Goddard . . . . Boxer
COMEDY Potteries. Sacked clerk rises to become Mayor and weds daughter of councillor who sacked him.

07425
MARRIED TO A MORMON (5800) (A)
Master (Astral)
P:DA: H.B. Parkinson
S: Frank Miller
Evelyn Brent . . . . Beryl Fane
Clive Brook . . . . Lionel Daventry
George Wynn . . . . Philip Lorimer
Booth Conway . . . . Bigelow
Molly Adair . . . .
DRAMA Mormon weds rich English girl, takes second wife in Utah, and is killed by first wife's lover.

MAY
07426
COCAINE (5100) retitled: WHILE LONDON SLEEPS (A)
Master Films (Astra)
P: H.B. Parkinson
D: Graham Cutts
S: Frank Miller
Hilda Bayley . . . . Madge Webster
Flora le Breton . . . . Jenny
Ward McAllister . . . . The Crook
Cyril Raymond . . . .
Tony Fraser . . . . Loki
Teddy Arundell . . . .
CRIME Drug king kills criminal for giving cocaine to his teenage daughter.

07427
CRUSHING THE DRUG TRAFFIC (2125) (A)
Master Films (BEF)
P: D: H.B. Parkinson
S: Frank MIller
James Knight . . . . Customs Officer
Dorothy Fane . . . . Actress
Cecil Morton York . . . . Baines
Tony Fraser . . . . Crook
CRIME Actress helps detective unmask fake theatrical agent as dope peddler.

07428
DIANA OF THE CROSSWAYS (4960) (A)
Ideal
D: Denison Clift
S: (NOVEL) George Meredith
SC: William Meredith
Fay Compton . . . . Diana
Henry Victor . . . . Hon Percy Dacier
J.R. Tozer . . . . Augustus Warwick
A. Harding Steerman . . . . Tonans
J. Fisher White . . . . Lord Dannisburgh
Reginald Fox . . . . Tom Redworth
Ivo Dawson . . . . Sir Lukyn Dunstane
Ernest A. Dagnall . . . . Prime Minister
Harvey Braban . . . . Radworth
Joyce Gayman . . . . Lady Emma
Pamela Cooper . . . . Princess
Hope Tilden . . . . Mary Paynham
DRAMA Barrister divorces wife after she has affair with prime minister and betrays cabinet secret.

07429
BOY WOODBURN (7300) (U)
George Clark Productions (Stoll)
D: SC: Guy Newall
S: (NOVEL) Alfred Olivant
Guy Newall . . . . Jim Silver
Ivy Duke . . . . Boy Woodburn
A. Bromley Davenport . . . . Matt Woodburn
Mary Rorke . . . . Ma Woodburn
Cameron Carr . . . . Jaggers
John Alexander . . . . Monkey Brand
SPORT Trainer's daughter agrees to wed broke banker if her foal wins race.

07430
THE WONDERFUL STORY (500) (A)
Graham-Wilcox (astra-National)
P: Herbert Wilcox
D: Graham Cutts
S: (NOVEL) I.A.R. Wylie
SC: Patrick L. Mannock
Lilian Hall Davis . . . .   Kate Richards
Herbert Langley . . . .   Robert Martin
Olaf Hytten . . . .   Jimmy Martin
DRAMA Paralytic dominates brother and wife
until their child reforms him.

07431
LONG ODDS (5430) (U)
Stoll
D: S: A.E. Coleby
A.E. Coleby . . . .   Gus Granville
Edith Bishop . . . .   Sally Walters
Sam Marsh . . . .   Jim Straker
Fred Paul . . . .   Hastings Floyd
Sam Austin . . . .   Tony Walters
H. Nicholls-Bates . . . .   Sam Marshall
Frank Wilson . . . .   Ned Boulter
Madge Royce . . . .   Mrs Granville
Harry Marsh . . . .   Pat Malone
SPORT Sick jockey rides winner when
substitute thrown and hurt.

07432
STABLE COMPANIONS (5960) (U)
British Super (Jury)
P: G.B. Samuelson
D: Albert Ward
S: Walter Summers
Clive Brook . . . .   James Pilkington
Lilian Hall Davis . . . .
Robert English . . . .   Sir Horace Pilkington
Arthur Pusey . . . .
Thomas Walters . . . .
James Wigham . . . .
Fred Mason . . . .
Chick Wongo . . . .
SPORT Rich man tests nephews by faking death
and leaving one stables and other his money.

07433
WITH FATHER'S HELP (1850) (U)
Peggy Hyland (Pioneer)
P: D: Peggy Hyland
Peggy Hyland . . . .   Kitty Gordon
Gibson Gowland . . . .   Mr Gordon
Donald Stuart . . . .   Dick Mason
COMEDY Girl's suitor tricks father into
consenting by posing as butler.

07434
THE COWGIRL QUEEN (420) (U)
Lily Long
P: Geoffrey Benstead
D: Hugh Croise
S: Patrick L. Mannock
Lily Long . . . .   Lily
Frank Grey . . . .   The Man
COMEDY

07435
WHEN GREEK MEETS GREEK (5400) (U)
Walter West (Butcher)
D: Walter West
S: (NOVEL) Paul Trent
Violet Hopson . . . .   Christine Ward
Stewart Rome . . . .   Cyrus Warner
Lillian Douglas . . . .   Julia Warner
Lewis Gilbert . . . .   Robert Craven
Arthur Walcott . . . .   Strike Leader
Marjorie Benson . . . .   Miss Lockwood
Tom Beaumont . . . .   Robertson
Bert Darley . . . .   Heller
DRAMA American magnate weds steelworks
heiress after saving her from strikers.

JUN
07436
THE PAUPER MILLIONAIRE (4993) (U)
Ideal
D: Frank H. Crane
S: (NOVEL) Austin Fryer
SC: Eliot Stannard
C.M. Hallard . . . .   Pye Smith
Katherine Blair . . . .   Hilda
John H. Roberts . . . .   Harry
Norma Whalley . . . .   Mrs Smith
George Goodwin . . . .   Crook
Pollie Emery . . . .   Sally
COMEDY Millionaire robbed, mistaken for
crook, and forced to work for living.

07437
A BACHELOR'S BABY (5200) (U)
I.B. Davidson (Granger)
D: Arthur Rooke
S: (NOVEL) Rolfe Bennett
SC: Lydia Hayward
Constance Woth . . . .   Peggy Woodward
Malcolm Tod . . . .   Lt Jimmy Barton
Tom Reymolds . . . .   Capt Rogers
Haidee Wright . . . .   Miss Fisher
Maud Yates . . . .   Mrs Prowse
COMEDY Lt plants baby on retired captain
to promote romance with neighbour's neice.

07438
A PRINCE OF LOVERS (7850) (U)
Gaumont-British Screencraft
D: C.C. Calvert
S: (PLAY) Alicia Ramsey (BYRON)
SC: Alicia Ramsey
Howard Gaye . . . .   Lord Byron
Marjorie Hume . . . .   Isabella Milbanke
Mary Clare . . . .   Lady Caroline Lamb
David Hawthorne . . . .   Cam Hobhouse
Marjorie Day . . . .   Augusta Leigh
George Foley . . . .   Sir Ralph Milbanke
H.R. Hignett . . . .   Fletcher
Windham Guise . . . .   Joe
Gladys Hamilton . . . .   Lady Milbanke
W.D.C. Knox . . . .   Sir Walter Scott
Viva Birkett . . . .   Lady Jersey
Eugene Leahy . . . .   Tom Moore
Bellenden Powell . . . .   Prince Regent
Saba Raleigh . . . .   Mme de Stael
Geoffrey Dunstan . . . .   Scrope Davis
Hector Abbas . . . .   Murray
Madge Tree . . . .   Mrs Clermont
Marie Ault . . . .   Nannie
HISTORY Lord's wife leaves him after jealous
lady plots ruin.

07439
TENSE MOMENTS FROM GREAT PLAYS
(series)
Master (BEF)
P: H.B. Parkinson
SC: Frank Miller

07440
1—MACBETH (1175) (U)
D: H.B. Parkinson
S: (PLAY) William Shakespeare
Russell Thorndike . . . .   Macbeth
Sybil Thorndike . . . .   Lady Macbeth

07441
2— BLEAK HOUSE (3100) (A)
D: H.B. Parkinson
S: (NOVEL) Charles Dickens
Sybil Thorndike . . . .   Lady Dedlock
Betty Doyle . . . .   Esther
Stacey Gaunt . . . .   Sir Leicester Dedlock
Harry J. Worth . . . .   Bucket
Alec Alexander . . . .   Joe

07442
3— IT'S NEVER TOO LATE TO MEND (1040)
(A)
D: George Wynn
S: (PLAY) Arthur Shirley, Charles Reade
Russell Thorndike . . . .   Squire Meadows
Ward McAllister . . . .   Tom Robinson
Alec Alexander . . . .

07443
4— JANE SHORE (950) (U)
D: Edwin J. Collins
S: (PLAY) W'G' Wills
Sybil Thorndike . . . .   Jane Shore
Booth Conway . . . .   Gloucester
Gordon Hopkirk . . . .   Matthew Shore
Lewis Gilbert . . . .   Edward IV

07444
5— THE LADY OF THE CAMELIAS (970) (A)
D: Edwin J. Collins
S: (PLAY) Alexandre Dumas
Sybil Thorndike . . . .   Marguerite Gautier
Ward McAllister . . . .   Armand Duval
Booth Conway . . . .   Baron de Varville
Clarence Blakiston . . . .   M. Duval

07445
6— THE MERCHANT OF VENICE (1170) (U)
D: Challis Sanderson
S: (PLAY) William Shakespeare
Sybil Thorndike . . . .   Portia
Ivan Berlyn . . . .   Shylock
R. McLeod . . . .   Bassiano

07446
7— ESMERALDA (1100) (A)
D: Edwin J. Collins
S: (NOVEL) Victor Hugo (THE HUNCHBACK
OF NOTRE DAME)
Sybil Thorndike . . . .   Esmeralda
Booth Conway . . . .   Quasimodo
Arthur Kingsley . . . .   Phoebus
Annesley Hely . . . .   Priest

07447
8— THE SCARLET LETTER (1198) (A)
D: Challis Sanderson
S: (NOVEL) Nathaniel Hawthorne
Sybil Thorndike . . . .   Hesther Prynne
Tony Fraser . . . .   Pastor Dimmesdale
Dick Webb . . . .   Roger Chillingworth
Rice Cassidy . . . .   Governor
DRAMAS Condensed versions of stage plays.

07448
DOWN ON THE FARM (2000)
Alldith Films
D: Eric l'Epine Smith
Ivy Siems . . . .   The Girl
Fred Howard . . . .   The Man
Jack Williams . . . .
COMEDY

07449
PERPETUA (6200) (A) USA: LOVE'S
BOOMERANG
Famous Players-Lasky (Par)
D: John S. Robertson, Tom Geraghty
S: (NOVEL) Dion Clayton Calthrop
(PERPETUA MARY)
SC: Josephine Levett, Helen Blizzard
David Powell . . . .   Brian McQueen
Ann Forrest . . . .   Perpetua Mary
Geoffrey Kerr. . . . .   Saville Mender
John Milterne . . . .   Russell Felton
Lionel D'Aragon . . . .   Christian
Frank Stanmore . . . .   Corn Chandler
Roy Byford . . . .   Lomballe
Polly Emery . . . .   Mme Tourtelle
Sara Sample . . . .   Mother
Bunty Fosse . . . .   Perpetua (child)
CRIME France. Man frames daughter for
poisoning rich husband.

07450
THE BOHEMIAN GIRL (7700) (U)
Alliance (Astra) *reissue:* 1924
D: Harley Knoles
S: (PLAY) William Balfe, Alfred Bunn
SC: Harley Knoles, Rosina Henley
Gladys Cooper . . . . Arlene Arnheim
Ivor Novello . . . . Thaddeus
C. Aubrey Smith . . . . Devilshoof
Ellen Terry . . . . Buda
Constance Collier . . . . Queen
Henry Vibart . . . . Count Arnheim
Gibb McLaughlin . . . . Capt Florenstein
ROMANCE Europe. Polish officer posing as gipsy
loves gipsy girl who is really count's daughter.

07451
THE HEAD OF THE FAMILY (5500)(U)
Artistic
P: George Redman
D: Manning Haynes
S: (STORY) W.W. Jacobs
SC: Lydia Hayward
Johnny Butt . . . . Green
Cynthia Murtagh . . . . Betty Foster
Charles Ashton . . . . Robert Letts
Daisy England . . . . Mrs Green
Bertie White . . . . Henry Whidden
Moore Marriott . . . . Mate
COMEDY Widow weds bully and tames him by
having sailor pose as long-lost son.

07452
THE MAN FROM HOME (6700) (A)
Famous Players-Lasky (Par)
D: George Fitzmaurice
S: (PLAY) Booth Tarkington, Harry Leon
Wilson
SC: Ouida Bergere
James Kirkwood . . . . Daniel Forbes Pike
Anna Q. Nillson . . . Genevieve Granger-Simpson
Norman Kerry . . . . Prince Leone Charmante
Dorothy Cumming . . . . Princess Sabina
Geoffrey Kerr . . . . Horace Granger-Simpson
John Milterne . . . . King
Annette Benson . . . . Faustina Riviere
Clifford Grey . . . . Secretary
Jose Rubens . . . . Riviere
Edward Dagnall . . . . Father
CRIME Italy. American heiress's fiance saves
fisherman accused of stabbing wife.

07453
THE GAME OF LIFE (10,000)
G:B. Samuelson *reissue:* 1924
D; G.B. Samuelson
S: G.B. Samuelson, Lauri Wylie
Isobel Elsom . . . . Alice Fletcher
Lilian Hall Davis . . . . Rose Wallingford
Dorothy Minto . . . . Betsy Rudd
Campbell Gullan . . . . Edwin Travers
Tom Reynolds . . . . Jim Cobbles
James Lindsay . . . . Reggie Walker
Allan Aynesworth . . . . John
Hubert Carter . . . . Marcus Benjamin
Windham Guise . . . . Abel Fletcher
Fred Lewis . . . . Richard Wallingford
C. Tilson-Chowne . . . . Richard Travers
Mickey Brantford . . . . Nipper
Mrs Henry Lytton . . . . Queen of Hearts
HISTORY Great events of Victoria's reign seen
through lives of three girls. (First British "ten-
reeler".)

07454
THE WEE MACGREGOR'S SWEETHEART
(5300) (U)
Welsh, Pearson (Jury)

D: SC: George Pearson
S: (STORIES) J.J. Bell (OH CHRISTINA;
COURTING CHRISTINA)
Betty Balfour . . . . Christina
Donald Macardle . . . . Wee MacGregor
Nora Swinburne . . . . Jessie Mary
Cyril Percival . . . . Uncle Baldwin
Minna Grey . . . . Mary Purvis
M.A. Wetherall . . . . John Robertson
Bryan Powley . . . . Uncle Purdie
Mabel Archdale . . . . Aunt Purdie
Lillian Christine . . . . Lizzie
Marie Ault . . . . Miss Todd
Bunty Fosse . . . . Christina (child)
ROMANCE Sctotland. Girl weds sweetheart
despite snobbish aunt.

07455
THE POINTING FINGER (5380) (U)
Stoll
D: George Ridgwell
S: (NOVEL) "Rita"
SC: Paul Rooff
Milton Rosmer . . . . Lord Rollestone/
                               Earl Edensore
Madge Stuart . . . . Lady Susan Silchester
J.R. Tozer . . . . Capt Jasper Mallory
Teddy Arundell . . . . Danny O'Shea
Irene Rooke . . . . Lady Anne Silchester
James English . . . . Earl of Edensore
Norma Whalley . . . . Mrs Ebury
Gibb McLaughlin . . . . The Monk
CRIME Captain kidnaps halfbrother to usurp
earldom.

07456
THE WHEELS OF CHANCE (5312) (U)
Stoll
D: Harold M.Shaw
S: (NOVEL) H.G. Wells
SC: Frank Miller
George K. Arthur . . . . Hoopdriver
Olwen Roose . . . . Jessie Milton
Gordon Parker . . . . Bechamel
Bertie Wright . . . . Briggs
Mabel Archdale . . . . Mrs Milton
Judd Green . . . . Wickens
Wallace Bosco . . . . Dangle
Clifford Marle . . . . Phipps
COMEDY Clerk on bicycle tour saves girl from
eloping with bully.

07457
HALF A TRUTH (4900) (A)
Stoll
D: Sinclair Hill
S: (NOVEL) "Rita"
SC: Leslie Howard Gordon
Margaret Hope . . . . Virginia
Lawford Davidson . . . . Chris Kennaway
Miles Mander . . . . Marquis Sallast
Norma Whalley . . . . Lady Lucille Altamont
Irene Rooke . . . . Octavia Madison
Percy Standing . . . . Sir Richard Madison
Philip Simmons . . . . Barry Connell
Stella Wood-Sims . . . . Doreen Madison
CRIME Blackmailing Lady tries to force
millionaire's daughter to marry crooked accomplice.

07458
MELODY OF DEATH (4771) (A)
Stoll
D: F. Martin Thornton
S: (NOVEL) Edgar Wallace
SC: Leslie Howard Gordon
Philip Anthony . . . . Gilbert Standerton
Enid R. Reed . . . . Enid Cathcart
Dick Sutherd . . . . George Wallis

H. Agar Lyons . . . . Sir John Standerton
Frank E. Petley . . . .
Hetta Bartlett . . . .
Bob Vallis . . . .
CRIME Man steals jewel back from gang and
saves captured wife.

07459
WALTER WINS A WAGER (2000)
British Comedies
D: Tom Seymour, Walter Forde
S: Walter Forde
Walter Forde . . . . Walter
Pauline Peters . . . . Miss Wager
Tubby Phillips . . . . Customer
Tom Seymour . . . .
Billy le Fre . . . .
COMEDY Floorwalker poses as crook to catch
coiners.

07460
WALTER'S TRYING FROLIC (2000)
British Comedies
D: Tom Seymour, Walter Forde
S: Walter Forde
Walter Forde . . . . Walter/Lord Gadabout
Pauline Peters . . . . Lady Victoria
Tubby Phillips . . . .
Tom Seymour . . . .
George Bishop . . . .
P.M. Marshall . . . .
COMEDY Car salesman dreams he is kidnapped
in mistake for his noble double.

07461
WALTER MAKES A MOVIE (2000)
British Comedies
D: Tom Seymour, Walter Forde
S: Walter Forde
Walter Forde . . . . Walter
Pauline Peters . . . . Pauline Highbrow
Tubby Phillips . . . . Farmer
Tom Seymour . . . . Cecil B. Gunns
COMEDY Walter finds actress's lost handbag
and spoils her film.

07462
WALTER WANTS WORK (2000)
British Comedies
D: Tom Syemour, Walter Forde
S: Walter Forde
Walter Forde . . . . Walter
Pauline Peters . . . . Mrs Walter
Tubby Phillips . . . . Employer
COMEDY Walter fails as organ-grinder and ends
up in workhouse.

JUL

07463
NO. 7, BRICK ROW (5500) (U)
Harma-Associated Exhibitors (Walturdaw)
D: Fred W. Durrant
S: (NOVEL) William Riley
Constance Worth . . . . Daisy Knox
Marjorie Villis . . . . Gertie Mellor
James Knight . . . . Dr Jonas Peacock
Bernard Dudley . . . . Bertram Lycester
H. Tyrrell-Davis . . . . Sam Mundy
Marguerita Leigh . . . . Mrs Tickle
George Williams . . . . Caleb Knox
Johnny Butt . . . . Sooty Bill
Sydney Lewis Ransome . . . Sgt Smith
Edith Morley . . . . Maud Annie Tickle
Marie d'Andara . . . . Cissie Tickle
Greta Wood . . . . Louisa
DRAMA Northern toy factory workman
framed by manager, who is thwarted by
forewoman.

07464
A SPORTING DOUBLE (4800) (U)
I.B. Davidson (Granger) *reissue:* 1926
(Butcher; 2 rls)
D: S: Arthur Rooke
John Stuart . . . . Will Blunt
Lillian Douglas . . . . Ethel Grimshaw
Douglas Munro . . . . John Brent
Humberston Wright . . . . . . Henry Maxwell
Terry Cavanagh . . . . Philip Harvey
Myrtle Vibart . . . . Aurora
Frank Gray . . . . Henry Grimshaw
Tom Coventry . . . . Bargee
SPORT Man wins Derby bet despite rival
framing him for theft.

07465
BROWN SUGAR (5600) (U)
British Super (Jury)
P: G.B. Samuelson
D: Fred Paul
S: (PLAY) Lady Arthur Lever
SC: Walter Summers
Owen Nares . . . . Lord Sloane
Lilian Hall-Davis . . . . Stella Deering
Eric Lewis . . . . .Earl of Knightsbridge
Henrietta Watson . . . .Countess of Knightsbridge
Margaret Halston . . . . Honoria Nesbitt
Cyril Dane . . . . Edmundson
Eric Leighton . . . . .Crowbie Carruthers
Gladys Harvey . . . . .Mrs Cunningham
Louise Hampton . . . . . . .Miss Gibson
ROMANCE Lord weds actress and she takes
blame for gambling brother.

07466
THE LILAC SUNBONNET (5180) (U)
Progress (Butcher)
P: Frank Spring
D: SC: Sidney Morgan
S: (NOVEL) S.R. Crockett
Joan Morgan . . . . .Winsome Charteris
Warwick Ward . . . . Ralph Peden
Pauline Peters . . . . Jess Kissock
Arthur Lennard . . . . Rev Allen Walsh
Lewis Dayton . . . . Capt Greatorix
Forrester Harvey . . . . Jock Gordon
Charles Levey . . . . Walter
A. Harding Steerman . . . . Rev Gilbert Peden
Nell Emerald . . . . Meg Kissock
ROMANCE Scotland. Girl wins cleric's
approval by revealing she is daughter by
runaway marriage.

07467
A SAILOR TRAMP (5593) (U)
Welsh-Pearson (Jury)
P: George Pearson
D: F. Martin Thornton
S: (NOVEL) Bart Kennedy
SC: Eliot Stannard
Victor McLaglan . . . . The Sailor Tramp
Pauline Johnson . . . . The Girl
Hugh E. Wright . . . . The Cockney
Bertie Wright . . . . The Proprietor
Ambrose Manning . . . . The Father
Kate Gurney . . . . The Mother
Harry J. Worth . . . . The Foreman
Mrs Hubert Willis . . . . . . The Aunt
ADVENTURE Robbed sailor turns tramp and
saves farmer's ship from burning.

07468
A SOUL'S AWAKENING (5993) (A)
Gaumont-Westminster
D: W.P. Kellino
S: Frank Fowell
David Hawthorne . . . . Ben Rackstraw
Flora le Breton . . . . Maggie Rackstraw
Ethel Oliver . . . . Sal Lee

Maurice Thompson . . . . Jim Rackstraw
Sylvia Caine . . . . Cynthia Dare
Tom Morriss . . . . Mike Nolan
Philip Desborough . . . . Cecil Wayne
DRAMA Rich girl pays dog thief £2 a week not
to illtreat daughter.

07469
THE TRUANTS (5550) (A)
Stoll
D: Sinclair Hill
S: (NOVEL) A.E. Mason
SC: Kinchen Wood
Joan Morgan . . . . Millie Stretton
Philip Simmonds . . . . Tony Stretton
Lawford Davidson . . . . . . Lionel Callam
Robert English . . . . John Mudge
George Bellamy . . . . Sir John Stretton
Lewis Gilbert . . . . Capt Tavernay
DRAMA Knight's son deserts Foreign Legion to
save wife from cad.

07470
FOX FARM (5850) (U)
George Clark (Stoll)
D: SC: Guy Newall
S: (NOVEL) Warwick Deeping
Guy Newall . . . . James Falconer
Ivy Duke . . . . Ann Wetherall
A. Bromley Davenport . . . . Sam Wetherall
Barbara Everest . . . . Kate Falconer
Cameron Carr . . . . Jack Rickaby
Charles Evemy . . . . Slim Wetherall
John Alexander . . . . Jacob Boase
ROMANCE Gipsy loves married farmer who is
blinded blowing up tree.

07471
THE WHITE RAT (1300) (A)
Quality Plays (Walturdaw)
D: George A. Cooper
S: (STORY) K.R.G. Browne
Sydney N. Folker . . . . Dick Barrington
Ernest A. Douglas . . . . Forsyth
Adeline Hayden-Coffin . . . Mrs Barrington
CRIME Usurer's pet rat brings killer to justice.

07472
A QUESTION OF PRINCIPLE (1987) (U)
Quality Plays (Walturdaw)
D: George A. Cooper
S: (STORY) Mayell Bannister
Sydney N. Folker . . . . Jim Cunninghame
Joan McLean . . . . Geraldine
Frank Stanmore . . . . Carman
COMEDY Newlyweds have trouble with gift of
grandfather clock.

07473
FALLEN LEAVES (1360) (U)
Quality Plays (Walturdaw)
D: George A. Cooper
S: (STORY) Will Scott
Chris Walker . . . . The Derelict
May Price . . . . Mrs Brown
Jeff Barlow . . . . Atkinson
John M. East . . . . P.C. Merridew
PATHOS Tramp comforts dying woman by
posing as her lost son.

07474
THE THIEF (1355) (U)
Quality Plays (Walturdaw)
D: George A. Cooper
S: (STORY) F.K. Junior
Malcolm Tod . . . . The Thief
Mildred Evelyn . . . . The Girl
Harry J. Worth . . . . PC Merridew
COMEDY Man's tale of robbery and murder is
elopement plot.

07475
GERALDINE'S FIRST YEAR (1365 (U)
Quality Plays (Walturdaw)
D: George A. Cooper
S: (STORY) Mayell Bannister
Sydney N. Folker . . . . Jim Cunninghame
Joan McLean . . . . Geraldine
Mrs L. March . . . . Mrs Venable
Betty Farquhar . . . . The Maid
COMEDY Busybody patches quarrel between
newlyweds.

07476
THE BIG STRONG MAN (1707) (U)
Quality Plays (Walturdaw)
D: George A. Cooper
S: (STORY) Christine Castle
George Turner . . . . George Herrick
Wyn Richmond . . . . Marrielle Herrick
Frank Stanmore . . . . Mr Thompson
COMEDY Plumber poses as artist to force fee
from publisher.

07477
TENSE MOMENTS FROM OPERA (series)
Master (Gaumont)
P: H.B. Parkinson
SC: Frank Miller

07478
1: MARTHA (1184) (A)
D: George Wynn
S: (OPERA) Friedrich Flotow
Dorothy Fane . . . . Lady Henrietta
Leslie Austin . . . . Lionel
James Knight . . . . Plunket

07479
2: RIGOLETTO (1124) (A)
D: George Wynn
S: (OPERA) Giuseppe Verdi
Wyn Richmond . . . . Gilda
Clive Brook . . . . Duke of Mantua
A.B. Imeson . . . . Rigoletto

07480
3: THE BRIDE OF LAMMERMOOR (779) (A)
D: Challis Sanderson
S: (OPERA) Gaetano Donizetti
Vivian Gibson . . . . Lucy Ashton
Gordon Hopkirk . . . . Edgar
Olaf Hytten . . . . Lord Bucklaw

07481
4: IL TROVATORE (842) (A)
D: Edwin J. Collins
S: (OPERA) Giuseppe Verdi
Bertram Burleigh . . . . Manrico
Lillian Douglas . . . . Countess Leonora
Cyril Dane . . . . Count di Luna
Ada Grier . . . . Azucena

07482
5: SAMSON AND DELILAH (1100) (A)
D: Edwin J. Collins
S: (OPERA) Charles Saint-Saens
Valia . . . . Delilah
M.D. Waxman . . . . Samson

07483
6: MARITANA (1183) (U)
D: George Wynn
S: (OPERA) W.V.Wallace
Vivian Gibson . . . . Maritana
Wallace Bosco . . . . King Charles
Gordon Hopkirk . . . . Don Cesar de Bazan

07484
7: THE LILY OF KILLARNEY (1067) (U)
D: Challis Sanderson
S: (OPERA) Charles Benedict

Betty Farquhar . . . . Eily O'Connor
Bertram Burleigh . . . . Hardress Creegan
Booth Conway . . . . Myles na Coppaleen
Miriam Merry . . . . Ann Chute
Alec Hunter . . . . Tom

07485
8: LA TRAVIATA (1274) (A)
D: Challis Sanderson
S: (OPERA) Giuseppe Verdi
Thelma Murray . . . . Violetta
Clive Brook . . . . Alfred Germont

07486
9: CARMEN (1061) (A)
D: George Wynn
S: (OPERA) Georges Bizet
Patricia Fitzgerald . . . . Carmen
Ward McAllister . . . . Don Jose
Maresco Maresini . . . . Escamillo

07487
10: FAUST (1152) (A)
D: Challis Sanderson
S: (OPERA) Charles Gounod
Dick Webb . . . . Faust
Sylvia Caine . . . . Marguerite
Lawford Davidson . . . . Mephistopheles
Gordon Hopkirk . . . . Valentine
Minnie Rayner . . . . Martha

07488
11: FRA DIAVOLO (1294) (U)
D: Challis Sanderson
S: (OPERA) Daniel Auber
Vivian Gibson . . . . Zerlina
Gordon Hopkirk . . . . Fra Diavolo
Lionelle Howard . . . . Lorenzo
Amy Willard . . . . Mrs Allcash

07489
12: DON JUAN (1000) (A)
D: Edwin J. Collins
S: (OPERA) Wolfgang Mozart
Pauline Peters . . . . Zerlina
J.R. Tozer . . . . Don Juan
Lillian Douglas . . . . Anna Pedro
Kathleen Vaughan . . . . Donna Elvira
DRAMAS Condensations of operas.

AUG
07490
FAMOUS POEMS BY GEORGE R. SIMS
("DAGONET") (series)
Master (W&F)
P: H.B. Parkinson
S: (POEMS) George R. Sims
SC: Frank Miller

07491
1—BILLIE'S ROSE (950) (A)
D: Challis Sanderson

07492
2—TICKET O' LEAVE (1104) (A)
D: Edwin J. Collins
Betty Doyle . . . . Eve
Ward McAllister . . . .
James Knight . . . .

07493
3— THE OLD ACTOR'S STORY (1000) (A)
D: H.B. Parkinson
Stella Muir . . . . Nell
James Knight . . . . The Actor
Booth Conway . . . . The Captain

07494
4— FALLEN BY THE WAY (1210) (U)
D: Challis Sanderson

Judd Green . . . .
Jeff Barlow . . . .
Kitty Van Loo . . . .

07495
5— SIR RUPERT'S WIFE (1000) (U)
D: Challis Sanderson
Clive Brook . . . . Sir Rupert Leigh
Maria Minetti . . . . Polly
Olaf Hytten . . . . Julian

07496
6— THE LIGHTS O' LONDON (1000) (U)
D: Edwin J. Collins
Florence Turner . . . .
James Knight . . . .
Stella Muir . . . .
William Freshman . . . .
Micky Brantford . . . .

07497
7— THE STREET TUMBLERS (1000) (U)
D: George Wynn
Florence Turner . . . . Gypsy
Tom Morriss . . . . Busker

07498
8— THE MAGIC WAND (1000) (U)
D: George Wynn
Stella Muir . . . .
Joan Whalley . . . .

07499— IN THE SIGNAL BOX (1065) (U)
D: H.B. Parkinson
George Wynn . . . . Father
Thelma Murray . . . . Mother
Baby Rayner . . . . Child

07500
10— THE ROAD TO HEAVEN (1000) (U)
D: Challis Sanderson
Micky Brantford . . . . Cripple
Ida Fane . . . .
Miriam Merry . . . .

07501
11— THE PARSON'S FIGHT (1000) (U)
D: Edwin J. Collins
Clive Brook . . . . Parson
Lillian Douglas . . . . Rector's Daughter
Ward McAllister . . . .
Ida Fane . . . . Spinster

07502
12— SAL GROGAN'S FACE (975) (A)
D: Edwin J. Collins
Ward McAllister . . . . The Man
Margaret Dean . . . . The Woman
Micky Brantford . . . . The Boy
Tom Morriss . . . .
DRAMAS Stories based on narrative poems.

07503
CREATION (5000)
Raleigh King
D: Humberston Wright
S: (NOVEL) May Edington THE MAN WHO
DARED)
Dorothy Fane . . . . Zena Hammond
Frank Dane . . . . Faux Evermore
Sir Simeon Stuart . . . . Dr Ganally
Thelma Murray . . . .
William Freshman . . . .
Kate Gurney . . . .
Raleigh King . . . .
Beryl Norton . . . .
DRAMA Man poses as reincarnation of
woman's drowned husband.

07504
SPANISH JADE (6700) (U)
Famous Players-Lasky (Par)
D: John S. Robertson, Tom Geraghty
S: (PLAY) Louis Joseph Vance
SC: Josephine Lovett
David Powell . . . . Perez
Evelyn Brent . . . . Manuela
Marc McDermott . . . . Grandee
Charles de Rochefort . . . . . Estban
Harry Ham . . . . Manvers
Frank Stanmore . . . . Donkins
Lionel d'Aragon . . . . Stepfather
Roy Byford . . . . Spy
CRIME Spain. When girl's lover kills her
husband she offers herself to father-in-law in
exchange for his freedom.

07505
A GIPSY CAVALIER (6752) (U)
International Artists (Gaumont)
P: D: J. Stuart Blackton
S: (NOVEL) John Overton (MY LADY APRIL)
Georges Carpentier . . . . . . Valerius Carew
Flora le Breton . . . . Dorothy Forrest
Rex McDougall . . . . Ralph Carew
Mary Clare . . . . Janet
Hubert Carter . . . . Bartholomew Grig
William Luff . . . . Beydach
Sir Simeon Stuart . . . . Sir Julian Carew
W.D.C. Knox . . . . Sir George Forrest
Norma Whalley . . . . Lady Forrest
Percy Standing . . . . Stirrett
Tom Coventry . . . . Ballard
Charles Blackton . . . . Valerius (child)
ADVENTURE Period. Fop posing as gipsy
boxer saves girl when gipsy king floods valley.

07506
A BILL FOR DIVORCEMENT (6109) (A)
Ideal
D: SC: Denison Clift
S: (PLAY) Clemence Dane
Constance Binney . . . . Sidney Fairfield
Fay Compton . . . . Margaret Fairfield
Malcolm Keen . . . . Hilary Fairfield
Henry Victor . . . . Grey Meredith
Henry Vibart . . . . Dr Aliot
Martin Walker . . . . Kit Pumphrey
Fewlass Llewellyn .Rev Christopher Pumphrey
Dora Gregory . . . . Hester Fairfield
Sylvia Young . . . . Bassett
DRAMA Girl renounces love to care for
insane father so that mother may marry again.

07507
TIT FOR TAT (5100) (U)
Hepworth
D: SC: Henry Edwards
S: Jessie Robertson
Henry Edwards . . . . Roger
Chrissie White . . . . Peggy Smith
Eileen Dennes . . . . Clove
Gwynne Herbert . . . . Auntie
Christine Rayner . . . . Muriel
Annie Esmond . . . . Mrs Speedwell
Mary Brough . . . . Gladys Slattery
COMEDY Girl posing as old housekeeper acts
as her own daughter to win employer's love.

07508
WAS SHE GUILTY ? (4891) (A)
Granger-Binger
D: George Andre Beranger
S: Maurits Binger
Gertrude McCoy . . . . Ruth Hewood
Zoe Palmer . . . . Mary
Lewis Willoughby . . . . George Midhurst

William Freshman . . . . Bobby
Kitty Kluppul . . . . Palmira Hurst
Paul de Groot . . . . John Hewood
Norman Doxat-Pratt . . . . . . Bobby (child)
CRIME Woman adopts her own bastard and
poison lover, letting husband take blame.

07509
THE FAITHFUL HEART (5600) (U)
British Super (Jury)
P: G.B. Samuelson
D: Fred Paul
S: (PLAY) Monckton Hoffe
SC: Walter Summers
Owen Nares . . . . Waverley Ango
Lilian Hall Davis . . . . Blackie Anderway
Cathleen Nesbitt . . . . Diana Oughterson
A.B. Imeson . . . . Maj Lestrade
Euth Maitland . . . . Mrs Gattiscombe
Cyril Raymond . . . . Albert Oughterson
Victor Tandy . . . . Sgt Brabazon
Charles Thursby . . . . Capt Ralkjam
Lois Heatherley . . . . Ginger
ROMANCE Naval capt returns and jilts
socialite to take care of his bastard daughter.

07510
SON OF KISSING CUP (5600) (U)
Walter West Productions (Butcher) reissue:
1926 (2 rls)
D: Walter West
S: Campbell Rae Brown
SC: J. Bertram Brown
Violet Hopson . . . . Gladys
Stewart Rome . . . . Sir Kenneth Stirling
Cameron Carr . . . . Norman Brady
Arthur Walcott . . . . Richard Marney
Lewis Gilbert . . . . Sir Bennett Grote
Adeline Hayden Coffin. . . . Mrs Sheldridge
Judd Green . . . . Joe Clarke
Bob Vallis . . . . Ezra Gilmer
SPORT Bookmaker bribes sick racehorse owner
to conceal impending death.

07511
MAN AND HIS KINGDOM (5438) (U)
Stoll
D: Maurice Elvey
S: (NOVEL) A.E.W. Mason
SC: Kinchen Wood
Valia . . . . Lucia Rimarez
Harvey Braban . . . . Sagasta
Bertram Burleigh . . . . Eugene Rimarez
Lewis Gilbert . . . . President Rimarez
Gladys Jennings . . . . .Terhissa Dennison
M.A. Wetherell . . . . Gregory Dene
ADVENTURE South America. Wife of
president's son loves leader of revolution.

SEP

07512
THE EXPERIMENT (4900) (U)
Stoll
D: Sinclair Hill
S: (NOVEL) Ethel M. Dell
SC: William J. Elliott
Evelyn Brent . . . . Doris Fielding
Clive Brook . . . . Vivian Caryll
Templar Powell . . . . Maj Maurice Brandon
Norma Whalley . . . . Mrs Lockyard
C.H. Croker-King . . . . Philip Abingdon
Hilda Sims . . . . Vera Abingdon
Cecil Kerr . . . . Fricker
Laura Walker . . . . Nurse
ROMANCE Rich girl's fiance poses as
chauffeur to stop her eloping with major.

07513
FIRES OF INNOCENCE (4700) (U)
Progress (Butcher)

P: Frank E. Spring
D: SC: Sidney Morgan
S: (NOVEL) George Stevenson (A LITTLE
WORLD APART)
Joan Morgan . . . . Helen Dalmaine
Bobbie Andrews . . . . Arthur Dalmaine
Arthur Lennard . . . . Rev Dalmaine
Marie Illington . . . . Lady Crane
Madge Tree . . . . Bella Blackburn
Nell Emerald . . . . Lydia Blackburn
CRIME Village vicar's disowned son steals
brooch and blames sister.

07514
A ROGUE IN LOVE (5590) (U)
Diamond Super (Globe)
D: Albert Brouett
S: (NOVEL) Tom Gallon
SC: Harry Hughes
Frank Stanmore . . . . Frank Badgery
Ann Trevor . . . . Pattie Keable
Gregory Scott . . . . Joe Bradwick
Fred Rains . . . . Joseph Keable
Lawford Davidson . . . . . . Ray Carrell
Betty Farquhar . . . . Eudocia
Kate Gurney . . . . Landlady
'DRAMA Ex-convict cannot bring himself to
tell friend that the legacy is non-existent.

07515
REPENTANCE (5654) (A)
B &Z (Renters)
P: Geoffrey Benstead
D: S: Edward R. Gordon
Peggy Hathaway . . . . Queenie Creedon
Roy Raymond . . . . Frank Hepburn
Geoffrey Benstead . . . . . . Toby
Ward McAllister . . . .
Ray Lankester . . . . Dr Smith
Fabbie Benstead . . . .
CRIME Escaped convict blackmails daughter
and on death reveals her titled lover is her
adopted brother.

07516
DICK TURPIN'S RIDE TO YORK (7660) (U)
Stoll
D: Maurice Elvey
S: (NOVEL) Harrison Ainsworth (ROOKWOOD)
SC: Leslie Howard Gordon
Matheson Lang . . . . Dick Turpin
Isobel Elsom . . . . Esther Bevis
Cecil Humphreys . . . . Litton Glover
Norman Page . . . . Ferret Bevis
Lewis Gilbert . . . . Tom King
Lily Iris . . . . Sally Dutton
Tony Fraser . . . . Bow Street Runner
Malcolm Tod . . . . Sir Charles Weston
Mme d'Esterre . . . . Lady Weston
James English . . . . Godfather
Somers Bellamy . . . . Major Domo
ADVENTURE 1739. Highwayman rides to
York to stop lady marrying usurper.

07517
A LOST LEADER (5800) (U)
Stoll
D: George Ridgwell
S: (NOVEL) E. Phillips Oppenheim
SC: William J. Elliott
Robert English . . . . Lawrence Mannering
Dorothy Fane . . . . Duchess Berenice
Lily Iris . . . . Blanche Fillimore
Lionel D'Aragon . . . . Sir Leslie Borrowden
George Bellamy . . . . John Fardell
Teddy Arundell . . . . Henry Rochester
Cecil Ward . . . . Lord Redford
CRIME Labour MP kills man in fight and
blackmailer forces him to retire.

07518
DOWN UNDER DONOVAN (5900) (U)
Stoll
D: Harry Lambart
S: (NOVEL) Edgar Wallace
SC: Forbes Dawson
Cora Goffin . . . . Mary President
W.H. Benham . . . . Eric Stanton
Bertram Parnell . . . . Milton Sands
William Lugg. . . . . John President
W.H. Willitts . . . . Ivan Soltikoff
Cecil Rutledge . . . . John Partridge
Peggy Surtees . . . . Mrs Bud Kitson
John Monkhouse . . . . . . .Sir George Frodmere
CRIME Ex-crook's horse wins despite crooked
rival and regains formula for malleable glass
from Russian

07519
RUNNING WATER (6075) (U)
Stoll
D: Maurice Elvey
S: (NOVEL) A.E.W. Mason
SC: Kinchen Wood
Madge Stuart . . . . Sylvia Skinner
Lawford Davidson . . . . . . .Capt Hilary Cheyne
Julian Royce . . . . Garrett Skinner
A. Bromley Davenport . . . . Capt Barstow
Irene Rooke .. . . Mrs Thesiger
George Turner . . . . Wallie Hine
E. Lewis Waller . . . . Archie Parminter
George Harrington . . . . . . Michel
CRIME Switzerland. Girl stops gambling
father from killing partner for insurance.

07520
TELL YOUR CHILDREN (5532) (A)
International Artists (Gaumont)
P: Martin Sabine
D: Donald Crisp
S: (NOVEL) Rachel McNamara (LARK'S GATE)
SC: Leslie Howard Gordon
Doris Eaton . . . . Rosny Edwards
Walter Tennyson . . . . John Haslar
Margaret Halstan . . . . Lady Sybil Edwards
Gertrude McCoy . . . . Maudie
Warwick Ward . . . . Lord Belhurst
Mary Rorke . . . . Susan Haslar
Cecil Morton York . . . . . . Reuben Haslar
Adeline Hayden Coffin . . . Nanny Dyson
A. Harding Steerman . . . . . Vicar
ROMANCE Lady stops daughter from eloping
with farmer, takes away baby, and makes her
marry lord.

07521
THE SKIPPER'S WOOING (5200) (A)
Artistic
P: George Redman
D: Manning Haynes
S: (NOVEL) W.W. Jacobs
SC: Lydia Hayward
Gordon Hopkirk . . . . The Skipper
Cynthia Murtagh . . . . Annie Getting
Johnny Butt . . . . Sam
Thomas Marriott . . . . Dick
Bobbie Rudd . . . . The Child
Jeff Barlow . . . . Mr Dunn
COMEDY Schoolmistress sets rival lovers to
find father who is hiding in belief that he is
murderer.

07522
THE SPORTING INSTINCT (5200) (U)
I.B. Davidson (Granger)
D: S: Arthur Rooke
SC: Kinchen Wood
Lilian Douglas . . . . June Crisp
J.R. Tozer . . . . Jerry West
Mickey Brantford . . . . Tony

Tom Coventry . . . . The Burglar
Betty Chapman . . . . His Wife
Somers Bellamy . . . . The Colonel
Howard Symons . . . .
Billy Vernon . . . .
Hetty Chapman . . . .
Vivian Gosnell . . . .
DRAMA Girl jilts man with war-weakened heart but weds him when he gives blood to crook's crippled son.

07523
IF FOUR WALLS TOLD (6050) (U)
British Super (Jury)
P: G.B. Samuelson
D: Fred Paul
S: (PLAY) Edward Percy
SC: Walter Summers
Lilian Hall Davis . . . . Martha Tregoning
Fred Paul . . . . Jan Rysling/Tom
Campbell Gullan . . . . David Rysling
John Stuart . . . . Ned Mason
Minna Grey . . . . Elizabeth Rysling
Enid King . . . . Clare Sturgis
Pollie Emery . . . . Mrs Sturgis
Somers Bellamy . . . . Toby Crouch
Marie Ault . . . .
DRAMA Cornwall. Man adopts brother's bastard who inherits when body is washed ashore with will.

07524
SQUIBS WINS THE CALCUTTA SWEEP (5250) (U)
Welsh-Pearson (Jury) *reissue:* 1930 (JMG)
D:S: George Pearson
Betty Balfour . . . . Squibs Hopkins
Fred Groves . . . . PC Charlie Lee
Hugh E. Wright . . . . Sam Hopkins
Bertram Burleigh . . . . . . The Weasel
Annette Benson . . . . Ivy Hopkins
Mary Brough . . . . Mrs Lee
Hal Martin . . . . Detective Reeve
Donald Searle . . . . Reporter
Tom Morriss . . . . Bob
Sam Lewis . . . . Nosey
CRIME Flower girl wins £60,000 and takes family to Paris to save sister from murderous husband.

07525
ROB ROY (6100) (U)
Gaumont-Westminster
D: W.P. Kellino
S: Alicia Ramsey
David Hawthorne . . . . . . Rob Roy MacGregor
Gladys Jennings . . . . Helen Campbell
Sir Simeon Stuart . . . . . . .Duke of Montrose
Wallace Bosco . . . . James Grahame
Alec Hunter . . . . The Dougal Creatur
Eva Llewellyn . . . . Mother MacGregor
Tom Morriss . . . . Sandy the Biter
Roy Kellino . . . . Ronald MacGregor
ADVENTURE Scotland, 1712. Clan chief's revenge on jealous duke who outlawed him.

07526
PIMPLE'S THREE MUSKETEERS (2000)
Fred Evans (Shadow Plays)
D: S: Fred Evans, Joe Evans
Fred Evans . . . . Pimple
COMEDY Burlesque of "The Three Musketeers."

07527
THE DODDINGTON DIAMONDS (2000)
Screen Plays
P: Percy Nash
D: Jack Denton

S: (CHARACTER) Harry Blyth
Douglas Payne . . . . Sexton Blake
George Bellamy . . ..
Mildred Evelyn . . . .
Jeff Barlow . . . .
Cecil Burke . . . .
CRIME

07528
THE CRIMSON CIRCLE (5378) (A)
Kinema Club (Granger)
D: George Ridgwell
S: (NOVEL) Edgar Wallace
SC: Patrick L. Mannock
Madge Stuart . . . . Thalia Drummond
Rex Davis . . . . Jack Beardmore
Fred Groves . . . . Insp Parr
Clifton Boyne . . . . Derrick Yale
Eva Moore . . . . Aunt Prudence
Robert English . . . . Felix Marl
Lawford Davidson . . . . Raphael Willings
Sydney Paxton . . . . Harvey Froyant
Norma Walley . . . . Kitty Froyant
Harry J. Worth . . . .
Bertram Burleigh . . . .
Mary Odette . . . .
Joan Morgan . . . .
Henry Victor . . . .
Olaf Hytten . . . .
Victor McLaglen . . . .
George Dewhurst . . . .
Jack Hobbs . . . .
Henry Vibart . . . .
Kathleen Vaughan . . . .
Flora le Breton . . . .
Eille Norwood . . . .
Malcolm Tod . . . .
Sir Simeon Stuart . . . .
CRIME Inspector unmasks private detective as leader of blackmail gang.

OCT

07529
THE WHITE HOPE (6300) (U)
Walter West (Butcher) *reissue:* 1926 (2 rls)
D: Frank Wilson
S: (NOVEL) W.H. Trowbridge
Violet Hopson . . . . Claudia Carisbrooke
Stewart Rome . . . . Jack Delane
Frank Wilson . . . . Joe Shannon
John McAndrews . . . . Daddy Royce
Kid Gordon . . . . Sam Crowfoot
SPORT Heavyweight wins title after squire's daughter renounces duke.

07530
THE AFFECTED DETECTIVE (2000)
Revue
D: Bert Haldane
S: Susan Schofield
Cecil Mannering . . . . Detective
COMEDY Detective takes cocaine and dreams he is in Orient.

07531
AUNTIE'S WEDDING PRESENT (2000)
Revue
D: Bert Haldane
S: Susan Schofield
Louie Freear . . . . Auntie
Jeffrey Saville . . . . Husband
Betty Farquhar . . . . Wife
COMEDY Newlyweds try to drown rich aunt's black cat.

07532
ELIZA'S ROMEO (2000)
Revue
D: Bert Haldane

S: Susan Schofield
Louie Freear . . . . Eliza
Jeffrey Saville . . . . Playwright
Betty Farquhar . . . . Girl
COMEDY Playwright arrested for burglary when sweetheart tries to finance play.

07533
THE FIELD OF HONOUR (5000)
British Producers
P: John Bowman
D: Percy Moran
S: Felix Joubert
Felix Joubert . . . . Jacques de Labain
Percy Moran . . . . Thomas Que
HISTORY Bruges, 1445.Man recalls historic duel between Burgundian and English knight.

07534
RAINBOW COMEDIES (series)
Bertram Phillips-Harma
D: Bernard Dudley
S: (CARTOON) H. O'Neill (THE TWO PICKLES)
Georgie Brassard . . . . Peter
Myrtle Peters . . . . Pauline
Queenie Thomas . . . . Mother
James Knight . . . . Father
Gladys Hamer . . . . Mary
Fatty Phillips . . . . Uncle Marmaduke
Ida Fane . . . . Aunt Polly

07535
1 — THE SWEEP (990)

07536
2 — SPRING CLEANING (925)

07537
3 — PLAYING AT DOCTORS (850)

07538
4 — CUTTING OUT PICTURES (850)

07539
5 — PAPER HANGING (825)

07540
6 — MAKING PAPER MONEY (845)

07541
7 — PETER THE BARBER (775)

07542
8 — MAKING GOOD RESOLUTIONS (705)

07543
9 — BOY SCOUTS (875)

07544
10 — THE CONJURORS (650)

07545
11 — FOOTBALL FUN (810)

07546
12 — SOLD AND HEALED (875)
COMEDIES Misadventures of mischievous children.

07547
THE ROMANCE OF BRITISH HISTORY (series)
B & C (Incorporated)
P: Edward Godal
S: Eliot Stannard

07548
1 — MARY QUEEN OF SCOTS (1000)
D: Edwin Greenwood
Cathleen Nesbitt . . . . Queen Mary
Reginald Bach . . . .

07549
2—AN AFFAIR OF HONOUR (1000)
D: Edwin Greenwood
Gerald Lawrence . . . .
Sylvia Caine . . . .

07550
3— THE FLIGHT OF THE KING (2000)
D: George Ridgwell
Dennis Neilson-Terry . . . . .   Charles II
Cynthia Murtagh . . . .
Gordon Hopkirk . . . .
Kate Gurney . . . .
Sylvia Caine . . . .

07551
4 — THE GREAT TERROR (2160) (U)
D: George Ridgwell
Malvina Longfellow . . . . . . Theresa Cabarous
Murray Graham . . . .
Muriel Somerset . . . .

07552
5 — THE LAST CRUSADE (1000)
D: George Ridgwell
Malvina Longfellow. . . . . . Queen
Reginald Fox . . . . Edward I
Cynthia Murtagh . . . . Eleanor de Montfort
Charles Ashton . . . .
Gordon Hopkirk . . . .

07553
6 — THE THREEFOLD TRAGEDY (2340) (U)
D: Edwin Greenwood
Lauderdale Maitland . . . . . Henry VIII
Janet Alexander . . . .
Edith Morley . . . .··
Sylvia Caine . . . .

07554
7 — THE UNWANTED BRIDE (1172) (U)
D: Edwin Greenwood
Lauderdale Maitland . . . . . . Henry VIII
Margaret Yarde . . . . Anne of Cleves

07555
8 — THE QUEEN'S SECRET (2000)
D: Edwin Greenwood
Lauderdale Maitland . . . . . Henry VIII
Thelma Murray . . . .
Gordon Hopkirk . . . .

07556
9 — A STORY OF NELL GWYNNE (1100) (U)
D: George Ridgwell
Dennis Neilson-Terry . . . . . Charles II
Sylvia Caine . . . . Nell Gwynne
Fred Rains . . . .

07557
10 — THE LAST KING OF WALES (1960) (U)
D: George Ridgwell
Malvina Longfellow . . . . . . Queen Eleanor
Cynthia Murtagh . . . .
Charles Ashton . . . . Llewellyn

07558
11 — SEADOGS OF GOOD QUEEN BESS (1000)
D: Edwin Greenwood
Gregory Scott . . . . Francis Drake

07559
12 —THE STORY OF AMY ROBSART (2000)
D: George Ridgwell
Edith Morley . . . . Amy Robsart
Gregory Scott . . . .
Gordon Hopkirk . . . .
Harry J. Worth . . . .
HISTORY Dramatised episodes from British history.

07560
EXPIATION (6246) (A)
Stoll
D: SC: Sinclair Hill
S: (NOVEL) E. Phillips Oppenheim
Ivy Close . . . . Eva Mornington
Fred Raynham . . . . Cecil Braithwaite
Lionelle Howard . . . . Godfrey Mornington
Malcolm Tod . . . . Lord Dereham
Fred Rains . . . . Mr Woodruffe
Marcelle Truffy . . . . Maud Langton
Daisy Campbell . . . . Mrs Langton
CRIME Estate claimant cleared of murder but found to be imposter.

07561
THE ELEVENTH HOUR (5248) (U)
Stoll
D: George Ridgwell
S: (NOVEL) Ethel M. Dell
SC: Leslie Howard Gordon
Madge White . . . ., Doris Elliott
Dennis Wyndham . . . . Jeff Ironside
Philip Simmons . . . . Hugh Chesyl
M. Gray Murray . . . . ., . . . Col Elliott
Beatrice Chester . . . . Mrs Elliott
ROMANCE Colonel's daughter marries farmer in name only, but returns to him when her lover threatens suicide.

07562
THE ADVENTURES OF CAPTAIN KETTLE (5500) (U)
Captain Kettle Films
P: Austin Leigh
D: Meyrick Milton
S: (NOVEL) C.J. Cutcliffe-Hyne
Charles Kettle . . . . Captain Charles Kettle
Nina Grudgeon . . . . Pacquita
Austin Leigh . . . . Gen Salveston
E.L. Frewen. . . . . Martin Cranforth
ADVENTURE South America. Gunrunner is crowned king and saved from revolution by native girl.

07563
THE CALL OF THE EAST (5000)
International Artists (Curry) reissue: 1927,
HIS SUPREME SACRIFICE (UK)
P: D: SC: Bert Wynne
S: (NOVEL) Esther Whitehouse
Doris Eaton . . . . Mrs Burleigh
Warwick Ward . . . . Arthur Burleigh
Walter Tennyson . . . . Jack Verity
Dorinea Shirley . . . .
Francis Innys . . . . . ., ...
ADVENTURE Egypt. Man fails to shoot faithless wife and walks into sandstorm.

07564
A SISTER TO ASSIST 'ER (5200)
Baron Films (Gau)
P: John L. Baron
D: SC: George Dewhurst
S: (PLAY) John le Breton
Mary Brough . . . . Mrs Millie May
Pollie Emery . . . . Mrs McMull
Muriel Aked . . . . Mrs Crawley
Cecil Morton York . . . .
John McAndrews . . . .
Billy Baron . . . .
COMEDY Poor woman poses as own rich twin to fool mean landlady.

07565
FATTY'S OVERTIME (2000)
Evans-Phillips Productions
D: Edward D. Roberts
S: Muriel Alleyne, Christabel Lowndes-Yates
Kimber Phillips . . . . Fatty
COMEDY

07566
HIMS ANCIENT AND MODERN (2000)
Evans-Phillips Productions
D: Edward D. Roberts
S: Muriel Alleyne, Christabel Lowndes-Yates
Bertie Wright . . . .
Athalie Davis . . . .
Donald Searle . . . .
Sydney Paxton . . . .
William Freshman . . . .
COMEDY

07567
GIPSY BLOOD
Daisy Productions-Mascot
P:S: Daisy Agnew
D: Bert Haldane
Daisy Agnew . . . .
James Donatus . . . .   Paolo
Florence Ingram . . . .
DRAMA

NOV

07568
A MAID OF THE SILVER SEA (5000)(U)
George Clark Productions (Stoll)
D:SC: Guy Newall
S: (NOVEL) John Oxenham
Ivy Duke . . . . Nance Hamon
Guy Newall . . . . Stephen Gard
A. Bromley Davenport . . . . Old Tom Hamon
Cameron Carr . . . . Tom Hamon
Lilian Cavanagh . . . . Julie
Charles Evemy . . . . Berne Hamon
Winifred Sadler . . . . Mrs Hamon
Percy Morrish . . . . Peter Mauger
Marie Gerald . . . . Grannie
Charles Wood . . . . Seneschal
Norman Loring . . . . Doctor
CRIME Cornishman working in silver mine on French island is framed for killing girl's father and brother.

07569
PAGES OF LIFE (5300) (U)
Adelqui Millar Productions (Butcher)
D: S: Adelqui Migliar
Evelyn Brent . . . . Mitzi / Dolores
Luis Hildago . . . .·. . . Walter Swinburne
Richard Turner . . . . Valerius
Jack Trevor . . . . Lord Mainwaring
Sundae Wilshin . . . . Phyllis Mainwaring
Bardo de Mart . . . . Count Boris Malinski
ROMANCE Chelsea. Composer's neighbour rescues seduced waif and discovers she is his daughter.

07570
FLAMES OF PASSION (9000) (A) prizma seq
Graham-Wilcox Productions (Astra)
P: Herbert Wilcox
D: Graham Cutts
S: Herbert Wilcox, M.V. Wilcox
Mae Marsh . . . . Dorothy Hawke
C. Aubrey Smith . . . . Richard Hawke KC
Hilda Bayley . . . . Kate Watson
Herbert Langley . . . . Arthur Watson
Allan Aynesworth . . . . Mr Forbes
Eva Moore . . . . Aunt
George K. Arthur . . . . Friend
Henry Vibart . . . . Lord Chief Justice
A.G. Poulton . . . . Counsel
Alban Atwood . . . . Mayor
Harry J. Worth . . . . Sheriff
Tony Fraser . . . . Agitator
CRIME KC's wife forced to admit in court that child killed by drunken ex-chauffeur was hers.

07571
THE MISSIONER (6160) (U)
Stoll
D: George Ridgwell
S: (NOVEL) E. Phillips Oppenheim
SC: Paul Rooff
Cyril Percival . . . . Victor Manderson
Pauline Peters . . . . Wilhelmina Thorpe-Hatton
Olaf Hytten . . . . Stephen Hurd
Lewis Gilbert . . . . Jean de Roi
Allan Jeayes . . . . Gilbert Deyes
Alice Ridgwell . . . . Letty Fulton
CRIME Blackmailed woman marries rich
reformer on discovering convicted husband is
bigamist.

07572
THE NONENTITY (5250) (U)
Stoll
D: SC: Sinclair Hill
Annette Benson . . . . Beryl Danvers
Hugh Buckler . . . . Lord Ronald Prior
Gordon Rickarts . . . . Major Fletcher
Daisy Campbell . . . . Mrs Ellis
Bryan Powley . . . . Robert Ellis
DRAMA India. Lord poses as native to save rich
widow from gambling major.

07573
THE SPORTING TWELVE (series) (U)
Master Films (Walturdaw)
P: H.B. Parkinson
S: Patrick L. Mannock, Frank Miller

07574
1: A FOOTBALL FAVOURITE (1000)
D: George Wynn
Malcolm Tod . . . . Ned Forrest
Daisy England . . . . Mrs Forrest

07575
2: ROWING TO WIN (1100)
D: H.B. Parkinson
James Knight . . . . Donald Turk
Nan Wilde . . . . Elsie Turk
Booth Conway . . . . Dobbs
James Selfridge . . . . Carter

07576
3: WHEELS OF FATE (1120)
D: Challis Sanderson
Gregory Scott . . . . Ronald Manning
Ena Beaumont . . . . Joyce Vernon
Gordon Hopkirk . . . . Ralph Allison
Thomas Canning . . . . Robert Vernon

07577
4: WON BY WARR (800)
D: Edwin J. Collins
Bertram Burleigh . . . . Eric Warr
Jeff Barlow . . . . Silas Gregg

07578
5: THE MAKING OF THE GORDONS (942)
D: Challis Sanderson
Rex Davis . . . . Tom Gordon
Kathleen Vaughan . . . . Dorothy Strong
David Lytham . . . . Ivor Trevarth
George Bishop . . . . Owen Strong

07579
6: PLAYING THE GAME (1017)
D: George Wynn
James Knight . . . . Dick Foley
Ward McAllister . . . . Dudlye Hamlin

07580
7: PLUCK V PLOT (1000)
D: Edwin J. Collins
James Knight . . . . Sid Carter
Dick Butler . . . . Dick Straker

07581
8: QUITTER GRANT (1000)
D: Edwin J. Collins
Jack Bloomfield . . . . Mac Grant
Arthur McLaglen . . . . Kid Daley
Percy Morrish . . . . Hal Stuart
Arthur Bawtrey . . . . Millionaire Grant

07582
9: A RACE FOR A BRIDE (1100)
D: Challis Sanderson
Rex Davis . . . . Jack Holton
Peggy Carlisle . . . . Molly Latham
Pat O'Dare . . . . Oliver Parks
Dora Henwood . . . . Ethel Holton

07583
10: THE EXTRA KNOT (1000)
D: George Wynn
John Stuart . . . . Teddy Blythe
Betty Farquhar . . . . Jill
Jack Jarman . . . . Horace Lee
George Bishop . . . . Peter Kent

07584
11: THE LAST HUNDRED YARDS (1000)
D: Challis Sanderson
James Knight . . . . Fred Blackett
Athalie Davis . . . . Evelyn Landis
Booth Conway . . . . Harry Boon
Jack Jarman . . . . Arthur Farrant

07585
12: THE MASKED RIDER (1000)
D: Challis Sanderson
E.Lewis Waller . . . . Robert Ward
Betty Doyle . . . . Betty Seaton
Billy Vernon . . . . Jimmy Seaton
SPORT Stories featuring different sports.

07586
THE GREEN CARAVAN (5300) (U)
Master (Granger)
D: SC: Edwin J. Collins
S: (NOVEL) Oliver Sandys
Catherine Calvert . . . . Gipsy
Gregory Scott . . . . Hugo Drummond
Valia . . . . Lilian Vesey
Ivo Dawson . . . . Lord Listane
Wallace Bosco . . . . Sir Simeon Marks
Sundae Wilshin . . . . Maisie Gay
Harry Newman . . . . Hiram J. Mutt
ROMANCE Jealous girl compromises lord's
gipsy wife but confesses when gipsy cures her
baby's diphtheria.

07587
WAS SHE JUSTIFIED? (5600) (U)
Walter West (Butcher)
D: Walter West
S: (PLAY) Maud Williamson, Andrew Soutar
(THE PRUNING KNIFE)
Florence Turner . . . . Joan Crossby
Ivy Close . . . .
Lewis Gilbert . . . . John Crossby
Arthur Walcott . . . . Robert Quidman
George Bellamy . . . .
Jeff Barlow . . . .
Gwen Dickens . . . .
John Reid . . . .
Leonard Upton . . . .
DRAMA Jealous man's wife fakes death and
drives him mad by pretending daughter is bastard.

07588
SHIFTING SANDS (7454) (U)
Granville-Windsor (FBO)
P: D: Fred Leroy Granville
S: Ralph C. Wells
Peggy Hyland . . . . Barbara Thayer
Lewis Willoughby . . . . William Lindsay
Valia . . . . Yvonne Lindsay
Gibson Gowland . . . . Sam Thayer
Richard Attwood . . . . Pierre Moreau
Tony Melford . . . . Boy
Rosina White . . . . Nurse
Arthur Walcott . . . .
ADVENTURE Tripoli. Man has amnesia after
being attacked by wife's lover and saves
artist's daughter from Arabs.

07589
SILENT EVIDENCE (5700) (U)
Gaumont-British Screencraft
D: C.C. Calvert
S: Alicia Ramsey
David Hawthorne . . . . Mark Stanton
Marjorie Hume . . . . Rosamund
Frank Dane . . . . Raoul de Merincourt
H.R. Hignett . . . . Charles
Cecil du Gue . . . . Dr Hickson
Winifred Nelson . . . . Fiancee
FANTASY Inventor's Wireless-vision device
discloses wife's flirtation with French jewel
thief.

07590
THE GRASS ORPHAN (6000) (U)
Ideal
D: Frank H. Crane
S: (NOVEL) I.A.R. Wylie (THE PAUPERS OF
PORTMAN SQUARE)
SC: Eliot Stannard
Margaret Bannerman . . . . . Mrs St John
Reginald Owen . . . . Heathcote St John
Douglas Munro . . . . Uncle Jeremy
Lawford Davidson . . . . Aubrey Smythe
Ann Trevor . . . . Tilda
Hugh Clifton . . . . Lord Seldridge
Jack Trevor . . . . Mulford
Gertrude Sterroll . . . . Mrs Gresham
Peter Dear . . . . Peter St John
Marie Ault . . . . Landlady
COMEDY Rich uncle fakes death and poses as
friend to make extravagant couple earn own livin

DEC
07591
THE LION'S MOUSE (6100) (U)
Granger-Binger
D: Oscar Apfel
S: (NOVEL) A.N. & A.M. Williamson
Wyndham Standing . . . . . . Dick Sands
Mary Odette . . . . Mouse
Rex Davis . . . . Justin O'Reilly
Marguerite Marsh . . . . Olga Beverley
CRIME Secret society kidnaps man to force
his sister to steal plans.

07592
THE DOUBLES (2000)
Beehive (S & F)
P: Geoffrey Benstead
D: George Dewhurst
S: Percy Manton
James Reardon . . . . The Man
Margaret Hope . . . . The Girl
Arthur Walcott . . . .
Hal Martin . . . .
COMEDY

07593
LONESOME FARM (2000)
Beehive
P: Geoffrey Benstead
D: George Dewhurst
S: Percy Manton
James Reardon . . . . The Man
Margaret Hope . . . . The Girl
Donald Searle . . . .
Olive Sloane . . . .
Bert Darley . . . .
COMEDY

07594
PETTICOAT LOOSE (4845) (U)
Stoll
D: George Ridgwell
S: (NOVEL) Rita
SC: Sinclair Hill
Dorinea Shirley .... Brianna Lynch
Warwick Ward .... Ralmere Clive
Lionelle Howard .... Mickey Croome
Jack Trevor .... Max Lorraine
Margaret Hope ....Ray St Vincent
Kate Gurney .... Sally Dunne
Frank Goldsmith :...... Lord Farlingham
Mme D'Esterre .... Lady Kilmurran
ROMANCE Rejected playwright hypnotises
actress to ruin her career and hunchback who
loves her dies under operation.

07595
A DEBT OF HONOUR (4787) (A)
Stoll
D: Maurice Elvey
S: (NOVEL) Ethel M. Dell
Isobel Elsom .... Hope Carteret
Clive Brook .... Walter Hyde
Sydney Seaward .... Maj Baring
Lionelle Howard .... Ronald Carteret
Lewis Gilbert .... Proprietor
Frank Goldsmith ....Col Latimer
Frances Peyton .... Mrs Latimer
Hilda Sims .... Ayah
DRAMA India. Engineer blackmails girl over
her gambling brother and is killed by python.

07596
OPEN COUNTRY (4696) (A)
Stoll
D: SC: Sinclair Hill
S: (NOVEL) Maurice Hewlett
Dorinea Shirley .... Sanchia Percival
David Hawthorne .... Neville Ingram
Bertram Burleigh .... Jack Senhouse
George Bellamy .... Mr Percival
Norma Whalley .... Mrs Percival
Miles Mander .... Hon William Chevenix
Bryan Powley .... Roger Charnock
Isobel Lee .... Vicky Percival
Rosina Wright .... Mrs Percival
ROMANCE Rich man becomes wandering
artist and falls for girl who loves married man.

07597
Q-RIOSITIES BY 'Q' (series)
USA = GEMS OF THE SCREEN
Hepworth
D: S: Gaston Quiribet

07598
1 – IF MATCHES STRUCK (850)

07599
2 – DO YOU REMEMBER ? (850)

07600
3 – PEEPS INTO PUZZLE LAND (350)
Eileen Dennes .... Mother

07601
4 – ONE TOO-EXCITING NIGHT (850)
TRICK Comedies with trick photography.

07602
POETIC LICENSE (2300) (U)
Quality Plays (Walturdaw)
D: George A. Cooper
S: (STORY) F.K. Junior
Shayle Gardner .... Tony Hamilton
Winifred McCarthy .... Mrs Templeton
Ivo Dawson .... Mr Templeton
Wilfred Fletcher .... Philip Rhodes
COMEDY

07603
THE CUNNINGHAMES ECONOMISE
(2614) (U)
Quality Plays (Walturdaw)
D: George A. Cooper
S: (STORY) Mayell Bannister
Sydney N. Folker .... Jim Cunninghame
Joan McLean .... Geraldine
Donald Searle .... Ferdinand
COMEDY Girl hires out her husband's car and
he thinks it is stolen.

07604
KEEPING MAN INTERESTED (2140) (U)
Quality Plays (Walturdaw)
D: George A. Cooper
S: (STORY) Mayell Bannister
Sydney N. Folker .... Jim Cunninghame
Joan McLean .... Geraldine
COMEDY Couple change minds about
separate holidays and mistake each other
for burglars.

07605
THE LETTERS (1362) (U)
Quality Plays (Walturdaw)
D: George A. Cooper
S: (STORY) Maurice Leval
Hugh Miller .... Landier
Madge Stuart .... Mme Vincourt
ROMANCE Paris. Wife tries to get letters back
from ex-lover.

07606
HER DANCING PARTNER (2000) (U)
Quality Plays (Walturdaw)
D: George A. Cooper
S: (STORY) Mayell Bannister
Sydney N. Folker .... Jim Cunninghame
Joan McLean .... Geraldine
COMEDY Young husband jealous over wife's
dancing partner.

07607
PEARL FOR PEARL (1600) (A)
Quality Plays (Walturdaw)
D: George A. Cooper
S: (STORY) Atreus van Schraeder
A.B. Imeson .... Pierre Tastu
Dezma du May .... Tara
W.G. Saunders .... Chinaman
DRAMA South Seas. Kanaka wins halfcaste's
daughter by causing duel with pearl buyer.

07608
HIS WIFE'S HUSBAND (3880) (A)
Quality Plays (Walturdaw)
D: George A. Cooper
S: Adrian Johnson
Madge Stuart .... Madge Pearson
Olaf Hytten .... Fred Pearson
M.A. Wetherell .... Edgar Armstrong
Ralph Forster .... Butler
CRIME Rich man forces wife's blackmailing
ex-husband to choose pistols in suicide pact.

07609
WEAVERS OF FORTUNE (5500) (U)
reissue: 1927, RACING LUCK (2 rls; Butch)
I.B. Davidson (Granger)
D: Arthur Rooke
S: Kinchen Wood
Henry Vibart .... Jackson
Dacia .... Minna Vandyck
Derek Glynne .... Tom Winter
Myrtle Vibart .... Molly Jackson
SPORT Expelled student buys horse, becomes
carrier, and wins Grand National.

07610
LOVE AND A WHIRLWIND (6858) (U)
Alliance (Cosmograph)
D: Duncan Macrae, Harold Shaw
S: (NOVEL) Helen Prothero Lewis
Clive Brook .... Griffith
Marjorie Hume .... Dorinda Saurin
Reginald Fox .... John Hir
Edward O'Neill .... Sir Roderic
Frank Goldsmith .... Oswald
Arthur Cullin .... Madoc
Mabel Archdale .... Aunt Fribble
Agnes Brantford .... Mary
Daisy Campbell .... Lady Vychen
CRIME Wales. Lord's son poses as fisherman
when poacher frames him for shooting his
brother.

07611
THE SCOURGE (6930) Retitled: FORTUNE'S
FOOL (U)
Hardy (H & S)
P: Sam Hardy
D: Geoffrey H. Malins
S: (NOVEL) Rafael Sabatini
SC: Rafael Sabatini
Madge Stuart .... Sylvia Farquharson
J.R. Tozer .... Duke of Buckingham
William Stack .... Ned Holles
Sir Simeon Stuart ...... Gen Monk
A. Harding Steerman ..... Rev Sylvester
Ruth MacKay .... Mrs Quin
Frank Woolfe .... Tucker
Fothringham Lysons .... Bates
DRAMA 1665. Duke abducts actress then
nurses her through Plague.

07612
TREASURE TROVE (2000)
Punch Films (S & F)
D: S: Frank Miller
Roy Byford .... Downe
Frank Stanmore .... Owte
Pollie Emery .... Ma
Dorothy Eaton ....
Fred Percy ....
Ivy Booker ....
Jack Miller ....
COMEDY Misadventures of gentlemen
tramps.

07613
CASEY'S MILLIONS (5000)
Irish Photoplays
P: Norman Whitten
D: John MacDonagh
Jimmy O'Dea ....
Kathleen Drago ....
Fred Jeffs ....
Chris Sylvester ....
COMEDY (Not shown in England).

07614
CRUISKEEN LAWN (4500)
Irish Photoplays (Walker)
P: Norman Whitten
D: S: John MacDonagh
Tom Moran .... Boyle Roche
Kathleen Armstrong....... Nora Blake
Jimmy O'Dea .... Sam Silk
Fred Jeffs............. Mr Blake
Chris Sylvester .... The Groom
Fay Sargent .... His Wife
COMEDY Ireland. Poor squire's horse wins
cup after charlatan dopes it with exlixir of life.

07615
HIDE AND SEEK (2000)
Walker-Boyd Sunshine Productions
D: S: Martin Walker
Bert Darley . . . . Farmer
Jack Roberts . . . .
Molly Kerr . . . .
Pamela Bruce . . . .
COMEDY

07616
LOVE'S INFLUENCE (4600) (U)
Star Productions (Unity)
P: George K. Arthur
D: Edward R. Gordon, William S. Charlton
S: Edward R. Gordon
George K. Arthur . . . . Johnny O'Hara
Flora le Breton . . . . June
Sir Simon Stuart . . . .
Bertie White . . . .
George Turner . . . .
Doris Lloyd . . . .
William Lugg . . . .
Marie Gerald . . . .
ROMANCE Village vicar's daughter saves
wayward heir from city siren.

07617
LET'S PRETEND (4422) retitled:
CASTLES IN THE AIR
British Super (Jury)
P: G.B. Samuelson
D: Fred Paul
S: Walter Summers
Nelson Keys . . . .
Lilian Hall-Davis . . . .
Campbell Gullan . . . .
Mary Rorke . . . .
Julian Royce . . . .
COMEDY Swindler hires poor colonel to pose
as daughter's rich husband.(Not shown until
March 1935).

1923

JAN

07618
THE ROMANY (5800) (U)
Welsh-Pearson (Jury)
P: George Pearson
D: F. Martin Thornton
S: Eliot Stannard
Victor McLaglen . . . . The Chief
Irene Norman . . . . Valia
Harvey Braban . . . . Andrew MacDonald
Peggy Hathaway . . . . Flora
Hugh Wright . . . .
Malcolm Tod . . . . Robbie
Ida Fane . . . . Zilla
H. Agar Lyons . . . .
N. Watts-Phillips . . . .
ADVENTURE Scotland. Gipsy chief saves
runaway girl from rich fiance.

07619
THE VIRGIN QUEEN (7000) (U) *prizma*
J. Stuart Blackton (Rose)
D: J. Stuart Blackton
S: Harry Pirie Gordon
Lady Diana Manners . . . . .Queen Elizabeth
Carlyle Blackwell, ... Lord Robert Dudley
Walter Tennyson . . . . Viscount Hereford
Hubert Carrer . . . . Sir William Cecil
A.B. Imeson . . . . Borghese
William Luff . . . . Bishop de Quadra
Lionel d'Aragon . . . . . . Earl of Northumberland
Norma Whalley . . . . Countess Lennox
Maisie Fisher . . . . Queen Mary
Marian Blackton . . . . Mary Arundel
Violet Blackton . . . . Lettice Knollys
HISTORY Lord saves queen from countess's
assassination plot.

07620
PADDY THE NEXT BEST THING (7200)
Graham-Wilcox *reissue:* 1925
P: Herbert Wilcox
D: Graham Cutts
S: (NOVEL) Gertrude Page
SC: Herbert Wilcox, Eliot Stannard
Mae Marsh . . . . Paddy Adair
Darby Foster . . . . Lawrence Blake
Lilian Douglas . . . . Eileen Adair
George K. Arthur . . . . Kack O'Hara
Nina Boucicault . . . . Mrs Blake
Haidee Wright . . . . Jane O'Hara
Marie Wright . . . . Mary O'Hara
Marie Ault . . . . Mrs Adair
Sir Simeon Stuart . . . . Gen Adair
Mildred Evelyn . . . . Doreen Blake
Tom Coventry . . . . Mickey Doolan
ROMANCE. Girl aids sister's romance with
man who really prefers her.

07621
ROGUES OF THE TURF (5899) (U)
Carlton (Butcher) *reissue:* 1926 (2 rls)
D: SC: Wilfred Noy
S: (PLAY) John F. Preston
Fred Groves . . . . Bill Higgins
Olive Sloane . . . . .Marion Heathcote
James Lindsay . . . . Capt Clifton
Mavis Clare . . . . .Nellie Flaxman
Bobbie Andrews . . . . Arthur Somerton
Clarence Blakiston . . . . . Sir George Venning
Dora Lennox . . . . Rose
Nell Emerald . . . . Nurse
James Reardon . . . . Rogue
SPORT Trainer's ex-wife weds employer and
plots to kidnap horse.

07622
A ROYAL DIVORCE (10,000) (U)
Napoleon
P: G.B. Samuelson, S.W. Smith

D: Alexander Butler
S:(PLAY) W.G. Wills, G.C. Collingham
SC: Walter Summers
Gwylim Evans . . . . Napoleon
Gertrude McCoy . . . . Josephine
Lilian Hall Davis . . . . Stephanie
Gerald Ames . . . . .Marquis de Beaumont
Mary Dibley . . . . Marie-Louise
Jerrold Robertshaw . . . . . . Talleyrand
Tom Reynolds . . . . Grimand
Mercy Peters . . . . King of Rome
HISTORY France, 1809. Emperor divorces
wife to marry Austrian Queen and have heir.

07623
BULLDOG DRUMMOND (6000) (U)
Astra-National
P: Maurits Binger
D: Oscar Apfel
S: (PLAY) "Sapper" (H.C. McNeile)
SC: C.B. Doxat-Pratt
Carlyle Blackwell . . . . Capt Hugh Drummond
Evelyn Greeley . . . . Phyllis Benton
Dorothy Fane . . . . Irma Peterson
Warwick Ward . . . . Dr Lakington
Horace de Vere . . . . Carl Peterson
Gerald Dean . . . . Algy Longworth
Harry Bogarth . . . . Sparring Partner
William Browning . . . . . . .James Handley
CRIME Captain saves kidnapped magnate from
nursing home run by foreign agents. (Made in
Holland).

07624
THE RIGHT TO STRIKE (6170) (U)
British Super (Jury)
P: G.B. Samuelson
D: Fred Paul
S: (PLAY) Ernest Hutchinson
SC: Walter Summers
Lilian Hall Davis . . . . Mrs Ormerod
Fred Paul . . . . Dr Wrigley
Campbell Gullan . . . . Montague
Lauderdale Maitland . . . . . . Ben Ormerod
DRAMA Bolshevik incites miners to strike,
causing death of son of doctor, who then
strikes against miners.

FEB

07625
ALWAYS TELL YOUR WIFE (2000)
Seymour Hicks Productions
D: SC: Hugh Croise
S: (PLAY) Seymour Hicks
Seymour Hicks . . . . The Husband
Gertrude McCoy . . . . The Wife
COMEDY

07626
THE PRODIGAL SON (18454) (U)
Stoll *reissue:* 1929 (EB; 12,000 ft cut)
D: SC: A.E. Coleby
S: (NOVEL) Hall Caine
Stewart Rome . . . . Magnus Stephenson
Henry Victor . . . . Oscar Stephenson
Edith Bishop . . . . Helga Neilson
Colette Brettelle . . . . Thora Neilson / Elin
Adeline Hayden Coffin . . Anna Stephenson
Frank Wilson . . . . .Stephen Stephenson
Henry Nicholls-Bates . . . . . Oscar Neilson
Louise Conti . . . . Aunt Margaret
Peter Upcher . . . . Nils Finsen
Sam Austin . . . . Captain
DRAMA Iceland. Governor's son weds brother's
sweetheart and leaves her to die in childbirth
after forging father's name. he makes love to
her sister in Nice, loses money cheating, fakes
suicide and returns home. (Longest British film.
Released in two parts of 8 and 9 reels, part two
entitled: THE RETURN OF THE PRODIGAL.

07627
THROUGH FIRE AND WATER (6188) (A)
Ideal
D: Thomas Bentley
S: (NOVEL) Victor Bridges (GREENSEA
ISLAND)
SC: Eliot Stannard
Clive Brook . . . . John Dryden
Flora le Breton . . . . Christine de Rhoda
Lawford Davidson . . . . Dr Manning
Jerrold Robertshaw . . . . . . Jennaway
M.A. Wetherell . . . . Craill
Teddy Arundel . . . . Bascomb
Esme Hubbard . . . . Mrs Craill
Ian Wilson . . . . Jimmy
ADVENTURE Naval officer inherits island and
helps girl thwart doctor's search for diamonds.

07628
THE HARBOUR LIGHTS (5877) (U)
Ideal
D: Tom Terriss
S: (PLAY) George R. Sims
SC: Eliot Stannard
Tom Moore . . . . .Lt David Kingsley
Isobel Elsom . . . . Dora Nelson
Gerald McCarthy . . . . Frank Morland
Gibson Gowland . . . . Mark Helstone
Annette Benson . . . . Lina Nelson
A.B. Imeson . . . . Insp Wood
Percy Standing . . . . Nicholson
Mary Rorke . . . . Mrs Helstone
Judd Green . . . . Old Tom
Gordon Begg . . . . Capt Nelson
CRIME Lieut saves heiress from wicked squire
and is framed for murder.

07629
WONDER WOMEN OF THE WORLD (series)
B & C (Regent)
P: Edward Godal
D: Edwin Greenwood
S: Eliot Stannard

07630
1 — MADAME RECAMIER; OR, THE PRICE
OF VIRTUE (2000)
Malvina Longfellow . . . . Mme Recamier
Charles Barratt . . . . Napoleon
Margaret Yarde . . . . Mme de Stael
Gordon Hopkirk . . . . Prince Rupert
Reginald Bach . . . .
M. Gray Murray . . . .

07631
2—SIMONE EVRARD; OR, DEATHLESS
DEVOTION (2000)
Marjorie Hume . . . . Simonne Evrard
Charles Barratt . . . . .Jean-Paul Marat
Dacia Deane . . . . Charlotte Corday
Roy Beard . . . . Petoir
M. Gray Murray . . . . Archbishop

07632
3—HENRIETTA MARIA; OR, THE QUEEN
OF SORROW (2000)
Janet Alexander . . . . Henrietta Maria
Russell Thorndike . . . . Charles I
Lionel D'Aragon . . . .
Roy Beard . . . .
Herbert Trumper . . . .

07633
4 — LADY JANE GREY; OR, THE COURT
OF INTRIGUE (2000)
Nina Vanna . . . . .Lady Jane Grey
Charles Barratt . . . . . .Duke of Northumberland
Forbes Dawson . . . . Edward VII
Charles Dane . . . . .Duke of Suffolk
Johnny Reid . . . . Lord Dudley

07634
5 – LUCREZIA BORGIA; OR, PLAYTHING
OF POWER (2000)
Nina Vanna . . . . Lucrezia Borgia
Russell Thorndike . . . . Cesare Borgia

07635
6 – EMPRESS JOSEPHINE; OR, WIFE OF A
DEMIGOD (2000)
Janet Alexander . . . . Josephine
Charles Barratt . . . . Napoleon
Reginald Bach . . . . Fouche
HISTORY Dramatised episodes from world
history.

07636
THE HYPOCRITES (4500) (A)
Granger-Binger
D: Charles Giblyn
S: (PLAY) Henry Arthur Jones
SC: Eliot Stannard
Wyndham Standing . . . . . . Rev Edgar Linnell
Mary Odette . . . . Rachel Neve
Lillian Douglas . . . . Helen Plugenet
Sydney Paxton . . . . Henry Wilmore
Harold French . . . . Lennard Wilmore
Roy Travers . . . . Sir John Plugenet
Bertie White . . . . Aubrey Viveash
William Hunter . . . . .Rev Everard Daubeney
Gertrude Sterroll . . . . Mrs Wilmore
Vera Hargreave . . . . Mrs Linnell
DRAMA Squire tries to make son deny he
fathered villager's child and marry heiress.

07637
THE PIPES OF PAN (5932) (U)
Hepworth
D: Cecil M. Hepworth
S: George Dewhurst
Alma Taylor . . . . Polly Bunning
G.H. Mulcaster . . . . Irwin Farman
Eileen Dennes . . . . Enid Markham
Hugh Clifton . . . . Cyril Farman
John McAndrews . . . . Miles Bunning
Buena Bent . . . . Aunt Maggie
Lawrence Hanray . . . . James Flaxman
Leslie Attwood . . . . Derek Hulme
James Annand . . . . Irwin Farman
ROMANCE Girl weds widowed toymaker after
tinker father's patent polish fails.

07638
LILY OF THE ALLEY (6590) (U)
Hepworth
D: S: Henry Edwards
Henry Edwards . . . . Bill
Chrissie White . . . . Lily
Campbell Gullan . . . . Sharkey
Mary Brough . . . . Widow
Frank Stanmore . . . . Alf
Lionel d'Aragon . . . . Dad
DRAMA Coffee stall keeper's wife dreams he
goes blind and dies in fire. (First British
feature without subtitles).

07639
MIST IN THE VALLEY (6715) (U)
Hepworth
D: Cecil M. Hepworth
S: (NOVEL) Dorin Craig
SC: George Dewhurst
Alma Taylor . . . . Margaret Yeoland
G.H. Mulcaster . . . . Denis Marlow
James Carew . . . . Justin Courtney
Esme Hubbard . . . . Nurse Merrion
John McAndrews . . . . . . .Job Pennyquick
Gwynne Herbert . . . . Mrs Crick
Maud Cressall . . . . Mother Superior
Charles Vane . . . . Squire Yeoland

Douglas Munro . . . . Prosecution
Lionel D'Aragon . . . . Defence
Bertram Terry . . . . Mr Moon
Fred Rains . . . . Mr Warren
CRIME Ex-nun weds amnesia victim and is
framed for killing usurping uncle who posed
as father.

07640
THE MONKEY'S PAW (5700) (A)
Artistic
P: George Redman
D: Manning Haynes
S: (PLAY) W.W. Jacobs
SC: Lydia Hayward
Moore Marriott . . . . John White
Marie Ault . . . . Mrs White
Charles Ashton . . . . Herbert White
Johnny Butt . . . . Sgt Tom Morris
A.B.Imeson . . . .
George Wynn . . . .
Tom Coventry . . . . Engine Driver
FANTASY Couple dream that magic paw
returns their dead son.

MAR
07641
THE TEMPTATION OF CARLTON EARLYE
(6276) (A)
British Actors – C. Aubrey Smith Theatres
(Phillips)
D: Wilfred Noy
S: (NOVEL) Stella During
SC: S.H. Herkomer
C. Aubrey Smith . . . . Carlton Earle
Gertrude McCoy . . . . Margaret Royston
James Lindsay . . . . Royston
Sir Simeon Stuart . . . . . . Whitworth
Francis Innys. . . . . Pap
Lilian Gould . . . . Jenny Taylor
Beatrice Trouville . . . . . . Sylvia Conyers
Charles Poulton . . . . Dr Carr
CRIME Dr Poisons dying friend and is
framed by valet for poisoning wife's first
husband.

07642
HORNET'S NEST (6102) (U)
Walter West (Butcher) *reissue:* 1926 (2 rls)
D: Walter West
S: (NOVEL) Andrew Soutar
SC: W.C. Rowden
Florence Turner . . . . Mrs Cobb
Fred Wright . . . . .Capt Anthony Cobb
Nora Swinburne . . . . Lady Rona
James Knight . . . . Tony Cobb
Kathleen Vaughan . . . . . . Rachael Beach
Lewis Gilbert . . . . Joe Beach
Cecil Morton York . . . . . . Sir Oswald
Forbes Dawson . . . . Leycester Craig
Jeff Barlow . . . . Farmer Craig
Arthur Walcott . . . . Dicky Truslove
Somers Bellamy . . . . Landlord
DRAMA Village blacksmith's pregnant daughter
kills herself when squire's son rejects her.

07643
THE LAST ADVENTURES OF SHERLOCK
HOLMES (series)
Stoll
D: George Ridgwell
S: (STORIES) Arthur Conan Doyle
SC: Geoffrey H. Malins, P.L. Mannock
Eille Norwood . . . . Sherlock Holmes
Hubert Willis . . . . Dr John Watson

07644
1 – SILVER BLAZE (2100) (U)
Knighton Small . . . . .Col Ross

Sam Marsh . . . . Straker
Norma Whalley . . . . Mrs Straker
Sam Austin . . . . Silas Brown
Bert Barclay . . . . Groom
Tom Beaumont . . . . Insp Gregory

07645
2 – THE SPECKLED BAND (1800) (U)
Lewis Gilbert . . . . Dr Grimsby Roylott
Cynthia Murtagh . . . . Helen Stoner
Henry Wilson . . . . The Baboon
Mme d'Esterre . . . . Mrs Hudson

07646
3 – THE GLORIA SCOTT (2070) (U)
Reginald Fox . . . . Victor Trevor
Fred Raynham . . . . James Trevor
Roy Raymond . . . . Prendergast
Laurie Leslie . . . . Hudson
Ernest Shannon . . . . Evans

07647
4 – THE BLUE CARBUNCLE (2000) (U)
Douglas Payne . . . . Peterson
Gordon Hopkirk . . . . Ryder
Sebastian Smith . . . . Henry Barker
Mary Mackintosh . . . . . . Mrs Oakshott
Archie Hunter. . . . . Breckinbridge

07648
5 – THE ENGINEER'S THUMB (2000) (U)
Bertram Burleigh . . . . Hatherley
Ward McAllister . . . . Ferguson
Mercy Hatton . . . . Girl

07649
6 – HIS LAST BOW (1600) (U)
Nelson Ramsey . . . . Von Bork
Van Courtland . . . . Baron Herling
Kate Gurney . . . . Martha
Watts Phillips . . . . Officer

07650
7 – THE CARDBOARD BOX (1800) (U)
Tom Beaumont . . . . Insp Lestrade
Hilda Anthony . . . . Mary Browner
Johnny Butt . . . . James Browner
Eric Lugg . . . . Alec Fairbairn
Maud Wulff . . . . Miss Cushing

07651
8 – THE DISAPPEARANCE OF LADY
FRANCES CARFAX (1800) (U)
Tom Beaumont . . . . Insp Gregory
Evelyn Cecil . . . . .Lady Frances Carfax
David Hawthorne . . . . . . .Hon Phillip Green
Cecil Morton York . . . . . . Hily Peters
Madge Tree . . . . Mrs Peters

07652
9—THE THREE STUDENTS (2500) (U)
William Lugg . . . . Soames
A. Harding Steerman . . . . . Bannister
L. Verne . . . . Gilchrist

07653
10—THE MISSING THREE QUARTER
(2200) (U)
Hal Martin . . . . Overton
Jack Raymond . . . . Porter
Albert E. Rayner . . . . .Dr Leslie Armstrong
Leigh Gabell . . . . Staunton
Cliff Davies . . . . Lord Mount James

07654
11—THE MYSTERY OF THOR BRIDGE
(2200) (U)
A.B. Imeson . . . . Mr Gibson
Violet Graham . . . . Miss Dunbar
Noel Grahame . . . . Mrs Gibson
Harry J. Worth . . . . Inspector

07655
12—THE STONE OF MAZARIN (1878) (U)
Tom Beaumont . . . . Insp Gregory
Lionel d'Aragon . . . . Count Sylvius
Laurie Leslie . . . . Merton

07656
13—THE MYSTERY OF THE DANCING MEN (2600) (U)
Frank Goldsmith . . . . Hilton Cubitt
Wally Bosco . . . . Slaney
Dezma du May . . . . Mrs Cubitt

07657
14—THE CROOKED MAN (2228) (U)
Jack Hobbs . . . . Henry Wood
Gladys Jennings . . . . Mrs Barclay
Dora de Winton . . . . Miss Morrison
Richard Lindsay . . . . Maj Murphy

07658
15—THE FINAL PROBLEM (1686) (U)
Percy Standing . . . . Prof Moriarty
Tom Beaumont . . . . Insp Taylor
CRIME Private tec solves various crimes.

07659
ST ELMO (5840) (U)
R.W. Syndicate (Capitol)
D:SC: Rex Wilson
S: (NOVEL) Augusta J. Evans-Wilson
Shayle Gardner . . . . St. Elmo Murray
Gabrielle Gilroy . . . . Agnes Powell
Madge Tree . . . . Mrs Murray
Harding Thomas . . . . Rev Hammond
DRAMA Widow's son kills clerical rival in duel and becomes possessed by devil.

07660
THIS FREEDOM (7220) (A)
Ideal
D:SC: Denison Clift
S: (NOVEL) A.S.M. Hutchinson
Fay Compton . . . . Rosalie Aubyn
Clive Brook . . . . Harry Occleve
John Stuart . . . . Huggo Occleve
Athene Seyler . . . . Miss Keggs
Nancye Kenyon . . . . Doda Occleve
Gladys Hamer . . . . Gertrude
Fewlass Llewellyn . . . . Rev Aubyn
Adeline Hayden Coffin . . . . Mrs Aubyn
Mickey Brantford . . . . Robert
Bunty Fosse . . . . Rosalie (child)
Joan Maude . . . . Hilda
Charles Vane . . . . Uncle Pyke
Gladys Hamilton . . . . Aunt Belle
Robert English . . . . Mr Field
DRAMA Cleric's daughter marries but stays in business so that neglected children grow up perverted.

APR

07661
THE LADY OWNER (5750) (U)
Walter West (Butcher) reissue: 1926 (2 rls)
D: Walter West
S: J. Bertram Brown
Violet Hopson . . . . Pamela Morland
James Knight . . . . Dick Tressider
Warwick Ward . . . . Morton Buckstead
Arthur Walcott . . . . Joe Sluggett
Fred Rains . . . . Sir Richard Tressider
Marjorie Benson . . . . Mrs Sluggett
Edwin Ellis . . . . Jimmy Burton
Jeff Barlow . . . . Jenkins
SPORT Bart posing as poor rides girl's horse and thwarts mortgage-holder.

07662
HORACE OF PUTNEY (1441) (U)
Thespian Productions
COMEDY
MAY

07663
GEMS OF LITERATURE (series)
B & C (Walturdaw)
P: Edward Godal
SC: Eliot Stannard

07664
1—THE MISTLETOE BOUGH (2050) (A)
D: Edwin J. Collins
S: (PLAY) Charles Somerset
John Stuart . . . . Lord Lovel
Flora le Breton . . . . . . Lady Agnes de Clifford
Lionel D'Aragon . . . . Sir Reginald de Courcey
William Lugg . . . . Baron de Clifford

07665
2—THE TAMING OF THE SHREW (2016) (U)
D: Edwin J. Collins
S: (PLAY) William Shakespeare
Dacia Deane . . . . Katherina
Lauderdale Maitland . . . . . Petruchio
Cynthia Murtagh . . . . Bianca
M. Gray Murray . . . . Baptista
Somers Bellamy . . . . Gremio
Roy Beard . . . . Lucentio

07666
3—CURFEW MUST NOT RING TONIGHT (2700) (U)
D: Edwin J. Collins
S: (POEM) Rose Thorpe
Joan Morgan . . . . Elizabeth
M.A. Wetherell . . . . Oliver Cromwell
Ronald Buchanan . . . . The Man
Lionel D'Aragon . . . . The Captain
M. Gray Murray . . . . Col Penn

07667
4—THE DREAM OF EUGENE ARAM (1908) (U)
D: Edwin Greenwood
S: (POEM) Thomas Hood
Russell Thorndike . . . . Eugene Aram
Olive Sloane . . . . Mrs Aram
Wallace Bosco . . . .
Gerald Anderson . . . .

07668
5—SCROOGE (1600) (U)
D: Edwin Greenwood
S: (NOVEL) Charles Dickens (A CHRISTMAS CAROL)
Russell Thorndike . . . . Ebenezer Scrooge
Nina Vanna . . . . Alice
Jack Denton . . . . Bob Cratchit
Forbes Dawson . . . . Marley

07669
6—THE BELLS (2100) (A)
D: Edwin Greenwood
S: (PLAY) Leopold Lewis
Russell Thorndike . . . . Matthias
Arthur Walcott . . . . Hypnotist
Daisy Agnew . . . . Farmer's Wife

07670
7—THE SCHOOL FOR SCANDAL (2386) (U)
D: Edwin Greenwood
S: (PLAY) Richard Brinsley Sheridan
Russell Thorndike . . . . Sir Peter Teazle
Nina Vanna . . . . Lady Teazle
Florence Wulff . . . . Lady Sneerwell

07671
8—SHE STOOPS TO CONQUER (2362) (U)
D: Edwin Greenwood
S: (PLAY) Oliver Goldsmith
Madge Stuart . . . . Miss Hardcastle
Walter Tennyson . . . . Young Marlow

07672
9—THE TEST (2196) (U)
D: Edwin Greenwood
S: (STORY) Honore de Balzac (MADAME FIRMIANI)
Madge Stuart . . . . Mme Firmiani
Russell Thorndike . . . . De Bourbonne

07673
10—THE SINS OF A FATHER (2117) (U)
D: Edwin Greenwood
S: (NOVEL) Mrs Gaskell
Madge Stuart . . . .
Russell Thorndike . . . .

07674
11—FALSTAFF THE TAVERN KNIGHT (2493) (U)
D: Edwin Greenwood
S: (PLAY) William Shakespeare
Roy Byford . . . . Sir John Falstaff
Margaret Yarde . . . . Mistress Ford
Jack Denton . . . . Master Ford

07675
12—LOVE IN AN ATTIC (1796) (U)
D: Edwin Greenwood
S: (POEM) Robert Buchanan (THE LITTLE MILLINER)
Nina Vanna . . . . The Milliner
Russell Thorndike . . . . The Producer
Walter Tennyson . . . . The Dramatist
DRAMAS

07676
SYNCOPATED PICTURE PLAYS (series)
Bertram Phillips (Butcher)
D: Bertram Phillips
S: Frank Miller
Queenie Thomas
Peter Upcher
Frank Stanmore
Adeline Hayden Coffin
Jeff Barlow
Fatty Phillips

07677
1—ONE EXCITED ORPHAN (1800) (U)

07678
2—TUT-TUT AND HIS TERRIBLE TOMB (2000) (U)

07679
3—JULIET AND HER ROMEO (2000) (U)

07680
4—DICKENS UP-TO-DATE (1900) (U)

07681
5—FAUST (1790) (U)

07682
6—STUNG BY A WOMAN (2000) (U)
COMEDIES Burlesques.

07683
THE MYSTERY OF DR FU MANCHU (series)
Stoll reissue: 1926
D: A.E. Coleby
S: (STORIES) Sax Rohmer (Arthur Ward)
SC: A.E. Coleby, Frank Wilson
H. Agar Lyons . . . . Dr Fu Manchu

Fred Paul . . . . Nayland Smith
Joan Clarkson . . . . Karamaneh
Humberston Wright . . . . Dr Petrie
Frank Wilson . . . . Insp Weymouth

07684
1—THE SCENTED ENVELOPES (2400)(A)
Robert English . . . . Sir John Astley
Booth Conway . . . . Mordain
Charles Vane . . . . Sir Crichton Davey

07685
2—THE WEST CASE (1800)(U)
Wyngold Lawrence . . . . Frank West

07686
3—THE CLUE OF THE PIGTAIL (1700) (A)
Ernest Spalding . . . . Shen Yan

07687
4—THE CALL OF SIVA (1700) (A)

07688
5—THE MIRACLE (1712) (A)
Stacey Gaunt . . . . Lord Southery
Napier Barry . . . . Henderson
Austin Leigh . . . . Valet

07689
6—THE FUNGI CELLARS (1630) (A)
Pat Royale . . . . Aziz

07690
7—THE KNOCKING ON THE DOOR
(2228) (A)
W.G. Saunders . . . . James Weymouth

07691
8—THE CRY OF THE NIGHTHAWK (1773) (A)
H. Cundall . . . . Forsyth

07692
9—AARON'S ROD (1862)
Percy Standing . . . . Abel Slattin
Bob Vallis . . . . Busker

07693
10—THE FIERY HAND (2174) (A)
Pat Royale . . . . Aziz

07694
11—THE MAN WITH THE LIMP (2000) (U)
Julie Suedo . . . . Zarm
Roy Raymond . . . . Sgt Fletcher

07695
12—THE QUEEN OF HEARTS (1750) (U)
Fred Raynham . . . . Sir Frazer
Julie Suedo . . . . Zarmi
D. Bland . . . . Logan

07696
13—THE SILVER BUDDHA (1570) (U)
E. Lewis Waller . . . . Salaman

07697
14—THE SACRED ORDER (1700) (U)
Percy Clarbour . . . . Insp Wills
Laurie Leslie . . . . Dacoit
H. Manning . . . . Mandarin

07698
15—THE SHRINE OF THE SEVEN LAMPS
(1500) (U)
CRIMES Chinese criminal constantly eludes the
police.

07699
THE CAUSE OF ALL THE TROUBLE (2000)
(U)
Albanian (Globe)

D: Edward D. Roberts
S: Walter Summers
George K. Arthur . . . . Jimmy Rodney
Flora le Breton . . . . Mrs Rodney
Sydney Paxton . . . .
Olaf Hytten . . . .
Bertie Wright . . . .
COMEDY

07700
THE SIGN OF FOUR (6750) (A)
Stoll
D:SC: Maurice Elvey
S: (NOVEL) Arthur Conan Doyle
Eille Norwood . . . . Sherlock Holmes
Isobel Elsom . . . . Mary Morstan
Fred Raynham . . . . Prince Abdullah Khan
Arthur Cullin . . . . Dr Watson
Norman Page . . . . Jonathan Small
Humberston Wright . . . . Dr Sholto
Henry Wilson . . . . Pygmy
Mme D'Esterre . . . . Mrs Hudson
Arthur Bell . . . . Insp Athelney Jones
CRIME Convict's revenge on partners who
cheated him of treasure share.

07701
THE KNOCKOUT (6000) (U)
Napoleon (Jury)
P: G.B. Samuelson
D: Alexander Butler
S: Walter Summers
Lilian Hall Davis . . . . Polly Peach
Rex Davis . . . . Billy Berks
Josephine Earle . . . . Lady Clare
Tom Reynolds . . . . Manager
Julian Royce . . . . Guy Ballinger
Micky Brantford . . . . Scout
SPORT Unconscious boxer dreams he buys
racehorse, is kidnapped, and his wife kills
herself.

07702
MARRIED LOVE (5570) (A) retitled:
MAISIE'S MARRIAGE
Napoleon
P: G.B. Samuelson
D: Alexander Butler
S: Marie Stopes
SC: Walter Summers
Lillian Hall Davis . . . . Maisie Burrows
Rex Davis . . . . Dick Reading
Sydney Fairbrother . . . . Mrs Burrows
Sam Livesey . . . . Mr Burrows
Roger Livesey . . . . Henry Burrows
Mary Brough . . . . Mrs Reading
Bert Darley . . . . Mr Sterling
Gladys Harvey . . . . Mrs Sterling
DRAMA Fireman's fiancee, ejected by her
father, becomes maid and finds small families
happier than large ones.

07703
LOVE, LIFE AND LAUGHTER (6290) (U)
Welsh-Pearson (Gaumont) *reissue:* 1928
P:D:S: George Pearson
Betty Balfour . . . . Tip-Toes
Harry Jonas . . . . The Boy
Frank Stanmore . . . . The Balloon-blower
Annie Esmond . . . . His Wife
Nancy Price . . . . Her Friend
Sydney Fairbrother . . . . Lily
Eric Smith . . . . Charlie
Λ. Harding Steerman . . . . . . The Musician
Audrey Ridgwell . . . . His Daughter
Gordon Hopkirk . . . . The Rich Man
Dacia . . . . Dancer
ROMANCE Novelist tells girl story of how she
becomes famous dancer, and dies.

07704
GOD'S PRODIGAL (5000)
International Artists
D: Bert Wynne, Edward Jose
S: (NOVEL) A.J. Russell
SC: Louis Stevens
Gerald Ames . . . . Gentleman Jeff
Flora le Breton . . . .
Frank Stanmore . . . . Hickey
Ada Ford . . . . Flora
Judd Green . . . .
Reginald Fox . . . .
Beatrix Templeton . . . . Mrs Breck
Cyril Percival . . . .
Irene Ridgwell . . . .
Josephine Quest . . . . Maid
Nan Wild . . . .
CRIME

07705
THE SCANDAL (6370) (A)
I.B. Davidson (Granger)
D: Arthur Rooke
S: (PLAY) Henri Battaille
SC: Kinchen Wood
Hilda Bayley . . . . Charlotte Ferrioul
Henry Victor . . . . Artenezzo
Edward O'Neill . . . . Jeannetier
Vanni Marcoux . . . . Maurice Ferrioul
Mme de la Croix . . . . Mme Ferrioul
CRIME Nice. Singer accused of theft when
married woman lends him jewels to gamble with.

07706
THE WANDERING JEW (8300) (A)
Stoll
D: Maurice Elvey
S: (PLAY) E. Temple Thurston
SC: Alicia Ramsey
Matheson Lang . . . . Matathias
Hutin Britton . . . . Judith
Malvina Longfellow . . . . Gianella
Isobel Elsom . . . . Olalla Quintana
Florence Sanders . . . . Joanne
Shayle Gardner . . . . Pietro Morelli
Hubert Carter . . . . The Ruler
Jerrold Robertshaw . . . . Juan de Texada
Winifred Izard . . . . Rachel
Fred Raynham . . . . Inquisitor
Lewis Gilbert . . . . Mario
Hector Abbas . . . . Zapportas
Lionel D'Aragon . . . . Raymond
Gordon Hopkirk . . . . Lover
FANTASY Cursed Jew lives through
Crusades, Mediaeval Italy, and dies in Spanish
inquisition.

07707
A GAMBLE WITH HEARTS (5000) (U)
Master (W & F)
P: H.B. Parkinson
D: Edwin J. Collins
S: (NOVEL) Anthony Carlyle
SC: Lucita Squiers
Milton Rosmer . . . . Dallas Chalfont
Madge Stuart . . . . Morag Lannon
Valia . . . . Rosaleen Erle
Olaf Hytten . . . . Dallas Jr
Margaret Hope . . . . Fanette Fraser
Cecil Morton York . . . . . . Vickers
George Bishop . . . . Insp Duer
Mickey Brantford . . . .
Hargreave Mansell . . . .
Pat Fitzgerald . . . .
CRIME Runaway groom's amnesiac fiancee
proves detective framed him for stabbing actress

07708
LITTLE MISS NOBODY (5750)
Carlton Productions (Butcher)
D:SC: Wilfred Noy
S: (PLAY) John Graham
Flora le Breton . . . . Miss Nobody
John Stuart . . . . Guy Cheviot
Ben Field . . . . Potter
Gladys Jennings . . . . Lady Violet
Sydney Paxton . . . . Dominie
Eva Westlake . . . . Lady Stilton
Alfred Clark . . . . Earl of Cripplegate
Donald Searle . . . . Gussie
Aubrey Fitzgerald . . . . Jock
James Reardon . . . . Manager
COMEDY Scotland. Castle caretaker fools rich
aunt by having lodgers pose as earl's family.

JUL

07709
BEAUTIFUL KITTY (4480) (U)
Walter West Productions (Butcher)
D: Walter West
S: J. Bertram Brown
Violet Hopson . . . . Kitty
James Knight . . . . Jim Bennett
Robert Vallis . . . . Alf Briggs
Arthur Walcott . . . .
Pollie Emery . . . .
Fred Percy . . . .
SPORT Workman loses winnings on dud
racehorse bought from bookmaker.

07710
THE INDIAN LOVE LYRICS (6920) (U)
Stoll
D:SC: Sinclair Hill
S: (POEM) Laurence Hope (THE GARDEN OF
KARMA)
Catherine Calvert . . . . Queen Vashti
Owen Nares . . . . Prince Zahirudin
Malvina Longfellow . . . . Princess Nadira
Shayle Gardner . . . . Ahmed Khan
Fred Raynham . . . . Ibrahim-beg-Ismael
Roy Travers . . . . Hassan Ali Khan
William Parry . . . . Mustapha Khan
Nelson Ramsey . . . . Sultan Abdul Rahin
Daisy Campbell . . . . Sjltana Manavour
Fred Rains . . . . Selim
Pino Conti . . . . Youssef
Arthur McLaglen . . . . Champion
ROMANCE India. Princess poses as commoner
to escape forced marriage to prince.

07711
THE HOTEL MOUSE (6500) (A)
British Super (Jury)
P: G.B. Samuelson
D: Fred Paul
S: (PLAY) Gerbidon & Armat
SC: Walter Summers
Lilian Hall Davis. . . . . Mauricette
Campbell Gullan . . . . Marchant
Warwick Ward . . . . Estaban
Josephine Earle . . . . Lola
Morgan Wallace . . . . . . Hon Harry Hurlingham
CRIME Nice. Girl thief helps American recoup
gambling losses and letters from blackmailer.

07712
SHOULD A DOCTOR TELL? (7400) (A)
Napoleon
P: G.B. Samuelson
D: Alexander Butler
S: G.B. Samuelson, Walter Summers
Lillian Hall Davis . . . . Alisa
Henry Vibart . . . . . . Dr Thornton Davies
Moyna McGill . . . . The Woman on the Rack
Francis Lister . . . . Roger Davies

Jerrold Robertshaw . . . . Prosecution
Bert Darley . . . . Defence
Hugh Dempster . . . .
DRAMA Doctor learns his pregnant patient is
engaged to his son.

07713
EARLY BIRDS (3000) (A)
Brouett-Egrot (W & F)
P: Lucien Egrot
D: Albert Brouett
S: (SKETCH) Fred Karno
SC: P.L. Mannock
Harry Wright . . . . The Drunk
Fred Karno . . . . The Jew
Katherine Kilfoyle . . . . Liza
J. Edwards Barber . . . . Bill
George Turner . . . . The Lover
Charles Bell . . . . The Newsboy
COMEDY Dude's night out in East End streets,
pubs, and dosshouse.

07714
THE UNINVITED GUEST (4900) (U)
Dewhurst (Walker)
P: D:S: George Dewhurst
Stewart Rome . . . . Philip Orme
Madge Stuart . . . . Mavis Steele
Cameron Carr . . . . Denton
Arthur Walcott . . . . Spaling
Cecil Morton York . . . . . . Felix Steele
Linda Moore . . . . Hilda
Leal Douglas . . . . Baines
DRAMA Bankrupt financier bribes thief to pose
as missing heir; he turns out to be heir. (Made
in Berlin).

07715
FIRES OF FATE (7185) (U)
Gaumont-Westminster
D: Tom Terriss
S: (NOVEL) A. Conan Doyle (TRAGEDY OF
THE KOROSKO (PLAY) Lewis Waller
SC: Alicia Ramsey
Wanda Hawley . . . . Dorinne Adams
Nigel Barrie . . . . Col Egerton
Pedro de Corboba . . . . Prince Ibrahim
Stewart Rome . . . . Rev Samuel Roden
Edith Craig . . . . Miss Adams
Percy Standing . . . . Stephen Belmont
Arthur Cullin . . . . Sir Charles Rodin
Douglas Munro . . . . Mansoor
Cyril Smith . . . . Lord Howard Cecil
ADVENTURE Egypt. Colonel with year to live
saves girl from Arab Prince.

07716
THE STARLIT GARDEN (6418) (U)
George Clark (Stoll)
D:SC: Guy Newall
S: (NOVEL) H. De Vere Stacpoole
Guy Newall . . . . Richard Pinckney
Ivy Duke . . . . Phyllis Berknowles
Valia . . . . Frances Blett
A. Bromley Davenport . . . . . Col Grangerson
Lawford Davidson . . . . Silas Grangerson
Mary Rorke . . . . Aunt Maria
Cecil Morton York . . . . Hennessey
John Alexander . . . . Rafferty
Marie Ault . . . . Old Prue
ROMANCE Italy. Ward wins affianced guardian
by saving him from rival's knife.

AUG

07717
THE LITTLE DOOR INTO THE WORLD
(5000)
Dewhurst-Thompson (Astra-National)
reissue: 1924, THE EVIL THAT MEN DO
(Globe)

P:D:S: George Dewhurst
Lawford Davidson. . . . . Lefarge
Nancy Beard . . . . . Maria Jose/Celestine
Olaf Hytten . . . . Mountebank
Peggy Patterson . . . . Dancer
Victor Tandy . . . . Agent
Arthur Mayhew . . . . Troubadour
Robert Williamson . . . . Manager
DRAMA Austria, period. Nun saves dancer
from squire by luring him, then revealing
she is his bastard. (Made in Berlin).

07718
HUTCH STIRS 'EM UP (5200) (U)
Ideal
D: Frank H. Crane
S: (NOVEL) Harry Harding (THE HAWK OF
REDE)
SC: Eliot Stannard
Charles Hutchison. . . . Hurricane Hutch
Joan Barry . . . . Joan
Malcolm Tod . . . . Tom Grey
Gibson Gowland . . Sir Arthur Blackross
Sunday Wilshin . . . . Mrs Grey
Aubrey Fitzgerald . . . . . . Cruddas
Violet Forbes . . . . Mrs Cruddas
CRIME Cowboy saves village girl from
mad squire's torture chamber.

07719
OUT TO WIN (6000)
Ideal
D:SC: Denison Clift
S: (PLAY) Dion Clayton Calthrop, Roland
Pertwee
Catherine Calvert . . . . Auriole Craven
Clive Brook . . . . . . Barraclough/Altar
Irene Norman . . . . Isobel
Cameron Carr . . . . Harrison Smith
A. B. Imeson . . . . Ezra Phipps
Ivo Dawson . . . . Lawrence
Olaf Hytten . . . . Cumberston
Norman Page . . . . Van Diet
Robert English . . . Lord Almont Frayne
Ernest A. Douglas . . Hilbert Torrington
James McWilliams . . . . . . Doran
Daisy Campbell . . . . Mrs Barraclough
Ernest Dagnall . . . . Sydney
CRIME Tramp hired to pose as financier to
obtain Balkan radium concession.

07720
I'PAGLIACCI (6000) (A) *Prizma Seq*
Napoleon
P: G.B. Samuelson
D: G.B. Samuelson, Walter Summers
S: (OPERA) R. Leoncavallo
SC: Walter Summers
Lilian Hall-Davis. . . . . Nedda
Adelqui Millar . . . . Canio
Campbell Gullan . . . . Tonio
Frank Dane . . . . Silvio
Andre Beaulieu . . . .
G. Longoborde . . . .
DRAMA Italy. Jealous cripple switches
knives so that actor stabs faithless wife
during play.

07721
STRANGLING THREADS (6648) (U)
Hepworth (Ideal)
D: Cecil M. Hepworth
S: (PLAY) Leon M. Lion, Naunton Davies
(THE COBWEB)
Alma Taylor . . . . Irma Brian
Campbell Gullan . . . . . . Martin Forsdyke KC
James Carew . . . . Stephen Mallard
Mary Dibley . . . . Dolorosa
Eileen Dennes . . . . Miss Debb
Gwynne Herbert . . . . Mrs Brian

John McAndrews . . . . Insp Beall
Maud Cressall . . . . Coroner's Wife
Louis Goodrich . . . . Coroner
Lyell Johnston . . . .
CRIME Millionaire thinks he kills blackmailing
Mexican wife who dies of shock.

07722
GUY FAWKES (6600) (U)
Stoll
D: Maurice Elvey
S: (NOVEL) Harrison Ainsworth
SC: Alicia Ramsey
Matheson Lang . . . . Guy Fawkes
Nina Vanna . . . . Viviana Ratcliffe
Hugh Buckler . . . . Catesby
Shayle Gardner . . . . Humphrey
Lionel d'Aragon . . . . Earl of Salisbury
Edward O'Neill . . . . Father
Jerrold Robertshaw . . . . James I
Robert English . . . . Radcliffe
Dallas Cairns . . . . Mounteagle
Pino Conti . . . . Tresham
HISTORY 1605. Papists hire Dutchman to
blow up parliament in revenge for anti-catholic
decree.

07723
THE SCHOOL FOR SCANDAL (6350) (U)
BP Productions (Butcher)
P:D: Bertram Phillips
S: (PLAY) Richard Brinsley Sheridan
SC: Frank Miller
Queenie Thomas . . . . Lady Teazle
Frank Stanmore . . . . Sir Peter Teazle
Basil Rathbone . . . . Joseph Surface
John Stuart . . . . Charles Surface
Sydney Paxton . . . . Sir Oliver Surface
A.G.Poulton . . . . Moses
Elsie French . . . . Lady Sneerwell
Mary Brough . . . . Mrs Candour
Jack Miller . . . . Trip
Billie Shotter . . . . Maria
Lottie Blackford . . . . Aunt Agatha
Richard Turner . . . . | Sir Benjamin Backbite
James Reardon . . . . Crabtree
Wallace Bosco . . . . Snake
Kimber Philips . . . . Sir Harry Bumper
COMEDY 1777. Uncle poses as usurer to
learn which nephew deserves fortune.

07724
THE WOMAN WHO OBEYED (6400) (A)
Astra-National
D:S: Sidney Morgan
Hilda Bayley . . . . Marion Dorchester
Stewart Rome . . . . Dorchester
Henry de Vries . . . . Capt Conway
Valia . . . . Mrs Bruce Corrington
Gerald Ames . . : . . . . Raymond Straithmore
Ivo Dawson . . . . Duke of Rexford
Peter Dear . . . . Bobbie Dorchester
Nancy Price . . . . Governess
ROMANCE Jealous man reunited with
divorced wife after running over their son.

07725
CHU CHIN CHOW (12,250) (U)
Graham-Wilcox
P:D:SC: Herbert Wilcox
S: (PLAY) Oscar Asche, Frederick Norton
Betty Blythe . . . . Zahrat
Herbert Langley . . . . Abou Hassan
Randle Ayrton . . . . Kasim Baba
Eva Moore . . . . Alcolma
Judd Green . . . . Ali Baba
Olaf Hytten . . . . Mukbill
Jeff Barlow . . . . Mustafa
Jameson Thomas . . . . Omar

Dora Levis . . . . Mahbubah
Dacia . . . . Dancer
FANTASY Baghdad. Girl escapes from robber
sheikh and thwarts plot to rob merchant.
(Made in Berlin).

07726
AFTERGLOW (6900) (U)
Napoleon Films
P: G.B.Samuelson
D: G.B.Samuelson, Walter Summers
S: Walter Summers
Lilian Hall-Davis . . . . Ethel
Fred Hearne . . . . Bayard Delavel
James Lindsay . . . . . Howard Massingham
Minna Grey . . . . Grace Andover
Annette Benson . . . . . Myra Massingham
Sir Simeon Stuart . . . . . Judge Maitland
Walter McEwen . . . . Bob Farley
Caleb Porter . . . .
SPORT Postmistress saves swindling bookie by
influencing judge, her ex-lover.

07727
LIGHTS OF LONDON (7386) (U)
Gaumont-British Screencraft
D: C.C.Calvert
S: (PLAY) George R.Sims
SC: Louis Stevens
Wanda Hawley . . . . Bess Marks
Nigel Barrie . . . . Harold Armytage
Warburton Gamble . . . . . Clifford Armytage
James Lindsay . . . . Seth Preene
Mary Clare . . . . Hetty Preene
Cecil Morton York . . . Sir Oliver Armytage
Dorothy Fane . . . . Belle
A. Harding Steerman . . . . . Bertram Marks
H. R. Hignett . . . . Simon Jarvis
Mary Brough . . . . Mrs Jarvis
CRIME Heir, framed by cousin for killing
father, breaks jail and saves wife from fire.

07728
SQUIBS, MP (5989) (U)
Welsh-Pearson (Gaumont)
P:D: George Pearson
S: George Pearson, Leslie Hiscott, Will Dyson
Betty Balfour . . . . Squibs Hopkins
Hugh E. Wright . . . . Sam Hopkins
Fred Groves . . . . PC Charlie Lee
Irene Tripod . . . . Euphemia Fitzbulge
Frank Stanmore . . . . . Horace Honeybunn
Odette Myrtil . . . . Dancer
COMEDY Girl stands for parliament when
rival milk company accuses her fiance of
bribery.

OCT

07729
YOUNG LOCHINVAR (5300) (U)
Stoll
D: W.P.Kellino
S: (POEM) Sir Walter Scott (NOVEL)
J. Preston Muddick
SC: Alicia Ramsey
Owen Nares . . . . Lochinvar
Gladys Jennings . . . . Helen Graeme
Dick Webb . . . . : . . . . Musgrave
Cecil Morton York . . . . Johnstone
Charles Barratt . . . . Alick Johnstone
Bertie Wright . . . . : . . . Brookie
Lionel Braham . . . . Jamie the Ox
Dorothy Harris . . . . Cecilia Johnstone
J. Nelson Ramsey . . . . Graeme
ADVENTURE Scotland, period. Chief saves
beloved from being forced to marry rival's son.

07730
THE CONSTABLE'S MOVE (1900) (U)
Artistic reissue: 1926 (UK)

P: George Redman
D: Manning Haynes
S: (STORY) W.W.Jacobs (CAPTAINS ALL)
SC: Lydia Hayward
Charles Ashton . . . . PC Evans
Johnny Butt . . . . Bob Crummit
COMEDY Poacher feuds with neighbour, a
policeman.

07731
AN ODD FREAK (1900) (U)
Artistic reissue: 1926 (UK)
P: George Redman
D: Manning Haynes
S: (STORY) W.W.Jacobs (LIGHT FREIGHTS)
SC: Lydia Hayward
Johnny Butt . . . . Sam Small
Gladys Hamer . . . . Emmie
Moore Marriott . . . . Beauty
Wally Bosco . . . . Showman
Toby Cooper . . . . Sailor
COMEDY Sailor sells nephew to showman as
wild man from Borneo.

07732
THE CONVERT (1900) (U)
Artistic reissue: 1926 (UK)
P: George Redman
D: Manning Haynes
S: (STORY) W.W.Jacobs (DEEP WATERS)
SC: Lydia Hayward
Johnny Butt . . . . Joe Billings
Bob Vallis . . . . Bully
Cynthia Murtagh . . . . Girl
Walter Wichelow . . . . Preacher
COMEDY Reformed bully slips until preacher
fights for fiancee.

07733
WHAT PRICE LOVING CUP? (5100) (U)
West Productions (Butcher) reissue: 1926 (2 rls)
D: Walter West
S: Campbell Rae Brown
SC: J. Bertram Brown
Violet Hopson . . . . Lady Lorimer
James Knight . . . . Philip Denham
James Lindsay . . . . Sir John Lorimer
Marjorie Benson . . . . Tony Sheldon
Cecil Morton York . . . . Earl of Dalmore
Arthur Walcott . . . . Manager
Bob Vallis . . . . Hireling
Oliver Marks . . . . Steward
James Strachey . . . . Trainer
SPORT Horse owner saves girl jockey from
being kidnapped by knight.

07734
THE AUDACIOUS MR SQUIRE (4770) (U)
B & C
P: Edward Godal
D: Edwin Greenwood
S: (PLAY) Sydney Bowkett (SQUIRE THE
AUDACIOUS)
SC: Eliot Stannard
Jack Buchanan . . . . Tom Squire
Valia . . . . Constance
Russell Thorndike . . . . . Henry Smallwood
Malcolm Tod . . . . Edgar
Sydney Paxton . . . . John Howard
Dorinea Shirley . . . . Bessie
Forbes Dawson . . . . Pitt
Fred Rains . . . . Jupp
COMEDY Collector mistakes thief for
daughter's secret husband and vice versa.

07735
FINISHED (1808) (U)
Quality Plays (Gaumont)
D: George A. Cooper

S:(STORY) Guy de Maupassant (FINI)
Jerrold Robertshaw . . . Comte de Lormerin
Daisy Campbell . . . . . . Baroness de Vance
Eileen Magrath . . . . Renee
Chris Walker . . . . Valet
ROMANCE Comte realises age when he visits
childhood sweetheart.

07736
DARKNESS (2000) (A)
Quality Plays (Gaumont)
D: George A. Cooper
S: (STORY) Max Brand
Hugh Miller . . . . Keever
Hilda Sims . . . .
Gordon Craig . . . .
M.A.Wetherell . . . .
Wallace Bosco . . . .
CRIME Man tries to kill the man responsible
for father's death.

07737
THE REVERSE OF THE MEDAL (1945) (U)
Quality Plays (Gaumont)
D: George A. Cooper
S: (STORY) Lionel James
Clive Brook . . . . General
John Stuart . . . . Pilot
Olaf Hytten . . . . Strategist
Bertram Terry . . . .
WAR France. General sends pilot son to crash
in enemy territory.

07738
THE MAN WHO LIKED LEMONS (1614) (U)
Quality Plays (Gaumont)
D: George A. Cooper
S: (STORY) Will Scott (UNTOLD GOLD)
Forrester Harvey . . . . Burglar
Harry J. Worth . . . .
W. G. Saunders . . . .
COMEDY Burglar's liking for lemons
causes capture.

07739
CONSTANT HOT WATER (2157) (U)
Quality Plays (Gaumont)
D: George A. Cooper
S: (STORY) P.L.Mannock
Gladys Jennings . . . . . Rosina Tennant
John Stuart . . . . Cuthbert
Lawford Davidson . . . . . . Man
Nora Roylance . . . . . . Girl
Gibb McLaughlin . . . . Eardley Adams
John East . . . . Janitor
COMEDY Men and girls cause trouble by
entering wrong apartment.

07740
THREE TO ONE AGAINST (2343) (U)
Quality Plays (Gaumont)
D: George A. Cooper
S: (STORY)
Florence Wood . . . . Mrs Musquash
Cecil du Gue . . . . Soldier
Judd Green . . . . Sailor
Gibb McLaughlin . . . . . . Cleric
COMEDY Rich widow with pet parrot is
wooed by soldier, sailor and cleric.

07741
HEARTSTRINGS (5170) (U)
B & C
P: Edward Godal
D: Edwin Greenwood
S: (NOVEL) Mrs Gaskell (A MANCHESTER
MARRIAGE)
SC: Eliot Stannard
Gertrude McCoy . . . . Norah
Victor McLaglen . . . . Frank Wilson
Edith Bishop . . . . Alice Wilson

Russell Thorndike . . . . . . Tom Openshaw
Sydney Fairbrother . . . . . Mrs Chadwick
George Bishop . . . . Mr Chadwick
Kate Gurney . . . . Mrs Wilson
ROMANCE Sailor returns from "death" to
find his wife has remarried for sake of
crippled child.

07742
THE BELOVED VAGABOND (10,020) (U)
Astra-National
D: Fred Leroy Granville
S: (NOVEL) W.J.Locke
SC: Frank Miller
Carlyle Blackwell . . Gaston de Nerac
Madge Stuart . . . . Blanquette
Phyllis Titmuss . . . . Joanna Rushworth
Sydney Fairbrother . . . . . . Mrs Smith
Albert Chase . . . . Asticot
Owen Roughwood . . .Comte de Verneuil
Hubert Carter . . . . Dubosc
Cameron Carr . . . . Bradshaw
Irene Tripod . . . . Mme Bain
Ernest Hilliard . . . . Maj Walters
Alfred Woods . . . . Mr Rushworth
Emily Nicholls . . . . Mrs Rushworth
Jessie Matthews . . . . Pan
ROMANCE Brittany. Jilted rich man poses
as tramp and falls in love with orphan.

07743
BODEN'S BOY (5600) (U)
Hepworth
D: Henry Edwards
S (NOVEL) Tom Gallon
SC: Tom White
Henry Edwards . . . . Enery Boden
Chrissie White . . . . Barbara Pilgrim
Francis Lister . . . . David Wayne
Henry Vibart . . . . Flower
Stephen T. Ewart . . . . Christopher Pilgrim
Judd Green . . . . Swaddell
Bob Russell . . . . Tickner
ROMANCE Shopkeeper sends adopted son
to college on inheritance and rejects
secretary's love for his sake.

07744
THE ROYAL OAK (6170) (U)
Stoll *reissue:* 1929 (EB)
D: Maurice Elvey
S: (PLAY) Henry Hamilton, Augustus Harris
SC: Lucita Squier
Betty Compson . . . . Lady Mildred
Henry Ainley . . . . Oliver Cromwell
Henry Victor . . . Charles I/Charles II
Thurston Hall . . . . Col. Ancketell
Clive Brook . . . . Dorian Clavering
Bertie Wright . . . . Dearlove
Peter Dear . . . . Lord Cholmondeley
Dallas Cairns . . . . Pendrel
Blanche Walker . . . . Parry
Rolf Leslie. . . . . Melchizedek
HISTORY 1651. Royalist lady poses as king
to help him escape.

07745
THE REST CURE (4800) (U)
Stoll
D: SC: A. E. Coleby
S: (NOVEL) George Robey
George Robey . . . . George
Sydney Fairbrother . . . . . . Mrs George
Gladys Hamer . . . . The Maid
Bertie White . . . . The Idiot
Harry Preston . . . . The Squire
Bob Reed . . . . The Vicar
Micky Brantford . . . . The Boy
Joan Whalley . . . . The Girl
Minna Leslie . . . . The Friend
George Bishop . . . . The Cabman

Raymond Ellis . . . . The Landlord
COMEDY City man's rest in country is so
upsetting he returns home.

07746
BECKET (6450) (U)
Stoll
D: George Ridgwell
S: (PLAY) Alfred Tennyson
SC: Eliot Stannard
Sir Frank Benson . . . . . . Thomas a Becket
Gladys Jennings . . . . Rosamund de Clifford
Mary Clare . . . . Queen Eleanor
A.V. Bramble . . . . Henry II
Bertram Burleigh . . . . . . Lord Leicester
Sydney Paxton . . . . Archbishop of York
Percy Standing . . . . Sir Reginald Fitzurse
William Lugg . . . . John of Oxford
Sydney Folker . . . . de Broc
Clive Currie . . . . Herbert of Bosham
Hargrave Mansell . . . . . . Theobald of Canterbury
Alex G. Hunter . . . . . . John of Salisbury
Arthur Burne . . . . Grim
Bert Daley . . . . de Tracey
Harry J. Worth . . . . de Brito
HISTORY 1170. Archbishop forces king's
mistress to enter convent, and is murdered.

07747
THE LOVES OF MARY, QUEEN OF SCOTS
Ideal   (7684) (U)
D:S: Denison Clift
Fay Compton . . . . Mary Stuart
Gerald Ames . . . . Bothwell
Ivan Samson . . . . Lord Dudley
John Stuart . . . . George Douglas
Ellen Compton . . . . Queen Elizabeth
Lionel d'Aragon . . . . . . Moray
Harvey Braban . . . . Ruthven
Irene Rooke . . . . Catherine de Medici
Donald McCardle . . . . . . Francis II
Rene Maupre . . . . Rizzio
Ernest A. Douglas . . . . . . Cardinal
Sydney Seaward . . . . . . Lord Douglas
Edward Sorley . . . . John Knox
Betty Faire . . . . Mary Livingstone
Dorothy Fane . . . . Mary Beaton
Nancye Kenyon . . . . Mary Fleming
Julie Hartley-Milburn . . . . Mary Seaton
HISTORY 1542-87. Dauphin's widow weds lord
and is executed for plotting against queen.

07748
I WILL REPAY (6600) (U) USA: SWORDS
Ideal   AND THE WOMAN
D: Henry Kolker
S:(NOVEL) Baroness Orczy
SC: Kinchen Wood, Isabel Johnstone
Holmes Herbert . . . . . Sir Percy Blakeney
Flora le Breton . . . Juliette de Mornay
Pedro de Cordoba . . . . Paul Deroulede
Ivan Samson . . . . . Viscount de Mornay
A.B.Imeson . . . . Tinville
Georges Treville . . . . . . Duc de Mornay
Marquisette Bostley . . . . Anne-Marie
Robert Lang . . . . Villefranche
ADVENTURE France, 1793. Duc's daughter
learns rescuer killed her brother and
betrays his plan to save queen.

07749
TWO-CHINNED CHOW (679) (U)
Atlas Biocraft (NAR)
D:S: Adrian Brunel
COMEDY Burlesque of "Chu Chin Chow."

07750
M'LORD OF THE WHITE ROAD (6800) (U)
I.B. Davidson (Granger) *reissue:* 1926
                          (Butcher; 2 rls)
D: Arthur Rooke

S: (NOVEL) Cedric D.Fraser
SC: Kinchen Wood
Victor McLaglen . . . Lord Annerley/John
Marjorie Hume . . . . Lady Gloria
James Lindsay . . . . Sir Humphrey Clayville
Fred Wright . . . . Master Peter
Mary Rorke . . . . Lady Collingway
George Turner . . . . Tom Brown
Bert Osborne . . . . Grappletight
Bob Reed . . . . Greenleaf
Bertie White . . . . Bushworthy
Harry Newbold . . . . Aylesbury
ADVENTURE 1725. Dying lord asks tramp to
pose as him and marry lady, and he is later
accused of killing lord.

07751
ARMAGEDDON (6000) (U)
British Instructional (New Era)
P:D: H.Bruce Woolfe
WAR Reconstruction of Lord Allenby's
Palestine campaign.

07752
WOMAN TO WOMAN (7455) (A)
Balcon, Freedman & Saville (W & F)
P: Michael Balcon, Victor Saville
D: Graham Cutts
S: (PLAY) Michael Morton
SC: Alfred J Hitchcock
Betty Compson . . . . Louise
Clive Brook . . . . David Compton
Josephine Earle . . . . Mrs Anson-Pond
Marie Ault . . . . Henriette
Myrtle Peter . . . . Davy
A. Harding Steerman . . . . Doctor
Madge Tree . . . .
Donald Searle . . . .
Tom Coventry . . . .
George Turner . . . .
Aubrey Fitzgerald . . . . . .
ROMANCE 1914. Amnesiac officer weds
barren socialite and adopts his son by French
ballerina.

07753
THE NAKED MAN (6125) (U)
Hepworth (Ideal)
D: SC: Henry Edwards
S: (PLAY) Tom Gallon, Leon M. Lion
(FELIX GETS A MONTH)
Henry Edwards . . . . . . Felix Delaney
Chrissie White . . . . . . Ninette Monday
James Carew . . . . . Anthony Mapletoft
Maul Cressall . . . . Evelyn Garland
E. Holman Clark . . . Alderman Twentyman
Frank Stanmore . . . . Hopkins
Gwynne Herbert . . . . . Mrs Garland
Henry Vibart . . . . Mr Janson
Eric Maturin . . . . Adrian Redwood
Jean Cadell . . . . Miss Linnett
Stephen T. Ewart . . . . . . Mr Garland
COMEDY heir to £500,000 must live for one
month without assistance.

07754
COMIN' THRO' THE RYE (7900) (U)
Hepworth
D: Cecil M. Hepworth
S: (NOVEL) Helen Mathers
SC: Blanche McIntosh
Alma Taylor . . . . Helen Adair
Shayle Gardner . . . . Paul Vasher
Eileen Dennes . . . . Sylvia Fleming
Ralph Forbes . . . . George Tempest
James Carew . . . . Col Adair
Francis Lister . . . . Dick Fellowes
Gwynne Herbert . . . . . . Mrs Adair
Henry Vibart . . . . Mr Tempest

Christine Rayner . . . . . . Jane Peach
Nancy Price . . . . Mrs Titmouse
John MacAndrews . . . . . Simpkins
Margot Armstrong . . . . Alice Adair
ROMANCE 1862. Jealous girl breaks up
friend's engagement with fake wedding
announcement. (Extract in THE SMALLEST
SHOW ON EARTH, 1957).

07755
A COUPLE OF DOWN AND OUTS (5550) (U)
Napoleon Films
P: G. B. Samuelson
D:S: Walter Summers
Rex Davis . . . . Danny Creath
Edna Best . . . . Molly Roake
George Foley . . . . PC Roake
Philip Hewland
DRAMA 1916. Ex-soldier steals his horse
to save it from battlefield, and becomes tramp.

07756
BONNIE PRINCE CHARLIE (6540) (U)
Gaumont-British Screencraft
D: C.C.Calvert
S: Alicia Ramsey
Gladys Cooper . . . . Flora MacDonald
Ivor Novello . . . . . Prince Charles Stuart
Hugh Miller . . . . Robert Fraser
A.B.Imeson . . . . . . Duke of Cumberland
Sydney Seaward . . . . Neil McEachinn
Benson Kleve . . . . . . Donald McPherson
Adeline Hayden Coffin . . . . Lady Clanronald
Arthur Wontner . . . . . . Lord Kingsburgh
Nancy Price . . . . Lady Kingsburgh
Lewis Gilbert . . . . Charles II
A. Bromley Davenport . . Sir John Cope
Mollita Davies . . . . Betty Burke
Robert Laing . . . . MacDonald
Arthur McLaglan . . . . MacKintosh
HISTORY Scotland, 1745. Pretender to
throne defeated at Culloden and betrayed by
rival.

DEC

07757
IN THE BLOOD (6100) (A)
Walter West (Butcher) reissue: 1926 (2 rls)
D: Walter West
S: (NOVEL) Andrew Soutar
SC:J. Bertram Brown
Victor McLaglan . . . . Tony Crabtree
Lillian Douglas . . . . Marian
Cecil Morton York . . . Sir James Crabtree
Valia . . . . Lady Crabtree
John Glidden . . . . Ralph Hardy
Arthur Walcott . . . . Osman Shebe
George Foley . . . . Fleming
Humberston Wright . . . . . Malcolm Jove
Judd Green . . . . Stoney Isaac
Adeline Hayden Coffin . . Lady Crabtree
Clifford McLaglen . . . . . . Kansas Cat
Kennth McLaglen . . . . . . The Whaler
SPORT Period. Lady frames stepson for
theft and he takes place of father's drugged
champion and wins boxing match.

07758
WIDOW TWAN-KEE (6050) (U) retitled:
ONE ARABIAN NIGHT
Stoll
D:SC: Sinclair Hill
S: (PANTOMIME) (ALADDIN)
George Robey . . . . Widow Twan-Kee
Julia Kean . . . . Princess
Lionelle Howard . . . . . . Aladdin
Edward O'Neill . . . . Abanazar
W.G.Saunders . . . . Emperor
H. Agar Lyons . . . . Li-Pong

Aubrey Fitzgerald . . . . . Servant
Basil Saunders . . . . Slave of the Lamp
Julie Suedo . . . . Fairy of the Ring
COMEDY China. Washerwoman's son uses
magician's lamp to marry Princess.

07759
DON QUIXOTE (4200) (U)
Stoll
D: Maurice Elvey
S: (NOVEL) Miguel de Cervantes
SC: Sinclair Hill
George Robey . . . . Sancho Panza
Jerrold Robertshaw . . . . . Don Quixote
Bertram Burleigh . . . . Carrasco
Sydney Fairbrother . . . . . Terezo
Minna Leslie . . . . Dulcinea
Edward O'Neill . . . . The Duke
Marie Blanche . . . . The Duchess
Frank Arlton . . . . Father Perez
Adeline Hayden Coffin . . . . Housekeeper
COMEDY Spain, 1600. Episodic misadven-
tures of man who thinks he is knight.

07760
SALLY BISHOP (7400)(A)
Stoll
D: Maurice Elvey
S:(NOVEL) E. Temple Thurston
Marie Doro . . . . Sally Bishop
Henry Ainley . . . . John Traill
Florence Turner . . . . Janet
Sydney Fairbrother . . . . . Landlady
Valia . . . . Miss Standish Rowe
A. Bromley Davenport . . . Landlord
Mary Dibley . . . . Mrs Priestley
Maie Hanbury . . . . Mrs Durlacher
Stella StAudrie . . . . Mrs Bishop
Humberston Wright . . . . . Judge
Dallas Cairns . . . . Mr Durlacher
George Turner . . . . Arthur
ROMANCE Typist threatens to expose lover
when he prosecutes divorce of woman he
means to marry.

07761
MUMMING BIRDS (2000)(U)
Brouett-Egrot (W&F)
D: Albert Brouett
S: (SKETCH) Fred Karno, Charles Baldwin
SC: P.L. Mannock
Harry Wright . . . . The Drunk
George Turner . . . .
Cynthia Murtagh . . . . The Girl
J. Edwards Barber . . . . . . The Tough
Franzi Carlos . . . . The Woman
Charlie Bell . . . . The Schoolboy
COMEDY Drunk causes trouble at music
hall.

07762
JAIL BIRDS (2000)(U)
Brouett-Egrot (W&F)
D: Albert Brouett
S: (SKETCH) Fred Karno
SC: P.L. Mannock
Harry Wright . . . . The Dude
George Turner . . . . The Curate
Cynthia Murtagh . . . . The Girl
Charles Ashton . . . . The Man
Cyril Percival . . . . Convict
Donald Searle . . . . Convict
Tom Coventry . . . . Convict
COMEDY Dude wrongfully jailed for theft.

07763
SQUIBS' HONEYMOON (5400)(U)
Welsh-Pearson (Gaumont)
D: George Pearson

S: George Pearson, Betty Balfour, T.A.Welsh
Betty Balfour . . . . Squibs
Hugh E.Wright . . . . Sam Hopkins
Fred Groves . . . . Charlie Lee
Frank Stanmore . . . . . .Horace Honeybunn
Irene Tripod . . . . . . Euphemia Fitzbulge
Robert Vallis . . . . Bob
Maurice Redmund . . . . . . Jean
COMEDY Paris. Bride poses as man to
escape capture by apaches.

07764
THE MAN WITHOUT DESIRE (7000)(A)
Atlas Biocraft (Novello-Atlas)
P: Ivor Novello
D: Adrian Brunel
S: Monckton Hoffe
SC: Frank Fowell
Ivor Novello . . . . Vittorio Dandolo
Nina Vanna . . . . Leonora/Genevia
Sergio Mari . . . . Almoro/Gordi
Chris Walker . . . . Roger/Mawdesley
Jane Dryden . . . . Luigia
Dorothy Warren . . . . Foscolnia
Adrian Brunel . . . . Reporter
FANTASY Venice, 1723. Dr suspends life of
mourning lover and he is revived 200 years
later.

07765
THE JOSE COLLINS DRAMAS (series)
B&C (Moss)
P: Edward Godal
D: Thomas Bentley
S: Eliot Stannard

07766
1: SHADOW OF DEATH (2000)
Jose Collins . . . . Gyp
Arthur Wontner . . . . . Sir John Bellingham
Lionelle Howard . . . . Dandy
Lionel d'Aragon . . . . Jules

07767
2: THE VELVET WOMAN (2000)
Jose Collins . . . . Mrs Graham
Arthur Wontner . . . . Henry B.Graham
Lionelle Howard . . . . . . Jack Merton
Lewis Gilbert . . . . Joshua Mills

07768
3: THE BATTLE OF LOVE (2000)(U)
Jose Collins . . . . Isabella
Arthur Wontner . . . . Otto
George Foley . . . . Franz
Cecil du Gue . . . . Paul

07769
4: THE COURAGE OF DESPAIR (2000)(U)
Jose Collins . . . . Isabella
Arthur Wontner . . . . Carlos

07770
5: THE LAST STAKE (2000)
Jose Collins . . . . Rosina
Arthur Wontner . . . . Guido
George Foley . . . . Beppo
Lionel d'Aragon . . . . Luigi

07771
6: SECRET MISSION (2000)
Jose Collins . . . . Olga
Arthur Wontner . . . . Paul
Lionelle Howard . . . . Michael
Lionel d'Aragon . . . . Nicholas
DRAMAS

07772
JACK SHEPPARD (2000)(A)
Broadoak Picture Productions
P:D: Henry Cockraft Taylor
S:(NOVEL) Harrison Ainsworth
Will West . . . . Jack Sheppard
May Lavelle . . . .
John F. Pearson . . . .
Edward Darcy . . . .
William Garrett . . . .
CRIME 1724. Carpenter turns robber,
escapes jail several times, and is hanged.

07773
THE FAIR MAID OF PERTH (5500)(U)
Anglia Films (Page)
P: Jack Buchanan
D: Edwin Greenwood
S: (NOVEL) Sir Walter Scott
SC: Eliot Stannard
Russell Thorndike . . . . . . Dwining
Sylvia Caine . . . . Catherine
Lionel d'Aragon . . . . Black Douglas
Tristram Rawson . . . . Harry Gow
Lionelle Howard . . . .
Donald McCardle . . . .
Sydney Paxton . . . .
Charles Barratt . . . .
Jack Denton . . . .
Kate Gurney . . . .
Leal Douglas . . . .
Wallace Bosco . . . .
ADVENTURE Scotland, period. Orphan
competes with prince for chief's daughter
and saves her from wicked duke.

1924

JAN

07774
THE MONEY HABIT (6400)(U)
Commonwealth (Granger)
D: Walter Niebuhr
S: (NOVEL) Paul Potter
SC: Alicia Ramsey
Clive Brook . . . . Noel Jason
Annette Benson . . . . Diana Hastings
Nina Vanna . . . . Cecile d'Arcy
Warwick Ward . . . . Varian
Fred Rains . . . . Marley
Eva Westlake . . . . Duchess
Philip Hewland . . . . Mr Hastings
Muriel Gregory . . . . Typist
Kate Gurney . . . . Mrs Hastings
CRIME Manager's mistress vamps financier
into buying dud oil claim.

07775
THE GREAT TURF MYSTERY (5250)(A)
Walter West (Butcher) reissue: 1926 (2 rls)
D: Walter West
S: J. Bertram Brown
Violet Hopson . . . . Sheila Donovan
James Knight . . . . Luke Pomeroy
Warwick Ward . . . . Frank Pomeroy
Marjorie Benson . . . . Maisie
Arthur Walcott . . . . Mark Goodman
M. Evans . . . . James Goodman
SPORT Lady owner loves millionaire's son
whose horse is doped by her trainer.

07776
LAWYER QUINCE (2200)(U)
Artistic reissue: 1926 (UK)
P: George Redman
D: Manning Haynes
S: (STORY) W.W.Jacobs
SC: Lydia Hayward
Moore Marriott . . . . Quince
Cynthia Murtagh . . . . Celia Rose
Charles Ashton . . . . Ned Quince
George Wynn . . . . His Rival
Johnny Butt . . . . Farmer Rose
Ada Palmer . . . . Widow
J. Edwards Barber . . . . . . Bully
COMEDY Village cobbler helps son win
farmer's daughter.

07777
DIXON'S RETURN (1800)(U)
Artistic reissue: 1926 (UK)
P: George Redman
D: Manning Haynes
S: (STORY) W.W.Jacobs
SC: Lydia Hayward
Moore Marriott . . . . Bob Dixon
Leal Douglas . . . . Mrs Dixon
Tom Coventry . . . . Uncle
Harry Ashton . . . . Nightwatchman
Bob Vallis . . . .
J Edwards Barber . . . . . .
Toby Cooper . . . .
COMEDY Henpecked publican runs away to
sea and returns a new man.

07778
THE BOATSWAIN'S MATE (1900)(U)
Artistic reissue: 1926 (UK)
P: George Redman
D: Manning Haynes
S: (STORY) W.W.Jacobs
SC: Lydia Hayward
Florence Turner . . . . Mrs Walters
Victor McLaglen . . . . Ned Travers
Johnny Butt . . . . George Benn

J. Edwards Barber . . . . . . Policeman
COMEDY Retired boatswain hires ex-soldier
to rob widow's inn.

07779
THE COLLEEN BAWN (6650)(U)
Stoll reissue: 1929
THE LOVES OF COLLEEN BAWN (EB)
D: W.P.Kellino
S: (PLAY) Dion Boucicault
SC: Eliot Stannard
Henry Victor . . . . Hardress Cregan
Colette Brettell . . . . . . Eily O'Connor
Stewart Rome . . . . Myles na Coppaleen
Gladys Jennings . . . . Ann Chute
Clive Currie . . . . Danny Mann
Marie Ault . . . . Sheelah
Marguerite Leigh . . . . . . Mrs Cregan
Aubrey Fitzgerald . . . Sir Patrick Chute
Dave O'Toole . . . . Mike
CRIME Ireland, 1820. Poor aristocrat hires
halfwit to drown his secret wife so he can
wed heiress.

07780
SOUTHERN LOVE (7800)(A) USA:
A WOMAN'S SECRET
Graham-Wilcox
P;D:SC: Herbert Wilcox
S: (POEM) Henry Longfellow (THE SPANISH
STUDENT)
Betty Blythe . . . . Dolores
Herbert Langley . . . . Pedro
Randle Ayrton . . . . Count de Silva
Warwick Ward . . . . Dick Tennant
Liane Haid . . . . Countess de Silva
Hal Martin . . . . Gipsy
DRAMA Spain. Gipsies save dancer from jail
when her admirer kills count who ruined her
career. (Made in Vienna).

07781
THE WHITE SHADOW (5047)(U) USA:
WHITE SHADOWS
Balcon. Freedman & Saville (W&F)
P: Michael Balcon, Victor Saville
D: Graham Cutts
S: (NOVEL) Michael Morton (CHILDREN
OF CHANCE).
SC: Alfred J. Hitchcock
Betty Compson . . . . . . .Nancy/Georgina Brent
Clive Brook . . . . Robin Field
Henry Victor . . . . Louis Chadwick
A.B.Imeson . . . . Mr Brent
Olaf Hytten . . . . Herbert Barnes
Daisy Campbell . . . . . Elizabeth Brent
Bert Darley . . . .
Maresco Marisini . . . .
Donald Searle . . . .
Muriel Gregory . . . .
DRAMA Paris. Wild girl becomes possessed by
soul of twin who died to save her life.

FEB

07782
FIGHTS THROUGH THE AGES (series)
Regent Films
Gerald Ames

07783
1: HEREWARD THE WAKE (1000)

07784
2: ROBIN HOOD'S MEN (1000)

07785
3: IN TUDOR DAYS (1000)

07786
4: THE TAVERN BRAWL (1000)

07787
5: IN SHERIDAN'S DAYS (1000)

07788
6: FOR LOVE OF A LADY (1000)
HISTORY Famous fights reconstructed.

07789
LIEUTENANT DARING RN AND THE WATER
RATS (5400)
MacDowell
P: J.B.MacDowell
D: Edward R. Gordon, James Youngdeer,
Percy Moran.
S: James Youngdeer, Percy Moran
Percy Moran . . . . Lt Jack Daring
Leila King . . . . Lola
George Foley . . . . Fawcett
Muriel Gregory . . . . Fiancee
N. Watts Phillips . . . . Smuggler
CRIME Naval lieut saves fiancee from drug
smugglers.

07790
EUGENE ARAM (8000) (U)
I.B.Davidson (Granger)
D: Arthur Rooke
S: (NOVEL) Lord Lytton
SC: Kinchen Wood
Arthur Wontner . . . . Eugene Aram
Barbara Hoffe . . . . Madeleine Lester
Mary Odette . . . . Elinor Lester
James Carew . . . . Richard Houseman
C.V.France . . . . Squire Lester
Walter Tennyson . . . . Walter Lester
Lionel d'Aragon . . . . Daniel Clarke
A.Bromley Davenport . . . . Cpl Bunting
William Matthews . . . . John Courtland
CRIME 1757. Blackmailed ex-thief is executed
for murder he didn't commit.

MAR

07791
HURRICANE HUTCH IN MANY
ADVENTURES (6000)
Ideal
D: Charles Hutchinson
S: Eliot Stannard
Charles Hutchinson . . . . . . Hurricane Hutch
Warwick Ward . . . . Dick
Malcolm Tod . . . . Frank Mitchell
Edith Thornton . . . . Nancy Norris
Robert Vallis . . . . Hugh
Ernest A. Douglas . . . . Mr Mitchell
Daisy Campbell . . . . Mrs Mitchell
Cecil Rayne . . . . Butler
CRIME Friend poses as shipwrecked heir who
is later saved and poses as friend's secretary.

07792
TONS OF MONEY (6400) (U)
Walls & Henson (Stoll)
P: Tom Walls, Leslie Henson
D: Frank Crane
S: (PLAY) Will Evans, "Valentine"
SC: Lucita Squier, Tom Webster
Leslie Henson . . . . . Aubrey Allington
Flora le Breton . . . . . . Louise Allington
Mary Brough . . . . Mrs Mullet
Clifford Seyler . . . . . . George Maitland
Jack Denton . . . . Henry
Elsie Fuller . . . . Jean Everard
Douglas Munro . . . . Sprules
Roy Byford . . . . Cheeseman
Willie Warde . . . . Giles
Ena Mason . . . . Maid
COMEDY Bankrupt poses as heir whilst
butler's brother poses as he.

07793
STRAWS IN THE WIND (6320) (A)
BP (Gaumont)
P:D: Bertram Phillips
S: Burton George
SC: Lucita Squier, Frank Miller
Betty Ross Clarke . . . . The Wife
Queenie Thomas . . . . The Woman
Fred Paul . . . . The Husband
Ivo Dawson . . . . The Brute
Clifford Cobbe . . . . The Man
Daisy James . . . . The Friend
Hargrave Mansell . . . . The Thinker
DRAMA Benefactor ejects tramp who covets
his wife and later adopts child of girl the
tramp saved from suicide.

07794
OLD BILL THROUGH THE AGES (7800)(U)
Ideal
D: Thomas Bentley
S: (CARTOONS) Bruce Bairnsfather
Syd Walker . . . . Old Bill
Arthur Cleave . . . . Bert
Jack Denton . . . . Alf
Gladys Ffolliott . . . . . . Queen Elizabeth
Austin Leigh . . . . William Shakespeare
Franzi Carlos . . . . Ann Hathaway
William Pardue . . . . The Redskin
Douglas Payne . . . .
Cecil Morton York . . . .
Clive Currie . . . .
Wally Bosco . . . .
Cyril Dane . . . .
Bruce Bairnsfather . . . .
FANTASY Private dreams he is William the
Conqueror, at Runnymede, at Plymouth
Hoe, and a bootlegger at the Boston Tea Party.

07795
HENRY, KING OF NAVARRE (5250) (U)
Stoll Reissue: 1929 (EB)
D: Maurice Elvey
S: (PLAY) Lewis Waller (NOVEL) Alexandre
Dumas
SC: Isabel Johnstone
Matheson Lang . . . . Henry
Gladys Jennings . . . Marguerite de Valois
Henry Victor . . . . Duc de Guise
Stella StAudrie . . . . Catherine de Medici
Humberston Wright . . . . . Charles XI
H. Agar Lyons . . . . Pierre
Mme d'Esterre . . . . Jeanne d'Albert
HISTORY France, 1572. Queen poisons
Huguenot Queen and weds her son to King's
sister as part of extermination plan.

07796
MIRIAM ROZELLA (7500) (A)
Astra-National
D:SC: Sidney Morgan
S: (NOVEL) B.J.Farjeon
Moyna McGill . . . . Miriam Rozella
Owen Nares . . . . Rudolph
Gertrude McCoy . . . . Lura Wood
Ben Webster . . . . Lord Laverock
Nina Boucicault . . . . Mrs Rozella
Russell Thorndike . . . . Crewe Slevens
Mary Brough . . . . Housekeeper
Henrietta Watson . . . . Lady Laverock
Gordon Craig . . . . Cecil Rozella
Sydney Paxton . . . . Priest
DRAMA Suicide's daughter becomes mistress
of rich man who reforms after baby sister
appears during orgy.

07797
THE WORLD OF WONDERFUL REALITY
(4990) (U)
Hepworth

D:SC: Henry Edwards
S: (NOVEL) E.Temple Thurston (THE CITY
OF BEAUTIFUL NONSENSE)
Henry Edwards . . . . John Grey
Chrissie White . . . . Jill Dealtry
James Lindsay . . . . Skipworth
Henry Vibart . . . . Thomas Grey
Gwynne Herbert . . . . Mrs Grey
Stephen Ewart . . . . Mr Dealtry
Violet Elliott . . . . Mrs Dealtry
ROMANCE Poor author has engaged girl pose
as wife to please dying father.

07798
MOONBEAM MAGIC (-) colour
Spectrum Films
P: Claude Friese-Greene
D:S: Felix Orman
Arthur Pusey . . . .
Margot Greville . . . .
Tom Heslewood . . . .
Roy Travers . . . .
Mabel Poulton . . . .
Kitty Foster . . . .
Joan Carr . . . .
FANTASY "The legend of how colour came into
the world."

07799
SHEER TRICKERY (800)
Atlas-Biocraft (Novello-Atlas)
D:S: Adrian Brunel
TRICK Scenes in slow motion, acceleration,
reverse, etc.

07800
THE GREAT WELL (6400) (A) USA:
NEGLECTED WOMEN
Ideal
D: Henry Kolker
S: (PLAY) Alfred Sutro
SC: Louis Stevens
Thurston Hall . . . . Peter Starling
Seena Owen . . . . Camilla Challenor
Lawford Davidson . . . . Maj Darenth
Joan Morgan . . . . Annette
Eva Moore . . . . Mrs Starling
Cameron Carr . . . . John
Harvey Braban . . . . Eric
Sir Simeon Stuart . . . . Sir Wilmot
Hugh Dempster . . . . Dick
DRAMA India. Major tries to cash in on dry
oil well but shoots himself when oil returns.

07801
THE PREHISTORIC MAN (4500) (U)
Stoll
D: A.E. Coleby
S: George Robey
SC: Sinclair Hill
George Robey . . He-of-the-Beetle-Brow
Marie Blanche . . . She-of-the-Permanent-Wave
H.Agar Lyons . . . He-of-the-Clutching-Hand
W.G.Saunders . . . He-of-the-Knotty-Joints
Johnny Butt . . . He-of-the-O-Cedar-Mop
Elsie Marriot-Watson-She-of-the-Tireless-Tongue
Laurie Leslie . . . . He-of-the-Matted Beaver
COMEDY Caveman elopes in stolen car and
saves bride's father from kidnap.

APR

07802
FILM FAVOURITES (2000)
Hepworth (Ideal)
D: Cecil M. Hepworth
S: Florence Turner
Florence Turner
COMEDY Impersonations of William S.Hart,
Larry Semon, Mae Murray, Richard Barthel-
mess, Charles Chaplin and Felix.

07803
CLAUDE DUVAL (9180) (U)
Gaumont
D: George A. Cooper
S: Mary Bennett
SC: Louis Stevens
Nigel Barrie . . . . Claude Duval
Fay Compton . . . . Duchess Frances
Hugh Miller . . . . Lord Lionel Malyn
A.B.Imeson . . . . Lord Chesterton
Dorinea Shirley . . . . Moll Crisp
James Knight . . . . Capt Craddock
James Lindsay . . . . Duke of Brentleigh
Charles Ashton . . . . Tom Crisp
Betty Faire . . . . Lady Anne
Stella StAudrie . . . . Mrs Crisp
Tom Coventry . . . . Mr Crisp
ADVENTURE Period. Frenchman turns
highwayman after duchess's cousin frames
him for killing titled blackmailer.

07804
THE UNWANTED (7250) (A)
Napoleon Films
P: G.B.Samuelson
D:S: Walter Summers
C.Aubrey Smith . . . . Col Carrington
Lilian Hall-Davis . . . . Marianne Dearsley
Nora Swinburne . . . . Joyce Mannering
Francis Lister . . . . John Dearsley
Walter Sondes . . . . Kenneth Carrington
Mary Dibley . . . . Genevieve
DRAMA Colonel's bastard son pretends
cowardly brother died a hero.

07805
PETT RIDGE STORIES (series)
B & C (Ideal)
P: Edward Godal
S: (STORIES) W. Pett Ridge
SC: Eliot Stannard

07806
1: LOVE AND HATE (2000) (U)
D: Thomas Bentley
George Foley . . . . Apps
Eve Chambers . . . . Mrs Williams
Frank Perfitt . . . . Thompson

07807
2: THE HAPPY PRISONER (2100) (A)
D: Hugh Croise
Ben Field . . . . The PC
James Knight . . . . The Prisoner
Dorothy Easton . . . . . The Farmer's Daughter

07808
3: WANTED, A BOY (1750) (U)
D: Thomas Bentley
Sydney Fairbrother . . . . . . The Aunt
Lionelle Howard . . . . The Suitor
Pauline Johnson . . . . The Niece
COMEDIES

07809
SLAVES OF DESTINY (5150) (A)
Stoll
D: Maurice Elvey
S: (NOVEL) A.E.W.Mason
(MIRANDA OF THE BALCONY)
Matheson Lang. . . . . . . Luke Charnock
Valia . . . . Miranda Warriner
Henry Victor . . . . . . Ralph Warriner
Humberston Wright . . . . . . Hassan
H. Agar Lyons . . . . . . Wilbrahim
DRAMA Africa. Englishman sold as slave by
blind beggar weds girl after beggar kills her
crooked husband.

MAY

07810
LOVERS IN ARABY (5000)
Atlas-Biocraft (Novello-Atlas)
P: Ivor Novello
D: Adrian Brunel
S: Adrian Brunel, Miles Mander
Annette Benson ...... Nadine Melville
Miles Mander .... Derek Fane
Norman Penrose .... Paul Melville
Adrian Brunel.......... Martin Carme
ADVENTURE Arabia. Engineer escapes from
Moors and saves girl from cad.

07811
THE GREAT PRINCE SHAN (6450) (U)
Stoll
D:SC: A.E.Coleby
S: (NOVEL) E.Phillips Oppenheim
Sessue Hayakawa .... Prince Shan
Ivy Duke .... Lady Maggie Trent
Tsuru Aoki .... Nita
Valia .... Nadia Karetsky
David Hawthorne .... Nigel Dorminster
Fred Raynham .... Immelmann
Henry Vibart .... Earl of Dorminster
H.Nicholls-Bates .... Gilbert Jenson
A.E.Coleby .... Prime Minister
DRAMA Assassinated Lord's daughter refuses
to marry Chinese Prince but agrees to be his
mistress.

07812
THE WINE OF LIFE (5600) (A)
I.B. Davidson (Butcher)
D: Arthur Rooke
S: (NOVEL) Maude Annesley
Betty Carter .... Lady Branton
Clive Brook .... Michael Strong
James Carew .... Alva Cortez
Juliette Compton .... Regine
Gertrude Sterroll .... Mrs Mainwaring
Mildred Evelyn .... Dorrie Richards
Lucien Verne .... Brian Westleigh
ROMANCE Italy. Artist saves divorced Lady
from hypnotist.

07813
HIS GRACE GIVES NOTICE (5900) (U)
Stoll
D: W.P.Kellino
S: (NOVEL) Lady Trowbridge
SC: Lydia Hayward
Nora Swinburne .... Cynthia Bannock
Henry Victor .... George Berwick
John Stuart .... Joseph Longley
Eric Bransby Williams .... Ted Burlington
Mary Brough .... Mrs Smith
Gladys Hamer .... Flickers
Phyllis Lytton .... Mrs Stapleton
Knighton Small .... Butler
COMEDY Butler inherits dukedom but stays
in service to save Lord's daughter from eloping
with married cad.

07814
THE CONSPIRATORS (4700) (A)
Stoll *reissue:* 1930, THE BARNES MURDER
CASE (EB)
D:SC: Sinclair Hill
S: (NOVEL) E.Phillips Oppenheim
Betty Faire .... Louise Fitzmaurice
David Hawthorne .... Herbert Wrayson
Moore Marriott ...... Morris/Sydney Barnes
Edward O'Neill ...... Col Fitzmaurice
Margaret Hope .... Mrs Barnes
Winifred Izard .... Queen of Rexonia
Fred Rains .... Benham
CRIME Girl accused when father kills
blackmailer to save his son.

07815
THE PRUDE'S FALL (5675)
Gainsborough (W&F)
P: Michael Balcon
D: Graham Cutts
S: (PLAY) Rudolf Besier, May Edginton
SC: Alfred Hitchcock
Jane Novak .... Beatrice Audley
Julanne Johnson ... . Sonia Roubetsky
Warwick Ward .... Andre le Briquet
Hugh Miller .... Marquis de Rocqueville
Gladys Jennings ...... Laura Westonry
Miles Mander .... Sir Neville Moreton
Henry Vibart .... Dean Carey
Marie Ault .... Mrs Masters
ROMANCE French captain persuades rich
widow to become mistress, but it is scheme to
test love.

JUN

07816
WOMEN AND DIAMONDS (5250) (U)
George Clarke (Ducal)
D: F.Martin Thornton
S: Clifton Boyne
Victor McLaglen .... Brian Owen
Madge Stuart .... Olive Seaton
Florence Turner .... Mrs Seaton
Norman Whalley .... Ray Seaton
Cecil du Gue .... Jim Beverley
M.A.Wetherell .... Barry Seaton
Walter Tennyson .... Jimmy Foster
Sir Simeon Stuart .... Munro Clay
Clifton Boyne .... Sweeney
CRIME Africa. Typist framed for killing
diamond smuggler who betrayed her father.

07817
REVEILLE (8400) (U)
Welsh-Pearson (Gaumont)
P:D:S: George Pearson
Betty Balfour .... Mick
Stewart Rome .... Nutty
Ralph Forbes .... The Kid
Sydney Fairbrother ...... Sophie Fitch
Frank Stanmore .... Whelks
Henrietta Watson .... The Mother
Guy Phillips .... Fred
Walter Tennyson .... Captain
Charles Ashton .... Sam
Donald Searle .... Ted
Beuna Bent .... Amelia Fitch
Sir Simeon Stuart .... Colonel
WAR Sempstress stops poor ex-soldier from
becoming leftwing agitator.

07818
LOVE ON THE RIVIERA (1000)
Riviera Films
D:S: W.H. Sheppard
Tom Isaacs .... The Man
Ethel Curnow .... The Girl
COMEDY Paignton.

JUL

07819
CROSSING THE GREAT SAGRADA (800)
Atlas-Biocraft (Novello-Atlas)
D:S: Adrian Brunel
Adrian Brunel
COMEDY Burlesque of "Crossing The Great
Sahara."

07820
THE OLD MAN IN THE CORNER (series)
Stoll
D:SC: Hugh Croise
S: (STORIES) Baroness Orczy
Rolf Leslie .... The Old Man
Renee Wakefield .... Mary Hatley

07821
1: THE KENSINGTON MYSTERY (2150) (U)
Reginal Fox .... William Yale
Donald Macardle .... William Biggs
Kate Gurney .... Mrs Yale
Elsa Martini .... Mrs Biggs

07822
2: THE AFFAIR AT THE NOVELTY
THEATRE (2200) (U)
Charles Vane ....
Phyllis Lytton ....
Walter Tennyson ....
Moore Marriott ....

07823
3: THE TRAGEDY OF BARNSDALE MANOR
(2200) (U)
Cecil Mannering ...... Lord Barnsdale
Noel Grahame .... Alice Hall
Arthur Lumley ...... Sir Gilbert Culworth
Marion Benham .... Lady Barnsdale
Mme d'Esterre .... Mme Quesnard

07824
4: THE YORK MYSTERY (2150) (A)
Dallas Cairns .... Lord Arthur Skelmerdon
Minna Grey .... Lady Skelmerdon
Jack Denton .... George Higgins
John Osborne .... Chips

07825
5: THE BRIGHTON MYSTERY (2200) (U)

07826
6: THE NORTHERN MYSTERY (2075) (A)

07827
7: THE REGENT'S PARK MYSTERY (1930)
(A)

07828
8: THE MYSTERY OF DOGSTOOTH
CLIFF (1940) (U)

07829
9: THE MYSTERY OF BRUDENELL COURT
(1831) (A)
John Hamilton ....
Molly Johnson ....

07830
10: THE MYSTERY OF THE KHAKI TUNIC
(2280) (A)

07831
11: THE TREMARNE CASE (1900) (A)

07832
12: THE HOCUSSING OF CIGARETTE
(2150) (U)
Roy Travers ....
Ena Evans ....
Frank Perfitt ....
Bob Vallis ....
CRIMES Old man tells girl reporter how he
solved various crimes.

07833
THRILLING STORIES FROM THE STRAND
MAGAZINE (series)
Stoll

07834
1: THE DRUM (1731) (A)
D:SC: Sinclair Hill
S: (STORY) F. Britten Austin
James Carew .... Doc Stevens
Jameson Thomas .... Capt Bull
Molly Johnson .... Daphne

07835
2: HOLLOWAY'S TREASURE (1728) (U)
D:SC: Sinclair Hill
S: (STORY) Morley Roberts
Dallas Cairns . . . . Holloway
Kathleen Kilfoyle . . . Margery Thwaites
Jack Trevor . . . . Dr Mandeville
Amy Willard . . . . Mrs Holloway
Micky Brantford . . . . Master Holloway
Bardy Russell . . . . Maj Thompson

07836
3: THE ACID TEST (1798) (U)
D:SC: Sinclair Hill
S:(STORY) Austin Phillips
Eric Bransby Williams. Harry Blackwell
Betty Faire . . . . Daphne Colvannick
Eric Hardin . . . . Allan Carmael
Hal Martin . . . . Roger Treffy
James English . . . . The Dean
Edith Camille . . . . Housekeeper

07837
4: AFTER DARK (1580) (U)
D: Thomas Bentley
S: (STORY) Bertram Atkey
Eric Bransby Williams . . . . Lt Latham
Joyce Dearsley . . . . Lady Louise
John Hamilton . . . . Lord Bramshaw
Gertrude Sterroll . . . . Mrs Latham

07838
5: FIGHTING SNUB REILLY (2161) (U)
D: Andrew P. Wilson
S: (STORY) Edgar Wallace
David Hawthorne . . . . Barry
Ena Evans . . . . Vera
Fred Raynham . . . . Dr Shaw
Dallas Cairns . . . . . . Sir John Selinger
Minnie Leslie . . . . Housekeeper

07839
6: THE CAVERN SPIDER (1750) (A)
D: Thomas Bentley
S: (STORY) L J Beeston
Jameson Thomas . . . . Spalding
Fred Raynham . . . . Fricker
Winifred Izard . . . . Helen
Ian Wilson . . . .
DRAMAS Short stories from monthly
magazine.

07840
CHAPPY — THAT'S ALL (4650) (A)
Stoll
D: Thomas Bentley
S: (NOVEL) Oliver Sandys
SC: Eliot Stannard
Joyce Dearsley . . . . Chappy
Gertrude McCoy . . . . Bettina
Francis Lister . . . . Stephen Poynter
Lewis Gilbert . . . . Piper
Eva Westlake . . . . Mrs Cherry
Edwin Greenwood . . . . Slim Jim
ROMANCE Novelist employs burglar's
daughter and saves her from attack by ex-
accomplice.

07841
THE MATING OF MARCUS (6000) (U)
Stoll
D: W.P. Kellino
S: (NOVEL) Mabel Barnes Grundy
Dollie . . . . Vivi Chester
Billie . . . . Naomi Chester
David Hawthorne . . . . Marcus Netherby
George Bellamy . . . . Mr Chester
Molly Johnson . . . . . Valerie Westmacott
Moore Marriott . . . . Rev Cheffins
W.G.Saunders . . . .
ROMANCE Girl with sick sister weds jilted
townsman who saves them from floods.

07842
SEN YAN'S DEVOTION (5530) (U)
Stoll
D:S: A.E.Coleby
Sessue Hayakawa . . . . Sen Yan
Tsuru Aoki . . . . His Wife
Fred Raynham . . . . Lutan Singh
H.Agar Lyons . . . . High Priest
Jeff Barlow . . . . Prince Huo Sang
Tom Coventry . . . . Li Chang
Johnny Butt . . . . O Ming
H.Nicholls-Bates . . . . Wun Li
DRAMA Disguised servant of dying
Japanese prince saves articles of
succession from rival faction.

07843
THE NOTORIOUS MRS CARRICK (5500)(A)
Stoll
D: George Ridgwell
S: (NOVEL) Charles Proctor (POOLS OF THE
PAST)
Disa . . . . Sybil Tregarthen
Cameron Carr . . . . David Carrick
A.B.Imeson . . . . Tony Tregarthen
Sydney Folker . . . . David Arman
Gordon Hopkirk . . . . Gerald Rosario
Jack Denton . . . . Allen Richards
Peggy Lynn . . . . Honor Tregarthen
Basil Saunders . . . . Insp Samson
Arthur Lumley . . . . Owen Lawson
CRIME Man's second wife is blackmailed by
former husband for murder of lover.

07844
THE COST OF BEAUTY (6100) (A)
Napoleon Films
P: G.B. Samuelson
D:S: Walter Summers
Betty Ross Clarke . . . . . . Diana Faire
Lewis Dayton . . . . Garth Walters
James Lindsay. . . . . Henri Delatour
Tom Reynolds . . . .
Nina Vanna . . . .
Pat Aherne . . . .
Hippodrome Eight
ROMANCE Rich woman refuses to bear
husband a child, but adopts son by mistress
after her death.

07845
THE GAY CORINTHIAN (5300) (A)
I.B. Davidson (Butcher) reissue: 1926,
THE THREE WAGERS (2 rls)
D: Arthur Rooke
S: (NOVEL) Ben Bolt
SC: Eliot Stannard
Victor McLaglen . . . Squire Hardcastle
Betty Faire . . . . Lady Carrie Fanshawe
Cameron Carr.. . . . . . Lord Barrymore
Humberston Wright . . . Sir Thomas Apreece
Donald McCardle . . . . Harry Fanshawe
George Turner . . . . Jeremy
Jack Denton . . . . Dr Lee
Guardsman Penwill . . . . Flaming Tinman
Noel Arnott . . . . . . Gentleman Jeffries
SPORT Period. Boxer saves lady who joins
gipsies on learning she is subject of a bet.

07846
ODD TRICKS (2000)
Tubby Phillips Films
D: Fred Rains
Tubby Phillips . . . . Tubby
Gibb McLaughlin . . . .
Franzi Carlos . . . .
Donald Searle . . . .
COMEDY Misadventures of a plump
District Messenger.

07847
THE SACRAMENT OF CONFIRMATION (2000)
Doctrinal Films
D: John M. Payne
Anonymous cast
RELIGION History of sacrament from
earliest days of church.

07848
THE PASSIONATE ADVENTURE (7923) (A)
Gainsborough (Gaumont)
P: Michael Balcon
D: Graham Cutts
S: (NOVEL) Frank Stayton
SC: Alfred Hitchcock
Alice Joyce . . . . Drusilla Sinclair
Marjorie Daw . . . . Vickey
Clive Brook . . . . Adrien StClair
Lilian Hall Davis . . . . Pamela
Victor McLaglen . . . . Herb Harris
J.R.Tozer . . . . . . Insp Stewart Sladen
Mary Brough . . . . Lady Rolls
John Hamilton . . . . Bill
DRAMA Rich man leaves wife, poses as
coster, and saves factory girl from crook.

07849
THE ALLEY OF GOLDEN HEARTS (5600)
(U)
BP Productions (MP Sales)
P:D: Bertram Phillips
S: E.P. Kinsella
SC: Frank Miller
Queenie Thomas . . . . Charity
John Stuart . . . . Jack
Cecil Morton York . . . . . Sir James/Paul Manners
Frank Stanmore . . . . Grocer
Mary Brough . . . .
Bernard Vaughan . . . .
Adeline Hayden Coffin . . .
Judd Green . . . .
Pollie Emery . . . .
DRAMA .Lonely squire throws New Year party
for villagers and discloses that he is poor girl's
uncle.

07850
THE ELEVENTH COMMANDMENT (7600) (A)
Gaumont
D: George A. Cooper
S: (PLAY) Brandon Fleming
Fay Compton . . . . Ruth Barchester
Stewart Rome . . . . John Lynton
Lilian Hall Davis . . . . Marian Barchester
Charles Quartermaine . . . James Mountford
Jack Hobbs . . . . Robert Ransome
Dawson Millward . . . . Sir Noel Barchester
Louise Hampton . . . . Lady Barchester
Brian Aherne . . . . Norman Barchester
CRIME Actress thwarts blackmailer by taking
blame for sister's compromise.

AUG

07851
PIXIE AT THE WHEEL (series)
Phillips
D: Lee Morrison
S: (STORIES) Dudley Sturrock
Peggy Worth . . . . Pixie O'Hara
Walter Tennyson . . . . Charles Cromwell

07852
1: MILES AGAINST MINUTES (2000)

07853
2: SPEEDING INTO TROUBLE (2000)

07854
3: PEACETIME SPIES (2000)
CRIME American girl reporter assisted on
stories by English motorist.

07855
THE LOVE STORY OF ALIETTE BRUNTON
(7300) (A)
Stoll
D: Maurice Elvey
S: (NOVEL) Gilbert Frankau
SC: Alicia Ramsey
Isobel Elsom . . . . Aliette Brunton
Henry Victor . . . . Ronald Cavendish
James Carew . . . . Hector Brunton KC
Humberston Wright . . . . . Admiral Brunton
Lewis Gilbert . . . . William Towers
Minna Leslie . . . . Maggie Peterson
Adeline Hayden Coffin . . Julia Cavenaish
ROMANCE Faithless KC's wife elopes with
opponent in slum murder trial.

07856
THE FURTHER MYSTERIES OF DR FU
MANCHU (Series) (A)
Stoll
D: SC: Fred Paul
S: (STORIES) Sax Rohmer
H. Agar Lyons . . . . Dr Fu Manchu
Fred Paul . . . . Nayland Smith
Dorinea Shirley . . . . Karamaneh
Humberston Wright . . . . Dr Petrie

07857
1: THE MIDNIGHT SUMMONS (1791)

07858
2: THE COUGHING HORROR (1800)
Fred Morgan . . . . Antonio Strozza
Johnny Butt . . . . Farmer
Harry Rignold . . . . Coughing Horror

07859
3: CRAGMIRE TOWER (2040)
George Foley . . . . Hagar
Rolfe Leslie . . . . Van Room

07860
4: THE GREEN MIST (1734)

07861
5: THE CAFE L'EGYPTE (2270)

07862
6: THE GOLDEN POMEGRANATES (2100)
Frank Wilson . . . . Insp Weymouth
Julie Suedo . . . . Zarmi
Fred Hearn . . . . Waiter

07863
7: KARAMANEH (2366)

07864
8: GREYWATER PARK (2390)
CRIME Chinese arch-criminal constantly
eludes police.

07865
WHITE SLIPPERS (6180) (A)
Stoll reissue: 1929, THE PORT OF LOST
SOULS (EB)
D: SC: Sinclair Hill
S: (NOVEL) Charles Edholm
Matheson Lang . . . . Lionel Hazard
Joan Lockton . . . . Alice
Gordon Hopkirk . . . Ramon Guitterez
Arthur McLaglen . . . . Lorenzo
Nelson Ramsey . . . . Hairy Joe
Irene Tripod . . . . Dona Pilar
Jack McEwen . . . . Mexican Rat
Adeline Hayden Coffin . . . . Mother
ADVENTURE Mexico. Girl saves treasure
hunter from mutinous crew and he saves her
from gambling husband.

07866
HER REDEMPTION (5430) (A) retitled:
THE GAYEST OF THE GAY
BP Productions (MP Sales)
P: D: Bertram Phillips
S: (PLAY) Arthur Shirley
SC: Frank Miller
Queenie Thomas . . . Olivia/Sylvia Meredith
John Stuart . . . . Jack Latimer
Cecil Humphreys . . . . Hubert Steele
Juliette Compton . . . . Liane Vandry
Frank Stanmore . . . . Barney
Arthur Cleave . . . . Percy
Windham Guise . . . . Seth Howard
CRIME Gambler kills wife's twin sister by
mistake.

SEP

07867
DECAMERON NIGHTS (9650) (A)
Graham-Wilcox Productions-Decla
P: Herbert Wilcox, Erich Pommer
D: Herbert Wilcox
S: (PLAY) R. McLoughlin, B. Lawrence
(BOOK) Boccaccio (THE DECAMERON)
SC: Herbert Wilcox, Noel Rhys
Lionel Barrymore . . . . Saladin
Ivy Duke . . . . Perdita
Werner Krauss . . . . Soldan
Bernhard Goetzke . . . . Torello
Randle Ayrton . . . . Ricciardo
Xenia Desni . . . . Lady Teodora
Jameson Thomas . . . . Imliff
Hannah Ralph . . . . Lady Violante
Albert Steinruck . . . . King Algarve
ROMANCE Period. Saracen sultan's disguised
son loves amnesiac Moslem princess.
(Made in Berlin).

07868
THE STIRRUP CUP SENSATION (5300) (U)
Walter West Productions (Butcher) reissue:
1926 (2 rls)
D: Walter West
S: Campbell Rae Brown
SC: J. Bertram Brown
Violet Hopson . . . . Eileen Chelverley
Stewart Rome . . . . Hon Jack Bellenden
Cameron Carr . . . . Paul Frensham
Judd Green . . . . Lord Bellenden
Fred Hearne . . . . . . Arthur Rowlandson
Gertrude Sterroll . . . . Aunt Lucy
Bobb Vallis . . . . Nat Monday
James Strachey . . . . Joyce
SPORT Lady owner ruins financier who
fouls her horse in return.

07869
WHO IS THE MAN? (5700) (A)
Napoleon Films
P: G.B. Samuelson
D: SC: Walter Summers
S: (PLAY) Louis Verneuil (DANIEL)
Isobel Elsom . . . . Genevieve Ainault
Langhorne Burton . . . . Albert Ainault
Lewis Dayton . . . . Maurice Granger
John Gielgud . . . . Daniel
Mary Rorke . . . . Mrs Gerard
Henry Vibart . . . . Dr Juvenal
Hugh Dempster . . . . Robert Borden
DRAMA Paris. Addicted artist takes blame
for married sister's lover.

OCT

07870
THE DIAMOND MAN (5800) (A)
I.B.Davidson (Butcher)
D: Arthur Rooke
S: (NOVEL) Edgar Wallace
SC: Eliot Stannard
Arthur Wontner . . . . Lady Marshalt
Mary Odette . . . . Audrey Torrington
Reginald Fox . . . . Dick Shannon
Gertrude McCoy . . . . Mrs Marshalt
Philip Hewland . . . . . . Henry Torrington
George Turner . . . . Peter Tonger
CRIME Orphan takes blame for half-sister's
gem theft and later exposes her employer as
her crooked husband.

07871
WHAT THE BUTLER SAW (5855) (U)
Dewhurst (Gaumont)
PDSC: George Dewhurst
S: (PLAY) Edward Parry, Frederick Mouillot
Irene Rich . . . . Mrs. Barrington
Pauline Garon . . . . Joan Wyckham
Guy Newall . . . . Barrington
Cecil Morton York . . . . Prof Shall
A.B.Imeson . . . . Sir Charles Foden
Drusilla Wills . . . . Sophie Foden
John McAndrews . . . . Pink
A.Bromley Davenport . . . . Gen Dunlop
Peggy Patterson . . . . Miss Dunlop
Cecil Mannering . . . . Dr Boggins
Hilda Anthony . . . . Mrs Flemyng-Smith
COMEDY Hydro guest, compromised by
parrot bite, gets the parrot to bite every male
guest. (Made in Berlin).

07872
THE SINS YE DO (6340) (A)
Stoll
D: Fred Leroy Granville
S: (NOVEL) Emmeline Morrison
SC: Mary Murillo
Joan Lockton . . . . . Lady Athol/Nadine
Henry Victor . . . . Ronald Hillier
Eileen Dennes . . . . Lady Eslin
Maie Hanbury . . . . Muriel Allendale
Jameson Thomas . . . . . . Capt Barrington
Jerrold Robertshaw . . . . Sir Philip Athol
Eric Bransby Williams . . . . Neville Fane
Leslie Attwood . . . . Nadine
Edward O'Neill . . . . Bishop Hillier
Frank Perfitt . . . . Dr Rutherford
Annie Esmond . . . . Governess
ROMANCE Divorced knight nearly becomes
lover of his married daughter.

07873
Q—RIOSITIES BY "Q" (series)
Hepworth (Novello-Atlas)
P: Cecil M Hepworth
D: S: Gaston Quiribet

07874
5: IF A PICTURE TELLS A STORY (1000)

07875
6: LIZZIE'S LAST LAP (1000)
Peter Haddon . . . . Fibs-Gerald

07876
7: THE DEATH RAY (1000)

07877
8: LET'S PAINT (1000)

07878
9: THE FUGITIVE FUTURIST (1000)

07879
10: THE CHINA PERIL (1000)

07880
11: THE COVETED COAT (1000)

07881
12: WHICH SWITCH ? (1000)

07882
13: THE NIGHT OF THE KNIGHT (1000)

07883
14: PLOTS AND BLOTS (1000)
TRICK Comedies employing trick
photographic effects.

07884
ZEEBRUGGE (7000) (U)
British Instructional (New Era)
P: H. Bruce Woolfe
D: H. Bruce Woolfe, A.V.Bramble
S: Cdr W.M.Bruce
WAR 1918. Reconstruction of the Dover
Patrol's bottling-up of U-boat base.
(Extracts in HEARTS OF OAK; 1933).

07885
UNNATURAL LIFE STUDIES (1000)
Atlas-Biocraft (Novello-Atlas)
D: S: Harry Hughes
COMEDY Burlesque film; The Life of a Flapper
FLAPPER.

07886
ADAM'S FILM REVIEW (1000)
Atlas-Biocraft (Novello-Atlas)
D:S: Harry Hughes
COMEDY Burlesque of series "Eve's Film
Review."

07887
THE PATHETIC GAZETTE (1000)
Atlas-Biocraft (Novello-Atlas)
D:S: Adrian Brunel
Adrian Brunel
Henry Harris
COMEDY   Burlesque of the series "The Pathe
Gazette."

07888
THE CLICKING OF CUTHBERT (series)
Stoll
D: Andrew P. Wilson
S: (STORIES) P.G.Wodehouse
Harry Beasley . . . . The Caddie

07889
1: THE CLICKING OF CUTHBERT (1960) (U)
Peter Haddon . . . . Cuthbert
Helena Pickard . . . . Adeline
Moore Marriott .   Vladimir Brusiloff
Peter Upcher . . . . Raymond

07890
2: CHESTER FORGETS HIMSELF (2160)(U)
Jameson Thomas . . . . .   Chester Meredith
Ena Evans . . . .   Felicia Blakeney
J. Nelson Ramsey . . . . Vicar
Nell Emerald . . . .   Mrs Blakeley

07891
3: THE LONG HOLE (2450) (U)
reissue: THE MOVING HAZARD
Charles Courtneidge . . .   Ralph Bingham
Roger Keyes . . . .   Arthur Jukes
Daphne Williams . . . .   Amanda Trivett
Moore Marriott . . . .   Grocer

07892
4: ORDEAL BY GOLF (2000) (U)
Edwin Underhill . . . .   Rupert Dixon
Jean Jay . . . .   Millicent Boyd
Moore Marriott . . . .   Rev Heeza Jonah
Jack Rowell . . . .   Mitchell Holmes

07893
5: RODNEY FAILS TO QUALIFY (2100) (U)
Victor Robson . . . .   Rodney Spelvin
Lionelle Howard . . . .   William Bates
Phyllis Lytton . . . .   June Pickard
Dallas Cairns . . . .   Maj Patmore

07894
6: THE MAGIC PLUS FOURS (1930) (U)
COMEDIES Romantic and slapstick mishaps
on golf course.

07895
HINTS ON HORSEMANSHIP (series)
Geoffrey Benstead Films
D:S: Geoffrey Benstead
Geoffrey Benstead
Victor Smyth
George Duller
James Reardon
Bob Vallis
Roy Calvert
Sydney Paxton
Fatty Phillips
SPORT "The horse as a friend of man in
peace, war, and sport."

07896
NOT FOR SALE (6460) (U)
Stoll
D: W.P. Kellino
S: (NOVEL) Monica Ewer
SC: Lydia Hayward
Mary Odette . . . . . .   Annie Armstrong
Ian Hunter . . . .   Martin Dering
Gladys Hamer . . . .   Florrie
Mary Brough . . . .   Mrs Keane
Lionelle Howard . . . .   Bertie Strangeways
Phyllis Lytton . . . . . .   Virginia Strangeways
Edward O'Neill . . . . .   Earl of Rathbury
Mickey Brantford . . . .   John Armstrong
Julie Kean . . . .   Tibbles Armstrong
W.G.Saunders . . . .   Sunny Jim
Jack Trevor . . . .   Desmond North
Maud Gill . . . .   Miss Carter
Minna Leslie . . . .   Mrs Lovell
Robert Vallis . . . .   Roberts
Moore Marriott . . . .   Solicitor
George Bellamy . . . . .Boarder
ROMANCE Earl's disowned son becomes
chauffeur, loves landlady, and is jailed for
theft.

NOV

07897
OWD BOB (6300) (A)
Atlantic Union (Novello-Atlas)
D: Henry Edwards
S: (NOVEL) Alfred Olivant
SC: Hugh Maclean
J. Fisher White . . . .   Adam McAdam
Ralph Forbes . . . .   Davie McAdam
James Carew . . . .   James Moore
Yvonne Thomas . . . .   Maggie Moore
Frank Stanmore . . . .   Jim Burton
Grace Lane . . . .   Mrs Moore
Robert English . . . .   Squire
DRAMA Lake District. Old farmer's sheepdog
saved when rival's dog proved to be sheep
killer.

07898
NETS OF DESTINY (5600) (U)
I.B.Davidson (Butcher)
D: Arthur Rooke
S: (NOVEL) Maurice Drake (THE SALVING
OF A DERELICT)
SC: Eliot Stannard
Stewart Rome . . . . .   Lawrence Averil
Mary Odette . . . . . .   Marion Graham
Gertrude McCoy . . . . Constance
Cameron Carr . . . .   Reingold
Judd Green . . . .   Capt Menzies
Reginald Fox . . . .   Pat Dwyer
Benson Kleve . . . .   Jock Menzies
James English . . . .   Maj Graham
George Turner . . . .   Jerry Fisher
Laura Walker . . . .   Mrs Jardine
Eddie Dolly Dance Troupe
ADVENTURE Suicide's son becomes deckhand
and loves daughter of man his father ruined.

07899
THE SHADOW OF EGYPT (7700) (U)
Astra-National
D:SC: Sidney Morgan
S: (NOVEL) Nora Lorimer
Carlyle Blackwell . . . .   Sheik Hanan
Alma Taylor . . . .   Lilian Westcott
Milton Rosmer . . . . Harold Westcott
Joan Morgan . . . .   Moonface
John Hamilton . . . .   Apollo
Arthur Walcott . . . .   Abdullah
Charles Levey . . . .   Yusef
ADVENTURE Egypt. Sheik loves artist's
wife but is killed in a revolt following artist's
sale of treasures.

07900
HUMAN DESIRES (6789) (A)
Anglia (Gaumont)
P: F.J. Nettlefold
D:S: Burton George
SC: Louis Stevens
Marjorie Daw . . . .   Joan Thayer
Clive Brook . . . .   Georges Gautier
Juliette Compton . . . . . .   Andree de Vigne
Warwick Ward . . . .   Pierre Brandon
Russell Thorndike . . . .   Paul Perot
Jean di Limur . . . .   Henri Regnier
ROMANCE Paris. Actress divorces jealous
impresario and weds officer who once saved
her from suicide.

07901
THE MYSTERY FILM (1253) (U)
International Cine Corp reissue: 1926,
WHERE-U-SEER? (Maddox)
Ah-Ben-Aza
TRICK Magician comes from Bagdad in a sack
and reads the minds of the cinema audience.

07902
THE FLYING FIFTY—FIVE (4900) (U)
Stoll (EB)
D:SC: A.E.Coleby
S: (NOVEL) Edgar Wallace
Lionelle Howard . . . .   Reggie Cambray
Stephanie Stephens . . . .   Stella Barrington
Brian B. Lemon . . . .   Lord Fountwell
Lionel d'Aragon . . . .   Sir Jacques Gregory
Frank Perfitt . . . .   Josiah Urquhart
Bert Darley . . . .   Hon Claud Barrington
Adeline Hayden Coffin . . . .   Aunt
SPORT Lord poses as a stableboy and rides
girl's horse when crooked knight injures her
jockey.

1925

JAN

07903
MRS MAY COMEDIES (series) (U)
Quality Plays (FBO)
P: George A. Cooper
D: Leslie Hiscott
S: (CHARACTERS) John le Breton
SC: Thomas le Breton
Sydney Fairbrother . . . . . .   Mrs May
Irene Tripod . . . .   Mrs McMull
Frank Stanmore . . . .
Annie Esmond . . . .
Edward O'Neill . . . .
James Reardon . . . .
Percy Parsons . . . .

07904
1: CATS (1683)

07905
2: RAISING THE WIND (2098)

07906
3: A FOWL PROCEEDING (2031)

07907
4: BILLETS (2074)

07908
5: SPOTS (1829)

07909
6: A FRIEND OF CUPID (1826)
COMEDIES Adventures of impecunious widow.

07910
THE HAPPY ENDING (8100) (U)
Gaumont
D: George A. Cooper
S: (PLAY) Ian Hay
SC: P.L.Mannock
Fay Compton . . . . .   Mildred Craddock
Jack Buchanan . . . .   Capt Dale Conway
Joan Barry . . . .   Molly Craddock
Jack Hobbs . . . .   Denis Craddock
Gladys Jennings . . . .   Joan Craddock
Eric Lewis . . . .   Sir Anthony Fenwick
Donald Searle . . . . . .   Harold Bagby
Drusilla Wills . . . .   Laura Meakin
Pat Doyle . . . .   The Maid
A.G.Poulton . . . .   Mr Moon
Benita Hume . . . .   Miss Moon
Doris Mansell . . . .   Phyllis Harding
DRAMA Wastrel returns to blackmail wife,
who has told children that he died a hero.

07911
MUTINY (4250) (U)
George Clark (Ducal)
D: F. Martin Thornton
S: (NOVEL) Ben Bolt
(DIANA OF THE ISLANDS)
Nigel Barrie . . . .   John England
Doris Lytton . . . .   Diana
Walter Tennyson . . . .
Clifton Boyne . . . .
Donald Searle . . . .
ADVENTURE Escaped convict joins crew of
yacht of Lord who framed him, and saves his
daughter from shipwreck.

07912
THRILLING STORIES FROM THE STRAND
MAGAZINE (series)
Stoll

07913
7: THE PERFECT CRIME (2000) (U)
D: SC: Walter Summers
S: (STORY) "Seamark"
J. Fisher White . . . .   Bank Manager

07914
8: RAGAN IN RUINS (2100) (U)
D: Fred Paul
S: (STORY)
SC: Hugh Croise
Fred Paul
Prudence Ponsonby

07915
9: A MADONNA OF THE CELLS (2380) (U)
D: Fred Paul
S: (STORY) Morley Roberts
SC: Hugh Croise
Fred Paul
Betty Faire
Moore Marriott

07916
10: A DEAR LIAR (2000) (U)
D: Fred Leroy Granville
S: (STORY) Edgar Wallace
SC: Hugh   Croise
Eileen Dennes
James Knight
Edward O'Neill
Jean Colin
Humberston Wright

07917
11: THE HONOURABLE MEMBER FOR
OUTSIDE LEFT (2050) (U)
D: Sinclair Hill
S: (STORY) Sidney Horler
SC: Hugh Croise
Eric Bransby Williams
DRAMAS Short stories from popular
monthly magazine .

FEB

07918
WE WOMEN (5000) (A)
Stoll
D: W.P. Kellino
S: (NOVEL) Countess Barcynska
SC: W.J.Roberts, Lydia Hayward
Dollie . . . .   Beatrice
Billie . . . .   Pauline
John Stuart . . . .   Michael Rivven
Reginald Bach . . . .   Badderley
Nina Vanna . . . .   Kitty Pragnell
Charles Ashton . . . .   Bert Simmons
Cecil du Gue . . . .   Flash Wheeler
DRAMA Sacked skater drifts into clutches
of actor who abandoned girl and baby.

07919
A DAUGHTER OF LOVE (5050) (A)
Stoll
D: Walter West
S: (NOVEL) Mrs E.J.Key
SC: Lucita Squiers
Violet Hopson . . . .   Mary Tannerhill
John Stuart . . . .   Dudley Bellairs
Jameson Thomas . . . .   Dr Eden Brent
Fred Raynham . . . .   Lord StErth
Arthur Walcott . . . .   Mr Tannerhill
Ena Evans . . . .   Lillian
Gladys Mason . . . .   Lady StErth
Madge Tree . . . .   Mrs Tobin
Minna Grey . . . .   Mrs Diamond
Mrs Charles Beattie . . . .   Mme Korsikov
ROMANCE Lord objects to son's love for
bastard until society doctor is revealed as her
father.

07920
MONEY ISN'T EVERYTHING (4960) (A)
Stoll
D: Thomas Bentley
S: (NOVEL) Sophie Cole
SC: Isobel Johnstone

Olive Sloane . . . .   Elizabeth Tuter
Arthur Burne . . . .   James Rodgers
Gladys Hamer . . . .   Adele Rockwell
John Hamilton . . . .   William Channon
Lewis Gilbert . . . .
Gladys Crebbin . . . .
ROMANCE Clerk wins sweep and weds
secretary, who has affair with ex-employer.

07921
AFRAID OF LOVE (6600) (A)
Britannia (UK)
P: F.J.Nettlefold
D: Reginald West
S: Hon Mrs John Russell
Hon Mrs John Russell . . . .   Rosamund Bond
Leslie Faber . . . .   Anthony Bond
Juliette Compton . . . .   Ruth
Jameson Thomas . . . .   Philip Bryce
Mickey Brantford . . . .   Tony Bond
Moore Marriott . . . .   Father
Adeline Hayden Coffin . . .   Mother
ROMANCE Woman leaves faithless husband
to manage lover's dress shop.

07922
LIVINGSTONE (9600) (U)
Hero (Butcher) *reissue:* 1933, STANLEY (MGM)
D:S: M.A.Wetherell
M.A.Wetherell . . . . .   David Livingstone
Molly Rogers . . . .   Mary Moffatt
Henry Walton . . . .   H.M.Stanley
Reginald Fox . . . .   Gordon Bennett
Douglas Cator . . . .   Robert Moffat
Sir Simeon Stuart . . . . .   Neil Livingstone
Blanche Graham . . . .   Queen Victoria
Douglas Pierce . . . .   David (child)
HISTORY Africa, 1871. Biography of the Scots
explorer. (Sound added 1933).

MAR

07923
THE BLACKGUARD (9200) (U)
UFA-Gainsborough (W&F)
P: Michael Balcon, Erich Pommer
D: Graham Cutts
S: (NOVEL) Raymond Paton
SC: Alfred Hitchcock
June Novak . . . . .   Princess Marie Idourska
Walter Rilla . . . .   Michael Caviol
Frank Stanmore . . . .   Pompouard
Bernhard Goetzke . . . .   Adrian Levinski
Martin Hertzberg . . . .   Michael (child)
Rosa Valeki . . . .   Grandmother
DRAMA French violinist saves beloved
princess from Russian revolution, of which his
former tutor is leader. (Made in Berlin).

07924
TALL TIMBER TALES (series) (U)
Geoffrey Barkas (New Era)
P:D:S: Geoffrey Barkas

07925
1: PROSPECTIN' AROUND (1000)

07926
2: WHITE WATER MEN (1000)

07927
3: THE MANITOU TRAIL (1000)

07928
4: RANDOM FLAKES (1000)

07929
5: THE LUMBERJACK (1000)
ADVENTURE Canada. Dramatised documentaries with amateur actors.

APR

07930
Q-RIOSITIES BY "Q" (series)
Phillips
D:S: Gaston Quiribet

07931
10: THE QUAINT Q'S (1000)

07932
11: PLOTS AND BLOTS (1000)
TRICK

07933
THE PRESUMPTION OF STANLEY HAY,MP
(4275) (U)
Stoll
D: Sinclair Hill
S: (NOVEL) Nowell Kaye
SC: Alicia Ramsey
David Hawthorne . . . .   Stanley Hay
Betty Faire . . . .   Princess Berenice
Fred Raynham . . . .   Baron Hertzog
Eric Bransby Williams . Hon Bertie Sellinger
Kinsey Peile . . . .   The King
Nelson Ramsey . . . .   The Spy
Dora de Winton . . . .   Lady Barmouth
Mme d'Esterre . . . .   Mme de Vere
ADVENTURE Ruritania. MP weds princess and
saves her from abduction.

07934
A ROMANCE OF MAYFAIR (4750) (U)
Stoll
D: Thomas Bentley
S: (NOVEL) J.C.Snaith (THE CRIME OF
CONSTABLE KELLY)
Betty Faire . . . .   Mary Lawrence
Henry Victor . . . .   Jack Dinneford
Molly Johnson . . . .   Lady Blanche
Fred Raynham . . . .   Sir Dugald Maclean
Edward O'Neill . . . .   Duke of Bridport
George Foley . . . .   Sgt Kelly
Temple Bell . . . .   Millie Wren
Reginald Bach . . . .   Lord Wrexham
Gertrude Sterroll   . . . . . .   Lady Wargrave
Eva Westlake . . . .   Mrs Wren
ROMANCE Duke's son and daughter love
actress and socialist MP.

MAY

07935
THE SQUIRE OF LONG HADLEY (6250) (U)
Stoll *reissue:1930, A ROMANCE OF
RICHES (EB)*
D:SC: Sinclair Hill
S: (NOVEL) E. Newton Bungay
Marjorie Hume . . . . . .   Marjorie Clayton
Brian Aherne . . . .   Jim Luttrell
G.H.Mulcaster . . . .   Ronald Neilson
Eileen Dennes . . . .   Lucy
Albert E. Raynor . . . .   Robert Clayton
Tom Coventry . . . .   Barker
Humberston Wright . . . . . .   Solicitor
Mabel Penn . . . .   Mrs Mopps
Margaret Reeve . . . .   Liz
ROMANCE Coster inherits title, retaining
heir as his steward.

07936
CONFESSIONS (6324) (U)
Stoll
D: W.P.Kellino
S:(NOVEL) Mrs Baillie Reynolds
(CONFESSION CORNER)
SC: Lydia Hayward
Ian Hunter . . . .   Charles Oddy
Joan Lockton . . . .   Phoebe Vallings
Eric Bransby Williams . . . .   Percy Denham

Fred Raynham . . . .   E.H.Slack
Gladys Hamer . . . .   Ada Best
W.G.Saunders . . . .   James Barnes
Lewis Shaw . . . .   Henry
Dod Watts . . . .   Child
ROMANCE Woman's advice expert saves
typist from eloping with jewel-robbing artist.

07937
SHE (8250) (U)
Reciprocity Films
P: G.B.Samuelson
D: Leander de Cordova
S: (NOVEL) H. Rider Haggard
SC: Walter Summers.
Betty Blythe . . . .   Ayesha
Carlyle Blackwell. . Leo Vincy/Kallikrates
Mary Odette . . . .   Ustane
Tom Reynolds . . . .   Job
Heinrich George . . . .   Horace Holly
Jerrold Robertshaw . . . .   Billali
Marjorie Statler . . . .   Amenartes
Alexander Butler . . . .   Mahomet
FANTASY Africa. Explorer is reincarnated
lover of 2,000 year old White Queen.
(Made in Berlin).

07938
SATAN'S SISTER (7800) (U)
B.W.P.Films (W&F)
P: George Pearson, Betty Balfour
D:SC: George Pearson
S: (NOVEL) H. DeVere Stacpoole (SATAN)
Betty Balfour . . . .   Jude Tyler
Guy Phillips . . . .   Satan Tyler
Phillip Stevens . . . .   Bobbie Ratcliffe
James Carew . . . .   Tyler
Frank Stanmore . . . .   Cleary
Caleb Porter . . . .   Carquinez
Frank Perfitt . . . .   Sellers
Jeff Barlow . . . .   Bones
ADVENTURE Jamaica. Rich man saves
captain's son from pirates and finds he is a
girl.

JUL

07939
THE IMPATIENT PATIENT (1450) (U)
Royalty Comedies
D:S: Harcourt Templeman
James Knight
A. Bromley Davenport
Nancy Simpson
Pollie Emery
Walter Sondes
COMEDY Man extorts £500 from aunt by
feigning charitable interest in lunatic.

07940
AN INCONVENIENT INFANT (2000)
Royalty Comedies
D:S.: Harcourt Templeman
A. Bromley Davenport
Pauline Johnson
Walter Sondes
Adeline Hayden Coffin
COMEDY Husband returns home late and is
thought to have kidnapped baby.

07941
THERE'S MANY A SLIP (2600) (U)
Royalty Comedies
D:S: Harcourt Templeman
Moore Marriott
Gladys Hamer
Max Douglas
Cyril Dane
COMEDY Absent-minded professor thwarts
crooks seeking antique mug.

07942
A MEDICAL MYSTERY (1378) (U)
Royalty Comedies
D:S: Harcourt Templeman
COMEDY

07943
A MERCENARY MOTIVE (1350) (U)
Royalty Comedies
D:S: Harcourt Templeman
Ian Wilson . . . .
COMEDY

07944
THE WHITE LIE (1000) (U)
Royalty Comedies
D:S: Harcourt Templeman
COMEDY

07945
THE GENTLEMAN (sound)
DeForest Phonofilms
D:SC: William J. Elliott
S: (PLAY)
COMEDY (First British film with photographic
soundtrack.)

AUG

07946
THE LAST WITNESS (6100) (A)
Stoll
D: Fred Paul
S: (NOVEL) F.Britten Austin
Isobel Elsom . . . .   Letitia Brand
Fred Paul . . . .   Stephen Brand KC
Stella Arbenina . . . .   Mrs Stapleton
Queenie Thomas . . . .   Lady Somerville
John Hamilton . . .' . . . . . .   Eric Norton
Tom Nesbitt . . . . .   Maurice Tregarthen
Aubrey Fitzgerald . . . Lord Bunny Somerville
CRIME KC prosecutes own wife for
apparently killing her MP lover.

07947
THE SECRET KINGDOM (5930) (A)
Stoll *Reissue:* 1929, BEYOND THE VEIL (EB)
D: Sinclair Hill
S: (NOVEL) Bertram Atkey (HIDDEN FIRES)
SC: Alicia Ramsey
Matheson Lang . . . .   John Quarrain
Stella Arbenina . . . .   Mary Quarrain
Eric Bransby Williams . . . .   Philip Darent
Genevieve Townsend . . . . .   The Secretary
Rudolph de Cordova . . . . .   The Protege
Robin Irvine . . . .   The Son
Lillian Oldland . . . .   The Daughter
Frank Goldsmith . . . .   Henry
FANTASY Financier buys mind-reading
device but destroys it on learning of wife's
faithlessness.

07948
KING OF THE CASTLE (6950) (A)
Stoll
D: Henry Edwards
S: (PLAY) Keble Howard
SC: Alicia Ramsey
Marjorie Hume . . . .   Lady Oxborrow
Brian Aherne . . . .   Colin O'Farrell
Dawson Millward . . . .   Chris Furlong
Prudence Vanbrugh . . . . . .   Leslie Rain
Moore Marriott . . . .   Peter Coffin
Albert E. Raynor . . . .   Matlock
E.C.Matthews . . . .   Ezekiel Squence
ROMANCE Widowed Lady, forced into
marriage, grows to love husband when he
saves child from cliff.

07949
THE QUALIFIED ADVENTURER (6850) (U)
Stoll *reissue:* 1930 (EB)
D:SC: Sinclair Hill
S: (NOVEL) Selwyn Jepson
Matheson Lang . . . . Peter Duff
Genevieve Townsend . . Jimmy Fellowes
Fred Raynham . . . . Northcote
Kyoshi Tekase . . . . Yen San
Cameron Carr . . . . Weames
Nelson Ramsey . . . . McNab
Moore Marriott . . . . Bosun
Windham Guise . . . . Capt Fellowes
Dave O'Toole . . . . Evans
ADVENTURE South Seas. Chinese cook who
helps writer thwart mutiny is Manchu Prince.

07950
THE ONLY WAY (10,075) (U)
Herbert Wilcox (FN)
P:D:SC: Herbert Wilcox
S: (NOVEL) Charles Dickens (A TALE OF TWO
CITIES)
(PLAY) Freeman Wills, Frederick Longbridge
John Martin Harvey . . . . Sidney Carton
Madge Stuart . . . . Mimi
Betty Faire . . . . Lucie Manette
Ben Webster . . . Marquis StEvremonde
J. Fisher White . . . . Dr Manette
Frederick Cooper . . . . Charles Darnay
Mary Brough . . . . Miss Pross
Frank Stanmore . . . . Jarvis Lorry
Gibb McLaughlin . . . . Barsad
Gordon McLeod . . . . Ernest Defarge
Jean Jay . . . . Jeanne Defarge
Margaret Yarde . . . . The Vengeance
Judd Green . . . . Prosecution
Fred Rains . . . . President
Jack Raymond . . . . Jacques
Michael Martin Harvey . . . . No. 46
ADVENTURE Paris, 1790. Dissolute English
advocate goes to guillotine in place of
aristocratic double.

07951
FORBIDDEN CARGOES (6325) (U)
Granville (WI)
P:D: Fred Leroy Granville
S: Douglas Stuart
SC: Mary Murillo
Peggy Hyland . . . . Violet
Clifford McLaglen . . . John Tredennis
James Lindsay . . . . Sir Charles
Guy Tilden Wright . . . . Philip Sutton
Bob Vallis . . .` . . . . Black Mike
James Edwards Barber .William Trefusis
Daisy Campbell . . . . Lady Tredennis
ADVENTURE Cornwall, 1760. Son of
murdered squire saved from capture by
smuggler who loves his step-sister.

07952
THE APACHE (7400) (A)
Millar-Thompson (Napoleon)
P: Adelqui Millar, Herbert Thompson
D: Adelqui Millar
S: Michael Allard
Adelqui Millar . . . . The Panther
Mona Maris . . . . Lisette Blanchard
Jameson Thomas . . . . Gaston d'Harcourt
Jerrold Robertshaw . . . Albert d'Harcourt
Doris Mansell . . . . Armande
San Juana . . . . Mario
James Carrasco . . . . Gaspard
ROMANCE Paris. Apache weds ex-fiancee's
sister for revenge but learns love.

07953
TRAINER AND TEMPTRESS (7500) (U)
Astra-National
D:SC: Walter West
S: Atty Persse, R.J.Russell
Juliette Compton . . . . Lady Maurice
James Knight . . . . Peter Todd
Stephanie Stephens . . . . . . Stella Jordan
Cecil Morton York . . . .Sir Blundell Maurice
Sydney Seaward . . . . Major Snazle
Violet Graham . . . . Madge Jordan
Judd Green . . . . .Claud Wentworth
SPORT Lady tries to win Derby by
burning trainer's stables.

07954
THE RAT (7323) (A)
Gainsborough (W&F)
P: Michael Balcon
D:SC: Graham Cutts
S: (PLAY) Ivor Novello, Constance Collier
Ivor Novello . . . . . Pierre Boucheron
Mae Marsh . . . . Odile Etrange
Isobel Jeans . . . . Zelie de Chaumet
Robert Scholtz . . . . Hermann Stetz
James Lindsay . . . . Insp Caillard
Marie Ault . . . . Mere Colline
Julie Suedo . . . . Mou-Mou
Hugh Brook . . . . Paul
Esme Fitzgibbons . . . . Madeleine
Lambart Glasby . . . . American
Iris Grey . . . . Rose
CRIME Paris. Apache thief's sweetheart
arrested when he kills to save her from
socialite's lustful lover.

SEP

07955
SONS OF THE SEA (6000)
British Instructional (New Era)
P:D: H. Bruce Woolfe
S: "TAFFRAIL"
D.C.Kenderdine . . . . Derek Bray
E.Godfrey . . . . Bill Martin
Dorothy Barclay . . . . Diana
ADVENTURE Rich boy and gardener's
son join navy in 1914 and later save girl
from Mediterranean bandits.

07956
THE WONDERFUL WOOING (6250) (A)
Stoll *reissue:* 1930, THE WAY OF A WOMAN
(EB)
D. Geoffrey H. Malins
S: (NOVEL) Douglas Walshe
Marjorie Hume . . . . Edith Deering
G.H.Mulcaster . . . . Ronald West
Eric Bransby Williams . . . . . Martin Hayward
Genevieve Townsend . . . . . Barbara
Tom Coventry . . . . Jenkins
Daisy Campbell . . . . Mrs West
ROMANCE Rich orphan learns of salesman's
love whilst he is under anaesthetic following
accident.

OCT

07957
THE GOLD CURE (5700) (U)
Stoll
D: W.P.Kellino
S: (NOVEL) Sara J. Duncan
SC: Lydia Hayward
Queenie Thomas . . Betty Van Allen
Gladys Hamer . . . . Bella Box
Eric Bransby Williams . . . . . Lord Dinacre
Jameson Thomas . . . . Lansing Carter
Albert E. Raynor . . . . Mr Van Allen
Moore Marriott . . . . Janbois

Judd Green . . . . Mr Box
Leal Douglas . . . . Lady Dunacre
Johnny Butt . . . . Albert Horsey
Jefferson Gore . . . . Dennis O'Shamus
Nell Emerald . . . . Nora Flanagan
Dave O'Toole . . . . Mickey Mulvaney
COMEDY Crooks chase runaway American
heiress who poses as Irish girl wanted by
police.

07958
A GIRL OF LONDON (6500) (A)
Stoll
D: Henry Edwards
S: (NOVEL) Douglas Walshe
Genevieve Townsend Lil
Ian Hunter . . . . Peter Horniman
Harvey Braban . . . . George Duncan
G.H. Mulcaster . . . . Wilson
Nora Swinburne . . . . Vee-Vee
Edward Irwin . . . . Lionel Horniman
Bernard Dudley . . . . Lawton
Nell Emerald . . . . Mother
CRIME MP's disowned son weds factory
girl and saves her from stepfather's dope den.

07959
SETTLED OUT OF COURT (8500) (A)
Gaumont
D: George A. Cooper
S: Eliot Stannard
Fay Compton . . . . The Woman
Jack Buchanan . . . . The Husband
Jeanne de Casalis . . . . The Wife
Leon Quartermaine . . . . . . The Russian
Kinsey Piele . . . . The Count
Malcolm Keen . . . . The Detective
DRAMA Faithless woman's husband loves
poor woman hired to be co-respondent.

07960
YPRES (8000) (U)
British Instructional (New Era)
P: H. Bruce Woolfe
D:S. Walter Summers
WAR Reconstruction of various battles which
took place at Ypres.

07961
THE ART OF LOVE (series)
Godal International (ICC)
P: Edward Godal
D: Edwin Greenwood, W.P.Kellino
S: Eliot Stannard

07962
1: THE LADY IN SILK STOCKINGS (1550)
(U) retitled THE WEAKNESS OF MEN
Betty Faire
Margaret Yarde
Arthur Chesney

07963
2: THE PAINTED LADY (2) (A)
retitled RED LIPS
Gladys Jennings
Miles Mander
J.R.Tozer
Margaret Yarde
Lilia Lande

07964
3: THE LADY IN FURS (2) (A)
retitled: SABLES OF DEATH
Gertrude McCoy
Miles Mander
Margaret Yarde
Lilian Lande

07965
4: THE LADY IN LACE (1800) (U)
retitled: CAUGHT IN THE WEB
Mai Bacon
Laurence Ireland
Roy Travers
Norman le Strange . . . .

07966
5: THE LADY IN JEWELS (2) (A)
retitled: HEARTS TRUMP DIAMONDS

07967
6: THE LADY IN HIGH HEELS (2) (U)
retitled: HEEL TAPS
Haddon Mason
DRAMAS

07968
THE ONLY MAN (1500) (A)
retitled: THE LEADING MAN
H.B.Parkinson
D: H.B.Parkinson
Moore Marriot . . . . The Husband
COMEDY Canvey Island. Wife catches
husband flirting in bathing beauty contest.

07969
MEMORIES (1000) (U)
Innovation Productions (Argosy)
P: Castleton Knight
D:S. Arthur Backner
Minna Grey . . . . The Wife
Fred Groves . . . . The Husband
David Openshaw . . . . The Friend
MUSICAL Couple recall son's death
in war whilst singer (on stage) sings "Tommy
Lad," "Land of Hope and Glory," etc.

NOV

07970
TWISTED TALES (series)
Reciprocity Films
P: G.B. Samuelson
D: Alexander Butler

07971
1: HOW IT HAPPENED (750) (U)
S: (STORY) Arthur Conan Doyle
Sydney Seaward . . . . The Motorist

07972
2: PARTED (1200) (U)
John Stuart . . . . The Tourist
Mary Jerrold . . . . The Woman

07973
3: THE CHOICE (1000) (A)
David Hawthorne . . . . The Husband
Betty Faire . . . . The Wife
James Lindsay . . . . The Lover

07974
4: THE ETERNAL TRIANGLE (1186) (A)

07975
5: SHOULD A MOTHER TELL (1035) (U)

07976
6: OCTOBER 4TH (910) (A)

07977
7: HER GREAT MISTAKE (910) (A)

07978
8: HUNG WITHOUT EVIDENCE (1000)

07979
9: SKELETON KEYS (1000) (A)

07980
10: DRIVEN FROM HOME   (1000) (A)

07981
11: AT THE MERCY OF HIS WIFE (1000) (A)

07982
12: THE DEATH OF AGNES (800) (A)
DRAMAS Short stories with surprise
endings.

07983
PROVERBS (series)
Reciprocity Films
P: G.B. Samuelson
D: Alexander Butler

07984
1: IT IS NEVER TOO LATE TO MEND
Rex Davis . . . . The Burglar

07985
2: OUT OF SIGHT OUT OF MIND (2000)

07986
3: ABSENCE MAKES THE HEART GROW
FONDER (1000)

07987
4: ALL THAT GLISTENS IS NOT GOLD (1000)

07988
5: MAN PROPOSES GOD DISPOSES (1000)

07989
6: DO UNTO OTHERS (1000)

07990
7: THERE'S MANY A SLIP (1000)

07991
8: 'TIS A LONG LANE THAT HAS NO
TURNING (1000)

07992
9: THOSE WHO LIVE IN GLASS HOUSES
(1000)

07993
10: A STITCH IN TIME (1000)

07994
11: NEVER PUT OFF TILL TOMORROW
(1000)

07995
12: LAUGH AND THE WORLD LAUGHS
WITH YOU (1000)
DRAMAS Stories based on proberbs.

07996
MILESTONE MELODIES (series) (U)
Reciprocity Films
P: G.B. Samuelson
D: Alexander Butler

07997
1: AULD LANG SYNE (1000)

07998
2: LITTLE DOLLY DAYDREAM (1000)

07999
3: I DO LIKE TO BE BESIDE THE
SEASIDE (1000)

08000
4: HER GOLDEN HAIR WAS HANGING
DOWN HER BACK (1000)

08001
5: THEY WOULDN'T BELIEVE ME (1000)
Benita Hume

08002
6: (TITLE UNKNOWN) (1000)
MUSICAL Picturisations of lyrics shown
while songs are sung from cinema stage.

08003
FAMOUS MUSIC MELODIES (series) (U)
James A. Fitzpatrick (Film Distributors)
D:S: James A. Fitzpatrick

08004
1: SONGS OF ENGLAND (1000)
James Knight . . . . The Shepherd
Peggy Shaw . . . . The Maiden

08005
2: SONGS OF IRELAND (1000)
James Knight . . . . Rory O'More
Peggy Shaw . . . . Peggy

08006
3: SONGS OF SCOTLAND (1000)
James Knight . . . . Robin Adair
Peggy Shaw . . . . Annie Laurie

08007
4: SONGS OF THE BRITISH ISLES (1000)
James Knight . . . . The Lover
Peggy Shaw . . . . The Girl
MUSICAL Romantic stories illustrating
songs shown while songs are sung from cinema
stage.

08008
GAINSBOROUGH BURLESQUES (series) (U)
Gainsborough (W&F)
P: Michael Balcon
D: Adrian Brunel
S: Adrian Brunel, Edwin Greenwood,
J.O.C.Orton

08009
1: BATTLING BRUISERS (1200)

08010
2: SO THIS IS JOLLYGOOD (942)
Alf Goddard

08011
3: CUT IT OUT (1210)

08012
4: A TYPICAL BUDGET (1000)
Jack Buchanan

08013
5: THE BLUNDERLAND OF BIG GAME
(1100)
COMEDIES Burlesques of boxing, Hollywood,
censorship, newsreels, and hunting.

08014
SOMEBODY'S DARLING (8800) (U)
Gaumont
D: George A. Cooper
S: (NOVEL) Sidney Morgan
Betty Balfour . . . . Joan Meredith
Rex O'Malley . . . . Jack Esmonds
Fred Raynham . . . . J.W.Jordan
Forrester Harvey . . . . Oliver Jordan
J. Fisher White . . . . Grandfather
Minna Grey . . . . Miss Jordan
Clarence Blakiston . . Sir John Esmonds
A. Bromley Davenport . . . . Sleeper
Clifton Boyne . . . . Publisher
Jack Harris . . . . Potman
Arthur Walcott . . . .
Morton Selten . . . .
Gibb McLaughlin . . . .
COMEDY Squire's novelist son poses as
nurse to save heiress from guardian's private
asylum.

08015
BULLDOG DRUMMOND'S THIRD ROUND
(7300) (U)
Astra-National
D:SC: Sidney Morgan
S: (NOVEL) "Sapper" (THE THIRD ROUND)
Jack Buchanan .... Capt Hugh Drummond
Betty Faire .... Phyllis
Juliette Compton .... Irma Peterson
Allan Jeayes .... Carl Peterson
Austin Leigh .... Prof Goodman
Frank Goldsmith .. Sir Raymond Blayntree
Edward Sorley .... Julius Freyder
Phil Scott .... Sparring Partner
CRIME Merchants hire foreign criminal to
kidnap scientist for secret of manufacturing
diamonds.

DEC

08016
MR PREEDY AND THE COUNTESS
Welsh-Pearson (W&F)
D:SC: George Pearson
S: (PLAY) R. C. Carton
Frank Stanmore .... Mr Preedy
Mona Maris .... Countess
W. Cronin Wilson .... Bounsall

Beuna Bent ....
Gladys Hamer ....
Frank Perfitt ....
Annie Esmond ....
Gibb McLaughlin ....
A. Harding Steerman .....
COMEDY (Made in Paris; not shown).

08017
CHILDREN OF THE NIGHT (series)
Cosmopolitan Productions
P: George J. Banfield
D: Charles Calvert
S: (STORIES) W.B.Maxwell

08018
1: CHILDREN OF THE NIGHT No.1 (2000)
Gertrude McCoy
James Carew
Guy Phillips
Molly Wynne

08019
2: CHILDREN OF THE NIGHT No.2 (2000)
Clifford Humphries
Dorothy Seacombe
Marie Ault
Frank Dane
DRAMAS

08020
VENETIAN LOVERS (6439) (A)
British Screen Classics (Phillips)
D: Walter Niebuhr, Frank A.Tilley
Arlette Marechal .... Lola Astoni
Hugh Miller .... Count Astoni
John Stuart .... Goring
Ben Field .... William P. Bradshaw
Eva Westlake .... Mrs Bradshaw
George Schnell .... Sir Harcourt
DRAMA Venice. City prefect's mistress
saves wife from profiteer. (Made in Munich).

08021
IRISH DESTINY (5055) (U)
retitled: AN IRISH MOTHER
Eppel's Films (European)
P:D:S: I.J:Eppel
Denis O'Shea .... Denis O'Hara
Una Shiels .... Mona Barry
Daisy Campbell .... Mother
Brian Magowan .... Beecher
Clifford Pembroke ....
Kit O'Malley ....
Pat O'Rourke ....
CRIME Dublin. Wounded man breaks jail in
time to save fiancee from assault.

1926

JAN

08022
THE STEVE DONOGHUE SERIES
C & M Productions (Gainsborough)
D: Walter West

08023
1: RIDING FOR A KING (2700) (U)
Steve Donoghue . . . . Steve Baxter
Carlyle Blackwell . . Capt Harry Swinden
June . . . . Lady Betty Raleigh
Miles Mander . . . . Lord Steerwell
Cecil Morton York . . . . . Earl of Westchurch

08024
2: BEATING THE BOOK (3134) (U)
Steve Donoghue . . . . Steve
Carlyle Blackwell . . Hon Teddy Blackton
Violet Hopson . . . . Joan Marlow
James Lindsay . . . . Felix Morton
Clifford Heatherley . . . . Merryboy

08025
3: THE GOLDEN SPURS (2131) (U)
Steve Donoghue . . . . Steve
Irene Russell . . . . Helen Hardacre
Harvey Braban . . . . Smithson
Frank Perfitt . . . .
M. Gray Murray . . . .

08026
4: THE STOLEN FAVOURITE (2000)
Steve Donoghue . . . . Steve
Lillian Pitchford . . . . Rosalind Ramsgate
Robert English . . . . Sir Charles Ramsgate
Bellenden Powell . . . . Trotwell
Chick Farr . . . . Jack Smith
SPORT Racing dramas featuring famous jockey.

08027
HAUNTED HOUSES AND CASTLES OF
GREAT BRITAIN (series)
Cosmopolitan Productions (C&M)
P:S: George J. Banfield

08028
1: THE MISTLETOE BOUGH (1600) (A)
D: Charles Calvert
Gladys Jennings

08029
2: BADDESLEY MANOR - THE PHANTOM
GAMBLER (1900) (A)
D: Maurice Elvey
John Stuart . . . . Stephen Ellis
Hugh Miller . . . . Gambling Phantom
Fred Raynham . . . . Maj Hickley

08030
3: WINDSOR CASTLE (1700) (U)
D: Maurice Elvey
Isabel Jeans
Ian Wilson

08031
4: HAMPTON COURT PALACE (1500) (U)
D: Bert Cann
Gabrielle Morton . . . . Katharine Howard
Eric Cowley . . . . . Sir Thomas Culpepper
Shep Camp . . . . Henry VIII
Adeline Hayden Coffin . . . . Mary Lassells

08032
5: GLAMIS CASTLE (1500) (U)
D: Maurice Elvey
Isobel Elsom

08033
6: THE LEGEND OF TICHBORNE DOLE
(1840) (U)
D: Hugh Croise

Gabrielle Morton
James Knight
Dorinea Shirley
Adeline Hayden Coffin

08034
7: WOODCROFT CASTLE (1300) (U)
D: Walter West
James Knight

08035
8: ASHRIDGE CASTLE - THE MONMOUTH
REBELLION (1700) (A)
D: Charles Calvert
Betty Faire

08036
9: KENILWORTH CASTLE AND AMY
ROBSART (1800) (A)
D: Maurice Elvey
Gladys Jennings
John Stuart
Madge Stuart
Dick Webb

08037
10: GUY OF WARWICK (1417) (U)
D: Fred Paul
Godfrey Tearle . . . . Guy

08038
11: THE TOWER OF LONDON (1600) (A)
D: Maurice Elvey
Isobel Elsom
John Stuart

08039
12: BODIAM CASTLE AND ERIC THE
SLENDER (1500) (A)
D: A.V.Bramble
Madge Stuart
Gladys Jennings
HISTORY Ghostly episodes from English
history.

08040
EVERY MOTHER'S SON (7925) (U)
Britannia (UK)
P: F.J.Nettlefold
D: Robert J. Cullen
S: G. B. Samuelson, Harry Engholm
SC: Lydia Hayward
Rex Davis MC . . . . David Brent
Frederick Cooper MC . . . Tony Browning
Jean Jay . . . . Janet Shaw
Moore Marriott . . . . Nobby
Alf Goddard . . . . Bully
Haddon Mason . . . . Jonathan Brent
Gladys Hamer . . . . Minnie
Johnny Butt . . . . Tricky
Hubert Harben . . . . . . Sir Alfred Browning
Leal Douglas . . . . Lady Browning
WAR Ex-soldier turns tramp and weds ex-
sweetheat despite her child by squire's dead
son.

08041
THE SEA URCHIN (7340) (A)
Gainsborough (W&F)
P: Michael Balcon
D: Graham Cutts
S:(PLAY) John Hastings Turner
SC: Graham Cutts, Charles Lapworth
Betty Balfour . . . . Fay Wynchbeck
George Hackathorne . . . Jack Trebarrow
W. Cronin Wilson . . . . Rivoli
Haidee Wright . . . . . Minnie Wynchbeck
Marie Wright . . . . Mary Wynchbeck
Cecil Morton York . . Sir Trevor Trebarrow
Clifford Heatherley . . . . . . Sullivan

A.G.Poulton . . . . Janitor
ROMANCE Pilot saves dancer from Paris
nightclub owner and they stow away to
Cornwall.

FEB

08042
ONE COLOMBO NIGHT (4475) (U)
Stoll
D: Henry Edwards
S: (NOVEL) Austin Phillips
SC: Alicia Ramsey
Godfrey Tearle . . . . Jim Farnell
Marjorie Hume . . . . . . Rosemary Thurman
Nora Swinburne . . . . Jean Caldicott
James Carew . . . . . . Richard Baker
J. Fisher White . . . . Father Anthony
William Pardue . . . . Pabu
Julie Suedo . . . . Lalla
Dawson Millward . . . . Governor
Annie Esmond . . . . Wife
ROMANCE Ceylon. Ruined planter makes good
in Australia and returns in time to save fiancee
from nunnery.

08043
A WET NIGHT (10) (sound)
British Acoustic Films
D:SC: Harry Hughes
Arthur Chesney . . . .
COMEDY (Made in Berlin.)

08044
NELL GWYNNE (7760) (U)
W.M.Productions - British National (FN)
P;D:SC: Herbert Wilcox
S: (NOVEL) Marjorie Bowen
(MISTRESS NELL GWYNNE)
Dorothy Gish . . . . Nell Gwynne
Randle Ayrton . . . . Charles II
Juliette Compton . . . . Lady Castlemaine
Sydney Fairbrother . . . . Mrs Gwynne
Donald McCardle . . . . . . Duke of Monmouth
Johnny Butt . . . . Samuel Pepys
Gibb McLaughlin . . . . Duke of York
Judd Green . . . . Toby Clinker
Edward Sorley . . . . Dickon
Forrester Harvey . . . . Charles Hart
Fred Rains . . . . Earl of Shaftesbury
Rolf Leslie . . . . Evelyn
Aubrey Fitzgerald . . . . . . Tom Killigrew
Tom Coventry . . . . Innkeeper
Booth Conway . . . . Messenger
Dorinea Shirley . . . . Maid
HISTORY 1669. Actress becomes king's
mistress and persuades him to convert
palace to servicemen's home.

MAR

08045
SAHARA LOVE (7300) (A)
Stoll-Espanola
D: Sinclair Hill
S: (NOVEL) A.L.Vincent
SC: Geoffrey Malins
Marie Colette . . . . Eleanor Vallance
John Dehelly . . . . Hugh Trevor
Sybil Rhoda . . . . Melody Rourke
Gordon Hopkirk . . . . Sheik
Edward O'Neill . . . . Sir Max Droke
ROMANCE Knight's widow, saved from sheik
by ex-lover, learns he loves another and walks
into desert.

08046
OXFORD BAGS (1650) (U)
Norman Walker (Gaumont)
P:D:S: Norman Walker
Peter Haddon . . . . The Golfer

Ena Grossmith . . . .
Rosalind Courtneidge . . . . .
COMEDY Goring-on-Thames. Golfer tries
to dispose of baggy trousers.

08047
SILENCE (2000)
Oxford University
D: Hugh Brooke, John Greenidge
Ursula Jeans . . . . The Girl
Countess Ina Bubna . . . .
DRAMA Dumb girl cured by shock.

APR

08048
THE LITTLE PEOPLE (7100) (U)
Welsh-Pearson (Butcher)
P: Thomas Welsh, George Pearson
D:S: George Pearson
SC: George Pearson, Thorold Dickinson
Mona Maris . . . . Lucia Morelli
Frank Stanmore . . . . Paolo
Gerald Ames . . . . Walery
Barbara Gott . . . . Sala
Harry Furniss . . . . Gian
Randle Ayrton . . . . Lyn
James Reardon . . . . Manevski
ROMANCE Italy. Puppeteer's daughter gives
up a dancing career to marry poor stepbrother.

08049
THE ISLAND OF DESPAIR (6360) (A)
Stoll *reissue:* 1930 (EB)
D: Henry Edwards
S:(NOVEL) Margot Neville
Matheson Lang . . . . Stephen Rhodes
Marjorie Hume . . . . . . Christine Vereker
Gordon Hopkirk . . Don Felipe Trevares
Jean Bradin . . . . Colin Vereker
Cyril McLaglen . . . . Mate
J,Fisher White . . . . Dr Blake
ADVENTURE Shipwrecked captain saves girl
from Spanish murderer by threatening to
give him leprosy.

MAY

08050
THE PLEASURE GARDEN (7058) (A)
Gainsborough-Emelka (W&F)
P: Michael Balcon
D: Alfred Hitchcock
S: (NOVEL) Oliver Sandys
SC: Eliot Stannard
Virginia Valli . . . . Patsy Brand
Carmelita Geraghty . . . . . . Jill Cheyne
Miles Mander . . . . Levett
John Stuart . . . . Hugh Fielding
Nita Naldi . . . . Native Girl
George Schnell . . . . Oscar Hamilton
C. Falkenberg . . . . Prince Ivan
Ferdinand Martini . . . . . . Mr Sidey
Florence Helminger . . . . Mrs Sidey
DRAMA Africa. Dancer marries drunkard
who tries to kill her after drowning native
mistress. (Made in Munich).

08051
THE CHINESE BUNGALOW (6600) (A)
Stoll
D: Sinclair Hill
S: (PLAY) Marian Osmond, James Corbett
Matheson Lang . . . . Yuan Sing
Genevieve Townsend . . . . . Charlotte
Juliette Compton . . . . Sadie
Shayle Gardner . . . . . . Richard Marquess
George Thirlwell . . . . Harold Marquess
Malcolm Tod . . . . Vivian Dale
Clifford McLaglen . . . . Abdul
CRIME China. Mandarin marries English girl
and tries to poison her lover.

08052
JOHN HENRY CALLING (series)
George Redman (Gaumont)
D: Challis Sanderson, Widgey R. Newman
S: John Henry
SC: Eliot Stannard
John Henry . . . . John Henry
Blossom . . . . Blossom
Mary Brough . . . . Mother-in-law

08053
1: HOW I BEGAN (2000) (U)
Tom Coventry . . . . . Joe Murgatroyd
Franzi Carlos . . . . . . Mrs Murgatroyd

08054
2: BROADCASTING (1956) (A)
Cynthia Murtagh . . . . The Girl

08055
3: OSCILLATION (2000) (A)
Mabel Poulton . . . . The Maid

08056
4: LISTENING IN (2086) (U)

08057
5: THE LOUD SPEAKER (1936) (U)

08058
6: HOME CONSTRUCTION (2000) (A)
COMEDIES Misadventures of radio comedian
as tippling henpeck.

JUN

08059
BINDLE (series)
H.B.Parkinson
D: H.B.Parkinson
S: (STORIES) Herbert Jenkins
Tom Reynolds . . . . Bindle
Annie Esmond . . . . Mrs Bindle
Charles Garry . . . . Mr Hearty
Minnie Rayner . . . . Mrs Hearty
Lillian Oldland . . . . Millie

08060
1: BINDLE INTRODUCED (2200) (U)

08061
2: BINDLE IN CHARGE (2072) (U)

08062
3: BINDLE, MILLIONAIRE (2000) (A)

08063
4: BINDLE'S COCKTAIL (2300) (U)
Muriel Aked . . . . . . Lady Knobb-Kerrick

08064
5: BINDLE, MATCHMAKER (2000) (A)

08065
6: BINDLE AT THE PARTY (2000) (A)
COMEDIES Misadventures of unprincipled,
tippling coster.

08066
HORSEY (series)
H.B.Parkinson
D: H.B.Parkinson

08067
1: FUN AT THE FAIR (2000)

08068
2: THE SIMPLE LIFE (2000)
COMEDIES Misadventures of men dressed as
pantomime horse.

08069
ROMANCES OF THE PRIZE RING (series)
H.B. Parkinson (White)

D: H.B.Parkinson, Geoffrey Malins
S: (STORIES) Andrew Soutar
SC: B.E.Doxat-Pratt

08070
1: FOR MY LADY'S HAPPINESS (2274) (A)
D: Geoffrey Malins
Phil Scott . . . . Deaf Burke

08071
2: THE GAME CHICKEN (2000)
D: H.B.Parkinson
Billy Wells . . . . Hen Pearce
Pat Aherne . . . .

08072
3: WHEN GIANTS FOUGHT (2194) (A)
Joe Beckett . . . . Tom Cribb
Frank Craig . . . . Tom Molyneux
James Knight . . . . Grenadier
George Wynn . . . . Sailor
Windham Guise . . . . Storyteller

08073
4: FOR A WOMAN'S EYES (2360) (A)
Jack Stanley

08074
5: GYPSY COURAGE (2000)

08075
6: THE PHANTOM FOE (2000) (A)
Frank Goddard . . . . Hen Pearce

08076
7: FIND THE WOMAN (2000)
Dick Smith . . . . George Stevenson
Gladys Dunham . . . . Lady Sykes

08077
8: THE FIGHTING GLADIATOR (2000)
Tom Berry . . . . Tom Sayers
Ian Wilson . . . .
SPORT Period. Dramas woven around famous
bare-knuckle fights.

08078
THE AMOROUS ADVENTURES OF BUX
(2000)
Norman le Strange Productions
P:D:S: Norman le Strange
Norman le Strange . . . . Bux
Ninon Zaria . . . .
Beatie Olna . . . .
COMEDY Amorous exploits of gay man-about-
town.

08079
HUMAN LAW (7000) (A)
Astra-National
D: Maurice Elvey
Isobel Elsom. . . . . Louise Radcliffe
Alfred Abel . . . . Radcliffe
Paul Richter . . . . Mason
DRAMA Jealous husband leaves jail to find
wife loves his counsel. (Made in Germany).

08080
WALTER'S PAYING POLICY (2400) (U)
British Super Comedies (Wardour)
D: James B. Sloan
S: Walter Forde
Walter Forde . . . . Walter
Pauline Peters . . . . Miss Gruff
George Foley . . . . Max Gruff
COMEDY Insurance salesman pretends to
steal collector's vase and catches burglar.

08081
WALTER'S WORRIES (2100) (U)
British Super Comedies (Wardour)
D: James B.Sloan
S: Walter Forde

Walter Forde. . . . .   Walter
Pauline Peters . . . .   The Girl
George Foley . . . .   The Boss
COMEDY Tailor contrives to attend staff
dinner and wins employer's daughter.

08082
WALTER THE SLEUTH (1900) (U)
British Super Comedies (Wardour)
D: James B. Sloan
S: Walter Forde
Walter Forde . . . .   Walter
Pauline Peters . . . .   Pauline
George Foley . . . .   George
COMEDY Girl has Walter pose as tec to
save father's gem.

08083
WALTER'S DAY OUT (1900) (U)
British Super Comedies (Wardour)
D: James B. Sloan
S: Walter Forde
Walter Forde . . . .   Walter
Pauline Peters . . . .   Mrs Walter
George Foley . . . .   The Boss
COMEDY Clerk takes colleague's children
to sea and meets his employer there.

08084
WALTER TELLS THE TALE (2200) (U)
British Super Comedies (Wardour)
D: James B.Sloan
S: Walter Forde
Walter Forde . . . .   Walter
Pauline Peters . . . .   Connie Sewer
George Foley . . . .   Cortin Tabbs
COMEDY Broke architect takes actress out
to dinner.

08085
WALTER THE PRODIGAL (2300) (U)
British Super Comedies (Wardour)
D: James B. Sloan
S: Walter Forde
Walter Forde . . . .   Walter
Pauline Peters . . . .   The Girl
COMEDY Dancer dressed as convict for
ball is mistaken for real one.

08086
THE WOMAN TEMPTED (7417) (A)
M.E.Productions (Wardour)
P: John Maxwell, Maurice Elvey
D: Maurice Elvey
S: (NOVEL) Countess Vera Cathcart
SC: Sidney Morgan
Juliette Compton . . . .   Louise Harding
Warwick Ward . . . .   Jimmy Davier
Nina Vanna . . . .   Maud Edworth
Malcolm Tod . . . .   Basil Gilmore
Joan Morgan . . . .   Sybil Helmsley
Adeline Hayden Coffin . . .   Mrs Edworth
Judd Green . . . .
DRAMA Suicide's ex-fiancee shoots vamp
responsible and enters convent.

08087
THE BALL OF FORTUNE (6500) (U)
Mercury Film Service
P: Booth Grainge
D:SC: Hugh Croise
S: (NOVEL) Sidney Horler
Billy Meredith . . . .   Himself
James Knight . . . .   Dick Huish
Mabel Poulton . . . .   Mary Wayne
Geoffrey B. Partridge . . . . .   Mr Wayne
Dorothy Boyd . . . .
Mark Barker . . . .   Bent
John Longden . . . .
Pat Aherne . . . .
SPORT Ruined man joins football team and
weds magistrate's daughter.

08088
SPIRITUALISM EXPOSED (2800) (U)
retitled: FAKE SPIRITUALISM EXPOSED
FHC Productions (Pioneer)
P: A.E.Coleby, G.H.Cricks
D;S. A.E.Coleby
Arthur Prince . . . .   Doctor
Yvonne Thomas . . . .   Mrs Cathcart
Charles Ashton . . . .   Mr Cathcart
CRIME Obsessed woman cured by exposure
of fraudulent medium.

JUL

08089
LONDON LOVE (7560) (A)
Gaumont
D: Manning Haynes
S:(NOVEL) Arthur Applin (THE WHIRLPOOL)
SC: Lydia Hayward
Fay Compton . . . .   Sally Hope
John Stuart . . . .   Harry Raymond
Miles Mander . . . .   Sir James Daring
Moore Marriott . . . .   Aaron Levinsky
A.B.Imeson . . . .   Henry Worlock
Humberston Wright . . .   Sir Philip Brown
Leal Douglas . . . .   Mrs Hope
Arthur Walcott . . . .   Bersault
Grace Vicat . . . .   Mrs James
Laura Walker . . . .   Anna
CRIME Rich man's chauffeur kills mistress
and frames daughter's fiance.

08090
TWISTED TALES (series)
Reciprocity Films
P: G.B. Samuelson
D: Charles Barnett
David Hawthorne . . . .
Betty Faire . . . .
Dennis Wyndham . . . .
Napier Barry . . . .
Edward Sorley . . . .

08091
1 – THE GREATEST OF THESE (1208) (U)
S: Clive Thornton

08092
2 – THE GENTLEMAN BURGLAR (865) (U)
S: Clifford Mayne

08093
3 – THE ONLY WAY OUT (938) (A)

08094
4 – OIL ON TROUBLED WATERS (1525) (U)

08095
5 – OFF THE SCENT (1215) (U)

08096
6 – PATERNAL INSTINCT (1093) (U)

08097
7 – BETRAYED (1082) (U)

08098
8 – DEAD HEAT (1077) (U)

08099
9 – THE LAST SHOT (1080) (U)

08100
10 – THE PROCTOR INTERVENES (925) (U)

08101
11 – WITHOUT THE OPTION (1083) (U)
DRAMAS Short stories with surprise endings.

08102
EVERYDAY FRAUDS (series)
Unique Productions (Pioneer)
D: S: F.W. Engholm

08103
1 – MISCREANTS OF THE MOTOR WORLD
(1100) (U)

08104
2 – HONESTY IS THE BEST POLICY (1000)(A)

08105
3 – THE MOCK AUCTIONEER (1000) (A)

08106
4 – STREET CORNER FRAUDS (1680) (U)

08107
5 – THE CONFIDENCE TRICK (1500) (U)

08108
6 – DUD CHEQUE CHICANERY (986((U)

08109
7 – THE BOGUS HOUSE AGENT (1140) (U)

08110
8 – EMPLOYMENT WITH INVESTMENT
AND THE MASKED FRAUD (1100) (U)
CRIMES Exposures of confidence tricks,
swindles, and frauds.

08111
SWEENEY TODD (1000)
BMPA (NewEra)
D: George Dewhurst
S: (PLAY) George Dibdin Pitt
SC: P.L. Mannock
G.A. Baughan . . . .   Sweeney Todd
P.L. Mannock . . . .   Producer
Lionel Collier . . . .   Title Writer
COMEDY Burlesque made for the Kinematograph
Garden Party.

08112
IF YOUTH BUT KNEW (8095) (U)
Reciprocity Films
P: G.B.Samuelson
D: George A. Cooper
S: (PLAY) K.C. Spiers
SC: Harry Engholm
Godfrey Tearle . . . .   Dr Martin Summers
Lilian Hall-Davis . . . .   Dora / Doreen
Wyndham Standing . . . .   Sir Ormsby Ledger
Mary Odette . . . .   Loanda
Mary Rorke . . . .   Mrs Romney
Patrick Waddington . . . .   Arthur Noel-Vane
May Beamish . . . .   Mrs Sumner
Minnie Rayner . . . .   Martha
Forrester Harvey . . . .   Amos
Donald Walcott . . . .   Aulole
ROMANCE Nigeria. Dr loves ex-sweetheart's
daughter but gives her up to younger man.

SEP

08113
WHITE HEAT (7200) (A)
Graham-Wilcox
D: Thomas Bentley
S: (NOVEL) "Pan"
SC: Eliot Stannard
Juliette Compton . . . .   Helen
Wyndham Standing . . . . . .   Gilbert Gillman
Vesta Sylva . . . .   Eve Storer
Walter Butler . . . .   Julian Jefferson
Bertram Burleigh . . . .   Phil Storer
George Bellamy . . . .   Mr Storey
Estelle Brodey . . . .   Ninon
Wellington Briggs . . . .   Hall
Alf Goddard . . . .   Apache
DRAMA Man loves dancer who becomes
producer's mistress.

08114
THE TRIUMPH OF THE RAT (7550) (A)
Gainsborough-Piccadilly (W & F)
P: Carlyle Blackwell, Michael Balcon
D: Graham Cutts
S: (CHARACTERS) Ivor Novello, Constance Collier
SC: Graham Cutts, Reginald Fogwell, Roland Pertwee
Ivor Novello . . . . Pierre Boucheron
Isabel Jeans . . . . Zelie de chaumet
Nina Vanna . . . . Comtesse Madeleine
Julie Suedo . . . . Mou-Mou
Marie Ault . . . . Mere Colline
Lewin Mannering . . . . . Comte Henri Mercereau
Mrs Hayden Coffin . . . . . Duchesse de l'Orme
Charles Dormer . . . . Rene Duval
Gabriel Rosca . . . . Apache
ROMANCE Paris. Apache bets he can win girl in month and falls in love with her.
(First British use of "mobile camera".)

08115
THE LODGER (7500) (A) USA: THE CASE OF JONATHAN DREW
Gainsborough (W & F)
P: Michael Balcon
D: Alfred Hitchcock
S: (NOVEL) Mrs Belloc Lowndes
SC: Eliot Stannard, Alfred Hitchcock
Ivor Novello . . . . Jonathan Drew
June . . . . Daisy Bunting
Malcolm Keen . . . . Joe Chandler
Marie Ault . . . . Mrs Bunting
Arthur Chesney . . . . Mr Bunting
CRIME Girl loves lodger who is suspected of being murderous 'Avenger'.

08116
THE MOUNTAIN EAGLE (7503) (A) USA: FEAR O'GOD
Gainsborough-Emelka (W & F)
P: Michael Balcon
D: Alfred Hitchcock
S: Charles Lapworth
SC: Eliot Stannard
Nita Naldi . . . . Beatrice
Malcolm Keen . . . . Fear O'God Fulton
John Hamilton . . . . Edward Pettigrew
Bernhard Goetzke . . . . Mr Pettigrew
DRAMA USA. Mountain hermit teacher to save her from judge who thinks she killed his crippled son. (Made in Munich.)

08117
MADEMOISELLE FROM ARMENTIERES (7758) (U)
Gaumont
P: Victor Saville, Maurice Elvey
D: Maurice Elvey
S: Victor Saville
SC: V. Gareth Gundrey
Estelle Brody . . . . Mademoiselle
John Stuart . . . . Johnny
Alf Goddard . . . . Fred
Humberston Wright . . . . . . Old Soldier
John Hamilton . . . . Young Soldier
Marie Ault . . . . Aunt
Gabriel Rosca . . . . Carl Branz
Clifford Heatherley . . . . . . Interrogator
Albert Raynor . . . . GSOI
Boris Ranevsky . . . . Liason Officer
Sgt L. Smith V.C . . . . Sgt
WAR French girl meets captured British lover whilst acting as spy.

08118
BLINKEYES (7300) (A)
Welsh-Pearson (Gaumont)
P: D: SC: George Pearson
S: (NOVEL) Oliver Sandys
Betty Balfour . . . . Blinkeyes
Tom Douglas . . . . Ken Clay
Frank Stanmore . . . . Flowerpots
Pat Aherne . . . . The Basher
Hubert Carter . . . . Chang
Dorothy Seacombe . . . . . . Bella
J. Fisher White . . . . Uncle Dick
Mary Dibley . . . . Mrs Banning
Frank Vosper . . . . Seymour
DRAMA Cockney girl auctions herself to rich man who saves her from Chinese crook.

08119
BILLY MERSON (sound)
DeForest Phonofilms
(First "sound-on-film" film made in England.)
MUSICAL Comic song.

08120
JOSEPH TERMINI (sound)
DeForest Phonofilms
MUSICAL Eccentric violinist.

08121
GWEN FARRAR (sound)
DeForest Phonofilms
MUSICAL Comic song.

08122
DICK HENDERSON (sound)
DeForest Phonofilms
MUSICAL Comic song: "I love her all the more."

08123
RIGOLETTO, ACT TWO (sound)
DeForest Phonofilms
Musical Operatic sequence.

08124
MONS (7500) (U)
British Instructional (New Era)
P: H. Bruce Woolfe
D: S: Walter Summers
WAR Reconstruction of battle and subsequent retreat.

08125
CINDERS (7180) (U)
Societe des Cineromans — W & F (W & F)
D: Louis Mercanton
S: Fred Wright
Betty Balfour . . . . Cinders
Fred Wright . . . . Prof Pottiefax
Andre Reanne . . . . Richard Dalroy
Louis Baron . . . . Ferraro
Lucy Sibley . . . . Mrs Catchpole
Irene Tripod . . . . Boarder
Albert Decouer . . . . Manager
Louis Lerton . . . . Chef
Jean Mercanton . . . . Groom
COMEDY Nice. Professor inherits hotel and is saved from blackmail by drudge. (Made in France.)

OCT

08126
NELSON (7990) (U)
British Instructional (New Era)
P: H. Bruce Woolfe
D: SC: Walter Summers
S: (BOOK) Robert Southey (THE LIFE OF NELSON)
Cedric Hardwicke . . . . . . Horatio Nelson
Gertrude McCoy . . . . Lady Hamilton
Frank Perfitt . . . . Capt Hardy
Frank Arlton . . . . Governor
Pat Courtney . . . . Nelson (Child)
Gladys Harvey . . . .
Johnny Butt . . . .
HISTORY Married sailor has affair with Lady and dies in battle.

08127
PALAVER (7329) (U)
British Instructional (New Era)
P: H. Bruce Woolfe
D: S: Geoffrey Barkas
Haddon Mason . . . . Capt Peter Allison
Reginald Fox . . . . Mark Fernandez
Hilda Cowley . . . . Jean Stuart
Yiberr . . . . Dawiya
Yilkuba . . . . Himself
ADVENTURE Nigeria. Jealous tin miner arouses tribe against rival.

08128
SAFETY FIRST (6348) (U)
Stoll
D: Fred Paul
S: (NOVEL) Margot Neville
SC: Geoffrey H. Malins
Brian Aherne . . . . Hippocrates Rayne
Queenie Thomas . . . . Nanda Macdonald
Mary Brough . . . . Caroline Lowecraft
Patrick Susands . . . . Birdie Nightingale
Doreen Banks . . . . Angela StJaques
Humberston Wright . . . . . Butler
COMEDY Man has friends pose as asylum inmates to fool rich aunt.

08129
THE FLAG LIEUTENANT (8500) (U)
Astra-National
D: Maurice Elvey
S: (PLAY) W.P. Drury, Leo Tover
SC: Patrick L. Mannock
Henry Edwards . . . . Lt Dicky Lascelles
Lillian Oldland . . . . Sybil Wynne
Dorothy Seacombe . . . . . . Mrs Cameron
Fred Raynham . . . . Maj Thesiger
Fewlass Lewllyn . . . . Admiral Wynne
Hayford Hobbs . . . . . . Hon D'Arcy Penrose
Forrester Harvey . . . . Dusty Miller
Humberston Wright . . . . . Stiffy Steele
WAR Lieut branded coward after saving beleaguered fort for amnesiac Major. (Royal Command Performance.)

08130
THE LIFE OF ROBERT BURNS (7600) (U)
Scottish Film Academy reissue: 1928, IMMORTALS OF BONNIE SCOTLAND
D: Maurice Sandground
Wal Croft . . . . Robert Burns
George Campbell . . . .
HISTORY Scotland. Biography of Ploughboy poet.

08131
THE LIFE OF SIR WALTER SCOTT (7600((U)
Scottish Film Academy reissue: 1928, IMMORTALS OF BONNIE SCOTLAND
D: Maurice Sandground
HISTORY. Scotland. Biography of novelist.

08132
LONDON (5400) (A)
British National (Par)
P: J.D. Williams
D: Herbert Wilcox
S: Thomas Burke
Dorothy Gish . . . . Mavis Hogan
Adelqui Millar . . . . Paul Merlan
John Manners . . . . Geoffrey Malvern
Hubert Carter . . . . Charlie Down
Gibb McLaughlin . . . . Ah Kwang
Margaret Yarde . . . . Eliza Critten
Elissa Landi . . . . Alice Cranston
Daisy Campbell . . . . Lady Arbourfield
Paul Whiteman and his band
ROMANCE Lady adopts runaway slum girl who resembles her own dead daughter.

08133
THE BROTHERHOOD (2230) (U)
Frederick Alfred (AP & D)
D: Walter West
S: (STORY) Edgar Wallace (EDUCATED
EVANS)
John MacAndrews . . . .   Evans
Jameson Thomas . . . .
SPORT Windsor. Racing tipster succeeds for
clients but fails when bets himself.

08134
MEG (5000) (U)
Walter Shaw (Wardour)
P: D: Walter Shaw
S: Arnold Tolson
Mabel Armitage . . . .   Meg
Noel Greenwood . . . .   Jack Horton
Ruth Kalinsky . . . .   Constance Hope
DRAMA Dewsbury. Runaway girl nurses mine
owner's injured son who engaged to her sister.

08135
THE DAILY MIRROR COMPETITION
FILMS (series)
British Projects (BSC)
P: A.E. Bundy
D: Frank Tilley
SC: Ralph C. Wells

08136
1— THE PIED PIPER OF HAMELIN (2000) (U)
S: (POEM) Robert Browning
Edward Sorley . . . .   Pied Piper
Judd Green . . . .   Mayor

08137
2— CURFEW SHALL NOT RING TONIGHT
(2000) (U)
S: (POEM) Rose Thorpe
John Stuart . . . .   Basil
Ena Evans . . . .   Bessie

08138
3— THE PIPES OF LUCKNOW (2000)
S: (POEM)

08139
4— THE WRECK OF THE HESPERUS (2000)
S: (POEM) Henry Longfellow
Jean Colin . . . .
Darby Foster . . . .
Alexander Butler . . . .
DRAMAS Based on winning poems in
newspaper popularity contest.

08140
THE HAPPY RASCALS (series)
British Screen Classics
D: SC: Frank Miller
S: (STORIES) Morton Howard
Moore Marriott . . . .   Orace
Gregory Scott . . . .
Judd Green . . . .
James Knight . . . .
Wally Bosco . . . .
George Bellamy . . . .
Irene Tripod . . . .

08141
1— THE HAPPY RASCALS (2000)

08142
2— REGAINING THE WIND (2000)

08143
3— GOOSE AND STUFFING (2000)

08144
4— MINED AND COUNTER—MINED (2000)

08145
5— THE LITTLE SHOP IN FORE STREET
(2000)
COMEDIES Adventures of crew of small
fishing boat.

08146
FAMOUS SONG SCENAS (series)
Mercury Film Service
P: Booth Grainge
D: S: Hugh Croise

08147
1— THE VETERAN (1000) (U)
David Openshaw . . . .
Dorothy Boyd . . . .

08148
2— DREAM FACES (1000)
Walter Butler . . . .
Dorothy Boyd . . . .

08149
3— SHIPMATES (1000)
David Openshaw . . . .

08150
4— SONGS MY MOTHER SANG (1000)
Esther Coleman . . . .
Lillian Grange . . . .

08151
5— SONGS OF THE WEST COUNTREE (1000)
Mark Barker . . . .

08152
6— THE IRISH EMIGRANT (1000)
Stanley Kirk . . . .
MUSICAL Stories illustrating popular songs.

08153
LITTLE DRAMAS OF EVERYDAY LIFE
(series)
Raymond-Elliott British Photoplays
D: SC: William J. Elliott
Gladys Hamer . . . .
John Hamilton . . . .
Olive Meadows . . . .

08154
1— THE CAB (2078) (U)
S: William J. Elliott

08155
2— THE CONTRAST (1665) (A)
S: Jessica Bond . . . .

08156
3— THE TEST (1775) (U)
S: Ben Hurt
DRAMAS

NOV

08157
BOADICEA (7915) (U)
British Instructional (New Era)
P: H. Bruce Woolfe
D: Sinclair Hill
S: Sinclair Hill, Anthony Asquith
Phyllis Neilson-Terry . . . . .   Boadicea
Lilian Hall-Davis . . . .   Emmelyn
Clifford McLaglen . . . .   Marcus
Sybil Rhoda . . . .   Blondicca
Fred Raynham . . . .   Badwallon
Clifford Heatherley . . . . . .   Catus Decianus
Humberston Wright . . . .   Prasutagas
Edward O'Neill . . . .   Caradoc
Cyril McLaglen . . . .   Madoc
Roy Raymond . . . .   Burrus
HISTORY British Queen rouses Iceni but is
defeated by Romans.

08158
SECOND TO NONE (7674) (U)
Britannia (Gaumont)
P: Dinah Shurey
D: Jack Raymond
S: "Bartimeus"
SC: Lydia Hayward
Moore Marriott . . . .   Bill Hyde
Ian Fleming . . . .   Brian Douglas
Benita Hume . . . .   Ina
Micky Brantford . . . .   Bill (child)
Aggie Brantford . . . .   Ina (child)
Alf Goddard . . . .   Curley
Johnny Butt . . . .   Tubby
A.B. Imeson . . . .   Levine
Daisy Campbell . . . .   Mrs Hyde
Tom Coventry . . . .   Old Lemon
WAR Cdr's adopted son deserts Navy when his
sweetheart weds spy.

DEC

08159
THE JUNGLE WOMAN (5780) (U)
Stoll-Hurley
P: D: S: Frank Hurley
Eric Bransby Williams . . . .   Martin South
Lillian Douglas . . . .   Eleanor Mack
Jameson Thomas . . . .   Stephen Mordyke
W.G. Saunders . . . .   Peter Mack
Grace Savieri . . . .   Hurana
ADVENTURE New Guinea. Man escapes from
natives and saves girl from marrying crooked
partner.

08160
THE HOUSE OF MARNEY (6583) (U)
Nettlefold (Allied Artists)
P: Archibald Nettlefold
D: Cecil M. Hepworth
S: (NOVEL) John Goodwin
SC: Harry Hughes
Alma Taylor . . . .   Beatrice Maxon
John Longden . . . .   Richard
James Carew . . . .   Piers Marney
Patrick Susands . . . .   Stephen Marney
Gibb McLaughlin . . . .   Ezra
Cameron Carr . . . .   Mad Matt
Stephen T. Ewart . . . .   Gerald Maxon
John MacAndrews . . . .   Puggy
CRIME Essex.Sailor helps girl save heir from
crooked uncle.

08161
INSCRUTABLE DREW, INVESTIGATOR
(series)
FHC Productions (Pioneer)
P: G.H. Cricks
D: S: A.E. Coleby
SC: Eliot Stannard
Henry Ainley . . . .   Victor Drew

08162
1: THE COPPER CYLINDER (2000) (U)
Philip Valentine . . . .   Abdul

08163
2: THE CLUE OF THE OAK LEAF (2000) (A)
Bertram Burleigh . . . .
Molly Wynn . . . .
Cameron Carr . . . .
H. Agar Lyons . . . .
Harry Davo . . . .

08164
3: THE CURSE OF RAVENSCROFT (1900) (A)
Forbes Alexander . . . .   Lord Ravenscroft

08165
4: THE RIVER HOUSE MYSTERY (1715) (U)
Frank Stuart . . . .   Dracos

Doris Nicholls . . . . Violet Humphries
Ivor James . . . . Martin Howard
Enrico Lang . . . . Eric Langley
Warren Hastings . . . . Dr Humphries

08166
5: THE MOON DIAMOND (2000) (U)

08167
6: THE LOCKED DOOR (2000) (U)
CRIME Private detective solves various crimes.

08168
SCREEN PLAYLETS (series)
Gaumont

08169
1— CASH ON DELIVERY (2077) (U)
D: Milton Rosmer
S: (STORY) Alfred Barrett
Moore Marriott . . . .   Mr Popple
Forrester Harvey . . . .   Mr Nippit
Gabrielle Casartelli . . . .   Mary Popple
Charles Ashton . . . .   PC Jack
Pollie Emery . . . .   Mrs Jones

08170
2— THE ESCAPE (1610) (A)
D: Edwin Greenwood
S: (PLAY) E.F. Parr
Bertram Burleigh . . . .   Richard Manton
Gladys Jennings . . . .   Constance Manton
Barbara Blenn . . . .   Pamela Brabazon

08171
3—MISS BRACEGIRDLE DOES HER DUTY
(1543) (A)
D: Edwin Greenwood
S: (STORY) Stacy Aumonier
Janet Alexander . . . .   Millicent Bracegirdle
George Bellamy . . . .   Stephen Layburn
Humberston Wright . . . .   Boldru
P. Evremonde . . . .   The Dean
Sadie Speight . . . .   Mrs Rushbridger

08172
4—THE GREATER WAR (1725) (A)
D: Jack Raymond
S: (STORY) W. Townend
Moore Marriott . . . .   Lucas
Victor Fairley . . . .   Schmidt
Joan Vincent . . . .   Mrs Lucas

08173
5—BACK TO THE TREES (1960) (U)
D: Edwin Greenwood
S: (STORY) H. H. Bashford
Janet Alexander . . . .   Enid Brain-Marsh
John Stuart . . . .   Philip Brain-Marsh
Gladys Jennings . . . .   Barbara Wren
George Bellamy . . . . .   Sir Oliver Brain-Marsh
Eleanor Stewart . . . . . Dame Agnes Brain-Marsh

08174
6—THE WOMAN JUROR (1900) (U)
D: Milton Rosmer
S: (PLAY) E. F. Parr
Gladys Jennings . . . .   Jenefer Canynge
John Stuart . . . .   Michael
Frank Vosper . . . .   Morgan
Charles Ashton . . . .   Casey
Alexander Field . . . .   Bell
DRAMAS

08175
THE LIFE STORY OF CHARLES CHAPLIN
(2800) (U)
H. B. Parkinson (Pioneer)

D: S: H. B. Parkinson
Chick Wango . . . .   Charlie Chaplin
HISTORY "The story of a London youth and
his rise to fame as the world's greatest screen
artiste." (Not shown.)

08176
THE FAIR MAID OF PERTH (sound)
DeForest Phonofilms
D: Miles Mander
Louise Maurel . . . .
DRAMA

08177
THE WHISTLER (sound)
DeForest Phonofilms
D: Miles Mander
Louise Maurel . . . .
John Hamilton . . . .
Reginald Fox . . . .
DRAMA

08178
THE SHEIK OF ARABY (sound)
DeForest Phonofilms
D: Miles Mander
Paul England . . . :
MUSICAL

08179
THE HOUSTON SISTERS (sound)
reissue: 1932, MUSICAL MEDLEY No 5 (EB)
DeForest Phonofilms
Renee and Billie Houston . . .
MUSICAL

08180
NERVO AND KNOX (sound)
reissue: 1932, CAMERA COCKTALES
(Hallmark)
DeForest Phonofilms
D: Widgey R. Newman
Jimmy Nervo and Teddy Knox . . .
COMEDY Acrobatic dance.

08181
MARIE LLOYD JR (sound)
DeForest Phonofilms
MUSICAL

08182
ETHEL HOOK (sound)
DeForest Phonofilms
MUSICAL

08183
THORPE BATES (sound)
DeForest Phonofilms
MUSICAL

08184
FRED BARNES (sound)
DeForest Phonofilms
MUSICAL

08185
BETTY CHESTER (sound)
DeForest Phonofilms
MUSICAL

08186
GWEN FARRAR AND BILLY MAYERL (sound)
DeForest Phonofilms
MUSICAL Pianist and singer.

08187
WALTER WILLIAMS (sound)
DeForest Phonofilms
MUSICAL

08188
WINNIE COLLINS (sound)
DeForest Phonofilms
MUSICAL

08189
ALVIN AND KELVIN KEECH (sound)
DeForest Phonofilms
MUSICAL

08190
JULIUS CAESAR (sound)
DeForest Phonofilms
D: George A. Cooper
S: (PLAY) William Shakespeare
Basil Gill . . . .   Brutus
Malcolm Keen . . . .   Cassius
DRAMA Rome. Quarrel scene.

08191
SANTA CLAUS (sound)
DeForest Phonofilms
D: George A. Cooper
Basil Gill . . . .
DRAMA Christmas play.

08192
THE MAN IN THE STREET (9) (U) (sound)
retitled: MAN OF MYSTERY
DeForest Phonofilms (EB)
D: Thomas Bentley
S: (PLAY) Louis N. Parker
John McAndrews . . . .   The Busker
Wilbur Lenton . . . .   The Artist
Bunty O'Nolan . . . .   The Wife
DRAMA Artist hires a busker to pose for him
and finds he is his father-in-law.

08193
KNEE DEEP IN DAISIES (sound)
DeForest Phonofilms
D: Miles Mander
Paul England . . . .
Dorothy Boyd . . . . . .
MUSICAL Office scene.

08194
THE YIDDISHER BAND (sound)
DeForest Phonofilms
D: Robert Cullen
Teddy Elben
MUSICAL

08195
THE FLAT CHARLESTON (sound)
DeForest Phonofilms
D: Dudley Ponting
Santos Casani . . . .
Jose Lennard . . . .
MUSICAL Dance demonstration.

08196
THOU FOOL (5100) (U)
Stoll (EB)
D: Fred Paul
S: (NOVEL) J.J. Bell
Stewart Rome . . . .   Robert Baker
Marjorie Hume . . . .   Elsie Glen
Mary Rorke . . . . Lady MacDonald
J. Fisher White . . . .   James Scobie
Windham Guise . . . .   Duncan Glen
Pat Aherne . . . .
Mickey Brantford . . . .   Robert (child)
Darby Foster . . . .   Harry Clement
DRAMA Scots shopkeeper ruins ex-
employer, whose daughter marries man made
rich by father's tips.

1927

JAN

08197
A DAUGHTER IN REVOLT (7300) (U)
Nettlefold (Allied Artists)
P: Archibald Nettlefold
D: SC: Harry Hughes
S: (NOVEL) Sidney Gowing
Mabel Poulton . . . . Aimee Scroope
Edward O'Neill . . . . Lord Scroope
Patrick Susands . . . . Billy Spencer
Lilian Oldland . . . . Georgina Berners
Pat Aherne . . . . Jackie the Climber
Hermione Baddeley . . . . . . Calamity Kate
Ena Grossmith . . . . Snooks
Marie Ault . . . . Mrs Dale
Daisy Campbell . . . . Lady Scroope
Neil Curtis . . . . Alexander Lambe
Gertrude Sterroll . . . . . Lady Erythea Lambe
COMEDY Lord's daughter suspected of
burglary when she changes places with her
friend.

FEB

08198
HINDLE WAKES (8800) (A)
USA: FANNY HAWTHORNE
Gaumont
P: Maurice Elvey, Victor Saville
D: Maurice Elvey
S: (PLAY) Stanley Houghton
Estelle Brody . . . . .Fanny Hawthorne
John Stuart . . . . .Allan Jeffcoate
Norman McKinnel . . . . . . .Nathaniel Jeffcoate
Marie Ault . . . . Mrs Hawthorne
Humberston Wright . . . . . . Chris Hawthorne
Gladys Jennings . . . . .Beatrice Farrar
Irene Rooke . . . . Mrs Jeffcoate
Peggy Carlisle . . . . Mary Hollins
Arthur Chesney . . . . Sir Timothy Farrar
Alf Goddard . . . . Nobby
Cyril McLaglen . . . . Alf
Graham Soutten . . . . Mr Hollins
ROMANCE Lancs. Millgirl refuses to marry
employer's son after holiday together.

08199
PEARL OF THE SOUTH SEAS (5000) (U)
Stoll- Hurley Productions
P: D: S: Frank Hurley
Eric Bransby Williams . . . . John Strong
Lillian Douglas . . . . Marjorie Jones
Jameson Thomas . . . . John Darley
V.G. Saunders . . . . Cockeye Jones
Mollie Johnson . . . . Lady Cynthia
Dallas Cairns . . . . Mr Bullyer
ADVENTURE Thursday Island. Girl saves
pearl-diving heir when cousin cuts his air-tube.

MAR

08200
THE BOOK OF PSALMS (series)
Triangle British Films
P: Bernard Smith
D: S: Charles Barnett

08201
1— THE STRANGER — PSALM 119 (2000)
Julie Suedo . . . .
Reginald Fox . . . .

08202
2— THE TRAITOR — PSALM 25 (2000)
Mary Odette . . . .
Tom Helmore . . . .

08203
3— THE PARTING OF THE WAYS —
PSALM 57 (2000)

Sonnie Hale . . . .
Maudie Dunham . . . .
Sir Simeon Stuart . . . .

08204
4— MEMORIES — PSALM 46 (2000)
Michael Hogan . . . .

08205
5— THE SHEPHERD — PSALM 23 (2000)
Jack Raine . . . .

08206
6— A DAUGHTER OF THE NIGHT —
PSALM 69 (2000)
Eve Gray . . . .
DRAMAS Moral stories suggested by psalms.
(Extracts in PAINTED PICTURES, 1930.)

08207
SYNCOPATED MELODIES (series) (U)
H.B. Parkinson (White)
D: S: J. Steven Edwards
Jack Hylton and his Band
Sidney Firman and the London Radio Dance
Band
Reggie Batten and the Savoy Havana Band
Jack Payne and the Hotel Cecil Band
Teddy Brown and the Cafe de Paris Band
Jack Howard and the Royal Opera House Band
John Lester's Cowboy Syncopaters
W.F. DeMorny's Savoy Havana Band

08208
1— BARCELONA (850)

08209
2— BECAUSE I LOVE YOU (970)

08210
3— CHINESE MOON (850)

08211
4— HI DIDDLE DIDDLE (850)

08212
5— THE MORE WE ARE TOGETHER (850)

08213
Nos 6 — 12 (850 each)
MUSICAL Illustrated songs synchronise with
cinema orchestras.

08214
BLIGHTY (8397) (U)
Gainsborough-Piccadilly (W & F)
P: Michael Balcon, Carlyle Blackwell
D: Adrian Brunel
S: Charles McEvoy, Ivor Montagu
SC: Eliot Stannard
Ellaline Terriss . . . . Lady Villiers
Lilian Hall Davis . . . . Mrs Villiers
Jameson Thomas . . . . . .David Marshall
Nadia Sibirskaia . . . . . . .The Little Refugee
Godfrey Winn . . . . Robin Villiers
Annesley Hely . . . . . . Sir Francis Villiers
Wally Patch . . . .
Dino Galvani . . . .
Seymour Hicks . . . .
The Houston Sisters . . . . . .
WAR Chauffeur becomes officer and later cares
for master's widow and child.

APR

08215
THE QUEEN WAS IN THE PARLOUR
(7250) (A) USA: FORBIDDEN LOVE
Gainsborough-Piccadilly—UFA (W & F)
P: Michael Balcon, Herman Fellner
D: SC: Graham Cutts

S: (PLAY) Noel Coward
Lili Damita . . . . Nadya
Paul Richter . . . . Sabieri
Harry Leichke . . . . Prince Keri
Rosa Richards . . . . Zana
Klein Rogge . . . . Gen Krish
Trude Hesterberg . . . . . . Grand Duchess Emilie
ROMANCE Ruritania. Widowed princess loves
author who commits suicide when forced to
marry prince. (Made in Germany.)

08216
ROSES OF PICARDY (8500) (A)
Gaumont
P: Maurice Elvey, Victor Saville
D: Maurice Elvey
S: (STORIES) R.H. Mottram (THE SPANISH
FARM; 64-94)
SC: V. Gareth Gundrey
Lilian Hall-Davis . . Madeleine Vanderlynden
John Stuart . . . . Lt Skene
Humberston Wright . . . . .Jerome Vanderlynden
Jameson Thomas . . . . Georges d'Archeville
Marie Ault . . . . Baroness d'Archeville
A. Bromley Davenport . . .Baron d'Archeville
Clifford Heatherley . . . . . . Uncle
WAR France. Ex-lieut returns to find
sweetheart is caring for baron's blinded son.

08217
ROBINSON CRUSOE (6500) (U)
Epic Films *reissue:* 1932
P: D: SC: M.A. Wetherell
S: (NOVEL) Daniel Defoe
M.A. Wetherell . . . . Robinson Crusoe
Fay Compton . . . . Sophie
Herbert Waithe . . . . Man Friday
Reginald Fox . . . .
ADVENTURE Tobago, 1659. Shipwrecked
man's prolonged stay on desert island.
(Sound added 1932)

08218
AS WE LIE (9) (U) retitled: LOST ONE
WIFE sound
DeForest Phonofilms (EB)
D: S: Miles Mander
Miles Mander . . . . The Husband
Lilian Hall Davis . . . . The Wife
COMEDY Man cures neglectful wife by faking
affair over telephone.

08219
THE ANTIDOTE (9) (sound)
DeForest Phonofilms
D: Thomas Bentley
S: (PLAY) Ben Landeck
Jameson Thomas . . . .
DRAMA Malaya. "Snakebite drama".

08220
THE SENTENCE OF DEATH (9) (U) (sound)
retitled: HIS GREAT MOMENT
DeForest Phonofilms (EB)
D: Miles Mander
S: (PLAY) Edward Dignon, Cyril Campion
Owen Nares . . . . The Patient
Dorothy Boyd . . . . The Woman
Peter Evan Thomas . . . . . . The Doctor
DRAMA Sick musician doctor revealed as
actor and playwright.

08221
PACKING UP (9) (sound)
DeForest Phonofilms
D: Miles Mander
S: (PLAY) Roland Pertwee
Malcolm Keen . . . .
Mary Clare . . . .
DRAMA

08222
FALSE COLOURS (15) (sound)
DeForest Phonofilms
D: Miles Mander
Ursula Jeans . . . .
A.B. Imeson
DRAMA

08223
HIS REST DAY (9) (sound)
DeForest Phonofilms
D: George A. Cooper
S: (PLAY) Matthew Boulton
Matthew Boulton . . . .   Bill Gosling
COMEDY

08224
ARTHUR ROBERTS (sound)
DeForest Phonofilms
D: Bertram Phillips
MUSICAL Two comic songs.

08225
ARTHUR ROBERTS SKETCH (sound)
DeForest Phonofilms
D: George A. Cooper
S: (SKETCH) Arthur Roberts
SC: Harry J. Worth
Arthur Roberts . . . .
COMEDY

08226
EDITH SITWELL (sound)
DeForest Phonofilms
D: Widgey R. Newman
S: Edith Sitwell
Edith and Sacheverell Sitwell
DRAMA Two poems.

MAY

08227
DOWNHILL (7600) (A) USA: WHEN BOYS
LEAVE HOME
Gainsborough (W & F)
P: Michael Balcon
D: Alfred Hitchcock
S: (PLAY) Ivor Novello, Constance Collier
SC: Eliot Stannard
Ivor Novello . . . .   Roddy Berwick
Isabel Jeans . . . .   Julia
Ian Hunter . . . .   Archie
Ben Webster . . . .   Dr Dawson
Lilian Braithwaite . . . .   Lady Berwick
Norman McKinnel . . . . . Sir Thomas Berwick
Robin Irvine . . . .   Tim Walkeley
Sybil Rhoda . . . .   Sybil Walkeley
Annette Benson . . . .   Mabel
Alf Goddard . . . .   The Swede
Jerrold Robertshaw . . . . . Rev Henry Walkeley
Violet Fairbrother . . . .   The Poetess
Barbara Gott . . . .   Mme Michet
DRAMA Disowned youth becomes gigolo
after wife bankrupts him.

08228
THE ROLLING ROAD (8700) (A)
Gainsborough-Piccadilly (W & F)
P: Michael Balcon, Carlyle Blackwell
D: Graham Cutts
S: Boyd Cable (E.W. Ewart)
SC: Violet E. Powell
Carlyle Blackwell . . . .   Tom Forty
Flora le Breton . . . .   Nell
A.V. Bramble . . . .   John Christobel
Clifford Heatherley . . . . . .   John Ogilvie
Cameron Carr . . . .   Mate
Marie Ault . . . .   Grannie
Mickey Brantford . . . .   Nipper
Benson Kleve . . . .   Captain
ADVENTURE Marooned sailor and stowaway
sister-in-law rescued by her husband.

08229
PASSION ISLAND (7500) (A)
Film Manufacturing Co (FNP)
P: G.A. Atkinson
D: Manning Hanyes
S: (NOVEL) W.W. Jacobs
SC: Lydia Hayward
Lillian Oldland. . . . . .Josettes Bernatti
Moore Marriott . . . .   Beppo
Randle Ayrton . . . .   Paolo Bernatti
Walter Butler . . . .   Tony
Dacia Deane . . . .   Santa
Gladys Hamer . . . .   Clare
Leal Douglas . . . .   Desiree
Johnny Butt . . . .   Tomaso
CRIME Corsica. Man framed for murdering
priest poses as paralytic and strangles culprit.

JUN

08230
CAMEO OPERAS (series) (U)
Song Films
P: John E. Blakeley

08231
1— THE BOHEMIAN GIRL (1472)
D: H.B. Parkinson
S: (OPERA) William Balfe
Herbert Langley . . . .   Thaddeus
Pauline Johnson . . . .   Arlene

08232
2— LILY OF KILLARNEY (1690)
D: H.B. Parkinson
S:(OPERA) Charles Benedict
Herbert Langley . . . .   Hardress Cregan
Kathlyn Hilliard . . . .   Eily O'Connor

08233
3— MARITANA (1652)
D: H.B. Parkinson
S: (OPERA) W.V. Wallace
Herbert Langley . . . .   Don Cesar
Kathlyn Hilliard . . . . :   Maritana

08234
4— RIGOLETTO (1669)
D: H.B. Parkinson
S: (OPERA) Giuseppi Verdi
Herbert Langley . . . .   Rigoletto
Mme Karina . . . .   Gilda
A.B. Imeson . . . .   Don Jose

08235
5— FAUST (1657)
D: H.B. Parkinson
S: (OPERA) Charles Gounod
Herbert Langley . . . .   Faust
A.B. Imeson . . . .   Mephistopheles
Margot Lees . . . .   Marguerite

08236
6— CARMEN (1657)
D: H.B. Parkinson
S: (OPERA) Georges Bizet
Herbert Langley . . . .   Don Jose
Zeda Pascha . . . .   Carmen

08237
7— LA TRAVIATA (1605)
D: H.B. Parkinson
S: (OPERA) Giuseppi Verdi
Anthony Ireland . . . .   Alfredo Germont
Peggy Carlisle . . . .   Violetta Valery
Booth Conway . . . .   Baron Douphol

08238
8— DAUGHTER OF THE REGIMENT (1764)
D: H.B. Parkinson
S: (OPERA) Gastono Donizetti
Kitty Barling . . . .   Marie
Oscar Sosander . . . .   Tonio
Algernon Hicks . . . .   Baron Bertrand

08239
9— MARTHA (1608)
D: H.B. Parkinson
S: (OPERA) Friedrich Flotow
Grizelda Hervey . . . .   Lady Henrietta
Gerald Rawlinson . . . .   Lionel
Algernon Hicks . . . .   Plunket

08240
10 — IL TROVATORE (1130)
D: A.E. Coleby
S: (OPERA) Giuseppi Verdi

08241
11— THE RING (2000)
D: H.B. Parkinson
S: (OPERA) Richard Wagner

08242
12— SAMSON AND DELILAH (2000)
D: H.B. Parkinson
S: (OPERA) Charles Saint-Saens
William Anderson . . . .   Samson
MUSICALS Condensed stories of operas
synchronise with cinema orchestras and
vocalists.

08243
ON WITH THE DANCE (series) (U)
H.B. Parkinson (Pioneer)
D: H.B. Parkinson, J. Steven Edwards
Nos. 1 — 12 (600 ft each)
Binnie Hale . . . .
Laddie Cliff . . . .
Cyril Ritchard . . . .
Leslie Henson . . . .
Sid Tracey . . . .
Leslie Hatton . . . .
Devine & Charles . . . .
THe Tiller Girls . . . .
Sonnie Hale . . . .
Phyllis Monkman . . . .
Madge Elliott . . . .
Bobby Howes . . . .
Bessie Hay . . . .
Annie Croft . . . .
Reginald Sharland . . . .
MUSICALS Dances synchronise with cinema
orchestras.

08244
TIPTOES (6286) (U)
British National (Par0
P: J.D. Williams
D: Herbert Wilcox
S: (PLAY) Guy Bolton, Fred Thompson
Dorothy Gish . . . .   Tiptoes
Will Rogers . . . .   Hen Kaye
Nelson Keys . . . .   Al Kaye
John Manners . . . Lord William Montgomery
Miles Mander . . . .   Rollo Stevens
Annie Esmond . . . .   Aunt
Ivy Ellison . . . .   Sister
Dennis Hoey . . . .   Hotelier
Hubert Carter . . . .
Jerrold Robertshaw . . . . . .
Judd Green . . . .
Fred Rains . . . .
ROMANCE Stranded American dancer poses
as heiress to impress lord.

08245
THE GLAD EYE (7700) (U)
Gaumont
P: Maurice Elvey, Victor Saville
D: Maurice Elvey
S: (PLAY) Jose Levy. Paul Armont, Nicholas
Nancey (LE ZEBRE)
SC: V. Gareth Gundrey, Maurice Elvey, Victor
Saville
Estelle Brody . . . .   Kiki
Hal Sherman . . . .   Chausette

John Stuart . . . . Maurice
Mabel Poulton . . . . Suzanne
Jeanne de Casalis . . . . Lucienne
John Longden . . . . Floquet
Humberston Wright . . . . . . Gaston
A.Bromley Davenport . . . . Gallipax
Aubrey Fitzgerald . . . . Footman
COMEDY Paris. Men elude wives by
pretending to go on dirigible; it crashes.

JUL

08246
MADAME POMPADOUR (7245) (U)
British National (Par)
P: E.A. Dupont
D: Herbert Wilcox
S: (PLAY) Rudolph Schanzer, Ernst Wellish
SC: Frances Marion, E.A. Dupont
Dorothy Gish . . . . Mme Pompadour
Antonio Moreno . . . . Rene Laval
Nelson Keys . . . . .Duc de Courcelette
Henri Bosc . . . . Loius XV
Gibb McLaughlin . . . . Comte Maurepas
Cyril McLaglen . . . . Gogo
Marsa Beauplan . . . . Mme Poisson
Marie Ault . . . . Belotte
HISTORY France. King's mistress frees jailed
lover and makes him bodyguard.

08247
EASY VIRTUE (7392) (A)
Gainsborough (W & F)
P: Michael Balcon
D: Alfred Hitchcock
S: (PLAY) Noel Coward
SC: Eliot Stannard
Isabel Jeans . . . . Laurita Filton
Robin Irvine . . . . .John Whittaker
Franklin Dyall . . . . Mr Filton
Enid Stamp-Taylor . . . . . . Sarah
Violet Farebrother . . . . . . Mrs Whittaker
Frank Elliot . . . . Col Whittaker
Dacia Deane . . . . Marion Whittaker
Dorothy Boyd . . . . Hilda Whittaker
Ian Hunter . . . . Counsel
Eric Bransby Williams . . . . . Co-respondent
Benita Hume . . . . Telephonist
DRAMA Divorcee weds infatuated youth,
shocks him and parents, and leaves.

08248
THE GHOST TRAIN (6500) (U)
Gainsborough (W & F)
P: Michael Balcon, Herman Fellner
D: Geza M. Bolvary
S: (PLAY) Arnold Ridley
Guy Newall . . . . Teddy Deakin
Ilse Bois . . . . Miss Bourne
Louis Ralph . . . . Saul Hodgkin
Anna Jennings . . . . Peggy Murdock
John Manners . . . . Charles Murdock
Agnes Korolenko . . . . Elsie Winthrop
Ernest Verebes . . . . Richard Winthrop
Rosa Walter . . . . Julia Price
CRIME Detective poses as simpleton to uncover
gun-runners using abandoned railway line. (Made
in Germany)

08249
SAINT JOAN (5) (sound)
DeForest Phonofilms
D: Widgey R. Newman
S: (PLAY) George Bernard Shaw
Sybil Thorndike . . . . Joan
DRAMA Cathedral scene.

08250
NEXT GENTLEMAN PLEASE (3000)
Oxford University (Wardour)

D: John Greenidge, Rudolph Messell
S: Alan Titley
Joan Maude . . . . Fortune-teller
COMEDY French fortune-teller helps beau steal
jewels and elopes with local thug (Amateur film
commercially released).

08251
PRELUDE (600)
Castleton Knight
D:SC: Castleton Knight
S: (STORY) Edgar Allen Poe (THE
PREMATURE BURIAL)
Castleton Knight . . . . The Man
HORROR Man listening to Rachmaninoff's
'Prelude' dreams he is victim of premature
burial.

08252
THE SOMME (8100) (U)
New Era
P: Gordon Craig
D: M.A. Wetherell
S: Boyd Cable
SC: Geoffrey Barkas
WAR Reconstruction of several battles
which took place on the Somme.

08253
THE BATTLES OF THE CORONEL AND
FALKLAND ISLANDS (8300) (U)
British Instructional-British Projects *reissue:*
1932, THE DEEDS MEN DO
P: A.E. Bundy, H. Bruce Woolfe
D: Walter Summers
S: Harry Engholm, Frank Bowen,
John Buchan,
SC: Harry Engholm, John Buchan, Merritt
Crawford
Craighall Sherry . . . . Admiral Sturdee
WAR Reconstruction of the Navy's pursuit and
sinking of the 'Von Spee'. (Sound added 1932).

08254
MUMSIE (6858) (U)
Herbert Wilcox (W & F)
D: Herbert Wilcox
S: (PLAY) Edward Knoblock (MUMSEE)
Pauline Frederick . . . . Mumsie
Nelson Keys . . . . Spud Murphy
Herbert Marshall . . . . Col Armytage
Frank Stanmore . . . . Nobby Clarke
Donald McCardle . . . . Noel Symonds
Irene Russell . . . . Louise Symonds
Rolf Leslie . . . . Edgar Symonds
A. Barry . . . . Carl Kessler
Frank Perfitt . . . . Maj Bowen
Patrick Susands . . . .
Tom Coventry . . . .
WAR Pacifist gambler turns spy and gives
father's gas factory plans to enemy.

08255
A WOMAN REDEEMED (7800) (A)
Stoll (New Era)
D: Sinclair Hill
S: (NOVEL) F. Britten Austin (THE FINING
POT IS FOR SILVER)
SC: Mary Murillo
Joan Lockton . . . . Felice Annaway
Brian Aherne . . . . Geoffrey Maynefleet
Stella Arbenina . . . . Marta
James Carew . . . . Count Kalvestro
Gordon Hopkirk . . . . Angelo
Frank Denton . . . . Bug (Capt Courtney)
Robert English . . . . Col Mather
CRIME Count forces girl to marry inventor and
steal plans for wireless-controlled torpedo.

08256
REMEMBRANCE (7400) (U)
British Independent Productions (UK)
D: Bert Wynne
S: George King
P: Sidney Eaton
Rex Davis . . . . Jack Morgan
Enid Stamp Taylor . . . . Enid Marsland
Alf Goddard . . . . Alf Harris
Hayford Hobbs . . . . Frank Laurie
Violet Hopson . . . . Jane Morgan
Frederick Cooper . . . . Albert Clarke
Gladys Hamer . . . . Ada Wilson
Olive Rimmer . . . . Olive Harris
Prince of Wales . . . . Himself
Earl Haig . . . . Himself
WAR Miner, builder and clerk join army, are
wounded, and ultimately aided by British
Legion.

08257
THE FAKE (8500) (A)
Neo-Art Productions (WP)
P: Julius Hagen
D: George Jacoby
S: (PLAY) Frederick Lonsdale
SC: George A. Cooper
Henry Edwards . . . . Geoffrey Sands
Elga Brink . . . . Mavis Stanton
Juliette Compton . . . . . . .Mrs Hesketh Pointer
Norman McKinnel. . . . . Ernest Stanton
Miles Mander . . . . Hon Gerald Pillick
J. Fisher White . . . . Sir Thomas Moorgate
A. Bromley Davenport . . . . Hesketh Pointer
Julie Suedo . . . . Dancer
Ivan Samson . . . . Clifford Howe
Ursula Jeans . . . . Maid
DRAMA MP forces daughter to marry titled
drug addict who dies when her lover tries to
cure him.

08258
LOVE'S OLD SWEET SONG (3) (sound)
Synchofilms
P:D: S.H. Johnson
Elsie Kitt
MUSICAL Song.

08259
CHARLESTON DANCE (3) (sound)
Synchofilms
P:D: S.H. Johnson
MUSICAL Dance.

08260
THE VORTEX (6281) (A)
Gainsborough (W & F)
P: Michael Balcon
D: Adrian Brunel
S: (PLAY) Noel Coward
SC: Eliot Stannard
Ivor Novello . . . . Nicky Lancaster
Wilette Kershaw . . . . Florence Lancaster
Frances Doble . . . . Bunty Mainwaring
Alan Hollis . . . . Tom Veryan
Sir Simeon Stuart . . . . David Lancaster
Kinsey Peile . . . . Pauncefort Quentin
Julie Suedo . . . . Anna Volloff
Dorothy Fane . . . . Helen Saville
ROMANCE Youth discovers his fiancee is
mistress of mother's lover.

08261
A SISTER TO ASSIST 'ER (6000) (A)
Gaumont
P: Maurice Elvey, Victor Saville, Gareth
Gundrey
D:SC: George Dewhurst

S: (PLAY) John le Breton
Mary Brough . . . . Mrs May
Pollie Emery . . . . Mrs Mull
Humberston Wright . . . . Mr Mull
A. Bromley Davenport . . . . . Jim Harris
Alf Goddard . . . . Sailor
Jack Harris . . . . Alf
COMEDY Poor woman poses as rich twin to fool mean landlady.

08262
THE FLIGHT COMMANDER (8276) (U)
Gaumont
P: Maurice Elvey, Victor Saville, Gareth Gundrey
D: Maurice Elvey
S: John Travers
SC: Eugene Clifford
Sir Alan Cobham . . . . Himself
Estelle Brody . . . . Mary
John Stuart . . . . John Massey
Humberston Wright . . . . . . James Mortimer
Vesta Sylva . . . . Babette
Alf Goddard . . . . Tommy
John Longden . . . . Ivan
Cyril McLaglen . . . . Sammy
William Pardue . . . . Pierre
A. Bromley Davenport . . . . . Philosopher
Edward O'Neill . . . . Missionary
ADVENTURE China. Pilot saves British residents from Bolshevik's massacre plot.

OCT

08263
A WOMAN IN PAWN (6845) (A)
Gaumont
P: Maurice Elvey, Victor Saville, Gareth Gundrey
D: Edwin Greenwood
S: (PLAY) Frank Stayton (IN PAWN)
Gladys Jennings . . . . Diana Rawdon
John Stuart . . . . James Rawdon
Lauderdale Maitland . . . . . . George Zarantis
Chili Bouchier . . . . Elaine
Tarva Penna . . . . Phipps
Karen Petersen . . . . Mrs Phipps
Desmond Roberts . . . . David Courthill
CRIME Ruined stockbroker blamed for killing crooked financier who lured his wife.

08264
THE ARCADIANS (7000) (U)
Gaumont
P: Maurice Elvey, Victor Saville, Gareth Gundrey
D: Victor Saville
S: (PLAY) Mark Ambient, Alex Thompson
Ben Blue . . . . Simplicitas Smith
Jeanne de Casalis . . . . Mrs Smith
Vesta Sylva . . . . Eileen Cavanaugh
John Longden . . . . Jack Meadows
Gibb McLaughlin . . . . Peter Doody
Humberston Wright . . . . . . Sir George Paddock
Cyril McLaglen . . . . The Crook
Doris Bransgrove . . . . Sombra
Nancy Rigg . . . . Chrysea
Teddy Brown
Ivor Vintor
Lola & Luis
Tracey & Haye
Balliol & Merton
Donovan Sisters
Tiller Girls
12 Arcadian Nymphs
FANTASY Club-owner crashes plane in Arcady, land of truth and beauty.

08265
THE RING (8454) (A)
BIP (Wardour)

D:S: Alfred Hitchcock
SC: Alfred Hitchcock, Alma Reville
Carl Brisson . . . . Jack Sander
Lilian Hall Davis . . . . Mabel
Ian Hunter . . . . Bob Corby
Forrester Harvey . . . . James Ware
Gordon Harker . . . . George
Harry Terry . . . . Barker
Bdr Billy Wells . . . . Boxer
Charles Farrell . . . . Second
Clare Greet . . . . Gypsy
SPORT Fairground boxer's wife returns to help him win championship. (Extract in ELSTREE STORY; 1952).

08266
POPPIES OF FLANDERS (8750) (U)
BIP (Wardour)
D: Arthur Maude
S: (STORY) "Sapper" (H.C. McNeile) THE HOPELESS CASE
SC: Violet Powell
Jameson Thomas . . . . Jim Brown
Eve Gray . . . . Beryl Kingwood
Malcolm Tod . . . . Bob Standish
Gibb McLaughlin . . . . Shorty Bill
Henry Vibart . . . . Earl of Strangeways
Daisy Campbell . . . . Countess
Cameron Carr . . . . Merrick
Vivienne Whittaker . . . . Mrs Merrick
Tubby Phillips . . . . Fat Man
WAR 1914. Earl's reformed son fakes relapse on learning sweetheart loves another, and dies saving his life.

08267
THE SILVER LINING (7407) (U)
BIP (Wardour)
D: Thomas Bentley
S: Bai David
SC: Violet Powell
Marie Ault . . . . Mrs Hurst
Pat Aherne . . . . Tom Hurst
John Hamilton . . . . John Hurst
Eve Gray . . . . Lettie Deans
Sydney Fairbrother . . . . Mrs Akers
Moore Marriott . . . . Gipsy
Cameron Carr . . . . Constable
Mrs Fred Emney . . . . Mrs Deans
Bernard Vaughan . . . . Vicar
CRIME Gamekeeper takes blame when brother steals pearls.

08268
MOTHERLAND (7002) (A)
Reciprocity Films
D: G.B. Samuelson, Rex Davis
S: G.B. Samuelson
Rex Davis . . . . The Lonely Soldier
Eva Moore . . . . Mrs Edwards
James Knight . . . . Tom Edwards
Peggy Carlisle . . . . Grace Edwards
A. Harding Steerman . . . . . Mr Edwards
Hayman & Franklin . . . . Mr & Mrs Abrahamson
Alec Alexander jr . . . . Ikey
Marjorie Spiers . . . .
Lena Halliday . . . .
WAR Soldier poses as dead captain to comfort blind mother while girl poses as dead Jew's wife to comfort family.

08269
THE KING'S HIGHWAY (7900) (U)
Stoll
D: Sinclair Hill
S: (NOVEL) Lord Lytton (PAUL CLIFFORD)
SC: Leslie Howard Gordon, Harcourt Templeman
Matheson Lang . . . . Paul Clifford
Joan Lockton . . . . Lucy Brandon

James Carew . . . . Judge Brandon
Gerald Ames . . . . Lord Mauleverer
Mark Lupino . . . . Old Baggs
Henry Latimer . . . . Gentleman George
Sydney Seaward . . . . Augustus
Frank Goldsmith . . . . Squire John Brandon
Clifford Heatherley . . . . Beau Nash
Nell Emerald . . . . Lizzie Lob
Aubrey Fitzgerald . . . . Nathaniel
George Butler . . . . Long Ned
Frederick Ranalow . . . . MacHeath
Wally Patch . . . . Police Chief
ADVENTURE 1765. Judge sentences highwayman to die, then finds he is his son.

08270
SOMEHOW GOOD (7900) (A)
Film Manufacturing Co (Pathe)
P: John Sloane
D: Jack Raymond
S: (NOVEL) William de Morgan
SC: Lydia Hayward
Fay Compton . . . . Rosalind Nightingale
Stewart Rome . . . . Jerry Harrison
Dorothy Boyd . . . . Sally
Frank Perfitt . . . . Dederich
Colin Keith-Johnson . . . . . Doctor
J. Fisher White . . . . Old Fossil
DRAMA Amnesiac weds wife he ejected after she was assaulted in brothel.

NOV

08271
FURTHER ADVENTURES OF THE FLAG LIEUTENANT (8500) (U)
Neo-Art Productions (WP)
P: Julius Hagen
D: W.P. Kellino
S: W.P. Drury
SC: George A. Cooper
Henry Edwards . . . . Lt Dicky Lascelles
Isabel Jeans . . . . Pauline
Lilian Oldland . . . . Sybil Wynne
Lyn Harding . . . . The Sinister Influence
Fewlass Llewellyn . . . . . . Admiral Wynne
Fred Raynham . . . . Col William Thesiger
Albert Egbert . . . . Bill
Seth Egbert . . . . Walter
Vivian Baron . . . . Ah Loom
ADVENTURE Shanghai. Lieut escapes from spies and regains stolen plans.

08272
LAND OF HOPE AND GLORY (8300) (U)
Glory Films (Napoleon) reissue: 1929 (BL)
P: Samuel W. Smith
D: Harley Knoles
S: Valentine Williams
SC: Adrian Brunel
Ellaline Terriss . . . . Mrs Whiteford
Lyn Harding . . . . Roger Whiteford
Robin Irvine . . . . Ben Whiteford
Ruby Miller . . . . Myra Almazov
Enid Stamp Taylor . . . . Jane
Arthur Pusey . . . . Matt Whiteford
Henry Vibart . . . . Sir John Maxeter
Lewin Mannering . . . . Boris Snide
Kenneth McLaglen . . . . . . Stan Whiteford
WAR 1919. Girl saves fiance's aeroplane stabiliser plans from spies.

08273
ONE OF THE BEST (8271) (U)
Gainsborough-Piccadilly (W & F)
P: Michael Balcon, Carlyle Blackwell
D: T. Hayes Hunter
S: (PLAY) Seymour Hicks, George Edwardes
SC: Patrick L. Mannock

Carlyle Blackwell . . . . Philip Ellsworth
Walter Butler . . . . Lt Dudley Keppel
Eve Gray . . . . Mary Penrose
Randle Ayrton . . . . Gen Gregg
James Carew . . . . Col Gentry
Julie Suedo . . . . Claire Melville
James Lindsay . . . . Maurice de Gruchy
Pauline Johnson . . . . Esther
Elsa Lanchester . . . . Kitty
Charles Emerald . . . . Pte Jupp
Cecil Barry . . . . Lt Wynne
Sir Simeon Stuart . . . . Squire Penrose
Harold Huth . . . . Adjutant
CRIME 1820. Officer frames colleague when
gambler forces him to steal secrets.

08274
THE LUCK OF THE NAVY (8300) (U)
Graham-Wilcox Productions
P: Rudolph Solomon
D: Fred Paul
S: (PLAY) Clifford Mills
SC: Dion Clayton Calthrop
Evelyn Laye . . . . Cynthia Eden
Henry Victor . . . . Lt Clive Stanton
Hayford Hobbs . . . . Louis Peel
Robert Cunningham . . . . . Admiral Maybridge
Norma Whalley . . . . Mrs Peel
H. Agar Lyons . . . . Col Dupont
William Freshman . . . . Wing Eden
Basil Griffin . . . . Anna
Zoe Palmer . . . . Dora Green
H. Saxon Snell . . . . Francois
Douglas Herald . . . . Joe Briggs
Wally Patch . . . . Stoker Clark
Burton Craig . . . . Lord Nelson
Joan Langford Reed . . . . . . Dora (child)
WAR 1914. Spy has son steal Admiral's
submarine plans.

08275
CARRY ON! (7050) (U)
Britannia Films (Gaumont)
P: Dinah Shurey
D: Dinah Shurey, Victor Peers
S: "Taffrail"
SC: Dinah Shurey
Moore Marriott . . . . Mick Trevorn
Trilby Clark . . . . Sylvia
Alf Goddard . . . . Lumley
Johnny Butt . . . . Barker
Mickey Brantford . . . . Mick (child)
Aggie Brantford . . . . Molly (child)
Cynthia Murtagh . . . . Molly
C.M. Hallard . . . . John Peters
Pat Aherne . . . . Bob Halliday
Lewis Shaw . . . . Bob (child)
Frank Atherley . . . . Admiral Halliday
Griffith Humphreys . . . . . . Mr Freeman
Windham Guise . . . . Oliver Trevorn
Leal Douglas . . . . Mrs Trevorn
Wally Patch . . . . Andrews
WAR Admiral's son loves girl who becomes
spy, and dies foiling her schemes.

08276
THE MERCHANT OF VENICE (sound)
De Forest Phonofilms
D:SC: Widgey R. Newman
S: (PLAY) William Shakespeare
Lewis Casson . . . . Shylock
Joyce Lyons . . . .
Christine Murray . . . .
DRAMA Trial scene.

08277
NAN WILD (sound)
De Forest Phonofilms
D: George A. Cooper
MUSICAL

08278
OLLY OAKLEY (sound)
De Forest Phonofilms *reissue:* 1932, MUSICAL
MEDLEY NO. 5 (EB)
D: George A. Cooper
MUSICAL Banjo player.

08279
THE WESTMINSTER GLEE SINGERS (sound)
De Forest Phonofilms *reissue:* 1932, MUSICAL
MEDLEY NO. 3 (EB)
MUSICAL Songs.

08280
WITH THE AID OF A ROGUE (1517) (U)
J.H. Payne (European)
D: J.H. Payne
S: Mr Northcote
SC: W.H. Fleet
J.H. Payne . . . . Dick
ADVENTURE 18th C. Lord's son poses as
highwayman to aid sister's elopement.

DEC
08281
HUNTINGTOWER (7192) (U)
Welsh-Pearson-Elder (Par)
D: George Pearson
S: (NOVEL) John Buchan
SC: Charles Whittaker
Sir Harry Lauder . . . . Dickson McCunn
Vera Voronina . . . . Princess Saskia
Pat Aherne . . . . Capt John Heritage
Lilian Christine . . . . Mrs McCunn
John Manners . . . . Prince Paul
Moore Marriott . . . . Speidel
Douglas Herald . . . . Leon
Suzanne Morris . . . . Mother
W. Cronin Wilson . . . . Dobson
Nancy Price . . . . Mrs Moran
Jerrold Robertshaw . . . . . . Father
Harry Malonie . . . . Dougal
ADVENTURE Scotland. Retired grocer and
Gorbals boys save Russian prince from
Bolsheviks.

08282
QUINNEYS (8600) (U)
Gaumont
P: V. Gareth Gundrey
D: Maurice Elvey
S: (PLAY) Horace Annesley Vachell
SC: John Longden
Alma Taylor . . . . Susan Quinney
John Longden . . . . Joe Quinney
Frances Cuyler . . . . Posy Quinney
Cyril McLaglen . . . . James Miggott
Wallace Bosco . . . . Sam Tomlin
Henry Vibart . . . . Lord Melchester
Ursula Jeans . . . . Mabel Dredge
Lionel D'Aragon . . . . Dealer
Judd Green . . . . Dealer
ROMANCE Antique dealer's daughter loves
foreman who makes fakes for ex-partner.

08283
CONFETTI (6183) (U)
First National-Pathe
P: Harry Ham
D: Graham Cutts
S: Douglas Furber
Jack Buchanan . . . . Count Andrea Zorro
Annette Benson . . . . Dolores
Sydney Fairbrother . . . . Duchess Maxine
Robin Irvine . . . . Carlo
Audree Sayre . . . . Roxanne
Georges Teroff . . . . Confetti Maker
ROMANCE Nice. Duchess tries to divert
nephew's love from woman of own age to
younger girl.

08284
THIS MARRIAGE BUSINESS (6206) (U)
Film Booking Offices
P: F.A. Enders
D:S: Leslie Hiscott
Estelle Brody . . . . Annette
Owen Nares . . . . Robert
Marjorie Hume . . . . Pat
Jack Rutherford . . . . Duncan
Jeff Barlow . . . . Perkins
Polly Ward . . . . Maid
COMEDY Newlywed poses as burglar to scare
flighty wife.

08285
MY LORD THE CHAUFFEUR (5320) (U)
British Screen Classics (Fox)
D: B.E. Doxat-Pratt
S: Jack Hellier
Kim Peacock . . . . Philip Parr
Pauline Johnson . . . . Margaret
Sydney Fairbrother . . . . Lady Parr
Jerrold Robertshaw . . . . . . Lord Parr
Jack Hellier . . . . Thunder
Gladys Hamer . . . . Mrs Thunder
Diana Dare . . . . Girl
COMEDY Peer's disowned nephew becomes
charabanc chauffeur and joins 'Frothblowers'.

08286
MR NOBODY (4941) (U)
British Screen Classics (Fox)
D:SC: Frank Miller
S: Eric Strang
Frank Stanmore . . . . Mr Nobody
Pauline Johnson . . . . Alice Meadows
Pat Whitcombe . . . . Geoffrey Forbes
Cameron Carr . . . .
James Knight . . . .
George Bellamy . . . .
Windham Guise . . . .
DRAMA Student expelled for gambling returns
from abroad in time to claim inheritance.

08287
MOTORING (5500) (U)
Inter-Cine (ICC)
D: George Dewhurst
S: (SKETCH) Harry Tate
SC: Eliot Stannard
Harry Tate . . . . Harry
Violet Ellison . . . . Mary Flint
Henry Latimer . . . . Basil Love
Roy Travers . . . . Sir Stone Flint
Alice O'Day . . . .
Ronnie Tate . . . . Boy
COMEDY Motorist helps knight's ward elope
with lover.

08288
DAILY JESTERS (series) (U)
Inter-Cine (ICC)
D: Widgey R. Newman
SC: Eliot Stannard

08289
1—JOHN CITIZEN (1000)
S: (CARTOONS) George Strube
Charles Paton . . . . John Citizen

08290
2—DOT AND CARRIE (1089)
S: (CARTOONS) J.F. Horrabin
Yvonne Thomas . . . . Carrie
Wenonah Nutting . . . . Dot
A. Citroen . . . . Miss Vamp

08291
3—POP (1070)
S: (CARTOONS) J. Millar Watt
Mark Lupino . . . . Pop

08292
4—DILLY AND DALLY (1492)
S: (CARTOONS) "Poy" (Percy Fearon)
Molly Weekes . . . .   Dilly
William Phelps . . . .   Dally

08293
5—DORA (1541)
S: (CARTOONS) "Poy" (Percy Fearon)
Millicent Wolf . . . .   Dora
COMEDIES Stories based on popular newspaper
cartoons.

08294
SCREEN PLAYLETS (Series)
Gaumont

08295
7—WHISPERING GABLES (2100)(A)
D:SC: Edwin Greenwood
S: (STORY) Agnes Platt
Gladys Jennings . . . .   Diana Marsh
Reginald Bach . . . .   James Helmore
Frances Cuyler . . . .   Florence Marsh
Wallace Bosco . . . .   John Marsh

08296
8—FEAR (2004) (A)
retitled: FANGS OF DEATH
D:SC: Edwin Greenwood
Gladys Jennings . . . .   Miriam Hanworth
Charles Barratt . . . . Sir Richard Faseby
Irene Rooke . . . .   Lady Hanworth
Charles Vane . . . . Sir John Hanworth
Wallace Bosco . . . .   Physician

08297
9—BRIGHT YOUNG THINGS (2084) (U)
D:SC: George Dewhurst
S: V. Gareth Gundrey
John Longden . . . .   Jerry
Kitty Berling . . . .   Jean
Humberston Wright . . . . . Josiah Partridge
Charles Vane . . . .   Hawkes
Joan Pitt-Chatham . . . .   Nina
DRAMA Short stories.

1928

JAN

08298
SAILORS DON'T CARE (7500) (U)
Gaumont
P: Maurice Elvey, V. Gareth Gaundrey
D: W.P. Kellino
S: (NOVEL) "Seamark" (Austin Small)
SC: (Eliot Stannard
Estelle Brody .... Jenny Melrose
John Stuart .... Slinger Woods
Alf Goddard .... Nobby Clark
Humberston Wright .... Sir William Graham
Gladys Hamer .... Rose Bishop
Mary Brough .... Cook
George Thirlwell .... Lt Graham
Wallace Bosco .... Fink
Maud Cressall .... Lady Graham
Vivian Baron .... Cdr Forrester
Shayle Gardner .... Messenger
COMEDY 1914. Knight poses as rating aboard
son's cruiser and helps Q-ship sink U-boat.

08299
A WINDOW IN PICCADILLY (7843) (U)
Sidney Morgan (W & F)
P:D:S: Sidney Morgan
De Groot .... The Professor
Joan Morgan .... The Girl
John Hamilton .... Piccolo
James Carew .... The Father
Julie Suedo .... Sally
Maurice Braddell .... Harry
Edmund Willard .... The Fourth Party
Miss XX .... A Fraility
ROMANCE Rich man's son has affair with
vamp but returns to street-singer sweetheart.

08300
THE WHITE SHEIK (8980) (A)
BIP (Wardour)
D: Harley Knoles
S: (NOVEL) Rosita Forbes (KING'S MATE)
SC: Mary Murillo, Violet Powell
Lilian Hall Davis .... Rosemary Tregarthen
Jameson Thomas .... Westwyn
Warwick Ward .... Martengo
Clifford McLaglen .... Manhebbe
Gibb McLaughlin .... Jock
Forrester Harvey .... Pat
Julie Suedo .... Zarita
Laurie Leslie .... Child
ADVENTURE Sahara. British Riff chief weds
captured girl to save her from tribe (Extract
in ELSTREE STORY, 1952).

08301
PUNCH AND JUDY (10) (U) (sound)
De Forest Phonofilms
COMEDY

08302
MIRTH AND MAGIC (10) (U) (sound)
De Forest Phonofilms
COMEDY Conjuror.

08303
AN ATTEMPTED DUET (8) (U) (sound)
De Forest Phonofilms
MUSICAL

08304
THE HAWAIIAN REVELLERS (7) (U) (sound)
De Forest Phonofilms reissue: 1933, MUSIC
WITHOUT WORDS (WB) 1932: MUSICAL
MEDLEY NO. 4 (EB)
MUSICAL Kohala Marsh and his Hawaiian
Orchestra.

08305
THE NEW PARIS LIDO CLUB BAND (7) (U)
(sound)
De Forest Phonofilms
MUSICAL

08306
ALMOST A GENTLEMAN (9) (U) (sound)
De Forest Phonofilms
Billy Bennett
COMEDY Comedian.

FEB

08307
CANOODLING (9) (U) (sound)
De Forest Phonofilms
MUSICAL

08308
J.H. SQUIRES' CELESTE OCTET (5) (U)
(sound)
De Forest Phonofilms reissue: 1932, MUSICAL
MEDLEY NO. 2 (EB)
MUSICAL Memories of Tchaikovsky.

08309
WYN GLADWYN (8) (U) (sound)
De Forest Phonofilms
MUSICAL

08310
PERCY PRYDE AND HIS PHONOFIDDLE ON
THE PHONOFILM (8) (U) (sound)
De Forest Phonofilms
MUSICAL Selection from "William Tell"

08311
THE GUNS OF LOOS (7950) (U)
Stoll (New Era)
D: Sinclair Hill
S: Sinclair Hill, Joe Grossman
SC: Leslie Howard Gordon, Reginald Fogwell
Henry Victor .... John Grimlaw
Madeleine Carroll .... Diana Cheswick
Bobby Howes .... Danny
Hermione Baddeley .... Mavis
Donald McCardle .... Clive
Adeline Hayden Coffin .... Lady Cheswick
Jeanne le Vaye .... Arlette
Philip Hewland .... Stevens
Frank Goldsmith .... Col Jameson
Tom Coventry .... Tubby
William Freshman .... Officer
Wally Patch .... Sgt
David Laidlaw VC .... Himself
WAR 1915. Hard ironmaster blinded saving men
in war and returns home to thwart strike and
win lady's daughter.

08312
SHOOTING STARS (7089) (A)
British Instructional (New Era)
P: H. Bruce Woolf
D: A.V. Bramble, Anthony Asquith
S: Anthony Asquith
SC: John Orton, Anthony Asquith
Annette Benson .... Mae Feather
Brian Aherne .... Julian Gordon
Donald Calthrop .... Andy Wilkes
Wally Patch .... Property Man
David Brooks .... Turner
Ella Daincourt .... Asphodel Smythe
Chili Bouchier .... Winnie
Tubby Phillips .... Fatty
Ian Wilson .... Reporter
Judd Green .... Lighting Man
Jack Rawl .... Hero
DRAMA Film Star's faithless wife puts real
bullets in gun but her lover is killed by mistake.

08313
THE FARMER'S WIFE (8875) (U)
BIP (Wardour)
D: Alfred Hitchcock
S: (PLAY) Eden Philpotts
SC: Eliot Stannard, Alfred Hitchcock
Jameson Thomas .... Samuel Sweetland
Lilian Hall Davis .... Araminta Dench
Gordon Harker .... Churdles Ash
Gibb McLaughlin .... Dunnybrigg
Maud Gill .... Thirza Tapper
Louise Pounds .... Widow Windeatt
Olga Slade .... Mary Hearn
Antonia Brough .... Mary Bassett
COMEDY Devon. Widowed farmer searches for
new wife and finally realises that he loves
housekeeper.

08314
THE CONSTANT NYMPH (10600) (A)
Gainsborough (W&F)
P: Michael Balcon
D: Adrian Brunel
S: (PLAY) Margaret Kennedy, Basil Dean
SC: Basil Dean, Alma Reville
Ivor Novello .... Lewis Dodd
Mabel Poulton .... Tessa Sanger
Frances Doble .... Florence
Mary Clare .... Linda Sanger
George Heinrich .... Albert Sanger
Dorothy Boyd .... Pauline Sanger
Tony de Lungo .... Roberto
Benita Hume .... Antonia Sanger
Peter Evan Thomas ...... Ike
Yvonne Thomas .... Kate Sanger
J.H.Roberts .... Dr Churchill
Clifford Heatherley ..... Sir Berkeley
Elsa Lanchester .... Lady
ROMANCE Tyrol. Composer leaves
dominating wife for schoolgirl. (FWA: 1929)

08315
WAIT AND SEE (6352) (U)
Nettlefold (Butcher)
P: Archibald Nettlefold
D: Walter Forde
S: Walter Forde, Patrick L. Mannock
Walter Forde .... Monty Merton
Frank Stanmore .... Frankie
Pauline Johnson .... Jocelyn Winton
Sam Livesey .... Gregory Winton
Mary Brough .... Landlady
Charles Dormer .... Eustace Mottletoe
London's Thirty Fat Men
COMEDY Warehouse workman, tricked into
thinking he is heir to millions, locates
American financier to win boss's daughter.

08316
HIS HOUSE IN ORDER (7666) (A)
QTS (Ideal)
P: Mayrick Milton
D: Randle Ayrton
S: (PLAY) Arthur Wing Pinero
SC: Patrick L. Mannock
Tallulah Bankhead ..... Nina Graham
Ian Hunter .... Hilary Jesson
David Hawthorne .... Filmer Jesson
Eric Maturin .... Major Maurewarde
Mary Dibley .... Geraldine
Windham Guise .... Sir Daniel Ridgeley
Nancy Price .... Lady Ridgeley
Claude Beerbohm ...... Pryce Ridgeley
Sheila Courtney .... Annabel Jesson
Pat Courtney .... Derek Jesson
DRAMA Rich man's worship of first wife ends
when he learns their son is bastard.

08317
DAWN (7300) (A)
B & D (W&F)
P: Herbert Wilcox
D: Herbert Wilcox
S: (PLAY) Reginald Berkeley
SC: Herbert Wilcox, Robert J. Cullen
Sybil Thorndike . . . . Edith Cavell
Marie Ault . . . . Mme Rappard
Mary Brough . . . . Mme Pitou
Ada Bodart . . . . Herself
Dacia Deane . . . . Mlle Deveaux
Haddon Mason . . . . APM
Mickey Brantford . . . . Jacques Rappard
Cecil Barry . . . . Col Schultz
Frank Perfitt . . . Gen von Zauberzweig
Edward O'Neill . . . . Priest
Maurice Braddell . . . . Airman
Griffith Humphreys . . . . . . President
HISTORY Brussels, 1914. Nurse helps 210 men
escape to England before Germans catch and
execute her.

MAR

08318
THE HELLCAT (6559) (U)
Nettlefold (Butcher)
P: Archibald Nettlefold
D: Harry Hughes
S: (PLAY) Florence Kilpatrick
(WILDCAT HETTY)
SC: H. Fowler Mear
Mabel Poulton . . . . Hetty
Eric Bransby Williams . . . . Stephen Tredegar
John Hamilton . . . . Bert Stiles
Pauline Johnson . . . . Nancy Price
Frank Stanmore . . . . Butler
Gerald Rawlinson . . . . David Birkett
Mary Dibley . . . . Mrs Price
Johnny Butt . . . . Lloyd
Charles Dormer . . . . Gilded Youth
ROMANCE Scientist adopts slum girl and
she saves him from murderous lover.

08319
MARIA MARTEN (7430) (A)
QTS (Ideal)
P: Harry Rowson
D: Walter West
S: (PLAY) Anon.
Trilby Clark . . . . Maria Marten
Warwick Ward . . . . William Corder
James Knight . . . . Carlos
Charles Ashton . . . . Sam Giles
Vesta Sylva . . . . Ann Marten
Frank Perfitt . . . . John Marten
Dora Barton . . . . Ann Marten
Margot Armand . Lady Maude Derringham
Judd Green . . . . William Giles
Tom Morriss . . . . Ishmael
CRIME 1820. Squire kills pregnant mistress
to wed heiress and is exposed by mother's dream.

08320
CHARMAINE (13) (U) (sound)
DeForest Phonofilms
MUSICAL

08321
HOT WATER AND VEGETABUEL (8) (U)
(sound)
DeForest Phonofilms
COMEDY

08322
THE SUGAR STEP (7) (U) (sound)
DeForest Phonofilms
MUSICAL Dance.

08323
A.C.ASTOR WITH SENTIMENTAL MAC (10)
(U) (sound)
DeForest Phonofilms
ACT Ventriloquist.

08324
THE CITY OF YOUTH
British University Films
D: C.C.Calvert
S: (NOVEL) Oona Ball (BARBARA COMES TO
OXFORD)
SC: Muriel Alleyne
Betty Faire . . . . Barbara
Lillian Oldland . . . . Brownie
H.Fisher White . . . . Patrick Enderby
Desmond Roberts . . . .
DRAMA Oxford.

08325
VICTORY (8689) (U)
W & F Film Service
D: M.A.Wetherell
S: Boyd Cable (E.W. Ewart)
Moore Marriott . . . . Seth Lee
Walter Butler . . . . Maj King
Julie Suedo . . . . Marie Dulac
Marie Ault . . . . Mother
Griffith Humphries . . Gen Van Doorn
Douglas Herald . . . . Capt Wein
Marjorie Gaffney . . . . Julie
Victor Maxim Moorkins . . . Pierre
Sydney Seaward . . . .
Cameron Carr . . . .
Edward O'Neill . . . .
Fred Rains . . . .
James Reardon . . . .
WAR France, 1918. Armistice saves girl and
pilot from death, but not Canadian agent.

08326
MOULIN ROUGE (10368) (A)
BIP (Wardour)
P:D:S: E.A.Dupont
Olga Tschechowa . . . . Parysia
Eve Gray . . . . Camille
Jean Bradin . . . . Andre
Georges Treville . . . . Father
Marcel Vibert . . . . Marquis
Blanche Bernis . . . . Wardrobe Mistress
Ellen Pollock . . . . Girl
ROMANCE Paris. Baron's son tries to kill
himself upon realising he loves both dancer
and her mother.

APR

08327
DR SIN FANG DRAMAS (series)
Fred Paul & A.M.Brooks (Pioneer)
D: Fred Paul
S: Patrick K. Heale
H.Agar Lyons . . . . Dr Sin Fang
Fred Paul . . . . Lt John Byrne
Evelyn Arden . . . . Betty Harberry
Wally Patch . . . . Bill Riggers

08328
1: THE SCARRED FACE (1908)

08329
2: THE ZONE OF DEATH (1970)

08330
3: THE LIGHT ON THE WALL (1930)

08331
4: THE LIVING DEATH (1908) (U)

08332
5: THE TORTURE CAGE (1992)

08333
6: UNDER THE TIDE (1900)
CRIMES Naval Lieut versus Chinese criminal.

08334
THE BURGLAR AND THE GIRL (12) (U)
(sound)
DeForest Phonofilms
D: Hugh Croise
S: (PLAY) Matthew Boulton
Moore Marriott . . . . The Burglar
Dorothy Boyd . . . . The Girl
COMEDY Burglar held up by girl who is a
burglar herself.

08335
THE VICTORIA GIRLS (14) (U) (sound)
DeForest Phonofilms reissue: 1932,
MUSICAL MEDLEY NO. 1 (EB)
D: Hugh Croise
MUSICAL Doll dance.

08336
THE TOY SHOP (12) (U) (sound)
DeForest Phonofilms
MUSICAL

08337
CLONK ! (5) (sound)
DeForest Phonofilms
MUSICAL

08338
THE STAGE HANDS (16) (U) (sound)
DeForest Phonofilms
COMEDY

08339
GHOSTS OF YESTERDAY (series)
British Filmcraft (Ideal)
P: George J.Banfield
D: George J.Banfield, Leslie Eveleigh
S: George J.Banfield, George A.Cooper,
Anthony L.Ellis

08340
1: LADY GODIVA (1580)
Gladys Jennings . . . . Lady Godiva
Roy Travers . . . . Earl Leofric
Syd Ellery . . . . Peeping Tom

08341
2: THE MAN IN THE IRON MASK (2010)
G.H.Mulcaster . . . Louis XIV/The Unknown
Gabrielle Morton . . Louise de la Valliere
Annesley Hely . . . . Fouquet
Peggy Carlisle . . . . Reader of the Tale.

08342
3: DAVID GARRICK (2046)
S: (PLAY) T.W.Robertson
Gordon McLeod . . . . David Garrick
Gabrielle Morton . . . . Peg Woffington
Betty Faire . . . . Ada Ingot
Judd Green . . . . Simon Ingot
Charles Matthews . . . . Dr Johnson

08343
4: THE VANISHED HAND (1911)
S: (POEM) Lord Tennyson ((BREAK BREAK
BREAK)
Cynthia Murtagh . . . . Alys Fraser
Hugh Dempster . . . . John Fleming
Annesley Hely . . . . Sir George Ferguson
Albert Raynor . . . . Duncan Fraser

08344
5: THE DANCE OF DEATH (1821)
S: (MUSIC) Saint-Saens (DANSE MACABRE)
Gabrielle Morton . . . . Elizabeth
Desmond Roberts . . . . Capt Dick Lovell

Annesley Hely	Sir Charles Eden
Leonard Calvert	The Squire
Adeline Hayden Coffin . . .	The Mother

08345
6: THE PRINCES IN THE TOWER (1935)

G.H.Mulcaster	Duke of Gloucester
Mary Clare	Queen Elizabeth
Gabrielle Morton	Lady Anne
Albert Raynor	Edward IV
Connie Harris	Prince Edward
Bunty Fosse	Prince Richard

DRAMAS Historical ghost stories.

08346
THE UNSLEEPING EYE (6450) (A)
Seven Seas Screen Productions (BSP)
D: Alexander Macdonald, Walter Sully
S: Alexander Macdonald

David Wallace	Dick Holloway
Wendy Osborne	Marjorie Challoner
Charles Norman	John Challoner

ADVENTURE New Guinea. Drunken gold
miner saves wife and partner by fighting native
and feigning death.

MAY

08347
THE WARE CASE (7689) (A)
Film Manufacturing Co (NFP)
P: James Sloane
D: Manning Haynes
S: (PLAY) George Pleydell Bancroft
SC: Lydia Hayward

Stewart Rome	Sir Hubert Ware
Betty Carter	Lady Magda Ware
Ian Fleming	Michael Adye
Cameron Carr	Insp Watkins
Cynthia Murtagh	Celia Gurney
Patrick Ludlow	Eustace Ede
Wellington Briggs	Sir Henry Egerton
Patrick Stewart	Marston Gurney
Syd Ellery	Tommy Bold
John Valentine	Attorney General

CRIME Acquitted knight admits drowning
wife's rich brother and jumps to his death.

08348
VIRGINIA'S HUSBAND (6300) (U)
Nettlefold (Butcher)
P: Archibald Nettlefold
D: Harry Hughes
S: (PLAY) Florence Kilpatrick
SC: H.Fowler Mear

Mabel Poulton	Joyce
Lillian Oldland	Virginia Trevor
Pat Aherne	Bill Hemingway
Marie Ault	Aunt Janet
Fewlass Llewellyn	Uncle Donald
Ena Grossmith	Elizabeth
Charles Dormer	Freddy Parkinson

COMEDY Girl hires ex-officer to pose as her
husband to deceive rich relations.

08349
H. G. WELLS COMEDIES (series) (U)
Angle Pictures (Ideal)
P: Simon Rowson
D: Ivor Montagu
S: H.G.Wells
SC: Frank Wells

08350
1: BLUEBOTTLES (2285)

Elsa Lanchester	Elsa
Joe Beckett	PC Spiffkins
Dorice Fordred	Maggie
Marie Wright	Landlady
Charles Laughton	Burglar

08351
2: THE TONIC (2410)

Elsa Lanchester	Elsa
Renee de Vaux	Auntie

08352
3: DAYDREAMS (2224)

Elsa Lanchester	Elsa
Harold Warrender	Count Pornay
Charles Laughton	Ram Das
Dorice Fordred	Maggie
Marie Wright	Landlady

COMEDY Misadventures of a spinster
maidservant.

08353
ASHTON AND RAWSON (8) (U) (sound)
DeForest Phonofilms
ACT

08354
THE 'FLU THAT FLEW (9) (U) (sound)
DeForest Phonofilms
COMEDY

08355
SEXTON BLAKE (series) (U)
British Filmcraft (Par)
P: George J.Banfield
S: (STORIES) various authors.

Langhorne Burton	Sexton Blake
Mickey Brantford	Tinker

08356
1: THE CLUE OF THE SECOND GOBLET
(2246)
D: George A. Cooper

Fred Raynham . .	George Marsden Plummer
Gabrielle Morton	Helen
Leslie Perrins	Fairbairn

08357
2: BLAKE THE LAWBREAKER (1888)
D: George A. Cooper
Fred Raynham
Thelma Murray
Leslie Perrins
Philip Desborough

08358
3: SEXTON BLAKE, GAMBLER (1962)
D: George J. Banfield

Marjorie Hume	Joan Fairfield
Frank Atherley	Lord Fairfield
Adeline Hayden Coffin . . .	Lady Fairfield
Oscar Rosander	Ralph Garvin

08359
4: SILKEN THREADS (1832)
D: Leslie Eveleigh

Leslie Perrins	Stormcroft
Marjorie Hume	Nadia Petrowski
Frank Atherley	Man
Mrs Fred Emney	Mrs Bardell

08360
5: THE GREAT OFFICE MYSTERY (2060)

Fred Raynham	Gordon Wincliffe
Gabrielle Morton	Sadie
Ronald Curtis	Kestrel

08361
6: THE MYSTERY OF THE SILENT DEATH
(1965)
D: Leslie Eveleigh

Roy Travers	Mr Reece
Thelma Murray	Peggy
Ray Raymond	Ross
Mrs Fred Emney	Mrs Bardell

CRIME Private tec and young assistant solve
various crimes.

08362
THE PHYSICIAN (8260) (A)
Gaumont
P: Maurice Elvey, Gareth Gundrey
D: George Jacoby
S: (PLAY) Henry Arthur Jones
SC: Edwin Greenwood

Miles Mander	Walter Amphiel
Elga Brink	Edana Hinde
Ian Hunter	Dr Carey
Lissi Arna	Jessie Gurdon
Humberston Wright	Stephen Gurdon
Julie Suedo	Lady Valerie Camille
Mary Brough	Landlady
Henry Vibart	Rev Peregrine Hinde
Johnny Ashby	Jessie's Son

DRAMA Temperance lecturer's fiancee learns
he has child by ex-mistress, and that he is
incurable dipsomaniac.

08363
TWO LITTLE DRUMMER BOYS (7500) (U)
Samuelson (Victoria)
P: John E. Blakeley
D: G.B. Samuelson
S: (PLAY) Walter Howard

Wee Georgie Wood	Eric Carsdale
Alma Taylor	Alma Carsdale
Paul Cavanagh	Capt Darrell
Walter Butler	Capt Carsdale
Julie Suedo	Margaret
Cameron Carr	Gen Kingsley
Derrick de Marney	Jack
Roy Travers	Officer

DRAMA Boy soldier takes blame for theft by
captain's son, who later saves him from
drowning.

JUN

08364
MADEMOISELLE PARLEY-VOO (7300) (U)
Gaumont
P: V.Gareth Gundrey
D: Maurice Elvey
S: F.V.Merrick, Jack Harris
SC: John Longden

Estelle Brody	Mademoiselle
John Stuart	John
John Longden	le Beau
Alf Goddard	Fred
Humberston Wright	Old Soldier
Wallace Bosco	Bollinger
Johnnie Ashby	Child

CRIME Revue producer's wife suspected of
killing detective for whom she vamped jewel-
stealing conjuror.

08365
A LITTLE BIT OF FLUFF (7900) (A)
USA: SKIRTS
BIP (Wardour)
D: Jess Robbins, Wheeler Dryden
S: (PLAY) Walter Ellis
SC: Ben Travers, Ralph Spence, Wheeler Dryden

Syd Chaplin	Bertram Tully
Betty Balfour	Mamie Scott
Edmond Breon	John Ayres
Nancy Rigg	Violet Tully
Clifford McLaglen	Henry Hudson
Annie Esmond	Aunt Agatha
Enid Stamp-Taylor	Susie West
Cameron Carr	Fred Carter
Haddon Mason	The Wasp
Plaza Tiller Girls	

COMEDY Flirtatious husband tries to steal
dancer's necklace from wife, so does crook.
(Extract in ELSTREE STORY, 1952).

08366
TOMMY ATKINS (8363) (U)
BIP (Wardour)
D: Norman Walker
S: (PLAY) Arthur Shirley, Ben Landeck
SC: Eliot Stannard, Ian Hay
Lilian Hall Davis . . . . Ruth
Henry Victor . . . . Victor
Walter Butler . . . . Harold
Shayle Gardner . . . . Mason
Jerrold Robertshaw . . . . . . Earl
Pat Courtney . . . . Ruth(child)
Leslie Tomlinson . . . . Victor (child)
Alfred Leonard . . . . Harold (child)
WAR Cleric enlists on learning he loves
brother's sweetheart, saves his life, and finds he
is really earl.

08367
TONI (5548) (U)
BIP (Wardour)
D: Arthur Maude
S: (PLAY) Dion Titheradge
SC: Violet Powell
Jack Buchanan . . . . Toni Marr/Marini
Dorothy Boyd . . . . Princess Eugenie
W.Lawson Butt . . . . Mendel
Moore Marriott . . . . Meyer
Forrester Harvey . . . . Watts
Hayford Hobbs . . . . Delavine
Henry Vibart . . . . Gardo
Frank Goldsmith . . . . Olsen
COMEDY Rich man poses as detective double
to save princess from jewel thieves.

08368
Q-SHIPS (7800) (U)
New Era National reissue: 1932,
BLOCKADE (1429 ft cut)
P: Gordon Craig
D: Geoffrey Barkas, Michael Barringer
S: Michael Barringer
J.P.Kennedy . . . . Admiral Sims
Roy Travers . . . . Capt von Haag
Johnny Butt . . . .
Philip Hewland . . . .
Douglas Herald . . . .
Charles Emerald . . . .
George Turner . . . .
Lionel d'Aragon . . . .
Alec Hurley . . . .
Terence O'Brien . . . .
Hugh Douglas . . . .
Val Gielgud . . . .
Earl Jellicoe; Lt-Cdr Harold Auten;
WAR 1917. Warships disguised as merchant
vessels destroy U-boats at Flanders.
(sound added 1932).

08369
WHAT NEXT ? (7800) (U)
Nettlefold (Butcher)
P: Archibald Nettlefold
D: Walter Forde
S: Walter Forde, H.Fowler Mear
Walter Forde . . . . Walter
Pauline Johnson . . . . Violet Chippendale
Frank Stanmore . . . . . . Cedric Chippendale
Douglas Payne . . . . Cornelius Vandergilt
Charles Dormer . . . . . Nick Winterbottom
Frank Perfitt . . . . . Septimus Vandergilt
Ian Wilson . . . . Wilson
Tom Seymour . . . .
COMEDY Salesman buys old candlestick
sought by mad collector.

08370
THE BARRISTER (8) (U) (sound)
DeForest Phonofilms

D: Hugh Croise
S: George Robey
George Robey
COMEDY Character cameo.

08371
SAFETY FIRST (4) (U) (sound)
DeForest Phonofilms
D: Hugh Croise
S: George Robey
George Robey
MUSICAL Comic song.

JUL

08372
THE RAW RECRUIT (16) (U) (sound)
DeForest Phonofilms reissue: 1930 (FBO)
D: Hugh Croise
S: Con West
Ernie Lotinga . . . . Jimmy Josser
COMEDY Man joins army.

08373
THE ORDERLY ROOM (17) (U) (sound)
DeForest Phonofilms reissue: 1930 (FBO)
D: Hugh Croise
S: (PLAY) Ernest Lotinga (1914)
Ernie Lotinga . . . . Jimmy Josser
COMEDY Rookie officer has trouble with RSM.

08374
WHEN WE WERE VERY YOUNG (series) (U)
British Screen Classics (BSP)
D:SC: Frank Miller
S: (SONGS) A.A.Milne

08375
1: NURSERY CHAIRS (677)
Mary Brough . . . .

08376
2: THE KING'S BREAKFAST (1036)
Moore Marriott . . . . The King
Mary Brough . . . . The Queen

08377
3: BAD SIR BRIAN BOTANY (982)
James Knight . . . . Sir Brian Botany

08378
4: THE MARKET SQUARE (688)
Sydney Fairbrother . . . . Market Woman

08379
5: KNIGHTS AND LADIES (782)
Mabel Poulton . . . . Lady

08380
6: IN THE DARK (640)
COMEDIES Stories based songs for children.

08381
HOUP-LA ! (6722) (U)
British Screen Productions
reissue: THE LION TAMER
D: Frank Miller
S: Arthur Phillips
SC: Edward Dryhurst
George Bellamy . . . . Noah Swinley
Frank Stanmore . . . . Clown
Peggy Carlisle . . . . Spangles
James Knight . . . . Daniel
Charles Garry . . . . Proprietor
DRAMA Cornwall. Zoologist framed for
theft becomes lion-tamer and loves proprietor's
daughter.

08382
WHAT MONEY CAN BUY (6400) (A)
Gaumont

P: Maurice Elvey, V.Gareth Gundrey
D:SC: Edwin Greenwood
S: (PLAY) Arthur Shirley, Ben Landeck
Madeleine Carroll . . . . Rhoda Pearson
Humberston Wright . . . . . Rev Dennis Norton
John Longden . . . . Ralph Tresham
Cecil Barry . . . . James Lorrimer
Alf Goddard . . . . Alf
Maudie Dunham . . . . Mrs Lorrimer
Anita Sharp Bolster . . . . Cleaner
Judd Green . . . . Client
DRAMA Cleric alibis ex-convict mannequin
when she is blamed for death of wealthy
husband.

08383
BOLIBAR (7322) (U)
British Instructional (Pro Patria)
P: H. Bruce Woolfe
D:SC: Walter Summers
S: (NOVEL) Leo Perutz
(THE MARQUISE OF BOLIBAR)
Elissa Landi . . . . Francoise-Marie/La Monita
Michael Hogan . . . . Lt Donop
Hubert Carter . . . . Col Bellay
Carl Harbord . . . . Lt Gunther
Jerrold Robertshaw . . . . . . The Marquis
Cecil Barry . . . . Capt Egolstein
Evelyn Roberts . . . . . Capt Brockendorf
Gerald Pring . . . . Capt O'Callaghan
Charles Emerald . . . . Colonel
Hector Abbas . . . . Artist
WAR Spain, 1808. Hessian officers'
flirtations with artist's daughter accidentally
give signals to attacking English.

08384
UNDERGROUND (7282) (U)
British Instructional (Pro Patria)
P: H.Bruce Woolfe
D:S: Anthony Asquith
Elissa Landi . . . . Nell
Brian Aherne . . . . Bill
Norah Baring . . . . Kate
Cyril McLaglen . . . . Bert
DRAMA Electrician tries to win shopgirl by
having his mistress pretend rival assaulted her.

08385
THE PASSING OF MR QUIN (8520) (A)
Strand – Cecil Cattermoul (Argosy)
P: Julius Hagen
SC: Leslie Hiscott
S: (NOVEL) Agatha Christie
Stewart Rome . . . . Dr Alec Portal
Trilby Clark . . . . Eleanor Appleby
Ursula Jeans . . . . Vera
Clifford Heatherley . . . . . . Prof Appleby
Mary Brough . . . . Cook
Vivian Baron . . . . Derek Cappel
Kate Gurney . . . . Landlady
CRIME Dr proves wife's first husband was
killed by neighbour posing as tramp.

08386
A SOUTH SEA BUBBLE (8302) (U)
Gainsborough (W&F)
P: Michael Balcon
D: T.Hayes Hunter
S: (NOVEL) Roland Pertwee
SC: Angus Macphail, Alma Reville
Ivor Novello . . . . Vernon Winslow
Benita Hume . . . . Averil Rochester
Annette Benson . . . . Lydia la Rue
S.J.Warmington . . . . Frank Sullivan
Alma Taylor . . . . Mary Ottery
Ben Field . . . . Isinglass
John Hamilton . . . . Tony Gates

Sydney Seaward . . . . . . William Carpenter
Mary Dibley . . . . Olive Barbary
Harold Huth. . . . . Pirate
ADVENTURE Girl reporter and insane fiance
join pirate's descendant in treasure hunt.

08387
PALAIS DE DANSE (7697) (A)
Gaumont
P: V.Gareth Gundrey, Maurice Elvey
D: Maurice Elvey
S: Jean Jay
SC: John Longden
Mabel Poulton . . . . No. 16
John Longden . . . . No. 1
Robin Irvine . . . . Tony King
Hilda Moore . . . . Lady King
Chili Bouchier . . . . No. 2
Jerrold Robertshaw . . . . Sir William King
ROMANCE Dancehall gigolo blackmails Lady
to make her stop son's affair with dancer.

08388
NOT QUITE A LADY (7258) (A)
BIP (Wardour)
D: Thomas Bentley
S: (PLAY) St John Hankin
(THE CASSILIS ENGAGEMENT)
SC: Eliot Stannard
Mabel Poulton . . . . Ethel Borridge
Janet Alexander . . . . Mrs Cassilis
Barbara Gott . . . . Mrs Borridge
Maurice Braddell . . . . . . Geoffrey Cassilis
Dorothy Bartlam . . . . . . Mabel Marchmont
George Bellamy . . . . Maj Warrington
Gibb McLaughlin . . . . Vicar
Sam Wilkinson . . . . Mr Borridge
COMEDY Rich woman gets rid of son's
common fiancee by boring her with house party.

AUG

08389
CHAMPAGNE (8038) (U)
BIP (Wardour)
D: Alfred Hitchcock
S: Walter C. Mycroft
SC: Eliot Stannard, Alfred Hitchcock
Betty Balfour . . . . Betty
Jean Bradin . . . . Jean
Gordon Harker . . . . The Father
Theodore von Alten . . . . . . The Baron
Clifford Heatherley . . . . . . The Manager
Jack Trevor . . . . The Officer
Sunday Wilshin . . . . A Girl
Claude Hulbert . . . . A Guest
Balliol & Merton . . . . Dancers
COMEDY France. Millionaire feigns
bankruptcy to frustrate daughter's love
affair.

08390
TESHA (7826) (A)
BIP-Burlington Films (Wardour)
P:D: Victor Saville
S: (NOVEL) Countess Barcynska
SC: Victor Saville, Walter C.Mycroft
Maria Corda . . . . Tesha
Jameson Thomas . . . . Robert Dobree
Paul Cavanagh . . . . Lenane
Micky Brantford . . . . Simpson
Clifford Heatherley . . . . . . Doctor
ROMANCE Russian ballerina weds shellshock
victim and has child by his friend.
(Sound added June 1929).

08391
CHICK (7215) (U)
British Lion (Ideal)
D: A.V.Bramble

S: (NOVEL) Edgar Wallace
SC: Eliot Stannard
Bramwell Fletcher . . . . Chick Beane
Trilby Clark . . . . Gwenda Maynard
Chili Bouchier . . . . Minnie Jarvis
Rex Maurice . . . . Marquis of Mansar
Edward O'Neill . . . . Mr Leither
John Cromer . . . . Mr Jarvis
COMEDY Cockney inherits title, supports
child welfare bill, and weds girl posing as
widow.

08392
THE RINGER (7150) (A)
British Lion (Ideal)
D: Arthur Maude
S: (PLAY) Edgar Wallace
SC: Edgar Wallace
Leslie Faber . . . . Dr Lomond
Annette Benson . . . . Cora Ann Milton
Lawson Butt . . . . Maurice Meister
Nigel Barrie . . . . Insp Wembury
Hayford Hobbs . . . . Insp Bliss
John Hamilton . . . . John Lenley
Muriel Angelus . . . . Mary Lenley
Charles Emerald . . . . Sam Hackett
Esther Rhodes . . . . Gwenda Milton
CRIME Police fail to prevent disguised crook
from killing partner.

08393
GOD'S CLAY (6301) (A)
First National (FNP)
P: Harry Ham
D: Graham Cutts
S: (NOVEL) Claude & Alice Askew
SC: P. Maclean Rogers
Anny Ondra . . . . Angela Clifford
Trilby Clark . . . . Poppy Stone
Franklyn Bellamy . . . . . . Jasper Murgatroyd
Haddon Mason . . . . Geoffrey Vance
Marie Ault . . . . Hannah
Annie Esmond . . . .
Julian Royce . . . . The Duke
Bernard Vaughan . . . . The Butler
Antionette Brough . . . . . . Mary Robbins
CRIME Secretary blackmails business man for
spending night with girl, and is killed by
mistress.

08394
EILEEN OF THE TREES (7182) (U)
retitled: GLORIOUS YOUTH
First National (FNP)
P: Harry Ham
D: Graham Cutts
S: (NOVEL) H. DeVere Stacpoole
SC: Reginald Fogwell, P Maclean Rogers
Anny Ondra . . . . Eileen
William Freshman . . . . . Lord Patrick Spence
Randle Ayrton . . . . Mr Skrines
Gibb McLaughlin . . . . Giles
A.Bromley Davenport . . . . . Farmer Duffield
Barbara Gott . . . . Mrs Duffield
Forrester Harvey . . . . Simmonds
Jerrold Robertshaw . . . . . . Lord Treveson
Maud Gill . . . . Julia Portman
Dora Barton . . . . Mrs Skrines
Arthur Roberts . . . . Daddy Ambrose
ROMANCE Lord abducts girl to save her from
wicked guardian.

08395
ZERO (8159) (A)
Film Manufacturing Co (FNP)
P: James Sloan
D: Jack Raymond
S: (NOVEL) Collinson Owen

SC: Lydia Hayward
Stewart Rome . . . . John Garth
Fay Compton . . . . Mrs Garth
Jeanne de Casalis . . . . Julia Norton
Sam Livesey . . . . Monty Sterling
Dorinea Shirley . . . . . . Veronica Sterling
J.R.Tozer . . . . Maj Potterton
Lewis Shaw . . . . Victor Garth
ROMANCE Author feigns death so he can live
with mistress but returns to wife when she
falls ill.

SEP

08396
THE BURGOMASTER OF STILEMONDE
(7934) (A)
British Filmcraft (W&F)
P:D: George J. Banfield
S: (PLAY) Maurice Maeterlinck
SC: Fred Raynham

Sir John Martin Harvey . . Cyrille van Belle
Fern Andra . . . . Isabelle Hilmer
Robert Andrews . . . . Lt Otto Hilmer
John Hamilton . . . . Odilion van Belle
Fred Raynham . . . . Baron von Rochow
Wilfred Shine . . . . Claus
A.B.Imeson . . . Capt Karl von Schernberg
Oswald Lingard . . . . Father de Coninck
Kinsey. Peile . . . . Sheriff Vermandel
Mickey Brantford . . . . Flores
Adeline Hayden Coffin . . . .
C.V.France . . . .
WAR Belgium, 1914. Uhlans order burgomaster
to be shot by son-in-law.

08397
THE BLUE PETER (7665) (U)
British Filmcraft (W&F)
P: George J.Banfield
D: Arthur Rooke
S: (NOVEL) E. Temple Thurston
SC: Vivian Thompson
Matheson Lang . . . . David Hunter
Gladys Frazin . . . . Rosa Callaghan
Mary Dibley . . . . Emma
A.Bromley Davenport . . . . Mr Callaghan
Cameron Carr . . . . Edward Formby
Esmond Knight . . . . Wireless Operator
DRAMA Man decides to stay with family
instead of returning to Nigeria.

08398
ADAM'S APPLE (7200) (U) USA:
HONEYMOON AHEAD
BIP (Wardour)
D: Tim Whelan
S: Tim Whelan, Rex Taylor
Monty Banks . . . . Monty Adams
Gillian Dean . . . . Ruth Appleby
Lena Halliday . . . . Mrs Appleby
Judy Kelly . . . . Vamp
Colin Kenney . . . . Husband
Dino Galvani . . . . Crook
Hal Gordon . . . . Drunk
Charles O'Shaughnessy . . . Official
COMEDY Paris. Honeymooning American
hires crooks to kidnap mother-in-law.

08399
LOVE'S OPTION (5890) (U)
Welsh-Pearson-Elder (Par)
D:SC: George Pearson
S: (NOVEL) Douglas Newton
Dorothy Boyd . . . . Dorothy
Pat Aherne . . . . John Dacre
James Carew . . . . Simon Wake
Henry Vibart . . . . Simon Wake

Scotch Kelly . . . .   Pat Kelly
Philip Hewland . . . .   Tom Bartlett
Cecil Barry . . . .
ADVENTURE Spain. Miner thwarts crooked
rival in time to take up option on copper
mine.

08400
SWEENEY TODD (6500) (A)
QTS Productions (Ideal)
P: Harry Rowson
D: Walter West
S: (PLAY) George Dibdin Pitt, C.Hazleton
Moore Marriott . . . .   Sweeney Todd
Zoe Palmer . . . .   Johanna
Charles Ashton . . . .   Mark Ingestre
Iris Darbyshire . . . .   Amelia Lovett
Judd Green . . . .   Simon Podge
Philip Hewland . . . .   Ben Wagstaffe
Brian Glenny . . . .   Tobias Wragge
Harry Lorraine . . . .   Mick Todd
CRIME Man dreams he is 'demon barber' who
cuts sailors' throats for jewels and uses
corpses for pies.

OCT

08401
SMASHING THROUGH (7098) (U)
Gaumont
P: Maurice Elvey, V.Gareth Gundrey
D: W.P.Kellino
S: William Lees, John Hunter
SC: L'Estrange Fawcett
John Stuart . . . .   Richard Bristol
Alf Goddard . . . .   Alf
Eve Gray . . . .   Kitty Masters
Hayford Hobbs . . . .   James Masters
Julie Suedo . . . .   Miss Duprez
Gladys Hamer . . . .   Ethyl
Charles Ashton . . . .   Westlake
Mike Johnson . . . .   Mate
H.Saxon-Snell . . . .   Driver
SPORT Vamp persuades inventor of
supercharger to race against friend.

08402
THE FIRST BORN (7786) (A)
Mander Production Syndicate-Gainsborough (W&F)
P: Miles Mander, Michael Balcon
D: Miles Mander
S: (PLAY) Miles Mander (THOSE COMMON
PEOPLE)
SC: Miles Mander, Alma Reville, Ian Dalrymple
Miles Mander . . . .   Sir Hugo Boycott
Madeleine Carroll . . .   Lady Madeleine Boycott
John Loder . . . . .   Lord David Harborough
Ella Atherton . . . .   Nina de Lande
Margot Armand . . . .   Sylvia Findlay
Ivo Dawson . . . .   Derek Findlay
Marjorie Roach . . . .   Phoebe Chivers
John St John . . . .   Dicky
Naomi Jacob . . . .   Dot
Bernard Vaughan . . . .   Butler
Walter Wichelow . . . .   Impitt
Theodore Mander . . . .   Stephen Boycott
DRAMA Knight's mistress deceives him into
thinking his own son is by his wife's lover.

08403
YELLOW STOCKINGS (7836) (A)
Welsh-Pearson-Elder (Par)
P: George Pearson
D: Theodor Komisarjevsky
S: (NOVEL) Wilson McArthur
SC: Fred Paul, Alicia Ramsey
Percy Marmont . . . .   Gavin Sinclair
Marjorie Mars . . . .   Iris Selton
Georges Galli . . . .   Richard Trevor

Enid Stamp-Taylor . . . .   Nellie Jackson
J.R.Tozer . . . .   Tom Jackson
Marie Ault . . . .   Countess
Franklin Bellamy . . . .   Menelos
Lydia Sherwood . . . .   Erica
May Calvin . . . .   Mona
Elizabeth Kerr . . . .   Mrs Higgins
ROMANCE Paris. Artist saves orphan from
wastrel husband.

08404
THE PRICE OF DIVORCE (7519) (A)
P.O.D.Syndicate (Stoll)
P: Oswald Mitchell
D: Sinclair Hill
S: Reginald Fogwell
SC: Leslie Howard Gordon
Miriam Seegar . . . .   The Other Woman
Wyndham Standing . . . . . .   The Doctor
Frances Day . . . .   The Wife
Rex Maurice . . . .   The Other Man
Gibb McLaughlin . . . .   The Valet
Johnny Ashby . . . .   The Child
Nancy Price . . . .   The Aunt
Maud Gill . . . .   The Maid
Frances Ross Campbell . . . .   The Nurse
James Fenton . . . .   The Solicitor
DRAMA (Not shown. Extracts in SUCH IS THE
LAW, 1930).

08405
TROUBLESOME WIVES (5870) (U)
Nettlefold (Butcher)
P: Archibald Nettlefold
D: Harry Hughes
S: (PLAY) Ernest Denny (SUMMER LIGHT-
NING)
SC: H.Fowler Mear
Mabel Poulton . . . .   Betty Page
Lillian Oldland . . . .   Norah Cameron
Eric Bransby Williams . . . .   Capt Tony Paget
Reginald Fox . . . .   Alec Cameron
Marie Ault . . . .   Aunt Mary
Roy Russell . . . .   Mr Cameron
COMEDY Pilot's wife takes blame when
designer's wife compromised by spy.

08406
SIR OR MADAM (6421) (U)
Foremost Productions (WB)
P: Arthur Clavering
D: Carl Boese
S: (NOVEL) Berta Ruck
SC: Eliot Stannard
Percy Marmont . . . .   Sir Ralph Wellalone
Ossi Oswalda . . . .   Guelda Rhos
Annette Benson . . . .   Lady Day
Margot Armand . . . .   Patricia Lloyd
Charles Ashton . . . .
Gordon Begg . . . .
Eugenie Prescott . . . .
Harold Huth . . . .
COMEDY Girl posing as Knight's male valet
vamped by his fiancee.

08407
THE MAN IN THE SADDLE (4350) (U)
retitled: A RECKLESS GAMBLE
Cinema Exclusives (PDC)
P: Frank Wheatcroft
D: Widgey R.Newman
S: Larry Lotinga
Desmond Roberts . . . . .   Dick Beresford
Gladys Dunham . . . .   Eve Charteris
Sir Simeon Stuart . . .   Sir Miles Wellington
Wally Patch . . . .   Wally
Chubb Leach; C.Elliott; J.Sirrett
SPORT Heir wins fortune when friend
mistakenly backs rival.

08408
CARRIE FROM LANCASHEER (8) (sound)
DeForest Phonofilms
MUSICAL

08409
THE FIRE BRIGADE (9) (sound)
DeForest Phonofilms reissue: 1930 (FBO)
S: (SKETCH) Robb Wilton
Robb Wilton
COMEDY Inept fire brigade captain.

08410
PERCIVAL AND HILL (8) (U) (sound)
British Sound Film Productions (BIFD)
A.CT

08411
GRANDFATHER SMALLWEED (9) (U) (sound)
British Sound Film Productions (BIFD)
D: Hugh Croise
S: (NOVEL) Charles Dickens (BLEAK HOUSE)
Bransby Williams . . . .   Smallweed
COMEDY Character study of aged man.

08412
MINE (sound)
British Sound Film Productions (BIFD)
Dorothy Bartlam
MUSICAL

08413
THE TWO GRENADIERS (sound)
British Sound Film Productions (BIFD)
MUSICAL

08414
TANNHAUSER: ACT THREE (sound)
British Sound Film Productions (BIFD)
Eric Marshall
MUSICAL

08415
LAUGHTER AND TEARS (2000)
Song Films
P: John E.Blakeley
D: H.B.Parkinson
Pearl Hay . . . .   The Child
MUSICAL Synchronises with songs sung
from cinema stage.

08416
GONE TO THE DOGS (2000)
Film Artists' Guild
D:S: Fred V.Merrick
Billy Watts . . . .   The Hero
Vivian Gaye . . . .   The Heroine
Leonard Barry . . . .   The Villain
Major Barber . . . .   The Father
COMEDY Burlesque melodrama made for
Film Circus and Garden Fair.

08417
PARADISE (7247) (U)
BIP (Wardour)
D: Denison Clift
S: (NOVEL) Phillip Gibbs
(THE CROSSWORD PUZZLE)
SC: Violet Powell
Betty Balfour . . . .   Kitty Cranston
Joseph Striker . . . .   Dr John Halliday
Alexander d'Arcy . . . .   Spiridoff
Winter Hall . . . .   Rev Cranston
Barbara Gott . . . .   Lady Liverage
Dino Galvani . . . .   Manager
Boris Ranevsky . . . .   Commissionaire
Albert Brouett . . . .   Detective
Ena de la Haye . . . .   Douchka
ROMANCE Riviera. Doctor steals milliner's
winnings to save her from gigolo.

08418
COCKTAILS (6100) (U)
BIP (Wardour)
D: Monty Banks
S: Scott Sidney, Rex Taylor
SC: Roger Burford
Pat . . . . Gin
Patachon . . . . It
Enid Stamp-Taylor . . . . Betty
Tony Wylde . . . . Jerry
Nigel Barrie . . . . Giles
Harry Terry . . . . Bosco
Lorna Duveen . . . . Mary
Warren Hastings . . . . Judge
COMEDY Heiress's crooked guardian plants
cocaine on her lover.

08419
FOR VALOUR (6150) (U)
Samuelson-Victoria Films
P:D: G.B.Samuelson
Dallas Cairns . . . . The Husband
Marjorie Stallor . . . . The Girl
Roy Travers . . . .
Mary Rorke . . . . The Grandmother
Beatrice Greeke . . . . . . Queen Victoria
Mrs Lytton . . . . Queen Victoria
Millicent Wolf . . . . Nurse
Leonard Keysor; George Findlater
WAR Blind grandmother recounts how husband
won VC.

NOV

08420
THE TRIUMPH OF THE SCARLET
PIMPERNEL (7946) (U)
USA: THE SCARLET DAREDEVIL
B&D (W&F)
P: Herbert Wilcox
D: T. Hayes Hunter
S: (NOVEL) Baroness Orczy
SC: Angus Macphail
Matheson Lang . . . . Sir Percy Blakeney
Juliette Compton . . . . . . Theresa Cabbarrus
Nelson Keys . . . . Robespierre
Marjorie Hume . . . . Lady Blakeney
Haddon Mason . . . . Tallien
Douglas Payne . . . . Rateau
H.Fisher White . . . . StJust
Harold Huth . . . . Fouquier-Tinville
ADVENTURE France, 1794. Dandy saves
wife from guillotine by framing woman who
helped kidnap her.

08421
AFTERWARDS (6800) (A)
Bushey Studios (AP&D)
D: W.Lawson Butt
S: (NOVEL) Kathlyn Rhodes
SC: R.Byron Webber
Marjorie Hume . . . . Mrs Carstairs
Julie Suedo . . . . Tocati
J.R.Tozer . . . . Dr Anstice
Cecil Barry . . . . Bruce Cheniston
Dorinea Shirley . . . . Iris Wayne
Jean Jay . . . . Hilda Ryder
Pat Courtney . . . . Cherry
Fewlass Llewellyn . . . . . Sir Richard Wayne
Frank Perfitt . . . . Major Carstairs
DRAMA Doctor shoots girl to save her from
Indians and later finds her fiance is rival for
another girl.

08422
THE INFAMOUS LADY (7500) (A)
New Era-National
P: Gordon Craig
D: Geoffrey Barkas, Michael Barringer
S: Michael Barringer

Arthur Wontner . . . . The KC
Ruby Miller . . . . The Adventuress
Walter Tennyson . . . . The Man
Muriel Angelus . . . . The Girl
John Rowal . . . . The Tramp
Dora Barton . . . . The Wife
Ion Swinley . . . . The Explorer
CRIME KC kills blackmailing adventuress
and defends man accused.

08423
YOU KNOW WHAT SAILORS ARE (7598)(A)
Gaumont
P: Maurice Elvey, Gareth Gundrey
D: Maurice Elvey
S: (NOVEL) W.E.Townend (A LIGHT FOR
HIS PIPE)
SC: L'Estrange Fawcett, Angus Macphail,
John Longden
Alf Goddard . . . . The British Mate
Cyril McLaglen . . . . The Spanish Mate
Chili Bouchier . . The Spanish Captain's daughter
Jerrold Robertshaw . . . . . . The Spanish Captain
Mathilde Comont . . . The British Captain
Leonard Barry . . . . Her Husband
Mike Johnson . . . . Seaman
Wally Patch . . . . Seaman
ADVENTURE Mate of cargo steamer saves
Spanish rival and girl from burning ship.

08424
THE RISING GENERATION (7200) (U)
Westminster Pictures (WP)
D: Harley Knoles, George Dewhurst
S: (PLAY) Wyn Weaver, Laura Leycester
SC: Dion Titheradge
Alice Joyce . . . . Mrs Kent
Jameson Thomas . . . . Major Kent
Robin Irvine . . . . George Breese
William Freshman . . . . .Robert Kent
Joan Barry . . . . Peggy Kent
Betty Nuthall . . . . School Friend
Gerald Ames . . . . John Parmoor
Gerald Rawlinson . . . . Augustus
Pamela Deane . . . . Friend
Eric Findon . . . . Friend
Eugenie Prescott . . . . Maid
Clare Greet . . . . Cook
Nervo & Knox
COMEDY Major and wife return from abroad
and pose as servants to observe their
adolescent children.

08425
THE TALLYMAN (3200) (U)
Homeland Films (Film Distributors)
P:D: Maurice Sandground
Mark Lupino . . . . The Tallyman
Muriel Southern . . . . The Girl
COMEDY Blackpool. Tallyman's holiday
jaunt with blacksmith's daughter.

08426
THE MAN WHO CHANGED HIS MIND (2696)
School Productions Committee, Altrincham (U)
(European)
D: Ronald Gow, Captain Mee
Sir Robert Baden Powell . . . . Himself
DRAMA Urchin's friends emulate scouts and
save poet from burning house.

08427
WARNED OFF (6510) (U)
B & D (JMG)
P: Herbert Wilcox
D: Walter West
S:(NOVEL) Robert Sevier
SC: Reginald Fogwell
Tony Wylde . . . . Frank Cuthbert
Chili Bouchier . . . . Florrie Greville

Queenie Thomas . . . . Lady Violet
Evan Thomas . . . . Col Cornwallis
H.Forbes Dawson . . Lord Winterbottom
Wally Patch . . . . Miles
Bert Tracy . . . . Diggle
SPORT Expelled horse owner clears name and
wins Grand National.

08428
THE WARNING (6800) (A)
British Projects (Pro Patria)
P:S: A.E.Bundy
D:SC: Reginald Fogwell
Percy Marmont . . . . Jim
Fern Andra . . . . The Other Woman
Anne Grey . . . . Mary
Pearl Hay . . . . The Child
DRAMA Mother prevents daughter's
elopement by telling how a wife shot
faithless husband.

DEC

08429
ADVENTUROUS YOUTH (4868) (U)
Pall Mall (WB)
P:D: Edward Godal
Derrick de Marney . . . . The Englishman
Renee Clama . . . . Mary Fergusson
Dino Galvani . . . . Don Estaban
Sybil Wise . . . . The Vamp
Harry Bagge . . . .
Loftus Tottenham . . . . . . Mr Fergusson
Julius Kantorez . . . . Father O'Flannigan
Harry Peterson . . . .
Lionel d'Aragon . . . .
ADVENTURE Mexico. Miner saves banker's
daughter from revolutionary but surrenders
to save church from destruction.

08430
THE FORGER (7305) (A)
British Lion (Ideal)
P: S.W.Smith
D: G.B.Samuelson
S: (NOVEL) Edgar Wallace
SC: Edgar Wallace
Lillian Rich . . . . Jane Leith
James Raglan . . . . Peter Clifton
Nigel Barrie . . . . Dr Cheyne Wells
Winter Hall . . . . John Leith
Sam Livesey . . . . Insp Rouper
Ivo Dawson . . . . Supt Brooks
Derrick de Marney . . . . Basil Hale
CRIME Doctor helps crook frame daughter's
husband for forgery.

08431
SPANGLES (7425) (U)
British Filmcraft (Par)
P:D: George J. Banfield
S: Fred Raynham
SC: Edward Dryhurst
Fern Andra . . . . Spangles
Forrester Harvey . . . . Watty
Lewis Dayton . . . . Hugh Gridstone
A.Bromley Davenport . . . . . Romanovitch
James Knight . . . . Haggerston
A.B.Imeson . . . . Earl of Warborough
Gladys Frazin . . . . Countess
Carlton Chase . . . . Dennis Adderly
ROMANCE Circus wirewalker prefers humble
clown to earl's son.

08432
EMERALD OF THE EAST (5600) (U)
British Pacific - BIP (Wardour)
D:SC: Jean de Kuharski
S: (NOVEL) Jerbanu Kothawala
Joshua Kean . . . . . . Lt Desmond Armstrong

Mary Odette . . . . Nellum
Jean de Kuharski . . . . Maharajah
Lya Delvelez . . . . Maharanee
Gillian Dean . . . . Evelyn
Maria Forescu . . . . Chieftainess
Kennth Rive . . . . Maharaj Kumar
Promotha Bose . . . . Vaghi
ADVENTURE India. Lieut saves maharajah's
son from bandit chieftainess.

08433
WIDECOMBE FAIR (6418) (U)
BIP (Wardour)
D: Norman Walker
S: (NOVEL) Eden Philpotts
SC: Eliot Stannard
William Freshman . . . . The Lover
Marguerite Allan . . . . The Daughter
Wyndham Standing . . . . . . The Squire
Violet Hopson . . . . The Widow
Moore Marriott . . . . . . Uncle Tom Cobleigh
Aubrey Fitzgerald . . . . The Bailiff
George Cooper . . . . The Farmer
Eva Lewellyn . . . . The Wife
Judd Green . . . . The Landlord
ROMANCE Devon. Rich widow helps poor
squire by pretending his ancestor hid treasure.

08434
WEEKEND WIVES (7226) (A)
BIP (Wardour)
D: Harry Lachman
S: Victor Kendall
SC: Victor Kendall, Rex Taylor
Monty Banks . . . . Amman
Jameson Thomas . . . . Henri Monard
Estelle Brody . . . . Gaby le Grand
Annette Benson . . . . Helene Monard
George Gee . . . . M.le Grand
Ernest Thesiger . . . . Bertram
Bebe Brune-Taylor . . . . Yvette
COMEDY Deauville. Lawyer spends weekend
with married actress at the same hotel as his
wife and her lover.

08435
THE WRECKER (6670) (U)
Gainsborough (W & F)
P: Michael Balcon
D: Geza M. Bolvary
S: (PLAY) Arnold Ridley, Bernard Merivale
SC: Angus Macphail
Carlyle Blackwell . . . . Ambrose Barney
Benita Hume . . . . Mary Shelton
Joseph Striker . . . . Roger Doyle
Winter Hall . . . . Sir Gerald Bartlett
Gordon Harker . . . . William
Pauline Johnson . . . . Beryl Matchley
Leonard Thompson . . . . Rameses Ratchett
CRIME Director's nephew unmasks manager
as wrecker of trains. (Sound added July 1929).

08436
A LIGHT WOMAN (7300) (A)
Gainsborough (W&F) *reissue:* DOLORES
P: Michael Balcon
D: Adrian Brunel
S: Dale Laurence Brunel
SC: Adrian Brunel, Angus Macphail
Benita Hume . . . . . Dolores de Vargas
C.M.Hallard . . . . Marquis de Vargas
Gerald Ames . . . . Don Andrea
Betty Carter . . . . Pauline
Donald McCardle . . . . Ramiro
Lillian Christine . . . . Isabel
Kitty Austin . . . . la Frasquita
Dennis Ray . . . . Enrique
Sidney Baron . . . . Jose
Beaufoy Milton . . . . Arturo
ADVENTURE Spain. Explorer saves friend
from mountain and marrying a light woman.

08437
THE THOROUGHBRED (5608) (U)
London Screenplays (Gaumont)
P:D:S: Sidney Morgan
Ian Hunter . . . . Allen Stockbridge
Louise Prussing . . . . Constance Stockbridge
Richard Barclay . . . . Laddie Gray
H.Agar Lyons . . . . The Bookmaker
SPORT MP's gambling wife tries to force
jockey to lose Derby.

08438
S.O.S. (7251) (A)
Strand Films (Allied Artists)
P: Julius Hagen
D: Leslie Hiscott
S: (PLAY) Walter Ellis
Robert Loraine . . . . Owen Heriott
Bramwell Fletcher . . . . . . Heriott
Ursula Jeans . . . . Lady Weir
Lewis Dayton . . . . Sir Julian Weir
Audree Sayre . . . . Judy Weir
Campbell Gullan . . . . Karensky
Anita Sharp Bolster . . . . . . Mme Karensky
Viola Lyel . . . . Effie
CRIME Deauville. Man proves father was
framed by fiancee's mother.

08439
THE THREE PASSIONS (8500) (A)
St George's Productions (Allied Artists)
P: Rex Ingram, Alastair Mackintosh
D: SC: Rex Ingram
S: (NOVEL) Cosmo Hamilton
Alice Terry . . . . . Lady Victoria Burlington
Ivan Petrovitch . . . . Philip Burlington
Shayle Gardner . . . . Lord Bellamont
Leslie Faber . . . . . . Father Aloysius
Andrews Englemann . . . . . Hairless Man
Claire Eames . . . . Lady Bellamont
Gerald Fielding . . . . Bobbie
DRAMA Lord's son aids seamen's mission but
returns to save sick father's shipyard from
strikers. (Sound added Oct 1929).

08440
THE LADY OF THE LAKE (5168) (U)
Gainsborough (Select)
P: Michael Balcon
D: James A. Fitzpatrick
S: (POEM) Sir Walter Scott
SC: James A. Fitzpatrick, Angus Macphail
Percy Marmont . . . . James V
Benita Hume . . . . Ellen Douglas
Haddon Mason . . . . Malcolm Graeme
Lawson Butt . . . . Roderick Dhu
James Carew . . . . Moray
Douglas Payne . . . . Douglas
Leo Dryden . . . . Allen Bane
Hedda Bartlett . . . . Margaret
J. Nelson Ramsay . . . . Brian
ADVENTURE Scotland, period. Exiled girl
saves king from outlaws. (Sound added July
1931).

08441
NUMBER SEVENTEEN (6517) (A)
Fellner & Somlo (W&F)
D: Geza M. Bolvary
S: (PLAY) J.Jefferson Farjeon
Guy Newall . . . . Ben
Lien Dyers . . . . Elsie Ackroyd
Carl de Vogt . . . . Gilbert Fordyce
Fritz Greiner . . . . Shelldrake
Ernst Neicher . . . . Harold Brant
Hertha von Walter . . . . Nora Brant
Craighall Sherry . . . . Sam Ackroyd
Frederick Solm . . . . Henry Jobber
CRIME Seaman helps tec catch convicts
seeking hidden gems. (Made in Germany. Sound
added Aug. 1929).

08442
VALLEY OF THE GHOSTS (5204) (A)
British Lion (JMG)
P: S.W.Smith
D: G.B.Samuelson
S: (NOVEL) Edgar Wallace
SC: Edgar Wallace
Miriam Seegar . . . . Stella Nelson
Ian Hunter . . . . Andrew McLeod
Leo Sheffield . . . . Kenneth Nelson
Wallace Bosco . . . . Darricus Merrivan
George Bellamy . . . . Sleepwalker
Derrick de Marney . . . . . .:
CRIME Tec loves daughter of artist suspected
of murdering blackmailer

08443
W W JACOBS STORIES (series)
Welsh-Pearson
P: George Pearson
D: Geoffrey H.Malins
S:(STORIES) W.W.Jacobs
SC: Geoffrey H.Malins, Fenn Sherie

08444
1: DOUBLE DEALING (2000)
Pat Aherne
Dodo Watts
Philip Hewland
Ian Wilson

08445
2: THE BRAVO (2000)
Frank Stanmore . . . . . The Nightwatchman

08446
3: IN BORROWED PLUMES
Charles Paton . . . . Skipper
Harry Terry . . . .
Bobby Kerrigan . . . .

08447
4: TWO OF A TRADE (2000)
Charles Paton . . . . Mate
James Reardon . . . .
Fred Rains . . . .

08448
5: THE CHANGELING (2000)
Frank Stanmore
James Reardon
Annie Esmond
COMEDIES Tales of seamen. (Not shown)

08449
SACRED DRAMAS (series)
B & D (W&F)
P: Herbert Wilcox
D: H.P.Parkinson, J. Steven Edwards
S: Robert J. Cullen, Norman Lee

08450
1: THE ROSARY (2000)
Haddon Mason
Dacia Deane

08451
2: ROCK OF AGES (2000)
Eric Hales
Barbara Hood

08452
3: AVE MARIA (2000)
Eric Hales
Barbara Hood

08453
4: THE LOST CHORD
Edgar Vosper
Paddie Naismith

08454
5: ABIDE WITH ME (2000)
Edgar Vosper
Nellie Richards

08455
6: LEAD KINDLY LIGHT (2000)
Alfed Woods
Betty Astell
DRAMAS Moral stories inspired by hymns.

08456
THE BELLS OF ST. MARY'S (5500) (U)
GP Productions (JMG)
P: Arthur Phillips
D: Herbert 'Red' Davis
S: Herbert Davis, Claude Gill
SC: Arrar Jackson
Tubby Phillips. . . . .   The Parson
Barbara Hood . . . .   The Girl
Tom Gibson . . . .   The Lover
Hal Martin . . . .   The Bully
Eric Pavitt . . . .   The Urchin
Lena Halliday . . . .   The Widow
Nellie Bowman . . . .   The Woman
COMEDY Sussex. New parson converts villagers
by fighting local bully.

08457
BALACLAVA (8500) (U)
USA: JAWS OF HELL
Gainsborough (W&F)
P: Michael Balcon
D: Maurice Elvey, Milton Rosmer
S: (POEM) Alfred Tennyson (THE CHARGE
OF THE LIGHT BRIGADE)
SC: Boyd Cable, W.P.Lipscomb, Angus Macphail
Milton Rosmer, V.Gareth Gundrey, Robert
Stevenson.
Benita Hume . . . .   Jean McDonald
Cyril McLaglen . . . .   John Kennedy
Alf Goddard . . . .   Nobby
Miles Mander . . . .   Capt Gardner
J.Fisher White . . . .   Lord Raglan
Henry Mollison . . . . . .   Prisoner's Friend
Betty Bolton . . . .   Natasha
Robert Holmes . . . .   Father Nikolai
Harold Huth . . . .   Capt Nolan
Wally Patch . . . .   Trooper Strang
H. StBarbe West . . . .   Prosecutor
Bos Ranevsky . . . .   Tsar
Wallace Bosco . . . .   Lord Palmerston
Marian Drada . . . .   Queen Victoria
Eugene Leahy . . . .   Prince Albert
WAR 1854. Cashiered lieutenant enlists as
private and catches spy. (Sound added
April 1930).

08458
THE MAN WHO CHANGED HIS NAME (7134) (A)
British Lion
P: S.W.Smith
D: A.V.Bramble
S:(PLAY) Edgar Wallace
SC: Kathleen Hayden
Stewart Rome . . . .   Selby Clive
Betty Faire . . . .   Nita Clive
James Raglan . . . .   Frank O'Ryan
Ben Field . . . .   Sir Ralph Whitcombe
Wallace Bosco . . . .   Jerry Muller
Douglas Payne . . . .   Canadian
Phyllis & Helene Blackburn
CRIME Millionaire's faithless wife mistakes
him for murderer.

08459
LIFE (7147) (A)
Whitehall Films (New Era)
P:D: Adelqui Millar
S: (NOVEL) Joacquim Dicenta (JUAN JOSE)
Adelqui Millar . . . .   Juan Jose
Marie Ault . . . .   Isidora
Manuela del Rio . . . .   Rosa
Marcel Vibert . . . .   Paco
Jose Lucio . . . .   Andres
Denise Lorys . . . .   Tournela
CRIME Spain. Sacked bricklayer steals for
dancer and breaks jail to kill her when she
becomes ex-employer's mistress.

08460
THE GORNO MARIONETTES (Sound)
British Sound Film Productions (BIFD)
reissue: 1932, CAMERA COCKTALES No 2
(Hallmark).
Ottorino Gorno's Marionettes
MUSICAL Puppet performance.

08461
THE TRIAL TURN (sound)
British Sound Film Productions (BIFD)
S: (SKETCH) Horace Kenney
Horace Kenney
COMEDY Inept performer tries out at
music hall.

08462
THE NIGHTWATCHMAN (sound)
British Sound Film Productions (BIFD)
Wilkie Bard
COMEDY Music hall sketch.

08463
THE CLEANER (sound)
British Sound Film Productions (BIFD)
Wilkie Bard
COMEDY Music hall sketch.

08464
THE HYDE SISTERS (sound)
British Sound Film Productions (BIFD)
MUSICAL (Reissue in MUSICAL MEDLEY
No. 3, 1932, EB).

08465
MOUTH ORGAN SOLO (sound)
British Sound Film Productions (BIFD)
MUSICAL (Reissue in MUSICAL MEDLEY
No. 6, 1932, EB).

08466
NAP (15) (U) (Sound)
British Sound Film Productions (BIFD)
reissue: 1930 (FBO)
D: Hugh Croise
S: (PLAY) Ernest Lotinga (1914)
Ernie Lotinga . . . .   Jimmy Josser
COMEDY Soldier captures German and plays
cards with him.

08467
JOINING UP (13) (U) (sound)
British Sound Film Productions (BIFD)
reissue: 1930 (FBO)
D: Hugh Croise
S: (PLAY) Ernest Lotinga (1914)
Ernie Lotinga . . . .   Jimmy Josser
COMEDY Workshy obtains money by
repeatedly enlisting in disguise.

08468
CHRISTMAS PARTY (sound)
British Sound Film Productions (BIFD)
Fred Elizalde and his Orchestra
MUSICAL

08469
THAT BRUTE SIMMONS (10) (sound)
British Sound Film Productions (BIFD)
D:SC: Hugh Croise
S: (PLAY) Arthur Morrison, Herbert
Sargent
Frank Stanmore . . . . .Thomas Simmons
Forrester Harvey . . . .   Bob Ford
Barbara Gott . . . .   Mrs Ford
Alice O'Day. . . . .   Mrs Simmons
COMEDY (Reissue: 1932, CAMERA
COCKTALES, Hallmark).

08470
THE TALE-TELLER PHONE (10)(U)
(sound)
British Sound Film Productions (BIFD)
D: (PLAY) Arthur Stanley
Philip Desborough
Athalie Davies
Charles Tomlin
Nita Alvalez
COMEDY

08471
THE INTRUDER (9) (U) (sound)
British Sound Film Productions (EB)
S: R. Byron-Webber
Juliette Compton . . . .   The Wife
Robin Irvine . . . .   The Lover
George Bellamy . . . .   The Stranger
COMEDY Neglected woman's lover mistakes
stranger for husband and bribes him to allow
elopement.

08472
THE SUPERIOR SEX (9) (U) (sound)`
British Sound Film Productions (EB)
S: (SKETCH) John Henry
John Henry & Blossom
COMEDY Radio stars in domestic crosstalk.

08473
AN INTIMATE INTERLUDE (9) (U) (sound)
British Sound Film Productions (EB)
Albert Whelan
MUSICAL Songs and whistling.

08474
SCROOGE (9) (sound)
British Sound Film Productions
D: Hugh Croise
S: (NOVEL) Charles Dickens (A CHRISTMAS ,
CAROL)
SC: Bransby Williams
Bransby Williams . . . .   Ebenezer Scrooge
DRAMA Old miser haunted by dead partner.

08475
VICTORIA GIRLS SKIPPING (4) (U) (sound)
British Sound Film Productions (BIFD)
D: Hugh Croise
Victoria Theatre Dancers
MUSICAL (Reissue: 1932, MUSICAL MEDLEY
No. 6 [EB]).

08476
POCKET NOVELTIES (series) (U) (sound)
Blattner Picture Corporation (PDC)
D: Karl Freund
P: Ludwig Blattner
Joseph Nussbaum's Orchestra

08477
1: TUNE UP THE UKE

08478
2: A FASCINATING VAMP

08479
3: A SNOWMAN'S ROMANCE

08480
4: A CHINESE MOON (4)
Desiree Ellinger, Thorpe Bates

08481
5: IN A JAPANESE GARDEN

08482
6: ZULU LOVE (4)

08483
7: TODDLIN' ALONG

08484
8: MADELEINE

08485
9: THE KEYS OF HEAVEN
MUSICAL Song scenes with trick effects.
(Made in Germany).

08486
PHOTOTONE REELS (series) (U) (sound)
British Phototone (PDC)
P: Ludwig Blattner
D: John Harlow

08487
No. 1: (9)
Teddy Brown   Ethel Hook
MUSICAL Xylophonist:
"Dancing Tambourine"; contralto:
"Love's Old Sweet Song."

08488
No. 2: (10)
Albert Sandler   Al Starita
MUSICAL Violinist: "Schubert's Serenade";
saxophonist: "At Dawning."

08489
No. 3: (12)
Herschel Henlere   Ord Hamilton & Manny
Randle
MUSICAL Accordionist: "Lost Chord;"
"Song Melody and a Piano."

08490
No. 4: (9)
The Fayre Sisters   Tino Pattiera
MUSICAL Song: "Mammy's Little Fellow;"
tenor: "Tosca."

08491
No. 5: (10)
Four Admirals   Albert Sandler
MUSICAL "Melodious Melodies;"
violinist: "Czardas."

08492
No. 6: (9)
Teddy Brown   Pat & Terry Kendal
MUSICAL Xylophonist; "Virginia"

08493
No. 7: (10)
Al Starita   Ethel Hook
MUSICAL Saxophonist; contralto.

08494
No. 8: (11)
Herschel Henlere   Emmanuel List
MUSICAL Pianist: "Home Sweet Home;"
bass: "Asleep in the Deep."

08495
No. 9 (10)
Fayre Sisters   Ord Hamilton
MUSICAL Quartette; pianist.

08496
No. 10 (10)
Tino Pattiera Miguel Galvan   Emmanuel List
MUSICAL "Pagliacci;" "Don't Be Like That;"
"Drinking Song."

08497
No. 11: (9)
Miguel Galvan   Gloria Maravillas
Paquita & Bilbainita
MUSICAL "La Provinciana;" "La Violetera;"
"Halfway to Heaven."

08498
No. 12 (9)
Pat & Terry Kendal   Orloff & Casado de
Vinaran
Camaro & his Band   Frisco
MUSICAL "I Can't Give You Anything But
Love;" "La Cumparsita;" "Nobody Knows."

08499
No. 13: (10)
Arthur Young & Geoffrey Gaunt
Frisco   Lud Gluskin's Ambassadors
MUSICAL Piano duet; "I've Got a Robe;"
Jazz Band.

08500
No. 14: (9)
Arnaut Brothers
MUSICAL

08501
No. 15: (8)
Oumansky Ballet
MUSICAL

08502
No. 16: (9)
Jerry Steiner   Lud Gluskin's Ambassadors
MUSICAL

1929

JAN

08503
KITTY (8100) (U) (Silent)
BIP-Burlington (Wardour)
P:D: Victor Saville
S: (NOVEL) Warwick Deeping
SC: Violet Powell, Benn W.Levy
Estelle Brody . . . . Kitty Greenwood
John Stuart . . . . Alec StGeorge
Dorothy Cumming . . . . . . Mrs StGeorge
Marie Ault . . . . Mrs Greenwood
Winter Hall . . . . John Furnival
Olaf Hytten . . . . Leaper
Charles O'Shaughnessy . . . . Ruben
E.F.Bostwick . . . . Dr Dazeley
Jerrold Robertshaw . . . . . . Artist
Gibb McLaughlin . . . . Electrician
Rex Maurice . . . . Dr Drake
ROMANCE 1914. Shopgirl loves paralysed
amnesiac and kidnaps him from his
interfering mother. (Dialogue sequences filmed
in New York; added May 1929).

08504
THE THIRD EYE (7200) (A) (Silent)
Graham-Wilcox
P: Rudolph Salomon
D:S: P. Maclean Rogers
SC: P. Maclean Rogers, S.K.Winston
Dorothy Seaombe . . . . Marion Carstairs
Ian Harding . . . . Tom Kennedy
Hayford Hobbs . . . . Henry Fenton
John Hamilton . . . . Jim Carstairs
Cameron Carr . . . . Inspector
Jean Jay . . . . Flash Annie
Beatrice Bell . . . . Mrs Carstairs
Syd Ellery . . . . Piggott
Harry J. Worth . . . Commissioner Cosgrove
Patrick Ludlow. . . . . Arthur Redfern
Eric Wilton . . . . . . .Sir James Woodridge
CRIME Crooked financier instals inventor's
television sets in banks to discover safe
combinations.

08505
THE STREETS OF LONDON (3600) (A)
(Silent)
H.B.Parkinson (Pioneer)
D:SC: Norman Lee
S: (PLAY) Dion Boucicault
David Dunbar . . . . Gideon Bloodgood
Jack Rutherford . . . . Mark Livingstone
Charles Lincoln . . . . Paul Fairweather
Beatrice Duffy . . . . Lucy
Wera Engels . . . . Alida
CRIME Man embezzles fortune of dead
captain's daughter.

08506
THE SECOND MATE (3960) (A) (Silent)
H.B. Parkinson (Pioneer)
D:SC: J. Steven Edwards
S: (NOVEL) R.W.Rees
David Dunbar . . . . Jack Arkwright
Cecil Barry . . . . Capt Bywater
Lorna Duveen . . . . Ivy Bywater
Eric Hales . . . . Capt Petrie
ADVENTURE Dead captain's daughter
saves burning ship when it is abandoned by
mate.

08507
HUMAN CARGO (4380) (U) (Silent)
H.B. Parkinson (Pioneer)
D: J. Steven Edwards
S: Norman Lee
David Dunbar . . . . Insp Benson
Ella Atherton . . . . Sylvia Frescar

Eric Hales . . . . Slick Maxted
Lionel Roberts . . . . Convict 49
CRIME Girl poses as crook to expose police
inspector as chief of Thames gang.

08508
THE BONDMAN (8660) (U) (Silent)
B & D (W&F)
P:D: Herbert Wilcox
S: (NOVEL) Hall Caine
SC: T.A.Innes
Norman Kerry . . . . Jason
Frances Cuyler . . . . Greeba Fairbrother
Donald McCardle . . . . Michael
Henry Vibart . . . . Father Ferrati
H. Saxon- Snell . . . . Testa
Judd Green . . . . Adam Fairbrother
Florence Vie . . . . Mrs Fairbrother
Edward O'Neill . . . . Father
Dora Barton . . . . Mother
Charles Emerald . . . . Captain
ADVENTURE Sicily. Blinded revolutionary
escapes execution when his Manx halfbrother
takes his place.

08509
THE WOMAN IN WHITE (6702) (A) (Silent)
B & D (W&F)
P:D: Herbert Wilcox
S: (NOVEL) Wilkie Collins
SC: Herbert Wilcox, Robert J.Cullen
Blanche Sweet . . . . . Laura Fairlie/Anne
Haddon Mason . . . . Walter Hartwright
Cecil Humphreys . . . . . . Sir Percival Glyde
Louise Prussing . . . . Marian Fairlie
Frank Perfitt . . . . Count Fosco
Minna Grey . . . . Countess Fosco
CRIME Impostor confines his wife and kills
her insane double.

08510
A PEEP BEHIND THE SCENES (7372) (A)
(Silent)
B & D (W&F)
P: Herbert Wilcox
D: Jack Raymond
S: (NOVEL) Mrs O.F.Walton
SC: Lydia Hayward
Frances Cuyler . . . . Rosalie Joyce
Haddon Mason . . . . Toby Charlton
H. Saxon-Snell . . . . Augustus Joyce
Vera Stanton . . . . Gipsy Belle
Johnny Butt . . . . Jim
Renee Macready . . . . Norah Joyce
Ethel Irving . . . . Lucy Leslie
Clarence Blakiston . . . . . . Henry Leslie
Shirley Whyte . . . . Mother Manikin
DRAMA On her mother's death a circus girl
flees to her aunt, pursued by drunken father.

08511
AFTER THE VERDICT (9372) (A) (Silent)
Tschechowa (BIFD)
P: I.W.Schlesinger
D: Henrik Galeen
S: (NOVEL) Robert Hichens
SC:Alma Reville
Olga Tschechowa . . . . Vivian Denys
Warwick Ward . . . . Oliver Baratrie
Malcolm Tod . . . . Jim Gordon
Henry Victor . . . . Mr Sabine
Betty Carter . . . . Mrs Sabine
CRIME Tennis star's fiance framed for killing
flirtatious wife.

08512
THE LAST POST (8040) (A) (Silent)
Britannia (Gaumont)
P:D:S: Dinah Shurey

SC: Lydia Hayward
John Longden . . . . David/Martin
Frank Vosper . . . . Paul
Alf Goddard . . . . Tiny
Cynthia Murtagh Haynes . . Christine
J.Fisher White . . . . Mr Blair
A.B.Imeson . . . . Rollo
Johnny Butt . . . . Goodson
Rolf Leslie . . . . Stefan
Aggie Brantford . . . . Girl
DRAMA Soldier takes the blame when his
Bolshevik brother shoots a soldier during the
General Strike (Sound added: Jan 1930).

08513
THE FLYING SQUAD (7572) (A) (Silent)
British Lion (WB)
P: S.W.Smith
D: Arthur Maude
S: (NOVEL) Edgar Wallace
SC: Kathleen Hayden
Wyndham Standing . . . . Mark McGill
Dorothy Bartlam . . . . Ann Perryman
John Longden . . . . Insp John Bradley
Donald Calthrop . . . . Sederman
Henry Vibart . . . . Tiser
Eugenie Prescott . . . . Mrs Schifan
John Nedgnol . . . . Li Joseph
Laurence Ireland . . . . Ronnie Perryman
Bryan Edgar Wallace . . . . . . Offender
Carol Reed . . . . Offender
CRIME Tec poses as murdered Jew to force
smuggler to confess.

08514
THE SILENT HOUSE (9376) (A) (Silent)
Nettlefold (Butcher)
P: Archibald Nettlefold
D: Walter Forde
S: (PLAY) John G.Brandon, George Pickett
SC: H. Fowler Mear
Mabel Poulton . . . . T'Mala
Gibb McLaughlin . . . . Chang Fu
Arthur Pusey . . . . George Winsford
Gerald Rawlinson . . . . Capt Barty
Frank Perfitt . . . . Richard Winsford
Kiyoshe Takasi . . . . Ho Fang
Arthur Stratton . . . . Benson
Albert Brouett . . . . Peroda
Danny Green . . . . W'Hang
Rex Maurice . . . . Legarde
CRIME Mandarin hypnotises his partner's
daughter to locate hidden bonds.

FEB

08515
DOWN CHANNEL (Silent)
New Era
P: Gordon Craig
D:S: Michael Barringer
Henry Victor . . . . Smiler
Alf Goddard . . . . Nixon
Christopher Anthony . . . . . The Boy
Roy Travers . . . . Smuggler
ADVENTURE Yachtsman and son get
involved with smugglers. (Released on sub-
standard only).

08516
MR SMITH WAKES UP (25) (U)
BSFP
D: Sinclair Hill
S: (RADIO PLAY) Vivian Tidmarsh
Moore Marriott . . . . Mr Smith
Barbara Gott . . . . Mrs Smith
Elsa Lanchester . . . .
COMEDY Henpecked husband turns on
his bullying wife.

08517
AG AND BERT (12) (U)
BSFP
D: Bertram Phillips
S: (SKETCH) Mabel Constanduros
Mabel Constanduros...... Aggie Buggins
Michael Hogan......... Bert
COMEDY Domestic Sketch.

08518
PEACE AND QUIET (12)
BSFP
D: Sinclair Hill
S: (PLAY) Ronald Jeans
Ralph Lynn
Winifred Shotter
COMEDY

08519
JOSSER, KC (19) (U)
BSFP (BIFD) reissue: 1930 (FBO)
D: Hugh Croise
S: (PLAY) Ernest Lotinga, Norman Lee
Ernie Lotinga.......... Jimmy Josser
COMEDY Crook and friend steal jewels by
using chloroform.

08520
THE BRIDE (6) (U)
BSFP (BIFD)
D: Hugh Croise
S: (SONG) George Robey
George Robey
MUSICAL Comic song.

08521
MRS MEPHISTOPHELES (8) (U)
BSFP (BIFD)
D: Hugh Croise
S: George Robey
George Robey ... Mrs. Mephistopheles
COMEDY Character cameo of a boarding-
house keeper.

08522
MEDEVEDEFF'S BALALAIKA ORCHESTRA
(14) (U)
BSFP (BIFD) reissue: 1932,
CAMERA COCKTALES No. 1 (Hallmark).
MUSICAL

08523
JOSEPHINE EARLE (5)
BSFP (BIFD) reissue: 1932,
MUSICAL MEDLEY No. 4 (EB)
MUSICAL Songs: "You have no idea;"
"Shout Hallelujah !"

08524
YVETTE DARNAC (5)
BSFP (BIFD)
MUSICAL Songs.

08525
BILLIE BARNES (5)
BSFP (BIFD)
MUSICAL Song: "Sing me a baby song."

08526
TEDDY BROWN, XYLOPHONIST (5)
BSFP (BIFD)
MUSICAL

08527
CLAPHAM AND DWYER No. 1 (10) (U)
BSFP (BIFD) reissue: 1930 (FBO); 1932
MUSICAL MEDLEY No. 5 (EB)
COMEDY Crosstalk act.

08528
CLAPHAM AND DWYER No. 2 (10) (U)
BSFP (BIFD) reissue: 1930 (FBO)
COMEDY Crosstalk act.

08529
JOE THEISS SAXOTETTE (5) (U)
BSFP (BIFD) reissue: 1932,
MUSICAL MEDLEY No. 1 (EB)
MUSICAL Saxophone sextette.

08530
THE PERCIVAL MACKEY TRIO (15) (U)
BSFP (BIFD)
MUSICAL

08531
DOING HIS DUTY (13) (U)
BSFP (BIFD) reissue: 1930 (FBO)
D: Hugh Croise
S: (PLAY) Ernest Lotinga (THE POLICE
FORCE)
Ernie Lotinga.......... Jimmy Josser
COMEDY Man joins the police to attend
football matches and makes many arrests.

08532
SPIRITS (10) (sound)
BSFP (BIFD)
D: Hugh Croise
S: (PLAY) Ernest Lotinga, Norman Lee
(JOSSER, KC)
Ernie Lotinga.......... Jimmy Josser
COMEDY

08533
THE HOO-RAY KIDS (series) (U) (Silent)
British Screen Productions (Eur)
D:SC: Bobby Harman
S: T. Roy Jackson
Jackie Ray............. "Hoo" Ray
Edward John........... Virol
A.Sylvester............. Inky
John Common.......... Specs
Rolls Smith............. Rolls
June Potts............. June
Happy Robertson........ Happy
Pug Podger............ Pug

08534
1: A RUNAWAY HOLIDAY (1930)

08535
2: JACKIE'S NIGHTMARE (1938)

08536
3: THE BIG SHOW (1825)

08537
4: KOLLEGE KAPERS (1975)

08538
5: HOUSE WARMERS (1739)

08539
6: JACKIE AND THE BEANSTALK (1978)
COMEDIES Slapstick adventures of a gang
of children.

08540
THE MANXMAN (8163) (A) (Silent)
BIP (Wardour)
D: Alfred Hitchcock
S: (NOVEL) Hall Caine
SC: Eliot Stannard
Carl Brisson............ Pete Quilliam
Anny Ondra........... Kate Cregeen
Malcolm Keen......... Philip Christian
Randle Ayrton......... Mr Cregeen
Clare Greet............. Mrs Cregeen
Wilfred Shine.......... Doctor
Kim Peacock.......... Ross Christian
Harry Terry............ Man
Nellie Richards......... Wardress
DRAMA Isle of Man. "Dead" fisherman returns
to wed innkeeper's daughter not knowing she
is pregnant by his best friend.

08541
PICCADILLY (9500) (A) (Silent)
BIP (Wardour)
P:D: E.A.Dupont
S: Arnold Bennett
Gilda Gray........... Mabel Greenfield
Anna May Wong......... Shosho
Jameson Thomas....... Valentine Wilmot
Charles Laughton........ Visitor
Cyril Ritchard.......... Victor Smiles
King Ho-Chang.......... Jim
Hannah Jones........... Bessie
Ellen Pollock............ Vamp
Harry Terry........... Publican
Gordon Begg........... Coroner
Charles Paton........... Doorman
Debroy Somers and his Band
CRIME Club owner's fiancee accused of
killing Chinese mistress. (Sound added Oct 1929;
Extract in ELSTREE STORY, 1952):

08542
LILY OF KILLARNEY (6100) (U) (Silent)
BIP (Wardour)
D: SC: George Ridgwell
S: (PLAY) Dion Boucicault (THE COLLEEN
BAWN)
Cecil Landeau....... Hardress Cregan
Pamela Parr.......... Eily O'Connor
Dennis Wyndham...... Myles-na-Coppaleen
Barbara Gott........... Sheelah
Gillian Dean.......... Ann Chute
H.Fisher White.......... Kyrle Daly
Edward O'Neill......... Corrigan
Wilfred Shine.......... Father Tom
Henry Wilson.......... Danny Mann
CRIME Ireland. Poor aristocrat hires dwarf
to drown his secret wife so he may marry an
heiress.

08543
CUPID IN CLOVER (6471) (U) (Silent)
British Screen Productions
D:SC: Frank Miller
S: (NOVEL) Upton Grey (YELLOW CORN)
Betty Siddons........... Clary Simpson
Eric Findon........... George Dowey
Herbert Langley......... John Simpson
Charles Garry.......... Joe Dowey
Winifred Evans.......... Lyddy
George Wynn........... Fred Amyon
Marie Esterhazy......... Maggie
James Knight...........
Wyndham Guise.........
Jack Miller.............
ROMANCE Hants. Farmer objects to his
daughter's poor lover until he learns that the
man he favours covets his land.

08544
MASTER AND MAN (8700) (U) (Silent)
British Screen Productions
D;S: George A. Cooper
SC: Edward Dryhurst
Humberston Wright...... Thomas Blount
Henry de Vries......... Richard Waring
Betty Siddons.......... Dorothy Blount
Maurice Braddell........ Dick Waring
Anne Grey............ Celia Waring
Frank Stanmore........ Wilkes
Mary Brough.......... Mrs Wilkes
Olaf Hytten........... Lord Overbury
DRAMA Sacked workman rescues owner's
amnesiac son from factory fire and reports him
dead.

08545
THREE MEN IN A CART (5187) (U) (Silent)
British Screen Productions (U)
D:S: Arthur Phillips
SC: Edward Dryhurst

Frank Stanmore . . . .   Hobbs
Tony Wylde . . . .   Charles Stanley
Pat Morton . . . .   Frank Whiteley
Joan Morgan . . . .
David Dunbar . . . .
Celia Hughesden . . . .
Alice O'Day . . . .
COMEDY Three friends run marriage agency, garage, butcher shop, and find treasure. (Made as series of two-reelers but shown as a feature.)

08546
THE BROKEN MELODY (6414) (A) (Silent)
Welsh-Pearson-Elder (Par)
P: George Pearson
D: Fred Paul
S: (PLAY) Herbert Keith, James Leader
SC: Fred Paul, Thomas Coutts Elder
Georges Galli . . . .   Prince Paul
Audree Sayre . . . .   Bianca
Enid Stamp-Taylor . . . . . .   Gloria
Cecil Humphreys . . . .   Gen Delange
Mary Brough . . . .   Marthe
Albert Brouett . . . .   Jacques
ROMANCE Paris. Exiled prince returns to his shopgirl wife after writing opera for flirtatious singer.

08547
WHEN KNIGHTS WERE BOLD (7213) (U) (Silent)
B & D (W&F)
P: Herbert Wilcox
D: Tim Whelan
S: (PLAY) Charles Marlow
SC: Tim Whelan, Herbert Wilcox
Nelson Keys . . . .   Sir Guy de Vere
Miriam Seegar . . . .   Lady Rowena
Eric Bransby Williams . . .   Sir Brian Ballymote
Wellington Briggs . . . .   Widdicombe
Lena Halliday . . . .   Lady Walgrave
Martin Adeson . . . .   Barker
Hal Gordon . . . .   Whittle
Edith Kingdon . . . .   Aunt Thornridge
E.L. Frewen . . . .   Dean
COMEDY Unpopular heir dreams he lives in mediaeval days.

08548
THE LOST PATROL (7250) (A) (Silent)
British Instructional (Fox)
P: H. Bruce Woolfe
D:SC: Walter Summers
S: (NOVEL) Philip Macdonald (PATROL)
Cyril McLaglen . . . .   The Sergeant
Sam Wilkinson . . . .   Sanders
Terence Collier . . . .   Cpl Bell
Hamilton Keene . . . .   Morelli
Fred Dyer . . . .   Abelson
Charles Emerald . . . .   Hale
Anew McMaster . . . .   Brown
James Watts . . . .   Cook
John Valentine . . . .   Mackay
Frederick Long . . . .   Pearson
WAR Mesopotamia. Lost cavalry patrol gradually killed off by Arabs.

08549
THE THREE KINGS (6824) (U) (Silent)
British & Foreign Films
D: Hans Steinhoff
S: Henry Edwards
Henry Edwards . . . .   Edgar King
Evelyn Holt . . . .   Maria
Warwick Ward . . . .   Frank King
John Hamilton . . . .   Charlie King
Clifford McLaglen . . . .   Fredo

DRAMA Blackpool. Clown loves young housekeeper and saves her from fire caused by jealous lion-tamer.

MAR
08550
ELECTROCORD FILMS (3) (U)
Electrocord (Butcher)
D: Dave Aylott, E.F.Symmons
Nella Elsa; Reg Hanson; Jack Yorke; Phyllis Bryant; Dan Draper; Donald Aked; Isy de Roi; Mary Bryant; Hal Martin; Charles Picton; Mary O'Hara.

08551
MY BLUE HEAVEN

08552
DOES SHE DO-DO-DO

08553
WAS IT A DREAM

08554
THAT'S MY WEAKNESS NOW

08555
CARMENA

08556
BANANAS ARE COMING BACK AGAIN

08557
WHY DOES THE HYENA LAUGH

08558
THE GOOD LITTLE BOY AND THE BAD LITTLE BOY

08559
SONNY BOY

08560
I CAN'T GIVE YOU ANYTHING BUT LOVE

08561
PAGLIACCI

08562
THE DANCING LESSON

08563
BELOVED

08564
TOY TOWN ARTILLERY

08565
EE BY GUM

08566
OLE MAN RIVER

08567
MY OHIO HOME

08568
STAY OUT OF THE SOUTH

08569
ALL BY YOURSELF IN THE MOONLIGHT

08570
HUMORESQUE

08571
GET OUT AND GET UNDER THE MOON

08572
ONE HUNDRED YEARS FROM NOW

08573
CAN'T HELP LOVING DAT MAN

08574
TOREADOR

08575
ROLLING ALONG HAVING MY UPS AND DOWNS

08576
MAISIE LOU
MUSICAL Actors mime to gramophone records.

08577
LITTLE MISS LONDON (6912) (U) (Silent)
British Instructional (Fox)
P: H. Bruce Woolfe
D:S: Harry Hughes
Pamela Parr . . . .   Molly Carr
Eric Bransby Williams . . . . .   Jack
Frank Stanmore . . . .   Ephraim Smith
Pauline Johnson . . . .   Jill Smith
Marie Ault . . . .   Mrs Higgins
Reginald Fox . . . .   Burton Gregg
Charles Dormer . . . .   Lord Blurberry
Belle Austin . . . .   Landlady
Moira Lynd . . . .   Typist
COMEDY Pickle king feigns bankruptcy and poses as workman while his daughter loves salesman posing as lord.

08578
SACRIFICE (6602) (A) (Silent)
British Instructional (Fox)
P: H. Bruce Woolfe
D: Victor Peers
S: (PLAY) H.M.Harwood, F.Tennyson Jesse (THE PELICAN)
Andree Tourneur . . . .   Wanda
G.H.Mulcaster . . . .   Marcus Heriot
Lewis Dayton . . . .   Paul Lazan
Eveline Chipman . . . .   Lady Heriot
Frank Atherley . . . .   Lord Heriot
Mickey Brantford . . . .   Robin
Florence Wood . . . .   Anna
Gordon Begg . . . .   Cheriton
ROMANCE Lady persuades her son to divorce his acress wife by implying their baby is a bastard.

08579
THE RUNAWAY PRINCESS (7053) (U) (Silent)
British Instructional-Laenderfilm (JMG)
P: H. Bruce Woolfe
D: Frederick Wendhausen, Anthony Asquith
S: (NOVEL) Elizabeth Russell (PRINCESS PRISCILLA'S FORTNIGHT)
SC: Anthony Asquith
Mady Christians . . . . .   Princess Priscilla
Paul Cavanagh . . . . . .   Prince of Savonia
Norah Baring . . . .   The Forger
Fred Rains . . . .   The Professor
Claude H. Beerbohm . . . . . . .The Detective
CRIME Prince in disguise saves runaway princess from becoming forger's dupe. (Made in Berlin).

08580
THE CELESTIAL CITY (8768) (U) (Silent)
British Instructional (JMG)
P: H. Bruce Woolfe
D:SC: John Orton
S: (NOVEL) Baroness Orczy
Norah Baring . . . .   Lita
Cecil Fearnley . . . . .   Sir Philip Charteris
Lewis Dayton . . . .   Paul Sergine
Malvina Longfellow . . . . .   Princess Brokska
Henry de Vries . . . .   Bill
Frank Perfitt . . . .   Sir John Errick
Albert Rebla . . . .   Laddie

Gordon Begg . . . . Truscott
CRIME Russia. Detective loves girl whose father is a jewel thief.

08581
CHAMBER OF HORRORS (5014) (A) (Silent)
British Instructional (PDC)
P: H. Bruce Woolfe
D:S: Walter Summers
Frank Stanmore . . . . . . James Budgeforth
Elizabeth Hempel . . . . Ninette
Joan Maude . . . . Reporter
Leslie Holland . . . . Deaf Mute
Fanny Wright . . . . Lecturer
HORROR Man dreams he murders his mistress and goes mad during night in Madame Tussaud's Waxworks.

08582
A KNIGHT IN LONDON (6675) (A) (Silent)
Blattner Pictures (WB)
P: Ludwig Blattner
D: Lupu Pick
S: Mrs Horace Tremlett
SC: Charles Lincoln
Lilian Harvey . . . . Aline Morland
Ivy Duke . . . . Lady Morland
Robin Irvine . . . . Harry Erskine
Bernard Nedell . . . . Prince Zalnoff
Robert English . . . . Mr McComber
Zena Dare . . . .
Hon Angela Brett . . . .
ROMANCE Prince makes socialite think she spent night in his room. (Sound added - 1930)

08583
THE CLUE OF THE NEW PIN (7292) (A) (Silent)
British Lion (PDC)
P: S.W.Smith
D: Arthur Maude
S: (NOVEL) Edgar Wallace
SC: Kathleen Hayden
Benita Hume . . . . Ursula Ardfern
Kim Peacock . . . . Tab Holland
Donald Calthrop . . . . Yeh Ling
John Gielgud . . . . Rex Trasmere
H. Saxon-Snell . . . . Walters
Johnny Butt . . . . Wellington Briggs
Colin Kenney . . . . Insp Carver
Hippodrome Chorus
CRIME Rich recluse killed by nephew who tries to burn reporter.

08584
RINGING THE CHANGES (6915) (U) (Silent)
Strand Films (Argosy)
P: Julius Hagen
D:SC: Leslie Hiscott
S: (NOVEL) Raleigh King (JIX)
Henry Edwards . . . . Lord Bemerton
Margot Landa . . . . Jill Farrar
James Fenton . . . . Stinson
Charles Cautley . . . . Mr Kemp
Forrester Harvey . . . . Steve Blower
Philip Hewland . . . . Mr Guggleswick
Barbara Gott . . . . Mrs Guggleswick
Rex Maurice . . . . Henry Foxley
Jeff Barlow . . . . Dorcas
Bernard de Bressey . . . . Percy Guggleswick
COMEDY Lord rents castle and poses as butler, exposing lawyer as crook.

08585
THE INSEPARABLES (6586) (A) (Silent)
Whitehall Films (WB)
P: Adelqui Millar
D: Adelqui Millar, John Stafford
S: Adelqui Millar, Guarino Glavany
SC: John Stafford

Elissa Landi . . . . Velda
Pat Aherne . . . . Laurie Weston
Annette Benson . . . . Adrienne
Gabriel Gabrio . . . . Pietro
Jerrold Robertshaw . . . Sir Reginald Farleigh
Fred Rains . . . . Alexander Figg
ROMANCE Riviera. Smuggler loves gipsy he saves from storm, but she loves her wounded companion.

08586
THE ALLEY CAT (7229) (A) (Silent)
British & Foreign Films
D: Hans Steinhoff
S: (NOVEL) Anthony Carlyle
SC: Iris North (Joan Morgan)
Mabel Poulton . . . . Polly
Jack Trevor . . . . Jimmy Rice
Clifford McLaglen . . . . Simon Beck
Shayle Gardner . . . . Insp Fordham
Margit Manstead . . . . Melona Miller
Marie Ault . . . . Ma
DRAMA Man who thinks he killed millionaire is cared for by cockney girl and becomes composer.

APR

08587
AULD LANG SYNE (6800) (U) (Silent)
Welsh-Pearson-Elder (Par)
D:SC: George Pearson
S: Hugh E. Wright, Patrick L.Mannock
Sir Harry Lauder . . . . Sandy McTavish
Dorothy Boyd . . . . Jill Bray
Pat Aherne . . . . Angus McTavish
Dodo Watts . . . . Marie McTavish
Hugh E. Wright . . . . Wullie McNab
DRAMA Scots farmer visits London and finds his son is a boxer and his daughter a nurse. (Sound added: Sep 1929).

08588
YOUNG WOODLEY (8162) (A) (Silent)
Regal Pictures
P: E.A.Abrahams
D:SC: Thomas Bentley
S: (PLAY) John Van Druten
Robine Irvine . . . . Woodley
Marjorie Hume . . . . Laura Simmons
Sam Livesey . . . . Mr Simmons
Gerald Rawlinson . . . . Milner
Tom Helmore . . . . Vining
Dorothy Black . . . . Francesca
ROMANCE Schoolboy falls in love with his teacher's young wife. (Not Shown).

08589
THE FIGHTING FOOL (10) (U)
BSFP (BIFD) *reissue:* 1930 (FBO)
D: Jack Harrison
S: Chick Farr
Chick Farr . . . . The Dandy
Herbert Cyril . . . . The Referee
Harry Terry . . . . The Bruiser
COMEDY Piccadilly dandy beats Bloomsbury boxer without landing one blow.

08590
PEPPER ! (16) (U)
BSFP (BIFD)
COMEDY

08591
EMILE GRIMSHAW BANJO QUARTETTE (4) (U)
BSFP (BIFD) *reissue:* 1933, MUSIC WITHOUT WORDS (WB); 1932, MUSICAL MEDLEY No.3 (EB).
MUSICAL

08592
GORDON FREEMAN, NOVELTY ENTER-TAINER (7) (U)
BSFP (BIFD)
COMEDY Inventor of household gadgets.

08593
NORAH BLANEY No.I (6) (U)
BSFP (BIFD) *reissue:* 1932, MUSICAL MEDLEY No. 2 (EB)
MUSICAL Songs: "He ain't done right by Nell;" "Masculine women and feminine men."

08594
NORAH BLANEY No. 2 (6) (U)
BSFP (BIFD) *reissue:* 1932, MUSICAL MEDLEY No. 6 (EB).
MUSICAL Songs: "If you hadn't gone away;" "What about me."

08595
GENTLEMEN THE CHORUS No. 1 (6) (U)
BSFP (BIFD) *reissue:* 1930 (FBO); 1932 CAMERA COCKTALES No.3 (Hallmark).
Dale Smith; Salisbury Singers
MUSICAL Old English song scena: "Come Landlord;" "My bonnie."

08596
GENTLEMEN THE CHORUS No. 2 (4) (U)
BSFP (BIFD) *reissue:* 1932, MUSICAL MEDLEY No. 4 (EB)
Dale Smith; Salisbury Singers
MUSICAL Old English song scena: "John Peel;" "Who's that a-calling."

08597
HER CARDBOARD LOVER (5)
British Phototone
D: Clayton Hutton
S: (PLAY) Jacques Deval, Valerie Wyngate, P.G.Wodehouse
Tallulah Bankhead. . . . . . . Simone
COMEDY Girl undresses while talking on the telephone. (Made in Berlin).

08598
FAVOURITE AIRS (11) (U)
BSFP (WB)
Luella Paikin
MUSICAL "Rigoletto;" "Lo hear the gentle lark;" "Londonderry air."

08599
ELECTROCORD FILMS (3) (U)
Electrocord (Butcher)
D: Dave Aylott, E.F.Symmons

08600
SO TIRED

08601
I'VE ALWAYS WANTED TO CALL YOU MY SWEETHEART

08602
SHE'S A GREAT GREAT GIRL

08603
COHEN FORMS A NEW COMPANY

08604
LIKE THE BIG POTS DO

08605
DON'T HAVE ANY MORE MRS MOORE

08606
WE'RE LIVING AT THE CLOISTERS

08607
GERANIUM

08608
IN THE WOOD SHED SHE SAID SHE WOULD

08609
AT SANTA BARBARA

08610
THE ADMIRAL'S YARN

08611
TOSTI'S GOODBYE

08612
TAKE A LOOK AT ME

08613
THE LITTLE WHITE HOUSE

08614
ONE ALONE

08615
CHLOE

08616
IN CELLAR COOL

08617
EVER BRAVEST HEART

08618
TAMIAMI TRAIL

08619
HAPPY DAYS AND LONELY NIGHTS

08620
RAINBOW ROUND MY SHOULDER

08621
YOU ALONG O' ME

08622
OFF TO PHILADELPHIA

08623
ONE FINE DAY
MUSICAL Actors mime to gramophone records.

MAY

08624
POWER OVER MEN (6918) (A) (Silent)
British Filmcraft (Par)
P:D:SC: George J.Banfield
S: Denison Clift
Isabel Jeans . . . . Marion Delacour
Jameson Thomas . . . . . . Phillipe Garnier
Wyndham Standing . . . . . Emile Delacour
Gibb McLaughlin . . . . . Alexandre Billot
Jerrold Robertshaw . . . . . . Fournier
James Knight . . . . Cesa
Franklyn Bellamy . . . . Bottomley
Gabrielle Morton . . . . Maid
Judd Green . . . .
Hugh Crumplin
CRIME Diplomat's wife takes blame when a
spy kills her husband, thinking her lover did it.

08625
THE RETURN OF THE RAT (7612) (A)
(Silent)
Gainsborough (W&F)
P: Michael Balcon
D: Graham Cutts
S: (CHARACTERS) Ivor Novello, Constance
Collier
SC: Edgar C. Middleton, A Neil Lyons,
Angus McPhail
Ivor Novello . . . . Pierre Boucheron
Isabel Jeans . . . . Zelia de Chaumet
Mabel Poulton . . . . Lisette
Bernard Nedell . . . . Henri

Marie Ault . . . . Mere Colline
Gordon Harker . . . . Morell
Scotch Kelly . . . . Bill
Harry Terry . . . . Alf
CRIME Paris. "Dead" thief accused of
murdering his ex-wife (Sound added Oct 1929).

08626
WOULD YOU BELIEVE IT ! (5015) (U)
(Silent)
Nettlefold (Butcher)
P: Archibald Nettlefold
D: Walter Forde
S: Walter Forde, H. Fowler Mear
Walter Forde . . . . Walter
Pauline Johnson . . . . Pauline
Arthur Stratton . . . . Cuthbert
Albert Brouett . . . . Spy
Anita O'Day . . . . Farmer's Wife
Anita Sharp Bolster . . . . . . Presbyterian
COMEDY Man invents a wireless-controlled
tank and foils spies. (Sound added Oct 1929.)
Extract in HELTER-SKELTER; 1949)

08627
THE POACHER (2069) (U) (Silent)
Albert C. Bolton (Eur)
P:D:S: Albert C. Bolton
Roy Meredith . . . . Jack Jennings
Molly Wright . . . . Jean
CRIME Billericay. Poacher reforms after
being shot by gamekeepers.

08628
WHITE CARGO (7965) (A) (Silent)
Neo-Art Productions (WP)
P:D: J.B.Williams, Arthur Barnes
S: (PLAY) Leon Gordon (NOVEL)
Vera Simonton
SC: J.B.Williams
Leslie Faber . . . . Weston
Gypsy Rhouma . . . . Tondelayo
John Hamilton . . . . Ashley
Maurice Evans . . . . Langford
Henry de Vries . . . . Skipper
Humberston Wright . . . . . . Missioner
Sebastian Smith . . . . Doctor
Tom Helmore . . . . Worthing
George Turner . . . . Mate
DRAMA Tropics. Manager of rubber
plantation marries native and she tries to
poison him.

08629
THE SILVER KING (8462) (A) (Silent)
Welsh-Pearson-Elder (Par)
P: George Pearson
D: T.Hayes Hunter
S: (PLAY) Henry Arthur Jones, Henry Herman
SC: Fenn Sherie
Percy Marmont . . . . Wilfred Denver
Jean Jay . . . . Nellie Denver
Chili Bouchier . . . . Olive
Bernard Nedell . . . . . Capt "Spider" Skinner
Hugh E.Wright . . . . Jaikes
Henry Wenman . . . . Cripps
Ben Field . . . . Coombes
Harold Huth . . . . Geoffrey Ware
Donald Stuart . . . . Corkett
CRIME Man framed for murder returns
rich from exile and secretly helps his wife.

08630
THE CROOKED BILLET (7226) (A) (Silent)
Gainsborough (W&F)
P: Michael Balcon
D: Adrian Brunel
S: (PLAY) Dion Titherage
SC: Angus Macphail

Carlyle Blackwell . . . . . Dietrich Hebburn
Madeleine Carroll . . . . Joan Easton
Miles Mander . . . . Guy Morrow
Gordon Harker . . . . Slick
Kim Peacock . . . . Philip Easton
Danny Green . . . . Rogers
Frank Goldsmith . . . . . Sir William Easton
Alexander Field . . . . Alf
CRIME International spy seeks documents
hidden in old inn. (Sound added: March 1930).

08631
THE NIGHT PATROL (4379) retitled:
CITY OF SHADOWS (A) (Silent)
H.B.Parkinson (JMG)
D:S: Norman Lee
Elizabeth Baxter . . . . Herself
CRIME Unemployed miner helps the flying
squad capture a den of thieves.

08632
DICK TURPIN (series) (U) (Silent)
British Filmcraft (Par)
P: George J. Banfield
S: Reginald Fogwell
Kenneth McLaglen . . . . Dick Turpin
Wally Patch . . . . Jonathan Wild

08633
1: OUTLAWED (1856)
D: Reginald Fogwell
Betty Siddons . . . . Betty Leigh
J.R.Tozer . . . . .Sir Anthony Lethridge
Gabrielle Morton . . . Hon Mary Carrouthers

08634
2: THE IMPOSTER (1550)
D: Reginald Fogwell
Kenneth McLaglen . . . . Sir Simon Kyle
Eve Terry . . . . Dorothy
Wallace Bosco . . . . Uncle
Holland Bennett . . . . John Watkin

08635
3: THE SNARE (2132)
D: Leslie Eveleigh
James Knight . . . . Tom King
Betty Siddons . . . . Betty Leigh
J.R.Tozer . . . . . . Sir Anthony Lethridge
Gabrielle Morton . . . Hon Mary Carrouthers

08636
4: NEMESIS (2072)
D: Leslie Eveleigh
Betty Siddons . . . . Betty Leigh
ADVENTURE 1720. Exploits of a high-
wayman.

08637
CHRIS'S MRS (1864) (U) (Silent)
G & S Films
D:S: Wilfred Gannon
Wilf Gannon . . . . Chris
COMEDY

08638
AUNTIE'S ANTICS (5144) (U) (Silent)
G & S Films
D:S: Wilf Gannon
Wilf Gannon
Hilda Sayer
COMEDY

08639
LIFE'S A STAGE (5885) (A) (Silent)
Encore Films (Argosy)
P:D: Arthur Phillips
S: Kenneth Gibbs

SC: Arrar Jackson
Frank Stanmore . . . . Alf Nobbler
Joy Windsor . . . . Snippets Nobbler
Tony Wylde . . . . Dennis Neville
Gerald Rawlinson . . . . Ted Denham
Dino Galvani . . . . Michael Standing
Donald Castle . . . . Armfield Knight
CRIME Busker confesses to shooting
seducer to save his amnesiac film star daughter.

08640
A ROMANCE OF SEVILLE (5610) (U)
(Colour/ Silent)
BIP (FNP)
D: Norman Walker
S: (STORY) Arline Lord (THE MAJO)
SC: Garnett Weston, Alma Reville
Alexandre D'Arcy . . . . Ramon
Marguerite Allan . . . . Pepita
Randle Ayrton . . . . Estavian
Cecil Barry . . . . Estaban
Hugh Eden . . . . Juan
Eugenie Amami . . . . Dolores
Koblenzova
ROMANCE Spain. Betrothed artist loves girl
engaged to jewel thief. (Sound added: July
1930).

08641
HIGH SEAS (6355) (A) (Silent)
BIP (FNP)
D: Denison Clift
S: (STORY) Monckton Hoffe (THE SILVER
ROSARY)
SC: Denison Clift, Victor Kendall
Lillian Rich . . . . Faith Jeffrey
John Stuart . . . . Tony Bracklethorpe
Randle Ayrton . . . . Capt Jeffrey
Winter Hall . . . . Lord Bracklethorpe
Janet Alexander . . .Lady Bracklethorpe
James Carew . . . . Jaeger
Daisy Campbell . . . . Mrs Jeffrey
DRAMA Press lord ruins sailor father of son's
fiancee. (Sound added: Mar 1930).

08642
THE VAGABOND QUEEN (5610) (U) (Silent)
BIP (Wardour)
D: Geza von Bolvary
S: Douglas Furber
SC: Rex Taylor, Val Valentine
Betty Balfour . . . . . Sally/Princess Xonia
Glen Byam Shaw . . . . Jimmie
Ernest Thesiger . . . . Katoff
Harry Terry . . . . Winkleburg
Charles Dormer . . . . Prince Adolphe
Dino Galvani . . . . Ilmar
COMEDY Ruritania. Princess's cockney double
is crowned to thwart rebels. (Sound added
Aug 1930)

08643
THE FLYING SCOTSMAN (5502) (U) (Silent)
BIP (WB)
D: Castleton Knight
S: Joe Grossman
SC: Victor Kendall, Garnett Weston
Moore Marriott . . . . Bob White
Pauline Johnson . . . . Joan White
Raymond Milland . . . . Jim Edwards
Alec Hurley . . . . Crow
Dino Galvani . . . . Headwaiter
Billy Shine . . . . Barman
DRAMA Sacked fireman tries to wreck express
train on driver's last journey. (Sound added:
Mar 1930).

08644
THE LADY FROM THE SEA (5540) (U)
(Silent)

BIP (PAR)
D: Castleton Knight
S: Joe Grossman
SC: Garnett Weston, Victor Kendall
Moore Marriott . . . . Old Roberts
Mona Goya . . . . Claire le Grange
Raymond Milland . . . . Tom Roberts
Bruce Gordon . . . . Dick Roberts
Eugenie Amami . . . . Rose
Anita Graham . . . . Mrs Roberts
Wilfred Shine . . . . Doctor
ROMANCE Goodwin Sands lifeboatman
rescues shipwrecked girl who tries to win
him away from fiancee. (Sound added
Apr 1930).

08645
THE WOMAN HE SCORNED (8467) (U)
(Silent)
Charles Whittaker Productions (WB)
D:S: Paul Czinner
SC: Charles Whittaker
Pola Negri . . . . Louise
Hans Rehmann . . . . John
Warwick Ward . . . . Maxim
Cameron Carr . . . . Magistrate
Margaret Rawlings . . . . Woman
DRAMA Cornwall. Lighthouse keeper's wife
shelters fugitive lover. (Sound added: May 1930).

08646
RED ACES (7200) (A) (Silent)
British Lion
D:SC: Edgar Wallace
S: (NOVEL) Edgar Wallace
Janice Adair . . . . Margot Lynn
Muriel Angelus . . . . Ena Burslem
Geoffrey Gwyther . . . . . . Kenneth McKay
James Raglan . . . . Rufus Machfield
Nigel Bruce . . . . T.B.Kinsfeather
George Bellamy . . . . J.G.Reeder
W.Cronin Wilson . . . . . Walter Wentworth
Douglas Payne . . . . Insp Gaylor
CRIME Gambler frames banker for killing
man whose name he forged.

08647
ELECTROCORD FILMS (3) (U)
Electrocord (Butcher)
D: Dave Aylott, E.F.Symmons

08648
MINE ALL MINE
Nella Elsa

08649
IS THERE ANYTHING WRONG IN THAT?
Nella Elsa

08650
MISERY FARM
Hal Martin

08651
MY ONE AND ONLY
Nella Elsa

08652
THE EGG SONG

08653
O SOLE MIO
Charles Picton

08654
NIRVANA
Hal Martin

08655
MIGHTY LAK' A ROSE
Ivy de Roe

08656
NELL
Hal Martin

08657
BECAUSE

08658
WHEN THE LIGHT SHINES BRIGHTLY IN
THE LIGHTHOUSE

08659
COHEN ON THE TELEPHONE
Hal Martin

08660
IF I DIDN'T MISS YOU

08661
GETTING A MOTOR
Hal Martin; Nella Elsa

08662
IT TAKES A GOOD MAN TO DO THAT

08663
SO THIS IS SPRING

08664
DADA DADA

08665
THE GREEN TIE ON THE LITTLE
YELLOW DOG
Hal Martin

08666
I'M EIGHTY IN THE MORNING

08667
ME AND THE MAN IN THE MOON

08668
KATE IN THE CALL BOX
Nella Elsa

08669
IN THAT VILLAGE DOWN THE VALLEY
UP THE HILL

08670
JOE MURGATROYD SAYS
Hal Martin

08671
MARY'S MAMMY

08672
POPULAR JOCULAR DR BROWN

08673
UNDER THE BAZUMKA TREE

08674
A CURTAIN LECTURE
Hal Martin; Nella Elsa
MUSICAL Actors mime to gramophone
records.

08675
BUNKERED (1962) (U) (Silent)
GP Productions (Fox)
P: W.H.Pay
D: Herbert Davis
Tubby Phillips . . . . The Husband
CHASE Henpeck poses as golf champion
to escape from wife.

08676
ST. GEORGE AND THE DRAGON (1585)
(U) (Silent)
Whitehall Films (Fox)

COMEDY Modern dress St George fights dragon but rejects princess after seeing her face.

08677
FROZEN FATE (5080) (U) (Silent)
British Screen Productions (JMG)
D:S: Ben R. Hart, St John L.Clowes
ADVENTURE Lapland. Boy killed skiing, his brother killed by pet reindeer, and father killed, too.

08678
BLACK WATERS (79) (A)
British & Dominions-Sono Art World Wide (W & F)
P: Herbert Wilcox
D: Marshall Neilan
S: (PLAY) John Willard (FOG)
James Kirkwood . . .   Tiger Larabee/Kelly
Mary Brian . . . .   Eunice
John Loder . . . .   Charles
Hallam Cooley . . . .   Elmer
Frank Reicher . . . .   Randall
Lloyd Hamilton . . . .   Temple
Robert Ames . . . .   Darcy
Ben Hendricks . . . .   Olaf
Noble Johnson . . . .   Jeelo
CRIME Mad captain poses as cleric to murder people aboard fogbound ship. (Made in USA).

JUN

08679
THE UNWRITTEN LAW (30) (U)
BSFP (BIFD)
D: Sinclair Hill
S: (PLAY) Violet Heckstall Smith
SC: Leslie Howard Gordon
Ion Swinley . . . .   Jake
Rosalinde Fuller . . . .   Bess
Robert Bruce . . . .   Policeman
Pat Williams . . . .   Villager
Edwin M. Robson . . . .   Villager
CRIME Devon. Girl shelters escaped convict and then discovers he killed her husband.

08680
THE THIRD GUN (36) (A)
BSFP (U)
D: Geoffrey Barkas
S: Michael Barringer
Randle Ayrton . . . .   Joe
Dora Gregory . . . .   Hannah
Patrick Ludlow . . . .   Robin
H. Saxon-Snell . . . .   Man
CRIME Poacher accidentally kills husband of woman he loves.

08681
BLACKMAIL (96) (A)
BIP (Wardour)
D: Alfred Hitchcock
S: (PLAY) Charles Bennett
SC: Charles Bennett, Benn W.Levy, Garnett Weston, Alfred Hitchcock
Anny Ondra . . . .   Alice White
(spoken by Joan Barry)
John Longden . . . .   Frank Webber
Donald Calthrop . . . .   Tracy
Cyril Ritchard . . . .   The Artist
Sara Allgood . . . .   Mrs White
Charles Paton . . . .   Mr White
Harvey Braban . . . .   Inspector
(Sam Livesey in silent version)
Phyllis Monkman . . . .   Gossip
Hannah Jones . . . .   Landlady
Percy Parsons . . . .   Crook
Johnny Butt . . . .   Sergeant

CRIME Detective's fiancee blackmailed for stabbing lecherous artist. (FWA: 1930; extract in ELSTREE STORY, 1952).

08682
ACCI-DENTAL TREATMENT (17) (U)
BSFP (BIFD) *reissue:* 1930 (FBO)
D: Thomas Bentley
S: (PLAY) Con West, Herbert Sargent (THE MOUSE TRAP)
Ernie Lotinga . . . .   Jimmy Josser
COMEDY Slapstick mishaps in a dentist's surgery.

08683
ELECTROCORD FILMS (3) (U)
Electrocord (Butcher)
D: Dave Aylott, E.F.Symmons

08684
THE GAY CABALLERO

08685
MY BONNIE HIELAND MAGGIE

08686
YOU WENT AWAY TOO FAR

08687
SWEETHEARTS ON PARADE

08688
TWO BLACK CROWS

08689
OH YOU HAVE NO IDEA

08690
HINTON, DINTON AND MERE

08691
I LIFT UP MY FINGER AND I SAY TWEET TWEET

08692
HE LOVES AND SHE LOVES

08693
HOTPOT

08694
OH WHAT A HAPPY LAND

08695
IT ALL DEPENDS ON YOU

08696
MY AUSTIN SEVEN

08697
ONE KISS

08698
THAT'S WHAT PUT THE SWEET IN HOME SWEET HOME

08699
WOULD A MANX CAT WAG ITS TAIL IF IT HAD ONE ?

08700
SCENTED SOAP

08701
SOMEWHERE A VOICE IS CALLING

08702
I'LL TAKE YOU HOME AGAIN KATHLEEN
MUSICAL Actors mime to gramophone records.

JUL

08703
CITY OF PLAY (80) (A)
Gainsborough (W&F)
P: Michael Balcon
D:S: Denison Clift
SC: Denison Clift, Angus Macphail
Chili Bouchier . . . .   Ariel
Pat Aherne . . . .   Richard von Rolf
Lawson Butt . . . .   Tambourini
James Carew . . . .   Gen von Rolf
Andrews Englemann . . .   Col von Lessing
Leila Dresner . . . .   Zelah
Olaf Hytten . . . .   Schulz
Harold Huth . . . .   Arezzi
DRAMA Berlin. Circus hypnotist forces girl to do parachute jumps.

08704
TAXI FOR TWO (73) (U)
Gainsborough (W & F)
P: Michael Balcon
D: Alexander Esway, Denison Clift
S: Alexander Esway
Mabel Poulton . . . .   Molly
John Stuart . . . .   Jack Devenish
Gordon Harker . . . .   Albert
Renee Clama . . . .   Gladys
Anne Grey . . . .   Charlotte
Grace Lane . . . .   Lady Devenish
Claude Maxten . . . .   The Baron
COMEDY Lady's son poses as chauffeur to woo girl who buys taxi.

08705
DOWNSTREAM (6053) (U) (Silent)
Carlton Films (WB)
P:D:S: Guarino G.Glavany
SC: Jane Tarlo, Richard deKeyser
Chili Bouchier . . . .   Lena
Harold Huth . . . .   Peter Carras
Marie Ault . . . .   Martha Jaikes
David Dunbar . . . .   Digger Brent
Judd Green . . . .   Tug Morton
Frank Dane . . . .   Crook
CRIME Tec poses as bargee to save girl from suicide and capture her crooked lover.

08706
UP THE POLL (8) (U)
BIP (Wardour)
D: R.E.Jeffrey
Donald Calthrop . . . .   The Candidate
COMEDY Bibulous election candidate makes speech.

08707
AN OLD WORLD GARDEN (10) (U)
BIP (Wardour) D: R.E.Jeffrey
Paul England . . . .   The Man
Mimi Crawford . . . .   The Girl
MUSICAL Singing lovers exchange vows amid ghosts of the past

08708
CHELSEA NIGHTS (12) (U)
BIP (Wardour)
D: R.E.Jeffrey
Carl Brisson . . . .   The Artist
Mimi Crawford . . . . .The Girl
Eugenie Prescott . . . .
The Jackson Girls
MUSICAL Artist laments absence of his sweetheart, who returns.

08709
MUSICAL MOMENTS (10) (U)
BIP (Wardour)
D: R.E.Jeffrey
Eric Randolph
Alma Vane
Norman Hackforth

Harris Sisters
MUSICAL Singing, dancing, and divertisement
at the piano.

08710
A SONG OR TWO (10) (U)
BIP (Wardour)
D: R.E.Jeffrey
Alma Vane
Eric Randolph
Norman Hackforth
Mavis Smith
MUSICAL Pot-pourri of modern song and
dance numbers.

08711
ME AND THE BOYS (6) (U)
BIP (Wardour)
D: Victor Saville
Estelle Brody
MUSICAL Song and dance. (Made in New York).

08712
BLACK AND WHITE (9) (U)
BIP (Wardour)
D: R.E.Jeffrey
Jackson & Blake
MUSICAL White man and Negro in crosstalk
and burlesque song.

AUG

08713
AN ARABIAN KNIGHT (9) (U)
BIP (Wardour)
D: R.E.Jeffrey
Paul England . . . . The Englishman
Alma Vane . . . . The Princess
MUSICAL Arabia. Englishman falls in love
with Eastern princess.

08714
JAZZTIME (9) (U)
BIP (Wardour)
D: R.E.Jeffrey
Jack Payne and the BBC Dance Band
MUSICAL "My sin;" "Everso goosey;"
"I'll never ask for more."

08715
ODD NUMBERS (7((U)
BIP (Wardour)
D: R.E.Jeffrey
Gwen Farrar
Billy Mayerl
MUSICAL 'Cello solo; duet, "Rain;"
Edgar Wallace monologue.

08716
NOTES AND NOTIONS (6) (U)
BIP (Wardour)
D: R.E.Jeffrey
Gwen Farrar
Billy Mayerl
MUSICAL "An oldfashioned girl;" "He's a
dangerous man."

08717
SONG-COPATION (9) (U)
BIP (Wardour)
D: R.E.Jeffrey
Patricia Rossborough
Bobbie Anderson
MUSICAL "Walking with Susie;" "Funny that
way;" "You can't make me feel blue."

08718
FLORA LE BRETON (9) (U)
BSFP (BIFD)

MUSICAL Two sentimental songs and an
impersonation of a cockney servant.

08719
DIMPLES AND TEARS (7) (U)
BSFP (BIFD) *reissue:* 1932, CAMERA
COCKTALES No. 3 (Hallmark)
D: Jack Harrison
Ottorino Gorno's Marionettes
COMEDY Film star puppets including
Al Jolson.

08720
AUNT MATILDA'S NEPHEW (1642) (U)
(Silent)
Cambridge University (Butcher)
E.A.Milne . . . . The Nephew
Veronique Lager . . . . Aunt Matilda
Leonard Claughton . . . . Hon Ginger Gung
COMEDY University student avoids visit
from aunt by having friend take his place.
(Amateur film shown professionally).

08721
HIGH TREASON (90) (A)
Gaumont
P:SC: L'Estrange Fawcett
D: Maurice Elvey
S: (PLAY) Noel Pemberton- Billing
Jameson Thomas . . . . Michael Deane
Benita Hume . . . . Evelyn Seymour
Basil Gill . . . . . President Stephen Deane
Humberston Wright. . . Vicar-General Seymour
Henry Vibart . . . . Lord Sycamore
James Carew . . . . Lord Rowleigh
Hayford Hobbs . . . . Charles Falloway
Milton Rosmer . . . . Ernest Stratton
Judd Green . . . . James Groves
Alf Goddard . . . . Soldier
Irene Rooke . . . . Senator
Clifford Heatherley . . . . . . Delegate
Wally Patch. . . . . Commissionaire
FANTASY 1940. Women unite to prevent
financiers from engineering second world war.

08722
THAT LASS OF CHANDLER'S (2000) (Silent)
North Wales Screen Productions
P:D:S: W.J. Sargent
Doris Ffoulkes-Griffith . . . The Girl
J.Adams . . . . The Sailor
ROMANCE Conway. Captain tries to stop his
daughter from marrying sailor. (Amateur
film shown professionally).

SEP

08723
UNDER THE GREENWOOD TREE (100) (U)
BIP (Wardour)
D: Harry Lachman
S: (NOVEL) Thomas Hardy
SC: Harry Lachman, Rex Taylor, Frank Laun-
der, Monckton Hoffe
Marguerite Allan . . . . Fancy Day
(spoken by Peggie Robb-Smith)
John Batten . . . . Dick Dewey
Nigel Barrie . . . . Shinar
Maud Gill . . . . Old Maid
Wilfred Shine . . . . Parson Maybold
Robert Abel . . . . Penny
Antonia Brough . . . . Maid
Tom Coventry . . . . Tranter Dewey
Robison Page . . . . Grandfather Dewey
Tubby Phillips . . . . Tubby
Billy Shine . . . . Leaf
Gotham Singers . . . . Quartette
MUSICAL Dorset, 1870. Girl organist is
blamed for ousting village choir.

08724
THE PLAYTHING (78) (A)
BIP (Wardour)
D: Castleton Knight
S: (PLAY) Arthur Black (LIFE IS PRETTY
MUCH THE SAME)
SC: Violet Powell
Estelle Brody . . . . Joyce Bennett
Heather Thatcher . . . . . . Martyn Bennett
Nigel Barrie . . . . Wallace McKinnel
Marguerite Allan . . . . . . Madeleine McKinnel
John St John . . . . Claud
Raymond Milland . . . . Ian
ROMANCE Scot acquires sophistication
in order to spurn socialite who spurned him.

08725
THE AMERICAN PRISONER (75) (U)
BIP (Wardour)
D: Thomas Bentley
S: (PLAY) Eden Philpotts
SC: Eliot Stannard, Garnett Weston
Carl Brisson . . . . Lt Stark
Madeleine Carroll . . . . Grace Malherb
Cecil Barry . . . . Peter Norcutt
Carl Harbord . . . . Lt Burnham
A.Bromley Davenport . . . Squire Malherb
Nancy Price . . . . Lovey Lee
Reginald Fox . . . . Capt Mainwaring
Charles Ashton . . . . Carberry
Harry Terry . . . . Bosun Knapps
John Valentine . . . . Cdr Miller
Robert English . . . . Col Governor
Edmond Dignon . . . . Leverett
CRIME Dartmoor, 1815. American prisoner of
war escapes and saves squire's daughter.

OCT

08726
THE DEVIL'S MAZE (82) (A)
Gaumont
P:D: V.Gareth Gundrey
S: (PLAY) G.R.Malloch (MOSTLY FOOLS)
SC: Sewell Collins
Renee Clama . . . . Frances Mildmay
Trilby Clark . . . . Barbara Carlton
Ian Fleming . . . . Derek Riffington
Hayford Hobbs . . . . Hon James Carlton
Gerald Rawlinson . . . . Robin Masters
Davy Burnaby . . . . Mr Fry
DRAMA Seduced girl blames her stillborn
baby on 'dead' explorer, who then returns.

08727
DARK RED ROSES (65) (A)
BSFP (BIFD)
D: Sinclair Hill
S: (STORY) Stacy Aumonier
SC: Leslie Howard Gordon, Harcourt
Templeman
Stewart Rome . . . . David Cardew
Frances Doble . . . . Laura Cardew
Hugh Eden . . . . Anton Falk
Una O'Connor . . . . Mrs Weeks
Kate Cutler . . . . Mother
Sydney Morgan . . . . Gardener
Jack Clayton . . . . Son
Jill Clayton . . . . Daughter
Anton Dolin; Lydia Lopokova; Georges
Balanchine.
DRAMA Sculptor tries to chop hands off
wife's pianist lover.

08728
A BROKEN ROMANCE (6854) (A) (Silent)
H.B.Parkinson (Fox)
D:S: J. Steven Edwards
William Freshman . . . . Jack Worth
Blanche Adele . . . . Mary Davies

Paul Neville . . . .   John Shund
Laura Smithson . . . .   Lalla Watkins
Colin Crop . . . .   Joe Davies
Picot Schooling . . . .   Catspaw
ROMANCE Welsh cripple stars in film
biography and meets the author she loves at
the trade show.

08729
LURE OF THE ATLANTIC (4550) (A) (Silent)
H.B.Parkinson (Fox)
D:S: Norman Lee
Eric Hales . . . .   The Reporter
Iris Darbyshire . . . .   The Wife
John St John . . . .   The Gambler
Fletcher Lightfoot . . . .   Alcock
Rex Barnett . . . .   Brown
DRAMA While Alcock and Brown fly the
Atlantic a reporter is robbed and a broke
gambler wins bet.

08730
A COTTAGE ON DARTMOOR (75) (A)
USA: ESCAPED FROM DARTMOOR
British Instructional (Pro Patria)
P: H. Bruce Woolfe
D:SC: Anthony Asquith
S: Herbert Price
Norah Baring . . . .   Sally
Uno Henning . . . .   Joe Ward
Hans Schlettow . . . .   Harry Stevens
Judd Green . . . .   Customer
CRIME Dartmoor. Farmer's wife shelters her
ex-lover when he breaks jail.

08731
NICK'S KNICKERS (4984) (U) (Silent)
G & S Films
P: Wilfred Gannon, John Scarborow
D:S: Wilf Gannon
Wilf Gannon . . . .   Nick
Hilda Sayer . . . .
COMEDY

08732
MEMORIES (10) (U)
BIP (Wardour) *reissue:* 1930
D: R.E.Jeffrey
S: (POEM) John McCrae (IN FLANDERS
FIELDS)
Jameson Thomas
John Stuart
John Longden
Jack Raine
WAR Club members recall 1914-18 war and
hope for continuing peace.

08733
THE INFORMER (83) (A)
BIP (Wardour)
D: Arthur Robinson
S:(PLAY) Liam O'Flaherty
SC: Benn W.Levy, Rolfe E. Vanlo
Lya de Putti . . . .   Katie Fox
Lars Hansen . . . .   Gypo Nolan
Warwick Ward . . . .   Dan Gallagher
Carl Harbord . . . .   Francis McPhillip
Dennis Wyndham . . . .   Murphy
Janice Adair . . . .   Bessie
Daisy Campbell . . . .   Mrs McPhillip
Craighall Sherry . . . .   Mulholland
Ellen Pollock . . . .   Prostitute
Johnny Butt . . . .   Publican
CRIME Ireland, 1920. IRA man betrays a
killer to the police, thinking he is his
mistress's lover. (Extract in ELSTREE STORY,
1952).

08734
WHITE CARGO (88) (A)
Neo-Art Productions (WP)

P:D: J.B.Williams, Arthur Barnes
S: (PLAY) Leon Gordon (NOVEL) Vera
Simonton
SC: J.B.Williams
Leslie Faber . . . .   Weston
Gypsy Rhouma . . . .   Tondelayo
John Hamilton . . . .   Ashley
Maurice Evans . . . .   Langford
Henry de Vries . . . .   Skipper
Humberston Wright . . . . . .   Missioner
Sebastian Smith . . . .   Doctor
Tom Helmore . . . .   Worthing
George Turner . . . .   Mate
DRAMA Tropics. Manager of rubber plantation
marries native who tries to poison him.

08735
THE GLITTERING SWORD (1800) (U) (Silent)
Altrincham School
D:S: Ronald Gow
T.Hampson . . . .   Boy King
L.Galloway . . . .   Chancellor
H.Mitchell . . . .   Death
A.Gregory . . . .   Devil
FANTASY "High moral purpose conveyed
in entertaining fashion by apt allegory."
(Amateur film shown professionally).

NOV

08736
WOMAN TO WOMAN (90) (A)
Gainsborough-Burlington-Tiffany-Stahl (W&F)
P: Michael Balcon, Victor Saville
D:SC: Victor Saville
S: (PLAY) Michael Morton
Betty Compson . . . .   Lola
Juliette Compton . . . .   Vesta
George Barraud . . . .   David
Winter Hall . . . .   Dr Garvin
Marguerite Chambers . . . . .   Florence
George Billings . . . .   Little David
ROMANCE 1914. Amnesiac officer weds
barren socialite and adopts his son by French
ballerina. (Made in Hollywood).

08737
ROMANTIC ENGLAND (4538) (U) (Silent)
Cinema Exclusives (PDC)
P: Frank Wheatcroft
D: H.B.Parkinson
HISTORY Stories connected with six old inns.
(Shorts combined into feature)

08738
ALPINE MELODIES (7) (U)
BIP (Wardour)
D: R.E.Jeffrey
Mary & Ernst Frey-Bernharsgrutter
MUSICAL Yodelling songs.

08739
MUSICAL MEDLEY (8) (U)
BIP (Wardour)
D: R.E.Jeffrey
Patricia Rossborough   Charlot Girls
Bobbie Alderson   Teddy Brown
MUSICAL

08740
POT-POURRI (8) (U)
BIP (Wardour)
D: R.E.Jeffrey
Gladys Chalk & Partner   Teddy Brown
Margaret Donald   The Berkoffs
May & Ernst Grey-Bernharsgrutter
MUSICAL

08741
ARMISTICE (15) (U)
Gainsborough (W&F)

P: Michael Balcon
D: Victor Saville
S: (POEM) John McCrae (IN FLANDERS
FIELDS)
N: Henry Ainley
Bands of HM Coldstream and Welsh Guards
Male Voice Choir
MUSICAL Songs of the 1914-18 war.

08742
THE FEATHER (90) (A)
Strand Films (UA)
P: Julius Hagen
D:SC: Leslie Hiscott
S: (NOVEL) C.M.Matheson
Jameson Thomas . . . .   Roger Dalton
Vera Flory . . . .   Mavis Cottrell
Randle Ayrton . . . .   Rizzio
Mary Clare . . . .   Mrs Dalton
W.Cronin Wilson . . . .   Mr Cottrell
James Reardon . . . .   Quint
Charles Paton . . . .   Prof Vivian
Irene Tripod . . . .   Mrs Higgins
Grace Lane . . . .   Nun
ROMANCE Clerk embezzles to pay for girl's
singing lessons in Rome.

08743
THE CO-OPTIMISTS (83) (U)
New Era *reissue:* 1931 (as 6 shorts)
P: Gordon Craig
D: Edwin Greenwood, Laddie Cliff
S: (REVUE) Melville Gideon, Laddie Cliff
Davy Burnaby . . . . . .   Phyllis Monkman
Laddie Cliff . . . .   Betty Chester
Melville Gideon . . . . . .   Elsa MacFarlane
Gilbert Childs . . . . .   Peggy Petronella
Stanley Holloway . . . . . Harry S. Pepper
REVUE Film of stage performance.

08744
THOSE WHO LOVE (87) (A)
BIP (FN)
D: Manning Haynes
S: (NOVEL) Guy Fletcher (MARY WAS LOVE)
SC: Lydia Hayward
Blanche Adele . . . .   Mary/Lorna
William Freshman . . . .   David Mellor
Lawson Butt . . . .   Joe
Carol Goodner . . . .   Anne
Hannah Jones . . . .   Babe
Dino Galvani . . . .   Frenchman
ROMANCE Author marries married whore
because she resembles his dead fiancee.

08745
RIVERSIDE MELODIES (49) (U)
Electrocord (Butcher)
Alice Shepherd . . . .   The Girl
John Mustill . . . .   The Boy
MUSICAL Courting couple go boating on
Thames.

08746
YULE (16) (U)
Electrocord (Butcher)
D: Dave Aylott
Electrocord Choir
MUSICAL Old-fashioned choir sing carols
while children snowball old gentleman.

08747
THE PRIDE OF DONEGAL (6412) (U) (Silent)
H.B.Parkinson (Fox)
D: J. Steven Edwards
S: Norman Lee
Rex Sherren . . . .   Roland Terrence
Robina Maugham . . . .   Molly Cross
Syd Crossley . . . .   Mike O'Flanagan
Graeme Low . . . .   Blarney Stone

SPORT Ireland. Groom saves maimed racehorse from cruel carter and wins Grand National.

08748
OVER THE STICKS (3345) (U) (Silent)
Cinema Exclusives (Fox)
P: Frank Wheatcroft
D: G.B.Samuelson, A.E.Coleby
S: G.B.Samuelson
Tom Shelton . . . . Lord Burton
Molly Wright . . . .
Billy Phelps . . . .
SPORT Blackmailed owner feigns death and makes fortune as bookie.

08749
UNTO EACH OTHER (7564) (A) (Silent)
Cinema Exclusives (Fox)
P: Frank Wheatcroft
D:S: A.E.Coleby
Frederick Catling . . . . Capt Graham
Harry Lorraine . . . . Jim Webber
Yvonne Thomas . . . .
Josephine Earle . . . .
Frank Goldsmith. . . . .
Marie Wright . . . .
DRAMA Miner's life saved by man he saved during war.

08750
TO WHAT RED HELL (100) (A)
Strand Films -Twickenham (Tiffany)
P: Julius Hagen
D: Edwin Greenwood
S: (PLAY) Percy Robinson
SC: Leslie Hiscott
Sybil Thorndike . . . . Mrs Fairfield
John Hamilton . . . . Harold Fairfield
Bramwell Fletcher . . . . Jim Nolan
Jillian Sande . . . . Eleanor Dunham
Janice Adair . . . . Madge Barton
Arthur Pusey . . . . George Hope
Athole Stewart . . . . Mr Fairfield
Drusilla Wills . . . . Mrs Ellis
Wyn Weaver . . . . Dr Barton
Matthew Boulton . . . . Insp Jackson
CRIME Woman shelters epileptic son when he kills prostitute.

08751
ATLANTIC (90) (A) *trilingual*
BIP (Wardour) *reissue:* 1935 (EB)
P:D: E.A.Dupont
S: (PLAY) Ernest Raymond (THE BERG)
SC: Victor Kendall
Franklin Dyall . . . . John Rool
Madeleine Carroll . . . . Monica
John Stuart . . . . Lawrence
Ellaline Terriss . . . . Alice Rool
Monty Banks . . . . Dandy
Donald Calthrop . . . . Pointer
John Longden . . . . Lanchester
Arthur Hardy . . . . Maj Boldy
Helen Haye . . . . Clara Tate-Hughes
D.A.Clarke-Smith . . . . Freddie Tate-Hughes
Joan Barry . . . . Betty Tate-Hughes
Francis Lister . . . . Padre
Sydney Lynn . . . . Capt Collins
Syd Crossley . . . . Wireless Operator
Dino Galvani . . . . Steward
Danny Green . . . . Passenger
DRAMA Transatlantic passenger liner strikes iceberg and sinks. (Extract in ELSTREE STORY: 1952).

08752
ALF'S CARPET (65) (U)
BIP (Wardour)

D: W.P.Kellino
S: (NOVEL) W.A.Darlington
SC: Val Valentine, Arthur Leclerq, Blanche Metcalfe
Pat . . . . Bill
Patachon . . . . Alf
Janice Adair . . . . Joan
Gerald Rawlinson . . . . . Jimmy Donaldson
Gladys Hamer . . . . Lizzie Fletcher
Philip Hewland . . . . Djinn
Edward O'Neill . . . . Father
Frank Perfitt . . . . Caliph
COMEDY Busmen find magic carpet and save girl's father from caliph.

DEC

08753
THE HATE SHIP (83) (A) *bilingual*
BIP (FNP)
D: Norman Walker
S: (NOVEL) Bruce Graeme
SC: Monckton Hoffe, Eliot Stannard, Benn W.Levy
Jameson Thomas . . . . Vernon Wolfe
Jean Colin . . . . Sylvia Paget
Jack Raine . . . . Roger Peel
Henry Victor . . . . . . Count Boris Ivanoff
Randle Ayrton . . . . Capt MacDarrell
Edna Davies . . . . Lisette
Carl Harbord . . . . Arthur Wardell
Allan Jeayes . . . . Dr Saunders
Maria Minetti . . . . Countess Olga
Charles Dormer . . . . Nigel Menzies
Ivo Dawson . . . . Col Paget
Syd Crossley . . . . Rigby
CRIME Son of murdered Russian count invites suspects on revenge cruise.

08754
JUNO AND THE PAYCOCK (99) (A)
USA: THE SHAME OF MARY BOYLE
BIP (Wardour)
D: Alfred Hitchcock
S: (PLAY) Sean O'Casey
SC: Sean O'Casey, Alma Reville, Alfred Hitchcock
Sara Allgood , ... Juno Boyle
Edward Chapman . . . . . . .Capt John Boyle
Sydney Morgan . . . . Joxer Daly
John Longden . . . . Chris Bentham
Kathleen O'Regan . . . . Mary Boyle
John Laurie . . . . Johnny Boyle
Donald Calthrop . . . . Needle Nugent
Maire O'Neill . . . . Maisie Madigan
Dave Morris . . . . Jerry Devine
Fred Schwartz . . . . Kelly
Dennis Wyndham . . . . Mobiliser
Barry Fitzgerald . . . . Orator
DRAMA Dublin. Poor man's legacy fails to materialise and his armless son is shot as informer. (Extract in ELSTREE STORY, 1962).

08755
SPLINTERS (82) (U)
B&D (W&F)
P: Herbert Wilcox
D: Jack Raymond
S: W.P.Lipscomb
Nelson Keys
Sydney Howard
Lew Lake
Hal Jones
Reg Stone
George Baker
Wilfred Temple
Sidney Grantham
Walter Glynne

COMEDY France, 1915. Soldiers form concert party.

08756
THE LONE SCOUT (2500) (U) (Silent)
J.H.Martin Cross
D:S: J.H.Martin Cross
Cyril Chant . . . . The Scout
Ursula Chant . . . . His Sister
ADVENTURE Minehead. Boy Scouts. (Amateur film shown professionally).

08757
POPULAR PIECES (23) (U)
Electrocord (Butcher)
D: Dave Aylott
The Syncopation Wizards
Bill Sawyer
MUSICAL Songs and sketches, including "The Hole in the Road."

08758
AN OLD TIME MUSIC HALL (18) (U)
Electrocord (Butcher)
D: Dave Aylott
Nella Elsa
Hal Martin
Charles Picton
Sam B.Wood
MUSICAL Old actors recall days of Victorian music hall.

08759
MORE, PLEASE (27) (U)
Electrocord (Butcher)
D: Dave Aylott
MUSICAL Vaudeville numbers, dance band, and doll dance.

08760
EXPRESS LOVE (18) (U) ·
Alpha Film Corp
P: Maurice J. Wilson
D: Sasha Geneen
Heather Thatcher . . . . The Girl
Clifford Mollison . . . . The Man
COMEDY Rapid courtship in a railway train.

08761
THE KINGDOM OF TWILIGHT (8360) (U) (Silent)
Seven Seas (U)
P:D: Alexander Macdonald
Wendy Osborne . . . . . Dorothy Carrington
David Wallace . . . . . . Reginald Carewe
John Faulkner . . . . Jim Carrington
Rex Arnot . . . . McCrimmon
Len Norman . . . . Tanami
Laurel Macdonald . . . . Baby
Herrick Corbett . . . . Puggy Markham
ADVENTURE Australia. Explorer saves girl from natives and helps her find captured father.

1930

JAN

08762
GAINSBOROUGH GEMS (series) (U)
Gainsborough (JMG)
P: Michael Balcon

08763
1—MARTINI AND HIS BAND No. 1 (8)

08764
2—MARTINI AND HIS BAND No. 2 (9)

08765
3—BILLIE BARNES (9)

08766
4—GEORGE MOZART IN DOMESTIC
TROUBLES (6)

08767
5—HAL SWAIN AND HIS SAX-O-FIVE (8)

08768
6—ELSIE PERCIVAL AND RAY RAYMOND(8)

08769
7—PETE MANDELL AND HIS RHYTHM
MASTERS No. 1 (9)

08770
8—PETE MANDELL AND HIS RHYTHM
MASTERS No. 2 (8)

08771
9—DICK HENDERSON (9)

08772
10—THE BLUE BOYS No. 1 (9)

08773
11—THE BLUE BOYS No. 2 (8)

08774
12—LEWIS HARDCASTLE'S DUSKY
SYNCOPATERS (9)

08775
13—THE WALSH BROTHERS (9)

08776
14—THE VOLGA SINGERS (9)

08777
15—ENA REISS (9)
MUSICAL Songs, dances, comedy sketches.

08778
COMETS (68) (U)
Alpha (JMG)
P: Maurice J. Wilson
D: Sasha Geneen

Heather Thatcher	Billy Merson
Charles Laughton	Elsa Lanchester
Albert Sandler	Noni & Horace
Gladys Cruickshank	Gus McNaughton
Flora le Breton	Randle Ayrton
Jack Raine	Rex Evans
Tiller Girls	Strelsky's Cossacks
Melton Club Orchestra	Golden Serenaders

REVUE

FEB

08779
NAUGHTY HUSBANDS (5600) (A) (silent)
Geoffrey Benstead
P:D:S: Geoffrey Benstead

Patrick Ludlow	Willy
Nigel Cope	Dilly
James Reardon	Mr Luckylove
Sonia Kerr	Girl
Judd Green	Policeman

Claude Hulbert .... Client
COMEDY Convict dreams he runs marriage
agency and tries to supply wife for man already
married.

08780
SUGAR AND SPICE (series) (U)
Gainsborough (Ideal)
P: Michael Balcon
D: Alexander Oumansky

08781
1-AL FRESCO (17)
Hal Swain's Kit Kat Band
Elsie Carlisle
Prince Twins
Plaza Boys

08782
2—TOYLAND (17)
Bendetti Brothers
Kirke White
Sheila Fuller
Freddie Bartholomew

08783
3—BLACK AND WHITE (17)
Elsie Carlisle
Johnny Nit
Plaza Boys
Barrie Sisters
Hal Swain's Kit Kat Band

08784
4—CLASSIC V JAZZ (17)
Hal Swain's Kit Kat Band
Adajio Trio
Barrie Twins

08785
5—GYPSY LAND (17)
Balam
Sedelli
Valli
Adajio Trio

08786
6—DUSKY MELODIES (15)
Johnny Nit
Lew Hardcastle's Band
Gainsborough Girls
Iris Rowe
MUSICAL (Made as THE GAINSBOROUGH
PICTURE SHOW, but released as shorts only).

08787
STRANGER THAN FICTION (2336) (A)
silent
Mrs C.M. Wright (U)

George Foley	Farmer Denton
Nell Emerald	Mrs Denton
Harry Lorraine	Jack Denton
Margaret Hope	Mrs Thrale

DRAMA Farmer's sick wife dreams she shoots
housekeeper for flirting with husband and son.
(Date uncertain).

08788
LITTLE PEOPLE BURLESQUES (series) (U)
ASFI (Showman)
D: J. Elder Wills, Jack Harrison, John Grierson
Ottorino Gorno's Marionettes.

08789
1—DON DOUGIO FAIRABANCA (9)

08790
2—TOM MIXUP (10)

08791
3—KUSTER BEATON (10)

08792
4—KERRI CHEARTON IN JUNGLE-TUNGLE
(9)

08793
5—HERLOCK SHOLMES IN BE-A-LIVE
CROOK (8) retitled: ANNA WENT WRONG

08794
6—OUR DUMB FRIEND (15)
COMEDY Parodies of films and film stars
enacted by puppets.

08795
TAM O' SHANTER(9) (U)
BIP (Wardour)
D: R.E. Jeffrey
S: (POEM) Robert Burns
Gilbert McAllister
DRAMA Scotland. Man recites poem in village
inn.

08796
THE JOLLY FARMERS (9) (U)
BIP (Wardour)
D: R.E. Jeffrey
Tubby Phillips
Stanley Kirkby
Robert Chigwell
MUSICAL Sing-song in village inn.

08797
TELL TALES (10) (U)
BIP (Wardour)
D: R.E. Jeffrey
S: Seymour Hicks
Seymour Hicks
COMEDY Comedian tells funny stories.

08798
CHORAL CAMEOS (8) (U)
BIP (Wardour)
D: R.E. Jeffrey
Glasgow Orpheus Choir
MUSICAL

08799
A FEAST OF HARMONY (8) (U)
BIP (Wardour)
D: R.E. Jeffrey
Glasgow Orpheus Choir
MUSICAL

08800
GOODBYE TO ALL THAT (9) (U)
BIP (Wardour)
D: R.E. Jeffrey
MUSICAL Lovers quarrel over dancing.

08801
CLAUDE DEPUTISES (10) (U)
BIP (Wardour)
D: R.E. Jeffrey
S: (SKETCH) Claude Dampier
Claude Dampier .... The Pianist
Billie Carlisle .... The Singer
COMEDY Pianist accompanies stage singer at
short notice.

08802
THE COCKNEY SPIRIT IN THE WAR (series)(U)
Butcher's Film Service reissue: 1939, TOMMY
ATKINS (series)
P: F.W. Baker
D: Castleton Knight

08803
1—ALL RIOT ON THE WESTERN FRONT (22)
Donald Calthrop
Gordon Harker
Ambrose Thorne

Alexander Field
Melville Cooper
Whilfred Shine

08804
2—THE COCKNEY SPIRIT IN THE WAR
No. 2 (30)
John Hamilton
Donald Calthrop
Alf Goddard
Ambrose Thorne
Alexander Field

08805
3—THE COCKNEY SPIRIT IN THE WAR
No. 3 (21)
Donald Calthrop
John Hamilton
Aledander Field
Hal Gordon
Ambrose Thorne
COMEDIES Based on war stories by readers
of "Evening News". (Eps 1 and 2 combined
as 42-minute feature, July 1930).

08806
INFATUATION (35) (A)
Alpha
P: Maurice J. Wilson
D: Sascha Geneen
S: (PLAY) Julian Frank (THE CALL)
Godfrey Tearle . . . .   Gerald Norton
Jeanne de Casalis . . . .   Georgette
Jack Raine . . . .   David
Leslie Coles . . . .
Violet Campbell . . . .
Percy Williams . . . .
ROMANCE Youth falls for ageing actress and
discovers she is his mother.

08807
AN ELASTIC AFFAIR (10)
BIP (Film Weekly)
D: Alfred Hitchcock
Aileen Despard . . . .   The Girl
Cyril Butcher . . . .   The Boy
COMEDY Short sketch featuring winners of
the "Film Weekly" acting scholarship.

08808
THE SHAMING OF THE TRUE (5)
British Instructional (Cochran)
P: Charles B. Cochran
D: Walter Creighton
Maisie Gay . . . .   The Woman
Ada May . . . .
Charles B. Cochran's Young Ladies
COMEDY Woman in theatre audience objects to
film and joins in. (Made for "Charles B. Cochran's
1930 Revue").

08809
KNOWING MEN (88) (A) *Bilingual*
Talkicolor (UA)
P:D: Elinor Glyn
S: (NOVEL) Elinor Glyn
SC: Elinor Glyn, Edward Knoblock
Carl Brisson . . . .   George Vere
Elissa Landi . . . .   Korah Harley
Jeanne de Casalis . . . .   Delphine
Helen Haye . . . .   Marquise de Jarnais
C.M. Hallard . . . .   Marquis de Jarnais
Henry Mollison . . . .   Frank Bramber
Thomas Weguelin . . . .   Michelet
Marjorie Loring . . . .   Blanche
ROMANCE Paris. Heiress poses as marquise's
companion to avoid fortune-hunters. (Made in
colour but shown monochrome).

08810
AT THE VILLA ROSE (100) (A) *bilingual*

USA: MYSTERY AT THE VILLA ROSE
Twickenham (WB)
P: Julius Hagen, Henry Edwards
D:: Leslie Hiscott
S: (NOVEL) A.E.W. Mason
SC: Cyril Twyford
Norah Baring . . . .   Celia Harland
Austin Trevor . . . .   Insp Hanaud
Richard Cooper . . . .   Ricardo
Barbara Gott . . . .   Mme d'Avray
Francis Lister . . . .   Harry Wethermill
Amy Brandon Thomas . . . . . .Adele Starling
Violet Farebrother . . . .   Helen
CRIME France. Jewel thieves kill rich widow
and frame fake medium.

08811
AFTER MANY YEARS (6321) (U) (silent)
Savana (JMG)
P: Alvin Saxon
D:S: Lawrence,Huntington
Henry Thompson
Nancy Kenyon
Savoy Havana Band
CRIME Murdered policeman's son catches
drug-smuggling culprit in Peru.

08812
TERRORS (47) (U)
Erle O. Smith (U)
P:D:S: Erle O. Smith
Erle Smith jr
Ronald Smith
Graham Smith
FANTASY Scots boys tell how they tunnelled
to Australia and frighten prehistoric monsters
with bagpipes.

08813
ELSTREE CALLING (86) (U) *multilingual/
colour seq.*
BIP (Wardour)
D: Adrian Brunel, Alfred Hitchcock, Andre
Charlot, Jack Hulbert, Paul Murray
S: Adrian Brunel, Val Valentine, Walter C.
Mycroft
Will Fyffe   Cicely Courtneidge
Lily Morris   Jack Hulbert
Tommy Handley   Helen Burnell
Teddy Brown   Donald Calthrop
Anna May Wong   Jameson Thomas
Gordon Harker   John Longden
Bobbie Comber   Ivor McLaren
Hannah Jones   Three Eddies
Charlot Girls   Adelphi Girls
Berkoff Dancers   Kasbek Singers
REVUE Man strives to recieve television broadcast
from film studio.

08814
RAISE THE ROOF (77) (U)
BIP (FNP)
D: Walter Summers
Betty Balfour . . . .   Maisie Grey
Maurice Evans . . . .   Rodney Langford
Jack Raine . . . .   Atherley Armitage
Sam Livesey . . . .   Mr Langford
Ellis Jeffreys . . . .   Mrs Langford
Arthur Hardy . . . .   Croxley Bellairs
Dorothy Minto . . . .   Juanita
Charles Garry . . . .   Deighton Duff
Mike Johnson . . . .   Fred Frisco
Louie Emery . . . .   Mrs Warburton
Josephine Earle
Plaza Tiller Girls
MUSICAL Rich man bribes actress to ruin
son's touring revue.

08815
SLEEPING PARTNERS (87) (A)
Sageen (Par)

P: Sascha Geneen, Maurice J. Wilson
D:SC: Seymour Hicks
S: (PLAY) Sascha Guitry
Seymour Hicks . . . .   He
Edna Best . . . .   She
Lyn Harding . . . .   It
Herbert Waring . . . .   Emile
Marguerite Allan . . . .   Elise
David Paget . . . .   Virtuoso
COMEDY Neglected wife spends night with
roue after drinking sleeping draught.

08816
ROOKERY NOOK (76) (U) USA: ONE
EMBARRASSING NIGHT
B & D (W & F) reissue: 1932
P: Herbert Wilcox
D: Tom Walls, Byron Haskin
S: (PLAY) Ben Travers
SC: W.P. Lipscomb, Ben Travers
Ralph Lynn . . . .   Gerald Popkiss
Tom Walls . . . .   Clive Popkiss
Winifred Shotter . . . .   Rhoda Marley
Mary Brough . . . .   Mrs Leverett
J. Robertson Hare . . . .   Harold Twine
Ethel Coleridge . . . .   Mrs Twine
Griffith Humphreys . . . . . .   Mr Putz
Doreen Bendix . . . .   Poppy Dickey
Margot Grahame . . . .   Clara Popkiss
COMEDY Husband tries to hide runaway girl
from wife and mother-in-law (FWA: 1931).

08817
AMATEUR NIGHT IN LONDON (34) (U)
PDC
P: Gordon Bostock
D: Monty Banks
Billy Caryll . . . .   Man in the Box
Duncan & Godfrey . . . .   Sailor & Girl
Charlie Rego . . . .   Manager
Billie Rego . . . . Singing Fisherman
Plaza Boys . . . .   Highclass Hoofers
Don & Luis . . . .   Wouldbe Acrobats
Archie McCaig . . . .   Swell Comedian
Harry Rogers . . . .   Fiddler
Jessie Hitter . . . .   Serio Belle
James Barber . . . .   Swell
Tubby Phillips . . . .   Conductor
COMEDY Amateur talent competition held in
London theatre.

08818
EVE'S FALL (34) (U)
PDC
P: Gordon Bostock
D: Monty Banks
John Stuart . . . .   Jack Tremaine
Muriel Angelus . . . .   Eve Warren
Donald Stuart . . . .   Doctor
Joy Windsor . . . .
Irwin Twins
Happy Boys
Louise Blackburn
MUSICAL Girl with amnesia believes she is
bachelor's wife.

08819
RED PEARLS (6536) (A) (silent)
Nettlefold (Butcher)
P: Archibald Nettlefold
D: Walter Forde
S: (NOVEL) J. Randolph James (NEARER!
NEARER!)
SC: H. Fowler Mear
Lillian Rich . . . .   Sylvia Radshaw
Frank Perfitt . . . .   Gregory Marston
Arthur Pusey . . . .   Paul Gordon
Frank Stanmore . . . .   Martin Radshaw
Kyoshi Tekase . . . .   Tamira
CRIME Japanese merchant drives financier insane
by sending him letters from man he killed.

08820
THE DIZZY LIMIT (5722) (U) (silent)
Edward G. Whiting (PDC) reissue with sound:
KIDNAPPED
D:S: Edward Dryhurst
Jasper Maskeleyne . . . . Jasper Montague
Joy Windsor . . . . June
Wallace Bosco . . . . Woolf
Dino Galvani . . . . Pierpont
George Wilson . . . . Gus
Ian Wilson . . . . Callboy
COMEDY Jewel thief kidnaps conjuror's
assistant to win prize for box trick.

MAR

08821
THE COMPULSORY HUSBAND (84) (A)
BIP (Wardour)
D: Monty Banks
S: (NOVEL) John Glyder
SC: Rex Taylor, Val Valentine
Monty Banks . . . . Monty
Gladys Frazin . . . . Mrs Pilluski
Clifford Heatherley . . . . Mr Pilluski
Lillian Manton . . . . Joy
Trilby Clark . . . . Gilda
Reginald Fox . . . . Father
Janet Alexander . . . . Mother
Michael Powell . . . . Man
COMEDY Switzerland. Affianced man shelters
runaway wife and poses as her husband.

08822
SONG OF SOHO (96) (A)
BIP (ENP)
D: Harry Lachman
S: Harry Lachman, Val Valentine
SC: Arthur Wimperis, Randall Faye,
Frank Launder
Carl Brisson . . . . Carl
Edna Davies . . . . Camille
Donald Calthrop . . . . Nobby
Henry Victor . . . . Henry
Lucienne Herval . . . . Lucienne
Antonia Brough . . . . Antonia
Charles Farrell . . . . Legionnaire
Andrea Nijinski . . . . Dancer
MUSICAL Foreign legionnaire becomes cafe
singer in Soho and is framed for murder.

08823
HARMONY HEAVEN (61) (U) colour
BIP (Wardour)
D: Thomas Bentley
S: Arthur Wimperis, Randall Faye
Polly Ward . . . . Billie Breeze
Stuart Hall . . . . Bob Farrell
Trilby Clark . . . . Lady Violet Mistley
Jack Raine . . . . Stuart
Philip Hewland . . . . Beasley Cutting
Percy Standing . . . . Producer
Gus Sharland . . . . Stage Manager
Aubrey Fitzgerald . . . . Suggs
Edna Prince . . . . Singer
MUSICAL Girl helps composer win fame
despite flirtatious socialite.

08824
THE FLAME OF LOVE (82) (A) bilingual
BIP (Wardour)
P: Richard Eichberg
D: Richard Eichberg, Walter Summers
S: Monckton Hoffe, Ludwig Wolff
Anna May Wong . . . . Hai-tang
John Longden . . . . Lt Boris Boriskoff
George Schnell . . . . Grand Duke
Mona Goya . . . . Yvette
Percy Standing . . . . Col Moravjev

Fred Schwartz . . . . Birnbaum
J. Ley-On . . . . Wang Hu
MUSICAL Russia, 1913. Chinese dancer gives
herself to duke to save brother's life.

08825
THE LOVES OF ROBERT BURNS (96) (A)
B & D (W & F)
P:D: Herbert Wilcox
S: Reginald Berkeley
SC: Herbert Wilcox, P. Maclean Rogers
Joseph Hislop . . . . Robert Burns
Dorothy Seacombe . . . . Jean Armour
Eve Gray . . . . Mary Campbell
Nancy Price . . . . Posie Nancy
Jean Cadell . . . . Mrs Burns
C.V. France . . . . Lord Farquhar
Neil Kenyon . . . . Tam the Tinkler
George Baker . . . . Soldier
H. Saxon-Snell . . . . Gavin Hamilton
Craighall Sherry . . . . James Armour
Wilfred Shine . . . . Sailor
MUSICAL Scotland, 1786. Biography of
ploughboy poet.

08826
JUST FOR A SONG (94) (A) colour seq
Gainsborough (W & F)
P: Michael Balcon
D:SC: V. Gareth Gundrey
S: Desmond Carter
Lillian Davis . . . . Norma Wentworth
Roy Royston . . . . Jack
Constance Carpenter . . . . . . Jill
Cyril Ritchard . . . . Craddock
Nick Adams . . . . Agent
Syd Crossley . . . . Stage Manager
Dick Henderson
Rebla
Mangan Tillerettes
Syd Seymour's Mad Hatters
MUSICAL Jealous agent uses girl singer to
break up double act.

08827
ALF'S BUTTON (96) (U) colour seq
Gaumont
P:SC: L'Estrange Fawcett
D: W.P. Kellino
S: (PLAY) W.A. Darlington
Tubby Edlin . . . . Alf Higgins
Alf Goddard . . . . Bill Grant
Nora Swinburne . . . . Lady Isobel Fitzpeter
Polly Ward . . . . Liz
Humberston Wright . . . . Eustace
Gypsy Rhouma . . . . Lucy
Annie Esmond . . . . Mrs Gaskins
Peter Haddon . . . . Lt Allen
Cyril McLaglen . . . . Sgt-Major
Bruce Winston . . . . Mustapha
Spencer Trevor . . . . Lord Dunwater
Anton Dolin & Anna Ludmilla
Nervo & Knox
Gotham Quartette
COMEDY 1917. Soldier discovers button made
from Aladdin's lamp grants wishes when rubbed.

08828
THE NIGHT PORTER (55) (U)
Gaumont (Ideal)
P: L'Estrange Fawcett
D: Sewell Collins
S: (PLAY) Harry Wall
SC: Sewell Collins, L'Estrange Fawcett
Donald Calthrop . . . . The Porter
Trilby Clark . . . . The Wife
Gerald Rawlinson . . . . The Husband
Barbara Gott . . . .

Tom Shale . . . .
COMEDY Hotel porter mistakes honeymooners
for jewel thieves.

08829
A SISTER TO ASSIST 'ER (64) (U)
F.A. Thompson (Gau)
P: H.B. Parkinson
D:SC: George Dewhurst
S: (PLAY) John le Breton
Barbara Gott . . . . Mrs May
Pollie Emery . . . . Mrs McNash
Donald Stuart . . . . Alf
Alec Hunter . . . . Mr McNash
Charles Paton . . . . Thistlethwaite
Maud Gill . . . . Miss Pilbeam
Johnny Butt . . . . Sailor
COMEDY Poor woman poses as rich twin to
fool mean landlady.

08830
THE NEW WAITER (35) (U)
PDC
P: Andre Charlot
D: Monty Banks
Rebla . . . . The Waiter
Leonard Henry . . . . Fraser
Robert Hine . . . . Service
Quentin Tod . . . . Alphonse
Barrie Oliver
Betty Oliver
Joy Spring
Betty Frankiss
Charlot Girls
MUSICAL Drunken waiter unmasks nightclub
conjuror as thief.

08831
THE MUSICAL BEAUTY SHOP (35) (U)
PDC
P: Andre Charlot
D: Monty Banks
Leonard Henry . . . . Len
Ethel Baird . . . . Pam
Barrie Oliver . . . . Claribel
Pope Stamper . . . . John
Betty Oliver
Joy Spring
Charlot girls
MUSICAL Beauty salon owner puts on cabaret.

08832
THE HOUSE OF THE ARROW (76) (A)
Twickenham (WB)
P: Julius Hagen, Henry Edwards
D: Leslie Hiscott
S: (PLAY) A.E.W. Mason
SC: Cyril Twyford
Dennis Neilson Terry . . . . . . Insp Hanaud
Benita Hume . . . . Betty Harlow
Richard Cooper . . . . Jim Frobisher
Stella Freeman . . . . Ann Upcott
Wilfred Fletcher . . . . Wabersky
Toni de Lungo . . . . Maurice Thevent
Barbar Gott . . . . Mrs Harlow
Betty de Malero . . . . Francine
CRIME France. Inspector solves poisoning of
rich aunt.

08833
SCRAGS (5659) (U) (silent)
H.B. Parkinson (JMG)
D:SC: Challis Sanderson
S: Norman Lee
Eric Hales . . . . The Man
Bobbie Bradshaw . . . . The Girl
Augusto Sandoni . . . . The Tramp
ANIMAL Lost terrier saves man's daughter
and finds tramp master.

08834
THE WOMAN FROM CHINA (7410) (A)(silent)
Edward G. Whiting (JMG)
D:SC: Edward Dryhurst
S: Cory Sala (George Dewhurst)
Julie Suedo . . . . Laloe Berchmans
Gibb McLaughlin . . . . Chang-Li
Frances Cuyler . . . . Celia Thorburn
Tony Wylde . . . . Lt Jack Halliday
Kyoshe Takase . . . . Chinaman
R. Byron-Webber . . . . Berchmans
George Wynn . . . . Officer
Clifford Pembroke . . . . Snell
Laurie Leslie . . . . Garcia
CRIME Jealous wife helps Chinaman kidnap
lieutenant's fiancee.

08835
SOULS IN PAWN (2976) (U) (silent)
Cinema Exclusives (Fox)
P: Frank Wheatcroft
D: G.B. Samuelson
Robina Maugham . . . . The Woman
Biddy Phelps . . . . The Child
DRAMA Christmas causes rich man to forgive
daughter for marrying secretary.

08836
WE TWO (15) (U)
A.R. Morgan (JMG)
Pat & Eddy
MUSICAL Couple present dance act at audition.

08837
THE SAFE (11) (U)
Electrocord (Butcher)
D: Dave Aylott
S: (PLAY) W.P. Lipscomb
Phyllis Carr . . . . The Typist
Sam B. Wood . . . . The Lover
Bill Sawyer . . . . The Burglar
DRAMA Typist is shut in safe by married lover
and later freed by burglar.

08838
VARSITY (3852) (U) (silent)
Cambridge University
P: J.A. Combrinck Graaf
D: Stuart Legg
Geoffrey Beaumont . . . . Jack
J. Evans Hunter . . . . Bill
Barbara Lee . . . . Marjorie
Rene Ray . . . . Iris
DRAMA Cambridge. Student takes blame for
gambling brother. (Amateur film shown
professionally)

08839
PAINTED PICTURES (5158) (U) (silent)
Bernard Smith (Fox)
D:S: Charles Barnett
Haddon Mason . . . . John Marsh
Evelyn Spillsbury . . . . The Girl
Winifred Evans . . . . The Flirt
DRAMA Artist reforms weak friends by
painting their portraits. (Includes extracts
from THE BOOK OF PSALMS, 1927).

APR

08840
YOU'D BE SURPRISED! (64) (U)
Nettlefold (Butcher)
P: Archibald Nettlefold
D: Walter Forde
S: Walter Forde, H. Fowler Mear
Walter Forde . . . . Walter
Joy Windsor . . . . Maisie Vane
Frank Stanmore . . . . Frankie
Frank Perfitt . . . . Major

Douglas Payne . . . . Convict 99
COMEDY Songwriter in fancy dress mistaken
for escaped convict.

08841
NOT SO QUIET ON THE WESTERN FRONT
(50) (U)
BIP (Wardour)
D: Monty Banks
S: Syd Courtenay, Lola Harvey
SC: Victor Kendall
Leslie Fuller . . . . Bill Smith
Mona Goya . . . . Fifi
Wilfred Temple . . . . Bob
Stella Browne . . . . Yvonne
Gladys Cruickshank . . . . Mimi
Gerald Lyley . . . . Pte Very
Dmitri Vetter . . . . Pte John Willie
Syd Courtenay . . . . Lieut
Frank Melroyd . . . . Sgt
Marjorie Loring . . . . Diane
Olivette . . . . Dancer
MUSICAL Cook recalls night spent in French
estaminet in 1915.

08842
THE MESSAGE (28) (A)
Gaumont
P: L'Estrange Fawcett
D: Sewell Collins
S: (STORY) Brandon Fleming
SC: Sewell Collins, Ralph Gilbert Bettinson
Arthur Wontner . . . . Sir John Craig
Rosalinde Fuller . . . . Mrs Hamilton
Frederick Leister . . . . Insp Hudson
CRIME Jewel thief escapes from prison to
shoot crooked lawyer.

08843
JOURNEY'S END (120) (A)
Gainsborough-Welsh-Pearson-Tiffany (W & F)
P: George Pearson
D: James Whale
S: (PLAY) R.C. Sheriff
SC: Joseph Moncure March, V. Gareth Gundrey
Colin Clive . . . . Capt Denis Stanhope
Ian Maclaren . . . . Lt Osborne
David Manners . . . . .2nd Lt James Raleigh
Billy Bevan . . . . 2nd Lt Trotter
Anthony Bushell . . . . 2nd Lt Hibbert
Robert Adair . . . . Capt Hardy
Charles Gerrard . . . . Pte Mason
Tom Whiteley . . . . Sgt Major
Jack Pitcairn . . . . Colonel
Warner Klinger . . . . Prisoner
WAR France, 1917. Alcoholic captain afraid
that new replacement, his sweetheart's brother,
will betray his downfall (Made in Hollywood).

08844
THE JERRY BUILDERS (30) (U)
PDC
P: Gordon Bostock
D: Monty Banks
S: (PLAY) (JERRY & CO)
George Graves . . . . Nightwatchman
Barrie Oliver . . . . Husband
Collinson & Dean
Miles Clifton
Harry Taft
Tubby Phillips
Billy Reeves
The Rego Twins
COMEDY Newlyweds are old by the time their
house is built.

08845
PEACE OF MIND (4) (U)
B & D (W & F)

P: Herbert Wilcox
Walter Glynne
Sydney Coltham
George Baker
MUSICAL Pierrot trio.

MAY

08846
GREEK STREET (85) (A) USA: LATIN
LOVE
Gaumont
P: L'Estrange Fawcett
D: Sinclair Hill
S: Robert Stevenson
SC: Ralph Gilbert Bettinson, Leslie Howard
Gordon
Sari Maritza . . . . Anna
William Freshman . . . . Rikki
Martin Lewis . . . . Mansfield Yates
Bert Coote . . . . Sir George Ascot
Renee Clama . . . . Lucia
Bruce Winston . . . . Max
Peter Haddon . . . . Business Man
Rex Maurice . . . . Business Man
Stanelli . . . . Business Man
Max Rivers Trocadero Girls
MUSICAL Soho restaurateur's protege becomes
star.

08847
HIS FIRST CAR (35) (U)
PDC
D: Monty Banks
S: (SKETCH) Lauri Wylie
SC: Brock Williams
George Clarke . . . . George
Mamie Watson . . . . His Wife
Cyril Smith . . . . Salesman
Billy Tasker . . . . Manager
Norah Dwyer . . . . Customer
COMEDY Husband wins £200 and buys car.

08848
PICCADILLY NIGHTS (90) (U)
Kingsway General (FBO)
P:D: Albert H. Arch
S: Albert H. Arch, Roger Burford
Billie Rutherford . . . . Billie
Elsie Bower . . . . Eslie
Julian Hamilton . . . . Jackson
June Grey . . . . Dolly
Pat Courtney . . . . Eros
Maurice Winnick and his Orchestra
Ralph Goldsmith and his Band
MUSICAL Girl singer makes good when star
too drunk to appear.

08849
WOLVES (56) (U) USA: WANTED MEN
B & D (W & F)
P: Herbert Wilcox
D: Albert de Courville
S: (PLAY) Georges Toudouze
SC: Reginald Berkeley
Dorothy Gish . . . . Leila McDonald
Charles Laughton . . . . Job
Malcolm Keen . . . . Pierre
Arthur Margetson . . . . Mark
Andrews Engelmann . . . . . .
Franklyn Bellamy . . . . Pablo
Betty Bolton . . . .
CRIME Labrador. Outlaw leader fakes draw
for sick girl so he can help her escape.

JUN

08850
LOOSE ENDS (95) (A)
BIP (Wardour)

S: (PLAY) Dion Titherage
SC: Dion Titheradge, Norman Walker
Edna Best . . . . Nina Grant
Owen Nares . . . . Malcolm Forrest
Miles Mander . . . . Raymond Carteret
Adrianne Allen . . . . Brenda Fallon
Donald Calthrop . . . . Winton Penner
Edna Davies . . . . Deborah Price
Sybil Arundale . . . . Sally Britt
J. Fisher White . . . . Stranger
Gerard Lyley . . . . Cyril Gayling
CRIME Girl reporter blackmailed for learning
that man is freed murderer.

08851
THE 'W' PLAN (105) (U)
BIP Burlington (Wardour)
P:D: Victor Saville
S: (NOVEL) Graham Seton
SC: Victor Saville, Miles Malleson, Frank
Launder
Brian Aherne . . . . Col Duncan Grant
Madeleine Carroll . . . . Rosa Hartmann
Gordon Harker . . . . Pte Waller
Gibb McLaughlin . . . . Pte McTavish
George Merritt . . . . Ulrich Muller
Mary Jerrold . . . . Frau Muller
C.M. Hallard . . . . C-in-C
Frederick Lloyd . . . . Col Jervois
Clifford Heatherley . . . . Proprietor
Norah Howard . . . . Lady of the Town
Milton Rosmer . . . . President
Alfred Drayton . . . . Prosecution
Charles Paton . . . . Defence
Cameron Carr . . . . Otto Geddern
Robert Harris . . . . Subaltern
WAR British spy helps prisoners of war destroy
Germans' secret tunnels.

08852
THE NIPPER (84) (U) *trilingual*
retitled: THE BRAT
Betty Balfour Pictures (UA)
P: Betty Balfour
D: Louis Mercanton
S: (PLAY) Michel Carre, A. Acremont (LA
MOME)
SC: Reginald Berkeley, Donovan Parsons
Betty Balfour . . . . The Nipper
John Stuart . . . . Max Nicholson
Anne Grey . . . . Clarissa Wentworth
Alf Goddard . . . . Alf Green
Gibb McLaughlin . . . . Bill Henshaw
Percy Parsons . . . . Joubert
Helen Haye . . . . Lady Sevenoaks
Louis Goodrich . . . . Woolf
MUSICAL Producer makes star of cockney waif
who tried to rob him.

08853
BEDROCK (39) (A)
Piccadilly (Par)
P:D: Carlyle Blackwell
S: Michael Arabian
SC: Noel Shammon
Carlyle Blackwell . . . . Jim Parke
Sunday Wilshin . . . . Bella
Alexander Field . . . . Jonas
Wilfred Fletcher . . . . Andrew
Barbar Gott . . . . Proprietress
Jane Baxter . . . . Rosie
DRAMA Canadian returns to find fiancee
married and schemes revenge.

08854
THE WOODPIGEON PATROL (4000) (U)
(silent)
Pro Patria
D:S: Ralph Smart, F.R. Lucas

Arthur Villiesid
Maurice Walter
J.A. Hewson
Lord Baden-Powell . . . . Himself
ADVENTURE Adventures of Boy Scout patrol.

08855
THE SQUEAKER (90) (A)
British Lion
P:S.W. Smith
D:SC: Edgar Wallace
S: (PLAY) Edgar Wallace
Percy Marmont . . . . Capt Leslie
Anne Grey . . . . Beryl Stedman
Gordon Harker . . . . Bill Annerley
Trilby Clark . . . . Millie Trent
Alfred Drayton . . . . Lew Friedman
Eric Maturin . . . . Frank Sutton
Nigel Bruce . . . . Collie
W. Cronin Wilson . . . . Inspector
CRIME Tec poses as exconvict to expose head
of benevolent society as fence.

08856
THE LAST HOUR (75) (U)
Nettlefold (Butcher)
P: Archibald Nettlefold
D: Walter Forde
S: (PLAY) Charles Bennett
SC: H. Fowler Mear
Stewart Rome . . . . Prince Nicola
Richard Cooper . . . . Byron
Kathleen Vaughan . . . . Mary Tregellis
Alexander Field . . . . Smarty Walker
Wilfred Shine . . . . Tregellis
James Raglan . . . . Charles Lister
George Bealby . . . . Blumfeldt
Frank Arlton . . . . George
Billy Shine . . . . Ben
CRIME Crooked prince uses death ray to force
down airships and steal cargo.

JUL

08857
THE PRICE OF THINGS (84) (A)
Elinor Glyn (UA)
P:D: Elinor Glyn
S: (NOVEL) Elinor Glyn
SC: Lady Rhys Williams
Elissa Landi . . . . Anthea Dane
Stewart Rome . . . . Dick Hammond
Walter Tennyson . . . . . . John Courtenay Dare
Alfred Tennyson . . . . Courtenay John Dare
Mona Goya . . . . .Natasha Boleska
Dino Galvani . . . . Hunya
Marjorie Loring . . . . Daphne
CRIME Duke's twin takes place at wedding when
he is drugged by spies.

08858
ONE FAMILY (70) (U)
Empire Marketing Board (Pro Patria)
D: Walter Creighton
Douglas Beaumont . . . . The Boy
Sam Livesey . . . . The Policeman
Michael Hogan . . . . The Father
Joan Maude . . . . The Mother
Phyllis Neilson-Terry . . . . . Australia
Lady Keble . . . . Canada
Lady Ravensdale . . . . New Zealand
Lady Carlisle . . . . South Africa
Lady Lavery . . . . Irish Free State
Miss Dadabhoy . . . . India
ADVENTURE Schoolboy dreams PC takes him
around Buckingham Palace and the Empire.

08859
NO EXIT (69) (U)
Warner Bros

D:S: Charles Saunders
John Stuart . . . . Bill Alden
Muriel Angelus . . . . Ann Ansell
James Fenton . . . . Mr Ansell
Janet Alexander . . . . Mrs Ansell
John Rowal . . . . Harry Matthews
ROMANCE Publisher's daughter mistakes poor
author for rich novelist.

08860
SYMPHONY IN TWO FLATS (86) (A)
Gainsborough (Gaumont)
P: Michael Balcon
D: V. Gareth Gundrey
S: (PLAY) Ivor Novello
SC: V. Gareth Gundrey, Angus Macphail
Ivor Novello . . . . David Kennard
Benita Hume . . . . Leslie Fullerton
(Jacqueline Logan . . . . Leslie Fullerton in
USA version)
Cyril Ritchard . . . . Leo Chavasse
Renee Clama . . . . Elsie
Minnie Rayner . . . . Mabel
Maidie Andrews . . . . Miss Trebelly
Clifford Heatherley . . . . Wainwright
Ernest A. Dagnall . . . . Bradfield
Alex Scott-Gatty . . . . Dr Mortimer
Jack Payne and the BBC Dance Band
DRAMA Blind composer's wife does not tell
him his competition entry failed.

08861
SANDY THE FIREMAN (11) (U)
First National (WB)
S: (SKETCH) Sandy Powell
Sandy Powell . . . . Sandy
COMEDY Shopkeeper and small girl report
fire to reluctant fireman.

08862
SUSPENSE (81) (A)
BIP (Wardour)
D:SC: Walter Summers
S: (PLAY) Patrick MacGill
Mickey Brantford . . . . . . Pte Reggie Pettigrew
Cyril McLaglen . . . . Sgt McCluskey
Jack Raine . . . . Capt Wilson
D. Hay Petrie . . . . Scruffy
Fred Groves . . . . Pte Lomax
Percy Parsons . . . . Pte Alleluia Brett
Syd Crossley . . . . Cpl Brown
Hamilton Keene . . . . Officer
WAR France, 1914. Soldiers hide in dugout near
German mining operations.

08863
YOUNG WOODLEY (79) (A)
BIP (Wardour)
D: Thomas Bentley
S: (PLAY) John Van Druten
SC: John Van Druten, Victor Kendall
Madeleine Carroll . . . . Laura Simmons
Frank Lawton . . . . Woodley
Sam Livesey . . . . Mr Simmons
Gerald Rawlinson . . . . Milner
Billy Milton . . . . Vining
Aubrey Mather . . . . Mr Woodley
John Teed . . . . Ainger
Tony Halfpenny . . . . Cope
Rene Ray . . . . Kitty
DRAMA Schoolboy falls in love with teacher's
young wife.

08864
TWO WORLDS (110) (A) *trilingual*
BIP (Wardour) *reissue:* 1935 (EB)
P:D: E.A. Dupont
S: E.A. Dupont, Thekla von Bodo
SC: Miles Malleson, Norbert Falk, Franz Schulz

Norah Baring . . . . . . Esther Goldscheider
John Longden . . . . . . Lt Stanistaus von Zaminsky
Donald Calthrop . . . . Mendel
Randle Ayrton . . . . Simon Goldscheider
Constance Carpenter . . . . . . Mizzi
C.M. Hallard . . . . Col von Zaminsky
Jack Trevor . . . . Capt Stanislaus
Andrews Englemann . . . . . . Lieut
Gus Sharland . . . . Major
Boris Ranevsky . . . . Ensign
Georges Marakoff . . . . Colonel
John Harlow . . . . Corporal
Teddy Hill
Meinhard Juenger
Mirjam Elias
WAR Old Jew is forced to hide the Austrian lieut who killed his son and loves his daughter.

08865
LORD RICHARD IN THE PANTRY (95) (U) bilingual
Twickenham (WB)
P: Julius Hagen, Henry Edwards
D: Walter Forde
S: (PLAY) Sidney Blow, Douglas Hoare
SC: H. Fowler Mear
Richard Cooper . . . . Lord Richard Sandridge
Dorothy Seacombe . . . . Sylvia Garland
Marjorie Hume . . . . Lady Violet Elliott
Leo Sheffield . . . . Carter
Fred Volpe . . . . Sir Charles Bundleman
Barbara Gott . . . . Cook
Alexander Field . . . . Sam
Viola Lyel . . . . Evelyn Lovejoy
Gladys Hamer . . . . Gladys
COMEDY Poor lord poses as butler to avoid framed arrest for theft.

AUG
08866
TOO MANY CROOKS (38) (U)
George King (Fox)
D: George King
S: Basil Roscoe
SC: Billie Bristow
Laurence Olivier . . . . The Man
Dorothy Boyd . . . . The Girl
A. Bromley Davenport . . . . The Man Upstairs
Arthur Stratton . . . . The Burglar
Ellen Pollock . . . . Rose
Mina Burnett . . . . The Maid
COMEDY Broke playboy lets flat, burgles it, and catches spy.

08867
THE YELLOW MASK (95) (U)
BIP (Wardour) reissue: 1935 (EB)
D: Harry Lachman
S: (PLAY) Edgar Wallace (TRAITORS' GATE)
SC: Val Valentine, Miles Malleson, George Arthurs, Walter C. Mycroft, W. David
Lupino Lane . . . . Sam Slipper
Dorothy Seacombe . . . . Mary Trayne
Warwick Ward . . . . Li San
Haddon Mason . . . . Ralph Carn
Wilfred Temple . . . . John Carn
Frank Cochrane . . . . Ah Sing
Wallace Lupino . . . . Steward
William Shine . . . . Sunshine
Winnie Collins . . . . Molly
MUSICAL Chinese potentate seals crown jewels from Tower of London.

08868
MURDER (108) (A) bilingual
BIP (Wardour)
D: Alfred Hitchcock
S: (PLAY) Clemence Dane, Helen Simpson (ENTER SIR JOHN)

SC: Alfred Hitchcock, Alma Reville, Water C. Mycroft
Herbert Marshall . . . . Sir John Menier
Norah Baring . . . . Diana Baring
Phyllis Konstam . . . . Dulcie Markham
Edward Chapman . . . . Ted Markham
Miles Mander . . . . Gordon Druce
Esme Percy . . . . Handel Fane
Donald Calthrop . . . . Ion Stewart
Amy Brandon Thomas . . . . Defence
Marie Wright . . . . Miss Mitcham
Hannah Jones . . . . Mrs Didsome
Una O'Connor . . . . Mrs Grogram
R.E. Jeffrey . . . . Foreman
Violet Farebrother . . . . Mrs Ward
Kenneth Kove . . . . Matthews
Gus McNaughton . . . . Tom Trewitt
CRIME Juror investigates touring company to prove convicted actress did not kill actor's wife. (Extract in ELSTREE STORY).

08869
KISS ME SERGEANT (56) (U)
BIP (Wardour)
D: Monty Banks
S: (PLAY) Syd Courtenay, Lola Harvey (THE IDOL OF MOOLAH)
SC: Val Valentine
Leslie Fuller . . . . Bill Biggles
Gladys Cruickshank . . . . . . Kitty
Gladys Frazin . . . . Burahami
Syd Courtenay . . . . Lieut
Mamie Holland . . . . Fanny Adams
Frank Melroyd . . . . Colonel
Lola Harvey . . . . Colonel's Wife
Roy Travers . . . . Sgt
Olivette
Marika Rokk
Gotham Quartette
COMEDY India. Soldier saves jewelled eye of sacred idol.

08870
ASHES (23) (U)
Gainsborough (Ideal)
P: Michael Balcon
D: Frank Birch
S: M.D. Lyon, Claude Soman
SC: Angus Macphail
Ernest Thesiger . . . . Announcer
Herbert Mundin . . . . Cricketer
Babs Valerie . . . . Girl
M.D. Lyon . . . . Cricketer
Elsa Lanchester . . . . Girl
COMEDY Lords. Slow cricket match starts in 1940 and finishes in 2000.

08871
ON APPROVAL (98) (A)
B & D (W & F)
P: Herbert Wilcox
D: Tom Walls
S: (PLAY) Frederick Lonsdale
SC: W.P. Lipscomb
Tom Walls . . . . Duke of Bristol
Yvonne Arnaud . . . . Maria Wislak
Winifred Shotter . . . . Helen Hayle
Edmond Breon . . . . Richard Wemys
Mary Brough . . . . Emerald
Robertson Hare . . . . Hedworth
COMEDY Broke duke and millionairess try month of trial marriage.

SEP
08872
THE ROAD TO FORTUNE (60) (U)
Starcraft (Par)
P:D: Arthur Varney
S: (NOVEL) Hugh Broadbridge (MOORLAND TERROR)

SC: Hugh Broadbridge
Guy Newall . . . . Guy Seaton
Doria March . . . . June Eastman
Florence Desmond . . . . . . Toots Willoughby
Stanley Cooke . . . . Prof Kingsbury
George Vollaire . . . . Dr Killick
J.H. Wakefield . . . . Willard
Jean Lester . . . . Miss Lurcher
CRIME Cornwall. Girl is saved from crime by rejected lover.

08873
CROSS ROADS (58) (A)
British Projects (Par)
P:S: Reginald Fogwell, A.E. Bundy
D: Reginald Fogwell
Percy Marmont . . . . Jim Wyndham
Anne Grey . . . . Mary Wyndham
Betty Faire . . . . The Other Woman
Langhorne Burton . . . . . . The Lawyer
Wilfred Shine . . . . The Father
DRAMA Mother thwarts daughter's elopement with story of how wife shot her errant husband.

08874
SPANISH EYES (71) (U) bilingual
Julian Wylie-Ulargui (MGM)
D: G.B. Samuelson
Edna Davies . . . . Estrella
Dennis Noble . . . . Amalio
Donald Calthrop . . . . Mascoso
Anthony Ireland . . . . Chechester
Antonia Brough . . . . Landlady
MUSICAL Busker adopts blind child who is cured by impresario.

08875
FRENCH LEAVE (92) (U)
D & H Productions (Sterling)
P: Henry Defries, Sam Harrison
D: Jack Raymond
S: (PLAY) Reginald Berkeley
SC: Reginald Berkeley, W.P. Lipscomb
Madeleine Carroll . . . . Dorothy Glenister
Sydney Howard . . . . Cpl Sykes
Arthur Chesney . . . . Gen Root
Haddon Mason . . . . Capt Harry Glenister
Henry Kendall . . . . Lt George Graham
George de Warfaz . . . . Jules Marnier
May Agate . . . . Mme Denaux
George Owen . . . . Pte Jenks
COMEDY France, 1915. Girl poses as French maid to be near husband.

08876
THAT'S HIS WEAKNESS (1900) (U) (silent)
Argyle Art Pictures (EB)
P:D:S: John F. Argyle
Ernest Bakewell . . . . Professor
COMEDY Mad Prof's shrewish wife finds him at fair with actress.

08877
ESCAPE (69) (A)
ATP (Radio)
P:D:SC: Basil Dean
S: (PLAY) John Galsworthy
Sir Gerald du Maurier . . . . .Capt Matt Denant
Edna Best . . . . Shingled Lady
Gordon Harker . . . . Convict
Horace Hodges . . . . Gentleman
Madeleine Carroll . . . . Dora
Mabel Poulton . . . . Girl of the Town
Lewis Casson . . . . Farmer
Ian Hunter . . . . Detective
Austin Trevor . . . . Parson
Marie Ney . . . . Grace
Felix Aylmer . . . . Governor
Ben Field . . . . Captain
Fred Groves . . . . Shopkeeper

Nigel Bruce . . . . Constable
S.J. Warmington . . . . Warder
Phyllis Konstam . . . . Wife
Ann Casson . . . . Girl
George Curzon . . . . Constable
CRIME Dartmoor. Escaped convict helped by various people.

08878
LONDON MELODY (58) (U)
British Screen Productions (AF)
D:S: Geoffrey Malins, Donald Stuart
Lorraine La Fosse . . . . Molly Smith
Haddon Mason . . . . Sam Austin
Betty Naismith . . . . Betty Smith
Ballard Berkeley . . . . Jan Moor
David Openshaw . . . . Singer
MUSICAL Agent loves girl posing as French revue star.

08879
THE SCHOOL FOR SCANDAL (76) (U)
raycol
Albion (Par)
P:D: Maurice Elvey
S: (PLAY) Richard Brinsley Sheridan
SC: Jean Jay
Basil Gill . . . . Sir Peter Teazle
Madeleine Carroll . . . . Lady Teazle
Ian Fleming . . . . Joseph Surface
Henry Hewitt . . . . Charles Surface
Edgar K. Bruce . . . . Sir Oliver Surface
Hayden Coffin . . . . . Sir Harry Bumper
Hector Abbas . . . . , . . Moses
Dodo Watts . . . . Maria
Anne Grey . . . . Lady Sneerwell
John Charlton . . . . Benjamin Backbite
Stanley Lathbury . . . . Crabtree
Henry Vibart . . . . Squire Hunter
May Agate . . . . Mrs Candour
Maurice Braddell . . . . Careless
Gibb McLaughlin . . . . William
Wallace Bosco . . . . Rawley
COMEDY 1777. Rich man poses as usurer to decide who shall be his heir.

08880
CANARIES SOMETIMES SING (80) (A)
B & D (W & F)
P: Herbert Wilcox
D: Tom Walls
S: (PLAY) Frederick Lonsdale
SC: W.P. Lipscomb
Tom Walls . . . . Geoffrey Lymes
Yvonne Arnaud . . . . Elma Melton
Cathleen Nesbitt . . . . Anne Lymes
Athole Stewart . . . . Ernest Melton
COMEDY Married playwright falls in love with best friend's wife.

08881
CASTE (70) (U)
Harry Rowson (UA)
P: Jerome Jackson
D: Campbell Gullan
S: (PLAY) T.W. Robertson
SC: Michael Powell
Hermione Baddeley . . . . Polly Eccles
Nora Swinburne . . . . Esther Eccles
Alan Napier . . . . Capt Hawtree
Sebastian Shaw . . . . Hon George d'Alroy
Ben Field . . . . Albert Eccles
Edward Chapman . . . . Sam Gerridge
Mabel Terry-Lewis . . . . Marquise
COMEDY 1914. Cockney drunkard's daughter weds marquise's son who is presumed killed in war.

08882
FLAMES OF FEAR (5655) (U) (silent)
Argyle Art Pictures (EB)
P: S: John F. Argyle
D: Charles Barnett
John Argyle . . . . Bob
Nancy Stratford . . . . Mary
Ernest Bakewell . . . . Bert
Bessie Richards . . . . Mother
DRAMA Tamworth. Cowardly miner saves fiancee's brother from fire.

08883
BEYOND THE CITIES (70) (A)
Piccadilly (Par)
P: D: Carlyle Blackwell
S: Noel Shannon
Carlyle Blackwell . . . . Jim Campbell
Edna Best . . . . Mary Hayes
Alexander Field . . . . Sam
Lawrence Hanray . . . . Gregory Hayes
Helen Haye . . . . Amy Hayes
Eric Maturin . . . . Hector Braydon
Percy Parsons . . . . Boss
DRAMA Canada. Sportsman saves crooked lawyer's amnesiac daughter from marrying rich cad.

08884
THE WINDJAMMER (Pro Patria)
P: H. Bruce Woolfe
D: John Orton
S: (NOVEL) A.J. Villiers (BY WAY OF CAPE HORN)
SC: John Orton, A.P. Herbert
Tony Bruce . . . . Jack Mitchell
Michael Hogan . . . . Bert Hodges
Hal Gordon . . . . Alf
Roy Travers . . . . Old Ned
Gordon Craig . . . . Youth
Hal Booth . . . .
J. Baker . . . .
J. Cunningham . . . .
P. Russell . . . .
C. Christie . . . .
ADVENTURE Gentleman tramp joins crew of windjammer for seven month voyage from Australia.

08885
THE GREAT GAME (79) (U)
Gaumont
P: L'Estrange Fawcett
D: Jack Raymond
S: William Hunter, John Lees
SC: W.P. Lipscomb, Ralph Gilbert Bettinson
John Batten . . . . Dicky Brown
Renee Clama . . . . Peggy Jackson
Jack Cock . . . . Jim Blake
Randle Ayrton . . . . Henderson
Neil Kenyon . . . . Jackson
Kenneth Kove . . . . Bultitude
A.G. Poulton . . . . Banks
Billy Blyth . . . . Billy
Lew Lake . . . . Tubby
Wally Patch . . . . Joe Miller
Rex Harrison . . . . George
SPORT Football team wins Cup despite bungling management.

08886
BIG BUSINESS (76) (U)
Oscar M. Sheridan (Fox)
P: D: Oscar M. Sheridan
S: Oscar M. Sheridan, Hubert W. David
Frances Day . . . . Pamela Fenchurch
Barrie Oliver . . . . Barrie

Virginia Vaughan . . . . Kay
Anthony Ireland . . . . Jimmy
Ben Welden . . . . Fenchurch
Jimmy Godden . . . . Oppenheimer
Billy Fry . . . . Augustus
Leslie "Hutch" Hutchinson
Giggie & Cortez
Elsie Percival
Sherman Fisher Girls
Arthur Roseberry's Symphonic Syncopated Orchestra
MUSICAL Partners save night club by staging cabaret.

08887
THE CHINESE BUNGALOW (74) (A)
Neo-Art (WP)
P: D: J.B. Williams, Arthur W. Barnes
S: (PLAY) Marion Osmond, James Corbet
Matheson Lang . . . . Yuan Sing
Jill Esmond Moore . . . . . . Jean
Anna Neagle . . . . Charlotte
Ballard Berkeley . . . . Richard Marquess
Derek Williams . . . . Harold Marquess
DRAMA China. Mandarin plots to kill lover of English wife.

08888
WHY SAILORS LEAVE HOME (70) (U)
BIP (Wardour)
D: Monty Banks
S: Syd Courtenay, Lola Harvey
SC: Val Valentine
Leslie Fuller . . . . Bill
Peter Barnard . . . . George
Eve Gray . . . . Slave Girl
Gladys Cruickshank . . . . . Slave Girl
Dmitri Vetter . . . . Multhasa
Frank Melroyd . . . . Captain
Syd Courtenay . . . . Sheik Sidi Ben
Lola Harvey . . . . Maya
Olivette
Marika Rokk
COMEDY Cockney sailor placed in charge of Sheik's harem.

08889
A WARM CORNER (104) (A)
Gainsborough (Ideal)
P: Maicael Balcon
D: Victor Saville
S: (PLAY) Franz Arnold, Ernst Bach, Arthur Wimperis, Lauri Wylie
SC: Angus MacPhail, Victor Saville
Leslie Henson . . . . Charles Corner
Heather Thatcher . . . . Mimi Price
Connie Ediss . . . . Adela Corner
Austin Melford . . . . Peter Price
Belle Chrystal . . . . Peggy Corner
Kim Peacock . . . . Count Toscani
Alfred Wellesley . . . . Thomas Turner
Toni Edgar Bruce . . . . Lady Bayswater
George de Warfaz . . . . Waiter
COMEDY Monte Carlo. Cornplaster millionaire blackmailed for flirting with secret wife of friend's nephew.

OCT

08890
WHEN SCOUTING WON (4815) (U) (silent)
J.H. Martin Cross
D: S: J.H. Martin Cross
Cyril Chant . . . . Scout
Frankie Purnell . . . . Cub
CHILDREN Boy Scout's adventures with criminal gipsies.

08891
AN OBVIOUS SITUATION (65) (A) retitled:
HOURS OF LONELINESS
Carlton (WB)
P: D: S: G.G. Glavany
Sunday Wilshin . . . . Cella Stuart
Walter Sondes . . . . John Stuart
Carl Harbord . . . . Michael Turner
Marjorie Jennings . . . . Betty Chase
Michael Hogan . . . . Trimmett
Iris Ashley . . . . Babe Garson
Mina Burnett . . . . Manette
Harold Huth . . . . Gustave
CRIME Riviera. Married woman's lover
blackmailed for shooting burglar.

08892
REALITIES (13) (U)
BIP (Wardour)
D: Bernard Mainwaring
S: (PLAY) Eric D. Brand (THE LOVE
DOCTOR)
Dodo Watts . . . . The Wife
Laurence Ireland . . . . The Lover
Ian Harding . . . . The Husband
COMEDY Wife's lover poses as doctor to
deceive husband.

08893
WE TAKE OFF OUR HATS (10) (U)
BIP (Wardour)
D: SC: Harry Hughes
S: (SKETCH) Hartley Carrick
Donald Calthrop . . . . Erb
Frank Stanmore . . . . Alf
Mark Lester . . . . Arry
Winifred Hall . . . . Barmaid
COMEDY Drinker's cough resembles that of
recently deceased friend.

08894
THE TEMPORARY WIDOW (84) (U)
bilingual
UFA (Wardour)
P: Erich Pommer
D: Gustav Ucicky
S: (PLAY) Curt Goetz (HOKUSPOKUS)
SC: Karl Hartl, Walter Reisch, Benn W. Levy
Lilian Harvey . . . . Kitty Keller
Laurence Olivier . . . . Peter Bille
Athole Stewart . . . . President Grant
Gillian Dean . . . . Anny Sedal
Frank Stanmore . . . . Kulicke
Felix Aylmer . . . . Defence
Frederick Lloyd . . . . Prosecution
Henry Caine . . . . Lindberg
COMEDY Girl pretends to drown husband so
his paintings will sell. (Made in Germany.
Extract in ELSTREE STORY, 1952.)

08895
LEAVE IT TO ME (40) (U)
George King (Fox)
D: George King
S: Billie Bristow
SC: Patrick L. Mannock
Robin Irvine . . . . Larry
Dorothy Seacombe . . . . . . Mrs Jordan
A. Bromley Davenport . . . . Mr Jordan
Harold Huth . . . . Slade
Joan Wyndham . . . . Ann Jordan
Frank Stanmore . . . . Merton
Tom Helmore . . . . Tony
Fanny Wright . . . . Housekeeper
COMEDY Wastrel fakes theft of necklace to
raise promised £5000 and thwarts blackmailing
secretary.

08896
AURA No. 1 (9) (U)
Walter West (Col)
D: Walter West
Mme Aura
MUSICAL Soprano

08897
AURA No. 2 (9) (U)
Walter West (Col)
D: Walter West
Mme Aura
MUSICAL Soprano

08898
ME AND MYSELF (6) (U)
Lincoln E. Stoll
D: S: Lincoln Stoll
Lincoln Stoll
COMEDY

08899
ALMOST A HONEYMOON (100) (U)
BIP (Wardour) reissue: 1935 (EB)
D: Monty Banks
S: (PLAY) Walter Ellis
SC: Val Valentine, Monty Banks, Walter C.
Mycroft
Clifford Mollison . . . . Basil Dibley
Dodo Watts . . . . Rosalie Quilter
Lamont Dickson . . . . . . Cuthbert de Gray
Donald Calthrop . . . . Charles
C.M. Hallard . . . . Sir James Jephson
Winifred Hall . . . . Lavinia Pepper
Pamela Carme . . . . Margaret Brett
Edward Thane . . . . Clutterbuck
COMEDY Wastrel seeking wife unwittingly
spends night in girl's bedroom.

08900
THE MIDDLE WATCH (112) (A)
BIP (Wardour) reissue: 1933
D: Norman Walker
S: (PLAY) Ian Hay, Stephen King-Hall
SC: Norman Walker, Frank Launder
Owen Nares . . . . Capt Maitland
Jaqueline Logan . . . . Mary Carlton
Jack Raine . . . . Cdr Baddeley
Dodo Watts . . . . Fay Eaton
Fred Volpe . . . . . Sir Herbert Hewitt
Henry Wenman . . . . Marine Ogg
Reginald Purdell . . . . Cpl Duckett
Margaret Halstan . . . . . Lady Agatha Hewitt
Phyllis Loring . . . . Nancy Hewitt
Hamilton Keene . . . . Capt Randall
Muriel Aked . . . . Charlotte Hopkinson
George Carr . . . . Ah Pong
Syd Crossley . . . . Sentry
COMEDY Captain tries to hide accidental
female passengers from Admiral. (FWA: 1932.)

08901
THE BLACK HAND GANG (63) (U)
BIP (Wardour)
D: Monty Banks
S: (PLAY) R.P. Weston, Bert Lee (BLACK
HAND GEORGE)
SC: Victor Kendall
Wee Georgie Wood . . . . . Georgie Robinson
Dolly Harmer . . . . Mrs Robinson
Violet Young . . . . Winnie
Lionel Hoare . . . . The Other Man
Junior Banks . . . . Archibald
Viola Compton . . . . Mater
Alfred Woods . . . . Pater
COMEDY Children catch burglars at rich boy's
home.

08902
SHOULD A DOCTOR TELL ? (58) (A)
British Lion
P: S.W. Smith
D: Manning Haynes
S: G.B. Samuelson, Walter Summers
SC: Edgar Wallace
Basil Gill . . . . Dr Bruce Smith
Norah Baring . . . . Joan Murray
Maurice Evans . . . . Roger Smith
Gladys Jennings . . . . The Wife
Anna Neagle . . . . Muriel
A.G. Poulton . . . . Judge
Harvey Braban . . . . Prosecution
DRAMA Doctor's oath prevents him telling son
he is engaged to unmarried mother.

08903
NIGHT BIRDS (97) (A) bilingual
BIP (Wardour) reissue: 1935 (EB)
P: D: Richard Eichberg
S: Victor Kendall
SC: Miles Malleson
Muriel Angelus . . . . Dolly
Jack Raine . . . . Sgt Harry Cross
Jameson Thomas . . . . Deacon Lake
Eve Gray . . . . Mary Cross
Franklyn Bellamy . . . . Charlo Bianci
Garry Marsh . . . . Archibald Bunny
Frank Perfitt . . . . Insp Warrington
D. Hay Petrie . . . . Scotty
Harry Terry . . . . Toothpick Jeff
Margaret Yarde . . . . Mrs Hallick
Ellen Pollock . . . . Flossie
CRIME Detective unmasks Night Club owner
as head of gang of jewel robbers.

08904
COMPROMISING DAPHNE (86) (A)
USA: COMPROMISED !
BIP (Wardour) reissue: 1935 (EB)
D: Thomas Bentley
S: (PLAY) Edith Fitzgerald
SC: Val Valentine
Jean Colin . . . . Daphne Ponsonby
Charles Hickman . . . . George
C.M. Hallard . . . . Mr Ponsonby
Phyllis Konstam . . . . Sadie Bannister
Leo Sheffield . . . . Mr Bannister
Viola Compton . . . . Mrs Ponsonby
Frank Perfitt . . . . Hicks
Barbara Gott . . . . Martha
Margot Grahame . . . . Muriel
COMEDY Man compromises girl to force her
father to consent to marriage.

08905
STAR IMPERSONATIONS (10) (U)
Film Weekly
P: Herbert Thompson
D: Harry Hughes
Mabel Poulton . . . . Mary Pickford
Donald Calthrop . . . . George Arliss
William Freshman . . . . Ramon Novarro
Micky Brantford . . . . Lewis Ayres
Vanda Greville . . . . Greta Garbo
COMEDY £150 competition: re-enacted scenes
from "The Taming of the Shrew"; "The Call of
the Flesh"; "All Quiet on the Western Front";
"Anna Christie".

08906
THE MAN FROM CHICAGO (88) (A)
BIP (Wardour) reissue: 1935 (EB)
D: Walter Summers
S: (PLAY) Reginald Berkeley (SPEED)
SC: Walter Summers, Walter C. Mycroft

Bernard Nedell . . . .   Nick Dugan
Dodo Watts . . . .   Cherry Henderson
Joyce Kennedy . . . .   Irma Russell
Morris Harvey . . . .   Rossi
Albert Whelan . . . .   Sgt Mostyn
Austin Trevor . . . .   Insp Drew
Billy Milton . . . .   Barry Larwood
O.B. Clarence . . . .   John Larwood
Dennis Hoey . . . .   Jimmy Donovan
Ben Welden . . . .   Ted
CRIME American motor bandit takes over London garage and club.

NOV

08907
CHILDREN OF CHANCE (80) (A) bilingual
BIP (FN-P)
D: Alexander Esway
S: Miles Malleson, Frank Launder
Elissa Landi . . . .   Binnie/Lia Monta
Mabel Poulton . . . .   Molly
John Stuart . . . .   Gordon
John Longden . . . .   Jeffrey
Gus McNaughton . . . .   H.K. Zinkwell
Wallace Lupino . . . .   O.K. Johnson
Gus Sharland . . . .   Hugo
John Deverell . . . .   Harold
Charles Dormer . . . .   Dude
Dorothy Minto . . . .   Sally
Kay Hammond . . . .   Joyce
CRIME Girl is double of jewel thief's artist wife.

08908
BIRDS OF PREY (98) (A)
USA: THE PERFECT ALIBI
ATP (Radio)
P: D: Basil Dean
S: (PLAY) A.A. Milne (THE FOURTH WALL)
SC: A.A. Milne, Basil Dean
Robert Loraine . . . .   Carter
Warwick Ward . . . .   Laverick
Frank Lawton . . . .   Jimmy Hilton
C. Aubrey Smith . . . .   Arthur Hilton
Dorothy Boyd . . . .   Mollie
Ellis Jeffreys . . . .   Mrs Green
Nigel Bruce . . . .   Manager
David Hawthorne . . . .
Tom Reynolds . . . .
Jack Hawkins . . . .   Alfred
CRIME Young couple solve murder in country house.

08909
SUCH IS THE LAW
(88) (A)
Stoll (Butcher)
P: Oswald Mitchell
D: Sinclair Hill

S: Reginald Fogwell
SC: Leslie Howard Gordon
Lady Tree . . . .   Granny
C. Aubrey Smith . . . . . . Sir James Whittaker
Bert Coote . . . .   Sir George
Kate Cutler . . . .   Mother
Janice Adair . . . .   Marjorie Marjoribanks
Carl Harbord . . . .   Vivian Fairfax
Rex Maurice . . . .·. . .   Philip Carberry
Pamela Carme . . . .   Mrs Marjoribanks
ROMANCE Wife's story of divorce case saves daughter's marriage. (Includes extracts from THE PRICE OF DIVORCE, 1928.)

08910
ENTER THE QUEEN (42) (U)
Starcraft (Fox)
P: Harry Cohen
D: Arthur Varney-Serrao
S: Brock Williams
Richard Cooper . . . .   Bertie Bunter
Doria March . . . .   Queen of Moravia
Herbert Mundin . . . .   Goss
Chili Bouchier . . . .   Marjorie Manners
Frederick Culley . . . . . . Sir Horace Bunter
Margaret Damer . . . .   Lady Bunter
Lena Halliday . . . .   Lady Manners
Percy Walsh . . . .   Brood
COMEDY Ruritanian queen causes upset when she stays at Lady's house.

08911
THE CALL OF THE SEA (65) (U)
Twickenham (WB) reissue: 1938 (IFR)
P: Julius Hagen, Henry Edwards
D: Leslie Hiscott
S: Frank Shaw
SC: H. Fowler Mear
Henry Edwards . . . . Lt/Cdr Good
Chrissie White . . . .   Iris Tares
Bernard Nedell . . . .   Ramon Tares
Chili Bouchier . . . .   Poquita
Clifford McLaglen . . . .   Pedro
Alexander Field . . . .   Hooky Walker
ADVENTURE Naval officer investigates colleagues' disappearance on tropical island.

08912
KISSING CUP'S RACE (75) (A)
Butcher
D: Castleton Knight
S: (POEM) Campbell Rae Brown
SC: Castleton Knight, Blanche Metcalfe
Stewart Rome . . . .   Lord Rattlington
Madeleine Carroll . . . . . . Lady Mollie Adair
John Stuart . . . . Lord Jimmy Hilhoxton
Richard Cooper . . . .   Rollo Adair
Chili Bouchier . . . .   Gabrielle
Moore Marriott . . . .   Joe Tricker

J. Fisher White . . . . . . .Marquis of Hilhoxton
James Knight . . . .   Detective
Gladys Hamer . . . .   Maid
Wally Patch . . . .   Bookie
SPORT Lord's horse wins big race despite crooked rival.

08913
THREAD O' SCARLET (35) (A)
Gaumont
P: L'Estrange Fawcett
D: Peter Godfrey
S: (PLAY) J.J. Bell
SC: Ralph Gilbert Bettinson
George Merritt . . . .   Butters
Arthur Goullet . . . .   Breen
William Freshman . . . .   Traveller
Norman Shelley . . . .   Migsworth
Humberston Wright . . . . . .   Smith
Wally Patch . . . .   Ford
Ben Field . . . .   Landlord
Viola Lyel . . . .   Mrs Marsden
Pat Garrod . . . .   Mary
CRIME Innocent blacksmith hanged on circumstantial evidence.

DEC

08914
BED AND BREAKFAST (68) (U)
Gaumont
P: L'Estrange Fawcett
D: Walter Forde
S: (PLAY) Frederick Witney
SC: H. Fowler Mear
Jane Baxter . . . . .Audrey Corteline
Richard Cooper . . . . .Toby Entwhistle
Sari Maritza . . . . .Anne Entwhistle
Alf Goddard . . . .   Alf Dunning
David Hawthorne . . . . . . .Bernard Corteline
Cyril McLaglen . . . .   Bill
Ruth Maitland . . . .   Mimosa Dunning
Muriel Aked . . .·. . . . .   Mrs Boase
Frederick Volpe . . . .   Cannon Boase
Mike Johnson . . . .   Henry
Matthew Boutlon . . . .   Sgt
COMEDY Estranged honeymooners catch burglars in bungalow.

08915
O. K. CHIEF (20) (U)
BIP (Wardour)
D: Bernerd Mainwaring
Frances Day . . . .   Girl
Albert Whelan . . . .   Cop
Walter Armitage . . . .   Englishman
Percy Parsons . . . .   Kelly
W.T. Ellwanger . . . .   Chief
COMEDY Girl blackmails police chief into releasing murderer.

1931

JAN

08916
TONS OF MONEY (97) (U)
B&D (W&F) *reissue:* 1937 (EB)
P: Herbert Wilcox
D: Tom Walls
S: (PLA) Will Evans, Arthur Valentine
SC: Herbert Wilcox, Ralph Lynn
Ralph Lynn . . . . Aubrey Allington
Yvonne Arnaud. . . . . . Louise Allington
Mary Brough . . . . Benita Mullet
Robertson Hare . . . . Chesterman
Gordon James. . . . . George Maitland
Madge Saunders . . . . Jane Everard
Philip Hewland . . . . Henry
Willie Warde . . . . Giles
John Turnbull . . . . Sprules
Peggy Douglas . . . . Simpson
COMEDY Poor inventor fakes death to pose as
longlost cousin.

08917
PLUNDER (98) (U)
B&D (W&F) *reissue:* 1937 (EB)
P: Herbert Wilcox
D: Tom Walls
S: (PLAY) Ben Travers
SC: W.P. Lipscomb
Ralph Lynn . . . . Darcy Tuck
Tom Walls . . . . Freddie Malone
Winifred Shotter . . . . Joan Hewlett
Robertson Hare . . . . Oswald Veal
Doreen Bendix . . . . Prudence Malone
Sydney Lynn . . . . Simon Veal
Ethel Coleridge . . . . Mrs Orlock
Hubert Waring . . . . Insp Sibley
COMEDY Heiress's fiance steals gems inherited
by grandfather's housekeeper.

08918
P. C. JOSSER (90) (U)
Gainsborough (W&F) *reissue:* 1945 (EB)
P: Michael Balcon
D: Milton Rosmer
S: (PLAY) Ernest Lotinga (THE POLICE
FORCE)
SC: Con West, Herbert Sargent
Ernie Lotinga . . . . Jimmy Josser
Jack Frost . . . . Nobby
Maisie Darrell . . . . Violet Newsome
Robert Douglas . . . . Dick Summers
Garry Marsh . . . . Carson
Max Avieson . . . . Travers
COMEDY Sacked PC helps trainer break jail to
prove club owner doped racehorse.

08919
THE WRONG MR PERKINS (38) (U)
Starcraft (Fox)
P: Harry Cohen
D: Arthur Varney-Serrao
S: Brock Williams
Herbert Mundin . . . . Jimmy Perkins
Sonia Bellamy . . . . Betty Petersham
Frederick Volpe . . . . Sir Trevor Petersham
Percy Walsh . . . . Mr Mellows
William Daunt . . . . Arnold Perkins
COMEDY Banker mistakes poor man for rich
namesake and makes him partner.

08920
MIDNIGHT (44) (U)
George King (Fox)
P: Harry Cohen
D: George King
S: (PLAY) Charles Bennett
SC: Charles Bennett, Billie Bristow
John Stuart . . . . Larry Byrne

Eve Gray . . . . Dorothy Harding
George Bellamy . . . . Max Strubel
Ellen Pollock . . . . Sonia Strubel
Kyoshi Takase . . . . Ching
CRIME Girl helps man save secret plans from
spies.

08921
CITY OF SONG (101) (U) *trilingual*
USA: FAREWELL TO LOVE
ASFI (Sterling) *reissue:* 1934 (2410 ft cut)
P: Isidore Schlesinger
D: Carmine Gallone
S: C.H. Dand
SC: Miles Malleson, Hans Szekely
Jan Kiepura . . . . Giovanni Cavallone
Betty Stockfeld . . . . Claire Winter
Hugh Wakefield . . . . Hon Roddy Fielding
Heather Angel . . . . Carmela
Francesco Maldacea . . . . . . Chi
Philip Easton . . . . John Barlow
Miles Malleson . . . . Doorman
MUSICAL Neapolitan singer, brought to
London by socialite, returns to his sweetheart.

08922
THE LOVE HABIT (90) (A)
BIP (Wardour) *reissue:* 1935 (EB)
D: Harry Lachman
S: (PLAY) Louis Verneuil
SC: Seymour Hicks, Val Valentine
Seymour Hicks . . . . Justin Abelard
Margot Grahame . . . . Julie Dubois
Edmund Breon . . . . Alphonse Dubois
Ursula Jeans . . . . Rose Pom Pom
Clifford Heatherley . . . . . . Santorelli
Walter Armitage . . . . Max Quattro
Elsa Lanchester . . . . Mathilde
COMEDY Paris. Roue poses as secretary to
flirt with employee's wife.

08923
CAPE FORLORN (86) (A) *trilingual*
USA: THE LOVE STORM
BIP (Wardour)
P: D: E.A. Dupont
S: (PLAY) Frank Harvey
SC: E.A. Dupont, Victor Kendall
Fay Compton . . . . Eileen Kell
Frank Harvey . . . . William Kell
Ian Hunter . . . . Gordon Kingsley
Edmund Willard . . . . Henry Cass
Donald Calthrop . . . . Parsons
DRAMA Lighthouse keeper's wife has affair
with shipwrecked thief.

08924
HOW HE LIED TO HER HUSBAND (33) (U)
BIP (Wardour)
D: Cecil Lewis
S: (PLAY) George Bernard Shaw
SC: Cecil Lewis, Frank Launder
Edmund Gwenn . . . . Teddy Bompas
Vera Lennox . . . . Aurora Bompas
Robert Harris . . . . Henry Apjohn
COMEDY Rich man suspects wife loves poet.

08925
THE WOMAN BETWEEN (89) (A)
USA: THE WOMAN DECIDES
BIP (Wardour)
D: Miles Mander
S: (PLAY) Miles Mander (CONFLICT)
SC: Miles Mander, Frank Launder
Owen Nares . . . . Tom Smith
Adrianne Allen . . . . Lady Pamela
David Hawthorne . . . . Sir Clive Marlow
C.M. Hallard . . . . Earl Bellingdon
Barbara Hoffe . . . . Mrs Tremayne
Margaret Yarde . . . . Mrs Robinson

Winifred Oughton . . . . Mrs Jones
C. Disney Roebuck . . . . . . Daniels
ROMANCE Lady torn between opposing
parliamentary candidates.

08926
MORITA (39) (U)
Patrick K. Heale (Britivox)
P: S: Patrick K. Heale
D: Fred Paul
Daphne Lennard . . . . Morita
Jean Romaine . . . . Taibie
Claude Russell . . . . Beachcomber
MUSICAL Hawaii. Beachcomber saves pearl
diver's sweetheart from rival.

08927
GUILT (65) (A)
Reginald Fogwell (Par)
D: S: Reginald Fogwell
James Carew . . . . James Barrett
Anne Grey . . . . Anne Barrett
Harold Huth . . . . Tony Carleton
James Fenton . . . . Roy
Rex Curtis . . . . Jack
Anne Smiley . . . . Phyllis
Ernest Lester . . . . Jennings
ROMANCE Playwright's wife pretends affair
with actor is part of play.

08928
HARRY LAUDER SONGS (series) (U)
Gainsborough (Ideal)
P: Michael Balcon
D: George Pearson

08929
1— I LOVE A LASSIE (3)

08930
2 — SOMEBODY'S WAITING FOR ME (3)

08931
3 — I LOVE TO BE A SAILOR (3)

08932
4 — ROAMING IN THE GLOAMING (3)

08933
5 — TOBERMORY (3)

08934
6 — NANNY (3)

08935
7 — THE SAFTEST OF THE FAMILY (3)

08936
8 — SHE'S MY DAISY (3)
MUSICAL Scots star sings songs in music hall
setting.

08937
THIS OXFORD (2023) (U) (silent)
Merton Motion Picture Society (U)
D: S: Frank Bowden
J.T. Race . . . . The Man
Ruth Bowden . . . . The Girl
Stephen Hopkinson . . . . . . The Rival
COMEDY Oxford. Student must win blue
before he can win girl.
(Amateur film shown professionally.)

08938
ARIANE (70) (A) *trilingual* retitled:
THE LOVES OF ARIANE
Nerofilm-Pathe Natan (U)
P: D: Paul Czinner
S: (NOVEL) Claude Anet
SC: Paul Czinner, Carl Mayer
Elisabeth Bergner . . . . Ariane
Percy Marmont . . . . Anthony Fraser

Oriel Ross . . . . Duchess
Warwick Ward . . . .
Joan Matheson . . . . Olga
Elizabeth Vaughan . . . . Waravara
Charles Carson . . . . Professor
ROMANCE Paris. Student invents imaginary
lovers to impress English philanderer.
(Made in Paris).

FEB

08939
THE ETERNAL FEMININE (82) (U)
Starcraft (Par)
P: D: S: Arthur Varney
SC: Hugh Broadbridge, Brock Williams
Guy Newall . . . . Sir Charles Winthrop
Doria March . . . . Yvonne de la Roche
Jill Esmond . . . . Claire Lee
Garry Marsh . . . . Arthur Williams
Terence de Marney . . . . . . Michael Winthrop
Madge Snell . . . . Lady Winthrop
Arthur Varney . . . . Al Peters
ROMANCE Lady's sons fall in love with
actress and sister.

08940
BRACELETS (50) (U)
Gaumont
P: L'Estrange Fawcett
D: SC: Sewell Collins
S: (PLAY) Sewell Collins
Bert Coote . . . . Edwin Hobbett
Joyce Kennedy . . . . Annie Moran
D.A. Clarke-Smith . . . . Joe le Sage
Margaret Emden . . . . Mrs Hobbett
Frederick Leister . . . . Slim Symes
Stella Arbenina . . . . . . Countess Soumbatoff
Harold Huth . . . . Maurice Dupont
George Merritt . . . . Director
CRIME Old jeweller foils crooks posing as
Russian royalty.

08941
HOT HEIR (39) (U)
Gainsborough (Ideal)
P: Michael Balcon
D: W.P. Kellino
S: Angus Macphail, Chandos Balcon
Charles Austin . . . .
Bobbie Comber . . . .
Anita Casimir . . . .
Fred Kitchen jr . . . .
Seth Egbert . . . .
COMEDY Usurping King dethroned in favour
of dancing girl.

08942
BULL RUSHES (37) (U)
Gainsborough (Ideal)
P: Michael Balcon
D: W.P. Kellino
S: Angus Macphail, Charles Balcon
Wallace Lupino . . . .
Reginald Gardiner . . . .
Dorrie Deane . . . .
Gladys Hamer . . . .
Seth Egbert . . . .
Billy Milton . . . .
Guy Fane . . . .
COMEDY Spain. English tourist gets drunk and
fights bull.

08943
WHO KILLED DOC ROBIN ? (36) (U)
Gainsborough (Ideal)
P: Michael Balcon
D: W.P. Kellino
S: Angus Macphail, Chandos Balcon
Clifford Heatherley . . . . Luigi Scarlatti

Dorrie Deane . . . . Sadie Sucker
Dennis Wyndham . . . . . . .Pat O'Callaghan
Ben Welden . . . .
Queenie Leonard . . . .
Billy Milton . . . .
Max Rivers Dancing Girls
COMEDY Rival gangsters discover nightclub
hostess is their mother.

08944
THIRD TIME LUCKY (85) (A)
Gainsborough (W&F)
P: Michael Balcon
D: Walter Forde
S: (PLAY) Arnold Ridley
SC: Angus Macphail
Bobby Howes . . . . Rev Arthur Fear
Gordon Harker . . . . Meggitt
Dorothy Boyd . . . . Jennifer
Garry Marsh . . . . Crowther
Henry Mollison . . . . Crofts
Gibb McLaughlin . . . . Charlie
Clare Greet . . . . Mrs Scratton
Margaret Yarde . . . . Mrs Clutterbuck
Viola Compton . . . . Mrs Starkey
Marie Ault . . . . Mrs Midge
Alexander Field . . . . Snoopy
Harry Terry . . . . Gregg
Peter Godfrey . . . . Gus
Matthew Boulton . . . . Inspector
COMEDY Timid parson steals back ward's
letters from blackmailer.

08945
THE STRONGER SEX (80) (A)
Gainsborough (Ideal)
P: Michael Balcon
D: SC: V. Gareth Gundrey
S: (PLAY) J. Valentine
Colin Clive . . . . .Warren Barrington
Adrianne Allen . . . . Mary Thorpe
Gordon Harker . . . . Parker
Martin Lewis . . . . John Brent
Renee Clama . . . . Joan Merivale
Elsa Lanchester . . . . Thompson
DRAMA Man sacrifices himself to save wife's
lover in mine disaster.

08946
THE SPORT OF KINGS (98) (U)
Gainsborough (Ideal)
P: Michael Balcon
D: Victor Saville
S: (PLAY) Ian Hay
SC: Angus Macphail
Leslie Henson . . . . Amos Purdie
Hugh Wakefield . . . . Alfie Sprigge
Gordon Harker . . . . Bates
Dorothy Boyd . . . . Dulcie
Renee Clama . . . . Jane
Jack Melford . . . . Sir Reginald Toothill
Mary Jerrold . . . . Mrs Purdie
Barbara Gott . . . . Cook
Wally Patch . . . . Panama Pete
COMEDY Puritannical JP takes over bookmaking
business and welshes.

08947
MADAME GUILLOTINE (74) (A)
Reginald Fogwell (W&F)
P: Reginald Fogwell, Mansfield Markham
D: S: Reginald Fogwell
SC: Harold Huth
Madeleine Carroll . . . . . Lucille de Choisigne
Brian Aherne . . . . Louis Dubois
Henry Hewitt . . . . Vicomte d'Avennes
Frederick Culley . . . . Marquis
Hector Abbas . . . . le Blanc
Ian MacDonald . . . . Jacques

H. Fisher White . . . . le Farge
ROMANCE Paris, 1789. Tribune weds aristocrat
to save her from death.

08948
THE LAST TIDE (5200) (A) (silent)
Argyle Art Pictures (EB)
P: D: S: John Argyle
James Benton . . . . Bob
Margaret Delane . . . . Letty
Grace Johnson . . . . Miriam
ROMANCE Devon. Fisherman loves girl but
marries injured sister.

08949
IMMEDIATE POSSESSION (42) (U)
Starcraft (Fox)
P: Harry Cohen
D: Arthur Varney-Serrao
S: Brock Williams
Herbert Mundin . . . . Peter Bootle
Dorothy Bartlam . . . . Violet Fayre
Leslie Perrins . . . . Andrew Maitland
George Bellamy . . . . Daniel Grimm
Merle Tottenham . . . . Polly Baxter
COMEDY Estate agent has 24 hours in which to
sell "haunted" house.

08950
UNEASY VIRTUE (83) (U)
BIP (Wardour)
D: Norman Walker
S:)PLAY) Harrison Owens (THE HAPPY
HUSBAND)
Fay Compton . . . . Dorothy Rendell
Edmond Breon . . . . Harvey Townsend
Francis Lister . . . . Bill Rendell
Margot Grahame . . . . Stella Tolhurst
Donald Calthrop . . . . Burglar
Garry Marsh . . . . Arthur Tolhurst
Dodo Watts . . . . Sylvia Fullerton
Adele Dixon . . . . Consuelo Pratt
Hubert Harben . . . . Frank K. Pratt
Gerard Lyley . . . . Sosso Stephens
Margaret Yarde . . . . Mrs Robinson
Molly Lamont . . . . Ada
COMEDY Virtuous wife pretends she has had
affairs with other men.

08951
IN A LOTUS GARDEN (47) (U)
Patrick K. Heale
P: S: Patrick K. Heale
D: Fred Paul
Roy Galloway . . . . Lt Dick Waring
Jocelyn Yeo . . . . Margaret Leyland
H. Agar Lyons . . . . Mandarin
Rita Cave . . . . San Tu
Jack Barnes . . . . Chen Sang
Frank Lilliput . . . . Ching Chong
MUSICAL China. Naval officer's fiancee saves
him from mandarin.

08952
ROMANY LOVE (58) (U)
Patrick K. Heale (MGM)
P: S: Patrick K. Heale
D: Fred Paul
Esmond Knight . . . . Davy Summers
Florence McHugh . . . . Taraline
Roy Travers . . . . Joe Cayson
MUSICAL Gipsy defeats cruel rival and wins
girl.

08953
OTHER PEOPLE'S SINS (63) (A)
Associated Picture Productions (PDC)
D: Sinclair Hill
S: Leslie Howard Gordon

Horace Hodges . . . . Carfax
Stewart Rome . . . . Anthony Vernon
Anne Grey . . . . Anne Vernon
Arthur Margetson . . . . . Bernard Barrington
Mrs Hayden Coffin . . . . . . Mrs Vernon
A. Harding Steerman . . . . . Prosecution
Clifton Boyne . . . . Juror
Arthur Hambling . . . . Fireman
Sam Wilkinson . . . . Actor
CRIME Man takes blame for daughter's crime and is defended by her husband.

MAR

08954
SANDY THE LOST POLICEMAN (9) (U)
First National (WB)
S: (SKETCH) Sandy Powell
Sandy Powell . . . . Sandy
COMEDY Misadventures of inept constable.

08955
MOTLEY AND MELODY (8) (U)
First National (WB)
Max and Harry Nesbitt
The Maestro Singers
MUSICAL Patter, song, dance and quartette.

08956
THE FIDDLE FANATICS (8) (U)
First National (WB)
Stanelli and Edgar
MUSICAL Violinist and singer.

08957
PAYNE AND HILLIARD (7) (U)
First National (WB)
COMEDY Husband and wife crosstalk act.

08958
CUPBOARD LOVE (19) (U)
BIP (Wardour)
D: Bernard Mainwaring
S: Eliot Crawshay-Williams
Marjorie Mars . . . . The Girl
Maurice Evans . . . . The Man
Helena Pickard . . . .
COMEDY Girl locks lover in bedroom cupboard all night.

08959
THE LAME DUCK (13) (U)
BIP (Wardour)
D: Bernard Mainwaring
S: Clemence Dane
Lester Matthews : . . . . Capt Dallas
Boris Ranevsky . . . .
George Turner . . . .
Wallace Evenett . . . .
CRIME Crippled war veteran outwits foreign crooks seeking formula for new explosive.

08960
TO OBLIGE A LADY (75) (A)
British Lion
P: S.W. Smith
D: Manning Haynes
S: (PLAY) Edgar Wallace
Maisie Gay . . . . Mrs Harris
Warwick Ward . . . . George Pinder
Mary Newland . . . . Betty Pinder
Haddon Mason . . . . John Prendergast
James Carew . . . . Sir Henry Markham
Annie Esmond . . . . Mrs Higgins
COMEDY Wife lets husband's flat to couple who want to impress rich uncle.

08961
THE SLEEPING CARDINAL (84) (U)
USA: SHERLOCK HOLMES' FATAL HOUR

Twickenham (WB)
P: Julius Hagen
D: Leslie Hiscott
S: (STORIES) Arthur Conan Doyle (THE EMPTY HOUSE; THE FINAL PROBLEM)
SC: Cyril Twyford, H. Fowler Mear
Arthur Wontner . . . . Sherlock Holmes
Norman McKinnel . . . . Moriarty
Jane Welsh . . . . Kathleen Adair
Ian Fleming . . . . Dr Watson
Louis Goodrich . . . . . Col Sebastian Moran
Philip Hewland . . . . Insp Lestrade
Charles Paton . . . . J.J. Godfrey
Minnie Rayner . . . . Mrs Hudson
CRIME Gamblers force diplomat to smuggle stolen money into France.

08962
THE SPECKLED BAND (90) (A)
B&D (W&F)
P: Herbert Wilcox
D: Jack Raymond
S: (STORY) Arthur Conan Doyle
SC: W.P. Lipscomb
Lyn Harding . . . . Dr Grimesby Rylott
Raymond Massey . . . . . . Sherlock Holmes
Athole Stewart . . . . Dr Watson
Angela Baddeley . . . . Helen Stonor
Nancy Price . . . . Mrs Staunton
Marie Ault . . . . Mrs Hudson
Stanley Lathbury . . . . Rodgers
Charles Paton . . . . Builder
Joyce Moore . . . . Violet
CRIME Detective solves mystery of murder by snake-bite.

08963
OLD SOLDIERS NEVER DIE (58) (U)
BIP (Wardour)
D: Monty Banks
S: Syd Courtenay, Lola Harvey
SC: Val Valentine
Leslie Fuller . . . . Bill Smith
Max Nesbitt . . . . Sam Silverstein
Alf Goddard . . . . Sgt
Molly Lamont . . . . Ada
Mamie Holland . . . . Jane
Wellington Briggs . . . . Col
Wilfred Shine . . . . Padre
Nigel Barrie . . . . Doctor
Harry Nesbitt . . . . Harry Silverstein
Hal Gordon . . . . Recruit/Sentry
COMEDY Cockney and Jew enlist and cause demotion of sergeant.

08964
WHAT A NIGHT ! (58) (U)
BIP (FN—P)
D: Monty Banks
S: Syd Courtenay, Lola Harvey
Leslie Fuller . . . . Bill Grimshaw
Molly Lamont . . . . Nora Livingstone
Frank Stanmore . . . . Mr Livingstone
Charles Paton . . . . Grindle
Syd Courtenay . . . . Mr Merry
Ernest Fuller . . . . Landlord
Molly Hamley-Clifford . . . . Landlady
Olivette . . . . Rose
COMEDY Traveller catches burglar during night at 'haunted' inn.

08965
POTIPHAR'S WIFE (78) (A)
USA: HER STRANGE DESIRE
BIP (FN—P)
D: Maurice Elvey
S: (PLAY) Edgar C. Middleton
SC: Edgar C. Middleton

Nora Swinburne . . . . Lady Diana Bromford
Laurence Olivier . . . . Straker
Norman McKinnel . . . . Lord Bromford
Guy Newall . . . . Hon Maurice Worthington
Ronald Frankau . . . . Maj Tony Barlow,
Betty Schuster . . . . Rosita Worthington
Marjorie Brooks . . . . Sylvia Barlow
Walter Armitage . . . . Geoffrey Hayes
Henry Wenman . . . . Stevens
Elsa Lanchester . . . . Therese
ROMANCE Lord's wife fails to seduce her chauffeur.

08966
SHADOWS (57) (A)
BIP (FN—P)
D: Alexander Esway
S: Frank Miller
Jacqueline Logan . . . . Fay Melville
Bernard Nedell . . . . Press Rawlinson
Gordon Harker . . . . Ear'ole
Derrick de Marney . . . . . . Peter
Molly Lamont . . . . Jill Dexter
D.A. Clarke-Smith . . . . Gruhn
Wally Patch . . . . Cripps
Mary Clare . . . . Lily
Mark Lester . . . . Herb
Roy Emerton . . . . Captain
CRIME Press lord's son tracks down girl's American kidnapper.

08967
TELL ENGLAND (88) (A)
USA: THE BATTLE OF GALLIPOLI
British Instructional (Wardour)
P: H. Bruce Woolfe
D: Anthony Asquith, Geoffrey Barkas
S: (NOVEL) Ernest Raymond
SC: Anthony Asquith
Fay Compton . . . . Mrs Ray
Tony Bruce . . . . Rupert Ray
Carl Harbord . . . . Edgar Doe
Dennis Hoey . . . . Padre
C.M. Hallard . . . . Colonel
Gerald Rawlinson . . . . Lt Doon
Frederick Lloyd . . . . Capt Harding
Sam Wilkinson . . . . Pte Booth
Wally Patch . . . . Sgt
Hubert Harben . . . . Mr Ray
WAR 1914. Public school friends become army officers and fight at Gallipoli.

08968
DANGEROUS SEAS (53) (U)
Edward G. Whiting (Filmophone)
D:S: Edward Dryhurst
Julie Suedo . . . . Nan Penwardine
Sandy Irving . . . . Capt Muddle
Charles Garrey . . . . Penwardine
Gerald Rawlinson . . . . Standford
Wally Bosco . . . . Sunny Bantick
Gladys Dunham . . . . Polly
CRIME Cornwall. Excise officer loves innkeeper's daughter whose father is smuggler.

08969
NEVER TROUBLE TROUBLE (75) (U)
Lupino Lane (PDC)
D: Lupino Lane
S: Lauri Wylie
SC: George Dewhurst
Lupino Lane . . . . Oliver Crawford
Renee Clama . . . . Pam Tweet
Jack Hobbs . . . . Jimmie Dawson
Wallace Lupino . . . . Mr Tweet
Iris Ashley . . . . Gloria Baxter
Dennis Hoey . . . . Stranger
Wally Patch . . . . Bill Hainton
Lola Hunt . . . . Mrs Hainton

Barry Lupino . . . . Tompkins
George Dewhurst . . . . Insp Stevens
COMEDY Artist arranges for own assassination, then inherits fortune.

08970
THE HOUSE OF UNREST (58) (U)
Associated Picture Productions (PDC)
D: SC: Leslie Howard Gordon
S: (PLAY) Leslie Howard Gordon
Dorothy Boyd . . . . Diana
Malcolm Keen . . . . Hearne
Tom Helmore . . . . David
Leslie Perrins . . . . Cleaver
Hubert Carter . . . . Ben
Mary Mayfren . . . . Agnes
CRIME Crooks try to rob island home of diamond collector.

08971
PARADISE ALLEY (5097) (U) (silent)
Argyle Art Pictures (UK)
P: D: S: John Argyle
John Argyle . . . . Joe
Margaret Delane . . . . Clare Stellar
CRIME Miner takes blame when brother robs and shoots man.

APR

08972
CONTRABAND LOVE (67) (U)
British Screenplays (Par)
P: D: Sidney Morgan
S: Joan Wentworth Wood (Morgan)
C. Aubrey Smith . . . . Paul Machin, JP
Janice Adair . . . . Janice Machin
Haddon Mason . . . . Roger
Rosalinde Fuller . . . . Belle Sterling
Sydney Seaward . . . . Sampson
Charles Paton . . . . Jude Sterling
Marie Ault . . . . Sarah Sterling
ADVENTURE Cornwall. Tec poses as escaped convict to catch smugglers.

08973
AROMA OF THE SOUTH SEAS (35) (U)
Gainsborough (Ideal)
P: Michael Balcon
D: W.P. Kellino
S: Angus Macphail
Reginald Gardiner . . . . The Man
Wallace Lupino . . . . The Valet
Wyn Richmond . . . . The Girl
Moore Marriott . . . . The King
Warren Hastings . . . . .The Witchdoctor
COMEDY Shipwrecked valet saves affianced master from native girl.

08974
WE DINE AT SEVEN (44) (U)
GS Enterprises (Fox)
P: A. George Smith, Harry Cohen
D: Frank Richardson
S: Brock Williams
Herbert Mundin . . . . Henry Sweet
Dorothy Bartlam . . . . Mrs Sweet
Leslie Perrins . . . . Mr Chilworth
Molly Johnson . . . . Mrs Chilworth
Arthur Argent . . . . Sam Cutler
COMEDY Newlywed husband gets involved with another man's wife.

08975
THE SKIN GAME (88) (A)
BIP (Wardour) *reissue:* 1935 (EB)
D: Alfred Hitchcock
S: (PLAY) John Galsworthy
SC: Alfred Hitchcock, Alma Reville
Edmund Gwenn . . . . Hornblower

Phyllis Konstam . . . . Chloe Hornblower
John Longden . . . . .Charles Hornblower
Frank Lawton . . . . Rolf Hornblower
C.V. France . . . . Mr Hillcrest
Jill Esmond . . . . Jill Hillcrest
Edward Chapman . . . . Dawker
Helen Haye . . . . Mrs Hillcrest
Ronald Frankau . . . . Auctioneer
Herbert Ross . . . . Mr Jackman
Dora Gregory . . . . Mrs Jackman
R.E. Jeffrey . . . . Stranger
DRAMA Country family use blackmail to thwart rich tradesman's building plans.

08976
BROWN SUGAR (70) (A)
Twickenham (WB)
P: Julius Hagen
D: Leslie Hiscott
S: (PLAY) Lady Arthur Lever
SC: Cyril Twyford
Constance Carpenter . . . .Lady Stella Sloane
Francis Lister . . . . Lord Sloane
Allan Aynesworth . . . . . . Lord Knightsbridge
Helen Haye . . . . .Lady Knightsbridge
Cecily Byrne . . . . Lady Honoria Nesbitt
Eva Moore . . . . Mrs Cunningham
Chili Bouchier . . . . .Ninon de Veaux
Gerald Rawlinson . . . . . . .Archie Wentworth
Alfred Drayton . . . . Edmondson
Wallace Geoffrey . . . . . .Crawbie Carruthers
ROMANCE Lord's parents object to actress wife until she takes blame for gambler.

08977
THE LYONS MAIL (76) (A)
Twickenham (W&F)
P: Julius Hagen
D: Arthur Maude
S: (PLAY) Charles Reade
SC: H. Fowler Mear
Sir John Martin Harvey . Lesurques/Dubosc
Norah Baring . . . . Julie
Ben Webster . . . . Jerome Lesurques
Moore Marriott . . . . Choppard
George Thirlwell . . . . Jean Didier
Michael Hogan . . . . Courriole
Sheila Wray . . . . Mme Couriole
Eric Howard . . . . Fouinnard
CRIME France, period. Virtuous man mistaken for murderous double.

08978
ALIBI (75) (A)
Twickenham (W&F)
P: Julius Hagen
D: Leslie Hiscott
S: (PLAY) Michael Morton, Agatha Christie
SC: H. Fowler Mear
Austin Trevor . . . . Hercule Poirot
Franklin Dyall . . . . .Sir Roger Ackroyd
Elizabeth Allan . . . . Ursula Browne
J.H. Roberts . . . . Dr Sheppard
John Deverell . . . . .Lord Halliford
Ronald Ward . . . . Ralph Ackroyd
Mary Jerrold . . . . Mrs Ackroyd
Mercia Swinburne . . . . Caryll Sheppard
Harvey Braban . . . . Insp Davis
CRIME French detective solves faked suicide in country house.

MAY

08979
TILLY OF BLOOMSBURY (70) (U)
Sterling
D: Jack Raymond
S: (PLAY) Ian Hay
SC: W.P. Lipscomb

Sydney Howard . . . . . . .Samuel Stillbottle
Phyllis Konstam . . . . Tilly Welwyn
Richard Bird . . . . .Dick Mainwaring
Edward Chapman . . . . . . Percy Welwyn
Ellis Jeffreys . . . . . . Lady Marion Mainwaring
Marie Wright . . . . Mrs Banks
Mabel Russell . . . . Mrs Welwyn
H.R. Hignett . . . . Lucius Welwyn
Ena Grossmith . . . . Amelia Welwyn
Sebastian Smith . . . . Abel Mainwaring
Leila Page . . . . Sylvia
Olwen Roose . . . . .Constance Damery
COMEDY MP's lady wife objects to son's love for boarding house keeper's daughter.

08980
THE OUTSIDER (93) (U)
Cinema House (MGM)
P: Eric Hakim
D: Harry Lacham
S: (PLAY) Dorothy Brandon
SC: Harry Lachman, Alma Reville
Joan Barry . . . . Lalage Sturdee
Harold Huth . . . . Anton Ragatzy
Norman McKinnel . . . . Jasper Sturdee
Frank Lawton . . . . Basil Owen
Mary Clare . . . . Mrs Coates
Glenore Pointing . . . . Carol
Annie Esmond . . . . Pritchard
S.J. Gillett . . . . Dr Ladd
Randolph McLeod . . . . . .Sir Nathan Israel
Fewlass Llewellyn . . . . Sir Montague Tollemach
DRAMA Unqualified osteopath cures surgeon's paralysed daughter.

08981
DREYFUS (90) (U)
USA: THE DREYFUS CASE
BIP (Wardour)
P: F.W. Kraemer
D: F.W. Kraemer, Milton Rosmer
S: (PLAY) Herzog, Rehfisch (THE DREYFUS CASE)
SC: Reginald Berkeley, Walter C. Mycroft
Cedric Hardwicke . . . . Alfred Dreyfus
Charles Carson . . . . Col Picquart
George Merritt . . . . Emile Zola
Sam Livesey . . . . Labori
Beatrix Thomson . . . . Lucie Dreyfus
Garry Marsh . . . . Maj Esterhazy
Randle Ayrton . . . . President
Henry Caine . . . . Col Henry
George Skillan . . . . Maj Paty du Clam
Leonard Shepherd . . . . . .Georges Clemenceau
Arthur Hardy . . . . Gen Mercier
Alexander Sarner . . . . .Matthieu Dreyfus
Frederick Leister . . . . Demange
J. Fisher White . . . . Pellieux
Abraham Sofaer . . . . Dubois
Leslie Frith . . . . Bertillon
George Zucco . . . . Cavaignac
Nigel Barrie . . . . Lauth
HISTORY France, 1894. General staff uses forged evidence to convict Jewish officer of spying.

08982
LET'S LOVE AND LAUGH (85) (A) *bilingual*
USA: BRIDEGROOM FOR TWO
BIP (Wardour)
P: D: Richard Eichberg
S: (PLAY) Fred Thompson, Ernest Paulton (A WELCOME WIFE)
SC: Frederick Jackson, Walter C. Mycroft
Gene Gerrard . . . . Bridegroom
Muriel Angelus . . . . Bride
George Gee . . . . Detective
Ronald Frankau . . . . Father

Frank Stanmore . . . . Father
Denis Wyndham . . . . Fiance
Rita Page . . . . Bride-who-wasn't
Margaret Yarde . . . . Mother
Henry Wenman . . . . Butler
COMEDY Drunkard's wife returns on eve of marriage to another.

08983
THE OFFICER'S MESS (98) (U)
Harry Rowson (Par) *reissue:* 1939
D: Manning Haynes
S: (PLAY) Sidney Blow, Douglas Hoare
SC: Eliot Stannard, Douglas Hoare
Richard Cooper . . . . Tony Turnbull
Harold French . . . . Budge Harbottle
Elsa Lanchester . . . . Cora Melville
Mary Newland . . . . Kitty
Max Avieson . . . . Bolton
Margery Binner . . . . Phoebe
George Bellamy . . . . Insp Bedouin
Annie Esmond . . . . Mrs Makepiece
Fewlass Lewellyn . . . . . . Admiral Harbottle
Helen Haye . . . . Mrs Harbottle
Faith Bennett . . . . Ann Telford
COMEDY Flirtatious lieutenants involved with actress's stolen jewels.

08984
NO LADY (72) (U)
Gaumont *reissue:* 1943 (EB)
P: L'Estrange Fawcett
D: Lupino Lane
S: R.P. Weston, Bert Lee, Lupino Lane
SC: George Dewhurst
Lupino Lane . . . . Mr Pog
Renee Clama . . . . Sonia
Sari Maritza . . . . Greta Gherkinski
Wallace Lupino . . . . Ptomanian Ptough
Lola Hunt . . . . Mrs Pog
Denis O'Neil . . . . Singer
Herman Darewski and his Tower Band
COMEDY Blackpool. Henpeck mistaken for foreign crook wins race in wireless-controlled glider.

08985
DOWN RIVER (73) (A)
Gaumont
P: L'Estrange Fawcett
D: Peter Godfrey
S: (NOVEL) "Seamark" (Austin Small)
SC: Ralph Gilbert Bettinson
Charles Laughton . . . . Capt Grossman
Jane Baxter . . . . Hilary Gordon
Harold Huth . . . . John Durham
Kenneth Kove . . . . Ronnie Gordon
Hartley Power . . . . Lingard
Arthur Goullet . . . . Maxick
Norman Shelley . . . . Blind Rudley
Frederick Leister . . . . Insp Manning
Cyril McLaglen . . . . Sgt Proctor
Humberston Wright . . . . Sir Michael Gordon
Hugh E. Wright . . . . Charlie Wong
CRIME Customs agent unmasks Dutch-Chinese tramp-skipper as head of smuggling gang.

08986
THE RINGER (75) (A)
Gainsborough-British Lion (Ideal)
P: Michael Balcon
D: Walter Forde
S: (PLAY) Edgar Wallace
SC: Angus Macphail, Robert Stevenson
Gordon Harker . . . . Sam Hackett
Franklin Dyall . . . . Maurice Meister
John Longden . . . . Insp Wembury
Carol Goodner . . . . Cora Ann Milton
Patrick Curwen . . . . Dr Lomond

Dorothy Bartlam . . . . Mary Lenley
Esmond Knight . . . . John Lenley
Henry Hallett . . . . Insp Bliss
Arthur Stratton . . . . Sgt Carter
Kathleen Joyce . . . . Gwenda Milton
CRIME Disguised crook kills ex-partner despite Police protection.

08987
THE CHANCE OF A NIGHT TIME (74) (U)
B&D (W&F) *reissue:* 1937 (EB)
P: Herbert Wilcox
D: Herbert Wilcox, Ralph Lynn
S: (PLAY) Ben Travers (THE DIPPERS)
SC: W.P. Lipscomb
Ralph Lynn . . . . Henry
Winifred Shotter . . . . Pauline Gay
Kenneth Kove . . . . Swithin
Sunday Wilshin . . . . Stella
Robert English . . . . Gen Rackham
Dino Galvani . . . . Boris Bolero
COMEDY Affianced solicitor poses as partner of professional dancing girl.

08988
CAPTIVATION (76) (A)
John Harvel Productions (W&F)
D: John Harvel
S: (PLAY) Edgar C. Middleton
Conway Tearle . . . . Hugh Somerton
Betty Stockfield . . . . Ann Moore
Violet Vanbrugh . . . . Lady Froster
Robert Farquharson . . . . . . Graves
Marilyn Mawm . . . . Muriel Froster
A. Bromley Davenport . . . . Col Jordan
Louie Tinsley . . . . Fluffy
Frederick Volpe . . . . Skipper
George de Warfaz . . . . Clerk
Dorothy Black . . . . Adventuress
ROMANCE Riviera. Girl's scheme to force famous novelist into marriage.

JUN

08989
MY WIFE'S FAMILY (80) (A)
BIP (Wardour) *reissue:* 1933
D: Monty Banks
S: (PLAY) Fred Duprez, Hal Stephens, Harry B. Linton
SC: Fred Duprez, Val Valentine
Gene Gerrard . . . . Jack Gay
Muriel Angelus . . . . Peggy Gay
Jimmy Godden . . . . Doc Knott
Amy Veness . . . . Arabella Nagg
Charles Paton . . . . Noah Nagg
Dodo Watts . . . . Ima Nagg
Tom Helmore . . . . Willie Nagg
Molly Lamont . . . . Sally
Ellen Pollock . . . . Dolly White
COMEDY Wife mistakes piano hidden by husband for his bastard baby.

08990
STEPPING STONES (50) (U)
Geoffrey Benstead
D: S: Geoffrey Benstead
Jade Hales
George Bellamy
Celia Bird
Victoria Palace Girls
Alec Alexander's Melody Boys
Heather Thatcher
Charles Paton
Henderson & Lenox
Tom Stuart
Fred Rains
MUSICAL Old couple recall stars and songs of Victorian Music Halls.

08991
THE OTHER WOMAN (64) (A)
Majestic Films (UA)
P: Gordon Craig
D: G.B. Samuelson
S: (STORY) Olga Hall Brown (THE SLAVE BRACELET)
Isobel Elsom . . . . Roxanne Paget
David Hawthorne . . . . Anthony Paget
Eva Moore . . . . Mrs Wycherley
Pat Paterson . . . . Prudence Wycherley
Gladys Frazin . . . . Minerva Derwent
Jane Vaughan . . . . Marian
ROMANCE Socialite wins back neglected husband.

JUL

08992
77 PARK LANE (82) *trilingual* (A)
Famous Players Guild (UA)
P: John Harding
D: Albert de Courville
S: (PLAY) Walter Hackett
SC: Michael Powell, Reginald Berkeley
Dennis Neilson-Terry, ... Lord Brent
Betty Stockfeld . . . . Mary Connor
Malcolm Keen . . . . Sherringham
Ben Welden . . . . Sinclair
Cecil Humphreys . . . . Paul
Esmond Knight . . . . Philip Connor
Molly Johnson . . . . Eve Grayson
Roland Culver . . . . . Sir Richard Carrington
W. Molesworth Blow . . . . George Malton
John Turnbull . . . . Supt
CRIME Blackmailer using Lord's home for gambling den frames girl's brother for partner's murder.

08993
RODNEY STEPS IN (42) (U)
Real Art (Fox)
P: Julius Hagen, Harry Cohen
D: Guy Newall
S: Brock Williams
Richard Cooper . . . . Rodney Perch
Elizabeth Allan . . . . Masked Lady
Walter Piers . . . . Steven Dalton
Leo Sheffield . . . . Tapper
Alexander Field . . . . Billings
John Turnbull . . . . Insp
COMEDY Rich man helps girl who is posing as jewel thief.

08994
NUMBER PLEASE (41) (A)
George King (Fox)
P: Harry Cohen
D: George King
S: Charles Bennett, Billie Bristow
SC: H. Fowler Mear
Mabel Poulton . . . . Peggy
Warwick Ward . . . . Curtis Somers
Richard Bird . . . . Jimmy
Frank Perfitt . . . . McAllister
Iris Darbyshire . . . . Vamp
Gladys Hamer . . . . Darkie
Norman Pierce . . . . Insp
CRIME Telephonist flirts with crook to annoy fiance.

08995
PEACE AND QUIET (42) (U)
GS Enterprises (Fox)
P: A. George Smith, Harry Cohen
D: Frank Richardson
S: Brock Williams
Herbert Mundin . . . . Percy Wilberforce
Iris Darbyshire . . . . Countess Sonia

D.A. Clarke-Smith . . . . Capt Nash
Marie Ault . . . . Mrs Cherry
Rene Ray . . . . Beryl
COMEDY Nervous man inherits peerage and thwarts crooked captain.

08996
BIRDS OF A FEATHER (52) (A)
P. Macnamara (G&L)
D: Ben R. Hart
Haddon Mason . . . . Michael
Dorothy Bartlam . . . . Vera
Edith Saville . . . .
Robert Horton . . . .
Gladys Dunham . . . .
ROMANCE Bohemian reforms for love of widowed artist's daughter.

08997
THE ROSARY (70) (A)
Twickenham (WP)
P: Julius Hagen
D: Guy Newall
S: John McNally
Margot Grahame . . . . Mary Edwards
Elizabeth Allan . . . . Vera Mannering
Walter Piers . . . . Capt Mannering
Leslie Perrins . . . . Ronald Overton
Robert Holmes . . . . Dalmayne
Charles Groves . . . . Hornett
Irene Rooke . . . . Mother Superior
Les Allen . . . . The Singer
CRIME Girl takes blame when halfsister shoots forger.

08998
TWO CROWDED HOURS (42) (A)
Film Engineering Co (Fox)
P: Jerome Jackson, Harry Cohen
D: Michael Powell
S: J. Jefferson Farjeon
John Longden . . . . Harry Fielding
Jane Welsh . . . . Joyce Danton
Jerry Verno . . . . Jim
Michael Hogan . . . . Scammell
Edward Barber . . . . Tom Murray
CRIME Escaped convict tries to kill witness.

08999
SALLY IN OUR ALLEY (77) (A)
TV APT(Radio) reissue:1935
P: Basil Dean
D: Maurice Elvey
S: (PLAY) Charles McEvoy (THE LIKES OF 'ER)
SC: Miles Malleson, Alma Reville, Archie Pitt
Gracie Fields . . . . Sally Winch
Ian Hunter . . . . George Miles
Florence Desmond . . . . . . Florrie Small
Ivor Barnard . . . . Tod Small
Fred Groves. . . . . Alf Cope
Gibb McLaughlin . . . . Jim Sears
Ben Field . . . . Sam Bilson
Barbara Gott . . . . Mrs Pool
Renee Macready . . . . Lady Daphne
Helen Ferrers . . . . Duchess of Wexford
MUSICAL Jealous girl tries to spoil cafe singer's love for wounded soldier.

09000
KEEPERS OF YOUTH (70) (A)
BIP (Wardour)
D: Thomas Bentley
S: (PLAY) Arnold Ridley
SC: Thomas Bentley, Frank Launder, Walter C. Mycroft
Garry Marsh . . . . Knox
Ann Todd . . . . Millicent
Robin Irvine . . . . David Lake

John Turnbull . . . . Gordon Duff
O.B. Clarence . . . . Slade
Herbert Ross . . . . Sullivan
Mary Clare . . . . Mrs Venner
John Hunt . . . . Henry Venner
Ethel Warwick . . . . Matron
Rene Ray . . . . Kitty Williams
DRAMA Teacher saves assistant matron from blackmailing sports master.

09001
THE HOUSE OPPOSITE (66) (U)
BIP (Pathe)
D: SC: Walter Summers
S: (PLAY) J. Jefferson Farjeon
Henry Kendall . . . . Hobart
Frank Stanmore . . . . Ben
Celia Glyn . . . . Nadine
Arthur Macrae . . . . Randall
Wallace Geoffrey . . . . Clitheroe
Rene Macready . . . . Jessica
Abraham Sofaer . . . . Fahmy
Molly Lamont . . . . Doris
Charles Farrell . . . . Wharton
CRIME Girl tec and blackmail victim catch mad scientist's gang.

09002
POOR OLD BILL (52) (U)
BIP (Wardour)
D: Monty Banks
S: Syd Courtenay, Lola Harvey
SC: Val Valentine
Leslie Fuller . . . . Bill
Iris Ashley . . . . Emily
Syd Courtenay . . . . Harry
Peter Lawford . . . . Horace
Hal Gordon . . . . Jack
Robert Brooks-Turner . . . . . Mick
Dick Francis . . . . PC
COMEDY Husband tries to get rid of permanent guest.

09003
FASCINATION (70) (A)
Regina (Wardour)
P: Clayton Hutton
D: Miles Mander
S: (PLAY) Eliot Crawshay Williams
SC: Victor Kendall
Madeleine Carroll . . . . Gwenda Farrell
Carl Harbord . . . . Larry Maitland
Dorothy Bartlam . . . . Vera Maitland
Kay Hammond . . . . Kay
Kenneth Kove . . . . Bertie
Louis Goodrich . . . . Col Farrington
Roland Culver . . . . Ronnie
Freddie Bartholomew . . . . Child
ROMANCE Woman offers to share husband with infatuated actress.

09004
GLAMOUR (71) (A)
BIP (Wardour)
D: Seymour Hicks, Harry Hughes
S: Seymour Hicks
Seymour Hicks . . . . Henry Garthorne
Ellaline Terriss . . . . Lady Belton
Margot Grahame . . . . . . Lady Betty Enfield
Basil Gill . . . . Lord Westborough
A. Bromley Davenport . . . Lord Belton
Beverley Nichols . . . . Hon Richard Wells
Betty Hicks . . . . Lady Armadale
Clifford Heatherley . . . . . . Edward Crumbles
Naomi Jacob . . . . .Rosalind Crumbles
David Hawthorne . . . . Charlie Drummond
Philip Hewland . . . . Millett
Arthur Stratton . . . . Fireman
Charles Paton . . . . Clockwinder

Margery Binner . . . . Reede
Eric Marshall . . . . Singer
ROMANCE Ageing actor repels infatuated lady and returns to first love.

09005
EAST LYNNE ON THE WESTERN FRONT (82) (U)
Welsh-Pearson (Gaumont)
P: T.A. Welsh
D: George Pearson
S: George Pearson, T.A. Welsh
SC: Donovan Parsons, Mary Parsons
Herbert Mundin . . . . . . Bob Cox/Lady Isobel
Mark Daly . . . . Maurice/Levison
Alf Goddard . . . . Ben/Cornelia
Hugh E. Wright . . . . Fred
Edwin Ellis . . . . .Sam/Barbara Hare
Harold French . . . . Reggie Pitt
Blanche Adele . . . . Mimi
Wilfrid Lawson . . . . Dick Webb/Carlyle
Escott Davies . . . . Joe/Little Willie
Roger Livesey . . . . Sandy
Philip Godfrey . . . . Jack/Hare
COMEDY France, 1915. Soldiers billeted in empty theatre stage burlesque of "East Lynne".

09006
A NIGHT IN MONTMARTRE (70) (A)
Gaumont
P: Michael Balcon
D: Leslie Hiscott
S: (PLAY) Miles Malleson, Walter Peacock
SC: Angus Macphail
Horace Hodges . . . . Lucien Borell
Franklin Dyall . . . . Max Levine
Hugh Williams . . . . Philip Borell
Heather Angel . . . . .Annette Lefevre
Austin Trevor . . . . Paul de Lisle
Kay Hammond . . . . Margot
Edmund Willard . . . . Alexandre
Arthur Hambling . . . . Insp Brichot
Reginald Purdell . . . . Tino
Binnie Barnes . . . . Therese
CRIME Paris. Man proves son did not murder blackmailer.

09007
THE HOUND OF THE BASKERVILLES (75) (U)
Gaumont
P: Michael Balcon
D: V. Gareth Gundrey
S: (NOVEL) Arthur Conan Doyle
SC: Edgar Wallace, V. Gareth Gundrey
John Stuart . . . . . . .Sir Henry Baskerville
Robert Rendel , ... Sherlock Holmes
Reginald Bach . . . . Stapleton
Heather Angel . . . . Beryl Stapleton
Wilfred Shine . . . . Dr Mortimer
Frederick Lloyd . . . . Dr Watson
Sam Livesey . . . . . . .Sir Hugo Baskerville
Henry Hallett . . . . Barrymore
Sybil Jane . . . . Mrs Barrymore
CRIME Dartmoor. Farmer tries to gain inheritance by killing heir with phosphorescent hound.

09008
HER REPUTATION (67) (A)
London Screenplays (Par)
P: D: SC: Sidney Morgan
S: (PLAY) Jevan Brandon-Thomas (PASSING BROMPTON ROAD)
Iris Hoey . . . . Dultitia Sloane
Frank Cellier . . . . Henry Sloane
Malcolm Tearle . . . . George Harding
Lilian Hall Davis . . . . Miss Carruthers
Maurice Braddell . . . . Eric Sloane

Joan Morgan . . . . Veronica Sloane
Dorothy Black . . . . Georgina Pastell
Lawrence Hanray . . . . Mr Montgomery
COMEDY Wife's attempt to divorce husband
fails through her accomplice's timidity.

09009
THESE CHARMING PEOPLE (820) (A)
Paramount British
P: Walter Morosco
D: Louis Mercanton
S: (PLAY) Michael Arlen (DEAR FATHER)
SC: Hugh Perceval, Irving Howard
Cyril Maude . . . . Col Crawford
Godfrey Tearle . . . . James Berridge
Nora Swinburne . . . . Julia Berridge
Ann Todd . . . . Pamela Crawford
Anthony Ireland . . . . Geoffrey Allen
Cyril Raymond . . . . Miles Winter
C.V. France . . . . Minx
Billy Shine . . . . Ulysses Wiggins
ROMANCE Col thwarts affair between
married daughter and secretary.

AUG

09010
THE FLYING FOOL (76) (U)
BIP (Wardour) *reissue:* 1935 (EB)
D: SC: Walter Summers
S: (PLAY) Arnold Ridley, Bernard Merivale
Henry Kendall . . . . Vincent Floyd
Benita Hume . . . . Marion Lee
Wallace Geoffrey . . . . Michael Marlowe
Martin Walker . . . . Jim Lancer
Ursula Jeans . . . . Morella Arlen
Barbara Gott . . . . Mme Charron
Charles Farrell . . . . Ponder
Syd Crossley . . . . Hicks
CRIME Crook's mistress reforms and helps
secret service pilot.

09011
CREEPING SHADOWS (79) (A)
USA: THE LIMPING MAN
BIP (Wardour)
D: SC: John Orton
S: (PLAY) Will Scott (THE LIMPING MAN)
Franklin Dyall . . . . Disher
Arthur Hardy . . . . Sir Edwin Paget
Margot Grahame . . . . Gloria Paget
Lester Matthews . . . . Brian Nash
Jeanne Stuart . . . . Olga Hoyt
Gerald Rawlinson . . . . Paul Tegle
David Hawthorne . . . . Peter Hoyt
Charles Farrell . . . . Chicago Joe
Henrietta Watson . . . . Lady Paget
Matthew Boulton . . . . Insp Potter
Percy Parsons . . . . Limping Man
CRIME Three victims plot to kill retired
informer.

09012
THE MAN AT SIX (70) (U)
USA: THE GABLES MYSTERY
BIP (Wardour)
D: Harry Hughes
S: (PLAY) Jack De Leon, Jack Celestin
SC: Harry Hughes, Victor Kendall
Anne Grey . . . . Sybil Vane
Lester Matthews . . . . Campbell Edwards
Gerald Rawlinson . . . . Frank Pine
John Turnbull . . . . Insp Dawford
Kenneth Kove . . . . Joshua Atkinson
Charles Farrell . . . . George Wollmer
Arthur Stratton . . . . Sgt Hogan
Herbert Ross . . . . .Sir Joseph Pine
Minnie Rayner . . . . Mrs Cummerpatch
CRIME Girl tec unmasks colleague as killer
posing as woman to steal jewels.

09013
BILL AND COO (42) (U)
BIP (Wardour)
D: John Orton
S: John Orton, Billy Merson
Billy Merson . . . . Bendo
Nita Underwood . . . . Nita
Leslie Hamilton . . . . Leslie
Hal Gordon . . . . Harry
Nan Kennedy . . . . Impressionist
O.K. Wise . . . . Old Actor
Herman Darewski . . . . Guggenheim
COMEDY Strong man dreams of bungalow
honeymoon with revue star.

09014
LOVE LIES (70) (U)
BIP (Wardour)
D: Lupino Lane
S: (PLAY) Stanley Lupino
SC: Stanley Lupino, Arthur Rigby, Frank
Miller
Stanley Lupino . . . . Jerry Walker
Dorothy Boyd . . . . Joyce
Jack Hobbs . . . . Rolly Rider
Dennis Hoey . . . . Cyrus Watt
Binnie Barnes . . . . Junetta
Sebastian Smith . . . . Nicholas Wich
Wallace Lupino . . . . Lord Lletgoe
Arty Ash . . . . Butler
Charles Courtneidge . . . . . Inspector
COMEDY One rich uncle wants nephew to stay
bachelor, the other wants him to marry.

09015
THE MAN THEY COULD NOT ARREST
(74) (U)
Gainsborough (W&F)
P: Michael Balcon
D: T. Hayes Hunter
S: (NOVEL) Edgar Wallace
SC: Arthur Wimperis, Angus Macphail,
T. Hayes Hunter
Hugh Wakefield . . . . Dain
Gordon Harker . . . . Tansey
Renee Clama . . . . Marcia
Nicholas Hannen . . . . Lyall
Garry Marsh . . . . Delbury
Robert Farquharson . . . . . Count Lazard
Dennis Wyndham . . . . Shaughnessy
CRIME Scientist's "eavesdrop wireless" exposes
fiancee's father as gang leader.

09016
ALMOST A DIVORCE (59) (A)
B&D (W&F)
P: Herbert Wilcox
D: S: Arthur Varney Serrao
SC: Brock Williams
Nelson Keys . . . . Richard Leighton
Sydney Howard . . . . Mackintosh
Marjorie Binner . . . . Angela Leighton
Eva Moore . . . . Aunt Isobel
Kay Hammond . . . . Maisie
Kenneth Kove . . . . Detective
COMEDY Bibulous man almost ruins friend's
marriage.

09017
BLACK COFFEE (78) (U)
Twickenham (W&F)
P: Julius Hagen
D: Leslie Hiscott
S: (PLAY) Agatha Christie
SC: Brock Williams, H. Fowler Mear
Austin Trevor . . . . Hercule Poirot
Adrianne Allen . . . . Lucia Amory
Richard Cooper . . . . Capt Hastings
Elizabeth Allan . . . . Barbara Amory
C.V. France . . . . Sir Claude Amory

Philip Strange . . . . Richard Amory
Dino Galvani . . . . Dr Carelli
Michael Shepley . . . . Raynor
Melville Cooper . . . . Insp Japp
Marie Wright . . . . Miss Amory
CRIME French tec solves theft of secret
formula.

09018
MY OLD CHINA (35) (U)
Gainsborough (Ideal)
P: Michael Balcon
D: W.P. Kellino
S: Angus Macphail, Chandos Balcon
Clifford Heatherley . . . . . . Moo Kow
Constance Carpenter . . . . .
Reginald Gardiner . . . .
Gibb McLaughlin . . . . Ping Pong
Seth Egbert . . . .
Frank Stanmore . . . . Sam
COMEDY Newsreel cameramen wrest secret
papers from Chinese bandit.

SEP

09019
JEALOUSY (56) (A)
P: Gordon Craig
Majestic-New Era
D: G.B. Samuelson
S: (PLAY) John McNally (THE GREEN EYE)
Mary Newland . . . . Joyce Newcombe
Malcolm Keen . . . . Henry Garwood
Harold French . . . . Bernard Wingate
Gibb McLaughlin . . . . Littleton Pardmore
Sam Livesey . . . . Insp Thompson
Henrietta Watson . . . . Mrs Delahunt
Henry Carlisle . . . . Clayton
Frank Pettingell . . . . Prof Macguire
DRAMA Jealous guardian tries to ruin young
ward's romance.

09020
THE SHADOW BETWEEN (87) (A)
BIP (Wardour)
D: Norman Walker
S: Dion Titheradge
SC: Norman Walker, Dion Titheradge
Godfrey Tearle . . . . Paul Haddon
Kathleen O'Regan . . . . Margaret Haddon
Olga Lindo . . . . Nell Baker
Ann Casson . . . . Betty Fielder
Mary Jerrold . . . . Mrs Maddox
Hubert Harben . . . . Rev Simon Maddox
Henry Wenman . . . . Sgt Blake
Henry Caine . . . . Wincher
Morton Selten . . . . . . Sir George Fielder
Arthur Chesney . . . . Pug Wilson
Jerrold Robertshaw . . . . . . Mr Haddon
DRAMA Financier and wife learn love after
each serves prison sentence.

09021
CHIN CHIN CHINAMAN (52) (U)
USA : BOAT FROM SHANGHAI
Real Art (MGM)
P: Julius Hagen
D: Guy Newall
S: (PLAY) Percy Walsh
SC: Brock Williams, Guy Newall
Leon M. Lion . . . . The Mandarin
Elizabeth Allan . . . . The Countess
George Curzon . . . . Colley
Dino Galvani . . . . Dolange
Picot Schooling . . . . Marie
Douglas Blandford . . . . . . Captain
CRIME Tecs pose as mandarin and countess to
recover stolen jewels.

09022
DEADLOCK (85) (A)
George King (Butcher)
D: George King
S: Charles Bennett, Billie Bristow
SC: H. Fowler Mear
Stewart Rome . . . . James Whitelaw KC
Marjorie Hume . . . . Mrs Whitelaw
Warwick Ward . . . . Markham Savage
Annette Benson . . . . . . Madeleine d'Arblay
Esmond Knight . . . . John Tring
Janice Adair . . . . Joan Whitelaw
Alma Taylor . . . . Mrs Tring
Cameron Carr . . . . Tony Makepeace
Hay Plumb . . . . Publicist
Pauline Peters . . . . Maid
Kyoshi Tekase . . . . Taki
Philip Godfrey . . . . Nifty Weekes
H. Saxon-Snell . . . . Prosecution
CRIME Camera records actor's murder during
film scene.

09023
THE GIRL IN THE NIGHT (65) (U)
Henry Edwards (Wardour)
D: S: Henry Edwards
SC: Edwin Greenwood
Henry Edwards . . . . Billie
Dorothy Boyd . . . . Cecile
Sam Livesey . . . . Ephraim Tucker
Reginald Bach . . . . Schmidt
Eric Maturin . . . . Fenton
Diana Wilson . . . . Mrs Fenton
Charles Paton . . . . Prof Winthrop
Harvey Braban . . . . Inspector
CRIME Man shelters from storm in old house
used by diamond smugglers.

09024
THE WRITTEN LAW (79) (A)
Reginald Fogwell (Ideal)
P: Reginald Fogwell, Mansfield Markham
D: S: Reginald Fogwell
Madeleine Carroll . . . . . Lady Margaret Rochester
Percy Marmont . . . . Sir John Rochester
Henry Hewitt . . . . Harry Carlisle
James Fenton . . . . Dr Rawlinson
Barbara Barlowe . . . . Celia
DRAMA Devon. Doctor does not tell his wife
that his blindness is cured.

09025
UP FOR THE CUP (76) (U)
B&D (W&F) *reissue:* 1937 (EB)
P: Herbert Wilcox
D: Jack Raymond
S: Con West, R.P. Weston, Bert Lee
Sydney Howard . . . . . . John Willie Entwhistle
Joan Wyndham . . . . Mary Murgatroyd
Stanley Kirk . . . . Cyril Hardcastle
Sam Livesey . . . . John Cartwright
Marie Wright . . . . Mrs Entwhistle
Moore Marriott . . . . James Hardcastle
Hal Gordon . . . . Proprietor
Herbert Woodward . . . . . . Tom
Jack Raymond . . . . Railway Clerk
COMEDY Yorkshire loom-inventor comes to
London for Cup Final and loses money and
tickets.

09026
MY FRIEND THE KING (52) (U)
Film Engineering (Fox)
P: Jerome Jackson
D: Michael Powell
S: J. Jefferson Farjeon
Jerry Verno . . . . Jim
Robert Holmes . . . . Capt Felz

Tracey Holmes . . . . Count Huelin
Eric Pavitt . . . . King Ludwig
Phyllis Loring . . . . Princess Helma
Luli Hohenberg . . . . Countess Zena
H. Saxon Snell . . . . Karl
COMEDY Ruritania. Taxi-driver saves boy king
from revolutionaries.

09027
THE GHOST TRAIN (72) (U)
Gainsborough (W&F)
P: Michael Balcon
D: Walter Forde
S: (PLAY) Arnold Ridley
SC: Angus Macphail, Lajos Biro
Jack Hulbert . . . . Teddy Deakin
Cicely Courtneidge . . . . Miss Bourne
Donald Calthrop . . . . Saul Hodgkin
Ann Todd . . . . Peggy Murdock
Cyril Raymond . . . . Richard Winthrop
Angela Baddeley . . . . Julia Price
Allan Jeayes . . . . Dr Sterling
Henry Caine . . . . Herbert Price
Tracy Holmes . . . . Charles Bryant
Carol Coombe . . . . Elsie Bryant
COMEDY Tec posing as fool catches smugglers
using abandoned railway line.

09028
A HONEYMOON ADVENTURE (67) (U)
USA: FOOTSTEPS IN THE NIGHT
ATP (Radio)
P: Basil Dean
D: Maurice Elvey
S: (NOVEL) Cecily Fraser-Smith
SC: Rupert Downing, John Paddy Carstairs,
Basil Dean
Benita Hume . . . . Eve Martin
Harold Huth . . . . Walter Creason
Peter Hannen . . . . Peter Martin
Walter Armitage . . . . Judson
Margery Binner . . . . Josephine
Jack Lambert . . . . Chauffeur
Pollie Emery . . . . Old Woman
Robert English . . . . Mr Harvey
Frances Ross Campbell . . . Janet
CRIME Honeymoon wife saves inventor
husband from kidnappers.

OCT

09029
THE HAPPY ENDING (70) (A)
Gaumont
P: L'Estrange Fawcett
D: Millard Webb
S: (PLAY) Ian Hay
SC: H. Fowler Mear
Anne Grey . . . . Mildred Craddock
Benita Hume . . . . Yvonne
George Barraud . . . . Denis Craddock
Alf Goddard . . . . Alf
Cyril Raymond . . . . Anthony Fenwick
Daphne Courtenay . . . . . . Mollie Craddock
Alfred Drayton . . . . Life of the Party
Irene Russell . . . . Wife
DRAMA Faithless husband returns to wife, who
has told their children he died a hero.

09030
HINDLE WAKES (79) (A)
Gaumont
P: Michael Balcon
D: Victor Saville
S: (PLAY) Stanley Houghton
SC: Victor Saville, Angus Macphail
Sybil Thorndike . . . . Mrs Hawthorne
John Stuart . . . . Alan Jeffcoate
Norman McKinnel . . . . . . Nat Jeffcoate

Edmund Gwenn . . . . Chris Hawthorne
Belle Chrystal . . . . Fanny Hawthorne
Mary Clare . . . . Mrs Jeffcoate
Muriel Angelus . . . . Beatrice Farrar
A.G. Poulton . . . . Sir Timothy
Ruth Peterson . . . . Mary Hollins
ROMANCE Lancs. Millgirl refuses to marry
employer's son after their holiday together.

09031
MICHAEL AND MARY (85) (A)
Gaumont (Ideal)
P: Michael Balcon
D: Victor Saville
S: (PLAY) A.A. Milne
SC: Angus Macphail, Robert Stevenson,
Lajos Biro
Herbert Marshall . . . . Michael Rowe
Edna Best . . . . Mary Rowe
Elizabeth Allan . . . . Romo
Frank Lawton . . . . David
D.A. Clarke-Smith . . . . Price
Sunday Wilshin . . . . Violet Cunliffe
Ben Field . . . . Mr Tullivant
Margaret Yarde . . . . Mrs Tullivant
ROMANCE Husband returns after 31 years to
find his wife married again.

09032
THE CALENDAR (79) (A)
USA: BACHELOR'S FOLLY
Gainsborough-British Lion (W&F)
P: Michael Balcon
D: T. Hayes Hunter
S: (PLAY) Edgar Wallace
SC: Angus Macphail, Robert Stevenson
Herbert Marshall . . . . Garry Anson
Edna Best . . . . Jill Panniford
Gordon Harker . . . . Sam Hillcott
Anne Grey . . . . Wenda Panniford
Nigel Bruce . . . . Lord Willie Panniford
Alfred Drayton . . . . John Dory
Allan Aynesworth . . . . . . Edmund Garth
Leslie Perrins . . . . Henry Lascarne
Melville Cooper . . . . Mr Waye
SPORT Ex-convict butler helps bankrupt horse-
owner prove he did not deliberately lose race.

09033
HOBSON'S CHOICE (65) (U)
BIP (Wardour)
D: Thomas Bentley
S: (PLAY) Harold Brighouse
SC: Frank Launder
Viola Lyel . . . . Maggie Hobson
James Harcourt . . . . Hobson
Frank Pettingell . . . . Will Mossup
Belle Chrystal . . . . Vicky Hobson
Jay Laurier . . . . Tubby Wadlow
Joan Maude . . . . Alice Hobson
Amy Veness . . . . Mrs Hepworth
Reginald Bach . . . . Albert Prosser
Basil Moss . . . . Freddy Beenstock
Herbert Lomas . . . . Jim Heeler
Kathleen Harrison . . . . Ada Figgins
COMEDY Lancs. Boot maker's strong-willed
daughter weds meek cobbler.

09034
THE PROFESSIONAL GUEST (42) (U)
George King (Fox)
P: Harry Cohen
D: George King
S: (NOVEL) William Garrett
SC: H. Fowler Mear
Gordon Harker . . . . Joe
Pat Paterson . . . . Marjorie Phibsby
Richard Bird . . . . The Guest
Garry Marsh . . . . Seton Fanshawe

Barbara Gott . . . . Lady Phibsby
Hay Plumb . . . . Sir Alfred Phibsby
Syd Crossley . . . . Crump
COMEDY Newly rich knight hires poor socialite to advance them in society.

09035
THE WORLD'S WORST FILM (10) (U)
International Productions
COMPILATION Extracts from earlier films, mostly American.

09036
STRANGLEHOLD (66) (A)
Teddington (WB)
P: D: SC: Henry Edwards
S: Hugh G. Esse
Isobel Elsom . . . . Beatrice
Garry Marsh . . . . Bruce
Allan Jeayes . . . . King
Dorothy Bartlam . . . . Grace
Derrick de Marney . . . . Phillip
Hugh E. Wright . . . . Briggs
Henry Vibart . . . . Farren
Minnie Rayner . . . . Cook
DRAMA Chinese halfcaste ruins marriage of schoolmate who wronged his sweetheart.

09037
THE BELLS (75) (A) *trilingual*
BSFP (PDC)
P: Isidore Schlesinger, Sergei Nolbandov
D: Oscar M. Werndorff, Harcourt Templeman
S: (PLAY) Erckmann & Chatrian (LE JUIF POLONAIS)
SC: C.H. Dand
Donald Calthrop . . . . Mathias
Jane Welsh . . . . Annette
Edward Sinclair . . . . Sgt Christian Nash
O.B. Clarence . . . . Watchman
Wilfred Shine . . . . Philosopher
Ralph Truman . . . . Blacksmith
CRIME Alsace.Burgomaster's conscience makes him confess to killing Jew.

09038
THE WICKHAM MYSTERY (84) (A)
Samuelson (UA)
P: E. Gordon Craig
D: G.B. Smauelson
S: (PLAY) John McNally (THE PAPER CHASE)
Eve Gray . . . . Joan Hamilton
John Longden . . . . Harry Crawford
Lester Matthews . . . . Charles Wickham
Sam Livesey . . . . Insp Cobb
Walter Piers . . . . '. . . . . . . George Beverley
John Turnbull . . . . Howard Clayton
Wally Bosco . . . . Edward Hamilton
Doris Clemence . . . .·. . Mrs Wickham
CRIME Crooks steal pearls and helicopter plans.

09039
A SAFE AFFAIR (52) (A)
Langham (MGM)
P: Franklin Dyall, J.H. Roberts
D: Herbert Wynne
S: Douglas Hoare
SC: Eliot Stannard
Franklin Dyall . . . . Rupert Gay
Jeanne Stuart . . . . Olga Delgaroff
Nancy Welford . . . . Mary Bolton
J.H. Roberts . . . . Judd
J.Neil More . . . . Otto Crann
George Turner . . . . Jim
James Knight . . . . Tom
Douglas Jeffries . . . . Henry
Connie Emerald . . . . Blonde
CRIME Adventurer saves secret papers from Ruritanian Countess.

09040
NIGHT SHADOWS (A)
Nettlefold (UA)
P: Archibald Nettlefold
D: Albert de Courville
William Freshman . . . .
Pat Paterson . . . .
Ethel Warwick . . . .
CRIME Marseilles. (Not shown)

09041
THE GREAT GAY ROAD (88) (A)
Stoll (Butcher)
D: Sinclair Hill
S: (NOVEL) Tom Gallon
SC: Leslie Howard Gordon
Stewart Rome . . . . Hilary Kite
Frank Stanmore . . . . Crook Perkins
Kate Cutler . . . . Aunt Jessie
Arthur Hardy . . . . Sir Crispin
Pat Paterson . . . . Nancy
Billy Milton . . . . Rodney
Hugh E. Wright . . . . Backus
Frederick Lloyd . . . . Col Trigg
Ethel Warwick . . . . Lizzie
Wally Patch . . . . Joe
The Kirkby Sisters . . . . Showgirls
ROMANCE Tramp poses as bart's lost son but relinquishes his sweetheart to younger man.

09042
STAMBOUL (75) (A) *bilingual*
Paramount British
P: Walter Morosco
D: Dmitri Buchowetzki
S: (PLAY) Pierre Frondale (L'HOMME QUI ASSASSINA)
SC: Reginald Denham
Warwick Ward . . . . . . Col Andre de Sevigne
Rosita Moreno . . . . . Baroness von Strick
Margot Grahame . . . . . Countess Elsa Talven
Henry Hewitt . . . . Baron von Strick
Garry Marsh . . . . Prince Cernuwitz
Alan Napier . . . . Bouchier
Abraham Sofaer . . . . Mahmed Pasha
Stella Arbenina . . . . Mme Bouchier
Annie Esmond . . . . Nurse
Eric Pavitt . . . . Franz
CRIME Constantinople. French diplomat kills German Baron who framed him for affair.

NOV

09043
GIPSY BLOOD (79) (U) USA: CARMEN

BIP (Wardour)
D: Cecil Lewis
S: (OPERA) Georges Bizet (CARMEN)
SC: Cecil Lewis, Walter C. Mycroft
Marguerite Namara . . . . Carmen
Thomas Burke . . . . Don Jose
Lance Fairfax . . . . Escamillo
Lester Matthews . . . . Zuniga
Mary Clare . . . . Factory Girl
Dennis Wyndham . . . . Doncairo
D. Hay Petrie . . . . Remenado
Lewin Mannering . . . . Innkeeper
MUSICAL Seville. Soldier deserts and kills for love of gipsy cigarette-maker.

09044
DR JOSSER KC (71) (U)
BIP (Pathe)
D: SC: Norman Lee
S: (SKETCH) Ernest Lotinga, Norman Lee (HOUSE FULL)
Ernie Lotinga . . . . Jimmy Josser
Jack Hobbs . . . . Dick O'Neill

Molly Lamont . . . . Betty O'Neill
Joan Wyndham . . . . Suzette
Binnie Barnes . . . . Rosa Wopp
Harold Wilkinson . . . . Golightly
Arnold Bell . . . . Dick Morris
COMEDY Crook dons disguises to attempt blackmail.

09045
OUT OF THE BLUE (88) (U)
BIP (Pathe)
D: Gene Gerrard, John Orton
S: (PLAY) Caswell Garth, Desmond Carter (LITTLE TOMMY TUCKER)
SC: Frank Miller, R.P. Weston, Bert Lee
Gene Gerrard . . . . Bill Coverdale
Jessie Matthews . . . . Tommy Tucker
Kay Hammond . . . . Angela Tucker
Kenneth Kove . . . . Freddie
Binnie Barnes . . . . Rosa
David Miller . . . . Sir Jeremy Tucker
Fred Groves . . . . Bannister Blair
Averil Haley . . . . Judy Blair
Hal Gordon . . . . Videlop
Gordon Begg . . . . Mumford
John Reynders and his Band
MUSICAL Poor bart's daughter loves radio star engaged to her sister.

09046
MEN LIKE THESE (46) (A)
USA: TRAPPED IN A SUBMARINE
BIP (Wardour)
D: Walter Summers
S: John F. Meed, James A. Marchant
SC: Walter Summers, Walter C. Mycroft
John Batten . . . .
Sydney Seaward . . . .
James Enstone . . . .
Syd Crossley . . . .
John Hunt . . . . Commander
Edward Gee . . . .
Charles Peachey . . . .
Athol Fleming . . . . Lieut
Lesley Waring . . . . Wife
DRAMA Crew is trapped in sunken submarine. (Based on true story of CPO Williams of the "Poseidon".)

09047
THE PERFECT LADY (76) (A)
BIP (Wardour)
D: Milton Rosmer, Frederick Jackson
S: Frederick Jackson
Moira Lynd . . . . Anne Burnett
Harry Wilcoxon . . . . Larry Tindale
Reginald Gardiner . . . . . . .Lord Tony Carderay
Betty Amann . . . . .Jacqueline Dubarry
Athene Seyler . . . . Lady Westhaven
Frederick Lloyd . . . . Lord Westhaven
COMEDY Girl poses as maid of French actress who stole her fiance.

09048
MANY WATERS (76) (A)
Associated Metropolitan (Pathe)
P: J.A. Thorpe
D: Milton Rosmer
S: (PLAY) Leon M. Lion
SC: Monckton Hoffe
Lilian Hall Davis . . . . .Mabel Barcaldine
Arthur Margetson . . . . Jim Barcaldine
Elizabeth Allan . . . . Freda Barcaldine
Donald Calthrop . . . . .Compton Hardcastle
Sam Livesey . . . . Stanley Rosel
Mary Clare . . . . Mrs Rosel
Robert Douglas . . . . Godfrey Marvin
Charles Carson . . . . Henry Delauney
Ivan Samson . . . . Philip Sales
Renee Macready . . . . Dolly Sales

Herbert Lomas . . . . Everett
D. Hay Petrie . . . . Director
J. Fisher White . . . . Gentleman
Monckton Hoffe . . . . Registrar
DRAMA Old pair recall small dramas and
pleasures of thier lives.

09049
BILL'S LEGACY (57) (A)
Twickenham (Ideal)
P: Julius Hagen
D: Harry J. Revier
S: Leslie Fuller, Syd Courtenay
Leslie Full . . . . Bill Smithers
Mary Clare . . . . Mrs Smithers
Angela Joyce . . . . Countess
Syd Courtenay . . . . Count
Ethel Leslie . . . . Bride
Ivan Crowe . . . . Groom
COMEDY Paperhanger buys racehorse with
inheritance, and loses his all.

09050
RYNOX (47) (A)
Film Engineering (Ideal)
P: Jerome Jackson
D: Michael Powell
S: (NOVEL) Philip Macdonald
S:: J. Jefferson Farjeon
Stewart Rome . . . . F.X. Benedik
Dorothy Boyd . . . . Peter
John Longden . . . . Tony Benedik
Edmund Willard . . . . Capt James
Charles Paton . . . .
Fletcher Lightfoot . . . .
Sybil Grove . . . .
Leslie Mitchell . . . .
CRIME Bankrupt businessman fakes own murder
to obtain insurance.

09051
SPLINTERS IN THE NAVY (76) (U)
Twickenham (W&F)
P: Julius Hagen
D: Walter Forde
S: H. Fowler Mear
SC: R.P. Weston, Bert Lee, Jack Marks
Sydney Howard . . . . Joe Crabbs
Frederick Bentley . . . . Bill Miffins
Helena Pickard . . . . Lottie
Paddy Browne . . . . Mabel
Alf Goddard . . . . Spike Higgins
Rupert Lister . . . . Admiral
Harold Heath . . . . Master-at-Arms
Ian Wilson . . . . Call boy
Lew Lake
Hal Jones
Reg Stone
Wilfred Temple
COMEDY Sailor beats Naval boxing champion
and wins girl.

09052
CARNIVAL (88) (A)
USA: VENETIAN NIGHTS
B&D (W&F)
P: D: Herbert Wilcox
S: (PLAY) Matheson Lang, C.M. Hardinge
SC: Donald Macardle
Matheson Lang . . . . Silvio Steno
Joseph Schildkraut . . . . . . Count Andreas Scipio
Dorothy Bouchier . . . . Simonetta Steno
Lilian Braithwaite . . . . Italia
Kay Hammond . . . . Helen
Brian Buchel . . . . Lelio
Dickie Edwards . . . . Nino
Brember Wills . . . . Stage Manager
Alfred Rode and his Tzigane Band
ROMANCE Venice. Jealous actor tries to
strangle wife during "Othello".

DEC
09053
THE RASP (44) (A)
Film Engineering (Fox)
P: Jerome Jackson
D: Michael Powell
S: (NOVEL) Philip Macdonald
SC: J. Jefferson Farjeon
Claude Horton . . . . Anthony Gethryn
Phyllis Loring . . . . Lucia Masterson
C.M. Hallard . . . . Sir Arthur Coates
James Raglan . . . . Alan Deacon
Thomas Weguelin . . . . Insp Boyd
Carol Coombe . . . . Dora Masterson
Leonard Brett . . . . Jimmy Masterson
CRIME Reporter proves minister was killed by
business rival.

09054
THE STAR REPORTER (43) (A)
Film Engineering (Fox)
P: Jerome Jackson
D: Michael Powell
S: Philip Macdonald, Ralph Smart
Harold French . . . . Maj Starr
Isla Bevan . . . . Lady Susan Loman
Garry Marsh . . . . Mandel
Spencer Trevor . . . . Lord Longbourne
Antony Holles . . . . Bonzo
Noel Dainton . . . . Col
CRIME Reporter poses as chauffeur to regain
girl's stolen jewel.

09055
MAN OF MAYFAIR (83) (U) *bilingual*
Paramount British
P: Walter Morosco
D: Louis Mercanton
S: (NOVEL) May Edginton (A CHILD IN
THEIR MIDST)
SC: Eliot Crawshay Williams, Hugh Perceval
Jack Buchanan . . . . Lord William
Joan Barry . . . . Grace Irving
Warwick Ward . . . . Ferdinand Barclay
Nora Swinburne . . . . Elaine Barclay
Ellaline Terriss . . . . Old Grace
Lilian Braithwaite . . . . Lady Kingsland
Cyril Raymond . . . . Charles
Charles Quartermaine . . . . . Dalton
Sebastian Smith . . . . Macpherson
J. Fisher White . . . . Wilson
The Francis Mangan Girls
ROMANCE Lord poses as workman to win
dancer who works as waitress in her mother's
tea garden.

09056
TWO WAY STREET (43) (A)
Nettlefold (UA)
D: George King
S: Charles Bennett, Billie Bristow
Sari Maritza . . . . Jill Whistler
James Raglan . . . . Hon James Wentworth
Harry Wilcoxon . . . . Bert Adams
Quinton Macpherson . . . . . Old Whistler
ROMANCE Bird fancier's daughter loves
nobleman whom her cockney fiance robs of
necklace.

09057
INQUEST (95) (A)
Majestic-New Era (FN)
P: Gordon Craig
D: G.B. Samuelson
S: (PLAY) Michael Barringer
SC: Michael Barringer
Mary Glynne . . . . Margaret Hamilton
Campbell Gullan . . . . Norman Dennison KC
Sydney Morgan . . . . Coroner

Haddon Mason . . . . Richard Hanning
G.H. Mulcaster . . . . Charles Wyatt
Lena Halliday . . . . Mrs Wyatt
Peter Coleman . . . . Mr Hamilton
Reginald Tippett . . . . Sir Denton Hume
CRIME Biassed coroner suspects widow of
poisoning husband.

09058
SUNSHINE SUSIE (87) (U)
USA: THE OFFICE GIRL
Gainsborough (Ideal)
P: Michael Balcon
D: Victor Saville
S: (PLAY) Franz Schulz, Szomahazy (DIE
PRIVATSEKRETERIN)
S: Angus Macphail, Robert Stevenson, Victor
Saville, Noel Wood-Smith
Renate Muller . . . . Susie Surster
Jack Hulbert . . . . Herr Hasel
Owen Nares . . . . Herr Arvray
Morris Harvey . . . . Klapper
Sybil Grove . . . . Secretary
Gladys Hamer . . . . Maid
Daphne Scorer . . . . Elsa
MUSICAL Vienna. Banker poses as clerk to
win secretary. (FWA: 1932.)

09059
A GENTLEMAN OF PARIS (76) (A)
Gaumont
P: Michael Balcon
D: Sinclair Hill
S: (NOVEL) Niranjan Pal (HIS HONOUR
THE JUDGE)
SC: Sewell Collins, S. Gilbert
Arthur Wontner . . . . Judge le Fevre
Vanda Greville . . . . Paulette Gerrard
Hugh Williams . . . . Gaston Gerrard
Phyllis Konstam . . . . Madeleine
Sybil Thorndike . . . . Lola Duval
Arthur Goullet . . . . Bagot
George Merritt . . . . M. Duval
Frederick Lloyd . . . . Advocate-General
George de Warfaz . . . . Valet
Florence Wood . . . . Concierge
Peter Lawford . . . . Child
CRIME Paris. Judge tries ex-mistress for murder
knowing her innocent.

09060
MISCHIEF (69) (A)
B&D (W&F) *reissue:* 1937 (EB)
P: Herbert Wilcox
D: Jack Raymond
S: (PLAY) Ben Travers
SC: W.P. Lipscomb, Maclean Rogers
Ralph Lynn . . . . Arthur Gordon
Winifred Shotter . . . . Diana Birkett
Jeanne Stuart . . . . Eleanor Bingham
James Carew . . . . Reginald Bingham
Jack Hobbs . . . . Tom Birkett
Maud Gill . . . . Louise Piper
Kenneth Kove . . . . Bertie Pitts
Louie Emery . . . . Mrs Easy
COMEDY Absent financier's friend tries to
curb flighty wife.

09061
RICH AND STRANGE (92) (A)
USA: EAST OF SHANGHAI
BIP (Wardour)
D: Alfred Hitchcock
S: (NOVEL) Dale Collins
SC: Val Valentine, Alma Reville, Alfred
Hitchcock
Henry Kendall . . . . Fred Hill
Joan Barry . . . . Emily Hill
Percy Marmont . . . . Cdr Gordon
Betty Amann . . . . Princess

Elsie Randolph . . . .   Miss Imery
Hannah Jones . . . .   Mrs Porter
Aubrey Dexter . . . .   Colonel
COMEDY Clerk and wife take world cruise on legacy, and try flirtations.

09062
THE LOVE RACE (83) (U)
BIP (Pathe)
D: Lupino Lane, Pat Morton
S: (PLAY) Stanley Lupino
SC: Edwin Greenwood
Stanley Lupino . . . .   Reggie Powley
Jack Hobbs . . . . Bobbie Mostyn
Dorothy Boyd . . . .   Ida Mostyn
Dorothy Bartlam . . . .   Rita Payne
Frank Perfitt . . . . Mr Powley
Wallace Lupino . . . .   Ferdinand Fish
Artie Ash . . . . Eustace
Florence Vie . . . .   Mrs Mostyn
Doris Rogers . . . .   Nernice Dawn
COMEDY Car magnate's son wins Schroeder Cup and rival's daughter.

09063
THE OLD MAN (77) (A)
British Lion reissue: 1939 (EB)
P: S.W. Smith
D: Manning Haynes
S: (PLAY) Edgar Wallace
SC: Edgar Wallace
Maisie Gay . . . .   Mrs Harris
Anne Grey . . . .   Lady Arranways
Lester Matthews . . . .   Keith Keller
Cecil Humphreys . . . .   Lord Arranways
D.A. Clarke-Smith . . . .   John Lorney
Diana Beaumont . . . .   Millie Jeans
Gerald Rawlinson . . . .   Dick Mayford
Frank Stanmore . . . .   Charles
Finlay Currie . . . . Rennet
CRIME Charlady helps unmask man who stabbed Lady's blackmailer.

09064
THE BEGGAR STUDENT (66) (U) bilingual
Amalgamated Films Associated (BL)
P: John Harvel
D: John Harvel, Victor Hanbury
S: (OPERA) Carl Millocher, R. Gene (DER BETTELSTUDENT)
SC: John Stafford, Hans Zerlett
Shirley Dale . . . .   Tania
Lance Fairfax . . . .   Carl Romaine
Jerry Verno . . . . Jan Janski
Frederick Lloyd . . . .   Col Ollendorff
Mark Daly . . . .   Sgt
Jill Hands . . . . Broni
Margaret Halstan . . . . . . .Countess Novalska
Ashley Cooper . . . .   Nicki

Alfred Wellesley . . . .   Drunk
Millicent Wolf . . . .   Miss Slipinski
MUSICAL Polish captain posing as poor student forced to marry countess.

09065
LLOYD OF THE C. I. D. (serial) (U)
USA: DETECTIVE LLOYD
Mutual (U) reissue: 1932, THE GREEN SPOT MYSTERY
P: D: S: Henry MacRae
SC: Henry MacRae, Ella O'Neill
"Jack Lloyd" . . . . .Insp Jack Lloyd
(Claude Saunders)
Muriel Angelus . . . .   Sybil Craig
Wallace Geoffrey . .Giles Wade ("The Panther")
Emily Fitzroy . . . . .The Manor Ghost
Janice Adair . . . .   Diana Brooks
Lewis Dayton . . . .   Randall Hale
Tracey Holmes . . . .   Chester Dunn
Shayle Gardner . . . . Sgt Watkins
Gibb McLaughlin . . . .   Abdul
John Turnbull . . . .   Supt
Humberston Wright . . . . . .   Lodgekeeper
Kenneth McLaglen . . . .   Sam
09066
1— THE GREEN SPOT MURDER (21)

09067
2— THE PANTHER STRIKES (21)

09068
3— THE TRAP SPRINGS (21)

09069
4— TRAPPED BY WIRELESS (20)

09070
5— THE DEATH RAY (20)

09071
6— THE POISON DART (20)

09072
7— THE RACE WITH DEATH (20)

09073
8— THE PANTHER'S LAIR (19)

09074
9— IMPRISONED IN THE NORTH TOWER(19)

09075
10— THE PANTHER'S CUNNING (20)

09076
11— THE PANTHER AT BAY (20)

09077
12— HEROES OF THE LAW (21)
CRIME Inspector thwarts gang seeking

Egyptian jewelled armlet and saves heiress from murderous mad woman.

09078
THE OTHER MRS PHIPPS (38) (U)
Real Art (FN)
P: Julius Hagen
D: Guy Newall
S: Brock Williams
Sydney Fairbrother . . . . . .   Mrs Phipps
Richard Cooper . . . .   Lord Tooting
Jane Welsh . . . .   Vivienne
Charles Groves . . . . Munro
Charles Paton . . . . Jem
Arthur Webb . . . .   Lord Eustace
Ronald Frankau . . . .   Auctioneer
COMEDY Broke lord poses as widow's lady companion and saves girl from kidnap.

09079
M'BLIMEY
ASFI (UA)
D: J.Elder Wills
S: Hans Neiter, Fred Swann
SC: J. Elder Wills, C.H. Dand
Sam Blake . . . . . .
Eddie Martin . . . . . .
Kenneth Kove . . . . .
Arthur Sinclair . . . . .
Marie O'Neill . . . . .
Bernard Ansell . . . . .
COMEDY African natives come to Britain to make travelogue. (Not shown)

09080
CONGRESS DANCES (92) (A) bilingual
UFA (GB)
P: Erich Pommer
D: Eric Charell
S: Norbert Falk, Robert Liebmann
SC: Rowland V. Lee
Lilian Harvey . . . .   Chrystel
Conrad Veidt . . . . .Prince Metternich
Henri Garat . . . . .Tsar Alexander I
Lil Dagover . . . . Countess
Gibb McLaughlin . . . .   Bibikoff
Reginald Purdell . . . . Pepi
Philip Manning . . . . .King of Saxony
Humberston Wright . . . .Duke of Wellington
Helen Haye . . . .   Princess
Spencer Trevor . . . . .Finance Minister
Tarquini d'Or . . . . .Heurige Singer
MUSICAL Vienna, 1815. Tsar flirts with girl while double takes his place at Congress. (Made in Germany.)

1932

JAN

09081
MURDER ON THE SECOND FLOOR (68) (A)
WB–FN (FtI)
P: Irving Asher
D: William McGann
S: (PLAY) Frank Vosper
SC: Roland Pertwee, Challis Sanderson
John Longden . . . .   Hugh Bromilow
Pat Paterson . . . .   Sylvia Armitage
Sydney Fairbrother . . . . . .   Miss Snell
Ben Field . . . .   Mr Armitage
Florence Desmond . . . .   Lucy
Franklyn Bellamy . . . . .Joseph Reynolds
John Turnbull . . . .   Inspector
CRIME Novelist imagines murder involving
fellow boarders.

09082
TONIGHT'S THE NIGHT (74) (U)
BIP (Wardour)
D: Monty Banks
S: Syd Courtenay, Lola Harvey
SC: Syd Courtenay, Leslie Arliss
Leslie Fuller . . . .   Bill Smithers
Amy Veness . . . .   Emily Smithers
Charles Farrell . . . .   Williams
Frank Perfitt . . . .   Maj Allington
Syd Crossley . . . .   Warder Jackson
Hal Walters . . . .   Alf Hawkins
Hal Gordon . . . .   Smiler
Betty Fields . . . . Miss Winterbottom
Rene Ray . . . .   Rose Smithers
Monty Banks . . . .   Convict
COMEDY Slate club treasurer jailed for theft
escapes and catches culprit.

09083
MONEY FOR NOTHING (72) (U)
BIP (Pathe)
D: Monty Banks
S: Seymour Hicks
SC: Victor Kendall, Walter C. Mycroft
Seymour Hicks . . . .   Jay Cheddar
Betty Stockfeld . . . .   Joan Blossom
Edmund Gwenn . . . . Sir Henry Blossom
Donald Calthrop . . . .   Manager
Henry Wenman . . . .   Jay Cheddar
Philip Strange . . . .   Jackson
Amy Veness . . . .   Emma Bolt
Charles Farrell . . . .   Digger
Mike Johnson . . . .   Walter
Hal Gordon . . . .   Waiter
Renee Gadd . . . .   Maid
COMEDY Monte Carlo. Broke gambler
mistaken for financier.

09084
FRAIL WOMEN (72) (A)
Twickenham (Radio)
P: Julius Hagen
D: Maurice Elvey
S: Michael Barringer
Mary Newcome . . . . Lilian Hamilton
Owen Nares . . . . Col Leonard Harvey
Edmund Gwenn . . . .   Jim Willis
Jane Welsh . . . .   Sister
Frederick Peisley . . . .   Peter Farrar
Margaret Vines . . . .   Mary Willis
Athole Stewart . . . .   Father
Frank Pettingell . . . .   McWhirter
Herbert Lomas . . . .   Solicitor
Miles Mander. . . . .   Registrar
DRAMA Colonel weds wartime mistress to
give daughter name.

09085
THE BLUE DANUBE (72) (A) *bilingual*
B&D (W&F)
P: D: Herbert Wilcox
S: Doris Zinkeisen
SC: Miles Malleson
Brigitte Helm . . . . Countess Gabrielle
Joseph Schildkraut . . . .   Sandor
Dorothy Bouchier . . . .   Yutka
Desmond Jeans . . . .   Johann
Patrick Ludlow . . . .   Companion
Alfred Rode and his Tzigane Band
Masine & Nikitina
ROMANCE Hungary. Gipsy leaves sweetheart
for flirtatious countess.

09086
SERVICE FOR LADIES (93) (A)
USA: RESERVED FOR LADIES
Paramount British
P: D: Alexander Korda
S: (NOVEL) Ernst Vaida (THE HEAD WAITER)
SC: Eliot Crawshay-Williams, Lajos Biro
Leslie Howard . . . .   Max Tracey
George Grossmith . . . .   Mr Westlake
Benita Hume . . . . Countess Ricardi
Elizabeth Allan . . . . Sylvia Robertson
Morton Selten . . . .   Mr Robertson
Cyril Ritchard . . . . Sir William Carter
Ben Field . . . .   Breslmeyer
Annie Esmond . . . .   Duchess
COMEDY Austria. Incognito king helps waiter
woo millionairess.

09087
ABOVE RUBIES (43) (U)
Ralph J. Pugh (UA)
D: Frank A. Richardson
S: Douglas Hoare
SC: Eliot Stannard
Zoe Palmer . . . . Joan Wellingford
Robin Irvine . . . .   Philip
Tom Helmore . . . .   Paul
John Deverell . . . . Lord Middlehurst
Franklyn Bellamy . . . .   Dupont
Allan Jeayes . . . .   Lamont
Madge Snell . . . . Lady Wellingford
COMEDY Monte Carlo. Girl tries to recoup
necklace pawned to gambler.

09088
COLLISION (79) (A)
Samuelson (UA)
P: E. Gordon Craig
D: G.B. Samuelson
S: (PLAY) E.C. Pollard
Sunday Wilshin . . . .   Mrs Oliver
Gerald Rawlinson . . . . .Jack Carruthers
Wendy Barrie . . . .   Joyce Maynard
Henrietta Watson . . . . Mrs Carruthers
A.G. Poulton . . . .   Mr Maynard
Irene Rooke . . . .   Mrs Maynard
Peter Coleman . . . .   Brabazon
CRIME Widow frames bridegroom for
stealing mother-in-law's pearls.

09089
THE TEMPERANCE FETE (45) (A)
Fogwell Films (MGM)
P: SC: Reginald Fogwell
D: Graham Cutts
S: (STORY) Herbert Jenkins
George Robey . . . .   Bindle
Sydney Fairbrother . . . . . .   Mrs Bindle
Connie Ediss . . . .   Mrs Hearty
Gibb McLaughlin . . . .   Mr Hearty
Seth Egbert . . . .   Ginger
Anita Sharp-Bolster . . . . .   Teacher
COMEDY Workshy cockney puts alcohol in
lemonade at teetotal fete.

09090
CONDEMNED TO DEATH (75) (A)
Twickenham (W&F)
P: Julius Hagen
D: Walter Forde
S: (PLAY) George Goodchild (JACK
O' LANTERN)
SC: Bernard Merivale, H. Fowler Mear,
Brock Williams
Arthur Wontner . . . . .Sir Charles Wallington
Edmund Gwenn . . . .   Banting
Gordon Harker . . . .   Sam Knudge
Jane Welsh . . . . Sonia Wallington
Cyril Raymond . . . .   Jim Wrench
Norah Howard . . . .   Gwen Banting
Griffith Humphreys . . . . . .   Prof Michaels
Bernard Brunel . . . .   Tobias Lantern
H. StBarbe West . . . . . . .Sir Rudolph Cantler
CRIME Condemned killer hypnotises judge to
murder his betrayers.

FEB

09091
DANCE PRETTY LADY (64) (A)
British Instructional (Wardour)
P: H. Bruce Woolfe
D: SC: Anthony Asquith
S: (NOVEL) Compton Mackenzie (CARNIVAL)
Ann Casson . . . .   Jenny Pearl
Carl Harbord . . . .   Maurice Avery
Michael Hogan . . . .   Castleton
Moore Marriott . . . .   Mr Raeburn
Flora Robson . . . .   Mrs Raeburn
Leonard Brett . . . .   Alf
Norman Claridge . . . .   Jack Danby
Sunday Wilshin . . . .   Irene
Rene Ray . . . .   Elsie
Marie Rambert's Corps de Ballet
ROMANCE 1908. Cockney ballerina refuses to
become mistress of aristocratic artist she loves.

09092
STRICTLY BUSINESS (46) (U)
British Instructional (Pathe)
D: Mary Field, Jacqueline Logan
S: Jacqueline Logan
Betty Amann . . . . Theodora Smith
Carl Harbord . . . .   David Plummett
Molly Lamont . . . .   Maureen
Percy Parsons . . . .   Mr Smith
Philip Strange . . . .   Bartling
C.M. Hallard . . . .   Mr Plummett
Gordon Begg . . . .   Stormont
COMEDY Heiress poses as plain girl to fool
escort, who saves her from blackmailer.

09093
THE THIRD STRING (65) (U)
Welsh-Pearson (Gau)
P: T.A. Welsh, George Pearson
D: George Pearson
S: (STORY) W.W. Jacobs
SC: George Pearson, James Reardon,
A.R. Rawlinson
Sandy Powell . . . .   Ginger Dick
Kay Hammond . . . .   Hebe Tucker
Mark Daly . . . .   Pete Russett
Alf Goddard . . . .   Bill Lumm
Charles Paton . . . .   Sam Small
Sydney Fairbrother . . . . . .   Miss Peabody
Pollie Emery . . . .   Mrs Chip
James Knight . . . .   Webson
COMEDY Sailor posing as boxer is forced to
fight champion.

09094
THE MISSING REMBRANDT (84) (A)
Twickenham (PDC)
P: Julius Hagen
D: Leslie Hiscott

S: (STORY) A. Conan Doyle (CHARLES
AUGUST MILVERTON)
SC: Cyril Twyford, H. Fowler Mear
Arthur Wontner . . . . Sherlock Holmes
Jane Welsh . . . . Lady Violet Lumsden
Miles Mander . . . . Claude Holford
Francis L. Sullivan . . Baron von Guntermann
Ian Fleming . . . . Dr Watson
Dino Galvani . . . . Carlo Ravelli
Ben Welden . . . . Pinkerton Man
Philip Hewland . . . . Insp Lestrade
Minnie Rayner . . . . Mrs Hudson
Antony Holles . . . . Marquess de Chaminade
CRIME Drug-addicted artist steals painting and
compromising letters from lady.

09095
EBB TIDE (74) (A)
Paramount British
P: Walter Morosco
D: Arthur Rosson
S: (NOVEL) Dixie Wilson (GOD GAVE ME
20 CENTS)
SC: Basil Mason, Reginald Denham
Dorothy Bouchier . . . . Cassie
Joan Barry . . . . Mary
George Barraud . . . . Steve
Vanda Greville . . . . Millie
Alexander Field . . . . Barney
Annie Esmond . . . . Landlady
Merle Oberon . . . . Girl
DRAMA Sailor weds orphan whilst sweetheart
in prison.

09096
LORD BABS (65) (U)
Gainsborough (Ideal)
P: Michael Balcon
D: Walter Forde
S: (PLAY) Keble Howard
SC: Clifford Grey, Angus Macphail
Bobby Howes . . . . Lord Drayford
Jean Collin . . . . Nurse Foster
Pat Paterson . . . . Helen Parker
Alfred Drayton . . . . Ambrose Parker
Arthur Chesney . . . . Mr Turpin
Clare Greet . . . . Mrs Parker
Hugh Dempster . . . . Dr Neville
Joseph Cunningham . . . . . . Chief Steward
MUSICAL Steward inherits an earldom and
feigns reversion to childhood to repel unwanted
fiancee.

09097
MURDER AT COVENT GARDEN (68) (A)
Twickenham (W&F)
P: Julius Hagen
D: Michael Barringer, Leslie Hiscott
S: (NOVEL) W.J. Makin
SC: Michael Barringer, H. Fowler Mear
Dennis Neilson-Terry . . . . . Jack Trencham
Anne Grey . . . . Helen Osmond
Walter Fitzgerald . . . . Donald Walpace
Henri de Vries . . . . Van Blond
George Curzon . . . . Belmont
Fred Pease . . . . Snowball
Binnie Barnes . . . . Girl
CRIME Tec poses as crook who killed club
owner for smuggled gems.

MAR

09098
A GAME OF CHANCE (65) (U) (added sound)
Equity British
D: Charles Barnett
S: John F. Argyle
John F. Argyle . . . . Dick Weston
Margaret Delane . . . . Ruth
Jack Marriott . . . . Jack Andrews

Eileen Lloyd . . . . Mrs Weston
Thomas Moss . . . . Bookie
SPORT Trainer makes crooked bookie transfer
farmer's bet to winner.

09099
THOROUGHBRED (64) (U) (added sound)
Equity British
D: Charles Barnett
S: John F. Argyle
John F. Argyle . . . . Edward Foster
Margaret Delane . . . . Eleanor Halliford
James Benton . . . . Smithy
Jack Marriott . . . . Henry Hamilton
Thomas Moss . . . . David Foster
CRIME Amnesiac trainer revealed as heir in
time to save heiress from marrying guardian's
son.

09100
THE FINAL RECKONING (64) (A) (added
sound)
Equity British
D: S: John F. Argyle
James Benton . . . . Bill Williams
Margaret Delane . . . . Violet Williams
Will Marriott . . . . Arthur Harding
Bessie Richards . . . . Mrs Williams
CRIME Mine owner's son tries to kill miner
for love of wife.

09101
THREADS (76) (A)
Samuelson (UA)
P: Gordon Craig
D: G.B. Samuelson
S: (PLAY) Frank Stayton
Lawrence Anderson . . . . . . John Wynn
Dorothy Fane . . . . Amelia Wynn
Gerald Rawlinson . . . . Arthur
Wendy Barrie . . . . Olive
Ben Webster . . . . Lord Grantham
Irene Rooke . . . . Lady Grantham
Walter Piers . . . . Col Packinder
DRAMA Pardoned murderer returns home to
find family wealthy.

09102
THE CALLBOX MYSTERY (73) (A)
Samuelson (UA)
P: Gordon Craig
D: G.B. Samuelson
S: Joan Wentworth Wood (Morgan)
Warwick Ward . . . . Leo Mount
Harold French . . . . Insp Layton
Wendy Barrie . . . . Iris Banner
Gerald Rawlinson . . . . David Radnor
Harvey Braban . . . . Insp Brown
Daphne Mowbray . . . . Rose
CRIME Inspector loves dead man's daughter
who helps him prove suicides are murders.

09103
C.O.D. (64) (A)
Westminster (UA)
P: Jerome Jackson
D: Michael Powell
S: Philip MacDonald
SC: Ralph Smart
Garry Marsh . . . . Peter Cowen
Hope Davy . . . . Frances
Cecil Ramage . . . . Vyner
Arthur Stratton . . . . Mr Briggs
Sybil Grove . . . . Mrs Briggs
Bruce Belfrage . . . . Philip
Roland Culver . . . . Edward
Peter Gawthorne . . . . Detective
CRIME Framed girl hires gentleman thief to
help her hide stepfather's body.

09104
HOTEL SPLENDIDE (53) (U)
Film Engineering (Ideal)
P: Jerome Jackson
D: Michael Powell
S: Philip Macdonald
SC: Ralph Smart
Jerry Verno . . . . Jerry Mason
Vera Sherburne . . . . Joyce Dacre
Antony Holles . . . . Mrs leGrange
Edgar Norfolk . . . . Gentleman Charlie
Sybil Grove . . . . Mrs Harkness
Philip Morant . . . . Mr Meek
Paddy Browne . . . . Miss Meek
COMEDY Clerk inherits seaside hotel built on
field where ex-convict buried loot.

09105
IN A MONASTERY GARDEN (81) (A)
Twickenham (AP&D) *reissue:* 1937
P: Julius Hagen
D: Maurice Elvey
S: Michael Barringer
SC: H. Fowler Mear, Michael Barringer
John Stuart . . . . Michael Ferrier
Joan Maude . . . . Roma Romano
Gina Malo . . . . Nina
Alan Napier . . . . Count Romano
Dino Galvani . . . . Cesare Bonelli
Frank Pettingell . . . . Bertholdi
Humberston Wright . . . . . Abbot
DRAMA Italy. Musican steals brother's
compositions when he is jailed for shooting
prince, fiance of his beloved.

09106
THE CROOKED LADY (75) (U)
Real Art (MGM)
P: Julius Hagen
D: Leslie Hiscott
S: (NOVEL) William C. Stone
SC: H. Fowler Mear
George Graves . . . . Sir Charles Murdoch
Isobel Elsom . . . . Miriam Sinclair
Ursula Jeans . . . . Joan Collinson
Austin Trevor . . . . Capt James Kent
Alexander Field . . . . Slim Barrett
Edmund Willard . . . . Joseph Garstin
S.J. Warmington . . . . Insp Hilton
Frank Pettingell . . . . Hugh Weldon
Moore Marriott. . . . . Crabby
H.B. Longhurst . . . . John Morland
Paddy Browne . . . . Susie
CRIME Workless ex-officer steals actress's
pearls and falls for lady detective.

09107
ONCE BITTEN (47) (U)
Real Art (Fox)
P: Julius Hagen
D: Leslie Hiscott
S: John Barrow
SC: Michael Barringer, H. Fowler Mear
Ursula Jeans . . . . Clare
Richard Cooper . . . . Toby Galloway
Frank Pettingell . . . . . . Sir Timothy Blott
Jeanne Stuart . . . . Alicia
Dino Galvani . . . . Mario Fideli
Sidney King . . . . Jerry
Antony Holles . . . . Legros
Kathleen Kelly . . . . Anne
COMEDY Amnesiac's father-in-law poses as
waiter in belief that he killed blackmailer.

09108
THE MARRIAGE BOND (82) (A)
Twickenham (Radio)
P: Julius Hagen
D: Maurice Elvey

S: Muriel Stewart
SC: H. Fowler Mear

Mary Newcombe	Jacqueline Heron
Guy Newall	Toby Heron
Stewart Rome	Sir Paul Swaythling
Ann Casson	Binnie Heron
Florence Desmond	Elsie
Denys Blakelock	Alfred Dreisler
Lewis Shaw	Frere Heron
Humberston Wright	Jenkins
Amy Veness	Mrs Crust
A. Bromley Davenport	MFH

ROMANCE Wife leaves drunken husband for children's sake but returns when he reforms.

09109
THE CHINESE PUZZLE (81) (A)
Twickenham (W&F)
P: Julius Hagen
D: Guy Newall
S: (PLAY) Leon M. Lion, Frances Barclay
SC: H. Fowler Mear

Leon M. Lion	Marquis Li Chung
Lilian Braithwaite	Lady de la Haye
Elizabeth Allan	Naomi Melsham
Austin Trevor	Paul Markatel
James Raglan	Sir Charles/Sir Roger
Jane Welsh	Victoria
C.M. Hallard	Sir Aylmer Brent
Mabel Sealby	Mrs Melsham
Francis L. Sullivan	Herman Strumm
Charles Carson	Armand de Rochecorbon
George Carr	Dr Fu Yang

CRIME Mandarin takes blame when wife of friend's son steals secret treaty.

09110
A NIGHT LIKE THIS (74) (U)
B&D (W&F) reissue: 1937 (EB)
P: Herbert Wilcox
D: Tom Walls
S: (PLAY) Ben Travers

Ralph Lynn	Clifford Tope
Tom Walls	Michael Mahoney
Winifred Shotter	Cora Mellish
Mary Brough	Mrs Decent
Robertson Hare	Miles Tuckett
Claude Hulbert	Archie Slott
Boris Ranevsky	Kosky
C.V. France	The Mailer
Joan Brierley	Molly Dean
Norma Varden	Mrs Tuckett
Kay Hammond	Cocktail Shaker

COMEDY Irish PC recovers borrowed necklace from blackmailer who runs gambling club.

09111
GOODNIGHT VIENNA (76) (U)
USA: MAGIC NIGHT
B&D (W&F) reissue: 1937 (EB) 1945 (EB)
P:D: Herbert Wilcox
S: (RADIO PLAY) Holt Marvel, George Posford

Jack Buchanan	Capt Max Schlettoff
Anna Neagle	Viki
Gina Malo	Frieda
Clive Currie	Gen Schlettoff
William Kendall	Ernest
Joyce Bland	Countess Helga
Gibb McLaughlin	Fritz
Herbert Carrick	Johann
Clifford Heatherley	Donelli
O.B. Clarence	Manager
Peggy Cartwright	Greta
Muriel Aked	Marya

MUSICAL Austria, 1913. General's son, engaged to Countess, loves shopgirl who becomes opera star.

09112
TWO WHITE ARMS (81) (A)
USA: WIVES BEWARE
Cinema House (MGM)
P: Eric Hakim
D: Fred Niblo
S: (PLAY) Harold Dearden
SC: Harold Dearden

Adolphe Menjou	Maj Carey Liston
Margaret Bannerman	Lydia Charrington
Claud Allister	Dr Biggash
Jane Baxter	Alison Drury
Kenneth Kove	Bob Russell
Ellis Jeffreys	Lady Ellerslie
Rene Ray	Trixie
Jean Cadell	Mrs Drury
Henry Wenman	Mears
Spencer Trevor	Sir George
Melville Cooper	Mack

COMEDY Married major feigns amnesia to flirt with younger girl.

09113
COME INTO MY PARLOUR (45) (U)
GEM Productions (MGM)
P: Kenneth McLaglen, A.J. Marks
D: John Longden
S: Jean Jay, John Longden

Renee Houston	Jenny Macdonald
Pat Aherne	Gerry
Robert Holmes	Julius Markham
Hal Walters	Burglar
Fanny Wright	Mrs Macdonald

CRIME Manicurist shelters barber who thinks he killed burglar.

09114
WOMEN WHO PLAY (78) (A)
Paramount British
P: Walter Morosco
D: Arthur Rosson
S: (PLAY) Frederick Lonsdale (SPRING CLEANING)
SC: Gilbert Wakefield, Basil Mason

Mary Newcomb	Mona
Benita Hume	Margaret Sones
George Barraud	Richard Sones
Joan Barry	Fay
Barry Jones	Ernest Steele
Edmond Breon	Rachie Wells
Gerald Lyley	Bobby
Sylvia Lesley	Lady Jane
Peter Evan Thomas	Willie

COMEDY Novelist gets actress to pose as prostitute to teach flighty wife lesson.

09115
AREN'T WE ALL ? (80) (A)
Paramount British
P: Walter Morosco
D: Harry Lachman
S: (PLAY) Frederick Lonsdale
SC: Basil Mason, Gilbert Wakefield

Gertrude Lawrence	Margot
Hugh Wakefield	Lord Grenham
Owen Nares	Willie
Harold Huth	Karl van der Hyde
Marie Lohr	Lady Frinton
Renee Gadd	Kitty Lake
Emily Fitzroy	Angela
Aubrey Mather	Vicar
Rita Page	Dancer

COMEDY Lord saves philandering son's marriage by inviting his wife's lover.

09116
SORRY YOU'VE BEEN TROUBLED (78) (U)
retitled: LIFE GOES ON
B&D Paramount British

D: Jack Raymond
S: (PLAY) Walter Hackett

Hugh Wakefield	Ridgeway Emsworth
Elsie Randolph	Phoebe Selsey
Betty Stockfeld	Lady Sheridan
Wallace Geoffreys	Robert Kent
Warwick Ward	Ronald StJohn
Jeanne Stuart	Clare Armore
Dennis Hoey	Anthony Carlisle
Antony Holles	John Collis
Robert Horton	Sir George Sheridan

CRIME Crook manipulates shares by hiding dead financier and framing fiance for murder.

09117
THE WATER GIPSIES (80) (A)
ATP (Radio)
P: Basil Dean
D: Maurice Elvey
S: (NOVEL) A.P. Herbert
SC: Basil Dean, Miles Malleson, Alma Reville, John Paddy Carstairs

Ann Todd	Jane Bell
Sari Maritza	Lily Bell
Ian Hunter	Fred Green
Peter Hannen	Bryan
Richard Bird	Ernest
Frances Doble	Fay
Anthony Ireland	Moss
Barbara Gott	Mrs Green
Moore Marriott	Mr Pewtar
Harold Scott	Mr Bell
Charles Garry	Mr Green
Betty Shale	Mrs Higgins

ROMANCE Thames gypsy poses for society artist and acidentally drowns jealous fiance.

09118
NINE TILL SIX (75) (A)
ATP (Radio)
P: D: Basil Dean
S: (PLAY) Aimee & Philip Stuart
SC: Beverley Nicholls, Alma Reville, John Paddy Carstairs

Louise Hampton	Madam
Elizabeth Allan	Gracie Abbott
Florence Desmond	Daisy
Isla Bevan	Ailene Pennarth
Richard Bird	Jimmie Pennarth
Frances Doble	Clare
Jeanne de Casalis	Yvonne
Kay Hammond	Beatrice
Sunday Wilshin	Judy
Alison Leggatt	Freda
Moore Marriott	Doorman

ROMANCE Dressmaker borrows gown to attend dance with peer, and is accused of theft.

09119
THE STRANGLER (45) (A)
BIP—BIF (Pathe)
D: S: Norman Lee

Jack Morrison	Johnnie Scott
Moira Lynd	Rosie Platt
Lewis Dayton	Lee MacArthur
Molly Lamont	Frances Marsden
Cecil Ramage	Dr Bevan
Carol Coombe	Billie Southgate
Hal Gordon	Loveridge
Patrick Susands	Eckersley

CRIME Actor killed during murder play rehearsal.

09120
HELP YOURSELF (74) (A) bilingual
WB—FN (WB)
P: Irving Asher
D: John Daumery
S: (NOVEL) Jerome Kingston (SINNERS ALL)

SC: Roland Pertwee, John Hastings Turner
Benita Hume . . . . Mary Lamb
Martin Walker . . . . George Quinnock
D.A. Clarke-Smith . . . . Maj Fred Harris
Carol Coombe . . . . Dodie
Kenneth Kove . . . . Peter Ball
Clifford Heatherley . . . . . . Fox-Cardington
D. Hay Petrie . . . . Sam Short
Helen Ferrers . . . . Lady Hermione Quinnock
Marie Wright . . . . Sparrow
Hal Gordon . . . . Bobby Vane
COMEDY Man throws party in rich aunt's absence and crooks try to steal necklace.

09121
IMPROMPTU (12) (U)
WB-FN (WB)
P: Irving Asher
D: William McGann
S: Roland Pertwee, John Hastings Turner
Florence Desmond
Richard Bird
Dodo Watts
COMEDY Impersonator burlesques three actresses.

09122
POSTAL ORDERS (24) (U)
WB-FN (WB)
P: Irving Asher
D: John Daumery
S: (PLAY) Roland Pertwee
SC: Roland Pertwee
Margot Grahame
Garry Marsh
Sydney Fairbrother
Margaret Damer
Madge White
COMEDY Man tries to delay postal message whilst girl tries to hurry.

09123
SELF-MADE LADY (68) (A)
George King (UA)
D: George King
S: (NOVEL) Douglas Newton (SOOKEY)
SC: Billie Bristow
Heather Angel . . . . Sookey
Harry Wilcoxon . . . . Bert Taverner
Amy Veness . . . . Old Sookey
A. Bromley Davenport . . . Duke of Alchester
Louis Hayward . . . . Paul Geneste
Charles Cullum . . . . Lord Mariven
Ronald Ritchie . . . . Alf Naylor
Doris Gilmour . . . . Claudine
Oriol Ross . . . . Lady Poppy
Lola Duncan . . . . Mrs Stoach
Violet Hopson . . . . Assistant
ROMANCE Slum girl becomes dress designer and is wooed by medical student, lord, and boxer.

09124
CAMERA COCKTALES (series) (U)
Hall Mark BSFP (MGM)
D: Bernard Vorhaus

09125
No. 1 (11)

09126
No. 2 (11)

09127
No. 3 (12)

09128
No. 4 (11)

09129
No. 5 (13)

09130
No. 6 —VISIT TO A CINEMA ON AMATEUR NIGHT (11)
REVUE (Mostly compiled from DeForest Phonofilms and British Sound Film Productions shorts).

09131
A VOICE SAID GOODNIGHT (35) (U)
WB-FN (WB)
P: Irving Asher
D: William McGann
S: Roland Pertwee
SC: Roland Pertwee, John Hastings Turner
Nora Swinburne . . . . Joan Creighton
Jack Trevor . . . . Gerald Creighton
D.A. Clarke-Smith . . . . Philip Gaylor
John Turnbull . . . . Insp Lavory
Daphne Scorer . . . . Annie
Wilfred Caithness . . . . Beldon
Roland Culver . . . . Reporter
CRIME Usurer killed for causing married woman's suicide.

09132
A LETTER OF WARNING (33) (U)
WB-FN (WB)
P: Irving Asher
D: John Daumery
S: (PLAY) John Hastings Turner
SC: Roland Pertwee, John Hastings Turner, Roland Pertwee
Margot Grahame . . . . Cynthia Latham
Richard Bird . . . . Eric Waterlow
Sydney Fairbrother . . . . . . Miss Butterworth
D.A. Clarke-Smith . . . . Sir James Royd
Clifford Heatherley . . . . Mr Prendergast
Helen Ferrers . . . . Miss Rosebart
Charles Paton . . . . Vicar
Wilfred Caithness . . . . Montague
DRAMA Amatuer actors receive poison pen letters.

09133
A LUCKY SWEEP (58) (U)
National Talkies (PDC)
P: Harry Rowson
D: A.V. Bramble
John Longden . . . . Bill Higgins
Diana Beaumont . . . . Polly
A.G. Poulton . . . . Joshua
Marie Wright . . . . Martha
Sybil Jane . . . . Miss Grey
Elsie Prince . . . . Secretary
COMEDY Maid buys Irish Sweepstake ticket for anti-gambling fiance, who is accused of stealing it.

09134
THE SPARE ROOM (34) (A)
PDC
D: Redd Davis
S: (SKETCH) Marriott Edgar
Jimmy James . . . . Jimmy
Ruth Taylor . . . . Mrs James
Charles Paton . . . . Mr Webster
Alice O'Day . . . . Mrs Webster
Charles Courtneidge . . . . . . Jones
Roland Gillett . . . . Hiram Harris
Kathleen Joyce . . . . Rita
Charles Farrell . . . . Boxer
COMEDY Drunken henpeck comes home late after night out.

09135
PARTNERS PLEASE (34) (A)
PDC
D: Lloyd Richards
S: Charles Bennett
Pat Paterson . . . . Angela Grittlewood
Tony Sympson . . . . Archie Dawlish
Ronald Ward . . . . Eric Hatington
Alice O'Day . . . . Mrs Grittlewood
Binnie Barnes . . . . Billie
Frederick Moyes . . . . Mr Grittlewood
Tony de Lungo . . . . Marano
Hal Gordon . . . . Waiter
Ralph Truman . . . . CID Man
COMEDY Girl's fiance, forced to find job, becomes nightclub gigolo.

09136
ACCOUNT RENDERED (35) (A)
PDC
D:SC: Leslie Howard Gordon
S: (PLAY) Michael Joseph
Cecil Ramage . . . . Barry Barriter
Reginald Bach . . . . Hugh Preston
Marilyn Mawm . . . . Barbara Wayne
Jessie Bateman . . . . Mrs Wayne
Frederick Moyes . . . . Gen Firmstone
J. Hubert Leslie . . . . Parsons
Ronald Ritchie . . . . Jim
Arthur Prince . . . . Lawyer
CRIME Financier, bankrupted by crooked partner, is prosecuted by beloved's fiance.

09137
THE NEW HOTEL (49) (U)
PDC
D: Bernerd Mainwaring
Norman Long
Dan Young
Hal Gordon
Mickey Brantford
Blanche Adele
Alfred Wellesley
Basil Howes
Betty Norton
Hamilton Keene
Ruth Taylor
Al Davidson and his Band
MUSICAL Drunkard blackmailed and rich man vamped during gala opening of hotel.

09138
CASTLE SINISTER (50) (A)
Delta (Filmophone)
D: Widgey R. Newman
Haddon Mason . . . . Ronald Kemp
Eric Adeney . . . . Prof Bandov
Wally Patch . . . . Jorkins
Ilsa Kilpatrick . . . . Jean
Edmund Kennedy . . . . Father
HORROR Devon. Mad doctor tries to put girl's brain into apeman's head.

09139
THE FRIGHTENED LADY (87) (A) USA: CRIMINAL AT LARGE
Gainsborough-British Lion (Ideal)
P: Miachel Balcon
D: T. Hayes Hunter
S: (PLAY) Edgar Wallace (THE CASE OF THE FRIGHTENED LADY)
SC: Angus Macphail, Bryan Edgar Wallace
Norman McKinnell . . . . Insp Tanner
Cathleen Nesbitt . . . . Lady Lebanon
Emlyn Williams . . . . Lord Lebanon
Gordon Harker . . . . Sgt Totty
Belle Chrystal . . . . Aisla Crane
Cyril Raymond . . . . Sgt Ferraby
D.A. Clarke-Smith . . . . Dr Amersham
Percy Parsons . . . . Gilder
Finlay Currie . . . . Brooks
Julian Royce . . . . Kelver
CRIME Mad lord's mother tries to stop him strangling fiancee.

09140
JOSSER JOINS THE NAVY (69) (U)
BIP (Wardour)
D: Norman Lee
S: Con West, Herbert Sargent

Ernie Lotinga	Jimmy Josser
Cyril McLaglen	Langford
Jack Hobbs	Lt-Cdr Cole
Leslie Wareing	Lesley Beauchamp
Renee Gadd	Polly
Jack Frost	Spud
H. Saxon-Snell	Ling Foo
Charles Paton	Prof Black
Florence Vie	Mrs Black
Leslie Stiles	Admiral

COMEDY Hall porter forced to join navy while tracking spies.

APR

09141
BROTHER ALFRED (77) (U)
BIP (Wardour)
D: Henry Edwards
S: (PLAY) P.G. Wodehouse, Herbert Westbrook
SC: Henry Edwards, Claude Guerney

Gene Gerrard	George Lattaker
Molly Lamont	Stella
Elsie Randolph	Mamie
Bobbie Comber	Billy Marshall
Clifford Heatherley	Prince Sachsberg
Hal Gordon	Harold Voles
Henry Wenman	Uncle George
Blanche Adele	Pilbeam
James Carew	Mr Marshall
Hugh E. Wright	Sydney
Harvey Braban	Denis Sturgis
Maurice Colbourne	Equerry
Tonie Edgar Bruce	Mrs Vandaline

COMEDY Monte Carlo. Man poses as twin to win back ex-fiancee.

09142
THE INNOCENTS OF CHICAGO (68) (A) USA: WHY SAPS LEAVE HOME
BIP (Wardour)
D: Lupino Lane
S: (PLAY) Reginald Simpson, J.W. Drawbell (THE MILKY WAY)
SC: Leslie Arliss, Lupino Lane

Henry Kendall	Percy Lloyd
Betty Norton	Betty Woods
Margot Grahame	Lil
Bernard Nedell	Tony Costello
Binnie Barnes	Peg Guinan
Ben Welden	Spike Guinan
Wallace Lupino	Ganster
Charles Farrell	Smiler
Cyril Smith	Gangster
Ernest Sefton	Gangster
Peter Bernard	Gangster
Val Guest	Gangster

COMEDY Chicago. Briton inherits dairy used as front by bootleggers.

09143
TIN GODS (52) (A)
BIP (Pathe)
D: F.W. Kraemer
S: (PLAY) Edgar C. Middleton

Frank Cellier	Major Drake
Dorothy Bartlam	Daphne Drake
Peter Evan Thomas	Robert Staveley
Frank Royde	Cheng Chi Lung
Ben Welden	Cyrus P. Schroeder
Alexander Field	Lane
Margaret Damer	Mrs Drake
Ruth Maitland	Mrs Schroeder
Atholl Fleming	Padre

DRAMA Chinese pirates capture ship and demand death of best-bred passenger.

09144
THE BAD COMPANIONS (45) (U)
BIP-BIF (Pathe)
D: John Orton
S: Fred Karno
SC: Con West

Nor Kiddie	Pip
Renee Gadd	Josie
Wallace Lupino	Blinks
Hal Gordon	Narkie
Lesley Wareing	Secretary

COMEDY Sacked jam-maker wins girl back from foreman.

09145
THE FIRST MRS FRASER (95) (A)
Sterling *reissue:* 1944 (Ad; 13 mins cut)
P: Louis Zimmerman
D: Sinclair Hill
S: (PLAY) St John Irvine
SC: Leslie Howard Gordon

Henry Ainley	James Fraser
Joan Barry	Elsie Fraser
Dorothy Dix	Janet Fraser
Harold Huth	Mario
Richard Cooper	Lord Larne
Hargrave Pawson	Ninian Fraser
Henry Hewitt	Philip Logan
Arnold Riches	George
Gibb McLaughlin	Butler
Ivan Brandt	Murdo Fraser
Millicent Wolf	Mabel
Oriel Ross	Connie
Eileen Peel	Ellen Fraser
Naunton Wayne	
Frances Day	
Yvette	
Noel Leyland	
Billy Cotton's Band	

ROMANCE Rich man returns to first wife on finding second wife loves younger man.

09146
BETRAYAL (65) (A)
Fogwell Films (U)
D:SC: Reginald Fogwell
S: (PLAY) Hubert Griffith (NO CRIME OF PASSION)

Stewart Rome	John Armytage
Marjorie Hume	Diana Armytage
Leslie Perrins	Clive Wilson
Henry Hewitt	Sir Robert Blackburn KC
J. Fisher White	John Lawrence KC
Frank Atherley	Judge
E.H. Williams	Butler
Charles Childerstone	Doctor

CRIME Girl weds man for money and saves him when he is tried for shooting lover.

09147
DOUBLE DEALING (48) (A)
Real Art (Fox)
P: Julius Hagen
D: Leslie Hiscott
S: Michael Barringer, H. Fowler Mear

Frank Pettingell	Rufus Moon
Richard Cooper	Toby Traill
Sydney Fairbrother	Sarah Moon
Zoe Palmer	Dolly Simms
Jill Hands	Betty
Betty Astell	Flossie
Charles Groves	Crump
Eileen Despard	Rosie
Gladys Hamer	Clara

COMEDY Reporter finds watch committee censor spends gay weekends in London.

09148
LILY CHRISTINE (82) (A)
Paramount British
P: Walter Morosco
D: Paul Stein
S: (NOVEL) Michael Arlen
SC: Robert Gore-Brown

Corinne Griffith	Lily Christine Summerset
Colin Clive	Rupert Harvey
Margaret Bannerman	Mrs Abbey
Miles Mander	Ambatriadi
Jack Trevor	Ivor Summerset
Anne Grey	Muriel Harvey
Barbara Everest	Hempel

DRAMA Author loves short-sighted woman who learns husband loves widowed actress.

MAY

09149
MR BILL THE CONQUEROR (87) (U) USA: THE MAN WHO WON
BIP (Pathe)
D: Norman Walker
S: Dion Titheradge

Henry Kendall	Sir William Normand
Heather Angel	Rosemary Lannick
Nora Swinburne	Diana Trenchard
Sam Livesey	Dave Lannick
Moore Marriott	Tom Turtle
Louie Tinsley	Mrs Turtle
Helen Ferrers	Mrs Priddy
Sam Wilkinson	Noah
A. Bromley Davenport	Lord Blagden
Tonie Edgar Bruce	Lady Blagden
David Hawthorne	George Jelby

ROMANCE Sussex. Heir to farm falls for daughter of hostile neighbour.

09150
INDISCRETIONS OF EVE (63) (A)
BIP (Wardour)
D:S: Cecil Lewis

Steffi Duna	Eve
Fred Conyngham	Sir Peter Martin
Lester Matthews	Ralph
Tony Sympson	Pip
Jessica Tandy	Maid
Clifford Heatherley	Butler
Hal Gordon	Simms
Muriel Aked	Mother
Arthur Chesney	Father
George Mozart	Smart
Teddy Brown	Barman
Marius B. Winter and his Orchestra	

MUSICAL Earl loves girl who models for shop window dummies.

09151
BACHELOR'S BABY (58) (U)
BIP (Pathe)
D:SC: Harry Hughes
S: (NOVEL) Rolphe Bennett

Ann Casson	Peggy
William Freshman	Jimmy
Henry Wenman	Capt Rogers
Alma Taylor	Aunt Mary
Ethel Warwick	Mrs Prowse
Charles Paton	Mr Ponder
Connie Emerald	Mrs Ponder
Patrick Ludlow	Clarence

COMEDY Man wins girl by planting baby on bachelor ex-captain.

09152
ILLEGAL (83) (A)
WB-FN (WB)
P: Irving Asher
D: William McGann
S: Roland Pertwee
SC: Roland Pertwee, John Hastings Turner

Isobel Elsom	Evelyn Dean

D.A. Clarke-Smith . . . . Franklyn Dean
Margot Grahame . . . . Dorothy Dixon
Moira Lynd . . . . Ann Dixon
Edgar Norfolk . . . . . . Lord Alan Sevingdon
DRAMA Deserted wife jailed for running
gambling club for daughter's sake.

09153
THE FAITHFUL HEART (84) (A) USA:
FAITHFUL HEARTS
Gainsborough (Ideal)
P: Michael Balcon
D: Victor Saville
S: (PLAY) Monckton Hoffe
SC: Angus Macphail, Robert Stevenson,
Lajos Biro, Victor Saville
Herbert Marshall . . . . Waverley Ango
Edna Best . . . . Blackie
Anne Grey . . . . Diana Oughterson
Athole Stewart . . . . . . Sir Gilbert Oughterson
Lawrence Hanray . . . . Major Ango
Mignon O'Dogherty . . . . Miss Gattiscombe
ROMANCE Col renounces rich fiancee to adopt
bastard daughter.

09154
THE SIGN OF FOUR (75) (U)
ATP (Radio)
P: Basil Dean
D: Rowland V. Lee, Graham Cutts
S: (NOVEL) Arthur Conan Doyle
SC: W.P. Lipscomb
Arthur Wontner . . . . Sherlock Holmes
Isla Bevan . . . . Mary Marstan
Ian Hunter . . . . Dr Watson
Ben Soutten . . . . Jonathan Small
Miles Malleson . . . . Thaddeus Sholto
Herbert Lomas . . . . Maj Sholto
Gilbert Davis . . . . Athelney Jones
Roy Emerton . . . . Bailey
Kynaston Reeves . . . . Bartholomew Sholto
Edgar Norfolk . . . . Capt Marstan
Clare Greet . . . . Mrs Hudson
CRIME Ex-convict seeks revenge upon partners
who cheated him of share in loot.

09155
FLAT NO. 9 (42) (A)
V.E. Deuchar (Fox)
D: Frank Richardson
S: Patricia Bach
SC: Brock Williams, John Barrow
Jane Baxter . . . . Eileen Merridew
Reginald Gardiner . . . . Peter Merridew
Marjorie Brooks . . . . Dora Danvers
Arthur Margetson . . . . John Danvers
Amy Veness . . . . Mrs Brandon Partridge
Margaret Damer . . . . Mrs Finch
A. Bromley Davenport . . . . . Caretaker
COMEDY Runaway wife and runaway husband
both rent same flat.

09156
WHITE FACE (70) (A)
Gainsborough-British Lion (W & F)
P: Michael Balcon
D: T. Hayes Hunter
S: (PLAY) Edgar Wallace (PERSONS
UNKNOWN)
SC: Angus Macphail, Bryan Edgar Wallace
Hugh Williams . . . . Michael Seeley
Gordon Harker . . . . Sam Hackett
Norman McKinnel . . . . Insp Mason
Renee Gadd . . . . Janice Harman
Richard Bird . . . . Donald Bateman
Nora Swinburne . . . . Inez Landor
Leslie Perrins . . . . Louis Landor
John H. Roberts . . . . Dr Marford
D.A. Clarke-Smith . . . . Dr Rudd
Gibb McLaughlin . . . . Sgt Elk

Jeanne Stuart . . . . Gloria Gaye
Clare Greet . . . . Mrs Albert
CRIME Reporter solves murder of crook who
blackmailed his ex-wife's husband.

JUN
09157
HIS LORDSHIP (79) (U)
Westminster (UA)
P: Jerome Jackson
D: Michael Powell
S: (NOVEL) Oliver Heuffer (THE RIGHT
HONOURABLE)
SC: Ralph Smart
Jerry Verno . . . . Bert Gibbs
Janet Megrew . . . . Ilya Myona
Ben Welden . . . . Washington Lincoln
Polly Ward . . . . Leninia
Peter Gawthorne . . . . Ferguson
Michael Hogan . . . . Comrade Curzon
Muriel George . . . . Mrs Gibbs
V.C. Clinton-Baddeley . . . . Comarde Howard
MUSICAL Cockney plumber becomes peer and
engaged to Russian film star.

09158
DOWN OUR STREET (87) (A)
Paramount British
P: S.E. Fitzgibbon
D:SC: Harry Lachman
S: (PLAY) Ernest George
Nancy Price . . . . Annie Collins
Elizabeth Allan . . . . Maisie Collins
Morris Harvey . . . . Bill Collins
Hugh Williams . . . . Charlie Stubbs
Alexander Field . . . . Sam
Sydney Fairbrother . . . . . Maggie Anning
Binnie Barnes . . . . Tessie Bernstein
Frederick Burtwell . . . . Fred Anning
Merle Tottenham . . . . Rose
DRAMA Slum youth reforms for girl and is
framed by her uncle for smash-and-grab raid.

09159
LUCKY GIRL (75) (U)
BIP (Wardour)
D:SC: Gene Gerrard, Frank Miller
S: (PLAY) Reginald Berkeley, Douglas Furber,
R.P. Weston, Bert Lee (MR ABDULLA)
Gene Gerrard . . . . Stephan Gregorovitch
Molly Lamont . . .Lady Moira Cavendish-
Gascoyne
Gus McNaughton . . . . Hudson E. Greener
Spencer Trevor . . . . Duke Hugo
Tonie Edgar Bruce . . . . Duchess Amelia
Hal Gordon . . . . PC
Ian Fleming . . . . Lord Henry
Frank Stanmore . . . . Mullins
MUSICAL Ruritanian King mistaken for gem
thief at Duke's house-party.

09160
STRIP, STRIP, HOORAY! (36) (A)
BIP (Pathe)
D: Norman Lee
S: Leslie Arliss
Ken Douglas . . . . Benny
Betty Norton . . . . Janet
Binnie Barnes . . . . Spanish Lady
Hal Gordon . . . . Hoodlum
Albert Rayner . . . . Sir Hector
Charles Castella . . . . Supt
Eric Pavitt . . . . Boy
Freddie Bartholomew . . . . . Boy
Frank & Albert
COMEDY Photographer blackmails fiancee's
father with sunbathing snaps.

09161
JACK'S THE BOY (91) (U) USA: NIGHT AND
DAY
Gainsborough (W&F) reissue: 1940 (IFR)
P: Michael Balcon
D: Walter Forde
S: Jack Hulbert, Douglas Furber
SC: W.P. Lipscomb
Jack Hulbert . . . . Jack Brown
Cicely Courtneidge . . . . Mrs Bobday
Winifred Shotter . . . . Ivy
Francis Lister . . . . Jules Martin
Peter Gawthorne . . . . Mr Brown
Ben Field . . . . Mr Bobday
Charles Farrell . . . . Martin
COMEDY Commissioner's son, secretly
policeman, catches smash-and-grab gang.

09162
A SAFE PROPOSITION (45) (U)
Real Art (Fox)
P: Julius Hagen
D: Leslie Hiscott
S: Michael Barringer
A.W. Baskcomb . . . . Henry Woodford
Barbara Gott . . . . Emily Woodford
Harold French . . . . Reggie Holloway
Joyce Kirby . . . . MargáretWoodford
Austin Trevor . . . . Count Tonelli
Alexander Field . . . . Ginger Newton
Molly Fisher . . . . Mrs Newton
Henry B. Longhurst . . . . . . Sgt Crouch
COMEDY Man saves girl's pearls from phoney
Count.

09163
THE IMPASSIVE FOOTMAN (70) (A) USA:
WOMAN IN BONDAGE
ATP (Radio) reissues: 1948 (EB) 1956 (EB)
P:D: Basil Dean
S: (PLAY) Sapper (H.C. McNeile)
SC: John Farrow, John Paddy Carstairs,
Harold Dearden
Owen Nares . . . . Bryan Daventry
Betty Stockfeld . . . . Mrs Marwood
Allan Jeayes . . . . John Marwood
George Curzon . . . . Simpson
Aubrey Mather . . . . Dr Bartlett
Frances Ross-Campbell . . . . Mrs Angers
Florence Harwood . . . . Mrs Hoggs
DRAMA Spinal specialist loves wife of cruel
patient, who is killed by vengeful servant.

JUL
09164
AFTER OFFICE HOURS (78) (U)
BIP (Wardour)
D: Thomas Bentley
S: (PLAY) John Van Druten (LONDON WALL)
SC: Thomas Bentley, Frank Launder
Frank Lawton . . . . Hec
Heather Angel . . . . Pat
Viola Lyel . . . . Miss Janus
Garry Marsh . . . . Brewer
Eileen Peel . . . . Miss Bufton
Frank Royde . . . . Mr Walker
Katie Johnson . . . . Miss Willesden
Nadine March . . . . Miss Hooper
ROMANCE Solicitor's spinster secretary helps
clerk win flighty typist.

09165
NUMBER SEVENTEEN (63) (U)
BIP (Wardour)
D: Alfred Hitchcock
S: (PLAY) J. Jefferson Farjeon
SC: Alfred Hitchcock, Alma Reville, Rodney
Ackland
Anne Grey . . . . Nora Brant

John Stuart . . . . Gilbert Fordyce
Donald Calthrop . . . . Brant
Barry Jones . . . . Henry Doyle
Ann Casson . . . . Rose Ackroyd
Garry Marsh . . . . Sheldrake
Henry Caine . . . . Mr Ackroyd
Herbert Langley . . . . Guard
CRIME Girl jewel thief reforms and helps tec
foil gang's escape to France (Extract in
ELSTREE STORY, 1952).

09166
LOVE ON THE SPOT (64) (A)
ATP (Radio)
P: Basil Dean
D: Graham Cutts
S: (NOVEL) Sapper (THREE OF A KIND)
SC: John Paddy Carstairs, Reginald Purdell
Rosemary Ames . . . . Joan Prior
Richard Dolman . . . . Bill Maitland
Aubrey Mather . . . . Mr Prior
Helen Ferrers . . . . Lady Witchell
W. Cronin Wilson . . . . Insp MacAndrews
Patrick Ludlow . . . . Mr Terrington
J. Hubert Leslie . . . . Manager
Margery Binner . . . . Maid
Johnny Singer . . . . Pageboy
Patrick Susands . . . . Cartwright
MUSICAL Love reforms hotel thief and
confidence man's daughter.

09167
THE MAYOR'S NEST (74) (U)
B & D (W & F)
P: Herbert Wilcox
D:SC: Maclean Rogers
S: R.P. Weston, Bert Lee, Jack Marks
Sydney Howard . . . . Joe Pilgrim
Claude Hulbert . . . . Algernon Ashcroft
Al Bowlly . . . . George
Muriel Aked . . . . Mrs Ashcroft
Frank Harvey . . . . Councillor Blackett
Michael Hogan . . . . Tom Ackroyd
Miles Malleson . . . . Clerk
Cyril Smith . . . . Magistrate
Syd Crossley . . . . Milkman
COMEDY Rich welfare worker helps
trombonist become Mayor.

09168
THARK (79) (A)
B&D (W&F) reissues: 1937 (EB) 1945 (Stahl)
P: Herbert Wilcox
D: Tom Walls
S: (PLAY) Ben Travers
Tom Walls . . . . Sir Hector Benbow
Ralph Lynn . . . . Ronald Gamble
Mary Brough . . . . Mrs Todd
Robertson Hare . . . . Hook
Claude Hulbert . . . . Lionel Todd
Joan Brierley . . . . Cherry Buck
Gordon James . . . . Death
Evelyn Bostock . . . . Kitty Stratton
Beryl de Querton . . . . Lady Benbow
Marjorie Corbett . . . . Warner
COMEDY Friends spend night in old house to
prove it is not haunted.

09169
BLACK DIAMONDS (53) (U)
Hanmer Productions (Wardour)
P:D:S: Charles Hanmer
John Martin . . . . The MP
John Morgan . . . . The Miner
Mrs Morgan . . . . The Wife
Jenny Morgan . . . . The Child
The Harmonious Miners; Barnborough Colliery
Orchestra.
DRAMA Yorkshire. Old miner persuades film
producer to show the world hazards of pit life.

09170
MONTE CARLO MADNESS (83) bilingual (U)
UFA (Pathe)
P: Erich Pommer
D: Hanns Schwartz
S:(NOVEL) Reck-Malleczewen
SC: Franz Schulz, Hans Muller, Rowland V.Lee
Sari Maritza . . . . Queen Yola
Hans Albers . . . . Capt Erickson
Charles Redgie . . . . Peter
Helen Haye . . . . Isabel
John Deverell . . . . Consul
C.Hooper Trask . . . . Prime Minister
Comedian Harmonists; Carlo Minari Orchestra.
MUSICAL Monte Carlo. Captain gambles to pay
crew and falls in love with incognito queen.
(Made in Germany).

09171
THE LOVE CONTRACT (80) (A)
B & D (W&F)
P: Herbert Wilcox
D: Herbert Selpin
S: (PLAY) Letraz, Desty, Blum (CHAUFFEUR
ANTIONETTE)
Winifred Shotter . . . . Antionette
Owen Nares . . . . Neville Cardington
Sunday Wilshin . . . . Mrs Savage
Miles Malleson . . . . Peters
Gibb McLaughlin . . . . Hodge
Spencer Trevor . . . . Mr Savage
Frank Harvey . . . . Bank Manager
Cosmo Kyrle Bellew . . . . . Sir George
The Mangan Tillerettes
MUSICAL Girl acts as chauffeur to
broker who lost her savings.

09172
THE FLYING SQUAD (8)) (A)
British Lion
P: S.W.Smith
D: F.W. Kraemer
S: (NOVEL) Edgar Wallace
SC: Bryan Edgar Wallace
Harold Huth . . . . Mark McGill
Carol Goodner . . . . Ann Perryman
Edward Chapman . . . . Sedeman
Campbell Gullan . . . . Tiser
Harry Wilcoxon . . . . Insp Bradley
Abraham Sofaer . . . . Li Yoseph
Joseph Cunningham . . . . . . Simmonds
CRIME Dope smugglers use victim's sister
to outwit police.

09173
WHEN LONDON SLEEPS (78) (A)
Twickenham (AP&D) reissue: 1937
P: Julius Hagen
D: Leslie Hiscott
S: (PLAY) Charles Darrell
SC: Bernard Merivale, H.Fowler Mear
Harold French . . . . Tommy Blythe
Francis L.Sullivan . . . . Rodney Haines
Rene Ray . . . . Mary
A.Bromley Davenport . . . . . . Col Grahame
Alexander Field . . . . Sam
Diana Beaumont . . . . Hilda
Ben Field . . . . Lamberti
Barbara Everest . . . . Mme Lamberti
Herbert Lomas . . . . Pollard
CRIME Gambling den owner kidnaps cousin
to usurp title.

09174
INSULT (80) (A)
Paramount British
P: S. Fitzgibbon
D: Harry Lachman
S: (PLAY) Jean Fabricus

SC: Basil Mason
Elizabeth Allan . . . . Pola Dubois
John Gielgud. . . . . Henri Dubois
Hugh Williams . . . . Capt Ramon Nadir
Sam Livesey . . . . Maj Dubois
Sydney Fairbrother . . . . . . Arabella
Abraham Sofaer . . . . Ali Ben Achmed
Edgar Norfolk . . . . Capt Jean Conte
Hal Gordon . . . . Sgt
Dinh Gilly . . . . Singer
DRAMA Africa. Halfcaste legionnaire dies to
save Governor, the son of Major who hates him.

09175
LOVE ON WHEELS (87) (U)
Gainsborough (W&F)
P: Michael Balcon
D: Victor Saville
S: Franz Schulz, Ernst Angel
SC: Victor Saville, Angus Macphail,
Robert Stevenson, Douglas Furber
Jack Hulbert . . . . Fred Hopkins
Edmund Gwenn . . . . Philpotts
Leonora Corbett . . . . Jane Russell
Gordon Harker . . . . Briggs
Tony de Lungo . . . . Bronelli
Percy Parsons . . . . Crook
Roland Culver . . . . Salesman
Lawrence Hanray . . . . Commissionaire
Miles Malleson . . . . Porter
Martita Hunt . . . . Demonstrator
MUSICAL Shop assistant becomes publicity
manager and thwarts thieves.

09176
HIGH SOCIETY (5)) (U)
WB-FN (FN)
P: Irving Asher
D: John Rawlings
S: W.Scott Darling, Randall Faye
Florence Desmond . . . . Florrie
William Austin . . . Wilberforce Strangeways
Emily Fitzroy . . . . Mrs Strangeways
Tracy Holmes . . . . Hon Tommy Montgomery
Joan Wyndham . . . . Betty Cunningham-Smith
Margaret Damer . . Mrs Cunningham-Smith
Leo Sheffield . . . . Lord Halkirk
Syd Crossley . . . . Simeon
COMEDY Cockney maid poses as society Lady
to help mistress.

09177
WEDDING REHEARSAL (84) (U)
London (Ideal)
P:D: Alexander Korda
S: Robert Vansittart, Lajos Biro, George
Grossmith
SC: Arthur Wimperis
Roland Young . . . . Reggie Candysshe
George Grossmith . . . . . Lord Stokeshire
John Loder . . . . Bimbo
Maurice Evans . . . . Tootles
Lady Tree . . . . Lady Stokeshire
Edmond Breon . . . . Lord Fleet
Wendy Barrie . . . . . Lady Maryrose Wroxbury
Joan Gardner . . . . . Lady Rosemary Wroxbury
Merle Oberon . . . . Miss Hutchinson
Kate Cutler . . . . Marchioness of Buckminster
Diana Napier . . . . Mrs Dryden
Morton Selten . . . . Maj Harry Wroxbury
COMEDY Bachelor marquis contrives for
grandmother's wedding candidates to marry his
friends.

09178
A YELL OF A NIGHT (42) (A)
C. aBecket Williams, E.E.Wishart, M.Long,
Max Zeitlin, L.A.Nicholl (U)
D: Gustave Minzenty
S: Gustave Minzenty, C.aBecket Williams

Mickey Brantford . . . . The Boy
Mignon Swaffer . . . . The Girl
M. Huntington . . . . The Father
Sam Lee . . . . The Crook
COMEDY Crooks search for stolen jewels in
waxworks.

09179
THE LAST COUPON (84) (U)
BIP (Wardour)
D: Thomas Bentley
S: (PLAY) Ernest E.Bryan
SC: Frank Launder, Syd Courtenay
Leslie Fuller . . . . Bill Carter
Mary Jerrold . . . . Polly Carter
Molly Lamont . . . . Betty Carter
Binnie Barnes . . . . .Mrs Meredith
Gus McNaughton . . . . Lord Bedlington
Jack Hobbs . . . . Dr Sinclair
Marian Dawson . . . . Mrs Bates
Harry Carr . . . . Jocker
Jimmy Godden . . . . Geordie Bates
Hal Gordon . . . . Rusty Walker
COMEDY Collier's wife tries to stop him
wasting £20,000 pools prize.

AUG

09180
A TIGHT CORNER (49) (A)
Real Art (MGM)
P: Julius Hagen
D: Leslie Hiscott
S: Michael Barringer
Harold French . . . . Tony Titmouse
Frank Pettingell . . . . Oswald Blekinsop
Gina Malo. . . . .
Betty Astell . . . .
Madeleine Gibson . . . .
Charles Farrell . . . .
Arthur Stratton . . . .
COMEDY Tecs pose as PT instructors to
recoup baron's letters from blackmailer.

09181
HEROES OF THE MINE (48) (U)
Delta (Butcher)
P: Geoffrey Clarke
D: Widgey R.Newman
S: Geoffrey Clarke, Cdr Barwood
Moore Marriott . . . . Gaffer
Wally Patch . . . . Bob
Terence de Marney . . . . . . Youngster
John Milton . . . . Taffy
Eric Adeney . . . . Timberman
Agnes Brantford . . . . Mrs Latham
Ian Wilson . . . . Ponyboy
DRAMA Wales. Entombed miner confesses
to framing cockney for theft.

SEP

09182
MONEY MEANS NOTHING (70) (U)
B&D-Paramount British
D: Harcourt Templeman, Herbert Wilcox
S: Douglas Furber
SC: Miles Malleson, Harcourt Templeman
John Loder . . . . Earl Egbert
Irene Richards . . . . Livia Faringay
Gibb McLaughlin . . . . . Augustus Bethersyde
Dorothy Robinson . . . . Daysie de Lille
Kay Hammond . . . . Angel
Clive Currie . . . . Sir Percival Puttock
A.Bromley Davenport . Earl of Massingham
Miles Malleson . . . . Doorman
COMEDY Broke Earl engaged to actress loves
rich butler's daughter.

09183
ARMS AND THE MAN (85) (U)
BIP (Wardour)
D: SC: Cecil Lewis
S: (PLAY) George Bernard Shaw
Barry Jones . . . . Capt Bluntschli
Anne Grey . . . . Raina Petkoff
Maurice Colbourne. . . . . Sergius Seranoff
Angela Baddeley . . . . Louka
Frederick Lloyd . . . . . . Maj Paul Petkoff
Wallace Evenett . . . . Niccola
Margaret Scudamore . . . . . Catherine Petkoff
Charles Morton . . . . Plechanoff
COMEDY Bulgaria, 1885. Swiss soldier retreats
to affianced girl's bedroom. (Extract in
ELSTREE STORY, 1952).

09184
JOSSER ON THE RIVER (75) (A)
BIP-BIF (Wardour)
D: Norman Lee
S: Norman Lee, Leslie Arliss
Ernie Lotinga . . . . Jimmy Josser
Molly Lamont . . . . Julia Kaye
Charles Hickman . . . . Eddie Kaye
Reginald Gardiner . . . . Donald
Wallace Lupino . . . . Uncle Abel
Joan Wyndham . . . . A little Lady
Arty Ash . . . . Hank
COMEDY Houseboat couple force blackmailer
to pose as servant.

09185
FIRES OF FATE (74) (A)
BIP (Wardour)
D: Norman Walker
S: (NOVEL/PLAY) A.Conan Doyle
(THE TRAGEDY OF THE KOROSKO)
SC: Dion Titheradge
Lester Matthews . . . . Lt-Col Egerton
Dorothy Bartlam . . . . Kay Byrne
Kathleen O'Regan . . . . Nora Belmont
Donald Calthrop . . . Sir William Royden
Jack Raine . . . . Filbert Frayne
Garry Marsh . . . . Capt Archer
Clifford Heatherley . . . . . . Abdullah
Jean Cadell . . . . Miss Byrne
Hubert Harben . . . . . Rev Mark Royden
Arthur Chesney . . . . Mr Braddell
ADVENTURE Egypt. Col with year to live
saves travellers from Bedouins.

09186
OLD SPANISH CUSTOMERS (68) (U)
BIP (Wardour)
D: Lupino Lane
S: Syd Courtenay, Lola Harvey
Leslie Fuller . . . . Bill
Binnie Barnes . . . . Carmen
Drusilla Wills . . . . Martha
Wallace Lupino . . . . Pedro
Hal Gordon . . . . Manuelito
Ernest Sefton . . . . Tormillo
Betty Fields . . . .
Syd Courtenay . . . .
Hal Walters . . . .
COMEDY Spain. Henpeck on prize holiday
mistaken for toreador.

09187
THE MAID OF THE MOUNTAINS (80) (U)
BIP (Wardour) *reissue:* 1935
D: Lupino Lane
S: (PLAY) Frederick Lonsdale
SC: Lupino Lane, Douglas Furber,
Frank Miller, Victor Kendall, Edwin Greenwood
Nancy Brown . . . . Teresa
Harry Welchman . . . . Baldasarre

Betty Stockfeld . . . . Angela Malona
Albert Burdon . . . . Tonio
Gus McNaughton . . . . Gen Malona
Garry Marsh . . . . Beppo
Renee Gadd . . . . Vittoria
Wallace Lupino . . . . Crumpet
Dennis Hoey . . . . Orsino
Alfredo and his Gypsy Orchestra
MUSICAL Italy. Bandit posing as new
governor is betrayed by jealous sweetheart.

09188
THE LODGER (85) (A) USA: THE
PHANTOM FIEND
Twickenham (W&F)
P: Julius Hagen
D: Maurice Elvey
S: (NOVEL) Mrs Belloc Lowndes
SC: Ivor Novello, Miles Mander, Paul Rotha,
H.Fowler Mear
Ivor Novello . . . . Angeloff
Elizabeth Allan . . . . Daisy Bunting
A.W.Baskcomb . . . . Mr Bunting
Jack Hawkins . . . . Joe Martin
Barbara Everest . . . . Mrs Bunting
Peter Gawthorne . . . . Lord Southcliffe
P. Kynaston Reeves . . . . . . Bob Mitchell
Shayle Gardner . . . . Snell
Drusilla Wills . . . . Mrs Coles
Antony Holles . . . . Sylvano
George Merritt . . . . Commissioner
CRIME Girl loves lodger suspected of
murdering girls.

09189
MEN OF STEEL (71) (A)
Langham (UA)
P: Bray Wyndham
D: George King
S: (NOVEL) Douglas Newton
SC: Edward Knoblock, Billie Bristow
John Stuart . . . . . James 'Iron' Harg
Benita Hume . . . . Audrey Paxton
Franklin Dyall . . . . Charles Paxton
Heather Angel . . . . Ann Ford
Alexander Field . . . . Sweepy Ford
Sydney Benson . . . . Lodger
Mary Merrall . . . . Mrs Harg
Edward Ashley Cooper . . . Sylvano
DRAMA Sheffield. Steelworker becomes callous
manager and is humanised by secretary's
accident.

09190
DUAL CONTROL (20) (U)
BIP (Wardour)
D:S: Walter Summers
Amy Johnson . . . . Herself
Jim Mollison . . . . Himself
Lionel Hoare . . . . Boy
COMEDY Famous fliers land in field, take
children for flight, and are stopped by PC in an
autogyro.

09191
ON THE AIR (17) (U)
WB-FN (WB)
P: Irving Asher
D: William McGann
Carlyle Cousins
Helen Ferrers
Syd Crossley
Hal Walters
MUSICAL Old opera star converted to
jazz by daughters' broadcast.

09192
MUSICAL MEMORIES (series) (U)
Delta (Filmophone)
D:S: Widgey R.Newman

09193
1: RACHMANINOV'S PRELUDE (8)

09194
2: THE MOONLIGHT SONATA (7)

09195
3: LIEBESTRAUM (7)

09196
4: FUNERAL MARCH OF A MARIONETTE(8)

09197
5: DANSE MACABRE

09198
6: MELODY IN F (7)
MUSICAL Dramas illustrating popular
classics.

09199
CAPTURE (8) (U)
Sound City (MGM)
DRAMA
09200
THE SAFE (20) (U)
Sound City (MGM)
S: (PLAY) W.P.Lipscomb
Angela Baddeley .... The Girl
Michael Hogan .... Alfred
CRIME Married man locks infatuated typist in
safe but she is freed by burglar.

09201
THE MERRY MEN OF SHERWOOD (36) (U)
Delta (Filmophone)
D: Widgey R.Newman
John Thompson .... Robin Hood
Aileen Marson .... Maid Marian
Eric Adeney .... Sheriff of Nottingham
John Milton ..: ....
Terence de Marney ....
Patrick Barr .... Torturer
ADVENTURE Period. Outlaw rescues captive
cousin and restores King Richard to throne.

09202
LUCKY· LADIES (74) (U)
WB-FN (FN)
P: Irving Asher
D: John Rawlings
S: W.Scott Darling
SC: Randall Faye
Sydney Fairbrother ...... Angle Tuckett
Emily Fitzroy .... Cleo Honeycutt
Tracy Holmes .... Ted
Janice Adair .... Pearl
Syd Crossley .... Hector Ramsbottom
Charles Farrell .... Bookmaker
COMEDY Sisters running oyster bar win
£30,000 on Irish Sweep and lose it to bogus
Count.

09203
THE SILVER GREYHOUND (47) (U)
WB-FN (WB)
P: Irving Asher
D: William McGann
S: John Hastings Turner
SC: Roland Pertwee, John Hastings Turner
Percy Marmont .... Norton Fitzwarren
Anthony Bushell .... Gerald Varrick
Janice Adair .... Ira Laennic
Harry Hutchinson .... Regan
J.A.O'Rourke .... O'Brien
Dino Galvani .... Valdez
Eric Stanley .... Sir Wallace Cantripp
CRIME Uncle of King's Messenger recoups
stolen papers from female spy.

09204
LOOKING ON THE BRIGHT SIDE (81) (U)
ATP (Radio) reissue: 1937
P: Basil Dean
D: Basil Dean, Graham Cutts
S: Basil Dean, Archie Pitt, Brock Williams
Gracie Fields .... Gracie
Richard Dolman .... Laurie
Julian Rose .... Oscar Schultz
Wyn Richmond .... Miss Joy
Tony de Lungo .... Delmonico
Betty Shale .... Hetty Hunt
Viola Compton .... Sgt
MUSICAL Manicurist loves song-writing
hairdresser who falls for singer.

09205
DIAMOND CUT DIAMOND (70) USA:
BLAME THE WOMAN
Cinema House (MGM)
P: Eric Hakim
D: Fred Niblo, Maurice Elvey
S: Viscount Castlerosse
Adolphe Menjou......... Dan MacQueen
Benita Hume .... Marda Blackett
Claud Allister .... Joe Fragson
Kenneth Kove .... Reggie Dean
Desmond Jeans .... Mr Blackett
Tonie Edgar Bruce ...... Mrs Loftus
Shayle Gardner .... Spellman
Philip Strange .... Partierre
COMEDY Girl outwits jewel thieves at
country house party.

09206
HERE'S GEORGE (64) (U)
Thomas Charles Arnold (PDC)
D: Redd Davis
S: (PLAY) Marriott Edgar
(THE SERVICE FLAT)
George Clarke .... George Muffitt
Pat Paterson .... Laura Wentworth
Ruth Taylor .... Mrs Wentworth
Marriott Edgar .... Mr Wentworth
Syd Crossley .... Commissionaire
Alfred Wellesley .... Tenant
Merle Tottenham .... Perkins
Wally Patch .... Foreman
Rene Ray .... Telephonist
COMEDY Man borrows service flat to impress
girl's parents.

09207
THE RETURN OF RAFFLES (71) (A)
Markham (WP)
P:D: Mansfield Markham
S: (STORIES) E.W.Hornung
SC: W.J. Balef
George Barraud .... A.J.Raffles
Camilla Horn .... Elga
Claud Allister .... Bunny
A.Bromley Davenport . Sir John Truwode
Sydney Fairbrother ...... Lady Truwode
H. Saxon - Snell .... Von Spechen
CRIME Reformed burglar framed for gem
theft at Lady's house-party.

09208
MEN OF TOMORROW (88) (U)
London (Par)
P: Alexander Korda
D: Leontine Sagan
S: (NOVEL) Anthony Gibbs (YOUNG APOLLO)
SC: Arthur Wimperis, Anthony Gibbs
Maurice Braddell .... Allan Shepherd
Joan Gardner .... Jane Anderson *
Emlyn Williams .... Horners
Robert Donat .... Julian Angell
Merle Oberon .... Ysobel d'Aunay

John Traynor .... Mr Waters
Esther Kiss .... Maggie
Annie Esmond .... Mrs Oliphant
ROMANCE Oxford. Girl loves student who
rebels against tradition.

OCT

09209
HIS WIFE'S MOTHER (69) (U)
BIP (Wardour)
D:SC: Harry Hughes
S: (PLAY) Will Scott (THE QUEER FISH)
Gus McNaughton .... Joy
Jerry Verno .... Henry
Molly Lamont .... Cynthia
Jack Hobbs . ... Eustace
Marion Dawson .... Mrs Trout
Jimmy Godden .... Mr Trout
Renee Gadd .... Tony
Hal Gordon .... Munro
COMEDY Husband poses as double to fool
mother-in-law.

09210
JOSSER IN THE ARMY (79)
BIP (Wardour)
D: Norman Lee
S: Con West, Herbert Sargent
SC: Frank Launder
Ernie Lotinga .... Jimmy Josser
Betty Norton .... Joan
Jack Hobbs .... Paul Langdon
Hal Gordon .... Parker
Jack Frost .... Ginger
Arnold Bell .... Becker
Harold Wilkinson ...... Seeley
COMEDY 1914. Soldier escapes capture and
unmasks spy. (Extract in
ELSTREE STORY, 1952).

09211
VERDICT OF THE SEA (65) (U)
Regina (Pathe)
P: Clayton Hutton
D: Frank Miller, Sydney Northcote
S: Frank Miller
John Stuart .... Gentleman Burton
Moira Lynd .... Paddy
Cyril McLaglen .... Fenn
David Miller .... Captain
Hal Walters .... Shorty
H. Saxon-Snell .... Myers
Billy Shine .... Slim
Fred Rains .... Martin
ADVENTURE Ex-doctor joins tramp steamer
crew and thwarts mutiny.

09212
BLIND SPOT (75) (A)
WB-FN (WB)
P: Irving Asher
D: John Daumery
S: Roland Pertwee, John Hastings Turner
Percy Marmont .... Holland Janney
Muriel Angelus .... Marilyn Janney
Warwick Ward .... Hugh Conway
Laura Cowie .... Anna Wiltone
Ivor Barnard .... Mull
Mary Jerrold .... Mrs Herriott
George Merritt .... Insp Cadbury
CRIME Gentleman thief's amnesiac daughter
weds KC who prosecutes him.

09213
HER NIGHT OUT (45) (A)
WB-FN (WB)
P: Irving Asher
D: William McGann
S: W.Scott Darling

Dorothy Bartlam . . . . Kitty Vickery
Lester Matthews . . . . Gerald Vickery
Joan Marion . . . . Goldie
Jack Raine . . . . Jim Hanley
Dodo Watts . . . . Toots
COMEDY Golfer's jealous wife flirts with bank robber.

09214
LITTLE FELLA (45) (U)
WB-FN (FN)
P: Irving Asher
D: William McGann
S: W.Scott Darling
John Stuart . . . . Maj Tony Griffiths
Joan Marion . . . . Cynthia Knowles
Dodo Watts . . . . Pan
Glyn James . . . . Bubblekins
Marie Ault . . . . Mrs Turner
Hal Walters . . . . Dawes
George Merritt . . . . Detective
COMEDY Baby helps runaway orphan win major from fiancee.

09215
LEAP YEAR (91) (A)
B & D (W&F) *reissue:* 1937 (EB)
P: Herbert Wilcox
D: Tom Walls
S: A.R.Rawlinson
Tom Walls . . . . Sir Peter Traillon
Anne Grey . . . . Paula Zahren
Edmond Breon . . . . Jack Debrant
Ellis Jeffreys . . . . Mrs Debrant
Jeanne Stuart . . . . Angela Mallard
Charles Carson . . . . . Sir Archibald Mallard
Lawrence Hanray . . . . Hope
Joan Brierley . . . . Girl
Franklyn Bellamy . . . . .Silas
COMEDY Affianced FO agent searches for mystery woman he loves.

09216
THE FLAG LIEUTENANT (85) (U)
B & D (W&F) *reissue:* 1937 (EB)
P: Herbert Wilcox
D: Henry Edwards
S: (PLAY) W.P.Drury, Leo Tover
Henry Edwards . . . . .Lt Dicky Lascelles
Anna Neagle . . . . Hermione Wynne
Joyce Bland . . . . Mrs Cameron
Peter Gawthorne . . . . Maj Thesiger
Louis Goodrich . . . . Admiral Wynne
Sam Livesey . . . . Col McLeod
Michael Hogan . . . . Lt Palliser
O.B.Clarence . . . . Gen Gough-Bogle
Abraham Sofaer . . . . Meheti Salos
Peter Northcote . . . . Midshipman Lee
Tully Comber . . . . Midshipman Hood
WAR Lieut branded coward after saving beleaguered fort for amnesiac major.

09217
MARRY ME (85) (U) *bilingual*
Gainsborough (Ideal)
P: Michael Balcon
D: William Thiele
S: Stephen Zador, Franz Schulz, Ernst Angel
SC: Angus Macphail, Anthony Asquith
Renate Muller . . . . Ann Linden
Harry Green . . . . Sigurd Bernstein
George Robey . . . . Aloysius Novak
Ian Hunter . . . . Robert Hart
Maurice Evans . . . . Paul Hart
Billy Caryll . . . . Meyer
Charles Hawtrey jr . . . . . . Billy Hart
Charles Carson . . . . Korten
Viola Lyel . . . . Frau Krause
Sunday Wilshin . . . . Ida Brun
MUSICAL Berlin. Recordist wins social climber by becoming housekeeper.

09218
BAROUD (80) (A) *bilingual*
USA: LOVE IN MOROCCO
Rex Ingram (Ideal)
P: Rex Ingram, Mansfield Markham
D: Rex Ingram
S: Rex Ingram, Benno Vigny
Rex Ingram . . . . Sgt Andre Duval
Rosita Garcia . . . . Zinah
Dennis Hoey . . . . Capt Labry
Arabella Fields . . . . Mabrouka
Pierre Batchef . . . . Si Hamed
Andrews Engelman . . . . . . Si Amarok
Felipe Montes . . . . Si Allal
Laura Salerni . . . . Arlette
ADVENTURE Morocco. Foreign Legion sergeant loves Berber chieftain's daughter. (Made in Morocco).

09219
HAPPY EVER AFTER (86) (U) *bilingual*
UFA (W&F)
P: Erich Pommer
D: Paul Martin, Robert Stevenson
S: Walter Reisch, Billy Wilder
SC: Jack Hulbert, Douglas Furber
Lilian Harvey . . . . Jou-Jou
Jack Hulbert . . . . Willie
Cicely Courtneidge . . . . . . Illustrated Ida
Sonnie Hale . . . . Willie
Edward Chapman . . . . Colonel
Percy Parsons . . . . Merriman
Clifford Heatherley . . . . . . Commissionaire
Charles Redgie . . . . Secretary
MUSICAL Berlin. Window cleaners help poor girl find stardom. (Made in Germany).

09220
TELL ME TONIGHT (91) (U) *bilingual*
USA: BE MINE TONIGHT
Cine-Allianz (W&F)
P: Herman Fellner, Josef Somlo
D: Anatol Litwak
S: Irma von Cube, A.Joseph
SC: John Orton
Jan Kiepura . . . . Enrico Ferraro
Sonnie Hale . . . . Koretsky
Magda Schneider . . . . Mathilde
Edmund Gwenn . . . . Mayor Pategy
Athene Seyler . . . . Mrs Pategy
Betty Chester . . . . Nonstop Nora
Aubrey Mather . . . . Belthasar
MUSICAL Switzerland. Italian tenor changes places with fugitive and falls in love with mayor's adopted daughter. (Made in Germany).

09221
THERE GOES THE BRIDE (79) (U)
Gainsborough-British Lion (Ideal)
reissue: 1943 (EB)
P: Michael Balcon
D: Albert de Courville
S: Herman Kosterlitz, Wolfgang Wilhelm
SC: W.P. Lipscomb, Fred Raymond
Jessie Matthews . . . . . . Annette Marquand
Owen Nares . . . . Max
Carol Goodner . . . . Cora
Jerry Verno . . . . Clark
Charles Carson . . . . M.Marquand
Barbara Everest . . . . Mme Marquand
Basil Radford . . . . Rudolph
Winifred Oughton . . . . . . Housekeeper
Jack Morrison . . . . Alphonse
Roland Culver . . . . Jacques
Max Kirby . . . . Pierre
Gordon McLeod . . . . M.Duchaine
Lawrence Hanray . . . . Police Chief
George Zucco . . . . Prosecutor
COMEDY Paris. Girl flees from a forced marriage and is mistaken for helper's fiancee.

09222
THE FACE AT THE WINDOW (52) (A)
Real Art (Radio)
P: Julius Hagen
D: Leslie Hiscott
S: (PLAY) F.Brooke Warren
SC: H.Fowler Mear
Raymond Massey . . . . Paul le Gros
Isla Bevan . . . . Marie de Brisson
Claude Hulbert . . . . Peter Pomeroy
Eric Maturin . . . . Count Fournal
Henry Mollison . . . . Lucien Courtier
A.Bromley Davenport . . . Gaston de Brisson
Harold Meade . . . . Dr Renard
Dennis Wyndham . . . . Lafonde
Charles Groves . . . . Jacques
Berenoff & Charlot
CRIME Paris. Tec fakes revival of murdered man to expose count as bank robber.

09223
THE BAILIFFS (24) (U)
ATP (Ideal)
P: Clayton Hutton
D: Frank Cadman
S: (SKETCH) Fred Karno (THE BAILIFF)
Flanagan & Allen . . . . Bailiffs
Florence Harwood . . . . . . Mrs Templeman
Reginald Smith . . . . Manager
Ian Wilson . . . . Youth
COMEDY Broker's men take possession of the wrong house.

09224
WATCH BEVERLY (80) (U)
Sound City (Butcher)
P: Ivor Campbell
D: Arthur Maude
S: (PLAY) Cyril Campion
SC: N.W.Baring Pemberton, John Cousins
Henry Kendall . . . . Victor Beverly
Dorothy Bartlam . . . . . . Audrey Thurloe
Francis X. Bushman . . . . . President Orloff
Frederic de Lara . . . . Rachmann
Charles Mortimer . . . . . . Sir James Briden
Patrick Ludlow . . . . Patrick Nolan
Colin Pole . . . . George
Antony Holles . . . . Arthur Briden
Ernest Stidwell . . . . Insp Roberts
Aileen Pitt Marsden . . . . . Anne Markham
COMEDY Diplomat poses as Ruritanian president outwit crooked magnates.

09225
AFTER DARK (45) (U)
Fox British
P: Hugh Perceval
D: Albert Parker
S: (PLAY) J.Jefferson Farjeon
SC: John Barrow
Horace Hodges . . . . . Thaddeus C. Brompton
Grethe Hansen . . . . Alva Lea
Hugh Williams . . . . Richard Morton
George Barraud . . . . George Harvey
Ian Fleming . . . . Henry Lea
Henry Oscar . . . . Higgins
Pollie Emery . . . . Mrs Thirkettle
Lucille Lisle . . . . Vivienne Roberts
COMEDY Crooks seek stolen emeralds hidden in antique clock.

09226
THE WONDERFUL STORY (72) (A)
Fogwell (Sterling)
P:D:SC: Reginald Fogwell
S: (NOVEL) I.A.R.Wylie
Wyn Clare . . . . Mary Richards
John Batten . . . . John Martin
Eric Bransby Williams . . . . Bob Martin
Moore Marriott . . . . Zacky Richards

J. Fisher White . . . . Parson
Sam Livesey . . . . Doctor
Ernest Lester . . . . Amos
ROMANCE Devon. Young farmer and
crippled brother both love same girl.

NOV

09227
THAT NIGHT IN LONDON (78) (A)
USA: OVERNIGHT
London (Par)
P: Alexander Korda
D: Rowland V.Lee
S: Dorothy Greenhill, Arthur Wimperis
Robert Donat . . . . Dick Warren
Pearl Argyle . . . . Eve
Miles Mander . . . . Harry Tresham
Roy Emerton . . . . Capt Paulson
Graham Soutten . . . . Bert
Lawrence Hanray . . . . Ribbles
James Knight . . . . Insp Brody
Max Rivers Girls
CRIME Crook has dancer pose as sister to
entice absconding bank clerk.

09228
SALLY BISHOP (82) (A)
British Lion
P: S.W.Smith
D: T.Hayes Hunter
S: (NOVEL) E.Temple Thurston
SC: John Drinkwater, G.E.Wakefield
Joan Barry . . . . Sally Bishop
Harold Huth . . . . John Traill
Isabel Jeans . . . . Dolly Durlacher
Benita Hume . . . . Evelyn Standish
Kay Hammond . . . . Janet Hallard
Emlyn Williams . . . . Arthur Montague
Anthony Bushell . . . . Bart
Annie Esmond . . . . Landlady
Diana Churchill . . . . Typist
ROMANCE Typist becomes mistress to rich
man who rejects her to marry socialite.

09229
HOLIDAY LOVERS (46) (A)
Harry I. Cohen (Fox)
D: Jack Harrison
S: Leslie Arliss
Marjorie Pickard . . . .
George Vollaire . . . .
Pamela Carme . . . .
Boris Ranevsky . . . .
George Benson . . . . Oswald
Wyn Weaver . . . . Lord Winterton
Vincent Holman . . . . Salesman
ROMANCE Couple meet on holiday and each
pretends to be rich.

09230
SLEEPLESS NIGHTS (73) (A)
BIP (Wardour)
D: Thomas Bentley
S: Stanley Lupino
SC: Victor Kendall
Stanley Lupino . . . . Guy Raynor
Polly Walker . . . . Marjorie Drew
Gerald Rawlinson . . . . Gerald Ventnor
Frederick Lloyd . . . . Summers
Percy Parsons . . . . Mr Drew
Charlotte Parry . . . . Mrs Drew
David Miller . . . . Captain
Hal Gordon . . . . Gendarme
MUSICAL Nice. Reporter poses as heiress's
husband and saves her from eloping with thief.

09231
MONEY TALKS (73) (U)
BIP (Wardour)
D: Norman Lee
S: Norman Lee, Frank Miller, Edwin Green-
wood
Julian Rose . . . . Abe Pilstein
Kid Berg . . . . Kid Burke
Gladdy Sewell . . . . Anna
Judy Kelly . . . . Rosie Pilstein
Gus McNaughton . . . . Solly Sax
Griffith Jones . . . . Jimmy Dale
Bernard Ansell . . . . Hymie Burkowitz
Lena Maitland . . . . Mrs Blumberg
Hal Gordon . . . . Pug Wilson
Mary Charles . . . . Nellie Kelly
Jimmy Godden . . . . Joe Bell
Rich & Galvin . . . . .Dough & Wal Nut
COMEDY Jew must lose all his money
before he can inherit.

09232
REUNION (60) (U)
Sound City (MGM)
P: Norman Loudon
D: Ivar Campbell
S: (ARTICLE) Reginald Hargreaves
SC: Herbert Ayres
Stewart Rome . . . . Maj Tancred
Antony Holles . . . . Padre
Fred Schwartz . . . . Pawnbroker
Robert Dudley . . . . Sgt Dudley
Eric Pavitt . . . . Boy
George Bishop . . . . Jews-harpist
Kit Keen . . . . Bones
DRAMA Broke major attends reunion and
gives last pound to help corporal.

09233
SAY IT WITH MUSIC (69) (U)
B&D (W&F) reissue: 1937 (EB)
P: Herbert Wilcox
D: Jack Raymond
S: William Pollock
Jack Payne . . . . Himself
Percy Marmont . . . . Philip Weston
Joyce Kennedy . . . . Mrs Weston
Evelyn Roberts . . . . Dr Longfellow
Sybil Summerfield . . . . . . Betty Weston
BBC Dance Band
MUSICAL Ex-pilot bandleader helps starving
composer regain memory.

09234
WHERE IS THIS LADY ? (77) (U)
Amalgamated Films Associated (BL)
P: John Stafford
D: Laszlo Vajda, Victor Hanbury
S: Billy Wilder (ES WAR EINMAL EIN
WALZER)
SC: Sydney Blow, John Stafford
Marta Eggerth . . . . Steffi Pirringer
Owen Nares . . . . Rudi Miller
George K.Arthur . . . . Gustl Linze
Wendy Barrie . . . . Lucie Kleiner
Ellis Jeffreys . . . . Frau Kleiner
Gibb McLaughlin . . . . Dr Schilling
O.B.Clarence . . . . Dr Peffer
MUSICAL Vienna. Broke heiress helps broke
banker turn bank into nightclub.

09235
THE BARTON MYSTERY (77) (A)
B & D -Paramount British
D: Henry Edwards
S: (PLAY) Walter Hackett
Ursula Jeans . . . . Ethel Standish
Ellis Jeffreys . . . . Lady Marshall
Lyn Harding . . . . Beverley

Ion Swinley . . . . Richard Standish
Wendy Barrie. . . . . Phyllis Grey
Joyce Bland . . . . Helen Barton
Tom Helmore . . . . Harry Maitland
O.B.Clarence . . . . Sir Everard Marshall
Franklyn Bellamy . . . . . . Gerald Barton
Wilfred Noy . . . . Griffiths
CRIME Fake medium proves girl did not
murder blackmailer.

09236
THE WORLD,THE FLESH AND THE DEVIL
(53) (A)
Real Art (Radio)
P: Julius Hagen
D: George A. Cooper
S: (PLAY) Lawrence Cowen
SC: H.Fowler Mear
Harold Huth . . . . Nicholas Brophy
Isla Bevan . . . . Beatrice Elton
S.Victor Stanley . . . . Jim Stanger
Sara Allgood . . . . Emma Stanger
James Raglan . . . . Robert Hall
Fred Groves . . . . Dick Morgan
Frederick Leister . . . . Sir James Hall
Felix Aylmer . . . . Sir Henderson Trent
Barbara Everest . . . . Mrs Brophy
CRIME Baronet's bastard schemes to dispose
of true heir.

09237
ROME EXPRESS (94) (A)
Gaumont reissue: 1940 (IFR)
P: Michael Balcon
D: Walter Forde
S: Clifford Grey
SC: Clifford Grey, Sidney Gilliat,
Frank Vosper, Ralph Stock
Esther Ralston . . . . Asta Marvelle
Conrad Veidt . . . . Zurta
Joan Barry . . . . Mrs Maxted
Harold Huth . . . . Grant
Gordon Harker . . . . Tom Bishop
Cedric Hardwicke . . . . . . Alastair McBane
Donald Calthrop . . . . Poole
Hugh Williams . . . . Tony
Frank Vosper . . . . Insp Jolif
Muriel Aked . . . . Spinster
Eliot Makeham . . . . Mills
Finlay Currie . . . . Publicist
CRIME Blackmailed film star helps crooks
steal painting aboard continental train.

DEC

09238
AFTER THE BALL (70) (A)
Gaumont
P: Michael Balcon
D: Milton Rosmer
S: Max Neufeldt
SC: J.O.C.Orton, H.M.Harwood
Esther Ralston . . . . Elissa Strange
Basil Rathbone . . . . Jack Harrowby
Marie Burke . . . . Lavita
Jean Adrienne . . . . Victorine
George Curzon . . . . Peter Strange
Clifford Heatherley . . . . . . Albuera
COMEDY Geneva. Diplomat's wife poses as
maid to flirt with courier.

09239
THE MIDSHIPMAID (84) (U)
Gaumont (W&F)
P: Michael Balcon
D: Albert de Courville
S: (PLAY) Ian Hay, Stephen King-Hall
SC: Stafford Dickens
Jessie Matthews . . . . Celia Newbiggin

Fred Kerr . . . . Sir Percy Newbiggin
Basil Sydney . . . . Cdr Ffosberry
A.W.Baskcomb . . . . AB Pook
Claud Allister . . . . Chinley
Anthony Bushell . . . . Lt Valentine
Edwin Lawrence . . . . Tappett
Nigel Bruce . . . . Maj Spink
Archie Glen . . . . Bundy
Albert Rebla . . . . Robbins
John Mills . . . . Golightly
Antony Holles . . . . Lt Kingsford
George Zucco . . . . Lord Dore
Joyce Kirby . . . . Dora
Condos Brothers . . . . Horse
COMEDY Malta. Commander loves affianced
daughter of chairman of Naval Economy
Committee.

09240
LET ME EXPLAIN DEAR (82) (A)
BIP (Wardour)
D: SC: Gene Garrard, Frank Miller
S: (PLAY) Walter Ellis
(A LITTLE BIT OF FLUFF)
Gene Gerrard . . . . George Hunter
Viola Lyel . . . . Angela Hunter
Claude Hulbert . . . . Cyril Merryweather
Jane Carr . . . . Mamie
Amy Veness . . . . Aunt Fanny
Henry Longhurst . . . . Dr Coote
Hal Gordon . . . . Parrott
Reginald Bach . . . . Taxi-driver
C. Denier Warren . . . . Jeweller
COMEDY Man feigns accident injury to
swindle newspaper insurance to pay for
girl's necklace.

09241
LORD CAMBER'S LADIES (80) (A)
BIP (Wardour)
P: Alfred Hitchcock
D: Benn W.Levy
S: (PLAY) Horace Annesley Vachell
(THE CASE OF LADY CAMBER)
SC: Benn W. Levy, Edwin Greenwood,
Gilbert Wakefield
Gerald du Maurier . . . . Dr Napier
Gertrude Lawrence . . . . . . Shirley Neville
Benita Hume . . . . Janet King
Nigel Bruce . . . . Lord Camber
Clare Greet . . . . Peach
A.Bromley Davenport . . . Sir Bedford Slufter
Betty Norton . . . . Hetty
Harold Meade . . . . Ainley
Hugh E.Wright . . . . Old Man
Hal Gordon . . . . Stage Manager
Molly Lamont . . . . Actress
DRAMA Lord weds actress, and tries to
poison her to marry nurse.
(Extract in ELSTREE STORY, 1952).

09242
PYJAMAS PREFERRED (46) (A)
BIP- BIF (Pathe)
D:SC: Val Valentine
S: (PLAY) J.O. Twiss (THE RED DOG)
Jay Laurier . . . . Pierre Gautier
Betty Amann . . . . Violet Ray
Jack Morrison . . . . Gustave
Amy Veness . . . . Mme Gautier
Kenneth Kove . . . . Rev Samson Sneed
Fred Schwartz . . . . Orsoni
Hugh E. Wright . . . . Grock
COMEDY France. Purity League president's
husband secretly runs club.

09243
FOR THE LOVE OF MIKE (86) (U)
BIP (Wardour)
D: Monty Banks
S: (PLAY) H.F.Maltby

SC: Clifford Grey, Frank Launder
Bobby Howes . . . . Bobby Seymour
Constance Shotter . . . . Mike
Arthur Riscoe . . . . Conway Paton
Renee Macready . . . . Stella Rees
Jimmy Godden . . . . Henry Miller
Viola Tree . . . . Emma Miller
Wylie Watson . . . . Rev James
Hal Gordon . . . . PC
Syd Crossley . . . . Sullivan
Monty Banks; The Carlyle Cousins
MUSICAL Heiress asks guardian's secretary
to steal back her power of attorney.

09244
BORN LUCKY (78) (U)
Westminster (MGM)
P: Jerome Jackson
D: Michael Powell
S: (NOVEL) Oliver Sandys (MOPS)
SC: Ralph Smart
Talbot O'Farrell . . . . Turnips
Rene Ray . . . . Mops
John Longden . . . . Frank Dale
Ben Welden . . . . Harriman
Helen Ferrers . . . . Lady Chard
Barbara Gott . . . . Cook
Paddy Browne . . . . Patty
Roland Gillett . . . . John Chard
MUSICAL Cockney maidservant becomes
singing star.

09245
LITTLE WAITRESS (49) (U)
Delta (Ace)
P: Geoffrey Clarke
D: Widgey R. Newman
Elvi Keene . . . . Trudi
Claude Bailey . . . . John Farrell
Moore Marriott . . . . Baron Halfsburg
Noel Birkin . . . . Student
MUSICAL Rhineland. Tourist feigns wealth to
woo a waitress who is really a poor Baron's
daughter.

09246
HER FIRST AFFAIRE (72) (A)
StGeorge's Productions (Sterling)
P: Frank Richardson
D: Allan Dwan
S: (PLAY) Frederick Jackson, Merrill Rogers
SC: Dion Titheradge, Brock Williams
Ida Lupino . . . . Anne
George Curzon . . . . Carey Merton
Diana Napier . . . . Mrs Merton
Harry Tate . . . . Major Gore
Muriel Aked . . . . Agatha Brent
Arnold Riches . . . . Brian
Kenneth Kove . . . . Prof Hotspur
Helen Haye . . . . Lady Bragden
Roland Culver . . . . Drunk
Melville Gideon . . . . Himself
COMEDY Infatuated girl tries to have
affair with married author of sensational novels.

09247
THE RIVER HOUSE GHOST (52) (A)
WB-FN (FN)
P: Irving Asher
D: Frank Richardson
S: W. Scott Darling
Florence Desmond . . . . Flo
Hal Walters . . . . Walter
Joan Marion . . . . Sally
Mike Johnson . . . . Johnson
Shayle Gardner . . . . Skeleton
Erle Stanley . . . . Black Mask
Helen Ferrers . . . . Martha Usher
COMEDY Cockney girl unmasks crooks posing
as ghosts.

09248
DON'T BE A DUMMY (54) (U)
WB-FN (FN)
P: Irving Asher
D: Frank Richardson
S: Brock Williams
William Austin . . . . . . Lord Tony Probus
Muriel Angelus . . . . . . Lady Diana Summers
Garry Marsh . . . . Capt Fitzgerald
Georgie Harris . . . . Dodds
Mike Johnson . . . . Tramp
Sally Stewart . . . . Florrie
Katherine Watts . . . . . Connie Sylvester
COMEDY Lord, ruined through gambling,
becomes stage ventriloquist, using jockey as
'dummy.'

09249
IT'S A KING (68) (U) reissue: 1937 (EB)
B & D (W&F)
P: Herbert Wilcox
D: Jack Raymond
S: Claude Hulbert, Paul England
SC: R.P. Weston, Bert Lee, Jack Marks
Sydney Howard . . . Albert King/King Albert
Joan Maude . . . . Princess Yasma
Cecil Humphreys . . . . . . Count Yendoff
George de Warfaz . . . . Col Brandt
Arthur Goullet . . . . Leader
Franklyn Bellamy . . . . Salvatore
Lew Stone and the Monseigneur Orchestra;
Bela Berkes and his Gipsy Orchestra
COMEDY Ruritania. Insurance agent poses
as royal double and saves him from anarchists.

09250
SMILIN' ALONG (38) (U)
Argyle Talking Pictures (EB)
P:D:S: John Argyle
Rene Ray . . . . Theresa
James Benton . . . .
Margaret Delane . . . .
Sara Sarony . . . .
Bessie Richards . . . .
COMEDY Flowergirl poses as maid at
beloved's engagement party.

09251
THE CHANGING YEAR (30) (U)
BIF (Pathe)
D:S: Mary Field
Rene Ray . . . . The Girl
Eric Findon . . . . The Boy
ROMANCE Couple fall in love as seasons
change through year.

09252
MUSICAL MEDLEYS (series) (U)
BSFP (EB)

09253
No. 1 (9)

09254
No. 2 (9)

09255
No. 3 (9)

09256
No. 4 (9)

09257
No. 5 (9)

09258
No. 6 (10)
MUSICAL Compiled from DeForest Phonofilms
and BSFP shorts.

09259
LOVE ME, LOVE MY DOG (19) (U)
WB-FN (WB)
P: Irving Asher
S: Roland Pertwee, John Hastings Turner
Jane Carr . . . . The Singer
MUSICAL Singer stages dog show to get producer to see her act.

09260
WOMEN ARE THAT WAY (22) (U)
WB-FN (WB)
P: Irving Asher
S: Roland Pertwee, John Hastings Turner
John Stuart . . . . Geoffrey
Hal Walters . . . . Simmons
COMEDY psychoanalyst falls in love and so does her husband.

09261
A HONEYMOON IN DEVON (11) (U)
National Progress
Dodo Watts . . . . Bride
Jack Hobbs . . . . Groom
ROMANCE Honeymoon couple spend holiday in Devon.

1933

JAN

09262
PUPPETS OF FATE (72) (A)
USA: WOLVES OF THE UNDERWORLD
Real Art (UA)
P: Julius Hagen
D: George A. Cooper
S: Arthur Rigby, R.H.Douglas
SC: H. Fowler Mear
Godfrey Tearle . . . . Richard Sabine
Russell Thorndike . . . . Dr Munro
Isla Bevan . . . . Joan
Fred Groves . . . . Arthur Brandon
John Turnbull . . . . Inspector
Michael Hogan . . . .
Ben Welden . . . .
Kynaston Reeves . . . .
S. Victor Stanley . . . .
Roland Culver . . . .
CRIME Escaped convict blackmails murderous
doctor into helping him.

09263
HUNDRED TO ONE (45) (U)
Twickenham (Fox)
P: Julius Hagen, Harry Cohen
D: Walter West
S: Basil Mason
Arthur Sinclair . . . . Patrick Flynn
Dodo Watts . . . . Molly Flynn
Derek Williams . . . . Bob Dent
David Nichol . . . . Birchington
Edmund Hampton . . . . Luggett
SPORT Irish publican buys useless horse
whose foal wins Derby.

09264
THE IRON STAIR (51) (A)
Real Art (Radio)
P: Julius Hagen
D: Leslie Hiscott
S: (NOVEL) 'Rita'
SC: H. Fowler Mear
Henry Kendall . . . . Geoffrey/George Gale
Dorothy Boyd . . . . Eva Marshall
Michael Hogan . . . . Pat Derringham
Michael Sherbrooke . . . . . . Benjamin Marks
Steffi Duna . . . . Elsa Damond
A.Bromley Davenport . . . . . Sir Andrew Gale
S.Victor Stanley . . . . Ben
Charles Groves . . . . Sam
Charles Paton . . . . Sloan
John Turnbull . . . . Major Gordon
CRIME Rich man's son framed for forgery
by twin brother.

09265
DISCORD (80) (A)
B & D - Paramount British
D: Henry Edwards
S: (PLAY) E.Temple Thurston
(A ROOF AND FOUR WALLS)
Owen Nares . . . . Peter Stenning
Benita Hume . . . . Phil Stenning
Harold Huth . . . . Lord Quilhampton
Clifford Heatherley . . . . . . Mr Moody
Aubrey Fitzgerald . . . . Mr Bollom
O.B.Clarence . . . . Mr Hemming
Archibald Batty . . . .
Harold Scott . . . . Harold
Esme Hubbard . . . .
ROMANCE Poor composer saves rich wife
from philandering lord.

09266
YES MR BROWN (94) (A)
B&D (W&F) reissue: 1937 (EB)
P: Herbert Wilcox
D: Herbert Wilcox, Jack Buchanan

S: (PLAY) Paul Frank, Ludwig Hershfield
(GESCHAFT MIT AMERIKA)
SC: Douglas Furber
Jack Buchanan . . . . Nicholas Baumann
Elsie Randolph . . . . Anne Webber
Margot Grahame . . . . Clary Baumann
Hartley Power . . . . Mr Brown
Vera Pearce . . . . Franzi
Clifford Heatherley . . . . . . Carlos
MUSICAL Vienna. Manager's secretary poses
as absent wife to impress American boss.

09267
THE MAN FROM TORONTO (77) (U)
Gainsborough (Ideal) reissue: 1945 (EB)
P: Michael Balcon
D: Sinclair Hill
S: (PLAY) Douglas Murray
SC: W.P.Lipscomb
Jessie Matthews . . . . Leila Farrar
Ian Hunter . . . . Fergus Wimbush
Fred Kerr . . . . Bunston
Ben Field . . . . Jonathan
Margaret Yarde . . . . Mrs Hubbard
Kathleen Harrison . . . . Martha
George Turner . . . . Povey
Herbert Lomas . . . . Jake
Lawrence Hanray . . . . Duncan
Kenneth Kove . . . . Vicar
Sybil Grove . . . . Vicar's Wife
Percy Parsons . . . . Hogbin
George Zucco . . . . Squire
COMEDY Widow poses as maid to test man
she must marry to inherit fortune.

09268
STRANGE EVIDENCE (71) (A)
London (Par)
P: Alexander Korda
D: Robert Milton
S: Lajos Biro
SC: Miles Malleson
Leslie Banks . . . . Francis Relf
Carol Goodner . . . . . Marie/Barbara Relf
George Curzon . . . . Stephen Relf
Frank Vosper . . . . Andrew Relf
Norah Baring . . . . Clare Relf
Haidee Wright . . . . Mrs Relf
Lyonel Watts . . . . Henry Relf
Lewis Shaw . . . . Larry
Diana Napier . . . . Jean
CRIME Faithless wife suspected of poisoning
invalid husband.

09269
PERFECT UNDERSTANDING (80) (A)
Gloria Swanson British (UA)
D: Cyril Gardner
S: Miles Malleson
SC: Michael Powell
Gloria Swanson . . . . Judy Rogers
Laurence Olivier . . . . . Nicholas Randall
John Halliday . . . . Ronnson
Genevieve Tobin . . . . Kitty
Nigel Playfair . . . . Lord Portleigh
Michael Farmer . . . . George
Nora Swinburne . . Lady Stephanie Fitzmaurice
O.B.Clarence . . . . Dr Graham
Mary Jerrold . . . . Mrs Graham
Charles Cullum . . . . Sir John
DRAMA Couple's agreement to confess
affairs almost causes divorce.

09270
THE KING'S CUP (76) (U)
B & D (W&F)
P: Herbert Wilcox
D: Herbert Wilcox, Robert J.Cullen,
Alan Cobham, Donald Macardle

S: Sir Alan Cobham
Dorothy Bouchier . . . . Betty Conway
Harry Milton . . . . Dick Carter
William Kendall . . . . Capt Richards
Rene Ray . . . . Peggy
Tom Helmore . . . . Ronnie Helmore
Lewis Shaw . . . . Peter
Sydney King . . . . Crasher
Leila Page . . . . Lena
Syd Crossley . . . . Crossley
Lew Stone and his Band
ADVENTURE Girl helps unnerved pilot
win air race.

09271
JUST MY LUCK (77) (U)
B&D (W&F) reissue: 1937 (EB)
P: Herbert Wilcox
D: Jack Raymond
S: (PLAY) H.F. Maltby (FIFTY-FIFTY)
FIFTY)
SC: Ben Travers
Ralph Lynn . . . . David Blake
Winifred Shotter . . . . Peggy Croft
Davy Burnaby . . . . Sir Charles Croft
Robertson Hare . . . . Trigg
Vera Pearce . . . . Lady Croft
Frederick Burtwell . . . . . . Stromboli
Phyllis Clare . . . . Babs
COMEDY Shy music teacher takes over
hotel and foils crooked accountant.

FEB

09272
THE LITTLE DAMOZEL (73) (A)
B & D (W&F) reissue: 1937 (EB)
P:D: Herbert Wilcox
S: (PLAY) Monckton Hoffe
SC: Donovan Pedelty
Anna Neagle . . . . Julie Alardy
James Rennie . . . . Recky Poole
Benita Hume . . . . Sybil Craven
Athole Stewart . . . . Capt Partington
Alfred Drayton . . . . Walter Angel
Clifford Heatherley . . . . . . Papa Bertholdy
Peter Northcote . . . . Abraham
Franklyn Bellamy . . . . Franz
Aubrey Fitzgerald . . . . Fritz
MUSICAL Capt bribes gambler to marry
singer and later they fall in love.

09273
ONE PRECIOUS YEAR (76) (A)
B & D-Paramount British (Par)
D: Henry Edwards
S: (PLAY) E.Temple Thurston (DRIVEN)
Anne Grey . . . . Dierdre Carton
Basil Rathbone . . . . Derek Nagel
Owen Nares . . . . Stephen Carton
Flora Robson . . . . Julia Skene
Ben Webster . . . . . . Sir Richard Pakenham
Evelyn Roberts . . . . Mr Telford
H.G.Stoker . . . . Sir John Rome
Robert Horton . . . . Dr Hibbert
Violet Hopson . . . . . . Woman at Party
Western Brothers; Jennie Robins; Casa Nuova
Girls.
ROMANCE Cad tries to have affair with
neglected wife who has one year to live.

09274
TAXI TO PARADISE (44) (A)
George Smith (Fox)
P: Harry Cohen
D:SC: Adrian Brunel
S: (PLAY) Graham Hope (MISCONDUCT)
Binnie Barnes . . . . Joan Melhuish
Garry Marsh . . . . George Melhuish
Harry Wilcoxon . . . . Stephen Randall

Jane Carr . . . . Claire
Sebastian Shaw . . . . Tom Fanshawe
Picot Schooling . . . . Manson
Vincent Holman . . . . Dunning
COMEDY Wife learns her husband has
mistress and takes lover.

09275
MR QUINCEY OF MONTE CARLO (53) (U)
WB-FN (FN)
P: Irving Asher
D: John Daumery
S: Brock Williams
John Stuart . . . . Mr Quincey
Rosemary Ames . . . . Norma McLeod
Ben Welden . . . . Grover Jones
George Merritt . . . . Inspector
Victor Fairley . . . . Manager
COMEDY Bank clerk uses legacy to finance
film company.

09276
NAUGHTY CINDERELLA (56) (U)
WB-FN (WB)
P: Irving Asher
D: John Daumery
S: W.Scott Darling
SC: Randall Faye
John Stuart . . . . Michael Wynard
Winna Winfried . . . . Brita Rasmusson
Betty Huntley Wright . . . . Elinore
Marion Gerth . . . . Elsa
Marie Wright . . . . Mrs Barrow
Victor Fairley . . . . Herr Amsel
Catherine Watts . . . . Clara Field
COMEDY Danish girl fools guardian by
posing as tomboy and friend.

09277
LITTLE MISS NOBODY (52) (U)
WB-FN (WB)
P: Irving Asher
D: John Daumery
Winna Winifried . . . . Karen Bergen
Sebastian Shaw . . . . Pat Carey
Betty Huntley Wright . . . . . Tilly
Alice O'Day . . . . Mrs Merridew
A.Bromley Davenport . . . . . Mr Romary
Drusilla Wills . . . . Birdie May
Ben Field . . . . Sam Brightwell
Ernest Sefton . . . . Mr Morrison
Abraham Sofaer . . . . Mr Beal
COMEDY Man's publicity stunt helps girl win
film contract.

09278
THE STOLEN NECKLACE (48) (A)
WB-FN (WB)
P: Irving Asher
D: Leslie Hiscott
S: W. Scott Darling
Lester Matthews . . . . Clive Wingate
Joan Marion . . . . Diana Hunter
Mickey Brantford . . . . Tom Hunter
Wallace Lupino . . . . Sailor
Denis Wyndham . . . . Sailor
Charles Farrell . . . . Sailor
Victor Fairley . . . . Col Hunter
A.Bromley Davenport . . . . Priest
CRIME Rival gangs seek stolen jewels.

09279
OUT OF THE PAST (51) (A)
WB-FN (WB)
P: Irving Asher
D: Leslie Hiscott
Lester Matthews . . Capt Leslie Farebrother
Joan Marion . . . . Frances Dane
Jack Raine . . . . Eric Cotton
Henry Mollison . . . . Gerald Brassard

Eric Stanley . . . . Sir John Brassard
Margaret Damer . . . . Lady Brassard
Aubrey Dexter . . . . David Mannering
Wilfred Shine . . . . Richard Travers
CRIME Manageress blackmailed for posing as
co-respondent.

09280
CALLED BACK (5)) (A)
Real Art (Radio)
P: Julius Hagen
D: Reginald Denham, Jack Harris
S: (NOVEL) Hugh Conway
Franklin Dyall . . . . Dr Jose Manuel
Lester Matthews . . . . Gilbert Vaughan
Dorothy Boyd . . . . Pauline March
Alexander Sarner . . . . Santos Macari
Anthony Ireland . . . . Anthony March
Francis L. Sullivan . . . . Kaledin
Ian Fleming . . . . Dr Carter
Margaret Emden . . . . Priscilla
Geoffrey Goodhart . . . . . . Ivan
CRIME Spain. Revolutionary doctor foiled by
blind man and amnesiac girl.

09281
THE MEDICINE MAN (52) (A)
Real Art (Radio)
P: Julius Hagen
D: Redd Davis
S: Michael Barringer, Robert Edmunds
Claud Allister . . . . . Hon Freddie Wiltshire
Frank Pettingell . . . . Amos Wells
Pat Paterson . . . . Gwendoline Wells
Ben Welden . . . . Garbel
Jeanne Stuart . . . . Flossie
Viola Compton . . . . Mrs Wells
Drusilla Wills . . . . Boadicea Briggs
Ronald Simpson . . . . . . Dr Wesley Primus
S.Victor Stanley . . . . Bitoff
Betty Astell . . . . Patient
COMEDY Dude catches crooks whilst
posing as doctor.

09282
SIGN PLEASE (19) (U)
Gaumont (Ideal)
P: Clayton Hutton
D: John Rawlins
Naughton & Gold . . . . The Salesmen
COMEDY Adventures of two salesmen.

09283
THEY'RE OFF ! (18) (U)
Gaumont (Ideal)
P: Clayton Hutton
D: John Rawlins
Flanagan & Allen . . . . The Bookies
COMEDY Adventures of two bookmakers.

09284
THE DREAMERS (19) (U)
Gaumont (Ideal)
P: Clayton Hutton
D: Frank Cadman
Flanagan & Allen . . . . The Sailors
COMEDY Adventures of two sailors.

09285
POST HASTE (20) (U)
Gaumont (Ideal)
P: Clayton Hutton
D: Frank Cadman
Jack Williams . . . .
Joey Porter . . . .
COMEDY Advenures of two detectives in
post office.

09286
TOOTH WILL OUT (17) (U)

Gaumont (Ideal)
P: Clayton Hutton
D: Frank Cadman
Jack Williams . . . .
Joey Porter . . . .
COMEDY Dentist's assistant makes good.

09287
TOMMY HANDLEY IN MAKING A CHRIST-
MAS PUDDING (11) (U)
Winads (MGM)
Tommy Handley . . . . Himself
COMEDY Comedian's mishaps whilst making
a Christmas pudding.

09288
YES, MADAM (46) (U)
British Lion (Fox)
P: Herbert Smith
D: Leslie Hiscott
S: (NOVEL) K.R.G.Browne
SC: Michael Barringer
Frank Pettingell . . . . Albert Peabody
Kay Hammond . . . . Pansy Beresford
Harold French . . . . Bill Quinton
Muriel Aked . . . . Mrs Peabody
Peter Haddon . . . . Hugh Tolliver
Wyn Weaver . . . . Mr Mountain
Hal Walters . . . . Catlett
COMEDY Heir to £80,000 must act as
chauffeur for two months.

09289
ON THIN ICE (62) (A)
Hall Mark (EB)
D: Bernard Vorhaus
Ursula Jeans . . . . Lady Violet
Kenneth Law . . . . Harry Newman
Dorothy Bartlam . . . .
Viola Gault . . . . Mabel
Stewart Thompson . . . . Corry
Cameron Carr . . . . Mr Newman
CRIME Crook has girl compromise affianced
man to blackmail rich father.

09290
LETTING IN THE SUNSHINE (73) (U)
BIP (Wardour)
D: Lupino Lane
S: Anthony Asquith
SC: Con West, Herbert Sargent, Frank Miller
Albert Burdon . . . . Nobby Green
Renee Gadd . . . . Jane
Molly Lamont . . . . Lady Anne
Henry Mollison . . . . Duvine
Tonie Edgar Bruce . . . Lady Warminster
Herbert Langley . . . . Foreman
Eric le Fre . . . . Bill
Ethel Warwick . . . . Housekeeper
Syd Crossley . . . . Jenkyns
COMEDY Window cleaner and maid foil gem
thieves at Lady's ball.
09291
SHE WAS ONLY A VILLAGE MAIDEN (60) (A)
Sound City (MGM)
P: Ivar Campbell
D: Arthur Maude
S: (PLAY) Fanny Bowker
(PRISCILLA THE RAKE)
SC: John Cousins, N.W.Baring-Pemberton
Anne Grey . . . . Priscilla Protheroe
Lester Matthews . . . . Frampton
Carl Harbord . . . . Peter
Barbara Everest . . . . Agatha
Julian Royce . . . . Duke of Buckfast
Antony Holles . . . . Vicar
Gertrude Sterroll . . . . Lady Lodden
Daphne Scorer . . . . Emily
Ella Daincourt . . . . Mrs Cruickshank
COMEDY Girl must ignore strict sister's
advice if she is to inherit fortune.

09292
TO BRIGHTON WITH GLADYS (45) (U)
George King (Fox)
D: George King
P: Harry Cohen
S: John Quin, H.M. Raleigh
SC: Eliot Stannard
Harry Milton . . . . Bertie Penge
Constance Shotter . . . . Florrie
Kate Cutler . . . . Aunt Dorothy
Sunday Wilshin . . . . Daphne Fitzogle
Melville Cooper . . . . Slingsby
COMEDY Man must take rich uncle's pet
penguin from London to seaside.

MAR

09293
I'M AN EXPLOSIVE (50) (U)
George Smith (Fox)
P: Harry Cohen
D:SC: Adrian Brunel
S: (NOVEL) Gordon Phillips
Billy Hartnell . . . . . Edward Whimperley
Gladys Jennings . . . . Anne Pannell
Eliot Makeham . . . . . . Prof Whimperley
D.A.Clarke-Smith . . . . Lord Ferndale
Sybil Grove . . . . Miss Harriman
Harry Terry . . . . Mould
George Dillon . . . . Shilling
Blanche Adele . . . . French Girl
COMEDY Professor's son drinks liquid
explosive in mistake for whisky.

09294
FORGING AHEAD (49) (A)
Harry Cohen (Fox)
D: Norman Walker
S: (NOVEL) K.R.G.Browne (EASY MONEY)
SC: Brandon Fleming
Margot Grahame . . . . Crystal Grey
Garry Marsh . . Hon Horace Slimminger
Antony Holles . . . . Percival Custard
Clifford Heatherley . . . . . . Prof Bowe
Eliot Makeham . . . . Abraham Lombard
Melville Cooper . . . . Smedley
Edgar Norfolk . . . . Lt-Col Fair
Edith Saville . . . . Lady Leverton
Arthur Chesney . . . . Shutley
George Turner . . . . Hamilton Fortescue
Wallace Lupino . . . . Furniture Man
Gus Sharland . . . . Insp Green
COMEDY "Haunted" house is forgers'
den where girl runs crime school.

09295
DAUGHTERS OF TODAY (74) (U)
FWK Productions (UA)
P:D: F.W.Kraemer
S: Michael Barringer
George Barraud . . . . Forbes
Betty Amann · . . . . Joan
Marguerite Allan . . . . Mavis
Gerald Rawlinson . . . . . . Lionel Pendayre
Hay Petrie . . . . Sharpe
Herbert Lomas . . . . Lincoln
Marie Ault . . . . Mrs Tring
DRAMA Farm sisters come to London for
love and adventure.

09296
THE SHADOW (74) (A)
Real Art (UA)
P: Julius Hagen
D: George A. Cooper
S: (PLAY) Donald Stuart
SC: H. Fowler Mear, Terence Egan
Henry Kendall . . . . The Shadow
Elizabeth Allan . . . . Sonia Bryant

Sam Livesey . . . . Sir Richard Bryant
Jeanne Stuart . . . . Moya Silverton
Cyril Raymond . . . . Silverton
Viola Compton . . . . Mrs Bascomb
John Turnbull . . . . Inspector
CRIME Novelist helps police unmask
murderous blackmailer.

09297
EXCESS BAGGAGE (59) (U)
Real Art (Radio)
P: Julius Hagen
D: Redd Davis
S: (NOVEL) H.M.Raleigh
SC: H. Fowler Mear
Claud Allister . . . . Col Murgatroyd RSVP
Frank Pettingell . . . . Maj Booster SOS
Sydney Fairbrother . . . . . Miss Toop
Rene Ray . . . . Angela Murgatroyd
Gerald Rawlinson . . . . . . Clive Worthington
Viola Compton . . . . Martha Murgatroyd
O.B.Clarence . . . . Lord Grebe
Maud Gill . . . . Duchess of Dillwater
Finlay Currie . . . . Insp Toucan
COMEDY Col thinks he has killed superior
while hunting ghost.

09298
THE MELODY MAKER (56) (U)
WB-FN (FN)
P: Irving Asher
D: Leslie Hiscott
Lester Matthews . . . . . . Tony Borrodaile
Joan Marion . . . . Mary
Evelyn Roberts . . . Reggie Bumblethorpe
Wallace Lupino . . . . Clamart
A.Bromley Davenport . . . . . Jenks
Vera Gerald . . . . Grandma
Joan White . . . . Jerry
Charles Hawtrey . . . . Tom
Tonie Edgar Bruce . . . . Donna Lola
COMEDY Composer rewrites fiancee's
sonata as musical comedy.

09299
DOUBLE WEDDING (49) (U)
WB-FN (WB)
P: Irving Asher
D: Frank Richardson
Joan Marion . . . . Daisy
Jack Hobbs . . . . Dick
Viola Keats . . . . Mildred
Anthony Hankey . . . . Roger
Mike Johnson . . . . George
Ernest Sefton . . . . PC
COMEDY Honeymoon troubles of two couples
who married to silence gossip.

09300
GOING STRAIGHT (48) (U)
WB-FN (WB)
P: Irving Asher
D: John Rawlings
Moira Lynd . . . . Peggy
Helen Ferrers . . . . Lady Peckham
Tracy Holmes . . . .
Joan Marion . . . .
Hal Walters . . . .
Huntley Wright . . . .
Eric Stanley . . . .
George Merritt . . . .
Gilbert Davis . . . .
COMEDY Lady's ex-criminal servants try
to save novelist son from loving secretary.

09301
TOO MANY WIVES (58) (U)
WB-FN (WB)
P: Irving Asher

D: George King
S: W. Scott Darling
Nora Swinburne . . . . Hilary Wildeley
Jack Hobbs . . . . John Wildeley
Viola Keats . . . . Sally
Claud Fleming . . . . . Baron von Schlossen
Alf Goddard . . . . Jeff
COMEDY Man persuades maid to pose as
absent wife to entertain foreign client.

09302
AS GOOD AS NEW (48) (A)
WB-FN (WB)
P: Irving Asher
D: Graham Cutts
S: (PLAY) Thompson Buchanan
SC: Randall Faye
Winna Winifried . . . . Elsa
John Batten . . . . Tom
Sunday Wilshin . . . . Rosa
Tonie Edgar Bruce . . . . . . Nurse Adams
ROMANCE Jilted girl turns gold-digger until
ex-fiance is blinded.

09303
THE THIRTEENTH CANDLE (68) (A)
WB-FN (WB)
P: Irving Asher
D: John Daumery
S: Brock Williams
Isobel Elsom . . . . . . Lady Sylvia Meeton
Arthur Maude . . . . . Sir Charles Meeton
Gibb McLaughlin . . . . Capt Blyth
Joyce Kirby . . . . Marie
Louis Hayward . . . . Paul Marriott
Louis Goodrich . . . . Tarrant
D.A.Clarke-Smith . . . . Blades
Winifred Oughton . . . . Pettit
Claude Fleming . . . . Sgt Harris
Charles Childerstone . . . . . Insp Hart
CRIME Which of his many enemies killed
village squire ?

09304
COUNSEL'S OPINION (76) (A)
London (Par)
P: Alexander Korda
D: Allan Dwan
S: (PLAY) Gilbert Wakefield
SC: Dorothy Greenhill, Arthur Wimperis
Henry Kendall . . . . Logan
Binnie Barnes . . . . Leslie
Cyril Maude . . . . Willock
Lawrence Grossmith . . . . . . .Lord Rockburn
Harry Tate . . . . Taxi-driver
Francis Lister . . . . James Govan
Mary Charles . . . . Stella Marston
Margaret Baird . . . . Saunders
J.Fisher White . . . . Judge
C.Denier Warren . . . . Manager
COMEDY Widow wins barrister by posing as
Lord's faithless wife.

09305
THEIR NIGHT OUT (74) (U)
BIP (Wardour)
D:SC: Harry Hughes
S: (PLAY) George Arthurs, Arthur Miller
Claude Hulbert . . . . Jimmy Oliphant
Renee Houston . . . . Maggie Oliphant
Gus McNaughton . . . . Fred Simpson
Binnie Barnes . . . . Lola
Jimmy Godden . . . . Archibald Bunting
Amy Veness . . . . Gertrude Bunting
Judy Kelly . . . . Betty Oliphant
Ben Welden . . . . Crook
Hal Gordon . . . . Sgt Bert Simpson
Marie Ault . . . . Cook
COMEDY Husband mistaken for gem
thief as result of night out with Scots girl.

09306
THE WISHBONE (78) (U)
Sound City (MGM)
P: Ivar Campbell
D: Arthur Maude
S: (STORY) W.Townend (ONE CROWDED
HOUR)
SC: N.W. Baring-Pemberton
Nellie Wallace . . . . Mrs Beasley
Davy Burnaby . . . . Peters
A.Bromley Davenport . . . . Harry Stammer
Jane Wood . . . . Mrs Stammer
Renee Macready . . . . Grace Elliott
Geoffrey King . . . . Fred Elliott
Fred Schwartz . . . . Jeweller
Hugh Lethbridge . . . . Lord Westland
COMEDY Charlady inherits £50, goes on
spree and helps busker.

09307
SIDE STREETS (46) (A)
Sound City (MGM)
P: Norman Loudon
D: Ivar Campbell
S: Philip Godfrey
Jane Wood . . . . Mrs Brown
Diana Beaumont . . . . Nancy Brown
Arnold Riches . . . . Ted Swan
Paul Neville . . . . Mr Brown
Harry Terry . . . .
Dora Levis . . . .
Gunner Moir . . . .
DRAMA Ex-boxer saves fiancee's mother
from blackmailing husband.

09308
THE GOLDEN CAGE (62) (A)
Sound City (MGM)
P: Norman Loudon
D: Ivar Campbell
S: (PLAY) Lady Trowbridge
SC: D.B.Wyndham-Lewis, Pamela Frankau
Anne Grey . . . . Venetia Doxford
Anthony Kimmins . . . . . . Paul Mortimer
Frank Cellier . . . .
Jillian Sande . . . . Jane Morris
Mackenzie Ward . . . . Claude Barrington
Cecil Parker . . . .
Andrea Malandrinos . . . . . .
ROMANCE Girl marries rich man but still
loves poor hotel clerk.

09309
A MOORLAND TRAGEDY (38) (U)
GEM Productions (EB)
P: Hayford Hobbs
D: M.A.Wetherell
S: (STORY) Baroness Orczy
SC: Allen Francis
Haddon Mason . . . . Gerry Moville
Barbara Coombes . . . . Winnie Gooden
Moore Marriott . . . . The Old Man
Griffith Humphreys . . . . . . Gooden
Ian Colin . . . . Tom Lee
CRIME Rich man accidentally kills poacher who
is rival for publican's daughter.

09310
THE GOOD COMPANIONS (113) (U)
Gaumont-Welsh-Pearson
P: T.A.Welsh, George Pearson
D: Victor Saville
S: (PLAY) J.B.Priestley
SC: W.P. Lipscomb, Angus Macphail,
Ian Dalrymple
N: Henry Ainley
Jessie Matthews . . . . Susie Dean
Edmund Gwenn . . . . Jess Oakroyd
John Gielgud . . . . Inigo Jolifant
Mary Glynne . . . . Miss Trant

Percy Parsons . . . . Morton Mitcham
A.W.Baskcomb . . . . Jimmy Nunn
Dennis Hoey . . . . Joe Brundit
Viola Compton . . . . Mrs Brundit
Richard Dolman . . . . . . Jerry Jerningham
Margery Binner . . . . Elsie
D.A. Clarke-Smith . . . . Ridvers
Florence Gregson . . . . Mrs Oakroyd
Frank Pettingell . . . . Sam Oglethorpe
Alex Fraser . . . . Dr MacFarlane
Finlay Currie . . . . Monte Mortimer
Max Miller . . . . Milbrau
Ivor Barnard . . . . Eric Tipstead
Olive Sloane . . . . Effie
Muriel Aked . . . . Vicar's Wife
J. Fisher White . . . . Vicar
Jack Hawkins . . . . Albert
Cyril Smith . . . . Leonard Oakroyd
Lawrence Hanray . . . . Mr Tarvin
Annie Esmond . . . . Mrs Tarvin
Ben Field . . . . Mr Droke
George Zucco . . . . Fauntley
Arnold Riches . . . . Hilary
Wally Patch . . . . Driver
Barbara Gott . . . . Big Annie
Margaret Yarde . . . . Mrs Mounder
Hugh E. Wright . . . . Librarian
Pollie Emery . . . . Miss Thong
COMEDY Orphaned spinster, married joiner
and rebellious schoolmaster join concert party
and make it a success.

09311
THE CRIME AT BLOSSOMS (77) (A)
B & D-Paramount British
D: Maclean Rogers
S: (PLAY) Mordaunt Shairp
Hugh Wakefield . . . . Chris Merryman
Joyce Bland . . . . Valerie Merryman
Eileen Munro . . . . Mrs Woodman
Ivor Barnard . . . . A Late Visitor
Frederick Lloyd . . . . George Merryman
Iris Baker . . . . Lena Denny
Arthur Stratton . . . . Mr Woodman
Maud Gill . . . . Mrs Merryman
Wally Patch . . . . Palmer
Barbara Gott . . . . Fat Lady
Moore Marriott . . . . Driver
George Ridgwell . . . . . . Process-server
CRIME Wife becomes obsessed by death of
previous tenant of country cottage.

09312
UP FOR THE DERBY (70) (U)
B&D (W&F) reissue: 1937 (EB)
P: Herbert Wilcox
D: Maclean Rogers
S: R.P.Weston, Bert Lee, Jack Marks
Sydney Howard . . . . Joe Burton
Dorothy Bartlam . . . . Dorothy Gordon
Mark Daly . . . . Jerry Higgs
Tom Helmore . . . . Ronnie Gordon
Frederick Lloyd . . . . Maj Edwards
Frank Harvey . . . . George Moberley
Franklyn Bellamy . . . . Palmer
COMEDY Stableboy buys ruined employer's
horse and wins Derby.

09313
THE BLARNEY STONE (81) (U)
USA: THE BLARNEY KISS
B & D (W&F) reissue: 1937 (EB)
P: Herbert Wilcox
D: Tom Walls
S: A.R.Rawlinson
SC: A.R. Rawlinson, Lennox Robinson
Tom Walls . . . . Tim Fitzgerald
Anne Grey . . . . Lady Anne Cranton
Robert Douglas . . . . Lord Breethorpe

Haidee Wright . . . . Countess Eleanor
Dorothy Tetley . . . . Muriel Atkins
Louis Bradfield . . . . Mackintosh
W.G.Fay . . . . The Leader
Zoe Palmer . . . . Diana
J.A.O'Rourke . . . . Mick
Charles Carson . . . . Sir Arthur
COMEDY Broke Irishman becomes business
partner of gambling lord.

09314
SOLDIERS OF THE KING (80) (U)
USA: THE WOMAN IN COMMAND
Gainsborough (W&F) reissue: 1939 (GN)
P: Michael Balcon
D: Maurice Elvey
S: Douglas Furber
SC: W.P.Lipscomb, J.O.C.Orton, Jack Hulbert
Cicely Courtneidge . . . Jenny/Maisie Marvello
Edward Everett Horton . . Sebastian Marvello
Anthony Bushell . . . Lt Ronald Jamieson
Dorothy Hyson . . . . . . Judy Marvello
Frank Cellier . . . . Col Markham
Leslie Sarony . . . . Wally
Bransby Williams . . . . . . Dan Marvello
Rebla . . . . Albert Marvello
Herschel Henlere . . . . . . Mozart Marvello
Ivor McLaren . . . . Harry Marvello
Olive Sloane . . . . Sarah Marvello
Arty Ash . . . . Doug
O.B.Clarence . . . . Tom
MUSICAL Period. Guards colonel forbids
lieut to wed music hall star.

09315
KING OF THE RITZ (81) (U)
Gainsborough-British Lion (Gau)
D: Carmine Gallone
S: (PLAY) Henri Kistemaeckers
(LE ROI DES PALACES)
SC: Clifford Grey, Ivor Montagu
Stanley Lupino . . . . Claude
Betty Stockfeld . . . . Mrs Cooper
Hugh Wakefield . . . . . . King of Blitz
Henry Kendall . . . . Teddy Smith
Gina Malo . . . . Victoria
Gibb McLaughlin . . . . . . Baron Popov
Harry Milton . . . . Alonso
Johnny Singer . . . . Pageboy
MUSICAL Paris. Head porter saves widow's
jewels and is made duke.

09316
HIKING WITH MADEMOISELLE (40) (U)
International Productions
D: Edward Nakhimoff
Nina Bucknall . . . . Louise
Dennis Clive . . . . John
E.Bonichon . . . . Reporter
John Milton . . . . Crook
COMEDY French girl foils robbery whilst
touring London.

09317
DOUBLE BLUFF (35) (U)
British Pictorial (U)
P: William & Clifford Jeapes
D: R.E.Jeffrey
Charles Childerstone . . . . . . Mr Shaw
Carol Coombe . . . . Mrs Shaw
George Merritt . . . . Bruce
Juliet Mansell . . . . Wife
CRIME Cardsharper fakes own death and
poses as valet.

09318
MONEY FOR SPEED (72) (A)
Hall Mark (UA)
D:S: Bernard Vorhaus
SC: Vera Allinson, Lionel Hale, Monica Ewer

John Loder . . . . Mitch
Ida Lupino . . . . Jane
Cyril McLaglen . . . . Bill
Moore Marriott . . . . Shorty
Marie Ault . . . . Ma
John Hoskins; Ginger Lees; Cyclone Davis;
Lionel Van Praag.
SPORT Crook has girl friend make rival lose
speedway race.

09319
MATINEE IDOL (75) (A)
Wyndham (UA)
P: Bray Wyndham
D: George King
S: Charles Bennett
Camilla Horn . . . . Sonia Vance
Miles Mander . . . . Harley Travers
Marguerite Allan . . . . Christine Vance
Viola Keats . . . . Gladys Wheeler
Anthony Hankey . . . . . . Sir Brian Greville
Hay Petrie . . . . Mr Clappit
Margaret Yarde . . . . Mrs Clappit
Albert Whelan . . . . Barlow
CRIME Actress proves sister did not
murder actor lover.

09320
TILL THE BELLS RING (46) (U)
BSFP (Bayley)
D: Graham Moffatt
S: (PLAY) Graham Moffatt
SC: Graham Moffatt
Graham Moffatt . . . . John Snodgrass
Margaret Moffatt . . . . . . Jenny Struthers
Winifred Moffatt . . . . . . Aggie Turnbull
COMEDY Scots widower woos poor spinster
believing her to be wealthy.

09321
MUSICAL MOMENTS (series) (U)
BSFP (Bayley)
Nos. 1 - 5
MUSICAL Compiled from DeForest
Phonofilms and BSFP shorts made 1929,

09322
NO FUNNY BUSINESS (76) (A)
Stafford (UA) reissue: 1951 (Sun)
P: John Stafford
D: John Stafford, Victor Hanbury
S: Dorothy Hope
SC: Victor Hanbury, Frank Vosper
Gertrude Lawrence . . . . . . Yvonne
Laurence Olivier. . . . . Clive
Jill Esmond . . . . Anne
Edmond Breon . . . . Edward
Gibb McLaughlin . . . . Florey
Muriel Aked . . . . Mrs Fothergill
COMEDY Riviera. Professional co-respondents
mistake one another for clients.

09323
THAT'S MY WIFE (67) (A)
British Lion
P: Herbert Smith
D: Leslie Hiscott
S: William C.Stone
SC: Michael Barringer
Claud Allister . . . . Archie Trevor
Frank Pettingell . . . . Josiah Crump
Betty Astell . . . . Lilian Harbottle
Davy Burnaby . . . . Maj Harbottle
Helga Moray . . . . Queenie Sleeman
Hal Walters . . . . Bertie Griggs
Thomas Weguelin . . . . Mr Sleeman
Jack Vyvyan . . . . Sam Griggs
COMEDY Beauty expert poses as solicitor
to save rich uncle from scandal.

APR
09324
THE LOST CHORD (95) (A)
Twickenham (AP&D) reissue: 1937
P: Julius Hagen
D: Maurice Elvey
S: Reuben Gillmer
SC: H. Fowler Mear
John Stuart . . . . David Graham
Elizabeth Allan . . . . Joan Elton
Mary Glynne . . . . Countess Madeleine
Anne Grey . . . . Pauline
Leslie Perrins . . . . Count Zara
Jack Hawkins . . . . Dr Jim Selby
Garry Marsh . . . . Joseph Mendel
Betty Astell . . . . Madge
Frederick Ranalow . . . . Beppo
Barbara Everest . . . . Mother Superior
Tudor Davis; Billy Mayerl
ROMANCE Musician kills count in duel for
wife, and later falls in love with daughter.

09325
F.P.1 (93) (U) bilingual
UFA (GB) reissue: 1938, SECRETS OF F.P.1
(NR)
P: Erich Pommer
D: Karl Hartl
S: (NOVEL) Kurt Siodmak (FPI ANTWORTET
NICHT)
SC: Kurt Siodmak, Walter Reisch, Robert
Stevenson, Peter Macfarlane
Conrad Veidt . . . . Elissen
Leslie Fenton . . . . Droste
Jill Esmond . . . . Claire Lennartz
George Merritt . . . . Lubin
Donald Calthrop . . . . Photographer
Nicholas Hannen. . . . . Matthias
William Freshman . . . . Conrad
Warwick Ward . . . . Officer
Alexander Field . . . . Sailor
Francis L.Sullivan . . . . Sailor
FANTASY Financiers conspire to destroy
first floating aerodrome. (Made in Germany).

09326
NIGHT OF THE GARTER (86) (U)
B&D (UA) reissue: 1937 (EB)
P: Herbert Wilcox
D: Jack Raymond
S: (PLAY) Avery Hopwood, Wilson Collison
(GETTING GERTIE'S GARTER)
SC: Austin Melford, Marjorie Gaffney
Sydney Howard . . . . Bodger
Winifred Shotter . . . . Gwen Darling
Elsie Randolph . . . . Jenny Warwick
Connie Ediss . . . . Fish
Austin Melford . . . . Bunny Phipps
Harold French . . . . Teddy Darling
Jack Melford . . . . Kenneth Warwick
Marjorie Brooks . . . . Barbara Phipps
Arthur Chesney . . . . Vicar
COMEDY Newlywed tries to get back gift
garter from honeymoon bride.

09327
LONG LIVE THE KING (44) (U)
WB-FN (FN)
P: Irving Asher
D: William McGann
S: W.Scott Darling
Florence Desmond . . . . . . Florrie
Hal Walters . . . . Simmonds
Skipper Glyn James . . . . . . Crown Prince
Mike Johnson . . . . Prime Minister
Abraham Sofaer . . . . Alexis
Betty Bolton . . . . Red Anna
Charles Castella . . . . King

COMEDY Ruritania. Cockney charlady on
prize holiday saves baby prince from
revolutionaries.

09328
OH FOR A PLUMBER ! (19) (U)
Delta (EB)
D: Widgey R. Newman
S: Harry Angers
Harry Angers . . . . The Plumber
Phyllis Pearson . . . .
John Milton . . . .
Picot Schooling . . . .
Ian Wilson . . . .
COMEDY. Slapstick mishaps of a plumber.

09329
IN OUR TIME (23) (U)
David Mackane
D:S: Aveling Ginever
Ion Swinley . . . . The Voice
George Turner . . . . First Man
Harry Clifford . . . . Second Man
RELIGION Voice stops quarrel between men
of different classes by presenting faith as
cure.

09330
LEAVE IT TO ME (76) (U)
BIP (Wardour)
D: Monty Banks
S: (PLAY) P.G.Wodehouse, Ian Hay
(LEAVE IT TO PSMITH)
SC: Gene Gerrard, Frank Miller, Cecil Lewis
Gene Gerrard . . . . Sebastian Help
Olive Borden . . . . Peavey
Molly Lamont . . . . Eve Halliday
George Gee . . . . Coots
Gus McNaughton . . . . Baxter
Clive Currie . . . . Lord Emsworth
Tonie Edgar Bruce . . . . Lady Constance
Peter Godfrey . . . . Siegfried Velour
Syd Crossley . . . . Beach
Melville Cooper . . . . Hon Freddie
Wylie Watson . . . . Client
COMEDY Professional helper poses as poet
to steal lady's necklace and saves it from
thieves.

09331
RADIO PARADE (7)) (U)
BIP (Wardour)
D: Archie de Bear, Richard Beville
S: Claude Hulbert, Paul England
Clapham & Dwyer   Elsie & Doris Waters
Florence Desmond   Mabel Constanduros
Claude Hulbert   Jeanne de Casalis
Houston Sisters   Christopher Stone
Flotsam & Jetsam   Elsie Carlisle
Leonard Henry   Stainless Stephen
Keith Wilbur   Stanelli & Edgar
Harry Pepper   Doris Arnold
Tex McLeod   Reginald Gardiner
Carlyle Cousins   Mario Lorenzo
Roy Fox and his Band   Gus McNaughton
REVUE Aspiring actors eavesdrop on
professionals and perform in Chicago.

09332
TIMBUCTOO (72) (U)
BIP (Wardour)
D: Walter Summers, Arthur Woods
S: (BOOK) (AFRICA DANCES)
SC: Walter Summers
Henry Kendall . . . . . Benedict Tichbourne
Margot Grahame . . . . Elizabeth
Victor Stanley . . . . Henry
Rama Tahe . . . . Native Girl
Emily Fitzroy . . . . Aunt Agatha
Jean Cadell . . . . Wilhelmina

Una O'Connor	Myrtle
Hubert Harben	Uncle George
Edward Ashley Cooper	Steven

COMEDY Girl's wastrel cousin and his valet go to Timbuctoo.

MAY

09333
CASH (73) (U) USA: FOR LOVE OR MONEY
London (Par)
P: Alexander Korda
D: Zoltan Korda
S: Anthony Gibbs
SC: Arthur Wimperis, Dorothy Greenhill

Edmund Gwenn	Edmund Gilbert
Wendy Barrie	Lilian Gilbert
Robert Donat	Paul Martin
Morris Harvey	Meyer
Lawrence Grossmith	Joseph
Clifford Heatherley	Hunt
Hugh E.Wright	Jordan
Antony Holles	Inspector

COMEDY Bankrupt financier uses counterfeit dollars to promote company.

09334
CLEANING UP (70) (U)
British Lion *reissue:* 1937 (EB)
P: Herbert Smith
D: Leslie Hiscott
S: Michael Barringer

George Gee	Tony Pumpford
Betty Astell	Marian Brent
Davy Burnaby	Lord Pumpford
Barbara Gott	Lady Rudd
Alfred Wellesley	Sir Rickaby Rudd
Muriel George	Mrs Hoggenheim
Joan Matheson	Angela
Dorothy Vernon	Agatha

Rona Ricardo; Max Rivers Girls
COMEDY Lord's son becomes cleaner salesman and poses as dancer's husband to fool bart's wife.

09335
LORD OF THE MANOR (71) (U)
B & D - Paramount British
D: Henry Edwards
S: (PLAY) John Hastings Turner
SC: Dorothy Rowan

Betty Stockfeld	Barbara Fleeter
Fred Kerr	Sir Henry Bovey
Harry Wilcoxon	Jim Bridge
Kate Cutler	Lady Bovey
Frank Bertram	George Tover
Joan Marion	Kitty Carvell
April Dawn	Lily Tover
Deering Wells	Robert Bovey
David Horne	Gen Sir George Fleeter

COMEDY Lord forced to give shelter to three homeless people, one of whom loves his daughter.

09336
SUMMER LIGHTNING (78) (U)
B&D (UA) *reissue:* 1937 (EB)
P: Herbert Wilcox
D: Maclean Rogers
S: (NOVEL) P.G.Wodehouse

Ralph Lynn	Hugo Carmody
Winifred Shotter	Millicent Keable
Dorothy Bouchier	Sue Brown
Horace Hodges	Lord Emsworth
Helen Ferrers	Lady Emsworth
Esme Percy	Baxter
Miles Malleson	Beach
Gordon James	Pillbream
Joe Monkhouse	Pigman

COMEDY Man steals prize pig in order to return it to Lord and claim his daughter.

09337
LOYALTIES (74) (A)
ATP (ABFD)
P:D: Basil Dean
S: (PLAY) John Galsworthy
SC: W.P.Lipscomb

Basil Rathbone	Ferdinand de Levis
Heather Thatcher	Margaret Orme
Miles Mander	Capt Ronald Dancy
Joan Wyndham	Mabel Dancy
Philip Strange	Maj Colford
Alan Napier	Gen Canynge
Athole Stewart	Lord StErth
Cecily Byrne	Lady Adela Windsor
Ben Field	Gilman

CRIME Ambitious Jew charges a captain with theft after being rejected by a society club.

09338
THREE MEN IN A BOAT (60) (U)
ATP (ABFD)
P: Basil Dean
D: Graham Cutts
S: (NOVEL) Jerome K. Jerome
SC: D.B. Wyndham-Lewis, Reginald Purdell

William Austin	Harris
Edmond Breon	George
Billy Milton	Jimmy
Davy Burnaby	Sir Henry Harland
Iris March	Peggy
Griffith Humphreys	Sgt
Stephen Ewart	Doctor
Victor Stanley	Cockney
Frank Bertram	Fisherman
Sam Wilkinson	PC
Winifred Evans	Lady Harland

COMEDY Misadventures of three friends on boating holiday.

09339
SEND 'EM BACK HALF DEAD (44) (U)
Cecil Landeau (Fox)
D: Redd Davis

Nelson Keys	Hank Ruck
Polly Luce	Marie Ruck
Ben Welden	Mustapha
Kenneth Kove	Roland Peabody
Andrea Malandrinos	Tony

Jack Harris and his Band
COMEDY Hollywood film director finds film units have civilised Africa.

09340
BEWARE OF WOMEN (5)) (U)
WB-FN (FN)
P: Irving Asher
D: George King

Jack Hobbs	Andrew
Pat Paterson	Margery
Anthony Hankey	Tony
Clifford Heatherley	Lord Edeley
Helen Ferrers	Lady Edeley

COMEDY Lord's son steals jewels by mistake.

09341
THE MAN OUTSIDE (51) (A)
Real Art (Radio)
P: Julius Hagen
D: George A.Cooper
S: Donald Stuart
SC: H. Fowler Mear

Henry Kendall	Harry Wainwright
Gillian Lind	Ann
Joan Gardner	Peggy Fordyce
Michael Hogan	Shiner Talbot
Cyril Raymond	Capt Fordyce
John Turnbull	Insp Jukes
Louis Hayward	Frank Elford
Ethel Warwick	Georgina Yapp

CRIME Tec unmasks murderer seeking stolen jewels.

09342
KARMA (68) (U) *bilingual*
Indian and British Film Productions (Ideal)
(Ideal)
P:S: Himansu Rai
D: J.L.Freer-Hunt

Devika Rani	Maharani
Himansu Rai	Prince
Abraham Sofaer	Holy Man

ROMANCE India. Progressive maharani loves neighbouring prince despite father's objections.

09343
THE ONLY GIRL (84) (U) *bilingual*
USA: HEART SONG
UFA (GB)
P: Erich Pommer
D: Friedrich Hollaender
S: Walter Reisch, Robert Liebmann, Felix Salten
SC: Robert Stevenson, John Heygate

Lilian Harvey	Juliette
Charles Boyer	Duke
Mady Christians	Empress
Ernest Thesiger	Chamberlain
Maurice Evans	Didier
Friedel Schuster	Annabel
Julius Falkenstein	Offenbach
Huntley Wright	Doctor
Ruth Maitland	Marianne
O.B.Clarence	Etienne

MUSICAL Germany, 1890. Duke falls in love with voice which is not that of empress, but of hairdresser. (Made in Germany).

09344
DON QUIXOTE (80) (U) *trilingual*
Nelson-Vandor (UA)
D: G.W.Pabst
S: (NOVEL) Miguel de Cervantes
(DON QUIXOTE DE LA MANCHA)
SC: Paul Morand, Alexandre Arnoux, John Farrow

Feodor Chaliapin	Don Quixote
George Robey	Sancho Panza
Sidney Fox	The Niece
Miles Mander	The Duke
Oscar Asche	Police Captain
Dannio	Carrasco
Emily Fitzroy	Sancho's Wife
Frank Stanmore	Priest
Wally Patch	Gipsy King
Lydia Sherwood	Duchess
Renee Valliers	Dulcinea

COMEDY Spain, 16th C. Mad squire's attempts to restore chivalry to world. (Made in France).

JUN

09345
HAWLEYS OF HIGH STREET (68) (U)
BIP (Wardour)
D: Thomas Bentley
S: (PLAY) Walter Ellis
SC: Charles Bennett, Syd Courtenay, Frank Launder

Leslie Fuller	Bill Hawley
Judy Kelly	Millie Hawley
Francis Lister	Lord Roxton
Amy Veness	Mrs Hawley
Moore Marriott	Mr Busworth
Hal Gordon	Nicholls
Wylie Watson	Rev Potter
Faith Bennett	Edith Busworth
Elizabeth Vaughan	Lady Evelyn
Jimmy Godden	Mayor
Mabel Twemlow	Mrs Busworth

COMEDY Henpecked draper and butcher are rivals in council election.

09346
FACING THE MUSIC (69) (U)
BIP (Wardour)
D: Harry Hughes
S: Clifford Grey, Sidney Gilliat
SC: Clifford Grey, Frank Launder, Stanley
Lupino
Stanley Lupino . . . . Jack Foley
Jose Collins . . . . Mme Calvini
Nancy Brown . . . . Mme Rivers
Nancy Burne . . . . Nina Carson
Doris Woodall . . . . Mme d'Ava
Lester Matthews . . . . Becker
Dennis Hoey . . . . Capradossi
Morris Harvey . . . . de Breen
Hal Gordon . . . . Sim
MUSICAL Publicist's fake theft of
prima donna's jewels backfires.

09347
ANNE ONE HUNDRED (66) (U)
B&D Paramount British
D: Henry Edwards
S: (PLAY) Sewell Collins (ANNE 100%)
(NOVEL) Edgar Franklin (RESCUING ANNE)
Betty Stockfeld . . . . Anne Briston
Gyles Isham . . . . Nixon
Dennis Wyndham . . . . March
Evelyn Roberts . . . . Burton Fraim
Allan Jeayes . . . . Penvale
Eric Hales . . . . Masters
Quinton McPherson . . . . . . Mole
DRAMA Girl inherits soap factory and
thwarts unscrupulous rival.

09348
CALL ME MAME (59) (A)
WB-FN (WB)
P: Irving Asher
D: John Daumery
S: Randall Faye
Ethel Irving . . . . Mame
John Batten . . . . Gordon Roantree
Dorothy Bartlam . . . . Tess Lennox
Winifred Oughton . . . . Victoria
Julian Royce . . . . Poulton
Arthur Maude . . . . Father
Alice O'Day . . . . Mother
Pat Fitzpatrick . . . . Child
Carroll Gibbons and his Savoy Orpheans
COMEDY Man is about to inherit peerage when
hard-drinking mother arrives from Mexico.

09349
HIGH FINANCE (67) (A)
WB-FN (FN)
P: Irving Asher
D: George King
Gibb McLaughlin . . . . Sir Grant Rayburn
Ida Lupino . . . . Jill
John Batten . . . . Tom
John H.Roberts . . . . Ladcock
D.A.Clarke-Smith . . . . Dodman
Abraham Sofaer . . . . Myers
DRAMA Selfish magnate humanised by
sentence.

09350
SLEEPING CAR (82) (A)
Gaumont (Ideal) reissue: 1942 (EB; 1002 ft cut)
P: Michael Balcon
D: Anatole Litvak
S: Franz Schulz
Madeleine Carroll . . . . Anne
Ivor Novello . . . . Gaston
Laddie Cliff . . . . Pierre
Kay Hammond . . . . Simone
Claud Allister . . . . Baron Delande
Stanley Holloway . . . . Francois
Vera Bryer . . . . Jenny

Ivor Barnard . . . . Durande
COMEDY France. Widow forced to marry
sleeping car attendant to avoid police.

09351
WALTZ TIME (82) (A)
Gaumont (W&F)
P: Herman Fellner
D: William Thiele
S: (OPERA) Johann Strauss (DIE FLEDER-
MAUS)
SC: A.P.Herbert
Evelyn Laye . . . . Rosalinde
Fritz Schultz . . . . Eisenstein
Gina Malo . . . . Adele
Jay Laurier . . . . Frosch
Parry Jones . . . . Alfred
George Baker . . . . Orlovsky
Frank Titterton . . . . Fiacre Driver
Ivor Barnard . . . . Falke
D.A.Clarke-Smith . . . . Meyer
Edmund Breon . . . . Judge Bauer
MUSICAL Vienna. Flirtatious author foiled
by wife at masked ball.

09352
THE LUCKY NUMBER (72) (U)
Gainsborough (Ideal)
P: Michael Balcon
D: Anthony Asquith
S: Franz Schulz
Clifford Mollison . . . . Percy Gibbs
Gordon Harker . . . . Hackney Man
Joan Wyndham . . . . Winnie
Joe Hayman . . . . MacDonald
Frank Pettingell . . . . Brown
Esme Percy . . . . Chairman
Alfred Wellesley . . . . Pickpocket
D.Hay Petrie . . . . Photographer
Arsenal Football Club
COMEDY Footballer tries to recoup
winning lottery ticket from publican.

09353
I LIVED WITH YOU (100) (A)
Twickenham (W&F)
P: Julius Hagen
D: Maurice Elvey
S: (PLAY) Ivor Novello
SC: H.Fowler Mear
Ivor Novello. . . . Prince Felix Lenieff
Ursula Jeans . . . . Gladys Wallis
Ida Lupino . . . . Ada Wallis
Minnie Rayner . . . . Mrs Wallis
Eliot Makeham . . . . Mr Wallis
Jack Hawkins . . . . Mort
Cicely Oates . . . . Flossie Williams
Davina Craig . . . . Maggie
Douglas Beaumont . . . . Albert Wallis
ROMANCE Exiled Russian prince lodges with
cockney shopgirl's family.

09354
MY LUCKY STAR (63) (U)
Masquerader (W&F)
P: Louis Blattner
D: Louis Blattner, John Harlow
Florence Desmond . . . . Mlle de Capo
Oscar Asche . . . . President
Naughton & Gold . . . . Housepainters
Harry Tate . . . . Director
Harold Huth . . . . Hero
Carol Coombe . . . . Lucette
Reginald Purdell . . . . Artist
Herman Darewski . . . . Conductor
George Baker . . . . Foreman
Henry Longhurst . . . . Dudley Collins
COMEDY Shopgirl posing as film star loves
porter posing as artist.

09355
DORA (40) (U)
H & S Film Service
D:S: StJohn L.Clowes
Sydney Fairbrother
Moore Marriott
Dodo Watts
Kenneth Kove
COMEDY American tourist frustrated by the
Defence of the Realm Act.

09356
MAID HAPPY (75) (A)
Bendar (WP)
P:D: Mansfield Markham
S: Garrett Graham
SC: Jack King
Charlotte Ander . . . . Lena
Johannes Riemann . . . . Fritz
Dennis Hoey . . . . Sir Rudolph Bartlett
Marjory Mars . . . . Mary Loo
Sybil Grove . . . . Miss Warburton
Gerhard Damann . . . . Schmidt
Polly Luce . . . . Madge
H.Saxon-Snell . . . . Bruckmann
Marie Ault . . . . Miss Woods
MUSICAL Switzerland. Schoolgirl poses as
socialite to win diplomat.

09357
THE LOVE WAGER (64) (U)
Anglo-European (Par)
P: E.A.Fell
D: A.Cyran
S: Moira Dale
Pat Paterson . . . . Peggy
Frank Stanmore . . . . Shorty
Wallace Douglas . . . . Peter Neville
Morton Selten . . . . Gen Neville
Moira Dale . . . . Auntie Prue
H.Saxon-Snell . . . . Huxter
Hugh E.Wright . . . . Noakes
Philip Godfrey . . . . Ed Grimes
COMEDY Advice expert helps novelist find
father's stolen jewels.

09358
THE STICKPIN (44) (A)
British Lion (Fox)
P: Herbert Smith
D: Leslie Hiscott
S: Michael Barringer
Henry Kendall . . . . Paul Rayner
Betty Astell . . . . Eve Marshall
Francis L.Sullivan . . . . Jacob Volke
Lawrence Anderson . . . . . . Tom Marshall
Henry Caine . . . . Dixon
Pope Stamper . . . . Simms
CRIME Man framed for killing blackmailer of
friend's wife.

09359
GREAT STUFF (50) (U)
British Lion (Fox)
P: Herbert Smith
D: Leslie Hiscott
S: Brandon Fleming
SC: Michael Barringer
Henry Kendall . . . . Archie Brown
Betty Astell . . . . Vera Montgomery
Alfred Wellesley . . . . . Vernon Montgomery
Barbara Gott . . . . . Claudette Montgomery
Hal Walters . . . . Spud
Ernest Sefton . . . . Captain
Gladys Hamer . . . . Cook
COMEDY Parents pose as burglars to stop
daughter's wedding.

09360
FOLLOW THE LADY (49) (A)
George Smith (Fox)
P: A.George Smith
D:S: Adrian Brunel
Billy Hartnell . . . . .   Mike Martindale
Marguerite Allen . . . .   Suzette
D.A.Clarke-Smith . . . .   Flash Bob
Marie Hemingway . . . .   Lady Saffron
Vincent Holman . . . .   Parsons
Basil Moss . . . .   Paul Barlow
COMEDY French girl blackmails bachelor
after night out.

09361
DOSS HOUSE (53) (A)
Sound City (MGM) *reissue:* 1939 (660 ft cut)
P: Ivar Campbell
D: John Baxter
S: Herbert Ayres
Frank Cellier . . . .   Editor
Arnold Bell . . . .   Reporter
Herbert Franklyn . . . .   Detective
Mark Daly . . . .   Shoeblack
Edgar Driver . . . .   Catsmeat Man
J.Hubert Leslie . . . .   Murderer
Wilson Coleman . . . .   Strangler
Robert MacLachlan . . . . . .   Doctor
CRIME Reporter and detective pose as tramps
to catch escaped convict.

09362
THE TELEVISION FOLLIES (45) (U)
English Films
P:D: Geoffrey Benstead
George Carney . . . .   Father
Wynne Gibson . . . .
Leslie Day . . . .
Jock McKay . . . .
REVUE Lancashire family watch performers
on new television set.

JUL

09363
IT'S A BOY ! (80) (A)
Gainsborough (W&F) *reissue:* 1942 (EB)
P: Michael Balcon
D: Tim Whelan
S: (PLAY) Franz Arnold, Ernst Bach,
Austin Melford
SC: Austin Melford, Leslie Howard Gordon,
John Paddy Carstairs
Leslie Henson . . . .   James Skippett
Edward Everett Horton . . .   Dudley Leake
Heather Thatcher . . . .   Anita Gunn
Alfred Drayton . . . .   Eustace Bogle
Albert Burdon . . . .   Joe Piper
Robertson Hare . . . .   Allister
Joyce Kirby . . . .   Lillian
Wendy Barrie . . . .   Mary Bogle
Helen Haye . . . .   Mrs Bogle
J.H.Roberts . . . .   Registrar
COMEDY Groom blackmailed by man
claiming to be his bastard son.

09364
FALLING FOR YOU (88) (U)
Gainsborough (W&F) *reissue:* 1942
(EB; 11 mins cut)
P: Michael Balcon
D: Jack Hulbert, Robert Stevenson
S: Jack Hulbert, Sidney Gilliat
Jack Hulbert . . . .   Jack Hazleden
Cicely Courtneidge . . . . .   Minnie Tucker
Tamara Desni . . . . .   Sondra van Heyden
Garry Marsh . . . .   Archduke Karl
Alfred Drayton . . . .   Editor
Ivor McLaren . . . .   Sweep
Tonie Edgar Bruce . . . .   Aunt Alice

O.B.Clarence . . . .   Trubshawe
Morton Selten . . . .   Caldicott
Leo Sheffield . . . .   Butler
COMEDY Switzerland. Rival reporters don
disguises to catch runaway heiress.

09365
BRITANNIA OF BILLINGSGATE (80) (U)
Gaumont (Ideal)
P: Michael Balcon
D: Sinclair Hill
S: (PLAY) Christine Jope-Slade, Sewell Stokes
SC: Ralph Stock
Violet Loraine . . . .   Bessie Bolton
Gordon Harker . . . .   Bolton
Kay Hammond . . . .   Pearl Bolton
John Mills . . . .   Fred
Walter Sondes . . . .   Hogarth
Glennis Lorimer . . . .   Maud
Gibb McLaughlin . . . .   Westerbrook
Drusilla Wills . . . .   Mrs Wigglesworth
Antony Holles . . . .   Garibaldi
Joyce Kirby . . . .   Joan
Grethe Hansen . . . .   Gwen
Wally Patch . . . .   Harry
Ernest Sefton . . . .   Publicity Man
Jane Cornell . . . .   Fay
George Turner . . . .   Pal
Cecil Ramage . . . .   Producer
Roy Fox and his Band; Ron Johnson;
Gus Kuhn; Colin Watson; Tom Farndon
MUSICAL Cockney fishmonger's wife becomes
film star.

09366
PRINCE OF ARCADIA (80) (A)
Nettlefold-Fogwell (W&F)
D: Hans Schwartz
P: Archibald Nettlefold, Reginald Fogwell
S: (PLAY) Walter Reisch
(DER PRINZ VON ARKADIEN)
SC: Reginald Fogwell
Carl Brisson . . . .   Prince Peter
Margot Grahame . . . .   Mirana
Ida Lupino . . . .   Princess
Annie Esmond . . . .   Queen
Peter Gawthorne . . . .   Equerry
C.Denier Warren . . . .   Detective
MUSICAL Ruritania. Prince prefers girl
to Princess with acting ambitions.

09367
ORDERS IS ORDERS (88) (U)
Gaumont (Ideal)
P:: Michael Balcon
D: Walter Forde
S: (PLAY) Ian Hay, Anthony Armstrong
SC: Leslie Arliss, Sidney Gilliat, James Gleason
Charlotte Greenwood . . . . .   Wanda
James Gleason . . . .   Ed Waggermeyer
Cyril Maude . . . .   Col Bellamy
Cedric Hardwicke . . . .   Brigadier
Ian Hunter . . . .   Capt Harper
Ray Milland . . . .   Dashwood
Jane Carr . . . .   Patricia Bellamy
Donald Calthrop . . . .   Pavey
Eliot Makeham . . . .   Pte Slee
Hay Plumb . . . .   Pte Goffin
Wally Patch . . . .   RSM
Finlay Currie . . . .   Dave
COMEDY Hollywood film company take
over army barracks to make Foreign
Legion film.

09368
PURSE STRINGS (69) (A)
B & D-Paramount British
D: Henry Edwards
S: (PLAY) Bernard Parry (THE PURSE

STRINGS)
Dorothy Bouchier . . . . .   Mary Willmore
Gyles Isham . . . .   James Willmore
G.H.Mulcaster . . . .   Edward Ashby
Allan Jeayes . . . .   Walford
Joan Henley . . . .   Ida Bentley
Evelyn Roberts . . . .   Beauchamp
DRAMA Rich man's meanness makes wife
become shoplifter causing reverse of positions.

09369
BITTER SWEET (93) (A)
B & D (UA)
P:D: Herbert Wilcox
S: (OPERETTA) Noel Coward
SC: Lydia Hayward, Herbert Wilcox,
Monckton Hoffe
Anna Neagle . . . .   Sari Millick
Fernand Graavey . . . .   Carl Linden
Ivy St Helier . . . . . .   Manon la Grevette
Miles Mander . . . . Capt Auguste Lutte
Esme Percy . . . .   Hugh Devon
Stuart Robertson . . . .   Lt Tranisch
Hugh Williams . . . .   Vincent Howard
Pat Paterson . . . .   Dolly Chamberlain
Clifford Heatherley . . . . . .   Herr Schlick
Gibb McLaughlin . . . .   Footman
Kay Hammond . . . .   Gussi
Patrick Ludlow . . . .   Henry
Norma Whalley . . . .   Mrs Millick
Alan Napier . . . .   Lord Shayne
MUSICAL Vienna, 1875. Dancer weds
violinist and they work in cafe until he is
killed by gambler.

09370
EARLY TO BED (83) (U) *bilingual*
UFA (W&F)
P: Erich Pommer
D: Ludwig Berger
S: Hans Szekelyi, Robert Liebmann
SC: Robert Stevenson
Sonnie Hale . . . .   Helmut
Edmund Gwenn . . . .   Kruger
Fernand Graavey . . . .   Carl
Heather Angel . . . .   Grete
Donald Calthrop . . . .   Peschke
Lady Tree . . . .   Widow Seidelblast
Athene Seyler . . . .   Frau Weiser
Gillian Sande . . . .   Trude
Leslie Perrins . . . .   Meyer
Lewis Shaw . . . .   Wolf
MUSICAL Manicurist and night waiter fall
in love, not knowing they use same bedroom.
(Made in Germany).

09371
THE VETERAN OF WATERLOO (48) (U)
National Talkies (Par)
P: Harry Rowson
D: A.V.Bramble
S: (PLAY) Arthur Conan Doyle
(A STORY OF WATERLOO)
Jerrold Robertshaw . . Cpl Gregory Brewster
Roger Livesey . . . .   Sgt Macdonald
Joan Kemp-Welch . . . . . .   Norah Brewster
A.B.Imeson . . . .   Colonel
Minnie Rayner . . . .   Neighbour
DRAMA 1890. Old corporal recalls adventures
at battle of Waterloo.

09372
I'LL STICK TO YOU (66) (A)
British Lion
P: Herbert Smith
D: Leslie Hiscott
S: Michael Barringer
Jay Laurier . . . .   Adam Tipper
Betty Astell . . . .   Pauline Mason

Louis Hayward . . . . Ronnie Matthews
Ernest Sefton . . . . Mortimer Moody
Hal Walters . . . . Wilkins
Annie Esmond . . . . Eve Oglethorpe
Mary Gaskell . . . . Millie Wiggins
Charles Childerstone . . . . Pilgrim
COMEDY Girl thwarts rich man who cheated
beloved glue inventor.

09373
HEADS WE GO (86) (A)
USA: THE CHARMING DECEIVER
BIP (Wardour)
D: Monty Banks
S: Fred Thompson
SC: Victor Kendall
Constance Cummings . . . . Betty/Dorothy
Frank Lawton . . . . Toby Tyrrell
Binnie Barnes . . . . Lil Pickering
Claude Hulbert . . . . Reginald Coke
Gus McNaughton . . . . . . Otis Dove
Fred Duprez . . . . Anderson
Ellen Pollock . . . . Madame
Peter Godfrey . . . . Fancourt
Tonie Edgar Bruce . . . . Lady Abercrombie
COMEDY Deauville. Mannequin inherits and
poses as film star double.

09374
THE UMBRELLA (56) (A)
Real Art (Radio)
P: Julius Hagen
D: Redd Davis
S: Lawrence Meynell
SC: H.Fowler Mear
Kay Hammond . . . . Mabel
Harold French . . . . Freddie Wallace
S.Victor Stanley . . . . Victor Garnett
Dick Francis . . . . . . Michael Frankenstein
Barbara Everest . . . . Mrs Wynne
Kathleen Tremaine . . . . . . Mary Wynne
John Turnbull . . . . Governor
Syd Crossley . . . . PC
COMEDY Man takes wrong umbrella
containing pickpocket's spoils.

09375
HIS GRACE GIVES NOTICE (57) (A)
Real Art (Radio)
P: Julius Hagen
D: George A.Cooper
S: (NOVEL) Lady Trowbridge
SC: H. Fowler Mear
Arthur Margetson . . . . George Barwick
Viola Keats . . . . Barbara Rannock
S.Victor Stanley . . . . James Roper
Barrie Livesey . . . . Ted Burlington
Ben Welden . . . . Michael Collier
Edgar Norfolk . . . . Capt Langley
Dick Francis . . . . Mr Perks
Lawrence Hanray . . . . Mr Grayling
Charles Groves . . . . Henry Evans
O.B.Clarence . . . . Lord Rannock
Gertrude Sterroll . . . . Lady Rannock
COMEDY Butler inherits title but keeps it
secret to woo employer's daughter.

09376
THE GHOST CAMERA (68) (A)
Real Art (Radio)
P: Julius Hagen
D: Bernard Vorhaus
S: (STORY) J.Jefferson Farjeon
SC: H. Fowler Mear
Henry Kendall . . . . John Grey
Ida Lupino . . . . Mary Elton
John Mills . . . . Ernest Elton
S.Victor Stanley . . . . Albert Sims
George Merritt . . . . Inspector

Felix Aylmer . . . . Coroner
CRIME Chemist's accidental photograph of
murder saves girl's brother.

09377
THIS WEEK OF GRACE (92) (U)
Real Art (Radio)
P: Julius Hagen
D: Maurice Elvey
S: Maurice Braddell, Nell Emerald
SC: H. Fowler Mear, Jack Marks
Gracie Fields . . . . Grace Milroy
Henry Kendall . . . . Lord Clive Swinford
John Stuart . . . . Henry Baring
Frank Pettingell . . . . Mr Milroy
Minnie Rayner . . . . Mrs Milroy
Douglas Wakefield . . . . . . Joe Milroy
Vivian Foster . . . . Vicar
Marjorie Brooks . . . . . . Pearl Forrester
Helen Haye . . . . Lady Warmington
Nina Boucicault . . . . . Duchess of Swinford
COMEDY Sacked factory girl's family
manages duchess's castle.

09378
LOVE'S OLD SWEET SONG (79) (A)
Argyle Talking Pictures (Butcher)
reissue: 1940 THE MISSING WITNESS
P: John Argyle
D: Manning Haynes
S: Lydia Hayward
John Stuart . . . . Paul Kingslake
Joan Wyndham . . . . Mary Dean
William Freshman . . . . Jimmy Croft
Julie Suedo . . . . Iris Sinclair
Ronald Ward . . . . Eric Kingslake
Moore Marriott . . . . Old Tom
Marie Wright . . . . Sarah
Ivor Maxwell . . . . Podger Kingslake
Barbara Everest . . . . Nurse
Malcolm Tod . . . . Announcer
ROMANCE Farmer loves singer whom his
halfbrother marries and abandons with baby.

09379
LITTLE NAPOLEON (44) (U)
George Smith (Fox)
D:SC: Adrian Brunel
S: Marshall Reade
Nancy Burne . . . . Barbara Shenstone
Terence de Marney . . . . . Michael Alison
Eliot Makeham . . . . Tully
Allan Jeayes . . . . Shenstone
Janice Adair . . . . Joan Melvor
George Thirlwell . . . . Lord Melvor
ROMANCE Poor playwright exposes fiancee's
father as faker of antiques.

AUG

09380
STRICTLY IN CONFIDENCE (42) (A)
WB-FN (FN)
P: Irving Asher
D: Clyde Cook
James Finlayson . . . . Mac
Reginald Purdell . . . . Jim
Betty Amann . . . . Rita
Cecil Humphreys . . . . Count Mantala
Joseph Cunningham . . . . Brandon Williams
Katie Johnson . . . . Grannie
COMEDY Reporters catch confidence
trickster.

09381
HEAD OF THE FAMILY (66) (A)
WB-FN (FN)
P: Irving Asher
D: John Daumery
S: Brock Williams
Irene Vanbrugh . . . . Mrs Powis-Porter

Arthur Maude . . . . Mr Powis-Porter
John Stuart . . . . Bill Stanmore
Pat Paterson . . . . Geraldine Powis-Porter
D.A.Clarke-Smith . . . . Welsh
Alexander Field . . . . Bill Higgins
Roland Culver . . . . Manny
Glen Alyn . . . . Maisie
Annie Esmond . . . . Mrs Slade
DRAMA Bankrupt magnate becomes night
watchman for rival and catches son attempting
robbery.

09382
THE GHOUL (79) (A)
Gaumont (W&F)
P: Michael Balcon
D: T.Hayes Hunter
S: (NOVEL) Frank King
SC: Frank King, Leonard Hines, L.DuGarde
Peach, Roland Pertwee, John Hastings Turner,
Rupert Downing
Boris Karloff . . . . Prof Morlant
Cedric Hardwicke . . . . Broughton
Ernest Thesiger . . . . Laing
Dorothy Hyson . . . . Betty Harlow
Anthony Bushell . . . . Ralph Morlant
Harold Huth . . . . Ali Ben Drage
D.A.Clarke-Smith . . . . Mahmoud
Kathleen Harrison . . . . Kaney
Ralph Richardson . . . . Nigel Hartley
Jack Raine . . . . Chauffeur
HORROR Dead egyptologist returns from
tomb to recover stolen gems.

09383
I WAS A SPY (89) (A)
Gaumont (W&F) reissue: 1939 (GFD)
P: Michael Balcon
D: Victor Saville
S: (BOOK) Marthe Cnockhaert McKenna
SC: W.P.Lipscomb, Ian Hay
Madeleine Carroll . . Marthe Cnockhaert
Conrad Veidt . . . . . Commandant Oberaertz
Herbert Marshall . . . . Stephan
Gerald du Maurier . . . . Doctor
Edmund Gwenn . . . . Burgomaster
Donald Calthrop . . . . Cnockhaert
Anthony Bushell . . . . Otto
Eva Moore . . . . Canteen Ma
Nigel Bruce . . . . Scotty
May Agate . . . . Mme Cnockhaert
George Merritt . . . . Reichmann
Martita Hunt . . . . Aunt Lucille
WAR Belgium, 1914. True story of nurse who
became spy. (FWA: 1934).

09384
THE LOVE NEST (69) (A)
BIP (Wardour)
D: Thomas Bentley
S: H.F.Maltby
SC: H.F.Maltby, Frank Miller, Gene Gerrard
Gene Gerrard . . . . George
Camilla Horn . . . . Fifi
Nancy Burne . . . . Angela
Gus McNaughton . . . . Fox
Garry Marsh . . . . Hugo
Amy Veness . . . . Ma
Charles Paton . . . . Pa
Marion Dawson . . . . Mrs Drinkwater
Judy Kelly . . . . Girl
COMEDY Groom shelters neighbour's
runaway wife on wedding eve.

09385
THE SONG YOU GAVE ME (86) (U)
BIP (Wardour)
D: Paul Stein
S: (PLAY) Walter Reisch (THE SONG IS

ENDED)
SC: Clifford Grey

Bebe Daniels	Mitzi Hansen
Victor Varconi	Karl Linden
Claude Hulbert	Tony Brandt
Lester Matthews	Max Winter
Frederick Lloyd	Baron Bobo
Eva Moore	Grandmother
Iris Ashley	Emmy
Walter Widdop	Singer

MUSICAL Paris. Flirtatious singer tries to force proposal from secretary.

09386
THE PRIDE OF THE FORCE (75) (U)
BIP (Wardour)
D: Norman Lee
S: Syd Courtenay, Lola Harvey
SC: Norman Lee, Syd Courtenay, Arthur Woods

Leslie Fuller	Bill/Bob Porter
Faith Bennett	Peggy Ramsbottom
Alf Goddard	Sgt Brown
Hal Gordon	Dick Smith
Nan Bates	Sheila
Ben Welden	Tony Carlotti
Frank Perfitt	Insp Ramsbottom
Pat Aherne	Max Heinrich
King Curtis	Steve

COMEDY Farmer takes place of policeman twin who joins circus.

09387
MY OLD DUCHESS (65) (U) Retitled:
OH WHAT A DUCHESS !
BIP (Pathe)
D: Lupino Lane
S: (SKETCH) Fred Karno (MUMMING BIRDS)
SC: Con West, Herbert Sargent

George Lacy	Irving
Betty Davies	Sally Martin
Dennis Hoey	Montagu Neilson
Fred Duprez	Jesse Martin
Renee Macready	Valerie
Florence Vie	Mrs Neilson
Hugh E.Wright	Higgins
Pat Aherne	Gaston

COMEDY Stage manager poses as duchess to impress film producer.

09388
A TALE OF TAILS (19) (U)
Saturn -Inspiration (AP & D)
D: Horace Shepherd
N: Tommy Handley

Bert Coote	The Drunk

COMEDY Drunkard's dream of animated models. (Includes extracts from foreign film.)

09389
MEET MY SISTER (70) (A)
Pathe
P: Fred Watts
D: John Daumery

Clifford Mollison	Lord Victor Wilby
Constance Shotter	Joan Lynton
Enid Stamp-Taylor	Lulu Marsac
Fred Duprez	Hiram Sowerby
Frances Dean	Helen Sowerby
Jimmy Godden	Pogson
Helen Ferrers	Hon Christine Wilby
Patrick Barr	Bob Seymour
Syd Crossley	Butler

COMEDY Poor Lord tells future father-in-law that his ex-fiancee is his sister.

09390
THE LURE (65) (A)
Maude Productions (Par)
D: Arthur Maude

S: (PLAY) J.W. Sabben-Clare

Anne Grey	Julia Waring
Cyril Raymond	Paul Dane
Alec Fraser	John Baxter
Billy Hartnell	Billy
Philip Clarke	Peter Waring
P.G.Clark	Merritt
Doris Long	Dorothy

CRIME Widow's fiance fakes suicide to trap murderous diamond thief.

09391
A ROYAL DEMAND (62) (U)
Moorland Productions (Par)
P: Mrs C.P.Williams
D: Gustave Minzenty
S: Jane Moorland (Mrs C.P.Williams)

Cyril McLaglen	Lord Forrest
Marjorie Hume	Lady Forrest
Fred Rains	Walters
Vi Kaley	Nana
Powell Edwards	Gen Orring
Howard Fry	Lord Wentover
Tich Hunter	Robin
Gisela Leif Robinson	Lady Ann

DRAMA 1645. Royalist Lord avoids capture by posing as Roundhead.

09392
HEARTS OF OAK (49) (U)
International Productions
D: M.A.Wetherell, Graham Hewett
S: Reginald Hargreaves
Frank Cellier
Hilda Sims
Alison Drake
WAR 1918. The battle of Zeebrugge.
(Includes extract from ZEEBRUGGE; 1924).

09393
UP TO THE NECK (72) (U)
B&D (UA) reissue: 1937 (EB)
P: Herbert Wilcox
D: Jack Raymond
S: Ben Travers

Ralph Lynn	Norman B.Good
Winifred Shotter	April Dawne
Francis Lister	Eric Warwick
Reginald Purdell	Jimmy Catlin
Mary Brough	Landlady
Marjorie Hume	Vera Dane
Grizelda Hervey	Miss Fish

COMEDY Bank clerk uses legacy to finance drama which succeeds as burlesque.

09394
THE PRIVATE LIFE OF HENRY VIII (96)(A)
London (UA) reissue: 1946 (BL)
P: Alexander Korda, Ludovico Toeplitz
D: Alexander Korda
S: Lajos Biro, Arthur Wimperis
SC: Arthur Wimperis

Charles Laughton	Henry VIII
Robert Donat	Culpepper
Lady Tree	The Nurse
Binnie Barnes	Katheryn Howard
Elsa Lanchester	Anne of Cleves
Merle Oberon	Anne Boleyn
Franklin Dyall	Cromwell
Miles Mander	Wriothesley
John Loder	Thomas Peynell
Wendy Barrie	Jane Seymour
Claud Allister	Cornell
William Austin	Duke of Cleves
Gibb McLaughlin	French Executioner
Sam Livesey	Executioner
Lawrence Hanray	Cranmer
Everley Gregg	Catherine Parr
Judy Kelly	Lady Rochford

John Turnbull	Holbein
Frederick Culley	Duke of Norfolk

HISTORY The reasons why King Henry had six wives. (AA: Best Actor, 1933).

SEP

09395
THE GIRL FROM MAXIM'S (79) (A) bilingual
London (UA)
P: Alexander Korda, Ludovico Toeplitz
D: Alexander Korda
S: (PLAY) Georges Feydeau
(LA DAME CHEZ MAXIM)
SC: Arthur Wimperis, Harry Graham

Leslie Henson	Dr Petypon
Frances Day	la Mome
George Grossmith	The General
Lady Tree	Mme Petypon
Stanley Holloway	Mongincourt
Evan Thomas	Corignon
Gertrude Musgrove	Clementine
Desmond Jeans	Etienne

COMEDY Paris, 1904. Married doctor forced to pass off singer as his wife.

09396
MAYFAIR GIRL (67) (A)
WB-FN (WB)
P: Irving Asher
D: George King
S: Brandon Fleming

Sally Blane	Brenda Mason
John Stuart	Robert Blair
D.A.Clarke-Smith	Capt Merrow
Glen Alyn	Santa
Roland Culver	Dick Porter
James Carew	
Charles Hickman	
Winifred Oughton	
Philip Strange	
Lawrence Anderson	

CRIME American girl framed for killing cad while drunk

09397
LUCKY BLAZE (48) (U)
Ace
D:S: Widgey R. Newman

William Freshman	Cliff Ellis
Vera Sherbourne	Rose Benson
Moore Marriott	Sir James Benson
Freddie Fox	Freddie
J.Collins	Collingdean

SPORT Squire's daughter helps jockey win race.

09398
THIS IS THE LIFE (78) (U)
British Lion reissue: 1939 (EB)
P: Herbert Smith
D: Albert de Courville
S: Clifford Grey
SC: Clifford Grey, R.P.Weston, Bert Lee

Gordon Harker	Albert Tuttle
Binnie Hale	Sarah Tuttle
Betty Astell	Edna Wynne
Ray Milland	Bob Travers
Jack Barty	Bert Scroggins
Charles Heslop	Mr Diggs
Percy Parsons	Lefty Finn
Ben Welden	Two Gun Mullins
Norma Whalley	Miss Vavasour
Julian Royce	Bronson

Percival Mackey and his Band
COMEDY Teashop proprietors inherit fortune, crash society, and thwart Chicago gangsters.

09399
HOME SWEET HOME (72) (A)
Real Art (Radio)
P: Julius Hagen
D:S: George A. Cooper
SC: Terence Egan, H. Fowler Mear
John Stuart . . . . Richard Pelham
Marie Ney . . . . Constance Pelham
Richard Cooper . . . . Tupman
Sydney Fairbrother . . . . . . Mrs Bagshaw
Cyril Raymond . . . . John Falkirk
Eve Becke . . . . Betty Martin
Eliot Makeham . . . . James Merrick
Felix Aylmer . . . . Robert Wilding KC
Ben Welden . . . . Santos
ROMANCE Man returns from abroad and
accidentally kills wife's lover.

09400
HOUSE OF DREAMS
Danubia
P: N.R.Adams
D: Anthony Frenguelli
S: (NOVEL) Margaret Pedlar
(HOUSE OF DREAMS COME TRUE)
SC: A. Trendall
Lester Matthews
Jean Adrienne
Margot Grahame
Alma Taylor
Sebastian Shaw
Eva Moore
Charles Cullum
ROMANCE Budapest.(Made in Vienna:not shown.)

09401
MUSICAL FILM REVUES (series) (U)
British Lion (MGM)
P: S.W.Smith
D: Herbert Smith
Stanelli & Edgar   Albert Sandler
Phyllis Stanley   Arthur Travers
Nile Players   Modernique Quartette
Foster Richardson   Ten Tromboneers
Terence McGovan's Novelty Orchestra

09402
No. 1: (11)

09403
No. 2: (11)

09404
No. 3: (10)

09405
No. 4: (10)

09406
No. 5: (10)

09407
No. 6: (10)

09408
No. 7: (11)

09409
No. 8: (10)

09410
No. 9: (8)

09411
No. 10: (9)
REVUE

09412
I SPY (69) (U)
BIP (Wardour)
P: Walter C. Mycroft
D: Allan Dwan
S: Fred Thompson
SC: Allan Dwan, Arthur Woods
Sally Eilers . . . . Thelma Coldwater
Ben Lyon . . . . Wally Sawyer
Harry Tate . . . . George
H.F.Maltby . . . . Herr Doktor
Harold Warrender . . . . . . NBG
Andrews Engelmann. . . . . . CO
Dennis Hoey . . . . MNT
Henry Victor . . . . KPO
Marcelle Rogez . . . . Girl
COMEDY Ruritanian spies mistake playboy
for one of their number.

09413
TIGER BAY (70) (A)
Wyndham (ABFD)
P: Bray Wyndham
D: J.Elder Wills
S: J.Elder Wills, Eric Ansell
SC: John Quin
Anna May Wong . . . . Lui Chang
Henry Victor . . . . Olaf
Rene Ray . . . . Letty
Lawrence Grossmith . . . Whistling Rufus
Victor Garland . . . . Michael
Ben Soutten . . . . Stumpy
Margaret Yarde . . . . Fay
Wally Patch . . . . Wally
Ernest Jay . . . . Alf
Brian Buchel . . . . Tony
DRAMA Tropics. Briton saves Chinese cafe
proprietress and English ward from Swedish
crook.

09414
GOING GAY (79) (U)
USA: KISS ME GOODBYE
Windsor (Sterling)
P: Frank A. Richardson
D: Carmine Gallone
S: Selwyn Jepson
SC: Selwyn Jepson, Jack Marks, K.R.G.Browne
Arthur Riscoe . . . . Jack
Naunton Wayne . . . . Jim
Magda Schneider . . . . Grete
Grete Natzler . . . . Conductor's Daughter
Joe Hayman . . . . Impresario
Wilfred Noy . . . . Conductor
Ruth Maitland , ... Mother
Bertha Belmore . . . . . . Masculine Lady
MUSICAL Vienna. Rivals try to make beloved
a star of opera and ballet.

09415
PARIS PLANE (52) (U)
Sound City (MGM)
P: Ivar Campbell
D: John Paddy Carstairs
S: Charles Bennett
John Loder
Molly Lamont
Allan Jeayes
Barrie Livesey
Julie Suedo
Edwin Ellis
James Harcourt
Eileen Munro
CRIME Detective catches murderer aboard
London-leBourget plane.

09416
MIXED DOUBLES (69) (A)
B&D-Paramount British
D: Sidney Morgan
S: (PLAY) Frank Stayton
SC: Joan Wentworth Wood (Morgan)
Jeanne de Casalis . . . . Betty Irvine
Frederick Lloyd . . . . Sir John Doyle
Molly Johnson . . . . Lady Audrey
Cyril Raymond . . . . Reggie Irvine
Athol Fleming . . . . Ian MacConochie
Rani Waller . . . . Rose MacConochie
Quinton McPherson . . . . Rev Arthur Escott
Gordon McLeod . . . . Consul
George Bellamy . . . . Barrett
COMEDY Divorcees remarry, then find
decrees were not final.

09417
THAT'S A GOOD GIRL (83) (U)
B & D (UA) reissue: 1945 (EB)
P: Herbert Wilcox
D: Jack Buchanan
S: (PLAY) Douglas Furber
SC: Douglas Furber, Jack Buchanan,
Donovan Pedelty
Jack Buchanan . . . . Jack Barrow
Elsie Randolph . . . . Joy Dean
Dorothy Hyson . . . . Moya Malone
Garry Marsh . . . . Francis Moray
Vera Pearce . . . . Sunya Berata
William Kendall . . . . Timothy
Kate Cutler . . . . Helen Malone
Frank Stanmore . . . . Malone
Antony Holles . . . . Canzone
MUSICAL France. Poor heir schemes to
arrange marriage between cousin and affianced
friend.

09418
THE FIRE RAISERS (77) (A)
Gaumont (W&F)
P: Jerome Jackson
D: Michael Powell
S: Jerome Jackson, Michael Powell
Leslie Banks . . . . Jim Bronson
Anne Grey . . . . Arden Brent
Carol Goodner . . . . Helen Vaughan
Frank Cellier . . . . Brent
Francis L.Sullivan . . . . Stedman
Laurence Anderson . . . . . . Twist
Joyce Kirby . . . . Polly
Henry Caine . . . . Bates
George Merritt . . . . Sonners
CRIME Insurance assessor joins arson gang
but reforms.

09419
JUST SMITH (76) (A)
Gaumont (W&F)
P: Michael Balcon
D: Tom Walls
S: (PLAY) Frederick Lonsdale
(NEVER COME BACK)
SC: J.O.C.Orton
Tom Walls . . . . Smith
Carol Goodner . . . . Mary Linkley
Ann Grey . . . . Lady Moynton
Allan Aynesworth . . . . Lord Trench
Eva Moore . . . . Lady Trench
Hartley Power . . . . John Mortimer
Leslie Perrins . . . . Duke of Bristol
Reginald Gardiner . . . . Lord Redwood
Veronica Rose . . . . Lady Susan
Basil Radford . . . . Sir John Moynton
Peter Gawthorne . . . . Rolls
COMEDY Gentleman thief accused when
host's daughter steals necklace .

OCT

09420
THE FLAW (67) (A)
Patrick K.Heale (Par)
D: Norman Walker
S: Brandon Fleming
Henry Kendall . . . . John Millway

Eric Maturin . . . . James Kelver
Phyllis Clare . . . . Laura Kelver
Eve Gray . . . . Irene Nelson
Douglas Payne . . . . Insp Barnes
Sydney Seaward . . . . Sgt
Vera Gerald . . . . Mrs Mamby
CRIME Poisoner's victim turns tables.

09421
GENERAL JOHN REGAN (74) (U)
B & D-Paramount British
D: Henry Edwards
S: (PLAY) George A.Birmingham
SC: Lenox Robinson
Henry Edwards . . . . Dr O'Grady
Chrissie White . . . . Moya Kent
Ben Welden . . . . Billing
Pegeen Mair . . . . Mary Ellen
David Horne . . . . Major Kent
W.G.Fay . . . . Golligher
Fred O'Donovan . . . . Doyle
Denis O'Neil . . . . Kerrigan
Eugene Leahy . . . . Sgt Colgan
George Callaghan . . . . PC Moriarty
Mary O'Farrell . . . . Mrs Gregg
COMEDY Ireland. Villagers invent
mythical hero to fool rich American.

09422
YOU MADE ME LOVE YOU (70) (U)
BIP (Wardour)
D: Monty Banks
S: Stanley Lupino
SC: Frank Launder
Stanley Lupino . . . . Tom Daly
Thelma Todd . . . . Pamela Berne
John Loder . . . . Harry Berne
Gerald Rawlinson . . . . Jerry
James Carew . . . . Oliver Berne
Charles Mortimer . . . . Mr Daly
Hugh E.Wright . . . . Father
Charlotte Parry . . . . Mother
Arthur Rigby jr . . . . Brother
Syd Crossley . . . . Bleak
Monty Banks . . . . Taxi-driver
MUSICAL Rich American feigns bankruptcy
to force wild daughter to marry composer.

09423
A SOUTHERN MAID (85) (U)
BIP (Wardour)
D: Harry Hughes
S: (PLAY) Harry Graham, Dion Clayton
Calthrop
SC: Austin Melford, Arthur Woods,
Frank Miller, Frank Launder
Bebe Daniels . . . . . Dolores/Juanita
Clifford Mollison . . Jack Rawden/Willoughby
Harry Welchman . . Fransisco del Fuego
Lupino Lane . . . . Antonio Lopez
Hal Gordon . . . . Pedro
Morris Harvey . . . . Vasco
Amy Veness . . . . Donna Rosa
Nancy Brown . . . . Carola
Basil Radford . . . . Tom
MUSICAL Spain. Senorita weds Englishman
despite grandee favoured by father.
(Extract in ELSTREE STORY, 1952).

09424
THE RIGHT TO LIVE (72) (A)
Fox British
D: Albert Parker
S: Michael Barringer
SC: Gordon Wong Wellesley, Frank Atkinson,
R.J.Davis
Davy Burnaby . . . . . . Sir George Kessler
Pat Paterson . . . . June Kessler
Richard Bird . . . . Richard Fulton

Francis L.Sullivan . . . . . . Roger Stoneham
Lawrence Anderson . . . . Hugh Latimer
Frank Atkinson . . . . Harry Woods
CRIME Crooked financier schemes to get
chemical which will neutralise poison gas.

09425
THE LAUGHTER OF FOOLS (47) (U)
George Smith (Fox)
D:SC: Adrian Brunel
S: (PLAY) H.F.Maltby
Pat Paterson . . . . Doris Gregg
Derrick de Marney . . . . Capt Vidal
Helen Ferrers . . . . Mrs Gregg
Eliot Makeham . . . . Mr Gregg
D.A.Clarke-Smith . . . . Plunkett
Joan Melville . . . . Mabel Gregg
George Thirlwell . . . . Bertie Gregg
COMEDY Mercenary mother schemes to wed
daughter to rich captain who prefers her
niece.

09426
THE JEWEL (67) (U)
Venture Films (Par)
P: Hugh Percival
D: Reginald Denham
S:(NOVEL) Edgar Wallace
SC: Basil Mason
Hugh Williams . . . . Frank Hallam
Frances Dean . . Jenny Day/Lady Joan
Jack Hawkins . . . . Peter Roberts
Mary Newland . . . . Lady Carleigh
Eric Cowley . . . . Maj Brook
Annie Esmond . . . . Mme Vanheim
Geoffrey Goodheart . . . . . . Mr Day
Clare Harris . . . . Mrs Day
CRIME Socialite saves aunt's diamond
by having shopgirl pose as lady crook.

09427
CHANNEL CROSSING (70) (A)
Gaumont (W&F) reissue: 1942 (EB)
P: Angus Macphail, Ian Dalrymple
D: Milton Rosmer
S: W.P.Lipscomb, Angus Macphail
SC: W.P.Lipscomb, Cyril Campion
Matheson Lang . . . . Jacob van Eeden
Constance Cummings . . . . . Marion Slade
Edmund Gwenn . . . . Trotter
Anthony Bushell . . . . Peter Bradley
Max Miller . . . . James
Dorothy Dickson . . . . Vi Guthrie
Nigel Bruce . . . . Nigel Guthrie
Douglas Jeffries . . . . Dr Walkley
H.G. Stoker . . . . Captain
Viola Lyel . . . . Singer
Ellen Pollock . . . . Actress
Cyril Smith . . . . Beach
Gerald Barry . . . . Passenger
Hay Plumb . . . . Steward
Wally Patch . . . . Sailor
C.Denier Warren . . . . Purser
DRAMA Dutch financier fleeing to France
tries to drown secretary's fiance.

09428
A CUCKOO IN THE NEST (85) (A)
Gaumont (W&F) reissue: 1942 (EB; 11 mins.
cut)
P: Angus Macphail, Ian Dalrymple
D: Tom Walls
S: (PLAY) Ben Travers
SC: Ben Travers, A.R.Rawlinson
Tom Walls . . . . Major Bone
Ralph Lynn . . . . Peter Wyckham
Yvonne Arnaud . . . . Marguerite Hickett
Robertson Hare . . . . Rev Sloley-Jones
Mary Brough . . . . Mrs Spoker

Veronica Rose . . . . Barbara Wyckham
Gordon James . . . . Noony
Grace Edwin . . . . Mrs Bone
Mark Daly . . . . Pinhorn
Cecil Parker . . . . Claude Hickett
Roger Livesey . . . . Alfred
Frank Pettingell . . . . Landlord
Joan Brierley . . . . Maid
COMEDY Newlywed and married ex-fiance
forced to spend night in inn's only bedroom.

09429
ENEMY OF THE POLICE (51) (A)
WB-FN(WB)
P: Irving Asher
D: George King
John Stuart . . . . John Meakin
Viola Keats . . . . Preston
A.Bromley Davenport Sir Lemuel Tapleigh
Margaret Yarde . . . . Lady Tapleigh
Violet Farebrother . . . . Lady Salterton
Ernest Sefton . . . . Slingsby
Winifred Oughton . . . . Martha Teavle
Alf Goddard . . . . Gallagher
Molly Fisher . . . . Ann
Hal Walters . . . . Bagshaw
COMEDY Reform guild secretary mistaken
for crook and given psychological treatment.

09430
SMITHY (53) (A)
WB-FN (WB)
P: Irving Asher
D: George King
Edmund Gwenn . . . . John Smith
Peggy Novak . . . . Jane
D.A.Clarke-Smith . . . . Boyd

09431
THE FEAR SHIP (66) (A)
ASFI-J.Steven Edwards (Par)
D:SC: J. Steven Edwards
S: (NOVEL) R.F.W.Rees (THE SECOND
MATE)
Cyril McLaglen . . . . Capt Petrie
Dorothy Bartlam . . . . Ivy Bywater
Edmund Willard . . . . Jack Arkwright
William Holmes . . . . Capt Bywater
John Blake . . . . Buckeye
ADVENTURE Mate saves sailing ship and
wins girl owner.

09432
COMMISSIONAIRE (72) (U)
Granville (MGM)
P: Edward G. Whiting
D: Edward Dryhurst
S: Herbert Ayres
Sam Livesey . . . . Sgt George Brown
Barrie Livesey . . . . Tom Brown
George Carney . . . . Sgt Ted Seymour
Betty Huntley-Wright . . . . Betty Seymour
Julie Suedo . . . . Thelma Monsell
Robert English . . . . Col Gretton
Hannah Jones . . . . Mrs Brown
Granville Ferrier . . . . Desborough
Georgie Harris . . . . Briggs
Humberston Wright . . . . . . Quartermaster
CRIME Old commissionaire blamed when son
robs office.

NOV

09433
HER IMAGINARY LOVER (65) (U)
WB-FN (FN)
P: Irving Asher
D: George King
S: (NOVEL) A.E.W.Mason
(GREEN STOCKINGS)

Laura la Plante . . . . Celia
Percy Marmont . . . . Lord Michael Ware
Lady Tree . . . . Grandma
Bernard Nedell . . . . Davidson
Olive Blakeney . . . . Polly
Emily Fitzroy . . . . Aunt Lydia Raleigh
Roland Culver . . .. Raleigh Raleigh
COMEDY Heiress invents fiance to stave
off fortune-hunters.

09434
I ADORE YOU (74) (U)
WB-FN (WB)
P: Irving Asher
D: George King
S: W.Scott Darling
SC: Paul England
Margot Grahame . . . . Margot Grahame
Harold French . . . . Norman Young
Clifford Heatherley . . . . . . Louis B.Koenig
O.B. Clarence . . . . Mr Young
Peggy Novak . . . . Operator
Georgie Harris . . . . Peter Butcher
Ernest Sefton . . . . Pilbeam
Gavin Gordon . . . . . . Alphonso Bouillabaise
Carroll Gibbons and the Savoy Orpheans
MUSICAL Old actor mistaken for new owner
of film studio.

09435
THE BERMONDSEY KID (75) (A)
WB-FN (FN)
P: Irving Asher
D: Ralph Dawson
S: Bill Evans
SC: W. Scott Darling
Esmond Knight . . . . Eddie Martin
Pat Paterson . . . . Mary
Ellis Irving . . . . Joe Dougherty
Ernest Sefton . . . . Lou Rodman
Clifford McLaglen . . . . Bates
Eve Gray . . . . Toots
Syd Crossley . . . . Porky
Winifred Oughton . . . . Mrs Bodge
Len Harvey . . . . Himself
SPORT Boxing newsboy forced to fight sick
friend for championship.

09436
STRIKE IT RICH (72) (U)
British Lion
P: Herbert Smith
D: Leslie Hiscott
S: Michael Barringer
George Gee . . . . Eddie Smart
Gina Malo . . . . Mary
Davy Burnaby . . . . Humphrey Wells
Betty Astell . . . . Janet Wells
Ernest Sefton . . . . Sankey
Cyril Raymond . . . . Slaughter
Hal Walters . . . .
Wilfrid Lawson . . . . Raikes
Ethel Warwick . . . .
COMEDY Phrenology causes meek clerk to
take over firm and corner nutmegs.

09437
MAROONED (67) (U)
British Lion (Fox)
P: Herbert Smith
D: Leslie Hiscott
S: Michael Barringer
Edmund Gwenn . . . . Tom Roberts
Viola Lyel . . . . Sarah Roberts
Iris March . . . . Mary Roberts
Victor Garland . . . . Norman Bristowe
Hal Walters . . . . Joe
Griffith Humphreys . . . . . . Convict
Wally Patch . . . . Wilson

Philip Hewland . . . . Jacob
Wilfred Shine . . . . Maille
CRIME Lighthouse keeper shelters escaped
convict who is his adopted daughter's father.

09438
THE ROOF (58) (A)
Real Art (Radio)
P: Julius Hagen
D: George A. Cooper
S: (NOVEL) David Whitelaw
SC: H. Fowler Mear
Leslie Perrins . . . . Insp Darrow
Judy Gunn . . . . Carol Foster
Russell Thorndike . . . . Clive Bristow
Michael Hogan . . . . Samuel Morton
Ivor Barnard . . . . Arthur Stannard
Eliot Makeham . . . . John Rutherford
Barbara Everest . . . . Mrs Foster
George Zucco . . . . James Renton
Leo Britt . . . . Tony Freyne
CRIME Jewels left in trust with lawyer are
stolen.

09439
A SHOT IN THE DARK (53) (A)
Real Art (Radio)
P: Julius Hagen
D: George Pearson
S: (NOVEL) Gerard Fairlie
SC: H. Fowler Mear
Dorothy Boyd . . . . Alaris Browne
O.B.Clarence . . . . Rev John Malcolm
Jack Hawkins . . . . Norman Paul
Russell Thorndike . . . . Dr Stuart
Michael Shepley . . . . Vivian Waugh
Davy Burnaby . . . . . . Col Michael Browne
A.Bromley Davenport . . . . . . Peter Browne
Hugh E.Wright . . . . George Barrow
Henrietta Watson . . . . Angela Browne
CRIME Several people confess to murder of
hated recluse.

09440
SONG BIRDS (36) (U)
BIF (Pathe)
P: Fred Watts
D: John Harlow
S: Wallace Lupino
Wallace Lupino . . . . Wally
Barry Lupino . . . . Barry
Gus McNaughton . . . . Pedro
COMEDY Tramps at Christmas party cure
drunken host.

09441
FOR LOVE OF YOU (77) (U)
Windsor (Sterling) Reissue: 1944
(Ad; 450 ft cut)
P: Frank A. Richardson
D: Carmine Gallone
S: Selwyn Jepson
Arthur Riscoe . . . . Jack
Naunton Wayne . . . . Jim
Franco Foresta . . . . The Tenor
Diana Napier . . . . The Wife
Pearl Osgood . . . . The Girl
MUSICAL Venice. Man helps friend court
opera star's wife.

09442
DICK TURPIN (79) (U)
Stoll-Stafford (Gaumont)
P: Clyde Cook
D: John Stafford, Victor Hanbury
S: (NOVEL) Harrison Ainsworth (ROOK-
WOOD)
SC: Victor Kendall
Victor McLaglen . . . . Dick Turpin
Jane Carr . . . . Eleanor Mowbray

Frank Vosper . . . . Tom King
James Finlayson . . . . Jeremy
Cecil Humphreys . . . . Luke Rookwood
Gillian Lind . . . . Nan
Gibb McLaughlin . . . . Governor
Alexander Field . . . . Weazel Jones
Helen Ferrers . . . . Lady Rookwood
Lewis Gilbert . . . . Jem
ADVENTURE Highwayman rides to York to
prevent enforced marriage.

09443
A DICKENSIAN FANTASY (10) (U)
Gee Films (Mackane)
D: Aveling Ginever
S: (NOVEL) Charles Dickens
(A CHRISTMAS CAROL)
Lawrence Hanray . . . . All Characters
FANTASY Man reads 'A Christmas Carol' and
dreams characters come to life.

09444
SKIPPER OF THE OSPREY (29) (U) *raycol*
ATP (ABFD)
P: Basil Dean
D: Norman Walker
S: (STORY) W.W.Jacobs
SC: W.P. Lipscomb
Renee Gadd . . . . Maggie Cringle
Ian Hunter . . . . Charlie Lee
D.A.Clarke-Smith . . . . Mate
Clive Currie . . . . Captain Cringle
DRAMA Sacked mate saves girl barge captain
from lustful replacement.

09445
THE FORTUNATE FOOL (73) (A)
ABFD
P: Jack Eppel
D: Norman Walker
S: (PLAY) Dion Titheradge
Hugh Wakefield . . . . Jim Falconer
Joan Wyndham . . . . Helen
Jack Raine . . . . Gerald
Elizabeth Jenns . . . . Mildred
Arthur Chesney . . . . Batty
Sara Allgood . . . . Rose
Bobbie Comber . . . . Marlowe
Mary Mayfren . . . . Mrs Falconer
COMEDY Rich author feigns poverty to adopt
poor girl and ex-boxer.

09446
CHELSEA LIFE (69) (A)
B & D-Paramount British
D:S: Sidney Morgan
SC: Joan Wentworth Wood (Morgan)
Louis Hayward . . . . David Fenner
Molly Johnson . . . . Lulu
Anna Lee . . . . Hon Muriel Maxton
Kathleen Saxon . . . . Mrs Bonnington
Stanley Vilven . . . . Grillini
Gordon McLeod . . . . Lawton Hodge
Eric Hales . . . . Harry Gordon
Patrick Ludlow . . . . Lancelot Humphrey
Arthur Chesney . . . . Ambrose Lincoln
ROMANCE Painter steals work of absent
Italian and becomes engaged to socialite.

09447
SORRELL AND SON (97) (A)
B&D (UA) *reissue:* 1938 (Amb)
P: Herbert Wilcox
D: Jack Raymond
S: (NOVEL) Warwick Deeping
SC: Lydia Hayward
H.B.Warner . . . . Stephen Sorrell
Hugh Williams . . . . Kit Sorrell
Winifred Shotter . . . . Molly Pentreath
Margot Grahame . . . . Mrs Sorrell

Donald Calthrop . . . . . . Sir Richard Orange
Ruby Miller . . . . Mrs Palfrey
Louis Hayward . . . . Duncan
Evelyn Roberts . . . . Mr Roland
Arthur Chesney . . . . Mr Porteous
Wally Patch . . . . Buck
Hope Davy . . . . Ethel
DRAMA Ex-captain devotes life to son after
wife leaves him.

09449
TROUBLE (70) (U)
B&D (UA) *reissue:* 1937 (EB)
P: Herbert Wilcox
D: Maclean Rogers
S: Dudley Sturrock, Walter Tennyson
SC: R.P.Weston, Bert Lee, Jack Marks
Sydney Howard . . . . Horace Hollebone
George Curzon . . . . Capt Vansittart
Dorothy Robinson . . . . . . Cora Vansittart
Hope Davy . . . . Miss Carruthers
Muriel Aked . . . . Miss May
George Turner . . . . Nobby Clarke
Wally Patch . . . . Chief Steward
Betty Shale . . . . Mrs Orpington
Abraham Sofaer . . . . Ali
COMEDY Pleasure cruise stewards outwit
jewel thieves.

09449
THE WANDERING JEW (111) (A)
Twickenham (Gaumont)
P: Julius Hagen
D: Maurice Elvey
S: (PLAY) E.Temple Thurston
SC: H. Fowler Mear
Phase I:
Conrad Veidt . . . . Matathias
Marie Ney . . . . Judith
Cicely Oates . . . . Rachel
Basil Gill . . . . Pontius Pilate
Phase II:
Anne Grey . . . . Joanne de Beaudricourt
Dennis Hoey . . . . de Beaudricourt
Jack Livesey . . . . Duke Godfrey
Bertram Wallis . . . . Prince Boemund
Phase III:
Joan Maude . . . . Gianella
John Stuart . . . . Pietro Morelli
Arnold Lucy . . . . Andrea Michelotti
Phase IV:
Peggy Ashcroft . . . . Olalla Quintana
Francis L.Sullivan . . . . . Juan de Texada
Felix Aylmer . . . . Ferera
Ivor Barnard . . . . Castro
Abraham Sofaer . . . . Zapportas
FANTASY Jew, cursed to live through the ages,
dies in the Inquisition.

09450
FRIDAY THE THIRTEENTH (84) (A)
Gainsborough (Gaumont) *reissue:* 1941 (IFR)
P: Michael Balcon
D: Victor Saville
S: G.H.Moresby-White, Sidney Gilliat
SC: Emlyn Williams
ON THE BUS
Sonnie Hale . . . . Alf
Cyril Smith . . . . Fred
Muriel Aked . . . . Miss Twigg
JACKSON THE SHIPPING CLERK
Eliot Makeham . . . . Jackson
Ursula Jeans . . . . Eileen Jackson
D.A.Clarke-Smith . . . . . . Max
Gibb McLaughlin . . . . Florist
BLAKE THE GENTLEMAN OF FORTUNE
Emlyn Williams . . . . Blake
Frank Lawton . . . . Frank Parsons
Belle Chrystal . . . . Mary
JOE OF THE CALEDONIAN MARKET

Max Miller . . . . Joe
Alfred Drayton . . . . Detective
Hartley Power . . . . American
WAKEFIELD THE CITY MAN
Edmund Gwenn . . . . Wakefield
Mary Jerrold . . . . Flora Wakefield
Gordon Harker . . . . Hamilton Briggs
MR LIGHTFOOT IN THE PARK
Robertson Hare . . . . Mr Lightfoot
Martita Hunt . . . . Agnes Lightfoot
Leonora Corbett . . . . Dolly
MILLIE THE NON-STOP VARIETY GIRL
Jessie Matthews . . . . Millie
Ralph Richardson . . . . . . Schoolmaster
Donald Calthrop . . . . Hugh Nichols
Ivor McLaren . . . . Dance Instructor
DRAMA Stories of people involved in omnibus
crash.

09451
MRS DANE'S DEFENCE (67) (A)
National Talkies (Par)
P: Harry Rowson
D: A.V.Bramble
S: (PLAY) Henry Arthur Jones
SC: Lydia Hayward, Kenelm Foss
Joan Barry . . . . Mrs Dane
Basil Gill . . . . . . Sir Daniel Carteret
Francis James . . . . Lionel Carteret
Ben Field . . . . Mr Bulsom-Porter
Clare Greet . . . . Mrs Bulsom-Porter
Evan Thomas . . . . James Risby
Evelyn Walsh-Hall . . . . Lady Eastney
DRAMA Widow strives to keep past secret
from wealthy lover.

DEC
09452
THE HOUSE OF TRENT (75) (U)
B & H - Ensign (Butcher)
P: W.G.D.Hutchinson
D: Norman Walker
S: Charles Bennett, Billie Bristow
John Stuart . . . . .Dr Trent/John Trent
Anne Grey . . . . Rosemary Trent
Wendy Barrie . . . . Angela Fairdown
Norah Baring . . . . Barbara
Peter Gawthorne . . . . . Lord Fairdown
Hope Davy . . . . Joan
Jack Raine . . . . Peter
Moore Marriott . . . . Ferrier
Estelle Winwood . . . . Charlotte
Victor Stanley . . . . Spriggs
ROMANCE Doctor's patient dies while he is
with press lord's daughter.

09453
CRIME ON THE HILL (69) (A)
BIP (Wardour)
D: Bernard Vorhaus
S: (PLAY) Jack de Leon, Jack Celestin
SC: Michael Hankinson, Vera Allinson,
E.M.Delafield, Bernard Vorhaus
Sally Blane . . . . Sylvia Kennett
Nigel Playfair . . . . Dr Moody
Lewis Casson . . . . Rev Michael Gray
Anthony Bushell . . . . Tony Fields
Phyllis Dare . . . . Claire Winslow
Judy Kelly . . . . Alice Green
George Merritt . . . . Insp Wolf
Reginald Purdell . . . . Reporter
Gus McNaughton . . . . Collins
Hal Gordon . . . . Sgt Granger
Jimmy Godden . . . . Landlord
Hay Petrie . . . . Jevons
Kenneth Kove . . . . Tourist
CRIME Vicar proves convicted man did not
poison fiancée's rich uncle.

09454
SONG OF THE PLOUGH (68) (U)
Sound City (MGM) *reissue:* 1939;
COUNTY FAIR (Llb; 2195 ft cut).
P: Ivar Campbell
D: John Baxter
S: Reginald Pound
Stewart Rome . . . . Farmer Freeland
Rosalinde Fuller . . . . Miss Freeland
Allan Jeayes . . . . Joe Saxby
Hay Petrie . . . . Farmhand
Kenneth Kove . . . . Archie
Jack Livesey . . . . Squire's Son
Edgar Driver . . . . Barber
James Harcourt . . . . Doctor
Freddie Watts . . . . Bandsman
Albert Richardson . . . . Singer
DRAMA Sussex. Farmer saved from ruin by
winning sheepdog trials.

09455
SAILORS TAKE CARE (19) (U)
Premier (U)
COMEDY Two sailors fall in love with twins.

09456
DAY DREAMS (18) (U)
Premier (U)
COMEDY Two tramps dream of winning
screen contest.

09457
MANNEQUIN (54) (U)
Real Art (Radio)
P: Julius Hagen
D: George A. Cooper
S: Charles Bennett
Harold French . . . . Peter Tattersall
Judy Kelly . . . . Heather Trent
Diana Beaumont . . . . . Lady Diana Savage
Whitmore Humphries . . . . . . Billy Armstrong
Richard Cooper . . . Lord Bunny Carstairs
Ben Welden . . . . Chris Dempson
Faith Bennett . . . . Queenie
Vera Boggetti . . . . Nancy
Anna Lee . . . . Babette
ROMANCE Boxer leaves true love for
society lady, but returns.

09458
THE POINTING FINGER (68) (U)
Real Art (Radio)
P: Julius Hagen
D: George Pearson
S: (NOVEL) "Rita"
SC: H. Fowler Mear
John Stuart . . . . Lord Rollestone
Viola Keats . . . . Lady Mary Stuart
Leslie Perrins . . . . Hon James Mallory
Michael Hogan . . . . Patrick Lafone
A.Bromley Davenport . . . . Lord Edensore
Henrietta Watson . . . Lady Anne Rollestone
D.J.Williams . . . . Grimes
Clare Greet . . . . Landlady
CRIME Man tries to kill halfbrother to inherit
earldom.

09459
TAKING WAYS (40) (A)
Sound City (U)
P: Ivar Campbell
D: John Baxter
S: (SKETCH) Leonard Morris
Leonard Morris . . . . . Lightfingered Freddie
Daisy Crossley . . . . Flash Kate
Harry Terry . . . . Basher
Freddie Watts . . . . Gus
Charles Farrell . . . . Spike Davis
Julie Suedo . . . . Girl

Johnnie Nit; Bernard Dudley; Yola de Fraine;
Rigoletto Brothers
COMEDY Crook poses as dude to steal
necklace.

09460
EYES OF FATE (67) (A)
Sound City (U)
P: Norman Loudon
D: Ivar Campbell
S: (STORY) Holloway Horn
Allan Jeayes . . . . Knocker
Valerie Hobson . . . . Rene
Terence de Marney . . . . . . Edgar
Faith Bennett . . . . Betty
Nellie Bowman . . . . Mrs Knocker
O.B.Clarence . . . . Mr Oliver
Tony Halfpenny . . . . George
Edwin Ellis . . . . Jefferson
FANTASY Bookmaker is given tomorrow's
newspaper, wins a fortune, and reads of his
own death.

09461
THIS ACTING BUSINESS (54) (U)
WB-FN (WB)
P: Irving Asher
D: John Daumery
Hugh Williams . . . . Hugh
Wendy Barrie . . . . Joyce
Donald Calthrop . . . . Milton Stafford
Violet Farebrother . . . . Mary Kean
Marie Wright . . . . Mrs Dooley
Charles Paton . . . . Ward
Janaice Adair . . . .
Henry B.Longhurst . . . .
COMEDY Parents' interference causes
newlywed actors to separate.

09462
THE CONSTANT NYMPH (98) (A)
Gaumont
P: Michael Balcon
D: Basil Dean
S: (PLAY) Margaret Kennedy, Basil Dean
SC: Margaret Kennedy, Basil Dean,
Dorothy Farnum
Victoria Hopper . . . . Tessa Sanger
Brian Aherne . . . . Lewis Dodd
Leonora Corbett . . . . Florence
Lyn Harding . . . . Albert Sanger
Mary Clare . . . . Linda Sanger

Jane Baxter. . . . . Antonia Sanger
Fritz Schultz . . . . Jacob Birnbaum
Tony de Lungo . . . . Roberto
Jane Cornell . . . . Kate Sanger
Peggy Blythe . . . . Lena Sanger
Athole Stewart . . . . Charles Churchill
Beryl Laverick . . . . Susan Sanger
Jim Gerald . . . . Trigorin
ROMANCE Tyrol. Composer leaves rich wife
for schoolgirl.

09463
AUNT SALLY (84) (U)
USA: ALONG CAME SALLY
Gainsborough (Gaumont)
P: Michael Balcon
D:S: Tim Whelan
SC: Austin Melford, Guy Bolton, A.R.Rawlinson
Cicely Courtneidge . . . . . . Sally/Zaza
Sam Hardy . . . . Mike King Kelly
Phyllis Clare. . . . . Queenie Mills
Billy Milton . . . . Billy
Hartley Power . . .. Gloves Clarke
Ben Welden . . . . Casino
Enrico Naldi . . . . Little Joey
Ann Hope . . . . Joan
Ivor McLaren . . . . Madison
Rex Evans . . . . Percy
Leslie Holmes; The Carlyle Cousins; The
Three Admirals; Val Rosing; The Naldi Trio;
Debroy Somers and his Band; Reilly and Comfort
MUSICAL Stage-struck woman poses as French
star and saves American club-owner from
gangsters.

09464
TURKEY TIME (73) (A)
Gaumont *reissue:* 1943 (EB)
P: Michael Balcon
D: Tom Walls
S: (PLAY) Ben Travers
SC: Ben Travers
Tom Walls . . . . Max Wheeler
Ralph Lynn . . . . David Winterton
Dorothy Hyson . . . . Rose Adair
Robertson Hare . . . . Edwin Stoatt
Mary Brough . . . . Mrs Gather
Norma Varden . . . . Ernestine Stoatt
Veronica Rose . . . . Louise Stoatt
D.A.Clarke-Smith . . . . Westbourne
Marjorie Corbett . . . . Florence
COMEDY Engaged man blames indiscretion on
fiancee's father.

09465
ASK BECCLES (68) (A)
B & D-Paramount British
D: Redd Davis
S: (PLAY) Cyril Campion, Edward Dignon
SC: Cyril Campion
Garry Marsh . . . . Eustace Beccles
Mary Newland . . . . Marion Holforth
Abraham Sofaer . . . . Baki
Allan Jeayes . . . . Matthew Blaise
John Turnbull . . . . Insp Daniels
Evan Thomas . . . . Sir Frederick Boyne
Eileen Munro . . . . Mrs Rivers
Fewlass Llewellyn . . . . . Sir James Holforth
COMEDY Advice expert steals diamond but
returns it to save innocent man.

09466
TWO WIVES FOR HENRY (45) (A)
George Smith (Fox)
D: Adrian Brunel
Garry Marsh . . . . Henry Stetson
Dorothy Boyd . . . . Estelle Stetson
Jack Raine . . . . Hugo Horsfall
Millicent Wolf . . . . Vera
Paul Sheridan . . . . Alphonse Pujol
Andrea Malandrinos . . . . . Gonzalez
COMEDY Boot manufacturer takes on second
"wife" for business reasons.

09467
ON SECRET SERVICE (91) (U) USA:
SECRET AGENT
BIP (Wardour)
D: Arthur Woods
S: (NOVEL) Georg Kloren, Robert Baberske
(SPIONE AM WERK)
SC: Frank Vosper, Max Kimmich, Herbert
Juttke, Arthur Woods
Greta Nissen . . . . Marchesa Marcella
Carl Ludwig Diehl. . . . Hauptmann von Hombergk
Don Alvarado . . . . Valenti
Lester Matthews . . . Coronello Ramenelli
Esme Percy . . . . Bleuntzli
C.M.Hallard . . . . Waldmuller
Austin Trevor . . . . ADC Larco
Cecil Ramage . . . . Da Villa
Wallace Geoffrey B18
WAR The Alps. Austrian officer loves Italian
girl who is really a spy.

1934

JAN

09468
THE SILVER SPOON (64) (A)
WB-FN (WB)
P: Irving Asher
D: George King
S: Brock Williams

Ian Hunter	Capt Watts-Winyard
Garry Marsh	Hon Roland Stone
Binnie Barnes	Lady Perivale
Cecil Parker	Trevor
Cecil Humphreys	Lord Perivale
Joan Playfair	Denise
O.B.Clarence	Parker
George Merritt	Insp Innes

COMEDY Gentleman tramps confess to
Lord's murder to shield woman they both love.

09469
TROUBLE IN STORE (39) (U)
WB-FN (FN)
P: Irving Asher
D: Clyde Cook

James Finlayson	The Watchman
Jack Hobbs	Jack
Glen Alyn	Gloria
Anthony Hankey	Tony
Clifford Heatherley	Potts
Margaret Yarde	Landlady
Charles Carson	Sanderson
Millicent Wolf	Venese
Joan Hickson	Mabel

COMEDY Store assistants catch burglars when
they are accidentally locked in.

09470
THE LADY IS WILLING (74) (A)
Columbia British
P: Joseph Friedman
D: Gilbert Miller
S: (PLAY) Louis Verneuil
SC: Guy Bolton

Leslie Howard	Albert Latour
Cedric Hardwicke	Gustav Dupont
Binnie Barnes	Helene Dupont
Nigel Playfair	Prof Menard
Nigel Bruce	Welton
Claud Allister	Brevin
W.Graham Browne	Pignolet
Kendall Lee	Valerie
Arthur Howard	Dr Germont
Virginia Field	Maid

COMEDY Paris. Ex-officer becomes detective
and kidnaps wife of financier who ruined him.

09471
SCREEN VAUDEVILLE NUMBER ONE (24)
(U)
Screen Vaudeville

Davy Burnaby	Max & Harry Nesbitt
Carlyle Cousins	Tiller Girls
Geoffrey Goodhart and his Band	

REVUE

09472
LILY OF KILLARNEY (88) (U)
USA: BRIDE OF THE LAKE
Twickenham (AP&D) reissue: 1937
P: Julius Hagen
D: Maurice Elvey
S: (PLAY) Dion Boucicault (THE COLLEEN
BAWN)
SC: H. Fowler Mear

John Garrick	Sir Patrick Cregeen
Gina Malo	Eileen O'Connor
Stanley Holloway	Father O'Flynn
Leslie Perrins	Sir James Corrigan
Dennis Hoey	Myles-na-Coppaleen
Sara Allgood	Mrs. O'Connor

Dorothy Boyd	Norah Cregeen
D.J.Williams	Danny Mann
Hughes Macklin	Shan
Pamela May	Ann Chute
A.Bromley Davenport	Lord Kenmore

MUSICAL Ireland. Poor knight's rival frames
him for murder when beloved peasant is
kidnapped by smuggler.

09473
SAY IT WITH FLOWERS (71) (U)
Real Art (Radio)
P: Julius Hagen
D:S: John Baxter
SC: Wallace Orton, H.Fowler Mear

Mary Clare	Kate Bishop
Ben Field	Joe Bishop
George Carney	Bill Woods
Mark Daly	Scotty MacDonald
Edgar Driver	Titch
Freddie Watts	Steve
Edwin Ellis	Ted

Florrie Forde; Charles Coburn; Marie Kendall;
Tom Costello; Percy Honri; Kearney & Browning.
MUSICAL Cockneys stage concert to help sick
flower-woman.

09474
THE BLACK ABBOT (56) (A)
Real Art (Radio)
P: Julius Hagen
D: George A. Cooper
S: (NOVEL) Philip Godfrey
(THE GRANGE MYSTERY)
SC: H. Fowler Mear

John Stuart	Frank Brooks
Judy Kelly	Sylvia Hillcrist
Richard Cooper	Lord Jerry Pilkdown
Ben Welden	Charlie Marsh
Drusilla Wills	Mary Hillcrist
Edgar Norfolk	Brian Heslewood
Farren Soutar	John Hillcrist
Cyril Smith	Alf Higgins
John Turnbull	Insp Lockwood

CRIME Crooks hold rich man to ransom in
own house.

09475
THE RIVER WOLVES (56) (A)
Real Art (Radio)
P: Julius Hagen
D: George Pearson
S: (PLAY) Edward Dignon, Geoffrey Swaffer
(THE LION AND THE LAMB)
SC: Terence Egan

Helga Moray	Moira Clare
Michael Hogan	Capt Guest
John Mills	Peter Farrell
Ben Welden	Flash Lawson
Hope Davy	Heather Patton
Martin Walker	Trevor Rowe
Norman Shelley	Jim Spiller
D.J.Williams	Tod
Mark Daly	Jock Brodie
Edgar Driver	George

CRIME Tilbury. Merchant skipper saves landlady's daughter's sweetheart from blackmailer.

09476
COLONEL BLOOD (98) (A)
Sound City (MGM)
P: Norman Loudon
D:S: W.P.Lipscomb

Frank Cellier	Col Blood
Anne Grey	Lady Castlemaine
Mary Lawson	Susie
Allan Jeayes	Charles II
Hay Petrie	Mr Edwards

Hilda Trevelyan	Mrs Edwards
Arthur Chesney	Samuel Pepys
Stella Arbenina	Mrs Pepys
Desmond Jeans	Parrot
Robert Nainby	Desborough
Arthur Goullet	Tim
Percy Standing	Duke of Ormonde
Ena Grossmith	Jane

HISTORY 1670. Irish patriot caught stealing
Crown Jewels talks his way to pardon.

09477
ON THE AIR (78) (U)
British Lion reissue: 1939 (EB)
D: Herbert Smith
S: Samuel Woolf Smith
SC: Michael Barringer

Davy Burnaby	Davy
Reginald Purdell	Reggie
Betty Astell	Betty
Anona Winn	Chambermaid
Max Wall	Boots
Hugh E.Wright	Vicar
Clapham & Dwyer	Scott & Whaley
Derek Oldham	Mario de Pietro
Jane Carr	Teddy Brown
Eve Becke	Harry Champion
Edwin Styles	Roy Fox & his Band
Wilson, Keppel & Betty	
Buddy Bradley's Dancing Girls	

MUSICAL Radio stars on holiday help
village vicar stage concert.

09478
FLAT NO. 3 (46) (A)
British Lion (MGM)
P: Herbert Smith
D: Leslie Hiscott
S: Michael Barringer

Mary Glynne	Mrs Rivington
D.A.Clarke-Smith	Kettler
Betty Astell	Trixie
Lewis Shaw	Harry Rivington
Cecil Parker	Hilary Maine
Elizabeth English	Joan Maine
Dorothy Vernon	Mrs Crummitt

CRIME Lawyer helps widow who believes she
has killed blackmailer .

09479
RED WAGON (107) (A)
BIP (Wardour)
P: Walter C.Mycroft
D: Paul Stein
S: (NOVEL) Lady Eleanor Smith
SC: Roger Burford, Edward Knoblock,
Arthur Woods

Charles Bickford	Joe Price
Raquel Torres	Sheba Price/Starlina
Greta Nissen	Zara
Don Alvarado	Davey Heron
Anthony Bushell	Tony Griffiths
Paul Graetz	Max Schultze
Amy Veness	Petal Schultze
Jimmy Hanley	Joe (Boy)
Frank Pettingell	McGinty
Alexander Field	Harry Cronk
Francis L. Sullivan	Cranley
Percy Parsons	Cowboy Joe
Nancy Brown	Lamentina
Aubrey Mather	Blewett

DRAMA Tiger tamer loves circus owner who
marries worthless gipsy. (Extract in
ELSTREE STORY, 1952).

09480
THE SCOTLAND YARD MYSTERY (76) (A)
USA: THE LIVING DEAD
BIP (Wardour)
P: Walter C. Mycroft

D: Thomas Bentley
S: (PLAY) Wallace Geoffrey
SC: Frank Miller
Gerald du Maurier . . . . Insp Stanton
George Curzon . . . . Dr Masters
Grete Natzler . . . . Irene
Belle Chrystal . . . . Mary Stanton
Leslie Perrins . . . . John
Paul Graetz . . . . Paston
Wally Patch . . . . Sgt George
Henry Victor . . . . Floyd
CRIME Crook collects insurance by injecting victims with life-suspending serum.

09481
A POLITICAL PARTY (73) (U)
BIP (Pathe)
P: Walter C. Mycroft
D: Norman Lee
S: Syd Courtenay, Lola Harvey
Leslie Fuller . . .· . . . . Bill Smithers
John Mills . . . . Tony Smithers
Enid Stamp-Taylor . . . . . Elvira Whitman
H.F.Maltby . . . Sir James Barrington-Oakes
Viola Lyel . . . . Mary Smithers
Hal Gordon . . . . Alf Jenks
Marion Dawson . . . . Sarah Jenks
Charles Gerrard . . . . Mr Whitman
Daphne Courtenay . . . . Kathleen Jenks
Moore Marriott . . . . Jim Turner
COMEDY Chimney sweep's son inveigled into helping opponent in by-election.

09482
CATHERINE THE GREAT (96) (A)
London (UA) reissues: 1943 (Prem);
1946 (BL)
P: Alexander Korda, Ludovico Toeplitz
D: Paul Czinner
S: (PLAY) Melchior Lengyel, Lajos Biro
(THE CZARINA)
SC: Lajos Biro, Arthur Wimperis, Marjorie Deans
Elisabeth Bergner . . . . Catherine II
Douglas Fairbanks jr . . . . . Grand Duke Peter
Flora Robson . . . . Empress Elizabeth
Gerald du Maurier . . . . Lecocq
Irene Vanbrugh . . . . . Princess Anhalt-Zerbst
Griffith Jones . . . . Gregory Orlov
Joan Gardner . . . . Katuschenka
Dorothy Hale . . . .·. . . . . . Countess Olga
Diana Napier . . . . Countess Elizabeth
Gibb McLaughlin . . . . Bestujhev
Clifford Heatherley . . . . . . Ogarev
Lawrence Hanray . . . . Goudovitch
Allan Jeayes . . . . Col Karnilov
HISTORY Russia, 1745. Army ousts mad Grand Duke and makes his German wife Empress.

09483
FACES (68) (A)
B&D-Paramount British
D: Sidney Morgan
S: (PLAY) Patrick Ludlow, Walter Sondes
Anna Lee . . . . Madeleine Pelham
Harold French . . . . Ted
Walter Sondes . . . . Dick Morris
Dorothy Tetley . . . . Mrs Morris
Moore Marriott . . . . Robert Pelham
Kate Saxon . . . . Mrs Pelham
Beryl de Querton . . . . Amy Amor
Noel Shannon . . . .·. Alphonse
Olive Sloane . . . . Lady Wallingford
ROMANCE Suburban beautician almost elopes with rich client's husband.

FEB
09484
PART-TIME WIFE (45)
B & S Productions (EB)
COMEDY (Not shown.)

09485
OH NO DOCTOR ! (62) (A)
George King (MGM) reissue: 1943
(Fed; 160 ft cut).
D: George King
Jack Hobbs . . . . Montagu Kent
Dorothy Boyd . . . . Josephine Morrow
James Finlayson . . . . Axminster
Cecil Humphreys . . . . Dr Morrow
Peggy Novak . . . . Tessa Burnett
Jane Carr . . . . Protheroe
Abraham Sofaen . . . . Skelton
David Wilton . . . . Villain
COMEDY Doctor tries to frighten ward's fiancee to death.

09486
IMPORTANT PEOPLE (48) (A)
GS Enterprises (MGM) reissue: 1943 (Fed)
P: A. George Smith
D: Adrian Brunel
S: (PLAY) F.Wyndham Mallock
Stewart Rome . . . . Tony Westcott
Dorothy Boyd . . . . Margaret Westcott
Jack Raine . . . . George Pelling
Helen Goss . . . . Beryl Cardew
Henry Longhurst . . . . . . Col Clutterbuck
James Carrall . . . . Gen Harbottle
Fred Withers . . . . Ald Digley
May Hallatt . . . . Mrs Stenham
COMEDY Prohibitionary reverses policy when wife opposes election.

09487
THE CRIMSON CANDLE (48) (A)
Mainwaring (MGM)
P:D:S: Bernerd Mainwaring
Eve Gray . . . . Mavis
Eliot Makeham . . . . Doctor
Kenneth Kove. Hon Horatius Chillingsbotham
Derek Williams . . . . Leonard Duberley
Kynaston Reeves . . . .
Eugene Leahy . . . . Detective
Arthur Goullet . . . .
Audrey Cameron . . . . Maid
CRIME Doctor proves maid engineered ex-lover's death by curse.

09488
JACK AHOY ! (82) (U)
Gaumont reissue: 1940 (IFR)
P: Michael Balcon
D: Walter Forde
S: Sidney Gilliat, J.O.C.Orton
SC: Jack Hulbert, Leslie Arliss, Gerard Fairlie, Austin Melford
Jack Hulbert . . . . Jack Ponsonby
Nancy O'Neil . . . . Patricia Fraser
Alfred Drayton . . . . Admiral Fraser
Tamara Desni . . . . Conchita
Henry Peterson . . . . Larios
Sam Wilkinson . . . . Dodger
COMEDY Sailor saves submarine and admiral's daughter from bandits.

09489
THE NIGHT OF THE PARTY (62) (A)
Gaumont
P: Jerome Jackson
D: Michael Powell
S: (PLAY) Roland Pertwee, John Hastings Turner
SC: Ralph Smart
Leslie Banks. . . . . Sir John Holland
Ian Hunter . . . . Guy Kennington
Jane Baxter . . . . Peggy Studholme
Ernest Thesiger . . . . Chiddiatt
Viola Keats . . . . Joan Holland
Malcolm Keen . . . . Lord Studholme
Jane Millican . . . . Anna Chiddiatt
Muriel Aked . . . . Princess
John Turnbull . . . . Ramage
CRIME Press lord's secretary framed for killing him during game.

09490
RED ENSIGN (69) (U) USA: STRIKE !
Gaumont
P: Jerome Jackson
D: Michael Powell
S: Michael Powell, Jerome Jackson
SC: L. duGarde Peach
Leslie Banks . . . . David Barr
Carol Goodner . . . . June Mackinnon
Frank Vosper . . . . Lord Dean
Alfred Drayton . . . . Manning
Donald Calthrop . . . . Macleod
Allan Jeayes . . . .,. . . Emerson
Campbell Gullan . . . . Hannay
Percy Parsons . . . . Casey
Fewlass Llewellyn . . . . Sir Gregory
Henry Oscar . . . . Raglan
DRAMA Shipbuilder launches a new boat despite crooked rival.

09491
WALTZES FROM VIENNA (81) (U)
USA: STRAUSS'S GREAT WALTZ
Tom Arnold (Gau) reissue: 1942 (EB; 1006 ft cut).
D: Alfred Hitchcock
S: (PLAY) Heinz Reichart, Ernst Marischka, D.A.Willner (WALZERKREIG).
SC: Alma Reville, Guy Bolton
Jessie Matthews .·. . . . . . . Rasi
Edmund Gwenn . . . . Johann Strauss
Fay Compton . . Countess Helga von Stahl
Frank Vosper . . . . Count Gustav von Stahl
Esmond Knight . . . . Schani Strauss
Robert Hale . . . . Ebezeder
Charles Heslop . . . . Valet
Sybil Grove . . . . Mme Fouchet
Betty Huntley Wright . . . . . Maid
Cyril Smith . . . . Secretary
Berinoff & Charlot
MUSICAL Vienna, 1840. Countess helps composer succeed in spite of father.

09492
HAPPY (84) (U)
BIP (Wardour)
P:D: Fred Zelnik
S: Jacques Bachrach, Alfred Hahm, Karl Notl
SC: Austin Melford, Frank Launder, Arthur Woods, Stanley Lupino
Stanley Lupino . . . . Frank
Laddie Cliff . . . . George
Will Fyffe . . . . Simmy
Dorothy Hyson . . . . Lillian
Harry Tate . . . . Dupont
Renee Gadd . . . . Pauline
Gus McNaughton . . . . Waller
Jimmy Godden . . . . Brummelberg
Bertha Belmore . . . . Mrs Brummelberg
Hal Gordon . . . . Conjuror
MUSICAL Paris. Band Leader poses as millionaire to sell gadget for foiling car thieves.
09493
BOOTS ! BOOTS ! (80) (U)
Blakeley's Productions (Butcher)

reissue: 1938 (Amb; 25 mins cut).
P: John E. Blakeley
D: Bert Tracy
S: George Formby, Arthur Mertz
George Formby . . . . John Willie
Beryl Formby . . . . Beryl
Arthur Kingsley . . . . Manager
Tonie Forde . . . . Chambermaid
Lilian Keyes . . . . Lady Royston
Donald Reid . . . . . . Sir Alfred Royston
Betty Driver . . . . Betty
Harry Hudson and his Band
MUSICAL Hotel "boots" and scullery maid
star in cabaret. (Extracts in MUSIC HALL
PERSONALITIES — 4 (1938);
GEORGE FORMBY — 4 (1938).)

09494
AUTUMN CROCUS (86) (A)
ATP (ABFD)
P:D: Basil Dean
S: (PLAY) C.L.Anthony
SC: Basil Dean
Ivor Novello . . . . Andreas Steiner
Fay Compton . . . . Jenny Gray
Jack Hawkins . . . . Alaric
Diana Beaumont . . . . Audrey
Muriel Aked . . . . Miss Mayne
Esme Church . . . . Edith
Frederick Ranalow . . . . Feldmann
Mignon O'Doherty . . . . Frau Feldmann
George Zucco . . . . Rev Mayne
ROMANCE Tyrol. Teacher on holiday falls
in love with married innkeeper.

09495
FOUR MASKED MEN (81) (A)
Real Art (U)
P: Julius Hagen
D: George Pearson
S: (PLAY) Cyril Campion
(THE MASQUERADERS)
SC: H. Fowler Mear, Cyril Campion
John Stuart . . . . Trevor Phillips
Judy Kelly . . . . Patricia Brent
Miles Mander . . . . Rodney Fraser
Richard Cooper . . . . . Lord Richard Clyne
Athole Stewart . . . . Col StJohn Clive
Sebastian Shaw . . . . Arthur Phillips
Victor Stanley . . . . Potter
CRIME Barrister poses as thief to unmask
gang who shot brother.

09496
THE ADMIRAL'S SECRET (63) (U)
Real Art (Radio)
P: Julius Hagen
D: Guy Newall
S: (PLAY) Cyril Campion, Edward Dignon
SC: H. Fowler Mear
Edmund Gwenn . . . . Admiral Fitzporter
Hope Davy . . . . Pamela Fitzporter
James Raglan . . . . Frank Bruce
Aubrey Mather . . . . Capt Brooke
Edgar Driver . . . . Sam Hawkins
Abraham Sofaer . . . Don Pablo Y Gonzales
Dorothy Black . . . . Donna Teresa
Andrea Malandrinos . . . . . Guido d'Elvira
D.J.Williams . . . . Questa
COMEDY Spanish brigands search for gems
stolen by retired Admiral.

09497
SPOTTING (series) (U)
New Era
P: Gordon Craig
D: G.B.Samuelson

09498
1: THE ACE OF TROUBLE (16)
Barry Livesey . . . . The Man

09499
2: A TOUCHING STORY (17)
Sydney Fairbrother . . . . . . The Woman

09500
3: HUSBANDS ARE SO JEALOUS (18)
Jack Livesey . . . . The Husband

09501
4: JADE (15)
Godfrey Tearle . . . . The Man

09502
5: LIPSKY'S CHRISTMAS DINNER (13)
Joe Hayman . . . . Lipsky

09503
6: THE END OF THE ACT (16)
Jack Livesey . . . . The Man

09504
7: THE GREATEST OF THESE (14)
Barry Livesey . . . . The Man

09505
8: OFF THE SCENT (13)

09506
9: AN AFFAIR OF THE HEART (17)

09507
10: THE DELUSION (14)

09508
11: THE GREEN LEATHER NOTE CASE (16)

09509
12: SPOILS (12)
DRAMAS Competition films containing
deliberate errors.

09510
SEEING IS BELIEVING (70) (U)
B & D-Paramount British
D: Redd Davis
S: Donovan Pedelty
Billy Hartnell . . . . Ronald Gibson
Gus McNaughton . . . . Geoffrey Cooper
Faith Bennett . . . . Marion Harvey
Vera Boggetti . . . . Nita Leonard
Fewlass Llewellyn . . . Sir Robert Gibson
Joan Periera . . . . Mme Bellini
Elsie Irving . . . . Lady Mander
COMEDY Police recruit mistakes girl for
thief and trails her aboard father's cruise ship.

09511
MURDER AT THE INN (56) (A)
WB-FN (WB)
P: Irving Asher
D: George King
S: Randall Faye
Wendy Barrie . . . . Angela Worthing
Harold French . . . . Tony
Jane Carr . . . . Fifi
Davy Burnaby . . . . Col Worthing
Nicholas Hannen . . . . Dedreet
Minnie Rayner . . . . Aunt
H.Saxon-Snell . . . . Inspector
CRIME Elopers involved in murder of
blackmailing landlord.

09512
BORROWED CLOTHES (70) (A)
Maude Productions (Col)
D: Arthur Maude
S: (PLAY) Aimee & Philip Stuart (HER SHOP)
Anne Grey . . . . Lady Mary Torrent
Lester Matthews . . . . . Sir Harry Torrent
Sunday Wilshin . . . . Lottie Forrest
Joe Hayman . . . . Herman Jacob
Renee Macready . . . . Diana Arbuthnot
P.G.Clark . . . . Donald MacDonald
Philip Strange . . . . Clarence Ponsonby

Antony Holles . . . . Gilbert Pinkley
Elizabeth Inglis . . . . Barbara
Constance Shotter . . . . . . Babette
COMEDY Extravagant Lady accidentally buys
couturiers.

MAR

09513
THE MAN WHO CHANGED HIS NAME (80)
(A)
Real Art (U)
P: Julius Hagen
D: Henry Edwards
S: (PLAY) Edgar Wallace
SC: H. Fowler Mear
Lyn Harding . . . . Selby Clive
Betty Stockfeld . . . . Nita Clive
Leslie Perrins . . . . Frank Ryan
Ben Welden . . . . Jerry Muller
Aubrey Mather . . . . . . Sir Ralph Whitcomb
Richard Dolman . . . . . . John Boscombe
CRIME Husband poses as murderer to prevent
wife's elopement.

09514
NIGHT CLUB QUEEN (87) (A)
Real Art (U)
P: Julius Hagen
D: Bernard Vorhaus
S: (PLAY) Anthony Kimmins
SC: H. Fowler Mear
Mary Clare . . . . Mary Brown
Lewis Casson . . . . Edward Brown
Jane Carr . . . . Bobbie Lamont
George Carney . . . . Hale
Lewis Shaw . . . . Peter Brown
Merle Tottenham . . . . Alice Lamont
Drusilla Wills . . . . Aggie
Syd Crossley . . . . Jimmy
Felix Aylmer . . . . Prosecution
Eight Black Streaks; Sherman Fisher Girls
CRIME Paralysed counsel defends wife on
framed murder charge.

09515
TANGLED EVIDENCE (57) (A)
Real Art (Radio)
P: Julius Hagen
D: George A. Cooper
S: (NOVEL) Mrs Champion de Crespigny
SC: H. Fowler Mear
Sam Livesey . . . . Insp Drayton
Joan Marion . . . . Anne Wilmot
Michael Hogan . . . . Ingram Underhill
Michael Shepley . . . . . . Gilbert Morfield
Reginald Tate . . . . Ellaby
Dick Francis . . . . Frame
Edgar Norfolk . . . . Dr Ackland
John Turnbull . . . . Moore
Davina Craig . . . . Faith
CRIME Inspector proves girl did not kill
occultist uncle.

09516
WHISPERING TONGUES (55) (A)
Real Art (Radio)
P: Julius Hagen
D: George Pearson
S: Bernerd Mainwaring
SC: H. Fowler Mear
Reginald Tate . . . . Alan Norton
Jane Welsh . . . . Claudia Mayland
Russell Thorndike . . . . Fenwick
Malcolm Keen . . . . Insp Dawley
Felix Aylmer . . . . Supt Fulton
Charles Carson . . . . Roger Mayland
Tonie Edgar Bruce . . . . . Lady Weaver
Victor Stanley . . . . Steward
CRIME Man and butler steal gems from those
responsible for father's suicide.

09517
THE QUEEN'S AFFAIR (77) (U)
USA: RUNAWAY QUEEN
B & D (UA)
P:D: Herbert Wilcox
S: (PLAY) Ernst Marischa, Bruno Granichstaedten (DIE KONIGIN)
SC: Samson Raphaelson, Monckton Hoffe, Miles Malleson
Anna Neagle . . . . Queen Nadina
Fernand Graavey . . . . Carl
Muriel Aked . . . . Marie Soubrekoff
Michael Hogan . . . . The Leader
Gibb McLaughlin . . . . . General Korensky
Miles Malleson . . . . The Chancellor
Stuart Robertson . . . . .A Revolutionary
Hay Petrie . . . . A Revolutionary
Edward Chapman . . . . A Soldier
Reginald Purdell . . . . A Soldier
Clifford Heatherley . . . . . A Diplomat
David Burns . . . . Manager
Trefor Jones . . . . Singer
MUSICAL Ruritania. Incognito president falls in love with incognito Queen he deposed.

09518
IT'S A COP (86) (A)
B & D (UA)
P: Herbert Wilcox
D: Maclean Rogers
S: (SKETCH) Charles Austin (PARKER PC)
SC: R.P.Weston, Bert Lee, Jack Marks, John Paddy Carstairs, Robert Cullen
Sydney Howard . . . . PC Robert Spry
Dorothy Bouchier . . . . Babette
Donald Calthrop . . . . Charles Murray
Garry Marsh . . . . James Risden
Annie Esmond . . . . Mrs Spry
Cyril Smith . . . . Lewis
John Turnbull . . . . Insp Gray
Ronald Simpson . . . . Bates
COMEDY Sacked PC promoted when he accidentally catches crooks.

09519
LUCKY LOSER (68) (A)
B & D-Paramount British
D: Reginald Denham
S: (PLAY) Matthew Brennan (THE BIG SWEEP)
SC: Anne Smith, Basil Mason
Richard Dolman . . . . Tom O'Grady
Aileen Marson . . . . Kathleen Willoughby
Anna Lee . . . . Ursula Hamilton
Annie Esmond . . . . Mrs Hamilton
Roland Culver . . . . Pat Hayden
Noel Shannon . . . . Peters
Joan White . . . . Alice
Gordon McLeod . . . . Auctioneer
COMEDY Man tries to recover desk he sold containing winning sweep ticket.

09520
SWEET INNISCARRA (72) (U)
Emmett Moore (Col)
D:S: Emmett Moore
Sean Rogers . . . . Gerald O'Carroll
Mae Ryan . . . . Kate
ROMANCE Ireland. Millionaire poses as schoolmaster to win colonel's daughter.

09521
BOOMERANG (82) (A)
Maude Productions (Col)
D: Arthur Maude
S: (PLAY) David Evans
SC: John Paddy Carstairs
Nora Swinburne . . . . Elizabeth Stafford
Lester Matthews . . . . David Kennedy
DRAMA Blind author discovers his wife is being blackmailed.

09522
GRAND PRIX (70) (U)
StJohn. L. Clowes & L.S.Stock (Col)
D:S: StJohn L.Clowes
John Stuart . . . . Jack Holford
Gillian Sande . . . . Jean McIntyre
Milton Rosmer . . . .
Peter Gawthorne . . . . John McIntyre
SPORT Racing car driver accidentally kills fiancee's father.

09523
DANGEROUS COMPANIONS (44) (U)
A.N.C.Macklin (Beacon)
D:S: A.N.C.Macklin
A.N.C.Macklin . . . . Noel
CRIME Jewel thief reforms and saves Lady's daughter from kidnappers.

09524
WITHOUT YOU (65) (A)
British Lion (Fox)
P: Herbert Smith
D: John Daumery
S: W. Scott Darling
SC: Michael Barringer
Henry Kendall . . . . Tony Bannister
Wendy Barrie . . . . Molly Bannister
Margot Grahame . . . . Margot Gilbey
Fred Duprez . . . . . . Baron von Steinmeyer
Georgie Harris . . . . Harrigan
Joe Hayman . . . . Blodgett
Billy Mayerl . . . . Fink
COMEDY Composer and playwright wife have trial separation and he is hired as co-respondent by her lover.

09525
THE MAN I WANT (68) (A)
British Lion (MGM)
P: Herbert Smith
D: Leslie Hiscott
S: MIchael Barringer
Henry Kendall . . . . Peter Mason
Wendy Barrie . . . . Marion Round
Betty Astell . . . . Prue
Davy Burnaby . . . . Sir George Round
Wally Patch . . . . Ernie
Hal Walters . . . . Haddock
COMEDY Man finds knight's stolen jewels.

09526
KEEP IT QUIET (64) (U)
British Lion (MGM)
P: Herbert Smith
D: Leslie Hiscott
S: Michael Barringer
Frank Pettingell . . . . . . Joe Puddlefoot
Jane Carr . . . . Nancy
Davy Burnaby . . . . Sir Charles Good
Cyril Raymond . . . . Jack
D.A.Clarke-Smith . . . . Vendervell
Bertha Belmore . . . . Mrs Puddlefoot
COMEDY Gem thieves blackmail man to act as butler in nephew's house.

09527
LOVE, LIFE AND LAUGHTER (83) (U)
ATP (ABFD)
P: Basil Dean
D: Maurice Elvey
S: Maurice Braddell
SC: Robert Edmunds
Gracie Fields . . . . Nellie Gwyn
John Loder . . . . Prince Charles
Norah Howard . . . . . Princess Grapfel
Allan Aynesworth . . . . King
Esme Percy . . . . Goebschen
Veronica Brady . . . . Mrs Gwyn
Horace Kenney . . . . Mr Gwyn
Robb Wilton . . . . Magistrate
Fred Duprez . . . . Greenbaum

A.Bromley Davenport . . . . Menkenburg
Ivor Barnard . . . . Troubetski
Eric Maturin . . . . Director
Elizabeth Jenns . . . . Actress
COMEDY Film star relinquishes prince for sake of Ruritania.

09528
THE TELL-TALE HEART (49) (A)
USA: BUCKET OF BLOOD
Clifton-Hurst (Fox)
P: Harry Clifton
D: Brian Desmond Hurst
S: (STORY) Edgar Allan Poe
SC: David Plunkett Greene
Norman Dryden . . . . The Boy
John Kelt . . . . The Old Man
Yolande Terrell . . . . The Girl
Thomas Shenton . . . . . First Investigator
James Fleck . . . . Second Investigator
Colonel Cameron . . . . Doctor
HORROR Mad killer confesses upon hearing his victim's heartbeats.

09529
THE WARREN CASE (75) (A)
BIP (Pathe)
P: Walter C.Mycroft
D:SC: Walter Summers
S: (PLAY) Arnold Ridley (THE LAST CHANCE)
Richard Bird . . . . Louis Bevan
Nancy Burne . . . . Mary Clavering
Diana Napier . . . . Pauline Warren
Edward Underdown . . . . . Hugh Waddon
Iris Ashley . . . . Elaine de Lisle
A.Bromley Davenport . . . Sir Richard Clavering
CRIME Mad reporter strangles mistress and frames fiance of employer's daughter.

09530
MASTER AND MAN (54) (U)
BIP (Pathe)
P: Walter C.Mycroft
D: John Harlow
S: Wallace Lupino
Wallace Lupino . . . . Wally
Barry Lupino . . . . Barry
Gus McNaughton . . . . Blackmailer
Faith Bennett . . . . Lady Sinden
Syd Crossley . . . . Coffee Stall Keeper
Hal Gordon . . . . Gamekeeper
Harry Terry . . . . Tiny
George Humphries . . . . Slim
COMEDY Two tramps save lady's house from arsonists.

09531
THE PATH OF GLORY (68) (U)
Triumph (PDC)
D: Dallas Bower
S: (PLAY) L.DuGarde Peach
SC: L.DuGarde Peach
Maurice Evans . . . . Anton Maroni
Valerie Hobson . . . . Maria
Felix Aylmer . . . . President of Thalia
Henry Daniell . . . . King Maximillian
Athole Stewart . . . . Gen Ferranzi
Stafford Hilliard . . . . Ferraldi
John Deverell . . . . Paul
David Burns . . . . Ginsberg
Frederick Burtwell . . . . . . Pedro
Harvey Braban . . . . Col Conti
Frank Atkinson . . . . Karl
COMEDY Two Ruritanian countries declare war and each tries to lose.

09532
THE DOUBLE EVENT (68) (A)
Triumph (PDC)
D: Leslie Howard Gordon
S: (PLAY) Sidney Blow, Douglas Hoare
Jane Baxter . . . . Evelyn Martingale
Ruth Taylor . . . . Aunt Laura

O.B.Clarence . . . . Rev Martingale
Alexander Field . . . . Charlie Weir
Bernard Lee . . . . Dennison
Sebastian Smith . . . . Uncle James
COMEDY Gambling cleric's daughter
becomes bookmaker until gambling
fiance breaks her.

09533
LITTLE STRANGER (51) (A)
George King (MGM)
reissue: 1943 (Fed; 100 ft cut).
D: George King
Nigel Playfair . . . . Sam Collins
Eva Moore . . . . Jessie Collins
Norah Baring . . . . Millie Dent
Hamilton Keene . . . . Tom Hale
DRAMA Old clerk's lodger dies and he
adopts her bastard.

09534
BY-PASS TO HAPPINESS (74) (A)
Sound City (Fox)
P: Ivar Campbell
D:S: Anthony Kimmins
Tamara Desni . . . . Tamara
Maurice Evans . . . . Robin
Kay Hammond . . . . Dinah
Mark Daly . . . . Wallop
Eliot Makeham . . . . Miller
Nellie Bowman . . . . Jane
John Teed . . . . Stephen
Billy Holland . . . . Jim
ROMANCE Girl helps ex-pilot make
success of dilapidated garage.

09535
DESIGNING WOMEN (71) (A)
Sound City (MGM) reissue: 1939,
HOUSE OF CARDS (Fed; 2048 ft cut).
P: Norman Loudon
D: Ivar Campbell
S: George Robinson
SC: N.W.Baring-Pemberton
Stewart Rome . . . . Travers
Valerie Taylor . . . . Diana Dent
Tyrell Davis . . . . Hildebrand Way
D.A.Clarke-Smith . . . . Bowsfield
Cyril Gardner . . . . Alan Dent
Kathleen Kelly . . . . Molly
Edgar Driver . . . . Green
DRAMA Ne'er-do-well's widow becomes
success in fashion business.

09536
WHITE ENSIGN (84) (U)
Sound City (MGM)
P: Ivar Campbell
D:S: John Hunt
Anthony Kimmins . . . . . . Cdr Falcon
Molly Lamont . . . . Col's Daughter
Kenneth Villiers . . . . Terry
Ivan Sampson . . . . Captain
Victor Stanley . . . . Seaman Steele
Anthony Ireland . . . .
Ivo Dawson . . . .
Ballard Berkeley . . . .
Edgar Driver . . . .
ADVENTURE Santa Barbara. British battle-
ship quells revolution promoted by big
business.

09537
THE CRUCIFIX (48) (A)
New Era (U)
P: Gordon Craig
D: G.B.Samuelson
S: G.B.Samuelson, Roland Pertwee
Nancy Price . . . . Miss Bryany
Sydney Fairbrother . . . . . .Lavinia Brooker
Farren Soutar . . . . Lord Louis

Brenda Harvey . . . . . . Miss Bryany (1886)
Audrey Cameron . . . . Lavinia (1886)
Pollie Emery . . . . Landlady
DRAMA Browbeaten companion steals
crucifix without knowing her late
mistress repented and left her everything.

09538
GUEST OF HONOUR (53)(U)
WB-FN(FN)
P: Irving Asher
D: George King
S: (PLAY) F.Anstey (THE MAN FROM
BLANKLEYS)
SC: W. Scott Darling
Henry Kendall . . . Lord Strathpeffer
Miki Hood . . . . Marjorie
Edward Chapman . . ,, . . Montague Tidmarsh
Margaret Yarde . . . . Emma Tidmarsh
Eve Gray . . . . Cissie Poffley
Joan Playfair . . . . Mrs Bodfish
Hay Plumb . . . . Mr Bodfish
Helen Ferrers . . . . Mrs Gilwattle
Cecil Humphreys . . . . . . Mr Gilwattle
Louis Goodrich . . . . Butler
COMEDY Lord posing as professional dinner
guest unmasks blackmailer.

09539
THE GIRL IN POSSESSION (72) (U)
WB-FN (WB)
P: Irving Asher
D: Monty Banks
Laura la Plante . . . . Eve Chandler
Henry Kendall . . . . Sir Mortimer
Claude Hulbert . . . . Cedric
Monty Banks . . . . Caruso
Bernard Nedell . . . . de Courville
Millicent Wolf . . . . Julie Garner
Ernest Sefton . . . . Wagstaffe
Charles Paton . . . . Saunders
COMEDY American girl tricked into
thinking she owns estate in England.

09540
THE UNFINISHED SYMPHONY (90) (U)
bilingual
Cine-Allianz (Gaumont)
P: Arnold Pressburger
D: Willi Forst, Anthony Asquith
S: Walter Reisch
SC: Willi Forst, Benn W.Levy
Marta Eggerth . . . . Caroline Esterhazy
Hans Yaray . . . . Franz Schubert
Helen Chandler . . . . Emmie Passenter
Ronald Squire . . . . Count Esterhazy
Paul Wagner . . . . Lt Folliot
Esme Percy . . . . ,, ... Huettenbrenner
Hermine Sperler. . . . . . . Princess Kinsky
Eliot Makeham . . . . Joseph Passenter
Cecil Humphreys . . . . . . Salieri
Beryl Laverick . . . . Mary Esterhazy
Brember Wills . . . . Secretary
Vienna Boys Choir
MUSICAL Vienna, 1820. Composer leaves
symphony unfinished when he loses love of
count's daughter.

09541
THE BATTLE (85) (A) bilingual
USA: THUNDER IN THE EAST
Lionofilm (Gau) reissue: 1943, HARA-KIRI
(13 mins cut)
P: Leon Garganoff
D: Nicolas Farkas
S: (NOVEL) Claude Farrere (LA BATAILLE)
(LA BATAILLE)
SC: Nicolas Farkas, Bernard Zimmer,
Robert Stevenson
Charles Boyer . . . . Marquis Yorisaka

John Loder . . . . Fergan
Merle Oberon . . . . Marquise Yorisaka
Betty Stockfeld . . . . Betty Hockley
Valerie Inkijinoff . . . . Mirata
Miles Mander . . . . Felze
Henri Fabert . . . . Admiral
WAR Japan, 1904. Japanese naval commander
makes wife vamp British Attache for
strategic secrets, and they fall in love.
(Made in France).

09542
MAN OF ARAN (75) (U)
Gainsborough (Gau)
P: Michael Balcon
D: Robert J. Flaherty
S: Robert J.Flaherty, Frances Flaherty
Colman 'Tiger' King . . . . . . A Man
Maggie Dirrane . . . . His Wife
Michael Dillane . . . . Their Son
Pat Mullen . . . . Crewman
Patch Ruadh . . . . Crewman
Patcheen Faherty . . . . . . Crewman
Tommy O'Rourke . . . . Canoeman
DRAMA Dramatised documentary of life on
the island of Aran.

09543
ROLLING IN MONEY (85) (A)
Fox British
P: John Barrow
D: Al Parker
S: (PLAY) R.C.Carton (MR HOPKINSON)
SC: R.J.Davis, Sewell Stokes, Frank
Atkinson
Isabel Jeans . . . Duchess of Braceborough
Leslie Sarony . . . . Mr Hopkinson
Horace Hodges . . . . Earl of Addleton
John Loder . . . . Lord Gawthorpe
Lawrence Grossmith. . Duke of Braceborough
Garry Marsh . . . . Dursingham
Anna Lee . . . . Lady Eggleby
Rene Ray . . . . Eliza Dibbs
C.M.Hallard . . . . Carter
Frank Atkinson . . . . Wiggins
COMEDY Broke duchess schemes to marry
daughter to newlyrich cockney barber.

09544
THE UNHOLY QUEST (56) (A)
Widgey Newman, Reginald Wyer, Bert Hop-
kins (EB)
D: R.W.Lotinga
S: Widgey Newman
Claude Bailey . . . . Prof Sorotoff
Terence de Marney . . . . . . Frank Davis
Cristine Adrien . . . . Vera
John Milton . . . . Hawkins
Harry Terry . . . . Soapy
Ian Wilson . . . . Wilky
HORROR Ex-convict butler kills blackmailer,
who is then used by doctor to revive
embalmed Crusader.

APR

09545
TWO HEARTS IN WALTZTIME (80) (U)
Nettlefold-Fogwell (Gaumont)
P: Reginald Fogwell
D: Carmine Gallone, Joe May
S: Walter Reisch, Franz Schulz
SC: Reginald Fogwell, John McNally
Carl Brisson . . . . Carl Hoffman
Frances Day . . . . Helene Barry
Bert Coote . . . . Danielli
Oscar Asche . . . . Herman Greenbaum
C. Denier Warren . . . . Meyer
Roland Culver . . . . Freddie
William Jenkins . . . . Max
Peter Gawthorne . . . . Mr Joseph

Valerie Hobson . . . . Susie
MUSICAL Vienna. Composer loves girl who
is actually star of his operetta.

09546
MOTOR MAGNATE (14) (U)
Electa Films
John Tilley . . . .
COMEDY

09547
MASTERSHIP (22) (U)
Gee Films (MacKane)
D:S: Aveling Ginever
Vi Kaley . . . .
Dorothy Vernon . . . .
RELIGION

09548
SURPRISE ITEM (10) (U)
International Productions
Mrs Borrett   Eugene Goossens
Leonard Henry   Ambrose and his Orchestra
REVUE

09549
PRINCESS CHARMING (78) (A)
Gainsborough (Gaumont)
P: Michael Balcon
D: Maurice Elvey
S: (PLAY) F.Martos (ALEXANDRA)
SC: L.DuGarde Peach, Arthur Wimperis,
Lauri Wylie
Evelyn Laye . . . . Princess Elaine
Yvonne Arnaud . . . . Countess Annette
George Grossmith . . . . . . King Charles
Max Miller . . . . Chuff
Harry Wilcoxon . . . . Capt Launa
Ivor McLaren . . . . Ernest
Finlay Currie . . . . Seegman
Ivor Barnard . . . . Ivanoff
Francis L.Sullivan . . . . Alakiev
MUSICAL Ruritania. Affianced Princess
weds Captain to escape revolution.

09550
EVERGREEN (90) (A)
Gaumont
P: Michael Balcon
D: Victor Saville
S: (PLAY) Benn W.Levy
SC: Emlyn Williams, Marjorie Gaffney
Jessie Matthews . . . . Harriet Green
Sonnie Hale . . . . Leslie Benn
Betty Balfour . . . . Maudie
Barry Mackay . . . . Tommy Thompson
Ivor McLaren . . . . Marquis of Staines
Hartley Power . . . . Treadwell
Patrick Ludlow . . . . Lord Shropshire
Betty Shale . . . . Mrs Hawkes
Marjorie Brooks . . . . Marjorie Moore
MUSICAL Girl posing as "ageless" mother
falls for man posing as her son.

09551
LOVE AT SECOND SIGHT (72) (U)
USA: THE GIRL THIEF
Radius (Wardour)
P: Julius Haimann
D: Paul Merzbach
S: Harold Simpson
SC: Frank Miller, Jack Davies
Marian Marsh . . . . Juliet
Anthony Bushell . . . . Bill
Claude Hulbert . . . . Alan Parsley
Ralph Ince . . . . McIntosh
Joan Gardner . . . . Evelyn
Stanley Holloway . . . . PC
Neil Kenyon . . . . Uncle Angus
Vivian Reynolds . . . . Butler
COMEDY Match king's daughter feigns
love for inventor of everlasting match.

09552
THE OUTCAST (74) (U)
BIP (Wardour)
P: Walter C.Mycroft
D: Norman Lee
S: Syd Courtenay, Lola Harvey
Leslie Fuller . . . . Bill Potter
Mary Glynne . . . . Eve Baxter
Hal Gordon . . . . Jim Truman
Jane Carr . . . . Nancy Acton
Gladdy Sewell . . . . May Truman
Jimmy Godden . . . . Harry
Wallace Geoffrey . . . . Ted Morton
Pat Aherne . . . . Burke
COMEDY Bankrupt bookie's pet greyhound
wins race despite crooks.

09553
THOSE WERE THE DAYS (80) (U)
BIP (Wardour) *reissue*: 1938 (AMB)
P: Walter C.Mycroft
D: Thomas Bentley
S: (PLAY) Arthur Wing Pinero
(THE MAGISTRATE)
SC: Fred Thompson, Frank Miller, Frank
Launder, Jack Jordan
Will Hay . . . . Brutus Poskett
Iris Hoey . . . . Agatha Poskett
Angela Baddeley . . . . Charlotte
Claud Allister . . . . Capt Horace Vale
George Graves . . . . Col Alexander Lukyn
John Mills . . . . Bobby
Jane Carr . . . . Minnie Taylor
Marguerite Allan . . . . Eve Douglas
H.F.Maltby . . . . Mr Bullamy
Lawrence Hanray . . . . Wormington
Syd Crossley . . . . Wyke
Wally Patch . . . . Insp Briggs
Jimmy Godden . . . . Pat Maloney
Jimmy Hanley . . . . Boy
Lily Morris; Harry Bedford
COMEDY 1890. Magistrate's second wife
conceals age by having her teenage son pose
as boy.

09554
NINE FORTY-FIVE (59) (A)
WB-FN (WB)
P: Irving Asher
D: George King
S: (PLAY) Owen Davis, Sewell Collins
SC: Brock Williams
Binnie Barnes . . . . Ruth Jordan
Donald Calthrop . . . . Dr Venables
Violet Farebrother . . . . Mrs Randall
Malcolm Tod . . . . James Everett
James Finlayson . . . . PC Doyle
George Merritt . . . . Insp Dickson
Ellis Irving . . . . Turner
Cecil Parker . . . . Robert Clayton
Janice Adair . . . . Molly Clayton
Margaret Yarde . . . . Margaret Clancy
Rene Ray . . . . Mary Doane
CRIME Dr proves that crime to which
three people confess was suicide.

09555
DANGEROUS GROUND (68) (A)
B & D - Paramount British
D: Norman Walker
S: Dion Titheradge
SC: Dion Titheradge, Dorothy Rowan
Malcolm Keen . . . . Mark Lyndon
Jack Raine . . . . Philip Tarry
Joyce Kennedy . . . . Claire Breedon
Martin Lewis . . . . John Breedon
Kathleen Kelly . . . . Joan Breedon
Gordon Begg . . . . Holford
Henry Longhurst . . . . Insp Hurley
CRIME Dead detective's fiancee unmasks
socialite as murderous fence.

MAY

09556
A CUP OF KINDNESS (81) (A)
Gaumont
P: Michael Balcon
D: Tom Walls
S: (PLAY) Ben Travers
SC: Ben Travers
Tom Walls . . . . Fred Tutt
Ralph Lynn . . . . Charlie Tutt
Robertson Hare . . . . . Ernest Ramsbottom
Dorothy Hyson . . . . Betty Ramsbottom
Claude Hulbert . . . . Stanley Tutt
Marie Wright . . . . Mrs Ramsbottom
Eva Moore . . . . Mrs Tutt
Veronica Rose . . . . Tilly Wynn
Gordon James . . . . Nicholas Ramsbottom
D.A.Clarke-Smith . . . . Mr Finch
J.Fisher White . . . . Vicar
COMEDY Couple wed despite parental feud
and are suspected of fraud.

09557
WILD BOY (85) (U)
Gainsborough (Gau)
P: Michael Balcon
D: Albert de Courville
S: Albert de Courville, J.E.Bradford
SC: Stafford Dickens
Sonnie Hale . . . . Billy Grosvenor
Gwynneth Lloyd . . . . Maggie Warren
Flanagan & Allen . . . . Bookmakers
Lyn Harding . . . . Redfern
Leonora Corbett . . . . Gladys
Ronald Squire . . . . Rollo
Fred Kitchen . . . . Plumber
Arthur Sinclair . . . . Murphy
Cyril Smith . . . . Kennel-boy
Mick the Miller . . . . Wild Boy
SPORT Crook's secretary helps greyhound
owner win dog derby.

09558
THE LASH (63) (A)
Real Art (Radio)
P: Julius Hagen
D: Henry Edwards
S: (PLAY) Cyril Campion
SC: Vera Allinson, H.Fowler Mear
Lyn Harding . . . . Bronson Haughton
John Mills . . . . Arthur Haughton
Joan Maude . . . . Dora Bush
Leslie Perrins . . . . Alec Larkin
Mary Jerrold . . . . Margaret Haughton
Aubrey Mather . . . . Col Bush
D.J.Williams . . . . Mr Charles
Roy Emerton . . . . Steve
Victor Stanley . . . . Jake
DRAMA Selfmade millionaire horsewhips son
who owns nightclub and neglects secret wife.

09559
THE BROKEN MELODY (84) (A)
Twickenham (AP&D) *reissue*: 1939,
VAGABOND VIOLINIST (8 mins. cut).
P: Julius Hagen
D:S: Bernard Vorhaus
SC: Vera Allinson, Michael Hankinson,
H.Fowler Mear
John Garrick . . . . Paul Verlaine
Margot Grahame . . . . Simone StClair
Merle Oberon . . . . Germaine
Austin Trevor . . . . Pierre
Charles Carson . . . . Dubonnet
Harry Terry . . . . Henri
Andrea Malandrinos . . . . . . Brissard
Tonie Edgar Bruce . . . . . . Vera
MUSICAL France. Composer kills
wife's lover and writes opera after escaping
from Devil's Island.

09560
PASSING SHADOWS (67) (A)
British Lion (Fox)
P: Herbert Smith
D: Leslie Hiscott
S: Michael Barringer
Edmund Gwenn . . . . David Lawrence
Barry Mackay . . . . Jim Lawrence
Aileen Marson . . . . Mary Willett
D.A.Clarke-Smith . . . . Stranger
Viola Lyel . . . . Mrs Willett
Wally Patch . . . . Sgt
John Turnbull . . . . Insp Goodall
Barbara Everest . . . . Mrs Lawrence
CRIME Burglar tricks chemist into believing
he killed man.

09561
WARN LONDON (68) (U)
British Lion *reissue*: 1945 (Ren)
P: Herbert Smith
D: T.Hayes Hunter
S:(NOVEL) Denison Clift
SC: Charles Bennett, Billie Bristow
Edmund Gwenn . . . . . . Dr Herman Krauss
John Loder . . . . Insp Yorke/Barraclough
Leonora Corbett . . . . Jill
D.A.Clarke-Smith . . . . Dr Nicoletti
Garry Marsh . . . . Van Der Meer
John Turnbull . . . . Insp Frayne
Raymond Lovell . . . . Prefect
Douglas Stewart . . . . Davis
CRIME Insp poses as tramp double to thwart
German criminologist.

09562
YSANI THE PRIESTESS (32) (U)
International Productions
D: Gordon Sherry
S: Raven Wood
Raven Wood . . . . Himself
Vivienne Bell . . . . Ysani
Charles Hay . . . . The Man
FANTASY Mummified priestess tells
audience's fortune with aid of live actor on
stage.

09563
BRIDES TO BE (68) (A)
B & D-Paramount British
D: Reginald Denham
S: (STORY) Basil Mason (SIGN PLEASE)
SC: Basil Mason
Betty Stockfeld . . . . Audrey Bland
Constance Shotter . . . . . . Maisie Beringer
Ronald Ward . . . . George Hutton
Olive Sloane . . . . Phyllis Hopper
Henry Oscar . . . . Laurie Randall
Ivor Barnard . . . . John Boyle
Gordon McLeod . . . . Snell
CRIME Crooks frame shopgirl for theft to
spoil her love for millionaire.

09564
THE CHURCH MOUSE (76) (A)
WB-FN (FN)
P: Irving Asher
D: Monty Banks
S: (PLAY) Ladislas Fodor, Paul Frank
SC: W. Scott Darling, Tom Geraghty
Laura la Plante . . . . Betty Miller
Ian Hunter . . . . Jonathan Steele
Edward Chapman . . . . Wormwood
Jane Carr . . . . Sylvia James
Clifford Heatherley . . . Sir Oswald Bottomley
John Batten . . . . Geoffrey Steele
Gibb McLaughlin . . . . Stubbings
Monty Banks . . . . Harry Blump
ROMANCE Banker's prim secretary blossoms
into beauty

09565
THE LUCK OF A SAILOR (66) (U)
BIP (Wardour)
P: Walter C.Mycroft
D: Robert Milton
S: (PLAY) Horton Giddy (CONTRABAND)
SC: Clifford Grey, Wolfgang Wilhelm
Greta Nissen . . . . Queen Helena
David Manners . . . . Capt Colin
Clifford Mollison . . . . Shorty
Camilla Horn . . . . Louise
Hugh Wakefield . . . . King Karl
Lawrence Grossmith . . . . . Silvius
Reginald Purdell . . . . Jenkins
H.F.Maltby . . . . Admiral
Jimmy Godden . . . . Betz
Jean Cadell . . . . Princess Rosanna
Cecil Ramage . . . . Owner
Gus McNaughton . . . . Official
ROMANCE Ruritanian Queen abdicates for
love of English captain.

09566
THE RETURN OF BULLDOG DRUMMOND
(71) (U)
BIP(Wardour)
P: Walter C.Mycroft
D:SC: Walter Summers
S: (NOVEL) "Sapper" (H.C.McNeile)
(THE BLACK GANG)
Ralph Richardson . . . . . . Hugh Drummond
Ann Todd . . . . Phyllis Drummond
Joyce Kennedy . . . . Irma Peterson
Francis L.Sullivan . . . . . Carl Peterson
Claud Allister . . . . Algy Longworth
H.Saxon-Snell . . . . Zadowa
Spencer Trevor . . . . Sir Bryan Johnstone
Charles Mortimer . . . . Insp McIver
Wallace Geoffrey . . . . Charles Latter
Pat Aherne . . . . Jerry Seymour
CRIME Ex-officer forms Black Clan to
fight crooked foreigners. (Extract in
ELSTREE STORY, 1952).

09567
THE SECRET OF THE LOCH (80) (U)
Wyndham (ABFD)
P: Bray Wyndham
D: Milton Rosmer
S: Charles Bennett, Billie Bristow
Seymour Hicks . . . . Professor Heggie
Nancy O'Neil . . . . Angela Heggie
Gibson Gowland . . . . Angus
Frederick Peisley . . . . Jimmy Andrews
Eric Hales . . . . Diver
Ben Field . . . . Piermaster
Hubert Harben . . . . . . Prof Fothergill
Stafford Hilliard . . . . Macdonald
Rosamund Johns . . . . Maggie
FANTASY Scotland. Diver discovers
prehistoric monster in Loch Ness.

09568
NOT FOR PUBLICATION (series)
Ace Films
P: Frank Green, R.A.Hopwood
D: Edwin Greenwood
S: John Quin

09569
1: THE MAN DOWNSTAIRS (20) (A)

09570
2: THREE WOMEN (18) (A)

09571
3: THE BLACK SKULL (21) (A)
Moore Marriott
CRIMES

09572
THE KING OF WHALES (44) (U)
Argonaut (MGM)
D: Challis Sanderson
Barrie Livesey . . . . Dan
Esmond Knight . . . . Gideon
Constance Travers . . . . . . Peggy
Humberston Wright . . . . . . Burt
Fred Raynham . . . . Claw
ADVENTURE Africa. Whaleship captain secures
ambergris despite crooked harpooner.

09573
HOW'S CHANCES (73) (A)
Sound City (Fox) reissue: 1939,
THE DIPLOMATIC LOVER (Llb; 2128 ft cut)
P: Norman Loudon
D: Anthony Kimmins
S: (PLAY) E.B.Leuthege, Kurt Braun
(DER FRAUENDIPLOMAT)
SC: Ivar Campbell, Harry Graham
Harold French . . . . Nottingham
Tamara Desni . . . . Helen
Davy Burnaby . . . . Michelo
Morton Selten . . . . Sir Charles
Reginald Gardiner . . . . . . Dersingham
Carol Rees . . . . Dolores
Peggy Novak . . . . Olga
Percy Walsh . . . . Castellano
Andrea Malandrinos . . . . . Machulla Ahab
MUSICAL Ruritania. Ballerina poses as
diplomat's fiancee to make friends jealous.

09574
SOMETIMES GOOD (68) (A)
Grafton (Par)
P: Fred Browett
D: W.P.Kellino
S: Emily Rushforth
SC: Michael Barringer
Henry Kendall . . . . Paul Everard
Nancy O'Neil . . . . Millie Tarrant
Minnie Rayner . . . . Jessica Mallory
Hal Gordon . . . . Michael Trout
Charles Mortimer . . . . John Everard
Madeleine Seymour . . . . . Mrs Everard
Jimmy Godden . . . . Col Mortimer
Edna Davies . . . . Ella Tyfield
Gladys Jennings . . . . Mrs Smyth-Jenkins
COMEDY Girl posing as colonel's daughter
loves ex-employer's son.

09575
THE GIRL IN THE FLAT (65) (A)
B & D-Paramount British
D: Redd Davis
S: (STORY) Evelyn Winch
SC: Violet Powell
Stewart Rome . . . . Sir John Waterton
Belle Chrystal . . . . Mavis Tremayne
Vera Boggetti . . . . Girda Long
Jane Millican . . . . Kitty Fellows
John Turnbull . . . . Insp Grice
Noel Shannon . . . . Maj Crull
CRIME Barrister's fiancee blackmailed over
murder of host.

09576
FREEDOM OF THE SEAS (74) (U)
BIP (Wardour)
P: Walter C.Mycroft
D: Marcel Varnel
S: (PLAY) Walter Hackett
SC: Roger Burford
Clifford Mollison . . . . Smith
Wendy Barrie . . . . Phyllis
Zelma O'Neal . . . . Jennie

H.F.Maltby . . . . Harcourt
James Carew . . . . Bolton
Frank Atkinson . . . . O'Hara
Henry Wenman . . . . Wallace
Tyrell Davis . . . . Cavendish
Cecil Ramage . . . . Bergstrom
Charles Paton . . . . Gamp
COMEDY Meek clerk joins navy, outwits
spies, and sinks submarine.

09577
BAGGED (40) (U)
BIP (Pathe)
P: Walter C.Mycroft
D: John Harlow
S: Wallace Lupino
Wallace Lupino . . . . Wally
Barry Lupino . . . . Barry
Gus McNaughton . . . . Anarchist
Syd Crossley . . . Coffee-stall Keeper
Hal Walters . . . . Cockney
COMEDY Anarchist dupes tramps into
delivering bomb to minister.

09578
OVER THE GARDEN WALL (68) (U)
BIP (Wardour) reissue: 1938 (Amb)
P: Walter C.Mycroft
D: John Daumery
S: (PLAY) H.F.Maltby
(THE YOUNGEST OF THREE)
SC: H.F.Maltby, Gordon Wellesley
Bobby Howes . . . . Bunny
Marian Marsh . . . . Mary
Margaret Bannerman . . . . . Diana
Viola Lyel . . . . Gladys
Bertha Belmore . . . . Jennifer
Syd Crossley . . . . Podds
Mary Sheridan . . . . Tilda
Fred Watts . . . . Thorold
MUSICAL Aunt objects to nephew's love
for neighbour's niece.

09579
NO ESCAPE (70) (A)
WB-FN (WB)
P: Irving Asher
D: Ralph Ince
S: W.Scott Darling
Binnie Barnes . . . . Myra Fengler
Ralph Ince . . . . Lucky
Ian Hunter . . . . Jim Brandon
Molly Lamont . . . . Helen Arnold
Charles Carson . . . . Mr Arnold
Philip Strange . . . . Kirk Fengler
Madeleine Seymour . . . . . . Mrs Arnold
George Merritt . . . . Insp Matheson
CRIME Malaya. Pursuit of planter framed for
poisoning partner and suspected of
carrying plague.

09580
SOMETHING ALWAYS HAPPENS (69) (U)
WB-FN (WB)
P: Irving Asher
D: Michael Powell
S: Brock Williams
Ian Hunter . . . . Peter
Nancy O'Neil . . . . Cynthia Hatch
Peter Gawthorne . . . . Mr Hatch
Johnny Singer . . . . Billy
Muriel George . . . . Mrs Badger
Barry Livesey . . . . George Hamlin
Millicent Wolf . . . . Glenda
Louie Emery . . . . Mrs Tremlett
COMEDY Car salesman loves secretary who
is really daughter of wealthy rival.

09581
MUSIC HALL (73) (U)
Real Art (Radio)
P: Julius Hagen
D: John Baxter
George Carney
Ben Field
Mark Daly
Helena Pickard
Olive Sloane
Wally Patch
Derrick de Marney
Peggy Novak
Edgar Driver
C.Denier Warren
Macari's Dutch Serenaders; Gershom Parking-
ton Quintet; Debroy Somers and his Band;
Chester's Performing Dogs; Raymond Newell;
G.H.Elliott; Eve Chapman; Sherman Fisher
Girls.
MUSICAL Modern showmanship saves old
music hall.

09582
THE PERFECT FLAW (5)) (A)
Fox British
D: Manning Haynes
S: Michael Barringer
Naomi Waters . . . . Phyllis Kearns
D.A.Clarke-Smith . . . . Louis Maddox
Ralph Truman . . . . Richard Drexel
Wally Patch . . . . Bert
Charles Carson . . . . Henry Kearns
Romilly Lunge . . . . Jack Robbins
Billy Hartnell . . . . Vickers
Hal Walters . . . . Jennings
CRIME Crooked clerk thwarted in attempt to
kill stockbroker.

JUL

09583
DANNY BOY (83) (U)
Panther (Butcher) reissue: 1937 (1275 ft cut).
P:D: Oswald Mitchell, Challis Sanderson
S: Oswald Mitchell, H.Barr-Carson
SC: Oswald Mitchell, H.Barr-Carson,
Archie Pitt
Frank Forbes-Robertson . . Pat Clare
Dorothy Dickson . . . . Jane Kaye
Archie Pitt . . . . Silver Sam
Ronnie Hepworth . . . . Danny
Denis O'Neil . . . . Mike
Cyril Ritchard . . . . John Martin
Fred Duprez . . . . Leo Newman
Paul Neville . . . . Maloney
Marcel de Haes and his Band
MUSICAL Singer's search for estranged
husband and son who have become buskers.
(Extract in HIGHLIGHTS OF VARIETY
No. 19 (1940).)

09584
SONG AT EVENTIDE (83) (A)
Argyle Talking Films (Butcher) reissue: 1937
(4065 ft cut)
P: John Argyle
D: Harry Hughes
S: John Hastings Turner
Fay Compton . . . . Helen d'Alaste
Lester Matthews . . . . Lord Belsize
Nancy Burne . . . . Patricia Belsize
Leslie Perrins . . . . Ricardo
Tom Helmore . . . . Michael Law
Minnie Rayner . . . . Blondie
O.B.Clarence . . . . Registrar
Alfred Wellesley . . . . Rosenbaum
Tully Comber . . . . Jim
Barbara Gott . . . . Anna

Charles Paton . . . . Director
Frank Titterton . . . . Singer
MUSICAL Blackmailed cabaret star turns
nun to save daughter from scandal.

09585
GIVE HER A RING (79) (U)
BIP (Pathe)
P: Walter C.Mycroft
D: Arthur Woods
S: (PLAY) H.Rosenfeld
(FRAULEIN FALSCH VERBUNDEN)
SC: Clifford Grey, Ernst Wolff, Marjorie
Deans, Wolfgang Wilhelm
Clifford Mollison . . . . Paul Hendrick
Wendy Barrie . . . . Karen Svenson
Zelma O'Neal . . . . Trude Olsen
Eric Rhodes . . . . Otto Brune
Bertha Belmore . . . . Miss Hoffman
Olive Blakeney . . . . Mrs Brune
Diamond Brothers . . . . Repair Men
Nadine March . . . . Karen's Friend
Jimmy Godden . . . . Uncle Rifkin
Syd Crossley . . . . Gustav
Richard Hearne . . . . Drunk
Stewart Granger . . . . Diner
Maurice Winnick's Ciro's Club Band
MUSICAL Copenhagen. Telephonist loves man
who is her employer.

09586
THE PRIMROSE PATH (70) (A)
B & D-Paramount British
D: Reginald Denham
S: (STORY) Joan Temple
SC: Basil Mason
Isobel Elsom . . . . Brenda Dorland
Whitmore Humphries . . . . David Marlow
Max Adrian . . . . Julian Leigh
Virginia Field . . . . Ianthe Dorland
Gordon McLeod . . . . Dr Dorland
Helen Ferrers . . . . Mrs Hassee
Ethel Stuart . . . . Fortuna
ROMANCE Dr's wife loves author who loves
her daughter.

09587
TO BE A LADY (68) (A)
B & D-Paramount British
D: George King
S: (STORY) C.H.Nicholson
SC: Violet Powell
Dorothy Bouchier . . . . Diana Whitcombe
Bruce Lister . . . . Jerry Dean
Vera Boggetti . . . . Countess Delavel
Charles Cullum . . . . Dudley Chalfont
Ena Moon . . . . Annette
Florence Vie . . . . Mrs Jubb
Tony de Lungo . . . . Manager
DRAMA Country girl becomes London
hairdresser and is wrongly convicted of theft.

09588
LILIES OF THE FIELD (83) (U)
B & D (UA)
P: Herbert Wilcox
D: Norman Walker
S: (PLAY) John Hastings Turner
SC: Dion Titheradge
Winifred Shotter . . . . Betty Beverley
Ellis Jeffreys . . . . Mrs Carmichael
Anthony Bushell . . . . Guy Mallory
Claude Hulbert . . . . Bryan Rigby
Judy Gunn . . . . Kitty Beverley
Jack Raine . . . . George Belwood
Bobbie Comber . . . . Withers
Hubert Harben . . . . Rev John Beverley
Maud Gill . . . . Mrs Beverley
Tonie Edgar Bruce . . . . Lady Rocker
Gladys Jennings . . . . Hon Monica Flane

Elsie French & John Mott (The Aspidistras)
COMEDY Cleric's daughter wins connoisseur
by posing as Victorian maiden.

09589
GIRLS PLEASE ! (73) (A)
B&D (UA) *reissue:* 1945 (EB)
P: Herbert Wilcox
D: Jack Raymond
S: Michael Hankinson, Basil Mason
SC: R.P.Weston, Bert Lee, Jack Marks
Sydney Howard . . . . Trampleasure
Jane Baxter . . . . . Renee van Hoffenheim
Meriel Forbes . . . . Ann Arundel
Edward Underdown . . . . . . Jim Arundel
Peter Gawthorne . . . . . . Van Hoffenheim
Lena Halliday . . . . Miss Prout
Cecily Oates . . . . Miss Kinter
Sybil Arundale . . . . Matron
Moore Marriott . . . . Oldest Inhabitant
COMEDY PT instructor poses as absent
headmistress of girls' school.

09590
THE LIFE OF THE PARTY (53) (A)
WB-FN (FN)
P: Irving Asher
D: Ralph Dawson
S: (PLAY) Margaret Mayo, Salisbury Field
(TWIN BEDS)
SC: Brock Williams
Jerry Verno . . . . Arthur Bleeby
Betty Astell . . . . Blanche Hopkins
Eric Fawcett . . . . Harry Hopkins
Vera Boggetti . . . . Caroline Bleeby
Kenneth Kove . . . . Andrew Larkin
Hermione Hannen . . . . . . Dora Reeves
Phyllis Morris . . . . Clarice
COMEDY Wife tries to hide drunken neighbour
from husband.

09591
CHU CHIN CHOW (102) (U)
Gainsborough (Gaumont)
P: Michael Balcon
D: Walter Forde
S: (PLAY) Oscar Asche, Frederick Norton
SC: Edward Knoblock, L. DuGarde Peach,
Sidney Gilliat
George Robey . . . . Ali Baba
Fritz Kortner . . . . Abu Hassan
Anna May Wong . . . . Zahrat
John Garrick . . . . Nur-al-din
Pearl Argyle . . . . Marjanah
Malcolm MacEachern . . . . . . Abdullah
Dennis Hoey . . . . Rakham
Francis L.Sullivan . . . . Caliph
Sydney Fairbrother . . . . . . Mahbubah
Lawrence Hanray . . . . Kasim Baba
Frank Cochrane . . . . Mustafa
Thelma Tuson ....'... ... Alcolom
Kyoshi Takase . . . . Entertainer
MUSICAL Slave girl foils robber posing as
mandarin he killed.

09592
LEST WE FORGET (60) (U)
Sound City (MGM)
P: Norman Loudon
D: John Baxter
S: Herbert Ayres
Stewart Rome . . . . Capt Rayner
George Carney . . . . Sgt Jock
Esmond Knight . . . . Pat Doyle jr
Ann Yates . . . . Sylvia Rayner
Roddy Hughes . . . . Taffy
Tony Quinn . . . . Pat Doyle
Wilson Coleman . . . . Butler
DRAMA Poor ex-captain feigns wealth to
keep reunion pact.

AUG
09593
LORD EDGWARE DIES (81) (A)
Real Art (Radio)
P: Julius Hagen
D: Henry Edwards
S: (NOVEL) Agatha Christie
SC: H.Fowler Mear
Austin Trevor . . . . Hercule Poirot
Jane Carr . . . . Lady Edgware
Richard Cooper . . . . Capt Hastings
John Turnbull . . . . Insp Japp
Michael Shepley . . . . . . Capt Ronald Marsh
Leslie Perrins . . . . Bryan Martin
C.V.France . . . . Lord Edgware
Esme Percy . . . . Duke of Merton
CRIME French tec proves old Lord was not
killed by young wife.

09594
BELLA DONNA (9)) (A)
Twickenham (Gaumont)
P: Julius Hagen
D: Robert Milton
S: (PLAY) James B. Fagan (NOVEL) Robert
Hichens
SC: H. Fowler Mear
Conrad Veidt . . . . Mahmoud Baroudi
Mary Ellis . . . . Mona Chepstowe
Cedric Hardwicke . . . . Dr Isaacson
John Stuart . . . . Nigel Armine
Jeanne Stuart . . . . Lady Harwick
Michael Shepley . . . . Dr Hartley
Rodney Millington . . . . Ibrahim
Eve . . . . Dancer
ROMANCE Woman tries to poison husband
for love of Egyptian.

09595
ARE YOU A MASON ? (84) (U)
Real Art (U)
P: Julius Hagen
D: Henry Edwards
S: (PLAY) Leo Dietrichstein, Emmanuel
Lederer
SC: H. Fowler Mear
Sonnie Hale . . . . Frank Parry
Robertson Hare . . . . Amos Bloodgood
Davy Burnaby . . . . John Halton
Gwynneth Lloyd . . . . Eva Parry
Joyce Kirby . . . . Lulu
Bertha Belmore . . . . Mrs Bloodgood
Lewis Shaw . . . . George Fisher
Michael Shepley . . . . Ernest Morrison
Davina Craig . . . . Annie
May Agate . . . . Mrs Halton
COMEDY Fake freemason gets friend to
pose as illegitimate daughter of his father-in-
law.

09596
NELL GWYN (85) (A)
B&D (UA) *reissues:* 1941 (EB; 10 mins cut);
1948 (EB)
P:D: Herbert Wilcox
S: Miles Malleson, Charles II, Nell Gwyn,
Samuel Pepys
SC: Miles Malleson
Anna Neagle . . . . Nell Gwyn
Cedric Hardwicke . . . . Charles II
Jeanne de Casalis . . Duchess of Portsmouth
Muriel George . . . . Meg
Miles Malleson . . . . Chiffinch
Esme Percy . . . . Samuel Pepys
Moore Marriott . . . . Robin
Lawrence Anderson . . . . . Duke of York
Craighall Sherry . . . . Ben
Helena Pickard . . . . Mrs Pepys
Dorothy Robinson . . . . Mrs Knipp

Julie Suedo . . . . Hortense
HISTORY 1668. Cockney actress and duchess
are rivals for king's love.

09597
GET YOUR MAN (67) (A)
B & D-Paramount British
D: George King
S: (PLAY) Louis Verneuil
(TU M'ESPOUSERAS)
SC: George Dewhurst
Dorothy Boyd . . . . Nancy McAlpine
Sebastian Shaw . . . . Robert Halbeam
Clifford Heatherley . . . . . Parker Halbeam
Hugh E.Wright . . . . Rev John Vivien
Kay Walsh . . . . Mary Vivien
Helen Ferrers . . . . Agatha McAlpine
Rex Harrison . . . . Tom Jakes
COMEDY Toothpaste magnate tries to force
son to wed rival's daughter.

09598
EASY MONEY (69) (U)
B & D-Paramount British
D: Redd Davis
S: (PLAY) Basil Mason (THE GHOSTS OF
MR PIM)
SC: Basil Mason
Mary Newland . . . . Joan Letchworth
Gerald Rawlinson . . . . . . Jock Durrant
George Carney . . . . Boggle
Lawrence Hanray . . . . Mr Pim
Hubert Leslie . . . . Col Hinckley
Harvey Braban . . . . Williams
Gladys Hamer . . . . Maggie
Rene Ray . . . . The Typist
COMEDY Bookmaker schemes to win money
from assistant, an heir apparent.

09599
THE OFFICE WIFE (43) (A)
WB-FN (WB)
P: Irving Asher
D: George King
S: (NOVEL) Faith Baldwin
SC: Randall Faye
Nora Swinburne . . . . Anne
Dorothy Bouchier . . . . Linda
Cecil Parker . . . . Lawrence Bradley
Percy Walsh . . . . Simms
Violet Farebrother . . . . . . Aunt Cynthia
Hamilton Keene . . . . Gregory
ROMANCE Publisher's divorced wife wins him
back after he weds secretary.
09600
WHAT HAPPENED TO HARKNESS (53) (U)
WB-FN(FN)
P: Irving Asher
D: Milton Rosmer
S: Roland Brown
SC: Brock Williams
Robert Hale . . . . Sgt McCabe
James Finlayson . . . . PC Gallun
Brember Wills . . . . Bernard Harkness
John Turnbull . . . . Insp Marlow
Clare Harris . . . . Mrs Millett
Wally Patch . . . . Bullett
Morland Graham . . . . Billy
Veronica Brady . . . . Mrs Bullett
Aubrey Mallalieu . . . . Dr Powin
Kathleen Kelly . . . . Pat
COMEDY Village policemen investigate
apparent murder of miser.

09601
BLOSSOM TIME (90) (A) USA: APRIL
ROMANCE
BIP (Wardour)
P: Walter C.Mycroft

D: Paul Stein
S: Franz Schulz
SC: John Drinkwater, Roger Burford, Paul Perez, G.H. Clutsam

Richard Tauber	Franz Schubert
Jane Baxter	Vicki Wimpassinger
Carl Esmond	Rudi
Athene Seyler	Archduchess
Paul Graetz	Alois Wimpassinger
Charles Carson	Lafont
Marguerite Allan	Baroness
Edward Chapman	Meyerhoffer
Lester Matthews	Schwindt
Gibb McLaughlin	Bauernfield
Frederick Lloyd	Captain
Hugh Dempster	Willi
Bertha Belmore	Madame

MUSICAL Vienna, 1826. Composer loves girl but helps her win dragoon she loves.
(FWA: 1935; extract in ELSTREE STORY, 1952.)

09602
THE GREAT DEFENDER (74) (U)
BIP (Wardour)
P: Walter C.Mycroft
D: Thomas Bentley
S: John Hastings Turner
SC: Marjorie Deans, Paul Perez

Matheson Lang	Sir Douglas Rolls
Margaret Bannerman	Laura Locke
Arthur Margetson	Leslie Locke
Richard Bird	Eric Hammond
Jeanne Stuart	Phyllis Ware
J.Fisher White	Judge
Sam Livesey	Sir Henry Lingard
Lawrence Hanray	Parker
O.B.Clarence	Mr Hammond
Mary Jerrold	Mrs Hammond
Frank Atkinson	Pope
Kathleen Harrison	Maid
Jimmy Godden	Insp Holmes

CRIME Sick KC proves beloved's husband did not stab mistress.

09603
LOST IN THE LEGION (66) (U)
BIP (Wardour)
P: Walter C.Mycroft
D: Fred Newmeyer
S: Syd Courtenay, Lola Harvey
SC: Syd Courtenay, John Paddy Carstairs

Leslie Fuller	Bill
Renee Houston	Mary McFee
Betty Fields	Sally Hogg
Hal Gordon	Alf
H.F.Maltby	Kaid
Alf Goddard	Sgt Mulligan
James Knight	Ryan
Mike Johnson	Fritz
A.Bromley Davenport	Colonel

COMEDY Ship's cooks join legion and save girls from harem.

09604
PATHETONE PARADE (4)) (U)
Pathe
D: Fred Watts

Ronald Frankau	Compere
Robb Wilton	Lily Morris
Sandy Powell	Gus Elen
Sam Mayo	Dorrie Dene
Collinson & Dean	Max & Harry Nesbitt
Arthur Prince and Jim	

REVUE Extracts from "Pathetone Weekly."

09605
JAVA HEAD (85) (A)
ATP (ABFD) reissue: 1944 (Ren)

P: Basil Dean
D: J. Walter Ruben
S: (NOVEL) Joseph Hergesheimer
SC: Martin Brown, Gordon Wellesley

Anna May Wong	Taou Yen
Elizabeth Allan	Nettie Vollar
John Loder	Gerrit Ammidon
Edmund Gwenn	Jeremy Ammidon
Ralph Richardson	William Ammidon
Herbert Lomas	Barzil Dunsack
George Curzon	Edward Dunsack
Roy Emerton	Broadrick
John Marriner	John Stone
Grey Blake	Roger Brevard
Amy Brandon Thomas	Rhoda

ROMANCE Bristol, 1850. Shipbuilder marries Manchu who kills herself on learning he loves English girl.

09606
MY SONG FOR YOU (86) (U)
Gaumont reissue: 1941 (EB; cut)
P: Jerome Jackson
D: Maurice Elvey
S: Ernst Marischka, Irma Von Cube
(EIN LEID FUR DICH)
SC: Austin Melford, Robert Edmunds, Richard Benson

Jan Kiepura	Gatti
Sonnie Hale	Charlie
Emlyn Williams	Theodore
Aileen Marson	Mary Newberg
Gina Malo	Fifi
Muriel George	Mrs Newberg
George Merritt	Mr Newberg
Reginald Smith	Kleeberg

MUSICAL Vienna. Chorus girl uses tenor's love to get pianist sweetheart job in opera.

09607
LITTLE FRIEND (85) (A)
Gaumont
AP: Robert Stevenson
D: Berthold Viertel
S: (NOVEL) Ernst Lothar
SC: Margaret Kennedy, Christopher Isherwood, Berthold Viertel

Matheson Lang	John Hughes
Nova Pilbeam	Felicity Hughes
Lydia Sherwood	Helen Hughes
Arthur Margetson	Hilliard
Allan Aynesworth	Col Amberley
Jean Cadell	Miss Drew
Jimmy Hanley	Leonard Parry
Lewis Casson	Judge
Clare Greet	Mrs Parry
Cecil Parker	Mason
Finlay Currie	Grove
Gibb McLaughlin	Thompson
Jack Raine	Jeffries

DRAMA Child's attempted suicide stops parents' divorce.

09608
GAY LOVE (76) (A)
British Lion reissue: 1939 (EB)
P: Herbert Smith
D: Leslie Hiscott
S: (PLAY) Audrey & Waveney Carton
SC: Charles Bennett, Billie Bristow, John Paddy Carstairs

Florence Desmond	Gloria Fellowes
Sophie Tucker	Sophie Tucker
Sydney Fairbrother	Dukie
Enid Stamp-Taylor	Marie Hopkins
Ivor McLaren	Lord Tony Eaton
Garry Marsh	Freddie Milton
Leslie Perrins	Gerald Sparkes
Ben Welden	Ben

Finlay Currie	Highams

MUSICAL Singer loves lord and finds he is engaged to her sister.

SEP

09609
LEAVE IT TO BLANCHE (51) (U)
WB-FN (FN)
P: Irving Asher
D: Harold Young
S: Roland Brown
SC: Brock Williams

Henry Kendall	Peter Manners
Olive Blakeney	Blanche Wetherby
Miki Hood	Doris Manners
Griffith Jones	Philip Amesbury
Rex Harrison	Ronnie
Hamilton Keene	Brewster
Julian Royce	Patteridge
Elizabeth Jenns	Blossom
Harold Warrender	Guardee
Phyllis Stanley	Singer

COMEDY Husband pretends to kill wife's lover and is convinced he succeeded.

09610
TOO MANY MILLIONS (57) (U)
WB-FN (WB)
P: Irving Asher
D: Harold Young
SC: Brock Williams

Betty Compton	Anne
John Garrick	Bill
Viola Keats	Viola
Athole Stewart	Mr Olcott
James Carew	Mr Worthing
Martita Hunt	Mrs Pilcher
Phyllis Stanley	Tamara
Sybil Grove	Mrs Runcorn

ROMANCE Millionairess poses as maid to help and woo poor artist.

09611
THE BLUE SQUADRON (74) (A)
WB-FN-Steffano Pittaluga (FN)
P: Irving Asher
D: George King
SC: Brock Williams

Esmond Knight	Capt Carlo Banti
John Stuart	Col Mario Spada
Greta Hansen	Elene
Cecil Parker	Bianci
Ralph Reader	
Barrie Livesey	
Hay Plumb	
Hamilton Keene	

ADVENTURE Italy. Colonel loses girl to rival, but saves his life in Alps.

09612
FATHER AND SON (48) (A)
WB-FN (WB)
P: Irving Asher
D: Monty Banks
S: (NOVEL) Ben Ames Williams
(BARBER JOHN'S BOY)
SC: Randall Faye

Edmund Gwenn	John Bolton
Esmond Knight	Michael Bolton
James Finlayson	Bildad
Charles Carson	Colin Bolton
Daphne Courtney	Emily Yates
O.B. Clarence	Tom Yates
Margaret Yarde	Victoria
Roland Culver	Vincent

CRIME Bank clerk takes blame for theft which he thinks was committed by ex-convict father.

09613
THE PRIVATE LIFE OF DON JUAN (90) (A)
London (UA)
P:D: Alexander Korda
S: (PLAY) Henri Bataille
SC: Lajos Biro, Frederick Lonsdale

Douglas Fairbanks	Don Juan
Merle Oberon	Antonia
Benita Hume	Dolores
Binnie Barnes	Rosita
Joan Gardner	Carmen
Melville Cooper	Leporello
Athene Seyler	Theresa
Owen Nares	Actor
Patricia Hilliard	Girl in Castle
Gina Malo	Pepita
Heather Thatcher	Actress
Claud Allister	Duke
Barry Mackay	Roderigo
Lawrence Grossmith	Guardian
Edmund Breon	Author
Clifford Heatherley	Pedro
Diana Napier	Would-be Wife
Gibson Gowland	Don Ascanio
Hay Petrie	Manager
Natalie Paley	Wife

COMEDY Spain, 1650. Ageing lover fakes death and tries to stage come-back.

09614
FALLING IN LOVE (80) (U) USA:
TROUBLE AHEAD
Vogue (Pathe)
P: Howard Welsch
D: Monty Banks
S: E.Bard, A. Hyman, Lee Loeb
SC: Fred Thompson, Miles Malleson, John Paddy Carstairs

Charles Farrell	Howard Ellison
Gregory Ratoff	Oscar Marks
Margot Grahame	June Desmond
Mary Lawson	Ann Brent
H.F.Maltby	Cummins
Diana Napier	Winnie
Cathleen Nesbitt	Mother
Pat Aherne	Dick Turner

COMEDY Publicity man tries to stop Hollywood star from loving orphan.

09615
THERE GOES SUSIE (79) (A) USA:
SCANDALS OF PARIS
Stafford (Pathe)
D: John Stafford, Victor Hanbury

Gene Gerrard	Andre Cochet
Wendy Barrie	Madeleine Sarteaux
Zelma O'Neal	Bunny
Gus McNaughton	Brammell
Henry Wenman	Otto Sarteaux
Bobbie Comber	Uncle Oscar
Gibb McLaughlin	Manager
Mark Daly	Sunshine

MUSICAL Soap magnate's daughter poses as artist's model and her painting is sold as poster for rival.

09616
GIRLS WILL BE BOYS (70) (U)
BIP (Wardour)
P: Walter C. Mycroft
D: Marcel Varnel
S: (PLAY) Kurt Siodmak (THE LAST LORD)
SC: Kurt Siodmak, Clifford Grey, Roger Burford

Dolly Haas	Pat Caverley
Cyril Maude	Duke of Bridgwater
Esmond Knight	Geoffrey Dawson
Irene Vanbrugh	Princess of Ehrenstein
Edward Chapman	Grey
Ronald Ward	Bernard

Charles Paton	Sanders
H.F.Maltby	
Alfred Wellesley	

COMEDY Girl poses as grandson of noble misogynist.

09617
WHAT HAPPENED THEN ? (62) (A)
BIP (Wardour)
P: Walter C.Mycroft
D:SC: Walter Summers
S: (PLAY) Lilian Trimble Bradley

Richard Bird	Peter Bromley
Lorna Storm	Alicia Deverton
Francis L. Sullivan	Richard Bentley KC
Geoffrey Wardwell	Raymond Rudford
Richard Gray	Robert
Cecil Ramage	Defence
George Zucco	Insp Hull
J.Fisher White	Judge
Stella Arbenina	Mrs Bromley
Lawrence Hanray	Dr Bristol

CRIME Homicidal maniac kills uncle for interfering with romance.

09618
SING AS WE GO (80) (U)
ATP (ABFD) *reissue:* 1953 (EB)
P:D: Basil Dean
S: J.B.Priestley
SC: Gordon Wellesley

Gracie Fields	Gracie Platt
John Loder	Hugh Phillips
Dorothy Hyson	Phyllis Logan
Stanley Holloway	Policeman
Frank Pettingell	Murgatroyd Platt
Lawrence Grossmith	Sir William Upton
Morris Harvey	Cowboy
Arthur Sinclair	Maestro
Maire O'Neill	Mme Osiris
Ben Field	Nobby
Olive Sloane	Violet
Margaret Yarde	Mrs Clotty
Evelyn Roberts	Parkinson
Norman Walker	Hezekiah Crabtree

COMEDY. Blackpool. Unemployed millgirl tries various jobs during holiday season.

09619
LOVE — MIRTH — MELODY (64) (U)
Mancunian (U)
P: John E. Blakeley
D: Bert Tracy

Graham Payn	Arthur Pond
Annie Rooney	Billy Percy
Phil Strickland	Madge Stevens
Tony Prior	Little Teddy Grey
Royal Merry Four	Little Jean and Joan
Lionel Claff and his Band	
Duggie Ascot's Dancing Girls	

REVUE (Extracts in MUSIC HALL PERSONALITIES No. 14 (1940)

09620
VIRGINIA'S HUSBAND (71) (U)
George Smith (Fox)
D: Maclean Rogers
S: (PLAY) Florence Kilpatrick

Dorothy Boyd	Virginia Trevor
Reginald Gardiner	John Craddock
Enid Stamp-Taylor	June Haslett
Ena Grossmith	Elizabeth
Annie Esmond	Mrs Elkins
Sebastian Smith	Mr Ritchie
Wally Patch	Police Sgt
Tom Helmore	Barney Hammond
Andrea Malandrinos	Headwaiter
Hal Walters	Mechanic

COMEDY Girl hires bachelor to pose as her husband and fool rich aunt.

09621
ANYTHING MIGHT HAPPEN (66) (A)
Real Art (Radio)
P: Julius Hagen
D: George A. Cooper
S: (NOVEL) Lady Evelyn Balfour
SC: H. Fowler Mear

John Garrick	Nicholson/Raybourn
Judy Kelly	Kit Dundas
Martin Walker	Kenneth Waring
Aubrey Mather	Seymour
D.J.Williams	Brown
Albert Whelan	Strickland

CRIME Reformed gangster is double of criminal.

09622
BADGER'S GREEN (68) (U)
B & D-Paramount British
D: Adrian Brunel
S: (PLAY) R.C.Sheriff
SC: R.J.Davis, Violet Powell

Valerie Hobson	Molly Butler
Bruce Lister	Dickie Wetherby
Frank Moore	Dr Wetherby
David Horne	Maj Forrester
Sebastian Smith	Mr Twigg
John Turnbull	Thomas Butler
Wally Patch	Mr Rogers
Elsie Irving	Mrs Wetherby

COMEDY Villagers unite against business man's scheme to build on cricket green.

09623
THE MEDIUM (38) (A)
Film Tests (MGM)
P: Walter Tennyson
D:SC: Vernon Sewell
S: (PLAY) Pierre Mills, Celia de Vylars (L'ANGOISSE)

Nancy O'Neil	Carol
Shayle Gardner	Dr Petrov
Barbara Gott	Maria
Richard Littledale	Martin
Ben Welden	Deval
Sandra Lawson	Annette

CRIME Psychic model reveals that mad sculptor hid dead wife in statue.

09624
A MINIATURE BROADCAST (9) (U)
Harry B. Harrison (B & N)
MUSICAL

09625
MONEY MAD (68) (A)
Champion (MGM)
P: Basil Humphrys
D: Frank Richardson
S: Selwyn Jepson

Virginia Cherrill	Linda
Garry Marsh	Rutherford
D.A.Clarke-Smith	Phillips
Peter Gawthorne	Sir John Leyland
Helen Haye	Lady Leyland
Lawrence Anderson	Chauffeur
Dennis Wyndham	Assistant

DRAMA Government official stops financier from inflating pound.

09626
ROMANCE IN RHYTHM (73) (A)
Allied Film Productions (MGM) *reissue:* 1940,
NIGHT CLUB MURDER (Coronel)
P:D: Lawrence Huntingdon

Phyllis Clare	Ruth Lee
David Hutcheson	Bob Mervyn
David Burns	Mollari

Carroll Gibbons and his Savoy Orpheans
MUSICAL Songwriter suspected when nightclub owner kills manager.

09627
CRAZY PEOPLE (67) (U)
British Lion (MGM)
D: Leslie Hiscott
S: (NOVEL) Margot Neville (SAFETY FIRST)
SC: Michael Barringer
Henry Kendall .... Hippo Rayne
Nancy O'Neil .... Nanda Macdonald
Kenneth Kove ..... Birdie Nightingale
Helen Haye .... Aunt Caroline
Vera Bogetti ....
Wally Patch ....
Hal Walters ....
Hugh E.Wright ....
Herschel Henlere; Al Oakes and his Three
Stooges
COMEDY Man has friends pose as lunatics to
fool rich aunt.

OCT

09628
WISHES (35) (U)
BIP (Pathe)
P: Walter C.Mycroft
D: W.P.Kellino
S: Wallace Lupino
Wallace Lupino .... Wally
Barry Lupino .... Barry
Gus McNaughton ....
Hal Gordon
COMEDY Two tramps find talisman which
grants wishes.

09629
MY SONG GOES ROUND THE WORLD (68)
(U)
BIP (Wardour)
P:D: Richard Oswald
S: Ernst Neubach (EIN LEID GEHT UM DIE
WELT)
SC: Clifford Grey, Frank Miller
Joseph Schmidt .... Ricardo
John Loder .... Rico
Charlotte Ander .... Nina
Jack Barty .... Simoni
Jimmy Godden .... Manager
Hal Gordon .... Stage-manager
MUSICAL Venice. Small tenor loses
sweetheart to tall friend.

09630
MISTER CINDERS (72) (U)
BIP (Wardour)
P: Walter C.Mycroft
D: Fred Zelnik
S: (PLAY) Clifford Grey, Frank Miller,
Greatrex Newman
SC: Clifford Grey, Frank Miller, Jack Davies,
Western Brothers
Clifford Mollison .... Jim Lancaster
Zelma O'Neal .... Jill Kemp
Kenneth Western .... Lumley Lancaster
George Western .... Guy Lancaster
W.H.Berry .... PC Merks
Renee Houston .... Mrs Phipps
Edward Chapman .... Mr Gaunt
Edmond Breon ...... Sir George Lancaster
Finlay Currie .... Henry Kemp
Lorna Storm .... Minerva Kemp
Esme Church .... Lady Agatha Lancaster
Henry Mollison .... Cross
Ellen Pollock .... Donna Lucia
MUSICAL American heiress posing as servant
loves rich man's poor nephew who is framed for
theft.

09631
EVENSONG (84) (U)
Gaumont
P: Michael Balcon

D: Victor Saville
S: (NOVEL) Beverley Nicholls (PLAY)
Edward Knoblock
SC: Edward Knoblock, Dorothy Farnum
Evelyn Laye .... Irela
Fritz Kortner .... Kober
Alice Delysia .... Mme Valmond
Carl Esmond .... Archduke Theodore
Emlyn Williams .... George Murray
Conchita Supervia .... Baba
Muriel Aked .... Tremlowe
Dennis Val Norton .... Sovino
Arthur Sinclair .... Pa McNeill
Pat O'Moore .... Bob McNeill
Browning Mummery ...... Tenor
MUSICAL Austria, period. Irish prima donna
gives up career for love.

09632
MY OLD DUTCH (82) (U)
Gainsborough (Gaumont)
AP: Ivor Montagu
D: Sinclair Hill
S: Albert Chevalier, Arthur Shirley;
Leslie Arliss, Bryan Wallace
SC: Bryan Wallace, Marjorie Gaffney, Mary
Murillo, Michael Hogan.
Betty Balfour Lil
Gordon Harker .... Ernie
Michael Hogan .... Bert
Florrie Forde .... Aunt Bertha
Mickey Brantford .... Jim
Glennis Lorimer .... Valerie Paraday
Peter Gawthorne .... Mr Paraday
Frank Pettingell .... Uncle Alf
Robert Nainby .... Grandpa
Billy Shine .... Cousin Arry
Finlay Currie .... MO
Felix Aylmer .... Judge
John Singer .... Jim (child)
DRAMA Cockney couple's son weds rich
man's disowned daughter and dies in the
RFC. (Includes extract from 1915 version).

09633
THE CAMELS ARE COMING (80) (U)
Gainsborough (Gaumont) reissue: 1941 (Ex)
P: Michael Balcon
D: Tim Whelan
S: Tim Whelan, Russell Medcraft,
SC: Guy Bolton, Jack Hulbert, W.P.Lipscomb
Jack Hulbert .... Jack Campbell
Anna Lee .... Anita Rodgers
Hartley Power .... Nicholas
Harold Huth .... Dr Zhiga
Allan Jeayes .... Sheikh
Peter Gawthorne .... Col Fairley
Norma Whalley .... Tourist
Peggy Simpson .... Tourist
Percy Parsons .... Arab
Tony de Lungo .... Servant
COMEDY Egypt. Camel Corps officer poses
as sheik to catch drug smugglers.

09634
JEW SUSS (109) (A) USA: POWER
Gaumont
P: Michael Balcon
D: Lothar Mendes
S: (NOVEL) Leon Feuchtwangler
SC: Dorothy Farnum, A.R.Rawlinson
Conrad Veidt .... Joseph Oppenheimer
Benita Hume .... Marie Auguste
Frank Vosper .... Karl Alexander
Cedric Hardwicke .... Rabbi Gabriel
Gerald du Maurier .... Wessensee
Pamela Ostrer .... Naomi
Joan Maude .... Magdalene Sibylle
Paul Graetz .... Landauer

Mary Clare .... Countess Wurben
Haidee Wright .... Michele
Percy Parsons .... Pflug
Eva Moore .... Jantje
James Raglan .... Lord Suffolk
Sam Livesey .... Harprecht
Dennis Hoey .... Dieterle
Campbell Gullan .... Thurne-Taxis
Gibb McLaughlin .... Pancorgo
Hay Plumb .... Pfaeffle
DRAMA Wurtemburg, 1730. Jew attains power
to help race and then finds he is gentile.

09635
FORBIDDEN TERRITORY (82) (U)
Progress Pictures (Gaumont)
reissue: 1940 (Ex; 10 mins cut)
P: Richard Wainwright
D: Phil Rosen
S: (NOVEL) Dennis Wheatley
SC: Dorothy Farnum, Alma Reville
Gregory Ratoff .... Alexei Leshki
Ronald Squire ..... Sir Charles Farringdon
Binnie Barnes .... Valerie Petrovna
Tamara Desni .... Marie-Louise
Barry Mackay .... Michael Farringdon
Anthony Bushell .... Rex Farringdon
Anton Dolin .... Jack Straw
Marguerite Allan .... Fenya
Boris Ranevsky .... Runov
ADVENTURE Russia. Girl singer helps
British bart and son rescue second son
from Siberian prison.

09636
THE SCOOP (68) (A)
B & D-Paramount British
D: Maclean Rogers
S: (PLAY) Jack Heming
SC: Gerald Geraghty, Basil Mason
Anne Grey .... Mrs Banyon
Tom Helmore .... Scoop Moreton
Peggy Blythe .... Marion Melville
Wally Patch .... Harry Humphries
Arthur Hambling .... Insp Stephenson
Reginald Bach .... Daniels
Roland Culver .... Barney Somers
Cameron Carr .... Douglas Banyon
Marjorie Shotter .... Reporter
Moore Marriott .... Jim Stewart
CRIME Reporter reveals he killed jealous
traveller in self-defence.

09637
ADVENTURE LIMITED (69) (A)
B & D-Paramount British
D: George King
S: (PLAY) Cyril Campion (TRUST BERKELEY)
SC: George Dewhurst
Harry Milton .... Kim Berkeley
Pearl Argyle .... Anita Lorenzo
Sebastian Shaw ...... Bruce Blandford
Sam Wilkinson .... Reginald Purdie
Clifford Heatherley .. Sir Matthew Muller
Hugh E.Wright . Don Lorenzo/Montagu Phelps
Lawrence Hanray .... Simon Ledbury
Cecil Humphreys .... Gen Baroda
COMEDY South America. Group use actor
to rescue double, imprisoned ex-president.

09638
THE BROKEN ROSARY (85) (U)
Butcher reissue: 1937 (4068 ft cut)
P: Wilfred Noy
D: Harry Hughes
S: (POEM) Adelaide Proctor
(LEGEND OF PROVENCE)
Derek Oldham .... Giovanni
Jean Adrienne .... Maria
Vesta Victoria .... Vesta

Ronald Ward . . . . Jack
Marjorie Corbett . . . . Celia
Margaret Yarde . . . . Nanny
Evelyn Roberts . . . . Uncle Jack
Dino Galvani . . . . Carlo
Fred Rains . . . . Professor
Ian Wilson . . . . Hodge
MUSICAL Italian singer loses sweetheart
to best friend.

09639
BLIND JUSTICE (73) (A)
Real Art (U)
P: Julius Hagen
D: Bernard Vorhaus
S: (PLAY) Arnold Ridley
(RECIPE FOR MURDER)
SC: Vera Allinson
Eva Moore . . . . Fluffy
Frank Vosper . . . . Dick Cheriton
John Stuart . . . . John Summers
Geraldine Fitzgerald . . . . Peggy Summers
John Mills . . . . Ralph Summers
Lucy Beaumont . . . . Mrs Summers
Hay Petrie . . . . Harry
Roger Livesey . . . . Gilbert Jackson
Charles Carson . . . . Dr Naylor
CRIME Girl is blackmailed because
brother was shot as coward.

09640
OPEN ALL NIGHT (61) (A)
Real Art (Radio)
P: Julius Hagen
D: George Pearson
S: (PLAY) John Chancellor
SC: Gerard Fairlie
Frank Vosper . . . . Anton
Margaret Vines . . . . Elsie Warren
Gillian Lind . . . . Maysie
Lewis Shaw . . . . Bill Warren
Leslie Perrins . . . . Ranger
Colin Keith-Johnson . . . . . Henry
Geraldine Fitzgerald . . . . . . Jill
Michael Shepley . . . . Hilary
DRAMA Exiled Russian grand duke, night
manager of restaurant, kills himself to save
girl from murder charge.

09641
THE GREEN PACK (72) (A)
British Lion *reissue:* 1939 (EB)
P: Herbert Smith
D: T.Hayes Hunter
S: (PLAY) Edgar Wallace
SC: John Hunter
John Stuart . . . . Larry Dean
Aileen Marson . .. . Joan Thurston
Hugh Miller . . . . Martin Creet
Garry Marsh . . . . Tubby Storman
Michael Shepley . . . . Mark Elliott
J.H.Roberts . . . . Dr Thurston
Antony Holles . . . . Insp Aguilar
Percy Walsh . . . . Monty Carr
CRIME Tropics. Prospectors draw cards to
decide who shall kill cheating backer.

09642
A GLIMPSE OF PARADISE (56) (A)
WB-FN(FN)
P: Irving Asher
D: Ralph Ince
S: Sam Mintz
SC: Michael Barringer
George Carney . . . . Jim Bigsworth
Eve Lister . . . . Marion Fielding
Robert Cochran . . . . Norman Ware
Wally Patch . . . . Harry
Winifred Oughton . . . . Mrs Latter

Roddy Hughes . . .. Walter Fielding
Katie Johnson . . . . Mrs Fielding
Margaret Yarde . . . . Mrs Kidd
D.J.Williams . . . . Bert Kidd
Fred Groves . . . . Joshua Ware
CRIME Ex-convict saves daughter who
does not know him from blackmailer.

09643
BIG BUSINESS (53) (U)
WB-FN (WB)
P: Irving Asher
D: Cyril Gardner
Claude Hulbert . Reggie Pullett/Shayne Carter
Eve Gray . . . . Sylvia Brent
Ernest Sefton . . . . Mac
James Finlayson . . . . PC
Hal Walters . . . . Spike
Maude Zimbla . . . . Nina
COMEDY Businessman's unemployed double
puts firm back on its feet.

NOV

09644
THE WIGAN EXPRESS (15) (U)
Film Alliance (U)
Alexander Field
Arthur Chesney
COMEDY

09645
DEATH AT BROADCASTING HOUSE (71)(A)
Phoenix (ABFD) *reissue:* 1953 (EB)
P: Hugh Perceval
D: Reginald Denham
S: (NOVEL) Val Gielgud, Holt Marvel
SC: Basil Mason
Ian Hunter . . . . Insp Gregory
Austin Trevor . . . . Leopold Dryden
Mary Newland . . . . Joan Dryden
Henry Kendall . . . . Rodney Fleming
Val Gielgud . . . . Julian Caird
Peter Haddon . . . . Guy Bannister
Betty (Ann) Davies . . . . . . Poppy Levine
Jack Hawkins . . . . Herbert Evans
Donald Wolfit . . . . Sydney Parsons
Robert Rendel . . . . . . Sir Herbert Farquharson
Bruce Lister . . . . Peter Ridgwell
Hannen Swaffer; Vernon Bartlett; Eric
Dunstan; Gillie Potter; Eve Becke; Elisabeth
Welch; Gershom Parkington Quintet;
Percival Mackey and his Band; Ord Hamilton
and his Band.
CRIME Inspector investigates strangling
of radio actor during broadcast.

09646
IRISH HEARTS (69) (A) USA: NORAH
O'NEALE
Clifton-Hurst (MGM)
P: Harry Clifton
D: SC: Brian Desmond Hurst
S: (NOVEL) Dr Johnson Abrahams
(NIGHT NURSE)
Nancy Burne . . . . Norah O'Neale
Lester Matthews . . . . . . Dermot Fitzgerald
Patric Knowles . . . . Pip Fitzgerald
Molly Lamont . . . . Nurse Otway
Kyrle Bellew . . . . Matron
Mary Warren . . . .
Sara Allgood . . . .
Torin Thatcher . . . .
Arthur Sinclair . . . .
Patric Barr . . . .
DRAMA Ireland. Surgeon loving two nurses
fights typhus in seaside town.

09647
DOCTOR'S ORDERS (68) (U)
BIP (Wardour)

P: Walter C. Mycroft
D: Norman Lee
S: Clifford Grey, Syd Courtney, Lola Harvey
SC: Clifford Grey, R.P.Weston, Bert Lee
Leslie Fuller . . . . Bill Blake
John Mills . . . . Ronnie Blake
Marguerite Allan . . . Gwen Summerfield
Mary Jerrold . . . . Mary Blake
Ronald Shiner . . . . Miggs
Georgie Harris . . . . Duffin
Felix Aylmer . . . Sir Daniel Summerfield
William Kendall . . . . Jackson
D.J.Williams . . . . Napoleon
COMEDY Hospital doctor discovers father
is market quack.

09648
HYDE PARK (48) (U)
WB-FN (WB)
P: Irving Asher
D:S: Randall Faye
George Carney . . . . Joe Smith
Eve Lister . . . . Mary Smith
Barry Clifton . . . . Bill Lenbridge
Wallace Lupino . . . . Alf Turner
Charles Carson . . . . Lord Lenbridge
Phyllis Morris . . . . Mrs Smith
COMEDY Socialist refuses to let daughter
marry lord's son, but relents when he
inherits £1,000.

09649
THE KING OF PARIS (75) (A)
B & D (UA)
P: Herbert Wilcox
D: Jack Raymond
S: (PLAY) Alfred Savoir, John Van Druten
(LA VOIE LACTEE)
SC: John Drinkwater, W.P.Lipscomb, Paul
Gangelin
Cedric Hardwicke . . . . Max Till
Marie Glory . . . . Maika Tamara
Ralph Richardson . . . . Paul Lebrun
Phyllis Monkman . . . . Gismonde
John Deverell . . . . Bertrand
Lydia Sherwood . . . . Juliette Till
Jeanne Stuart . . . . Yvonne
Joan Maude . . . . Lea Rossignol
O.B.Clarence . . . . Mayor
ROMANCE Paris. Selfish impresario makes
star of Russian girl and tricks her into marriage.

09650
THE CASE FOR THE CROWN (70) (U)
B & D - Paramount British
D: George A.Cooper
S: (STORY) Anthony Gittins
(AN ERROR OF JUDGEMENT)
SC: Sherard Powell
Miles Mander . . . . James. L. Barton
Meriel Forbes . . . . Shirley Rainsford
Whitmore Humphries . . . Roy Matherson
Lawrence Anderson . . . . . . Roxy
David Horne . . . . James Rainsford
Gordon McLeod . . . . Prosecution
John Turnbull . . . . Prof Lawrence
CRIME Contractor makes partner's
"suicide" resemble murder to save daughter
from disgrace.

09651
THE WAY OF YOUTH (65) (A)
B & D-Paramount British
D:Norman Walker
S: (PLAY) Amy Kennedy Gould, Ralph Neale
(WAYWARD YOUTH)
SC: Sherard Powell
Aileen Marson . . . . Carol Bonnard
Irene Vanbrugh . . . . Mme Bonnard
Sebastian Shaw . . . . Alan Marmon

Henry Victor . . . . Sylvestre
Diana Wilson . . . . Grace Bonnard
Robert Rendel . . . . Sir Peter Marmon
Leslie Bradley . . . . Lt Burton
The Western Brothers
CRIME Casino owner saves grand-daughter
from blackmailing manager.

09652
YOUTHFUL FOLLY (72) (A)
Sound City (Col)
P: Norman Loudon
D: Miles Mander
S: (PLAY) Gordon Daviot
SC: Heinrich Fraenkel
Irene Vanbrugh . . . . Lady Wilmington
Jane Carr . . . . Ursula Wilmington
Mary Lawson . . . . Susan Grierson
Grey Blake . . . . Larry Wilmington
Arthur Chesney . . . . . . Lord Wilmington
Eric Maturin . . . . Tim Grierson
Fanny Wright . . . . Mrs Grierson
Betty Ann Davies. . . . . . .
Merle Tottenham . . . .
Belle Chrystal . . . .
Kenneth Kove
ROMANCE Lady's son and daughter love
musician and sister from Balham.

09653
KENTUCKY MINSTRELS (84) (U)
Real Art (U)
P: Julius Hagen
D: John Baxter
S: (RADIO SERIES) Harry S.Pepper,
C.Denier Warren
Scott & Whaley . . . . Mott & Bayley
C.Denier Warren . . . . Danny Goldman
April Vivian . . . . Maggie
Wilson Coleman . . . . Ben
Madge Brindley . . . . Landlady
Roddy Hughes . . . . Town Clerk
Norman Green . . . . Massa Johnson
Nina Mae McKinney; Terence Casey;
Leslie Hatton; Polly Ward; Eight Black
Streaks; Harry S.Pepper and his White
Coons; Debroy Somers and his Band.
MUSICAL Old time minstrel sinks to poverty
and rises to fresh stardom.

09654
FLOOD TIDE (63) (U)
Real Art (Radio)
P: Julius Hagen
D: John Baxter
S: Ernest Anson Dyer
George Carney. . . . . . Capt Bill Buckett
Peggy Novak . . . . Mabel
Leslie Hatton . . . . Ted Salter
Janice Adair . . . . Betty Buckett
Wilson Coleman . . . . Ben Salter
Minnie Rayner . . . . Sarah Salter
Mark Daly . . . . Scotty
Edgar Driver . . . . Titch
ROMANCE Thames lock keeper's officer son
weds bargee's daughter.

09655
JOSSER ON THE FARM (63) (U)
Fox British
D: T. Hayes Hunter
S: (PLAY) Con West, Herbert Sargent
Ernie Lotinga . . . . Jimmy Josser
Betty Astell . . . . Betty
Garry Marsh . . . . Granby
Muriel Aked . . . . Mrs Savage
John Gattrell . . . . Dennis
Hope Davy . . . . June
Hyde White . . . . Brooks
Edwin Ellis . . . . Spud

H.F.Maltby . . . . Luke
COMEDY Farmhand elected magistrate
tries to crash society.

DEC
09656
MY HEART IS CALLING (91) (U) *bilingual*
Cine-Allianz (Gaumont)
P: Arnold Pressburger
D: Carmine Gallone
S: Ernst Marischka
SC: Richard Benson, Robert Edmunds,
Sidney Gilliat
Jan Kiepura . . . . Mario Delmonte
Marta Eggerth. . . . . Carla
Sonnie Hale . . . . Alphonse Rosee
Hugh Wakefield . . . . Arvelle
Ernest Thesiger. . . . . Fevrier
Marie Lohr . . . . Manageress
Jeanne Stuart . . . . Margo
Johnny Singer . . . . Pageboy
Anthony Hankey . . . . Singer
Mickey Brantford . . . . Singer
Parry Jones; Hilde von Stolz
MUSICAL Monte Carlo. Tenor and girl
stowaway save itinerant opera company.

09657
LADY IN DANGER (68) (A)
Gaumont
P: Michael Balcon
D: Tom Walls
S: (PLAY) Ben Travers (O MISTRESS MINE)
SC: Ben Travers
Tom Walls . . . . Richard Dexter
Yvonne Arnaud . . . Queen of Ardenberg
Leon M. Lion . . . . Dittling
Anne Grey . . . . Lydia
Hugh Wakefield . . . . King
Marie Lohr . . . . Lady Brockley
Alfred Drayton . . . . Quill
Leonora Corbett . . . . Marcelle
Cecil Parker . . . . Liker
O.B.Clarence . . . . Nelson
Harold Warrender . . . . Clive
Hubert Harben . . . . Matterby
COMEDY Affianced Englishman protects
incognito Queen from revolutionaries.

09658
ROAD HOUSE (76) (A)
Gaumont
P: Michael Balcon
D: Maurice Elvey
S: (PLAY) Walter Hackett
SC: Austin Melford, Leslie Arliss
Violet Loraine . . . . Belle Tout
Gordon Harker . . . . Sam Pritchard
Emlyn Williams . . . . Chester
Aileen Marson . . . . Kitty
Hartley Power . . . . Darcy
Anne Grey . . . . Lady Chetwynde
Stanley Holloway . . . . Donovan
Marie Lohr . . . . Lady Hamble
Edwin Styles . . . . Archie Hamble
Romilly Lunge . . . . Romilly
Horace Kenney; Geraldo and his Band
MUSICAL Barmaid becomes star and saves
"unknown" daughter from charge of
killing crook.
09659
THE MAN WHO KNEW TOO MUCH (75) (A)
Gaumont
AP: Ivor Montagu
D: Alfred Hitchcock
S: Charles Bennett, D.B.Wyndham-Lewis
SC: A.R.Rawlinson, Edwin Greenwood,
Emlyn Williams
Leslie Banks . . . . Bob Lawrence

Edna Best . . . . Jill Lawrence
Peter Lorre . . . . Abbott
Nova Pilbeam . . . . Betty Lawrence
Frank Vosper . . . . Levine
Hugh Wakefield . . . . Clive
Pierre Fresnay . . . . Louis Bernard
Cicely Oates . . . . Nurse Agnes
D.A.Clarke-Smith . . . . Insp Binstead
George Curzon . . . . Gibson
Henry Oscar . . . . George Barbor
CRIME Couple save kidnapped daughter
from political assassins.

09660
DIRTY WORK (78) (A)
Gaumont
P: Michael Balcon
D: Tom Walls
S: (PLAY) Ben Travers
SC: Ben Travers
Ralph Lynn . . . . Jimmy Milligan
Gordon Harker . . . . Nettle
Robertson Hare . . . . Clement Peck
Lilian Bond . . . . Eve Wynne
Basil Sydney . . . . Hugh Stafford
Margaretta Scott . . . . Leonora Stafford
Cecil Parker . . . . Gordon Bray
Gordon James . . . . Toome
Peter Gawthorne . . . . Sgt Barlow
Louis Bradfield . . . . Charlie Wrench
COMEDY Jeweller's assistants pose as
crooks to catch thieves.

09661
SPRING IN THE AIR (74) (A)
Stafford (Pathe)
P: John Stafford
D: Victor Hanbury, Norman Lee
Edmund Gwenn . . . . Franz
Zelma O'Neal . . . . Ila
Theo Shall . . . . Paul
Lydia Sherwood . . . . Vilma
Gus McNaughton . . . . Max
Mary Jerrold . . . . Albertina
Winifred Oughton . . . . Minna
Jane Welsh . . . . Rosa
MUSICAL Budapest. Porter thinks he is
father of girl who poses as maid to win
experimenter.

09662
THE OLD CURIOSITY SHOP (95) (U)
BIP (Wardour)
P: Walter C. Mycroft
D: Thomas Bentley
S: (NOVEL) Charles Dickens
SC: Margaret Kennedy, Ralph Neale
Ben Webster . . . . Grandfather Trent
Elaine Benson . . . . Nell Trent
Hay Petrie . . . . Quilp
Beatrix Thompson . . . . Mrs Quilp
Gibb McLaughlin . . . . Sampson Brass
Reginald Purdell . . . . Dick Swiveller
Polly Ward . . . . Marchioness
James Harcourt . . . . . . Single Gentleman
J.Fisher White . . . . Schoolmaster
Lily Long . . . . Sally Brass
Dick Tubb . . . . Tommy Codlin
Roddy Hughes . . . . Short
Amy Veness . . . . Mrs Jarley
Peter Penrose . . . . Kit Nubbles
Wally Patch . . . . George
Fred Groves . . . . Showman
DRAMA Period. Gambler and granddaughter
evicted by dwarf usurer and die in poverty.

09663
RADIO PARADE OF 1935 (96) (A) *dufay seq*
USA: RADIO FOLLIES
BIP (Wardour)

P: Walter C.Mycroft
D: Arthur Woods
S: Reginald Purdell, John Watt
SC: Jack Davies, Paul Perez, James Bunting, Arthur Woods

Will Hay	William Garland
Helen Chandler	Joan Garland
Clifford Mollison	Jimmie Clare
Davy Burnaby	Sir Ffrederick Ffotheringhay
Alfred Drayton	Carl Graham
Billy Bennett	Commissionaire
Lily Morris	Charlady
Nellie Wallace	Charlady
Western Brothers	Announcers
Clapham & Dwyer	Reporters
Three Sailors	Assistants
Haver & Lee	Effects Men
Carlyle Cousins	Telephonists
Georgie Harris	Pageboy
Gerry Fitzgerald	Window Cleaner
Arthur Young	Window Cleaner
Claude Dampier	Piano Tuner
Hugh E.Wright	Algernon Bird
Robert Nainby	Col Featherstone Haugh-Haugh
Jimmy Godden	Vere de V. de Vere
Basil Foster	Capt Esme StJ. Entwhistle
Ivor McLaren	Eric Lyttle-Lyttle

Teddy Joyce and his Band; Eve Becke; Fay Carroll; Peggy Cochrane; Yvette Darnac; Ronald Frankau; Alberta Hunter; Ted Ray; Joyce Richardson; Buddy Bradley Girls; Beryl Orde; Fred Conyngham; Stanelli and his Hornchestra.
MUSICAL Complaints manager takes over radio station and uses amateur talent. (Extract in ELSTREE STORY; 1952).

09664
WOMANHOOD (61) (A)
Louis London (Butcher)
D: Harry Hughes
S: Brandon Fleming

Eve Gray	Leila Mason
Leslie Perrins	Richard Brent
Esmond Knight	Jack Gordon
Christine Adrian	Ann Gordon
MacArthur Gordon	Bolton
Charles Castella	Klein

CRIME Reporter convicts bandit who breaks jail and is killed by his ex-mistress.

09665
BORROW A MILLION (50) (U)
Fox British
D: Reginald Denham
S: Margaret McDonnell

Reginald Gardiner	Alastair Cartwright
Vera Bogetti	Adele Cartwright
Charles Cullum	Michael Trent
Wally Patch	Bodgers
Meriel Forbes	Eileen Dacres
Robert Rendel	Struthers
Roland Culver	Charles Nutford
Wilson Coleman	Blake
Gordon McLeod	Bowers

COMEDY Teashop proprietor opens restaurant chain with backing from millionaire.

09666
THE THIRD CLUE (72) (A)
Fox British
D: Albert Parker
S: (NOVEL) Neil Gordon
(THE SHAKESPEARE MURDERS)
SC: Michael Barringer, Lance Sieveking, Frank Atkinson

Basil Sydney	Reinhardt/James Conway
Molly Lamont	Rosemary Clayton
Robert Cochran	Peter Kerrigan
Alfred Sangster	Rupert Clayton
C.M.Hallard	Gabriel Wells
Raymond Lovell	Robinson

Frank Atkinson	Lefty
Ernest Sefton	Newman
Ian Fleming	Mark Clayton
Quinton McPherson	Reuben
Eric Fawcett	Jack Tully
Bruce Lister	Derek Clayton

CRIME Rival crooks seek stolen jewels hidden in old house.

09667
THE GIRL IN THE CROWD (52) (U)
WB-FN (FN)
P: Irving Asher
D: Michael Powell

Barry Clifton	David
Googie Withers	Sally
Patricia Hilliard	Marian
Harold French	Bob
Clarence Blakiston	Peabody
Margaret Gunn	Joyce
Richard Littledale	Bill Manners
Phyllis Morris	Mrs Lewis
Patric Knowles	Tom Burrows
Eve Lister	Ruby
Betty Lynne	Phyllis
John Wood	Harry

COMEDY Man decides to wed girl picked at random, and lands in jail.

09668
WHAT'S IN A NAME ? (47) (U)
WB-FN (FN)
P: Irving Asher
D: Ralph Ince

Carol Goodner	Marta Radovic
Barry Clifton	George Andrews
Reginald Purdell	Harry Stubbs
Gyles Isham	Schultz
Eve Gray	Mrs Schultz
Ernest Sefton	Light
George Zucco	Foot
Winifred Oughton	Maid

COMEDY Clerk posing as foreign composer loves girl posing as film star.

09669
THE FEATHERED SERPENT (72) (A)
GS Enterprises (Col)
P: A.George Smith
D: Maclean Rogers
S: (NOVEL) Edgar Wallace
SC: Maclean Rogers, Kathleen Butler

Enid Stamp-Taylor	Ella Crewe
Tom Helmore	Peter Dewin
D.A.Clarke-Smith	Joe Farmer
Moore Marriott	Harry Hugg
Molly Fisher	Daphne Olroyd
Vincent Holman	Insp Clarke
Evelyn Roberts	Leicester Crewe
Iris Baker	Paula Ricks
O.B.Clarence	George Beale

CRIME Reporter proves actress did not murder fence.

09670
EIGHT CYLINDER LOVE (42) (U)
Tribune (Col)
P:D: Peter Saunders

Pat Aherne	Bill Gardner
Dodo Watts	Vivian
Klifton Court	Friend
Vincent Lawson	Danvers
Max Adrian	
Norman Hackforth	

SPORT Racing driver eludes kidnappers in time to win race.

09671
THE POISONED DIAMOND (73) (A)
Grafton (Col)
P: Fred Browett
D: W.P.Kellino

Anne Grey	Mary Davidson
Lester Matthews	John Reader
Patric Knowles	Jack Dane
Raymond Raikes	
Bryan Powley	
Lucius Blake	
D.J.Williams	

DRAMA Bankrupt finds diamond mine and uses wealth to destroy those who ruined him.

09672
LOST OVER LONDON (38) (U)
Rex Graves (Col)
D:S: Rex Graves
Wally Patch
Vi Kaley
Girda Terry
DRAMA Travels of stolen pound note until it returns to counterfeiter.

09673
MENACE (70) (A) retitled:
SABOTAGE
USA: WHEN LONDON SLEEPS
Sound City (Reunion)
P: Norman Loudon
D: Adrian Brunel
S: Victor Varconi
SC: Heinrich Fraenkel, A.R.Rawlinson

Victor Varconi	Stephen Ronsart
Joan Maude	Lady Conway
D.A.Clarke-Smith	Sir Robert Conway
J.Hubert Leslie	Mr Jones
Joan Matheson	Mrs Jones
J.A.O'Rourke	O'Leary
Shayle Gardner	Commissioner
Wilfred Noy	Dean

CRIME Railway magnate wrecks trains during brainstorms.

09674
WEDDING ANNIVERSARY (11) (A)
Sound City (MGM)

Molly Lamont	The Wife
Martin Lewis	The Husband

DRAMA "Story with logical but unhappy ending."

09675
KNIFE NUMBER SIX (11) (A)
Sound City (MGM)
DRAMA

09676
NO QUARTER (12) (U)
Sound City (MGM)
George Hayes .... The Gangster
CRIME Shot gangster repents.

09677
THE WAY OUT (11) (U)
Sound City (MGM)
COMEDY Three suitors love one girl.

09678
BUTTONS (13) (A)
Sound City (MGM)
CRIME Mother changes son's coat buttons when she suspects him of murder.

09679
THE LOVING CUP (12) (A)
Sound City (MGM)
DRAMA "Triangle drama with a subtle climax."

09680
A GARLAND OF SONG (20) (U)
A P & D
Alfred Piccaver
MUSICAL Tenor sings to background of famous paintings.

09681
TELL ME IF IT HURTS (20)
Richard Massingham (Denning)
P:D:S: Richard Massingham
Russell Waters . . . .   The Patient
Patrick Ross . . . .   The Dentist
Freda Silcock . . . .   The Nurse
Peter Copley . . . .   The Waiter
COMEDY Man gets toothache during
dinner and visits dentist.

09682
TEMPTATION (77) (U) *bilingual*
Milofilm (Gau)
D: Max Neufeld
S: (PLAY) Melchior Lengyel (ANTONIA)
Frances Day . . . .   Antonia Palmay
Stewart Rome . . . .   Paul Palmay
Anthony Hankey . . . .   William Parker
Peggy Simpson . . . .   Piri
Mickey Brantford . . . .   Johnny
Lucy Beaumont . . . .   Headmistress
Billy Watts . . . .   Gus
C.Denier Warren . . . .   Director
Effie Atherton . . . .   Vera Hanka
Molly Hamley-Clifford . . . .   Maresa
Alfred Rode and his Tzigane Orchestra
MUSICAL Hungary. Retired singer flirts
with niece's fiance to annoy husband.
(Made in France).

1935

JAN

09683
LORNA DOONE (90) (A)
ATP (ABFD) *reissue:* 1945 (Ren)
P:D: Basil Dean
S: (NOVEL) R.D.Blackmore
SC: Dorothy Farnum, Miles Malleson,
Gordon Wellesley
Victoria Hopper . . . . Lorna Doone
John Loder . . . . Jan Ridd
Margaret Lockwood . . . . . . Annie Ridd
Roy Emerton . . . . Carver Doone
Mary Clare . . . . Mistress Ridd
Edward Rigby . . . . Reuben Huckaback
Roger Livesey . . . . Tom Faggus
George Curzon . . . . King James II
D.A.Clarke-Smith . . . . . Counsellor Doone
Lawrence Hanray . . . . . Parson Bowden
Amy Veness . . . . Betty Muxworthy
Eliot Makeham . . . . John Fry
Wyndham Goldie . . . . . . Judge Jeffries
Frank Cellier . . . . Jeremy Stickles
Herbert Lomas . . . . . . Sir Ensor Doone
ADVENTURE Exmoor, 1625. Yeoman loves
an outlaw's daughter who is really a
stolen heiress.

09684
THE SCARLET PIMPERNEL (98) (A)
London (UA) *reissues:* 1942 (AA) 1947 (BL)
P: Alexander Korda
D: Harold Young
S: (NOVEL) Baroness Orczy
SC: Robert E.Sherwood, Sam Berman,
Arthur Wimperis, Lajos Biro
Leslie Howard . . . . . . Sir Percy Blakeney
Merle Oberon . . . . Marguerite Blakeney
Raymond Massey . . . . . . Chauvelin
Nigel Bruce . . . . Prince of Wales
Bramwell Fletcher . . . . . . Priest
Anthony Bushell . . . . Sir Andrew Ffoulkes
Joan Gardner . . . . Suzanne de Tournay
Walter Rilla . . . . Armand StJust
Mabel Terry-Lewis . . Countess de Tournay
O.B.Clarence . . . . Count de Tournay
Ernest Milton . . . . Robespierre
Edmund Breon . . . . Winterbottom
Melville Cooper . . . . Romney
Gibb McLaughlin . . . . Barber
Morland Graham . . . . Treadle
Allan Jeayes . . . . Lord Greville
William Freshman . . . . . . Lord Hastings
ADVENTURE 1793. Fop dons disguises to
save aristocrats from French revolution.
(PGAA: 1938).

09685
THE LOVE TEST (63) (U)
Fox British
D: Michael Powell
S: Jack Celestin
SC: Selwyn Jepson
Judy Gunn . . . . Mary
Louis Hayward . . . . John
David Hutcheson . . . . Thompson
Morris Harvey . . . . President
Googie Withers . . . . Minnie
Aubrey Dexter . . . . Vice-President
Eve Turner . . . . Kathleen
Bernard Miles . . . . Allan
COMEDY Research chemists choose one
to make love to new supervisor.

09686
ONCE IN A NEW MOON (63) (U)
Fox British
D: Anthony Kimmins
S: (NOVEL) Owen Rutter (LUCKY STAR)
Eliot Makeham . . . . Harold Drake
Rene Ray . . . . Stella Drake

Morton Selten . . . . Lord Bravington
Wally Patch . . . . Syd Parrott
Derrick de Marney . . . . . Hon Bryan Grant
John Clements . . . . Edward Teale
Mary Hinton . . . . Lady Bravington
Gerald Barry . . . . Col Fitzgeorge
Richard Goolden . . . . . Rev Benjamin Buffett
H.Saxon-Snell . . . . K.Pilkington-Bigge
John Turnbull . . . . Capt Crump
FANTASY Socialist postmaster elected
governor of village thrown into space when
moon collides with star.

09687
HIS MAJESTY AND CO (66) (U)
Fox British
D: Anthony Kimmins
S: Sally Sutherland
John Garrick . . . . John
Barbara Waring . . . . Princess Sandra
Morton Selten . . . . King of Poldavia
Wally Patch . . . . Bert Hicks
Mary Grey . . . . Queen
Jean Gillie . . . . Nina
Desmond Jeans . . . . Michael
H.Saxon-Snell . . . . Ferguson
Howard Douglas . . . . Sam Bloom
Alfredo Campoli and his Tzigane Orchestra
MUSICAL Rich man's nephew and exiled
Ruritanian royalty open restaurant.

09688
BARNACLE BILL (90) (U)
City (Butcher)
P: Basil Humphrys
D: Harry Hughes
S: Archie Pitt
SC: Aveling Ginever
Archie Pitt . . . . Bill Harris
Joan Gardner . . . . Jill Harris
Gus McNaughton . . . . Jack Barton
Jean Adrienne . . . . Mary Bailey
Sybil Jason . . . . Jill (child)
Denis O'Neil . . . . Shorty
O.B.Clarence . . . . Uncle George
Henrietta Watson . . . . Aunt Julia
Minnie Rayner . . . . Mrs Bailey
Iris Darbyshire . . . . Florrie
Tully Comber . . . . Harry Fordyce
Frank Atkinson . . . . Arthur Neal
Frank Titterton; Donna le Bourdais
DRAMA Widowed sailor's sacrifices for young
daughter.

09689
THE IRON DUKE (88) (U)
Gaumont
P: Michael Balcon
D: Victor Saville
S: H.M.Harwood
SC: Bess Meredyth
George Arliss . . . . Duke of Wellington
Gladys Cooper . . . Duchess of Angouleme
Emlyn Williams . . . . Bates
Ellaline Terriss . . . . Duchess Kitty
A.E.Matthews . . . . Lord Hill
Allan Aynesworth . . . . . . Louis XVIII
Lesley Wareing . . . . Lady Frances Webster
Edmund Willard . . . . Marshal Ney
Franklin Dyall . . . . Blucher
Felix Aylmer . . . . Lord Uxbridge
Gibb McLaughlin . . . . Talleyrand
Peter Gawthorne . . . . . Duke of Richmond
Norma Varden . . . Duchess of Richmond
Walter Sondes . . . . Wedderburn Webster
Campbell Gullan . . . . D'Artois
Gyles Isham . . . . Castlereagh
Frederick Leister . . . . King of Prussia
Gerald Lawrence . . . . Czar
HISTORY France, 1816. French Duchess uses

infatuated Lady to scheme against Duke of
Wellington.

09690
THINGS ARE LOOKING UP (78) (U)
Gaumont
P: Michael Balcon
D: Albert de Courville
S: Albert de Courville, Daisy Fisher
SC: Stafford Dickens, Con West
Cicely Courtneidge . . . . Cicely/Bertha Fytte
Max Miller . . . . Joey
William Gargan . . . . Van Guard
Mary Lawson . . . . Mary Fytte
Dick Henderson . . . . Mr Money
Dick Henderson jr . . . . . . Money jr
Mark Lester . . . . Chairman
Henrietta Watson . . . . . . Miss MacTavish
Cicely Oates . . . . Miss Crabbe
Judy Kelly . . . . Opal
Danny Green . . . . Big Black Fox
Wyn Weaver . . . . Governor
Alma Taylor . . . . Schoolmistress
Suzanne Lenglen . . . . Herself
COMEDY Circus equestrienne poses as
schoolmistress while sister elopes.

09691
THE PHANTOM LIGHT (75) (U)
Gainsborough (Gaumont)
reissue: 1950 (EB; 10 mins cut)
P: Jerome Jackson
D: Michael Powell
S: (PLAY) Evadne Price, Joan Roy Byford
(THE HAUNTED LIGHT)
SC: Austin Melford, Ralph Smart
Binnie Hale . . . . Alice Bright
Gordon Harker . . . . Sam Higgins
Ian Hunter . . . . Jim Pierce
Donald Calthrop . . . . David Owen
Milton Rosmer . . . . Dr Carey
Reginald Tate . . . . Tom Evans
Mickey Brantford . . . . . . Bob Peters
Herbert Lomas . . . . Claff Owen
Fewlass Llewellyn . . . . . . Griffith Owen
Alice O'Day . . . . Mrs Owen
CRIME Wales. Wreckers pose as ghosts to scare
new lighthouse-keeper.

09692
D'YE KEN JOHN PEEL ? (81) (A)
USA: CAPTAIN MOONLIGHT
Twickenham (AP&D)
P: Julius Hagen
D: Henry Edwards
S: Charles Cullum
SC: H. Fowler Mear
John Garrick . . . . Maj John Peel
Winifred Shotter . . . . Lucy Merrall
Stanley Holloway . . . . Sam Small
John Stuart . . . . Capt Moonlight
Mary Lawson . . . . Toinette
Leslie Perrins . . . . . Sir Charles Hawksley
Morris Harvey . . . . Glover
Charles Carson . . . . Francis Merrall
MUSICAL 1815. Major exposes beloved's
husband as bigamous gambler.

09693
THE ROCKS OF VALPRE (73) (A)
USA: HIGH TREASON
Real Art (Radio)
P: Julius Hagen
D: Henry Edwards
S: (NOVEL) Ethel M.Dell
SC: H. Fowler Mear
John Garrick . . . . Louis de Monteville
Winifred Shotter . . . . . Christine Wyndham
Leslie Perrins . . . . Capt Rodolphe
Michael Shepley . . . . . . Trevor Mordaunt

Lewis Shaw .... Noel Wyndham
Athene Seyler .... Aunt Philippa
Agnes Imlay .... Mlle Gautier
CRIME Belgium, 1860. Court-martialled officer freed from Devil's Island in time to save beloved from blackmailing spy.

09694
LAZYBONES (65) (U)
Real Art (Radio)
P: Julius Hagen
D: Michael Powell
S: (PLAY) Ernest Denny
SC: Gerard Fairlie
Claire Luce .... Kitty McCarthy
Ian Hunter .... Sir Reginald Ford
Sara Allgood .... Bridget
Bernard Nedell .... Mike McCarthy
Michael Shepley .... Hildebrand Pope
Bobbie Comber .... Kemp
Denys Blakelock .... Hugh Ford
Marjory Gaskell .... Marjory Ford
Pamela Carme .... Lottie Pope
Harold Warrender .... Lord Melton
Miles Malleson .... Pessimist
COMEDY Broke bart weds American heiress whose cousin frames her for stealing official papers.

09695
WIDOW'S MIGHT (77) (U)
WB-FN (WB)
P: Irving Asher
D: Cyril Gardner
S: (PLAY) Frederick Jackson
SC: Roland Brown, Brock Williams
Laura la Plante .... Nancy Tweesdale
Yvonne Arnaud .... Princess Suzanne
Garry Marsh .... Barry Carrington
George Curzon .... Champion
Barry Clifton .... Cyril Monks
Margaret Yarde .... Cook
Davina Craig .... Amelia
Joan Hickson .... Burroughs
Hugh E. Wright .... Peasgood
Hay Plumb .... Sgt Dawkins
COMEDY Widows fake burglary to win back ex-sweethearts.

09696
MURDER AT MONTE CARLO (70) (A)
WB-FN (FN)
P: Irving Asher
D: Ralph Ince
S: (NOVEL) Tom Van Dyke
SC: John Hastings Turner, Michael Barringer
Errol Flynn .... Dyter
Eve Gray .... Gillian
Paul Graetz ...... Dr Heinrich Becker
Molly Lamont ...... Margaret Becker
Ellis Irving .... Marc Orton
Lawrence Hanray .... Collum
Henry Victor .... Major
Brian Buchel .... Yates
Peter Gawthorne .... Duprez
CRIME Monte Carlo. Reporter solves murder of professor for his winning roulette system.

09697
BREWSTER'S MILLIONS (84) (U)
B & D (UA) reissue: 1941 (EB)
P: Herbert Wilcox
D: Thornton Freeland
S: (PLAY) George Barr McCutcheon, Winchell Smith
SC: Arthur Wimperis, Paul Gangelin, Douglas Furber, Clifford Grey, Donovan Pedelty, Wolfgang Wilhelm
Jack Buchanan .... Jack Brewster

Lili Damita .... Rosalie
Nancy O'Neil .... Cynthia
Amy Veness .... Mrs Barry
Sydney Fairbrother ...... Miss Plimsole
Ian McLean .... McLeod
Fred Emney .... Freddie
Sebastian Shaw .... Frank
Allan Aynesworth .... Rawles
Antony Holles .... Ferago
Henry Wenman .... Pedro
Dennis Hoey .... Mario
MUSICAL Heir must spend £500,000 in two months to inherit £6,000,000.

09698
IN TOWN TONIGHT (81) (U)
British Lion reissue: 1938 (1237 ft cut)
P:D: Herbert Smith
Jack Barty .... The Agent
Dave Apollon and his Romantic Serenaders
Billy Merrin and his Commanders
Howard Jacobs and his Orchestra
Kneller Hall Military Band
Stanley Holloway   Three Radio Rogues
Wilson, Keppel & Betty Arthur Prince and Jim
Olive Groves   Carson Sisters
Nora Williams   Finlay Currie
Melissa Mason   Val Rosing
Tessa Deane   The Dynamites
Seven Thunderbolts   Beryl Orde
Bob Lively   Howard Jacobs
REVUE Unemployed agent seeks stars for new recording company.

09699
EQUITY MUSICAL REVUE (series) (U)
British Lion (MGM)
P: Herbert Smith
Roy Fox and his Band
Reggie Bristow's Band
Terence McGovern's Band
The Moderniques   Nat Mills and Bobbie
Betty Astell   Harry Champion
Davy Burnaby   Seven Lady Harpists
Mario de Pietro   Teddy Brown
Albert Sandler Trio Freddie Bamberger

09700
No. 1: (9)

09701
No. 2: (9)

09702
No. 3: (9)

09703
No. 4: (10)

09704
No. 5: (10)

09705
No. 6: (10)

09706
No. 7: (10)

09707
No. 8: (9)

09708
No. 9: (10)

09709
No. 10: (8)
REVUE

09710
THE PUBLIC LIFE OF HENRY THE NINTH (60) (U)
Hammer (MGM) reissue: 1940 (Ex)
D: Bernerd Mainwaring
Leonard Henry .... Henry

Betty Frankiss .... Maggie
George Mozart .... Draughts Player
Wally Patch .... Landlord
Aileen Latham .... Liz
Mai Bacon .... Landlady
Herbert Langley .... PC
Dorothy Vernon .... Mrs Fickle
COMEDY Potman and drudge bring fame to pub and win contract.

09711
SWINGING THE LEAD (63) (U)
Weiner, MacKane and Rogers (U)
D: David MacKane
Billy Hartnell .... Freddy Fordum
Moira Lynd .... Joan Swid
Gibb McLaughlin .... Inigo Larsen
Marie Ault .... Mrs Swid
George Rogers .... Benjamin Brown
Nita Harvey .... Peggy
COMEDY Crooks smuggle drug that changes personality.

FEB

09712
TEN MINUTE ALIBI (76) (A)
British Lion-Transatlantic (BL)
reissue: 1939 (EB)
P: Paul Soskin
D: Bernard Vorhaus
S: (PLAY) Anthony Armstrong
SC: Michael Hankinson, Vera Allinson
Phillips Holmes .... Colin Derwent
Aileen Marson .... Betty Findon
Theo Shall .... Philip Sevilla
Morton Selten ...... Sir Miles Standish
George Merritt .... Insp Pemper
Charles Hickman .... Sgt Brace
Philip Hatfield .... Hunter
CRIME Man dreams perfect murder and uses it to kill foreign rival.

09713
THE PRICE OF WISDOM (64) (U)
B&D-Paramount British reissue: 1948 (Amb)
P: Anthony Havelock-Allan
D: Reginald Denham
S: (PLAY) Lionel Brown
SC: Basil Mason, George Dewhurst
Mary Jerrold .... Mary Temple
Roger Livesey .... Peter North
Mary Newland .... Jean Temple
Robert Rendel .... Alfred Blake
Eric Cowley .... Col Layton
Ann Codrington .... Miss Stokes
Ivor Barnard .... Bonny
Cecily Oates .... Pollitt
ROMANCE Handbag designer loved by employer and young inventor.

09714
THE TRIUMPH OF SHERLOCK HOLMES (84) (A)
Real Art (Gaumont)
P: Julius Hagen
D: Leslie Hiscott
S: (NOVEL) Arthur Conan Doyle (THE VALLEY OF FEAR)
SC: H. Fowler Mear
Arthur Wontner .... Sherlock Holmes
Lyn Harding .... Prof Moriarty
Jane Carr .... Ettie Douglas
Leslie Perrins .... John Douglas
Ian Fleming .... Dr Watson
Michael Shepley .... Cecil Barker
Ben Welden .... Ted Baldwin
Roy Emerton .... Boss McGinty
Wilfred Caithness ... Col Sebastian Moran
Charles Mortimer .... Insp Lestrade
Minnie Rayner .... Mrs Hudson

CRIME Detective uncovers American secret society behind revenge killing.

09715
ANNIE, LEAVE THE ROOM ! (76) (A)
Twickenham (U)
P: Julius Hagen
D: Leslie Hiscott
S: (PLAY) Norman Cannon
(SPENDLOVE HALL)
SC: Michael Barringer
Eva Moore . . . . Mrs Morley
Morton Selten . . . . Lord Spendlove
Jane Carr . . . . Adrienne Ditmar
Davina Craig . . . . Annie
Richard Cooper . . . . Hon Algernon Lacey
Jane Welsh . . . . Lady Mary
Ben Welden . . . . Raisins
Arthur Finn . . . . Al Gates
Edward Underdown . . . . John Brandon
COMEDY Broke lord rents house to film company and his maid becomes star.

09716
THE LAD (74) (A)
Twickenham (U)
P: Julius Hagen
D: Henry Edwards
S: (NOVEL) Edgar Wallace
SC: Gerard Fairlie
Gordon Harker . . . . Bill Shane
Betty Stockfeld . . . . Lady Fandon
Jane Carr . . . . Pauline Carruthers
Michael Shepley . . . . Arthur Madderley
Gerald Barry . . . . Lord Fandon
Geraldine Fitzgerald . . . .. Joan Fandon
Sebastian Shaw . . . . Jimmy Elford
John Turnbull . . . . Insp Martin
Ralph Truman . . . . Nifty O'Shea
David Hawthorne . . . . . . Maj Grannitt
COMEDY Jailbird mistaken for detective saves lord's gems from theft.

09717
THE ACE OF SPADES (66) (U)
Real Art (Radio)
P: Julius Hagen
D: George Pearson
S: (NOVEL) John Crawford Fraser
SC: Gerard Fairlie
Michael Hogan . . . . Nick Trent
Dorothy Boyd . . . . Nita
Richard Cooper . . . . Tony
Jane Carr . . . . Cleo Despard
Michael Shepley . . . . George Despard
Geraldine Fitzgerald . . . .. Evelyn
Sebastian Shaw . . . . Trent
Felix Aylmer . . . . Lord Yardleigh
Bobbie Comber . . . . Andrews
CRIME Jealous girl blackmails sister's fiance for death of political rival.

09718
EMIL AND THE DETECTIVES (70) (U)
USA: EMIL
Wainwright (Gau)
P: Richard Wainwright
D: Milton Rosmer
S: (NOVEL) Erich Kastner (EMIL UND DIE DETEKTIVEN)
SC: Cyrus Brooks, Margaret Carter, Frank Launder
George Hayes . . . . The Man
Mary Glynne . . . . Mrs Blake
John Williams . . . . Emil Blake
Clare Greet . . . . Grandmother
George Merritt . . . . PC
Marion Foster . . . . .Polly
Donald Pittman . . . . Gussy
Bobby Rietti . .. . Professor

John Singer . . . . Tuesday
Derek Blomfield . . . . Jerry
CRIME Gang of children pursue thief.

09719
STRICTLY ILLEGAL (69) (U)
Leslie Fuller (Gau) *reissue:* 1940,
HERE COMES A POLICEMAN (24 mins cut)
P: Joe Rock
D: Ralph Ceder
S: (PLAY) Con West, Herbert Sargent
(THE NAUGHTY AGE)
SC: Syd Courtenay, Georgie Harris
Leslie Fuller . . . . Bill the Bookie
Betty Astell . . . . Mrs Bill
Georgie Harris . . . . Bert the Runner
Cissie Fitzgerald . . . . Lady Percival
Glennis Lorimer . . . . The Girl
Mickey Brantford . . . . . . The Boy
Ernest Sefton . . . . The Colonel
Alf Goddard . . . . The Cop
Humberston Wright . . . . . The Reverend
COMEDY Street bookie posing as cleric saves Lady's gems from theft.

09720
THE DICTATOR (86) (A) retitled:
THE LOVE AFFAIR OF THE DICTATOR
USA: THE LOVES OF A DICTATOR
reissues: 1943, 1947, 1955, FOR LOVE OF A QUEEN (NR)
Toeplitz (Gau)
P: Ludovico Toeplitz
D: Victor Saville, Alfred Santell
S: H.G.Lustig, Hans Wilhelm, Michael Hogan
SC: Benn W.Levy
Clive Brook . . . . Dr Struensee
Madeleine Carroll . . . . . Caroline Mathilde
Emlyn Williams . . . King Christian VII
Helen Haye . . . . Queen Juliana
Isabel Jeans . . . . Von Eyben
Alfred Drayton . . . . Brandt
Nicholas Hannen . . . . Guldberg
Ruby Miller . . . . Hilda
Frank Cellier . . . . Sir Murray Keith
Heather Thatcher . . . . Lady
Gibb McLaughlin . . . .
HISTORY Denmark, 1776. Country doctor usurps power of mad King and has affair with Queen.

09721
OH DADDY ! (77) (A)
Gainsborough (Gaumont) *reissue:* 1941 (Ex)
P: Michael Balcon
D: Graham Cutts, Austin Melford
S: (PLAY) Austin Melford
SC: Austin Melford
Leslie Henson . . . . Lord Pye
Frances Day . . . . Benita de Lys
Robertson Hare . . . . Rupert Boddy
Barry Mackay . . . . Jimmy Ellison
Marie Lohr . . . . Lady Pye
Alfred Drayton . . . . Uncle Samson
Tony de Lungo . . . . Count Duval
Daphne Courtney . . . . Phyllis Pye
COMEDY Purity League lord led astray by showgirl who turns out to be his stepdaughter.

09722
OPENING NIGHT (68) (A)
Olympic (Col) *reissue:* 1937 DRESS REHEARSAL (20); RHYTHM AND SONG (17)
P: Charles Alexander
D: Alex Brown
Douglas Byng   Dolores Dalgarno
Walter Crisham   Edward Cooper
Reginald Gardiner   Doris Hare
REVUE First night cabaret at night club.

09723
BREAKERS AHEAD (58) (U)
Anglo-Cosmopolitan (Reunion)
P: Fraser Foulsham
D:S: Anthony Gilkison
Barrie Livesey . . . . George Kenyon
April Vivian . . . . Stella Trevarthen
Billy Holland . . . . Bob Pentreath
Roddy Hughes . . . . Will
Cicely Oates . . . . Aunt Martha
Richard Worth . . . . Skipper
Francis Gregory . . . . Champion
ADVENTURE Cornwall. Fisherman tries to drown rival, then dies to save him from storm.

09724
SMITH'S WIVES (59) (A)
Fox British
D: Manning Haynes
S: (PLAY) James Darnley
(FACING THE MUSIC)
SC: Con West, Herbert Sargent
Ernie Lotinga . . . . Jimmy Smith
Beryl de Querton . . . . Norah Smith
Tyrell Davies . . . . Dick Desmond
Richard Ritchie . . . . Rev James Smith
Kay Walsh . . . . Mabel Smith
Jean Gillie . . . . Anne
Vashti Taylor . . . . Dierdre Fotheringay
COMEDY bookie and parson, both named Smith, live in opposite flats.

09725
DANDY DICK (72) (U)
BIP (Wardour) *reissue:* 1938 (Amb)
P: Walter C.Mycroft
D: William Beaudine
S: (PLAY) Arthur Wing Pinero
SC: Frank Miller, William Beaudine, Clifford Grey, Will Hay
Will Hay . . . . Rev Richard Jedd
Nancy Burne . . . . Pamela Jedd
Esmond Knight . . . . Tony Mardon
Davy Burnaby . . . . . Sir William Mardon
Mignon O'Doherty . . . . Georgiana Jedd
Syd Crossley . . . . Wilkins
Robert Nainby . . . . Bale
Hal Gordon . . . . Mullins
Jimmy Godden . . . . Creecher
John Singer . . . . Freddie
Wally Patch . . . . PC Topping
Moore Marriott . . . . Stableboy
COMEDY Village vicar tries to raise funds for steeple and is accused of racehorse doping.

09726
IT'S A BET (69) (U)
BIP (Wardour)
P: Walter C. Mycroft
D: Alexander Esway
S: (NOVEL) Marcus McGill
(HIDE AND I'LL FIND YOU)
SC: L. DuGarde Peach, Frank Miller, Kurt Siodmak
Gene Gerrard . . . . Rollo Briggs
Helen Chandler . . . . Clare
Judy Kelly . . . . Anne
Allen Vincent . . . . Norman
Dudley Rolph . . . . Harry
Nadine March . . . . Miss Parsons
Polly Ward . . . . Maudie
Alf Goddard . . . . Joe
Jimmy Godden . . . . Mayor
Frank Stanmore . . . . Tramp
Ronald Shiner . . . . Fair Man
Ellen Pollock . . . . Mrs Joe
Violet Farebrother . . . . . . Lady Allway
George Zucco . . . . Convict
COMEDY Devon. Reporter hides for month to win bet from editor.

09727
WE'VE GOT TO HAVE LOVE (35) (U)
B & N Productions
P: Baron Nahum
D:S: Patrick O'Brien (Brunner)

Nelson Keys	Lord Bingo
Hilda Moreno	Anita
Davy Burnaby	The Man

COMEDY Live actor on cinema stage helps film actors' romance.

09728
WEDDING EVE (39) (U)
National Progress - Astor (Radio)
D:S: Charles Barnett

Clapham & Dwyer	Motorists
Frank Titterton	Joe Gulliver
Dodo Watts	Jessie Gulliver
Muriel George	Mrs Gulliver
Ernest Butcher	George
Leslie Sarony	Sam
Charles Fletcher	Lt Jim Hamilton
Orpheum Octet	Guests

MUSICAL Devon. Singsong on eve of publican's daughter's wedding.

MAR

09729
DEATH ON THE SET (73) (A)
USA: MURDER ON THE SET
Twickenham (U)
P: Julius Hagen
D: Leslie Hiscott
S: (NOVEL) Victor MacClure
SC: Michael Barringer

Henry Kendall	Morden/Marsh
Eve Gray	Laura Lane
Jeanne Stuart	Lady Blanche
Garry Marsh	Insp Burford
Wally Patch	Sgt Crowther
Lewis Shaw	Jimmy Frayle
Ben Welden	Freshman
Rita Helsham	Constance Lyon
Robert Nainby	Lord Umbridge
Hal Walters	Albert

CRIME Film director kills gangster double, takes place and frames actress.

09730
THREE WITNESSES (68) (A)
Twickenham (U)
P: Julius Hagen
D: Leslie Hiscott
S: (NOVEL) S. Fowler Wright
SC: Michael Barringer

Henry Kendall	Leslie Trent
Eve Gray	Margaret Truscott
Sebastian Shaw	Roger Truscott
Garry Marsh	Charles Rowton
Richard Cooper	Claude Pember
Geraldine Fitzgerald	Diane Morton
Noel Dryden	Cyril Truscott
Ralph Truman	Mr Bellman
Gladys Hamer	Mrs Bellman

CRIME Solicitor unmasks partner as murderer of fiancee's brother.

09731
INSIDE THE ROOM (66) (A)
Twickenham (U)
P: Julius Hagen
D: Leslie Hiscott
S: (PLAY) Marten Cumberland
SC: H. Fowler Mear

Austin Trevor	Pierre Santos
Dorothy Boyd	Dorothy Ayres
Garry Marsh	Geoffrey Lucas
George Hayes	Henry Otisse
Brian Buchell	Adam Steele
Robert Horton	Sir George Frame

Frederick Burtwell	Insp Grant
Marjorie Chard	Lady Groombridge
Vera Boggetti	Agnes Judd
Dorothy Minto	Lilian Hope

CRIME French tec unmasks singer as killer avenging dead mother.

09732
THAT'S MY UNCLE (58) (U)
Twickenham (U)
P: Julius Hagen
D: George Pearson
S: (PLAY) Frederick Jackson
(THE IRON WOMAN)
SC: Michael Barringer

Mark Daly	Walter Frisbee
Richard Cooper	Arthur Twindle
Betty Astell	Maudie
Margaret Yarde	Mrs Frisbee
Michael Shepley	Charlie Cookson
Wally Patch	Splinty Woods
David Horne	Col Marlowe
Hope Davy	Betty Marlowe
Ralph Truman	Monty

COMEDY Crooks plant stolen wallet on henpecked uplifter posing as butler.

09733
STREET SONG (64) (A)
Real Art (Radio)
P: Julius Hagen
D: Bernard Vorhaus
S: Bernard Vorhaus, Paul Gangelin

John Garrick	Tom Tucker
Rene Ray	Lucy
Wally Patch	Wally
Lawrence Hanray	Tuttle
Johnny Singer	Billy

MUSICAL Crooks reform for girl's sake and become radio stars.

09734
THE MORALS OF MARCUS (76) (A)
Real Art (Gaumont)
P: Julius Hagen
D: Miles Mander
S: (NOVEL) W.J.Locke
(THE MORALS OF MARCUS ORDEYNE)
SC: Miles Mander, Guy Bolton, H.Fowler Mear

Lupe Velez	Carlotta
Ian Hunter	Sir Marcus Ordeyne
Adrianne Allen	Judith Mainwaring
Noel Madison	Tony Pasquale
J.H.Roberts	
H.F.Maltby	
Arnold Lucy	
Frank Atkinson	
D.J.Williams	
James Raglan	
Johnny Nit	

COMEDY Harem escapee loves aristocratic archaeologist who saves her from cad in Paris.

09735
DEATH DRIVES THROUGH (63) (U)
Clifford Taylor (ABFD)
D: Edward L. Cahn
S: Katherine Strueby, John Huston
SC: Gordon Wellesley

Dorothy Bouchier	Kay Lord
Robert Douglas	Kit Woods
Miles Mander	Garry Ames
Percy Walsh	Mr Lord
Frank Atkinson	Nigger Larson
Lillian Gunns	Binnie

SPORT Racing car designer wins magnate's daughter from crooked rival.

09736
RADIO PIRATES (89) (U)
Sound City (AP & D) *reissue:* 1940,

BIG BEN CALLING (44 mins cut)
P: Norman Loudon
D: Ivar Campbell
S: Donovan Pedelty

Leslie French	Leslie
Mary Lawson	Mary
Warren Jenkins	Willie Brooks
Enid Stamp-Taylor	
Kenneth Kove	
Edgar Driver	
Frederick Lloyd	
John Turnbull	
Fanny Wright	

Hughie Green; Teddy Brown; Roy Fox and his Band
MUSICAL Cafe proprietress, radio salesman, and composer set up pirate radio station.

09737
THE RIVERSIDE MURDER (64) (A)
Fox British
D: Albert Parker
S: (NOVEL) Andre Steedman
(SIX DEAD MEN)
SC: Selwyn Jepson, Leslie Landau

Basil Sydney	Insp Winton
Judy Gunn	Claire Harris
Alastair Sim	Sgt McKay
Tom Helmore	Jerome
Ian Fleming	Sanders
Reginald Tate	Perrin
Martin Lewis	Gregg
Aubrey Mallalieu	Norman
Zoe Davis	Mrs Harris

CRIME Girl reporter helps inspector solve deaths of three financiers on eve of group shareout.

09738
PITY THE POOR RICH (22) (U)
Walker (ABFD)
D: Ian Walker
Nat Gonella and his Georgians

Dorothy Thomas	Queenie Leonard
Arthur Young	Julian Vedey

MUSICAL Romantic couple's evening out at nightclub.

09739
OH, WHAT A NIGHT ! (58) (A)
BSFP (U)
P: Edward G. Whiting
D: Frank Richardson
S: (PLAY) Ernest Denny
(THE IRRESISTIBLE MARMADUKE)

Molly Lamont	Pat
James Carew	Mortimer B.Gregory
Valerie Hobson	Susan
Martin Walker	Marmaduke
Nina Boucicault	Althea Gregory
Roland Culver	Marmaduke
Kathleen Kelly	Miss Wyley
Ernest Stidwell	Dawson

COMEDY Relatives persuade amnesia victim that he is son of missing millionaire.

09740
KEY TO HARMONY (68) (A)
B & D-Paramount British
P: Anthony Havelock-Allan
D: Norman Walker
S: (NOVEL) John B.Wilson
(SUBURBAN RETREAT)
SC: Basil Mason

Belle Chrystal	Mary Meynell
Fred Conyngham	Victor Barnett
Reginald Purdell	Tom Kirkwood
Olive Sloane	Nonia Sande
Ernest Butcher	Mr Meynell

Muriel George . . . .   Mrs Meynell
D.A.Clarke-Smith . . . .   Rupert Golder
Cyril Smith . . . .   Fred
ROMANCE Composer attains success after
marrying actress and is tempted to leave her.

09741
SAY IT WITH DIAMONDS (64) (A)
Davis (MGM)
D: Redd Davis
S: Jack Marks
Frank Pettingell . . . .   Ezra Hopkins
Eve Becke . . . .   Sylvia
Vera Bogetti . . . .   Kay
Gerald Rawlinson . . . .   Richard
Eileen Munro . . . .   Fanny Hopkins
Ernest Sefton . . . .   Mocket
Arthur Finn . . . .   Montana
COMEDY Mancunian brassfounder saves
necklace from crooks posing as detectives.

09742
A LITTLE BIT OF BLUFF (61) (U)
GS Enterprises (MGM)
P: A.George Smith
D: Maclean Rogers
S: H.F.Maltby, Kathleen Butler
Reginald Gardiner . . . .   Hugh Rigby
Marjorie Shotter . . . .   Joyce Simcox
H.F.Maltby . . . .   Admiral Simcox
Margaret Watson . . . .   Mrs Simcox
Clifford Heatherley . . . . . .
Clifford McLaglen . . . .
Molly Fisher . . . .
Peggy Novak . . . .
COMEDY Girl's fiancee poses as tec to
find father's lost jewels.

09743
A REAL BLOKE (70) (U)
Baxter & Barter (MGM)
P: John Barter
D: John Baxter
S: Herbert Ayres
George Carney . . . .   Bill
Mary Clare . . . .   Kate
Diana Beaumont . . . .   Mary
Peggy Novak   Lil
Mark Daly . . . .   Scotty
Billy Holland . . . .   Joe
Wilson Coleman . . . .   Watchman
Roddy Hughes . . . .   Taffy
Edgar Driver . . . .   Titch
C.Denier Warren . . . .   Tailor
DRAMA Navvy keeps unemployment secret
until after daughter's wedding.

09744
THE SMALL MAN (71) (U)
Baxter & Barter (U)
P: John Barter
D: John Baxter
S: Con West
George Carney . . . .   Bill Edwards
Minnie Rayner . . . .   Alice Roberts
Mary Newland . . . .   Mary Roberts
Ernest Butcher . . . .   Arthur
Mark Daly . . . .   Scotty
Edgar Driver . . . .   Titch
Charles Mortimer . . . .   Director
Ian Colin . . . .   His Son
Roddy Hughes . . . .   David
C.Denier Warren . . . .   Manager
Albert Sandler; Haydn Wood; Thorpe Bates;
Gresham Singers; Foden's Band
DRAMA Small shopkeepers unite to fight
chain store.

09745
WHO'S YOUR FATHER ? (63) (A)
Lupino Lane-St George's Pictures (Col)
D: Henry W.George
S: (PLAY) Mark Melford (TURNED UP)
SC: Lupino Lane, Arthur Rigby, Reginald Long
Lupino Lane . . . .   George Medway
Peter Haddon . . . .   Frank Steadley
Nita Harvey . . . .   Bina Medway
James Finlayson . . . .
Jean Kent . . . .   Mary Radcliffe
Margaret Yarde . . . .   Mrs Medway
James Carew . . . .   Elmer J.Radcliffe
Peter Gawthorne . . . .   Capt Medway
COMEDY Affianced man's mother weds
undertaker and father weds Negress.

09746
SO YOU WON'T TALK ? (84) (U)
WB-FN (FN)
P: Irving Asher
D: Monty Banks
S: Tom Geraghty
SC: Russell Medcraft, Frank Launder
Monty Banks . . . .   Tony Cazari
Claude Dampier . . . .   Wilbur Whistle
Ralph Ince . . . .   Ralph Younger
Vera Pearce . . . .   Edith
Bertha Belmore . . . .   Harriet
Enid Stamp-Taylor . . . .   Pauline
Muriel Angelus . . . .   Katrina
A.Bromley Davenport . . . . .   Fielding
Julian Royce . . . .   Peebles
COMEDY Heir to £100,000 must not speak
or write for one month.

09747
VARIETY (86) (U)
Argyle Talking Films (Butcher)
P: John Argyle
D: Adrian Brunel
S: Oswald Mitchell
SC: Oswald Mitchell, Adrian Brunel
Sam Livesey . . . .   Charlie Boyd
Cassie Livesey . . . .   Maggie Boyd
Jack Livesey . . . .   Matt Boyd
Barry Livesey . . . .   Victor Boyd
April Vivian . . . .   Joan
Bertha Wilmott   Nellie Wallace
Tessa Deane   Houston Sisters
George Carney   Harry Brunning
Phyllis Robins   Bobbie "Uke" Henshaw
Denis O'Neil   Sam Barton
John Rorke   Sherman Fisher Girls
Olsen's Sea Lions   Horace Sheldon's Orchestra
Billy Cotton and his Band
MUSICAL Forty years of family-owned
Music Hall. (Extracts in HIGHLIGHTS OF
VARIETY Nos. 1 - 6 (1937).

09748
HANDLE WITH CARE (55) (U)
Embassy (Radio) *reissue:* 1941,
LOOK OUT MR HAGGIS (Fed)
P: George King, Randall Faye
D: Redd Davis
S: Randall Faye
Molly Lamont . . . .   Patricia
Jack Hobbs . . . .   Jack
James Finlayson . . . .   Jimmy
Henry Victor . . . .   Count Paul
Vera Bogetti . . . .   Fifi
Margaret Yarde . . . .   Mrs Tunbody
Tonie Edgar Bruce . . . .   Lady Deeping
Stafford Hilliard . . . .   Prof Deeping
COMEDY Ex-crook takes strength pill and
thwarts spies.

09749
CLAP HANDS (18) (U)
Fidelity (LMB)
D: Frank Dormand
Charlie Kunz
Teddy Brown
MUSICAL Dance tunes played by pianist
and xylophonist.

09750
KIDDIES ON PARADE (22) (U)
Majestic Enterprises (MGM)
P: Bertram H. Hyams
D: Stewart B. Moss
S: Fay Glenn
Charles Hawtrey   Tommie Hayes
Rosie Youngman   Dan Rowles
Italia Conti's Juveniles
Pat Rose and his Majestic Orchestra
MUSICAL Children sing and dance.

09751
IMMORTAL GENTLEMAN (61) (U)
Bernard Smith (EB)
D:S: Widgey Newman
SC: John Quin
Basil Gill.. William Shakespeare/Malvolio
Rosalinde Fuller.. Ophelia/Juliet/Lady
Dennis Hoey . . . . . Soldier/Toby Belch
Anne Bolt . . . .   Jane/Maria
Edgar Owen . . . . . Ben Jonson/Mercutio
J. Hubert Leslie . . . .   Michael Drayton
Laidman Browne .. Gambler/Petruchio/Feste
Terence de Marney..Harry Morton/Hamlet/Romeo
Derrick de Marney . . . James Carter/Tybalt
Fred Rains . . . .   Miser
Dennis Wyndham . . . .   Voyager
Ivan Berlyn . . . . . . Father/Aguecheek
Leo Genn . . . . Merchant/Shylock
Roy Byford . . . .   Squire
DRAMA 1606. Playwright discusses
work with friends.

09752
THE MOUNTAIN (82) (A)
Jackatoon (EB)
D: Travis Jackson
Maurice Jones . . . .   David Rodgers
Hope Sharpe . . . .   Sylvia Goodhall
Alan F. Elliott . . . . .   Rev Brian Goodhall
J. Vyne Clarke . . . .   Old Sam
Rosemary Lee Booker . . . . .   Rose Harding
Sydney Dench . . . .   John Rodgers
ADVENTURE Lakeland. Jealous cleric
goes mad and kills wife's mountaineering
lover.

09753
DISCIPLINE (18) (A)
Monarch (Zenifilms)
P: Fraser Foulsham
D: James Riddell, A.B. Imeson
S: (STORY) Lesley Storm
SC: James Riddell
Charles Mortimer . . . .   Businessman
A.B.Imeson . . . .   Watchman
April Vivian . . . .
Eric Dance . . . .
Clifford Cobb . . . .
Mary Mackintosh . . . .
Natalie Nova . . . .
DRAMA Psychic watchman warns
businessman that his train will crash, and
it kills his blackmailer.

09754
THE OBVIOUS THING (20) (A)
Monarch (U)
P: Fraser Foulsham D: James Riddell
A.B.Imeson . . . . Embezzler
CRIME Embezzler's plan to kill associate
fails when door handle comes off.

09755
JUST FOR TONIGHT (11) (A)
Patrick K. Heale (MGM)
D: Patrick K. Heale
Eve Gray . . . . Girl
COMEDY Alleged burglar forced to pose
as girl's husband.

09756
MURDER AT TEN (8) (A)
Patrick K. Heale (MGM)
D: Patrick K.Heale
CRIME Jealous husband tries to kill
wife's lover.

09757
FIGHTING STOCK (68) (A)
Gainsborough (Gaumont)
P: Michael Balcon
D: Tom Walls
S: Ben Travers
Tom Walls . . . . Sir Donald Rowley
Ralph Lynn . . . . Sidney
Robertson Hare . . . . Duck
Marie Lohr . . . . Barbara Rivers
Lesley Wareing . . . . Eileen Rivers
Veronica Rose . . . . Diana Rivers
Herbert Lomas . . . . Murlow
Hubert Harben . . . . Mr Rivers
Mary Jerrold . . . . Emmie
Sybil Grove . . . . Mrs Peacock
Norah Howard . . . . Ada
COMEDY Brigadier and nephew save niece
from blackmailer.

APR

09758
ABDUL THE DAMNED (111) (A)
BIP-Capitol (Wardour)
P: Max Schach
D: Karl Grune
S: (NOVEL) Robert Neumann
SC: Ashley Dukes, Warren Chetham
Strode, Roger Burford
Fritz Kortner . . Abdul Hamid II/Kislar
Nils Asther . . . . Kadar Pash
Adrienne Ames . . . . Therese Alder
John Stuart . . . . Talak Pash
Esme Percy . . . . Ali the Eunuch
Walter Rilla . . . . Hassan Bey
Charles Carson . . . . Halmi Pasha
Patric Knowles . . . . Omar
Eric Portman . . . . Conspirator
Clifford Heatherley . . . . . . Doctor
Annie Esmond . . . . Lady
Arthur Hardy . . . . Ambassador
Robert Naylor; Warren Jenkins
DRAMA Turkey, 1900. Viennese opera
star saves lover's life by joining Sultan's
harem.

09759
ROYAL CAVALCADE (104) (U)
USA: REGAL CAVALCADE
BIP (Wardour)
P: Walter C. Mycroft
D: Thomas Bentley, Herbert Brenon,
Norman Lee, Walter Summers, Will Kellino,
Marcel Varnel
S: Val Gielgud, Holt Marvel, Eric Maschwitz
SC: Marjorie Deans
N: Roy Russell, Edward Chapman,
D.A.Clarke-Smith
Marie Lohr . . . . Mother
Hermione Baddeley . . . . . . Barmaid
Robert Hale . . . . Drinker
J.H.Roberts . . . . Drinker
Charles Paton . . . . Taxidriver
C.V.France . . . . Father
John Singer . . . . Boy
Esme Percy . . . . Lloyd George
Frederick Lloyd . . . . Neighbour
C.Denier Warren . . . . Smith
Pearl Argyle . . . . Anna Pavlova
Frank Vosper . . . . Capt Scott
Austin Trevor . . . . Capt Oates
John Stuart . . . . Explorer
Jane Baxter . . . . Girl
John Mills . . . . Boy
Jimmy Hanley . . . . Newsboy
Wally Bosco . . . . MP
Alice Lloyd . . . . Marie Lloyd
Amy Veness . . . . Suffragette
Antionette Cellier . . . . . . Marjorie Wilkinson
Jimmy Godden . . . . Harry
Chili Bouchier . . . . Landgirl
Renee Macready . . . . Landgirl
Annie Esmond . . . . Lady
Bertha Belmore . . . . Schoolmistress
C.M.Hallard . . . . Winston Churchill
H.Saxon Snell . . . . Sir Edward Grey
Fred Groves . . . . Soldier
George Graves . . . . Old Bill
Ronald Shiner . . . . Soldier
Iris Ashley . . . . Girl
Constance Shotter . . . . . . Girl
Patric Knowles . . . . Officer
Judy Kelly . . . . Girl
Billy Caryll . . . . Agent
Hilda Mundy . . . . Girl
Gus McNaughton . . . . Workman
W.H.Berry . . . . Bob
Clifford Mollison . . . . Customer
Gene Gerrard . . . . Passenger
Vera Pearce . . . . Wife
Reginald Gardiner . . . . . . Conductor
Reginald Purdell . . . . Listener
Ellen Pollock . . . . Wife
Diana Napier . . . . Actress
Syd Walker . . . . Doorman
Rene Ray . . . . Girl
Elaine Benson . . . . Child
Leonora Corbett . . . . Nurse
Olga Lindo . . . . Tourist
Mary Glynne . . . . Waitress
Sam Livesey . . . . Drinker
Robert Nainby . . . . Drinker
Seymour Hicks . . . . Gentleman
Ellaline Terriss . . . . Wife
Owen Nares . . . . Gentleman
Aileen Marson . . . . Lady
Gyles Isham . . . . Officer
Arthur Margetson . . . . . . Officer
Basil Gill . . . . Bishop
Jerry Verno . . . . Taxpayer
Craighall Sherry . . . . Chancellor
Ivan Samson . . . . Man
Carol Goodner . . . . Tourist
James Carew . . . . Tourist
Ben Welden . . . . Businessman
Matheson Lang . . . . Henry V
Athene Seyler . . . . Queen Elizabeth
George Robey; Arthur Prince; Harry Tate;
Lady Astor; Jack Judge; Florrie Forde;
Bert Feldman; Norman Long; Stanton
Jefferies; Stuart Hibberd; Leonard Henry;
Debroy Somers and his Band; Sydney
Baines and his Band; Band of HM Scots
Guards.
HISTORY 1910-1935. Events during the
reign of King George V through the
travels of a penny. (Includes extracts from
ATLANTIC; DRAKE OF ENGLAND;
and newsreels).

09760
ESCAPE ME NEVER (95) (A)
B&D (UA) reissue: 1941 (Ex)
P: Herbert Wilcox
D: Paul Czinner
S: (PLAY) Margaret Kennedy
SC: Carl Zuckerman, Robert Cullen
Elisabeth Bergner . . . . Gemma Jones
Hugh Sinclair . . . . Sebastian Sanger
Griffith Jones . . . . Caryl Sanger
Penelope Dudley Ward . .Fenella McClean
Irene Vanbrugh . . . . Mrs McClean
Leon Quartermaine . . . . . . Mr McClean
Lyn Harding . . . . Heinrich
Rosalinde Fuller . . . . Teremtcherva
ROMANCE Vienna. Girl stranded with baby
weds composer who loves his brother's
fiancee.

09761
THE VILLAGE SQUIRE (66) (U)
B & D-Paramount British
P: Anthony Havelock-Allan
D: Reginald Denham
S: (PLAY) Arthur Jarvis Black
SC: Sherard Powell
David Horne . . . . Squire Hollis
Leslie Perrins . . . . Richard Venables
Moira Lynd . . . . Mary Hollis
Vivien Leigh . . . . Rose Venables
Margaret Watson . . . . Aunt Caroline
Haddon Mason . . . . Dr Blake
Ivor Barnard . . . . Mr Worsfold
COMEDY Film star saves squire's production
of "Macbeth" and weds his daughter.

09762
GENTLEMAN'S AGREEMENT (71) (A)
B & D-Paramount British
P: Anthony Havelock-Allan
D: George Pearson
S: (STORY) Jennifer Howard (THE WAGER)
SC: Basil Mason
Frederick Peisley . . . . Guy Carfax
Vivien Leigh . . . . Phil Stanley
Antony Holles . . . . Bill Bentley
David Horne . . . . Sir Charles Lysle
Vera Bogetti . . . . Dora Deleamere
Victor Stanley . . . . Williams
Ronald Shiner . . . . Jim Ferrin
Kate Saxon . . . . Mrs Ferrin
COMEDY Educated wastrel changes
places with down-and-out.

09763
MARIA MARTEN; OR, THE MURDER IN THE
RED BARN (67) (A)
George King (MGM) reissue: 1940 (Amb)
D: George King
S: (PLAY) Unknown
SC: Randall Faye
Tod Slaughter . . . . William Corder
Sophie Stewart . . . . Maria Marten
Eric Portman . . . . Carlos
Ann Trevor . . . . Nan
D.J.Williams . . . . Farmer Marten
Clare Greet . . . . Mrs Marten
Quinton McPherson . . . . . . Mr Serret
Antonia Brough . . . . Mrs Serret
Dennis Hoey . . . . Gambler
CRIME 1820. Squire kills his pregnant
mistress to marry heiress.

09764
MR WHAT'S-HIS-NAME (67) (A)
WB-FN (FN)
P: Irving Asher

D: Ralph Ince
S: (PLAY) Yves Mirande, Seymour Hicks
SC: Tom Geraghty, Frank Launder
Seymour Hicks . . . . Alfred Henfield
Olive Blakeney . . . . Ann Henfield
Enid Stamp-Taylor . . . . Corinne Henfield
Garry Marsh . . . . Yates
Tonie Edgar Bruce . . . . Sylvia
Martita Hunt . . . . Mrs Davies
Henry Longhurst . . . . Mr Bullen
Louis Broughton . . . . Mr Holt
COMEDY Married millionaire weds
beautician while suffering amnesia.

09765
FULL CIRCLE (55) (A)
WB-FN (WB)
P: Irving Asher
D: George King
S: Michael Barringer
Rene Ray . . . . Margery Boyd
Garry Marsh . . . . Max Reeves
Graham Pocket . . . . Mark Boyd
Betty Shale . . . . Mrs Boyd
Margaret Yarde . . . . Agatha
Patricia Hilliard . . . . Jeanne Westover
Bruce Belfrage . . . . Clyde Warren
John Wood . . . . Tony Warren
Elizabeth Jenns . . . . Leonora Allway
CRIME Burglar steals will, then steals it
again to return it to heiress.

MAY

09766
OFF THE DOLE (89) (A)
Mancunian reissue: 1938 (Amb; cut)
P: John E. Blakeley
D:S: Arthur Mertz
George Formby . . . . John Willie
Beryl Formby . . . Grace, Charm and Ability
Constance Shotter . . . . Irene
Dan Young . . . . The Inimitable Dude
James Plant . . . Crisp and Debonair
Stan Pell . The Most Inoffensive Parson
Stan Little . . . . Little Jack
Tully Comber . . . Measured for his Part
Clifford McLaglen. . A Villain and Proud of it
Wally Patch . . . . . . Revels in his Part
Twilight Blondes; Boy Choristers; London
Babes; Arthur L.Ward and his Band
MUSICAL Workshy takes over uncle's
detective agency and catches crooks.
(Extracts in MUSIC HALL PERSONALITIES
Nos. 2; 5; 6; GEORGE FORMBY Nos. 2; 6.
(1938).)

09767
SANDERS OF THE RIVER (98) (U)
London (UA) reissues: 1938 (564 ft cut)
1943 (AA) 1947 (BL)
P: Alexander Korda
D: Zoltan Korda
S: (NOVEL) Edgar Wallace
SC: Lajos Biro, Jeffrey Dell, Arthur
Wimperis
Paul Robeson . . . . Bosambo
Leslie Banks . . . . R.G.Sanders
Nina Mae McKinney . . . . . . Lilongo
Robert Cochran . . . . Tibbets
Martin Walker . . . . Ferguson
Richard Grey . . . . Hamilton
Marquis de Portago . . . . . . Farini
Eric Maturin . . . . Smith
Allan Jeayes . . . . Father O'Leary
Charles Carson . . . . Governor
Orlando Martins . . . . K'Lova
Chiefs and members of the Wagenia,
Acholi, Sesi, Teffik, Juruba, Mendi & Kroo
tribes.

ADVENTURE Nigeria. African ex-convict
helps British commissioner quell slavery
and thwart crooked deputy.

09768
HEAT WAVE (75) (U)
Gainsborough (Gaumont)
P: Jerome Jackson
D: Maurice Elvey
S: Austin Melford
SC: Austin Melford, Leslie Arliss, Jerome
Jackson
Albert Burdon . . . . Albert Speed
Cyril Maude . . . . President Allison
Les Allen . . . . Tom Brown
Anna Lee . . . . Jane Allison
Vera Pearce . . . . Gloria Spania
Bernard Nedell . . . . Gen de Costa
C.Denier Warren . . . . . . Col d'Alvarez
Bruce Winston . . . . Lenane
Edmund Willard . . . . Hoffman
Lecuona Cuban Boys; Grace Poggi
MUSICAL Ruritania. Greengrocer mistaken
for gunrunner thwarts revolution.

09769
BULLDOG JACK (72) (U) USA: ALIAS
BULLDOG DRUMMOND
Gaumont
P: Michael Balcon
D: Walter Forde
S: Jack Hulbert; (CHARACTERS) H.C.
McNeile (BULLDOG DRUMMOND)
SC: H.C.McNeile, Gerard Fairlie, J.O.C.Orton,
Sidney Gilliat
Jack Hulbert . . . . Jack Pennington
Fay Wray . . . . Ann Manders
Claude Hulbert . . . . Algy Longworth
Ralph Richardson . . . . Morelle
Paul Graetz . . . . Salvini
Gibb McLaughlin . . . . Denny
Athol Fleming . . . . Bulldog Drummond
Cyril Smith . . . . Henchman
Harvey Braban . . . . Sgt Robinson
COMEDY Playboy posing as detective catches
gang using old underground station to raid
British Museum.

09770
BROWN ON RESOLUTION (80) (A)
retitled: FOREVER ENGLAND
USA: BORN FOR GLORY
Gaumont reissue: 1941 (IFR; II mins cut)
P: Michael Balcon
D: Walter Forde
S: (NOVEL) C.S.Forester
SC: Michael Hogan, Gerard Fairlie,
J.O.C.Orton
Betty Balfour . . . . Elizabeth Brown
John Mills . . . . Albert Brown
Barry McKay . . . . Lt Somerville
Jimmy Hanley . . . . Ginger
Howard Marion Crawford . . Max
H.G.Stoker . . . . Capt Holt
Percy Walsh . . . . Kapitan von Lutz
George Merritt . . . . William Brown
Cyril Smith . . . . William Brown jr
WAR 1914. Captain's bastard son holds
German cruiser at bay with rifle.

09771
THE BIG SPLASH (66) (U)
British Lion (MGM)
P: Herbert Smith
D: Leslie Hiscott
S: Michael Barringer
Frank Pettingell . . . . Bodkin
Finlay Currie . . . . Hartley Bassett
Marguerite Allan . . . . Germaine

Drusilla Wills . . . . Mrs Bodkin
Roy Royston . . . . Jack Trent
Ben Welden . . . . Crook
Percy Parsons . . . . Crook
COMEDY Affianced millionaire hires
married man to pose as him.

09772
THE CASE OF GABRIEL PERRY (78) (A)
British Lion reissue: 1939 (EB)
P: Herbert Smith
D: Albert de Courville
S: (PLAY) James Dale (WILD JUSTICE)
(WILD JUSTICE)
SC: L. DuGarde Peach
Henry Oscar . . . . Gabriel Perry
Olga Lindo . . . . Mrs Perry
Margaret Lockwood . . . . . Mildred Perry
Franklin Dyall . . . . Prosecution
Raymond Lovell . . . . Defence
John Wood . . . . Godfrey Perry
Martita Hunt . . . . Mrs Read
Rodney Ackland . . . . Tommy Read
Percy Walsh . . . . William Read
Ralph Truman . . . . Insp White
CRIME 1885. Wife learns that her JP
husband has killed local woman.

09773
MARRY THE GIRL (69) (A)
British Lion reissue: 1939 (EB)
P: Herbert Smith
D: Maclean Rogers
S: (PLAY) George Arthurs, Arthur Miller
SC: Maclean Rogers, Kathleen Butler
Sonnie Hale . . . . Wally Gibbs
Winifred Shotter . . . . . . Doris Chattaway
Hugh Wakefield . . . . Hugh Delafield
Judy Kelly . . . . Jane Elliott
C.Denier Warren . . . . Banks
Kenneth Kove . . . . Cyril Chattaway
Maidie Hope . . . . Mrs Elliott
Wally Patch . . . . Bookmaker
John Deverell . . . . Judge
COMEDY Woman makes daughter sue
her fiance although they love one another.

09774
NIGHT MAIL (53) (A)
British Lion (MGM)
P:D: Herbert Smith
S: Charles Bennett, Billie Bristow
Henry Oscar . . . . Mancini
Hope Davy . . . . Wendy March
C.M.Hallard . . . . Sir Walter March
Richard Bird . . . . Billy
Jane Carr . . . . Lady Angela Savage
Garry Marsh . . . . . . Capt Ronnie Evans
Edmond Breon . . . . Lord Ticehurst
Doris Hare . . . .
Tonie Edgar Bruce . . . .
Frank Atkinson . . . .
Viola Lyel. . . . .
Wilfrid Hyde White . . . .
CRIME Co-respondent thwarts violinist's
attempt to kill judge aboard Aberdonian
express.

09775
THE CITY OF BEAUTIFUL NONSENSE (88)
(U)
Butcher's Film Service
P: Wilfred Noy
D: Adrian Brunel
S: (NOVEL) E.Temple Thurston
SC: Donovan Pedelty
Emlyn Williams . . . . Jack Grey
Sophie Stesart . . . . Jill Dealtry
Eve Lister . . . . Amber
George Carney . . . . Chesterton

Marie Wright . . . . Dorothy Grey
Eric Maturin . . . . Robert Downing
J.Fisher White . . . . Thomas Grey
Daisy Dormer . . . . Mrs Deakin
Hubert Harben . . . . Mr Dealtry
Margaret Damer . . . . Mrs Dealtry
Derek Oldham . . . . Singer
ROMANCE Poor composer loves girl
pledged to rich man for her father's sake.

09776
BARGAIN BASEMENT (65) (A)
retitled: DEPARTMENT STORE
Real Art (Radio)
P: Julius Hagen
D: Leslie Hiscott
S: H.F.Maltby
SC: H. Fowler Mear
Garry Marsh . . . . Timothy Bradbury
Eve Gray . . . . Dolly Flint
Sebastian Shaw . . . John Goodman Johnson
Geraldine Fitzgerald . . . . . Jane Grey
Jack Melford . . . . Bob Goodman
Patrick Curwen . . . . James Goodman
Henry Hallett . . . . Mr Buxton
Hal Walters . . . . Sam Slack
CRIME Crooked manager mistakes
ex-convict for employer's incognito heir.

09777
BE CAREFUL MR SMITH (72) (U)
Union (Apex) reissue: 1940,
SINGING THROUGH (22 mins cut)
D: Max Mack
S: Frank Atkinson, Ernest Longstaffe
Bobbie Comber . . . . Geoffrey Smith
Bertha Belmore . . . . Jenny Smith
Frank Atkinson . . . .
Cecil Ramage . . . .
Bertha Ricardo . . . .
C.Denier Warren . . . .
Warren C.Jenkins . . . .
MUSICAL Retired henpeck buys bookmaker's
and foils sharepushers.

09778
MIMI (94) (A)
BIP (Wardour)
P: Walter C.Mycroft
D: Paul Stein
S: (NOVEL) Henri Murger
(LA VIE BOHEME)
SC: Clifford Grey, Paul Merzbach, Jack Davies,
Denis Waldock
Douglas Fairbanks jr . . . . . . Rodolphe
Gertrude Lawrence . . . . . . Mimi
Diana Napier . . . . Sidonie
Harold Warrender . . . . Marcel
Carol Goodner . . . . Musette
Richard Bird . . . . Colline
Martin Walker . . . . Schaunard
Austin Trevor . . . . Lamotte
Lawrence Hanray . . . . Barbemouche
Paul Graetz . . . . Durand
Jack Raine . . . . Duke
ROMANCE France, 1850. Poor girl helps
playwright to succeed, then dies.
(Extract in ELSTREE STORY, 1952).

09779
SCHOOL FOR STARS (70) (A)
B & D- Paramount British
P: Anthony Havelock-Allan
D:SC: Donovan Pedelty
S: Arthur Austin
Fred Conyngham . . . . Frank Murray
Jean Gillie . . . . Joan Martin
Torin Thatcher . . . . Guy Mannering
Peggy Novak . . . . Phyllis Dawn

Ian Fleming . . . . . Sir Geoffrey Hilliard
Frank Birch . . . . Robert Blake
Winifred Oughton . . . . Mrs Dealtry
Victor Stanley . . . . Bill
Geraldo and his Music
ROMANCE Waitress joins drama school,
becomes dancer and finds love.

09780
THE PRICE OF A SONG (67) (A)
Fox British
D: Michael Powell
S: Anthony Gittins
Campbell Gullan . . . . . . Arnold Grierson
Marjorie Corbett . . . . . . Margaret Nevern
Eric Maturin . . . . Nevern
Gerald Fielding . . . . . . Michael Hardwicke
Dora Barton . . . . Letty Grierson
Charles Mortimer . . . . Oliver Bloom
Oriel Ross . . , ... Elsie
Henry Caine . . . . Stringer
Sybil Grove . . . . Mrs Bancroft
CRIME Bookmaker inherits fortune by
killing step-daughter's husband and
framing her lover.

JUN

09781
HELLO SWEETHEART (70) (U)
WB-FN (WB)
P: Irving Asher
D: Monty Banks
S: (PLAY) George M.Cohan (THE BUTTER
AND EGG MAN)
SC: Brock Williams
Claude Hulbert . . . . Henry Pennyfeather
Gregory Ratoff . . . . Joseph Lewis
Jane Carr . . . . Babs Beverley
Nancy O'Neil . . . . Helen Taylor
Olive Blakeney . . . . Daisy Montrose
Cyril Smith . . . . Mac McQuire
Morris Harvey . . . . F.Q.Morse
Felix Aylmer . . . . Peabody
Phyllis Stanley; Johnnie Nit; Three Ginx;
Marriott Edgar; Carroll Gibbons.
MUSICAL Americans persuade farmer to use
inheritance to finance film.

09782
DRAKE OF ENGLAND (104) (U)
USA: DRAKE THE PIRATE
BIP (Wardour)
P: Walter C.Mycroft
D: Arthur Woods
S: (PLAY) Louis N.Parker
SC: Clifford Grey, Akos Tolnay,
Marjorie Deans, Norman Watson
Matheson Lang . . . . Francis Drake
Athene Seyler . . . . Queen Elizabeth
Jane Baxter . . . . Elizabeth Sydenham
Henry Mollison . . . . John Doughty
Donald Wolfit . . . . Thomas Doughty
George Merritt . . . . Tom Moone
Amy Veness . . . . Mother Moone
Ben Webster . . . . Lord Burghley
Sam Livesey . . . . Sir George Sydenham
Margaret Halstan . . . . . . Lady Sydenham
Charles Quartermaine . . . Parson Fletcher
Allan Jeayes . . . . Don Bernardino
Gibb McLaughlin . . . . Don Enriquez
Helen Haye . . . . Lady Lennox
Moore Marriott . . . . Bright
HISTORY 1567-88. Francis Drake plunders
Spanish ships, is knighted, and defeats Armada.

09783
LEND ME YOUR HUSBAND (61) (U)
Embassy (Radio) reissue: 1941 (Fed)
P: George King, Randall Faye

D: Frederick Hayward
S: Michael Trevellyan
SC: Randall Faye
John Stuart . . . . Jeff Green
Nora Swinburne . . . . Virgie Green
Nancy Burne . . . . Baba Green
Evan Thomas . . . . Tony Green
Annie Esmond . . . . Mother
COMEDY Married man spends trial weekend
with his friend's wife.

09784
ADMIRALS ALL (75) (U)
Stafford (Radio) P: John Stafford
D: Victor Hanbury
S: (PLAY) Stephen King-Hall, Ian Hay
Wynne Gibson . . . . .Gloria Gunn
Gordon Harker . . . . PO Dingle
Anthony Bushell . . . . . Lt Steve Langham
George Curzon . . . . Jeff Barclay
Joan White . . . . . Prudence Stallybrass
Henry Hewitt. . . . . Capt Knox
Percy Walsh . . . . Admiral Westerham
Ben Welden . . . . Adolph Klotz
Gwynneth Lloyd . . . . . Jean Stallybrass
Wilfrid Hyde White . . . . . . Mr Stallybrass
COMEDY American star aboard battleship
is kidnapped by pirates.

09785
THE RIGHT AGE TO MARRY (69) (U)
GS Enterprises (Radio)
P: A.George Smith
D: Maclean Rogers
S: (PLAY) H.F.Maltby
SC: H.F.Maltby, Kathleen Butler
Frank Pettingell . . . . Lomas
Joyce Bland . . . . Ellen
Tom Helmore . . . . Stephen
Ruby Miller . . . . Mrs Carlisle
Moira Lynd . . . . Carol
Hal Walters . . . . Crowther
H.F.Maltby . . . . Tetley
Gerald Barry . . . . Maj Locke
Isobel Scaife . . . . Clara
COMEDY Retired mill-owner vamped by
gold-digging widow.

09786
WHITE LILAC (67) (A)
Fox British
D: Albert Parker
S: (PLAY) Ladislas Fodor
Basil Sydney . . . . Ian Mackie
Judy Gunn . . . . Mollie
Claude Dampier . . . . Percy
Percy Marmont . . . . Tollitt
Gwenllian Gill . . . . Muriel
Leslie Perrins . . . . Iredale
Constance Travers . . . . Jessie
Billy Holland . . . . Harvey
Marjorie Hume . . . . Mrs Lyall
CRIME Various people suspected of
murdering unpopular villager.

09787
ONCE A THIEF (67) (A)
B & D-Paramount British
P: Anthony Havelock-Allan
D: George Pearson
S: Robert Dargavel
SC: Basil Mason
John Stuart . . . . Roger Drummond
Nancy Burne . . . . Marion Ashley
Lewis Shaw . . . . Frank Ashley
Derek Gorst . . . . George Marston
Frederick Culley . . . . . Sir John Chirwin
Lola Dauncan . . . . Mrs Eagle
Joan Kemp-Welch . . . . Alice
Ronald Shiner . . . . Man

CRIME Manager steals chemist's paint formula while he is in jail for gem theft.

09788
JUBILEE WINDOW (61) (A)
B & D-Paramount British
P: Anthony Havelock-Allan
D: George Pearson
S: Gerald Elliott
SC: Gerald Elliott, George Pearson
Sebastian Shaw .... Peter Ward
Ralph Truman .... Dan Stevens
Olive Melville .... Margery Holroyd
Frank Birch .... Ambrose Holroyd
Margaret Yarde .... Mrs Holroyd
Michael Shepley .... Dacres
Winifred Oughton ...... Mrs Tribbets
Robert Horton ..... Sir Edward Musgrove
Dorothy Hammond ...... Lady Musgrove
Mark Daly .... Dave
COMEDY Crooks try to steal hidden jewels on Jubilee Day.

09789
ROLLING HOME (68) (U)
Sound City (AP&D)
P: Norman Loudon
D: Ralph Ince
Will Fyffe .... John McGregor
Ralph Ince .... Wally
Molly Lamont .... Ann
James Raglan.......... Capt Pengelly
Ruth Maitland .... Mrs Murray
Mrs Graham Moffatt ..... Mrs McGregor
H.Saxon-Snell .... Callaghan
Jock McKay .... Jock
COMEDY Stowaway engineer stops officer from smuggling his crooked brother.

09790
THE 39 STEPS (86) (A)
Gaumont reissues: 1939 (GFD) 1942 (IFR)
AP: Ivor Montagu
D: Alfred Hitchcock
S: (NOVEL) John Buchan
SC: Charles Bennett, Ian Hay, Alma Reville
Robert Donat .... Richard Hannay
Madeleine Carroll .... Pamela
Godfrey Tearle .... Prof Jordan
Lucie Mannheim .... Anabella Smith
Peggy Ashcroft .... Margaret
John Laurie .... John
Helen Haye .... Mrs Jordan
Wylie Watson .... Memory
Frank Cellier .... Sheriff Watson
Jerry Verno .... Traveller
Gus McNaughton .... Traveller
Hilda Trevelyan .... Innkeeper's Wife
CRIME Spies pursue framed man and girl through Scotland.

09791
SQUIBS (77) (U)
Twickenham (Gaumont)
P: Julius Hagen
D: Henry Edwards
S: (PLAY) Clifford Seyler; George Pearson
SC: Michael Hogan, H.Fowler Mear
Betty Balfour .... Squibs Hopkins
Gordon Harker .... Sam Hopkins
Stanley Holloway....... PC Charley Lee
Margaret Yarde .... Mrs Lee
Morris Harvey .... Inspector Lee
Michael Shepley .... Colin Barrett
Drusilla Wills .... Mrs Parker
O.B.Clarence .... Sir John Barrett
Ronald Shiner .... Bill
Thomas Weguelin .... Alf
MUSICAL Gambler's flowergirl daughter wins sweepstake and weds PC.

09792
VINTAGE WINE (80) (A)
Real Art (Gaumont)
P: Julius Hagen
D: Henry Edwards
S: (PLAY) Alexander Engel
(DER EWIGE JUNGELING)
SC: Seymour Hicks, Ashley Dukes,
H.Fowler Mear
Seymour Hicks .... Charles Popinot
Claire Luce .... Nina Popinot
Eva Moore .... Josephine Popinot
Judy Gunn .... Blanche Popinot
Miles Malleson .... Henri Popinot
Kynaston Reeves .... Benedict Popinot
Michael Shepley .... Richard Emsley
A.Bromley Davenport .... Pierre
Amy Brandon Thomas .....
Meriel Forbes ....
Brian Buchel ....
COMEDY Rome. Girl finds her husband is twenty years older than he claims.

09793
THE DIVINE SPARK (81) (U) bilingual
Alleanza Cinematografica Italiana (GB)
P: Arnold Pressburger
D: Carmine Gallone
S: Walter Reisch
SC: Emlyn Williams, Richard Benson
Marta Eggerth.... Maddalena Fumaroli
Phillips Holmes .... Vincenzo Bellini
Benita Hume .... Giriditta Pasta
Donald Calthrop .... Judge Fumarolli
Arthur Margetson .... Ernesto Tosi
Edmund Breon .... Rossini
Basil Gill .... Romani
Hugh Miller .... Paganini
Edward Chapman .... Mercadanti
John Clements .... Florimo
Felix Aylmer .... Butler
John Deverell .... King
MUSICAL Naples, period. Affianced girl loves composer but rejects him lest he spoil his chances of success. (Made in Italy).

09794
THE SILENT PASSENGER (75) (A)
Phoenix Films (ABFD)
P: Hugh Perceval
D: Reginald Denham
S: (NOVEL) Dorothy L. Sayers
SC: Basil Mason
John Loder .... John Ryder
Peter Haddon .... Lord Peter Wimsey
Mary Newland .... Mollie Ryder
Austin Trevor .... Insp Parker
Donald Wolfit .... Henry Camberley
Leslie Perrins .... Maurice Windermere
Aubrey Mather .... Bunter
Robb Wilton .... Porter
Ralph Truman .... Saunders
CRIME Lord proves man did not kill wife's blackmailer.

09795
JOY RIDE (78) (A)
City (ABFD)
P: Basil Humphreys
D: Harry Hughes
S: Vernon Harris
Gene Gerrard .... Bill Shepherd
Zelma O'Neal.......... Virgy Maxwell
Betty Anne Davies .... Anne Maxwell
Paul Blake .... Dippy
Gus McNaughton .... String
Violet Vanbrugh .... Duchess
Cynthia Stock .... Selina Prune
Charles Sewell ..Sir Aubrey Mutch-Twistleton
Amy Veness .... Lady Clara

W.G.Saunders .... Bishop
Buddy Bradley Rythm Girls
COMEDY Man and cabaret girls pose as amnesiacs to fool rich aunt.

09796
IT HAPPENED IN PARIS (68) (U) bilingual
Wyndham (ABFD)
P: Bray Wyndham
D: Robert Wyler, Carol Reed
S: (PLAY) Yves Mirande (L'ARPETE)
SC: John Huston, H.F.Maltby
John Loder .... Paul
Nancy Burne .... Jacqueline
Edward H.Robbins .... Knight
Esme Percy .... Pommier
Lawrence Grossmith ..... Bernard
Dorothy Boyd .... Patricia
Jean Gillie .... Musette
Bernard Ansell .... Simon
Paul Sheridan .... Baptiste
Warren Jenkins .... Raymond
Kyrle Bellew .... Ernestine
Margaret Yarde .... Marthe
ROMANCE Paris. Rich American poses as poor artist to win poor girl.

09797
LOOK UP AND LAUGH (80) (U)
ATP (ABFD) reissue: 1942 (EB: 6 mins cut)
P:D: Basil Dean
S: J.B.Priestley
SC: Gordon Wellesley
Gracie Fields........... Grace Pearson
Douglas Wakefield .... Joe Chirk
Harry Tate .... Turnpenny
Alfred Drayton .... Belfer
Morris Harvey .... Rosenbloom
Vivien Leigh .... Marjorie Belfer
Robb Wilton .... Mayor
Huntley Wright .... Ketley
Tommy Fields .... Sidney Pearson
Billy Nelson .... Alf Chirk
D.J.Williams .... Maplas
Kenneth Kove .... Assistant
Jack Melford .... Reporter
Maud Gill .... Miss Canvey
Helen Ferrers .... Lady Buster
COMEDY Market stallholders thwart chainstore by discovering Royal Charter.

JUL

09798
DANCE BAND (74) (U)
BIP (Wardour)
P: Walter C.Mycroft
D: Marcel Varnel
S: Roger Burford, Jack Davies, Denis Waldock
Charles Buddy Rogers ..... Buddy Morgan
June Clyde .... Pat Shelley
Steven Geray .... Steve Sarel
Magda Kun .... Anny Ginger
Fred Duprez .... Lewis
Leon Sherkot .... Jim
Richard Hearne .... Drunk
Hal Gordon .... Spike
Albert Whelan .... Bourne
Fred Groves .... Mason
Jack Holland & June Hart
MUSICAL Dance band leader loves leader of all-girl orchestra.

09799
McGLUSKY THE SEA ROVER (58) (U)
USA: HELL'S CARGO
BIP (Wardour)
P: Walter C.Mycroft
D:SC: Walter Summers
S: (NOVEL) A.G.Hales
Jack Doyle .... McGlusky

Tamara Desni . . . . Flame
Henry Mollison . . . . Mazarin
Cecil Ramage . . . . Auda
Frank Cochrane . . . . Abu
Hugh Miller . . . . Karim
Jackie Short . . . . Govan
ADVENTURE Stowaway involved with
gunrunners falls in love with Arab girl.
(Extract in ELSTREE STORY, 1952).

09800
THE STOKER (69) (A)
Leslie Fuller (Gaumont) *reissue:* 1940
SHOVEL UP A BIT MORE COAL (cut)
P: Joe Rock
D: Leslie Pearce
S: Wallace Geoffrey
SC: Syd Courtenay, George Harris
Leslie Fuller . . . . Bill
Georgie Harris . . . . Oswald
Phyllis Clare . . . . Nita
Leslie Bradley . . . . Frank Munro
Olive Melville . . . . Alice
Pat Aherne . . . . Russell Gilham
Gibson Gowland . . . . Steve
Robert English . . . . Sir Richard Munro
COMEDY Stoker saves magnate's son from
wiles of gold-digger.

09801
COCK O' THE NORTH (84) (U)
Mitchell Films-Panther (Butcher)
P:S: Oswald Mitchell
D: Oswald Mitchell, Challis Sanderson
George Carney . . . . George Barton
Marie Lohr . . . . Mary Barton
Ronnie Hepworth . . . . Danny Barton
Horace Kenney . . . . Alf Coggins
Frederick Peisley . . . . Fred Coggins
Eve Lister . . . . Edna Barton
Peggy Novak . . . . Maggie Harris
Johnnie Schofield . . . . Bert Harris
Roddy Hughes . . . . Taffy
Leslie "Hutch" Hutchinson; Naughton & Gold;
Robert Chisholm; Simone Rogers
MUSICAL Engine driver retired after crash
finds consolation in his son. (Extracts in
HIGHLIGHTS OF VARIETY 11 & 12 (1937).)

09802
CROSS CURRENTS (66) (U)
B & D-Paramount British
P: Anthony Havelock-Allan
D: Adrian Brunel
S: (NOVEL) Gerald Elliott
(NINE DAYS BLUNDER)
SC: Adrian Brunel, Pelham Leigh Amann
Ian Colin . . . . . . Tony Brocklehurst
Marjorie Hume . . . . . . Mrs Stepping-Drayton
Evelyn Foster . . . . Margery Weston
Frank Birch . . . . Rev Eustace Hickling
Aubrey Mallalieu . . . . Gen Trumpington
Kate Saxon . . . . Miss Cruickshank
Aubrey Dexter . . . . Col Bagge-Grant
Bryan Powley . . . . Cdr Mannering
Sally Gray . . . . Sally Croker
COMEDY Devon. Village vicar suspected of
killing rival for widow.

09803
THE MAD HATTERS (68) (U)
B & D-Paramount British
P: Anthony Havelock-Allan
D: Ivar Campbell
S: (STORY) James Stewart (THE ONLY SON)
SC: Christine Jope-Slade
Chili Bouchier . . . . Vicki
Sidney King . . . . Tim St anhope
Evelyn Foster . . . . Ruth Stanhope
Kim Peacock . . . . Joe

Grace Lane . . . . Mrs Stanhope
Bellenden Clarke . . . . Gen Stanhope
Toska von Bissing . . . . Duchess
Vera Bogetti . . . . Lady Felicity
COMEDY Ex-Sandhurst cadet and sister's
fiance both fall for French neighbour when
they open hat shop.

09804
SEXTON BLAKE AND THE BEARDED
DOCTOR (64) (U)
Fox British (MGM)
D: George A.Cooper
S: (NOVEL) Rex Hardinge
(THE BLAZING LAUNCH MURDER)
George Curzon . . . . Sexton Blake
Henry Oscar . . . . Dr Gibbs
Tony Sympson . . . . Tinker
Gillian Maude . . . . Janet
Phil Ray . . . . Jim Cameron
John Turnbull . . . . Insp Donnell
Edward Dignon . . . . Hawkins
James Knight . . . . Red
Donald Wolfit . . . . Percy
CRIME Doctor kills violinist to defraud
insurance company.

09805
OLD ROSES (60) (A)
Fox British
D: Bernerd Mainwaring
S: Anthony Richardson
Horace Hodges . . . . Johnnie Lee
Nancy Burne . . . . Jenny Erroll
Bruce Lister . . . . Chris Morgan
Charles Mortimer . . . . John Morgan
Felix Aylmer . . . . Lord Sandebury
Wilfrid Walter . . . . Sweeton
Esma Church . . . . Mrs Erroll
George Hayes . . . . Simes
Eric Portman . . . . Lou
Trefor Jones . . . . Singing Gypsy
CRIME Old villager confesses to murder to
save rich man's suspected son.

09806
CHARING CROSS ROAD (72) (U)
British Lion *reissue:* 1939 (EB)
P: Herbert Smith
D: Albert de Courville
S: (RADIO PLAY) Gladys & Clay Keyes
SC: Con West, Clifford Grey
John Mills . . . . Tony
June Clyde . . . . Pam
Derek Oldham . . . . Jimmy O'Connell
Jean Colin . . . . Cherry
Belle Baker . . . . Belle
Arthur Sinclair . . . . Mac
Garry Marsh . . . . Berry
Judy Kelly . . . . Vera
Charles Heslop . . . . Langdon
Coral Brown . . . . Lady Ruston
C.Denier Warren . . . . Salesman
MUSICAL Landlord tells dancers how
social aspirations spoiled the success of
duettists.

09807
SOME DAY (68) (A)
WB-FN (WB)
P: Irving Asher
D: Michael Powell
S: (NOVEL) I.A.R.Wylie (YOUNG
NOWHERES)
SC: Brock Williams
Esmond Knight . . . . Curly Blake
Margaret Lockwood . . . . . Emily
Henry Mollison . . . . Canley
Sunday Wilshin . . . . Betty

Raymond Lovell . . . . Carr
Ivor Barnard . . . . Hope
George Pughe . . . . Milkman
ROMANCE Playboy helps poor lift operator
marry cleaner.

09808
WINDFALL (65) (U)
Embassy (Radio)
P: George King, Randall Faye
D: George King
S: (PLAY) R.C.Sheriff
SC: Randall Faye, Jack Celestin
Edward Rigby . . . . Sam Spooner
Marie Ault . . . . Maggie Spooner
George Carney . . . . Syd
Marjorie Corbett . . . . Mary
Derrick de Marney . . . . . . Tom Spooner
Googie Withers . . . . Dodie
DRAMA Ironmonger's inheritance turns son
into society loafer.

AUG

09809
THE CLAIRVOYANT (80) (A)
Gainsborough (Gau)
P: Michael Balcon
D: Maurice Elvey
S: (NOVEL) Ernst Lothar
SC: Charles Bennett, Bryan Edgar Wallace,
Robert Edmunds
Claude Rains . . . . Maximus
Fay Wray . . . . Rene
Jane Baxter . . . . Christine
Mary Clare . . . . Mother
Ben Field . . . . Simon
Athole Stewart . . . . Lord Southwood
Felix Aylmer . . . . Counsel
Donald Calthrop . . . .
Jack Raine . . . .
Margaret Davidge . . . .
C.Denier Warren . . . .
DRAMA Fraudulent mind-reader predicts
tunnel disaster that comes true.

09810
ME AND MARLBOROUGH (84) (U)
Gaumont
P: Michael Balcon
D: Victor Saville
S: W.P.Lipscomb, Reginald Pound
SC: Ian Hay, Marjorie Gaffney
Cicely Courtneidge . . . . . . Kit Ross
Tom Walls . . . . Duke of Marlborough
Barry McKay . . . . Dick Welch
Alfred Drayton . . . . Sgt Bull
Iris Ashley . . . . Josephine
Ivor McLaren . . . . Sgt Cummings
Gibb McLaughlin . . . . Old Soldier
Peter Gawthorne . . . . Colonel
Cecil Parker . . . . Colonel
George Merritt . . . . Harley
Micky Brantford . . . . Ensign Coke
Randle Ayrton . . . . Louis XIV
Henry Oscar . . . . Goultier
COMEDY Flanders, 1709. Woman poses as
soldier husband to prove he is not a spy.

09811
18 MINUTES (84) (A)
Allied (Pathe)
D: Monty Banks
S: Gregory Ratoff
SC: Fred Thompson
Gregory Ratoff . . . . Nikita
John Loder . . . . Clive Trelawney
Benita Hume . . . . Lady Phyllis Pilcott
Katherine Sergava . . . . Lida
Richard Bennett . . . . Korn
Hugh Wakefield . . . . Lord Cyril Pilcott

Paul Graetz . . . . Pietro
Carl Harbord . . . . Jacques
Rosamund Barnes . . . . . . Lida (child)
Hal Gordon . . . .
Margaret Yarde . . . .
ROMANCE Paris. Lion tamer adopts an
orphan, marries her, and learns that she
loves a magician.

09812
SCROOGE (78) (U)
Twickenham (TFD) *reissues:* 1947 (Amb)
1951 (Pi)
P: Julius Hagen, Hans Brahm
D: Henry Edwards
S: (NOVEL) Charles Dickens
(A CHRISTMAS CAROL)
SC: Seymour Hicks, H.Fowler Mear
Seymour Hicks . . . . . Ebenezer Scrooge
Donald Calthrop . . . . Bob Cratchit
Robert Cochran . . . . Fred
Mary Glynne . . . . Belle
Oscar Asche . . . . Christmas Present
Athene Seyler . . . . Charwoman
Mary Lawson . . . . Poor Man's Wife
Maurice Evans . . . . Poor Man
Garry Marsh . . . . Belle's Husband
Barbara Everest . . . . Mrs Cratchit
Eve Gray . . . . Fred's Wife
C.V.France . . . . Christmas Future
Morris Harvey . . . . Poulterer
Philip Frost . . . . Tiny Tim Cratchit
D.J.Williams . . . . Undertaker
Margaret Yarde . . . . Laundress
Hugh E.Wright . . . . Joe
Charles Carson . . . . Middlemark
Marie Ney . . . . Christmas Past
FANTASY 1843. Miser reforms after visions
of past, present and future.

09813
ALIBI INN (53) (A)
Central (MGM)
P:D: Walter Tennyson
S: Sydney Box, Muriel Box
Molly Lamont . . . . Mary Talbot
Frederick Bradshaw . . . . . . Jack Lawton
Ben Welden . . . . Saunders
Gladys Jennings . . . . Anne
Olive Sloane . . . . Queenie
Brian Buchel . . . . Masters
Wilfrid Hyde White . . . . . . Husband
CRIME Inventor breaks jail to prove jewel
thieves framed him for killing watchman.

09814
THE HALF-DAY EXCURSION (30) (U)
Q Films (U)
D: A.L.Dean
Wally Patch . . . . Cockney
Frank Stanmore . . . . Cockney
Moore Marriott . . . . Captain
COMEDY Holiday visitors get drunk
while old captain describes his experiences.

09815
OUR HUSBAND (15) (A)
Patrick K. Heale (U)
D: Patrick K. Heale
Clifford Heatherley . . . . . . The Husband
COMEDY Lord invites his ex-wives to dinner
and finds butler is bigamist.

09816
WHEN THE CAT'S AWAY (34) (U)
Central (Zenifilms)
P:D: Walter Tennyson
Davy Burnaby . . . . George
John Miller . . . . Will

COMEDY Henpecks go punting and try
to photograph bathing girls for competition.

09817
THE GHOST WALKS (22) (U)
Central (Zenifilms)
P:D: Walter Tennyson
George Bass
Barbara Gott
COMEDY

09818
THE STRANGE CASE OF MR TODMORDEN
(20) (U)
Central (Zenifilms)
P:D: Walter Tennyson
CRIME Lawyer kills rich old lady while walking
in his sleep.

09819
STORMY WEATHER (74) (A)
Gainsborough (Gaumont)
P: Michael Balcon
D: Tom Walls
S: (PLAY) Ben Travers
SC: Ben Travers
Tom Walls . . . . Sir Duncan Craggs
Ralph Lynn . . . . Mr Penny
Yvonne Arnaud . . . . Louise Craggs
Robertson Hare . . . . Mr Bullock
Andrews Engelmann . . . . . Polotsky
Stella Moya . . . . Moya
Gordon James . . . . Salt Jasper
Louis Bradfield . . . . Lacey
Fewlass Llewellyn. . . . . . . Pullman
Peter Gawthorne . . . . Inspector
Graham Moffatt . . . . Office Boy
COMEDY Chain store proprietor foils
Russian blackmailer in Chinatown.

09820
BOYS WILL BE BOYS (75) (A)
Gainsborough (Gaumont)
P: Michael Balcon
D: William Beaudine
S: (CHARACTERS) J.B.Morton
(BY THE WAY)
SC: Will Hay, Robert Edmunds
Will Hay . . . . Dr Alec Smart
Gordon Harker . . . . Faker Brown
Claude Dampier . . . . Theo P.Finch
Jimmy Hanley . . . . Cyril Brown
Davy Burnaby . . . . Col Crableigh
Norma Varden . . . . Lady Dorking
Charles Farrell . . . . Louis Brown
Percy Walsh . . . . Governor
COMEDY Headmaster thwarts pupil's
jewel-robbing father.

09821
CRIME UNLIMITED (72) (A)
WB-FN (FN)
P: Irving Asher
D: Ralph Ince
S: (NOVEL) David Hume
SC: Brock Williams, Ralph Smart
Esmond Knight . . . . Pete Borden
Lilli Palmer . . . . Natasha
Cecil Parker . . . . Asst-Commissioner
George Merritt . . . . Insp Cardby
Raymond Lovell . . . . Delaney
Wyndham Goldie . . . . Conway Addison
Peter Gawthorne . . . . Newall
Jane Millican . . . . Lady Sybil
Stella Arbenina . . . . Lady Mead
CRIME Tec poses as crook to unmask the
leader of gang of jewel thieves.

09822
THE STUDENT'S ROMANCE (78) (U)
BIP (Wardour)

P: Walter C. Mycroft
D: Otto Kanturek
S: (PLAY) Beda & Ernst Neumann
(I LOST MY HEART IN HEIDELBURG)
SC: Clifford Grey, Norman Watson,
Richard Hutter
Grete Natzler . . . . Princess Helene
Patric Knowles . . . . Max Brandt
Carol Goodner . . . . Veronika
W.H.Berry . . . . Pedell
Haver & Lee . . . . Hans & Otto
Steven Geray . . . . Mickey
Mackenzie Ward . . . . Karl
Iris Ashley . . . . Desiree
Ivan Samson . . . . Grand Duke
Wallace Lupino . . . . Sportsman
Hugh Dempster . . . . Bruno
MUSICAL Austria, 1830. Student loves
princess posing as poor girl.

09823
HONOURS EASY (62) (A)
BIP (Wardour)
P: Walter C.Mycroft
D: Herbert Brenon
S: (PLAY) Roland Pertwee
Greta Nissen . . . . Ursula Barton
Patric Knowles . . . . Harry Markham
Margaret Lockwood . . . . . Ann
George Graves . . . . Col Bagnall
W.H.Berry . . . . Joe Budd
Chili Bouchier . . . . Kate
Robert Rendel . . . . . Sir Henry Markham
Ivan Samson . . . . William Barton
DRAMA Art dealer frames client's son for
theft, not knowing his own wife can alibi
him. (Extract in ELSTREE STORY, 1952).

09824
HEART'S DESIRE (82) (U)
BIP (Wardour)
P: Walter C. Mycroft
D: Paul Stein
S: Lioni Pickard
SC: Clifford Grey, L. DuGarde Peach,
Jack Davies, Roger Burford, Bruno Frank
Richard Tauber . . . . Joseph Steidler
Leonora Corbett . . . . Frances Wilson
Diana Napier . . . . Diana Sheraton
Frank Vosper . . . . Van Straten
Kathleen Kelly . . . . Anna
George Graves . . . . Granville Wilson
Paul Graetz . . . . Florian
Viola Tree . . . . Lady Bennington
Carl Harbord . . . . Oliver Desmond
C.Denier Warren . . . . Ted Mayer
MUSICAL Tenor returns to Viennese
sweetheart on learning socialite vamped him
for sake of her fiance's opera.

09825
JIMMY BOY (71) (U)
Baxter & Barter (U)
P: John Barter
D: John Baxter
S: Con West, Harry O'Donovan
Jimmy O'Dea . . . . Jimmy
Guy Middleton . . . . The Count
Vera Sherburne . . . . Nora
Enid Stamp-Taylor . . . . . . The Star
Elizabeth Jenns . . . . The Princess
Harold Williams . . . . The Prince
Edgar Driver . . . . The Liftman
Harry O'Donovan . . . . O'Brien
Peggy Novak . . . . The Maid
Sherman Fisher Girls; Mackay Twins;
Reginald Forsyth and his Band
COMEDY Irish bootboy unmasks foreign
film star as spy.

09826
LUCKY DAYS (67) (U)
B&D-Paramount British
P: Anthony Havelock-Allan
D: Reginald Denham
S: Margaret & Gordon MacDonnell
SC: Margaret MacDonnell
Chili Bouchier . . . . Patsy Cartwright
Whitmore Humphries . . . . . . Paul Cartwright
Leslie Perrins . . . . Jack Hurst
Ann Codrington . . . . Eve Tandring
Derek Gorst . . . . Prosser
Ronald Simpson . . . . Smedley
Eric Cowley . . . . Eric
Alexander Archdale . . . . . . Alec
Sally Gray . . . . Alice
COMEDY Superstitious wife tries to help
her husband with tips from an Eastern
astrologer.

09827
WHERE'S GEORGE ? (69) (U)
retitled: THE HOPE OF HIS SIDE
B & D (UA)
P: Herbert Wilcox
D: Jack Raymond
S: R.P.Weston, Bert Lee, Jack Marks,
John Paddy Carstairs
Sydney Howard . . . . Alf Scodger
Mabel Constanduros. . . . . . . Mrs Scodger
Leslie Sarony . . . . Willy Yates
Frank Pettingell . . . . Harry Swan
Sam Livesey . . . . . Sir Richard Lancaster
Wally Patch . . . . Ted Sloane
COMEDY Henpecked blacksmith becomes
football hero.

09828
PEG OF OLD DRURY (76) (U)
B&D (UA) reissues: 1941 (EB) 1948 (EB)
P:D: Herbert Wilcox
S: (PLAY) Charles Reade, Tom Taylor
(MASKS AND FACES)
SC: Miles Malleson
Anna Neagle . . . . Peg Woffington
Cedric Hardwicke . . . . David Garrick
Jack Hawkins . . . . Michael O'Taffe
Margaretta Scott . . . . Kitty Clive
Hay Petrie . . . . Mr Rich
Maire O'Neill . . . . Mother
Arthur Sinclair . . . . Father
Robert Atkins . . . . Dr Johnson
Stuart Robertson . . . . Singer
Dorothy Robinson . . . . Miss Dalloway
Leslie French . . . . Pope
Tom Heslewood . . . . William Pitt
Christopher Steele . . . . . Oliver Goldsmith
Aubrey Fitzgerald . . . . Digby
Eliot Makeham . . . . Dr Bowdler
Sara Allgood . . . . Irishwoman
Pollie Emery . . . . Martha
HISTORY 1740. Actor makes star of Irish
girl and falls in love with her.

09829
WHAT THE PARROT SAW (40) (U)
Newman (Butcher)
D:S: Widgey R.Newman
SC: John Quin
Roma Beaumont . . . . The Girl
Bill Muirhead . . . . The Man
Wally Patch . . . .
Stan Paskin . . . .
ROMANCE Macaw helps couple's romance
during visit to Zoo.

09830
THE CROUCHING BEAST (80) (A)
Stafford (Radio) P: John Stafford
D: Victor Hanbury
S: (NOVEL) Valentine Williams (CLUBFOOT)
Fritz Kortner . . . . Ahmed Bey
Wynne Gibson . . . . Gail Dunbar
Richard Bird . . . . Nigel Druce
Isabel Jeans . . . . Pellegrini
Andrews Engelmann . . . . . . Prince Dmitri
Fred Conyngham . . . . Rudi von Linz
Peter Gawthorne . . . . Kadir Pasha
Ian Fleming . . . . Maj Abbott
Marjorie Mars . . . . Ottillie
Gus McNaughton . . . .
A.Bromley Davenport . . . .
Margaret Vyner . . . .
CRIME American girl reporter helps British
spy steal plans of Dardanelles fortifications.

SEP

09831
OLD FAITHFUL (67) (A)
GS Enterprises (Radio)
P: A.George Smith
D: Maclean Rogers
S: Irving Dennes, Harry Dawes
SC: Kathleen Butler
Horace Hodges . . . . Bill Brunning
Glennis Lorimer . . . . Lucy Brunning
Bruce Lister . . . . Alf Haines
Wally Patch . . . . Joe Riley
Isobel Scaife . . . . Lily
Muriel George . . . . Martha Brown
Edward Ashley Cooper . . . Edwards
ROMANCE Taxi driver poses as plumber to
woo old cabman's daughter.

09832
WHILE PARENTS SLEEP (72) (A)
Transatlantic-B&D (UA) reissue: 1941 (EB)
P: Paul Soskin
D: Adrian Brunel
S: (PLAY) Anthony Kimmins
SC: Anthony Kimmins, Edwin Greenwood,
John Paddy Carstairs, Jack Marks
Jean Gillie . . . . .Bubbles Thompson
Ellis Jeffreys . . . . Mrs Hammond
Enid Stamp-Taylor . . . . . . Lady Cattering
Mackenzie Ward . . . . Jerry Hammond
Davy Burnaby . . . . Lord Cattering
Athole Stewart . . . . Col Hammond
Romilly Lunge . . . . Neville Hammond
Albert Rebla . . . . Bedworth
Wally Patch . . . . Taxi-driver
Billy Hartnell . . . . George
COMEDY Snobbish family accept shopgirl
after she keeps their intrigues secret.

09833
THE DEPUTY DRUMMER (71) (U)
St George's Pictures (Col)
P: Ian Sutherland
D: Henry W.George
S: Reginald Long, Arthur Rigby
Lupino Lane . . . . Adolphus Miggs
Jean Denis . . . . Bubbles O'Hara
Kathleen Kelly . . . . Peggy Sylvester
Wallace Lupino . . . . Robbins
Margaret Yarde . . . . Lady Sylvester
Arthur Rigby . . . . Sir Henry Sylvester
Syd Crossley . . . . Curtis
Reginald Long . . . . Capt Hindlemarsh
Fred Leslie . . . . Kabitzer
Hal Gordon . . . . Yokel
MUSICAL Poor composer posing as lord
at lady's house-party catches jewel thieves.

09834
CAR OF DREAMS (68) (U)
Gaumont
P: Michael Balcon

D: Graham Cutts, Austin Melford
S: Miklos, Vitez, Laszlo Vadnai.(MESAUTO)
SC: Austin Melford
John Mills . . . . Robert Miller
Grete Mosheim . . . . Vera Hart
Robertson Hare . . . . . Henry Butterworth
Norah Howard . . . . Anne Fisher
Paul Graetz . . . . Mr Hart
Jack Hobbs . . . . Peters
Glennis Lorimer . . . . Molly
Mark Lester . . . . Mr Miller
Margaret Withers . . . . Mrs Hart
MUSICAL Antique dealer's daughter
loves employer's son posing as chauffeur.

09835
THE PASSING OF THE THIRD FLOOR BACK
(90) (A)
Gaumont
AP: Ivor Montagu
D: Berthold Viertel
S: (PLAY) Jerome K. Jerome
SC: Michael Hogan, Alma Reville
Conrad Veidt . . . . The Stranger
Anna Lee . . . . Vivian Tompkin
Rene Ray . . . . Stasia
Frank Cellier . . . . Mr Wright
Mary Clare . . . . Mrs Sharpe
Beatrix Lehmann . . . . Miss Kite
John Turnbull . . . . Major Tompkin
Cathleen Nesbitt . . . . Mrs Tompkin
Ronald Ward . . . . Chris Penny
Jack Livesey . . . . Larkcomb
Sara Allgood . . . . Mrs de Hooley
Barbara Everest . . . . Cook
FANTASY Christ-like visitor reforms
inhabitants of boardinghouse.

09836
MAN OF THE MOMENT (81) (A)
WB-FN (FN)
P: Irving Asher
D: Monty Banks
S: (PLAY) Yves Mirande (WATER NYMPH)
SC: Roland Pertwee, Guy Bolton,
A.R.Rawlinson
Douglas Fairbanks jr . . . . . Tony
Laura la Plante . . . . Mary
Claude Hulbert . . . . Rufus
Margaret Lockwood . . . . . . Vera
Donald Calthrop . . . . Butler
Peter Gawthorne . . . . Father
Monty Banks . . . . Doctor
COMEDY Prospective groom falls in love
with girl he saves from suicide.

09837
THE PRIVATE SECRETARY (70) (U)
Twickenham (TFD)
P: Julius Hagen
D: Henry Edwards
S: (PLAY) Van Moser (DER BIBLIOTHEKER)
SC: George Broadhurst, Arthur Macrae,
H. Fowler Mear
Edward Everett Horton. Rev Robert Spalding
Barry Mackay . . . . Douglas Cattermole
Judy Gunn . . . . Edith Marsland
Oscar Asche . . . . Robert Cattermole
Sydney Fairbrother . . . . Miss Ashford
Michael Shepley . . . . Henry Marsland
Alastair Sim . . . . Mr Nebulae
Aubrey Dexter . . . . Gibson
O.B.Clarence . . . . ‧. . . Thomas Marsland
Davina Craig . . . . Annie
COMEDY Rich man's nephew dupes meek
cleric to avoid creditors.

09838
FLAME IN THE HEATHER (66) (A)
Crusade (Par)

P: Victor M. Greene
D:SC: Donovan Pedelty
S: (NOVEL) Esson Maule (THE FIERY CROSS)

Gwenllian Gill	Alison
Barry Clifton	Col Stafford
Bruce Seton	Murray
Richard Hayward	Fassiefern
Ben Williams	Rushton
Kenneth McLaglen	Donald
Rani Waller	Myrat
Francis de Wolff	Hawley

ADVENTURE Scotland, 1745. English spy saves Scots chieftain's daughter.

09839
CHECKMATE (68) (A)
B & D - Paramount British
P: Anthony Havelock-Allan
D: George Pearson
S: (NOVEL) Amy Kennedy Gould
SC: Basil Mason

Maurice Evans	Philip Allen
Felix Aylmer	Henry Nicholls
Evelyn Foster	Mary Nicholls
Sally Gray	Jean Nicholls
Donald Wolfit	Jack Barton
Wilfrid Caithness	Insp Smith
Percy Walsh	Mr Curtaill
Ernest Jay	Huntly

CRIME Detective exposes fiancee's father as leader of gang of jewel thieves.

09840
THE MAN WITHOUT A FACE (62) (A)
Embassy (Radio) reissues: 1941 (Fed; 490 ft cut) 1950 (Butch)
P: George King, Randall Faye
D: George King
S: StJohn Irvine
SC: Randall Faye

Carol Coombe	Joan Ellis
Cyril Chosack	Billy Desmond
Moore Marriott	Tinker John
Ronald Ritchie	Paul Keefe
Billy Holland	Detective
Ben Williams	Warder
Vi Kaley	Landlady

CRIME Framed man breaks jail and changes places with man thought dead, who is the real culprit.

09841
HONEYMOON FOR THREE (81) (A)
Gaiety Films (ABFD) reissue: 1940 (EB)
P:S: Stanley Lupino
D: Leo Mittler
SC: Frank Miller

Stanley Lupino	Jack Denver
Aileen Marson	Yvonne Daumery
Jack Melford	Raymond Dirk
Robert English	Herbert Denver
Dennis Hoey	M. Daumery
Arty Ash	Herbert Jones
Roddy Hughes	Toomes
Syd Crossley	PC Smithers
Doris Rogers	Mme Daumery
Barry Clifton	Crooner

Percival Mackey and his Band
MUSICAL French banker forces affianced daughter to wed broke playboy who compromised her.

OCT

09842
THE GUV'NOR (88) (U) USA: MISTER HOBO
Gaumont reissues: 1944 (Sherwood; 760 ft cut) 1949
P: Michael Balcon
D: Milton Rosmer

S: Paul Lafitte (ROTHSCHILD)
SC: Maude Howell, Guy Bolton

George Arliss	Francois Rothschild
Gene Gerrard	Flit
Viola Keats	Madeleine
Patric Knowles	Paul
Frank Cellier	Barsac
George Hayes	Dubois
Mary Clare	Mme Barsac
Henrietta Watson	Mrs Granville

COMEDY France. Tramp is made director of failing bank because he bears financier's surname.

09843
LIEUTENANT DARING, RN (85) (U)
Butcher's Film Service
P: Lawrence Huntington
D: Reginald Denham
S: Frank H. Shaw
SC: Gerald Elliott

Hugh Williams	Lt Bob Daring
Geraldine Fitzgerald	Joan Fayre
Frederick Lloyd	Capt Mayne
Jerry Verno	AB Swallow
John Rorke	Marine Fish
Ernest Butcher	AB Singer
Martin Walker	Neville Mayne
Ralph Truman	Mung
Richard Norris	Briggs
Edwin Ellis	Sgt

Su Yee Troupe; Neil McKay; Horace Sheldon and his Orchestra
ADVENTURE Lieut, framed for theft by captain's son, is cleared after defeating Chinese pirates.

09844
THE LAST JOURNEY (66) (A)
Twickenham (TFD)
P: Julius Hagen
D: Bernard Vorhaus
S: J. Jefferson Farjeon
SC: John Soutar, H. Fowler Mear

Hugh Williams	Gerald Winter
Godfrey Tearle	Sir Wilfred Rhodes
Judy Gunn	Diana Gregory
Julien Mitchell	Bob Holt
Nelson Keys	Frenchman
Michael Hogan	Charlie
Frank Pettingell	Goddard
Olga Lindo	Emily Holt
Sydney Fairbrother	Crank
Eliot Makeham	Pip
Eve Gray	Daisy
Mickey Brantford	Tom

DRAMA Express train driver goes mad thinking his fireman is having affair with his wife.

09845
A FIRE HAS BEEN ARRANGED (70) (U)
Twickenham (TFD)
P: Julius Hagen
D: Leslie Hiscott
S: H. Fowler Mear, James Carter
SC: H. Fowler Mear, Michael Barringer

Bud Flanagan	Bud
Chesney Allen	Ches
Mary Lawson	Betty
Robb Wilton	Oswald
Harold French	Toby
C.Denier Warren	Shuffle
Alastair Sim	Cutte
Hal Walters	Hal
Buddy Bradley Girls	Shopgirls

COMEDY Ex-convicts find store built on field where they buried jewels, and try to burn it down.

09846
SEXTON BLAKE AND THE MADEMOISELLE (63) (U)
Fox British (MGM)
D: Alex Bryce
S: (NOVEL) G.H.Teed (THEY SHALL REPAY)
SC: Michael Barringer

George Curzon	Sexton Blake
Lorraine Grey	Mlle Roxanne
Tony Sympson	Tinker
Edgar Norfolk	Insp Thomas
Raymond Lovell	Captain
Ian Fleming	Henry Norman
Vincent Holman	Carruthers
Wilson Coleman	Pierre

CRIME Girl robs crooked financier who ruined her father.

09847
LEND ME YOUR WIFE (61) (A)
Grafton (MGM)
P: Fred Browett
D: W.P.Kellino
S: (PLAY) Fred Duprez, Edmund Dalby

Henry Kendall	Tony Radford
Kathleen Kelly	Grace Harwood
Cyril Smith	Charles Harwood
Jimmy Godden	Uncle Jerry
Marie Ault	Aunt Jane
Hal Gordon	Nick Larkin
Gillian Maude	Ruth

COMEDY Bachelor has his friend's wife pose as his own to fool rich uncle.

09848
INVITATION TO THE WALTZ (77) (A)
BIP (Wardour)
P: Walter C. Mycroft
D: Paul Merzbach
S: (RADIO PLAY) Eric Maschwitz, Holt Marvel, George Posford
SC: Paul Merzbach, Clifford Grey, Roger Burford

Lilian Harvey	Jennie Peachey
Carl Esmond	Carl
Harold Warrender	Duke of Wirtemberg
Wendy Toye	Signora Picci
Richard Bird	Weber
Esme Percy	Napoleon
Gus McNaughton	Valet
Charles Carson	Lombardi
Alexander Field	George Peachey
Hay Petrie	Periteau
Eric Stanley	Sir Francis
Hal Gordon	Sgt
Anton Dolin	Dancer

MUSICAL 1803. British ballerina becomes German duke's mistress to make him renew treaty.

09849
MUSIC HATH CHARMS (70) (U)
BIP (Wardour)
P: Walter C. Mycroft
D: Thomas Bentley, Alexander Esway, Walter Summers, Arthur Woods
S: L. DuGarde Peach
SC: Jack Davies, Courtney Terrett

Henry Hall	Himself
W.H.Berry	Basil Turner
Carol Goodner	Mrs. Norbray
Arthur Margetson	Alan Sterling
Lorna Hubbard	Marjorie Turner
Antoinette Cellier	Joan
Billy Milton	Jack Lawton
Aubrey Mallalieu	Judge
Wallace Douglas	George Sheridan
Edith Sharpe	Miss Wilkinson
Gus McNaughton	Goodwin
Hugh Dempster	Tony Blower

Hildegarde; Dan Donovan; Len Berman;
BBC Dance Orchestra
MUSICAL Effect of dance band's broadcast on
listeners in the jungle, aboard ship, etc.
(Extract in ELSTREE STORY, 1952).

09850
THE RIVER HOUSE MYSTERY (56) (U)
Imeson-Foulsham (U)
P: A.B.Imeson
D: Fraser Foulsham
S: F.G.Robertson
G.H.Mulcaster . . . . Sir John Harpenden
Ena Moon . . . . Anna
Bernard Lee . . . . Wade Belloc
A.B.Imeson . . . . Drang
Roddy Hughes . . . . Higgins
Boris Ranevsky . . . . Krilloff
Clifford Evans . . . . Ivan
CRIME Tec saves girl's jewels from gang
and finds he has been hoaxed.

09851
A GANGSTER NIGHTMARE (18) (U)
Omega (Ace)
Charles Hill . . . . The Man
COMEDY Crime magazine enthusiast
dreams he is Chicago gangster.

09852
HANGING RAIN (14) (A)
Patrick K. Heale (ABFD)
D: Patrick K.Heale
CRIME Sneak murderer trapped by rain
on his car tyres.

09853
CHEERIO ! (17) (U)
Fidelity Films
Billy Merrin and his Commanders
Ken Crowley   Alice & Jimmy Day
MUSICAL

09854
LOOPYTONE NEWS (10) (U)
International Productions
COMEDY Burlesque newsreel.

09855
HIS APOLOGIES (18) (U)
Westanmor (Famous)
D: Widgey R.Newman
S: (POEM) Rudyard Kipling
N: Laidman Brown
Moore Marriott . . . . Colonel
Violet Hopson . . . . Wife
ANIMAL Life of Aberdeen terrier from
puppy to death.

09856
LANGFORD REED'S LIMERICKS (6) (U)
A.F.C.Barrington (EB)
D: A.F.C.Barrington
S: (BOOK) Langford Reed
MUSICAL Picturisations of comic limericks.

09857
KOENIGSMARK (96) (A) *bilingual*
Capitol (GFD) *reissue:* 1942 (Pi)
P: Roger Richebe, Max Schach
D: Maurice Tourneur
S: (NOVEL) Pierre Benoit
Elissa Landi . . . . Princess Aurore
John Lodge . . . Grand Duke Frederick
Pierre Fresnay . . . . Raoul Vignerte
Frank Vosper . . . Major Baron de Boise
Marcelle Rogez . . . . Comtesse Melusine
Allan Jeayes . . . Grand Duke Rodolphe
Romilly Lunge . . . . Lt de Hagen
Cecil Humphreys . . . . . . de Marcais
P: A. George Smith
D: Maclean Rogers
CRIME Ruritania. Tutor solves murder of
Princess's unloved husband. (Made in France).

09858
HER LAST AFFAIRE (78) (A)
New Ideal (PDC)
P: Simon & Geoffrey Rowson
D: Michael Powell
S: (PLAY) Walter Ellis (SOS)
SC: Ian Dalrymple
Hugh Williams . . . . Alan Heriot
Viola Keats . . . . Lady Avril Weyre
Francis L. Sullivan . . . . . Sir Julian Weyre
Sophie Stewart . . . . Judy Weyre
Felix Aylmer . . . . Lord Carnforth
Cecil Parker . . . . Sir Arthur Harding
John Laurie . . . . Robb
Eliot Makeham . . . . Dr Rudd
Googie Withers . . . . Effie
Shayle Gardner . . . . Boxall
DRAMA Secretary clears father's name after
compromising employer's wife and causing
her death.

09859
MIDSHIPMAN EASY (77) (U)
USA: MEN OF THE SEA
ATP (ABFD)
P: Basil Dean, Thorold Dickinson
D: Carol Reed
S: (NOVEL) Captain Marryatt
(MR MIDSHIPMAN EASY)
SC: Anthony Kimmins
Hughie Green . . . . Jack Easy
Margaret Lockwood . . . . . Donna Agnes
Harry Tate . . . . Mr Biggs
W. Robert Adams . . . . Mesty
Roger Livesey . . . . Capt Wilson
Dennis Wyndham . . . . Don Silvio
Lewis Casson . . . . Mr Easy
Tom Gill . . . . Gascoine
Frederick Burtwell . . . . . . Mr Easthupp
Desmond Tester . . . . Gossett
Dorothy Holmes-Gore . . . . Mrs Easy
ADVENTURE 1790. Midshipmen rescue
girl from Spanish ship and Italian bandits.

09860
EXPERT'S OPINION (71) (A)
B & D- Paramount British
P: Anthony Havelock-Allan
D: Ivar Campbell
S: Guillan Hopper
SC: Ivar & Sheila Campbell
Lucille Lisle . . . . Marian Steele
Leslie Perrins . . . . Richard Steele
Molly Fisher . . . . Kay Frost
Franklyn Bellamy . . . . Keller
Kim Peacock . . . . Desmond Carter
John Kevan . . . . Jay Frost
Lawrence Hanray . . . . Coroner
CRIME Gunnery expert's wife suspected of
killing assistant, spy seeking aircraft gun plans.

NOV

09861
ALL AT SEA (60) (U)
Fox British
D: Anthony Kimmins
S: (PLAY) Ian Hay
Tyrell Davis . . . . Joe Finch
Googie Withers . . . . Daphne Tomkins
James Carew . . . . Julius Mablethorpe
Cecily Byrne . . . . Mary Maggs
Rex Harrison . . . . Aubrey Bellingham
Dorothy Vernon . . . . Mrs Humphrey
James Harcourt . . . . Mr Humphrey
Colin Lesslie . . . . Tony Lambert
COMEDY Timid clerk spends legacy on sea
cruise and poses as author.

09862
LATE EXTRA (69) (A)
Fox British
D: Albert Parker
S: Anthony Richardson
SC: Fenn Sherie, Ingram d'Abbes
Virginia Cherrill . . . . Janet
James Mason . . . . Jim Martin
Alastair Sim . . . . Mac
Ian Colin . . . . Carson
Clifford McLaglen . . . . . . Weinhardt
Cyril Chosack . . . . Jules
David Horne . . . . Editor
Antoinette Cellier . . . . Sylvia
Donald Wolfit . . . . Insp Greville
Hannen Swaffer . . . . Himself
CRIME Cub reporter catches fugitive
gunman.

09863
NO LIMIT (79) (U)
ATP (ABFD) *reissue:* 1946
P: Basil Dean
D: Monty Banks
S: Walter Greenwood
SC: Tom Geraghty, Fred Thompson
George Formby . . . . . George Shuttleworth
Florence Desmond . . . . . . Florence Dibney
Edward Rigby . . . . Grandfather
Jack Hobbs . . . . Bert Tyldesley
Peter Gawthorne . . . . Higgins
Alf Goddard . . . . Norton
Betrix Fielden-Kaye . . . . . . Mrs Horrocks
Howard Douglas . . . . Turner
Evelyn Roberts . . . . Commentator
Florence Gregson . . . . . Mrs Shuttleworth
COMEDY Isle of Man. Yorkshire motorcycle
enthusiast wins Tourist Trophy race.

09864
TURN OF THE TIDE (80) (U)
British National (Gau)
P: John Corfield
D: Norman Walker
S: (NOVEL) Leo Walmsley (THREE FEVERS)
SC: L. DuGarde Peach, J.O.C.Orton
John Garrick . . . . Marney Lunn
Geraldine Fitzgerald . . . . . Ruth Fosdyck
Niall McGinnis . . . . John Lunn
J.Fisher White . . . . Isaac Fosdyck
Joan Maude . . . . Amy
Sam Livesey . . . . Henry Lunn
Wilfrid Lawson . . . . Luke Fosdyck
Moore Marriott . . . . Tindall Fosdyck
DRAMA Yorks. Love ends a feud between
two fishing families.

09865
BIRDS OF A FEATHER (69) (U)
Baxter & Barter (U)
P: John Barter
D: John Baxter
S: (PLAY) George Foster
(A RIFT IN THE LOOT)
SC: Con West, Gerald Elliott
George Robey . . . . Henry Wortle
Horace Hodges . . . . Lord Cheverton
Jack Melford . . . . Rudolph
Eve Lister . . . . Lady Susan
Diana Beaumont . . . . May Wortle
Veronica Brady . . . . Mrs Wortle
Sebastian Shaw . . . . Jack Wortle
Julian Royce . . . . Warrington
C.Denier Warren . . . . Tailor
COMEDY Poor lord rents castle to sausage
magnate and poses as servant to seek hidden
treasure.

09866
THE SHADOW OF MIKE EMERALD (61) (A)
GS Enterprises (Radio)

S: Anthony Richardson
SC: Kathleen Butler, Anthony Richardson

Leslie Perrins	Mike Emerald
Marjorie Mars	Lucia Emerald
Martin Lewis	Lee Cooper
Vincent Holman	John Ellman
Atholl Fleming	Clive Warner
Neville Brook	Ryder March
Basil Langton	Rollo Graham

CRIME Swindling financier sought by cheated partners.

09867
GET OFF MY FOOT (82) (A)
WB-FN (FN)
P: Irving Asher
D: William Beaudine
S: (PLAY) Edward Paulton
(MONEY BY WIRE)
SC: Frank Launder, Robert Edmunds

Max Miller	Herbert Cronk
Jane Carr	Helen Rawlingcourt
Chili Bouchier	Mrs Rawlingcourt
Norma Varden	Mrs Rawlingcourt
Morland Graham	Maj Rawlingcourt
Anthony Hankey	Algy
Reginald Purdell	Joe
Vera Bogetti	Matilda
Wally Patch	Tramp

COMEDY Major schemes to marry his daughter to his butler, heir to a fortune.

09868
LINE ENGAGED (68) (U)
British Lion
P: Herbert Smith
D: Bernerd Mainwaring
S: (PLAY) Jack de Leon, Jack Celestin

Bramwell Fletcher	David Morland
Jane Baxter	Eva Rutland
Arthur Wontner	Insp Morland
Mary Clare	Mrs Gardner
Leslie Perrins	Gordon Rutland
George Merritt	Sgt Thomas
Kathleen Harrison	Maid
John Turnbull	Supt Harrison
Coral Browne	Doreen
Ronald Shiner	Ryan

CRIME Insp proves his son did not kill his beloved's blackmailing husband.

09869
FATHER O'FLYNN (82) (U)
Butcher's Film Service
P: Wilfred Noy
D: Wilfred Noy, Walter Tennyson

Tom Burke	Father O'Flynn
Jean Adrienne	Macushlah
Robert Chisholm	Nigel
Henry Oscar	Westmacott
Denis O'Neil	Flannigan
Ralph Truman	Fawcett
Johnnie Schofield	Cassidy
Dorothy Vernon	Bridget O'Loveley
Billy Holland	Muldoon

Ethel Revnell & Gracie West; Stanley Kirkby; Sherman Fisher Girls
MUSICAL Ireland. Jailbird's daughter, adopted by priest, loves squire's son.

09870
FIRST A GIRL (94) (A)
Gaumont
P: Michael Balcon
D: Victor Saville
S: (PLAY) Reinhold Schunzel
(VIKTOR UND VIKTORIA)
SC: Marjorie Gaffney

Jessie Matthews	Elizabeth
Sonnie Hale	Victor

Griffith Jones	Robert
Anna Lee	Princess
Alfred Drayton	McIntosh
Constance Godridge	Darryl
Martita Hunt	Seraphina
Eddie Gray	GooseTrainer

MUSICAL Riviera. Messenger girl becomes star by posing as male female impersonator.

09871
THE TUNNEL (94) (U)
USA: TRANSATLANTIC TUNNEL
Gaumont
P: Michael Balcon
D: Maurice Elvey
S: (NOVEL) Bernhard Kellerman
(DER TUNNEL)
SC: Kurt Siodmak, L. DuGarde Peach, Clemence Dane

Richard Dix	McAllan
Leslie Banks	Robbie
Madge Evans	Ruth McAllan
Helen Vinson	Varlia
C. Aubrey Smith	Lloyd
George Arliss	Prime Minister
Walter Huston	President
Basil Sydney	Mostyn
Jimmy Hanley	Geoffrey
Henry Oscar	Grellier
Cyril Raymond	Harriman
Hilda Trevelyan	Mary

FANTASY Undersea tunnel to America built despite financial trickery.

09872
I GIVE MY HEART (90) (A)
BIP (Wardour)
P: Walter C. Mycroft
D: Marcel Varnel
S: (OPERA) Paul Knepler,
J.M.Welleminsky (THE DUBARRY)
SC: Frank Launder, Roger Burford,
Kurt Siodmak, Paul Perez

Gitta Alpar	Jeanne
Patrick Waddington	Rene
Owen Nares	Louis XV
Arthur Margetson	Count Dubarry
Margaret Bannerman	Marechale
Hugh Miller	Choiseul
Gibb McLaughlin	de Brissac
Iris Ashley	Margot
Hay Petrie	Cascal

MUSICAL France, 1769. Milliner weds count in order to become King's mistress.
(Extract in ELSTREE STORY, 1952).

09873
NO MONKEY BUSINESS (78) (U)
Radius (GFD)
P: Julius Haemann
D: Marcel Varnel
S: Joe May, Karl Notl
SC: Roger Burford, Val Guest

Gene Gerrard	Jim Carroll
June Clyde	Clare Barrington
Renee Houston	Jessie
Peter Haddon	Arthur
Claude Dampier	Roberts
Hugh Wakefield	Prof Barrington
Richard Hearne	Charlie
Fred Duprez	Manager
Clifford Heatherley	Bailiff
O.B.Clarence	Professor
Alexander Field	Greengrocer

Reuben Castang and his Apes
COMEDY Actor poses as intelligent ape to help partner win anthropologist's daughter.

09874
THE MYSTERY OF THE MARY CELESTE
(80) (A) USA: PHANTOM SHIP

Hammer (GFD)
P: H. Fraser Passmore
D:S: Denison Clift

Bela Lugosi	Anton Lorenzen
Shirley Grey	Sarah Briggs
Arthur Margetson	Capt Briggs
Edmund Willard	Toby Bilson
George Mozart	Tommy Duggan
Ben Welden	Boas Hoffman
Dennis Hoey	Tom Goodschard
Gibson Gowland	Andy Gillings
Clifford McLaglen	Capt Marchant
James Carew	James Winchester
Terence de Marney	Charlie Kaye
Ben Soutten	Jack Samson
Gunner Moir	Ponta Katz

DRAMA 1872. Mad sailor kills everyone aboard ship, then jumps into sea.

09875
CAPTAIN BILL (81) (U)
Leslie Fuller (ABFD) *reissue:* 1956 (EB)
P: Joe Rock
D: Ralph Ceder
S: Val Valentine, Syd Courtenay, George Harris

Leslie Fuller	Bill
Judy Kelly	Polly
Hal Gordon	Tim
O.B.Clarence	Sir Anthony Kipps
Georgie Harris	Georgie
D.J.Williams	Cheerful
Tonie Edgar Bruce	Lady Kipps
Ralph Truman	Red

COMEDY Bargee saves schoolmistress from capture by gunrunners.

09876
PLAY UP THE BAND (71) (U)
City (ABFD)
P: Basil Humphreys
D: Harry Hughes
S: Frank Atkinson

Stanley Holloway	Sam Small
Betty Ann Davies	Betty Small
Leslie Bradley	Jack
Frank Atkinson	Alf Ramsbottom
Charles Sewell	Lord Heckdyke
Amy Veness	Lady Heckdyke
Cynthia Stock	Vera
Julie Suedo	Marquise de Vaux
Arthur Gomez	Marquis de Vaux
Hal Gordon	Bandmaster

Louise Selkirk's Ladies Orchestra; London Brass Band
COMEDY Northern euphonium player framed for theft during visit to Crystal Palace band contest.

09877
HYDE PARK CORNER (84) (A)
Grosvenor (Pathe)
P: Harcourt Templeman
D: Sinclair Hill
S: (PLAY) Walter Hackett
SC: D.B.Wyndham-Lewis

Gordon Harker	PC Cheatle
Binnie Hale	Sophie
Gibb McLaughlin	Sir Arthur Gannett
Harry Tate	Taxi Driver
Eric Portman	Chester
Robert Holmes	Concannon
Eileen Peel	Barbara Ainsworth
Donald Wolfit	Howard

COMEDY Duelling death of 1780 repeats itself in 1935.

09878
COME OUT OF THE PANTRY (71) (U)
B&D (UA) *reissue:* 1941 (EB)
P: Herbert Wilcox

D: Jack Raymond
S: (PLAY) Alice Duer Miller
(COME OUT OF THE KITCHEN)
SC: Austin Parker, Douglas Furber

Jack Buchanan	Lord Robert Brent
Fay Wray	Hilda Beach-Howard
James Carew	Mr Beach-Howard
Olive Blakeney	Mrs Beach-Howard
Ronald Squire	Eccles
Fred Emney	Lord Axminster
Kate Cutler	Lady Axminster
Ethel Stewart	Rosie
Maire O'Neill	Mrs Gore
Ben Welden	Tramp
W.T.Ellwanger	Porteous

MUSICAL New York. Broke lord acting as butler falls in love with brother's rich fiancee.

09879
GAY OLD DOG (62) (A)
Embassy (Radio)
P: George King, Randall Faye
D: George King
S: Enid Fabia
SC: Randall Faye

Edward Rigby	Tom Bliss
Moore Marriott	George Bliss
Ruby Miller	Mrs Vernon
Marguerite Allan	Judith
Annie Esmond	Mrs Gambit
Joan Wyndham	Betty
Patrick Barr	Phillip
Johnny Singer	Andrew V.Oakes
Billy Holland	Capt Black

COMEDY Country doctor saves veterinary brother from marrying scheming widow.

DEC

09880
SHE SHALL HAVE MUSIC (91) (U)
Twickenham (TFD)
P: Julius Hagen
D: Leslie Hiscott
S: Paul England, C. Denier Warren
SC: Arthur Macrae, H.Fowler Mear

Jack Hylton	Jack Hylton
June Clyde	Dorothy Drew
Claude Dampier	Eddie
Bryan Lawrence	Brian Gates
Gwen Farrar	Miss Peachum
Marjorie Brooks	Mrs Marlow
Edmond Breon	Freddie Gates
Felix Aylmer	Black

Mathea Merryfield; Magda Neeld; Diana Ward; Two Mackays; Carmona; Baby Terry; Leon Woizikowski Ballet; Dalmora Cancan Dancers; Terry' Juveniles; Freddie Schweitzer; Sonny Farrar; Billie Carlisle
MUSICAL Magnate hires dance band to broadcast from cruise.

09881
TWO HEARTS IN HARMONY (75) (A)
Time Pictures (Wardour)
P: John Clein
D: William Beaudine
S: Samuel Gibson Browne
SC: Robert Edmunds, A.R.Rawlinson

Bernice Clare	Micky
George Curzon	Lord Sheldon
Enid Stamp-Taylor	Sheila
Nora Williams	Lil
Gordon Little	Joe
Guy Middleton	Mario
Paul Hartley	Bobby
Eliot Makeham	Wagstaffe
Julian Royce	Carstairs

Charles Farrell & Chick Endor; Jack

Harris and his Band
MUSICAL Cabaret singer weds lord after becoming his son's governess.

09882
VANITY (76) (U)
George Smith (Col)
D: Adrian Brunel
S: (PLAY) Ernest Denny

Jane Cain	Vanity Faire
Percy Marmont	Jefferson Brown
John Counsell	Dick Broderick
H.F.Maltby	Lord Cazalet
Moira Lynd	
Nita Harvey	

COMEDY Conceited actress feigns death to enjoy her public's sorrow.

09883
CAN YOU HEAR ME MOTHER ? (77) (U)
New Ideal (PDC)
P: Simon Rowson, Geoffrey Rowson
D: Leslie Pearce
S: Sandy Powell
SC: Sandy Powell, Paul Thomson

Sandy Powell	Sandy
Mary Lawson	Mary Warner
Paul Thomson	Mike Arnold
Muriel Aked	Mother
Elsie Irving	Mrs Wilkinson
Katie Kay	Lucy
Norman Pierce	Joe
Raymond Huntley	Dolan
Hal Walters	Taxi-driver
Henry Victor	Father
Cingalee	Himself

COMEDY Yorkshireman adopts lost baby and dancer helps him become comedian.

09884
FOREIGN AFFAIRES (71) (U)
Gainsborough (Gau)
P: Michael Balcon
D: Tom Walls
S: Ben Travers

Tom Walls	Capt Archibald Gore
Ralph Lynn	Jefferson Darby
Robertson Hare	Hardy Hornett
Norma Varden	Mrs Hornett
Marie Lohr	Mrs Cope
Diana Churchill	Sophie
Cecil Parker	Lord Wormington
Kathleen Kelly	Millicent
Gordon James	Rope
Ivor Barnard	Count

COMEDY Nice. Broke gambler and car salesman become touts for phoney count's casino.

09885
THE LUCK OF THE IRISH (81) (U)
RH Films (Par)
P: Richard Hayward, Donovan Pedelty
D:SC: Donovan Pedelty
S: (NOVEL) Victor Haddick

Richard Hayward	Sam Mulhern
Kay Walsh	Eileen O'Donnell
Niall McGinnis	Derek O'Neill
Jimmy Mageean	Sir Brian O'Neill
R.H.MacCanless	Gavin Grogan
Charles Fagan	Sgt Doyle
Harold Griffen	Simon Reid
Charlotte Tedlie	Hortense O'Neill

SPORT Antrim. Poor squire pawns castle to bet on his racehorse.

09886
MOSCOW NIGHTS (75) (A)
USA: I STAND CONDEMNED
London Films-Capitol (GFD)

reissue: 1942 (Pi)
P: Alexander Korda, Alexis Granowski, Max Schach
D: Anthony Asquith
S: (NOVEL) Pierre Benoit
(LES NUITS DE MOSCOU)
SC: Erich Seipmann

Harry Baur	Brioukow
Laurence Olivier	Capt Ignatoff
Penelope Dudley Ward	Natasha
Robert Cochran	Polonsky
Morton Selten	Kovrin
Athene Seyler	Mme Sabline
Walter Hudd	Doctor
Kate Cutler	Mme Kovrin
C.M. Hallard	President
Edmund Willard	Prosecution
Charles Carson	Defence
Morland Graham	Servant
Hay Petrie	Spy

WAR Russia, 1916. Girl gives herself to profiteer to save captain from being shot as spy.

09887
DARK WORLD (73) (A)
Fox British
P: Leslie Landau
D: Bernard Vorhaus
S: Leslie Landau, Selwyn Jepson
SC: Hugh Brooke

Tamara Desni	Brigitta
Leon Quartermaine	Stephen
Hugh Brooke	Philip
Olga Lindo	Eleanor
Morton Selten	Colonel
Fred Duprez	Schwartz
Viola Compton	Auntie
Googie Withers	Annie
Kynaston Reeves	John

CRIME Jealous man tries to electrocute his brother and kills wrong man.

09888
BLUE SMOKE (74) (U)
Fox British
P: John Barrow
D: Ralph Ince
S: Charles Bennett
SC: Fenn Sherie, Ingram d'Abbes

Tamara Desni	Belle Chinko
Ralph Ince	Al Dempson
Bruce Seton	Don Chinko
Ian Colin	Chris Steele
Eric Hales	Tawno Herne
Hal Walters	Stiffy Williams
Beryl de Querton	Anna Steele
Wilson Cochran	Jasper Chinko
Jock McKay	Mac

SPORT Gipsy boxer and rival both love same girl.

09889
MR COHEN TAKES A WALK (82) (U)
WB-FN (WB)
P: Irving Asher
D: William Beaudine
S: (NOVEL) Mary Roberts Rinehart
SC: Brock Williams

Paul Graetz	Jake Cohen
Violet Farebrother	Rachel Cohen
Chili Bouchier	Julie Levine
Barry Livesey	Joe Levine
Mickey Brantford	Jack Cohen
Ralph Truman	Sam Cohen
Meriel Forbes	Sally O'Connor
George Merritt	Pat O'Connor
Kenneth Villiers	Bob West

DRAMA Store founder poses as pedlar but returns in time to save business.

09890
BLACK MASK (67) (A)
WB-FN(WB)
P: Irving Asher
D: Ralph Ince
S: (NOVEL) Bruce Graeme (BLACKSHIRT)
SC: Paul Gangelin, Frank Launder, Michael Barringer

Wylie Watson	Jimmie Glass
Aileen Marson	Jean McTavish
Ellis Irving	Verrell
Wyndham Goldie	Davidson
Joyce Kennedy	Lady McTavish
Herbert Lomas	Sir John McTavish
John Turnbull	Insp Murray
Kate Cutler	Lady Mincott

CRIME Gentleman crook who steals for charity is framed for killing press knight.

09891
TRUST THE NAVY (71) (U)
St George's Pictures (Col)
P: Ian Sutherland
D: Henry W.George
S: Arthur Rose
SC: Reginald Long, Arthur Rigby

Lupino Lane	Nip Briggs
Nancy Burne	Susie
Wallace Lupino	Wally Wopping
Guy Middleton	Lt Richmond

Miki Hood	Andree Terraine
Ben Welden	Scar
Fred Leslie	CPO
Doris Rogers	Martha
Reginald Long	Serge Chungster
Arthur Rigby	Lambert Terrain

COMEDY Portsmouth. Sailors catch smugglers during annual Navy Week.

09892
RIDERS TO THE SEA (40) (A)
Flanagan-Hurst (MGM)
P: John P. Flanagan, Gracie Fields
D: Brian Desmond Hurst
S: (PLAY) J.M. Synge
SC: Brian Desmond Hurst, Wolfgang Wilhelm, Patrick Kirwan, Francis Stewart

Sara Allgood	Maurya
Denis Johnstone	Michael
Kevin Guthrie	Bartley
Ria Mooney	Shelagh Richards

DRAMA Ireland. Old woman loses her husband and sons to the sea.

09893
RUNAWAY LADIES (56) (A)
International Players (Ex)
P: M. Haworth Booth
D: Jean de Limur
S: Tristram Bernard
(LE VOYAGE IMPERVU)

Betty Stockfeld	Betty

Hugh Wakefield	Lord Ramsden
Edna Searle	Lady Ramsden
Roger Treville	Georges
Raymond Cordy	

COMEDY France. Girl tries to return compromising slipper to Lady who is mistaken for crook.

09894
CHILDREN OF THE FOG (59) (A)
Jesba Films (NPFD)
D: Leopold Jessner, John Quin
S: John Cousins, Stephen Clarkson

Barbara Gott	Mrs Jenner
Ben Soutten	Butcher
Rani Waller	Alice Crimson
Marjorie Corbett	Joan
Kenneth Guthrie	Butcher
Linden Travers	Polly Mortimer
Laurence Hepworth	Bert Jenner
Eric Pavitt	Syd Butcher
Vi Kaley	Charwoman

DRAMA Drunken docker's son weds late stepmother's bastard and they take his sick brother to Australia.

09895
LITTLE PAPER PEOPLE (7) (U)
Margaret Hoyland (ABFD)
P:D:S: Margaret Hoyland
TRICK Paper marionettes: Victorian foibles and seaside characters.

1936

JAN

09896
STARS ON PARADE (82) (U)
Butcher *reissues*: 1940; 1950;
STAR PARADE (2560 ft cut)
P: D: Oswald Mitchell, Challis Sanderson
Edwin Lawrence   Horace Goldin
Albert Whelan   Sherman Fisher Girls
Syd & Max Harrison   Pat O'Brien
The Act Superb   Mabel Constanduros
John Rorke   Navarre
Jimmy James   Robb Wilton
Lucan & McShane   Sam Barton
Debroy Somers and his Band
REVUE

09897
DON'T RUSH ME ! (72) (U)
Fred Karno Films (PDC)
D: Norman Lee
S: (SKETCH) Fred Karno
(WHEN WE ARE MARRIED)
SC: Con West, Michael Barringer
Robb Wilton . . . . Samuel Honey
Muriel Aked . . . . Amy Andrews
Haver & Lee . . . . Detectives
Peter Haddon . . . . Adolphe
Bobbie Comber . . . . Louis
Kathleen Kelly . . . . Tilly
Kenneth Kove . . . . Bertie Moon
Wallace Douglas . . . . Jack Honey
Dino Galvani . . . . Tony
Hal Walters . . . . Hal
Nor Kiddie . . . . Commissionaire
COMEDY Anti-gambling society president
forced to become dogtrack bookie.

09898
TWICE BRANDED (72) (A)
GS Enterprises (Radio)
P: A. George Smith
D: Maclean Rogers
S: (NOVEL) Anthony Richardson
(TROUBLE IN THE HOUSE)
SC: Kathleen Butler
Robert Rendel . . . . Charles Hamilton
Lucille Lisle . . . . Betty Hamilton
James Mason . . . . Henry Hamilton
Eve Gray . . . . Sylvia Hamilton
Mickey Brantford . . . . Dennis
Ethel Griffies . . . . Mrs Hamilton
Isobel Scaife . . . . Mary
Paul Blake . . . . Lord Hugo
CRIME Father framed for fraud returns from
prison and is forced to pose as his family's
uncle.

09899
THE VANDERGILT DIAMOND MYSTERY
(60) (A)
Randall Faye (Radio)
P: D: Randall Faye
S: Michael Crombie
SC: Margaret Houghton
Elizabeth Astell . . . . Mary
Bruce Seton . . . . Hardcastle
Hilary Pritchard . . . . Briggs
Charles Paton . . . . Mr Throstle
Ethel Royale . . . . Mrs Throstle
Ben Graham Soutten . . . . . The Boss
William Holland . . . . Carponi
Henry B. Longhurst . . . . . . Insp Greig
COMEDY Girl and gang seek pendant
secreted in golf bag.

09900
BALL AT SAVOY (74) (U)
Stafford (Radio)
D: Victor Hanbury
S: (PLAY) Alfred Grunwald,

Fritz Lohner-Beda
SC: Akos Tolnay, Reginald Long
Conrad Nagel . . . . John Egan
Marta Labarr . . . .… . Anita
Fred Conyngham . . . . George
Lu-Anne Meredith . . . . Mary
Aubrey Mather . . . . Herbert
Fred Duprez . . . . Mason
Bela Mila . . . .… . Therese
Dino Galvani . . . . Manager
Monte de Lisle . . . . Stranger
Tony de Lungo . . . . Maitre d'Hotel
Esther Kiss . . . .… . . Suzanne
MUSICAL Cannes. Baron poses as waiter
to woo opera star and is accused of stealing
necklace.

09901
JURY'S EVIDENCE (74) (A)
British Lion *reissue*: 1946 (NR)
P: Herbert Smith
D: Ralph Ince
S: (PLAY) Jack de Leon, Jack Celestin
SC: Ian Dalrymple
Hartley Power . . . . Edgar Trent
Margaret Lockwood . . . .… . Betty Stanton
Nora Swinburne . . . . Mary Trent
Eve Gray . . . . Ruby
Sebastian Shaw . . . . Philip
Tracy Holmes . . . . John Stanton
Jane Millican . . . . Agatha
Patrick Ludlow . . . . Cyril
Charles Paton . . . . Crowther
CRIME Foreman of Old Bailey jury
refuses to accept circumstantial evidence
and helps solve murder case.

09902
A WIFE OR TWO (63) (A)
British Lion
P: Herbert Smith
D: Maclean Rogers
S: (PLAY) C.B.Poultney, Roland Daniel
SC: Maclean Rogers, Kathleen Butler
Henry Kendall . . . . Charles Marlowe
Nancy Burne . . . . Margaret Marlowe
Betty Astell . . . .… . . Mary Marlowe
Fred Duprez . . . . Sam Hickleberry
Garry Marsh . . . . George Hamilton
Ena Grossmith . . . .
Wally Patch . . . .
Leo Sheffield . . . .
COMEDY Newlywed tries to make rich uncle
believe he is still married to his first wife,
who has since married again.

09903
TICKET OF LEAVE (69) (A)
B & D-Paramount British
P: Anthony Havelock-Allan
D: Michael Hankinson
S: Michael Hankinson, Vera Allinson
SC: Margaret McDonell
Dorothy Boyd . . . . Lillian Walters
John Clements . . . . Lucky Fisher
George Merritt . . . . Insp Black
Max Kirby . . . . Goodman
Wally Patch . . . . Sgt Knott
Enid Lindsay . . . . Edith Groves
Neil More . . . . Sir Richard Groves
Molly Hamley-Clifford . . . Old Rose
CRIME Thief robs girl's flat and they
become partners in crime.

09904
POLLY'S TWO FATHERS (23) (U)
WH Films (Exclusive)
P: D: Will Hammer
S: George Mozart
George Mozart . . . .… . Jack

Will Hammer . . . . Bill
April Vivian . . . . Polly
Pat Aherne . . . . Fred
Ian Wilson . . . . Lord Stockridge
DRAMA Norfolk. Girl adopted by fishermen
saves lord from drowning and weds poor seaman.

09905
OLD TIMERS (24) (U)
WB-FN (FN)
P: Irving Asher
Harry Champion   Charles Coburn
Lottie Lennox   Harry Bedford
Marie Lloyd jr   Brothers Egbert
REVUE Music hall stars.

09906
MISS BRACEGIRDLE DOES HER DUTY (20)
London
P: Alexander Korda
D: Lee Garmes
S: (STORY) Stacy Aumonier
Elsa Lanchester . . Millicent Bracegirdle
COMEDY Paris. Dean's daughter gets
involved with murder and white slavers.

09907
THE BELLES OF ST CLEMENT'S (68) (A)
B & D-Paramount British
P: Anthony Havelock-Allan
D: Ivar Campbell
S: Ivar & Sheila Campbell
SC: Terence Rattigan
Evelyn Foster . . . . Eve Chester
Meriel Forbes . . Natalie de Mailliere
Basil Langton . . . .… . Billy Grant
Isobel Scaife . . . . Maisie Carstairs
Enid Lindsey . . . . Miss Nelson
Sonia Somers . . . . Miss Grant
Heather White . . . . Betty Green
Tosca von Bissing . Countess de Mailliere
DRAMA Schoolgirl flees from enforced
marriage and gets involved with car theft.

09908
THE INVADER (61) (U) bilingual
USA: AN OLD SPANISH CUSTOM
British & Continental (MGM)
P: Sam Spiegel, Harold Richman
D: Adrian Brunel
S: Edwin Greenwood
Buster Keaton . . . . Leander Proudfoot
Lupita Tova . . . . Lupita Malez
Esme Percy . . . . Jose
Lyn Harding . . . . Gonzalo Gonzalez
Webster Booth . . . . Serenader
Andrea Malandrinos . . . . . Carlos
Hilda Moreno . . . . Carmita
Clifford Heatherley . . . . . David Cheeseman
COMEDY Spain. Girl feigns love for rich
tourist so that her fiance's rival will murder him.

09909
KING OF THE DAMNED (76) (A)
Gaumont
P: Michael Balcon
D: Walter Forde
S: (PLAY) John Chancellor
SC: Charles Bennett, A.R.Rawlinson,
Sidney Gilliat
Conrad Veidt . . . . Convict 83
Helen Vincent . . . . Anna
Noah Beery . . . . Mooche
Cecil Ramage . . . . Ramon
Edmund Willard . . . . The Greek
Percy Parsons . . . . Lumberjack
Peter Croft . . . . Boy
Raymond Lovell . . . . Capt Torres
C.M. Hallard. . . . . Commandant

Allan Jeayes . . . . Dr Prada
Percy Walsh . . . . Capt Perez
CRIME Caribbean island. Cultured convict
leads prison mutiny.

09910
LIMELIGHT (80) (U) USA: BACKSTAGE
Wilcox (GFD)
D: Herbert Wilcox
S: Laura Whetter
Anna Neagle . . . . Marjorie Kaye
Arthur Tracy . . . . Bob Grant
Jane Winton . . . . Ray Madison
Ellis Jeffreys . . . . Lady Madeleine
Muriel George . . . . Mrs Kaye
Alexander Field . . . . Alf Sparkes
Antony Holles . . . . Impresario
William Freshman . . . . Joe
Helena Pickard . . . . Pixie
Queenie Leonard . . . . Queenie
Ralph Reader . . . . Ralph
Tilly Losch; Jack Buchanan; W. MacQueen
Pope; Bobbie & Virginia; 24 Hippodrome Girls;
Geraldo and his Sweet Music
MUSICAL Chorus girl helps busker become
star and he becomes infatuated with
socialite.

09911
THE GHOST GOES WEST (90) (A)
London (UA)
reissues: 1941 (BL) 1947 (BL)
P: Alexander Korda
D: Rene Clair
S: (STORY) Eric Keown
(SIR TRISTRAM GOES WEST)
SC: Robert E. Sherwood, Geoffrey Kerr
Robert Donat . . . . Murdoch/Donald Glourie
Jean Parker . . . . Peggy Martin
Eugene Pallette . . . . Joe Martin
Elsa Lanchester . . . . Lady Shepperton
Ralph Bunker . . . . Ed Bigelow
Patricia Hilliard . . . . Shepherdess
Everley Gregg . . . . Gladys Martin
Morton Selten . . . . Gavin Glourie
Chili Bouchier . . . . Cleopatra
Mark Daly . . . . Groom
Herbert Lomas . . . . Fergus
Elliot Mason . . . . Mrs McNiff
Jack Lambert . . . . MacLaggan
FANTASY American millionaire takes Scots
castle to Florida, and the ghost goes too.
(FWA: 1937; Top Moneymaker: 1936).

09912
SUNSHINE AHEAD (64) (U)
Baxter & Barter (U)
P: John Baxter
D: Wallace Orton
S: Con West, Geoffrey Orme
Eddie Pola . . . . The Producer
Betty Astell . . . . The Girl
Leslie Perrins . . . . The Critic
Eve Lister . . . . The Secretary
Jack Payne and his Band
Leonard Henry   The Two Leslies
Harry S. Pepper   Doris Arnold
Harold Ramsay   George Baker
Ruth Naylor   Webster Booth
Troise and his Mandoliers
Sherman Fisher Girls
MUSICAL Producer stages outside broadcast
despite jealous critic.

09913
THE AMATEUR GENTLEMAN (102) (A)
Criterion (UA)
P: Marcel Hellman, Douglas Fairbanks jr
D: Thornton Freeland

S: (NOVEL) Jeffrey Farnol
SC: Clemence Dane, Edward Knoblock,
Sergei Nolbandov
Douglas Fairbanks jr . . . . . . Barnabas Barty
Elissa Landi . . . . Lady Cleone
Gordon Harker . . . . Natty Bell
Basil Sydney . . . . Chichester
Hugh Williams . . . . Ronald
Irene Browne . . . . . . Lady Huntstanton
Athole Stewart . . . Marquess of Camberhurst
Coral Brown . . . . Pauline d'Arville
Margaret Lockwood . . Georgina Huntstanton
Frank Pettingell . . . . John Barty
Esme Percy . . . . Townsend
Gilbert Davis . . . . Prince Regent
ADVENTURE Regency. Innkeeper's son
poses as boxing 'buck' to prove his father
did not steal marquis's jewels.

09914
THE IMPROPER DUCHESS (80) (A)
City (GFD)
P: Maurice Browne
D: Harry Hughes
S: (PLAY) James B. Fagan
SC: Harry Hughes, Vernon Harris
Yvonne Arnaud . . . . Duchess of Tann
Hugh Wakefield . . . . King of Poldavia
James Carew . . . . . Montgomery Curtis
Felix Aylmer . . . . Count Seidel
Arthur Finn . . . . Senator Corcoran
Gerald Barry . . . . Baron Kamp
Finlay Currie . . . . Milton Lee
Wilfred Caithness . . . . Rev Adam McAdam
Ben Welden . . . . McCabe
Annie Esmond . . . . Baroness Kamp
COMEDY Washington. Oil executives
scheme to compromise Ruritanian duchess
to prevent loan.

09915
ON TOP OF THE WORLD (79) (U)
City (AP & D) *reissue:* 1940,
EVERYTHING OKAY (cut)
P: Basil Humphrys
D: Redd Davis
S: H.B.Parkinson
SC: Evelyn Barrie
Betty Fields . . . . Betty Schofield
Frank Pettingell . . . . Albert Hicks
Leslie Bradley . . . . Jimmy Priestley
Ben Field . . . . Old Harry
Charles Sewell . . . . Mr Preston
Eileen Latham . . . . Anne
Wally Patch . . . . Cardsharper
Fewlass Llewellyn . . . . Soames
COMEDY Lancs. Millgirl uses winnings
from greyhound race to help strikers.

FEB

09916
KING OF THE CASTLE (69) (U)
City (GFD)
P: Basil Humphrys
D: Redd Davis
S: Frank Atkinson
SC: George Dewhurst
June Clyde . . . . Marilyn Bean
Claude Dampier . . . . Pullen
Billy Milton . . . . Monty King
Cynthia Stock . . . . Elsie
Wally Patch . . . . Trout
Arthur Finn . . . . Henry Bean
Paul Balke . . . . . . Sir Percival Trellis
H.F.Maltby . . . . Mr Crow
Mavis Villiers . . . . Billie
Jimmy Godden . . . . Bailiff
COMEDY Family butler is missing heir
to title.

09917
EXCUSE MY GLOVE (75) (A)
Alexander (ABFD)
P: R. Howard Alexander, Joe Rock
D: Redd Davis
S: R. Howard Alexander
SC: Val Valentine, Katherine Strueby
Len Harvey . . . . Don Carter
Archie Pitt . . . . Bill Adams
Betty Ann Davies . . . . Ann Haydon
Olive Blakeney . . .. Aunt Fanny Stafford
Wally Patch . . . . Hurricane Harry
Ronald Shiner . . . . Perky Pat
Arthur Finn . . . . Madigan
Vera Bogetti . . . . Lucille
Bobbie Comber . . . . Bivex
Don McCorkindale; Tommy Farr; Jimmy Wilde;
Bdr Billy Wells; Gunner Moir
SPORT Glass collector becomes boxer and
wins championship at Albert Hall despite
crooked manager.

09918
CHEER UP ! (72) (U)
Stanley Lupino (ABFD)
D: Leo Mittler
S: Stanley Lupino
SC: Michael Barringer
Stanley Lupino . . . . Tom Denham
Sally Gray . . . . Sally Gray
Roddy Hughes . . . . Dick Dirk
Gerald Barry . . . . John Harman
Kenneth Kove . . . . Wilfred Harman
Wyn Weaver . . . . Mr Carter
Marjorie Chard . . . . Mrs Carter
Ernest Sefton . . . . Tom Page
Syd Crossley . . . . Waiter
MUSICAL Author finances show by
being mistaken for millionaire.

09919
QUEEN OF HEARTS (80) (U)
ATP (ABFD) *reissue:* 1945 (EB)
P: Basil Dean
D: Monty Banks
S: Clifford Grey, H.F.Maltby, Anthony
Kimmins, Douglas Furber, Gordon Wellesley
Gracie Fields . . . . Grace Perkins
John Loder . . . . Derek Cooper
Enid Stamp-Taylor . . . . Yvonne
Fred Duprez . . . . Zulenberg
Edward Rigby . . . . Perkins
Julie Suedo . . . . Rita Dow
Jean Lister . . . . Mrs Perkins
Hal Gordon . . . . Stage Manager
Syd Crossley . . . . PC
Madeleine Seymour . . . . . . Mrs Vandeleur
H.F.Maltby . . . . Solicitor
Margaret Yarde . . . . Mrs Porter
MUSICAL Seamstress wins matinee idol by
posing as rich woman.

09920
WHOM THE GODS LOVE (82) (U) USA:
MOZART
ATP (ABFD) *reissue:* 1949 (EB)
P:D: Basil Dean
S: Margaret Kennedy
Victoria Hopper . . . . . . Constance Mozart
John Loder . . . . Prince Lopkonitz
Stephen Haggard . . . . Wolfgang Mozart
Liane Haid . . . . Aloysia
Marie Lohr . . . . Empress
George Curzon . . . . Da Ponte
Jean Cadell . . . . Frau Mozart
Hubert Harben . . . . Leopold Mozart
Frederick Leister . . . . Emperor
Lawrence Hanray . . . . Archbishop
Richard Goolden . . . . Weber

Muriel George .... Frau Weber
Leueen Magrath .... Josefa Weber
Oda Slobodskaya; Percy Hemming;
Tudor Davies; Enid James; Sylvia Nells;
Sir Thomas Beecham and the London
Philharmonic Orchestra
MUSICAL Austria, 1790. Composer's wife
remains faithful to him despite attentions
of Prince.

09921
WHAT THE PUPPY SAID (39) (U)
Newman (Butcher)
D:S. Widgey Newman
SC: John Quin
Moore Marriott .... Sir John
Wally Patch .... Wally
Vera Sherburne .... Vera Benson
Joe Hayman .... Benson
Margaret Yarde .... Mrs Benson
Stan Paskin ....
Herbert Langley ....
ANIMAL Collie dog aids romance of
farmer's daughter and squire's son.

09922
TROUBLED WATERS (70) (A)
Fox British
P: John Findlay
D: Albert Parker
S: W.P.Lipscomb, Reginald Pound
SC: Gerard Fairlie
Virginia Cherrill. .... June Elkhardt
James Mason .... John Merriman
Alastair Sim .... Mac MacTavish
Raymond Lovell .... Carter
Bellenden Powell .... Dr Garthwaite
Sam Wilkinson .... Lightning
Peter Popp .... Timothy Golightly
William T. Ellwanger .... Ezra Elkhardt
CRIME Secret agent saves villager's liquid
explosive from crooks.

09923
UNDER PROOF (50) (U)
Fox British
D: Roland Gillett
S: (PLAY) Tod Waller (DUDLEY DOES IT)
Betty Stockfeld .... Vivian
Tyrell Davis .... Dudley
Judy Kelly .... Corone
Guy Middleton .... Bruce
Charles Farrell .... Spike
Viola Compton .... Mrs Richards
David Horne .... Dr Walton
Edward Ashley .... Ward Delaney
Henry Longhurst .... Insp Holt
COMEDY Brandy gives coward courage to
catch smugglers.

09924
FAUST (43) (A) *spectra*
Publicity Picture Productions-National
Interest (Reunion)
P: Fred A. Swann
D: Albert Hopkins
S: (OPERA) Charles Gounod
Webster Booth .... Faust
Anne Zeigler .... Marguerite
Dennis Hoey .... Mephistopheles
MUSICAL Period. Old man gives soul to
devil in return for youth.

09925
PATHETONE PARADE OF 1936 (36) (U)
Pathe
D: Fred Watts
Leonard Henry .... Compere
Charlie Kunz .... Scott & Whaley
Carson Sisters .... Arthur Prince & Jim
Robb Wilton .... Norman Long

Nosmo King .... Charles Coborn
Troise and his Mandoliers
REVUE Extracts from Pathetone Weekly.

09926
PRISON BREAKER (69) (A)
George Smith (Col) *reissue:* 1948
D: Adrian Brunel
S: (NOVEL) Edgar Wallace
SC: Frank Witty
James Mason .... Bunny Barnes
Marguerite Allan .... Veronica
Wally Patch .... Villars
Andrews Engelmann .... Steigelmann
Ian Fleming .... Stephen Shand
George Merritt .... Goldring
Vincent Holman .... Jackman
Tarva Penna .... Macallum
Aubrey Mallalieu .... Sir Douglas Mergin
CRIME Man rescues secret agent friend
when he is jailed for killing crook.

09927
THE SECRET VOICE (68) (A)
B & D-Paramount British
P: Anthony Havelock-Allan
D: George Pearson
S: Frances Warren
SC: Margaret McDonnell
John Stuart .... Jim Knowles
Diana Beaumont .... Helen Allinson
John Kevan .... Dick Allinson
Henry Victor .... Brandt
Ruth Gower .... Joan Grayson
Monte de Lyle .... Perez
Charles Carew .... Scotty
CRIME Crooks seek photograph of
formula for non-inflammable petrol.

09928
WHEN KNIGHTS WERE BOLD (75) (U)
Capitol (GFD) *reissues:* 1942 (Pi) 1947 (Amb)
P: Max Schach
D: Jack Raymond
S: (PLAY) Charles Marlow
SC: Austin Parker, Douglas Furber
Jack Buchanan .... Sir Guy de Vere
Fay Wray .... Lady Rowena
Garry Marsh .... Brian Ballymote
Kate Cutler .... Aunt Agatha
Martita Hunt .... Aunt Esther
Robert Horton .... Cousin Bertie
Aubrey Mather .... Canon
Aubrey Fitzgerald .... Barker
Robert Nainby .... Whittle
Moore Marriott .... Tramp
MUSICAL Lieut inherits title and wins
cousin after dreaming of mediaeval days.

09929
SOFT LIGHTS AND SWEET MUSIC (86) (U)
British Lion *reissue:* 1946 (NR; cut)
P:D: Herbert Smith
Ambrose and his Orchestra
Evelyn Dall .... Western Brothers
Harry Tate .... Billy Bennett
Turner Layton .... Elisabeth Welch
Max Bacon .... Wilson, Keppel & Betty
Donald Stewart .... Karina
3 Rhythm Brothers .... 4 Flash Devils
4 Robinas .... 5 Charladies
Sandy Powell's Harmonica Band
REVUE

09930
A TOUCH OF THE MOON (67) (U)
GS Enterprises (Radio)
P: A.George Smith
D: Maclean Rogers
S: (PLAY) Cyril Campion
SC: Kathleen Butler, H.F.Maltby

John Garrick .... Martin Barnaby
Dorothy Boyd .... Mona Dupare
Joyce Bland .... Mrs Fairclough
David Horne .... Col Plattner
Max Adrian .... Francis Leverton
Aubrey Mallalieu .... Mr Dupare
W.T.Ellwanger .... Garfield
Wally Patch .... PC
COMEDY Alcoholic wins girl away
from rich American fiance.

09931
JACK OF ALL TRADES (76) (U)
USA: THE TWO OF US
Gainsborough (Gaumont) *reissue:* 1943
P: Michael Balcon
D: Jack Hulbert, Robert Stevenson
S: (PLAY) Paul Vulpuis
(YOUTH AT THE HELM)
SC: Jack Hulbert, Austin Melford, J.O.C.Orton
Jack Hulbert .... Jack Warrender
Gina Malo .... Frances Wilson
Robertson Hare .... Lionel Fitch
Athole Stewart .... Huckle
Felix Aylmer .... Benton
H.F.Maltby .... Holman
Fewlass Llewellyn .... Nicholson
Mary Jerrold .... Old Lady
C.M.Hallard .... Henry Kilner
Cecil Parker .... Barrington
Ian McLean .... Gangster
Betty Astell & Bruce Seton
MUSICAL Unemployed man talks his way
into high finance and catches arsonists.

09932
THINGS TO COME (100) (U)
London Films (UA)
reissues: 1943 (Ex; 2931 ft cut) 1948 (BL)
P: Alexander Korda
D: William Cameron Menzies
S: H.G.Wells
Raymond Massey .. John Cabal/Oswald Cabal
Cedric Hardwicke .... Theotocopulos
Margaretta Scott .... Roxana
Ralph Richardson .... The Boss
Edward Chapman.. Pippa Passworthy/Raymond
Maurice Braddell .... Dr Harding
Sophie Stewart .... Mrs Cabal
Derrick de Marney .... Richard Gordon
Ann Todd .... Mary Gordon
Pearl Argyle .... Katherine Cabal
Kenneth Villiers .... Maurice Passworthy
Ivan Brandt .... Mitani
Anthony Holles .... Simon Burton
Allan Jeayes .... Mr Cabal
John Clements .... Airman
FANTASY 1940-2036. Scientists rebuild
wartorn world and aim for the moon.

09933
PUBLIC NUISANCE No. 1 (78) (A)
Cecil Films (GFD) *reissue:* 1952 (Pi)
P: Herman Fellner, Max Schach
D: Marcel Varnel
S: Franz Arnold
SC: Roger Burford, Robert Edmunds,
Val Guest
Frances Day .... Frances Travers
Arthur Riscoe .... Arthur Rawlings
Claude Dampier .... Feather
Muriel Aked .... Miss Trumps
Peter Haddon .... Richard Trelawney
Sebastian Smith .... Mr Snelling
Robert Nainby .... Mr Rawlings
Antony Holles .... Waiter
MUSICAL Riviera. Shopgirl helps wastrel
acting as waiter to save rich uncle's hotel.

MAR

09934
BELOVED IMPOSTOR (86) (A)
Stafford (Radio)
P: John Stafford
D: Victor Hanbury
S: (NOVEL) Ethel Mannin (DANCING BOY)
SC: Connery Chappell
Rene Ray . . . . Mary
Fred Conyngham . . . . George
Germaine Aussey . . . . La Lumiere
Penelope Parkes . . . . Connie
Edwin Ellis . . . . Herbert
Charles Oliver . . . . Pierre
Fred Groves . . . . Jack Harding
Bela Mila . . . . Mona
Tony de Lungo . . . . Gavani
Lawrence Hanray . . . . Arthur
Leslie "Hutch" Hutchinson; Gwen Farrar;
Caligary Brothers
MUSICAL Boastful waiter thinks he kills
the singer who spurned him.

09935
SWEENEY TODD. THE DEMON BARBER
OF FLEET STREET (68) (A)
George King (MGM) *reissue:* 1940 (Amb)
D: George King
S: (PLAY) George Dibdin-Pitt
SC: Frederick Hayward, H.F.Maltby
Tod Slaughter . . . . Sweeney Todd
Bruce Seton. . . . . Mark Ingestre
Eve Lister . . . . Johanna Oakley
Stella Rho . . . . Mrs Lovatt
Ben Soutten . . . . Beadle
D.J.Williams . . . . Stephen Oakley
Jerry Verno . . . . Fearnley
John Singer . . . . Tobias Wragg
CRIME 1760. Barber cuts sailors' throats,
steals their gems, and uses their corpses for
pies.

09936
21 TODAY (34) (U)
Albany Studios (MGM)
P: Herbert Kemplen
D: John H. Taylor
Arthur Prince & Jim   Ian Fleming
Frank Titterton   Garda Hall
Rebla   Mary Honri
MUSICAL Stars and buskers perform
at a birthday party.

09937
THE MUSIC MAKER (52) (U)
Inspiration (MGM)
P: Horace Shepherd, Holt Turner
D: "Hugh Kairs" (Horace Shepherd)
S: Horace Shepherd
Arthur Young . . . . The Musician
Violet Loxley . . . . His Wife
MUSICAL Old violinist finishes symphony and
dies.

09938
THE BROWN WALLET (68) (A)
WB-FN (FN)
P: Irving Asher
D: Michael Powell
S: (STORY) Stacy Aumonier
SC: Ian Dalrymple
Patric Knowles . . . . John Gillespie
Nancy O'Neil . . . . Eleanor
Henry Caine . . . . Simmonds
Henrietta Watson . . . . Aunt Mary
Charlotte Leigh . . . . Miss Barton
Shayle Gardner . . . . Wotherspoone
Edward Dalby . . . . Minting
Eliot Makeham . . . . Hobday
CRIME Bankrupt publisher is suspected
of killing rich aunt when he finds £2,000.

09939
FAITHFUL (78) (U)
WB-FN (WB)
P: Irving Asher
D: Paul Stein
S: Brock Williams
Jean Muir . . . . Marilyn Koster
Gene Gerrard . . . . Danny Reeves
Hans Sonker . . . . Carl Koster
Chili Bouchier . . . . Pamela Carson
Margaret Yarde . . . . Mrs Kemp
MUSICAL Viennese singer poses as bachelor
and is tempted by socialite.

09940
GAOL BREAK (64) (A)
WB-FN (WB)
P: Irving Asher
D: Ralph Ince
S: Michael Barringer
Ralph Ince . . . . Jim Oakley
Pat Fitzpatrick . . . . Mickie Oakley
Basil Gill . . . . Dr Walter Merian
Raymond Lovell . . . . Duke
Lorna Hubbard . . . . Daisy Oakley
Roy Findlay . . . . Louie
Elliot Mason . . . . Euphie
Desmond Roberts . . . . Paul Kendall
CRIME Convict escapes jail to save
son from kidnap by his old associates.

09941
CROWN V STEVENS (66) (A)
WB-FN (WB)
P: Irving Asher
D: Michael Powell
S: (NOVEL) Laurence Maynell
(THIRD TIME UNLUCKY)
SC: Brock Williams
Beatrix Thomson . . . . Doris Stevens
Patric Knowles . . . . Chris Jansen
Reginald Purdell . . . . Alf
Glennis Lorimer . . . . Molly
Allan Jeayes . . . . Insp Carter
Frederick Piper . . . . Arthur Stevens
Googie Withers . . . . Ella
Mabel Poulton . . . . Mamie
Morris Harvey . . . . Julius Bayleck
CRIME Ex-dancer kills usurer and her husband,
framing his employee.

09942
TWELVE GOOD MEN (64) (A)
WB-FN (WB)
P: Irving Asher
D: Ralph Ince
S: (NOVEL) John Rhodes
(MURDERS IN PRAED STREET)
SC: Frank Launder, Sidney Gilliat
Henry Kendall . . . . Charles Drew
Nancy O'Neil . . . . Ann
Joyce Kennedy . . . . Lady Thora
Percy Parsons . . . . Hopwood
Morland Graham . . . . Victor Day
Bernard Miles . . . . Insp Pine
Philip Ray . . . . Higgs
Frederick Burtwell . . . . . . Fotheringay
CRIME Actor foils a convict who escapes to
murder his jury.

09943
WEDDING GROUP (69) (U) USA: WRATH OF
JEALOUSY
Fox British
P: Leslie Landau
D: Alex Bryce, Campbell Gullan
S: (RADIO PLAY) Philip Wade
SC: Selwyn Jepson, Hugh Brooke
Fay Compton . . . . . Florence Nightingale
Barbara Greene . . . . Janet Graham
Patric Knowles . . . . Robert Smith

Alastair Sim . . . . Angus Graham
Bruce Seton . . . . Dr Jock Carnegie
Ethel Glendinning . . . Margaret Graham
David Hutcheson . . . . George Harkness
Arthur Young . . . . Dr Granger
ROMANCE Scotland, 1855. Minister's daughter
becomes nurse to follow beloved officer to
Crimea.

09944
THE BIG NOISE (65) (U)
Fox British
P: John Findlay
D: Alex Bryce
S: Gene Markey, Harry Ruskin
SC: Gerard Fairlie
Alastair Sim . . . . Finny
Norah Howard . . . . Mary Miller
Fred Duprez . . . . Henry Hadley
Grizelda Hervey . . . . Consuelo
C.Denier Warren . . E. Pinkerton Gale
Viola Compton . . . . Mrs Dayton
Peter Popp . . . . Jenkins
Howard Douglas . . . . Gluckstein
Reginald Forsyth and his Band
COMEDY Oil company directors promote
clerk to make him their scapegoat.

09945
BLIND MAN'S BLUFF (72) (A)
Fox British
D: Albert Parker
S: (PLAY) William Foster, B.Scott-Elder
(SMOKED GLASSES)
SC: Cecil Maiden
Basil Sydney . . . . Dr Peter Fairfax
Enid Stamp-Taylor . . . . . . Sylvia Fairfax
Barbara Greene . . . . Vicki Sheridan
James Mason . . . . Stephen Neville
Iris Ashley . . . . Claire
Ian Colin . . . . Philip Stanhope
Wilson Coleman . . Dr Franz Morgenhardt
Warburton Gamble . . . . . . Tracy
DRAMA Blind scientist cured by secret ray
but does not tell his unfaithful wife.

09946
FIND THE LADY (70) (A)
Fox British
D: Roland Gillett
S: (PLAY) Tod Waller (THE FAKERS)
SC: Roland Gillett, Edward Dryhurst
Jack Melford . . . . Schemer Doyle
Althea Henley . . . . Venus Doyle
George Sanders . . . . Curly Randall
Viola Compton . . . . Lady Waldron
Violet Loxley . . . . Vilma Waldron
Dorothy Vernon. . . . .
Eric Pavitt . . . .
John Warwick . . . .
COMEDY American trickster posing as
faith healer loves poor man who loves a
lady's daughter.

09947
KING OF HEARTS (82) (U)
Butcher *reissue:* 1940, LITTLE GEL
(2462 ft cut)
P:D: Oswald Mitchell, Walter Tennyson
S: (PLAY) Matthew Boulton
(THE CORDUROY DIPLOMAT)
Will Fyffe . . . . Bill Saunders
Gwenllian Gill . . . . May Saunders
Richard Dolman . . . . Jack Ponsonby
Amy Veness . . . . Mrs Ponsonby
O.B.Clarence . . . . Mr Ponsonby
Jock McKay . . . . George
Googie Withers . . . . Elaine
Margaret Davidge . . . . . . Mrs Saunders
Ronald Shiner . . . . Tomkins
Patrick Ludlow . . . . Reggie

Frakson; Java's Tzigane Band; Constance,
Lilyan & Malo
MUSICAL Rich woman bribes docker to
spoil his daughter's romance with her son.
(Extracts in HIGHLIGHTS OF VARIETY
No. 21 (1940).)

09948
FIRST OFFENCE (66) (A)
Gainsborough (Gau)
P: Michael Balcon
D: Herbert Mason
S: Stafford Dickens
SC: Austin Melford

John Mills	Johnnie Penrose
Lilli Palmer	Jeanette
Bernard Nedell	The Boss
Michael Andre	Michel
H.G.Stoker	Dr Penrose
Jean Wall	The Zebra
Paul Velsa	Peanuts
Maupi	Man in Panama
Judy Kelly	Girl in Garage

CRIME France. Doctor's spoiled son
joins gang of car thieves.

09949
RHODES OF AFRICA 991) (U)
USA: RHODES
Gaumont
AP: Geoffrey Barkas
D: Berthold Viertel
S: (BOOK) Sarah Millin
SC: Michael Barringer, Miles Malleson,
Leslie Arliss

Walter Huston	Cecil Rhodes
Oscar Homolka	Paul Kruger
Basil Sydney	Dr Jamison
Peggy Ashcroft	Ann Carpenter
Frank Cellier	Barney Barnato
Renee de Veaux	Mrs Kruger
Bernard Lee	Cartwright
Lewis Casson	Helm
Ndaniso Kumala	King Lobengula
Glennis Lorimer	Fiancee

HISTORY Africa. Diamond miner rises to
become Prime Minister of Cape Colony.

09950
STRANGE CARGO (68) (A)
Lawrence Huntington (Par)
D: Lawrence Huntington
S: Gerald Elliott

Kathleen Kelly	Sonia
George Mozart	'Orace
Moore Marriott	Capt Burch
George Sanders	Roddy Burch
Richard Norris	Travers
Geoffrey Clarke	Rev Twiddell
Kenneth Warrington	Capt Mandara
Julien Vedey	Customs Officer

Alvin Saxon's Murray Club Band;
Matt Davidson & Adele
CRIME Stowaway dancer helps cargo
captain's son catch gunrunners.

09951
HAPPY DAYS ARE HERE AGAIN (87) (U)
Argyle Talking Pictures (AP&D)
reissue: 1938, HAPPY DAYS REVUE
(BIED; 4931 ft cut)
P: John Argyle
D: Norman Lee
S: Renee Houston
SC: Dan Birt, FH.Bickerton, Alan Rennie

Renee Houston	Kitty Seymour
Billie Houston	Mickey Seymour
Shirley Houston	Nita
Harry Milton	Chris
Billy Watts	Reg Jarvis

Georgie Harris	Brainwave
Viola Compton	Lil Grayson
Sally McBride	Ella
Mark Stone	Alf
Ida Barr	Girlie

Marie Kendall; Bert & Michael Kidd;
Syd Seymour and his Mad Hatters
MUSICAL Singing sisters become stars.

09952
FAME (68) (U)
Wilcox (GFD)
P: Herbert Wilcox
D: Leslie Hiscott
S: John Harding, William Hargreaves
SC: Michael Barringer, R.P.Weston, Bert Lee,
Jack Marks

Sydney Howard	Oswald Bertwhistle
Muriel Aked	Mrs Bertwhistle
Miki Hood	Joan Riley
Brian Lawrance	Douglas Cameron
Guy Middleton	Lester Cordwell
Geraldine Hislop	Geraldine
Arthur Finn	Director
H.F.Maltby	Mayor
Herbert Lomas	Rumbold Wakefield
Russell Thorndike	Judge
Frank Pettingell	Reuben Pendleton
Sydney Fairbrother	Passenger
Maire O'Neill	Mrs Docker
Henry Victor	Actor

Geraldo and his Orchestra
COMEDY Shopwalker wins competition
and becomes film star.

09953
PAL O' MINE (41) (U)
Film Sales (Radio)
P:D:S: Widgey R.Newman
SC: John Quin

Herbert Langley	Bombasso
Stan Paskin	Beano
Charles Paton	Macready Phelps
Arthur Gomez	Guvnor
Doris Long	Millie
Peter Cotes	Archie

Marie Lloyd jr; Harold Heath; Freddy
Summers; Peter the Dog.
MUSICAL Stage doorman takes blame for
robbing safe, thinking his son is the culprit.

09954
ONCE IN A MILLION (77) (U)
USA: WEEKEND MILLIONAIRE
BIP (Wardour)
P: Walter C. Mycroft
D: Arthur Woods
S: Jack Davies, Geoffrey Kerr, Max Kester

Charles 'Buddy' Rogers	Pierre
Mary Brian	Suzanne
W.H.Berry	Gallivert
Billy Milton	Prince
Haver & Lee	Joe & Chief
Charles Carson	President
Norah Gale	Princess
Nadine March	Josette
Iris Hoey	Mrs Fenwick
Veronica Rose	Caroline
Jimmy Godden	Plume

COMEDY Paris. Bank clerk mistaken for
millionaire loves mannequin posing as
countess.

09955
LIVING DANGEROUSLY (72) (A)
BIP (Wardour)
P: Walter C. Mycroft
D: Herbert Brenon
S: (PLAY) Reginald Simpson, Frank
Gregory
SC: Geoffrey Kerr, Marjorie Deans,

Dudley Leslie

Otto Kruger	Dr Stanley Norton
Leonora Corbett	Helen Pryor
Francis Lister	Dr Henry Pryor
Aileen Marson	Vera Kennedy
Hartley Power	District Attorney
Lawrence Anderson	Lloyd
James Carew	Lingard
Iris Hoey	Lady Annesley
Jimmy Godden	Council Member
Charles Mortimer	Insp Webster
Eric Stanley	Sir George Parker

CRIME Doctor trafficking in morphia
frames ex-partner for adultery with his
ex-wife and blackmails him.

09956
THE CRIMSON CIRCLE (76) (A)
Wainwright (U)
P: Richard Wainwright
D: Reginald Denham
S:(NOVEL) Edgar Wallace
SC: Howard Irving Young

Hugh Wakefield	Derrick Yale
Alfred Drayton	Insp Parr
Noah Beery	Felix Marl
June Duprez	Sylvia Howard
Niall McGinnis	Jack Beardmore
Renee Gadd	Millie MacRoy
Basil Gill	James Beardmore
Paul Blake	Sgt Webster
Gordon McLeod	Insp Brabazon
Ralph Truman	Lawrence Fuller

CRIME Inspector unmasks mysterious
leader of blackmail gang.

09957
WOLF'S CLOTHING (80) (A)
Wainwright (U)
P: Richard Wainwright
D: Andrew Marton
S: (PLAY)(THE EMANCIPATION OF
AMBROSE)
SC: Evadne Price, Brock Williams

Claude Hulbert	Ambrose Girling
Gordon Harker	Prosser
George Graves	Sir Roger Balmayne
Lilli Palmer	Lydia
Helen Haye	Mildred Girling
Shayle Gardner	Babo
Peter Gawthorne	Sir Hector
George Hayes	Yassiov
Joan Swinstead	Mary Laming
Frank Birch	Rev Laming
Ernest Sefton	Finden Charvet

COMEDY Paris. Spy gang mistake timid FO man
for famous assassin.

09958
THE HOWARD CASE (62) (U)
Sovereign (U)
P: Fraser Foulsham
D: Frank Richardson
S: (PLAY) H.F.Maltby (FRAUD)

Jack Livesey	Jerry
Olive Melville	Pat
Arthur Seaton	Howard/Phillips
Olive Sloane	Lena Maxwell
David Keir	Barnes
Jack Vyvyan	Sgt Halliday

CRIME Lawyer kills twin cousin and frames
partner.

09959
THIS GREEN HELL (71) (A)
Randall Faye (Radio)
P:D:SC: Randall Faye

Edward Rigby	Dan Foyle
Sybil Grove	Mrs Foyle
Richard Dolman	Andy
Roxie Russell	Peggy Foyle

John Singer . . . . Billy Foyle
Billy Watts . . . . Barton
Norman Pierce . . . . Willington
COMEDY Train crash makes daydreamer
think he is famous explorer.

09960
PICTORIAL REVUE (40) (U)
Pathe
D: Fred Watts
Ronald Frankau . . . . Compere
Robb Wilton   Eric Woodburn
Charles Coburn   Dave & Joe O'Gorman
Collinson & Dean .Rupert Hazell & Elsie Day
Sereno & June   Jaconelli
Geraldo and his Orchestra
REVUE Extracts from "Pathe Pictorial"
series.

09961
THE MAN BEHIND THE MASK (79) (A)
Joe Rock (MGM)
D: Michael Powell
S: (NOVEL) Jacques Futrelle
(THE CHASE OF THE GOLDEN PLATE)
SC: Ian Hay, Syd Courtenay, Jack Byrd,
Stanley Haynes
Hugh Williams . . . . Nick Barclay
Jane Baxter . . . . June Slade
Maurice Schwartz . . . . The Master
Donald Calthrop . . . . Dr Walpole
Henry Oscar . . . . Officer
Peter Gawthorne . . . . Lord Slade
Kitty Kelly . . . . Miss Weeks
Ronald Ward . . . : . . . . Jimmy Slade
George Merritt . . . . Mallory
Reginald Tate . . . . Hayden
Ivor Barnard . . . . Hewitt
Hal Gordon . . . . Sgt
CRIME Mad astronomer kidnaps Lord's
daughter to obtain oriental shield.

09962
THE CARDINAL (75) (A)
Grosvenor (Pathe)
P: Harcourt Templeman
D: Sinclair Hill
S: (PLAY) Louis N. Parker
SC: D.B.Wyndham-Lewis
Matheson Lang . . . Cardinal de Medici
June Duprez . . . . . Francesca Monterosa
Eric Portman . . . . . Guiliano de Medici
Robert Atkins . . . . Gen Belmont
Henrietta Watson . . . . . Donna de Medici
O.B.Clarence . . . . Monterosa
Douglas Jeffries . . . . Baglioni
F.B.J.Sharpe . . . . Pope Julius II
Wilfred Fletcher . . . . Michael Angelo
A.Bromley Davenport . . . . Bramante
HISTORY Rome, 16th C. Cardinal feigns
madness to wrest confession from general
who framed his brother for murder.

09963
HOT NEWS (77) (U)
St George's Pictures (Col)
P: Ian Sutherland
D: W.P.Kellino
S: Reginald Long, Arthur Rigby
Lupino Lane . . . . Jimmy Selby
Phyllis Clare . . . . Betty Mason
Wallace Lupino . . . . Horace Wells
Barbara Kilner . . . . Princess Ina
Ben Welden . . . . Slug Wilson
Glen Raynham . . . . . . Barbara O'Neill
Reginald Long . . . . Prince Stephen
Fred Leslie . . . . Leslie Fredericks
George Pughe . . . . Slim McGill

The Dorchester Girls
COMEDY Chicago gangsters kidnap
cabaret star in mistake for heiress.

09964
CHINESE CABARET (44) (U)
Bijou (Col)
P: Moy Long, Rae Saloman
D: Buddy Harris
S: S.E.Reynolds
Robert Hobbs . . . . Blackstone
Douglas Stewart . . . . Insp Brand
Lillian Graham . . . . Peggy Brand
Tony Gerrard . . . .
Lai Foun Troupe; Anne Zeigler; Hal Fox
and his Band; Dinah Lee; Grant & Moseley
MUSICAL Detective's daughter unmasks
Chinatown restaurateur as silk-smuggler.

09965
DEBT OF HONOUR (83) (A)
British National (GFD)
reissue: 1939 (NR; 22 mins cut)
P: John Corfield
D: Norman Walker
S: "Sapper" (H.C.McNeile)
SC: Tom Geraghty, Cyril Campion
Leslie Banks . . . . Maj Jimmy Stanton
Will Fyffe . . . . `Fergus McAndrews
Geraldine Fitzgerald . . . . . Peggy Mayhew
Niall McGinnis . . . . Lt Peter Stretton
Reginald Purdell . . . . Pedro Salvas
Garry Marsh . . . . Bill
Stewart Rome . . . . Maj Purvis
Phyllis Dare . . . . Mrs Stretton
Joyce Kennedy . : . . . . . . Lady Bracebury
William Kendall . . . . Paul Martin
Randle Ayrton . . . . Capt Turner
Eric Cowley . . . . Richard Denman
David Horne . . . . Col Mayhew
DRAMA Africa. Major takes blame when
friend steals for sake of gambling girl.

09966
RAILROAD RHYTHM (43) spectra (U)
Carnival (Ex)
P: W. Devenport Hackney
D: A.E.C.Hopkins
S: Raymond Fish
Jack Browning . . . . Pilot
Vilma Vanne . . . . Girl
Foster Richardson . . . .
Pat Baring . . . .
MUSICAL Pilot brings success to derelict
railway station with jazz.

09967
THE VOICE OF IRELAND (49) (U)
Victor Haddick (ICC)
D:S: Victor Haddick
Richard Hayward . . . .
Victor Haddick . . . .
Barney O'Hara . . . .
MUSICAL Ireland. Traveller returns
home and meets old friends.

09968
FORGET-ME-NOT (72) (U) bilingual
USA: FOREVER YOURS
London (UA)
P: Alberto Giacalone, Alexander Korda
D: Zoltan Korda, Stanley Irving
S: Hugh Gray, Arthur Wimperis
Beniamino Gigli . . . . Enzo Curti
Joan Gardner . . . . Helen Carlton
Ivan Brandt . . . . Hugh Anderson
Hugh Wakefield . . . . Jackson
Jeanne Stuart . . . . Irene Desborough
Allan Jeayes . . . . London Manager
Hay Petrie . . . . New York Manager

Charles Carson . . . . George Arnold
Richard Gofe . . . . Benvenuto
MUSICAL Girl weds widowed tenor and
stays true despite return of her ex-fiance.

09969
BRITISH LION VARIETIES (U) (series)
British Lion (MGM)
P:D: Herbert Smith

09970
No. 1: (10)
Radio Rogues   Petite Ascots
Stanelli and Edgar Joe Loss and his Band

09971
No. 2: (11)
Four Aces   3 Australian Boys
Anita, Charles & Jack
                    Joe Loss and his Band

09972
No. 3: (10)
Radio Rogues   Petite Ascots
3 Accordion Kings   Joe Loss and his Band

09973
No. 4: (11)
Four Aces   Petite Ascots
Harriette Hutchinson
                    Joe Loss and his Band

09974
No. 5: (11)
Four Aces   Stewart & Vale
Tessa Deane   Anita, Charles & Jack

09975
No. 6: (11)
Bob Lively   Carson Sisters
Radio Rogues   Roy Fox and his Band

09976
No. 7: (10)
3 Accordion Kings   3 Australian Boys
Petite Ascots   Joe Loss and his Band

09977
No. 8: (11)
Harriette Hutchinson   7 Thunderbolts
Radio Rogues   Joe Loss and his Band

09978
No. 9: (11)
Four Aces   3 Australian Boys
Harriette Hutchinson
                    Joe Loss and his Band

REVUE

09979
CABARET NIGHTS (series) (U)
Highbury (MGM)

09980
No. 1: (10)
Haver & Lee   Oliver & Wicks
Natasha & Lorenz

09981
No. 2: (10)
Haver & Lee   3 Australian Boys
Carmelita & Malaquita El Cubanos Orchestra

09982
No. 3: (10)
Haver & Lee   Al Boxy
Nora Colton   Berndardi & Bernice

09983
No. 4: (10)
Haver & Lee   Milton Rhodes
Weston & Vine   Rosina Dixon

09984
No. 5: (10)
Haver & Lee — El Cubanos Orchestra
Mai Bacon — Bernard Bedford

09985
No. 6: (10)
Haver & Lee — 3 Australian Boys
Rita Bernard — El Cubanos Orchestra

09986
No. 7: (10)
Haver & Lee — Frank Cram
Rita Bernard — Norah Colton
REVUE

09987
HERE AND THERE (14) (U)
Baxter & Barter (U)
P: John Barter
D: John Baxter
Eve Lister — Albert Sandler
Gresham Singers — Two Leslies
REVUE

09988
THE MOTHER (10) (U)
Joe Rock (ABFD)
S: (PICTURE) James Whistler
(THE ARTIST'S MOTHER)
John Garrick .... The Artist
MUSICAL Song scene: ballads sung to a
baby and a mother.

09989
THE BEAUTY DOCTOR (16) (U) *spectra*
Beaumont (Viking)
D: L.C.Beaumont
Bruce Seton .... The Man
Joy Worth .... The Girl
Bobbie Whitehall ....
Jim Stadden ....
MUSICAL Moribund beauty parlour
pepped up by song and dance.

09990
COCKTAIL (27) (U) *spectra*
Beaumont (Colmore)
D: L.C.Beaumont
Bruce Seton .... The Man
Joy Worth .... The Girl
MUSICAL

09991
TALKING HANDS (20) (A) *harmoni*
Harmonicolor Films *reissue:* 1937,
HANDS IN HARMONY (Lib)
D: Ivar Campbell
S: Herbert Ayres
SC: Ronald Frankau
Ronald Frankau .... The Man
Ruby Miller .... The Woman
COMEDY Business man weds typist and is
vamped by manicurist.

09992
SIGN PLEASE (15) (U)
Burt Hyman Hyams (Col)
Vic Wise Vic
Stan Paskin .... Stan
Sydney Monckton .... Shopwalker
COMEDY Slapstick mishaps of two shop
assistants and their supervisor.

09993
HARD LABOUR (15) (U)
Burt Hyman Hyams (Col)
Vic Wise Vic
Stan Paskin .... Stan
Sydney Monckton .... Warder
COMEDY Slapstick mishaps of two convicts
and crooked warder.

APR

09994
ELIZA COMES TO STAY (69) (A)
Twickenham (TFD)
P: Julius Hagen
D: Henry Edwards
S: (PLAY) H.V.Esmond
SC: H. Fowler Mear
Betty Balfour .... Eliza Vandan
Seymour Hicks .... Sandy Verrall
Oscar Asche .... Herbert
Ellis Jeffreys .... Lady Elizabeth
Nelson Keys .... Sir Gregory
A.R.Whatmore .... Monty Jordan
Vera Bogetti .... Vera Laurence
Ben Webster
COMEDY Dowdy girl falls in love with
ageing bachelor guardian.

09995
IN THE SOUP (72) (U)
Twickenham (TFD)
P: Julius Hagen
D: Henry Edwards
S: (PLAY) Ralph Lumley
SC: H. Fowler Mear
Ralph Lynn .... Horace
Judy Gunn .... Kitty
Morton Selten. . Abernathy Ruppershaw
Nelson Keys .... Emile Moppert
Bertha Belmore .... Mme Moppert
Michael Shepley .... Paul Hemming
Olive Melville .... Delphine Moppert
Morris Harvey .... Bates
Margaret Yarde .... Mrs Bates
Felix Aylmer .... Counsel
Mervyn Johns .... Meakin
Olive Sloane .... Defendant
COMEDY Solicitor and wife pose as butler
and maid to fool his rich uncle.

09996
POT LUCK (71) (A)
Gainsborough (Gaumont)
P: Michael Balcon
D: Tom Walls
S: Ben Travers
Tom Walls .... Insp Pat Fitzpatrick
Ralph Lynn .... Reggie Bathbrick
Robertson Hare .... Mr Pye
Diana Churchill .... Jane Bathbrick
Gordon James .... Cream
Martita Hunt .... Mrs Cream
J.A.O'Rorke .... Kelly
Sara Allgood .... Mrs Kelly
J.H.Roberts .... Bevis
H.G.Stoker .... Davey
Sam Wilkinson .... Lever
Peter Gawthorne ...... Chief Constable
COMEDY Ex-inspector recovers Chinese
vase from gang hiding in old abbey.

09997
SERVANTS ALL (34) (U)
Fox British
D: Alex Bryce
S: Tod Waller
Robb Wilton .... Watkins
Eve Lister .... Priscilla
Ian Colin .... Gale
Viola Compton .... Lady Agatha Grant
Arthur Young .... Sir Phineas Grant
Edie Martin .... Mrs Watkins
Cyril Chosack .... Billy
Francesca Bahrle .... Gloria
Alan d'Egville .... Mr Horton-Pratt
COMEDY Penniless aristrocrats change
places with servants.

09998
THE AVENGING HAND (64) (A)
Stafford (Radio) *reissue:* 1951 (Sun)
P: John Stafford
D: Victor Hanbury
S: Akos Tolnay, Reginald Long
Noah Beery .... Lee Barwell
Kathleen Kelly .... Gwen Taylor
Louis Borell .... Pierre Charrell
James Harcourt .... Sam Hupp
Charles Oliver .... Toni Visetti
Reginald Long .... Charles Mason
Ben Welden .... Slug Clarke
Tarver Penna .... Conrad Colter
Penelope Parkes .... Elizabeth
Billie de la Volta .... Muriel
Bela Mila .... Mrs Penworthy
CRIME Hotel guests are crooks searching
for hidden money.

09999
LOVE AT SEA (70) (A)
B & D-Paramount British
P: Anthony Havelock-Allan
D: Adrian Brunel
S: Jane Browne
SC: Beaufoy Milton
Rosalyn Boulter .... Betty Foster
Carl Harbord .... Dick Holmes
Aubrey Mallalieu .... John Brighton
Frank Birch .... Mr Godwin
Dorothy Dewhurst ... Mrs Hackworth Pratt
Maud Gill .... Emily Foster
Beatrix Fielden-Kaye .... Katherine Foster
Billy Bray .... Slippery Joe
George Merritt .... Insp
COMEDY Girl on cruise loves reporter
accused of robbing her elderly suitor.

10000
MELODY OF MY HEART (82) (A)
Incorporated Talking Films (Butcher)
P: Brandon Fleming, George Barclay
D: Wilfred Noy
S: Brandon Fleming
Derek Oldham .... Joe Montfort
Lorraine La Fosse .... Carmel
Bruce Seton .... Jim Brent
Hughes Macklin .... Mr Smith
Dorothy Vernon .... Mrs Dearwell
Macarthur Gordon ...... Manager
Colin Cunningham..... Ramenado/Jose
Joe Velitch .... Pastias
Joyce StClair .... Mercedes
Clelia Matania; Adriana Otero; Covent
Garden Chorus
MUSICAL Man tries to kill rival during
amateur production of "Carmen."

10001
BLOW BUGLES BLOW (74)
Progressive Film Institute
D: Rudolph Messel
George Hicks
DRAMA Unions call for general strike and avert
prime minister's war on France.
(Refused certificate by BBFC.)

10002
THEY DIDN'T KNOW (67) (A)
British Lion (MGM)
P: D: Herbert Smith
S: Brock Williams
Eve Gray .... Cutie
Leslie Perrins .... Duval
Kenneth Villiers .... Basil Conway
Hope Davy .... Ursula
John Deverell .... Lord Budmarsh
Diana Beaumont .... Pamela Budmarsh
C. Denier Warren .... Padre
Patrick Ludlow .... Charles Rockway

22

Maidie Hope . . . . Lady Charfield
COMEDY Couple blackmailed on wedding eve
by ex-lovers.

MAY

10003
WHERE'S SALLY ? (71) (A)
WB—FN (FN)
P: Irving Asher
D: Arthur Woods
S: Brock Williams, Frank Launder
Gene Gerrard . . . . Jimmy Findlay
Claude Hulbert . . . . Tony Chivers
Reginald Purdell . . . . Dick Burgess
Renee Gadd . . . . Sally
Chili Bouchier . . . . Sonia
Violet Farebrother . . . . Mrs Hickory
Athole Stewart . . . . Lord Mullion
Morland Graham . . . . Polkinhorne
COMEDY Honeymoon wife learns of husband's
past and runs away.

10004
TWO ON A DOORSTEP (71) (U)
B&D Paramount British
P: Anthony Havelock-Allan
D: Lawrence Huntington
S: Donovan Pedelty
SC: Gerald Elliott, George Barraud
Kay Hammond . . . . Jill Day
Harold French . . . . Jimmy Blair
Anthony Hankey . . . . Peter Day
George Mozart. . . . . George
Dorothy Dewhurst . . . . Mrs Beamish
Frank Tickle . . . . Mr Beamish
Walter Tobias . . . . Diggle
COMEDY Bailiff becomes bookie to help girl's
gambling brother.

10005
WEDNESDAY'S LUCK (68) (A)
B&D Paramount British
P: Anthony Havelock-Allan
D: George Pearson
S: Edythe Pryce
SC: Ralph Neale
Wilson Coleman . . . . Stevens
Susan Bligh . . . . Sheila
Patrick Barr . . . . Jim Carfax
Moore Marriott . . . . Nobby
Paul Neville . . . . Waddington
Linden Travers . . . . Mimi
George Dewhurst . . . . Wood
CRIME Detective poses as ex-convict to unmask
head of benevolent society as receiver.

10006
TUDOR ROSE (78) (U)
USA: NINE DAYS A QUEEN
Gainsborough (Gau) reissue: 1948 (ABFD)
P: Michael Balcon
D: Robert Stevenson
S: Robert Stevenson, Miles Malleson
Cedric Hardwick . . . . .Earl of Warwick
Nova Pilbeam . . . . Lady Jane Grey
John Mills . . . . Lord Guildford
Felix Aylmer . . . . Edward Seymour
Leslie Perrins . . . . Thomas Seymour
Frank Cellier . . . . Henry VIII
Desmond Tester . . . . Edward VI
Gwen Ffrancon Davies . . . . Mary Tudor
Sybil Thorndike . . . . Ellen
Martita Hunt . . . . Mother
Miles Malleson . . . . Father
John Laurie . . . . John Knox
Roy Emerton . . . . Executioner
HISTORY 1553. Young queen is executed for
treason after reign of 9 days. (PGAA: 1937)

10007
IT'S LOVE AGAIN (83) (U)
Gaumont
P: Michael Balcon
D: Victor Saville
S: Marian Dix
SC: Lesser Samuels, Marian Dix, Austin Melford
Jessie Matthews . . . . Elaine Bradford
Robert Young . . . . Peter Carlton
Sonnie Hale . . . . Freddie
Ernest Milton . . . . Raymond
Robb Wilton . . . . Boys
Sara Allgood . . . . Mrs Hopkins
Warren Jenkins . . . . Geoffrey
Athene Seyler . . . . Mrs Durand
Glennis Lorimer . . . . Typist
Cyril Raymond . . . . Montague
MUSICAL Chorus girl poses as socialite invented
by gossip writer.

10008
THE SECRET AGENT (85) (A)
Gaumont
P: Ivor Montagu
D: Alfred Hitchcock
S: (PLAY) Campbell Dixon (STORIES)
Somerset Maugham (TRITON; THE HAIRLESS
MEXICAN)
SC: Charles Bennett, Ian Hay, Jesse Lasky jr,
Alma Reville
Madeleine Carroll . . . . Elsa
Peter Lorre . . . . The General
Robert Young . . . . Marvin
John Gielgud . . . . Edgar Brodie
Percy Marmont . . . . Mr Caypor
Florence Kahn . . . . Mrs Caypor
Charles Carson . . . . R
Lilli Palmer Lilli
Michel Saint-Denis . . . . Coachman
Andrea Malandrinos . . . . . . Manager
Tom Helmore . . . . Capt Anderson
CRIME Geneva , 1916. Author and girl agent
pose as man and wife to find and kill spy.

10009
LABURNUM GROVE (73) (A)
ATP (ABFD) reissue: 1943
P: Basil Dean
D: Carol Reed
S: (PLAY) J.B. Priestley
SC: Gordon Wellesley, Anthony Kimmins
Edmund Gwen . . . . Mr Radfern
Cedric Hardwicke . . . . Mr Baxley
Victoria Hopper . . . . Elsie Radfern
Ethel Coleridge . . . . Mrs Baxley
Katie Johnson . . . . Mrs Radfern
Francis James . . . . Harold Russ
James Harcourt . . . . Joe Fletten
David Hawthorne . . . . Insp Stack
Frederick Burtwell . . . . Simpson
COMEDY Suburban father reveals he is forger
to get rid of sponging brother-in-law.

10010
TWO'S COMPANY (74) (U)
B&D—Soskin (UA) reissue: 1943 (EB)
P: Paul Soskin
D: Tim Whelan
S: (NOVEL) Sidney Horler (ROMEO AND
JULIA)
SC: Tom Geraghty, Roland Pertwee, J.B.
Morton, John Paddy Carstairs, Tim Whelan
Ned Sparks . . . . Al
Gordon Harker . . . . Muggridge
Mary Brian . . . . Julia Madison
Patric Knowles . . . . .Lord Jerry Wendover
Harry Holman . . . . B.G. Madison
Olive Blakeney . . . . Mrs Madison
Morton Selten . . . . Earl of Warke

Robb Wilton . . . . .Mr Muddlecombe JP
Gibb McLaughlin . . . . Toombes
H.F. Maltby . . . . Otto Stump
Syd Crossley . . . . Ives
COMEDY Prejudiced Earl's son loves daughter
of neighbouring American millionaire.

10011
THE CRIMES OF STEPHEN HAWKE (69) (A)
George King (MGM) reissue: 1940 (Amb)
D: George King
S: Jack Celestin
SC: H.F. Maltby
Tod Slaughter . . . . Stephen Hawke
Marjorie Taylor . . . . Julia Hawke
Eric Portman . . . . Matthew Trimble
Gerald Barry . . . . Miles Archer
Ben Soutten . . . . Nathaniel
D.J. Williams . . . . Joshua Trimble
Charles Penrose . . . . Sir Franklyn
Norman Pierce . . . . Landlord
Mr Flotsam & Mr Jetsam
CRIME Regency usurer is also mysterious spine-
breaker.

10012
LOVE IN EXILE (78) (A)
Capitol (GFD) reissue: 1942 (Pi)
P: Max Schach
D: Alfred L. Werker
S: (NOVEL) Gene Markey (HIS MAJESTY'S
PYJAMAS)
SC: Herman Mankiewicz, Roger Burford, Ernest
Betts
Clive Brook . . . . King Regis VI
Helen Vinson . . . . Countess Zandra
Mary Carlisle . . . . Emily Stewart
Will Fyffe . . . . Doc Tate
Ronald Squire . . . . Paul
Tamara Desni . . . . Tanya
Henry Oscar . . . . Dictator
Edmond Breon . . . . Zarroy
Cecil Ramage . . . . Weston
Barbara Everest . . . . Anna
COMEDY Ruritania. Abdicated king thwarts oil
magnate and regains throne.

10013
SOMEONE AT THE DOOR (74) (A)
BIP (Wardour)
P: Walter C. Mycroft
D; Herbert Brenon
S: (PLAY) Dorothy & Campbell Christie
SC: Jack Davies, Marjorie Deans
Billy Milton . . . . Ronald Martin
Aileen Marson . . . . Sally Martin
Noah Beery . . . . Harry Kapel
Edward Chapman . . . . Price
John Irwin . . . . Bill Reid
Hermione Gingold . . . . Mrs Appleby
Charles Mortimer . . . . Sgt Spedding
Edward Dignon . . . . Soames
Lawrence Hanray . . . . Poole
Jimmy Godden . . . . PC O'Brien
COMEDY Reporter inherits house and fakes
murder that comes true.

10014
OURSELVES ALONE (68) (A)
USA: RIVER OF UNREST
BIP (Wardour)
P: Walter C. Mycroft
D: Walter Summers, Brian Desmond Hurst
S: (PLAY) Dudley Sturrock, Noel Scott
(THE TROUBLE)
SC: Dudley Leslie, Marjorie Deans, Dennis
Johnstone, Philip Macdonald
John Lodge . . . . Insp Hannay
John Loder . . . . Capt Wiltshire

Antonette Cellier . . . . Maureen Elliott
Niall McGinnis . . . . Terence Elliott
Clifford Evans . . . . Commandant Connolly
Jerry Verno . . . . Pte Parsley
Bruce Lister . . . . Lt Lingard
Maire O'Neill . . . . Nanny
Pat Noonan . . . . Sgt Halloran
Fred O' Donovan . . . . Publican
Cavan O'Connor . . . . Singer
CRIME Ireland, 1921. Two policemen love
sister of IRA fugitive.

10015
UNLUCKY JIM (44) (U)
Master (Radio)
P: Harry Marks, Fay Davis
D: Harry Marks
S: "A Schoolboy"
Bob Stevens . . . . Father
Agnes Lenton . . . . Mother
Tony Jones . . . . Jimmy
Alma Aston . . . . Sister
George Beck . . . . Sweetheart
Chris Hawkes . . . . Pal
COMEDY Adventures of two boys on half
day's holiday.

10016
NOT SO DUSTY (69) (U)
GS Enterprises—Bow Bell (Radio)
P: George Smith
D: Maclean Rogers
S: Wally Patch, Frank Atkinson
SC: Kathleen Butler, H.F. Maltby
Wally Patch . . . . Dusty Grey
Gus McNaughton . . . . Nobby Clark
Muriel George . . . . Mrs Clark
Phil Ray . . . . Dan Stevens
Johnny Singer . . . . Johnny Clark
Isobel Scaife . . . . Mary
Ethel Griffies . . . . Miss Miller
H.F. Maltby . . . . Mr Armstrong
Raymond Lovell . . . . Mr Holding
COMEDY Crooks seek rare book given to two
dustmen.

10017
IF I WERE RICH (58) (U)
Randall Faye (Radio)
P: D: Randall Faye
S: (PLAY) Horace Annesley Vachell
(HUMPTY—DUMPTY)
SC: Brandon Fleming
Jack Melford . . . . Albert Mott
Kay Walsh . . . . .Chrissie de la Mothe
Clifford Heatherley . . . . . Gen de la Mothe
Minnie Rayner . . . . Mrs Mott
Henry Carlisle . . . . Puttick
Frederick Bradshaw . . . . . Jack de la Mothe
Ruth Haven . . . . Nancy
Quinton McPherson . . . . . Higginbotham
COMEDY Socialist barber is "converted" after
inheriting earldom.

10018
SHIPMATES O' MINE (87) (U)
T.A. Welsh Productions (Butcher)
D: Oswald Mitchell
S: Ivor Bellas .
SC: Oswald Mitchell, George Pearson
John Garrick . . . . Jack Denton
Jean Adrienne . . . . Lorna Denton
Wallace Lupino . . . . Bill Webb
Mark Daly . . . . Andrew McFee
Frank Atkinson . . . . Oliver Bright
Cynthia Stock . . . . Angela Bright
Richard Hayward . . . . Mike Dooley
Derek Blomfield . . . . Tony Denton
John Turnbull . . . . Capt Roberts
Polly Ward; Navarre; Jack Hodges; Sherman.

Fisher Girls; Radio Male Voice Chior; Horace
Sheldon and his Orchestra.
MUSICAL Sacked war hero regains command
of old ship. (Extracts in HIGHLIGHTS OF
VARIETY No. 22(1940).)

10019
MEN OF YESTERDAY (82) (U)
UK Films (AP&D)
P: John Barter
D: John Baxter
S: Gerald Elliott, Jack Francis
Stewart Rome . . . . Maj Radford
Sam Livesey . . . .
Hay Petrie . . . .
Eve Lister . . . .
Cecil Parker . . . .
Roddy Hughes . . . . .
Ian Colin . . . .
George Robey; Will Fyffe; Ella Shields; Dick
Henderson.
MUSICAL Retired major and ex-enemies pledge
peace at reunion. (Extracts released as short,
CAMP CONCERT (New Realm). 1/1941.)

10020
BROKEN BLOSSOMS (78) (A)
Twickenham (TFD)
P: Julius Hagen
D: Hans Brahm
S: (STORY) Thomas Burke (THE CHINK AND
THE CHILD) (SCREENPLAY) D.W. Griffith
SC: Emlyn Williams
Dolly Haas . . . . Lucy Burrows
Emlyn Williams . . . . Chen
Arthur Margetson . . . . . . Battling Burrows
Gibb McLaughlin . . . . Evil Eye
Donald Calthrop . . . . Old Chinaman
Ernest Sefton . . . . Manager
Jerry Verno . . . . Bert
Bertha Belmore . . . . Daisy
Ernest Jay . . . . Alf
C.V.France . . . . High Priest
Kathleen Harrison . . . . . . Mrs Lossy
Basil Radford . . . . Mr Reed
DRAMA Limehouse. Brutal boxer kills
daughter when Chinaman gives her shelter.

JUN

10021
ONE GOOD TURN (72) (U)
Leslie Fuller (ABFD)
P: Joe Rock
D: Alfred Goulding
S: Con West, Herbert Sargent
SC: Syd Courtenay, Georgie Harris, Jack Byrd
Leslie Fuller . . . . Bill Parsons
Georgie Harris . . . . Georgie
Hal Gordon . . . . Bert
Molly Fisher . . . . Dolly Pearson
Basil Langton . . . . Jack Pearson
Clarissa Selwyn . . . . Ma Pearson
Arthur Finn . . . . Townsend
Faith Bennett . . . . Violet
COMEDY Coffee stall keepers save girl from
bogus film producer.

10022
EVERYTHING IS RHYTHM (73) (U)
Joe Rock (ABFD)
D: Alfred Goulding
S: Tom Geraghty
SC: Syd Courtenay, Jack Byrd, Stanley Haynes
Harry Roy , ... Harry Wade
Princess Pearl . . . . Princess Paula
Ivor Moreton . . . . Joe
Dave Kaye . . . . Sam
Dorothy Boyd . . . . Grethe
Clarissa Selwyn . . . . Miss Mimms
Robert English . . . . The Duke

Gerald Barry . . . . Count Rudolph
Phyllis Thackery . . . . Lucy
Johnnie Nit; Bill Currie; Mabel Mercer;
Harry Roy's Band;
MUSICAL Ruritanian princess defies her court
and elopes with dance band leader.

10023
ROYAL EAGLE (69) (A)
Quality (Col)
P: Clive Loehnis
D: George A. Cooper, Arnold Ridley
S: Arnold Ridley
John Garrick . . . . Jim Hornby
Nancy Burne . . . . Sally Marshall
Edmund Willard . . . . Burnock
Lawrence Anderson . . . . . Vale
Hugh E. Wright . . . . Albert Marshall
Muriel Aked . . . . Miss Mimm
Fred Groves . . . . Sam Waldock
Felix Aylmer . . . . Windridge
Betty Shale . . . . Mrs Marshall
CRIME Clerk suspected of warehouse robbery
catches thieves aboard pleasure boat.

10024
THE MARRIAGE OF CORBAL (93) (U)
USA: PRISONER OF CORBAL
Capitol (GFD) reissue: 1942 (Pi; cut)
P: Max Schach
D: Karl Grune
S: (NOVEL) Rafael Sabatini (THE NUPTIALS
OF CORBAL)
SC: S. Fullman
Nils Asther . . . . Varennes
Hugh Sinclair . . . . Marquis of Corbal
Hazel Terry . . . . Cleonie
Noah Beery . . . . Sergeant
Ernest Deutsch . . . . Fugitive
Davy Burnaby . . . . Pierre
Clifford McLaglen . . . . . . Jean
Ralph Truman . . . . Charles
Brian Buchel . . . . Roger
Walter Sondes . . . . Chaplain
Arthur Rigby jr . . . . Major
Moira Lynd . . . . Hostess
ADVENTURE France, 1790.Deputy loves
aristocrat and makes her marry Marquis to
escape revolution.

10025
THE INTERRUPTED HONEYMOON (72) (A)
British Lion
P: Herbert Smith
D: Leslie Hiscott
S: (PLAY) Ernst Bach, Franz Arnold
SC: Michael Barringer, Wyndham Brown,
Neil Tyfield
Claude Hulbert . . . . Victor
Francis L. Sullivan . . . . Alphonse
Hugh Wakefield . . . . Uncle John
Jane Carr . . . . Greta
Glennis Lorimer . . . . Edith Hobson
Robb Wilton . . . . Henry Briggs
Jack Hobbs . . . . George
David Horne . . . . Col Craddock
Martita Hunt . . . . Nora Briggs
Wally Patch . . . . PC
Helen Haye . . . . Aunt Harriet
Hal Walters . . . . Valet
COMEDY Quarreling newlyweds return from
Paris to find flat occupied friends.

10026
SHE KNEW WHAT SHE WANTED (74) (U)
Rialto (Wardour)
P: D: Thomas Bentley
S: (PLAY) Paul Gerard Smith, Fred Thompson
(FUNNY FACE)

SC: Tom Geraghty, Frank Miller
Albert Burdon . . . . Dugsie
Betty Ann Davies . . . . Frankie
Claude Dampier . . . . Jimmy Reeves
W.H. Berry . . . . Herbert
Fred Conyngham . . . . Peter Thurston
Ben Welden . . . . Chester
Googie Withers . . . . Dora
Hope Davy . . . . June
Sybil Grove . . . . Mme Piccard
Albert le Fre . . . . Butler
MUSICAL Band leader steals girl's diary of lies
from her guardian and catches jewel thieves.

10027
A STAR FELL FROM HEAVEN (70) (U)
BIP (Wardour)
P: Walter C. Mycroft
D: Paul Merzbach
S: Marjorie Deans, Dudley Leslie, Jack Davies,
Gerald Elloitt, Val Guest, Geoffrey Kerr
Joseph Schmidt . . . . Josef
Florine McKinney . . . . Anne Heinmeyer
Billy Milton . . . . Douglas Lincoln
W.H. Berry . . . . Tomson
George Graves . . . . Fischer
Steven Geray . . . . Willi Wass
Judy Kelly . . . . Flora
C. Denier Warren . . . . Starfel
Iris Hoey . . . . Frau Heinmeyer
Bruce Lister . . . . Winkler
Eliot Makeham . . . . Professor
MUSICAL Austria. Singing student loses
actress to film star whose voice he dubs.

10028
PLAYBOX ADVENTURE (68) (U)
B&D Paramount British
P: Anthony Havelock-Allan
D: W.P. Kellino
S: Gerald Elliott
Syd Crossley . . . . Tom Furlong
Marjorie Corbett . . . . Mary Blake
Roxie Russell . . . . Enid Soames
Billy Watts . . . . Jimmy Trevor
Eric Fawcett . . . . Sidney Parke
Molly Hamley Clifford . . . . Mrs Bartlett
George Turner . . . . Gus
CRIME Lawyer schemes to destroy cinema
where cashier is an heiress.

10029
HOUSE BROKEN (74) (A)
B&D Paramount British
P: Anthony Havelock-Allan
D: Michael Hankinson
S: Paul Hervey Fox
SC: Vera Allinson
Mary Lawson . . . . Angela Macgregor
Enid Stamp Taylor . . . . Peggy Allen
Louis Borell . . . . Charles Delmont
Jack Lambert . . . . Jock Macgregor
COMEDY Newlywed tries to make husband
jealous by eloping with French friend.

10030
HIGHLAND FLING (68) (U)
Fox British
P: John Findlay
D: Manning Haynes
S: Alan d'Egville
SC: Alan d'Egville, Ralph Stock
Charlie Naughton . . . . Smith
Jimmy Gold . . . . Smythe
Eve Foster . . . . Jean
Frederick Bradshaw . . . . . . Tony
Gibson Gowland . . . . Delphos
Naomi Plaskett . . . . Katherine
Billy Shine . . . . Lizards
Peter Popp . . . . Clockmender
COMEDY Detectives seek lost will during
Highland Games.

10031
THE ROBBER SYMPHONY (136) (U) *bilingual*
Concordia
P: Robert Weine
D: S: Friedrich Feher
SC: Friedrich Feher, Anton Kun, Jack Trendall
Hans Feher . . . . Giannino
Magda Sonja . . . . Mother
Michael Martin Harvey . . . . Straw Hat
Webster Booth . . . . Singer
George Graves . . . . Grandfather
Oscar Asche . . . . Police Chief
Alexandre Rignault . . . . Black Devil
Vinette
Ivor Wilmot
MUSICAL Tyrol. Robber gang seek money
hidden in boy's street-piano.

10032
TO CATCH A THIEF (66) (U)
GS Enterprises (Radio)
P: A. George Smith
D: Maclean Rogers
S: (PLAY) Margaret & Gordon MacDonnell
SC: Kathleen Butler, H.F. Maltby
John Garrick . . . . John
Mary Lawson . . . . Anne
H.F. Maltby . . . . Sir Herbert Condine
John Wood . . . . Bill Lowther
Vincent Holman . . . . Galloway
Eliot Makeham . . . . Secretary
Max Adrian . . . . Salesman
Gordon McLeod . . . . Detective
COMEDY Man invents device to foil car
thieves and catches smash-and-grab bandits.

10033
WHERE THERE'S A WILL (80) (A)
Gainsborough (Gaumont)
P: Michael Balcon
D: William Beaudine
S: Leslie Arliss, Sidney Gilliat
SC: Will Hay, Ralph Spence, Robert Edmunds,
William Beaudine
Will Hay . . . . Benjamin Stubbins
Gina Malo . . . . Goldie Kelly
Hartley Power . . . . Duke Wilson
Graham Moffatt . . . . Willie
H.F. Maltby . . . . Sir Roger Wimpleton
Norma Varden . . . . .Lady Margaret Wimpleton
Peggy Simpson . . . . Barbara Stubbins
Gibb McLaughlin . . . . Martin
Hal Walters . . . . Nick
John Turnbull . . . . Sgt Collins
Mickey Brantford . . . . Jimmy
Davina Craig . . . . Lucy
COMEDY Shyster lawyer duped by crooks who
cut through his office into bank vault.

JUL

10034
SEVEN SINNERS (70) (A)
USA: DOOMED CARGO
Gaumont *reissue:* 1947 (IFR)
P: Michael Balcon
D: Albert de Courville
S: (PLAY) Arnold Ridley, Bernard Merivale
(THE WRECKER)
SC: Frank Launder, Sidney Gilliat, L.DuGarde
Peach, Austin Melford
Edmund Lowe . . . . John Harwood
Constance Cummings . . . . . Caryl Fenton
Thomy Bourdelle . . . . Paul Turbe
Henry Oscar . . . . Axel Hoyt
Felix Aylmer . . . . Sir Charles Webber
Joyce Kennedy . . . . Elizabeth Wentworth
Allan Jeayes . . . . Karl Wagner
O.B. Clarence . . . . Registrar
Mark Lester . . . . Chief Constable
Antony Holles . . . . Receptionist

David Horne . . . . Manager
CRIME France. American detectives expose
gunrunners who wreck train to hide murder.

10035
FAIR EXCHANGE (63) (U)
WB—FN (WB)
P: Irving Asher
D: Ralph Ince
S: Brock Williams, Russell Medcraft
Patric Knowles . . . . Tony Meredith
Roscoe Ates . . . . Elmer Goodge
Isla Bevan . . . . Elsie Randall
Raymond Lovell . . . . . Sir Reeves Willoughby
Cecil Humphreys . . . . Matthew Randall
Louis Goodrich . . . . James Meredith
Morland Graham . . . . Dr Franz Schmidt
COMEDY Criminologist stages picture theft to
thwart son's detective ambitions.

10036
DODGING THE DOLE (95) (U)
Mancunian
P: D: John E. Blakeley
S: Arthur Mertz
Roy Barbour . . . . . . .The Simplicity of Genius
Dan Young . . . . .The Charming Fool
Jenny Howard . . . The Generator of Electric
                            Radiance.
Barry K. Barnes . . . . The Dole Dodger
Fred Walmsley . . . . . The Lancashire Favourite
Tot Sloan . . . . . . The Little Bundle of Fun
Bertha Ricardo . . . . .Dainty and Demure
Hatton & Manners; Barry Twins; Two Jays;
Steffani's Silver Songsters; Archie's Juvenile
Band; Bertini and the Tower Blackpool Band.
MUSICAL Workshies thwart supervisor's
attempts to find them jobs. (Extracts in
MUSIC HALL PERSONALITIES Nos 1; 3
(1938).

10037
THE THREE MAXIMS (87) (U)
USA: THE SHOW GOES ON
Cie Pathe Consortium (GFD)
D: Herbert Wilcox
S: Nicolas Farkas
SC: Herman Mankiewicz
Anna Neagle. . . . . Pat
Tullio Carminati . . . . Toni
Leslie Banks . . . . Mac
Horace Hodges . . . . Mike
Arthur Finn . . . . Hiram K. Winston
Olive Blakeney . . . . Mrs Winston
Anthony Ireland . . . . Val
Miki Hood . . . . Valentine
Nicolas Koline . . . . Niki
12 Hippodrome Girls; Gaston Palmer; Leonard
Snelling.
Leonard Snelling
ROMANCE Paris. Trapeze star tries to kill girl
who prefers his partner.

10038
APRON FOOLS (34) (U)
Marks Picture Corp (Radio)
P: Harry S. Marks
D: Widgey R. Newman
S: John Quin
Wally Patch
Hal Walters
Frederick Bradshaw
Anne Bolt
Kate Saxon
Elsie Wagstaffe
Ben Williams
COMEDY Knighted profiteer's son mistakes
squire's actress daughter for servant.

10039
ANNIE LAURIE (82) (U)
Mondover (Butcher) *reissue:* 1943

(Kinograph; 2369 ft cut)
P: Walter Tennyson, Wilfred Noy
D: Walter Tennyson
S: Frank Miller

Will Fyffe	Will Laurie
Polly Ward	Annie Laurie
Bruce Seton	Jamie Turner
Vivienne Chatterton	Maggie Laurie
Romilly Lunge	John Anderson
Percy Walsh	Alec Laurie
Frederick Culley	Robert Anderson
Evelyn Barnard	Elspeth McAlpine
Quinton McPherson	Small

Rodney Hudson Girls; Doris and her Zebra;
Horace Sheldon's Orchestra.
MUSICAL Sacked bargee's adopted daughter
finds fame as dancer. (Extract in HIGHLIGHTS
OF VARIETY No. 18 (1938).)

10040
CALLING THE TUNE (71) (U)
Phoenix—IFP (ABFD)
P: Hugh Perceval
D: Reginald Denham
S: Basil Mason

Adele Dixon	Julia Harbord
Clifford Evans	Peter Mallory
Sam Livesey	Bob Gordon
Sally Gray	Margaret Gordon
Donald Wolfit	Dick Finlay
Eliot Makeham	Stephen Harbord
Lewis Casson	John Mallory
Ronald Simpson	Bramwell
H.F. Maltby	Stubbins

Cedric Hardwicke; George Robey; Charles
Penrose; Reginald Forsyth; Sir Henry Wood
and the Queen's Hall Light Orchestra; English
Quartette.
MUSICAL Record manufacturer's daughter
loves the son of the man he cheated.

10041
CAFE MASCOT (77) (U)
Pascal Films (Par)
P: Gabriel Pascal
D: Lawrence Huntington
S: Cecil Lewis
SC: Gerald Elliott

Geraldine Fitzgerald	Moira O'Flynn
Derrick de Marney	Jerry Wilson
George Mozart	George Juppley
Clifford Heatherley	Dudhope
Richard Norris	Nat Dawson
Paul Neville	Peters
Julien Vedey	Francois
George Turner	Miles
Geoffrey Clark	Benton

COMEDY Man finds £1000 in taxi and uses it
to help Irish girl.

10042
THE GAY ADVENTURE (74) (A)
Grosvenor (Pathe)
P: Harcourt Templeman
D: Sinclair Hill
S: (PLAY) Walter Hackett
SC: D.B. Wyndham-Lewis

Yvonne Arnaud	Julie
Barry Jones	Darnton
Nora Swinburne	Fay d'Allary
Finlay Currie	Porter
Robert Holmes	d'Allary
Guy Middleton	Aram
Percy Parsons	Pete
Keith Warrington	Mickey Blane
Antony Holles	Charles
Ralph Truman	Buck
Sybil Grove	Miss Darnton

COMEDY Swindlers persuade mild man that he
is d'Artagnan's descendant.

10043
THE MAN WHO COULD WORK MIRACLES
(82) (U)
London (UA) reissue: 1948 (EB)
P: Alexander Korda
D: Lothar Mendes
S: (STORY) H.G. Wells
SC: Lajos Biro

Roland Young	George Fotheringay
Ralph Richardson	Col Winstanley
Edward Chapman	Maj Grigsby
Ernest Thesiger	Mr Maydig
Joan Gardner	Ada Price
Sophie Stewart	Maggie Hooper
Robert Cochrane	Bill Stoker
Lawrence Hanray	Mr Bamfylde
George Zucco	Moody
Wallace Lupino	PC Winch
Lady Tree	Housekeeper
Joan Hickson	Effie Brickman
Wally Patch	Supt Smithells
Bernard Nedell	Reporter
Bruce Winston	Cox
George Sanders	Indifference

FANTASY Gods give humble shop-assistant
power to work miracles.

10044
BORN THAT WAY (640 (U)
Randall Faye (Radio)
D: Randall Faye
S: V.C. Clinton-Baddeley, Diana Bourbon

Elliott Mason	Aunt Emily
Kathleen Gibson	Pamela Gearing
Terence de Marney	Richard Gearing
Eliot Makeham	Prof Gearing
Ian Colin	Hugh
Conway Palmer	Kenneth Danvers
John Laurie	McTavish

COMEDY Scottish spinster supervises children
of her absent-minded brother-in-law.

10045
A WOMAN ALONE (78) (A)
USA: TWO WHO DARED
Garrett—Klement Pictures (UA)
reissues: 1942 (Amb) 1947 (ABFD)
P: Robert Garrett, Otto Klement
D: Eugene Frenke
S: Fedor Otzep
SC: Leo Lania, Warren Chetham Strode

Anna Sten	Maria
Henry Wilcoxon	Nicolai Ilyinski
Viola Keats	Olga Karoff
John Garrick	Yakov Sharialev
Romilly Lunge	Lt Tuzenbach
Esme Percy	General
Francis L. Sullivan	Prosecutor
Guy Middleton	Alioshka
Peter Gawthorne	President
Minnie Rayner	Lousha
Frank Atkinson	Porter

Ballets de Leon Woizikovski
ROMANCE Russia, 1896. Married captain has
affair with peasant and frames her soldier fiance.

10046
THE AMAZING QUEST OF ERNEST BLISS
(80) (U) USA: ROMANCE AND RICHES
Garrett—Klement Pictures (UA)
reissues: 1942 (Amb) 1947 (ABFD)
P: Robert Garrett, Otto Klement
D: Alfred Zeisler
S: (NOVEL) E. Phillips Oppenheim
SC: John L. Balderston

Cary Grant	Ernest Bliss
Mary Brian	Frances
Henry Kendall	Lord Honiton
Leon M. Lion	Donnington

Garry Marsh	Buyer
John Turnbull	Masters
Iris Ashley	Clare
Arthur Hardy	Crawley
Frank Stanmore	Mr Mott
Beuna Bent	Mrs Mott
Marie Wright	Mrs Heath
Hal Gordon	Bill Bronson
Alf Goddard	Butcher Bill
Moore Marriott	Edwards

COMEDY Millionaire bets he can live for one
year on his own earnings.

10047
ACCUSED (85) (A)
Criterion (UA) reissue: 1944 (Anglo)
P: Marcel Hellman, Douglas Fairbanks jr
D: Thornton Freeland
S: Zoe Atkins
SC: Zoe Atkins, George Barraud, Harold French

Douglas Fairbanks jr	Tony Seymour
Dolores del Rio	Gaby Seymour
Florence Desmond	Yvette de Lange
Basil Sydney	Eugene Roget
Googie Withers	Ninette
Athole Stewart	President
J.H. Roberts	Defence
Cecil Humphreys	Prosecution
Esme Percy	Morel
Moore Marriott	Dubec
Edward Rigby	Alphonse
Cyril Raymond	Guy Henry
Roland Culver	Henry Capelle

CRIME Paris. Dancer's jealous wife accused of
stabbing partner.

AUG

10048
THE DAWN (89) (A)
USA: DAWN OVER IRELAND
Hibernia (IP)
P: D: Thomas G. Cooper
S: Thomas G. Cooper, Donal O'Cahill,
D.A. Moriarty

Tom Cooper	Dan O'Donovan
Eileen Davis	Eileen O'Donovan
Brian O'Sullivan	Brian Malone
Donal O'Cahill	Jerry Malone
Jerry O'Mahoney	OC
Bill Murphy	Sgt Geary
James Gleeson	John Malone
Marion O'Connell	Mrs Malone

CRIME 1866/1919. Man expelled from IRA
joins RIC.

10049
BED AND BREAKFAST (58) (A)
Walter West (Coronel)
D: Walter West
S: Frank Miller

Barry Lupino	Bert Fink
Mabel Poulton	The Maid
Frank Miller	Charles Blake
Daphne Courtney	Margaret Reynolds
Florence leRoy	Landlady

DRAMA Old actor solves problems of author,
composer, typist.

10050
EVERYTHING IS THUNDER (77) (A)
Gaumont
AP: S.C. Balcon
D: Milton Rosmer
S: (NOVEL) Jocelyn Hardy
SC: Marian Dix, J.O.C. Orton

Constance Bennett	Anna von Stucknadel
Oscar Homolka	Schenck Goertz
Douglass Montgomery	Hugh McGrath
Roy Emerton	Kostner

Frederick Lloyd . . . . Muller
George Merritt . . . . Webber
Peggy Simpson . . . . Mitzi
Robert Atkins . . . . Adjutant
H.F. Maltby . . . . Burgomaster
WAR Germany. Prostitute helps escaped
British lieut elude detective.

10051
GUILTY MELODY (75) (A) *bilingual*
Franco-London (ABFD)
P: F. Deutschmeister
D: Richard Potter
S: (NOVEL) Hans Rehfisch
SC: G.F. Salmony
Nils Asther . . . . Galloni
Gitta Alpar . . . . Marguerite Salvini
John Loder . . . . Richard Carter
Don Alcaide . . . . Duke of Mantua
Coral Brown . . . . Cecile
Ethel Griffies . . . . Lady Rochester
Arty Ash . . . . Insp Bartle
Robert English . . . . Chief Inspector
F.Rendell . . . . Rigoletto
MUSICAL Opera star's spy husband feigns death
and poses as impresario.

10052
THE EARLY BIRD (69) (U)
Crusade (Par)
P: Victor M. Greene
D: SC: Donovan Pedelty
S: (PLAY) J. McGregor Douglas
Richard Hayward . . . . Daniel Duff
Jimmy Mageean . . . . Charlie Simpson
Charlotte Tedlie . . . . Mrs Gordon
Myrtle Adams . . . . Lizzie
Nan Cullen . . . . Mrs Madill
Elma Hayward . . . . Susan Duff
Terence Grainger . . . . Archie Macready
Charles Fagan . . . . Harold Gordon
COMEDY Ireland. Villagers rebel against
puritannical woman.

10053
MURDER BY ROPE (64) (A)
B&D Paramount British *reissue:* 1948 (Amb)
P: Anthony Havelock-Allan
D: George Pearson
S: Ralph Neale
Constance Godridge . . . . Daphne Farrow
D.A. Clarke-Smith . . . . Hanson
Sunday Wilshin . . . . Lucille Davine
Wilfred Hyde White . . . . Alastair Dane
Donald Read . . . . Peter Paxton
Daphne Courtney . . . . Flora
Dorothy Hamilton . . . . Mrs Mulcaire
Guy Belmore . . . . Simpson
Philip Hewland . . . . Judge Paxton
CRIME Apparent return of hanged man to kill
judge and hangman.

10054
THE HAPPY FAMILY (67) (A)
British Lion
P: Herbert Smith
D: Maclean Rogers
S: (PLAY) Max Cotto (FRENCH SALAD)
SC: Maclean Rogers, Kathleen Butler
Hugh Williams . . . . Victor Hutt
Leonora Corbett . . . . Barbara Hutt
Eve Gray . . . . Nina Harrison
Maidie Hope . . . . Mrs Hutt
Ellen Pollock . . . . Leo Hutt
Glennis Lorimer . . . . Robina Hutt
Max Adrian . . . . Noel Hutt
D.A. Clarke-Smith . . . . Mr Harrison
Dick Francis . . . . Mr Hutt
Muriel George . . . . Housekeeper
COMEDY Father feigns bankruptcy to cure his
lazy family.

SEP

10055
THE LONELY ROAD (80) (A)
USA: SCOTLAND YARD COMMANDS
ATP (ABFD)
P: Basil Dean
D: James Flood
S: (NOVEL) Nevil Shute
SC: James Flood, Gerard Fairlie, Anthony
Kimmins
Clive Brook . . . . Malcolm Stevenson
Victoria Hopper . . . . Molly Gordon
Nora Swinburne . . . . Lady Anne
Malcolm Keen . . . . Professor
Cecil Ramage . . . . Maj Norman
Charles Farrell . . . . Palmer
Lawrence Hanray . . . . Jenkinson
Frederick Peisley . . . . Bill Gordon
Ethel Coleridge . . . . Mrs Rogers
Warburton Gamble . . . . Fedden
CRIME Court martialled commander tracks
down gunrunners.

10056
KEEP YOUR SEATS PLEASE (82) (U)
ATP (ABFD) *reissue:* 1939
P: Basil Dean
D: Monty Banks
S: (PLAY) Elie Ilf, Eugene Petrov
(TWELVE CHAIRS)
SC: Tom Geraghty, Ian Hay, Anthony Kimmins
George Formby . . . . George
Florence Desmond . . . . Flo
Gus McNaughton . . . . Max
Alastair Sim . . . . Drayton
Harry Tate . . . . Auctioneer
Fiona Stuart . . . . Bimkie
Hal Gordon . . . . Sailor
Fred Culpitt . . . . Magician
Margaret Moffatt . . . . Landlady
Maud Gill . . . . Spinster
Mike Johnson . . . . Landlord
COMEDY Heir and crooked lawyer seek gems
hidden in one of six chairs.

10057
EDUCATED EVANS (86) (U)
WB—FN (FN)
P: Irving Asher
D: William Beaudine
S: (NOVEL) Edgar Wallace
SC: Frank Launder, Robert Edmunds
Max Miller . . . . Evans
Nancy O'Neil . . . . Mary
Clarice Mayne . . . . Emily Hackitt
Albert Whelan . . . . Sgt Challoner
Hal Walters . . . . Nobby
George Merritt . . . . Joe Markham
Julien Mitchell . . . . Arthur Hackitt
Frederick Burtwell . . . . Hubert
Anthony Shaw . . . . Lord Appleby
Percy Walsh . . . . Capt Reid
Robert English . . . . Lord Brickett
COMEDY Racing tipster becomes trainer for
newly-rich stable owner.

10058
IT'S IN THE BAG (80) (U)
WB—FN (WB)
P: Irving Asher
D: William Beaudine
S: Russell Medcraft
SC: Brock Williams
Jimmy Nervo . . . . Jimmy
Teddy Knox . . . . Teddy
Jack Barty . . . . Bert
George Carney . . . . Blumfield
Rene Hunter . . . . Ethel
Ursula Hirst Vi
Aubrey Dexter . . . . Peters

Hal Gordon . . . . Boss
Ernest Sefton . . . . Jerry Gee
C. Denier Warren . . . . Emery
Glen Alyn . . . . Fifi
Gaston & Andree
Charles B. Cochran's Young Ladies
COMEDY Covent Garden porters find forged
money and finance night club.

10059
RHYTHM IN THE AIR (72) (U)
Fox British *reissue:* 1941 (Fed)
P: John Findlay
D: Arthur Woods
S: Jack Donohoe, Vina de Vesci
Jack Donohoe . . . . Jack Donovan
Tutta Rolf . . . . Mary
Vic Oliver . . . . Tremayne
Leslie Perrins . . . . Director
Kitty Kelly . . . . Celia
Tony Sympson . . . . Alf
MUSICAL Riveter breaks ankles and becomes
star tap dancer.

10060
SONG OF FREEDOM (80) (U)
Hammer (BL) *reissue:* 1946 (Ex)
P: H. Fraser Passmore
D: J. Elder Wills
S: Claude Wallace, Dorothy Holloway
SC: Fenn Sherie, Ingram d'Abbes, Michael
Barringer, Philip Lindsay
Paul Robeson . . . . John Zinga
Elisabeth Welch . . . . Ruth Zinga
George Mozart . . . . Bert Puddick
Esme Percy . . . . Donezetti
Joan Fred Emney . . . . Nell
Arthur Williams . . . . Witch Doctor
Ronald Simpson . . . . Blane
Robert Adams . . . . Monty
Cornelia Smith . . . . Queen Zinga
Alf Goddard . . . . Alf
Will Hammer . . . . Potman
MUSICAL Negro docker renounces career in
opera to help backward tribe.

10061
EAST MEETS WEST (74) (A)
Gaumont
AP: Haworth Bromley
D: Herbert Mason
S: (PLAY) Edwin Greenwood (THE LAKE OF
LIFE)
SC: Maude Howell
George Arliss . . . . Sultan
Lucie Mannheim . . . . Marguerite
Godfrey Tearle . . . . Sir Henry Mallory
Romney Brent . . . . Dr Shagu
Ballard Berkeley . . . . Nazim
Ronald Ward . . . . Carter
Norma Varden . . . . Lady Mallory
John Laurie . . . . Dr Ferguson
O.B. Clarence . . . . Osmin
Campbell Gullan . . . . Takasoto
Eliot Makeham . . . . Goodsen
Ralph Truman . . . . Abdul
Patrick Barr . . . . O'Flaherty
Stella Moya . . . . Suleeka
DRAMA Sultan wrangling with diplomat over
treaty learns his son loves crook's wife.

10062
THE MAN WHO CHANGED HIS MIND (66) (A)
USA: THE MAN WHO LIVED AGAIN
Gainsborough (Gaumont) *reissue:* 1949 (ABFD)
P: Michael Balcon
D: Robert Stevenson
S: John L. Balderston, L.duGarde Peach,
Sidney Gilliat
Boris Karloff . . . . Dr Laurience

Anna Lee . . . . Claire Wyatt
John Loder . . . . Dick Haslewood
Frank Cellier . . . . Lord Laslewood
Donald Calthrop . . . . Clayton
Cecil Parker . . . . Dr Gratton
Lyn Harding . . . . Prof Holloway
HORROR Doctor exchanges mind of press Lord with mind of cripple.

10063
GYPSY MELODY (77) (A)
British Artistic (Wardour)
P: Leon Hepner, Emil E. Reinert
D: Edmond T. Greville
S: Alfred Rode (JUANITA)
SC: Irving Leroy, Dan Weldon
Lupe Velez . . . . Mila
Alfred Rode . . . . Eric Danilo
Jerry Verno . . . . Madam Beatrice
Fred Duprez . . . . Herbert P. Melon
Wyn Weaver . . . . Grand Duke
Raymond Lovell . . . . Chamberlain
Margaret Yarde . . . . Duchess
Monti de Lyle . . . . Marco
MUSICAL Ruritania. Captain and gypsy dancer come to london as cabaret stars.

10064
THE TENTH MAN (68) (A)
BIP (Wardour)
P: Walter C. Mycroft
D: Brian Desmond Hurst
S: (PLAY) W. Somerset Maugham
SC: Geoffrey Kerr, Dudley Leslie, Marjorie Deans, Jack Davies
John Lodge . . . . George Winter
Antoinette Cellier . . . . Catherine Winter
Aileen Marson . . . . Anne Etchingham
Clifford Evans , ... Ford
George Graves . . . . Col Trent
Frank Cochrane . . . . Bennett
Athole Stewart . . . . Lord Etchingham
Iris Hoey . . . . Lady Etchingham
Bruce Lister . . . . Edward O'Donnell
Barry Sinclair . . . . Robert Colby
Antony Holles . . . . Swalescliffe
DRAMA Crooked financier's wife stays with him so that his parliamentary career will not be harmed.

10065
AS YOU LIKE IT (96) (U)
Inter-Allied (20th)
P: Joseph M. Schenck, Paul Czinner
D: Paul Czinner
S: (PLAY) William Shakespeare
SC: J.M. Barrie, Robert Cullen
Elizabeth Bergner . . . . Rosalind
Laurence Olivier . . . . Orlando
Sophie Stewart . . . . Celia
Henry Ainley . . . . Exiled Duke
Leon Quartermaine . . . . . . Jacques
Mackenzie Ward. . . . . Touchstone
Richard Ainley . . . . Sylvius
Felix Aylmer . . . . Duke Frederick
Aubrey Mather . . . . Corin
Austin Trevor . . . . le Beau
J. Fisher White . . . . Adam
John Laurie . . . . Oliver
Dorice Fordred . . . . Audrey
Stuart Robertson . . . . Amiens
Peter Bull . . . . William
Joan White . . . . Phebe
COMEDY Period. Banished duke's daughter posing as man loves disowned man who loves 'sister'.

10066
THE BELOVED VAGABOND (78) (A) bilingual
Toeplitz Productions (ABDF)

reissues: 1946; 1950 (EB; 10 mins cut)
P: Ludovico Toeplitz
D: Kurt Bernhardt
S: (NOVEL) W.J. Locke
SC: Wells Root, Arthur Wimperis, Hugh Mills, Walter Creighton
Maurice Chevalier . . . . Gaston de Nerac
Betty Stockfeld . . . . Joanna Rushworth
Margaret Lockwood . . . . . . Blanquette
Desmond Tester . . . . Asticot
Austin Trevor . . . . Count Verneuil
Peter Haddon . . . . Major Walters
Charles Carson . . . . Charles Ruchworth
Cathleen Nesbitt . . . . Mme Boin
Barbara Gott . . . . Concierge
D.J. Williams . . . . Undertaker
C. Denier Warren . . . . Railway Clerk
MUSICAL France, 1900. Jilted architect poses as tramp and falls in love with orphan.

10067
LOVE UP THE POLE (82) (A)
British Comedies (Butcher)
P: Norman Hope-Bell
D: Clifford Gulliver
S: (PLAY) Con West, Herbert Sargent
Ernie Lotinga . . . . Jimmy Josser
Vivienne Chatterton . . . . . . Mrs Berwick
Wallace Lupino . . . . Major Toulonge
Jack Frost . . . . Spud Walker
Davina Craig . . . . Annie Noakes
Lorna Hubbard . . . . Joan
John Kevan . . . . Jack
Harold Wilkinson . . . . Ramolini
Fred Schwartz . . . . Mosenstein
Phyllis Dixey . . . . Patient
COMEDY Waiters fleeing from police don disguise to catch gem thieves.

10068
SPY OF NAPOLEON (101) (U)
JH Productions (Wardour)
P: Julius Hagen
D: Maurice Elvey
S: (NOVEL) Baroness Orczy
SC: L.duGarde Peach, Frederick Merrick, Harold Simpson
Richard Barthelmess . . . . . Gerard de Lancy
Dolly Haas . . . . Eloise
Frank Vosper . . . . . . .Louis NapoleonIII
Francis L. Sullivan . . . . Toulon
Joyce Bland . . . . Empress
Lyn Harding . . . . Bismark
Henry Oscar . . . . Hugo Biot
Marjorie Mars . . . . Anna
Brian Buchel . . . . Philippe StPaul
C. Denier Warren . . . . Nicolet
HISTORY France, 1852. Dancer poses as emperor's bastard to uncover assassination plot.

10069
DUSTY ERMINE (84) (A)
USA: HIDEOUT IN THE ALPS
Twickenham (Wardour) reissue: 1947 (Amb)
P: Julius Hagen
D: Bernard Vorhaus
S: (PLAY) Neil Grant
SC: L. duGarde Peach, Michael Hankinson, Arthur Macrae, Paul Hervey Fox, H. Fowler Mear
Ronald Squire . . . . Jim Kent
Anthony Bushell . . . . Insp Forsythe
Jane Baxter . . . . Linda Kent
Arthur Macrae . . . . Gilbert Kent
Athole Stewart . . . . Mr Kent
Austin Trevor . . . . Hotelier
Margaret Rutherford . . . . . Miss Butterby
Katie Johnson . . . . Mrs Kent
Felix Aylmer . . . . Commissioner
Hal Gordon . . . . Sgt Helmsley
CRIME Austria. Jailbird forger takes blame when nephew joins gang of counterfeiters.

10070
JUGGERNAUT (74) (A)
JH Productions (Wardour)
P: Julius Hagen
D: Henry Edwards
S: (NOVEL) Alice Campbell
SC: Heinrich Fraenkel, Cyril Campion, H. Fowler Mear
Boris Karloff . . . . Dr Sartorius
Mona Goya . . . . .Lady Yvonne Clifford
Arthur Margetson . . . . Roger Clifford
Joan Wyndham . . . . Eve Rowe
Morton Selton . . . . Sir Charles Clifford
Gibb McLaughlin . . . . Jacques
Anthony Ireland . . . . Arthur Halliday
Nina Boucicault . . . . Mary Clifford
J.H. Roberts . . . . Chalmers
CRIME Doctor kills lady's aged husband in return for research money.

10071
NOTHING LIKE PUBLICITY (64) (U)
GS Enterprises (Radio)
P: A. George Smith
D: Maclean Rogers
S: Arthur Cooper
SC: Kathleen Butler, H.F. Maltby
Billy Hartnell . . . . Pat Spencer
Marjorie Taylor . . . . Denise Delorme
Moira Lynd . . . . Miss Bradley
Ruby Miller . . . . Sadie Sunshine
Max Adrian . . . . Bob Wharncliffe
Isobel Scaife . . . . Maid
Gordon McLeod . . . . .Sir Arthur Wharncliffe
Dorothy Hammond . . . . . . Lady Wharncliffe
Aubrey Mallalieu . . . . Mr Dines
COMEDY Press agent has dud actress pose as American heiress, who is also impersonated by crook.

10072
WINGS OVER AFRICA (63) (U)
Premier-Stafford (Radio)
P: John Stafford
D: Ladislaus Vajda
S: Akos Tolnay
Joan Gardner . . . . Carol Reade
Ian Colin . . . . Terry Cooper
James Harcourt . . . . Wilkins
James Carew . . . . Norton
Alan Napier . . . . Redfern
James Craven . . . . John Trevor
Charles Oliver . . . . Collins
Phil Thomas . . . . Quincey
ADVENTURE Africa. Murder ensues when rival parties search for hidden jewels.

10073
LUCK OF THE TURF (64)(A)
Randall Faye (Radio)
P: D: Randall Faye
S: John Hunter
Jack Melford . . . . Sid Smith
Moira Lynd . . . . Letty Jackson
Wally Patch . . . . Bill Harris
Moore Marriott . . . . Mr Jackson
Sybil Grove . . . . Mrs Jackson
Tom Helmore . . . . Lord Broadwater
Peggy Novak . . . . Maisie
COMEDY Tipster loses first bet when he gambles to pay for his wedding

10074
CHICK (72) (U)
B&D (UA) reissue: 1943 (EB)
P: Jack Raymond
D: Michael Hankinson
S: (NOVEL)Edgar Wallace
SC: Irving Leroy, Daniel Wheddon, Gerard Fairlie, Cyril Gardner, D.B. Wyndham-Lewis
Sydney Howard . . . . Chick Beane

Betty Ann Davies . . . . Peggy
Fred Conyngham . . . . . Sir Anthony Monsard
Cecil Humphreys . . . . Sturgis
Mai Bacon . . . . Gert
Wallace Geoffrey . . . . Latimer
Aubrey Mather . . . . The Dean
Arthur Chesney . . . . Lord Frensham
Edmund Dalby . . . . Rennie
Robert Nainby . . . . Mr Beane
Merle Tottenham . . . . Maid
Aubrey Fitzgerald . . . . Banks
Fred Rains . . . . Warden
COMEDY College porter inherits earldom and
thwarts crooks who pretend to find oil on his
estate.

10075
GRAND FINALE (71) (A)
B&D Paramount British
P: Anthony Havelock-Allan
D: Ivar Campbell
S: Paul Hervey Fox
SC: Vera Allinson
Mary Glynne . . . . Lina Parsons
Guy Newall . . . . Hugo Trench
Eric Cowley . . . . Sir Thomas Portland
Glen Alyn . . . . Pat Mainwaring
Douglas Rhodes . . . . Peter Trench
Philip Holles . . . . Collins
Dorothy Dewhurst . . . . Miss Pittaway
Kim Peacock . . . . Editor
Afrique . . . . Himself
COMEDY Two ex-husbands try to win back
divorced actress.

10076
DISHONOUR BRIGHT (82) (A)
Cecil (GFD) reissue: 1942 (Pi)
P: Herman Fellner, Max Schach
D: Tom Walls
S: Ben Travers
Tom Walls . . . . Stephen Champion
Eugene Pallette . . . . Busby
Betty Stockfeld . . . . Stella
Diana Churchill . . . . Ivy Lamb
Arthur Wontner . . . . Judge
Cecil Parker . . . . Vincent Lamb
George Sanders . . . . Lisle
Hubert Harben . . . . Lamb
Henry Oscar . . . . Blenkinsop
Mabel Terry-Lewis . . . . Lady Melbury
Basil Radford . . . . Henry Crane
Jeni le Gon; Bernardi.
COMEDY Rich corespondent weds divorcee and
is blackmailed for affair with his prosecutor's
wife.

10077
MILLIONS (70) (U)
Wilcox (GFD)
P: Herbert Wilcox
D: Leslie Hiscott
S: Michael Barringer
Gordon Harker. . . . . Otto Forbes
Frank Pettingell . . . . Sir Charles Rimmer
Richard Hearne . . . . Jimmy Forbes
Jane Carr . . . . Jane Rimmer
Stuart Robertson . . . . Bastian
Antony Holles . . . . Billy Todd
Ellen Pollock . . . . Janet Mason
Jack Hobbs . . . . Parsons
Ernest Sefton . . . . Naseby
COMEDY Millionaire discovers rival's wastrel
son is posing as composer.

10078
SOUTHERN ROSES (78) (U)
Grafton (GFD) reissue: 1942 (Pi)
P: Isidore Goldschmidt, Max Schach
D: Fred Zelnik

S: (PLAY) Rudolph Bernauer
SC: Ronald Gow
George Robey . . . . Higgins
Neil Hamilton . . . . Reggie
Gina Malo . . . . Mary Rowland
Chili Bouchier . . . . Estrella
Vera Pearce . . . . Carrie
Richard Dolman . . . . Bill Higgins
Leslie Perrins . . . . Don Ramon
Sara Allgood . . . . Florence
Athene Seyler . . . . Miss Rowland
D.A. Clarke-Smith . . . . Senor Estrello
Gus McNaughton . . . . Parker
Hal Gordon . . . . Mountford
MUSICAL Naval officer loves star who poses as
his best friend's wife.

10079
THE DREAM DOCTOR (41) (A)
Bernard Smith & Widgey Newman (MGM)
D: R.W. Lotinga
Sydney Monckton . . . . Doctor
Julie Suedo . . . . Gipsy
Yvonne Murray . . . . Patient
Leo Genn . . . . Husband
DRAMA Psychic gipsy interprets dreams of
doctor's patient.

10080
INTERNATIONAL REVUE (40) (U)
Medway (NPFD)
P: Lai Foun
D: Buddy Harris
Ronald Frankau
Fred Duprey
Bernard de Gautier
Marcella Saltzer
Lai Foun and his Chinese Wonders
Peter Bernard
Frank Braidwood
Jessica Merton
Two Jays
REVUE

OCT

10081
TROPICAL TROUBLE (70) (A)
City (GFD)
P: Basil Humphrys
D: Harry Hughes
S: (NOVEL) Stephen King-Hall (BUNGA—
BUNGA)
SC: Vernon Harris
Douglass Montgomery . . . . George Masterman
Betty Ann Davis . . . . Mary Masterman
Alfred Drayton . . . . . . Sir Montagu Thumpeter
Natalie Hall . . . . . . Louise van der Houten
Sybil Grove . . . . Lady Thumperter
Victor Stanley . . . . Albert
Gerald Barry . . . . . Sir Pomfrey Pogglethwaite
Morris Harvey . . . . Chief of the Bungs
Marie Ault . . . . Nonnie
Vernon Harris . . . . Martindale
Mabel Mercer
Chela & Doray
COMEDY Island governor's aide poses as
bachelor while his wife poses as his secretary.

10082
THE SECRET OF STAMBOUL (93) (A)
Wainwright (GFD) reissue: 1940, THE SPY
IN WHITE
P: Richard Wainwright
D: Andrew Marton
S: (NOVEL) Dennis Wheatley (EUNUCH OF
STAMBOUL)
SC: Richard Wainwright, Howard Irving Young,
Noel Langley
Valerie Hobson . . . . Tania
Frank Vosper . . . . Kazdim

James Mason . . . . Larry
Kay Walsh . . . . Diana
Peter Haddon . . . . Peter
Laura Cowie . . . . Baroness
Cecil Ramage . . . . Prince Ali
Robert English . . . . Sir George
Emilio Cargher . . . . Renouf
Leonard Sachs . . . . Arif
CRIME Turkey. Englishman investigates trouble
at tobacco factory and foils revolution.

10083
LAND WITHOUT MUSIC (80) (U)
USA: FORBIDDEN MUSIC
Capitol (GFD) reissue: 1947 (Amb)
P: Max Schach
D: Walter Forde
S: Fritz Koselka, Armin Robinson
SC: Rudolph Bernauer, Marian Dix, LduGarde
Peach
Richard Tauber . . . . Mario Carlini
Jimmy Durante . . . . Jonah J. Whistler
Diana Napier . . . . Princess Regent
June Clyde . . . . Sadie Whistler
Derrick de Marney . . . . Rudolpho Strozzi
Esme Percy . . . . Ambassador
George Hayes . . . . Capt Strozzi
John Hepworth . . . . Pedro
Edward Rigby . . . . Maestro
George Carney . . . . Warder
Ivan Wilmot . . . . Chief Bandit
MUSICAL Ruritania. Tenor incites revolt against
princess's ban on music.

10084
SHOW FLAT (70) (U)
B&D Paramount British
P: Anthony Havelock-Allan
D: Bernerd Mainwaring
S: (PLAY) Cecil Maiden, Martha Robinson
SC: Sherard Powell, George Barraud
Eileen Munro . . . . Aunt Louisa
Anthony Hankey . . . . Paul Collett
Clifford Heatherley . . . . . . Ginnsberg
Max Faber . . . . Ronnie Chubb
Polly Ward . . . . Mary Blake
Vernon Harris . . . . Tom Vernon
Miki Decima . . . . Miss Jube
Billy Bray . . . . Fox
COMEDY Playwright and girl use vacant show
flat to impress producer.

10085
AND SO TO WORK (17) (U)
Massingham (Kinograph)
D: S: Richard Massingham
Russell Waters . . . . Mr Glen
COMEDY Morning routine of bachelor in
boarding house.

10086
HAIL AND FAREWELL (73) (A)
WB—FN (FN)
D: Ralph Ince
S: Paul Merzbach
SC: Reginald Purdell, John Dighton,
Brock Williams
Claude Hulbert . . . . Bert
Reginald Purdell . . . . Nobby
Nicholas Hannen . . . . Col Harvey
Joyce Kennedy . . . . Mrs Harvey
Moira Reed . . . . Annie Turner
Bruce Lister . . . . Peter Dove
Ivan Samson . . . . Col Oldham
Wally Patch . . . . Sgt-Major
Henry Caine . . . . Joe Perkins
Marie Wright . . . . Mrs Perkins
Joyce Kirby . . . . Ruby
DRAMA Intertwined adventures of privates and
officers during six hour leave in Southampton.

10087
EVERYBODY DANCE (74) (A)
Gainsborough (Gaumont)
P: Michael Balcon
D: Charles Reisner
S: Stafford Dickens, Ralph Spence, Leslie Arliss
Cicely Courtneidge . . . . Lady Kate
Ernest Truex . . . . Wilbur Spurgeon
Charles Reisner jr . . . . Tony Spurgeon
Billie de la Volta . . . . Shirley Spurgeon
Percy Parsons . . . . Josiah Spurgeon
Alma Taylor . . . . Rosemary Spurgeon
Peter Gawthorne . . . . . Sir Rowland Morton
Helen Haye . . . . Lady Morton
Kathleen Harrison . . . . Lucy
Bruce Winston . . . . Pierre
C. Denier Warren . . . . Dan Fleming
Janet Johnson . . . . Lilian
MUSICAL Nightclub singer poses as rural
social worker to look after her American neice
and nephew.

10088
IT'S YOU I WANT (73) (A)
British Lion *reissue:* 1946 (NR)
P: Herbert Smith
D: Ralph Ince
S: (PLAY) Maurice Braddell
SC: Cyril Campion
Seymour Hicks . . . . Victor Delaney
Marie Lohr . . . . Constance Gilbert
Hugh Wakefield . . . . Otto Gilbert
Jane Carr . . . . Melisande
Lesley Wareing . . . . Anne Vernon
H.G. Stoker. . . . . Braille
Gerald Barry . . . . Maj Entwhistle
Ronald Waters . . . . Jimmy Watts
COMEDY Old philanderer finds his flat occupied
by his married friend and his mistress.

10089
DIGGING FOR GOLD (43) (U)
Ace Films
D: R.A. Hopwood
Eric Woodburn   Edna Thompson
Afrique   Dick Tubb
Alan d'Albert   Windmill Girls
REVUE Windmill Theatre production.

10090
THE MAN IN THE MIRROR (82) (A)
JH Productions (Wardour)
P: Julius Hagen
D: Maurice Elvey
S: (NOVEL) William Garrett
SC: F. McGrew Willis, Hugh Mills
Edward Everett Horton . . . . Jeremy Dike
Genevieve Tobin . . . . Helen
Garry Marsh . . . . Tarkington
Ursula Jeans . . . . Veronica
Alastair Sim . . . . Interpreter
Aubrey Mather . . . . Bogus of Bokhara
Renee Gadd . . . . Miss Blake
Viola Compton . . . . Mrs Massiter
Felix Aylmer . . . . Earl of Wigan
Stafford Hilliard . . . . Dr Graves
FANTASY Timid businessman's reflection
emerges from mirror and takes over his life.

10091
THE END OF THE ROAD (71) (U)
Fox British
D: Alex Bryce
S: Edward Dryhurst
Harry Lauder . . . . John MacGregor
Ruth Haven . . . . Shelia MacGregor
Ethel Glendinning . . . . Jean MacGregor
Bruce Seton . . . . Donald Carson
Margaret Moffatt . . . . Maggie
Campbell Gullan . . . . David

Vera Lennox . . . . Flo
Tully Comber . . . . Alan Cameron
MUSICAL Scotland. Travelling minstrel loses
savings after death of his daughter.

10092
CRIME OVER LONDON (80) (A) *bilingual*
Criterion (UA) *reissues:* 1944 (Anglo)
1946 (Picc; cut)
P: Marcel Hellman, Douglas Fairbanks jr
D: Alfred Zeisler
S: (NOVEL) Louis de Wohl (HOUSE OF A
THOUSAND WINDOWS)
SC: Norman Alexander, Harold French
Margot Grahame . . . . Pearl Dupres
Paul Cavanagh . . . . Insp Gary
Joseph Cawthorn . . . . Sherwood/Riley
Basil Sydney . . . . Joker Finnegan
Rene Ray . . . . Joan Vane
Bruce Lister . . . . Ronald Martin
David Burns . . . . Sniffy
Edmon Ryan . . . . Spider
John Darrow . . . . Jim
Danny Green . . . . Klemm
Googie Withers . . . . Miss Dupree
CRIME American blackmailer forces double of
store owner to help him rob store.

NOV

10093
SUCH IS LIFE (80) (A)
Incorporated Talking Films (NPFD) *reissue:*
1949, MUSIC AND MILLIONS
P: Brandon Fleming, Reginald Gottwaltz
D: Randall Faye
S: Brandon Fleming
Gene Gerrard . . . . Jack Rayner
Claude Dampier . . . . Green
Jean Colin . . . . Betty Blair
Eve Gray . . . . Vicky
Frank Birch . . . . Mockett
McArthur Gordon . . . . Chapman
Aubrey Mallalieu . . . . Sallust
Paul Sheridan . . . . Mandeville
Billie Carlyle . . . . Secretary
Robert Ashley
Chela & Dorvay
COMEDY Millionaire poses as clerk to help
typist become singer.

10094
LIVE AGAIN (74) (A)
Morgan (NPFD)
P: G.B. Morgan
D: Arthur Maude
S: John Quin
Noah Beery . . . . Morton Meredith
Bessie Love . . . . Kathleen Vernon
John Garrick . . . . John Wayne
Stan Paskin . . . . Joshua Bloggs
Vi Kaley . . . . Jane Bloggs
Cecil Gray . . . . Vivian Turnbull
Pamela Randall . . . . Grace Felton
Lynwood Roberts . . . . Maj Cannon
Frank Stanmore . . . . Magistrate
MUSICAL Old opera star tries to live again
through young protege.

10095
FULL STEAM (47) (U)
Ace films
D: R.A. Hopwood
Edna Thompson   Maggie Eaton
Warden & West   Gus Chevalier
Ken Douglas   Eric Woodburn
REVUE Windmill Theatre production.

10096
BOTTLE PARTY (45) (U)
Ace Films

D: R.A. Hopwood
Meggie Eaton   Edna Wood
Paddy Browne   Olive del Mar
Gus Chevalier   Warden & West
REVUE Windmill Theatre production.

10097
RADIO LOVER (64) (U)
City (ABDF) *reissue:* 1953 (EB)
P: Ernest King
D: Austin Melford, Paul Capon
S: Elma Dangerfield
SC: Ian Dalrymple
Wylie Watson . . . . Joe Morrison
Ann Penn . . . . Miss Oliphant
Betty Ann Davies . . . . Wendy Maradyck
Jack Melford . . . . Reggie Clifford
Cynthia Stock . . . . Miss Swindon
Gerald Barry . . . . Sir Hector
Max Faber . . . . Brian Maradyck
COMEDY Plain singer has handsome friend mime
for television appearances.

10098
THE HOUSE OF THE SPANIARD (70) (U)
IFP-Phoenix (ABFD)
P: Hugh Perceval
D: Reginald Denham
S: (NOVEL) Arthur Behrend
SC: Basil Mason
Brigitte Horney . . . . Margarita de Guzman
Petter Haddon . . . . David Grey
Jean Galland . . . . Ignacio
Allan Jeayes . . . Don Pedro de Guzman
Gyles Isham . . . . John Gilchrist
Hay Petrie . . . . Orlando
Ivor Barnard . . . . Mott
David Horne . . . . Captain
Minnie Rayner . . . . Mrs Blossom
Fred O'Donovan . . . . McNail
CRIME Liverpool. Clerk unmasks employer
as Spanish revolutionary counterfeiting money
in marshbound house.

10099
TOMORROW WE LIVE (72) (A)
Conquest (ABFD)
P: Clayton Hutton
D:S: Manning Haynes
Godfrey Tearle . . . . Sir Charles Hendra
Haidee Wright . . . . Mrs Gill
Renee Gadd . . . . Patricia Gordon
Sebastian Shaw . . . . Eric Morton
Eliot Makeham . . . . Henry Blossom
Thea Holme . . . . Mary Leighton
George Carney . . . . Mr Taylor
Rosalind Atkinson . . . . . . Mrs Taylor
Jessica Black. . . . . Mrs Carter
Fred Withers . . . . Mr Carter
Cyril Raymond . . . . George Warner
DRAMA Ruined financier presents £50 each
to twelve desperate down-and-outs.

10100
THE LIMPING MAN (72) (A)
Welwyn (Pathe)
D:SC: Walter Summers
S: (PLAY) Will Scott
Francis L. Sullivan. . . . . . . Theodore Disher
Hugh Wakefield . . . . Col Paget
Patricia Hilliard . . . . Gloria Paget
Robert Cochran . . . . Philip Nash
Leslie Perrins . . . . Paul Hoyt
Judy Kelly . . . . Olga Hoyt
Iris Hoey . . . . Mrs Paget
Frank Atkinson . . . . Insp Cable
George Pughe . . . . Chicago Joe
John Turnbull . . . . Insp Potts
CRIME Three people hatch different plots
to murder retired traitor.

10101
IRISH AND PROUD OF IT (72) (U)
Crusade (Par)
P: Victor M. Greene
D: Donovan Pedelty
S: (STORY) Dorothea Donn Byrne
SC: David Evans, Donovan Pedelty
Richard Hayward . . . . Donogh O'Connor
Dinah Sheridan . . . . Moira Flaherty
Gwenllian Gill . . . . Mary Johnson
George Pembroke . . . . . . Mike Finnegan
Liam Gaffney . . . . Sean Casey
Herbert Thorpe . . . . Benito Colombo
Jimmy Mageean . . . . Flaherty
COMEDY Ireland. Food tablet manufacturer
thwarts Chicago gangster's moonshiners.

10102
HEAD OFFICE (90) (A)
WB-FN (WB)
P: Irving Asher
D: Melville Brown
S: (NOVEL) Hugh Preston
Owen Nares . . . . Henry Crossman
Nancy O'Neil . . . . Margaret
Arthur Margetson . . . . Dixon
Eileen Peel . . . . Sheila
Alexis France . . . . Janie Clutterbuck
Philip Ray . . . . Gerrard
Ronald Simpson . . . . Knott
Charles Carson . . . . Armstrong
Hilda Bayley . . . . Mrs Braham
Bruce Lister . . . . Halliday
H.F.Maltby . . . . Blenkinsop
DRAMA Clerk knows employer's son died
a coward and blackmails colleague.

10103
DAVID LIVINGSTONE (71) (U)
Fitzpatrick Pictures (MGM)
D: James A. Fitzpatrick
S: W.K.Williamson
Percy Marmont . . . . David Livingstone
Marian Spencer . . . . Mary Moffatt
James Carew . . . . Gordon Bennett
Pamela Stanley . . . . Queen Victoria
Hugh McDermott . . . . H.M.Stanley
HISTORY Africa, 1871. Explorer seeking
source of Nile is found by American
reporter.

10104
THE CAPTAIN'S TABLE (55) (A)
Fitzpatrick Pictures (MGM)
P: James A. Fitzpatrick
D: Percy Marmont
S: John Paddy Carstairs
Percy Marmont . . . . John Brooke
Marian Spencer . . . . Ruth Manning
Louis Goodrich . . . . Capt Henderson
Mark Daly . . . . Sanders
Philip Brandon . . . . Eric Manning
Daphne Courtenay . . . . . . Mary Vaughan
Hugh McDermott . . . . Insp Mooney
CRIME Detective poses as steward to find
cruise passenger's killer.

10105
HEARTS OF HUMANITY (75) (U)
UK Films (AP&D) reissue: 1942,
THE CRYPT (cut); 1948 (Amb)
P: John Barter
D: John Baxter
S: Herbert Ayres
Bransby Williams . . . . Mike
Wilfrid Walter . . . . . Rev John Maitland
Cathleen Nesbitt . . . . Mrs Bamford
Pamela Randall . . . . Ann Bamford
Eric Portman . . . . Jack Clinton
Hay Petrie . . . . Alf

J.Fisher White . . . . Dad
Fred Duprez . . . . Manager
Stanelli; Teddy Reilly; Romilly Choir;
Teddy Joyce and his Band
DRAMA Village cleric fleeing gossip
helps tramps and catches gang.

10106
THE LAST WALTZ (74) (U) bilingual
Warwick (AP&D) reissue: 1940
(NR; 11 m cut)
P: Gina Carlton
D: Leo Mittler, Gerald Barry
S: (OPERA) Oscar Strauss, Max Wallner,
Georg Weber (DER LETZEWALZER)
SC: Reginald Arkell
Jarmilla Novotna . . Countess Vera Lizavetta
Harry Welchman . . . . Count Dmitri
Gerald Barry . . . . Prince Paul
Josephine Huntley Wright . . . Babushka
Tonie Edgar Bruce . . . . . . Countess
Betty Huntley Wright . . . . .
Bruce Winston . . . .
Jack Hellier . . . .
Paul Sheridan . . . .
MUSICAL Ruritania. Jealous prince jails
rival for treason. (Made in Paris).

10107
DREAMS COME TRUE (78) (A)
London & Continental (Reunion)
reissue: 1943 (BAP)
P: Ilya Salkind, John Gossage
D: Reginald Denham
S: (OPERA) Franz Lehar (CLO-CLO)
SC: Bruce Sevier, Donald Bull
Frances Day . . . . Ilona Ratkay
Nelson Keys . . . . Anton
Hugh Wakefield . . . Albert von Waldenau
Frederick Bradshaw . . . . . . Peter
Marie Lohr . . . . Helen von Waldenau
Morris Harvey . . . . Waldemar
Arthur Finn . . . . Manager
Minnie Rayner . . . . Dresser
Ivor Barnard . . . .
Molly Hamley Clifford . . .
MUSICAL Vienna. Rich farmer learns the
actress he and his son love is his own daughter.

10108
SKYLARKS (73) (U)
Reunion
P: John Gossage
D: Thornton Freeland
Jimmy Nervo . . . . Jimmy Doakes
Teddy Knox . . . . Teddy Cook
Nancy Burne . . . . Marion Hicks
Queenie Leonard . . . . Maggie Hicks
Eddie Gray . . . .
Amy Veness . . . .
COMEDY Drunken airmen accidentally
break air endurance record.

10109
BUSMAN'S HOLIDAY (64) (U)
GS Enterprises-Bow Bell (Radio)
P: A.George Smith
D: Maclean Rogers
S: Wally Patch
SC: Kathleen Butler, H.F.Maltby
Wally Patch . . . . Jeff Pinkerton
Gus McNaughton . . . . . . Alf Green
Muriel George . . . . Mrs Green
H.F.Maltby . . . . Mr Bulger
Isobel Scaife . . . . Daisy
Robert Hobbs . . . . Harry Blake
Norman Pierce . . . . Crook
Michael Ripper . . . . Crook
COMEDY Busmen mistaken for burglars
catch culprits.

10110
THE HEIRLOOM MYSTERY (72) (A)
GS Enterprises (Radio)
P: A.George Smith
D: Maclean Rogers
S: G.H. Moresby-White
SC: Kathleen Butler
Edward Rigby . . . . Charles Marriott
Mary Glynne . . . . Lady Benton
Gus McNaughton . . . . . . Alfred Fisher
Marjorie Taylor . . . . Mary
John Robinson . . . . Dick Marriott
Martin Lewis . . . . Sir Arthur Benton
Kathleen Gibson . . . . Doris
Louanne Shaw . . . . Millie
Bruce Lister . . . . Alf Dene
H.F.Maltby . . . . Mr Lewis
DRAMA Cabinet maker's fake antique
causes trouble for his progressive son.

10111
HIS LORDSHIP (71) (U)
USA: MAN OF AFFAIRES
Gaumont reissue: 1942 (Ren)
AP: S.C.Balcon
D: Herbert Mason
S: (PLAY) Neil Grant (THE NELSON TOUCH)
SC: Maude Howell, Edwin Greenwood,
L. DuGarde Peach
George Arliss . . . Lord Dunchester/Richard
Rene Ray . . . . Vera
Romilly Lunge . . . . Bill Howard
Jessie Winter . . . . Lady Dunchester
John Ford . . . . Ibrahim
Allan Jeayes . . . . Barak
Lawrence Anderson . . . . . . Nahil
John Turnbull . . . . Stevenson
Basil Gill . . . . Abdullah
DRAMA Foreign Secretary's twin takes
his place to prove sheik killed emir.

10112
ALL IN (71) (A)
Gainsborough (Gau)
P: Michael Balcon
D: Marcel Varnel
S: (PLAY) Bernard Merivale, Brandon Fleming
(TATTENHAM CORNER)
SC: Leslie Arliss, Val Guest
Ralph Lynn . . . . Archie Slott
Gina Malo . . . . Kay Slott
Jack Barty . . . . Tingaling Tom
Claude Dampier . . . . Toop
Sydney Fairbrother . . . . . . Genesta Slott
Garry Marsh . . . . Lilleywhite
Robert Nainby . . . . Eustace Slott
O.B.Clarence . . . . Hemingway
Gibb McLaughlin. . . . .Rev Cuppleditch
Glennis Lorimer . . . . Kitty
Fewlass Llewellyn . . . . . Dean of Plinge
COMEDY Anti-gambling crusader's nephew
inherits racing stable and buys wrestling
stadium.

10113
STRANGERS ON A HONEYMOON (70) (A)
Gaumont
AP: Haworth Bromley
D: Albert de Courville
S: (NOVEL) Edgar Wallace
(THE NORTHING TRAMP)
SC: Ralph Spence, Bryan Wallace,
Sidney Gilliat
Constance Cummings . . . October Jones
Hugh Sinclair . . . . Quigley
Noah Beery . . . . Redbeard
Beatrix Lehmann . . . . Elfrida

David Burns . . . . Lennie
Butler Hixon . . . . Sam Wasser
James Arnold . . . . Groom
Ann Tucker McGuire . . . . . Bride
Edmund Breon . . . . Sir Gregory
COMEDY Canada. Titled man posing as
tramp weds girl and saves her deed
from crooks.

10114
THIS'LL MAKE YOU WHISTLE (79) (A)
Wilcox (GFD)
P:D: Herbert Wilcox
S: (PLAY) Guy Bolton, Paul Thompson
SC: Guy Bolton, Paul Thompson
Jack Buchanan . . . . Bill Hopping
Elsie Randolph . . . . Bobbie Rivers
Jean Gillie . . . . Joan Longhurst
William Kendall . . . . Reggie Benson
David Hutcheson . . . . . Archie Codrington
Antony Holles . . . . . . Sebastian Venables
Marjorie Brooks . . . . Laura Buxton
Maidie Hope . . . . Mrs Longhurst
Miki Hood . . . . Clarice
MUSICAL Riviera. Playboy poses as
forger to shock his unwanted fiancee's
guardian.

10115
EVERYTHING IN LIFE (70) (U)
Tudor (Col) reissue: 1944 (Prem)
P: Marquis of Ely
D: J. Elder Wills
S: Courtney Terrett
SC: James E.Lewis
Gitta Alpar . . . . Rita Bonya
Neil Hamilton . . . . Geoffrey Loring
Lawrence Grossmith . . . . . Lewis Radford
H.F.Maltby . . . . Sir Algernon Spindle
Gerald Barry . . . . Vere Ponsonby
Dorothy Boyd . . . . Miss Winstone
Wyn Weaver . . . . William Tewkes
Clarissa Selwyn . . . . Matilda Tewkes
Bruce Winston . . . . Franz Graumann
Vera Bogetti . . . . Carolyn Dexter
John Deverell . . . . Johns
MUSICAL Temperamental opera star
feigns poverty to win composer.

10116
REMBRANDT (85) (A)
London (UA) reissue: 1943 (BL)
P:D: Alexander Korda
S: Carl Zuckmayer
SC: Lajos Biro, June Head
Charles Laughton . Rembrandt van Rijn
Gertrude Lawrence . . . . . . Geertke Dirx
Elsa Lanchester . . . . Henrikje Stoffels
Edward Chapman . . . . Fabrizius
Walter Hudd . . . . Banning Cocq
Roger Livesey . . . . Beggar Saul
John Bryning . . . . Titus van Rijn
Sam Livesey . . . . Auctioneer
Herbert Lomas . . . . . . Harmen van Rijn
Allan Jeayes . . . . Dr Tulp
John Clements . . . . Gavaert Flink
Raymond Huntley . . . . Ludwig
Abraham Sofaer. . . . . Dr Monasseh
Lawrence Hanray . . . . Hertzsbeeke
Austin Trevor . . . . Marquis
Henry Hewitt . . . . Jan Six
Gertrude Musgrove . . . . . . Agelintje
Basil Gill . . . . Adrien
Edmund Willard . . . . Van Seeland
Marius Goring . . . . Baron Leivens
HISTORY Amsterdam, 1642-69. Painter loses
his faith on wife's death and has it restored
by his housekeeper.

10117
MEN ARE NOT GODS (90) (A)
London (UA) reissue: 1943 (BL)
P: Alexander Korda
D:S: Walter Reisch
SC: G.B.Stern, Iris Wright
Miriam Hopkins . . . . Ann Williams
Gertrude Lawrence . . . . . . Barbara Halford
Sebastian Shaw . . . . Edmond Davey
Rex Harrison . . . . Tommy Stapleton
A.E.Matthews . . . . Skeates
Val Gielgud . . . . Producer
Laura Smithson . . . . Katherine
Lawrence Grossmith . . . . . . .Stanley
Sybil Grove . . . . Painter
Wally Patch . . . . Attendant
ROMANCE Actor's mistress stops him
strangling his pregnant wife during "Othello."

10118
VARIETY PARADE (83) (U)
Malcolm (Butcher)
P: Ian Sutherland, Reginald Long
D: Oswald Mitchell
S: Con West
Mrs Jack Hylton and her Boys
Sam Browne   Harry Tate
Teddy Brown   Dave & Joe O'Gorman
G.S.Melvin   Nini & Partner
Archie Glen   Radio Three
Ernest Shannon Ivor Vintnor & Ann Gordon
Corona Kids   Sherman Fisher Girls
REVUE (Extracts in HIGHLIGHTS OF
VARIETY No. 13-17 (1938);
CAVALCADE OF VARIETY (1940).)

10119
FULL SPEED AHEAD (71) (U)
Huntington (Par)
D: Lawrence Huntington
S: Lawrence Huntington, Gerald Elliott
SC: Gerald Elliott
Paul Neville . . . . Capt Murton
Moira Lynd . . . . Jean Hunter
Richard Norris . . . . Tim Brent
George Mozart . . . . Chief Smith
Geoffrey Clark . . . . Dunn
Victor Hagen . . . . Smith
George Turner . . . . Oily Short
Arthur Seaton . . . . Irving Hunter
Julien Vedey . . . . Mendoza
Syd Crossley . . . . Moggridge
ADVENTURE Rich girl elopes with
chauffeur aboard ship which captain
plans to scuttle.

10120
THE SCARAB MURDER CASE (68) (A)
B & D- Paramount British
P: Anthony Havelock-Allan
D: Michael Hankinson
S: (NOVEL) S.S.Van Dine
SC: Selwyn Jepson
Kathleen Kelly . . . . Angela Hargreaves
Wilfrid Hyde White . . . . . . Philo Vance
Wally Patch . . . . Insp Moor
Henri de Vries . . . . Dr Bliss
John Robinson . . . . Donald Scarlett
Wallace Geoffrey . . . . Salveter
Stella Moya . . . . Meryt Amen
Grahame Chesewright . . . . Makeham
CRIME Tec proves archaeologist killed
rich backer.

DEC

10121
NO ESCAPE (80) (A)
Welwyn (Pathe)

D: Norman Lee
S: (PLAY) George Goodchild, Frank
Witty (NO EXIT)
Valerie Hobson . . . . Laura Anstey
Billy Milton . . . . Billy West
Robert Cochran . . . . Beeston
Leslie Perrins . . . . Anthony Wild
Henry Oscar . . . . Cyril Anstey
Ronald Simpson . . . . Scoop Martin
Margaret Yarde . . . . Bunty
Hal Gordon . . . . PC
CRIME Novelist bets he can hide his
friend from the police for one month.

10122
YOU MUST GET MARRIED (68) (A)
City (GFD)
P: Basil Humphreys
D: Leslie Pearce
S: (NOVEL) David Evans
SC: F.McGrew Willis, Richard Fisher
Frances Day . . . . Fenella Dane
Neil Hamilton . . . . Michael Brown
Robertson Hare . . . . Percy Phut
Wally Patch . . . . Chief Blow
Gus McNaughton . . . . Bosun
Fred Duprez . . . . Cyrus P. Hankin
Dennis Wyndham . . . . Albert Gull
C.Denier Warren . . . . Mr Wurtsell
James Carew . . . . Mr Schillinger
COMEDY Captain abducts American wife
on learning she only married him to become
naturalised.

10123
REASONABLE DOUBT (73) (A)
Pascal (MGM)
P: Gabriel Pascal
D: George King
SC: Ewart Brooks
John Stuart . . . . Noel Hampton
Nancy Burne . . . . Pat
Marjorie Taylor . . . .
Ivan Brandt . . . . Tony
Marie Lohr . . . .
Clifford Heatherley . . . . . .
H.F.Maltby . . . .
Cecil Humphreys . . . .
Fred Duprez . . . .
Cynthia Stock . . . .
CRIME KC loves girl and defends her fiance,
who turns out to be his own son, an
hereditary neurasthenic.

10124
PICCADILLY PLAYTIME (50) (U)
Ace Films
D: Frank Green
Walden & West   Paddy Brown
Olive Del Mar   Eric Woodburn
Meggie Eaton   Leslie Spurling
REVUE "Windmill Theatre" Revuedeville show.

10125
SPORTING LOVE (70) (U)
Hammer (BL) reissue: 1941 (Ex)
H: H. Fraser Passmore
D: J. Elder Wills
S: (PLAY) Stanley Lupino
SC: Fenn Sherie, Ingram d'Abbes
Stanley Lupino . . . . Percy Brace
Laddie Cliff . . . . Peter Brace
Eda Peel . . . . Maud Dane
Lu-Anne Meredith . . . . Nellie Gray
Bobbie Comber . . . . Gerald Dane
Henry Carlisle . . . . Lord Dimsdale
Clarissa Selwyn . . . . Aunt Fanny
Wyn Weaver . . . . Wilfred Wimple
COMEDY Broke racehorse-owners forced to
produce "wives" to please rich aunt.

10126
SECOND BUREAU (76) (A)
Premier-Stafford (Radio)
P: John Stafford
D: Victor Hanbury
S: (NOVEL) Charles Robert Dumas
(DEUXIEME BUREAU)
SC: Akos Tolnay

Marta Labarr	Erna Fielder
Charles Oliver	Paul Benoit
Arthur Wontner	Col Gueraud
Meinhart Maur	Gen von Raugwitz
Fred Groves	Sgt Colleret
Joan White	Dorothy Muller
Anthony Eustrel	von Stranmer
G.H.Mulcaster	Brosilaw
Leo von Porkony	Dr Weygellman

WAR France, 1918. German spy falls in love
with French spy she is ordered to trap.

10127
ALL THAT GLITTERS (72) (U)
GS Enterprises (Radio)
P: A. George Smith
D: Maclean Rogers
S: Denison Clift

Jack Hobbs	Jack Tolley
Moira Lynd	Angela Burrows
Aubrey Mallalieu	Flint
Kay Walsh	Eve Payne-Coade
Annie Esmond	Mrs Payne-Coade
Fred Duprez	Mortimer
John Robinson	Taylor
Dick Francis	Derek Montague

COMEDY Part owner of gold mine foils
swindlers.

10128
TALK OF THE DEVIL (78) (U)
B&D (UA) reissue: 1943 (EB)
P: Jack Raymond
D: Carol Reed
S: Carol Reed, Anthony Kimmins
SC: Carol Reed, George Barraud, Anthony
Kimmins

Ricardo Cortez	Ray Allen
Sally Eilers	Ann Marlow
Basil Sydney	Stephen Findlay
Randle Ayrton	John Findlay
Frederick Culley	Alderson
Charles Carson	Lord Dymchurch
Gordon McLeod	Inspector
Dennis Cowles	Philip Couls
Quinton MacPherson	Angus
Margaret Rutherford	Housekeeper
Moore Marriott	Dart-thrower

CRIME Shipping magnate kills himself after
brother uses American impersonator to
frame him for crooked deal.

10129
SABOTAGE (76) (A)
USA: THE WOMAN ALONE
Gaumont
AP: Ivor Montagu
D: Alfred Hitchcock
S: (NOVEL) Joseph Conrad
(THE SECRET AGENT)
SC: Charles Bennett, Ian Hay, Alma
Reville, Helen Simpson, EVH Emmett

Sylvia Sidney	Sylvia Verloc
Oscar Homolka	Carl Verloc
John Loder	Ted Spencer
Desmond Tester	Steve
Joyce Barbour	Renee
Matthew Boulton	Supt Talbot
S.J.Warmington	Hollingshead
William Dewhurst	A.S.Chatman
Austin Trevor	Vladimir
Torin Thatcher	Yunct

Aubrey Mather	Greengrocer
Peter Bull	Michaelis
Charles Hawtrey	Youth

CRIME Tec poses as greengrocer to unmask
cinema owner as foreign saboteur.

10130
WINDBAG THE SAILOR (85) (U)
Gainsborough (Gau)
P: Michael Balcon
D: William Beaudine
S: Leslie Arliss, Robert Edmunds,
Marriott Edgar, Val Guest

Will Hay	Ben Cutlett
Moore Marriott	Jeremiah Harbottle
Graham Moffatt	Albert
Dennis Wyndham	Marryatt
Norma Varden	Olivia Potter-Porter
Amy Veness	Emma Harbottle
Kenneth Warrington	Yates

COMEDY Inept braggart put in charge of a
ship destined for scuttling.

10131
PAGLIACCI (92) (A) chemi seq
USA: A CLOWN MUST LAUGH
Trafalgar (UA)
P: Max Schach
D: Karl Grune
S: (OPERA) Ruggiero Leoncavallo
SC: Monckton Hoffe, John Drinkwater,
Roger Burford, Ernest Betts

Richard Tauber	Canio Tonini
Steffi Duna	Nedda Tonini
Diana Napier	Trina
Arthur Margetson	Tonio
Esmond Knight	Silvio
Jerry Verno	Beppo
Gordon James	Leone
Harry Milton	Officer

MUSICAL Cremona. Jealous actor kills wife
and soldier lover.

10132
MURDER AT THE CABARET (67) (A)
MB Productions (Par)
P: Reginald Fogwell, Nell Emerald
D:S: Reginald Fogwell
SC: Reginald Fogwell, Percy Robinson

Phyllis Robins	Jean
Freddie Forbes	Freddie
James Carew	Husband
Frederick Peisley	Jimmie
Kenneth Warrington	Toni
Peggy Crawford	Wife
Miska	Tash
Douglas Phillips	Inspector

Chick Farr & Farland; Bernardi; Michael
Ronni; Clifford Seagrave; Rosarita; Nina;
Alvis & Capla; Holland's Magyar Band
MUSICAL Singer kills crooner by substituting
live cartridges in cabaret act.

10133
MIDNIGHT AT MADAME TUSSAUD'S (66) (A)
USA: MIDNIGHT AT THE WAX MUSEUM
Premier Sound Films (Par)
P: J. Steven Edwards
D: George Pearson
S: James Edwards, Roger MacDougall
SC: Roger MacDougall, Kim Peacock

Lucille Lisle	Carol Cheyne
James Carew	Sir Clive Cheyne
Charles Oliver	Harry Newton
Kim Peacock	Nick Frome
Patrick Barr	Gerry Melville
Billy Hartnell	Stubbs
Lydia Sherwood	Brenda
Bernard Miles	Modeller

CRIME Embezzler tries to kill explorer during
a night in the Chamber of Horrors.

10134
NOT WANTED ON VOYAGE (72) (A)
USA: TREACHERY ON THE HIGH SEAS
Dela Films (BL)
P: Alexandre de Lasta
D: Emil E. Reinert
S: (PLAY) Maurice Messenger
(MURDER IN THE STALLS)
SC: Harold Simpson, Charles Lincoln

Bebe Daniels	May Hardy
Ben Lyon	Johnny Hammond
Tom Helmore	Edward Brailstone
Charles Farrell	Logan
Hay Petrie	Brainie
Gordon McLeod	Fleming
James Carew	Chief

COMEDY Singer and crooks seek ruby
necklace during transatlantic voyage.

10135
IRISH FOR LUCK (68) (U)
WB-FN (FN)
P: Irving Asher
D: Arthur Woods
S: (NOVEL) L.A.G.Strong

Athene Seyler	Duchess
Margaret Lockwood	Ellen O'Hare
Patric Knowles	Terry O'Ryan
Gibb McLaughlin	Thady
Edward Rigby	Hon Denis Maguire
Eugene Leahy	O'Callaghan
George Dillon	Mooney
Terry Conlin	Costello

COMEDY Ireland. Poor duchess, orphan niece,
and busker win fame on BBC.

10136
MY PARTNER MR DAVIS (58) (U)
retitled: THE MYSTERIOUS MR DAVIS
Oxford Films (RKO)
D: Claude Autant-Lara
S: (NOVEL) Jenaro Prieto

Henry Kendall	Julian Roscoe
Kathleen Kelly	Audrey Roscoe
Morris Harvey	Cecil Goldenburg
A.Bromley Davenport	Sir George Miller
Alastair Sim	Theodore G.Wilcox
Guy Middleton	Martin

COMEDY Unemployed man creates
imaginary business partner to thwart
fraudulent financier.

10137
OLYMPIC HONEYMOON (63) (U)
retitled: HONEYMOON MERRY-GO-ROUND
London Screenplays-Fanfare (RKO)
P: Sidney Morgan
D: Alfred Goulding
S: (NOVEL) F. Dawson Gratrix (HE AND SKI)
SC: Alfred Goulding, Monty Banks,
Chetwynd Strode, Joan Morgan

Claude Hulbert	Bob Bennett
Monty Banks	Orban
Princess Pearl	Bunny
Sally Gray	Miss America
Tully Comber	Cosmo
Bob Bowman	Announcer

Wembley Lions Ice Hockey Team
COMEDY Switzerland. Estranged honeymooner, mistaken for ice hockey champion,
helps England win international match.

10138
THE BANK MESSENGER MYSTERY (56) (A)
Hammer (Renown)
P: Will Hammer
D: Lawrence Huntington

George Mozart	George Brown
Francesca Bahrle	Miss Brown
Paul Neville	Harper
Marilyn Love	

Frank Tickle . . . .
Kenneth Kove . . . .
CRIME Sacked cashier joins gang and
robs old bank.

10139
TERROR ON TIPTOE (58) (A)
MB Productions (New Realm)
P: Reginald Fogwell, Nell Emerald
D: Louis Renoir
S: (PLAY) Fenn Sherie, Ingram d'Abbes
(SHADOW MAN)
SC: Fenn Sherie, Ingram d'Abbes
Bernard Nedell . . . .   Clive Morell
Mabel Poulton . . . .   Poppy
Jasper Maskeleyne . . . .   Vivian
Stella Bonheur . . . .   Mrs Morell
Joe Hayman . . . .   Sol Hyman
Victor Fairley . . . .   Dr Strauss
CRIME Attempted murder of American
film star's double.

10140
CONQUEST OF THE AIR (71) (U)
London (UA)
reissue: 1944 (Key; 1860 ft cut)
P: Alexander Korda
D: Zoltan Korda, Alexander Esway,
Donald Taylor, Alexander Shaw,
John Monk Saunders
S: John Monk Saunders
SC: Hugh Gray, Peter Bezencenet
Laurence Olivier . . . .   Vincent Lunardi
Franklin Dyall . . . .   Jerome de Ascoli
Henry Victor. . . . .   Otto Lilienthal
Hay Petrie . . . .   Tiberius Cavallo
John Turnbull . . . .   Von Zeppelin
Charles Lefaux. . . . .   Louis Bleriot
Bryan Powley . . . .   Sir George Cayley
Frederick Culley . . . .   Roger Bacon
Alan Wheatley . . . .   Borelli
John Abbott . . . .   De Rozier
Ben Webster . . . .   Leonardo da Vinci
Percy Marmont . . . .   Wilbur Wright
Dick Vernon . . . . . .   Simon the Magician
Denville Bond . . . .   Oliver the Monk
Charles Hickman . . . .   Orville Wright
HISTORY Man's attempts to fly, from 57 Ad
to date.

10141
TOILERS OF THE SEA (83) (U)

Beaumont (Col)
P: L.C.Beaumont
D: Selwyn Jepson, Ted Fox
S: (NOVEL) Victor Hugo
SC: Selwyn Jepson
Cyril McLaglen . . . .   Gilliatt
Mary Lawson . . . .   Deruchette
Ian Colin . . . .   Peter Caudray
Andrews Engelmann . . . . .   Capt Clubin
Walter Sondes . . . .   Rataine
Wilson Coleman . . . .   Lethierry
William Dewhurst . . . .   Landois
ADVENTURE Guernsey, 1824. Seaman
salvages the first steamship after it is
abandoned by its crooked captain.

10142
MUSICAL MERRYTONE No.1 (11) (U)
Hammer (Exclusive)
D: Will Hammer
Will Hammer
REVUE Songs, dances and comedy.

10143
THE SHOW'S THE THING (17) (U)
Sturt-Stross Metropolitan (Fidelity)
D: Raymond Stross
Ronald Frankau   Rita Willis
Dorchester Girls   Billy Merrin and his
                         Commanders

REVUE

10144
B B C   MUSICALS (series) (U)
Inspiration (Col)
P:D: Horace Shepherd

10145
1: CEDRIC SHARPE AND HIS SEXTETTE
(17)
Edwin Styles

10146
2; LESLIE JEFFRIES AND HIS ORCHESTRA
(17)
Tommy Handley
Esther Coleman
Wyn Clare

10147
3: MARIO DE PIETRO AND HIS
ESTUDIANTINA (17)

Trevor Watkins
Ella Drummond

10148
4: REGINALD KING AND HIS ORCHESTRA (17)

10149
5: ALFREDO CAMPOLI AND HIS
ORCHESTRA (15)

10150
6: EUGENE PINI AND HIS TANGO
ORCHESTRA (15)
Terry & Doris Kendall
MUSICAL (Extracts reissued as short,
RADIO NIGHTS)

10151
DID I BETRAY ? (93) (A) bilingual
UFA (Reunion) *reissue:* 1938,
BLACK ROSES (NPFD)
D: Paul Martin
S: Paul Martin, Curt Braun, Walter Supper
SC: John Heygate, Peter MacFarlane
Lilian Harvey . . . .   Tania Fedorovna
Esmond Knight . . . .   Pavo Collin
Robert Rendel . . . .   Prince Avarov
Dennis Hoey . . . .   Niklander
Amy Veness . . . .   Annushka
Henry Wolston . . . .   Police Chief
Beatrice Munro . . . .   Maid
DRAMA Finland, 1900. Russian ballerina
saves rebel sculptor she loves by becoming
mistress of Tsarist governor. (Made in Berlin).

10152
THE FLYING DOCTOR (92) (U)
Gaumont-National Productions (GFD)
D: Miles Mander
S: Robert Waldron
SC: J.O.C.Orton
Charles Farrell . . . .   Sandy Nelson
Mary Maguire . . . .   Jenny Rutherford
James Raglan . . . .   Dr John Vaughan
Margaret Vyner . . . .   Betty Webb
Joe Valli . . . .   Dodger Green
Eric Colman . . . .   Geoffrey Webb
Maudie Edwards . . . .   Phyllis
ADVENTURE Australia. Man abandons
bride, fakes suicide, finds gold, is shot,
blinded and dies. (Made in Australia).

1937

JAN

10153
GYPSY (78) (A)
WB-FN (WB)
P: Irving Asher
D: Roy William Neill
S: (NOVEL) Lady Eleanor Smith (TZIGANE)
SC: Brock Williams, Terence Rattigan
Roland Young .... Alan Brooks
Chili Bouchier .... Hassina
Hugh Williams .... Brazil
Frederick Burtwell .... Pim
Glen Alyn Lilli
Brian Buchel .... Vicot
Andrea Malandrinos ...... Hunyadi
Victor Fairley .... Strauss
Emilio Colombo's Tzigane Band
ROMANCE Gipsy girl weds ageing socialite
believing beloved lion tamer dead.

10154
SONG IN SOHO (48) (A)
Ace Films
P: Frank Green
D: R.A. Hopwood
Meggie Eaton   Edna Wood
Paddy Browne   Olive del Mar
Gus Chevalier   Warden & West
REVUE Windmill Theatre production,
including "Escalator Squiggle" and
Hollywood premiere burlesque.

10155
WELL DONE, HENRY (86) (A)
Neville Clarke (Butcher)
D: Wilfred Noy
S: Selwyn Jepson
SC: Wilfred Noy, A. Barr-Smith
Will Fyffe .... Henry McNab
Cathleen Nesbitt ...... Mrs McNab
Charles Hawtrey .... Rupert McNab
Iris March .... Mary McNab
Donald Gray .... Jimmy Dale
Marjorie Taylor .... Celia Canford
Torin Thatcher .... George Canford
Edward Wild .... Peter Dill
Hugh McDermott .... Sevier
Paul Sheridan .... Leroux
COMEDY Henpeck outwits crooked
financier and helps his daughter to elope.

10156
SENSATION (67) (A)
BIP (ABPC)
P: Walter C. Mycroft
D: Brian Desmond Hurst
S: (PLAY) Basil Dean, George Munro
(MURDER GANG)
SC: Dudley Leslie, Marjorie Deans,
William Freshman
John Lodge .... Pat Heaton
Diana Churchill .... Maisie Turnpit
Francis Lister .... Richard Grainger
Joan Marion .... Mrs Grainger
Margaret Vyner .... Claire Lindsay
Athene Seyler .... Mme Henry
Richard Bird .... Henry Belcher
Jerry Verno .... Spikey
Martin Walker .... Dimmitt
Leslie Perrins .... Strange
Henry Oscar .... Supt Stainer
Felix Aylmer .... Lord Bouverie
James Hayter .... Jock
CRIME Reporter solves the murder of
waitress at village inn.

10157
AREN'T MEN BEASTS ! (66) (A)
BIP (ABPC)
P: Walter C. Mycroft

D: Graham Cutts
S: (PLAY) Vernon Sylvaine
SC: Marjorie Deans, William Freshman
Robertson Hare .... Herbert Holly
Alfred Drayton .... Thomas Potter
June Clyde .... Marie Potter
Billy Milton .... Roger Holly
Judy Kelly .... Yvette Bingham
Ellen Pollock .... The Vamp
Amy Veness .... Mrs Flower
Ruth Maitland .... Selina Potter
Frank Royde .... PC
Victor Stanley .... Harry Harper
Kathleen Harrison .... Annie
COMEDY Dentist poses as aunt to thwart
French vamp's plot to stop son's marriage.

10158
THE DOMINANT SEX (74) (A)
BIP(ABPC)
P: Walter C. Mycroft
D: Herbert Brenon
S: (PLAY) Michael Egan
SC: Vina de Vesci, John Fernald
Phillips Holmes .... Nick Shale
Diana Churchill .... Angela Shale
Romney Brent .... Joe Clayton
Carol Goodner .... Gwen Clayton
Billy Milton .... Alec Winstone
Hugh Miller .... Philip Carson
Kathleen Kelly .... Mary
Olga Edwardes .... Lucy Webster
Charles Paton .... Mr Webster
COMEDY Inventive farmer's wife strives
for equality while her friend almost loses her
husband.

10159
THE MILL ON THE FLOSS (94) (A)
Morgan (NPFD) reissue: 1948 (1631 ft cut)
P: John Clein
D: Tim Whelan
S: (NOVEL) George Eliot
SC: John Drinkwater, Garnett Weston,
Austin Melford, Tim Whelan
Frank Lawton .... Philip Wakem
Victoria Hopper .... Lucy Deane
Fay Compton .... Mrs Tulliver
Geraldine Fitzgerald ..... Maggie Tulliver
Griffith Jones .... Stephen Guest
Mary Clare .... Mrs Moss
James Mason .... Stephen Tulliver
Athene Seyler .... Mrs Pullet
Sam Livesey .... Mr Tulliver
Amy Veness .... Mrs Deane
Felix Aylmer .... Mr Wakem
Eliot Makeham .... Mr Pullet
William Devlin .... Bob Jakin
Ivor Barnard .... Mr Moss
David Horne .... Mr Deane
O.B.Clarence .... Mr Gore
Cecil Ramage .... Luke
DRAMA Lincoln, 19th C. Feud between mill
owners and lawyer's family ends when
married children drown.

10160
LOVE FROM A STRANGER (90) (A)
Trafalgar (UA)
P: Max Schach
D: Rowland V.Lee
S: (PLAY) Frank Vosper
(NOVEL) Agatha Christie
SC: Frances Marion
Ann Harding .... Carol Howard
Basil Rathbone.......... Gerald Lovell
Binnie Hale .... Kate Meadows
Bruce Seton .... Ronald Bruce
Jean Cadell .... Aunt Lou
Bryan Powley .... Dr Gribble

Joan Hickson .... Emmy
Donald Calthrop .... Hobson
CRIME Lottery winner realises she has
married wife-killing maniac.

10161
LANDSLIDE (67) (A)
Crusade (Par)
P: Victor M. Greene
D:S: Donovan Pedelty
Jimmy Hanley .... Jimmy Haddon
Dinah Sheridan .... Dinah Shaw
Jimmy Mageean .... Harry McGovern
Ann Cavanagh .... Lena Petrie
Elizabeth Inglis .... Vera Grant
Bruno Barnabe .... Bob White
David Arnold .... Sgt Lewellyn
CRIME Wales. Sgt investigates death of
cashier when landslide traps actors in theatre.

10162
FIRE OVER ENGLAND (92) (U)
Pendennis (UA) reissue: 1949 (Adelphi)
P: Erich Pommer
D: William K. Howard
S: (NOVEL) A.E.W.Mason
SC: Clemence Dane, Sergei Nolbandov
Laurence Olivier .... Michael Ingolby
Flora Robson .... Queen Elizabeth
Leslie Banks .... Earl of Leicester
Raymond Massey .... Philip of Spain
Vivien Leigh .... Cynthia
Tamara Desni .... Elena
Morton Selten .... Burleigh
Lyn Harding .... Sir Richard
George Thirlwell .... Gregory
Henry Oscar .... Ambassador
Robert Rendel .... Don Miguel
Robert Newton .... Don Pedro
Donald Calthrop .... Don Escobal
Charles Carson .... Admiral Valdez
James Mason ....
HISTORY 1580. Lieutenant poses as
conspirator to uncover Spain's plans for
Armada. (Extract in THE LION HAS WINGS,
1939).

10163
STRANGE EXPERIMENT (74) (A)
Fox British
D: Albert Parker
S: (PLAY) Hubert Osborne, John Golden
(TWO WORLDS)
SC: Edward Dryhurst
Donald Gray .... James Martin
Ann Wemyss .... Joan
Mary Newcomb .... Helen Rollins
Ronald Ward .... Waring
Henri de Vries .... Prof Bauer
Alastair Sim .... Lawler
James Carew .... Dr Rollins
CRIME Chemist feigns amnesia to catch
gang who forced him to help in robbery.

10164
CAFE COLETTE (71) (A) USA: DANGER
IN PARIS
Garrick (ABFD)
P: W. Devenport Hackney
D: Paul Stein
S: (RADIO SERIES) Walford Hyden,
Eric Maschwitz
SC: Eric Maschwitz, Val Gielgud, Val
Valentine, Katherine Struely
Paul Cavanagh .... Ryan
Greta Nissen .... Vanda Muroff
Walford Hyden .... Himself
Sally Gray .... Jill Manning
Bruce Seton .... Roger Manning
Donald Calthrop .... Nick
Dino Galvani .... Josef

Paul Blake . . . . Ethelred Burke
Fred Duprez . . . . Burnes
Cecil Ramage . . . . Petrov
C.Denier Warren . . . . Compere
D.A.Clarke-Smith . . . .
Charles Carson . . . .
Olive Sloane . . . .
Cafe Colette Orchestra; Tzigansky Choir;
Ronnie Boyer; Cleo Nordi
MUSICAL Paris. Russian spy poses as
singer to steal formula of new explosive.

10165
TAKE A CHANCE (73) (A)
Grosvenor (ABFD)
P: Harcourt Templeman
D: Sinclair Hill
S: (PLAY) Walter Hackett
SC: D.B. Wyndham-Lewis, G.H.Moresby-White
Claude Hulbert . . . . Alastair Pallivant
Binnie Hale . . . . Wilhelmina Ryde
Henry Kendall . . . . Archie Burton
Enid Stamp-Taylor . . . . Cicely Burton
Gwen Farrar . . . . Lady Meriton
Jack Barty . . . . Joe Cooper
Harry Tate . . . . Sgt Tugday
Guy Middleton . . . . Richard Carfax
Kynaston Reeves . . . . Blinkers Grayson
COMEDY Racing tipster discovers horse
owner's wife leaking information.

10166
CROSS MY HEART (65) (A)
B & D-Paramount British
reissue: 194-, LOADED DICE
P: Anthony Havelock-Allan
D: Bernerd Mainwaring
S: Robert Skinner
SC: Basil N. Keyes
Kathleen Gibson . . . . Sally Nichols
Kenneth Duncan . . . . Steve King
Tully Comber . . . . Chesty Barlow
Aubrey Fitzgerald . . . . The Major
Robert Field . . . . Mabardi
Muriel Johnston . . . . Miss Bly
Eric Hales . . . . Mr Bland
Sylvia Coleridge . . . . Alice
ROMANCE Girl turns boarding house
into nightclub and is loved by musician and
gambler.

10167
WAKE UP FAMOUS (68) (U)
Premier-Stafford (Radio)
P: John Stafford
D: Gene Gerrard
S: Basil Mason
Nelson Keys . . . . Alfred Dimbleden
Gene Gerrard . . . . Fink
Bela Mila . . . . Agatha Dimbleden
Josephine Huntley Wright . . Daisy
Fred Conyngham . . . . Jack
H.F.Maltby . . . . Sir Weatherby Watts
MUSICAL Cannes. Hotel clerk framed for
jewel theft mistaken for song writer by
film producer.

10168
WINDMILL REVELS (47) (A)
Ace Films
P: Frank Green
D: R.A.Hopwood
Meggie Eaton . . . . Edna Wood
Paddy Browne . . . . Gus Chevalier
Warden & West . . . . Kenneth More
REVUE Windmill Theatre production:
sketches, dances, juggling, contortionist.

10169
O.H.M.S. (86) (U) USA: YOU'RE IN THE
ARMY NOW

Gaumont *reissue*: 1942 (Ren; 1000 ft cut)
AP: Geoffrey Barkas
D: Raoul Walsh
S: Lesser Samuels, Ralph Gilbert Bettinson
SC: Bryan Edgar Wallace, Austin Melford,
A.R.Rawlinson
Wallace Ford . . . . Jim Tracey
John Mills . . . . Bert Dawson
Anna Lee . . . . Sally Bridges
Grace Bradley . . . . Jean Burdett
Frank Cellier . . . . Sgt Briggs
Frederick Leister . . . . Vice Consul
Lawrence Anderson . . . . . Trader
Athol Fleming . . . . Schoolmaster
Peter Evan Thomas . . . . . . General
Cyril Smith . . . . Steward
Arnold Bell . . . . Matthews
Peter Croft . . . . Student
Arthur Chesney . . . . Sugar Daddy
Leslie Roberts . . . . Dance Instructor
WAR China. American gangster joins British
army to escape justice and dies a hero.

10170
THUNDER IN THE CITY (88) (A)
Atlantic (UA) *reissue*: 1948 (Stahl)
P: Alexander Esway, Akos Tolnay
D: Marion Gerling
S: Robert E. Sherwood
SC: Akos Tolnay, Aben Kandel,
Walter Hackett
Edward G. Robinson . . . . . Dan Armstrong
Luli Deste . . . . Lady Patricia
Nigel Bruce . . . . Duke of Glenavon
Constance Collier . . . . . Duchess of Glenavon
Arthur Wontner . . . . . . Sir Peter Challoner
Ralph Richardson . . . Henry Manningdale
Nancy Burne . . . . Edna
Annie Esmond . . . . Lady Challoner
Elizabeth Inglis . . . . Dolly Challoner
Cyril Raymond . . . . James Challoner
James Carew . . . . Snyderling
Everley Gregg . . . . Millie
COMEDY American publicist helps
penniless duke float company to promote
'magnelite.'

FEB

10171
GOOD MORNING, BOYS (79) (A)
USA: WHERE THERE'S A WILL
Gainsborough (Gaumont)
reissue: 1948 (ABFD)
P: Edward Black
D: Marcel Varnel
S: Anthony Kimmins
SC: Marriott Edgar, Val Guest
Will Hay . . . . Dr Benjamin Twist
Graham Moffatt . . . . Albert
Lilli Palmer . . . . Yvette
Mark Daly . . . . Arty Jones
Peter Gawthorne. . Col Willoughby-Gore
Martita Hunt . . . . Lady Bagshot
Charles Hawtrey . . . . Septimus
Will Hay jr. . . . . Clarence
Basil McGrail . . . . Watson
Peter Godfrey . . . . Cliquot
Fewlass Llewellyn . . . . Dean
C.Denier Warren . . . . Henri Duval
COMEDY Schoolmaster and pupils visit Paris
and save Mona Lisa from thieves. (Top
moneymaker: 1937).

10172
DARK JOURNEY (77) (U)
London-Victor Saville Productions (UA)
reissues: 1943 (Anglo) 1953,
THE ANXIOUS YEARS (G&S)
P: Alexander Korda
D: Victor Saville
S: Lajos Biro

SC: Arthur Wimperis
Conrad Veidt . . . . Baron Karl von Marwitz
Vivien Leigh . . . . Madeleine Goddard
Joan Gardner . . . . Lupita
Anthony Bushell . . . . Bob Carter
Ursula Jeans . . . . Gertrude
Margery Pickard . . . . Colette
Eliot Makeham . . . . Anatole
Austin Trevor . . . . Dr Muller
Sam Livesey . . . . Maj Schaffer
Cecil Parker . . . . Captain
Edmund Willard . . . . . . German Intelligence
Charles Carson . . . . Fifth Bureau
Henry Oscar . . . . Magistrate
Reginald Tate . . . . Mate
Robert Newton . . . . Officer
William Dewhurst . . . . Killer
WAR Stockholm, 1915. French spy posing
as traitor loves German spy.

10173
ELEPHANT BOY (80) (U)
London (UA) *reissues*: 1943 (Anglo)
1946 (BL)
P: Alexander Korda
D: Robert Flaherty, Zoltan Korda
S: (NOVEL) Rudyard Kipling
(TOOMAI OF THE ELEPHANTS)
SC: John Collier, Akos Tolnay, Marcia de Sylva
Sabu . . . . Toomai
Walter Hudd . . . . Petersen
Allan Jeayes . . . . Machua Appa
W.E.Holloway . . . . Father
Bruce Gordon . . . . Ram Lal
D.J. Williams . . . . Hunter
Wilfrid Hyde White . . . . . . Commissioner
ADVENTURE India. Boy leads Government
hunters to dancing ground of migrating
elephants.

10174
THE INSPECTOR (34) (U)
Ace Films (WB)
D:S: Widgey Newman
Stan Paskin . . . . Inspector
Roma Beaumont . . . . Girl
Wally Patch
COMEDY Uplift society's investigator
enjoys himself at holiday camp.

10175
CARRY ON LONDON (46) (A)
Ace Films
P: Frank Green
D: D.R.Frazer
Lucy Loupe . . . . Warden & West
Paddy Browne . . . . Meggie Eaton
Gus Chevalier . . . . Eric Barker
Leslie Spurling . . . . Kenneth More
Windmill Theatre "Revuedeville" production.
REVUE

10176
WINGS OF THE MORNING (85) *tech* (U)
New World (20) *reissue*: 1945
P: Robert T. Kane
D: Harold Schuster
S: (STORY) Donn Byrne
(THE TALE OF A GYPSY HORSE)
SC: Tom Geraghty, John Meehan, Brinsley
Macnamara
Annabella . . . . Maria
Henry Fonda . . . . Kerry Gilfallen
Leslie Banks . . . . Earl of Clontarf
Stewart Rome . . . . Valentine
Harry Tate . . . . Paddy
Irene Vanbrugh . . . . Marie
Helen Haye . . . . Jenepher
Edward Underdown . . . . . Don Diego
Mark Daly . . . . Jimmy
Sam Livesey . . . . Angelo

John McCormack; Steve Donoghue;
Hermione Darnborough; Emmanuelo;
E.V.H.Emmett
SPORT Ireland. Spanish gipsy posing as boy
loves Earl's Canadian nephew. (First British
feature in Technicolor).

10177
THE BLACK TULIP (57) (A)
Fox British
D: Alex Bryce
S: (NOVEL) Alexandre Dumas
(LA TULIPE NOIRE)

Patrick Waddington . . .	Cornelius
Ann Soreen	Rosa
Campbell Gullan	Boxtel
Jay Laurier	Gryphus
Wilson Coleman	Cornelius de Witte
Bernard Lee	William of Orange
Florence Hunt	Julia Boxtel
Ronald Shiner	Hendrik
Aubrey Mallalieu	Col Marnix

ADVENTURE Holland, period. Merchant
frames cultivator to obtain secret of
black tulips.

10178
DOUBLE ALIBI (40) (A)
Fox British reissue: 1941
P: Edward Dryhurst
D: David Macdonald
S: Harold Weston
SC: Edward Dryhurst, Laurie Webb

Ernest Sefton	Crayshaw
John Warwick	Charlie
Paul Neville	Dawkin
Linden Travers	Rita
Mavis Villiers	Miss Grant
Margaret Scudamore	Mrs Havilland
Charles Eaton	Davidson
Eric Hales	Chauffeur

CRIME Factory robber's alibi ruined by
rival's girlfriend.

10179
SPLINTERS IN THE AIR (71) (U)
Wilcox (GFD)
P: Herbert Wilcox
D: Alfred Goulding
S: K.R.G.Browne, Ralph Reader
SC: R.P.Weston, Bert Lee, Jack Marks

Sydney Howard . .	George/Sydney Metcalfe
Richard Hearne	Sgt Hearne
Stuart Robertson	Sgt Robertson
Ralph Reader	Sgt Reader
Ellen Pollock	CO's Wife
D.A.Clarke-Smith	WO
Franklyn Bellamy	CO
Ronald Ward	Richards
Binkie Stuart	Mary
Lew Lake	Stage-manager

COMEDY Helicoptor inventor takes
twin's place in RAF and saves CO's wife
from cad.

10180
LONDON MELODY (75) (A)
USA: GIRLS IN THE STREET
Wilcox (GFD)
P:D: Herbert Wilcox
S: Ray Lewis
SC: Florence Tranter, Monckton Hoffe

Anna Neagle	Jacqueline
Tullio Carminati	Marius Andreani
Robert Douglas	Nigel Taplow
Horace Hodges	Father Donnelly
Grizelda Hervey	Friend
Miki Hood	Friend
Davina Craig	Maid
Joan Kemp-Welch	Maid

Arthur Chesney	Butler

MUSICAL Diplomat thinks dancer prefers
his friend, so he takes the blame for friend's
error.

10181
AULD LANG SYNE (72) (A)
Fitzpatrick Pictures (MGM)
P:D: James A. Fitzpatrick
S: W.K. Williamson

Andrew Cruickshank	Robert Burns
Christine Adrian	Jean Armour
Richard Ross	Gavin Hamilton
Marian Spencer	Clarinda
Malcolm Graham	Gilbert Burns
Doris Palette	Highland Mary
Jenny Laird	Alison Begbie

HISTORY Scotland, 1780. Life and loves
of ploughboy poet.

10182
IT'S A GRAND OLD WORLD (71) (U)
Tom Arnold (BL) reissue: 1947 (Ren)
D: Herbert Smith
S: Tom Arnold, Sandy Powell

Sandy Powell	Sandy
Gina Malo	Joan
Cyril Ritchard	Brian
Frank Pettingell	Bull
Garry Marsh	Stage-manager
Ralph Truman	Banks
Fewlass Llewellyn.	Father
John Turnbull	Auctioneer

COMEDY Workshy man wins football
pool and helps actress save her home.

10183
THE ELDER BROTHER (67) (A)
Triangle (Par)
P: George King
D: Frederick Hayward
S: (NOVEL) Anthony Gibbs
SC: Dorothy Greenhill

John Stuart	Ronald Bellairs
Marjorie Taylor	Susan Woodward
Basil Langton	Hugo Bellairs
Stella Bonheur	Lady Hobbs
Hilary Pritchard	Sir Frederick Hobbs
Claude Horton	Doctor

DRAMA Affianced man takes blame for
brother's affair with married woman, who
is murdered.

10184
STARLIGHT PARADE (38) (U)
Viking Films
P:D: Eric Humphris

Norman Long	Veronica
Teddy Brown	Metaxa Girls

REVUE

10185
BEAUTY AND THE BARGE (71) (U)
Twickenham (Wardour)
P: Julius Hagen
D: Henry Edwards
S: (PLAY) W.W.Jacobs
SC: H Fowler Mear

Gordon Harker	Capt Barley
Judy Gunn	Ethel Smedley
Jack Hawkins	Lt Seton Boyne
George Carney	Tom Codd
Margaret Rutherford	Mrs Baldwin
Ronald Shiner	Augustus
Michael Shepley	Herbert Manners
Margaret Yarde	Mrs Porton
Sebastian Smith	Maj Smedley
Margaret Scudamore	Mrs Smedley
Anne Wemys	Lucy Dallas

COMEDY Bargee adopts major's runaway
daughter who falls for lieut posing as mate.

10186
UNDERNEATH THE ARCHES (71) (U)
Twickenham (Wardour)
reissue: 1948 (19 mins cut)
P: Julius Hagen
D: Redd Davis
S: Alison Booth
SC: H. Fowler Mear

Bud Flanagan	Bud
Chesney Allen	Ches
Stella Moya	Anna
Lyn Harding	Pedro
Enid Stamp-Taylor	Dolores
Edmund Willard	Chief Steward
Edward Ashley	Carlos
Aubrey Mather	Professor

COMEDY Stowaways stop revolutionaries
from stealing peace gas.

10187
PLEASE TEACHER (76) (U)
ABPC (Wardour)
P: Walter C. Mycroft
D:SC: Stafford Dickens
S: (PLAY) K.R.G.Browne, R.P.Weston,
Bert Lee

Bobby Howes	Tommy Deacon
Rene Ray	Ann Trent
Wylie Watson	Oswald Clutterbuck
Bertha Belmore	Agatha Pink
Vera Pearce	Petunia Trundle
Lyn Harding	Wing Foo
Aubrey Dexter	Reeves
Arthur Chesney	Round

MUSICAL Heir poses as girl's explorer
brother to find will hidden in Girls' school.

10188
HEAD OVER HEELS (81) (U)
USA: HEAD OVER HEELS IN LOVE
Gaumont
AP: S.C.Balcon
D: Sonnie Hale
S: (PLAY) Francois de Crosset
(PIERRE OU JAC)
SC: Dwight Taylor, Fred Thompson,
Marjorie Gaffney

Jessie Matthews	Jeanne
Louis Borell	Marcel
Robert Flemyng	Pierre
Helen Whitney Bourne	Norma
Romney Brent	Matty
Buddy Bradley	Instructor
Eliot Makeham	Martin
Paul Leyssac	Max
Edward Cooper	Charles
Fred Duprez	Manager

MUSICAL France. Engineer loves singer
who loves playboy who loves film star.

10189
THE GREAT BARRIER (82) (U)
USA: SILENT BARRIERS
Gaumont reissue: 1942 (Ren)
AP: Gunther Stapenhorst
D: Milton Rosmer, Geoffrey Barkas
S: (NOVEL) Alan Sullivan
(THE GREAT DIVIDE)
SC: Ralph Spence, Michael Barringer,
Milton Rosmer

Richard Arlen	Hickey
Antionette Cellier	Mary Moody
Barry Mackay	Steve
Lilli Palmer	Lou
J Farrell MacDonald . .	Hells Bells Rogers
Jock McKay	Bates
Roy Emerton	Moody
Ben Welden	Joe

ADVENTURE British Columbia. Wastrels
reform and help build Canadian Pacific
Railway.

10190
MOONLIGHT SONATA (90) (U)
Pall Mall (UA) *reissues:* 1943, THE CHARMER
(Anglo; 40 mins cut) 1946 (Eal)
P:D: Lothar Mendes
S: Hans Rameau
SC: Edward Knoblock, E.M. Delafield
Ignace Jan Paderewski . . . . . Himself
Charles Farrell . . . . Eric Molnar
Marie Tempest . . . . Baroness Lindenburg
Barbara Greene . . . . Ingrid
Eric Portman . . . . Mario de la Costa
Graham Browne . . . . Dr Bowman
Queenie Leonard . . . . Margit
Lawrence Hanray . . . . Bishop
Binkie Stuart . . . . Child
Bryan Powley . . . . Nils
MUSICAL Sweden. Pianist's art reforms
stranded victims of plane crash.

10191
WANTED (71) (U)
Embassy (SC)
P:D: George King
S: (PLAY) Brock Williams
SC: Brock Williams
ZaSu Pitts . . . . Winnie Oatfield
Claude Dampier . . . . Henry Oatfield
Finlay Currie . . . . . . Uncle Mart
Norma Varden . . . . Mrs Smithers
Mark Daly . . . . Mr Smithers
Kathleen Harrison . . . . Belinda
Billy Holland . . . . . . Harry the Hick
Stella Bonheur . . . . Babyface
Arthur Wellesley . . . . Lord Hotbury
Mabel Twemlow . . . . Lady Hotbury
COMEDY Crooks mistake shipping clerk for
American jewel-thief.

10192
SONG OF THE ROAD (71) (U)
UK Films (SC)
P: John Barter
D: SC: John Baxter
S: Michael Kent
Bransby Williams . . . . Bill
Ernest Butcher . . . . Foreman
Muriel George . . . . Mrs Trelawney
Davy Burnaby . . . . Mr Keppel
Tod Slaughter . . . . Showman
John Turnbull . . . . Bristow
Edgar Driver . . . . Titch
Fred Schwartz . . . . Solomon
Percy Parsons . . . . Showman
Peggy Novak . . . . Wife
H.F.Maltby . . . . Proprietor
DRAMA Sussex. Mechanization causes
old labourer and horse to search for work.

10193
KATHLEEN MAVOURNEEN (77) (U)
USA: KATHLEEN
Argyle-British (Wardour)
P: John Argyle
D: Norman Lee
S: (NOVEL) Clara Mulholland
SC: Marjorie Deans, John Glen
Sally O'Neil . . . . Kathleen O'Moore
Tom Burke . . . . Mike Rooney
Sara Allgood . . . . . Mary Ellen O'Dwyer
Jack Daly . . . . Denis O'Dwyer
Talbot O'Farrell . . . . Dan Milligan
Denis O'Neil . . . . Mat Cooney
Fred Duprez . . . . Walter Bryant
Pat Noonan . . . . Sean O'Dwyer
Jeanne Stuart . . . . . . Barbara Fitzpatrick
John Forbes-Robertson . . Pat O'Moore
Lucan & McShane; Rory O'Connor;
Sean Dempsey; Frank Lee's Tara Ceilidh Band
MUSICAL Ireland. Waitress rejects rich man
for singing stevedore.

10194
THE SCAT BURGLARS (45) (A)
New Ideal (MGM)
P: Simon Rowson, Geoffrey Rowson
D: Leslie Rowson
S: Fenn Sherie, Ingram d'Abbes
Harry Haver . . . . Hank
Frank Lee . . . . Haye
Shayle Gardner . . . . The Crook
Ann Ibbitson . . . . The Child
Craigie Doon . . . .
Constance Godridge . . . . . . The Star
COMEDY Crooks persuade ideas-men
to steal star's gems for publicity.

10195
DARBY AND JOAN (75) (A)
Rock Studios (MGM)
P: Nat Ross
D: SC: Syd Courtenay
S: (NOVEL) "Rita"
Peggy Simpson . . . . Joan Templeton
Ian Fleming . . . . . . Sir Ralph Ferris
Mickey Brantford . . . . . . Yorke Ferris
Tod Slaughter . . . . Mr Templeton
Audrene Brier . . . . Connie
Pamela Bevan . . . . Darby Templeton
Ella Retford . . . . Nurse
Harvey Braban . . . . Coroner
ROMANCE Girl weds rich bart for sake
of her blind sister, then her fiance returns.

10196
THE VULTURE (67) (A)
WB-FN (FN)
D: Ralph Ince
S: Stafford Dickens
Claude Hulbert . . . . Cedric Gull
Lesley Brook . . . . Sylvia
Hal Walters . . . . Stiffy Mason
Frederick Burtwell . . . . Jenkinson
George Merritt . . . . Spicer
Arthur Hardy . . . . Li Fu
Archibald Batty . . . . McBride
George Carr . . . . Charlie Yen
COMEDY Tec poses as Chinaman to catch
jewel thieves.

MAR

10197
THE PRICE OF FOLLY (52) (A)
Welwyn (Pathe)
D: Walter Summers
S: (PLAY) John Lee-Thompson
(DOUBLE ERROR)
SC: John Lee-Thompson, Walter Summers,
Ruth Landon
Leonora Corbett . . . . Christine
Colin Keith-Johnson . . . . . Martin
Leslie Perrins . . . . Owen
Judy Kelly . . . . Frances
Andrea Malandrinos . . . . . Gomez
Wally Patch . . . .
The Trocadero Girls
CRIME Barrister kills blackmailing landlord
who faked girl's death.

10198
LUCKY JADE (69) (A)
Welwyn Studios (Par)
P: Fred Browett
D:SC: Walter Summers
S: Jane Brown
Betty Ann Davies . . . . Betsy Bunn
John Warwick . . . . John Marsden
Claire Arnold . . . . Mrs Sparsley
Syd Crossley . . . . Rickets
Derek Gorst . . . . Bob Grant
Gordon Court . . . . Ricky Rickhart
Richard Littledale . . . . Dingbat Eisan

Tony Wylde . . . . Whitebait
Boyer & Ravel
CRIME Maid poses as actress in employer's
absence and is framed for stealing jade.

10199
HOLIDAY'S END (70) (A)
B & D- Paramount British
P: Anthony Havelock-Allan
D: John Paddy Carstairs
S: Gerald Elliott
Sally Stewart . . . . Betty Sulgrave
Wally Patch . . . . Sgt Yerbury
Rosalyn Boulter . . . . Joyce Deane
Aubrey Mallalieu . . . . Bellamy
Kenneth Buckley . . . . Arthur Marsh
Henry Victor . . . . . Maj Zwanenberg
Leslie Bradley . . . . Peter Hurst
Robert Field . . . . Des Voeux
DRAMA School teacher unmasks revolutionary
attempting to kill boy king.

10200
THE CAVALIER OF THE STREETS (70) (A)
B & D-Paramount British
P: Anthony Havelock-Allan
D: Harold French
S: (STORY) Michael Arlen
SC: Ralph Neale, George Barraud
Margaret Vyner . . . . Fay Avalon
Patrick Barr . . . . The Cavalier
Carl Harbord . . . . Prince Karanov
James Craven . . . . Sir John Avalon
Laura Smithson . . . . Mrs Rudd
Renee de Vaux . . . . Lady Carnal
Peggy Chester . . . . Daphne Brook
Leo Genn . . . . Attorney-general
CRIME Blackmailer confesses to killing partner
to save barrister's accused wife.

10201
DREAMING LIPS (94) (A)
Trafalgar (UA) *reissue:* 1944 (NR; 1500 ft cut)
P: Max Schach, Paul Czinner
D: Paul Czinner, Lee Garmes
S: (PLAY) Henry Bernstein (MELO)
SC: Margaret Kennedy, Carl Mayer,
Lady Cynthia Asquith
Elizabeth Bergner . . . . Gaby Lawrence
Raymond Massey . . . . . Miguel del Vayo
Romney Brent . . . . Peter Lawrence
Joyce Bland . . . . Christine
Sydney Fairbrother . . . . . . Mrs Stanway
Felix Aylmer . . . . Sir Robert Blaker
J. Fisher White . . . . Dr Wilson
Charles Carson . . . . Impresario
Donald Calthrop . . . . Philosopher
Ronald Shiner . . . . Friend
Cyril Raymond . . . . PC
George Carney . . . . Rescuer
ROMANCE Sick violinist's neurotic wife
falls in love with friend and drowns herself.

10202
JUMP FOR GLORY (89) (A)
USA: WHEN THIEF MEETS THIEF
Criterion (UA) *reissues:* 1944 (Anglo)
1946 (Picc; 19 mins cut)
P: Douglas Fairbanks jr, Marcel Hellman
D: Raoul Walsh
S: (NOVEL) Gordon MacDonnell
SC: John Meehan jr, Harold French
Douglas Fairbanks jr . . . . . . Ricky Morgan
Valerie Hobson . . . . Glory Howard
Alan Hale . . . . Jim Dial
Edward Rigby . . . . Sanders
Barbara Everest . . . . Mrs Nolan
Jack Melford . . . . Thompson
Anthony Ireland . . . . Sir Timothy Haddon
Esme Percy . . . . Robinson
Basil Radford . . . . Defence

Leo Genn . . . . Prosecution
Ian Fleming . . . . Coroner
CRIME Burglar kills ex-partner who is wed
to his own ex-fiancee.

10203
FEATHER YOUR NEST (86) (U)
ATP (ABFD)
P: Basil Dean
D: William Beaudine
S: Ivar & Sheila Campbell
SC: Austin Melford, Robert Edmunds,
Anthony Kimmins
George Formby . . . . Willie
Polly Ward . . . . Mary Taylor
Enid Stamp-Taylor . . . . Daphne Randall
Val Rosing . . . . Rex Randall
Davy Burnaby . . . . Sir Martin
Jack Barty . . . . Mr Chester
Clifford Heatherley . . . . . . Valet
Frederick Burtwell . . . . . . Murgatroyd
Ethel Coleridge . . . . . . Mrs Taylor
Jimmy Godden . . . . Mr Higgins
Moore Marriott . . . . Mr Jenkins
Syd Crossley . . . . PC
Frank Perfitt . . . . Manager
Three Rhythm Sisters
COMEDY Record maker becomes star when
he substitutes disc of himself for broken matrix.

10204
MAYFAIR MELODY (83) (U)
WB-FN (WB)
P: Irving Asher
D: Arthur Woods
S: James Dyrenforth
Keith Falkner . . . . Mark
Joyce Kirby . . . . Brenda
Chili Bouchier . . . . Carmen
Bruce Lister . . . . Dickie
Glen Alyn . . . . Daphne
George Galleon . . . . Lord Chester
Louis Goodrich . . . . Ludborough
Ian McLean . . . . Collecchi
Vivienne Chatterton . . . . . Mme Collecchi
MUSICAL Car magnate's spoiled daughter
helps mechanic become opera star.

10205
SIDE STREET ANGEL (63) (A)
WB-FN (WB)
P: Irving Asher
D: Ralph Ince
Hugh Williams . . . . Peter
Lesley Brook . . . . Anne
Henry Kendall . . . . Boscomb
Reginald Purdell . . . . McGill
Phyllis Stanley . . . . Laura
Madeleine Seymour . . . . . Mrs Kane
Edna Davies . . . . Loretta
COMEDY Rich man poses as gem thief to
woo girl who runs reformatory.

10206
IT'S NOT CRICKET (63) (A)
WB-FN (FN)
P: Irving Asher
D: Ralph Ince
S: Henry Kendall
Claude Hulbert . . . . Willie
Henry Kendall . . . . Henry
Betty Lynne . . . . Yvonne
Sylvia Marriott . . . . Jane
Clifford Heatherley . . . Sir George Harlow
Violet Farebrother . . . . . . Lady Harlow
Frederick Burtwell . . . . . . Morton
COMEDY Affianced man tries to elope
with best friend's wife.

10207
DON'T GET ME WRONG (80) (U)
WB-FN (FN)
P: Irving Asher
D: Arthur Woods, Reginald Purdell
S: Reginald Purdell, Brock Williams,
Frank Launder
Max Miller . . . . Wellington Lincoln
George E. Stone . . . . Chuck
Olive Blakeney . . . . Frankie
Glen Alyn . . . . Christine
Clifford Heatherley . . . Sir George Baffin
Wallace Evennett . . . . Dr Rudolph Pepper
Alexander Field . . . . Gray
COMEDY Fair-ground entertainer promotes
tabloid petrol substitute invented by
mad chemist.

10208
PATRICIA GETS HER MAN (68) (A)
WB-FN (FN)
P: Irving Asher
D: Reginald Purdell
S: Max Merritt, Maurice Kusell
Hans Sonker . . . . Count Stephan d'Orlet
Lesley Brook . . . . Patricia Fitzroy
Edwin Styles . . . . Brian Maxwell
Aubrey Mallalieu . . . . Col Fitzroy
Cissy Fitzgerald . . . . . Duchess Banning
Betty Lynne . . . . Marie
Yoshihide Yanai . . . . Suki
COMEDY Girl tries to make star jealous by
hiring gigolo who is really a Count.

10209
THE WINDMILL (62) (A)
WB-FN (FN)
P: Irving Asher
D: Arthur Woods
S: (NOVEL) John Drabble
Hugh Williams . . . . Lt Peter Ellington
Glen Alyn . . . . Clodine Asticot
Henry Mollison . . . . Gaston Lefarge
Anthony Shaw . . . . Col Richardson
George Galleon . . . . Maj Arbuthnot
William Dewhurst . . . . . . M. Asticot
Winifred Oughton . . . . . . Mme Asticot
John Laurie . . . . M. Coutard
John Carol . . . . Pte Goggle
Bruce Lister . . . . Officer
WAR France, 1916. Spy blackmails
innkeeper's adopted German daughter.

10210
THE COMPULSORY WIFE (57) (A)
WB-FN (WB)
P: Irving Asher
D: Arthur Woods
S: (PLAY) John Glyder
SC: Reginald Purdell, John Dighton
Henry Kendall . . . . Rupert Sinclair
Joyce Kirby . . . . Bobby Carr
Margaret Yarde . . . . Mrs Thackery
Robert Hale . . . . Col Craven
Agnes Lauchlan . . . . Mrs Craven
George Merritt . . . . Mr Thackery
Anthony Shaw . . . . George Bittleston
Mercia Swinburne . . . . . Mrs Bittleston
COMEDY Burglar steals clothes of
couple forced to spend night together in
cottage.

10211
CALLING ALL MA'S (49) (A)
retitled: THE BITER BIT
Fox British
P: Ivor McLaren
D: Redd Davis
S: Al Booth

Billy Caryll . . . . Billy Smith
Hilda Munday . . . . Hilda Smith
Margaret Yarde . . . . Ma-in-law
Anthony Shaw . . . . Arthur Parkins
Julien Vedey . . . . Italian
Charles Castella . . . . Barman
COMEDY Henpeck's attempts to escape
nagging wife.

10212
CONCERNING MR MARTIN (59) (A)
Fox British
D: Roy Kellino
S: Ernest Dudley
Wilson Barrett . . . . Leo Martin
William Devlin . . . . Martell
Marjorie Peacock . . . . Gloria
Derek Williams . . . . Robin
Lionel Montgomery . . . . . Foo
Herbert Cameron . . . . Detective
Bdr Billy Wells . . . . Commissionaire
CRIME Gentleman thief frames club owner
who swindled girl.

10213
VARIETY HOUR (66) (A)
Fox British reissue: 1941 (18 mins cut)
D: Redd Davis
Clapham & Dwyer   Weir Brothers
Carson Robison and his Pioneers
Brian Lawrence and his Lansdowne Band
Jack Donohue   Helen Howard
Kay, Katya & Kay   Norwich Tio
Raymond Newell   Music Hall Boys
REVUE Comedians try to make good as radio
commentators.

10214
AGAINST THE TIDE (67) (U)
Fox British
P:SC: Victor M. Greene
D: Alex Bryce
Robert Cockran . . . . Jim Leigh
Cathleen Nesbitt . . . . Margaret Leigh
Linden Travers . . . . Mary Poole
Jimmy Mageean . . . . Tom Jenkins
Herbert Cameron . . . . William Poole
Neil Carlton . . . . Bert Poole
Dorothy Vernon . . . . Mrs Brewer
DRAMA Cornwall. Fisherman's widowed
mother is jealous of his fiancee.

10215
THE £5 MAN (76) (A)
Fox British
D: Albert Parker
S: David Evans
Judy Gunn . . . . Margaret Fenton
Edwin Styles . . . . Richard Fordyce
Frank Allenby . . . . Claud Fenton
Charles Bannister . . . . Eustace Grant
Esma Cannon . . . . Lucy
G.H.Mulcaster . . . . Sinclair
Paul Blake . . . . Bennett
Norman Wooland . . . . Lodge Keeper
COMEDY Framed ex-convict poses as
butler to unmask counterfeiter.

10216
MEMBER OF THE JURY (61) (A)
Fox British
D: Bernerd Mainwaring
S: (NOVEL) John Millard
SC: David Evans
Ellis Irving . . . . Walter Maitland
Marjorie Hume . . . . Mary Maitland
Franklyn Bellamy . . . . Sir John Sloane
Arnold Lucy . . . . Uncle
Roy Russell . . . . Attorney General
Aubrey Pollock . . . . Defence

W.E.Holloway .... Judge
CRIME The problem of juror whose rich
employer is on trial.

10217
CALLING ALL STARS (75) (U)
British Lion reissue: 1945 (Ren; 1329 ft cut)
P: D: Herbert Smith
Ambrose and his Orchestra
Carroll Gibbons and the Savoy Orpheans
Evelyn Dall .... Max Bacon
Sam Browne .... Larry Adler
Elisabeth Welch .... Billy Bennett
Turner Layton .... Davy Burnaby
Nicholas Bros ... Billy "Popeye" Costello
Buck & Bubbles ...... Flotsam & Jetsam
Arren & Broderick ...... Revnell & West
Leon Cortez and his Coster Pals
Eugene Pini and his Tango Band
REVUE

10218
FOR VALOUR (95) (A)
Capitol (GFD) reissues: 1942 (Pi) 1947
(Amb; cut)
P: Max Schach
D: Tom Walls
S: Ben Travers
Tom Walls¡ ...... George/Charlie Chisholm
Ralph Lynn .... Hilary/Willie Pyke
Veronica Rose .... Phyllis Chisholm
Joan Marion .... Clare Chisholm
Hubert Harben .... Mr Gallop
Henry Longhurst .... Insp Harding
Gordon James .... Fowle
Reginald Tate .... Chester
Alan Napier .... Governor
Joyce Barbour .... Barmaid
Romilly Lunge .... Stafford
COMEDY Respectable major has crooked
son while his crooked friend has respectable son.

10219
PEARLS BRING TEARS (63) (U)
GS Enterprises (Col) reissue: 1943 (Ren)
P: A. George Smith
D: Manning Haynes
S: Clifford Grey
SC: Roy Lockwood
John Stuart .... Harry Willshire
Dorothy Boyd .... Madge Hart
Eve Gray .... Pamela Vane
Mark Stone .... George Hart
Googie Withers .... Doreen
Aubrey Mallalieu .... Mr Vane
Annie Esmond .... Mrs Vane
H.F.Maltby .... Mr Duffield
Hal Walters .... Herbert
Syd Crossley .... Bankes
Isobel Scaife .... Mary
COMEDY Ex-fiance of business man's
wife and ex-convict try to recoup lost pearls.

10220
WHEN THE DEVIL WAS WELL (67) (U)
George Smith Productions (Col)
P: A. George Smith
D: Maclean Rogers
S: W. Lane Crawford
Jack Hobbs .... Jack Lawson
Vera Lennox .... Betty Painton
Eve Gray .... Ann
Gerald Rawlinson .... Bob
Annie Esmond .... Mrs Lawson
Max Adrian .... David
Aubrey Mallalieu .... Banks
Bryan Powley .... Col Piper
COMEDY Ambitious mother tries to make
her son marry heiress.

10221
IT'S NEVER TOO LATE TO MEND (67) (A)
George King (MGM) reissue: 1942 (Amb)
D: David Macdonald
S: (PLAY) Charles Reade, Arthur Shirley
SC: H.F.Maltby
Tod Slaughter .... Squire Meadows
Marjorie Taylor .... Susan Merton
Jack Livesey .... Tom Robinson
Ian Colin .... George Fielding
Lawrence Hanray .... Lawyer Crawley
D.J.Williams .... Farmer Merton
Roy Russell .... Rev Eden
Johnny Singer .... Joseph
CRIME 1860. JP schemes to wed farmer's
daughter by jailing her fiance.

10222
THE HOUSE OF SILENCE (43) (A)
George King (MGM)
D: R.K. Neilson-Baxter
S: Paul White
Tom Helmore .... Jack Ramsden
Terence de Marney ...... Him Hallam
Jenny Laird .... Joan Hallam
Roddy Hughes .... Photographer
D.J. Williams .... Landlord
Dorothy Vernon .... Landlady
Isobel Scaife .... Barmaid
Howard Douglas .... Smuggler
CRIME Cornwall. Reporter unmasks
innkeeper as chief smuggler.

10223
OVERCOAT SAM (43) (A)
UK Films (MGM)
P: John Barter, John Baxter
D: Wallace Orton
S: (STORY) W.J. Makin
George Mozart .... Sam
Vera Sherbourne ....
Frederick Peisley ....
Olive Sloane ....
Edwin Ellis ....
Ernest Butcher ....
Muriel Sedgwick ....
CRIME Thief steals coat containing ticket
for trunk which is believed to hold a corpse.

10224
THE ACADEMY DECIDES (49) (A)
UK Films (MGM)
P: John Barter, John Baxter
D: John Baxter
S: Stuart Jackson
Henry Oscar .... Kyke
April Vivian .... Mary
John Oxford ....
Wensley Russell ....
Boris Ranevsky ....
Frank Birch ....
Walter Tobias ....
DRAMA Orphan girl adopted by buskers tries
to kill her seducer.

10225
SCREEN STRUCK (38) (U)
UK Films (MGM)
P: John Barter, John Baxter
D: Lawrence Huntington
S: Herbert Ayres
Julian Vedey .... Al Sugarman
Diana Beaumont .... Marjorie
Richard Norris ....
John Oxford ....
Royston Taylor ....
George Turner ....
Dorothy Hogben Singers
COMEDY Film company tries to make the
best of an American production supervisor.

10226
THE LOCAL TRAIN MYSTERY (14) (U)
Anthony Baerlin (WB)
D: Anthony Baerlin
CRIME Detective invites audience to solve
mystery.

10227
BULLDOG DRUMMOND AT BAY (78) (U)
ABPC (Wardour)
P: Walter C. Mycroft
D: Norman Lee
S: (NOVEL) "Sapper" (H.C. McNeile)
SC: Patrick Kirwan, James Parrish
John Lodge .... Hugh Drummond
Dorothy Mackaill .... Doris
Victor Jory .... Gregoroff
Claud Allister .... Algy Longworth
Richard Bird .... Caldwell
Hugh Miller .... Ivan Kalinsky
Leslie Perrins .... Grayson
Brian Buchel .... Meredith
Jim Gerald .... Veight
Maire O'Neill .... Norah
Annie Esmond .... Mrs Caldwell
Frank Cochrane .... Dr Belfrus
William Dewhurst ..... Reginald Portside
Wilfrid Hyde White ...... Conrad
CRIME Foreign crooks use peace club as
front to steal wireless-controlled aeroplane.

10228
KNIGHTS FOR A DAY (69) (U)
Pearl Productions (Pathe)
reissue: 1949 (H&S)
P: Aveling Ginever
D: Norman Lee, Aveling Ginever
S: Aveling Ginever, Frank Atkinson,
Charles Bray
Nelson Keys .... Bert Wrigley
John Garrick .... Prince Nicholas
Nancy Burne .... Sally Wrigley
Frank Atkinson .... Timothy Trout
Cathleen Nesbitt .... Lady Agatha
Billy Bray .... Brandt
Fred Duprez .... Custer
Gerald Barry .... Krampf
Wyn Weaver .... Lord Croke
Percy Walsh .... Lord Southdown
3 Diamond Brothers
COMEDY Ruritania. Barber wins motor
caravan and saves Prince from revolutionaries.

10229
WEST END FROLICS (46) (U)
Ace Films
P: Frank Green
D: R.A.Hopwood
Meggie Eaton .... Eric Barker
Warden & West .... Edna Wood
Eric Woodburn .... Eddie Hooper
REVUE Windmill Theatre production.

10230
THE FROG (75) (A)
Wilcox (GFD)
P: Herbert Wilcox
D: Jack Raymond
S: (PLAY) Ian Hay (NOVEL) Edgar Wallace
(THE FELLOWSHIP OF THE FROG)
SC: Ian Hay, Gerald Elliott
Gordon Harker .... Sgt Elk
Carol Goodner .... Lola Bassano
Noah Beery .... Joshua Broad
Jack Hawkins .... Capt Gordon
Richard Ainley .... Ray Bennett
Felix Aylmer .... John Bennett
Vivian Gaye .... Stella Bennett
Esme Percy .... Philo Johnson

Cyril Smith . . . . PC Balder
Gordon McLeod . . . . Commissioner
Julien Mitchell . . . . John Maitland
CRIME Tecs unmask leader of criminals'
organisation.

APR

10231
SECRET LIVES (80) (A)
USA: I MARRIED A SPY
IFP-Phoenix (ABFD) *reissue:* 1953 (EB)
P: Hugh Perceval
D: Edmond T. Greville
S: (NOVEL) Paul de Saint-Colombe
SC: Basil Mason
Brigitte Horney . . . . Lena Schmidt
Neil Hamilton . . Lt Pierre de Montmalion
Gyles Isham . . . . Franz Abel
Ivor Barnard . . . . Baldhead
Charles Carson . . . . Henri
Raymond Lovell . . . . . . German SS Chief
Frederick Lloyd . . . . French SS Chief
Ben Field . . . . Karl Schmidt
Hay Petrie . . . . Robert Pigeon
Leslie Perrins . . . . J 14
WAR 1915. German girl, forced to spy for
France, loves French lieutenant.

10232
THE HIGH COMMAND (90) (A)
Fanfare (ABFD) *reissue:* 1945 (Ren)
P: Gordon Wong Wellesley
D: Thorold Dickinson
S: (NOVEL) Lewis Robinson
(THE GENERAL GOES TOO FAR)
SC: Katharine Strueby, Walter Meade,
Val Valentine
Lionel Atwill . . . . Sir John Savage VC
Lucie Mannheim . . . . Diana Cloam
Steven Geray . . . . Martin Cloam
James Mason . . . . Heverell
Allan Jeayes . . . . Governor
Wally Patch . . . . Crawford
Kathleen Gibson . . . . Belinda
Henry Hewitt . . . . Defence
Leslie Perrins . . . . Carson
Michael Lambart . . . . Lorne
CRIME Africa. General traps blackmailer's
murderer to save daughter from scandal.

10233
THE SHOW GOES ON (93) (U)
ATP (ABFD) *reissue:* 1943 (EB; 232 ft cut)
P:D:S: Basil Dean
SC: Austin Melford, Anthony Kimmins,
E.G. Valentine
Gracie Fields . . . . Sally Scowcroft
Owen Nares . . . . Martin Fraser
John Stuart . . . . Mack
Horace Hodges . . . . Sam Bishop
Edward Rigby . . . . Mr Scowcroft
Amy Veness . . . . Mrs Scowcroft
Arthur Sinclair . . . . Mike O'Hara
Cyril Ritchard . . . . Jimmy
Jack Hobbs . . . . Nicholson
Dennis Arundell . . . . Felix Flack
Billy Merson . . . . Manager
Frederick Leister . . . . O.B.Dalton
Patrick Barr . . . . Designer
Nina Vanna . . . . Maniana
Olsen's Sea Lions
MUSICAL Consumptive composer helps
millgirl become star singer.

10234
MR STRINGFELLOW SAYS NO (76) (U)
Incorporated Talking Films (NPFD)
reissue: 1948, ACCIDENTAL SPY

P: Brandon Fleming, Reginald Gottwaltz
D: Randall Faye
S: Brandon Fleming, Randall Faye
Neil Hamilton . . . . . Jeremy Stringfellow
Claude Dampier . . . . Mr Piper
Muriel Aked . . . . Mrs Piper
Kathleen Gibson . . . . Miss Piper
Marcelle Rogez . . . . Marta
Franklin Dyall . . . . Count Hokana
Peter Gawthorne . . . . Prime Minister
COMEDY Government and spies believe
Church Lads Brigade leader possesses
important secret.

10235
WIFE OF GENERAL LING (72) (A)
Premier-Stafford (Radio)
P: John Stafford
D: Ladislas Vajda
S: Peter Cheyney, Dorothy Hope
SC: Akos Tolnay, Reginald Long
Griffith Jones . . . . John Fenton
Valery Inkijinoff . . . . Gen Ling
Adrianne Renn . . . . Tai
Alan Napier . . . . Governor
Anthony Eustrel . . . . See Long
Gibson Gowland . . . . Mike
Jino Soneya . . . . Yuan
Hugh McDermott . . . . Tracy
Gabrielle Brune . . . . Germaine
ADVENTURE China. Merchant's white
wife helps British agent unmask him as
head of bandit gang.

10236
FAREWELL TO CINDERELLA (64) (U)
GS Enterprises (Radio)
P: A. George Smith
D: Maclean Rogers
S: Arthur Richardson
SC: Kathleen Butler, Maclean Rogers,
H.F.Maltby
Anne Pichon . . . . Margaret
John Robinson . . . . Stephen Morley
Arthur Rees . . . . Betty Temperley
Glennis Lorimer . . . . . . Betty Temperley
Sebastian Smith . . . . Andy Weir
Ivor Barnard . . . . Mr Temperley
Margaret Damer . . . . Mrs Temperley
Ena Grossmith . . . . Emily
ROMANCE Australian uncle helps family
drudge win artist.

10237
THE STREET SINGER (86) (U)
British National (ABPC)
P: Dora Nirva
D: Jean de Marguenat
S: Paul Schiller, Jean de Marguenat
SC: Reginald Arkell
Arthur Tracy . . . . Richard King
Arthur Riscoe . . . . Sam Green
Margaret Lockwood. . . . . . Jenny Green
Hugh Wakefield . . . . Hugh Newman
Emil Boreo . . . . Luigi
Ellen Pollock . . . . Gloria Weston
Wally Patch . . . . PC
Ian MacLean . . . . Inspector
John Deverell . . . . James
Rawicz & Landauer; Car Hyson Dancers;
Lew Stone and his Band
MUSICAL Tenor posing as busker loves
ward of ex-Music Hall star.

10238
SHIP'S CONCERT (44) (U)
WB-FN (WB)
P: Irving Asher
D: Leslie Hiscott

S: Reginald Purdell, John Dighton
Claude Hulbert . . . . Claude Stork
Joyce Kirby . . . . Joyce
Henry Kendall . . . . Harry Bolton
Enid Trevor . . . . Enid Stork
Jack Donahue . . . . Jack
Jackie Heller . . . . Dickie
Glen Alyn . . . . Plasta Seene
Bruce Lister . . . . Purser
Reginald Purdell . . . . Reggie
George Galleon . . . . Wireless Officer
Gibson Gowland . . . . Purser
Patricia Burke . . . . Geraldine Jackson
Albert le Fre . . . . Privett
MUSICAL Luxury cruise passengers put
on show to aid stowaway actors.

10239
THE PERFECT CRIME (69) (A)
WB-FN (WB)
P: Irving Asher
D: Ralph Ince
S: Basil Woon
Hugh Williams . . . . Charles Brown
Glen Alyn . . . . Sylvia Burton
Ralph Ince . . . . Jim Lanahan
Iris Hoey . . . . Mrs Pennypacker
Philip Ray . . . . Newbold
James Stephenson . . . . . . Parker
Wilfrid Caithness . . . . Rawhouse
John Carol . . . . Snodgrass
CRIME Clerk is framed for murder after he
fakes his own suicide and robs office.

10240
THE GANG SHOW (69) (U)
Wilcox (GFD)
P: Herbert Wilcox
D: Alfred Goulding
S: Ralph Reader
SC: Marjorie Gaffney
Ralph Reader . . . . Skipper
Gina Malo . . . . Marie
Stuart Robertson . . . . Raydon
Richard Ainley . . . . : . . . . Whipple
Leonard Snelling . . . . Len
Syd Palmer . . . . Syd
Roy Emerton . . . . Proprietor
Percy Walsh . . . . McCullough
MUSICAL Manager's secretary helps
scoutmaster put on boy scout show.

10241
OUR FIGHTING NAVY (75) (U)
USA: TORPEDOED !
Wilcox (GFD)
P: Herbert Wilcox
D: Norman Walker
S: "Bartimeus", Guy Pollock, H.T.Bishop
SC: Gerald Elliott, Harrison Owens
H.B.Warner . . . . Mr Brent
Richard Cromwell . . . . Bill Armstrong
Robert Douglas . . . . Capt Markham
Noah Beery . . . . The President
Hazel Terry . . . . Pamela Brent
Esme Percy . . . . Da Costa
Richard Ainley . . . . Lieut
Henry Victor . . . . Enricquo
Frederick Culley . . . . Admiral
Binkie Stuart . . . . Jennifer
Julie Suedo . . . . Juanita
ADVENTURE South America. British Captain
uses smoke-screen to save Consul's daughter
from revolutionary's battleship.

10242
ROSE OF TRALEE (80) (U)
Butcher *reissue:* 1940 (NR; 24 mins cut)
P: Norman Hope-Bell
D: SC: Oswald Mitchell

S: Oswald Mitchell, Ian Walker,
Kathleen Tyrone

Binkie Stuart	Rose O'Malley
Fred Conyngham	Paddy O'Malley
Kathleen O'Regan	Mary O'Malley
Sydney Fairbrother	Mrs Thompson
Talbot O'Farrell	Tim Kelly
Patrick Ludlow	Frank
Dorothy Dare	Jean Hale
Danny Malone	Singer
C.Denier Warren	Henry Collett
Scott Harold	Gleeson

MUSICAL Irish singer returns from
America to seek wife and child.

10243
UPTOWN REVUE (45) (U)
Ace Films
P: Frank Green
D: R.A.Hopwood

Meggie Eaton	Gus Chevalier
Warden & West	Edna Wood
Eddie Kelland	Keith Wilbur

REVUE Windmill Theatre production.

10244
MUSEUM MYSTERY (69) (U)
B &D- Paramount British
P: Anthony Havelock-Allan
D: Clifford Gulliver
S: Gerald Elliott

Jock McKay	Jock
Elizabeth Inglis	Ruth Carter
Gerald Case	Peter Redding
Tony Wylde	Mr Varleigh
Charles Paton	Clutters
Alfred Wellesley	Mayor
Sebastian Smith	Dr Trapnell
Roy Byford	Prof Wickstead

CRIME Student and curator's daughter
save Burmese idol from crooks.

10245
BEHIND YOUR BACK (70) (A)
Crusade (Par)
P: Victor M. Greene
D: SC: Donovan Pedelty
S: (PLAY) Charles Landstone

Jack Livesey	Archie Bentley
Dinah Sheridan	Kitty Hugon
Elizabeth Astell	Gwen Bingham
Stella Bonheur	Lady Millicent Coombe
Desmond Marshall	Leslie Woodford
Rani Waller	Mary Woodford
Kenneth Buckley	Albert Clifford
Toni Edgar Bruce	Clara Bradley
Raymond Lovell	Adam Adams
Jimmy Mageean . . .	Man from the Stalls

DRAMA Authoress solves actors' problems
during first night of her play.

10246
THE GAP (38) (A)
GB Instructional (GFD)
D: Donald Carter

G.H.Mulcaster	Air Vice Marshal
Patric Curwen	Major General
Carleton Hobbs	Cabinet Minister
Jack Vyvyan	Butcher
Charles Denville	Baker
Norman Wooland	Candlestick Maker
Foster Carlin	Apothecary

WAR What may happen in the event of
an air raid on London.

10247
OKAY FOR SOUND (85) (A)
Gainsborough (GFD) *reissue:* 1942 (Ren)
P: Edward Black
D: Marcel Varnel

S: (SHOW)
SC: Marriott Edgar, Val Guest
Bud Flanagan & Chesney Allen
Jimmy Nervo & Teddy Knox
Charlie Naughton & Jimmy Gold

Fred Duprez	Hyman Goldberger
Enid Stamp-Taylor	Jill Smith
Graham Moffatt	Albert
Meinhart Maur	Guggenheimer
H.F.Maltby	John Rigby

Lucienne & Ashour; Patricia Bowman;
Radio Three; The Robenis; Peter Dawson;
Sherman Fisher Girls; Jan Gotch & Louis
Pergantes
COMEDY Workshy brothers mistaken for
financiers and put in charge of film studio.

10248
GLAMOROUS NIGHT (81) (U)
ABPC
P: Walter C. Mycroft
D: Brian Desmond Hurst
S: (PLAY) Ivor Novello
SC: Dudley Leslie, Hugh Brooke,
William Freshman

Mary Ellis	Melitza Hjos
Otto Kruger	King Stefan
Victor Jory	Baron Lyadeff
Barry Mackay	Anthony Allan
Trefor Jones	Lorenti
Maire O'Neill	Phoebe
Antony Holles	Maestro
Charles Carson	Otto
Felix Aylmer	Diplomat
Finlay Currie	Angus Mackintosh

MUSICAL Ruritania. Opera singer leads
gipsy people to save beloved king from his
prime minister.

MAY

10249
SONG OF THE FORGE (82) (U)
Butcher *reissue:* 1939
THE VILLAGE BLACKSMITH (25 mins cut)
P: Wilfred Noy, Norman Hope-Bell
D: Henry Edwards
S: J.D.Lewin
SC: H. Fowler Mear

Stanley Holloway	Joe/Sir William Barrett
Lawrence Grossmith	Ben Dalton
Eleanor Fayre	Sylvia Brent
Davy Burnaby	Auctioneer
C.Denier Warren	Farmer George
Arthur Chesney	Huckleberry
Aubrey Fitzgerald	Oldest Inhabitant
Hal Walters	Sam Tucker
Charles Hayes	Mayor
Ian Wilson	Albert Meek
Hay Plumb	Assistant
Bruce Gordon	Ted Salter

Rodney Hudson Dancing Girls
MUSICAL 1906-1927. Village blacksmith
offended when progressive son enters
car business. (Extracts in HIGHLIGHTS
OF VARIETY No.23).

10250
THE VICAR OF BRAY (68) (U)
JH Productions (ABPC)
P: Julius Hagen
D: Henry Edwards
S: Anson Dyer
SC: H. Fowler Mear

Stanley Holloway	The Vicar
Margaret Vines	Lady Nora Brendon
Esmond Knight	Dennis Melross
Eve Gray	Meg Clancy
Felix Aylmer	Earl of Brendon
Hugh Miller	Charles I

Garry Marsh	Sir Richard Melross
Martin Walker	Sir Patrick Condon
George Merritt	Oliver Cromwell
K. Hamilton Price	Prince Charles Stuart
Fred O'Donovan	Tim Connor

HISTORY King's ex-tutor persuades
him to pardon a man imprisoned for treason.

10251
TAKE MY TIP (74) (U)
Gaumont (GFD *reissue:* 1942 (Ren)
D: Herbert Mason
S: Sidney Gillatt, Michael Hogan, Jack Hulbert

Jack Hulbert	Lord George Pilkington
Cicely Courtneidge . .	Lady Hattie Pilkington
Harold Huth	Buchan
Frank Cellier	Paradine
Robb Wilton	Foreman
Frank Pettingell	Willis
H.F.Maltby	Patchett
Eliot Makeham	Digworthy

MUSICAL Lord and lady catch swindler
while acting as servants in their rich
butler's hotel.

10252
THE STRANGE ADVENTURES OF MR
SMITH (71) (U)
George Smith Productions (Radio)
D: Maclean Rogers
S: H.F.Maltby, Kathleen Butler

Gus McNaughton	Will Smith
Norma Varden	Mrs Broadbent
Eve Gray	Mrs Smith
Aubrey Mallalieu	Mr Broadbent
Billy Shine	Rodney Broadbent
Hal Walters	Lobby
Isobel Scaife	Birkenstraw

COMEDY Pavement artist posing as
business man is accused of murdering
himself.

10253
FIFTY-SHILLING BOXER (74) (U)
George Smith (Radio)
D: Maclean Rogers
S: Guy Fletcher

Bruce Seton	Jack Foster
Nancy O'Neil	Moira Regan
Moore Marriott	Tim Regan
Eve Gray	Miriam Steele
Charles Oliver	Jim Pollett
Aubrey Mallalieu	Charles Day

SPORT Cockney boxer returns to ring
after failing as an actor.

10254
RETURN OF A STRANGER (69) (A)
USA: THE FACE BEHIND THE SCAR
Premier-Stafford (Radio)
Reissue: 1950 (Sun)
P: John Stafford
D: Victor Hanbury
S: (PLAY) Rudolph Lothar
SC: Akos Tolnay, Reginald Long

Griffith Jones	James Martin
Ellis Jeffreys	Lady Wall
Athole Stewart	Sir Patrick Wall
Rosalyn Boulter	Carol
Constance Godridge	Esme
Cecil Ramage	John Forbes
Sylvia Marriott	Mary
James Harcourt	Johnson
Harold Scott	Peters

CRIME Disfigured man returns from exile
to find fiancee married.

10255
SPRING HANDICAP (68) (U)
ABPC

P: Walter C. Mycroft
D: Herbert Brenon
S: (PLAY) Ernest E. Bryan (THE LAST COUPON)
SC: Elizabeth Meehan, William Freshman

Will Fyffe	Jack Clayton
Maire O'Neill	Meg Clayton
Billy Milton	Len Redpath
Aileen Marson	Barbara Clayton
Frank Pettingell	Scullion
David Burns	Amos
Hugh Miller	Selby
Beatrice Varley	Mrs Tulip

COMEDY Miner's wife stops him from wasting legacy on betting and bookmaking.

10256
FAREWELL AGAIN (85) (U)
USA: TROOPSHIP
Pendennis-London (UA)
reissues: 1942 (BL) 1944 (Anglo)
P: Erich Pommer
D: Tim Whelan
S: Wolfgang Wilhelm
SC: Clemence Dane, Patrick Kirwan

Flora Robson	Lucy Blair
Leslie Banks	Col Harry Blair
Patricia Hilliard	Ann Harrison
Sebastian Shaw	Capt Gilbert Reed
Robert Cochrane	Carlisle
Leonora Corbett	Lady Joan
Rene Ray	Elsie Wainwright
Anthony Bushell	Roddy Hammond
Robert Newton	Jim Carter
Edward Lexy	Sgt Brough
Edmund Willard	Pte Withers
Alf Goddard	Pte Bulger
Wally Patch	Sgt Maj Billings
Jerry Verno	Pte Judd
Martita Hunt	Adela Swayle
Maire O'Neill	Mrs Brough
John Laurie	Pte McAllister
Eliot Makeham	Maj Swayle
David Horne	John Carlisle

DRAMA Soldiers returning from India have home leave cut to six hours.

10257
WHEN THE POPPIES BLOOM AGAIN (44) (U)
George King (MGM)
D: David Macdonald
S: Herbert Ayres
SC: Evadne Price

John Warwick	Squire's Son
Nancy Burne	Postmistress
Jack Livesey	Labourer
Derek Gorst	
Billy Percy	

WAR 1918. Nurse loves blinded soldier suspected of being a spy.

10258
DOUBLE EXPOSURES (67) (U)
Triangle (Par) reissue: ALIBI BREAKER
P: George King
D: John Paddy Carstairs
S: Gerald Elliott

Julien Mitchell	Hector Rodman
Ruby Miller	Mrs Rodman
Basil Langton	Peter Bradfield
Mavis Clare	Jill Rodman
Brian Buchel	Geoffrey Cranswick
George Astley	George Rodman
Frank Birch	Kempton
Ivor Barnard	Mather

CRIME Sacked reporter's photograph proves manufacturer's secretary killed crooked solicitor.

10259
MERRY COMES TO TOWN (79) (U)
Embassy (SC)
P:D: George King
S: Evadne Price
SC: Brock Williams

ZaSu Pitts	Winnie Oatfield
Guy Newall	Prof John Stafford
Betty Ann Davies	Marjorie Stafford
Stella Arbenina	Mme Saroni
Bernard Clifton	Dennis Stafford
Margaret Watson	Grandmother
Basil Langton	Noel Slater
Muriel George	Cook
Tom Helmore	Peter Bell
Cecil Mannering	Horace Bell
W.T.Ellwanger	Mr Ramp
Arthur Finn	Mr Walheimer
Hermione Gingold	Ida Witherspoon

COMEDY Spinster's relatives think her small legacy is a fortune.

10260
CONCERT PARTY (45) (U)
Ace Films
D: R.A.Hopwood

Gus Chevalier	Warden & West
Eric Barker	Hal Bryan
Rabello	Dick Tubb

REVUE Windmill Theatre production.

10261
FINE FEATHERS (68) (U)
British Lion
P: Herbert Smith
D: Leslie Hiscott
S: Michael Barringer

Renee Houston	Teenie McPherson
Donald Stewart	Jim
Francis L. Sullivan	Hugo Steinway
Robb Wilton	Tim McPherson
Jack Hobbs	Felix
Marcelle Rogez	Mme Barescon
Henry Victor	Gibbons
Stella Arbenina	Elizabeth

MUSICAL Paris. Scots shopgirl poses as mistress of Ruritanian Prince.

10262
THE FATAL HOUR (66) (A)
B & D - Paramount British
P: Anthony Havelock-Allan
D: George Pearson
S: (NOVEL) Cicely Frazer-Simpson (THE CLOCK)
SC: Ralph Neale, Gerald Elliott

Edward Rigby	Cready
Moira Reed	Mary Denston
Moore Marriott	Dixon
Dick Hunter	Peter
Derek Gorst	James West
D.J.Williams	Evangelist
J.H. Lockwood	Sir George Bell
Ernest Sefton	Pat

CRIME Secret agent poses as wastrel to save uncle's anti-gas formula from spies' timebomb.

10263
HEAVILY MARRIED (35) (A)
Krackerjack Komedies (MGM)
P: Gerald Hobbs
D: Clayton Hutton
S: Will Collinson, Mai Bacon

Will Collinson	Will Peabody
Alfie Dean	Perks
Mai Bacon	La Juno
Mawby Triplets	Daughters

COMEDY Man weds circus strong-woman and finds she has triplets.

10264
STORM IN A TEACUP (87) (A)
London-Victor Saville (UA)
reissues: 1943 (Anglo) 1946 (Eal)
P: Victor Saville
D: Victor Saville, Ian Dalrymple
S: (PLAY) Bruno Frank (STURM IN WASSERGLASS); James Bridle
SC: Ian Dalrymple, Donald Bull

Vivien Leigh	Victoria Gow
Rex Harrison	Frank Burdon
Sara Allgood	Mrs Hegarty
Cecil Parker	Provost Gow
Ursula Jeans	Lisbet Skirving
Gus McNaughton	Horace Skirving
Arthur Wontner	Fiscal
Edgar K. Bruce	McKellar
Robert Hale	Lord Skerryvore
Quinton McPherson	Baillie Callender
Eliot Makeham	Sheriff
Ivor Barnard	Watkins
W.G.Fay	Cassidy

COMEDY Scotland. Reporter ruins ambitious provost after his callous treatment of widow's dog.

JUN

10265
KNIGHT WITHOUT ARMOUR (108) (A)
London (UA)
P: Alexander Korda
D: Jacques Feyder
S: (NOVEL) James Hilton (WITHOUT ARMOUR)
SC: Frances Marion, Lajos Biro, Arthur Wimperis

Marlene Dietrich	Alexandra Vladinoff
Robert Donat	Ainsley Fothergill
Irene Vanbrugh	Duchess of Zorin
Herbert Lomas	Gen Gregor Vladinoff
Austin Trevor	Count Adraxine
Basil Gill	Axelstein
John Clements	Poushkoff
Hay Petrie	Station Master
Miles Malleson	Drunken Soldier
David Tree	Alexis Maronin
Lyn Harding	Bargee
Frederick Culley	Stanfield
Lawrence Hanray	Forrester
Lisa d'Esterre	Czarina

ADVENTURE Russia. British spy saves Countess from revolutionaries.

10266
THE ANGELUS (76) (A)
Retitled: WHO KILLED FEN MARKHAM ?
St Margarets (Amb)
P: Julius Hagen
D: Thomas Bentley
S: Michael Barringer

Anthony Bushell	Brian Ware
Nancy O'Neil	June Rowland
Eve Gray	Maisie Blake
Mary Glynne	Sister Angelica
Garry Marsh	Fen Markham
Zoe Wynn	Gina Lock
Richard Cooper	Kenneth Blake
Joyce Evans	Jill Ware
Charles Carson	John Ware
Amy Veness	Mrs Grimes

CRIME Nun proves actress and fiance did not kill producer.

10267
COTTON QUEEN (80) (U)
Rock Studios (BIED) *reissue:* 1941, CRYING OUT LOUD (cut)
P: Joe Rock
D: Bernard Vorhaus
S: Syd Courtenay, Barry Peake

SC: Louis Golding, Scott Pembroke
Will Fyffe .... Bob Todcastle
Stanley Holloway .... Sam Owen
Mary Lawson .... Joan
Helen Haye .... Margaret Owen
Marcelle Rogez .... Zita de la Rue
Jimmy Hanley .... Johnny Owen
C. Denier Warren .... Joseph Cotter
Syd Courtenay .... Mayor
Gibson Gowland .... Jailer
COMEDY Lancs. Mill owner's novelist
daughter poses as worker in rival's mill.

10268
FATHER STEPS OUT (64) (U)
George Smith Productions (Radio)
D: Maclean Rogers
S: Henry Holt, Irving Leroy
SC: Kathleen Butler
George Carney .... Joe Hardcastle
Dinah Sheridan .... Helen Hardcastle
Bruce Seton .... Johnnie Miller
Vivienne Chatterton. .... Mrs Hardcastle
Basil Langton ...... Philip Fitzwilliam
Peter Gawthorne .... Mr Fitzwilliam
Zillah Bateman .... Mrs Fitzwilliam
Elizabeth Kent .... Joan
Isobel Scaife .... Alice
COMEDY Cheese manufacturer's chauffeur
saves him from society swindlers.

10269
NIGHT RIDE (70) (U)
B & D-Paramount British
P: Anthony Havelock-Allan
D: John Paddy Carstairs
S: Julien Vedey
SC: Ralph Gilbert Bettinson
Julien Vedey .... Tony Spinelli
Wally Patch .... Alf Higgins
Jimmy Hanley .... Dick Benson
Joan Ponsford .... Jean Morley
Frank Petley .... Mr Wilson
Elizabeth Kent .... Ruth Wilson
Kenneth Buckley .... Claude
Clelia Matania .... Lucia Spinelli
Moore Marriott .... Miner
DRAMA Sacked lorry drivers start up
their own business and help save trapped miners.

10270
THE MAN WHO MADE DIAMONDS (73) (A)
WB-FN (FN)
P: Irving Asher
D: Ralph Ince
S: Frank A. Richardson
SC: Michael Barringer, Anthony Hankey
Noel Madison .... Joseph
James Stephenson .... Ben
Lesley Brook .... Helen Calthrop
George Galleon .... Tony
Renee Gadd .... Marianne
Wilfrid Lawson .... Gallanie
Philip Ray .... Tompkins
J. Fisher White .... Prof Calthrop
Hector Abbas .... Nichols
CRIME Assistant kills scientist to market
his manufactured diamonds.

10271
SUNSET IN VIENNA (73) (U)
USA: SUICIDE LEGION
Wilcox (GFD)
P: Herbert Wilcox
D: Norman Walker
S: Florence Tranter
SC: Marjorie Gaffney, Harrison Owens
Tullio Carminati .... Toni
John Garrick .... Adolphe
Lilli Palmer .... Gelda

Edgar Driver .... Batman
Geraldine Hislop .... Wanda
Alice O'Day .... Maddalena
Hubert Harben .... General
MUSICAL Italy, 1914. Austrian wife leaves
Italian husband when he shoots her brother
for spying.

10272
THE PENNY POOL (85) (U)
Mancunian *reissue:* 1938 (Amb; cut)
P: John E. Blakeley
D: George Black
S: Arthur Mertz
Duggie Wakefield .... Duggie
Billy Nelson .... Billy
Tommy Fields .... Tommy Bancroft
Luanne Shaw .... Renee Harland
Charles Sewell .... Henry Bancroft
Harry Terry .... Jerry Rogers
Chuck O'Neil .... Chuck
Jack Butler .... Jack
Mascotte; Marie Louise Sisters; Macari and
his Dutch Serenaders
COMEDY Crook steals girl's winning pools
coupon (Extract in MUSIC HALL PERSON-
ALITIES Nos. 7; 8; 9; 10; 11; 12; (1939).)

10273
BIG FELLA (73) (U)
Fortune Films (BL)
P:D: James Elder Wills
S: (NOVEL) Claude McKay (BANJO)
SC: Fenn Sherie, Ingram d'Abbes
Paul Robeson .... Joe
Elisabeth Welch .... Miranda
Roy Emerton .... Spike
Marcelle Rogez .... Marietta
Eldon Grant .... Roy Oliphant
Joyce Kennedy .... Mrs Oliphant
Eric Cowley .... Mr Oliphant
James Hayter .... Chuck
MUSICAL Marseilles. Negro returns runaway
boy to his English parents.

10274
FRENCH LEAVE (86) (A)
Welwyn (Pathe) *reissue:* 1939
P: Warwick Ward
D: Norman Lee
S: (PLAY) Reginald Berkeley
SC: Vernon Clancey
Betty Lynne .... Dorothy Glennister
Edmond Breon .... Col Root
John Longden .... Lt Glennister
John Wickham .... Lt Graham
Arthur Hambling .... Cpl Sykes
Frederick Burtwell .... Nobby
Michael Morel .... Jules Marnier
Margaret Yarde .... Mme Denaux
Oliver Wakefield; The Roosters
COMEDY France, 1915. Actress poses as
landlady's French niece to be near her
officer husband.

10275
FOOTLIGHTS (44) (U)
Ace Films
P: Frank Green
D: R.A.Hopwood
Gus Chevalier .... Meggie Eaton
Edna Wood .... Warden & West
Alec Shaw .... Eric Woodburn
REVUE Windmill Theatre production.

10276
FIRST NIGHT (69) (U)
Crusade (Par)
P: Victor M. Greene
D: SC: Donovan Pedelty

S: (PLAY) Sheila Donisthorpe
Jack Livesey .... Richard Garnet
Rani Waller .... Judith Armstrong
Sunday Wilshin .... Rosalind Faber
Ernest Mainwaring .... Henry Armstrong
Margaret Damer ...... Elaine Armstrong
Ann Wilton .... Ivy
Felix Irwin .... Patterson Luke
ROMANCE Producer helps family drudge
become playwright.

JUL
10277
LET'S MAKE A NIGHT OF IT (94) (U)
ABPC
P: Walter C. Mycroft
D: Graham Cutts
S: (RADIO PLAY) Henrik N Ege
(THE SILVER SPOON)
SC: F. McGrew Willis, Hugh Brooke
Charles "Buddy" Rogers ... Jack Kent
June Clyde .... Peggy Boydell
Claire Luce .... Viola Vandere
Fred Emney .... Henry Boydell
Steve Geray ....:.. Luigi
Zelma O'Neal .... Kitty
Iris Hoey .... Laura Boydell
Jack Melford .... Count Castelli
Claud Allister .... Monty
Bertha Belmore .... PCW
Syd Walker .... PC
Oliver Wakefield .... Wedding Guest
Afrique; Brian Michie; Dan Donovan;
Irene Prador; Molly Picon; Four Franks;
Peggy & Ready; Four Aces; Josephine Bradley;
Percy Athos Follies; Jack Jackson & his Band;
Jack Harris & his Band; Sydney Lipton & his Band
Joe Loss & his Band; Eddie Carroll & his Band;
Harry Acres & his Band; Rudy Starita's
Marimba Band.
MUSICAL Nice. Man and wife do not tell
each other they own rival nightclubs.

10278
CATCH AS CATCH CAN (71) (A)
*Fox British *reissues:* 1943 (200 ft cut)
1947, ATLANTIC EPISODE (Stahl)
D: Roy Kellino
S: Alexander George
SC: Richard Llewellyn
James Mason .... Robert Leyland
Viki Dobson .... Barbara Standish
Eddie Pola .... Tony Canzari
Finlay Currie .... Al Parsons
John Warwick .... Eddie Fallon
Margaret Rutherford ..... Maggie Carberry
Paul Blake .... Cornwallis
Jimmy Mageean .... Ben
Paul Sheridan .... Fournival
Zoe Wynn .... Mrs Kendall
CRIME Girl smuggles diamond aboard
transatlantic liner and crooks try to steal it.

10279
PASSENGER TO LONDON (57) (A)
Fox British
D: Lawrence Huntington
S: David Evans
John Warwick .... Frank Drayton
Jenny Laird .... Barbara Lane
Paul Neville .... Vautel
Ivan Wilmot .... Veinberg
Aubrey Pollock .... Sir James Garfield
Victor Hagen .... Carlton
Nigel Barrie .... Sir Donald Frame
CRIME British agent saves secret documents
from spies.

10280
KING SOLOMON'S MINES (80) (U)
Gaumont (GFD) *reissue:* 1942 (Ren)
AP: Geoffrey Barkas
D: Robert Stevenson
S: (NOVEL) H. Rider Haggard
SC: Michael Hogan, Roland Pertwee,
A.R.Rawlinson, Charles Bennett, Ralph
Spence

Paul Robeson	Umbopa
Cedric Hardwicke	Allan Quartermaine
Roland Young	Cdr Good
John Loder	Henry Curtis
Anna Lee	Kathy O'Brien
Sydney Fairbrother	Gagool
Majabalo Hlubi	Kapsie
Ecce Homo Toto	Infadoos
Robert Adams	Twala
Frederick Leister	Wholesaler
Alf Goddard	Red
Arthur Sinclair	O'Brien

ADVENTURE Africa. Exiled chief helps
explorers find diamond mine.

10281
SAID O'REILLY TO MCNAB (85) (U)
USA: SEZ O'REILLY TO MCNAB
Gainsborough (GFD)
P: Edward Black
D: William Beaudine
S: Howard Irving Young
SC: Leslie Arliss, Marriott Edgar

Will Mahoney	Tim O'Reilly
Will Fyffe	Malcolm McNab
Ellis Drake	Mrs McNab
Jock McKay	Sandy McDougal
Jean Winstanley	Mary McNab
James Carney	Terry O'Reilly
Marianne Davis	Sophie
Robert Gall	Jock McNab

COMEDY Irish sharepusher and Scots
businessman promote slimming pills.

10282
TALKING FEET (79) (U)
UK Films (SC)
P: John Barter
D: John Baxter
S: Geoffrey Orme, Jack Francis
SC: H. Fowler Mear

Hazel Ascot	Hazel Barker
Jack Barty	Joe Barker
Davy Burnaby	Mr Shirley
Enid Stamp-Taylor	Sylvia Shirley
John Stuart	Dr Roger Hood
Ernest Butcher	Thomas
Edgar Driver	Titch
Muriel George	Mrs Gumley
Kenneth Kove	Lord Cedric Scattery
Robert English	Lord Langdale
Scott Sanders	Scotty McDonald
Jennie Gregson	Mrs Barker

Mark Hambourg; Billy Thorburn; Scots
Kilties Band; Dagenham Girl Pipers;
William Heughen; Corona Babes; Gordon Ray
Girls; Sonny Farrar Band; Band of the
Royal Marines; Minipiano Ensemble of
Juveniles; Variety Proteges.
MUSICAL Fishmonger's young daughter
stages a show to save a hospital.
(Extracts in short TWINKLING FINGERS
(New Realm), 8/1940).

10283
MAKE UP (70) (U) *bilingual*
Standard International (ABFD)
reissue: 1948 (EB)
P: K.C. Alexander, C.M. Origo
D: Alfred Zeisler
S: (NOVEL) Hans Passendorf (BUX)

SC: Reginald Long, Jeffrey Dell

Nils Asther	Bux
June Clyde	Joy
Judy Kelly	Marion Hutton
Kenneth Duncan	Lorenzo
Lawrence Grossmith	Sir Edward Hutton
John Turnbull	Karo
Lawrence Anderson	Goro
Norma Varden	Hostess
Jill Craigie	Tania

Chapman's Circus
DRAMA Milan. Surgeon becomes clown
and proves his ward did not kill jealous
lion-tamer.

10284
WHO'S YOUR LADY FRIEND ? (73) (A)
Dorian (ABFD)
P: Martin Sabine
D: Carol Reed
S: (PLAY) Oesterreicher & Jenbach
(DER HERR OHNE WORNUNG)
SC: Anthony Kimmins, Julius Hoest

Frances Day	Lulu
Vic Oliver	Dr Mangold
Betty Stockfeld	Mrs Mangold
Romney Brent	Fred
Margaret Lockwood	Mimi
Sarah Churchill	Maid
Marcelle Rogez	Yvonne Fatigay
Muriel George	Mrs Somers
Frederick Ranalow	The Cabby

COMEDY Vienna. Plastic surgeon mistakes
singer for rich patient.

10285
MIDNIGHT MENACE (79) (U)
USA: BOMBS OVER LONDON
Grosvenor (ABFD)
P: Harcourt Templeman
D: Sinclair Hill
S: Roger Macdougall, Alexander Mackendrick
SC: G.H. Moresby-White, D.B. Wyndham Lewis

Charles Farrell	Briant Gaunt
Fritz Kortner	Peters
Margaret Vyner	Mary Stevens
Danny Green	Socks
Wallace Evennett	Smith
Monte de Lyle	Pierre
Dino Galvani	Tony
Dennis Val Norton	Vronsky
Arthur Finn	Mac
Lawrence Hanray	Sir George
Raymond Lovell	Harris

WAR Cartoonist exposes Ruritanian
minister's plot to use wireless-controlled
airplanes to bomb London.

10286
SILVER BLAZE (70) (U)
USA: MURDER AT THE BASKERVILLES
Twickenham (ABPC)
P: Julius Hagen
D: Thomas Bentley
S: (NOVEL) A. Conan Doyle
SC: Arthur Macrae, H. Fowler Mear

Arthur Wontner	Sherlock Holmes
Lyn Harding	Prof Moriarty
Judy Gunn	Diana Baskerville
Ian Fleming	Dr Watson
Lawrence Grossmith	Sir Henry Baskerville
Arthur Macrae	Jack Trevor
Eve Gray	Mrs Straker
Martin Walker	John Straker
John Turnbull	Insp Lestrade
Robert Horton	Col Ross
Arthur Goullet	Col Sebastian Moran
Minnie Rayner	Mrs Hudson

CRIME Dartmoor. Tec proves racehorse
did not kill groom and trainer.

10287
THE EDGE OF THE WORLD (80) (A)
Rock Studios (BIED) *reissue:* 1948 (GFD)
P: Joe Rock
D:S: Michael Powell

Niall MacGinnis	Andrew Gray
Belle Chrystal	Ruth
John Laurie	Peter Manson
Finlay Currie	James Gray
Eric Berry	Bobby Manson
Kitty Kirwan	Jean Manson
Grant Sutherland	The Catechist

DRAMA Foura. Life and death on desolate
Shetland island.

10288
SING AS YOU SWING (82) (U)
Rock Studios (BIED) *reissue:* 1941,
LET THE PEOPLE LAUGH (cut)
P: Joe Rock
D: Redd Davis
S: Clifford Grey
SC: Syd Courtenay

Evelyn Dall	Cora Fane
Claude Dampier	Pomphrey Featherstone-Chaw
Luanne Meredith	Sally Bevan
Brian Lawrance	Jimmy King
Clapham & Dwyer	Four Mills Brothers
Beryl Orde	Billie Carlisle

Mantovani and his Tipicas
Nat Gonella and his Georgians
Sherman Fisher Girls
MUSICAL National radio station competes
with commercial station broadcasting
from the continent. (Extracts released as
short films SWING TEASE and THE
MUSIC BOX (New Realm), 8/1940).

10289
BOYS WILL BE GIRLS (66) (U)
Leslie Fuller (BIED)
P: Joe Rock
D: Gilbert Pratt
S: Evelyn Barrie
SC: Clifford Grey, H.F.Maltby

Leslie Fuller	Bill Jenkins
Nellie Wallace	Bertha Luff
Greta Woxholt	Roberta
Georgie Harris	Roscoe
Judy Kelly	Thelma
D.J.Williams	George Luff
Tonie Edgar Bruce	Mrs Jenkins
Constance Godridge	Ernestine
Syd Crossley	Nolan
Syd Courtenay	Bookum
Olivette	Dancer

COMEDY Heir must stop smoking and
drinking if he is to inherit fortune.

10290
UNDER THE RED ROBE (82) (U)
New World (20th) *reissues:* 1943 (Anglo)
1945 (Key) 1948 (ABFD)
P: Robert T.Kane
D: Victor Seastrom
S: (PLAY) Edward Rose (NOVEL)
Stanley Weyman
SC: Lajos Biro, Philip Lindsay, J.L.Hodgson,
Arthur Wimperis

Conrad Veidt	Gil de Berault
Annabella	Lady Marguerite
Raymond Massey	Cardinal Richelieu
Romney Brent	Marius
Sophie Stewart	Duchess Elise
F. Wyndham Goldie	Duke Edmond
Lawrence Grant	Father Joseph
Baliol Holloway	Clon
Haddon Mason	Count Rossignac
J. Fisher White	Bron Breteuil
Ben Soutten	Leval

Anthony Eustrel . . . .   Lt Brissac
Shayle Gardner . . . .   Louis
ADVENTURE France, 1630. Cardinal's
emissary falls in love with revolutionary's
sister.

10291
THE LILAC DOMINO (79) (U)
Grafton-Capitol-Cecil (UA)
P: Max Schach, Isadore Goldschmidt,
Lee Garmes
D: Fred Zelnik
S: (PLAY) Rudolf Bernauer, E.Gatti,
B. Jenbach
SC: Basil Mason, Neil Gow, R. Hutter,
Derek Neame
June Knight . . . .   Shari de Gonda
Michael Bartlett . . . .   Count Anatole
Athene Seyler . . . .   Mme Alary
Richard Dolman . . . .   Stephen
Szocke Sakall . . . .   Sandor
Fred Emney . . . .   Baron de Gonda
Jane Carr . . . .   Leonie
Morris Harvey . . . .   Janosh
Paul Blake . . . .   Andor
Joan Hickson . . . .   Maid
MUSICAL Budapest. Gambling count
falls in love with masked girl, daughter
of baron.

10292
ACTION FOR SLANDER (83) (A)
London Saville (UA)
reissues: 1944 (Anglo) 1949 (ABFD)
P: Victor Saville
D: Tim Whelan
S: (NOVEL) Mary Borden
SC: Ian Dalrymple, Miles Malleson
Clive Brook. . . . .   Maj Gordon Daviot
Ann Todd . . . .   Ann Daviot
Margaretta Scott . . . .   Josie Bradford
Arthur Margetson . . . .   Capt Bradford
Ronald Squire . . . .   Charles Cinderford
Athole Stewart . . . .   Lord Pontefract
Percy Marmont . . . .   William Cowbit
Frank Cellier . . . .   Sir Bernard Roper
Morton Selten . . . .   Judge Trotter
Gus McNaughton . . . .   Tandy
Francis L. Sullivan. . .   Sir Quinton Jessops
Antony Holles . . . .   Grant
Enid Stamp-Taylor . . . .   Jenny
Kate Cutler . . . .   Dowager
Felix Aylmer . . . . . .   Sir Eustace Cunningham
CRIME Bankrupt major brings suit against
allegation that he cheated at cards.

10293
COMMAND PERFORMANCE (19) (U)
Ajax (Exclusive)
Roy Royston
Louanne Shaw
MUSICAL

10294
FUNERAL MARCH OF A MARIONETTE
(9) (U)
British Screen Services (Winads)
P: Maurice J. Wilson
D: Widgey R. Newman
Reginald Foort . . . .   Himself
MUSICAL Organist tells how sick child
is cured by Punch and Judy show in her
bedroom.

10295
LULLABY (10) (U)
British Screen Services (Winads)
P: Maurice J. Wilson
D: Widgey R.Newman
Reginald Foort . . . .   Himself
MUSICAL Organist tells how peasant is

arrested for bringing illegal white bread
to his family.

10296
SPIRIT OF VARIETY (16) (U)
Studio Sound Services (Exclusive)
D: Hal Wilson
Eddie Carroll and his Radio Boys
Alan Kane   Pat Hurran
Nola Reid   Joan Coleridge
REVUE

10297
WHY PICK ON ME ? (64) (A)
GS Enterprises (Radio)
P: A. George Smith
D: Maclean Rogers
S: Con West, Jack Marks
SC: H.F.Maltby, Kathleen Butler
Wylie Watson . . . .   Sam Tippett
Jack Hobbs . . . .   Stretton
Sybil Grove . . . .   Mrs Tippett
Max Adrian . . . .   Jack Mills
Isobel Scaife . . . .   Daisy Mog
Elizabeth Kent . . . .   Bubbles
COMEDY Henpecked bank clerk gets
drunk and is mistaken for crooked double.

10298
THE LAST CURTAIN (67) (U)
B & D-Paramount British
P: Anthony Havelock-Allan
D: David Macdonald
S: Derek B. Mayne
SC: A.R.Rawlinson
Campbell Gullan. . .   Sir Alan Masterville
Kenneth Duncan . . . .   Joe Garsatti
Greta Gynt . . . .   Julie Rendle
John Wickham . . . .   Bob Fenton
Sara Seagar . . . .   Molly
Joss Ambler . . . .   Ellis
W.G.Fay . . . .   Milligan
Eric Hales . . . .   Barrington
CRIME Insurance tec poses as crook to
expose actor-manager as fence.

AUG

10299
BRIEF ECSTASY (71) (A)
IFP-Phoenix (ABFD) *reissue:* 1947 (BAP)
P: Hugh Perceval
D: Edmond T. Greville
S: Basil Mason
Paul Lukas. . . . .   Prof Paul Bernardy
Hugh Williams . . . .   Jim Wyndham
Linden Travers . . . .   Helen Norwood
Marie Ney . . . .   Martha Russell
Renee Gadd . . . .   Girl Friend
Fred Withers . . . .   Gardener
Howard Douglas . . . .   Coleman
Fewlass Llewellyn . . . .   Director
Peter Gawthorne . . . .   Director
ROMANCE Scientist's young wife falls
in love with his ward, a pilot.

10300
KEEP FIT (82) (U)
ATP (ABFD) *reissue:* 1947
P: Basil Dean
D: Anthony Kimmins
S: Anthony Kimmins, Austin Melford
George Formby . . . .   George Green
Kay Walsh . . . .   Joan Allen
Guy Middleton . . . .   Hector Kent
Gus McNaughton . . . .   Publicity Man
Edmund Breon . . . . .   Sir Augustus Marks
George Benson . . . .   Ernie Gill
Evelyn Roberts . . . .   Barker
C. Denier Warren . . . .   Editor
Hal Walters . . . .   Racing Tough

Leo Franklyn . . . .   Racing Tough
Hal Gordon . . . .   Reporter
Aubrey Mallalieu . . . .   Magistrate
COMEDY Weak barber mistaken for
athlete exposes sporting salesman as thief..

10301
THE GIRL IN THE TAXI (72) (A) *bilingual*
British Unity (ABFD) *reissue:* 1943
P: Kurt Bernhardt, Eugene Tuscherer
D: Andre Berthomieu
S: (PLAY) Georg.Okonowski
SC: Austin Melford, Val Valentine,
Fritz Gottfurcht
Frances Day . . . .   Suzanne Pommarel
Henri Garat . . . .   Rene Boiseurette
Lawrence Grossmith . . . .   Baron des Aubrais
Jean Gillie . . . .   Jacqueline des Aubrais
Mackenzie Ward . . . . . .   Robert des Aubrais
John Deverell . . . .   Capt Emile Pommarel
Helen Haye . . . .   Baroness Delphine
Ben Field . . . .   Dominique
Albert Whelan . . . .   Alexis
Lawrence Hanray . . . .   Charency
Joan Kemp-Welch . . . . . .   Suzanne Dupont
MUSICAL Paris. Captain's wife flirts with
head of purity league and his son.

10302
WISE GUYS (67) (A)
Fox British *reissue:* 1943 (FED)
P: Ivor McLaren
D: Harry Langdon
S: Alison Booth
SC: David Evans
Charlie Naughton . . . .   Charlie
Jimmy Gold . . . .   Jimmy
Audrene Brier . . . .   Flo
Robert Nainby. . . . . . .   Phineas McNaughton
Walter Roy . . . .   Drake
Sydney Keith . . . .   Eddie
David Kier . . . .   Lawyer
COMEDY Edinburgh. Couple must
raise £500 before they can inherit uncle's
loan company.

10303
CLOTHES AND THE WOMAN (70) (A)
JH Productions (ABPC)
P: Julius Hagen
D: Albert de Courville
S: Franz Schulz
SC: F. McGrew Willis
Rod la Rocque . . . .   Eric Thrale
Tucker McGuire . . . .   Joan Moore
Constance Collier . . . .   Eugenia
George E. Stone . . . .   Count Bernhardt
Dorothy Dare . . . .   Carol Dixon
Alastair Sim . . . .   Francois
Mona Goya . . . .   Cecilie
Mary Cole . . . .   Marie Thrale
Jim Gerald . . . .   Enrico Castigliani
Renee Gadd . . . .   Schoolmistress
ROMANCE Runaway schoolgirl poses as
sophisticate to win airman.

10304
GANGWAY (89) (U)
Gaumont (GFD)
D: Sonnie Hale
S: Dwight Taylor
SC: Lesser Samuels, Sonnie Hale
Jessie Matthews . . . .   Pat Wayne
Barry Mackay . . . .   Insp Bob Deering
Nat Pendleton. . . . .   Smiles Hogan
Noel Madison . . . .   Mike Qtterman
Olive Blakeney . . . .   Nedda Beaumont
Alastair Sim . . . .   Taggett
Graham Moffatt . . . .   Joe
Edmon Ryan . . . .   Red Mike
Danny Green . . . .   Shorty

Patrick Ludlow . . . . Carl Freemason
Liane Ordeyne . . . . Greta Brand
MUSICAL New York. Girl reporter poses
as star's maid and is mistaken for jewel thief.

10305
DR SYN (80) (U)
Gaumont (GFD)
D: Roy William Neill
S: (NOVEL) Russell Thorndike
SC: Michael Hogan, Roger Burford
George Arliss . . . . Dr Syn
John Loder . . . . Denis Cobtree
Margaret Lockwood . . . . . . Imogene
Roy Emerton . . . . Capt Howard Collyer
Graham Moffatt . . . . Jerry Jerk
Frederick Burtwell . . . . Rash
George Merritt . . . . Mipps
Athole Stewart . . . . . Sir Anthony Cobtree
Wally Patch . . . . Bosun
Meinhart Maur . . . . Mulatto
Muriel George . . . . Mrs Waggetts
Wilson Coleman . . . . Dr Pepper
ADVENTURE Dymchurch, 1780. Revenue
agent unmasks vicar as "dead" pirate
leading gang of smugglers.

10306
COMMAND PERFORMANCE (84) (U)
Grosvenor (GFD)
P: Harcourt Templeman
D: Sinclair Hill
S: (PLAY) Stafford Dickens
SC: George Pearson, Michael Hankinson,
Sinclair Hill
Arthur Tracy . . . . Street Singer
Lilli Palmer . . . . Susan
Mark Daly . . . . Joe
Rae Collett . . . . Betty
Finlay Currie . . . . Manager
Jack Melford . . . . Reporter
Stafford Hilliard . . . . Sam
Julien Vedey . . . . Toni
Phyllis Stanley . . . . Olga
MUSICAL Film star posing as tramp
falls for gipsy girl.

10307
SCHOOL FOR HUSBANDS (71) (A)
Wainwright (GFD) reissue: 1945 (Carlyle)
P: Richard Wainwright
D: Andrew Marton
S: (PLAY) Frederick Jackson
SC: Frederick Jackson, Austin Melford,
Gordon Sherry
Diana Churchill . . . . Marion Carter
June Clyde . . . . Diana Cheswick
Rex Harrison . . . . Leonard Drummond
Romney Brent . . . . Morgan Cheswick
Henry Kendall . . . . Geoffrey Carter
Roxie Russell . . . . Kate
Richard Goolden . . . . Whittaker
COMEDY Husbands scheme to trap
their wives who both flirt with an author.

10308
THE SQUEAKER (77) (A) USA: MURDER
ON DIAMOND ROW
London-Denham (UA) reissue: 1943 (Key)
P: Alexander Korda
D: William K. Howard
S: (NOVEL) Edgar Wallace
SC: Edward O. Berkman, Bryan Wallace
Edmund Lowe . . . . Insp Barrabal
Sebastian Shaw . . . . Frank Sutton
Ann Todd . . . . Carol Stedman
Tamara Desni . . . . Tamara
Robert Newton . . . . Larry Graeme
Allan Jeayes . . . . Insp Elford
Alastair Sim . . . . Joshua Collie

Stewart Rome . . . . Supt Marshall
Mabel Terry-Lewis . . . . Mrs Stedman
CRIME Discredited tec poses as ex-convict
to unmask shipper as fence.

10309
TWIN FACES (67) (A)
Premier Sound·Films (Par)
P: J. Steven Edwards
D: Lawrence Huntington
S: Douglas Reekie
SC: Gerald Elliott
Anthony Ireland..Jimmy/Michael Strangeways
Francesca Bahrle . . . . Judy Strangeways
Frank Birch . . . . Ben Zwigi
Paul Neville . . . . Cdr Strangeways
Victor Hagen . . . . Insp Coates
George Turner . . . . Maurice
Ivan Wilmot . . . . Levenstein
Frank Tickle . . . . John Cedar
CRIME Art dealer's nephew is jewel
thief's double.

10310
UNDER A CLOUD (67) (A)
Triangle (Par)
P:D: George King
S: Gordon Francis
SC: M.B. Parsons
Edward Rigby . . . . Jimmy Forbes
Betty Ann Davies . . . . Diana Forbes
Bernard Clifton . . . . George Forbes
Renee Gadd . . . . Judy StJohn
Hilda Bayley . . . . Mrs Forbes
Moira Reed . . . . Mary Jessyl
Brian Buchel . . . . Arnold Gill
Peter Gawthorne . . . . . Sir Edmund Jessyl
Jack Vyvyan . . . . Insp Bryan
CRIME Husband returns after 20 years
and proves his son did not kill his
fiancee's blackmailer.

10311
OLD MOTHER RILEY (75) (U)
Butcher-Hope-Bell reissues: 1940; 1941;
1945; 1949 (Sherwood; 931 ft cut)
THE RETURN OF OLD MOTHER RILEY;
THE ORIGINAL OLD MOTHER RILEY
P: Norman Hope-Bell
D: Oswald Mitchell
S: John Argyle
SC: Con West
Arthur Lucan . . . . Mrs Riley
Kitty McShane . . . . Kitty Riley
Barbara Everest . . . . Mrs Briggs
Patrick Ludlow . . . . Edwin Briggs
J. Hubert Leslie . . . . Capt Lawson
Edith Sharpe . . . . Matilda Lawson
Syd Crossley . . . . Butler
Edgar Driver . . . . Bill Jones
Dorothy Vernon . . . . Aggie Sparks
Zoe Wynn . . . . Kay Stewart
G.H.Mulcaster . . . . Prosecution
Charles Carson . . . . Defence
Balliol & Tiller
COMEDY Widow must shelter old match-
seller for six months or lose legacy.

10312
OVER SHE GOES (74) (A)
ABPC
P: Walter C. Mycroft
D: Graham Cutts
S: (PLAY) Stanley Lupino
SC: Elizabeth Meehan, Hugh Brooke
Stanley Lupino . . . . Tommy Teacher
Laddie Cliff . . . . Billy Bowler
Claire Luce . . . . Pamela
Gina Malo . . . . Dolly Jordan
Max Baer . . . . Silas Morner

Sally Grey . . . . Kitty
Judy Kelly . . . . Alice Mayhill
John Wood . . . . . Lord Harry Drewsden
Syd Walker . . . . Insp Giffnock
Bertha Belmore . . . . Lady Drewsden
Richard Murdoch . . . . Sgt Oliver
MUSICAL Lord's ex-partner poses as his
uncle to thwart blackmailing girl.

SEP

10313
A ROMANCE IN FLANDERS (73) (A)
bilingual USA: LOST ON THE WESTERN
FRONT
Franco-London (BL)
P: F. Deutschmeister
D: Maurice Elvey
S: (NOVEL) Mario Fort, Ralph Vanlo
(WIDOW'S ISLAND)
SC: Harold Simpson
Paul Cavanagh . . . . John Morley
Marcelle Chantal . . . . Yvonne Berry
Garry Marsh . . . . Rod Berry
Olga Lindo . . . . Mme Vlandermaere
Alastair Sim . . . . Col Wexton
Evelyn Roberts . . . . Capt Stanford
Kynaston Reeves . . . . Maj Burke
Arthur Hambling . . . . Col Kennedy
C.Denier Warren . . . . Bill Johnson
Frank Atkinson . . . . Joe Stuggins
Bobbie Comber . . . . Chauffeur
Muriel Pavlow . . . . Bessie
DRAMA Amnesiac soldier returns after
20 years to find his wife married to the
man who ordered him to his "death."

10314
YOU LIVE AND LEARN (80) (U)
WB-FN (WB)
P: Irving Asher
D: Arthur Woods
S: (NOVEL) Norma Patterson
(HAVE YOU COME FOR ME)
SC: Brock Williams, Tom Phipps
Glenda Farrell . . . . Mamie Wallis
Claude Hulbert . . . . Peter Millett
Glen Ayln . . . . Dot Harris
John Carol . . . . George
James Stephenson . . . . Sam Brooks
George Galleon . . . . . Lord Haverstock
Arthur Finn . . . . Joseph P.Munro
Margaret Yarde . . . . Mrs Biddle
Pat Fitzpatrick . . . . Jimmy Miller
Gibb McLaughlin . . . . Duval
COMEDY American showgirl thinks she
is marrying rich landowner and finds he
is widowed farmer with children.

10315
THE MINSTREL BOY (79) (A)
Dreadnought (Butcher)
P:D: Sidney Morgan
S: Joan Wentworth Wood (Morgan)
Fred Conyngham . . . . Mike
Chili Bouchier . . . . Dee Dawn
Lucille Lisle . . . . Angela
Kenneth Buckley . . . . Austin Ravensbourne
Basil Langton . . . . Ed
Marjorie Chard . . . . . Lady Ravensbourne
Mabel Twemlow . . . . Lady Pont
Granville Darling . . . . Pat
Xenia & Boyer; Ronald Walters
MUSICAL Irish bandleader weds socialite
who thinks he loves his singer.

10316
THE LAST ROSE OF SUMMER (60) (U)
Fitzpatrick Pictures (MGM)
P:D: James A. Fitzpatrick
S: W.K.Williamson

John Garrick . . . . Thomas More
Kathleen Gibson . . . . His Sweetheart
Malcolm Graham . . . . Lord Byron
Marian Spencer . . . .
Cecil Ramage . . . .
Meadows White . . . .
MUSICAL Ireland. Life and love of poet.

10317
RACING ROMANCE (63) (U)
GS Enterprises (Radio)
P: George Smith
D: Maclean Rogers
S: John Hunter
Bruce Seton . . . . Harry Stone
Marjorie Taylor . . . . Peggy Lanstone
Eliot Makeham . . . . George Hanway
Sybil Grove . . . . Mrs Hanway
Elizabeth Kent . . . . Muriel Hanway
Ian Fleming . . . . Martin Royce
Robert Hobbs . . . . James Archer
Charles Sewell . . . . Mr Lanstone
SPORT Garage proprietor buys girl
trainer's filly and wins Oaks.

10318
MR SMITH CARRIES ON (68) (U)
B & D-Paramount British
P: Anthony Havelock-Allan
D: Lister Laurance
S: John Cousins, Stephen Clarkson
SC: Ronald Gow
Edward Rigby . . . . Mr Smith
Julien Mitchell . . . . Mr Minox
H.F.Maltby . . . . Sir Felix
Dorothy Oldfield . . . . Hilary Smith
Basil Langton . . . . Jerry Stone
Franklyn Bellamy . . . . Mr Williams
Margaret Emden . . . . Mrs Smith
Frederick Culley . . . . Mr Fane
DRAMA Secretary accidentally shoots
magnate and completes pending deal
before disclosure.

10319
MISSING, BELIEVED MARRIED (66) (A)
B & D-Paramount British
P: Anthony Havelock-Allan
D: John Paddy Carstairs
S: A.R.Rawlinson
Wally Patch . . . . Flatiron Stubbs
Julien Vedey . . . . Mario Maroni
Hazel Terry . . . . Hermione Blakiston
Emilio Cargher . . . . Emilio Graffia
Peter Coke . . . . Peter
Margaret Rutherford . . . . . Lady Parke
Charles Paton . . . . Mr Horton
Irene Handl . . . . Chambermaid
COMEDY Cockney and Italian stall-
holders adopt amnesiac heiress and save
her from fortune hunters.

10320
DR SIN FANG (60) (A)
Victory (MGM)
P: Nell Emerald
D: Tony Frenguelli
S: Kaye Mason
SC: Nigel Byass, Frederick Reynolds
H. Agar Lyons . . . . Dr Sin Fang
Anne Grey . . . . Sonia Graham
Robert Hobbs . . . . John Byrne
George Mozart . . . . Bill
Nell Emerald . . . . Mrs Higgins
Arty Ash . . . . Prof Graham
Louis Darnley . . . .
Ernest Sefton . . . .
CRIME Chinese crook tries to obtain
professor's formula for curing cancer.

10321
CHANGE FOR A SOVEREIGN (72) (A)
WB-FN (FN)
P: Irving Asher
D: Maurice Elvey
S: Seymour Hicks
Seymour Hicks . . . . King Hugo
Chili Bouchier . . . . Countess Rita
Bruce Lister . . . . Prince William
Violet Farebrother . . . . Queen Agatha
Aubrey Mallalieu . . . . Baron Breit
Ralph Truman . . . . Archduke Paul
Wilfrid Hyde White . . . . . Charles
C. Denier Warren . . . . Mr Heller
Florence Vie . . . . Mrs Heller
Daphne Raglan . . . . Katrina Heller
COMEDY Ruritania. Drunken double takes
place of king on holiday.

10322
TRANSATLANTIC TROUBLE (78) (U)
retitled: TAKE IT FROM ME
WB-FN (FN)
P: Irving Asher
D: William Beaudine
S: John Meehan jr, J.O.C. Orton
Max Miller . . . . Albert Hall
Betty Lynne . . . . Lilli Maguet
Buddy Baer . . . . Kid Brody
Clem Lawrence . . . . Timber Wood
Zillah Bateman . . . . Lady Foxham
James Stephenson . . . . Lewis
Charlotte Parry . . . . Mrs Murphy
Joan Miller . . . . Secretary
COMEDY Dud boxer elopes on liner with
lady and his pursuing manager is mistaken for
millionaire.

10323
VICTORIA THE GREAT (112) (U) tech seq
Imperator (Radio) reissue: 1950 (BL)
P:D: Herbert Wilcox
S: (PLAY) Laurence Houseman
(VICTORIA REGINA)
SC: Robert Vansittart, Miles Malleson
Anna Neagle . . . . Queen Victoria
Anton Walbrook . . . . Prince Albert
Walter Rilla . . . . Prince Ernest
Mary Morris . . . . Duchess of Kent
H.B.Warner . . . . Lord Melbourne
Grete Wegener . . . . Baroness Lehzen
C.V.France . . . . Archbishop of Canterbury
James Dale . . . . Duke of Wellington
Charles Carson . . . . Sir Robert Peel
Hubert Harben . . . . Lord Conyngham
Felix Aylmer . . . . Lord Palmerston
Arthur Young . . . . Mr Gladstone
Derrick de Marney . . . . . Disraeli (young)
Hugh Miller . . . . Disraeli (old)
Percy Parsons . . . . Abraham Lincoln
Lewis Casson . . . . Archbishop
Henry Hallatt . . . . Joseph Chamberlain
Gordon McLeod . . . . John Brown
Wyndham Goldie . . . . Cecil Rhodes
Tom Hesslewood . . . . . . Sir Francis Grant
Miles Malleson . . . . Physician
HISTORY 1837-1901. Life of Queen Victoria.
(PGA: 1938; FWA: 1938).

10324
JERICHO (77) (U) USA: DARK SANDS
Buckingham (GFD) reissues: 1942 (Pi)
1947 (Amb)
P: Walter Futter, Max Schach
D: Thornton Freeland
S: Walter Futter
SC: Frances Marion, George Barraud,
Robert N. Lee, Peter Ruric
Paul Robeson . . . . Jericho Jackson

Henry Wilcoxon . . . . Capt Mack
Wallace Ford . . . . Mike Clancy
Princess Kouka . . . . Gara
John Laurie . . . . Hassan
James Carew . . . . Maj Barnes
Laurence Brown . . . . Pte Fane
Rufus Rennell . . . . Sgt Garney
Ike Hatch . . . . Tag
Frank Cochrane . . . . Agouba
Frederick Cooper . . . . Explorer
George Barraud . . . . Explorer
ADVENTURE Africa. Court-martialled
captain pursues murderous deserter.

10325
NON-STOP NEW YORK (71) (A)
Gaumont (GFD) reissue: 1947 (NR)
D: Robert Stevenson
S: (NOVEL) Ken Attiwill
(SKY STEWARD)
SC: Kurt Siodmak, Roland Pertwee,
J.O.C.Orton, Derek Twist
John Loder . . . . Insp Jim Grant
Anna Lee . . . . Jennie Carr
Francis L. Sullivan . . . . Hugo Brandt
Frank Cellier . . . . Sam Pryor
Desmond Tester . . . . Arnold James
William Dewhurst . . . . Mortimer
James Pirrie . . . . Billy Cowper
Drusilla Wills . . . . Ma Carr
Jerry Verno . . . . Steward
Athene Seyler . . . . Aunt Veronica
Ellen Pollock . . . . Miss Harvey
Arthur Goullet . . . . Henry Abel
CRIME 1940. Gangsters try to kill chorus
girl witness who stows away in trans-
atlantic airliner.

10326
SMASH AND GRAB (76) (A)
Jack Buchanan (GFD) reissue: 1949 (ABFD)
D:S: Tim Whelan
SC: Ralph Spence
Jack Buchanan . . . . Jack Forrest
Elsie Randolph . . . . Alice Thornby
Arthur Margetson . . . . Julius Malvern
Antony Holles . . . . Palino
Zoe Wynn . . . . Carole
Edmund Willard . . . . Cappelano
David Burns . . . . Bellini
Lawrence Grossmith . . . . . Rankin
Edward Lexy . . . . Insp McInery
Lawrence Hanray . . . . Praskins
Sara Seegar . . . . Miss Quincey
COMEDY Tec's wife helps him unmask
philandering jeweller as head of smash
and grab gang.

10327
LEAVE IT TO ME (71) (A)
Tom Arnold (BL)
D: Herbert Smith
S: Fenn Sherie, Ingram d'Abbes
Sandy Powell . . . . Sandy
Iris March . . . . Joan
Franklin Dyall . . . . Sing
Garry Marsh . . . . Sergeant
Davy Burnaby . . . . Sir William
Jack Hobbs . . . . Guest
Claude Horton . . . . Butler
Dora Hibbert & Nicholas Bird
COMEDY Ambitious PC saves jewel from
Chinese gang.

10328
THERE WAS A YOUNG MAN (63) (U)
Fox British
D: Albert Parker
S: Dudley Clark
SC: David Evans

Oliver Wakefield . . . . George Peabody
Nancy O'Neil . . . . Barbara Blake
Clifford Heatherley . . . . Wallop
Robert Nainby . . . . Vicar
Molly Hamley Clifford . . . Mrs Blake
Eric Hales . . . . Vernon
Brian Buchel . . . . Prince Bunkhadin
John Laurie . . . . Stranger
Syd Crossley . . . . Slim
COMEDY Poor man mistaken for heir
foils Orientals seeking sacred bone.

OCT

10329
RHYTHM RACKETEER (84) (A)
Rock Productions (BIED)
P: Joe Rock
D: James Seymour
S: Betty Laidlaw, Robert Lively
SC: John Byrd
Harry Roy . . . Harry Grand/Nap Connors
Princess Pearl . . . . Karen Vosper
James Carew . . . . Clinton Vosper
Norma Varden . . . . Della Nash
Johnny Hines . . . . Nifty
Johnny Schofield . . . . Spike
Judith Wood . . . . Lola
Georgie Harris . . . . The Rat
Pamela Randall; Harry Roy's Band
MUSICAL Chicago gangster steals jewels
aboard line and frames band leader double.

10330
THE SCHOONER GANG (72) (U)
New Garrick (Butcher)
P:D: W. Devenport Hackney
S: W. Devenport & M.L.Hackney
SC: Frank Atkinson, Ralph Dawson, Iris Terry
Vesta Victoria . . . . Mrs Truman
Billy Percy . . . . Freddie Fellowes
Gerald Barry . . . . Carleton
Percy Honri . . . . Adam
Mary Honri . . . . Mary
Betty Norton . . . . Mary Truman
Basil Broadbent . . . . Jack Norris
Frank Atkinson . . . . Ben Worton.
The Gerrard Quartet
CRIME Gang force ex-convict innkeeper
to help them steal necklace.

10331
LITTLE MISS SOMEBODY (78) (U)
Mondover (Butcher)
P: Walter Tennyson, Alfred D'Eyncourt
D:S: Walter Tennyson
SC: H. Fowler Mear, Mary Dunn
Binkie Stuart . . . . Binkie Sladen
John Longden . . . . Jim Trevor
Kathleen Kelly . . . . Mary Grey
Jane Carr . . . . Mrs Borden
George Carney . . . . Angus Duncan
D.A.Clarke-Smith . . . . Mr Borden
Margaret Emden . . . . Mrs Peacher
Vivienne Chatterton . . . . . Amelia Sparkes
C. Denier Warren . . . . Jonas
Hal Walters . . . . Albert Sims
J. Fisher White . . . . Tom Shirley
DRAMA Wicked squire learns farmer's adopted
orphan is heiress.

10332
PATHETONE PARADE OF 1938 (36) (U)
Pathe
D: Fred Watts
Ronald Frankau . . . . Compere
Stanelli . . . . Charlie Kunz
Patrick Colbert . . . . Lance Fairfax
Norman Long . . . . Sandy Rowan
Hillbillies . . . . Danny Lipton Trio

Collinson & Dean . . . . Myles Sisters
Billy Reid and his Accordian Band
REVUE

10333
JENIFER HALE (66) (A)
Fox British *reissue:* 1941 (147 ft cut)
D: Bernerd Mainwaring
S: (NOVEL) Rob Eden
SC: Ralph Stock, Bernerd Mainwaring,
Edward Dryhurst
Rene Ray . . . . Jenifer Hale
Ballard Berkeley . . . . Richard
John Longden . . . . Insp Merton
Paul Blake . . . . Ives
Frank Birch . . . . Sharman
Richard Parry . . . . Jim Watson
Ernest Sefton . . . . Sgt Owen
Kay Seely . . . . Mr Joyce
CRIME Architect proves chorus girl did
not kill producer.

10334
OH, MR PORTER ! (84) (U)
Gainsborough (GFD)
Reissue: 1947 (IFR)
P: Edward Black
D: Marcel Varnel
S: Frank Launder
SC: Marriott Edgar, Val Guest, J.O.C.Orton
Will Hay . . . . William Porter
Moore Marriott . . . . Jerry Harbottle
Graham Moffatt . . . . Albert Brown
Sebastian Smith . . . . Charles Trimbletow
Agnes Lauchlan . . . . Mrs Trimbletow
Percy Walsh . . . . Supt
Dennis Wyndham . . . . Grogan
Dave O'Toole . . . . Postman
COMEDY Ireland. Stationmaster of a
disused halt catches gun-runners.

10335
THE BELLS OF ST MARY'S (44) (U)
Fitzpatrick Pictures (MGM)
D: James A. Fitzpatrick
S: W.K.Williamson
John Garrick . . . . John Warren
Kathleen Gibson . . . . Kathleen
Sylvia Marriott . . . .
J. Fisher White . . . .
Stella Bonheur . . . .
R. Meadows White . . . . . .
Evelyn Ankers . . . .
MUSICAL Devon, 1880. Chorister returns from
training in Rome to marry sexton's daughter.

10336
THE TICKET OF LEAVE MAN (71) (A)
George King (MGM) *reissue:* 1942 (Amb)
D: George King
S: (PLAY) Tom Taylor
SC: H.F.Maltby, A.R.Rawlinson
Tod Slaughter . . . . The Tiger
Marjorie Taylor . . . . May Edwards
John Warwick . . . . Bob Brierly
Robert Adair . . . . Hawkshaw
Frank Cochran . . . . Melter Moss
Peter Gawthorne . . . . Joshua Gibson
Jenny Lynn . . . . Mrs Willoughby
Arthur Payne . . . . Sam Willoughby
CRIME Head of Prisoners' Aid Society
frames his rival for forgery.

10337
FALSE EVIDENCE (71) (A)
Crusade (Par)
P: Victor M. Greene
D:SC: Donovan Pedelty
S: (NOVEL) Roy Vickers (I'LL NEVER TELL)
(I'LL NEVER TELL)

Gwenllian Gill . . . . · Judy Endale
George Pembroke . . . . John Massiter
Michael Hogarth . . . . Gerald Wickham
Daphne Raglan . . . . . Annabelle Stirling
George Pughe . . . . Tom Vanderlam
Francis Roberts . . . . Insp Jones
Langley Howard . . . . Julius Wickham
Ralph Michael . . . . PC Barlow
CRIME Secretary proves her ex-fiance,
married to a jewel thief, innocent of murder.

10338
SHOOTING STARS (69) (U)
Viking Films *reissue:* 1939 (2324 ft cut)
P:D: Eric Humphris
S: Fred Duprez
Scott & Whaley   Fred Duprez
Phyllis Robins   Karina
Sherman Fisher Girls   Harry Robin
Debroy Somers and his Band
REVUE'

10339
DEATH CROONS THE BLUES (74) (A)
St Margarets (MGM)
P: Julius Hagen
D: David Macdonald
S: (NOVEL) James Ronald
SC: H. Fowler Mear
Hugh Wakefield . . . . Jim Martin
Antoinette Cellier.. Lady Constance Gaye
George Hayes . . . . Hugo Branker
Gillian Lind . . . .
John Turnbull . . . .
Hugh Burden . . . .
Barbara Everest . . . .
CRIME Drunken reporter proves Lady's
missing brother did not kill girl singer.

10340
THE LAST ADVENTURERS (77) (U)
Conway (SC) *reissues:* 1940 ,
DOWN TO THE SEA IN SHIPS; 1947 (Amb)
P: H. Fraser Passmore
D: Roy Kellino
S: Denison Clift
Niall McGinnis . . . . Jeremy Bowker
Roy Emerton . . . . John Arkell
Linden Travers . . . . Ann Arkell
Kay Walsh . . . . Margaret Arkell
Peter Gawthorne . . . . Fergus Arkell
Katie Johnson . . . . Susan Arkell
Johnnie Schofield . . . . Stalky
Norah Howard . . . . Mary Allen
Ballard Berkeley . . . . Fred Delvin
Esma Cannon . . . . Polly Shepherd
Tony Wylde . . . . Glory Be
ADVENTURE Trawlerman loves daughter
of captain who saves him from shipwreck.

10341
SATURDAY NIGHT REVUE (77) (A)
Welwyn (Pathe) *reissue:* 1939
P: Warwick Ward
D: Norman Lee
S: Vernon Clancey
Billy Milton . . . . Jimmy Hanson
Sally Gray . . . . Mary Dorland
John Watt . . . . Himself
Betty Lynne . . . . Ann
Edward Ashley . . . . Duke O'Brien
Georgie Harris . . . . Plug
Julien Vedey . . . . Monty
Charles Carson . . . . Mr Dorland
Mary Jerrold . . . . Mrs Dorland
Hillbillies; Gerry Fitzgerald; Bennett &
Williams; Reg Bolton; Webster Booth;
Stanford & McNaughton; Sydney Kyte
and his Band; Scots Kilties Band; John
Reynders and his BBC Orchestra; Billy

Reid's Band; Strad and his Newsboys.
MUSICAL Crooked club-owner reforms
and reunites blind busker with ex-partner.

10342
THE LIVE WIRE (69) (U)
Tudor-Olympic (BL) reissue: 1946 (NR)
P: Herbert Wynne
D: Herbert Brenon
S: (PLAY) Stafford Dickens
(PLUNDER IN THE AIR)
SC: Stafford Dickens
Bernard Nedell . . . . James Cody
Jean Gillie . . . . Sally Barton
Hugh Wakefield . . . . Grantham
Arthur Wontner . . . . Montell
Kathleen Kelly . . . . Phoebe
Irene Ware . . . . Jane
David Burns . . . . Snakey
Felix Aylmer . . . . Wilton
H.F.Maltby . . . . Hodgson
C.M.Hallard . . . . Sir George Dawson
COMEDY Yankee trickster reforms and
turns worthless land into spa.

NOV

10343
THE RETURN OF THE SCARLET
PIMPERNEL (94) (U)
London (UA) reissue: 1943 (Key; 11 mins cut)
P: Alexander Korda, Arnold Pressburger
D: Hans Schwartz
S: (NOVEL) Baroness Orczy
SC: Lajos Biro, Arthur Wimperis, Adrian Brunel
Barry K. Barnes . . . . . . Sir Percy Blakeney
Sophie Stewart . . . . Marguerite Blakeney
Margaretta Scott . . . . . . Theresa Cabarrus
James Mason . . . . Jean Tallien
Francis Lister . . . . Chauvelin
Anthony Bushell . . . . . Sir Andrew ffoulkes
Patrick Barr . . . . Lord Hastings
David Tree . . . . Lord Denning
Henry Oscar . . . . Robespierre
Hugh Miller . . . . de Calmet
Allan Jeayes . . . . Judge
O.B.Clarence . . . . de Marre
George Merritt . . . . Chief of Police
Evelyn Roberts . . . . Prince of Wales
Esme Percy . . . . Richard Sheridan
Edmund Breon . . . . Col Winterbottom
ADVENTURE Paris, 1797. Fop dons
disguises to save wife from guillotine.

10344
PARADISE FOR TWO (77) (U) USA:
THE GAIETY GIRLS
London-Denham (UA) reissue: 1943
(Key; 9 mins cut)
P: Alexander Korda, Gunther Stapenhorst
D: Thornton Freeland
S: Robert Stevenson, Arthur Macrae
Jack Hulbert . . . . Rene Martin
Patricia Ellis . . . . Jeannette
Arthur Riscoe . . . . Jacques Thibaud
Googie Withers . . . . Miki
Sydney Fairbrother . . . . . Miss Clare
Wylie Watson . . . . Clarence
David Tree . . . . Marcel
Cecil Bevan . . . . Renaud
Antony Holles . . . . Brand
Roland Culver . . . . Paul Duval
H.F.Maltby . . . . Director
Finlay Currie . . . . Creditor
MUSICAL Paris. Singer persuades millionaire
posing as reporter to pose as millionaire
husband.

10345
THE RAT (72) (A)
Imperator (Radio) Reissue: 1944 (Anglo)
P: Herbert Wilcox
D: Jack Raymond
S: (PLAY) Ivor Novello, Constance Collier
SC: Hans Rameau, Marjorie Gaffney,
Miles Malleson, Romney Brent.
Ruth Chatterton . . . . . . Zelia de Chaumont
Anton Walbrook . . . . Jean Boucheron
Rene Ray . . . . Odile Verdier
Beatrix Lehmann . . . . Marguerite
Mary Clare . . . . Mere Colline
Felix Aylmer . . . . Attorney General
Hugh Miller . . . . Luis Stets
Gordon McLeod . . . . Caillard
Frederick Culley . . . . Judge
Nadine March . . . . Rose
George Merritt . . . . Pierre Verdier
Leo Genn . . . . Defence
Fanny Wright . . . . Therese
CRIME Paris. Thief takes blame when
ward shoots millionaire; he is saved by socialite.

10346
SAM SMALL LEAVES TOWN (79) (U)
British Screen Service
Reissue: 1942, IT'S SAM SMALL AGAIN
(Fed; 9 mins cut)
P: Maurice J. Wilson
D: Alfred Goulding
Stanley Holloway . . . . . . Richard Manning
June Clyde . . . . Sally Elton
Fred Conyngham . . . . Jimmy West
Harry Tate . . . . Camper
Johnnie Schofield . . . . . . Sam Small
Robert English . . . . Robert Harrison
James Craven . . . . Steve Watt
Brookins & Van
COMEDY Actor bets editor he can escape
capture and poses as holiday camp handyman

10347
THE SKY'S THE LIMIT (79) (U)
Jack Buchanan (GFD)
D: Lee Garmes, Jack Buchanan
S: Ralph Spence
SC: Jack Buchanan, Douglas Furber
Jack Buchanan . . . . Dave Harber
Mara Loseff . . . . Isobella
William Kendall . . . . Thornwell Beamish
David Hutcheson . . . . Teddy Carson
H.F.Maltby . . . . Lord Beckley
Athene Seyler . . . . Miss Prinney
Sara Allgood . . . . Mrs O'Reilly
Antony Holles . . . . Marillo
David Burns . . . . Ballyhoo Bangs
Wally Patch . . . . Commissionaire
Barry Lupino . . . . Drunk
Morris Harvey . . . . Ambassador
C.M.Hallard . . . . Lord Morgan
Rawicz & Landauer; Four New Yorkers;
Leslie Mitchell
MUSICAL Opera star and aircraft manu-
facturer seek sacked designer.

10348
LANCASHIRE LUCK (74) (U)
B & D-Paramount British reissue: 1948 (Amb)
P: Anthony Havelock-Allan
D: Henry Cass
S: Ronald Gow
SC: A.R.Rawlinson
George Carney . . . . George Lovejoy
Wendy Hiller . . . . Betty Lovejoy
Muriel George . . . . Mrs Lovejoy
Nigel Stock . . . . Joe Lovejoy
George Galleon . . . . Sir Gerald Maydew
Margaret Damer . . . . Lady Maydew
Bett Huth . . . . Lady Evelyn Brenton
COMEDY Lancs. Girl's father wins pools
and buys roadside cafe, and she falls in
love with lady's son.

10349
THE LAST CHANCE (74) (A)
Welwyn (Pathe)
P: Warwick Ward
D: Thomas Bentley
S: (PLAY) Frank Stayton
SC: Harry Hughes
Frank Leighton . . . . . . Alan Burminster
Judy Kelly . . . . Mary Perrin
Billy Milton . . . . Michael Worrall
Wyndham Goldie . . . . John Worrall
Aubrey Mallalieu . . . . Judge Croyle
Jenny Laird . . . . Betty
Franklyn Bellamy . . . . Insp Cutts
Lawrence Hanray . . . . Perrin
Alfred Wellesley . . . . Ivor Connell
CRIME Gunrunner breaks jail to prove
barrister framed him for killing usurer.

10350
INTIMATE RELATIONS (66) (A)
Tudor Films (ABFD) reissue: 1944 (Ren)
P: Herbert Wynne
D: Clayton Hutton
S: (PLAY) Stafford Dickens
SC: Frank Atkinson
June Clyde . . . . Molly Morrell
Garry Marsh . . . . George Gommery
Jack Hobbs . . . . Freddie Hall
Vera Bogetti . . . . Jane Gommery
Cynthia Stock . . . . Maggie
Moore Marriott . . . . Toomley
Arthur Finn . . . . Goldfish
Bruce Winston . . . . Stetson
Lew Stone and his Band
COMEDY Married man flirts with film
star who poses as friend's fiancee.

10351
THE MUTINY OF THE ELSINORE (79) (A)
Argyle British (ABPC) reissue: 1948 (IFR)
P: John Argyle
D: Roy Lockwood
S: (NOVEL) Jack London
SC: Walter Summers, Beaufoy Milton
Paul Lukas . . . . Jack Pathurst
Lyn Harding . . . . Mr Pike
Kathleen Kelly . . . . Margaret West
Clifford Evans . . . . Bert Rhyme
Michael Martin-Harvey . . . . . Charles Davis
Pat Noonan . . . . Murphy
Hamilton Keene . . . . Twist
William Devlin . . . . O'Sullivan
Ben Soutten . . . . Mr Mellaire
Conway Dixon . . . . Capt West
Tony Sympson . . . . Shorty
ADVENTURE Reporter aboard sailing
ship gets involved in mutiny.

10352
WHO KILLED JOHN SAVAGE ? (69) (A)
WB-FN (WB)
P: Irving Asher
D: Maurice Elvey
S: (NOVEL) Philip Macdonald (RYNOX)
SC: Basil Dillon
Nicholas Hannen . . . . John Savage
Barry Mackay . . . . Anthony Benedick
Edward Chapman . . . . Insp Chortley
Kathleen Kelly . . . . Kate Savage
Henry Oscar . . . . Woolrich
Ross Landon . . . . Smith
George Kirby . . . . Prout

C. Denier Warren . . . . Scruggs
CRIME Head of chemical firm fakes
his own murder to collect insurance.

10353
YOUNG AND INNOCENT (82) (A)
USA: A GIRL WAS YOUNG
Gaumont (GFD)
D: Alfred Hitchcock
S: (NOVEL) Josephine Tey (A SHILLING
FOR CANDLES)
SC: Charles Bennett, Alma Reville,
Antony Armstrong, Edwin Greenwood,
Gerald Savory.
Nova Pilbeam . . . . Erica Burgoyne
Derrick de Marney . . . . Robert Tisdall
Percy Marmont . . . . Col Burgoyne
Edward Rigby . . . . Old Will
Mary Clare . . . . Aunt Margaret
John Longden . . . . Insp Kent
George Curzon . . . . Guy
Basil Radford . . . . Uncle Basil
Pamela Carme . . . . Christine Clay
George Merritt . . . . Sgt Miller
J.H.Roberts . . . . Henry Briggs
Jerry Verno . . . . Driver
H.F.Maltby . . . . Sgt
Gerry Fitzgerald . . . . Singer
CRIME Chief Constable's daughter helps
fugitive prove he did not strangle film star.

10354
TELEVISION TALENT (56) (U)
Alexander Film Productions (Amb)
P:S: R. Howard Alexander
D: SC: Robert Edmunds
Richard Goolden . . . . Prof Langley
Polly Ward . . . . Mary Hilton
Gene Sheldon . . . . Herbert Dingle
Hal Walters . . . . Steve Bagley
COMEDY Music teacher wins drama
school competition despite being framed
for forgery. (Extracts as short film
THE BANJO FOOL (New Realm), 8/1940).

DEC

10355
MACUSHLA (59) (U)
Fox British
P: Victor M. Greene
D: S: Alex Bryce
SC: David Evans
Pamela Wood . . . . Kathleen Muldoon
Liam Gaffney . . . . Jim O'Grady
Jimmy Mageean . . . . Pat Muldoon
Max Adrian . . . . Kerry Muldoon
E.J.Kennedy . . . . Hugh Connolly
Kitty Kirwan . . . . Bridget
Brian Herbert . . . . Pat Rooney
Edgar K. Bruce . . . . Dean McLaglen
CRIME Ireland. Farmer's daughter loves
policeman who is seeking her gunrunning
brother.

10356
EAST OF LUDGATE HILL (47) (U)
Fox British
D: Manning Haynes
S: (PLAY) Arnold Ridley
SC: Edward Dryhurst, Stanley Jackson
Robert Cochran . . . . Derek Holt
Nancy O'Neil . . . . Norah Applin
Eliot Makeham . . . . Mr Tallweather
Hal Gordon . . . . Bert Bickley
Aubrey Mallalieu . . . . James McIntyre
Pamela Wood . . . . Minnie Hazell
Vernon Harris . . . . Martin Bland
Paul Blake . . . . Hilary McIntyre
Charles Hawtrey . . . . Edwin Tallweather

Annie Esmond . . . . Miss Monkton
DRAMA Effect on office staff when the
loss of some bonds threatens promised bonus.

10357
DINNER AT THE RITZ (77) (U)
New World (20th) I reissue: 1948 (GN)
P: Robert T. Kane
D: Harold Schuster
S: Roland Pertwee, Romney Brent
SC: Roland Pertwee
Annabella . . . . Ranie Racine
Paul Lukas . . . . Baron Philip
David Niven . . . . Paul de Brack
Romney Brent . . . . Jimmy Raine
Francis L. Sullivan . . . . . . Brogard
Stewart Rome . . . . Racine
Nora Swinburne . . . . Lady Railton
Tyrell Davis . . . . Duval
Frederick Leister . . . . Tarade
William Dewhurst . . . . Devine
Vivienne Chatterton . . . . . Marthe
Ronald Shiner . . . . Sidney
CRIME Riviera. French girl poses as
Marquesa to unmask swindlers who
faked her father's suicide.

10358
MELODY AND ROMANCE (71) (U)
British Lion reissue: 1946 (NR)
P: Herbert Smith
D: Maurice Elvey
S: Leslie Howard Gordon, Maurice Elvey
SC: L. duGarde Peach
Hughie Green . . . . Hughie Hawkins
Margaret Lockwood . . . . Margaret Williams
Jane Carr . . . . Kay Williams
Alastair Sim . . . . Prof Williams
Garry Marsh . . . . Warwick Mortimer
C. Denier Warren . . . . . . Capt Hawkins
Julien Vedey . . . . Jacob
Margaret Scudamore . . . . . Mrs Hawkins
Rex Roper and Maisie; Hughie Green's Gang
MUSICAL Bargee's son and gang rise to
stardom on radio.

10359
DANGEROUS FINGERS (79) (A)
USA: WANTED BY SCOTLAND YARD
Rialto (Pathe)
P:John Argyle
D: Norman Lee
S: (NOVEL) Vernon Clancey (MAN HUNT)
SC: Vernon Clancey
James Stephenson . . . . Fingers
Betty Lynne . . . . Doris
Leslie Perrins . . . . Standish
D.A.Clarke-Smith . . . . Insp Williams
Nadine March . . . . Mabel
Sally Stewart . . . . Molly
George Merritt . . . . Charlie
Phil Ray . . . . Ben
CRIME Cracksman framed for killing
man who caused his sister's suicide.

10360
THE DERELICT (57) (U)
M.V.Gover (IFD)
P: Victor Gover, Joe Rosenthal
D: SC: Harold Simpson
S: James Spence
Malcolm Morley . . . . Toby Merriman
Jane Griffiths . . . . Mary
Charles Penrose . . . . Toby's Pal
Frank Strickland . . . . Sir Benjamin
Peter Kernohan . . . . Sonny
DRAMA Old tramp sells his drawings to
pay for operation on widow's crippled son.

10361
CAPTAIN'S ORDERS (75) (U)

Liberty Films reissue: 1952 (H&S)
D: Ivar Campbell
S: Frank Shaw
Henry Edwards . . . . Capt Trent
Jane Carr . . . . Belle Mandeville
Marie Lavarre . . . . Violet Potts
Franklyn Dyall . . . . Newton
Wally Patch . . . . Johnstone
C.Denier Warren . . . . Lawson
Mark Daly . . . . Scotty
Roddy Hughes . . . . Cookie
Basil Radford . . . . Murdoch
Kim Peacock . . . . Aubrey Chaytor
Joss Ambler . . . . Randolph Potts
H.F.Maltby . . . . Director
Rae Collet; Sherman Fisher Girls; Jack Hart
and his Band
DRAMA Merchant captain almost loses
race to New York when he rescues star
from her wrecked yacht.

10362
MADEMOISELLE DOCTEUR (84) (A)
Grafton-Trafalgar (UA)
reissues: 1942 (Maj) 1947 (Amb)
P: Max Schach
D: Edmond T. Greville
S: Georges Hereaux, Irma Von Cube
SC: Jacques Natanson, Marcel Archard,
Ernest Betts
Dita Parlo . . . . Anne-Marie Lesser
John Loder . . . . Lt Peter Carr
Erich von Stroheim . . Col Mathesius Simonis
Claire Luce . . . . Gaby
Gyles Isham . . . . Lt Hans Hoffman
Clifford Evans . . . . Condoyan
John Abbott . . . . Armand
Antony Holles . . . . Mario
Edward Lexy . . . . Orderly
Raymond Lovell . . . . Col von Steinberg
Frederick Lloyd . . . . Col Marchand
WAR Salonika. German spy falls in love
with British officer.

10363
OVER THE MOON (78) (A) tech
London-Denham (UA) reissue: 1946 (BL)
P: Alexander Korda
D: Thornton Freeland, William K. Howard
S: Robert E. Sherwood, Lajos Biro
SC: Anthony Pelissier, Arthur Wimperis,
Alec Coppel
Merle Oberon . . . . June Benson
Rex Harrison . . . . Dr Freddie Jarvis
Ursula Jeans . . . . . . Lady Millie Parsmill
Robert Douglas . . . . John Flight
Louis Borell . . . Count Pietro d'Altamura
Zena Dare . . . . Julie Deethorpe
Peter Haddon . . . . Lord Petcliffe
David Tree . . . . Journalist
Mackenzie Ward . . . . Lord Guy Carstairs
Carl Jaffe . . . . Michel
Elisabeth Welch . . . . Singer
ROMANCE Girl tours Europe on huge
legacy but returns to wed poor doctor.

10364
FOUR DARK HOURS (65) (A)
Retitled: THE GREEN COCKATOO
New World (20th) reissues: 1942, RACE GANG
(Ren; 600 ft cut) 1948 (GN) 1953 (G&S)
P: Robert T. Kane
D: William Cameron Menzies
S: (STORY) Graham Greene
SC: Edward O. Berkman, Arthur Wimperis
John Mills . . . . Jim Connor
Rene Ray . . . . Eileen
Robert Newton . . . . Dave Connor
Charles Oliver . . . . Terence

Bruce Seton . . . . Madison
Julien Vedey . . . . Steve
Allan Jeayes . . . . Inspector
Frank Atkinson . . . . Butler
CRIME Country girl helps dancer whose brother is killed by race gang.

10365
STARDUST (78) Retitled: MAD ABOUT MONEY USA: HE LOVED AN ACTRESS
Morgan (BL)
P: William Rowland
D: Melville Brown
S: John F. Harding
SC: John Meehan jr
Lupe Velez . . . . Carla de Huleva
Ben Lyon . . . . . . `. . . . . . Roy Harley
Wallace Ford . . . . Peter Jackson
Harry Langdon . . . . Otto
Jean Colin . . . . Diana West
Mary Cole . . . . Peggy
Cyril Raymond . . . . Jerry Sears
Ronald Ward . . . . Eric Williams
Olive Sloane . . . . Floria Dane
Arthur Finn . . . . J.D.Meyers
Peggy Novak . . . . Secretary
MUSICAL Bankrupt film producers seek finance from Mexican heiress who is really a poor actress.

10366
WHAT A MAN ! (74)
IFP-Phoenix (BL)
P: Hugh Perceval

D: Edmond T. Greville
S: Basil Mason
SC: Basil Mason, Jack Marks
Sydney Howard . . . Samuel Pennyfeather
Vera Pearce . . . . Emily Pennyfeather
Ivor Barnard . . . . Mayor
Jenny Laird . . . . . Daisy Pennyfeather
Frederick Bradshaw . . . . . Walter Walkeling
H.F.Maltby . . . . Sgt Bull
John Singer . . . . Harold Bull
Robert Adair . . . . Lord Bromwich
Frank Cochrane . . . . Simpkins
COMEDY Photographer's search for bureau containing slate club funds.

10367
THE FIRST AND THE LAST (75)
retitled 21 DAYS; USA: 21 DAYS TOGETHER
London-Denham (Col) *reissue:* 1944 (Key)
P: Alexander Korda
D: Basil Dean
S: (PLAY) John Galsworthy
SC: Graham Greene
Vivien Leigh . . . . Wanda
Leslie Banks . . . . Keith Durrant
Laurence Olivier . . . . Larry Durrant
Francis L. Sullivan . . . . Mander
Hay Petrie . . . . John Aloysius Evan
Esme Percy . . . . Henry Walenn
Robert Newton . . . . Tolly
Victor Rietti . . . . Antonio
Morris Harvey . . . . Alexander Macpherson
Meinhart Maur . . . . Carl Grunlich

David Horne . . . . Beavis
Wallace Lupino . . . . Father
Muriel George . . . . Mother
CRIME KC's brother kills girl's brother and lets ex-parson take blame.

10368
REMEMBER WHEN (68) (U) retitled:
RIDING HIGH
Embassy (BL)
P: George King
D: David Macdonald
S: H. Fowler Mear
Claude Dampier. . . . . Septimus Earwicker
John Garrick . . . . Tom Blake
Kathleen Gibson . . . . Grace Meadows
Helen Haye . . . . Miss Broadbent
John Warwick . . . . George Davenport
Billy Merson . . . . Popping
Mai Bacon . . . . Mrs Winterbottom
Peter Gawthorne . . . . Sir Joseph Wilmot
Billy Holland . . . . Jack Adamson
Billy Bray . . . . Ted Rance
Georgian Singers; Mansell & Ling; Bertie Kendrick
COMEDY 1879. Solicitor helps a village blacksmith win race on his bicycle invention.

10369
THE NEW FRONTIERSMEN (18)
Positive Productions
P: George Fraser
D: Eric Parfitt
Cecil Broadhurst . . . . Cowboy
MUSICAL Saskatchewan . Singing cowboy

1938

JAN

10370
THE LONDONDERRY AIR (47) (U)
Fox British
P: Victor M. Greene
D: Alex Bryce
S: (PLAY) Rachel Field
SC: David Evans, Alex Bryce
Sara Allgood .... Widow Rafferty
Liam Gaffney .... The Pedlar
Phyllis Ryan............ Rose Martha
Jimmy Mageean.......... Sheamus
Maureen Moore .... Mrs Murphy
Grenville Darling .... Auctioneer
Kitty Kirwan .... Deaf Woman
ROMANCE Ireland. Pedlar persuades
widow's servant to run away with him.

10371
SOUTH RIDING (91) (A)
London (UA) *reissues:* 1943 (Anglo)
1946 (Eal)
P: Alexander Korda, Victor Saville
D: Victor Saville
S: (NOVEL) Winifred Holtby
SC: Ian Dalrymple, Donald Bull
Ralph Richardson. .... Robert Carne
Edna Best .... Sarah Burton
Edmund Gwenn .... Alfred Huggins
Ann Todd .... Madge Carne
John Clements .... Joe Astell
Marie Lohr .... Mrs Beddows
Milton Rosmer .... Snaith
Edward Lexy .... Mr Holly
Josephine Wilson .... Mrs Holly
Joan Ellum .... Lydia Holly
Gus McNaughton .... Tadman
Glynis Johns .... Midge Carne
Lewis Casson .... Lord Sedgemire
DRAMA Yorks. Teacher loves married
squire who exposes crooked councillors.

10372
THE DIVORCE OF LADY X (92) (A) *tech*
London-Denham Films (UA) *reissue:*
1944 (Eal)
P: Alexander Korda
D: Tim Whelan
S: (PLAY) Gilbert Wakefield (COUNSEL'S
OPINION)
SC: Lajos Biro, Arthur Wimperis,
Ian Dalrymple
Merle Oberon .... Leslie
Laurence Olivier .... Logan
Binnie Barnes .... Lady Mere
Ralph Richardson .... Lord Mere
Morton Selten .... Lord Steele
J.H.Roberts .... Slade
Gertrude Musgrove .... Saunders
Gus McNaughton .... Waiter
COMEDY Lord's daughter wins barrister
by posing as divorce client.

10373
EASY RICHES (67) (U)
GS Enterprises (RKO)
P: A. George Smith
D: Maclean Rogers
S: John Hunter
George Carney .... Sam Miller
Gus McNaughton .... Joe Hicks
Marjorie Taylor .... Dorothy Hicks
Tom Helmore .... Harry Miller
Peter Gawthorne .... Stacey Lang
Aubrey Mallalieu
COMEDY Rival cement manufacturers
combine against confidence tricksters.

10374
A DREAM OF LOVE (37) (U)
Fitzpatrick Pictures (MGM)
P:D: James A. Fitzpatrick
S: W.K.Williamson
Ian Colin .... Franz Liszt
Sylvia Marriott .... Catherine
Cathleen Nesbitt ...... Baroness StCricq
Julie Suedo ....
Cecil Ramage .... Baron StCricq
Fanny Wright ....
Bertram Wallis .... Liszt (old)
MUSICAL Composer writes "Liebestraum"
when thwarted in love for baron's daughter.

10375
GEORGE BIZET, COMPOSER OF CARMEN
(37) (U)
Fitzpatrick Pictures (MGM)
P:D: James A. Fitzpatrick
S: W.K.Williamson
Dino Galvani........... George Bizet
Madeleine Gibson .... Mme Bizet
Webster Booth .... Don Jose
Julie Suedo .... Carmen
Peter Gawthorne ....
Howard Douglas ....
Fanny Wright ....
MUSICAL Starving composer dies after
new opera fails.

10376
THE LIFE OF CHOPIN (36) (A)
Fitzpatrick Pictures (MGM)
P:D: James A Fitzpatrick
S: W.K. Williamson
Frank Henderson .... Frederick Chopin
Julie Suedo............ George Sand
Ian Colin .... Franz Liszt
Sylvia Marriott ....
John Wickham ....
Leo von Porkony ....
MUSICAL Jilted composer becomes lover
of authoress.

10377
LILY OF LAGUNA (84) (A)
Butcher's Film Service
P: Sidney Morgan
D: Oswald Mitchell
S: Joan Wentworth Wood (Morgan)
SC: Oswald Mitchell, Ian Walker
Nora Swinburne .... Gloria Grey
Richard Ainley .... Roger Fielding
Talbot O'Farrell .... Mike
G.H. Mulcaster .... Gerald Marshall
Jenny Laird .... Jane Marshall
Edgar Driver .... Tommy Thompson
Desmond Roberts .... Arnold Egerton
Violet Graham .... Margaret Marshall
John Payne's Negro Choir; Dudley Rolph
MUSICAL Divorcee discovers the man
she loves engaged to her daughter.

10378
THE DARK STAIRWAY (72) (A)
WB-FN (WB)
P: Irving Asher
D: Arthur Woods
S: (NOVEL) Mignon G. Eberhart
(FROM WHAT DARK STAIRWAY)
SC: Brock Williams, Basil Dillon
Hugh Williams .... Dr Thurlow
Chili Bouchier .... Betty Trimmer
Garry Marsh .... Dr Mortimer
Reginald Purdell .... Askew
James Stephenson .... Insp Clarke
Glen Alyn .... Isabel Simmonds
John Carol .... Merridew
Lesley Brook .... Mary Cresswell

Robert Rendel .... Dr Fletcher
CRIME Hospital doctor murdered for
new anaesthetic.

10379
THE SINGING COP (78) (U)
WB-FN (WB)
P: Irving Asher
D: Arthur Woods
S: James Dyrenforth, Kenneth Leslie-Smith
SC: Brock Williams, Tom Phipps
Keith Falkner .... Jack Richards
Marta Labarr .... Maria Santova
Chili Bouchier .... Kit Fitzwillow
Ivy StHelier .... Sonia Kassona
Glen Alyn .... Bunty Waring
Athole Stewart ... Sir Algernon Fitzwillow
George Galleon ..... Drips Foster-Hanley
Ian Maclean .... Zabisti
Bobbie Comber .... Bombosa
Robert Rendel .... Sir Treves Hallam
Vera Bogetti .... Rosa
Brian Buchel .... Pemberton
Derek Gorst .... Capt Farquhar
Chorus of the Royal Opera House Covent
Garden
MUSICAL Policeman poses as opera singer
to expose prima donna as spy.

10380
SWEET DEVIL (79) (U)
Jack Buchanan (GFD)
D: Rene Guissart
S: (PLAY) (QUELLE DROLE DE GOSSE)
SC: Ralph Spence, Geoffrey Kerr
Bobby Howes .... Tony Brent
Jean Gillie .... Jill Turner
William Kendall .... Edward Bane
Syd Walker .... Belton
Ellis Jeffreys .... Lady Tonbridge
Glen Alyn .... Sylvia Tonbridge
Anthony Ireland .... Flores
Hazel Terry .... Rose
Sylvia Leslie .... Frances
Syd Crossley .... PC
4 New Yorkers
MUSICAL Affianced playboy falls for
typist he saves from faked suicide.

10381
OWD BOB (78) (U) USA: TO THE VICTOR
Gainsborough (GFD)
P: Edward Black
D: Robert Stevenson
S: (NOVEL) Alfred Olivant
SC: Michael Hogan, J.B.Williams
Will Fyffe .... Adam McAdam
John Loder .... David Moore
Margaret Lockwood ...... Jeannie McAdam
Moore Marriott ....,..... Samuel
Graham Moffatt .... Tammas
Wilfred Walter .... Thwaites
Eliot Mason .... Mrs Winthrop
A. Bromley Davenport .... Magistrate
H.F.Maltby .... Sgt Musgrave
Edmund Breon .... Lord Meredale
Wally Patch .... Bookie
Alf Goddard .... Bookie
DRAMA Cumberland. Old Scots farmer's
dog accused of killing sheep.

10382
BANK HOLIDAY (86) (A) USA: THREE ON
A WEEKEND
Gainsborough (GFD) *reissue:* 1951 (GFD)
(18 mins cut)
P: Edward Black
D: Carol Reed
S: Hans Wilhelm, Rodney Ackland

SC: Rodney Ackland, Roger Burford

John Lodge	Stephen Howard
Margaret Lockwood	Catherine Lawrence
Hugh Williams	Geoffrey
Rene Ray	Doreen Richards
Linden Travers	Ann Howard
Merle Tottenham	Milly
Wally Patch	Arthur
Kathleen Harrison	May
Garry Marsh	Manager
Jeanne Stuart	Miss Mayfair
Wilfrid Lawson	Sgt
Felix Aylmer	Surgeon
Alf Goddard	Man on Beach
Michael Rennie	Guardsman

DRAMA Day at seaside with nurse,
her poor fiance, widower, beauty queen,
cockney family, and embezzler.

10383
SECOND BEST BED (74) (A)
Capitol (GFD) *reissues:* 1942 (Pi) 1947 (Amb)
P: Max Schach
D: Tom Walls
S: Ben Travers

Tom Walls	Victor Garnett
Jane Baxter	Patricia Lynton
Veronica Rose	Jenny Murdoch
Carl Jaffé	Georges Dubonnet
Greta Gynt	Yvonne
Edward Lexy	Murdoch
Tyrell Davis	Whittaker
Mai Bacon	Mrs Whittaker
Ethel Coleridge	Mrs Knuckle
Davy Burnaby	Lord Kingston
Martita Hunt	Mrs Mather
Gordon James	Judge

COMEDY Magistrate's new wife thinks
he loves villager's daughter.

10384
SILVER TOP (66) (U)
Triangle (Par)
P:D: George King
S: Evadne Price
SC: Gerald Elliott, Dorothy Greenhill

Marie Wright	Mrs Deeping
Betty Ann Davies	Dushka Vernon
Marjorie Taylor	Hazel Summers
David Farrar	Babe
Brian Buchel	Flash Gerald
Brian Herbert	Jem Withers
Polly Emery	Martha Bains
Isobel Scaife	Aggie Murbles

CRIME Rich old lady reforms crook who
poses as her long-lost son.

10385
INCIDENT IN SHANGHAI (67) (A)
B&D-Paramount British *reissue:* 1949 (Amb)
P: Anthony Havelock-Allan
D:S: John Paddy Carstairs
SC: A.R.Rawlinson

Margaret Vyner	Madeleine Linden
Patrick Barr	Pat Avon
Ralph Roberts	Robert Barlow
Derek Gorst	Brian Linden
John Deverell	Weepie
George Courtney	Mel Purdue
Lotus Fragrance	Butterfly Ku
Rita Davies	Ada Newell
Johnnie Schofield	Ted Higgins

WAR China. Red Cross chief's wife loves
British pilot flying for Chinese.

10386
DIAL 999 (46) (A)
Fox British *reissue:* 1942 (Ex)
P: Edward Dryhurst

D: Lawrence Huntington
S: Lawrence Huntington, Gerald Elliott
SC: Ernest Dudley

John Longden	Bill Waring
Elizabeth Kent	Margot Curtis
Neville Brook	Hicks
Ian Fleming	Sir Edward Rigg
Paul Neville	Insp Morris
Ivan Wilmot	Gelder
Victor Hagen	Brandon

CRIME Insp unmasks head of international
gang of counterfeiters.

10387
THE REVERSE BE MY LOT (68) (A)
Rock Productions (Col)
P: Nat Ross
D: Raymond Stross
S: (NOVEL) Margaret Morrison
SC: Syd Courtenay

Ian Fleming	Dr Murray
Marjorie Corbett	Margaret
Mickey Brantford	Ralph
Georgie Harris	George
Jackie Heller	Jackie
Helen Goss	Helen
Audrene Brier	Bubbles
Aubrey Mallalieu	Dr Davidson

ROMANCE Inventor of influenza serum
and his son both love girl guinea-pig.

FEB

10388
HOUSEMASTER (95) (U)
ABPC
P: Walter C. Mycroft
D: Herbert Brenon
S: (PLAY) Ian Hay (BACHELOR BORN)
SC: Dudley Leslie, Elizabeth Meehan

Otto Kruger	Charles Donkin
Diana Churchill	Rosemary Faringdon
Phillips Holmes	Philip de Courville
Joyce Barbour	Barbara Fane
Rene Ray	Chris Faringdon
Kynaston Reeves	Rev Edmund Ovington
Walter Hudd	Frank Hastings
John Wood	Flossie Nightingale
Cecil Parker	Sir Berkeley Nightingale
Henry Hepworth	Bimbo Faringdon
Michael Shepley	Victor Beamish
Jimmy Hanley	Travers

COMEDY New headmaster demands
teacher's resignation when boys rebel
against his reforms.

10389
QUIET PLEASE (67) (A)
WB-FN (FN)
P: Irving Asher
D: Roy William Neill
S: Reginald Purdell, Anthony Hankey

Reginald Purdell	Algy Beresford
Lesley Brook	Margery Meadows
Wally Patch	Bill
Julien Mitchell	Holloway
Ian McLean	Woods
Bruce Lister	Dr Faversham
Winifred Izard	Lady Winterley
Clem Lawrance	Johnson
Ian Fleming	Dr Craven

COMEDY Buskers posing as patient and
valet save lady's gems from theft.

10390
MR SATAN (79) (A)
WB-FN(FN)
P: William Collier
D: Arthur Woods
S: John Meehan jr, J.O.C. Orton

Skeets Gallagher	Connelly
James Stephenson	Tim Garnett
Chili Bouchier	Jacqueline Manet
Franklin Dyall	Zubova
Betty Lynne	Conchita
Mary Cole	Billy
Robert Rendel	Seymour
Eric Clavering	Wilson
Dino Galvani	Scipio

CRIME War correspondent loves agent
of "dead" armaments king.

10391
MERELY MR HAWKINS (71) (U)
George Smith Productions (RKO)
D: Maclean Rogers
S: John Hunter

Eliot Makeham	Alfred Hawkins
Sybil Grove	Charlotte Hawkins
Dinah Sheridan	Betty Hawkins
George Pembroke	John Fuller
Jonathan Field	Richard
Jack Vyvyan	Harry
Max Adrian	Mr Fletcher

COMEDY Henpeck wins wife's respect by
outwitting tricksters.

10392
PAID IN ERROR (68) (U)
George Smith Productions (Col)
D: Maclean Rogers
S: John Chancellor
SC: Basil Mason, H.F.Maltby

George Carney	Will Baker
Lillian Christine	Joan Atherton
Tom Helmore	Jimmy Randle
Marjorie Taylor	Penny Victor
Googie Withers	Jean Mason
Molly Hamley-Clifford	Mrs Jenkins
Jonathan Field	Jonathan Green
Aubrey Mallalieu	George

COMEDY Boarder tries to recover £600
credited to him in error.

10393
THE VILLIERS DIAMOND (50) (A)
Fox British *reissue:* 1942 (Ex)
D: Bernerd Mainwaring
S: F. Wyndham-Mallock
SC: David Evans

Edward Ashley	Capt Dawson
Evelyn Ankers	Joan
Frank Birch	Silas Wade
Liam Gaffney	Alan O'Connel
Leslie Harcourt	Barker
Julie Suedo	Mrs Forbes
Sybil Brooke	Miss Waring
Billy Shine	Joe

CRIME Old ex-crook, blackmailed by
former partner, fakes robbery.

10394
MURDER IN THE FAMILY (75) (A)
Fox British *reissue:* 1942 (Ex)
D: Albert Parker
S: (NOVEL) James Ronald
SC: David Evans

Barry Jones	Stephen Osborne
Jessica Tandy	Ann Osborne
Evelyn Ankers	Dorothy Osborne
Donald Gray	Ted Fleming
Jessie Winter	Edith Osborne
David Markham	Michael Osborne
Glynis Johns	Marjorie Osborne
Roddy McDowell	Peter Osborne
Annie Esmond	Aunt Octavia
Rani Waller	Miss Mimms

CRIME Seven members of family have
motives for killing rich aunt.

10395
MR REEDER IN ROOM 13 (78) (A)
USA: MYSTERY OF ROOM 13
British National (ABPC)
P: John Corfield
D: Norman Lee
S: (NOVEL) Edgar Wallace (ROOM 13)
SC: Doreen Montgomery, Victor Kendall,
Elizabeth Meehan
Gibb McLaughlin . . . . J.G.Reeder
Sara Seegar . . . . Lila
Peter Murray Hill . . . . Johnnie Gray
Sally Gray . . . . Claire Kane
Malcolm Keen . . . . Peter Kane
Leslie Perrins . . . . Jeff Legge
D.J.Williams . . . . Emmanuel Legge
Robert Cochran . . . . Barker
George Merritt . . . . Stevens
CRIME Tec poses as ex-convict to catch
counterfeiters using old jail as den.

10396
SEXTON BLAKE AND THE HOODED
TERROR (70) (A)
George King (MGM) reissue: 1942 (Amb)
D: George King
S: (NOVEL) Pierre Quiroule
SC: A.R.Rawlinson
Tod Slaughter . . . . Michael Larron
George Curzon . . . . Sexton Blake
Greta Gynt . . . . Mlle Julie
Charles Oliver . . . . Max Fleming
Tony Sympson . . . . Tinker
Marie Wright . . . . Mrs Bardell
Norman Pierce . . . . Insp Bramley
David Farrar . . . . Granite Grant
CRIME Tec unmasks millionaire as head
of hooded gang.

10397
MAKE IT THREE (78) (U)
St Margarets (MGM)
P: Julius Hagen
D: David Macdonald
S: Vernon Sylvaine
Hugh Wakefield . . . . Percy Higgin
Edmund Willard . . . . Big Ed
Diana Beaumont . . . . Annie
Sydney Fairbrother . . . . . . Aunt Aggie
Jack Hobbs . . . . Charlie
Olive Sloane . . . . Kate
Alexander Field . . . . Sam
C.Denier Warren . . . . Mr Cackleberry
COMEDY Henpecked clerk must spend
three months in jail to inherit fortune.

10398
MURDER TOMORROW (69) (A)
Crusade (Par)
P: Victor M. Greene
D:SC: Donovan Pedelty
S: (PLAY) Frank Harvey
Gwenllian Gill . . . . Jean Andrews
Jack Livesey . . . . Peter Wilton
Molly Hamley-Clifford . . . . Miss Fitch
Rani Waller . . . . Miss Canning
Francis Roberts . . . . Sgt Enfield
Raymond Lovell . . . . Insp Travers
Jonathan Field . . . . PC Sanders
CRIME Solicitor helps girl who accidentally
killed her husband.

10399
SAILING ALONG (90) (U)
Gaumont (GFD)
D: Sonnie Hale
S: Selwyn Jepson
SC: Lesser Samuels, Sonnie Hale
Jessie Matthews . . . . Kay Martin
Roland Young . . . . . . Anthony Gulliver

Barry Mackay . . . . Steve Barnes
Jack Whiting . . . . Dick Randall
Alastair Sim . . . . Sylvester
Noel Madison . . . . Windy
Athene Seyler . . . . Victoria Gulliver
Frank Pettingell . . . . Skipper Barnes
Margaret Vyner . . . . Stephanie
Peggy Novak . . . . Jill
William Dewhurst . . . . Winton
Patrick Barr . . . .
MUSICAL Bargee's adopted daughter
gives up stardom for love of his son.

10400
I SEE ICE (81) (U)
ATP (ABFD) reissues: 1943; 1945; 1959 (EB)
P: Basil Dean
D: Anthony Kimmins
S: Anthony Kimmins, Austin Melford
George Formby . . . . George Bright
Kay Walsh . . . . Judy Gaye
Betty Stockfeld . . . . Mrs Hunter
Cyril Ritchard . . . . Paul Martine
Garry Marsh . . . . Galloway
Frederick Burtwell . . . . . . Detective
Ernest Sefton . . . . Outhwaite
Gavin Gordon . . . . Singer
Gordon McLeod . . . . Lord Felstead
Archibald Batty. . . . . Col Hunter
Frank Leighton . . . . Manager
COMEDY Property man in ice ballet
becomes newspaper photographer.

MAR

10401
GLAMOUR GIRL (68) (U)
WB-FN (WB)
P: William Collier
D: Arthur Woods
S: John Meehan jr, Tom Phipps
Gene Gerrard . . . . Dean Webster
Lesley Brook . . . . Connie Stevens
Ross Landon . . . . Taylor Brooks
Betty Lynne . . . . Vicki
Leslie Weston . . . . Murphy
Robert Rendel . . . . J.J.Andex
Dennis Arundell . . . . Sir Raymond Bell
James Carew . . . . Collins
Jimmy Godden . . . . Arnold
COMEDY Conceited photographer reformed
by loving secretary.

10402
SIMPLY TERRIFIC (73) (A)
WB-FN (WB)
P: Irving Asher
D: Roy William Neill
S: Basil Woon
SC: Anthony Hankey, Basil Dillon
Claude Hulbert . . . . Rodney Cherridew
Reginald Purdell . . . . Sam Todd
Zoe Wynn . . . . Goldie Divine
Patricia Medina . . . . . . Heather Carfax
Aubrey Mallalieu . . . . Sir Walter Carfax
Glen Alyn . . . . Stella Hemingway
Hugh French . . . . Dickie
Laura Wright . . . . . . Annie Hemingway
Ian McLean . . . . Foster
COMEDY Broke playboys promote
flower-seller's hangover cure.

10403
THE VIPER (75) (U)
WB-FN (FN)
P: Irving Asher
D: Roy William Neill
S: Reginald Purdell, John Dighton, J.O.C.Orton
Claude Hulbert . . . . Cedric Gull
Betty Lynne . . . . Gaby Toulong
Hal Walters . . . . Stiffy Mason

Lesley Brook . . . . Jenny
Fred Groves . . . . Insp Bradawl
Dino Galvani . . . . The Viper
Boris Ranevsky . . . . Carlos
Harvey Braban . . . . Jagger
Reginald Purdell . . . . Announcer
COMEDY Tec dons disguises to save girl's
diamond from escaped convict.

10404
IT'S IN THE BLOOD (56) (U)
WB-FN (FN)
P: Irving Asher
D: Gene Gerrard
S:(NOVEL) David Whitelaw (THE BIG
PICTURE)
SC: Reginald Purdell, John Dighton,
J.O.C.Orton, Brock Williams, Basil Dillon
Claude Hulbert . . . . Edwin Povey
Lesley Brook . . . . Jill Borden
James Stephenson . . . . Milky Joe
Max Leeds . . . . James Renton
Clem Lawrence . . . . . . Dave Grimmett
Glen Alyn . . . . Celestin
Percy Walsh . . . . Jules Barres
George Galleon . . . . Gendarme
COMEDY Film fan on day trip to Bologne
catches jewel thieves.

10405
DOUBLE OR QUITS (72) (A)
WB-FN (WB)
P: Irving Asher
D: Roy William Neill
S: Michael Barringer
Frank Fox. . . Bill Brooks/Scotty Tucker
Patricia Medina . . . . Caroline
Hal Walters . . . . Alf
Ian Fleming . . . . Sir Frederick Beal
Gordon McLeod . . . . School
Jack Raine . . . . Roland
Philip Ray . . . . Hepworth
Charles Paton . . . . Mr Binks
Mai Bacon. . . . . Mrs Binks
CRIME Reporter is double of thief who
steals rare stamps on transatlantic liner.

10406
THISTLEDOWN (79) (U)
WB-FN (WB)
P: Irving Asher
D: Arthur Woods
S: John Meehan jr, J.O.C.Orton
SC: Brock Williams
Aino Bergo . . . . Therese Glenloch
Keith Falkner . . . . Sir Ian Glenloch
Athole Stewart . . . . . Duke of Invergower
Sharon Lynne . . . . Ivy Winter
Bruce Lister . . . . Lord James Dunfoyle
Ian Maclean . . . . Rossini
Amy Veness . . . . Mary Glenloch
Vera Bogetti . . . . Simmonds
Gordon McLeod . . . . Gallagher
MUSICAL Scotland. Laird believes continental
wife is unfaithful.

10407
DARTS ARE TRUMPS (72) (U)
George Smith Productions (RKO)
D: Maclean Rogers
S: Gordon Bushell
SC: Kathleen Butler, H.F.Maltby
Eliot Makeham . . . . Joe Stone
Nancy O'Neil . . . . Mary Drake
Ian Colin . . . . Harry
Muriel George . . . . Mrs Drake
H.F.Maltby . . . . Stephen Sims
Paul Blake . . . . Hon Bernard Jaye
Johnny Singer . . . . Jimmy
COMEDY Clerk's skill as dart player helps
him catch jewel thief.

10408
ROMANCE A LA CARTE (72) (U)
GS Enterprises (RKO)
P: George Smith
D: Maclean Rogers
S: Paul Hervey Fox
SC: Vera Allinson
Leslie Perrins .... Louis
Dorothy Boyd .... Anne
Antony Holles .... Rudolph
Charles Sewell .... Roberto
Michael Bazalgette .... Tony
Paul Sheridan .... Strelini
Betty Shale .... Lady Eleanor Clure
COMEDY Rivalry between manager of
restaurant and chef.

10409
IF I WERE BOSS (72) (A)
GS Enterprises (Col)
P: George Smith
D: Maclean Rogers
S: Basil Mason
Bruce Seton .... Steve
Googie Withers .... Pat
Ian Fleming .... Mr Biltmore
Zillah Bateman .... Mrs Biltmore
Julie Suedo .... Irma
Charles Oliver .... Owen Reeves
DRAMA Conceited clerk inherits firm
and becomes pawn of crooks.

10410
COMING OF AGE (68) (U)
GS Enterprises (Col)
P: George Smith
D: Manning Haynes
S: Paul White, Rowan Kennedy
Eliot Makeham .... Henry Strudwick
Joyce Bland .... Isobel Strudwick
Jack Melford .... Roger Squire
Ruby Miller .... Julia Knight
Jimmy Hanley .... Arthur Strudwick
Evelyn Ankers .... Christine Squire
Annie Esmond .... Mrs Crowther
Aubrey Mallalieu .... Mr Myers
COMEDY Husband flirts with singer,
his wife with singer's husband.

10411
THE CLAYDON TREASURE MYSTERY
(63) (A)
Fox British
D: Manning Haynes
S: (NOVEL) Neil Gordon
(THE SHAKESPEARE MURDERS)
SC: Edward Dryhurst
John Stuart .... Peter Kerrigan
Garry Marsh .... Sir George Ilford
Evelyn Ankers .... Rosemary Claydon
Annie Esmond .... Lady Caroline
Campbell Gullan .... Tollemach
Aubrey Mallalieu .... Lord Claydon
Finlay Currie .... Rubin
Joss Ambler .... Insp Fleming
Vernon Harris .... Rhodes
CRIME Novelist solves librarian's death
and locates hidden treasure.

10412
THE LAST BARRICADE (58) (U)
Fox British reissue: 1943 (200 ft cut)
D: SC: Alex Bryce
S: R.F. Gore-Brown, Lawrence Green
Frank Fox .... Michael Donovan
Greta Gynt .... Maria
Paul Sheridan .... Valdez
Meinhart Maur .... Don Jose

Dino Galvani .... Lopez
Vernon Harris .... Capt Lee
Hay Petrie .... Capt MacTavish
Andrea Malandrinos ..... General
WAR Spain. Reporter saves spy's daughter
from prison.

10413
SECOND THOUGHTS (61) (A)
Fox British reissue: 1941,
THE CRIME OF PETER FRAME (Fed)
D: Albert Parker
S: David Evans
Frank Fox .... Tony Gordon
Evelyn Ankers .... Molly Frame
Frank Allenby .... Peter Frame
A.Bromley Davenport .... George Gaunt
Marjorie Fielding .... Mrs Gaunt
Joan Hickson .... Ellen
DRAMA Disfigured chemist suspects his
wife loves playwright.

10414
FATHER O' NINE (47) (U)
Fox British
P: Ivor McLaren
D: Roy Kellino
S: Harold G.Brown
Hal Gordon .... Eddie Mills
Dorothy Dewhurst ...... Mill Wilson
Jimmy Godden .... Col Briggs
Claire Arnold .... Miss Pipp
Denis Cowles .... Blenkinsop
Jo Monkhouse .... Albert
COMEDY Sacked man must find nine
children to prove claim for sympathy.

10415
WHO GOES NEXT ? (85) (A)
Fox British
P: Ivor McLaren
D: Maurice Elvey
S: (PLAY) Reginald Simpson, James
W. Drawbell
SC: David Evans, Lawrence Green
Barry K. Barnes .... Maj Hamilton
Sophie Steward .... Sarah Hamilton
Jack Hawkins .... Capt Beck
Charles Eaton .... Capt Royde
Andrew Osborn .... F/O Stevens
Frank Birch .... Capt Grover
Roy Findlay .... Lt Williams
Alastair Macintyre .... Lt Mackenzie
Meinhart Maur .... Commandant
WAR Germany, 1916. POW Major supervising
tunnelling learns that a captain is in
love with his wife.

10416
DEAD MEN TELL NO TALES (80) (A)
British National (ABPC)
P: John Corfield
D: David Macdonald
S: (NOVEL) Francis Beeding
(THE NORWICH VICTIMS)
SC: Walter Summers, Stafford Dickens,
Doreen Montgomery, Emlyn Williams
Emlyn Williams .. Dr Robert Headlam/
Friedberg
Hugh Williams .... Insp Martin
Sara Seegar .... Marjorie
Marius Goring .... Greening
Lesley Brook .... Elizabeth Orme
Christine Silver .... Miss Haslett
Clive Morton .... Frank Fielding
Anne Wilton .... Bridget
Hal Gordon .... Sgt
CRIME Boys' School matron murdered
when she wins French lottery.

10417
CHIPS (80) (U)
British Fine Arts reissue: 1939 (1246 ft cut)
P:D: Edward Godal
S: Vivian Tidmarsh
Tony Wyckham .... Chips
Robb Wilton .... PC Chester
Davy Burnaby .... Alderman
Billy Merson .... Harbour-Master
Peter Dawson .... Salty Sam
Joyce Bland .... Lady
Bertram Wallis .... Smuggler
Terry's Juveniles; Twenty Tiny Tappers
MUSICAL Suspended sea scout reinstated
after he catches smugglers.

10418
BLONDES FOR DANGER (68) (A)
Wilcox (BL) reissue: 1946 (NR)
P: Herbert Wilcox
D: Jack Raymond
S: (NOVEL) Evadne Price
(RED FOR DANGER)
SC: Gerald Elliott
Gordon Harker .... Alf Huggins
Enid Stamp-Taylor .... Valerie
Ivan Brandt .... Capt Berkeley
Janet Johnson .... Ann Penny
Percy Parsons .... Quintin Hearne
Everley Gregg .... Hetty Hopper
Charles Eaton .... Prince Boris
CRIME Taxi driver saves wounded prince
from assassins.

10419
DEVIL'S ROCK (54) (U)
Germain Gerard Burger (Col)
D: Germain Burger
S: Richard Hayward
Richard Hayward .... Sam Mulhern
Geraldine Mitchell ... Geraldine Larmour
Gloria Grainger ...... Veronica Larmour
Terence Grainger .... John Browne
Nancy Cullen .... Mrs Huggins
Charles Fagan .... Sgt Davis
Tom Casement .... Dandy Dick
Stendal Todd; Lambeg Folk Dance Society;
St Gall's School Choir
MUSICAL Ireland. Concert party takings
stolen from box office.

10420
HORSE SENSE (39) (U)
AIP (Col)
D: S: Widgey Newman
Jennie Lovelace .... Ann
W.E.Hodge .... Donald
Roy Byford .... Magistrate
Bob Able .... Governor
Bob Earle .... Alf
DRAMA Old farm mare ousted by
mechanisation but saved from shipment to
France.

10421
GOVERNOR BRADFORD (33) (U)
USA: GOVERNOR WILLIAM BRADFORD
AIP (Col)
P: Widgey Newman
D: Hugh Parry
S: (PAGEANT) Hugh Parry; John Nathaniel
Ruffin (RHETORLOGUE)
Hetty Sawyer .... Meg
A.M.Cowlard .... William Bradford
Frank Parker .... Bartholomew
Kenneth Maggs .... Poynes
Henry J. Gamble .... John Robinson
Marjorie Johnson ...... Bridget Robinson
Reuben Dory .... Myles Standish
Eric Price Holmes .... John Alden
Leo Genn .... Prologue

HISTORY Persecution causes pilgrims to set sail in "Mayflower."

10422
ON VELVET (70) (A)
AIP (Col) *reissue:* 1941 (Ex; 18 mins cut)
D: Widgey Newman
S: John Quin

Wally Patch	Harry Higgs
Joe Hayman	Sam Cohen
Vi Kaley	Mrs Higgs
Mildred Franklin	Mrs Cohen
Jennifer Skinner	Mary
Leslie Bradley	Monty
Ambrose Day.	Waterbury

Nina Mae McKinney; Julie Suedo; Gordon Little; Eric Barker; Collinson & Dean; Mark Stone; Helga & Jo; Belling's Dogs; Rex Burrows' Orchestra
MUSICAL Cockney bookie and Jewish punter set up their own television station.

10423
A SISTER TO ASSIST 'ER (72) (U)
AIP (Col) *reissue:* 1941 (Ex; 22 mins cut)
P: Widgey Newman
D: Widgey Newman, George Dewhurst
S: (PLAY) John le Breton
SC: George Dewhurst

Muriel George	Mrs May
Pollie Emery	Mrs Getch
Charles Paton	Mr Harris
Billy Percy	Alf
Harry Herbert	Mr Getch
Dorothy Vernon	Mrs Thistlethwaite
Dora Levis	Mrs Hawkes

COMEDY Poor old woman poses as rich twin to fool mean landlady.

10424
CROWN TRIAL (35) (U)
AIP (Ex)
P: Widgey R. Newman
D: SC: John Ruffin
S: (ORATIONS) Demosthenes; Aeschines

John Nathaniel. .Demosthenes/Aeschines	
Tubby Hayes	Adipose
Ambrose Day	

COMEDY Greece, 300 BC. Youth-restoring weed leads to treason trial.

10425
BAD BOY (69) (A)
Radius Films *reissue:* 1940, BRANDED (RKO)
P: Vaughan N. Dean
D: SC: Lawrence Huntington
S: R. Astley Richards

John Warwick	Nick Bryan
John Longden	Insp Thompson
Kathleen Kelly	Ann Travers
Gabrielle Brune	Ena Bryan
Brian Buchel	Tony Santell
Richard Norris	Joe Morgan
Edie Martin	Mrs Bryan
Ernest Sefton	Sam Barnes

CRIME Reformed thief saves sister from capture by old boss.

10426
SPECIAL EDITION (68) (A)
Redd Davis (Par)
D: Redd Davis
S: Derek Neame
SC: Katharine Strueby

Lucille Lisle	Sheila Pearson
John Garrick	Frank Warde
Norman Pierce	Aiken
Johnny Schofield	Horatio Adams
Frederick Culley	Dr Pearson
Vera Bogetti	Mrs Howard

Mabel Twemlow	Mrs Cavendish
Vincent Holman	Insp Bourne
Dino Galvani	Toni Lang
Fewlass Llewellyn	Coroner

CRIME Reporter proves photographer stabbed doctor and blackmailer.

10427
OH BOY ! (73) (U)
ABPC
P: Walter C. Mycroft
D: Albert de Courville
S: Douglas Furber
SC: Dudley Leslie

Albert Burdon	Percy Flower
Mary Lawson	June Messenger
Bernard Nedell	Angelo Tonelli
Jay Laurier	Horatio Flower
Robert Cochran	Albert Bolsover
Edmon Ryan	Butch
Maire O'Neill	Mrs Baggs
Syd Walker	Sgt
Charles Carson	Governor
Jerry Verno	Shopwalker
John Wood	Man
Billy Milton	Conductor

COMEDY Chemist reverts to childhood and saves Crown Jewels from gangsters.

10428
JUST LIKE A WOMAN (79) (A)
ABPC
P: Walter C. Mycroft
D: Paul Stein
S: Paul Hervery Fox
SC: Alec Coppel

John Lodge	Tony Walsh
Gertrude Michael	Ann Heston
Jeanne de Casalis	Poppy Mayne
Fred Emney	Sir Charles Devoir
Arthur Wontner	Escubar
Hartley Power	Al
Anthony Ireland	Roderique
David Burns	Pedro
Felix Aylmer	Sir Robert Hummell
Henry Hewitt	Simpson
Ralph Truman	Maharajah

COMEDY Jeweller's agent seeking black pearls saves girl rival from crooks.

10429
ALMOST A HONEYMOON (80) (A)
Welwyn (Pathe) *reissue:* 1942 (Amb)
P: Warwick Ward
D: Norman Lee
S: (PLAY) Walter Ellis
SC: Kenneth Horne, Ralph Neale

Tommy Trinder	Peter Dibley
Linden Travers ..	Patricia Quilter
Edmond Breon	Aubrey Lovitt
Frederick Burtwell	Charles
Vivienne Bennett	Rita Brent
Arthur Hambling	Adolphus
Aubrey Mallalieu	Clutterbuck
Betty Jardine	Lavinia Pepper
Ian Fleming	Sir James Hopper
Wally Patch	Bailiff

COMEDY Poor playboy forgets he has let flat to girl and spends night there.

10430
THE GABLES MYSTERY (66) (A)
Welwyn (MGM)
P: Warwick Ward
D: Harry Hughes
S: (PLAY) Jack Celestin, Jack de Leon (THE MAN AT SIX)
SC: Victor Kendall, Harry Hughes

Francis L. Sullivan	Power
Antoinette Cellier	Helen Vane

Leslie Perrins	Insp Lloyd
Derek Gorst	Frank Rider
Jerry Verno	Potts
Aubrey Mallalieu	Sir James Rider
Sidney King	Mortimer
Laura Wright	Mrs Mullins

CRIME Girl tec unmasks colleague as killer who posed as woman to steal jewels.

10431
THE SKY RAIDERS (57) (A)
Sovereign (FN)
D: Fraser Foulsham

Nita Harvey	June Welwyn
Ambrose Day	Crealand Wake
Ronald Braden	David Welwyn
Michael Hogarth	Jack Weatherby
Beatrice Marsden	Miss Quarm
Harry Newman	Hawkins
David Keir	Dr Martin

CRIME Bullion thieves kidnap girl to force her pilot brother's help.

10432
JOHN HALIFAX, GENTLEMAN (69) (U)
George King (MGM) *reissue:* 1940 (Amb)
D: George King
S: (NOVEL) Mrs Craik
SC: A.R. Rawlinson

John Warwick	John Halifax
Nancy Burne	Ursula March
Ralph Michael	Phineas Fletcher
D.J.Williams	Abel Fletcher
Brian Buchel	Lord Luxmore
Billy Bray	Tully
Elsie Wagstaffe	Jael

DRAMA 1790. Apprentice inherits mill and weds Lord's disowned ward.

10433
SMUGGLERS' HARVEST (43) (U)
Cantaphone (Ex)
P: D.F. Cantley
D: John R. Phipps

Hope Davy	
Mike Nono	
Katherine Ferraz	
Harry Cultance	

ADVENTURE Cornwall. Coastguard catches rum smugglers.

10434
THE AWAKENING (64) (A)
Cosmopolitan
D: Alfonse Frenguelli

Eric Elliott	Dr Christian Adrian
Eve Gray	
Rex Walker	

ROMANCE Girl doctor loved by old doctor and young partner.

10435
CHINATOWN NIGHTS (70) (U)
Victory (Col)
D: Tony Frenguelli
S: Nigel Byass

H. Agar Lyons	Dr Sin Fang
Anne Grey	Sonia Graham
Robert Hobbs	John Bryne
Nell Emerald	Mrs Higgins

CRIME Chinese crook kidnaps girl for her brother's "Silver Ray."

10436
THE DANCE OF DEATH (64) (A)
Glenrose (Fidelity)
D: Gerald Blake
S: Ralph Dawson

Vesta Victoria	Lady Lander
Stewart Rome	Armand Chabrier

Julie Suedo . . . .   Mara Gessner
Elizabeth Kent . . . .
Jimmy Godden . . . .
Betty Norton . . . .
Billy Merrin and his Commanders
CRIME Ex-convict steals Lord's cursed
jewel and kills dancer.

10437
ON TOP OF THE UNDERWORLD (series) (A)
Century Films (BSS)
P: Charles Leeds
D: Mickey Delamar, Denis Kavanagh
S: (BOOK) Ex Detective Inspector Leach
SC: Rupert Downing
Andre Morell . . . .   Insp Simmonds

10438
1: THE MURDERED CONSTABLE (14)

10439
2: RECEIVERS (15)
Andrew Lawrence
David Pringle
Johnny Scofield
George Turner

10440
3: THE KITE MOB (16)
David Pringle
Andrew Lawrence
George Turner
Nita Harvey

10441
4: CONFIDENCE TRICKSTERS (17)
Roddy Hughes
David Pringle
Edna Davies
Reg Hunt

10442
5: CRIMINALS ALWAYS BLUNDER (14)
CRIME Based on cases solved by an
ex Detective Inspector.

10443
WEST END NIGHTS (12) (U)
British Foundation (Col)
D:S: Ronald Haines
MUSICAL Football pools winner takes
friends to cabaret.

10444
SINK OR SWIM (15) (U)
Fidelity
Norman Taylor . . . .   The Man
COMEDY Fat man acts in his first film
and gets blown up.

10445
SECOND SIGHT (15) (U)
Fidelity
DRAMA Dreamed warning indirectly saves
the life of magnate

10446
UNCLE NICK (60)
Hibernia Film Studios
P:D:S: Tom Cooper
Val Vousden . . . .   Nick
COMEDY Ireland.

10447
BEDTIME STORY (71) (U)
Admiral (GN)
P. Victor M. Greene
D:SC: Donovan Pedelty
S: (PLAY) Walter Ellis
Jack Livesey . . . . Sir John Shale
Lesley Wareing . . . .   Judy
Eliot Makeham . . . .   Uncle Toby

Dorothy Dewhurst . . . . . .   Lady Blundell
Margery Morris . . . .   Isabel
Michael Balzagerre . . . .   Prince
Jonathan Field . . . .   Butler
COMEDY Lady's orphan niece poses as
American heiress to win cousin's fiance.

10448
WEST OF KERRY (48) (U) USA: MEN OF
IRELAND Retitled: ISLAND MAN
Irish National (Butcher)
P: Victor Taylor
D: Dick Bird
S: Donal O'Cahil, John Duffy
SC: Patrick Keenan Heale
Eileen Curran . . . .   Eileen Guheen
Cecil Ford . . . .   Neale O'Moore
Brian O'Sullivan . . . .
Gabriel Fallon . . . .
Daisy Murphy . . . .
Gerard Duffy . . . .
Josephine Fitzgerald . . . . . .
ROMANCE Blasket Island girl falls in love
with visiting medical student.

10449
TWO MEN IN A BOX (49) (A)
Ace Films
D: R.A.Hopwood
Ronald Frankau   Tommy Handley
Warden & West   Paddy Browne
Gus Chevalier   Bruno Hoffman
REVUE Windmill Theatre production.

10450
SWING (37) (A)
Ace Films
D: R.A.Hopwood
Meggie Eaton   Gus Chevalier
Warden & West   Eric Woodburn
Dick Hurran   Edna Wood
REVUE Windmill Theatre production.

10451
REVUE PARADE (35) (A)
Ace Films
D: R.A.Hopwood
Gus Chevalier   Meggie Eaton
Mollie Halliwell   Leslie Spurling
Ken Douglas   Barry Seymour
REVUE Windmill Theatre production.

10452
THE INTERRUPTED REHEARSAL (39)
Ace Films
D: R.A.Hopwood
Windmill Theatre cast
REVUE Windmill Theatre production.

10453
BEHIND THE TABS (48)
Ace Films
D: R.A. Hopwood
Windmill Theatre cast
REVUE Windmill Theatre production.

10454
SPOTLIGHT (39)
Ace Films
D: R.A.Hopwood
Windmill Theatre cast
REVUE Windmill Theatre production.

APR

10455
A YANK AT OXFORD (105) (U)
MGM British reissue: 1945
P: Michael Balcon
D: Jack Conway
S: John Monk Saunders, Leon Gordon,
Sidney Gilliat, Michael Hogan

SC: Malcolm Stuart Boylan, Walter Ferris,
George Oppenheimer, Leon Gordon,
Roland Pertwee.
Robert Taylor . . . .   Lee Sheridan
Lionel Barrymore . . . .   Dan Sheridan
Vivien Leigh . . . .   Elsa Craddock
Maureen O'Sullivan . . . .   Molly Beaumont
Edmund Gwenn . . . .   The Dean
Griffith Jones . . . .   Paul Beaumont
C.V.France . . . .   Dean Snodgrass
Edward Rigby . . . .   Scatters
Morton Selten . . . .   Cecil Davidson
Claud Gillingwater . . . .   Ben Dalton
Tully Marshall . . . .   Cephas
Walter Kingsford . . . .   Dean Williams
Robert Coote . . . .   Wavertree
Peter Croft . . . .   Ramsey
Edmond Breon . . . .   Capt Wavertree
COMEDY Cocksure American student
loves the sister of his English rival.
(Top Moneymaker: 1938).

MAY

10456
KATE PLUS TEN (81) (U)
Wainwright (GFD) reissue: 1942 (Maj)
P: Richard Wainwright
D: Reginald Denham
S: (NOVEL) Edgar Wallace
SC: Jack Hulbert, Jeffrey Dell
Jack Hulbert . . . .   Mike Pemberton
Genevieve Tobin . . . .   Kate Westhanger
Noel Madison . . . .   Gregori
Francis L. Sullivan . . . .   Lord Flamborough
Arthur Wontner . . . .   Col Westhanger
Frank Cellier . . . .   Sir Ralph Sapson
Peter Haddon . . . .   Boltover
Googie Withers . . . .   Lady Moya
Edward Lexy . . . .   Sgt
Felix Aylmer . . . .   Bishop
Leo Genn . . . .   Dr Gurdon
Queenie Leonard . . . .
Walter Sondes . . . .
CRIME Inspector falls for a girl whose
gang steals a bullion train.

10457
BLARNEY (68) (U) USA: IRELAND'S
BORDER LINE
O.D.Productions (ABFD)
reissue: 1949 (25 mins cut)
P:S: Jimmy O'Dea, Harry O'Donovan
D: Harry O'Donovan
Jimmy O'Dea . . . .   Billy Brannigan
Myrètte Morven . . . .   Annie
Ronald Malcolmson . . . . . .   Sgt MacAleer
Hazel Hughes . . . .   Maura
Julie Suedo . . . .   Sadie Tyler
Kenneth Warrington . . . . .   Albert Tyler
Noel Purcell . . . .   Sgt Hogan
COMEDY Ireland. Salesman mistakenly
takes bag containing stolen gems.

10458
STAR OF THE CIRCUS (68) (U)
USA: HIDDEN MENACE
ABPC Reissue: 1942 (IFR)
P: Walter C. Mycroft
D: Albert de Courville
S: (NOVEL) Heinrich Zeiler
(DECEMBER WITH TRUXA)
SC: John Monk Saunders, Hans Zerlett,
Elizabeth Meehan, Dudley Leslie
Gertrude Michael . . . .   Yesta
Otto Kruger . . . .   Garvin
John Clements . . . .   Paul Huston
Barbara Blair . . . .   Hilda
Gene Sheldon . . . .   Peters
Patrick Barr . . . .   Truxa

Norah Howard . . . .   Frau Schlipp
John Turnbull . . . .   Tenzler
Alfred Wellesley . . . .   Ackermann
ROMANCE Germany. Sailor posing as
tightrope walker loves dancer coveted
by illusionist.

10459
THE TERROR (73) (A)
ABPC *reissue:* 1942 (IFR)
P: Walter C. Mycroft
D: Richard Bird
S: (PLAY) Edgar Wallace
SC: William Freshman
Wilfrid Lawson . . . .   Mr Goodman
Arthur Wontner . . . .   Col Redmayne
Linden Travers . . . .   Mary Redmayne
Bernard Lee . . . .   Ferdy Fane
Alastair Sim . . . .   Soapy Marks
Henry Oscar . . . .   Connor
Iris Hoey . . . .   Mrs Elvery
Lesley Wareing . . . .   Veronica Elvery
Edward Lexy . . . .   Insp Dobie
Richard Murdoch . . . .   PC Lewis
John Turnbull . . . .   Insp Hallick
CRIME Ex-convict searches for bullion
hidden in old guest-house.

10460
JANE STEPS OUT (71) (A)
ABPC *reissue:* 1942 (IFR)
P: Walter C. Mycroft
D: Paul Stein
S: (PLAY) Kenneth Horne
SC: Dudley Leslie, William Freshman
Jean Muir . . . .   Beatrice Wilton
Diana Churchill . . . .   Jane Wilton
Peter Murray Hill . . . .   Basil Gilbert
Fred Emney . . . .   Gen Wilton
Judy Kelly . . . .   Margot Kent
Athene Seyler . . . .   Grandma
Iris Hoey . . . .   Mrs Wilton
COMEDY Family drudge revolts after
falling for sister's fiance.

JUN
10461
THE DRUM (104) (U) tech USA: DRUMS
London-Denham (UA) *reissues:* 1944
(Eal) 1948 (BL)
P: Alexander Korda
D: Zoltan Korda
S: Lajos Biro, Arthur Wimperis, Patrick
Kirwan, Hugh Gray
Sabu . . . .   Prince Azim
Raymond Massey . . . .   Prince Ghul
Valerie Hobson . . . .   Mrs Carruthers
Roger Livesey . . . .   Capt Carruthers
Desmond Tester . . . .   Bill Holder
Martin Walker . . . .   Herrick
David Tree . . . .   Lt Escott
Francis L. Sullivan . . . .   Governor
Roy Emerton . . . .   Wafadar
Edward Lexy . . . .   Sgt-Maj Kernel
Julien Mitchell . . . .   Sgt
Amid Taftazani . . . .   Mohammed Khan
Archibald Batty . . . .   Maj Bond
Frederick Culley . . . .   Dr Murphy
Charles Oliver . . . .   Rajab
Alf Goddard . . . .   Pte Kelly
ADVENTURE India. Boy Prince summons
army friends to thwart frontier rising by
his usurping uncle.

10462
THE CHALLENGE (75) (U)
London-Denham (UA) *reissue:* 1944 (Key)
P: Gunther Stapenhorst, Alexander Korda
D: Milton Rosmer, Luis Trenker

SC: Emeric Pressburger, Patrick Kirwan,
Milton Rosmer
Luis Trenker . . . .   Jean Carrell
Robert Douglas . . . .   Edward Whymper
Joan Gardner . . . .   Felicitas Favre
Mary Clare . . . .   Mme Carrell
Fred Groves . . . .   Favre
Lawrence Baskcomb . . . . .   Podestra
Ralph Truman . . . .   Giordano
Tony Sympson . . . .   Luc Meynet
Cyril Smith . . . .   Customs Officer
Frank Birch . . . .   Rev Charles Hudson
Geoffrey Wardwell . . . Lord Francis Douglas
ADVENTURE Matterhorn, 1865. Guide proves
that English climber did not sacrifice friends.

10463
AROUND THE TOWN (68) (U)
British Lion *reissue:* 1946 (NR)
P:D: Herbert Smith
S: Fenn Sherie, Ingram d'Abbes
Vic Oliver . . . .   Ollie
Irene Ware . . . .   Norma Wyngold
Finlay Currie . . . .   Sam Wyngold
Jimmy Kennedy . . . .   Michael Carr
Tin Pan Alley Trio . . . . . .   Leslie Carew
3 Hillbillies . . . .   Rhythm Sisters
Terry's Juveniles . . . .   2 Charladies
Al & Bob Harvey . . . . . .   Pat McCormack
Maurice Winnick and his Band
MUSICAL Agent escorts American
producer and his daughter around London
shows.

10464
WE'RE GOING TO BE RICH (80) (A)
20th Century Productions (20)
P: Robert T. Kane, Samuel G. Engel
D: Monty Banks
S: James Edward Grant
SC: Rohama Siegel, Sam Hellman
Gracie Fields . . . .   Kit Dobson
Victor McLaglen . . . .   Dobbie Dobson
Brian Donlevy . . . .   Yankee Gordon
Coral Browne . . . .   Pearl
Ted Smith . . . .   Tim
Gus McNaughton . . . .   Broderick
Charles Carson . . . .   Keeler
Syd Crossley . . . .   Jake
Hal Gordon . . . .   Charlie
Don McCorkindale . . . . . .   Killer
DRAMA Africa, 1880. Singer leaves worthless
boxer husband for saloon keeper.

10465
STRANGE BOARDERS (79) (A)
Gainsborough (GFD)
P: Edward Black
D: Herbert Mason
S: (NOVEL) E. Phillips Oppenheim
(STRANGE BOARDERS OF PARADISE
CRESCENT)
SC: A.R.Rawlinson, Sidney Gilliat
Tom Walls . . . .   Tommy Blythe
Renee Saint-Cyr . . . .   Louise Blythe
Leon M. Lion . . . .   Luke
Googie Withers . . . .   Elsie
Ronald Adam . . . .   Barstow
C.V.France . . . .   Col Anstruther
Nina Boucicault . . . .   Mrs Anstruther
Tyrell Davis . . . .   Hayes
C. Denier Warren . . . .   Fry
Irene Handl . . . .   Mrs Dewar
George Curzon . . . .   Sir Charles
Martita Hunt . . . .   Miss Pitter
CRIME Secret agent and newlywed
wife stay at boarding house full of spies.

10466
CONVICT 99 (91) (A)
Gainsborough (GFD)
P: Edward Black
D: Marcel Varnel
S: Cyril Campion,
SC: Marriott Edgar, Val Guest,
Jack Davies, Ralph Smart
Will Hay . . . .   Benjamin Twist
Moore Marriott . . . .   Jerry the Mole
Graham Moffatt . . . .   Albert
Googie Withers . . . .   Lottie
Garry Marsh . . . .   Johnson
Peter Gawthorne . . . . . Sir Cyril Wagstaffe
Basil Radford . . . .   Governor
Denis Wyndham . . . .   Warder
Wilfrid Walter . . . .   Max Slessor
Alf Goddard . . . .   Sykes
Teddy Brown . . . .   Slim Charlie
Kathleen Harrison . . . .   Mabel
Roy Emerton . . . .   Charles Benjamin
COMEDY Teacher made prison governor
in error lets convicts run stock corporation.

10467
VESSEL OF WRATH (93) (A)
USA: THE BEACHCOMBER
Mayflower (ABPC) *reissue:* 1949 (Ren)
P:D: Erich Pommer
S: (STORY) W. Somerset Maugham
SC: Bartlett Cormack, B. Van Thal
Charles Laughton . . . .   Ginger Ted Wilson
Elsa Lanchester . . . .   Martha Jones
Robert Newton . . . .   Controleur
Tyrone Guthrie . . . .   Rev Jones
Dolly Mollinger . . . .   Lia
Rosita Garcia . . . . . , ...   Kati
Fred Groves . . . .   Captain
Eliot Makeham . . . .   Clerk
Ley On . . . .   Ah King
COMEDY South Seas. Missionary's sister
reforms drunken beachcomber.

10468
ALMOST A GENTLEMAN (78) (U)
Butcher's Film Service
P: Sidney Morgan
D: Oswald Mitchell
S: Willie Singer
SC: Sidney Morgan, Oswald Mitchell,
Billy Bennett
Billy Bennett . . . .   Bill Barker
Kathleen Harrison . . . .   Mrs Barker
Gibb McLaughlin . . . . Bartholomew Quist
Marcelle Rogez . . . .   Mimi
Mervyn Johns . . . .   Percival Clicker
Basil Langton . . . .   Andrew Sinker
Harry Terry . . . .   Jim
Dorothy Vernon . . . .   Mrs Garrett
COMEDY Sharepushers mistake night
watchman for glue magnate

10469
MOUNTAINS 'O' MOURNE (85) (U)
Rembrandt (Butcher)
D: Harry Hughes
S: Daisy L. Fielding
SC: Gerlad Brosnan
Rene Ray . . . .   Mary Macree
Niall MacGinnis . . . .   Paddy Kelly
Jerry Verno . . . .   Dip Evans
Betty Ann Davies . . . .   Violet Mayfair
Charles Oliver . . . .   Errol Finnegan
Kaye Seely . . . .   Peter O'Loughlin
Maire O'Neill . . . .   Maura Macree
Eve Lynd . . . .   Nikita Finchley
Pat Noonan . . . .   Murty Macree
Freda Jackson . . . .   Biddy O'Hara

Alexandér Butler . . . . Tim Kelly
Leonard Henry; Andre & Curtis; Cornelia
& Eddie; Percival Mackey's Band
MUSICAL Ireland. Farmer dallies with
socialite but returns to village sweetheart.

10470
LITTLE DOLLY DAYDREAM (82) (U)
Argyle-British (Butcher)
Reissue: 1943 (Sherwood; 1381 ft cut)
P: John Argyle
D: Oswald Mitchell
S: Ian Walker
SC: Oswald Mitchell
Binkie Stuart . . . . Dolly
Talbot O'Farrell . . . . Old Moe
Jane Welsh . . . . Claire
Warren Jenkins . . . . Jack Kelly
Eric Fawcett . . . . Richard
Cathleen Nesbitt . . . . Miss Parker
Sydney Fairbrother . . . . . . Mrs Harris
G.H. Mulcaster . . . . Warton
Arthur E. Owen . . . . Spider
Guy Jones and his Band
MUSICAL Street organist saves lost girl
from crooks and returns her to mother.
(Extracts in HIGHLIGHTS OF VARIETY
No. 24 (1940).)

10471
SCRUFFY (61) (U)
Vulcan (BIED)
D: Randall Faye
S: Margaret Houghton
Jack Melford . . . . Jim
Billy Merson . . . . Golly
Tonie Edgar Bruce . . . . . . Mrs Pottinger
Michael Gainsborough . . . . Michael
McArthur Gordon . . . . Hoskins
Chris McMaster . . . . Adam
Peter Gawthorne . . . . Chairman
Joan Ponsford . . . . Judy
DRAMA Two burglars reform to adopt
runaway orphan and mongrel.

10472
MEET MR PENNY (70) (U)
British National (ABPC)
P: John Corfield
D: David Macdonald
S: (RADIO SERIES) Maurice
Moisiewitsch (MR PENNY)
SC: Victor Kendall, Doreen Montgomery
Richard Goolden . . . . Henry Penny
Vic Oliver . . . . Allgood
Fabia Drake . . . . Annie Penny
Kay Walsh . . . . Peggy Allgood
Patrick Barr . . . . Clive Roberts
Hermione Gingold . . . . . . Mrs Wilson
Wilfrid Hyde White . . . . . . Mr Wilson
Charles Farrell . . . . Jackson
Hal Walters . . . . Cecil
Joss Ambler . . . . Gridley
Jack Raine . . . . Preston
Renee Gadd . . . . Mrs Brown
COMEDY Henpecked clerk stops chainstore
chief from building on local allotments.

10473
THANK EVANS (78) (U)
WB-FN (FN)
P: Irving Asher
D: Roy William Neill
S: (NOVEL) Edgar Wallace (GOOD EVANS)
SC: Austin Melford, John Dighton,
John Meehan jr
Max Miller . . . . Evans
Hal Walters . . . . Nobby
Polly Ward . . . . Rosie

Albert Whelan . . . . Sgt Challoner
John Carol . . . . Harry
Robert Rendel . . . . Lord Claverley
Glen Alyn . . . . Brenda
Freddie Watts . . . . Mulcay
Harvey Braban . . . . Insp Pine
Aubrey Mallalieu . . . . Magistrate
COMEDY Broke tipster saves Lord's
racehorse from crooked trainer.

10474
BLACK LIMELIGHT (70) (A)
ABPC reissue: 1942 (IFR)!
P: Walter C. Mycroft
D: Paul Stein
S: (PLAY) Gordon Sherry
SC: Dudley Leslie, Walter Summers
Raymond Massey . . . . . Peter Charrington
Joan Marion . . . . Mary Charrington
Walter Hudd . . . . Lawrence Crawford
Henry Oscar . . . . Insp Tanner
Coral Browne . . . . Lily James
Diana Beaumont . . . . Gwen
Elliot Mason . . . . Jemima
Dan Tobin . . . . Reporter
Leslie Bradley . . . . Detective
CRIME Convicted man's wife proves he
did not kill mistress.

10475
KICKING THE MOON AROUND (78) (U)
Vogue (GFD) reissue: 1944 (GN)
P: Herbert Wynne
D: Walter Forde
S: Tom Geraghty
SC: Angus Macphail, Roland Pertwee,
Michael Hogan, H. Fowler Mear
Ambrose . . . . Ambrose
Evelyn Dall . . . . Pepper Martin
Harry Richman . . . . Harry
Florence Desmond . . . . . . Flo Hadley
Hal Thompson . . . . Bobbie Hawkes
C. Denier Warren . . . . Mark Browd
Julien Vedey . . . . Herbert Stoker
Max Bacon . . . . Gus
Leslie Carew . . . . Streamline
Davy Burnaby . . . . Magistrate
George Carney . . . . PC Truscott
Edward Rigby . . . . . . Prof Scattlebury
Ambrose's Orchestra
MUSICAL. Gold digger tries to thwart
millionaire's plans to star the cabaret
singer he loves.

10476
BREAK THE NEWS (78) (U)
Jack Buchanan Productions (GFD)
D: Rene Clair
S: (NOVEL) Loic de Gouriadec
(LE MORT EN FUITE)
SC: Geoffrey Kerr
Jack Buchanan . . . . Teddy Enton
Maurice Chevalier . . . . . . Francois Verrier
June Knight . . . . Grace Gatwick
Marta Labarr . . . . Sonia
Gertrude Musgrove . . . . . . Helena
Garry Marsh . . . . Producer
Felix Aylmer . . . . Sir George Bickory
C. Denier Warren . . . . . Sir Edward Phring
Robb Wilton . . . . Taxi-driver
Gibb McLaughlin . . . . Porter
Athole Stewart . . . . Governor
Guy Middleton . . . . Englishman
George Hayes . . . . President
Wally Patch . . . . Guard
MUSICAL Dancer "kills" his partner for
publicity and is jailed while he is involved
in Ruritanian revolution.

10477
DENTISTS (18) (U)
Coronel Films
COMEDY Sailors try their hands as dentists.

10478
CALVALCADE OF THE STARS (19) (U)
Coronel Films
D:S: Geoffrey Benstead
Nervo & Knox . . . . Ella Shields
Jack Buchanan . . . . Nellie Wallace
Billy Merson . . . . George Formby
Mary Glynne . . . . Lucille Benstead
Fay Compton . . . . Beatrice Lillie
Gertrude Lawrence
COMPILATION. Extracts from earlier
films woven into a story.

10479
FOOLS STEP IN (13) (U)
Fraternity Films (BSS)
P: Toni Frenguelli
D: Nigel Byass
S: (STORY) B.O. Byass (THING HIDDEN)
Betty Dorian . . . . The Girl
Douglas Vine . . . . The Man
CRIME Strangers investigate fogbound
mansion murder – which is a radio play.

10480
STEPPING TOES (85) (U)
UK Films-Two Cities (BIED)
P: John Barter
D: John Baxter
S: Jack Francis, Barbara K. Emary
SC: H. Fowler Mear
Hazel Ascot . . . . Hazel Warrington
Enid Stamp-Taylor . . . . . . Mrs Warrington
Jack Barty . . . . Joe
Edgar Driver . . . . Tich
Ernest Butcher . . . . Stringer
Richard Cooper . . . . . . Kenneth Warrington
Ivan Samson . . . . Mr Warrington
Wilson Coleman . . . . Bob Burnham
John Turnbull . . . . Representative
Gerry Fitzgerald; Bill Thorburn; Alfredo
Campoli; Sanders Twins; Three Dots;
Cone School Girls; Duke of York's School Boys
MUSICAL Showman's grand-daughter becomes
tap-dancer and reconciles parted parents.
(Extracts in short FIDDLERS ALL
(New Realm), 8/1940).

10481
13 MEN AND A GUN (64) (U) bilingual
Two Cities-Pisorno (BIED)
P:D: Mario Zampi
S: Giovanni Forzano
SC: Basil Dillon, Kathleen Connors
Arthur Wontner . . . . Captain
Clifford Evans . . . . Jorg
Howard Marion-Crawford . . . . Kramer
Allan Jeayes . . . . Gen Vloty
Gibb McLaughlin . . . . Col Vlatin
Wally Patch . . . . Hans
Scott Harold . . . . Ludwig
Donald Gray . . . . Johann
Bernard Miles . . . . Schultz
Andre Morell . . . . Kroty
John Kevan . . . . Peder
WAR Austria, 1914. Search for member of
German gun crew who betrayed their
position to Russians. (Made in Italy).

JUL

10482
ALF'S BUTTON AFLOAT (89) (U)
Gainsborough (GFD) reissue: 1943
reissue: 1943
P: Edward Black

D: Marcel Varnel
S: (PLAY) W.A. Darlington (ALF'S BUTTON)
SC: Marriott Edgar, Val Guest, Ralph Smart

Bud Flanagan	Alf Higgins
Chesney Allen	Ches
Jimmy Nervo	Cecil
Teddy Knox	Teddy
Charlie Naughton	Charlie
Jimmy Gold	Jimmy
Alastair Sim	Eustace
Wally Patch	Sgt Hawkins
Peter Gawthorne	Capt Driscol
Glennis Lorimer	Frankie Driscol
James Carney	Lt Hardy
Agnes Laughlin	Lady Driscol
Bruce Winston	Mustapha

COMEDY Marine's button made from
Aladdin's lamp grants wishes when rubbed.

10483
HIS LORDSHIP REGRETS (78) (U)
Canterbury (RKO) *reissue:* 1945
(Ex; 1566 ft cut)
P: A. George Smith
D: Maclean Rogers
S: (PLAY) H.F.Maltby (BEES AND HONEY)
SC: Kathleen Butler, H.F.Maltby

Claude Hulbert	Lord Cavender
Winifred Shotter	Mary (Mabel)
Gina Malo	Mabel van Morgan
Aubrey Mallalieu	Dawkins
Antony Holles	Guy Reading
Eve Gray	Enid
Athole Stewart	Sir Timothy Kentford
Annie Esmond	Lady Kentford
Sally Stewart	Sally
Derek Gorst	Hon Percy Hartlock
Gerald Rawlinson	Capt Arthur Gregson

COMEDY Poor Lord woos fake heiress
and finds his secretary, whom he loves,
is true one.

10484
FOLLOW YOUR STAR (80) (U)
Belgrave (GFD)
P: Harcourt Templeman
D: Sinclair Hill
S: Sinclair Hill, Arthur Tracy
SC: George Pearson, Stafford Dickens

Arthur Tracy	Arthur Tee
Belle Chrystal	Mary
Mark Daly	Shorty
Horace Hodges	Mr Wilmot
Nina Boucicault	Mrs Tee
James Harcourt	Mr Tee
Dick Tubb	Freddy
Finlay Currie	Maxie

MUSICAL Factory hand becomes busker
and thence a radio star.

10485
YELLOW SANDS (68) (U)
ABPC
P: Walter C. Mycroft
D: Herbert Brenon
S: (PLAY) Eden & Adelaide Philpotts
SC: Michael Barringer, Rodney Ackland

Marie Tempest	Jennifer Varwell
Belle Chrystal	Lydia Blake
Wilfrid Lawson	Richard Varwell
Robert Newton	Joe Varwell
Patrick Barr	Arthur Varwell
Edward Rigby	Tom Major
Amy Veness	Mary Varwell
Coral Browne	Emma Copplestone
Drusilla Wills	Minnie Masters

COMEDY Cornwall. Old aunt leaves her
money to communistic fisherman.

10486
ST. MARTIN'S LANE (85) (U)
USA: SIDEWALKS OF LONDON

Mayflower (ABPC) *reissue:* 1949 (Ren)
P: Erich Pommer
D: Tim Whelan
S: Clemence Dane

Charles Laughton	Charles Saggers
Vivien Leigh	Libby
Rex Harrison	Harley Prentiss
Larry Adler	Constantine
Tyrone Guthrie	Gentry
Gus McNaughton	Arthur Smith
Basil Gill	Magistrate
David Burns	Hackett
Edward Lexy	Mr Such
Alf Goddard	Doggie
Romilly Lunge	Duchesi
Maire O'Neill	Mrs Such
Polly Ward	Frankie
Helen Haye	Lady Selena
Phyllis Stanley	Della Fordingbridge

Carroll Gibbons and his Orchestra;
The Luna Boys
ROMANCE Cockney busker loves girl
thief whom a socialite makes a dancing star.

10487
TAKE OFF THAT HAT (86) (U)
Viking Films *reissue:* 1939 (2495 ft cut)
P:D: Eric Humphris
S: Edmund Dalby. C. Denier Warren

Scott & Whaley	Cuthbert & Pussyfoot
C.Denier Warren	Ginsberg
Fred Duprez	Burroughs

Olly Aston and his Band; Inga Andersen;
Gipsy Nina; Billy Russell; Noni;
Sherman Fisher Girls.
COMEDY Negro buskers rise to stardom
after faking football pool win.

10488
BREAKERS AHEAD (37) (U)
G.B.Instructional (GFD)
Reissue: AS WE FORGIVE
D: Vernon Sewell
S: Leo Walmesley

Belle Chrystal	Mary
J.Fisher White	Harry
Arthur Seaton	Silas
Grant Sutherland	Joe
Michael Hogarth	Davy

DRAMA Cornwall. Fisherman's marriage
estranges him from his brother until he
saves him from wreck.

10489
NO PARKING (72) (A)
Wilcox (BL)
P: Herbert Wilcox
D: Jack Raymond
S: Carol Reed
SC: Gerald Elliott

Gordon Harker	Albert
Leslie Perrins	Capt Sneyd
Irene Ware	Olga
Cyril Smith	Stanley
Charles Carson	Hardcastle
Fred Groves	Walsh
George Hayes	James Selby
Frank Stanmore	Gus

Geraldo and his Orchestra
COMEDY Gem thieves mistake car park
attendant for American assassin.

AUG

10490
HOLD MY HAND (76) (U)
ABPC *reissue:* 1942 (IFR)
P: Walter C. Mycroft
D: Thornton Freeland
SC: Clifford Grey, Bert Lee, William Freshman

Stanley Lupino	Eddie Marston
Fred Emney	Lord Milchester

Barbara Blair	Jane Howard
Sally Gray	Helen
Polly Ward	Paula Pond
Bertha Belmore	Lady Millchester
Jack Melford	Pop Currie
John Wood	Bob Crane
Syd Walker	Insp Rogers
Arthur Rigby	Norman Love
Gibb McLaughlin	Bank Manager

MUSICAL Ward suspects guardian of
embezzling newspaper profits.

10491
QUEER CARGO (61) (U)
USA: PIRATES OF THE SEVEN SEAS
ABPC *reissue:* 1942 (IFR)
P: Walter C. Mycroft
D: Harold Schuster
S: (PLAY) Noel Langley
SC: Patrick Kirwan, Walter Summers

John Lodge	Capt Harley
Judy Kelly	Ann Warren
Keneth Kent	Monty Cabini
Bertha Belmore	Henrietta Travers
Louis Borell	Benson
Wylie Watson	Rev James Travers
Geoffrey Toone	Lt Stocken
Jerry Verno	Slops
Frank Pettingell	Dan
Frank Cochrane	Ho-Tang

ADVENTURE China. Pirate takes over
merchant ship to obtain captain's smuggled
pearls.

10492
LASSIE FROM LANCASHIRE (81) (U)
British National (ABPC)
P: John Corfield
D: John Paddy Carstairs
S: Doreen Montgomery, Ernest Dudley

Marjorie Browne	Jenny
Hal Thompson	Tom
Marjorie Sandford	Margie
Mark Daly	Dad
Vera Lennox	Daisy
Elsie Wagstaffe	Aunt Hetty
Johnnie Schofield	Cyril

Billy Caryll & Hilda Mundy
COMEDY Isle of Man. Landlady's niece
wins songwriter despite jealous pierrette.

10493
THE ROMANCE OF DANCING (series) (U)
Highbury Studios (MGM)
D: Herbert R. Parsons

Julie Suedo	Michael Ronni
Harry Gordon	Bob Busby
Anna Marita	Edna Squire-Brown
John Wells	Sergius Margolinski

10494
1: TAPPING THE TEMPO (16)

10495
2: TROUPES ON PARADE (20)

10496
3: ROMANY RHYTHM (19)

10497
4: THERE'S REASON IN RHUMBA (18)

10498
5: TEMPO ON TIPTOE (18)

10499
6: FROM MINUET TO FOXTROT (15)
MUSICAL Filmed in Parsons Multiscene
system.

10500
ONCE UPON A TIME (14) (U) *dufay*
Short Films (Technique)
ROMANCE Frustrated love beside the sea.

10501
THE LITTLE BOY THAT SANTA CLAUS
FORGOT (10) (U)
Avenue Films (Technique)
D: Harold Simpson
MUSICAL Boy cannot get toy from big
store because his father is dead.

10502
MARCH OF THE MOVIES (45) (U)
Argyle British (ABPC)
P: John Argyle
D:S: Howard Gaye
N: Kent Stevenson
COMPILATION Extracts from earlier films.

10503
A SPOT OF BOTHER (70) (U)
Pinebrook (GFD)
P: Anthony Havelock-Allan
D: David MacDonald
S: (PLAY) Vernon Sylvaine
SC: John Cousins, Stephen Clarkson,
A.R.Rawlinson
Robertson Hare . . . .   Mr Rudd
Alfred Drayton . . . .   Mr Watney
Sandra Storme . . . .   Sadie
Kathleen Joyce . . . .   Margaret Watney
Ruth Maitland . . . .   Mrs Watney
Gordon James . . . .   Joe
Robert Hale . . . .   Col Pigge
Fewlass Llewellyn . . .   Bishop of Barchester
Drusilla Wills . . . .   Miss Hagworthy
Julien Vedey . . . .   Scheipman
COMEDY Bishop's secretary buys smuggled
goods with cathedral funds.

10504
DANGEROUS MEDICINE (72) (A)
WB—FN (FN)
P: Jerome Jackson
D: Arthur Woods
S: (NOVEL) Edmond Deland
SC: Paul Gangelin, Connery Chappell
Elizabeth Allan . . . .   Victoria Ainswell
Cyril Ritchard . . . .   Dr Noel Penwood
Edmond Breon . . . .   Totsie Mainwaring
Antony Holles . . . .   Alistair Hoard
Aubrey Mallalieu . . . .   Judge
Basil Gill . . . .   Sir Francis
Leo Genn . . . .   Murdoch
Gordon McLeod . . . .   Mr Buller
Allan Jeayes . . . .   Supt Fox
CRIME Dr helps girl escape jail and trap real
murderer.

10505
THE RETURN OF CAROL DEANE (77) (A)
WB—FN (WB)
P: Jerome Jackson
D: Arthur Woods
S: Joseph Santley (THE HOUSE ON 56th
STREET)
SC: John Meehan jr, Paul Gangelin, Tom Phipps
Bebe Daniels . . . .   Carol Deane
Arthur Margetson . . . .   Mark Poynton
Zena Dare . . . .   Lady Brenning
Chili Bouchier . . . .   Anne Dempster
Michael Drake . . . .   Lord Robert Brenning
Wyndham Goldie . . . . .Francis Scott-Vaughan
Peter Coke . . . .   Lord David Brenning
Lesley Brook . . . .   Diana
David Burns . . . .   Nick Wellington
Ian Maclean . . . .   Prosecution
Aubrey Mallalieu . . . .   Lamont
CRIME Woman ex-convict weds gambler to
keep her secret from her son.

10506
CALLING ALL CROOKS (85) (A)
Mancunian

P: John E. Blakeley
D: George Black
S: Arthur Mertz
Duggie Wakefield . . . .   Duggie
Billy Nelson . . . .   Billy
Leslie Perrins . . . .   Duvane
Helen Barnes . . . .   Joan Bellamy
Chuck O'Neil . . . .   Chuck
Jack Butler . . . .   Jack
Dan Young; Howard Rogers; Raymond Smith;
7 Royal Hindustanis; Hal Wright and his Circus;
60 Sherman Fisher Girls; 10 Master Singers; 30
Gypsy Revellers
COMEDY Tecs don disguises to unmask
crooked company promoter. (Extracts in
MUSIC HALL PERSONALITIES Nos 13—18
(1940).)

SEP

10507
THIS MAN IS NEWS (77) (A)
Pinebrook (Par)
P: Anthony Havelock-Allan
D: David Macdonald
S: Allan Mackinnon, Roger Macdougal
SC: Allan Mackinnon, Roger Macdougal,
Basil Dearden
Barry K. Barnes . . . .   Simon Drake
Valerie Hobson . . . .   Pat Drake
Alastair Sim . . . .   Macgregor
John Warwick . . . .   Johnnie Clayton
Garry Marsh . . . .   Sgt Bright
Edward Lexy . . . .   Insp Hollis
Kenneth Buckley . . . .   Ken Marquis
Philip Leaver . . . .   Harelip Murphy
CRIME Wife helps framed reporter unmask gem
thieves.

10508
THE LADY VANISHES (95) (A)
Gainsborough (MGM) reissues: 1942;
1948 (ABFD)
P: Edward Black
D: Alfred Hitchcock
S: (NOVEL) Ethel Lina White (THE WHEEL
SPINS)
SC: Frank Launder, Sidney Gilliat
Margaret Lockwood . . . . . .   Iris Henderson
Michael Redgrave . . . .   Gilbert Redman
Paul Lukas . . . .   Dr Hartz
Dame May Whitty . . . .   Miss Froy
Cecil Parker . . . .   Eric Todhunter
Linden Travers . . . .   Margaret
Mary Clare . . . .   Baroness
Naunton Wayne . . . .   Caldicott
Basil Radford . . . .   Charters
Emile Boreo . . . .   Manager
Googie Withers . . . .   Blanche
Philip Leaver . . . .   Doppo
Catherine Lacey . . . .   Nun
Charles Oliver . . . .   Officer
CRIME Europe. Girl suspects spies kidnapped
an old lady (secret agent) aboard train.

10509
I'VE GOT A HORSE (77) (U)
British Lion reissue: 1945 (Ren)
P: D: Herbert Smith
S: Fenn Sherie, Ingram d'Abbes, Sandy Powell
Sandy Powell . . . .   Sandy
Norah Howard . . . .   Alice
Felix Aylmer . . . .   Lovatt
Evelyn Roberts . . . .   Thomas
Leo Franklyn . . . .   Joe
D.A. Clarke-Smith . . . .   Fowler KC
Kathleen Harrison . . . .   Mabel
Edward Chapman . . . .   George
Wilfrid Hyde White . . . .   PC
Frank Atkinson . . . .   Bunker
COMEDY Punter acquires horse as settlement
for bet and trains it to win big race.

10510
NIGHT ALONE (76) (A)
Welwyn (Pathe) reissue: 1942 (Amb)
P: Warwick Ward
D: Thomas Bentley
S: (PLAY) Jeffrey Dell
SC: Victor Kendall, Vernon Clancey
Emlyn Williams . . . .   Charles Seaton
Leonora Corbett   Vi
Lesley Brook . . . .   Barbara Seaton
Cyril Raymond . . . .   Tommy
Margot Landa . . . .   Celia
Julie Suedo . . . .   Gloria
John Turnbull . . . .   Supt
Wally Patch . . . .   Policeman
COMEDY Newlywed drunk awakens in wrong
flat and is mistaken for forger.

10511
THE LANDLADY (35) (U)
Charter (Fidelity)
P: John Boulting
D: Roy Boulting
S: Francis Miller
Vi Kaley . . . .   Mrs Cooper
Dorothy Vernon . . . .
Marie Wright . . . .
DRAMA Bayswater landlady ejects poor girl
who later becomes actress.

10512
WEDDINGS ARE WONDERFUL (79) (A)
Canterbury (RKO)
P: A. George Smith
D: Maclean Rogers
S: (PLAY) Sidney Blow, Douglas Hoare
(PEACHES)
SC: Kathleen Butler, H.F. Maltby
June Clyde .. . .   Cora Sutherland
Esmond Knight . . . .   Guy Rogers
Rene Ray . . . .   Betty Leadbetter
Bertha Belmore . . . .   Mrs Leadbetter
Frederick Lloyd . . . .   Mr Leadbetter
Bruce Seton . . . .   John Smith
Antony Holles . . . .   Adolph
George Carney . . . .   Rogers
COMEDY Singer blackmails socialite and
prospective father-in-law.

OCT

10513
FLASHBACKS (70) (U)
Charles B. Cochran (Anglo)
D: N: R.E. Jeffrey
S: A. Barr-Smith, Lester Powell
COMPILATION Extracts from earlier films.

10514
PENNY PARADISE (72) (U)
ATP (ABFD) reissue :1948 (EB)
P: Basil Dean, Jack Kitchin
D: Carol Reed
S: Basil Dean
SC: Thomas Thompson, W.L. Meade,
Thomas Browne
Edmund Gwenn . . . .   Joe Higgins
Jimmy O'Dea . . . .   Pat
Betty Driver . . . .   Betty Higgins
Maire O'Neill . . . .   Widow Clegg
Jack Livesey . . . .   Bert
Ethel Coleridge . . . .   Aunt Agnes
Syd Crossley . . . .   Uncle Lancelot
James Harcourt . . . .   Amos Cook
COMEDY Liverpool. Tug captain wins football
pool—but his mate forgot to post coupon.

10515
SAVE A LITTLE SUNSHINE (75) (A)
Welwyn (Pathe) reissue: 1942 (Ren)
P: Warwick Ward
D: Norman Lee
S: (PLAY) W. Armitage Owen (LIGHTS OUT

AT ELEVEN)
SC: Victor Kendall, Vernon J. Clancey,
Gilbert Gunn
Dave Willis . . . . Dave Smalley
Pat Kirkwood . . . . Pat
Tommy Trinder . . . . Will
Max Wall . . . . Walter
Ruth Dunning . . . . Miss Dickson
Peggy Novak . . . . Clara Timpson
Roger Maxwell . . . . Hector Stanley
Annie Esmond . . . . Mrs Melworthy
Marian Dawson . . . . Mrs Winterbottom
Aubrey Mallalieu . . . . Official
MUSICAL Lodger buys boarding-house and
turns it into nightclub.

10516
SIXTY GLORIOUS YEARS (95) (U) *tech*
USA: QUEEN OF DESTINY
Imperator (RKO) *reissue:* 1942,
QUEEN VICTORIA (Ren)
P: D: Herbert Wilcox
S: Robert Vansittart, Miles Malleson
SC: Charles de Grandcourt
Anna Neagle . . . . Queen Victoria
Anton Walbrook . . . . Prince Albert
C. Aubrey Smith . . . . Duke of Wellington
Walter Rilla . . . . Prince Ernest
Charles Carson . . . . Sir Robert Peel
Grete Wegener . . . . Baroness Lehzen
Felix Aylmer . . . . Lord Palmerston
Lewis Casson. . . . . Lord John Russell
Pamela Standish . . . . Princess Royal
Gordon McLeod . . . . John Brown
Stuart Robertson . . . . Mr Anson
Olaf Olsen . . . . Prince Frederick
Henry Hallett . . . . Joseph Chamberlain
Wyndham Goldie . . . . A.J. Balfour
Malcolm Kenn . . . . W.E. Gladstone
Frederick Leister . . . . H.H. Asquith
Derrick de Marney . . . . . . Benjamin Disraeli
Marie Wright . . . . Maggie
Joyce Bland . . . . Florence Nightingale
Frank Cellier . . . . Lord Derby
Laidman Browne . . . . Gen Gordon
HISTORY 1840-1901. Events during the reign
of Queen Victoria.

10517
YOU'RE THE DOCTOR (78) (U)
New Georgian (BIED) *reissue:* 1941
(Butch; 973 ft cut)
P: A, George Smith
D: Roy Lockwood
S: Guy Beauchamp
SC: Beaufoy Milton, H.F. Maltby
Barry K. Barnes . . . . John Meriden
Googie Withers . . . . Helen Firmstone
Norma Varden . . . . Lady Beatrice
Joan White . . . . Jane
Gus McNaughton . . . . Kemp
Paul Blake . . . . Reggie Bissett
James Harcourt . . . . William Firmstone
Margaret Yarde . . . . Mrs Taggart
Aubrey Mallalieu . . . . Vicar
Bruce Seton . . . . Appleby
Eliot Makeham . . . . Prout
COMEDY Chemist poses as a doctor to help an
heiress fleeing from a forced marriage.

10518
HIS LORDSHIP GOES TO PRESS (80) (U)
Canterbury (RKO)
P: George Smith
D: Maclean Rogers
S: Margaret & Gordon McDonnell
SC: Kathleen Butler, H.F. Maltby
June Clyde . . . . Valerie Lee
Hugh Williams . . . . Lord Bill Wilmer
Romney Brent . . . . Pinkie Butler

Louise Hampton . . . . Mrs Hodges
Leslie Perrins . . . . Sir Richard Swingleton
H.F. Maltby . . . . Gen Tukes
Zillah Bateman . . . . Mrs Tukes
Aubrey Mallalieu . . . . Hardcastle
COMEDY Lord poses as farmer to fool brash
American girl reporter.

10519
PRISON WITHOUT BARS (80) (A)
London (UA) *reissue:* 1944 (Key)
P: Alexander Korda, Irving Asher
D: Brian Desmond Hurst
S: (PLAY) Gina Kaus, E. & O. Eis, Hilde
Koveloff (PRISON SANS BARREAUX)
SC: Hans Wilhelm, Margaret Kennedy,
Arthur Wimperis
Corinne Luchaire . . . . Susanne
Edna Best . . . . Yvonne Chanel
Barry K. Barnes . . . . George Marechal
Mary Morris . . . . Renee
Lorraine Clewes . . . . Alice
Sally Wisher . . . . Julie
Martita Hunt . . . . Mme Appel
Margaret Yarde . . . . Mlle Artemise
Elsie Shelton . . . . Mme Remy
Glynis Johns . . . . Nina
Phyllis Morris . . . . Mlle Pauline
Nancy Roberts . . . . Mlle Dupont
DRAMA France. Reform school girl loves
doctor who is secretly engaged to new
superintendent.

10520
HEY! HEY! U.S.A.! (92) (U)
Gainsborough (GFD) *reissue:* 1951
(17 mins cut)
P: Edward Black
D: Marcel Varnel
S: Howard Irving Young, Jack Swain,
Ralph Smart
SC: Marriott Edgar, Val Guest, J.O.C. Orton
Will Hay . . . . Benjamin Twist
Edgar Kennedy . . . . Bugs Leary
Tommy Bupp . . . . Bertie Schultz
David Burns . . . . Tony Ricardo
Edmon Ryan . . . . Ace Marco
Fred Duprez . . . . Cyrus Schultz
Paddy Reynolds . . . . Mrs Schultz
Peter Gawthorne . . . . Captain
Gibb McLaughlin . . . . Steward
Arthur Goullet . . . . Gloves Johnson
Eddie Pola . . . . Announcer
COMEDY Tutor on transatlantic liner mistaken
for gangster saves millionaire's son from
kidnappers.

10521
CRACKERJACK (79) (A)
USA: THE MAN WITH A HUNDRED FACES
Gainsborough (GFD)
P: Edward Black
D: Albert de Courville
S: (NOVEL) W.B. Ferguson
SC: A.R. Rawlinson,Michael Pertwee,
Basil Mason
Tom Walls . . . . Jack Drake
Lilli Palmer . . . . Baroness von Haltze
Noel Madison . . . . Sculpie
Leon M. Lion . . . . Hanbro Golding
Edmond Breon . . . . Tony Davenport
Charles Heslop . . . . Burdge
Ethel Griffies . . . . Annie
H.G. Stoker . . . . Insp Benting
Michael Shepley . . . . Wally Astill
Henry B. Longhurst . . . . Insp Lunt
Muriel George . . . . Mrs Humbold
COMEDY Gentleman thief loves baroness and
poses as butler to catch gang out to catch him.

NOV

10522
LUCK OF THE NAVY (72) (U)
USA: NORTH SEA PATROL
ABPC *reissue:* 1942 (IFR)
P: Walter C. Mycroft
D: Norman Lee
S: (PLAY) Clifford Mills
SC: Clifford Grey
Geoffrey Toone . . . . Cdr Clive Stanton
Judy Kelly . . . . Cynthia Maybridge
Keneth Kent . . . . Prof Suvaroff
Albert Burdon . . . . Noakes
Clifford Evans . . . . Lt Peel
John Wood . . . . Lt Wing Eden
Olga Lindo . . . . Mrs Rance
Edmond Breon . . . . Admiral Maybridge
Marguerite Allan . . . . Anna Suvaroff
Leslie Perrins . . . . Briggs
Henry Oscar . . . . Cdr Perrin
Diana Beaumont . . . . Millie
Alf Goddard . . . . Tomkins
Frank Fox . . . . Francois
Doris Hare . . . . Mrs Maybridge
CRIME Spies pose as admiral's guests to steal
secret orders.

10523
YES, MADAM ? (77) (U)
ABPC *reissue:* 1942 (IFR)
P: Walter C. Mycroft
D: Norman Lee
S: (NOVEL) K.R.G. Browne
SC: Clifford Grey, Bert Lee, William Freshman
Bobby Howes. . . . . Bill Quinton
Diana Churchill . . . . Sally Gault
Wylie Watson . . . . Albert Peabody
Bertha Belmore . . . . Emily Peabody
Vera Pearce . . . . Pansy Beresford
Billy Milton . . . . Tony.Tolliver
Fred Emney . . . . . . Sir Charles Drake—Drake
Cameron Hall . . . . Catlett
MUSICAL Heirs to £160,000 must act as
servants for a month.

10524
GHOST TALES RETOLD (series) (A)
AIP (WB)
D: Widgey R. Newman
S: Widgey & Joan Newman
SC: George A. Cooper
Hal Walters . . .
Ian Fleming
Howard Douglas
W.E. Hodge
Vi Kaley
D.J. Williams
Claude Bailey
Jenny Lovelace

10525
1— THE MISTLETOE BOUGH (25)

10526
2 — PROOF POSITIVE (16)

10527
3 — THE LIGHT (20)

10528
4 — THE STONE (17)

10529
5 — BE NOT AFRAID (18)

10530
6 — WOULD YOU BELIEVE IT ! (17)
FANTASY Up-to-date versions of traditional
ghost stories.

10531
MARIGOLD (73) (U)
ABPC
P: Walter C. Mycroft
D: Thomas Bentley
S: (PLAY) Charles Garvice, Allen Harker,
F. Prior
SC: Dudley Leslie

Sophie Stewart	Marigold Sellar
Patrick Barr	Lt Archie Forsyth
Phyllis Dare	Mme Marly
Edward Chapman	Mordan
Nicholas Hannen	Maj Sellar
Hugh Dempster	Bobbie Townsend
Pamela Stanley	Queen Victoria
Ian Maclean	James Paton
Elliot Mason	Beenie
Katie Johnson	Sarita Dunlop
James Hayter	Peter Cloag

ROMANCE Scotland, 1842. Girl flees from
father's choice of husband and discovers her
mother was an actress.

10532
PREMIERE (71) (A)
USA: ONE NIGHT IN PARIS
ABPC
P: Walter C. Mycroft
D: Walter Summers
S: (SCREENPLAY) Max Wallner, F.D. Andam
SC: F. McGrew Willis

John Lodge	Insp Bonnard
Judy Kelly	Carmen Daviot
Joan Marion	Lydia Lavalle
Hugh Williams	Rene Nissen
Edward Chapman	Lohrmann
Steven Geray	Frohlich
Edmond Breon	Morel
Wallace Geoffrey	Renoir
Geoffrey Sumner	Capt Curry

CRIME Paris. Revue backer shot in theatre box
during first performance.

10533
THE GAUNT STRANGER (73) (A)
USA: THE PHANTOM STRIKES
Ealing—CAPAD—Northwood (ABFD)
reissue: 1945 (Ren)
P: Michael Balcon
D: Walter Forde
S: (PLAY) Edgar Wallace (THE RINGER)
SC: Sidney Gilliat

Sonnie Hale	Sam Hackett
Wilfrid Lawson	Maurice Meister
Louise Henry	Cora Ann Milton
Alexander Knox	Dr Lomond
Patricia Roc	Mary Lenley
Patrick Barr	Insp Wembury
John Longden	Insp Bliss
Peter Croft	John Lenley
George Merritt	Sgt Carter

CRIME Disguised crook kills ex-partner despite
police protection.

10534
IT'S IN THE AIR (86) (U)
USA: GEORGE TAKES THE AIR
ATP-Eltham (ABFD) reissues:
1945, 1959 (EB)
P: Basil Dean
D: S: Anthony Kimmins

George Formby	George Brown
Polly Ward	Peggy
Garry Marsh	CO
Julien Mitchell	Sgt—Major
Jack Hobbs	Cpl Craig
C. Denier Warren	Sir Philip Bargrave
Jack Melford	Pilot
Hal Gordon	Nobby Clark

Michael Shepley	Adjutant
Frank Leighton	Bob Bullock
Ilena Sylva	Anne Brown
O.B. Clarence	Gardener
Esma Cannon	Maid

COMEDY Motor cycle enthusiast poses as
sister's fiance, an RAF dispatch rider.

10535
LIGHTNING CONDUCTOR (79) (A)
Pinebrook (GFD)
P: Anthony Havelock-Allan
D: Maurice Elvey
S: Evadne Price
SC: J. Jefferson Farjeon, Ivor McLaren,
Laurence Green

Gordon Harker	Albert Rughouse
John Lodge	Anderson
Sally Gray	Mary
Ernest Thesiger	Professor
George Moon	George
Steven Geray	Morley
Charles Eaton	Royle
Arthur Hambling	Bus Inspector

COMEDY Spy tries to recoup barrage-balloon
plans planted on bus conductor.

10536
PYGMALION (96) (A)
Pascal (GFD) reissues: 1944; 1949
(IFR) 1953 (Amb)
P: Gabriel Pascal
D: Anthony Asquith, Leslie Howard
S: (PLAY) George Bernard Shaw
SC: Anatole de Grunwald, W.P. Lipscomb,
Cecil Lewis, Ian Dalrymple

Leslie Howard	Prof Henry Higgins
Wendy Hiller	Eliza Doolittle
Wilfrid Lawson	Doolittle
Marie Lohr	Mrs Higgins
Scott Sunderland	Col Pickering
Jean Cadell	Mrs Pearce
David Tree	Freddy
Everley Gregg	Mrs Eynsford Hill
Leueen McGrath	Clara
Esme Percy	Count Karpathy
Violet Vanbrugh	Ambassadress
Iris Hoey	Ysabel
Viola Tree	Perfide
Irene Browne	Duchess
Wally Patch	Bystander
H.F. Maltby	Bystander
Stephen Murray	PC

COMEDY Professor turns cockney dustman's
daughter into socialite.
(FWA: 1939; Top Moneymaker: 1939.)

10537
TEA LEAVES IN THE WIND (62) (A)
Chesterfield (BSS) reissue: HATE IN
PARADISE
P: Neville Clarke, A. Barr-Smith
D: Ward Wing
S: Loni Bara

Nils Asther	Tony Drake
Eve Shelley	Margot Hastings
Gibson Gowland	David Webster
Cyril Chadwick	

CRIME Ceylon. Planter's assistant schemes to
get control of plantation.

10538
OLD MOTHER RILEY IN PARIS (76) (U)
Butcher Reissue: 1942, OLD MOTHER RILEY
CATCHES A QUISLING (Sherwood; 760 ft cut)
D: Oswald Mitchell
S: Con West

Arthur Lucan	Mrs Riley
Kitty McShane	Kitty Riley
Jerry Verno	Joe

Magda Kun	Mme Zero
C. Denier Warren	Commissioner
Stanley Vilven	Hotelier
George Wolkowsky	Apache

COMEDY Paris. Charlady searching for
daughter's fiance mistaken for spy but catches
real one.

DEC

10539
A ROYAL DIVORCE (85) (A)
Imperator (Par)
P: Herbert Wilcox
D: Jack Raymond
S: (NOVEL) Jacques Thery (JOSEPHINE)
SC: Miles Malleson

Ruth Chatterton	Josephine de Beauharnais
Pierre Blanchar	Napoleon Bonaparte
Frank Cellier	Talleyrand
Carol Goodner	Mme Tallien
Auriol Lee	Napoleon's Mother
George Curzon	Barras
Lawrence Hanray	Metternich
John Laurie	Joseph
Jack Hawkins	Capt Charles
Rosalyn Boulter	Hortense
Allan Jeayes	Murat
Romilly Lunge	Junot
David Farrar	Louis

HISTORY Paris, 1809. Emperor weds widow
who has affair during his absence in Italy.

10540
THE RETURN OF THE FROG (75) (A)
Imperator (BL) reissue: 1944 (Anglo)
P: Herbert Wilcox
D: Maurice Elvey
S: (NOVEL) Edgar Wallace (THE INDIA—
RUBBER MEN)
SC: Ian Hay, Gerald Elliott

Gordon Harker	Insp Elk
Una O'Connor	Mum Oaks
Rene Ray	Lila
Hartley Power	Sandford
Cyril Smith	Maggs
Charles Lefeaux	Golly Oaks
Charles Carson	Commissioner
George Hayes	Lane
Aubrey Mallalieu	Banker
Meinhart Maur	Alkman

CRIME Insp and American tec unmask man
behind crime organisation.

10541
OLD IRON (80) (U)
TW Productions (BL) reissue: 1945 (Ren)
P: D: Tom Walls
S: Ben Travers

Tom Walls	Sir Henry Woodstock
Eva Moore	Lady Woodstock
Cecil Parker	Barnett
Richard Ainley	Harry Woodstock
David Tree	Michael
Veronica Rose	Lorna Barnett
Enid Stamp-Taylor	Eileen Penshaw
Leslie Perrins	Richard Penshaw
Arthur Wontner	Judge
Henry Hewitt	Wilfred
O.B. Clarence	Gordon

DRAMA Shipping magnate reconciled with
eloping son after car accident.

10542
CLIMBING HIGH (78) (U)
Gaumont (MGM) reissue: 1942 (ABFD)
D: Carol Reed
S: Lesser Samuels, Marian Dix
SC: Stephen Clarkson

Jessie Matthews	Diana Castle
Michael Redgrave	Dicky Brooke

Noel Madison . . . . Gibson
Alastair Sim . . . . Max Tolliver
Margaret Vyner . . . . .Lady Constance Westacre
Mary Clare . . . . Lady Emily
Francis L. Sullivan . . . . Madman
Enid Stamp-Taylor . . . . Winnie
Torin Thatcher . . . . Jim Castle
Tucker McGuire . . . . Patsy
Basil Radford . . . . Reggie
Athole Stewart . . . . Uncle
COMEDY Rich man poses as advertising model
to win girl model.

10543
OLD BONES OF THE RIVER (90) (U)
Gainsborough (GFD)
P: Edward Black
D: Marcel Varnel
S: (NOVELS) Edgar Wallace (BONES;
LIEUTENANT BONES)
SC: Marriott Edgar, Val Guest, J.O.C. Orton
Will Hay . . . . Benjamin Tibbetts
Moore Marriott . . . . Jerry Harbottle
Graham Moffatt . . . . Albert
Robert Adams . . . . Bosambo
Jack Livesey . . . . Capt Hamilton
Jack London . . . . M'Bapi
Wyndham Goldie . . . . Comm Sanders
COMEDY Africa. Teacher acting as commissioner
quells native rising.

10544
THE CITADEL (110) (A)
MGM British *reissue:* 1948
P: Victor Saville
D: King Vidor
S: (NOVEL) A.J. Cronin
SC: Frank Wead, Emlyn Williams, Ian Dalrymple,
Elizabeth Hill, John Van Druten
Robert Donat . . . . Dr Andrew Manson
Rosalind Russell . . . . Christine
Ralph Richardson . . . . Denny
Rex Harrison . . . . Dr Lawford
Emlyn Williams . . . . Owen
Mary Clare . . . . Mrs Orlando
Cecil Parker . . . . Charles Emery
Nora Swinburne . . . . Mrs Thornton
Athene Seyler . . . . Lady Raeburn
Francis L. Sullivan . . . . Ben Chenkin
Edward Chapman . . . . Joe Morgan
Felix Aylmer . . . . Boon
Penelope Dudley-Ward . . . . Toppy Leroy
DRAMA Wales. Doctor takes up society ·
practice when superstitious miners wreck his
TB research laboratory.

10545
KEEP SMILING (91) (U)
USA: SMILING ALONG
20th Century Productions (20)
P: Robert T. Kane
D: Monty Banks
S: William Conselman
SC: Val Valentine, Rodney Ackland
Gracie Fields . . . . Gracie Gray
Roger Livesey . . . . Bert Wattle
Mary Maguire . . . . Avis Maguire
Peter Coke . . . . Rene Sigani
Jack Donohue . . . . Denis Wilson
Eddie Gray . . . . Silvo
Tommy Fields . . . . Bola
Edward Rigby . . . . Silas Gray
Hay Petrie . . . . Jock
Joe Mott . . . . Bill Sneed
Gus McNaughton . . . . Eddie Perkins
MUSICAL Ex-manager tries to ruin touring
revue by kidnapping the pianist.

10546
ANTHING TO DECLARE ? (76) (U)
Rembrandt (Butcher)
P: Ralph C. Wells, Neville Carter
D: Redd Davis

S: Hayter Preston
John Loder . . . . Capt Rufus Grant
Noel Madison . . . . Dr Heinz Klee
Belle Chrystal . . . . Nora Grayson
Leonora Corbett . . . . Helaine Frank
Davina Craig . . . . Polly
Jerry Verno . . . . Hugo Guppy
Eliot Makeham . . . . Prof Grayson
Alexander Sarner . . . . Mr Vander
Nigel Barrie . . . . Col Lockwood
CRIME Intelligence officer saves professor's
formula from doctor spy.

10547
CONSIDER YOUR VERDICT (37) (A)
Charter (Anglo)
P: John Boulting
D: Roy Boulting
S: (RADIO PLAY) Laurence Houseman
SC: Francis Miller
Marius Goring . . . . The Novelist
Manning Whiley . . . . The Prisoner
George Carney . . . . The Butcher
Hay Petrie . . . . The Undertaker
Olive Sloane . . . . The Sex
CRIME Juror falsely confesses to murder to
prove accused man did not kill blackmailer.

10548
IN YOUR GARDEN (series) (U) *dufay seq*
Newhall Films
P: Leslie Barber
D: John Alderson
S: (RADIO SERIES) C.H. Middleton
C.H. Middleton
Mavis Villiers
Roddy Hughes
Molly Raynor

10549
1 – PASTURES NEW (11)

10550
2 – A GARDENER'S LOT (9)

10551
3 – STONY GROUND (11)

10552
4 – 'ISTORY AND 'ORTICULTURE 910)

10553
5 – CABBAGES AND KINGS (10)

10554
6 – NATURE'S NURSERY (10)
COMEDY BBC radio gardening expert gives
advice.

10555
MELODIES OF THE MOMENT (16) (U)
Inspiration (Butcher)
P: D: Horace Shepherd
S: Philip Oakes
Alfredo Campoli   Leslie Jeffries
Eugene Pini   Arthur Dulay
Esther Coleman   Terry & Doris Kendal
MUSICAL

10556
TAKE COVER (27) (U)
Scotia Films
P: Harry S. Marks, Donald Stuart
D: Leslie Hiscott
S: Michael Barringer
Jerry Verno
William Gaunt
Charles Childerstone
Hubert Leslie
Andrea Malandrinos
COMEDY ARP burlesque.

10557
MANY TANKS MR ATKINS (68) (U)
WB—FN (FN)

P: Jerome Jackson
D: Roy William Neill
S: Austin Melford, Reginald Purdell,
John Dighton, J.O. C. Orton
Claude Hulbert . . . . Claude Fishlock
Reginald Purdell . . . . Pte Nutter
Barbara Greene . . . . Rosemary Edghill
Davy Burnaby . . . . Lord Fishlock
Frederick Burtwell . . . . Col Edghill
Jack Melford . . . . Capt Torrent
Arthur Hambling . . . . Sgt-Maj Hornett
Edward Lexy . . . . Sgt Butterworth
Edmond Breon . . . . Col
Ralph Truman . . . . Zanner
Dorothy Seacombe . . . . Mrs Hornett
COMEDY Cavalry trooper invents tank
supercharger and saves it from spies.

10558
THEY DRIVE BY NIGHT (84) (A)
WB—FN (FN)
P: Jerome Jackson
D: Arthur Woods
S: (NOVEL) James Curtis
SC: Derek Twist
Emlyn Williams . . . . Shorty Matthews
Ernest Thesiger . . . . Walter Hoover
Anna Konstam . . . . Molly O'Neill
Allan Jeayes . . . . Wally Mason
Antony Holles . . . . Murray
Ronald Shiner . . . . Charlie
Yolande Terrell . . . . Marge
Julie Barrie . . . . Pauline
Kitty de Legh . . . . Mrs Mason
CRIME Lorry driver and girl help fugitive
ex-convict catch silk-stocking strangler.

10559
EVERYTHING HAPPENS TO ME (82) (A)
WB—FN (WB)
P: Jerome Jackson
D: Roy William Neill
S: Austin Melford, John Dighton
Max Miller . . . . Charles Cromwell
Chili Bouchier . . . . Sally Green
H.F. Maltby . . . . Arthur Gusty
Frederick Burtwell . . . . Norman Prodder
Norma Varden . . . . Mrs Prodder
Winifred Izard . . . . Mrs Gusty
Adin Weeks . . . . Johnny
Ivor Barnard . . . . Martin
Nell Emerald . . . . Matron
COMEDY Cleaner salesman becomes
electioneer for both sides.

10560
TOO MANY HUSBANDS (59) (A)
Liberty Films *reissue:* 1951 (H&S)
D: Ivar Campbell
S: (PLAY) Guy Pelham Bolton (MIRABELLE)
Jack Melford . . . . Stephen Brinkway
Iris Baker . . . . Clare Brinkway
Geoffrey Sumner . . . . Capt Corrie
Philip Leaver . . . . Francois
David Baxter . . . . le Fletange
Brian Oulton . . . . Pottleby
Suzanne Lenglen . . . . Ruth
COMEDY Riviera. When sharepusher fakes his
own death his 'widow' poses as flirtatious
countess.

10561
MY IRISH MOLLY (69) (U)
UAS: LITTLE MISS MOLLY
Argyle British (ABPC)
P: S: John Argyle
D: Alex Bryce
SC: Alex Bryce, Ian Walker, W.G. Fay
Binkie Stuart . . . . Molly Martin
Tom Burke . . . . Sonny Gallagher
Philip Reed . . . . Bob
Maureen Fitzsimmons . . . . Eileen O'Shea
Maire O'Neill . . . . Mrs O'Shea

C.Denier Warren . . . . Chuck
Maureen Moore . . . . Hannah Delaney
MUSICAL Ireland. Orphan girl becomes radio star.

10562
NIGHT JOURNEY (76) (A)
British National-Butcher (Butcher)
P: John Corfield
D: Oswald Mitchell
S: (NOVEL) Jim Phelan (TENAPENNY PEOPLE)
SC: Jim Phelan, Maisie Sharman
Geoffrey Toone . . . . Johnny Carson
Patricia Hilliard. . . . . Mary Prentice
Alf Goddard . . . . Tiny
Edward Lexy . . . . Milstone Mike
Ronald Ritchie . . . . Lemmy
Zillah Bateman . . . . Nan
Charles Farrell . . . . Dave
Richard Norris . . . . Harry
Phyllis Morris . . . . Mrs Prentice
CRIME Driver of high-explosives lorry saves girl from fur thieves.

10563
THE WARE CASE (79) (A)
Ealing—CAPAD—Associated Star (ABFD)
reissue: 1946 (NR)
AP: S.C. Balcon
D: Robert Stevenson
S: (PLAY) George Pleydell Bancroft
SC: Robert Stevenson, Roland Pertwee, E.V.H. Emmett
Clive Brook . . . . Sir Hubert Ware
Jane Baxter . . . . Lady Margaret Ware
Barry K. Barnes . . . . Michael Adye
C.V. France . . . . Judge

Francis L. Sullivan . . . . Attorney-General
Frank Cellier . . . . Skinner
Edward Rigby .. . . Tommy Bold
Peter Bull . . . . Eustace Ede
Dorothy Seacombe . . . . Mrs Slade
Athene Seyler . . . . Mrs Pinto
Elliot Mason . . . . Juror
John Laurie . . . . Hewson
Wally Patch . . . . Taxi-driver
Glen Alyn . . . . Clare
Ernest Thesiger . . . . Carter
CRIME Acquitted bart admits he murdered wife's rich brother and jumps from a high window.

10564
SOUVENIRS (17) (U) *dufay*
Harcourt-Pearson (GFD)
P: Harcourt Templeman
D: George Pearson
John Wickham . . . . John
Carol Lynne . . . . Mary
Renaud Lockwood . . . . John (old)
Pamela Hope . . . . Mary (old)
Howard Douglas . . . . Father
Frank Drew . . . . Singer
ROMANCE Old man recalls elopement to Gretna Green.

10565
OLD SOLDIERS (19) (U) *dufay*
Harcourt-Pearson (GFD)
P: Harcourt Templeman
D: George Pearson
Fred Sinclair . . . . Grandad
Rex Alderman .. . . Dad
Johnny Singer . . . . Boy

Brooks Turner . . . . Bill
John Lovering . . . . Fred
Harry Herbert . . . . Joe
Beryl Walkeley . . . . Mother
MUSICAL Chelsea Pensioner recalls songs of Great War.

10566
MOTHER OF MEN (20) (U) *dufay*
Harcourt-Pearson (GFD)
P: Harcourt Templeman
D: George Pearson
Paul Neville . . . . Cap'n Ben
Frank Drew . . . . Ped'lar Joe
Johnny Singer . . . . Young Ben
Charles Paton . . . . Sam
John Lovering . . . . John
George Sims . . . . Dan
Beryl Walkeley . . . . Mother
MUSICAL Fishermen sing in village inn, then go to sea in storm.

10567
MIRACLES DO HAPPEN (59) (U)
George Smith Enterprises (NR)
D: Maclean Rogers
S: Con West, Jack Marks
SC: Kathleen Butler
Jack Hobbs . . . . Barry Strangeways
Bruce Seton . . . . Rodney
Marjorie Taylor . . . . Peggy
Aubrey Mallalieu . . . . Prof Gilmore
George Carney . . . . Greenlaw
Molly Hamley-Clifford . . . . Mrs Greenlaw
Antony Holles . . . . Proctor
COMEDY Prof's nephew poses as financier to obtain backing for artificial milk.

1939

JAN

10568
STOLEN LIFE (91) (A)
Orion Productions (Par) *reissue:* 1942 (ABFD)
P: Anthony Havelock-Allan
D: Paul Czinner
S: (NOVEL) Karel J. Benes
SC: Margaret Kennedy, George Barraud
Elisabeth Bergner . . . Sylvina/Martina Lawrence
Michael Redgrave . . . . Alex Mackenzie
Wilfrid Lawson . . . . Thomas E. Lawrence
Richard Ainley . . . . Morgan
Mabel Terry-Lewis . . . . Aunt Helen
Clement McCallin . . . . Karl Anderson
Kenneth Buckley . . . . Garrett
Dorice Fordred . . . . Martine
Annie Esmond . . . . Cook
Oliver Johnston . . . . Prof Bardesley
Stella Arbenina . . . . Nurse
ROMANCE Brittany. Girl swaps identities with
dead twin to deceive her husband.

10569
THE MIKADO (91) (U) *tech*
G & S Films (GFD)
P: Geoffrey Toye, Josef Somio
D: Victor Schertzinger
S: (OPERS) W.S. Gilbert, Arthur Sullivan
SC: Geoffrey Toye
Kenny Baker . . . . Nanki-Poo
Jean Colin . . . . Yum-Yum
Martyn Green . . . . Ko-Ko
Sydney Granville . . . . Pooh-Bah
John Barclay . . . . The Mikado
Gregory Stroud . . . . Pish-Tush
Constance Willis . . . . Katisha
Elizabeth Paynter . . . . Pitti-Simg
Kathleen Naylor . . . . Peep-Bo
MUSICAL Japan. Emperor's son poses as poor
minstrel to look for love.
(AA: Best colour photography, 1940.)

FEB

10570
MURDER IN SOHO (70) (A)
USA: MURDER IN THE NIGHT
ABPC
P: Walter C. Mycroft
D: Norman Lee
S: F. McGrew Willis
Jack la Rue . . . . Steve Marco
Sandra Storme . . . . Ruby Lane
Bernard Lee . . . . Roy Barnes
Googie Withers . . . . Lola Matthews
Francis Lister . . . . Joe
Martin Walker . . . . Insp Hammond
Arthur O'Connell . . . . Lefty
Edmon Ryan . . . . Spike
James Hayter . . . . Nick Green
Alf Goddard . . . . Mike
Diana Beaumont . . . . Girl
CRIME American racketeer runs Soho nightclub,
kills partner and is trapped by dance hostess
widow.

10571
ALL LIVING THINGS (22) (U)
GB Instructional (Ex)
D: Andrew Buchanan
S: (STORY) Nell StJohn Montague
(THE HALLMARK OF CAIN)
SC: Andrew Buchanan, Oswald Skilbeck
G.H. Mulcaster . . . . Sir Bernerd Deye
Catherine Lacey . . . . Lady Deye
Michael Gainsborough . . . . Peter Deye
J. Fisher White . . . . Clergyman
DRAMA Ambitious vivisectionist seeking cure
for disease almost causes the death of his son.

10572
OH DEAR UNCLE ! (22) (U)
Sun Films (Renown)
D: SC: Richard Llewellyn
S: (STORY) W.W. Jacobs (PETER'S PENCE)
Frank O'Brian . . . . Peter Russett
Syd Crossley . . . . Ginger Dick
Scott Harold . . . . Sam Small
Ivor Barnard . . . . Uncle Goodman
COMEDY Sailor's uncle absconds with
collection for 'drowned' seaman.

10573
THE BARBER'S SHOP (16) (U)
Sun Films (Renown)
D: Richard Llewellyn
S: Frank O'Brian
Frank O.Brian . . . . Barber
Ernest Bee . . . .
Henry Latimer . . . .
Sonja Carol . . . .
Frank Terry . . . .
Stephanie Head . . . .
D: S: Richard Llewellyn
Frank O'Brian . . . . Barber
COMEDY Sacked barber takes over shop while
his ex-boss is away.

10574
EYE WITNESS (10) (A)
Sun Films (Renown)
D: S: Richard Llewellyn
Jack Raine . . . . The Man
Curigwen Lewis . . . . The Witness
Ivor Barnard . . . .
CRIME Balckmail victim shoots photographer
and is 'seen' by blind girl.

10575
PRINCE OF PEACE (23) (U)
GB Instructional (Ex)
D: Donald Carter
Pamela Kellino . . . . Mary
RELIGION Birth of Jesus according to Saint
Luke.

10576
SHADOW OF DEATH (25) (A)
MM Films (ABFD) *reissue:* 1948 (H&S)
P: Harry S. Marks, Oswald Moor
D: Harry S. Marks
S: (PLAY) John Quin
Donald Calthrop . . . . Henry Wilson
Ellen Pollock . . . . Mrs Wilson
Simon Lack . . . .
Winifred Evans . . . .
Alice Astaire . . . .
CRIME Henpeck cures wife by posing as
murderer.

10577
ME AND MY PAL (74) (U)
Welwyn (Pathe) *reissue:* 1942 (Amb)
P: Warwick Ward
D: Thomas Bentley
Dave Willis . . . . Dave Craig
Pat Kirkwood . . . . Peggy
George Moon . . . . Hal Thomson
A. Giovanni . . . . Giovanni
John Warwick . . . . Charlie
Arthur Margetson . . . . Andrews
Aubrey Mallalieu . . . . Governor
Eliot Makeham . . . . Cripps
O.B. Clarence . . . . Judge
Ernest Butcher . . . . Webb
Hugh Dempster . . . . Joe
Gerry Fitzgerald . . . . Singing Convict
COMEDY Dupes pose as convicts to help police
expose insurance crooks.

10578
DEAD MEN ARE DANGEROUS (69) (A)
Welwyn (Pathe) *reissue:* 1942 (Amb)
P: Warwick Ward
D: Harold French
S: (NOVEL) H.C. Armstrong (HIDDEN)
SC' Victor Kendall, Harry Hughes, Vernon
Clancey
Robert Newton . . . . Aylmer Franklyn
Betty Lynne . . . . Nina
John Warwick . . . . Goddard
Peter Gawthorne . . . . Conroy
Merle Tottenham . . . . Gladys
John Turnbull . . . . Detective
Aubrey Mallalieu . . . . Coroner
Kynaston Reeves . . . . Uncle
CRIME Broke author changes clothes with
corpse and is accused of murder.

MAR

10579
THE MIND OF MR REEDER (75) (U)
USA: THE MYSTERIOUS MR REEDER
Jack Raymond (GN) *reissue:* 1943 (Ex)
P: Charles Q. Steele
D: Jack Raymond
S: (NOVEL) Edgar Wallace
SC: Bryan Wallace, Marjorie Gaffney,
Michael Hogan
Will Fyffe . . . . J.G. Reeder
Kay Walsh . . . . Peggy Gillette
George Curzon . . . . Welford
Chili Bouchier . . . . Elsa Welford
John Warwick . . . . Ted Bracher
Lesley Wareing . . . . Mrs Gaylor
Romilly Lunge . . . . Insp Gaylor
Derek Gorst . . . . Langdon
Ronald Shiner . . . . Sam Hackett
Wally Patch . . . . Lomer
George Hayes . . . . Brady
Betty Astell . . . . Barmaid
CRIME Old tec unmasks chief forger as club
owner's killer.

10580
THE NURSEMAID WHO DISAPPEARED
(86) (A)
WB—FN (WB)
P: Jerome Jackson
D: Arthur Woods
S: (NOVEL) Philip Macdonald
SC: Paul Gangelin, Connery Chappell
Arthur Margetson . . . . Antony Gethryn
Peter Coke . . . . Tom Sheldon
Lesley Brook . . . . Avis Bellingham
Edward Chapman . . . . Jenks
Coral Browne . . . . Mabel Barnes
Joyce Kennedy . . . . Lucia Gethryn
Dorice Fordred . . . . Janet Murch
Martita Hunt . . . . Lady Ballister
Marion Gerth . . . . Ada Brent
Ian Maclean . . . . Insp Pike
Ian Fleming . . . . Sir Egbert Lucas
CRIME Playwright helps tec catch kidnappers
posing as domestic agency.

10581
TOO DANGEROUS TO LIVE (74) (A)
WB—FN (FN)
P: Jerome Jackson
D: Anthony Hankey, Leslie Norman
S: (NOVEL) David Hume (CRIME UNLIMITED)
SC: Paul Gangelin, Connery Chappell, Leslie Arliss
Sebastian Shaw . . . . Jacques Leclerq
Greta Gynt . . . . Marjorie
Reginald Tate . . . . Collins
Anna Konstam . . . . Lou
Ronald Adam . . . . Murbridge/Wills
Edward Lexy . . . . Insp Cardby

Ian Maclean . . . . Saunders
Henry Caine . . . . Selford
George Relph . . . . Manners
Tonie Edgar Bruce . . . . Mrs Herbert
CRIME French tec poses as crook to unmask
jewel thieves' leader.

10582
Q PLANES (82) (U)
USA: CLOUDS OVER EUROPE
Harefield (Col) *reissue*: 1944 (Key)
P: Irving Asher, Alexander Korda
D: Tim Whelan
S: Brock Williams, Jack Whittingham,
Arthur Wimperis
SC: Ian Dalrymple
Laurence Olivier . . . . Tony McVane
Valerie Hobson . . . . Kay Hammond
Ralph Richardson . . . . Charles Hammond
George Curzon . . . . Jenkins
George Merritt . . . . Barrett
Gus McNaughton . . . . Blenkinsop
David Tree . . . . Mackenzie
Sandra Storme . . . . Daphne
Hay Petrie . . . . Stage-doorman
Frank Fox . . . . Karl
Gordon McLeod . . . . Baron
John Longden . . . . John Peters
Reginald Purdell . . . . Pilot
John Laurie . . . . Editor
Pat Aherne . . . . Officer
CRIME Spies use secret ray to steal new aircraft
during test flights.

10583
THE SPY IN BLACK (82) (U)
USA: U—BOAT 29
Harefield (Col) *reissue*: 1944 (Key)
P: Irving Asher, Alexander Korda
D: Michael Powell
S: (NOVEL) J. Storer Clouston
SC: Emeric Pressburger, Roland Pertwee
Conrad Veidt . . . . Capt Hardt
Sebastian Shaw . . . . Cdr David Blacklock
Valerie Hobson . . . . Joan
Marius Goring . . . . Lt Schuster
June Duprez . . . . Anne Burnett
Athole Stewart . . . . Rev Hector Matthews
Agnes Lauchlan . . . . Mrs Matthews
Helen Haye . . . . Mrs Sedley
Cyril Raymond . . . . Rev John Harris
Hay Petrie . . . . Engineer
Grant Sutherland . . . . Bob Bratt
Robert Rendel . . . . Admiral
Mary Morris . . . . Chauffeuse
WAR Orkneys, 1917. Spy posing as German
spy posing as schoolmistress catches U—Boat
captain acting as spy.

10584
SO THIS IS LONDON (89)
20th Century Productions (20) *reissue*: 1949 (cut)
P: Robert T. Kane
D: Thornton Freeland
S: (PLAY) Arthur Goodrich
SC: William Conselman, Ben Travers, Tom
Phipps, Douglas Furber
Robertson Hare . . . . Henry Honeycutt
Alfred Drayton . . . . Lord Worthing
George Sanders . . . . Dr de Reszke
Berton Churchill . . . . Hiram Draper
Fay Compton . . . . Lady Worthing
Carla Lehmann . . . . Elinor Draper
Stewart Granger . . . . Laurence
Ethel Revnell . . . . Dodie
Gracie West . . . . Liz
Lily Cahill . . . . Mrs Draper
Mavis Clair . . . . Mrs Honeycutt
Aubrey Mallalieu . . . . Butler
COMEDY Bakery magnate vies with American
magnate for an impostor's vitamin B4 flour.

10585
INSPECTOR HORNLEIGH (87) (A)
20th Century Productions (20)
P: Robert T. Kane
D: Eugene Ford
S: (RADIO SERIES) Hans Wolfgang Priwin
SC: Bryan Wallace, Gerald Elliott, Richard
Llewellyn
Gordon Harker . . . . Insp Hornleigh
Alastair Sim . . . . Sgt Bingham
Hugh Williams . . . . Bill Gordon
Steve Geray . . . . Kavanos
Wally Patch . . . . Sam Holt
Edward Underdown . . . . . . Peter Dench
Miki Hood . . . . Ann Gordon
Gibb McLaughlin . . . . Alfred Cooper
Ronald Adam . . . . Wittens
CRIME Insp suspects foreign millionaire of
stealing the Chancellor of the Exchequer's bag.

10586
LET'S BE FAMOUS (83) (U)
ATP (ABFD) *reissue*: 1945 (Prem)
P: Michael Balcon
D: Walter Forde
S: Roger Macdougal, Allan Mackinnon
Jimmy O'Dea . . . . Jimmy Houlinan
Betty Driver . . . . Betty Pinbright
Sonnie Hale . . . . Finch
Patrick Barr . . . . Johnnie Blake
Basil Radford . . . . Watson
Milton Rosmer . . . . Albert Pinbright
Lena Brown . . . . Polly Pinbright
Garry Marsh . . . . BBC Official
Alf Goddard. . . . . Battling Bulger
Henry Hallett . . . . Grenville
Hay Plumb . . . . Announcer
COMEDY Commercial radio talent scout tries
to publicise Irish singer.

10587
TROUBLE BREWING (87) (U)
ATP (ABFD) *reissue*: 1942
P: Jack Kitchin
D: Anthony Kimmins
S: Anthony Kimmins, Angus Macphail,
Michael Hogan
George Formby . . . . George Gullip
Googie Withers . . . . Mary Brown
Gus McNaughton . . . . Bill Pike
Garry Marsh . . . . A.G. Brady
Joss Ambler . . . . Lord Redhill
Ronald Shiner . . . . Bridgwater
Martita Hunt . . . . Mme Berdi
C. Denier Warren . . . . Maj Hopkins
Beatrix Fielden-Kaye . . . . . Housekeeper
Basil Radford . . . . Guest
Esma Cannon . . . . Maid
COMEDY Newspaper printer catches
counterfeiters using brewery as cover.

10588
THE SILENT BATTLE (84) (U)
USA: CONTINENTAL EXPRESS
Pinebrook (Par)
P: Anthony Havelock-Allan
D: Herbert Mason
S: (NOVEL) Jean Bommart (LE POISSON
CHINOIS)
SC: Wolfgang Wilhelm, Rodney Ackland
Rex Harrison . . . . Jacques Sauvin
Valerie Hobson . . . . Draguisha Montescu
John Loder . . . . Rene Bordier
Muriel Aked . . . . Mme Duvivier
George Devine . . . . Sonneman
John Salew . . . . Ernest
Kaye Seeley . . . . Bartoff
Carl Jaffe . . . . Rykoff
Megs Jenkins . . . . Louise
Arthur Maude . . . . Editor
CRIME Balkans, 1938. French agent stops
revolutionaries from blowing up train with
President aboard.

10589
TWO MINUTES (42) (A) USA: THE SILENCE
GB Instructional (Ex)
D: Donald Taylor
Walter Hudd . . . . James Selworthy
Edana Romney . . . . Molly Selworthy
Patric Curwen . . . . Padre
Margaret Hanson . . . .
Jeanne Macintyre . . . .
DRAMA Armistice Day silence decides man
against leaving war-injured wife.

10590
BEYOND OUR HORIZON (42) (U)
GHW Productions (Unity)
D: Norman Walker
Milton Rosmer . . . . Pastor Brandt
Josephine Wilson . . . . Mrs Brandt
Jimmy Hanley . . . .
Mavis Clair . . . .
Carl Harbord . . . .
RELIGION Norway. Pastor with the gift of
healing is unable to cure his wife's paralysis.

10591
MEN WITHOUT HONOUR (59) (A)
Smith & Newman (EB)
P: Bernard Smith
D: S: Widgey Newman
SC: George A. Cooper
Ian Fleming . . . . Franl Hardy
Grace Arnold . . . . Mrs Hardy
Howard Douglas . . . . Fayne
W.T. Hodge . . . . Vigor
Charles Paton . . . . Vicar
CRIME Lawyer poses as crook to help police
trap sharepushers.

APR
10592
I MET A MURDERER (78) (A)
Gamma (GN) *reissue*: 1947 (Ex)
P: Roy Kellino, Pamela Kellino, James Mason
D: Roy Kellino
S: Pamela Kellino
SC: Pamela Kellino, James Mason
James Mason . . . . Mark Warrow
Pamela Kellino . . . . Jo
Sylvia Coleridge . . . . Martha Warrow
William Devlin . . . . Warrow
Peter Coke . . . . Horseman
Esma Cannon . . . . Hiker
James Harcourt . . . . Cart-driver
CRIME Authoress shelters fugitive farmer who
killed nagging wife.

10593
THE LAMBETH WALK (84) (U)
CAPAD-Pinebrook (MGM) *reissue*: 1943 (BL)
P: Anthony Havelock-Allan
D: Albert de Courville
S: (PLAY) Louis Rose, Douglas Furber,
Noel Gay (ME AND MY GIRL)
SC: Clifford Grey, Robert Edmunds,
John Paddy Carstairs
Lupino Lane . . . . Bill Snibson
Sally Gray . . . . Sally
Seymour Hicks . . . . Sir John
Norah Howard . . . . The Duchess
Enid Stamp-Taylor . . . . Jacqueline
Wallace Lupino . . . . Parchester
Wilfrid Hyde White . . . . Lord Battersby
May Hallatt . . . . Lady Battersby
Mark Lester . . . . Sir Roger
Charles Heslop . . . . Oswald
MUSICAL Cockney inherits dukedom but
stays true to sweetheart.

10594
HOME FROM HOME (73) (U)
British Lion *reissue*: 1946 (Ren)
P: D: Herbert Smith
S: Fenn Sherie, Ingram d'Abbes

Sandy Powell . . . . Sandy
Rene Ray . . . . Gladys Burton
Roy Emerton . . . . Bill Burton
Kathleen Harrison . . . . Mabel
Bruce Lister . . . . Jim
Wally Patch . . . . .Banks
Norma Varden . . . . Mrs Fairweather
Peter Gawthorne . . . . Governor
5 Harmonica Rascals
Gaillard Brothers
COMEDY Henpeck helps bank-robbers return to prison to escape wife and work.

10595
TRUNK CRIME (51) (A)
USA: DESIGN FOR MURDER
Charter (Anglo)
P: John Boulting
D: Roy Boulting
S: (PLAY) Edward Percy, Reginald Denham
SC: Francis Miller
Manning Whiley . . . . Bentley
Barbara Everest . . . . Ursula
Michael Drake . . . . Grierson
Hay Petrie . . . . Old Dan
Thorley Walters . . . . Frazier
Eileen Bennett . . . . Eve
Lewis Stringer . . . . Hearty
CRIME Taunted student goes mad and tries to bury tormentor alive.

10596
THE FACE AT THE WINDOW (65) (A)
Pennant (BL) reissue: 1942 (Amb)
P: D: George King
S: (PLAY) F. Brooke Warren
SC: A.R. Rawlinson, Randall Faye
Tod Slaughter . . . . Chevalier del Gardo
Marjorie Taylor . . . . Cecile de Brisson
John Warwick . . . . Lucien Cortier
Leonard Henry . . . . Gaston
Aubrey Mallalieu . . . . de Brisson
Robert Adair . . . . Insp Guffert
Wallace Evennett . . . . Prof le Blanc
Kay Lewis . . . . Babette
Margaret Yarde . . . . Le Pinan
Harry Terry . . . . The Face
CRIME Paris, 1880. Fake revival of corpse exposes chevalier and his mad half-brother as bank robbers.

MAY
10597
BLACK EYES (70) (A)
ABPC Remake: 1937 (Milo)
P: Walter C. Mycroft
D: Herbert Brenon
S: V. Tourjansky (LES YEUX NOIRS)
SC: Dudley Leslie
Otto Kruger . . . . Petrov
Mary Maguire . . . . Tania Petrov
Walter Rilla . . . . Roudine
John Wood . . . . Karlo
Marie Wright . . . . Miss Brown
Cecil Ramage . . . .
Kenneth Kove . . . .
Jenny Laird . . . .
O.B. Clarence . . . .
DRAMA Moscow. Waiter saves girl from philandering banker by revealing that he is her father.

10598
JAMAICA INN (107) (A)
Mayflower (ABPC) reissues: 1944; 1948 (Ren) 1948 (Ren)
P: Erich Pommer
D: Alfred Hitchcock
S: (NOVEL) Daphne du Maurier
SC: Sidney Gilliat, Joan Harrison, J.B. Priestley
Charles Laughton . . .Sir Humphrey Pengallan
Maureen O'Hara . . . . Mary Yelland
Leslie Banks . . . . Joss Merlyn
Emlyn Williams . . . . Harry Pedlar
Robert Newton . . . . Jem Trehearne
Wylie Watson . . . . .Salvation Watkins
Marie Ney . . . . Patience Merlyn
Morland Graham . . . . Sea-lawyer Sydney
Stephen Haggard . . . . Boy
Mervyn Johns . . . . Thomas
Edwin Greenwood . . . . Dandy
Horace Hodges . . . . Chadwick
Jeanne de Casalis . . . . Guest
Basil Radford . . . . Guest
George Curzon . . . . Guest
John Longden . . . . Capt Johnson
ADVENTURE Cornwall, period. Government agent poses as wrecker to unmask JP as ringleader.

10599
SPIES OF THE AIR (77) (A)
British National (ABPC)
P: John Corfield
D: David Macdonald
S: (PLAY) Jeffrey Dell (OFFICIAL SECRETS)
SC: A.R. Rawlinson, Bridget Boland
Barry K. Barnes . . . . Jim Thurloe
Roger Livesey . . . . Houghton
Joan Marion . . . . .Dorothy Houghton
Basil Radford . . . . Madison
Felix Aylmer . . . . Col Cairns
John Turnbull . . . . .Sir Andrew Hamilton
Henry Oscar . . . . Porter
Edward Ashley . . . . Stuart
Wallace Douglas . . . . Hooper
Everley Gregg . . . . Mrs Madison
CRIME Test pilot kills blackmailer and betrays designer's plans.

10600
PATHETONE PARADE OF 1939 (39) (U)
Pathe
D: Fred Watts
Robb Wilton   Albert Sandler
Raymond Newell   Leonard Henry
Mario de Pietro   Arthur Prince & Jim
Rupert Hazell & Elsie Day
6 Lai Founs
Mantovani and his Tipica Orchestra
Rudy Starita and his Marimba Band
REVUE

10601
FLYING FIFTY FIVE (72) (U)
Admiral (RKO)
P: Victor M. Greene
D: Reginald Denham
S: (NOVEL) Edgar Wallace
SC: Victor Greene, Vernon Clancey, Kenneth Horne
Derrick de Marney . . . . Bill Urquhart
Nancy Burne . . . . Stella Barrington
Marius Goring . . . . .Charles Barrington
John Warwick . . . . Jebson
Peter Gawthorne . . . . Jonas Urquhart
D.A. Clarke-Smith . . . . . . Jacques Gregory
Amy Veness . . . . Aunt Eliza
Ronald Shiner . . . . Scrubby Oaks
Billy Bray . . . . Cheerful
Francesca Bahrle . . . . Clare
SPORT Owner's son posing as trainer blackmailed to lose race.

10602
ASK A POLICEMAN (82) (U)
Gainsborough (MGM) reissue: 1942

(ABFD; 8 mins cut)
P: Edward Black
D: Marcel Varnel
S: Sidney Gilliat
SC: Marriott Edgar, Val Guest, J.O.C. Orton
Will Hay . . . . Sgt Samuel Dudfoot
Moore Marriott . . . . . .Jerry Harbottle/His Dad
Graham Moffatt . . . .'. . Albert Brown
Glennis Lorimer . . . . Emily Martin
Peter Gawthorne . . . . John Cronshaw
Charles Oliver . . . . Montague Pennington
Herbert Lomas . . . . Coastguard
Pat Aherne. . . . . Motorist
COMEDY Village police try to stimulate crime and unmask squire as smuggler.

10603
A GIRL MUST LIVE (92) (A)
Gainsborough (20) reissue: 1948 (GFD)
P: Edward Black
D: Carol Reed
S: (NOVEL) Emery Bonnet
SC: Frank Launder, Austin Melford
Margaret Lockwood . . . . . . Leslie James
Renee Houston . . . . Gloria Lind
Lilli Palmer . . . . Clyte Devine
George Robey . . . . Horace Blount
Hugh Sinclair . . . . Earl of Pangborough
Naunton Wayne . . . . Hugo Smythe
Moore Marriott . . . . Bretherton-Hythe/
                                 Lord Grandonald
Mary Clare . . . . Mrs Wallis
David Burns . . . . Joe Gold
Kathleen Harrison . . . . Penelope
Drusilla Wills . . . . Miss Polkinghorne
Wilson Coleman . . . . Mr Joliffe
Helen Haye . . . . Aunt Primrose
Frederick Burtwell . . . . Hodder
Martita Hunt . . . . Mme Dupont
COMEDY Runaway schoolgirl posing as actress's daughter foils dancer's plot to blackmail Earl.

10604
A GENTLEMAN'S GENTLEMAN (70) (U)
WB—FN (WB)
P: Jerome Jackson
D: Roy William Neill
S: (PLAY) Philip Macdonald
SC: Austin Melford, Elizabeth Meehan
Eric Blore . . . . Heppelwhite
Marie Lohr . . . . Mrs Handside-Lane
Peter Coke . . . . Tony
Patricia Hilliard . . . . Judy
David Hutcheson . . . . Bassy
David Burns . . . . Alfred
Ian Maclean . . . . Fox
Wallace Evennett . . . . Magnus Pomeroy
C. Denier Warren . . . . Dr Bottom
COMEDY Switzerland. Valet blackmails master for supposed poisoning.

10605
TUNES OF THE TIMES (17) (U)
Inspiration (Par)
D: Horace Shepherd
Mario de Pietro
Alfredo Campoli
MUSICAL Vocal, dance, violin and orchestral items.

10606
JUDY BUYS A HORSE (17) (U)
P & W Films (Butcher)
D: Lance Comfort
Judy Dick . . . . Judy
ANIMAL Girl persuades father to buy horse, trains it, and wins race.

10607
THE FOUR FEATHERS (130) (A) *tech*
London (UA) *reissues:* 1943 (Eal; 25 mins cut)
1948 (BL)
P: Alexander Korda, Irving Asher
D: Zoltan Korda
S: (NOVEL) A.E.W. Mason
SC: R.C. Sheriff, Lajos Biro, Arthur Wimperis
John Clements . . . . Harry Faversham
Ralph Richardson . . . . . . Capt John Durrance
C. Aubrey Smith . . . . Gen Burroughs
Allan Jeayes . . . . Gen Faversham
Jack Allen . . . . Lt Willoughby
Donald Gray . . . . .Peter Burroughs
Frederick Culley . . . . Dr Sutton
Amid Taftazani . . . . Karaga Pasha
Henry Oscar . . . . Dr Harraz
John Laurie . . . . Khalifa
Robert Rendel . . . . Colonel
Hal Walters , ... Joe
WAR Egypt. Coward redeems himself by
posing as Arab to save captured friends.

10608
FULL SPEED AHEAD (60) (U)
Trading Corp for Education & General
Services (GFD)
D; John Hunt
S: "Bartimeus"
Michael Osler . . . . John Elwood
Frederick Peisley . . . . Michael Elwood
Dinah Sheridan . . . . Joan Barrymore
Morland Graham . . . . Gordon Tweedie
H.G. Stoker . . . . Sir Robert Barrymore
Betty Shale . . . . Mrs Elwood
DRAMA New destroyer's commander saves
shipping magnate's daughter from burning
cargo-boat.

10609
SWORD OF HONOUR (83) (U)
Butcher *reissue::* 1941 (Sherwood; 1350 ft cut)
P: D: Maurice Elvey
S: Dudley Sturrock
SC: Gerald Elliott
Geoffrey Toone . . . . Bill Brown
Sally Gray . . . . Lady Moira Talmadge
Dorothy Dickson . . . . Mrs Stanhope
Donald Gray . . . . Stukeley
Wally Patch . . . . Pomeroy Brown
Peter Gawthorne . . . . . . Lord Carhampton
Frederick Culley . . . . Duke of Honiton
Maire O'Neill . . . . Biddy
Gordon Begg . . . . Grandpa Brown
Cyril Smith . . . . Bright
Patrick Susands . . . . Adjutant
Tommy Woodrooffe . . . . . Commentator
DRAMA Sandhurst. Royal Military College
student proves he is no coward.

10610
THE MISSING PEOPLE (71) (A)
Jack Raymond (GN) *reissue:* 1943 (Ex)
P: Charles Q. Steele
D: Jack Raymond
S: (NOVEL) Edgar Wallace (THE MIND OF
MR REEDER)
SC: Lydia Hayward
Will Fyffe . . . . J.G. Reeder
Lyn Harding . . . . Joseph Branstone
Kay Walsh . . . . Peggy Gillette
Ronald Shiner . . . . Sam Hackett
Patricia Roc . . . . Doris Bevan
Ronald Adam . . . . Surtees
Antony Holles . . . . Ernest Branstone
Reginald Purdell . . . . Harry Morgan
Maire O'Neill . . . . Housekeeper
CRIME Old tec unmasks solicitor brothers
behind the drowning of rich old women.

JUN
10611
I KILLED THE COUNT (89) (A)
USA: WHO IS GUILTY ?
Grafton (GN) *reissues:* 1942 (Maj) 1948 (GN)
P: Isidore Goldschmidt
D: Fred Zelnik
S: (PLAY) Alec Coppel
SC: Alec Coppel, Lawrence Huntington
Syd Walker . . . . Insp Davidson
Ben Lyon . . . . Bernard Froy
Terence de Marney . . . . Det-Sgt Raines
Barbara Blair . . . . Renee la Lune
Antoinette Cellier . . . . Louise Rogers
Athole Stewart . . . . Lord Sorrington
Leslie Perrins . . . . Count Mattoni
Ronald Shiner . . . . Mullet
David Burns . . . . Diamond
Kathleen Harrison . . . . . . Polly
Gus McNaughton . . . . Martin
Aubrey Mallalieu . . . . Johnson
CRIME Four people confess to killing
philandering Count.

10612
TWO DAYS TO LIVE (44) (U)
Venture (Anglo)
P: Alfred d'Eyncourt
D: Walter Tennyson
S: Ian Walker
Richard Goolden . . . . Mr Jackson
Phyllis Calvert . . . . Joyce
Ernest Sefton . . . . The Burglar
Frank Atkinson . . . . Wilkie
Andrea Malandrinos . . . . . . Duvaliti
Arthur Seaton . . . . Reginald Newbould
Douglas Stewart . . . . Trevor Williams
COMEDY Hypochondriac seeking excitement
becomes burglar.

10613
TROUBLE FOR TWO (46) (U)
Venture (Anglo)
P: Alfred d'Eyncourt
D: Walter Tennyson
S: Ian Walker
Anthony Hulme . . . . Rodney Paine
Mavis Claire . . . . Carol Hanson
C. Denier Warren . . . . Pip Piper
Jack Knight . . . . Mr Craven
Bryan Herbert . . . . Corrigan
CRIME Tec poses as jeweller to catch gem
thieves at house party.

10614
GOODBYE, MR CHIPS (113) (U)
MGM-British *reissues:* 1944 (MGM) 1954 (Eros)
P: Victor Saville
D: Sam Wood
S: (NOVEL) James Hilton
SC: Eric Maschwitz, R.C. Sheriff, Claudine West,
Sidney Franklin
Robert Donat . . . . Charles Chipping
Greer Garson . . . . Katherine Ellis
Terry Kilburn . . . . John/Peter Colley
John Mills . . . . Peter Colley
Paul von Hernreid . . . . Max Staefel
Judith Furse . . . . Flora
Lyn Harding . . . . Dr Wetherby
Milton Rosmer . . . . Charteris
Frederick Leister . . . . Marsham
Louis Hampton . . . . Mrs Wickett
Austin Trevor . . . . Ralston
David Tree . . . . Jackson
Edmond Breon . . . . Col Morgan
Jill Furse . . . . Helen Colley
Guy Middleton . . . . McCulloch
Nigel Stock . . . . John Forrester

DRAMA 1870—1919. Teacher humanised by
wife becomes the oldest inhabitant at public
school. (AA: Best Actor 1939; PGAA: 1940.)

10615
THE GANG'S ALL HERE (77) (A)
USA: THE AMAZING MR FORREST
ABPC
P: Walter C. Mycroft, Jack Buchanan
D: Thornton Freeland
S: Ralph Spence
Jack Buchanan . . . . John Forrest
Syd Walker . . . . Younce
Edward Everett Horton . . . Treadwell
Googie Withers . . . . Alice Forrest
Otto Kruger . . . . Mike Chadwick
Jack la Rue . . . . Alberni
Walter Rilla . . . . Prince Homouska
David Burns . . . . Beretti
Charles Carson . . . . Charles Cartwright
Leslie Perrins . . . . Harper
Ronald Shiner . . . . Spider Ferris
Robb Wilton . . . . Barman
Edward Lexy . . . . Insp Holroyd
COMEDY Insurance tec poses as American
gunman to unmask club owner as jewel thief.
(Extract in ELSTREE STORY, 1952.)

10616
THE GOOD OLD DAYS (79) (U)
WB-FN (FN)
P: Jerome Jackson
D: Roy William Neill
S: Ralph Smart
SC: Austin Melford, John Dighton
Max Miller . . . . Alexander the Greatest
Hal Walters . . . . Titch
Kathleen Gibson . . . . Polly
H.F. Maltby . . . . Randolph Macaulay
Martita Hunt . . . . Sarah Macaulay
Anthony Shaw . . . . Lovelace
Allan Jeayes . . . . Shadwell
Sam Wilkinson . . . . Croker
Roy Emerton . . . . Grimes
Phyllis Monkman . . . . Mrs Bennett
COMEDY 1840. Persecuted players save Lord's
son from chimney sweep.

10617
MUSIC HALL PARADE (80) (U)
Butcher *reissue:* 1948
D: Oswald Mitchell
S: Con West, Oswald Mitchell
Glen Raynham . . . . Jean Parker
Richard Norris . . . . Dick Smart
Charles Sewell . . . . Stage Manager
Rita Grant . . . . Mrs Whipsnade
Frank E. Franks . . . . Tom Gamble
Hughie Green . . . . Eve Becke
Freddie Forbes . . . . Jack Stanford
Australian Motor Air Aces
Billy Cotton and his Band
Macari and his Dutch Serenaders
REVUE Commissionaire saves music hall by
finding amateur talent. (Extracts in
CAVALCADE OF VARIETY (1940)
HIGHLIGHTS OF VARIETY No. 25 (1940).)

10618
SECRET JOURNEY (72) (U)
USA: AMONG HUMAN WOLVES
British National (Anglo)
P: John Corfield
D: John Baxter
S: (NOVEL) Charles Dumas (LONE WOLVES)
SC: Michael Hogan
Basil Radford . . . . John Richardson
Sylvie StClaire . . . . Helen Richardson
Thorley Walters . . . . . . Max von Raugwitz

Peter Gawthorne . . . . . . Gen von Raugwitz
Patricia Medina . . . .
George Hayes . . . .
Tom Helmore . . . .
Joss Ambler . . . .
C. Denier Warren . . . . . .
CRIME Paris. Spy's sister loves son of German general, who stole formula for explosive.

10619
THE FOUR JUST MEN (85) (A)
USA: THE SECRET FOUR
Ealing-CAPAD (ABFD) *reissue:* 1944 (Ren)
AP: S.C. Balcon
D: Walter Forde
S: (NOVEL) Edgar Wallace
SC: Roland Pertwee, Angus Macphail, Sergei Nolbandov
Hugh Sinclair . . . . Humphrey Mansfield
Griffith Jones . . . . James Brodie
Francis L. Sullivan .. . . Leon Poiccard
Frank Lawton . . . . Terry
Anna Lee . . . . Ann Lodge
Basil Sydney . . . . Frank Snell
Alan Napier . . . . Sir Hamar Ryman
Lydia Sherwood . . . . Myra Hastings
Athole Stewart . . . . Commissioner
Edward Chapman . . . . B.J. Burrell
George Merritt . .. . Insp Falmouth
Garry Marsh . . . . Bill Grant
Ellaline Terriss . . . . Lady Willoughby
CRIME Actor, producer, costumier, and millionaire kill MP to save Empire from aliens.

10620
THERE AIN'T NO JUSTICE (83) (A)
Ealing-CAPAD (ABFD) *reissue:* 1949
(EB; 155 ft cut)
AP: Sergei Nolbandov
D: Pen Tennyson
S: (NOVEL) James Curtis
SC: Pen Tennyson, James Curtis, Sergei Nolbandov
Jimmy Hanley . . . . Tommy Mutch
Edward Rigby . . . . Pa Mutch
Mary Clare . . . . Ma Mutch
Edward Chapman . . . . Sammy Sanders
Phyllis Stanley . . . . Elsie Mutch
Jill Furse . . . . Connie Fletcher
Nan Hopkins . . . . Dot Ducrow
Richard Ainley . . . . Billy Frost
Michael Wilding . . . . Len Charteris
Gus McNaughton . . . . Alfie Norton
Richard Norris . . . . Stan
SPORT Boxing mechanic, bribed to lose match, wins.

JUL

10621
THIS MAN IN PARIS (86) (A)
Pinebrook (Par)
P: S: Anthony Havelock-Allan
D: David Macdonald
SC: Allan Mackinnon, Roger Macdougall
Barry K. Barnes . . . . Simon Drake
Valerie Hobson . . . . Pat Drake
Alastair Sim . . . . Macgregor
Edward Lexy . . . . Insp Holly
Garry Marsh . . . . Sgt. Bright
Jacques Max Michel . . . . . . Emile Beranger
Mona Goya . . . . Torch Bernal
Anthony Shaw . . . . Gen Craysham
Cyril Chamberlain . . . . Swindon
Charles Oliver . . . . Gaston
CRIME Paris. Wife helps reporter unmask banknote forger.

10622
THE SAINT IN LONDON (77) (A)
RKO—Radio

P: William Sistrom
D: John Paddy Carstairs
S: (NOVEL) Leslie Charteris (THE MILLION POUND DAY)
SC: Lynn Root, Frank Fenton
George Sanders . . . . Simon Templar
Sally Gray . . . . Penelope Parker
Ballard Berkeley . . . . Richard Blake
David Burns . . . . Dugan
Gordon McLeod . . . . Insp Teal
Henry Oscar . . . . Bruno Lang
Ralph Truman . . . . Jusella
Carl Jaffe . . . . Stengler
Nora Howard . . . . Mrs Morgan
Charles Carson . . . . Mr Morgan
John Abbott . . . . Count Duni
Athene Seyler . . . . Mrs Buckley
CRIME Ex-crook exposes gangster's attempt to defraud foreign government.

10623
POISON PEN (79) (A)
ABPC
P: Walter C. Mycroft
D: Paul Stein
S: (PLAY) Richard Llewellyn
SC: Doreen Montgomery, William Freshman, N.C. Hunter, Esther McCracken
Flora Robson . . . . Mary Rider
Robert Newton . . . . Sam Hurrin
Ann Todd . . . . Ann Rider
Geoffrey Toone . . . . David
Reginald Tate . . . . Rev Rider
Belle Chrystal . . . . Sucal Hurrin
Edward Chapman . . . . Len Griffin
Edward Rigby . . . . Badham
Athole Stewart . . . . Col Cashelton
Mary Hinton . . . . Mrs Cashelton
Cyril Chamberlain . . . . Peter Cashelton
Catherine Lacey . . . . Connie Fateley
Wally Patch . . . . Mr Suggs
Ella Retford . . . . Mrs Suggs
Jean Clyde . . . . Mrs Griffin
Wilfrid Hyde White . . . . . . Postman
Marjorie Rhodes . . . . Mrs Scaife
CRIME Village vicar finds his spinster sister is the writer of poison pen letters. (Extract in ELSTREE STORY, 1952.)

10624
DOWN OUR ALLEY (56) (U)
British Screen Service *reissue:* 1943,
GANG SHOW (Fed)
D: George A. Cooper
Hughie Green . . . . Hughie Dunstable
Wally Patch . . . . Mr Dunstable
Vivienne Chatterton . . . . . . Mrs Dunstable
Sylvia Saetre . . . . Sally
Antony Holles . . . . Tony
Daphne Raglan . . . . Mary
Philip Morant . . . . Eustace
Johnnie Schofield . . . . Waiter
Hughie Green's Gang
MUSICAL Music shop manager's slum gang substitutes for nightclub crooner.

10625
SHIPYARD SALLY (79) (U)
20th Century Productions (20)
P: Robert T. Kane
D: Monty Banks
S: Gracie Fields, Tom Geraghty, Val Valentine
SC: Karl Tunberg, Don Ettlinger
Gracie Fields . . . . Sally Fitzgerald
Sydney Howard . . . . Major Fitzgerald
Morton Selten . . . . Lord Randall
Norma Varden . . . . Lady Patricia
Oliver Wakefield . . . . Forsyth
Tucker McGuire . . . . Linda Marsh
MacDonald Parke . . . . Diggs

Richard Cooper . . . . . . Sir John Treacher
MUSICAL Clydeside publican poses as American singer to persuade Lord to reopen shipyard.

AUG
10626
DEAD MAN'S SHOES (70) (A)
ABPC
P: Walter C. Mycroft
D: Thomas Bentley
S: (STORY) Hans Kafka (CARREFOUR)
SC: Nina Jarvis
Leslie Banks . . . . Roger de Vetheuil
Wilfrid Lawson . . . . Lucien Sarrou
Judy Kelly . . . . Michele Allein
Joan Marion . . . . Viola de Vetheuil
Nancy Price . . . . Mme Pelletier
Walter Hudd . . . . Gaston Alexandri
Peter Bull . . . . Defence
Henry Oscar . . . . President
Ludwig Stossel . . . . Dr Breithaut
Geoffrey Atkins. . . . . Paul de Vetheuil
CRIME Paris. Amnesiac industrialist blackmailed for his past life as a thief.

10627
THE OUTSIDER (90) (A)
ABPC
P: Walter C. Mycroft
D: Paul Stein
S: (PLAY) Dorothy Brandon
SC: Dudley Leslie
George Sanders . . . . Anton Ragatzy
Mary Maguire . . . . Lalage Sturdee
Barbara Blair . . . . Wendy
Peter Murray Hill . . . . Basil Owen
Frederick Leister . . . . Joseph Sturdee
Walter Hudd . . . . Dr Helmore
Kathleen Harrison . . . . Mrs Coates
Kynaston Reeves . . . . Sir Montague Tollemach
Edmond Breon . . . . Dr Ladd
Ralph Truman . . . . Sir Nathan Israel
Martin Walker . . . .
Ian Colin . . . .
Lesley Waring . . . . . .
Edward Lexy . . . . . .
Eddie Pola . . . .
DRAMA Unqualified osteopath cures surgeon's paralysed daughter.

10628
JUST WILLIAM (72) (U)
ABPC
P: Walter C. Mycroft
D: Graham Cutts
S: (STORIES) Richmal Crompton
SC: Doreen Montgomery, Ireland Wood, Graham Cutts
Dicky Lupino . . . . William Brown
Fred Emney . . . . Mr Brown
Basil Radford . . . . Mr Sidway
Amy Veness . . . . Mrs Bott
Iris Hoey . . . . Mrs Brown
Roddy McDowell . . . . Ginger
Norman Robinson . . . . Douglas
Peter Miles . . . . Henry
David Tree . . . . Marmaduke Bott
Jenny Laird . . . . Ethel Brown
Simon Lack . . . . Robert Brown
Aubrey Mather . . . . Fletcher
COMEDY Village boy exposes father's election rival as sharepusher. (Extract in ELSTREE STORY, 1952.)

10629
WHERE'S THAT FIRE ? (73) (U)
20th Century Productions (20)
P: Edward Black
D: Marcel Varnel
S: Maurice Braddell
SC: Marriott Edgar, Val Guest, J.O.C. Orton

Will Hay . . . . Capt Benjamin Viking
Moore Marriott . . . . Jerry Harbottle
Graham Moffatt . . . . Albert Brown
Peter Gawthorne . . . . Chief Officer
Eric Clavering . . . . Hank Sullivan
Hugh McDermott . . . . Jim Baker
Charles Hawtrey . . . . Youth
COMEDY Village fire brigade saves crown
jewels from gangsters.

10630
PANDAMONIUM (27) (U)
AIP (ABFD)
D: S: Widgey R. Newman
Hal Walters
Jane Griffiths
Howard Douglas
COMEDY Newlyrich pair buy animal hostel in
mistake for guest house.

10631
CHEER BOYS CHEER (84) (U)
ATP (ABFD) reissue: 1956 (EB)
AP: S.C. Balcon
D: Walter Forde
S: Ian Dalrymple, Donald Bull
SC: Roger Macdougall, Allan Mackinnon
Nova Pilbeam . . . . Margaret Greenleaf
Edmund Gwenn . . . . Edward Ironside
Jimmy O'Dea . . . . Matt Boyle
Moore Marriott . . . . Geordie
Graham Moffatt . . . . Albert
C.V. France . . . . Tom Greenleaf
Peter Coke . . . . John Ironside
Alexander Knox . . . . Saunders
Ivor Barnard . . . . Naseby
Jean Webster Brough . . . . . . Belle
COMEDY Brewery owner's son joins rival to
ruin him but falls in love with his daughter.

10632
YOUNG MAN'S FANCY (77) (A)
Ealing-CAPAD (ABFD) reissue: 1944
(Ren; 8 mins cut)
AP: S.C. Balcon
D: S: Robert Stevenson
SC: Roland Pertwee, Rodney Ackland,
E.V.H. Emmett
Griffith Jones . . . . Lord Alban
Anna Lee . . . . Ada
Seymour Hicks . . . . Duke of Beaumont
Billy Bennett . . . . Capt Boumphrey
Edward Rigby . . . . Gray
Francis L. Sullivan . . . . Blackbeard
Martita Hunt. . . . . Duchess of Beaumont
Meriel Forbes . . . . Miss Crowther
Felix Aylmer . . . . Sir Caleb Crowther
Aimos . . . . Tramp
Phyllis Monkman . . . . Esme
Morton Selten . . . . Fothergill
George Carney . . . . Chairman
COMEDY 1868. Lord escapes brewery heiress
by eloping to Paris with human cannonball.

10633
OLD MOTHER RILEY MP (76) (U)
Butcher's Film Service reissue: 1942
(Sherwood; 7 mins cut)
P: F.W. Baker
D: Oswald Mitchell
S: Oswald Mitchell, Con West
Arthur Lucan . . . . Mrs Riley
Kitty McShane . . . . Kitty Riley
Torin Thatcher . . . . Jack Nelson
Henry Longhurst . . . . Wicker
Patrick Ludlow . . . . Archie
Dennis Wyndham . . . . . Emperor of Rocavia
Cynthia Stock . . . . Supervisor
COMEDY Washerwoman elected to parliament
by tenement tenants, is made minister and
recovers foreign loan.

10634
CONFIDENTIAL LADY (75) (U)
WB—FN (FN)
P: Sam Sax
D: Arthur Woods
S: Brock Williams, Derek Twist
Ben Lyon . . . . Jim Brent
Jane Baxter . . . . Jill Trevor
Athole Stewart . . . . Sir Joshua Morple
Ronald Ward . . . . John Carter
Jean Cadell . . . . Amy Boswell
Frederick Burtwell . . . . Phillips
Gibb McLaughlin . . . . Sherriffe
Vera Bogetti . . . . Rose
Gordon McLeod . . . . Somers
Stewart Rome . . . . Alfred Trevor
ROMANCE Jilted reporter helps jilted girl
thwart press lord who ruined her father.

SEP

10635
MURDER WILL OUT (65) (A)
WB—FN (WB)
P: Sam Sax
D: Roy William Neill
S: Roy William Neill, Austin Melford, Brock
Williams, Derek Twist
John Loder . . . . Dr Paul Raymond
Jane Baxter . . . . Pamela Raymond
Jack Hawkins . . . . Stamp
Hartley Power . . . . Campbell
Peter Croft . . . . Nigel
Frederick Burtwell . . . . Morgan
Billy Hartnell . . . . Dick
Ian Maclean . . . . Inspector
CRIME Crooks fake murder to blackmail rich
doctor's neglected wife.

10636
HIS BROTHER'S KEEPER (70) (A)
WB—FN (FN)
P: Sam Sax
D: Roy William Neill
S: Roy William Neill, Austin Melford,
Brock Williams
Clifford Evans . . . . Jack Cornell
Tamara Desni . . . . Olga
Una O'Connor . . . . Eva
Peter Glenville . . . . Hicky Cornell
Reginald Purdell . . . . Bunny Reeves
Ronald Frankau . . . . George Hollis
Antoinette Lupino . . . . Pat
Aubrey Dexter . . . . Sylvester
Frederick Burtwell . . . . Harry
DRAMA Sharpshooting brothers quarrel over
gold-digging blues singer.

10637
WHAT WOULD YOU DO CHUMS ? (75) (A)
British National (Anglo)
P: John Corfield
D: John Baxter
-S: (RADIO SERIES) Gordon Crier
(MR WALKER WANTS TO KNOW)
SC: David Evans, Geoffrey Orme, Con West
Syd Walker . . . . Himself
Jean Gillie . . . . Lucy
Cyril Chamberlain. . . . . Mike
Jack Barty . . . . Joe
Wally Patch . . . . Tom
Gus McNaughton . . . . Harry
Peter Gawthorne . . . . . . Sir Douglas Gordon
Julien Vedey . . . . Mossy
Arthur Finn . . . . Slim
CRIME Junk dealer forced to convict girl's
fiance when fails to reform and robs bank.

10638
SHADOWED EYES (68) (A)
Savoy—GS Enterprises (RKO)
P: Kurt Sternberg, A. George Smith

D: Maclean Rogers
S: Arnold Ridley
SC: Roy Carter, Herbert Hill
Basil Sydney . . . . Dr Zander
Patricia Hilliard . . . . Dr Diana Barnes
Stewart Rome . . . . Sir John Barnes
Dorothy Boyd . . . .
Ian Fleming . . . . Dr McKane
Tom Helmore . . . . Ian
Dorothy Calve . . . . Mariorie
Ruby Miller . . . . Mrs. Clarke-Fenwick
Brian Buchel . . . .
DRAMA Amnesiac eye surgeon operates on
counsel who convicted him for killing wife's
lover.

10639
DISCOVERIES (68) (U)
Vogue (GN) reissues: 1942 (Maj) 1948 (GN)
D: Redd Davis
S: (RADIO SERIES) Carroll Levis
SC: Redd Davis, Cyril Campion, Anatole de
Grunwald
Carroll Levis . . . . Himself
Afrique . . . . Alfredo
Issy Bonn . . . . Mr Schwitzer
Julien Vedey . . . . Mr Spinelli
Bertha Belmore . . . . PCW Duggan
Ronald Shiner . . . . Jim Pike
Doris Hare . . . . Bella Brown
Kathleen Harrison . . . . Maid
Zoe Wynn . . . . Susie
Barbara Everest . . . . Mrs Venters
Shayle Gardner . . . . Manager
Cyril Levis; Three Ginx; Dump & Tony;
George Meaton; Radio Rascals; Pearl
Venters; Archie Galbraith; Glyn Davies;
Tony Vaughan; David Delmonte
Radio Rascals
Pearl Venters
Archie Galbraith
Glyn Davies
Tony Vaughan
David Delmonte
MUSICAL Rival manufacturers vie to sponsor
radio talent show.

10640
THE MIDAS TOUCH (68) (A)
WB—FN (WB)
P: Sam Sax
D: David Macdonald
S: (NOVEL) Margaret Kennedy
Barry K. Barnes . . . . Evan Jones
Judy Kelly . . . . Lydia Brenton
Frank Cellier . . . . Corris Morgan
Bertha Belmore . . . . Mrs Carter-Blake
Iris Hoey . . . . Ellie Morgan
Philip Friend . . . . David Morgan
Anna Konstam . . . . Mamie
Evelyn Roberts . . . . Maj Arnold
Eileen Erskine . . . . Rosalie
DRAMA Medium predicts faithless financier
will die in car accident involving his son.

OCT

10641
AN ENGLISHMAN'S HOME (79) (A)
USA: MADMEN OF EUROPE
Aldwych (UA)
P: Neville E. Neville
D: Albert de Courville
S: (PLAY) Guy du Maurier
SC: Edward Knoblock, Ian Hay, Dennis
Wheatley, Robert Edmunds, Dora Nirva,
Clifford Grey, Richard Llewellyn, Rodney
Ackland
Edmund Gwenn . . . . William Brown
Mary Maguire . . . . Betty Brown
Paul von Hernried . . . . Victor Brandt
Geoffrey Toone . . . . Peter Templeton
Richard Ainley . . . . Geoffrey Brown

Desmond Tester . . . . Billy Brown
John Wood . . . . Jimmy
Carl Jaffe . . . . Martin
Meinhart Maur . . . . Waldo
Mavis Villiers . . . . Dolly
Mark Lester . . . . Uncle Ben
WAR Foreign spy lives with English family and radios invaders.

10642
DARK EYES OF LONDON (75) (H)
USA: THE HUMAN MONSTER
Argyle Productions (Pathe) reissues: 1945
1950 (AA)
P: John Argyle
D: Walter Summers
S: (NOVEL) Edgar Wallace
SC: John Argyle, Walter Summers, Patrick Kirwan
Bella Lugosi . . . . Dr Orloff
Hugh Williams . . . . Insp Holt
Greta Gynt . . . . Diana Stewart
Wilfrid Walter . . . . Jake
Edmon Ryan . . . . Lt O'Reilly
Julie Suedo . . . . Secretary
Alexander Field . . . . Grogan
Arthur E. Owen . . . . Dumb Lew
Gerald Pring . . . . Henry Stuart
Charles Penrose . . . . Drunk
HORROR Blind home proprietor uses mute giant to drown insured victims.

10643
RADIO NIGHTS (16 (U)
Inspiration (Par)
P: D: Horace Shepherd
Leslie Jeffries and his Orchestra
Reginald King and his Orchestra
Eugene Pini and his Tango Orchestra
Horace Shepherd and his Symphony Orchestra
Terry & Doris Kendall
MUSICAL

10644
EDDIE CARROLL AND HIS BOYS (14) (U)
Inspiration (Par)
O: D: Horace Shepherd
Gwen Jones; Billy Day; Curly Ormerod
MUSICAL Radio dance band.

10645
PAPER PEOPLE LAND (17) (U)
C. Jenkins (ABFD)
D: C. Jenkins
TRICK Paper cutout marionettes perform with choral commentary.

10646
A TRAMP IN KILLARNEY (14) (U)
Fraternity— Victory (Col)
D: Nigel Byass
Patrick Ward . . . . The Tramp
MUSICAL Eire. Singing tramp finds former sweetheart but prefers open road.

10647
AT THE VILLA ROSE (74) (A)
USA: HOUSE OF MYSTERY
ABPC
P: Walter C. Mycroft
D: Walter Summers
S: (NOVEL) A.E.W. Mason
SC: Doreen Montgomery
Keneth Kent . . . . Insp Hanaud
Judy Kelly . . . . Celia Harland
Walter Rilla . . . . Ricardo
Peter Murray Hill . . . . Harry Wethermill
Antoinette Cellier . . . . Adele Rossignol
Clifford Evans . . . . Tace

Martita Hunt . . . . Helen Vaquier
Ruth Maitland . . . . Mme Dauvray
Ronald Adam . . . . Besnard
CRIME Aix-les-Bains. Gem thieves kidnap fake medium and frame her for killing rich widow.

10648
TEN DAYS IN PARIS (82) (A)
USA: MISSING TEN DAYS
Irving Asher Productions (Col) reissue:
1944 (BAP)
D: Tim Whelan
S: (NOVEL) Bruce Graeme (THE DISAPPEARANCE OF ROGER TREMAYNE)
SC: John Meehan jr, James Curtis
Rex Harrison . . . . Bob Stevens
Karen Verne . . . . Diane de Guermantes
C.V. France . . . . .Gen de Guermantes
Leo Genn . . . . Lanson
Joan Marion . . . . Denise
Antony Holles . . . . Francois
John Abbott . . . . Andre
Robert Rendel . . . . Sir James Stevens
Mavis Clair . . . . Marie
Andre Morell . . . . Victor
Hay Petrie . . . . Benoit
Frank Atkinson . . . . Pierre
CRIME Paris. Amnesiac working as general's chauffeur mistaken for spy, saves munitions train from destruction.

10649
MEET MAXWELL ARCHER (74) (A)
USA: MAXWELL ARCHER DETECTIVE
RKO Radio
P: William Sistrom
D: John Paddy Carstairs
S: (NOVEL) Hugh Cleveley (ARCHER PLUS 20)
SC: Hugh Cleveley, Katherine Strueby
John Loder . . . . Maxwell Archer
Leueen McGrath . . . . Sarah
Marta Labarr . . . . Nina
Athole Stewart . . . . Supt Gordon
George Merritt . . . . Insp Cornell
Ronald Adam . . . . Nicolides
Peter Halliwell Hobbs . . . . . George Gull
Syd Crossley . . . . Parkins
Barbara Everest . . . . Miss Duke
CRIME Private tec proves pilot did not kill spyring's contact-man.

10650
FRENCH WITHOUT TEARS (85) (A)
Two Cities (Par) reissues: 1943; 1948
P: David E. Rose
D: Anthony Asquith
S: (PLAY) Terence Rattigan
SC: Terence Rattigan, Ian Dalrymple, Anatole de Grunwald
Ray Milland . . . . Alan Howard
Ellen Drew . . . . Diana Lake
Janine Darcy . . . . Jacqueline Maingot
Roland Culver . . . . Cdr Rogers
David Tree . . . . Chris Neilan
Jim Gerald . . . . Maingot
Guy Middleton . . . . Brian Curtis
Kenneth Morgan . . . . Kenneth Lake
COMEDY France. Student's sister flirts with students to win diplomat.

10651
MRS PYM OF SCOTLAND YARD (65) (A)
Hurley Productions (GN) reissue: 1942 (Maj)
P: Victor Katona
D: Fred Elles
S: (NOVEL) Nigel Morland
SC: Fred Elles, Nigel Morland, Peggy Barwell
Mary Clare . . . . Mrs Pym
Edward Lexy . . . . Insp Shott

Nigel Patrick . . . . Richard Loddon
Janet Johnson . . . . Maraday Wood
Anthony Ireland . . . . Henry Menchen
Irene Handl . . . . Miss Bell
Vernon Kelso . . . . Frank Wood
Robert English . . . . Commissioner
CRIME Woman detective unmasks fake medium and saves heiress from murder.

NOV

10652
THE LION HAS WINGS (76) (U)
London—Korda (UA)
P: Alexander Korda
D: Michael Powell, Brian Desmond Hurst, Adrian Brunel
S: Ian Dalrymple
SC: Adrian Brunel, E.V.H. Emmett
N: E.V.H. Emmett
Merle Oberon . . . . Mrs Richardson
Ralph Richardson . . . . WC Richardson
June Duprez . . . . June
Robert Douglas . . . . Briefing Officer
Anthony Bushell . . . . Pilot
Derrick de Marney . . . . Bill
Brian Worth . . . . Bobby
Austin Trevor . . . . Schulemburg
Ivan Brandt . . . . Officer
G.H. Mulcaster . . . . Controller
Herbert Lomas . . . . Holveg
Milton Rosmer . . . . Observer
Robert Rendel . . . . Chief of Air Staff
John Longden . . . .
Bernard Miles . . . .
WAR Events leading to outbreak of war and RAF raid on Kiel canal. (Includes excerpts from FIRE OVER ENGLAND and THE GAP.)

10653
A WINDOW IN LONDON (77) (A)
USA: LADY IN DISTRESS
G&S Films (GFD)
P: Josef Somlo, Richard Norton
D: Herbert Mason
S: (SCREENPLAY) Herbert & Manet (METROPOLITAN)
SC: Ian Dalrymple, Brigid Cooper
Michael Redgrave . . . . Peter
Sally Gray . . . . Vivienne
Paul Lukas . . . . Zoltini
Hartley Power . . . . Preston
Patricia Roc . . . . Pat
Glen Alyn . . . . Andrea
Gertrude Musgrove . . . . . . Telephonist
George Carney . . . . Watchman
Alf Goddard . . . . Tiny
Wilfred Walter . . . . Foreman
George Merritt . . . . Manager
Kimberley & Page; Pamela Randall
DRAMA Married crane-driver falls for girl, who is killed by her illusionist husband.

10654
THE ARSENAL STADIUM MYSTERY (84) (A)
G&S Films (GFD)
P: Josef Somlo, Richard Norton
D: Thorold Dickinson
S: (NOVEL) Leonard Gribble
SC: Thorold Dickinson, Donald Bull
Leslie Banks . . . . Insp Slade
Greta Gynt . . . . Gwen Lee
Ian Maclean . . . . Sgt Clinton
Esmond Knight . . . . Raille
Liane Linden . . . . Inga
Brian Worth . . . . Philip Morring
Anthony Bushell . . . . Jack Dyce
Richard Norris . . . . Setchley
Wyndham Goldie . . . . Kindilett

Dennis Wyndham . . . . Commissionaire
Maire O'Neill . . . . Mrs Kirwan
George Allison; Tom Whittaker; E.V.H.
Emmett; Arsenal Football Team
CRIME Star footballer poisoned during vital
match.

10655
ON THE NIGHT OF THE FIRE (94) (A)
USA: THE FUGITIVE
G&S Films (GFD)
P: Josef Somlo
D: Brian Desmond Hurst
S: (NOVEL) F.L. Green
SC: Brian Desmond Hurst, Terence Young,
Patrick Kirwan
Ralph Richardson . . . . Will Kobling
Diana Wynyard . . . . Kit Kobling
Romney Brent . . . . Jimsey Jones
Mary Clare . . . . Lizzie Crane
Henry Oscar . . . . Pilleger
Dave Crowley . . . . Jim Smith
Gertrude Musgrove . . . . . . Dors Smith
Frederick Leister . . . . Insp Carr
Ivan Brandt . . . . Sgt Wilson
Sara Allgood . . . . Charlady
Glynis Johns . . . . Mary
CRIME Barber steals for wife's sake and is
forced to kill her blackmailer.

10656
THE FROZEN LIMITS (84) (U)
Gainsborough (GFD)
P: Edward Black
D: Marcel Varnel
S: Marriott Edgar, Val Guest, J.O.C. Orton
Flanagan & Allen . . . . Bud & Ches
Nervo & Knox . . . . Cecil & Teddy
Naughton & Gold . . . . Charlie & Jimmy
Moore Marriott . . . . Tom Tiddler
Eileen Bell . . . . Jill
Anthony Hulme . . . . Tex O'Brien
Bernard Lee . . . . Bill McGrew
Eric Clavering . . . . Foxy
COMEDY Alaska. Broke actors, late for the
gold rush, help prospector locate lost mine.

10657
INSPECTOR HORNLEIGH ON HOLIDAY
(87) (A)
20th Century Productions (20)
P: Edward Black
D: Walter Forde
S: (RADIO SERIES) Hans W. Priwin
(NOVEL) Leo Grex (STOLEN DEATH)
SC: Frank Launder, Sidney Gilliat
Gordon Harker . . . . Insp Hornleigh
Alastair Sim . . . . Sgt Bingham
Linden Travers . . . . Miss Meadows
Wally Patch . . . . Sgt
Edward Chapman . . . . Capt Fraser
Philip Leaver . . . . Bradfield
Kynaston Reeves . . . . Dr Manners
John Turnbull . . . . Chief Constable
Wyndham Goldie . . . . Sir George Winbeck
CRIME Gang use substitute corpses to defraud
insurance company.

10658
COME ON GEORGE (88) (U)
ATP (ABFD) reissues: 1943; 1950 (EB)
P: Jack Kitchin
D: Anthony Kimmins
S: Anthony Kimmins, Leslie Arliss,
Val Valentine
George Formby . . . . George
Pat Kirkwood . . . . Ann Johnson
Joss Ambler . . . . Sir Charles Bailey
Meriel Forbes . . . . Monica Bailey

Cyril Raymond . . . . Jimmy Taylor
George Hayes . . . . Bannerman
George Carney . . . . Sgt Johnson
Ronald Shiner . . . . Nat
Gibb McLaughlin . . . . Dr MacGregor
Hal Gordon . . . . Stableboy
Davy Burnaby . . . . Col Bollinger
C. Denier Warren . . . . Barker
James Hayter . . . . Banker
Syd Crossley . . . . PC
COMEDY Nervous stableboy rides fractious
racehorse to victory.

10659
ALL AT SEA (75) (U)
British Lion reissue: 1944
P: D: Herbert Smith
S: Gerald Elliott, Reginald Long
Sandy Powell . . . . Sandy Skipton
Kay Walsh . . . . Diana
John Warwick . . . . Brown
Gus McNaughton . . . . Nobby
George Merritt . . . . Bull
Leslie Perrins . . . . Williams
Franklin Dyall . . . . Dr Stolk
Robert Rendel . . . . Sir Herbert
Aubrey Mallalieu . . . . Prof Myles
COMEDY Chemical factory messenger
accidentally joins navy and saves new explosive
from spies.

10660
THE GIRL WHO FORGOT (79) (U)
Daniel Birt (Butcher) reissue: 1948
P: Daniel Birt, Louise Birt
D: Adrian Brunel
S: (PLAY) Gertrude Jennings (THE YOUNG
PERSON IN PINK)
SC: Louise Birt
Elizabeth Allan . . . . Leonora Barradine
Ralph Michael . . . . Tony Stevenage
Enid Stamp Taylor . . . . . . Caroline Tonbridge
Basil Radford . . . . Mr Barradine
Jeanne de Casalis . . . . Mrs Barradine
Muriel Aked . . . . Mrs Badger
David Keir . . . . Drawbridge
COMEDY Old crook poses as amnesiac girl's
mother to usurp her trust fund.

10661
OLD MOTHER RILEY JOINS UP (75) (U)
British National (Anglo)
P: John Corfield
D: Maclean Rogers
S: Jack Marks, Con West
Arthur Lucan . . . . Mrs Riley
Kitty McShane . . . . Kitty Riley
Bruce Seton . . . . Lt Travers
Martita Hunt . . . . Commandant
H.F. Maltby . . . . Gen Hogsley
Garry Marsh . . . . Rayful
Jeanne Stuart . . . .
Bryan Powley . . . .
COMEDY District nurse joins ATS and saves
munitions magnate's formula from spies.

10662
BLIND FOLLY (78) (U)
George Smith Productions (RKO)
D: Reginald Denham
S: John Hunter
SC: H.F. Maltby
Clifford Mollison . . . . George Bunyard
Lilli Palmer . . . . Valerie
Leslie Perrins . . . . Deverell
William Kendall . . . . Raine
Gus McNaughton . . . . Prof Zozo
Elliot Mason . . . . Aunt Mona
David Horne . . . . Mr Steel

Gertrude Musgrove . . . . . . Agnes
Roland Culver . . . . Ford
Antony Holles . . . . Louis
COMEDY Man inherits roadhouse where crooks
have secreted jewels.

10663
HOOTS MON ! (77) (A)
WB–FN (WB)
P: Sam Sax
D: Roy William Neill
S: Roy William Neill, Jack Henley, John Dighton
Max Miller . . . . Harry Hawkins
Florence Desmond . . . . . . Jenny McTavish
Hal Walters . . . . Chips
Davina Craig . . . . Annie
Garry Marsh . . . . Charlie Thompson
Edmund Willard . . . . Sandy McBride
Gordon McLeod . . . . McDonald
Mark Daly . . . . Campbell
COMEDY Rivalry between cockney comedian
and Scots impressionist ends in love.

10664
HELL'S CARGO (82) (A)
USA: DANGEROUS CARGO
ABPC
P: Walter C. Mycroft
D: Harold Huth
S: (SCREENPLAY) Leo Joannon
(ALERTE EN MEDITERANEE)
SC: Dudley Leslie
Robert Newton . . . . Cdr Tomasov
Walter Rilla . . . . Cdr Lestailleur
Kim Peacock . . . . Cdr Falcon
Penelope Dudley Ward . . Annette Lestailleur
Geoffrey Atkins . . . . Pierre Lestailleur
Ronald Adam . . . . Capt Dukes
Martin Walker . . . . Dr Laurence
Henry Oscar . . . . Capt
Charles Victor . . . . Mr Martin
Henry Morell . . . . Father Blanc
ADVENTURE Tangier. British, French and
Russian commanders unite to pursue oil tanker
loaded with poison gas.

10665
LUCKY TO ME (69) (A)
ABPC
P: Walter C. Mycroft
D: Thomas Bentley
S: Stanley Lupino, Arthur Rigby
SC: Clifford Grey
Stanley Lupino . . . . Potty
Phyllis Brooks . . . . Pamela
Barbara Blair . . . . Minnie
Gene Sheldon . . . . Hap Hazard
Antoinette Cellier . . . . Kay
David Hutcheson . . . . Peter Malden
Bruce Seton . . . . Lord Tyneside
COMEDY Clerk, secretly wed to secretary, is
forced to aid rich client's affair.

10666
SHE COULDN'T SAY NO (72) (U)
ABPC
P: Walter C. Mycroft
D: Graham Cutts
S: (PLAY) Paul Smith, Fred Thompson
(FUNNY FACE)
SC: Clifford Grey, Elizabeth Meehan, Bert Lee
Tommy Trinder . . . . Dugsie Gibbs
Fred Emney . . . . Herbert
Googie Withers . . . . Dora
Greta Gynt . . . . Frankie Barnes
David Hutcheson . . . . Peter Thurston
Bertha Belmore . . . . Dr Grimstone
Basil Radford . . . . Lord Pilton
Cecil Parker . . . . Jimmy Reeves

David Burns . . . . Chester
Wylie Watson . . . . Thrumgood
Doris Hare . . . . Amelia Reeves
Geoffrey Sumner . . . . Announcer
COMEDY Couple posing as doctor and patient catch gem thieves while seeking a girl's false diary.

10667
WHAT MEN LIVE BY (42) (U)
GB Instructional (Ex)
D: Donald Taylor
S: (STORY) Leo Tolstoy
Esmond Knight . . . . Michael
Eliot Makeham . . . . Simon
Olga Lindo . . . . Martha
Grant Sutherland . . . . . .
Arthur Seaton . . . .
Charles Cauntley . . . . . .
Anna Russell . . . .
RELIGION Sussex, 1803. Disobedient angel becomes carpenter's apprentice.

DEC

10668
TRAITOR SPY (75) (A)
USA: THE TORSO MURDER MYSTERY
Rialto (Pathe)
P: John Argyle
D: Walter Summers
S: (NOVEL) T.C.H. Jacobs
SC: Walter Summers, John Argyle, Jan Van Lusil, Ralph Gilbert Bettinson
Bruce Cabot . . . . Beyersdorf
Marta Labarr . . . . Freyda Beyersdorf
Tamara Desni . . . . Marie Dufreyene
Romilly Lunge . . . . Beverley Blake
Edward Lexy . . . . Insp Barnard
Cyril Smith . . . . Sgt Trotter
Percy Walsh . . . . Lemnel
Eve Lynd . . . . Florrie McGowan
Alexander Field . . . . Yorky Meane
Peter Gawthorne . . . . Commissioner
CRIME German spies and British agents seek traitor with plans of anti-submarine patrol boat.

10669
PATHETONE PARADE OF 1940 (42) (U)
Pathe
D: Fred Watts   Nosmo King
Robb Wilton   Norman Long
Two Leslies   Bashful Boys
Patricia Rossborough
Murgatroyd & Winterbottom
Teddy Brown
Albert Sandler   Robert Wilson
Three New Yorkers   Winnie Ryland
Mantovani and his Tipica Orchestra
REVUE

10670
THE MIDDLE WATCH (87) (U)
ABPC
P: Walter C. Mycroft
D: Thomas Bentley
S: (PLAY) Ian Hay, Stephen King-Hall
SC: Clifford Grey, J. Lee-Thompson
Jack Buchanan . . . . Capt Maitland
Greta Gynt . . . . Mary Carlton
Fred Emney . . . . Sir Reginald Hewett
Kay Walsh . . . . Fay Eaton
David Hutcheson . . . . Cdr Baddeley
Leslie Fuller . . . . Marine Ogg
Reginald Purdell . . . . Cpl Blackett
Jean Gillie . . . . Betty Hewett
Bruce Seton . . . . Capt Randall
Martita Hunt . . . . Lady Elizabeth Hewett
Louise Hampton . . . . . . .Charlotte Hopkinson
Romney Brent . . . . Ah Fong
Ronald Shiner . .' . . . . Engineer
COMEDY Girls accidentally taken to sea aboard battleship must be hidden from Admiral.

10671
JAILBIRDS (73) (U)
Butcher *reissue:* 1943 (Sherwood; 591 ft cut)
P: F.W. Baker
D: Oswald Mitchell
S: (SKETCH) Fred Karno
SC: Con West
Albert Burdon . . . . Bill Smith
Shaun Glenville . . . . Col Pepper
Charles Farrell . . . . Spike Nelson
Charles Hawtrey . . . . Nick
Lorraine Clewes . . . . Mary Smith
Sylvia Coleridge . . . . Mrs Smith
Harry Terry . . . . Narky
Cyril Chamberlain . . . . Bob
Nat Mills & Bobbie . . . Mr & Mrs Popodopulous
COMEDY Tough jewel thief forces meek convict to join him in jail break.

10672
THE STARS LOOK DOWN (104) (A)
Grafton (GN) *reissues:* 1942 (Maj) 1947 (Ex) 1952 (GN)
P: Isadore Goldsmidt
D: Carol Reed
S: (NOVEL) A.J. Cronin
SC: J.B. Williams, A.J. Cronin
Michael Redgrave . . . . David Fenwick
Margaret Lockwood . . . . . . Jenny Sunley
Emlyn Williams . . . . Joe Gowan
Nancy Price . . . . Martha Fenwick
Allan Jeayes . . . . Richard Barras
Edward Rigby . . . . Robert Fenwick
Cecil Parker . . . . .Stanley Millington
Linden Travers . . . . Laura Millington
Milton Rosmer . . . . Harry Nugent
George Carney . . . . Slogger Gowan
Ivor Barnard . . . . Wept
Olga Lindo . . . . Mrs Sunley
Desmond Tester . . . . Hughie Fenwick
David Markham . . . . Arthur Barras
DRAMA Wales. Coal miner's son weds worthless girl and struggles to become an MP.

10673
HAPPY EVENT (36) (U) *dufay*
Anglo-French Productions (GN) *reissue:* 1942 (Maj)
P: S: Leon Hepner
D: Patrick Brunner
SC: D.B. Wyndham-Lewis
N: E.V.H. Emmett
Diana Magwood . . . . Diana Lambert
H. Seaton . . . .
Gordon Leslie . . . .
SPORT Trainer's daughter raises colt to win Grand National.

10674
SONS OF THE SEA (82) (U) *dufay*
British Consolidated (GN) *reissue:* 1942 (Maj)
P: K.C. Alexander
D: Maurice Elvey
S: Maurice Elvey, Gerald Elliott, William Woolf
Leslie Banks . . . . Capt Hyde
Kay Walsh . . . . Alison Dewar
Mackenzie Ward . . . . Newton Hulls
Cecil Parker . . . . Cdr Herbert
Simon Lack . . . . Philip Hyde
Ellen Pollock . . . . Margaret Hulls
Peter Shaw . . . . Lt John Streete
Nigel Stock . . . . Rudd
Kynaston Reeves . . . . Prof Dewar
WAR Dartmouth Naval College. Commander's cadet son unwittingly aids enemy spy.

10675
INQUEST (60) (A)
Charter (GN) *reissues:* 1942 (Maj) 1948 (Prem)
P: John Boulting

D: Roy Boulting
S: (PLAY) Michael Barringer
SC: Francis Miller
Elizabeth Allan . . . . Margaret Hamilton
Herbert Lomas . . . . Mr Knight
Hay Petrie . . . . Stephen Neale KC
Barbara Everest . . . . Mrs Wyatt
Olive Sloane . . . . Lily Prudence
Philip Friend . . . . Richard Neale
Harold Anstruther . . . . Sir Denton Hulme
Malcolm Morley . . . . Dr MacFarlane
CRIME Biassed coroner suspects widow of poisoning her husband.

10676
THE SPIDER (81) (A)
Admiral—Wembley (GFD)
P: Victor M. Greene
D: Maurice Elvey
S: (NOVEL) Henry Holt (NIGHT MAIL)
SC: Victor M. Greene, Kenneth Horne, Reginald Long
Diana Churchill . . . . Sally Silver
Derrick de Marney . . . . Gilbert Silver
Jean Gillie . . . . Clare Morley
Cecil Parker . . . . Lawrence Bruce
Frank Cellier . . . . Julian Ismay
Edward Lexy . . . . Insp Horridge
Allan Jeayes . . . . George Hackett
Jack Melford . . . . Duke
Jack Lambert . . . . Smith
Antony Holles . . . . Manager
Moira Lynd . . . . Nurse
CRIME Tec's wife helps him foil gem-stealing agent's attempt to kill amnesiac actress.

10677
MISTAKEN IDENTITY (48) (U)
Venture (NR)
P: Alfred D'Eyncourt
D: Walter Tennyson
S: Ian Walker
Richard Goolden . . . . Edward Benson
Gillian Maude . . . . Ann Waterhouse
Julien Vedey . . . . Max Wenda
COMEDY Producer mistakes shy composer for millionaire.

10678
THE BODY VANISHES (45) (U)
Venture Films (NR)
P: Alfred D'Eyncourt
D: Walter Tennyson
S: Ian Walker
Anthony Hulme . . . . Rodney Paine
C. Denier Warren . . . . Pip Piper
Ernest Sefton . . . . Sgt Hopkins
Eve Foster . . . . Miss Casson
Frank Atkinson . . . . Hobbleberry
Wilfred Noy . . . . Snelling
CRIME Picture thief fakes own death to escape partner's vengeance

10679
BLACKOUT TIME (17) (U)
Fraternity Films (Butcher)
D: Nigel Byass
COMEDY Mishaps of husband trying to black out villa windows.

10680
HOSPITAL HOSPITALITY (25)(U)
Christy—Bass (Renown)
P: William Christy, George Bass jr
D: William Christy
George Bass jr . . . . George
Wally Patch . . . . Doorman
Finlay Currie . . . . Doctor
Charles Penrose. . . . . Patient
Eve Shelley . . . . Nurse
June Martin . . . . Assistant
COMEDY Scientist mislays briefcase containing elixir of life.

1940

JAN

10681
RETURN TO YESTERDAY (68) (U)
Ealing-CAPAD (ABFD) *reissue:* 1944 (Ren)
AP: S.C. Balcon
D: Robert Stevenson
S: (PLAY) Robert Morley (GOODNESS
HOW SAD)
SC: Robert Stevenson, Margaret Kennedy,
Roland Pertwee, Angus Macphail
Clive Brook . . . .   Robert Maine
Anna Lee . . . .   Carol Sands
Dame May Whitty . . . .   Mrs Truscott
Hartley Power . . . .   Regan
Milton Rosmer . . . .   Sambourne
David Tree . . . .   Peter Thropp
Arthur Margetson . . . .   Osbert
Olga Lindo . . . . Grace Sambourne
Garry Marsh . . . .   Charlie Miller
Elliot Mason . . . .   Mrs Priskin
O.B. Clarence . . . .   Mr Truscott
Frank Pettingell . . . .   Prendergast
David Horne . . . .   Morrison
Wally Patch . . . .   Watchman .
ROMANCE Hollywood star posing as actor
joins seaside rep company and falls for affianced
leading lady.

10682
THE PROUD VALLEY (76) (A)
Ealing-CAPAD (ABFD) *reissue:* 1948
AP: Sergei Nolbandov
D: Pen Tennyson
S: Herbert Marshall, Alfredda Brilliant
SC: Roland Pertwee, Louis Golding, Jack Jones
Paul Robeson . . . .   David Goliath
Edward Chapman . . . .   Dick Parry
Edward Rigby . . . .   Bert
Simon Lack . . . .   Emlyn Parry
Rachel Thomas . . . .   Mrs Parry
Janet Johnson. . . . .   Gwen Owen
Clifford Evans . . . .   Seth Jones
Allan Jeayes . . . .   Mr Trevor
Jack Jones . . . .   Thomas
George Merritt . . . .   Mr Lewis
Edward Lexy . . . .   Commissionaire
DRAMA Wales. Negro stoker loses life helping
unemployed miners reopen pits.

10683
SPY FOR A DAY (71) (U)
Two Cities (Par)
P: Mario Zampi
D: Mario Zampi
S: (STORY) Stacy Aumonier (SOURCE OF
IRRITATION)
SC: Anatole de Grunwald, Hans Wilhelm,
Emeric Pressburger, Ralph Block, Tommy
Thompson
Duggie Wakefield . . . .   Sam Gates
Paddy Browne . . . .   Martha Clowes
Jack Allen . . . .   Capt Bradshaw
Albert Lieven . . . .   Capt Hausemann
Nicholas Hannen . . . .   Col Pemberton
Gibb McLaughlin . . . .   Col Ludwig
Allan Jeayes . . . .   Col Roberts
Alf Goddard . . . .   Sgt Bryan
George Hayes . . . .   Cpl Boehme
Eliot Makeham . . . .   Mr Trufitt
Hay Petrie . . . .   Mr Britt
O.B. Clarence . . . .   MO
COMEDY Germans abduct farm hand who is
double of spy.

10684
LAUGH IT OFF (78) (U)
British National (Anglo) *reissue:* 1943
P: John Corfield
D: John Baxter

S: Bridget Boland
SC: Bridget Boland, Austin Melford
Tommy Trinder . . . .   Tommy Towers
Jean Colin . . . .   Sally
Anthony Hulme . . . .   Lt Somers
Marjorie Browne . . . .   Peggy
Edward Lexy . . . . Sgt-Maj Slaughter
Ida Barr . . . .   Mrs McNab
Charles Victor . . . .   Col
Peter Gawthorne . . . .   Gen
Wally Patch . . . .   Sgt
Warren Jenkins . . . .   Pat
John Laurie . . . .   Jock
Geraldo and his Orchestra; Darville & Shires;
Three Maxwells; Joan Davis Dancers; Julias
Ladies Choir; Sydney Burchell; Georgian
Singers
MUSICAL Private stages concert and is
promoted to entertainments officer.

10685
THE CHINESE BUNGALOW (72) (A)
USA: CHINESE DEN
Pennant (BL) *reissues:* 1944 (BL) 1946 (Ren)
P: D: George King
S: (PLAY) Matheson Lang, Marian Osmond
SC: A.R. Rawlinson, George Wellesley
Paul Lukas . . . .   Yuan Sing
Jane Baxter . . . . Charlotte Merrivale
Robert Douglas . . . .   Richard Marquess
Kay Walsh . . . .   Sadie Merrivale
Wallace Douglas . . . .   Harold Marquess
Jerry Verno . . . .   Stubbins
Mayura . . . .   Ayah
CRIME China. Merchant kills his English wife's
planter lover.

10686
BAND WAGGON (85) (U)
Gainsborough (GFD)
P: Edward Black
D: Marcel Varnel
S: (RADIO SERIES) Harry S. Pepper,
Gordon Crier; Vernon Harris
SC: Marriott Edgar, Val Guest
Arthur Askey .. . . Big Hearted Arthur
Jack Hylton . . . .   Himself
Richard Murdoch . . . .   Stinker
Pat Kirkwood .. . .   Pat
Moore Marriott . . . .   Jasper
Peter Gawthorne . . . .   Claude Pilkington
Wally Patch . . . .   Commissionaire
Donald Calthrop . . . .   Hobday
Jack Hylton's Band; Freddy Schweitzer;
Bruce Trent; Sherman Fisher Girls; Michael
Standing; C.H. Middleton; Jasmine Bligh;
Jonah Barrington
MUSICAL Would-be comedians catch spies
while running pirate tv station in 'haunted'
castle.

10687
DR O'DOWD (76) (A)
WB—FN (WB)
P: Sam Sax
D: Herbert Mason
S: (NOVEL) L.A.G. Strong
SC: Austin Melford, Derek Twist
Shaun Glenville . . . .   Marius O'Dowd
Peggy Cummins . . . .   Pat O'Dowd
Mary Merrall . . . .   Constantia
Liam Gaffney . . . .   Stephen O'Dowd
Patricia Roc . . . .   Rosemary
James Carney . . . .   O'Hara
Walter Hudd . . . .   Dr Crowther
Charles Victor . . . .   Dooley
Pat Noonan . . . .   Mulvaney
Maire O'Neill . . . .   Mrs Mulvaney
Irene Handl . . . .   Sarah

Pamela Wood . . . .   Moira
Felix Aylmer . . . .   President
DRAMA Ireland. Drunkard doctor reinstated
after saving engineer son from diphtheria
epidemic.

FEB

10688
THEY CAME BY NIGHT (72) (A)
20th Century Productions (20)
P: Edward Black
D: Harry Lachman
S: (PLAY) Barre Lyndon
SC: Frank Launder, Sidney Gilliat, Michael
Hogan, Roland Pertwee
Will Fyffe . . . . James Fothergill
Phyllis Calvert . . . .   Sally
Anthony Hulme . . . .   Sgt Tolley
George Merritt . . . .   Insp Metcalfe
John Glyn Jones . . . .   Llewellyn Jones
Athole Stewart . . . .   Lord Netherley
Cees Laseur . . . .   Vollaire
Kathleen Harrison . . . .   Mrs Lightbody
Wally Patch . . . .   Bugsie
Hal Walters . . . .   Hopkins
Kuda Bux . . . .   Ali
Sylvia StClaire . . . .   Claire
Peter Gawthorne . . . .   Commissionaire
CRIME Scots jeweller poses as thief to catch
gang responsible for brother's suicide.

10689
CRIMES AT THE DARK HOUSE (69) (A)-
Pennant (BL) *reissues:* 1944 (BL) 1947 (Amb)
P: D: George King
S: (NOVEL) Wilkie Collins (THE WOMAN
IN WHITE)
SC: Edward Dryhurst, Frederick Hayward,
H.F. Maltby
Tod Slaughter . . . . Sir Percival Glyde
Hilary Eaves . . . .   Marian Fairlie
Sylvia Marriott . . . .   Laura Fairlie
Hay Petrie . . . .   Dr Fosco
Geoffrey Wardwell . . . . . .   Paul Hartwright
David Horne . . . .   Mr Fairlie
Margaret Yarde . . . .   Mrs Bullen
CRIME 1850. Imposter kills rich wife and
substitutes her for her double, an escaped
lunatic.

MAR

10690
LET GEORGE DO IT (82) (U)
Ealing-ATP (ABFD) *reissues:* 1944 (EB)
1962 (EB)
AP: Basil Dearden
D: Marcel Varnel
S: John Dighton, Austin Melford, Angus
Macphail, Basil Dearden
George Formby . . . .   George
Phyllis Calvert . . . .   Mary
Garry Marsh . . . .   Mendez
Romney Brent . . . .   Slim
Bernard Lee . . . .   Nelson
Coral Browne . . . .   Ivy
Diana Beaumont . . . .   Greta
Torin Thatcher . . . .   U—boat Cdr
Hal Gordon . . . .   Arbuckle
Donald Calthrop . . . .   Strickland
COMEDY Norway. Ukelele player, mistaken
for secret agent, unmasks band leader as spy.

10691
TWO FOR DANGER (73) (A)
WB—FN (WB)
P: A.M. Salomon
D: George King
S: Brock Williams
SC: Brock Williams, Basil Woon, Hugh Gray

Barry K. Barnes . . . .   Tony Grigson
Greta Gynt . . . .   Diana
Cecil Parker . . . .   Sir Richard Frencham
George Merritt . . . .   Insp Canway
Henry Oscar . . . .   Claude Frencham
Vera Boggetti . . . .   The Lady
Peter Gawthorne . . . .   Commissioner Grigson
Gus McNaughton . . . .   Braithwaite
Kynaston Reeves . . . .   Dr George Frencham
Ian Maclean . . . .   The Australian
Leslie Weston . . . .   The Welshman
Gordon McLeod . . . .   The German
CRIME Barrister and fiance save private art
collection from international thieves.

10692
THE BACKYARD FRONT (15) (U)
British Films (GN)
D: S: Andrew Buchanan
C.H. Middleton . . . .   Himself
Claude Dampier . . . .   Claude
COMEDY Gardening expert explains how to
grow vegetables in wartime.

10693
ALL HANDS (10) (U)
Ealing (MGM)
P: Michael Balcon
D: John Paddy Carstairs
John Mills . . . .   Sailor
Leureen McGrath . . . .   Waitress
Eliot Makeham . . . .
Gertrude Musgrove . . . .
Annie Esmond . . . .
Carl Jaffe . . . .   German
WAR Sailor's talk of recall overheard by
waitress who betrays his ship to U boat.

10694
DANGEROUS COMMENT (13) (U)
Ealing (MGM)
P: Michael Balcon
D: John Paddy Carstairs
Frank Lawton
Penelope Dudley Ward
Milton Rosmer
Margaret Vyner
Roland Culver
WAR Officer's wife betrays RAF raid on
German base.

10695
NOW YOU'RE TALKING (11) (U)
Ealing (MGM)
P: Michael Balcon
D: John Paddy Carstairs
Sebastian Shaw . . . .   Driver
Dorothy Hyson . . . .   Girl
Edward Chapman . . . .
WAR Lorry driver's talk of overtime causes
munition factory scientists to be blown up.

10696
THE BRIGGS FAMILY (69) (U)
WB—FN (WB)
P: A.M. Salomon
D: Herbert Mason
S: Brock Williams
SC: John Dighton
Edward Chapman . . . .   Charley Briggs
Jane Baxter . . . .   Sylvia Briggs
Oliver Wakefield . . . .   Ronnie Perch
Mary Clare . . . .   Mrs Briggs
Peter Croft . . . .   Bob Briggs
Lesley Brook . . . .   Alice
Felix Aylmer . . . .   Mr Sand
Jack Melford . . . .   Jerry Tulse
Austin Trevor . . . .   John Smith
George Carney . . . .   George Downing
Glynis Johns . . . .   Sheila Briggs

Muriel George . . . .   Mrs Brokenshaw
Aubrey Mallalieu . . . .   Milward
CRIME Lawyer's clerk defends crippled son
and exposes real burglar.

10697
THAT'S THE TICKET (63) (A)
WB—FN (WB)
P: A.M. Salomon
D: Redd Davis
S: Jack Henley, John Dighton
Sid Field . . . .   Ben Baker
Betty Lynne . . . .   Fifi
Hal Walters . . . .   Nosey
Gus McNaughton . . . .   Milkbar Monty
Gordon McLeod . . . .   Ferdinand
Charles Castella . . . .   The Bull
Gibb McLaughlin . . . .   The Count
Ian Maclean . . . .   Hercule
Ernest Sefton . . . .   Marchand
COMEDY Cloakroom attendants don disguises
to save blueprints from spies in Paris.

10698
GEORGE AND MARGARET (77) (U)
WB—FN (WB)
P: A.M. Salomon
D: George King
S: (PLAY) Gerald Savory
SC: Brock Williams, Rodney Ackland
Judy Kelly . . . .   Frankie Garth-Binder
Marie Lohr . . . .   Alice Garth-Binder
Oliver Wakefield . . . .   Roger
Noel Howlett . . . .   Malcolm Garth-Binder
Ann Casson . . . .   Gladys
Arthur Macrae . . . .   Dudley Garth-Binder
John Boxer . . . .   Claude Garth-Binder
Irene Handl . . . .   Beer
Margaret Yarde . . . .   Cook
Gus McNaughton . . . .   Wolverton
COMEDY Suburban family's problems sorted
out by their maid.

10699
PACK UP YOUR TROUBLES (75) (U)
Butcher's Film Service
P: F.W. Baker
D: Oswald Mitchell
S: Con West
SC: Reginald Purdell, Milton Hayward
Reginald Purdell . . . .   Tommy Perkins
Wylie Watson . . . .   Eric Sampson
Patricia Roc . . . .   Sally Brown
Wally Patch . . . .   Sgt Barker
Muriel George . . . .   Mrs Perkins
Ernest Butcher. . . . .   Jack Perkins
Manning Whiley . . . .   Muller
G.H. Mulcaster . . . .   Col Diehard
COMEDY France. Ventroloquist enlists and
uses his gift to avoid capture.

10700
LAW AND DISORDER (73) (A)
British Consolidated (RKO) *reissues:*
1943 (IPC) 1952 (Ad)
P: K.C. Alexander
D: David Macdonald
S: Roger Macdonald
Barry K. Barnes . . . .   Larry Preston
Diana Churchill . . . .   Janet Preston
Alastair Sim . . . .   Samuel Blight
Edward Chapman . . . .   Insp Bray
Austin Trevor . . . .   Heinrichs
Ruby Miller . . . .
Leo Genn . . . .
Geoffrey Sumner . . . . . .
Glen Alyn . . . .
Torin Thatcher . . . .
Carl Jaffe . . . .
Cyril Smith . . . .
CRIME Solicitor's partner unmasks saboteurs
who use portable radios to direct bombers.

10701
TILLY OF BLOOMSBURY (83) (U)
Hammersmith (RKO)
P: Kurt Sternberg, A. Barr-Smith
D: Leslie Hiscott
S: (PLAY) Ian Hay
SC: Nils Holstius, Jack Marks
Sydney Howard . . . .   Samuel Stillbottle
Jean Gillie . . . .   Tilly Welwyn
Henry Oscar . . . .   Lucius Welwyn
Athene Seyler . . . .   Mrs Banks
Michael Wilding . . . .   Percy Welwyn
Kathleen Harrison . . . . . .   Mrs Welwyn
Athole Stewart . . . .   Abel Mainwaring
Michael Denison . . . .   Dick Mainwaring
Martita Hunt . . . . . .   Lady Marion Mainwaring
Joy Frankau . . . .   Amelia Mainwaring
Eve Shelley . . . .   Diana
COMEDY Lady objects to son's love for
boardinghouse-keeper's daughter.

10702
THE SECOND MR BUSH (56) (U)
British National (Anglo)
P: John Corfield
D: John Paddy Carstairs
S: (PLAY) Stafford Dickens
SC: Doreen Montgomery, Leslie Arliss
Derrick de Marney . . . .   Tony
Kay Walsh . . . .   Angela Windel-Todd
Barbara Everest . . . .   Mrs Windel-Todd
Evelyn Roberts . . . .   Maj Dawson
Wallace Evennett . . . .   Mr Bush
COMEDY Poor author hired to pose as meek
millionaire in boarding house.

10703
CONTRABAND (92) (U)
USA: BLACKOUT
British National (Anglo)
P: John Corfield
D: Michael Powell
S: Emeric Pressburger
SC: Michael Powell, Brock Williams
Conrad Veidt . . . .   Capt Andersen
Valerie Hobson . . . .   Mrs Sorenson
Esmond Knight . . . .   Mr Pidgeon
Hay Petrie . . . .   Mate Skold/Chief Skold
Raymond Lovell . . . .   Van Dyne
Harold Warrender . . . .   Lt/Cdr Ellis
Charles Victor . . . .   Hendrick
Manning Whiley . . . .   Manager
Peter Bull . . . .   Grimm
Stuart Latham . . . .   Grimm
Leo Genn . . . .   Grimm
Dennis Arundell . . . .   Leimann
Julien Vedey . . . .   Waiter
Paddy Browne . . . .   Singer
WAR Danish merchant captain and waiters help
girl agent thwart spies who use cinema as front.

APR

10704
FOR FREEDOM (87) (U)
Gainsborough (GFD)
P: Edward Black, Castleton Knight
D: Maurice Elvey
S: Castleton Knight
SC: Miles Malleson, Leslie Arliss
Will Fyffe . . . .   Chief
Anthony Hulme . . . .   Steve
E.V.H. Emmett . . . .   Himself
Guy Middleton . . . .   Pierre
Albert Lieven . . . .   Fritz
Hugh McDermott . . . .   Sam
Billy Russell . . . .   Adolf Hitler
Capt Dove
Capt Pottinger
FO Murphy
WAR HMS Exeter and Ajax save prisoners
from the Altmark and sink the Graf Spee.

10705
CHARLEY'S (BIG HEARTED) AUNT (76) (U)
Gainsborough (GFD)
P: Edward Black
D: Walter Forde
S: (PLAY) Brandon Thomas (CHARLEY'S AUNT)
SC: Marriott Edgar, Val Guest

Arthur Askey	Arthur Linden-Jones
Richard Murdoch	Stinker Burton
Moore Marriott	Jerry
Graham Moffatt	Albert Brown
Phyllis Calvert	Betty Forsythe
Jeanne de Casalis	Aunt Lucy
J.H. Roberts	Dean of Bargate
Felix Aylmer	Proctor
Wally Patch	Butler

COMEDY Oxford student poses as his rich aunt and the real one arrives.

10706
THE FLYING SQUAD (64) (A)
ABPC
P: Walter C. Mycroft
D: Herbert Brenon
S: (NOVEL) Edgar Wallace
SC: Doreen Montgomery

Sebastian Shaw	Insp Bradley
Phyllis Brooks	Ann Perryman
Jack Hawkins	Mark McGill
Basil Radford	Sederman
Ludwig Stossel	Li Yoseph
Manning Whiley	Ronnie Perryman
Kathleen Harrison	Mrs Schifan
Cyril Smith	Tiser
Henry Oscar	Commissioner
Kynaston Reeves	Magistrate

CRIME Girl unmasks her employer as the drug smuggler who killed her brother.

10707
THE HOUSE OF THE ARROW (66) (A)
USA: CASTLE OF CRIMES
ABPC
P: Walter C. Mycroft
D: Harold French
S: (NOVEL) A.E.W. Mason
SC: Doreen Montgomery

Keneth Kent	Insp Hanaud
Diana Churchill	Betty Harlowe
Belle Chrystal	Ann Upcott
Peter Murray Hill	Jim Frobisher
Clifford Evans	Maurice Thevenet
Catherine Lacey	Francine Rollard
James Harcourt	Boris Raviart
Louise Hampton	Mme Harlowe

CRIME France. Blackmailing girl poisons rich widow and frames her English companion.

10708
BULLDOG SEES IT THROUGH (77) (A)
ABPC
P: Walter C. Mycroft
D: Harold Huth
S: (NOVEL) Gerald Fairlie (SCISSORS CUT PAPER)
SC: Doreen Montgomery

Jack Buchanan	Bill Watson
Greta Gynt	Jane Sinclair
Sebastian Shaw	Derek Sinclair
David Hutcheson	Freddie Caryll
Googie Withers	Toots
Robert Newton	Watkins
Arthur Hambling	Insp Horn
Wylie Watson	Dancing Professor
Polly Ward	Miss Fortescue
Nadine March	Gladys
Ronald Shiner	Pug
Aubrey Mallalieu	Magistrate

CRIME Test pilot and his secret agent butler unmask his ex-fiancee's husband as an armaments saboteur.

10709
OLD MOTHER RILEY IN SOCIETY (81) (U)
British National (Anglo) *reissue:* 1941 (12 mins cut)
P: John Corfield
D: John Baxter
S: Kitty McShane, Bridget Boland
SC: Austin Melford, Barbara K. Emary, Mary Cathcart Borer

Arthur Lucan	Mrs Riley
Kitty McShane	Kitty Riley
John Stuart	Tony Morgan
Dennis Wyndham	Tug Mulligan
Minnie Rayner	
Athole Stewart	
Charles Victor	
Ruth Maitland	
Margaret Halstan	
Peggy Novak	
Diana Beaumont	

COMEDY When chorus girl weds nobleman's son her washerwoman mother poses as her maid.

MAY

10710
PASTOR HALL (97) (A)
Charter (GN) *reissue:* 1942 (Maj)
P: John Boulting
D: Roy Boulting
S: (PLAY) Ernst Toller
SC: Leslie Arliss, Anna Reiner, Haworth Bromley

Nova Pilbeam	Christine Hall
Seymour Hicks	Gen von Grotjahn
Wilfrid Lawson	Pastor Frederick Hall
Marius Goring	Gerte
Percy Walsh	Veit
Brian Worth	Werner von Grotjahn
Peter Cotes	Erwin Kohn
Hay Petrie	Nazi Pastor
Eliot Makeham	Pipperman
Edmund Willard	Freundlich
Manning Whiley	Vogel
Lina Barrie	Lina Veit
J. Fisher White	Johann Herder
Barbara Gott	Frau Kemp
Bernard Miles	Degan

DRAMA Germany, 1934. Village pastor denounces Nazism and is shot.

10711
GESTAPO (95) (A) retitled: NIGHT TRAIN TO MUNICH, USA: NIGHT TRAIN
20th Century Productions (MGM) *reissue:* 1948
P: Edward Black
D: Carol Reed
S: (NOVEL) Gordon Wellesley
SC: Frank Launder, Sidney Gilliat

Margaret Lockwood	Anna Bomasch
Rex Harrison	Gus Bennett
Paul Von Hernried	Karl Marsen
Basil Radford	Charters
Naunton Wayne	Caldicott
Keneth Kent	Controller
Felix Aylmer	Dr Fredericks
James Harcourt	Axel Bomasch
Wyndham Goldie	Dryton
Roland Culver	Roberts
Eliot Makeham	Schwab
Raymond Huntley	Kampenfeldt
Austin Trevor	Capt Prada
C.V. France	Admiral Hassenger
Morland Graham	Attendant

WAR Germany. British agent poses as Nazi officer to rescue Czech inventor and his daughter.

10712
GENTLEMAN OF VENTURE (80) (A)
USA: IT HAPPENED TO ONE MAN

British Eagle (RKO)
P: Victor Hanbury
D: Paul Stein
S: (PLAY) Roland Pertwee, John Hastings Turner
SC: Paul Merzbach, Nina Jarvis

Wilfrid Lawson	Felton Quair
Nora Swinburne	Alice Quair
Marta Labarr	Rita
Ivan Brandt	Leonard Drayton
Reginald Tate	Ackroyd
Brian Worth	Jack Quair
Edmond Breon	Admiral Drayton
Patricia Roc	Betty Quair
Athole Stewart	Lord Kenley
Thorley Walters	Ronnie

DRAMA Devon. Swindler returns from abroad and reforms for sake of his estranged family.

10713
GASLIGHT (88) (A)
USA: ANGEL STREET
British National (Anglo)
P: John Corfield
D: Thorold Dickinson
S: (PLAY) Patrick Hamilton
SC: A.R. Rawlinson, Bridget Boland

Anton Walbrook	Paul Mallen
Diana Wynyard	Bella Mallen
Frank Pettingell	Rough
Cathleen Cordell	Nancy
Robert Newton	Vincent Ullswater
Jimmy Hanley	Cobb
Minnie Rayner	Elizabeth
Mary Hinton	Lady Winterbourne
Marie Wright	Alice Barlow
Jack Barty	Chairman
Darmora Ballet	

CRIME 1880. Ex-policeman prevents murderous bigamist from driving his wife insane.

10714
CONVOY (90) (A)
Ealing (ABFD) *reissue:* 1943 (140 ft cut)
AP: Sergei Nolbandov
D: Pen Tennyson
S: Pen Tennyson, Patrick Kirwan

Clive Brook	Capt Tom Armitage
John Clements	Lt David Cranford
Edward Chapman	Capt Eckersley
Judy Campbell	Lucy Armitage
Penelope Dudley Ward	Mabel
Edward Rigby	Mr Matthews
Charles Williams	Shorty Howard
Allan Jeayes	Cdr Blount
Albert Lieven	Cdr, U—37
Michael Wilding	Dot
Harold Warrender	Lt-Cdr Martin
David Hutcheson	Capt Sandeman
George Carney	Bates
Al Millen	Knowles
Charles Farrell	Walker
John Laurie	Gates
Hay Petrie	Skipper
Mervyn Johns	Mate
Edward Lexy	Skipper
John Glyn Jones	Mate
Stewart Granger	Sutton

WAR Merchant skipper loses his life and ship warning convoy of German pocket-battleship. (Top moneymaker: 1940)

10715
SALOON BAR (76) (A)
Ealing (ABFD) *reissue:* 1943
AP: Culley Forde
D: Walter Forde
S: (PLAY) Frank Harvey jr
SC: Angus Macphail, John Dighton

Gordon Harker	Joe Harris
Elizabeth Allan	Queenie

Mervyn Johns . . . . Wickers
Joyce Barbour . . . . Sally
Judy Campbell . . . . Doris
Anna Konstam . . . . Ivy
Cyril Raymond . . . . Harry Small
Alec Clunes . . . . Eddie Graves
Al Millen . . . . Fred
Norman Pierce . . . . Bill Hoskins
Mavis Villiers . . . . Joan
Felix Aylmer . . . . Mayor
O.B. Clarence . . . . Sir Archibald
Manning Whiley . . . . Evangelist
CRIME Bookmaker proves barmaid's fiance did
not kill girl.

10716
THE DOOR WITH SEVEN LOCKS (89) (A)
USA: CHAMBER OF HORRORS
Rialto (Pathe)
P: John Argyle
D: Norman Lee
S: (NOVEL) Edgar Wallace
SC: Norman Lee, John Argyle, Gilbert Gunn
Leslie Banks . . . . Dr Manetta
Lilli Palmer . . . . June Lansdowne
Romilly Lunge . . . . Dick Martin
Gina Malo . . . . Glenda Blake
David Horne . . . . Edward Havelock
Richard Bird . . . . Insp Sneed
Cathleen Nesbitt . . . . Ann Cody
J.H. Roberts . . . . Luis Silva
Aubrey Mallalieu . . . . Lord Selford
Harry Hutchinson . . . . Bevan Cody
Ross Landon . . . . John Selford
CRIME Inspector unmasks mad doctor's
conspiracy to obtain heiress's jewels in old mill.

JUN

10717
THREE SILENT MEN (72) (A)
Butcher reissues: 1942 (Sherwood; 1009 ft cut)
1947 (Butch)
P: F.W. Baker
D: Daniel Birt
S:(NOVEL) E.P. Thorne
SC: Dudley Leslie, John Byrd
Sebastian Shaw . . . . Sir James Quentin
Derrick de Marney . . . . . . Capt John Mellish
Patricia Roc . . . . Pat Quentin
Arthur Hambling. . . . . Ginger Brown
Meinhart Maur . . . . Karl Zaroff
John Turnbull . . . . Insp Gill
Peter Gawthorne . . . . Gen Bullington
Andre Morell . . . . Klein
CRIME Pacifist surgeon framed for killing
inventor of a secret weapon.

10718
THE CASE OF THE FRIGHTENED LADY
(81) (A) USA: THE FRIGHTENED LADY
Pennant Pictures (BL) reissues: 1944 (BL)
1946 (Ren)
P: D: George King
S: (NOVEL) Edgar Wallace
SC: Edward Dryhurst
Marius Goring . . . . Lord Lebanon
Penelope Dudley Ward . . . . Isla Crane
Helen Haye . . . . Lady Lebanon
Patrick Barr . . . . Dick Ferraby
Felix Aylmer. . . . . Dr Amersham
John Warwick . . . . Studd
George Merritt . . . . Insp Tanner
Ronald Shiner . . . . Sgt Totty
Roy Emerton . . . . Gilder
CRIME Lady tries to stop her mad son from
strangling his cousin.

10719
HULLO FAME ! (45) (U)
British Films

P: D: Andrew Buchanan
S: Gerard Bryant
Sutherland Felce . . . . Hedli Anderson
Jean Carr (Kent) . . . . Gordon Little
Roberta Huby . . . . Davina Craig
Pola Nirenska . . . . Peter Ustinov
Wilbur Hall . . . . Joe Hayman
REVUE "New faces" in entertainment.

JUL

10720
ROOM FOR TWO (77) (A)
Hurley (GN) reissue: 1942 (Maj)
P: Victor Katona
D: Maurice Elvey
S: (PLAY) Gilbert Wakefield
Frances Day . . . . Clare Spencer
Vic Oliver . . . . Michael Brent
Basil Radford . . . . Robert Spencer
Greta Gynt . . . . Hilda Westby
Hilda Bayley . . . . Dressmaker
Leo de Porkony . . . . Manager
Magda Kun . . . . Mimi
Victor Rietti . . . . Gaston
Andrea Malandrinos . . . . . Gondolier
COMEDY Venice. Playboy poses as maid to
flirt with philanderer's wife.

10721
GARRISON FOLLIES (64) (U)
Signet (Butch) reissue: 1943 (Sherwood;
714 ft cut)
P: Hugh Perceval, Ernest Gartside
D: Maclean Rogers
S: Maclean Rogers, Kathleen Butler, H.F.Maltby
Barry Lupino . . . . Alf Shufflebotham
Nancy O'Neil . . . . Sally Richards
H.F. Maltby . . . . Maj Hall-Vett
John Kevan . . . . Dick Munro
Hugh Dempster . . . . Adjutant
Gabrielle Brune . . . . Lady Cynthia Clayton
Neville Brook . . . . CO
Dennis Val Norton . . . . . . Plummer
Harry Herbert; Sylvia Kellaway & Leslie; Ann
Lenner; Joan Davis Eight; Rose Petals; Percival
Mackey's Band
COMEDY Plumber mistaken for impresario
saves RAF camp's plate from theft.

10722
SOMEWHERE IN ENGLAND (79) (U)
Mancunian (Butch) reissues: 1944 (621 ft cut)
1948 (Sherwood)
P: D: John E. Blakeley
S: Arthur Mertz, Roney Parsons
Harry Korris . . . . Sgt Korris
Frank Randle . . . . Pte Randle
Winki Turner . . . . Irene Morant
Dan Young . . . . Pte Young
Robbie Vincent . . . . Pte Enoch
Harry Kemble . . . . Jack Vernon
John Singer . . . . Bert Smith
Sidney Monkton . . . . Adjutant
Stanley King; Eight Master Singers; Percival
Mackey's Orchestra
COMEDY Episodic misadventures of army
conscripts who stage a show.

10723
TWO SMART MEN (52) (U)
Clive Films—AIP (EB)
P: D: Widgey R. Newman
Leslie Fuller. . . . . Jimmy
Wally Patch . . . . Wally
Margaret Yarde . . . . Mrs Smith
Pamela Bevan . . . . Pamela
George Turner. . . . . Henry Smith
COMEDY Men posing as butler and cook catch
jewel thief at party.

10724
BUSMAN'S HONEYMOON (99) (A)
USA: HAUNTED HONEYMOON
MGM British
P: Harold Huth
D: Arthur Woods
S: (PLAY) Dorothy L. Sayers, Muriel StClare
Byrne
SC: Monckton Hoffe, Angus Macphail,
Harold Goldman
Robert Montgomery . . . . . Lord Peter Wimsey
Constance Cummings . . . . . Harriet Vane
Leslie Banks . . . . Insp Kirk
Seymour Hicks . . . . Bunter
Robert Newton . . . . Frank Crutchley
Googie Withers . . . . Polly
Frank Pettingell . . . . Puffett
Joan Kemp-Welsh . . . . . . Aggie Twitterton
Aubrey Mallalieu . . . . Rev Simon Goodacre
James Carney . . . . PC Sellon
Roy Emerton . . . . Noakes
Louise Hampton . . . . Mrs Ruddle
Eliot Makeham . . . . Simpson
Reginald Purdell . . . . McBride
CRIME Devon. Titled tec solves murder of the
former tenant of his honeymoon cottage.

10725
BRINGING IT HOME (19) (U)
Strand (Anglo)
P: A.R. Taylor
D: J.E. Lewis
N: Patric Curwen
Percy Marmont . . . . The Man
Barbara Everest . . . . The Woman
WAR Navy's convoy system ensures safe
arrival of supply ships.

10726
AT THE HAVANA (28) (U)
Mishiku (NR)
P: Denis Kavanagh
D: Richard Mishiku
Sylvia Sartre
Paddy Kelly
Cyril Blake
Vivienne Paget
Howard de Courcy
Victor Garland
Jack Davis and the Havana Club Band
REVUE Cabaret at the Havana Club.

10727
THE THIRTEENTH INSTANT (17) (U)
British Foundation (Kinograph)
D: Ronald Haines
N: Lionel Gamelin
COMEDY Man finds magic ring at zoo and is
turned into monkey.

10728
A CALL FOR ARMS (6) (U)
Denham & Pinewood (NSS)
D: Brian Desmond Hurst
S: Rodney Ackland
Jean Gillie . . . . Chorus Girl
Rene Ray . . . . Chorus Girl
DRAMA Two chorus girls give up theatre to
become munitions workers.

10729
FOOD FOR THOUGHT (5) (U)
Ealing (NSS)
P: Michael Balcon
D: Adrian Brunel
Mabel Constanduros
Muriel George
Eliot Makeham
Hal Gordon
COMEDY Guests bring their own sugar to tea
party.

10730
FEAR AND PETER BROWN (15) (U)
Spectator (Denning)
P: Ivan Scott
D: Richard Massingham
S: Lewis Grant Wallace
Nicholas Hannen
Stephen Haggard . . . .   Peter Brown
Wendy Weddell . . . .   Mrs Brown
DRAMA Doting mother raises her son to grow
up without knowing fear.

AUG

10731
FOR GOODNESS SAKE (7) (U)
New Realm
COMEDY Silent film melodrama with comic
commentary.

10732
MISS GRANT GOES TO THE DOOR (6) (U)
Denham & Pinewood (NSS)
D: Brian Desmond Hurst
S: Rodney Ackland
Mary Clare
Martita Hunt
WAR German parachutist lands in English
village.

10733
ALBERT'S SAVINGS (5) (U)
Merton Park (NSS)
D: Harold Purcell
S: Stanley Holloway
COMEDY Boy's efforts to raise money to buy
National Savings certificates.

10734
SALVAGE WITH A SMILE (6) (U)
Ealing (NSS)
P: Michael Balcon
D: Adrian Brunel
Aubrey Mallalieu . . . .   Professor
Ronald Shiner . . . .   Dustman
Kathleen Harrison . . . .   Housekeeper
COMEDY Professor explains how household
salvage can be utilised in war.

10735
MR BORLAND THINKS AGAIN (6) (U)
British Films (NSS)
D: Paul Rotha
Emlyn Williams
Herbert Lomas
Beatrix Lehmann
DRAMA Farmer realises need to make silage
for winter feeding of cattle.

10736
CROOK'S TOUR (84) (U)
British National (Anglo) *reissue:* 1945
P: John Corfield
D: John Baxter
S: (RADIO SERIAL) John Watt, Max Kester
Basil Radford . . . .   Charters
Naunton Wayne . . . .   Caldicott
Greta Gynt . . . .   La Palermo
Abraham Sofaer . . . .   Ali
Charles Oliver . . . .   Sheik
Gordon McLeod . . . .   Rossenger
Bernard Rebel . . . .   Klacken
Cyril Gardner K7
Morris Harvey . . . .   Waiter
COMEDY English tourists pursued from
Baghdad by Nazis who mistake them for spies.

10737
THE GIRL IN THE NEWS (78) (A)
20th Century Productions (MGM) *reissue:* 1948

P: Edward Black
D: Carol Reed
S: (NOVEL) Roy Vickers
SC: Frank Launder, Sidney Gilliat
Margaret Lockwood . . . . . .   Anne Graham
Barry K. Barnes . . . .   Stephen Farringdon
Emlyn Williams . . . .   Tracy
Margaretta Scott . . . .   Judith Bentley
Roger Livesey . . . .   Bill Mather
Basil Radford . . . .   Dr Treadgrove
Wyndham Goldie . . . .   Edward Bentley
Irene Handl . . . .   Miss Blaker
Mervyn Johns . . . .   James Fetherwood
Kathleen Harrison . . . .   Cook
Felix Aylmer . . . .   Prosecution
CRIME Butler poisons employer and frames
nurse previously acquitted of poisoning a
patient.

SEP

10738
SAILORS DON'T CARE (79) (U)
Butcher's Film Service
P: F.W. Baker
D: Oswald Mitchell
Tom Gamble . . . .   Nobby Clark
Edward Rigby . . . .   Joe Clark
Jean Gillie · . . . .   Nancy
Michael Wilding . . . .   Dick
Marion Gerth . . . .   Mimi
Mavis Villiers . . . .   Blondie
G.H. Mulcaster . . . .   Admiral Reynolds
John Salew . . . .   Henri
Henry B. Longhurst . . . . .   Admiral Drake
Denis Wyndham . . . .   Capt Raleigh
COMEDY River Patrol Service men catch
spies who think their barge is secret radio
station.

10739
THE GREAT CONWAY (10) (A)
S.E. Reynolds (MGM)
D: S.E. Reynolds
Jerrold Robertshaw . . . . . .   Conway
CRIME Shakespearean actor becomes obsessed
and murders his dresser.

10740
YESTERDAY IS OVER YOUR SHOULDER
(7) (U)
Denham & Pinewood (NSS)
D: Thorold Dickinson
Robertson Hare . . . .   The Man
COMEDY Unlikely people become craftsmen
at Government Training Centres.

10741
CHANNEL INCIDENT (8) (U)
Denham & Pinewood (NSS)
P: D: Anthony Asquith
S: "Bartimeus"
SC: Dallas Bower
Peggy Ashcroft . . . .   The Woman
Gordon Harker
Robert Newton
WAR Incident at Dunkirk.

10742
MISS KNOWALL (5) (U) *reissue:* 1941,
THE SCAREMONGERS
Denham & Pinewood (NSS)
D: Graham Cutts
WAR Incorrect information about air raids
causes anguish.

10743
OLD MOTHER RILEY IN BUSINESS (80) (U)
British National (Anglo)
P: John Corfield

D: John Baxter
S: Geoffrey Orme
Arthur Lucan . . . .   Mrs Riley
Kitty McShane . . . .   Kitty Riley
Cyril Chamberlain . . . .   John Halliwell
Charles Victor . . . .
Wally Patch . . . .
Ernest Butcher . . . . . .
Ernest Sefton . . . .
O.B. Clarence . . . .
Edgar Driver . . . .
Edie Martin . . . .
Roddy Hughes . . . .
COMEDY Small-town Shopkeeper helps
traders fight chain-stores.

10744
UNDER YOUR HAT (79) (U)
Grand National (BL) *reissues:* 1943 (Maj)
1947 (GN)
P: Jack Hulbert
D: Maurice Elvey
S: (PLAY) Jack Hulbert, Archie Menzies,
Geoffrey Kerr, Arthur Macrae
SC: Rodney Ackland, Anthony Kimmins,
L. Green
Jack Hulbert . . . .   Jack Millett
Cicely Courtneidge . . . .   Kay Millett
Austin Trevor . . . .   Boris Vladimir
Leonora Corbett . . . .   Carole Markoff
Cecil Parker . . . .   Sir Geoffrey Arlington
Charles Oliver . . . .   Carl
H.F. Maltby . . . .   Col Sheepshanks
Glynis Johns . . . .   Winnie
Myrette Morven . . . .   Miss Stevens
MUSICAL Cannes. Film stars don disguises to
recover carburettor from spies.

10745
JOHN SMITH WAKES UP (42) (U)
Pioneer (BL)
P: Dora Nirva
D: Jiri Weiss
S: Jeffrey Dell
Eliot Makeham . . . .   John Smith
Percy Parsons . . . .   Fred Brown
Leslie Perrins . . . .   Mr Greenwood
Amy Veness . . . .   Emily Smith
Derek Blomfield . . . .   Jimmy Smith
Joan Greenwood . . . .   Joan Greenwood
WAR London bookseller dreams his son
betrays him to the Nazis.

OCT

10746
SAILORS THREE (86) (U)
USA: THREE COCKEYED SAILORS
Ealing (ABFD) *reissue:* 1943
AP: Culley Forde
D: Walter Forde
S: Angus Macphail, John Dighton, Austin
Melford
Tommy Trinder . . . .   Tommy Taylor
Claude Hulbert . . . .   Admiral
Michael Wilding . . . .   Johnny
Carla Lehmann . . . .   Jane
Jeanne de Casalis . . . .   Mrs Pilkington
James Hayter . . . .   Hans
Henry Hewitt . . . .   Prof Pilkington
John Laurie . . . .   McNab
Harold Warrender . . . .   Mate
John Glyn Jones . . . .   Best Man
Julien Vedey . . . .   Resident
Manning Whiley . . . .   German Cdr
Robert Rendel . . . .   Capt
Allan Jeayes . . . .   Cdr
Alec Clunes . . . .   Pilot
COMEDY Drunken sailors board German
battleship by mistake and capture it.

NOV

10747
OLD BILL AND SON (96) (U)
Legeran Films (GFD)
P: Josef Somlo, Harold Boxall, Alexander Korda
D: Ian Dalrymple
S: (CARTOONS) Bruce Bairnsfather
SC: Bruce Bairnsfather, Ian Dalrymple
Morland Graham . . . .   Old Bill Busby
John Mills . . . .   Young Bill Busby
Mary Clare . . . .   Maggie Busby
Renee Houston . . . .   Stella Malloy
Rene Ray . . . .   Sally
Janine Darcey . . . .   Francoise
Roland Culver . . . .   Colonel
Gus McNaughton . . . .   Alf
Ronald Shiner . . . .   Bert
Manning Whiley . . . .   Chimp
Nicholas Phipps . . . .   Commentator
COMEDY Old soldier joins Pioneer Corps and
follows his son to France.

10748
FINGERS (69) (A)
WB—FN (WB)
P: A.M. Salomon
D: Herbert Mason
S: Brock Williams
Clifford Evans . . . .   Fingers
Leonora Corbett . . . .   Bonita Grant
Esmond Knight . . . .   Sid Harris
Edward Rigby . . . .   Sam Bromley
Elizabeth Scott . . . .   Meg
Roland Culver . . . .   Hugo Allen
Reginald Purdell . . . .   Creeper
Joss Ambler . . . .   Inspector
CRIME East End fence falls for socialite but
returns to girl of his own class.

10749
THE OWNER COMES ABOARD (5) (U)
Spectator (NSS)
P: Ivan Scott
D: Alex Bryce
WAR Taxpayer boards warship and demands
to be shown how his money is spent.

10750
HENRY STEPS OUT (52) (U)
Clive Films—AIP (EB)
P: D: Widgey R. Newman
George Turner . . . .   Henry Smith
Margaret Yarde . . . .   Cynthia Smith
Wally Patch . . . .   Wally
COMEDY Crooks seeking hidden loot mistake
caretaker for colonel.

10751
YOU WILL REMEMBER (86) (U)
Jack Raymond (BL) reissue: 1943 (Ex)
P: Charles Q. Steele
D: Jack Raymond
S: Lydia Hayward
Robert Morley . . . .   Leslie Stuart
Emlyn Williams . . . .   Bob Slater
Dorothy Hyson . . . . .Ellaline Terriss
Tom E. Finglass . . . .   Eugene Stratton

Nicholas Phipps . . . .   Earl of Potter
Allan Jeayes . . . .   Signor Foli
Charles Victor . . . .   Pat Barrett
Maire O'Neill . . . .   Mrs Barrett
Maurice Kelly . . . .   Tom Barrett
Roddy McDowell . . . .   Bob (child)
Band of HM Grenadier Guards
MUSICAL Biography of poor composer's rise
to fame.

10752
GASBAGS (77) (U)
Gainsborough (GFD)
P: Edward Black
D: Marcel Varnel
S: Val Valentine, Ralph Smart
SC: Val Guest, Marriott Edgar
Flanagan & Allen . . . .   Bud & Ches
Nervo & Knox . . . .   Cecil & Knoxy
Naughton & Gold . . . .   Charlie & Goldy
Moore Marriott . . . .   Jerry Jenkins
Wally Patch . . . .   Sgt-Major
Peter Gawthorne . . . .   CO
Frederick Valk . . . .   Sturmfuehrer
Eric Clavering . . . .   Scharffuehrer
Anthony Eustrel . . . .   Gestapo Officer
Carl Jaffe . . . .   Gestapo Chief
Manning Whiley . . . .   OP Colonel
Torin Thatcher. . . . .   SS Man
Irene Handl . . . .   Wife
COMEDY Airmen blown to Germany on
barrage balloon return in captured tunnel-
borer.

10753
NEUTRAL PORT (92) (U)
Gainsborough (GFD)
P: Edward Black
D: Marcel Varnel
S: J.B. Williams, T.J. Morrison
Will Fyffe . . . .   Capt Ferguson
Leslie Banks . . . .   George Carter
Yvonne Arnaud . . . .   Rosa Pirenti
Phyllis Calvert . . . .   Helen Carter
Hugh McDermott . . . .   Jim Gray
John Salew . . . .   Wilson
Cameron Hall . . . .   Charlie Baxter
Frederick Valk . . . .   Capt Traumer
Albert Lieven . . . .   Capt Henkel
Anthony Holles. . . . .   Police Chief
Wally Patch . . . .   Fred
Denis Wyndham . . . .   Terry
Jack Raine . . . .   Alf
WAR Merchant skipper avenges ship by stealing
German supply boat and ramming U-boat.

DEC

10754
SPARE A COPPER (77) (U)
Ealing—ATP (ABFD) reissues: 1944 (ABFD)
1956 (EB)
AP: Basil Dearden
D: John Paddy Carstairs
S: Roger Macdougall, Austin Melford,
Basil Dearden
George Formby . . . .   George Carter
Dorothy Hyson . . . .   Jane Grey

Bernard Lee . . . .   Jake
John Warwick . . . .   Shaw
Warburton Gamble . . . . .   Sir Robert Dyer
John Turnbull . . . .   Insp Richards
George Merritt . . . .   Edward Brewster
Eliot Makeham . . . .   Fuller
Ellen Pollock . . . .   Lady Hardstaff
Edward Lexy . . . .   Nightwatchman
Jack Melford . . . .   Dame
Hal Gordon . . . .   Sergeant
Jimmy Godden . . . .   Manager
COMEDY Merseyside. Police war reservist
catches shipyard saboteurs using fairground as
front.

10755
THE THIEF OF BAGDAD (106) (U) tech
London-Korda (UA) reissues: 1944 (Eal)
1948 (BL)
P: Alexander Korda
D: Michael Powell, Ludwig Berger, Tim Whelan
S: Lajos Biro, Miles Malleson
Conrad Veidt . . . .   Jaffar
Sabu . . . .   Abu
June Duprez . . . .   Princess
John Justin . . . .   Ahmad
Rex Ingram . . . .   Djinni
Miles Malleson . . . .   Sultan
Morton Selten . . . .   King
Mary Morris . . . .   Halima
Bruce Winston . . . .   Merchant
Hay Petrie . . . .   Astrologer
Roy Emerton . . . .   Jailer
Allan Jeayes . . . .   Storyteller
Adelaide Hall . . . .   Singer
FANTASY Boy thief and genie help deposed
king thwart usurping magician. (Completed in
Hollywood. AA 1940: Best Photography, Art
Direction, Special Effects, Sound Effects.)

10756
CAVALCADE OF VARIETY (68) (U)
Butcher's Film Service
P: F.W. Baker
D: Thomas Bentley
Peter Brough & Jimmy
COMPILATION Extracts from VARIETY
PARADE (1936), MUSIC HALL PARADE
(1939).

10757
HER FATHER'S DAUGHTER (8) (U)
Butcher (NSS)
D: Desmond Dickinson
Alastair Sim . . . .   Father
Viola Lyel . . . .   Mother
Jennifer Gray . . . .   Daughter
DRAMA Need for women trainees for
munitions work.

10758
GOOFER TROUBLE (8) (U)
Denham & Pinewood (NSS)
D: Maurice Elvey
Fred Emney
Edward Chapman
COMEDY Folly of neglecting to take cover
during air battles.

1941

JAN

10759
SPELLBOUND (82) (A)
USA: THE SPELL OF AMY NUGENT
Pyramid Amalgamated (UA) *reissue:* 1946,
PASSING CLOUDS (FR; 14 mins cut)
P: R. Murray Leslie
D: John Harlow
S: (NOVEL) Robert Benson (THE
NECROMANCERS)
SC: Miles Malleson
Derek Farr . . . . Laurie Baxter
Vera Linsday . . . . Diana Hilton
Frederick Leister . . . . Mr Vincent
Hay Petrie . . . . Cathcart
Felix Aylmer . . . . Mr Morton
Diana King . . . . Amy Nugent
W.G. Fay . . . . Johnnie
Gibb McLaughlin . . . . Gibb
Marian Spencer . . . . Mrs Stapleton
Hannen Swaffer . . . . Himself
FANTASY Love saves man from madness when
spiritualist materialises his dead fiancee.

10760
EAST OF PICCADILLY (79) (A)
USA: THE STRANGLER
ABPC (Pathe) *reissue:* 1945
P: Walter C. Mycroft
D: Harold Huth
S: (NOVEL) Gordon Beckles
SC: Lesley Storm, J. Lee-Thompson
Judy Campbell . . . . Penny Sutton
Sebastian Shaw . . . . Tamsie Green
Henry Edwards . . . . Insp
Niall MacGinnis . . . . Joe
George Pughe . . . . Oscar Juloff
Martita Hunt . . . . Ma
George Hayes . . . . Mark Struberg
Cameron Hall . . . . George
Edana Romney . . . . Sadie Jones
Bunty Payne . . . . Tania
Charles Victor . . . . Editor
CRIME Soho. Novelist and girl reporter
unmask silk-stocking strangler.

10761
THE FARMER'S WIFE (82) (U)
ABPC (Pathe) *reissue:* 1945
P: Walter C. Mycroft
D: Norman Lee, Leslie Arliss
S: (PLAY) Eden Philpotts
SC: Norman Lee, Leslie Arliss, J.E. Hunter
Basil Sydney . . . . Samuel Sweetland
Wilfrid Lawson . . . . Churdles Ash
Nora Swinburne . . . . Araminta Grey
Patricia Roc . . . . Sibley
Michael Wilding . . . . Richard Coaker
Bunty Payne . . . . Petronell
Enid Stamp Taylor . . . . Mary Hearne
Betty Warren . . . . Lovisa Windeatt
Viola Lyel . . . . Thirza Tapper
Edward Rigby . . . . Tom Gurney
Kenneth Griffith . . . . George Smerdon
A. Bormley Davenport . . . . . . Henry Coaker
Jimmy Godden . . . . Sgt
Gilbert Gunn . . . . Pianist
COMEDY Devon. Widowed farmer woos
several women before realising he loves his
housekeeper.

10762
DAWN GUARD (5) (U)
Charter (NSS)
P: John Boulting
D: Roy Boulting
Bernard Miles . . . . Farmer
Percy Walsh
WAR Farmers serving in Home Guard discuss
war and peace.

10763
TELEFOOTLERS (6) (U)
Verity (NSS)
P: Sidney Box
D: John Paddy Carstairs
Muriel George . . . . Woman
Barbara Everest . . . . Woman
WAR Thoughtless telephone gossipers give
information to enemy.

10764
SPRING MEETING (93) (U)
ABPC (Pathe) *reissue:* 1945
P: D: Walter C. Mycroft
S: (PLAY) M.J. Farrell, John Percy
SC: Walter C. Mycroft, Norman Lee
Nova Pilbeam . . . . Baby Furze
Basil Sydney . . . . James
Henry Edwards . . . . Sir Richard Furze
Sarah Churchill . . . . Joan Furze
Enid Stamp Taylor . . . . . Tiny Fox-Collier
Michael Wilding . . . . Tony Fox-Collier
Margaret Rutherford . . . . . Aunt Bijou
Hugh McDermott . . . . Michael Byrne
W.G. Fay . . . . Johnny
COMEDY Ireland. Widow schemes to wed her
son to the daughter of her rich, mean ex-fiance.

10765
THE MAN AT THE GATE (48) (U)
USA: MEN OF THE SEA
GHW Productions (GFD)
P: James B. Sloan
D: Norman Walker
S: (POEM) Louise Haskin
SC: Manning Haynes, Lydia Hayward,
Harold Simpson
Wilfrid Lawson . . . . Henry Foley
Mary Jerrold . . . . Mrs Foley
William Freshman . . . . George Foley
Kathleen O'Regan . . . . Ruth
DRAMA Cornwall. Fisherman's wife loses
faith when her sailor son is reported drowned.

FEB

10766
THE GHOST OF ST MICHAEL'S (82) (A)
Ealing (ABFD) *reissues:* 1944; 1947; 1955 (NR)
AP: Basil Dearden
D: Marcel Varnel
S: Angus Macphail, John Dighton
Will Hay . . . . William Lamb
Claude Hulbert . . . . Hilary Teasdale
Charles Hawtrey . . . . Percy Thorne
Raymond Huntley . . . . Mr Humphries
Felix Aylmer . . . . Dr Winter
Elliot Mason . . . . Mrs Wigmore
John Laurie . . . . Jamie
Hay Petrie . . . . Procurator Fiscal
Roddy Hughes . . . . Amberley
Manning Whiley . . . . Stock
Derek Blomfield . . . . Sunshine
Brefni O'Rorke . . . . Sgt MacFarlane
COMEDY Skye. Evacuated teacher and his
pupils catch spies in a "haunted" castle.

10767
THE SAINT'S VACATION (75) (A)
RKO—Radio
P: William Sistrom
D: Leslie Fenton
S: (NOVEL) Leslie Charteris (GETAWAY)
SC: Jeffrey Dell
Hugh Sinclair . . . . Simon Templar
Sally Gray . . . . Mary Langdon
Arthur Macrae . . . . Monty Howard
Cecil Parker . . . . Rudolph
Leueen McGrath . . . . Valerie
Gordon McLeod . . . . Insp Teal
John Warwick . . . . Gregory

Ivor Barnard . . . . Emil
Manning Whiley . . . . Marko
Felix Aylmer . . . . Leighton
CRIME Switzerland. Girl reporter helps tec
save sound detector from spies.

10768
FREEDOM RADIO (95) (A)
USA: A VOICE IN THE NIGHT
Two Cities (Col)
P: Mario Zampi
D: Anthony Asquith
S: Wolfgang Wilhelm, George Campbell
SC: Basil Woon, Gordon Wellesley, Louis
Golding, Anatole de Grunwald, Jeffrey Dell,
Bridget Boland, Roland Pertwee
Clive Brook . . . . Dr Karl Roder
Diana Wynyard . . . . Irene Roder
Raymond Huntley . . . . Rabenau
Derek Farr . . . . Hans
Joyce Howard . . . . Elly
Howard Marion Crawford . . Kummer
John Penrose . . . . Otto
Morland Graham . . . . Father Landbach
Ronald Squire . . . . Spiedler
Reginald Beckwith . . . . . . Fenner
Clifford Evans . . . . Dressler
Bernard Miles . . . . Muller
Gibb McLaughlin . . . . Dr Weiner
Muriel George . . . . Hanna
Martita Hunt . . . . Concierge
Hay Petrie . . . . Sebastian
Manning Whiley . . . . Trooper
WAR Vienna. Throat specialist married to Nazi
actress runs secret radio transmitter.

MAR

10769
THE PRIME MINISTER (109) (U)
WB—FN (WB)
P: Max Milder
D: Thorold Dickinson
S: Brock Williams, Michael Hogan
John Gielgud . . . . Benjamin Disraeli
Diana Wynyard . . . Mary Anne Wyndham-Lewis
Will Fyffe . . . . Agitator
Stephen Murray . . . . W.E. Gladstone
Owen Nares . . . . Lord Derby
Fay Compton . . . . Queen Victoria
Lyn Harding . . . . Bismark
Pamela Standish . . . . Princess Victoria
Leslie Perrins . . . . Earl of Salisbury
Vera Bogetta . . . . Lady Blessington
Anthony Ireland . . . . Capt d'Orsay
Irene Browne . . . . Lady Londonderry
Frederick Leister . . . . Lord Melbourne
Nicolas Hannan . . . . Sir Robert Peel
Barbara Everest . . . . Baroness Lehzen
Kynaston Reeves . . . . Lord Stanley
Gordon McLeod . . . . John Brown
Glynis Johns . . . . Miss Sheridan
Margaret Johnston . . . . . . Miss Sheridan
HISTORY 1837—1878. Jewish novelist's wife
helps his political career.

10770
THE GHOST TRAIN (85) (A)
Gainsborough (GFD) *reissue:* 1947
(ABFD; 126 ft cut)
P: Edward Black
D: Walter Forde
S: (PLAY) Arnold Ridley
SC: Marriott Edgar, Val Guest, J.O.C. Orton
Arthur Askey . . . . Tommy Gander
Richard Murdoch . . . . Teddy Deakin
Kathleen Harrison . . . . Miss Bourne
Morland Graham . . . . Dr Sterling
Linden Travers . . . . Julie Price
Peter Murray Hill . . . . Richard Winthrop
Carole Lynn . . . . Jackie Winthrop
Herbert Lomas . . . . Saul Hodgkin

Raymond Huntley . . . . . . John Price
Betty Jardine . . . . Edna
Stuart Latham . . . . Herbert
D.J. Williams . . . . Ben Isaacs
COMEDY Tec poses as passenger to catch
spies using abandoned track.

10771
THIS ENGLAND (84) (U)
Scotland: OUR HERITAGE
British National (Anglo)
P: John Corfield
D: David Macdonald
S: A.R. Rawlinson, Bridget Boland
SC: Emlyn Williams
Emlyn Williams . . . . Appleyard
John Clements . . . . John Rokeby
Constance Cummings . . . .
Frank Pettingell . . . . . .
Esmond Knight . . . . . .
Roland Culver . . . .
Morland Graham . . . . . .
Leslie French . . . .
Martin Walker . . . .
Ronald Ward . . . .
James Harcourt . . . .
Walter Fitzgerald . . . . . .
Charles Victor . . . .
Roddy McDowall . . . . .
HISTORY Land owner and labourer fight
through Norman conquest, Spanish armada,
Napoleonic wars, Great War, and 1940.

10772
DANGEROUS AQUAINTANCE (27) (A)
Inspiration (Exclusive)
P: D: Horace Shepherd
DRAMA Soldier on leave quarrels with fiancee
and goes with prostitute responsible for her
brother's death.

10773
A MUSICAL COCKTAIL (15) (U)
Inspiration (Par)
P: D: Horace Shepherd
Alfredo Campoli
Frank Drew
"Dawn"
MUSICAL

10774
ONCE UPON A TIME (15) (U)
Inspiration (Par)
P: D: Horace Shepherd
COMEDY Fire-watcher dreams of pre-war days.

10775
YOU'RE TELLING ME ! (5) (U)
Paul Rotha (NSS)
P: Paul Rotha
D: Bladon Peake
COMEDY Gossipers magnify boy breaking
window to destruction of factory.

10776
MR PROUDFOOT SHOWS A LIGHT (7) (U)
20th Century Productions (NSS)
P: Edward Black
D: Herbert Mason
Sydney Howard . . . . Mr Proudfoot
COMEDY Danger of showing lights during
blackout.

10777
THE FINE FEATHERS (12) (U)
British Films (GFD)
D: S: Andrew Buchanan
Jeanne de Casalis . . . . Mrs Feather
Aubrey Mallalieu . . . . Mr Feather
COMEDY Doctor tries to explain balanced
diets to henpeck's wife.

10778
QUIET WEDDING (80) (A)
Conqueror (Par) |reissues: 1943; 1947
P: Paul Soskin
D: Anthony Asquith
S: (PLAY) Esther McCracken
SC: Terence Rattigan, Anatole de Grunwald
Margaret Lockwood. . . . . . Janet Royd
Derek Farr . . . . Dallas Chaytor
Marjorie Fielding . . . . Mrs Royd
A.E. Matthews . . . . Mr Royd
Athene Seyler . . . . Aunt Mary
Margaretta Scott . . . . Marcia Royd
Peggy Ashcroft . . . . Flower Lisle
Frank Cellier . . . . Mr Chaytor
Roland Culver . . . . Boofy Ponsonby
Jean Cadell . . . . Aunt Florence
David Tomlinson . . . . John Royd
Sidney King . . . . Denys Royd
Michael Shepley . . . . Jim
Muriel Pavlow . . . . Miranda
Roddy Hughes . . . . Vicar
O. B. Clarence . . . . Magistrate
Margaret Rutherford . . . . . Magistrate
Wally Patch . . . . Magistrate
Bernard Miles . . . . PC
Martita Hunt . . . . Mme Mirelle
COMEDY Family complications almost upset
country wedding.

10779
INSPECTOR HORNLEIGH GOES TO IT
(87) (U) USA: MAIL TRAIN
20th Century Productions (20)
P: Edward Black
D: Walter Forde
S: (RADIO SERIES) Hans Priwin
SC: Frank Launder, Val Guest, J.O.C. Orton
Gordon Harker . . . . Insp Hornleigh
Alastair Sim . . . . Sgt Bingham
Phyllis Calvert . . . . Mrs Wilkinson
Edward Chapman . . . . Mr Blenkinsop
Raymond Huntley . . . . Dr Kerbishley
Charles Oliver . . . . Mr Wilkinson
Percy Walsh . . . . Insp Blow
David Horne . . . . Commissioner
Peter Gawthorne . . . . Col
Wally Patch . . . . Sgt-Maj
Betty Jardine . . . . Daisy
O.B. Clarence . . . . Prof Mackenzie
CRIME Tecs pose as teachers, postmen and
soldiers to unmask fifth-columnists.

10780
KIPPS (112) (U)
USA: THE REMARKABLE MR KIPPS
20th Century Productions reissue: 1944
(2455 ft cut)
P: Edward Black
D: Carol Reed
S: (NOVEL) H.G. Wells
SC: Frank Launder, Sidney Gilliat
Michael Redgrave . . . . Arthur Kipps
Diana Wynyard . . . . . . Helen Walshingham
Phyllis Calvert. . . . . Ann Pornick
Arthur Riscoe . . . . Chitterlow
Max Adrian . . . . Chester Coote
Helen Haye . . . . Mrs Walshingham
Michael Wilding . . . . Ronnie Walshingham
Lloyd Pearson. . . . . Shalford
Edward Rigby . . . . Buggins
Mackenzie Ward . . . . Pearce
Hermione Baddeley . . . . . Miss Mergle
Betty Ann Davies . . . . Flo Bates
Betty Jardine . . . . Doris
Frank Pettingell . . . . Mr Kipps
Beatrice Varley . . . . Mrs Kipps
George Carney . . . . Mr Pornick
Irene Browne . . . . Mrs Bindon-Botting
Peter Graves . . . . Sidney Revel

Vis Castlerosse . . . . . . Man in Bathchair
COMEDY 1906. Shopkeeper loses legacy
attempting to crash society and returns to girl
of his own class.

10781
THIS MAN IS DANGEROUS (82) (A)
retitled: THE PATIENT VANISHES
Rialto (Pathe) |reissue: 1945
P: John Argyle
D: Lawrence Huntington
S: (NOVEL) David Hume (THEY CALLED
HIM DEATH)
SC: John Argyle, Edward Dryhurst
James Mason . . . . Mick Cardby
Mary Clare . . . . Matron
Margaret Vyner . . . . Mollie Bennett
Gordon McLeod . . . . Insp Cardby
Frederick Valk . . . . Dr Moger
Barbara Everest . . . . Mrs Cardby
Barbara James . . . . Lena Morne
G.H. Mulcaster . . . . Lord Morne
Eric Clavering . . . . Al Meason
Brefni O'Rorke . . . . Dr Crosbie
Michael Rennie . . . . Inspector
CRIME Insp's son saves Lord's daughter from
fake doctor's nursing home.

APR

10782
MAJOR BARBARA (121) (A)
Pascal (GFD)
P: Gabriel Pascal
D: Gabriel Pascal, Harold French, David Lean
S: (PLAY) George Bernard Shaw
SC: Anatole de Grunwald,George Bernard Shaw
Wendy Hiller . . . . .Maj Barbara Undershaft
Rex Harrison . . . . Adolphus Cusins
Robert Morley . . . . Mr Undershaft
Emlyn Williams . . . . Snobby Price
Robert Newton . . . . Bill Walker
Sybil Thorndike . . . . The General
Deborah Kerr . . . . .Jenny Hill
David Tree . . . . Charles Lomax
Penelope Dudley-Ward . . . . Sarah Undershaft
Marie Lohr . . . . Lady Brittomart
Walter Hudd . . . . Stephen Undershaft
Marie Ault . . . . Rummy Mitchens
Donald Calthrop. . . . . . . Peter Shirley
Felix Aylmer . . . . James
Stanley Holloway . . . . PC
DRAMA Armaments millionaire's daughter
resigns from Salvation Army when it accepts
her father's donation.

10783
OLD MOTHER RILEY'S GHOSTS (82) (U)
British National (Anglo)
P: D: John Baxter
S: Con West, Geoffrey Orme, Arthur Lucan
Arthur Lucan . . . . Mrs Riley
Kitty McShane . . . . Kitty Riley
John Stuart . . . . John Cartwright
A. Bromley Davenport . . . Warrender
Dennis Wyndham . . . . Jem
John Laurie . . . . McAdam
Peter Gawthorne . . . . Mr Cartwright
Henry Longhurst . . . . .
Ben Williams . . . .
Charles Paton . . . .
COMEDY Charwoman foils spies seeking
inventor's plans in "haunted" castle.

10784
LOVE ON THE DOLE (100) (A)
British National (Anglo) reissue:1948 (Pathe)
P: D: John Baxter
S: (PLAY) Ronald Gow (NOVEL) Walter
Greenwood
SC: Walter Greenwood, Barbara K. Emary,

Rollo Gamble
Deborah Kerr	Sally Hardcastle
Clifford Evans	Larry Meath
Joyce Howard	Helen Hawkins
Frank Cellier	Sam Grundy
Mary Merrall	Mrs Hardcastle
George Carney	Mr Hardcastle
Geoffrey Hibbert	Harry Hardcastle
Maire O'Neill	Mrs Dorbell
A. Bromley Davenport	Pawnbroker
Peter Gawthorne	Supt
Martin Walker	Ned Narkey
Iris Vandeleur	Mrs Nattle
Marie Ault	Mrs Jilke
Marjorie Rhodes	Mrs Bull
Kenneth Griffith	Tom Hare
B. John Slater	Jackson
Muriel George	Landlady

DRAMA Lancs; 1930. Girl becomes bookie's mistress to help her workless family.

MAY

10785
DANNY BOY (80) (U)
Signet (Butcher) *reissue:* 1943
(Sherwood; 546 ft cut)
P: Hugh Perceval
D: Oswald Mitchell
S: Oswald Mitchell, A. Barr-Carson
Ann Todd	Jane Kaye
Wilfrid Lawson	Jack Newton
John Warwick	Carter
Grant Tyler	Danny
David Farrar	Martin
Wylie Watson	Fiddlesticks
Albert Whelan	Scotty
Tony Quinn	Maloney
Norah Gordon	Mrs Maloney
Percy Manchester	Vocalist

MUSICAL Singer searches for estranged husband and son who have become buskers.

10786
THE SAVING SONG (5) (U) *tech*
National Savings (NSS)
Jack Hylton and his Band
George Baker
MUSICAL Parody of "Sailing, Sailing" to promote National Savings.

10787
HOME GUARD (7) (U) *reissue:*
CITIZEN'S ARMY
Strand (NSS)
D: Donald Taylor
Bernard Miles . . . . Home Guard
WAR Village Home Guard describes duties to pals in pub.

10788
EATING OUT WITH TOMMY (6) (U)
Strand (NSS)
D: Desmond Dickinson
Tommy Trinder	Tommy
Jean Colin	Girl
Edward Chapman	Father

COMEDY Comedian takes girl's family to eat in "British Restaurant".

JUN

10789
TURNED OUT NICE AGAIN (81) (U)
ATP (UA) *reissues:* 1945 (10 mins cut)
1949 (EB)
AP: Basil Dearden
D: Marcel Varnel
S: (PLAY) Hugh Mills, Wells Root
(AS YOU ARE)

SC: Austin Melford, John Dighton, Basil Dearden
George Formby	George Pearson
Peggy Bryan	Lydia Pearson
Edward Chapman	Uncle Arnold
Elliot Mason	Mrs Pearson
Mackenzie Ward	Gerald Dawson
O.B. Clarence	Mr Dawson
Ronald Ward	Nelson
John Salew	Largos
Wilfrid Hyde White	Remover
Hay Petrie	Drunk
Michael Rennie	Diner

COMEDY Buyer's purchase of new material saves old-fashioned underwear firm.

10790
ATLANTIC FERRY (108) (U)
USA: SONS OF THE SEA
WB—FN (WB)
P: Max Milder
D: Walter Forde
S: Derek MacIver, Wynne MacIver
SC: Gordon Wellesley, Edward Dryhurst, Emeric Pressburger
Michael Redgrave	Charles MacIver
Valerie Hobson	Mary Anne Morrison
Griffith Jones	David MacIver
Margaretta Scott	Susan Donaldson
Hartley Power	Samuel Cunard
Bessie Love	Begonia Baggott
Milton Rosmer	George Burns
Frederick Leister	Morrison
Henry Oscar	Eagles
Edmund Willard	Robert Napier
Charles Victor	Grogan
Leslie Bradley	Elmer
Felix Aylmer	Banker

ADVENTURE Liverpool, 1837. Brothers build first steam packet to cross Atlantic.

10791
ONCE A CROOK (81) (A)
20th Century Productions (20)
P: Edward Black
D: Herbert Mason
S: (PLAY) Evadne Price, Ken Attiwill
SC: Roger Burford
Gordon Harker	Charlie Hopkins
Sydney Howard	Hallelujah Harry
Frank Pettingell	Captain
Carla Lehmann	Estelle
Bernard Lee	Duke
Kathleen Harrison	Auntie
Cyril Cusack	Bill Hopkins
Diana King	Bessie
Joss Ambler	Insp Marsh
Raymond Huntley	Governor
Felix Aylmer	KC
Wally Patch	Warder

CRIME Ex-cracksman publican's son framed by his ex-partner for shooting girl accomplice in jewel robbery.

10792
PATHETONE PARADE OF 1941 (35) (U)
Pathe
D: Fred Watts
Ronald Frankau	Compere
Robb Wilton	Teddy Brown
Sandy Macpherson	Mantovani
Norman Evans	Sidney Burchell
Beryl Orde	Jeanne de Casalis
Jack Jackson and his Band	

REVUE

10793
PIMPERNEL SMITH (121) (U)
USA: MISTER V

British National (Anglo)
P: D: Leslie Howard
S: A.G. MacDonell, Wolfgang Wilhelm
SC: Anatole de Grunwald, Roland Pertwee, Ian Dalrymple
Leslie Howard	Prof Horatio Smith
Francis L. Sullivan	Gen von Graum
Mary Morris	Ludmilla Koslowski
Hugh McDermott	David Maxwell
Raymond Huntley	Marx
Manning Whiley	Bertie Gregson
Peter Gawthorne	Sidimir Koslowski
Allan Jeayes	Dr Beckendorf
Dennis Arundell	Hoffman
Joan Kemp-Welch	Teacher
Philip Friend	Spencer
Lawrence Kitchen	Clarence Elstead
David Tomlinson	Steve
Basil Appleby	Jock McIntyre
Percy Walsh	Dvorak
Roland Pertwee	Sir George Smith
A.E. Matthews	Earl of Meadowbrook

WAR "Absent-minded" archaeologist helps Polish journalist escape Nazis.

JUL

10794
DANGEROUS MOONLIGHT (98) (U)
USA: SUICIDE SQUADRON
RKO—Radio *reissue:* 1958
P: William Sistrom
D: Brian Desmond Hurst
S: Shaun Terence Young
SC: Shaun Terence Young, Brian Desmond Hurst, Rodney Ackland
Anton Walbrook	Stefan Radetzky
Sally Gray	Carole Peters
Derrick de Marney	Mike Carroll
Cecil Parker	Specialist
Percy Parsons	Bill Peters
Keneth Kent	de Guise
J.H. Roberts	Physician
Guy Middleton	Shorty
John Laurie	Cdr
Frederick Valk	Polish Cdr
Philip Friend	Pete
Michael Rennie	Pilot

WAR Polish pianist escapes to New York, weds rich reporter, and has amnesia after flying in Battle of Britain.

10795
NIGHT WATCH (7) (U)
Strand (NSS)
D: Donald Taylor
S: Rodney Ackland, Reg Graves
Anne Firth	The Girl
Cyril Chamberlain	The Man

WAR Night duty with Civil Defence workers.

10796
LADY BE KIND (7) (U)
John Corfield (NSS)
D: Rodney Ackland
S: Rodney Ackland, Arthur Boys
Muriel George . . . . Landlady
COMEDY Landlady eventually realises lodger's munitions work is important.

10797
AN AIRMAN'S LETTER TO HIS MOTHER (5) (U)
Michael Powell (MGM)
D: Michael Powell
WAR Officer reads dead airman's last letter to his mother.

10798
SURPRISE BROADCAST (18) (U)
Andrew Buchanan (Ex)

D: Andrew Buchanan
A.E. Matthews . . . . Husband
Jean Colin . . . . Singer
Adela Manten . . . . Wife
COMEDY Wife cures husband of infatuation with radio singer.

10799
MY WIFE'S FAMILY (82) (A)
ABPC (Pathe) *reissue:* 1945
P: D: Walter C. Mycroft
S: (PLAY) Fred Duprez
SC: Norman Lee, Clifford Grey
Charlie Clapham . . . . Doc Knott
John Warwick . . . . Jack Gay
Patricia Roc . . . . Peggy Gay
Wylie Watson . . . . Noah Bagshott
Chili Bouchier . . . . Rosa Latour
Peggy Bryan . . . . Sally
Margaret Scudamore . . . . . Arabella Bagshott
Leslie Fuller . . . . Policeman
David Tomlinson . . . . Willie Bagshott
Joan Greenwood . . . . Irma Bagshott
COMEDY Newlywed mistakes husband's hidden piano for his bastard baby.

10800
FACING THE MUSIC (79) (U)
Butcher *reissue:* 1944 (Sherwood; 1087 ft cut)
D: Maclean Rogers
S: Maclean Rogers, Kathleen Butler
Bunny Doyle . . . . Wilfred Hollebone
Betty Driver . . . . Mary Matthews
H.F. Maltby . . . . Mr Bulger
Chili Bouchier . . . . Anna Braun
Wally Patch . . . . Briggs
Gus Mc Naughton . . . . Illusionist
Ruby Miller . . . . Gloria Lynn
Eliot Makeham . . . . Secretary
Gordon McLeod . . . . Mr Kelly
Ronald Chesney; Paddy Drew; Percival Mackey's Band
COMEDY Munitions worker put in charge of fake factory to fool spies.

AUG

10801
COTTAGE TO LET (90) (A)
USA: BOMBSIGHT STOLEN
Gainsborough (GFD) *reissue:* 1948 (Ex)
P: Edward Black
D: Anthony Asquith
S: (PLAY) Geoffrey Kerr
SC: Anatole de Grunwald, J.O.C. Orton
Leslie Banks. . . . . John Barrington
Alastair Sim . . . . Charles Dimble
John Mills . . . . Lt George Perrey
Jeanne de Casalis . . . . Mrs Barrington
Carla Lehmann . . . . Helen Barrington
George Cole . . . . Ronald Mittsby
Michael Wilding . . . . Alan Trentley
Frank Cellier . . . . John Forrest
Wally Patch . . . . Evans
Muriel Aked . . . . Miss Fernery
Muriel George . . . . Mrs Trimm
Hay Petrie . . . . Dr Truscott
Catherine Lacey . . . . Mrs Stokes
CRIME Scotland. Evacuee thwarts spies' plot to kidnap inventor of bombsight.

10802
PENN OF PENNSYLVANIA (79) (A)
USA: THE COURAGEOUS MR PENN
British National (Anglo)
P: Richard Vernon
D: Lance Comfort
S: (BOOK) C.E. Vulliamy (WILLIAM PENN)
SC: Anatole de Grunwald
Clifford Evans . . . . William Penn

Deborah Kerr . . . . Gugliema
Dennis Arundell . . . . Charles II
Aubrey Mallalieu . . . . Chaplain
D.J. Williams . . . . Lord Arlington
O.B. Clarence . . . . Lord Cecil
James Harcourt . . . . Fox
Charles Carson . . . . Admiral Penn
Henry Oscar . . . . Samuel Pepys
Max Adrian . . . . Elton
John Stuart . . . . Bindle
Maire O'Neill . . . . Cook
Edward Rigby . . . . Bushell
Joss Ambler . . . . Lord Mayor
J.H. Roberts . . . . Ford
Edmund Willard . . . . Captain
Percy Marmont . . . . Holme
Gibb McLaughlin . . . . Indian Chief
Herbert Lomas . . . . Cockle
Gus McNaughton . . . . Mate
David Farrar . . . .
HISTORY Persecution of Quakers leads to founding of Pennsylvania.

SEP

10803
HE FOUND A STAR (88) (U)
John Corfield (GFD)
D: John Paddy Carstairs
S: (NOVEL) Monica Ewer (RING O'ROSES)
SC: Austin Melford, Bridget Boland
Vic Oliver . . . . Lucky Lyndon
Sarah Churchill . . . . Ruth Cavour
Evelyn Dall . . . . Susanne
Robert Sanson . . . . Dick Hargreaves
Robert Atkins . . . . Frank Forrester
George Merritt . . . . Max Nagel
Uriel Porter . . . . . . .George Washington Brown
Raymond Lovell . . . . Maurier
J.H. Roberts . . . . Mr Cavour
Barbara Everest . . . . Mrs Cavour
Joan Greenwood . . . . Babe Cavour
Peter Saunders . . . . Ryamond
Charles Victor . . . . Ben Marsh
The Kellaways . . . . Elsie & Jack
MUSICAL Secretary wins theatrical agent when his star singer lets him down.

10804
JEANNIE (101) (U)
Tansa Films (GFD) *reissue:* 1949
(Er; 1663 ft cut)
P: Marcel Hellman
D: Harold French
S: (PLAY) Aimee Stuart
SC: Anatole de Grunwald, Roland Pertwee
Michael Redgrave . . . . Stanley Smith
Barbara Mullen . . . . Jeannie McLean
Wilfrid Lawson . . . . James McLean
Kay Hammond . . . . Margaret
Albert Lieven . . .Count Erich von Wittgenstein
Edward Chapman . . . . Mr Jansen
Googie Withers . . . . Laundress
Gus McNaughton . . . . Angus Whitelaw
Phyllis Stanley . . . . Mrs Whitelaw
Hilda Bayley . . . . Mrs Jansen
Marjorie Fielding. . . . . Mrs Murdoch
Frank Cellier . . . .
Anne Shelton . . . .
ROMANCE Vienna. Salesman wins Scots girl from Count who thinks her legacy is larger than it is.

10805
I THANK YOU (81) (U)
Gainsborough (GFD)
P: Edward Black
D: Marcel Varnel
S: Howard Irving Young, Val Guest, Marriott Edgar

Arthur Askey . . . . Arthur
Richard Murdoch . . . . Stinker
Lily Morris . . . . Lady Randall
Moore Marriott . . . . Pop Bennett
Graham Moffatt . . . . Albert
Kathleen Harrison . . . . . . Cook
Wally Patch . . . . Bill
Felix Aylmer . . . . Henry Potter
Cameron Hall . . . . Lomas
Issy Bonn; Forsythe, Seamon & Farrell
COMEDY Actors pose as cook and footman to get titled ex-star to back show.

10806
THE SEVENTH SURVIVOR (75) (U)
British National-Shaftesbury (Anglo)
P: Elizabeth Hiscott
D: Leslie Hiscott
S: Michael Barringer
Austin Trevor . . . . Capt Hartzmann
Linden Travers . . . . Gillian Chase
John Stuart . . . . Robert Cooper
Martita Hunt . . . . Mrs Lindley
Frank Pettingell . . . . Thomas Pettifer
Jane Carr . . . . Diane Winters
Wally Patch . . . . Bob Sutton
Felix Aylmer . . . . Sir Elmer Norton
Henry Oscar . . . . Goodenough
Ralph Truman . . . . Captain
Ronald Shiner . . . . Ernie
WAR One of torpedoed group stranded in lighthouse is Nazi agent.

OCT

10807
SHEEPDOG OF THE HILLS (76) (U)
Butcher *reissues:* 1943 (Sherwood; 5 mins cut)
1948 (Butch)
D: Germain Burger   P: F.W. Baker
David Farrar . . . . Rev Michael Verney
Philip Friend . . . . Dr Peter Hammond
Helen Perry . . . . Frances Miller
Dennis Wyndham . . . . Riggy Teasdale
Len Sharp . . . . Geordie Scott
Jack Vyvyan . . . . Constable Scott
Arthur Denton . . . . Hawkins
Philip Godfrey . . . . Sam Worrow
Johnnie Schofield . . . . Tom Abbott
DRAMA Devon. Village vicar loses nurse to new doctor and adopts mad farmer's sheepdog.

10808
GERT AND DAISY'S WEEKEND (79) (U)
Butcher *reissue:* 1945 (Sherwood; 10 mins cut)
P: F.W. Baker
D: Maclean Rogers
S: Maclean Rogers, Kathleen Butler, H.F. Maltby
Elsie Waters . . . . Gert
Doris Waters . . . . Daisy
Iris Vandeleur . . . . Ma Butler
John Slater . . . . Jack Densham
Elizabeth Hunt . . . . Maisie Smith
Wally Patch . . . . Charlie Peters
Annie Esmond . . . . Lady Plumtree
Aubrey Mallalieu . . . . Barnes
Gerald Rex . . . . George the Terror
COMEDY Cockney sisters in charge of evacuees framed for stealing Lady's jewels.

10809
THE TOWER OF TERROR (78) (A)
ABPC (Pathe)
P: John Argyle
D: Lawrence Huntington
S: John Reinhart
SC: John Argyle, John Reinhart
Wilfrid Lawson . . . . Wolfe Kristan
Movita . . . . Marie Durand

Michael Rennie . . . . Anthony Hale
Morland Graham . . . . Kleber
George Woodbridge . . . . . . Jurgens
Edward Sinclair . . . . Fletcher
Richard George . . . . Capt Borkman
Charles Rolfe . . . . Albers
John Longden . . . . Commander
Victor Weske . . . . Peters
Olive Sloane . . . . Florist
DRAMA Germany. British agent poses as mate to mad lighthouse-keeper and helps French girl escape Gestapo.

10810
THE SAINT MEETS THE TIGER (79) (A)
RKO-Radio
P: William Sistrom
D: Paul Stein
S: (NOVEL) Leslie Charteris (MEET THE TIGER)
SC: Leslie Arliss, Wolfgang Wilhelm, James Seymour
Hugh Sinclair . . . . Simon Templar
Jean Gillie . . . . Patricia Holm
Clifford Evans . . . . Tidmarsh
Wylie Watson . . . . Horace
Gordon McLeod . . . . Insp Teal
Dennis Arundell . . . . Bentley
Charles Victor . . . . Bittle
Louise Hampton . . . . Aunt Agatha
Eric Clavering . . . . Frankie
CRIME Cornwall. Tec stops gang from taking stolen bullion to South Africa.

10811
THE COMMON TOUCH (104) (U)
British National (Anglo) reissue: 1945 (cut)
P:D: John Baxter
S: Herbert Ayres
SC: Barbara K. Emary, Geoffrey Orme
Greta Gynt . . . . Sylvia Meadows
Geoffrey Hibbert . . . . Peter Henderson
Joyce Howard . . . . Mary Weatherby
Harry Welchman . . . . Lincoln's Inn
Edward Rigby . . . . Tich
George Carney . . . . Charlie
Bransby Williams . . . . Old Ben
Wally Patch . . . . Nobby
Eliot Makeham . . . . Inky
John Longden . . . . Stuart Gordon
Raymond Lovell . . . . Cartwright
Percy Walsh . . . . McFarlane
Bernard Miles . . . . Perkins
Charles Carson . . . . Haywood
Bill Fraser . . . . Harris
Arthur Maude . . . . Martin
Jerry Verno . . . . Messenger
Mark Hambourg; Carroll Gibbons; Sandy Macpherson; Scott Sanders
DRAMA Youth inherits business and poses as tramp to save dosshouse from demolition.

10812
49th PARALLEL (123) (U)
Ortus Films (GFD)
P: John Sutro, Michael Powell
D: Michael Powell
S: Emeric Pressburger
SC: Emeric Pressburger, Rodney Ackland
Leslie Howard . . . . Philip A. Scott
Raymond Massey . . . . Andy Brock
Laurence Olivier . . . . Johnnie
Anton Walbrook . . . . Peter
Eric Portman . . . . Lt Hirth
Glynis Johns . . . . Anna
Niall MacGinnis . . . . Vogel
Finlay Currie . . . . Factor
Raymond Lovell . . . . Lt Kuhnecke
John Chandos . . . . Lohrmann
Basil Appleby . . . . Jahner

Eric Clavering . . . . Art
Charles Victor . . . . Andreas
Ley On . . . . Nick the Eskimo
WAR Canada. Stranded U-boat crew try to escape into America. (Top Moneymaker: 1942).

NOV

10813
SHIPS WITH WINGS (103) (A)
Ealing (UA) reissue: 1946 (Cut)
AP: S.C. Balcon
D: Sergei Nolbandov
S: Sergei Nolbandov, Patrick Kirwan, Austin Melford, Diana Morgan
John Clements . . . . Lt Dick Stacey
Leslie Banks . . . . Admiral Wetherby
Jane Baxter . . . . Celia Wetherby
Ann Todd . . . . Kay Gordon
Basil Sydney . . . . Capt Fairfax
Edward Chapman . . . . Papadopulous
Hugh Williams . . . . Wagner
Frank Pettingell . . . . Fields
Michael Wilding . . . . Lt Grant
Michael Rennie . . . . Lt Peter Maxwell
Frank Cellier . . . . Gen Scarappa
Cecil Parker . . . . Air Marshal
John Stuart . . . . Cdr Hood
Morland Graham . . . . CPO Marsden
Charles Victor . . . . MacDermott
Hugh Burden . . . . Lt Wetherby
John Laurie . . . . Lt Cdr Reid
WAR 1936-9. Cashiered pilot helps his old aircraft carrier attack German dam.

10814
THE BLACK SHEEP OF WHITEHALL (80) (U)
Ealing (UA) reissue: 1945 (Eal)
AP: S.C. Balcon
D: Will Hay, Basil Dearden
S: Angus Macphail, John Dighton
Will Hay . . . . William Davis
John Mills . . . . Bobby
Basil Sydney . . . . Costello
Frank Cellier . . . . Dr Innsbach
Felix Aylmer . . . . Crabtree
Henry Hewitt . . . . Prof Davys
Joss Ambler . . . . Sir John
Thora Hird . . . . Joyce
Leslie Mitchell . . . . Interviewer
COMEDY Teacher mistaken for economics expert saves him from nursing home run by spies.

10815
OLD MOTHER RILEY'S CIRCUS (80) (U)
British National (Anglo)
P: Wallace Orton
D: Thomas Bentley
S: Con West, Geoffrey Orme, Barbara K. Emary, Arthur Lucan
Arthur Lucan . . . . Mrs Riley
Kitty McShane . . . . Kitty Riley
John Longden . . . . Bill
Roy Emerton . . . . Santley
Edgar Driver . . . . Bobo
Beckett Bould . . . . Davis
O.B. Clarence . . . . Lawyer
Syd Crossley . . . . Bailiff
Hector Abbas . . . . Wizista
The Hindustans; The Balstons; The Carsons; Reading & Grant; Medlock & Marlow; Speedy; Isabel & Emma; Eve & Joan Banyard; Harry Koady; Jean Black
COMEDY Old woman saves bankrupt circus and finds her longlost daughter.

10816
HATTER'S CASTLE (102) (A)
Paramont British reissue: 1947

P: Isadore Goldsmith
D: Lance Comfort
S: (NOVEL) A.J. Cronin
SC: Paul Merzbach, Rudolf Bernauer, Rodney Ackland
Robert Newton . . . . James Brodie
Deborah Kerr . . . . Mary Brodie
Emlyn Williams . . . . Dennis
James Mason . . . . Dr Renwick
Enid Stamp-Taylor . . . . Nancy
Beatrice Varley . . . . Mrs Brodie
Henry Oscar . . . . Emerson
Lawrence Hanray . . . . Dr Lawrie
Brefni O'Rorke . . . . Foyle
Claude Bailey . . . . Paxton
Gordon McLeod . . . . Sir John Latta
Roddy Hughes . . . . Gordon
Mary Hinton . . . . Lady Winton
Milton Rosmer . . . . Gibson
DRAMA Scotland, 1879. Tyrannical hatter goes mad after his assistant seduces his daughter and his wife dies of cancer.

10817
BOB'S YOUR UNCLE (76) (U)
Butcher's Film Service reissue: 1945
(Sherwood 8 mins cut)
P: F.W. Baker
D: Oswald Mitchell
S: Vera Allinson
SC: Oswald Mitchell, Vera Allinson
Albert Modley . . . . Albert Smith
Jean Colin . . . . Dolly Diehard
George Bolton . . . . Jeff Smith
Wally Patch . . . . Sgt Brownfoot
H.F. Maltby . . . . Maj Diehard
Bert Linden . . . . Cpl Nelson
Clifford Cobbe . . . . Butler
Johnnie Schofield . . . . Stationmaster
Alfred Wright & Co.; Pim's Comedy Navy
COMEDY Village Home Guard wins his CO's daughter by staging show to buy tank.

DEC

10818
HI GANG! (100) (U)
Gainsborough (GFD)
P: Edward Black
D: Marcel Varnel
S: (RADIO SERIES) Bebe Daniels, Ben Lyon
SC: Val Guest, Marriott Edgar, J.O.C. Orton, Howard Irving Young
Bebe Daniels . . . . The Victory Girl
Ben Lyon . . . . Her Other Half
Vic Oliver . . . . . . The Nuisance with the Ideas
Moore Marriott . . . . Uncle Jerry
Graham Moffatt . . . . Albert
Felix Aylmer . . . . Lord Amersham
Georgina Mackinnon . . . . . Mrs Endicott
Maurice Rhodes . . . . Little Ben
Percy Parsons . . . . Hergensheimer
Diana Beaumont . . . . Secretary
Jacques Brown . . . . Botticelli
Sam Browne; The Green Sisters; Jay Wilbur and his Band
MUSICAL Married radio rivals come from America believing publican's evacuated nephew to be lord's son.

10819
SAM PEPYS JOINS THE NAVY (7) (U)
GB Screen Services (NSS)
D: Francis Searle
COMEDY Pepys' portrait comes to life and is amazed by today's costs.

10820
RUSH HOUR (5) (U)
20th Century Productions (NSS)

P: Edward Black
D: Anthony Asquith
S: Rodney Ackland, Arthur Boys
Muriel George . . . . Shopper
Joan Sterndale Bennett . . . . Shopper
COMEDY War workers suffer from selfish
shoppers during rush hour.

10821
SOUTH AMERICAN GEORGE (93) (U)
Columbia British *reissues:* 1947; 1950 (GN)
P: Ben Henry
D: Marcel Varnel
S: Leslie Arliss, Norman Lee, Austin Melford
George Formby . . . . . . .George Butters/Gilli
                                          Vanetti
Linden Travers . . . . Carole Dean
Enid Stamp-Taylor . . . . Frances Martinique
Jacques Brown . . . . Enrico Richardo
Felix Aylmer . . . . Mr Appleby
Ronald Shiner . . . . Swifty
Alf Goddard . . . . Slappy
Gus McNaughton . . . . George White

Mavis Villiers . . . . Mrs Durrant
Eric Clavering . . . . Mr Durrant
Beatrice Varley . . . . Mrs Butters
Herbert Lomas . . . . Mr Butters
COMEDY Sacked singer poses as Mexican opera
star and wins press agent.

10822
BREACH OF PROMISE (79) (A) USA:
ADVENTURE IN BLACKMAIL
British Mercury (MGM)
P: Richard Norton, Michael Brooke
D: Harold Huth, Roland Pertwee
S: Emeric Pressburger
SC: Roland Pertwee
Clive Brook . . . . Peter
Judy Campbell . . . . Pamela Lawrence
C.V. France . . . . Morgan
Marguerite Allan . . . . Pamela Rose
Percy Walsh . . . . Saxon Rose
Dennis Arundell . . . . Phillip
George Merritt . . . . Professor
David Horne . . . . Sir Hamar

Charles Victor . . . . Sir William
Aubrey Mallalieu . . . . Judge
COMEDY Playwright weds girl who fakes
breach of promise suit against him.

10823
BANANA RIDGE (87) (A)
ABPC (Pathe) *reissue:* 1945
P:D: Walter C. Mycroft
S: (PLAY) Ben Travers
SC: Walter C. Mycroft, Lesley Storm, Ben
Travers
Robertson Hare . . . . Willoughby Pink
Alfred Drayton . . . . Mr Pound
Isabel Jeans . . . . Sue Long
Nova Pilbeam . . . . Cora Pound
Adele Dixon . . . . Mrs Pound
Patrick Kinsella. . . . . Jones
Valentine Dunn . . . . Mrs Pink
Stewart Rome . . . . Sir Ramsey Flight
John Stuart . . . . Staples
COMEDY Partners' former flame pretends her
son is their bastard.

1942

JAN

10824
THIS WAS PARIS (88) (U)
WB-FN (WB)
D: John Harlow
S: Gordon Wellesley, Basil Woon
SC: Brock Williams, Edward Dryhurst

Ann Dvorak	Anne Morgan
Ben Lyon	Butch
Griffith Jones	Bill Hamilton
Robert Morley	Van Der Stuyl
Harold Huth	De La Vague
Mary Maguire	Blossom Leroy
Vera Bogetti	Mme Florien
Harry Welchman	Forsythe
Frederick Burtwell	Entwhistle
Marian Spencer	Lady Muriel
Miles Malleson	Watson
Hay Petrie	Popinard

WAR Paris, 1940. British agent suspects American fashion designer is a spy.

10825
HARD STEEL (86) (A)
GHW Productions (GFD) *reissue:* 1952, WHAT SHALL IT PROFIT (cut)
P: James B. Sloan
D: Norman Walker
S: (NOVEL) Roger Dataller (STEEL SARABAND)
SC: Lydia Hayward

Wilfrid Lawson	Walter Haddon
Betty Stockfeld	Freda Haddon
John Stuart	Alan Saunders
George Carney	Bert Mortimer
Joan Kemp-Welch	Janet Mortimer
James Harcourt	Jim Calver
Frank Atkinson	Dick Sefton
Arthur Hambling	Lamport
John Turnbull	Rowlandson
Hay Petrie	Kissack
Clifton Boyne	Carter
Angela Glynne	Bunty Phillips

DRAMA Steel worker turns tough when raised to manager, but is humanised when his wife leaves him.

10826
THE BIG BLOCKADE (73) (U)
Ealing (UA) *reissue:* 1947 (Eal)
AP: Alberto Cavalcanti
D: Charles Frend
S: Charles Frend, Angus Macphail

Leslie Banks	Taylor
Michael Redgrave	Russian
Will Hay	Skipper
John Mills	Tom
Frank Cellier	Schneider
Robert Morley	Von Geiselbrecht
Alfred Drayton	Direktor
Bernard Miles	Mate
Marius Goring	Propaganda Officer
Austin Trevor	U-boat Captain
Michael Rennie	George
Morland Graham	Dock Official
Albert Lieven	Gunter
John Stuart	Naval Officer
Joss Ambler	Stoltenhoff
Michael Wilding	Captain
David Evans	David
George Woodbridge	Quisling

Quentin Reynolds; Frank Owen; Hon David Bowes-Lyon; Hugh Dalton
WAR Blockade of Germany by the Ministry of Economic Warfare, Navy and RAF.

FEB

10827
SOMEWHERE IN CAMP (88) (U)
Mancunian (Butcher) I*reissues:* 1944 (cut)

1949 (Sherwood)
P:D: John E. Blakeley
S: Roney Parsons, Anthony Toner, Frank Randle

Harry Korris	Sgt Korris
Frank Randle	Pte Randle
Robbie Vincent	Pte Enoch
Dan Young	Pte Young
John Singer	Pte Jack Trevor
Toni Lupino	Jean Rivers
Peggy Novak	Mrs Rivers
Clifford Buckton	Col Rivers
Gus Aubrey	Pte Lofty
Betty Wheatley	Mrs Randle
Evie Carcroft	Mrs Korris

COMEDY Episodic misadventures of army recruits who stage concert.

MAR

10828
UNPUBLISHED STORY (92) (A)
Two Cities (Col)
P: Anthony Havelock-Allan
D: Harold French
S: Anthony Havelock-Allan, Allan Mackinnon
SC: Anatole de Grunwald, Patrick Kirwan

Richard Greene	Bob Randall
Valerie Hobson	Carol Bennett
Basil Radford	Lamb
Roland Culver	Stannard
Brefni O'Rorke	Denton
Miles Malleson	Farmfield
George Carney	Landlord
Muriel George	Landlady
Andre Morell	Marchand
Frederick Cooper	Trapes
Renee Gadd	Miss Hartley
Aubrey Mallalieu	Warden
George Thorpe	Maj Edwards

WAR 1940. Reporter exposes pacifist organisation as Nazi saboteurs.

10829
FLYING FORTRESS (109) (U)
WB-FN
D: Walter Forde
S: Brock Williams
SC: Gordon Wellesley, Edward Dryhurst, Brock Williams

Richard Greene	Jim Spence
Carla Lehmann	Sidney Kelly
Betty Stockfeld	Lady Deborah Ottershaw
Donald Stewart	Sky Kelly
Charles Heslop	Harrington
Sidney King	Lord Ottershaw
Basil Radford	Wilkinson
Joss Ambler	Sheepshead
Edward Rigby	Dan Billings
Billy Hartnell	Taxi-driver

WAR Cocksure American pilot joins RAF and helps bomb Berlin.

10830
THE MISSING MILLION (84) (A)
Signet (ABFD) *reissue:* 1945 (Ren)
P: Hugh Perceval
D: Phil Brandon
S: (NOVEL) Edgar Wallace
SC: James Seymour

Linden Travers	Joan Walton
John Warwick	Bennett
Patricia Hilliard	Dora Coleman
John Stuart	Insp Dicker
Ivan Brandt	Rex Walton
Brefni O'Rorke	Coleman
Charles Victor	Nobb Knowles
Marie Ault	Mrs Tweedle

CRIME Millionaire's blackmailed fiancee helps police save him from kidnapper.

10831
THEY FLEW ALONE (103) USA: WINGS AND THE WOMAN (U)
Imperator (RKO)
P:D: Herbert Wilcox
S: Lord Castlerosse
SC: Miles Malleson

Anna Neagle	Amy Johnson
Robert Newton	Jim Mollison
Edward Chapman	Mr Johnson
Nora Swinburne	ATA Commandant
Joan Kemp-Welch	Mrs Johnson
Charles Carson	Lord Wakefield
Brefni O'Rorke	Mac
Muriel George	Housekeeper
Martita Hunt	Schoolmistress
Eliot Makeham	Mayor
Ronald Shiner	Mechanic
David Horne	Solicitor
Charles Victor	Postmaster
Miles Malleson	Salesman
Charles Maxwell	BBC Commentator

HISTORY 1930 - 1941. Flying pioneers marry, divorce, and join ATA.

10832
THE NIGHT HAS EYES (79) (A) USA: TERROR HOUSE
ABPC (Pathe)
P: John Argyle
D: Leslie Arliss
S: (NOVEL) Alan Kennington
SC: John Argyle, Leslie Arliss

James Mason	Stephen Deremid
Wilfrid Lawson	Jim Sturrock
Mary Clare	Mrs Ranger
Joyce Howard	Marian Ives
Tucker McGuire	Doris
John Fernald	Dr Barry Randall

CRIME Yorks. Schoolmistress proves housekeeper framed Spanish War veteran for killing her friend.

10833
ONE OF OUR AIRCRAFT IS MISSING (102) (U)
British National (Anglo) I*reissues:* 1945; 1949 (Pat)
P:D:S: Michael Powell, Emeric Pressburger

Godfrey Tearle	Sir George Corbett
Eric Portman	Tom Earnshaw
Hugh Williams	Frank Shelley
Bernard Miles	Geoff Hickman
Hugh Burden	John Glyn Haggard
Emrys Jones	Bob Ashley
Googie Withers	Jo de Vries
Pamela Browne	Else Meertens
Joyce Redman	Jet van Dieren
Hay Petrie	Burgomeister
Arnold Marle	Pieter Sluys
Robert Helpmann	de Jong
Peter Ustinov	Priest
Alec Clunes	Organist
Roland Culver	Officer
Stewart Rome	Cmdr

WAR Holland. Patriots smuggle crew of crashed bomber to freedom.

APR

10834
THOSE KIDS FROM TOWN (82) (U)
British National (Anglo)
P: Richard Vernon
D: Lance Comfort
S: (NOVEL) Adrian Arlington (THESE OUR STRANGERS)
SC: Adrian Arlington

Shirley Lenner	Liz Burns
Jeanne de Casalis	Sheila

Percy Marmont . . . . Earl
D.J. Williams . . . . Butler
Maire O'Neill . . . . Housekeeper
Charles Victor . . . . Vicar
Angela Glynne . . . . Maud Burns
George Cole . . . . Charlie
Harry Fowler . . . . Ern
Olive Sloane . . . . Vicar's Wife
Sydney King . . . . Donald
Bransby Williams . . . . Uncle Sid
Ronald Shiner . . . . Mr Burns
Josephine Wilson . . . . Mrs Burns
A. Bromley Davenport . . . . Egworth
COMEDY Cockney evacuees billeted on
country Earl.

10835
BACK ROOM BOY (82) (U)
Gainsborough (GFD)
P: Edward Black
D: Herbert Mason
S: Val Guest, Marriott Edgar
Arthur Askey . . . . Arthur Pilbeam
Moore Marriott . . . . Jerry
Graham Moffatt . . . . Albert
Googie Withers . . . . Bobbie
Vera Francis . . . . Jane
Joyce Howard . . . . Betty
John Salew . . . . Steve Mason
George Merritt . . . . Uncle
COMEDY Meteorologist unmasks spy in
desolate Scots lighthouse.

10836
THE OWNER GOES ALOFT (6) (U)
Spectator (NSS)
P: Michael Hankinson
D: Gilbert Gunn
G.B. Mulcaster . . . . The Owner
WAR citizen demands to be shown how his
National Savings are spent.

10837
THE FOREMAN WENT TO FRANCE (87) (A)
USA: SOMEWHERE IN FRANCE
Ealing (UA) reissue: 1945
AP: Alberto Cavalcanti
D: Charles Frend
S: J.B. Priestley
SC: John Dighton, Angus Macphail, Leslie
Arliss, Roger Macdougall, Diana Morgan
Tommy Trinder . . . . Tommy
Constance Evans . . . . Fred Carrick
Robert Morley . . . . Mayor
Gordon Jackson . . . . Jock
Ernest Milton . . . . Stationmaster
Charles Victor . . . . Spotter
John Williams . . . . Captain
Paul Bonifas . . . . Prefect
Anita Palacine . . . . Barmaid
Ronald Adam . . . . Sir Charles Fawcett
Francis L. Sullivan . . . . Skipper
Bill Blewett . . . . Spotter
Mervyn Johns . . . . Official
WAR France, 1940. Soldiers help Welsh fore-
man salvage secret machinery (Based on the true
story of Melbourne Johns).

10838
FRONT LINE KIDS (80) (U)
Signet (Butcher)
P: Hugh Perceval
D: Maclean Rogers
S: John Byrd
SC: Kathleen Butler, H.F. Maltby
Leslie Fuller . . . . Nobby Clarkson
Marion Gerth . . . . Elsa la Rue
Antony Holles . . . . Hotelier

Kay Lewis . . . .
Gerald Rex . . . . Bert Wragg
John Singer . . . . Ginger Smith
George Pughe . . . . Pinski
Ralph Michael . . . . Paul
Eric Clavering . . . . Carl
O.B. Clarence . . . .
COMEDY Hotel porter and pageboy's gang
catch foreign jewel thieves.

10839
LET THE PEOPLE SING (105) (U)
British National (Anglo) reissue: 1948
(1162 ft cut)
P:D: John Baxter
S: (NOVEL) J.B. Priestley
SC: John Baxter, Barbara K. Emary,
Geoffrey Orme
Alastair Sim . . . . The Professor
Fred Emney . . . . . . Sir George Denberry-Baxter
Edward Rigby . . . . Timmy Tiverton
Oliver Wakefield . . . . . . Sir Reginald Foxfield
Patricia Roc . . . . Hope Ollerton
Annie Esmond . . . . Lady Foxfield
Marian Spencer . . . . Lady Shepshod
Olive Sloane . . . . Daisy Barley
Maire O'Neill . . . . Mrs Mitterley
Gus McNaughton . . . . Ketley
Charles Hawtrey . . . . Orton
Peter Gawthorne . . . . Maj Shiptonthorpe
Aubrey Mallalieu . . . . Cdr Spofforth
G.H. Mulcaster . . . . Inspector
Wally Patch . . . . Sam
Horace Kenney . . . . Walter
Morris Harvey . . . . Jim Flagg
Ida Barr . . . . Katie
COMEDY Unemployed comedian and drunken
bart stop village council from closing public hall.
MAY
10840
THE DAY WILL DAWN (98) (U) USA: THE
AVENGERS
Niksos Films (GFD) reissue: 1948 (GN)
P: Paul Soskin
D: Harold French
S: Frank Owen
SC: Terence Rattigan, Anatole de Grunwald,
Patrick Kirwan
Ralph Richardson . . . . Lockwood
Deborah Kerr . . . . Kari Alstead
Hugh Williams . . . . Colin Metcalfe
Griffiths Jones . . . . Inspector Gunter
Francis L. Sullivan . . . . Wettau
Roland Culver . . . . Naval Attache
Niall McGinnis . . . . Olaf
Finlay Currie . . . . Alstead
Bernard Miles . . . . McAllister
Patricia Medina . . . . Ingrid
Elizabeth Mann . . . . Gerda
Henry Oscar . . . . Editor
John Warwick . . . . Milligan
David Horne . . . . Editor
WAR Norway. Reporter and skipper's daughter
destroy U-boat base, and are saved by
commandos.

10841
THE NEXT OF KIN (102) (A)
Ealing (UA) reissue: 1954 (NR)
AP: S.C. Balcon
D: Thorold Dickinson
S: Thorold Dickinson, Basil Bartlett, Angus
Macphail, John Dighton
Mervyn Johns . . . . Mr Davis
Nova Pilbeam . . . . Beppie Leemans
Reginald Tate . . . . Maj Richards
Stephen Murray . . . . Mr Barratt
Geoffrey Hibbert . . . . Pte John

Philip Friend . . . . Lt Cummins
Phyllis Stanley . . . . Miss Clare
Mary Clare . . . . Ma Webster
Basil Sydney . . . . Capt
Joss Ambler . . . . Mr Vernon
Brefni O'Rorke . . . . Brigadier
Alexander Field . . . . Pte Durnford
David Hutcheson . . . . Intelligence Officer
Jack Hawkins . . . . Major
Frederick Leister . . . . Colonel
Torin Thatcher . . . . General
Charles Victor . . . . Seaman
WAR Careless talk betrays commando raid to
fifth columnists.

10842
ALIBI (82) (A)
Corona Productions (BL) reissue: 1945 (Ren; 6
mins cut)
P: Josef Somlo,
D: Brian Desmond Hurst
S: (NOVEL) Marcel Archard (L'ALIBI)
SC: Lesley Storm, Jacques Companeez, Justine
& Carter
Margaret Lockwood . . . . . . Helene Ardouin
Hugh Sinclair . . . . Insp Calas
James Mason . . . . Andre Laurent
Raymond Lovell . . . . Prof Winkler
Enid Stamp Taylor . . . . Dany
Hartley Power . . . . Gordon
Jane Carr . . . . Delia
Rodney Ackland . . . . Kretz
Edana Romney . . . . Assistant
Elizabeth Welch . . . . Singer
Olga Lindo . . . . Mme Laureau
Muriel George . . . . Mme Bertonnet
George Merritt . . . . Bourdille
CRIME Paris, 1937. Night club hostess helps
inspector trap murderous mind-reader.

JUN
10843
THE YOUNG MR PITT (118) (U)
20th Century Productions (20)
P: Edward Black
D: Carol Reed
S: Viscount Castlerosse
SC: Frank Launder, Sidney Gilliat
Robert Donat . . . . William Pitt /Earl of
                                        Chatham
Robert Morley . . . . Charles Fox
Phyllis Calvert . . . . Eleanor Eden
John Mills . . . . William Wilberforce
Raymond Lovell . . . . George III
Max Adrian . . . . Richard Sheridan
Felix Aylmer . . . . Lord North
Albert Lieven . . . . Talleyrand
Stephen Haggard . . . . Horatio Nelson
Geoffrey Atkins . . . . Pitt (child)
Jean Cadell . . . . Mrs Sparry
Agnes Lauchlan . . . . Queen Charlotte
A. Bromley Davenport . . . . Sir Evan Nepean
Frank Pettingell . . . . Coachman
Leslie Bradley . . . . Gentleman Jackson
Roy Emerton . . . . Dan Mendoza
Hugh McDermott . . . . Mr Melvill
HISTORY 1776-1805. Earl's son rises to become
Prime Minister.

10844
SUSPECTED PERSON (75) (A)
ABPC (Pathe)
P: Warwick Ward
D:S: Lawrence Huntington
Clifford Evans . . . . Jim Raynor
Patricia Roc . . . . Joan Raynor
David Farrar . . . . Insp Thompson
Anne Firth . . . . Carol

Robert Beatty . . . . Franklin
Eric Clavering . . . . Dolan
Leslie Perrins . . . . Tony Garrett
Eliot Makeham . . . . David
John Salew . . . . Jones
CRIME Swindled reporter finds American bank
robber's loot and is stopped from keeping it by
sister.

10845
GO TO BLAZES! (8) (U)
Ealing (NSS)
P: Michael Balcon
D: Walter Forde
S: Angus Macphail, Diana Morgan
Will Hay . . . . Father
COMEDY Father demonstrates how to deal
with incendiaries.

10846
PARTNERS IN CRIME (8) (U)
Gainsborough (NSS)
P: Edward Black
D:S: Frank Launder, Sidney Gilliat
Basil Radford . . . . Charters
Naunton Wayne . . . . Caldicott
COMEDY Purchasers in Black Market are as
guilty as sellers.

JUL

10847
PATHETONE PARADE OF 1942 (41) (U)
Pathe
D: Fred Watts
Roy Rich . . . . Compere
Two Leslies . . . . Arthur Prince & Jim
Eric Woodburn . . . . Jeanne de Casaslis
Robert Wilson . . . . Jasper Maskeleyne
Robb Wilton . . . . Florence de Jong
Foden's Prize Band . . . . . . Gipsy Nina
REVUE

10848
GERT AND DAISY CLEAN UP (85) (U)
Butcher's Film Service
P: F.W. Baker
D: Maclean Rogers
S: Kathleen Butler, H.F. Maltby
Elsie Waters . . . . Gert
Doris Waters . . . . Daisy
Iris Vandeleur . . . . Ma Butler
Elizabeth Hunt . . . . Hettie
Joss Ambler . . . . Mr Perry
Ralph Michael . . . . Jack Gregory
Tonie Edgar Bruce . . . . Mrs Wilberforce
Douglas Stewart . . . . Mayor
Harry Herbert . . . . Old Cheerful
Angela Glynne . . . . Girl
Uriel Porter . . . . Snow White
MUSICAL Sisters stop black marketeer from
cornering canned fruit cargo.

10849
SABOTAGE AT SEA (74) (U)
British National-Shaftesbury (Anglo)
P: Elizabeth Hiscott
D: Leslie Hiscott
S: Michael Barringer
Jane Carr . . . . Diane
David Hutcheson . . . . Capt Tracey
Margaretta Scott . . . . Jane Dighton
Wally Patch . . . . Steward
Ronald Shiner . . . . Cook
Felix Aylmer . . . . John Dighton
Martita Hunt . . . . Daphne Faber
Ralph Truman . . . . Chandler
Billy Hartnell . . . . Digby
Arthur Maude . . . . Engineer
WAR Merchant captain sails with sabotaged
screwshaft to force saboteur to confess.

10850
UNCENSORED (108) (U)
Gainsborough (GFD)
P: Edward Black
D: Anthony Asquith
S: (NOVEL) Oscar Millard
SC: Wolfgang Wilhelm, Terence Rattigan, Rodney
Ackland
Eric Portman . . . . Andre Delange
Phyllis Calvert . . . . Julie Lanvin
Griffith Jones . . . . Father de Gruyte
Raymond Lovell . . . . Von Koerlner
Peter Glenville . . . . Charles Neels
Frederick Culley . . . . Victor Lanvin
Irene Handl . . . . Frau von Koerner
Carl Jaffe . . . . Kohlmeier
Felix Aylmer . . . . Col Hohenstein
Eliot Makeham . . . . Abbede Moor
J.H. Roberts . . . . Father Corot
Walter Hudd . . . . Van Heemskirk
Phyllis Monkman . . . . Pony Girl
WAR Brussels. Editor writes for Nazi paper and
secret news-sheet run by patriots.

10851
MUCH TOO SHY (92) (U)
Columbia British *reissues:* 1947; 1950 (GN)
P: Ben Henry
D: Marcel Varnel
S: Ronald Frankau
George Formby . . . . George Andy
Kathleen Harrison . . . . Amelia Peabody
Hilda Bayley . . . . Lady Driscoll
Eileen Bennett . . . . Jackie Somers
Joss Ambler . . . . Sir George Driscoll
Jimmy Clitheroe . . . . Jimmy
Frederick Burtwell . . . . Mr Harefield
Brefni O'Rorke . . . . Mr Somers
Eric Clavering . . . . Robert Latimer
Gibb McLaughlin . . . . Rev Sheepshanks
Peter Gawthorne . . . . Counsel
Gus McNaughton . . . . Manager
COMEDY Student adds nude bodies to handyman's
portraits and sells them as soap advertisements.

10852
SALUTE JOHN CITIZEN (98) (A)
British National (Anglo)
P: Wallace Orton
D: Maurice Elvey
S: (NOVELS) Robert Greenwood (MR
BUNTING; MR BUNTING AT WAR)
SC: Clemence Dane, Elizabeth Baron
Edward Rigby . . . . Mr Bunting
Stanley Holloway . . . . Oskey
George Robey . . . . Corder
Mabel Constanduros . . . . . . Mrs Bunting
Jimmy Hanley . . . . Ernest Bunting
Dinah Sheridan . . . . Evie
Eric Micklewood . . . . Chris Bunting
Peggy Cummins . . . . Julie Bunting
Charles Deane . . . . Bert Rollo
Stewart Rome . . . . Col Saunders
WAR Sacked clerk returns to work, and his
pacifist son is 'cured' by the blitz.

10853
TALK ABOUT JACQUELINE (84) (A)
Excelsior (MGM)
P: Marcel Hellman
D: Harold French
S: (NOVEL) Katherine Holland
SC: Roland Pertwee, Marjorie Deans
Hugh Williams . . . . Dr Michael Thomas
Carla Lehmann . . . . Jacqueline Marlow
Joyce Howard . . . . June Marlow
Roland Culver . . . . .Leslie Waddington
John Warwick . . . . Donald Clark
Mary Jerrold . . . . Aunt Helen

Guy Middleton . . . . Capt Tony Brock
Max Adrian . . . . Lionel
Antony Holles . . . . Attendant
Katie Johnson . . . . Ethel
COMEDY Girl takes blame for sister's past
when she weds doctor.

AUG

10854
THE GOOSE STEPS OUT (79) (U)
Ealing (UA) *reissues:* 1946 (ABFD) 1955 (NR)
1961 (EB)
AP: S.C. Balcon
D: Will Hay, Basil Dearden
S: Bernard Miles, Reginald Groves
SC: Angus Macphail, John Dighton
Will Hay . . . . William Potts/Muller
Frank Pettingell . . . . Prof Hoffman
Julien Mitchell . . . . Gen von Glotz
Charles Hawtrey . . . . Max
Peter Croft . . . . Hans
Anne Firth . . . . Lena
Leslie Harcourt . . . . Vagel
Jeremy Hawk . . . . ADC
Raymond Lovell . . . . Schmidt
Aubrey Mallalieu . . . . Rector
Barry Morse . . . . Kurt
Lawrence O'Madden . . . . . . Col Truscott
Peter Ustinov . . . . Krauss
COMEDY Teacher sent to Germany in place
of his Nazi double, to steal secret weapon.

10855
THE NOSE HAS IT (7) (U)
Gainsborough (NSS)
P: Edward Black
D:S: Val Guest
Arthur Askey . . . . Himself
COMEDY Comedian lectures on dangers of
sneezing.

10856
ROSE OF TRALEE (77) (U)
Butcher *reissues:* 1944 (Sherwood; 1365 ft cut)
1948 (Butch)
D: Germain Burger
S: Oswald Mitchell, Ian Walker   P: F.W. Baker
SC: Kathleen Butler, H.F. Maltby
John Longden . . . . Paddy O'Brien
Lesley Brook . . . . Mary O'Brien
Angela Glynne . . . . Rose O'Brien
Mabel Constanduros . . . . Mrs Thompson
Talbot O'Farrell . . . . Tim Kelly
Gus McNaughton . . . . Gleeson
George Carney . . . . Collett
Virginia Keily . . . . Jean Hale
Iris Vandeleur . . . . Mrs Crawley
Morris Harvey . . . . McIsaac
MUSICAL Irish singer reunites with his wife
and child after making good in America.

10857
THE PETERVILLE DIAMOND (85) (U)
WB-FN
D: Walter Forde
S: Brock Williams, Gordon Wellesley
Ann Crawford . . . . Teri
Donald Stewart . . . . Charles
Renee Houston . . . . Lady Margaret
Oliver Wakefield . . . . The Robber
Charles Heslop . . . . Dilfallow
Bill Hartnell . . . . Joseph
Felix Aylmer . . . . President
Charles Victor . . . . Dan
Joss Ambler . . . . Police Chief
Paul Sheridan . . . . Luis
COMEDY Mexico. Neglected wife flirts with
gentleman jewel thief.

10858
THE FIRST OF THE FEW (117) (U) USA:
SPITFIRE
Misbourne-British Aviation (GFD) *reissues:*
1947 (Eal; 27 mins cut) 1953 (EB)
P: Leslie Howard, George King, John Stafford,
Adrian Brunel
D: Leslie Howard
S: Henry C. James, Katherine Strueby
SC: Anatole de Grunwald, Miles Malleson
Leslie Howard . . . . R.J. Mitchell
David Niven . . . . Geoffrey Crisp
Rosamund John . . . . Diana Mitchell
Roland Culver . . . . Cdr Bride
Anne Firth . . . . Miss Harper
David Horne . . . . Higgins
John H. Roberts . . . . Sir Robert Maclean
Derrick de Marney . . . . S/L Jefferson
Rosalyn Boulter . . . . Mable Livesey
Tonie Edgar Bruce . . . . Lady Houston
Gordon McLeod . . . . Maj Buchan
Erik Freund . . . . Messerschmidt
Filippo del Guidice . . . . Bertorelli
Brefni O'Rourke . . . . Specialist
Gerry Wilmott . . . . Announcer
HISTORY 1922-1940. Biography of designer of
Spitfire fighter.

SEP

10859
SECRET MISSION(94) (U)
IP-Excelsior (GFD) *reissue:* 1947 (Eros)
P: Marcel Hellman
D: Harold French
S: Shaun Terence Young
SC: Anatole de Grunwald, Basil Bartlett
Hugh Williams . . . . Peter Garnett
James Mason . . . . Raoul de Carnet
Michael Wilding . . . . Nobby Clark
Carla Lehmann . . . . Michele de Carnet
Nancy Price . . . . Violette
Roland Culver . . . . Red Gowan
Betty Warren . . . . Mrs Clark
Karel Stepanek . . . . Maj Lang
Percy Walsh . . . . Fayolle
Beatrice Varley . . . . Mrs Donkin
Brefni O'Rourke . . . . Father Jouvet
F.R. Wendhausen . . . . Gen von Reichmann
John Salew . . . . Capt Grune
Herbert Lom . . . . MO
Stewart Granger . . . . Lt Jackson
WAR France. Four agents don disguises to rescue
captured colleague.

10860
THE GREAT MR HANDEL (103) (U) *tech*
IP-GHW (Productions GFD)
P: James B. Sloan
D: Norman Walker
S: (RADIO PLAY) L. Du Garde Peach
SC: Gerald Elliott, Victor MacClure
Wilfrid Lawson . . . . George Handel
Elizabeth Allan . . . . Mrs Cibber
Malcolm Keen . . . . Lord Chesterfield
Michael Shepley . . . . Sir Charles
Morris Harvey . . . . Heidegger
Hay Petrie . . . . Phineas
Max Kirby . . . . Prince Frederick
A.E. Matthews . . . . Charles Jennens
Frederick Cooper . . . . Pooley
Robert Atkins . . . .
H.F. Maltby . . . .
Trefor Jones . . . . Singer
HISTORY Composer offends Prince of Wales but
is restored to favour after writing "The Messiah"

10861
LADY FROM LISBON (75) (U)
British National-Shaftesbury (Anglo)

P: Elizabeth Hiscott
D: Leslie Hiscott
S: Michael Barringer
Francis L. Sullivan . . . . Minghetti
Jane Carr . . . . Tamara
Martita Hunt . . . . .Susan Wellington-Smythe
Charles Victor . . . . Porter
Antony Holles . . . . Anzoni
George Street . . . . Hauptmann
Gerhard Kempinsky . . . . . . Flugel
Leo de Porkony . . . . Mario
Wilfrid Hyde White . . . . Ganier
COMEDY Lisbon. Millionaire agrees to spy for
Nazis in return for the "Mona Lisa".

10862
THUNDER ROCK (112) (A)
Charter (MGM) *reissue:* 1947
P: John Boulting
D: Roy Boulting
S: (PLAY) Robert Ardrey
SC: Wolfgang Wilhelm, Jeffrey Dell, Bernard Miles,
Anna Reiner
Michael Redgrave . . . . David Charleston
Barbara Mullen . . . . Ellen Kirby
James Mason . . . . Streeter
Lilli Palmer . . . . Melanie Kurtz
Finlay Currie . . . . Capt Joshua
Frederick Valk . . . . Dr Kurtz
Sybilla Binder . . . . Anne-Marie
Frederick Cooper . . . . Ted Briggs
Jean Sheperd . . . . Mrs Briggs
Barry Morse . . . . Robert
George Carney . . . . Harry
Miles Malleson . . . . Chairman
A.E. Matthews . . . . Kirby
Olive Sloane . . . . Director
FANTASY Canada, 1939. Writer rejects world
and peoples his lighthouse with victims of 1849
shipwreck.

OCT

10863
IN WHICH WE SERVE (114) (U)
Two Cities (BL) *reissue:* 1947 (1187 ft cut)
P: Noel Coward
D: Noel Coward, David Lean
S: Noel Coward
Noel Coward . . . . Capt Kinross
John Mills . . . . Shorty Blake
Bernard Miles . . . . Walter Hardy
Celia Johnson . . . . Alix Kinross
Kay Walsh . . . . Freda Lewis
Joyce Carey . . . . Kath Hardy
Michael Wilding . . . . Flags
Penelope Dudley Ward . . . . . Maureen Fenwick
Philip Friend . . . . Torps
Derek Elphinstone . . . . No. 1
Frederick Piper . . . . Edgecombe
Geoffrey Hibbert . . . . Joey Mackridge
George Carney . . . . Mr Blake
Kathleen Harrison . . . . Mrs Blake
George Carney . . . . Uncle Fred
James Donald . . . . Doctor
Richard Attenborough . . . . . Stoker
Walter Fitzgerald . . . . Col Lumsden
Ann Stephens . . . . Lavinia Kinross
Daniel Massey . . . . Bobby Kinross
WAR Crete, 1941. Story of destroyer told
through memories of her wrecked crew. (Top
moneymaker: 1943).

10864
ESCAPE TO JUSTICE (45) (A)
Piccadilly (Renown)
P: Thelma Svenson
D: C. Pattinson Knight
S: Henry Halstead
Kent Stevenson . . . . Carl Banner

Van Boolen . . . . Charles
Johnny Claes . . . . Frederick Stack
CRIME Nightclub owner escapes from
internment camp and is killed in air raid.

10865
WE'LL SMILE AGAIN (93) (U)
British National (Anglo)
P:D: John Baxter
S: Austin Melford, Barbara K. Emary, Bud
Flanagan
Bud Flanagan . . . . Bob Parker
Chesney Allen . . . . Gordon Maxwell
Phyllis Stanley . . . . Gina Cavendish
Horace Kenney . . . . George
Charles Austin . . . . Butler
Edgar Driver . . . . Porter
Wally Patch . . . . Porter
Peggy Dexter . . . . Googie
C. Denier Warren . . . . Waiter
Meinhart Maur . . . . Steiner
Julien Vedey . . . . Hoffman
Gordon McLeod . . . . Holtzman
Gwen Catley; Billy Mayerl; Malcolm (Jetsam)
McEachern
COMEDY Unemployed man becomes film star
and unmasks foreign studio employees as spies.

NOV

10866
SOMEWHERE ON LEAVE (96) (U)
Mancunian (Butcher) *reissue:* 1946 (cut)
P:D: John E. Blakeley
S: Roney Parsons, Anthony Toner, Frank
Randle
Frank Randle . . . . Pte Randle
Harry Korris . . . . Sgt Korris
Robbie Vincent . . . . Pte Enoch
Dan Young . . . . Pte Young
Toni Lupino . . . . Toni Beaumont
Pat McGrath . . . . Roy Desmond
Noel Dainton . . . . Capt Delvaine
Tonie Edgar Bruce . . . . Mrs Delvaine
Percival Mackey and his Orchestra
COMEDY Episodic mishaps of soldiers on leave
at rich friend's home.

10867
WE'LL MEET AGAIN (84) (U)
Columbia British
P: Ben Henry, George Formby
D: Phil Brandon
S: Derek Sheils
SC: James Seymour, Howard Thomas
Vera Lynn . . . . Peggy Brown
Geraldo . . . . Gerry
Patricia Roc . . . . Ruth
Ronald Ward . . . . Frank
Donald Gray . . . . Bruce McIntosh
Frederick Leister . . . . Mr Hastropp
Betty Jardine . . . . Miss Bohne
Brefni O'Rorke . . . . Dr Drake
Marian Spencer . . . . Mrs Crump
Lesley Osmond . . . . Sally
Geraldo's Orchestra; John Watt; John Sharman;
Alvar Liddell
MUSICAL Radio singer loses Scots soldier to
her best friend.

10868
WENT THE DAY WELL? (92) (A) USA:
48 HOURS
Ealing (UA) *reissue:* 1948
AP: S.C. Balcon
D: Cavalcanti
S: Graham Greene
SC: Angus Macphail, John Dighton, Diana
Morgan
Leslie Banks . . . . Oliver Winsford

Elizabeth Allan . . . . Peggy
Frank Lawton . . . . Tom Sturry
Basil Sydney . . . . Ortler
Valier Taylor . . . . Nora Ashton
Mervyn Johns . . . . Sims
Edward Rigby . . . . Poacher
Marie Lohr . . . . Mrs Frazer
C.V. France . . . . Vicar
David Farrar . . . . Jung
Muriel George . . . . Mrs Collins
Thora Hird . . . . Land Girl
Harry Fowler . . . . George Truscott
WAR Villagers fight back when their squire helps
German paratroopers take over.

10869
SQUADRON LEADER X (100) (A)
RKO—Radio
P: Victor Hanbury
D: Lance Comfort
S: Emeric Pressburger
SC: Wolfgang Wilhelm, Miles Malleson
Eric Portman . . . . Erich Korner
Ann Dovrak . . . . Barbara Lucas
Walter Fitzgerald . . . . Inspector Milne
Barry Jones . . . . Bruce Fenwick
Henry Oscar . . . . Dr Schultz
Beatrice Varley . . . . Mrs Krohn
David Peel . . . . Michael Berthlot
Martin Miller . . . . Mr Krohn
Frederick Richter . . . . Insp Seigel
Charles Victor . . . . Marks
Marjorie Rhodes . . . . Mrs Agnew
Mary Merrall . . . . Miss Thorndike
WAR Nazi hero posing as British pilot tries to
contact agents and return to Germany.

10870
WOMEN AREN'T ANGELS (85) (A)
ABPC (Pathe)
P: Warwick Ward
D: Lawrence Huntington
S: (PLAY) Vernon Sylvaine
SC: Vernon Sylvaine, Bernerd Mainwaring,
Lawrence Huntington
Robertson Hare . . . . Wilmer Popday
Alfred Drayton . . . . Alfred Bandle
Polly Ward . . . . Frankie Delane
Joyce Heron . . . . Karen
Mary Hinton . . . . Thelma Bandle
Peggy Novak . . . . Elizabeth Popday
Ethel Coleridge . . . . Mrs Featherstone

Charles Murray . . . . Bertie
Ralph Michael . . . . Jack
John Stuart . . . . Maj Gaunt
Leslie Perrins . . . . Schaffer
COMEDY Music publishers join Home Guard
and catch fifth columnists.

10871
ASKING FOR TROUBLE (81) (U)
British National (Anglo)
P: Wallace Orton
D: Oswald Mitchell
S: Oswald Mitchell, Con West
Max Miller . . . . Dick Smith
Carol Lynne . . . . Jane Smythe
Mark Lester . . . . Gen Smythe
Wilfrid Hyde White . . : . . . . Pettifer
Billy Percy . . . . George
Eleanor Hallam . . . . Margarita
Aubrey Mallalieu . . . . Gen Fortescue
Kenneth Kove . . . . Capt Fortescue
Chick Elliott . . . . Mandy Lou
Raymond Glendenning . . . . Commentator
COMEDY Bookie poses as big game hunter to
save General's daughter from marrying real
hunter.

DEC

10872
TOMORROW WE LIVE (85) (U) USA: AT
DAWN WE DIE
British Aviation (BL) reissue: 1946 (NR)
P: George King, John Stafford
D: George King
S: "Jean Baptiste"
SC: Anatole de Grunwald, Katherine Strueby
John Clements . . . . Jean Baptiste
Greta Gynt . . . . Maria Duchesne
Hugh Sinclair . . . . Maj von Kleist
Judy Kelly . . . . Germaine
Godfrey Tearle . . . . Pierre Duchesne
Yvonne Arnaud . . . . Mme Labouche
Bransby Williams . . . . Matthieu
Gabrielle Brune . . . . Frisette
Karel Stepanek . . . . Seitz
F.R. Wendhausen . . . . Commandant
Allan Jeayes . . . . Pogo
Brefni O'Rorke . . . . Moreau
Gibb McLaughlin . . . . Dupont
WAR France. Mayor's daughter poses as
collaborator to help man escape to England
with U-Boat information.

10873
KING ARTHUR WAS A GENTLEMAN (99) (U)
Gainsborough (GFD)
P: Edward Black
D: Marcel Varnel
S: Val Guest, Marriott Edgar
Arthur Askey . . . . Arthur King
Evelyn Dall . . . . Susan Ashley
Anne Shelton . . . . Gwen Duncannon
Max Bacon . . . . Maxie
Jack Train . . . . Jack
Peter Graves . . . . Lance
Vera Frances . . . . Vera
Al Burnett . . . . Slim
Brefni O'Rorke . . . . Col Duncannon
Ronald Shiner . . . . Sgt
Freddie Crump; Ernie (Victor) Feldman
COMEDY Africa. Meek soldier, believing he has
King Arthur's magic sword, saves friends from
captivity.

10874
THE BALLOON GOES UP (58) (U)
New Realm
P: E.J. Fancey
D: Redd Davis
S: Val Valentine
Ethel Revnell . . . . Ethel
Gracie West . . . . Gracie
Donald Peers . . . . Sgt Jim
Ronald Shiner . . . . Sgt Shiner
Elsie Wagstaffe . . . . Welfare Officer
Mrs Masemore Morris . . . . . . Lady Hurst
Gordon McLeod . . . . Doctor
MUSICAL Entertainers catch spies while posing
as WAAFS on balloon site.

10875
WHAT PRICE CRIME? (series) (A)
British Foundation (20th)
P:D: Ronald Haines.

10876
1—THE SOHO MURDERS (16)

10877
2—MURDER IN MAYFAIR (17)

10878
3—THE SAFE BLOWER (20)

10879
4—VENDETTA (18)
CRIME

1943

JAN

10880
OLD MOTHER RILEY DETECTIVE (80) (U)
British National (Anglo)
P: John Baxter
D: Lance Comfort
S: Austin Melford, Geoffrey Orme,
Barbara K. Emary, Arthur Lucan
Arthur Lucan . . . . Mrs Riley
Kitty McShane . . . . Kitty Riley
Ivan Brandt . . . . Insp Victor Cole
Owen Reynolds . . . . Kenworthy
George Street . . . . Insp Moresby
Johnnie Schofield . . . . PC Jimmy Green
Hal Gordon . . . . Bill
Valentine Dunn . . . . Elsie
Marjorie Rhodes . . . . Cook
H.F. Maltby . . . . H.G. Popplethwaite
Peggy Cummins . . . . Lily
Alfredo Campoli
COMEDY Food office cleaner helps police
catch black marketeers.

FEB

10881
IT'S THAT MAN AGAIN (84) (U)
Gainsborough (GFD)
P: Edward Black
D: Walter Forde
S: (RADIO SERIES) Ted Kavanagh
SC: Howard Irving Young, Ted Kavanagh
Tommy Handley . . . . Mayor Handley
Greta Gynt . . . . Stella Ferris
Jack Train . . . . Lefty/Funf
Sidney Keith . . . . Sam Scram
Horace Percival . . . . Ali Oop/Cecil
Dorothy Summers . . . . Mrs Mop
Dino Galvani . . . . Signor Soso
Clarence Wright . . . . Clarence
Leonard Sharp . . . . Claude
Claude Bailey . . . . C.B. Cato
Vera Frances . . . . Daisy
Jean Kent . . . . Kitty
COMEDY Mayor and Swindled students put on
show to save bombed theatre.

10882
NINE MEN (68) (A)
Ealing (UA) reissue: 1946 (ABFD)
AP: Charles Crichton
D: SC: Harry Watt
S: Gerald Kersh
Jack Lambert . . . . Sgt Jack Watson
Gordon Jackson . . . . Young 'Un
Frederick Piper . . . . Banger Hill
Grant Sutherland. . . . . Jock Scott
Bill Blewett . . . . Bill Parker
Eric Micklewood . . . . Booky Lee
John Varley . . . . Dusty Johnstone
Jack Horsman . . . . Joe Harvey
Richard Wilkinson . . . . John Crawford
WAR Libya. Sgt and seven soldiers in desert
tomb hold off Italians until help arrives.

MAR

10883
THE SILVER FLEET (87) (U)
IP—Archers (GFD) reissue: 1949 (Eros)
P: Michael Powell, Emeric Pressburger,
Ralph Richardson
D: S: Vernon Sewell, Gordon Wellesley
Ralph Richardson. . . . . . . Jaap van Leyden
Googie Withers . . . . Helene van Leyden
Esmond Knight . . . . Von Schiller
Beresford Egan . . . . Kramf
Frederick Burtwell . . . . . . Capt Muller
Kathleen Byron . . . . Schoolmistress

Willem Akkerman .. . . Willem van Leyden
Dorothy Gordon . . . . Janni Peters
Charles Victor . . . . Bastiaan Peters
John Longden . . . . Jost Meertens
Joss Ambler . . . . Cornelius Smit
Margaret Emden . . . . Bertha
Ivor Barnard . . . . Admiral von Rapp
Valentine Dyall . . . . Markgraf
WAR Holland. Shipping magnate poses as
traitor to destroy his new U Boat.

10884
VARIETY JUBILEE (92) (U)
Butcher reissues: 1945 (2042) ft cut); 1949
D: Maclean Rogers   P: F.W. Baker
S: Mabel Constanduros
SC: Kathleen Butler
Reginald Purdell . . . . Joe Swan
Ellis Irving . . . . Kit Burns
Lesley Brook . . . . Evelyn Vincent
Marie Lloyd jr . . . . Marie Lloyd
Tom E. Finglass . . . . Eugene Stratton
John Rorke . . . . Gus Elen
Betty Warren . . . . Florrie Forde
George Robey
Charles Coborn
Ella Retford
Charles Shadwell
Joan Winters
Nat D. Ayer
Slim Rhyder
Tessa Deane
Ganjou Bros & Juanita
Wilson, Keppel & Betty
Band of HM Coldstream Guards
MUSICAL Love behind the scenes at a Music
Hall from Boer War to date.

10885
GET CRACKING (96) (U)
Columbia British
P: Ben Henry
D: Marcel Varnel
S: L. DuGarde Peach
George Formby . . . . George Singleton
Edward Rigby . . . . Sam Elliott
Frank Pettingell . . . . Alf Pemberton
Ronald Shiner . . . . Everett Manley
Dinah Sheridan . . . . Mary Pemberton
Wally Patch . . . . Sgt Joe Preston
Mike Johnson . . . . Josh
Irene Handl . . . . Maggie Turner
Vera Frances . . . . Irene
COMEDY Village Home Guard wins manoeuvres
against rival village.

10886
THURSDAY'S CHILD (81) (U)
ABPC (Pathe) reissue: 1946
P: John Argyle
D: Rodney Ackland
S: (NOVEL) Donald Macardle
SC: Donald Macardle, Rodney Ackland
Sally Ann Howes . . . . Fennis Wilson
Wilfrid Lawson . . . . Frank Wilson
Kathleen O'Regan . . . . Ellen Wilson
Eileen Bennett . . . . Phoebe Wilson
Stewart Granger . . . . David Penley
Marianne Davis . . . . Gloria Dewey
Gerhardt Kempinski . . . . . Rudi Kaufmann
Felix Aylmer . . . . Mr Keith
Margaret Yarde . . . . Mrs Chard
Vera Bogetti . . . . Mme Felicia
Percy Walsh . . . . Charles Lennox
Ronald Shiner . . . . Joe
Pat Aherne . . . . Lance Sheridan
DRAMA Child's success in films causes trouble
for her family.

10887
THE NIGHT INVADER (81) (U)
WB—FN
D: Herbert Mason
S: (NOVEL) John Bentley (RENDEZVOUS
WITH DEATH)
SC: Brock Williams, Edward Dryhurst,
Roland Pertwee
Anne Crawford . . . . Karen Lindley
David Farrar . . . . Dick Marlow
Carl Jaffe . . . . Count von Biebrich
Sybilla Binder . . . . Baroness von Klaveren
Jenny Lovelace . . . . Liesje von Klaveren
Marius Goring . . . . Oberleutenant
Martin Walker . . . . Jimmy Archer
John Salew . . . . Witsen
George Carney . . . . Conductor
Kynaston Reeves . . . . Sir Michael
WAR Holland. American girl helps British
agent capture Nazi Count.

10888
WHEN WE ARE MARRIED (98) (U)
British National (Anglo)
P: John Baxter
D: Lance Comfort
S: (PLAY) J.B. Priestley
SC: Austin Melford, Barbara K. Emary
Sydney Howard . . . . .Henry Ormonroyd
Raymond Huntley . . . . Albert Parker
Olga Lindo . . . . Maria Helliwell
Marian Spencer . . . . Annie Parker
Ethel Coleridge . . . . Clara Soppitt
Lloyd Pearson . . . . Joe Helliwell
Ernest Butcher . . . . Herbert Soppitt
Barry Morse . . . . Gerald Forbes
Lesley Brook . . . . Nancy Holmes
Marjorie Rhodes . . . . Mrs Northrup
Charles Voctor . . . . Mr Northrup
Cyril Smith . . . . Fred Dyson
George Carney . . . . Landlord
A. Bromley Davenport . . . . . Mayor
COMEDY Yorks, 1890. Three couples
celebrating Silver Weddings learn their
marriages are void.

10889
THE DUMMY TALKS (85) (A)
British National (Anglo)
P: Wallace Orton
D: Oswald Mitchell
S: Con West, Jack Clifford
SC: Michael Barringer
Jack Warner . . . . Jack
Claude Hulbert . . . . Victor Harbord
Beryl Orde . . . . Beryl
Derna Hazel . . . . Maya
Ivy Benson . . . . Ivy
Manning Whiley . . . . Russell Warren
Charles Carson . . . . Marvello
G.H. Mulcaster . . . . Piers Harriman
John Carol . . . . Jimmy Royce
Ivy Benson's All Ladies Orchestra
Manley & Austin   Skating Avalons
Sylvester & Nephew   5 Lai Founs
CRIME Midget poses as dummy to unmask
killer of blackmailing ventroloquist.

APR

10890
PLAYTIME FOR WORKERS (51) (U)
Federated reissue: 1949 (28 mins cut)
P: D: Harold Baim
Gerry Wilmot   Kay Cavendish
Scott Sanders   Bill Smith
Stan Shedden and his Orchestra
REVUE.

10891
HAPPIDROME (87) (U)
Aldwych (MGM)
P: Harold Boxall, Jack Buchanan, Tom Arnold
D: Phil Brandon
S: (RADIO SERIES) Harry Korris
SC: Tom Arnold, James Seymour
Harry Korris . . . .   Mr Lovejoy
Robbie Vincent . . . .   Enoch
Cecil Frederick . . . .   Ramsbottom
Bunty Meadows . . . .   Bunty Mossup
Lisa Lee . . . . .Tanya/Josephine
Jennie Gregson . . . .   Mrs Bane
Joss Ambler . . . .   Mr Mossup
Valentine Dunn . . . .   Mrs Mossup
Leslie "Hutch" Hutchinson
Cairoli Brothers
COMEDY Rich Man finances his daughter in a
tragedy that achieves success as a burlesque.

10892
WE DIVE AT DAWN (98) (U)
Gainsborough (GFD)
P: Edward Black
D: Anthony Asquith
S: J.B. Williams, Val Valentine, Frank Launder
Eric Portman . . . .   James Hobson
John Mills . . . . Lt Freddie Taylor
Reginald Purdell . . . . .CPO Dicky Dabbs
Niall MacGinnis . . . . PO Mike Corrigan
Joan Hopkins . . . .   Ethel Dabbs
Josephine Wilson . . . .   Alice Hobson
Louis Bradfield . . . .   Lt Brace
Ronald Millar . . . .   Lt Johnson
Jack Watling . . . .   Lt Gordon
Caven Watson . . . .   CPO Duncan
Leslie Weston . . . .   Tug Wilson
Norman Williams . . . .   Canada
Lionel Grose . . . .   Spud
Beatrice Varley . . . .   Mrs Dabbs
Frederick Burtwell . . . .   Sidney Biggs
Marie Ault . . . .   Mrs Metcalfe
John Salew . . . .   Drake
Philip Friend . . . .   Humphries
WAR Submarine, disabled after sinking
battleship in Kiel Canal, is refuelled by Danes.

10893
THE GENTLE SEX (93) (U)
Two Cities—Concanen (GFD) Ireissue: 1948
(Eros; 620 ft cut)
P: Derrick de Marney, Leslie Howard
D: Leslie Howard, Maurice Elvey
S: Moie Charles
SC: Moie Charles, Aimee Stuart, Roland
Pertwee, Phyllis Rose
Joan Gates . . . .   Gwen
Jean Gillie . . . .   Good Time Dot
Joan Greenwood . . . .   Betty
Joyce Howard . . . .   Ann Lawrence
Rosamund John . . . .   Maggie Frazer
Lilli Palmer . . . .   Erna
Barbara Waring . . . .   Joan
John Justin . . . . FO David Sheridan
Frederick Leister . . . .   Col Lawrence
Mary Jerrold . . . .   Mrs Sheridan
Everley Gregg . . . .   Mrs Simpson
Anthony Bazell . . . .   Ted
Elliot Mason . . . .   Mrs Frazer
John Laurie . . . .   Cpl
Rosalyn Boulter . . . .   Sally
Meriel Forbes . . . .   Cmdr
Harry Welchman . . . .   Capt
Ronald Shiner . . . .   Racegoer
Jimmy Hanley . . . .   Soldier
Miles Malleson . . . .   Guard
Peter Cotes . . . .   Taffy
WAR Experiences of seven assorted girls
conscripted into ATS.

10894
THE BELLS GO DOWN (90) (U)
Ealing (UA) *reissue:* 1946
AP: S.C. Balcon
D: Basil Dearden
S: (BOOK) Anonymous
SC: Stephen Black, Roger Macdougall
Tommy Trinder . . . .   Tommy Turk
James Mason . . . .   Ted Robbins
Mervyn Johns . . . .   Sam
Philippa Hiatt . . . .   Nan
Finlay Currie . . . .   McFarlane
Philip Friend . . . .   Bob
Meriel Forbes . . . .   Susie
Beatrice Varley . . . .   Ma Turk
Billy Hartnell . . . .   Brooks
Norman Pierce . . . .   Pa Robbins
Muriel George . . . .   Ma Robbins
Julien Vedey . . . .   Lou Freeman
Lesley Brook . . . .   June
WAR Love rivals in AFS fight fire in 1940
blitz .

10895
SWINGONOMETRY (17) (U)
Inspiration (Par)
D: Horace Shepherd
Harry Parry and his Radio Rhythm Club Septet
MUSICAL

10896
HARRY PARRY AND HIS RADIO
RHYTHM CLUB SEPTET (15) (U)
Inspiration (Par)
D: Horace Shepherd
MUSICAL

10897
I'LL WALK BESIDE YOU (88) (U)
Butcher *reissues:* 1945; 1948
(Sherwood; 16 mins cut)
P: F.W. Baker
D: Maclean Rogers
S: Mabel Constanduros
SC: Kathleen Butler
Richard Bird . . . .   John Brent
Lesley Brook . . . .   Ann Johnson
Percy Marmont . . . .   Vicar
Leslie Bradley . . . .   Tom Booth
Sylvia Marriott . . . .   Joan Trematne
Hugh Miller . . . .   Dr Stevenson
Beatrice Varley . . . .   Miss McKenzie
Irene Handl . . . .   Ma Perkins
George Merritt . . . .   Hancock
Hilda Bayley . . . .   Mrs Tremayne
John McHugh; St David's Singers; London
Symphony Orchestra
ROMANCE Amnesiac naval officer returns
from "death" to find his fiancee engaged to
doctor.

MAY

10898
MISS LONDON LTD (99) (U)
Gainsborough (GFD)
P: Edward Black
D: Val Guest
S: Val Guest, Marriott Edgar
Arthur Askey . . . .   Arthur Bowman
Evelyn Dall . . . .   Terry Arden
Anne Shelton . . . .   Gail Martin
Richard Hearne . . . .   Commodore
Max Bacon . . . .   Romeo
Jack Train . . . .   Joe Nelson
Peter Graves . . . . Capt Rory O'More
Jean Kent . . . . The Encyclopaedia
Ronald Shiner . . . .   Sailor
MUSICAL Girl modernises escort agency for
lonely officers on leave.

10899
THEATRE ROYAL (92) (U)
British National (Anglo)
P: D: John Baxter
S: Bud Flanagan, Austin Melford, Geoffrey Orme
Bud Flanagan . . . .   Bob Parker
Chesney Allen . . . .   Gordon Maxwell
Peggy Dexter . . . .   Connie Webster
Lydia Sherwood . . . .   Claudia Brent
Horace Kenney . . . .   George
Marjorie Rhodes . . . .   Agnes
Finlay Currie . . . .   Clement J. Earle
Owen Reynolds . . . .   Harding
Maire O'Neill . . . .   Mrs Cope
Gwen Catley . . . .   Singer
Jack Melford . . . .
Buddy Flanagan . . . .   Callboy
COMEDY Prop man stages revue and saves
theatre owner from bankruptcy.

JUN

10900
THE DARK TOWER (93) (A)
WB—FN *reissue:* 1949 (20 mins cut)
D: John Harlow
S: (PLAY) Alexander Woolcott, George S.
Kaufman
SC: Brock Williams, Reginald Purdell
Ben Lyon . . . .   Phil Danton
Anne Crawford . . . .   Mary
David Farrar . . . .   Tom Danton
Herbert Lom . . . .   Torg
Billy Hartnell . . . .   Towers
Frederick Burtwell . . . .   Willie
Josephine Wilson . . . .   Mme Shogun
Elsie Wagstaffe . . . .   Eve
J.H. Roberts . . . .   Dr Wilson
DRAMA Hypnotist makes circus girl perform
trapeze stunts and tries to force her from her
lover.

10901
THE LIFE AND DEATH OF COLONEL
BLIMP (163) (U) *tech* USA: COLONEL
BLIMP
IP-Archers (GFD) *reissue:* 1948 (2983 ft cut)
P:D:S: Michael Powell, Emeric Pressburger
Anton Walbrook . . Theo Kretschmar-Schuldorff
Deborah Kerr . . . . Edith/Barbara/Johnny
Roger Livesey . . . .   Clive Candy
Roland Culver . . . .   Col Bettridge
James McKechnie . . . .   Spud Wilson
Albert Lieven . . . .   von Ritter
Arthur Wontner . . . .   Counsellor
David Hutcheson . . . .   Hoppy
Ursula Jeans . . . . Frau Kalteneck
John Laurie . . . .   Murdoch
Harry Welchman . . . .   Maj Davis
Reginald Tate . . . .   van Zijl
A.E.Matthews . . . .   President
Carl Jaffe . . . .   von Reumann
Valentine Dyall . . . .   von Schonborn
Muriel Aked . . . .   Aunt Margaret
Felix Aylmer . . . .   Bishop
Frith Banbury . . . . Babyface Fitzroy
WAR 1902 - 1943. Loves and life of a
professional soldier.

10902
UNDERCOVER (80) (A) USA:
UNDERGROUND GUERILLAS
Ealing (UA) *reissue:* 1949 (ABFD)
AP: S.C.Balcon
D: Sergei Nolbandov
S: George Slocombe
SC: John Dighton, Monja Danischewsky,
Sergei Nolbandov, Milosh Sokulich
John Clements . . . . Milosh Petrovitch
Godfrey Tearle . . . Gen von Staengel

Tom Walls ...... Kossan Petrovitch
Michael Wilding .... Constantine
Mary Morris .... Anna Petrovitch
Stephen Murray ... Dr Stevan Petrovitch
Robert Harris .... Col von Brock
Rachel Thomas .... Maria Petrovitch
Charles Victor .... Sergeant
Niall MacGinnis .... Dr Jordan
Finlay Currie .... Father
Ivor Barnard .... Tosha
Stanley Baker .... Peter
WAR Jugoslavia, 1941. Doctor poses as
collaborator to help guerilla family.

10903
IT'S JUST THE WAY IT IS (10) (U)
Two Cities (NSS)
WAR Wing Commander persuades parents
their son's death in a raid was accidental.

10904
DEATH BY DESIGN (18) (U)
Guild Films (Butcher)
D: Geoffrey Faithfull
S: (STORY) Leonard Gribble
John Longden .... Insp Slade
Wally Patch .... Sgt
CRIME Insp solves murder mystery.

JUL

10905
KING OF THE KEYBOARD (15) (U)
Delman (RKO)
D: Horace Shepherd
Arthur Dulay
MUSICAL Pianist.

10906
WARN THAT MAN (82) (A)
ABPC (Pathe)
P: Warwick Ward
D: Lawrence Huntington
S: (PLAY) Vernon Sylvaine
SC: Vernon Sylvaine, Lawrence Huntington
Gordon Harker ...... George Hawkins
Raymond Lovell .. Hausemann/Lord Buckley
Finlay Currie .... Capt Andrew Fletcher
Philip Friend......... PO John Cooper
Jean Kent .... Frances Lane
Frederick Cooper...... Charles/Frampton
Carl Jaffe .... Schultz
John Salew .... Wilson
Veronica Rose .... Miss Conway
Anthony Hawtrey .... Brent
Antony Holles .... Waiter
Pat Aherne .... Mellows
CRIME Spies pose as Lord and staff to
kidnap Prime Minister.

10907
THE MAN IN GREY (116) (A)
Gainsborough (GFD) reissues: 1946;
1950 (Eros)
P: Edward Black
D: Leslie Arliss
S: (NOVEL) Lady Eleanor Smith
SC: Margaret Kennedy, Leslie Arliss,
Doreen Montgomery
Margaret Lockwood ...... Hesther Shaw
Phyllis Clavert .... Clarissa Rohan
James Mason .... Marquis of Rohan
Stewart Granger .... Peter Rokeby
Raymond Lovell .... Prince Regent
Nora Swinburne .... Mrs Fitzherbert
Helen Haye .... Lady Rohan
Martita Hunt .... Miss Patchett
Amy Veness .... Mrs Armstrong
Diana King .... Jane Seymour
Beatrice Varley .... Gipsy
Roy Emerton .... Gamekeeper

A.E.Matthews .... Auctioneer
ROMANCE Regency. Marquis's unloved wife
loves an actor and is killed by her jealous
friend. (PGAA: 1944).

10908
ESCAPE TO DANGER (92) (A)
RKO-Radio
P: William Sistrom
D: Lance Comfort, Mutz Greenbaum
S: Patrick Kirwan
SC: Wolfgang Wilhelm, Jack Whittingham
Eric Portman .... Arthur Lawrence
Ann Dvorak .... Joan Grahame
Karel Stepanek ..... Franz von Brinkman
Ronald Ward .... Rupert Chessman
Ronald Adam .... George Merrick
Lily Kann .... Karin Moeller
David Peel .... Lt Peter Leighton
Felix Aylmer .... Sir Alfred Horton
Brefni O'Rorke .... Security Officer
A.E.Matthews .... Sir Thomas Leighton
Charles Victor .... PO Flanagan
Marjorie Rhodes .... Mrs Pickles
Frederick Cooper .... Goesta
Ivor Barnard .... Henry Waud
WAR English schoolmistress poses as
Danish quisling and helps catch German agent.

10909
RHYTHM SERENADE (87) (U)
Columbia British
P: Ben Henry, George Formby
D: Gordon Wellesley
S: Marjorie Deans
SC: Marjorie Deans, Basil Woon, Margaret
Kennedy, Edward Dryhurst
Vera Lynn .... Ann Martin
Peter Murray Hill........ John Drover
Julien Mitchell .... Mr Jimson
Charles Victor .... Mr Martin
Jimmy Jewel .... Jimmy Martin
Ben Warriss .... Ben Martin
Joss Ambler .... Mr Preston
Rosalyn Boulter .... Monica Jimson
Betty Jardine .... Helen
Irene Handl .... Mrs Crumbling
Lloyd Pearson .... Mr Simkins
Jimmy Clitheroe .... Joey
MUSICAL Factory girl helps wealthy
ex-sailor recover his courage.

10910
MY LEARNED FRIEND (76) (U)
Ealing reissues: 1946; 1948 (Ren)
AP: Robert Hamer
D: Will Hay, Basil Dearden
S: John Dighton, Angus Macphail
Will Hay .... William Fitch
Claude Hulbert ...... Claude Babbington
Mervyn Johns .... Grimshaw
Ernest Thesiger .... Ferris
Charles Victor .... Safety Wilson
Derna Hazel .... Gloria
Lloyd Pearson .... Col Chudleigh
Maudie Edwards .... Aladdin
G.H.Mulcaster .... Dr Scrudamore
Gibb McLaughlin .... Carstairs
Aubrey Mallalieu ...... Magistrate
COMEDY Disbarred lawyer is sixth on an
ex-convict's murder list.

AUG

10911
THE BUTLER'S DILEMMA (83) (U)
British National-Shaftesbury (Anglo)
P: Elizabeth Hiscott
D: Leslie Hiscott
S: Michael Barringer
Richard Hearne .... Rodney Playfair

Francis L. Sullivan .... Leo Carrington
Judy Kelly .... Ann Carrington
Hermione Gingold ...... Aunt Sophie
Henry Kendall .... Carmichael
Wally Patch .... Tom
Ronald Shiner .... Ernie
Andre Randall .... Vitello
Ralph Truman .... Bishop
Ian Fleming ...... Sir Hubert Playfair
Marjorie Rhodes .... Mrs Plumb
COMEDY Gamblers force gem thief's
double to pose as his fiancee's butler.

10912
THEY MET IN THE DARK (104) (U)
IP-Excelsior (GFD) reissue: 1948 (Eros; cut)
P: Marcel Hellman
D: Karel Lamac
S: (NOVEL) Anthony Gilbert
(THE VANISHING CORPSE)
SC: Anatole de Grunwald, Miles Malleson,
Basil Bartlett, Victor Maclure, James Seymour
James Mason ..... Cdr Richard Heritage
Joyce Howard .... Laura Verity
Tom Walls .... Christopher Child
Phyllis Stanley .... Lily Bernard
Edward Rigby .... Mansell
Ronald Ward .... Carter
David Farrar .... Cdr Lippinscott
Karel Stepanek .... Riccardo
Betty Warren .... Fay
Walter Crisham .... Charlie
George Robey .... Pawnbroker
Peggy Dexter .... Bobby
Finlay Currie .... Capt
Brefni O'Rorke .... Insp Burrows
Jeanne de Casalis .... Lady with Dog
Patricia Medina .... Pat
Charles Victor .... Publican
Ronald Chesney; Alvar Liddell
CRIME Court-martialled cmdr unmasks
spies posing as theatrical agents.

10913
DEAR OCTOPUS (86) (A) USA:
THE RANDOLPH FAMILY
Gainsborough (GFD) reissue: 1946
P: Edward Black
D: Harold French
S: (PLAY) Dodie Smith
SC: R.J.Minney, Patrick Kirwan
Margaret Lockwood ... Penny Randolph
Michael Wilding .... Nicholas
Celia Johnson .... Cynthia
Roland Culver .... Felix Martin
Helen Haye .... Dora Randolph
Athene Seyler .... Aunt Belle
Basil Radford .... Kenneth
Frederick Leister....... Charles Randolph
Nora Swinburne .... Edna
Antoinette Cellier ...... Hilda
Jean Cadell .... Mrs Vicar
Madge Compton .... Marjorie
Kathleen Harrison ...... Mrs Glossop
Ann Stephens .... Scrap
Muriel George .... Maggie
Graham Moffatt .... Fred
ROMANCE Family reunite for their
parents' Golden Wedding celebrations.

10914
PICTORIAL REVUE OF 1943 (39) (U)
Pathe
D: Fred Watts
Tommy Handley   Robb Wilton
Collinson & Dean   Suzette Tarri
Oliver Wakefield   Leslie Hutchinson
Percival Mackey   Rebla
Albert Sandler   Lavanda
Oscar Rabin and his Band

Big Bill Campbell and his Rocky
Mountaineers
REVUE Extracts from "Pathe Pictorial."

10915
SCHWEIK'S NEW ADVENTURES (84) (U)
Eden Films (Coronel) *reissue:* 1945,
IT STARTED AT MIDNIGHT (Ren)
P: Walter Sors, Edward G.Whiting
D: Karel Lamac
S: (NOVEL) Jaroslav Hasek
SC: Karel Lamac, Con West
Lloyd Pearson . . . . Schweik
Julien Mitchell . . . . Gestapo Chief
George Carney . . . . Gendarme
Richard Attenborough . . . . Worker
Margaret McGrath . . . . Karova
COMEDY Czechoslovakia. Humorist becomes
a Gestapo Chief's bodyguard and saves his
friends from concentration camp.

10916
THE FLEMISH FARM (82) (U)
Two Cities (GFD) *reissue:* 1949 (ABFD)
P: Sydney Box
D: Jeffrey Dell
S: Jeffrey Dell, Jill Craigie Dell
Clive Brook . . . . Maj Lessart
Clifford Evans . . . . Jean Duclos
Jane Baxter . . . . Tresha
Philip Friend. . . . . Fernand Matagne
Brefni O'Rorke . . . . Minister
Wylie Watson . . . . Farmer
Ronald Squire . . . . S/L Hardwicke
Mary Jerrold . . . . Mme Duclos
Charles Compton . . . . Ledoux
Richard George . . . . Scheldheimer
Lili Kann . . . . Farmwife
Irene Handl . . . . Frau
WAR Belgium. Airman returns to occupied
country to retrieve buried flag.

10917
STRANGE TO RELATE (33) (U)
Film Sales (NR)
P:D: Widgey Newman
Wally Patch
Mabel Poulton
Hal Walters
COMEDY Sweepstake winner buys guest
house and boards wild animals.
(Includes extracts from PANDAMONIUM
(1939).)

10918
SOMEWHERE IN CIVVIES (87) (U)
T.A. Welsh (Butcher) *reissues:* 1947;
1951 (Sherwood; cut)
D: Maclean Rogers
S: Con West
Frank Randle . . . . Pte Randle
George Doonan . . . . Sgt Doonan
Suzette Tarri . . . . Mrs Spam
Joss Ambler . . . . Matthews
H.F.Maltby . . . . Col Tyldesley
Nancy O'Neil . . . . Mary Randle
Grey Blake . . . . Ralph Tyldesley
COMEDY Cousin tries to drive ex-soldier
mad to usurp his inheritance.

SEP

10919
ADVENTURES OF TARTU (103) (A)
USA: TARTU
MGM British
P: Irving Asher
D: Harold S.Bucquet
S: John C.Higgins
SC: Howard Emmet Rogers, John Lee Mahin,

Miles Malleson
Robert Donat . . . . Capt Terence Stevenson
Valerie Hobson . . . . Maruschka
Walter Rills. . . . . Insp Otto Vogel
Glynis Johns . . . . Paula Palacek
Phyllis Morris . . . . Anna Palacek
Martin Miller . . . . Dr Novothy
Anthony Eustrel . . . . Officer
Percy Walsh . . . . Dr Willendorf
Frederic Richter . . . . Nestor
John Penrose . . . . Lt Krantz
Mabel Terry Lewis . . . . . . Mrs Stevenson
WAR Czechoslovakia. British officer poses
as Rumanian ex-diplomat to blow up poison
gas plant.

10920
MILLIONS LIKE US (103) (U)
Gainsborough (GFD) *reissue:* 1947 (ABFD; cut)
P: Edward Black
D:S: Frank Launder, Sidney Gilliat
Eric Portman . . . . Charlie Forbes
Patricia Roc . . . . Celia Crowson
Anne Crawford . . . . Jennifer Knowles
Gordon Jackson . . . . Fred Blake
Basil Radford . . . . Charters
Naunton Wayne . . . . Caldicott
Moore Marriott . . . . Jim Crowson
Joy Shelton . . . . Phyllis Crowson
Megs Jenkins . . . . Gwen Price
Terry Randall . . . . Annie Earnshaw
John Boxer . . . . Tom Crowson
Valentine Dunn . . . . Elsie Crowson
John Salew . . . . Dr Gill
Irene Handl . . . . Landlady
Amy Veness . . . . Mrs Blythe
WAR 1939 - 1941. Aircraft factory worker
weds air gunner who is killed in action.

OCT

10921
YELLOW CANARY (98) (U)
Imperator (RKO)
P:D: Herbert Wilcox
S: Pamela Bower
SC: Miles Malleson, Dewitt Bodeen
Anna Neagle . . . . Sally Maitland
Richard Greene . . . . Jim Garrick
Nova Pilbeam . . . . Betty Maitland
Lucie Mannheim . . . . Mme Orlock
Albert Lieven . . . . Jan Orlock
Cyril Fletcher . . . . Himself
Margaret Rutherford . . . . . Mrs Towcester
Claude Bailey . . . . Maj Fothergill
Patric Curwen. . . . Sir William Maitland
Marjorie Fielding . . . . Lady Maitland
Aubrey Mallalieu. . . . . Reynolds
David Horne . . . . Admiral
Franklin Dyall . . . . Captain
George Thorpe . . . . Col Hargreaves
WAR Socialite suspected of Nazi sympathies
thwarts a plot to destroy Halifax harbour.

NOV

10922
DEADLOCK (59) (A)
British Foundation (IFR)
P:D: Ronald Haines
John Slater . . . . Fred/Allan Bamber
Cecile Chevreau . . . . Eileen
Hugh Morton . . . . Arkell
Molly Hamley-Clifford . . . Martha
CRIME Twin helps his brother, a convicted
killer, break jail.

10923
THE LAMP STILL BURNS (90) (A)
Two Cities (GFD) *reissues:* 1946; 1951 (Eros)

P: Leslie Howard
D: Maurice Elvey
S: (NOVEL) Monica Dickens
(ONE PAIR OF FEET)
SC: Elizabeth Baron, Roland Pertwee, Major
Neilson
Rosamund John . . . . Hilary Clarke
Stewart Granger . . . . Larry Rains
Godfrey Tearle . . . Sir Marshall Frayne
Sophie Stewart . . . . Christine Morris
John Laurie . . . . Mr Hervey
Margaret Vyner . . . . Pamela Siddell
Cathleen Nesbitt . . . . Matron
Eric Micklewood . . . . Dr Trevor
Joyce Grenfell . . . . Dr Barratt
Joan Maude . . . . Sister Catley
Grace Arnold . . . . Sister Sprock
Jenny Laird . . . . Ginger Watkins
Megs Jenkins . . . . Nurse
Wylie Watson . . . . Diabetic
Ernest Thesiger . . . . Chairman
Brefni O'Rorke . . . . Lorimer
DRAMA Probationer nurse fights restrictions
in country hospital.

10924
HEADLINE (76) (A)
John Corfield (Ealing) *reissue:* 1946 (Ren)
D: John Harlow
S: (NOVEL) Ken Attiwill (THE REPORTER)
SC: Ralph Gilbert Bettinson, Maisie Sharman
Anne Crawford . . . . Anne
David Farrar . . . . Brookie
John Stuart . . . . L.B.Ellington
Antoinette Cellier . . . . Mrs Ellington
Billy Hartnell . . . . Dell
Anthony Hawtrey . . . . Paul Grayson
Nancy O'Neil . . . . Betty
Merle Tottenham . . . . Mrs Deans
Joss Ambler . . . . Sub-editor
Richard Goolden . . . . Jones
CRIME Reporter finds his editor's wife
is missing witness to girl's murder.

10925
THE VOLUNTEER (46) (U)
Archers (Anglo)
P:D:S: Michael Powell, Emeric Pressburger
Ralph Richardson . . . . Himself
Pat McGrath . . . . Fred Davey
WAR Actor's dresser joins Fleet Air Arm, and
wins DSM.

10926
THE HUNDRED POUND WINDOW (84) (U)
WB-FN
D: Brian Desmond Hurst
S: Mark Hellinger
SC: Abem Finkel, Brock Williams, Rodney
Ackland
Anne Crawford . . . . Joan Draper
David Farrar . . . . George Graham
Frederick Leister . . . . Ernest Draper
Mary Clare . . . . Millie Draper
Richard Attenborough . . . . Tommy Draper
Niall MacGinnis . . . . Chick Slater
David Hutcheson . . . . Steve Halligan
Francis Lister . . . . Capt Johnson
Claud Allister . . . . Hon Freddie
Claude Bailey . . . . John D.Humphries
Peter Gawthorne . . . . Van Rayden
John Slater . . . . O'Neil
David Horne . . . . Baldwin
Anthony Hawtrey . . . . Evans
Ruby Miller . . . . Mrs Remington
CRIME Totalisator clerk involved with
crooked gamblers repents and exposes them
as black marketeers.

DEC

10927
UP WITH THE LARK (83) (U)
New Realm *reissue:* 1947 (2381 ft cut)
P: E.J.Fancey
D: Phil Brandon
S: Val Valentine
Ethel Revnell . . . .   Ethel
Gracie West . . . .   Gracie
Anthony Hulme . . . .   Mr Britt
Lesley Osmond . . . .   Mabel
Alan Kane . . . .   Fred Tomkins
Antony Holles . . . .   Martel
Ian Fleming . . . .   Rev Swallow
Alma & Bobby; Van Straten's Piccadilly Dance Band
MUSICAL Land Army girls unmask hotelier as black marketeer.

10928
DOWN MELODY LANE (60) (U)
New Realm
D: (Uncredited)
Johnnie Schofield . . . . . .   Sam Mitchell
Lesley Osmond . . . .   Trixie
Naughton & Gold   Leslie "Hutch" Hutchinson
Houston Sisters   Australian Air Aces
Phyllis Robins   G.S.Melvin
Sherman Fisher Girls
Billy Cotton and his Band
REVUE Music Hall stage manager recalls stars and his wooing of barmaid. (Includes extracts from earlier films).

10929
THE DEMI-PARADISE (115) (U)
USA: ADVENTURE FOR TWO
Two Cities (GFD) *reissue:* 1948 (Eros; 2728 ft cut)
P: Anatole de Grunwald
D: Anthony Asquith
S: Anatole de Grunwald
Laurence Olivier . . .   Ivan Kouznetsoff
Penelope Dudley Ward . . . .   Ann Tisdall
Leslie Henson . . . .   Himself
Marjorie Fielding . . . .   Mrs Tisdall
Margaret Rutherford . . . . .   Rowena Ventnor
Felix Aylmer . . . .   Mr Runalow
George Thorpe . . . .   Herbert Tisdall
Guy Middleton . . . .   Richard Christie
Michael Shepley . . . .   Mr Walford
Edie Martin . . . .   Aunt Winnie
Muriel Aked . . . .   Mrs Tisdall-Stanton
Joyce Grenfell . . . .   Mrs Pawson
Jack Watling . . . .   Tom Sellars
Everley Gregg . . . .   Mrs Flannel
Aubrey Mallalieu . . . .   Toomes
Brian Nissen . . . .   George Tisdall
John Laurie . . . .   Sailor
COMEDY 1939. Russian inventor of an ice-breaking propeller is befriended by ship-builder's family.

10930
CANDLELIGHT IN ALGERIA (85) (U)
British Aviation (BL) *reissue:* 1946 (NR)
P:D: George King
S: Dorothy Hope
SC: Katherine Strueby, Brock Williams
James Mason . . . .   Alan Thurston
Carla Lehmann . . . .   Susan Foster
Walter Rilla . . . .   Dr Muller
Raymond Lovell . . . .   Von Alven
Enid Stamp Taylor . . . . . .   Maritza
Pamela Stirling . . . .   Yvette
Lea Seidl . . . .   Sister
Leslie Bradley . . . .   Henri de Lange
Michel Morel . . . .   Commissioner
Albert Whelan . . . .   Kadour
Meinhart Maur . . . .   Schultz
Harold Berens . . . .   Toni

WAR American girl helps British agent save photograph of Allied rendezvous from spies.

10931
SAN DEMETRIO-LONDON (105) (U)
Ealing *reissue:* 1948 (671 ft cut)
AP: Robert Hamer
D: Charles Frend
S: F. Tennyson Jesse
SC: Robert Hamer, Charles Frend
Walter Fitzgerald. . . . .   Charles Pollard
Mervyn Johns . . . .   John Boyle
Ralph Michael . . . .   Hawkins
Robert Beatty . . . .   Yank Preston
Charles Victor . . . .   Deckhand
Frederick Piper . . . .   Bosun Fletcher
Gordon Jackson . . . .   John Jamieson
Arthur Young. . . . .   Capt George Waite
Barry Letts . . . .   John Jones
James McKechnie . . . .   Colum McNeil
Nigel Clarke . . . .   R.J.E.Dodds
Lawrence O'Madden . . . .   Capt Fogarty Fegan
David Horne . . . .   Mr Justice Langton
WAR 1940. Survivors of crippled tanker bring ship home to port.

10932
IT'S IN THE BAG (80) (U)
Butcher's Film Service
P: F.W. Baker
D: Herbert Mason
S: Con West
Elsie Waters . . . .   Gert
Doris Waters . . . .   Daisy
Ernest Butcher . . . .   Sam Braithwaite
Lesley Osmond . . . .   April Vaughan
Gordon Edwards . . . .   Alan West
Reginald Purdell . . . .   Joe
Irene Handl . . . .   Mrs Beam
Antony Holles . . . .   Costumier
Tony Quinn . . . .   Prendergast
Vera Bogetti . . . .   Rose Trelawney
Megs Jenkins . . . .   Peach StClair
COMEDY Sisters search for grandmother's dress which has fortune hidden in bustle.

10933
QUIZ CRIMES (series)
British Foundation (Par)
P:D: Ronald Haines

10934
No. 1: (13) (A)
10935
No. 2: (18) (U)
10936
No. 3: (17) (A)
10937
No. 4: (17) (A)
10938
No. 5: (19) (A)
10939
No. 6: (19) (A)
CRIME Detective investigates murders and invites audience to solve them.

10940
THERE'S A FUTURE IN IT (36) (U)
Strand Films (Par)
P: Donald Taylor
D: Leslie Fenton
S: H.E.Bates
Ann Dvorak . . . .   Kitty
Barry Morse . . . .   Johnny O'Connor
Beatrice Varley . . . .   Mother
John Turnbull . . . .   Father
Richard George . . . .   Publican
Mattie Heft . . . .   Pianist
WAR Girl's father objects to her love for bomber pilot.

10941
BATTLE FOR MUSIC (87) (U)
Strand Films (Anglo)
P:D: Donald Taylor
Hay Petrie . . . .
Mavis Claire . . . .
Joss Ambler . . . .
Charles Carson . . . .
Dennis Wyndham . . . .
Ben Williams . . . .
Antony Holles . . . .
Jack Hylton; J.B.Priestley; Brian Michie; Eileen Joyce; Moiseiwitsch; Sir Adrian Boult: Warwick Braithwaite; Constant Lambert; Sir Malcolm Sargent; London Philharmonic Orchestra
MUSICAL Orchestra sticks together through bankruptcy and war.

10942
OLD MOTHER RILEY OVERSEAS (80) (U)
British National (Anglo)
P:D: Oswald Mitchell
S: L.S.Deacon, Albert Mee
SC: H. Fowler Mear, Arthur Lucan
Arthur Lucan . . . .   Mrs Riley
Kitty McShane . . . .   Kitty Riley
Morris Harvey . . . .   Barnacle Bill
Fred Kitchen jr . . . .   Pedro Quentos
Magda Kun . . . .
Antony Holles . . . .
Ferdy Mayne . . . .
"Freddie"; Stanelli; Rosarito & Paula
COMEDY Portugal. Wine-house licensee rescues kidnapped daughter from port wine thieves.

10943
THE SHIPBUILDERS (89) (A)
British National (Anglo)
P:D: John Baxter
S: George Blake
SC: Gordon Wellesley, Reginald Pound, Stephen Potter
Clive Brook . . . .   Leslie Pagan
Morland Graham . . . .   Danny Shields
Nell Ballantyne . . . .   Mrs Shields
Finlay Currie . . . .   McWain
Maudie Edwards . . . .   Lizzie
Geoffrey Hibbert . . . .   Peter Shields
Allan Jeayes . . . .   Ralph
Moire Lister . . . .   Rita
Frederick Leister . . . .   Mr Villier
Gus McNaughton . . . .   Jim
John Turnbull . . . .   Baird
DRAMA 1931 - 9. Clydeside shipbuilder and a loyal rivetter fight to keep Britain a sea power.

10944
BELL-BOTTOM GEORGE (97) (U)
Columbia British
P: Ben Henry
D: Marcel Varnel
S: Richard Fisher, Peter Cresswell
SC: Peter Fraser, Edward Dryhurst, John L. Arthur
George Formby . . . .   George
Anne Firth . . . .   Pat
Reginald Purdell . . . .   Birdie Edwards
Peter Murray Hill . . . .   Shapley
Charles Farrell . . . .   Jim Benson
Eliot Makeham . . . .   Johnson
Manning Whiley . . . .   Church
Hugh Dempster . . . .   White
Dennis Wyndham . . . .   Black
Jane Welsh . . . .   Rita
Peter Gawthorne . . . .   Admiral Coltham
COMEDY Unfit waiter poses as sailor and catches spies.

1944

JAN

10945
STARLIGHT SERENADE (45) (U)
Federated *reissue:* as 2 shorts
P: Harold Baim
D. Denis Kavanagh
S: Syd Colin
Bryan Michie   Bonar Colleano
Beryl Davis   Ted Hockridge
Ike Hatch   Billy deHaven & Dandy Page
Wilson, Keppel & Betty
Eddie Palmer and his Novachord
Oscar Rabin and his Band
Johnny Denis and his Ranchers
REVUE

FEB

10946
THE HALFWAY HOUSE (95) (A)
Ealing
AP: Cavalcanti
D: Basil Dearden
S: (PLAY) Denis Ogden
(THE PEACEFUL INN)
SC: Angus Macphail, Diana Morgan
Francoise Rosay . . . . Alice Meadows
Tom Walls . . . . Capt Harry Meadows
Mervyn Johns . . . . Rhys
Glynis Johns . . . . Gwyneth
Alfred Drayton . . . . Oakley
Esmond Knight . . . . David Davies
Richard Bird . . . . S/L Richard French
Philippa Hiatt . . . . Margaret
Sally Ann Howes . . . . Joanna French
Guy Middleton . . . . Fortescue
Valerie White . . . . Jill French
Pat McGrath . . . . Terence
C.V.France . . . . Solicitor
FANTASY Wales. Group of travellers
reform after night at phantom inn.

10947
DEMOBBED (96) (U)
Mancunian (Butcher) *reissue:* 1947 (cut)
P: D: John E.Blakeley
S: Julius Cantor, Max Zorlini
SC: Roney Parsons, Anthony Toner
Nat Jackley . . . . Nat
Norman Evans . . . . Norman
Dan Young . . . . Dan
Betty Jumel . . . . Betty
Tony Dalton . . . . Billy Brown
Jimmy Plant . . . . Graham
Anne Firth . . . . Norma Deane
Neville Mapp . . . . John Bentley
George Merritt . . . . James Bentley
Fred Kitchen jr . . . . Black
Gus McNaughton . . . . Capt Gregson
Anne Ziegler & Webster Booth; Felix
Mendelssohn's Hawaiian Serenaders
COMEDY Demobilised soldiers expose
factory secretary as thief.

10948
RAINBOW ROUND THE CORNER (52) (U)
Berkeley (Premier) *reissue:* 1946,
RAINBOW RHYTHM
P: Burt Hyams
D: Victor M. Gover
S: Robin Richmond, Edward Eve
Billy "Uke" Scott   Daphne Day
Vera Bradley   Boswell Twins
Gordon Ray Girls   Chappie d'Amato
REVUE

10949
TIME FLIES (88) (U)
Gainsborough (GFD)
P: Edward Black

D: Walter Forde
S: Howard Irving Young, J.O.C.Orton,
Ted Kavanagh
Tommy Handley . . . . Tommy
Evelyn Dall . . . . Susie Barton
George Moon . . . . Bill Barton
Felix Aylmer . . . . Professor
Moore Marriott . . . . Soothsayer
Graham Moffatt . . . . His Nephew
John Salew . . . . William Shakespeare
Leslie Bradley . . . . Walter Raleigh
Olga Lindo . . . . Queen Elizabeth
Roy Emerton . . . . Capt John Smith
Iris Lang . . . . Princess Pocohontas
Stephane Grappelly . . . . . . Troubadour
COMEDY Tricksters return to Mediaeval
days in prof's time machine.

MAR

10950
BEES IN PARADISE (75) (A)
Gainsborough (GFD)
P: Edward Black
D: Val Guest
S: Val Guest, Marriott Edgar
Arthur Askey . . . . Arthur Tucker
Anne Shelton . . . . Rouana
Peter Graves . . . . Peter Lovell
Max Bacon . . . . Max Holer
Jean Kent . . . . Jani
Ronald Shiner . . . . Ronald Wild
Antoinette Cellier . . . . Queen
Joy Shelton . . . . Almura
Beatrice Varley . . . . Moagga
MUSICAL Four airmen bale out on
South Atlantic island ruled by girls, where
men must commit suicide after their
honeymoons.

10951
ON APPROVAL (80) (A)
IP (GFD)
P: Sydney Box, Clive Brooke
D: Clive Brook
S: (PLAY) Frederick Lonsdale
SC: Clive Brook, Terence Young
Clive Brook . . . . Duke of Bristol
Beatrice Lillie . . . . Maria Wislak
Googie Withers . . . . Helen Hale
Roland Culver . . . . Richard Halton
O.B.Clarence . . . . Dr Graham
Lawrence Hanray . . . . Parkes
Elliot Mason . . . . Mrs McCosh
Hay Petrie . . . . Landlord
Marjorie Rhodes . . . . Cook
Molly Munks . . . . Jeannie
COMEDY Edwardian. Bankrupt Duke and
American heiress spend trial month together
in Scots castle.

10952
BROWNED OFF (35) (U)
Strand Films (IFR)
P:D: Donald Taylor
John Martin . . . . Jim Hardy
Jenny Laird . . . . Alice
Arthur Hambling . . . . Fowler
WAR Bombardier on lonely searchlight
unit cheers up when he is posted nearer to his
girl.

10953
IT HAPPENED ONE SUNDAY (99) (A)
ABPC (Pathe)
P: Victor Skutezky
D: Karel Lamac
S: (PLAY) Victor Skutezky
(SHE MET HIM ONE SUNDAY)
SC: Victor Skutezky, Frederic Gotfurt,

Stephen Black
Robert Beatty . . . . Tom Stevens
Barbara White . . . . Moya Malone
Marjorie Rhodes . . . . Mrs Buckland
Ernest Butcher . . . . Mr Buckland
Judy Kelly . . . . Violet
Irene Vanbrugh . . . . Mrs Bellamy
Kathleen Harrison . . . . Mrs Purkiss
C.V.France . . . . Magistrate
Paul Demel . . . . Cassio
Marie Ault . . . . Madame
Brefni O'Rorke . . . . Engineer
Charles Victor . . . . Frisco Joe
Moore Marriott . . . . Porter
ROMANCE Liverpool. Irish maid loves
Canadian seaman involved with crooks.

10954
HEAVEN IS ROUND THE CORNER (94) (U)
British National (Anglo)
P: Fred Zelnik
D: Maclean Rogers
S: A. Hilarius, Paul Knepler
SC: Austin Melford
Will Fyffe . . . . Dougal
Leni Lynn . . . . Joan Sedley
Austin Trevor . . . . John Cardew
Magda Kun . . . . Musette
Peter Glenville . . . . Donald Mackay
Barbara Waring . . . . Dorothy Trevor
Leslie Perrins . . . . Robert Sedley
Barbara Couper . . . . Mrs Trevor
Tonie Edgar Bruce . . . . Mrs Harcourt
Hugh Dempster . . . . Capt Crowe
MUSICAL Old farmhand reunites soprano
with war-wounded diplomat.

APR

10955
FOR THOSE IN PERIL (67) (U)
Ealing
AP: S.C.Balcon
D: Charles Crichton
S: Richard Hillary
SC: Harry Watt, J.O.C.Orton, T.E.B.Clarke
David Farrar . . . . Murray
Ralph Michael. . . . . Rawlings
Robert Wyndham . . . . Leverett
John Slater . . . . Wilkie
John Batten . . . . Wireless Op
Robert Griffith . . . . Griffith
WAR Unfit officer joins Air/Sea rescue and
saves dinghy from minefield.

MAY

10956
TAWNY PIPIT (85) (U) *sepia*
Two Cities (GFD) *reissue:* 1948 (ABFD;
309 ft cut)
D: SC: Bernard Miles, Charles Saunders
S: Bernard Miles
Bernard Miles . . . . Col Barton-Barrington
Rosamund John . . . . Hazel Brooke
Niall MacGinnis . . . . Jimmy Bancroft
Jean Gillie . . . . Nancy Forrester
Christopher Steele . . . . Rev Kingsley
Lucie Mannheim . . . . Russian Sniper
Brefni O'Rorke . . . . Uncle Arthur
George Carney . . . . Whimbrel
Wylie Watson . . . . Croaker
John Salew . . . . Pickering
Marjorie Rhodes . . . . Mrs Pickering
Ernest Butcher . . . . Tommy Fairchild
Grey Blake . . . . Capt Dawson
Joan Sterndale-Bennett . . . Rose
COMEDY Convalescent pilot, nurse, and
village vicar save pair of nesting pipits.

10957
THIS HAPPY BREED (114) (A) *tech*
Two Cities-Cineguild (EL)
P: Noel Coward, Anthony Havelock-Allan
D: David Lean
S: (PLAY) Noel Coward
SC: David Lean, Ronald Neame, Anthony
Havelock-Allan
Robert Newton	Frank Gibbons
Celia Johnson	Ethel Gibbons
John Mills	Billy Mitchell
Kay Walsh	Queenie Gibbons
Stanley Holloway	Bob Mitchell
Amy Veness	Mrs Flint
Alison Leggatt	Aunt Sylvia
Eileen Erskine	Vi
John Blythe	Reg
Guy Verney	Sam Leadbitter
Merle Tottenham	Edie
DRAMA Lives and loves of suburban
family from 1919 to 1939. (Top Moneymaker:
1944.)

10958
FANNY BY GASLIGHT (108) (A)
USA: MAN OF EVIL
Gainsborough (GFD) *reissues:* 1945;
1948 (Eros; cut)
P: Edward Black
D: Anthony Asquith
S: (NOVEL) Michael Sadleir
SC: Doreen Montgomery, Aimee Stuart
Phyllis Calvert	Fanny Hopwood
James Mason	Lord Manderstoke
Wilfrid Lawson	Chunks
Stewart Granger	Harry Somerford
Margaretta Scott	Alicia
Jean Kent	Lucy Beckett
John Laurie	Mr Hopwood
Stuart Lindsell	Clive Seymour
Nora Swinburne	Mrs Hopwood
Amy Veness	Mrs Heaviside
Ann Wilton	Carver
Helen Haye	Mrs Somerford
Cathleen Nesbitt	Kate Somerford
ROMANCE 1870. Minister's bastard loves
his secretary, who saves her from lustful Lord.

10959
A CANTERBURY TALE (124) (U)
IP-Archers (EL) *reissue:* 1948 (Eros; cut)
P:D:S: Michael Powell, Emeric Pressburger
Eric Portman	Thomas Colpepper
Sheila Sim	Joan Webster
Dennis Price	Sgt Peter Gibbs
Sgt John Sweet	Bob Johnson
Esmond Knight	Narrator/Soldier/Idiot
Charles Hawtrey	Thomas Duckett
Hay Petrie	Woodcock
George Merritt	Ned Horton
Edward Rigby	Jim Horton
Freda Jackson	Prudence Honeywood
Betty Jardine	Fee Baker
Eliot Makeham	Organist
DRAMA Land girl, sgt, and GI unmask JP
as man who pours glue on girls' hair during
blackouts.

10960
TOM'S RIDE (11) (U)
GB Instructional (GFD)
P: H.Bruce Woolfe
D: Darrell Catling
S: Darrell Catling, Mary Cathcart Borer
Colin Simpson	Tom
Angela Glynne	
Stewart Rome	
Valentine Dunn	
CHILDREN Schoolboy finds old lady's
wallet and returns it to her.

10961
VICTORY WEDDING (20)
Gainsborough
D: Jessie Matthews
John Mills	Soldier
Dulcie Gray	Girl
Beatrice Varley	Mother
Vincent Holman	Father
ROMANCE Soldier returns after three years
and thinks his fiancee loves another.

10962
WELCOME MR WASHINGTON (90) (U)
British National-Shaftesbury (Anglo)
P: Elizabeth Hiscott
D: Leslie Hiscott
S: Noel Streatfeild
SC: Jack Whittingham
Barbara Mullen	Jane Willoughby
Donald Stewart	Lt Johnny Grant
Peggy Cummins	Sarah Willoughby
Graham Moffatt	Albert
Leslie Bradley	Capt Abbott
Martita Hunt	Miss Finch
Arthur Sinclair	Murphy
Roy Emerton	Selby
Shelagh Frazer	Millie
Louise Lord	Katherine Willoughby
Paul Blake	Vernon
Beatrice Varley	Martha
George Carney	Publican
CRIME Lady of the Manor falls for US sergeant
billeted in village.

10963
CANDLES AT NINE (86) (A)
British National (Anglo)
P: Wallace Orton
D: John Harlow
S: (NOVEL) Anthony Gilbert
(THE MOUSE WHO WOULDN'T PLAY BALL)
SC: John Harlow, Basil Mason
Jessie Matthews	Dorothea Capper
Beatrix Lehmann	Miss Carberry
John Stuart	William Gordon
Winifred Shotter	Brenda Tempest
Reginald Purdell	Charles Lacey
Hugh Dempster	Hugh Lacey
Joss Ambler	Garth Hope
Eliot Makeham	Everard Hope
Vera Bogetti	Lucille Hope
Ernest Butcher	Gardener
Guy Fielding	Gerry Wilmot
CRIME Housekeeper tries to kill heiress
who is forced to live in old mansion.

JUN

10964
HOTEL RESERVE (89) (U)
RKO-Radio
P: Victor Hanbury
D: Lance Comfort, Max Greene
S: (NOVEL) Eric Ambler
(EPITAPH FOR A SPY)
SC: John Davenport
James Mason	Peter Vedassey
Lucie Mannheim	Suzanne Koch
Raymond Lovell	Robert Duclos
Julien Mitchell	Beghin
Clare Hamilton	Mary Skelton
Martin Miller	Walter Vogel
Herbert Lom	Andre Roux
Frederick Valk	Emil Schimler
Patricia Medina	Odette Roux
Ivor Barnard	Chemist
Valentine Dyall	Warren Skelton
David Ward	Henri Asticot
Anthony Shaw	Maj Clandon-Hartlett
CRIME France, 1938. Hotel guest unmasks spy
who used his camera by mistake.

10965
THE WAY AHEAD (115) (U)
Two Cities (EL) *reissue:* 1948 (ABFD)
P: John Sutro, Norman Walker
D: Carol Reed
S: Eric Ambler
SC: Eric Ambler, Peter Ustinov
David Niven	Lt Jim Perry
Raymond Huntley	Davenport
Billy Hartnell	Sgt Fletcher
Stanley Holloway	Brewer
James Donald	Lloyd
John Laurie	Luke
Leslie Dwyer	Beck
Hugh Burden	Parsons
Jimmy Hanley	Stainer
Renee Asherson	Marjorie Gillingham
Penelope Dudley Ward	Mrs Perry
Reginald Tate	CO
Leo Genn	Cdr
Mary Jerrold	Mrs Gillingham
Raymond Lovell	Garage Proprietor
Alf Goddard	Instructor
A.E.Matthews	Col Walmsley
Peter Ustinov	Rispoli
Tessie O'Shea	Herself
WAR Group of infantrymen from
conscription to North Africa.

10966
MEDAL FOR THE GENERAL (99) (U)
British National (Anglo)
P: Louis H. Jackson
D: Maurice Elvey
S: (NOVEL) James Ronald
SC: Elizabeth Baron
Godfrey Tearle	Gen Church
Jeanne de Casalis	Lady Frome
Morland Graham	Bates
Mabel Constanduros	Mrs Bates
John Laurie	McNab
Maureen Glynne	Cynara
Gerald Moore	Harry
Brian Weske	Limpy
Petula Clarke	Irma
Patrick Curwen	Dr Sargeant
Thorley Walters	Andrew
H.F.Maltby	Mayor
DRAMA Cockney evacuees billeted on old
General give him new interest in life.

JUL

10967
GIVE US THE MOON (95) (U)
Gainsborough (GFD)
P: Edward Black
D:SC: Val Guest
S: (NOVEL) Caryl Brahms, S.J.Simon
(THE ELEPHANT IS WHITE)
Margaret Lockwood	Nina
Vic Oliver	Sascha
Peter Graves	Peter Pyke
Roland Culver	Ferdinand
Max Bacon	Jacobus
Frank Cellier	Pyke
Jean Simmons	Heidi
Eliot Makeham	Dumka
Iris Lang	Tania
George Relph	Otto
Gibb McLaughlin	Marcel
Irene Handl	Miss Haddock
Henry Hewitt	Announcer
COMEDY Postwar Soho. Russians form club
to promote idleness.

10968
ONE EXCITING NIGHT (89) (A)
USA: YOU CAN'T DO WITHOUT LOVE
Columbia British
P: Ben Henry, Culley Forde

D: Walter Forde
S: Peter Fraser
SC: Howard Irving Young, Peter Fraser, Margaret Kennedy, Emery Bonnet

Vera Lynn	Vera Baker
Donald Stewart	Michael Thorne
Mary Clare	Mrs Trout
Frederick Leister	Hampton
Richard Murdoch	Illusionist
Phyllis Stanley	Lucille
Cyril Smith	Joe
Mabel Villiers	Mabel

MUSICAL Welfare worker foils plot to steal Rembrandt from producer.

AUG

10969
ENGLISH WITHOUT TEARS (89) (A)
USA: HER MAN GILBEY
Two Cities (GFD) *reissue:* 1949 (ABFD)
P: Anatole de Grunwald, Sydney Box, William Sassoon
D: Harold French
S: Terence Rattigan, Anatole de Grunwald

Michael Wilding	Tom Gilbey
Penelope Ward	Joan Heseltine
Lilli Palmer	Brigid Knudsen
Claude Dauphin	Jean de Freysinet
Roland Culver	Sir Cosmo Brandon
Albert Lieven	Felix Dembowski
Peggy Cummins	Bobby Heseltine
Margaret Rutherford	Lady Christabel Beauderk
Martin Miller	Schmidt
Felix Aylmer	Spagott
Beryl Measor	Miss Foljambe
Judith Furse	Elsie Batter-Jones
Guy Middleton	
Afrique; Albert Whelan	

COMEDY Rich girl joins ATS and falls for her butler who has become a lieutenant.

10970
CHAMPAGNE CHARLIE (105) (A)
Ealing reissue: *reissue:* 1956 (EB; cut)
AP: John Croydon
D: Alberto Cavalcanti
S: Austin Melford, Angus Macphail, John Dighton

Tommy Trinder	George Leybourne
Stanley Holloway	Alfred Vance
Betty Warren	Bessie Bellwood
Austin Trevor	Duke
Jean Kent	Dolly Bellwood
Guy Middleton	Tipsy Swell
Frederick Piper	Learoyd
Harry Fowler	Orace
Robert Wyndham	Duckworth
Peter de Greeff	Lord Petersfield
Andrea Malandrinos	Gatti

MUSICAL 1860. Feud between rival singers is ended by music hall proprietress.

10971
THEY CAME TO A CITY (77) (U)
Ealing *reissue:* 1948
AP: Sidney Cole
D: Basil Dearden
S: (PLAY) J.B.Priestley
SC: Basil Dearden, Sidney Cole

John Clements	Joe Dinmore
Googie Withers	Alice
Raymond Huntley	Malcolm Stritton
Renee Gadd	Mrs Stritton
A.E.Matthews	Sir George Gedney
Mabel Terry-Lewis	Lady Loxfield
Ada Reeve	Mrs Batley
Norman Shelley	Cudworth
Frances Rowe	Philippa Loxfield

FANTASY Assorted group of people find themselves outside the gates of a mysterious city.

10972
2,000 WOMEN (97) (A)
Gainsborough (GFD) *reissue:* 1947 (Eros)
P: Edward Black
D: Frank Launder
S: Frank Launder, Sidney Gilliat

Phyllis Calvert	Freda Thompson
Flora Robson	Miss Manningford
Patricia Roc	Rosemary Brown
Renee Houston	Maud Wright
Anne Crawford	Margaret Long
Jean Kent	Bridie Johnson
Reginald Purdell	Alec Harvey
James Mackechnie	Jimmy Moore
Bob Arden	Dave Kennedy
Carl Jaffe	Sgt Hentzner
Muriel Aked	Miss Meredith
Kathleen Boutall	Mrs Hadfield
Thora Hird	Mrs Burtshaw
Dulcie Gray	Nellie Skinner

WAR France. Two British pilots parachute into women's internment camp.

SEP

10973
THE MAN FROM SCOTLAND YARD (36) (A)
British Foundation
P:D:S: Ronald Haines

Franklyn Scott	Sir Richard Pellis
Muriel George	Agatha Dewsbury
Walter Piers	Col Dewsbury
Geoffrey Heathcote	Inspector Maclean
Elizabeth Wilson	Ethel Dewsbury

CRIME Girl loves man who poses as knight to steal her aunt's jewels.

10974
MR EMMANUEL (97) (A)
Two Cities (EL)
P: William Sistrom
D: Harold French
S: (NOVEL) Louis Golding
SC: Gordon Wellesley, Norman Ginsberg

Felix Aylmer	Mr Emmanuel
Greta Gynt	Elsie Silver
Walter Rilla	Willi Brockenburg
Peter Mullins	Bruno
Ursula Jeans	Frau Heinkes
Elspeth March	Rose Cooper
Frederick Richter	Heikes
Frederick Schiller	Examiner
Maria Berger	Frau Kahn
Charles Goldner	Secretary
Irene Handl	Trude
Meier Tzelniker	Silver
Arnold Marle	Kahn

DRAMA 1936. Old Jew visits Germany to find refugee boy's mother, who has wed a Nazi.

10975
GIVE ME THE STARS (90) (A)
British National (Anglo)
P: Fred Zelnik
D: Maclean Rogers
S: A. Hilarius, Rudolf Bernauer
SC: Maclean Rogers, Austin Melford

Leni Lynn	Toni Martin
Will Fyffe	Hector McTavish
Jackie Hunter	Lyle Mitchell
Olga Lindo	Lady Lester
Emrys Jones	Jack Ross
Margaret Vyner	Patricia Worth
Antony Holles	Achille Lebrun
Grace Arnold	Mrs Gossage
Patric Curwen	Sir John Worth

Joss Ambler	George Burns
Hilda Bayley	Mrs Ross
Angela Glynne	Janie
Guy Fielding; Eda Peel; Ronald Chesney; Stanelli	

MUSICAL 1939. American girl cures Scots grandfather of drunkenness.

OCT

10976
LOVE STORY (108) (U) USA: A LADY
SURRENDERS
Gainsborough (EL) *reissue:* 1949
(Eros; 10 mins cut)
P: Harold Huth
D: Leslie Arliss
S: (NOVEL) J.W.Drawbell
SC: Leslie Arliss, Doreen Montgomery, Rodney Ackland

Margaret Lockwood	Lissa Cambell
Stewart Granger	Kit Firth
Patricia Roc	Judy Martin
Tom Walls	Tom Tanner
Reginald Purdell	Albert
Moira Lister	Carol
Dorothy Bramhall	Susie
Vincent Holman	Prospero
Joan Rees	Ariel
Walter Hudd	Ray
A.E.Matthews	Col Pitt Smith
Beatrice Varley	Mrs Rossiter
Harriet Cohen	Pianist

ROMANCE Cornwall. Pianist with weak heart loves pilot with failing sight.

10977
KISS THE BRIDE GOODBYE (89) (A)
Butcher *reissues:* 1946; 1949 (Sherwood; cut)
P:D:S: Paul Stein
SC: Jack Whittingham

Patricia Medina	Joan Dodd
Jimmy Hanley	Jack Fowler
Frederick Leister	Capt Blood
Marie Lohr	Emma Blood
Claud Allister	Adolphus Pickering
Ellen Pollock	Gladys Dodd
Wylie Watson	David Dodd
Jean Simmons	Molly Dodd
Muriel George	Mrs Fowler
Irene Handl	Mrs Victory
Aubrey Mallalieu	Rev Glory
Hay Petrie	Fraser
C. Denier Warren	Reporter
Julie Suedo	Part time Worker

COMEDY Uncle thinks runaway niece and soldier are newlyweds.

10978
DON'T TAKE IT TO HEART (91) (U)
Two Cities (GFD) *reissue:* 1948 (ABFD)
P: Sydney Box
D:S: Jeffrey Dell

Richard Greene	Peter Hayward
Patricia Medina	Lady Mary
Alfred Drayton	Pike
Edward Rigby	Butler
Richard Bird	Ghost/Arthur
Wylie Watson	Harry Bucket
Moore Marriott	Granfer
Brefni O'Rorke	Earl of Chaunduyt
Amy Veness	Cook
Claude Dampier	Loopy
Joan Hickson	Mrs Pike
Joyce Barbour	Harriet
Ronald Squire	Music Lover
Ernest Thesiger	Clerk
David Horne	Sir Henry Wade

COMEDY Lawyer proves village poacher is rightful Earl.

10979
A NIGHT OF MAGIC (56) (U)
Berkeley (Premier)
P: Burt Hyams
D: Herbert Wynne
S: Eversley Bracken
Robert Griffith . . . . Reggie
Billy "Uke" Scott . . . . His Pal
Marian Olive . . . . Princess Raviola
Broadway Boys; Dot Delavine; Vera Bradley;
Gordon Ray Girls
MUSICAL Playboy dreams 3,000-year old
Egyptian Princess revives.

10980
FIDDLERS THREE (88) (A)
Ealing *reissue:* 1948
AP: Robert Hamer
D: Harry Watt
S: Diana Morgan, Angus Macphail
Tommy Trinder . . . . Tommy
Frances Day . . . . Poppaea
Sonnie Hale . . . . Professor
Francis L. Sullivan . . . . . . Nero
Diana Decker . . . . Lydia
Elisabeth Welch . . . . Thora
Mary Clare . . . . Volumnia
Ernest Milton . . . . Titus
Frederick Piper . . . . Auctioneer
Robert Wyndham . . . . . . .Lion-keeper
Russell Thorndike . . . . High Priest
FANTASY Sailors save Wren from
Nero's orgy when lighting sends them back
to Ancient Rome.

10981
TWILIGHT HOUR (85) (U)
British National (Anglo)
P: Louis H. Jackson
D: Paul Stein
S: (NOVEL) Arthur Valentine
SC: Jack Whittingham
Mervyn Johns . . . . John Smith
Basil Radford . . . . Lord Chetwood
Marie Lohr . . . . Lady Chetwood
A.E.Matthews . . . . Gen Fitzhenry
Lesley Brook . . . . Virginia
Grey Blake . . . . Michael
Ian Maclean . . . . Hemingway
Barbara Waring . . . . Gladys
Brefni O'Rorke . . . . Richard Melville
Margaret Vyner . . . . Angela
Joyce Heron . . . . Diana
DRAMA Lord's amnesiac gardener is a
rich Major, father of the Lord's son's fiancee.

10982
MEET SEXTON BLAKE (80) (A)
British National-Strand (Anglo)
P: Louis H. Jackson
D: SC: John Harlow
S: (CHARACTERS) Harry Blyth
David Farrar . . . . Sexton Blake
John Varley . . . . Tinker
Magda Kun . . . . Yvonne
Gordon McLeod . . . . Insp Venner
Manning Whiley . . . . Raoul Sudd
Kathleen Harrison . . . . Mrs Bardell
Dennis Arundell . . . . Johann Sudd
Cyril Smith . . . . Belford
Ferdi Mayne . . . . Slant-eyes
Betty Huntley-Wright . . . . . Nobby
Jean Simmons . . . . Eva Watkins
CRIME Crook steals brother's formula
for airplane alloy.

NOV

10983
MY AIN FOLK (75) (U)
Butcher *reissues:* 1946; 1949 (Sherwood)
P: F.W. Baker
D: Germain Burger
S: Kathleen Butler
Mabel Constanduros . . . . . . Mrs Mackenzie
Moira Lister . . . . Joan Mackenzie
Norman Prince . . . . Malcolm Keir
Herbert Cameron . . . . Mr Keir
Nicolette Roeg . . . . Betty Stewart
John Turner . . . . Robertson
Ben Williams . . . . Jack McAllister
Charles Rolfe . . . . Alan Macgregor
Walter Midgeley; Lowry & Richardson;
Lorna Martin
MUSICAL Glasgow. Factory girl loves
wireless operator in Merchant Navy.

10984
DREAMING (78) (U)
John Baxter (Ealing)
D: John Baxter
S: Bud Flanagan, Reginald Purdell
Flanagan & Allen . . . . Bud & Ches
Hazel Court . . . . . . Wren/Avalah/Miss Grey
Dick Francis . . . . Sir Charles Paddock
Philip Wade . . . . Dr Goebbels
Gerry Wilmot . . . . US General
Peter Bernard . . . . US Soldier
Ian Maclean . . . . General
Roy Russell . . . . Trainer
Robert Adams . . . . Prince
Teddy Brown; Reginald Foort; Gordon
Richards; Raymond Glendenning; Bobby
Jones; Alfredo Campoli; Band of HM Col-
stream Guards; Donald McCullough
COMEDY Soldier dreams of Ascot races,
Africa, Germany, and Stage Door Canteen.

DEC

10985
HE SNOOPS TO CONQUER (103) (U)
Columbia British
P: Ben Henry, Marcel Varnel
D: Marcel Varnel
S: Stephen Black, Howard Irving Young,
Norman Lee, Michael Vaughan, Langford Reed
George Formby . . . . George Gribble
Robertson Hare . . . Sir Timothy Strawbridge
Elizabeth Allan . . . . . Jane Strawbridge
Claude Bailey . . . . Councillor Oxbold
James Harcourt . . . . . . Councillor Hopkins
Aubrey Mallalieu . . . . . .Councillor Stubbins
Gordon McLeod . . . . Angus McGluee
Vincent Holman . . . . Butler
COMEDY Handyman and inventor expose
council's fraudulent plebiscite.

10986
MADONNA OF THE SEVEN MOONS (110) (A)
Gainsborough (EL) *reissue:* 1949 (Eros)
P: R.J. Minney
D: Arthur Crabtree
S: (NOVEL) Margery Lawrence
SC: Roland Pertwee, Brock Williams
Phyllis Calvert . . . . Maddalena (Rosanna)
Stewart Granger . . . . Nino Barucci
Patricia Roc . . . . Angela
Peter Glenville . . . . Sandro Barucci
John Stuart . . . . Guiseppi
Jean Kent . . . . Vittoria
Nancy Price . . . . Mme Barucci
Peter Murray Hill . . . . Logan
Reginald Tate . . . . Ackroyd
Dulcie Gray . . . . Nesta
Amy Veness . . . . Tessa
Hilda Bayley . . . . Mrs Fiske
ROMANCE Italy. Childhood rape makes
prim wife become gipsy thief's mistress.

10987
THE TWO FATHERS (13) (U)
Crown Film Unit (WB)
P: Arthur Elton
D:SC: Anthony Asquith
S: V.S.Pritchett
Bernard Miles . . . . Englishman
Paul Bonifas . . . . Frenchman
Margaret Yarde . . . .
Paulette Pruny . . . .
Arthur Young . . . .
Everley Gregg . . . .
David Keir . . . .
WAR Englishman with son in RAF shares
room with Frenchman whose daughter is
nurse in Maquis.

1945

JAN

10988
WATERLOO ROAD (76) (A)
Gainsborough (GFD)
P: Edward Black
D:S: Sidney Gilliatt
SC: Val Valentine

John Mills	Jim Colter
Stewart Granger	Ted Purvis
Alastair Sim	Dr Montgomery
Joy Shelton	Tillie Colter
Beatrice Varley	Mrs Colter
Alison Leggatt	Ruby
Leslie Bradley	Mike Duggan
Jean Kent	Toni
George Carney	Tom Mason
Wylie Watson	Tattooist
Arthur Denton	Fred
Vera Frances	Vera
Ben Williams	Cpl Lewis
Anna Konstam	May
Wallace Lupino	Uncle

DRAMA Cockney private goes AWOL to save his wife from a spiv.

10989
THE WORLD OWES ME A LIVING (91) (A)
British National (Anglo)
P: Louis H. Jackson
D: Vernon Sewell
S: (NOVEL) John Llewellyn-Rhys
SC: Vernon Sewell, Erwin Reiner

David Farrar	Paul Collyer
Judy Campbell	Moira Barrett
Sonia Dresdel	Eve Heatherley
Jack Livesey	Jack Graves
Jack Barker	Chuck Rockley
John Laurie	Matthews
Anthony Hawtrey	Jerry
Wylie Watson	Conductor

WAR Amnesiac commodore recalls how, as a flying circus pilot, he helped to devise a troop-carrying glider.

10990
STRAWBERRY ROAN (84) (U)
British National (Anglo)
P: Louis H. Jackson
D: Maurice Elvey
S: (NOVEL) A.G.Street
SC: Elizabeth Baron

Billy Hartnell	Chris Lowe
Carole Raye	Molly Lowe
Walter Fitzgerald	Morley
Sophie Stewart	Mrs Morley
John Ruddock	Dibben
Wylie Watson	Bill Gurd
Petula Clark	Emily
Joan Maude	Gladys Moon
Joan Young	Mrs Dibben
Ellis Irving	Auctioneer
Kynaston Reeves	Dealer
Norman Shelley	Dr Lambert

Jack Simpson and his Sextet
DRAMA Farmer weds extravagant showgirl who ruins his farm and himself.

10991
THE AGITATOR (104) (U)
British National (Anglo) reissue: 1948 (Pathe; cut)
P: Louis H. Jackson
D: John Harlow
S: (NOVEL) William Riley (PETER PETTINGER)
S: (NOVEL) William Riley (PETER PETTINGER)
SC: Edward Dryhurst

Billy Hartnell	Peter Pettinger
Mary Morris	Lettie Shackleton
John Laurie	Tom Tetley
Moore Marriott	Ben Duckett
George Carney	
Edward Rigby	Charlie Bromfield
Elliot Mason	
Frederick Leister	Mark Overend
J.H.Roberts	
Cathleen Nesbitt	Mrs Montrose
Moira Lister	Joan Shackleton

DRAMA Socialist agitator inherits factory on employer's death.

10992
HENRY V (137) tech (U)
Two Cities (EL)
P:D: Laurence Olivier
S: (PLAY) William Shakespeare
SC: Laurence Olivier, Alan Dent

Laurence Olivier	Henry V
Robert Newton	Ancient Pistol
Leslie Banks	Chorus
Renee Asherson	Katherine
Esmond Knight	Fluellen
Leo Genn	Constable
Ralph Truman	Mountjoy
Harcourt Williams	Charles VI
Ivy StHelier	Alice
Ernest Thesiger	Duke of Bedford
Max Adrian	Dauphin
Francis Lister	Duke of Orleans
Valentine Dyall	Duke of Burgundy
Russell Thorndike	Duke of Bourbon
Morland Graham	Sir Thomas Erpingham
George Cole	Boy
Felix Aylmer	Archbishop of Canterbury
Nicholas Hannen	Duke of Exeter
Robert Helpmann	Bishop of Ely
Freda Jackson	Mistress Quickly
Jimmy Hanley	Williams
John Laurie	Jamy
Niall MacGinnis	McMorris
George Robey	Sir John Falstaff
Roy Emerton	Bardolph
Griffith Jones	Earl of Salisbury
Frederick Cooper	Cpl Nym

HISTORY 1415. King of England leads army to win at Agincourt. (AA: Special Award, 1946; PGAA: 1946).

FEB

10993
FLIGHT FROM FOLLY (94) (A)
WB-FN
D: Herbert Mason
S: Edmund Goulding
SC: Basil Woon, Lesley Storm, Katherine Strueby

Pat Kirkwood	Sue Brown
Hugh Sinclair	Clinton Gray
Sydney Howard	Dr Wylie
Marian Spencer	Harriet
Tamara Desni	Nina
A.E.Matthews	Neville
Jean Gillie	Millicent
Leslie Bradley	Bomber
Charles Goldner	Ramon

Edmundo Ros and his Band; Halamar & Konarski
MUSICAL Showgirl poses as nurse to cure playwright of amnesia.

10994
THE MAN FROM MOROCCO (115) (A)
ABPC (Pathe)
P: Warwick Ward
D: Max Greene
S: Rudolph Cartier
SC: Warwick Ward, Edward Dryhurst, Margaret Steen

Anton Walbrook	Karel Langer
Margaretta Scott	Manuela
Mary Morris	Sarah Duboste
Reginald Tate	Ricardi
Peter Sinclair	Joack Sinclair
David Horne	Dr Duboste
Hartley Power	Cql Bagley
Sybilla Binder	Erna
Charles Victor	Bourdelle
Dennis Arundell	Galzini
Orlando Martins	Jeremiah

WAR Czech leader of international Brigade escapes to London with secret information.

MAR

10995
FOR YOU ALONE (98) (U)
Butcher reissue: 1948 (Sherwood; 22 mins cut)
P: F.W. Baker
D: Geoffrey Faithfull
S: Kathleen Butler
SC: Montgomery Tully

Lesley Brook	Katherine Britton
Jimmy Hanley	Dennis Britton
Dinah Sheridan	Stella White
G.H.Mulcaster	Rev Peter Britton
Robert Griffith	John Bradshaw
Olive Walter	Lady Markham
Manning Whiley	Max Borrow
Irene Handl	Miss Trotter
George Merritt	PC Blundell
Muriel George	Mrs Johns

Helen Hill; Heddle Nash; Albert Sandler; London Symphony Orchestra
MUSICAL Naval officer loves cleric's daughter promised to another.

10996
JUDGE JEFFERSON REMEMBERS (16) (A)
British Foundation (Col)
D: Ronald Haines
CRIME Criminal Court judge recalls three crimes.

10997
SPORTS DAY (24) (U)
GB Instructional (GFD)
reissue: THE COLONEL'S CUP

Jean Simmons	Girl

CHILDREN Boy wrongly accused of maltreating dog is cleared in time to win swimming cup.

10998
THE TELL-TALE TAPS (20) (A)
B.S.Productions (20)
P:D: Paul Barralet
Richard Goolden
Ida Reece
CRIME Dancer uses tap routine to broadcast RAF's plan to bomb Keil canal.

10999
A PLACE OF ONE'S OWN (92) (A)
Gainsborough (EL) reissue: 1949 (Eros)
P: R.J.Minney
D: Bernard Knowles
S: (NOVEL) Osbert Sitwell
SC: Brock Williams

Margaret Lockwood	Annette
James Mason	Mr Smedhurst
Barbara Mullen	Mrs Smedhurst
Dennis Price	Dr Selbie
Helen Haye	Mrs Manning-Tuthorn
Michael Shepley	Maj Manning-Tuthorn
Dulcie Gray	Sarah
Moore Marriott	George
Gus McNaughton	PC Hargreaves
Ernest Thesiger	Dr Marsham
O.B.Clarence	Perkins
John Turnbull	Sir Roland Jarvis
Clarence Wright	Brighouse

FANTASY Companion of old couple is possessed by spirit of murdered girl.

11000
I LIVE IN GROSVENOR SQUARE (113) (U)
USA: A YANK IN LONDON
ABPC (Pathe)
P:D: Herbert Wilcox
S: Maurice Cowan
SC: Nicholas Phipps, William D. Bayles

Anna Neagle	Lady Pat Fairfax
Rex Harrison	Maj David Bruce
Dean Jagger	Sgt John Patterson
Robert Morley	Duke of Exmoor
Jane Darwell	Mrs Patterson
Nancy Price	Mrs Wilson
Irene Vanbrugh	Mrs Catchpole
Edward Rigby	Innkeeper
Walter Hudd	Vicar
Elliott Arluck	Benjie Greenburg
Francis Pierlot	Postman
Aubrey Mallalieu	Bates
Michael Shepley	Lt Lutyens
Charles Victor	Taxidriver
Ronald Shiner	Paratrooper

Irene Manning; Alvar Liddell; Gerry Wilmot;
Carroll Gibbons and his Orchestra
ROMANCE Duke's daughter engaged to
Major falls in love with USAAF sergeant.

APR

11001
GREAT DAY (79) (U)
RKO-Radio
P: Victor Hanbury
D: Lance Comfort
S: (PLAY) Lesley Storm
SC: Wolfgang Wilhelm, John Davenport

Eric Portman	Capt Ellis
Flora Robson	Mrs Ellis
Sheila Sim	Margaret Ellis
Isabel Jeans	Lady Mott
Walter Fitzgerald	John Tyndale
Philip Friend	Geoffrey Winthrop
Marjorie Rhodes	Mrs Mumford
Margaret Withers	Mrs Tyndale
Maire O'Neill	Mrs Walsh
Beatrice Varley	Miss Tracy

DRAMA Village Women's Institute prepares
for visit by Mrs Roosevelt.

11002
BLITHE SPIRIT (96) (A) *tech*
Two Cities-Cineguild (GFD)
P: Anthony Havelock-Allan
D: David Lean
S: (PLAY) Noel Coward
SC: David Lean, Anthony Havelock-Allan,
Ronald Neame

Rex Harrison	Charles Condomine
Constance Cummings	Ruth Condomine
Kay Hammond	Elvira Condomine
Margaret Rutherford	Mme Arcati
Hugh Wakefield	George Bradman
Joyce Carey	Violet Bradman
Jacqueline Clark	Edith

FANTASY Man's second marriage upset
by return of his first wife's ghost.

11003
THEY WERE SISTERS (115) (A)
Gainsborough (GFD)
reissue: 1947 (Eros; cut)
P: Harold Huth
D: Arthur Crabtree
S: (NOVEL) Dorothy Whipple
SC: Roland Pertwee, Katherine Strueby

Phyllis Calvert	Lucy
James Mason	Geoffrey
Hugh Sinclair	Terry
Anne Crawford	Vera
Dulcie Gray	Charlotte
Peter Murray Hill	William
Barrie Livesey	Brian
Pamela Kellino	Margaret
Ann Stephens	Judith
Helen Stephens	Sarah
John Gilpin	Stephen
Brian Nissen	John
David Horne	Mr Field
Brefni O'Rorke	Coroner
Amy Veness	Mrs Purley

ROMANCE Three sisters and their respective
marriages.

MAY

11004
OLD MOTHER RILEY AT HOME (76) (A)
British National (Anglo)
P: Louis H. Jackson
D: Oswald Mitchell
S: Joan Butler, Ralph Temple
SC: Oswald Mitchell, George A. Cooper

Arthur Lucan	Mrs Riley
Kitty McShane	Kitty Riley
Freddie Forbes	Mr Bumpron
Richard George	Dan
Willer Neal	Bill
Wally Patch	Bouncer
Kenneth Warrington	Boss
Angela Barrie	Duchess
Janet Morrison	Mary
Elsie Wagstaffe	Mrs Ginochie

COMEDY Girl becomes hostess in country
house used as gambling den.

11005
DON CHICAGO (80) (A)
British National (Anglo)
P: Louis H. Jackson
D: Maclean Rogers
S: (NOVEL) C.E.Bechhofer-Roberts
SC: Austin Melford

Jackie Hunter	Don Chicago
Eddie Gray	PC Gray
Joyce Heron	Kitty Mannering
Claud Allister	Lord Piccadilly
Amy Veness	Bowie Knife Bella
Wylie Watson	Peabody
Don Stannard	Ken Cressing
Charles Farrell	Don Dooley
Finlay Currie	Bugs Mulligan
Cyril Smith	Flash Kelly
Ellen Pollock	Lady Vanessa
Moira Lister	Telephone Operator
Wally Patch	Sgt

Eric Winstone and his Band; The Modernaires
COMEDY PC thwarts gangster's attempt
to steal Crown Jewels.

11006
29 ACACIA AVENUE (83) (A)
USA: THE FACTS OF LOVE
Boca (Col)
P: Sydney Box
D: Henry Cass
S: (PLAY Mabel & Denis Constanduros
(ACACIA AVENUE)
SC: Muriel & Sydney Box

Gordon Harker	Mr Robinson
Carla Lehmann	Fay
Jimmy Hanley	Peter Robinson
Betty Balfour	Mrs Robinson
Jill Evans	Joan
Hubert Gregg	Michael
Dinah Sheridan	Pepper Robinson
Henry Kendall	Wilson
Guy Middleton	Gerald
Megs Jenkins	Shirley
Noele Gordon	Mrs Wilson

COMEDY Youth falls for married flirt
and his sister has trial marriage.

JUN

11007
THE MAN WITH THE MAGNETIC EYES
(51) (A)
British Foundation *reissue:* 1951 (G&S)
P:D: Ronald Haines
S: (NOVEL) Roland Daniel

Robert Bradfield	Norman Wade
Henry Norman	Van Deerman
Joan Carter	Diana Wilbur
Peter Lilley	Harry Wilbur
Charles Penrose	Roberts
Mabel Twemlow	Mrs Morton Rose
Andre Belhomme	Count Arno

CRIME Tec poses as playboy to catch
the head of spy ring.

11008
CAMERA REFLECTIONS (38) (A)
Ariston (Ambassador)
D: Julia Woolf
S: Yvonne Thomas
N: John Stuart
COMPILATION Extracts from silent films.

11009
JULIUS CAESAR (19) (U)
Theatrecraft (20)
P: Sidney Box
D: Compton Bennett
S: (PLAY) William Shakespeare

Felix Aylmer	Brutus
Leo Genn	Mark Antony

DRAMA Forum scene.

11010
MACBETH (16) (U)
Theatrecraft (20)
P: Sidney Box
D: Henry Cass
S: (PLAY) William Shakespeare

Wilfrid Lawson	Macbeth
Cathleen Nesbitt	Lady Macbeth

DRAMA Murder scene; sleepwalking scene.

11011
THE WAY TO THE STARS (109) (U)
USA: JOHNNY IN THE CLOUDS
Two Cities (UA)
P: Anatole de Grunwald
D: Anthony Asquith
S: Terence Rattigan, Richard Sherman
SC: Terence Rattigan, Anatole de Grunwald

Michael Redgrave	David Archdale
John Mills	Peter Penrose
Rosamund John	Toddy Todd
Douglass Montgomery	Johnny Hollis
Stanley Holloway	Mr Palmer
Renee Asherson	Iris Winterton
Felix Aylmer	Rev Charles Moss
Basil Radford	Tiny Williams
Bonar Colleano jr	Joe Friselli
Trevor Howard	S/L Carter
Joyce Carey	Miss Winterton
Jean Simmons	Singer
Bill Rowbotham	Nobby Clarke
Charles Victor	Fitter
David Tomlinson	Prune Parsons
Hartley Power	Col Hope
Alf Goddard	Sgt

WAR 1940. Pilot postpones marriage when
his comrades are killed. (DMNFA:
Best British Film 1939-1945).

11012
I'LL BE YOUR SWEETHEART (104) (A)
Gainsborough (GFD) *reissue:* 1948
P: Louis Levy
D: Val Guest
S: Val Guest, Val Valentine

Margaret Lockwood	Edie Storey
Vic Oliver	Sammy Kahn
Michael Rennie	Bob Fielding
Peter Graves	Jim Knight
Moore Marriott.	George le Brunn
Frederick Burtwell	Pacey
Maudie Edwards	Mrs Jones
Garry Marsh	Wallace
George Merritt	T.P. O'Connor
Muriel George	Mrs le Brunn
Eliot Makeham	John Friar
Ella Retford	Dresser
Alf Goddard	Henchman

MUSICAL 1900. Songwriters' fight with
music pirates brings about Copyright Act.

11013
I DIDN'T DO IT (97) (A)
Columbia British
P: Marcel Varnel, Ben Henry
D: Marcel Varnel
S: Howard Irving Young, Stephen Black,
Norman Lee, Peter Fraser, Michael Vaughan

George Formby	George Trotter
Billy Caryll	Pa Tubbs
Hilda Mundy	Ma Tubbs
Gaston Palmer	le Grand Gaston
Jack Daly	Terry O'Rourke
Carl Jaffe	Hilary Vance
Marjorie Browne	Jill Dixon
Wally Patch	Sgt Carp
Ian Fleming	Insp Twyning
Vincent Holman	Erasmus Montague
Dennis Wyndham	Tom Driscoll
Jack Raine	J.B.Cato
The Boswell Twins	

COMEDY Stage-struck boarder proves he
did not kill Australian acrobat.

JUL

11014
WALTZ TIME (100) (A)
British National (Anglo)
P: Louis H. Jackson
D: Paul Stein
S: Henry C.James, Karl Rossler
SC: Montgomery Tully, Jack Whittingham

Carole Raye	Empress Maria
Peter Graves . . .	Count Franz von Hofer
Patricia Medina	Cenci Prohaska
Thorley Walters	Stephan Ravenne
Richard Tauber	Shepherd
Harry Welchman.	Count Rodzanka
George Robey	Vogel
John Ruddock	Count Prohaska
Hugh Dempster	Ferdinand Hohenlohe
Brefni O'Rorke	Emperor
Wylie Watson	Josef
Tonie Edgar Bruce	Augustine
Kay Kendall	Lady-in-waiting
Anne Zeigler; Webster Booth; Albert	
Sandler; Hans May	

MUSICAL Vienna, period. Empress poses as
her masked friend to win philandering Count.

11015
JOHNNY FRENCHMAN (105) (U)
Ealing (EL)
AP: S.C.Balcon
D: Charles Frend
S: T.E.B.Clarke

Francoise Rosay	Lanec Florrie
Tom Walls	Nat Pomeroy
Patricia Roc	Sue Pomeroy
Ralph Michael	Bob Tremayne
Paul Dupuis	Yan Kervarec
Frederick Piper	Zacky Penrose
Arthur Hambling	Steve Matthews
Richard George	Charlie West
Bill Blewett	Dick Trewhiddie
James Harcourt	Joe Pender

Grace Arnold	Mrs Matthews
Beatrice Varley	Mrs Tremayne
Judith Furse	Jane Matthews
Stan Paskin	Tim Bassett

DRAMA Cornwall. Evacuated Breton
fisherwoman saves village from mine,
settling an ancient feud.

AUG

11016
THEY KNEW MR KNIGHT (93) (A)
IP-GHW Productions (GFD)
reissue: 1949 (ABFD)
P: James B. Sloan
D: Norman Walker
S: (NOVEL) Dorothy Whipple
SC: Norman Walker, Victor MacClure

Mervyn Johns	Tom Blake
Nora Swinburne	Celia Blake
Alfred Drayton	Mr Knight
Joyce Howard	Freda Blake
Joan Greenwood	Ruth Blake
Olive Sloane	Mrs Blake
Joan Maude	Carrie Porritt
Peter Hammond	Douglas Knight
Marie Ault	Grandma Knight
Frederick Cooper	Edward Knight
Grace Arnold	Isabel Knight
Kenneth Kove	Coggie Selby
Frederick Burtwell	Mr Berry

DRAMA Financier's tips bring wealth and
then ruin to clerk's family.

11017
HOME SWEET HOME (92) (A)
Mancunian (Butcher)
reissue: 1948 (11 mins cut)
P:D: John E.Blakeley
S: Roney Parsons, Anthony Toner,
Frank Randle

Frank Randle	Frank
Nicolette Roeg	Jacqueline Chantry
Tony Pendrell	Eric Wright
H.F.Maltby	Col Wright
Hilda Bayley	Mrs Wright
Cecil Fredericks	Webster
Stan Little	Young Herbert
Bunty Meadows	Bunty
Gerhard Kempinski	Pagoli
George Merritt	Dr Handy
Rawicz & Landauer; Helen Hill; Donovan & Byl;	
Arnley & Gloria	

COMEDY Doorman aids romance of boss's
son and Jersey evacuee. (Extract in
RANDLE AND ALL THAT.)

SEP

11018
PERFECT STRANGERS (102) (A)
USA: VACATION FROM MARRIAGE
MGM-London *reissue:* 1948
P:D: Alexander Korda
S: Clemence Dane
SC: Clemence Dane, Anthony Pelissier

Robert Donat	Robert Wilson
Deborah Kerr	Catherine Wilson
Glynis Johns	Dizzy Clayton
Ann Todd	Elena
Roland Culver	Richard
Elliot Mason	Mrs Hemmings
Eliot Makeham	Mr Staines
Brefni O'Rorke	Mr Hargrove
Edward Rigby	Charlie
Muriel George	Minnie
Allan Jeayes	Cmdr
Ivor Barnard	Chemist

ROMANCE Naval war service improves
characters of clerk and dowdy wife.
(AA: Best Story 1946).

11019
PAINTED BOATS (63) (U)
USA: THE GIRL ON THE CANAL
Ealing
AP: Henry Cornelius
D: Charles Crichton
S: Stephen Black
SC: Louis MacNeice, Michael McCarthy
N: James McKechnie

Jenny Laird	Mary Smith
Robert Griffith	Ted Stoner
Bill Blewett	Pa Smith
May Hallatt	Ma Smith
Harry Fowler	Alf Stoner
Madoline Thomas	Mrs Stoner
Megs Jenkins	Barmaid

DRAMA Canal girl loves bargee who joins
the army without knowing she is pregnant.

11020
THE ECHO MURDERS (75) (A)
British National-Strand (Anglo)
P: Louis H. Jackson
D:SC: John Harlow
S: (CHARACTERS) Harry Blyth

David Farrar	Sexton Blake
Dennis Price	Dick Warren
Pamela Stirling	Stella Duncan
Julien Mitchell	James Duncan
Dennis Arundell	Rainsford
Cyril Smith	PC Morgan
Ferdi Mayne	Dacier
Kynaston Reeves	Beales
Patric Curwen	Dr Grey

CRIME Cornwall. Tec stages own death
to catch Nazis using tin mines.

11021
HERE WE COME GATHERING (21) (U)
Wallace Productions (GFD)
P:D: Barry Delmaine
CHILDREN Kent. Unpopular boy on
fruit picking holiday rescues girl from sandpit.

11022
DEAD OF NIGHT (1)4) (A)
Ealing (EL) *reissue:* 1949 (ABFD); 10 mins cut)
AP: Sidney Cole, John Croydon
SC: Angus Macphail, John Baines, T.E.B.
Clarke
The Linking Story
D: Basil Dearden
S: (STORY) E.F.Benson

Mervyn Johns	Walter Craig
Roland Culver	Eliot Foley
Mary Merrall.	Mrs Foley
Frederick Valk	Dr Van Straaten
Renee Gadd	Mrs Craig

The Hearse Driver
D: Basil Dearden
S: (STORY) E.F.Benson

Antony Baird	Hugh Grainger
Judy Kelly	Joyce Grainger
Miles Malleson	Hearse Driver

The Christmas Story
D: Cavalcanti
S: Angus Macphail

Sally Ann Howes	Sally O'Hara
Michael Allan	Jimmy Watson
Robert Wyndham	Dr Albury

The Haunted Mirror
D: Robert Hamer
S: John V. Baines

Googie Withers	Joan Courtland
Ralph Michael	Peter Courtland
Esme Percy	Dealer

The Ventriloquist's Dummy
D: Cavalcanti
S: John V. Baines

Michael Redgrave	Maxwell Frere

Hartley Power . . . . Sylvester Kee
Elisabeth Welch . . . . Beulah
Magda Kun . . . . Mitzi
Garry Marsh . . . . Harry Parker
The Golfing Story
D: Charles Crichton
S: (STORY) H.G.Wells
Basil Radford . . . . George Parratt
Naunton Wayne . . . . Larry Potter
Peggy Bryan . . . . Mary Lee
FANTASY Characters in architect's
recurring nightmare narrate their supernatural
experiences.

OCT

11023
MURDER IN REVERSE (88) (A)
British National (Anglo)
P: Louis H.Jackson
D:SC: Montgomery Tully
S: (NOVEL) "Seamark" (QUERY)
Billy Hartnell . . . . Tom Masterick
Jimmy Hanley . . . . Peter Rogers
Chili Bouchier . . . . Doris Masterick
John Slater . . . . Fred Smith
Dinah Sheridan . . . . Jill Masterick
Wylie Watson . . . . Tailor
Edward Rigby . . . . Spike
Brefni O'Rorke . . . . Sullivan
Maire O'Neill . . . . Mrs Moore
Ellis Irving . . . . Sgt Howell
Petula Clark . . . . Jill (child)
Kynaston Reeves . . . . Crossley KC
John Salew . . . . Blake KC
Aubrey Mallalieu . . . . Judge
Scott Sanders . . . . Landlord
Maudie Edwards . . . . Customer
CRIME Ex-convict tracks down the man
he was supposed to have killed.

11024
JOURNEY TOGETHER (95) (U)
RAF Film Unit (RKO) *reissue:* 1949 (Premier)
D: SC: John Boulting
S: Terence Rattigan
Richard Attenborough . . . . David Wilton
Edward G.Robinson . . . . . . Dean McWilliams
Bessie Love . . . . Mary McWilliams
Ronald Squire . . . . Selection Officer
Jack Watling . . . . John Aynesworth
David Tomlinson . . . . Smith
Hugh Wakefield . . . . Adjutant
John Justin . . . . Instructor
George Cole . . . . Curley
Stuart Latham . . . . · Fitter
WAR R A F trainee fails as pilot but
becomes successful navigator.

11025
MEN OF THE MINES (42) (U)
Bruton (Premier)
P: John Sutro, Eric Cosby
D: David MacKane
S: Edward Cork
Ernest Butcher . . . . Joe Cartwright
Gladys Young . . . . Maggie Cartwright
John McLaren . . . . Ted Flinton
Monica Mallory . . . . Mary Cartwright
Don Avory . . . . Bill Oakland
DRAMA Yorks. Reporter falls for miner's
daughter.

11026
THE SEVENTH VEIL (94) (A)
Theatrecraft-Ortus (GFD)
reissues: 1948; 1950 (ABFD)
P: John Sutro, Sydney Box

D: Compton Bennett
S: Muriel & Sydney Box
James Mason . . . . Nicholas
Ann Todd . . . . Francesca Cunningham
Herbert Lom . . . . Dr Larsen
Hugh McDermott . . . . Peter Gay
Albert Lieven . . . . Maxwell Leyden
Yvonne Owen . . . . Susan Brooks
David Horne . . . . Dr Kendal
Manning Whiley . . . . Dr Irving
John Slater . . . . James
Eileen Joyce; Muir Matheson; Arnold
Goldsborough
ROMANCE After psychiatric treatment a
suicidal pianist prefers cruel guardian to
artist or band leader. (AA: Best Screenplay
1946; PGAA: 1946; Top Moneymaker:
1945).

NOV

11027
SWEETHEARTS FOR EVER (33) (U)
Empire Films (Renown)
P: Moss Goodman, Victor C.Harvey
D: S: Frank Richardson
Carl Carlisle   Jules Reuben
Rosalind Melville   Johnny Denis
Frank King and his Band
MUSICAL Proprietors of actors' home
celebrate 50th anniversary.

11028
LATIN QUARTER (80) (A)
British National (Anglo)
P: Louis H.Jackson, Derrick de Marney
D: SC: Vernon Sewell
S: (PLAY) Pierre Mills, C. de Vylars
(L'ANGOISE)
Derrick de Marney . . . . Charles Garrie
Frederick Valk . . . . Dr Krasner
Joan Greenwood . . . . . . Christine Minetti
Joan Seton . . . . Lucille
Beresford Egan . . . . Minetti'
Lilly Kann . . . . Maria
Martin Miller . . . . Morgue Keeper
Valentine Dyall . . . . Prefect
Anthony Hawtrey . . . . Specialist
Bruce Winston . . . . Friend
Sybilla Binder . . . . Medium
CRIME Paris, 1893. Psychic model reveals
mad sculptor killed his wife and put her
inside statue.

11029
I KNOW WHERE I'M GOING (92) (U)
IP-Archers (GFD) *reissue:* 1949
(Eros; 10 mins cut)
P:D:S: Michael Powell, Emeric Pressburger
Roger Livesey . . . . Torquil McNeil
Wendy Hiller . . . . Joan Webster
Pamela Brown . . . . Catriona Potts
Nancy Price . . . . Mrs Crozier
Finlay Currie . . . . Ruairidh Mur
John Laurie . . . . John Campbell
George Carney . . . . Mr Webster
Walter Hudd . . . . Hunter
Murdo Morrison . . . . Kenny
Margot Fitzsimmons . . . . . Bridie
Jean Cadell . . . . Postmistress
Norman Shelley . . . . . Sir Robert Bellinger
Petula Clark . . . . Cheril
Catherine Lacey . . . . Mrs Robinson
Valentine Dyall . . . . Mr Robinson
Herbert Lomas . . . . Mr Campbell
Graham Moffatt . . . . Sgt
ROMANCE Hebrides. Girl travelling to wed
rich man falls for poor laird while stranded
in storm.

11030
CABARET (33) (A)
Empire Films (Premier)
P: Moss Goodman, Victor C.Harvey
D: Frank Richardson
Harry Seltzer
Rosalinde Melville
Frank King and his Orchestra
REVUE

DEC

11031
BRIEF ENCOUNTER (86) (A)
IP-Cineguild (GFD) *reissue:* 1948 (ABFD)
P: Anthony Havelock-Allan, Ronald Neame
D: David Lean
S: (PLAY) Noel Coward (STILL LIFE)
SC: David Lean, Ronald Neame
Celia Johnson . . . . Laura Jesson
Trevor Howard . . . . Dr Alec Harvey
Stanley Holloway . . . . Albert Godby
Joyce Carey . . . . Myrtle Bagot
Cyril Raymond . . . . Fred Jesson
Everley Gregg . . . . Dolly Messiter
Margaret Barton . . . . Beryl Walters
Dennis Harkin . . . . Stanley
Valentine Dyall . . . . Stephen Lynn
Marjorie Mars . . . . Mary Norton
Irene Handl . . . . Organist
ROMANCE Married woman and married
doctor fall in love but agree to part.

11032
THE WICKED LADY (104) (A)
Gainsborough (EL) *reissue:* 1949 (ABFD)
P: R.J.Minney
D: Leslie Arliss
S: (NOVEL) Magdalen King-Hall
(LIFE AND DEATH OF THE WICKED
LADY SKELTON)
SC: Leslie Arliss, Aimee Stuart, Gordon
Glennon
Margaret Lockwood . . . . . Barbara Worth
James Mason . . . . Capt Jerry Jackson
Patricia Roc . . . . Caroline
Griffith Jones . . . . Sir Ralph Skelton
Michael Rennie . . . . Kit Locksby
Felix Aylmer . . . . Hogarth
Enid Stamp Taylor . . . . Henrietta Kingsclere

Jean Kent . . . . Doxy
Martita Hunt . . . . Agatha Trimble
Francis Lister . . . . Lord Kingsclere
Emrys Jones . . . . Ned Cottrell
David Horne . . . . Martin Worth
CRIME 1683. Orphan contrives to wed
nobleman and becomes highway robber
by night. (Top Moneymaker: 1946).

11033
PINK STRING AND SEALING WAX (89) (A)
Ealing (EL) *reissue:* 1949 (ABFD)
AP: S.C.Balcon
D: Robert Hamer
S: (PLAY) Roland Pertwee
SC: Diana Morgan, Robert Hamer
Mervyn Johns . . . . Edward Sutton
Googie Withers . . . . Pearl Bond
Gordon Jackson . . . . David Sutton
Sally Ann Howes . . . . Peggy Sutton
Mary Merrall . . . . Ellen Sutton
John Carol . . . . Dan Powell
Catherine Lacey . . . . Miss Porter
Jean Ireland . . . . Victoria Sutton
Garry Marsh . . . . Joe Bond
Frederick Piper . . . . Dr Pepper
Maudie Edwards . . . . Mrs Webster
Pauline Letts . . . . Louise

Margaret Ritchie . . . .   Mme Patti
Don Stannard . . . .   John Bevan
CRIME Brighton, 1880. Publican's wife
blackmails chemist by involving his son in her
husband's death.

11034
THE RAKE'S PROGRESS (123) (A)
USA: NOTORIOUS GENTLEMAN
IP-Individual (EL)
P: Frank Launder, Sidney Gillat
D: Sidney Gillat
S: Val Valentine
SC: Frank Launder, Sidney Gillat
Rex Harrison . . . .   Vivian Kenway
Lilli Palmer . . . .   Rikki Krausner
Godfrey Tearle . . . .   Col Kenway
Griffith Jones . . . .   Sandy Duncan
Margaret Johnston . . . . ..   Jennifer Calthrop
Guy Middleton . . . .   Fogroy
Jean Kent . . . .   Jill Duncan
Marie Lohr . . . .   Lady Parks
Garry Marsh . . . .   Sir Hubert Parks
David Horne . . . .   Sir John Brockley
Alan Wheatley . . . .   Edwards
Brefni O'Rorke . . . .   Bromhead
Charles Victor . . . .   Old Sweat
Joan Maude . . . .   Alice
Patricia Laffan . . . .   Miss Fernandez
Howard Marion Crawford. .   Guardsman
Emrys Jones . . . .   Bateson
DRAMA Disgraced student has affair with
his friend's wife, weds for payment, becomes
gigolo, and redeems himself in war.

11035
HERE COMES THE SUN (91) (U)
John Baxter (GFD) *reissue:* 1949 (ABFD)
D: John Baxter

S: Bud Flanagan, Reginald Purdell
SC: Geoffrey Orme
Bud Flanagan . . . .   Corona Flanagan
Chesney Allen . . . .   Ches Allen
Elsa Tee . . . .   Helen Blare
Joss Ambler . . ..   Bradshaw
Dick Francis . . . .   Governor
John Dodsworth . . . .   Roy Lucas
Gus McNaughton . . . .   Barrett
Roddy Hughes . . . .   Simpson
Horace Kenney . . . .   Gatekeeper
Edie Martin . . . .   Mrs Galloway
Peter Barnard . . . .   Barker
Harry Terry . . . .   Bill
Peter; Iris Kirkwhite Dancers; Dudley and his
Midgets
MUSICAL Tipster breaks jail to prove he
was framed by crooked newspaper proprietor.

11036
THE VOICE WITHIN (74) (A)
GN Film Productions (GN)
reissue: 1949 (30 mins cut)
P: Isadore Goldsmith
D: Maurice J. Wilson
S: Michael Goldsmith
SC: Stafford Dickens, Herbert Victor,
B. Charles-Deane
Barbara White . . . .   Kathleen
Keiron O'Hanrahan . . . . . .   Denis O'Shea
Shaun Noble . . . .   Roy O'Shane
Violet Farebrother . . . . . .   Grandma
Olive Sloane . . . .   Fair Owner's Wife
Brefni O'Rorke . . . .   Sgt Sullivan
George Merritt . . . .   McDonnell
Paul Merton . . . .   Patrick O'Day
Hay Petrie . . . .   Fair Owner
CRIME Ireland. Smuggler frames brother
for killing policeman.

11037
WHAT DO WE DO NOW ? (74) (A)
GN Films (GN) *reissue:* 1947 (906 ft cut)
P: Maurice J. Wilson
D: Charles Hawtrey
S: George A. Cooper
George Moon . . . .   Wesley
Burton Brown . . . .   Lesley
Gloria Brent . . . .   Diana
Jill Summers . . . .   Birdie Maudlin
Ronald Frankau . . . .   Drunk
Leslie Fuller . . . .   Cabby
Barry Lupino . . . .   Jeff
Harry Parry's Swing Band; Edmundo Ros'
Conga Band; Steffani and his Silver Songsters;
Monte Crick; Gail Page
MUSICAL Comedians turn detective to find
lost brooch.

11038
DUMB DORA DISCOVERS TOBACCO (40)(U)
Hurley (GN) *reissue:* 1947, FAG END
(8 mins cut)
P: Victor Katona
D: Charles Hawtrey
S: J. Szenas, Robin Robinson
SC: Victor Katona, Henry King
Henry Kendall . . . .   Mackenzie
Pamela Stirling . . . .   Dora
Gene Gerrard . . . .   Smoking Tutor
Claud Allister . . . .   Sir Percival
Hugh Dempster . . . . .   Peter Pottlebury
Phillip King . . . .   Justice Hare
Wally Patch . . . .   Heckler
COMEDY Girl reporter researches into
history of smoking (includes extracts from
REMBRANDT (1936) RETURN OF THE
SCARLET PIMPERNEL (1937) FIRE OVER
ENGLAND (1937).)

1946

JAN

11039
BAD COMPANY (44) (U)
Barralet (NR)
D: Paul Barralet
S: R. Walkeley
Mabel Constanduros ...... Ma White
Diana Dawson .... Mary Jeans
Gordon Begg .... Joe Graham
Kenneth Mosley .... Tom Gilmore
Bob Elsom .... Peter Graham
Granville Squires & Elmer; Pauline Grant
Ballet Co
DRAMA Crippled girl who wants to be
ballerina loves jewel thief.

11040
THE TROJAN BROTHERS (86) (A)
British National (Anglo)
reissue: MURDER IN THE FOOTLIGHTS
P: Louis H. Jackson
D: Maclean Rogers
S: (NOVEL) Pamela Hansford Johnson
SC: Maclean Rogers, Irwin Reiner
Patricia Burke .... Betty Todd
David Farrar .... Sid Nicholls
Barbara Mullen .... Maggie Castelli
Bobby Howes .... Benny Castelli
Lesley Brook .... Ann Devon
David Hutcheson .... Cyril Todd
Finlay Currie .... W.H.Maxwell
George Robey .... Old Sam
Wylie Watson .... Stage Manager
Gus McNaughton .... Frank
Hugh Dempster .... Tommy
Bransby Williams .... Tom Hockaby
H.F.Maltby .... Col Robbins
Joyce Blair .... Beryl Johnson
DRAMA Rear end of comic horse act
stops mad partner from killing socialite he
loves.

11041
NIGHT BOAT TO DUBLIN (99) (A)
ABPC (Pathe)
P: Hamilton G. Inglis
D: Lawrence Huntington
S: Lawrence Huntington, Robert Hall
Robert Newton .... Capt David Grant
Raymond Lovell .... Paul Faber
Guy Middleton .... Capt Tony Hunter
Muriel Pavlow .... Marion Decker
Herbert Lom .... Keitel
John Ruddock .... Bowman
Martin Miller .... Prof Hansen
Marius Goring .... Frederick Jannings
Brenda Bruce .... Lily Leggett
Gerald Case .... Insp Emerson
Julian Dallas .... Lt Allen
Leslie Dwyer .... George Leggett
Olga Lindo .... Mrs Coleman
Joan Maude .... Sidney Vane
Carroll Gibbons; Edmundo Ros and his
Rumba Band
WAR Secret agent saves Swedish atom
scientist from German spies.

11042
ECHO OF APPLAUSE (47) (U)
Burt Hyams (WB)
D:S: James M. Anderson
N: Frederick Grisewood
Anne Wrigg
Kenneth Firth
Max Melford
COMPILATION Extracts from silent films.

11043
TROUBLE AT TOWNSEND (23) (U)
GB Instructional (GFD)

D: Darrell Catling
Petula Clark .... The Girl
CHILDREN Two London children get
up to mischief on uncle's farm.

11044
BOTHERED BY A BEARD (36) (A)
GB INstructional (GFD)
P:D:S: E.V.H.Emmett
Tod Slaughter .... Sweeney Todd
Jerry Verno ....
John Salew ....
Franklyn Bennett ....
Dorothy Bramhall ....
Arthur Baird ....
Arthur Denton ....
HISTORY Story of shaving from Bronze
Age to date.

11045
HANDS ACROSS THE OCEAN (37) (U)
Harry Gordon (BL)
D: Gordon Myers
S: Edward Eve
Pearl Cameron .... Helen
Bill Swyre .... Joe
ROMANCE GI and English girl fall in love
and tour England.

11046
CAESAR AND CLEOPATRA (138) *tech* (A)
IP-Pascal (EL) *reissue:* 1948 (459 ft cut)
D: Gabriel Pascal
S: (PLAY) George Bernard Shaw
SC: George Bernard Shaw, Marjorie Deans,
W.P.Lipscomb
Vivien Leigh .... Cleopatra
Claude Rains .... Julius Caesar
Stewart Granger .... Apollodorus
Flora Robson .... Ftatateeta
Francis L. Sullivan .... Pothinus
Renee Asherson .... Iras
Basil Sydney .... Rufio
Cecil Parker .... Britannus
Olga Edwardes .... Charmian
Ernest Thesiger .... Theodotus
Raymond Lovell .... Lucius Septimus
Stanley Holloway .... Belzanor
Anthony Eustral .... Achillas
Leo Genn .... Bel Affris
Alan Wheatley .... The Persian
Esme Percy .... Major Domo
Gibb McLaughlin .... High Priest
James McKechnie .... Centurion
Michael Rennie .... Centurion
Jean Simmons .... Girl
HISTORY Egypt, 45 BC. Ageing Roman
conqueror loves young Queen.

FEB

11047
UNDER NEW MANAGEMENT (90) (A)
Mancunian (Butcher) *reissue:* 1948,
HONEYMOON HOTEL (cut)
P: D: John E.Blakeley
S: Roney Parsons, Anthony Toner
Nat Jackley .... Nat
Norman Evans .... Joe Evans
Dan Young .... Dan
Betty Jumel .... Betty
Nicolette Roeg .... Brenda Evans
Tony Dalton .... Tony
Marianne Lincoln .... Marianne
Bunty Meadows .... Bunty
Aubrey Mallalieu .... John Marshall
G.H.Mulcaster .... William Barclay
John Rorke .... Father Flannery
Hay Petrie .... Groom
Cavan O'Connor; Lynda Ross; Donovan Octette;
Mendel's Female Sextette; Percival Mackey

and his Orchestra
COMEDY Sweep inherits hotel and
staffs it with army pals.

MAR

11048
LISBON STORY (103) (A)
British National (Anglo)
P: Louis H. Jackson
D: Paul Stein
S: (PLAY) Harold Purcell, Harry Parr-Davis
SC: Jack Whittingham
Patricia Burke .... Gabrielle Girard
David Farrar .... David Warren
Walter Rilla .... Karl von Schrine
Richard Tauber .... Andre Joubert
Lawrence O'Madden ... Michael O'Rourke
Austin Trevor .... Maj Lutzen
Paul Bonifas .... Stephan Corelle
Harry Welchman .... George Duncan
Esme Percy .... Mariot
Noele Gordon .... Panache
John Ruddock .... Pierre Sargon
Joan Seton .... Lisette
Allan Jeayes .... Dr Cartier
Stephane Grappelly; Lorely Dyer; Halamar
& Konarski
MUSICAL Lisbon, 1940. Singer poses as
collaborator to help British agent rescue
French atom scientist.

11049
LOYAL HEART (80) (U)
British National-Strand (Anglo)
P: Louis H.Jackson
D: Oswald Mitchell
S: (NOVEL) Ernest Lewis
(BETH THE SHEEPDOG)
SC: George A. Cooper
Percy Marmont .... John Armstrong
Harry Welchman .... Sir Ian
Patricia Marmont .... Joan Stewart
Philip Kay .... Tommy
Eleanor Hallam .... Mary Armstrong
Beckett Bould .... Burton
Valentine Dunn .... Alice Burton
Cameron Hall .... Edwards
Alexander Field .... Blinkers
James Knight .... Police Sgt
DRAMA Cumberland. Jealous farmer
accuses rival's dog of stealing sheep.

11050
LATE AT NIGHT (69) (A)
Bruton Films (Premier)
P: Herbert Wynne
D: Michael Chorlton
S: Henry C. James
Daphne Day .... Jill Esdaile
Barry Morse .... Dave Jackson
Noel Dryden .... Tony Cunningham
Paul Demel .... The Spider
CRIME Singer helps a reporter catch the
leader of a wood-alcohol gang.

11051
QUIET WEEKEND (93) (U)
ABPC (Pathe)
P: Warwick Ward
D: Harold French
S: (PLAY) Esther McCracken
SC: Warwick Ward, Victor Skutezky,
Stephen Black, T.J.Morrison
Derek Farr .... Denys Royd
Barbara White .... Miranda Bute
Frank Cellier ...... Adrian Barrasford
Marjorie Fielding .... Mildred Royd
George Thorpe .... Arthur Royd
Helen Shingler .... Rowena Hyde
Edward Rigby .... Sam Pecker

Josephine Wilson . . . . Mary Jarrow
Gwen Whitby . . . . Marcia Brent
Ballard Berkeley . . . . Jim Brent
Judith Furse . . . . Ella Spender
COMEDY Family spend hectic weekend of romance and poaching at country cottage.

11052
GEORGE IN CIVVY STREET (79) (A)
Columbia British
P: Marcel Varnel, Ben Henry
D: Marcel Varnel
S: Howard Irving Young
SC: Peter Fraser, Ted Kavanagh, Max Kester, Gale Pedrick
George Formby . . . . George Harper
Rosalyn Boulter . . . . Mary Colton
Ronald Shiner . . . . Fingers
Ian Fleming . . . . Uncle Shad
Wally Patch . . . . Sprout
Philippa Hiatt . . . . Lavender
Enid Cruickshank . . . . . Miss Gummidge
Mike Johnson . . . . Toby
Moore Raymond; Johnny Claes and his Claepigeons
COMEDY Ex-soldier returns to country pub and thwarts crooked rival.

11053
GAIETY GEORGE (98) (A) USA: SHOWTIME
Embassy (WB) reissue: 1953 (WB)
P:D: George King
S: Richard Fisher, Peter Cresswell
SC: Katherine Strueby
Richard Greene . . . . George Howard
Ann Todd . . . . Kathryn Davis
Peter Graves . . . . Carter
Hazel Court . . . . Elizabeth Brown
Leni Lynn . . . . Florence Stephens
Ursula Jeans . . . . Isobel Forbes
Morland Graham . . . . Morris
Frank Pettingell . . . . Grindley
Charles Victor . . . . Collier
Daphne Barker . . . . Miss de Courtney
Jack Train . . . . Hastings
Maire O'Neill . . . . Mrs Murphy
Phyllis Robins . . . . Chubbs
John Laurie . . . . McTavish
Frederick Burtwell . . . . Jenkins
Antony Holles . . . . Wade
David Horne . . . . Lord Mountsby
Patrick Waddington . . . . . . Lt Travers
Claud Allister . . . . Archie
Wally Patch . . . . Commissionaire
MUSICAL 1900 - 1920. Irish producer weds actress, promotes musical comedies, loses fortune, and comes back.

MAR
11054
WANTED FOR MURDER (103) (A)
Excelsior (20) reissue: 1952,
A VOICE IN THE NIGHT (Ex)
P: Marcel Hellman
D: Lawrence Huntington
S: (PLAY) Percy Robinson, Terence de Marney
SC: Emeric Pressburger, Rodney Ackland, Maurice Cowan
Eric Portman . . . . Victor Coleman
Dulcie Gray . . . . Anne Fielding
Derek Farr . . . . Jack Williams
Roland Culver . . . . Insp Conway
Stanley Holloway . . . . Sgt Sullivan
Barbara Everest . . . . Mrs Colebrook
Bonar Colleano . . . . Cpl Mappolo
Jenny Laird . . . . Jeannie McLaren
Kathleen Harrison . . . . Florrie
Viola Lyel . . . . Mrs Cooper
John Ruddock . . . . Tramp

Moira Lister . . . . Miss Willis
George Carney . . . . Boatman
CRIME Man strangles girls because his father was a public hangman.

APR
11055
MUSICAL MASQUERADE (39) (U)
Inspiration (20)
P:D:S: Horace Shepherd
John Burch . . . . Harry Smith
Norma Webb . . . . Mrs Smith
Alfredo Campoli
MUSICAL Poor composer pretends his symphony is by Tchaikowsky.

11056
THE CAPTIVE HEART (98) (A)
Ealing (GFD) reissue: 1949 (ABFD)
AP: Michael Relph
D: Basil Dearden
S: Patrick Kirwan
SC: Angus Macphail, Guy Morgan
Michael Redgrave . . . . . Capt Karel Hasek
Mervyn Johns . . . . Pte Dai Evans
Basil Radford . . . . Maj Ossy Dalrymple
Jack Warner . . . . Cpl Horsfall
Jimmy Hanley . . . . Pte Matthews
Gordon Jackson . . . . Lt David Lennox
Karel Stepanek . . . . Forster
Ralph Michael . . . . Capt Thurston
Derek Bond . . . . Lt Hartley
Guy Middleton . . . . Capt Jim Grayson
Jack Lambert . . . . Padre
Rachel Kempson . . . . Celia Mitchell
Frederick Leister . . . . Mr Mowbray
Meriel Forbes . . . . Beryl Curtess
Robert Wyndham . . Lt-Cdr Robert Marsden
Jane Barrett . . . . Caroline Hartley
Gladys Henson . . . . Mrs Horsfall
Rachel Thomas . . . . Mrs Evans
Margot Fitzsimmons . . . Elspeth McDougall
WAR Germany, 1940. Lives of various prisoners of war, including Czech captain who poses as British officer.

11057
CARAVAN (122) (A)
Gainsborough (GFD) reissue: 1949 (ABFD)
P: Harold Huth
D: Arthur Crabtree
S: (NOVEL) Lady Eleanor Smith
SC: Roland Pertwee
Stewart Granger . . . . Richard Darrell
Jean Kent . . . . Rosal
Anne Crawford . . . . . Oriana Camperdene
Dennis Price . . . Sir Francis Castleton
Robert Helpmann . . . . Wycroft
Gerard Heinz . . . . Don Carlos
Enid Stamp-Taylor . . . . Bertha
David Horne . . . . Charles Camperdene
John Salew . . . . Diego
Arthur Goullet . . . . Suiza
Julian Somers . . . . Manoel
Peter Murray . . . . Juan
Sylvie StClair . . . . Marie
Mabel Constanduros . . . . . Woman
Jusef Ramart . . . . Jose
Gypsy Petulengro . . . . Paco
ROMANCE 1840. Nobleman tries to kill author who gets amnesia and weds Spanish gipsy.

MAY
11058
I'LL TURN TO YOU (96) (U)
Butcher reissue: 1949 (Sherwood; cut)
D: Geoffrey Faithfull
S: Kathleen Butler

SC: David Evans
Terry Randal . . . . Aileen Meredith
Don Stannard . . . . Roger Meredith
Harry Welchman . . . . Mr Collins
Ann Codrington . . . . Mrs Collins
George Merritt . . . . Cecil Joy
Irene Handl . . . . Mrs Gammon
Ellis Irving . . . . Henry Browning
Nicolette Roeg . . . . Flora Fenton
Tony Pendrell . . . . Dick Fenton
Leslie Perrins . . . . Chigwell
Albert Sandler and his Palm Court Orchestra;
Sandy MacPherson; Sylvia Welling; Choir of the Welsh Guards; John McHugh;
London Symphony Orchestra
MUSICAL Ex-RAF sgt is jealous of his rich friend.

11059
DANCING THRU (35) (A)
Angel Productions (Pi)
P: Daniel Angel
D: Victor M. Gover
Ronnie Waldman   Avis Gill
Jack Billings   Diana Chase
Sammy Curtis   Charles Thebault
Lou Preager and his Orchestra
REVUE

11060
APPOINTMENT WITH CRIME (97) (A)
British National (Anglo)
P: Louis H.Jackson
D: SC: John Harlow
S: Michael Leighton, Vernon Sewell
William Hartnell . . . . Leo Martin
Robert Beatty . . . . Insp Rogers
Joyce Howard . . . . Carol Dane
Raymond Lovell . . . . Gus Loman
Herbert Lom . . . . Gregory Lang
Alan Wheatley . . . . Noel Penn
Cyril Smith . . . . Sgt Charlie Weeks
Ivor Barnard . . . . Jonah Crackle
Wally Patch . . . . Joe Fisher
John Rorke . . . . Casson
Ernest Butcher . . . . John Brown
Kenneth Warrington . . . . . . Winkle
Wilfrid Hyde White . . . . . . Cleaner
Albert Chevalier . . . . Spearman
Gaston & Helen; Elizabeth Webb; Lew Stone and his Band; Buddy Featherstonehaugh and his Sextette
CRIME Ex-convict avenges himself on former partners in smash-and-grab raid.

JUN
11061
MEET THE NAVY (82) (U) tech seq
British National (Anglo)
P: Louis H.Jackson
D: Alfred Travers
S: (SHOW)
SC: Lester Cooper, James Seymour
Lionel Murton . . . . Johnny
Margaret Hurst . . . . Midge
John Pratt . . . . Horace
Bob Goodier . . . . Tommy
Bill Oliver . . . . CPO Oliver
Phyllis Hudson . . . . Jennie
Oscar Natzke . . . . Fisherman
MUSICAL Story behind staging of Royal Canadian Navy show.

11062
BEDELIA (90) (A)
John Corfield (GFD) reissue: 1948
P: Isadore Goldsmith
D: Lance Comfort
S: (NOVEL) Vera Caspary
SC: Vera Caspary, Herbert Victor,

Moie Charles, Roy Ridley, Isadore Goldsmith
Margaret Lockwood . . . .   Bedelia Carrington
Ian Hunter . . . .   Charles Carrington
Barry K. Barnes . . . .   Ben Chaney
Anne Crawford . . . .   Ellen Walker
Jill Esmond . . . .   Nurse Harris
Barbara Blair . . . .   Sylvia Johnstone
Ellen Pollock . . . .   Housekeeper
Louise Hampton . . . .   Hannah
Julien Mitchell . . . .   Dr McAbee
Kynaston Reeves . . . .   Mr Bennett
Beatrice Varley . . . .   Mary
Olga Lindo . . . .   Mrs Bennett
John Salew . . . .   Alec Johnstone
Al Gold & Lola Cordell
CRIME 1938. Tec discovers friend's wife
poisoned three husbands.

11063
THE YEARS BETWEEN (100) (A)
Sydney Box (GFD) *reissue:* 1949 (ABFD)
D: Compton Bennett
S: (PLAY) Daphne du Maurier
SC: Muriel & Sydney Box
Michael Redgrave . . . . . .   Michael Wentworth
Valerie Hobson . . . .   Diana Wentworth
Flora Robson . . . .   Nanny
Felix Aylmer . . . .   Sir Ernest Foster
James McKechnie . . . . .   Richard Llewellyn
Dulcie Gray . . . .   Jill
Edward Rigby . . . .   Postman
John Gilpin . . . .   Robin Wentworth
Yvonne Owen . . . .   Alice
Wylie Watson . . . .   Vining
Esma Cannon . . . .   Effie
Muriel George . . . .   Mrs May
Ernest Butcher . . . .   Old Man
DRAMA MP returns from ''death'' to
find his wife standing in his stead.

11064
BEWARE OF PITY (106) (A)
Two Cities (EL)
P: W.P.Lipscomb
D: Maurice Elvey
S: (NOVEL) Stefan Zweig
SC: W.P.Lipscomb, Elizabeth Baron,
Margaret Steen
Lilli Palmer . . . .   Baroness Edith
Albert Lieven . . . .   Lt Anton Marek
Cedric Hardwicke . . . . . .   Dr Albert Condor
Gladys Cooper . . . .   Kiara Condor
Linden Travers . . . .   Ilona Domansky
Ernest Thesiger . .Baron Emil de Kekesfalva
Emrys Jones . . . .   Lt Joszi Molnar
Gerhard Kempinski . . . Mayor Jan Nivak
Ralph Truman . . . Maj Sandor Balinsky
John Salew . . . . . .   Col Franz Bubenic
Peter Cotes . . . .   Cusma
Freda Jackson . . . .   Gypsy
Kenneth Warrington. .Archduke Franz Ferdinand
Jenny Laird . . . .   Trudi
ROMANCE Period. Crippled girl realises
that lieutenant's love is pity.

JUL

11065
JEAN'S PLAN (30) (U)
Merton Park (GFD)
P: Frank Hoare
D: William C.Hammond
S: J.O.Thomas
Vivienne Pickles . . . .   Jean Fairfax
Tony Hillman . . . .   Johnny Higgs
Billie Brooks . . . .   Elsie Higgs
Edward Robson . . . .   Mr Fairfax
Lyn Evans . . . .   Mr Higgs
Gerald Case . . . .   Inspector
CHILDREN Girl hides gems in teddy
bear and is chased by crooks.

11066
RIDERS OF THE NEW FOREST (serial) (U)
GB Instructional (GFD)
P: H. Bruce Woolfe
D: Philip Leacock
S: (NOVEL) Ruth Clark (BONNY THE PONY)
SC: Patricia Latham
Ivor Bowyer . . . .   John Rivers
Jill Gibbs . . . .   Vikki Rivers
Michael Cabon . . . .   Danny
Geoffrey Keen . . . .   Mr Rivers
Ben Williams . . . .   Thief
Eps. 1 - 5 (15 each)
CHILDREN Farm children raise wild pony
and rescue it from thief. (also released as
a 60 minute feature).

11067
APPOINTMENT WITH FEAR (series) (A)
British Foundation (20)
P:D: Ronald Haines
S: (STORIES) John Dickson Carr
N: Valentine Dyall

11068
1: THE CLOCK STRIKES EIGHT (27)
Mary Shaw
Millicent Wolf
Mona Wynne

11069
2: THE GONG CRIED MURDER (29)
Ivan Wilmott
Diana Decker
Keith Shepherd

11070
3: THE HOUSE IN RUE RAPP (31)
Mary Waterman
Herbert Walton
Robert Bradfield
CRIME

11071
I SEE A DARK STRANGER (111) (A)
USA: THE ADVENTURESS
IP-Individual (GFD)
P: Frank Launder, Sidney Gilliat
D: Frank Launder
S: Frank Launder, Sidney Gilliat, Wolfgang
Wilhelm
Deborah Kerr . . . .   Bridie Quilty
Trevor Howard . . . .   Lt David Bayne
Raymond Huntley . . . .   Miller
Michael Howard . . . .   Hawkins
Norman Shelley . . . . Man in Straw Hat
Brenda Bruce . . . .
Liam Redmond . . . .   Timothy
Brefni O'Rorke . . . ..   Michael O'Callaghan
James Harcourt . . . .   Grandfather
W.G.O'Gorman . . . .   Danny Quilty
George Woodbridge . . . . . .   Steve
Garry Marsh . . . . Capt Goodhusband
Olga Lindo . . . .   Mrs Edwards
Kathleen Harrison . . . .   Waitress
WAR Ireland. IRA girl regrets spying for
Nazis and helps British officer escape.

11072
AMATEUR NIGHT (35) (U)
Radnor (Renown)
P: Moss Goodman, Victor C. Harvey
D:S: Frank Richardson
Ernest Sefton . . . .   Stage Manager
Geraldine Farrar . . . .   Carl Carlisle
Halstan Crimmins . . . .   Lorna Martin
Borstal Boys . . . . . .   Primrose Milligan
Frank King's Orchestra
MUSICAL Buskers put on show in fogbound
theatre.

11073
HAPPY FAMILY (39) (U)
British Foundation
P:D: Ronald Haines
S: Harry Alan Towers, Stuart Jackson
Frederick Morant . . . .   Mr Portland
Doris Rodgers . . . .   Mrs Portland
Sally Rogers . . . .   Miss Portland
Peter Scott . . . .   Master Portland
Frank Weir and his Band; Gail Kendall
COMEDY Family dream of how they
will spend father's football pool win.

11074
A GIRL IN A MILLION (90) (A)
Boca Productions (BL)
P: Sydney Box
D: Francis Searle
S: Muriel & Sydney Box
Hugh Williams . . . .   Tony
Joan Greenwood . . . .   Gay
Basil Radford . . . .   Prendergast
Naunton Wayne . . . .   Fotheringham
Wylie Watson . . . .   Peabody
Yvonne Owen . . . .   Molly
Hartley Power . . . .   Col Saltzman
Garry Marsh . . . .   General
Edward Lexy . . . . ,,   PC
Eileen Joyce . . . .   Pianist
COMEDY Chemist divorces nagging wife
and weds dumb girl, but makes the mistake
of curing her.

AUG

11075
MEN OF TWO WORLDS (109) *tech* (A)
Two Cities (GFD) *reissues:* 1948; 1961
P: John Sutro
D: Thorold Dickinson
S: E. Arnot Robertson, Joyce Cary
SC: Thorold Dickinson, Herbert W.Victor
Phyllis Calvert . . . . Dr Catherine Munro
Eric Portman . . . .   Comm Randall
Robert Adams . . . .   Kisenga
Orlando Martins . . . .   Magole
Arnold Marle . . . .   Prof Gollner
Cathleen Nesbitt . . . .   Mrs Upjohn
David Horne . . . .   Agent
Cyril Raymond . . . .   Education Officer
Sam Blake . . . .   Rafi
Uriel Porter . . . .   Saidi
ADVENTURE Tanganyika. Educated native
helps commissioner persuade villagers
to leave tsetse area.

11076
PICCADILLY INCIDENT (102) (A)
ABPC (Pathe)
P:D: Herbert Wilcox
S: Florence Tranter
SC: Nicholas Phipps
Anna Neagle . . . .   Diana Fraser
Michael Wilding . . . .   Capt Alan Pearson
Michael Laurence . . . .   Bill Weston
Frances Mercer . . . .   Joan Draper
Coral Browne . . . .:.   Virginia Pearson
A.E.Matthews . . . .   Sir Charles Pearson
Edward Rigby . . . .   Judd
Brenda Bruce . . . .   Sally Benton
Leslie Dwyer . . . .   Sam
Maire O'Neill . . . .   Mrs Milligan
ROMANCE 1941. ''Drowned'' Wren returns
to find husband remarried. (DMNFA: 1946;
PGAA: 1947).

SEP

11077
THE GRAND ESCAPADE (7)) (U)
Elstree Independent (BL)

P:D: John Baxter
S: Geoffrey Orme, Barbara K. Emary
Peter .... Tom
Philip .... Dick
Jackie .... Harry
Patric Curwen .... The Author
James Harcourt .... Mr Robbins
Peter Bull .... Jennings
Ernest Sefton .... Archer
Edgar Driver .... Watchman
Ben Williams .... Barrow
Bobbie & Nornie Dwyer
ADVENTURE Boys travel with old junk
dealer whose son was drowned whilst
smuggling.

11078
LONDON TOWN (126) (U) *tech*
USA: MY HEART GOES CRAZY
Wesley Ruggles (EL) *reissue*: 1948
(1913 ft cut)
D: S: Wesley Ruggles
SC: Elliot Paul, Sigfried Herzig, Val Guest
Sid Field .... Jerry Sanford
Greta Gynt .... Mrs Barry
Tessie O'Shea .... Tessie
Claude Hulbert .... Belgrave
Sonnie Hale .... Charlie
Mary Clare .... Mrs Gates
Petula Clark .... Peggy Sanford
Kay Kendall .... Patsy
Jerry Desmonde .... George
Beryl Davis .... Paula
Scotty McHarg .... Bill
Reginald Purdell .... Stage Manager
W.G.Fay .... Mike
Lucas Hovinga; Marion Saunders; Jack Parnell;
Pamela Carroll
MUSICAL Understudy's daughter tricks
star so that her father may win success.

11079
SEND FOR PAUL TEMPLE (83) (A)
Butcher *reissue*: 1950
P:D: John Argyle
S: (RADIO SERIAL) Francis Durbridge
SC: Francis Durbridge, John Argyle
Anthony Hulme .... Paul Temple
Joy Shelton .... Steve Trent
Tamara Desni .... Diana Thornley
Jack Raine .... Sir Graham Forbes
Beatrice Varley .... Miss Marchmont
Hylton Allen .... Dr Milton
Maire O'Neill .... Mrs Neddy
Phil Ray .... Horace Daley
Olive Sloane .... Ruby
CRIME Novelist helps dead detective's
sister unmask leader of smash-and-grab gang.

11080
THIS MAN IS MINE (103) (A)
Columbia British
P:D: Marcel Varnel
S: (PLAY) Reginald Beckwith
(A SOLDIER FOR CHRISTMAS)
SC: Doreen Montgomery, Nicholas Phipps,
Reginald Beckwith, Mabel Constanduros,
Val Valentine, David Evans
Tom Walls .... Philip Ferguson
Glynis Johns .... Millie
Jeanne de Casalis ..... Mrs Ferguson
Hugh McDermott .... Bill Mackenzie
Nova Pilbeam .... Phoebe Ferguson
Barry Morse .... Ronnie
Rosalyn Boulter .... Brenda Ferguson
Ambrosine Philpotts ... Lady Daubney
Mary Merrall .... Mrs Jarvis
Agnes Lauchlan .... Cook
Bernard Lee .... James Nicholls

Charles Victor .... Hi-jacker
Peter Gawthorne .... Businessman
Capt Bob Farnon and the Canadian Army
Orchestra
COMEDY Girl and ex-maid compete for
visiting Canadian soldier.

11081
THOSE WERE THE DAYS (38) (U)
Bishu Sen (Butcher)
P: Henry W.Fisher
D:S: James M. Anderson
N: Kenneth Horne
COMPILATION Extracts from earlier films,
including Muggins VC (1909); Variety Jubilee
(1943).

11082
THE ADVENTURES OF PARKER (35) (A)
Defender (Carlyle)
D: W.F.Elliott
Arthur Brander .... Parker
Luanne Shaw .... Veronica
COMEDY Man helps couple win approval
from girl's uncle.

11083
THE CURSE OF THE WRAYDONS (94) (A)
Bushey (Ambassador)
P: Gilbert Church
D: Victor M. Gover
S: (PLAY) (SPRINGHEELED JACK THE
TERROR OF LONDON)
SC: Michael Barringer
Tod Slaughter .... Phillip Wraydon
Bruce Seton .... Capt Jack Clayton
Gabriel Toyne .... Lt Payne
Andrew Laurence ...... George Heeningham
Lorraine Clewes ...... Helen Sedgefield
Pearl Cameron .... Rose Wraydon
Ben Williams .... John Rickers
Barry O'Neill .... George Wraydon
CRIME Period. Mad inventor, ex-spy for
Napoleon, wreaks revenge on brother's
family. (Extract in A GHOST FOR SALE
(1952).)

OCT

11084
THE MAGIC BOW (106) (U)
Gainsborough (GFD)
P: R.J.Minney
D: Bernard Knowles
S: (NOVEL) Manuel Komroff
SC: Roland Pertwee, Norman Ginsbury
Stewart Granger .... Paganini
Phyllis Calvert .... Jeanne
Jean Kent .... Bianchi
Dennis Price .... Paul de la Roche
Cecil Parker .... Germi
Felix Aylmer .... Pasini
Frank Cellier .... Antonio
Marie Lohr .... Countess de Vermand
Henry Edwards ...... Count de Vermand
Mary Jerrold .... Teresa
Betty Warren .... Landlady
Antony Holles .... Manager
David Horne .... Rizzi
Charles Victor .... Peasant
Eliot Makeham .... Giuseppe
Yehudi Menuhin .... Soloist
MUSICAL Violinist's childhood sweetheart
lets him wed French aristocrat.

11085
THE OVERLANDERS (91) (U)
Ealing (EL)
AP: Ralph Smart
D: S: Harry Watt

Chips Rafferty .... Dan McAlpine
John Nugent Hayward .... Bill Parsons
Daphne Campbell .... Mary Parsons
John Fernside .... Corky
Jean Blue .... Mrs Parsons
Peter Pagan .... Sinbad
Helen Grieve .... Helen Parsons
Frank Ransome .... Charlie
Clyde Combo .... Jacky
ADVENTURE Australia, 1942. Drovers drive
cattle 1600 miles to escape Japanese
invasion threat.

11086
CARNIVAL (93) (A)
Two Cities (GFD) *reissue*: 1949 (ABFD)
P: John Sutro, William Sassoon
D: Stanley Haynes
S: (NOVEL) Compton Mackenzie
SC: Stanley Haynes, Peter Ustinov,
Eric Maschwitz, Guy Green
Sally Gray .... Jenny Pearl
Michael Wilding .... Maurice Avery
Stanley Holloway ...... Charlie Raeburn
Bernard Miles .... Trewhalla
Jean Kent .... Irene Dale
Catherine Lacey .... Florrie Raeburn
Nancy Price .... Mrs Trewhalla
Hazel Court .... Mae Raeburn
Brenda Bruce .... Maudie Chapman
Antony Holles .... Corentin
Ronald Ward .... Jack Danby
Mackenzie Ward .... Arthur Danby
Dennis Arundell .... Studholme
Phyllis Monkman .... Barmaid
Amy Veness .... Aunt Fanny
Bebe de Roland; Carpenter Corps de Ballet
ROMANCE 1890. Ballerina loves selfish
artist but weds Cornish farmer.

NOV
11087
OTHELLO (45) (A)
Henry Halstead (Ex)
D: David Mackane
S: (PLAY) William Shakespeare
John Slater .... Othello
Luanne Shaw .... Desdemona
Sebastian Cabot .... Iago
Sheila Raynor .... Emilio
DRAMA Jealous moor murders his wife.

11088
SPRING SONG (86) (A) USA: SPRINGTIME
British National (Anglo)
P: Louis H.Jackson
D: Montgomery Tully
S: Lore & Maurice Cowan
SC: Montgomery Tully, James Seymour
Carol Raye .... Janet Hill/Janet Ware
Peter Graves .... Tony Winster
Leni Lynn .... Vera Dale
Lawrence O'Madden ..... Johnnie Ware
Alan Wheatley .... Menelli
George Carney .... Stage Doorman
Finlay Currie .... Cobb
Jack Billings .... Dancer
Maire O'Neill .... Dresser
Netta Westcott .... Lady Norchester
David Horne .... Sir Anthony
Lois Maxwell .... Penelope Cobb
MUSICAL Irish comic objects to daughter
loving descendant of cad who jilted her
mother.

11089
THE LAUGHING LADY (93) *tech* (A)
British National (Anglo)

P: Louis H. Jackson
D: Paul Stein
S: (PLAY) Ingram d'Abbes
SC: Jack Whittingham
Ann Ziegler . . . .   Denise Tremayne
Webster Booth . . . .   Andre
Peter Graves . . . .   Prince of Wales
Felix Aylmer . . . .   Sir Felix Mountroyal
Francis L. Sullivan . .   Sir William Tremayne
Paul Dupuis . . . .   Pierre
Ralph Truman . . . .   Lord Mandeville
Chili Bouchier . . . .   Louise
Charles Goldner . . . .   Robespierre
John Ruddock . . . .   Gilliatt
Jack Melford . . . .   Lord Barrymore
Hay Petrie . . . : . . . . . .   Tom
Frederick Burtwell . . . .   Jenkins
Anthony Nicholls . . . .   Mr Pitt
MUSICAL 1790. French artist will be
spared guillotine if he steals English Lady's
pearls.

11090
WOMAN TO WOMAN (99) (A)
British National (Anglo)
P: Louis H. Jackson
D: Maclean Rogers
S: (PLAY) Michael Morton
SC: James Seymour, Marjorie Deans
Douglass Montgomery . . . . .   David Anson
Joyce Howard . . . .   Nicole Bonnet
Adele Dixon . . . .   Sylvia Anson
Yvonne Arnaud . . . .   Henriette
Paul Collins . . . .   David jr
John Warwick . . . .   Dr Gavron
Eugene Deckers . . . .   de Rillac
Lily Kahn . . . .   Concierge
Martin Miller . . . .   Postman
George Carney . . . .   Taxi-driver
Carole Coombe . . . .   Secretary
Ralph Truman . . . .   Colonel
Charles Victor . . . .   Stage Manager
Finlay Currie . . . .   Manager
Daisy Burrell . . . . Committee Member
Ballet Rambert
ROMANCE Married officer with amnesia
recalls he was son by French ballerina.

11091
THE VOYAGE OF PETER JOE (series) (U)
GB Instructional (GFD)
P: Henry Passmore
D: Harry Hughes
S: Marriott Edgar
Brian Peck . . . .   Peter Joe
Graham Moffatt . . . .   Albert
Mark Daly . . . .   Nobby
Knox Crichton . . . .   Grinder

11092
1: A SMASHING JOB (20)

11093
2: GHOSTESSES (20)

11094
3: ALL'S FAIR (20)

11095
4: THE SOLDIER'S COTTAGE (20)
retitled: COTTAGE PIE

11096
5: THE LAUNDRY (20) retitled: LOST
IN THE WASH

11097
6: STAMP RAMP (20)
CHILDREN Slapstick comedies.

11098
WALKING ON AIR (61) (U)
Michael H. Goodman (Piccadilly)
D: Aveling Ginever
S: Aveling Ginever, Johnny Worthy,
Val Guest
Johnny Worthy . . . .   Johnny
Bertie Jarrett . . . .   Bertie
Susan Shaw . . . .
Billy Thatcher . . . .
Jasmine Dee . . . .
Maudie Edwards . . . .
Miki Hood . . . . :. . . . .
Gordon Edwards . . . .
Ray Ellington Quartet; Skating Avalons;
Freddie Crump
MUSICAL Girl playing hind legs of
skating horse wants to be a ballerina.

11099
A MATTER OF LIFE AND DEATH (104) (A)
tech USA: STAIRWAY TO HEAVEN
IP-Archers (GFD) *reissue:* 1948
P:D:S: Michael Powell, Emeric Pressburger
David Niven . . . .   S/L Peter Carter
Roger Livesey . . . .   Dr. Reeves
Raymond Massey . . . .   Abraham Farlan
Kim Hunter . . . .   June
Marius Goring . . . .   Conductor 71
Robert Coote . . . .   Bob
Robert Atkins . . . . :.   Vicar
Edwin Max . . . .   Dr McEwen
Abraham Sofaer . . . .   Judge
Kathleen Byron . . . .   Angel
Richard Attenborough . . . .   Pilot
Bonar Colleano jr . . . .   Pilot
Joan Maude . . . .   Recorder
FANTASY WAC's love helps dead pilot
win his life from Heavenly court. (RFP:
1946).

11100
SCHOOL FOR SECRETS (108) (A)
Two Cities (GFD)
P: Peter Ustinov, George H.Brown
D:S: Peter Ustinov
Ralph Richardson . . . .   Prof Heatherville
Raymond Huntley . . .   Prof Laxton-Jones
Richard Attenborough . . . . .   Jack Arnold
Marjorie Rhodes . . . .   Mrs Arnold
John Laurie . . . .   Dr McVitie
Ernest Jay . . . .   Dr Dainty
David Hutcheson . . . .   S/L Sowerby
Finlay Currie . . . .   Sir Duncan Wills
David Tomlinson . . . .   Mr Watlington
Michael Hordern . . . . . .   Lt/Cdr Lowther
Pamela Matthews . . . .   Mrs Watlington
Joan Young . . . .   Mrs McVitie
Cyril Smith . . . .   F/Sgt Cox
Hugh Dempster . . . .   S/Ldr Slatter
Peggy Evans . . . .   Daphne Adams
Edward Lexy . . . . . .   Sir Desmond Prosser
Bill Rowbotham . . . .   Sgt
Paul Carpenter . . . .   F/L Argylle
Robin Bailey . . . . Billeting Officer
Dagenham Girl Pipers; Alvar Liddell
WAR Secret group of scientists develop
radar.

DEC

11101
GREEN FOR DANGER (91) (A)
IP-Individual (GFD)
reissues: 1948; 1956 (Ex)
P: Frank Launder, Sidney Gilliat
D: Sidney Gilliat
S: (NOVEL) Christianna Brand
SC: Sidney Gilliat, Claude Guerney

Sally Gray . . . .   Freddie Linley
Trevor Howard . . . .   Dr Barney Barnes
Rosamund John . . . .   Esther Sanson
Alastair Sim . . . .   Insp Cockrill
Leo Genn . . . .   Mr Eden
Judy Campbell . . . .   Marian Bates
Megs Jenkins . . . .   Nurse Woods
Moore Marriott . . . .   Joe Higgins
Henry Edwards . . . .   Mr Purdy
Ronald Adam . . . .   Dr White
George Woodbridge . . . . . .   Sgt Hendricks
CRIME Air raid victim and nurse murdered
in an emergency hospital.

11102
GREAT EXPECTATIONS (118) (A)
IP-Cineguild (GFD) *reissue:* 1948
P: Anthony Havelock-Allan, Ronald Neame
D: David Lean
S: (NOVEL) Charles Dickens
SC: Ronald Neame, David Lean, Kay Walsh,
Cecil McGivern, Anthony Havelock-Allan
John Mills . . . .   Pip Pirrip
Valerie Hobson . . . .   Estella/Her Mother
Bernard Miles . . . .   Joe Gargery
Francis L. Sullivan . . . .   Jaggers
Martita Hunt . . . .   Miss Havisham
Finlay Currie . . . .   Abel Magwitch
Anthony Wager . . . .   Pip (child)
Jean Simmons . . . .   Estella (child)
Alec Guinness . . . . . .   Herbert Pocket
Ivor Barnard . . . .   Wemmick
Freda Jackson . . . .   Mrs Gargery
Torin Thatcher . . . .   Bentley Drummle
Eileen Erskine . . . .   Biddy
Hay Petrie . . . .   Uncle Pumblechook
George Hayes . . . .   Compeyson
O.B.Clarence . . . .   Aged Parent
DRAMA Period. Orphan becomes a gentleman
as the heir of a convict he once helped.
(AA: Best Photography, Art Direction,
Interiors, 1947; PGAA: 1947; DEFA: 1947).

11103
DAYBREAK (81) (A)
Triton (GFD)
P: Sydney Box
D: Compton Bennett
S: (PLAY) Monckton Hoffe
SC: Muriel & Sydney Box
Ann Todd . . . .   Frankie
Eric Portman . . . .   Eddie Tribe
Maxwell Reed . . . .   Olaf
Edward Rigby . . . .   Bill Shackle
Bill Owen . . . .   Ron
Jane Hylton . . . .   Doris
Maurice Denham . . . .   Inspector
John Turnbull . . . .   Superintendent
Eliot Makeham . . . .   Bigley
Milton Rosmer . . . .   Governor
CRIME Public hangman fakes own death to
frame wife's lover.

11104
WOT ! NO GANGSTERS ? (46) (A)
Cine-Film-Tex (NR)
P:S: Cecil H. Williamson
D: E.W.White
Mark Hambourg   Ronald Frankau
Claude Dampier   Billie Carlisle
George Pughe   Miki Decima
Bettina Richman   Corona Babes
Harry Owen's Band   Minipiano Ensemble
REVUE Inventors demonstrate television
set with world-wide scope. (Includes
extracts from earlier films).

1947

JAN

11105
HUNGRY HILL (109) (A)
Two Cities (GFD) *reissue:* 1948
P: William Sistrom
D: Brian Desmond Hurst
S: (NOVEL) Daphne du Maurier
SC: Daphne du Maurier, Terence Young, Francis Crowdy

Margaret Lockwood	Fanny Ross
Dennis Price	Greyhound John
Cecil Parker	Copper John
Michael Denison	Henry Brodrick
F.J.McCormick	Old Tim
Dermot Walsh	Wild Johnnie
Eileen Crowe	Bridget
Jean Simmons	Jane Brodrick
Peter Murray	Lt Fox
Eileen Herlie	Katherine
Siobhan McKenna	Kate Donovan
Arthur Sinclair	Morty Donovan
Barbara Waring	Barbara Brodrick
Dan O'Herlihy	Harry Brodrick
Anthony Wager	Johnnie
Henry Mollison	Dr Armstrong

DRAMA Ireland. Family feud over copper mine spans three generations.

11106
THE SHOP AT SLY CORNER (92) (A)
USA: THE CODE OF SCOTLAND YARD
Pennant Pictures (BL)
P:D: George King
S: (PLAY) Edward Percy
SC: Katherine Strueby

Oscar Homolka	Descius Heiss
Derek Farr	Robert Graham
Muriel Pavlow	Margaret Heiss
Manning Whiley	Morris
Kathleen Harrison	Mrs Catt
Kenneth Griffith	Archie Fellowes
Garry Marsh	Maj Elliott
Irene Handl	Ruby Towser
Johnnie Schofield	Insp Robson

CRIME Fence posing as antique dealer kills blackmailing assistant to save violinist daughter.

FEB

11107
ODD MAN OUT (116) (A)
Two Cities (GFD) *reissues:* 1948; 1956 (Ex)
P:D: Carol Reed
S: (NOVEL) F.L.Green
SC: F.L.Green, R.C.Sheriff

James Mason	Johnny
Robert Newton	Lukey
Kathleen Ryan	Kathleen
Robert Beatty	Dennis
Cyril Cusack	Pat
F.J.McCormick	Shell
William Hartnell	Fencie
Fay Compton	Rosie
Denis O'Dea	Constable
W.G. Fay	Father Tom
Maureen Delany	Theresa
Elwyn Brook-Jones	Tober
Dan O'Herlihy	Nolan
Kitty Kirwan	Granny
Beryl Measor	Maudie
Joseph Tomelty	Cabbie

CRIME Ireland. Wounded IRA leader hunted by police. (BFA: Best British Film 1947).

11108
WHILE THE SUN SHINES (81) (A)
ABPC-International Screenplays (Pathe)
P: Anatole de Grunwald
D: Anthony Asquith
S: (PLAY) Terence Rattigan
SC: Terence Rattigan, Anatole de Grunwald

Barbara White	Lady Elizabeth Randall
Ronald Squire	Duke of Ayr and Stirling
Ronald Howard	Earl of Harpenden
Brenda Bruce	Mabel Crum
Bonar Colleano jr	Joe Mulvaney
Margaret Rutherford	Dr Winifred Frye
Cyril Maude	Admiral
Michael Allan	Colbert
Miles Malleson	Horton
Garry Marsh	Mr Jordan
Joyce Grenfell	Daphne
Charles Victor	Conductor
Wilfrid Hyde White	Receptionist
Geoffrey Sumner	Peer
O.B.Clarence	Old Gentleman
Gordon Begg	Ancient Porter

COMEDY Sailor Earl and GI both love poor Duke's daughter.

11109
THE MYSTERIOUS MR NICHOLSON (78) (A)
Bushey (Ambassador) *reissue:* 1949 (10 mins cut)
P: Gilbert Church
D: Oswald Mitchell
S: Francis Miller
SC: Francis Miller, Oswald Mitchell

Anthony Hulme	Nicholson/Raeburn
Lesley Osmond	Peggy Dundas
Frank Hawkins	Insp Morley
Andrew Laurence	Waring
Douglas Stewart	Seymour
George Bishop	Mr Browne
Josie Bradley	Freda

CRIME Gentleman thief tracks down murderous double.

11110
MEET ME AT DAWN (99) (A)
Excelsior (20) *reissue:* 1953,
THE GAY DUELLIST (Ex; cut)
P: Marcel Hellman
D: Thornton Freeland
S: Anatole Litvak, Marcel Archard (LE TEUER)
SC: James Seymour, Lesley Storm, Maurice Cowan

William Eythe	Charles Morton
Hazel Court	Gabrielle Vernorel
Margaret Rutherford	Mme Vernorel
Stanley Holloway	Emile
Basil Sydney	Georges Vernorel
Irene Browne	Mme Renault
George Thorpe	Senator Renault
Ada Reeve	Concierge
Graham Muir	Count de Brissac
Beatrice Campbell	Margot
John Salew	Client
Charles Victor	Client
Hy Hazell	Girl
Wilfrid Hyde White	Editor
James Harcourt	Butler
Diana Decker	Girl
Lind Joyce	Yvonne Jadin

COMEDY Paris, 1900. Professional duellist loves editor's daughter.

11111
TEMPTATION HARBOUR (104) (A)
ABPC (Pathe)
P: Victor Skutezky
D: Lance Comfort
S: (NOVEL) Georges Simenon (NEWHAVEN-DIEPPE)
SC: Victor Skutezky, Frederic Gotfurt, Rodney Ackland

Robert Newton	Bert Mallinson
Simone Simon	Camelia
William Hartnell	Jim Brown
Marcel Dalio	Insp Dupre
Margaret Barton	Betty Mallinson
Edward Rigby	Tatem
Joan Hopkins	Beryl Brown
Charles Victor	Gowshall
Kathleen Harrison	Mabel
Irene Handl	Mrs Gowshall
Wylie Watson	Fred
Leslie Dwyer	Reg
W.G.Fay	Porter

CRIME Signalman finds stolen money and spends it on his daughter.

11112
GREEN FINGERS (83) (A)
British National (Anglo)
P: Louis H. Jackson
D: John Harlow
S: (NOVEL) Edith Arundel (PERSISTENT WARRIOR)
SC: Jack Whittingham

Robert Beatty	Thomas Stone
Carol Raye	Jeannie Marshall
Nova Pilbeam	Alexandra Baxter
Felix Aylmer	Daniel Booth
Moore Marriott	Pickles
Brefni O'Rorke	Coroner
Charles Victor	Joe Mansell
Harry Welchman	Dr Baxter
Edward Rigby	Albert Goodman
Ellis Irving	Jones
Olive Walters	Mrs Mansell
Wally Patch	Dawson
Daisy Burrell	Receptionist

DRAMA Socialite patient almost ruins an unqualified osteopath's marriage.

11113
THE ROOT OF ALL EVIL (110) (A)
Gainsborough (GFD)
P: Harold Huth
D: SC: Brock Williams
S: (NOVEL) J.S.Fletcher

Phyllis Calvert	Jeckie Farnish
Michael Rennie	Charles Mortimer
John McCallum	Joe Bartle
Moore Marriott	Scholes
Brefni O'Rorke	Farnish
Hazel Court	Rushie Farnish
Arthur Young	George Grice
Hubert Gregg	Albert Grice
Reginald Purdell	Perkins
George Carney	Bowser
George Merritt	Landlord

DRAMA Jilted woman breaks her ex-fiance, becomes unscrupulous in business, and cheats farmer to get oil land.

11114
HUE AND CRY (82) (U)
Ealing (GFD) *reissue:* 1948
AP: Henry Cornelius
D: Charles Crichton
S: T.E.B.Clarke

Alastair Sim	Felix H. Wilkinson
Jack Warner	Jim Nightingale
Valerie White	Rhona Davis
Jack Lambert	Insp Ford
Harry Fowler	Joe Kirby
Joan Dowling	Clarry
Douglas Barr	Alec
Stanley Escane	Roy
Ian Dawson	Norman
Gerald Fox	Dicky
Frederick Piper	Mr Kirby
Bruce Belfrage	BBC Announcer

COMEDY Gang of cockney kids catch black marketeers who send messages through boys' magazine.

MAR

11115
NICHOLAS NICKLEBY (105) (A)
Ealing (GFD) *reissue:* 1953
AP: John Croydon
D: Cavalcanti
S: (NOVEL) Charles Dickens
SC: John Dighton
Cedric Hardwicke . . . . Ralph Nickleby
Stanley Holloway . . . . Vincent Crummles
Alfred Drayton . . . . Wackford Squeers
Cyril Fletcher . . . . Alfred Mantalini
Bernard Miles . . . . Newman Noggs
Derek Bond . . . . Nicholas Nickleby
Sally Ann Howes . . . . Kate Nickleby
Mary Merrall . . . . Mrs Nickleby
Sybil Thorndike . . . . Mrs Squeers
Vera Pearce . . . . Mrs Crummles
Cathleen Nesbitt . . . . Miss Knagg
Athene Seyler . . . . Miss la Creevy
Cecil Ramage . . . . . . Sir Mulberry Hawke
George Relph . . . . Mr Bray
Emrys Jones . . . . Frank Cheeryble
Fay Compton . . . . Mme Mantalini
Jill Balcon . . . . Madeleine Bray
Aubrey Woods . . . . Smike
James Hayter . . . . Ned/Charles
Vida Hope . . . . Fanny Squeers
Roddy Hughes . . . . . Tim Linkinwater
Timothy Bateson . . . . . . Lord Verisopht
Frederick Burtwell . . . . . . Mercury
DRAMA 1831. Adventures of young
teacher hounded by wicked uncle.

11116
WHITE CRADLE INN (83) (A)
USA: HIGH FURY
Peak Films (BL)
P: Ivor McLaren, A.E.Hardman
D: Harold French
S: Harold French, Lesley Storm
Madeleine Carroll . . . . Magda
Ian Hunter . . . . Anton
Michael Rennie . . . . Rudolph
Anne Marie Blanc . . . . Louise
Michael MacKeag . . . . Roger
Arnold Marle . . . . Joseph
Willy Feuter . . . . Benno
Max Haufler . . . . Frederick
DRAMA Switzerland. Philanderer forces
wife to give up her inn when she adopts
refugee boy.

11117
THE SILVER DARLINGS (84) (U)
Holyrood (Pathe)
P: Karl Grune, William Elder
D: Clarence Elder, Clifford Evans
S: (NOVEL) Neil Gunn
SC: Clarence Elder
Clifford Evans . . . . Roddy
Helen Shingler . . . . Catrine
Carl Bernard . . . . Angus
Norman Shelley . . . . Hendry
Simon Lack . . . . Don
Norman Williams . . . . Tormad
Murdo Morrison . . . . Finn
Josephine Stuart . . . . Una
Hugh Griffith . . . . Packman
Carole Lesley . . . . Una (child)
ADVENTURE Hebrides islanders save homes
by taking to herring fishing.

11118
WHEN YOU COME HOME (97) (U)
Butcher *reissue:* 1951 (cut)
P:D: John Baxter
S: David Evans, Geoffrey Orme, Frank Randle
Frank Randle . . . . Himself

Leslie Sarony . . . . Maestro
Leslie Holmes . . . . Fingers
Diana Decker . . . . . . Paula Ryngelbaum
Fred Conyngham . . . . . . Mike O'Flaherty
Lynda Parker . . . . Singer
Tony Heaton . . . . Mr Ryngelbaum
Lesley Osmond . . . . Delia
Jack Melford . . . . Dr Dormer Franklyn
Lily Lapidus . . . . Mrs Ryngelbaum
Hilda Bayley . . . . Lady Langfield
COMEDY 1908. Theatre handyman exposes
fraudulent hypnotist.

11119
SO WELL REMEMBERED (114) (A)
Alliance (RKO)
P: Adrian Scott
D: Edward Dmytryk
S: (NOVEL) James Hilton
SC: John Paxton
John Mills . . . . George Boswell
Martha Scott . . . . Olivia Channing
Patricia Roc . . . . Julie Whiteside
Trevor Howard . . . . Dr Whiteside
Richard Carson . . . . Charles Winslow
Reginald Tate . . . . Mangin
Beatrice Varley . . . . Annie
Frederick Leister . . . . Channing
Ivor Barnard . . . . Spivey
John Turnbull . . . . Morris
Juliet Mills . . . . Baby Julie
DRAMA Lancs. Idealistic editor marries
and divorces an ambitious mill-owner.

11120
THE TURNERS OF PROSPECT ROAD (88)
(A) Grand National *reissue:* 1950 (AA)
P: Victor Katona
D: Maurice J. Wilson
S: Victor Katona, Patrick Kirwan
Wilfrid Lawson . . . . Will Turner
Jeanne de Casalis . . . . Mrs Webster
Maureen Glynne . . . . Betty Turner
Helena Pickard . . . . Lil Turner
Leslie Perrins . . . . Webster
Peter Bull . . . . J.G.Clarkson
Amy Veness . . . . Grandma
Shamus Locke . . . . Terence
Desmond Tester . . . . Nicky
Gus McNaughton . . . . Knocker
SPORT Taxi-driver's daugher's pet greyhound
wins Dog Derby despite crooks.

11121
WE DO BELIEVE IN GHOSTS (36) (A)
WW British (Ex)
D: Walter West
John Latham . . . . Gray
Arthur Dibbs . . . . Henry VIII
Valerie Carlish . . . . Anne Boleyn
FANTASY Ghosts of Charles I, Fred Archer
and Anne Boleyn.

APR

11122
THE MAN WITHIN (90) (A) *tech*
USA: THE SMUGGLERS
Production Film Service (GFD) *reissue:* 1948
P: Muriel & Sydney Box
D: Bernard Knowles
S: (NOVEL) Graham Greene
SC: Muriel & Sydney Box
Michael Redgrave . . . . Richard Carlyon
Jean Kent . . . . Lucy
Joan Greenwood . . . . Elizabeth
Richard Attenborough . . . Francis Andrews
Francis L. Sullivan . . . . Braddock
Felix Aylmer . . . . Priest
Ronald Shiner . . . . Cockney Harry
Ernest Thesiger . . . . Farne

Basil Sydney . . . . Sir Henry Merriman
David Horne . . . . Dr Stanton
Ralph Truman . . . . Interrogator
Allan Jeayes . . . . Judge
George Merritt . . . . Hilliard
Maurice Denham . . . . Smuggler
ADVENTURE Sussex, 1820. Coward betrays
his smuggling guardian but later refuses to
give evidence.

11123
TEHERAN (86) (U)
USA: THE PLOT TO KILL ROOSEVELT
Pendennis (GFD) *reissue:* 1953,
APPOINTMENT IN PERSIA (G & S)
P: Steven Pallos, John Stafford
D: William Freshman, Giacomo Gentilomo
S: Dorothy Hope
SC: Akos Tolnay, William Freshman
Derek Farr . . . . Pemberton Grant
Marta Labarr . . . . . . Natalie Trubetzin
Manning Whiley . . . . Paul Sherek
Pamela Stirling . . . . Hali
John Slater . . . . Maj Sobieski
John Warwick . . . . Maj McIntyre
Macdonald Parke . . . . Maj Wellman
Sebastian Cabot . . . . Caretaker
Phillip Ridgeway jr. . . . . . . Razed
WAR Corespondent loves Russian ballerina
who is forced to help spies in assassination plot.

11124
CRIME REPORTER (35) (A)
Knightsbridge-Hammer (Exclusive)
P: Hal Wilson
D: Ben R.Hart
S: James Corbett
John Blythe . . . . Reporter
George Dewhurst . . . . Inspector
Stan Paskin . . . . Taxi-driver
Jackie Brent . . . . Girl
Van Boolen . . . . Crook
Agnes Brantford . . . . Landlady
CRIME Reporter unmasks Soho black
marketeer behind taxicab murder.

MAY

11125
BLACK NARCISSUS (100) tech (A)
IP-Archers (GFD)
P:D:SC: Michael Powell, Emeric Pressburger
S: (NOVEL) Rumer Godden
Deborah Kerr . . . . Sister Clodagh
Sabu . . . . Dulip Rai
David Farrar . . . . Mr Dean
Flora Robson . . . . Sister Philippa
Esmond Knight . . . . General
Jean Simmons . . . . Kanchi
Kathleen Byron . . . . Sister Ruth
Jenny Laird . . . . Sister Honey
Judith Furse . . . . Sister Briony
May Hallatt . . . . Angu Ayah
Shaun Noble . . . . Con
Nancy Roberts . . . . Mother Dorothea
DRAMA India. Anglo-Catholic nuns open
school/hospital in hill village. (AA: Best
Colour Photography, Best Art Direction, 1948).

11126
THE COURTNEYS OF CURZON STREET
(120) (U) USA: THE COURTNEY AFFAIR
Imperadio (BL) *reissue:* 1950 (30 mins cut)
P:D: Herbert Wilcox
S: Florence Tranter
SC: Nicholas Phipps
Anna Neagle . . . . Catherine O'Hallo
Michael Wilding . . . . Sir Edward Court
Gladys Young . . . . Lady Courtney

Coral Browne . . . . Valerie
Michael Medwin . . . . Edward Courtney
Daphne Slater . . . . Cynthia
Jack Watling . . . . Teddy Courtney
Helen Cherry . . . . Mary Courtney
Bernard Lee . . . . Col Cascoyne
Percy Walsh . . . . . . Sir Frank Murchison
Thora Hird . . . . Kate
Max Kirby . . . . Algie Longworth
MUSICAL 1899-1945. Saga of family founded
by nobleman and Irish maid. (DMNFA: 1947;
PGAA: 1948; Top Moneymaker: 1947).

11127
BANK HOLIDAY LUCK (42) (U)
John Baxter (ABFD)
D: Baynham Honri
S: Geoffrey Orme
Fred Wynne . . . . Bill
Olive Sloane . . . . Mrs Bill
Arthur Denton . . . . Gus
Billy Thatcher . . . . Joe
Michael Aldridge . . . . Fred
COMEDY Builders recount adventures on
previous bank holiday.

11128
TAKE MY LIFE (79) (A)
IP—Cineguild (GFD)
P: Anthony Havelock-Allan
D: David Lean
S: Winston Graham, Valerie Taylor
SC: Winston Graham, Valerie Taylor,
Margaret Kennedy
Hugh Williams . . . . Nicholas Talbot
Greta Gynt . . . . Philippa Bentley
Marius Goring . . . . Sidney Fleming
Francis L. Sullivan . . . . Prosecution
Rosalie Crutchley . . . . Liz Rusman
Henry Edwards . . . . Insp Archer
Marjorie Mars . . . . Mrs Newcome
Ronald Adam . . . . Deaf Man
Maurice Denham . . . . Defence
CRIME Opera star proves her husband
did not kill her ex-fiancee.

11129
THE BROTHERS (98) (A)
Triton (GFD) *reissue:* 1948
P: Sydney Box
D: David Macdonald
S: (NOVEL) L.A.G.Strong
SC: Muriel & Sydney Box, David Macdonald,
Paul Vincent Carroll
Patricia Roc . . . . Mary
Will Fyffe . . . . Aeneas McGrath
Maxwell Reed . . . . Fergus Macrae
Finlay Currie . . . . Hector Macrae
John Laurie . . . . Dugald
Andrew Crawford . . . . . Willie McFarish
Duncan Macrae . . . . John Macrae
Morland Graham . . . . Angus McFarish
Megs Jenkins . . . . Angusi McFarish
DRAMA Scotland. Servant girl loved by two
brothers and clan rival.

JUN

11130
BUSH CHRISTMAS (77) (U)
Ralph Smart (GFD) *reissue:* 1950 (ABFD)
D:S: Ralph Smart
N: John McCallum
Chips Rafferty . . . . Long Bill
John Fernside . . . . Jim
Stan Tolshurst . . . . Blue
Helen Grieve . . . . Helen
Nicky Yardley . . . . Snow
Michael Yardley . . . . Michael
Morris Unicombe . . . . John
Clyde Combo . . . . Old Jack
CHILDREN New South Wales. Children on
holiday pursue and catch horse thieves.

11131
DEAR MURDERER (94) (A)
Gainsborough (GFD)
P: Betty Box
D: Arthur Crabtree
S: (PLAY) StJohn Legh Clowes
SC: Muriel & Sydney Box, Peter Rogers
Eric Portman . . . . Lee Warren
Greta Gynt . . . . Vivien Warren
Dennis Price . . . . Richard Fenton
Jack Warner . . . . Insp Pembury
Maxwell Reed . . . . Jimmy Martin
Hazel Court . . . . Avis Fenton
Andrew Crawford . . . . Sgt Fox
Jane Hylton . . . . Rita
Ernest Butcher . . . . Porter
John Blythe . . . .·. . . . Ernie
CRIME Circumstances thwart husband's
perfect murder of his wife's lover.

11132
THE LOVES OF JOANNA GODDEN (89) (A)
Ealing (GFD)
AP: Sidney Cole
D: Charles Frend
S: (NOVEL) Sheila Kaye-Smith (JOANNA
GODDEN)
SC: H.E.Bates, Angus Macphail
Googie Withers . . . . Joanna Godden
Jean Kent . . . . Ellen Godden
John McCallum . . . . Arthur Alce
Derek Bond . . . . Martin Trevor
Chips Rafferty . . . . Collard
Henry Mollison . . . . Harry Trevor
Sonia Holm . . . . Louise
Josephine Stuart . . . . Grace Wickens
Edward Rigby . . . . Stuppen
Frederick Piper . . . . Isaac Turk
ROMANCE Romney Marsh, 1905. Three loves
of woman farm-owner.

11133
FRIEDA (98) (A)
Ealing (GFD) *reissue:* 1954 (Mon; 15 mins cut)
AP: Michael Relph
D: Basil Dearden
S: (PLAY) Ronald Millar
SC: Ronald Millar, Angus Macphail
David Farrar . . . . Robert Dawson
Glynis Johns . . . . Judy Dawson
Mai Zetterling . . . . Frieda Dawson
Flora Robson . . . . Nell Dawson
Albert Lieven . . . . Richard Mannsfeld
Barbara Everest . . . . Mrs Dawson
Gladys Henson . . . . Edith
Ray Jackson . . . .·. . . Tony Dawson
Patrick Holt . . . .·. ... Alan Dawson
Milton Rosmer . . . . Tom Merrick
Barry Letts . . . . Jim Merrick
Barry Jones . . . . Holliday
Garry Marsh . . . . Beckwith
DRAMA 1945. German girl's marriage
to British pilot upset by her Nazi brother.

11134
THE UPTURNED GLASS (86) (A)
Triton (GFD) *reissue:* 1948
P: Sydney Box, James Mason
D: Lawrence Huntington
S: Jno P. Monaghan
SC: Jno P. Monaghan, Pamela Kellino
James Mason . . . . Michael Joyce
Rosamund John . . . . Emma Wright
Pamela Kellino . . . . Kate Howard
Ann Stephens . . . . Ann Wright
Henry Oscar . . . . Coroner
Morland Graham . . . . Clay
Brefni O'Rorke . . . . Dr Farrell
Jane Hylton . . . . Miss Marsh
Susan Shaw . . . . Student
Richard Afton . . . .·. Mate
Peter Cotes . . . . Questioner

Cyril Chamberlain . . . . Doctor
Jno P. Monaghan . . . . Driver
Maurice Dénham . . . . Policeman
Beatrice Varley . . . . Mother
CRIME Surgeon kills sister-in-law whose
jealousy caused his wife's death.

11135
THE HANGMAN WAITS (63) (A)
Five Star (Butcher)
P: A. Barr-Smith, Roger Proudlock
D:S: A. Barr-Smith
John Turnbull . . . . Inspector
Anthony Baird . . . . Sinclair
Beatrice Campbell . . . . Usherette
Kenneth Warrington . . . . . .
Michael Balzagette . . . .
Edwin Ellis . . . .
Leonard Sharp . . .·. .. ..
CRIME Inspector and reporter track down
organist who killed usherette.

11136
DUAL ALIBI (81) (A)
British National (Pathe)
P: Louis H.Jackson
D: Alfred Travers
S: Renault Capes
SC: Alfred Travers, Stephen Clarkson,
Vivienne Ades
Herbert Lom. . . Jules/Georges de Lisle
Phyllis Dixey . . . . Penny
Terence de Marney . . . . . . Mike Bergen
Ronald Frankau . . . . Vincent Barney
Abraham Sofaer . . . . Judge
Eugene Deckers . . . . Ringmaster
Ben Williams . . . . Charlie
Clarence Wright . . . . Mangin
Beryl Measor . . . . Gwen
Harold Berens . . . . Ali
Sebastian Cabot . . . . Official
Cromwell Brothers Trapeze Act
CRIME Trapeze star poses as twin to recoup
stolen lottery ticket.

11137
DEATH IN HIGH HEELS (47) (A)
Marylebone (Ex)
P: Henry Halstead
D: Lionel Tomlinson
S: (NOVEL) Christianna Brand
Don Stannard . . . . Insp Charlesworth
Bill Hodge . . . . Mr Cecil
Veronica Rose . . . . Agnes Gregory
Patricia Laffan . . . . Magda Doon
Denise Anthony . . . . Aileen
Elsa Tee . . . . Victoria
Diana Wong . . . . Almond Blossom
Leslie Spurling . . . . Sgt Bedd
Kenneth Warrington . . . . . . Frank Bevan
CRIME Inspector solves poisoning of
Bond Street mannequin.

11138
DANCING WITH CRIME (83) (A)
Coronet-Alliance (Par)
P: James A.Carter
D: John Paddy Carstairs
S: Peter Fraser
SC: Brock Williams
Richard Attenborough . . . . . Ted Peters
Barry K. Barnes . . . . Paul Baker
Sheila Sim . . . . Joy Goodall
Garry Marsh . . . . Sgt Murray
John Warwick . . . . Insp Carter
Judy Kelly . . . . Toni
Barry Jones . . . . Gregory
Bill Rowbotham . . . . Dave Robinson
Cyril Chamberlain . . . . Sniffy
John Salew . . . . Pogson
Hamish Menzies . . . . Orchestra Leader
CRIME Taxi-driver and girl thwart black
marketeers using dance hall as front.

11139
THE PHANTOM SHOT (49) (A)
International Talking Pictures (IFR)
P:D: Mario Zampi
S: Walter C. Mycroft, Norman Lee
John Stuart . . . . Insp Webb
Olga Lindo . . . . Mrs Robson
Howard Marion Crawford . . Sgt Clapper
Louise Lord . . . . Anne Horder
Ronald Adam . . . . Caleb Horder
John Varley . . . . Peter Robson
Cyril Conway . . . . Philip Grahame
Jock McKay . . . . Angus
CRIME Inspector invites audience to solve
death of hated man.

JUL

11140
THEY MADE ME A FUGITIVE (103) (A)
USA: I BECAME A CRIMINAL
Gloria-Alliance (WB) *reissue:* 1950
(10 mins cut)
P: Nat Bronsten, James Carter
D: Cavalcanti
S: (NOVEL) Jackson Budd
(A CONVICT HAS ESCAPED)
SC: Noel Langley
Sally Gray . . . . Sally
Trevor Howard . . . . Clem Morgan
Griffith Jones . . . . Narcey
Rene Ray . . . . Cora
Mary Merrall . . . . Aggie
Vida Hope . . . . Mrs Fenshawe
Ballard Berkeley . . . . Insp Rockliffe
Phyllis Robins . . . . Olga
Eve Ashley . . . . Ellen
Charles Farrell . . . . Curley
Jack McNaughton . . . . . . Soapy
CRIME Framed crook breaks jail to
avenge himself on Soho dope-peddlers.

11141
BLACK MEMORY (73) (A)
Bushey (Ambassador) *reissue:* 1953 (Pi)
P: Gilbert Church
D: Oswald Mitchell
S: John Gilling
Michael Atkinson . . . . . . Danny Cruff
Myra O'Connell . . . . Joan Davidson
Jane Arden . . . . Sally Davidson
Michael Medwin . . . . Johnnie Fletcher
Frank Hawkins . . . . Alf Davidson
Winifred Melville . . . . . . Mrs Davidson
Sidney James . . . . Eddie Clinton
CRIME Youth poses as delinquent to clear
father of murder charge.

11142
SWISS HONEYMOON (63) (U)
International Artists (NR)
P:S: W.M.Sibley
D: Jan Sikorsky, Henry C.James
SC: Henry C.James
Percy Marmont . . . . The Man
Pat Mainwaring . . . . The Girl

ADVENTURE Switzerland. Honeymoon
couple are rescued from mountain.

AUG

11143
BEYOND PRICE (34) (U)
DUK Films (NR)
P:D:S: Cecil H. Williamson
Frederick Allen . . . . David Jones
Arnold Bell . . . . Insp Morgan
ADVENTURE Shipwrecked sailor tells
how he obtained pearl from native girl in
South Seas.

11144
JIM THE PENMAN (45) (A)
Frank Chisnell (NR)
D: Frank Chisnell
S: (RADIO PLAY) (ROGUES AND
VAGABONDS)
SC: Terry Sanford, Edward Eve
Mark Dignam . . . . James T. Saward
Beatrice Kane . . . . Amy
Campbell Singer . . . . Sutro
Alec Ross . . . . Insp Atwell
George Street . . . . Sir George
Daphne Maddox. . . . . . . Belle Cartwright
Theodore Tree . . . . Threefingered John
Colin Gordon . . . . Roberts
CRIME 1870. True story of barrister who
turned to forgery.

11145
MAKING THE GRADE (33) (U)
Inspiration (NR)
P:D:S: Horace Shepherd
Edwin Styles .   Jenny Laird
Jessie Matthews   Alfredo Campoli
Tommy Handley   Arthur Dulay
REVUE Producer shows early scenes of
famous stars to budding actress.(Includes
extracts from earlier films).

11146
A MAN ABOUT THE HOUSE (99) (A)
BLPA (BL)
P: Edward Black
D: Leslie Arliss
S: (NOVEL) Francis Brett Young
(PLAY) John Perry
SC: Leslie Arliss, J.B.Williams
Margaret Johnston . . . . Agnes Isit
Dulcie Gray . . . . Ellen Isit
Kieron Moore . . . . Salvatore
Guy Middleton . . . . Sir Benjamin Dench
Felix Aylmer . . . . Richard Sanctuary
Lilian Braithwaite . . . . . . Mrs Armitage
Jone Salinas . . . . Maria
Maria Fimiani . . . . Assunta
Reginald Purdell . . . . Higgs
CRIME Italy, 1907. Handsome butler plans
to kill two rich English spinsters.

11147
HOLIDAY CAMP (97) (A)
Gainsborough (GFD) *reissues:* 1948;
1954; (Mon; 12 mins cut)
P: Sydney Box
D: Ken Annakin
S: Godfrey Winn
SC: Muriel Box, Sydney Box, Peter Rogers,
Mabel Constanduros, Denis Constanduros,
Ted Willis
Flora Robson . . . . Esther Harman
Dennis Price . . . . S/L Hardwicke
Jack Warner . . . . Joe Huggett
Hazel Court . . . . Joan Martin
Emrys Jones . . . . Michael Halliday
Kathleen Harrison . . . . Ethel Huggett
Yvonne Owen . . . . Angela Kirby
Esmond Knight . . . . Announcer
Jimmy Hanley . . . . Jimmy Gardner
Peter Hammond . . . . Harry Huggett
Dennis Harkin . . . . Charlie
Esma Cannon . . . . Elsie Dawson
John Blythe . . . . Steve
Jeannette Tregarthen. . . . Valerie Thompson
Beatrice Varley . . . . Aunt
Susan Shaw . . . . Patsy Crawford
Maurice Denham . . . . Doctor
Jane Hylton . . . . Receptionist
Jack Raine . . . . Detective
Reginald Purdell . . . . Redcoat

Alfie Bass . . . . Redcoat
Patricia Roc; Cheerful Charlie Chester;
Gerry Wilmot
COMEDY Adventures and romances of
varied group including murderer at summer
holiday camp.

11148
JASSY (102) *tech* (A)
Gainsborough (GFD) *reissue:* 1948
P: Sydney Box
D: Bernard Knowles
S: (NOVEL) Norah Lofts
SC: Dorothy & Campbell Christie, Geoffrey
Kerr
Margaret Lockwood . . . . . Jassy Woodroffe
Patricia Roc . . . . Dilys Helmar
Dennis Price . . . . . Christopher Hatton
Dermot Walsh . . . . Barney Cannon
Basil Sydney . . . . Nick Helmar
Nora Swinburne . . . . Mrs Hatton
Linden Travers . . . . Mrs Helmar
Ernest Thesiger . . . . Sir Edward Follesmark
Cathleen Nesbitt . . . . . . Elizabeth Twisdale
Jean Cadell . . . . Meggie
John Laurie . . . . Woodroffe
Grey Blake . . . . Stephen Fennell
Clive Morton . . . . . Sir William Fennell
Torin Thatcher . . . . Bob Wicks
Beatrice Varley . . . . Mrs Wicks
Maurice Denham . . . . Jim Stoner
Alan Wheatley . . . . Sir Edward Walker
ROMANCE 1830. Psychic gipsy weds
gambler in exchange for return of the
house he won to the man she loves.

11149
MASTER OF BANKDAM (105) (A)
Holbein (GFD)
P: Nat Bronsten, Walter Forde,
Edward Dryhurst
D: Walter Forde
S: (NOVEL) Thomas Armstrong
(THE CROWTHERS OF BANKDAM)
SC: Edward Dryhurst, Moie Charles
Anne Crawford . . . . . . Annie Pickersgill
Dennis Price . . . . Joshua Crowther
Tom Walls . . . . Simeon Crowther
Stephen Murray . . . . . . Zebediah Crowther
Linden Travers . . . . Clara Baker
Jimmy Hanley . . . . . . Simeon Crowther jr.
Nancy Price . . . . Lydia Crowther
David Tomlinson . . . . Lancelot Crowther
Patrick Holt . . . . . Lemuel Pickersgill
Herbert Lomas . . . . Tom France
Frederick Piper . . . . . Ben Pickersgill
Beatrice Varley . . . . . . Mrs Pickersgill
Raymond Rollett . . . . Handel Baker
April Stride . . . . Sophie Crowther
Avis Scutt . . . . Mary Crowther
Nicholas Parsons . . . . Edgar Hoylehouse
DRAMA Yorkshire, 1854-1900. Saga of
three generations of mill-owners.

SEP

11150
THE HILLS OF DONEGAL (85) (A)
Butcher *reissue:* 1951 (Sherwood)
P:D: John Argyle
S: John Dryden
Dinah Sheridan . . . . Eileen Hannay
James Etherington. . . . . Michael O'Keefe
Moore Marriott . . . . Old Jake
John Bentley . . . . Terry O'Keefe
Brendan Clegg . . . . Paddy Hannay
Irene Handl . . . . Mrs McTavish
Tamara Desni . . . . Carole Wells
Maire O'Neill . . . . Hannah
Gaelic Irish Dancers; Green Flag Ceilidh

Band
MUSICAL Ireland. Opera star weds cousin when her caddish husband dies.

11151
CAPTAIN BOYCOTT (93) (A)
IP-Individual (GFD) *reissue:* 1954
(Mon; 17 mins cut)
P: Frank Launder, Sidney Gillat
D: Frank Launder
S: (NOVEL) Philip Rooney
SC: Frank Launder, Wolfgang Wilhelm,
Paul Vincent Carroll, Patrick Campbell
Stewart Granger . . . . Hugh Davin
Kathleen Ryan . . . . Anne Killain
Cecil Parker . . . . Capt Charles Boycott
Robert Donat . . . . Charles Parnell
Alastair Sim . . . . Father McKeogh
Mervyn Johns . . . . Watty Connell
Noel Purcell . . . . Daniel McGinty
Niall McGinnis . . . . Mark Killain
Maureen Delaney . . . . Mrs Davin
Eddie Byrne . . . . Sean Kerrin
Liam Gaffney . . . . Michael Fagan
Liam Redmond . . . . Martin Egan
Edward Lexy . . . . Sgt Demsey
Maurice Denham . . . . Col Strickland
Joe Linane . . . . Auctioneer
Bernadette O'Farrell . . . . . Mrs Fagan
Ian Fleming . . . . Reporter
Reginald Purdell . . . . Reporter
HISTORY Ireland, 1880. Persecuted
farmers ostracise absentee landlord's agent.

11152
THE LITTLE BALLERINA (60) (U)
GB Instructional (GFD)
P: Geoffrey Barkas
D: Lewis Gilbert
S: Michael Barringer
SC: Lewis Gilbert, Mary Cathcart Borer
Yvonne Marsh . . . . Joan
Marian Chapman . . . . Sally
Doreen Richards . . . . Lydia
Kay Henderson . . . . Pamela
Beatrice Varley . . . . Mrs Field
Herbert C.Walton . . . . Grandpa
George Carney . . . . Bill
Anthony Newley . . . . Johnny
Martita Hunt . . . . Miss Crichton
Leslie Dwyer . . . . Barney
Eliot Makeham . . . . Mr Maggs
Margot Fonteyn; Michael Soes
CHILDREN Poor girl realises ambition to
be ballet dancer.

11153
DUSTY BATES (serial) (U)
GB Instructional (GFD)
P: Geoffrey Barkas
D: Darrell Catling
S: Michael Barringer
Anthony Newley . . . . Dusty Bates
Billie Brooks . . . . Gil Ford
Michael McKeag . . . . David Ford
John Longden . . . . Capt Ford
Dennis Harkin . . . .
Wally Patch . . . .
Eps 1-5 (20)
CHILDREN Stowaway boy helps captain's
children catch jewel thieves.

11154
CIRCUS BOY (50) (U)
Merton Park (GFD)
P: Frank Hoare
D: Cecil Musk
S: Patita Nicholson
SC: Cecil Musk, Mary Cathcart Borer
James Kenney . . . . Michael Scott

Florence Stephenson . . . . . . Florence
George Stephenson . . . . . . George
Denver Hall . . . . Bailey
Dennis Gilbert . . . . Borden
Peter Scott . . . . Stewart
Gwen Bacon . . . . Mrs Scott
Jock Easton . . . . Jeff
Robert Raglan . . . . Trevor
Bertram Mills' Circus
CHILDREN Schoolboy swimmer loses
nervousness after becoming circus clown.

11155
THE OCTOBER MAN (110) (A)
Two Cities (GFD) *reissue:* 1954
(Mon; 22 mins cut)
P:SC: Eric Ambler
D: Roy Baker
S: (NOVEL) Eric Ambler
John Mills . . . . Jim Ackland
Joan Greenwood . . . . Jenny Carden
Edward Chapman . . . . Mr Peachey
Joyce Carey . . . . Mrs Vinton
Kay Walsh . . . . Molly Newman
Adrianne Allen . . . . Joyce Carden
Catherine Lacey . . . . Miss Selby
Frederick Piper . . . . Godby
Felix Aylmer . . . . Dr Martin
Patrick Holt . . . . Harry
George Benson . . . . Mr Pope
Jack Melford . . . . Wilcox
John Boxer . . . . Troth
Edward Underdown . . . . . . Official
Juliet Mills . . . . Girl
CRIME Brain-injured neurotic proves he
did not strangle fashion model.

11156
EYES THAT KILL (55) (A)
Condor (Butcher)
P: Harry Goodman
D:SC: Richard M. Grey
S: Warwick Charlton
Robert Berkeley . . . . Martin Bormann
Sandra Dorne . . . . Joan
William Price . . . . Maj Redway
CRIME MI5 man tracks down escaped Nazi's
underground organisation.

11157
FAME IS THE SPUR (116) (A)
Two Cities (GFD)
P: John Boulting
D: Roy Boulting
S: (NOVEL) Howard Spring
SC: Nigel Balchin
Michael Redgrave . . . . Hamer Radshaw
Rosamund John . . . . Ann Radshaw
Bernard Miles . . . . Tom Hanaway
Carla Lehmann . . . . Lady Lettice
Hugh Burden . . . . Arnold Ryerson
Marjorie Fielding . . . . Aunt Lizzie
Seymour Hicks . . . . Lord Lostwithiel
Anthony Wager . . . . Hamer (child)
Brian Weske . . . . Arnold (child)
Gerald Fox . . . . Tom (child)
David Tomlinson . . . . Lord Liskeard
Milton Rosmer . . . . Magistrate
Wylie Watson . . . . Pendleton
DRAMA 1870 - 1935. Northern socialist's
career in politics.

11158
UNCLE SILAS (103) (A)
USA: THE INHERITANCE
Two Cities (GFD)
P: Josef Somlo, Laurence Irving
D: Charles Frank
S: (NOVEL) Sheridan le Fanu

SC: Ben Travers
Jean Simmons . . . . Caroline Ruthyn
Katina Paxinou . . . . Mme de la Rougierre
Derrick de Marney . . . . Uncle Silas
Derek Bond . . . . Lord Richard Ibury
Esmond Knight . . . . Dr Bryerley
Sophie Stewart . . . . Lady Monica Waring
Manning Whiley . . . . Dudley Ruthyn
Reginald Tate . . . . Austin Ruthyn
Marjorie Rhodes . . . . Mrs Rusk
John Laurie . . . . Giles
Frederick Burtwell . . . . Branston
George Curzon . . . . Sleigh
O.B.Clarence . . . . Vicar
Guy Rolfe . . . . Sepulchre Hawkes
CRIME 1890. Guardian plots with housekeeper
to kill young heiress.

11159
THE WHITE UNICORN (97) (A)
USA: BAD SISTER
John Corfield (GFD)
P: Harold Huth
D: Bernard Knowles
S: (NOVEL) Flora Sandstrom
(THE MILKWHITE UNICORN)
SC: Robert Westerby, A.R.Rawlinson,
Moie Charles
Margaret Lockwood . . . . . . Lucy
Dennis Price . . . . Richard Glover
Ian Hunter . . . . Philip Templar
Joan Greenwood . . . . Lottie Smith
Guy Middleton . . . . Fobey
Catherine Lacey . . . . Miss Carter
Mabel Constanduros . . . . . Nurse
Paul Dupuis . . . . Paul
Eileen Peel . . . . Joan
Toots Lockwood . . . . Norey
Lily Kann . . . . Shura
Valentine Dyall . . . . Storton
Joan Rees . . . . Alice Waters
Stewart Rome . . . . Charles Madden
ROMANCE Remand home matron and slum
girl inmate recount unhappy love affairs.

11160
THE GHOSTS OF BERKELEY SQUARE (89)
(A) British National (Pathe)
P: Louis H. Jackson
D: Vernon Sewell
S: (NOVEL) Caryl Brahms, S.J.Simon
(NO NIGHTINGALES)
SC: James Seymour
Robert Morley . . . . Gen Burlap
Felix Aylmer . . . . Col Kelsoe
Yvonne Arnaud . . . . Millie
Claude Hulbert . . . . Merryweather
Abraham Sofaer . . . . Disraeli
Ernest Thesiger . . . . Investigator
Marie Lohr . . . . Lottie
Martita Hunt . . . . Lady Mary
A.E.Matthews . . . . Gen Bristow
John Longden . . . . Mortimer Digby
Ronald Frankau . . . . Tex Farnham
Wilfrid Hyde White . . . . . . Capt
Martin Miller . . . . Professor
Wally Patch . . . . Foreman
Esme Percy . . . . Vizier
Mary Jerrold . . . . Lettie
FANTASY Two 18th-century ghosts
doomed to haunt house until Royalty
comes to visit.

11161
MRS FITZHERBERT (99) (A)
British National (Pathe)
P: Louis H. Jackson
D: Montgomery Tully
S: (NOVEL) Winifred Carter

(PRINCESS FITZ)
SC: Montgomery Tully

Peter Graves	Prince of Wales
Joyce Howard	Maria Fitzherbert
Leslie Banks	Charles Fox
Margaretta Scott	Lady Jersey
Wanda Rotha	Princess Caroline
Mary Clare	Duchess of Devonshire
Frederick Valk	George III
Ralph Truman	Richard Sheridan
John Stuart	Duke of Bedford
Helen Haye	Lady Sefton
Chili Bouchier	Norris
Lily Kann	Queen Charlotte
Lawrence O'Madden	Lord Southampton
Frederick Leister	Henry Errington
Julian Dallas	Prince William
Barry Morse	Beau Brummell

HISTORY Prince Regent, secretly wed to
Catholic widow, is forced to marry
Princess of Brunswick.

NOV

11162
THE END OF THE RIVER (83) (A)
IP-Archers (GFD)
P: Michael Powell, Emeric Pressburger
D: Derek Twist
S: (NOVEL) Desmond Holdridge
SC: Wolfgang Wilhelm

Sabu	Manoel
Bibi Ferreira	Teresa
Esmond Knight	Dantos
Robert Douglas	Mr Jones
Antoinette Cellier	Conceicao
Torin Thatcher	Lisboa
Orlando Martins	Harrigan
Raymond Lovell	Col Porpino
James Hayter	Chico
Nicolette Bernard	Dona Serafina
Maurice Denham	Defence
Alan Wheatley	Irygoyen
Charles Hawtrey	Raphael
Zena Marshall	Sante
Dennis Arundell	Continho
Milton Rosmer	Judge

ADVENTURE South America. Indian boy
returns to his people after being made
the dupe of revolutionaries.

11163
THE WOMAN IN THE HALL (93) (A)
IP-Wessex (GFD)
P: Ian Dalrymple
D: Jack Lee
S: (NOVEL) G.B.Stern
SC: G.B.Stern, Ian Dalrymple, Jack Lee

Ursula Jeans	Lorna Blake
Jean Simmons	Jay Blake
Cecil Parker	Sir Hamar Barnard
Jill Raymond	Molly Blake
Edward Underdown	Neil Inglefield
Joan Miller	Susan
Nigel Buchanan	Toby
Ruth Dunning	Shirley
Russell Walters	Alfred
Terry Randal	Ann
Lily Kann	Baroness
Martin Walker	Judge

DRAMA Woman obtains money and
marriage by lies, causing her daughter to
become a thief.

11164
IT ALWAYS RAINS ON SUNDAY (92) (A)
Ealing (GFD)
AP: Henry Cornelius
D: Robert Hamer
S: (NOVEL) Arthur La Bern

SC: Robert Hamer, Henry Cornelius,
Angus Macphail

Googie Withers	Rose Sandigate
Jack Warner	Sgt Fothergill
John McCallum	Tommy Swann
Edward Chapman	George Sandigate
Jimmy Hanley	Whitey Williams
John Carol	Freddie Price
John Slater	Lou Hyams
Susan Shaw	Vi Sandigate
Sydney Tafler	Morry Hyams
Alfie Bass	Dicey Perkins
Patricia Plunkett	Doris Sandigate
Betty Ann Davies	Sadie Hyams
Michael Howard	Soapy Collins
Jane Hylton	Bessie Hyams
Frederick Piper	Sgt Leech
Hermione Baddeley	Mrs Spry
Nigel Stock	Ted Edwards
Gladys Henson	Mrs Neesley

CRIME Bethnal Green. Escaped convict
sheltered by married ex-fiancee.

11165
WHEN THE BOUGH BREAKS (81) (A)
Gainsborough (GFD)
P: Betty Box
D: Lawrence Huntington
S: Moie Charles, Herbert Victor
SC: Muriel & Sydney Box, Peter Rogers

Patricia Roc	Lily Bates
Rosamund John	Frances Norman
Bill Owen	Bill Collins
Patrick Holt	Robert Norman
Brenda Bruce	Ruby Chapman
Leslie Dwyer	George
Jane Hylton	Maid
Sonia Holm	Nurse
Cavan Malone	Jimmy
Torin Thatcher	Adams
Catherine Lacey	Almoner
Muriel George	Landlady
Ada Reeve	Landlady

DRAMA Bigamist abandons wife who
then lets her child be adopted.

11166
MUSICAL ROMANCE (35) (U)
Inspiration (NR)
P:D:S: Horace Shepherd
Bruce Belfrage
MUSICAL   Old Busker writes symphony
after wife dies.

11167
THE WAY OF THE WORLD (33) (U)
Bishu Sen Films (Butcher)
D: James Komisarjevsky
S: Simon Stone

Hamilton Deane	Grandpa
Mary Perkins	Jane
Graham Russell	Dick

COMPILATION Grandfather forces girl's
suitor to watch silent films.
(Includes extracts from earlier films).

11168
WHILE I LIVE (85) (A)
Edward Dryhurst (20) *reissue:* 1950,
DREAM OF OLWEN
D: John Harlow
S: (PLAY) Robert Bell
(THIS SAME GARDEN)
SC: John Harlow, Doreen Montgomery

Tom Walls	Nehemiah
Sonia Dresdel	Julia Trevelyan
Clifford Evans	Peter
Carol Raye	Sally Warwick
Patricia Burke	Christine
John Warwick	George Warwick

Edward Lexy	Selby
Audrey Fildes	Olwen
Charles Victor	Sgt Pearne
Ernest Butcher	Ambrose
Sally Rogers	Hannah

DRAMA Cornwall. Woman believes
amnesiac wife of reporter to be the
reincarnation of her sister.

11169
JOURNEY AHEAD (62) (U)
Random (IFR)
P:D: Peter Mills
S: Warren Tute

Ruth Haven	Anne Franklin
John Stevens	Mike Baxter
Nora Gordon	Mrs Deacon
Howard Douglas	Adam Baxter

CRIME Cornwall. War widow loves
smuggler who turns out to be tec.

DEC

11170
BRIGHTON ROCK (91) (A)
ABPC (Pathe)
P: Roy Boulting
D: John Boulting
S: (NOVEL) Graham Greene
SC: Graham Greene, Terence Rattigan

Richard Attenborough	Pinkie Brown
Hermione Baddeley	Ida Arnold
William Hartnell	Dallow
Carol Marsh	Rose Brown
Nigel Stock	Cubitt
Wylie Watson	Spicer
Harcourt Williams	Prewitt
Alan Wheatley	Fred Hale
George Carney	Phil Corkery
Charles Goldner	Colleoni
Reginald Purdell	Frank

Constance Smith; Norman Griffiths and his
Orchestra
CRIME Brighton, 1938. Teenage leader of
race gang weds waitress to silence her,
and tries to cause her suicide.

11171
MINE OWN EXECUTIONER (108) (A)
London-Harefield (BL)
reissue: '1953 (22 mins cut)
P: Anthony Kimmins, Jack Kitchin
D: Anthony Kimmins
S: (NOVEL) Nigel Balchin
SC: Nigel Balchin

Burgess Meredith	Felix Milne
Dulcie Gray	Patricia Milne
Kieron Moore	Adam Lucian
Barbara White	Molly Lucian
Christine Norden	Barbara Edge
John Laurie	Dr James Garsten
Michael Shepley	Peter Edge
Lawrence Hanray	Dr le Farge
Walter Fitzgerald	Dr Norris Pile
Martin Miller	Dr Hans Tautz
Jack Raine	Insp Pierce
Helen Haye	Lady Maresfield
John Stuart	Dr John Hayling

CRIME Psychiatrist fails to cure ex-POW,
who then kills his wife.

11172
JUST WILLIAM'S LUCK (92) (U)
Diadem-Alliance (UA)
P: David Coplan, James Carter
D: SC: Val Guest
S: (STORIES) Richmal Crompton

William Graham	William Brown
Leslie Bradley	The Boss
A.E.Matthews	The Tramp

Garry Marsh . . . . MrBrown
Jane Welsh . . . . Mrs Brown
Muriel Aked . . . . Emily
Hugh Cross . . . . Robert Brown
Kathleen Stuart . . . . Ethel Brown
Jack Raine . . . . Policeman
Hy Hazel . . . . Gloria Gail
Brian Roper . . . . Ginger
James Crabbe . . . . Douglas
Brian Weske . . . . Henry
COMEDY Village boys catch fur thieves
in 'haunted' house.

11173
THE SECRET TUNNEL (49) (U)
Merton Park (GFD)
P: Frank A.Hoare
D:SC: William C.Hammond
S: (NOVEL) Mary Borer
(THE HOUSE WITH THE BLUE DOOR)
Anthony Wager . . . . Roger Henderson
Ivor Bowyer . . . . John Wilson
Murray Matheson . . . . Mr Henderson
Gerald Pring . . . . Mr Wilson
Thelma Rea . . . . Mrs Matthews
Frank Henderson . . . . Mr Harvey
John H. Sullivan . . . . Insp Bell
Michael Kelly . . . . Slim
CHILDREN Boys discover secret passage
used by painting smugglers.

11174
STAGE FRIGHTS (34) (U)
GB Instructional (GFD)
P: Henry Passmore
D: Harry Hughes
S: Marriott Edgar
Mark Daly . . . . Nobby
Graham Moffatt . . . . Albert
Knox Crichton . . . . Kedge
Agnes Lauchlan . . . . Mrs Catchpole
CHILDREN Pantomime property men use
stolen money for "snow."

11175
FORTUNE LANE (60) (U)
Elstree Independent (GFD)
P:D: John Baxter
S: Geoffrey Orme, Mary Cathcart Borer
Douglas Barr . . . . Peter Quentin
Billy Thatcher . . . . John
Brian Weske . . . . Tim
Angela Glynne . . . . Margaret Quentin
George Carney . . . . Mr Quentin
Nell Ballantyne . . . . Mrs Quentin
Antony Holles . . . . Mr Carpenter
CHILDREN Gardener's son cleans windows
to achieve ambition to drive train.

11176
COMIN' THRO' THE RYE (61) (U)
Advance (Adelphi)
P: Arthur Dent
D: Walter C. Mycroft
S: Gilbert McAllister
Terence Alexander . . . . . . Robert Burns
Olivia Barley . . . . Jean Armour
Patricia Burleigh . . . . Highland Mary
Trefor Jones; Sylvia Welling; Walter Saull's
Scotia Singers
MUSICAL Scotland, 1780.
Life and loves of ploughboy poet.

11177
ESCAPE DANGEROUS (62) (A)
DS Films (H & S)
P: John Denny, Digby Smith
D: Digby Smith
S: Oswell Blakeston
Beresford Egan . . . . Dr Belhomme
Mary Stone . . . . Jacqueline Fabre
Lily Lapidus . . . . Mme Angeline
Daphne Day . . . . Blanche de Vigny
Peter Noble . . . . Michel
Humberston Wright . . . . . Aristide Fabre
DRAMA France, 1793. Doctor helps aristos
escape guillotine for a fee, then betrays them.

1948

JAN

11178
THE MARK OF CAIN (88) (A)
Two Cities (GFD)
P: W.P.Lipscomb
D: Brian Desmond Hurst
S: (NOVEL) Joseph Shearing
(AIRING IN A CLOSED CARRIAGE)
SC: W.P.Lipscomb, Francis Crowdy,
Christianna Brand

Eric Portman	Richard Howard
Sally Gray	Sarah Bonheur
Patrick Holt	John Howard
Dermot Walsh	Jerome Thorne
Denis O'Dea	Sir William Godfrey
Edward Lexy	Lord Rochford
Therese Giehse	Sister Seraphine
Maureen Delany	Daisy Cobb
Helen Cherry	Mary
Vida Hope	Jennie
James Hayter	Dr White
Andrew Cruickshank	Sir Jonathan
Miles Malleson	Mr Burden

John Hollingsworth; Albert Ferber
CRIME 1900. Jealous man kills his younger
brother and frames his wife.

11179
VICE VERSA (111) (U)
Two Cities (GFD)
P: Peter Ustinov, George H.Brown
D: Peter Ustinov
S: (NOVEL) F. Anstey
SC: Peter Ustinov

Roger Livesey	Paul Bultitude
Kay Walsh	Mrs Verlayne
Anthony Newley	Dick Bultitude
David Hutcheson	Marmaduke Paradine
Petula Clark	Dulcie Grimstone
James Robertson Justice	Dr Grimstone
Joan Young	Mrs Grimstone
Patricia Raine	Alice
Kynaston Reeves	Dr Challoner
Vida Hope	Nanny
Harcourt Williams	Judge
Robert Eddison	Mr Blinkhorn
James Hayter	Headmaster
Alfie Bass	Urchin
Hugh Dempster	Col Ambrose
Peter Jones	Chawner jr
James Kenney	Coggs

FANTASY 1907. Magic stone makes
pompous father change places with
his schoolboy son.

11180
EASY MONEY (94) (A)
Gainsborough (GFD)
P: A. Frank Bundy
D: Bernard Knowles
S: (PLAY) Arnold Ridley
SC: Muriel & Sydney Box

Greta Gynt	Pat Parsons
Dennis Price	Joe Henry
Jack Warner	Philip Stafford
Mervyn Johns	Herbert Atkins
Petula Clark	Jackie Stafford
Edward Rigby	Teddy Ball
Marjorie Fielding	Ruth Stafford
Bill Owen	Mr Lee
Raymond Lovell	Mr Cyprus
Guy Rolfe	Archie
Yvonne Owen	Carol Stafford
David Tomlinson	Martin Latham
Frank Cellier	Director
Mabel Constanduros	Grandma
Jack Watling	Dennis Stafford
Joan Young	Agnes Atkins
Maurice Denham	Insp Kirby

Frederick Piper	Martin

London Casino Dancers
DRAMA Linked stories of four people
who win football pool.

11181
AN IDEAL HUSBAND (96) tech (A)
London (BL)
P:D: Alexander Korda
S: (PLAY) Oscar Wilde
SC: Lajos Biro

Paulette Goddard	Mrs Cheveley
Michael Wilding	Viscount Goring
Diana Wynyard	Lady Chiltern
C.Aubrey Smith	Earl of Caversham
Glynis Johns	Mabel Chiltern
Hugh Williams	Sir Robert Chiltern
Constance Collier	Lady Markby
Christine Norden	Mrs Marchmont
Harriette Johns	Lady Basildon
Michael Medwin	Duke of Nonsuch
Michael Anthony	Vicomte de Nanjac
Fred Groves	Phipps

COMEDY 1895. Viscount foils blackmailing
widow.

11182
NIGHT COMES TOO SOON (52) (A)
Federated (Butcher)
P: Harold Baim
D: Denis Kavanagh
S: (PLAY) Lord Lytton
(THE HAUNTED AND THE HAUNTERS)
SC: Pat Dixon

Valentine Dyall	Doctor

Anne Howard
Alec Faversham
Howard Douglas
Beatrice Marsden
Arthur Brander
Anthony Baird
David Keir
FANTASY Doctor rids old house of the
ghosts of sailor, his wife, and her lover.

11183
DAUGHTER OF DARKNESS (91) (A)
Kenilworth-Alliance (Par) reissue: 1955 (Ren)

P: Victor Hanbury
D: Lance Comfort
S: (PLAY) Max Catto (THEY WALK ALONE)
SC: Max Catto

Anne Crawford	Bess Stanforth
Maxwell Reed	Dan
Siobhan McKenna	Emily Beaudine
George Thorpe	Mr Tallent
Barry Morse	Robert Stanforth
Liam Redmond	Father Corcoran
Honor Blackman	Julie Tallent
Grant Tyler	Larry Tallent
David Greene	David Price
Denis Gordon	Saul Trevethick
Arthur Hambling	Jacob

CRIME Yorkshire. Passionate Irish peasant
kills her lovers.

11184
CHORUS GIRL (46) (U)
R.J.Tomson-St James (Renown)
D: Randolph Tomson
S: Raphael Knappett
SC: Alan Cullimore

Jacquelyn Dunbar	Valerie
Alex Wright	Father
Beth Ross	Joyce
Beryl Trent	Grandma
Maud Long	Mother
Charmian Innes	Dresser

DRAMA Ex-stage star helps her
granddaughter become dancer.

11185
NOTHING VENTURE (73) (U)
John Baxter (BL)
D: John Baxter
S: Geoffrey Orme

The Artemus Boys	Tom, Dick & Harry
Terry Randal	Diana Chaice
Patric Curwen	The Author
Michael Aldridge	Michael Garrod
Paul Blake	The Boss
Wilfred Caithness	The Professor
Howard Douglas	Badger
Ben Williams	Spike
Peter Gawthorne	Official

Jack Simpson and his Sextet
CRIME Boys save plans of prof's secret
ray and catch crooks.

FEB

11186
MY BROTHER JONATHAN (107) (A)
ABPC (Pathe)
P: Warwick Ward
D: Harold French
S: (NOVEL) Francis Brett Young
SC: Leslie Landau, Adrian Arlington

Michael Denison	Jonathan Dakers
Dulcie Gray	Rachel Hammond
Ronald Howard	Harold Dakers
Stephen Murray	Dr Craig
Mary Clare	Mrs Dakers
Finlay Currie	Dr Hamilton
Beatrice Campbell	Edie Martyn
Arthur Young	Sir Joseph Higgins
Beatrice Varley	Mrs Hodgkiss
James Robertson Justice	Eugene Dakers
James Hayter	Tom Morse
Jessica Spencer	Connie
John Salew	Wilburn
Peter Murray	Tony Dakers
Wylie Watson	Bagley
Hilda Bayley	Mrs Perry
Josephine Stuart	Lily
Wilfrid Hyde White	Mr Gaige

DRAMA Slum doctor gives up fiancee to
marry his dead brother's mistress for the
sake of her child.

11187
CALL OF THE BLOOD (88) (A)
Pendennis Pictures (BL)
P: John Stafford, Steven Pallos
D: John Clements, Ladislas Vajda
S: (NOVEL) Robert Hichens
SC: John Clements, Akos Tolnay, Basil Mason

Kay Hammond	Dr Anne Lester
John Clements	Julius Ikon
John Justin	David Erskine
Lea Padovani	Maddelena
Robert Rietti	Gaspari
Carlo Ninchi	Salvatore
Hilton Edwards	Dr Robert Blake
Jelo Filippo	Sebastiano
H.G.Stoker	Uncle
Michael Medwin	Student
Eliot Makeham	Assistant

DRAMA Sicily, 1900. Honeymoon husband
seduces villager and is killed by her fisherman
father.

11188
NIGHT BEAT (91) (A)
BLPA (BL) reissue: 1951 (11 mins cut)
P:D: Harold Huth
S: Guy Morgan
SC: T.J.Morrison, Roland Pertwee,
Robert Westerby

Anne Crawford	Julie Kendall
Maxwell Reed	Felix Fenton

Ronald Howard	Andy Kendall
Christine Norden	Jackie
Hector Ross	Don Brady
Fred Groves	PC Kendall
Sidney James	Nixon
Nicholas Stuart	Rocky
Frederick Leister	Magistrate
Michael Medwin	Spider

CRIME Ex-commando joins police while
his friend becomes crooked club-owner.

11189
DEATH IN THE HAND (43) (A)
Four Star (GFD)
P: A. Barr-Smith, Roger Proudlock
D: A. Barr-Smith
S: (STORY) Max Beerbohm
SC: Douglas Cleverdon

Esme Percy	Cosmo Vaughan
Ernest Jay	MacRae
Cecile Chevreau	Sylvia Mottram
Carleton Hobbs	Chairman
John le Mesurier	Jack Mottram
Shelagh Fraser	Penelope MacRae
Norman Shelley	Businessman
Wilfred Caithness	Rowlandson

DRAMA Neurotic predicts train crash
from his fellow passengers' palms.

11190
AGAINST THE WIND (96) (A)
Ealing (GFD)
AP: Sidney Cole
D: Charles Crichton
S: J. Elder Wills
SC: T.E.B.Clarke, Michael Pertwee,
Paul Vincent Carroll

Robert Beatty	Father Phillip
Jack Warner	Max Cronk
Simone Signoret	Michele
Gordon Jackson	Johnny Duncan
Paul Dupuis	Jacques Picquart
Gisele Preville	Julie
John Slater	Emile Meyer
Peter Illing	Andrew
James Robertson Justice . .	Ackerman
Sybilla Binder	Malou
Helen Hanson	Marie Berlot
Eugene Deckers	Marcel van Hecke
Andre Morell	Abbot

WAR 1943. Canadian priest, Scot, Belgian
girl, Jew, adventurer and patriot sent to
Belgium to play practical jokes on Germans.

11191
BLANCHE FURY (95) tech (A)
IP-Cineguild (GFD) reissue: 1950 (ABFD)
P: Anthony Havelock-Allan
D: Marc Allegret
S: (NOVEL) Joseph Shearing
SC: Audrey Erskine Lindop, Hugh Mills,
Cecil McGivern

Stewart Granger	Philip Thorn
Valerie Hobson	Blanche Fury
Walter Fitzgerald	Simon Fury
Michael Gough	Lawrence Fury
Maurice Denham	Maj Frazer
Sybilla Binder	Louisa
Edward Lexy	Col Jenkins
Allan Jeayes	Wetherby
Suzanne Gibbs	Lavinia Fury
Ernest Jay	Calamy
George Woodbridge	Aimes
Arthur Wontner	Lord Rudford
Amy Veness	Mrs Winterbourne
M.E.Clifton-James . .	Prison Governor

CRIME Derby, period. Governess weds rich
landowner who is killed by ambitious steward.

11192
MOVIE MEMORIES (14) (A)
Inspiration (20)
P:D:S: Horace Shepherd
N: Ronald Waldman
COMPILATION Extracts from silent films.

11193
THE FLAMINGO AFFAIR (58) (A)
Inspiration (GN) reissue: 1952
BLONDE FOR DANGER (EB; 7 mins cut)
P:D: Horace Shepherd
S: Maurice Moisiewitsch

Denis Webb	Dick Tarleton
Colette Melville	Paula Danvers
Arthur Chesney	Roberts
Eddie Matthews	Eddie Williams
Michael Anthony	Reynolds
Geoffrey Wilmer	Schultz

Stephane Grappelly and his Quintet;
Charmian Innes; Eugene Pini and his Tango
Orchestra
CRIME Ex-commando, infatuated with girl
black-marketeer, robs his employer.

11194
CASTLE SINISTER (49) (A)
Unicorn (EB)
P: W. Howard Borer
D: Oscar Burn

Mara Russell-Tavernan . . .	Lady Glennye
Robert Essex	Nigel Craven
Karl Mier	Maj Selwyn
Alistair Hunter	McTavish
John Gauntley	Michael
James Liggatt	Neale
Maureen O'Moor	Maggie

CRIME Scotland. Marchioness's stepson
unmasks MO as Nazi spy.

11195
IDOL OF PARIS (105) (A)
Premier (WB)
P: R.J.Minney
D: Leslie Arliss
S: (NOVEL) Alfred Shirkauer
(PAIVA QUEEN OF LOVE)
SC: Norman Lee, Stafford Dickens, Harry Ostrer

Michael Rennie	Hertz
Beryl Baxter	Theresa
Christine Norden	Cora Pearl
Margaretta Scott	Empress Eugene
Keneth Kent	Napoleon
Miles Malleson	Offenbach
Henry Oscar	Lachman
Andrew Osborne	Antoine
Andrew Cruickshank	Prince Nicholas
Sybilla Binder	Mrs Lachman
Leslie Perrins	Count Paiva
Patti Morgan	Bellanger
Donald Gray	Inspector

DRAMA Paris, period. Ill-used daughter of
ragman achieves notoriety without actual
blemish.

11196
WHO KILLED VAN LOON ? (51) (A)
Gordon Kyle (Ex)
P: Gordon Kyle, James Carreras
D: Lionel Tomlinson, Gordon Kyle
S: Peter Cresswell

Raymond Lovell	Johann Schmidt
Kay Bannerman	Anna Kreuger
Robert Wyndham	Insp Oxley
John Dodsworth	Ian Ferguson
Milton Rosmer	Simmonds
Patricia Laffan	Peggy Osborn

CRIME Rich man frames Dutch girl for
killing diamond merchant.

11197
THE THREE WEIRD SISTERS (82) (A)
British National (Pathe)
P: Louis H. Jackson
D: Dan Birt
S: (NOVEL) Charlotte Armstrong
(THE CASE OF THE THREE WEIRD
SISTERS)
SC: Louise Birt, David Evans, Dylan Thomas

Nancy Price	Gertrude Morgan-Vaughan
Mary Clare	Maud Morgan-Vaughan
Mary Merrall	Isobel Morgan-Vaughan
Nova Pilbeam	Claire Prentiss
Anthony Hulme	David Davies
Raymond Lovell . . .	Owen Morgan-Vaughan
Elwyn Brook-Jones	Thomas
Edward Rigby	Waldo
Hugh Griffith	Mabli Hughes
Marie Ault	Beattie

CRIME Wales. Crippled sisters plot to kill
their rich halfbrother and his secretary.

11198
SO EVIL MY LOVE (109) (A)
Paramount British
P: Hal B. Wallis
D: Lewis Allen
S: (NOVEL) Joseph Shearing
SC: Leonard Spiegelglass, Ronald Millar

Ray Milland	Mark Bellis
Ann Todd	Olivia Harwood
Geraldine Fitzgerald	Susan Courtney
Leo G. Carroll	Jarvis
Raymond Huntley	Henry Courtney
Martita Hunt	Edgar Bellamy
Raymond Lovell	Edgar Bellamy
Moira Lister	Kitty Feathers
Finlay Currie	Dr Kyrlie
Roderick Lovell . . .	Sir John Curle
Muriel Aked	Hattie Shoebridge

CRIME 1866. Artist involves missionary's
widow in blackmail and murder.

11199
THIS WAS A WOMAN (104) (A)
Excelsior (20)
P: Marcel Hellman
D: Tim Whelan
S: (PLAY) Joan Morgan
SC: Val Valentine

Sonia Dresdel	Sylvia Russell
Barbara White	Fenella Russell
Walter Fitzgerald	Arthur Russell
Cyril Raymond	Austin Penrose
Marjorie Rhodes	Mrs Holmes
Emrys Jones	Terry Russell
Celia Lipton	Effie
Julian Dallas	Val Christie
Lesley Osmond	Sally
Kynaston Reeves	Dr Morrison

CRIME Power-mad wife tries to poison
her husband and ruin her daughter's marriage.

11200
DICK BARTON - SPECIAL AGENT (70) (U)
Marylebone (Ex)
P: Henry Halstead
D: Alfred Goulding
S: (RADIO SERIAL) Edward J.Mason
SC: Alan Stranks, Alfred Goulding

Don Stannard	Dick Barton
George Ford	Snowey White
Jack Shaw	Jock
Gillian Maude	Jean Hunter
Geoffrey Wincott	Dr Caspar
Beatrice Kane	Miss Horrock
Ivor Danvers	Snub

CRIME Tec thwarts smugglers and foreign agent intent on destroying England with germ bombs placed in reservoirs.

Also released as a serial in six parts:

11201
1: SPECIAL AGENT (1)

11202
2: THE POISONED DART (1500)

11203
3: THE SMUGGLER'S SECRET (1500)

11204
4: TRAPPED (1300)

11205
5: NITRIC ACID (900)

11206
6: FIGHT TO THE FORTUNE (900)

11207
RIVER PATROL (45) (A)
Knightsbridge
P: Hal Wilson
D: Ben R. Hart
S: James Corbett
John Blythe . . . . Robby
Lorna Dean . . . . Jean
Wally Patch . . . .
Stan Paskin . . . .
CRIME Customs agent catches nylon smugglers.

11208
THE FIRST GENTLEMAN (111) (A)
USA: AFFAIRS OF A ROGUE
Columbia British
P: Joseph Friedman
D: Cavalcanti
S: (PLAY) Norman Ginsbury
SC: Nicholas Phipps, Reginald Long
Jean-Pierre Aumont . . . . . . Prince Leopold
Joan Hopkins . . . . Princess Charlotte
Cecil Parker . . . . Prince Regent
Margaretta Scott . . . . Lady Hertford
Jack Livesey . . . . Duke of Kent
Ronald Squire . . . . Mr Brougham
Athene Seyler . . . . Miss Knight
Anthony Hawtrey . . . . . . Sir Richard Croft
Hugh Griffith . . . . . . Bishop of Salisbury
Gerard Heinz . . . . Dr Stockman
George Curzon . . . . Duke of York
Betty Huntley-Wright . . Princess Elizabeth
Tom Gill . . . . Prince William
Lydia Sherwood . . . . Princess Augusta
Frances Waring . . . . Queen Charlotte
Amy Frank . . . . Princess Caroline
HISTORY Prince Regent tries to make his daughter marry Prince of Orange instead of Prince of Saxe-Coburg.

11209
ANNA KARENINA (123) (A)
London (BL)
P: Alexander Korda
D: Julien Duvivier
S: (NOVEL) Leo Tolstoy
SC: Julien Duvivier, Jean Anouilh, Guy Morgan
Vivien Leigh . . . . Anna Karenina
Ralph Richardson . . . . Alexei Karenin
Kieron Moore . . . . Count Vronsky
Sally Ann Howes . . . . . Kitty Scherbatsky
Niall MacGinnis . . . . Levin
Martita Hunt . . Princess Betsy Tversky
Marie Lohr . . . . . . Princess Scherbatsky
Michael Gough . . . . Nicholai
Hugh Dempster . . . . Stefan Oblonsky

Marry Kerridge . . . . Dolly Oblonsky
Heather Thatcher . . Countess Lydia Ivanovna
Helen Haye . . . . Countess Vronsky
Austin Trevor . . . . Col Vronsky
Ruby Miller . . . . Countess Meskov
John Longden . . . . . . Gen Serpuhousky
Leslie Bradley . . . . Korsunsky
Michael Medwin . . . . Doctor
Jeremy Spenser . . . . Giuseppe
Gino Cervi . . . . Enrico
ROMANCE Russia, 1875. Count rejects army career to live with official's wife.

11210
BORN OF THE SEA (38) (U)
Duchy (EB)
P: Albert Stanley Williamson
D: Anthony Mavrogordato
S: Howard Douglas, Frank Phillips
Cedric Staples . . . . George
Dorothea Paul . . . . Mary
Betty Williams . . . . Betty
Archie Rowe . . . . Sam
ADVENTURE Cornwall. Widow adopts shipwrecked waif who later loses his life to save another.

11211
THE GENTLEMEN GO BY (39) (A)
AIP (Electa)
P: Joan Widgey Newman
D: Joan Widgey Newman, John Calthrop
S: John Calthrop
Conrad Phillips
Alaistair Bannerman
CRIME Ex-sailor joins smuggling gang using Holiday Camp as front.

11212
THE GOODWIN SANDS (34) (U)
D.G. & S. Productions (WB)
P: Carlyn Dixie
D: Rudall C. Hayward
S: John Swift
Kent Walton . . . . O'Malley
Pamela Saxby . . . . Jean Kirkaldie
Joseph Cunningham . . . . . Capt Erickson
Jack Anton . . . . Whitey
Douglas Kirkaldie . . . . . David Kirkaldie
ADVENTURE Ramsgate. Lifeboatmen save stubborn captain and girl stowaway from shipwreck.

11213
THE GIRL FROM SCOTLAND YARD (35) (A)
Barralet (Sherwood)
D:S: Paul Barralet
Susan Carol . . . . Dorothy Shepperd
Ivan Craig . . . .
Hope Carr . . . .
CRIME Girl joins police and catches car thieves.

11214
FOR OLD TIMES' SAKE (34) (U)
Barralet (Butcher)
D:S: Paul Barralet
Vic Oliver   Lionel Marson
Marie Lloyd jr   Albert Chevalier
Florrie Forde   Wilson, Keppel & Betty
REVUE (Includes extracts from earlier films).

11215
MERRY- GO-ROUND (53) (U)
Federated
P: Margaret Cordin
D: Josh Binney
Bonar Colleano jr
Beryl Davis

Leon Sherkot
COMEDY Producer searches for new ideas for film.

11216
TAILS YOU LOSE (35) (A)
Laurie Freedman (Aladdin)
D: Laurie Freedman
Will E. Russell . . . . The Man
COMEDY Drunk tries to get stained shirt cleaned at laundry.

11217
SNOWBOUND (85) (A)
Gainsborough (RKO)
P: Aubrey Baring
D: David Macdonald
S: (NOVEL) Hammond Innes
(THE LONELY SKIER)
SC: David Evans, Keith Campbell
Robert Newton . . . . Derek Engels
Dennis Price . . . . Neil Blair
Herbert Lom . . . . Keramikos
Mila Parely . . . . Carla Rometta
Marcel Dalio . . . . Valdini
Stanley Holloway . . . . Joe Wesson
Guy Middleton . . . . Albert Mayne
Willy Feuter . . . . Aldo
Richard Molinas . . . . Mancini
Catherine Ferraz . . . . Emilia
William Price . . . . Stelben
Zena Marshall . . . . Italian Girl
ADVENTURE Alps. Scriptwriter discovers snowbound group seeking hidden gold.

11218
ESCAPE (79) (A)
20th Century Productions (20)
P: William Perlberg
D: Joseph L. Mankiewicz
S: (PLAY) John Galsworthy
SC: Phillip Dunne
Rex Harrison . . . . Matt Denant
Peggy Cummins . . . . Dora Winton
William Hartnell . . . . Insp Harris

Betty Ann Davies . . . . Girl
Norman Wooland . . . . Parson
Jill Esmond . . . . Grace Winton
Frederick Piper . . . . Convict
Cyril Cusack . . . . Rogers
Marjorie Rhodes . . . . Mrs Pinkem
John Slater . . . . Salesman
Frank Pettingell . . . . PC
Frederick Leister . . . . Judge
Walter Hudd . . . . Defence
Maurice Denham . . . . Crown
George Woodbridge . . . . . Farmer Browning
CRIME Various people help RAF officer escape from Dartmoor.

11219
UNDER THE FROZEN FALLS (44) (U)
GB Instructional (GFD)
P: Donald B. Wilson
D: Darrell Catling
S: (NOVEL) J.H. Martin-Cross
SC: Donald B. Wilson, Frank Wilson
Harold Warrender . . . . Carlington
Jacques Brown . . . . Prof Bell-Wrightson
Ivan Brandt . . . . Thompson
Claude Hulbert . . . . Riley
Mary Kerridge . . . . Mrs Roseby
Ray Jackson . . . . David Roseby
Peter Scott . . . . Bob

Tony Richardson . . . .   Peter
CHILDREN Scouts catch crooks seeking secret
formula hidden in cave.

11220
THE GREED OF WILLIAM HART (78) (A)
Bushey (Ambassador)
P: Gilbert Church
D: Oswald Mitchell
S: John Gilling
Tod Slaughter . . . .   William Hart
Henry Oscar . . . .   Mr Moore
Aubrey Woods . . . .   Daft Jamie
Jenny Lynn . . . .   Helen Moore
Arnold Bell . . . .   Dr Cox
Mary Love . . . .   Mary Patterson
Winifred Melville . . . .   Meg Hart
Patrick Addison . . . .   Hugh Alston
Ann Trego . . . .   Janet Brown
CRIME Edinburgh, 1820. Resurrectionists kill
halfwit and sell his corpse to anatomist.

APR

11221
MIRANDA (80) (A)
Gainsborough (GFD)
P: Betty Box
D: Ken Annakin
S: (PLAY) Peter Blackmore
SC: Peter Blackmore, Denis Waldock
Googie Withers . . . .   Clare Marten
Glynis Johns . . . .   Miranda
Griffith Jones . . . .   Paul Marten
John McCallum . . . .   Nigel Hood
David Tomlinson . . . .   Charles
Margaret Rutherford . . . .   Nurse Cary
Yvonne Owen . . . .   Betty
Sonia Holm . . . .   Isobel
Maurice Denham . . . .   Cockle Man
Brian Oulton . . . .   Manell
Zena Marshall . . . .   Secretary
Charles Penrose . . . .   Stage Manager
FANTASY Married doctor falls for mermaid
and tries to keep her tail secret.

11222
THE FATAL NIGHT (50) (A)
Anglofilm (Col)
P: D: Mario Zampi
S: (STORY) Michael Arlen
(THE GENTLEMAN FROM AMERICA)
SC: Gerald Butler, Kathleen Connors
Lester Ferguson . . . .   Puce
Jean Short . . . .   Geraldine
Leslie Armstrong . . . .   Cyril
Brenda Hogan . . . .   Julia
Patrick Macnee . . . .   Tony
Aubrey Mallalieu . . . .   Yokel
FANTASY American spends night in haunted
house and is scared to death.

11223
BROKEN JOURNEY (89) (A)
Gainsborough (GFD) *reissue:* 1952 (ABFD)
P: Sydney Box
D: Ken Annakin
S: Robert Westerby
Phyllis Calvert . . . .   Mary Johnstone
Margot Grahame . . . .   Joanna Dane
James Donald . . . .   Bill Haverton
Francis L. Sullivan . . . .   Anton Perami
Raymond Huntley . . . .   Edward Marshall
Derek Bond . . . .   Richard Faber
Guy Rolfe . . . .   Capt Fox
Sonia Holm . . . .   Anne Stevens
David Tomlinson . . . .   Jimmy Marshall
Andrew Crawford . . . .   Kid Cormack
Charles Victor . . . .   Harry Gunn
Grey Blake . . . .   John Barber
Gerard Heinz . . . .   Joseph Romer

ADVENTURE Alps. Dakota crashes with
thirteen aboard, including film star, boxer,
opera star singer, DP, etc.

11224
ONE NIGHT WITH YOU (92) (U)
Two Cities (GFD)
P: Josef Somlo
D: Terence Young
S: Carlo Bragaglia
SC: Caryl Brahms, S.J. Simon
Nino Martini . . . .   Giulio Moris
Patricia Roc . . . .   Mary Santell
Bonar Colleano . . . .   Piero Santellini
Hugh Wakefield . . . .   Santell
Guy Middleton . . . .   Matty
Stanley Holloway . . . .   Tramp
Charles Goldner . . . .   Fogliati
Irene Worth . . . .   Lina Linari
Willy Feuter . . . .   Pirelli
Miles Malleson . . . .   Jailer
Richard Hearne . . . .   Station Master
MUSICAL Italy. Stranded girl and tenor
mistaken for forgers.

11225
JIVIN' AND JAMMIN' (17) (U)
Piccadilly Cinematograph Films
P: C. Pattinson-Knight
Dinah Kaye
Maurice Arnold Sextet
MUSICAL

11226
SPRING IN PARK LANE (92) (U)
Imperadio (BL)
P: D: Herbert Wilcox
S: (PLAY) Alice Duer Miller
(COME OUT OF THE KITCHEN)
SC: Nicholas Phipps
Anna Neagle . . . .   Judy Howard
Michael Wilding . . . .   Lord Richard
Tom Walls . . . .   Joshua Howard
Peter Graves . . . .   Basil Maitland
Marjorie Fielding . . . .   Mildred Howard
Nicholas Phipps . . . . . .   Marquis of Borechester
G.H. Mulcaster . . . .   Perkins
Josephine Fitzgerald . . . . . .   Kate O'Malley
Nigel Patrick . . . .   Mr Bacon
Lana Morris . . . .   Rosie
H.R. Hignett . . . .   Higgins
COMEDY Poor Lord posing as footman loves
diamond magnate's niece.
(DMNFA: 1948; PGAA: 1949; Top
Moneymaker: 1948.)

MAY

11227
GOOD TIME GIRL (93) (A)
Triton (GFD)
P: Sydney Box, Samuel Goldwyn jr
D: David Macdonald
S: (NOVEL) Arthur la Bern
(NIGHT DARKENS THE STREET)
SC: Muriel & Sydney Box, Ted Willis
Jean Kent . . . .   Gwen Rawlings
Dennis Price . . . .   Red Farrell
Flora Robson . . . .   Miss Thorpe
Griffith Jones . . . .   Danny Martin
Herbert Lom . . . .   Max
Bonar Colleano . . . .   Micky
Hugh McDermott . . . .   Al
Peter Glenville . . . .   Jimmy Rosso
Nora Swinburne . . . .   Miss Mills
Elwyn Brook-Jones . . . . . .   Pottinger
Jill Balcon . . . .   Roberta
Beatrice Varley . . . .   Mrs Rawlings
Margaret Barton . . . .   Agnes
Diana Dors . . . .   Lyla Lawrence
Garry Marsh . . . .   Mr Hawkins

Amy Veness . . . .   Mrs Chalk
George Carney . . . .   Mr Rawlings
Zena Marshall . . . .   Mrs Farrell
John Blythe . . . .   Art Moody
CRIME Remand home escapee joins American
deserters in robberies.

11228
PENNY AND THE POWNALL CASE (47) (A)
Production Facilities (GFD)
P: John Corfield
D: Slim Hand
S: William Fairchild
Peggy Evans . . . .   Penny Justin
Ralph Michael . . . .   Michael Carson
Christopher Lee . . . .   Jonathon Blair
Diana Dors . . . .   Molly James
Frederick Piper . . . .   PC
Olaf Pooley . . . .   von Leicher
Ethel Coleridge . . . .   Mrs Hodgson
Sam Costa . . . .   Receptionist
Dennis Vance . . . .   Crawford
Duncan Carse . . . .   Boatman
CRIME Model girl helps solve murder.

11229
CORRIDOR OF MIRRORS (105) (A)
Apollo Films (GFD)
P: Rudolph Cartier
D: Terence Young
S: (NOVEL) Chris Massie
SC: Rudolph Cartier, Edana Romney
Eric Portman . . . .   Paul Mangin
Edana Romney . . . .   Mifanwy Conway
Barbara Mullen . . . .   Veronica
Hugh Sinclair . . . .   Owen Rhys
Bruce Belfrage . . . .   Sir David Conway
Joan Maude . . . .   Caroline Hart
Alan Wheatley . . . .   Edgar Orsen
Leslie Weston . . . .   Mortimer
Lois Maxwell . . . .   Imogen
Valentine Dyall . . . .   Defence
Christopher Lee . . . .   Charles
CRIME Rich artist obsessed by the Renaissance
takes blame when his jealous housekeeper
strangles his mistress.

11230
A SISTER TO ASSIST 'ER (60) (A)
Bruton–Trytel (Premier)
P: W.L. Trytel
D: SC: George Dewhurst
S: (PLAY) John le Breton
Muriel Aked . . . .   Daisy Crawley
Muriel George . . . .   Gladys May
Michael Howard . . . .   Alf
COMEDY Poor old woman poses as rich twin
to fool mean landlady.

11231
COUNTERBLAST (99) (A)
British National (Pathe)
P: Louis H. Jackson
D: Paul Stein
S: Guy Morgan
SC: Jack Whitingham
Robert Beatty . . . .   Dr Rankin
Mervyn Johns . . . .   Dr Bruckner
Nova Pilbeam . . . .   Tracy Shaw
Margaretta Scott . . . .   Sister Johnson
Sybilla Binder . . . .   Martha
Marie Lohr . . . .   Mrs Coles
Karel Stepanek . . . .   Prof Inman
Alan Wheatley . . . .   Kennedy
Gladys Henson . . . .   Mrs Plum
John Salew . . . .   Padre
Antony Eustrel . . . .   Dr Forrester
Karl Jaffe . . . .   Heinz
Ronald Adam . . . .   Col Ingram
Martin Miller . . . .   Seaman

Aubrey Mallalieu . . . .   Maj Walsh
Horace Kenney . . . .   Taxi-driver
CRIME Escaped Nazi scientist poses as
British scientist in bacteria research laboratory.

JUN

11232
THE CALENDAR (80) (A)
Gainsborough (GFD) *remake:* 1931
P: Anthony Darnborough
D: Arthur Crabtree
S: (PLAY) Edgar Wallace
SC: Geoffrey Kerr
Greta Gynt . . . . Wenda Panniford
John McCallum . . . .   Gerry Anson
Raymond Lovell . . . .   Lord Willie
Sonia Holm . . . .   Molly Panniford
Leslie Dwyer . . . .   Sam Hillcott
Charles Victor . . . .   John Dory
Barry Jones . . . . Sir John Garth
Felix Aylmer . . . . Lord Forlingham
Sydney King . . . .   Tony
Diana Dors . . . .   Hawkins
SPORT Girl trainer helps broke owner to prove
he did not nobble his horse.

11233
HAMLET (155) (U)
Two Cities (GFD)
P: D: Laurence Olivier
S: (PLAY) William Shakespeare
Laurence Olivier . . . .   Hamlet
Eileen Herlie . . . .   Queen Gertrude
Basil Sydney . . . .   King Claudius
Jean Simmons . . . .   Ophelia
Norman Wooland . . . .   Horatio
Felix Aylmer . . . .   Polonius
Terence Morgan . . . .   Laertes
Stanley Holloway . . . .   Gravedigger
John Laurie . . . .   Francisco
Esmond Knight . . . .   Bernado
Anthony Quayle . . . .   Marcellus
Niall McGinnis . . . .   Captain
Harcourt Williams . . . .   Player
Peter Cushing . . . .   Osric
Russell Thorndike . . . .   Priest
DRAMA Denmark. Murdered king's ghost
inspires his son to vengeance.
(AA: Best Film, Actor, Photography, Art
Direction, Costumes, 1949; PGAA: 1949.)

11234
TROUBLE IN THE AIR (55) (A)
Production Facilities (GFD)
P: George & Alfred Black
D: Charles Saunders
S: George & Alfred Black, Jack Davies
SC: Michael Pertwee, Martin Lane
Jimmy Edwards . . . . B. Barrington Crockett
Freddie Frinton . . . .   Fred Somers
Joyce Golding . . . .   Miss Clinch
Bill Owen . . . .   Spiv
Sam Costa . . . .   Spiv
Dennis Vance . . . .   Larry Somers
Laurence Naismith . . . .   Tom Hunt
Jon Pertwee . . . .   Truelove
COMEDY BBC commentator broadcasts village
bellringers and foils spivs.

11235
A SONG FOR TOMORROW (62) (A)
Production Facilities (GFD)
P: Ralph Nunn-May
D: Terence Fisher
S: William Fairchild
Evelyn McCabe . . . .   Helen Maxwell
Ralph Michael . . . .   Roger Stanton
Shaun Noble . . . .   Derek Wardwell
Valentine Dunn . . . .   Mrs Wardwell
James Hayter . . . .   Klausemann

Christopher Lee . . . .   Auguste
Conrad Phillips . . . .   Lt Fenton
ROMANCE Amnesiac pilot loves opera star
until he regains his memory.

11236
MY SISTER AND I (97) (A)
Burnham (GFD)
P: John Corfield, Harold Huth
D: Harold Huth
S: (NOVEL) Emery Bonnet
(HIGH PAVEMENT)
SC: A.R. Rawlinson, Joan Rees, Michael
Medwin, Robert Westerby
Sally Ann Howes . . . .   Robina Adams
Barbara Mullen . . . .   Hypatia Foley
Dermot Walsh . . . .   Graham Forbes
Hazel Court . . . .   Helena Forsythe
Martita Hunt . . . .   Mrs Camelot
Patrick Holt . . . .   Roger Crisp
Jane Hylton . . . .   Elsie
Joan Rees . . . .   Ardarth Bondage
Michael Medwin . . . .   Charlie
Helen Goss . . . .   Mrs Pomfret
Hugh Miller . . . .   Hubert Bondage
Stewart Rome . . . .   Col Thrusby
Diana Dors . . . .   Dreary Girl
James Knight . . . .   Dustman
CRIME Widow learns her husband fathered her
sister's daughter.

11237
BOND STREET (108) (A)
ABPC—World Screenplays (Pathe)
P: Anatole de Grunwald
D: Gordon Parry
S: J.G. Brown
SC: Anatole de Grunwald, Terence Rattigan,
Rodney Ackland
Jean Kent . . . .   Ricki Merritt
Roland Young . . . . George Chester-Barrett
Kathleen Harrison . . . .   Mrs Brawn
Derek Farr . . . .   Joe Marsh
Hazel Court . . . . Julia Chester-Barrett
Ronald Howard . . . .   Steve Winter
Paula Valenska . . . .   Elsa
Patricia Plunkett . . . .   Mary
Robert Flemyng . . . .   Frank Moody
Adrianne Allen . . . .   Mrs Taverner
Kenneth Griffith . . . .   Len Phillips
Joan Dowling . . . .   Norma
Charles Goldner . . . .   Waiter
James McKechnie . . . .   Yarrow
Leslie Dwyer . . . .   Barman
Mary Jerrold . . . .   Miss Slennett
ROMANCE Stories of theft, blackmail, romance,
and comedy woven around a trousseau.

11238
THE LAST LOAD (57) (U)
Elstree Independent (GFD)
P: D: John Baxter
S: Geoffrey Orme, Mary Cathcart Borer
Douglas Barr . . . .   David Eden
Ivor Bowyer . . . .   Monty
Angela Glynne . . . .   Susan Potter
Angela Foulds . . . .   Betty Potter
David Hannaford . . . .   Bobby
Ian Colin . . . .   Mr Eden
John Longden . . . .   Mr Potter
Frank Atkinson . . . .   Jenkins
CHILDREN Lorry owner's chidren catch lorry
thieves.

11239
NO ORCHIDS FOR MISS BLANDISH (104) (A)
Tudor—Alliance (Renown)
P: A.R. Shipman, Oswald Mitchell
D: SC: StJohn L. Clowes
S: (NOVEL) James Hadley Chase
Jack la Rue . . . .   Slim Grisson

Linden Travers . . . .   Miss Blandish
Hugh McDermott . . . .   Fenner
Walter Crisham . . . .   Eddie
Leslie Bradley . . . .   Bailey
Zoe Gail . . . .   Margo
Charles Goldner . . . .   Louis
Macdonald Parke . . . .   Doc
Lily Molnar . . . .   Ma Grisson
Danny Green . . . .   Flyn
Percy Marmont . . . .   Mr Blandish
Michael Balfour . . . .   Barney
Frances Marsden . . . .   Ann Borg
Irene Prador . . . .   Olga
Jack Durant; Halamar & Konarski; Toy & Wing
CRIME America. Gangster falls in love with
the millionaire's daughter he kidnaps.

11240
UNEASY TERMS (91) (A)
British National (Pathe)
P: Louis H. Jackson
D: Vernon Sewell
S: (NOVEL) Peter Cheyney
Michael Rennie . . . .   Slim Callaghan
Moira Lister . . . . Corinne Allardyce
Faith Brook . . . .   Viola Allardyce
Joy Shelton . . . .   Effie
Nigel Patrick . . . .   Lucien Donnelly
Paul Carpenter . . . .   Windy Nicholls
Marie Ney . . . .   Honoria Wymering
Barry Jones . . . .   Insp Gringall
Patricia Goddard . . . . Patricia Allardyce
Sydney Tafler . . . .   Maysin
J.H. Roberts . . . .   Sallins
John Robinson . . . .   Inspector
CRIME Private tec proves blackmail victim did
not kill her stepfather.

11241
CUP—TIE HONEYMOON (93) (A)
Film Studios Manchester (Mancunian)
P: D: John E. Blakeley
S: Anthony Toner, Harry Jackson
Sandy Powell . . . .   Joe Butler
Dan Young . . . .   Cecil Alistair
Betty Jumel . . . .   Betty
Pat McGrath . . . .   Eric Chambers
Violet Farebrother . . . .   Mary Chambers
Frank Groves . . . .   Jimmy Owen
Joyanne Bracewell . . . . . .   Pauline May
Vic Arnley . . . .   Grandad
Harold Walden . . . .   Himself
COMEDY Chairman's son wins secretary by
playing in the football final at Manchester.

11242
HOLIDAYS WITH PAY (115) (A)
Film Studios Manchester (Mancunian)
reissue: 1950 (cut)
P: D: John E. Blakeley
S: Anthony Toner
SC: Harry Jackson, Frank Randle
Frank Randle . . . .   Jack Rogers
Tessie O'Shea . . . .   Pansy Rogers
Dan Young . . . .   Phil Rogers
Josef Locke . . . .   Himself
Sally Barnes . . . .   Pamela Rogers
Joyanne Bracewell . . . . . .   Joyanne Rogers
Sonny Burke . . . .   Michael Sandford
Bert Tracy . . . .   Ephraim
Pat Heywood Troupe
COMEDY Family spend a holiday at the
haunted castle of the daughter's fiance.
(Extracts in SEASIDE FROLICS; TONIGHT'S
THE NITE (1960).)

11243
HOUSE OF DARKNESS (77) (A)
International Motion Pictures (BL)
P: Harry Reynolds
D: Oswald Mitchell

S: (PLAY) Batty Davies (DUET)
SC: John Gilling, Robin Estridge

Lawrence Harvey	Francis Merivale
Lesley Brook	Lucy
John Stuart	Lawyer
George Melachrino	Himself
Lesley Osmond	Elaine Merivale
Henry Oscar	Film Director
Alexander Archdale	John

FANTASY Period. Murdered man's ghost seeks vengeance on his stepbrother.

11244
THE CLOUDED CRYSTAL (57) (A)
Grossmar—Cullimore—Arbeid (Butcher)
P: Ben Arbeid, A. Grossman
D: S: Alan J. Cullimore

Patrick Wadddington	Jack
Lind Joyce	Cathy Butler
Dorothy Bramhall	Paula
Frank Muir	Frank Butler
Dino Galvani	Manzetti
Ethel Coleridge	Mme Zamba

COMEDY Fortune teller predicts that a girl's husband has a month to live.

11245
MY HANDS ARE CLAY (60) (U)
Dublin Films (Monarch)
P: Patrick McCrossan
D: Lionel Tomlinson
S: Paul Trippe

Richard Aherne	Shean Regan
Bernardette Leahy	Mary
Robert Dawson	Michael
Sheila Richards	Lady Killane
Terry Wilson	Father O'Brien
Cecil Brock	Peter
Francis Riedy	Singer

DRAMA Ireland. Sculptor wrongly suspects his wife is unfaithful.

11246
A GUNMAN HAS ESCAPED (58) (A)
Condor Films (Monarch)
P: Harry Goodman, Richard Grey
D: Richard Grey
S: John Gilling

John Harvey	Eddie
John Fitzgerald	Sinclair
Robert Cartland	Bill Grant
Frank Hawkins	Mr Cranston
Jane Arden	Jane
Hope Carr	Mrs Cranston
Maria Charles	Goldie

CRIME Mutual distrust among robbers in hiding leads to their undoing.

11247
THE MONKEY'S PAW (64) (A)
Kay Films (Butcher)
P: Ernest G. Roy
D: Norman Lee
S: (PLAY) W.W. Jacobs
SC: Norman Lee, Barbara Toy

Milton Rosmer	Mr Trelawne
Megs Jenkins	Mrs Trelawne
Joan Seton	Dorothy Lang
Norman Shelley	Monoghan
Michael Martin Harvey	Kelly
Eric Micklewood	Tom Trelawne
Brenda Hogan	Beryl
Mackenzie Ward	Noel Lang
Alfie Bass	Manager
Hay Petrie	Grimshaw

FANTASY Old pair use magic paw to wish for their dead son's return.

11248
CALLING PAUL TEMPLE (92) (A)
Nettlefold (Butcher) *reissue:* 1952

P: Ernest G. Roy
D: Maclean Rogers
S: (RADIO SERIAL) Francis Durbridge
(PAUL TEMPLE & THE CANTERBURY CASE)
SC: Francis Durbridge, A.R. Rawlinson, Kathleen Butler

John Bentley	Paul Temple
Dinah Sheridan	Steve Temple
Margaretta Scott	Mrs Trevellyan
Abraham Sofaer	Dr Kohima
Celia Lipton	Norma Rice
Jack Raine	Sir Graham Forbes
Alan Wheatley	Edward Lathom
Hugh Pryse	Wilfred Davies
Wally Patch	Spider Williams

CRIME Tec unmasks "Rex", killer of nerve specialist's rich female patients.

JUL

11249
OLIVER TWIST (116) (A)
IP—Cineguild (GFD)
P: Anthony Havelock-Allan
D: David Lean
S: (NOVEL) Charles Dickens
SC: David Lean, Stanley Haynes

Robert Newton	Bill Sikes
Alec Guiness	Fagin
Kay Walsh	Nancy
Francis L. Sullivan	Mr Bumble
John Howard Davies	Oliver Twist
Henry Stephenson	Mr Brownlow
Mary Clare	Mrs Corney
Anthony Newley	Artful Dodger
Josephine Stuart	Oliver's Mother
Ralph Truman	Monks
Kathleen Harrison	Mrs Sowerberry
Gibb McLaughlin	Mr Sowerberry
Amy Veness	Mrs Bedwin
Diana Dors	Charlotte
Frederick Lloyd	Mr Grimwig
Maurice Denham	Chief of Police
W.G. Fay	Bookseller
Henry Edwards	Official
Hattie Jacques	Singer

CRIME Period. Workhouse foundling flees and is trained as pickpocket.

11250
MY BROTHER'S KEEPER (91) (A)
Gainsborough (GFD)
P: Anthony Darnborough
D: Alfred Roome, Roy Rich
S: Maurice Wiltshire
SC: Frank Harvey

Jack Warner	George Martin
Jane Hylton	Nora Lawrence
David Tomlinson	Ronnie Waring
Bill Owen	Syd Evans
George Cole	Willie Stannard
Yvonne Owen	Meg Waring
Raymond Lovell	Wainwright
Beatrice Varley	Mrs Martin
Amy Veness	Mrs Gulley
Brenda Bruce	Winnie Foreman
Susan Shaw	Beryl
John Boxer	Bert Foreman
Fred Groves	Landlord
Garry Marsh	Brewster
Wilfrid Hyde White	Harding
Frederick Piper	Caretaker
Maurice Denham	Trent
Jack Raine	Chief Constable

CRIME Pursuit of escaped killer handcuffed to innocent youth.

11251
THE RED SHOES (134) *tech* (A)
IP—Archers (GFD)

P: D: Michael Powell, Emeric Pressburger
S: (STORY) Hans Andersen
SC: Emeric Pressburger, Keith Winter

Anton Walbrook	Boris Lermontov
Marius Goring	Julian Craster
Moira Shearer	Victoria Page
Robert Helpmann	Boleslawsky
Leonide Massine	Ljubov
Albert Basserman	Ratov
Ludmilla Tcherina	Boronskaja
Esmond Knight	Livy
Irene Browne	Lady Nelson
Austin Trevor	Prof Palmer
Marcel Poncin	Boudin
Jerry Verno	George
Madame Rambert	Herself

MUSICAL Ballerina torn between marriage and career.   (AA 1948: Best Colour Photography, Art Direction, Interiors.)

11252
IT HAPPENED IN SOHO (55) (A)
FC Films (ABFD)
P: D: Frank Chisnell
S: Terry Sanford

Richard Murdoch	Bill Scott
Patricia Raine	Susan Marsh
John Bailey	Paul Sayers
Henry Oscar	Insp Carp

CRIME Reporter unmasks Soho Strangler.

AUG

11253
LONDON BELONGS TO ME (112) (A)
USA: DULCIMER STREET
IP—Individual (GFD)
P: Frank Launder, Sidney Gilliat
D: Sidney Gilliat
S: (NOVEL) Norman Collins
SC: Sidney Gilliat, J. B. Williams

Richard Attenborough	Percy Boon
Alastair Sim	Mr Squales
Fay Compton	Mrs Josser
Stephen Murray	Uncle Henry
Wylie Watson	Mr Josser
Susan Shaw	Doris Josser
Ivy StHellier	Connie
Joyce Carey	Mrs Vizzard
Andrew Crawford	Bill Todds
Eleanor Summerfield	Myrna
Gladys Henson	Mrs Boon
Hugh Griffith	Headlam Fynne
Maurice Denham	Jack Rufus
Jack McNaughton	Jimmy
Henry Edwards	Supt

CRIME 1939. Garage hand steals car and is accused of murdering girl.

11254
THAT GOLF GAME (18) (U)
Comet Productions (GFD)
COMEDY Amateur golfer demonstrates how not to play golf.

11255
MR PERRIN AND MR TRAILL (92) (A)
Two Cities (GFD)
P: Alexander Galperson
D: Lawrence Huntington
S: (NOVEL) Hugh Walpole
SC: L.A.G. Strong, T.J. Morrison

Marius Goring	Vincent Perrin
David Farrar	David Traill
Greta Gynt	Isabel Lester
Raymond Huntley	Moy-Thompson
Edward Chapman	Birkland
Mary Jerrold	Mrs Perrin
Finlay Currie	Sir Joshua Varley
Ralph Truman	Mr Comber
Lloyd Pearson	Mr Dormer

Archie Harradine . . . . Mr White
Viola Lyel . . . . Mrs Comber
Donald Barclay . . . . Rogers
DRAMA Old teacher tries to kill young sports
master over school nurse.

11256
THE DARK ROAD (72) (A)
Marylebone (Exclusive)
P: Henry Halstead
D: Alfred Goulding
Charles Stuart . . . . Sidney Robertson
Joyce Linden . . . . Ann
Antony Holles . . . .
Roddy Hughes . . . .
Patricia Hicks . . . .
Mackenzie Ward . . . .
CRIME Ex-Borstal boy uses girl to help him in
robbery.

11257
NOOSE (95) (A) USA: THE SILK NOOSE
Edward Dryhurst (Pathe) *reissue:* 1951 (12
mins cut)
D: Edmond T. Greville
S: (PLAY) Richard Llewellyn
SC: Richard Llewellyn, Edward Dryhurst
Carole Landis . . . . Linda Medbury
Derek Farr . . . . Capt Jumbo Hoyle
Joseph Calleia . . . . Sugiani
Stanley Holloway . . . . Insp Rendall
Nigel Patrick . . . . Bar Gorman
John Slater . . . . Puddn Bason
Edward Rigby . . . . Slush
Leslie Bradley . . . . Basher
Ruth Nixon . . . . Annie Foss
Carol Van Derman . . . . Mercia Lane
Reginald Tate . . . . Editor
Hay Petrie . . . . Barber
John Salew . . . . Greasy Anderson
Ella Retford . . . . Nelly
Ronald Boyer & Jeanne Ravel; Olive Lucius
CRIME Ex-commando and tough pals help girl
reporter smash Soho club-owner's black market.

SEP
11258
SARABAND FOR DEAD LOVERS (96) tech (A)
Ealing (GFD)
AP: Michael Relph
D: Michael Relph, Basil Dearden
S: (NOVEL) Helen Simpson
SC: John Dighton, Alexander Mackendrick
Stewart Granger . . . . Count Philip
              Koenigsmark
Joan Greenwood . . . . Sophie-Dorothea
Francoise Rosay . . . . Electress Sophie
Flora Robson . . . . Countess Platen
Frederick Valk . . . . Ernest Augustus
Peter Bull . . . . .Prince George-Louis
Anthony Quayle . . . . Durer
Megs Jenkins . . . . Frau Busche
Michael Gough . . . . Prince Charles
Jill Balcon . . . . Knesbeck
Cecil Trouncer . . . . Maj Eck
David Horne . . . . .Duke George William
Mercia Swinburne . . . . Countess Eleanore
Miles Malleson . . . . Lord of Misrule
Allan Jeayes . . . . Governor
Guy Rolfe . . . . Envoy
HISTORY Hanover, 1689. Countess's favourite
Count loves Prince's unloved wife.

11259
COLONEL BOGEY (51) (U)
Production Facilities (GFD)
P: John Croydon
D: Terence Fisher
S: William Fairchild
SC: William Fairchild, John Baines

Jack Train . . . . Uncle James (voice)
Mary Jerrold . . . . Aunt Mabel
Jane Barrett . . . . Alice Graham
John Stone . . . . .Wilfred Barriteau
Ethel Coleridge . . . . Emily
Hedli Anderson . . . . Millicent
FANTASY 1912. Dead uncle's ghost refuses
to leave his home.

11260
TO THE PUBLIC DANGER (44)(A)
Production Facilities (GFD)
P: John Croydon
D: Terence Fisher
S: (PLAY) Patrick Hamilton
SC: T.J. Morrison, Arthur Reid
Dermot Walsh . . . . Capt Cole
Susan Shaw . . . . Nancy Bedford
Barry Letts . . . . Fred Lane
Roy Plomley . . . . Reggie
Frederick Piper . . . . Labourer
Betty Ann Davies . . . . Barmaid
DRAMA Hit-and-run driver crashes while
fleeing from police.

11261
THE WEAKER SEX (84) (U)
Two Cities (GFD)
P: Paul Soskin
D: Roy Baker
S: (PLAY) Esther McCracken (NO MEDALS)
SC: Esther McCracken, Paul Soskin
Ursula Jeans . . . . Martha Dacre
Cecil Parker . . . . Geoffrey Radcliffe
Joan Hopkins . . . . Helen
Derek Bond . . . . Nigel
Lana Morris . . . . Lolly
John Stone . . . . Roddy
Thora Hird . . . . Mrs Gaye
Marian Spencer . . . . Harriet Lessing
Digby Wolfe . . . . Benjie
Kynaston Reeves . . . . Capt Wishart
Eleanor Summerfield . . . . . Clippie
Gladys Henson . . . . Woman
COMEDY 1944. Widow's troubles with her
daughters and billeted sailors.

11262
THE BLIND GODDESS (87) (A)
Gainsborough (GFD)
P: Betty Box
D: Harold French
S: (PLAY) Patrick Hastings
SC: Muriel & Sydney Fox
Eric Portman . . . . Sir John Dearing KC
Anne Crawford . . . . Lady Brasted
Hugh Williams . . . . Lord Brasted
Michael Denison . . . . Derek Waterhouse
Nora Swinburne . . . . Lady Dearing
Claire Bloom . . . . Mary Dearing
Raymond Lovell . . . . .Mr Mainwaring KC
Frank Cellier . . . . Judge
Clive Morton . . . . Mersel
Elspet Gray . . . . Daphne Dearing
Maurice Denham . . . . Butler
Martin Benson . . . . Count Mikla
Carl Jaffe . . . . Meyer
CRIME Secretary accuses fiancee's father of
embezzling public funds.

11263
THE FALLEN IDOL (95) (A)
London-Reed (BL)
P: David O. Selznick, Carol Reed
D: Carol Reed
S: (STORY) Graham Greene (THE BASEMENT
ROOM)
SC: Graham Greene, Lesley Storm, William
Templeton
Ralph Richardson . . . . Baines

Michele Morgan . . . . Julie
Sonia Dresdel . . . . Mrs Baines
Bobby Henrey . . . . Felipe
Denis O'Dea . . . . Insp Crowe
Jack Hawkins . . . . Det Ames
Dora Bryan . . . . Rose
Walter Fitzgerald . . . . Dr Fenton
Bernard Lee . . . . Det Hart
Karel Stepanek . . . . Secretary
Joan Young . . . . Mrs Barrow
Geoffrey Keen . . . . Det Davis
James Hayter . . . . Perry
DRAMA Ambassador's son thinks his hero the
butler has murdered his wife (BFA: Best
British Film 1948; DEFA: 1948).

11264
THAT DAY OF REST (17) (U)
Fairbairn (GFD)
P:D: Kenneth Fairbairn
Eddie Leslie . . . . The Man
COMEDY A working man's day off.

11265
EUGENE PINI AND HIS ORCHESTRA (14)(U)
Inspiration (Eros)
P:D: Horace Shepherd
N: Ronnie Waldman
Eugene Pini
Charmian Innes
MUSICAL

11266
STEPHANE GRAPPELLY AND HIS QUINTET
(14) (U)
Inspiration (Eros)
P:D: Horace Shepherd
Stephane Grappelly
George Shearing
Ray Ellington
MUSICAL

11267
THE WINSLOW BOY (117) (U)
London-BLPA (BL) *reissue:* 1952 (33 mins cut)
P: Anatole de Grunwald
D: Anthony Asquith
S: (PLAY) Terence Rattigan
SC: Terence Rattigan, Antole de Grunwald,
Anthony Asquith
Robert Donat . . . . .Sir Robert Morton
Margaret Leighton . . . . Catherine Winslow
Cedric Hardwicke . . . . Arthur Winslow
Basil Radford . . . . Esmond Curry
Kathleen Harrison . . . . Violet
Francis L. Sullivan . . . . Attorney General
Marie Lohr . . . . Grace Winslow
Jack Watling . . . . Dickie Winslow
Frank Lawton . . . . John Watherstone
Neil North . . . . Ronnie Winslow
Walter Fitzgerald . . . . First Lord
Wilfrid Hyde White . . . . . . Watkinson
Kynaston Reeves . . . . Lord Chief Justice
Ernest Thesiger . . . . Mr Ridgeley-Pearce
Lewis Casson . . . . Admiral Springfield
Stanley Holloway; Cyril Ritchard
CRIME 1912. Barrister proves Osborne naval
cadet did not steal postal-order.

OCT
11268
NO ROOM AT THE INN (82) (A)
British National (Pathe)
P: Ivan Foxwell
D: Dan Birt
S: (PLAY) Joan Temple
SC: Ivan Foxwell, Dylan Thomas
Freda Jackson . . . . Mrs Voray
Joy Shelton . . . . Judith Drave
Hermione Baddeley . . . . Mrs Waters

Joan Dowling . . . . Norma Bates
Harcourt Williams . . . . Rev Allworth
Niall MacGinnis . . . . O'Rane
Sydney Tafler . . . . Spiv
Ann Stephens . . . . Mary O'Rane
Frank Pettingell . . . . Burrells
Robin Netscher . . . . Ronnie
Betty Blackler . . . . Lily
Jill Gibbs . . . . Irene
Wylie Watson . . . . Councillor Green
Beatrice Varley . . . . Mrs Jarvis
DRAMA Vicious woman deprives four evacuees
for her own comforts.

11269
ESTHER WATERS (109) (A)
IP-Wessex (GFD)
P: Ian Dalrymple
D: Ian Dalrymple, Peter Proud
S: (NOVEL) George Moore
SC: Michael Gordon, William Rose, Gerard
Tyrrell
Kathleen Ryan . . . . Esther Waters
Dirk Bogarde . . . . William Latch
Cyril Cusack . . . . Fred Parsons
Ivor Barnard . . . . Mr Randall
Fay Compton . . . . Mrs Barfield
Mary Clare . . . . Mrs Latch
Julian d'Albie . . . . Mr Barfield
Morland Graham . . . . Mr Ketley
Shelagh Fraser . . . . Margaret Gale
Margaret Withers . . . . Miss Grover
Lalage Lewis . . . . Miss Peggy
George Hayes . . . . Journeyman
Alex Parker . . . . Fred Archer
DRAMA 1873-85. Squire's gambling groom
seduces maid who then refuses to wed lay
preacher and brings up her child alone.

11270
FLY AWAY PETER (60) (U)
Production Facilities (GFD)
P: Henry Passmore
D: Charles Saunders
S: (PLAY) A.P. Dearsley
SC: Arthur Reid
Frederick Piper . . . . Mr Hapgood
Kathleen Boutall . . . . Mrs Hapgood
Margaret Barton . . . . Myra Hapgood
Patrick Holt . . . . John Neilson
Elspet Gray . . . . Phyllis Hapgood
Peter Hammond . . . . George Harris
Nigel Buchanan . . . . Arthur Hapgood
John Singer . . . . Ted Hapgood
COMEDY Family breaks up as the children
mature and leave home.

11271
LOVE IN WAITING (60) (U)
Production Facilities (GFD)
P: Henry Passmore
D: Douglas Pierce
S: Monica Dickens
SC: Arthur Reid, Martin Lane
David Tomlinson . . . . Clitheroe
Andrew Crawford . . . . Dick Lambert
Peggy Evans . . . . Goldy
Elspet Gray . . . . Brenda
Patsy Drake . . . . Mary
John Witty . . . . Harry
Linda Grey . . . . Miss Bell
George Merritt . . . . Pepperfield
Johnnie Schofield . . . . Insp Bates
COMEDY Restaurateur's son poses as dustman
to woo waitress who catches black marketeers.

11272
SLEEPING CAR TO TRIESTE (95) (A)
Two Cities (GFD)

P: George H. Brown
D: John Paddy Carstairs
S: Clifford Grey (ROME EXPRESS)
SC: Allan Mackinnon, William Douglas Home
Jean Kent . . . . Valya
Albert Lieven . . . . Zurta
Derrick de Marney . . . . George Grant
Paul Dupuis . . . . Insp Jolif
Rona Anderson . . . . Joan Maxted
Bonar Colleano . . . . Top-Sgt West
David Tomlinson . . . . Tom Bishop
Alan Wheatley . . . . Poole
Finlay Currie . . . . Alastair McBain
Hugh Burden . . . . Mills
Coco Aslan . . . . Poirier
David Hutcheson . . . . Denning
Zena Marshall . . . . Suzanne
CRIME Spies search for diary aboard Orient
Express.

11273
WOMAN HATER (105) (A)
Two Cities (GFD)
P: William Sistrom
D: Terence Young
S: Alec Coppel
SC: Robert Westerby, Nicholas Phipps
Stewart Granger . . . . . . Lord Terence Datchett
Edwige Feuillere . . . . Colette Marly
Ronald Squire . . . . Jameson
Jeanne de Casalis . . . . Claire
Mary Jerrold . . . . Lady Datchett
David Hutcheson . . . . Robert
W.A. Kelly . . . . Patrick
Georgina Cookson . . . . Julia
Henry Edwards . . . . Major
Stewart Rome . . . . Col Weston
Valentine Dyall . . . . George Spencer
Richard Hearne . . . . Reveller
Cyril Ritchard . . . . Reveller
Graham Moffatt . . . . Fat Boy
Miles Malleson . . . . Vicar
COMEDY Lord poses as agent to woo
recuperating film star.

11274
QUARTET (120) (A)
Gainsborough (GFD)
P: Anthony Darnborough
S: (STORIES) W. Somerset Maugham
SC: R.C. Sheriff

THE COLONEL'S LADY
D: Ken Annakin
Cecil Parker . . . . Col Peregrine
Norma Swinburne . . . . Eve Peregrine
Linden Travers . . . . Daphne
Ernest Thesiger . . . . Henry Dashwood
Felix Aylmer . . . . Martin
Henry Edwards . . . . Duke of Cleverel
Claud Allister . . . . Clubman

THE KITE
D: Arthur Crabtree
George Cole . . . . Herbert Sunbury
Susan Shaw . . . . Betty
Mervyn Johns . . . . Samuel Sunbury
Hermione Baddeley . . . . . . Mrs Sunbury
Bernard Lee . . . . Visitor
Frederick Leister . . . . Governor

THE ALIEN CORN
D: Harold French
Dirk Bogarde . . . . George Bland
Francoise Rosay . . . . Lea Makart
Raymond Lovell . . . . . . Sir Frederick Bland
Honor Blackman . . . . Paula
Irene Browne . . . . Lady Bland
George Thorpe . . . . Uncle John

THE FACTS OF LIFE
D: Ralph Smart
Basil Radford . . . . Henry Garnet
Naunton Wayne . . . . Leslie
Jack Watling . . . . Nicky
Mai Zetterling . . . . Jeanne
James Robertson Justice . . . . Branksome
Angela Baddeley . . . . Mrs Garnet
Jean Cavall . . . . Singer
DRAMA Four short stories.

11275
A DATE WITH A DREAM (55) (U)
Tempean (GN)
P: Robert S.Baker, Monty Berman
D: Dicky Leeman
S: Carl Nystrom
SC: Dicky Leeman, Robert S. Baker, Monty
Berman
Terry-Thomas . . . . Terry
Jean Carson . . . . Jean
Len Lowe . . . . Len
Bill Lowe . . . . Bill
Wally Patch . . . . Uncle
Norman Wisdom; Elton Hayes
COMEDY Reunion of wartime concert party
leads to nightclub success.

NOV

11276
THE GUINEA PIG (97) (U)
Pilgrim (Pathe) *reissue:* 1951 (15 mins cut)
P: John Boulting
D: Roy Boulting
S: (PLAY) Warren Chetham Strode
SC: Warren Chetham Strode, Bernard Miles,
Roy Boulting
Richard Attenborough . . . . . Jack Read
Sheila Sim . . . . Lynne Hartley
Bernard Miles . . . . Mr Read
Cecil Trouncer . . . . Mr Hartley
Robert Fleming . . . . Nigel Lorraine
Edith Sharpe . . . . Mrs Hartley
Joan Hickson . . . . Mrs Read
Peter Reynolds . . . . Grimmett
Timothy Bateson . . . . Ronald Tracey
Clive Baxter . . . . Gregory
Basil Cunard . . . . Buckton
John Forrest . . . . Fitch
Maureen Glynne . . . . Bessie
Brenda Hogan . . . . Lorna Beckett
Herbert Lomas . . . . Sir James Corfield
Anthony Newley . . . . Miles Minor
Anthony Nicholls . . . . Mr Stringer
Wally Patch . . . . Uncle Percy
DRAMA Walthamstow tobacconist's son wins
place at posh public school.

11277
A PIECE OF CAKE (45) (U)
Production Facilities (GFD)
P: Adrian Worker
D: John Irwin
S: John Croydon, Betty Astell
SC: Bernard McNab, Lyn Lockwood,
Dick Pepper
Cyril Fletcher . . . . Cyril Clarke
Betty Astell . . . . Betty Clarke
Laurence Naismith . . . . Merlin Mound
Jon Pertwee . . . . Mr Short
Harry Fowler . . . . Spiv
Sam Costa . . . . Bandleader
Tamara Lees . . . . Guest
FANTASY Conjuror dreams magic tricks cause
trouble with authorities.

11278
HERE COME THE HUGGETTS (93) (A)
Gainsborough (GFD)

P: Betty Box
D: Ken Annakin
S: (CHARACTERS) Godfrey Winn
SC: Mabel & Denis Constanduros, Peter Rogers,
Muriel & Sydney Box

Jack Warner	Joe Huggett
Kathleen Harrison	Ethel Huggett
Jane Hylton	Jane Huggett
Susan Shaw	Susan Huggett
Petula Clark	Pat Huggett
Jimmy Hanley	Jimmy
David Tomlinson	Harold Hinchley
Diana Dors	Diana Hopkins
Peter Hammond	Peter Hawtrey
John Blythe	Gowan
Amy Veness	Grandma
Clive Morton	Mr Campbell
Maurice Denham	Mechanic

COMEDY Suburban family upset by flashy
blonde niece.

11279
IT'S HARD TO BE GOOD (93) (U)
Two Cities (GFD)
P: John Gossage
D: S: Jeffrey Dell

Anne Crawford	Mary
Jimmy Hanley	James
Raymond Huntley	Williams
Lana Morris	Daphne
Edward Rigby	Parkinson
Geoffrey Keen	Sgt Todd
Elwyn Brook-Jones	Budibent
David Horne	Edward Beckett
Joyce Carey	Alice Beckett
Muriel Aked	Ellen Beckett

COMEDY Demobilised war hero tries to
promote peace and goodwill.

11280
THE SMALL VOICE (85) (A) USA: HIDEOUT
Constellation (BL)
P: Anthony Havelock-Allan
D: Fergus McDonnell
S: (NOVEL) Robert Westerby
SC: Derek Neame, Julian Orde, George Barraud

Valerie Hobson	Eleanor Byrne
James Donald	Murray Byrne
Harold Keel	Boke
David Greene	Jim
Michael Balfour	Frankie
Joan Young	Potter
Angela Foulds	Jenny
Glyn Dearman	Ken
Norman Claridge	Supt
Edward Evans	Insp

CRIME Wales. Escaped convicts force crippled
playwright to shelter them.

11281
THE STORY OF SHIRLEY YORKE (92) (A)
Nettlefold (Butcher) *reissue:* 1952
(Regent; 16 mins cut)
P: Ernest G. Roy
D: Maclean Rogers
S: (PLAY) H.A. Vachell (THE CASE OF
LADY CAMBER)
SC: A.R. Rawlinson, Kathleen Butler,
Maclean Rogers

Derek Farr	Gerald Ryton
Dinah Sheridan	Shirley Yorke
Margaretta Scott	Alison Gwynne
John Robinson	Dr Bruce Napier
Barbara Couper	Muriel Peach
Beatrix Thomson	Lady Camber
Ian Maclean	Dr Harris
Jack Raine	Stansfield Yorke
Lesley Osmond	Jennifer Ware
Valentine Dyall	Edward Holt
Eleanor Summerfield	Doris

Bruce Seton	Capt Sharp

CRIME Lord implicates nurse in poisoning of
his invalid wife.

11282
BONNIE PRINCE CHARLIE (136) *tech* (A)
London—BLPA (BL)
P: Edward Black
D: SC: Anthony Kimmins
S: Clemence Dane

David Niven	Prince Charles Stuart
Margaret Leighton	Flora Macdonald
Judy Campbell	Clementine Walkinshaw
Jack Hawkins	Lord George Murray
Morland Graham	Donald
Finlay Currie	Marquis of Tullibardine
Elwyn Brook-Jones	Duke of Cumberland
John Laurie	Blind Jamie
Hector Ross	Glenaladale
Hugh Kelly	Lt Ingleby
Charles Goldner	Capt Ferguson
Henry Oscar	James III
Martin Miller	George II
Franklin Dyall	Macdonald
Herbert Lomas	Kinloch Moidart
Ronald Adam	Macleod
John Longden	Col O'Sullivan
James Hayter	Kingsburgh
Julien Mitchell	Gen Cope

HISTORY Scotland, 1745. Pretender fails in
his bid to restore Stuarts to English throne.

DEC

11283
ANOTHER SHORE (91) (U)
Ealing (GFD)
AP: Ivor Montagu
D: Charles Crichton
S: (NOVEL) Kenneth Reddin
SC: Walter Meade

Robert Beatty	Gulliver Shiels
Stanley Holloway	Alastair McNeil
Moira Lister	Jennifer Stockley
Michael Medwin	Yellow Bingham
Maureen Delany	Mrs Gleeson
Fred O'Donovan	Coghlan
Sheila Manahan	Nora
Desmond Veane	Parkes
Dermot Kelly	Boxer
Michael Golden	Broderick
W.A. Kelly	Roger
Wilfred Brambell	Moore

COMEDY Dublin. Girl schemes to stop
dreamer from going to South Seas with rich
friend.

11284
SCOTT OF THE ANTARCTIC (111) *tech* (U)
Ealing (GFD)
AP: Sidney Cole
D: Charles Frend
S: Ivor Montagu, Walter Meade, Mary
Hayley Bell

John Mills	Capt R.F. Scott
Derek Bond	Capt L.E.G. Gates
Harold Warrender	Dr E.A. Wilson
James Robertson Justice	PO Taff Evans
Reginald Beckwith	Lt H.R. Bowers
Kenneth More	Lt Teddy Evans
James McKechnie	Lt Atkinson
John Gregson	PO Green
Norman Williams	Stoker Lashley
Barry Letts	Apsley Cherry-Gerrard
Clive Morton	Herbert Ponting
Anne Firth	Oriana Wilson
Diana Churchill	Kathleen Scott
Dennis Vance	Charles Wright
Christopher Lee	Bernard Day

Bruce Seton	Lt Pennell

HISTORY 1909—1912. Captain's expedition
to South Pole ends in death. (RFP: 1948.)

11285
THE FOOL AND THE PRINCESS (72) (A)
Merton Park (GFD)
P: Frank Hoare
D: SC: William C. Hammond
S: (NOVEL) Stephen Spender

Bruce Lester	Harry Granville
Lesley Brook	Kate Granville
Adina Mandlova	Moura
Irene Handl	Mrs Wicker
Murray Matheson	Graham Ballard
Macdonald Parke	Wingfield
Vi Kaley	Mrs Jenkins

ROMANCE Germany. Married officer falls for
DP in the belief that she is Russian Princess.

11286
LOOK BEFORE YOU LOVE (96) (A)
Burnham Productions (GFD)
P: John Corfield, Harold Huth
D: Harold Huth
S: Ketti Frings
SC: Reginald Long

Margaret Lockwood	Ann Markham
Griffith Jones	Charles Kent
Norman Wooland	Ashley Moorhouse
Phyllis Stanley	Bettina Colby
Michael Medwin	Emile
Maurice Denham	Fosser
Frederick Piper	Miller
Violet Farebrother	Dowager
Bruce Seton	Johns
Peggy Evans	Typist

ROMANCE Embassy girl in Rio weds gambler
who blackmails millionaire who loves her.

11287
ONCE A JOLLY SWAGMAN (100) (A)
USA: MANIACS ON WHEELS
Pinewood—Wessex (GFD)
P: Ian Dalrymple
D: Jack Lee
S: (NOVEL) Montagu Slater
SC: Jack Lee, William Rose, Cliff Gordon

Dirk Bogarde	Bill Fox
Bonar Colleano	Tommy Fossey
Renee Asherton	Pat
Bill Owen	Lag Gibbon
Moira Lister	Dorothy Liz
Thora Hird	Ma Fox
James Hayter	Pa Fox
Patric Doonan	Dick
Cyril Cusack	Duggie
Sandra Dorne	Kay Fox
Sidney James	Rowton
Anthony Oliver	Derek

SPORT Speedway champion loses conceit
during war service.

11288
PORTRAIT FROM LIFE (90) (A)
USA: THE GIRL IN THE PAINTING
Gainsborough (GFD)
P: Anthony Darnborough
D: Terence Fisher
S: David Evans
SC: Muriel & Sidney Box, Frank Harvey

Mai Zetterling	Hildegarde
Robert Beatty	Campbell Reid
Guy Rolfe	Maj Lawrence
Herbert Lom	Hendlemann
Patrick Holt	Ferguson
Arnold Marle	Prof Menzel
Sybilla Binder	Eitel
Thora Hird	Mrs Skinner

Gerard Heinz . . . .   Heine
Yvonne Owen . . . .   Helen
Ernest Thesiger . . . .   Bloomfield
John Blythe . . . .   Johnnie
DRAMA Germany.Major searches DP camp
for amnesiac girl in painting.

11289
PANIC AT MADAM TUSSAUD'S (49) (A)
Vandyke (Ex)
P: Roger Proudlock
D: Peter Graham Scott
S: Sam Lee, Roger Proudlock, Peter
Graham Scott
Harry Locke . . . .   Gladstone Green
Harry Fine . . . .   Bugs Maloney
Patricia Owens . . . .
Frances Clare . . . .
Ivan Craig . . . .
Sam Lee . . . .
COMEDY Crooks search for stolen gems
hidden in waxworks chamber of horrors.

11290
THINGS HAPPEN AT NIGHT (79) (A)
Tudor-Alliance (Renown) *reissue:* 1953
P: A.R. Shipman, James Carter
D: Francis Searle
S: (PLAY) Frank Harvey (THE POLTERGEIST)
SC: StJohn Legh Clowes
Gordon Harker . . . .   Joe Harris
Alfred Drayton . . . .   Wilfred Prescott
Robertson Hare . . . .   Vincent Ebury
Gwyneth Vaughan . . . . . .   Audrey Prescott
Olga Lindo . . . .   Mrs Ebury
Garry Marsh . . . .   Spender
Wylie Watson . . . .   Watson
Joan Young . . . .   Mrs Venning
Beatrice Campbell . . . .   Joyce Prescott
Knox Crichton; Eric Robinson; George
Melachrino and his Orchestra
George Melachrino and his Orchestra
FANTASY Insurance agent finds psychic maid
is activating poltergeist.

11291
OPERATION DIAMOND (53) (U)
Cine—Industrial Productions (Renown)
P: Patrick Matthews
D: Ronnie Pilgrim
S: Anthony Richardson
Frank Hawkins . . . .   Major Dane
Michael Medwin . . . .   Sullivan
Beth Ross . . . .   Hilda

Campbell Singer . . . .   Bert
Gerik Schelderupp . . . .   Jan van der Meer
WAR Mission to Holland saves world's largest
diamond from Nazis.

11292
ESCAPE FROM BROADMOOR (37) (A)
International Motion Pictures (GN)
P: Harry Reynolds
D: S: John Gilling
John Stuart . . . .   Insp Thornton
Victoria Hopper . . . .   Susan
John le Mesurier . . . .   Pendicot
Frank Hawkins . . . .   Roger Trent
Anthony Doonan . . . .   Jenkins
T. Gilly Fenwick . . . .   Sandy
FANTASY Murdered girl's ghost seeks
vengeance on madman.

11293
WILLIAM COMES TO TOWN (89)(U)
Diadem-Alliance (UA) *reissue:* 1953,
WILLIAM AT THE CIRCUS (Ren)
P: John R. Sloan, David Coplan
D: SC: Val Guest
S: (STORIES) Richmal Crompton
William Graham . . . .   William Brown
Garry Marsh . . . .   Mr Brown
Jane Welsh . . . .   Mrs Brown
A.E. Matthews . . . .   Minister
Muriel Aked . . . .   Emily
Hugh Cross . . . .   Robert Brown
Kathleen Stuart . . . .   Ethel Brown
Michael Medwin . . . .   Reporter
Jon Pertwee . . . .   Supt
Brian Roper . . . .   Ginger
James Crabbe . . . .   Douglas
Brian Weske . . . .   Henry
COMEDY Village boys cause trouble at
Downing Street and circus.

11294
THE BRASS MONKEY (84) *retitled:*
LUCKY MASCOT (A)
Diadem-Alliance (UA) *reissue:* 1954 (Ren)
P: Nat A. Bronsten, David Coplan
D: Thornton Freeland
S: Alec Coppel
SC: Alec Coppel, Thornton Freeland,
C. Denis Freeman
Carole Landis . . . .   Kay Sheldon
Carroll Levis . . . .   Himself

Herbert Lom . . . .   Peter Hobart
Avril Angers . . . .   Herself
Ernest Thesiger . . . .   Ryder-Harris
Henry Edwards . . . .   Insp Miller
Edward Underdown . . . . . .   Max Taylor
Terry Thomas; Carroll Levis's Discoveries;
Albert & Les Ward; Leslie "Hutch" Hutchinson
CRIME Radio star thwarts Buddhist
connoisseur seeking brass monkey.

11295
THE TRIAL OF MADAME X (54) (A)
Invicta—Wyndham T. Vint (EB)
D: SC: Paul England
S: (PLAY) Alexandre Bisson (MADAME X)
Mara Russell-Tavernan . . . .   Jacqueline
Paul England . . . .   Perrisard
Edward Leslie . . . .   Raymond
Frank Hawkins . . . .   la Roque
Hamilton Deane . . . .   Noel
Hamilton Keene . . . .   Louis
Jean le Roy . . . .   Madeleine
CRIME France. Woman's unknown son
defends her for shooting blackmailer.

11296
WHAT A LIFE ! (12) (U)
Public Relationship (NSS)
P: Richard Massingham
D: S: Michael Law
Richard Massingham . . . . . .   Mr A
Russell Waters . . . .   Mr B
Ella Milne . . . .
Arthur Brander . . . .
Kenneth Buckle . . . .
Dorothy Gray . . . . .
COMEDY Two businessmen, depressed by state
of country, attempt suicide and fail.

11297
BUT NOT IN VAIN (73) (A)
Anglo—Dutch (Butcher)
P: Guus E. Ostwalt, Geoffrey Goodheart
D: Edmond T. Greville
S: (PLAY) Ben Van Eeslyn
Raymond Lovell . . . .   Jan Alting
Carol Van Derman . . . . . .   Elly Alting
Martin Benson . . . .   Mark Meyer
Agnes Bernelle . . . .   Mary Meyer
Julian Dallas . . . .   Willem Bakker
Bruce Lister . . . .   Fred Van Nespen
WAR Holland. Farmer's son threatens to betray
hidden patriots.

1949

JAN

11298
WARNING TO WANTONS (104) (A)
Aquila (GFD)
P: D: Donald B. Wilson
S: (NOVEL) Mary Mitchell
SC: Donald B. Wilson, James Laver
Harold Warrender . . . . . . Count Anton Kardak
Anne Vernon . . . . Renee de Vaillant
David Tomlinson . . . . Count Max Kardak
Sonia Holm . . . . Maria
Marie Burke . . . . Therese
Judy Kelly . . . . Mimi de Vaillant
Hugh Cross . . . . Pauli
Ellen Pollock . . . . Baroness
Andre van Gyseghem . . . . . Oblensky
Bruce Belfrage . . . . Archimandrite
Dennis Vance . . . . Franklin Budd
Jack Melford . . . . Maurice Lugard
Vincent Ball . . . . Footman
ROMANCE France. Runaway schoolgirl flirts
with Count and his son.

11299
THIRD TIME LUCKY (91) (A)
Kenilworth—Alliance (GFD)
P: Mario Zampi
D: Gordon Parry
S: (NOVEL) Gerald Butler (THEY
CRACKED HER GLASS SLIPPER)
SC: Gerald Butler
Glynis Johns . . . . Joan
Dermot Walsh . . . . Lucky
Charles Goldner . . . . Flash
Harcourt Williams . . . . Doc
Yvonne Owen . . . . Peggy
Helen Haye . . . . Old Lady
John Stuart . . . . Inspector
Harold Berens . . . . Waiter
Ballard Berkeley . . . . Bertram
Sebastian Cabot . . . . Benny
Millicent Wolf . . . . Matron
CRIME Gambler hires girl to bring him luck;
his rival lusts after her.

11300
BADGER'S GREEN (62) (U)
Production Facilities (GFD)
P: John Croydon
D: John Irwin
S: (PLAY) R.C. Sheriff
SC: William Fairchild
Barbara Murray . . . . Jane Morton
Brian Nissen . . . . Dickie Wetherby
Garry Marsh . . . . Maj Forrester
Kynaston Reeves . . . . Dr Wetherby
Laurence Naismith . . . . . . Mr Butler
Mary Merrall . . . . Mrs Wetherby
Jack McNaughton . . . . Mr Twigg
Norman Pierce . . . . Sam Rogers
COMEDY Village cricket rivals unite against
proposed building scheme.

11301
EUREKA STOCKADE (103) (U)
Ealing (GFD)
AP: Leslie Norman
D: S: Harry Watt
SC: Harry Watt, Walter Greenwood,
Ralph Smart
Chips Rafferty . . . . Peter Lalor
Jane Barrett . . . . Alicia Dunn
Gordon Jackson . . . . Tom Kennedy
Jack Lambert . . . . Commissioner Rede
Peter Illing . . . . Rafaello
Ralph Truman . . . . Governor Hotham
Sydney Loder . . . . Vern
John Fernside . . . . Sly Grog Seller
Grant Tyler . . . . Sgt Milne

Peter Finch . . . . Humffray
ADVENTURE Australia, 1850. Gold diggers
revolt against harsh governor.

11302
ROVER AND ME (45) (U)
F.C. Films (EB)
P: D: Frank Chisnell
S: Terry Sanford
Edward Rigby . . . . Mr Maggott
Keith Bartlett . . . . Tommy
Judy Edwards . . . . Susan Jackson
Cambell Singer . . . . Mr Jackson
Ninian Brodie . . . . Mr Morgan
Pat Nye . . . . Mrs O'Brien
DRAMA Orphan boy and dog help old tramp
catch smugglers.

11303
ELIZABETH OF LADYMEAD (97) *tech* (A)
Imperadio (BL)
P: D: Herbert Wilcox
S: (PLAY) Frank Harvey
SC: Frank Harvey
Anna Neagle . . . . . . Beth/Elizabeth/Betty/Liz
Hugh Williams . . . . John (1946)
Bernard Lee . . . . John (1903)
Michael Laurence . . . . John (1919)
Nicholas Phipps . . . . John (1854)
Isobel Jeans . . . . Mother (1903)
Hilda Bayley . . . . Mother (1946)
Michael Shepley . . . . . . Maj Wrigley (1903)
Jack Allen . . . . Maj Wrigley (1946)
ROMANCE Four generations of husbands
return from war to find their wives are more
independent.

FEB

11304
THE SMALL BACK ROOM (108) (A)
London-BLPA-Archers (BL) *reissue:*
1952 (23 mins cut)
P: D: SC: Michael Powell, Emeric Pressburger
S: (NOVEL) Nigel Balchin
David Farrar . . . . Sammy Rice
Kathleen Byron . . . . Susan
Jack Hawkins . . . . Waring
Leslie Banks . . . . Col Holland
Cyril Cusack . . . . Cpl Taylor
Robert Morley . . . . Minister
Emrys Jones . . . . Joe
Renee Asherson . . . . ATS Cpl
Walter Fitzgerald . . . . Brine
Anthony Bushell . . . . Maj Stang
Milton Rosmer . . . . Prof Mair
Michael Gough . . . . Capt Stewart
Michael Goodliffe . . . . . . Till
WAR Man with tin foot regains faith after
disposing of boobytrap.

11305
ONCE UPON A DREAM (84) (A)
Triton (GFD)
P: Anthony Darnborough
D: Ralph Thomas
S: Patrick Kirwan, Victor Katona
Googie Withers . . . . Carol Gilbert
Griffith Jones . . . . Jackson
Guy Middleton . . . . Maj Gilbert
Raymond Lovell . . . . Mr Trout
Agnes Lauchlan . . . . Aunt Agnes
Hubert Gregg . . . . Capt Williams
Maurice Denham . . . . Vicar
Betty Lynne . . . . Mlle Louise
David Horne . . . . Registrar
Gibb McLaughlin . . . . Pontefact
Dora Bryan . . . . Barmaid
COMEDY Major's wife dreams his batman is
her lover and thinks it is true.

11306
THE PASSIONATE FRIENDS (95) (A)
USA: ONE WOMAN'S STORY
Pinewood—Cineguild (GFD)
P: Eric Ambler
D: David Lean
S: (NOVEL) H.G. Wells
SC: Eric Ambler, David Lean, Stanley Haynes
Ann Todd . . . . Mary Justin
Claude Rains . . . . Howard Justin
Trevor Howard . . . . Steven Stratton
Betty Ann Davies . . . . Miss Layton
Isabel Dean . . . . Pat Moore
Arthur Howard . . . . Manservant
Wilfrid Hyde White . . . . . . Solicitor
Guido Lorraine . . . . Manager
ROMANCE 1939. Woman weds rich banker
and then meets her first love in Switzerland.

11307
VOTE FOR HUGGETT (84) (A)
Gainsborough (GFD)
P: Betty Box
D: Ken Annakin
S: Mabel & Denis Constanduros, Allan
Mackinnon
Jack Warner . . . . Joe Huggett
Kathleen Harrison . . . . . Ethel Huggett
Susan Shaw . . . . Susan Huggett
Petula Clark . . . . Pet Huggett
David Tomlinson . . . . Harold Hinchley
Diana Dors . . . . Diana
Peter Hammond . . . . Peter Hawtrey
Amy Veness . . . . Grandma
Hubert Gregg . . . . Maurice Lever
John Blythe . . . . Gowan
Anthony Newley . . . . Dudley
Charles Victor . . . . Mr Hall
Adrianne Allen . . . . Mrs Hall
Frederick Piper . . . . Mr Bentley
Empsie, Isa & Nellie Bowman . . . Old Ladies
COMEDY Estate agent wants builder's wife's
land for war memorial.

11308
THE HISTORY OF MR POLLY (95) (A)
Two Cities (GFD)
P: John Mills
D: SC: Anthony Pelissier
S: (NOVEL) H.G. Wells
John Mills . . . . Alfred Polly
Sally Ann Howes . . . . Christabel
Finlay Currie . . . . Uncle Jim
Betty Ann Davies . . . . Miriam Larkins
Edward Chapman . . . . Mr Jackson
Megs Jenkins . . . . Plump Woman
Diana Churchill . . . . Annie Larkins
Gladys Henson . . . . Mrs Larkins
Shelagh Fraser . . . . Minnie
Miles Malleson . . . . Old Gentleman
Moore Marriott . . . . Uncle Pentstemon
David Horne . . . . Mr Garvace
Ernest Jay . . . . Mr Hinks
Edie Martin . . . . Old Lady
Dandy Nichols . . . . Mrs Johnson
Wally Patch . . . . Customer
Lawrence Baskcomb . . . . . . Mr Rumbold
Juliet Mills . . . . Polly
Wylie Watson . . . . Mr Rusper
COMEDY 1900. Draper rebels against his wife
and becomes handyman at country inn.

11309
ALL OVER TOWN (88) (U)
Pinewood—Wessex (GFD)
P: Ian Dalrymple
D: Derek Twist
S: R.F. Delderfield
SC: Derek Twist, Michael Gordon, Inez Holden,
Stafford Byrne

Norman Wooland . . . . Nat Hearne
Sarah Churchill . . . . Sally Thorpe
Cyril Cusack . . . . Gerald Vane
Fabia Drake . . . . Miss Gelding
James Hayter . . . . Baines
Edward Rigby . . . . Grimmett
Patric Doonan . . . . Burton
Eleanor Summerfield . . . . . . Beryl Hooper
Bryan Forbes . . . . Trumble
John Salew . . . . Sleek
Henry Edwards . . . . Maj Martindale
Sandra Dorne . . . . Marlene
Frederick Leister . . . . Wainer
Ronald Adam . . . . Sam Vane
Trefor Jones . . . . Tenor
COMEDY Ex-pilot buys seaside newspaper
and attacks council's housing scheme.

11310
SILENT DUST (82) (A)
Independent Sovereign (ABP)
P: Nat A. Bronsten
D: Lance Comfort
S: (PLAY) Roland and Michael Pertwee
(THE PARAGON)
SC: Michael Pertwee
Sally Gray . . . . Angela Rawley
Stephen Murray . . . . Robert Rawley
Derek Farr . . . . Maxwell Oliver
Nigel Patrick . . . . Simon Rawley
Beatrice Campbell . . . . Joan Rawley
Seymour Hicks . . . . Lord Clandon
Marie Lohr . . . . Lady Clandon
Yvonne Owen . . . . Nellie
James Hayter . . . . Pringle
Maria Var . . . . Singer
CRIME Blind man's son returns from "heroic
death" a coward, blackmailer and killer.

11311
THE GLASS MOUNTAIN (98) (A)
Victoria (Renown) reissues: 1950; 1953
P: John Sutro, Fred Zelnik, Joseph Janni
D: Henry Cass
S: Joseph Janni, John Hunter, Emery Bonnet,
Henry Cass, John Cousins
Michael Denison . . . . . . , . . Richard Wilder
Dulcie Gray . . . . Ann Wilder
Valentine Cortese . . . . Alida
Tito Gobbi . . . . Tito
Sebastian Shaw . . . . Bruce McLeod
Antonio Centa . . . . Gino
Sidney King . . . . Charles
Elena Rizzieri . . . . Singer
Venice Opera House Orchestra and Chorus
ROMANCE Dolomites. Married composer loves
Italian girl who saved his life during the war.

11312
FORBIDDEN (87) (A)
Pennant Pictures (BL)
P: D: George King
S: Val Valentine
SC: Katherine Strueby
Douglass Mongomery . . . . . Jim Harding
Hazel Court . . . . Jane Thompson
Patricia Burke . . . . Diana Harding
Garry Marsh . . . . Jerry Burns
Ronald Shiner . . . . Dan Collins
Kenneth Griffith . . . . Johnny
Eliot Makeham . . . . Mr Thompson
Frederick Leister . . . . Dr Franklin
Richard Bird . . . . Jennings
Michael Medwin . . . . Cabby
Andrew Cruickshank . . . . . Baxter
CRIME Blackpool. Chemist tries to poison
extravagant wife.

11313
SOMEWHERE IN POLITICS (108) (A)
Film Studios Manchester (Mancunian)
P: D: John E. Blakele.
S: Harry Jackson, Arthur Mertz, Frank Randle
Frank Randle . . . . Joe Smart
Tessie O'Shea . . . . Daisy Smart
Josef Locke . . . . Willoughby
Sally Barnes . . . . Marjorie Willoughby
Syd Harrison . . . . Tommy Parker
Max Harrison . . . . Arthur Parker
Bunty Meadows . . . . Pat Parker
Jimmy Clitheroe . . . . Sonny
Sonny Burke . . . . Reggie Smart
COMEDY Radio repair man puts up for
Council election against his boss.
(Extract in FULL HOUSE (1960).)

MAR
11314
THE BLUE LAGOON (103) tech (A)
Pinewood—Individual (GFD)
P: Frank Launder, Sidney Gilliat
D: Frank Launder
S: (NOVEL) H. DeVere Stacpoole
SC: Frank Launder, John Baines, Michael Hogan
Jean Simmons . . . . Emmeline Foster
Donald Houston . . . . Michael Reynolds
Noel Purcell . . . . Paddy Button
Cyril Cusack . . . . James Carter
James Hayter . . . . Dr Murdock
Susan Stranks . . . . Emmeline (child)
Peter Jones . . . . Michael (child)
Maurice Denham . . . . Captain
Patrick Barr . . . . Mr Bruce
Russell Waters . . . . Craggs
ROMANCE Shipwrecked children grow up on
desert island and learn love.

11315
TRAPPED BY THE TERROR (56) (U)
Merton Park (GFD)
P: Frank Hoare
D: Cecil Musk
S: Ion Grundy
SC: Sherard Powell, Mary Cathcart Borer
James Kenney . . . . Philip Dupois
Colin Stephens . . . . Maurice
Valerie Carlton . . . . Marie
Ian Colin . . . . Count Dupois
Louise Gainsborough . . . . Countess Dupois
Alastair Bannerman . . . . . . Marcel
John Longdon . . . . Pierre
Martin Benson . . . . Governor
CHILDREN France. Baker's children help
Count's son save parents from Bastille.

11316
FOOLS RUSH IN (82) (A)
Pinewood (GFD)
P: Aubrey Baring
D: John Paddy Carstairs
S: (PLAY) Kenneth Horne
SC: Geoffrey Kerr
Sally Ann Howes . . . . Pamela Dickson
Guy Rolfe . . . . Paul Dickson
Nora Swinburne . . . . Angela Dickson
Nigel Buchanan . . . . Joe Trent
Raymond Lovell . . . . Sir Charles Leigh
Thora Hird . . . . Mrs Coot
Patricia Raine . . . . Millicent
Nora Nicholson . . . . Mrs Mandrake
Peter Hammond . . . . Tommy
Charles Victor . . . . Mr Atkins
Esma Cannon . . . . Mrs Atkins
COMEDY Wife makes up with her divorced
husband when their daughter cancels her
wedding.

11317
THE BAD LORD BYRON (85) (A)
Triton (GFD)
P: Aubrey Baring
D: David Macdonald
S: Terence Young, Anthony Thorne, Peter
Quennell, Lawrence Kitchin, Paul Holt
Dennis Price . . . . Lord Byron
Mai Zetterling . . . . Teresa Guiccioli
Joan Greenwood .. . . . . .Lady Caroline Lamb
Linden Travers . . . . Augusta Leigh
Sonia Holm . . . . .Arabella Millbank
Raymond Lovell . . . . John Hobhouse
Leslie Dwyer . . . . Fletcher
Denis O'Dea . . . . Prosecution
Nora Swinburne . . . . Lady Jersey
Ernest Thesiger . . . . Count Guiccioli
Irene Browne . . . . Lady Melbourne
Barry Jones . . . . Col Stanhope
Henry Oscar . . . . Count Gamba
Archie Duncan . . . . John Murray
Liam Gaffney . . . . Tom Moore
John Salew . . . . Samuel Rogers
Wilfrid Hyde White . . . . . . Mr Hopton
Betty Lynne . . . . Signora Segati
Zena Marshall . . . . Italian
HISTORY Life and loves of noble poet.

11318
FLOODTIDE (90) (A)
Aquila (GFD)
P: Donald B. Wilson
D: Frederick Wilson
S: George Blake
SC: George Blake, Donald B. Wilson
Frederick Wilson
Gordon Jackson . . . . David Shields
Rona Anderson . . . . Mary Anstruther
John Laurie . . . . Joe Drummond
Jack Lambert . . . . Mr Anstruther
Jimmy Logan . . . . Tim Brogan
Elizabeth Sellars . . . . Judy
Janet Brown . . . . Rosie
Gordon McLeod . . . . Pursey
Ian Maclean . . . . Sir John
Archie Duncan . . . . Charlie Campbell
Molly Weir . . . . Mrs McTavish
Ian Wallace . . . . Director
Kitty Kirwan . . . . Granny Shields
Peter Illing. . . . . Senor Arandha
DRAMA Clydebank. Shipyard apprentice rises
to become designer.

11319
BRITANNIA MEWS (91) (A)
USA:. FORBIDDEN STREET
20th Century Productions (20) reissue: 1952
(29 mins cut)
P: William Perlberg
D: Jean Negulesco
S: (NOVEL) Margery Sharp
SC: Ring Lardner jr
Dana Andrews . . . . Gilbert/Henry
Maureen O'Hara . . . . Adelaide Culver
Sybil Thorndike . . . . Mrs Mounsey
Fay Compton . . . . Mrs Culver
A.E. Matthews . . . . Mr Bly
Anne Butchart . . . . Alice Hambo
Diane Hart . . . . The Blazer
Wilfrid Hyde White . . . . . . Mr Culver
Anthony Tancred . . . . Treff Culver
Herbert C. Walton . . . . . . The Old'Un
Mary Martlew . . . . Milly Lauderdale
Neil North . . . . Jimmy Hambro
Suzanne Gibbs . . . . Alice Hambro
John Wright's Marionettes
ROMANCE Period. Rich girl marries poor
artist, and, after his death, marries his double.

11320
THE JACK OF DIAMONDS (73) (U)
V.S. Productions (Ex)
P: Walter d'Eyncourt
D: Vernon Sewell
S: Nigel Patrick, Cyril Raymond

Nigel Patrick	Alan Butler
Cyril Raymond	Roger Keen
Joan Carol	Joan Keen
Darcy Conyers	Colin Campbell
Vernon Sewell	Engineer

ADVENTURE Couple charter yacht to search
for sunken treasure.

11321
A MAN'S AFFAIR (62) (U)
Concord (Exclusive)
P: D: Jay Gardner Lewis
S: Jay Gardner Lewis, Harold Stewart

Hamish Menzies	Jim
Cliff Gordon	Ted
Diana Decker	Sheila
Joan Dowling	Joan
Wallas Eaton	Leonard

ROMANCE Ramsgate. Playboy tries to spoil
miners' holiday romances.

11322
HELD IN TRUST (58) (A)
Productions No. 1 (DUK)
P: D: S: Cecil H. Williamson

Ian Proctor	Charles Ross
Dorothy Shaw	Bess Lovell
Guy Verney	

CRIME Skipper adopts stowaway artist whose
former friends force him into crime.

11323
BLESS 'EM ALL (79) (U)
Advance (Adelphi)
P: D: Robert Jordan Hill
S: Aileen Burke, Leone Stuart, Arthur Dent
SC: C. Boganny, Hal Monty

Hal Monty	Skimpy Carter
Max Bygraves	Tommy Anderson
Les Ritchie	Sgt Willis
Stanley White	Cpl
Jack Milroy	Jock
Patricia Linova	Val Willis
Sibyl Amiel	Lisette

COMEDY France, 1940. Private and sgt are
rivals for girl.

11324
MELODY IN THE DARK (68) (A)
Advent (Adelphi)
P: D: Robert Jordan Hill
S: John Guillermin

Ben Wrigley	Ben
Eunice Gayson	Pat
Richard Thorp	Dick
Dawn Lesley	Dawn

Alan Dean; Carl Carlisle; Maisie Weldon; The
Keynotes; The Stardusters
MUSICAL Actress inherits old house where
crooks hold owner captive.

11325
THE NITWITS ON PARADE (42) (A)
Advance (Adelphi)
P: D: Robert Jordan Hill

Syd Millward	Norah Moody
Max Bygraves	The Nitwits
Rex Reymer	Josephine & Payne
Wally Stewart	Men About Town

REVUE

11326
I WAS A DANCER (49) (A)
Richardson (Adelphi)
D: S: Frank Richardson

Diana Napier	Mme Dupont

Primrose Rhead	Molly

CRIME Knife killer at ballet school unmasked
thirty years later.

11327
EDWARD MY SON (112) (A)
MGM British *reissue:* 1952 (23 mins cut)
P: Edwin H. Knopf
D: George Cukor
S: (PLAY) Robert Morley, Noel Langley
SC: Donald Ogden Stuart

Spencer Tracy	Arnold Bolt
Deborah Kerr	Evelyn Bolt
Ian Hunter	Dr Larry Woodhope
Leueen McGrath	Eileen Perrin
James Donald	Bronton
Mervyn Johns	Harry Simpkin
Harriette Johns	Phyllis Mayden
Felix Aylmer	Mr Hanray
Walter Fitzgerald	Mr Kednar
Ernest Jay	Walter Prothin
Colin Gordon	Ellerby

DRAMA Ambitious Lord's love for son drives
wife to drink.

11328
THE CASE OF CHARLES PEACE (88) (A)
Argyle (Monarch) *reissue:* 1952 (30 mins cut)
P: John Argyle
D: Norman Lee
S: Doris Davison, Norman Lee

Michael Martin Harvey	Charles Peace
Chili Bouchier	Katherine Dyson
Valentine Dyall	Storyteller
Bruce Belfrage	Prosecution
Ronald Adam	Defence
Robert Huby	Sue Thompson
Peter Forbes-Robertson	William Habron
Richard Shayne	Arthur Dyson
Peter Gawthorne	Mr Justice Lopes

CRIME 1870. True story of picture-framer
who became burglar.

11329
MOVIE—GO—ROUND (45) (U)
Fama Films (Ambassador)
D: Fred Weiss
S: Jim Phelan, Patrick Burke

Donald Biset	Old Time Projector
Rene Goddard	Modern Projector
Sam Kydd	Repair Man

COMPILATION Repair-man dreams old and
new projectors become human and discuss
films. (Includes extracts from earlier films.)

11330
THE GREEDY BOY'S DREAM (22) (U)
Public Relationship (GFD)
P: D: Richard Massingham
S: Richard Massingham, John Waterhouse

Dennis Carey	The Boy
Richard Massingham	

CHILDREN Ireland. Small boy overeats and
has nightmare.

11331
THREE BAGS FULL (serial) (U)
Elstree Independent (GFD)
P: D: John Baxter
S: Sybil Clarke

Perlita Neilson	Maria
Freddie Mason	Tony
Graham Moffatt	Albert
Mark Daly	Jock

Eps 1 — 3 (19 each)
CHILDREN Children save foreign
ambassador's despatches from spies.

APR

11332
CARDBOARD CAVALIER (96) (U)
Two Cities (GFD)

P: D: Walter Forde
S: Noel Langley
N: John Snagge

Sid Field	Sidcup Buttermeadow
Margaret Lockwood	Nell Gwynne
Mary Clare	Milady Doverhouse
Jerry Desmonde	Col Lovelace
Claude Hulbert	Sylvester Clutterbuck
Brian Worth	Tom Pride
Anthony Hulme	Charles II
Edmund Willard	Oliver Cromwell
Irene Handl	Lady Agnes
Miles Malleson	Judge Gorebucket
Joan Young	Maggie
Jack McNaughton	Uriah Croup
Alfie Dean	Murdercasket
Michael Brennan	Barebones

COMEDY 1658. Barrow-boy gets involved in
plot against Cromwell.

11333
IT'S NOT CRICKET (77) (U)
Gainsborough (GFD)
P: Betty Box
D: Alfred Roome, Roy Rich
S: Bernard McNab, Lyn Lockwood,
Gerard Bryant

Basil Radford	Maj Bright
Naunton Wayne	Capt Early
Susan Shaw	Primrose Brown
Maurice Denham	Otto Fisch
Alan Wheatley	Felix
Nigel Buchanan	Gerald Lawson
Jane Carr	Virginia Briscoe
Leslie Dwyer	Batman
Patrick Waddington	Valentine Christmas
Edward Lexy	Brig Falcon
Frederick Piper	Yokel
Diana Dors	Blonde
Mary Hinton	Lady Lawson

COMEDY Private tecs catch Nazi seeking
cricket ball containing diamond.

11334
A BOY, A GIRL AND A BIKE (92) (U)
Gainsborough (GFD)
P: Ralph Keene
D: Ralph Smart
S: Ted Willis

John McCallum	David Howarth
Honor Blackman	Susie Bates
Patrick Holt	Sam Walters
Diana Dors	Ada Foster
Leslie Dwyer	Steve Hall
Thora Hird	Mrs Bates
Anthony Newley	Charlie Ritchie
Megs Jenkins	Nan Ritchie
Maurice Denham	Bill Martin
John Blythe	Frankie Martin
Alison Leggatt	Mrs Howarth
Julien Mitchell	Mr Howarth
Amy Veness	Grandma Bates

DRAMA Yorks. Romantic and criminal
adventures of mill town cycle club.

11335
PASSPORT TO PIMLICO (84) (U)
Ealing (GFD)
AP: E.V.H. Emmett
D: Henry Cornelius
S: Henry Cornelius, T.E.B. Clarke

Stanley Holloway	Arthur Pemberton
Hermione Baddeley	Edie Randall
Margaret Rutherford	Prof Hatton-Jones
Paul Dupuis	Duke of Burgundy
Basil Radford	Gregg
Naunton Wayne	Straker
Jane Hylton	Molly
Raymond Huntley	Mr Wix
Betty Warren	Connie Pemberton
Barbara Murray	Shirley Pemberton

John Slater . . . . Frank Huggins
Frederick Piper . . . . Garland
Sydney Tafler . . . . Fred Cowan
Charles Hawtrey . . . . Bert Fitch
James Hayter . . . . Commissionaire
COMEDY Ironmonger finds papers proving
Pimlico part of Burgundy.

11336
THE QUEEN OF SPADES (95) (A)
ABPC—World Screenplays (ABP)
P: Anatole de Grunwald
D: Thorold Dickinson
S: (NOVEL) Alexander Pushkin
SC: Rodney Ackland, Arthur Boys
Anton Walbrook . . . . Herman Suvorin
Edith Evans . . . . Countess Ranevskaya
Ronald Howard . . . . Andrei
Mary Jerrold . . . . Vavarushka
Yvonne Mitchell . . . . Lizavetta Ivanouna
Anthony Dawson . . . . Fyodor
Pauline Tennant . . . . Countess (young)
Miles Malleson . . . . Tchybukin
Athene Seyler . . . . Princess Ivashin
Michael Medwin . . . . Ilovaisky
Ivor Barnard . . . . Bookseller
Yusef Ramart . . . . Lover
Valentine Dyall . . . . Messenger
Gibb McLaughlin . . . . Birdseller
Violetta Elvin
Maroussia Dmitravitch
FANTASY Russia, 1806. Poor captain wrests
Devil's card-winning secret from aged Countess.

11337
FOR THEM THAT TRESPASS (95) (A)
ABPC (ABP)
P: Victor Skatezky
D: Cavalcanti
S: (NOVEL) Ernest Raymond
SC: J. Lee-Thompson, William Douglas Home
Stephen Murray . . . . Christopher Drew
Patricia Plunkett . . . . Rosie
Richard Todd . . . . Herb Logan
Rosalyn Boulter . . . . Frankie
Michael Laurence . . . . . . Jim Heal
Joan Dowling . . . . Gracie
Mary Merrall . . . . Mrs Drew
Frederick Leister . . . . Mr Drew
Helen Cherry . . . . Mary Drew
Michael Medwin . . . . Len Stevens
Vida Hope . . . . Olive Mockson
Harry Fowler . . . . Dave
Irene Handl . . . . Mrs Sams
James Hayter . . . . Jocko
George Curzon . . . . Clark Hall
Valentine Dyall . . . . Sir Archibald
Harcourt Williams . . . . . . Judge
CRIME Ex-convict proves he did not kill tart
despite cowardice of author witness.

11338
PAPER ORCHID (86) (A)
Ganesh (Col)
P: William Collier, John R. Sloan
D: Roy Baker
S: (NOVEL) Arthur la Berne
SC: Val Guest
Hugh Williams . . . . Frank McSweeney
Hy Hazell . . . . Stella Mason
Sidney James . . . . Freddy Evans
Garry Marsh . . . . Johnson
Andrew Cruickshank . . . . Insp Clement Pill
Ivor Barnard . . . . Eustace Crabb
Walter Hudd . . . . Briggs
Ella Retford . . . . Lady Croup
Hughie Green . . . . Harold Croup
Vida Hope . . . . Jonquil Jones
Frederick Leister . . . . . . .Walter Wibberley

Ray Ellington Quartet
CRIME Reporter's confession clears girl
colleague from charge of killing star.

11339
THE TEMPTRESS (85) (A)
Bushey (Ambassador)
P: Gilbert Church
D: Oswald Mitchell
S: (NOVEL) Alice Campbell (JUGGERNAUT)
SC: Kathleen Butler
Joan Maude . . . . Lady Clifford
Arnold Bell . . . . Dr Leroy
Don Stannard . . . . Derek Clifford
Shirley Quentin . . . . Nurse Rowe
John Stuart . . . . Sir Charles Clifford
Ferdy Mayne . . . . Julian
Conrad Phillips . . . . Capt Green
CRIME Lady gives doctor research money in
return for killing her husband.

11340
DICK BARTON STRIKES BACK (71) (U)
Exclusive
P: Anthony Hinds, Mae Murray
D: Godfrey Grayson
S: (RADIO SERIAL) Edward J. Mason
SC: Ambrose Grayson
Don Stannard . . . . Dick Barton
Sebastian Cabot . . . . Fouracada
Jean Lodge . . . . Tina
James Raglan . . . . Lord Armadale
Bruce Walker . . . . Snowey White
Humphrey Kent . . . . Col Gardner
John Harvey . . . . Maj Henderson
CRIME Blackpool. Foreign agents beam atomic
rays from top of Tower.

11341
THE GOLDEN MADONNA (88) (A)
IFP (WB) *reissue:* 1953 (JPD)
P: John Stafford
D: Ladislas Vajda
S: Akos Tolnay
Phyllis Calvert . . . . Patricia Chandler
Michael Rennie . . . . Mike Christie
Tullio Carminati . . . . Migone
David Greene . . . . Johnny Lester
Aldo Silvani . . . . Don Vincenzo
Pippo Bonucci . . . . Pippo
Francesca Bondi . . . . Maria
ROMANCE Italy. Couple search for religious
painting hidden by Nazis.

MAY

11342
MAN ON THE RUN (82) (A)
ABPC (ABP)
P: D: S: Lawrence Huntington
Derek Farr . . . . Peter Burdon
Joan Hopkins . . . . Jean Adams
Edward Chapman . . . . Insp Mitchell
Laurence Harvey . . . . Sgt Lawson
John Bailey . . . . Dan Underwood
John Stuart . . . . Insp McBain
Edward Underdown . . . . . . Slim
Leslie Perrins . . . . Charlie
Kenneth More . . . . Cpl Newman
Martyn Miller . . . . Proprietor
Eleanor Summerfield . . . . May Baker
Anthony Nicholls . . . . Inspector
CRIME Shopgirl helps deserter who gets
involved in jewel robbery.

11343
IT HAPPENED IN LEICESTER SQUARE (49)
(U)
Benstead & Sharp (Benstead)
P: Norman Sharp
D: S: Geoffrey Benstead

Harry Tate jr . . . . Harry
Slim Allen . . . . Slim
Joe Davis . . . . Himself
COMEDY Two Yorkshiremen spend day
seeing London.

11344
THE HUGGETTS ABROAD (87) (U)
Gainsborough (GFD)
P: Betty Box
D: Ken Annakin
S: Mabel & Denis Constanduros, Ted Willis,
Gerard Bryant
Jack Warner . . . . Joe Huggett
Kathleen Harrison . . . . Ethel Huggett
Susan Shaw . . . . Susan Huggett
Petula Clark . . . . Pet Huggett
Dinah Sheridan . . . . Jane Huggett
Hugh McDermott . . . . Bob McCoy
Jimmy Hanley . . . . Jimmy
Peter Hammond . . . . Peter Hawtrey
Amy Veness . . . . Grandma
John Blythe . . . . Gowan
Esma Cannon . . . . Brown Owl
COMEDY Africa. Family emigrates and gets
involved with diamond smugglers.

11345
ADAM AND EVELYNE (92) (A)
USA: ADAM AND EVALYN
Two Cities (GFD)
P: D: Harold French
S: Noel Langley
SC: Noel Langley, Lesley Storm, George
Barraud, Nicholas Phipps
Stewart Granger . . . . Adam Black
Jean Simmons . . . . Evelyne Wallace
Helen Cherry . . . . Moira Hannen
Joan Swinstead . . . . Molly
Edwin Styles . . . . Bill Murray
Raymond Young . . . . Roddy Black
Beatrice Varley . . . . Mrs Parker
Wilfrid Hyde White . . . . . . Col Bradley
Fred Johnson . . . . Chris Kirby
Geoffrey Denton . . . . Insp Collins
Peter Reynolds . . . . David
Irene Handl . . . . Manageress
ROMANCE Society gambler adopts dead
friend's daughter, and they fall in love.

11346
THE PERFECT WOMAN (89) (A)
Two Cities (GFD)
P: George Black, Alfred Black
D: Bernard Knowles
S: (PLAY) Wallace Geoffrey, Basil Mitchell
SC: Bernard Knowles, George Black,
J.B. Boothroyd
Patricia Roc . . . . Penelope
Stanley Holloway . . . . Ramshead
Nigel Patrick . . . . Roger Cavendish
Miles Malleson . . . . Prof Belmon
Irene Handl . . . . Mrs Butter
Anita Sharp-Bolster . . . . . . Lady Diana
Fred Berger . . . . Farini
David Hurst . . . . Wolfgang Winkel
Pamela Devis . . . . Olga the Robot
Constance Smith . . . . Receptionist
COMEDY Girl poses as robot woman invented
by her uncle.

11347
SLICK TARTAN (37) (U)
Frank Chisnell (EB)
P: D: Frank Chisnell
S: Rex Diamond
Dave Willis . . . . Slick Tartan
Billy Howard . . . . Insp Snatchem
Denise Anthony . . . . Baby
COMEDY Special agent investigates kidnapping
of nobleman's baby.

11348
IT'S A WONDERFUL DAY (50) (U)
Knightsbridge (EB)
P: D: Hal Wilson
John Blythe
Dorothee Baroone
Eva Benyon
7 Imeson Brothers; Jack Hodges; Lew Sherman
George Mitchell and his Swing Choir
MUSICAL West Country. Convalescent band leader discovers local talent and love on farm.

11349
HAUNTED PALACE (34) (U)
Gwynne (Premier) *reissue:* 1952 (EB)
D: S: Richard Fisher
Shaw Desmond . . . .   Himself
Ian Russell
John Warren
John Singer
Helene Cooney
Anne Wrigg
Hilary Pritchard
William Holloway
FANTASY Ghost expert reconstructs legends of phantom monk, St James Palace, Hampton Court Palace, etc.

11350
BORN OF THE SEA (38) (U)
Duchy Productions (EB)
P: Albert Stanley Williamson
D: Anthony Mavrogordato
S: Howard Douglas
Cedric Staples . . . .   George
Dorothea Paul . . . .   Mary
Archie Rowe . . . .   Sam
ADVENTURE Cornwall. Widow adopts shipwrecked waif who later loses his life saving another.

11351
MEET THE DUKE (64) (U)
New Park (ABFD)
P: Link Neale
D: James Corbett
S: (PLAY) Temple Saxe (ICE ON THE COFFIN)
SC: Farnham Baxter
Farnham Baxter . . . .   Duke Hogan
Heather Chasen . . . .   Carol
Gale Douglas . . . .   Van Gard
COMEDY Brooklyn boxer inherits Dukedom and finds his servants are crooks searching for treasure.

11352
THE MAN FROM YESTERDAY (68) (A)
International Motion Pictures (Renown)
P: Harry Reynolds
D: Oswald Mitchell
S: John Gilling
John Stuart . . . .   Gerald Amersley
Henry Oscar . . . .   Julius Rickman
Gwyneth Vaughan . . . .   Doreen Amersley
Marie Burke . . . .   Doris
Laurence Harvey . . . .   John Matthews
CRIME Dead man's brother seeks vengeance by posing as family friend.

11353
DR MORELLE — THE CASE OF THE MISSING HEIRESS (73) (A)
Exclusive
P: Anthony Hinds
D: Godfrey Grayson
S: (RADIO SERIES) Ernest Dudley; (PLAY) Wilfred Burr
SC: Ambrose Grayson, Roy Plomley

Valentine Dyall . . . .   Dr Morelle
Julia Lang . . . .   Miss Frayle
Philip Leaver . . . .   Samuel Kimber
Jean Lodge . . . .   Cynthia Mason
Peter Drury . . . .   Peter
CRIME Tec solves cremation of secretary's sister.

11354
THAT DANGEROUS AGE (99) (A)
USA: IF THIS BE SIN
London (BL)
P: D: Gregory Ratoff
S: (PLAY) Margaret Kennedy, Ilya Surgutchoff (AUTUMN)
SC: Gene Markey
Myrna Loy . . . .   Lady Cathy Brooke
Roger Livesey . . . .   Sir Brian Brooke
Peggy Cummins . . . .   Monica Brooke
Richard Greene . . . .   Michael Barclaigh
Elizabeth Allan . . . .   Lady Sybil
Gerard Heinz . . . .   Dr Thorvald
Jean Cadell . . . .   Nannie
G.H. Mulcaster . . . .   Simmons
Margaret Withers . . . .   May Drummond
Robert Atkins . . . .   George Drummond
Barry Jones . . . .   Arnold Cane
George Curzon . . . .   Selby
Wilfrid Hyde White . . . . . .   Mr Potts
Phyllis Stanley . . . .   Jane
ROMANCE Capri. KC cured of blindness learns his wife loves his partner.

11355
THE LAST DAYS OF DOLWYN (95) (U)
USA: WOMAN OF DOLWYN
London—BLPA (BL)
P: Anatole de Grunwald
D:S: Emlyn Williams
Edith Evans . . . .   Merri
Emlyn Williams . . . .   Rob
Richard Burton . . . .   Gareth
Anthony James . . . .   Dafydd
Barbara Couper . . . .   Lady Dolwyn
Allan Aynesworth . . . . . .   Lord Lancashire
Andrea Lea . . . .   Margaret
Hugh Griffith . . . .   Minister
Roddy Hughes . . . .   Caradoc
David Davies . . . .   Septimus
DRAMA Wales, 1892. Old woman tries to stop industrialist from flooding her valley village.

11356
MURDER AT THE WINDMILL (70) (A)
USA: MURDER AT THE BURLESQUE
Daniel Angel, Nat Cohen
D: S: Val Guest
Garry Marsh . . . .   Inspector
Jack Livesey . . . .   Vivian Van Damm
Jon Pertwee . . . .   Sgt
Diana Decker . . . .   Frankie
Donald Clive . . . .   Donald
Eliot Makeham . . . .   Gimpy
Jill Anstey . . . .   Patsy
Margot Johns . . . .   Box Office Girl
Genine Graham . . . .   Usherette
Peter Butterworth . . . . . .   PC
Jimmy Edwards; Robin Richmond; Christine Welsford; Johnnie Gale; Ron Perriam; Anita d'Ray; Johnnie McGregor; The Windmill Girls
MUSICAL Murder of revue patron in front row of stalls.

11357
BLUE SCAR (90) (U)
Outlook (BL)
P: William MacQuitty
D: S: Jill Craigie

Emrys Jones . . . .   Tom Thomas
Gwyneth Vaughan . . . .   Olwen Williams
Rachel Thomas . . . .   Gweneth Williams
Anthony Pendrell . . . .   Alfred Collins
Prysor Williams . . . .   Ted Williams
Madoline Thomas . . . .   Granny
Jack James . . . .   Dai Morgan
Kenneth Griffith . . . .   Thomas Williams
DRAMA Wales. Mine Manager finds that village life is better than the city.

JUN

11358
STOP PRESS GIRL (78) (U)
Aquila Films (GFD)
P: Donald B. Wilson
D: Michael Barry
S: T.J. Morrison, Basil Thomas
Sally Ann Howes . . . .   Jennifer Peters
Gordon Jackson . . . .   Jock Melville
Basil Radford . . . . .   Engine Driver/Bus Driver/
                                              Fred/Projectionist/Pilot
Naunton Wayne . .Fireman/Conductor/Fred's Boy
                                              Projectionist/Copilot
James Robertson Justice . .   Mr Peters
Sonia Holm . . . .   Angela Carew
Nigel Buchanan . . . .   Roy Fairfax
Joyce Barbour . . . .   Miss Peters
Julia Lang . . . .   Carole Saunders
Campbell Cotts . . . .   Mr Fairfax
Cyril Chamberlain . . . .   Johnnie
Michael Goodliffe . . . .   McPherson
Humphrey Lestocq . . . . . .   Commentator
Kenneth More . . . .   Sgt
Vincent Ball . . . .   Hero
Ann Valery . . . .   Heroine
FANTASY Everything mechanical stops working when a girl is near.

11359
MARRY ME (97) (A)
Gainsborough (GFD)
P: Betty Box
D: Terence Fisher
S: Lewis Gilbert, Denis Waldock
Derek Bond . . . .   Andrew Scott
Susan Shaw . . . .   Pat
Patrick Holt . . . .   Martin Roberts
Carol Marsh . . . .   Doris
David Tomlinson . . . .   David Haig
Zena Marshall . . . .   Marcelle
Guy Middleton . . . .   Sir Gordon Blake
Nora Swinburne . . . .   Enid Lawson
Brenda Bruce . . . .   Brenda
Denis O'Dea . . . .   Sanders
Jean Cadell . . . .   Hestor Parsons
Mary Jerrold . . . .   Emily Parsons
Yvonne Owen . . . .   Sue Carson
Alison Leggatt . . . .   Miss Beamish
Beatrice Varley . . . .   Mrs Perrins
Anthony Steel . . . .   Jack Harris
ROMANCE Four couples united by spinsters' marriage bureau.

11360
CHRISTOPHER COLUMBUS (104) *tech* (U)
Gainsborough (GFD)
P: A. Frank Bundy
D: David Macdonald
S: Cyril Roberts, Muriel & Sydney Box
N: Valentine Dyall
Frederick March . . . .   Christopher Columbus
Florence Eldridge . . . .   Queen Isabella
Francis L. Sullivan . . . .   de Bobadilla
Linden Travers . . . .   Beatriz de Peranza
Kathleen Ryan . . . .   Beatriz
Derek Bond . . . .   Diego de Arana
James Robertson Justice . . .   Martin Pinzon

Felix Aylmer . . . . **Father Perez**
Nora Swinburne . . . . Juana de Torres
Edward Rigby . . . . Pedro
Francis Lister . . . . King Ferdinand
Niall MacGinnis . . . . Juan de laCosta
Abraham Sofaer . . . . .Luis de Santangel
Dennis Vance . . . . Francisco Pinzon
Ralph Truman . . . . Captain
HISTORY 1492. Columbus eventually sails to discover the New World.

11361
WHISKY GALORE! (82) (A)
USA: TIGHT LITTLE ISLAND
Ealing (GFD)
AP: Monja Danischewsky
D: Alexander Mackendrick
S: (NOVEL) Compton Mackenzie
SC: Compton Mackenzie, Angus Macphail
N: Finlay Currie
Basil Radford . . . . Capt Paul Waggett
Joan Greenwood . . . . . . Peggy Maccroon
James Robertson Justice   Dr Maclaren
Gordon Jackson . . . . George Campbell
Wylie Watson . . . . Joseph Maccroon
Catherine Lacey . . . . Mrs Waggett
Jean Cadell . . . . Mrs Campbell
Bruce Seton . . . . Sgt Odd
Henry Mollison . . . . Mr Farquharson
Morland Graham . . . . The Biffer
John Gregson . . . . Sammy MacCodrum
Gabrielle Blunt . . . . Catriona Maccroon
Duncan Macrae . . . . Angus MacCormac
James Woodburn . . . . . .Roderick MacBurie
Compton Mackenzie . . . . . Capt Buncher
A.E. Matthews . . . . Col Linsey-Woolsey
COMEDY Hebrides, 1943. Islanders salvage shipwrecked whisky.

11362
KIND HEARTS AND CORONETS (106) (A)
Ealing (GFD)
AP: Michael Relph
D: Robert Hamer
S: (NOVEL) Roy Horniman (ISRAEL RANK)
SC: Robert Hamer, John Dighton
Dennis Price . . . . Louis Mazzini
Valerie Hobson . . . . Edith d'Ascoyne
Joan Greenwood . . . . . . Sibella
Alec Guinness . . . . Lord d'Ascoyne
Alec Guinness . . . . Henry d'Ascoyne
Alec Guinness . . . . Canon d'Ascoyne
Alec Guinness . . . . Generàl d'Ascoyne
Alec Guinness . . . . Admiral d'Ascoyne
Alec Guinness . . . . Ascoyne d'Ascoyne
Alec Guinness . . . . Duke of Chalfont
Alec Guinness . . . . Lady Agatha d'Ascoyne
Audrey Fildes . . . . Mama
Miles Malleson . . . . Hangman
Clive Morton . . . . Governor
Cecil Ramage . . . . Counsel
John Penrose . . . . Lionel
Hugh Griffith . . . . Lord High Steward
COMEDY Period. Disowned man kills eight relatives to inherit dukedom.

11363
NOW BARABBAS was a robber . . . (87) (A)
Anatole de Grunwald (WB) *reissue:*
1953 (22 mins cut)
D: Gordon Parry
S: (PLAY) William Douglas Home
SC: Gordon Parry
Richard Greene . . . . Tufnell
Cedric Hardwicke . . . . . . Governor
Kathleen Harrison . . . . Mrs Brown
Ronald Howard . . . . Roberts
Stephen Murray . . . . Chaplain

William Hartnell . . . . Warder Jackson
Beatrice Campbell . . . . Kitty
Richard Burton . . . . Paddy
Betty Ann Davies . . . . Rosie
Leslie Dwyer . . . . Brown
Alec Clunes . . . . Gale
Harry Fowler . . . . Smith
Kenneth More . . . . Spencer
Dora Bryan . . . . Winnie
Constance Smith . . . . Jean
Lily Kahn . . . . Woman
David Hannaford . . . . Erb Brown
CRIME Various episodes in the lives of prisoners.

11364
THE LAST WISH (34) (U)
Vandyke Pictures (GN)
P: Roger Proudlock
D: Sam Lee
Felix Deebank . . . . The Man
Jacqueline Hunt . . . . The Girl
DRAMA Paris. Englishman searches for son of exiled Frenchman.

11365
JOURNEY FOR JEREMY (33) (U)
GB Instructional (NR)
D: S: James Hill
Robin Netscher . . . . Jeremy
Audrey Manning . . . . . .
Katherine Page . . . . . .
Harry Douglas . . . . . .
CHILDREN Boy dreams he drives a Scots express train.

11366
MAYTIME IN MAYFAIR (96) *tech* (U)
Imperadio (BL)
P: D: Herbert Wilcox
S: Nicholas Phipps
Anna Neagle . . . . Eileen Grahame
Michael Wilding . . . . . . Michael Gore-Brown
Tom Walls . . . . Inspector
Peter Graves . . . . Darcy Davenport
Nicholas Phipps . . . . . . Sir Henry Hazelrigg
Thora Hird . . . . Janet
Michael Shepley . . . . Shepherd
Max Kirby . . . . Keats
Desmond Walter-Ellis . . . . . Shelley
Tom Walls jr . . . . PC
MUSICAL Manageress of dress shop and new owner thwart rivals.

11367
SAINTS AND SINNERS (85) (A)
London—BLPA (BL)
P: D: Leslie Arliss
S: Paul Vincent Carroll, Leslie Arliss
Kieron Moore . . . . Michael Kissane
Christine Norden . . . . Blanche
Sheila Manahan . . . . Sheila Flaherty
Michael Dolan . . . . Canon
Maire O'Neill . . . . Ma Murnaghan
Tom Dillon . . . . O'Brien
Noel Purcell . . . . Flaherty
Pamela Arliss . . . . Betty
Tony Quinn . . . . Berry
Eddie Byrne . . . . Norreys
Liam Redmond . . . . O'Driscoll
COMEDY Ireland. Ex-convict reveals true characters of those who condemned him.

JUL

11368
POET'S PUB (79) (U)
Aquila Films (GFD)
P: Donald B. Wilson
D: Frederick Wilson

S: (NOVEL) Eric Linklater
SC: Diana Morgan
Derek Bond . . . . .Saturday Keith
Rona Anderson . . . . Joanna Benbow
James Robertson Justice . . . Prof Benbow
Barbara Murray . . . . Nellie Bly
Leslie Dwyer . . . . Holly
Joyce Grenfell . . . . . . Miss Horsefell-Hughes
John McLaren . . . . Van Buren
Peter Croft . . . . Quentin Cotton
Fabia Drake . . . . Lady Cotton
Iris Hoey . . . . Lady Keith
Andrew Osborn . . . . Williams
Kay Cavendish . . . . Jean Forbes
Maurice Denham . . . . PC
COMEDY Poet takes over country inn and foils crooks seeking antique glove.

11369
WHICH WILL YOU HAVE ? (36) (U)
USA: BARABBAS THE ROBBER
GB Instructional (GFD)
P: Clifford Jeapes
D: Donald Taylor
S: S.N. Sedgewick
SC: Lawrence Barratt
Niall MacGinnis . . . . Barabbas
Betty Ann Davies . . . . Mary Magdalene
Elspeth March . . . . .
Henry Oscar . . . . . .
RELIGION Arrest and release of robber and Christ's crucifixion.

11370
HELTER SKELTER (84) (A)
Gainsborough (GFD)
P: Antony Darnborough
D: Ralph Thomas
S: Patrick Campbell
SC: Patrick Campbell, Jan Read, Gerard Bryant
Carol Marsh . . . . Susan Graham
David Tomlinson . . . . Nick Martin
Mervyn Johns . . . . Ernest Bennett
Peter Hammond . . . . Spencer Stone
Richard Hearne . . . . Prof Pastry
Peter Haddon . . . . Maj Basil Beagle
Geoffrey Sumner . . . . Humphrey Beagle
Henry Kendall . . . . . . Lord Bruce Carlton
John Pertwee . . . . Headwaiter/Charles II
Zena Marshall . . . . Giselle
Terry-Thomas . . . . Announcer
Jimmy Edwards . . . . .Dr James Edwards
Patricia Raine . . . . Amber
Colin Gordon . . . . Chadbeater Longwick
Judith Furse . . . . Mrs Martin
Wilfrid Hyde White . . . Dr B. Jekyll/Mr Hyde
Harry Secombe . . . . Alf
Robert Lamouret; Shirl Conway; Glynis Johns; Valentine Dyall; Dennis Price
COMEDY Mother-ridden radio detective tries to cure heiress's hiccups. (Includes extracts from WOULD YOU BELIEVE IT, 1929.)

11371
DON'T EVER LEAVE ME (85) (U)
Triton Films (GFD)
P: Sydney Box
D: Arthur Crabtree
S: (NOVEL) Anthony Armstrong
(THE WIDE GUY)
SC: Robert Westerby
Jimmy Hanley . . . . Jack Denton
Petula Clark . . . . Sheila Farlane
Hugh Sinclair . . . . Michael Farlane
Linden Travers . . . . Mary Lamont
Edward Rigby . . . . Harry Denton
Anthony Newley . . . . Jimmy Knowles
Barbara Murray . . . . Joan Robbins
Brenda Bruce . . . . Miss Smith

Maurice Denham . . . . Mr Knowles
Frederick Piper . . . . Max Marshall
Sandra Dorne . . . . Miss Baines
Antony Steel . . . . Harris
Patricia Dainton . . . . Girl
COMEDY Old crook and grandson kidnap
actress's daughter who then refuses to be
ransomed.

11372
PRIVATE ANGELO (106) (A)
Pilgrim Pictures (ABP)
P: Peter Ustinov
D: Peter Ustinov, Michael Anderson
S: (NOVEL) Eric Linklater
SC: Peter Ustinov, Mcihael Anderson
Godfrey Tearle . . . . . . Count Piccolo-Grando
Maria Denis . . . . Lucrezia
Peter Ustinov . . . . Angelo
James Robertson Justice . . . . .Feste
Robin Bailey . . . . Simon Telfer
Marjorie Rhodes . . . . Countess
Moyna McGill . . . . Marchesa Dolce
Harry Locke . . . . Cpl Trivet
Bill Shine . . . . Col Michael
John Harvey . . . . Cpl McCunn
COMEDY Italy. Count's cowardly soldier son
helps British army pursue retreating Germans.

11373
VENGEANCE IS MINE (59) (A)
Cullimore-Arbeid (Eros)
P: Ben Arbeid
D: S: Alan Cullimore
Valentine Dyall . . . . Charles Heywood
Anne Forth . . . . Linda Farrell
Richard Goolden . . . . Sammy Parsons
Sam Kydd . . . . Stacey
Arthur Brander . . . . Richard Kemp
Alex Wright . . . . Doctor
Ethel Coleridge . . . . Caretaker
CRIME Man with six months to live hires
assassin to kill him.

11374
MELODY CLUB (63) (A)
Tempean Films (Eros)
P: Robert Baker, Monty Berman
D: Monty Berman
S: Carl Nystrom
Terry-Thomas . . . . Freddy Forrester
Gwyneth Vaughan . . . . Jean
Len Lowe . . . . Tony
Bill Lowe . . . . Birdie
Michael Balfour . . . . Max
COMEDY Inept tec catches crooks in
nightclub.

11375
NO WAY BACK (72) (A)
Concanen Recordings (Eros)
P: Derrick de Marney
D: Stefan Osiecki
S: (STORY) Thomas Burke (BERYL AND
THE CROUCHER)
SC: Stefan Osiecki, Derrick de Marney
Terence de Marney . . . . . . Croucher
Eleanor Summerfield . . . . . Beryl
Jack Raine . . . . Joe Sleet
John Salew . . . . Sammy Linkman
Shirley Quentin . . . . Sally
Denys Val Norton . . . . Harry
Gerald Lawson . . . . Mike
Tommy McGovern . . . . . . Himself
CRIME Gangster's girl loves one-eyed boxer
who is framed for robbery.

11376
OLD MOTHER RILEY'S NEW VENTURE
(79) (U)
Harry Reynolds (Renown) *reissue*: 1953,

MOTHER RILEY'S NEW VENTURE
D: John Harlow
S: Con West, Jack Marks
Arthur Lucan . . . . Mrs Riley
Kitty McShane . . . . Kitty Riley
Chili Bouchier . . . . Cora
Maureen Riscoe . . . . Mabel
Willer Neal . . . . David
Sebastian Cabot . . . . Potentate
Wilfred Babbage . . . . Major
John le Mesurier . . . . Karl
C. Denier Warren . . . . Hillick
COMEDY Dishwasher becomes hotelier and is
framed for gem theft.

11377
OBSESSION (98) (A)
USA: THE HIDDEN ROOM
Independent Sovereign (GFD)
P: Nat A. Bronsten
D: Edward Dmytryk
S: (NOVEL) Alec Coppel (A MAN ABOUT
A DOG)
SC: Alec Coppel
Robert Newton . . . . Dr Clive Riordan
Sally Gray . . . . Storm Riordan
Naunton Wayne . . . . Supt Finsbury
Phil Brown . . . . Bill Kronin
Olga Lindo . . . . Mrs Humphreys
Ronald Adam . . . . Clubman
James Harcourt . . . . Aitkin
Allan Jeayes . . . . Clubman
Russell Waters . . . . Detective
CRIME Doctor plans to kill his wife's lover in
an acid bath.

11378
MADNESS OF THE HEART (105) (A)
Two Cities (GFD)
P: Richard Wainwright
D: SC: Charles Bennett
S: (NOVEL) Flora Sandstrom
Margaret Lockwood . . . . . . Lydia Garth
Maxwell Reed . . . . Joseph Rondolet
Kathleen Byron . . . . Veritee Faimont
Paul Dupuis . . . . Paul de Vandiere
Thora Hird . . . . Rosa
Raymond Lovell . . . . . . Comte de Vandiere
Maurice Denham . . . . Dr Simon Blake
David Hutcheson . . . . Max Ffoliott
Cathleen Nesbitt . . . . . . Mother Superior
Peter Illing . . . . Dr Matthieu
Jack McNaughton . . . . Attendant
Pamela Stirling . . . . Felicite
Marie Burke . . . . Comtesse de Vandiere
Marie Ault . . . .
Kynaston Reeves . . . . . .Sir Robert Hammond
ROMANCE Blind woman incurs rival's hatred
when she weds Comte's son.

11379
TROTTIE TRUE (96) *tech* (A)
USA: GAY LADY
Two Cities (GFD)
P: Hugh Stewart
D: Brian Desmond Hurst
S: (NOVEL) Caryl Brahms, S.J. Simon
SC: C. Denis Freeman
Jean Kent . . . . Trottie True
James Donald . . . . . . Lord Digby Landon
Hugh Sinclair . . . . .Maurice Beckenham
Lana Morris . . . . Bouncie Barrington
Andrew Crawford . . . . Skid Skinner
Bill Owen . . . . Joe Jugg
Harcourt Williams . . . . . Duke of Wellwater
Michael Medwin . . . . Marquis Monty
Hattie Jacques . . . . Daisy Delaware
Joan Young . . . . Mrs True
Heather Thatcher . . . . .Angela Platt-Brown
Mary Hinton . . . . Duchess
Francis de Wolff . . . .
Harold Scott . . . . Mr True

Dilys Laye . . . . Trottie (child)
Daphne Anderson. . . . . . . Bertha
Carol Lesley . . . . Clare
ROMANCE Edwardian. Gaiety girl weds Peer
and flouts conventions.

11380
TRAIN OF EVENTS (88) (A)
Ealing (GFD)
AP: Michael Relph
D: Sidney Cole, Charles Crichton,
Basil Dearden
S: Basil Dearden, T.E.B. Clarke, Angus Macphail
Ronald Millar
Valerie Hobson . . . . Stella Hilary
Jack Warner . . . . Jim Hardcastle
John Clements . . . . Raymond Hilary
Irina Baronova . . . . Irma Norozova
Susan Shaw . . . . Doris Hardcastle
Joan Dowling . . . . Ella
Patric Doonan . . . . Ron Stacey
Mary Morris . . . . Louise Mason
Gladys Henson . . . . Mrs Hardcastle
Miles Malleson . . . . Johnson
John Gregson . . . . Malcolm Murray-Bruce
Peter Finch . . . . Philip Mason
Laurence Payne . . . . Richard
Olga Lindo . . . . Mrs Bailey
Neal Arden . . . . Compere
Lyndon Brook . . . . Actor
DRAMA Four stories about victims of train
crash.

11381
THE LOST PEOPLE (88) (A)
Gainsborough (GFD)
P: Gordon Wellesley
D: Bernard Knowles, Muriel Box
S: (PLAY) Bridget Boland (COCKPIT)
SC: Bridget Boland, Muriel Box
Dennis Price . . . . Capt Ridley
Mai Zetterling Lili
Richard Attenborough . . . . . .Jan
Siobhan McKenna . . . . Marie
Maxwell Reed . . . . Peter
William Hartnell . . . . Sgt Barnes
Gerard Heinz . . . . Professor
Zena Marshall . . . . Anna
Olaf Pooley . . . . Milosh
Harcourt Williams . . . . Priest
Philo Hauser . . . . Draja
Jill Balcon . . . . Rebecca
Grey Blake . . . . Capt Saunders
Marcel Poncin . . . . Duval
WAR British captain and sgt try to keep peace
among displaced persons in German theatre.

11382
DEAR MR PROHACK (91) (U)
Pinewood Films-Wessex (GFD)
P: Ian Dalrymple
D: Thornton Freeland
S: (PLAY) Edward Knoblock (NOVEL)
Arnold Bennett (MR PROHACK)
SC: Ian Dalrymple, Donald Bull
Cecil Parker . . . . Arthur Prohack
Glynis Johns . . . . Mimi Warburton
Hermione Baddeley . . . . . . Eve Prohack
Dirk Bogarde . . . . Charles Prohack
Sheila Sim . . . . Mary Prohack
Heather Thatcher . . . . Lady Maslam
Frances Waring . . . . Nursie
Charles Goldner . . . . Manservant
Campbell Cotts . . . . Sir Paul Spinner
Denholm Elliott . . . . Ozzie Morfrey
Russell Waters . . . . Cartwright
Henry Edwards . . . . Sir Digby Bunce
Frederick Valk . . . . Dr Veiga
James Hayter . . . . Carrell Quire
Bryan Forbes . . . . Tony
Jon Pertwee . . . . Plover

Ada Reeve . . . . Mrs Griggs
COMEDY Treasury official is incapable of handling his own inheritance.

11383
THE INTERRUPTED JOURNEY (80) (A)
Valiant Films (BL)
P: Anthony Havelock-Allan
D: Dan Birt
S: Michael Pertwee
Valerie Hobson . . . . Carol North
Richard Todd . . . . John North
Christine Norden . . . . Susan Wilding
Tom Walls . . . . Mr Clayton
Ralph Truman . . . . Insp Waterson
Vida Hope . . . . Miss Marchmont
Alexander Gauge . . . . Jerves Wilding
Dora Bryan . . . . Waitress
Arnold Ridley . . . . Saunders
CRIME Married author proves he did not kill mistress in train crash.

11384
A TOUCH OF SHAMROCK (30) (U)
Delman (NR)
D: Horace Shepherd
Cavan O'Connor . . . . The Vagabond
MUSICAL Irish singer wanders through Hertfordshire.

11385
THE ONE CYLINDER WONDER (15) (U)
Falcon Films (Arrow)
COMEDY Drunkard's dream of ancient motor cycle.

11386
CONSPIRATOR (87) (U)
MGM British
P: Ben Goetz, Arthur Hornblow jr
D: Victor Saville
S: (NOVEL) Humphrey Slater
CS: Gerard Fairlie, Sally Benson
Robert Taylor . . . . Michael Curragh
Elizabeth Taylor . . . . Melinda Greyton
Robert Flemyng . . . . . . Capt Gugh Ladholme
Harold Warrender . . . . . . Col Hammerbrook
Honor Blackman . . . . Joyce
Marjorie Fielding . . . . Aunt Jessica
Marie Ney . . . . Lady Pennistone
Thora Hird . . . . Broaders
Jack Allen . . . . Raglan
Wilfrid Hyde White . . . . . Lord Pennistone
Helen Haye . . . . Lady Witheringham
Karel Stepanek . . . . Radek
Cyril Smith . . . . Inspector
CRIME Guards officer is ordered to kill his wife when she discovers he is communist spy.

11387
CELIA (67) (A)
Exclusive
P: Anthony Hinds
D: Francis Searle
S: (RADIO SERIAL) Edward J. Mason
SC: Francis Searle, Edward J. Mason, A.R. Rawlinson
Hy Hazell . . . . Celia
Bruce Lister . . . . Larry Peters
John Bailey . . . . Lester Martin
James Raglan . . . . Insp Parker
Elsie Wagstaffe . . . . Aunt Nora
Lockwood West . . . . Dr Cresswell
CRIME Actress poses as her aunt to prove her step-uncle is poisoner.

SEP

11388
THE THIRD MAN (104) (A)
London—BLPA (BL)
P: David O. Selznick, Alexander Korda

D: Carol Reed
SC: Graham Greene
S: (NOVEL) Graham Greene
Joseph Cotten . . . . Holly Martins
Alida Valli . . . . Anna Schmidt
Orson Welles . . . . Harry Lime
Trevor Howard . . . . Maj Galloway
Paul Hoerbiger . . . . Porter
Ernst Deutsch . . . . Baron Kurtz
Erich Ponto . . . . Dr Winkel
Siegfried Brever . . . . Poposcu
Bernard Lee . . . . Sgt Paine
Wilfrid Hyde White . . . . Crabbin
Paul Hardtmuth . . . . Porter
CRIME Vienna. Novelist helps authorities seek black marketeer supposed dead. (BFA: Best British Film 1949; DEFA: 1949; Top Money-maker: 1949.)

11389
WHAT A CARRY ON! (94) (U)
Film Studios Manchester (Mancunian)
P: D: John E. Blakeley
S: Anthony Toner
Jimmy Jewel . . . . Jimmy Jervis
Ben Warriss . . . . Ben Watts
Josef Locke . . . . Sgt Locke
Terry Randall . . . . Cpl Joan Watts
Anthony Pendrell . . . . . . Capt Derek Whitfield
Kitty Blewett . . . . Maid
Eva Eacott . . . . Daisybell
COMEDY Episodic misadventures of clumsy soldiers. (Extract as short: JOINING THE ARMY, 1953.)

11390
THE CHILTERN HUNDREDS (84) (U)
USA: THE AMAZING MR BEECHAM
Two Cities (GFD)
P: George H. Brown
D: John Paddy Carstairs
S: (PLAY) William Douglas Home
SC: William Douglas Home, Patrick Kirwan
Cecil Parker . . . . Benjamin Beecham
A.E. Matthews . . . . Lord Lister
David Tomlinson . . . . Lord Tony Pym
Lana Morris . . . . Bessie Sykes
Helen Backlin . . . . June Farrell
Marjorie Fielding . . . . . . Lady Molly
Tom Macaulay . . . . Jack Cleghorn
Joyce Carey . . . . Lady Caroline
Charles Cullum . . . . Colonel
Anthony Steel . . . . Adjutant
COMEDY Tory butler stands for election against employer's son.

OCT

11391
DIAMOND CITY (90) (U)
Gainsborough (GFD)
P: A. Frank Bundy
D: David Macdonald
S: Roger Bray
SC: Roger Bray, Roland Pertwee
David Farrar . . . . Stafford Parker
Honor Blackman . . . . Mary Hart
Diana Dors . . . . Dora Bracken
Niall Macginnis . . . . Muller
Andrew Crawford . . . . . . David Raymond
Mervyn Johns . . . . Hart
Phyllis Monkman . . . . . . Ma Bracken
Bill Owen . . . . Pinto
Hal Osmond . . . . Brandy Bill
Philo Hauser . . . . Plet Quleman
John Blythe . . . . Izzy Cohen
Reginald Tate . . . . Longden
Ronald Adam . . . . Robert Southey
ADVENTURE Africa, 1870. Gambling miner brings law to diamond diggings.

11392
DARK SECRET (85) (A)
Nettlefold (Butcher) *reissue:* 1952 (10 mins cut)
P: Ernest G. Roy
D: Maclean Rogers
S: (PLAY) Mordaunt Shairp
(CRIME AT BLOSSOMS)
SC: A.R. Rawlinson, Moie Charles
Dinah Sheridan . . . . Valerie Merryman
Emrys Jones . . . . Chris Merryman
Irene Handl . . . . "Woody" Woodman
Hugh Pryse . . . . A Very Late Visitor
Barbara Couper . . . . Mrs Barrington
Percy Marmont . . . . Vicar
Geoffrey Sumner . . . . Jack Farrell
Mackenzie Ward . . . . Artist
Charles Hawtrey . . . . Arthur Figson
John Salew . . . . Mr Barrington
George Merritt . . . . Mr Lumley
Stanley Vilven . . . . Mr Woodman
CRIME Ex-pilot's wife obsessed by murder of their cottage's previous tenant.

11393
THE HASTY HEART (107) (U)
ABPC (ABP)
P: D: Vincent Sherman
S: (PLAY) John Patrick
SC: Ronald MacDougall
Ronald Reagan . . . . Yank
Patricia Neal . . . . Sister Margaret
Richard Todd . . . . Cpl Lachlan McLachlan
Anthony Nicholls . . . . . . Lt-Col Dunn
Howard Marion Crawford . . . . Tommy
Ralph Michael . . . . Kiwi
Orlando Martins . . . . Blossom
Alfie Bass . . . . Orderly
John Sherman . . . . Digger
WAR Burma, 1945. Dying Scots soldier learns meaning of friendship. (DMNFA: 1950; PGAA: 1950; Extract in ELSTREE STORY, 1952.)

11394
LANDFALL (88) (U)
ABPC (ABP)
P: Victor Skutezky
D: Ken Annakin
S: (NOVEL) Nevil Shute
SC: Talbot Jennings, Gilbert Gunn, Anne Burnaby
Michael Denison . . . . Rick
Patricia Plunkett . . . . Mona Stevens
Kathleen Harrison . . . . . . Mrs Stevens
David Tomlinson . . . . Binks
Joan Dowling . . . . Miriam
Maurice Denham . . . . W/C Hewitt
A.E. Matthews . . . . Warden
Denis O'Dea . . . . Capt Burnaby
Margaretta Scott . . . . Mrs Burnaby
Sebastian Shaw . . . . W/C Dickens
Nora Swinburne . . . . Admiral's Wife
Charles Victor . . . . Mr Stevens
Laurence Harvey . . . . P/O Hooper
Paul Carpenter . . . . F/O Morgan
Frederick Leister . . . . Admiral
Hubert Gregg . . . . L/C Dale
Walter Hudd . . . . Prof Legge
Margaret Barton . . . . Sister
Teddy Foster and his Band
WAR 1940. Girl proves test pilot is mistaken in thinking he accidentally sank British submarine.

11395
UNDER CAPRICORN (116) (A) *tech*
Capricorn—Transatlantic (WB)
P: Sydney M. Bernstein, Alfred Hitchcock
D: Alfred Hitchcock
S: (NOVEL) Helen Simpson (PLAY)
John Colton, Margaret Linden

SC: James Bridie, Hume Cronyn
Ingrid Bergman . . . . . . Lady Henrietta Flusky
Joseph Cotten . . . . Sam Flusky
Michael Wilding . . . . .Hon Charles Adare
Margaret Leighton . . . . Milly
Cecil Parker . . . . Governor
Denis O'Dea . . . . Corrigan
Jack Watling . . . . Winter
Harcourt Williams . . . . Coachman
John Ruddock . . . . Mr Potter
Ronald Adam . . . . Mr Riggs
Francis de Wolff . . . . Commissioner
G.H. Mulcaster . . . . Dr McAllister
Olive Sloane . . . . Sal
Maureen Delany . . . . Flo
ROMANCE Australia, 1830. Housekeeper
tries to ruin dipsomaniac Lady's marriage to
rich ex-convict.

11396
THE ADVENTURES OF PC 49 — THE CASE
OF THE GUARDIAN ANGEL (67) (A)
Exclusive—Hammer
P: Anthony Hinds
D: Godfrey Grayson
S: (RADIO SERIES) Alan Stranks
SC: Alan Stranks, Vernon Harris
Hugh Latimer . . . . . . Archibald Berkeley-
Willoughby
John Penrose . . . . Barney
Annette Simmonds. . . . . . . Carrots
Pat Nye . . . . Ma Benson
Patricia Cutts . . . . Joan
Arthur Brander . . . . Insp Wilson
Eric Phillips . . . . Sgt Wright
Martin Benson . . . . Skinny
CRIME PC Poses as gangster to catch lorry
thieves.

11397
CHILDREN OF CHANCE (99) (A)
Ortus Films (BL)
P: Ludovico Toeplitz, John Sutro
D: Luigi Zampa
S: Piero Tellini
SC: Piero Tellini, Michael Medwin
Patricia Medina . . . . Agostina
Manning Whiley . . . . Don Andrea
Yvonne Mitchell . . . . Australia
Barbara Everest . . . . Francesca
Eliot Makeham . . . . Vicar
George Woodbridge . . . . . . Butcher
Frank Tickle . . . . Mayor
Eric Pohlmann . . . . Sgt
Edward Lexy . . . . Doctor
Carlo Giustini . . . . Marco
DRAMA Ischia. Priest spends girl's black
market profits on home for bastards.

11398
GIVE US THIS DAY (120) (A)
USA: SALT TO THE DEVIL
Plantaganet (GFD)
P: Rod E. Geiger, Nat A. Bronsten
D: Edward Dmytryk
S: (NOVEL) Pietro di Donato
(CHRIST IN CONCRETE)
SC: Ben Barzman, John Penn
Sam Wanamaker . . . . Geremio
Lea Padovani . . . . Annunzia
Kathleen Ryan . . . . Kathleen
Bonar Colleano . . . . Julio
Charles Goldner . . . . Luigi
Bill Sylvester . . . . Giovanni
Nino Pastellides . . . . The Lucy
Philo Hauser . . . . Head of Pig
Sidney James . . . . Mundin
Karel Stepanek . . . . Jaroslav
Ina de la Haye . . . . Katerina
Rosalie Crutchley . . . . Julio's Wife
Ronan O'Casey . . . . Bastian

DRAMA Brooklyn. Italian bricklayer dies
attempting to give his wife a home of her own.

11399
ARTFUL DODGERS (39)(A)
Dresden (Adelphi)
D: Renault Capes
S: Hilary Long
Gillian Maude
Richard Foate
CRIME Various frauds and confidence tricks.

NOV
11400
SKIMPY IN THE NAVY (84) (A)
Advance (Adelphi)
P: David Dent
D: Stafford Dickens
S: Aileen Burke, Leone Stuart, Hal Monty
Hal Monty . . . . Skimpy Carter
Max Bygraves . . . . Tommy Anderson
Avril Angers. . . . . Sheila
Les Ritchie . . . . Lickett
Chris Sheen . . . . Joe
Vic Ford . . . . Spud
COMEDY Friends join navy to seek treasure on
Mediterranean island.

11401
TORMENT (78) (A)
USA: PAPER GALLOWS
Advance (Adelphi)
P: Robert Jordan Hill, John Guillermin
D: S: John Guillermin
Dermot Walsh . . . . Cliff Brandon
Rona Anderson . . . . Joan
John Bentley . . . . Jim Brandon
Michael Martin-Harvey . . . . . .Curley Wilson
Valentine Dunn . . . . Mrs Crier
Dilys Laye . . . . Violet Crier
CRIME Jealous novelist tries to put perfect
murder plot into operation.

11402
THE SPIDER AND THE FLY (95) (A)
Pinewood-Mayflower (GFD)
P: Maxwell Setton, Aubrey Baring
D: Robert Hamer
S: Robert Westerby
Eric Portman . . . . Insp Fernand Maubert
Guy Rolfe . . . . Philippe de Ledocq
Nadia Gray . . . . Madeleine Saincaize
Edward Chapman . . . . War Minister
Maurice Denham . . . . .Col de la Roche
George Cole . . . . Marc
John Carol . . . . Jean/Alfred Louis
Harold Lang . . . . Belfort
May Hallatt . . . . Monique
James Hayter . . . . Mayor
Jeremy Spenser . . . . Jacques
Sebastian Cabot . . . . Inspector
Natasha Sokolova . . . . Nicole Porte
CRIME France, 1914. Inspector frees thief to
crack German safe in Berne.

11403
A RUN FOR YOUR MONEY (85) (A)
Ealing (GFD)
AP: Leslie Norman
D: Charles Frend
S: Clifford Evans
SC: Charles Frend, Leslie Norman,
Richard Hughes, Diana Morgan
Donald Houston . . . . Dai Jones
Moira Lister . . . . Jo
Alec Guiness . . . . Whimple
Meredith Edwards . . . . Twm Jones
Hugh Griffith . . . . Huw Price
Clive Morton . . . . Editor
Leslie Perrins. . . . . Barney
Joyce Grenfell . . . . Mrs Pargiter
Edward Rigby . . . . Beefeater

Julie Milton . . . . Bronwen
Peter Edwards . . . . Davies
Dorothy Bramhall . . . . Jane Benson
Desmond Walter-Ellis . . . . Announcer
Mackenzie Ward . . . . Photographer
Patric Doonan . . . . Conductor
COMEDY Welsh miners win £220 and visit
London to see rugby match.

11404
MEET SIMON CHERRY (67) (A)
Hammer (Ex)
P: Anthony Hinds
D: Godfrey Grayson
S: (RADIO SERIES) Gale Pedrick
(MEET THE REV)
SC: Gale Pedrick, Godfrey Grayson,
A.R. Rawlinson
Zena Marshall . . . . Lisa Colville
John Bailey . . . . Henry Dantry
Hugh Moxey . . . . .Rev Simon Cherry
Anthony Forwood . . . . Alan Colville
Ernest Butcher . . . . Young
Jeanette Tregarthen . . . . . Monica Harling
Courtney Hope . . . . Lady Harling
Arthur Lovegrove . . . . Charlie
CRIME Cleric proves invalid woman died of
heart failure.

11405
TINKER (70) (U)
Citizen (Eros)
P: S: Herbert Marshall, Alfredda Brilliant
D: Herbert Marshall
Derek Smith . . . . Tinker
DRAMA Durham. Gypsy boy becomes mining
trainee and flees when framed for theft.

DEC
11406
THE ADVENTURES OF JANE (55) (A)
New World—Keystone (Eros)
P: Edward G. Whiting
D: Edward G. Whiting, Alf Goulding
S: (COMIC STRIP) Norman Pett
SC: Edward Whiting, Alf Goulding, Con West
Christabel Leighton-Porter . . Jane
Stanelli . . . . Hotelier
Michael Hogarth . . . . Tom Hawke
Wally Patch . . . . Customs Officer
Ian Colin . . . . Capt Cleaver
Sonya O'Shea . . . . Ruby
Peter Butterworth . . . . Drunk
Sebastian Cabot . . . . Traveller
COMEDY Phoney captain smuggles diamond
in actress's bracelet.

11407
THE ROMANTIC AGE (86) (A)
USA: NAUGHTY ARLETTE
Pinnacle Productions (GFD)
P: Edward Dryhurst, Eric l'Epine Smith
D: Edmond T. Greville
S: (NOVEL) Serge Weber
(LYCEE DES JEAUNES FILLES)
SC: Edward Dryhurst, Peggy Barwell
Mai Zetterling . . . . Arlette
Hugh Williams . . . . Arnold Dickson
Margot Grahame . . . . Helen Dickson
Petula Clark . . . . Julie Dickson
Carol Marsh . . . . Patricia
Raymond Lovell . . . . Hedges
Paul Dupuis . . . . Henri Sinclair
Margaret Barton . . . . Bessie
Marie Ney . . . . Miss Hallam
Mark Daly . . . . Withers
Judith Furse . . . . Miss Adams
Betty Impey . . . . Jill
Adrienne Corri . . . . Nora
ROMANCE Art teacher falls for daughter's
flirty French classmate.

11408
BOYS IN BROWN (85) (A)
Gainsborough (GFD)
P: Anthony Darnborough
D: SC: Montgomery Tully
S: (PLAY) Reginald Beckwith

Jack Warner	Governor
Richard Attenborough	Jackie Knowles
Dirk Bogarde	Alfie Rawlins
Jimmy Hanley	Bill Foster
Barbara Murray	Kitty Hurst
Patrick Holt	Tigson
Andrew Crawford	Casey
Thora Hird	Mrs Knowles
Graham Payn	Plato Cartwright
Michael Medwin	Sparrow
John Blythe	Bossy
Alfie Bass	Basher
Cyril Chamberlain	Johnson

CRIME Borstal governor tries to reform teenage delinquents.

11409
THE ROCKING HORSE WINNER (90) (A)
Two Cities (GFD)
P: John Mills
D: SC: Anthony Pelissier
S: (STORY) D.H. Lawrence

John Mills	Bassett
Valerie Hobson	Hester Grahame
John Howard Davies	Paul Grahame
Ronald Squire	Oscar Cresswell
Hugh Sinclair	Richard Grahame
Charles Goldner	Mr Tsaldouris
Susan Richards	Nannie
Cyril Smith	Bailiff
Antony Holles	Bowler Hat

FANTASY Boy who predicts winners while riding horse is driven to death by his greedy mother.

11410
SCHOOL FOR RANDLE (89) (A)
Film Studios Manchester (Mancunian)
P: D: John E. Blakeley

Frank Randle	Flatfoot Mason
Dan Young	Clarence
Alec Pleon	Blackhead
Terry Randal	Betty Andrews
Maudie Edwards	Bella Donna
John Singer	Ted Parker
Hilda Bayley	Mrs Andrews
Jimmy Clitheroe	Jimmy
Elsa Tee	Miss Weston

COMEDY Schoolgirl does not know the janitor is her father. (Extracts released as shorts: TEACHER'S PEST (1950); THE THREE WHO—FLUNGS (1950); BELLA'S BIRTHDAY (1950).)

11411
THE STRANGERS CAME (71) (A)
USA: YOU CAN'T FOOL AN IRISHMAN
Vandyke (GN)
P: Roger Proudlock, Michael Healy
D: Alfred Travers
S: Michael Healy
SC: Michael Healy, Alfred Travers, Tommy Duggan

Tommy Duggan	Stefan Wurlitz
Shirl Conway	Jane McDonald
Shamus Locke	Tom O'Flaherty
Tony Quinn	Hotelier
Reed de Rouen	Manager
Eve Eacott	Dona del Monte
Josephine Fitzgerald	Widow McDermott
Sheila Martin	Mary Laffey
Geoffrey Goodheart	Joe Bantham

COMEDY Dublin. American film director schemes to obtain finance from mean millionaire.

11412
A MATTER OF MURDER (59) (A)
Vandyke (GN)
P: Roger Proudlock, Sam Lee
D: S: John Gilling

Maureen Riscoe	Julie McKelvin
John Barry	Geoffrey Dent
Charles Clapham	Col Peabody
Ivan Craig	Tony
Ian Fleming	Insp McKelvin
John le Mesurier	Ginter
Peter Madden	Sgt Bex

CRIME Embezzling bank clerk in hiding is framed for killing woman.

11413
HIGH JINKS IN SOCIETY (78) (U)
Advent (Adelphi)
P: S: Robert Jordan Hill, John Guillermin
D: Robert Jordan Hill

Ben Wrigley	Ben
Barbara Shaw	Angela
Moore Marriott	Grandpa
Basil Appleby	Hector
Netta Westcott	Lady Barr-Nunn
Michael Ward	Watkins
Peter Gawthorne	Jenkins

COMEDY Lady hires window cleaner to save jewels from thieves.

11414
TRAVELLER'S JOY (78) (A)
Gainsborough (GFD)
P: Anthony Darnborough
D: Ralph Thomas
S: (PLAY) Arthur Macrae
SC: Allan Mackinnon, Bernard Quayle

John McCullum	Reggie Pelham
Googie Withers	Bumble Pelham
Yolande Donlan	Lil Fowler
Maurice Denham	Fowler
Geoffrey Sumner	Lord Tilbrook
Colin Gordon	Tony Wright
Dora Bryan	Eva
Gerard Heinz	Helstrom
Anthony Forwood	Mick Rafferty

COMEDY Sweden. Divorced couple try to raise money when their travel allowances are spent.

11415
THREE MEN AND A GIRL (82) *retitled:*
GOLDEN ARROW
Anatole de Gurnwald (Renown)
D: Gordon Parry
S: Anatole de Grunwald
SC: Paul Darcy, Sid Colin

Burgess Meredith	Dick
Jean-Pierre Aumont	Andre Marchand
Richard Murdoch	David Felton
Paula Valenska	Suzy/Sonia/Hedy
Kathleen Harrison	Isobel
Karel Stepanek	Schroeder
Edward Lexy	Colonel
Hilda Bayley	Mrs Felton
Ernest Jay	Mr Felton
Natasha Parry	Betty FElton
Sandra Dorne	Club Girl
Colin Gordon	Connolly
Philip Slessor	Himself

ROMANCE Riviera; Berlin; Twickenham. Three men daydream a girl is model, club singer, and film star.

11416
ALGERNON BLACKWOOD STORIES
(series) (A)
Rayant Pictures (20)
P: D: Anthony Gilkison
S: (STORIES) Algernon Blackwood

Algernon Blackwood	Himself

11417
1—CONFESSION (16)

11418
2—THE REFORMATION OF ST JULES (12)

11419
3—THE RENDEZVOUS (12)

11420
4—THE DRESS REHEARSAL (12)

11421
5—LOCK OUR DOOR (12)

11422
6—TWO OF A KIND (12)
DRAMA Author tells stories of crime, murder and mystery.

1950

JAN

11423
MISS PILGRIM'S PROGRESS (82) (U)
Angel Productions (GN)
P: Daniel M. Angel, Nat Cohen
D:S: Val Guest
Michael Rennie . . . . Bob Thane
Yolande Donlan. . . . . Laramie Pilgrim
Garry Marsh . . . . Mayor
Emrys Jones . . . . Vicar
Reginald Beckwith . . . . Mr Jenkins
Helena Pickard . . . . Mrs Jenkins
Jon Pertwee . . . . .Postman Perkins
Richard Littledale . . . . Mr Thane
Bruce Belfrage . . . . Manager
Valentine Dyall . . . . Superintendent
Peter Butterworth . . . . Jonathan
Avril Angers . . . . Factory Girl
COMEDY American exchange worker in
factory saves village from Planning Act.

11424
THE TWENTY QUESTIONS MURDER
MYSTERY (95) (A)
Pax-Pendennis (GN) *reissue:* 1952,
MURDER ON THE AIR (Ren)
P: Steven Pallos, Victor Katona
D: Paul Stein
S: Charles Leeds
SC: Patrick Kirwan, Victor Katona
Robert Beatty . . . . Bob Beacham
Rona Anderson . . . . Mary Game
Clifford Evans . . . . Tom Harmon
Edward Lexy . . . . Insp Charlton
Olga Lindo . . . . Olive Tavy
Frederick Leister . . . . Commissioner
Harold Scott . . . . Maurice Emery KC
Wally Patch . . . . Tiny White
Meadows White . . . . Frederick Tavy
Kynaston Reeves . . . . . Gen Maitland Webb
Stewart MacPherson; Daphne Padel;
Jack Train; Richard Dimbleby; Jeanne de
Casalis; Norman Hackforth
CRIME Reporter unmasks killer who sends
clues to radio quiz show.

11425
THE CURE FOR LOVE (98) (U)
London-Island (BL)
P:D: Robert Donat
S: (PLAY) Walter Greenwood
SC: Walter Greenwood, Robert Donat,
Alexander Shaw, Albert Fennell
Robert Donat . . . . Jack Hardacre
Renee Asherson . . . . Milly
Marjorie Rhodes . . . . Mrs Hardacre
Charles Victor . . . . Harry
Dora Bryan. . . . . Jenny Jenkins
Thora Hird . . . . Mrs Dorbell
Gladys Henson . . . . Mrs Jenkins
John Stratton . . . . Sam
Francis Wignall . . . . Claude
COMEDY Lancs, 1942. Affianced soldier
falls for cockney evacuee.

11426
BAIT (73) (A)
Advance (Adelphi)
D: Frank Richarson
S: (PLAY) Frank Richardson
SC: Mary Bendetta, Francis Miller
Diana Napier . . . . Eleanor Panton
John Bentley . . . . Ducane
John Oxford . . . . Bromley
Patricia Owens . . . . Anne Hastings
Kenneth Hyde . . . . Jim Prentiss
Sheila Robins . . . . Nina Revere
Willoughby Goddard . . . . . John Hartley
CRIME Woman gang leader frames man for
death of halfbrother.

11427
HANGMAN'S WHARF (73) (U)
DUK Films
P:D: Cecil H. Williamson
S: (RADIO SERIAL) John Beldon
John Witty . . . . Dr David Galloway
Genine Graham . . . . Alison Maxwell
Patience Rentoul . . . . Mrs Williams
Gerald Nodin . . . . Sir Brian Roderick
Campbell Singer . . . . Insp Prebble
Max Brimmell . . . . Krim
Patricia Laffan . . . . Rosa Warren
CRIME Girl reporter helps doctor prove
he did not kill rich man.

11428
THE GIRL WHO COULDN'T QUITE (85) (A)
John Argyle (Monarch)
D: Norman Lee
S: (PLAY) Leo Marks
SC: Norman Lee, Marjorie Deans
Bill Owen . . . . Tim
Elizabeth Henson . . . . Ruth
Iris Hoey . . . . Janet
Betty Stockfeld . . . . Pamela
Stuart Lindsell . . . . John Pelham
Vernon Kelso . . . . Paul Evans
Rose Howlett . . . . Rosa
Fred Groves . . . . Tony
DRAMA Tramp cures teenager's amnesia
and she fails to recognise him.

11429
THE GORBALS STORY (74) (A)
New World (Eros)
P: Ernest Gartside
D:SC: David MacKane
S: (PLAY) Robert McLeish
Howard Connell . . . . Willie Mutrie
Betty Henderson . . . . Peggie Anderson
Russell Hunter . . . . Johnnie Martin
Marjorie Thomson . . . . Jean Mutrie
Roddy McMillan . . . . Hector
Isobel Campbell . . . . Nora Reilly
Jack Stewart . . . . Peter Reilly
Archie Duncan . . . . Bull
DRAMA Glasgow. Artist recalls slum
tenement life that almost caused him to
murder.

11430
THE BLUE LAMP (84) (A)
Ealing (GFD)
P: Michael Relph
D: Basil Dearden
S: Jan Read, Ted Willis
SC: T.E.B.Clarke, Alexander Mackendrick
Jack Warner . . . . PC George Dixon
Jimmy Hanley . . . . PC Andy Mitchell
Dirk Bogarde . . . . Tom Riley
Robert Flemyng . . . . Sgt Roberts
Bernard Lee . . . . Insp Cherry
Peggy Evans . . . . Diana Lewis
Patric Doonan . . . . Spud
Gladys Henson . . . . Emily Dixon
Bruce Seton . . . . PC Campbell
Meredith Edwards . . . . PC Hughes
Clive Morton . . . . Sgt Brooks
Frederick Piper . . . . Lewis
Dora Bryan . . . . Maisie
Norman Shelley . . . . Jordan
Campbell Singer . . . . Sgt
Tessie O'Shea . . . . Herself
CRIME Police track down thief who shot
policeman during cinema robbery. (BFA:
Best British Film 1950; Top moneymaker:
1950).

11431
THE MAN IN BLACK (75) (A)
Hammer (Ex)
P: Anthony Hinds
D: Francis Searle
S: (RADIO SERIES) John Dickson Carr
(APPOINTMENT WITH FEAR)
SC: John Gilling, Francis Searle
Betty Anne Davies . . . . . Bertha Clavering
Sidney James . . . . Henry Clavering
Anthony Forwood . . . . Victor Harrington
Sheila Burrell . . . . Janice
Hazel Penwarden . . . . Joan
Courtney Hope . . . . Mrs Carter
Lawrence Baskcomb . . . . . Sandford
Valentine Dyall . . . . Storyteller
CRIME Yoga expert fakes death and
poses as gardener to stop his wife driving his
daughter insane.

FEB

11432
NO PLACE FOR JENNIFER (90) (A)
ABPC (ABP)
P: Hamilton G. Inglis
D: Henry Cass
S: (NOVEL) Phyllis Hambledon
(NO DIFFERENCE TO ME)
SC: J. Lee-Thompson
Leo Genn . . . . William
Rosamund John . . . . Rachel Kershaw
Beatrice Campbell . . . . Paula
Guy Middleton . . . . Brian Stewart
Janette Scott . . . . Jennifer
Anthony Nicholls . . . . Baxter
Jean Cadell . . . . Aunt Jacqueline
Megs Jenkins . . . . Mrs Marshall
Edith Sharpe . . . . Doctor
Ann Codrington . . . . Miss Hancock
Brian Smith . . . . Martin Marshall
Andre Morell . . . . Counsel
Macdonald Hobley . . . . Salesman
Harold Scott . . . . Man
DRAMA 12-year old girl runs away
when her parents divorce.

11433
YOUR WITNESS (100) (A)
USA: EYE WITNESS
Coronado (WB)
P: David E. Rose, Joan Harrison
D: Robert Montgomery
S: Hugo Butler
SC: Hugo Butler, Ian Hunter, William
Douglas Home
Robert Montgomery . . . . . Adam Heywood
Leslie Banks . . . . Col Summerfield
Felix Aylmer . . . . Judge
Andrew Cruickshank . . . Sir Adrian North KC
Patricia Wayne . . . . Alex Summerfield
Harcourt Williams . . . . Beamish
Jenny Laird . . . . Mary Baxter
Michael Ripper . . . . Sam Baxter
Ann Stephens . . . . Sandy Summerfield
Wylie Watson . . . . Widgery
Noel Howlett . . . . Martin Foxglove KC
James Hayter . . . . Prouty
CRIME American lawyer's search for
witness to prove innocence of wartime friend.

11434
GOLDEN SALAMANDER (87) (U)
Pinewood (GFD)
P: Alexander Galperson
D: Ronald Neame
S: (NOVEL) Victor Canning
SC: Victor Canning, Ronald Neame,
Lesley Storm
Trevor Howard . . . . David Redfern
Anouk Aimee . . . . Anna
Herbert Lom . . . . Rankl
Walter Rilla . . . . Paul Serafis
Miles Malleson . . . . Supt Douvet

Jacques Sernas . . . . Max
Wilfrid Hyde White . . . . . . Agno
Peter Copley . . . . Aribi
Marcel Poncin . . . . Dominic
Kathleen Boutall . . . . Mme Guillard
Eugene Deckers . . . . Police Chief
Sybilla Binder . . . . Mme Labree
Henry Edwards . . . . Jeffries
CRIME Tunis. Archaeologist and hotel
proprietress thwart gunrunners.

11435
MADELEINE (114) (A)
Pinewood-Cineguild (GFD)
P: Stanley Haynes
D: David Lean
S: Stanley Haynes, Nicholas Phipps
N: James McKechnie
Ann Todd . . . . Madeleine Smith
Norman Wooland . . . . William Minnoch
Ivan Desny . . . . Emile l'Angelier
Leslie Banks . . . . James Smith
Edward Chapman . . . . Dr Thompson
Barbara Everest . . . . Mrs Smith
Andre Morell . . . . Dean
Barry Jones . . . . Lord Advocate
Elizabeth Sellars . . . . Christina
Jean Cadell . . . . Mrs Jenkins
Ivor Barnard . . . . Mr Murdoch
Patricia Raine . . . . Bessie Smith
Eugene Deckers . . . . Mr Thau
Amy Veness . . . . Miss Aiken
John Laurie . . . . Divine
Irene Browne . . . . Miss Grant
Henry Edwards . . . . Clerk
Moira Fraser . . . . Dancer
CRIME Glasgow, 1857. True story of affianced
girl who may have given arsenic to her
blackmailing French lover.

11436
THE ANGEL WITH THE TRUMPET (98) (U)
London-BLPA (BL)
P: Karl Hartl
D: Anthony Bushell
S: (NOVEL) Ernst Lothar
(DER ENGEL MIT DER POSAUNE)
SC: Karl Hartl, Franz Tassie, Clemence Dane
Eileen Herlie . . . . Henrietta Stein
Norman Wooland . . . . Prince Rudolf
Basil Sydney . . . . Francis Alt
Maria Schell . . . . Anna Linden
Olga Edwardes . . . . Monica Alt
John Justin . . . . Paul Alt
Andrew Cruickshank . . . . . Otto Alt
Oscar Werner . . . . Herman Alt
Anthony Bushell . . . . .Baron Hugo Traun
Wilfrid Hyde White . . . . . . Simmerl
Campbell Cotts . . . . Gen Paskiewicz
Dorothy Batley . . . . Pauline Drauffer
DRAMA Austria, 1889-1939. Girl gives
up Prince to wed rich piano maker and watches
their sons grow up and marry.

MAR

11437
MORNING DEPARTURE (102) (A)
USA: OPERATION DISASTER
Jay Lewis (GFD)
P: Leslie Parkyn
D: Roy Baker
S: (PLAY) Kenneth Woollard
SC: William Fairchild
John Mills . . . . Lt-Cdr Armstrong
Richard Attenborough . . . . Stoker Snipe
Nigel Patrick . . . . Lt Manson
Lana Morris . . . . Rose Snipe
Peter Hammond . . . . Sub-Lt Oakley

Helen Cherry . . . . Helen
James Hayter . . . . AB Higgins
Andrew Crawford . . . . WO McFee
Zena Marshall . . . . WREN
George Cole . . . . ERA Marks
Michael Brennan . . . . CPO Barlow
Wylie Watson . . . . Nobby Clarke
Bernard Lee . . . . Cdr Gates
Kenneth More . . . . Lt-Cdr James
George Thorpe . . . . Capt Fenton
DRAMA Crew trapped when submarine
strikes mine and sinks.

11438
THE ASTONISHED HEART (89) (U)
Gainsborough (GFD)
P: Anthony Darnborough
D: Anthony Darnborough, Terence Fisher
S: (PLAY) Noel Coward
SC: Noel Coward
Noel Coward . . . . Christian Faber
Celia Johnson . . . . Barbara Faber
Margaret Leighton . . . . Leonora Vail
Joyce Carey . . . . Susan Birch
Graham Payn . . . . Tim Verney
Amy Veness . . . . Alice Smith
Ralph Michael . . . . Philip Lucas
Michael Hordern . . . . Ernest
Patricia Glyn . . . . Helen
Everley Gregg . . . . Miss Harper
ROMANCE Psychiatrist's wife sends him
on world tour with his mistress.

11439
THEY WERE NOT DIVIDED (102) (A)
Two Cities (GFD) *reissue:* 1961 (GEFD)
P: Herbert Smith
D:S: Terence Young
Edward Underdown . . . . . Philip
Ralph Clanton . . . . David
Helen Cherry . . . . Wilhelmina
Stella Andrews . . . . Jane
Michael Brennan . . . . Smoke O'Connor
Michael Trubshawe . . . . Maj Bushy Noble
John Wynn . . . . 45 Jones
Desmond Llewellyn . . . . . . 77 Jones
Rufus Cruickshank . . . . . . Sgt Dean
Estelle Brody . . . . Correspondent
Christopher Lee . . . . Lewis
R.S.M.Brittain . . . . Himself
WAR 1940-44. American officer and British
officer in Guards Armoured Division die in
Ardennes.

11440
THE HAPPIEST DAYS OF YOUR LIFE (91)
(U) BLPA-Individual (BL)
P: Frank Launder, Sidney Gilliat
D: Frank Launder
S: (PLAY) John Dighton
SC: John Dighton, Frank Launder
Alastair Sim . . . . Wetherby Pond
Margaret Rutherford . . . . . Miss Whitchurch
Joyce Grenfell . . . . Miss Gossage
Edward Rigby . . . . Rainbow
Guy Middleton . . . . Victor Hyde-Brown
John Bentley . . . . Richard Tassell
Bernardette O'Farrell . . . . Miss Harper
Muriel Aked . . . . Miss Jezzard
John Turnbull . . . . Conrad Matthews
Richard Wattis . . . . Arnold Billings
Arthur Howard . . . . Anthony Ramsden
Millicent Wolf . . . . Miss Curtis
Myrette Morven . . . . Miss Chappell
Russell Waters . . . . Mr West
COMEDY Girls' School mistakenly
billeted on Boys' School.

11441
CHANCE OF A LIFETIME (89) (U)
Pilgrim Pictures (BL)
P: Bernard Miles, John Palmer
D: Bernard Miles, Alan Osbiston
S: Bernard Miles, Walter Greenwood
Basil Radford . . . . Dickinson
Niall MacGinnis . . . . Baxter
Bernard Miles . . . . Stevens
Julien Mitchell . . . . Morris
Kenneth More . . . . Adam
Geoffrey Keen . . . . Bolger
Josephine Wilson . . . . Miss Cooper
John Harvey . . . . Bland
Russell Waters . . . . Palmer
Patrick Troughton . . . . Kettle
Hattie Jacques . . . . Alice
Amy Veness . . . . Lady Dysart
Compton Mackenzie . . . . Sir Robert Dysart
Peter Jones . . . . Xenobian
DRAMA Plough manufacturer lets his
striking employees take over his factory.

11442
ROOM TO LET (68) (A)
Hammer (Exclusive)
P: Anthony Hinds
D: Godfrey Grayson
S: (RADIO PLAY) Margery Allingham
SC: John Gilling, Godfrey Grayson
Jimmy Hanley . . . . Curley Minter
Valentine Dyall . . . . Dr Fell
Christine Silver . . . . Mrs Musgrave
Merle Tottenham . . . . Alice
Charles Hawtrey . . . . Mike Atkinson
Constance Smith . . . . Molly Musgrave
J. Anthony la Penna . . . . . J.J.
Reginald Dyson . . . . Sgt Cranbourne
CRIME 1904. Reporter learns crippled
widow's lodger is Jack the Ripper.

11443
THE MYSTERY OF THE SNAKESKIN BELT
(serial) (U)
GB INstructional (GFD)
P:D: Frank Cadman
S: Lewis Jackson
SC: Mary Cathcart Borer
Cyril Wentzel . . . . Jim Travers
Ursula Strachey . . . .
Colin Barlow . . . .
Episodes 1. - 8 (16)
CHILDREN Rhodesia. Children help foil
crooks who steal treasure map to lost city.

11444
AN INTERNATIONAL AFFAIR (27) (A)
John Austin (ABFD)
CRIME American agent tracks down
gang of jewel smugglers.

11445
NEVER SAY DIE (61) (U)
retitled: DON'T SAY DIE
X Productions (IFD)
P: Vivian Milroy, Margot Lovell
D: Vivian Milroy
S: Dido & Vivian Milroy
Desmond Walter-Ellis .. Ron Bertie Blarney
Sandra Dorne . . . . Sandra
Charles Heslop. . . . . Charles Choosey
Constance Smith . . . . Red Biddy
Tony Quinn . . . . Mike Murphy
Stanley Rose . . . . Gus
Derek Tansley . . . . Potts
Thomas Gallagher . . . . . . Gorilla
Kenneth Connor . . . . Pat O'Neill
COMEDY Ireland. Heir to old castle finds
it is being used by smugglers.

11446
GUILT IS MY SHADOW (86) (A)
ABPC (ABP)
P: Ivan Foxwell
D: Roy Kellino
S: (NOVEL) Peter Curtis
(YOU'RE BEST ALONE)
SC: Ivan Foxwell, Roy Kellino, John Gilling
Patrick Holt . . . . Kit
Elizabeth Sellars . . . . Linda
Lana Morris . . . . Betty
Peter Reynolds . . . . Jamie
Laurence O'Madden . . . . . . Tom
Avice Landone . . . . Eva
Esma Cannon . . . . Peggy
Wensley Pithey . . . . Tillingham
CRIME Devon. Farmer helps girl who killed
her crooked husband in fight.

11447
THE DRAGON OF PENDRAGON CASTLE
(52) (U)
Elstree Independent (GFD)
P:D: John Baxter
S: Janet M. Smith
SC: Mary Cathcart Borer
Robin Netscher . . . . Peter Fielding
Hilary Rennie . . . . Judy Fielding
Jane Welsh . . . . Mrs Fielding
J. Hubert Leslie . . . . Sir William Magnus
Graham Moffatt . . . . Paddy
David Hannaford . . . . Bobby
Leslie Bradley . . . . Mr Ferber
C.Denier Warren . . . . Mr Morgan
Lily Lapidus . . . . Mrs Morgan
CHILDREN Broke knight's grandchildren
find sea dragon and use it to heat castle.

APR

11448
THE GIRL IS MINE (51) (U)
Touchstone (BL)
P: Freda Stock
D:SC: Marjorie Deans
S: Ralph Stock
Patrick Macnee . . . . Hugh Hurcombe
Pamela Deeming . . . . Betty Marriott
Lionel Murton . . . . James Rutt
Arthur Melton . . . . Pringle
Richard Pearson . . . . Sgt
Ben Williams . . . . Policeman
Len Sharp . . . . Watchman
DRAMA GI helps couple save pinnace
from dock owner.

11449
STRANGER AT MY DOOR (80) (A)
Leinster Films (Monarch)
P: Paul King
D: Brendan J.Stafford, Desmond Leslie
S: Desmond Leslie
Valentine Dyall . . . . Paul Wheeler
Joseph O'Connor . . . . Michael Foley
Agnes Bernelle . . . . Laura Riordan
Maire O'Neill . . . . Clarissa Finnegan
Jill Raymond . . . . Kate
Liam O'Leary . . . . Kelly
Michael Moore . . . . Septimus Small
CRIME Dublin. Ex-commando becomes
burglar to help blackmailed girl.

11450
DOUBLE CONFESSION (85) (A)
Harry Reynolds (ABP)
D: Ken Annakin
S: (NOVEL) John Garden
(ALL ON A SUMMER'S DAY)
SC: William Templeton, Ralph Keene
Derek Farr . . . . Jim Medway

Joan Hopkins . . . . Ann Corday
Peter Lorre . . . . Paynter
William Hartnell . . . . Charlie Durham
Kathleen Harrison . . . . Kate
Naunton Wayne . . . . Insp Tenby
Ronald Howard . . . . Hilary Boscombe
Leslie Dwyer . . . . Leonard
Edward Rigby . . . . Fisherman
George Woodbridge . . . . . . Sgt Sawnton
Henry Edwards . . . . Man in Shelter
Vida Hope . . . . Mme Zilia
Esma Cannon . . . . Mme Cleo
CRIME Margate. Estranged husband kills
his wife and frames her lover.

11451
THE RELUCTANT WIDOW (91) (A)
Two Cities (GFD)
P: Gordon Wellesley
D: Bernard Knowles
S: (NOVEL) Georgette Heyer
SC: Gordon Wellesley, J.B.Boothroyd
Jean Kent . . . . Elinor
Guy Rolfe . . . . Lord Carlyon
Paul Dupuis . . . . Lord Nivelle
Lana Morris . . . . Becky
Kathleen Byron . . . . Mme de Chevreaux
Julian Dallas . . . . Francois Cheviot
Anthony Tancred . . . . Nicky
Peter Hammond . . . . Eustace Cheviot
Jean Cadell . . . . Mrs Barrows
Andrew Cruickshank . . . . Lord Bedlington
George Thorpe . . . . Col Strong
Ralph Truman . . . . Scowler
James Carney . . . . Maj Forbes
Allan Jeayes . . . . Col
DRAMA Governess weds dying Lord, loves
his cousin, and saves papers from Napoleon's
spies.

11452
UP FOR THE CUP (76) (U)
Citadel-Byron (ABFD) *reissue:* 1955 (NR)
P: Henry Halstead
D: Jack Raymond
S: R.P.Weston, Bert Lee
SC: Con West, Jack Marks
Albert Modley . . . . Albert Entwhistle
Mai Bacon . . . . Maggie Entwhistle
Helen Christie . . . . Jane
Harold Berens . . . . Auctioneer
Wallas Eaton . . . . Barrowboy
Jack Melford . . . . Barrowboy
Charmian Innes . . . . ,. . . . Clippie
Fred Groves . . . . Hardcastle
John Warren . . . . Cartwright
COMEDY Misadventures of Yorkshire
loom inventor in London on Cup Final Day.

11453
NIGHT AND THE CITY (101) (A)
20th Century Productions
P: Samuel G. Engel
D: Jules Dassin
S: (NOVEL) Gerald Kersh
SC: Jo Eisinger
Richard Widmark . . . . Harry Fabian
Gene Tierney . . . . Mary Bristol
Googie Withers . . . . Helen Nosseross
Hugh Marlowe . . . . Adam Dunne
Francis L. Sullivan . . . . Phil Nosseross
Herbert Lom . . . . Kristo
Stanley Zbysko . . . . Gregorius
Mike Mazurki . . . . Strangler
Charles Farrell . . . . Beer
Ada Reeve . . . . Molly
Ken Richmond . . . . Nikolas
Edward Chapman . . . . Hoskins
James Hayter . . . . Figler

Gibb McLaughlin . . . . Googin
CRIME Spiv tries to promote wrestling in
opposition to Greek gangster.

11454
THE BODY SAID NO ! (75) (U)
New World-Angel (Eros)
P: Daniel M. Angel
D:S: Val Guest
Michael Rennie . . . . Himself
Yolande Donlan . . . . Mikki Brent
Hy Hazell . . . . Sue
Jon Pertwee . . . . Watchman
Valentine Dyall . . . . John Sutherland
Reginald Beckwith . . . . Benton
Arthur Hill . . . . Robin King
Cyril Smith . . . . Sgt
Jack Billings . . . . Eddie
Peter Butterworth . . . . Driver
Margaret McGrath . . . . Mrs Rennie
Winifred Shotter . . . . TV Announcer
COMEDY Singer mistakes accidental
televising of rehearsal for plot to murder actor.

11455
STATE SECRET (104) (U) USA: THE GREAT
MANHUNT
London-BLPA (BL) reissue: 1964 (10 mins cut)
P: Frank Launder, Sidney Gilliatt
D: SC: Sidney Gilliatt
S: (NOVEL) Roy Huggins
(APPOINTMENT WITH FEAR)
Douglas Fairbanks jr . . . . Dr John Marlowe
Glynis Johns . . . . Lisa
Jack Hawkins . . . . Col Galcon
Herbert Lom . . . . Theodor
Walter Rilla . . . . Gen Niva
Karel Stepanek . . . . Dr Revo
Carl Jaffe . . . . Janovik Prada
Gerard Heinz . . . . Bendel
Hans Moser . . . . Sigrist
Gerik Schjelderup . . . . Bartorek
Guido Lorraine . . . . Lt Prachi
Anton Diffring . . . . Policeman
Peter Illing . . . . Macco
ADVENTURE Europe. Dead general's
supporters pursue surgeon in order to
silence him.

11456
THE DANCING YEARS (97) (A) *tech*
ABPC (ABP)
P: Warwick Ward
D: Harold French
S: (PLAY) Ivor Novello
SC: Warwick Ward, Jack Whittingham
Dennis Price . . . . Rudi Kleiber
Giselle Preville . . . . Maria Zeitler
Patricia Dainton . . . . Grete
Anthony Nicholls . . . . Prince Reinaldt
Olive Gilbert . . . . Frau Kurt
Grey Blake . . . . Franzl
Muriel George . . . . Hatti
Jeremy Spenser . . . . Maria's Son
Moyra Frazer; Pamela Foster; Igo Barcinszki;
Barry Ashton
MUSICAL Vienna, 1910. Composer loves
opera star who weds Prince but loves the
composer's son. (Extract in
ELSTREE STORY, 1952).

11457
SOMEONE AT THE DOOR (65) (U)
Hammer (Ex)
P: Anthony Hinds
D: Francis Searle
S: (PLAY) Dorothy & Campbell Christie
SC: A.R.Rawlinson
Michael Medwin . . . . Ronnie Martin
Garry Marsh . . . . Kapel

Yvonne Owen . . . . Sally Martin
Hugh Latimer . . . . Bill Reid
Danny Green . . . . Price
Campbell Singer . . . . Insp Spedding
John Kelly . . . . PC O'Brien
COMEDY Reporter and sister inherit old
house and invent a murder that comes true.

MAY

11458
PRELUDE TO FAME (88) (U)
Two Cities (GFD)
P: Donald B. Wilson
D: Fergus McDonnell
S: (NOVEL) Aldous Huxley
(YOUNG ARCHIMEDES)
SC: Robert Westerby
Guy Rolfe . . . . John Morell
Kathleen Ryan . . . . Catherine Morell
Kathleen Byron . . . . Signora Bondini
Jeremy Spenser . . . . Guido
James Robertson Justice. . Sir Arthur Harold
Henry Oscar . . . . Signor Bondini
Rosalie Crutchley . . . . Carlotta
John Slater . . . . Dr Lorenzo
Ferdy Mayne . . . . Carlo
Robert Rietti . . . . Giuseppe
DRAMA Professor saves Italian boy
conductor from exploitation.

11459
SO LONG AT THE FAIR (86) (U)
Gainsborough (GFD)
P: Betty Box
D: Anthony Darnborough, Terence Fisher
S: (NOVEL) Anthony Thorne
SC: Hugh Mills, Anthony Thorne
Jean Simmons . . . . Vicky Barton
Dirk Bogarde . . . . George Hathaway
David Tomlinson . . . . John Barton
Honor Blackman . . . . . . Rhoda O'Donovan
Cathleen Nesbitt . . . . Mme Herve
Felix Aylmer . . . . Consul
Betty Warren . . . . Mrs O'Donovan
Marcel Poncin . . . . Narcisse
Austin Trevor . . . . Commissaire
Andre Morell . . . . Dr Hart
Zena Marshall . . . . Nina
DRAMA Paris, 1889. English girl's brother
and his room vanish from hotel.

11460
LAST HOLIDAY (88) (U)
ABPC-Watergate (ABP)
P: Stephen Mitchell, A.D.Peters, J.B.Priestley.
D: Henry Cass
S: J.B. Priestley
Alec Guinness . . . . George Bird
Beatrice Campbell . . . . Sheila Rockingham
Kay Walsh . . . . Mrs Poole
Bernard Lee . . . . Insp Wilton
Wilfrid Hyde White . . . . . . Chalfont
Muriel George . . . . Lady Oswington
Helen Cherry . . . . Miss Mellows
Jean Colin . . . . Daisy Clarence
Brian Worth . . . . Derek Rockingham
Sidney James . . . . Joe Clarence
Coco Aslan . . . . Gambini
Ernest Thesiger . . . Sir Trevor Lampington
David McCallum . . . . Blind Fiddler
COMEDY Man with one month to live
spends it at seaside hotel.

11461
STAGE FRIGHT (111) (A)
WB-FN (WB)
P:D: Alfred Hitchcock
S: (NOVEL) Selwyn Jepson (MAN RUNNING)
SC: Whitfield Cook, Alma Reville, James Bridie

Jane Wyman . . . . Eve Gill
Marlene Dietrich . . . . Charlotte Inwood
Michael Wilding . . . . Insp Wilfred Smith
Richard Todd . . . . Jonathan Penrose
Alastair Sim . . . . Commodore Gill
Sybil Thorndike . . . . Mrs Gill
Kay Walsh . . . . Nellie Good
Miles Malleson . . . . Fortescue
Hector MacGregor . . . . . Freddie Williams
Joyce Grenfell . . . . Attendant
Andre Morell . . . . Insp Byard
Patricia Hitchcock . . . . . Chubby Bannister
CRIME Actress tries to help fugitive
dancer prove singer killed her husband.

11462
FAKE'S PROGRESS (52) (U)
Falcon Films (Arrow)
P: Hilary Long
D: Ken Fairbairn
S: Ken Fairbairn, Hilary Long
Lou Cass . . . . Clerk
Harry Nova . . . . Spiv
COMEDY Clerk and spiv try various
schemes to make money.

11463
OLD MOTHER RILEY, HEADMISTRESS (75)
(U) Harry Reynolds (Renown)
D: John Harlow
S: Con West, Jack Marks
Arthur Lucan . . . . Mrs Riley
Kitty McShane . . . . Kitty Riley
Enid Hewitt . . . . Miss Carruthers
Jenny Mathot . . . . Mlle Leblanc
Ethel Royale . . . . Lady Meersham
Harry Herbert . . . . Simon
Cyril Smith . . . . Maltby
Paul Sheridan . . . . Nixon
Willer Neal . . . . Travers
C.Denier Warren . . . . Clifton Hill
Luton Girls Choir; George Melachrino
Orchestra
COMEDY Washerwoman inherits laundry
and exchanges it for Girls' School, where
she thwarts railway speculators.

11464
THE LONE CLIMBER (59) (U)
GB Instructional (GFD)
P: Mary Field
D: William C. Hammond
S: Patricia Latham
Gerty Jobstmann . . . . Fraulein Huber
Fritz Langer . . . . Karl Behrens
Elesnore Kulicek . . . . Lisel Bauer
Herbert Nitsch . . . . Hans Schneider
Fritz von Friedl . . . . Rudi
CHILDREN Austria. Search party seeks
child with broken leg.

11465
THE MYSTERIOUS POACHER (49) (U)
GB Instructional (GFD)
P: Mary Field
D: Don Chaffey
S: Simon Braydon
SC: Patricia Latham
Herbert Leidinger . . . . Hans Veit
Herbert Nawratil-Edgar . . . Kurt Burger
Vera Kulicek . . . . Marta
Fritz von Friedl . . . . Willi
Karl Gallasch . . . . Poacher
CHILDREN Austria. Holiday children
help gamekeeper trap poacher.

11466
PAUL TEMPLE'S TRIUMPH (80) (U)
Nettlefold (Butcher)

Reissues: 1953; 1958 (Winart)
P: Ernest G. Roy
D: Maclean Rogers
S: (RADIO SERIAL) Francis Durbridge
(NEWS OF PAUL TEMPLE)
SC: A.R.Rawlinson
John Bentley . . . . Paul Temple
Dinah Sheridan . . . . Steve Temple
Jack Livesey . . . . Sir Graham Forbes
Beatrice Varley . . . . Mrs Weston
Barbara Couper . . . . Mrs Morgan
Jenny Mathot . . . . Jacqueline Giraud
Andrew Leigh . . . . Prof Hardwicke
Hugh Dempster . . . . Oliver Ffollett
Bruce Seton . . . . Bill Bryant
Ivan Samson . . . . Maj Murray
CRIME "Z" kidnaps an atomic scientist
in the New Forest.

11467
SHADOW OF THE PAST (83) (A)
Anglofilm (Col)
P: Mario Zampi, Mae Murray
D: Mario Zampi
S: Aldo di Benedetti
SC: Aldo di Benedetti, Ian Stuart Black
Joyce Howard . . . . Lady in Black
Terence Morgan . . . . John Harding
Michael Medwin . . . . Dick Stevens
Andrew Osborn . . . . George Bentley
Wylie Watson . . . . Caretaker
Marie Ney . . . . Mrs Bentley
Ella Retford . . . . Daily Help
Ronald Adam . . . . Solicitor
Louise Gainsborough . . . . Susie
CRIME "Ghost" of murderer's wife is
her twin sister seeking vengeance.

11468
COME DANCE WITH ME (58) (U)
Anglofilm (Col)
P:D: Mario Zampi
S: Cyril Roberts
Max Wall . . . . Manager
Gordon Humphris . . . . Boy
Yvonne Marsh . . . . Girl
Barbara Hamilton . . . . Stage Girl
Vincent Ball . . . . Secretary
Anne Shelton; Derek Roy; Anton Karas;
Marquis Trio; Aida Foster Girls
MUSICAL Valet posing as bart and maid
posing as Lady fall in love at nightclub.

JUN

11469
TREASURE ISLAND (96) (U) *tech*
Walt Disney (RKO)
P: Perce Pearce
D: Byron Haskin
S: (NOVEL) Robert Louis Stevenson
SC: Lawrence E. Watkin
Bobby Driscoll . . . . Jim Hawkins
Robert Newton . . . . . . Long John Silver
Basil Sydney . . . . Capt Smollett
Walter Fitzgerald . . . . . . Squire Trelawney
Denis O'Dea . . . . Dr Livesey
Finlay Currie . . . . Capt Billy Bones
Ralph Truman . . . . George Merry
Geoffrey Keen . . . . Israel Hands
Geoffrey Wilkinson . . . . . . Ben Gunn
John Laurie . . . . Blind Pew
Francis de Wolff . . . . Black Dog
John Gregson . . . . Redruth
William Devlin . . . . Morgan
Harry Locke . . . . Haggott
Eddie Moran . . . . Bart
ADVENTURE Period. Widow's son joins
expedition to find pirate's treasure.

11470
DANCE HALL (80) (A)
Ealing (GFD) *reissue:* 1961 (GEFD)
AP: E.V.H.Emmett
D: Charles Crichton
S: E.V.H.Emmett, Diana Morgan, Alexander Mackendrick

Donald Houston	Phil
Bonar Colleano	Alec
Petula Clark	Georgie Wilson
Natasha Parry	Eve
Jane Hylton	Mary
Diana Dors	Carol
Gladys Henson	Mrs Wilson
Sydney Tafler	Manager
Douglas Barr	Peter
Fred Johnson	Mr Wilson
James Carney	Mike
Kay Kendall	Doreen
Eunice Gayson	Mona

Geraldo and his Orchestra; Ted Heath and his Music; Hy Hazell; Wally Fryer & Margaret Barnes
ROMANCE Stories of four factory girls who visit Palais de Danse.

11471
TONY DRAWS A HORSE (91) (A)
Pinnacle (GFD)
P: Brock Williams, Harold Richmond
D: John Paddy Carstairs
S: (PLAY) Lesley Storm
SC: Brock Williams

Cecil Parker	Dr Howard Fleming
Anne Crawford	Clare Fleming
Derek Bond	Tim Shields
Barbara Murray	Joan Parsons
Mervyn Johns	Alfred Parsons
Edward Rigby	Grandfather
Barbara Everest	Mrs Parsons
Dandy Nichols	Mrs Smith
Kynaston Reeves	Dr Bletchley
David Hurst	Ivan

COMEDY Psychiatrist disagrees with doctor husband over their son and goes to France with her sister's fiance.

11472
WHAT THE BUTLER SAW (61) (U)
Hammer (Ex)
P: Anthony Hinds
D: Godfrey Grayson
S: Roger & Donald Good
SC: A.R.Rawlinson, Edward J.Mason

Edward Rigby	The Earl
Henry Mollison	Bembridge
Mercy Haystead	Lapis
Michael Ward	Gerald
Eleanor Hallam	Lady Mary
Peter Burton	Bill Fenton
Anne Valery	Elaine

COMEDY Earl tries to hide the native Princess who loves his butler.

11473
MY DAUGHTER JOY (81) (A)
USA: OPERATION X
London-BLPA (BL)
P:D: Gregory Ratoff
S: (NOVEL) Irene Nemirowsky
(DAVID GOLDER)
SC: Robert Theoren, William Rose

Edward G. Robinson	George Constantin
Peggy Cummins	Georgette Constantin
Richard Greene	Larry
Nora Swinburne	Ava Constantin
Walter Rilla	Andrews
Finlay Currie	Sir Thomas MacTavish
James Robertson Justice	Prof Keval

Ronald Adam	Col Fogarty
David Hutcheson	Annix
Peter Illing	Sultan
Ronald Ward	Dr Schindler

DRAMA Financier plans to start dynasty by marrying his daughter to Sultan.

11474
CAIRO ROAD (95) (A)
Mayflower (ABP)
P: Aubrey Baring, Maxwell Setton
D: David Macdonald
S: Robert Westerby

Eric Portman	Col Youssef Bey
Laurence Harvey	Lt Mourad
Maria Mauban	Marie
Camelia	Anna Michelis
Harold Lang	Humble
Coco Aslan	Lombardi
Karel Stepanek	Edouardo Pavlis
John Bailey	Doctor
Martin Boddey	Maj Ahmed Mustafa
John Gregson	Coastguard
Marne Maitland	Gohari
Abraham Sofaer	Commandant

ADVENTURE Egypt. Police colonel catches narcotics smugglers.

11475
MR H.C. ANDERSEN (62) (U)
British Foundation
P:D: Ronald Haines
S: (BOOK) Hans Christian Andersen
(THE TRUE STORY OF MY LIFE)
SC: Ronald & Jean Haines

Ashley Glynne	Hans Andersen
Constance Lewis	Mrs Andersen
Terence Noble	Mr Andersen
Stuart Sanders	Bailiff
June Elvin	Jenny Lind
Edward Sullivan	Charles Dickens
Victor Rietty	King Frederick

HISTORY Denmark. Biography of author, with fairy tales in animation.

11476
THE FALL OF THE HOUSE OF USHER (70)
(H)GIB Films (Vigilant)
Reissues: 1955; 1961 (EB)
P:D: George Ivan Barnett
S: (STORY) Edgar Allan Poe
SC: Kenneth Thompson, Dorothy Catt

Gwendoline Watford	Lady Medeleine Usher
Kay Tendeter	Lord Roderick Usher
Irving Steen	Jonathan
Lucy Pavey	Hag
Vernon Charles	Dr Cordwell
Gavin Lee	Butler

HORROR Period. Lord's sister revives after being buried alive.

JUL

11477
WATERFRONT (80) (A) USA: WATERFRONT WOMEN
Conqueror (GFD)
P: Paul Soskin
D: Michael Anderson
S: (NOVEL) John Brophy
SC: John Brophy, Paul Soskin

Robert Newton	Peter McCabe
Kathleen Harrison	Mrs McCabe
Susan Shaw	Connie McCabe
Richard Burton	Ben Satterthwaite
Avis Scott	Nora McCabe
Kenneth Griffith	Maurice Bruno
Robin Netscher	George Alexander
Olive Sloane	Mrs Gibson
Charles Victor	Bill
James Hayter	Captain

Michael Brennan	Engineer
Allan Jeayes	Prison Officer
Hattie Jacques	Singer

CRIME Liverpool, 1930. Drunkard seaman returns to his family after 14 years and kills engineer.

11478
BITTER SPRINGS (89) (U)
Ealing (GFD)
AP: Leslie Norman
D:S: Ralph Smart
SC: W.P. Lipscomb, Monja Danischewsky

Tommy Trinder	Tommy
Chips Rafferty	Wally King
Gordon Jackson	Mac
Jean Blue	Ma King
Charles Tingwell	John King
Nonnie Piper	Emma King
Nicky Yardley	Charlie
Michael Pate	Trooper
Henry Murdoch	Black Jack

ADVENTURE Australia, 1900. Sheep farmer and his family fight Aborigines.

11479
TRIO (91) (A)
Gainsborough (GFD)
P: Anthony Darnborough
S:(STORIES) W.Somerset Maugham
SC: R.C.Sheriff, Noel Langley
The Verger
D: Ken Annakin

James Hayter	Albert Foreman
Kathleen Harrison	Emma Foreman
Felix Aylmer	Banker
Lana Morris	Gladys
Michael Hordern	Vicar
Henry Edwards	Warden

Mr Knowall
D: Ken Annakin

Anne Crawford	Mrs Ramsay
Nigel Patrick	Kelada
Naunton Wayne	Mr Ramsay
Wilfrid Hyde White	Grey
Clive Morton	Captain
Michael Medwin	Steward

Sanatorium
D: Harold French

Jean Simmons	Eve Bishop
Michael Rennie	Templeton
Roland Culver	Ashenden
Raymond Huntley	Mr Chester
Betty Ann Davies	Mrs Chester
Andre Morell	Dr Lennox
John Laurie	Mr Campbell
Finlay Currie	Mr McLeod
Mary Merrall	Miss Atkin
Marjorie Fielding	Mrs Whitbread

DRAMA Three short stories.

11480
OVER THE GARDEN WALL (94) (U)
Film Studios Manchester (Mancunian)
reissue: 1959 (39 mins cut)
P:D: John E.Blakeley

Norman Evans	Fanny Lawton
Jimmy James	Joe Lawton
Dan Young	Dan
Alec Pleon	Alec
Sonya O'Shea	Mary Harrison
John Wynn	Tony Harrison
Frederick Bradshaw	Ken Smith

COMEDY Boss's son tries to flirt with employee's married daughter.
(Extract in EVANS ABOVE (1959).)

11481
ROUND RAINBOW CORNER (32) (U)
Squire Strong Saunders (H&S Films)

D: Frank Neall
Ronald Frankau
Judy Allen
Neal Arden
REVUE (Includes extracts from earlier films).

11482
ODETTE (123) (A)
Imperadio (BL)
P:D: Herbert Wilcox
S: (BOOK) Jerrard Tickell
SC: Warren Chetham Strode
Anna Neagle . . . . Odette
Trevor Howard . . . . Capt Peter Churchill
Marius Goring . . . . Henri
Peter Ustinov . . . . Arnaud
Bernard Lee . . . . Jack
Maurice Buckmaster . . . . . Himself
Alfred Shieske . . . . Commandant
Gilles Queant . . . . Jacques
Marianne Waller . . . . Wardress
Frederick Wendhausen . . . . . Colonel
Marie Burke . . . . Mme Gliere
WAR 1942. True story of woman agent
captured and tortured by Germans.
(DMNFA: 1950; PGAA: 1951).

11483
ONCE A SINNER (80) (A)
John Argyle (Butcher)
D: Lewis Gilbert
S: (NOVEL) Ronald Marsh (IRENE)
SC: David Evans
Pat Kirkwood . . . . Irene James
Jack Watling . . . . . . , . . . John Ross
Joy Shelton . . . . Vera Lamb
Sydney Tafler . . . . Jimmy Smart
Thora Hird . . . . Mrs James
Humphrey Lestocq . . . . . Lewis Canfield
Harry Fowler . . . . Bill James
CRIME Ex-crook gives her life to save
banker husband from former partner.

AUG

11484
PORTRAIT OF CLARE (98) (A)
ABPC (ABP)
P: Leslie Landau
D: Lance Comfort
S: (NOVEL) Francis Brett Young
SC: Leslie Laundau, Adrian Arlington
Margaret Johnston . . . . Clare
Richard Todd . . . . Robert Hart
Robin Bailey . . . . Dudley Wilburn
Ronald Howard . . . . Ralph Hingston
Mary Clare . . . . Lady Hingston
Marjorie Fielding . . . . Aunt Cathie
Anthony Nicholls . . . . Dr Boyd
Lloyd Pearson . . . . Sir Joseph Hingston
Jeremy Spenser . . . . Steven
Bruce Seton . . . . . Lord Steven Wolverbury
Campbell Copelin . . . . . . Insp Cunningham
ROMANCE 1900. Woman weds dull
solicitor, rich man, and barrister.

11485
THE LADY CRAVED EXCITEMENT (69) (U)
Hammer (Ex)
P: Anthony Hinds
D: Francis Searle
S: (RADIO SERIAL) Edward J.Mason
SC: Edward J.Mason, John Gilling, Francis
Searle
Hy Hazell . . . . Pat
Michael Medwin . . . . Johnny
Sidney James . . . . Carlo
Thelma Grigg . . . . Julia
Andrew Keir . . . . Peterson
Danny Green . . . . Boris

John Longden . . . . Insp James
Ian Wilson . . . . Mugsy
COMEDY Caberet stars save old paintings
from lunatic art smuggler.

11486
THE WOODEN HORSE (101) (U)
BLPA-Wessex (BL)
P: Ian Dalrymple
D: Jack Lee
S: (BOOK) Eric Williams
SC: Eric Williams
Leo Genn . . . . Peter
David Tomlinson . . . . Phil
Anthony Steel . . . . John
David Greene . . . . Bennett
Peter Burton . . . . Nigel
Patrick Waddington . . . . . . CO
Michael Goodliffe . . . . Robbie
Anthony Dawson . . . . Pomfret
Bryan Forbes . . . . Paul
Franz Schaftheitlin . . . . . . Commandant
Hans Meyer . . . . Charles
Jacques Brunius . . . . Andre
Peter Finch . . . . Australian
WAR True story of POWs who tunnel
out of Stalag Luft III.

11487
SEVEN DAYS TO NOON (94) (A)
London-BLPA (BL) reissue: 195-.
P: John Boulting
D: Roy Boulting
S: Paul Dehn, James Bernard
SC: Roy Boulting, Frank Harvey
Barry Jones . . . . Prof Willingdon
Andre Morell . . . . Supt Folland
Olive Sloane . . . . Goldie
Sheila Manahan . . . . Ann Willingdon
Hugh Cross . . . . Stephen Lane
Joan Hickson . . . . Mrs Peckett
Ronald Adam . . . . Prime Minister
Marie Ney . . . . Mrs Willingdon
Geoffrey Keen . . . .
Merrill Mueller . . . . American Commentator
FANTASY Mad professor threatens to
destroy London with an atomic bomb.
(AA: Best Story 1951).

11488
LET'S HAVE A MURDER (95) (U)
Film Studios Manchester (Mancunian)
reissue: 1959; STICK'EM UP (cut)
P:D: John E. Blakeley
Jimmy Jewel . . . . Jimmy Jewsbury
Ben Warriss . . . . Ben Warren
Lesley Osmond . . . . Marjorie Gordon
Stewart Rome . . . . Col Gordon
COMEDY Tecs expose psychiatrist as
jewel thief and the killer of singer.

11489
THE BLACK ROSE (121) (U) tech
20th Century Productions
reissue: 1954 (30 mins cut)
P: Louis D. Lighton
D: Henry Hathaway
S: (NOVEL) Thomas B. Costain
SC: Talbot Jennings
Tyrone Power . . . . Walter of Gurnie
Orson Welles . . . . Bayan
Cecile Aubrey . . . . Maryam
Jack Hawkins . . . . Tristram Griffen
Michael Rennie . . . . King Edwards
Finlay Currie . . . . Alfgar
Herbert Lom . . . . Anemus
Mary Clare . . . . Countess of Lenford
James Robertson Justice . . . .Simeon Beautrie
Laurence Harvey . . . . Edmond
Alfonso Bedoya . . . . Lu Chung

Valery Inkijinoff . . . . Minister
Gibb McLaughlin . . . . Wilderkin
Henry Oscar . . . . Roger Bacon
ADVENTURE 1250. Saxon scholar saves captive
girl from Mongol chief.

11490
SHADOW OF THE EAGLE (92) (U)
Valiant-Tuscania (IFD)
P: Anthony Havelock-Allan
D: Sidney Salkow
S: Jacques Companeez
SC: Doreen Montgomery, Hagar Wilde
Richard Greene . . . . Count Alexei Orloff
Valentina Cortesa . . . . Princess Tarakanova
Greta Gynt . . . . Countess Camponiello
Binnie Barnes . . . . .'. . . Empress Catherine
Charles Goldner . . . . . . Gen Korsakoff
Walter Rilla . . . . Prince Rasiwill
Hugh French . . . . Capt Nikolsky
Dennis Vance . . . . Vaska
ADVENTURE Venice, 1770. Russian envoy
falls in love with Princess he is ordered to kidnap.

11491
A RAY OF SUNSHINE (55) (U)
Delman-Phyllis Shepherd (Adelphi)
D: Horace Shepherd
Ted Ray   Lucille Gaye
Freddie Bamberger   Wilson, Keppel & Betty
Janet Brown   Morton Frazer's Harmonica Gang
Ivy Benson and her Girls Band
REVUE

11492
RETURN FARE TO LAUGHTER (38) (U)
Butcher's
P: Henry W.Fisher
D:S: James M. Anderson
N: Frederick Grisewood
COMPILATION (Extracts from earlier films).

SEP

11493
THE MINIVER STORY (104) (U)
MGM British
P: Sidney Franklin
D: H.C.Potter
S: (CHARACTERS) Jan Struther (MRS
MINIVER)
SC: Ronald Millar, George Froeschel
Greer Garson . . . . Kay Miniver
Walter Pidgeon . . . . Clem Miniver
John Hodiak . . . . Spike
Leo Genn . . . . Steve Brunswick
Cathy O'Donnell . . . . Judy Miniver
Henry Wilcoxon . . . . Vicar
Reginald Owen . . . . Mr Foley
Anthony Bushell . . . . Dr Kaneson
Richard Gale . . . . Tom Foley
Peter Finch . . . . Polish Officer
William Fox . . . . Toby Miniver
Alison Leggatt . . . . Mrs Foley
DRAMA Wife with year to live clears
up her family's problems.

11494
NO TRACE (76) (A)
Tempean (Eros)
P: Robert Baker, Monty Berman
D:S: John Gilling
Hugh Sinclair . . . . Robert Southley
Dinah Sheridan . . . . Linda
John Laurie . . . . Insp McDougall
Barry Morse . . . . Harrison
Dora Bryan . . . . Maisie
Michael Brennan . . . . Fenton
Michael Ward . . . . Salesman
CRIME Crime novelist kills blackmailer
and pretends to help police.

11495
BLACKOUT (73) (A)
Tempean (Eros)
P: Robert Baker, Monty Berman
D: Robert S.Baker
S: Robert S.Baker, John Gilling
Maxwell Reed . . . . Chris Pelley
Dinah Sheridan . . . . Patricia Dale
Patric Doonan . . . . Chalky
Eric Pohlmann . . . . Otto
Annette Simmonds . . . . . . Lila Drew
Kynaston Reeves . . . . Dale
Michael Brennan . . . . Mickey
CRIME Once-blind man discovers girl's
'dead' brother running smuggling gang.

11496
CAGE OF GOLD (83) (A)
Ealing (GFD)
AP: Michael Relph
D: Basil Dearden
S: Jack Whittingham
SC: Jack Whittingham, Paul Stein
Jean Simmons . . . . Judith Moray
David Farrar . . . . Bill Brennan
James Donald . . . . Alan Keane
Herbert Lom . . . . Rahman
Madeleine Lebeau . . . . Madeleine
Bernard Lee . . . . Insp Grey
Gladys Henson . . . . Waddy
Maria Mauban . . . . Antoinette
Gregoire Aslan . . . . Dupont
Harcout Williams . . . . Dr Kearns
CRIME "Dead" man returns to blackmail
his fiancee and is killed.

11497
SOMETHING IN THE CITY (76) (U)
Nettlefold (Butcher)
P: Ernest G. Roy
D: Maclean Rogers
S: H.F.Maltby
Richard Hearne . . . . Mr Ningle
Garry Marsh . . . . Mr Holley
Ellen Pollock . . . . Mrs Holley
Betty Sinclair . . . . Mrs Ningle
Tom Gill . . . . Richard Holley
Diana Calderwood . . . . Beryl Ningle
Bill Shine . . . . Reporter
Dora Bryan . . . . Waitress
George Merritt . . . . Inspector
Horace Kenney . . . . Squeaker Man
COMEDY Pavement artist who poses as
businessman is accused of his own murder.

11498
GONE TO EARTH (110) (A) tech
USA: THE WILD HEART
London-BLPA-Vanguard (BL)
P: David O. Selznick
D:SC: Michael Powell, Emeric Pressburger
S: (NOVEL) Mary Webb
N: Joseph Cotten
Jennifer Jones . . . . Hazel Woodus
David Farrar . . . . Jack Reddin
Cyril Cusack . . . . Edward Marston
Sybil Thorndike . . . . Mrs Marston
Edward Chapman . . . . Mr James
Esmond Knight . . . . Abel Woodus
Hugh Griffith . . . . Andrew Vessons
George Cole . . . . Albert
Beatrice Varley . . . . Aunt Prowde
Frances Clare . . . . Amelia Comber
Raymond Rollett . . . . Elder/Landlord
Gerald Lawson. . . . . Elder/Roadmender
ROMANCE Shropshire, 1897. Gipsy weds
cleric and becomes squire's mistress.

11499
HER FAVOURITE HUSBAND (79) (A)
USA: THE TAMING OF DOROTHY

Orlux Films (Renown)-
P: John Sutro, Colin Lesslie
D: Mario Soldati
S: (PLAY) Pepine de Felipe
SC: Noel Langley, W.F.Templeton
Jean Kent . . . . Dorothy
Robert Beatty . . . . Antonio/Leo
Gordon Harker . . . . Mr Dotherington
Margaret Rutherford . . . Mrs Dotherington
Rona Anderson . . . . Stellina
Walter Crisham . . . . Caradotti
Max Adrian . . . . Catoni
Tamara Lees . . . . Rosana
Norman Shelley . . . . Dobson
Michael Balfour . . . . Pete
Jack McNaughton . . . . El Greco
Danny Green . . . . Angelface
COMEDY Italy. Gangster kidnaps his
double and takes his place to rob bank.

OCT

11500
THE WOMAN IN QUESTION (88) (A)
USA: FIVE ANGLES ON MURDER
Javelin (GFD)
P: Teddy Baird
D: Anthony Asquith
S: John Cresswell
Jean Kent . . . . Astra
Dirk Bogarde . . . . Bob Baker
John McCallum . . . . Murray
Susan Shaw . . . . Catherine
Hermione Baddeley . . . . . . Mrs Finch
Charles Victor . . . . Pollard
Duncan Macrae . . . . Supt Lodge
Lana Morris . . . . Lana
Joe Linnane . . . . Insp Butler
Vida Hope . . . . Shirley
Bobbie Scroggins . . . . Alfie Finch
Duncan Lamont . . . . Barney
Anthony Dawson . . . . Wilson
Albert Chevalier . . . . Gunter
CRIME Dead fortune-teller as seen through
the eyes of her sister, fiance, charlady,
shopkeeper, and sailor.

11501
THE MAGNET (79) (A)
Ealing (GFD)
AP: Sidney Cole
D: Charles Frend
S: T.E.B.Clarke
Stephen Murray . . . . Dr Brent
Kay Walsh . . . . Mrs Brent
William Fox . . . . Johnny Brent
Meredith Edwards . . . . Harper
Gladys Henson . . . . Nannie
Wylie Watson . . . . Pickering
Thora Hird . . . . Nannie
Julien Mitchell . . . . Mayor Hancock
Michael Brooke jr. . . . . Kit
Keith Robinson . . . . Spike
Thomas Johnson . . . . Perce
Bryan Michie . . . . Announcer
Seamus Mor Na Feasag . . . Tramp
COMEDY Mersey. Psychiatrist's son runs
away thinking he has killed a boy for history.

11502
MURDER WITHOUT CRIME (76) (A)
ABPC (ABP)
P: Victor Skutezky
D:SC: J. Lee-Thompson
S: (PLAY) J.Lee-Thompson (DOUBLE ERROR)
Dennis Price . . . . Matthew
Derek Farr . . . . Stephen
Patricia Plunkett . . . . Jan
Joan Dowling . . . . Grena
CRIME Landlord blackmails author for
apparent death of nightclub girl.
(Extract in ELSTREE STORY, 1952).

11503
THE WOMAN WITH NO NAME (83) (A)
USA: HER PANELLED DOOR
IFP(ABP)
P: John Stafford
D: Ladislas Vajda, George More O'Ferrall
S: (NOVEL) Theresa Charles (HAPPY NOW I
GO)
SC: Ladislas Vajda, Guy Morgan
Phyllis Calvert . . . . Yvonne Winter
Edward Underdown . . . . . . Luke Winter
Helen Cherry . . . . Sybil
Richard Burton . . . . Nick Chamerd
Anthony Nicholls . . . . Doctor
James Hayter . . . . Capt Bradshaw
Betty Ann Davies . . . . Beatrice
Amy Veness . . . . Sophie
Andrew Osborn . . . . Paul Hammond
Patric Troughton . . . . Colin
DRAMA Morose cripple's amnesiac wife
learns her sister is scheming to destroy her
marriage.

11504
DICK BARTON AT BAY (68) (U)
Marylebone-Hammer (Ex)
P: Henry Halstead
D: Godfrey Grayson
S: (RADIO SERIAL) Edward J.Mason
SC: Ambrose Grayson
Don Stannard . . . . Dick Barton
Tamara Desni . . . . Anna
George Ford . . . . Snowey White
Meinhart Maur . . . . Serg Volkoff
Percy Walsh . . . . Prof Mitchell
Joyce Linden . . . . Mary Mitchell
Campbell Singer . . . . Insp Cavendish
John Arnatt . . . . Jackson
Richard George . . . . Insp Slade
CRIME Anarchist kidnaps inventor and
instals death ray atop lighthouse at Beachy Head.

11505
SOHO CONSPIRACY (85) (U)
DUK Films
P: E.J. Fancey
D: Cecil H. Williamson
S: S & M. Monicelli
SC: Cecil H. Williamson, Ralph Dawson
Zena Marshall . . . . Dora
Jacques Labreque . . . . Carlo Scala
Peter Gawthorne . . . . Father Shaney
Syd & Max Harrison . . . . . Gondotti Bros
John Witty . . . . Guy
Tito Gobbi; Beniamino Gigli; Tito Schipa;
Gino Becchi
MUSICAL Concert saves Soho restaurateur
from lawyer's crooked plot. (Includes
extracts from earlier films).

11506
THE CLOWN (34) (A)
DUK Films
P: D: Cecil H. Williamson
S: Ken Cleveland
Ken Cleveland . . . . Andre Prezzo
Raymond Dawes . . . . Maitland
Arthur Lovegrove . . . . Steve
DRAMA New circus owner accuses old
clown of causing wife's death.

11507
THE CURE (18) (U)
Public Relationship
P: Richard & Betty Massingham
D: Richard Massingham, Michael Law
S: Richard & Betty Massingham
Richard Massingham . . . . . John
Barbara Lott . . . . Elsie
Nicholas Bentley . . . . Dr Stoss
Russell Waters . . . . Specialist
Hugh Massingham . . . . Masseur
COMEDY Health fiend falls victim to
lumbago and tries every known cure.

11508
METHOD AND MADNESS (29) (U)
also: MR PASTRY DOES THE LAUNDRY
Regent (AA)
P: Herbert Marshall, James Wilson
D: Herbert Marshall
S: Herbert Marshall, Richard Hearne
Richard Hearne . . . . Sidney Pastry
Guy Fane . . . . Charlie
Lilian Hinton . . . . Mrs Pastry
COMEDY Husband's slapstick mishaps
trying to do the week's washing.

11509
THE MAGIC CHALKS (10) (U) tech
GB Instructional (GFD)
CHILDREN Girl draws animal with magic
chalk and it comes to life.

11510
IRISH MELODY (37) (U)
Barralet (IFD)
D: Paul Barralet
S: Isobel StVincent
Barry Keegan . . . .
Albert Tee . . . .
Seamus Cavanaugh . . . . . .
MUSICAL Ireland. Wandering balladeer
rises to fame.

NOV

11511
DARK INTERVAL (60) (A)
Present Day (Apex)
P: Charles Reynolds
D: Charles Saunders
S: John Gilling
Zena Marshall . . . . Sonia Jordan
Andrew Osborn . . . . Walter Jordan
John Barry . . . . Trevor
John le Mesurier . . . .
Mona Washbourne . . . .
Wallas Eaton . . . .
Charmian Innes . . . .
CRIME Honeymoon wife learns her
husband is jealous madman.

11512
DANGEROUS ASSIGNMENT (58) (A)
Target (Apex)
P: Miriam Crowdy
D: Ben R. Hart
S: Chick Messina
Lionel Murton . . . . Joe Wilson
Pamela Deeming . . . . Laura
Ivan Craig . . . . Frank Mayer
Macdonald Parke . . . . B.G.Bradley
Michael Hogarth . . . .
Bill Hodge . . . .
CRIME Girl helps American reporter clean
up stolen car racket.

11513
THE CLOUDED YELLOW (96) (A)
Carillon (GFD) *reissue:* 1958 (8 mins cut)
P: Betty Box
D: Ralph Thomas
S: Janet Green
SC: Eric Ambler
Jean Simmons . . . . Sophie Malraux
Trevor Howard . . . . David Somers
Sonia Dresdel . . . . Jess Fenton
Maxwell Reed . . . . Nick
Barry Jones . . . . Nicholas Fenton
Kenneth More . . . . Willy
Geoffrey Keen . . . . Inspector
Andre Morell . . . . Chubb
Michael Brennan . . . . Supt Rolls
Gerard Heinz . . . . Karl
Lily Kann . . . . Minna

Sandra Dorne . . . . Kyra
Gabrielle Blunt . . . . Addie
CRIME Sacked agent helps unbalanced girl
prove she did not kill handyman.

11514
THE MUDLARK (100) (U)
20th Century Productions
P:SC: Nunally Johnson
D: Jean Negulesco
S: (NOVEL) Theodore Bonnet
Irene Dunne . . . . Queen Victoria
Alec Guinness . . . . Benjamin Disraeli
Andrew Ray . . . . Wheeler
Beatrice Campbell . . . . . . Lady Emily Prior
Finlay Currie . . . . John Brown
Anthony Steel . . . . Lt Charles McHatten
Raymond Lovell. . . . . Sgt Footman Naseby
Marjorie Fielding . . . . Lady Margaret Prior
Constance Smith . . . . Kate Noonan
Ronan O'Casey . . . . Slattery
Edward Rigby . . . . Watchman
Kynaston Reeves . . . . . . Sir Henry Ponsonby
Wilfrid Hyde White . . . . . . Tucker
HISTORY 1876. Urchin breaks into Windsor
Castle, humanising the mourning Queen.
(RFP: 1950; PGAA: 1951).

11515
THE ELUSIVE PIMPERNEL (109) (U) tech
London-BLPA-Archers (BL)
P: Samuel Goldwyn, Alexander Korda
D:SC: Michael Powell, Emeric Pressburger
S: (NOVEL) Baroness Orczy (THE SCARLET
PIMPERNEL)
David Niven . . . . Sir Percy Blakeney
Margaret Leighton . . . . Marguerite Blakeney
Jack Hawkins . . . . Prince of Wales
Cyril Cusack . . . . Chauvelin
Robert Coote . . . . Sir Andrew ffoulkes
Edmond Audran . . . . Armand StJuste
Danielle Godet . . . . . Suzanne de Tournai
Arlette Marchal . . . Comtesse de Tournai
Gerard Nery . . . . . Philippe de Tournai
Charles Victor . . . . Col Winterbottom
David Hutcheson . . . . Lord Anthony Dewhurst
Eugene Deckers . . . . . Capt Merieres
John Longden . . . . Abbot
Arthur Wontner . . . . Lord Grenville
ADVENTURE 1792. English fop dons
disguises to save French aristrocrats from
guillotine.

11516
THE NAKED EARTH (96) (U)
Everest (BL)
P: Nelson Scott
D: Marc Allegret
S: (NOVEL) Louis Hemon (MARIA
CHAPDELAINE)
SC: Marc Allegret, Roger Vadim, Hugh
Mills, J. McLaren-Ross, C.K. Jaeger
Michele Morgan . . . . . Maria Chapdelaine
Kieron Moore . . . . . Lorenzo Suprenant
Francoise Rosay . . . . Laura Chapdelaine
Jack Watling . . . . Robert Gagnon
Nancy Price . . . . Theresa Suprenant
Philippe Lemaire . . . . . . Francois Paradis
Francis de Wolff . . . . . . Papa Suprenant
George Woodbridge . . . . . . Samuel
ROMANCE Canada, 1912. Convent girl is
loved by fugitive, trapper, and childhood
sweetheart.

11517
SHE SHALL HAVE MURDER (90) (U)
Concanen Recordings (IFD)
P: Derrick de Marney, Guido Coen
D: Daniel Birt
S: (NOVEL) Delano Ames

SC: Allan Mackinnon
Rosamund John . . . . Jane Hamish
Derrick de Marney . . . . . . Dagobert Brown
Mary Jerrold . . . . Mrs Robjohn
Felix Aylmer . . . . Mr Playfair
Joyce Heron . . . . Rosemary Proctor
Jack Allen . . . . Maj Stewart
Henryetta Edwards . . . . . Sarah Swinburne
Harry Fowler . . . . Albert Oates
John Bentley . . . . Douglas Robjohn
Beatrice Varley . . . . Mrs Hawthorne
June Elvin . . . . Barbara Jennings
CRIME Novelist and law clerk solve death
of old lady client.

DEC

11518
LILLI MARLENE (85) (U)
Monarch
P: William Gell
D: Arthur Crabtree
S: Leslie Wood
Lisa Daniely . . . . Lilli Marlene
Hugh McDermott . . . . Steve Moray
Richard Murdoch . . . . Capt Wimpole
Leslie Dwyer . . . . Berry
John Blythe . . . . Holt
Rufus Cruickshank . . . . Sgt Bull
Michael Ward . . . . Winterton
Carl Jaffe . . . . Propaganda Chief
Irene Prador . . . . Nurse Schmidt
Estelle Brody . . . . Estelle
WAR Africa. Germans kidnap French girl
and force her to sing.

11519
HA'PENNY BREEZE (72) (U)
Storytellers (ABP)
P: Darcy Conyers, Don Sharp
D: Frank Worth
S: Don Sharp, Frank Worth
Don Sharp . . . . Johnny Craig
Edwin Richfield . . . . David King
Gwyneth Vaughan . . . . Joan King
Terry Everett . . . . Brian King
Eva Rowland . . . . Mrs King
Roger Maxwell . . . . Mr Simmonds
John Powe . . . . Barney
Darcy Conyers . . . . Richard Martin
DRAMA Suffolk. Ex-soldier turns 'dead'
village into yachting centre.

11520
HIGHLY DANGEROUS (88) (U)
Two Cities (GFD)
P: Anthony Darnborough
D: Roy Baker
S: Eric Ambler
Margaret Lockwood . . . . . . Frances Gray
Dane Clark . . . . Bill Casey
Marius Goring . . . . Anton Razinski
Naunton Wayne . . . . Hedgerley
Wilfrid Hyde White . . . . . . Luke
Eugene Deckers . . . . Alf
Olaf Pooley . . . . Assistant
Gladys Henson . . . . Attendant
Paul Hardtmuth . . . . Priest
Michael Hordern . . . . Rawlings
George Benson . . . . Customer
Eric Pohlmann . . . . Joe
Joan Haythorne . . . . Judy
Patric Doonan . . . . Customs Man
Anthony Newley . . . . Operator
Noel Johnson . . . . . . Frank Conway (voice)
ADVENTURE Balkans. American press agent
helps drugged entomoligist steal disease-
carrying insects.

11521
MIDNIGHT EPISODE (78) (A)
Triangle (Col) *reissue:* 1955 (11 mins cut)
P: Theo Lageard
D: Gordon Parry
S: (NOVEL) Georges Simenon (MONSIEUR
LA SOURIS)

SC: Rita Barisse, Reeve Taylor, Paul Vincent
Carroll, David Evans, William Templeton
Stanley Holloway . . . . Prof Prince
Leslie Dwyer . . . . Albert
Reginald Tate . . . . Insp Lucas
Meredith Edwards . . . . Sgt Tate
Wilfrid Hyde White . . . . . . Mr Knight

Joy Shelton . . . . Mrs Arnold
Natasha Parry . . . . Jill Harris
Raymond Young . . . . Miller
Leslie Perrins . . . . Charles Mason
Sebastian Cabot . . . . Benno
CRIME Tramp finds stolen wallet and
is used by police to trap murderer.

1951

JAN

11522
INTO THE BLUE (83) (U)
USA: THE MAN IN THE DINGHY
Imperadio (BL)
P: Herbert Wilcox, Michael Wilding
D: Herbert Wilcox
S: Nicholas Phipps
SC: Pamela Wilcox Bower, Donald Taylor
Michael Wilding . . . . Nicholas Foster
Odile Versois . . . . Jackie
Jack Hulbert . . . . John Ferguson
Constance Cummings . . . . . Kate Ferguson
Edward Rigby . . . . Bill
COMEDY Yachting couple and stowaway
catch French watch-smuggler.

11523
TAKE ME TO PARIS (72) (U)
Byron (ABFD)
P: Henry Halstead
D: Jack Raymond
S: Max Catto
Albert Modley . . . . Albert
Roberta Huby . . . . Linda Vane
Bruce Seton . . . . Gerald Vane
Claire Guilbert . . . . Annette
Richard Molinas . . . . Pojo
George Bishop . . . . Mr Armstrong
Leonard Sharp . . . . Walter
Jim Gerald . . . . Butcher
Argus . . . . Jules
COMEDY Crooks use jockey's horse blanket
to smuggle gems into France.

11524
THE SECOND MATE (76) (U)
Elstree Independent (ABFD)
P:D: John Baxter
S: Anson Dyer
SC: Barbara K. Emary, Jack Francis
Gordon Harker . . . . Bill Tomkins
Graham Moffatt . . . . Paddy
David Hannaford . . . . Bobby
Beryl Walkley . . . . Kate
Charles Sewell . . . . Joe
Anne Blake . . . . Fortune Teller
Charles Heslop . . . . Hogan
Jane Welsh . . . . Mrs Mead
Howard Douglas . . . . Dusty
CRIME Thames bargee poses as crook to
catch jewel smugglers.

11525
THE ADVENTURERS (86) (A)
USA: THE GREAT ADVENTURE
Mayflower (GFD)
P: Maxwell Setton, Aubrey Baring
D: David Macdonald
S: Robert Westerby
Dennis Price . . . . Clive Hunter
Jack Hawkins . . . . Pieter Brandt
Siobhan McKenna . . . . Anne Hunter
Peter Hammond . . . . Hendrik van Thaal
Gregoire Aslan . . . . Dominic
Bernard Lee . . . . O'Connell
Ronald Adam . . . . Van Thaal
Charles Paton . . . . Barman
ADVENTURE Africa, 1902. Boers trek to
recover hidden diamonds.

11526
BLACKMAILED (85) (A)
HH Films (GFD)
P: Harold Huth
D: Marc Allegret
S: (NOVEL) Elizabeth Myers
(MRS CHRISTOPHER)
SC: Hugh Mills, Roger Vadim
Mai Zetterling . . . . Carol Edwards
Dirk Bogarde . . . . Stephen Mundy

Fay Compton . . . . Mrs Christopher
Robert Flemyng . . . . . . Dr Giles Freeman
Michael Gough . . . . Maurice Edwards
James Robertson Justice . . Mr Sine
Joan Rice . . . . Alma
Harold Huth . . . . Hugh Saintsbury
Wilfrid Hyde White . . . . Lord Dearsley
Bruce Seton . . . . Supt Crowe
Cyril Chamberlain . . . . PC
CRIME Victims of dead blackmailer
conspire to conceal the crime.

11527
MR DRAKE'S DUCK (85) (U)
Angel Productions (Eros)
P: Daniel Angel, Douglas Fairbanks jr
D: SC: Val Guest
S: (RADIO PLAY) Ian Messiter
Douglas Fairbanks jr . . . . . Don Drake
Yolande Donlan . . . . Penny Drake
A.E.Matthews . . . . Brigadier
Jon Pertwee . . . . Reuben
Reginald Beckwith . . . . Mr Boothby
Wilfrid Hyde White . . . . . . Mr May
Howard Marion-Crawford . . Maj Travers
Peter Butterworth . . . . Higgins
Tom Gill . . . . Capt White
COMEDY. The services occupy farm to
find which duck lays uranium eggs.

FEB

11528
THE DARK MAN (91) (A)
Independent Artists (GFD)
P: Julian Wintle
D:S: Jeffrey Dell
Edward Underdown . . . Insp Jack Viner
Maxwell Reed . . . . The Dark Man
Natasha Parry . . . . Molly Lester
William Hartnell . . . . Supt
Barbara Murray . . . . Carol Burns
Cyril Smith . . . . Samuel Denny
Leonard White . . . . Det Evans
John Singer . . . . Adjutant
Geoffrey Sumner . . . . Major
CRIME Killer pursues actress who saw
him kill black marketeer.

11529
POOL OF LONDON (85) (A)
Ealing (GFD)
AP: Michael Relph
D: Basil Dearden
S: Jack Whittingham, John Eldridge
Bonar Colleano . . . . Dan MacDonald
Susan Shaw . . . . Pat
Renee Asherson . . . . Sally
Earl Cameron . . . . Johnny
Moira Lister . . . . Maisie
Max Adrian . . . . Vernon/George
Joan Dowling . . . . Pamela
James Robertson Justice . . . Trotter
Michael Golden . . . . Andrews
John Longden . . . . Insp Williamson
Alfie Bass . . . . Alf
Leslie Phillips . . . . Harry
CRIME Merchant seaman get his negro
friend to help him smuggle diamonds
stolen by acrobat.

11530
THE FRANCHISE AFFAIR (88) (A)
ABPC (ABP)
P: Robert Hall
D: Lawrence Huntington
S: (NOVEL) Josephine Tey
SC: Lawrence Huntington, Robert Hall
Michael Denison . . . . Robert Blair
Dulcie Gray . . . . Marion Sharpe
Anthony Nicholls . . . . . Kevin McDermott
Marjorie Fielding . . . . Mrs Sharpe

Athene Seyler . . . . Aunt Lin
John Bailey . . . . Insp Grant
Ann Stephens . . . . Betty Kane
Hy Hazell . . . . Mrs Chadwick
Kenneth More . . . . Stanley Peters
Avice Landone . . . . Mrs Wynn
Maureen Glynne . . . . Rose Glynn
Peter Jones . . . . Bernard Chadwick
Moultrie Kelsall . . . . Judge
John Warwick . . . . Carley
CRIME Teenage girl accuses widow and
daughter of kidnapping her.

11531
THE THIRD VISITOR (85) (A)
Elvey-Gartside (Eros)
P: Ernest Gartside
D: Maurice Elvey
S: (PLAY) Gerald Anstruther
SC: Gerald Anstruther, David Evans
Sonia Dresdel . . . . Steffy Millington
Guy Middleton . . . . Insp Mallory
Hubert Gregg . . . . Jack Kurton
Colin Gordon . . . . Bill Millington
Karel Stepanek . . . . Richard Carling
Eleanor Summerfield . . . . . Vera Kurton
John Slater . . . . James Oliver
Cyril Smith . . . . Horton
Michael Martin-Harvey . . . . Hewson
CRIME Crooked German kills ex-partner
and fakes his own death.

11532
THE LATE EDWINA BLACK (78) (A)
USA: OBSESSED
Elvey-Gartside (IFD)
P: Ernest Gartside
D: Maurice Elvey
S: (PLAY) William Dinner, William Morum
SC: Charles Frank, David Evans
David Farrar . . . . Gregory Black
Geraldine Fitzgerald . . . . . Elizabeth
Roland Culver . . . . Inspector
Jean Cadell . . . . Ellen
Mary Merrall . . . . Lady Southdale
Harcourt Williams . . . . Dr Prendergast
Charles Heslop . . . . Vicar
Ronald Adam . . . . Schoolmaster
Sydney Monckton . . . . Horace
CRIME 1890. Housekeeper and lover
suspect each other of poisoning his sadistic
wife.

11533
PANDORA AND THE FLYING DUTCHMAN
(112) (A) *tech*
Dorkay-Romulus (IFD) *reissue:* 1955 (Ren)
P:D:S: Albert Lewin
James Mason . . . Hendrick van der Zee
Ava Gardner . . . . Pandora Reynolds
Nigel Patrick . . . . Stephen Cameron
Sheila Sim . . . . Janet Fielding
Harold Warrender . . . . . . Geoffrey Fielding
Mario Cabre . . . . Juan Montalvo
Marius Goring . . . . Reggie Demarest
John Laurie . . . . Angus
Pamela Kellino . . . . Jenny Ford
Patricia Raine . . . . Peggy Ford
Margarita d'Alvarez. . . . . . Senora Montalvo
La Pillina . . . . Dancer
Abraham Sofaer . . . . Judge
FANTASY Spain, 1930. Rich, selfish
American girl gives her life to free Dutch
captain from curse of eternal life.

11534
I'LL GET YOU FOR THIS (83) (A)
USA: LUCKY NICK CAIN
Kaydor-Romulus (IFD) *reissue:* 1955 (Ren)
P: Joseph Kaufman
D: Joseph M. Newman
S: (NOVEL) James Hadley Chase (HIGH

STAKES)
SC: George Callahan, William Rose
George Raft . . . . Nick Cain
Coleen Gray . . . . Kay Wonderley
Charles Goldner . . . . Massine
Walter Rilla . . . . Mueller
Greta Gynt . . . . Claudette Ambling
Enzo Staiola . . . . Tony
Hugh French . . . . Travers
Elwyn Book-Jones . . . . Fence
Martin Benson . . . . Speranza
Peter Illing . . . . Ceralde
Peter Bull . . . . Hans
Constance Smith . . . . Nina
CRIME Italy. American gambler catches
forgers who framed him for killing T-Man.

11535
THE ROSSITER CASE (75) (A)
Hammer (Ex)
P: Anthony Hinds
D: Francis Searle
S: (PLAY) Kenneth Hyde (THE ROSSITERS)
SC: Kenneth Hyde, John Gilling, Francis
Searle
Helen Shingler . . . . Liz Rossiter
Clement McCallin . . . . Peter Rossiter
Sheila Burrell . . . . Honor
Frederick Leister . . . . Sir James Ferguson
Henry Edwards . . . . Dr Bendix
Ann Codrington . . . . Marty
Dorothy Batley . . . . Nurse West
Gabrielle Blunt . . . . Alice
Stanley Baker . . . . Joe
CRIME Man accused when paralysed
wife shoots his mistress.

11536
THE LONG DARK HALL (86) (A)
Five Ocean-Cusick International (BL)
P: Peter Cusick
D: Anthony Bushell, Reginald Beck
S: Nunnally Johnson
SC: Nunnally Johnson, William Fairchild
Rex Harrison . . . . Arthur Groome
Lilli Palmer . . . . Mary Groome
Denis O'Dea . . . . Sir Charles Morton
Raymond Huntley . . . . Insp Sullivan
Patricia Wayne . . . . Rose Mallory
Anthony Dawson . . . . The Man
Anthony Bushell . . . . Clive Bedford
Meriel Forbes . . . . Marjorie
Brenda de Banzie . . . . Mrs Rogers
William Squires . . . . Sgt Cochran
Michael Medwin . . . . Leslie Scott
Colin Gordon . . . . Pound
Eric Pohlmann . . . . Polaris
CRIME Suspension of death sentence
saves innocent father from hanging for
death of his mistress.

11537
ONE WILD OAT (78) (A)
Coronet (Eros)
P: John Croydon
D: Charles Saunders
S: (PLAY) Vernon Sylvaine
SC: Vernon Sylvaine, Lawrence Huntington
Robertson Hare . . . . . . Humphrey Proudfoot
Stanley Holloway . . . . Alfred Gilbey
Sam Costa . . . . Mr Pepys
Andrew Crawford . . . . Fred Gilbey
Vera Pearce . . . . Mrs Gilbey
June Sylvaine . . . . Cherrie Proudfoot
Robert Moreton . . . . Throstle
Constance Lorne . . . . Mrs Proudfoot
Irene Handl . . . . Audrey Cuttle
Ingeborg Wells . . . . Gloria Samson
Charles Groves . . . . Charles
Joan Rice . . . . Annie

COMEDY Greyhound owner poses as
solicitor's wife to save him from blackmailing
ex-mistress.

11538
FILES FROM SCOTLAND YARD (57) (U)
Parthian (IFD)
P: Henry Hobhouse
D: Anthony Squire
John Harvey . . . . Jim Hardy
Moira Lister . . . . Joanna Goring
Louise Hampton . . . . Agatha Steele
Reginald Purdell . . . . Insp Gower
Dora Bryan . . . . Minnie Robinson
CRIME "The Lady's Companion;" "The
Telephone;" "The Interrogation."

MAR

11539
TO HAVE AND TO HOLD (63) (A)
Hammer (Ex)
P: Anthony Hinds
D: Godfrey Grayson
S: (PLAY) Lionel Brown
SC: Reginald Long
Avis Scott . . . . June de Winter
Patrick Barr . . . . Brian Harding
Robert Ayres . . . . Max
Eunice Gayson . . . . Peggy Harding
Ellen Pollock . . . . Roberta
Harry Fine . . . . Robert
Richard Warner . . . . Cyril
DRAMA Cripple tries to force his wife to
love his divorced friend.

11540
A TALE OF FIVE CITIES (99) (A)
USA: A TALE OF FIVE WOMEN
Grand National
P: Alexander Paal, Borris Morros
D: Montgomery Tully, R. Marcellini,
M. Stuadte, Emil E. Reinert, Gvon Cziffra
S: Patrick Kirwan, Maurice J. Wilson
Bonar Colleano . . . . Bob Mitchell
Barbara Kelly . . . . Lesley
Lana Morris . . . . Dealia
Anne Vernon . . . . Jeannine
Eva Bartok . . . . Katalin
Gina Lollobrigida . . . . Maria
Karin Himbold . . . . Charlotte
Geoffrey Sumner . . . . Wingco
Lily Kahn . . . . Charlady
Danny Green . . . . Levinsky
Carl Jaffe . . . . Brother
ROMANCE Amnesiac GI searches for girl in
Paris, Vienna, Rome, Berlin and London.

11541
SMART ALEC (58) (A)
Vandyke (GN)
P: Roger Proudlock
D: John Guillermin
S: Alec Coppel
Peter Reynolds . . . . Alec Albion
Mercy Haystead . . . . Judith
Leslie Dwyer . . . . Gossage
Edward Lexy . . . . Inspector
Kynaston Reeves . . . . Uncle Edward
CRIME Man predicts rich uncle's death
and shoots him with an ice bullet.

11542
FLESH AND BLOOD (102) (A)
Harefield (BL)
P: Anatole de Grunwald
D: Anthony Kimmins
S: (PLAY) James Bridie (THE SLEEPING
CLERGYMAN)
SC: Anatole de Grunwald
Richard Todd . . . Charles Cameron/Sutherland
Glynis Johns . . . . Katherine

Joan Greenwood . . . . . . Wilhelmina Cameron
Andre Morell . . . . Dr Marshall
Freda Jackson . . . . Mrs Hannah
James Hayter . . . . Sir Douglas Manley
George Cole . . . . John Hannah
Ursula Howells . . . . Harriet Marshall
Ronald Howard . . . . Purley
Walter Fitzgerald . . . . Dr Cooper
Muriel Aked . . . . Mrs Walker
Michael Hordern . . . . Webster
DRAMA Glasgow, 1867-1927. Doctor sees
dead friend's genius reappear in his grandson.

11543
THE QUIET WOMAN (71) (U)
Tempean (Eros)
P: Robert Baker, Monty Berman
D:SC: John Gilling
S: Ruth Adam
Derek Bond . . . . Duncan McLeod
Jane Hylton . . . . Janie Foster
Dora Bryan . . . . Elsie
Michael Balfour . . . . Lefty
Dianne Foster . . . . Helen
John Horsley . . . . Insp Bromley
Harry Towb . . . . Jim Cranshaw
Campbell Singer . . . . Willis
CRIME Romney Marsh. Smuggler helps
publican's husband who is escaped convict.

11544
THE BROWNING VERSION (90) (A)
Javelin (GFD)
P: Teddy Baird
D: Anthony Asquith
S: (PLAY) Terence Rattigan
SC: Terence Rattigan
Michael Redgrave . . . . Andrew Crocker-Harris
Jean Kent . . . . . Millie Crocker-Harris
Nigel Patrick . . . . Frank Hunter
Ronald Howard . . . . Gilbert
Wilfrid Hyde White . . . . . . Frobisher
Brian Smith . . . . Taplow
Bill Travers . . . . Fletcher
Paul Medland . . . . Wilson
Ivan Samson . . . . Lord Baxter
Josephine Middleton . . . . . Mrs Frobisher
Peter Jones . . . . Carstairs
Sarah Lawson . . . . Betty Carstairs
DRAMA Retiring schoolmaster realises
he is complete failure.

11545
HAPPY-GO-LOVELY (97) tech (U)
Excelsior (ABP)
P: Marcel Hellman
D: Bruce Humberstone
S: F. Damman, H. Rosenfeld
SC: Val Guest, Arthur Macrae
David Niven . . . . B.G.Bruno
Vera-Ellen . . . . Janet Jones
Cesar Romero . . . . John Frost
Bobby Howes . . . . Charlie
Diane Hart . . . . Mae
Sandra Dorne . . . . Betty
Gordon Jackson . . . . Paul Tracey
Barbara Couper . . . . Mme Amanda
Henry Hewitt . . . . Dodds
Gladys Henson . . . . Mrs Urquhart
Hugh Dempster . . . . Bates
Joyce Carey . . . . Secretary
John Laurie . . . . Jonskill
Wylie Watson . . . . Stage-doorman
Kay Kendall . . . . Secretary
MUSICAL Edinburgh. Dancer mistaken for
fiancee of millionaire who is posing as
reporter.

11546
TALK OF A MILLION (78) (U)
USA: YOU CAN'T BEAT THE IRISH
ABPC (ABP)
P: Alex Boyd
D: John Paddy Carstairs
S: (PLAY) Louis d'Alton
(THEY GOT WHAT THEY WANTED)
SC: Frederic Gotfurt
Jack Warner . . . . . Bartley Murnahan
Barbara Mullen . . . . . Bessie Murnahan
Noel Purcell . . . . Matty McGrath
Ronan O'Casey . . . . Derry Murnahan
Michael Dolan . . . . Turbidy
Niall McGinnis . . . . Tom Cassidy
Vincent Ball . . . . Jack Murnahan
Joan Kenney . . . . Sally Murnahan
Elizabeth Erskine . . . . . Norah Murnahan
Sidney James . . . . John C. Moody
Alfie Bass . . . . Lorcan
Milo O'Shea . . . . Signwriter
COMEDY Ireland. Workshy father poses as
heir to £500.000.

APR

11547
THE GALLOPING MAJOR (82) (U)
Sirius-Romulus (IFD) *reissue:* 1955 (Ren)
P: Monja Danischewsky
D: Henry Cornelius
S: Basil Radford
SC: Monja Danischewsky, Henry Cornelius
Basil Radford . . . . Maj Arthur Hill
Jimmy Hanley . . . . Bill Collins
Janette Scott . . . . Susan Hill
A.E.Matthews . . . . . . Sir Robert Medleigh
Rene Ray . . . . Pam Riley
Charles Victor . . . . Sam Fisher
Joyce Grenfell . . . . Maggie
Hugh Griffith . . . . Harold Temple
Julien Mitchell . . . . Sgt Adair
Sydney Tafler . . . . Mr Leon
Charles Hawtrey . . . . Lew Rimmel
Sidney James . . . . Bookie
Alfie Bass . . . . Newsboy
Charlie Smirke; Raymond Glendenning;
Bruce Belfrage; Marion Harris jr.
COMEDY Pet shop owner's syndicate buys
racehorse and wins Grand National .

11548
THE MAN WITH THE TWISTED LIP (35) (U)
Telecine Films (GN)
P: Rudolph Cartier
D: Richard M. Grey
S: (STORY) A. Conan Doyle
John Longden . . . . Sherlock Holmes
Campbell Singer . . . . Dr Watson
Hector Ross . . . . Neville StClair
Beryl Baxter . . . . Doreen
Walter Gotell . . . . Luzatto
CRIME Tec tracks missing husband to
Wapping opium den.

11549
WORM'S EYE VIEW (77) (U)
Byron (ABFD) *reissue:* 1955 (Ren)
P: Henry Halstead
D: Jack Raymond
S: (PLAY) R.F. Delderfield
SC: R.F. Delderfield, Jack Marks
Ronald Shiner . . . . Sam Porter
Garry Marsh . . . . Pop Brownlow
Diana Dors . . . . Thelma
John Blythe . . . . Duke
Bruce Seton . . . . SL Briarly
Digby Wolfe . . . . . Cpl Mark Trelawney
Eric Davies . . . . Taffy
Everley Gregg . . . . Mrs Bounty

Christina Forrest . . . . Bella Bounty
COMEDY 1942. Adventures of group of
airmen billeted on seaside land-lady.

11550
THE CASE OF THE MISSING SCENE (47) (U)
GB Instructional (GFD)
P: William D'Arcy
D: Don Chaffey
S: Mary Cathcart Borer
Ivor Bowyer . . . . Tony
Peter Butterworth . . . . George
CHILDREN Norfolk. Children help
photographer catch bird poachers.

11551
TREK TO MASHOMBA (46) (U)
GB Instructional (GFD)
P: Brian Salt
D: Vernon Sewell
S: Mary Cathcart Borer
Ivor Bowyer . . . . Dick Martin
John Longden . . . . Dr Martin
Bruce Meredith-Smith . . . . Hargreaves
CHILDREN Africa, 1890. Crooked miners
give lives to save British trekkers from
Matabele.

11552
NIGHT WITHOUT STARS (86) (A)
Europa (GFD)
P: Hugh Stewart
D: Anthony Pelissier
S: (NOVEL) Winston Graham
SC: Winston Graham
David Farrar . . . . Giles Gordon
Nadia Gray . . . . Alix Delaisse
Maurice Teynac . . . . Louis Malinay
Gilles Queyant . . . . Deffond
Gerard Landry . . . . Pierre Cheval
June Clyde . . . . Claire
Robert Ayres . . . . Walter
Clive Morton . . . . Dr Carlson
Eugene Deckers . . . . Armand
Martin Benson . . . . White Cap
CRIME Nice. Blind lawyer solves death
of traitor who turned smuggler.

11553
LAUGHTER IN PARADISE (93) (U)
Transocean (ABP)
P:D: Mario Zampi
S: Michael Pertwee, Jack Davies
Alastair Sim . . . . Deniston Russell
Fay Compton . . . . Agnes Russell
Beatrice Campbell . . . . . . .Lucille Grayson
Veronica Hurst . . . . Joan Webb
Guy Middleton . . . . Simon Russell
George Cole . . . . Herbert Russell
A.E.Matthews . . . . . . Sir Charles Robson
Joyce Grenfell . . . . Elizabeth Robson
Anthony Steel . . . . Roger Godfrey
John Laurie . . . . Gordon Webb
Eleanor Summerfield . . . . . Sheila Wilcott
Ronald Adam . . . . Mr Wagstaffe
Leslie Dwyer . . . . Sgt
Ernest Thesiger . . . . Endicott
Hugh Griffith . . . . Henry Russell
Michael Pertwee . . . . Stuart
Audrey Hepburn . . . . Cigarette Girl
COMEDY Practical joker leaves his fortune
on strange conditions.(Top Moneymaker: 1951).

11554
ASSASSIN FOR HIRE (67) (A)
Merton Park (AA)
P: Julian Wintle
D: Michael McCarthy
S: (TV PLAY) Rex Rienits
SC: Rex Rienits
Sydney Tafler . . . . Antonio Riccardi
Ronald Howard . . . . Insp Carson

John Hewer . . . . Guiseppi Riccardi
Kathryn Blake . . . . Maria Riccardi
Gerald Case . . . . Sgt Stott
Ian Wallace . . . . Charlie
Martin Benson . . . . Catesby
Ewen Solon . . . . Fred
CRIME Inspector tricks professional
killer into thinking he killed his brother.

11555
CIRCLE OF DANGER (86) (U)
Coronado (RKO)
P: David E. Rose, Joan Harrison
D: Jacques Tourneur
S: (NOVEL) Philip Macdonald
SC: Philip Macdonald
Ray Milland . . . . Clay Douglas
Patricia Roc . . . . Elspeth Graham
Marius Goring . . . . Sholto Lewis
Hugh Sinclair . . . . Hamish McArran
Naunton Wayne . . . . Reggie Sinclair
Marjorie Fielding . . . . Mrs McArran
Edward Rigby . . . . Idwal Llewellyn
John Bailey . . . . Pape Llewellyn
Colin Gordon . . . . Col Fairbairn
Dora Bryan . . . . Bubbles
Michael Brennan . . . . Bert Oakshott
Reginald Beckwith . . . . . . Oliver
David Hutcheson . . . . Tony Wrexham
DRAMA American searches Wales and Scotland
for the truth of his brother's wartime death.

11556
CAPTAIN HORATIO HORNBLOWER RN
(118) (U) tech
WB-FN *reissue:* 1954
P:D: Raoul Walsh
S: (NOVEL) C.S.Forester
SC: Ivan Goff, Ben Roberts, Aeneas
Mackenzie
Gregory Peck . . . Horatio Hornblower
Virginia Mayo . . . Lady Barbara Wellesley
Robert Beatty . . . . . Lt William Bush
James Robertson Justice . . . Quist
Denis O'Dea . . . . Admiral Leighton
Terence Morgan . . . . Lt Gerard
Richard Hearne . . . . Polwheal
James Kenney . . . . Midshipman Longley
Moultrie R. Kelsall . . . . . . Lt Crystal
Michael Dolan . . . . Gundarson
Stanley Baker . . . . Mr Harrison
John Witty . . . . Capt Etenza
Christopher Lee . . . . Captain
Kynaston Reeves . . . . Lord Hood
Ingeborg Wells . . . . Hebe
Ronald Adam . . . . Admiral Macartney
Michael Goodliffe . . . . Caillard
Amy Veness . . . . Mrs McPhee
ADVENTURE Captain finds love during
battles with ships of Spain, France and
Holland.

11557
THERE IS ANOTHER SUN (95) (A)
Nettlefold (Butcher) *reissue:* 1953,
WALL OF DEATH
P: Ernest G. Roy
D: Lewis Gilbert
S: James Raisin
SC: Guy Morgan
Maxwell Reed . . . . Racer
Susan Shaw . . . . Lillian
Laurence Harvey . . . . Maguire
Hermione Baddeley . . . . . . Gypsy Sarah
Leslie Dwyer . . . . Foley
Meredith Edwards . . . . Sgt Bratcher
Robert Adair . . . . Sarno
Earl Cameron . . . . Ginger Jones
CRIME Fairground boxer helps wall of
death rider rob boss.

MAY

11558
TOM BROWN'S SCHOOLDAYS (96) (U)
Talisman (Renown) *reissue:* 1957 (cut)
P: Brian Desmond Hurst
D: Gordon Parry
S: (NOVEL) Thomas Hughes
SC: Noel Langley

John Howard Davies	Tom Brown
Robert Newton	Dr Arnold
Diana Wynyard	Mrs Arnold
Hermione Baddeley	Sally Harrowell
Kathleen Byron	Mrs Brown
James Hayter	Thomas
John Charlesworth	East
John Forrest	Flashman
Michael Hordern	Wilkes
Max Bygraves	Coach Guard
Francis de Wolff	Squire Brown
Amy Veness	Mrs Wixie
Brian Worth	Judd
Rachel Gurney	Mrs Arthur
Michael Brennan	Black Bart

DRAMA 1834. New headmaster tries to
reform the bad traditions of Rugby School.

11559
OLD MOTHER RILEY'S JUNGLE
TREASURE (75) (U)
Oakland Films (Renown)
P: George Minter
D: Maclean Rogers
S: Val Valentine

Arthur Lucan	Mrs Riley
Kitty McShane	Kitty Riley
Garry Marsh	Kim
Sebastian Cabot	Morgan
Cyril Chamberlain	Capt Daincourt
Anita d'Ray	Estelle
Willer Neal	Harry Benson
Robert Adams	Chief Stinker
Roddy Hughes	Mr Orders
Peter Butterworth	Steve

COMEDY Cleaner finds old map and goes
to jungle to seek treasure.

11560
PENNY POINTS TO PARADISE (77) (U)
Advance-PYL Productions (Adelphi)
P: Alan Cullimore
D: Tony Young
S: John Ormonde

Harry Secombe	Harry Flakers
Alfred Marks	Edward Haynes
Peter Sellers . . .	The Major/Arnold P'Fringe
Paddy O'Neil	Christine Russell
Spike Milligan	Spike Donnelly
Bill Kerr	Digger Graves
Freddie Frinton	Drunk
Vicki Page	Sheila Gilroy
Joe Linnane	Policeman
Sam Kydd	Porter/Taxi Driver

Felix Mendelssohn and his Hawaiian
Serenaders
COMEDY Brighton. Forger tries to exchange
false banknotes for pool winner's fortune.

11561
THE DARK LIGHT (66) (A)
Hammer (EX)
P: Michael Carreras
D:S: Vernon Sewell

Albert Lieven	Mark
David Greene	Johnny
Norman MacOwan	Rigby
Martin Benson	Luigi
Catherine Blake	Linda
Jack Stewart	Matt

John Harvey	Roger
John Longden	Stephen

CRIME Lighthouse keepers rescue bank
robbers and are tempted to help them escape.

11562
A SOLID EXPLANATION (10) (U) (3D)
Pathe Documentary Unit (Stereo Techniques)
P: Peter Baylis
D: Peter Bradford
S: Godfrey Harrison
Desmond Walter-Ellis . . . . . Himself
COMEDY Television comedian explains
stereoscopy.

11563
THE TALES OF HOFFMAN (127) (U) *tech*
London-BLPA (BL)
P:D:SC Michael Powell, Emeric Pressburger
S: (OPERA) Offenbach; Dennis Arundell
Prologue & Epilogue

Moira Shearer	Stella
Robert Rounseville	Hoffmann
Robert Helpmann	Lindorff
Pamela Brown	Nicklaus
Frederick Ashton	Kleinzack
Meinhart Maur	Luther
Edmond Audran	Cancer

The Tale of Olympia

Moira Shearer	Olympia
Robert Helpmann	Coppelius
Leonide Massine	Spalanzani

The Tale of Giulietta

Ludmilla Tcherina	Giulietta
Robert Helpmann	Dapertutto
Leonide Massine	Schlemil

The Tale of Antonia

Ann Ayars	Antonia
Robert Helpmann	Dr Miracle
Leonide Massine	Franz

VOICES: Owen Brannigan; Monica Sinclair;
Rene Soames; Bruce Dargavel; Dorothy Bond;
Margherita Grandi; Grahame Clifford
MUSICAL The three loves of a poet.

11564
THE MAGIC MARBLE (13) (U)
GB Instructional (GFD)
D: Darrell Catling
CHILDREN Marble comes to life and
plays tricks around the house.

11565
THE MARBLE RETURNS (11) (U)
GB Instructional (GFD)
D: Darrell Catling
CHILDREN Marble changes boy into
fairy and father into midget, Indian and
Sherlock Holmes.

11566
BILLY MAYERL ENTERTAINS (series) (U)
Bushey Film Studios (Ambassador)
P: Gilbert Church

11567
No. 1: (9)

11568
No. 2: (8)
MUSICAL Pianist.

11569
CHANGE OF HEART (21) (U)
British Movietonews (Butcher)
D: Peter Whale
Henry Mollison . . . . The Man
Cecile Chevreau . . . . The Girl
DRAMA Disabled soldier's love for animals
leads to romance with farmer's daughter.

11570
SCARLET THREAD (84) (A)
Nettlefold-International Realist (Butcher)
reissue: 1953
P: Ernest G. Roy
D: Lewis Gilbert
S: (PLAY) A.R.Rawlinson, Moie Charles
SC: A.R.Rawlinson

Kathleen Byron	Josephine
Laurence Harvey	Freddie
Sydney Tafler	Marcon
Arthur Hill	Shaw
Dora Bryan	Maggie
Eliot Makeham	Jason
Harry Fowler	Sam
Cyril Chamberlain	Mason
Renee Kelly	Eleanor

CRIME Cambridge. Crooks hiding in
university try to steal jewels.

11571
MIRTH AND MELODY (36) (U)
Inspiration (20)
P:D: Horace Shepherd
Max Wall   Terry & Dorrie Kendall
Stephane Grappelly and his Quintet
Alfredo Campoli
Eugene Pini and his Orchestra
REVUE (Includes extracts from earlier films).

11572
LOOKING FOR TROUBLE (46) (U)
Merton Park (GFD)
P: Frank Hoare
D: William C. Hammond
S: Patricia Latham
Perlita Neilson . . . . Pamela
CHILDREN Germany. Sgt's daughter tries
to get herself expelled from school.

11573
YOUNG WIVES' TALE (79) (A)
ABPC (ABP)
P: Victor Skutezky
D: Henry Cass
S: (PLAY) Ronald Jeans
SC: Anne Burnaby

Joan Greenwood	Sabina Pennant
Nigel Patrick	Rodney Pennant
Derek Farr	Bruce Banning
Guy Middleton	Victor Manifold
Athene Seyler	Nanny Gallop
Helen Cherry	Mary Banning
Audrey Hepburn	Eve Lester
Fabia Drake	Nurse Blott
Irene Handl	Nurse

COMEDY Playwright and helpless wife
share house with efficient couple.

11574
LET'S GO CRAZY (32)
Advance (Adelphi)
D: Alan Cullimore

Peter Sellers	Groucho/Guiseppe/
	Cedric/Izzy Gozzunk/
	Crystal Jollibottom
Spike Milligan	Eccles

Wallas Eaton; Manly & Austin; Freddie
Mirfield's Garbage Men
REVUE

JUN

11575
OUT OF TRUE (40) (A)
Crown Film Unit (Regent)
P: Frederick Wilson
D: Philip Leacock
S: Jay & Stephen Black
SC: Montagu Slater

Jane Hylton . . . . Molly Slade
David Evans . . . . Arthur Slade
Muriel Pavlow . . . . Betty
Mary Merrall . . . . Granny
Beatrice Varley . . . . Mrs Green
Robert Bloom . . . . Dr Dale
Jean Anderson . . . . Dr Bell
DRAMA Suicidal housewife cured after
treatment in mental home.

11576
LIFE IN HER HANDS (58) (A)
Crown Film Unit (UA)
P: Frederick Wilson
D: Philip Leacock
S: Monica Dickens, Anthony Stevens
Kathleen Byron . . . . Ann Peters
Bernadette O'Farrell . . . . Mary Gordon
Jacqueline Charles . . . . Michele Rennie
Jenny Laird. . . . . Matron
Robert Long . . . . Jack Wilson
Grace Gaven . . . . Sister McTavish
Jean Anderson . . . . Night Sister
Joan Maude . . . . . . Sister Tutor
Elwyn Brook-Jones . . . . . . Surgeon
DRAMA Wife blames herself for husband's
death and becomes nurse.

11577
WHITE CORRIDORS (102) (A)
Vic Films (GFD) reissue: 1963 (cut)
P: Joseph Janni, John Croydon
D: Pat Jackson
S: (NOVEL) Helen Ashton (YEOMAN'S
HOSPITAL)
SC: Pat Jackson, Jan Read
Googie Withers . . . . Dr Sophie Dean
James Donald . . . . Dr Neil Marriner
Godfrey Tearle . . . . Groom
Petula Clark . . . . Joan Shepherd
Moira Lister . . . . Dolly Clark
Jack Watling . . . . Dick Groom
Barry Jones . . . . Shoesmith
Basil Radford . . . . Civil Servant
Megs Jenkins . . . . Mrs Briggs
Henry Edwards . . . . Philip Brewster
Dagmar Wynter . . . . Marjorie Brewster
Gerard Heinz . . . . Dr Macuzek
Avice Landone . . . . Sister Jenkins
Jean Anderson . . . . Sister Gater
Fabia Drake . . . . Miss Farmer
DRAMA Various events during few days
at Midland hospital.

11578
HELL IS SOLD OUT (84) (A)
Zelstro (Eros)
P: Raymond Stross
D: Michael Anderson
S: (NOVEL) Maurice Dekobra
SC: Guy Morgan, Moie Charles
Richard Attenborough . . . . . Pierre Bonnet
Mai Zetterling . . . . Valerie Martin
Herbert Lom . . . . Dominic Danges
Kathleen Byron . . . . Arlette de Balzamann
Hermione Baddeley . . . . . Mme Menstrier
Zena Marshall . . . . Honeychild
Nicholas Hannen . . . . Francois
Joan Hickson . . . . Hortense
Eric Pohlmann . . . . Louis
Laurence Naismith . . . . . . Dr Monceau
Joan Young . . . . Gertrude Cole
COMEDY France. "Dead" novelist returns
to find Swedish authoress posing as his widow.
widow.

11579
THE LAVENDER HILL MOB (78) (U)
Ealing (GFD)
AP: Michael Truman
D: Charles Crichton

S: T.E.B.Clarke
Alec Guinness . . . . Holland
Stanley Holloway . . . . Pendlebury
Sidney James . . . . Lackery
Alfie Bass . . . . Shorty
Marjorie Fielding . . . . Mrs Chalk
John Gregson . . . . Farrow
Clive Morton . . . . Sgt
Ronald Adam . . . . Turner
Sydney Tafler . . . . Clayton
Edie Martin . . . . Miss Evesham
Jacques Brunius . . . . Official
Meredith Edwards . . . . PC Edwards
Gibb McLaughlin . . . . Godwin
Patrick Barr . . . . Inspector
Marie Burke . . . . Senora Gallardo
Audrey Hepburn . . . . Chiquita
COMEDY Bank clerk steals million in gold
and makes it into paper-weights. (AA: Best
Screenplay 1951; BFA: Best British Film 1951).

JUL

11580
BLACK WIDOW (62) (A)
Hammer (Exclusive)
P: Anthony Hinds
D: Vernon Sewell
S: (RADIO SERIAL) Lester Powell
(RETURN FROM DARKNESS)
SC: Allan Mackinnon
Christine Norden . . . . .Christine Sherwin
Robert Ayres . . . . Mark Sherwin
Anthony Forwood . . . . . . Paul
Jennifer Jayne . . . . Sheila Kemp
John Longden . . . . Kemp
John Harvey . . . . Dr Wallace
CRIME Amnesiac realises that his wife
and her lover intend to kill him.

11581
CHELSEA STORY (65) (A)
Present Day (Apex)
P: Charles Reynolds
D: Charles Saunders
S: John Gilling
Henry Mollison . . . . Mike Harvey
Sydney Tafler . . . . . . Fletcher Gilchrist
Ingeborg Wells . . . . Janice
Lesley Osmond . . . . Louise
Michael Moore . . . . George
Wallas Eaton . . . . Danny
Laurence Naismith . . . . . . Sgt Matthews
Michael Ward . . . . Chris Fawcett
CRIME Reporter robs house for bet and
is framed for killing occupier.

11582
CALLING BULLDOG DRUMMOND (80) (U)
MGM British
P: Hayes Goetz
D: Victor Saville
S: (NOVEL) Gerard Fairlie
SC: Gerard Fairlie, Howard Emmett Rogers,
Arthur Wimperis
Walter Pidgeon . . . . Hugh Drummond
Margaret Leighton . . . . . . Sgt Helen Smith
Robert Beatty . . . . Guns
David Tomlinson . . . . . Algy Longworth
Peggy Evans . . . . Molly
Charles Victor . . . . Insp McIver
Bernard Lee . . . . Col Webson
James Hayter . . . . Bill
Patric Doonan . . . . Alec
Harold Lang . . . . Stan
CRIME Policewoman and tecs pose as
crooks to catch gang of organised robbers.

11583
CLOUDBURST (92) (A)
Hammer (Ex)
P: Anthony Hinds, Alexander Paal

D: Francis Searle
S: (PLAY) Leo Marks
SC: Leo Marks, Francis Searle
Robert Preston . . . . John Graham
Elizabeth Sellars . . . . Carol Graham
Colin Tapley . . . . Insp Davis
Sheila Burrell . . . . Lorna
Harold Lang . . . . Mickie Fraser
Mary Germaine . . . . Peggy
George Woodbridge . . . . . . Sgt Ritchie
Lyn Evans . . . . Chuck Peters
Daphne Anderson . . . . Kate
Edward Lexy . . . . Cardew
CRIME Cipher expert tracks down thieves
who ran over his crippled wife.

11584
DAVID (38)
World Wide (Regent)
P: James Carr
D:S: Paul Dickson
D.R.Griffiths . . . . Dafydd Rhys
John Davies . . . . Ifor Morgan
Mary Griffiths . . . . Mary Rhys
Sam Jones . . . . Rev Mr Morgan
DRAMA Wales. School caretaker's elegy on
his son's death wins Eisteddfodd.

11585
NO RESTING PLACE (77) (A)
Colin Lesslie (ABFD)
D: Paul Rotha
S: (NOVEL) Ian Niall
SC: Paul Rotha, Colin Lesslie, Michael Orrom,
Gerard Healy
Michael Gough . . . . Alec Kyle
Eithne Dunne . . . . Meg Kyle
Noel Purcell . . . . Mannigan
Brian O'Higgins . . . . Tom Kyle
Jack MacGowran . . . . Billy Kyle
Christy Lawrence . . . . Paddy Kyle
CRIME Ireland. Civil Guard pursues
tinker who accidentally killed gamekeeper.

11586
HOTEL SAHARA (96) (U)
Tower (GFD) reissue: 1959 (20 mins cut)
P: George H. Brown
D: Ken Annakin
S: George H.Brown, Patrick Kirwan
Yvonne de Carlo . . . . Yasmin Pallas
Peter Ustinov . . . . Emad
David Tomlinson . . . . . Capt Puffin Cheyne
Roland Culver . . . . Maj Bill Randall
Albert Lieven . . . Lieut Gunther von Heilicke
Bill Owen . . . . Pte Binns
Sydney Tafler . . . . Cpl Pullar
Tom Gill . . . . Pte O'Brien
Mireille Perrey . . . . Mme Pallas
Ferdy Mayne . . . . Yusef
Guido Lorraine . . . . Capitano Guiseppi
Anton Diffring . . . . German
AC2 Lewis . . . . Suleiman the Goat
COMEDY Africa, 1942. Hotel staff change
loyalties to suit their occupiers.

AUG

11587
NO HIGHWAY (99) (U)
USA: NO HIGHWAY IN THE SKY
20th Century Productions
P: Louis D.Lighton
D: Henry Koster
S: (NOVEL) Nevil Shute
SC: Oscar Millard, R.C.Sheriff, Alec Coppel
James Stewart . . . . Theodore Honey
Marlene Dietrich . . . . . . Monica Teasdale
Glynis Johns . . . . Marjorie Corder
Jack Hawkins . . . . Denis Scott
Janette Scott . . . . Elspeth Honey
Elizabeth Allan . . . . Shirley Scott

Ronald Squire . . . . Sir John
Niall MacGinnis . . . . . . Capt Samuelson
Kenneth More . . . . Dobson
Maurice Denham . . . . Maj Pearl
Wilfrid Hyde White . . . . . . Fisher
David Hutcheson . . . . Bill Penworthy
Dora Bryan . . . . Rosie
DRAMA Eccentric scientist crashes air
liner to prove stress theory correct.

11588
HONEYMOON DEFERRED (79) (A)
Vic Films (BL)
P: John Sutro, Joseph Janni
D: Mario Camerini
S: Suso d'Amici, A. Pietrangelli
SC: John Hunter, C. Denis Freeman,
F. Brusati
Sally Ann Howes . . . . Katherine
Griffith Jones . . . . David
Kieron Moore . . . . Rocco
Lea Padovani . . . . Rosina
Anna Dondini . . . . Mama Pia
Moneta . . . . Grandpa Maggini
David Keir . . . . Professor
Freddie Meloni . . . . Churchill
COMEDY Italy. Ex-soldier spends honeymoon
in village he helped to liberate.

11589
THE MAN IN THE WHITE SUIT (85) (U)
Ealing (GFD)
AP: Sidney Cole
D: Alexander Mackendrick
S: (PLAY) Roger Macdougall
SC: Roger Macdougall, Alexander Macken-
drick, John Dighton
Alec Guinness . . . . Sidney Stratton
Joan Greenwood . . . . Daphne Birnley
Cecil Parker . . . . Alan Birnley
Michael Gough . . . . Michael Corland
Ernest Thesiger . . . . Sir John Kierlaw
Vida Hope . . . . Bertha
Howard Marion Crawford . . . .Cranford
Miles Malleson . . . . Tailor
Henry Mollison . . . . Hoskins
Patric Doonan . . . . Frank
Duncan Lamont . . . . Harry
Harold Goodwin . . . . Wilkins
Colin Gordon . . . . Bill
Joan Harben . . . . Miss Johnson
Mandy Miller . . . . Gladdie
Brian Worth . . . . King
Billy Russell . . . . Watchman
COMEDY Textile industry tries to suppress
inventor's everlasting fabric.

11590
A CASE FOR PC 49 (80) (A)
Hammer (Ex)
P: Anthony Hinds
D: Francis Searle
S: (RADIO SERIES) Alan Stranks, Vernon
Harris
SC: Alan Stranks, Vernon Harris
Brian Reece . . . Archibald Berkeley-Willoughby
Joy Shelton . . . . Joan Carr
Christine Norden . . . . Della Dainton
Leslie Bradley . . . . Victor Palantine
Gordon McLeod . . . . Insp Wilson
Campbell Singer . . . . Sgt Wright
Jack Stewart . . . . Cutler
Michael Balfour . . . . Chubby Price
CRIME PC proves artist's model killed
millionaire.

11591
HOME TO DANGER (66) (A)
New World (Eros)
P: Lance Comfort
D: Terence Fisher

S: John Temple-Smith, Francis Edge
Guy Rolfe . . . . Robert
Rona Anderson . . . . Barbara
Francis Lister . . . . Wainwright
Alan Wheatley . . . . Hughes
Bruce Belfrage . . . . Solicitor
Stanley Baker . . . . Willie Dougan
Dennis Harkin . . . . Jimmy the One
Peter Jones . . . . Lips Leonard
CRIME Dope peddler tries to kill dead
partner's daughter when she inherits old
house.

11592
THE SIX MEN (65) (A)
Planet Productions (Eros)
P: Roger Proudlock
D: Michael Law
S: E. & M A Radford
SC: Reed de Rouen, Michael Law, Richard
Eastham
Harold Warrender . . . . Supt Holroyd
Olga Edwardes . . . . Christina Frazer
Peter Bull . . . . Walkeley
Avril Angers . . . . Herself
Desmond Jeans . . . . Colonel
Michael Evans . . . . Hunter
Ivan Craig . . . . Wainwright
Reed de Rouen . . . . Lewis
CRIME Supt poses as blind informer
to destroy gang of jewel thieves.

11593
CHEER THE BRAVE (62) (U)
SWH-Piccadilly (Apex)
P: John Sutro, David Webster
D:S: Kenneth Hume
Elsie Randolph . . . . Doris Wilson
Jack McNaughton . . . . Bill Potter
Vida Hope . . . .
Geoffrey Keen . . . . Wilson
Marie Ault . . . . Mother-in-law
COMEDY Henpeck leaves nagging wife
when her first husband returns.

11594
VALLEY OF THE EAGLES (86) (U)
Independent Sovereign (GFD)
P: Nat A. Bronsten, George Willoughby
D: SC: Terence Young
S: Paul Tabori, Nat A Bronsten
Jack Warner . . . . Insp Petersen
Nadia Gray . . . . Kara Niemann
John McCallum . . . . Dr Nils Ahlen
Anthony Dawson . . . . Sven Nystrom
Mary Laura Wood . . . . Helga Ahlen
Norman MacOwan . . . . McTavish
Alfred Maurstad . . . . Trerik
Martin Boddey . . . . Headman
Christopher Lee . . . . Detective
Ewen Solon . . . . Detective
Niama Wiwstrand . . . . . . Baroness Erland
George Willoughby . . . . . Bertil
ADVENTURE Lapland. Swedish scientist
chases wife and assistant who stole invention
for producing power from sound.

SEP

11595
TWO ON THE TILES (72) (A)
Vandyke (GN)
P: Roger Proudlock
D: John Guillermin
S: Alec Coppel
Herbert Lom . . . . Ford
Hugh McDermott . . . . Dick Lawson
Brenda Bruce . . . . Janet Lawson
Ingeborg Wells . . . . Madeleine
Humphrey Lestocq . . . . . . Jimmy Bradley
G.A.Guinle . . . . Pierre
COMEDY Newlyweds blackmailed by
their butler and his wife.

11596
THE MAGIC BOX (118) tech (U)
Festival (BL)
P: Ronald Neame
D: John Boulting
S: (BOOK) Ray Allister (FRIESE-GREENE)
SC: Eric Ambler
Robert Donat . . . . William Friese-Greene
Margaret Johnston. . . . . . . Edith Harrison
Maria Schell. . . . . . Helen Friese-Greene
John Howard Davies . . Maurice Friese-Greene
David Oake . . . . . . Claude Friese-Greene
Renee Asherson . . . . Miss Tagg
Richard Attenborough . . . . . Jack Carter
Robert Beatty . . . . Lord Beaverbrook
Michael Denison . . . . Reporter
Henry Edwards . . . . Butler
Leo Genn . . . . Dacres
Marius Goring . . . . House Agent
Joyce Grenfell . . . . Mrs Clare
Robertson Hare . . . . Sitter
Kathleen Harrison . . . . Mother
William Hartnell . . . . Sgt
Stanley Holloway . . . . Broker's Man
Jack Hulbert . . . . Sgt
Glynis Johns . . . . May Jones
Mervyn Johns . . . . Pawnbroker
Barry Jones . . . . Doctor
Miles Malleson . . . . Conductor
Muir Matheson . . . . . . Sir Arthur Sullivan
A.E.Matthews . . . . Colonel
John McCallum . . . . Sitter
Bernard Miles . . . . Alfred
Laurence Olivier . . . . PC 94 B
Cecil Parker . . . . Platform Man
Eric Portman . . . . Arthur Collings
Dennis Price . . . . Assistant
Michael Redgrave . . . . Mr Lege
Margaret Rutherford . . . . . Lady Pond
Ronald Shiner . . . . Fairground Barker
Sheila Sim . . . . Nurse
Basil Sydney . . . . . . William Fox-Talbot
Sybil Thorndike . . . . Sitter
David Tomlinson . . . . Bob
Cecil Trouncer . . . . John Rudge
Peter Ustinov . . . . Industry Man
Frederick Valk . . . . Guttenberg
Kay Walsh . . . . Receptionist
Emlyn Williams . . . . Bank Manager
Harcourt Williams . . . . Tom
Googie Withers . . . . Sitter
HISTORY Biography of a cinematograph
pioneer (1855-1921).

11597
THE WESTMINSTER PASSION PLAY —
BEHOLD THE MAN (75) (U)
Film Reports-Companions of the Cross
(Philomena)
P: Susan Dallison, Fred T. Swann
D: Walter Rilla
S: (PLAY) Walter Meyjes, Charles P. Carr
(ECCE HOMO)
SC: Walter Meyjes, Walter Rilla
Charles P. Carr . . . . Jesus
RELIGION Story of Jesus Christ.

11598
MYSTERY JUNCTION (67) (A)
Merton Park (AA)
P: William H. Williams
D:S: Michael McCarthy
Sydney Tafler . . . . Larry Gordon
Barbara Murray . . . . Pat Dawn
Pat Owens . . . . Mabel Dawn
Martin Benson . . . . Steve Harding
Christine Silver . . . . Miss Owens
Philip Dale . . . . Elliot Fisher
Pearl Cameron . . . . Helen Mason
John Salew . . . . John Martin
Denis Webb . . . . Insp Clarke
CRIME Novelist solves murders in snowbound
railway station.

OCT

11599
MADAME LOUISE (83) (U)
Nettlefold (Butcher) *reissue:* 1953
(1117 ft cut)
P: Ernest G. Roy
D: Maclean Rogers
S: (PLAY) Vernon Sylvaine
SC: Michael Pertwee
Richard Hearne . . . . Mr Pastry
Petula Clark . . . . Penny
Garry Marsh . . . . Mr Trout
Richard Gale . . . . Lt Edwards
Doris Rogers . . . . Mrs Trout
Hilda Bayley . . . . Mme Louise
Charles Farrell . . . . Felling
Vic Wise . . . . Curly
Harry Fowler . . . . Clerk
COMEDY Bookie wins dress shop and
modernises it.

11600
FOUR DAYS (55) (A)
Vandyke (GN)
P: Roger Proudlock
D: John Guillermin
S: (PLAY) Monckton Hoffe
SC: Lindsay Galloway, J. McLaren Ross
Hugh McDermott . . . . . . Francis Templar
Kathleen Byron . . . . Lucienne Templar
Peter Reynolds . . . . Johnny Keylin
Gordon McLeod . . . . Mr Keylin
H.G.Stoker . . . . Baxter
John Harvey . . . . Hammond Stubbs
Petra Davies . . . . Helen
DRAMA Deceived husband has amnesia
following attempted suicide.

11601
APPOINTMENT WITH VENUS (89) (U)
USA: ISLAND RESCUE
British Film Makers (GFD) *reissue* 1960 (cut)
P: Betty Box
D: Ralph Thomas
S: (NOVEL) Jerrard Tickell
SC: Nicholas Phipps
David Niven . . . . Maj Valentine Morland
Glynis Johns . . . . Nicola Fallaize
George Coulouris . . . . Capt Weiss
Barry Jones . . . . Provost
Noel Purcell . . . . Trawler Langley
Kenneth More . . . . Lionel Fallaize
Martin Boddey . . . . Sgt Vogel
Bernard Lee . . . . Brigadier
Jeremy Spenser . . . . Georges
Patric Doonan . . . . Sgt Forbes
Richard Wattis . . . . Executive
David Horne . . . . Magistrate
Geoffrey Sumner . . . . Major
Peter Butterworth . . . . . . Rating
Anton Diffring . . . . German
COMEDY Channel Islands, 1940. Major and girl
rescue prize cow.

11602
THE LADY WITH THE LAMP (110) (U)
Imperadio (BL)
P:D: Herbert Wilcox
S: (PLAY) Reginald Berkeley
SC: Warren Chetham Strode
Anna Neagle . . . . . Florence Nightingale
Michael Wilding . . . . Sidney Herbert
Gladys Young . . . . Mrs Bracebridge
Felix Aylmer . . . . Lord Palmerston
Sybil Thorndike . . . . Miss Bosanquet
Peter Graves . . . . Prince Albert
Julian D'Albie . . . . Mr Bracebridge
Arthur Young . . . . W.E.Gladstone
Edwin Styles . . . . Mr Nightingale
Barbara Couper . . . . Mrs Nightingale

Helen Shingler . . . . . . Parthenope Nightingale
Helena Pickard . . . . Queen Victoria
Rosalie Crutchley . . . . Mrs Herbert
Maureen Pryor . . . . Sister Wheeler
Henry Edwards . . . . . . Howard Russell
Andrew Osborn . . . . . . Dr Sutherland
Clement McCallin . . . . . Richard Milnes
Monckton Hoffe . . . . Lord Stratford
HISTORY 1854. Nurse helps wounded in
Crimea and champions hospital reform.

11603
THE HOUSE IN THE SQUARE (91) (U) *tech*
USA: I'LL NEVER FORGET YOU
20th Century Productions
P: Sol C. Seigel
D: Roy Baker
S: (PLAY) John L. Balderston
(BERKELEY SQUARE)
SC: Ranald MacDougall
Tyrone Power . . . . Peter Standish
Ann Blyth . . . . Helen Pettigrew
Michael Rennie . . . . Roger Forsyth
Dennis Price . . . . Tom Pettigrew
Beatrice Campbell . . . . . . Kate Pettigrew
Raymond Huntley . . . . . . Mr Throsle
Kathleen Byron . . . . . Duchess of Devonshire
Irene Browne . . . . . . Lady Ann Pettigrew
Robert Atkins . . . . Samuel Johnson
Alex McCrindle . . . . James Boswell
Felix Aylmer . . . . Physician
Gibb McLaughlin . . . . Jacob
FANTASY American atomic chemist
becomes his own ancestor in the London
of 1784.

11604
SCROOGE (86) (U)
Renown *reissue:* 1955
P: George Minter
D: Brian Desmond Hurst
S: (NOVEL) Charles Dickens (A CHRISTMAS
CAROL)
SC: Noel Langley
Alastair Sim . . . . Ebenezer Scrooge
Kathleen Harrison . . . . Mrs Dilber
Jack Warner . . . . Mr Jorkins
Mervyn Johns . . . . Bob Cratchit
Hermione Baddeley . . . . . . Mrs Cratchit
Clifford Mollison . . . . Mr Wilkins
Michael Hordern . . . . Jacob Marley
George Cole . . . . Scrooge (youth)
Rona Anderson . . . . Alice
John Charlesworth . . . . . . Peter Cratchit
Glyn Dearman . . . . Tiny Tim
Francis de Wolff. . . . . . Christmas Present
Carol Marsh . . . . Fan
Brian Worth . . . . Fred
Miles Malleson . . . . Old Joe
Ernest Thesiger . . . . Undertaker
Michael Dolan . . . . Christmas Past
Roddy Hughes . . . . Mr Fezziwig
FANTASY Old miser is reformed by
visions of his past, present, and future.

NOV

11605
HIGH TREASON (93) (U)
Conqueror (GFD)
P: Paul Soskin
D: Roy Boulting
S: Frank Harvey, Roy Boulting
Andre Morell . . . . Supt Folland
Liam Redmond . . . . Cdr Brennan
Mary Morris . . . . Ann Braun
Kenneth Griffith . . . . Jimmy Ellis
Patric Doonan . . . . George Ellis
Anthony Bushell . . . . Maj Elliott
Joan Hickson . . . . Mrs Ellis
Anthony Nicholls . . . . . Grant Mansfield

Geoffrey Keen . . . . Morgan Williams
John Bailey . . . . Stringer
Dora Bryan . . . . Mrs Bowers
Charles Lloyd Pack . . . . . . Percy Ward
Laurence Naismith . . . . . . Gordon Wells
CRIME Police track down saboteurs before
they can blow up Battersea power station.

11606
GREEN GROW THE RUSHES (79) (U)
ACT Films (BL) *reissue:* 1954
BRANDY ASHORE (EB; 1060 ft cut).
P: John Gossage
D: Derek Twist
S: (NOVEL) Howard Clewes
SC: Howard Clewes, Derek Twist
Roger Livesey . . . . Capt Biddle
Honor Blackman . . . . Meg
Richard Burton . . . . Hammond
Frederick Leister . . . . Col Gill
John Salew . . . . Finch
Colin Gordon . . . . Fisherwick
Geoffrey Keen . . . . Prudhoe
Cyril Smith . . . . Hewitt
Eliot Makeham . . . . Urquhart
Vida Hope . . . . Polly
Russell Waters . . . . Bainbridge
Archie Duncan . . . . Pettigrew
COMEDY Kent marsh men smuggle brandy
under protection of ancient charter.

11607
ANOTHER MAN'S POISON (89) (A)
Daniel Angel (Eros)
P: Daniel Angel, Douglas Fairbanks jr
D: Irving Rapper
S: (PLAY) Leslie Sands (DEADLOCK)
SC: Val Guest
Bette Davis . . . . Janet Frobisher
Gary Merrill . . . . George Bates
Emlyn Williams . . . . Dr Henderson
Anthony Steel . . . . Larry Stevens
Barbara Murray . . . . Chris Dale
Reginald Beckwith . . . . . . Mr Bigley
Edna Morris . . . . Mrs Bunting
CRIME Yorks. Novelist uses horse-pill
to kill bankrobbing husband.

11608
MR DENNING DRIVES NORTH (93) (A)
London-BLPA (BL) *reissue:* 1960 (Orb)
P: Anthony Kimmins, Stephen Mitchell
D: Anthony Kimmins
S: (NOVEL) Alec Coppel
SC: Alec Coppel
John Mills . . . . Tom Denning
Phyllis Calvert . . . . Kay Denning
Sam Wanamaker . . . . Chick Eddowes
Herbert Lom . . . . Mados
Eileen Moore . . . . Liz Denning
Raymond Huntley . . . . . . Wright
Bernard Lee . . . . Insp Dodds
Wilfrid Hyde White . . . . . . Woods
Freda Jackson . . . . Ma Smith
Sheila Shand Gibbs . . . . . Matilda
Trader Faulkner . . . . Ted Smith
Russell Waters . . . . Harry Stopes
Michael Shepley . . . . Chairman
John Stuart . . . . Wilson
CRIME Man accidentally kills daughter's
lover, hides the body, and loses it.

11609
LADY GODIVA RIDES AGAIN (90) (U)
London-BLPA (BL)
P: Frank Launder, Sidney Gilliat
D: Frank Launder
S: Frank Launder, Val Valentine
Dennis Price . . . . Simon Abbott
John McCallum . . . . Larry Burns
Stanley Holloway . . . . Mr Clark

Pauline Stroud . . . . Marjorie Clark
Gladys Henson . . . . Mrs Clark
Bernardette O'Farrell . . . . Janie
George Cole . . . . Johnny
Diana Dors . . . . Dolores August
Eddie Byrne . . . . Eddie Mooney
Kay Kendall . . . . Sylvie
Renee Houston . . . . Beattie
Dora Bryan . . . . Publicity Woman
Sidney James . . . . Lew Beeson
Dagmar Wynter . . . . Myrtle Shaw
Tommy Duggan; Eddie Leslie; Walford Hyden;
Edward Forsyth; Lisa Lee
COMEDY Waitress wins phoney beauty
contest but flops in show business.

11610
THE WONDER KID (85) *Bilingual* (U)
London-BLPA (BL)
P:D:S: Karl Hartl
SC: Gene Markey
Bobby Henrey . . . . Sebastian Giro
Robert Shackleton . . . . . . Rocks Cooley
Christa Winter . . . . Anni
Muriel Aked . . . . Miss Frisbie
Elwyn Brook-Jones . . . . . . Mr Gorik
Paul Hardtmuth . . . . Prof Bindl
Oscar Werner . . . . Rudi
Sebastian Cabot . . . . Pizzo
June Elvin . . . . Miss Kirsch
DRAMA Austria. Governess hires crooks to
kidnap boy pianist from his cruel manager.

11611
WHERE NO VULTURES FLY (107) (U) *tech*
USA: IVORY HUNTER
Ealing (GFD)
AP: Leslie Norman
D:S: Harry Watt
SC: Ralph Smart, W.P.Lipscomb, Leslie Norman
Anthony Steel . . . . Bob Payton
Dinah Sheridan . . . . Mrs Payton
Harold Warrender . . . . Mannering
Meredith Edwards . . . . Gwyl
William Simons . . . . Tim Payton
Orlando Martins . . . . M'Kwongi
Philip Birkinshaw . . . . DC
ADVENTURE Africa. Game warden starts
national park despite ivory poachers.
(RFP: 1951; Top Moneymaker: 1952).

11612
ENCORE (86) (A)
Two Cities-Paramount (GFD)
P: Anthony Darnborough
S: (STORIES) W.Somerset Maugham
The Ant and the Grasshopper
D: Harold French
SC: T.E.B.Clarke
Nigel Patrick . . . . Tom Ramsey
Roland Culver . . . . George Ramsey
Alison Leggatt . . . . Freda Ramsey
Charles Victor . . . . Mr Bateman
Peter Graves . . . . Philip Cronshaw
Margaret Vyner . . . . Gertrude Wilmot
Winter Cruise
D: Pat Jackson
SC: Arthur Macrae
Kay Walsh . . . . Miss Reid
Noel Purcell . . . . Captain
Ronald Squire . . . . Doctor
John Laurie . . . . Engineer
Jacques Francois . . . . Pierre
Gigolo and Gigolette
D: Anthony Pelissier
SC: Eric Ambler
Glynis Johns . . . . Stella Cotman
Terence Morgan . . . . Syd Cotman
David Hutcheson . . . . . . Sandy Wescott
Charles Goldner . . . . Paco Espinal

Mary Merrall . . . . Flora Penezzi
Heather Thatcher . . . . Eva Barrett
Daphne Barker . . . . Countess
DRAMA Three short stories.

11613
DEATH IS A NUMBER (50)
Delman (Adelphi)
P: Phyllis Shepherd
D: Horace Shepherd
S: Charles K. Shaw
Terence Alexander . . . . Alan Robert
Lesley Osmond . . . . Joan Robert
Denis Webb . . . . John Bridgnorth
Ingeborg Wells . . . . Gipsy
Peter Gawthorne . . . . James Gregson
Isabel George . . . . Nurse
FANTASY Racing driver's death in crash
fulfils 300-year old curse.

11614
THE KILTIES ARE COMING (52) (U)
Advance (Adelphi) *reissue:* LADS AND
LASSES ON PARADE (cut)
P:D: Robert Jordan Hill
Peter Sinclair   Macdonald Hobley
Royal Kiltie Juniors
Margaret Thomson   Molly Booth
Agnes Quinn   Ralph Bryson
REVUE

DEC

11615
RELUCTANT HEROES (80) (U)
Byron (ABFD) *reissue:* 1955 (Ren)
P: Henry Halstead
D: Jack Raymond
S: (PLAY) Colin Morris
SC: Colin Morris
Ronald Shiner . . . . Sgt Bell
Derek Farr . . . . Michael Tone
Christine Norden . . . . Gloria Dennis
Brian Rix . . . . Horace Gregory
Larry Noble . . . . Trooper Morgan
Betty Impey . . . . Pat Thompson
Angela Whitehead . . . . . . Penny Roberts
Anthony Baird . . . . Sgt McKenzie
Colin Morris . . . . Capt Percy
Elspet Gray . . . . Lt Virginia
COMEDY Episodic misadventures of army
conscripts.

11616
NIGHT WAS OUR FRIEND (61) (A)
ACT Films (Monarch)
P: Gordon Parry
D: Michael Anderson
S: (PLAY) Michael Pertwee
SC: Michael Pertwee
Elizabeth Sellars . . . . .Sally Raynor
Michael Gough . . . . Martin Raynor
Ronald Howard . . . . Dr John Harper
Marie Ney. . . . . Emily Raynor
Edward Lexy . . . . Arthur Glenville
Nora Gordon . . . . Kate
John Salew . . . . Mr Lloyd
Cyril Smith . . . . Reporter
Michael Pertwee . . . . Young Man
CRIME Wife accused when her mad husband
kills himself.

11617
OUTCAST OF THE ISLANDS (102) (A)
London-BLPA (BL)
P:D: Carol Reed
S: (NOVEL) Joseph Conrad
SC: William Fairchild
Ralph Richardson . . . . Capt Lingard
Trevor Howard . . . . Peter Willems
Robert Morley . . . . Mr Almayer

Wendy Hiller . . . . Mrs Almayer
Kerima . . . . Aissa
George Coulouris . . . . Babalatchi
Wilfrid Hyde White . . . . . . Vinck
Frederick Valk . . . . Hudig
Betty Ann Davies . . . . Mrs Willems
Peter Illing . . . . Alagappan
James Kenney . . . . Ramsey
A.V.Bramble . . . . Badavi
ADVENTURE Far East, period. Crook
betrays trader's secret channel for love
of native Princess.

11618
RETURN TO GLANNASCAUL (23) (U)
Elliman (GFD)
P: Louis Elliman, Michael MacLiammoir
D:S: Hilton Edwards
Orson Welles . . . . Traveller
Michael Lawrence . . . . Passenger
Helena Hughes . . . . Woman
Sheila Richards . . . . Woman
FANTASY Ireland. Man helps two women
who turn out to be ghosts.

11619
ONE GOOD TURN (28) (U)
Majestic-Bushey (Ambassador)
P:D: Arthur Maude
S: Valerie Villiers-Bolton
Billy Mayerl . . . . Billy Lowery
Eve Gray . . . . Mrs Lowery
Douglas Barr . . . . Tom Horne
Angela Glynne . . . . Mary Lowery
Angela Faulds . . . . Felicity Carter
Hugh Buckner . . . . Frank Lowery
Frank Hawkins . . . . Mr Horne
DRAMA Boy saves girl from car accident
and is invited to her party.

11620
GLASGOW ORPHEUS CHOIR (13) (U)
Film Traders
P:D: George Hoellering
Glasgow Orpheus Choir
MUSICAL Choir sings five songs.

11621
COOKERY NOOK (28) (U)
Regent
P: James Wilson
Terry-Thomas . . . . The Man
Michael Bentine . . . . The Friend
COMEDY Husband and friend instal electric
cooker and prepare a meal.

11622
LONDON ENTERTAINS (48) (U)
E.J. Fancey Productions
D: E.J.Fancey
S: Jimmy Grafton
Eamonn Andrews . . . . Himself
Christine Forrest . . . . Christine
Pamela Bygrave . . . . Pamela
Vincent Ball . . . . Hiram
Eastbourne Girls Choir
Bobby Breen   Paul Adam
Diana Coupland   Tony Fayne
David Evans   Peter Sellars
Harry Secombe   Spike Milligan
MUSICAL Girls from Swiss finishing
school set up London escort agency and
fall in love with clients.

11623
THE QUEEN STEPS OUT (19) (U)
Carisbrooke (EJ Fancey)
P:D: Robert Henryson
Terry-Thomas
COMEDY Comedian narrates to drawings
of Queen of Sheba and King Solomon.

1952

JAN

11624
THE ARMCHAIR DETECTIVE (60) (A)
Meridian (Apex)
P: Donald Ginsberg, Derek Elphinstone
D: Brendan J. Stafford
S: (RADIO SERIES) Ernest Dudley
SC: Ernest Dudley, Derek Elphinstone
Ernest Dudley .... Himself
Hartley Power .... Nicco
Sally Newton .... Penny
Derek Elphinstone .... Insp Carter
Iris Russell .... Jane
David Oxley .... Terry
Lionel Grose .... Sgt
CRIME Radio tec proves nightclub singer
did not kill employer.

11625
BLIND MAN'S BLUFF (67) (A)
Present Day (Apex)
P: Charles Reynolds
D: Charles Saunders
S: John Gilling
Zena Marshall ...... Christine Stevens
Sydney Tafler .... Rikki Martin
Anthony Pendrell .... Roger Morley
Russell Napier .... Stevens
Norman Shelley .... Insp Morley
John le Mesurier .... Lefty Jones
Anthony Doonan .... Charley
Barbara Shaw .... Clare Raven
CRIME Inspector's novelist son breaks up
crime ring in boarding house.

11626
SALUTE THE TOFF (75) (A)
Nettlefold Films (Butcher)
P: Ernest G. Roy
D: Maclean Rogers
S: (NOVEL) John Creasey
John Bentley ...... Hon Richard Rollison
Carol Marsh .... Fay Gretton
Valentine Dyall .... Insp Grice
Shelagh Fraser .... Myra Lorne
June Elvin .... Lady Anthea
Arthur Hill .... Ted Harrison
Michael Golden .... Benny Kless
Jill Allen .... Singer
Roddy Hughes .... Jolly
Wally Patch .... Bert Ebbutt
John Forbes-Robertson ..... Gerald Harvey
Tony Britton .... Draycott
CRIME Tec saves girl's boss from being
kidnapped by insurance swindler.

11627
HIS EXCELLENCY (84) (U)
Ealing (GFD)
P: Michael Truman
D: Robert Hamer
S: (PLAY) Dorothy & Campbell Christie
SC: Robert Hamer, W.P.Lipscomb
Eric Portman .... George Harrison
Cecil Parker ...... Sir James Kirkman
Helen Cherry .... Lady Kirkman
Susan Stephen .... Peggy Harrison
Edward Chapman .... Admiral
Clive Morton .... GOC
Geoffrey Keen .... Morellos
Alec Mango .... Jackie
John Salew .... Fernando
Robin Bailey .... Charles
Eric Pohlmann .... Dobrieda
Howard Marion Crawford .... Proprietor
DRAMA Mediterranean. Yorkshire docker
becomes island governor and fights corrupt
leader of dock strike.

11628
NEVER TAKE NO FOR AN ANSWER (82)
(U) *bilingual*
Constellation (IFD)
P: Anthony Havelock-Allan
D: Maurice Cloche, Ralph Smart
S: (NOVEL) Paul Gallico
(THE SMALL MIRACLE)
SC: Paul Gallico, Pauline Gallico, Maurice
Cloche, Ralph Smart
Vittorio Manunta .... Peppino
Denis O'Dea .... Father Damico
Frank Coulson .... Dr Bartolo
Guido Celano .... Strotti
Nerio Bernardi .... Father Superior
Robert Adamina .... Gianni
John Murphy .... Father O'Brien
DRAMA Italy. Country boy seeks Pope's
permission to take sick donkey into crypt
of St Francis.

11629
DEATH OF AN ANGEL (64) (A)
Hammer-Lesser (Ex)
P: Anthony Hinds, Julian Lesser
D: Charles Saunders
S: (PLAY) Frank King
(THIS IS MARY'S CHAIR)
SC: Reginald Long
Jane Baxter .... Mary Welling
Patrick Barr .... Robert Welling
Julie Somers .... Judy Welling
Jean Lodge .... Ann Marlow
Raymond Young .... Chris Boswell
Russell Waters .... Walter Grannage
Russell Napier .... Supt Walshaw
Katie Johnson .... Sarah Oddy
CRIME Locum solves poisoning of village
doctor's wife.

11630
WHISPERING SMITH HITS LONDON (82)
(A) USA: WHISPERING SMITH VERSUS
SCOTLAND YARD.
Hammer-Lesser (Ex)
P: Anthony Hinds, Julian Lesser
D: Francis Searle
S: Steve Fisher
SC: John Gilling
Richard Carlson .... Whispering Smith
Greta Gynt .... Louise
Herbert Lom .... Ford
Rona Anderson .... Anne
Alan Wheatley .... Hector Reith
Dora Bryan .... la Fosse
Reginald Beckwith .... Manson
Danny Green .... Cecil
James Raglan .... Supt Meaker
CRIME American tec unmasks blackmail
gang behind girl's "suicide."

FEB

11631
THE AFRICAN QUEEN (103) (U) *tech*
Romulus-Horizon (IFD)
P: Sam Spiegel
D: John Huston
S: (NOVEL) C.S.Forester
SC: John Huston, James Agee
Humphrey Bogart .... Charlie Allnutt
Katharine Hepburn ...... Rose Sayer
Robert Morley .... Samuel Sayer
Peter Bull .... Captain
Theodore Bikel .... First Officer
Walter Gotell .... Second Officer
Peter Swanwick .... First Officer
Richard Marner .... Second Officer
ADVENTURE Africa, 1914. Rough captain
takes missionary's sister to safety by
riverboat. (AA: Best Actor 1952; PGAA: 1953).

11632
HOME AT SEVEN (85) (U)
USA: MURDER ON MONDAY
London-BLPA (BL)
P: Maurice Cowan
D: Ralph Richardson
S: (PLAY) R.C.Sheriff
SC: Anatole de Grunwald
Ralph Richardson .... David Preston
Margaret Leighton .... Janet Preston
Jack Hawkins .... Dr Sparling
Campbell Singer .... Insp Hemingway
Frederick Piper .... Mr Petherbridge
Diana Beaumont .... Ellen
Meriel Forbes .... Peggy Dobson
Michael Shepley .... Maj Watson
Margaret Withers .... Mrs Watson
CRIME Amnesiac bank clerk accused of
robbing social club.

11633
SECRET PEOPLE (96) (A)
Ealing (GFD)
P: Sidney Cole
D: Thorold Dickinson
S: Thorold Dickinson, Joyce Cary
SC: Thorold Dickinson, Wolfgang Wilhelm,
Christianna Brand
Valentina Cortesa .... Maria
Serge Reggiani .... Louis
Audrey Hepburn .... Nora Brent
Charles Goldner .... Anselmo
Megs Jenkins .... Penny
Irene Worth .... Miss Jackson
Reginald Tate .... Insp Eliot
Michael Shepley .... Manager
Athene Seyler .... Mrs Kellick
Geoffrey Hibbert .... Steenie
Sydney Tafler .... Syd Burnett
John Ruddock .... Daly
Michael Allan .... Rodd
John Field .... Fedor Luki
Norman Williams .... Sgt Newcome
Bob Monkhouse .... Barber
Charlie Cairoli & Paul
CRIME London, 1937. Political exiles plot
to assassinate tyrant leader.

11634
THE WOMAN'S ANGLE (86) (A)
Bow Bells (ABP)
P: Walter C.Mycroft
D: Leslie Arliss
S: (NOVEL) Ruth Feiner
(THREE CUPS OF COFFEE)
SC: Leslie Arliss, Mabbie Poole
Edward Underdown...... Robert Mansell
Cathy O'Donnell .... Nina Van Rhyne
Lois Maxwell .... Enid Mansell
Claude Farell .... Delysia Veronova
Peter Reynolds .... Brian Mansell
Marjorie Fielding .... Mrs Mansell
Anthony Nicholls ...... Dr Nigel Jarvis
Isabel Dean .... Isobel Mansell
John Bentley .... Renfro Mansell
Olaf Pooley .... Rudolf Mansell
Ernest Thesiger .... Judge
Eric Pohlmann .... Steffano
Joan Collins .... Marina
Dagmar Wynter .... Elaine
Geoffrey Toone .... Count Cambia
Anton Diffring .... Peasant
Miles Malleson .... Secrett
ROMANCE Musical director. loves nurse,
ballerina, and secretary.

11635
HUNTED (84) (A) USA: THE STRANGER
IN BETWEEN
BFM-Independent Artists (GFD)
reissue: 1961 (GEFD)

P: Julian Wintle
D: Charles Crichton
S: Michael McCarthy
SC: Jack Whittingham

Dirk Bogarde	Chris Lloyd
Kay Walsh	Mrs Sykes
Elizabeth Sellars	Magda Lloyd
Jon Whiteley	Robbie
Frederick Piper	Mr Sykes
Julian Somers	Jack Lloyd
Jane Aird	Mrs Campbell
Jack Stewart	Mr Campbell
Geoffrey Keen	Insp Deakin
Joe Linnane	Pawnbroker

CRIME Fugitive murderer abducts 6-year old orphan as protection.

11636
SONG OF PARIS (80) (A) USA: BACHELOR IN PARIS
Vandyke (Adelphi)
P: Roger Proudlock
D: John Guillermin
S: William Rose
SC: Allan Mackinnon, Frank Muir, Denis Norden

Dennis Price	Matthew Ibbetson
Anne Vernon	Clementine
Mischa Auer	Comte de Sarliac
Hermione Baddeley	Mrs Ibbetson
Brian Worth	Jim Barrett
Joan Kenney	Jenny Ibbetson

COMEDY French star engaged to phoney Comte loves English businessman with domineering mother.

11637
SING ALONG WITH ME (79) (U)
HH Film-Challenge (BL)
P: John Croydon, Harold Huth
D: Peter Graham Scott
S: Peter Graham Scott, Dennis Vance

Donald Peers	David Parry
Dodo Watts	Gwynneth Evans
Dennis Vance	Harry Humphries
Jill Clifford	Sheila
Mercy Haystead	Gloria
Cyril Chamberlain	Jack Bates
Humphrey Morton	Syd Maxton
George Curzon	Mr Palmer
Leonard Morris	Uncle Ebeneezer

MUSICAL Wales. Grocer wins composing contest and thwarts crooked music publisher.

11638
JUDGMENT DEFERRED (88) (A)
Group 3 (ABFD)
P: John Baxter, John Grierson
D: John Baxter
S: Herbert Ayres (DOSS HOUSE)
SC: Geoffrey Orme, Barbara K. Emary, Walter Meade

Hugh Sinclair	David Kennedy
Helen Shingler	Kay Kennedy
Abraham Sofaer	Chancellor
Leslie Dwyer	Flowers
Joan Collins	Lil Carter
Harry Locke	Bert
Elwyn Brook-Jones	Coxon
Marcel Poncin	Stranger
Martin Benson	Pierre Desportes
Bransby Williams	Dad
Michael Martin Harvey	Martin
Harry Welchman	Doc
Wilfrid Walter	Judge
Maire O'Neill	Mrs O'Halloran
Mary Merrall	Lady Musterby
Edgar Driver	Blackie
Billy Russell	Ginger

Bud Flanagan; Edmundo Ros and his Orchestra
CRIME Escaped convict's friends try dope smuggler who framed him.

11639
BRANDY FOR THE PARSON (78) (U)
Group 3 (ABFD)
P: John Grierson, Alfred O'Shaughnessy
D: John Eldridge
S: (NOVEL) Geoffrey Household
SC: John Dighton, Walter Meade, Alfred O'Shaughnessy

James Donald	Bill Harper
Kenneth More	Tony Rackham
Jean Lodge	Petronella Brand
Frederick Piper	Insp Marle
Charles Hawtrey	George Crumb
Michael Trubshawe	Redworth
Alfie Bass	Dallyn
Wilfred Caithness	Minch
Reginald Beckwith	Scoutmaster
Arthur Wontner	Maj Glockleigh

COMEDY Couple on yachting holiday get involved with brandy smugglers.

MAR

11640
SATURDAY ISLAND (102) (A) *tech*
USA: ISLAND OF DESIRE
Coronado (RKO)
P: David E. Rose
D: Stuart Heisler
S: (NOVEL) Hugh Brooke
SC: Stuart Heisler, Stephanie Nordli

Linda Darnell	Elizabeth Smythe
Tab Hunter	Chicken Dugan
Donald Gray	William Peck
John Laurie	Grimshaw
Sheila Chong	Tukua
Russell Waters	Dr Snyder
Macdonald Parke	Capt
Peter Butterworth	Marine
Diana Decker	Nurse

ROMANCE Tropics, 1943. Shipwrecked marine and crashed pilot love nurse on desert island.

11641
SO LITTLE TIME (88) (U)
Mayflower (ABP)
P: Maxwell Setton, Aubrey Baring
D: Compton Bennett
S: (NOVEL) Noelle Henry
(JE NE SUIS PAS UNE HEROINE)
SC: John Cresswell

Marius Goring	Col Hohensee
Maria Schell	Nicole de Malvines
Gabrielle Dorzat	Mme de Malvines
Barbara Mullen	Anna
John Bailey	Philippe de Malvines
Lucie Mannheim	Lotte Schonberg
Harold Lang	Lt Seger
David Hurst	Blumel
Oscar Quitak	Gerard
Stanley van Beers	Prof Perronet
Andree Melly	Paulette

WAR Belgium. Pianist forced to betray German governor she loves.

11642
THE CARD (91) (U) USA: THE PROMOTER
British Film Makers (GFD)
P: John Bryan
D: Ronald Neame
S: (NOVEL) Arnold Bennett
SC: Eric Ambler

Alec Guinness	Edward Henry Machin
Glynis Johns	Ruth Earp
Valerie Hobson	Countess of Chell
Petula Clark	Nellie Cotterill
Edward Chapman	Herbert Duncalf
Veronica Turleigh	Mrs Machin
George Devine	Herbert Calvert
Joan Hickson	Mrs Codleyn
Frank Pettingell	Supt Barlow
Gibb McLaughlin	Emery
Michael Hordern	Banker
Alison Leggatt	Mrs Cotterill
Wilfrid Hyde White	Lord

COMEDY Five Towns , 1890. Washerwoman's son rises to become Mayor.

11643
I BELIEVE IN YOU (95) (U)
Ealing (GFD)
P: Michael Relph
D: Basil Dearden
S: (BOOK) Sewell Stokes (COURT CIRCULAR)
SC: Michael Relph, Basil Dearden, Jack Whittingham, Nicholas Phipps

Celia Johnson	Matty
Cecil Parker	Henry Phipps
Godfrey Tearle	Mr Pyke
Harry Fowler	Hooker
George Relph	Mr Dove
Joan Collins	Norma
Laurence Harvey	Jordie
Ernest Jay	Mr Quayle
Ursula Howells	Hon Ursula
Sidney James	Sgt Brodie
Katie Johnson	Miss Macklin
Ada Reeve	Mrs Crockett
Brenda de Banzie	Mrs Hooker
Alex McCrindle	Mr Haines
Laurence Naismith	Sgt Braxton
Gladys Henson	Mrs Stevens

CRIME Probation officer tries to stop youth from returning to crime.

11644
13 EAST STREET (71) (A)
Tempean (Eros)
P: Robert Baker, Monty Berman
D:S: Robert Baker
SC: John Gilling

Patrick Holt	Gerald Blake
Sandra Dorne	Judy
Robert Ayres	Larry Conn
Sonia Holm	Joan
Dora Bryan	Valerie
Michael Balfour	Joey Long
Michael Brennan	George Mack

CRIME Tec poses as escaped convict to catch gang of warehouse robbers.

11645
THE FRIGHTENED MAN (69) (A)
Tempean (Eros)
P: Robert Baker, Monty Berman
D:S: John Gilling

Dermot Walsh	Julius Roselli
Barbara Murray	Amanda
Charles Victor	Mr Roselli
John Blythe	Maxie
Michael Ward	Cornelius
Thora Hird	Vera
John Horsley	Harry
Annette Simmonds	Marcella

CRIME Junk dealer's son joins gang and robs diamond merchant.

11646
MURDER IN THE CATHEDRAL (136) (U)
Film Traders
P:D:SC: George Hoellering
S: (PLAY) T.S.Eliot

Father John Groser	Thomas a Becket
Alexander Gauge	Henry II
Donald Bisset	First Priest
Clement McCallin	Second Priest
Michael Groser	Third Priest
Mark Dignam	First Knight
Michael Aldridge	Second Knight
Leo McKern	Third Knight
Paul Rogers	Fourth Knight
Niall MacGinnis	Herald
George Woodbridge	Tempter

T.S.Eliot . . . . Voice
RELIGION 1149. Archbishop of Canterbury
struggles with his conscience and is
assassinated.

11647
ANGELS ONE FIVE (98) (U)
Templar (ABP)
P: John Gossage, Derek Twist
D: George More O'Ferrall
S: Pelham Groom
SC: Derek Twist
Jack Hawkins . . . . G/C Tiger Small
Michael Denison . . . . S/L Peter Moon
Dulcie Gray. . . . . Nadine Clinton
John Gregson . . . . P/O Septic Baird
Cyril Raymond . . . . S/L Barry Clinton
Humphrey Lestocq. . . . . F/L Batchy Salter
Andrew Osborn . . . . S/L Bill Ponsford
Veronica Hurst . . . . Betty Carfax
Harold Goodwin . . . . AC2 Wailes
Norman Pierce . . . . Bonzo
Geoffrey Keen . . . . CSM
Harry Locke . . . . Lookout
Philip Stainton . . . . PC
Vida Hope . . . . Waaf
Amy Veness . . . . Aunt Tabitha
Ronald Adam . . . . Controller
WAR 1940. Fighter pilot's career from training
to death in action.

11648
THE STORY OF ROBIN HOOD AND HIS
MERRIE MEN (84) (U) *tech reissue: 1972*
Walt Disney (RKO)
P: Perce Pearce
D: Ken Annakin
S: Lawrence E. Watkin
Richard Todd . . . . Robin Hood
Joan Rice . . . . Maid Marian
Martita Hunt . . . . Queen Eleanor
Peter Finch . . . . Sheriff of Nottingham
James Robertson Justice . . . Little John
James Hayter . . . . Friar Tuck
Hubert Gregg . . . . Prince John
Elton Hayes . . . . Alan-a-Dale
Patrick Barr . . . . King Richard
Bill Owen . . . . Stutely
Michael Hordern . . . . Scathelock
Reginald Tate . . . . Hugh Fitzooth
Hal Osmond . . . . Midge
Anthony Forwood . . . . . Will Scarlett
ADVENTURE 1194. Outlawed Earl leads
Sherwood outlaws against corrupt authorities

11649
THE HAPPY FAMILY (86) (U)
USA: MR LORD SAYS NO
London Independent (Apex)
P: Sydney Box, William MacQuitty
D: Muriel Box
S: (PLAY) Michael Clayton Hutton
SC: Muriel & Sydney Box
Stanley Holloway . . . . Henry Lord
Kathleen Harrison . . . . Lillian Lord
Naunton Wayne . . . . Mr Filch
Dandy Nichols . . . . Ada
George Cole . . . . Cyril
Margaret Barton . . . . Anne
Tom Gill . . . . Maurice Hennessey
Miles Malleson . . . . Mr Thwaites
Eileen Moore . . . . Joan Lord
Geoffrey Sumner . . . . Sir Charles Spaniell
John Stratton . . . . David
COMEDY Cockney grocer refuses to
surrender shop as site for Festival of Britain.

APR
11650
TALL HEADLINES (100) (A)
Raymond Stross (GN) *reissue 1954,*
THE FRIGHTENED BRIDE   (NR)

D: Terence Young
S: (NOVEL) Audrey Erskine Lindop
SC: Audrey Erskine Lindop, Dudley Leslie
Mai Zetterling . . . . Doris Richardson
Michael Denison . . . . Philip Rackham
Flora Robson . . . . Mary Rackham
Dennis Price . . . . Maurice Fletcher
Andre Morell . . . . George Rackham
Jane Hylton . . . . Frankie Rackham
Naunton Wayne . . . . Inspector
Mervyn Johns . . . . Uncle Ted
Celia Lipton . . . . Sandra
Hugh Dempster . . . . Inspector
Olive Sloane . . . . Mrs Baker
Barbara Blair . . . . Nancy Richardson
CRIME Effect on suburban family when
the son is hanged for murder.

11651
HAMMER THE TOFF (71) (U)
Nettlefold (Butcher)
P: Ernest G. Roy
D: Maclean Rogers
S: (NOVEL) John Creasey
John Bentley . . . . . . Hon Richard Rollison
Patricia Dainton . . . . . . Susan Lancaster
Valentine Dyall . . . . Insp Grice
John Robinson . . . . Linnett
Wally Patch . . . . Bert Ebbutt
Katherine Blake . . . . Janet Lord
Roddy Hughes . . . . Jolly
Basil Dignam . . . . Supt
Lockwood West . . . . Kennedy
Charles Hawtrey . . . . Cashier
CRIME Tec proves "robin hood" crook
did not steal metal formula.

MAY
11652
PRIVATE INFORMATION (65) (U)
ACT FILMS (Monarch)
P: Ronald Kinnoch
D: Fergus McDonnel
S: (PLAY) Gordon Glennon (GARDEN CITY)
SC: Gordon Glennon, John Baines, Ronald
Kinnoch
Jill Esmond . . . . Charlotte
Jack Watling . . . . Hugh
Carol Marsh . . . . Georgie
Garard Heinz . . . . Alex
Norman Shelley . . . . Freemantle
Mercy Haystead . . . . Iris
Lloyd Pearson . . . . Mayor
Henry Caine . . . . Forrester
Brenda de Banzie . . . . Dolly
DRAMA Architect's mother discovers
the council estate is unsafe.

11653
NEVER LOOK BACK (73) (A)
Hammer (Ex)
P: Michael Carreras, James Brennan
D: Francis Searle
S: John Hunter, Guy Morgan, Francis Searle
Rosamund John . . . . . . Anne Maitland KC
Hugh Sinclair . . . . Nigel Stuart
Guy Middleton . . . . Guy Ransome
Henry Edwards . . . . Whitcomb
Terence Longdon . . . . Alan
John Warwick . . . . Raynor
Brenda de Banzie . . . . Molly Wheeler
Arthur Howard . . . . Vaughan
Bruce Belfrage . . . . Judge
Frances Rowe . . . . Liz
CRIME Woman KC forced to alibi her
ex-fiance when he kills his mistress.

11654
THE LAST PAGE (84) (A) USA: MANBAIT
Hammer-Lippert (Ex)
P: Anthony Hinds

D: Terence Fisher
S: (PLAY) James Hadley Chase
SC: Frederick Knott
George Brent . . . . John Harman
Marguerite Chapman . . . . . Stella
Raymond Huntley . . . . Clive
Peter Reynolds . . . . Jeff
Diana Dors . . . . Ruby
Eleanor Summerfield Vi
Meredith Edwards . . . . Dave
Harry Fowler . . . . Joe
Conrad Phillips . . . . Todd
Isabel Dean . . . . May
CRIME Bookseller framed for death of
blackmailing blonde.

11655
STOLEN FACE 972) (A)
Hammer-Lippert (Ex)
P: Anthony Hinds
D: Terence Fisher
S: Martin Berkeley, Richard Landau
Lisabeth Scott . . . . Alice Brent/Lily
Paul Henreid . . . . . . Dr Philip Ritter
Andre Morell . . . . David
Susan Stephen . . . . Betty
Mary Mackenzie . . . . Lily
John Wood . . . . Dr Jack Wilson
Arnold Ridley . . . . Dr Russell
Everley Gregg . . . . Lady Haringay
Cyril Smith . . . . Alf
Diana Beaumont . . . . May
DRAMA Plastic surgeon gives girl criminal
face of dead pianist he loved.

11656
WINGS OF DANGER (73) (U) USA:
DEAD ON COURSE
Hammer-Lippert (Ex)
P: Anthony Hinds
D: Terence Fisher
S: NOVEL) Elleston Trevor (DEAD ON
COURSE)
SC: John Gilling
Zachary Scott . . . . Van
Robert Beatty . . . . Nick Talbot
Kay Kendall . . . . Alexia
Colin Tapley . . . . Maxwell
Naomi Chance . . . . Avril
Arthur Lane . . . . Boyd Spencer
Diane Cilento . . . . Jeannette
Harold Lang . . . . Snell
CRIME Charter pilot saves blackmailed
friend from gold smugglers.

11657
WIDE BOY (67) (A)
Merton Park (AA)
P: W.H.Williams
D: Ken Hughes
S: Rex Rienits
Sydney Tafler . . . . Benny
Susan Shaw . . . . Molly
Ronald Howard . . . . Insp Carson
Melissa Stribling . . . . Caroline
Colin Tapley . . . . Mannering
Laidman Brown . . . . Pop
Helen Christie . . . . Sally
Martin Benson . . . . Rocco
CRIME Girl tracks down blackmailer who
killed her lover.

11658
CURTAIN UP (82) (U)
Constellation (GFD) *reissue: 1958 (Arch)*
P: Robert Garrett
D: Ralph Smart
S: (PLAY) Philip King (ON MONDAY NEXT)
SC: Michael Pertwee, Jack Davies
Robert Morley . . . . Harry Blacker

Margaret Rutherford . . . . Jeremy St Clare
Kay Kendall . . . . Sandra
Olive Sloane . . . . Maude
Joan Rice . . . . Avis
Michael Medwin . . . . Jerry
Charlotte Mitchell . . . . Daphne
Lloyd Lamble . . . . Jackson
Liam Gaffney . . . . Norwood Bellamy
Constance Lorne. . . . . Sarah Stebbins
COMEDY Suburban repertory company has
trouble rehearsing new play.

11659
EMERGENCY CALL (90) (U)
USA: THE HUNDRED HOUR HUNT
Nettlefold (Butcher)
P: Ernest G. Roy
D: Lewis Gilbert
S: Lewis Gilbert, Vernon Harris
Jack Warner . . . . Insp Lane
Anthony Steel . . . . Dr Carter
Joy Shelton . . . . Laura Bishop
Freddie Mills . . . . Tim Mahoney
Sydney Tafler . . . . Brett
Eric Pohlmann . . . . Flash Harry
John Robinson . . . . Dr Braithwaite
Earl Cameron . . . . George Robinson
Sidney James . . . . Danny Marks
Henry Hewitt . . . . Mr Wilberforce
Geoffrey Hibbert . . . . Jackson
Thora Hird . . . . Mrs Cornelius
Avis Scott . . . . Marie
Bruce Seton . . . . Sgt Bellamy
DRAMA Police search for rare blood to
save child leads to Negro stoker, boxer,
and murderer.

11660
CRY, THE BELOVED COUNTRY (103) (A)
USA: AFRICAN FURY
London-BLPA (BL)
P: Zoltan Korda, Alan Paton
D: Zoltan Korda
S: (NOVEL) Alan Paton
SC: Alan Paton
Canada Lee . . . . Stephen Kumalo
Charles Carson . . . . James Jarvis
Sidney Poitier. . . . . Rev Maimangu
Joyce Carey . . . . Margaret Jarvis
Edric Connor . . . . John Kumalo
Geoffrey Keen . . . . Father Vincent
Vivien Clinton . . . . Mary
Michael Goodliffe . . . . Masters
Albertina Temba . . . . Mrs Kumalo
Edric Connor . . . . John Jumalo
Lionel Ngakare . . . . Absalom
CRIME Africa. Native preacher's son kills
son of rich white man. (BFA: UN Award 1952).

11661
THE WALLET (64) (A)
Sunset (Archway) *reissue:* 1953;
BLUEPRINT FOR DANGER
P:D: Morton M. Lewis
S: Ted Willis
John Longden . . . . Man with Pipe
Chil Bouchier . . . . Babs
Roberta Huby . . . . Dot Johnson
Alfred Farrell . . . . Harry Maythorpe
Hilda Fenemore . . . . . . Alice Maythorpe
Diana Calderwood . . . . May Jenkins
CRIME Lost wallet with £100 passes
through hands of dancer, crooked cashier,
and blackmailer.

11662
THE BLACK SWAN (13) (U) (3D)
Anglo-Scottish (Stereo Techniques)
P: Jack Ralph
D: Leonard Reeve

S: (BALLET) Tschaikovsky (SWAN LAKE)
Beryl Grey . . . . John Field
David Paltenghi . . . . . . Margaret King-Farlow
Peter Brinson
MUSICAL Ballet in three dimensions.

11663
GISELLE (31) (U)
Craft (Ex)
P:D: Henry Caldwell
S: (BALLET) Adolphe Adam
N: Jack Buchanan
Alicia Markova
Anton Dolin
Festival Ballet
MUSICAL Ballet.

11664
WHAT A HUSBAND ! (20) (U)
Regent
P: James Wilson
D: Donald Taylor
Richard Hearne . . . . Mr Pastry
Gilbert Harding . . . . Himself
COMEDY Slapstick misadventures of
clumsy husband.

11665
MELODIES FROM GRAND HOTEL (14) (U)
Carisbrooke (WB)
D: Robert Henryson
Leslie Jeffries and his Orchestra
MUSICAL From BBC radio series "Grand Hotel."

11666
SAY ABRACADABRA (28) (U)
Harold Baim
D: Harold Baim
N: Frank Phillips
Col Ling Soo   Percy Press
Robert Harbin   Geoffrey Buckingham
Weaver Smith
REVUE Magicians and conjurors.

JUN

11667
THE IMPORTANCE OF BEING EARNEST (95)
(U) *tech*
BFM-Javelin (GFD)
P: Teddy Baird
D: Anthony Asquith
S: (PLAY) Oscar Wilde
SC: Anthony Asquith
Michael Redgrave . . . . Jack Worthing
Michael Denison . . . . Algernon Moncrieff
Edith Evans . . . . Lady Bracknell
Joan Greenwood . . . . . . Gwendolen Fairfax
Dorothy Tutin . . . . Cecily Cardew
Margaret Rutherford . . . . . Miss Prism
Miles Malleson . . . . Rev Cahsuble
Richard Wattis . . . . Seton
Aubrey Mather . . . . Merriman
COMEDY 1895. Friends woo girls by
posing as same non-existant brother.

11668
IVANHOE (106) *tech* (U)
MGM British
P: Pandro S. Berman
D: Richard Thorpe
S: (NOVEL) Walter Scott
SC: Aeneas Mackenzie, Noel Langley
Robert Taylor . . . . Ivanhoe
Elizabeth Taylor . . . . Rebecca
Joan Fontaine . . . . Rowena
George Sanders . . Sir Brian Bois-de-Guilbert
Emlyn Williams . . . . Wamba
Guy Rolfe . . . . Prince John
Robert Douglas . . . . Sir Hugh de Bracy
Finlay Currie . . . . Cedric
Felix Aylmer . . . . Isaac of York

Norman Wooland . . . . . . King Richard
Basil Sydney . . . . Waldemar Fitzurse
Harold Warrender . . . . Locksley
Patrick Holt . . . . . Philip de Malvaisin
Francis de Wolff . . . . . . Front-de-Boeuf
Sebastian Cabot . . . . Clerk
ADVENTURE 1190. Saxon knight saves
king's ransom money from Normans.

11669
TREASURE HUNT (79) (U)
Romulus (IFD)
P:SC: Anatole de Grunwald
D: John Paddy Carstairs
S: (PLAY) M.J.Farrell, John Perry
Jimmy Edwards . . Hercules Ryall/Sir Roderick
Martita Hunt . . . . Aunt Anna Rose
Naunton Wayne . . . . Eustace Mills
Athene Seyler . . . . Consuelo Howard
June Clyde . . . . Mrs Cleghorn-Thomas
Miles Malleson . . . . Mr Walsh
Susan Stephen . . . . Mary O'Leary
Brian Worth . . . . Philip
Mara Lane . . . . Yvonne
Maire O'Neill . . . . Brigid
Toke Townley . . . . William Burke
COMEDY Ireland. Bart's heirs take in
boarders while they search for a mad
aunt's lost rubies.

11670
WHO GOES THERE ! (85) (U)
USA: THE PASSIONATE SENTRY
London-BLPA (BL)
P:D: Anthony Kimmins
S: (PLAY) John Dighton
SC: John Dighton
Nigel Patrick . . . . Miles Cornwall
Valerie Hobson . . . . Alex Cornwall
Peggy Cummins . . . . Christine Deed
George Cole . . . . Arthur Crisp
A.E.Matthews . . . . . . Sir Hubert Cornwall
Anthony Bushell . . . . Maj Guy Ashley
Joss Ambler . . . . Guide
COMEDY Guardsman's Irish fiancee causes
trouble in Grace and Favour House.

11671
DERBY DAY (84) (U) USA: FOUR AGAINST
FATE
Imperadío (BL)
P: Herbert Wilcox, Maurice Cowan
D: Herbert Wilcox
S: Arthur Austie
SC: Monckton Hoffe, John Baines, Alan
Melville
Anna Neagle . . . . Lady Helen Forbes
Michael Wilding . . . . David Scott
Googie Withers . . . . Betty Molloy
John McCallum . . . . Tommy Dillon
Peter Graves . . . . Gerald Berkeley
Suzanne Cloutier . . . . Michele Jolivet
Gordon Harker . . . . Joe Jenkins
Edwin Styles . . . . Sir George Forbes
Gladys Henson . . . . Gladys Jenkins
Nigel Stock . . . . Jim Molloy
Ralph Reader . . . . Bill Hammond
Tom Walls Jr . . . . Gilpin
Josephine Fitzgerald . . . . . Cook
Alfie Bass . . . . Spider Wilkes
Raymond Glendenning; Bryan Johnstone
DRAMA Day at races with widow, cartoonist,
taxi driver, film star, French maid, and
murderer.

11672
CASTLE IN THE AIR (90) (U)
Hallmark (ABP)
P: Edward Dryhurst, Ernest Gartside
D: Henry Cass
S: (PLAY) Alan Melville
SC: Alan Melville, Edward Dryhurst

David Tomlinson . . . . .   Earl of Locharne
Helen Cherry . . . .   Boss Trent
Margaret Rutherford . . . .   Miss Nicholson
Barbara Kelly . . . .   Mrs Clodfelter Dunne
A.E.Matthews . . . .   Blair
Patricia Dainton . . . .   Ermyntrude
Brian Oulton . . . .   Phillips
Ewan Roberts . . . .   Menzies
Clive Morton . . . .   MacFee
Gordon Jackson . . . .   Hiker
Russell Waters . . . .   Moffatt
COMEDY Rich American and Coal Board
vie to buy poor Earl's Scots castle.

JUL

11673
I'M A STRANGER (60) (U)
Corsair (Apex)
P: Harold Richmond
D:S: Brock Williams
Greta Gynt . . . .   Herself
James Hayter . . . .   Horatio Flowerdew
Hector Ross . . . .   Insp Craddock
Jean Cadell . . . .   Hannah Mackenzie
Patric Doonan . . . .   George Westcott
Charles Lloyd Pack . . . . . .   Mr Cringle
Martina Mayne . . . .   Mary
Fulton Mackay . . . .   Alastair Campbell
CRIME Film star and window cleaner help
heir find missing will.

11674
NO HAUNT FOR A GENTLEMAN (58) (U)
Anglo-Scottish (Apex)
P: Charles Reynolds
D: Leonard Reeve
S: Frederick Allwood
SC: Julian Caunter, Gerard Bryant, Leonard
Reeve
Anthony Pendrell . . . .   John Northwick
Sally Newton . . . .   Miriam Northwick
Jack MacNaughton . . . .   FitzCholmondley
Patience Rentoul . . . .   Mother
Dorothy Summers . . . .   Mrs Mallett
Peter Swanwick . . . .   Brother Ravioli
Rufus Cruickshank . . . . . .   Angus McDingle
Barbara Shaw . .   Lady Medeline de Boudoir
Joan Hickson . . . .   Mme Omskaya
Hattie Jacques . . .   Mrs FitzCholmondley
Joan Sterndale-Bennett . . .   Mother Skipton
FANTASY Ghost helps newlywed frighten
away mother-in-law.

DISTANT TRUMPET (63) (U)
Meridian (Apex)
P: Harold Richmond, Derek Elphinstone
D: Terence Fisher
S: Derek Elphinstone
Derek Bond . . . .   David Anthony
Jean Patterson . . . .   Valerie Maitland
Derek Elphinstone . . . .   Richard Anthony
Anne Brooke . . . .   Beryl Jeffries
Grace Gavin . . . .   Mrs Phillips
Keith Pyott . . . .   Sir Rudolph Gettins
Jean Webster-Brough . . . .   Mrs Waterhouse
Grace Denbigh-Russell . . . .   Mrs Hallett
DRAMA Society doctor changes places
with sick missionary brother.

11676
KING OF THE UNDERWORLD (82) (A)
Bushey (Ambassador)
P: Gilbert Church
D: Victor M. Gover
S: John Gilling
Tod Slaughter . . . .   Terence Riley
Patrick Barr . . . .   Insp Morley
Tucker McGuire . . . .   Eileen Trotter
Ingeborg Wells . . . .   Marie
Frank Hawkins . . . .   Insp Cranshaw
Len Sharp . . . .   Mullins

Ann Valery . . . .   Susan
CRIME Three stories of gang boss: blackmail;
jewel theft; stolen formula.

11677
WHERE'S CHARLEY? (97) (U) *tech*
WB-FN
D: David Butler
S: (PLAY) Brandon Thomas (CHARLEY'S
AUNT)
(PLAY) Frank Loesser, George Abbott
SC: John Monks jr
Ray Bolger . . . .   Charley Wykeham
Allyn McLerie . . . .   Amy Spettigue
Robert Shackleton . . . .   Jack Chesney
Mary Germaine . . . .   Kitty Verdun
Horace Cooper . . . .   Stephen Spettigue
Margaretta Scott . . . .   Donna Lucia
Howard Marion Crawford .Sir Francis Chesney
Henry Hewitt . . . .   Brassett
H.G.Stoker . . . .   Wilkinson
Martin Miller . . . .   Photographer
MUSICAL Oxford, 1890. Student poses as
aunt to chaperone girls, then his aunt turns up.

11678
MADE FOR LAUGHS (34) (U)
Hammer (Ex) *reissue:* 1958 (17 mins cut;
Winart)
D:S: James M. Anderson
N: Bryan Michie
COMPILATION Extracts from silent films,
mostly American.

11679
THE CASE OF THE OLD ROPE MAN (18) (U)
G.B.Instructional (GFD)
P: Frank Wells
D: Darrell Catling
S: Alastair Scobie
James Carney . . . .   Ken Casey
Howell Davies . . . .   Jack Spice
David Tearle . . . .   Kroller
Philip Lennard . . . .   Snaith
Brian Campbell . . . .   Insp Dunwoodie
CRIME Reporter solves murder of
dockside nightwatchman.

11680
THE GIFT HORSE (100) (U)
USA: GLORY AT SEA
Molton (IFD)
P: George Pitcher
D: Compton Bennett
S: Ivan Goff, Ben Roberts
SC: William Fairchild, Hugh Hastings,
William Rose
Trevor Howard   L/C Hugh Fraser
Richard Attenborough   Dripper Daniels
Sonny Tufts   Yank Flanagan
James Donald   Lt Richard Jennings
Joan Rice   June Mallory
Bernard Lee   Stripey Wood
Dora Bryan   Glad
Hugh Williams   Capt (D)
Robin Bailey   Lt Michael Grant
Meredith Edwards   Jones
John Forrest   Appleby
Patric Doonan   PO Martin
Sidney James   Ned Hardy
James Kenney   John Fraser
James Carney   Bone
Russell Enoch   Adams
WAR 1940. Strict officer takes command of
an old US destroyer, given to Britain in
exchange for a base.

11681
TIME GENTLEMEN PLEASE ! (83) (U)
Group 3 (ABFD)
P: John Grierson, Herbert Mason
D: Lewis Gilbert
S: (NOVEL) R.J.Minney (NOTHING TO LOSE)

SC: Peter Blackmore, Val Guest
Eddie Byrne . . . .   Dan Dance
Raymond Lovell . . . . . .   Sir Digby Montague
Hermione Baddeley . . . . . .   Emma Stebbins
Sidney James . . . .   Eric Hace
Jane Barrett . . . .   Sally
Dora Bryan . . . .   Peggy Stebbins
Sydney Tafler . . . .   Joseph Spink
Robert Brown . . . .   Bill Jordan
Marjorie Rhodes . . . .   Miss Mouncey
Patrick McAlinney . . . .   Rev Soater
Thora Hird . . . .   Alice Crouch
Ivor Barnard . . . .   Timothy Crouch
Edie Martin . . . .   Mary Wade
Joan Young . . . .   Mrs Round
Peter Jones . . . .   Lionel Batts
Ian Carmichael . . . .   PRO
COMEDY Whimsical Irish tramp versus
council of "Perfect Village."

11682
YOU'RE ONLY YOUNG TWICE ! (81) (U)
Group 3 (ABFD)
P: John Grierson, Barbara K. Emary
D: Terry Bishop
S: (PLAY) James Bridie (WHAT SAY THEY)
SC: Reginald Beckwith, Lindsay Galloway,
Terry Bishop
Duncan Macrae . . . .   Prof Hayman
Joseph Tomelty . . . .   Dan McEntee
Patrick Barr . . . .   Sir Archibald Asher
Charles Hawtrey . . . .   Adolphus Hayman
Diane Hart . . . .   Ada Shore
Robert Urquhart . . . .   Sheltie
Edward Lexy . . . .   Lord Carshennie
Jacqueline Mackenzie . . . .   Nellie
Eric Woodburn . . . .   The Bedellus
Molly Urquhart . . . .   Lady Duffy
Reginald Beckwith . . . .   BBC Commentator
COMEDY Scotland. Famed Irish poet poses
as university gatekeeper.

11683
LITTLE BIG SHOT 990) (U)
Byron (ABFD)
P: Henry Halstead
D: Jack Raymond
S: (PLAY) Janet Allan
SC: John Paddy Carstairs
Ronald Shiner . . . .   Henry Hawkwood
Marie Lohr . . . .   Mrs Maddox
Derek Farr . . . .   Sgt Wilson
Manning Whiley . . . .   Mike Connor
Danny Green . . . .   Big Mo
Yvette Wyatt . . . .   Ann
Digby Wolfe . . . .   Peter Carton
Marjorie Stewart . . . .   Mrs Crane
Victor Baring . . . .   Little Mo
COMEDY Nervous heir to father's gang
forced to steal jewels.

11684
SOMETHING MONEY CAN'T BUY (83) (U)
BFM-Vic (GFD)
P: Joseph Janni
D: Pat Jackson
S: James Lansdale Hodson, Pat Jackson
Patricia Roc . . . .   Anne Wilding
Anthony Steel . . . .   Harry Wilding
Moira Lister . . . .   Diana Haverstock
A.E.Matthews . . . .   Lord Haverstock
David Hutcheson . . . .   Buster
Michael Trubshawe . . . . . .   Willy
Diane Hart . . . .   Joan
Charles Victor . . . .   Treasurer
Henry Edwards . . . .   Gerald Forbes
Mary Hinton . . . .   Mrs Forbes
D.A.Clarke-Smith . . . .   Critic
Mara Lane . . . .   Film Star
John Barry . . . .   Film Star
Dennis Arundell . . . .   Director
COMEDY Ex-officer runs mobile canteen;
his wife runs agency.

11685
PENNY PRINCESS (94) *tech* (U)
Conquest (GFD)
P: Val Guest, Frank Godwin
D:S: Val Guest

Yolande Donlan	Lindy Smith
Dirk Bogarde	Tony Craig
Mary Clare	Maria
A.E.Matthews	Selby
Edwin Styles	Chancellor
Reginald Beckwith	Finance Minister
Kynaston Reeves	Burgomaster
Peter Butterworth	Julien
Desmond Walter-Ellis	Alberto
Laurence Naismith	Louis
Paul Sheridan	French Attache
Eric Pohlmann	Paul

COMEDY American girl inherits European state and stops smuggling by exporting alcoholic cheese.

11686
MANDY (93) (A) USA: CRASH OF SILENCE
Ealing (GFD)
P: Leslie Norman
D: Alexander Mackendrick
S: (NOVEL) Hilda Lewis (THE DAY IS OURS)
SC: Jack Whittingham, Nigel Balchin

Phyllis Calvert	Christine Garland
Jack Hawkins	Richard Searle
Terence Morgan	Henry Garland
Godfrey Tearle	Mr Garland
Mandy Miller	Mandy Garland
Nancy Price	Jane Ellis
Edward Chapman	Ackland
Marjorie Fielding	Mrs Garland
Patricia Plunkett	Mrs Crocker
Dorothy Alison	Miss Stockton
Eleanor Summerfield	Lily Tabor
Colin Gordon	Woolard
Julian Amyes	Jimmy Tabor
Jane Asher	Nina

DRAMA Strained parents send deaf child to oral education school.

11687
MOTHER RILEY MEETS THE VAMPIRE (74) (U) USA: VAMPIRE OVER LONDON
Fernwood (Renown)
P:D: John Gilling
S: Val Valentine

Arthur Lucan	Mrs Riley
Bela Lugosi	Von Housen
Dora Bryan	Tillie
Richard Wattis	PC Freddie
Judith Furse	Freda
Philip Leaver	Anton
Maria Mercedes	Julia Loretti
Roderick Lovell	Douglas
David Hurst	Mugsy
Hattie Jacques	Mrs Jenks
Graham Moffatt	Yokel

COMEDY Housekeeper thwarts vampiric inventor and his robot.

AUG
11688
MY DEATH IS A MOCKERY (75) (A)
Park Lane (Adelphi)
P: David Dent
D: Tony Young
S: (NOVEL) Douglas Baber

Donald Houston	John Bradley
Kathleen Byron	Helen Bradley
Bill Kerr	Hansen
Edward Leslie	le Cambre

CRIME Fisherman hanged for accidentally killing partner in smuggling.

11689
THE SOUND BARRIER (118) (U)
USA: BREAKING THE SOUND BARRIER
London-BLPA (BL) *reissue:* 1960 (Orb)
P:D: David Lean
S: Terence Rattigan

Ralph Richardson	John Ridgefield
Ann Todd	Susan Garthwaite
Nigel Patrick	Tony Garthwaite
John Justin	Philip Peel
Dinah Sheridan	Jess Peel
Joseph Tomelty	Will Sparks
Denholm Elliott	Chris Ridgefield
Jack Allen	Windy Williams
Ralph Michael	Fletcher
Leslie Phillips	Controller
Jolyon Jackley	Baby

DRAMA Aircraft magnate's son-in-law dies trying to break sound barrier. (AA: Best Sound 1952; BFA: Best Film, Best Actor 1952).

11690
THE BRAVE DON'T CRY (90) (U)
Group 3 (ABFD)
P: John Grierson
D: Philip Leacock
S: Montagu Slater

John Gregson	John Cameron
Meg Buchanan	Margaret Wishart
Andrew Keir	Charlie Ross
Fulton Mackay	Dan Wishart
Jack Stewart	Willie Duncan
John Rae	Donald Sloan
Wendy Noel	Jean Knox
Russell Waters	Hughie Aitken
Jameson Clark	Dr Andrew Keir
Archie Duncan	Walter Hardie
Jock McKay	Jock Woods

DRAMA Scotland. 118 men rescued after 36 hours in gas-filled coal mine.

11691
FATHER'S DOING FINE (83) *tech* (U)
Marble Arch (ABP)
P: Victor Skutezky
D: Henry Cass
S: (PLAY) Noel Langley (LITTLE LAMBS EAT IVY)
SC: Anne Burnaby

Richard Attenborough	Dougall
Heather Thatcher	Lady Buckering
Noel Purcell	Shaughnessy
George Thorpe	Dr Drew
Diane Hart	Doreen
Susan Stephen	Bicky
Mary Germaine	Gerda
Virginia McKenna	Catherine
Jack Watling	Clifford Magill
Peter Hammond	Roly
Brian Worth	Wilfred
Sidney James	Taxi-driver

COMEDY Troubles of impoverished, widowed Lady and her four daughters.

11692
24 HOURS OF A WOMAN'S LIFE (90) (A) *tech*
USA: AFFAIR IN MONTE CARLO
ABPC (ABP)
P: Ivan Foxwell
D: Victor Saville
S: (NOVEL) Stefan Zewig
SC: Warren Chetham Strode

Merle Oberon	Linda Venning
Richard Todd	Young Man
Leo Genn	Robert Stirling
Stephen Murray	Abbe Benoit
Peter Reynolds	Peter
Joan Dowling	Mrs Barry
June Clyde	Mrs Rohe
Peter Illing	M.Blanc
Jacques Brunius	Francois
Isabel Dean	Miss Johnson
Peter Jones	Bill
Yvonne Furneaux	Henriette
Mara Lane	Alice Brown
Robert Ayres	Frank Brown

ROMANCE Monte Carlo. Novelist tells how rich widow failed to reform gambler.

11693
CROW HOLLOW (69) (A)
Merton Park-Bruton (AA)
P: William Williams
D: Michael McCarthy
S: Vivian Milroy

Donald Houston	Robert
Natasha Parry	Ann
Nora Nicholson	Opal
Esma Cannon	Judith
Susan Richmond	Hester
Pat Owens	Willow
Melissa Stribling	Diana

CRIME Surrey. Aunt tries to secure inheritance by poisoning nephew's new wife.

11694
THE HOLLY AND THE IVY (83) (U)
London-BLPA (BL)
P: Anatole de Grunwald, Hugh Perceval
D: George More O'Ferrall
S: (PLAY) Wynyard Browne
SC: Anatole de Grunwald

Ralph Richardson	Rev Martin Gregory
Celia Johnson	Jenny Gregory
Margaret Leighton	Margaret Gregory
Denholm Elliott	Michael Gregory
John Gregson	David Patterson
Hugh Williams	Richard Wyndham
William Hartnell	CSM
Robert Flemyng	Major
Roland Culver	Lord B
Margaret Halstan	Aunt Lydia
Maureen Delany	Aunt Bridget

DRAMA Parson learns truth about lives and loves of his daughters.

SEP
11695
THE LOST HOURS (72) (U) USA: THE BIG FRAME
Tempean (Eros)
P: Robert Baker, Monty Berman
D: David Macdonald
S: Steve Fisher
SC: John Gilling

Mark Stevens	Paul Smith
Jean Kent	Louise Parker
Garry Marsh	Foster
John Bentley	Clark Sutton
Dianne Foster	Dianne Wrigley
Jack Lambert	John Parker
Leslie Perrins	Dr Morrison
Brian Coleman	Tom Wrigley
Duncan Lamont	Bristow
Cyril Smith	Roper
Thora Hird	Maid

CRIME American test pilot proves he was drugged and framed for killing wartime comrade.

11696
GIRDLE OF GOLD (66) (U)
Screenplays London (Eros)
P: Audrey Hirst, D'Arcy Conyers
D: Montomery Tully
S: Jack Dawe

Esmond Knight	William Evans
Maudie Edwards	Mrs Griffiths
Meredith Edwards	Mr Griffiths
Petra Davies	Mary Rees
Glyn Houston	Dai Thomas
Tonie MacMillan	Mrs Macie
Kenneth Evans	Sgt Mortimer

COMEDY Wales. Undertaker searches for money sewn in wife's old corsets.

11697
PAUL TEMPLE RETURNS (71) (U)
Nettlefold (Butcher)
P: Ernest G. Roy
D: Maclean Rogers

S: (RADIO SERIAL) Francis Durbridge
SC: Francis Durbridge
John Bentley . . . . Paul Temple
Patricia Dainton . . . . Steve Temple
Valentine Dyall . . . . Supt Bradley
Christopher Lee . . . . Sir Felix Reybourne
Ronald Leigh Hunt . . . . . . Insp Ross
Ben Williams . . . . Roddy Carson
Grey Blake . . . . Storey
Arthur Hill . . . . Cranmer Guest
Robert Urquhart . . . . Slater
Dan Jackson . . . . Sakki
Peter Gawthorne . . . . . . Sir Graham Forbes
CRIME Novelist unmasks "The Marquis."

11698
AT HOME WITH THE HARDWICKES
(series) (U)
British Movietonews (20)
Cameron Hall . . . . Mr Hardwicke
Everley Gregg . . . . Mrs Hardwicke
Harry Fowler . . . . Harry Hardwicke
John Sharp . . . . Mr Arkwright

11699
1: A SPOT OF BOTHER (19)

11700
2: THE PAPER CHASE (20)

11701
3: A SWEEPING STATEMENT (17)

11702
4: SHEDDING THE LOAD (17)

11703
5: FOOD FOR THOUGHT (18)

11704
6: HEIGHT OF AMBITION (17)
COMEDY Slapstick misadventures of
clumsy husband and his son.

11705
HIGHLIGHTS OF RADIO (20) (U)
S & R Productions (Arrow)
Eric Winstone and his Band
REVUE

11706
LADY IN THE FOG (82) (A) USA:
SCOTLAND YARD INSPECTOR
Hammer-Lippert (Ex)
P: Anthony Hinds
D: Sam Newfield
S: (RADIO SERIAL) Lester Powell
SC: Orville Hampton
Cesar Romero . . . . Philip Odell
Lois Maxwell . . . . Peggy
Bernadette O'Farrell . . . . Heather
Geoffrey Keen . . . . Hampden
Campbell Singer . . . . Insp Rigby
Lloyd Lamble . . . . Sorroway
Mary Mackenzie . . . . Marilyn
Alastair Hunter . . . . Sgt Reilly
Frank Birch . . . . Boswell
Lisa Lee . . . . , ... Donna Devore
CRIME American reporter proves girl's
brother was not run over accidentally.

11707
MEET ME TONIGHT (85) tech (A)
British Film Makers (GFD)
P: Anthony Havelock-Allan
D: Anthony Pelissier
S: (PLAYS) Noel Coward (TONIGHT AT 8-30)
Ways and Means
Valerie Hobson . . . . Stella Cartwright
Nigel Patrick . . . . Toby Cartwright
Jack Warner . . . . Murdoch
Jessie Royce Landis . . . . . . Olive

Michael Trubshawe . . . . . . Chaps
Mary Jerrold . . . . Nanny
Yvonne Furneaux . . . . Elena
Red Papers
Kay Walsh . . . . Lily Pepper
Ted Ray . . . . George Pepper
Martita Hunt . . . . Mabel Grace
Frank Pettingell . . . . Mr Edwards
Bill Fraser . . . . Bert Bentley
Frank's Fox Terriers; Young China Troupe
Fumed Oak
Stanley Holloway . . . . Henry Gow
Betty Ann Davies . . . . Doris Gow
Mary Merrall . . . . Grandma Rockett
Dorothy Gordon . . . . Elsie
DRAMA Three short stories.

11708
THE PLANTER'S WIFE (91) (A)
USA: OUTPOST IN MALAYA
Pinnacle (GFD)
P: John Stafford
D: Ken Annakin
S: Peter Proud, Guy Elmes
Claudette Colbert . . . . Liz Frazer
Jack Hawkins . . . . Jim Frazer
Anthony Steel . . . . Insp Hugh Dobson
Ram Gopal . . . . Nair
Jeremy Spenser . . . . Mat
Tom Macauley . . . . Jack Bushell
Helen Goss . . . . Eleanor Bushell
Sonya Hana . . . . Ah Moy
Andy Ho . . . . Wan Li
Peter Asher . . . . Mike Frazer
Bryan Coleman . . . . Capt Dell
Don Sharp . . . . Lt Summers
Bill Travers . . . . Planter
Alfie Bass . . . . Soldier
WAR Malaya. Rubber planter neglects
wife and child in fight against the terrorists.

OCT

11709
MY WIFE'S LODGER (80) (A)
Advance (Adelphi) *reissue:* 1956 (GN)
P: David Dent
D: Maurice Elvey
S: (PLAY) Dominic Roche
SC: Dominic Roche, Stafford Dickens
Dominic Roche . . . . Willie Higginbotham
Olive Sloane . . . . Maggie Higginbotham
Leslie Dwyer . . . . Roger the Lodger
Diana Dors . . . . Eunice Higginbotham
Alan Sedgwick . . . . Tex
Vincent Downing . . . . Norman Higginbotham
Vi Kaley . . . . Mother-in-law
COMEDY Ex-soldier unmasks favoured
lodger as crook.

11710
CIRCUMSTANTIAL EVIDENCE (61) (A)
ACT Films (Monarch)
P: Phil Brandon
D: Dan Birt
S: (STORY) Allan Mackinnon
(THE JUDGE SEES THE LIGHT)
SC: Allan Mackinnon
Rona Anderson . . . . Linda Harrison
Patrick Holt . . . . Michael Carteret
John Arnatt . . . . Steve Harrison
John Warwick . . . . Pete Hanken
Frederick Leister . . . . . . Sir Edward Carteret
Ronald Adam . . . . . Sir William Harrison QC
June Ashley . . . . Rita Hanken
Peter Swanwick . . . . Charley Pott
Lisa Lee . . . . Gladys Vavasour
Ballard Berkeley . . . . Insp Hall
CRIME Blackmailed doctor accused of
killing fiancee's husband.

11711
A KILLER WALKS (57) (A)
Leontine Entertainments (GN)
P:D:SC: Ronald Drake
S: (PLAY) Gordon Glennon
(GATHERING STORM)
(NOVEL) Rayner Barton
(ENVY MY SIMPLICITY)
Laurence Harvey . . . . Ned
Susan Shaw . . . . Joan Gray
Trader Faulkner . . . . Frankie
Laurence Naismith . . . . . . Doctor
Sheila Shand Gibbs . . . . . . Brenda
Ethel Edwards . . . . Gran
CRIME Man kills grandmother for her
farm and frames his brother.

11712
VENETIAN BIRD (95) (A)
USA: THE ASSASSIN
British Film Makers (GFD)
P: Betty Box
D: Ralph Thomas
S: (NOVEL) Victor Canning
SC: Victor Canning
Richard Todd . . . . Edward Mercer
Eva Bartok . . . . Adrianna Medova
John Gregson . . . . Cassana
George Coulouris . . . . Spadoni
Margot Grahame . . . . Rosa Melitus
Walter Rilla . . . . Count Boria
John Bailey . . . . Lt Longo
Sidney James . . . . Bernardo
Martin Boddey . . . . Gufo
Michael Balfour . . . . Moretto
Sydney Tafler . . . . Boldesca
Miles Malleson . . . . Crespi
Eric Pohlmann . . . . Gostini
CRIME Venice. Tec searches for ex-partisan
who has become an assassin.

11713
THE GENTLE GUNMAN (86) (A)
Ealing (GFD)
P: Michael Relph
D: Basil Dearden
S: (PLAY) Roger Macdougall
SC: Roger Macdougall
John Mills . . . . Terence Sullivan
Dirk Bogarde . . . . Matt Sullivan
Robert Beatty . . . . Shinto
Elizabeth Sellars . . . . Maureen Fagan
Gilbert Harding . . . . Henry Truethorne
Barbara Mullen . . . . Molly Fagan
Eddie Byrne . . . . Flynn
Joseph Tomelty . . . . Dr Brannigan
Liam Redmond . . . . Tim Connolly
James Kenney . . . . Johnny Fagan
Michael Golden . . . . Murphy
Jack MacGowran . . . . Patsy McGuire
Patric Doonan . . . . Sentry
CRIME Ireland, 1941. IRA man, disgusted
by violence, rescues prisoners to thwart his
brother's gang.

11714
IT STARTED IN PARADISE (94) tech (U)
British Film Makers (GFD)
P: Sergei Nolbandov, Leslie Parkyn
D: Compton Bennett
S: Marghanita Laski
SC: Marghanita Laski, Hugh Hastings
Jane Hylton . . . . Martha Watkins
Ian Hunter . . . . Arthur Turner
Terence Morgan . . . . Edouard
Muriel Pavlow . . . . Alison
Martita Hunt . . . . Mme Alice
Kay Kendall . . . . Lady Caroline
Ronald Squire . . . . Mary Jane
Brian Worth . . . . Michael

Joyce Barbour	Lady Burridge
Diana Decker	Crystal Leroy
Jack Allen	Lord Chandos
Harold Lang	Louis
Mara Lane	Popsie
Naomi Chance	Model

DRAMA Ambitious designer's salon ruined by phoney Count's bad taste.

11715
TRENT'S LAST CASE (90) (U)
Imperadio (BL)
P:D: Herbert Wilcox
S: (NOVEL) E.C.Bentley
SC: Pamela Wilcox Bower

Margaret Lockwood	Margaret Manderson
Michael Wilding	Philip Trent
Orson Welles	Sigsbee Manderson
John McCallum	John Marlowe
Miles Malleson	Burton Cupples
Hugh McDermott	Calvin C. Bunner
Sam Kydd	Insp Murch
Jack McNaughton	Martin

CRIME Financier kills himself and framed his secretary for murder.

11716
THE NIGHT WON'T TALK (60) (U)
Corsair (ABP)
P: Harold Richmond
D: Daniel Birt
S: Roger Burford
SC: Brock Williams

Hy Hazell	Theo Castle
John Bailey	Clayton Hawkins
Mary Germaine	Hazel Carr
Ballard Berkeley	Insp West
Elwyn Brook-Jones	Martin Soames
Grey Blake	Kenneth Wills
Duncan Lamont	Sgt Robbins
Sarah Lawson	Susan

CRIME Chelsea. Artist, war hero, and ex-husband suspected of killing model.

11717
TOP SECRET (94) (U)
USA: MR POTTS GOES TO MOSCOW
Transocean (ABP)
P:D: Mario Zampi
S: Michael Pertwee, Jack Davies

Oscar Homolka	Zekov
Nadia Gray	Tania Ivanova
George Cole	George Potts
Wilfrid Hyde White	Sir Hubert
Charles Goldner	Gaston
Irene Handl	Mrs Tidmarsh
Gerard Heinz	Director
Frederick Leister	Prime Minister
Michael Medwin	Smedley
Olaf Pooley	Roblettski
Edwin Styles	Supt
Geoffrey Sumner	Pike
Frederick Valk	Rakov
Eleanor Summerfield	Cecilia
Kynaston Reeves	Director
Richard Wattis	Barnes

COMEDY Soviet spies kidnap sanitary engineer in mistake for atom scientist.

11718
DOWN AMONG THE Z MEN (71) (U)
E.J.Fancey Productions (NR)
D: Maclean Rogers
S: Jimmy Grafton, Francis Charles

Harry Secombe	Harry Jones
Carole Carr	Carole Gayley
Peter Sellers	Maj Bloodnock
Michael Bentine	Prof Osrick Purehart
Spike Milligan	Pte Eccles
Television Toppers	WRACs

COMEDY Conscripted grover helps an M15 girl save an atomic formula from spies.

11719
GHOST SHIP (74) (A)
Anglo-Amalgamated
P:D:S: Vernon Sewell

Dermot Walsh	Guy
Hazel Court	Margaret
Hugh Burden	Dr Fawcett
John Robinson	Dr Martineau
Hugh Latimer	Peter
Pat Owens	Joyce
Joan Carol	Mrs Martineau
Joss Ambler	Manager
Mignon O'Doherty	Mrs Manley

FANTASY Couple buy motor yacht haunted by previous owner's wife and her lover.

11720
HINDLE WAKES (82) (A) USA: HOLIDAY WEEK
Monarch
P: William J. Gell
D: Arthur Crabtree
S: (PLAY) Stanley Houghton
SC: John Baines

Lisa Daniely	Jenny Hawthorne
Leslie Dwyer	Chris Hawthorne
Brian Worth	Alan Jeffcoate
Sandra Dorne	Mary Hollins
Ronald Adam	Nat Jeffcoate
Joan Hickson	Mrs Hawthorne
Michael Medwin	George Ramsbottom
Mary Clare	Mrs Jeffcoate
Bill Travers	Bob
Tim Turner	Tommy Dykes
Lloyd Pearson	Tim Farrar
Diana Hope	Betty Farrar

ROMANCE Lancs. Millgirl spends holiday with employer's son and then refuses to wed him.

11721
LOVE'S A LUXURY (89) (A)
USA: THE CARETAKER'S DAUGHTER
Film Studios Manchester (Mancunian)
P: Tom Blakeley
D: Francis Searle
S: (PLAY) Guy Paxton, Edward V. Hole
SC: Hugh Wakefield, Elwyn Ambrose

Hugh Wakefield	Charles Pentwick
Derek Bond	Robert Bentley
Michael Medwin	Dick Pentwick
Helen Shingler	Mrs Pentwick
Zena Marshall	Fritzi Villiers
Bill Shine	Clarence Mole
Patricia Raine	Molly Harris
Grace Arnold	Mrs Harris

COMEDY Actors pose as various people to fool impresario's jealous wife.

11722
THE HOUR OF 13 (78) (A)
MGM British
P: Hayes Goetz
D: Harold French
S: (NOVEL) Philip Macdonald (X V REX)
SC: Howard Emmett Rogers, Leon Gordon

Peter Lawford	Nicholas Revel
Dawn Addams	Jane Frensham
Roland Culver	Insp Connor
Derek Bond	Sir Christopher Lenhurst
Heather Thatcher	Mrs Chumley Orr
Leslie Dwyer	Ernie Perker
Colin Gordon	MacStreet
Fabia Drake	Lady Elbridge
Michael Hordern	Sir Herbert
Jack McNaughton	Ford
Campbell Cotts	Mr Chumley Orr
Richard Shaw	The Terror

CRIME Edwardian. Gentleman thief proves he is not "The Terror" who kills constables.

11723
THE STARFISH (38) (A)
Mount Pleasant (JPD)
P:D:S: Alan Cooke, John Schlesinger

Kenneth Griffith	Jack Trevennick
Nigel Finzi	Tim Wilson
Susan Schlesinger	Jill
Ursula Wood	Mrs Wilson
Christopher Finzi	Michael
Margaret Webber	Witch Meg

FANTASY Cornwall. Fisherman helps children rescue child from witch.

11724
THE CRIMSON PIRATE (104) tech (U)
WB-FN-Norma (WB) *reissue:* 1963 (11 mins cut)
D: Robert Siodmak
S: Roland Kibbee

Burt Lancaster	Vallo
Nick Cravat	Ojo
Eva Bartok	Consuelo
Torin Thatcher	Humble Bellows
James Hayter	Prudence
Margot Grahame	Bianca
Leslie Bradley	Baron Gruda
Noel Purcell	Pablo Murphy
Eliot Makeham	Governor
Frederick Leister	El Libre
Frank Pettingell	Col
Dagmar Wynter	Signorita

ADVENTURE Caribbean, 18th C. Pirates help islanders rebel against their oppressors.

11725
SOUTH OF ALGIERS (95) (U) tech
USA: THE GOLDEN MASK
Mayflower (ABP)
P: Maxwell Setton, Aubrey Baring
D: Jack Lee
S: Robert Westerby

Van Heflin	Nick Chapman
Wanda Hendrix	Anne Burnett
Eric Portman	Dr Burnett
Charles Goldner	Petris
Jacques Francois	Jacques Farnod
Jacques Brunius	Kress
Alec Mango	Mahmoud
Marne Maitland	Thank You
George Pastell	Hassan
Marie France	Yasmin
Aubrey Mather	Sir Arthur Young
Noelle Middleton	Stewardess
Simone Silva	Zara
Maxwell Setton	Donkey Buyer
Aubrey Baring	Camel Rider

ADVENTURE Africa. Archaeologist and crooks seek Mask of Moloch.

11726
ELSTREE STORY (61) (U)
ABPC (ABP)
P:D: Gilbert Gunn
S: Jack Howells

Richard Todd	Himself

VOICES: Norman Shelley; Georgie Henschel; Kenneth Connor; Leonard Sachs; Peter Jones; Warwick Ward; Peter du Roch
COMPILATION Extracts from earlier films.

11727
COME BACK PETER (80) (U)
Present Day (Apex)
P: Charles Reynolds
D:SC: Charles Saunders
S: (PLAY) A.P.Dearsley

Patrick Holt	John Neilson
Peter Hammond	George Harris
Humphrey Lestocq	Arthur Hapgood
Kathleen Boutall	Mrs Hapgood
Charles Lamb	Mr Hapgood

Pamela Bygrave . . . . Myrna Hapgood
Aud Johansen . . . . Virginia
Dorothy Primrose . . . . . . Phyllis Hapgood
Doris Groves . . . . Dandy
John Singer . . . . Ted
COMEDY Married children return to live with parents in new small house.

11728
THE STOLEN PLANS (57) (U)
GB Instructional (ABFD-CFF)
P: Frank Wells
D:SC: James Hill
S: Michael Poole
Mavis Sage . . . . .Nicolette Renaud
Lance Secretan . . . . Michael Foster
Peter Neil . . . . Tony Burton
Pamela Edmunds . . . . Mrs Foster
Peter Burton . . . . Dr Foster
Patrick Boxill . . . . Mr Palmer
Len Sharp . . . . Tod
Geoffrey Goodheart . . . . . The Boss
Ludmilla Tchakalova . . . . .
CHILDREN French girl helps boy catch spies seeking aircraft designer's plans.

11729
THE GAMBLER AND THE LADY (74) (A)
Hammer (Ex)
P: Anthony Hinds
D: Pat Jenkins, Sam Newfield
Dane Clark . . . . Jim Forster
Kathleen Byron . . . . Pat
Naomi Chance . . . . . Lady Susan Willens
Meredith Edwards . . . . Dave
Anthony Forwood . . . . . . Peter Willens
Eric Pohlmann . . . . Arturo Colonna
Julian Somers . . . . Licasi
Anthony Ireland . . . . Farning
Enzo Cottichia . . . . Angelo Colonna
Thomas Gallagher . . . . Sam
Max Bacon . . . . Maxie
Jane Griffiths . . . . Janey Greer
Percy Marmont . . . . Lord Hortland
Eric Boon . . . . Boxer
CRIME American gambler tries to crash society and is framed when crooked brothers kill his nightclub manager.

11730
MADE IN HEAVEN (981) tech (U)
BFM-Fanfare (GFD)
P: George H. Brown
D: John Paddy Carstairs
S: George H.Brown
SC: William Douglas Home
David Tomlinson . . . . Basil Topham
Petula Clark . . . . Julie Topham
Sonja Ziemann . . . . Marta
A.E.Matthews . . . . Grandpa
Charles Victor . . . . Mr Topham
Sophie Stewart . . . . Mrs Topham
Richard Wattis . . . . Vicar
Athene Seyler . . . . Miss Honeycroft
Philip Stainton . . . . Mr Grimes
Ferdy Mayne . . . . Istfan
Alfie Bass . . . . Mr Jenkins
Dora Bryan . . . . Mrs Jenkins
Michael Brennan . . . . Sgt Marne
COMEDY Couple win Dunmow Flitch and it is stolen while husband is kissing Hungarian maid.

11731
THE PICKWICK PAPERS (115) (U)
Renown
P: George Minter, Noel Langley
D:SC: Noel Langley
S: (NOVEL) Charles Dickens
James Hayter . . . . Samuel Pickwick
Nigel Patrick . . . . Mr Jingle

James Donald . . . . Mr Winkle
Kathleen Harrison . . . . Rachel Wardle
Joyce Grenfell . . . . Mrs Leo Hunter
Hermione Gingold . . . . . . Miss Tomkins
Donald Wolfit . . . . Sgt Buzfuz
Hermione Baddeley . . . . . Mrs Bardell
Harry Fowler . . . . Sam Weller
Diane Hart . . . . Emily Wardle
George Robey . . . . Tony Weller
William Hartnell . . . . Irate Cabman
Joan Heal . . . . Isabel
Walter Fitzgerald . . . . Mr Wardle
Sam Costa . . . . Job Trotter
Alexander Gauge . . . . Mr Tupman
Lionel Murton . . . . Mr Snodgrass
Athene Seyler . . . . Miss Witherfield
D.A.Clarke-Smith . . . . Dodson
Alan Wheatley . . . . Fogg
June Thorburn . . . . Arabella
Gerald Campion . . . . Fat Boy
Mary Merrall. . . . . Grandma Wardle
Raymond Lovell . . . . Surgeon
Cecil Trouncer . . . Mr Justice Stareleigh
Felix Felton . . . . Dr Slammer
Max Adrian . . . . Aide
Barry Mackey . . . . Mr Snubbins
Hattie Jacques . . . . Mrs Nupkins
Noel Purcell . . . . Roker
Gibb McLaughlin . . . . Foreman
COMEDY 1830. Adventures of group of friends on country jaunt.

11732
WOMEN OF TWILIGHT (89) (X)
USA: TWILIGHT WOMEN
Daniel Angel-Romulus (IFD)
D: Gordon Parry
S: (PLAY) Sylvia Rayman
SC: Anatole de Grunwald
Freda Jackson . . . . Helen Alastair
Rene Ray . . . . Vivianne Bruce
Lois Maxwell . . . . Christine Ralston
Laurence Harvey . . . . Jerry Nolan
Joan Dowling . . . . Rose Gordon
Dora Bryan . . . . Olga Lambert
Vida Hope . . . . Jess Smithson
Mary Germaine . . . . Veronica
Ingeborg Wells . . . . Lilly
Dorothy Gordon . . . . Sally
Clare James . . . . Molly
Cyril Smith . . . . Mr Flinton
CRIME Woman baby-farmer victimises unmarried mothers.

DEC
11733
THE RINGER (78) (U)
London-BLPA (BL) reissue: 1964
P: Hugh Perceval
D: Guy Hamilton
S: (PLAY) Edgar Wallace
SC: Val Valentine, Lesley Storm
Herbert Lom . . . . Maurice Meister
Donald Wolfit . . . . Dr Lomond
Mai Zetterling . . . . Lisa
Greta Gynt . . . . Cora Ann Milton
William Hartnell . . . . Sam Hackett
Norman Wooland . . . . Insp Bliss
Denholm Elliott . . . . John Lenley
Dora Bryan . . . . Mrs Hackett
Charles Victor . . . . Insp Wembury
Walter Fitzgerald . . . . Commissioner
John Stuart . . . . Gardener
John Slater . . . . Bell
CRIME Master of disguise kills ex-partner despite police protection.

11734
FOLLY TO BE WISE (91) (U)
London-BLPA (BL)

P: Frank Launder, Sidney Gilliatt
D: Frank Launder
S: (PLAY) James Bridie
(IT DEPENDS WHAT YOU MEAN)
SC: Frank Launder, John Dighton
Alastair Sim . . . . Capt Paris
Roland Culver . . . . George Prout
Elizabeth Allan . . . . Angela Prout
Martita Hunt . . . . Lady Dodds
Colin Gordon . . . . Prof James Mutch
Janet Brown . . . . Pte Jessie Killigrew
Miles Malleson . . . . . . Dr Hector McAdam
Edward Chapman . . . . Joseph Byres
Peter Martyn . . . . Walter
Robin Bailey . . . . Corporal
George Cole . . . . Private
COMEDY Army Brains Trust asked if marriage is a good idea.

11735
THE VOICE OF MERRILL (84) (A)
USA: MURDER WILL OUT
Tempean (Eros)
P: Robert Baker, Monty Berman
D: SC: John Gilling
S: Gerald Landeau, Terence Austin
Valerie Hobson . . . . Alycia Roach
Edward Underdown . . . . . . Hugh Allen
James Robertson Justice . .Jonathan Roach
Henry Kendall . . . . Ronald Parker
Garry Marsh . . . . Insp Thornton
Daniel Wherry . . . . Pierce
Sam Kydd . . . . Sgt Baker
Daphne Newton . . . . Miss Quinn
Ian Fleming . . . . Dr Forrest
CRIME Dying author frames radio narrator for killing his secretary;

11736
DECAMERON NIGHTS (94) tech (A)
Film Locations (Eros)
P: M.J.Frankovitch, William Szekeley
D: Hugo Fregonese
S: (STORIES) Giovanni Boccaccio
(THE DECAMERON)
SC: George Oppenheimer
Main Story
Joan Fontaine . . . . Fiamette
Louis Jourdan . . . . Boccaccio
Binnie Barnes . . . . Contessa
Joan Collins . . . . Pampinea
Mara Lane . . . . Girl
Paganino the Pirate
Joan Fontaine . . . . Bartolomea
Louis Jourdan . . . . Paganino
Binnie Barnes . . . . Countess
Godfrey Tearle . . . . Ricciardo
Eliot Makeham . . . . Governor
Wager for Virtue
Joan Fontaine . . . . Ginevra
Louis Jourdan . . . . Guilio
Binnie Barnes . . . . Nerina
Godfrey Tearle . . . . Bernabo
Meinhart Maur . . . . Sultan
George & Bert Bernard . . . . Messengers
The Doctor's Daughter
Joan Fontaine . . . . Isabella
Louis Jourdan . . . . Bertrando
Joan Collins . . . . Maria
Binnie Barnes . . . . Witch
Noel Purcell . . . . Father Francisco
Marjorie Rhodes . . . . Signora Bucca
ROMANCE 1350. Poet's stories lead to his marriage to a widow.

11737
THE YELLOW BALLOON (80) (X)
Marble Arch (ABP)
P: Victor Skutezky
D: J. Lee-Thompson
S: Anne Burnaby

SC: J. Lee-Thompson, Anne Burnaby
William Sylvester . . . .   Len
Kenneth More . . . .   Ted
Kathleen Ryan . . . .   Em
Andrew Ray . . . .   Frankie
Bernard Lee . . . . PC Chapman
Hy Hazell . . . . Mary
Veronica Hurst . . . .   Teacher
Sandra Dorne . . . .   Iris
Campbell Singer . . . .   Potter
Sidney James . . . .   Barrowboy
Marjorie Rhodes . . . .   Mrs Stokes
Elliot Makeham . . . .   Pawnbroker
CRIME Crook uses boy in robbery by
telling him he killed his chum.

11738
THE SECOND MRS TANQUERAY (75) (A)
Vandyke (ABFD)
P: Roger Proudlock
D: Dallas Bower
S: (PLAY) Arthur Wing Pinero
Pamela Brown . . . .   Paula Tanqueray
Hugh Sinclair . . . .   Aubrey Tanqueray
Ronald Ward . . . .   Cayley Drummle
Virginia McKenna . . . . . .   Ellean Tanqueray
Andrew Osborn . . . .   Capt Ardale
Mary Hinton . . . .   Mrs Cortellion
Peter Haddon . . . .   Sir George Orreyed
Peter Bull . . . . Misquith
Bruce Seton . . . .   Gordon Jayne
DRAMA Man's second wife learns his
daughter loves her own ex-lover.

11739
TREAD SOFTLY (70) (A)
Albany (Apex)
P: Donald Ginsberg, Vivian A. Cox
D: David Macdonald
S: (RADIO SERIAL) Gerald Verner
(THE SHOW MUST GO ON)
SC: Gerald Verner
Frances Day . . . .   Madeleine Peters
Patricia Dainton . . . .   Tangye Ward
John Bentley . . . .   Keith Gilbert
John Laurie . . . .   Angus MacDonald
Olaf Olsen . . . .   Philip Defoe
Nora Nicholson . . . .   Isobel Mayne
Harry Locke . . . .   Nutty Potts
Betty Baskcomb . . . .   Olivia Winter
Robert Urquhart . . . .   Clifford Brett
CRIME Murder in old theatre owned by mad
woman whose husband was killed years
before.

11740
HOT ICE (65) (A)
Present Day-SWH Piccadilly (Apex)
P: Charles Reynolds
D:SC: Kenneth Hume
S: (PLAY) Alan Melville
(A WEEKEND AT THRACKLEY)
John Justin . . . .   Jim Henderson
Barbara Murray . . . .   Mary
Ivor Barnard . . . .   Edwin Carson
John Penrose . . . .   Freddie Usher
Michael Balfour . . . .   Jacobson
Gabrielle Brune . . . .   Marcella
Anthony Pendrell . . . .   Burroughs
Bill Shine . . . .   Henry
CRIME Jewel thief invites rich guests to
house party in order to rob them.

11741
POTTER OF THE YARD (30) (U)
Collingwood (NR)
P: E.J.Fancey
D: John Wall, Oscar Burn
John Laurie . . . .   Edward Potter
Hector Ross . . . .   Insp Greenaway

Avis Scott . . . .   Eloise Tremaine
CRIME Scotland Yard clerk poses as
mechanic to catch escaped bank-robber.

11742
THE GREAT DAY (9) (U)
Carlyle
P: Olive Negus
D: Oscar Burn
Chris & Jennifer . . . .   The Children
CHILDREN Girl wins four first prizes
at local gymkhana.

11743
FUN ON THE FARM (11) (U)
Carlyle
P: Olive Negus
D: Oscar Burn
Chris & Jennifer . . . .   The Children
CHILDREN Children look after farm while
father is away.

11744
MISS ROBIN HOOD (78) (U)
Group 3 (ABFD)
P: John Grierson, Donald Wilson
D: John Guillermin
S: Reed de Rouen
SC: Val Valentine, Patrick Campbell,
Geoffrey Orme
Margaret Rutherford . . . . .   Miss Honey
Richard Hearne . . . . Henry Wrigley
Michael Medwin . . . .   Ernest
Peter Jones . . . . Lidstone
James Robertson Justice . .   McAllister
Sidney James . . . . Sidney
Dora Bryan . . . . Pearl
Frances Rowe . . . . Marion
Eunice Gayson . . . .   Pam
Edward Lexy . . . .   Wilson
Eric Berry . . . . Lord Otterbourne
COMEDY Author of girls' stories helps
old lady recover stolen formula for whiskey.

11745
JOHN OF THE FAIR (62) (U)
Merton Park (ABFD-CFF)
P: Frank Hoare
D: SC: Michael McCarthy
S: Arthur Groom
John Charlesworth . . . . . .   John Claydon
Arthur Young . . . . Doc Claydon
Richard George . . . .   William Samuels
Michael Mulcaster . . . .   Jasper Sly
Hilda Barry . . . . Ma Miggs
Carol Wolveridge . . . .   Jill
Sidney Bland . . . . Gilroy
David Garth . . . .   Sir Thomas Renton
Fanny Wright . . . . Sarah Wilcott
CHILDREN 18th C. Uncle seeks to usurp
the inheritance of quack's son.

11746
MURDER AT SCOTLAND YARD (75) (U)
Bushey (Ambassador) reissue: 1962
(as two films)
P: Gilbert Church
D: Victor M. Gover
S: John Gilling
Tod Slaughter . . . . Terence Riley
Patrick Barr . . . . Insp Morley
Tucker McGuire . . . .   Eileen Trotter
Dorothy Bramhall . . . . Maria Flame
Tom Macauley . . . .   Insp Grant
CRIME Three stories of gang boss: explosive
radio sets; diamond robbery.

11747
MURDER AT THE GRANGE (31) (A)
Bushey (Famous)
P: Gilbert Church
D: Victor M. Gover

S: John Gilling
Tod Slaughter . . . . The Butler
Patrick Barr . . . . Insp Morley
Margaret Boyd . . . .   Agatha Quelch
CRIME Cripple persuades butler to
strangle her sister.

11748
A GHOST FOR SALE (31) (A)
Bushey (Famous)
P: Gilbert Church
D: Victor M. Gover
S: John Gilling
Tod Slaughter . . . . Caretaker
Patrick Barr . . . . Man
Tucker McGuire . . . .   Wife
FANTASY Manor caretaker relates tale of
mad squire, and vanishes. (Includes extracts
from THE CURSE OF THE WRAYDONS
(1946).)

11749
SWIFT WATER (16) (U)
Data Film Unit (CFF-ABFD)
P: J.D.Chambers
D: Tony Thompson
S: Wolfgang Wilhelm
Guthrie Mason . . . .   Terry
Sally Sanderson . . . . Ann
Jasper Jewitt . . . . Jeff
Dorothy Hannaford . . . .   Aunt
George Passmore . . . .   Piermaster
CHILDREN Devon. Town boy on holiday
joins bird watchers and saves aunt's
spaniel from river.

11750
TO THE RESCUE (21) (U)
Massingham (CFF-ABFD)
P: S: Richard Massingham
D: Jacques Brunius
Richard Massingham . . . . .   Mr Polly
Jacques Brunius . . . . Mr Black
Fella Edmonds . . . .   George
John Ruddock
John Stuart
Christina Chevreau
CHILDREN Village grocer helps boy whose
poodle is stolen by rich rival.

11751
FOR YOUR ENTERTAINMENT (series) (U)
Gaumont British (GFD)
P: Frank Wells
D: Colin Bell

11752
No. 1: (15)
Ericson   Three Jokers
Levanda & Van   Three Monarchs

11753
No. 2: (15)
Chris Sands   Seven Volantes
Cynthia & Gladys   Twelve Jackson Girls

11754
No. 3: (14)
Boyer & Ravel   Seven Volantes
Cynthia   Swan & Leigh
Levanda & Van   Syd Millward and
                                  the Nitwits

11755
No. 4: (14)
Ted & George Durante   Levanda & Van
Barbour Brothers   Cynthia & Le Roys
Syd Millward and the Nitwits
REVUE

1953

JAN

11756
THERE WAS A YOUNG LADY (84) (U)
Nettlefold (Butcher)
P: Ernest G. Roy, A.R. Rawlinson
D: SC: Lawrence Huntington
S: (RADIO SERIAL) Vernon Harris,
John Jowett

Michael Denison	David Walsh
Dulcie Gray	Elizabeth Foster
Sydney Tafler	Johnny
Bill Owen	Joe
Geraldine McEwen	Irene
Charles Farrell	Arthur
Robert Adair	Basher
Bill Shine	Duke of Chiddingford
Kenneth Connor	Countryman
Tommy Duggan	Weatherspoon

COMEDY Smash and grab gang kidnap an
efficient secretary who then organises them.

11757
COSH BOY (75) (X)
USA: THE SLASHER
Daniel Angel—Romulus (IFD)
D: Lewis Gilbert
S: (PLAY) Bruce Walker (MASTER CROOK)
SC: Lewis Gilbert, Vernon Harris

James Kenney	Roy Walsh
Joan Collins	Rene Collins
Hermione Baddeley	Mrs Collins
Hermione Gingold	Queenie
Betty Ann Davies	Elsie Walsh
Robert Ayres	Bob Stevens
Nancy Roberts	Gran Walsh
Ian Whittaker	Alfie Collins
Stanley Escane	Pete
Sean Lynch	Darkey
Michael McKeag	Brian
Edward Evans	Sgt Woods
Laurence Naismith	Insp Donaldson
Frederick Piper	Mr Easter
Walter Hudd	Magistrate
Sidney James	Sgt

CRIME Teenage gang leader on probation robs,
coshes old woman, seduces pal's sister, and is
thrashed by his stepfather.

11758
THE LONG MEMORY (96) (A)
Europa (GFD)
P: Hugh Stewart
D: Robert Hamer
S: (NOVEL) Howard Clewes
SC: Robert Hamer, Frank Harvey

John Mills	Davidson
John McCallum	Insp Lowther
Elizabeth Sellars	Fay Lowther
Eva Berg	Elsa
Geoffrey Keen	Craig
Michael Martin-Harvey ...	Jackson
John Chandos	Boyd
John Slater	Pewsey
Thora Hird	Mrs Pewsey
Vida Hope	Alice Gedge
Harold Lang	Chauffeur
Mary Mackenzie	Gladys
Laurence Naismith	Asprey
Peter Jones	Fisher
Henry Edwards	Judge

CRIME Framed ex-convict's desire for
vengeance quelled by his love for refugee.

11759
THE NET (86) (U)
USA: PROJECT M7
Two Cities (GFD)
P: Anthony Darnborough
D: Anthony Asquith
S: (NOVEL) John Pudney
SC: William Fairchild

Phyllis Calvert	Lydia Heathley
James Donald	Michael Heathley
Robert Beatty	Sam Seagram
Herbert Lom	Alex Leon
Muriel Pavlow	Caroline Cartier
Noel Willman	Dr Dennis Bord
Walter Fitzgerald	Sir Charles Craddock
Patric Doonan	Brian Jackson
Maurice Denham	Carrington
Marjorie Fielding	Mama
Cavan Watson	Ferguson
Herbert Lomas	George Jackson
Cyril Chamberlain	Insp Carter
Tucker McGuire	Myrna

CRIME Inventor of 2000 mph jet plane
thwarts spy during test flight.

11760
THE GREAT GAME (80) (U)
Advance (Adelphi) *reissue*: 1956 (GN)
P: David Dent
D: Maurice Elvey
S: (PLAY) Basil Thomas (SHOOTING STAR)
SC: Wolfgang Wilhelm

James Hayter	Joe Lawson
Thora Hird	Miss Rawlings
Diana Dors	Lulu Smith
Sheila Shand Gibbs	Mavis Pink
John Laurie............	Wells
Glyn Houston	Ned Rutter
Geoffrey Toone	Jack Bannerman
Jack Lambert	Mr Blake
Meredith Edwards	Skid Evans
Alexander Gauge	Ben Woodhall
Frank Pettingell	Sir Julius
Glenn Melvyn	Heckler
Tommy Lawton	Himself

Brentford Football Club
SPORT Club manager tries to acquire rival
team's centre forward.

11761
THE MAN WHO WATCHED TRAINS GO BY
(80) *tech* (A)
USA: PARIS EXPRESS
Raymond Stross (Eros) *reissue*: 1962
(Compton)
P: Joseph Shaftel
D: SC: Harold French
S: (NOVEL) Georges Simenon

Claude Rains	Kees Popinga
Marta Toren	Michele
Marius Goring	Insp Lucas
Anouk Aimee	Jeanne
Herbert Lom	Julius de Koster
Lucie Mannheim	Mme Popinga
Felix Aylmer	Merkemans
Ferdy Mayne	Louis
Eric Pohlmann	Goin
Gibb McLaughlin	de Koster
Mary Mackenzie	Mrs Lucas

CRIME Holland. Old clerk steals money and
flees to Paris.

11762
ESCAPE ROUTE (79) (U)
USA: I'LL GET YOU
Banner (Eros)
P: Bernard Luber, Ronald Kinnoch
D: Seymour Friedman, Peter Graham Scott
S: John Baines
SC: John Baines, Nicholas Phipps

George Raft	Steve Rossi
Sally Gray	Joan Miller
Clifford Evans	Michael Grand
Reginald Tate	Col Wilkes
Patricia Laffan	Miss Brooks
Frederick Piper	Insp Reed
Roddy Hughes	Porter
June Ashley	Girl
John Warwick	Brice

CRIME FBI agent poses as fugitive to save
kidnapped scientists from spies.

FEB

11763
ALF'S BABY (75) (U)
ACT Films (Adelphi)
P: John Harlow
D: Maclean Rogers
S: (PLAY) A. P. Dearsley (IT WON'T BE A
STYLISH MARRIAGE)
SC: A.P. Dearsley

Jerry Desmonde	Alf Donkin
Pauline Stroud	Pamela Weston
Olive Sloane	Mrs Matthews
Peter Hammond	Tim Barton
Sandra Dorne	Enid
Roy Purcell	Sgt Bob Mackett
C. Denier Warren	Cedric Donkin
Mark Daly	Will Donkin
Roddy Hughes	Mr Prendergast

COMEDY Three bachelor brothers adopt girl
who later falls for crooked garage-man.

11764
THOSE PEOPLE NEXT DOOR (77) (U)
Film Studios Manchester (Eros)
P: Tom Blakeley
D: John Harlow
S: (PLAY) Zelda Davees (WEARING THE
PANTS)

Jack Warner	Sam Twigg
Charles Victor	Joe Higgins
Marjorie Rhodes	Mary Twigg
Gladys Henson	Emma Higgins
Garry Marsh	Sir Andrew Stevens
Jimmy James	Drunk
Patricia Cutts	Anne Twigg
Peter Forbes-Robertson ...	Victor Stevens
Anthony Newley	Bob Twigg

COMEDY 1941. S/L's titled parents object to
his working-class fiancee.

11765
TOP OF THE FORM (75) (U)
BFM (GFD)
P: Paul Soskin
D: John Paddy Carstairs
S: Anthony Kimmins, Leslie Arliss.
Val Guest, Marriott Edgar (GOOD MORNING BOYS)
SC: John Paddy Carstairs, Patrick Kirwan,
Ted Willis

Ronald Shiner	Ronnie Fortescue
Harry Fowler	Albert
Alfie Bass	Arty Jones
Jacqueline Pierreux	Yvette
Anthony Newley	Percy
Mary Jerrold	Mrs Bagshott
Richard Wattis	Willoughby-Gore
Howard Marion-Crawford ..	Dickson
Roland Curram	Terence
Terence Mitchell	Clarence
Gerald Campion	Pugley
Oscar Quitak	Septimus
Kynaston Reeves	The Dean
Martin Benson	Cliquet

COMEDY Bookie poses as teacher and helps
pupils save Mona Lisa from thieves.

11766
BLACK ORCHID (60) (A)
Kenilworth (GFD)
P: Robert Baker, Monty Berman
D: Charles Saunders
S: John Temple-Smith, Francis Edge

Ronald Howard	Dr John Winnington
Olga Edwardes	Christine Shaw
John Bentley	Eric Blair
Mary Laura Wood	Sophie Winnington
Patrick Barr	Vincent Humphries
Sheila Burrell	Annette Durrant
Russell Napier	Insp Markham
Mary Jones	Mrs Humphries

CRIME Doctor accused of poisoning his wife
for the love of her sister.

11767
APPOINTMENT IN LONDON (96) (U)
Mayflower (BL)
P: Maxwell Setoon, Aubrey Baring
D: Philip Leacock
S: Robert Westerby, John Wooldridge
Dirk Bogarde . . . . W/C Tim Mason
Ian Hunter . . . . G/C Logan
Dinah Sheridan . . . . Eve Canyon
William Sylvester . . . . Mac
Walter Fitzgerald . . . . Doc Mulvaney
Bryan Forbes . . . . P/O Greeno
Bill Kerr . . . . F/L Bill Brown
Charles Victor . . . . Dobbie
Anne Leon. . . . . Pamela Greeno
Richard Wattis . . . . Pascal
Terence Longden . . . . Dr Buchanan
Sam Kydd . . . . A/C Ackroyd
Campbell Singer . . . . F/Sgt
Donovan Winter . . . . Navigator
Don Sharp . . . . Gunner
Anthony Shaw . . . . Smithy
Carl Jaffe . . . . General
WAR 1943. Strained officer goes on bombing raid against orders.

11768
TOO MANY DETECTIVES (33) (U)
Collingwood (New Realm)
P: D: S: Oscar Burn, John Wall
John Laurie . . . . Edward Potter
Hector Ross . . . . Insp Greenaway
Mavis Villiers
Jack Stewart
Howard Connell
CRIME Scotland Yard clerk proves missing embezzler was murdered.

11769
THE DRAYTON CASE (26) (U)
Merton Park (AA)
P: Alec Snowden
D: S: Kenneth Hughes
N: Edgar Lustgarten
Victor Platt
Hilda Barry
John le Mesurier
CRIME Killer uses air raids to dispose of his victims.

11770
THE STRANGER LEFT NO CARD (23) (A)
Meteor (BL)
P: George K. Arthur
D: Wendy Toye
S: Sidney Carroll
Alan Badel . . . . The Stranger
Cameron Hall . . . . Latham
Eileen Way . . . . Secretary
CRIME Weird eccentric murders man who framed him.

11771
MISSING PERSONS (15) (U)
Rayant (GFD)
P: Anthony Gilkison
D: Alun Falconer
N: Robert Robinson
DRAMA Political disappearance; army deserter; student's suicide; boy who stole airplane.

11772
ROVER MAKES GOOD (16) (U)
Plymouth (ABFD—CFF)
P: D: S: John Dooley
Felicity Alway . . . . The Girl
Malcolm Doney . . . . The Boy
CHILDREN Cornwall. Useless sheepdog brings help to children trapped in mine.

11773
STABLE RIVALS (16) (U)
Anglo—Scottish (ABFD—CFF)
P: D: S: Leonard Reeve
Sheila Muir . . . . Betty
Kerrin Masterman . . . . Jim
Kim Pickup . . . . Dick
CHILDREN Baker's children and riding school owner's son compete in pony gymkhana.

11774
BUNTY WINS A PUP (26) (U)
Bushey (Ambassador)
D: S: Victor M. Gover
Yvonne Prestige . . . . Bunty Brown
Desmond Llewellyn . . . . . . Mr Brown
Helen Christie . . . . Peggy Brown
Frank Hawkins . . . . Uncle George
Paul Adrian . . . . Harry Brown
CHILDREN Small girl wins prize, buys terrier, and loses it.

11775
SKID KIDS (65) (U)
Bushey (ABFD—CFF)
P: Gilbert Church
D: Don Chaffey
S: Jack Howells
Barry McGregor . . . . Swankey Clarke
Anthony Lang . . . . Bobby Reynolds
Peter Neil . . . . PC
Tom Walls . . . . Mr Clarke
Angela Monk . . . . Sylvia Clarke
A.E. Matthews . . . . Man in Taxi
CHILDREN East End cycle-racing children catch bicycle thieves.

11776
HEIGHTS OF DANGER (60) (U)
ABPC (ABFD—CFF)
P: Howard Thomas
D: Peter Bradford
S: Betty Davies
Basil Appleby . . . . Mr Burton
Freda Bamford . . . . Mrs Burton
Wilfrid Downing . . . . Wilfrid Burton
Annette Cabot . . . . Annette Burton
Christopher Cabot . . . . . . Christopher Burton
Richard Goolden . . . . Mr Henderson
Jack Melford . . . . Mr Croudson
Roger Snowden . . . . Wolfing
Sebastian Cabot . . . . Jakes
CHILDREN Alps. Garage man wins car rally despite crooked rival.

11777
TIME BOMB (72) (U)
USA: TERROR ON A TRAIN
MGM British
P: Richard Goldstone
D: Ted Tetzlaff
S: (NOVEL) Kem Bennett (DEATH AT ATTENTION)
SC: Kem Bennett
Glenn Ford . . . . Peter Lyncourt
Anne Vernon . . . . Janine Lyncourt
Maurice Denham . . . . Jim Warrilow
Harcourt Williams . . . . Vicar
Victor Maddern . . . . Saboteur
Harold Warrender . . . . . . Sir Evelyn Jordan
John Horsley . . . . PC Charles Baron
Campbell Singer . . . . Insp Branson
Bill Fraser . . . . PC Reed
Herbert C. Walton . . . . Old Charlie
Frank Atkinson . . . . Guard
Ernest Butcher . . . . Martindale
Ada Reeve . . . . Old Lady
CRIME Birmingham. Canadian engineer dismantles time bomb planted in trainload of naval mines.

11778
ROUGH SHOOT (86) (U)
USA: SHOOT FIRST
United Artists (UA)
P: Joseph Shaftel, Raymond Stross
D: Robert Parrish
S: (NOVEL) Geoffrey Household (A ROUGH SHOOT)
SC: Eric Ambler
Joel McCrea . . . . Col Bob Taine
Evelyn Keyes . . . . Cecily Taine
Herbert Lom . . . . Peter Sandorski
Marius Goring . . . . Hiart
Roland Culver . . . . Randall
Karel Stepanek . . . . Diss
David Hurst . . . . Lex
Frank Lawton . . . . Richard Hassingham
Patricia Laffan . . . . . . Magda Hassingham
Megs Jenkins . . . . Mrs Powell
Laurence Naismith . . . . . . Blossom
Cyril Raymond . . . . Col Cartwright
Ellis Irving . . . . PC Wharton
CRIME Dorset. US Army colonel poses as agent to help Polish MI5 man catch spies seeking atom secrets.

11779
VALLEY OF SONG (74) (U)
USA: MEN ARE CHILDREN TWICE
ABPC (ABP)
P: Vaughan N. Dean
D: Gilbert Gunn
S: (RADIO PLAY) Cliff Gordon (CHOIR PRACTICE)
SC: Cliff Gordon, Phil Park
Mervyn Johns . . . . Griffiths Minister
Clifford Evans . . . . Geraint Llewellyn
Maureen Swanson . . . . . . Olwn Davies
John Fraser . . . . Cliff Lloyd
Rachel Thomas . . . . Mrs Lloyd
Betty Cooper . . . . Mrs Davies
Rachel Roberts . . . . Bessie Lewis
Hugh Pryse . . . . Lloyd Undertaker
Edward Evans . . . . Davies Shop
Kenneth Williams . . . . . . Lloyd Haulage
Alun Owen . . . . Pritchard
COMEDY Wales. Villagers feud over contralto part in "The Messiah".

MAR

11780
THE ORACLE (84) (U)
USA: THE HORSE'S MOUTH
Group 3 (ABFD)
P: John Grierson, Colin Lesslie
D: C. Pennington Richards
S: (RADIO PLAY) Robert Barr (TO TELL YOU THE TRUTH)
SC: Patrick Campbell
Robert Beatty . . . . Bob Jefferson
Joseph Tomelty . . . . Terry Roche
Mervyn Johns . . . . Tom Mitchum
Michael Medwin . . . . Timothy Blake
Virginia McKenna . . . . Shelagh
Gillian Lind . . . . Jane Bond
Ursula Howells . . . . Peggy
Arthur Macrae . . . . Alan Digby
Louise Hampton . . . . Miss Turner
John Charlesworth . . . . . . Denis
Maire O'Neill . . . . Mrs Lenham
Gilbert Harding . . . . Oracle
FANTASY Ireland. Reporter cashes in on predictions of oracle in well.

11781
MANTRAP (78) (A)
USA: WOMAN IN HIDING
Hammer
P: Michael Carreras, Alexander Paal
D: Terence Fisher

S: (NOVEL) Elleston Trevor
(QUEEN IN DANGER)
SC: Paul Tabori, Terence Fisher
Paul Henreid . . . . Hugo Bishop
Lois Maxwell . . . . Thelma Tasman
Kieron Moore . . . . Mervyn Speight
Hugh Sinclair . . . . Maurice Jerrard
Lloyd Lamble . . . . Frisnay
Anthony Forwood . . . . Rex
Bill Travers . . . . Victor Tasman
Mary Laura Wood . . . . Susie
Kay Kendall . . . . Vera
John Penrose . . . . du Vancet
CRIME Tec helps escaped madman prove he is
not murderer.

11782
THE TITFIELD THUNDERBOLT (84) tech (U)
Ealing (GFD)
P: Michael Truman
D: Charles Crichton
S: T.E.B. Clarke
Stanley Holloway . . . . Valentine
George Relph . . . . Rev Weech
Naunton Wayne . . . . Blakeworth
John Gregson . . . . Gordon
Godfrey Tearle . . . . The Bishop
Hugh Griffith . . . . Dan
Gabrielle Brune . . . . Joan
Sidney James . . . . Hawkins
Reginald Beckwith . . . . . . Coggett
Edie Martin . . . . Emily
Michael Trubshawe . . . . . . Ruddock
Nancy O'Neil . . . . Mrs Blakeworth
COMEDY Rich eccentric helps villagers take
over closed railway line.

11783
DEADLY NIGHTSHADE (61) (U)
Kenilworth (GFD)
P: Robert Baker, Monty Berman
D: John Gilling
S: Lawrence Huntington
Emrys Jones . . . . Matthews/Barlow
Zena Marshall . . . . Ann Farrington
John Horsley . . . . Insp Clements
Joan Hickson . . . . Mrs Fenton
Hector Ross . . . . Canning
Victor Platt . . . . Sgt
Roger Maxwell . . . . Col Smythe
Lesley Deane . . . . Mrs Smythe
CRIME Cornwall. Escaped convict poses as
dead double, then finds he was a spy.

11784
STREET CORNER (94) (U)
USA: BOTH SIDES OF THE LAW
London Independent (GFD) reissue:
1961 (GEFD)
P: Sydney Box, William MacQuitty
D: Muriel Box
S: Jan Read
SC: Muriel & Sydney Box
Anne Crawford . . . . Susan
Peggy Cummins . . . . Briget Foster
Rosamund John . . . Sgt Pauline Ramsey
Terence Morgan . . . . Ray
Barbara Murray . . . . WPC Lucy
Ronald Howard . . . . David Evans
Eleanor Summerfield . . . . . Edna
Michael Medwin . . . . Chick Farrar
Sarah Lawson . . . . Joyce
Charles Victor . . . . Muller
Dora Bryan . . . . Daughter of Joy
Eunice Gayson . . . . Janet
Yvonne Marsh . . . . Elsa
Michael Hordern . . . . Insp Heron
Lloyd Lamble . . . . Sgt Weston
John Warwick . . . . Insp Gray
Joyce Carey . . . . Miss Hopkins
Maurice Denham . . . . Mr Dawson

Thora Hird . . . . Mrs Perkins
Marjorie Rhodes . . . . Mrs Foster
Anthony Oliver . . . . Stanley Foster
David Horne . . . . Judge
John Stuart . . . . Magistrate
CRIME Chelsea. Various adventures of
several policewomen.

11785
DESPERATE MOMENT (88) (U)
BFM—Fanfare (GFD)
P: George H. Brown
D: Compton Bennett
S: (NOVEL) Martha Albrand
SC: George H. Brown, Patrick Kirwan
Dirk Bogarde . . . . Simon van Hallder
Mai Zetterling . . . . Anna de bergh
Philip Friend . . . . Robert Sawyer
Albert Lieven . . . . Paul Fliege
Walter Rilla . . . . Col Bertrand
Simone Silva . . . . Mink
Frederick Wendhousen . . . . . Grote
Carl Jaffe . . . . Becker
Gerard Heinz . . . . Bones
Andre Mikhelson . . . . Insp
Harold Ayer . . . . Trevor Wood
Theodore Bikel . . . . Anton
CRIME Berlin. Dutchman tracks down black
marketeer who framed him for murder.

11786
THE WEDDING OF LILLI MARLENE (87) (U)
Monarch
P: William Gell
D: Arthur Crabtree
S: John Baines
Lisa Daniely . . . . Jenny Hawthorne
Hugh McDermott . . . . Steve Moray
Sidney James . . . . Fennimore Hunt
Gabrielle Brune . . . . Maggie Lennox
Jack Billings . . . . Hal Marvel
Robert Ayres . . . . Andrew Jackson
Joan Heal . . . . Linda
Wally Patch . . . . Wally
Irene Handl . . . . Daisy
John Blythe . . . . Holt
MUSICAL French singer rises to stardom
despite machinations of her rival.

11787
HOUSE OF BLACKMAIL (72) (U)
ACT Films (Monarch)
P: Phil Brandon
D: Maurice Elvey
S: Allan Mackinnon
Mary Germaine . . . . Carol Blane
William Sylvester . . . . Jimmy
Alexander Gauge . . . . John Markham
John Arnatt . . . . Pete Carter
Denis Shaw . . . . Bassett
Ingeborg Wells . . . . Emma
Patricia Owens . . . . Joan
C. Denier Warren . . . . Jock
CRIME Murder of blackmailer in house
surrounded by high-tension wires.

11788
MOULIN ROUGE (120) tech (A)
Romulus—Moulin (IFD)
P: D: John Huston
S: (NOVEL) Pierre la Mure
SC: John Huston, Anthony Veiller
Jose Ferrer . . . . . Henri de Toulouse-Lautrec/
The Count
Colette Marchand . . . . Marie Charlet
Zsa Zsa Gabor . . . . Jane Avril
Suzanne Flon . . . . Myriamme Hayem
Claude Nollier . . . . The Countess
Katherine Kath . . . . la Goulue
Muriel Smith . . . . Aicha
Mary Clare . . . . Mme Loubet

Walter Crisham . . . . Valetin 'le Desosse
Harold Kasket . . . . Zidler
Jim Gerald . . . . Pere Cotelle
Georges Lannes . . . . Patou
Lee Montague . . . . Maurice Joyant
Maureen Swanson . . . . Denise
Tutte Lemkow . . . . Partner
Jill Bennett . . . . Sarah
Theodore Bikel . . . . King
Peter Cushing . . . . .Marcel de la Voisier
HISTORY Paris, 1890. Biography of a
crippled artist.

11789
INTIMATE RELATIONS (86) (X)
Advance (Adelphi) reissue: 1956 (GN)
P: David Dent
D: SC: Charles Frank
S: (PLAY) Jean Cocteau (LES PARENTS
TERRIBLES)
Harold Warrender . . . . George
Elsy Albiin . . . . Madeleine
Marian Spencer . . . . Yvonne
Ruth Dunning . . . . Leonie
Russell Enoch . . . . Michael
DRAMA Invalid's husband learns his son loves
his own ex-mistress.

APR
11790
SEA DEVILS (90) tech (U)
Coronado (RKO)
P: David E. Rose, John R. Sloan
D: Raoul Walsh
S: (NOVEL) Victor Hugo TOILERS OF
THE SEA)
SC: Borden Chase
Yvonne de Carlo . . . . Drouette
Rock Hudson . . . . Gilliatt
Maxwell Reed . . . . Rantaine
Denis O'Dea . . . . Lethierry
Michael Goodliffe . . . . Ragan
Bryan Forbes . . . . Willie
Jacques Brunius . . . . Fouche
Ivor Barnard . . . . Benson
Arthur Wontner . . . . Baron de Vaudrez
Gerard Oury . . . . Napoleon
Keith Pyott . . . . Gen Latour
ADVENTURE France. Smuggler saves English
girl spy from Napoleon.

11791
THE FINAL TEST (91) (U)
ACT Films (GFD)
P: R.J. Minney
D: Anthony Asquith
S: (TV PLAY) Terence Rattigan
SC: Terence Rattigan
Jack Warner . . . . Sam Palmer
Robert Morley . . . . Alexander Whitehead
Brenda Bruce . . . . Cora
Ray Jackson . . . . Reggie Palmer
George Relph . . . . Syd Thompson
Adrianne Allen . . . . Aunt Ethel
Stanley Maxted . . . . Senator
Joan Swinstead . . . . Miss Fanshawe
Richard Bebb . . . . Frank Weller
Valentine Dyall . . . . Man in Black
Len Hutton; Denis Compton; Alec Bedser;
Godfrey Evans; Jim Laker; Cyril Washbrook
SPORT Poet is not interested in his father's
last cricket Test Match.

11792
THE CRUEL SEA (126) (U)
Ealing (GFD) reissues: 1958 (Ren)
1961 (GEFD)
P: Leslie Norman
D: Charles Frend
S: (NOVEL) Nicholas Monsarrat
SC: Eric Ambler

Jack Hawkins . . . . LtCdr Ericson
Donald Sinden . . . . Lt Lockhart
Denholm Elliott . . . . Lt Morell
John Stratton . . . . Ferraby
Stanley Baker . . . . Bennett
Virginia McKenna . . . . Julie Hallam
Moira Lister . . . . Elaine Morell
Liam Redmond . . . . Jim Watts
Meredith Edwards . . . . Yeoman Wells
Bruce Seton . . . . Bob Tallow
Megs Jenkins . . . . Glad Tallow
June Thorburn . . . . Doris Ferraby
John Warner . . . . Baker
Glyn Houston . . . . Phillips
Alec McCowen . . . . Tonbridge
Andrew Cruickshank . . . . . Scott Brown
Walter Fitzgerald . . . . Warden
WAR 1941. Corvette captain sinks U—Boat by
running down British survivors.
(PGAA: 1954; Top Moneymaker: 1953.)

11793
GRAND NATIONAL NIGHT (81) (A)
USA: WICKED WIFE
Talisman (Renown)
P: Phil C. Samuel
D: Bob McNaught
S: (PLAY) Dorothy & Campbell Christie
SC: Dorothy & Campbell Christie
Nigel Patrick . . . . Gerald Coates
Moira Lister . . . . Babs Coates
Beatrice Campbell . . . . . . Joyce Penrose
Betty Ann Davies . . . . . . Pinkie Collins
Michael Hordern . . . . Insp Ayling
Noel Purcell . . . . Philip Balfour
Colin Gordon . . . . Buns Darling
Gibb McLaughlin . . . . Morton
Barry Mackay . . . . Sgt Gibson
Leslie Mitchell . . . . Jack Donovan
Maria Mercedes . . . . Maria
CRIME Insp tries to convict stable-owner for
accidental death of his faithless wife.

11794
STREET OF SHADOWS (84) (A)
USA: SHADOW MAN
Merton Park—William Nassour (AA)
P: W.H. Williams
D: S: Richard Vernon
S: (NOVEL) Lawrence Meynall
(THE CREAKING CHAIR)
Cesar Remero . . . . Luigi
Kay Kendall . . . . Barbara Gale
Edward Underdown . . . . . . Insp Johnstone
Victor Maddern . . . . Limpy
Simone Silva . . . . Angele
John Penrose . . . . Capt Gerald Gale
Molly Hamley-Clifford . . . . Starry Darrell
Annaconda . . . . Darrell
Bill Travers . . . . Nigel Langley
CRIME Soho arcade owner framed for killing
former mistress.

11795
NOOSE FOR A LADY (73) (A)
Insignia (AA)
P: Victor Hanbury
D: Wolf Rilla
S: (NOVEL) Gerald Verner (WHISPERING
WOMAN)
SC: Rex Rienits
Dennis Price . . . . Simon Gale
Rona Anderson . . . . Jill Hallam
Ronald Howard . . . . Dr Evershed
Pamela Allan . . . . Margaret Allan
Alison Leggatt . . . . . Mrs Langdon-Humphries
Melissa Stribling . . . . Vanessa Lane
Charles Lloyd Pack . . . . . Robert Upcott
Colin Tapley . . . . Maj Fergusson
George Merritt . . . . Insp Frost
CRIME Tec proves his convicted cousin did
not poison her blackmailer husband.

11796
LAXDALE HALL (77) (U)
USA: SCOTCH ON THE ROCKS
Group 3 (ABFD)
P: John Grierson, Alfred Shaughnessy
D: John Eldridge
S: (NOVEL) Eric Linklater
SC: John Eldridge, Alfred Shaughnessy
Ronald Squire . . . . Gen Matheson
Kathleen Ryan . . . . Catriona Matheson
Raymond Huntley . . . . . . Samuel Pettigrew MP
Sebastian Shaw . . . . Hugh Marvel MP
Jameson Clark . . . . Roderick McLeod
Jean Colin . . . . Lady Pettigrew
Kynaston Reeves . . . . . Rev Ian Macauley
Fulton Mackay . . . . Andrew Flett
Prunella Scales . . . . Moraig McLeod
Andrew Keir . . . . McKillaig
Keith Falkner . . . . Peter McLeod
Rikki Fulton . . . . Poacher
COMEDY Hebrides. Village's five car owners
refuse to pay tax until road is built.

11797
NEVER LET ME GO (94) (U)
MGM British
P: Clarence Brown
D: Delmer Daves
S: (NOVEL) Roger Bax (CAME THE DAWN)
SC: Ronald Millar, George Froeschel
Clark Gable . . . . Philip Sutherland
Gene Tierney . . . . Marya Lamarkina
Bernard Miles . . . . Joe Brooks
Richard Haydn . . . . Christopher Denny
Belita . . . . Valentina Alexandrovna
Kenneth More . . . . Steve Quillan
Frederick Valk . . . . Kuragin
Karel Stepanek . . . . Commissar
Theodore Bikel . . . . Lieut
Anna Valentina . . . . Svetlana Mikhailovna
Peter Illing . . . . NKVD Man
Meinhart Maur . . . . Lemkov
Anton Dolin
London Festival Ballet
ADVENTURE American reporter and British
sergeant smuggle their Russian wives to
England.

MAY

11798
THE STEEL KEY (69) (A)
Tempean (Eros)
P: Robert Baker, Monty Berman
D: Robert Baker
S: Roy Chanslor
SC: John Gilling
Terence Morgan . . . . Johnny O'Flynn
Joan Rice . . . . Doreen Wilson
Raymond Lovell . . . . Insp Forsythe
Dianne Foster . . . . Sylvia Newman
Hector Ross . . . . Beroni
Colin Tapley . . . . Dr Crabtree
Esmond Knight . . . . Prof Newman
Arthur Lovegrove . . . . . . Gilchrist
CRIME Ex-crook saves inventor of steel-
hardening process from sanatorium run by
spies.

11799
DEATH GOES TO SCHOOL (65) (U)
Independent Artists (Eros)
P: Victor Hanbury
D: Stephen Clarkson
S: (NOVEL) Maisie Sharman
SC: Maisie Sharman, Stephen Clarkson
Barbara Murray . . . . Miss Shepherd
Gordon Jackson . . . . Insp Campbell
Pamela Allan . . . . Helen Cooper
Jane Aird . . . . Miss Halstead
Beatrice Varley . . . . Miss Hopkinson
Stanley Rose . . . . Insp Burgess

Robert Long . . . . Mr Lawley
Sam Kydd . . . . Sgt Harvey
CRIME Girls' School music mistress proves
colleague is a strangler.

11800
TURN THE KEY SOFTLY (81) (A)
Chiltern (GFD)
P: Maurice Cowan
D: Jack Lee
S: (NOVEL) John Brophy
SC: John Brophy, Maurice Cowan
Yvonne Mitchell . . . . Monica Marsden
Terence Morgan . . . . David
Joan Collins . . . . Stella Jarvis
Kathleen Harrison . . . . Mrs Quilliam
Thora Hird . . . . Landlady
Dorothy Alison . . . . Joan
Glyn Houston . . . . Bob
Geoffrey Keen . . . . Gregory
Russell Waters . . . . Jenkins
Clive Morton . . . . Walters
Richard Massingham . . . . . Bystander
CRIME Burglar, shoplifter, and prostitute
released from Holloway on same day.

11801
FOUR SIDED TRIANGLE (81) (A)
Hammer (Exclusive)
P: Michael Carreras, Alexander Paal
D: Terence Fisher
S: (NOVEL) William F. Temple
SC: Terence Fisher, Paul Tabori
Barbara Payton . . . . Lena/Helen
James Hayter . . . . Dr Harvey
Stephen Murray . . . . Bill
John Van Eyssen . . . . Robin
Percy Marmont . . . . Sir Walter
Jennifer Dearman . . . . . . Lena (child)
Glyn Dearman . . . . Bill (child)
Sean Barrett . . . . Robin (child)
Kynaston Reeves . . . . Lord Grant
John Stuart . . . . Solicitor
FANTASY Scientist creates duplicate of his
friend's wife.

11802
THE STORY OF GILBERT AND SULLIVAN
(109) tech (U) USA: THE GREAT
GILBERT AND SULLIVAN
London—BLPA (BL)
P: Frank Launder, Sidney Gilliat
D: Sidney Gilliat
S: (BOOK) Leslie Bailey
(THE GILBERT AND SULLIVAN BOOK)
SC: Leslie Bailey, Sidney Gilliat, Vincent Korda
Robert Morley . . . . W.S. Gilbert
Maurice Evans . . . . Arthur Sullivan
Eileen Herlie . . . . Helen Lenoir
Martyn Green . . . . George Grossmith
Peter Finch . . . . . . Richard D'Oyley Carte
Dinah Sheridan . . . . Grace Marston
Isabel Dean . . . . Mrs Gilbert
Wilfrid Hyde White . . . . . Mr Marston
Muriel Aked . . . . Queen Victoria
Michael Ripper . . . . Louis
Bernadette O'Farrell . . . . . Jessie Bond
Ann Haslip . . . . Bride
Eric Berry . . . . Rutland Barrington
Yvonne Marsh . . . . Bride
Lloyd Lamble . . . . Joseph Bennett
Ian Wallace . . . . Captain
Owen Brannigan; Webster Booth, Thomas
Round; Elsie Morison; Marjorie Thomas; John
Cameron; Gordon Clinton; Harold Williams;
Muriel Brunskill; Jennifer Vyvyan; Joan
Gillingham
MUSICAL 1875—1907. Biography of writers
of comic operas.

11803
WILL ANY GENTLEMAN? (84) *tech* (U)
ABPC (ABP)
P: Hamilton G. Inglis
D: Michael Anderson
S: (PLAY) Vernon Sylvaine
SC: Vernon Sylvaine
George Cole . . . . Henry
Veronica Hurst . . . . Florence
Jon Pertwee . . . . Charley
Heather Thatcher . . . . Mrs Whittle
James Hayter . . . . Dr Smith
William Hartnell . . . . Insp Martin
Diana Decker . . . . Angel
Joan Sims . . . . Beryl
Alan Badel . . . . The Great Mendoza
Sidney James . . . . Hobson
Brian Oulton . . . . Mr Jackson
Alexander Gauge . . . . Mr Billing
Josephine Douglas . . . . Receptionist
Peter Butterworth . . . . Stage Manager
Wally Patch . . . . Bookmaker
Lionel Jeffries . . . . Mr Frobisher
Richard Massingham . . . . . Stout Man
COMEDY Meek bank clerk becomes
philanderer after hypnosis.

11804
GENEVIEVE (86) *tech* (U)
Sirius (GFD) *reissue:* 1960
P: D: Henry Cornelius
S: William Rose
Dinah Sheridan . . . . Wendy McKim
John Gregson . . . . Alan McKim
Kay Kendall . . . . Rosalind Peters
Kenneth More . . . . Ambrose Claverhouse
Geoffrey Keen . . . . Speed Cop
Reginald Beckwith . . . . . . J.C. Callahan
Arthur Wontner . . . . Gentleman
Joyce Grenfell . . . . Proprietress
Leslie Mitchell . . . . Himself
Michael Medwin . . . . Husband
Michael Balfour . . . . Conductor
Edie Martin . . . . Guest
Harold Siddons . . . . Speed Cop
COMEDY Two couples in veteran cars race
from London to Brighton.
(BFA: Best British Film 1953.)

11805
JUNO HELPS OUT (19) (U)
British Films (CFF-ABFD) *reissue:* 196-,
JUNO, HOME HELP
P: William Weedon
D: S: William C. Hammond
CHILDREN Children's Great Dane helps them
do housework while their mother is ill.

11806
THE NUTCRACKER (11) (U) *ferrania*
Group Three (BL)
P: John Grierson
D: Cyril Frankel
S: (BALLET) Tchaikowsky
John Gilpin
Belinda Wright
MUSICAL Excerpts from ballet.

11807
VINTAGE '28 (14) (U) (3D)
Film Partnership (Stereo Techniques)
D: Robert Angell
S: Christopher Barry
Desmond Montgomery . . . Hank
Julian Orchard . . . . James Featherstone
COMEDY American becomes enthusiastic after
visiting Vintage Car Rally.

JUN

11808
THE FAKE (81) (U)
Pax (UA)

P: Steven Pallos, Ambrose Grayson
D: Godfrey Grayson
S: James Daplyn
SC: Patrick Kirwan, Bridget Boland
Dennis O'Keefe . . . . Paul Mitchell
Coleen Gray . . . . Mary Mason
Hugh Williams . . . . Sir Richard Aldingham
Guy Middleton . . . . Smith
John Laurie . . . . Henry Mason
Gerald Case . . . . Randall
Eliot Makeham . . . . George
Ellen Pollock . . . . Miss Fossett
Dora Bryan . . . . Barmaid
Billie Whitelaw . . . . Waitress
CRIME American tec proves knight hired artist
to fake a da Vinci, and killed him.

11809
ISN'T LIFE WONDERFUL! (83) (U) *tech*
ABPC (ABP)
P: Patrick Ward
D: Harold French
S: (NOVEL) Brock Williams (UNCLE WILLIE
AND THE BICYCLE SHOP)
SC: Brock Williams
Eileen Herlie . . . . Mother
Cecil Parker . . . . Father
Donald Wolfit . . . . Uncle Willie
Robert Urquhart . . . . Frank
Eleanor Summerfield . . . . . Aunt Kate
Dianne Foster . . . . Virginia van Stuyden
Peter Asher . . . . Charles
Cecil Trouncer . . . . Dr Barsmith
Russell Waters . . . . Green
Edwin Styles . . . . Bamboula
Fabia Drake . . . . Lady Probus
Arthur Young . . . . .Sir George Probus
Viola Lyel . . . . Aunt Jane
COMEDY 1902. Family set up drunken uncle
in bicycle business.

11810
THE MISSING MAN (30) (U)
Merton Park (AA)
P: Alex Snowden
D: S: Ken Hughes
N: Edgar Lustgarten
Tristan Rawson
Evelyn Moore
CRIME Insp traces killer of cleric's son
through his mother's dream.

11811
TWICE UPON A TIME (75) (U)
London—BLPA (BL)
P: D: SC: Emeric Pressburger
S: (NOVEL) Erich Kastner
(DAS DOPPELTE LOTTCHEN)
Hugh Williams . . . . James Turner
Elizabeth Allan . . . . Carol-Anne Bailey
Jack Hawkins . . . . Dr Matthews
Yolande Larthe . . . . Carol Turner
Charmain Larthe . . . . Anne Nailey
Violette Elvin . . . . Florence la Roche
Isabel Dean . . . . Miss Burke
Michael Gough . . . . Mr Lloyd
Walter Fitzgerald . . . . Prof Reynolds
Eileen Elton
Kenneth Melville
ROMANCE Tyrol. Twin sisters meet for the
first time and reconcile their divorced parents.

11812
THE CAPTAIN'S PARADISE (93) (A)
London—BLPA (BL) *reissue:* 1957 (cut)
P: D: Anthony Kimmins
S: Alec Coppel
SC: Alec Coppel. Nicholas Phipps,
Anthony Kimmins
Alec Guinness . . . . Capt Henry St James
Yvonne de Carlo . . . . Nita StJames
Celia Johnson . . . . Maud StJames

Charles Goldner . . . . Ricco
Miles Malleson . . . . Lawrence StJames
Bill Fraser . . . . Absalom
Walter Crisham . . . . Bob
Ferdy Mayne . . . . Sheikh
Nicholas Phipps . . . . Major
Sebastian Cabot . . . . Ali
Claudia Gray . . . . Susan Dailey
George Benson . . . . Salmon
Joss Ambler . . . . Prof Ebbart
Joyce Barbour . . . . Mrs Reid
COMEDY Steamer captain has one wife in
Gibraltar, another in Africa.

11813
JOHNNY ON THE RUN (68) (U)
International Realist (ABFD—CFF)
P: Victor Lyndon
D: Lewis Gilbert, Vernon Harris,
Patricia Latham
Eugeniusz Chylek . . . . Johnny
Sydney Tafler . . . . Harry
Michael Balfour . . . . Fingers
Jean Anderson . . . . Mrs MacIntyre
Moultrie Kelsall . . . . Mr MacIntyre
Mona Washbourne . . . . . . Mrs MacGregor
Margaret McCourt . . . . . . Janet MacGregor
CHILDREN Scotland. Runaway Polish orphan
gets involved with jewel thieves.

11814
INNOCENTS IN PARIS (102) (A)
Romulus (IFD) *reissue:* 1956
(Ren; 10 mins cut)
P: SC: Anatole de Grunwald
D: Gordon Parry
Alastair Sim . . . . Sir Norman Barker
Ronald Shiner . . . . Dicky Bird
Claire Bloom . . . . Susan Robbins
Margaret Rutherford . . . . . Gwladwys Inglott
Claude Dauphin . . . . Max de Lorne
Laurence Harvey . . . . Francois
Jimmy Edwards . . . . .Capt George Stilton
James Copeland . . . . Andy MacGregor
Gaby Bruyere . . . . Josette
Monique Gerard . . . . Raymonde
Mara Lane . . . . Gloria Delaney
Gregoire Aslan . . . . Carpet Seller
Peter Illing . . . . Panitov
Colin Gordon . . . . Customs Officer
Kenneth Kove . . . . Bickerstaff
Frank Muir . . . . Hearty Man
Philip Stainton . . . . Nobby Clarke
Peter Jones . . . . Langton
Richard Wattis . . . . Secretary
Reginald Beckwith . . . . . . Photographer
Alf Goddard . . . . Sgt-Major
Louis de Funes . . . . Celestin
Plymouth Royal Marines Band
Hungaria Gypsy Orchestra
Moulin Rouge Can-Can Dancers
COMEDY Seven stories of British tourists on
weekend trip to Paris.

11815
SINGLE—HANDED (85) (U)
USA: SAILOR OF THE KING
20th Century Productions (20)
P: Frank McCarthy
D: Roy Boulting
S: (NOVEL) C.S. Forester
(BROWN ON RESOLUTION)
SC: Valentine Davies
Jeffrey Hunter . . . . Andrew Brown
Michael Rennie . . . . Richard Saville
Wendy Hiller . . . . Lucinda Bentley
Bernard Lee . . . . Stoker Wheatley
Peter Van Eyck . . . . Kapitan von Falk
Victor Maddern . . . . Earnshaw
John Horsley . . . . Cdr Willis
Patrick Barr . . . . Capt Ashley
Robin Bailey . . . . Lt Stafford
James Copeland . . . . Cdr Laughton

WAR 1940. Captain's bastard sailor son holds German ship at bay with his rifle.

JUL

11816
TAKE A POWDER (58) (U)
RLT Productions (Apex)
P: Lionel Tomlinson
D: Lionel Tomlinson, Julien Vedey
S: Julien Vedey

Julien Vedey	Prof Schultz
Max Bacon	Maxie
Isabel George	Betty
Maudie Edwards	Matron
Neville Gates	Bill
Fred Kitchen jr	Dr Fowler
Alexis Chesnakov	Dr Stroganoff
Larry Taylor	Spike

COMEDY Market medicine man poses as atom scientist to catch spies.

11817
MR BEAMISH GOES SOUTH (33) (U)
Collingwood (NR)
P: D: John Wall, Oscar Burn

John Laurie	Edward Potter
Hector Ross	Insp Greenaway
Molly Raynor	
Catherine Campbell	
Jack Stewart	

CRIME Police clerk unmasks hotel guest who kills women in acid baths.

11818
MALTA STORY (103) (U)
BFM Theta (GFD) reissue: 1961 (GEFD)
P: Peter de Sarigny
D: Brian Desmond Hurst
S: Peter de Sarigny, Thorold Dickinson, William Fairchild
SC: William Fairchild, Nigel Balchin

Alec Guinness	F/L Peter Rose
Jack Hawkins	AOC
Anthony Steel	W/C John Bartlett
Flora Robson	Melita
Muriel Pavlow	Maria
Renee Asherson	Joan Rivers
Hugh Burden	Eden
Nigel Stock	Guiseppe
Reginald Tate	Payne
Ralph Truman	Vice Admiral Banks
Rosalie Crutchley	Carmella
Michael Medwin	Ramsay
Ronald Adam	Operator
Stuart Burge	Paolo
Jerry Desmonde	General
Ivor Barnard	Old Man

WAR Malta, 1942. Pilot loves Maltese whose brother spies for Italians.

11819
THE SQUARE RING (83) (A)
Ealing (GFD)
P: Michael Relph
D: Basil Dearden
S: (PLAY) Ralph Peterson
SC: Robert Westerby, Peter Myers, Alec Grahame

Jack Warner	Danny Felton
Robert Beatty	Kid Curtis
Maxwell Reed	Rick Martell
Bill Owen	Happy Burns
Joan Collins	Frankie
Kay Kendall	Eve Lewis
Bernadette O'Farrell	Peg Curtis
Eddie Byrne	Lou Lewis
Sidney James	Adams
Alfie Bass	Frank Forbes
George Rose	Whitey Johnson
Bill Travers	Rowdie Rawlings
Ronald Lewis	Eddie Lloyd
Joan Sims	Bunty
Sydney Tafler	Wiseacre
Kid Berg	Referee

SPORT Several stories woven around one night at boxing stadium.

11820
WHEEL OF FATE (70) (A)
Kenilworth (GFD)
P: D: Francis Searle
S: (PLAY) Alex Atkinson
SC: Guy Elmes

Patric Doonan	Johnny Burrows
Sandra Dorne	Lucky Price
Bryan Forbes	Ted Reid
John Horsley	Sgt Simpson
Johnnie Schofield	Len Bright
Martin Benson	Riscoe
Cyril Smith	Perce

CRIME Artistic garage hand's stepbrother robs and kills his paralysed father.

11821
THREE STEPS IN THE DARK (60) (A)
Corsair (ABP)
P: Harold Richmond
D: Daniel Birt
S: Roger East
SC: Brock Williams

Greta Gynt	Sophy Burgoyne
Hugh Sinclair	Philip Burgoyne
Sarah Lawson	Dorothy
Helene Cordet	Esme
Elwyn Brook-Jones	Wilbrahim
John Van Eyssen	Henry Burgoyne
Nicholas Hannen	Arnold Burgoyne
Alistair Hunter	Insp Forbes
Katie Johnson	Mrs Riddle

CRIME Crime authoress unmasks rich uncle's killer.

11822
SPACEWAYS (76) (U)
Hammer—WH Productions (Ex)
P: Michael Carreras
D: Terence Fisher
S: (RADIO PLAY) Charles Eric Maine
SC: Paul Tabori, Richard Landau

Howard Duff	Steve Mitchell
Eva Bartok	Lisa Frank
Alan Wheatley	Smith
Philip Leaver	Dr Keppler
Michael Medwin	Toby Andrews
Andrew Osborn	Philip Crenshaw
Cecile Chevreau	Vanessa Mitchell
Anthony Ireland	Gen Hayes
Hugh Moxey	Col Daniels
David Horne	Minister

FANTASY US scientist accused of stowing his wife's corpse in space rocket.

11823
THE FLANAGAN BOY (81) (A)
USA: BAD BLONDE
Hammer (Ex)
P: Anthony Hinds
D: Reginald Leborg
S: (NOVEL) Max Catto
SC: Richard Landau, Guy Elmes

Barbara Payton	Lorna Vecchi
Frederick Valk	Guiseppe Vecchi
John Slater	Charlie
Sidney James	Sharkey
Tony Wright	Johnny Flanagan
Marie Burke	Mrs Vecchi
Selma Vaz Dias	Mrs Corelli
George Woodbridge	Inspector

CRIME Wife of old promoter persuades boxing protege to drown him.

11824
THE BROKEN HORSESHOE (79) (U)
Nettlefold (Butcher)
P: Ernest G. Roy
D: Martyn C. Webster
S: (TV SERIAL) Francis Durbridge
SC: A.R. Rawlinson

Robert Beatty	Dr Mark Fenton
Elizabeth Sellars	Della Freman
Peter Coke	Insp Bellamy
Vida Hope	Jackie Leroy
Ferdy Mayne	Charles Constance
James Raglan	Supt Grayson
Hugh Pryse	Mr Rattray
Hugh Kelly	Dr Craig
Janet Butler	Sister Rogers
George Benson	Prescott
Ronald Leigh Hunt	Sgt Lewis

CRIME Dr involved with dope smugglers cleared by woman crook.

11825
THE BEGGAR'S OPERA (94) tech (U)
Imperadio (BL)
P: Herbert Wilcox, Laurence Olivier
D: Peter Brook
S: (PLAY) John Gay
SC: Dennis Cannan, Christopher Fry

Laurence Olivier	MacHeath
Dorothy Tutin	Polly Peachum
Stanley Holloway	Lockit
Daphne Anderson	Lucy Lockit
George Devine	Peachum
Mary Clare	Mrs Peachum
Hugh Griffith	The Beggar
Yvonne Furneaux	Jenny Diver
Sandra Dorne	Sukey Tawdrey
Athene Seyler	Mrs Trapes
George Rose	Turnkey
Margot Grahame	Actress
Kenneth Williams	Jack
Dennis Cannan	Footman
Bdr Billy Wells	Hangman

VOICES: Adele Leigh; Jennifre Vyvyan; Edith Coates; Joan Cross; Bruce Boyce; John Cameron
MUSICAL 1741. Betrayed Highwayman torn between his wife and jailer's daughter.

11826
THE MASTER OF BALLANTRAE (88) tech (U)
WB—FN (WB)
D: William Keighley
S: (NOVEL) Robert Louis Stevenson
SC: Herb Meadow, Harold Medford, Robert Hall, T.J. Morrison
N: Robert Beatty

Errol Flynn	James Durisdeer
Roger Livesey	Col Francis Burke
Anthony Steel	Henry Durisdeer
Beatrice Campbell	Lady Alison
Yvonne Furneaux	Jessie Brown
Jacques Berthier	Arnaud
Felix Aylmer	Lord Durisdeer
Mervyn Johns	MacKellar
Charles Goldner	Mendoza
Ralph Truman	Maj Clarendon
Francis de Wolff	Matthew Bull
Moultrie Kelsall	MacCauley
Charles Carson	Col Banks

ADVENTURE Scotland, 1745. Rebel becomes buccaneer thinking his brother has betrayed him.

11827
COUNTERSPY (88) (U)
USA: UNDERCOVER AGENT
Merton Park (AA)
P: W.H. Williams
D: Vernon Sewell
S: (NOVEL) Julian Symons
(CRISS CROSS CODE)

SC: Guy Elmes, Michael le Fevre

Dermot Walsh	Manning
Hazel Court	Clare Manning
Hermione Baddeley	Del Mar
Alexander Gauge	Smith
James Vivian	Larry
Archie Duncan	Jim
Frederick Schrecker	Plattnauer
Hugh Latimer	Barlow
Bill Travers	Rex
Beryl Baxter	Girl

CRIME Auditor gets involved with spy ring running nursing home.

11828
MURDER AT 3 AM (60) (U)
David Henley (Renown)
P: John Ainsworth
D: Francis Searle
S: John Ainsworth

Dennis Price	Insp Peter Lawton
Peggy Evans	Joan Lawton
Philip Saville	Edward/Jim King
Greta Mayaro	Lena
Rex Garner	Sgt Bill Todd
Arnold Bell	McMann
Leonard Sharp	Old Skip
Nora Gordon	Nanna

CRIME Inspector uses his sister to trap her fiance's halfbrother.

AUG

11829
ALWAYS A BRIDE (83) (A)
Clarion (GFD)
P: Robert Garrett
D: Ralph Smart
S: Ralph Smart, Peter Jones

Peggy Cummins	Clare Hemsley
Terence Morgan	Terence Winch
Ronald Squire	Victor Hemsley
James Hayter	Dutton
Marie Lohr	Dowager
Geoffrey Sumner	Teddy
Charles Goldner	Manager
David Hurst	Beckstein
Jacques Brunius	Inspector
Jill Day	Singer
Sebastian Cabot	Taxidriver
Jacques Brown	Manager
Dino Galvani	Magistrate

COMEDY Monte Carlo. Treasury agent loves confidence trickster's daughter.

11830
THE GIRL ON THE PIER (65) (A)
Major (Apex)
P: Lance Comfort, John Temple-Smith
D: Lance Comfort
S: Guy Morgan

Veronica Hurst	Rita Hammond
Ron Randell	Nick Lane
Charles Victor	Insp Chubb
Marjorie Rhodes	Mrs Chubb
Campbell Singer	Joe Hammond
Eileen Moore	Cathy Chubb
Brian Roper	Ronnie Hall
Anthony Valentine	Charlie Chubb

CRIME Brighton. Waxworks exhibitor kills blackmailing ex-convict.

11831
THE SWORD AND THE ROSE (91) tech (U)
Walt Disney (RKO)
P: Perce Pearce
D: Ken Annakin
S: (NOVEL) Charles Major
(WHEN KNIGHTHOOD WAS IN FLOWER)
SC: Lawrence E. Watkin

Richard Todd	Charles Brandon
Glynis Johns	Mary Tudor
James Robertson Justice	Henry VII
Michael Gough	Duke of Buckingham
Jane Barrett	Lady Margaret
Peter Copley	Sir Edwin Caskoden
Rosalie Crutchley	Katherine of Aragon
D.A. Clarke-Smith	Cardinal Wolsey
Ernest Jay	Lord Chamberlain
Jean Mercure	Louis XII
Gerard Oury	Dauphin

HISTORY 1514. Commoner weds King's sister despite jealous Duke.

11832
THE HOUSE OF THE ARROW (73) (A)
ABPC (ABP)
P: Vaughan N. Dean
D: Michael Anderson
S: (NOVEL) A.E.W. Mason
SC: Edward Dryhurst

Oscar Homolka	Insp Hanaud
Yvonne Furneaux	Betty Harlowe
Robert Urquhart	Jim Frobisher
Anthony Nicholls	Jeremy Haslett
Josephine Griffin	Ann Upcott
Pierre le Fevre	Thevenet
Andrea Lea	Francine
Harold Kasket	Boris Wabersky
Jeanne Pali	Mme Harlowe

CRIME Dijon. Lawyer helps inspector prove English girl did not poison her rich aunt.

11833
THE BOSUN'S MATE (30) (U)
Anvil (GFD)
P: Ralph May
D: Richard Warren
S: (STORY) W.W. Jacobs

Cameron Hall	George Benn
Barbara Mullen	Mrs Waters
Edwin Richfield	Ned Travers
George Woodbridge	PC

COMEDY Barge skipper fakes burglary to impress widowed innkeeper.

11834
BETTY SLOW DRAG (26)
Half Moon
P: E.D. Kayton
D: S: Ernest Borneman
Lynne Cole
Ted Monson
Dinah Kaye
MUSICAL

11835
THE SUPER SECRET SERVICE (25) (U)
SGR Productions (NR)
D: Charles W. Green
S: Spike Milligan
Peter Sellers
Graham Stark
Dick Emery
Ray Ellington Quartet
COMEDY MI5 thwart foreign power seeking secret formula.

11836
OUT OF THE BANDBOX (30) (U)
Norman Redhead (NR)
D: Norman Redhead
Cyril Chamberlain
David Welch
John Blythe
Lisa Lee
Lyn Mason
Tony Fayne & David Evans
Billy Ternent and his Orchestra
REVUE

11837
GLAD TIDINGS (67) (U)
Insignia (Eros)
P: Victor Hanbury
D: SC: Wolf Rilla
S: (PLAY) R.F. Delderfield

Barbara Kelly	Kay Stuart
Raymond Huntley	Tom Forester
Ronald Howard	Cpl Nicholas Brayne
Jean Lodge	Celia Forester
Terence Alexander	F/L Spud Cusack
Diana Calderwood	Josephine Forester
Laurence Payne	Clive Askham
Arthur Howard	Mr Roddington
Brian Smith	Derek Forester
Harry Green	Golfer

COMEDY Colonel's adult children object to youthful fiancee.

11838
RECOIL (79) (A)
Tempean (Eros)
P: Robert Baker, Monty Berman
D: S: John Gilling

Kieron Moore	Nicholas Conway
Elizabeth Sellars	Jean Talbot
Edward Underdown	Michael Conway
John Horsley	Insp Tunbridge
Robert Raglan	Sgt Perkins
Ethel O'Shea	Mrs Conway
Martin Benson	Farnborough
Michael Kelly	Crouch
Ian Fleming	Talbot
Bill Lowe	Walters

CRIME Dead jeweller's daughter poses as crook to catch doctor's burglar brother.

11839
BACKGROUND (82) (A)
Group 3 (ABFD)
P: Herbert Mason
D: Daniel Birt
S: (PLAY) Warren Chetham Strode
SC: Warren Chetham Strode, Don Sharp

Valerie Hobson	Barbie Lomax
Philip Friend	John Lomax
Norman Wooland	Bill Ogden
Janette Scott	Jess Lomax
Mandy Miller	Linda Lomax
Jeremy Spenser	Adrian Lomax
Lilly Kann	Brownie
Helen Shingler	Mary Wallace
Thora Hird	Mrs Humphries
Louise Hampton	Miss Russell
Jack Melford	Mackay
Richard Wattis	David Wallace

DRAMA Son of divorcing couple tries to kill mother's lover with air gun.

11840
ALL HALLOWE'EN (34) (A)
Joan Maude & Michael Warre (ABFD)
D: Michael Gordon
S: Joan Maude, Michael Warre

Sally Gilmour	Rowena
Oleg Briansky	Gervase
Jane Baxter	Lady Delville
Diane Cilento	Harriet
Clive Morton	Sir Arthur
Walter Hudd	Mr Wilberforce
Hattie Jacques	Miss Quibble
Ferdy Mayne	Soldier

FANTASY Lovers born 200 years apart united on Hallowe'en.

11841
THE RED BERET (88) (U) tech
USA: PARATROOPER
Warwick (Col) reissue: 1961 (Unifilms)
P: Irving Allen, Albert R. Broccoli,

Anthony Bushell
D: Terence Young
S: (BOOK) Hilary StGeorge Sanders
SC: Richard Maibaum, Frank Nugent
Alan Ladd . . . . Canada Mackendrick
Leo Genn . . . . Maj Snow
Susan Stephen . . . . Penny Gardner
Harry Andrews . . . . RSM
Donald Houston . . . . Taffy
Anthony Bushell . . . . Gen Whiting
Patric Doonan . . . . Flash
Stanley Baker . . . . Breton
Lana Morris . . . . Pinky
Tim Turner . . . . Rupert
Michael Kelly . . . . Dawes
Anton Diffring . . . . The Pole
WAR 1940. US Army officer posing as
Canadian refuses commission in paratroops in
belief that he killed his friend.

11842
MELBA (113) *tech* (U)
Horizon (UA)
P: Sam Spiegel
D: Lewis Milestone
S: Harry Kurnitz
Patrice Munsel . . . . Nellie Melba
Robert Morley . . . . .Oscar Hammerstein
John McCallum . . . . Charles Armstrong
John Justin . . . . Eric Walton
Alec Clunes . . . . Cesar Carlton
Martita Hunt . . . . Mme Marchesi
Sybil Thorndike . . . . Queen Victoria
Joseph Tomelty . . . . Thomas Mitchell
Beatrice Varley . . . . Aunt Catherine
Cecile Chevreau . . . . Annette
Violetta Elvin
Charles Craig
MUSICAL Australian soprano's success in
Europe spoils her marriage.

SEP

11843
IS YOUR HONEYMOON REALLY
NECESSARY? (80) (A)
Advance (Adelphi) *reissue:* 1956 (GN)
P: David Dent
D: Maurice Elvey
S: (PLAY) E.V. Tidmarsh
SC: Talbot Rothwell
David Tomlinson . . . . Frank Betterton
Diana Dors . . . . Candy
Bonar Colleano . . . . Laurie Vining
Diana Decker . . . . Gillian
Sidney James . . . . Hank Hamilton
McDonald Parke . . . . Admiral Fields
Audrey Freeman . . . . Lucy
COMEDY Honeymoon husband tries to hide
his first wife from his second.

11844
LAUGHING ANNE (90) *tech* (A)
Imperadio (Rep)
P: D: Herbert Wilcox
S: (NOVEL) Joseph Conrad
(BETWEEN THE TIDES)
SC: Pamela Wilcox Bower
Wendell Corey . . . . Capt Davidson
Margaret Lockwood . . . . . Anne
Forrest Tucker . . . . Jem Farrell
Ronald Shiner . . . . Nobby Clark
Robert Harris . . . . Joseph Conrad
Jacques Brunius . . . . Frenchie
Daphne Anderson . . . . Singer
Helen Shingler . . . . Susan Davidson
Danny Green . . . . Nicholas
Harold Lang . . . . Jacques
Maurice Bush . . . . Battling Brunius
Dave Crowley . . . . Boxer
ADVENTURE Java, 1890. Singer leaves
ex-boxer for sea captain.

11845
BLOOD ORANGE (76) (A)
Hammer (Ex)
P: Michael Carreras
D: Terence Fisher
S: Jan Read
Tom Conway . . . . Himself
Mila Parely . . . . Helen Pascall
Naomi Chance. . . . . Gina
Eric Pohlmann . . . . Mercedes
Andrew Osborn . . . . Capt Simpson
Richard Wattis . . . . Macleod
Margaret Halstan . . . . Lady Marchant
Eileen Way . . . . Fernande
Delphi Lawrence . . . . Chelsea
CRIME Ex-FBI man solves jewel robbery and
death of model.

11846
THE SAINT'S RETURN (73) (U)
USA: THE SAINT'S GIRL FRIDAY
Hammer (Ex)
P: Julian Lesser, Anthony Hinds
D: Seymour Friedman
S: (CHARACTERS) Leslie Charteris
SC: Allan Mackinnon
Louis Hayward . . . . Simon Templar
Sydney Tafler . . . . Lennar
Naomi Chance . . . . Lady Carol Denbigh
Charles Victor . . . . Insp Teal
Harold Lang . . . .'. . . . . . Jarvis
Thomas Gallagher . . . . Hoppy Uniatz
Jane Carr . . . . '. . Katie
Fred Johnson . . . . Irish Cassidy
Russell Enoch . . . . Keith Merton
Diana Dors . . . . Girl
CRIME Tec unmasks blackmailer behind
gambling den.

11847
A PRINCE FOR CYNTHIA (28) (U)
Go Pictures (BL)
P: George K. Arthur
D: Muriel Box
S: Sidney Carroll
Elizabeth Henson . . . . Cynthia
Paul Rogers . . . . Prince
ROMANCE Secretary dreams she is kidnapped
by foreign prince.

11848
BOUNCER BREAKS UP (9) (U) *tech*
SADFAS (CFF—ABFD)
D: Don Chaffey
S: Winifred Holmes
Bunny May . . . . John
Mavis Sage . . . . Mary
Hilda Fenemore . . . . Mother
CHILDREN Cartoon dog in scrapbook comes
to life when children play musical box.

11849
MARDI AND THE MONKEY (19) (U)
Peregrine (CFF—ABFD)
P: Deborah Chessmire
D: S: Kay Mander
Wasmin . . . . Mardi
Watmadiredja . . . . . .
Narisah . . . .
CHILDREN West Java. Boy's pet monkey leads
search party when he is lost in forest.

11850
LOONIZOO (14) (U)
New Realm
P: E.J. Fancey
S: Michael Bentine
Michael Bentine . . . . Himself
COMEDY Comedian's impressions of animals
and their languages.

11851
ALBERT RN (88) (U)
USA: BREAK TO FREEDOM
Dial (Eros)
P: Daniel M. Angel
D: Lewis Gilbert
S: (PLAY) Edward Sammis, Guy Morgan
SC: Guy Morgan, Vernon Harris
Anthony Steel . . . . Lt Geoffrey Ainsworth
Jack Warner . . . . Capt Maddox
Robert Beatty . . . . Lt Jim Reid
William Sylvester . . . . Lt Texas Norton
Anton Diffring . . . . Hauptmann Schultz
Eddie Byrne . . . . Lt-Cdr Brennan
Guy Middleton . . . . Capt Bongo Barton
Paul Carpenter . . . . Lt Fred Erickson
Michael Balfour . . . . Lt Henry Adams
Moultrie Kelsall . . . . Lt-Cdr Dawson
Frederick Valk . . . . Commandant
Frederick Schiller . . . . Hermann
Peter Jones . . . . Lt Browne
WAR 1944. True story of naval POWs who use
dummy to cover their escapes.

11852
LOVE IN PAWN (81) (U)
Tempean (Eros)
P: Robert Baker, Monty Berman
D: Charles Saunders
S: Humphrey Knight
SC: Guy Morgan, Frank Muir, Denis Norden
Bernard Braden . . . . Roger Fox
Barbara Kelly . . . . Jean Fox
Jean Carson . . . . Amber Trusslove
Reg Dixon . . . . Albert Trusslove
John Laurie . . . . Mr McCutcheon
Walter Crisham . . . . Hilary Stitfall
Avice Landone . . . . Amelia Trusslove
Laurence Naismith . . . . Uncle Amos
COMEDY Wife pawns her husband, heir to
£10,000 and loses ticket.

11853
THE MAN BETWEEN (101) (U)
London—BLPA (BL)
P: D: Carol Reed
S: (NOVEL) Walter Ebert (SUSANNE IN
BERLIN)
SC: Harry Kurnitz, Eric Linklater
James Mason . . . . Ivo Kern
Claire Bloom . . . . Susan Mallinson
Hildegarde Neff . . . . Bettina Mallinson
Geoffrey Toone . . . . Martin Mallinson
Albert Waescher . . . . Haladar
Ernst Schroeder . . . . Kastner
Karl John . . . . Insp Kleiber
Dieter Krause . . . . Horst
CRIME Berlin. Lawyer kidnaps West Berliner's
who are wanted in Eastern Zone.

OCT

11854
THE INTRUDER (84) (U)
Ivan Foxwell (BL)
D: Guy Hamilton
S: (NOVEL) Robin Maugham
(LINE ON GINGER)
SC: Robin Maugham, John Hunter,
Anthony Squire
Jack Hawkins . . . . Wolf Merton
George Cole . . . . John Summers
Dennis Price . . . . Leonard Pirry
Michael Medwin . . . . Ginger Edwards
Susan Shaw . . . . Nina
Dora Bryan . . . . Dora Bee
Edward Chapman . . . . Walter Lowden
Nicholas Phipps . . . . Capt Featherstonehaugh
Hugh Williams . . . . Tim Ross
Duncan Lamont . . . . Donald Cope
Arthur Howard . . . . Bertram Slake

George Baker . . . . Adjutant
Richard Wattis . . . . Schoolmaster
Gene Anderson . . . . June Maple
Patrick Barr . . . . Insp Williams
CRIME Ex-Colonel searches for tank corps trooper who has become thief.

11855
THE HEART OF THE MATTER (105) (A)
London—BLPA (BL)
P: Ian Dalrymple
D: George More O'Farrell
S: (NOVEL) Graham Greene
SC: Ian Dalrymple, Lesley Storm
Trevor Howard . . . . Harry Scobie
Elizabeth Allan . . . . Louise Scobie
Maria Schell . . . . Helen Rolt
Denholm Elliott . . . . Wilson
Gerard Oury . . . . Yusef
Peter Finch . . . . Father Rank
George Couloris . . . . Captain
Earl Cameron . . . . Ali
Michael Hordern . . . . Commissioner
Colin Gordon . . . . Secretary
Cyril Raymond . . . . Carter
Orlando Martins . . . . Rev Clay
Evelyn Roberts . . . . Col Wright
Gillian Lind . . . . Mrs Carter
DRAMA Sierra Leone, 1942. Trader blackmails Catholic Police Commissioner over his love for refugee.

11856
PERSONAL AFFAIR (83) (A)
Two Cities (GFD)
P: Anthony Darnborough
D: SC: Anthony Pelissier
S: (PLAY) Lesley Storm (A DAY'S MISCHIEF)
Gene Tierney . . . . Kay Barlow
Leo Genn . . . . Stephen Barlow
Glynis Johns . . . . Barbara Vining
Pamela Brown . . . . Evelyn
Walter Fitzgerald . . . . Henry Vining
Megs Jenkins . . . . Vi Vining
Michael Hordern . . . . Headmaster
Thora Hird . . . . Mrs Usher
Martin Boddey . . . . Inspector
Norah Gorsen . . . . Phoebe
Nanette Newman . . . . Sally
DRAMA School teacher accused of having affair with his vanished pupil.

11857
A DAY TO REMEMBER (92) (U)
Group (GFD)
P: Betty Box
D: Ralph Thomas
S: (NOVEL) Jerrard Tickell (THE HAND AND THE FLOWER)
SC: Robin Estridge
Stanley Holloway . . . . Charlie Porter
Joan Rice . . . . Vera Mitchell
Odile Versois . . . . Martine Berthier
Donald Sinden . . . . Jim Carver
James Hayter . . . . Fred Collins
Harry Fowler . . . . Stan Harvey
Edward Chapman . . . . Mr Robinson
Bill Owen . . . . Shorty Sharpe
Peter Jones . . . . Percy Goodall
Meredith Edwards . . . . Bert Tripp
George Couloris . . . . Captain
Vernon Gray . . . . Marvin
Thora Hird . . . . Mrs Trott
Theodore Bikel . . . . Henri Dubot
Brenda de Banzie . . . . Mrs Collins
COMEDY Adventures of public house darts team on day trip to Boulogne.

11858
THE BLUE PARROT (69) (A)
ACT Films (Monarch)
P: Stanley Haynes
D: John Harlow
S: (STORY) Percy Hoskins (GUNMAN)
SC: Allan Mackinnon
Dermot Walsh . . . . Bob Herrick
Jacqueline Hill . . . . Maureen
Ballard Berkeley . . . . Supt Chester
June Ashley . . . . Gloria
Richard Pearson . . . . Quincey
Ferdy Mayne . . . . Stevens
Victor Lucas . . . . Rocks Owen
Edwin Richfield . . . . Taps Campbell
John le Mesurier . . . . Carson
CRIME American tec and PCW posing as hostess solve nightclub killing.

11859
THE GOOD BEGINNING (64) (U)
ABPC (ABP)
P: Robert Hall
D: Gilbert Gunn
S: Janet Green
SC: Robert Hall, Gilbert Gunn, Janet Green
John Fraser . . . . Johnny Lipson
Eileen Moore . . . . Kit Lipton
Peter Reynolds . . . . Brian Watson
Lana Morris . . . . Evie Watson
Humphrey Lestocq . . . . Thorogood
Hugh Pryse . . . . Braithwaite
Anne Stephens . . . . Polly
Peter Jones . . . . Furrier
Robert Raglan . . . . Shelley
David Kossoff . . . . Dealer
CRIME Newlywed husband robs office to buy fur coat for his wife.

11860
THE CANDLELIGHT MURDER (32) (U)
Merton Park (AA)
P: Alec C. Snowden
D: S: Ken Hughes
N: Edgar Lustgarten
Jack Lambert
Gerald Case
Robert Cawdron
Clifford Buckton
CRIME Inspector unmasks blacksmith as killer of old hermit.

11861
THE STRAW MAN (74) (A)
Hedgerley (UA)
P: D: SC: Donald Taylor
S: (NOVEL) Doris Miles Disney
Dermot Walsh . . . . Mal Farris
Clifford Evans . . . . Jeff Howard
Lana Morris . . . . Ruth Hunter
Amy Dalby . . . . Lucy Graham
Ronald Ward . . . . Clay Rushlow
Josephine Stuart . . . . Miss Ward
Peter Williams . . . . Insp Conrad
Philip Saville . . . . Link Hunter
CRIME Tec proves assistant strangled girl and framed mistress's husband.

NOV

11862
FLANNELFOOT (74) (A)
E.J. Fancey (NR)
D: Maclean Rogers
S: Jack Henry
SC: Carl Heck
Ronald Howard . . . . Sgt Fitzgerald
Mary Germaine . . . . Kathleen Fraser
Jack Watling . . . . Frank Mitchell

Gene Anderson . . . . Rene Wexford
Ronald Adam . . . . Insp Duggan
Adrienne Scott . . . . Cynthia Leyland
CRIME Reporter helps inspector catch jewel thief at house party.

11863
BEHIND THE HEADLINES (46) (U)
E.J. Fancey (NR)
D: S: Maclean Rogers
Gilbert Harding
John Fitzgerald
Adrienne Scott
Vi Kaley
Michael McCarthy
Jack May
CRIME Scotland Yard tracks down lorry thieves who killed watchman.

11864
FORCES' SWEETHEART (76) (U)
E.J. Fancey (NR)
D: Maclean Rogers
Hy Hazell . . . . Judy James
Harry Secombe . . . . Harry Llewellyn
Michael Bentine . . . . F/L John Robinson
Freddie Frinton . . . . Aloysius Dimwitty
John Ainsworth . . . . Lt John Robinson
Molly Weir . . . . The Maid
Adrienne Scott . . . . Audrey
Kenneth Henry . . . . Tommy Tupp
Graham Stark . . . . Simmonds
John Fitzgerald . . . . Producer
Michael McCarthy . . . . Plumber
Leslie Roberts Television Girls
COMEDY Three servicemen use the same name to woo singer.

11865
MARILYN (70) (A)
Nettlefold (Butcher) *reissue:* 1954,
ROADHOUSE GIRL
P: Ernest G. Roy
D: SC: Wolf Rilla
S: (PLAY) Peter Jones (MARIAN)
Maxwell Reed . . . . Tom Price
Sandra Dorne . . . . Marilyn Saunders
Leslie Dwyer . . . . George Saunders
Vida Hope . . . . Rosie
Ferdy Mayne . . . . Nicky Everton
Hugh Pryse . . . . Coroner
Kenneth Connor . . . . Driver
Ben Williams . . . . Foreman
CRIME Garage mechanic loves wife of boss and kills him in brawl.

11866
BLACK 13 (77) (A)
Vandyke (Archway)
P: Roger Proudlock
D: SC: Ken Hughes
S: (SCREENPLAY) Pietro Germi (GIOVENTU PERDUTA)
Peter Reynolds . . . . Stephen Barclay
Rona Anderson . . . . Claire Barclay
Patrick Barr . . . . Robert
Lana Morris . . . . Marion
Genine Graham . . . . Stella
Michael Balfour . . . . Joe
John Forrest . . . . Wally
Viola Lyel . . . . Mrs Barclay
Martin Walker . . . . Prof Barclay
John le Mesurier . . . . Inspector
CRIME Sister of neurotic girl-killer loves detective on the case.

11867
THE DOG AND THE DIAMONDS (55) (U)
London Independent (ABFD—CFF)

P: Peter Rogers
D: Ralph Thomas
S: Mary Cathcart Borer
SC: Patricia Latham

Kathleen Harrison	Mrs Fossett
George Coulouris	Forbes
Geoffrey Sumner	Mr Gayford
Brian Oulton	Mr Plumpton
Michael McGuire	Jimmy
Robert Sandford	Peter
Robert Scroggins	Ginger
Dennis Wyndham	Crook

CHILDREN Children make zoo in garden of old house used as den by thieves.

11868
GIBRALTAR ADVENTURE (58) (U) retitled:
THE CLUE OF THE MISSING APE
Gaumont (ABFD—CFF)
P: Frank Wells
D: SC: James Hill
S: Frank Wells, Donald Carter,
Cdr Hackforth-Jones

Nati Banda	Pliar Ellis
Roy Savage	Jimmy Sutton
George Cole	Gobo
Patrick Boxill	Mr Palmer
William Patrick	Lt-Cdr Collie
Marcus Simpson	PO Ellis

CHILDREN Gibraltar. Sea cadet saves British fleet from saboteurs.

11869
THE LIMPING MAN (74) (U)
Banner (Eros)
P: Donald Ginsberg
D: Charles de la Tour, Cy Endfield
S: Anthony Verney
SC: Ian Stuart Black, Reginald Long

Lloyd Bridges	Frank Prior
Moira Lister	Pauline French
Helene Cordet	Helene Castle
Alan Wheatley	Insp Braddock
Leslie Phillips	Cameron
Bruce Beeby	Kendal Brown
Andre Van Gysegham	Stage-doorman
Rachel Roberts	Barmaid

Robert Harben; Lionel Blair
CRIME American proves actress did not kill blackmailing smuggler.

11870
SMALL TOWN STORY (69) (U)
Almanak (GFD)
P: Otto Kreisler, Ken Bennett
D: Montgomery Tully
S: Franz Marischka, Maurice Weissberger
SC: George Fisher

Donald Houston	Tony Warren
Susan Shaw	Patricia Lane
Alan Wheatley	Nick Hammond
Kent Walton	Bob Regan
George Merritt	Michael Collins
Margaret Harrison	Jackie Collins
Norman Williams	Elton
Arthur Rigby	Alf Benson

Denis Compton; Raymond Glendenning;
Middlesex Cricket Club; Arsenal Football
Club; Millwall Football Club
SPORT Midland football club will inherit
fortune if it wins promotion to third division.

11871
ROB ROY THE HIGHLAND ROGUE
(81) *tech* (U)
Walt Disney (RKO)
P: Perce Pearce
D: Harold French

S: Lawrence E. Watkin

Richard Todd	Rob Roy Macgregor
Glynis Johns	Helen Mary
James Robertson Justice	Duke of Argyll
Michael Gough	Duke of Montrose
Finlay Currie	Hamish McPherson
Jean Taylor Smith	Lady Glengyll
Geoffrey Keen	Killearn
Archie Duncan	Dougal Macgregor
Michael Goodliffe	Robert Walpole
Marjorie Fielding	Maggie MacPherson
Russell Waters	Hugh Macgregor
Eric Pohlmann	George I
Malcolm Keen	Duke of Montrose
Kitty & Marietta McLeod	Mouth Music Singers

ADVENTURE Scotland, 1715. Clan chief rebels against King. (RFP: 1953)

11872
IT'S A GRAND LIFE (102) (U)
Film Studios Manchester (Mancunian)
P: D: John E. Blakeley
S: H. F. Maltby
SC: H. F. Maltby, Frank Randle

Frank Randle	Pte Randle
Diana Dors	Cpl Paula Clements
Dan Young	Pte Young
Michael Brennan	Sgt Maj O'Reilly
Jennifer Jayne	Pte Desmond
John Blythe	Pte Philip Green
Anthony Hulme	Capt Saunders
Charles Peters	Pte Rubenstein
Arthur White	Pte Prendergast
Ian Fleming	Mr Clements
Ruth Taylor	Mrs Clements

Winifred Attwell; Jack Pye
COMEDY Private saves WRAC Corporal from
lecherous sergeant.

DEC

11873
PARK PLAZA 605 (75) (U)
USA: NORMAN CONQUEST
B & A Productions (Eros)
P: Bertram Ostrer, Albert Fennell
D: Bernard Knowles
S: (NOVEL) Berkeley Gray
(DAREDEVIL CONQUEST)
SC: Bernard Knowles, Albert Fennell,
Bertram Ostrer, Clifford Witting

Tom Conway	Norman Conquest
Eva Bartok	Nadina Rodin
Joy Shelton	Pixie Everard
Sidney James	Supt Williams
Richard Wattis	Theodore Feather
Carl Jaffe	Boris Roff
Frederick Schiller	Ivan Burgin
Robert Adair	Baron von Henschel
Anton Diffring	Gregor

CRIME Suspected tec stops Nazi Baron and girl from smuggling gems.

11874
MEET MR LUCIFER (83) (U)
Ealing (GFD)
P: Monja Danischewsky
D: Anthony Pelissier
S: (PLAY) Arnold Ridley
(BEGGAR MY NEIGHBOUR)
SC: Monja Danischewsky, Peter Myers,
Alec Graham

Stanley Holloway	Sam Hollingsworth /Lucifer
Peggy Cummins	Kitty Norton
Jack Watling	Jim Norton
Barbara Murray	Patricia Pedelty
Joseph Tomelty	Mr Pedelty
Kay Kendall	Lonely Hearts Singer

Gordon Jackson	Hector McPhee
Charles Victor	Mr Elder
Humphrey Lestocq	Arthur Simmonds
Jean Cadell	Mrs Macdonald
Raymond Huntley	Mr Patterson
Ernest Thesiger	Eun Macdonald
Frank Pettingell	Mr Roberts
Olive Sloane	Mrs Stannard
Joan Sims	Fairy Queen
Ian Carmichael	Man Friday

Gilbert Harding; McDonald Hobley; Philip
Harben; David Miller
FANTASY Pantomime comic helps Satan make
television a curse.

11875
TROUBLE IN STORE (85) (U)
Two Cities (GFD)
P: Maurice Cowan
D: John Paddy Carstairs
S: John Paddy Carstairs, Maurice Cowan,
Ted Willis

Norman Wisdom	Norman
Margaret Rutherford	Miss Bacon
Moira Lister	Peggy
Derek Bond	Gerald
Lana Morris	Sally
Jerry Desmonde	Mr Freeman
Megs Jenkins	Miss Gibson
Joan Sims	Edna
Michael Ward	Wilbur
Michael Brennan	Davis
John Warwick	Robson
Perlita Neilson	Mabel
Eddie Leslie	Bill

COMEDY Zealous stockroom clerk outwits
department store robbers.

11876
THE KIDNAPPERS (95) (U)
USA: THE LITTLE KIDNAPPERS
Group (GFD) Reissue: 1957 (cut)
P: Sergei Nolbandov, Leslie Parkyn
D: Philip Leacock
S: Neil Paterson

Duncan Macrae	Jim Mackenzie
Adrienne Corri	Kirst Mackenzie
Jon Whiteley	Harry
Vincent Winter	Davy
Jean Anderson	Grandma
Theodore Bikel	Willem Bloem
Francis de Wolff	Jan Hooft
James Sutherland	Aaron McNab
John Rae	Andrew McLeod
Jack Stewart	Dominie
Jameson Clark	Tom Cameron
Howard Connell	Archibald Jenkins

DRAMA Nova Scotia, 1900. Orphans steal
baby when stern grandfather refuses them a
dog. (AA: Best Juvenile Actors 1954.)

11877
THE LARGE ROPE (72) (A)
Insignia (UA)
P: Victor Hanbury
D: Wolf Rilla
S: Ted Willis

Donald Houston	Tom Penney
Susan Shaw	Susan Hamble
Robert Brown	Mick Jordan
Vanda Godsell	Amy Jordan
Peter Byrne	Jeff Stribling
Richard Warner	Insp Harmer
Christine Finn	May
Thomas Heathcote	James Gore
Carl Bernard	Alfred Hamble
Douglas Herald	Simon Penney

CRIME Ex-convict returns to home village and
is suspected of murder.

11878
BEAT THE DEVIL (100) (A)
Romulus—Santana (IFD)
P: D: John Huston
S: (NOVEL) James Helvick
SC: John Huston, Truman Capote
Humphrey Bogart . . . . . Billy Dannreuther
Jennifer Jones . . . . Gwendolen Chelm
Gina Lollobrigidia . . . . . Maria Dannreuther
Robert Morley . . . . Petersen
Peter Lorre . . . . O'Hara
Edward Underdown . . . . Harry Chelm
Ivor Barnard . . . . Maj Ross
Bernard Lee . . . . Insp Jack Clayton
Marco Tulli . . . . Ravello
COMEDY Italy. Crooks conspire to acquire
uranium deposit.

11879
3 STEPS TO THE GALLOWS (81) (A)
USA: WHITE FIRE
Tempean (Eros)
P: Robert Baker, Monty Berman
D: SC: John Gilling
S: Paul Erickson
Scott Brady . . . . Gregor Stevens
Mary Castle . . . . Yvonne Durante
John Blythe . . . . Dave Leary
Gabrielle Brune . . . . Lorna Dryhurst
Colin Tapley . . . . Winslow
Ferdy Mayne . . . . Sartago
Lloyd Lamble . . . . James Smith
Ballard Berkeley . . . . Insp Haley
Paul Erickson . . . . Larry
CRIME American seaman proves gem
smugglers framed his brother for killing
club owner.

11880
THE FLOATING DUTCHMAN (76) (A)
Merton Park (AA) reissue: 1958 (Winart)
P: W.H. Williams
D: SC: Vernon Sewell
S: (NOVEL) Nicolas Bentley
Dermot Walsh . . . . Alexander James
Sydney Tafler . . . . Victor Skinner
Mary Germaine . . . . Rose Reid
Guy Verney . . . . Snow White
Hugh Morton . . . . Insp Cathie
James Raglan . . . . Mr Wynn
Nicolas Bentley . . . . Collis
Arnold Marle . . . . Otto
Derek Blomfield . . . . Philip Reid
CRIME CID man poses as crook to unmask
club owner as jewel thief.

11881
STRANGE STORIES (45) (U)
Vandyke (Archway)
P: Roger Proudlock
THE STRANGE MR BARTLEBY
D: John Guillermin
John Laurie . . . . Mr Bartleby
Norman Shelley . . . . Mr Gilkie
Naomi Chance . . . . Young Woman
STRANGE JOURNEY
D: Don Chaffey
Colin Tapley . . . . Charles Kellerton
Peter Bull . . . . Capt Breen
Helen Horton . . . . Marie Kellerton
DRAMA Tramp is girl's lost father;
Man robs employer and takes his identity
aboard ship.

11882
OPERATION DIPLOMAT (70) (U)
Nettlefold (Butcher)
P: Ernest G. Roy
D: John Guillermin
S: (TV SERIAL) Francis Durbridge
SC: A.R. Rawlinson, John Guillermin
Guy Rolfe . . . . Dr Mark Fenton
Lisa Daniely . . . . Lisa Durand
Patricia Dainton . . . . Sister Rogers
Sydney Tafler . . . . Wade
Brian Worth . . . . Geoffrey Terry
Anton Diffring . . . . Shroder
Ballard Berkeley . . . . Insp Austin
James Raglan . . . . Sir Oliver Peters
CRIME Dr saves kidnapped diplomat upon
whom he was forced to operate.

11883
THE SECRET CAVE (62) (U)
Merton Park (ABFD—CFF)
P: Frank Hoare
D: John Durst
S: (NOVEL) Thomas Hardy
(OUR EXPLOITS AT WEST POLEY)
SC: Joe Mendoza
David Coote . . . . Steve Draycott
Susan Ford . . . . Margaret Merriman
Nicholas Emdett . . . . Lennie Hawkins
Lewis Gedge . . . . Miller Griffin
Johnny Morris . . . . Charlie Bassett
Trevor Hill . . . . Job Tray
CHILDREN Boys divert village stream and are
trapped in Mendip cave.

11884
A GOOD PULL—UP (17) (U)
Grendon (ABFD—CFF)
P: Frank Cadman
D: Don Chaffey
S: Patricia Latham
Peter Butterworth . . . . Dickie Duffle
John Levitt . . . . Tom
Humphrey Kent . . . . Mr Crossington
Kurt Wagener . . . . Joe
CHILDREN Slapstick mishaps of clumsy
helper in wayside cafe.

11885
WATCH OUT! (17) (U)
Grendon (ABFD—CFF)
P: Frank Cadman
D: Don Chaffey
S: Patricia Latham
Peter Butterworth . . . . Dickie Duffle
John Levitt . . . . Tom
Harry Lane . . . . Commissionaire
Humphrey Kent . . . . Mr Crossington
CHILDREN Clapper boy tries to return watch
to bullying manager.

11886
A LETTER FROM EAST ANGLIA (11) (U)
Clarke & Hornby (ABFD-CFF)
D:S: Cynthia Whitby
CHILDREN Thatcher's children rescue lost
brother from wreck.

11887
A LETTER FROM WALES (15) (U)
Brunner, Lloyd (ABFD—CFF)
D: George Lloyd
S: Gwylim Jones
Evie Wyn Jones . . . . Rhys
Katie Wyn Jones . . . . Mother
Sam Wyn Jones . . . . Mr Williams
Vera Wyn Jones . . . . Mai
Olga Wyn Jones . . . . Luned
CHILDREN Welsh boy catches trout, rescues
lamb, and goes out in new lifeboat.

11888
MASTER OF LAUGHTER (33) (U)
Harold Baim
S: Marcel Cornelis
N: Roy Rich
Marcel Cornelis . . . . Himself
COMEDY Belgian mime in sketches The
Dentist, The Big Fight, The Concert Pianist,
At The Cinema.

11889
THE TELL—TALE HEART (20) (X)
Film Alliance (Adelphi)
P: I. G. Goldsmith
D: J.B. Williams
S: (STORY) Edgar Allan Poe
SC: J.B. Williams
Stanley Baker . . . . Edgar Allan Poe
HORROR Madman betrays himself when he hears
heartbeats of his victim's corpse.

11890
THE MASK (28) (X)
Vandyke (Archway)
P: Roger Proudlock
D: Don Chaffey
Robert Ayres . . . . The Miller
Cecile Chevreau . . . . The Wife
CRIME Cornwall, 1909. Miller's wife and her
lover conspire to murder her disfigured
husband.

11891
THE WORLD'S A STAGE (series) (U)
Emil Katzke (NR)
P: D: Charles Deane
S: (PLAYS) William Shakespeare
N: Ronald Howard
Young Vic Theatre Company

11892
1—JULIUS CAESAR (13)

11893
2—OTHELLO (13)

11894
3—A WINTER'S TALE (13)

11895
4—TWELFTH NIGHT (12)

11896
5—MACBETH (13)

11897
6—A MIDSUMMER NIGHT'S DREAM (12)
DRAMA Scenes from Shakespeare's plays.

1954

JAN

11898
FRONT PAGE STORY (99) (A)
Jay Lewis (BL)
D: Gordon Parry
S: (NOVEL) Robert Gaines (FINAL NIGHT)
SC: Jay Lewis, Jack Howells, William Fairchild,
Guy Morgan

Jack Hawkins	John Grant
Elizabeth Allan	Susan Grant
Eva Bartok	Mrs Thorpe
Derek Farr	Teale
Martin Miller	Dr Bruckman
Jenny Jones	Jenny
Walter Fitzgerald	Black
Joseph Tomelty	Dan
Michael Howard	Barrow
Michael Goodliffe	Kennedy
Patricia Marmont	Julie
Helen Haye	Mother
Guy Middleton	Gentle
Henry Mollison	Lester
Ronald Adam	Editor
John Stuart	Prosecution

DRAMA News editor deals with several
stories: traitorous scientist; homeless children;
euthanasia.

11899
ESCAPE BY NIGHT (79) (A)
Tempean (Eros)
P: Robert Baker, Monty Berman
D: S: John Gilling

Bonar Colleano	Tom Buchan
Andrew Ray	Joey Weston
Sidney James	Gino Rossi
Ted Ray	Mr Weston
Simone Silva	Rosetta Mantania
Patrick Barr	Insp Frampton
Peter Sinclair	MacNaughton
Avice Landone	Mrs Weston
Ronald Adam	Tallboy

CRIME Reporter catches fugitive vice king by
pretending to help him.

11900
DON'T BLAME THE STORK (80) (A)
Advance—Objective (Adelphi)
P: David Dent, Victor Katona
D: Akos Rathony
S: Wolfgang Wilhelm, E. Silas
SC: Talbot Rothwell, Victor Katona

Veronica Hurst	Katie O'Connor
Ian Hunter	Sir Goerge Redway
Reginald Beckwith	Jonathan
Patricia Laffan	Lilian Angel
Brenda de Banzie	Evelyn Steele
Harry Fowler	Harry Fenn
Thora Hird	Agnes O'Connor
Mark Daly	Michael O'Connor
Howard Marion Crawford	Fluffy Faversham
Avril Angers	Renee O'Connor

COMEDY Actress poses as mother of child
left on actor's step.

11901
THE BLAKES SLEPT HERE (38) tech (U)
Martin Films (Apex) reissue: FAMILY ALBUM
P: John Martin, Richard Massingham
D: Jacques Brunius, Richard Massingham
S: Roy Plomley
SC: Roy Plomley, Jacques Brunius

David King-Wood	Richard Blake
Dorothy Gordon	Laura Blake
Peter Coke	William
Ursula Howells	Emily
John Richmond	Albert
Pamela Stirling	Vicky
David Markham	Edward
Rachel Gurney	Betty
Harcourt Williams	Narrator

HISTORY 100 years of change through five
generations of London family.

11902 INTO THE UNKNOWN (34) (U)
E. J. Fancey (NR)
D: E.J. Fancey
N: Andrew Timothy, Leslie Mitchell

Klaus Helberg	Dr Claud Parg
James Sharkey	

ADVENTURE Norway. Flying doctor crashes
in mountains after operating for appendicitis.

11903
THE MIRROR AND MARKHEIM (28) (A)
Motley (Ex)
P: Norman Williams
D: SC: John Lamont
S: (STORY) Robert Louis Stevenson
N: Marius Goring

Philip Saville	Markheim
Arthur Lowe	Arthur Henry
Christopher Lee	Visitant
Lloyd Lamble	Kelly
Ruth Sheil	Maid

FANTASY Period. Mirror figure shows man
what would happen if he stabbed an antique
dealer.

11904
THE MILLION POUND NOTE (91) (U) tech
USA: MAN WITH A MILLION
Group (GFD) reissue: 1961 (Uni)
P: John Bryan
D: Ronald Neame
S: (STORY) Mark Twain
SC: Jill Craigie

Gregory Peck	Henry Adams
Jane Griffiths	Portia Lansdowne
Ronald Squire	Oliver Montpelier
A.E. Matthews	Duke of Frognall
Wilfrid Hyde White	Roderick Montpelier
Joyce Grenfell	Duchess of Cromarty
Maurice Denham	Reid
Reginald Beckwith	Rock
Brian Oulton	Lloyd
John Slater	Parsons
Wilbur Evans	Ambassador
Hartley Power	Hastings
George Devine	Proprietor
Bryan Forbes	Tod
Ann Gudrun	Renie
Hugh Wakefield	Duke of Cromarty
Ronald Adam	Samuel Clements
Ernest Thesiger	Director

COMEDY 1900. Poor American's rise to
fortune with unchanged banknote for million
pounds.

11905
MEET MR MALCOLM (65) (U)
Corsair (APB)
P: Theo Lageard
D: Daniel Birt
S: Brock Williams

Adrianne Allen	Mrs Durant
Sarah Lawson	Louie Knowles
Richard Gale	Colin Knowles
Duncan Lamont	Supt Simmons
Meredith Edwards	Whistler Grant
Pamela Galloway	Andria Durant
John Horsley	Tony Barlow
John Blythe	Carrington-Phelps
Claude Dampier	Joe Tutt

CRIME Police prove producer killed ex-wife's
husband.

11906
THE WEAK AND THE WICKED (88) (A)
Marble Arch (ABP)
P: Victor Skutezky
D: J. Lee-Thompson
S: (NOVEL) Joan Henry (WHO LIE IN GAOL)
SC: J. Lee-Thompson, Joan Henry,
Anne Burnaby

Glynis Johns	Jean Raymond
John Gregson	Michael
Jane Hylton	Babs
Diana Dors	Betty
Sidney James	Sid Baden
A.E. Matthews	Harry Wicks
Anthony Nichols	Chaplain
Athene Seyler	Millie
Olive Sloane	Nellie Baden
Sybil Thorndike	Mabel
Barbara Couper	Doctor
Joyce Heron	PO Arnold
Ursula Howells	Pam
Mary Merrall	Mrs Skinner
Rachel Roberts	Pat
Marjorie Rhodes	Susie
Josephine Griffin	Miriam
Simone Silva	Tina
Josephine Stuart	Andy
Edwin Styles	Seymour
Cecil Trouncer	Judge
Paul Carpenter	Joe
Sandra Dorne	Prisoner
Bessie Love	Prisoner

CRIME Woman gambler spends year in jail
and open prison.

11907
OUR GIRL FRIDAY (87) (U) Eastman
USA: THE ADVENTURES OF SADIE
Renown reissue: 1957
P: George Minter
D: SC: Noel Langley
S: (NOVEL) Norman Lindsay
(THE CAUTIOUS AMORIST)

Joan Collins	Sadie Patch
George Cole	Jimmy Carroll
Kenneth More	Pat Plunkett
Robertson Hare	Prof Gibble
Hermione Gingold	Spinster
Walter Fitzgerald	Captain
Hattie Jacques	Mrs Patch
Felix Felton	Mr Patch
Lionel Murton	Barman

COMEDY Three men and millionaire's daughter
wrecked on desert isle.

11908
HELL BELOW ZERO (90) tech (U)
Warwick (Col) reissue: 1961 (Unifilms)
P: Irving Allen, Albert Broccoli,
George Willoughby
D: Mark Robson
S: (NOVEL) Hammond Innes
(THE WHITE SOUTH)
SC: Alec Coppel, Max Trell, Richard Maibaum

Alan Ladd	Duncan Craig
Joan Tetzel	Judy Nordahl
Basil Sydney	Col Bland
Stanley Baker	Erik Bland
Joseph Tomelty	Capt McPhee
Niall MacGinnis	Dr Howe
Jill Bennett	Gerda Petersen
Peter Dyneley	Miller
Susan Rayne	Kathleen
Philo Hauser	Sandeborg
John Witty	Martens
Genine Graham	Stewardess

ADVENTURE Antarctica. Mate helps girl
owner of whaling ship find father's murderer.

11909
EIGHT O'CLOCK WALK (87) (A)
British Aviation (BL)
P: George King
D: Lance Comfort
S: Jack Roffey, Gordon Harbord
SC: Guy Morgan, Katherine Strueby

Richard Attenborough	Tom Manning
Cathy O'Donnell	Jill Manning
Derek Farr	Peter Tanner

Ian Hunter .... Geoffrey Tanner
Maurice Denham .... Horace Clifton
Bruce Seton .... DCI
Lily Kann .... Mrs Zunz
Harry Welchman .... Harrington
Kynaston Reeves .... Munro
Eithene Dunne .... Mrs Evans
David Hannaford .... Ernie Higgs
CRIME QC saves taxi-driver who is accused of killing child.

FEB

11910
THE LOVE LOTTERY (89) *tech* (U)
Ealing (GFD)
P: Monja Danischewsky
D: Charles Crichton
S: Charles Neilson-Terry, Zelma Bramley-Moore
SC: Harry Kurnitz
David Niven .... Rex Allerton
Peggy Cummins .... Sally
Anne Vernon .... Jane
Herbert Lom .... Amico
Charles Victor .... Jennings
Gordon Jackson .... Ralph
Felix Aylmer .... Winant
Hugh McDermott .... Rodney Wheeler
Stanley Maxted .... Stanton
June Clyde .... Viola
John Chandos .... Gulliver Kee
Theodore Bikel .... Parsimomious
Sebastian Cabot .... Suarez
Eugene Deckers .... Vernet
Hattie Jacques .... Chambermaid
COMEDY Human computer loves film star won by typist in lottery.

11911
THE MAGGIE (92) (U)
USA: HIGH AND DRY
Ealing (GFD)
P: Michael Truman
D: Alexander Mackendrick
S: William Rose
Paul Douglas .... Calvin B. Marshall
Alex Mackenzie .... Capt MacTaggart
James Copeland .... Mate
Abe Barker .... Engineer
Tommy Kearins .... The Wee Boy
Hubert Gregg .... Pusey
Geoffrey Keen .... Campbell
Dorothy Alison .... Miss Peterson
Andrew Keir .... Reporter
Meg Buchanan .... Sarah
Jameson Clark .... Dirty Dan
COMEDY Scotland. Pufferboat captain insists on delivering American's cargo.

11912
YOU KNOW WHAT SAILORS ARE (89) *tech* (U)
Group (GFD)
P: Julian Wintle, Peter Rogers
D: Ken Annakin
S: (NOVEL) Edward Hyams (SYLVESTER)
SC: Peter Rogers
Akim Tamiroff ...... President of Agraria
Donald Sinden .... Lt Sylvester Green
Sarah Lawson .... Betty
Naunton Wayne .... Capt Owbridge
Bill Kerr .... Lt Smart
Dora Bryan .... Gladys
Martin Miller .... Prof Pfumbaum
Michael Shepley .... Admiral
Michael Hordern .... Capt Hamilton
Ferdy Mayne .... Stanislaus Voritz
Bryan Coleman .... Lt-Cdr Voles
Peter Arne .... Ahmed
Peter Martyn .... Lt Ross
COMEDY Prof averts war by fooling President with lieut's fake radar device.

11913
FAST AND LOOSE (75) (A)
Group (GFD)
P: Teddy Baird
D: Gordon Parry
S: (PLAY) Ben Travers
(A CUCKOO IN THE NEST)
SC: A.R. Rawlinson, Ben Travers
Stanley Holloway .... Mr Crabb
Kay Kendall .... Carol
Brian Reece .... Peter
Charles Victor .... Lumper
June Thorburn .... Barbara
Reginald Beckwith .... Tripp-Johnson
Vida Hope .... Gladys
Joan Young .... Mrs Gullett
Fabia Drake .... Mrs Crabb
Dora Bryan .... Rawlings
Aubrey Mather .... Noony
Toke Townley .... Alfred
COMEDY Married man forced to spend night at inn with his ex-fiancee.

11914
STAR OF MY NIGHT (71) (U)
Kenilworth (GFD)
P: Edward J. & Harry Lee Danziger
D: Paul Dickson
S: Paul Tabori
Griffith Jones .... Michael Donovan
Kathleen Byron .... Eve Malone
Hugh Williams .... Arnold Whitman
Pauline Olsen .... Iris
Harold Lang .... Carl
Andre Mikhelson .... Papa Condor
Ilona Ference .... Daisy
Malcolm Mitchell Trio
ROMANCE Sculptor engaged to ballerina feigns love for actress on learning he is losing his sight.

11915
FACE THE MUSIC (84) (A)
USA: THE BLACK GLOVE
Hammer (Ex)
P: Michale Carreras
D: Terence Fisher
S: (NOVEL) Ernest Bornemann
SC: Ernest Bornemann
Alex Nicol .... James Bradley
Eleanor Summerfield .... Barbara Quigley
John Salew .... Max Margulis
Paul Carpenter .... John Sutherland
Geoffrey Keen .... Maurice Green
Ann Hanslip .... Maxine
Fred Johnson .... Insp Mackenzie
Martin Boddey .... Sgt Mulrooney
Arthur Lane .... Jeff Colt
Gordon Crier .... Vic Parsons
Kenny Baker's Dozen
CRIME American trumpeter proves he did not kill girl singer.

11916
LIFE WITH THE LYONS (81) (U)
USA: FAMILY AFFAIR
Hammer (Ex)
P: Robert Dunbar
D: Val Guest
S: (RADIO SERIES) Bebe Daniels, Bob Block, Bill Harding
SC: Val Guest, Robert Dunbar
Bebe Daniels .... Bebe Lyon
Ben Lyon .... Ben Lyon
Barbara Lyon .... Barbara Lyon
Richard Lyon .... Richard
Horace Percival .... Mr Wimple
Molly Weir .... Aggie
Hugh Morton .... Mr Hemingway
Arthur Hill .... Slim Cassidy
Doris Rogers .... Florrie Wainwright

Gwen Lewis .... Mrs Wimple
Belinda Lee .... Violet Hemingway
COMEDY Family try to get their landlord to sign lease.
Reissued in 1957 as a serial:

11917
ADVENTURES WITH THE LYONS (serial)

11918
1. MOVING IN (11)

11919
2. DINNER FOR MR HEMINGWAY (13)

11920
3. AN IDEA FOR BEN (10)

11921
4. CHAOS IN THE ROCKERY (13)

11922
5. BARBARA'S BOY FRIEND (15)

11923
6. ROUNDUP (13)

11924
THE RUNAWAY BUS (78) (U)
Conquest—Guest (Eros)
P:D:S: Val Guest
Frankie Howerd .... Percy Lamb
Margaret Rutherford ...... Cynthia Beeston
Petula Clark .... Lee Nichols
George Coulouris .... Edward Schroeder
Belinda Lee .... Janie Grey
Reginald Beckwith .... Collector
Toke Townley .... Henry Waterman
Terence Alexander .... Peter Jones
John Horsley .... Insp Henley
Anthony Oliver .... Duty Officer
Stringer Davis .... Admin Officer
Lisa Gastone .... Receptionist
Frank Phillips .... Newsreader
COMEDY Crooks hide £200,000 gold bullion in fogbound airport bus.

11925
STAR OF INDIA (97) *tech* (U)
Raymond Stross (Eros)
D: Arthur Lubin
S: Herbert Dalmas
SC: Seton I. Miller, C. Denis Freeman
Cornel Wilde .... Pierre St Laurent
Jean Wallace .... Katrina
Herbert Lom .... Vicomte de Narbonne
Yvonne Sanson .... Mme de Montespan
Basil Sydney .... Louis XIV
Walter Rilla .... Van Horst
John Slater .... Emile
Leslie Linder .... Moulai
Arnold Bell .... Captain
ADVENTURE France, 1690. Usurped nobleman helps Dutch widow recover stolen jewel from Governor.

11926
RIVER BEAT (70) (U)
Insignia (Eros)
P: Victor Hanbury
D: Guy Green
S: Rex Rienits
Phyllis Kirk .... Judy Roberts
John Bentley .... Insp Dan Barker
Robert Ayres .... Capt Waterford
Ewan Roberts .... Blake
Leonard White .... Sgt McLeod
Harold Ayer .... Gordon
Glyn Houston .... Charlie Williamson
Charles Lloyd Pack .... Hendrick
David Hurst .... Paddy Maclure
CRIME American girl wireless-operator unmasks captain as diamond smuggler.

11927
THEY WHO DARE (107) *tech* (U)
Mayflower (BL)
P: Maxwell Setton, Aubrey Baring
D: Lewis Milestone
S: Robert Westerby
Dirk Bogarde . . . . Lt Graham
Denholm Elliott . . . . Sgt Corcoran
Akim Tamiroff . . . . Capt George One
Gerard Oury . . . . Capt George Two
Eric Pohlmann . . . . Capt Raplinis
Alec Mango . . . . Patroklis
Kay Callard . . . . Singer
Russell Enoch . . . . Lt Poole
David Peel . . . . Sgt Evans
Sam Kydd . . . . Marine Boyd
Lisa Gastoni . . . . Girl
WAR Rhodes. Special Boat Service blow up island
airfield.

11928
HOBSON'S CHOICE (107) (U)
London-BLPA (BL) *reissues:* 1958 (BL)
1960 (Orb)
P:D: David Lean
S: (PLAY) Harold Brighouse
SC: David Lean, Wynyard Browne, Norman
Spencer
Charles Laughton . . . . Henry Hobson
John Mills . . . . Willie Mossup
Brenda de Banzie . . . . Maggie Hobson
Daphne Anderson . . . . Alice Hobson
Prunella Scales . . . . Vicky Hobson
Richard Wattis . . . . Albert Prosser
Derek Blomfield . . . . Freddy Breenstock
Helen Haye . . . . Mrs Hepworth
Joseph Tomelty . . . . Jim Heeler
Julien Mitchell . . . . Sam Minns
Gibb McLaughlin . . . . Tudsbury
Dorothy Gordon . . . . Ada Figgins
John Laurie . . . . Dr MacFarlene
Raymond Huntley . . . . Nathaniel Breenstock
Jack Howarth . . . . Tubby Wadlow
COMEDY Salford, 1900. Tyrannical bootmaker's
strong-willed daughter weds timid assistant.
(BFA: Best British Film 1954).

11929
AN INSPECTOR CALLS (79) (A)
Watergate (BL)
P: A.D. Peters
D: Guy Hamilton
S: (PLAY) J.B. Priestley
SC: Desmond Davis
Alastair Sim . . . . Insp Poole
Arthur Young . . . . Arthur Birling
Olga Lindo . . . . Sybil Birling
Eileen Moore . . . . Sheila Birling
Bryan Forbes . . . . Eric Birling
Brian Worth . . . . Gerald Croft
Jane Wenham . . . . Eva Smith
Pat Neal . . . . Maid
Norman Bird . . . . Foreman
John Welsh . . . . Shopwalker
Barbara Everest . . . . Committee Member
Jenny Jones . . . . Girl
DRAMA 1913. "Inspector" proves that prosperous
family share responsibility for girl's suicide.

11930
SOLUTION BY PHONE (60) (A)
Pan Productions (ABP)
P: Geoffrey Goodhart, Brandon Fleming
D: Alfred Travers
S: Brandon Fleming
Clifford Evans . . . . Richard Hanborough
Thea Gregory . . . . Ann Selby
John Witty . . . . Peter Wayne
Georgina Cookson . . . . . . Frances Hanborough

Enid Hewitt . . . . Mrs Garner
Geoffrey Goodhart . . . . Insp Kirby
Max Brimmell . . . . Sgt Woods
CRIME Actor kills his mistress and frames her
novelist husband.

11931
THE BLAZING CARAVAN (32) (U)
Merton Park (AA)
P: Alec Snowden
D:S: Ken Hughes
N: Edgar Lustgarten
Alexander Gauge
Edgar Driver
Alan Robinson
Betty Carter
CRIME Man kills partner in football pool win
and exchanges identities.

MAR

11932
THE GOOD DIE YOUNG (98) (A)
Remus (IFD)
P: Jack Clayton
D: Lewis Gilbert
S: (NOVEL) Richard Macauley
SC: Lewis Gilbert, Vernon Harris
Laurence Harvey . . . . Miles Ravenscourt
Gloria Grahame . . . . Denise
Richard Basehart . . . . Joe
Joan Collins . . . . Mary
John Ireland . . . . Eddie
Rene Ray . . . . Angela
Stanley Baker . . . . Mike
Margaret Leighton . . . . . Eve Ravenscourt
Robert Morley . . . . Sir Francis Ravenscourt
Freda Jackson . . . . Mrs Freeman
James Kenney . . . . David
Susan Shaw . . . . Doris
Lee Patterson . . . . Tod Maslin
Sandra Dorne . . . . Girl
Leslie Dwyer . . . . Stookey
Walter Hudd . . . . Dr Reed
CRIME Broke playboy persuades three men to
help him rob bank.

11933
BANG! YOU'RE DEAD (88) (A) USA: GAME
OF DANGER
Wellington (BL)
P:D: Lance Comfort
S: Guy Elmes
SC: Guy Elmes, Ernest Borneman
Jack Warner . . . . Mr Bonsell
Derek Farr . . . . Grey
Veronica Hurst . . . . Hilda
Michael Medwin . . . . Bob Carter
Gordon Harker . . . . Mr Hare
Anthony Richmond . . . . . . Cliff Bonsell
Sean Barrett . . . . Willy
Beatrice Varley . . . . Mrs Maxted
Philip Saville . . . . Ben Jones
John Warwick . . . . Sgt Gurney
Toke Townley . . . . Jimmy Knuckle
CRIME Boy shoots man in play and his father's
friend is accused.

11934
DOUBLE EXPOSURE (63) (U)
Kenilworth (GFD)
P: Robert Baker, Monty Berman
D:SC: John Gilling
S: John Roddick
John Bentley . . . . Pete Fleming
Rona Anderson . . . . Barbara Leyland
Garry Marsh . . . . Daniel Beaumont
Alexander Gauge . . . . Denis Clayton

Ingeborg Wells . . . . Maxine Goldner
John Horsley . . . . Lamport
Rick Rydon . . . . Trixon
Frank Forsyth . . . . Insp Grayle
CRIME Tec proves bookmaker faked the suicide
of an executive's wife.

11935
DOCTOR IN THE HOUSE (91) *tech* (U)
Group (GFD)
P: Betty Box
D: Ralph Thomas
S: (NOVEL) Richard Gordon
SC: Richard Gordon, Nicholas Phipps, Ronald
Wilkinson
Dirk Bogarde . . . . Simon Sparrow
Muriel Pavlow . . . . Joy
Kenneth More . . . . Benskin
Kay Kendall . . . . Isobel
James Robertson Justice . . . Sir Lancelot
Donald Houston . . . . Taffy Evans
Suzanne Cloutier . . . . Stella
Geoffrey Keen . . . . Dean
George Coulouris . . . . Briggs
Harry Locke . . . . Jessup
Ann Gudrun . . . . May
Joan Sims . . . . Rigor Mortis
Shirley Eaton . . . . Milly Groaker
Nicholas Phipps . . . . Magistrate
Amy Veness . . . . Grandma
Richard Wattis . . . . Salesman
COMEDY Adventures of medical students
during five year training. (BFA: Best Actor
1954; Top Moneymaker: 1954).

11936
DANGEROUS VOYAGE (72) (U) USA:
TERROR SHIP
Merton Park (AA) *reissue:* 1958 (Winart)
P: W.H. Williams
D:S: Vernon Sewell
SC: Julian Ward
William Lundigan . . . . Peter Duncan
Naomi Chance . . . . Joan Drew
Vincent Ball . . . . John Drew
Jean Lodge . . . . Vivian Bolton
Kenneth Henry . . . . Insp Neal
Richard Stewart . . . . Sgt French
John Warwick . . . . Carter
Beresford Egan . . . . Hartnell
CRIME Gang steal uranium derivative and hide
it in mast of abandoned yacht.

11937
THE DARK STAIRWAY (32) (U)
Merton Park (AA)
P: Alec Snowden
D:S: Ken Hughes
N: Edgar Lustgarten
Russell Napier . . . . Insp Hammond
Edwin Richfield . . . . Joe Lloyd
George Manship . . . . George Benson
Vincent Ball . . . . Sgt Gifford
CRIME Blind man identifies the man who
stabbed a mail robber.

11938
THE DEVIL'S JEST (60) (A)
Terra Nova (EB)
P: Paul King
D: Alfred Goulding
S: Vance Uhden
Mara Russell-Tavernan . . . Lady Irma Enderby
Ivan Craig . . . . Maj Seton
Valentine Dyall . . . . Intelligence Director
Derek Aylwood . . . . Victor
Julian Sherrier . . . . Tony
Lee Fox . . . . Maj Malcolm
Hamilton Keene . . . . Col Lorimer

Edward Leslie . . . . Capt Blynne
CRIME Lady's ex-lover is a Nazi spy, posing as a British MO.

11939
THE MISSING PRINCESS (31) (U)
Capitol (EB)
P: Brendan J. Stafford
D: Alastair Scobie, Desmond Leslie
S: Alastair Scobie
Agnes Bernelle . . . . Trudy
Linda Victoria . . . . Princess Lindi
David Locke . . . . Bert
Michael Seavers . . . . Tramp
CHILDREN Ruritanian Princess, age 10, wanders off with boy and dog.

11940
A LETTER FROM THE ISLE OF WIGHT (11) (U)
Rayant (ABFD-CFF)
P: Anthony Gilkison
D: Brian Salt
Robin Doyer . . . . Dick
Joy Ray . . . . Mary
CHILDREN Coastguard's son and visiting cousin saved from the sea by lighthouse keepers.

11941
WINSTON LEE AND HIS ORCHESTRA (series) (U)
Carisbrooke
P: D: Horace Shepherd
Max Geldray; Alan Loveday

11942
1—A MUSICAL MEDLEY (11) (Par)

11943
2—TIME FOR MUSIC (12) Saxon)

11944
3—HANDS IN HARMONY (12) (Saxon)

11945
4—TAKE A FEW NOTES (12) (Par)

11946
5—MELODY MIXTURE (11) (UA)

11947
6—ON WITH THE DANCE (13) (UA)

11948
7—WINSTON LEE AND HIS ORCHESTRA (11) (Rep)

11949
8—THE MAGIC OF MUSIC (12) (UA)
MUSICAL

11950
THE HARRASSED HERO (61) (U)
Corsair (ABP)
P: Clive Nicholas
D: Maurice Elvey
S: (NOVEL) Ernest Dudley
SC: Brock Williams

Guy Middleton . . . . Murray Selwyn
Joan Winmill . . . . Nurse Brooks
Elwyn Brook-Jones . . . . . . Logan
Mary Mackenzie . . . . Estelle Logan
Harold Goodwin . . . . Twigg
Joss Ambler . . . . Dr Grice
Clive Morton . . . . Archer
Hugh Moxey . . . . Willis
COMEDY Rich bachelor in nursing home foils gang seeking counterfeit plates.

11951
DEVIL ON HORSEBACK (89) (U)
Group 3 (BL)
P: Isobel Pargiter
D: Cyril Frankel
S: James Curtis
SC: Neil Paterson, Montagu Slater, Geoffrey Orme
Googie Withers . . . . Jane Cadell
John McCallum . . . . Charles Roberts
Jeremy Spenser . . . . Moppy Parfitt
Liam Redmond . . . . Scarlett O'Hara
Meredith Edwards . . . . Ted Fellowes
Sam Kydd . . . . Darky
Vic Wise . . . . Fred Cole
George Rose . . . . Blacksmith
Malcolm Knight . . . . Squib
SPORT Ex-jockey helps suspended boy jockey lose his conceit.

APR

11952
CONFLICT OF WINGS (84) *eastman*
Group 3 (BL)
P: Herbert Mason
D: John Eldridge
S: (NOVEL) Don Sharp
SC: Don Sharp, John Pudney
John Gregson . . . . Bill Morris
Muriel Pavlow . . . . Sally
Kieron Moore . . . . S/L Parsons
Niall MacGinnis . . . . Harry Tilney
Harry Fowler . . . . Buster
Guy Middleton . . . . Adjutant
Sheila Sweet . . . . Fanny Bates
Campbell Singer . . . . F/S Campbell
Frederick Piper . . . . Joe Bates
George Woodbridge . . . . . . Old Circular
Russell Napier . . . . W/C Rogers
William Mervyn. . . Mr Wentworth/Col Wentworth
Charles Lloyd Pack . . . . . . Bookie
DRAMA Norfolk. Villagers save island bird sanctuary from becoming RAF rocket range.

11953
WEST OF ZANZIBAR (94) *tech* (U)
Ealing-Schlesinger (GFD)
P: Leslie Norman
D:S: Harry Watt
SC: Jack Whittingham, Max Catto
Anthony Steel . . . . Bob Payton
Sheila Sim . . . . Mary Payton
Edric Connor . . . . Ushingo
Orlando Martins . . . . M'Kwongwi
William Simons . . . . Tim Payton
Martin Benson . . . . Dhofar
Peter Illing . . . . Khingoni
Juma . . . . Juma
Howard Marion-Crawford . Wood
R. Stuart Lindsell . . . . Col Ryan
ADVENTURE Africa. National Park warden catches ivory smugglers.

11954
THE DIAMOND (83) (A) (3D)
USA: THE DIAMOND WIZARD
Gibraltar (UA)
P: Steven Pallos
D: Montgomery Tully
S: (NOVEL) Maurice Procter
(RICH IS THE TREASURE)
SC: John C. Higgins
Dennis O'Keefe . . . . Joe Dennison
Margaret Sheridan . . . . . . Marlene Miller
Philip Friend . . . . Insp McLaren
Alan Wheatley . . . . Thompson Blake
Francis de Wolff . . . . Yeo
Eric Berry . . . . Hunzinger
Ann Gudrun . . . . Sgt Smith
Paul Hardtmuth . . . . Dr Eric Miller
Colin Tapley . . . . Sir Stafford Beach
Donald Gray . . . . Cdr Gillies
Cyril Chamberlain . . . . . . Castle
CRIME T-Man helps inspector save diamond-maker from kidnappers. (First British stereoscopic feature, but shown "flat").

11955
THE NIGHT OF THE FULL MOON (67) (U)
Hedgerley (UA)
P:D:SC: Donald Taylor
S: Carl Koch
Dermot Walsh . . . . Robby
Kathleen Byron . . . . Jane
Philip Saville . . . . Dale Merritt
Anthony Ireland . . . . Watercan Man
Tim Turner . . . . George
Everley Gregg . . . . Mrs Jeans
Elizabeth Wallace . . . . Helen
George Merritt . . . . Charlie
CRIME Spies trap FBI agent in country farmhouse.

11956
CALLING ALL CARS (44) (U)
E.J.Fancey (NR)
D:S: Maclean Rogers
Cardew Robinson . . . . . . Reggie
John Fitzgerald . . . . Tom
Adrienne Scott . . . . Beryl
Pauline Olsen . . . . Marjorie
COMEDY Friends on motoring holiday pursue two girls.

11957
JOHNNY ON THE SPOT (72) (U)
E.J.Fancey (NR)
D:SC: Maclean Rogers
S: (NOVEL) Michael Cronin (PAID IN FULL)
Hugh McDermott . . . . Johnny Breakes
Elspet Gray . . . . Joan Ingram
Paul Carpenter . . . . Paul Carrington
Jean Lodge . . . . Sally Erskine
Ronald Adam . . . . Insp Beveridge
Valentine Dyall . . . . Tyneley
CRIME Framed ex-convict proves innocence and saves kidnapped girl.

11958
ADVENTURE IN THE HOPFIELDS (60) (U)
Vandyke (BL-CFF)
P: Roger Proudlock
D: John Guillermin
S: (NOVEL) Nora Lavin, Molly Thorp
(THE HOP DOG)
SC: John Cresswell
Mandy Miller . . . . Jenny Quin
Mona Washbourne . . . . . . Mrs McBain
Hilda Fenemore . . . . Mrs Quin
Russell Waters . . . . Mr Quin
Melvyn Hayes . . . . Reilly

Harold Lang . . . . Sam Hines
Wallas Eaton . . . . Postman
CHILDREN Kent. Runaway girl picks hops to
pay for broken china dog.

MAY

11959
HIS MAJESTY O'KEEFE (90) *tech* (U)
WB-FN (WB)
D: Byron Haskin
S: (NOVEL) Lawrence Kingman, Gerald Green
SC: Borden Chase, James Hill
Burt Lancaster . . . . Capt David O'Keefe
Joan Rice . . . . Dalabo
Andre Morell . . . . Alfred Tetens
Abraham Sofaer . . . . Fatumak
Archie Savage . . . . Boogulroo
Benson Fong . . . . Mr Chou
Tessa Prendergast . . . . Kakofel
Charles Horvath . . . . Bully Hayes
Philip Ahn . . . . Sien Tang
Guy Doleman . . . . Weber
Grant Taylor . . . . Lt Brenner
Alexander Archdale . . . . . . Harris
ADVENTURE Jap. Copra trader thwarts
pirates and is made king by islanders.

11960
DANGEROUS CARGO (61) (U)
ACT Films (Monarch)
P:SC: Stanley Haynes
D: John Harlow
S: (STORY) Percy Hoskins
Susan Stephen . . . . Janie Matthews
Jack Watling . . . . Tom Matthews
Karel Stepanek . . . . Pliny
Richard Pearson . . . . Noel
Terence Alexander . . . . Harry
John le Mesurier . . . . Luigi
Ballard Berkeley . . . . Findley
Genine Graham . . . . Diana
John Longden . . . . Worthington
CRIME London Airport security man
blackmailed into helping bullion robbers.

11961
BURNT EVIDENCE (61) (A)
ACT Films (Monarch)
P: Ronald Kinnoch
D: Dan Birt
S: (STORY) Percy Hoskins
(BURN THE EVIDENCE)
SC: Ted Willis
Jane Hylton . . . . Diana Taylor
Duncan Lamont . . . . Jack Taylor
Donald Gray . . . . Jimmy Thompson
Meredith Edwards . . . . Bob Edwards
Cyril Smith . . . . Alf Quinney
Iren Handl . . . . Mrs Raymond
Hugo Shuster . . . . Hartl
Kynaston Reeves . . . . Pathologist
CRIME Husband flees after accidentally
shooting wife's lover.

11962
THE LARK STILL SINGS (45) (U)
Waverley (EB)
P:D:S: Hugh Wedderburn
Hugh Wedderburn . . . . Michael
Dorothy Dewhurst . . . . . . Mary
Iris Vandeleur . . . .
Roddy Hughes . . . .
Peggy Ann Clifford . . . .
ROMANCE Waiter finds that farm home of
Irish dishwasher is imaginary.

11963
KNAVE OF HEARTS (103) (X)
USA: LOVERS, HAPPY LOVERS
Transcontinental (ABP)
P: Paul Graetz

D: Rene Clement
S: (NOVEL) Louis Hemon
(M.RIPOIS AND HIS NEMESIS)
SC: Rene Clement, Hugh Mills, Raymond
Queneau
Gerard Philipe . . . . Andre Ripois
Valerie Hobson . . . . Catherine
Joan Greenwood . . . . Norah
Margaret Johnston . . . . Anne
Natasha Parry . . . . Patricia
Germaine Montero . . . . Marcelle
Percy Marmont . . . . Father
Diana Decker . . . . Diana
Eric Pohlmann . . . . Proprietor
Bill Shine . . . . Barman
Mai Bacon . . . . Mrs Rose
COMEDY Frenchman tries to seduce
his wife's friend by recounting affairs
with various English girls.

11964
THE HOUSE ACROSS THE LAKE (69) (A)
USA: HEATWAVE
Hammer (ABP)
P: Anthony Hinds
D:SC: Ken Hughes
S: (NOVEL) Ken Hughes (HIGH WRAY)
Alex Nicol . . . . Mark Kendrick
Hilary Brooke . . . . Carol Forrest
Sidney James . . . . Beverley Forrest
Susan Stephen . . . . Andrea Forrest
Paul Carpenter . . . . Vincent Gordon
Alan Wheatley . . . . Insp MacLennan
Cleo Rose . . . . Abigail
Peter Illing . . . . Harry Stevens
Hugh Dempster . . . . Frank
CRIME Windermere. Rich woman drowns her
husband for love of novelist.

11965
FIVE DAYS (72) (A) USA: PAID TO KILL
Hammer (Ex)
P: Anthony Hinds
D: Montgomery Tully
S: Paul Tabori
Dane Clark . . . . James Nevill
Thea Gregory . . . . Andrea Nevill
Paul Carpenter . . . . Paul Kirby
Cecile Chevreau . . . . Joan
Anthony Forwood . . . . Glanville
Howard Marion Crawford . . . .McGowan
Avis Scott . . . . Eileen
Peter Gawthorne . . . . Bowman
Charles Hawtrey . . . . Bill
CRIME Ruined financier blackmails friend
to kill him for insurance.

11966
FORBIDDEN CARGO (85) (U)
London Independent (GFD)
P:S: Sydney Box
D: Harold French
Nigel Patrick . . . . Michael Kenyon
Elizabeth Sellars . . . . Rita Compton
Terence Morgan . . . . Roger Compton
Greta Gynt . . . . Simonetta
Jack Warner . . . . Alec White
Joyce Grenfell . . . . . . Lady Flavia Queensway
Theodore Bikel . . . . Max
James Gilbert . . . . Larkins
Eric Pohlmann . . . . Lasovin
Michael Hordern . . . . Director
Martin Boddey . . . . Holt
Jacques Brunius . . . . Pierre Valence
CRIME Customs officer tracks down
French drug smugglers.

11967
THE RAINBOW JACKET (99) *tech* (U)
Ealing (GFD)
P: Michael Relph
D: Basil Dearden

S: T.E.B.Clarke
Kay Walsh . . . . Barbara Crain
Bill Owen. . . . . Sam Lilley
Edward Underdown . . . . . . Geoffrey Tyler
Fella Edmonds. . . . . Georgie Crane
Robert Morley . . . . Lord Logan
Wilfrid Hyde White . . . . . . Lord Stoneleigh
Charles Victor . . . . Ross
Ronald Ward . . . . Bornie Rudd
Howard Marion Crawford . . Travers
Honor Blackman . . . . Mrs Tyler
Sidney James. . . . . Harry
Michael Trubshawe. . . . . . . Gresham
Frederick Piper . . . . Lukey
Brian Roper . . . . Ron Saunders
SPORT Crooks blackmail boy jockey into
losing St Leger for sake of veteran jockey.

11968
DEVIL GIRL FROM MARS (76) (U)
Gigi (BL)
P: Harry Lee & Edward J. Danziger
D: David Macdonald
S: John C. Maher
SC: James Eastwood
Hugh McDermott . . . . Michael Carter
Hazel Court . . . . Eileen Prestwick
Patricia Laffan . . . . Nyah
Peter Reynolds . . .'. . . . . . Albert
Adrienne Corri . . . . Doris
Joseph Tomelty . . . . Prof Hennessey
Sophie Stewart . . . . Mrs Jamieson
John Laurie . . . . Mr Jamieson
Anthony Richmond . . . . . . Tommy
FANTASY Scotland. Queen of Mars comes
with robot to abduct males for breeding
purposes.

JUN

11969
FATHER BROWN (91) (U) USA: THE
DETECTIVE
Facet (Col)
P: Paul Finder Moss, Vivian A. Cox
D: Robert Hamer
S: (STORIES) G.K.Chesterton
SC: Thelma Schnee, Robert Hamer
Alec Guinness . . . . Father Brown
Joan Greenwood . . . . Lady Warren
Peter Finch . . . . Gustave Flambeau
Cecil Parker . . . . The Bishop
Bernard Lee . . . . Insp Valentine
Sidney James . . . . Bert Parkinson
Gerard Oury . . . . Insp Dubois
Ernest Thesiger . . . . Vicomte
Ernest Clark . . . . Secretary
Everley Gregg . . . . Governess
Austin Trevor . . . . Herald
Marne Maitland . . . . Maharajah
Eugene Deckers . . . . Officer
Jim Gerald . . . . Station Master
Matisconia de Macon Singers and Dancers
CRIME Paris. Catholic priest saves sacred
cross from French thief.

11970
THE SCARLET WEB (63) (A)
Fortress (Eros)
P: Frank Bevis
D: Charles Saunders
S: Doreen Montgomery
Griffith Jones . . . . Jake Winter
Hazel Court . . . . Susan Honeywell
Zena Marshall . . . . Laura Vane
Robert Percival . . . . Charles Dexter
Molly Raynor . . . . Miss Riggs
Ronald Stevens . . . . Simpson
John Fitzgerald . . . . Bert
CRIME Insurance agent posing as ex-
convict framed for stabbing girl.

11971
MEET MR CALLAGHAN (88) (A)
Pinnacle (Eros)
P: Guido Coen, Derrick de Marney
D: Charles Saunders
S: (PLAY) Gerald Verner (NOVEL)
Peter Cheyney (THE URGENT HANGMAN)
SC: Brock Williams
Derrick de Marney . . . . . . Slim Callaghan
Harriette Johns . . . . Cynthia Meraulton
Peter Neil . . . . William Meraulton
Adrienne Corri . . . . Mayola
Delphi Lawrence . . . . Effie
Belinda Lee . . . . Jenny Appleby
Larry Burns . . . . Darkey
Trevor Reid . . . . Insp Gringall
John Longden . . . . Jeremy Meraulton
Roger Williams . . . . Bellamy Meraulton
CRIME Private tec unmasks killer of rich
uncle of crooked brothers.

11972
THE GAY DOG (87) (U)
Coronet (Eros)
P: Ernest Gartside
D: Maurice Elvey
S: (PLAY) Joseph Colton
SC: Peter Rogers
Wilfred Pickles . . . . Jim Gay
Petula Clark . . . . Sally Gray
Megs Jenkins . . . . Maggie Gay
John Blythe . . . . Peter Nightingale
Margaret Barton . . . . Peggy Gowland
Russell Enoch . . . . Leslie Gowland
Cyril Raymond . . . . Vicar
Harold Goodwin . . . . Bert Gay
Jon Pertwee; Peter Butterworth
COMEDY Miner uses underhand methods
to win races with his greyhound.

11973
WHAT EVERY WOMAN WANTS (88) (A)
Advance (Adelphi)
P: David Dent
D: Maurice Elvey
S: (PLAY) Edwin Lewis (RELATIONS ARE
BEST APART)
SC: Talbot Rothwell
William Sylvester . . . . Jim Barnes
Elsy Albiin . . . . Jane
Brenda de Banzie . . . . Sarah Brown
Patric Doonan . . . . Mark
Dominic Roche . . . . Bill Brown
Joan Hickson . . . . Polly Ann
Brian Rix . . . . Herbert Brown
Joan Sims . . . . Doll
Beckett Bould . . . . Tom
DRAMA Midlands. Grandfather encourages
neglected wife to have affair with her
war-wounded cousin.

11974
KNIGHTS OF THE ROUND TABLE (115) (U)
eastman/scope
MGM British
P: Pandro S. Berman
D: Richard Thorpe
S: (NOVEL) Sir Thomas Malory
(LE MORT D'ARTHUR)
SC: Talbot Jennings, Jan Lustig, Noel Langley
Robert Taylor . . . . Lancelot
Ava Gardner . . . . Queen Guinevere
Mel Ferrer . . . . King Arthur
Anne Crawford . . . . Morgan le Fay
Stanley Baker . . . . Mordred
Felix Aylmer . . . . Merlin
Maureen Swanson . . . . Elaine
Gabriel Woolf . . . . Percival
Anthony Forwood . . . . . . Gareth
Robert Urquhart. . . . . Gawaine

Niall MacGinnis . . . . Green Knight
Ann Hanslip . . . . Nan
HISTORY Camelot, 6th C. Knight's love
for Queen is used by King's rival. (First
British Film in Cinemascope).

11975
TROUBLE IN THE GLEN (91) (U) *TRU*
Everest (Rep)
P:D: Herbert Wilcox
S: Maurice Walsh
SC: Frank S. Nugent
Margaret Lockwood . . . . Marissa Mengues
Orson Welles . . . . Sanin Mengues
Forrest Tucker . . . . Lance Lansing
Victor McLaglen . . . . Parlan
John McCallum . . . . Malcolm
Eddie Byrne . . . . Dinny Sullivan
Archie Duncan . . . . Nolly Dukes
Ann Gudrun . . . . Dandy Dinmont
Moultrie Kelsall . . . . Luke Carnoch
Margaret McCourt . . . . . . Alguin
Alex McCrindle . . . . Keegan
Mary Mackenzie . . . . Kate Kurnoch
Peter Sinclair . . . . Gillie
Jack Watling . . . . Sammy Weller
COMEDY Scotland. American major leads
tinkers against new laird from Mexico.

11976
HAPPY EVER AFTER (91) (U) *tech*
USA: TONIGHT'S THE NIGHT
Anglofilm (ABP)
P:D: Mario Zampi
S: Michael Pertwee, Jack Davies
David Niven . . . . Jasper O'Leary
Yvonne de Carlo . . . . . . Serena McGlusky
Barry Fitzgerald . . . . Thady O'Heggarty
George Cole . . . . Terence
Robert Urquhart . . . . . . Dr Michael Flynn
A.E.Matthews . . . . Gen O'Leary
Michael Shepley . . . . Maj McGlusky
Anthony Nicholls . . . . . . Solicitor
Joseph Tomelty . . . . Dooley
Eddie Byrne . . . . Lannigan
Liam Redmond . . . . Regan
Noelle Middleton . . . . . . Kathy McGluskey
COMEDY Ireland. Villagers try to kill
unpopular new squire.

11977
DUEL IN THE JUNGLE (101) *tech* (U)
Marcel Hellman (ABP)
D: George Marshall
S: S.K.Kennedy
SC: Sam Marx, T.J. Morrison
Jeanne Crain . . . . Marian Taylor
Dana Andrews . . . . Scott Walters
David Farrar . . . . .Perry/Arthur Henderson
Patrick Barr . . . . Supt Roberts
George Coulouris . . . . . . Capt Malburn
Charles Goldner . . . . Martell
Wilfrid Hyde White . . . . . . Pitt
Mary Merrall . . . . Mrs Henderson
Heather Thatcher . . . . . . Lady
Michael Mataka . . . . Vincent
Mary Mackenzie . . . . Secretary
Paul Carpenter . . . . Clerk
ADVENTURE Africa. Diamond diver
fakes his own death to claim insurance.

11978
THE STRANGER'S HAND (85) (U)
bilingual
IFP(BL)
P: John Stafford, Graham Greene
D: Mario Soldati
S: Graham Greene
SC: Guy Elmes, Georgino Bassani
Trevor Howard . . . . Maj Court
Alida Valli . . . . Roberta

Richard Basehart . . . . . Joe Hamstringer
Eduardo Cianelli . . . . Dr Vivaldi
Richard O'Sullivan . . . . . . Roger Court
Stephen Murray . . . . Consul
Giorgio Constantini. . . . . Pescovitch
CRIME Venice. Schoolboy searches for
his father, kidnapped by Communist spies.

JUL

11979
THE SLEEPING TIGER (89) (A)
Insignia (AA)
P: Victor Hanbury
D: Joseph Losey
S: (NOVEL) Maurice Moisiewitsch
SC: Carl Foreman
Dirk Bogarde . . . . Frank Clements
Alexis Smith . . . . Glenda Esmond
Alexander Knox . . . . Dr Clive Esmond
Hugh Griffith . . . . Insp Simmonds
Patricia MacCarron . . . . . . Sally
Maxine Audley . . . . Carol
Glyn Houston . . . . Bailey
Harry Towb . . . . Harry
Billie Whitelaw . . . . Receptionist
CRIME Psychiatrist's wife falls for thief he
is using as guinea-pig.

11980
LATE NIGHT FINAL (29) (U)
Merton Park (AA)
P: Alec Snowden
D: Montgomery Tully
S: Gaston Charpentier
SC: Montgomery Tully
N: Edgar Lustgarten
Stanley Van Beers. . Burrage/Crawford
Colin Tapley . . . . Insp Turner
John Wynn . . . . Sgt Conway
Richard Shaw . . . . Wooland
CRIME Missing crippled witness turns
out to be drug smuggler's disguise.

11981
THE SEEKERS (90) (A) *eastman*
USA: LAND OF FURY
Group-Fanfare (GFD)
P: George H.Brown
D: Ken Annakin
S: (NOVEL) John Guthrie
SC: William Fairchild
Jack Hawkins . . . . Philip Wayne
Glynis Johns . . . . Marion Southey
Noel Purcell . . . . Paddy Clarke
Inia Te Wiata . . . . Hongi Tepe
Laya Raki . . . . Moana
Patrick Warbrick . . . . Awarua
Francis de Wolff . . . . Capt Bryce
Thomas Heathcote . . . . . . Sgt Paul
Kenneth Williams . . . . . . Peter Wishart
James Copeland . . . . Mackay
Norman Mitchell . . . . Grayson
Ian Fleming . . . . Mr Southey
ADVENTURE New Zealand, 1800. English
sailor and wife settle down despite Maoris.

11982
UP TO HIS NECK (90) (U)
Group (GFD)
P: Hugh Stewart
D: John Paddy Carstairs
S: Sidney Gilliat, John Orton (JACK AHOY)
SC: John Paddy Carstairs, Patrick Kirwan,
Ted Willis, Maurice Cowan,
Hugh Stewart, Peter Rogers
Ronald Shiner . . . . Jack Carter
Laya Raki . . . . Lao Win Tan
Harry Fowler . . . . Smudge
Brian Rix . . . . Wiggy
Michael Brennan . . . . CPO Brazier
Gerald Campion. . . . . Skinny

Anthony Newley . . . . Tommy
Bryan Forbes . . . . Subby
Colin Gordon . . . . Lt-Cdr Sterning
John Warwick . . . . Lt Truman
Martin Boddey . . . . Chang
Alec Mango . . . . Bandit General
Hattie Jacques . . . . Rakiki
COMEDY Girl spy helps sailor save
submarine from Chinese pirates.

11983
THE EMBEZZLER (61) (A)
Kenilworth (GFD)
P: Robert Baker, Monty Berman
D:S: John Gilling
Charles Victor . . . . Henry Paulson
Zena Marshall . . . . Mrs Forrest
Cyril Chamberlain . . . . Johnson
Leslie Weston . . . . Piggott
Avice Landone . . . . Miss Ackroyd
Peggy Mount . . . . Mrs Larkin
Michael Gregson . . . . Dr Forrest
Frank Forsyth . . . . Insp Gale
CRIME Old cashier absconds and uses
money to help blackmailed widow.

11984
DELAYED ACTION (60) (A)
Kenilworth (GFD)
P: Robert Baker, Monty Berman
D: John Harlow
S: Geoffrey Orme
Robert Ayres . . . . Ned Ellison
Alan Wheatley . . . . Mark Cruden
June Thorburn . . . . Anne Curlew
Michael Kelly . . . . Lob
Bruce Seton . . . . Sellars
Michael Balfour . . . . Honey
Ballard Berkeley . . . . Insp Crane
John Horsley . . . . Worsley
CRIME Crooks pay suicidal novelist to kill
himself if their scheme goes wrong.

11985
SEAGULLS OVER SORRENTO (92) (U)
USA: CREST OF THE WAVE
MGM British
P:D: John & Roy Boulting
S: (PLAY) Hugh Hastings
SC: Roy Boulting, Frank Harvey
Gene Kelly . . . . Lt Bradville
John Justin . . . . Lt Wharton
Bernard Lee . . . . Lofty Turner
Jeff Richards . . . . Butch Cleland
Sidney James . . . . Charlie Badger
Patric Doonan . . . . PO Herbert
Ray Jackson . . . . Sprog Simms
Fredd Wayne . . . . Shorty Karminsky
Patrick Barr . . . . Cdr Sinclair
WAR British and American naval personnel
on remote Scots isle test new torpedo.

11986
THE MASTER PLAN (78) (U)
Gibraltar (GN)
P: Steven Pallos, Charles A.Leeds
D: Hugh Raker (Cy Endfield)
S: (TV PLAY) Harold Bratt
(OPERATION NORTH STAR)
SC: Hugh Raker (Cy Endfield), Donald Bull
Wayne Morris . . . . Maj Brent
Tilda Thamar . . . . Helen
Norman Wooland . . . . Col Cleaver
Mary Mackenzie . . . . Miss Gray
Arnold Bell . . . . Gen Goulding
Marjorie Stewart . . . . Yvonne
Laurie Main . . . . Johnny Orwell
Frederick Schrecker . . . . . Dr Morgan Stern
CRIME Germany. Spy drugs US Major
and makes him photograph files.

11987
VARIETY HALF HOUR (30) (U)
Harold Baim (Butcher)
D: Harold Baim
David Nixon . . . . Frank Pepper
Savoir . . . . Windy Blow
Marcel Cornelis . . . . Reading & Grantley
REVUE

11988
CHILDREN'S CABARET (14) (U)
Carlyle
P:D: Olive Negus
CHILDREN Children dance and sing.

11989
DANCE LITTLE LADY (87) (A) eastman
Alderdale (Renown) reissue: 1958
P: George Minter
D: Val Guest
S: R. Howard Alexander, Alfred Dunning
SC: Val Guest, Doreen Montgomery
Terence Morgan . . . . Mack Gordon
Mai Zetterling . . . . Nina Gordon
Guy Rolfe . . . . Dr John Ransome
Mandy Miller . . . . Jill Gordon
Eunice Gayson . . . . Adele
Reginald Beckwith . . . . . . Poldi
Ina de la Haye. . . . . Mme Bayanova
Harold Lang . . . . Mr Bridson
Richard O'Sullivan . . . . . . Peter
Jane Aird . . . . Mary
William Kendall . . . . Mr Matthews
Alexander Gauge . . . . Joseph Miller
Lisa Gastoni . . . . Amaryllis
David Poole; Maryon Lane
DRAMA When ballerina breaks leg her
faithless husband tries to make their
daughter a Hollywood star.

11990
MALAGA (84) (U) tech USA: FIRE OVER
AFRICA
Film Locations (BL)
P: M.J. Fankovitch, Colin Lesslie
D: Richard Sale
S: Robert Westerby
Maureen O'Hara . . . . Joanna Dale
Macdonald Carey . . . . Van Logan
Binnie Barnes . . . . Frisco
Guy Middleton . . . . Soames Howard
James Lilburn . . . . Danny Boy
Leonard Sachs . . . . Paul Dupont
Harry Lane . . . . Augie
Bruce Beeby . . . . Potts
Meinhart Maur . . . . Jakie
Hugh McDermott . . . . . . Richard Farrell
Ferdy Mayne . . . . Mustapha
ADVENTURE Tangier. American woman
agent poses as singer to catch drug smugglers.

11991
BEAUTIFUL STRANGER (89) (A)
USA: TWIST OF FATE
Marksman (BL)
P: Maxwell Setton, John R. Sloan
D: David Miller
S: David Miller, Rip Van Ronkel
SC: Robert Westerby, Carl Nystrom
Ginger Rogers . . . . Johnny Victor
Herbert Lom . . . . Emil Landosh
Stanley Baker . . . . Louis Galt
Jacques Berberac . . . . Pierre Clement
Margaret Rawlings . . . . . . Marie Galt
Eddie Byrne . . . . Luigi
Coral Browne . . . . Helen
Lisa Gastoni . . . . Yvette
Lily Kann . . . . Nicole
Ferdy Mayne . . . . Police Chief
Keith Pyott . . . . Georges
CRIME Cannes. Counterfeiter frames artist
for killing his mistress's lover.

11992
THE GREEN SCARF (96) (A)
B & A Productions (BL)
P: Bertram Ostrer, Albert Fennell
D: George More O'Ferrall
S: (NOVEL) Guy des Cars (THE BRUTE)
SC: Gordon Wellesley
Michael Redgrave . . . . Maitre Deloit
Leo Genn . . . . Brother Redolec
Ann Todd . . . . Solande Vauthier
Kieron Moore . . . . Jacques Vauthier
Michael Medwin . . . . Henri Teral
Jane Griffiths . . . . Daniele
Anthony Nicholls . . . . Maitre Goirin
Phil Brown . . . . John Bell
Evelyn Roberts . . . . President
George Merritt . . . . Advocate General
Ella Milne . . . . Louise
Jane Henderson . . . . Mme Vauthier
Richard O'Sullivan . . . . . Jacques (child)
CRIME France. Aged lawyer proves blind,
deaf, and dumb man innocent.

11993
THE STRANGER CAME HOME (80) (A)
USA: THE UNHOLY FOUR
Hammer (Ex)
P: SC: Michael Carreras
D: Terence Fisher
S: (NOVEL) George Sanders (STRANGER
AT HOME)
Paulette Goddard . . . . Angie Vickers
William Sylvester . . . . Philip Vickers
Patrick Holt . . . . Job Crandall
Paul Carpenter . . . . Bill Saul
Alvys Maben . . . . Joan Merrill
Russell Napier . . . . Insp Treherne
Pat Owens . . . . Blonde
David King-Wood . . . . Sessions
Kay Callard . . . . Jenny
Jeremy Hawk . . . . Sgt Johnson
CRIME Amnesiac financier returns from
"death" and is framed for murder.

AUG
11994
THE GOLDEN LINK (83) (A)
Parkside (Archway)
P: Guido Coen
D: Charles Saunders
S: Allan Mackinnon
Andre Morell . . . . Supt Blake
Patrick Holt . . . . Terry Maguire
Thea Gregory . . . . Joan Blake
Jack Watling . . . . Bill Howard
Arnold Bell . . . . Insp Harris
Olive Sloane . . . . Mrs Pullman
Bruce Beeby . . . . Sgt Fred Baker
Alexander Gauge . . . . Arnold Debenham
Ellen Pollock . . . . Mme Sonia
Dorinda Stevens . . . . Norma Sheridan
Charlie Drake . . . . Joe
CRIME Inspector's daughter framed for
killing lover's wife.

11995
THE BEACHCOMBER (90) tech (A)
London Independent (GFD)
P: William MacQuitty
D: Muriel Box
S: (STORY) Somerset Maugham
(VESSEL OF WRATH)
SC: Sydney Box
Robert Newton . . . . Hon Ted Wilson
Glynis Johns . . . . Martha Jones
Donald Sinden . . . . Ewart Grey
Paul Rogers . . . . Owen Jones
Donald Pleasence . . . . Tromp
Walter Crisham . . . . Vedalaya

Michael Hordern . . . . Headman
Auric Lorand . . . . Alfred
Tony Quinn . . . . Captain
Ah Chong Choy . . . . Wang
Ronald Lewis . . . . Headman's Son
COMEDY Welcome Islands. Missionary's
sister reforms drunkard beachcomber.

11996
THE YOUNG LOVERS (96) (A)
USA: CHANCE MEETING
Group (GFD)
P: Anthony Havelock-Allan
D: Anthony Asquith
S: George Tabori
SC: Robin Estridge
Odile Versois. . . . . Anna Szobeck
David Knight . . . . Ted Hutchens
Joseph Tomelty . . . . Moffatt
David Kossoff . . . . Geza Szobeck
Paul Carpenter . . . . Gregg Pearson
Thoedore Bikel . . . . Joseph
Jill Adams . . . . Judy
John McClaren . . . . Col Margetson
Betty Marsden . . . . Mrs Forrester
Peter Illing . . . . Dr Weissbrod
Peter Dyneley . . . . Regan
ROMANCE US Embassy employee thought
a traitor for loving daughter of Iron Curtain
minister. (BFA: Best Screenplay 1954).

11997
FATAL JOURNEY (30) (U)
Merton Park (AA)
P: Alec Snowden
D: Paul Gherzo
S: James Eastwood
N: Edgar Lustgarten
Gordon Bell . . . . Insp Durrant
Edward Forsyth . . . . Detective
Jack Melford . . . . Mr Preston
Jane Welsh . . . . Mrs Preston
Julian Somers . . . . Goff
CRIME Inspector exposes amnesiac as
blackmailer who killed woman who
jailed him.

11998
PROFILE (65) (A)
Major (Monarch)
P: John Temple-Smith, Francis Edge
D: Francis Searle
S: John & Maurice Temple-Smith
SC: John Gilling
John Bentley . . . . Peter Armstrong
Kathleen Byron . . . . Margot Holland
Thea Gregory . . . . Susan Holland
Stuart Lindsell . . . . Aubrey Holland
Garard Green . . . . Charlie Pearson
Ivan Craig . . . . Jerry
Lloyd Lamble . . . . Michael
Arnold Bell . . . . Insp Crawford
CRIME Editor proves he did not kill
publisher to cover forged cheque.

SEP

11999
ROMEO AND JULIET (138) *tech* (U)
Verona (GFD)
P: Joseph Janni, Sandro Ghenzi
D: SC: Renato Castellani
S: (PLAY) William Shakespeare
Laurence Harvey . . . . Romeo
Susan Shentall . . . . Juliet
Flora Robson . . . . Nurse
Norman Wooland . . . . Paris
Mervyn Johns . . . . Friar Laurence
John Gielgud . . . . Chorus
Bill Travers . . . . Benvolio
Sebastian Cabot . . . . Capulet

Lydia Sherwood . . . . Lady Capulet
Aldo Zollo . . . . Mercutio
Enzo Fiermonte . . . . Tybalt
ROMANCE Italy. Youth and girl love each
other despite feuding families.

12000
THE BLACK KNIGHT (85) *tech* (U)
Warwick (Col) *reissue:* 1961 (Unifilms)
P: Irving Allen, Albert Broccoli, Phil C.
Samuel
D: Tay Garnett
S: Alec Coppel
Alan Ladd . . . . John
Patricia Medina . . . . Linet
Andre Morell . . . . Sir Ontzlake
Harry Andrews . . . . Earl of Yeonil
Peter Cushing . . . . Sir Palamides
Anthony Bushell . . . . King Arthur
Laurence Naismith . . . . . . Major Domo
Patrick Troughton . . . . . . King Mark
Ronald Adam . . . . The Abbot
Basil Appleby . . . . Sir Hal
Jean Lodge . . . . Queen Guinevere
John Laurie . . . . James
David Paltenghi . . . . High Priest
Elton Hayes . . . . Troubadour
ADVENTURE 6th C. Sword maker poses as
knight to unmask "Vikings" as army of rival
king.

12001
DEVIL'S POINT (65) (U) USA: DEVIL'S
HARBOUR
Charles Deane (Monarch)
D: Montgomery Tully
S: Charles Deane
Richard Arlen . . . . John Martin
Greta Gynt . . . . Peggy
Donald Houston . . . . Michael Mallard
Mary Germaine . . . . Margaret
Victor Baring . . . . Enson'
Michael Balfour . . . . Bennett
John Dunbar . . . . Sam
Vincent Ball . . . . Williams
CRIME American launch-owner catches
cortizone thieves.

12002
THIRTY-SIX HOURS (80) (A)
USA: TERROR STREET
Hammer (Ex)
P: Anthony Hinds
D: Montgomery Tully
S: Steve Fisher
Dan Duryea . . . . Bill
Elsy Albiin . . . . Katie
Ann Gudrun . . . . Jenny
Eric Pohlmann . . . . Slauson
John Chandos . . . . Neville Hart
Kenneth Griffith . . . . Henry
Jane Carr . . . . Sister Clair
Michael Golden . . . . Insp Kevin
Harold Lang . . . . Harry
Lee Patterson . . . . Joe
CRIME USAAF pilot on leave proves he
did not kill wife.

12003
TIME IS MY ENEMY (64) (A)
Vandyke (IFD)
P: Roger Proudlock
D: Don Chaffey
S: (PLAY) Ella Adkins (SECOND CHANCE)
SC: Allan Mackinnon
Dennis Price . . . . Martin Radley
Renee Asherson . . . . Barbara Everton
Susan Shaw . . . . Evelyn Gower
Patrick Barr . . . . John Everton
Bona Colleano . . . . Room-mate
Duncan Lamont . . . . Charles Wayne

Brenda Hogan . . . . Diana
Alfie Bass . . . . Ernie Gordon
Agnes Lauchlan . . . . Aunt Laura
William Franklyn . . . . Peter Thompson
CRIME Crook blackmails ex-wife and
frames her for his murder.

12004
THE BELLES OF ST. TRINIAN'S (91) (U)
British Lion
P: Frank Launder, Sidney Gilliat
D: Frank Launder
S: (CARTOONS) Ronald Searle
SC: Frank Launder, Sidney Gilliat, Val
Valentine
Alastair Sim. . . . . . Miss Fitton/Clarence
Joyce Grenfell. . . . . PW Ruby Gates
George Cole . . . . Flash Harry
Hermione Baddeley . . . . . . Miss Drownder
Betty Ann Davies . . . . Miss Waters
Beryl Reid . . . . Miss Wilson
Mary Merrall . . . . Miss Buckland
Renee Houston . . . . Miss Brimmer
Irene Handl . . . . Miss Gale
Joan Sims . . . . Miss Dawn
Balbina . . . . . . Mlle de St Emillion
Guy Middleton . . . Eric Rowbottom Smith
Sidney James . . . . Benny
Arthur Howard . . . . Wilfred Woodley
Richard Wattis . . . . Manton Bassett
Eric Pohlmann . . . . Sultan
Lloyd Lamble . . . . Supt Kemp-Bird
Andree Melly . . . . Lucretia
Belinda Lee . . . . Amanda
Jerry Verno . . . . Alf
Jack Doyle . . . . Trainer
COMEDY Schoolgirls hide racehorse from
gang of headmistress's brother.

12005
THE ANGEL WHO PAWNED HER HARP (76)
(U)
Group 3 (BL)
P: Sidney Cole
D: Alan Bromly
S: (TV PLAY) Charles Terrot
SC: Charles Terrot, Sidney Cole
Felix Aylmer . . . . Joshua Webman
Diane Cilento . . . . The Angel
Jerry Desmonde . . . . Parker
Joe Linnane . . . . Ned Sullivan
Alfie Bass . . . . Lennox
David Kossoff . . . . Schwartz
Sheila Sweet . . . . Jenny Lane
Raymond Rollett . . . . Stillvane
Robert Eddison . . . . The Voice
FANTASY Islington. Visiting angel helps
pawnbroker and friends.

OCT

12006
THE PURPLE PLAIN (100) (A) *tech*
Two Cities (GFD) *reissue:* 1960 (cut)
P: John Bryan
D: Robert Parrish
S: (NOVEL) H.E.Bates
SC: Eric Ambler
Gregory Peck . . . . S/L Forrester
Win Min Than . . . . Anna
Brenda de Banzie . . . . Miss McNab
Bernard Lee . . . . Dr Harris
Maurice Denham. . . . . F/L Blore
Lyndon Brook . . . . F/O Carrington
Anthony Bushell . . . . Cdr Aldridge
Josephine Griffin . . . . Mrs Forrester
Ram Gopal . . . . Mr Phang
Jack McNaughton . . . . Sgt Brown
Peter Arne . . . . F/L
Dorothy Alison . . . . Nurse

WAR Burma, 1945. Widowed Canadian S/L crashes and helps carry injured navigator to safety.

12007
LEASE OF LIFE (94) (U) *eastman*
Ealing (GFD)
P: Jack Rix
D: Charles Frend
S: Frank Baker, Patrick Jenkins
SC: Eric Ambler

Robert Donat	Rev William Thorne
Kay Walsh	Vera Thorne
Denholm Elliott	Martin Blake
Adrienne Corri	Susan Thorne
Walter Fitzgerald	Dean
Reginald Beckwith	Foley
Vida Hope	Mrs Sproatley
Cyril Raymond	Headmaster
Jean Anderson	Mrs Calthorpe
Mark Daly	Spooner
Russell Waters	Russell
Richard Wattis	Solicitor
Beckett Bould	Mr Sproatley
Frank Atkinson	Verger

DRAMA Village vicar with year to live gives controversial sermon.

12008
THE CROWDED DAY (82) (A)
Advance (Adelphi)
P: David Dent
D: John Guillermin
S: John Paddy Carstairs, Moie Charles
SC: Talbot Rothwell

John Gregson	Leslie
Joan Rice	Peggy
Freda Jackson	Mrs Morgan
Patricia Marmont	Eve
Josephine Griffin	Yvonne
Sonia Holm	Moira
Patricia Plunkett	Alice
Rachel Roberts	Maggie
Vera Day	Suzy
Thora Hird	Woman
Dora Bryan	Marge
Sydney Tafler	Alex
Edward Chapman	Mr Bunting
Cyril Raymond	Philip Stanton
Sidney James	Watchman
Richard Wattis	Mr Christopher
Kynaston Reeves	Mr Ronson

DRAMA Stories of five girl assistants in department store during Christmas.

12009
THE END OF THE ROAD (76) (U)
Group 3 (BL)
P: Alfred Shaughnessy
D: Wolf Rilla
S: (RADIO PLAY) James Forsyth
(OLD MICK-MACK)
SC: James Forsyth, Geoffrey Orme

Finlay Currie	Old Mick-Mack
Duncan Lamont	Barney
Naomi Chance	Molly
David Hannaford	Barney Wee
Edward Chapman	Manager
George Merritt	Timekeeper
Edie Martin	Gloomy Gertie
Gordon Whiting	Young Kennie
Hilda Fenemore	Madge
Herbert C. Walton	Old Man

DRAMA Scotland. Old plater resents retirement and wanders off with small grandson.

12010
ORDERS ARE ORDERS (78) (U)
Group 3 (BL)
P: Donald Taylor
D: David Paltenghi
S: (PLAY) Ian Hay, Anthony Armstrong
SC: Donald Taylor, Geoffrey Orme, Eric Sykes

Brian Reece	Capt Harper
Margot Grahame	Wanda Sinclair
Raymond Huntley	Col Bellamy
Sidney James	Ed Waggermeyer
Tony Hancock	Lt Wilfred Cartroad
Peter Sellers	Pte Goffin
Clive Morton	Gen Grahame-Foxe
June Thorburn	Veronica Bellamy
Maureen Swanson	Joanne Delamere
Peter Martyn	Lt Broke
Bill Fraser	Pte Slee
Edward Lexy	Capt Ledger
Barry Mackay	RSM Benson
Donald Pleasence	L/Cpl Martin
Eric Sykes	Pte Waterhouse

COMEDY Hollywood company takes over army barracks to make science-fiction film.

12011
CHILD'S PLAY (68) (U)
Group 3 (BL)
P: Herbert Mason
D: Margaret Thomson
S: Don Sharp
SC: Peter Blackmore

Mona Washbourne	Miss Goslett
Peter Martyn	PC Parker
Dorothy Alison	Margery Chappell
Ingeborg Wells	Lea Blotz
Carl Jaffe	Carl Blotz
Ballard Berkeley	Dr Nightingale
Joan Young	Mrs Chizzler
Robert Raglan	Supt
Christopher Beeny	Horatio Flynn
Wendy Westcott	Mary Huxley
Ian Smith	Tom Chizzler
Patrick Wells	Hans Einstein Blotz

COMEDY Son of research scientist invents Atomic Popcorn.

12012
FINAL APPOINTMENT (61) (U)
ACT Films (Monarch)
P: Francis Searle
D: Terence Fisher
S: Sidney Nelson, Maurice Harrison
SC: Kenneth R. Hayles

John Bentley	Mike Billings
Eleanor Summerfield	Jenny Drew
Hubert Gregg	Hartnell
Jean Lodge	Laura Robens
Sam Kydd	Vickery
Meredith Edwards	Tom Martin
Liam Redmond	Insp Corcoran
Charles Farrell	Percy

CRIME Reporter saves lawyer from being killed by victim of wartime court-martial.

12013
FOR BETTER, FOR WORSE (84) (U) *eastman*
USA: COCKTAILS IN THE KITCHEN
Kenwood (ABP)
P: Kenneth Harper
D: J. Lee-Thompson
S: (PLAY) Arthur Watkyn
SC: J. Lee-Thompson, Peter Myers, Alec Grahame

Dirk Bogarde	Tony Howard
Susan Stephen	Anne Purves
Cecil Parker	Mr Purves
Dennis Price	Debenham
Eileen Herlie	Mrs Purves
Athene Seyler	Miss Mainbrace
Thora Hird	Mrs Doyle
Charles Victor	Fred
James Hayter	Plumber
Sidney James	Foreman
Pia Terri	Mrs Debenham
Robin Bailey	Salesman
Peter Jones	Dealer
Digby Wolfe	Grocer

COMEDY The troubles of newlyweds in one-room flat.

12014
GOLDEN IVORY (86) (U) *tech*
USA: WHITE HUNTRESS
Summit (ABP)
P: John Croydon, Peter Crane, George Breakston, Ray Stahl
D: George Breakston
S: Dermot Quinn

Robert Urquhart	Jim Dobson
John Bentley	Paul Dobson
Susan Stephen	Ruth Meecham
Alan Tarlton	Seth
Howarth Wood	Meecham
Maureen Connell	Elizabeth Johnson
Tom Lithgow	Peter Johnson
Kip Kamoi	Kip

ADVENTURE Kenya, 1890. Rival brothers search for elephants' burial ground.

12015
STRANGER FROM VENUS (75) (U)
USA: IMMEDIATE DECISION
Rich & Rich-Princess (Eros)
P: Burt Balaban, Gene Martel
D: Burt Balaban
S: Desmond Leslie
SC: Hans Jacoby

Patricia Neal	Susan North
Helmut Dantine	Stranger
Derek Bond	Arthur Walker
Cyril Luckham	Dr Meinard
Willoughby Gray	Tom
Marigold Russell	Gretchen
Arthur Young	Scientist

FANTASY Visiting Venusian wants Earth to abandon atomic experiments.

12016
DIPLOMATIC PASSPORT (64) (U)
Rich & Rich-Princess (Eros)
P: Burt Balaban, Gene Martel
D: Gene Martel
S: Paul Tabori

Marsha Hunt	Judy Anderson
Paul Carpenter	Roy Anderson
Henry Oscar	Chief
Honor Blackman	Marcelle
Marne Maitland	Philip
John MacLaren	Jack Gordon

CRIME Paris. Gang smuggle jewels in American diplomat's car.

12017
RADIO CAB MURDER (70) (A)
Insignia (Eros)
P: George Maynard
D:SC: Vernon Sewell
S: Pat McGrath

Jimmy Hanley	Fred Martin
Lana Morris	Myra
Sonia Holm	Jean
Jack Allen	Parker
Sam Kydd	Spencer
Pat McGrath	Henry
Bruce Beeby	Insp Rawlings
Elizabeth Seal	Gwen

CRIME Ex-convict taxi-driver poses as crook to catch bank robbers.

12018
HARMONY LANE (25) (U) (3D)
Dial (Eros)
P: Morris Talbot, Lewis Gilbert, Daniel Angel
D: Byron Gill

Max Bygraves	Beverley Sisters
Svetlana Beriosova	David Paltenghi
Jack Billings Trio	Skating Sayers
Television Toppers	Dora Bryan

REVUE

12019
THE SEA SHALL NOT HAVE THEM (93) (U)
Apollo (Eros)
P: Daniel Angel
D: Lewis Gilbert
S: (NOVEL) John Harris
SC: Lewis Gilbert, Vernon Harris

Michael Redgrave	Air Commodore Waltby
Dirk Bogarde	F/Sgt Mackay
Anthony Steel	F/O Trehearne
Nigel Patrick	F/Sgt Slingsby
Bonar Colleano	Sgt Kirby
James Kenney	Cpl Skinner
Sydney Tafler	Cpl Robb
Griffith Jones	G/C Todd
Jack Watling	F/O Harding
Guy Middleton	S/L Scott
Paul Carpenter	Lt Pat Boyle
Ian Whittaker	AC2 Milliken
Anton Diffring	Pilot
Rachel Kempson	Mrs Waltby

WAR 1944. Air/Sea Rescue search for
crew of crashed Hudson.

12020
THE GREEN BUDDHA (62) (U)
Republic Productions
P: William N. Boyle
D: John Lemont
S: Paul Erickson

Wayne Morris	Gary Holden
Mary Germaine	Vivien Blake
Walter Rilla	Frank Olsen
Mary Merrall	Mrs Rydon-Smith
Arnold Marle	Vittorio Miranda
Lloyd Lamble	Insp Flynn
Kenneth Griffith	Nobby
Leslie Linder	Harry Marsh
George Woodbridge	Farmer
Percy Herbert	Casey O'Rourke

CRIME American charter pilot saves nightclub
singer from international jewel thieves.

12021
THE STRANGE CASE OF BLONDIE (32) (U)
Merton Park (AA)
P: Alec Snowden
D: Ken Hughes
S: Basil Francis
N: Edgar Lustgarten

Russell Napier	Insp Harmer
Derek Aylward	Langham
Lee Sinclair	Eddie Leroy
Cyril Smith	Wilson
Barbara James	Mrs Dexter

CRIME Murderous blonde cat-burglar
is man in disguise.

12022
THE SILENT WITNESS (32) (U)
Merton Park (AA)
P: Alec Snowden
D: Montgomery Tully
S: James Eastwood
N: Edgar Lustgarten

Ivan Craig	Stafford
Kenneth Henry	Insp Baker
Namara Michael	Ann Stafford
Jean Lodge	Mrs Price
Molly Weir	Mum

CRIME Man is forced to kill again to
cover up wife's murder.

12023
AUNT CLARA (84) (U)
Colin Lesslie (BL)
P:D: Anthony Kimmins
S: (NOVEL) Noel Streatfeild
SC: Kenneth Horne, Roy Miller

Ronald Shiner	Henry Martin
Margaret Rutherford	Clara Hilton
A.E.Matthews	Simon Hilton
Fay Compton	Gladys Smith
Nigel Stock	Charles Willis
Jill Bennett	Julie
Reginald Beckwith	Alfie Pearce
Raymond Huntley	Rev Maurice Hilton
Eddie Byrne	Fosdick
Sidney James	Honest Sid
Diana Beaumont	Dorrie
Garry Marsh	Arthur Cole
Gillian Lind	Doris Hilton
Ronald Ward	Cyril Mason

COMEDY Pious old lady inherits
greyhounds, pub, and brothel.

12024
THE TECKMAN MYSTERY (90) (U)
Corona (BL)
P: Josef Somlo
D: Wendy Toye
S: (TV SERIAL) Francis Durbridge
(THE TECKMAN BIOGRAPHY)
SC: Francis Durbridge, James Matthews

Margaret Leighton	Helen Teckman
John Justin	Philip Chance
Roland Culver	Insp Harris
Michael Medwin	Martin Teckman
George Coulouris	Garvin
Duncan Lamont	Insp Hilton
Raymond Huntley	Maurice Miller
Jane Wenham	Ruth Wade
Meier Tzelniker	John Rice
Harry Locke	Leonard
Frances Rowe	Eileen Miller
Barbara Murray	Girl in Plane

CRIME Pilot's biographer catches spies.

NOV

12025
THE HAPPINESS OF 3 WOMEN (78) (U)
Advance (Adelphi)
P: David Dent
D: Maurice Elvey
S: (PLAY) E.Eynon Evans
(THE WISHING WELL)
SC: E.Eynon Evans, Maufy Davis

Brenda de Banzie	Jane Price
Petula Clark	Delith
Donald Houston	John
Patricia Cutts	Irene
Eynon Evans	Amos
Patricia Burke	Ann
Bill O'Connor	Peter
Gladys Hay	Amelia
Glyn Houston	Morgan

ROMANCE Wales. Postman restores
happiness to three women visitors at
an inn.

12026
MYSTERY AT MONSTEIN (28) (U)
Greenpark (Monarch)
D: Joe Mendoza
CRIME Switzerland. Ski champion tries
to kill orphan ward to inherit fortune.

12027
PARDON ME (8) (U)
Eton Films (Astral)
COMEDY Slapstick between waiter and
diners in restaurant.

12028
MAD ABOUT MEN (90) *tech* (U)
Group (GFD)
P: Betty Box
D: Ralph Thomas
S: Peter Blackmore

Glynis Johns	Miranda/Caroline
Donald Sinden	Jeff Saunders
Anne Crawford	Barbara
Margaret Rutherford	Nurse Carey
Dora Bryan	Berengaria
Noel Purcell	Old Salt
Peter Martyn	Ronald
Nicholas Phipps	Barclay Sutton
Joan Hickson	Mrs Forster
Judith Furse	Viola
Irene Handl	Mme Blanche
David Hurst	Mantalini
Martin Miller	Dr Fergus
Harry Welchman	Symes
Meredith Edwards	PC

FANTASY Cornwall. Mermaid changes
places with sports mistress double.

12029
TO DOROTHY A SON (84) (U)
USA: CASH ON DELIVERY
Welbeck (IFD)
P: Ben Schrift, Sydney Box
D: Muriel Box
S: (PLAY) Roger Macdougall
SC: Peter Rogers

Shelley Winters	Myrtle LaMar
Peggy Cummins	Dorothy Rapallo
John Gregson	Tony Rapallo
Wilfrid Hyde White	Mr Starke
Mona Washbourne	Nurse Appleby
Hartley Power	Cy Daniel
Martin Miller	Brodcynsky
Anthony Olivier	Reporter
Joan Sims	Telephonist
Hal Osmond	Livingstone Potts
Aubrey Mather	Dr Cameron
Ronald Adam	Parsons
Charles Hawtrey	Potman
Alfie Bass	Taxi-driver
Meredith Edwards	Owner
Marjorie Rhodes	Landlady

COMEDY American singer will inherit
£2,000,000 if her ex-husband fails to
become father.

12030
THE PASSING STRANGER (84) (A)
Harlequin (IFD)
P: Anthony Simmons, Leon Clore, Ian
Gibson-Smith
D: John Arnold
S: Anthony Simmons
SC: Anthony Simmons, John Arnold

Lee Patterson	Chick
Diane Cilento	Jill
Duncan Lamont	Fred
Olive Gregg	Meg
Liam Redmond	Barney
Harold Lang	Spicer
Mark Digham	Inspector
Paul Whitsun-Jones	Lloyd
Alfie Bass	Harry
Cameron Hall	Maxie
George Cooper	Charlie
Lyndon Brook	Mike

CRIME American deserter rejoins old
gang to raise money to marry cafe girl.

12031
CARRINGTON VC (106) (A)
USA: COURT-MARTIAL
Remus (IFD)

P: Teddy Baird
D: Anthony Asquith
S: (PLAY) Dorothy & Campbell Christie
SC: John Hunter

David Niven	Maj Carrington
Margaret Leighton	Valerie Carrington
Noelle Middleton	Capt Alison Graham
Maurice Denham	Lt-Col B.R. Reeve
Geoffrey Keen	President
Laurence Naismith	Maj R.E. Panton
Clive Morton	Lt Col T.B. Huxford
Mark Dignam	Prosecutor
Allan Cuthbertson	Lt Col Henniker
Victor Maddern	Sgt Owen
John Glyn-Jones	Evans
Newton Blick	Mr Tester-Terry
Raymond Francis	Maj Mitchell
John Chandos	Rawlinson
R.S.M. Brittain	Sergeant Major

CRIME Major court-martialled for taking money due to him from company safe.

12032
MEN OF SHERWOOD FOREST (77) (U)
eastman
Hammer (Ex) *reissue:* 1961 (RFI)
P: Michael Carreras
D: Val Guest
S: Allan Mackinnon

Don Taylor	Robin Hood
Reginald Beckwith	Friar Tuck
Eileen Moore	Lady Alys
David King-Wood	Sir Guy Belton
Patrick Holt	King Richard
John Van Eyssen	Will Scarlett
Douglas Wilmer	Sir Nigel Saltire
Harold Lang	Hubert
Leslie Linder	Little John
Vera Pearce	Elvira
John Kerr	Brian of Eskdale
John Stuart	Moraine
Raymond Rollett	Abbot St Jude
Leonard Sachs	Sheriff of Nottingham
Bernard Bresslaw	Outlaw

ADVENTURE 1149. Outlaw searches for lost plan to rescue the King.

12033
PASSENGER TO TOKYO (32) (U)
Merton Park (AA)
P: Alec Snowden
D: Ken Hughes
S: James Eastwood
N: Edgar Lustgarten

Kenneth Henry	Insp Ross
Ken Marshall	Sgt
Peter Penn	Geoffrey Craig
Dorothy Bramhall	Mrs Craig
Genine Graham	Miss Summers

CRIME Rare operation helps track killer of rich woman sent to Tokyo in trunk.

12034
BEAU BRUMMELL (111) *eastman* (U)
MGM British
P: Sam Zimbalist
D: Curtis Bernhardt
S: (PLAY) Clyde Fitch
SC: Karl Tunberg

Stewart Granger	Capt George Brummell
Elizabeth Taylor	Lady Patricia Belham
Peter Ustinov	Prince of Wales
Robert Morley	George III
James Donald	Lord Edwin Mercer
James Hayter	Mortimer
Rosemary Harris	Mrs Fitzherbert
Paul Rogers	William Pitt
Noel Willman	Lord Byron
Peter Dyneley	Midger
Charles Carson	Sir Geoffrey Baker

Finlay Currie	McIver
Peter Bull	Mr Fox

HISTORY 1816. Dandy's frankness loses him Prince's favour . (RFP: 1954).

12035
THE DIVIDED HEART (89) (U)
Ealing (GFD)
P: Michael Truman
D: Charles Crichton
S: Jack Whittingham, Richard Hughes

Cornell Borchers	Inga Hartl
Yvonne Mitchell	Sonja Slavko
Armin Dahlen	Franz Hartl
Alexander Knox	Chief Justice
Michel Ray	Toni
Geoffrey Keen	Marks
Eddie Byrne	Justice
Liam Redmond	Justice
Theodore Bikel	Josip Slavko
Ferdy Mayne	Dr Muller
Andre Mikhelson	Prof Miran
Pamela Stirling	Mlle Poncet
Martin Stephens	Hans
John Schlesinger	Ticket Collector

DRAMA Yugoslav mother claims her son back from Austrian foster-parents. (BFA: UN Award, Best Actress, 1954).

DEC

12036
LILACS IN THE SPRING (94) (U) *tru*
USA: LET'S MAKE UP
Everest (Republic)
P: D: Herbert Wilcox
S: (PLAY) Harold Purcell (THE GLORIOUS DAYS)
SC: Miles Malleson

Anna Neagle	Carole/Lilian/Nell Gwyn/ Queen Victoria
Errol Flynn	John Beaumont
David Farrar	Charles King/King Charles II
Kathleen Harrison	Kate
Peter Graves	Albert Gutman/Prince Albert
Helen Haye	Lady Dayton
Scott Sanders	Old George
Alan Gifford	Director
George Margo	Reporter
Alma Taylor	Woman in Circle
Hetty King	Woman in Circle

MUSICAL 1944. ENSA star hurt by bomb dreams of living in the past.

12037
MAKE ME AN OFFER (88) (U) *eastman*
Group 3 (BL)
P: W.P.Lipscomb
D: Cyril Frankel
S: (NOVEL) Wolf Mankowitz
SC: Wolf Mankowitz, W.P.Lipscomb

Peter Finch	Charlie
Adrienne Corri	Nicky
Rosalie Crutchley	Bella
Finlay Currie	Abe Sparta
Ernest Thesiger	Sir John
Wilfrid Lawson	Father
Anthony Nicholls	Auctioneer
Guy Middleton	Armstrong
Alfie Bass	Fred Frames
Vic Wise	Sweeting
Meier Tzelniker	Wendl
Richard O'Sullivan	Charlie (child)

COMEDY Antique dealer tries to raise £100 to buy Portland vase.

12038
MYSTERY ON BIRD ISLAND (57) (U)
Rayant (BL-CFF)
P: Anthony Gilkison

D: John Haggerty
S: Mary Dunn
SC: Mary Cathcart Borer, John Haggerty

Mavis Sage	Marion
Jennifer Beach	Jeanne
Nicky Emdett	Victor
Alexander Gauge	Bronson
Vernon Morris	John
Peter Arne	Henri
Roddy Hughes	Grumpy
Howard Connell	Gaston

CHILDREN Alderney. Holiday children catch smugglers using bird sanctuary.

12039
MASK OF DUST (79) (U)
USA: RACE FOR LIFE
Hammer (Ex)
P: Mickey Delamar
D: Terence Fisher
S: (NOVEL) Jon Manchip White
SC: Paul Tabori

Richard Conte	Peter Wells
Mari Aldon	Pat Wells
George Coulouris	Dallapiccola
Peter Illing	Bellario
Alec Mango	Guido Rizetti
Meredith Edwards	Lawrence
James Copeland	Johnny
Jeremy Hawk	Martin

Stirling Moss; Reg Parnell; John Cooper; Alan Brown; Geoffrey Taylor
SPORT Italy. Racing driver fights way to the top against his wife's wishes.

12040
THE BLACK RIDER (66) (U)
Balblair (Butcher)
P:S: A.R.Rawlinson
D: Wolf Rilla

Jimmy Hanley	Jerry Marsh
Rona Anderson	Mary
Leslie Dwyer	Robert
Lionel Jeffries	Brennan
Beatrice Varley	Mrs Marsh
Michael Golden	Rakov
Valerie Hanson	Karen
Vincent Ball	Ted Lintott
Edwin Richfield	Geoff Morgan
Kenneth Connor	George Amble

CRIME Reporter and motor-cycle club catch smugglers "haunting" ruined castle.

12041
THE DELAVINE AFFAIR (64) (U)
Croydon-Passmore (Monarch)
P: John Croydon, Henry Passmore
D: Douglas Pierce
S: (NOVEL) Robert Chapman
(WINTER WEARS A SHROUD)
SC: George Fisher

Peter Reynolds	Rex Banner
Honor Blackman	Maxine Banner
Gordon Jackson	Florian
Valerie Vernon	Lola
Michael Balfour	Sammy
Peter Neil	Insp Johnson
Laurie Main	Summit
Katie Johnson	Mrs Blissett
Mark Daly	Mr Blissett

CRIME Reporter framed for killing jewel robbery informant.

12042
CHILDREN GALORE (60) (U)
Grendon (GFD)
P: Henry Passmore
D: Terence Fisher
S: John & Emery Bonnet, Peter Plaskett

Eddie Byrne	Zacky Jones
Marjorie Rhodes	Ada Jones

June Thorburn . . . . Milly Ark
Richard Leach . . . . Harry Bunnion
Betty Ann Davies . . . . Mrs Ark
Jack McNaughton . . . . Pat Ark
Peter Evan Thomas . . . . . Lord Redscarfe
Marjorie Hume . . . . Lady Redscarfe
Lucy Griffiths . . . . Miss Prescott
Henry Caine . . . . Bert Bunnion
COMEDY Squire offers cottage to villager
with most grand-children.

12043
ONE GOOD TURN (90) (U)
Two Cities (GFD)
P: Maurice Cowan
D: John Paddy Carstairs
S: Dorothy Whipple, Sid Colin, Talbot
Rothwell
SC: Maurice Cowan, John Paddy Carstairs,
Ted Willis
Norman Wisdom . . . . Norman
Joan Rice . . . . Iris
Shirley Abicair . . . . Mary

Thora Hird . . . . Cook
William Russell . . . . Alec
Joan Ingram . . . . Matron
Richard Caldicott . . . . Bigley
David Hurst . . . . Prof Dofee
Harold Kasket . . . . Ivor Petrovitch
Keith Gilman . . . . Jimmy
COMEDY Orphan odd job man raises money
to buy car for boy.

12044
SVENGALI (82) (A) *eastman*
Alderdale (Renown)
P: George Minter
D: SC: Noel Langley
S: (NOVEL) George du Maurier (TRILBY)
Hildegarde Neff . . . . Trilby O'Ferrall
Donald Wolfit . . . . Svengali
Terence Morgan . . . . Billy Bagot
Derek Bond . . . . The Laird
Paul Rogers . . . . Taffy
David Kossoff . . . . Gecko
Hubert Gregg . . . . Durien

Noel Purcell . . . . Patrick O'Ferrall
Alfie Bass . . . . Carrell
Harry Secombe . . . . Barizel
Peter Illing . . . . Inspector
Hugh Cross . . . . Dubose
Toots Pounds . . . . Mama Martin
Michael Craig . . . . Zouzou
Elizabeth Schwarzkopf
ROMANCE Paris, 1890. Hypnotist makes
artist's model sing, but cannot force her love.

12045
FIVE O'CLOCK FINISH (19) (U)
Grendon (BL-CFF)
P: John Croydon
D: John Irwin
S: J.B.Boothroyd, John Croydon
Peter Butterworth . . . . Dickie Duffle
Humphrey Kent . . . . Mr Crossington
Lloyd Pearson . . . . Mr Piper
CHILDREN Garage hand repairs motor
cycle and delivers it to rich owner.

1955

JAN

12046
TIM DRISCOLL'S DONKEY (59) (U)
Bushey Films (BL-CFF)
P: Gilbert Church
D: Terry Bishop
S: Mary Cathcart Borer
SC: Terry Bishop, Patricia Latham
David Coote . . . . Tim Driscoll
John Kelly . . . . Mike Driscoll
Hugh Latimer . . . . Mr Marshall
Peggy Marshall . . . . Mrs Riordan
Carole Lorimer . . . . Sheila Riordan
Anthony Green . . . . Pat Reilly
Shay Gorman . . . . Mr Sullivan
CHILDREN Irish tinker and son search for
pet donkey exported by mistake.

12047
THE LYONS IN PARIS (81) (U)
Hammer (Ex)
P: Robert Dunbar
D: SC: Val Guest
S: (RADIO SERIES) Bebe Daniels, Bob Block,
Bill Harding (LIFE WITH THE LYONS)
Bebe Daniels . . . . Bebe Lyon
Ben Lyon . . . . Ben Lyon
Barbara Lyon . . . . Barbara Lyon
Richard Lyon . . . . Richard Lyon
Reginald Beckwith . . . . Capt le Grand
Martine Alexis . . . . Fifi le Fleur
Pierre Dudan . . . . Charles
Dino Galvani . . . . Gerrard
Horace Percival . . . . Mr Wimple
Molly Weir . . . . Aggie
Doris Rogers . . . . Florrie Wainwright
Gwen Lewis . . . . Mrs Wimple
Hugh Morton . . . . Col Price
COMEDY Complications when family spend
holiday in Paris.

12048
THE BRAIN MACHINE (83) (A)
Merton Park (AA)
P: Alec Snowden
D:S: Ken Hughes
Patrick Barr . . . . .Dr Geoffrey Allen
Elizabeth Allan . . . . Dr Philippa Roberts
Maxwell Reed . . . . Frank Smith
Russell Napier . . . . Insp Durham
Gibb McLaughlin . . . . Spencer Simon
Edwin Richfield . . . . Ryan
Neil Hallett . . . . Sgt John Harris
Vanda Godsell . . . . Mae
Bill Nagy . . . . Charlie
CRIME Psychopathic drug-thief kidnaps
woman psychiatrist.

12049
LITTLE RED MONKEY (74) (A)
USA: THE CASE OF THE RED MONKEY
Merton Park (AA)
P: Alec Snowden
D: Ken Hughes
S: (TV SERIAL) Eric Maschwitz
SC: Ken Hughes, James Eastwood
Richard Conte . . . . Bill Locklin
Rona Anderson . . . . Julia
Russell Napier . . . . Insp Harrington
Colin Gordon . . . . Martin
Arnold Marle . . . . Dushenko
Sylvia Langova . . . . Hilde
Bernard Rebel . . . . Vinson
Noel Johnson . . . . Sgt Hawkins
John Horsley . . . . Sgt Gibson
Colin Tapley . . . . Sir Clive Raglan
CRIME Spy ring poses as friendship club
to assassinate scientists.

12050
NIGHT PLANE TO AMSTERDAM (31) (U)
Merton Park (AA)
P: Alec Snowden
D: Ken Hughes
S: James Eastwood
N: Edgar Lustgarten
Gerald Case . . . . Insp Carron
Shay Gorman . . . . Sgt
Selma vaz Diaz . . . . Mme Langer
Andrea Malandrinos . . . . . . Pierce
Guy Deghy . . . . Capt Haas
CRIME Diamond.robbery traced to woman
fence using hotel as front.

12051
TO PARIS WITH LOVE (78) tech (A)
Two Cities (GFD)
P: Anthony Darnborough
D: Robert Hamer
S: Robert Buckner
Alec Guinness . . . . Sir Edgar Fraser
Odile Versois . . . . Lizette Marconette
Vernon Gray . . . . John Fraser
Elina Labourdette . . . . . . Sylvia Gilbert
Claude Romain . . . . Georges
Jacques Francois . . . . Victor
Maureen Davis . . . . Suzanne
Austin Trevor . . . . . Gen Leon de Colville
Jacques Brunius . . . . . Aristide Marconette
COMEDY Paris. Widower and son scheme
to marry each other off.

12052
THE MAN WHO LOVED REDHEADS (90)
(A) eastman
British Lion
P: Josef Somlo
D: Harold French
S: (PLAY) Terence Rattigan (WHO IS SYLVIA?)
SC: Terence Rattigan
Moira Shearer . . . . . Sylvia/Daphne/Olga/Colette
John Justin . . . . Mark StNeots
Roland Culver . . . . Oscar
Gladys Cooper . . . . Caroline
Denholm Elliott . . . . Dennis
Harry Andrews . . . . Williams
Patricia Cutts . . . . Bubbles
Moyra Fraser . . . . Ethel
John Hart . . . . Sergei
Jeremy Spenser . . . . Young Mark
Melvyn Hayes . . . . Sydney
COMEDY Husband recalls affairs with
girls resembling his first love.

12053
THE COLDITZ STORY (97) (U)
Ivan Foxwell (BL)
D: Guy Hamilton
S: (BOOKS) P.R.Reid (THE COLDITZ STORY;
THE LATTER DAYS)
SC: P.R.Reid, Ivan Foxwell, William Douglas
Home, Guy Hamilton
John Mills . . . . Pat Reid
Eric Portman . . . . Col Richmond
Frederick Valk . . . . Kommandant
Denis Shaw. . . . . Priem
Lionel Jeffries . . . . Harry Tyler
Christopher Rhodes . . . . Mac MacGill
Richard Wattis . . . . Richard Gordon
Ian Carmichael . . . . Robin Cartwright
Bryan Forbes . . . . Jimmy Winslow
Theodore Bikel . . . . Vandy
Eugene Deckers . . . . Latour
Anton Diffring . . . . Capt Fischer
WAR Saxony, 1940. Recaptured POWs
escape from castle.

12054
SOULS IN CONFLICT (75) (U) eastman
Anglo-Scottish (Great Commission)
P: Billy Graham
D: Dick Ross, Leonard Reeve
S: Dick Ross
Joan Winmill . . . . Ann Woodbridge
Eric Micklewood . . . . Geoff Bradley
Charles Leno. . . . . Tom Stock
Hilda Fenemore . . . . Ruth Stock
Frederick Leister . . . . . Rev Alan Woodbridge
Neal Arden . . . . Frank
Billy Graham; Colleen Townsend Evans;
Don Moomaw
RELIGION American evangelist converts
vicar's daughter, test pilot, and factory hand.

12055
TRACK THE MAN DOWN (75) (A)
Republic Productions
P: William N. Boyle
D: R.G.Springsteen
S: Paul Erickson, Kenneth R.Hayles
Kent Taylor . . . . Don Ford
Petula Clark . . . . June Dennis
Renee Houston . . . . Pat Sherwood
Walter Rilla . . . . Austin Melford
George Rose . . . . Rick Lambert
Mary Mackenzie . . . . Mrs Norman
Kenneth Griffith . . . . Ken Orwell
Ursula Howells . . . . Mary Dennis
Lloyd Lamble . . . . Insp Barnet
CRIME Reporter catches dogtrack takings thief
on long distance bus.

12056
SHADOW OF A MAN (69) (A)
E.J.Fancey (NR)
D: Michael McCarthy
S: (PLAY) Paul Erickson
SC: Paul Erickson, Michael McCarthy
Paul Carpenter . . . . Gene
Rona Anderson . . . . Linda
Jane Griffiths . . . . Carol
Ronald Leigh Hunt . . . . . . Norman
Tony Quinn . . . . Inspector
Jack Taylor . . . . Sgt McBride
Robert O'Neill . . . . Max
Rose Alba . . . . Singer
CRIME Hastings. Author proves crooked
friend was killed by diabetic.

12057
SIMBA (99) (A) eastman
Group (GFD) reissue: 1961 (Unifilms)
P: Peter de Sarigny
D: Brian Desmond Hurst
S: (NOVEL) Anthony Perry
SC: John Baines, Robin Estridge
Dirk Bogarde . . . . Allan Howard
Donald Sinden . . . . Tom Drummond
Virginia McKenna . . . . Mary Crawford
Earl Cameron . . . . Karanja
Basil Sydney . . . . Mr Crawford
Marie Ney . . . . Mrs Crawford
Joseph Tomelty . . . . Dr Hughes
Orlando Martins . . . . Headman
Frank Sanguineau . . . . Waweru
ADVENTURE Kenya. Father of African
doctor is secret leader of Mau-Mau.

FEB

12058
OUT OF THE CLOUDS (88) (U) eastman
Ealing (GFD)
P: Michael Relph
D: Basil Dearden
S: (NOVEL) John Fores (THE SPRINGBOARD)
SC: Michael Relph, John Eldridge, Rex Reinits

Anthony Steel	Gus Randall
Robert Beatty	Nick Melbourne
David Knight	Bill Steiner
Margo Lorenz	Leah Roche
James Robertson Justice . . .	Capt Brent
Eunice Gayson	Penny Henson
Gordon Harker	Taxi-driver
Marie Lohr	Rich Woman
Bernard Lee	Customs Officer
Isabel Dean	Mrs Malcolm
Abraham Sofaer	Indian
Megs Jenkins	Landlady
Melissa Stribling	Jean Osmond
Michael Howard	Purvis
Sidney James	Gambler
Nicholas Phipps	Hilton Davidson

DRAMA Several stories of smuggling, romance, etc., in fogbound London Airport.

12059
IMPULSE (80) (A)
Tempean (Eros)
P: Robert Baker, Monty Berman
D: Charles de la Tour, Cy Endfield
S: Carl Nystrom, Robert Baker
SC: Lawrence Huntingdon, "Jonathan Roach"

Arthur Kennedy	Alan Curtis
Constance Smith	Lila
Joy Shelton	Elizabeth Curtis
Jack Allen	Freddie
James Carney	Jack Forrester
Cyril Chamberlain	Gray
Cameron Hall	Joe

CRIME Nightclub singer tricks American estate agent into thinking he killed jewel thief.

12060
THE GILDED CAGE (77) (A)
Tempean (Eros)
P: Robert Baker, Monty Berman
D: John Gilling
S: Paul Erickson
SC: Brock Williams

Alex Nicol	Steve Anderson
Veronica Hurst	Marcia Farrell
Clifford Evans	Ken Aimes
Ursula Howells	Brenda Lucas
Elwyn Brook-Jones	Bruno
John Stuart	Harding
Michael Alexander	Harry Anderson
Trevor Reid	Insp Brace

CRIME USAAF security man proves brother was framed by art smuggler.

12061
BEFORE I WAKE (78) (A)
USA: SHADOW OF FEAR
Gibraltar (GN)
P: Steven Pallos, Charles A. Leeds
D: Albert S. Rogell
S: (NOVEL) Hal Debrett
SC: Robert Westerby

Mona Freeman	April Haddon
Jean Kent	Florence Haddon
Maxwell Reed	Dr Simon Elder
Frederick Leister	Dr Elder
Hugh Miller	Driscoll
Gretchen Franklin	Elsie
Alexander Gauge	Sgt
Josephine Middleton	Mrs Harrison

CRIME Nurse kills husband and tries to kill stepdaughter.

12062
BREAK IN THE CIRCLE (91) (U) eastman
Hammer-Concanen Recordings (EX)
P: Mickey Delamar
D: Val Guest
S: (NOVEL) Philip Lorraine
SC: Robert Westerby. Val Guest

Forrest Tucker	Skip Morgan
Eva Bartok	Lisa
Marius Goring	Baron Keller
Reginald Beckwith	Dusty
Guy Middleton	Hobart
Eric Pohlmann	Emile
Arnold Marle	Kudnic
Fred Johnson	Farquarson
David King-Wood	Patchway
Guido Lorraine	Franz

ADVENTURE Contraband gang smuggle scientist out of East Germany.

12063
SECRET VENTURE (68) (U)
Republic Productions
P: William N. Boyle
D: R.G.Springsteen
S: Paul Erickson, Kenneth R.Hayles

Kent Taylor	Ted O'Hara
Jane Hylton	Joan Butler
Kathleen Byron	Renee l'Epine
Karel Stepanek	Zelinsky
Frederick Valk	Otto Weber
Maurice Kaufmann	Dan Fleming
Martin Boddey	Squire Marlowe
Arthur Lane	Bob Hendon
Michael Balfour	Stevens
John Boxer	Insp Dalton

CRIME Bodyguard saves inventor of jet fuel from being kidnapped by spies.

12064
THE LOVE MATCH (85) (U)
Group 3 (BL)
P: John Baxter, Maclean Rogers
D: David Paltenghi
S: (PLAY) Glenn Melvyn
SC: Geoffrey Orme, Glenn Melvyn

Arthur Askey	Bill Brown
Thora Hird	Sal Brown
Glenn Melvyn	Wally Binns
Robb Wilton	Mr Muddlecombe
Shirley Eaton	Rose Brown
James Kenney	Percy Brown
Edward Chapman	Mr Longworth
Danny Ross	Alf Hall
Anthea Askey	Vera
William Franklyn	Arthur Ford
Maurice Kaufmann	Harry Longworth

COMEDY Lancs. Football fans try to replace stolen holiday fund.

12065
BLACK IN THE FACE (15) (U)
Grendon (BL-CFF)
P: John Croydon
D: John Irwin
S: J.B.Bothroyd

Peter Butterworth	Dickie Duffle
Humphrey Kent	Mr Crossington
Lloyd Pearson	Mr Tompkins
Celia Cavendish	Mrs Tompkins

CHILDREN Sweeps try to clean client's chimney before mayor arrives.

12066
PLAYGROUND EXPRESS (17) (U)
Grendon (BL-CFF)
P: John Croydon
D: John Irwin
S: J.B.Boothroyd

Peter Butterworth	Peter
Humphrey Kent	Mr Crossington

CHILDREN Brighton. Playground manager and children prevent angry man from locking playground.

12067
ALL LIVING THINGS (30) (U)
Pioneer Exclusives (Famous)
P: Gilbert Church
D: Victor M. Gover
S: (STORY) Nell Montagu
(HALLMARK OF CAIN)

Patrick Barr	Sir Bernard Deye
Kit Terrington	Peter Deye

DRAMA Sick boy cured when vivisectionist father restores his stolen dog.

12068
BETTY AND THE GAMBLER (19) (U)
Sunset (Archway)
DRAMA

12069
CROSSROADS (19) (A)
Bartlett (Butcher)
D: John Fitchen

Christopher Lee	The Ghost
Ferdy Mayne	The Impresario
Mercy Haystead	The Girl

FANTASY Dead man returns to cause death of impresario who killed his sister.

12070
BODY LIKE MINE (12) (U)
Faro Films (Ex)
COMEDY Frail youth takes muscle building course to win back girl from strong rival.

12071
SONG OF NORWAY (32) (U)
E.J.Fancey (NR)
D: Maclean Rogers
N: Eamonn Andrews
Eric Micklewood
Adrienne Scott
Vanda Godsell
Graham Stark
Andrew Timothy
ADVENTURE Oslo. English girl becomes hotel receptionist, enters ski race, and is rescued from crevasse.

12072
RAISING A RIOT (91) tech (U)
London-Dalrymple (BL) reissue: 1960
P: Ian Dalrymple, Hugh Perceval
D: Wendy Toye
S: (NOVEL) Alfred Toombs
SC: Ian Dalrymple, Hugh Perceval, James Matthews

Kenneth More	Tony Kent
Ronald Squire	Grampy
Mandy Miller	Anne Kent
Jan Miller	Sue
Lionel Murton	Harry
Mary Laura Wood	Jacqueline
Olga Lindo	Aunt Maud
Shelagh Fraser	Mary Kent
Gary Billings	Peter Kent
Fusty Bentine	Fusty Kent
Nora Nicholson	Miss Pettigrew
Anita Sharp Bolster	Mrs Buttons
Michael Bentine	Museum Official
Dorothy Dewhurst	Mother

COMEDY Father copes with children on holiday in old windmill.

12073
A PRIZE OF GOLD (100) tech (A)
Warwick (Col) reissue: 1961 (Unifilms)
P: Irving Allen, Albert Broccoli, Phil Samuel
D: Mark Robson
S: (NOVEL) Max Catto
SC: Robert Buckner, John Paxton

Richard Widmark	Sgt Joe Lawrence
Mai Zetterling	Maria

Nigel Patrick . . . . Brian Hammell
George Cole . . . . Sgt Roger Morris
Donald Wolfit . . . . Alfie Scratton
Andrew Ray . . . . Conrad
Joseph Tomelty . . . . Uncle Dan
Karel Stepanek . . . . Dr Zachman
Robert Ayres . . . . Tex
Eric Pohlmann . . . . Hans Fischer
Olive Sloane . . . . Mavis
CRIME Berlin. US Sgt steals cargo of
gold for sake of German girl.

MAR

12074
THE END OF THE AFFAIR (105) (A)
Coronado (Col)
P: David E. Rose, David Lewis
D: Edward Dmytryk
S: (NOVEL) Graham Greene
SC: Lenore Coffee
Deborah Kerr . . . . Sarah Miles
Van Johnson . . . . Maurice Bendix
John Mills . . . . Albert Parkis
Peter Cushing . . . . Henry Miles
Stephen Murray . . . . Father Crompton
Nora Swinburne . . . . Mrs Bertram
Charles Goldner . . . . Savage
Michael Goodliffe . . . . Smythe
Joyce Carey . . . . Mrs Palmer
Frederick Leister . . . . Dr Collingwood
ROMANCE 1944. Married woman promises
God she will leave her lover if he survives
bomb wound.

12075
WHERE THERE'S A WILL (79) (U)
Film Locations (Eros)
P: George Maynard
D: Vernon Sewell
S: (PLAY) R.F.Delderfield
SC: R.F.Delderfield
Kathleen Harrison . . . . Annie Yeo
George Cole . . . . Fred Slater
Leslie Dwyer . . . . Alfie Brewer
Ann Hanslip . . . . June Hodge
Michael Shepley . . . . Mr Cogent
Dandy Nichols . . . . Maud Hodge
Thelma Ruby . . . . Amy Slater
Norman MacOwan . . . . Cagey
Hugh Morton . . . . Arscott
Edward Lexy . . . . Mafeking
COMEDY Devon. Cockney family inherit
farm mortgaged to rival.

12076
AS LONG AS THEY'RE HAPPY (91) (U)
eastman
Group (GFD)
P: Raymond Stross
D: J. Lee-Thompson
S: (PLAY) Vernon Sylvaine
SC: Alan Melville
Jack Buchanan . . . . John Bentley
Jean Carson . . . . Pat Bentley
Janette Scott . . . . Gwen Bentley
Brenda de Banzie . . . . Stella Bentley
Susan Stephen . . . . Corinne
Jerry Wayne . . . . Bobby Denver
Diana Dors . . . . Pearl
Hugh McDermott . . . . Barnaby
Nigel Greene . . . . Peter
David Hurst . . . . Dr Schneider
Athene Seyler . . . . Mrs Arbuthnot
Joan Sims . . . . Linda
Dora Bryan . . . . Mavis
Charles Hawtrey . . . . Teddyboy
Gilbert Harding . . . . Himself
COMEDY Father tries to cure family's
passion for visiting American pop-singer.

12077
MURDER BY PROXY (87) (A)
USA: BLACKOUT
Hammer (Ex)
P: Michael Carreras
D: Terence Fisher
S: (NOVEL) Helen Neilson
SC: Richard Landau
Dane Clark . . . . Casey Morrow
Belinda Lee . . . . Phyllis Brunner
Betty Ann Davies . . . . Alicia Brunner
Eleanor Summerfield . . . . . Maggie Doone
Andrew Osborn . . . . Lance Gorden
Harold Lang . . . . Travis
Michael Golden . . . . Insp Johnson
Jill Melford . . . . Miss Nardis
Delphi Lawrence . . . . Linda
Alfie Bass . . . . Ernie
Cleo Laine . . . . Singer
CRIME Broke American bribed to wed
heiress is framed for killing her father.

12078
THIRD PARTY RISK (70) (U)
USA: THE DEADLY GAME
Hammer (Ex)
P: Robert Dunbar
D: SC: Daniel Birt
S: (NOVEL) Nicolas Bentley
Lloyd Bridges . . . . Philip Graham
Finlay Currie . . . . Mr Darius
Maureen Swanson . . . . Lolita
Simone Silva . . . . Mitzi
Ferdy Mayne . . . . Maxwell Carey
Peter Dyneley . . . . Tony Roscoe
Roger Delgardo . . . . Gonzales
George Woodbridge . . . . . . Insp Goldfinch
Russell Waters . . . . Dr Zeissman
Mary Parker . . . . Mrs Zeissman
CRIME Spain. American suspected of killing
wartime friend for microfilm.

12079
ONE JUMP AHEAD (66) (A)
Kenilworth (GFD)
P: Guido Coen
D: Charles Saunders
S: (NOVEL) Robert Chapman
SC: Doreen Montgomery
Paul Carpenter . . . . Paul Banner
Diane Hart . . . . Maxine
Jill Adams . . . . Judy
Freddie Mills . . . . : . . . Bert Tarrant
Peter Sinclair . . . . Old Tarrant
Arnold Bell . . . . Supt Faro
David Hannaford . . . . Brian
Roddy Hughes . . . . Mac
CRIME Reporter solves deaths of
blackmailing girl and schoolboy witness.

12080
THAT LADY (100) (A)
eastman/scope
Atalanta (20)
P: Sy Bartlett
D: Terence Young
S: (NOVEL) Kate O'Brien
SC: Sy Bartlett, Anthony Veiller
Olivia De Havilland . . . . Ana de Mendoza
Gilbert Roland . . . . Antonio Perez
Paul Scofield . . . . Philip II
Francoise Rosay . . . . Bernardina
Dennis Price . . . . Mateo Vasquez
Anthony Dawson . . . . Don Inigo
Robert Harris . . . . Cardinal
Peter Illing . . . . Diego
Jose Nieto . . . . Don Escovedo
Christopher Lee . . . . Captain
DRAMA Madrid, 1580. Widow loves minister
accused of plotting against King.

12081
TANGIER ASSIGNMENT (64) (U)
Rock Pictures (NR)
P: Cyril Parker
D:S: Ted Leversuch
Robert Simmons . . . . Valentine
June Powell . . . . Vicky
Fernando Rey . . . . Inspector
CRIME Tangier. Secret agent and nightclub
singer catch gun runners.

APR

12082
THE NIGHT MY NUMBER CAME UP (94) (U)
Ealing (GFD)
P: Tom Morahan
D: Leslie Norman
S: (ARTICLE) Victor Goddard
SC: R.C.Sheriff
Michael Redgrave . . Air Marshal John Hardie
Sheila Sim . . . . Mary Campbell
Alexander Knox . . . . Owen Robertson
Denholm Elliott . . . . F/L Mackenzie
Ursula Jeans . . . . Mrs Robertson
Ralph Truman . . . . Lord Wainwright
Michael Hordern . . . . Cdr Lindsay
Nigel Stock . . . . SL Walker
George Rose . . . . Walter Bennett
Bill Kerr . . . . Soldier
Alfie Bass . . . . Soldier
Victor Maddern . . . . Engineer
DRAMA Commander's dream of thirteen
people crashing during Hong Kong-Tokio
flight comes true.

12083
ABOVE US THE WAVES (99) (U)
London Independent (GFD) *reissue:* 1959
(25 mins cut)
P: Sydney Box, William MacQuitty
D: Ralph Thomas
S: (BOOK) C.E.T.Warren, James Benson
SC: Robin Estridge
John Mills . . . . Cdr Fraser
John Gregson . . . . Lt Alec Duffy
Donald Sinden . . . . Lt Tom Corbett
James Robertson Justice . . . Admiral Ryder
Michael Medwin . . . . Smart
James Kenney . . . . Abercrombie
O.E.Hasse . . . . Tirpitz Capt
William Russell . . . . Ramsey
Thomas Heathcote . . . . Hutchins
Lee Patterson . . . . Cox
Theodore Bikel . . . . German Officer
WAR Norway. Commander's midget
submarines sink German battleship "Tirpitz."

12084
PASSAGE HOME (102) (A)
Group (GFD)
P: Julian Wintle
D: Roy Baker
S: (NOVEL) Richard Armstrong
SC: William Fairchild
Anthony Steel . . . . Vosper
Peter Finch . . . . Capt Lucky Ryland
Diane Cilento . . . . Ruth Elton
Cyril Cusack . . . . Bohannon
Geoffrey Keen . . . . Ike
Hugh Griffith . . . . Pettigrew
Duncan Lamont . . . . Llewellyn
Gordon Jackson . . . . Burne
Bryan Forbes . . . . Shorty
Michael Craig . . . . Burton
Robert Brown . . . . Shane
Martin Benson . . . . Guiterres
Patrick McGoohan . . . . McIsaacs
DRAMA 1931. Drunken cargo ship
captain and his mate fall for enforced
passenger.

12085
CONTRABAND SPAIN (82) (U) eastman
Diadem (ABP)
P: Ernest Gartside
D:S: Lawrence Huntington
Richard Greene .... Lee Scott
Anouk Aimee .... Elena Vargas
Michael Denison .... Ricky Metcalfe
Jose Nieto .... Pierre
John Warwick .... Bryan
Philip Saville .... Martin Scott
Alfonso Estella .... Marcos
G.H.Mulcaster .... Col Ingleby
Robert Ayres .... Official
CRIME Spain. Singer helps FBI agent catch
dollar forgers who killed his brother.

12086
THE DAM BUSTERS (125) (U)
ABPC
P: Robert Clark, W.A.Whittaker
D: Michael Anderson
S: (BOOKS) Paul Brickhill; Guy Gibson
(ENEMY COAST AHEAD)
SC: R.C.Sheriff
Richard Todd .... W/C Guy Gibson
Michael Redgrave ...... Barnes N. Wallis
Derek Farr .... G/C Whitworth
Ursula Jeans .... Mrs Wallis
Basil Sydney .... Sir Arthur Harris
Patrick Barr .... Capt Joseph Summers
Ernest Clark .... AVM Ralph Cochrane
John Fraser .... F/L Hopgood
Nigel Stock .... F/L Spofford
Bill Kerr .... F/L Martin
George Baker .... F/L Maltby
Robert Shaw .... F/Sgt Pulford
Raymond Huntley .... Official
Anthony Doonan ...... F/L Hutchinson
Harold Goodwin .... Crosby
Laurence Naismith ...... Farmer
Frank Phillips .... BBC Announcer
WAR 1943. Scientist's riccochet bomb
enables RAF to destroy Ruhr dams. (Top
Moneymaker: 1955).

12087
THE CONSTANT HUSBAND (88) tech (U)
Individual (BL)
P: Frank Launder, Sidney Gillat
D: Sidney Gillat
S: Sidney Gillat, Val Valentine
Rex Harrison .... Charles Hathaway
Margaret Leighton ...... Miss Chesterman
Kay Kendall .... Monica
Cecil Parker .... Llewellyn
Nicole Maurey .... Lola
George Cole .... Luigi Sopranelli
Raymond Huntley ...... J.F.Hassett
Michael Hordern .... Judge
Robert Coote .... Jack Carter
Eric Pohlmann .... Papa Sopranelli
Marie Burke .... Mama Sopranelli
Valerie French .... Bridget
Jill Adams .... Miss Brent
Muriel Young .... Clara
John Robinson .... Secretary
COMEDY Amnesiac discovers he has six homes
and six wives.

12088
THE PRISONER (95) (A)
Facet-London Independent (Col)
P: Sydney Box, Vivian A. Cox
D: Peter Glenville
S: (PLAY) Bridget Boland
SC: Bridget Boland
Alec Guinness .... The Cardinal
Jack Hawkins .... The Interrogator
Wilfrid Lawson .... The Jailer
Raymond Huntley ...... The General

Jeannette Sterke .... The Girl
Ronald Lewis .... The Warder
Kenneth Griffith .... The Secretary
DRAMA Europe. Interrogator's methods
eventually make Cardinal confess to treason.

12089
THE DARK AVENGER (85) (U)
eastman/scope USA: THE WARRIORS
Monogram (20)
P: Vaughan N. Dean
D: Henry Levin
S: Daniel B. Ullman
SC: Daniel B. Ullman, Phil Park
Errol Flynn .... Prince Edward
Joanne Dru .... Lady Joan Holland
Peter Finch .... Count de Ville
Yvonne Furneaux .... Marie
Patrick Holt .... Sir Ellys
Michael Hordern .... Edward III
Moultrie Kelsall .... Sir Bruce
Robert Urquhart .... Sir Phillip
Vincent Winter .... John Holland
Noel Willman .... De Guesclin
Frances Rowe .... Genevieve
Richard O'Sullivan ...... Thomas Holland
ADVENTURE France, 1350. Black Prince poses
as French knight to rescue captive Lady.

12090
A KID FOR TWO FARTHINGS (96)
eastman (U)
Big Ben-London (IFD)
P:D: Carol Reed
S: (NOVEL) Wolf Mankowitz
SC: Wolf Mankowitz
Celia Johnson .... Joanna
Diana Dors .... Sonia
David Kossoff .... Kandinsky
Joe Robinson .... Sam
Jonathan Ashmore .... Joe
Brenda de Banzie .... Ruby
Vera Day .... Mimi
Primo Carnera .... Python Macklin
Sydney Tafler .... Madam Rita
Sidney James .... Ice Berg
Daphne Anderson .... Dora
Lou Jacobi .... Blackie Isaacs
Harold Berens .... Oliver
Danny Green .... Bason
Irene Handl .... Mrs Abramowitz
Alfie Bass .... Alf
Eddie Byrne .... Sylvester
Joseph Tomelty .... Vagrant
DRAMA Petticoat Lane boy believes
one-horned goat is a wish-granting unicorn.

MAY

12091
TIGER BY THE TAIL (85) (A)
USA: CROSSUP
Tempean (Eros)
P: Robert Baker, Monty Berman
D: John Gilling
S: (NOVEL) John Mair (NEVER COME BACK)
SC: Willis Goldbeck, John Gilling
Larry Parks .... John Desmond
Constance Smith .... Jane Claymore
Lisa Daniely .... Anna Ray
Cyril Chamberlain .... Foster
Donald Stewart .... Macaulay
Thora Hird .... Mary
Joan Heal .... Annabelle
Alexander Gauge .... Fitzgerald
Ronan O'Casey .... Mick
Marie Bryant .... Melodie
CRIME Counterfeiters kidnap American
reporter to obtain dead girl's diary.

12092
POLICE DOG (70) (U)
Westridge Fairbanks (Eros)
P: Harold Huth
D:S: Derek Twist
Joan Rice .... Pat Lewis
Tim Turner .... Frank Mason
Sandra Dorne .... Blonde
Charles Victor .... Sergeant
Jimmy Gilbert .... Ken Lade
Nora Gordon .... Mrs Lewis
John le Mesurier .... Inspector
CRIME PC trains stray Alsatian dog and
catches friend's killer.

12093
CYRIL STAPLETON AND THE SHOW BAND
(28) (U) eastman/scope
Hammer (Ex)
P:D: Michael Carreras
Cyril Stapleton's Show Band
Lita Roza .... Ray Burns
Bill McGuffie
MUSICAL

12094
DEAD ON TIME (27) (A)
Vandyke (Archway)
P: Roger Proudlock
D: Don Chaffey
Patrick Allen
Greta Gynt
John Loder
CRIME Secret agent tracks atomic spies who
kidnap girl.

12095
THE SHIP THAT DIED OF SHAME (95) (A)
USA: PT RAIDERS
Ealing (GFD) reissue: 1959 (cut)
P: Michel Relph
D: Basil Dearden
S: (NOVEL) Nicholas Monsarrat
SC: Michael Relph, Basil Dearden, John Whiting
Richard Attenborough ..... George Hoskins
George Baker .... Bill Randall
Bill Owen .... Birdie Dick
Virginia McKenna .... Helen Randall
Roland Culver .... Fordyce
Bernard Lee .... Sam Brewster
Ralph Truman .... Sir Richard
John Chandos .... Raines
Harold Goodwin .... Customs Officer
John Longden .... Detective
CRIME Ex-officers buy old motor gunboat
and become smugglers.

12096
THE HORNET'S NEST (64) (U)
Kenilworth (GFD)
P: Guido Coen
D: Charles Saunders
S: John Roddick
SC: Allan Mackinnon
Paul Carpenter .... Bob Bartlett
June Thorburn .... Pat
Marla Landi .... Terry Savarese
Charles Farrell .... Posh Peterson
Larry Burns .... Alfie
Alexander Gauge .... Mr Arnold
Christine Silver .... Becky Crumb
Nora Nicholson .... Rachel Crumb
COMEDY Model girls buy houseboat in
which crooks have cached jewels.

12097
THE STATELESS MAN (29) (U)
Merton Park (AA)
P: Alec Snowden
D: Paul Gherzo
S: James Eastwood

Frank Leighton . . . . Insp Parry
May Hallett . . . . Mrs Fenton
Robin Wentworth . . . . Sgt
Theodore Wilhelm . . . . Slavik
Tom Clegg . . . . Bill Fenton
CRIME Police prove landlady's docker son
stabbed girl lodger.

12098
CONFESSION (90) (A) USA: THE DEADLIEST
SIN
Anglo-Guild (AA)
P: Alec Snowden
D:SC: Ken Hughes
S: (PLAY) Don Martin
Sydney Chaplin . . . . Mike Nelson
Audrey Dalton . . . . Louise Nelson
John Bentley . . . . Insp Kessler
Peter Hammond . . . . Alan
John Welsh . . . . Father Neil
Jefferson Clifford . . . . Pop
Pat McGrath . . . . Williams
Robert Raglan . . . . Becklan
Patrick Allan . . . . Corey
CRIME American thief tries to kill Catholic
priest who knows his secret.

12099
THREE CASES OF MURDER (99) (A)
Wessex (BL)
P: Ian Dalrymple, Alexander Paal, Hugh Perceval
LORD MOUNTDRAGO
D: George More O'Ferrall
S: (STORY) W. Somerset Maugham
SC: Ian Dalrymple
Orson Welles . . . . Lord Mountdrago
Alan Badel . . . . Owen
Helen Cherry . . . . Lady Mountdrago
Andre Morell . . . . Dr Audlin
YOU KILLED ELIZABETH
D: David Eady
S: (STORY) Brett Halliday
SC: Sidney Carroll
Elizabeth Sellars . . . . Elizabeth
John Gregson . . . . Edgar Curtain
Emrys Jones . . . . George Wheeler
Jack Lambert . . . . Insp Acheson
IN THE PICTURE
D: Wendy Toye
S: (STORY) Roderick Wilkinson
SC: Donald Wilson
Alan Badel . . . . Mr X
Hugh Pryse . . . . Jarvis
Leueen MacGrath . . . . The Woman
Eddie Byrne . . . . Snyder
CRIME Three murder stories, two with elements
of fantasy.

JUN

12100
THE SECRET (80) (A) *eastman*
Laureate-Golden Era (Eros)
P: S.Benjamin Fisz
D: C.Raker Endfield
S: (PLAY) Robert Brenon
SC: C.Raker Endfield
Sam Wanamaker . . . . Nick Delaney
Mandy Miller . . . . Katie Martin
Andre Morell . . . . Insp Lake
Harold Berens . . . . Frank Farmer
Jan Miller . . . . Margaret
Wyndham Goldie . . . . Dr Scott
Marian Spencer . . . . Aunt Doris
Richard O'Sullivan . . . . John Martin
Henry Caine . . . . Superintendent
CRIME Brighton. American thief tries to get
orphan's teddy bear which contains stolen gems.
gems.

12101
JOHN AND JULIE (82) (U) *eastman*
Group 3 (BL)
P: Herbert Mason
D:S: William Fairchild
Moira Lister . . . . Dora
Noelle Middleton . . . . Miss Stokes
Constance Cummings . . . . . Mrs Davidson
Wilfrid Hyde White . . . . . . Sir James
Sidney James . . . . Mr Pritchett
Joseph Tomelty . . . . Mr Davidson
Colin Gibson . . . . John Pritchett
Lesley Dudley . . . . Julie
Megs Jenkins . . .'. . . . . . . Mrs Pritchett
Patric Doonan . . . . Jim Webber
Peter Sellers . . . . PC Diamond
Richard Dimbleby; Wynford Vaughan Thomas
COMEDY Two six-year old children walk
to London to see Coronation.

12102
SEE HOW THEY RUN (84) (U)
Winwell (BL)
P: Bill Luckwell
D: Leslie Arliss
S: (PLAY) Philip King
SC: Leslie Arliss, Philip King, Val Valentine
Ronald Shiner . . . . Wally Winton
Greta Gynt . . . .'. . . . . . . Penelope Toop
James Hayter . . . . Bishop of Lax
Wilfrid Hyde White . . . . . . Brigadier Buskin
Dora Bryan . . . . Ida
Richard Wattis . . . . Rev Lionel Toop
Viola Lyel . . . . Miss Skilton
Charles Farrell . . . . Basher
Michael Brennan . . . . Sgt-Maj Towers
Roddy Hughes . . . Rev Arthur Humphrey
Ballard Berkeley . . . . Col Warrington
COMEDY Soldier seeking promotion to
fulfil will poses as cleric and catches convict.

12103
DON GIOVANNI (170) (U) *eastman*
Harmony (Maxwell)
P: Paul Czinner, Fred Swann
D: Paul Czinner, Alfred Travers
S: (OPERA) Wolfgang Mozart, Lorenzo da Ponte
Cesare Siepi . . . . Don Giovanni
Otto Edelmann . . . . Leporello
Elizabeth Grummer . . . . . . Donna Anna
Lisa Della Casa . . . . Donna Elvira
Anton Dermota . . . . Don Ottavio
Erna Berger . . . . Zerlina
Walter Berry . . . . Masetto
Deszo Ernster . . . . Commendatore
MUSICAL 1954 Salzburg Festival production.

12104
THE TIME OF HIS LIFE (74) (U)
Shaftesbury (Renown)
P: Elizabeth Hiscott, W.A.Smith
D: Leslie Hiscott
S: Leslie Hiscott, Brock Williams
SC: Leslie Hiscott, Richard Hearne
N: Macdonald Hobley
Richard Hearne . . . . Charles Pastry
Ellen Pollock . . . . Lady Florence
Richard Wattis . . . . Edgar
Robert Moreton . . . . Humphrey
Frederick Leister . . . . Sir John
Peter Sinclair . . . . Kane
John Downing . . . . Simon
Anne Smith . . . . Penelope
Darcy Conyers . . . . Morgan
Yvonne Hearne . . . . Guest
COMEDY Lady secretary to prisoners'
aid society locks away her ex-convict father.

12105
YOU LUCKY PEOPLE (79) (U) *scope*
Advance (Adelphi)
P: David Dent
D: Maurice Elvey
S: Maurice Harrison, Sidney Wilson
SC: Anthony Verney, Tommy Trinder
Tommy Trinder . . . . Tommy Smart
Mary Parker . . . . Pte Sally Briggs
Dora Bryan . . . . Sgt Hortense Tipp
RSM Brittain . . . . Himself
James Copeland . . . . Pte Jim Campbell
Michael Kelly . . . . Sgt Manners
Mark Singleton . . . . Lt Robson
Charles Rolfe . . . . Hooky
Rolf Harris . . . . Pte Proudfoot
Rufus Cruickshank . . . Sgt-Maj Thickpenny
Michael Trubshawe. . . Col Barkstone-Gadsby
COMEDY Army surplus profiteer has to do
two weeks' army training.

JUL

12106
BARBADOS QUEST (70) (U)
USA: MURDER ON APPROVAL
Cipa (RKO)
P: Robert Baker, Monty Berman
D: Bernard Knowles
S: Kenneth R. Hayles
Tom Conway . . . . Tom "Duke" Martin
Delphi Lawrence . . . . Jean Larsen
Brian Worth . . . . Geoffrey Blake
Michael Balfour . . . . Barney
Campbell Cotts . . . . Coburn
John Horsley . . . . Insp Taylor
Ronan O'Casey . . . . Stefan Gordoni
Launce Maraschal . . . . Everleigh
Colin Tapley . . . . Lord Valcrist
CRIME Private tec proves Lady's nephew
is behind forgery of rare stamp.

12107
FOOTSTEPS IN THE FOG (90) (A) *tech*
Film Locations (Col)
P: M.J. Frankovich, Maxwell Setton
D: Arthur Lubin
S: (NOVEL) W.W.Jacobs (THE INTERRUPTION)
SC: Lenore Coffee, Dorothy Reid, Arthur Pierson
Stewart Granger . . . . Stephen Lowry
Jean Simmons . . . . Lily Watkins
Bill Travers . . . . David MacDonald
Ronald Squire . . . . Alfred Travers
Finlay Currie . . . . Insp Peters
Belinda Lee . . . . Elizabeth Travers
William Hartnell . . . . Herbert Moresby
Barry Keegan . . . . Matthew Burke
Marjorie Rhodes . . . . Mrs Park
Sheila Manahan . . . . Rose Moresby
Peter Bull . . . . Brasher
Frederick Leister . . . . Dr Simpson
Victor Maddern . . . . Jones
Percy Marmont . . . . Magistrate
CRIME 1905. Blackmailing maid weds
man who killed wife and is framed for own
murder.

12108
MISS TULIP STAYS THE NIGHT (68) (U)
Jaywell (Adelphi)
P: John O.Douglas, Bill Luckwell
D: Leslie Arliss
S: John O. Douglas
Diana Dors . . . . Kate Dax
Patrick Holt . . . . Andrew Dax
Jack Hulbert . . . . PC Feathers
Cicely Courtneidge . . . . . Millicent Tulip
A.E.Matthews . . . . Mr Potts

Joss Ambler . . . . Insp Thorne
Pat Terry-Thomas . . . . . . Judith Gale
COMEDY Novelist proves spinster shot
twin for inheritance.

12109
ROOM IN THE HOUSE (74) (U)
ACT Films (Monarch)
P:SC: Alfred Shaughnessy
D: Maurice Elvey
S: (PLAY) E.Eynon Evans
(BLESS THIS HOUSE)
Patrick Barr . . . . Jack Richards
Hubert Gregg . . . . Hugh Richards
Marjorie Rhodes . . . . Betsy Richards
Leslie Dwyer . . . . Benji Pugh
Rachel Gurney . . . . Mary
Margaret Anderson . . . . . . Christine
Josephine Griffin . . . . Julia
Helen Shingler . . . . Ethel
Anthony Marlowe . . . . David Richards
COMEDY Wales. Widow finds happiness after
visiting homes of three married sons.

12110
NO LOVE FOR JUDY (51) (U)
De Lane Lea (Archway)
D:S: Jacques de Lane Lea
Ellet Mauret . . . . June
Zoe Newton . . . . Judy
COMEDY Riviera. Model on holiday steals
companion's boy friends.

12111
CROSS CHANNEL (61) (A)
Republic Productions
P: William N. Boyle
D: R.G. Springsteen
S: Rex Rienits
Wayne Morris . . . . Tex Parker
Yvonne Furneaux . . . . . Jacqueline Moreau
Arnold Marle . . . . Papa Moreau
Patrick Allen . . . . Hugo Platt
Carl Jaffe . . . . Otto Dagoff
Peter Sinclair . . . . Soapy
Charles Laurence . . . . Jean-Pierre
Michael Golden . . . . Carrick
CRIME Jewel smugglers frame charter
boat skipper for faked murder.

12112
DOLLARS FOR SALE (35) (U)
Ascot House (Adelphi)
P: S: Robert Hartford Davis
D: SC: Denis Kavanagh
Robert Ayres . . . . Ray Blanchard
Earl Cameron . . . . Earl Rutters
John Slater . . . . Loudmouth Willetts
Victor Platt . . . . Insp Mann
Magda Miller . . . . Girl
Larry Cross . . . . Mike Stevens
Bernie Winters . . . . Suspect
Robert Hartford Davis . . . Cop
CRIME FBI agent tracks down Negro
counterfeiter.

12113
DOCTOR AT SEA (93) tech (U)
Group (RFD)
P: Betty E. Box
D: Ralph Thomas
S: (NOVEL) Richard Gordon
SC: Richard Gordon, Nicholas Phipps,
Jack Davies
Dirk Bogarde . . . . Simon Sparrow
Brenda de Banzie . . . . . . Muriel Mallett
Brigitte Bardot . . . . Helene Colbert
James Robertson Justice . . Capt Hogg
Maurice Denham . . . . Easter
Michael Medwin . . . . Traill
Hubert Gregg . . . . Archer

James Kenney . . . . Fellowes
Raymond Huntley . . . . . . Capt Beamish
Geoffrey Keen . . . . Hornbeam
George Coulouris . . . . Carpenter
Noel Purcell . . . . Corbie
Jill Adams . . . . Jill
Joan Sims . . . . Wendy
Frederick Piper . . . . Sandyman
Paul Carpenter . . . . Captain
COMEDY Misadventures of medical officer
aboard passenger-carrying cargo steamer.

12114
ESCAPADE (87) (U)
Pinnacle (Eros)
P: Daniel Angel, Hannah Weinstein
D: Philip Leacock
S: (PLAY) Roger Macdougall
SC: Gilbert Holland
John Mills . . . . John Hampden
Yvonne Mitchell . . . . Stella Hampden
Alastair Sim . . . . Dr Skillingsworth
Jeremy Spenser . . . . Daventry
Andrew Ray . . . . Max Hampden
Marie Lohr . . . . Mrs Hampden
Colin Gordon . . . . Deeson
Peter Asher . . . . Johnny Hampden
COMEDY Schoolboy steals plane and flies
to Vienna to plea for peace.

12115
THAT'S AN ORDER (18) (U)
Grendon (BL-CFF)
P: John Croydon
D: John Irwin
S: J.B.Boothroyd
Peter Butterworth
CHILDREN Slapstick mishaps of grocer's
clumsy assistant.

12116
ERIC WINSTONE BAND SHOW (28) (U)
eastman/scope
Hammer (Ex)
P:D: Michael Carreras
Eric Winstone and his Band
Kenny Baker   Alma Cogan
George Mitchell Singers
MUSICAL

12117
WINDFALL (64) (U)
Mid-Century (Eros)
P: Robert Baker, Monty Berman
D: Henry Cass
S: John Gilling
Lionel Jeffries . . . . Arthur Lee
Jack Watling . . . . John Lee
Gordon Jackson . . . . Leonard
Avice Landone . . . . Mary Lee
Brian Worth . . . . Michael Collins
Patricia Owens . . . . Connie Lee
Cyril Chamberlain . . . . . . Clarkson
COMEDY Draper finds £2,000, his daughter's
fiance steals it, and it turns out to be
counterfeit.

12118
THE MYSTERIOUS BULLET (31) (U)
Merton Park (AA)
P: Alec Snowden
D: Paul Gherzo
S: James Eastwood
Robert Raglan . . . . Insp Dexter
John Warwick . . . . Robert Churchill
Christine Adrian . . . . Emily Thatcher
Carol Marsh . . . . Julie Thatcher
Howard Lang . . . . Patterson
CRIME Ballistic expert traces killer of
widow's fiance.

12119
THE GLASS CAGE (59) (A)
USA: THE GLASS TOMB
Hammer (Ex)
P: Anthony Hinds
D: Montgomery Tully
S: (NOVEL) A.E.Martin (THE OUTSIDERS)
SC: Richard Landau
John Ireland . . . . Pel
Honor Blackman . . . . Jenny
Geoffrey Keen . . . . Stanton
Eric Pohlmann . . . . Sapolio
Sidney James . . . . Tony Lewis
Liam Redmond . . . . Lindley
Sydney Tafler . . . . Rorke
Valerie Vernon . . . . Bella
Arnold Marle . . . . Pop Manoni
Stan Little . . . . Mickelwitz
CRIME World's Champion Starving Man
sees blackmailer murdered and is killed.

AUG

12120
GEORDIE (99) (U) tech USA: WEE GEORDIE
Argonaut (BL)
P: Frank Launder, Sidney Gilliat
D: Frank Launder
S: (NOVEL) David Walker
SC: Frank Launder, Sidney Gilliat
Alastair Sim . . . . The Laird
Bill Travers . . . . . . Geordie MacTaggart
Norah Gorsen . . . . Jean Donaldson
Brian Reece . . . . Dick Harley
Raymond Huntley . . . . . . Rawlins
Miles Malleson . . . . Lord Paunseton
Jack Radcliffe . . . . Rev McNab
Francis de Wolff . . . . Henry Samson
Jameson Clark . . . . Mr MacTaggart
Duncan Macrae. . . . . Schoolmaster
Molly Urquhart . . . . Mrs MacTaggart
Stanley Baxter . . . . Postman
COMEDY Frail Scot takes muscle-building
course and wins Olympics at Melbourne.

12121
STOLEN ASSIGNMENT (62) (U)
ACT Films-Unit (BL)
P: Francis Searle
D: Terence Fisher
S: Sidney Nelson, Maurice Harrison
SC: Kenneth R. Hayles
John Bentley . . . . Mike Billings
Hy Hazell . . . . Jenny Drew
Eddie Byrne . . . . Insp Corcoran
Patrick Holt . . . . Henry Crossley
Joyce Carey . . . . Ida Garnett
Kay Callard . . . . Stella Watson
Jessica Cairns . . . . Marilyn Dawn
Charles Farrell . . . . Percy Simpson
CRIME Reporter and girl prove woman did
not kill her niece.

12122
VALUE FOR MONEY (93) (A) tech
Group (RFD)
P: Sergei Nolbandov
D: Ken Annakin
S: (NOVEL) Derrick Boothroyd
SC: R.F.Delderfield, William Fairchild
John Gregson . . . . Chayley Broadbent
Diana Dors . . . . Ruthine West
Susan Stephen . . . . Ethel
Derek Farr . . . . Duke Popplewell
Frank Pettingell . . . . Mayor Higgins
Charles Victor . . . . Lunn
Ernest Thesiger . . . . Lord Drewsbury
Hal Osmond . . . . Mr Hall
Jill Adams . . . . Joy
Joan Hickson . . . . Mrs Perkins

James Gregson . . . . Oldroyd
Donald Pleasence . . . . Limpy
Leslie Phillips . . . . Robjohns
Ronald Chesney; Paddy Stone; Irving Davis;
Hanwell Silver Band
COMEDY London showgirl spurns Yorkshire
ragman, thinking he is poor.

12123
THE GOLD EXPRESS (58) (U)
Gaumont (RFD)
P: Frank Wells
D: Guy Fergusson
S: Jackson Budd
Vernon Gray . . . . Bob Wright
Ann Walford . . . . Mary Wright
May Hallatt . . . . Agatha Merton
Ivy St Helier . . . . Emma Merton
Patrick Boxill . . . . Mr Rover
John Serrett . . . . Luke Dubois
Delphi Lawrence . . . . Pearl
CRIME Reporter and wife thwart plot to
rob train of gold shipment.

12124
THE FLAW (61) (A)
Cybex (Renown)
P: Geoffrey Goodheart
D: Terence Fisher
S: Brandon Fleming
John Bentley . . . . Paul Oliveri
Donald Houston . . . . John Millway
Rona Anderson . . . . Monica Oliveri
Tonia Berne . . . . Vera
Doris Yorke . . . . Mrs Bower
J. Trevor Davies . . . . . . Sir George Bentham
Cecilia Cavendish . . . . Lady Bentham
CRIME Solicitor foils racing driver's plot
to kill his wife.

12125
CAST A DARK SHADOW (82) (A)
Frobisher (Eros)
P: Daniel Angel
D: Lewis Gilbert
S: (PLAY) Janet Green (MURDER MISTAKEN)
SC: John Cresswell
Dirk Bogarde . . . . Edward Bare
Margaret Lockwood . . . . Freda Jeffries
Kay Walsh . . . . Charlotte Young
Kathleen Harrison . . . . Emmie
Robert Flemyng . . . . Peter Mortimer
Mona Washbourne . . . . . . Monica Bare
Walter Hudd . . . . Coroner
Philip Stainton . . . . Charlie Mann
Lita Roza . . . . Singer
CRIME Brighton. Clerk kills rich wife,
fails to inherit, weds rich barmaid and
tries again.

12126
THE RELUCTANT BRIDE (72) (A)
USA: TWO GROOMS FOR A BRIDE
Tempean (Eros)
P: Robert Baker, Monty Berman
D: Henry Cass
S: Frederick Stephani
John Carroll . . . . Jeff Longstreet
Virginia Bruce . . . . Laura Weeks
Brian Oulton . . . . Prof Baker
Kay Callard . . . . Lola Sinclair
Michael Caridia . . . . Tony Longstreet
Barbara Brown . . . . Ra Longstreet
Kit Terrington . . . . Big Longstreet
Alexander Gauge . . . . Humbold
Donald Stewart . . . . Cadwell
Ann Doran . . . . Violet Blue
COMEDY American millionaire and
entomoligist fall in love while caring
for children of missing relatives.

12127
THE DEEP BLUE SEA (99) (A)
eastman/scope
London (20)
P: Alexander Korda, Anatole Litvak
D: Anatole Litvak
S: (PLAY) Terence Rattigan
SC: Terence Rattigan
Vivien Leigh . . . . Hester Collyer
Kenneth More . . . . Freddie Page
Eric Portman . . . . Miller
Emlyn Williams . . . . . Sir William Collyer
Moira Lister . . . . Dawn Maxwell
Arthur Hill . . . . Jackie Jackson
Dandy Nichols . . . . Mrs Elton
Alec McCowen . . . . Ken Thompson
Jimmy Hanley . . . . Dicer Durston
Miriam Karlin . . . . Barmaid
Heather Thatcher . . . . Lady Dawson
Bill Shine . . . . Golfer
Sidney James . . . . Man
Gibb McLaughlin . . . . Clerk
ROMANCE Judge's wife tries to kill herself
after affair with unreliable pilot.

12128
THE QUATERMASS EXPERIMENT (82) (X)
USA: THE CREEPING UNKNOWN
Hammer-Concanen Recordings (Ex)
P: Anthony Hinds
D: Val Guest
S: (TV SERIAL) Nigel Kneale
(THE QUATERMASS EXPERIMENT)
SC: Val Guest, Richard Landau
Brian Donlevy . . . Prof Bernard Quatermass
Jack Warner . . . . Insp Lomax
Margia Dean . . . . Judith Caroon
Richard Wordsworth . . . . . . Victor Carroon
David King Wood . . . . . . Dr Gordon Briscoe
Thora Hird . . . . Rosie
Gordon Jackson . . . . TV Producer
Harold Lang . . . . Christie
Lionel Jeffries . . . . Blake
Maurice Kaufmann . . . . . . Marsh
Frank Phillips . . . . BBC Announcer
HORROR Sole survivor of first space
rocket becomes vegetable thing.

SEP

12129
THE FLYING EYE (53) (U)
British Films (BL-CFF)
P: William Weedon
D: William C. Hammond
S: (NOVEL) John Newton Chance
SC: William C. Hammond, Ken Hughes,
Darrell Catling
David Hannaford . . . . Bunstuffer
Julia Lockwood . . . . Angela
Harcourt Williams . . . . Professor
Ivan Craig . . . . Mayer
Geoffrey Sumner . . . . . . Colonel Audacious
CHILDREN Model plane with television eye
helps children catch spies.

12130
THE WOMAN FOR JOE (91) *tech* (U)
Group (RFD)
P: Leslie Parkyn
D: George More O'Ferrall
S: (STORY) Neil Paterson (AND DELILAH)
SC: Neil Paterson
Diane Cilento . . . . Mary
George Baker . . . . Joe Harrap
David Kossoff . . . . Max
Jimmy Kairoubi . . . . George Wilson
Violet Farebrother . . . . Ma Gollatz
Man Mountain Dean . . . . . . Vendini
Earl Cameron . . . . Lemmie
Sydney Tafler . . . . Butch

Patrick Westwood . . . . Freddie the Kid
Derek Sydney . . . . Harry the Spice
Verna Gilmore . . . . Princess Circassy
Martin Miller . . . . Iggy Pulitzer
Meier Tzelniker . . . . Sol Goldstein
Miriam Karlin . . . . Gladys
Frank Paulo . . . . Stephan
Amy Veness . . . . Landlady
ROMANCE Midget loves foreign singer who
loves fairground owner.

12131
MAN OF THE MOMENT (88) (U)
Group (RFD)
P: Hugh Stewart
D: John Paddy Carstairs
S: Maurice Cowan
SC: John Paddy Carstairs, Vernon Sylvaine
Norman Wisdom . . . . Norman
Lana Morris . . . . Penny
Belinda Lee . . . . Sonia
Jerry Desmonde . . . . Jackson
Karel Stepanek . . . . Lom
Garry Marsh . . . . Delegate
Inia te Wiata . . . . Toki
Evelyn Roberts . . . . Sir Horace
Violet Farebrother . . . . Queen Tawaki
Martin Miller . . . . Tailor
Lisa Gastoni . . . . Chambermaid
Charles Hawtrey . . . . Producer
Man Mountain Dean . . . . . Bodyguard
Beverley Sisters; Macdonald Hobley;
Phillip Harben; Ronnie Waldman; "The
Grove Family"; Bruce Seton
COMEDY Geneva. Foreign powers try to
kill minor UN clerk who is accidentally
important.

12132
ONE WAY OUT (61) (U)
Major (RFD)
P: John Temple-Smith, Francis Edge
D: Francis Searle
S: John Temple-Smith, Jean Scott-Rogers
SC: Jonathan Roche
Jill Adams . . . . Shirley Harcourt
Eddie Byrne . . . . Supt Harcourt
Lyndon Brook . . . . Leslie Parrish
John Chandos . . . . Danvers
Olive Milbourne . . . . Mrs Harcourt
Arthur Howard . . . . Marriott
Ryck Rydon . . . . Harry
Anne Valery . . . . Carol Martin
CRIME Jewel thieves blackmail detective
by incriminating his daughter.

12133
I AM A CAMERA (99) (X)
Remus (IFD)
P: Jack Clayton
D: Henry Cornelius
S: (PLAY) John Van Druten (STORIES)
Christopher Isherwood
SC: John Collier
Julie Harris . . . . Sally Bowles
Laurence Harvey . . . . Christopher Isherwood
Shelley Winters . . . . Natalie Landauer
Ron Randell . . . . Clive
Lea Seidl . . . . Frau Schneider
Anton Diffring . . . . Fritz
Jean Gargoet . . . . Pierre
Frederick Valk . . . . Doctor
Tutte Lemkow . . . . Electro-Therapist
Patrick McGoohan . . . . Swede
Stanley Maxted . . . . Editor
Julia Arnall . . . . Model
Zoe Newton . . . . Cigarette Girl
Stan Bernard Trio
COMEDY Berlin, 1932. Poor writer shares room
with American girl singer who feigns pregnancy.

OCT

12134
TOUCH AND GO (85) (U) *tech*
USA: THE LIGHT TOUCH
Ealing (RFD)
P: Seth Holt
D: Michael Truman
S: William & Tania Rose
SC: William Rose

Jack Hawkins	Jim Fletcher
Margaret Johnston	Helen Fletcher
Roland Culver	Reg Fairbright
John Fraser	Richard Kenyon
June Thorburn	Peggy Fletcher
James Hayter	M.B.Kimball
Alison Leggatt	Alice Fairbright
Margaret Halstan	Mrs Pritchett
Henry Longhurst	Mr Pritchett
Basil Dignam	Stevens
Bessie Love	Mrs Baxter

COMEDY Furniture designer prepares to emigrate to Australia, but events change his mind.

12135
THE MAN ON THE CLIFF (23) (U)
E.J.Fancey (NR)
D: Robert Hartford Davis
S: Maxwell Munden
Ronald Leigh-Hunt
Adrienne Scott
Billie Lane
Russell Carr
CRIME Amnesiac changes identities with corpse of atomic scientist.

12136
TIMESLIP (93) (A) USA: THE ATOMIC MAN
Anglo-Guild (AA)
P: Alec Snowden
D:SC: Ken Hughes
S: (TV PLAY) Charles Eric Maine

Gene Nelson	Mike Delaney
Faith Domergue	Jill Friday
Joseph Tomelty	Insp Cleary
Donald Gray	Maitland
Vic Perry	Vasquo
Peter Arne	Stephen Maitland
Launce Maraschal	Editor
Charles Hawtrey	Scruffy
Martin Wyldeck	Dr Preston
Carl Jaffe	Dr Marks
Barry Mackay	Insp Hammond

CRIME Spies injure nuclear physicist and replace him with his double.

12137
STOCK CAR (68) (A)
Balblair (Butcher)
P: A.R.Rawlinson
D: Wolf Rilla
S: A.R.Rawlinson, Victor Lyndon

Paul Carpenter	Larry Duke
Rona Anderson	Katie Glebe
Susan Shaw	Gina
Harry Fowler	Monty Allbright
Robert Rietty	Roberto
Paul Whitsun Jones	Turk McNeil
Sabrina	Trixie
Alma Taylor	Nurse Sprott
Lorrae Desmond	Singer

SPORT American driver thwarts crooks and wins stock car race and girl garage-owner.

12138
STOLEN TIME (69) (A)
USA: BLONDE BLACKMAILER
Charles Deane (BL)
D:S: Charles Deane

Richard Arlen	Tony Pelassier
Susan Shaw	Carole Carlton
Constance Leigh	Marie
Vincent Ball	Johnson
Andrea Malandrinos	Papa Pelassier
Alathea Siddons	Mama Pelassier

CRIME Ex-convict tracks down man who framed him for killing blackmailing woman.

12139
THE STOLEN AIRLINER (59) (U)
ABPC (BL-CFF)
P: Howard Thomas
D: SC: Don Sharp
S: (NOVEL) John Pudney (THURSDAY ADVENTURE)

Fella Edmunds	Fred
Diana Day	Anne
Peter Dyneley	Uncle George
Michael Macguire	John
Nicola Braithwaite	Kitty
Ballard Berkeley	Mr Head
Iris Russell	Mrs Head
David King-Wood	Controller

CHILDREN Air cadets save uncle and airliner from spies.

12140
THEY CAN'T HANG ME (75) (A)
Vandyke (IFD)
P: Roger Proudlock
D: Val Guest
S: (NOVEL) Leonard Moseley
SC: Val Guest, Val Valentine

Terence Morgan	Insp Brown
Yolande Donlan	Jill
Andre Morell	Robert Pitt
Ursula Howells	Antonia Pitt
Anthony Oliver	Newcome
Reginald Beckwith	Harold
Guido Lorraine	Piotr Revsky
Basil Dignam	WC Riddle
Raymond Rollett	Sir Robert Rosper

CRIME Inspector unmasks scientist behind spy ring seeking atom secrets.

12141
JOE MACBETH (90) (A)
Film Locations (Columbia)
P: M.J.Frankovich, George Maynard
D: Ken Hughes
S: (PLAY) William Shakespeare (MACBETH)
SC: Philip Yordan

Paul Douglas	Joe Macbeth
Ruth Roman	Lily Macbeth
Bonar Colleano	Lennie
Gregoire Aslan	Duca
Sidney James	Banky
Harry Green	Big Dutch
Walter Crisham	Angus
Kay Callard	Ruth
Robert Arden	Ross
George Margo	Assassin
Minerva Pious	Rosie
Nicholas Stuart	Duffy

CRIME America. Gangster's wife urges him to kill his boss and take over.

NOV

12142
A TIME TO KILL (65) (A)
Fortress (ABP)
P: Clive Nicholas
D: Charles Saunders
S: Doreen Montgomery

Jack Watling	Dennis Willows
Rona Anderson	Sallie Harbord
John Horsley	Peter Hastings
Russell Napier	Insp Simmons
Keneth Kent	Dr Cole

Mary Jones	Florence Cole
Alastair Hunter	Sgt Thorpe
Joan Hickson	Miss Edinger
John le Mesurier	Phineas

CRIME Chemist's fiancee proves he did not poison blackmailing girl.

12143
OH ROSALINDA !! (101) (U) *tech/scope*
Powell & Pressburger (ABP)
P:D:SC: Michael Powell, Emeric Pressburger
S: (OPERA) Johann Strauss (DIE FLEDERMAUS)

Michael Redgrave	Col Eisenstein
Ludmilla Tcherina	Rosalinda
Anton Walbrook	Dr Falke
Mel Ferrer	Capt Westerman
Dennis Price	Maj Frank
Anthony Quayle	Gen Orlofsky
Anneliese Rothenberger	Adele
Oska Sima	Frosh
Richard Marner	Judge

VOICES: Sari Barabas; Alexander Young; Denis Dowling; Walter Berry
MUSICAL Vienna. French colonel escapes arrest and flirts with his own wife at masked ball.

12144
KING'S RHAPSODY (93) (U) *eastman/scope*
Everest (BL)
P:D: Herbert Wilcox
S: (PLAY) Ivor Novello
SC: Pamela Bower, Christopher Hassall, A.P.Herbert

Anna Neagle	Marta Karillos
Errol Flynn	Prince Richard
Patrice Wymore	Princess Christiane
Martita Hunt	Queen Mother
Finlay Currie	King Paul
Francis de Wolff	Prime Minister
Joan Benham	Countess Astrid
Reginald Tate	King Peter
Miles Malleson	Jules

Edmund Hockridge; Lionel Blair; Jon Gregory; Terence Theobald.
MUSICAL Ruritania. Abdicated King's mistress feigns marriage to force him back to wife.

12145
THE BLUE PETER (93) (U) *eastman*
USA: NAVY HEROES
Group 3 (BL)
P: Herbert Mason
D: Wolf Rilla
S: Don Sharp
SC: Don Sharp, John Pudney

Kieron Moore	Mike Merriworth
Greta Gynt	Mary Griffith
Sarah Lawson	Gwyneth Thomas
Mervyn Johns	Capt Snow
John Charlesworth	Andrew Griffin
Harry Fowler	Charlie Barton
Mary Kerridge	Mrs Snow
Ram Gopal	Dr Tigara
Russell Napier	Raymond Curtiss
Brian Roper	Tony Mullins
Anthony Newley	Sparrow
Vincent Ball	Digger

DRAMA Aberdovy. Naval hero, brainwashed in Korea, becomes instructor at Sea School.

12146
NO SMOKING (72) (U)
Tempean (Eros)
P: Robert Baker, Monty Berman
D: Henry Cass
S: (TV PLAY) Rex Rienits, George Moresby-White

SC: Kenneth R. Hayles
Reg Dixon . . . . Reg Bates
Belinda Lee . . . . Miss Tonkins
Lionel Jeffries . . . . George Pogson
Myrtle Rowe . . . . Milly
Ruth Trouncer . . . . Joyce
Peter Martyn . . . . Hal
COMEDY Village chemist invents anti-
smoking pill and thwarts tobacco magnate.

12147
STORM OVER THE NILE (107) (U)
tech/scope
London-Big Ben (IFD)
P: Zoltan Korda
D: Zoltan Korda, Terence Young
S: (NOVEL) A.E.W.Mason
(THE FOUR FEATHERS)
SC: R.C.Sheriff, Lajos Biro, Arthur Wimperis
Anthony Steel . . . . Harry Faversham
Laurence Harvey . . . . . John Durrance
James Robertson Justice . . . Gen Burroughs
Mary Ure . . . . Mary Burroughs
Geoffrey Keen . . . . Dr Sutton
Ronald Lewis . . . . Peter Burroughs
Ian Carmichael . . . . Tom Willoughby
Michael Hordern . . . . Gen Faversham
Jack Lambert . . . . Colonel
Christopher Lee . . . . Karaga Pasha
Ferdy Mayne . . . . Dr Harraz
Sam Kydd . . . . Joe
WAR 1895. Coward redeems himself by
saving friends from capture in Sudan.

12148
THE BESPOKE OVERCOAT (32) (A)
Remus (IFD)
P:D: Jack Clayton
S: (STORY) Nikolai Gogol (THE CLOAK)
(PLAY) Wolf Mankowitz
SC: Wolf Mankowitz
Alfie Bass . . . . Fender
David Kossoff . . . . Morry
Alan Tilvern . . . . Ranting
Alfie Dean . . . . Gravedigger
FANTASY Old Jew dies from cold and
returns for promised overcoat. (AA: Best
short, 1957; BFA: Special award, 1958).

12149
PORTRAIT OF ALISON (84) (A)
USA: POSTMARK FOR DANGER
Insignia (AA)
P: Frank Godwin
D: Guy Green
S: (TV SERIAL) Francis Durbridge
SC: Guy Green, Ken Hughes
Robert Beatty . . . . Tim Forrester
Terry Moore . . . . Alison Ford
William Sylvester . . . . David Forrester
Geoffrey Keen . . . . Insp Colby
Josephine Griffin . . . . Jill Stewart
Allan Cuthbertson . . . . . . Henry Carmichael
Henry Oscar . . . . Smith
William Lucas . . . . Dorking
Terence Alexander . . . . . . Fenby
CRIME Diamond smuggler kills artist's
brother and model.

12150
MURDER ANONYMOUS (31) (A)
Merton Park (AA)
P: Alec Snowden
D: Ken Hughes
S: James Eastwood
N: Edgar Lustgarten
Peter Arne . . . . Douglas Sheldon
Jill Bennett . . . . Mrs Sheldon
Ewen Solon . . . . Insp Conway
CRIME Inspector proves blind man
murdered wife's lover.

DEC
12151
A YANK IN ERMINE (85) (U) eastman
Monarch
P: William Gell
D: Gordon Parry
S: (NOVEL) John Paddy Carstairs
(SOLID SAID THE EARL)
SC: John Paddy Carstairs
Peter Thompson . . . . Joe Turner
Noelle Middleton . . . . Angela
Harold Lloyd jr . . . . Butch
Diana Decker . . . . Gloria
Jon Pertwee . . . . Slowburn
Reginald Beckwith . . . . . . Kimp
Edward Chapman . . . . . Duke of Fontenham
Richard Wattis . . . . Boone
Guy Middleton . . . . Bertram Maltravers
Harry Locke . . . . Clayton
Jennifer Jayne . . . . Enid
Sidney James . . . . Manager
COMEDY USAAF pilot inherits earldom
and falls for duke's daughter.

12152
SIMON AND LAURA (91) (U) tech
Group (RFD)
P: Teddy Baird
D: Muriel Box
S: (PLAY) Alan Melville
SC: Peter Blackmore
Peter Finch . . . . Simon Foster
Kay Kendall . . . . Laura Foster
Muriel Pavlow . . . . Janet Honeyman
Hubert Gregg . . . . Bertie Burton
Maurice Denham . . . . Wilson
Ian Carmichael . . . . David Prentice
Richard Wattis . . . . Controller
Thora Hird . . . . Jessie
Terence Longdon . . . . Barney
Clive Parritt . . . . Timothy
Alan Wheatley . . . . Adrian Lee
Joan Hickson . . . . Barmaid
Cyril Chamberlain . . . . . . Bert
Marianne Stone . . . . Elsie
Muriel George . . . . Grandma
Charles Hawtrey . . . . Porter
Gilbert Harding; Lady Barnet; John Ellison;
George Cansdale; Peter Haigh.
COMEDY Actors verging on divorce feign
happy marriage for TV serial.

12153
AN ALLIGATOR NAMED DAISY (88) (U) tech
Group (RFD)
P: Raymond Stross
D: J. Lee-Thompson
S: (NOVEL) Charles Terrot
SC: Jack Davies
Donald Sinden . . . . Peter Weston
Diana Dors . . . . Vanessa Colebrook
Jean Carson . . . . Moira
James Robertson Justice . . . Sir James
Stanley Holloway . . . . General
Roland Culver . . . . Col Weston
Margaret Rutherford . . . . . Prudence Croquet
Avice Landone . . . . Mrs Weston
Stephen Boyd . . . . Albert
Richard Wattis . . . . Hoskins
Henry Kendall . . . . Valet
Michael Shepley . . . . Judge
Charles Victor . . . . Sgt
Ernest Thesiger . . . . Notcher
Wilfrid Lawson . . . . Irishman
George Moon . . . . Al
Jimmy Edwards; Gilbert Harding; Frankie
Howerd; Ronnie Stevens; Ken Mackintosh
and his Band
COMEDY Songwriter with pet alligator
prefers Irish girl to heiress.

12154
THE LADYKILLERS (97) (U) tech
Ealing (RFD)
P: Seth Holt
D: Alexander Mackendrick
S: William Rose
Alec Guinness . . . . Prof Marcus
Cecil Parker . . . . The Major
Herbert Lom . . . . Louis
Peter Sellers . . . . Harry
Danny Green . . . . One-Round
Jack Warner . . . . Supt
Frankie Howerd . . . . Barrow Boy
Katie Johnson . . . . Mrs Wilberforce
Philip Stainton . . . . Sgt
Fred Griffiths . . . . Junk Man
Kenneth Connor . . . . Cab Driver
Edie Martin . . . . Lettice
Jack Melford . . . . Detective
COMEDY Old lady's musical lodgers are
bank robbers. (BFA: 1955; Best screenplay,
Best actress).

12155
ALL FOR MARY (79) (U) eastman
Rank (RFD)
P: Paul Soskin
D: Wendy Toye
S: (PLAY) Harold Brock, Kay Bannerman
SC: Paul Soskin, Peter Blackmore,
Alan Melville
Nigel Patrick . . . . Clive Morton
Kathleen Harrison . . . . . . Nannie Cartwright
David Tomlinson . . . . Humpy Miller
Jill Day . . . . Mary
David Hurst . . . . M. Victor
Leo McKern . . . . Gaston Nikopopoulos
Nicholas Phipps . . . . General
Joan Young . . . . Mrs Hackenfleuger
Lionel Jeffries . . . . Maitre d'Hotel
Paul Hardtmuth . . . . Porter
Fabia Drake . . . . Opulent Lady
Tommy Farr . . . . Bruiser
COMEDY Switzerland. Old nanny nurses two
love-rivals with chicken pox.

12156
DIAL 999 (86) (A) USA: THE WAY OUT
Merton Park (AA)
P: Alec Snowden
D:-SC: Montgomery Tully
S: (NOVEL) Bruce Graeme (THE WAY OUT)
Gene Nelson . . . . Greg Carradine
Mona Freeman . . . . Terry Carradine
John Bentley . . . . Sgt Seagrave
Michael Goodliffe . . . . John Moffatt
Sydney Tafler . . . . Cressett
Charles Victor . . . . Tom Smithers
Paula Byrne . . . . Vera Bellamy
Michael Golden . . . . Insp Keyes
Arthur Lovegrove . . . . George
Charles Mortimer . . . . Harding
CRIME Bookie's killer tries to leave England
by secret escape route for criminals.

12157
JOSEPHINE AND MEN (98) (U) eastman
Charter (BL)
P: John Boulting
D: Roy Boulting
S: Nigel Balchin
SC: Roy Boulting, Frank Harvey, Nigel Balchin
Glynis Johns . . . . Josephine Luton
Jack Buchanan . . . . Charles Luton
Donald Sinden . . . . Alan Hartley
Peter Finch . . . . David Hewer
William Hartnell . . . . Insp Parsons
Ronald Squire . . . . Frederick Luton
Victor Maddern . . . . Henry
Heather Thatcher . . . . May Luton
Thorley Walters . . . . Salesman

Hugh Moxey . . . . Inspector
Laurence Naismith . . . . Porter
John le Mesurier . . . . Registrar
Lisa Gastoni . . . . Girl
COMEDY Playwright's wife hides fugitive
ex-fiance.

12158
COCKLESHELL HEROES (98) (U)
tech/scope
Warwick (Col) reissue: 1964 (14 mins cut)
P: Irving Allen, Albert Broccoli,
Phil C. Samuel
D: Jose Ferrer
S: (BOOK) George Kent
SC: Richard Maibaum, Bryan Forbes
Jose Ferrer . . . . Maj Stringer
Trevor Howard . . . . Capt Thompson
Dora Bryan . . . . Myrtle
Victor Maddern . . . . Sgt Craig
Anthony Newley . . . . Marine Clarke
David Lodge . . . . Marine Ruddock
Peter Arne . . . . Marine Stephens
Percy Herbert . . . . Lomas
Walter Fitzgerald . . . . Commandant
Beatrice Campbell . . . . Mrs Ruddock

Karel Stepanek . . . . Assistant
Sydney Tafler . . . . PC
Gladys Henson . . . . Barmaid
Patric Doonan. . . . . Sailor
WAR 1942. Ten marines in canoe raid
Bordeaux docks with limpet mines.

12159
RICHARD III (161) (U) *tech*
London-Big Ben (IFD)
P: Laurence Olivier
D: Laurence Olivier, Anthony Bushell
S: (PLAY) William Shakespeare
SC: Alan Dent
Laurence Olivier . . . . Richard III
John Gielgud . . . . Clarence
Claire Bloom . . . . Lady Anne
Ralph Richardson . . . . Buckingham
Alec Clunes . . . . Hastings
Cedric Hardwicke . . . . Edward IV
Stanley Baker . . . . Henry Tudor
Laurence Naismith . . . . . . Stanley
Norman Wooland . . . . Catesby
Mary Kerridge . . . . Queen Elizabeth
Pamela Brown . . . . Jane Shore
Helen Haye . . . . Duchess of York

John Laurie . . . . Lovel
Esmond Knight . . . . Ratcliffe
Michael Gough . . . . Dighton
Andrew Cruickshank . . . . . Brakenbury
Clive Morton . . . . Rivers
Nicholas Hannen . . . . Archbishop
Russell Thorndike . . . . Priest
HISTORY Richard murders his way to
the throne of England (BFA: 1955: Best
British Film, Best Film, Best Actor).

12160
THE RIGHT PERSON (30) (A) *eastman/scope*
Hammer (Ex)
P: Michael Carreras
D: Peter Cotes
S: Philip Mackie
Margo Lorenz . . . . Martha Jorgensen
Douglas Wilmer . . . . Mr Rasmussen
David Markham . . . . Mr Jorgensen
DRAMA Copenhagen. Man suspects newlywed
husband is wartime traitor who stole
Resistance funds.

1956

JAN

12161
JUST FOR YOU (31) (U) *eastman/scope*
Hammer (Ex)
P:D: Michael Carreras
Cyril Stapleton and the Show Band
Joan Regan; Ronnie Harris
MUSICAL

12162
IT'S A GREAT DAY (71) (U)
Grove (Butcher)
P: Victor Lyndon
D: John Warrington
S: (TV SERIAL) Roland & Michael
Pertwee (THE GROVES)
SC: Roland & Michael Pertwee
Ruth Dunning . . . .   Gladys Grove
Edward Evans . . . .   Bob Grove
Sidney James . . . .   Harry Mason
Vera Day . . . .   Blondie
Sheila Sweet . . . .   Pat Grove
Peter Bryant . . . .   Jack Grove
Nancy Roberts . . . .   Gran
Margaret Downs . . . .   Daphne Grove
Christopher Beeny . . . .   Lennie Grove
Victor Maddern . . . .   Charlie Mead
John Stuart . . . .   Inspector
Henry Oscar . . . .   Surveyor
Marjorie Rhodes . . . .   Landlady
COMEDY Builder suspected of stealing
tiles for new estate.

12163
FUN AT ST FANNY'S (80) (U) *scope*
Grand Alliance (BL)
P: David Dent
D: Maurice Elvey
S: (CHARACTERS) Douglas Robinson
SC: Peter Noble, Denis Waldock, Anthony
Verney, Fred Emney
Fred Emney . . . .   Dr Jankers
Cardew Robinson . . . .   Cardew the Cad
Vera Day . . . .   Maisie
Johnny Brandon . . . .   Fanshawe
Davy Kaye . . . .   Ferdy
Freddie Mills . . . .   Harry the Scar
Gerald Campion . . . .   Fatty Gilbert
Miriam Karlin . . . .   Mildred
Claude Hulbert . . . .   Winkle
Kynaston Reeves . . . .   McTavish
Gabrielle Brune . . . .   Matron
Stanley Unwin . . . .   The Guide
Dino Galvani . . . .   Pumpernickel
Peter Butterworth . . . .   The Potter
Francis Langford's Singing Scholars
COMEDY Gambling master will inherit if
he expels his 25-year old pupil.

12164
JOHNNY, YOU'RE WANTED (71) (A)
Anglo-Amalgamated
P: George Maynard
D: Vernon Sewell
S: (TV SERIES) Maurice McLoughlin
SC: Michael Leighton, Frank Driscoll
John Slater . . . .   Johnny
Alfred Marks . . . .   Marks
Garry Marsh . . . .   Balsamo
Chris Halward . . . .   Julie
Joan Rhodes . . . .   Herself
Jack Stewart . . . .   Insp Bennett
John Stuart . . . .   Surgeon
Thelma Ruby . . . .   PCW/Smuggler
Ann Lynn . . . .   Chorus Girl
CRIME Lorry driver unmasks joke salesmen as
drug smugglers.

12165
FLIGHT FROM VIENNA (58) (U)
E.J.Fancey (NR)
D:S: Denis Kavanagh
John Bentley . . . .   Capt Lawson
Theodore Bikel . . . .   Kosice
Adrienne Scott . . . .
Carina Helm . . . .
Donald Scott . . . .
DRAMA Hungarian escapes and proves his
sincerity by returning to save scientist.

12166
YOU CAN'T ESCAPE (77) (A)
Forth Films (ABP)
P: Robert Hall
D: Wilfred Eades
S: (NOVEL) Alan Kennington
(SHE DIED YOUNG)
SC: Robert Hall, Doreen Montgomery
Noelle Middleton . . . .   Kay March
Guy Rolfe . . . .   David Anstruther
Robert Urquhart   . . . .   Peter Darwin
Peter Reynolds . . . .   Rodney Nixon
Elizabeth Kentish . . . .   Claire Segar
Barbara Cavan . . . .   Aunt Sue
Martin Boddey . . . .   Insp Crane
Thorley Walters . . . .   Chadwick
Jacqueline Mackenzie . . . . . .   Mrs Baggerley
CRIME Heiress's fiance kills his ex-fiancee
and blackmailer.

12167
THE CASE OF THE MUKKINESE BATTLE-
HORN (30) (U)
Cinead-Marlborough (Archway)
P: Jon Pennington, Harry Booth, Michael
Deeley
D: Joseph Stirling
S: Larry Stephens
SC: Jon Pennington, Harry Booth, Spike
Milligan, Peter Sellers
Peter Sellers . . . .   Insp Quilt/Henry
                    Crun/Sid Crimp/Sir Jervis Fruit
Spike Milligan . . . .   Sgt Brown/Eccles/
                    Catchpole Burkington/Minnie
Dick Emery . . . . . .   Nodule/Maurice Ponk
COMEDY Inspector unmasks museum
curator as head of horn-smuggling ring.

12168
THE GAMMA PEOPLE (79) (A)
Warwick (Col) *reissue:* 1961 (Unifilms)
P: Irving Allen, Albert Broccoli, John
Gossage
D: John Gilling
S: Louis Pollack
SC: John Gilling, John Gossage
Paul Douglas . . . .   Mike Wilson
Eva Bartok . . . .   Paula Wendt
Leslie Phillips . . . .   Howard Meade
Walter Rilla . . . .   Boronski
Philip Leaver . . . .   Koerner
Martin Miller . . . .   Lochner
Michael Caridia . . . .   Hugo
Pauline Drewett . . . .   Hedda
Jackie Lane . . . .   Anna
Rosalie Crutchley . . . .   Frau Bikstein
St John Stuart . . . .   Goon
FANTASY Europe. Scientist's rays turn
adults into idiots and children into geniuses.

12169
THE ADVENTURES OF QUENTIN DURWARD
(100) (U) *eastman/scope*
MGM British
P: Pandro S. Berman
D: Richard Thorpe
S: (NOVEL) Sir Walter Scott
(QUENTIN DURWARD)
SC: George Froeschel, Robert Ardrey
Robert Taylor . . . .   Quentin Durward
Kay Kendall . . . .   Isabelle de Croye
Robert Morley . . . .   Louis XI
George Cole . . . .   Hayraddin
Alec Clunes . . . .   Duke of Burgundy
Duncan Lamont . .   Count William de la Marck
Laya Raki . . . .   Gipsy Dancer
Marius Goring . . . .   Count de Creville
Wilfrid Hyde White . . . . . .   Master Oliver
Eric Pohlmann . . . .   Gluckmeister
Harcourt Williams . . . .   Bishop
Michael Goodliffe . . . . . .   Count de Dunois
Nicholas Hannen . . . .   Cardinal Banue
Ernest Thesiger . . . .   Lord Crawford
ADVENTURE France, 1465. Lord's nephew
saves Duke's ward from political kidnapping.

12170
LOST (89) (A) *eastman* USA: TEARS FOR
SIMON
Rank (RFD)
P: Vivian A. Cox, Sydney Box
D: Guy Green
S: Janet Green
David Farrar . . . .   Insp Craig
David Knight . . . .   Lee Cochrane
Julia Arnall . . . .   Sue Cochrane
Eleanor Summerfield . . . .   Sgt Cook
Anthony Oliver . . . .   Sgt Lyel
Thora Hird . . . .   Landlady
Anne Paige . . . .   Nanny
Marjorie Rhodes . . . .   Mrs Jeffries
Anna Turner . . . .   Mrs Robey
Everley Gregg . . . .   Viscountess
Meredith Edwards . .. .   Sgt Davies
Irene Prador . . . .   Mitzi
Shirley Anne Field . . . .   Girl
Eileen Peel . . . .   Henrietta Gay
Barbara Shotter . . . .   Mrs Martin
Alma Taylor . . . .   Mrs Bellamy
CRIME Inspector finds neurotic widow
who stole young couple's baby.

FEB

12171
CLOAK WITHOUT DAGGER (68) (A)
USA: OPERATION CONSPIRACY
Balblair (Butcher)
P: S: A.R.Rawlinson
D: Joseph Stirling
Philip Friend . . . .   Felix Gretton
Mary Mackenzie . . . .   Kyra Gabaine
Leslie Dwyer . . . .   Fred Borcombe
Allan Cuthbertson . . . .   Col Packham
John G. Heller . . . .   Peppi Gilroudian
Chin Yu . . . .   Yan Chu
Bill Nagy . . . .   Mario Oromonda
Patrick Jordan . . . .   Capt Wallis
CRIME Intelligence man and fashion
reporter catch spies.

12172
ON SUCH A NIGHT (37) (U) *eastman*
Screen Audiences (RFD)
D: Anthony Asquith
S: Paul Dehn
David Knight . . . .   Cornell
Josephine Griffin . . . .   Virginia
Marie Lohr . . . .   Lady Falconbridge
MUSICAL Glyndebourne. US tourist falls
in love at opera.

12173
JUMPING FOR JOY (88) (U)
Rank (RFD)
P: Raymond Stross

D: John Paddy Carstairs
S: Jack Davies, Henry E.Blyth

Frankie Howerd	Willie Joy
Stanley Holloway	Jack Montague
A.E.Matthews	Lord Cranfield
Tony Wright	Vincent
Susan Beaumont	Susan
Alfie Bass	Blagg
Joan Hickson	Lady Cranfield
Lionel Jeffries	Bert Benton
Terence Longdon	John
Colin Gordon	Max
Richard Wattis	Carruthers
Ewen Solon	Haines

COMEDY Sacked sweeper's greyhound wins race and he catches doping gang.

12174
NOW AND FOREVER (91) *tech* (U)
Anglofilm (ABP)
P:D: Mario Zampi
S: (PLAY) R.F.Delderfield
(THE ORCHARD WALLS)
SC: R.F.Delderfield, Michael Pertwee

Janette Scott	Janette Grant
Vernon Gray	Mike Pritchard
Kay Walsh	Miss Muir
Jack Warner	Mr Pritchard
Pamela Brown	Mrs Grant
David Kossoff	Pawnbroker
Wilfrid Lawson	Gossage
Ronald Squire	Waiter
Sonia Dresdel	Miss Fox
Guy Middleton	Hector
Charles Victor	Farmer
Marjorie Rhodes	Farmer's Wife
Bryan Forbes	Frisby
Michael Pertwee	Reporter

ROMANCE Schoolgirl leaves divorced mother and elopes to Gretna.

12175
1984 (90) (X)
Holiday (ABP)
P: N. Peter Rathvon
D: Michael Anderson
S: (NOVEL) George Orwell
SC: William Templeton, Ralph Gilbert Bettinson

Edmond O'Brien	Winston Smith
Jan Sterling	Julia
Michael Redgrave	O'Connor
David Kossoff	Charrington
Mervyn Johns	Jones
Donald Pleasence	Parsons
Carol Wolveridge	Selina Parsons
Ernest Clark	Announcer
Ronan O'Casey	Rutherford
Kenneth Griffith	Prisoner

FANTASY History reviser falls in love and rebels against Big Brother's regime.

12176
DOUBLECROSS (71) (U)
Beaconsfield (BL)
P: Donald Taylor
D: Anthony Squire
S: (NOVEL) Kem Bennett
(THE QUEER FISH)
SC: Kem Bennett, Anthony Squire

Donald Houston	Albert Pascoe
William Hartnell	Whiteway
Fay Compton	Alice Pascoe
Delphi Lawrence	Anna Krassin
Anton Diffring	Dmitri Krassin
Frank Lawton	Chief Constable
John Blythe	Fred Trewin
Allan Cuthbertson	Clifford
Bruce Gordon	Harry Simms
Raymond Francis	Insp Harris
Ann Stephens	Rose

CRIME Cornwall. Salmon poacher finds passengers are Soviet spies.

12177
THE SECRET TENT (69) (A)
Forward (BL)
P: Nat Miller, Frank Bevis
D: Don Chaffey
S: (PLAY) Elizabeth Addeyman
SC: Jan Read

Donald Gray	Chris Martyn
Andree Melly	Ruth Martyn
Jean Anderson	Mrs Martyn
Sonia Dresdel	Miss Mitchum-Browne
Andrew Cruickshank	Insp Thornton
Dinah Ann Rogers	Sally
Peter Hammond	Smith
Conrad Phillips	Sgt

CRIME Man finds missing wife helping her burglar brother escape justice.

12178
NOT SO DUSTY (81) (U)
Jaywell (Eros)
P: Bill Luckwell, D.E.A.Winn
D:SC: Maclean Rogers
S: Wally Patch, Frank Atkinson, Kathleen Butler, H.F.Maltby

Joy Nichols	Lobelia
Bill Owen	Dusty
Leslie Dwyer	Nobby Clark
Harold Berens	Driver
Roddy Hughes	Mr Layton
Ellen Pollock	Agatha
Wally Patch	Porter
Dandy Nichols	Mrs Clark
William Simons	Derek Clark
Totti Trueman Taylor	Miss Duncan
Bill Shine	Alistair

COMEDY Two dustmen search for valuable old book wanted by collector.

12179
THE NARROWING CIRCLE (66) (A)
Fortress (Eros)
P: Frank Bevis
D: Charles Saunders
S: (NOVEL) Julian Symonds
SC: Doreen Montgomery

Paul Carpenter	Dave Nelson
Hazel Court	Rosemary Speed
Russell Napier	Sir Henry Dimmock
Trevor Reid	Insp "Dumb" Crambo
Paula Byrne	Laura Martin
June Ashley	Christy
Ferdy Mayne	Bill Strayte
Basil Dignam	George Pacey

CRIME Crime writer proves he did not kill rival for editorial post.

12180
THE MESSAGE (31) (A)
Clara Urquhart (Curzon)
D: S: Enrico Pratt

Michael Grover	John Russell
William Patrick	Bill Jackson
Michael Nightingale	The German
Peter Brinson	The Officer

WAR Wounded British soldier carrying vital message meets wounded German soldier.

12181
THE MAN WHO NEVER WAS (103) (U)
eastman/scope
Sumar (20) *reissue:* 1960 (20 mins cut)
P: Andre Hakim, Maxwell Setton
D: Ronald Neame
S: (BOOK) Ewen Montagu
SC: Nigel Balchin

Clifton Webb	Cdr Ewen Montagu
Gloria Grahame	Lucy Sherwood
Robert Flemyng	Lt George Acres
Josephine Griffin	Pam
Stephen Boyd	Patrick O'Reilly
Laurence Naismith	Admiral Cross
Geoffrey Keen	Gen Nye
Moultrie Kelsall	Father
Cyril Cusack	Taxi-driver
Andre Morell	Sir Bernard Spillsbury
Michael Hordern	Gen Coburn
Allan Cuthbertson	Vice Admiral
Joan Hickson	Landlady
Terence Longden	Larry
Gibb McLaughlin	Porter
Miles Malleson	Scientist
William Russell	Joe
Richard Wattis	Assistant
Peter Williams	Admiral Mountbatten
Wolf Frees	Admiral Canaris
Peter Sellers	Winston Churchill (voice)

WAR 1943. True story of false plans for invasion of Sicily planted on corpse to deceive Germans. (BFA: Best Screenplay 1956).

12182
THE GELIGNITE GANG (75) (U)
Cybex (Renown)
P: Geoffrey Goodheart
D: Terence Fisher
S: Brandon Fleming

Wayne Morris	Jimmy Baxter
James Kenney	Chapman
Patrick Holt	Rutherford
Sandra Dorne	Sally Morton
Simone Silva	Simone
Arthur Young	Scobie
Eric Pohlmann	Popoulos
Lloyd Lamble	Insp Felby
Hugh Miller	Crosby

CRIME Private tec and secretary unmask client as chief of jewel robbing gang.

MAR

12183
A TOWN LIKE ALICE (117) (A)
Vic Films (RFD) *reissue:* 1960
P: Joseph Janni
D: Jack Lee
S: (NOVEL) Nevil Shute
SC: W.P.Lipscomb, Richard Mason

Virginia McKenna	Jean Paget
Peter Finch	Joe Harman
Marie Lohr	Mrs Frost
Renee Houston	Ebbey
Eileen Moore	Mrs Holland
Jean Anderson	Mrs Horsfall
Maureen Swanson	Ellen
Nora Nicholson	Mrs Frith
Tagaki	Sergeant
Tran Van Khe	Capt Sugaya
Vu Ngoc Tuan	Capt Yanata
John Fabian	Mr Holland
Geoffrey Keen	Solicitor
Vincent Ball	Ben
Tim Turner	Sergeant

WAR Malaya. Group of women forced to march to Japanese camp. (BFA: Best Actor, Best Actress, 1956).

12184
WHO DONE IT ? (85) (U)
Ealing (RFD) *reissue:* 1961 (GEFD)
P: Michael Relph
D: Basil Dearden
S: T.E.B.Clarke

Benny Hill	Hugo Dill
Belinda Lee	Frankie Mayne
David Kossoff	Zacco
Garry Marsh	Insp Hancock
George Margo	Barakov
Ernest Thesiger	Sir Walter Finch
Denis Shaw	Otto Stumpf
Frederick Schiller	Gruber

Thorley Walters . . . . Raymond Courtney
Nicholas Phipps . . . . Scientist
Gibb McLaughlin . . . . Scientist
Irene Handl . . . . Customer
Charles Hawtrey . . . . Disc-jockey
Jeremy Hawk; Robert McDermott; Dagenham
Girl Pipers
COMEDY Strong girl helps amateur tec
save weather control device from spies.

12185
THE BLACK TENT (93) (U) tech
Rank (RFD)
P: William MacQuitty
D: Brian Desmond Hurst
S: Robin Maugham, Bryan Forbes
Anthony Steel . . . . Capt David Holland
Donald Sinden . . . . Charles Holland
Anna Maria Sandri . . . . :. . Mabrouka
Andre Morell . . . . Sheik Salem
Ralph Truman . . . . Croft
Donald Pleasence . . . . Ali
Anthony Bushell . . . . Baring
Michael Craig . . . . Faris
Anton Diffring . . . . German Officer
WAR Tripoli. Man searches for brother who
wed Sheik's daughter and was betrayed
to Germans.

12186
PRIVATE'S PROGRESS (102) (U)
Charter (BL) reissue: 1957 (5 mins cut)
P: Roy Boulting
D: John Boulting
S: (NOVEL) Alan Hackney
SC: John Boulting, Frank Harvey
N: E.V.H.Emmett
Richard Attenborough . . . . . Cox
Dennis Price . . . . . . Bertram Tracepurcel
Terry-Thomas . . . . Maj Hitchcock
Ian Carmichael . . . . Stanley Windrush
Peter Jones . . . . Egan
William Hartnell . . . . Sgt Sutton
Thorley Walters . . . . Capt Bootle
Jill Adams . . . . Prudence Greenslade
Ian Bannen . . . . Pte Horrocks
Victor Maddern . . . . Pte George Blake
Kenneth Griffith . . . . Pte Dai Jones
John Warren . . . . Sgt-maj Gradwick
George Coulouris . . . . Padre
Derrick de Marney . . . . . . Pat
Miles Malleson . . . . Mr Windrush
Michael Trubshawe . . . . . Col Panshawe
John le Mesurier . . . . Psychiatrist
COMEDY 1942. Inept student enlists and
unwittingly helps commissioned uncle
loot German art treasures.

12187
CHARELY MOON (92) (U) eastman
Colin Lesslie (BL)
P: Aubrey Baring
D: Guy Hamilton
S: (NOVEL) Reginald Arkell
SC: Leslie Bricusse, John Cresswell
Max Bygraves . . . . Charley Moon
Dennis Price . . . . Harold Armytage
Michael Medwin . . . . Alf Higgins
Florence Desmond . . . . . . Mary Minton
Shirley Eaton . . . . Angel Dream
Patricia Driscoll . . . . Rose
Reginald Beckwith . . . . Vicar
Cyril Raymond . . . . Bill
Charles Victor . . . . Miller Moon
Peter Jones . . . . Stewart
Newton Blick . . . . Monty Brass
Vic Wise . . . . Solly Silvers
Eric Sykes . . . . Brother-in-law
Bill Fraser . . . . Marber
MUSICAL Ex-soldier finds stage stardom
shallow and returns to circus.

12188
SOHO INCIDENT (77) (A)
USA: SPIN A DARK WEB
Film Locations (Col)
P: M.J.Frankovich, George Maynard
D: Vernon Sewell
S: (NOVEL) Robert Westerby
(WIDE BOYS NEVER WORK)
SC: Ian Stuart Black
Faith Domergue . . . . Bella Francesi
Lee Patterson . . . . Jim Bankley
Rona Anderson . . . . Betty Walker
Martin Benson . . . . Ricco Francesi
Robert Arden . . . . Buddy
Joss Ambler . . . . Tom Walker
Peter Hammond . . . . Bill Walker
Peter Burton . . . . Insp Collis
Sam Kydd . . . . Sam
CRIME Gang boss's sister tries to stop her
lover from quitting crime.

12189
THE SECRET OF THE FOREST (61) (U)
Rayant (BL-CFF)
P: Anthony Gilkison
D: Darcy Conyers
S: George Ewart Evans
SC: Darcy Conyers, Gerard Bryant
Kit Terrington . . . . Henry
Diana Day . . . . Mary
Jacqueline Cox . . . . Caroline
Barry Knight . . . . Johnny
Vincent Ball . . . . Mr Lawson
Michael Balfour . . . . Len
Arthur Lovegrove . . . . Wally
CHILDREN Suffolk. Archaeologist's niece
and nephew catch gold cup thieves.

12190
SUPERSONIC SAUCER (50) (U)
Gaumont (BL-CFF)
P: S: Frank Wells
D: S.G.Ferguson
SC: Dallas Bower
Fella Edmonds . . . . Rodney
Donald Gray . . . . Headmaster
Marcia Monolescu . . . . . . Sumac
Raymond Rollett . . . . No. 1
Gillian Harrison . . . . Greta
Tony Lyons . . . . No. 13
Hilda Fenemore . . . . Mother
CHILDREN Children save Venusian flying
saucer from crooks.

12191
TONS OF TROUBLE (77) (U)
Shaftesbury (Renown)
P: Elizabeth Hiscott, Richard Hearne
D: Leslie Hiscott
S: John Barrow
SC: Leslie Hiscott, Richard Hearne
Richard Hearne . . . . Mr Pastry
William Hartnell . . . . Bert
Austin Trevor . . . . Sir Hervey Shaw
Joan Marion . . . . Angela Shaw
Robert Moreton . . . . Jevons
Ralph Truman . . . . Insp Bridger
Ronald Adam . . . . Psychiatrist
Junia Crawford . . . . Diana Little
Tony Quinn . . . . Cracknell
John Stuart . . . . Doctor
COMEDY Financier's search for sacked
hotel boiler-man with vital information.

12192
WALL OF DEATH (30) (U)
Merton Park (AA)
P: Alec Snowden
D: Montgomery Tully
S: James Eastwood
N: Edgar Lustgarten

Cyril Chamberlain . . . . Insp Harris
Vernon Greeves . . . . Schmidt
Vanda Godsell . . . . Mrs Hartier
CRIME Insp proves woman caused death
of her fairground rider husband.

12193
A MAN ON THE BEACH (29) (U) eastman
Hammer (Ex)
P: Anthony Hinds
D: Joseph Losey
S: (STORY) Victor Canning
(CHANCE AT THE WHEEL)
SC: Jimmy Sangster
Donald Wolfit . . . . Carter
Michael Medwin . . . . Max
Michael Ripper . . . . Chauffeur
Edward Forsyth . . . . Insp Clement
Alex de Gallier . . . . Casino Manager
Barry Shawzin . . . . American
Corinne Grey . . . . Blonde
CRIME France. Man poses as woman to rob
casino and is caught by blind doctor.

12194
THE GENTLE CORSICAN (25) (U) tru
Harlequin (Republic)
P: Leon Clore, John Arnold
D:S: Anthony Simmons
N: Nigel Stock
Toussain Maraninchi . . . . Maurin
Jackie Maraninchi . . . . Nico
DRAMA Corsica. Old fisherman worried
by small son's interest in underwater
swimming equipment.

12195
FUN ON A WEEKEND (10) (U)
Carlyle
P:D: Olive Negus
Chris & Jennifer . . . . The Children
CHILDREN Cornwall. Children rescue boy
stranded on beach.

12196
PARADE OF THE BANDS (28) (U)
eastman/scope
Hammer (Ex)
P:D: Michael Carreras
Malcolm Mitchell   Johnny Dankworth
                    & Cleo Laine
Frank Weir & Lisa Ashwood   Freddy Randall
Eric Jupp   Francisco Cavez
MUSICAL Six dance orchestras.

12197
INVITATION TO MAGIC (20) (U)
Harold Baim (UA)
D: Harold Baim
N: Franklyn Engelmann
David Berglas . . . . Himself
REVUE Conjuror performs at party.

12198
THE MAN IN THE ROAD (84) (U)
Gibraltar (GN)
P: Charles A. Leeds
D: Lance Comfort
S: (NOVEL) Anthony Armstrong
(HE WAS FOUND IN THE ROAD)
SC: Guy Morgan
Derek Farr . . . . Ivan Mason
Ella Raines . . . . Rhona Ellison
Donald Wolfit . . . . Prof Cattrell
Lisa Daniely . . . . Mitzi
Karel Stepanek . . . . Dmitri Balenkov
Cyril Cusack . . . . Dr Kelly
Olive Sloane . . . . Mrs Lemming
Bruce Beeby . . . . Dr Manning
Russell Napier . . . . Supt Davidson
Frederick Piper . . . . Insp Hayman
CRIME Girl novelist saves amnesiac
scientist from spy's nursing-home.

APR

12199
THE FEMININE TOUCH (91) (U) *tech*
USA: THE GENTLE TOUCH
Ealing (RFD)
P: Jack Rix
D: Pat Jackson
S: (NOVEL) Sheila Mackay Russell
(A LAMP IS HEAVY)
SC: Ian McCormick

George Baker	Jim Alcott
Belinda Lee	Susan Richards
Delphi Lawrence	Pat Martin
Adrienne Corri	Maureen O'Brien
Mandy Miller	Jessie
Diana Wynyard	Matron
Dorothy Alison	The Suicide
Henryetta Edwards	Ann Bowland
Christopher Rhodes	Ted Russell
Barbara Archer	Liz Jenkins
Newton Blick	Lofty
Joss Ambler	Bateman
Joan Haythorne	Home Sister
Beatrice Varley	Sister Snow

DRAMA Lives and loves of group of nurses
from training to hospital duty.

12200
SAFARI (92) (A) *tech/scope*
Warwick (Col) *reissue:* 1961 (Unifilms)
P: Irving Allen, Albert Broccoli, Adrian
Worker
D: Terence Young
S: (NOVEL) Robert Buckner
SC: Anthony Veiller

Victor Mature	Ken Duffield
Janet Leigh	Linda Latham
John Justin	Brian Sinden
Roland Culver	Sir Vincent Brandon
Liam Redmond	Roy Shaw
Earl Cameron	Jeroge
Orlando Martins	Jerusalem
Juma	Odongo
Lionel Ngakane	Makora
Cy Grant	Chief Massaj
Estelle Brody	Aunty May

ADVENTURE Africa. Hunter leads lion
safari to track down Mau Mau leader.

12201
THE EXTRA DAY (83) (U) *eastman*
William Fairchild (BL)
P: E.M.Smedley-Aston
D:S: William Fairchild

Richard Basehart	Joe Blake
Simone Simon	Michele Blanchard
George Baker	Steven Marlow
Josephine Griffin	Toni Howard
Sidney James	Barney West
Dennis Lotis	Ronnie Baker
Shani Wallis	Shirley
Beryl Reid	Beryl
Colin Gordon	Sir George Howard
Laurence Naismith	Kurt Vorn
Jill Bennett	Susan
Olga Lindo	Mrs Bliss
Philip Ray	Mr Bliss
Charles Victor	Bert
David Hannaford	Buster West
Meier Tzelniker	Lou Skeat
Bryan Forbes	Harry
Eddie Byrne	Robin
Doreen Dawn	Beauty Queen

DRAMA Stories of five extras recalled
for additional film scenes.

12202
THE MARCH HARE (85) (U) *eastman/scope*
Achilles (BL)
P: Bertram Ostrer, Albert Fennell
D: George More O'Ferrall
S: (NOVEL) T.H.Bird
(GAMBLERS SOMETIMES WIN)
SC: Gordon Wellesley, Allan Mackinnon,
Paul Vincent Carroll

Peggy Cummins	Pat Maguire
Terence Morgan	Sir Charles Hare
Wilfrid Hyde White	Col Keene
Martita Hunt	Lady Anne
Cyril Cusack	Lazy Mangan
Derrick de Marney	Capt Marlow
Charles Hawtrey	Fisher
Maureen Delany	Bridget
Ivan Samson	Hardwicke
Macdonald Parke	Maguire
Reginald Beckwith	Broker

FANTASY Ireland. Fairy gives trainer
magic word that makes his horse win Derby.

12203
RAIDERS OF THE RIVER (serial) (U)
Merton Park (BL-CFF)
P: Frank Hoare
D: SC: John Haggarty
S: (STORIES) Robin Martin
N: John Slater

Richard O'Sullivan	Joey
Jenny Jones	Patsy
Jack McGowran	Alf Barber
John Longden	Prof Dykes
Vic Perry	Talbot
John Stuart	Mr Hampton
Larry Cross	Mr Wilberforce
Larry Burns	Boxer

12204
1: MYSTERY IN COVENT GARDEN (18)

12205
2: THE SECRET OF THE CELLAR (19)

12206
3: THE RAIDERS' HIDE-OUT (20)

12207
4: THE THING IN THE BASEMENT (20)

12208
5: CAUGHT BY THE GANG (18)

12209
6: TRAPPED IN THE TUNNEL (18)

12210
7: HOT ON THE TRAIL (16)

12211
8: THE GANG AT BAY (18)
CHILDREN Children trap gang using
landing craft and electronic brain to rob
bank.

12212
BOND OF FEAR (66) (A)
Mid-Century (Eros)
P: Robert Baker, Monty Berman
D: Henry Cass
S: Digby Wolfe
SC: John Gilling, Norman Hudis

Dermot Walsh	John Sewell
Jane Barrett	Mary Sewell
John Colicos	Dewar
Jameson Clark	Scotty
John Horsley	PC
Anthony Pavey	Michael Sewell
Marilyn Baker	Ann Sewell
Avril Angers	Hiker

CRIME Escaped killer forces family to
hide him in caravan.

MAY

12213
KEEP IT CLEAN (75) (U)
Marksman (Eros)
P: Maxwell Setton, John R. Sloan
D: David Paltenghi
S: R.F.Delderfield
SC: Carl Nystrom, R.F.Delderfield

Ronald Shiner	Bert Lane
James Hayter	Mr Bouncenboy
Ursula Howells	Pat Anstey
Diane Hart	Kitty
Jean Cadell	Mrs Anstey
Tonia Bern	Colette Dare
Colin Gordon	Peter
Benny Lee	Tarbottom
Joan Sims	Vi Tarbottom
Gerald Campion	Rasher
Albert Whelan	Gregson

COMEDY Publicity man tries to get
Purity Leaguer to finance cleaner.

12214
IT'S NEVER TOO LATE (95) (U) *eastman*
Park Lane (ABP)
P: Jules Simmons, George Pitcher
D: Michael McCarthy
S: (PLAY) Felicity Douglas
SC: Edward Dryhurst

Phyllis Calvert	Laura Hammond
Guy Rolfe	Stephen Hodgson
Patrick Barr	Charles Hammond
Susan Stephen	Tessa Hammond
Sarah Lawson	Anne
Delphi Lawrence	Mrs Dixon
Peter Hammond	Tony
Richard Leech	John
Jean Taylor Smith	Grannie
Robert Ayres	Crane
Irene Handl	Neighbour

COMEDY Family troubles ensue when
mother goes to Hollywood as script-writer.

12215
IT'S GREAT TO BE YOUNG (93) (u) *tech*
Marble Arch (ABP)
P: Victor Skutezky
D: Cyril Frankel
S: Ted Willis

John Mills	Mr Dingle
Cecil Parker	Mr Frome
Jeremy Spenser	Nicky
Dorothy Bromiley	Paulette
Eleanor Summerfield	Barmaid
John Salew	Mr Routledge
Bryan Forbes	Salesman
Brian Smith	Ginger
Carole Shelley	Peggy
Richard O'Sullivan	Lawson
Mary Merrall	Miss Wyvern
Derek Blomfield	Mr Patterson
Marjorie Rhodes	Landlady
Eddie Byrne	Morris

Ruby Murray; Humphrey Lyttelton;
Coronets
MUSICAL Co-ed school mutinies when
popular music master sacked.

12216
RAMSBOTTOM RIDES AGAIN (93) (U)
Jack Hylton (BL)
P:D: John Baxter
S: (PLAY) Harold G. Robert
SC: John Baxter, Basil Thomas, Arthur Askey,
Glenn Melvyn, Geoffrey Orme

Arthur Askey	Bill Ramsbottom
Glenn Melvyn	Charlie
Sidney James	Black Jake
Shani Wallis	Joan Ramsbottom
Frankie Vaughan	Elmer
Betty Marsden	Florrie Ramsbottom
Jerry Desmonde	Blue Eagle
Sabrina	Girl
Danny Ross	Danny
Anthea Askey	Susie Ramsbottom

Billy Percy . . . . Reuben
Gary Wayne . . . . Tombstone
Denis Wyndham . . . . Dan
COMEDY Timid grandson of tough
sheriff inherits property in Wild West.

12217
PACIFIC DESTINY (97) (U) *eastman/scope*
Lawrie (BL)
P: James H. Lawrie
D: Wolf Rilla
S: (BOOK) Sir Arthur Grimble
(A PATTERN OF ISLANDS)
SC: Richard Mason
Denholm Elliott . . . . Arthur Grimble
Susan Stephen . . . . Olivia Grimble
Michael Hordern . . . . . Commissioner Gregory
Gordon Jackson . . . . DO
Inia Te Wiata . . . . Tauvela
Felix Felton . . . . Uncle
Mona McDonald . . . . . Voice-of-the-tide
ADVENTURE 1912. True story of
Colonial Service cadet in South Seas.

12218
MY TEENAGE DAUGHTER (100) (A)
USA: TEENAGE BAD GIRL
Everest (BL)
P:D: Herbert Wilcox
S: Felicity Douglas
Anna Neagle . . . . Valerie Carr
Sylvia Sims . . . . Janet Carr
Norman Wooland . . . . Hugh Manning
Wilfrid Hyde White . . . . Sir Joseph
Kenneth Haigh . . . . . . Tony Ward Black
Julia Lockwood . . . . Poppet Carr
Helen Haye . . . . Aunt Louisa
Josephine Fitzgerald . . . . . . Aunt Bella
Wanda Ventham . . . . Gina
Michael Shepley . . . . Sir Henry
CRIME Widow's daughter and crooked
boyfriend cause death of his aunt.

12219
PORT OF ESCAPE (76) (A)
Wellington (Renown)
P: Lance Comfort
D: Tony Young
S: (STORY) Barbara Harper
(SAFE HARBOUR)
SC: Barbara Harper, Tony Young, Abby Mann
Googie Withers . . . . Anne Stirling
John McCallum . . . . Mitchell Gillie
Bill Kerr . . . . Dinty Missouri
Joan Hickson . . . . Rosalie Watchett
Wendy Danielli . . . . Daphne Stirling
Hugh Pryse . . . . Skinner
Alexander Gauge . . . . Insp Levins
Ingeborg Wells . . . . Lucy
Ewan Roberts . . . . Sgt Rutherford
CRIME Fugitive and insane comrade force
girl reporter to shelter them on her barge.

12220
PORT AFRIQUE (92) *tech* (A)
Coronado (Col)
P: David E. Rose, John R. Sloan
D: Rudolph Mate
S: (NOVEL) Bernard Victor Dyer
SC: Frank Partos, John Cresswell
Pier Angeli . . . . Ynez
Phil Carey . . . . Rip Reardon
Dennis Price . . . . Robert Blackton
Eugene Deckers . . . . Col Moussac
James Hayter . . . . Nino
Rachel Gurney . . . . Diane Blackton
Anthony Newley . . . . Pedro
Guido Lorraine . . . . Abdul
Christopher Lee . . . . Franz Vermes
CRIME Morocco. Crippled USAAF
pilot solves shooting of his wife.

12221
WICKED AS THEY COME (94) (A)
Film Locations (Col)
P: M.J.Frankovich, Maxwell Setton
D: Ken Hughes
S: (NOVEL) Bill S. Ballinger
(PORTRAIT IN SMOKE)
SC: Ken Hughes, Robert Westerby, Sigmund
Miller
Arlene Dahl. . . . . Kathy Allen
Phil Carey . . . . Tim O'Bannion
Herbert Marshall . . . . Stephen Collins
Michael Goodliffe . . . . Larry Buckman
Ralph Truman . . . . John Dowling
Sidney James . . . . Frank Allen
David Kossoff . . . . Sam Lewis
Faith Brook . . . . Virginia Collins
Marvin Kane . . . . Mike Lewis
Patrick Allen . . . . Willie
Jacques Brunius . . . . Insp Caron
DRAMA American slum girl wins beauty
contest and ruins men's lives.

12222
THE INTIMATE STRANGER (95) (A)
USA: FINGER OF GUILT
Anglo-Guild-Merton Park (AA)
P: Alec C. Snowden
D: Joseph Losey
S: (NOVEL) Peter Howard (PAY THE PIPER)
SC: Peter Howard
Richard Basehart . . . . Reggie Wilson
Mary Murphy . . . . Evelyn Stewart
Constance Cummings . . . . . Kay Wallace
Roger Livesey . . . . Ben Case
Mervyn Johns . . . . Ernest Chapple
Faith Brook . . . . Lesley Wilson
Vernon Greeves . . . . George Mearns
Andre Mikhelson. . . . . Steve Vadney
Basil Dignam . . . . Dr Gray
David Lodge . . . . Sgt Brown
CRIME Married film producer's rival
bribes girl to pose as his ex-fiancee.

12223
THE LONG ARM (96) (U) USA: THE THIRD
KEY
Ealing (RFD)
P: Tom Morahan
D: Charles Frend
S: Robert Barr
SC: Robert Barr, Janet Green, Dorothy &
Campbell Christie
Jack Hawkins . . . . Supt Tom Halliday
John Stratton . . . . Sgt Ward
Dorothy Alison . . . . Mary Halliday
Geoffrey Keen . . . . Supt Jim Malcolm
Ursula Howells . . . . Mrs Gilson
Newton Blick . . . . Cdr Harris
Sydney Tafler . . . . Stone
Ralph Truman . . . . Col Blenkinsop
Maureen Delany . . . . Mrs. Stevens
Richard Leech . . . . Gilson
Meredith Edwards . . . . Thomas
George Rose . . . . Slob
Ian Bannen . . . . Workman
Alec McCowen . . . . Surgeon
CRIME Superintendent and his new sergeant
track down safe robber.

12224
GUILTY ? (93) (A)
Gibraltar (GN)
P: Charles A. Leeds
D: Edmond T.Greville
S: (NOVEL) Michael Gilbert
(DEATH HAS DEEP ROOTS)
SC: Maurice J. Wilson, Ernest Dudley
John Justin . . . . Nap Rumbold
Barbara Laage . . . . Jacqueline Delbois
Donald Wolfit . . . . The Judge

Stephen Murray . . . . Summers
Norman Wooland . . . . Pelton
Andree Debar . . . . Vicki Martin
Frank Villard . . . . Pierre Lemaire
Betty Stockfeld . . . . Mrs Roper
Sydney Tafler . . . . Camino
Leslie Perrins . . . . Poynter
Kynaston Reeves . . . . Col Wright
Russell Napier . . . . Insp Hobson
CRIME France. French policewoman helps
lawyer prove resistance heroine framed by
forgers.

JUN

12225
TOGETHER (52) (U)
BFI (Connoisseur)
D: Lorenza Mazzetti
S: Denis Horne
Michael Andrews
Eduardo Paolozzi
Valy
Denis Richardson
Cecilia May
DRAMA Deaf mute dock-workers live
together and one is accidentally killed.

12226
REACH FOR THE SKY (135) (U)
Pinnacle (RFD) *reissue:* 1959
P: Daniel M. Angel
D: Lewis Gilbert
S: (BOOK) Paul Brickhill
SC: Lewis Gilbert, Vernon Harris
Kenneth More . . . . Douglas Bader
Muriel Pavlow . . . . Thelma Bader
Lyndon Brook . . . . Johnny Sanderson
Lee Patterson . . . . Stan Turner
Alexander Knox . . . . Mr Joyce
Dorothy Alison . . . . Nurse Brace
Michael Warre . . . . Harry Day
Sydney Tafler . . . . Robert Desoutter
Howard Marion Crawford ..Woody Woodhall
Jack Watling . . . . Peel
Walter Hudd . . . . AVM Halahan
Eddie Byrne . . . . F/Sgt Mills
Nigel Green . . . . Streatfield
Charles Carson . . . . ACM Sir Hugh Dowding
Ronald Adam. . . . . AVM Leigh Mallory
Eric Pohlmann . . . . Adjutant
Michael Gough . . . . Pearson
HISTORY 1931-1945. Biography of pilot
who loses legs yet returns to fly fighters
in war. (BFA: Best British Film, 1956;
Top Moneymaker: 1956; PGAA: 1957).

12227
JACQUELINE (93) (U)
Rank (RFD) *reissue:* 1959 (22 mins cut)
P: George H. Brown
D: Roy Baker
S: Patrick Kirwan, Liam O'Flaherty,
Patrick Campbell, Catherine Cookson
John Gregson . . . . Mike McNeil
Kathleen Ryan . . . . Elizabeth McNeil
Jacqueline Ryan . . . . . . Jacqueline McNeil
Noel Purcell . . . . Owen
Cyril Cusack . . . . Flanagan
Tony Wright . . . . Jack McBride
Maureen Swanson . . . . Maggie
Liam Redmond . . . . Mr Lord
Maureen Delany . . . . Mrs McBride
Marie Kean . . . . Mrs Flanagan
Richard O'Sullivan . . . . . . Michael
DRAMA Ireland. Drunkard shipbuilder's
child helps him get farm work.

12228
WOMEN WITHOUT MEN (73) (A)
USA: BLONDE BAIT
Hammer (Ex)
P: Anthony Hinds
D: Elmo Williams
S: Richard Landau
SC: Richard Landau, Val Guest
Beverley Michaels .... Angie Booth
Joan Rice .... Cleo
Avril Angers .... Bessie
Thora Hird .... Granny
Hermione Baddeley ...... Grace
Paul Carpenter .... Nick
Gordon Jackson .... Percy
Ralph Michael .... Julian
Sheila Burrell .... Babs
April Olrich .... Marguerite
CRIME Police let showgirl break jail to
lead them to murderer.

12229
THE DOOR IN THE WALL (29) (U) *tech*
BFI (ABP)
P: Howard Thomas
D: SC: Glenn H. Alvey jr
S: (STORY) H.G.Wells
Stephen Murray .... Sir Frank Wallace
Ian Hunter .... Henry Redmond
Leonard Sachs .... Father
Ann Blake .... Aunt
Kit Terrington .... Frank (child)
Brian Leslie .... Henry (child)
FANTASY Minister's childhood memory of
enchanted garden causes his death. (First
film in "Dynamic Frame.")

12230
ERIC WINSTONE'S STAGECOACH (30) (U)
eastman/scope
Hammer (Ex)
P:D: Michael Carreras
Eric Winstone and his Orchestra
Alma Cogan   Marion Ryan
Ray Ellington Quartet
MUSICAL

12231
FAITHFUL TO THE RESCUE (25) (U)
Carlyle
P:D: Olive Negus
Chris & Jennifer .... The Children
Ross Salmon .... The Cowboy
CHILDREN Devon. Children help cowboy
foil horse rustlers.

12232
WAS IT A DREAM? (16) (U)
Carlyle
P:D: Olive Negus
Chris & Jennifer .... The Children
CHILDREN Children fancy they are turned
into a cowboy and cowgirl.

12233
THE MAGIC RING (14) (U)
Carlyle
P:D: Olive Negus
Chris & Jennifer .... The Children
CHILDREN Children make wish at Chancton-
bury Ring and have cowboy adventure with
horse thieves.

12234
ALIAS JOHN PRESTON (66) (A)
Danziger (BL)
P: Edward J, Harry Lee Danziger
D: David Macdonald
S: Paul Tabori
Betta StJohn .... Sally Sandford
Alexander Knox .... Dr Walton

Christopher Lee .... John Preston
Sandra Dorne .... Maria
Patrick Holt .... Stranger
Betty Anne Davies ...... Mrs Sandford
John Longden .... Mr Sandford
Bill Fraser .... Joe Newton
John Stuart .... Dr Underwood
CRIME Psychiatrist proves schizophrenic's
nightmare of murder was true.

12235
THE CASE OF THE RIVER MORGUE (34) (A)
Merton Park (AA)
P: Alec Snowden
D: Montgomery Tully
S: James Eastwood
N: Edgar Lustgarten
Hugh Moxey .... Inspector
Gordon Needham .... Hiller
Jane Welsh .... Mrs Hiller
CRIME Diabetic steals corpse and 'drowns'
it to swindle insurance co.

12236
YIELD TO THE NIGHT (99) (X)
USA: BLONDE SINNER
Kenwood (ABP)
P: Kenneth Harper
D: J. Lee Thompson
S: (NOVEL) Joan Henry
SC: Joan Henry, John Cresswell
Diana Dors .... Mary Hilton
Yvonne Mitchell .... Macfarlane
Michael Craig .... Jim Lancaster
Geoffrey Keen .... Chaplain
Olga Lindo .... Hill
Mary Mackenzie .... Maxwell
Joan Miller .... Barker
Marie Ney .... Governor
Liam Redmond .... Doctor
Marjorie Rhodes .... Brandon
Athene Seyler .... Miss Bligh
Molly Urquhart .... Mason
Harry Locke .... Fred Hilton
Michael Ripper .... Roy
CRIME Condemned woman recalls why she
shot rich mistress of her pianist lover.

JUL
12237
SMILEY (97) (U) *deluxe/scope*
London (20)
P:D: Anthony Kimmins
S: (NOVEL) Moore Raymond
SC: Moore Raymond, Anthony Kimmins
Ralph Richardson .... Rev Lambeth
John McCallum .... Rankin
Chips Rafferty .... Sgt Flaxman
Colin Petersen .... Smiley Greevins
Bruce Archer .... Joey
Jocelyn Hernfield .... Miss Waterman
Charles Tingwell .... Stevens
Margaret Christensen ...... Ma Greevins
Guy Doleman .... Rider
Reg Lye .... Pa Greevins
ADVENTURE Australia. Drunkard's son
helps stop publican from smuggling opium
to Aborigines.

12238
PERIL FOR THE GUY (55) (U)
World Wide (BL-CFF)
P: Hindle Edgar
D:SC: James Hill
S: (NOVEL) John Kennett
Christopher Warbey ...... Freddie
Frazer Hines .... Kim
Ali Alleney .... Ali
Katherine Kath .... Anita Fox
Meredith Edwards .... PC Durrant
Amanda Coxall .... Pat

Peter Copley .... Ritter
CHILDREN Children save inventor of
oil detector from being kidnapped by spies.

12239
BREAKAWAY (72) (U)
Cipa (RKO)
P: Robert Baker, Monty Berman
D: Henry Cass
S: Manning O'Brine
SC: Norman Hudis
Tom Conway .... Tom "Duke" Martin
Honor Blackman .... Paula Grant
Michael Balfour .... Barney
Bruce Seton .... Webb
Brian Worth .... Johnny Matlock
Freddie Mills .... Pat
Alexander Gauge .... McAllister
John Horsley .... Michael Matlock
CRIME Gang kidnaps girl to obtain
formula to eliminate metal fatigue.

12240
ODONGO (85) (U) *tech/scope*
Warwick (Col)
P: Irving Allen, Albert Broccoli, Islin Ausler
D:SC: John Gilling
S: Islin Ausler
Rhonda Fleming .... Pamela Muir
Macdonald Carey .... Steve Stratton
Juma .... Odongo
Eleanor Summerfield ..... Celia Watford
Francis de Wolff .... George Watford
Earl Cameron .... Hassan
Michael Caridia .... Lester Watford
Leonard Sachs .... Warden
Dan Jackson .... Walla
Bartholomew Sketch .... Leni
ADVENTURE Africa. Circus trapper
suspects native boy of freeing his animals.

12241
INVITATION TO THE DANCE (62) (U) *tech*
MGM British
P: Arthur Freed
D:S: Gene Kelly
CIRCUS
Gene Kelly .... The Clown
Claire Sombert .... The Loved
Igor Youskevitch .... The Lover
RING AROUND THE ROSY
Gene Kelly .... The Marine
Tamara Toumanova ...... The Girl
Tommy Rall .... Stagedoor Johnny
Belita .... Femme Fatale
David Paltenghi .... The Husband
MUSICAL Two ballets.

12242
BHOWANI JUNCTION (109) (A)
eastman/scope
MGM British
P: Pandro S. Berman
D: George Cukor
S: (NOVEL) John Masters
SC: Sonya Levien, Ivan Moffatt
Ava Gardner .... Victoria Jones
Stewart Granger .... Col Rodney Savage
Bill Travers .... Patrick Taylor
Abraham Sofaer .... Surabhai
Francis Matthews .... Ranjit Kasel
Marne Maitland .... Govindaswami
Peter Illing .... Ghanshayam
Edward Chapman .... Thomas Jones
Freda Jackson .... The Sadani
Lionel Jeffries ..... Lt Graham McDaniel
Alan Tilvern .... Ted Dunphy
DRAMA India, 1947. Halfcaste girl torn
between her love for British colonel and her
country.

12243
FIRE MAIDENS FROM OUTER SPACE (80) (U)
Criterion (Eros)
P: George Fowler, Cy Roth
D: S: Cy Roth
Anthony Dexter . . . . Luther Blair
Susan Shaw . . . . Hestia
Paul Carpenter . . . . Larson
Harry Fowler . . . . Sydney Stanhope
Jacqueline Curtis . . . . Duessa
Sydney Tafler . . . . Dr Higgins
Owen Berry . . . . Prasus
Rodney Diak . . . . Anderson
FANTASY Space explorers kill creature to
save girls of Jupiter's thirteenth moon.

12244
CHILD IN THE HOUSE (88) (U)
Laureate (Eros)
P: S. Benjamin Fisz
D: C. Raker Endfield, Charles de la Tour
S: (NOVEL) Janet McNeil
SC: C. Raker Endfield
Phyllis Calvert . . . . Evelyn Acheson
Eric Portman . . . . Henry Acheson
Stanley Baker . . . . Stephen Lorimer
Mandy Miller . . . . Elizabeth Lorimer
Dora Bryan . . . . Cassie
Percy Herbert . . . . Sgt Taylor
Joan Benham . . . . Vera McNally
Victor Maddern . . . . Bert
Martin Miller . . . . Prof Topolsky
Joan Hickson . . . . Cook
Alfie Bass . . . . Ticket Collector
CRIME Rich woman tricks niece into
disclosing her fugitive father.

12245
PASSPORT TO TREASON (80) (U)
Mid-Century (Eros)
P: Robert S. Baker, Monty Berman
D: Robert S. Baker
S: (NOVEL) Manning O'Brine
SC: Norman Hudis, Kenneth R.Hayles
Rod Cameron . . . . Mike O'Kelly
Lois Maxwell . . . . Diane Boyd
Clifford Evans . . . . Orlando Sims
Peter Illing . . . . Giorgio Sacchi
Marianne Stone . . . . Miss Jones
Douglas Wilmer . . . . Dr Randolph
John Colicos . . . . Pietro
Ballard Berkeley . . . . Insp Threadgold
Andrew Faulds . . . . Barrett
CRIME American tec and MI5 girl expose
fascists behind peace league.

12246
BEHIND THE HEADLINES (67) (U)
Kenilworth (RFD)
P: Guido Coen
D: Charles Saunders
S: (NOVEL) Robert Chapman
SC: Allan Mackinnon
Paul Carpenter . . . . Paul Banner
Hazel Court . . . . Maxine
Adrienne Corri . . . . Pam Barnes
Alfie Bass . . . . Sammy
Ewen Solon . . . . Supt Faro
Harry Fowler . . . . Alfie
Trevor Reid . . . . Mr Bunting
Olive Gregg . . . . Mrs Bunting
CRIME Reporters solve murder of black-
mailing blonde.

12247
EYEWITNESS (82) (A)
Rank (RFD)
P: Sydney Box
D: Muriel Box
S: Janet Green

Donald Sinden . . . . Wade
Muriel Pavlow . . . . Lucy Church
Belinda Lee . . . . Penny Mander
David Knight . . . . Mike
Nigel Stock . . . . Barney
Michael Craig . . . . Jay Church
Susan Beaumont . . . . Nurse
Ada Reeve . . . . Mrs Hudson
Leslie Dwyer . . . . Mr Cammon
Allan Cuthbertson . . . . Insp Reardon
Avice Landone . . . . Sister
Nicholas Parsons . . . . Dr Bright
John Stuart . . . . Chief Constable
Richard Wattis . . . . Anaesthetist
Charles Victor . . . . Sgt
CRIME Playboy and deaf partner try to
kill hospitalised witness.

12248
THE BABY AND THE BATTLESHIP (96) (U)
eastman
Jay Lewis (BL)
P: Antony Darnborough
D: Jay Lewis
S: (NOVEL) Anthony Thorne
SC: Jay Lewis, Gilbert Hackforth-Jones,
Bryan Forbes
John Mills . . . . Puncher Roberts
Richard Attenborough . . . . . Knocker White
Andre Morell . . . . Marshal
Bryan Forbes . . . . Professor
Michael Howard . . . . Joe
Lisa Gastoni . . . . Maria Vespucci
Ernest Clark . . . . Cdr Digby
Harry Locke . . . . CPO Blades
Michael Hordern . . . . Captain
Lionel Jeffries . . . . George
Clifford Mollison . . . . Sails
Thorley Walters . . . . Lt Setley
Duncan Lamont . . . . Master at Arms
Cyril Raymond . . . . PMO
D.A.Clarke-Smith . . . . Admiral
Kenneth Griffith . . . . Sub-Lt
John le Mesurier . . . . Aide
Gordon Jackson . . . . Harry
COMEDY Sailors hide Italian baby aboard
battleship.

AUG

12249
IT'S A WONDERFUL WORLD (89) (U)
tech/scope
George Minter (Renown)
P: Denis O'Dell
D:S: Val Guest
Terence Morgan . . . . Ray Thompson
George Cole . . . . Ken Miller
Kathleen Harrison . . . . Mrs Gilly
Mylene Demongeot . . . . . Georgie Dubois
James Hayter . . . . Bert Fielding
Harold Lang . . . . Mervyn Wade
Maurice Kaufman . . . . Paul Taylor
Richard Wattis . . . . Harold
Reginald Beckwith . . . . Manager
Derek Blomfield . . . . Arranger
Maya Koumani . . . . Henrietta
Walter Crisham . . . . American
Dennis Lotis; Ted Heath and his Music
MUSICAL Composers win popular success by
reversing songs.

12250
ALL IN GOOD FUN (47) (U)
Butcher
P: Henry W.Fisher
D:S: James M. Anderson
SC: James M. Anderson, Bob Monkhouse
Bob Monkhouse . . . . Himself
COMPILATION Extracts from silent films,
including CHARLIE SMILER TAKES
UP JU-JITSU (1911); DR BRIAN PELLIE AND

THE SECRET DESPATCH (1912); LT DARING
AND THE MYSTERY OF ROOM 41 (1913);
BUNNY AT THE DERBY (1913).

12251
SAILOR BEWARE ! (80) (U)
USA: PANIC IN THE PARLOUR
Remus (IFD)
P: Jack Clayton
D: Gordon Parry
S: (PLAY) Philip King, Falkland Cary
SC: Philip King, Falkland Cary
Peggy Mount . . . . Emma Hornett
Shirley Eaton . . . . Shirley Hornett
Ronald Lewis . . . . Albert Tufnell
Gordon Jackson . . . . Carnoustie Bligh
Cyril Smith . . . . Henry Hornett
Thora Hird . . . . Mrs Lack
Esma Cannon . . . . Edie Hornett
Joy Webster . . . . Daphne
Geoffrey Keen . . . . Mr Purefoy
Jack McGowran . . . . Toddy
Eliot Makeham . . . . Uncle Brummell
COMEDY Nagging woman almost ruins her
daughter's chances of marrying sailor.

12252
THE IRON PETTICOAT (90) (A) *tech*
Remus - Setafilm (IFD)
P: Harry Saltzman, Betty E. Box
D: Ralph Thomas
S: Ben Hecht
Bob Hope . . . . Lt Chuck/Lockwood
Katharine Hepburn . . . . . Vinka Kovlenko
Noelle Middleton . . Lady Connie Warburton-
Watts
James Robertson Justice . . . Col Sklarnoff
Robert Helpmann . . . . Ivan Kropotkin
David Kossoff . . . . Dr Dubratz
Alan Gifford . . . . . Col Newton Tarbell
Nicholas Phipps . . . . Tony Mallard
Paul Carpenter . . . . Maj Lewis
Sidney James . . . . Paul
Alexander Gauge . . . . Senator Holly
Sandra Dorne . . . . Tityana
Richard Wattis . . . . Clerk
Tutte Lemkow . . . . Sutsiyawa
Martin Boddey . . . . Grisha
COMEDY Berlin. USAAF pilot tries to
convince Russian woman pilot western
democracy is best.

12253
THE SHIELD OF FAITH (56) (U)
GHW-Church & Chapel (RFD)
D: Norman Walker
S: Joseph Arthur Rank, R.N.F.Evans
SC: Lawrence Barrett
Mervyn Johns
Adrienne Corri
Emrys Jones
RELIGION Survivors of air crash start
life again with renewed faith.

12254
X THE UNKNOWN (78) (X)
Hammer (Ex)
P: Anthony Hinds
D: Leslie Norman
S: Jimmy Sangster
Dean Jagger . . . . Dr Adam Royston
Edward Chapman . . . . Elliott
Leo McKern . . . . McGill
Anthony Newley . . . . Pte Spider Webb
Jameson Clark . . . . Jack Harding
William Lucas . . . . Peter Elliott
Peter Hammond . . . . Lt Bannerman
Marianne Brauns . . . . Zena
Ian MacNaughton . . . . Haggis
Michael Ripper . . . . Sgt Grimsdyke
John Harvey . . . . Maj Cartwright

Edward Judd . . . . Soldier
HORROR Scotland. Seeping mass enlarges
as it absorbs radiation.

12255
THE LAST MAN TO HANG ? (75) (A)
ACT Films-Warwick (Col)
P: John W. Gossage
D: Terence Fisher
S: (NOVEL) Gerald Bullett (THE JURY)
SC: Gerald Bullett, Maurice Elvey, Ivor
Montagu, Max Trell
Tom Conway . . . . . . Sir Roderick Strood
Elizabeth Sellars . . . . Daphne Strood
Eunice Gayson . . . . Elizabeth Anders
Freda Jackson . . . . Mrs Tucker
Raymond Huntley . . . . . . Attorney-Gen
David Horne . . . . Anthony Harcombe
Victor Maddern . . . . Bonaker
Margaretta Scott . . . . Mrs Cranshaw
Walter Hudd . . . . Judge
Anthony Newley . . . . Cyril Gaskin
Anna Turner . . . . Lucy Prynne
Hugh Latimer . . . . Mark Perryman
Russell Napier . . . . Sgt Bolton
Olive Sloane . . . . Mrs Bayfield
CRIME Juror convinces his fellows that a
knight did not poison possessive wife.

12256
THE HIGH TERRACE (82) (A)
Cipa (RKO)
P: Robert Baker, Monty Berman
D: Henry Cass
S: A.T.Weisman
SC: Brock Williams, Alfred Shaughnessy,
Norman Hudis
Dale Robertson . . . . Bill Lang
Lois Maxwell . . . . Stephanie Blake
Derek Bond . . . . John Mansfield
Eric Pohlmann . . . . Otto Kellner
Mary Laura Wood . . . . . . Molly Kellner
Lionel Jeffries . . . . Monckton
Jameson Clark . . . . Insp Mackay
Carl Bernard . . . . Jock Dunmow
CRIME American playwright takes blame
for actress who killed producer.

SEP
12257
A HILL IN KOREA (81) (A) USA:
HELL IN KOREA
Wessex-Dalrymple (BL) reissue: 1960 (cut)
P: Anthony Squire
D: Julian Amyes
S: (NOVEL) Max Catto
SC: Ian Dalrymple, Anthony Squire,
Ronald Spencer
George Baker . . . . Lt Butler
Stanley Baker . . . . Cpl Ryker
Harry Andrews . . . . Sgt Payne
Michael Medwin . . . . Pte Docker
Ronald Lewis . . . . Pte Wyatt
Stephen Boyd . . . . Pte Sims
Victor Maddern . . . . Pte Lindop
Harry Landis . . . . Pte Rabin
Robert Brown . . . . Pte O'Brien
Robert Shaw . . . . L/Cpl Hodge
Percy Herbert . . . . Pte Moon
Michael Caine . . . . Pte Lockyer
WAR Korea. Army patrol hold hill temple
against Chinese.

12258
THE GREEN MAN (90) (A)
Granadier (BL)
P: Frank Launder, Sidney Gillat
D: Robert Day
S: (PLAY) Frank Launder, Sidney Gillat
(MEET A BODY)
SC: Frank Launder, Sidney Gillat

Alastair Sim . . . . Hawkins
George Cole . . . . William Blake
Terry-Thomas . . . . Boughtflower
Jill Adams . . . . Ann Vincent
Avril Angers . . . . Marigold
Dora Bryan . . . . Lily
Eileen Moore . . . . Joan Wood
Raymond Huntley . . . Sir Gregory Upshott
John Chandos . . . . McKecknie
Colin Gordon . . . . Reginald
Cyril Chamberlain . . . . . . Sgt Bassett
COMEDY Retired assassin fails to kill
expert on Middle East.

12259
SATELLITE IN THE SKY (84) (U)
warner/scope
Tridelta (WB)
P: Edward J.& Harry Lee Danziger
D: Paul Dickson
S: John C. Mather, J.T.McIntosh, Edith Dell
Kieron Moore . . . . Michael
Lois Maxwell . . . . Kim
Donald Wolfit . . . . Merrity
Bryan Forbes . . . . Jimmy
Jimmy Hanley . . . . Larry
Thea Gregory . . . . Barbara
Barry Keegan . . . . Lefty
Alan Gifford . . . . Col Galloway
Walter Hudd . . . . Blandford
Donald Gray . . . . Capt Ross
Carl Jaffe . . . . Bechstein
FANTASY Scientists sacrifice lives to
lloosen tritonium bomb from side of spaceship.

12260
HOME AND AWAY (81) (U)
Conquest-Guest (Eros)
P: George Maynard
D: Vernon Sewell
S: (PLAY) Heather McIntyre
(TREBLE TROUBLE)
SC: Vernon Sewell, R.F.Delderfield
Jack Warner . . . . George Knowles
Kathleen Harrison . . . . . . Elsie Knowles
Lana Morris . . . . Mary Knowles
Charles Victor . . . . Ted Groves
Thora Hird . . . . Margie Groves
Leslie Henson . . . . Uncle Tom
Valerie White . . . . Mrs Jarvis
Harry Fowler . . . . Syd Jarvis
Merrie Carroll . . . . Annie Knowles
Margaret StBarbe West . . . . Aunt Jean
COMEDY Widow kidnaps son to cheat
partner in football pool prize.

12261
THE WEAPON (81) (A) scope
Periclean (Eros)
P: Hal E.Chester, Frank Bevis
D: Val Guest
S: Hal E. Chester
SC: Fred Freiberger
Steve Cochran . . . . Mark Andrews
Lizabeth Scott . . . . Elsa Jenner
George Cole . . . . Joshua Henry
Herbert Marshall . . . . . . Insp Mackenzie
Nicole Maurey . . . . Vivienne
Jon Whiteley . . . . Eric Jenner
Laurence Naismith . . . . . . Jamison
Stanley Maxted . . . . Colonel
John Horsley . . . . Johnson
Denis Shaw . . . . Groggins
Richard Goolden . . . . Man
Joe Aston & Renee
CRIME Runaway boy finds gun and
is chased by police and murderer.

12262
DESTINATION DEATH (31) (A)
Merton Park (AA)

P: Alec Snowden
D: Montgomery Tully
S: Colin S. Reid
SC: James Eastwood
N: Edgar Lustgarten
Russell Napier . . . . Insp Duggan
Paula Byrne . . . . Mrs Carden
Melissa Stribling . . . . Helen Challoner
Arthur Gomez . . . . Supt Mason
Raymond Young . . . . Mr Carden
CRIME Scotland Yard track down ring
smuggling currency to Lisbon.

12263
LOSER TAKES ALL (88) (A) eastman/scope
IFP (BL)
P: John Stafford
D: Ken Annakin
S: (NOVEL) Graham Greene
SC: Graham Greene
Glynis Johns . . . . Cary
Rossano Brazzi . . . . Bertrand
Robert Morley . . . . Dreuther
Tony Britton . . . . Phillip
Felix Aylmer . . . . The Other
Albert Lieven . . . . The Manager
A.E.Matthews . . . . Elderly Man
Joyce Carey . . . . Birds' Nest
Geoffrey Keen . . . . Receptionist
Peter Illing . . . . Stranger
Walter Hudd . . . . Arnold
Charles Lloyd Pack . . . . Sir Walter Blixon
COMEDY Monte Carlo. Honeymooner
deserts his wife for gambling.

12264
ONE WISH TOO MANY (56) (U)
Realist (BL-CFF)
P: Basil Wright
D: John Durst
S: Norah Pulling
SC: John Eldridge, Mary Cathcart Borer
Anthony Richmond . . . . . Peter Brown
Rosalind Gougey . . . . Nancy
John Pike . . . . Ian
Terry Cooke . . . . Bert
Arthur Howard . . . . Headmaster
Gladys Young . . . . Miss Mint
Sam Costa . . . . Mr Pomfret
CHILDREN Boy finds magic marble
which grants wishes.

12265
CIRCUS FRIENDS (63) (U)
LIP-Femina Films (BL-CFF)
P:S: Peter Rogers
D: Gerald Thomas
Alan Coleshill . . . . Nicky
Carole White . . . . Nan
David Tilley . . . . Martin
Pat Belcher . . . . Beryl
Meredith Edwards . . . . Farmer Beasley
John Horsley . . . . Bert Marlow
Sam Kydd . . . . George
CHILDREN Children hide pony when
uncle gives it to farmer.

12266
BEYOND MOMBASA (90) tech (U)
Todon-Hemisphere (Col)
P: M.J.Frankovich, Adrian Worker
D: George Marshall
S: (NOVEL) James Eastwood
(MARK OF THE LEOPARD)
SC: Richard English, Gene Levitt
Cornel Wilde . . . . Matt Campbell
Donna Reed . . . . Ann Wilson
Leo Genn . . . . Ralph Hoyt
Ron Randell . . . . Eliot Hastings
Eddie Calvert . . . . Trumpeter
Christopher Lee . . . . Gil Rossi
Dan Jackson . . . . Ketimi
Bartholomew Sketch . . . . . Native Boss

Clive Morton . . . .   Irate Man
ADVENTURE Africa. Missionary in party
of uranium seekers is leader of native
terrorist group.

12267
THE SILKEN AFFAIR (96) (U)
Dragon (RKO)
P: Douglas Fairbanks, Fred Feldkamp
D: Roy Kellino
S: John McCarten
SC: Robert Lewis Taylor
David Niven . . . .   Roger Tweakham
Genevieve Page . . . . . .   Genevieve Gerard
Ronald Squire . . . .   Marberry
Beatrice Straight . . . .   Theora
Wilfrid Hyde White . . . . .   Sir Horace Hogg
Howard Marion-Crawford .   Baggott
Dorothy Alison . . . .   Mrs Tweakham
Richard Wattis . . . .   Worthington
Miles Malleson . . . .   Mr Blucher
Joan Sims . . . .   Lady Barber
Irene Handl . . . .   Receptionist
Charles Carson . . . .   Judge
COMEDY Staid accountant rebels and
juggles accounts of two stocking
manufacturers.

12268
ASSIGNMENT REDHEAD (79) (A)
Butcher's Films
P: W.G.Chalmers
D:SC: Maclean Rogers
S: Lindsay Hardy
Richard Denning . . . .   Keen
Carole Matthews . . . .   Hedy
Ronald Adam . . . .   Scammel
Danny Green . . . .   Yottie
Brian Worth . . . .   Ridgway
Jan Holden . . . .   Sally
Hugh Moxey . . . .   Sgt Coutts
Elwyn Brook-Jones . . . . . .   Mitchell
CRIME German singer helps FBI agent
catch gang seeking twelve million dollars
counterfeited by Nazis.

12269
FIND THE LADY (56) (U)
Major (RFD)
P: John Temple-Smith, Francis Edge
D: Charles Saunders
S: Paul Erickson, Dermot Palmer
SC: Kenneth R. Hayles
Donald Houston . . . .   Bill
Beverley Brooks . . . .   June Weston
Melvyn Johns . . . .   Hurst
Kay Callard . . . .   Rita
Maurice Kaufmann . . . . . .   Nicky
Edwin Richfield . . . .   Max
Moray Watson . . . .   Jimmy
Ferdy Mayne . . . . . .   Tony Del Roma
Anne Heywood . . . .   Receptionist
CRIME Bank robbers hide in old lady's
house and kidnap her niece.

12270
HOUSE OF SECRETS (97) (A) *tech*
USA: TRIPLE DECEPTION
Rank (RFD) *reissue:* 1960
P: Julian Wintle, Vivian A. Cox
D: Guy Green
S: (NOVEL) Sterling Noel
SC: Robert Buckner, Bryan Forbes
Michael Craig . . . .   Larry Ellis
Julia Arnall . . . .   Diane
Brenda de Banzie . . . .   Mme Ballu
Barbara Bates . . . .   Judy
David Kossoff . . . .   Van de Heide
Gerard Oury . . . .   Pindar
Geoffrey Keen . . . .   Burleigh

Anton Diffring . . . .   Lauderbach
Eric Pohlmann . . . .   Gratz
Eugene Deckers . . . .   Vidal
Jacques Brunius . . . .   Lessage
Carl Jaffe . . . .   Dorffman
Balbina . . . .   Maid
CRIME Paris. Naval officer catches forgers
by posing as dead double.

12271
THEY NEVER LEARN (47) (U)
E.J.Fancey (NR)
D:S: Denis Kavanagh
John Blythe . . . .   Frankie
Jackie Collins . . . .   Lil Smith
Adrienne Scott . . . .   PCW Watson
Graham Stark . . . .   Plum
CRIME Police woman catches forgers by
posing as ex-convict.

12272
A TOUCH OF THE SUN (80) (U)
Raystro Films (Eros)
P: Raymond Stross
D: Gordon Parry
S: Alfred Shaughnessy
Frankie Howerd . . . .   William Darling
Ruby Murray . . . .   Ruby
Dennis Price . . . .   Hatchard
Dorothy Bromiley . . . .   Rose
Katherine Kath . . . .   Lucienne
Gordon Harker . . . .   Sid
Reginald Beckwith . . . . . .   Hardcastle
Pierre Dudan . . . .   Louis
Colin Gordon . . . .   Cecil Flick
Richard Wattis . . . .   Purchase
Alfie Bass . . . .   May
Naomi Chance . . . .   Miss Lovejoy
COMEDY Hotel porter inherits £10,000
and has staff pose as guests to impress
prospective purchasers.

12273
DRY ROT (87) (U)
Remus (IFD)
P: Jack Clayton
D: Maurice Elvey
S: (PLAY) John Chapman
SC: John Chapman
Ronald Shiner . . . .   Alf Tubbs
Brian Rix . . . .   Fred Phipps
Peggy Mount . . . .   Sgt Fire
Lee Patterson . . . .   Danby
Sidney James . . . .   Flash Harry
Christian Duvaleix . . . .   Polignac
Joan Sims . . . .   Beth
Heather Sears . . . .   Susan
Michale Shepley . . . .   Col Wagstaffe
Joan Haythorne . . . .   Mrs Wagstaffe
Miles Malleson . . . .   Yokel
Raymond Glendenning . . . .   Himself
COMEDY Broke bookies scheme to
switch doped horse for favourite.

NOV

12274
ON THE TWELFTH DAY (23) (U) *eastman*
eastman
Bahamian (BL)
P: George K. Arthur
D: Wendy Toye
S: James Matthews, Val Valentine
Wendy Toye . . . .   Miss Tilly
David O'Brien . . . .   True Love
Franklin Bennett . . . .   Butler
MUSICAL Period. Suitor courts girl with
the items recounted in song, "The Twelve
Days of Christmas."

12275
MOBY DICK (115) *tech* (U)
Moulin (WB)
P: John Huston, Vaughan N. Dean
D: John Huston
S: (NOVEL) Herman Melville
SC: John Huston, Ray Bradbury
Gregory Peck . . . .   Capt Ahab
Richard Basehart . . . .   Ishmael
Leo Genn . . . .   Starbuck
Orson Welles . . . .   Father Mapple
James Robertson Justice . .   Capt Boomer
Harry Andrews . . . .   Stubb
Bernard Miles . . . .   Manxman
Noel Purcell . . . .   Carpenter
Edric Connor . . . .   Daggoo
Mervyn Johns . . . .   Peleg
Joseph Tomelty . . . .   Peter Coffin
Francis de Wolff . . . .   Capt Gardiner
Philip Stainton . . . .   Bildad
Royal Dano . . . .   Elijah
Friedrich Ledebur . . . .   Queequeg
ADVENTURE 1840. Obsessed captain
searches for white whale that took off
his leg.

12276
PERSON UNKNOWN (32) (U)
Merton Park (AA)
P: Alec Snowden
D: Montgomery Tully
S: James Eastwood
N: Edgar Lustgarten
Russell Napier . . . .   Insp Duggan
Marianne Stone . . . .   Mrs Cusick
CRIME Polish spy changes places with
would-be assassin.

12277
MY WIFE'S FAMILY (76) (U) *eastman*
Forth Films (ABP)
P: Hamilton G. Inglis
D: Gilbert Gunn
S: (PLAY) Fred Duprez
SC: Gilbert Gunn, Talbot Rothwell
Ronald Shiner . . . .   Doc Knott
Ted Ray . . . .   Jack Gay
Greta Gynt . . . .   Gloria Marsh
Robertson Hare . . . .   Noah Parker
Fabia Drake . . . .   Arabella Parker
Diane Hart . . . .   Stella Gay
Zena Marshall . . . .   Hilda
Benny Lee . . . .   Arnold
Jessica Cairns . . . .   Irma Parker
Jimmy Mageean . . . .   Dobson
Gilbert Harding . . . .   Himself
COMEDY Wife mistakes her husband's hidden
piano for his bastard baby.

12278
CHECKPOINT (84) (U) *eastman*
Rank (RFD)
P: Betty E. Box
D: Ralph Thomas
S: Robin Estridge
Anthony Steel . . . .   Bill Fraser
Odile Versois . . . .   Francesca
Stanley Baker . . . .   O'Donovan
James Robertson Justice . .   Warren Ingram
Maurice Denham . . . . . .   Ted Thornhill
Michael Medwin . . . .   Ginger
Paul Muller . . . .   Petersen
Lee Patterson . . . .   Johnny Carpenter
Anne Heywood . . . .   Gabriella
Anthony Oliver . . . .   Michael
McDonald Hobley . . . .   Commentator
SPORT Italy. Driver in Florence-Locarno
race learns his partner is a crook.

12279
THE BATTLE OF THE RIVER PLATE (119)
(U) *tech* USA: PURSUIT OF THE GRAF SPEE
Arcturus (RFD) *reissue:* 1961 (cut)
P:D:S: Michael Powell, Emeric Pressburger
John Gregson .... Capt Bell
Anthony Quayle .... Cdr Harwood
Peter Finch .... Capt Langsdorff
Bernard Lee .... Capt Dove
Ian Hunter .... Capt Woodhouse
Jack Gwillim .... Capt Parry
Lionel Murton .... Mike Fowler
Anthony Bushell ...... Millington-Drake
Peter Illing .... Dr Guani
Michael Goodliffe .... Capt McCall
William Squire .... Ray Martin
Andrew Cruickshank ..... Capt Stubs
Christopher Lee .... Manola
WAR Montevideo, 1939. British cruisers
sink German pocket battleship . (RFP: 1956).

12280
THE SPANISH GARDENER (97) *tech* (U)
Rank (RFD)
P: John Bryan
D: Philip Leacock
S: (NOVEL) A.J.Cronin
SC: John Bryan, Lesley Storm
Dirk Bogarde .... Jose Santero
Jon Whiteley .... Nicholas Brande
Michael Hordern .... Harrington Brande
Cyril Cusack .... Garcia
Maureen Swanson .... Maria
Lyndon Brook .... Robert Burton
Josephine Griffin .... Carol Burton
Bernard Lee .... Leighton Bailey
Rosalie Crutchley .... Magdalena
Ina de la Haye .... Mrs Santero
Geoffrey Keen .... Dr Harvey
CRIME Spain. British consul's young
son helps gardener who is jailed for
chauffeur's theft.

12281
TIGER IN THE SMOKE (94) (A)
Rank (RFD)
P: Leslie Parkyn
D: Roy Baker
S: (NOVEL) Margery Allingham
SC: Anthony Pelissier
Donald Sinden .... Geoffrey Levett
Muriel Pavlow .... Meg Elkin
Tony Wright .... Jack Havoc
Bernard Miles .... Tiddy Doll
Alec Clunes .... Oates
Laurence Naismith .... Canon Avril
Christopher Rhodes ...... Insp Luke
Charles Victor .... Will Talisman
Thomas Heathcote ...... Rolly Gripper
Sam Kydd .... Tom Gripper
Kenneth Griffith .... Crutches
Beatrice Varley .... Mrs Cash
CRIME Police and gang seek escaped
convict searching for treasure.

12282
STARS IN YOUR EYES (96) (U)
eastman/scope
Grand Alliance (BL)
P: David Dent
D: Maurice Elvey
S: Francis Miller
SC: Talbot Rothwell, Hubert Gregg
Nat Jackley .... Jimmy Knowles
Pat Kirkwood .... Sally Bishop
Bonar Colleano .... David Laws
Dorothy Squires .... Ann Hart
Jack Jackson .... Rigby
Hubert Gregg .... Crawley Walters
Meier Tzelniker .... Maxie Jago
Vera Day .... Maureen Temple
Joan Sims .... Secretary
Jimmy Clitheroe .... Joey

Freddie Frinton .... Publican
Reginald Forsythe .... Pianist
MUSICAL Unemployed artistes put on
show despite crooked agents.

DEC

12283
THE HIDEOUT (57) (U)
Major (RFD)
P: John Temple-Smith, Francis Edge
D: Peter Graham Scott
S: Kenneth R. Hayles
Dermot Walsh .... Steve Curry
Rona Anderson .... Helen Grant
Ronald Howard .... Robert Grant
Sam Kydd .... Tim Bowers
Howard Lang .... Greeko
Edwin Richfield .... Teacher
Trevor Reid .... Fraser
Frank Hawkins .... Insp Ryan
CRIME Broker buys stolen furs and
finds them diseased with anthrax.

12284
UP IN THE WORLD (91) (U)
Rank (RFD)
P: Hugh Stewart
D: John Paddy Carstairs
S: Jack Davies, Henry Blyth, Peter Blackmore
Norman Wisdom .... Norman
Maureen Swanson .... Jeannie Andrews
Jerry Desmonde .... Maj Willoughby
Michael Caridia ..... Sir Reginald Banderville
Colin Gordon ..... Fletcher Hethrington
Ambrosine Philpotts .. Lady Banderville
Michael Ward .... Maurice
Jill Dixon .... Sylvia
Edwin Styles .... Conjuror
Hy Hazell .... Yvonne
William Lucas .... Mick Bellman
Lionel Jeffries .... Wilson
Cyril Chamberlain ...... Harper
Eddie Leslie .... Max
Bernard Bresslaw .... Williams
COMEDY Lady's window cleaner saves
mischievous son from kidnappers.

12285
THE HOSTAGE (80) (A)
Douglas Fairbanks-Westridge (Eros)
P: Thomas Clyde
D: Harold Huth
S: Alfred Shaughnessy
Ron Randell .... Bill Trailer
Mary Parker .... Rosa Gonzuelo
John Bailey .... Dr Main
Carl Jaffe .... Dr Pablo Gonzuelo
Anne Blake .... Mrs Steen
Cyril Luckham .... Hugh Ferguson
Margaret Diamond ...... Mme Gonzuelo
Victor Brooks .... Insp Clifford
CRIME Pilot saves president's daughter
from revolutionary.

12286
THREE MEN IN A BOAT (94) (U)
eastman/scope
Remus (IFD)
P: Jack Clayton
D: Ken Annakin
S: (NOVEL) Jerome K. Jerome
SC: Hubert Gregg, Vernon Harris
Laurence Harvey .... George
Jimmy Edwards .... Harris
David Tomlinson .... J
Shirley Eaton .... Sophie Clutterbuck
Jill Ireland ...... Bluebell Porterhouse
Lisa Gastoni...... Primrose Porterhouse
Martita Hunt .... Mrs Willis
Adrienne Corri .... Clara Willis
Noelle Middleton .... Ethelbertha
Robertson Hare .... Photographer
Campbell Cotts ...... Ambrose Porterhouse

A.E.Matthews .... Crabtree
Miles Malleson .... Baskcomb
Ernest Thesiger .... Old Gent
Joan Haythorne .... Mrs Porterhouse
COMEDY Period. Misadventures of three
friends on boating holiday.

12287
ANASTASIA (105) (U) *eastman/scope*
20th Century Fox
P: Buddy Adler
D: Anatole Litvak
S: (PLAY) Marcelle Maurette, Guy Bolton
SC: Arthur Laurents
Ingrid Bergman .... Anastasia
Yul Brynner .... Bounine
Helen Hayes .... Dowager Empress
Akim Tamiroff .... Chernov
Martita Hunt .... Baroness Livenbaum
Felix Aylmer .... Chamberlain
Serge Pitoeff .... Petrovin
Ivan Desny .... Prince Paul
Natalie Schaefer .... Lissenskaia
Karel Stepanek .... Vlados
Katherine Kath.......... Maxime
Hy Hazell .... Blonde
DRAMA Paris, 1928. Is an amnesiac girl
really the Czar's daughter ?
(AA: Best Actress, 1957).

12288
THE BIG MONEY (86) (U) *tech*
Rank (RFD)
P: Joseph Janni
D: John Paddy Carstairs
S: John Baines
SC: John Baines, Patrick Campbell
Ian Carmichael .... Willie Frith
Belinda Lee .... Gloria
Kathleen Harrison .... Mrs Frith
Robert Helpmann .... Reverend
James Hayter .... Mr Frith
George Coulouris .... Colonel
Renee Houston .... Bobby
Michael Brennan .... Bluey
Jill Ireland .... Doreen Frith
Leslie Phillips .... Receptionist
Harold Berens .... Bookie
Digby Wolfe .... Harry Mason
COMEDY Crooked family's inept son steals
counterfeit money from gang leader.

12289
DICK TURPIN – HIGHWAYMAN (25) (U)
eastman/scope
Hammer
P: Michael Carreras
D: David Paltenghi
S:Joel Murcott
Philip Friend .... Dick Turpin
Diane Hart .... Liz
Allan Cuthbertson ...... Jonathan Redgrove
Raymond Rollett .... Hawkins
Hal Osmond .... Mac
Norman Mitchell .... Rooks
Gabrielle May .... Genevieve
ADVENTURE Period. Highwayman steals girl's
dowry and exposes her fiance as decoy for robber
gang.

12290
FIVE GUINEAS A WEEK (33) (U) *eastman/scope*
De Lane Lea (Archway)
P: Jacques de Lane Lea
D: Donald Monat
S: Donald Monat, Martinson James, Donald
Cotton
Sally Bazeley .... Georgia Brown
Sheila O'Neill .... Glen Wilcox
Nevil Whiting .... Eileen Elton
Len Mayne .... Barbara Ferris
MUSICAL Life in Chelsea apartment house.

1957

JAN

12291
OPERATION MURDER (66) (A)
Danziger (ABP)
P: Edward J. & Harry Lee Danziger
D: Ernest Morris
S: Brian Clemens

Tom Conway	Dr Wayne
Sandra Dorne	Pat Wayne
Patrick Holt	Dr Bowen
Rosamund John	Head Nurse
Robert Ayres	Larry Winton
Virginia Keiley	Julie
John Stone	Insp Price
Alastair Hunter	Williams

CRIME Surgeon changes places with colleague so he may kill his rich cousin to save private hospital.

12292
THE LONELY HOUSE (33) (A)
Merton Park (AA)
P: Alec Snowden
D: Montgomery Tully
S: James Eastwood
N: Edgar Lustgarten

Russell Napier	Inspector Duggan
Dorothy Bramhall	
Bettina Dickson	

CRIME Man and wife run phoney marriage bureau.

12293
THE COUNTERFEIT PLAN (87) (A)
Merton Park (AA)
P: Alec Snowden
D: Montgomery Tully
S: James Eastwood

Zachary Scott	Max Brandt
Peggie Castle	Carol
Mervyn Johns	Louis
Sydney Tafler	Flint
Lee Patterson	Duke
Chili Bouchier	Housekeeper
Eric Pohlmann	Wandermann
Robert Arden	Bob
John Welsh	Insp Grant
David Lodge	Watson
Alvar Lidell	Newsreader

CRIME Escaped murderer forces ex-forger to counterfeit £5 banknotes.

12294
THE GIRL IN THE PICTURE (63) (U)
Cresswell (Eros)
P: Edward Lloyd
D: Don Chaffey
S: Paul Rogers

Donald Houston	John Deering
Patrick Holt	Insp Bliss
Maurice Kaufmann	Rod Molloy
Junia Crawford	Pat Dryden
Paddy Joyce	Jack Bates
John Miller	Duncan
Tom Chatto	George Keefe

CRIME Reporter seeks girl witness to murder of policeman.

12295
THE MAN IN THE SKY (87) (U)
USA: DECISION AGAINST TIME
Ealing (MGM)
P: Seth Holt
D: Charles Crichton
S: William Rose
SC: William Rose, John Eldridge

Jack Hawkins	John Mitchell
Elizabeth Sellars	Mary Mitchell
Walter Fitzgerald	Conway
Eddie Byrne	Ashmore
John Stratton	Peter Hook
Victor Maddern	Joe Biggs
Lionel Jeffries	Keith
Donald Pleasence	Crabtree
Catherine Lacey	Mother
Megs Jenkins	Mrs Snowden
Ernest Clark	Maine
Russell Waters	Sim
Howard Marion-Crawford	Ingram

DRAMA Test pilot saves small avaition company by landing damaged freighter.

12296
ZARAK (95) (A) *tech/scope*
Warwick (Col) *reissue:* 1961 (Unifilms)
P: Phil C. Samuel
D: Terence Young, Yakima Canutt, John Gilling
S: (BOOK) A.C. Bevan
(THE STORY OF ZARAK KHAN)
SC: Richard Maibaum

Victor Mature	Zarak Khan
Michael Wilding	Maj Ingram
Anita Ekberg	Salma
Bonar Colleano	Biri
Finlay Currie	Mullah
Bernard Miles	Hassu
Eunice Gayson	Cathy Ingram
Peter Illing	Ahmad
Eddie Byrne	Kasim
Yana	Singer
Frederick Valk	Haji Khan
Patrick McGoohan	Larkin
Harold Goodwin	Higgins
Andre Morell	Atherton
Geoffrey Keen	Carruthers

ADVENTURE India, period. Bandit chief saves life of British major who captured him.

12297
TOWN ON TRIAL (96) (A)
Marksman (Col)
P: Maxwell Setton
D: John Guillermin
S: Robert Westerby, Ken Hughes

John Mills	Supt Mike Halloran
Charles Coburn	Dr John Fenner
Barbara Bates	Elizabeth Fenner
Derek Farr	Mark Roper
Elizabeth Seal	Fiona Dixon
Alec McCowen	Peter Crowley
Fay Compton	Mrs Crowley
Geoffrey Keen	Mr Dixon
Margaretta Scott	Helen Dixon
Meredith Edwards	Sgt Rogers
Harry Locke	Sgt Beale
Raymond Huntley	Dr Reese
Maureen Connell	Mary Roper
Magda Miller	Molly Stevens

CRIME CID supt suspects nurse's uncle strangled pregnant girl.

12298
TREASURE AT THE MILL (60) (U)
Wallace (BL—CFF)
P: A.V. Curtice
D: Max Anderson
S: Malcolm Saville
SC: Mary Cathcart Borer

Richard Palmer	John Adams
John Ruddock	Mr Wilson
Hilda Fenemore	Mrs Adams
The Pettit Family	Themselves

CHILDREN Children help widow's son search old mill for cavalier's treasure.

12299
BULLET FROM THE PAST (33) (U)
Merton Park (AA)
P: Alec Snowden
D: Kenneth Hume
S: Donovan Winter
N: Edgar Lustgarten

Ballard Berkeley
Robert Sansom
Philippa Hiatt

CRIME Insp solves 27—year old murder whilst investigating the shooting of insurance agent.

FEB

12300
NO ROAD BACK (83) (A)
Gibraltar (RKO)
P: Steven Pallos, Charles Leeds
D: Montgomery Tully
S: (PLAY) Falkland Cary, Philip Weathers
(MADAME TICTAC)
SC: Charles Leeds, Montgomery Tully

Skip Homier	John Railton
Paul Carpenter	Clem Hayes
Patricia Dainton	Beth
Norman Wooland	Insp Harris
Margaret Rawlings	Mrs Railton
Eleanor Summerfield	Marguerite
Alfie Bass	Rudge Haven
Sean Connery	Spike

CRIME Blind and deaf club-owner saves son from being framed by jewel thieves.

12301
ILL MET BY MOONLIGHT (104) (U)
USA: NIGHT AMBUSH
Vega (RFD) *reissue:* 1961 (Unifilms)
P:D:SC: Michael Powell, Emeric Pressburger
S: (BOOK) W. Stanley Moss
N: E.V.H. Emmett

Dirk Bogarde	Maj Patrick Leigh Fermor
Marius Goring	Gen Karl Kreipe
David Oxley	Capt W. Stanley Moss
Demitri Andreas	Nikko
Cyril Cusack	Sandy
Laurence Payne	Manoli
Wolfe Morris	George
Michael Gough	Andoni Zoidakis
John Cairney	Elias
Brian Worth	Stratis Saviolkis
Rowland Bartrop	Micky Akouianakis

WAR Crete, 1944. True story of capture of German general.

12302
THE SECRET PLACE (98) (A)
Rank (RFD)
P: John Bryan, Anthony Perry
D: Clive Donner
S: Linette Perry

Belinda Lee	Molly Wilson
Ronald Lewis	Gerry Carter
Michael Brooke	Freddie Haywood
Michael Gwynn	Stephen Waring
Geoffrey Keen	PC Haywood
David McCullum	Mike Wilson
Maureen Pryor	Mrs Haywood
George Selway	Paddy
George A. Cooper	Harry

CRIME Crooks use PC's young son as dupe and he hides their stolen diamond.

12303
TRUE AS TURTLE (96) (U) *eastman*
Rank (RFD)
P: Peter de Sarigny
D: Wendy Toye
S: (NOVEL) John Coates
SC: John Coates, Jack Davies, Nicholas Phipps

John Gregson	Tony Hudson
June Thorburn	Jane Hudson
Cecil Parker	Dudley
Keith Michell	Harry Bell
Elvi Hale	Anne
Avice Landone	Valerie
Jacques Brunius	Charbonnier

Gabrielle Brune .... Mary
Charles Clay .... Sir Harold Brazier
Betty Stockfeld .... Lady Brazier
COMEDY Honeymooners aboard old yacht
mistake insurance man for crook.

12304
THE BARRETTS OF WIMPOLE STREET
(105) (U) *metro/scope*
MGM British
P: Sam Zimbalist
D: Sidney Franklin
S: (PLAY) Rudolph Besier
SC: John Dighton
Jennifer Jones .... Elizabeth
John Gielgud .... Edward Moulton-Barrett
Bill Travers .... Robert Browning
Virginia McKenna .... Henrietta
Susan Stephen .... Bella
Vernon Gray .... Capt Surtees-Cook
Jean Anderson .... Wilson
Maxine Audley .... Arabel
Leslie Phillips .... Harry Bevan
Laurence Naismith .... Dr Chambers
ROMANCE 1845. Sick authoress weds poet
despite her tyrannical father.

12305
SUSPENDED ALIBI (64) (U)
ACT Films (RFD)
P: Robert Dunbar
D: Alfred Shaughnessy
S: Kenneth R. Hayles
Patrick Holt .... Paul Pearson
Honor Blackman .... Lynn Pearson
Valentine Dyall .... Insp Kayes
Naomi Chance .... Diana
Lloyd Lamble .... Waller
Andrew Keir .... Sandy
CRIME Editor accused of stabbing friend he
used as an alibi while visiting mistress.

12306
ALIVE ON SATURDAY (58) (U)
C & G Films (ABP)
P: Geoffrey Goodhart, Brandon Fleming
D: Afred Travers
S: Brandon Fleming
Guy Middleton .... George Pilbeam
Patricia Owens .... Sally Parker
Geoffrey Goodhart ..... Joseph H. Parker
John Witty .... Slade
Jessica Cairns .... Maisie
John Salew .... Melito
Charles Lloyd Pack ...... Gorman
Wallas Eaton .... Garton
COMEDY American millionaire financing
revolution mistakes broke man for Ruritanian
Prince.

12307
THE PASSIONATE STRANGER (97) (A)
USA: A NOVEL AFFAIR *eastman seq*
Beaconsfield (BL)
P: Peter Rogers, Gerald Thomas
D: Muriel Box
S: Muriel & Sydney Box
Ralph Richardson .... Roger Wynter/
                          Sir Clement
Margaret Leighton ... Judith Wynter/Leonie
Patricia Dainton .... Emily/Betty
Carlo Justini .... Carlo/Mario
Marjorie Rhodes .... Mrs Poldy
Thorley Walters .... Jimmy
Frederick Piper .... Mr Poldy
Megs Jenkins .... Millie
Alexander Gauge .... MC
John Arnatt .... Maurice
George Woodbridge ...... Landlord

Allan Cuthbertson .... Miles Easter
Ada Reeve .... Old Woman
COMEDY Prof's wife writes romance which
her Sicilian chauffeur believes is true.

12308
BROTHERS IN LAW (94) (U)
Tudor (BL)
P: John Boulting
D: Roy Boulting
S: (NOVEL) Henry Cecil
SC: Roy Boulting, Frank Harvey, Jeffrey Dell
Richard Attenborough .... Henry Marshall
Ian Carmichael .... Roger Thursby
Terry-Thomas .... Alfred Green
Jill Adams .... Sally Smith
Miles Malleson .... Kendall Grimes
Raymond Huntley .... Tatlock
Eric Barker .... Alec Blair
Nicholas Parsons .... Charles Poole
Kynaston Reeves .... Judge Lawson
John le Mesurier .... Judge Ryman
Irene Handl .... Mrs Potter
Olive Sloane .... Mrs Newent
Edith Sharpe .... Mrs Thursby
Leslie Phillips .... Shopman
Brian Oulton .... Solicitor
George Rose .... Frost
Kenneth Griffith .... Undertaker
COMEDY Episodic misadventures of pupil
barrister.

12309
YOU PAY YOUR MONEY (67) (U)
Butcher's Films
P: W.G. Chalmers
D:SC: Maclean Rogers
S: (NOVEL) Michael Cronin
Hugh McDermott .... Bob Westlake
Jane Hylton .... Rosemary Delgardo
Honor Blackman .... Susie Westlake
Hugh Moxey ..... Tom Cookson
Ivan Samson .... Steve Mordaunt
Ferdy Mayne .... Delal
Shirley Deane .... Doris Squire
Gerard Heinze .... Dr Burger
CRIME Arab league kidnaps girl for rare books
smuggled by financier.

MAR

12310
SEVEN WAVES AWAY (95) (A)
USA: ABANDON SHIP !
Copa (Col)
P: Ted Richmond, John R. Sloan
D:S: Richard Sale
Tyrone Power .... Alec Holmes
Mai Zetterling .... Julie White
Lloyd Nolan .... Frank Kelly
Stephen Boyd .... Will McKinley
Moira Lister .... Edith Middleton
James Hayter .... Cookie Morrow
Marie Lohr .... Mrs Knudsen
Finlay Currie .... Weedon
John Stratton .... Sparks Cleary
Victor Maddern .... Willy Hawkins
Eddie Byrne .... Michael Faroni
Noel William .... Aubrey Clark
Moultrie Kelsall .... Daniel Cane
Ralph Michael .... George Kilgore
Gordon Jackson .... John Merritt
Clive Morton .... Maj-Gen Barrington
Laurence Naismith .... Captain
Orlando Martins .... Sam Holly
DRAMA Officer of mined liner must cast some
passengers overboard to save lifeboat.

12311
FORTUNE IS A WOMAN (95) (A)
USA: SHE PLAYED WITH FIRE
John Harvel (Col)
P: Frank Launder, Sidney Gilliat
D: Sidney Gilliat
S:(NOVEL) Winston Graham
SC: Frank Launder,Sidney Gilliat,
Val Valentine
Jack Hawkins .... Oliver Branwell
Arlene Dahl .... Sarah Morton
Dennis Price .... Tracey Morton
Ian Hunter .... Clive Fisher
Greta Gynt .... Vere Lychen
Bernard Miles .... Jerome
Patrick Holt .... Fred Connor
Violet Farebrother .... Mrs Morton
Malcolm Keen .... Abercrombie
Geoffrey Keen .... Michael Abercrombie
John Robinson .... Berkeley Reckitt
Michael Goodliffe .... Sgt Barnes
Christopher Lee .... Charles Highbury
CRIME Insurance investigator learns painting
burned in fire was a fake.

12312
THE GOOD COMPANIONS (104) (U)
tech/scope
ABPC
P: Hamilton G. Inglis
D: J. Lee-Thompson
S: (NOVEL) J.B. Priestley
SC: T.J. Morrison, J.L. Hodgson, John Whiting
Eric Portman .... Jews Oakroyd
Celia Johnson .... Miss Trant
Hugh Griffith .... Morton Mitcham
Janette Scott .... Susie Dean
John Fraser .... Inigo Jolifant
Joyce Grenfell .... Lady Parlett
Bobby Howes .... Jimmy Nunn
Rachel Roberts .... Elsie/Effie Longstaffe
Thora Hird .... Mrs Oakroyd
Mona Washbourne .... Mrs Brundit
John Salew .... Joe Brundit
Paddy Stone ....Jerry Jerningham
Beatrice Varley .... Mrs Nunn
Alec McCowen .... Albert
John le Mesurier ....Monte Mortimer
Fabia Drake .... Mrs Tarvin
Anthony Newley .... Milbrau
MUSICAL Middle-aged woman finances failing
concert party.

12313
TIME WITHOUT PITY (88) (A)
Harlequin (Eros)
P: Leon Clore, John Arnold, Anthony Simmons
D: Joseph Losey
S: (PLAY) Emlyn Williams

(SOMEONE WAITING)
SC: Ben Barzman
Michael Redgrave .... David Graham
Ann Todd .... Honor Stanford
Leo McKern .... Robert Stanford
Peter Cushing .... Jeremy Clayton
Lois Maxwell .... Vicky Harker
Renee Houston .... Mrs Harker
Alec McCowen .... Alan Graham
Paul Daneman .... Brian Stanford
Richard Wordsworth ...... Maxwell
George Devine .... Barnes
Joan Plowright .... Agnes Cole
Dickie Henderson .... Comedian
CRIME Alcoholic gives life to trap killer who
framed his son.

12314
WEST OF SUEZ (75) (A)
USA: FIGHTING WILDCATS
Winwell (Astral)
P: Bill & Kay Luckwell, Derek Winn
D: Arthur Crabtree
S: Lance Z. Hargreaves
SC: Norman Hudis
Keefe Brasselle .... Brett Manders
Kay Callard .... Pat
Karel Stepanek .... Langford
Maya Koumani .... Men Hassa
Bruce Seton .... Maj Osborne
Harry Fowler .... Tommy
Ursula Howells .... Eileen
Richard Shaw........... Cross
Sheldon Lawrence .... Jeff
CRIME Gun traffickers hire American explosives expert to blow up Arab leader in London.

12315
THERE'S ALWAYS THURSDAY (62) (A)
ASFI (RFD)
P: Guido Coen
D: Charles Saunders
S: Brandon Fleming
Charles Victor .... George Potter
Marjorie Rhodes .... Marjorie Potter
Frances Day .... Vera Clanton
Patrick Holt .... Middleton
Jill Ireland .... Jennifer
Bruce Seton .... James Pelley
Ewen Solon .... Insp Bradley
Lloyd Lamble .... Sgt Bolton
Glen Alyn .... Mrs Middleton
Alex Macintosh .... TV Interviewer
COMEDY Henpecked bank clerk mistaken for philanderer is made director of lingerie firm.

12316
DOCTOR AT LARGE (104) (eastman) (U)
Rank (RFD)
P: Betty E. Box
D: Ralph Thomas
S: (NOVEL) Richard Gordon
SC: Richard Gordon, Nicholas Phipps
Dirk Bogarde .... Simon Sparrow
Muriel Pavlow .... Joy
Donald Sinden .... Benskin
James Robertson Justice . Sir Lancelot Spratt
Shirley Eaton .... Nan
Derek Farr .... Dr Potter-Shine
Michael Medwin .... Bingham
Edward Chapman .... Wilkins
George Coulouris .... Pascoe
Gladys Henson .... Mrs Wilkins
Ann Heywood .... Emerald
Lionel Jeffries .... Dr Hatchett
Mervyn Johns .... Smith
Geoffrey Keen .... Examiner
Dilys Laye .... Jasmine
A.E. Matthews .... Duke of Skye and Lewes
Guy Middleton .... Major
Barbara Murray .... Kitty
Nicholas Phipps .... Mr Wayland
Frederick Piper .... Ernest
George Relph .... Dr Farquarson
Athene Seyler .... Lady Howkins
Ernest Thesiger .... Examiner
Noel Purcell .... Bartender
COMEDY Episodic misadventures of doctor after leaving hospital.
(Top Moneymaker: 1957.)

12317
QUATERMASS II (85) (X)
USA: ENEMY FROM SPACE
Hammer–Clarion (UA)
P: Anthony Hinds
D: Val Guest
S: (TV SERIAL) Nigel Kneale
SC: Nigel Kneale, Val Guest
Brian Donlevy .... Bernard Quatermass
Sidney James .... Jimmy Hall
John Longden .... Insp Lomax
Bryan Forbes .... Marsh
Vera Day .... Sheila
William Franklyn .... Brand
Charles Lloyd Pack .... Dawson
Tom Chatto .... Vincent Broadhead
John Van Eyssen .... PRO
Percy Herbert .... Gorman
HORROR Space organisms take over humans and build huge food plant.

12318
SEAWIFE (82) (A) tech/scope
Sumar Films (20) Reissue: 1961 (cut)
P: Andre Hakim
D: Bob McNaught
S: (NOVEL) J.M. Scott
(SEAWYF AND BISCUIT)
SC: George K. Burke
Joan Collins .... Seawife
Richard Burton .... Biscuit
Basil Sydney .... Bulldog
Cy Grant .... No. 4
Ronald Squire .... Clubman
Harold Goodwin .... Clerk
Roddy Hughes .... Barman
Gibb McLaughlin .... Porter
Lloyd Lamble .... Captain
Nicholas Hannen .... Passenger
Ronald Adam .... Padre
Beatrice Varley .... Nun
ADVENTURE Far East, 1942. Three men survive torpedoed ship and learn girl with them is a nun.

12319
TROUBLE FOR JUNO (13) (U)
Gateway (Saxon)
P:D:S: Barbara Woodhouse
ANIMAL Children's Great Dane pet rescues baby.

12320
JUNO MAKES FRIENDS (19) (U)
Gateway Films (Saxon)
P:D:S: Barbara Woodhouse
ANIMAL Great Dane leaves home and befriends tramp when children adopt puppy.

APR

12321
FIGHTING MAD (53) (U)
Border (NR)
P:Edwin Scott
D: Denis Kavanagh
S: Jeniffer Wyatt
Joe Robinson .... Muscles Tanner
Adrienne Scott .... Paula
Beckett Bould .... Uncle Jake
Jack Taylor .... Walker
CRIME Canada. Boxer and wife save uncle's oil claim from crooks.

12322
THE TRAITORS (88) (A)
USA: THE ACCUSED
Fantur Films (NR) reissue: 1960
P: E.J. Fancey
D:S: Michael McCarthy
Donald Wolfit .... Col Price
Robert Bray .... Maj Shane
Jane Griffiths .... Vicki Toller
Anton Diffring .... Joseph Brezzini
Oscar Quitak .... Thomas Rilke
John Van Eyssen .... Lt Grant
Rupert Davies .... Clinton
Christopher Lee ....
Carl Jaffe .... Prof Toller
Karel Stepanek ......
CRIME Col unmasks Nazi agent at reunion of resistance group.

12323
HI–JACK (50) (U) retitled:
ACTION STATIONS
Aqua Films (NR)
P:D:S: Cecil H. Williamson
Paul Carpenter .... Bob Reynolds
Mary Martin .... Anna Braun
Joe Robinson .... Pete Archer
Ronald Leigh Hunt ...... Kleivar
CRIME Spain. Smuggler saves engraver's daughter from counterfeiters.

12324
HIGH TIDE AT NOON (109) (A)
Rank (RFD)
P: Julian Wintle
D: Philip Leacock
S: (NOVEL) Elizabeth Oglivie
SC: Neil Paterson
Betta StJohn .... Joanna Mackenzie
William Sylvester .... Alec Douglas
Michael Craig .... Nils
Flora Robson .... Donna Mackenzie
Alexander Knox .... Stephen Mackenzie
Peter Arne .... Owen Mackenzie
Patrick McGoohan .... Simon Breck
Patrick Allen .... Charles Mackenzie
Jill Dixon .... Mateel
Susan Beaumont .... Kristi
Stella Bonheur .... Aunt Mary
Bernard Bresslaw .... Tom Robey
DRAMA Nova Scotia. Girl weds gambling fisherman who is drowned.

12325
THE SMALLEST SHOW ON EARTH (81) (U)
Hallmark (BL) reissue: 1960 (cut)
P: Frank Launder, Sidney Gillat, Michael Relph
D: Basil Dearden
S: William Rose
SC: William Rose, John Eldridge
Virginia McKenna .... Jean Spencer
Bill Travers .... Matt Spencer
Peter Sellers .... Percy Quill
Margaret Rutherford .... Mrs Fazackerlee
Bernard Miles .... Old Tom
Leslie Phillips .... Robin Carter
Francis de Wolff .... Hardcastle
Sidney James .... Hogg
June Cunningham .... Marlene Hogg
COMEDY Couple inherit fleapit cinema and staff, who help them thwart their rival.
(Includes extract from COMIN' THRO' THE RYE, 1923)

12326
YANGTSE INCIDENT (113) (U)
USA: BATTLE HELL
Everest (BL) reissue: 1960,
ESCAPE OF THE AMETHYST (20 mins cut)
P: Herbert Wilcox
D: Michael Anderson
S: (BOOK) Laurence Earl (ESCAPE OF THE AMETHYST); Franklin Gollings
SC: Eric Ambler
Richard Todd .... Lt/Cdr Kearns
William Hartnell .... L/S Frank
Akim Tamiroff .... Col Peng
Donald Houston .... Lt Weston
Keye Luke .... Capt Kuo Tai
Sophie Stewart .... Charlotte Dunlap
Robert Urquhart .... F/Lt Fearnley
James Kenney .... Lt Hett
Richard Leach .... Lt Strain
Michael Brill .... Lt Berger
Barry Foster .... PO McCarthy
Thomas Heathcote .... Mr Monaghan
Sam Kydd .... AB Walker
Ewen Solon .... Williams

Ian Bannen .... Bannister
Gene Anderson .... Ruth Worth
WAR China, 1949. Communist army traps
HMS Amethyst in Yangtse river.

12327
CARRY ON ADMIRAL (82) (U) *scope*
USA: THE SHIP WAS LOADED
George Minter (Renown) *reissue:* 1959
P: Denis O'Dell
D:SC: Val Guest
S: (PLAY) Ian Hay, Stephen King-Hall
(OFF THE RECORD)
David Tomlinson .... Tom Baker
Peggy Cummins .... Susan Lashwood
Brian Reece .... Lt/Cdr Peter Fraser
Eunice Gayson .... Jane Godfrey
A.E. Matthews .... Admiral Godfrey
Ronald Shiner .... Salty Simpson
Joan Sims .... Mary
Lionel Murton .... Psychiatrist
Reginald Beckwith .... Receptionist
Desmond Walter-Ellis . Willy Oughton-Formby
Peter Coke .... Lt Simpson
Derek Blomfield .... Lt Dobson
George Moon .... Casey
Alfie Bass .... Orderley
COMEDY Parliamentary private secretary
mistaken for naval officer when he changes
clothes with friend.

12328
THE CROOKED SKY (77) (U)
Luckwin (RFD)
P: Bill Luckwell, Derek Winn
D: Henry Cass
S: Lance Z. Hargreaves, Maclean Rogers
SC: Norman Hudis
Wayne Morris .... Mike Conlin
Karin Booth .... Sandra Hastings
Anton Diffring .... Fraser
Bruce Seton .... Mac
Sheldon Lawrence .... Bill
Collette Barthrop .... Penny
Frank Hawkins .... Robson
Murray Kash .... Lewis
Wally Peterson .... Wilson
CRIME American tec unmasks gambler as head
of banknote counterfeiters.

12329
INTERPOL (92) (A) *scope*
USA: PICKUP ALLEY
Warwick (Col) *reissue:* 1961 (Unifilms)
P: Irving Allen, Albert Broccoli, Phil C. Samuel
D: John Gilling
S: (BOOK) A.J. Forrest
SC: John Paxton
Victor Mature .... Charles Sturgis
Anita Ekberg .... Gina Broger
Trevor Howard .... Frank McNally
Bonar Colleano .... Amalio
Dorothy Alison .... Helen
Andre Morell .... Breckner
Martin Benson .... Varolli
Eric Pohlmann .... Fayala
Peter Illing .... Capt Baris
Sydney Tafler .... Curtis
Lionel Murton .... Murphy
Danny Green .... Bartender
Sidney James .... Joe
Yana .... Singer
CRIME American tec chases dope smuggler
around London, Paris, Rome, Athens, and
New York.

12330
THE DEVIL'S PASS (56) (U)
Darcy Conyers (ABP)
P: David Henley
D:S: Darcy Conyers

John Slater .... Bill Buckle
Christopher Warbey ...... Jim
Richard George .... Ted Trelawney
Joan Newell .... Mrs Trelawney
Archie Duncan .... George Jolley
Charles Leno .... Headmaster
ADVENTURE Devon. Boy stowaway helps
fisherman save boat from wreckers.

12331
MURDER REPORTED (58) (A)
Fortress (Col)
P: Guido Coen
D: Charles Saunders
S: (NOVEL) Robert Chapman
(MURDER FOR THE MILLIONS)
SC: Doreen Montgomery
Paul Carpenter .... Jeff Holly
Melissa Stribling .... Amanda North
Patrick Holt .... Bill Stevens
John Laurie .... Mac
Peter Swanwick .... Hatter
Maurice Durant .... Carmady
Georgia Brown .... Myra
Trevor Reid .... Insp Palisay
CRIME Reporter and boss's daughter solve
death of local councillor.

12332
FUN AT THE MOVIES (12) (U)
Danziger (BL)
P: Harry & Edward Danziger
D: Paul Dickson
S: Michael Bentine
Michael Bentine .... Himself
COMEDY Comedian satirises various types of
films.

12333
ALL SQUARE AFT (29) (U) *eastman*
AB—Pathe
D: Gerry Bryant
Anthony Sagar .... Bill Rogers
Norman Pierca .... Sam Rogers
Charles Lamb ....
Robert Desmond .....
John Harvey ....
ADVENTURE Trawler skipper rescues his son
from storm off Iceland.

MAY

12334
HEAVEN KNOWS, MR ALLISON (106) (U)
tech/scope
20th Century Fox
P: Buddy Adler, Eugene Frenke
D: John Huston
S: (NOVEL) Charles Shaw
SC: John Huston, John Lee Mahin
Deborah Kerr .... Sister Angela
Robert Mitcham .... Cpl Allison
WAR Pacific. Marine cpl and nun hide from
Japanese task force.

12335
THE MAN WITHOUT A BODY (80) (X)
Filmplays (Eros)
P: W. Lee Wilder, Guido Coen
D: W. Lee Wilder, Charles Saunders
S: William Grote
Robert Hutton .... Dr Merritt
George Coulouris .... Karl Brussard
Julia Arnall .... Jean Kramer
Nadja Regin .... Odette Vernay
Sheldon Lawrence ..... Dr Lew Waldenhaus
Michael Golden .... Nostradamus
Peter Copley .... Leslie
Kim Parker .... Maid
HORROR Doctor revives prophet's head and
grafts it to body of an American financier.

12336
HOUR OF DECISION (81) (A)
Tempean (Eros)
P: Robert Baker, Monty Berman
D: Pennington Richards
S: Norman Hudis
Jeff Morrow .... Joe Sanders
Hazel Court .... Peggy Sanders
Lionel Jeffries .... Elvin Main
Anthony Dawson .... Garry Bax
Mary Laura Wood .... Olive Bax
Carl Bernard , ... Insp Gower
Vanda Godsell .... Eileen Chadwick
Alan Gifford .... J. Foster Green
CRIME American reporter proves wife did not
poison blackmailer.

12337
STRANGER IN TOWN (73) (U)
Tempean (Eros)
P: Robert Baker, Monty Berman
D: George Pollock
S: (NOVEL) Frank Chittenden
(THE UNINVITED)
SC: Norman Hudis, Edward Dryhurst
Alex Nicol .... Jihn Madison
Anne Page .... Vicky Leigh
Mary Laura Wood .... Lorna Ryland
Mona Washbourne .... Agnes Smith
Charles Lloyd Pack ...... Capt Nash
Bruce Beeby .... William Ryland
John Horsley .... Insp Powell
Colin Tapley .... Henry Ryland
Betty Impey .... Geraldine Nash
CRIME American reporter solves shooting of
blackmailer.

12338
KILL ME TOMORROW (80) (U)
Delta (Renown)
P: Francis Searle
D: Terence Fisher
S: Robert Falconer, Manning O'Brine
Pat O'Brien .... Bart Crosbie
Lois Maxwell .... Jill Brook
George Coulouris .... Heinz Webber
Wensley Pithey .... Insp Lane
Freddie Mills .... Waxy
Ronald Adam .... Brook
Robert Brown .... Steve
Richard Pascoe .... Dr Fisher
April Olrich .... Bella Braganza
Tommy Steele .... Himself
CRIME Sacked reporter confesses to killing
editor in return for cash for son's operation.

12339
LET'S BE HAPPY (106) (U) *tech/scope*
Marcel Hellman (ABP)
D: Henry Levin
S: (PLAY) Aimee Stuart (JEANNIE)
SC: Diana Morgan
Tony Martin .... Stanley Smith
Vera Ellen .... Jeannie McLean
Robert Flemyng ..... Lord James McNairn
Zena Marshall .... Helene
Guy Middleton .... Mr Fielding
Katherine Kath .... Mrs Fielding
Carl Duering .... Customs Insp
Helen Horton .... Sadie Whitelaw
Jean Cadell ...:........ Mrs Cathie
Molly Weir .... Flower Girl
Peter Sinclair .... Mr MacTavish
Gordon Jackson .....'.... Dougal McLean
MUSICAL Edinburgh. Poor Lord woos
American girl in belief that her legacy is large.

12340
THE STEEL BAYONET (85) *scope* (A)
Hammer—Clarion (UA)
P:D: Michael Carreras
S: Howard Clewes

Leo Genn . . . . Maj Gerrard
Kieron Moore . . . . Capt Mead
Michael Medwin . . . . Lt Vernon
Robert Brown . . . . Sgt-Maj Gill
Michael Ripper . . . . Pte Middleditch
John Paul . . . . Lt-Col Derry
Shay Gorman . . . . Sgt Gates
Tom Bowman . . . . Sgt Nicholls
Percy Herbert . . . . Pte Clark
WAR Tunis, 1943. Soldiers hold farmhouse
observation post against tank attack.

12341
THE CURSE OF FRANKENSTEIN (83) (X)
eastman/scope
Hammer-Clarion (WB) *reissue:* 1961 (RFI)
P: Anthony Hinds
D: Terence Fisher
S: (NOVEL) Mary Shelley (FRANKENSTEIN)
SC: Jimmy Sangster
Peter Cushing . . . . Victor Frankenstein
Christopher Lee . . . . The Creature
Hazel Court . . . . Elizabeth
Robert Urquhart . . . . Paul Krempe
Valerie Gaunt . . . . Justine
Paul Hardtmuth . . . . Prof Bernstein
Hugh Dempster . . . . Burgomaster
Melvyn Hayes . . . . Victor (child)
Noel Hood . . . . Aunt Sophia
Marjorie Hume . . . . Mother
HORROR Europe, period. Baron uses
corpses to create man but damaged brain makes
it mad killer.

12342
THE AWAKENING HOUR (21) (U)
Falcon (AA)
P:D:S: Donovan Winter
Donovan Winter . . . . The Man
CRIME Burglars shoot policeman and are
caught by Flying Squad.

12343
INSOMNIA IS GOOD FOR YOU (26) (U)
Park Lane (ABP)
P: Jules Simmons
D: Leslie Arliss
S: Lewis Greifer, Mordecai Richler
Peter Sellers . . . . Hector Dimwiddie
COMEDY Married man cultivates insomnia
preparatory to impending interview with his
employer.

12344
DEARTH OF A SALESMAN (29) (U)
Park Lane (ABP)
P: Jules Simmons
D: Leslie Arliss
S: Lewis Greifer, Mordecai Richler
Peter Sellers . . . . Hector Dimwiddie
COMEDY Inept salesman tries to sell
dishwashing machine.

12345
DAY OF GRACE (26) (U) *scope/eastman*
Hammer (Ex)
P:D: Francis Searle
S: Jon Manchip White
SC: Jon Manchip White, Francis Searle
Vincent Winter . . . . Ian
John Laurie . . . . Uncle Henry
Grace Arnold . . . . Aunt Helen
George Woodbridge . . . . Mr Kemp
Nora Gordon . . . . Mrs Kemp
DRAMA Man hires poacher to drown
nephew's sheepdog but kindly farmer saves
him.

12346
EDMUNDO ROS HALF HOUR (28) (U)
eastman
Hammer (Ex)
P:D: Michael Carreras
Edmundo Ros and his Latin-American
Orchestra.
Morton Frazer Harmonica Gang
Buddy Bradley Dancers
MUSICAL

12347
THAT WOMAN OPPOSITE (85) (A)
USA: CITY AFTER MIDNIGHT
Monarch
P: William Gell
D:SC: Compton Bennett
S: (NOVEL) John Dickson Carr
(THE EMPEROR'S SNUFFBOX)
Phyllis Kirk . . . . Eve Atwood
Dan O'Herlihy . . . . Dermot Kinross
Wilfrid Hyde White . . . Sir Maurice Lawes
Petula Clark . . . . Janice
Jack Watling . . . . Toby
William Franklyn . . . . Ned
Guido Lorraine . . . . Goron
Margaret Withers . . . . Lady Lawes
Balbina . . . . Prue
CRIME France. Jewel thief's ex-wife accused of
killing her fiance's father.

12348
FIRE DOWN BELOW (115) (A) *tech/scope*
Warwick (Col)
P: Irving Allen, Albert Broccoli,
Ronald Kinnoch
D: Robert Parrish
S: (NOVEL) Max Catto
SC: Irwin Shaw
Rita Hayworth . . . . Irena
Robert Mitchum . . . . Felix
Jack Lemmon . . . . Tony
Herbert Lom . . . . Harbour Master
Bernard Lee . . . . Dr Sam
Bonar Colleano . . . . Nat Sellars
Peter Illing . . . . Captain
Edric Connor . . . . Jimmy Jean
Joan Miller . . . . Mrs Canaday
Anthony Newley . . . . Miguel
ADVENTURE Caribbean. Cargo vessel
partners fall for girl of ill repute.

12349
THE ADMIRABLE CRICHTON (93) (U) *tech*
USA: PARADISE LAGOON
Modern Screenplays
P: Ian Dalrymple
D: Lewis Gilbert
S: (PLAY) J.M. Barrie
SC: Vernon Harris
Kenneth More . . . . Bill Crichton
Diane Cilento . . . . Eliza
Cecil Parker . . . . Lord Loam
Sally Ann Howes . . . . Lady Mary
Martita Hunt . . . . Lady Brocklehurst
Jack Watling . . . . John Treherne
Peter Graves . . . . Lord Brocklehurst
Miles Malleson . . . . Vicar
Eddie Byrne . . . . Captain
Gerald Harper . . . . Ernest Wooley
Mercy Haystead . . . . Lady Catherine
Miranda Connell . . . . Lady Agatha
COMEDY 1905. When aristocrats are
shipwrecked their butler becomes their leader.

12350
THE SHIRALEE (99) (U)
Ealing (MGM)
P: Jack Rix

D: Leslie Norman
S: (NOVEL) Darcy Niland
SC: Leslie Norman, Neil Paterson
Peter Finch . . . . Jim Macauley
Elizabeth Sellars . . . . Marge Macauley
Dana Wilson . . . . Buster Macauley
Rosemary Harris . . . . Lily Parker
Tessie O'Shea . . . . Bella
Sidney James . . . . Luke
George Rose . . . . Donny
Russell Napier . . . . Parker
Niall MacGinnis . . . . Beauty Kelly
Reg Lye . . . . Desmond
Barbara Archer . . . . Shopgirl
Charles Tingwell . . . . Jim Muldoon
DRAMA Australia. Travels of swagman with
unwanted daughter.

JUN

12351
THE KID FROM CANADA (57) (U)
Anvil (BL—CFF)
P: Ralph May
D: Kay Mander
S: John Eldridge
Christopher Braden . . . . Andy Cameron
Bernard Braden . . . . Joe
Bobby Stevenson . . . . Neil
Eleanor Laing . . . . Margaret
Pamela Stirling . . . . Jean
David Caldwell . . . . Ian
Alex Mackenzie . . . . Macfarlane
CHILDREN Scotland. Canadian braggart
proves courage by rescuing shepherd.

12352
FIVE CLUES TO FORTUNE (serial) (U)
Merton Park (BL—CFF)
P: Frank Hoare
D:SC: Joe Mendoza
S: Geoffrey Bond
John Rogers . . . . Michael Strong
Roberta Paterson . . . . Jill Strong
Peter Godsell . . . . Mark Strong
David Hemmings . . . . Ken
Dafydd Havard . . . . Jonas Wrench
Norman Mitchell . . . . Bert Dakin
David Cameron . . . . Mr King
Peter Welch . . . . Mr Strong

12353
1: THE DEAD MAN'S MESSAGE (15)

12354
2: THE SECRET OF THE ANTLER (18)

12355
3: RAIDERS AT MIDNIGHT (16)

12356
4: A TIGHT SPOT (17)

12357
5: RACE AGAINST TIME (16)

12358
6: STAMPEDE (15)

12359
7: THE FIFTH CLUE (15)

12360
8: THE TREASURE CHEST (17)
CHILDREN Woburn Abbey. Steward's
children foil crooks seeking buried teasure.

12361
THE TOMMY STEELE STORY (82) (U)
USA: ROCK AROUND THE WORLD
Insignia (AA)

P: Herbert Smith
D: Gerard Bryant
S: Norman Hudis
Tommy Steele .... Himself
Lisa Daniely .... Nurse
Patrick Westwood .... Brushes
Hilda Fenemore .... Mrs Steele
Charles Lamb .... Mr Steele
Peter Lawison .... John Kennedy
John Boxer .... Paul Lincoln
Mark Daly .... Junkshop Man
Cyril Chamberlain .... Steward
The Steelmen
Humphrey Lyttleton and his Band
Chas McDevitt Skiffle Group
Nancy Whiskey
Tommy Eytle Calypso Band
Chris O'Brien's Caribbeans
MUSICAL Teenage merchant seaman rises to
fame as rock'n'roll singer.

12362
INSIDE INFORMATION (32) (U)
Merton Park (AA)
P: Alec Snowden
D: Montgomery Tully
S: James Eastwood
N: Edgar Lustgarten
Ronald Adam .... Insp Duggan
Basil Henson .... Tony Neilson
Colette Wilde .... Ellie
CRIME Insp tracks killer of Negro crook burned
on bonfire as a "guy".

12363
THE KEY MAN (63) (U)
Insignia (AA)
P: Alex Snowden
D: Montgomery Tully
S: (PLAY) J. McLaren Ross
SC: J. McLaren Ross
Lee Patterson .... Lionel Hulme
Hy Hazell .... Gaby (Eva)
Colin Gordon .... Larry Parr
Philip Leaver .... Smithers
Henry Vidon .... Hallow
Harold Kasket .... Dimitriadi
Paula Byrne .... Pauline
Maudie Edwards .... Mrs Glass
CRIME Radio reporter tracks robbery loot to
safe deposit.

12364
ROCK YOU SINNERS (59) (U)
Small Films
P: Jeffrey Kruger, B.C. Fancey
D: Denis Kavanagh
S: Beatrice Scott
Philip Gilbert .... Johnny
Adrienne Scott .... Carol
Colin Croft .... Pete
Jackie Collins .... Jackie
Michael Duffield .... Selway
Beckett Bould .... McIver
Tony Crombie & his Rockets
Art Baxter & his Rockin' Sinners
Dickie Bennett
Joan Small
Rory Blackwell & the Blackjacks
George Browne
Don Sollash & his Rockin' Horses
Curly Pat Barry
Tony Hall
MUSICAL Radio disc jockey sells rock'n'roll
show to television.

12365
AT THE STROKE OF NINE (72) (U)
Tower (GN)
P:SC: Harry Booth, Michael Deeley,

Jon Pennington
D: Lance Comfort
S: Tony O'Grady
Patricia Dainton .... Sally Bryant
Stephen Murray .... Stephen Garrett
Patrick Barr .... Frank
Dermot Walsh .... MacDonnell
Clifford Evans .... Insp Hudgell
Leonard White .... Thompson
Reg Green .... Toby
Frank Atkinson .... Porter
CRIME Mad pianist kidnaps girl reporter and
announces he will kill her in five days' time.

12366
FACE IN THE NIGHT (75) (A)
USA: MENACE IN THE NIGHT
Gibraltar (GN)
P: Charles Leeds
D: Lance Comfort
S: (NOVEL) Bruce Graeme (SUSPENSE)
SC: Norman Hudis, John Sherman
Griffith Jones .... Rapson
Lisa Gastoni .... Jean Francis
Vincent Ball .... Bob Meredith
Eddie Byrne .... Art
Victor Maddern .... Ted
Clifford Evans .... Insp Ford
Joan Miller .... Mrs Victor
Leslie Dwyer .... Toby
Leonard Sachs .... Victor
Barbara Couper .... Mrs Francis
CRIME Mail van robbers intimidate girl witness.

12367
THE RISING OF THE MOON (81) (U)
Four Provinces (WB)
P: Michael Killanin
D: John Ford
SC: Frank Nugent

THE MAJESTY OF THE LAW
S: (PLAY) Frank O'Connor
Noel Purcell .... Dan O'Flaherty
Cyril Cusack .... Insp Michael Dillon
John Cowley .... Phelim O'Feaney
Jack MacGowran .... Mickey J

A MINUTE'S WAIT
S: (PLAY) Martin McHugh
Jimmy O'Dea .... Paddy Morrissey
Tony Quinn .... Andrew Rourke
Paul Farrell .... Jim O'Brien
Maureen Potter .... Pegeen Mallory
Michael Trubshawe ... Col Charles Frobisher
Maureen Connell ...... Mary Ann McMahon
Michael O'Duffy .... Singer

1921
S: (PLAY) Lady Gregory
Denis O'Dea .... Sgt
Maureen Cusack .... Sister Therese
Frank Lawton .... Major
Edward Lexy .... RQMS
Donal Donelly .... Sean Curren
Martin Thornton .... Sgt
COMEDY Ireland. Arrest of potheen maker;
delay of train; rescue of prisoner.

12368
HOW TO MURDER A RICH UNCLE (79) (A)
scope
Warwick (Col)
P: Irving Allen, Albert Broccoli, John Paxton
D: Nigel Patrick, Max Varnel
S: (PLAY) Didier Daix
(IL FAUT TUER JULIE)
SC: John Paxton
Nigel Patrick .... Sir Henry Clitterburn
Charles Coburn .... Uncle George
Wendy Hiller .... Edith Clitterburn

Anthony Newley .... Edwards
Athene Seyler .... Grannie
Kenneth Fortescue .... Albert
Katie Johnson .... Aunt Alice
Noel Hood .... Aunt Marjorie
Patricia Webster .... Constance
Trevor Reid .... Insp Harries
COMEDY Poor bart set traps for rich American
uncle but kills other members of his family.

12369
SAINT JOAN (110) (A) *tech/scope*
Wheel (UA)
P:D: Otto Preminger
S: (PLAY) George Bernard Shaw
SC: Graham Greene
Richard Widmark ..... Charles the Dauphin
Richard Todd .... Dunois
Anton Walbrook .... Bishop Cauchon
John Gielgud .... Earl of Warwick
Jean Seberg .... Joan
Felix Aylmer .... Inquisitor
Harry Andrews .... John de Stogumber
Barry Jones .... de Courcelles
Finlay Currie .... Archbishop
Bernard Miles .... Executioner
Kenneth Haigh .... Brother Martin
Archie Duncan .... de Baudricourt
Margot Grahame .... Duchesse
Francis de Wolff .... le Trenouille
Victor Maddern .... Soldier
Patrick Barr .... Capt le Hire
David Oxley .... Gilles de Rais
HISTORY France, 1429. Militant maid's
refusal to confess leads to her death at stake.

12370
THE PRINCE AND THE SHOWGIRL (114)
(A) *tech*
Laurence Olivier—Marilyn Monroe (WB)
D: Laurence Olivier, Anthony Bushell
S: (PLAY) Terence Rattigan
(THE SLEEPING PRINCE)
SC: Terence Rattigan
Laurence Olivier .... Grand Duke Charles
Marilyn Monroe .... Elsie Marina
Sybil Thorndike .... Queen Dowager
Richard Wattis .... Northbrooke
Jeremy Spenser .... Prince Nicholas
Jean Kent .... Maisie Springfield
Esmond Knight .... Hoffman
David Horne ...... The Foreign Office
Charles Victor .... Manager
Daphne Anderson .... Fanny
Vera Day .... Betty
Gillian Owen .... Maggie
Maxine Audley .... Lady Sunningdale
Gladys Henson .... Dresser
COMEDY 1911. Showgirl flirts with
Ruritanian Duke during coronation week.

12371
MIRACLE IN SOHO (98) (U) *eastman*
Rank (RFD)
P:S: Emeric Pressburger
D: Julian Amyes
John Gregson .... Michael Morgan
Belinda Lee .... Julia Gozzi
Cyril Cusack .... Sam Bishop
Peter Illing .... Papa Gozzi
Rosalie Crutchley .... Mafalda Gozzi
Marie Burke .... Mama Gozzi
Ian Bannen .... Filippo Gozzi
Brian Bedford .... Johnny
Barbara Archer .... Gwladwys
John Cairney .... Tom
Billie Whitelaw .... Maggie
ROMANCE Road gang worker is loved by
barmaid Italian girl contemplating emigration.

12372
SECOND FIDDLE (73) (U)
ACT Films (BL)
P: Robert Dunbar
D: Maurice Elvey
S: Robert Dunbar, Mary Cathcart Borer
SC: Robert Dunbar, Allan Mackinnon
Adrienne Corri . . . . Deborah
Thorley Walters . . . . Charles
Lisa Gastoni . . . . Pauline
Richard Wattis . . . . Bill Turner
Bill Fraser . . . . Nixon
Aud Johansen . . . . Greta
Madoline Thomas . . . . Fenny
Brian Nissen . . . . Jack Carter
Ryck Rydon . . . . Chuck
COMEDY Publicist falls for secretary while his
wife is abroad.

JUL

12373
AFTER THE BALL (89) (U) *eastman*
Beaconsfield (IFD)
P: Peter Rogers
D: Compton Bennett
S: (TV PLAY) Hubert Gregg (BOOK) Lady de
Frece (RECOLLECTIONS OF VESTA
TILLEY)
SC: Hubert Gregg, Peter Blackmore
Laurence Harvey . . . . Walter de Frece
Pat Kirkwood . . . . Vesta Tilley
Clive Morton . . . . Henry de Frece
Jerry Verno . . . . Harry Ball
June Clyde . . . . Lottie Gilson
Charles Victor . . . . Stagehand
Marjorie Rhodes . . . . Bessie
Jerry Stovin . . . . Frank Tanhill
Tom Gill . . . . Manager
Peter Carlisle . . . . Oscar Hammerstein
George Margo . . . . Tony Pastor
Leonard Sachs . . . . Richard Warner
Mark Baker . . . . George M. Cohan
Terry Cooke . . . . Dan Leno jr
The Television Toppers
MUSICAL 1868—1920. Career and love story
of music hall singer.

12374
TIME LOCK (73) (A)
Beaconsfield (IFD)
P:SC: Peter Rogers
D: Gerald Thomas
S: (TV PLAY) Arthur Hailey
Robert Beatty . . . . Pete Dawson
Lee Patterson . . . . Colin Walker
Betty McDowall . . . . Lucille Walker
Vincent Winter . . . . Steven Walker
Robert Ayres . . . . Insp Andrews
Alan Gifford . . . . George Foster
Larry Cross . . . . Reporter
Sandra Francis . . . . Evelyn Webb
Gordon Tanner . . . . Dr Hewitson
DRAMA Toronto. Boy trapped in time-locked
bank vault.

12375
ISLAND IN THE SUN (123) (A) *tech/scope*
20th Century Fox
P: Darryl F. Zanuck
D: Robert Rossen
S: (NOVEL) Alec Waugh
SC: Alfred Hayes
James Mason . . . . Maxwell Fleury
Joan Fontaine . . . . Mavis Norman
Harry Belafonte . . . . David Boyeur
Dorothy Dandridge . . . . . . Margot Seaton
Joan Collins . . . . Jocelyn Fleury
Michael Rennie . . . . Hilary Carson
Diana Wynyard . . . . Mrs Fleury

John Williams . . . . .Col Whittingham
Stephen Boyd . . . . Eun Templeton
Patricia Owens . . . . Sylvia Fleury
Basil Sydney . . . . Julian Fleury
John Justin . . . . Denis Archer
Ronald Squire . . . . The Governor
Hartley Power . . . . Bradshaw
DRAMA Caribbean. Planter learns his
grandmother had Negro blood and kills his
wife's supposed lover.

12376
BOOBY TRAP (71) (A)
Jaywell (Eros)
P: Bill Luckwell, Derek Winn
D: Henry Cass
S: Peter Bryan
SC: Peter Bryan, Bill Luckwell
Sydney Tafler . . . . Hunter
Patti Morgan . . . . Jackie
Harry Fowler . . . . Sammy
Tony Quinn . . . . Prof Hasdane
Richard Shaw . . . . Richards
Jacques Cey . . . . Bentley
John Watson . . . . Maj Cunliffe
Michael Moore . . . . Curate
CRIME Drug peddler does not know he has
taken an explosive pen activated by broadcast
time signal.

12377
DATE WITH DISASTER (61) (U)
Fortress (Eros)
P: Guido Coen
D: Charles Saunders
S: Brock Williams
Tom Drake . . . . Miles
William Hartnell . . . . Tracy
Shirley Eaton . . . . Sue
Maurice Kaufmann . . . . . . Don
Michael Golden . . . . Insp Matthews
Richard Shaw . . . . Ken
CRIME Car salesman suspected of safe
breaking saves his fiancee from kidnappers.

12378
THE HYPNOTIST (88) (A)
USA: SCOTLAND YARD DRAGNET
Merton Park (AA)
P: Alec Snowden
D:SC: Montgomery Tully
S: (PLAY) Falkland Cary
Roland Culver . . . . .Dr Francis Pelham
Patricia Roc . . . . Mary Foster
Paul Carpenter . . . . Val Neal
William Hartnell . . . . Insp Rose
Kay Callard . . . . Susie
Ellen Pollock . . . . Barbara Barton
Gordon Needham . . . . Sgt Davies
Martin Wyldeck . . . . Dr Bradford
Oliver Johnston . . . . Dr Kenyon
CRIME Psychiatrist hypnotises pilot into
killing his secret wife.

12379
MAN FROM TANGIER (67) (U)
USA: THUNDER OVER TANGIER
Butcher's Films
P: W.G. Chalmers
D: Lance Comfort
S: Manning O'Brine
Robert Hutton . . . . Chuck Collins
Lisa Gastoni . . . . Michele
Martin Benson . . . . Voss
Derek Sydney . . . . Darracq
Jack Allen . . . . Rex
Leonard Sachs . . . . Heinrich
Robert Raglan . . . . Insp Meredith
Harold Berens . . . . Sammy
CRIME Film stuntman is framed by crooks
seeking plates for forging passports.

12380
THESE DANGEROUS YEARS (108) (A)
USA: DANGEROUS YOUTH
Everest (ABP)
P: Anna Neagle
D: Herbert Wilcox
S: Jack Trevor Story
George Baker . . . . Padre
Frankie Vaughan . . . . . . :. . . Dave Wyman
Carole Lesley . . . . Dinah Brown
Jackie Lane . . . . Maureen
Katherine Kath . . . . Mrs Wyman
Thora Hird . . . . Mrs Larkin
Eddie Byrne . . . . Danny
Kenneth Cope . . . . Juggler
Robert Desmond . . . . Cream O'Casey
John le Mesurier . . . . CO
David Lodge . . . . Sgt Lockwood
Reginald Beckwith . . . . Hairdresser
Ralph Reader; Eric Morley
CRIME Liverpool. Teenage gang leader
conscripted into army, deserts after wounding
a bully.

12381
HELL DRIVERS (108) (A)
Rank-Aqua (RFD) *reissue:* 1961 (24 mins cut)
P: S.Benjamin Fisz
D: C. Raker Endfield
S: (STORY) John Kruse
SC: C. Raker Endfield, John Kruse
Stanley Baker . . . . Tom Yately
Herbert Lom . . . . Gino
Peggy Cummins . . . . Lucy
Patrick McGoohan . . . . Red
William Hartnell . . . . Cartley
Wilfrid Lawson . . . . Ed
Sidney James . . . . Dusty
Jill Ireland . . . . Jill
Alfie Bass . . . . Tinker
Gordon Jackson . . . . Scotty
David McCallum . . . . Jimmy Yately
Sean Connery . . . . Johnny
Marjorie Rhodes . . . . Ma West
Vera Day . . . . Blonde
Robin Bailey . . . . Assistant
CRIME Ex-convict becomes lorry driver
hauling ballast and thwarts his foreman's
racket.

12382
THE HEART WITHIN (61) (U)
Penington—Eady (RFD)
P: Jon Penington
D: David Eady
S: John Baxter
SC: Geoffrey Orme
James Hayter . . . . Mr Willard
Earl Cameron . . . . Voctor Conway
David Hemmings . . . . Danny Willard
Clifford Evans . . . . Matthew Johnson
Betty Cooper . . . . Miss Trevor
Dan Jackson . . . . Joe Martell
Jack Stewart . . . . Insp Matheson
Frank Sanguineau . . . . Bobo
Kings of the Caribbean Steel Band
CRIME Junkman and grandson prove West
Indian is not drug smuggler.

12383
MANUELA (95) (A)
USA: STOWAWAY GIRL
Foxwell Films (RFD)
D: Guy Hamilton
S: (NOVEL) William Woods
SC: William Woods, Guy Hamilton,
Ivan Foxwell
Trevor Howard . . . . James Prothero
Pedro Armendariz . . . . Mario Constanza
Elsa Martinelli . . . . Manuela Hunt

Donald Pleasence	Evans
Peter Illing	Agent
Leslie Weston	Bleloch
Jack MacGowran	Tommy
Roger Delgardo	Stranger
Warren Mitchell	Moss
Harold Kasket	Jose Periera
Barry Lowe	Murphy
Max Butterfield	Bliss

ADVENTURE Drunkard captain and brutish engineer fall for South American stowaway.

AUG

12384
FIVE ON A TREASURE ISLAND (serial) (U)
Rank Screen Services (BL—CFF)
P: Frank Wells
D: Gerald Landau
S: (NOVEL) Enid Blyton
SC: Frank Wells, Michael Barnes

Rel Grainer	George Kirrin
Richard Palmer	Julian
Gillian Harrison	Ann
John Bailey	Dick
Daga	Tim
Robert Cawdron	Luke Undown
Nicholas Bruce	Jim
John Charlesworth	Jan
Rufus Cruickshank	Capt Zachary

12385
1: THE FAMOUS FIVE (16)

12386
2: DIVING TO DANGER (16)

12387
3: THE SECRET OF THE WRECK (18)

12388
4: ON THE TRACK OF THE TREASURE (16)

12389
5: TRAPPED IN THE DUNGEONS (14)

12390
6: ESCAPE TO DANGER (15)

12391
7: AT THE MERCY OF THE WAVES (15)

12392
8: THE FIVE TRIUMPHANT (16)
CHILDREN Naval engineer's tomboy daughter and cousins foil crooks seeking sunken treasure.

12393
THE FLESH IS WEAK (88) (X)
Raystro (Eros) reissue: 1961 (Gala)
P: Raymond Stross
D: Don Chaffey
S: Leigh Vance

John Derek	Tony Giani
Milly Vitale	Marissa Cooper
Freda Jackson	Trixie
William Franklyn	Lloyd Buxton
Martin Benson	Angelo Giani
Vera Day	Edna
Shirley Ann Field	Susan
Norman Wooland	Insp Kingcomb
Harold Lang	Harry
Patricia Jessel	Millie
John Paul	Sgt Franks
Denis Shaw	Saradine
Joe Robinson	Lofty
Patricia Plunkett	Doris Newman

CRIME Soho vice king uses handsome brother to lure girls into prostitution.

12394
ROGUE'S YARN (80) (A)
Cresswell (Eros)
P: George Maynard
D: Vernon Sewell
S: Ernie Bradford, Vernon Sewell

Nicole Maurey	Michele Cartier
Derek Bond	John Marsden
Elwyn Brook-Jones	Insp Walker
Hugh Latimer	Sgt Adams
John Serret	Insp Lefarge
John Salew	Sam Youles
Joan Carol	Nurse

CRIME Shoreham. Insp breaks yachting alibi of man who killed rich, invalid wife.

12395
ACROSS THE BRIDGE (103) (A)
IPF (RFD)
P: John Stafford
D: Ken Annakin
S: (NOVEL) Graham Greene
SC: Guy Elmes, Denis Freeman

Rod Steiger	Carl Schaffer
David Knight	Johnny
Marla Landi	Mary
Noel Willman	Police Chief
Bernard Lee	Insp Hadden
Eric Pohlmann	Sgt
Alan Gifford	Cooper
Ingeborg Wells	Mrs Scarff
Bill Nagy	Paul Scarff
Faith Brook	Kay
Marianne Deeming	Anna

CRIME Mexico. Fugitive financier poses as man he killed, who turns out to have been a murderer.

12396
ACCOUNT RENDERED (61) (A)
Major (RFD)
P: John Temple-Smith, Francis Edge
D: Peter Graham Scott
S: (NOVEL) Pamela Barrington
SC: Barbara S. Harper

Griffiths Jones	Robert Ainsworth
Ursula Howells	Lucille Ainsworth
Honor Blackman	Sarah Hayward
Ewen Solon	Insp Marshall
Robert Raikes	Sgt Berry
John Van Eyssen	Clive Franklin
Philip Gilbert	John Langford
Carl Bernard	Gilbert Morgan

CRIME Man proves he did not murder faithless wife.

12397
ACTION OF THE TIGER (93) (U) tech/scope
Claridge (MGM)
P: Kenneth Harper
D: Terence Young
S: (NOVEL) James Wellard
SC: Robert Carson, Peter Myers

Van Johnson	Capt Carson
Martine Carol	Tracy Mallambert
Herbert Lom	Trifon
Gustavo Rocco	Henri Mallambert
Jose Nieto	Kol Stendho
Helen Haye	Countess
Anna Gerber	Mara
Anthony Dawson	Guard
Sean Connery	Mike
Yvonne Warren	Katina

ADVENTURE Albania. American launch-owner helps French girl rescue brother from communists.

12398
THE CASE OF THE SMILING WIDOW (31) (A)
Merton Park (AA)

P: Alec Snowden	
D: Montgomery Tully	
S: Gil Saunders	
N: Edgar Lustgarten	
Russell Napier	Insp Duggan
Carl Jaffe	Christopher Nicholls
Sylvia Marriott	Mrs Nicholls

CRIME Insp proves crippled collector's wife gassed blackmailing artist.

12399
THE ABOMINABLE SNOWMAN (91) (A) scope
Hammer-Clarion (WB) reissue: 1961 (RFI)
P: Aubrey Baring
D: Val Guest
S: (TV PLAY) Nigel Kneale (THE CREATURE)
SC: Nigel Kneale

Forrest Tucker	Tom Friend
Peter Cushing	Dr John Rollason
Maureen Conell	Helen Rollason
Richard Wattis	Peter Fox
Robert Brown	Ed Shelley
Michael Brill	Andrew McNee
Arnold Marle	Lhama
Wolfe Morris	Kusang

FANTASY Himalayas. Botanist and adventurer discover intelligent Yeti.

12400
NO TIME FOR TEARS (86) (U) eastman/scope
ABPC
P: W.A. Whittaker
D: Cyril Frankel
S: Anne Burnaby

Anna Neagle	Eleanor Hammond
George Baker	Nigel Barnes
Sylvia Syms	Margaret
Anthony Quayle	Dr Seagrave
Flora Robson	Sister Birch
Alan White	Dr Hugh Storey
Daphne Anderson	Marion
Michael Hordern	Surgeon
Joan Hickson	Sister Duckworth
Sophie Stewart	Sister Willis
Patricia Marmont	Sister Davies
Rosalie Crutchley	Theatre Sister
Joan Sims	Sister O'Malley
Angela Baddeley	Mrs Harris
Christopher Witty	George
Lucille Mapp	Maya
Marjorie Rhodes	Cleaner

DRAMA Various episodes involving staff and patients in Children's Hospital.

12401
DANGER LIST (22) (A)
Hammer (Ex)
P: Anthony Hinds
D: Leslie Arliss
S: J.D. Scott

Philip Friend	Dr Jim Bennett
Honor Blackman	Gillian Freeman
Mervyn Johns	Mr Ellis
Constance Fraser	Mrs Ellis
Alexander Field	Mr Carlton
Muriel Zillah	Mrs Coombe
Amanda Coxell	Laura Coombe

DRAMA Doctor and police trace three people mistakenly given poisonous tablets.

12402
COLD COMFORT (16) (U)
C.M. George (Saxon)
P: Theo Lageard
D: James Hill
S: Lewis Greifer, Maurice Wiltshire

Peter Sellers	Hector Dimwittie
Louise Granger	Mrs Dimwittie
Kathleen St John	Mrs Parkins

COMEDY Average man takes advice on how to cure cold.

12403
THE STORY OF ESTHER COSTELLO (104) (A)
USA: GOLDEN VIRGIN
Valiant-Romulus (Col)
P: David Miller, Jack Clayton
D: David Miller
S: (NOVEL) Nicholas Monsarrat
SC: Charles Kaufman, Lesley Storm
Joan Crawford . . . . Margaret Landi
Rossano Brazzi . . . . Carlo Landi
Heather Sears . . . . Esther Costello
Lee Patterson . . . . Harry Grant
Ron Randell . . . . Frank Wenzel
Fay Compton . . . . Mother Superior
John Loder . . . . Paul Marchant
Denis O'Dea . . . . Father Devlin
Sidney James . . . . Ryan
Bessie Love . . . . Woman
Robert Ayres . . . . Wilson
Maureen Delany . . . . Jenny Costello
Estelle Brody . . . . Tammy
June Clyde . . . . Mrs Forbes
Megs Jenkins . . . . Nurse Evans
Andrew Cruickshank . . . . . . Dr Stein
DRAMA Rich American woman uses blind, and
dumb and deaf Irish girl to raise funds for
charity. (BFA: Best Actress, 1957; PGAA:

12404
LIGHT FINGERS (86) (U)
Parkside (Archway)
P: Roger Proudlock
D: Terry Bishop
S: Alfred Shaughnessy
Roland Culver . . . . Humphrey Levenham
Eunice Gayson . . . . Rose Levenham
Guy Rolfe . . . . Dennis Payne
Ronald Howard . . . . Michael
Hy Hazell . . . . Cynthia
Avril Angers . . . . Miss Manley
Lonnie Donegan . . . . Himself
COMEDY Mean man thinks his junk-buying wife
has kleptomania.

12405
LADY OF VENGEANCE (74) (A)
Rich & Rich (UA)
P: William N. Boyle, Burt Balaban, Bernard
Donnenfield
D: Burt Balaban
S: Irve Tunick
Dennis O'Keefe . . . . William T. Marshall
Patrick Barr . . . . Insp Madden
Anton Diffring . . . . Karnak
Ann Sears . . . . Katie Whiteside
Vernon Greeves . . . . Larry Shaw
Eileen Elton . . . . Melissa
Frederick Schiller . . . . Schtegel
G.H. Mulcaster . . . . Bennett
CRIME Philatelist plots to kill man responsible
for his ward's suicide.

SEP

12406
THE LONG HAUL (100) (A)
Marksman (Col)
P: Maxwell Setton
D:SC: Ken Hughes
S: (NOVEL) Mervyn Mills
Victor Mature . . . . Harry Miller
Diana Dors . . . . Lynn
Patrick Allen . . . . Joe Easy
Gene Anderson . . . . Connie Miller
Peter Reynolds . . . . Frank
Liam Redmond . . . . Casey
John Welsh . . . . Doctor
Meier Tzelniker . . . . Nat Fine
Dervis Ward . . . . Mutt
Murray Kash . . . . Jeff

John Harvey . . . . Supt Macrea
CRIME Liverpool. Married ex-GI becomes truck
driver and falls for fur-smuggler's girl.

12407
THE VICIOUS CIRCLE (84) (U) USA: THE
CIRCLE
Beanconsfield (IFD)
P: Peter Rogers
D: Gerald Thomas
S: (TV SERIAL) Francis Durbridge (THE BRASS
CANDLESTICK)
SC: Francis Durbridge
John Mills . . . . Dr Howard Latimer
Derek Farr . . . . Ken Palmer
Noele Middleton . . . . Laura James
Wilfrid Hyde White . . . . Robert Brady
Roland Culver . . . . Insp Dane
Mervyn Johns . . . . Dr George Kimber
Rene Ray . . . . Mrs Amber
Lionel Jeffries . . . . Jeffrey Windsor
Lisa Daniely . . . . Frieda Veldon
CRIME Police use framed doctor to trap
actress's murderer.

12408
SEVEN THUNDERS (100) (A) USA: THE
BEASTS OF MARSEILLES
Dial (RFD)
P: Daniel M. Angel
D: Hugo Fregonese
S: (NOVEL) Rupert Croft-Cooke
SC: John Baines
Stephen Boyd . . . . Dave
James Robertson Justice . . . Dr Martout
Kathleen Harrison . . . . Mme Abou
Tony Wright . . . . Jim
Anna Gaylor . . . . Lise
Eugene Deckers . . . . Emile Blanchard
Rosalie Crutchley . . . . Therese Blanchard
Katherine Kath . . . . Mme Parfait
James Kenney . . . . Eric Triebel
Anton Diffring . . . . Col Trautman
Martin Miller . . . . Schlip
George Coulouris . . . . Bourdin
Carl Duering . . . . Maj Grautner
Edric Connor . . . . Abou
WAR Marseilles. Escaped POWs expose doctor
helper as thief and poisoner.

12409
CAMPBELL'S KINGDOM (100) (U) eastman
Rank (RFD) reissue: 1960 (22 mins cut)
P: Betty E. Box
D: Ralph Thomas
S: (NOVEL) Hammond Innes
SC: Robin Estridge, Hammond Innes
Dirk Bogarde . . . . Bruce Campbell
Stanley Baker . . . . Owen Morgan
Michael Craig . . . . Boy Bladen
Barbara Murray . . . . Jean Lucas
James Robertson Justice . . . . James Macdonald
Athene Seyler . . . . Miss Abigail
Robert Brown . . . . Creasey
John Laurie . . . . Mac
Sidney James . . . . Timid Driver
Mary Merrall . . . . Miss Ruth
George Murcell . . . . Max
Finlay Currie . . . . Old Man
ADVENTURE Canada. Sick man inherits oil
valley which crooked contractor plans to flood.
(PGAA: 1958).

12410
THE BIG CHANCE (61) (U)
Major (RFD)
P: John Temple-Smith, Francis Edge
D:SC: Peter Graham Scott
S: (NOVEL) Pamela Barrington

Adrienne Corri . . . . Diana
William Russell . . . . Bill
Ian Colin . . . . Adam
Penelope Bartley . . . . Betty
Ferdy Mayne . . . . Alpherghis
John Rae . . . . Jarvis
Douglas Ives . . . . Stan Willett
Robert Raglan . . . . Inspector
CRIME Married clerk robs travel agency to flee
to Panama with socialite.

12411
A KING IN NEW YORK (109) (U)
Attica (Archway)
P:D:S: Charles Chaplin
Charles Chaplin . . . . King Shahdov
Dawn Adams . . . . Ann Kay
Oliver Johnston . . . . Ambassador
Maxine Audley . . . . Queen Irene
Harry Green . . . . Lawyer Green
Phil Brown . . . . Headmaster
John McLaren . . . . Macabee
Alan Gifford . . . . Supt
Michael Chaplin . . . . Rupert Macabee
Sidney James . . . . Johnson
Jerry Desmonde . . . . Prime Minister
Shani Wallis; Joy Nichols; Lauri Lupino Lane &
George Truzzi.
COMEDY America. Deposed King makes TV
commercials and is accused of being a
communist.

12412
JACK TRENT INVESTIGATES (28) (U)
Carlyle
P: D: Olive Negus
Chris & Jennifer . . . . The Children
CHILDREN Children foil cattle thieves and
illicit gold diggers.

12413
THE BLACK ICE (51) (U)
Parkside (Archway)
P: Jacques de Lane Lea
D: Godfrey Grayson
S: John Sherman
SC: Roger Proudlock, John Sherman
Paul Carpenter . . . . Greenslade
Gordon Jackson . . . . Bert Harris
Ewen Solon . . . . Capt John Dodds
David Oxley . . . . Tom
ADVENTURE Trawler trapped while saving
ship from fog and ice.

12414
HIGH FLIGHT (102) (U) tech/scope
Warwick (Col) reissue: 1961 (Unifilms)
P: Irving Allen, Albert Broccoli, Phil C. Samuel
D: John Gilling
S: Jack Davies
SC: Joseph Landon, Ken Hughes, John Gilling
Ray Milland . . . . W/C Rudge
Anthony Newley . . . . Roger Endicott
Helen Cherry . . . . Louise
Leslie Phillips . . . . S/L Blake
Bernard Lee . . . . F/S Harris
Kenneth Haigh . . . . Tony Winchester
Kenneth Fortescue . . . . John Fletcher
Sean Kelly . . . . Cadet Day
Duncan Lamont . . . . Cpl
Kynaston Reeves . . . . Air Minister
John le Mesurier . . . . Commandant
Jan Brooks . . . . Diana
Jan Holden . . . . Jackie
Anne Aubrey . . . . Susan
DRAMA Cranwell. RAF cadet blames CO for
father's wartime death.

12415
MAN IN THE SHADOW (84) (U)
Merton Park (AA)

P: Alec Snowden
D: Montgomery Tully
S: Stratford Davis
Zachary Scott . . . . John Sullivan
Faith Domergue . . . . Barbara Peters
Faith Brook . . . . Joan Lennox
Peter Illing . . . . Carl Raffone
Gordon Jackson . . . . Jimmy Norris
Kay Callard . . . . Pamela Norris
John Welsh . . . . Insp Hunt
John Horsley . . . . Alan Peters
Fabia Drake . . . . Sister Veronica
CRIME Blackmailed woman proves convicted husband innocent of murder.

12416
LUCKY JIM (95) (U)
Charter (BL)
P: Roy Boulting
D: John Boulting
S: (NOVEL) Kingsley Amis
SC: Jeffrey Dell, Patrick Campbell
Ian Carmichael . . . . Jim Dixon
Terry Thomas . . . . Bertrand Welch
Hugh Griffith . . . . Prof Welch
Sharon Acker . . . . Christine Callaghan
Jean Anderson . . . . Mrs Welch
Maureen Connell . . . . Margaret Peel
Clive Morton . . . . Sir Hector Gore-Urquhart
John Welch . . . . Principal
Reginald Beckwith . . . . Porter
Kenneth Griffith . . . . Cyril Jones
Jeremy Hawk . . . . Bill Atkinson
Harry Fowler . . . . Taxi-driver
COMEDY University lecturer's troubles at professor's party and ceremonial weekend.

OCT

12417
THE MAIL VAN MURDER (29) (U)
Merton Park (AA)
P: Alec Snowden
D: John Knight
S: James Eastwood
N: Edgar Lustgarten
Hy Hazell . . . . Carla
Denis Castle . . . . Insp Duggan
Gordon Needham . . . . Sgt Wilson
CRIME Insp tracks gang boss behind theft of mail van.

12418
THE TYBURN CASE (32) (U)
Merton Park (AA)
P: Alec Snowden
D: David Paltenghi
S: James Eastwood
N: Edgar Lustgarten
John Warwick . . . . Supt Reynolds
Patricia Marmont . . . . Nora Sims
Howard Marion Crawford . . . Peter Shilling
Genine Graham . . . . Mrs Sandford
CRIME Supt proves lawyer drowned widow for insurance.

12419
THE WHITE CLIFFS MYSTERY (32) (U)
Merton Park (AA)
P: Alec Snowden
D: Montgomery Tully
S: James Eastwood
N: Edgar Lustgarten
Russell Napier . . . . Insp Duggan
CRIME Dead rocket engineer blackmailed by his secretary under pressure from foreigners.

12420
NIGHT CROSSING (32) (U)

Merton Park (AA)
P: Alec Snowden
D: Montgomery Tully
S: James Eastwood
N: Edgar Lustgarten
Russell Napier . . . . Insp Duggan
CRIME USAAF Lt helps police catch Hungarian knife-thrower who killed his drug-addicted partner.

12421
WOMAN IN A DRESSING GOWN (94) (A)
Godwin-Willis (ABP)
P: Frank Godwin, J. Lee-Thompson
D: J. Lee-Thompson
S: (TV PLAY) Ted Willis
SC: Ted Willis
Yvonne Mitchell . . . . Amy Preston
Sylvia Syms . . . . Georgie Harlow
Anthony Quayle . . . . Jim Preston
Andrew Ray . . . . Brian Preston
Carole Lesley . . . . Hilda
Olga Lindo . . . . Manageress
Harry Locke . . . . Merchant
Marianne Stone . . . . Hairdresser
Michael Ripper . . . . Pawnbroker
Nora Gordon . . . . Mrs Williams
DRAMA Middle-aged father is torn between slatternly wife and young secretary.

12422
THE SCAMP (88) (A)
Lawrie (GN) *reissue:* 1960 (1276 ft cut)
P: James H. Lawrie
D:SC: Wolf Rilla
S: (PLAY) Charlotte Hastings (UNCERTAIN JOY)
Richard Attenborough . . . . Stephen Leigh
Terence Morgan . . . . Mike Dawson
Colin Petersen . . . . Ted Dawson
Dorothy Alison . . . . Barbara Leigh
Jill Adams . . . . Julie Dawson
Geoffrey Keen . . . . Headmaster
Margaretta Scott . . . . Mrs Blundell
Maureen Delany . . . . Mrs Perryman
Charles Lloyd Pack . . . . Beamish
Victor Brooks . . . . Insp Burch
June Cunningham . . . . Annette
DRAMA Teacher adopts unruly boy who "kills" his drunkard father.

12423
ROBBERY UNDER ARMS (99) (A) *eastman*
Rank (RFD)
P: Joseph Janni
D: Jack Lee
S: (NOVEL) Rolf Boldrewood
SC: W.P. Lipscomb, Alexander Baron
Peter Finch . . . . Capt Starlight
Ronald Lewis . . . . Dick Marston
Maureen Swanson . . . . Kate Morrison
David McCallum . . . . Jim Marston
Jill Ireland . . . . Jean
Laurence Naismith . . . . Ben Marston
Jean Anderson . . . . Ma
Vincent Ball . . . . George Storefield
Dudy Nimmo . . . . Eileen
Ursula Finlay . . . . Grace Storefield
Russell Napier . . . . Mr Green
ADVENTURE Australia, 1850. Backwoods family join bushranger's rustling gang.

12424
THE ONE THAT GOT AWAY (111) (U)
Rank (RFD)
P: Julian Wintle
D: Roy Baker
S: (BOOK) Kendal Burt, James Leasor

SC: Howard Clewes
Hardy Kruger . . . . Franz von Werra
Colin Gordon . . . . Army Interrogator
Michael Goodliffe . . . . RAF Interrogator
Terence Alexander . . . . Intelligence Officer
Jack Gwillim . . . . Commandant
Andrew Faulds . . . . Lieut
Julian Somers . . . . Clerk
Alec McCowen . . . . Duty Officer
John Van Eyssen . . . . Prisoner
WAR True Story of Luftwaffe pilot's escape from Britain to Canada.

12425
THE BOLSHOI BALLET (100) (U) *eastman*
Harmony (RFD)
P: I.R. Maxwell, Paul Czinner
D: Paul Czinner

SPANISH DANCE
S: (BALLET) Peter Tchaikovsky
S. Zvyagina
A. Neresova

SPRING WATER
S: (BALLET) Sergei Rachmaninov
L. Bogomolova
S. Vlasov

POLONAISE AND CRACOVIENNE
S: (BALLET) Michael Glinka
Y. Sangovich
S. Zyvagina

WALPURGISNACHT
S: (BALLET) Gounod
Raissa Struchkova
A. Lapauri

THE DYING SWAN
S: (BALLET) Saint-Saens
Galina Ulanova

GISELLE
S: (BALLET) A. Adam
Galina Ulanova . . . . Giselle
Nikolai Fadeyechev . . . . Albrecht
Taisia Monakhova . . . . Berthe
Alexander Radunsky . . . . . Duke
Bournemouth Symphony Orchestra; Royal Opera House Orchestra.
MUSICAL (Filmed at Covent Garden and Davis Theatre).

12426
STRANGERS' MEETING (64) (A)
Parroch (RFD)
P: Jack Parsons, E. Smedley Aston
D: Robert Day
S: David Gordon
Peter Arne . . . . Harry Bellair
Delphi Lawrence . . . . Margot Sanders
Conrad Phillips . . . . David Sanders
Barbara Archer . . . . Rosie Foster
David Ritch . . . . Giovanni
David Lodge . . . . Fred
Selma Vaz Diaz . . . . Magda Mayer
Victor Maddern . . . . WillieFisher
CRIME Acrobat escapes from prison to prove his partner was killed by jealous girl.

12427
PROFESSOR TIM (57) (U)
Emmett-Dalton-Dublin Films (RKO)
P: Robert Baker, Monty Berman
D: Henry Cass
S: (PLAY) George Shiels
SC: Robert S. Baker
Ray McAnally . . . . Hugh O'Cahan

Maire O'Donnell . . . . Peggy Scally
Seamus Kavanagh . . . . Prof Tim
Maire Kean . . . . Bridget Scally
Philip O'Flynn . . . . John Scally
John Hoey . . . . Paddy Kinney
Geoffrey Golden . . . . James Kilroy
COMEDY Ireland. Wanderer returns to family
after 20 years, keeping his inheritance secret.

12428
SMALL HOTEL (59) (U)
Welwyn (ABP)
P: Robert Hall
D: David Macdonald
S: (PLAY) Rex Frost
SC: Wilfred Eades
Gordon Harker . . . . Albert
Marie Lohr . . . . Mrs Samson-Fox
John Loder . . . . Mr Finch
Irene Handl . . . . Mrs Gammon
Janet Munro . . . . Caroline Mallet
Billie Whitelaw . . . . Caroline
Ruth Trouncer . . . . Sheila
Francis Matthews . . . . Alan Pryor
COMEDY Old hotel waiter refuses to be
replaced by young girl.

12429
THE BRIDGE ON THE RIVER KWAI (101)
(U) *tech/scope reissues:* 1962, 1967
Horizon (Col)
P: Samuel Spiegel
D: David Lean
S: (NOVEL) Pierre Boulle
SC: Pierre Boulle, Carl Foreman, Michael
Wilson
William Holden . . . . Shears
Alec Guinness . . . . Col Nicholson
Jack Hawkins . . . . Maj Warden
Sessue Hayakawa . . . . Col Saito
James Donald . . . . Maj Clipton
Geoffrey Horne . . . . Lt Joyce
Ann Sears . . . . Nurse
Andre Morell . . . . Col Green
Peter Williams . . . . Capt Reeves
John Boxer . . . . Maj Hughes
Percy Herbert . . . . Pte Grogan
Harold Goodwin . . . . Pte Baker
Henry Okawa . . . . Capt Kanematsu
WAR Burma, 1943. POW col persuades men to
build railway bridge for Japanese. (AA: 1958,
Best Film, Director, Actor, Screenplay,
Photography, Music, Editor; BFA: 1958, Best
Film, Screenplay, Actor; Top Moneymaker:
1958).

12430
THE BIRTHDAY PRESENT (100) (U)
Whittingham (BL)
P: GeorgePitcher
D: Pat Jackson
S: Jack Whittingham
Tony Britton . . . . Simon Scott
Sylvia Syms . . . . Jean Scott
Jack Watling . . . . Bill Thompson
Geoffrey Keen . . . . Col Wilson
Walter Fitzgerald . . . . Sir John Dell
Howard Marion Crawford . . . George Bates
John Welsh . . . . Customs Officer
Ian Bannen . . . . Assistant
Lockwood West . . . . Barraclough
Harry Fowler . . . . Charlie
Thorley Walters . . . . Photographer
Malcolm Keen . . . . Bristow
CRIME Toy salesman sacked after serving three
months for watch smuggling.

12431
THE SURGEON'S KNIFE (83) (A)
Gibraltar (GN)
P: Charles Leeds
D: Gordon Parry

S: (NOVEL) Anne Hocking (THE WICKED
FLEE)
SC: Robert Westerby
Donald Houston . . . . Dr Alex Waring
Adrienne Corri . . . . Laura Shelton
Lyndon Brook . . . . Dr Ian Breck
Jean Cadell . . . . Henrietta Sevens
Sydney Tafler . . . . Dr Hearne
Mervyn Johns . . . . Mr Waring
Marie Ney . . . . Matron Fiske
Ronald Adam . . . . Maj Tilling
John Welsh . . . . Insp Austen
Beatrice Varley . . . . Mrs Waring
CRIME Surgeon achieves social success and kills
blackmailer.

12432
THREE SUNDAYS TO LIVE (71) (U)
Danziger (UA)
P: Edward J. & Harry Lee Danziger
D: Ernest Morris
S: Brian Clemens
Kieron Moore . . . . Frank Martin
Jane Griffiths . . . . Judy Allen
Sandra Dorne . . . . Ruth Chapman
Basil Dignam . . . . Davitt
Hay Ayer . . . . Al Murray
John Stone . . . . Detective
John Longden . . . . Warder
CRIME Band leader breaks jail to find girl
witness who can prove his innocence.

NOV

12433
NIGHT OF THE DEMON (82) (X) USA:
CURSE OF THE DEMON
Sabre (Col)
P: Hal E. Chester
D: Jacques Tourneur
S: (STORY) Montagu R. James (CASTING THE
RUNES)
SC: Hal E. Chester, Charles Bennett
Dana Andrews . . . . Dr John Holden
Peggy Cummins . . . . Joanna Harrington
Niall MacGinnis . . . . Dr Karswell
Athene Seyler . . . . Mrs Karswell
Maurice Denham . . . . Prof Harrington
Ewan Roberts . . . . Williamson
Liam Redmond . . . . Prof Mark O'Brien
Peter Elliott . . . . Kumar
Reginald Beckwith . . . . Mr Meek
Richard Leech . . . . Insp Mottram
HORROR American psychologist defeats
doctor's demon conjured from hell.

12434
THE DEPRAVED (70) (A)
Danziger (UA)
P: Edward J. & Harry Lee Danziger
D: Paul Dickson
S: Edith Dell
SC: Brian Clemens
Anne Heywood . . . . Laura Wilton
Robert Arden . . . . Dave Dillon
Carroll Levis . . . . Maj Kellaway
Basil Dignam . . . . Tom Wilton
Denis Shaw . . . . Insp Flynn
Robert Ayres . . . . Colonel
Gary Thorne . . . . Kaufmann
CRIME US Army officer helps beloved kill
drunkard husband.

12435
TARZAN AND THE LOST SAFARI (81) (U)
tech/scope
Solar (MGM)
P: Sy Weintraub, Harvey Hayutin, John
Croydon
D: H. Bruce Humberstone, Victor Stoloff
S: (CHARACTERS) Edgar Rice Burroughs
SC: Lillie Hayward, Montgomery Pittman

Gordon Scott . . . . Tarzan
Robert Beatty . . . . Tusker Hawkins
Yolande Donlan . . . . Gamage Dean
Betta St John . . . . Diane Penrod
Wilfrid Hyde White . . . . . . Doodles Fletcher
George Coulouris . . . . Carl Kraski
Peter Arne . . . . Dick Penrod
Orlando Martins . . . . Chief Ogonoore
ADVENTURE Africa. Jungle man saves plane
crash victims from being bartered for ivory by
crooked hunter.

12436
NOT WANTED ON VOYAGE (82) (U)
Byron-Ronald Shiner (Renown)
P: Henry Halstead, Jack Marks
D: Maclean Rogers
S: Dudley Sturrock (PLAY) Evadne Price, Ken
Attiwill (WANTED ON VOYAGE)
SC: Evadne Price, Roland Pertwee, Jack Marks
Ronald Shiner . . . . Albert Higgins
Brian Rix . . . . Cecil Hollebone
Griffith Jones . . . . Guy Harding
Catherine Boyle . . . . Julia Haynes
Fabia Drake . . . . Mrs Brough
Michael Brennan . . . . Chief Steward
Michael Shepley . . . . Col Blewton-Fawcet
Dorinda Stevens . . . . Pat
Martin Boddey . . . . Captain
Therese Burton . . . . Mrs Rose
COMEDY Stewards thwart jewel thieves on
cruise to Tangiers.

12437
CAT GIRL (75) (X)
Insignia (AA)
P: Herbert Smith, Peter Rogers
D: Alfred Shaughnessy
S: Lou Rusoff
Barbara Shelley . . . . Leonora
Robert Ayres . . . . Dr Marlowe
Kay Callard . . . . Dorothy Marlowe
Paddy Webster . . . . Cathy
Ernest Milton . . . . Edmund Brandt
Lilly Kann . . . . Anna
Jack May . . . . Richard
HORROR Girl suffering from "leopard curse"
kills husband and tries to kill psychiatrist's wife.

12438
THE FLYING SCOT (69) (U) USA: MAILBAG
ROBBERY
Insignia (AA) *reissue:* 1963 (Compton)
P: D: Compton Bennett
S: Ralph Smart, Jan Read
SC: Norman Hudis
Lee Patterson . . . . Ronnie
Kay Callard . . . . Jackie
Alan Gifford . . . . Phil
Margaret Withers . . . . Lady
Mark Baker . . . . Gibbs
Jeremy Bodkin . . . . Charlie
Gerald Case . . . . Guard
CRIME Trio's plan to rob express train works
perfectly in imagination but fails in fact.

12439
SAIL INTO DANGER (72) (U)
Patria (GN)
P: Steven Pallos
D:S: Kenneth Hume
Dennis O'Keefe . . . . Steve Ryman
Kathleen Ryan . . . . Lana
James Hayter . . . . Monty
Ana Luisa Peluffo . . . . . . Josafina
Pedro de Cordoba . . . . . . Luis
BartaBarry . . . . Emil
Felix de Pommes . . . . Insp Gomez
CRIME Barcelona. American launch owner
foils plot to steal Madonna.

12440
THE HOUSE IN THE WOODS (60) (A)
Film Workshop (Archway)
P: Geoffrey Goodhart
D:SC: Maxwell Munden
S: (STORY) Walter C. Brown (PRELUDE TO MURDER)
Ronald Howard . . . . Spencer Rowland
Patricia Roc . . . . Carol Carter
Michael Gough . . . . Geoffrey Carter
Andrea Trowbridge . . . . Mrs Shellaby
Bill Shine . . . . Col Shellaby
Norah Hammond . . . . Mrs Bletchley
CRIME Author learns landlord plans to kill his wife.

12441
JUST MY LUCK (86) (U)
Rank (RFD)
P: Hugh Stewart
D: John Paddy Carstairs
S: Alfred Shaughnessy, Peter Blackmore
Norman Wisdom . . . . Norman
Margaret Rutherford . . . . . . Mrs Dooley
Jill Dixon . . . . Anne
Leslie Phillips . . . . Hon Richard Lumb
Delphi Lawrence . . . . Miss Daviot
Edward Chapman . . . . .Mrs Hackett
Joan Sims . . . . Phoebe
Peter Copley . . . . Weaver
Michael Ward . . . . Cranley
Bill Fraser . . . . Powell
Campbell Cotts . . . . Lord Beale
Robin Bailey . . . . Sir George
Sabrina . . . . Herself
COMEDY Bookies welsh when punter's accumulator bet succeeds.

12442
DANGEROUS EXILE (90) (A) *eastman*
Rank (RFD)
P: George H. Brown
D: Brian Desmond Hurst
S: (NOVEL) Vaughan Wilkins (A KING RELUCTANT)
SC: Robin Estridge
Louis Jourdan . . . . Duc de Beauvais
Belinda Lee . . . . Virginia Traill
Keith Michell . . . . Col St Gerard
Richard O'Sullivan . . . . Louis XVII
Martita Hunt . . . . Aunt Fell
Finlay Currie . . . . Mr Patient
Anne Heywood . . . . Glynis
Jean Mercure . . . . Chief of Police
Jean Claudio . . . . De Castres
Terence Longdon . . . . .Sir Frederick Venner
Frederick Leister . . . . Ogden
Laurence Payne . . . . Lautrec
Austin Trevor . . . . Petival
Jacques Brunius . . . . De Chassagne
ADVENTURE Pembroke 1795. Girl helps Duc save Louis XVI's son from revolutionaries.

12443
BARNACLE BILL (87) (U) USA: ALL AT SEA
Ealing (MGM)
P: Dennis Van Thal
D: Charles Frend
S: T.E.B. Clarke
Alec Guinness . . . . .William Ambrose/
Six Ancestors
Irene Browne . . . . Mrs Barrington
Maurice Denham . . . . Mayor Crowley
Victor Maddern . . . . Figg
Percy Herbert . . . . Tommy
George Rose . . . . Bullen
Lionel Jeffries . . . . Garrod
Harold Goodwin . . . . Duckworth
Lloyd Lamble . . . . Supt Browning
Warren Mitchell . . . . Artie White

Jackie Collins . . . . June
Miles Malleson . . . . Angler
Frederick Piper . . . . Harry
Richard Wattis . . . . Registrar
Eric Pohlmann . . . . Consul
Donald Pleasence . . . . Teller
COMEDY Seasick sailor runs stationary cruise on old pier in spite of council opposition.

DEC

12444
DAVY (83) (U) *tech/scope*
Ealing (MGM)
P: Basil Dearden
D: Michael Relph
S: William Rose
Harry Seccombe . . . . Davy Morgan
Alexander Knox . . . . Sir Giles
Ron Randell . . . . George
George Relph . . . . Uncle Pat
Susan Shaw . . . . Gwen
Bill Owen . . . . Eric
Isabel Dean . . . . Miss Carstairs
Adele Leigh . . . . Joanna
Peter Frampton . . . . Tim
Joan Sims . . . . Waitress
Gladys Henson . . . . Waitress
George Moon . . . . Jerry
Clarkson Rose . . . . Mrs MacGillicuddy
Kenneth Connor . . . . Herbie
Principals and Chorus of the Royal Opera House
COMEDY Welsh comedian forgoes chances in opera to remain in family act.

12445
BLUE MURDER AT ST TRINIAN'S (86) (U)
John Harvel (BL)
P: Frank Lauder, Sidney Gilliat
D: Frank Launder,
S: (CARTOONS) Ronald Searle
SC: Frank Launder, Sidney Gilliat, Val Valentine
Terry Thomas . . . . . .Capt Romney Carlton-
Ricketts
George Cole . . . . Flash Harry
Joyce Grenfell . . . . Sgt Ruby Gates
Alastair Sim . . . . Miss Fritton
Sabrina . . . . Virginia
Lionel Jeffries . . . . Joe Mangan
Eric Barker . . . . Culpepper Brown
Richard Wattis . . . . Bassett
Thorley Walters . . . . Major
Lloyd Lamble . . . . Supt Kemp-Bird
Lisa Gastoni . . . . Myrna Mangan
Dilys Laye . . . . Bridget
Judith Furse . . . . Maud Hackstraw
Kenneth Griffith . . . . Charlie Bull
Guido Lorraine . . . . Prince Bruno
Peter Jones . . . . Prestwick
Alma Taylor . . . . Mother
COMEDY Gem Thief poses as headmistress of girls' school on UNESCO tour of Europe.

12446
THE NAKED TRUTH (92) (U) USA: YOUR PAST IS SHOWING
Anglofilm-Rank (RFD)
P:D: Mario Zampi
S: Michael Pertwee
Terry Thomas . . . . Lord Mayley
Peter Sellers . . . . Sonny Macgregor
Peggy Mount . . . . Flora Ransom
Shirley Eaton . . . . Belinda Wright
Dennis Price . . . . Michael Dennis
Georgina Cookson . . . . Lady Mayley
Joan Sims . . . . Ethel Ransom
Miles Malleson . . . . Rev Bastaple
Kenneth Griffith . . . . Porter
Moutrie Kelsall . . . . Mactavish

Wilfrid Lawson . . . . Sgt Rumbold
Bill Edwards . . . . Bill
Wally Patch . . . . Fred
Henry Hewitt . . . . Gunsmith
John Stuart . . . . Inspector
George Benson . . . . Photographer
Peter Noble . . . . TV Announcer
COMEDY Blackmail victims try to murder blackmailing publisher of scandal magazine.

12447
WINDOM'S WAY (108) (U) *eastman*
Rank (RFD)
P: John Bryan
D: Ronald Neame
S: (NOVEL) James Ramsey Ullman
SC: Jill Craigie
Peter Finch . . . . Dr Alec Windom
Mary Ure . . . . Lee Windom
Natasha Parry . . . . Anna Vidal
Robert Fleming . . . . George Hasbrook
Michael Hordern . . . . Patterson
Gregoire Aslan . . . . Lollivar
John Cairney . . . . Jan Vidal
Marne Maitland . . . . Belhedron
Kurt Siegenberg . . . . Kosti
George Margo . . . . Lansang
Martin Benson . . . . Commander
ADVENTURE Malaya. Government troops thwart doctor's attempt to aid rebels.

12448
THE END OF THE LINE (64) (A)
Fortress (Eros)
P: Guido Coen
D: Charles Saunders
S: Paul Erickson
Alan Baxter . . . . Mike Selby
Barbara Shelley . . . . Lilliane Crawford
Ferdy Mayne . . . . Edwards
Jennifer Jayne . . . . Ann Bruce
Arthur Gomez . . . . John Crawford
Geoffrey Hibbert . . . . Max Perrin
Jack Melford . . . . Insp Gates
Marianne Braun . . . . Desk Clerk
CRIME Wife of night club owner frames American writer for his murder.

12449
MORNING CALL (75) (A)
Winwell (Astral)
P: Bill Luckwell, Derek Winn
D: Arthur Crabtree
S: Leo Townsend
SC: Paul Tabori, Bill Luckwell, Tom Waldron
Ron Randell . . . . Nick Logan
Greta Gynt . . . . Annette Manning
Bruce Seton . . . . Insp Brown
Charles Farrell . . . . Karver
Virginia Keily . . . . Vera Clark
Garard Green . . . . Stevens
Wally Patch . . . . Wally
CRIME Doctor's wife tries to ransom kidnapped husband despite police.

12450
SON OF A STRANGER (68) (A)
Danziger (UA)
P: Edward J. & Harry Lee Danziger
D: Ernest Morris
S: Stanley Miller
James Kenney . . . . Tom Adams
Ann Stephens . . . . Joannie
Victor Maddern . . . . Lenny
Basil Dignam . . . . Dr Delaney
Catharine Finn . . . . Mrs Adams
Diana Chesney . . . . Mrs Peck
CRIME Cornwall. Slum teenager's obsessive search for "rich" father.

12451
ZOO BABY (59) (U)
Penington-Eady (RFD)
P: Jon Penington
D: David Eady
S: Jan Read
Angela Baddeley . . . .   Mrs Ramsey
Gerard Lohan . . . .   Pip
Maurice Kaufmann . . . .   Steve
Dorothy Bromiley . . . .   Sarah
Bruce Seton . . . .   Zoo Supt
Ronald Leigh-Hunt . . . . . .   Supt Copton
Peter Sinclair . . . .   Benham
DRAMA Newsreel cameraman suspected when
hunter's son steals Coati Mundi bear from
Chessington Zoo.

12452
KILL HER GENTLY (63) (A)
Fortress (Col)
P: Guido Coen
D: Charles Saunders
S: Paul Erickson
Griffith Jones . . . .   Jeff Martin
Maureen Connell . . . .   Kay Martin
Marc Lawrence . . . .   William Connors

George Mikell . . . .   Lars Svenson
Shay Gorman . . . .   Dr Landers
Marianne Brauns . . . .   Raina
Frank Hawkins . . . .   Inspector
CRIME Man hires escaped convicts to kill wife
for certifying him insane.

12453
ACCUSED (83) *tech/scope* USA: MARK OF
THE HAWK
Film Productions International
P: Burton Martin, Lloyd Young
D: Michael Audley, Gilbert Gunn
S: Lloyd Young
SC: H. Ken Carmichael
Eartha Kitt . . . .   Renee
Juano Hernandez . . . .   Amugo
John McIntyre . . . .   Craig
Sidney Poitier . . . .   Oban
Patrick Allen . . . .   Gregory
Earl Cameron . . . .   Preacher
Gerard Heinz . . . .   Governor-General
Helen Horton . . . .   Barbara
Clifton Macklin . . . .   Kanda
Ewen Solon . . . .   Inspector
Marne Maitland . . . .   Sunday

Lockwood West . . . .   Magistrate
Francis Matthews . . . .   Overholt
DRAMA Nigeria. American missionary
influences workers' representative torn
between duty and brother's terrorist gang.

12454
BITTER VICTORY (90) (A) *scope/bilingual*
Transcontinental — Robert Laffont (Col)
P: Paul Graetz
D: Nicholas Ray
S: (NOVEL) Rene Hardy (Amere Victoire)
SC: Nicholas Ray, Rene Hardy, Gavin Lambert,
Paul Gallico
Richard Burton . . . .   Capt Jimmy Leith
Curt Jurgens . . . .   Maj David Brand
Ruth Roman . . . .   Jane Brand
Raymond Pellegrin . . . .   Mokrane
Anthony Busell . . . .   Gen Patterson
Sean Kelly . . . .   Lt Barton
Christopher Lee . . . .   Sgt Barney
Andrew Crawford . . . .   Pte Roberts
Nigel Green . . . .   Wilkins
Ronan O'Casey . . . .   Sgt Dunnigan
WAR Benghazi. Cowardly major on raid
discovers his wife loves his captain.

1958

JAN

12455
COUNT FIVE AND DIE (92) (A) *scope*
Zonic (20)
P: Ernest Gartside
D: Victor Vicas
S: Jack Seddon, David Pursall
Jeffrey Hunter . . . . Capt Bill Ranson
Nigel Patrick . . . . Maj Julien Howard
Annemarie Duringer . . . . . . Rolande Hertog
David Kossoff . . . . Dr Mulder
Rolf LeFebvre . . . . Hans Faber
Larry Burns . . . . Martins
Otto Diamant . . . . Hendrijk
Philip Bond . . . . Piet
Wolf Frees . . . . Brauner
Arthur Gross . . . . Jan
WAR 1944. Dutch girl spy foils scheme to feed
false information to Germans.

12456
SOAPBOX DERBY (64) (U)
Rayant (CFF)
P: Anthony Gilison
D:SC: Darcy Conyers
S: Robert Martin
Michael Crawford . . . . PeterToms
Keith Davis . . . . Legs Johnson
Roy Townsend . . . . Foureyes Fulton
Alan Coleshill . . . . Lew Lender
Malcolm Kirby . . . . John
Carla Challoner . . . . Betty
Mark Daly . . . . Grandpa
Denis Shaw . . . . Lender
Harry Fowler . . . . Barrow Boy
CHILDREN Battersea gang's soapbox car stolen by
rivals.

12457
TOTO AND THE POACHERS (50) (U)
eastman
World Safari (CFF)
P: Henry Geddes
D: Brian Salt
S: Brian Salt, John Coquillon, Michael Johns
John Aloisi . . . . Toto
Mpigano . . . . Baaba
Shabani Hamisi . . . . Shabani
David Betts . . . . Warden
Obago . . . . Poacher
CHILDREN Africa. Native boy helps game
warden catch ivory poachers.

12458
VIOLENT PLAYGROUND (108) (A)
Rank (RFD)
P: Michael Relph
D: Basil Dearden
S: (NOVEL) James Kennaway
SC: James Kennaway
Stanley Baker . . . . Sgt Truman
Peter Cushing . . . . The Priest
Anne Heywood . . . . Cathie Murphy
David McCallum . . . . Johnny Murphy
John Slater . . . . Sgt Walker
Clifford Evans . . . . Heaven Evans
Moultrie Kelsall . . . . Supt
George A. Cooper . . . . Chief Insp
Brona Boland . . . . Mary Murphy
Fergal Boland . . . . Patrick Murphy
Michael Chow . . . . Alexander
Tsai Chin . . . . Primrose
CRIME Liverpool. Detective loves sister of
psychotic teenage arsonist.

12459
THE GYPSY AND THE GENTLEMAN (107)
(A) *eastman*
Rank (RFD)
P: Maurice Cowan

D: Joseph Losey
S: (NOVEL) Nina Warner Hooke (DARKNESS
I LEAVE YOU)
SC: Janet Green
Melina Mercouri . . . . Belle
Keith Michell . . . . Sir Paul Deverill
Flora Robson . . . . Mrs Haggard
Patrick McGoohan . . . . Jess
June Laverick . . . . Sarah Deverill
Lyndon Brook . . . . John Patterson
Clare Austin . . . . Vanessa
Helen Haye . . . . Lady Ayrton
Newton Blick . . . . Ruddock
Mervyn Johns . . . . Brook
John Salew . . . . Duffin
Catherine Feller . . . . Hattie
Laurence Naismith . . . . Forrester
DRAMA Regency. Poor nobleman's gypsy wife
claims sister is insane to obtain her legacy.

12460
CHASE A CROOKED SHADOW (87) (U)
Associated Dragon (ABP)
P: Douglas Fairbanks jr, Thomas Clyde
D: Michael Anderson
S: David D. Osborn, Charles Sinclair
Richard Todd . . . . Ward Prescott
Anne Baxter . . . . Kim Prescott
Herbert Lom . . . . Insp Vargas
Alexander Knox . . . . Chandler Bridson
Faith Brook . . . . Mrs Whitman
Alan Tilvern . . . . Carlos
Thelma d'Aguiar . . . . Maria
CRIME Costa Brava. Tec poses as heiress's dead
brother to prove she has missing diamonds.

12461
THE MAN WHO WOULDN'T TALK (97) (U)
Everest (BL)
P:D: Herbert Wilcox
S: (NOVEL) Stanley Jackson
SC: Edgar Lustgarten
Anna Neagle . . . . Mary Randall QC
Anthony Quayle . . . . Dr Frank Smith
Katherine Kath . . . . Yvonne Delbeau
Dora Bryan . . . . Telephonist
Patrick Allen . . . . Jim Kennedy
Lloyd Lamble . . . . Bellamy
Hugh McDermott . . . . Bernie
John Welsh . . . . George Fraser
Leonard Sachs . . . . Prof Horvard
John Paul . . . . John Castle
John le Mesurier . . . . Judge
Edward Lexy . . . . Hobbs
CRIME Woman QC defends American virologist
charged with killing the secret agent he loved.

12462
DEATH OVER MY SHOULDER (89) (A)
Vicar (Orb)
P: Frank Bevis
D: Arthur Crabtree
S: Alyce Canfield
SC: Norman Hudis
Keefe Brasselle . . . . Jack Regan
Bonar Colleano . . . . Joe Longo
Jill Adams . . . . Evelyn Connors
Arlene de Marco . . . . Julie
Charles Farrell . . . . Shiv Maitland
Al Mulock . . . . Brainy Peterson
Sonia Dresdel . . . . Miss Upton
CRIME American tec hires gangster to kill him
so his insurance will pay for sick son's cure.

12463
UNDERCOVER GIRL (68) (A)
Bill & Michael Luckwell (Butcher)
P: Kay Luckwell, Derek Winn
D: Francis Searle
S: Bernard Lewis,
SC: Bernard Lewis, Bill Luckwell

Paul Carpenter . . . . Johnny Carter
Kay Callard . . . . Joan Foster
Monica Grey . . . . Evelyn King
Bruce Seton . . . . Ted Austin
Jackie Collins . . . . Peggy Foster
Maya Koumani . . . . Miss Brazil
Kim Parker . . . . Maid
Tony Quinn. . . . . Mike O'Sullivan
CRIME Dead reporter's brother unmasks
nightclub owner as black-mailing drug peddler.

FEB

12464
THE BETRAYAL (82) (U)
Danziger (UA)
P: Edward J & Harry Lee Danziger
D: Ernest Morris
S: Brian Clemens, Eldon Howard
Philip Friend . . . . Michael McCall
Diana Decker . . . . Janet Hillyer
Philip Saville . . . . Bartel
Peter Bathurst . . . . Insp Baring
Peter Burton . . . . Tony Adams
Ballard Berkeley . . . . Lawson
Harold Lang . . . . Clay
CRIME Model helps blind pilot track man who
betrayed him to Germans.

12465
A TALE OF TWO CITIES (117) (A)
Rank (RFD)
P: Betty E. Box
D: Ralph Thomas
S: (NOVEL) Charles Dickens
SC: T.E.B. Clarke
Dirk Bogarde . . . . Sidney Carton
Dorothy Tutin . . . . Lucie Manette
Cecil Parker . . . . Jarvis Lorry
Stephen Murray . . . . Dr Manette
Athene Seyler . . . . Miss Pross
Paul Guers . . . . Charles Darnay
Marie Versini . . . . Marie Gabelle
Ian Bannen . . . . Gabelle
Alfie Bass . . . . Jerry Cruncher
Ernest Clark . . . . Stryver
Rosalie Crutchley . . . . Mme Defarge
Freda Jackson . . . . The Vengeance
Duncan Lamont . . . . Ernest Defarge
Christopher Lee . . . . . . Marquis St Evremonde
Leo McKern . . . . Attorney General
Donald Pleasence . . . . Barsad
ADVENTURE France, 1795. English lawyer goes
to guillotine in place of his aristocratic double.

12466
CARVE HER NAME WITH PRIDE (119)(U)
Keyboard (RFD)
P: Daniel M. Angel
D: Lewis Gilbert
S: (BOOK) R.J. Minney
SC: Lewis Gilbert, Vernon Harris
Virginia McKenna . . . . Violet Szabo
Paul Scofield . . . . Tony Fraser
Jack Warner . . . . Mr Bushell
Denise Grey . . . . Mrs Bushell
Maurice Ronet . . . . Jacques
Avice Landone . . . . Vera Atkins
Anne Leon . . . . Lilliane Rolfe
Nicole Stephane . . . . Denise Bloch
Billie Whitelaw . . . . Winnie
William Mervyn . . . . Col Buckmaster
Michael Goodliffe . . . . Coding Expert
Bill Owen . . . . Instructor
Sydney Tafler . . . . Potter
Noel Willman . . . . Interrogator
WAR True story of shopgirl who worked with
resistance in France and died in Ravensbruck.
(PGAA: 1958).

12467
THE DIPLOMATIC CORPSE (65) (U)
ACT Films (RFD)
P: Francis Searle
D: Montgomery Tully
S: Sidney Nelson, Maurice Harrison
Robin Bailey . . . . Mike Billings
Susan Shaw . . . . Jenny Drew
Liam Redmond . . . . Insp Corcoran
Harry Fowler . . . . Knocker Parsons
Maya Koumani . . . . Marian Weaver
Andre Mikhelson . . . . Hamid
Bill Shine . . . . Humphrey Garrad
Charles Farrell . . . . Percy Simpson
CRIME Reporter solves diplomat's murder and
rescues kidnapped fiancee from foreign embassy.

12468
THE SUPREME SECRET (56) (U)
GHW Productions (Church & Chapel) *reissue:*
1965, GOD SPEAKS TODAY (26 mins cut)
D: Norman Walker
S: Lawrence Barratt
Hugh David
Meredith Edwards
Anthony Green
Harry Fowler
RELIGION Youth involved in dock robbery
converted by Mission.

12469
HAPPY IS THE BRIDE (84) (U)
Panther (BL) *reissue:* 1962 (cut)
P: Paul Soskin
D: Roy Boulting
S: (PLAY) Esther McCracken (QUIET
WEDDING)
SC: Roy Boulting, Jeffrey Dell
Ian Carmichael . . . . David Chaytor
Janette Scott . . . . Janet Royd
Cecil Parker . . . . Arthur Royd
Terry Thomas . . . . PC
Joyce Grenfell . . . . Florence Bute
Eric Barker . . . . Vicar
Edith Sharpe . . . . Mildred Royd
Elvi Hale . . . . Petula
Miles Malleson . . . . Magistrate
Athene Seyler . . . . Aunt Harriet
Irene Handl . . . . Mme Edna
John le Mesurier . . . . Mr Chaytor
Thorley Walters . . . . Jim
Nicholas Parsons . . . . John Royd
Virginia Maskell . . . . Marcia
COMEDY Family complications precede a country
wedding.

12470
THE TRUTH ABOUT WOMEN (107) (A)
eastman
Beaconsfield (BL)
P: Sydney Box
D: Muriel Box
S: Muriel & Sydney Box
Laurence Harvey . . . . Humphrey Tavistock
Julie Harris . . . . Helen Cooper
Diane Cilento . . . . Ambrosine Viney
Mai Zetterling . . . . Julie
Eva Gabor . . . . Louise
Roland Culver . . . . Charles
Wilfrid Hyde White . . . . Sir George Tavistock
Marius Goring . . . . Otto Kerstein
Michael Denison . . . . Rollo
Jackie Lane . . . . Saida
Derek Farr . . . . Anthony
Elina Labourdette . . . . Comtesse
Griffith Jones . . . . Sir Jeremy
Catherine Boyle . . . . Diana
Lisa Gastoni . . . . Mary Maguire
Thorley Walters . . . . Trevor
Ambrosine Philpotts . . . . . Lady Tavistock

Ernest Thesiger . . . . Judge
Christopher Lee . . . . Francois
COMEDY Diplomat tells son-in-law of affairs
in Yekrut, Paris, America, London, and World
War 1.

12471
FAMILY DOCTOR (85) (A) *scope* USA: RX
MURDER
Templar (20)
P: John Gossage
D: Derek Twist
S: (NOVEL) Joan Fleming (THE DEEDS OF
DR DEADCERT)
SC: Derek Twist
Rick Jason . . . . Jethro Jones
Marius Goring . . . . Dr Henry Dysert
Lisa Gastoni . . . . Kitty Mortlock
Sandu Scott . . . . Stella Dysert
Mary Merrall . . . . Miss Bettyhill
Vida Hope . . . . Louise
Helen Shingler . . . . Charlotte
Phyllis Neilson-Terry . . . . . Lady Lacy
Nicholas Hannen . . . . Colonel
Kynaston Reeves . . . . Mr Sparrow
Avice Landone . . . . **Mrs Mortlock**
Frederick Leister . . . . Dr Alexander
Patrick Waddington . . . . . Sir George Watson
CRIME American poses as tourist to prove
seaside doctor killed his ex-wife.

12472
THE NAKED EARTH (96) (A) *scope*
Foray (20)
P: Adrian Worker
D: Vincent Sherman
S: Milton Holmes
Richard Todd . . . . Danny Halloran
Juliette Greco . . . . Maria Boyle
John Kitzmiller . . . . David
Finlay Currie . . . . Father Verity
Laurence Naismith . . . . . . Trader
Christopher Rhodes . . . . . . Al
Orlando Martins . . . . Tribesman
Harold Kasket . . . . Arab Captain
ADVENTURE Africa, 1894. Poor Irishman
weds dead friend's mistress and has
crocodile skins stolen by traders.

12473
THE STRANGE WORLD OF PLANET X (75)
(X) retitled: THE STRANGE WORLD USA:
COSMIC MONSTERS
Artistes Alliance-WNW (Eros)
P: George Maynard
D: Gilbert Gunn
S: (TV SERIAL) Rene Ray
SC: Paul Ryder, Joe Ambor
Forrest Tucker . . . . Gil Graham
Gaby Andre . . . . Michele Dupont
Martin Benson . . . . Smith
Alec Mango . . . . Dr Laird
Wyndham Goldie . . . . Brig Cartwright
Hugh Latimer . . . . Jimmy Murray
Richard Warner . . . . Insp Burns
Patricia Sinclair . . . . Helen Forsythe
Geoffrey Chater . . . . Gerald Wilson
HORROR Extra-terrestial emissary destroys
doctor's insect-enlarger.

12474
THE GOLDEN DISC (78) (U) USA: THE
INBETWEEN AGE
Butcher's Films (ABP)
P: W.G. Chalmers
D: Don Sharp
S: Gee Nichol
Lee Patterson . . . . Harry Blair
Mary Steele . . . . Joan Farmer
Terry Dene . . . . Himself
Linda Gray . . . . Aunt Sarah
Ronald Adam . . . . Mr Dryden

Peter Dyneley . . . . Mr Washington
David Jacobs . . . . Himself
Dennis Lotis; Nancy Whiskey; Les Hobeaux;
Murray Campbell; Sheila Buxton; Phil Seamon's
Jazz Group; Sonny Stewart's Skiffle Kings
MUSICAL Couple start coffee bar and record
company with teenage callboy as their singing
star.

12475
I ACCUSE! (99) (U) *scope*
MGM British
P: Sam Zimbalist
D: Jose Ferrer
S: (BOOK) Nicholas Halasz
SC: Gore Vidal
Jose Ferrer . . . . Alfred Dreyfus
Anton Walbrook . . . . Maj Esterhazy
Viveca Lindors . . . . Lucie Dreyfus
Leo Genn . . . . Maj Picquart
Emlyn Williams . . . . Emile Zola
David Farrar . . . . Matthieu Dreyfus
Donald Wolfit . . . . Gen Mercier
Herbert Lom . . . . Maj du Paty de Clam
Harry Andrews . . . . Maj Henry
Felix Aylmer . . . . Edgar Demange
Ronald Howard . . . . Capt Lauth
Peter Illing . . . . Georges Clemnceau
George Coulouris . . . . Col Sandherr
Eric Pohlmann . . . . Bertillon
HISTORY France, 1894. General staff convicts
Jew as spy on forged evidence.

12476
ESCAPEMENT (76) (A) USA: THE
ELECTRIC MONSTER
Anglo-Guild (AA)
P: Alec Snowden
D: Montgomery Tully
S: (NOVEL) Charles Eric Maine
SC: Charles Eric Maine, J. McLaren Ross
Rod Cameron . . . . Kennan
Mary Murphy . . . . Ruth
Meredith Edwards . . . . Dr Maxwell
Peter Illing . . . . Zakon
Carl Jaffe . . . . Dr Erich Hoff
Kay Callard . . . . Laura Maxwell
Carl Duering . . . . Blore
Larry Cross . . . . Brad Somers
FANTASY France. Magnate uses clinic's tape-
recorded "dreams" to brainwash VIPs.

MAR

12477
ROONEY (88) (U)
Rank (RFD)
P: George H. Brown
D: George Pollock
S: (NOVEL) Catherine Cookson
SC: Patrick Kirwan
John Gregson . . . . James Rooney
Muriel Pavlow . . . . Maire Hogan
Barry Fitzgerald . . . . . . Grandfather O'Flynn
June Thorburn . . . . Doreen O'Flynn
Noel Purcell . . . . Tim Hennessey
Maire Kean . . . . Mrs O'Flynn
Eddie Byrne . . . . Micky Hart
Liam Redmond . . . . Mr Doolan
Jack MacGowran . . . . Joe O'Connor
Irene Browne . . . . Mrs Manning-French
COMEDY Dublin. Dustman loves family
Cinderella accused of gem theft.

12478
INNOCENT SINNERS (95) (U)
Rank (RFD)
P: Hugh Stewart
D: Philip Leacock
S: (NOVEL) Rumer Godden (AN EPISODE
OF SPARROWS)
SC: Rumer Godden, Neil Patterson
Flora Robson . . . . Olivia Chesney

David Kossoff . . . . Mr Vincent
Barbara Mullen . . . . Mrs Vincent
Catherine Lacey . . . . Angela Chesney
Susan Beaumont . . . . Liz
Lyndon Brook . . . . Charles
Edward Chapman . . . . Morley
June Archer . . . . Lovejoy Mason
Christopher Hey . . . . Tip Malone
Brian Hammond . . . . Sparkey
Vanda Godsell . . . . Mrs Mason
Andrew Cruickshank . . . . Doctor
DRAMA Neglected girl tries to build garden on bombsite.

12479
A CLEAN SWEEP (27) (U)
Hammer (RKO)
P: Anthony Hinds
D: Maclean Rogers
Eric Barker . . . . George Watson
Thora Hird . . . . Vera Watson
Vera Day . . . . Beryl Watson
Wallas Eaton . . . . Ted
Bill Fraser . . . . Bookmaker
Ian Whittaker . . . . Dick Watson
COMEDY Wife tries to cure gambling husband until he wins Irish Sweepstake.

12480
MAN WITH A DOG (24) (U)
Hammer (Ex)
P: Anthony Hinds
D: Leslie Arliss
Maurice Denham . . . . Mr Keeble
Sarah Lawson . . . . Vicky Alexander
Clifford Evans . . . . Dr Bennett
John Van Eyssen . . . . Dr Langham
Marianne Stone . . . . Mrs Stephens
Jan Holden . . . . Nurse
DRAMA Almoner and neighbours look after old man's dog and home while he undergoes operation.

12481
THE SAFECRACKER (96) (U)
Coronado (MGM)
P: David E. Rose, John R. Sloan
D: Ray Milland
S: (BOOK) Rhys Davis, Bruce Thomas
SC: Paul Monash
Ray Milland . . . . Colley Dawson
Barry Jones . . . . Bennett Canfield
Jeannette Sterke . . . . Irene
Victor Maddern . . . . Morris
Ernest Clark . . . . Maj Adbury
Cyril Raymond . . . . Insp Frankham
Melissa Stribling . . . . Angela
Percy Herbert . . . . Sgt Harper
Barbara Everest . . . . Mrs Dawson
Anthony Nicholls . . . . Gen Prior
David Horne . . . . Herbert Fenwright
Colin Gordon . . . . Dakers
Clive Morton . . . . Sir George Turvey
Colin Tapley . . . . Col Charles Mercer
WAR 1940. Burglar offered freedom in exchange for cracking German safe in Belgium.

12482
6.5 SPECIAL (85) (U) *reissue:* 1962, CALLING ALL CATS (27 mins cut)
Insignia (AA)
P: Herbert Smith
D: Alfred Shaughnessy
S: (TV SERIES)
SC: Norman Hudis
Diane Todd . . . . Anne
Avril Leslie . . . . Judy
Finlay Currie . . . . Himself
Josephine Douglas . . . . Herself
Pete Murray . . . . Himself

Freddie Mills . . . . Himself
Lonnie Donegan; Dickie Valentine; Jim Dale; Petula Clark; Russ Hamilton; Joan Regan; King Brothers; Don Lang and his Frantic Five; **Johnny Dankworth and his Orchestra; Cleo Laine; Jackie Dennis; The Kentones; Desmond Lane; John Barry Seven; Mike & Bernie Winters;** Victor Soverall
MUSICAL Girl gets chance to sing on BBC-TV teenage programme.

12483
THE DUKE WORE JEANS (89) (U)
Insignia (AA)
P: Peter Rogers
D: Gerald Thomas
S: Lionel Bart, Michael Pratt
SC: Norman Hudis
Tommy Steele . . . . Tommy Hudson/Tony
                        Whitecliffe
June Laverick . . . . Princess Maria
Michael Medwin . . . . Cooper
Alan Wheatley . . . . King of Ritallia
Eric Pohlmann . . . . Bastini
Clive Morton . . . . Duke
Mary Kerridge . . . . Queen
Ambrosine Philpotts . . . . . Duchess
Elwyn Brook-Jones . . . . . . Bartolomeo
MUSICAL Nobleman's son gets his cockney double to woo Ruritanian Princess.

12484
THE STRANGE AWAKENING (69) (U)
Merton Park (AA)
P: Alec Snowden
D: Montgomery Tully
S: (NOVEL) Pattrick Quentin (PUZZLE FOR FIENDS)
SC: J. McLaren Ross
Lex Barker . . . . Peter Chance
Carole Matthews . . . . Selena Friend
Lisa Castoni . . . . Marny Friend
Nora Swinburne . . . . Mrs Friend
Peter Dyneley . . . . Dr Rene Normand
Joe Robinson . . . . Sven
Malou Pantera . . . . Isabella
John Serrat . . . . Commissaire Sagain
CRIME France. Scheming family convince amensiac that he is heir to fortune.

12485
THE YOUNG AND THE GUILTY (67) (A)
Welwyn (ABP)
P: Warwick Ward
D: Peter Cotes
S: (TV PLAY) Ted Willis
SC: Ted Willis
Phyllis Calvert . . . . Mrs Connor
Andrew Ray . . . . Eddie Marshall
Edward Chapman . . . . Mr Connor
Janet Munro . . . . Sue Connor
Campbell Singer . . . . Mr Marshall
Jean St Clair . . . . Mrs Humbolt
Hilda Fenemore . . . . Mrs Marshall
ROMANCE Rich man objects to daughter's love for poor student.

12486
THE MOONRAKER (82) *tech* (U)
ABPC
P: Hamilton G. Inglis
D: David Macdonald
S: (PLAY) Arthur Watkyn
SC: Robert Hall, Wilfred Eades, Alistair Bell
George Baker . . . . Earl Anthony
Sylvia Syms . . . . Anne Wyndham
Peter Arne. . . . . Edmund Tyler
Marius Goring . . . . Col Beaumont
Richard Leech . . . . Henry Strangeways
Clive Morton . . . . Lord Harcourt
Paul Whitsun-Jones . . . . Parfitt

Gary Raymond . . . . Charles Stuart
Iris Russell . . . . Judith Strangeways
John le Mesurier . . . . Cromwell
Patrick Troughton . . . . Capt Wilcox
Michael Anderson jr. . . . . . . Martin Strangeways
ADVENTURE 1651. Noble highwayman gets King's son to France despite Roundheads.

12487
ORDERS TO KILL (111) (A)
Lynx (BL)
P: Anthony Havelock-Allan
D: Anthony Asquith
S: Donald C. Downes
SC: Paul Dehn, George St George
Eddie Albert . . . . Maj McMahon
Paul Massie . . . . Gene Summers
Lilian Gish . . . . Mrs Summers
James Robertson Justice . . . . Cmdr
Leslie French . . . . Marcel Lafitte
Irene Worth . . . . Leonie
John Crawford . . . . Kimball
Lionel Jeffries . . . . Interrogator
Nicholas Phipps . . . . Lieut
Sandra Dorne . . . . Blonde
Jacques Brunius . . . . Comm Morand
WAR Paris, 1944. USAAF pilot trained to kill agent suspected of being Nazi. (BFA: Best Screenplay, Best Actress, 1958).

12488
THE SILENT ENEMY (112) (U)
Romulus (IFD)
P: Bertram Ostrer
D: William Fairchild
S: (BOOK) Marshall Pugh (COMMANDER CRABB)
SC: William Fairchild
Laurence Harvey . . . . Lt Lionel Crabb
Dawn Addams . . . . Jill Masters
John Clements . . . . Admiral
Michael Craig . . . . LS Knowles
Gianna Maria Canale . . . . Conchita Tomolino
Arnoldo Foa . . . . Tomolino
Massimo Serato . . . . Forzellini
Sidney James . . . . CPO Thorpe
Howard Marion Crawford . . . . WC
Alec McCowen . . . . AB Morgan
Ewen Solon . . . . Captain
Nigel Stock . . . . AB Fraser
Brian Oulton . . . . Holford
Giacomo Rossi-Stuart . . . . . Rosati
Carlo Justini . . . . Fellini
WAR Gibraltar 1941. True story of lieutenant who foils Italian underwater attack on invasion convoy.

12489
GIDEON'S DAY (91) (A) *tech* USA:
GIDEON OF SCOTLAND YARD
Columbia British
P: Michael Killanin
D: John Ford
S: (NOVEL) J.J. Marric (John Creasey)
SC: T.E.B. Clarke
Jack Hawkins . . . . Insp George Gideon
Dianne Foster . . . . Joanna Delafield
Cyril Cusack . . . . Birdy Sparrow
Andrew Ray . . . . Simon Farnaby-Green
James Hayter . . . . Mason
Ronald Howard . . . . Paul Delafield
Anna Massey . . . . Sally Gideon
Howard Marion-Crawford . . . Chief
Laurence Naismith . . . . Arthur Sayer
Derek Bond . . . . Sgt Kirby
Grizelda Hervey . . . . Mrs Kirby
Frank Lawton . . . . Sgt Liggott
Anna Lee . . . . Kate Gideon
John Loder . . . . Ponsford
Doreen Madden . . . . Miss Courtney
Miles Malleson . . . . Judge
Marjorie Rhodes . . . . Mrs Saporelli

Michael Shepley . . . . . . Sir Rupert Bellamy
Michael Trubshawe . . . . Sgt Golightly
Jack Watling . . . . Rev Julian Small
CRIME Inspector deals with bribery, a mad miller, society thieves, etc.

APR

12490
DUNKIRK (135) (U)
Ealing (MGM)
P: Michael Forlong
D: Leslie Norman
S: (NOVEL) Elleston Trevor (THE BIG PICKUP)
(BOOK) Ewen Butler, J.S. Bradford (DUNKIRK)
SC: W.P. Lipscomb, David Divine
John Mills . . . . Cpl Tubby Binns
Richard Attenborough . . . . . . John Holden
Bernard Lee . . . . Charles Foreman
Robert Urquhart . . . . Mike
Ray Jackson . . . . Barlow
Ronald Hines . . . . Miles
Sean Barrett . . . . Frankie
Roland Curram . . . . Harper
Meredith Edwards . . . . Dave Bellman
Patricia Plunkett . . . . Grace Holden
Rodney Diak . . . . Pannet
Michael Shillo. . . . . Jouvet
Eddie Byrne . . . . Commander
Maxine Audley . . . . Diana Foreman
Lionel Jeffries . . . . Colonel
Victor Maddern . . . . Seaman
Flanagan & Allen
WAR France, 1940. Civillians' boats rescue retreating British army.

12491
A WOMAN OF MYSTERY (71) (U)
Danziger (UA)
P: Edward & Harry Lee Danziger
D: Ernest Morris
S: Brian Clemens, Eldon Howard
Dermot Walsh . . . . Ray Savage
Hazel Court . . . . Joy Grant
Jennifer Jayne . . . . Ruby Ames
Ferdy Mayne . . . . Andre
Ernest Clark . . . . Harvey
Diana Chesney . . . . Mrs Bassett
Paul Dickson . . . . Winter
CRIME Reporter unmasks counterfeit gang behind girl's "suicide".

12492
HEART OF A CHILD (77) (U)
Beaconsfield (RFD)
P: Alfred Shaughnessy
D: Clive Donner
S: (NOVEL) Phyllis Bottome
SC: Leigh Vance
Jean Anderson . . . . Maria Heiss
Donald Pleasence . . . . Speil
Richard Williams . . . . Karl Speil
Maureen Pryor . . . . Frau Speil
John Glyn Jones . . . . Priest
Andrew Keir . . . . Constable
Norman MacOwan . . . . . . Heiss
Carla Challoner . . . . Elsa
Willoughby Goddard . . . . . Sott
DRAMA Austria, 1918. Boy runs away when his father sells his St Bernard.

12493
THE CAMP ON BLOOD ISLAND (91)(X)
Hammer-Clarion (Col) reissue: 1961 (RFI)
P: Anthony Hinds
D: Val Guest
S: Val Guest, Jon Manchip White
Andre Morell . . . . Col Lambert
Carl Mohner . . . . Piet van Elst

Edward Underdown . . . . . . Maj Dawes
Walter Fitzgerlad . . . . Cyril Beattie
Phil Brown . . . . Lt Bellamy
Barbara Shelley . . . . Kate Keiller
Michael Goodliffe . . . . Father Anjou
Richard Wordsworth . . . . . . Dr Keiller
Mary Merrall . . . . Mrs Beattie
WAR Japan. POW colonel tries to keep news of surrender from camp commandant.

12494
WOMANEATER (71) (X)
Fortress (Eros)
P: Guido Coen
D: Charles Saunders
S: Brandon Fleming
George Coulouris . . . . Dr James Moran
Vera Day . . . . Sally
Peter Wayn . . . . Jack Venner
Joyce Gregg . . . . Margaret Santer
Joy Webster . . . . Judy Ryan
Jimmy Vaughan . . . . Tanga
Sara Leighton . . . . Susan Curtis
Maxwell Foster . . . . Insp Brownlow
HORROR Mad doctor feeds girls to Amazonian tree to obtain fluid to revive dead housekeeper.

12495
BONJOUR TRISTESSE (93) (A) tech/scope
Wheel Productions (Col)
P:D: Otto Preminger
S: (NOVEL) Francoise Sagan
SC: Arthur Laurents
Deborah Kerr . . . . Anne
David Niven. . . . . Raymond
Jean Seberg . . . . Cecile
Mylene Demongeot . . . . Elsa
Geoffrey Horne . . . . Philippe
Juliette Greco . . . . Singer
Walter Chiari . . . . Pablo
Martita Hunt . . . . Mother
Roland Culver . . . . Mr Lombard
Jean Kent . . . . Mrs Lombard
David Oxley . . . . Jacques
Elga Andersen . . . . Denise
ROMANCE Riviera. Girl's attempt to reinstate father's mistress causes the death of a widow.

12496
NO TIME TO DIE (103) (U) tech/scope USA: TANK FORCE
Warwick (Col)
P: Phil C. Samuel
D: Terence Young
S: Merle Miller
SC: Richard Maibaum, Terence Young
Victor Mature . . . . Sgt David Thatcher
Leo Genn . . . . Sgt Kendall
Anthony Newley . . . . Tiger Noakes
Bonar Colleano . . . . Pole
Luciana Paluzzi . . . . Carola
Sean Kelly . . . . Bartlett
Kenneth Fortescue . . . . Cpl Johnson
Anne Aubrey . . . . Italian Girl
George Coulouris . . . . Commandant
Alfred Burke . . . . Capt Ritter
David Lodge . . . . Sgt Fred Patterson
George Pravda . . . . Sergeant
Percy Herbert . . . . Soldier
WAR Libya. Five soldiers escape from Italian camp but are caught by pro-Nazi sheikh.

12497
UP THE CREEK (83) (U) scope
Byron Exclusive (WB) reissue: 1961 (RFI)
P: Henry Halstead
D: Val Guest
S: Val Guest, Len Heath, John Warren
David Tomlinson . . . . . Lt Humphrey Fairweather

Peter Sellers . . . . CPO Docherty
Wilfrid Hyde White . . . . Admiral Foley
Liliane Sottane . . . . Susanne
Lionel Jeffries . . . . Steady Barker
Lionel Murton . . . . Perkins
Sam Kydd . . . . Bates
John Warren . . . . Cooky
David Lodge . . . . Scouse
Reginald Beckwith . . . . Publican
Vera Day . . . . Millie
Michael Goodliffe . . . . Nelson
Frank Pettingell . . . . Station Master
COMEDY Missile-mad lieut in charge of old destroyer finds bosun runs it as cutprice shop.

12498
SMILEY GETS A GUN (90) (U) tech/scope
Canberra (20)
P:D: Anthony Kimmins
S: (NOVEL) Moore Raymond
SC: Anthony Kimmins, Rex Rienits
Keith Calvert . . . . Smiley Greevins
Sybil Thorndike . . . . Granny McKinley
Chips Rafferty . . . . Sgt Flaxman
Bruce Archer . . . . Joey
Margaret Christensen . . . . . Ma Greevins
Reg Lye . . . . Pa Greevins
Grant Taylor . . . . Stiffy
Verena Kimmins . . . . Miss McCowan
Guy Doleman . . . . Quirk
ADVENTURE Australia. Blacksmith's son tries to earn rifle and is blamed for stealing old woman's gold.

12499
PRINT OF DEATH (26) (U)
Merton Park (AA)
P: Jack Greenwood
D: Montgomery Tully
S: James Eastwood
N: Edgar Lustgarten
John Warwick . . . . Supt Reynolds
Tim Turner . . . . Webber
Phil Brown . . . . Kovacs
CRIME Tecs prove payroll robbers dismembered ex-convict and grafted his fingertips on to rubber gloves.

MAY

12500
BATTLE OF THE V.1 (85) (A) USA: UNSEEN HEROES
Criterion (Eros)
P: George Maynard, John Bash
D: Vernon Sewell
S: (BOOK) Bernard Newman (THEY SAVED LONDON)
SC: Jack Hanley, Eryk Wlodek
Michael Rennie . . . . Stefan
Patricia Medina . . . . Zofia
Milly Vitale . . . . Anna
David Knight . . . . Tadek
Esmond Knight . . . . Stricker
Christopher Lee . . . . Brunner
Carl Jaffe . . . . General
John G. Heller . . . . Fritz
Peter Madden . . . . Stanislaw
Gordon Sterne . . . . Margraaf
George Pravda . . . . Karewski
Julian Somers . . . . Himmler
WAR Poland, 1942. Escapees from labour camp capture robot bomb and get it to England.

12501
ANOTHER TIME, ANOTHER PLACE (95) (A)
Kaydor (Par)
P: Joseph Kaufman, Lewis Allen
D: Lewis Allen
S: (NOVEL) Lenore Coffee
SC: Stanley Mann

Lana Turner . . . . Sara Scott
Barry Sullivan . . . . Carter Reynolds
Glynis Johns . . . . Kay Trevor
Sean Connery . . . . Martin Trevor
Sidney James . . . . Jake Klein
Terence Longden . . . . Alan Thompson
Martin Stephens .. . . Brian Trevor
Doris Hare . . . . Mrs Bunker
ROMANCE 1944. Girl reporter assures
correspondent's widow that she did not love
him.

12502
DRACULA (82) (X) *eastman* USA: HORROR
OF DRACULA
Hammer-Cadogan (UI)
P: Anthony Hinds
D: Terence Fisher
S: (NOVEL) Bram Stoker
SC: Jimmy Sangster
Peter Cushing . . . . Dr Van Helsing
Christopher Lee . . . . Count Dracula
Michael Gough . . . . Arthur
Melissa Stribling . . . . Mina
John Van Eyssen . . . . Jonathan Harker
Carol Marsh . . . . Lucy
Olga Dickie . . . . Gerda
Valerie Gaunt . . . . Vampire
HORROR Period. Doctor tracks vampiric
Count to England and destroys him.

JUN

12503
WONDERFUL THINGS! (84) (U)
Everest (ABP)
P: Anna Neagle
D: Herbert Wilcox
S: Jack Trevor Story
Frankie Vaughan . . . . Carmello
Jeremy Spenser . . . . Mario
Jackie Lane . . . . Pepita
Wilfrid Hyde White . . . . . . Sir Bertram
Jean Dawnay . . . . Anne
Eddie Byrne . . . . Harry
Harold Kasket . . . . Poppa
Christopher Rhodes . . . . . . Codger
Cyril Chamberlain . . . . . . Butler
Barbara Goalen . . . . Herself
ROMANCE Catalan fisherman comes to
London to make fortune and weds socialite.

12504
SHE DIDN'T SAY NO! (97) (A) *tech*
GW Films (ABP)
P: Josef Somlo, Sergei Nolbandov
D: Cyril Frankel
S: (NOVEL) Una Troy (WE ARE SEVEN)
SC: Una Troy, T.J. Morrison
Eileen Herlie . . . . Bridget Monahan
Niall MacGinnis . . . . Jamesey Casey
Ray McAnally . . . . Jim Power
Perlita Neilson . . . . Mary Monahan
Liam Redmond . . . . Dr Cassidy
Betty McDowell . . . . Mrs Power
Ian Bannen . . . . Peter Howard
Raymond Manthorpe . . . . . Toughy Monahan
Ann Dickins . . . . Poppy Monahan
Jack MacGowran . . . . William Bates
COMEDY Ireland. Villagers seek to expel widow
and her five children by different lovers.

12505
ON THE RUN (70) (A)
Danziger (UA)
P: Edward J & Harry Lee Danziger
D: Ernest Morris
S: Brian Clemens, Eldon Howard
Neil McCallum . . . . Wesley
Susan Beaumont . . . . Kitty Casey
William Hartnell . . . . Tom Casey
Gordon Tanner . . . . Bart Taylor

Philip Saville . . . . Driscol
Gilbert Winfield . . . . Joe
CRIME Boxer refuses to lose match and hides
from crooks in country garage.

12506
THE KEY (134) *scope* (A)
Open Road (Col)
P: Carl Foreman, Aubrey Baring
D: Carol Reed
S: (NOVEL) Jan de Hartog (STELLA)
SC: Carl Foreman
William Holden . . . . David Rose
Sophia Loren . . . . Stella
Trevor Howard . . . . Chris Ford
Oscar Homolka . . . . Van Dam
Kieron Moore . . . . Kane
Bernard Lee . . . . Wadlow
Beatrix Lehmann . . . . Housekeeper
Noel Purcell . . . . Porter
Bryan Forbes . . . . Weaver
Russell Waters . . . . Sparks
James Hayter . . . . Locksmith
Irene Handl . . . . Clerk
John Crawford . . . . Captain
WAR Swiss refugee proves fatal to successive
tugboat skippers who live with her. (BFA: Best
Actor, 1958).

12507
THE SPANIARD'S CURSE (80) (U)
Wentworth (IFD)
P. Roger Proudlock
D: Ralph Kemplen
S: (NOVEL) Edith Pargiter (THE ASSIZE OF
THE DYING)
SC: Kenneth Hyde
Tony Wright . . . . Charlie Manton
Lee Patterson . . . . **Mark Brett**
Michael Hordern . . . . Judge Manton
Susan Beaumont . . . . Margaret Manton
Ralph Truman . . . . Sir Robert Wyvern
Henry Oscar . . . . Mr Fredericks
Brian Oulton . . . . Frank Porter
Olga Dickie . . . . Hannah
Roddy Hughes . . . . Jody
Basil Dignam . . . . Guy Stevenson
CRIME Innocent man curses his judge and jury
and one by one they die.

12508
THE SNORKEL (90) (A)
Hammer-Clarion (Col)
P: Michael Carreras
D: Guy Green
S: (NOVEL) Anthony Dawson
SC: Jimmy Sangster, Peter Myers
Peter Van Eyck . . . . Jacques Duval
Betta St John . . . . Jean Duval
Mandy Miller . . . . Candy Duval
Gregoire Aslan . . . . Inspector
William Franklyn . . . . Wilson
Marie Burke . . . . Daily Woman
Irene Prador . . . . French Woman
CRIME Spain. Teenage girl causes death of
stepfather who drowned her father and gassed
her mother.

12509
THE WHOLE TRUTH (85) (A)
Valiant (Col)
P: Jack Clayton
D: John Guillermin
S: (TV PLAY) Philip Mackie
SC: Jonathan Latimer
Stewart Granger . . . . Max Poulton
Donna Reed . . . . Carol Poulton
George Sanders . . . . Carliss
Gianna Maria Canale . . . . . Gina Bertini
Michael Shillo . . . . Insp Simon
Peter Dyneley . . . . Willy Reichel
Hy Hazell . . . . American

Jimmy Thompson . . . . Assistant
Richard Molinas . . . . Gilbert
John Van Eyssen . . . . Archer
Philip Vickers . . . . Jack Leslie
Carlo Justini . . . . Leading Man
CRIME Riviera. Producer's wife proves he did
not kill mistress.

12510
THE WIND CANNOT READ (115) (U) *eastman*
Rank (RFD)
P: Betty E. Box
D: Ralph Thomas
S: (NOVEL) Richard Mason
SC: Richard Mason
Dirk Bogarde . . . . F/L Michael Quinn
Yoko Tani . . . . Suzuki San
John Fraser . . . . F/O Peter Munro
Ronald Lewis . . . . S/L Fenwick
Anthony Bushell . . . . Brigadier
Henry Okawa . . . . Lt Nakamura
Marne Maitland . . . . Bahadur
Michael Medwin . . . . F/O Lamb
Richard Leech . . . . Hobson
Anthony Wager . . . . Moss
Donald Pleasence . . . . Doctor
WAR Burma. Pilot escapes from POW camp to
return to sick Japanese wife (PGAA: 1959).

12511
LAW AND DISORDER (76) (U)
Hotspur (BL)
P: Paul Soskin, George Pitcher
D: Charles Crichton
S: (NOVEL) Denys Roberts (SMUGGLERS'
CIRCUIT)
SC: T.E.B. Clarke, Patrick Campbell,
Vivienne Knight
Michael Redgrave . . . . Percy Brand
Robert Morley . . . . Sir Edward Crichton
Elizabeth Sellars . . . . Gina Lasalle
Ronald Squire . . . . Col Masters
George Coulouris . . . . Bennie
Joan Hickson . . . . Aunt Florence
Lionel Jeffries . . . . Maj Proudfoot
Jeremy Burnham . . . . Colin Brand
Harold Goodwin . . . . Blacky
Meredith Edwards . . . . Sgt Bolton
Brenda Bruce . . . . Mary Cooper
David Hutcheson . . . . Freddie Cooper
John Le Mesurier . . . . . . Sir Humphrey Pomfret
COMEDY Smuggler posing as cleric tries to
prevent his son, a judge's marshal, from
learning truth.

JUL

12512
A NIGHT TO REMEMBER (123) (U)
Rank (RFD)
P: William MacQuitty
D: Roy Baker
S: (BOOK) Walter Lord
SC: Eric Ambler
Kenneth More . . . . Herbert Lightoller
David McCallum . . . . Bride
Jill Dixon . . . . Mrs Clarke
Laurence Naismith . . . . . . Capt Lord
Frank Lawton . . . . Chairman
John Cairney . . . . Murphy
Michael Goodliffe . . . . Andrews
Joseph Tomelty . . . . Dr O'Loughlin
Anthony Bushell . . . . Capt Rostron
Jack Watling . . . . Boxall
Honor Blackman . . . . Mrs Lucas
Alec McCowen . . . . Cottam
Richard Clarke . . . . Gallagher
George Rose . . . . Joghlin
Ralph Michael . . . . Yates
Kenneth Griffith . . . . Phillips
HISTORY 1912. "Titanic" sinks on maiden
voyage to New York.

12513
NOR THE MOON BY NIGHT (92) (U)
eastman USA: ELEPHANT GUN
IFP (RFD)
P: John Stafford
D: Ken Annakin
S: (NOVEL) Joy Packer
SC: Guy Elmes

Belinda Lee	Alice Lang
Michael Craig	Rusty Miller
Patrick McGoohan	Andrew Miller
Anna Gaylor	Thea Boryslawski
Eric Pohlmann	Anton Boryslawski
Pamela Stirling	Mrs Boryslawski
Lionel Ngakane	Nimrod
Joan Brickhill	Harriet Carver
Ben Heydenrych	Sgt Van Wyck

ADVENTURE Africa. Game warden's correspondence bride prefers his brother.

12514
HIGH HELL (85) (A)
Rich & Rich-Barbara (Par)
P: Arthur Mayer, William N. Boyle
D: Burt Balaban
S: (NOVEL) Steve Frazee
SC: Irve Tunick

John Derek	Craig Rhodes
Elaine Stewart	Lenore Davidson
Patrick Allen	Luke Fulgham
Rodney Burke	Danny Rhodes
Jerold Wells	Charlie Spence
Al Mulock	Frank Davidson
Colin Croft	Dell Malverne
Nicholas Stuart	Jed Thomas

ADVENTURE Canada. Gold prospectors, and one of their wives, are snowed in.

12515
ICE COLD IN ALEX (129) (A)
ABPC
P: W.A. Whittaker
D: J. Lee-Thompson
S: (NOVEL) Christopher Landon
SC: Christopher Landon, J. Lee-Thompson

John Mills	Capt Anson
Sylvia Syms	Diane Murdoch
Anthony Quayle	Capt Van Der Peol
Harry Andrews	Sgt Tom Pugh
Liam Redmond	Brigadier
Peter Arne	Officer
Diane Clare	Denise Norton
Richard Leech	Capt Crosbie
Allan Cuthbertson	Staff Officer
David Lodge	CMP Captain

WAR Libya, 1942. Captain taking nurses by ambulance to Alexandra learns African passenger is spy.

12516
HARRY BLACK (117) (U) *tech/scope* USA: HARRY BLACK AND THE TIGER
Mersham (20)
P: John Brabourne
D: Hugo Fregonese
S: (NOVEL) David Walker
SC: Sydney Boehm

Stewart Granger	Harry Black
Barbara Rush	Christian Tanner
Anthony Steel	Desmond Tanner
I.S. Johar	Bapu
Martin Stephens	Michael Tanner
Frank Olegario	Dr Chwodhury
Kamala Devi	Nurse Somola
Gladys Boot	Mrs Tanner
George Curzon	Philip Tanner
Archie Duncan	Woosley

ADVENTURE Africa, 1895. Hunter loves wife of coward who caused him to lose leg.

12517
INTENT TO KILL (89) *scope* (A)
Zonic (20)
P: Adrian Worker
D: Jack Cardiff
S: (NOVEL) Michael Bryan
SC: Jimmy Sangster

Richard Todd	Bob McLaurin
Betsy Drake	Nancy Ferguson
Herbert Lom	Juan Menda
Warren Stevens	Finch
Carlo Justini	Francisco Flores
Paul Carpenter	O'Brien
Alexander Knox	Mr McNeil
Lisa Gastoni	Carla Menda
Peter Arne	Kral
Catherine Boyle	Margaret McLaurin
John Crawford	Boyd
Kay Callard	Friend
Jackie Collins	Carol Freeman

CRIME Montreal. Doctor saves South American president from assassins.

12518
BLIND SPOT (71) (U)
Butcher's Films
P: Robert Baker, Monty Berman
D: Peter Maxwell
S: Robert Baker, John Gilling
SC: Kenneth R. Hayles

Robert Mackenzie	Dan Adams
Delphi Lawrence	Yvonne
Gordon Jackson	Chalky
Anne Sharp	June
John le Mesurier	Brent
George Pastell	Schreider
Ernest Clark	Fielding
Ronan O'Casey	Rushford

CRIME US Army officer tracks down gem smugglers who framed him when he was blind.

12519
THEM NICE AMERICANS (62) (U)
Chelsea (Butcher)
P: Anthony Young, Richard Griffith
D: Anthony Young
S: Gilbert Winfield

Bonar Colleano	Joe
Vera Day	Ann Adams
Renee Houston	Mrs Adams
Sheldon Lawrence	Johnny
Basil Dignam	Insp Adams
Patti Morgan	Lady Theodora
Michael Wade	Billy Adams
Ryck Ryden	Butch
Gilbert Winfield	Captain

COMEDY GI wins village policeman's daughter by saving young brother from minefield.

12520
A QUESTION OF ADULTERY (85) (A)
Connaught Place (Eros) *reissue:* 1961 (Gala)
P: Raymond Stross
D: Don Chaffey
S: (PLAY) Dan Sutherland (A BREACH OF MARRIAGE)
SC: Anne Edwards, Denis Freeman

Julie London	Mary Loring
Anthony Steel	Mark Loring
Basil Sydney	Sir John Loring
Donald Houston	Mr Jacobus
Anton Diffring	Carl Dieter
Andrew Cruickshank	Dr Cameron
Frank Thring	Mr Stanley
Conrad Phillips	Mario
Kynaston Reeves	Judge
Mary Mackenzie	Nurse Parsons
Georgina Cookson	Mrs Duncan

Trader Faulkner & Vola Van Dere
DRAMA Sterile man brings divorce action when his wife has A.I.D.

12521
DEATH WAS A PASSENGER (18) (U)
Supra Films (Mondial)
P:D: Theodore Zichy
Harriet Johns
Terence Alexander
Marigold Russell
WAR Flashback story of wartime escape by train.

12522
PORTRAIT OF A MATADOR (23) (U)
Supra Films (Mondial)
P:D: Theodore Zichy
Anthony Tancred
Sandra Dorne
Yvonne Warren
David Rich
DRAMA The effect of portrait on its painter and model.

12523
MINGALOO (20) (U)
Supra Films (Mondial)
P:D: Theodore Zichy
DRAMA Sculptor dreams of Chinese dog and models it.

12524
NEXT TO NO TIME (93) (U) *eastman*
Montpelier (BL)
P: Albert Fennell
D:SC: Henry Cornelius
S: (NOVEL) Paul Gallico (THE ENCHANTED HOUR)

Kenneth More	David Webb
Betsy Drake	Sir Godfrey Cowan
Harry Green	Saul
Patrick Barr	Jerry
Maureen Connell	Mary
Bessie Love	Becky
Reginald Beckwith	Warren
John Welsh	Steve
Howard Marion-Crawford	Hobbs
Clive Morton	Wallis
John Laurie	Abercrombie
Irene Handl	Mrs Cowley
Raymond Huntley	Forbes
Ferdy Mayne	Mario
Sidney James	Albert

COMEDY Shy designer gains confidence during nightly "lost hour" aboard "Queen Elizabeth".

AUG

12525
CARRY ON SERGEANT (83) (U)
Insignia (AA)
P: Peter Rogers
D: Gerald Thomas
S: R.F. Delderfield (THE BULL BOYS)
SC: Norman Hudis, John Antrobus

William Hartnell	Sgt Grimshaw
Bob Monkhouse	Charlie Sage
Shirley Eaton	Mary Sage
Eric Barker	Capt Potts
Dora Bryan	Nora
Bill Owen	Cpl Copping
Charles Hawtrey	Peter Golightly
Kenneth Connor	Horace Strong
Terence Longdon	Miles Heywood
Norman Rossington	Herbert Brown
Gerald Campion	Andy Galloway
Hattie Jacques	Capt Clark

COMEDY National Servicemen come out top for their sergeant's last parade.

12526
CRIME OF HONOUR (27) (U)
Merton Park (AA)
P: Jack Greenwood
D: Montgomery Tully
S: James Eastwood
N: Edgar Lustgarten
Russell Napier . . . . Supt Duggan
Ivan Craig . . . . Richard Watts
Jean Lodge . . . . Julia Branston
CRIME Supt proves wine-shipper was killed by
his partner.

12527
THE CROSSROAD GALLOWS (29) (U)
Merton Park (AA)
P: Jack Greenwood
D: Montgomery Tully
S: James Eastwood
N: Edgar Lustgarten
John Warwick . . . . Supt Reynolds
David Lodge . . . . Insp Travers
Tim Turner . . . . Sgt Hale
Genine Graham . . . . Miss Penny
John Stuart . . . . Mr Simmons
CRIME Tecs track down German ex-POW who
killed caravanners.

12528
THE LONG KNIFE (57) (U)
Merton Park (AA)
P: Jack Greenwood
D: Montgomery Tully
S: (NOVEL) Seldon Truss (THE LONG NIGHT)
SC: Ian Stuart Black
Joan Rice . . . . Jill Holden
Sheldon Lawrence . . . . . . Ross Waters
Dorothy Brewster . . . . . .Angela/ The Boy
Ellen Pollock . . . . Mrs Cheam
Victor Brooks . . . . Supt Leigh
Alan Keith . . . . Dr Ian Probus
Arthur Gomez . . . . Sgt Bowles
CRIME American lawyer proves suspected nurse
did not stab her rich patient.

12529
MAN WITH A GUN (60) (U)
Merton Park (AA)
P: Jack Greenwood
D: Montgomery Tully
S: Michael Winner
Lee Patterson . . . . Mike Davies
Rona Anderson . . . . Stella
John le Mesurier . . . . Harry Drayson
Warren Mitchell . . . . Joe Harris
Glen Mason . . . . Steve Riley
Carlo Borelli . . . . Carlo
Harold Lang . . . . John Drayson
Cyril Chamberlain . . . . . . Supt Wood
CRIME Insurance investigator exposes gang behind
burning of nightclub.

12530
TREAD SOFTLY STRANGER (90) (A)
Alderdale (Renown)
P: Denis O'Dell
D: Gordon Parry
S: (PLAY) Jack Popplewell (BLIND ALLEY)
SC: George Minter, Denis O'Dell
Diana Dors . . . . Calico
George Baker . . . . Johnny Mansell
Terence Morgan . . . . Dave Mansell
Patrick Allen . . . . Paddy Ryan
Jane Griffiths . . . . Sylvia
Maureen Delany . . . . Mrs Finnegan
Betty Warren . . . . Flo
Thomas Heathcote . . . . . . Sgt Lamb
Russell Napier . . . . Potter
Norman MacOwen . . . . . . Danny

Wilfrid Lawson . . . . Holroyd
CRIME Gambler's staid brother robs steel mill
for girl's sake.

12531
INDISCREET (98) *tech* (A)
Grandon (WB) *reissue:* 1961
P: Cary Grant, Stanley Donen
D: Stanley Donen
S: (PLAY) Norman Krasna (KIND SIR)
SC: Norman Krasna
Cary Grant . . . . Philip Adams
Ingrid Bergman . . . . Anna Kalman
Cecil Parker . . . . Alfred Munson
Phyllis Calvert . . . . Margaret Munson
David Kossoff . . . . Carl Banks
Megs Jenkins . . . . Doris Banks
Oliver Johnston . . . . Mr Fingleigh
Michael Anthony . . . . Oscar
COMEDY NATO man pretends he has wife to
avoid marrying actress.

12532
A WOMAN POSSESSED (68) (U)
Danziger (UA)
P: Edward J & Harry Lee Danziger
D: Max Varnel
S: Brian Clemens, Eldon Howard
Margaretta Scott . . . . . .Katherine Winthrop
Francis Matthews . . . . John Winthrop
Kay Callard . . . . Ann Winthrop
Alison Leggatt . . . . Emma
Ian Fleming . . . . Walter
Jan Holden . . . . Mary
Denis Shaw . . . . Bishop
Totti Truman Taylor . . . . . Miss Frobisher
CRIME Doctor suspects widowed mother of
trying to poison his wife.

12533
BLOOD OF THE VAMPIRE (85) *eastman* (X)
Artistes Alliance-WNW (Eros)
P: Robert Baker, Monty Berman
D: Henry Cass
S: Jimmy Sangster
Donald Wolfit . . . . Dr Callistratus
Barbara Shelley . . . . Madeleine
Vincent Ball . . . . Dr John Pierre
Victor Maddern . . . . Carl
William Devlin . . . . Kurt Urach
Andrew Faulds . . . . Wetzler
John le Mesurier . . . . Chief Justice
George Murcell . . . . Guard
Bryan Coleman . . . . Herr Auron
Bernard Bresslaw . . . . Sneakthief
Colin Tapley . . . . Judge
HORROR Bavaria 1885. Vampiric head of
criminal asylum uses inmates for blood
experiments.

12534
STORMY CROSSING (69) (U)
Tempean (Eros)
P: Robert Baker, Monty Berman
D: Pennington Richards
S: Sid Harris, Lou Dyer
SC: Brock Williams
John Ireland . . . . Griff Parker
Derek Bond . . . . Paul Seymour
Leslie Dwyer . . . . Bill Harris
Maureen Connell . . . . . . Shelley Baxter
Sheldon Lawrence . . . . . . Danny Parker
Sam Rockett . . . . Himself
Jack Taylor . . . . Navigator
Joy Webster . . . . Kitty Tyndall
Cameron Hall . . . . Insp Parry
MURDER American trainer proves sponsor
drowned girl during cross-channel swim.

12535
A CRY FROM THE STREETS (100) (U)
Film Traders (Eros)
P: Ian Dalrymple
D: Lewis Gilbert
S: (NOVEL) Elizabeth Coxhead (THE FRIEND
IN NEED)
SC: Vernon Harris
Max Bygraves . . . . Bill Lowther
Barbara Murray . . . . Ann Fairlie
Colin Petersen . . . . Georgie Murray
Dana Wilson . . . . Barbie Taylor
Kathleen Harrison . . . . . . Mrs Farrer
Eleanor Summerfield . . . . Gloria Murray
Mona Washbourne . . . . . . Mrs Daniels
Sean Barrett . . . . Don Farrer
Toke Townley . . . . Mr Daniels
Gillian Vaughan . . . . Sally
David Bushell . . . . Alec
Dandy Nicholls . . . . Mrs Jenks
Avice Landone . . . . Rachel Seymour
DRAMA Girl welfare officer and electrician help
deprived children.

12536
CAT AND MOUSE (79) (A) retitled: THE
DESPERATE MEN
Anvil (Eros)
D:SC: Paul Rotha
S: (NOVEL) Michael Halliday
Lee Patterson . . . . Rod Fenner
Ann Sears . . . . Ann Coltby
Victor Maddern . . . . Supt Harding
Hilton Edwards . . . . Mr Scruby
Roddy McMillan . . . . Mr Pomeroy
George Rose . . . . Dealer
CRIME GI deserter frames girl for killing
blackmailer and holds her captive while
seeking gems.

12537
THE REVENGE OF FRANKENSTEIN (89)
tech (X)
Hammer-Cadogan (Col)
P: Anthony Hinds
D: Terence Fisher
S: (CHARACTERS) Mary Shelley
SC: Jimmy Sangster, Hurford Janes
Peter Cushing . . . . . . Victor Frankenstein
Eunice Gayson . . . . Margaret
Francis Matthews . . . . Dr Hans Kleve
Michael Gwynn . . . . Karl
John Welsh . . . . Bergman
Lionel Jeffries . . . . Fritz
Oscar Quitak . . . . Karl (dwarf)
Richard Wordsworth . . . . . Up Patient
Charles Lloyd Pack . . . . . . President
John Stuart . . . . Inspector
Margery Cresley . . . . . .Countess Barscynska
HORROR Period. Doctor running charity
hospital creates cannibalistic creature from
amputations and dwarf's brain.

12538
THE MAN INSIDE (97) *scope* (A)
Warwick (Col)
P: Irving Allen, Albert Broccoli, Harold Huth
D: John Gilling
S: (NOVEL) M.E. Chaber
SC: Richard Maibaum, John Gilling,
David Shaw
Jack Palance . . . . Milo March
Anita Ekberg . . . . Trudie Hall
Nigel Patrick . . . . Sam Carter
Bonar Colleano . . . . Martin Lomer
Anthony Newley . . . . Ernesto
Sean Kelly . . . . Rizzio

Sidney James . . . . Franklin
Donald Pleasence . . . . Organ Grinder
Eric Pohlmann . . . . Tristao
Josephine Brown . . . . Mrs Frazur
Gerard Heinz . . . . Stone
Anne Aubrey . . . . Girl
Naomi Chance . . . . Jane Leyton
CRIME Tec and girl trail gem thief from New
York to London, via Lisbon, Madrid, and
Paris.

SEP

12539
THE CARRINGFORD SCHOOL MYSTERY
(serial) (U)
British Films (CFF)
P:SC: John Haggarty
D: William C. Hammond
S: Anthony Wilson
Jenny Jones . . . . Jane Selwyn
Derek Freeman . . . . Maurice Anderson
Anthony Richmond . . . . Brian Kendall
Richard James . . . . Peter Hastings
Eric Corrie . . . . Beaumont
Jack Stewart . . . . Gibson
Keith Marsh . . . . Ben Brundle
Gerald Case . . . . Mr Ashworth
Shaw Taylor . . . . Insp Bradfield

12540
1: CRISIS IN THE CLASSROOM (18)

12541
2: EVENING OF DANGER (18)

12542
3: GUNPLAY (19)

12543
4: KIDNAPPED (18)

12544
5: ORDEAL UNDER WATER (17)

12545
6: DANGER UNDER GROUND (16)

12546
7: PERIL AT SEA (14)

12547
8: THE FATAL SLIP (14)
CHILDREN Crook poses as science teacher to
steal gold necklace from museum.

12548
THE SALVAGE GANG (52) (U)
World Wide (CFF)
P: Hindle Edgar
D:SC: John Krish
S: Mary Cathcart Borer
Christopher Warbey . . . . . . Borer
Ali Allen . . . . Ali
Amanda Coxell . . . . Pat
Fraser Hines . . . . Kim
Richard Molinas . . . . Mr Caspanelli
CHILDREN Children sell bed for scrap iron and
then try to track it down.

12549
SEA FURY (97) (A)
Rank -Aqua (RFD)
P: S. Benjamin Fisz
D: C. Raker Endfield
S: C. Raker Endfield, John Kruse
Stanley Baker . . . . Abel Hewson
Victor McLaglen . . . . Capt Bellew
Luciana Paluzzi . . . . Josita
Gregoire Aslan . . . . Fernando
Francis de Wolff . . . . Mulder

David Oxley . . . . Blanco
George Murcell . . . . Lludon
Percy Herbert . . . . Walker
Rupert Davies . . . . Bosun
Robert Shaw . . . . Gorman
Joe Robinson . . . . Hendrik
Dermot Walsh . . . . Kelso
ADVENTURE Spain. Mate of salvage tug
saves wrecked ship despite drunken captain.

12550
THE MAN UPSTAIRS (88) (A)
ACT Films (BL)
P: Robert Dunbar
D: Don Chaffey
S: Alun Falconer
SC: Robert Dunbar, Don Chaffey
Richard Attenborough . . . . . Peter Watson
Bernard Lee . . . . Thompson
Donald Houston . . . . Sanderson
Dorothy Alison . . . . Mrs Barnes
Virginia Maskell . . . . Helen Grey
Kenneth Griffith . . . . Pollen
Patricia Jessel . . . . Mrs Lawrence
Charles Houston . . . . Nicholas
Maureen Connell . . . . Eunice Blair
Walter Hudd . . . . Supt
Edward Judd . . . . PC Stevens
CRIME Police try to persuade neurotic scientist
to leave locked room.

12551
CHAIN OF EVENTS (62) (A)
Beaconsfield (BL)
P: Peter Rogers
D: Gerald Thomas
S: (RADIO PLAY) Leo McKern (LONDON
STORY)
SC: Patrick Brawn
Dermot Walsh . . . . Quinn
Susan Shaw . . . . Jill
Lisa Gastoni . . . . Simone
Jack Watling . . . . Freddie
Alan Gifford . . . . Lord Fenchurch
Harold Lang . . . . Jimmy Boy
Kenneth Griffith . . . . Clarke
Ballard Berkeley . . . . Stockman
Freddie Mills . . . . Tiny
CRIME Bank clerk's lie to avoid bus fare starts
series of events leading to blackmail and death.

12552
MOMENT OF INDISCRETION (71) (U)
Danziger (UA)
P: Edward J & Harry Lee Danziger
D: Max Varnel
S: Brian Clemens, Eldon Howard
Ronald Howard . . . . John Miller
Lana Morris . . . . Janet Miller
John Van Eyssen . . . . Corby
John Witty . . . . Bryan
Denis Shaw . . . . Insp Marsh
Ann Lynn . . . . Pauline
John Stone . . . . Eric
Arnold Bell . . . . Surgeon
CRIME Lawyer proves convicted wife did not
stab ex-fiance's mistress.

12553
ROCKETS GALORE (94) *eastman* (U)
Rank (RFD)
P: Basil Dearden
D: Michael Relph
S: (NOVEL) Compton Mackenzie
SC: Monja Danischewsky
N: Finlay Currie
Jeannie Carson . . . . Janet McLeod
Donald Sinden . . . . S/L Hugh Mander
Roland Culver . . . . Capt Paul Waggett

Noel Purcell . . . . Father James McAllister
Ian Hunter . . . . A/C Watchorn
Duncan Macrae . . . . Duncan Ban
Jean Cadell . . . . Mrs Campbell
Gordon Jackson . . . . George Campbell
Alex Mackenzie . . . . Joseph McLeod
James Copeland . . . . Kenny McLeod
Carl Jaffe . . . . Dr Emile Hamburger
Nicholas Phipps . . . . Andrew Wishart
Catherine Lacey . . . . Mrs Waggett
John Laurie . . . . Capt MacKechnie
Reginald Beckwith . . . . Mumford
Richard Dimbleby; Michael Foot; W.J. Brown;
A.J.P. Taylor; Robert Boothby; Edgar Lustgarten;
Daniel Farson
COMEDY Hebridean islanders create pink seagull
to stop building of rocket base.

OCT

12554
LINKS OF JUSTICE (68) (U)
Danziger (Par)
P: Edward J & Harry Lee Danziger
D: Max Varnel
S: Brian Clemens, Eldon Howard
Jack Watling . . . . Edgar Mills
Sarah Lawson . . . . Clare Mills
Robert Raikes . . . . Averill
Denis Shaw . . . . Heath
Kay Callard . . . . Stella
Michael Kelly . . . . Robert Lane
Jacques Cey . . . . Dr Zelderman
Jan Holden . . . . Elsie
Geoffrey Hibbert . . . . Edward Manning
CRIME Burglar witness proves girl killed her
husband in self defence.

12555
THREE CROOKED MEN (71) (U)
Danziger (Par)
P: Edward J. & Harry Lee Danziger
D: Ernest Morris
S: Brian Clemens, Eldon Howard
Gordon Jackson . . . . Don Wescott
Sarah Lawson . . . . May Wescott
Warren Mitchell . . . . Prinn
Philip Saville . . . . Seppy
Michael Mellinger . . . . Vince
Eric Pohlmann . . . . Masters
Kenneth Edwards . . . . Insp Wheeler
Arnold Bell . . . . Mr Brady
CRIME Suspect tracks down robbers who
broke into bank through his shop.

12556
THE BANK RAIDERS (60) (U)
Film Workshop (RFD)
P: Geoffrey Goodhart
D:Maxwell Munden
S: Brandon Fleming
Peter Reynolds . . . . Terry
Sandra Dorne . . . . Della
Sydney Tafler . . . . Shelton
Lloyd Lamble . . . . Insp Mason
Rose Hill . . . . Mrs Marling
Arthur Mullard . . . . Linders
CRIME Petty crook joins gang of bank robbers
who kidnap girl to silence witness.

12557
PASSIONATE SUMMER (104) *eastman* (A)
Briar (RFD)
P: Kenneth Harper, George Willoughby
D: Rudolph Cartier
S: (NOVEL) Richard Mason (THE SHADOW
AND THE PEAK)
SC: Joan Henry
Virginia McKenna . . . . Judy
Bill Travers . . . . Douglas Lockwood

Yvonne Mitchell . . . . Mrs Pawley
AlexanderKnox . . . . Mr Pawley
Carl Mohner . . . . Louis
Ellen Barrie . . . . Sylvia
Guy Middleton . . . . Duffield
Bruce Pitt . . . . John
Martin Stephens . . . . Alan
ROMANCE Jamaica. Headmaster's wife causes
death of infatuated schoolgirl.

12558
SEA OF SAND (97) (U)
Tempean (RFD)
P: Robert Baker, Monty Berman
D: Guy Green
S: Sean Fielding
SC: Robert Westerby
Richard Attenborough . . . . Trooper Brody
John Gregson . . . . Capt Williams
Michael Craig . . . . Capt Cotton
Vincent Ball . . . . Sgt Nesbitt
Dermot Walsh . . . . Maj Jeffries
Percy Herbert . . . . Trooper White
Barry Foster . . . . Cpl Matheson
Andrew Faulds . . . . Sgt Parker
George Murcell . . . . Cpl Simms
Ray McAnally . . . . Sgt Hardy
WAR Africa, 1943. Long Range Desert Group
blow up German petrol dump.

12559
DUBLIN NIGHTMARE (64) (U)
Penington-Eady (RFD)
P: Jon Penington, David Eady
D: John Pomeroy
S: John Tully
William Sylvester . . . . John Kevin
Marla Landi . . . . Anna
Richard Leech . . . . Steven Lawlor
William Sherwood . . . . Edward Dillon
Harry Hutchinson . . . . The Vulture
Jack Cunningham . . . . Insp O'Connor
Pat O'Sullivan . . . . O'Callaghan
CRIME Dublin. Photographer discovers his
"murdered" friend is an IRA leader.

12560
THE TROLLENBERG TERROR (84) (X)
USA: THE CRAWLING EYE
Tempean (Eros)
P: Robert Baker, Monty Berman
D: Quentin Lawrence
S: (TV SERIAL) Peter Key
SC: Jimmy Sangster
Forrest Tucker. . . . . Alan Brooks
Laurence Payne . . . . Philip Truscott
Janet Munro . . . . Anne Pilgrim
Jennifer Jayne . . . . Sarah Pilgrim
Warren Mitchell . . . . Prof Crevett
Andrew Faulds . . . . Brett
Stuart Sanders . . . . Dewhurst
Frederick Schiller . . . . Klein
HORROR Switzerland. UNO scientist destroys
extra-terrestrials intent on killing girl mind-
reader.

12561
GRIP OF THE STRANGLER (78) (X) USA
THE HAUNTED STRANGLER
MLC Producers Associates (Eros)
P: John Croydon
D: Robert Day
S: Jan Read
SC: Jan Read, John C. Cooper
Boris Karloff . . . . James Rankin
Jean Kent . . . . Cora Seth
Elizabeth Allan . . . . Mrs Rankin
Anthony Dawson . . . . Supt Burke
Vera Day . . . . Pearl
Tim Turner . . . . Kenneth MacColl
Diane Aubrey . . . . Lily

Dorothy Gordon . . . . Hannah
Leslie Perrins . . . . Governor
HORROR 1880. Novelist realises he is the
paralytic Haymarket Strangler.

12562
I WAS MONTY'S DOUBLE (100) (U)
Film Traders-Setfair (ABP)
P: Maxwell Setton
D: John Guillermin
S: (BOOK) M.E. Clifton-James
SC: Bryan Forbes
John Mills . . . . Maj Harvey
Cecil Parker . . . . Col Logan
M.E. Clifton-James . . . . Himself/Montgomery
Marius Goring . . . . Carl Neilson
Michael Hordern . . . . Governor
Leslie Phillips . . . . Maj Tennant
Bryan Forbes . . . . Lt Butterfield
Barbara Hicks . . . . Hester
James Hayter . . . . Sgt Adams
Sidney James . . . . Porter
Patrick Allen . . . . Col Matthews
Vera Day . . . . Angela Cook
Victor Maddern . . . . Sgt
Marne Maitland . . . . Arab
Alfie Bass . . . . Man
MacDonald Parke . . . . General
Duncan Lamont . . . . W/C Bates
Patrick Holt . . . . Col Dawson
John le Mesurier . . . . Adjutant
WAR 1944. True story of actor persuaded to
pose as General Montgomery to fool Nazis in
Africa.

12563
GIRLS AT SEA (80) *tech* **(U)**
ABPC
P: Vaughan N. Dean, Gilbert Gunn
D: Gilbert Gunn
S: (PLAY) Stephen King-Hall, Ian Hay (THE
MIDDLE WATCH)
SC: T.J. Morrison, Gilbert Gunn, Walter C.
Mycroft
Guy Rolfe . . . . Capt Alwyn Maitland
Ronald Shiner . . . . Marine Ogg
Alan White . . . . Cmdr
Michael Hordern . . . . . . .Sir Reginald Hewitt
Anne Kimbell . . . . Mary Carlton
Nadine Tallier . . . . Antoinette
Fabia Drake . . . . Lady Kitty Hewitt
Mary Steele . . . . Jill Eaton
Richard Coleman . . . . Capt Bobby Randall
Lionel Jeffries . . . . Tourist
Daniel Massey . . . . Flag Lieut Courtney
David Lodge . . . . Cpl Duckett
Teddy Johnson . . . . The Singer
COMEDY Girls taken to sea on battleship must be
hidden from admiral.

12564
FURTHER UP THE CREEK (91) *scope* **(U)**
Byron-Hammer (Col)
P: Henry Halstead
D: Val Guest
S: Val Guest, John Warren, Len Heath
David Tomlinson . . . . . . Lt Fairweather
Frankie Howard . . . . Bosun
Shirley Eaton . . . . Jane
Thora Hird . . . . Mrs Galloway
Lionel Jeffries . . . . Steady Barker
Lionel Murton . . . . Perkins
David Lodge . . . . Scouse
John Warren . . . . Cooky
Sam Kydd . . . . Bates
Edwin Richfield . . . . Bennett
Eric Pohlmann . . . . President
Stanley Unwin . . . . Porter
Michael Goodliffe . . . . . Lt/Cdr Blakeley
Patrick Holt . . . . Lt
Walter Hudd . . . . Consul

COMEDY Lieut, put in charge of old frigate, is
unaware that bosun is hiding paying passengers.

12565
VIRGIN ISLAND (94) *eastman* **(U)**
Countryman (BL)
P: Leon Clore, Grahame Tharp
D: Pat Jackson
S: (NOVEL) Robb White (OUR VIRGIN
ISLAND)
SC: Pat Jackson, Philip Rush
John Cassavetes . . . . Evan
Virginia Maskell . . . . Tina Lomax
Sidney Poitier . . . . Marcus
Isabel Dean . . . . Mrs Lomax
Colin Gordon . . . . Commissioner
Howard Marion-Crawford . . . Prescott
Edric Connor . . . . Capt Jason
Ruby Dee . . . . Ruth
Gladys Boot . . . . Mrs Carruthers
ROMANCE Archaeologist buys Caribbean island for
honeymoon home.

12566
BEHIND THE MASK (99) *eastman* **(A)**
GW Films (BL)
P: Sergei Nolbandov, Josef Somlo
D: Brian Desmond Hurst
S: (NOVEL) John Rowan Wilson (THE PACK)
SC: John Hunter
Michael Redgrave . . . . .Sir Arthur Benson Gray
Tony Britton . . . . Philip Selwood
Carl Mohner . . . . Dr Carl Romek
Niall MacGinnis . . . . Neil Isherwood
Vanessa Redgrave . . . . Pamela Gray
Ian Bannen . . . . Alan Crabtree
Brenda Bruce . . . . Elizabeth Fallon
Lionel Jeffries . . . . Walter Froy
Miles Malleson . . . . Sir Oswald Pettiford
John Welsh . . . . Col Langley
Ann Firbank . . . . Mrs Judson
Jack Hedley . . . . Dr Galbraith
Hugh Miller . . . . Examiner
DRAMA Young surgeon takes blame for Polish
drug addict when patient dies from neglect.

12567
THE ADVENTURES OF HAL 5 (59) (U)
Bushey (CFF)
P: Gilbert Church
D:SC: Don Sharp
S: (NOVEL) Henry Donald (HAL 5 AND THE
HAYWARDS)
Peter Godsell . . . . Charles
William Russell . . . . Vicar
John Glyn Jones . . . . Mr Goorlie
Janina Faye . . . . Moira
John Charlesworth . . . . . . Ralph
Edwin Richfield . . . . Cooper
David Morrell . . . . Dicey
CHILDREN Swindling garage owner tries to
steal family's old car.

12568
BLOW YOUR OWN TRUMPET (56) (U)
Cecil Musk (CFF)
D: Cecil Musk
S: Geoffrey Bond
SC: Mary Cathcart Borer
Michael Crawford . . . . Jim Fenn
Peter Butterworth . . . . Mr Duff
Gillian Harrison . . . . Helen Fenn
Martyn Shields . . . . Tony Holroyd
Arley Welfare Band
CHILDREN Lancs. Sacked band conductor helps
boy win cornet contest.

12569
NODDY IN TOYLAND (87) *eastman* **(U)**
Bill & Michael Luckwell (Luckwell)
P: Kay Luckwell
D: Maclean Rogers

S: (PLAY) Enid Blyton
Colin Spaull . . . . Noddy
Gloria Johnson . . . . Silky
Leslie Sarony . . . . Mr Pinkwhistle
Peter Elliott . . . . PC Plod
FANTASY Toyland boy blamed for crimes of
Red Goblins.

NOV

12570
SON OF ROBIN HOOD (77) *eastman/scope* (U)
Argo (20)
P: Jack Lamont
D: George Sherman
S: George W. George, George Slavin
Al Hedison . . . . Jamie
June Laverick . . . . Deering Hood
David Farrar . . . . , ... Des Roches
Marius Goring . . . . Chester
Philip Friend . . . . Dorchester
Delphi Lawrence . . . . Sylvia
George Coulouris . . . . Alan a Dale
George Woodbridge . . . . . . Little John
Humphrey Lestocq . . . . Blunt
Shelagh Fraser . . . . Constance
Jack Lambert . . . . Will Scarlet
Maya Koumani . . . . .Lady in Waiting
ADVENTURE 1200. Outlaw's daughter saves boy
Prince from evil Duke.

12571
THE SHERIFF OF FRACTURED JAW (110)
eastman/scope
Apollo (20)
P: Daniel M. Angel
D: Raoul Walsh
S: (STORY) Jacob Hay
SC: Arthur Dales
Kenneth More . . . . Jonathan Tibbs
Jayne Mansfield . . . . Kate
Henry Hull . . . . Mayor Masters
Bruce Cabot . . . . Jack
Ronald Squire . . . . Toynbee
William Campbell . . . . Keeno
Sidney James . . . . Drunk
Reed de Rouen . . . . Claybourne
Charles Irwin . . . . Luke
Donald Stewart . . . . Drummer
Robert Morley . , ... Uncle Lucius
David Horne . . . . James
Gordon Tanner . . . . Wilkins
Sheldon Lawrence . . . . Johnny
COMEDY Nervous English gunsmith elected
sheriff of Western town.

12572
MARK OF THE PHOENIX (64) (U)
Butcher's Films
P: W.G. Chalmers
D: Maclean Rogers
S: Desmond Cory
SC: Norman Hudis
Julia Arnall . . . . Petra
Sheldon Lawrence . . . . Chuck Martin
Anton Diffring . . . . Insp Schell
Eric Pohlmann . . . . Duser
George Margo . . . . Emilson
Michael Peake . . . . Koos
Martin Miller . . . . Brunet
CRIME Germany. American jewel thief foils art
collector seeking rare alloy.

12573
A LADY MISLAID (59) (U)
Welwyn (ABP)
P: Robert Hall
D: David Macdonald
S: (PLAY) Kenneth Horne
SC: Frederick Gotfurt
Phyllis Calvert . . . . Esther Williams

Alan White . . . . Sgt Bullock
Thorley Walters . . . . Smith
Gillian Owen . . . . Jennifer Williams
Richard Leech . . . . George
Constance Fraser . . . . Mrs Small
Sheila Shand Gibbs . . . . . , . Betty
COMEDY Sisters rent cottage and suspect
former tenant killed his wife.

12574
I ONLY ARSKED! (82) (U)
Hammer-Lawrie (Col)
P: Anthony Hinds
D: Montgomery Tully
S: (TV SERIES) Sid Colin (THE ARMY GAME)
SC: Sid Colin, Jack Davies
Bernard Bresslaw . . . . Popeye Popplewell
Michael Medwin . . . . Cpl Springer
Alfie Bass . . . . Excused Boots Bisley
Geoffrey Sumner . . . . . . Maj Upshott-Bagley
Charles Hawtrey . . . . Professor
Norman Rossington . . . . . Cupcake Cook
David Lodge . . . . Sgt Potty Chambers
Michael Bentine . . . . Fred
Arthur Howard . . . . Sir Redvers
Francis Matthews . . . . Mahmoud
Marne Maitland . . . . King Fazim
Marie Devereux . . . . Harem Girl
COMEDY Soldiers and harem girls thwart
revolution and find oil.

12575
SALLY'S IRISH ROGUE (74) (U)
Emmett Dalton (BL)
P: Robert Baker, Monty Berman
D: George Pollock
S: (PLAY) George Shiels (THE NEW
GOSSOON)
SC: Patrick Kirwan, Blanaid Irvine
Julie Harris . . . . Sally Hamil
Tim Seely . . . . Luke Carey
Harry Brogan . . . . Rabit Hamil
Maire Kean . . . . Ellen Carey
Bridie Lynch . . . . Mag Kehoe
Eddie Golden . . . . Ned Shay
Philip O'Flynn . . . . John Henley
COMEDY Ireland. Poacher's daughter tames
wild inheritor of farm.

12576
FLOODS OF FEAR (84) (A)
Rank (RFD)
P: Sydney Fox
D: Charles Crichton
S: (NOVEL) John & Ward Hawkins
SC: Charles Crichton, Vivienne Knight
Howard Keel . . . . Donovan
Anne Heywood . . . . Elizabeth Matthews
Cyril Cusack . . . . : . . . . . Peebles
Harry H. Corbett . . . . Sharkey
John Crawford . . . . Jack Murphy
Eddie Bryne . . . . Sheriff
John Phillips . . . . Dr Matthews
James Dyrenforth . . . . . . Mayor
Peter Madden . . . . Banker
Guy Kingsley Poynter . . . . . Deputy
CRIME USA. Girl trapped in flood with framed
convict and moronic thief.

DEC

12577
FIEND WITHOUT A FACE (73) (X)
MLC Producers Associates (Eros)
P: John Croydon
D: Arthur Crabtree
S: (STORY) Amelia Reynolds Long (THE
THOUGHT MONSTER)
SC: Herbert J. Leder
Marshall Thompson . . . . .Maj Jeff Cummings
Kim Parker . . . . Barbara Grisselle

Kynaston Reeves . . . . Prof Walgate
Stanley Maxted . . . . Col Butler
Terence Kilburn . . . . Capt Al Chester
James Dyrenforth . . . . . . Maj Hawkins
Peter Madden . . . . Dr Bradley
Gilbert Winfield . . . . Capt Warren
Michael Balfour . . . . Sgt Kasper
HORROR Manitoba. Scientist's thoughts
materialise as life-sucking brains.

12578
NOWHERE TO GO (97) (U)
Ealing (MGM)
P: Eric Williams
D: Seth Holt
S: (NOVEL) Donald Mackenzie
SC: Seth Holt, Kenneth Tynan
George Nader . . . . Paul Gregory
Maggie Smith . . . . Bridget Howard
Bernard Lee . . . . Vic Sloane
Geoffrey Keen . . . . Insp Scott
Bessie Love . . . . Harriet Jefferson
Andree Melly . . . . Rosa
Howard Marion Crawford . . . Cameron
Arthur Howard . . . . Dodds
Margaret McGrath . . . . . . Rosemary
Harry H. Corbett . . . . Sullivan
Harry Locke . . . . Bendel
Lionel Jeffries . . . . Pet Shop Man
CRIME Socialite helps escaped Canadian thief
seek safety deposit key.

12579
TOM THUMB (92) *eastman* (U)
Galaxy (MGM)
P-D: George Pal
S: (STORY) Brothers Grimm
SC: Ladislas Fodor
Russ Tamblyn . . . . Tom Thumb
Alan Young . . . . Woody
Terry Thomas . . . . Ivan
Peter Sellers . . . . Tony
June Thorburn . . . . Forest Queen
Jessie Matthews . . . . Anna
Bernard Miles . . . . Jonathan
Ian Wallace . . . . Cobbler
Stan Freberg . . . . Puppetoon Voices
FANTASY Two-inch boy saves father by catch-
ing men who stole town's treasure (AA: Best
special effects, 1958).

12580
THE INN OF THE SIXTH HAPPINESS (159)
eastman/scope (U)
20th Century Fox
P: Buddy Adler
D: Mark Robson
S: (NOVEL) Alan Burgess (THE SMALL
WOMAN)
SC: Isobel Lennart
Ingrid Bergman . . . . Gladys Aylward
Curt Jurgens . . . . Capt Lin Nan
Robert Donat . . . . Mandarin
Ronald Squire . . . . Sir Francis Jamison
Athene Seyler . . . . Mrs Lawson
Noel Hood . . . . Miss Thompson
Richard Wattis . . . . Mr Murfin
Joan Young . . . . Cook
Moultrie Kelsall . . . . Dr Robinson
Peter Chong . . . . Yang
Michael David . . . . Ho Ka
DRAMA China, 1930. True story of English
servant who became missionary and saved
children from Japanese attack.

12581
THE SOLITARY CHILD (64) (A)
Beaconsfield (BL)
P: Peter Rogers
D: Gerald Thomas

S: (NOVEL) Nina Bawden
SC: Robert Dunbar

Philip Friend	James Random
Barbara Shelley	Harriet Random
Rona Anderson	Jean Dennison
Jack Watling	Cyril Sully
Sarah Lawson	Ann Random
Julia Lockwood	Maggie Random
Catherine Lacey	Mrs Evans
Violet Farebrother	Mrs Denison

CRIME Girl weds farmer and suspects him of shooting first wife.

12582
THE SQUARE PEG (89) (U)
Rank (RFD)
P: Hugh Stewart
D: John Paddy Carstairs
S: Jack Davies, Henry E. Blyth, Norman Wisdom, Eddie Leslie

Norman Wisdom	Norman Pitkin/Gen Schreiber
Honor Blackman	Lesley Cartland
Edward Chapman	Wilfred Grimsdale
Campbell Singer	Sgt Loder
Hattie Jacques	Gretchen von Schmetterling
Brian Worth	Henri LeBlanc
Terence Alexander	Capt Wharton
John Warwick	Col Layton
Arnold Bell	Gen Hunt
Eddie Leslie	MO

COMEDY Captured parachutist saves friends by posing as German double.

12583
BACHELOR OF HEARTS (94) *eastman* **(U)**
Independent Artists (RFD)
P: Vivian A. Cox, Julian Wintle, Leslie Parkyn
D: Wolf Rilla
S: Leslie Bricusse, Frederic Raphael

Hardy Kruger	Wolf Hauser
Sylvia Syms	Ann Wainwright
Ronald Lewis	Hugo Foster
Eric Barker	Dr Butson
Newton Blick	Morgan
Jeremy Burnham	Adrian Baskerville
Peter Myers	Jeremy
Philip Gilbert	Conrad Lewis
Charles Kay	Tom Clark
Gillian Vaughan	Virginia
Sandra Francis	Lois
Barbara Steele	Fiona

COMEDY Cambridge. Episodic adventures of German exchange student.

12584
THE TWO-HEADED SPY (93) (U)
Sabre (Col)
P: Hal E. Chester, Bill Kirby
D: Andre de Toth
S: J. Alvin Kugelmass

SC: James O'Donnell

Jack Hawkins	Gen Alex Scottland
Gia Scala	Lili Geyr
Erik Schumann	Capt Kurt Reinisch
Alexander Knox	Mueller
Felix Aylmer	Cornaz
Laurence Naismith	Gen Hauser
Edward Underdown	Kaltenbrunner
Donald Pleasence	Gen Hardt
Martin Benson	Gen Wagner
Kenneth Griffith	Adolph Hitler
Walter Hudd	Admiral Canaris
Harriette Johns	Karen Corscher
Geoffrey Bayldon	Dietz
Richard Grey	Marshal Keitel

WAR Berlin, 1939-45, True story of British spy serving on German general staff.

12585
ALIVE AND KICKING (94) (U)
Diador (ABF)
P: Victor Skutezky
D: Cyril Frankel
S: (PLAY) William Dinner, William Morum

Sybil Thorndike	Dora
Kathleen Harrison	Rosie
Estelle Winwood	Mabel
Stanley Holloway	MacDonagh
Liam Redmond	OldMan
Marjorie Rhodes	Old Woman
Richard Harris	Lover
Olive McFarland	Lover
John Salew	Solicitor
Eric Pohlmann	Captain
Colin Gordon	Birdwatcher
Joyce Carey	Matron

COMEDY Ireland. Three escapees from old ladies' home pose as millionaire's nieces and organise knitting industry.

12586
THE SECRET MAN (68) (U)
Producers Associates-Amalgamated (Butcher)
P:D: Ronald Kinnoch
S: Tony O'Grady

Marshall Thompson	Dr Cliff Mitchell
John Loder	Maj Anderson
Anne Aubrey	Jill Warren
Madga Miller	Ruth
John Stuart	Dr Warren
Henry Oscar	John Manning
Murray Kash	Waldo
Michael Mellinger	Tony

CRIME American missile expert poses as runaway idealist to unmask spy.

12587
HELLO LONDON (78) *eastman* **(U)**
Kinran (RFI)
P: George Fowler
D: Sidney Smith
S: George Fowler, Herb Sargent, Ken Englund,

Guv Elmes

Sonja Henie	Herself
Michael Wilding	
Ronnie Graham	
Eunice Gayson	
Lisa Gastoni	
Charles Heslop	
Oliver Johnston	

TreforJones; Stanley Holloway; Dennis Price; Dora Bryan; Robert Coote; Roy Castle; Joan Regan
MUSICAL Stars conspire to make American skaters miss their plane and appear at charity show.

12588
CORRIDORS OF BLOOD (86) (X)
Producers Associates (MGM)
P: John Croydon
D: Robert Day
S: Jean Scott Rogers

Boris Karloff	Dr Thomas Bolton
Betta St John	Susan
Finlay Currie	Dr Matheson
Christopher Lee	Ressurection Joe
Francis Matthews	Dr Jonathan Bolton
Adrienne Corri	Rachel
Francis de Wolff	Black Ben
Basil Dignam	Chairman
Frank Pettingell	Dr Blount
Carl Bernard	Ned the Crow
Marian Spencer	Mrs Matheson
Nigel Green	Insp Donovan

DRAMA 1844. Surgeon seeking anaesthesia becomes addict and pawn of criminals.

12589
LIFE IS A CIRCUS (84) (U) *scope*
Vale (BL)
P: E.M. Smedley Aston
D: Val Guest
S: Val Guest, John Warren, Len Heath

Bud Flanagan	Bud
Jimmy Nervo	Cecil
Teddy Knox	Sebastian
Charlie Naughton	Charlie
Jimmy Gold	Goldie
Eddie Gray	Eddie
Shirley Eaton	Shirley Winter
Michael Holliday	Carl Rickenback
Lionel Jeffries	Genie
Joseph Tomelty	Joe Winter
Eric Pohlmann	Rickenback
Chesney Allen	Ches
Maureen Moore	Rose of Bagdad

COMEDY Aladdin's lamp helps bankrupt circus thwart rivals.

1959

JAN

12590
THE CAPTAIN'S TABLE (89) (A) *eastman*
Rank Film
P: Joseph Janni
D: Jack Lee
S: (NOVEL) Richard Gordon
SC: John Whiting, Bryan Forbes, Nicholas Phipps

John Gregson	Capt Albert Ebbs
Peggy Cummings	Mrs Judd
Donald Sinden	Shawe-Wilson
Nadia Gray	Mrs Porteous
Maurice Denham	Maj Broster
Richard Wattis	Prittlewood
Reginald Beckwith	Burtweed
Bill Kerr	Bill Coke
Nicholas Phipps	Reddish
John le Mesurier	Sir Angus
Lionel Murton	Bernie Floate
Joan Sims	Maude Prichett
Miles Malleson	Canon Swingler
James Hayter	Earnshaw
Joseph Tomelty	Dalrymple

COMEDY Cargo captain takes over luxury cruise and gets involved with widow and adventuress.

12591
OPERATION AMSTERDAM (104) (U)
Rank (RFD)
P: Maurice Cowan
D: Michael McCarthy
S: (NOVEL) David E. Walker (ADVENTURE IN DIAMONDS)
SC: Michael McCarthy, John Eldridge

Peter Finch	Jan Smit
Eva Bartok	Anna
Tony Britton	Maj Dillon
Alexander Knox	Walter Keyser
Malcolm Keen	Johann Smit
Christopher Rhodes	Alex
Tim Turner	Lieut
John Horsley	Cdr Bowerman
Keith Pyott	Dealer
Melvyn Hayes	Willem Lubka
Oscar Quitak	Dealer
John Bailey	Officer

WAR Holland, 1940. Girl helps British intelligence man remove million in diamonds from time vault.

12592
HIDDEN HOMICIDE (72) (U)
Bill & Michael Luckwell (RFD)
P: Derek Winn
D: Tony Young
S: (NOVEL) Paul Capon (MURDER AT SHINGLESTRAND)
SC: Tony Young, Bill Luckwell

Griffith Jones	Michael Cornforth
James Kenney	Oswald/Mrs Dodge/Kate
Patricia Laffan	Jean
Bruce Seton	Bill Dodd
Maya Koumani	Marian
Robert Raglan	Ashbury
Richard Shaw	Wright
Charles Farrell	Mungo Peddey

CRIME Girl hiker proves female impersonator killed author's uncle.

12593
THE MAN WHO LIKED FUNERALS (60) (U)
Penington-Eady (RFD)
P: Jon Penington
D: David Eady
S: Cicely Finn, Joan O'Connor
SC: Margot Bennett

Leslie Phillips	Simon Hurd
Susan Beaumont	Stella

Bill Fraser	Jeremy Bentham
Mary Mackenzie	Hester Waring
Jimmy Thompson	Lt Hunter
Anita Sharp Bolster	Lady Hunter
Lily Lapidus	Ma Morelli

COMEDY Printer forges memoirs of dead celebrities to blackmail their relatives and save bankrupt Boys' Club.

12594
THE CAT GANG (50) (U)
Realist (CFF)
P: Arthur T. Viliesid
D: Darrell Catling
S: G. Ewart Evans
SC: John Eldridge

Francesca Annis	Sylvia
John Pike	John
Jeremy Bullock	Bill
John Gabriel	Mason
John Stacy	Dodds
Paddy Joyce	Banks

CHILDREN Children help customs officer trap smuggling gang.

12595
ROOM AT THE TOP (117) (X)
Remus (IFD) *reissue:* 1961
P: John & James Woolf
D: Jack Clayton
S: (NOVEL) John Braine
SC: Neil Paterson

Simone Signoret	Alice Aisgill
Laurence Harvey	Joe Lampton
Heather Sears	Susan Brown
Donald Wolfit	Mr Brown
Donald Houston	Charlie Soames
Hermione Baddeley	Elspeth
Allan Cuthbertson	George Aisgill
Raymond Huntley	Mr Hoylake
John Westbrook	Jack Wales
Ambrosine Philpotts	Mrs Brown
Richard Pasco	Teddy
Beatrice Varley	Aunt
Delena Kidd	Eva
Ian Hendry	Cyril
Mary Peach	June Samso
Miriam Karlin	Gertrude
Wilfrid Lawson	Uncle Nat

DRAMA Yorks. Ambitious clerk weds pregnant heiress, causing death of his married mistress. (BFA: Best Film, 1958. Extract in THE LOVE GODDESSES).

12596
THE GREAT VAN ROBBERY (70) (U)
Danziger (UA)
P: Edward J & Harry Lee Danziger
D: Max Varnel
S: Brian Clemens, Eldon Howard

Denis Shaw	Caesar Smith
Kay Callard	Ellen
Tony Quinn	Mercer
Philip Saville	Carter
Tony Doonan	Wally
Geoffrey Hibbert	Venner
Vera Fusek	Mara
Carl Duering	Delgano

CRIME Interpol agent travels to Rio, Rome and Paris to prove London coffee importer robbed Royal Mint van.

12597
SHAMUS (54) *eastman* (U)
Border (NR)
P: O. Negus-Fancey
D:S: Eric Marquis

John Francis Rooney	Seamus Rooney
Tiny Littler	Leprechaun

FANTASY Ireland. Leprechaun's magic gives orphan boy tail until he finds donkey.

FEB

12598
TOO MANY CROOKS (87) (U)
Rank (RFD)
P: Mario & Giulio Zampi
D: Mario Zampi
S: Jean Nery, Christiane Rochefort
SC: Michael Pertwee

Terry Thomas	Billy Gordon
George Cole	Fingers
Brenda de Banzie	Lucy Gordon
Bernard Bresslaw	Snowdrop
Sidney James	Sid
Vera Day	Charmaine
Joe Melia	Whisper
Delphi Lawrence	Beryl
John le Mesurier	Magistrate
Sydney Tafler	Solicitor
Nicholas Parsons	Tommy Weston
Terry Scott	PC Smith
John Stuart	Insp Jenson

COMEDY Neglected wife helps inept kidnappers rob tax-evading husband.

12599
THE HORSE'S MOUTH (95) *tech* (U)
Knightsbridge (UA)
P: John Bryan
D: Ronald Neame
S: (NOVEL) Joyce Cary
SC: Alec Guinness

Alec Guinness	Gulley Jimson
Kay Walsh	Coker
Renee Houston	Sarah
Mike Morgan	Nosey
Robert Coote	Sir William Beeder
Arthur Macrae	Alabaster
Veronica Turleigh	Lady Beeder
Michael Gough	Abel
Reginald Beckwith	Capt Jones
Ernest Thesiger	Hickson

COMEDY Penniless painter cheats and swindles to obtain walls for murals. (RFP: 1959).

12600
THE LADY IS A SQUARE (99) (U)
Everest (ABP)
P: Herbert Wilcox, Anna Neagle
D: Herbert Wilcox
S: Harold Purcell
SC: Harold Purcell, Pamela Bower, Nicholas Phipps

Anna Neagle	Frances Baring
Frankie Vaughan	Johnny Burns
Janette Scott	Joanna Baring
Anthony Newley	Freddie
Wilfrid Hyde White	Charles
Ted Lune	Harry Shuttleworth
Christopher Rhodes	Greenslade
Kenneth Cope	Derek
Josephine Fitzgerald	Mrs Eady
Mary Peach	Mrs Freddy
National Youth Orchestra	

MUSICAL Singer posing as Lady's butler secretly finances her concerts.

12601
NUDIST PARADISE (72) *eastman/scope* (A)
Orb International (AA)
Reissue: 1962
P: Nat Miller, Frank Bevis
D: Charles Saunders
S: Leslie Bell
SC: Leslie Bell, Denise Kaye

Anita Love	Joan Stanton
Carl Conway	Mike Malone
Katy Cashfield	Pat Beatty
Dennis Carnell	Jimmy Ross
Celia Hewitt	Interviewer

Emma Young . . . . Receptionist
NUDIST Spielplatz. American art student falls
for girl and joins nudist camp to be near her.

12602
THE UNSEEING EYE (28) (U)
Merton Park (AA)
P: Jack Greenwood
D: Geoffrey Muller
S: James Eastwood
N: Edgar Lustgarten
Russell Napier . . . . Supt Duggan
John Stone
Denny Dayviss . . . .
CRIME Glass eye leads to capture of murderous
arsonist.

12603
DANGER WITHIN (101) (U)
Colin Lesslie (BL)
D: Don Chaffey
S: (NOVEL) Michael Gilbert (DEATH IN
CAPTIVITY)
SC: Bryan Forbes, Frank Harvey
Richard Todd . . . . Lt/Col David Baird
Richard Attenborough . . . .Capt Bunter Phillips
Bernard Lee . . . . Lt/Col Huxley
Michael Wilding . . . . Major CharlesMarquand
Dennis Price . . . . Capt Roger Callender
Donald Houston . . . . Capt Roger Byford
Peter Arne . . . . Capt Benucci
William Franklyn . . . . Capt Tony Long
Vincent Ball . . . . Capt Pat Foster
Ronnie Stevens . . . . Lt Meynell
Peter Jones . . . . Capt Alfred Parker
Terence Alexander . . . . Lt Gibbs
Andrew Faulds . . . . Lt/Cdr Dopey Gibbon
WAR Italy, 1942. POWs try to discover which
officer betrays their escape plans.

12604
PASSPORT TO SHAME (91) (X) USA: ROOM
43
United Co-Productions (BL)
P: John Clein
D: Alvin Rakoff
S: Patrick Alexander
Odile Versois . . . . Malou
Diana Dors . . . . Vicki
Herbert Lom . . . . Nick
Eddie Constantine . . . . Johnny
Brenda de Banzie . . . . Aggie
Robert Brown . . . . Mike
Elwyn Brook-Jones . . . . Heath
Cyril Shaps . . . . Willie
Denis Shaw . . . . Mac
Joan Sims . . . . Miriam
Lana Morris . . . . Girl
Robert Fabian . . . . Himself
CRIME Taxi driver weds French girl for money
but later saves her from brother proprietor.

12605
SUBWAY IN THE SKY (86) (A)
Orbit (Britannia)
P: Sydney Box, John Temple-Smith, Patrick
Filmer-Sankey
D: Muriel Box
S: (PLAY) Ian Main
SC: Jack Andress
Van Johnson . . . . Maj Baxter Grant
Hildegarde Neff . . . . Lilli Hoffman
Albert Lieven . . . . Carl von Schecht
Cec Linder . . . . Capt Carson
Katherine Kath . . . . Anna Grant
Vivian Matalon . . . . Stefan
Carl Jaffe . . . . Adler
Chuck Keyser . . . . Harwell
Edward Judd . . . . Molloy

CRIME Berlin. Singer helps US Army deserter
prove he is not drug trafficker and did not kill
wife.

12606
MAKE MINE A MILLION (82) (U)
Jack Hylton (BL)
P: John Baxter
D: Lance Comfort
S: Jack Francis
SC: Peter Blackmore, Talbot Rothwell,
Arthur Askey
Arthur Askey . . . . Arthur Ashton
Sidney James . . . . Sid Gibson
Dermot Walsh . . . . Martin Russell
Olga Lindo . . . . Mrs Burgess
Clive Morton . . . . Director General
Sally Barnes . . . . Sally
George Margo . . . . Assistant
Lionel Murton . . . . TV Director
Bernard Cribbins . . . . Jack
Kenneth Connor . . . . Husband
Martin Benson . . . . Chairman
David Nettheim . . . . Professor
Bruce Seton . . . . Supt James
Tommy Trinder; Dickie Henderson; Evelyn
Laye; Dennis Lotis; Anthea Askey; Raymond
Glendenning; Patricia Bredin; Leonard Weir;
Sabrina; Television Toppers; Gillian Lynne;
Penge Formation Dancers; Peter Noble
COMEDY Salesman and makeup man use
mobile TV transmitter to advertise detergent.

12607
BROTH OF A BOY (77) (U)
Emmett Dalton (BL)
P: Alec Snowden
D: George Pollock
S: (PLAY) Hugh Leonard (THE BIG
BIRTHDAY)
SC: Patrick Kirwan, Blanaid Irvine
Barry Fitzgerald . . . . Patrick Farrell
Tony Wright . . . . Randall
June Thorburn . . . . Silin Lehane
Harry Brogan . . . . Willie
Eddie Golden . . . . Martin Lehane
Maire Kean . . . . Molly Lehane
Godfrey Quigley . . . . Desmond Phillips
Dermot Kelly . . . . Tim
Josephine Fitzgerald . . . . Mrs O'Shaughnessy
COMEDY Poacher refuses to be televised on his
110th birday.

12608
MODEL FOR MURDER (73) (U)
Parroch (BL)
P: C. Jack Parsons, Robert Dunbar
D: Terry Bishop
S: Peter Fraser
SC: Terry Bishop, Robert Dunbar
Keith Andes . . . . David Martens
Hazel Court . . . . Sally Meadows
Jean Aubrey . . . . Annabel Meadows
Michael Gough . . . . Kingsley Beauchamp
Julia Arnall . . . . Diana Leigh
Patricia Jessel . . . . Mme Dupont
Peter Hammond . . . . George
Howard Marion-Crawford . . . Insp Duncan
CRIME Gem smugglers frame US Navy officer
for stabbing fashion model.

12609
FIRST MAN INTO SPACE (77) (X)
Producers Associates (MGM)
P: Charles Vetter jr, John Croydon
D: Robert Day
S: Wyott Ordung
SC: John C. Cooper, Lance Z. Hargreaves
Marshall Thompson . . . . . . Chuck Prescott

Marla Landi . . . . Tia Francesca
Bill Edwards . . . . Dan Prescott
Robert Ayres . . . . Ben Richards
Bill Nagy . . . . Wilson
Carl Jaffe . . . . Dr von Essen
Roger Delgardo . . . . Mexican Consul
HORROR New Mexico. Meteor dust changes
first space pilot into vampiric monster.

12610
ROBBERY WITH VIOLENCE (67) (A)
GIB Films (RFI)
P:D: George Ivan Barnett
S: Edith M. Barnett
SC: David Cumming
Ivan Craig . . . . Peter Frayne
Sally Day . . . . Brenda Bailey
Michael Golden . . . . Insp Wilson
John Martin Lewis . . . . Derek Bailey
John Trevor Davis . . . . Insp Greenway
CRIME Bank robber posing as hop picket shoots
mistress's husband.

12611
THE CHILD AND THE KILLER (65) (A)
Danziger (UA)
P: Edward J & Harry Lee Danziger
D: Max Varnel
S: Brian Clemens, Eldon Howard
Patricia Driscoll . . . . Peggy Martin
Robert Arden . . . . Capt Joe Marsh
Richard Williams . . . . Tommy Martin
Ryck Rydon . . . . Mather
Gordon Sterne . . . . Sgt
John McLaren . . . . Maj Finch
Robert Raglan . . . . Insp
CRIME US Army deserter forces widow's
7-year old son to help him.

MAR

12612
CARRY ON NURSE (86) (U)
Beaconsfield (AA)
P: Peter Rogers
D: Gerald Thomas
S: (PLAY) Patrick Cargill, Jack Beale (RING
FOR CATTY)
SC: Norman Hudis
Shirley Eaton . . . . Dorothy Denton
Kenneth Connor . . . . Ernie Bishop
Charles Hawtrey . . . . Mr Hinton
Hattie Jacques . . . . Matron
Wilfrid Hyde White . . . . . . Colonel
Terence Longdon . . . . Ted York
Bill Owen . . . . Percy Hickson
Leslie Phillips . . . . Jack Bell
Joan Sims . . . . Stella Dawson
Susan Stephen . . . . Georgie Axwell
Kenneth Williams . . . . Oliver Reckitt
Michael Medwin . . . . Ginger
Susan Beaumont . . . . Frances James
Ann Firbank . . . . Helen Lloyd
Joan Hickson . . . . Sister
Cyril Chamberlain . . . . Bert Able
Harry Locke . . . . Mick
Irene Handl . . . . Marge Hickson
COMEDY Episodic misadventures in men's
surgical ward. (Top Moneymaker: 1959).

12613
VIOLENT MOMENT (61) (A)
Independent Artists (AA)
P: Bernard Coote
D: Sidney Hayers
S: Peter Barnes
Lyndon Brook . . . . Douglas Baines
Jane Hylton . . . . Daisy Harker
Jill Browne . . . . Janet Greenway
John Paul . . . . Sgt Ranson

Rupert Davies . . . .   Bert Glennon
Moira Redmond . . . .   Kate Glennon
Bruce Seton . . . .   Insp Davis
Martin Miller . . . .   Hendricks
CRIME Army deserter strangles mistress when she has their son adopted, and becomes garage owner.

12614
BREAKOUT (62) (U)
Independent Artistis (AA)
P: Julian Wintle, Leslie Parkyn
D: Peter Graham Scott
S: (BOOK) Frederick Oughton
SC: Peter Barnes
Lee Patterson . . . .   George Munro
Hazel Court . . . .   Rita Arkwright
Terence Alexander . . . .   Farrow
Dermot Kelly . . . .   O'Quinn
John Paul . . . .   Arkwright
Billie Whitelaw . . . .   Rose Munro
William Lucas . . . .   Chandler
Estelle Brody . . . .   Maureen O'Quinn
CRIME Architect poses as lorry driver to help embezzler break jail.

12615
LIFE IN EMERGENCY WARD 10 (86) (U)
Artistes Alliance-WNW (Eros)
P: Edward Lloyd
D: Robert Day
S: (TV SERIAL) Tessa Diamond (EMERGENCY WARD 10)
SC: Tessa Diamond, Hazel Adair
Michael Craig . . . .   Dr Stephen Russell
Wilfrid Hyde White . . . .   Prof Bourne-Evans
Dorothy Allison . . . .   Sister Janet Fraser
Glyn Owen . . . .   Dr Paddy O'Meara
Rosemary Miller . . . .   Pat Roberts
Charles Tingwell . . . .   Dr Alan Dawson
Frederick Bartman . . . .   Dr Simon Forrester
Joan Sims . . . .   Mrs Pryor
Rupert Davies . . . .   Dr Tim Hunter
Sheila Sweet . . . .   Anne Hunter
David Lodge . . . .   Mr Phillips
Dorothy Gordon . . . .   Mrs Phillips
Christopher Witty . . . .   David Phillips
Douglas Ives . . . .   Potter
Pauline Stroud . . . . . . : . . .   Nurse Vincent
DRAMA Hospital doctor's heart-lung machine fails with old man but helps boy with hole in heart.

12616
THE 39 STEPS (93) *eastman* (U)
Rank (RFD)
P: Betty E. Box
D: Ralph Thomas
S: (NOVEL) John Buchan
SC: Frank Harvey, Charles Bennett, Ian Hay, Alma Reville
Kenneth More . . . .   Richard Hannay
Taina Elg . . . .   Miss Fisher
Brenda de Banzie . . . .   Nellie Lumsden
Barry Jones . . . .   Prof Logan
Reginald Beckwith . . . .   Lumsden
Sidney James . . . .   Perce
Faith Brook . . . .   Nannie
Jameson Clark . . . .   McDougal
Michael Goodliffe . . . .   Brown
James Hayter . . . .   Mr Memory
Duncan Lamont . . . .   Kennedy
Andrew Cruickshank . . . . .   Sheriff
Leslie Dwyer . . . .   Milkman
CRIME Framed man and sports mistress track down spy ring in Scotland.

12617
TIGER BAY (105) (A)
Independent Artists (RFD)
P: John Hawkesworth

D: J. Lee-Thompson
S: (NOVEL) Noel Calef (RODOLPHE ET LE REVOLVEUR)
SC: John Hawkesworth, Shelley Smith
John Mills . . . .   Supt Graham
Horst Buchholz . . . .   Korchinsky
Hayley Mills . . . .   Gillie
Yvonne Mitchell . . . .   Anya
Megs Jenkins . . . .   Mrs Phillips
Anthony Dawson . . . .   Barclay
Meredith Edwards . . . . . .PC George Williams
Shari . . . .   Christine
Christopher Rhodes . . . . . .   Insp Bridges
Kenneth Griffith . . . .   Choirmaster
George Pastell . . . .   Captain
Paul Stassino . . . .   Officer
George Selway . . . .   Sgt Harvey
Edward Cast . . . .   Det Thomas
E. Eynon Evans . . . .   Mr Morgan
Rachel Thomas . . . .   Mrs Parry
CRIME Cardiff. Polish seaman kills girl and kidnaps child witness (Extract in THE LOVE GODDESSES)

12618
WHIRLPOOL (95) *eastman* (A)
Rank (RFD)
P: George Pitcher
D: Lewis Allen
S: (NOVEL) Lawrence P. Bachmann (THE LORELEI)
SC: Lawrence P. Bachmann
Juliette Greco . . . .   Lora
O.W. Fischer . . . .   Rolph
Muriel Pavlow . . . .   Dina
William Sylvester . . . .   Herman
Marius Goring . . . .   George
Richard Palmer . . . .   Derek
Lily Kann . . . .   Mrs Steen
Peter Illing . . . .   Braun
Geoffrey Bayldon . . . .   Wendel
Harold Kasket . . . .   Steibel
CRIME Rhineland. Barge cpatain shelters accomplice of pursued killer.

12619
THE ANGRY HILLS (105) (A)
Raymond (MGM)
P: Raymond Stross
D: Robert Aldrich
S: (NOVEL) Leon Uris
SC: A.I. Bezzerides
Robert Mitchum . . . .   Mike Morrison
Stanley Baker . . . .   Konrad Heisler
Elizabeth Muller . . . .   Lisa
Gia Scala . . . .   Eleftheria
Theodore Bikel . . . .   Tassos
Kieron Moore . . . .   Andreas
Sebastian Cabot . . . .   Chessey
Donald Wolfitt . . . .   Stergiou
Marius Goring . . . .   Col Oberg
Leslie Phillips . . . .   Ray Taylor
Jackie Lane . . . .   Maria
WAR Greece, 1940. Girl helps wounded American correspondent escape with list of resistance agents.

12620
THE DOCTOR'S DILEMMA (99) *metro* (U)
Comet (MGM)
P: Anatole de Grunwald
D: Anthony Asquith
S: (PLAY) George Bernard Shaw
SC: Anatole de Grunwald
Leslie Caron . . . .   Jennifer Dubedat
Dirk Bogarde . . . .   Louis Dubedat
Alastair Sim . . . .   Cutler Walpole
Robert Morley . . . . .Sir Ralph Bonnington
John Robinson . . . .   Sir Colenso Ridgeon
Felix Aylmer . . . . Sir Patrick Cullen

Michael Gwynn . . . .   Dr Blenkinsop
Maureen Delany . . . .   Emmy
Alec McCowen . . . .   Redpenny
Colin Gordon . . . .   Newspaper Man
Terence Alexander . . . .   Mr Lanchester
COMEDY Should doctor cure TB of immoral artist or dull doctor?

12621
CARLTON-BROWNE OF THE F.O. (88) (U)
USA: MAN IN A COCKED HAT
Charter (BL)
P: John Boulting
D: Roy Boulting, Jeffrey Dell
S: Roy Boulting, Jeffrey Dell
Terry Thomas . . . . .Cadogan deVere Carlton-Browne
Peter Sellers . . . .   Amphibulous
Luciana Paoluzzi . . . .   Princess Ilyena
Ian Bannen . . . .   King Loris
Thorley Walters . . . .   Col Bellingham
Miles Malleson . . . .   Davidson
Raymond Huntley . . . .   Tufton-Slade
John le Mesurier . . . . . . .Grand Duke Alex
Marie Lohr . . . . .Lady Carlton-Browne
Kynaston Reeves . . . . .Sir Arthur Carlton-Browne
Ronald Adam . . . .   Sir John Farthing
John Van Eyssen . . . .   Hewitt
Nicholas Parsons . . . .   Rodgers
Irene Handl . . . .   Mrs Carter
Kenneth Griffith . . . .   Griffiths
Marne Maitland . . . .   Archipolagos
COMEDY Inept Foreign Office man tries to stop ex-colony's civil war over cobalt rights.

12622
NO TREES IN THE STREET (96) (X)
Allegro (ABP)
P: Frank Godwin
D: J. Lee Thompson
S: (PLAY) Ted Willis
SC: Ted Willis
Sylvia Syms . . . .   Hetty
Herbert Lom . . . .   Wilkie
Ronald Howard . . . .   Frank
Stanley Holloway . . . .   Kipper
Joan Miller . . . .   Jess
Liam Redmond . . . .   Bill
Carole Lesley . . . .   Lova
Lana Morris . . . .   Marje
Melvyn Hayes . . . .   Tommy
Lilly Kann . . . .   Mrs Jacobson
Marianne Stone . . . .   Mrs Jokel
Edwin Richfield . . . .   Jackie
Campbell Singer . . . .   Inspector
David Hemmings . . . .   Kenny
CRIME 1938. Slum mother lets crooked bookie seduce her daughter and turn her son into killer.

12623
THE HOUND OF THE BASKERVILLES (87) (A) *tech*
Hammer (UA)
P: Anthony Hinds
D: Terence Fisher
S: (NOVEL) Arthur Conan Doyle
SC: Peter Bryan
Peter Cushing . . . .   Sherlock Holmes
Andre Morell . . . .   Dr Watson
Christopher Lee . . . . .Sir Henry Baskerville
Marla Landi . . . .   Cecile Stapleton
David Oxley . . . . .Sir Hugo Baskerville
Miles Malleson . . . .   Bishop Frankland
Francis de Wolff . . . .   Dr Mortimer
Ewen Solon . . . .   Stapleton
John le Mesurier . . . .   Barrymore
Sam Kydd . . . . : .   Perkins
Helen Goss . . . .   Mrs Barrymore
CRIME Dartmoor 1897. Tec unmasks farmer as heir trying to kill titled relative with phosphorescent dog.

12624
IDOL ON PARADE (92) *scope* (U)
Warwick (Col)
P: Harold Huth
D: John Gilling
S: (NOVEL) William Camp
SC: John Antrobus

William Bendix	Sgt Lush
Anne Aubrey	Caroline
Anthony Newley	Jeep Jackson
Lionel Jeffries	BB
David Lodge	Shorty
William Kendall	CO
Sidney James	Herbie
Dilys Laye	Renee
Bernie Winters	Joe Jackson
Harry Fowler	Ron

MUSICAL Conscripted singer's agent smuggles him out of camp to give concerts.

APR

12625
MEN OF TOMORROW (40) (U)
Border (NR)
P: O. Negus-Fancey
D: Alfred Travers
S: Alfred Travers, Vernon Greeves

Vernon Greeves	Bill Hanley
Janet Smith	Helen
David Hemmings	Ted

DRAMA Reporter helps orphan teenagers lose aggressiveness.

12626
SERIOUS CHARGE (99) (X)
Alva (Eros)
P: Mickey Delamar
D: Terence Young
S: (PLAY) Philip King
SC: Mickey Delamar, Guy Elmes

Anthony Quayle	Howard Phillips
Sarah Churchill	Hester Peters
Andrew Ray	Larry Thompson
Cliff Richard	Curly Thompson
Liliane Brousse	Michele
Irene Browne	Mrs Phillips
Percy Herbert	Mr Thompson
Noel Howlett	Mr Peters
Wensley Pithey	Sgt
Leigh Madison	Mary Williams
Wilfred Pickles	Magistrate
Jean Cadell	Matron
Olive Sloane	Mrs Browning

DRAMA Soured woman supports teenager's false charge that new vicar is homosexual.

12627
INNOCENT MEETING (62) (A)
Danziger (UA)
P: Edward J & Harry Lee Danziger
D: Godfrey Grayson
S: Brian Clemens, Eldon Howard

Sean Lynch	Johnny Brent
Beth Rogan	Connie
Raymond Huntley	Harold
Ian Fleming	Garside
Howard Lang	Macey
Arnold Bell	Fry
Colin Tapley	Stannard
Robert Raglan	Martin
Denis Shaw	Uncle

CRIME Teenager turns gunman when girl's rich father accuses him of theft.

12628
HORRORS OF THE BLACK MUSEUM (80) (X)
eastman/scope
Merton Park (AA) *reissue:* 1962
P: Herman Cohen, Jack Greenwood
D: Arthur Crabtree
S: Herman Cohen, Aben Kandel

Michael Gough	Edmond Bancroft
June Cunningham	Joan Berkeley
Graham Curnow	Rick
Shirley Ann Field	Angela
Geoffrey Keen	Supt Graham
Beatrice Varley	Aggie
John Warwick	Insp Lodge
Austin Trevor	Comm Wayne

HORROR Crippled crime writer turns his teenage assistant into murderous monster.

12629
THE BANDIT OF ZHOBE (81) *tech/scope* (U)
Warwick (Col)
P: Harold Huth
D:SC: John Gilling
S: Richard Maibaum

Victor Mature	Kasim
Anthony Newley	Cpl Stokes
Anne Aubrey	Zena Crowley
Norman Wooland	Maj Corlwey
Dermot Walsh	Capt Saunders
Walter Gotell	Ahzad
Sean Kelley	Lt Wylie
Paul Stassino	Hatti
Denis Shaw	Hussu
Maya Koumani	Tamara

ADVENTURE India, period. Chieftain kidnaps Major's daughter when rebels posing as British soldiers kill wife.

12630
SAPPHIRE (92) *eastman* (A)
Artna (RFD)
P: Michael Relph
D: Basil Dearden
S: Janet Green
SC: Janet Green, Lukas Heller

Nigel Patrick	Supt Hazard
Yvonne Mitchell	Mildred
Michael Craig	Insp Learoyd
Paul Massie	David Harris
Bernard Miles	Ted Harris
Olga Lindo	Mrs Harris
Earl Cameron	Dr Robbins
Gordon Heath	Paul Slade
Jocelyn Britton	Patsy
Harry Baird	Johnny Fiddle
Orlando Martins	Barman
Rupert Davies	Ferris
Robert Adams	Horace Big Cigar
Yvonne Buckingham	Sapphire

CRIME Supt investigates stabbing of pregnant halfcaste art student who passed for white. (BFA: Best British Film, 1959).

12631
BEYOND THIS PLACE (90) (A) USA: WEB OF EVIDENCE
Georgefield (Renown)
P: Maxwell Setton, John R. Sloan
D: Jack Cardiff
S: (NOVEL) A.J. Cronin
SC: Kenneth Taylor

Van Johnson	Paul Mathry
Vera Miles	Lena Anderson
Emlyn Williams	Enoch Oswald
Bernard Lee	Patrick Mathry
Jean Kent	Louise Birt
Leo McKern	McEvoy
Rosalie Crutchley	Ella Mathry
Vincent Winter	Paul (child)
Moultrie Kelsall	Insp Dale
Ralph Truman	Sir Matthew Sprott
Geoffrey Keen	Governor
Jameson Clark	Swann
Joyce Heron	Lady Catherine Sprott
Henry Oscar	Sharpe

CRIME Liverpool. Ex-evacuee proves convicted father did not kill girl during 1940 blitz.

MAY

12632
WEB OF SUSPICION (70) (A)
Danziger (Par)
P: Edward J & Harry Lee Danziger
D: Max Varnel
S: Brian Clemens, Eldon Howard

Philip Friend	Bradley Wells
Susan Beaumont	Janet Shenley
John Martin	Eric Turner
Peter Sinclair	Tom Wright
Robert Raglan	Insp Clark
Peter Elliot	Watson
Ian Fleming	Forbes
Rolf Harris	Ben
Hal Osmond	Charlie

CRIME Art mistress helps accused games master prove music teacher killed girl.

12633
TOP FLOOR GIRL (71) (U)
Danziger (Par)
P: Edward J & Harry Lee Danziger
D: Max Varnel
S: Brian Clemens, Eldon Howard

Kay Callard	Connie
Neil Hallett	Dave
Robert Raikes	Bob
Maurice Kaufmann	Peter Farnite
Brian Nissen	Stevens jr
Diana Chesney	Miss Prentice
Elizabeth Fraser	Mabel
Arnold Bell	Stevens sr.

ROMANCE Ambitious clerk gives up car magnate's son for advertising agent.

12634
NO SAFETY AHEAD (68) (U)
Danziger (Par)
P: Edward J & Harry Lee Danziger
D: Max Varnel
S: Robert Hurst

James Kenney	Clem
Susan Beaumont	Jean
Denis Shaw	Inspector
Gordon Needham	Richardson
Tony Doonan	Don
John Charlesworth	Jeff
Brian Weske	Bill
Robert Raglan	Langton

CRIME Poor clerk joins fiancee's brother's gang, robs bank, goes on run, and surrenders.

12635
LOOK BACK IN ANGER (101) (X)
Woodfall (ABP)
P: Harry Saltzman, Gordon L.T. Scott
D: Tony Richardson
S: (PLAY) John Osborne
SC: Nigel Kneale, John Osborne

Richard Burton	Jimmy Porter
Claire Bloom	Helena Charles
Mary Ure	Alison Porter
Edith Evans	Mrs Tanner
Gary Raymond	Cliff Lewis
Glen Byam Shaw	Col Redfern
George Devine	Doctor
Donald Pleasence	Hurst
Phyllis Neilson-Terry	Mrs Redfern

Chris Barber and his Jazz Band
DRAMA Frustrated working-class intellectual drives away pregnant middle-class wife and has affair with her friend.

JUNE

12636
SHAKE HANDS WITH THE DEVIL (111) (A)
Troy Pennebaker (UA)
P: George Glass, Walter Seltzer
D: Michael Anderosn
S: (NOVEL) Reardon Conner
SC: Ivan Goff, Ben Roberts, Marian Thompson

James Cagney	Sean Lenihan
Don Murray	Kerry O'Shea
Dana Wynter	Jennifer Curtis
Glynis Johns	Kitty O'Brady
Cyril Cusack	Chris Noonan
Michael Redgrave	The General
Sybil Thorndike	Lady Fitzhugh
Marianne Benet	Mary Madigan
John Breslin	McGrath
Harry Borgan	Cassidy
Lewis Casson	Judge
John Cairney	Mike O'Callaghan
Harry H. Corbett	Clancy
Richard Harris	Terence O'Brien
William Hartnell	Sgt Jenkins
Niall MacGinnis	Michael O'Leary
Ray McAnally	Paddy Nolan
Noel Purcell	Liam O'Sullivan
Peter Reynolds	Captain
Alan White	Capt Flemming

CRIME Dublin, 1921. American student revolts against IRA doctor after helping him kidnap English official.

12637
THE HEADLESS GHOST (61) (U) *scope*
Merton Park (AA)
P: Herman Cohen, Jack Greenwood
D: Peter Graham Scott
S: Herman Cohen, Kenneth Langtry

Richard Lyon	Bill
Liliane Sottane	Ingrid
David Rose	Ronnie
Clive Revill	The Fourth Earl
Jack Allen	Earl of Ambrose
Alexander Archdale	Randolph
Carl Bernard	Sgt Grayson

FANTASY American students help ghost recover lost head.

12638
DEADLY RECORD (58) (A)
Independent Artists (AA)
P: Vivian A. Cox
D: Lawrence Huntington
S: (NOVEL) Nina Warner Hooke
SC: Vivian A. Cox, Lawrence Hungtington

Lee Patterson	Trevor Hamilton
Barbara Shelley	Susan Webb
Jane Hylton	Ann Garfield
Peter Dyneley	Dr Morrow
Geoffrey Keen	Supt Ambrose
John Paul	Phil Gamage
Everly Gregg	Mrs Mac
Edward Cast	PC Ryder
George Pastell	Angelo
Ferdy Mayne	Ramon Casadas
April Olrich	Carmela

CRIME Accused pilot proves jealous receptionist killed wife.

12639
IN THE WAKE OF A STRANGER (64) (U)
Crest (Butcher)
P: Jacques de Lane Lea, Jon Penington
D: David Eady
S: (NOVEL) Ian Stuart Black
SC: John Tully

Tony Wright	Tom Cassidy
Shirley Eaton	Joyce Edwards
Danny Green	Barnes

Willoughby Goddard	Shafto
Harry H. Corbett	McCabe
Peter Sinclair	Captain
Tom Bowman	Spike
Alun Owen	Ferris

CRIME Liverpool. Schoolmistress helps sailor prove he did not kill man while drunk.

12640
THE CROWNING TOUCH (75) (U)
Crescent (Butcher)
P: Charles Leeds, Jon Penington
D: David Eady
S: Cecily Finn, Joan O'Connor
SC: Margot Bennett

Ted Ray	Bert
Greta Gynt	Rosie
Griffith Jones	Mark
Sydney Tafler	Joe
Dermot Walsh	Aubrey Drake
Maureen Connell	Julia
Colin Gordon	Stacey
Irene Handl	Bebe
Allan Cuthbertson	Philip
Diane Hart	Tess

COMEDY Three people conjecture as to why girl's hat was sold but not collected.

12641
CRASH DRIVE (65) (A)
Danziger (UA)
P: Edward J & Harry Lee Danziger
D: Max Varne l
S: Brian Clemens, Eldon Howard

Dermot Walsh	Paul Dixon
Wendy Williams	Ann Dixon
Ian Fleming	Dr Marshall
Anton Rodgers	Tomson
Grace Arnols	Mrs Dixon
Ann Sears	Nurse Phillips
George Roderick	Manotti
Rolf Harris	Bart
Geoffrey Hibbert	Henry

DRAMA Wife returns to paralysed racing driver and cures his self-pity.

12642
HIGH JUMP (66) (A)
Danziger (UA)
P: Edward J & Harry Lee Danziger
D: Godfrey Grayson
S: Brian Clemens, Eldon Howard

Richard Wyler	Bill Ryan
Lisa Daniely	Jackie Field
Leigh Madison	Kitty
Michael Peake	Ray Shaw
Arnold Bell	Tom Rowton
Nora Gordon	Mrs Barlow
Tony Doonan	Frank
Robert Raglan	Inspector

CRIME Widow feigns love for ex-trapeze artist to get him to help gem thieves.

12643
YESTERDAY'S ENEMY (95) (A)
Hammer (Col)
P: Michael Carreras
D: Val Guest
S: (TV PLAY) Peter Newman
SC: Peter Newman

Stanley Baker	Capt Langford
Guy Rolfe	Padre
Leo McKern	Max
Gordon Jackson	Sgt Mackenzie
David Oxley	Doctor
Richard Pasco	Lt Hastings
Philip Ahn	Yamazaki
Bryan Forbes	Dawson
Percy Herbert	Wilson
Edwina Carroll	Suni

WAR Burma, 1942. Captain shoots hostages for information and later the situation is reversed.

12644
THE MAN WHO COULD CHEAT DEATH (83) *tech* (X)
Hammer-Cadogan (Par)
P: Anthony Hinds
D: Terence Fisher
S: (PLAY) Barre Lyndon (THE MAN IN HALFMOON STREET)
SC: Jimmy Sangster

Anton Diffring	Dr Georges Bonner
Hazel Court	Janine Dubois
Christopher Lee	Dr Pierre Gerard
Arnold Marle	Dr Ludwig Weisz
Delphi Lawrence	Margo Philippe
Francis de Wolff	Insp Legris
Gerda Larsen	Street Girl

HORROR Paris, 1890. 104-year old doctor keeps youthful with gland operations which disfigure female victims.

12645
THE HEART OF A MAN (92) (U)
Everest (RFD)
P: Anna Neagle
D: Herbert Wilcox
S: Rex North
SC: Jack Trevor Story, Pamela Bower

Frankie Vaughan	Frankie Martin
Anne Heywood	Julie
Tony Britton	Tony Carlisle
Anthony Newley	Johnnie Ten Percent
Michael Medwin	Sid the Sausage
George Rose	Charlie Boy
Peter Sinclair	Bud
Harold Kasket	Oscar
Harry Fowler	Razor

Leslie Mitchell; Kent Walton; Hogan "Kid" Bassey

MUSICAL Ex-seaman tries to earn £100 by becoming bouncer on gambler's yacht, boxer, commissionaire, etc.

12646
JACK THE RIPPER (84) (X)
Mid Century (RFI)
P: Robert Baker, Monty Berman
D: Robert S. Baker
S: Peter Hammond, Colin Craig
SC: Jimmy Sangster

Lee Patterson	Sam Lowry
Eddie Byrne	Insp O'Neill
Betty McDowall	Anne Ford
Ewen Solon	Sir David Rodgers
John le Mesurier	Dr Tranter
Philip Leaver	Manager
George Rose	Clarke
Barbara Burke	Kitty Knowles
Denis Shaw	Simes
Endre Muller	Louis Benz

Montparnasse Ballet
CRIME 1888. American tec loves niece of surgeon he suspects of stabbing girls with scalpel.

12647
THE BRIDAL PATH (95) *tech* (U)
Vale (BL)
P: Frank Launder . Sidney Gilliat
D: Frank Launder
S: (NOVEL) Nigel Tranter
SC: Frank Launder, Geoffrey Willans

Bill Travers	Ewan McEwan
George Cole	Sgt Bruce
Bernardette O'Farrell	Fiona
Patricia Bredin	Margaret
Fiona Clyne	Katie

Alex Mackenzie . . . . Finlay
Gordon Jackson . . . . Constable Alec
Dilys Laye . . . . Isobel
Vincent Winter . . . . Neal
Eddie Byrne . . . . Mike Flanagan
Duncan Macrae . . . . Sgt
Charlotte Mitchell . . . . Sgt's Wife
COMEDY Hebridean islander seeking wife
is mistaken for salmon poacher.

12648
LEFT, RIGHT AND CENTRE (95) (U)
Vale (BL)
P: Frank Launder, Sidney Gilliat
D: Sidney Gilliat
S: Sidney Gilliat, Val Valentine
Ian Carmichael . . . . Robert Wilcott
Alastair Sim . . . . Lord Wilcott
Patricia Bredin . . . . Stella Stoker
Richard Wattis . . . . Harding-Pratt
Eric Barker . . . . Bert Glimmer
Moyra Fraser . . . . Annabel Brentwood
Jack Hendley . . . . Bill Hemmingway
Gordon Harker . . . . Hardy
William Kendall . . . . Pottle
Anthony Sharpe . . . . Peterson
George Benson . . . . Egerton
Leslie Dwyer . . . . Alf Stoker
Irene Handl . . . . Mrs Maggs
Jeremy Hawke; Eamonn Andrews; Gilbert
Harding; Carole Carr; Josephine Douglas
COMEDY TV star stands as Tory candidate
and falls for opponent.

12649
MORE DEADLY THAN THE MALE (60)
eastman (X)
U.N.A. (Cross Channel)
D: Robert Bucknell
S: (NOVEL) Paul Chevalier
Jeremy White . . . . Saul Coe
Ann Davy . . . . Estelle le Fol
Edna Dore . . . . Ruth
Lorraine Peters . . . . Rita
John Mahoney . . . . Godfrey le Fol
CRIME American tourist kills fruitgrower for
wife who then kills tourist's fiancee.

12650
THE GREAT EXPEDITION (29) (U)
Falcon Films (AA)
P:D:S: Donovan Winter
Loretta Parry . . . . The Girl
John Parsons . . . . The Boy
CHILDREN Boy and girl get lost while
Christmas shopping.

12651
MUSIC WITH MAX JAFFA (19) (U)
Zonic (Hillcrest)
P: Adrian Worker
D: Francis Searle
Max Jaffa Trio; Bobby Watson
George Mitchell Singers
MUSICAL Violin, songs and sword dance.

12652
TARZAN'S GREATEST ADVENTURE (84)
tech (U)
Solar (Par)
P: Sy Weintraub, Harvey Hayutin
D: John Guillermin
S: (CHARACTERS) Edgar Rice Burroughs
SC: Les Crutchfield, Berne Giler, John
Guillermin
Gordon Scott . . . . Tarzan
Anthony Quayle . . . . Slade
Sara Shane . . . . Angie
Sean Connery . . . . O'Bannion

Niall MacGinnis . . . . Kruger
Scilla Gabel . . . . Toni
Al Mulock . . . . Dino
ADVENTURE Kenya. Jungle man and
plane-crashed girl pursue crooks searching for
diamond mine.

12653
FERRY TO HONG KONG (113) eastman/scope
(U)
Rank (RFD)
P: George Maynard
D: Lewis Gilbert
S: (NOVEL) Max Catto
SC: Lewis Gilbert, Vernon Harris,
John Mortimer
Curt Jurgens . . . . Mark Conrad
Orson Welles . . . . Capt Cecil Hart
Sylvia Syms . . . . Liz Ferrers
Jeremy Spenser . . . . Miguel Henriques
Noel Purcell . . . . Joe Skinner
Margaret Withers . . . . Miss Carter
John Wallace . . . . Inspector
Milton Reid . . . . Yen
Roy Chiao . . . . Johnny Singup
Shelley Shen . . . . Foo Soo
ADVENTURE China. Exiled Austrian forced
to stay aboard ferry and save it from pirates
and storm.

12654
OPERATION BULLSHINE (84) tech (U)
ABPC
P: Frank Godwin
D: Gilbert Gunn
S: Anne Burnaby
SC: Anne Burnaby, Rupert Lang, Gilbert Gunn
Donald Sinden . . . . Lt Gordon Brown
Barbara Murray . . . . Pte Betty Brown
Carole Lesley . . . . Pte Marge White
Ronald Shiner . . . . Gnr Slocum
Naunton Wayne . . . . Maj Pym
Dora Bryan . . . . Pte Cox
Judy Grinham . . . . PT Instructress
John Cairney . . . . Gnr Willie Ross
Daniel Massey . . . . Bdr Palmer
Peter Jones . . . . Gnr Perkins
Fabia Drake . . . . Cdr Maddox
Joan Rice . . . . Pte Finch
COMEDY 1942. ATS private suspects
fidelity of secret husband, an anti-aircraft
lieutenant.

12655
THE BOY AND THE BRIDGE (91) (U)
Xanadu (Col)
P: Kevin McClory, David Eady
D: Kevin McClory
S: (STORY) Leon Ware
SC: Kevin McClory, Desmond O'Donovan,
Geoffrey Orme
Ian MacLaine . . . . Tommy Doyle
Liam Redmond . . . . Pat Doyle
James Hayter . . . . Skipper
Geoffrey Keen . . . . Bridge Master
Royal Dano . . . . Evangelist
Norman MacOwan . . . . Engineer
Jack MacGowran . . . . Porter
Bill Shine . . . . Mechanic
Jocelyn Britton . . . . Girl
Andreas Malandrinos . . . . . . Organist
Chili Bouchier . . . . Publican's Wife
DRAMA Bermondsey boy hides in Tower
Bridge thinking his father is a murderer.

12656
LIFE IN DANGER (63) (A)
Parroch (Butcher)
P: C. Jack Parsons
D: Terry Bishop

S: Malcolm Hulke, Eric Paice
Derren Nesbitt . . . . The Man
Julie Hopkins . . . . Hazel Ashley
Howard Marion Crawford . . Maj Peters
Victor Brooks . . . . Tom Baldwin
Jack Allen . . . . Jack Ashley
Christopher Witty . . . . Johnny Ashley
Mary Manson . . . . Jill Shadwell
Bruce Seton . . . . Landlord
DRAMA Major leads villagers against workman
whom they mistake for escaped child-killer.

12657
WRONG NUMBER (59) (U)
Merton Park (AA)
P: Jack Greenwood
D: Vernon Sewell
S: (PLAY) Norman Edwards
SC: James Eastwood
Peter Reynolds . . . . Angelo
Lisa Gastoni . . . . Maria
Peter Elliot . . . . Dr Pole
Olive Sloane . . . . Miss Crystal
Paul Whitsun-Jones . . . . . . Cyril
Barry Keegan . . . . Max
John Horsley . . . . Supt Blake
Harold Goodwin . . . . Bates
CRIME Old lady's telephone mistake helps
police track mail van robbers.

12658
THE MOUSE THAT ROARED (90) tech (U)
Open Road (Col)
P: Walter Shenson, Jon Penington
D: Jack Arnold
S: (NOVEL) Leonard Wibberley
(THE WRATH OF THE GRAPES)
SC: Stanley Mann, Roger Macdougall
Peter Sellers . . . . . Tully Bascombe/Gloriana/
                               Count Mountjoy
Jean Seberg . . . . Helen Kokintz
William Hartnell . . . . Will
David Kossoff . . . . Kokintz
Leo McKern . . . . Benter
Macdonald Parke . . . . Snippet
Austin Willis . . . . Secretary of Defence
Timothy Bateson . . . . Roger
Monty Landis . . . . Cobbley
Robin Gatehouse . . . . Mulligan
Colin Gordon . . . . Announcer
George Margo . . . . O'Hara
COMEDY Bankrupt Duchy invades America—
and wins.

12659
THE UGLY DUCKLING (84) (U)
Hammer (Col)
P: Tommy Lyndon-Hayes
D: Lance Comfort
S: (NOVEL) Robert Louis Stevenson
(DR JEKYLL AND MR HYDE)
SC: Sid Colin, Jack Davies
Bernard Bresslaw . . Henry Jekyll/Teddy Hyde
Reginald Beckwith . . . . Reginald
Jon Pertwee . . . . Victor Jekyll
Maudie Edwards . . . . Henrietta Jekyll
Jean Muir . . . . Snout
Richard Wattis . . . . Barclay
Elwyn Brook-Jones . . . . . . Dandy
Michael Ripper . . . . Benny
David Lodge . . . . Peewee
COMEDY Chemist's assistant becomes jewel
thief under influence of great-grandfather's
formula.

12660
A WOMAN'S TEMPTATION (60) (U)
Danziger (BL)
P: Edward J. & Harry Lee Danziger
D: Godfrey Grayson
S: Brian Clemens, Eldon Howard

Patricia Driscoll . . . . Betty
Robert Ayres . . . . Mike
John Pike . . . . Jimmy
Neil Hallett . . . . Glyn
John Longden . . . . Insp Syms
Kenneth Warren . . . . Warner
Robert Raglan . . . . PC
CRIME Seaman saves widow from crooks who
hid stolen money in her dustbin.

12661
BOBBIKINS (90) *scope* (U)
20th Century Fox
P:S: Oscar Brodney
D: Robert Day
Shirley Jones . . . . Betty Barnaby
Max Bygraves . . . . Benjamin Barnaby
Billie Whitelaw . . . . Lydia Simmons
Barbara Shelley . . . . Valerie
Colin Gordon . . . . Dr Phillips
Charles Tingwell . . . . Luke Packer
Lionel Jeffries . . . . Gregory Mason
Charles Carson . . . . . Sir Jason Crandall
Rupert Davies . . . . Jock Fleming
Steven Stocker . . . . Bobbikins Barnaby
Charles Lloyd Pack . . . . . . Stebbins
FANTASY Talking baby makes father rich
with tips from Chancellor of Exchequer.

AUG
12662
THE SCAPEGOAT (92) (A)
Du Maurier-Guinness (MGM)
P: Michael Balcon
D: Robert Hamer
S: (NOVEL) Daphne du Maurier
SC: Gore Vidal, Robert Hamer
Alec Guinness . . . John Barratt/Count Jacques
Bette Davis . . . . Countess de Gue
Nicole Maurey . . . . Bela
Irene Worth . . . . Francoise de Gue
Pamela Browne . . . . Blanche
Annabel Bartlett . . . . . . Marie-Noel de Gue
Geoffrey Keen . . . . Gaston
Leslie French . . . . Lacoste
Noel Howlett . . . . Dr Aloin
Peter Bull . . . . Aristide
CRIME France. Count persuades teacher
double to take place and then kills rich wife.

12663
MURDER AT SITE THREE (67) (U)
Francis Searle (Ex) *reissue:* 1961 (RFI)
P: Charles Leeds
D: Francis Searle
S: (NOVEL) W. Howard Baker
(CRIME IS MY BUSINESS)
SC: Manning O'Brine
Geoffrey Toone . . . . Sexton Blake
Barbara Shelley . . . . Susan
Jill Melford . . . . Paula Dane
John Warwick . . . . Cdr Chambers
Richard Burrell . . . . Tinker
Reed de Rouen . . . . McGill
Harry Towb . . . . Kenney
CRIME Tec uses truth drug to expose missile
security chief as spy.

12664
THE MUMMY (88) *tech* (X)
Hammer (UI)
P: Michael Carreras
D: Terence Fisher
S: (SCREENPLAYS) Nina Wilcox Putnam
(THE MUMMY) Griffin Jay
(THE MUMMY'S TOMB)
SC: Jimmy Sangster
Peter Cushing . . . . John Banning
Christopher Lee . . . . Kharis

Yvonne Furneaux . . . . Isobel/Ananka
Eddie Byrne . . . . Mulrooney
Felix Aylmer . . . . Stephen Banning
Raymond Huntley . . . . Joseph Whemple
George Pastell . . . . Mehemet
John Stuart . . . . Coroner
Harold Goodwin . . . . Pat
Dennis Shaw . . . . Mike
HORROR 1896. Egyptian priest brings
revived mummy to England to kill
archaeologists.

12665
CARRY ON TEACHER (86) (U)
Beaconsfield (AA)
P: Peter Rogers
D: Gerald Thomas
S: Norman Hudis
Ted Ray . . . . William Wakefield
Kenneth Connor . . . . Gregory Adams
Charles Hawtrey . . . . Michael Bean
Leslie Phillips . . . . Alastair Crigg
Joan Sims . . . . Sarah Allcock
Kenneth Williams . . . . Edwin Milton
Hattie Jacques . . . . Grace Short
Rosalind Knight . . . . Felicity Wheeler
Cyril Chamberlain . . . . Alf
Richard O'Sullivan . . . . . . Robin Stevens
Carol White . . . . Sheila Dale
COMEDY Pupils play tricks on inspectors so
that their headmaster's transfer will be
rejected.

12666
THE WHITE TRAP (58) (U)
Independent Artists (AA)
P: Julian Wintle, Leslie Parkyn
D: Sidney Hayers
S: Peter Barnes
Lee Patterson . . . . Paul Langley
Conrad Phillips . . . . Sgt Morrison
Michael Goodliffe . . . . Insp Walters
Jack Allen . . . . Dr Hayden
Yvette Wyatt . . . . Ann Fisher
Gillian Vaughan . . . . Wendy
Felicity Young . . . . Joan Langley
Trevor Maskell . . . . Dr Lucas
CRIME Wartime friend helps escaped convict
reach his wife as she dies in childbirth.

12667
I'M ALL RIGHT JACK (105) (U)
Charter (BL)
P: Roy Boulting
D: John Boulting
S: (NOVEL) Alan Hackney
(PRIVATE LIFE)
SC: John Boulting, Frank Harvey, Alan Hackney
N: E.V.H. Emmett
Ian Carmichael . . . . Stanley Windrush
Terry-Thomas . . . . Maj Hitchcock
Peter Sellers . . . . Fred Kite
Richard Attenborough . Sidney de Vere Cox
Margaret Rutherford . . . . . Aunt Dolly
Dennis Price . . . . Bertram Tracepurcel
Irene Handl . . . . Mrs Kite
Miles Malleson . . . . Mr Windrush
Victor Maddern . . . . Knowles
Liz Fraser . . . . Cynthia Kite
John le Mesurier . . . . Waters
Marnes Maitland . . . . Mr Mohammed
Kenneth Griffith . . . . Dai
Raymond Huntley . . . . Magistrate
Cardew Robinson . . . . Shop Steward
Terry Scott . . . . Crawley
Malcolm Muggeridge; Frank Phillips; Muriel
Young
COMEDY Missile manufacturer uses his keen
nephew to cause a strike to increase a contract.
(BFA 1959: Best Actor, Screenplay.)

12668
UPSTAIRS AND DOWNSTAIRS (101)
eastman (A)
Rank (RFD)
P: Betty E. Box
D: Ralph Thomas
S: (NOVEL) Ronald Scott Thorne
SC: Frank Harvey
Michael Craig . . . . Richard Barry
Anne Heywood . . . . Kate Barry
Mylene Demongeot . . . . Ingrid Gunnar
James Robertson Justice . . . Mansfield
Sidney James . . . . PC Edwards
Daniel Massey . . . . Wesley Cotes
Claudia Cardinale . . . . Maria
Joan Hickson . . . . Rosemary
Joan Sims . . . . Blodwen
Joseph Tomelty . . . . Arthue Farringdon
Nora Nicholson . . . . Edith Farringdon
COMEDY Newlywed businessman has maid
trouble: one throws parties, others rob bank, etc.

12669
BLIND DATE (95) (A)
Independent Artists (RFD)
P: David Deutsch
D: Joseph Losey
S: (NOVEL) Leigh Howard
SC: Ben Barzman, Millard Lampell
Hardy Kruger . . . . Jan Van Rooyen
Stanley Baker . . . . Insp Morgan
Micheline Presle . . . . Jacqueline Cousteau
Robert Flemyng . . . . Sir Brian Lewis
Gordon Jackson . . . . Sgt
John Van Eyssen . . . . Westover
Jack MacGowran . . . . Postman
George Roubicek . . . . PC
CRIME Inspector proves diplomat's wife
framed Dutch Artist for his mistress's death.

12670
THIS OTHER EDEN (80) (U)
Emmett Dalton (RFI)
P: Alec Snowden
D: Muriel Box
S: (PLAY) Louis d'Alton
SC: Patrick Kirwan, Blanaid Irvine
Audrey Dalton . . . . Maire McRoarty
Leslie Phillips . . . . Crispin Brown
Niall MacGinnis . . . . Devereaux
Geoffrey Golden . . . . McRoarty
Norman Rodway . . . . Conor Heaphy
Milo O'Shea . . . . Pat Tweedy
Harry Brogan . . . . Clannery
Eddie Golden . . . . Sgt Grilly
COMEDY Ireland. British colonel's bastard
blamed when church student destroys statue
on learning his father led IRA.

12671
THE SIEGE OF PINCHGUT (100) (U)
Ealing (ABP)
P: Eric Williams
D: Harry Watt
S: Inman Hunter, Lee Robinson
SC: Harry Watt, Jon Cleary, Alexander Baron
Aldo Ray . . . . Matt Kirk
Heather Sears . . . . Ann Fulton
Neil McCallum . . . . Johnny Kirk
Victor Maddern . . . . Bert
Carlo Justini . . . . Luke
Alan Tilvern . . . . Supt Hanna
Barbara Mullen . . . . Mrs Fulton
Gerry Duggan . . . . Pat Fulton
Kenneth J. Warren . . . . . . Commissioner
Grant Taylor . . . . Macey
CRIME Australia. Escaped convict siezes
armoured island off Sydney harbour to force
retrial.

12672
JET STORM (99) (A)
Pendennis (Britannia)
P: Steven Pallos
D: C. Raker Endfield
S: Sigmund Miller
SC: Sigmund Miller, C. Raker Endfield
Richard Attenborough .... Ernest Tilley
Stanley Baker............ Capt Bardow
Diane Cilento .... Angelica Como
Virginia Maskell .... Pam Leyton
Marty Wilde .... Billy Forrester
Mai Zetterling .... Carol Tilley
Hermione Baddeley .... Mrs Satterley
Bernard Braden .... Otis Randolf
Barbara Kelly .... Edwina Randolf
David Kossoff .... Dr Bergstein
Harry Secombe .... Binky Meadows
Elizabeth Sellars .... Inez Barrington
Sybil Thorndike .... Emma Morgan
Patrick Allen .... Mulliner
Paul Carpenter .... George Towers
Megs Jenkins .... Rose Brock
Jackie Lane .... Clara Forrester
Cec Linder .... Col Coe
Neil McCallum .... Gil Gilbert
Lana Morris .... Jane Turner
DRAMA Mad scientist plants bomb aboard transatlantic jet to kill man who ran over his child.

SEP

12673
THE DEVIL'S DISCIPLE (83) (U)
Hecht—Hill—Lancaster—Brynaprod (UA)
P: Harold Hecht
D: Guy Hamilton
S: (PLAY) George Bernard Shaw
SC: John Dighton, Roland Kibbee
Burt Lancaster .... Pastor Anderson
Kirk Douglas .... Dick Dudgeon
Laurence Olivier .... Gen Burgoyne
Janette Scott .... Judith
Eva le Gallienne .... Mrs Dudgeon
Harry Andrews .... Maj Swindon
Basil Sydney .... Lawyer Hawkins
George Rose .... Sgt
Neil McCallum .... Chris Dudgeon
David Horne .... William
Mervyn Johns .... Maindeck Parshotter
Erik Chitty .... Titus
WAR New Hampshire, 1777. Pastor saves scapegrace from gallows where he has taken place of parson.

12674
THE ADVENTURES OF REX (serial) (U)
P:D: Leonard Reeve
S: Leonard Reeve, Tom Twigge
John Pike .... Ted
Shirley Joy .... Vicky
Ralph Lynn .... Fisherman
Kenneth Earl .... Teddy Boy
Christopher Witty .... Cripple Boy

12675
1: FEATHERS FLYING (14)

12676
2: TEDDY TROUBLE (13)

12677
3: THE SILVER STREAK (14)

12678
4: THE PAINTED TRAIL (15)

12679
5: GOOD SHOW REX (12)
CHILDREN Episodic adventures of two children and their Alsatian dog.

12680
THE DAWN KILLER (serial) (U)
ABPC (CFF)
P: Terry Ashwood
D: Donald Taylor
S: Monica Edwards
SC: Vivian Milroy
Jeremy Bulloch .... Colin Hawkes
Sally Bulloch .... Anne Hawkes
Suzan Farmer .... Cathy Hawkes
David Markham .... Mr Hawkes
Michael Saunders .... Joe Hoddy
Brian Weske .... Fred Hoddy
Richard Warner .... Mr Hoddy
Sheila Burrell .... Mrs Hoddy
Harry Fowler .... Bert Irons

12681
1: THE KILLER STRIKES (16)

12682
2: UNDER SUSPICION (13)

12683
3: THE STOLEN SHEEP (14)

12684
4: THE KILLER STRIKES AGAIN (14)

12685
5: A HARD CHOICE (15)

12686
6: TRACKING THE THIEF (13)

12687
7: RACE AGAINST TIME (12)

12688
8: THE CHAMPION DOG (10)
CHILDREN Romney Marsh. Dogs of two families are suspected of killing sheep.

12689
MYSTERY IN THE MINE (serial) (U)
Merton Park (CFF)
P: Frank Hoare
D: James Hill
S: Peter Ling
SC: Dallas Bower, James Hill
Ingrid Cardon .... Jane Trelawney
Stewart Guidotti .... Tom Lee
Howard Greene .... Mr Collins
Peter Copley .... Mr Abbott
David Rose .... Ray Pentreath
Elwyn Brook-Jones .... Grimblatt

12690
1: SECRET AGENT (15)

12691
2: DANGER IN THE DARK (18)

12692
3: TRAPPED UNDERGROUND (15)

12693
4: POISON GAS (14)

12694
5: SUDDEN PERIL (17)

12695
6: HOT ON THE TRAIL (16)

12696
7: OUT OF CONTROL (16)

12697
8: DESPERATE FINISH (17)
CHILDREN Cornwall. Cousins foil crook seeking rare mineral to fuel space-mirror.

12698
THE NIGHT WE DROPPED A CLANGER (86) (U)
Four Star (RFD)
P: David Henley
D: Darcy Conyers
S: John Chapman
Brian Rix .. WC Blenkinsop/Arthur Atwood
Cecil Parker ...... Sir Bertram Bukpasser
William Hartnell .... Sgt Bright
Leslie Phillips .... SL Thomas
Leo Franklyn .... Belling
Hattie Jacques .... ADA
Liz Fraser .... Lulu
John Welsh .... SL Grant
Toby Perkins .... FL Spendal
Vera Pearce .... Mme Grilby
Sarah Branch .... WAAF Hawkins
COMEDY Latrine orderly sent on mission to France in mistake for his double, a wing commander.

OCT

12699
KILLERS OF KILIMANJARO (91)
eastman/scope (U)
Warwick (Col)
P: John R. Sloan
D: Richard Thorpe
S: (BOOK) John A. Hunter, Dan P. Mannix (AFRICAN BUSH ADVENTURES)
SC: Richard Maibaum, Cyril Hume, John Gilling, Earl Fenton
Robert Taylor .... Robert Adamson
Anthony Newley ....Hooky Hook
Anne Aubrey .... Jane Carlton
Gregoire Aslan .... Ben Ahmed
Alan Cuthbertson .... Sexton
Martin Benson .... Ali
Orlando Martins .... Chief
Donald Pleasence .... Captain
John Dimech .... Pasha
Martin Boddey .... Gunther
Earl Cameron .... Witchdoctor
ADVENTURE Africa, period. Engineer surveys first railway despite rivals and slave traders.

12700
THE ROUGH AND THE SMOOTH (99) (X)
USA: PORTRAIT OF A SINNER
George Minter (Renown)
P:D: Robert Siodmak
S: (NOVEL) Robin Maugham
SC: Audrey Erskine Lindop, Dudley Leslie
Nadja Tiller .... Ila Hanssen
Tony Britton .... Mike Thompson
William Bendix .... Reg Barker
Natasha Parry .... Margaret Goreham
Norman Wooland .... David Fraser
Donald Wolfit .... Lord Drewell
Tony Wright .... Jack
Adrienne Corri .... Jane Buller
Joyce Carey .... Mrs Thompson
John Welsh .... Mr Thompson
Martin Miller ....Piggy
Edward Chapman .... Willy Catch
Beatrice Varley .... Manageress
ROMANCE Archaeologist leaves press heiress for German nyphomaniac.

12701
NORTH WEST FRONTIER (129)
eastman/scope (U)
USA: FLAME OVER INDIA
Rank (RFD) reissue: 1961 (31 mins cut)
P: Marcel Hellman
D: J. Lee-Thompson
S: Robin Estridge
Kenneth More .... Capt Scott
Lauren Bacall .... Catherine Wyatt

Herbert Lom . . . . Van Leyden
Wilfrid Hyde White . . . . Bridie
I.S. Johar . . . . Gupta
Ursula Jeans . . . . Lady Wyndham
Ian Hunter . . . . Sir John Wyndham
Eugene Deckers . . . . Peters
Jack Gwillim . . . . Brig Ames
Govind Raja Ross . . . . Prince Kishnan
ADVENTURE India, 1905. Captain takes
over train to help Hindu boy prince and
American governess escape Moslem rebels.

12702
S.O.S. PACIFIC (91) (A)
Remfield (RFD)
P: John Nasht, Patrick Filmer-Sankey
D: Guy Green
S: Robert Westerby
Richard Attenborough . . . . . Whitey
Pier Angeli . . . . Teresa
John Gregson . . . . Jack Bennett
Eva Bartok . . . . Maria
Eddie Constantine . . . . Mark Reisener
Jean Anderson . . . . Miss Shaw
Cec Linder . . . . Willy
Clifford Evans . . . . Peterson
Gunnar Moller . . . . Dr Strauss
ADVENTURE American smuggler saves
passengers of crashed plane from H—bomb test
island.

12703
THE NAVY LARK (90) scope (U)
Everest (20)
P: Herbert Wilcox
D: Gordon Parry
S: (RADIO SERIES) Laurie Wyman
SC: Laurie Wyman, Sid Colin
Cecil Parker . . . . Cdr Stanton
Ronald Shiner . . . . CPO Banyard
Leslie Phillips . . . . Lt Pouter
Elvi Hale . . . . WREN Heather
Nicholas Phipps . . . . Capt Povey
Harold Kasket . . . . Gaston Higgins
Cardew Robinson . . . . Lt Binns
Hattie Jacques . . . . Fortune Teller
Gordon Jackson . . . . LS Johnson
Reginald Beckwith . . . . CNI
Kenneth J. Warren . . . . Brown
COMEDY Sailors thwart new captain's attempts
to close their island base.

12704
LIBEL (100) (A)
Anatole de Grunwald (MGM)
D: Anthony Asquith
S: (PLAY) Edward Wooll
SC: Karl Tunberg, Anatole de Grunwald
Dirk Bogarde . Sir Mark Loddon/Frank Welney/
No. 13
Olivia de Havilland . . . . Lady Loddon
Paul Massie . . . . Jeffrey Buckenham
Robert Morley . . . . Sir Wilfred
Wilfrid Hyde White . . . . Foxley
Anthony Dawson . . . . Gerrald Loddon
Richard Wattis . . . . Judge
Martin Miller . . . . Dr Schrott
Millicent Martin . . . . Maisie
Richard Dimbleby . . . . Himself
CRIME Amnesiac bart's court battle to prove
he is not his POW double.

12705
MAN ACCUSED (58) (U)
Danziger (UA)
P: Edward J. & Harry Lee Danziger
D: Montgomery Tully
S: Mark Grantham
Ronald Howard . . . . Bob Jenson
Carol Marsh . . . . Kathy Riddle

Ian Fleming . . . . Sir Thomas
Catherina Ferraz . . . . Anna
Brian Nissen . . . . Derek
Robert Dorning . . . . Beckett
Stuart Saunders . . . . Curran
Colin Tapley . . . . Inspector
CRIME Rich widow's butler helps fiance break
jail and prove he did not kill girls for jewels.

12706
BEHEMOTH THE SEA MONSTER (70) (X)
USA: THE GIANT BEHEMOTH
Artistes Alliance-WNW-Stratford (Eros)
P: David Diamond, Edward Lloyd
D: Eugene Lourie, Douglas Hickox
S: Robert Abel, Allen Adler
SC: Eugene Lourie
Gene Evans . . . . Steve Karnes
Andre Morell . . . . .Prof James Bickford
Leigh Madison . . . . Jeanie Trevethan
John Turner . . . . Ian Duncan
Jack MacGowran . . . . Dr Sampson
Maurice Kaufmann . . . . . . Officer
Henry Vidon . . . . Tom MacDougal
Leonard Sachs . . . . Scientist
Neal Arden . . . . Announcer
HORROR American scientist uses radium-tipped
torpedo to kill radioactive paleosaurus.

NOV

12707
STRICTLY CONFIDENTIAL (62) (U)
Twickenham (RFD)
P: Guido Coen
D: Charles Saunders
S: Brock Williams
Richard Murdoch . . . . Cdr Bissham-Ryley
William Kendall . . . . . Maj Rory MacQuarry
Maya Koumani . . . . Maxine Millard
William Hartnell . . . . Grimshaw
Bruce Seton . . . . Insp Shearing
Neil Hallett . . . . Basil Wantage
Ellis Irving . . . . Capt Sharples
Colin Rix . . . . Warder
Beresford Egan . . . . O'Connor
COMEDY Widow hires ex-convicts as
factory directors to cover share-juggling.

12708
THE WITNESS (58) (U)
Merton Park (AA)
P: Jack Greenwood
D: Geoffrey Muller
S: John Salt
SC: Julian Bond
Dermot Walsh . . . . Richard Brinton
Greta Gynt . . . . May
Russell Napier . . . . Insp Rosewarne
Martin Stephens . . . . Peter Brindon
John Chandos . . . . Lodden
Derek Sydney . . . . Manny
Hedger Wallace . . . . Manbre
CRIME Boy betrays ex-convict father to
police.

12709
SWEET BEAT (55) (U)
Flamingo (Archway)
P: Jeffrey S. Kruger, H.B.Conn
D: Ronnie Albert
S: Ron Ahran
Julie Amber . . . . Ronnie Martin
Sheldon Lawrence . . . . Bill Lacey
Irv Bauer . . . . Dave Lefferts
Leonie Page . . . . Tina Miller
David Browning . . . . Gerry Turner
MUSICAL Singer wins beauty contest and
is tricked into visiting New York.

12710
TREASURE OF SAN TERESA (81) (A)
Beaconsfield (Britannia)
P: John Nasht, Patrick Filmer-Sankey
D: Alvin Rakoff
S: Jeffrey Dell
SC: Jack Andrews
Eddie Constantine . . . . Larry Brennan
Dawn Addams . . . . Hedi von Hartmann
Marius Goring . . . . Rudi Seibert
Nadine Tallier . . . . Zizi
Christopher Lee . . . . Jaeger
Walter Gotell . . . . Inspector
Gaylord Cavallaro . . . . Mike Jones
Georgina Cookson . . . . Billie
Willy Witte . . . . Gen von Hartmann
Clive Dunn . . . . Cemetery Keeper
Sheldon Lawrence . . . . Patrolman
Leslie "Hutch" Hutchinson. . Himself
CRIME Hamburg. Ex-OSS man and German
callgirl regain gems from Czech convent
despite crooked lawyer.

12711
FRIENDS AND NEIGHBOURS (79) (U)
Valiant (BL)
P: Bertram Ostrer
D: Gordon Parry
S: (PLAY) Austin Steele
SC: Val Valentine, Talbot Rothwell
Arthur Askey . . . . Albert Grimshaw
Megs Jenkins . . . . Lily Grimshaw
Tilda Thamar . . . . Olga
Peter Illing . . . . Nikita
Reginald Beckwith . . . . . . Wilf Holmes
Danny Ross . . . . Sebastian Green
June Whitfield . . . . Doris Holmes
Catherine Feller . . . . Susan Grimshaw
Jess Conrad. . . . . Buddy Fisher
Linda Castle . . . . Gloria Stockwell
Max Robertson . . . . Himself
COMEDY Bus conductor's lottery prize
is to entertain two Russian social workers in
his home.

12712
THIRD MAN ON THE MOUNTAIN (103)
tech (U)
Walt Disney
P: William H. Anderson
D: Ken Annakin
S: (NOVEL) James Ramsay Ullman
(BANNER IN THE SKY)
SC: Eleanor Griffin
Michael Rennie . . . . Capt John Winter
James MacArthur . . . . Rudi Matt
Janet Munro . . . . Lizbeth Hempel
James Donald . . . . Franz Lerner
Herbert Lom . . . . Emil Saxo
Laurence Naismith . . . . Teo Zurbriggen
Lee Patterson . . . . Klaus Wesselhoft
Walter Fitzgerald . . . . Herr Hempel
Nora Swinburne . . . . Frau Matt
Ferdy Mayne . . . . Andreas
ADVENTURE Switzerland, 1865.
Boy guide saves rival by climbing peak
on which his father died.

12713
THE HOUSE OF THE SEVEN HAWKS (92)
(U)
Coronado (MGM)
P: David E.Rose
D: Richard Thorpe
S: (NOVEL) Victor Canning
(THE HOUSE OF THE SEVEN FLIES)
SC: Jo Eisinger
Robert Taylor . . . . John Nordley
Nicole Maurey . . . . Constanta
Linda Christian . . . . Elsa

Donald Wolfit . . . . Van Der Stoor
David Kossoff . . . . Wilhelm Dekker
Eric Pohlmann . . . . Capt Rohner
Philo Hauser . . . . Charlie Ponz
Gerard Heinz . . . . Insp Sluiter
CRIME Holland. American charterboat
skipper seeks million in gems hidden
in river by Nazi looters.

12714
DON'T PANIC CHAPS ! (85) (U)
ACT Films-Hammer (Col)
P: Ralph Bond, Teddy Baird
D: George Pollock
S: (RADIO PLAY) Michael Corston,
Ronald Holroyd
SC: Jack Davies
Dennis Price . . . . Capt Edward von Krisling
George Cole . . . . Pte Eric Finch
Thorley Walters . . . . . . Lt Percy Brown
Nadja Regin . . . . Elsa
Harry Fowler . . . . Pte Fred Ackroyd
Percy Herbert . . . . Sgt Bolter
George Murcell . . . . Meister
Nicholas Phipps . . . . Maj Mortimer
Terence Alexander . . . . . Lt Babbington
COMEDY British observation unit
becomes friendly with German unit
on Adriatic island.

12715
THE STRANGLERS OF BOMBAY (80)
scope (A)
Hammer (Col)
P: Anthony Hinds
D: Terence Fisher
S: David Z. Goodman
Guy Rolfe . . . . Capt Lewis
Allan Cutherbertson . . . Capt Connaught-Smith
Andrew Cruickshank . . . . Col Henderson
George Pastell . . . . High Priest
Marne Maitland . . . . Patel Shan
Jan Holden . . . . Mary
Paul Stassino . . . . Silver
Tutti Lemkow . . . . Ram Das
David Spenser . . . . Gopali
Marie Devereaux . . . . Karim
CRIME India, 1820. British captain unmasks
officials behind Kali-worshipping sect
of murderers.

12716
NAKED FURY (60) (A)
Coenda (Butcher)
P: Guido Coen
D: Charles Saunders
S: Guido Coen
SC: Brock Williams
Reed de Rouen . . . . Eddy
Kenneth Cope . . . . Johnny
Leigh Madison . . . . Carol
Arthur Lovegrove . . . . Syd
Thomas Eytle . . . . Steve
Alexander Field Vic
Ann Lynn . . . . Judy
Marianne Brauns . . . . . . Joy
Katy Cashfield . . . . Commere
CRIME Safe robbers kill watchman and hold
daughter captive in crumbling warehouse.

12717
TOMMY THE TOREADOR (86) *tech* (U)
Fanfare (WPD) *reissue:* 1963 (10 mins cut)
P: George H. Brown
D: John Paddy Carstairs
S: George H. Brown, Patrick Kirwan
SC: Nicholas Phipps, Sid Colin, Talbot Rothwell
Tommy Steele . . . . Tommy Tomkins
Janet Munro . . . . Amanda

Sidney James . . . . Cadena
Virgillio Texeira . . . . Parilla
Pepe Nieto . . . . Insp Quintero
Noel Purcell . . . . Captain
Kenneth Williams . . . . Vice Consul
Eric Sykes . . . . Martin
Bernard Cribbins . . . . Paco
Harold Kasket . . . . Jose
Francis de Wolff . . . . Proprietor
Ferdy Mayne . . . . Lopez
MUSICAL Spain. Poor seaman takes the
place of bullfighter framed for smuggling.

DEC
12718
A TOUCH OF LARCENY (91) (U)
Foxwell (Par)
P: Ivan Foxwell
D: Guy Hamilton
S: (NOVEL) Andrew Garve
(THE MEGSTONE PLOT)
SC: Paul Winterton, Roger Macdougall,
Ivan Foxwell, Guy Hamilton
James Mason . . . . Cdr Max Easton
Vera Miles . . . . Virginia Killain
George Sanders . . . . Sir Charles Holland
Harry Andrews . . . . Capt Graham
Robert Flemyng . . . . Cdr Larkin
Ernest Clark . . . . Cdr Bates
Duncan Lamont . . . . Special
Barbara Hicks . . . . Miss Price
Peter Barkworth . . . . Lt Brown
Mavis Villiers . . . . Adele Parrish
Macdonald Parke . . . . Jason Parrish
John le Mesurier . . . . Admiral
Rachel Gurney . . . . Clare Holland
Charles Carson . . . . Robert Holland
Martin Stephens . . . . John Holland
William Kendall . . . . Husband
COMEDY Naval commander pretends to sell
secrets to Russia to sue press and win widow.

12719
DESERT MICE (83) (U)
Artna (RFD)
P: Michael Relph, Sydney Box
D: Basil Dearden
S: David Climie
Alfred Marks . . . . Maj Poskett
Sidney James . . . . Bert Bennett
Dick Bentley . . . . Gavin O'Toole
Patricia Bredin . . . . Susan
Marius Goring . . . . German Major
Dora Bryan . . . . Gay
Reginald Beckwith . . . . Fred
Irene Handl . . . . Miss Patch
Kenneth Fortescue . . . . . . Lt Peter Ribstone
Joan Benham . . . . Una
Liz Fraser . . . . Edie
COMEDY Africa, 1941. ENSA troupe catch
German major posing as Briton.

12720
FOLLOW A STAR (104) (U)
Rank (RFD)
P: Hugh Stewart
D: Robert Asher
S: Jack Davies, Henry E. Blyth, Norman Wisdom
Norman Wisdom . . . . . . Norman Truscott
June Laverick . . . . Judy
Jerry Desmonde . . . . Vernon Carew
Hattie Jacques . . . . Dymphna Dobson
Eddie Leslie . . . . Harold Franklin
John le Mesurier . . . . Birkett
Richard Wattis . . . . Dr Chatterway
Sydney Tafler . . . . Pendlebury
Fenella Fielding . . . . Lady Finchinton
Charles Heslop . . . . General

Joe Melia . . . . Stage Manager
Ron Moody . . . . Violinist
MUSICAL Ageing singer mimes to his
pupil who can only sing to cripple girl.

12721
DEVIL'S BAIT (58) (U)
Independent Artists (RFD)
P: Arthur Alcott
D: Peter Graham Scott
S: Peter Johnston, Diana Watson
Geoffrey Keen . . . . Joe Frisby
Jane Hylton . . . . Ellen Frisby
Gordon Jackson . . . . Sgt Malcolm
Dermot Kelly . . . . Mr Love
Shirley Lawrence . . . . Shirley
Eileen Moore . . . . Barbara
Molly Urquhart . . . . Mrs Tanner
Rupert Davies . . . . Landlord
DRAMA Baker helps police seek loaf
baked in poisoned tin.

12722
EXPRESSO BONGO (111) *scope* (A)
Val Guest (Britannia) *reissue:* 1962
P: Jon Penington, Val Guest
D: Val Guest
S: (PLAY) Wolf Mankowitz, Julian More
SC: Wolf Mankowitz
Laurence Harvey . . . . Johnny Jackson
Sylvia Syms . . . . Maisie King
Yolande Donlan . . . . Dixie Collins
Cliff Richard . . . . Bongo Herbert
Meier Tzelniker . . . . Mayer
Ambrosine Philpotts . . . . . Lady Rosemary
Eric Pohlmann . . . . Leon
Gilbert Harding . . . . Himself
Hermione Baddeley . . . . . . Penelope
Reginald Beckwith . . . . . Rev Tobias Craven
Wilfrid Lawson . . . . Mr Rudge
Martin Miller . . . . Kakky
Kenneth Griffith . . . . Charlie
Wolf Mankowitz . . . . Sandwich-man
MUSICAL Soho. American singer breaks
unscrupulous agent's contract with teenage
pop singer. (Extract in THE LOVE
GODDESSES).

12723
PLEASE TURN OVER (87) (A)
Beaconsfield (AA)
P: Peter Rogers
D: Gerald Thomas
S: (PLAY) Basil Thomas
(BOOK OF THE MONTH)
SC: Norman Hudis
Ted Ray . . . . Edward Halliday
Jean Kent . . . . Janet Halliday
Leslie Phillips . . . . Dr Henry Manners
Joan Sims . . . . Beryl
Julia Lockwood . . . . Jo Halliday
Tim Seely . . . . Robert Hughes
Charles Hawtrey . . . . Jeweller
Dilys Laye . . . . Millicent Jones
Lionel Jeffries . . . . Ian Howard
June Jago . . . . Gladys Worth
Colin Gordon . . . . Maurice
Victor Maddern . . . . Smithy
Ronald Adam . . . . Appleton
COMEDY Teenage girl writes sexy
best-seller featuring her family.

12724
THE DESPERATE MAN (57) (U)
Merton Park (AA)
P: Jack Greenwood
D: Peter Maxwell
S: (NOVEL) Paul Somers
(BEGINNER'S LUCK)
SC: James Eastwood

Jill Ireland . . . . Carol Bourne
Conrad Phillips . . . . Curtis
William Hartnell . . . . Smith
Charles Gray . . . . Lawson
Peter Swanwick . . . . Hoad
Arthur Gomez . . . . Landlord
John Warwick . . . . Insp Cobley
Patricia Burke . . . . Miss Prew
Ernest Butcher . . . . Grocer
CRIME Sussex. Gem thief holds girl
hostage in old castle to force reporter
to help him.

12725
THE GHOST TRAIN MURDER (32) (A)
Merton Park (AA)
P: Jack Greenwood
D: Peter Maxwell
S: James Eastwood
N: Edgar Lustgarten
Russell Napier . . . . Supt Duggan
Jill Ireland . . . . Nora
Mary Laura Wood . . . . Mrs Williams
Gordon Needham . . . . Sgt Wallace
CRIME Insp unmasks shoplifters behind
stabbing of Hungarian girl.

12726
WITNESS IN THE DARK (62) (U)
Ethiro (RFD)
P: Norman Williams
D: Wolf Rilla

S: Leigh Vance, John Lemont
Patricia Dainton . . . . Jane Pringle
Conrad Phillips . . . . Insp Coates
Madge Ryan . . . . Mrs Finch
Nigel Green . . . . Intruder
Enid Lorimer . . . . Mrs Temple
Richard O'Sullivan . . . . Don Theobold
Stuart Saunders . . . . Mr Finch
Ian Colin . . . . Supt Thompson
CRIME Blind girl helps police trap old
lady's killer.

12727
HOME IS THE HERO (83) (U)
Emmett Dalton (BL)
P: Robert Baker, Monty Berman
D: J. Fielder Cook
S: (PLAY) Walter Macken
SC: Henry Keating
Arthur Kennedy . . . . . . Willie O'Reilly
Walter Macken . . . . Paddo O'Reilly
Eileen Crowe . . . . Daylia O'Reilly
Joan O'Hara . . . . Josie
Maire O'Donnell . . . . Maura Green
Harry Brogan . . . . Dovetail
Maire Kean . . . . Bid
Eddie Golden . . . . Shannon
DRAMA Ireland. Crippled cobbler subdues
ex-convict father.

12728
THE BATTLE OF THE SEXES (84) (U)
Prometheus (Bryanston)

P: SC: Monja Danischewsky
D: Charles Crichton
S: (STORY) James Thurber
(THE CATBIRD SEAT)
N: Sam Wanamaker
Peter Sellers . . . . Mr Martin
Robert Morley . . . . Robert Macpherson
Constance Cummings . . . . . Angela Barrows
Jameson Clark . . . . Andrew Darling
Ernest Thesiger . . . . Macpherson
Donald Pleasence . . . . Irwin Hoffman
Moultrie Kelsall . . . . Graham
Alex Mackenzie . . . . Robertson
Roddy McMillan . . . . Macleod
Michael Goodliffe . . .. Detective
Norman MacOwan . . . . Jock Munro
William Mervyn . . . . Detective's Friend
COMEDY Edinburgh. Tweed maker's
accountant tries to kill American woman
efficiency expert.

12729
STARS OF A SUMMER NIGHT (24) (U)
eastman
Triangle (Unifilms)
P: Theodora Olembert
D: Gerard Bryant
John Van Eyssen . . . .
Liliane Robin . . . .
Olaf Pooley . . . .
DRAMA Venice. Young actress is brought
to the notice of director during Film Festival.

1960

JAN

12730
OUR MAN IN HAVANA (111) *scope* (A)
Kingsmead (Col)
P: Carol Reed, Raymond Anzarut
D: Carol Reed
S: (NOVEL) Graham Greene
SC: Graham Greene
Alec Guinness . . . .   Jim Wormald
Burl Ives . . . .   Carl Hasselbacher
Maureen O'Hara . . . .   Beatrice Evans
Ernie Kovacs . . . .   Capt Segura
Noel Coward . . . .   Hawthorne
Ralph Richardson   C
Jo Morrow . . . .   Milly Wormald
Gregoire Aslan . . . .   Cifuentes
Paul Rogers . . . .   Hubert Carter
Jose Prieto . . . .   Lopez
Duncan Macrae . . . .   MacDougal
Maurice Denham . . . .   Admiral
Raymond Huntley . . . . . .   General
COMEDY Cuba. Salesman becomes
spy and invents plans to impress his superiors.

12731
TOO YOUNG TO LOVE (88) (X)
Beaconsfield (RFD)
P: Herbert Smith, Sydney Box
D: Muriel Box
S: (PLAY) Elsa Shelley (PICKUP GIRL)
SC: Muriel & Sydney Box
Thomas Mitchell . . . .   Judge Bentley
Pauline Hahn . . . .   Elizabeth Collins
Joan Miller . . . .   Mrs Collins
Austin Willis . . . .   Mr Collins
Cec Linder . . . .   Mr Brill
Jess Conrad . . . .   Peter Martin
Alan Gifford . . . .   Mr Elliot
Bessie Love . . . .   Mrs Busch
Vivian Matalon . . . .   Larry Webster
Sheila Gallagher . . . .   Ruby Lockwood
Cal McCord . . . .   Owens
DRAMA Brooklyn. 15-year old girl reforms
after seduction, abortion and syphilis.

12732
THE SHAKEDOWN (92) (X)
Ethiro (RFD)
P: Norman Williams
D: John Lemont
S: John Lemont, Leigh Vance
Terence Morgan . . . .   Augie Cortona
Hazel Court . . . .   Mildred Hyde
Donald Pleasence . . . .   Jessel
Robert Beatty . . . .   Insp Jarvis
Bill Owen . . . .   Spettigue
Sheila Buxton . . . .   Nadia
Harry H. Corbett . . . .   Gollar
Gene Anderson . . . .   Zena
Eddie Byrne . . . .   George
Georgina Cookson . . . . . .   Miss Firbank
Dorinda Stevens . . . .   Grace
John Salew . . . .   Mr Arnold
CRIME Policewoman poses as model to
thwart Soho blackmailer's nude photography
and prostitution racket.

12733
THE ROYAL BALLET (132) *eastman* (U)
Poetic (RFD)
P:D: Paul Czinner
SWAN LAKE
S: (BALLET) Peter Tchaikovsky
Margot Fonteyn . . . .   Princess Odette
Michael Somes . . . .   Prince Siegfried
Bryan Ashbridge . . . .   Benno

THE FIREBIRD
S: (BALLET) Igor Stravinsky
Margot Fonteyn . . . .   Firebird
Michael Somes . . . .   Prince Ivan

Rosemary Lindsay . . . .   Tsarevna
ONDINE
S: (BALLET) Hans Henze
Margot Fonteyn . . . .   Ondine
Michael Somes . . . .   Palemon
Julia Farron . . . .   Berta
MUSICAL Three ballets.

12734
SENTENCED FOR LIFE (64) (U)
Danziger (UA)
P: Edward J & Harry Lee Danziger
D: Max Varnel
S: Eldon Howard, Mark Grantham
Francis Matthews . . . .   Jim Richards
Jill Williams . . . .   Sue Thompson
Basil Dignam . . . .   Ralph Thompson
Jack Gwillim . . . .   John Richards
Lorraine Clewes . . . .   Mrs Richards
Mark Singleton . . . .   Edward Thompson
Nyree Dawn Porter . . . .   Betty
Arnold Bell . . . .   Williams
CRIME Lawyer proves convicted father
was framed by partner for selling
blueprints to enemy.

12735
TWO-WAY STRETCH (87) (U)
Shepperton-Vale-John Harvel (BL)
P: E.M.Smedley Aston
D: Robert Day
S: John Warren, Len Heath
SC: John Warren, Len Heath, Alan Hackney
Peter Sellers . . . .   Dodger Lane
Wilfrid Hyde White . .   Basil 'Soapy' Fowler
Maurice Denham . . . . . .   Cdr Horatio Bennett
Irene Handl . . . .   Mrs Price
David Lodge . . . .   Jelly Knight
Lionel Jeffries . . . .   Sidney Crout
Liz Fraser . . . .   Ethel
Bernard Cribbins . . . .   Lennie Price
Thorley Walters . . . .   Col Arkwright
Beryl Reid . . . .   Miss Pringle
Walter Hudd . . . .   Rev Butterworth
George Woodbridge . . . . . .   Jenkins
Cyril Chamberlain . . . .   George
John Wood . . . .   Captain
COMEDY Three convicts escape, steal
jewels and return to jail.

12736
NIGHT TRAIN FOR INVERNESS (69) (U)
Danziger (Par)
P: Edward J & Harry Lee Danziger
D: Ernest Morris
S: Mark Grantham
Norman Wooland . . . .   Roy Lewis
Jane Hylton . . . .   Marion
Denis Waterman . . . .   Ted Lewis
Silvia Francis . . . .   Ann Lewis
Irene Arnold . . . .   Mrs Wall
Valentine Dyall . . . .   Ken
Howard Lang . . . .   Sgt
Colin Tapley . . . .   Jackson
DRAMA Ex-embezzler abducts son
without knowing he is diabetic.

12737
SINK THE BISMARCK! (98) *scope* (U)
20th Century Fox
P: John Brabourne
D: Lewis Gilbert
S: (BOOK) C.S.Forester
SC: Edmund H. North
Kenneth More . . . . . .   Capt Jonathan Shephard
Dana Wynter . . . .   Anne Davis
Carl Mohner . . . .   Capt Lindemann
Laurence Naismith . . . . .   First Sea Lord
Karel Stepanek . . . .   Admiral Lutjens
Maurice Denham . . . .   Cdr Richards

Michael Goodliffe . . . . . .   Capt Bannister
Michael Hordern . . . .   C in C
Geoffrey Keen . . . .   ACNS
Esmond Knight . . . .   Captain
Jack Watling . . . .   Signals
Sydney Tafler . . . .   Workman
John Stuart . . . .   Captain
Ed Morrow . . . .   Himself
WAR 1941. Director of Naval Operations
humanised by his secretary during pursuit
of German battleship.

FEB

12738
THE ANGRY SILENCE (95) (A)
Beaver (BL)
P: Richard Attenborough, Bryan Forbes
D: Guy Green
S: Michael Craig, Richard Gregson
SC: Bryan Forbes
Richard Attenborough . . . .   Tom Curtis
Pier Angeli . . . .   Anna Curtis
Michael Craig. . . . .   Joe Wallace
Bernard Lee . . . .   Bert Connolly
Geoffrey Keen . . . .   Davis
Laurence Naismith . . . .   Martindale
Russell Napier . . . .   Sid Thompson
Penelope Horner . . . .   Pat
Alfred Burke . . . .   Phil Travers
Brian Bedford . . . .   Eddie Barrett
Brian Murray . . . .   Gladys
Norman Bird . . . .   Roberts
Beckett Bould . . . .   Billy Armstrong
Oliver Reed . . . .   Mick
Daniel Farson; Alan Whicker
DRAMA Factory worker and family are
"sent to Coventry" by wildcat strikers.
(BFA: Best Screenplay, 1960).

12739
DATE AT MIDNIGHT (57) (A)
Danziger (Par)
P: Edward J & Harry Lee Danziger
D: Godfrey Grayson
S: Mark Grantham
Paul Carpenter . . . .   Bob Dillon
Jean Aubrey . . . .   Paula Burroughs
Harriette Johns . . . .   Lady Leyton
Ralph Michael . . . .   Sir Edward Leyton
John Charlesworth . . . .   Tommy
Philip Ray . . . .   Jenkins
Howard Lang . . . .   Inspector
Robert Ayres . . . .   Gordon Baines
CRIME American reporter proves lawyer's
nephew did not kill girl.

12740
COVER GIRL KILLER (61) (A)
Butcher-Parroch (Eros)
P: C. Jack Parsons
D:S: Terry Bishop
Harry H. Corbett . . . .   The Man
Felicity Young . . . .   June Rawson
Spencer Teakle . . . .   John Mason
Victor Brooks . . . .   Insp Brunner
Tony Doonan . . . .   Sgt
Bernadette Milne . . . .   Gloria
Christina Gregg . . . .   Joy
Charles Lloyd Pack . . . . . .   Capt Adams
CRIME Pinup magazine publisher and
model help police trap maniac.

12741
CONSCIENCE BAY (60) (A)
Rickra (Cross Channel)
P: Norman Thaddeus Vane, Henry Passmore
D:S: Norman Thaddeus Vane
John Brown . . . .   Ben
Rosemary Anderson . . . . . .   Nelly
Mark Dignam . . . .   Caleb
Catherine Wilmer . . . .   Aunt Boo

Marc Sheldon . . . . Fred
DRAMA Nova Scotia. Preacher's adopted
daughter loves his hunchbacked bastard
who steals lobsters.

12742
CONSPIRACY OF HEARTS (113) (U)
Rank (RFD)
P: Betty E. Box
D: Ralph Thomas
S: Dale Pitt
SC: Robert Presnell jr
Lilli Palmer . . . . Mother Katherine
Sylvia Syms . . . . Sister Mitya
Yvonne Mitchell . . . . Sister Gerta
Ronald Lewis . . . . Maj Spoletti
Albert Lieven . . . . Col Horsten
Peter Arne . . . . Lt Schmidt
Nora Swinburne . . . . Sister Tia
Michael Goodliffe . . . . . Father Desmaines
Megs Jenkins . . . . Sister Constance
David Kossoff . . . . Rabbi
Jenny Laird . . . . Sister Honoria
George Coulouris . . . . Petrelli
Phyllis Neilson-Terry . . . Sister Elisaveta
Rebecca Dignam . . . . Anna
WAR Italy, 1943. Nuns help Jewish
children escape from concentration camp.

12743
THE DOVER ROAD MYSTERY (30) (U)
Merton Park (AA)
P: Jack Greenwood
D: Gerard Bryant
S: James Eastwood
N: Edgar Lustgarten
Geoffrey Keen . . . . Supt Graham
Leonard Sachs . . . . Herbert Roberts
Cyril Chamberlain . . . . . . Jack Chambers
CRIME Police unmask racing motorist
behind car thefts and bank robbery.

12744
CARRY ON CONSTABLE (86) (U)
GHW (AA)
P: Peter Rogers
D: Gerald Thomas
S: Brock Williams
SC: Norman Hudis
Sidney James . . . . Sgt Frank Wilkins
Eric Barker . . . . Insp Mills
Kenneth Connor . . . . . . Charlie Constable
Charles Hawtrey . . . . Timothy Gorse
Kenneth Williams . . . . . . Stanley Benson
Leslie Phillips . . . . Tom Potter
Joan Sims . . . . Gloria Passworthy
Hattie Jacques . . . . Laura Moon
Shirley Eaton . . . . Sally Barry
Cyril Chamberlain . . . . PC Thurston
Joan Hickson . . . . Mrs May
Irene Handl . . . . Distraught Woman
Terence Longdon . . . . Herbert Hall
Jill Adams . . . . PCW Harrison
Freddie Mills . . . . Crook
COMEDY Episodic misadventures of
police college graduates.

12745
THE FLESH AND THE FIENDS (97) scope
USA: MANIA
Triad (RFI)
P: Robert Baker, Monty Berman
D:S: John Gilling
SC: John Gilling, Leon Griffiths
Peter Cushing . . . . Dr Robert Knox
June Laverick . . . . Martha
Donald Pleasence . . . . William Hare
Dermot Walsh . . . . Dr Geoffrey Mitchell
Renee Houston . . . . Helen Burke

George Rose . . . . William Burke
Billie Whitelaw. . . . . Mary Patterson
John Cairney . . . . Chris Jackson
Melvyn Hayes . . . . Daft Jamie
CRIME Edinburgh, 1820. Resurrectionists
kill whore and halfwit and sell corpses
to doctor.

12746
JAZZBOAT (96) scope (A)
Warwick (Col)
P: Harold Huth
D: Ken Hughes
S: Rex Rienits
SC: Ken Hughes, John Antrobus
Anthony Newley . . . . Bert Harris
Anne Aubrey . . . . Doll
Bernie Winters . . . . Jinx
James Booth . . . . Spider Kelly
Leo McKern . . . . Inspector
Lionel Jeffries . . . . Sgt Thompson
David Lodge . . . . Holy Mike
Al Mulock . . . . Dancer
Joyce Blair . . . . Renee
Jean Philippe . . . . Jean
Ted Heath and his Music
MUSICAL Electrician poses as cat
burglar and is forced to help jewel robbers.

12747
LET'S GET MARRIED (91) scope (A)
Viceroy (Eros)
P: John R. Sloan
D: Peter Graham Scott
S: (NOVEL) Gina Klausen
(CONFESSIONS OF A KEPT WOMAN)
SC: Ken Taylor
Anthony Newley . . . ., . Dickie Bird
Anne Aubrey . . . . Anne Linton
Bernie Winters . . . . Bernie
Hermione Baddeley . . . . . Mrs O'Grady
James Booth . . . . Photographer
Lionel Jeffries . . . . Marsh
Diane Clare . . . . Glad
John le Mesurier . . . . Dean
Victor Maddern . . . . Manager
Joyce Carey . . . . Miss Finch
Sydney Tafler . . . . Pendle
Betty Marsden . . . . Miss Kaplan
Cardew Robinson . . . . . . Salesman
Meier Tzelniker . . . . Schutzberger
COMEDY Doctor working as laundryman
weds pregnant model and conquers
nerves by delivering her baby.

12748
INN FOR TROUBLE (90) (U)
Film Locations (Eros)
P: Norman J. Hyams, Edward Lloyd
D: C.M.Pennington-Richards
S: (TV SERIES) Fred Robinson
(THE LARKINS)
SC: Fred Robinson
Peggy Mount . . . . Ada Larkins
David Kossoff . . . . Alf Larkins
Leslie Phillips . . . . John Belcher
Glyn Owen . . . . Lord Bill Osborne
Yvonne Monlaur . . . . Yvette
Charles Hawtrey . . . . Silas
A.E.Matthews . . . . . Sir Hector Gore-Blandish
Shaun O'Riordan . . . . Eddie Larkins
Ronan O'Casey . . . . Jeff Rogers
Alan Wheatley . . . . Harold Gaskin
Graham Moffatt . . . . Jumbo Gudge
Willoughby Goddard . . . . . Sgt Saunders
Gerald Campion . . . . George
Stanley Unwin . . . . Farmer
Irene Handl . . . . Lily

Fred Robinson . . . . Fred
COMEDY Publican uses Lord's home brew
to thwart rival brewery.

12749
AND THE SAME TO YOU (70) (U)
Monarch (Eros)
P: William Gell
D: George Pollock
S: (PLAY) A.P.Dearsley
(THE CHIGWELL CHICKEN)
SC: John Paddy Carstairs, John Junkin,
Terry Nation
Brian Rix. . . . . . . Dickie Dreadnought
Leo Franklyn . . . . Rev Sydney Mullett
William Hartnell . . . . Wally Burton
Vera Day . . . . Cynthia
Tommy Cooper . . . . Horace
Dick Bentley . . . . George Nibbs
Tony Wright . . . . Percy Gibbons
Renee Houston . . . . Mildred
John Robinson . . . . Pomphret
Sidney James . . . . Sammy Gatt
Miles Malleson . . . . Bishop
Ronald Adam . . . . Trout
Shirley Ann Field . . . . Iris
Terry Scott . . . . PC
COMEDY Vicar's nephew becomes
boxer and his promoter poses as clerk
to fool archdeacon.

12750
MOMENT OF DANGER (96) (A)
USA: MALAGA
Cavalcade (WPD)
P:Thomas Clyde
D: Laslo Benedek
S:(NOVEL) Donald Mackenzie
SC:David Osborn, Donald Ogden Stewart
Trevor Howard . . . . John Bain
Dorothy Dandridge . . . . . . Gianna
Edmund Purdom . . . . Peter Carran
Michael Hordern . . . . Insp Farrell
Paul Stassino . . . . Juan Montoya
John Bailey . . . . Cecil
Alfred Burke . . . . Shapley
Peter Illing . . . . Pawnbroker
Barry Keegan . . . . Corrigan
Brian Worth . . . . Guard
CRIME Cheated crook pursues jewel
thief to Spain, accompanied by thief's
mistress.

12751
NEVER TAKE SWEETS FROM A STRANGER
(81) (X) scope USA: NEVER TAKE CANDY
FROM A STRANGER
Hammer (Col)
P: Anthony Hinds
D: Cyril Frankel
S: (PLAY) Roger Garis (THE PONY CART)
SC: John Hunter
Gwen Watford . . . . Sally Carter
Patrick Allen . . . . Peter Carter
Felix Aylmer . . . . Clarence Olderberry
Niall MacGinnis . . . . Defence Counsel
Bill Nagy . . . . Clarence jr
Janina Faye . . . . Jean Carter
Macdonald Parke. . . . . Judge
Michael Gwynn . . . . Prosecutor
Frances Green . . . . Lucille Demarest
Alison Leggatt . . . . Martha
Robert Arden . . . . Tom Demarest
Cal McCord . . . . Charles Kalliduke
Estelle Brody . . . . Eunice Kalliduke
CRIME Canada. British teacher fails to
convict town founder for making his
9-year old daughter dance naked.

MAR

12752
GIRLS OF LATIN QUARTER (69) *tech* (A)
Border (NR)
P: O'Negus Fancey
D: Alfred Travers
S: Alfred Travers, Bernard Hunter
SC: Dick Vosburgh, Brad Ashton
Bernard Hunter . . . . Clive Smedley
Jill Ireland . . . . Jill
Sheldon Lawrence . . . . Mac
Danny Green . . . . Hodgson
Joe Baker . . . . Finch
Mimi Pearce; Cherry Wainer; Sonya Cordeaux;
Cuddly Dudley
MUSICAL Timid heir is forced to run
farm and visit nightclub.

12753
BLUEBEARD'S TEN HONEYMOONS (92) (A)
Anglo-Allied (WPD)
P: Roy Parkinson
D: W.Lee Wilder
S: Myles Wilder
George Sanders . . . . Henri Landru
Corinne Calvet . . . . Odette
Jean Kent . . . . Julienne Guillin
Patricia Roc . . . . Vivienne Dureaux
Greta Gynt . . . . Jeannette Tissot
Maxine Audley . . . . Cynthis Phillips
Ingrid Hafner . . . . Giselle
Selma Vaz Diaz . . . . Mme Boyer
Peter Illing . . . . Lefevre
George Coulouris . . . . Lacoste
Sheldon Lawrence . . . . Pepi
Jack Melford . . . . Concierge
Harold Berens . . . . Jeweller
CRIME Paris, period. Antique dealer
weds wealthy women and kills them.

12754
FACES IN THE DARK (85) (A)
Penington-Eady (RFD)
P: Jon Penington
D: David Eady
S: (NOVEL) Pierre Boileau, Thomas Narcejac
SC: Ephraim Kogan, John Tully
John Gregson . . . . Richard Hammond
Mai Zetterling . . . . . . Christine Hammond
John Ireland . . . . Max Hammond
Michael Denison . . . . David Merton
Tony Wright . . . . Clem
Nanette Newman . . . . Janet
Valerie Taylor . . . . Miss Hopkins
CRIME Man helps mistress drive her
blind husband mad by moving his house
from Cornwall to France.

12755
YOUR MONEY OR YOUR WIFE (91) (A)
Ethiro (RFD)
P: Norman Williams
D: Anthony Simmons
S: Ronald Jeans
Donald Sinden . . . . Pelham Butterworth
Peggy Cummins . . . . . . Gay Butterworth
Richard Wattis . . . . Hubert Fry
Peter Reynolds . . . . Theodore Malek
Georgina Cookson . . . Thelma Cressington
Gladys Boot . . Mrs Compton-Chamberlain
Barbara Steele . . . . Juliet Frost
Betty Baskcomb . . . . Janet Fry
Olive Sloane . . . . Mrs Withers
Ian Fleming . . . . Judge
COMEDY Couple take in lodgers and
fake divorce to comply with will terms.

12756
JACKPOT (71) (A)
Eternal (GN)

P: Maurice J. Wilson
D: Montgomery Tully
S: John Sherman
SC: Maurice J. Wilson, Montgomery Tully
William Hartnell . . . . Supt Frawley
Betty McDowell . . . . Kay Stock
Eddie Byrne . . . . Sam Hare
George Mikell . . . . Carl Stock
Michael Ripper . . . . Lenny Lane
Victor Brooks . . . . Sgt Jacks
Tim Turner . . . . Peter
CRIME Ex-convict gets ex-safecracker to
help him rob nightclub.

12757
THE PRICE OF SILENCE (73) (U)
Eternal (GN)
P: Maurice J. Wilson
D: Montgomery Tully
S: (NOVEL) Laurence Meynell
(ONE STEP FROM MURDER)
SC: Maurice J. Wilson
Gordon Jackson . . . . Roger Fenton
June Thorburn . . . . Audrey Truscott
Maya Koumani . . . . Maria Shipley
Terence Alexander . . . . John Braine
Mary Clare . . . . Mrs West
Victor Brooks . . . . Supt Wilson
Joan Heal . . . . Ethel
Olive Sloane . . . . Landlady
CRIME Ex-convict estate agent suspected
when cellmate strangles rich client.

12758
TROUBLE WITH EVE (64) (A)
Blakeley's Films (Butcher)
P: Tom Blakeley
D: Francis Searle
S: (PLAY) June Garland
(WIDOWS ARE DANGEROUS)
SC: Brock Williams
Robert Urquhart . . . . Brian Maitland
Hy Hazell . . . . Louise Kingston
Garry Marsh . . . . Roland
Vera Day . . . . Daisy
Sally Smith . . . . Eve
Tony Quinn . . . . Bellchambers
Denis Shaw . . . . George
Brenda Hogan . . . . Angela
Bruce Seton . . . . Digby Philpotts
COMEDY Village councillor loves widow
with teashop and beatnik daughter.

12759
HELL IS A CITY (98) *scope* (A)
Hammer (WPD)
P: Michael Carreras
D:SC: Val Guest
S: (NOVEL) Maurice Procter
Stanley Baker . . . . Insp Martineau
John Crawford . . . . Don Starling
Donald Pleasence . . . . Gus Hawkins
Maxine Audley . . . . Julia Martineau
Billie Whitelaw . . . . Chloe Hawkins
Joseph Tomelty . . . . . Furnisher Steele
George A. Cooper . . . . . . Doug Savage
Geoffrey Frederick . . . . Deverey
Vanda Godsell . . . . Lucky Lusk
Charles Houston . . . . Clogger Roach
Sarah Branch . . . . Silver Steele
Russell Napier . . . . Supt
CRIME Manchester. Malachite on stolen
banknotes helps inspector track escaped
convict.

12760
BOTTOMS UP ! (89) (U)
Transocean (WPD)
P:D: Mario Zampi
S: (TV SERIES) Frank Muir, Denis Norden
(WHACKO!)

SC: Michael Pertwee, Frank Muir, Denis Norden
Jimmy Edwards . . . . . . Prof Jim Edwards
Arthur Howard .. . . Oliver Pettigrew
Martita Hunt . . . . . . Lady Gore-Willoughby
Sydney Tafler . . . . Sid Biggs
Raymond Huntley . . . . . Carrick-Jones
Reginald Beckwith . . . . Bishop Wendover
Vanda Hudson . . . . Matron Carlini
Melvyn Hayes . . . . Cecil Biggs
John Mitchell . . . . Wendover
Richard Briars . . . . Caldwell
Gordon Phillot. . . . . Dinwiddie
COMEDY Schoolmaster has his bookie's
son pose as a prince from the Middle East.

12761
URGE TO KILL (58) (A)
Merton Park (AA)
P: Jack Greenwood
D: Vernon Sewell
S: (STORY) Gerald Savory, Charles
Freeman (HAND IN GLOVE)
SC: James Eastwood
Patrick Barr . . . . Supt Allen
Howard Pays . . . . Charles Ramskill
Ruth Dunning . . . . Auntie B
Terence Knapp . . . . Hughie
Anna Turner . . . . Lily Willis
Christopher Trace . . . . Sgt Grey
Margaret StBarbe West . . . . . Mrs Willis
Yvonne Buckingham. . . . . . Gwen
CRIME Supt proves lodger framed
retarded orphan youth for killing and
mutilating girl.

APR

12762
THE LEAGUE OF GENTLEMEN (113) (A)
Allied Film Makers (RFD)
P: Michael Relph
D: Basil Dearden
S: (NOVEL) John Boland
SC: Bryan Forbes
Jack Hawkins . . . . Norman Hyde
Nigel Patrick . . . . Peter Graham Race
Roger Livesey . . . . Mycroft
Richard Attenborough . . . . . Edward Lexy
Bryan Forbes . . . . Martin Porthill
Kieron Moore . . . . Stevens
Robert Coote . . . . Bunny Warren
Terence Alexander . . . . . Rupert Rutland-Smith
Melissa Stribling . . . . Peggy
Norman Bird . . . . Frank Weaver
Nanette Newman . . . . Elizabeth
David Lodge . . . . CSM
Doris Hare . . . . Molly Weaver
CRIME Ex-colonel blackmails group
of cashiered officers into helping him rob bank.

12763
OPERATION CUPID (65) (U)
Twickenham (RFD)
P: Guido Coen
D: Charles Saunders
S: Jack Taylor
SC: Brock Williams
Charles Farrell . . . . Charlie Stevens
Wallas Eaton . . . . Cecil
Avice Landone . . . . Mrs Mountjoy
Wally Patch . . . . Bookmaker
Harold Goodwin . . . . Mervyn
David Saire . . . . Claude
Beth Rogan . . . . Barmaid
Bruce Seton . . . . Representative
COMEDY Man wins marriage bureau
and poses as millionaire to woo widow
posing as millionairess.

12764
AND WOMEN SHALL WEEP (65) (A)
Ethiro (RFD)
P: Norman Williams
D: John Lemont
S: John Lemont, Leigh Vance
Ruth Dunning . . . . Mrs Lumsden
Max Butterfield . . . . Terry Lumsden
Gillian Vaughan . . . . Brenda Wilkes
Richard O'Sullivan . . . . Godfrey Lumsden
Claire Gordon . . . . Sadie MacDougall
David Gregory . . . . Desmond Peel
David Rose . . . . Woody Forrest
Leon Garcia . . . . Ossie Green
CRIME Widow saves teenage son from
crime by exposing his brother as pawnbroker's
killer.

12765
BEYOND THE CURTAIN (88) (U)
Martin (RFD)
P: John Martin
D: Compton Bennett
S: (NOVEL) Charles Blair, A.J.Wallis
(THUNDER ABOVE)
SC: Compton Bennett, John Cresswell
Richard Greene . . . . Jim Kyle
Eva Bartok . . . . . . Karin von Seefeldt
Marius Goring . . . . Hans Koertner
Lucie Mannheim . . . . . Frau von Seefeldt
Andree Melly . . . . Linda
George Mikell . . . . Pieter
John Welsh . . . . Turner
Denis Shaw . . . . Krumm
Annette Karell . . . . Governor
Gaylord Cavallaro . . . . Twining
Leonard Sachs . . . . Waiter
DRAMA Berlin. Airline pilot rescues
German hostess from Russian zone.

12766
PEEPING TOM (109) eastman (X)
Michael Powell Theatre (AA)
P: Michael Powell, Albert Fennell
D: Michael Powell
S: Leo Marks
Carl Boehm. . . . . Mark Lewis
Moira Shearer . . . . Vivian
Anna Massey . . . . Helen Stephens
Maxine Audley . . . . Mrs Stephens
Brenda Bruce . . . . Dora
Martin Miller. . . . . Dr Rosan
Esmond Knight . . . . Arthur Baden
Bartlett Mullins . . . . Mr Peters
Michael Goodliffe . . . . Don Jarvis
Jack Watson . . . . Insp Gregg
Shirley Ann Field . . . . Diane Ashley
Pamela Green . . . . Milly
Michael Powell . . . . Mr Lewis
CRIME Scientist's son films girls as he
stabs them with his camera-leg.

12767
THE RUNNING, JUMPING AND
STANDING STILL FILM (11) (U) sepia
Sellers Productions (BL)
D: Dick Lester
S: Peter Sellers, Spike Milligan
Peter Sellers
Spike Milligan
Leo McKern
David Lodge
Graham Stark
Bruce Lacey
Mario Fabrizi
COMEDY Unlikely occurences in a field.

12768
THE LAST TRAIN (31) (U)
Merton Park (AA)

P: Jack Greenwood
D: Geoffrey Muller
S: James Eastwood
N: Edgar Lustgarten
Russell Napier . . . . Supt Duggan
Lisa Daniely . . . .
John Sloane. . . . .
CRIME Police investigate murder in
Underground and catch watch smugglers.

12769
CIRCUS OF HORRORS (91) eastman (X)
Independent Artists-Lynx (AA) reissue: 1962

P: Norman Priggen
D: Sidney Hayers
S: George Baxt
Anton Diffring . . . . Dr Bernard Schuler
Erika Remberg . . . . Elissa
Yvonne Monlaur . . . . Nicole Vanet
Donald Pleasence . . . . Vanet
Jane Hylton . . . . Angela Webb
Kenneth Griffith . . . . Martin Webb
Conrad Phillips . . . . Insp Arthur Ames
Jack Gwillim . . . . Supt Andrews
Vanda Hudson . . . . Magda von Meck
Yvonne Romain . . . . Melina
CRIME France. Plastic surgeon cures
criminal girls and stars them in his circus.

12770
SCHOOL FOR SCOUNDRELS (94) (U)
Guardsman (WPD)
P: Hal E.Chester, Douglas Rankin
D: Robert Hamer
S: (BOOKS) Stephen Potter
(GAMESMANSHIP; LIFEMANSHIP;
ONEUPMANSHIP)
SC: Patricia Moyes, Hal E. Chester, Peter Ustinov
Peter Ustinov
Ian Carmichael . . . . Henry Palfrey
Terry-Thomas . . . . Raymond Delauney
Janette Scott . . . . April Smith
Alastair Sim . . . . Stephen Potter
Dennis Price . . . . Dunstan Dorchester
Edward Chapman . . . . Gloatbridge
Kynaston Reeves . . . . General
Irene Handl . . . . Mrs Stringer
John le Mesurier . . . . Skinner
Hugh Paddick . . . . Instructor
Peter Jones . . . . Dudley Dorchester
COMEDY Weak businessman wins girl
back from cad after taking course in
Lifemanship.

12771
CAUGHT IN THE NET (64) (U)
Wallace (CFF)
P: A. Frank Bundy
D: John Haggarty
S: (NOVEL) Sutherland Ross
(THE LAZY SALMON MYSTERY)
SC: Max Anderson
Jeremy Bulloch . . . . Bob Ketley
Joanna Horlock . . . . Susan
James Luck . . . . Simon
Anthony Parker . . . . Peter Ketley
Larry Burns . . . . George
Bruce Wightman . . . . Tom
Michael Collins . . . . Arnold
CHILDREN Devon. Fishing researcher's
brother captures salmon dynamiters.

12772
DANGER TOMORROW (61) (A)
Parroch (AA)
P: C. Jack Parsons
D: Terry Bishop
S: Frank Charles
SC: Guy Deghy

Zena Walker . . . . Ginny Murray
Robert Urquhart . . . . Bob Murray
Rupert Davies . . . . Dr Robert Campbell
Annabel Maule . . . . Helen
Russell Waters . . . . Steve
Lisa Daniely . . . . Marie
FANTASY Doctor's wife with ESP has
vision of murder in attic.

12773
CONE OF SILENCE (92) (U)
USA: TROUBLE IN THE SKY
Aubrey Baring (Bry)
D: Charles Frend
S: (NOVEL) David Beaty
SC: Robert Westerby, Jeffrey Dell
Michael Craig. . . . . Capt Hugh Dallas
Peter Cushing . . . . Capt Clive Judd
Bernard Lee . . . . Capt George Gort
Elizabeth Seal . . . . Charlotte Gort
George Sanders . . . Sir Arnold Hobbes QC
Andre Morell . . . . . Capt Edward Manningham
Gordon Jackson . . . . . Capt Bateson
Charles Tingwell . . . . Capt Braddock
Noel Willman . . . . Nigel Pickering
Delphi Lawrence . . . . . . Joyce Mitchell
Marne Maitland . . . . Mr Robinson
DRAMA Training captain proves design
weakness caused death of his fiancee's
jet pilot father.

12774
THE HAND (60) (A)
Bill & Michael Luckwell (Butcher)
P: Bill Luckwell, Derek Winn
D: Henry Cass
S: Ray Cooney, Tony Hilton
Derek Bond . . . . Roberts/Crawshaw
Ronald Leigh Hunt . . . . Insp Munyard
Reed de Rouen . . . . Michael Brodie
Bryan Coleman . . . . Adams
Ray Cooney . . . . Pollitt
Tony Hilton . . . . Foster
Harold Scott . . . . Charlie Taplow
CRIME Inspector unmasks wartime
traitor as man who stabbed one-armed man.

MAY

12775
AN HONOURABLE MURDER (69) (U)
Danziger (WPD)
P: Edward J & Harry Lee Danziger
D: Godfrey Grayson
S: (PLAY) William Shakespeare
(JULIUS CAESAR)
SC: Brian Clemens, Eldon Howard
Norman Wooland . . . . Brutus Smith
Margaretta Scott . . . . Claudia Caesar
Lisa Daniely . . . . Paula
Douglas Wilmer . . . . R.Cassius
Philip Saville . . . . Mark Anthony
John Longden . . . . Julian Caesar
Marion Mathie . . . . Portia Smith
Colin Tapley . . . . Casca
Kenneth Edwards . . . . Trebon
Arnold Bell . . . . Ligar
DRAMA Director persuades board to vote
chairman out of office, causing his death.

12776
SONS AND LOVERS (100) scope (A)
20th Century Fox reissue: 1962
P: Jerry Wald
D: Jack Cardiff
S: (NOVEL) D.H.Lawrence
SC: Gavin Lambert, T.E.B.Clarke
Trevor Howard . . . . Walter Morel
Dean Stockwell . . . . Paul Morel
Wendy Hiller . . . . Gertrude Morel

Mary Ure . . . . Clara Dawes
Heather Sears . . . . Miriam Leivers
William Lucas. . . . . William Morel
Conrad Phillips . . . . Baxter Dawes
Donald Pleasence . . . . Pappleworth
Ernest Thesiger . . . . Henry Hadlock
Rosalie Crutchley . . . . Mrs Leivers
Elizabeth Begley . . . . Mrs Radford
ROMANCE Nottingham, 1905. Coarse miner's
artistic son has affairs with religious
neighbour and married suffragette. (AA:
Best Photography, 1961).

12777
OSCAR WILDE (98) (X)
Vantage (20)
P: Jo Eisinger, William Kirby
D: Gregory Ratoff
S: Jo Eisinger
Robert Morley . . . . Oscar Wilde
Ralph Richardson . . . . . Sir Edward Carson
Phyllis Calvert . . . . Constance Wilde
John Neville . . . . Lord Alfred Douglas
Dennis Price . . . . Robbie Ross
Alexander Knox . . . . . . Sir Edward Clarke
Edward Chapman . . . . . . Marquis of Queensbury
Martin Benson . . . . George Alexander
Robert Harris . . . . Justice Collins
Henry Oscar . . . . Justice Wills
William Devlin . . . . Solicitor General
Ronald Leigh Hunt . . . . . Lionel Johnson
Martin Boddey . . . . Insp Richards
Leonard Sachs . . . . . . Richard Legallienne
Tony Doonan . . . . Wood
HISTORY 1895. Marquis's slander
action leads to playwright's imprisonment
for sodomy.

12778
THE TRIALS OF OSCAR WILDE (123) (X)
tech/scope USA: THE MAN WITH THE GREEN
CARNATION
Viceroy-Warwick (Eros)
P: Harold Huth
D: SC: Ken Hughes
S: (BOOK) Montgomery Hyde
(PLAY) John Fernald (THE STRINGED LUTE)
Peter Finch . . . . Oscar Wilde
Yvonne Mitchell . . . . . . Constance Wilde
James Mason . . . . Sir Edward Carson
Nigel Patrick . . . . Sir Edward Clarke
James Fraser . . . . Lord Alfred Douglas
Lionel Jeffries . . . . . . Marquess of Queensbury
Emrys Jones . . . . Robbie Ross
James Booth . . . . Alfred Wood
Sonia Dresdel . . . . Lady Wilde
Maxine Audley . . . . Ada Leverson
Lloyd Lamble . . . . . Charles Humphries
Paul Rogers . . . . Frank Harris
Ian Fleming . . . . Arthur
Laurence Naismith . . . . . . Prince of Wales
Naomi Chance . . . . Lily Langtry
Meredith Edwards . . . . . . Auctioneer
Michael Goodliffe . . . . Charles Gill
Liam Gaffney . . . . Willie Wilde
A.J.Brown . . . . Justice Collins
David Ensor . . . . Justice Wills
HISTORY 1895. Marquis's slander action
leads to playwright's imprisonment for
sodomy. (BFA: Best Actor, 1960).

12779
THE PROFESSIONALS (61) (U)
Independent Artists (AA)
P: Norman Priggen
D: Don Sharp
S: Peter Barnes
William Lucas . . . . Philip Bowman
Andrew Faulds . . . . Insp Rankin

Colette Wilde . . . . Ruth
Stratford Johns . . . . Lawson
Vilma Ann Leslie . . . . Mabel
Edward Cast . . . . Clayton
Charles Vince . . . . Holden
CRIME Gang raids bank through sewers but
is betrayed by chance.

12780
CLIMB UP THE WALL (65) (U)
Border (NR)
P: O.Negus-Fancey
D: Michael Winner
S: Michael Winner, Jack Jackson

Jack Jackson   Glen Mason
Russ Conway   Mike Preston
Cherry Wainer   Libby Morris
Neville Taylor   George Browne
Tommy Yeardye   Malcolm Jackson
Peter Sellers   Michael Bentine
Frances Day   Claude Dampier
Charlie Kunz   Antonio
REVUE (includes extracts from earlier films).

12781
KIDNAPPED (97) tech (U)
Walt Disney
P: Hugh Attwoole
D:SC: Robert Stevenson
S: (NOVEL) Robert Louis Stevenson
Peter Finch. . . . . . Alan Breck Stewart
James MacArthur . . . . . . David Balfour
Bernard Lee . . . . Capt Hoseason
John Laurie . . . . Ebenezer Balfour
Niall MacGinnis. . . . . Shuan
Finlay Currie . . . . Cluny MacPherson
Miles Malleson . . . . Mr Rankeillor
Duncan Macrae . . . . Highlander
Andrew Cruickshank . . . Colin Roy Campbell
Peter O'Toole . . . . Robin Oig MacGregor
Alex Mackenzie . . . . Ferryman
Oliver Johnston . . . . Mr Campbell
Norman MacOwan . . . . . . Tinker
Eileen Way . . . . Jennet Clouston
ADVENTURE Scotland, 1751. Jacobite rebel
saves youth from being kidnapped by uncle.

12782
A TERRIBLE BEAUTY (89) (U)
USA: THE NIGHT FIGHTERS
Raymond Stross-DRM-Cineman (UA)
P: Raymond Stross
D: Tay Garnett
S: (NOVEL) Arthur Roth
SC: Robert Wright Campbell
Robert Mitchum . . . . Dermot O'Neill
Anne Heywood . . . . Neeve Donnelly
Dan O'Herlihy . . . . Don McGinnis
Cyril Cusack . . . . Jimmy Hannafin
Richard Harris . . . . Sean O'Reilly
Niall MacGinnis . . . . Ned O'Neill
Marianne Benet . . . . Bella O'Neill
Christopher Rhodes . . . . . . Malone
Harry Brogan . . . . Patrick O'Neill
Eileen Crowe . . . . Kathleen O'Neill
Geoffrey Golden . . . . Sgt Crawley
WAR Ireland, 1941. Recruit informs on IRA
when it affiliates with Nazi Germany.

12783
THE CHALLENGE (89) (A)
Alexandra (RFD)
P: John Temple-Smith
D: S: John Gilling
Jayne Mansfield . . . . Billy Lacrosse
Anthony Quayle . . . . Jim Maxton
Car Mohner . . . . Kristy
Peter Reynolds . . . . Buddy
Barbara Mullen . . . . Ma Piper

Robert Brown . . . . Bob Crowther
Dermot Walsh . . . . Insp Willis
Patrick Holt . .: . .. . Max
Edward Judd . . . . Sgt Gittens
John Bennett . . . . Spider
Lorraine Clewes . . . . Mr Rick
Perdy Herbert . . . . Shop Steward
John Stratton . . . . Rick
Peter Pike . . . . Joey
Bill McGuffie; Liane Marelli
CRIME Woman's gang kidnap widowed
ex-convict's son to force him to surrender
buried loot.

12784
DENTIST IN THE CHAIR (88) (U)
Briand (Renown)
P: Bertram Ostrer
D: Don Chaffey
S: (NOVEL) Matthew Finch
SC: Val Guest, Bob Monkhouse,
George Wadmore
Bob Monkhouse . . . . David Cookson
Peggy Cummins . . . . Peggy Travers
Kenneth Connor . . . . Sam Field
Eric Barker . . . . The Dean
Ronnie Stevens . . . . Brian Dexter
Vincent Ball . . . . Michaels
Eleanor Summerfield . . . . . Ethel Field
Reginald Beckwith . . . . . . Watling
Stuart Saunders . . . . Insp Richardson
Avril Angers . . . . Rosie Lee
Ian Wallace . . . . Dentist
Jeremy Hawk . . . . Instructor
COMEDY Dental students help crook pose
as one of them to recoup stolen instruments.

12785
THE DAY THEY ROBBED THE BANK OF
ENGLAND (85) (U)
Summit (MGM)
P: Jules Buck
D: John Guillermin
S: (NOVEL) John Brophy
SC: Howard Clewes, Richard Maibaum
Aldo Ray . . . . Charles Norgate
Elizabeth Sellars . . . . Iris Medoon
Peter O'Toole . . . . Capt Fitch
Kieron Moore . . . . Walsh
Hugh Griffith . . . . O'Shea
Albert Sharpe . . . . Tosher
John le Mesurier . . . . Green
Joseph Tomelty . . . . Cohoun
Wolf Frees . . . . Dr Hagen
Miles Malleson . . . . Curator
Colin Gordon . . . . Keeper
CRIME 1901. American adventurer helps Irish
rebels raid Bank of England through disused
sewer.

12786
THE NUDIST STORY (90) tech (A)
Danziger (Eros)
P: John P. Wyler
D: Ramsey Herrington
S: Norman Armstrong
Shelley Martin . . . . Jane Robinson
Brian Cobby . . . . Bob Sutton
Anthony Oliver . . . . Blake
Natalie Lynn . . . . Aunt Meg
Jacqueline d'Orsay . . . . . . Gloria
Joy Hinton . . . . Carol
Paul Hendrick . . . . Tim
NUDIST Rich girl inherits nudist camp and
falls for director despite flirtatious foreigner.

12787
DILL JONES AND HIS ALL STARS (9) (U)
Carisbrooke Films (GN)
P:D: Robert Henryson
MUSICAL

12788-12829

12788
ERIC DELANEY AND HIS NEW BAND (9) (U)
Carisbrooke Films (AA)
P:D:Robert Henryson
MUSICAL

12789
SIXTEEN FLYING FINGERS (9) (U)
Carisbrooke Films (AA)
P:D:Robert Henryson
MUSICAL

12790
FREE AND EASY (9) (U)
Carisbrooke Films (GN)
P:D:Robert Henryson
MUSICAL

12791
BLUE TUNES (9) (U)
Carisbrooke Films (BL)
P:D:Robert Henryson
Ray Ellington Quartet
Eric Delaney and his Band
Dill Jones and his All Stars
MUSICAL

12792
MAKING MUSIC (9) (U)
Carisbrooke Films (BL)
P:D:Robert Henryson
Eric Delaney and his Band
MUSICAL

12793
RAY ELLINGTON AND HIS QUARTET (9)
(U)
Carisbrooke Films (BL)
P:D:Robert Henryson
MUSICAL

12794
CALL BACK YESTERDAY (25) (U)
Derick Williams (BL)
DRAMA

JUN

12795
SUDDENLY, LAST SUMMER (114) (X)
Horizon (Col)
P: Samuel Spiegel, Bill Kirby
D: Joseph L. Mankiewicz
S: (PLAY) Tennessee Williams
SC: Gore Vidal, Tennessee Williams
Elizabeth Taylor . . . . Catherine Holly
Montgomery Clift . . . . . . Dr Cukrowicz
Katharine Hepburn . . . . Violet Venable
Albert Dekker . . . . Dr Hockstader
Mercedes McCambridge . . . . Mrs Holly
Gary Raymond . . . . George Holly
Mavis Villiers . . . . Miss Foxhill
Patricia Marmont . . . . Nurse Benson
Joan Young . . . . Sister Felicity
DRAMA New Orleans. Insane girl tells neuro-
surgeon how her homosexual cousin was
killed by Spanish beggars.

12796
BOYD'S SHOP (55) (U)
Emmett Dalton (RFD)
P: Robert S. Baker, Monty Berman
D: Henry Cass
S: (PLAY) StJohn G.Ervine
SC: Philip Howard
Eileen Crowe . . . . Miss McClure
Geoffrey Golden . . . . Andrew Boyd
Aideen O'Kelly . . . . Agnes Boyd
Vincent Dowling . . . . John Haslett
Aiden Crenwell . . . . Rev Dunwoody
Rita O'Dea . . . . Miss Logan

May Craig . . . . Mrs Clotworthy
COMEDY Ireland. New grocer falls for
rival's daughter.

12797
NEVER LET GO (91) (X)
Independent Artists (RFD)
P: Peter de Sarigny
D: John Guillermin
S: John Guillermin, Peter de Sarigny
SC: Alun Falconer
Richard Todd . . . . John Cummings
Peter Sellers . . . . Lionel Meadows
Elizabeth Sellars . . . . Anne Cummings
Adam Faith . . . . Tommy Towers
Carol White . . . . Jackie
Mervyn Johns . . . . Alfie Barnes
Noel Willman . . . . Insp Thomas
David Lodge . . . . Cliff
Peter Jones . . . . Alec Berger
John Bailey . . . . Mackinnon
Nigel Stock . . . . Regan
John le Mesurier . . . . Pennington
CRIME Weak salesman rejects police
help and fights sadistic boss of gang
of car thieves.

12798
MAKE MINE MINK (101) (U)
Rank (RFD) *reissue:* 1964 (21 mins cut)
P: Hugh Stewart
D: Robert Asher
S: (PLAY) Peter Coke (BREATH OF
SPRING) SC: Michael Pertwee, Peter Blackmore
Terry-Thomas . . . . Maj Albert Rayne
Athene Seyler . . . . . . Dame Beatrice Appleby
Hattie Jacques . . . . Nanette Parry
Billie Whitelaw . . . . Lily
Elspeth Duxbury . . . . . . Elizabeth Pinkerton
Jack Hedley . . . . PC Jim Benham
Raymond Huntley . . . . Insp Pape
Irene Handl . . . . Mme Spolinsky
Kenneth Williams . . Hon Freddie Warrington
Noel Purcell . . . . Burglar
Sydney Tafler . . . . Lionel Spanager
Joan Heal . . . . Dora Spanager
Penny Morell . . . . Gertrude
Freddie Frinton . . . . Drunk
Ron Moody . . . . Jelks
Clement Freud . . . . Croupier
COMEDY Dame and lodgers steal furs to
aid charities.

12799
VILLAGE OF THE DAMNED (77) (A)
MGM British
P: Ronald Kinnoch
D: Wolf Rilla
S: (NOVEL) John Wyndham
(THE MIDWICH CUCKOOS)
SC: Sterling Silliphant, George Harley,
Wolf Rilla
George Sanders . . . . Gordon Zellaby
Barbara Shelley . . . . Anthea Zellaby
Martin Stephens . . . . David Zellaby
Michael Gwynn . . . . Alan Bernard
Laurence Naismith . . . . . . Dr Willers
Richard Warner . . . . Harrington
Jenny Laird . . . . Mrs Harrington
Sarah Long . . . . Evelyn
Thomas Heathcote . . . . . . James Pawle
Charlotte Mitchell . . . . . . Janet Pawle
Bernard Archard . . . . Vicar
FANTASY Physicist versus "space
children" born of village women.

12800
TARZAN THE MAGNIFICENT (86)
eastman (U)
Solar (Par)

P: Sy Weintraub, Harvey Hayutin
D: Robert Day
S: (CHARACTERS) Edgar Rice Burroughs
SC: Berne Giler, Robert Day
Gordon Scott . . . . Tarzan
Jock Mahoney . . . . Coy Benton
Betta StJohn . . . . Fay Ames
John Carradine . . . . Abel Banton
Lionel Jeffries . . . . Ames
Alexandra Stewart . . . . Laurie
Gary Cockrell . . . . Johnny Banton
Earl Cameron . . . . Tate
Charles Tingwell . . . . Conway
Al Mulock . . . . Martin Banton
ADVENTURE Africa. Jungle man brings
thief to justice despite murderous family.

12801
FOLLOW THAT HORSE ! (79) (U)
Cavalcade (WPD)
P: Thomas Clyde
D: Alan Bromly
S: (NOVEL) Howard Mason (PHOTO FINISH)
SC: Howard Mason, Alfred Shaughnessy,
William Douglas Home
David Tomlinson . . . . . . Dick Lanchester
Cecil Parker . . . . Sir William Crane
Richard Wattis . . . . Hugh Porlock
Dora Bryan . . . . Miss Bradstock
Mary Peach . . . . Susan Turner
Raymond Huntley . . . . . Special Branch Chief
Sam Kydd . . . . Farrell
George Pravda . . . . Hammler
John Welsh . . . . Maj Turner
Peter Copley . . . . Garrod
Victor Brooks . . . . Blake
COMEDY Civil servants, spies, and traitorous
scientist seek race-horse that swallowed
microfilm.

12802
IDENTITY UNKNOWN (66) (U)
Danziger (Par)
P: Edward J & Harry Lee Danziger
D: Frank Marshall
S: Brian Clemens
Richard Wyler . . . . John
Pauline Yates . . . . Jenny
Patricia Plunkett . . . . Betty
Beatrice Varley . . . . Matron
Valentine Dyall . . . . Ambrose
Kenneth Edwards . . . . Reynolds
John Gabriel . . . . Jamieson
Nyree Dawn Porter . . . . . . Pam
Vincent Ball . . . . Ken
Sheldon Lawrence . . . . Larry
DRAMA Reporters inverview relatives
of survivors of plane crash.

12803
LIGHT UP THE SKY (90) (A)
Criterion (Bry)
P:D: Lewis Gilbert
S: (PLAY) Robert Storey (TOUCH IT LIGHT)
SC: Vernon Harris
Ian Carmichael . . . . Lt Ogleby
Tommy Steele . . . . Eric McCaffey
Benny Hill . . . . Syd McCaffey
Sydney Tafler . . . . Ted Green
Victor Maddern . . . . Tomlinson
Harry Locke . . . . Roland Kenyon
Johnny Briggs . . . . Leslie Smith
Cyril Smith . . . . Spinner Rice
Dick Emery . . . . Harry
Susan Burnet . . . . Jean
Cardew Robinson . . . . Compere
COMEDY 1941. Episodic misadventures of
searchlight battery.

12804
DEAD LUCKY (64) (U)
ACT Films (BL)
P: Ralph Bond, Robert Dunbar
D: Montgomery Tully
S: Sidney Nelson, Maurice Harrison
Vincent Ball . . . . Mike Billings
Betty McDowall . . . . Jenny Drew
John le Mesurier . . . . Insp Corcoran
Alfred Burke . . . . Knocker Parsons
Michael Ripper . . . . Percy Simpson
Sam Kydd . . . . Harry Winston
Chili Bouchier . . . . Mrs Winston
John Charlesworth . . . Hon Stanley Dewsbury
Brian Worth . . . . Lucky Lewis
Frederick Piper . . . . Harvey Walters
Joan Heal . . . . Barmaid
CRIME Reporter proves girl friend did not
kill amorous gambler.

12805
ALI AND THE CAMEL (serial) *eastman* (U)
World Safari (CFF)
P:D:S: Henry Geddes
Mohamed Rifai . . . . Ali
Haj Mohamed . . . . Father
Alan Rodman . . . . Professor
Abdul Daabub . . . . Inspector
Mohamed Cinema . . . . Big Black
Mike Pirotta . . . . Three-finger
Maurice Denham . . . . Camel's Voice

12806
1: TALK OF A CAMEL (17)

12807
2: INTO THE DESERT (17)

12808
3: SAND STORM (16)

12809
4: THE MAN WITH THREE FINGERS (17)

12810
5: THE BOMB (17)

12811
6: DANGER AHEAD (17)

12812
7: THE FROG MAN (16)

12813
8: THE CAMEL TAKES A HAND (18)
CHILDREN Arabia. Talking camel helps
boy track down jewel robbers.

12814
THE YOUNG JACOBITES (serial) (U)
Rayant (CFF)
P: Anthony Gilkinson
D: John Reeve
S: Kenneth MacFarlane
SC: Paul Tabori, Gordon Wellesley
Francesca Annis . . . . Jean
Jeremy Bulloch . . . . Hamish
Frazer Hines . . . . Angus
John Pike . . . . Willie
Gareth Tandy . . . . Alistair
John Woodnut . . . . Lieut
Michael O'Brien . . . . Anderson
David Stuart . . . . Prince Charles
Michael Nightingale . . . . . . Col O'Sullivan

12815
1: JOURNEY INTO THE PAST (15)

12816
2: THE TRAITOR (16)

12817
3: THE LEAGUE IN ACTION (14)

12818
4: THE AMBUSH (15)

12819
5: THE PRINCE MUST BE WARNED (14)

12820
6: THE RESCUE (17)

12821
7: THE ENEMY CLOSES IN (15)

12822
8: OVER THE THRESHOLD (20)
CHILDREN Skye. Threshold Stone transports
children back in time to help Prince Charles
escape to France.

JUL
12823
IN THE NICK (105) *scope* (U)
Warwick (Col)
P: Harold Huth
D: SC: Ken Hughes
S: Frank Norman
Anthony Newley . . . . Dr Newcome
Anne Aubrey . . . . Doll
Bernie Winters . . . . Jinx Shortbottom
James Booth . . . . Spider Kelly
Harry Andrews . . . . Chief Williams
Al Mulock . . . . Dancer
Derren Nesbitt . . . . Nick
Niall MacGinnis . . . . Governor
Victor Brooks . . . . Screw Smith
Ian Hendry . . . . Ted Ross
Kynaston Reeves . . . . Judge
COMEDY Prison psychiatrist reforms
gangster who is then framed for theft.

12824
THE BRIDES OF DRACULA (85) *tech* (X)
Hammer-Hotspur (UI)
P: Anthony Hinds
D: Terence Fisher
S: (CHARACTERS) Bram Stoker
SC: Jimmy Sangster, Peter Bryan, Edward Percy
Peter Cushing . . . . Dr·Van Helsing
Freda Jackson . . . . Greta
Martita Hunt . . . . Baroness Meinster
Yvonne Monlaur . . . . . Marianne Danielle
Andree Melly . . . . Gina
Miles Malleson . . . . Dr Tobler
Henry Oscar . . . . Lang
David Peel . . . . Baron Meinster
Victor Brooks . . . . Hans
Mona Washbourne . . . . Mrs Lang
Marie Devereux . . . . Villager
Michael Mulcaster . . . . Latour
HORROR Transylvania, period. Doctor
saves Parisienne by destroying vampiric fiance.

12825
JUST JOE (73) (U)
Parkside (Archway)
P: Roger Proudlock
D: Maclean Rogers
S: Donald Bull
SC: Raymond Drewe
Leslie Randall . . . . Joe
Joan Reynolds . . . . Sybil
Michael Shepley . . . . Fowler
Anna May Wong . . . . Peach Blossom
Jon Pertwee . . . . Prendergast
Howard Pays . . . . Rodney
Martin Wyldeck . . . . Bill
Bruce Seton . . . . Charlie
Betty Huntley Wright . . . . Miss Appleby
COMEDY Blackmailer tries to obtain
phoney hero's detergent formula.

12826
THE BIG DAY (62) (A)
Independent Artists (Bryanston)
P: Arthur Alcott
D: Peter Graham Scott
S: Bill MacIlwraith
Donald Pleasence . . . . . Victor Partridge
Andree Melly . . . . Nina Wentworth
Colin Gordon . . . . George Baker
Harry H. Corbett . . . . Jackson
William Franklyn . . . . Selkirk
Susan Shaw . . . . Phyllis Selkirk
Molly Urquhart . . . . Mrs Deeping
Betty Marsden . . . . Mabel Jackson
DRAMA Weak husband with mistress
competes for directorship with manager's
brother-in-law and keen salesman.

12827
SNOWBALL (69) (U)
Independent Artists (RFD)
P: Julian Wintle, Leslie Parkyn
D: Pat Jackson
S: (NOVEL) James Lake
SC: Anne Francis
Gordon Jackson . . . . Bill Donovan
Kenneth Griffith . . . . Phil Hart
Zena Walker . . . . Mary Donovan
Daphne Anderson . . . . Nora Hart
Denis Waterman . . . . Mickey Donovan
John Welsh . . . . Ted Wylie
Myrtle Reed . . . . Betty Martin
Wensley Pithey . . . . Jim Adams
Eric Pohlmann . . . . Editor
Ronald Adam . . . . Mr King
DRAMA 11-year old boy's lie eventually
causes the death of amnesiac ex-POW.

12828
DOCTOR IN LOVE (98) *eastman* (A)
Rank (RFD)
P: Betty E. Box
D: Ralph Thomas
S: (NOVEL) Richard Gordon
SC: Nicholas Phipps
Michael Craig . . . . Dr Richard Hare
James Robertson Justice . . Sir Lancelot Spratt
Virginia Maskell . . . . Nicola Barrington
Carole Lesley . . . . Kitten Strudwick
Leslie Phillips . . . . Tony Burke
Reginald Beckwith . . . . . . Wildwinde
Joan Sims . . . . Dawn
Liz Fraser . . . . Leonora
Nicholas Phipps . . . . Dr Clive Cardew
Ambrosine Philpotts . . . . . Lady Spratt
Irene Handl . . . . .Prof MacRitchie
Fenella Fielding . . . . Mrs Tadwich
Nicholas Parsons . . . . Dr Hinxman
Moira Redmond . . . . . Sally Nightingale
Ronnie Stevens . . . . Harold Green
Michael Ward . . . . Dr Flower
John Le Mesurier . . . . Dr Mincing
Meredith Edwards . . . . . . Parker
COMEDY Episodic misadventures of two
hospital doctors who take over country
practice. (Top Moneymaker 1960).

12829
THE ENTERTAINER (96) (X)
Woodfall-Holly (Bry)
P: Harry Saltzman
D: Tony Richardson
S: (PLAY) John Osborne
SC: John Osborne, Nigel Kneale
Laurence Olivier . . . . Archie Rice
Brenda de Banzie . . . . Phoebe Rice
Roger Livesey . . . . Billy Rice
Joan Plowright . . . . Jean Rice
Alan Bates . . . . Frank Rice
Daniel Massey . . . . Graham

Shirley Anne Field . . . . Tina Lapford
Albert Finney . . . . Mick Rice
Thora Hird . . . . Ada Lapford
Miriam Karlin . . . . Soubrette
Geoffrey Toone . . . . Harold Hubbard
Max Bacon . . . . Charlie Klein
George Doonan . . . . Eddie Trimmer
Macdonald Hobley, Beryl & Bobo, The Clippers
DRAMA Morecambe. Bankrupt comic
seduces beauty queen and causes his father's
death in staging a comeback.

12830
SANDS OF THE DESERT (92) *tech* (U)
ABPC (WPD)
P: Gordon L.T.Scott
D: John Paddy Carstairs
S: Robert Hall, Anne Burnaby, Stafford Byrne
SC: John Paddy Carstairs, Charlie Drake
Charlie Drake . . . . Charlie Sands
Peter Arne . . . . Sheikh El Jabez
Sarah Branch . . . . Janet Brown
Raymond Huntley . . . . Bossom
Rebecca Dignam . . . . Nerima
Peter Illing . . . . Sheikh Ibrahim
Harold Kasket . . . . Abdulla
Marne Maitland . . . . Adviser
Neil McCarthy . . . . Hassan
Derek Sydney . . . . Mamud
Alan Tilvern . . . . Mustafa
Martin Benson . . . . Selim
Eric Pohlmann . . . . Scrobin
William Kendall . . . . Consul
Inia te Wiata . . . . Fahid
COMEDY Travel agent saves girl reporter
from Sheikh and opens holiday camp in desert.

AUG

12831
THE MAN WHO COULDN'T WALK (63) (A)
Bill & Michael Luckwell (Butcher)
P: Jock MacGregor, Umesh Mallik
D: Henry Cass
S: Umesh Mallik
Peter Reynolds . . . . Keefe Brand
Eric Pohlmann . . . . The Consul
Pat Clavin . . . . Carol
Reed de Rouen . . . . Luigi
Bernadette Milnes . . . . Cora
Richard Shaw . . . . Enrico
Martin Cass . . . . Beppo
CRIME Cracksman discovers his father
was killed by crippled diplomat.

12832
LIES MY FATHER TOLD ME (60)
Emmet Dalton
P: Don Chaffey, Charles Leeds
D: Don Chaffey
S: (STORY) Ted Allan
SC: Ted Allan
Harry Brogan . . . . Grandfather
Betsy Blair . . . . Mother
Edward Golden . . . . Father
Rita O'Dea.. . . . . Grandmother
Terry Raven . . . . David
Gearold O'Lochlain . . . . . . Old Gentleman
John Cowley . . . . Old Gentleman
DRAMA Dublin. Parents try to win love of
their nine-year-old son away from his grand-
father, a rag and bone man.

12833
JOEY KNOWS A VILLAIN (16) (U)
Beacon (NR)
P:D:S: James Richards
ANIMAL Thieves lock children in van and
they are saved by their pet donkey.

12834
JOEY'S NO ASS (15) (U)
Beacon (NR)
P:D:S: James Richards
ANIMAL Children build bridge to island
to save pets from angry neighbour.

12835
JOEY LEADS THE WAY (15) (U)
Beacon (NR)
P:D:S: James Richards
ANIMAL Pet donkey saves farm children
from well.

12836
DEPTH CHARGE (55) (A)
President Pictures (BL)
P: James Mellor
D: Jeremy Summers
S: Jeremy Summers, Kenneth Talbot
Alex McCrindle . . . . Skipper
David Orr . . . . Lt Forrester
Elliot Playfair . . . . Jamie
J. Mark Roberts . . . . Bob
Alex Allen . . . . Secretary
ADVENTURE Scotland. Coxswain helps
expert dismantle depth charge hauled
aboard trawler.

12837
TUNES OF GLORY (107) *tech* (A)
HM Films (UA)
P: Albert Fennell, Colin Lesslie
D: Ronald Neame
S: (NOVEL) James Kennaway
SC: James Kennaway
Alec Guinness . . . Lt/Col Jock Sinclair
John Mills . . . . Lt/Col Basil Barrow
Dennis Price . . . . Maj Charles Scott
Kay Walsh . . . . Mary
John Fraser . . . . Cpl/Piper Fraser
Susannah York . . . . Morag Sinclair
Gordon Jackson . . . . . . Capt Jimmy Cairns
Duncan Macrae . . . . . Pipe/Major Maclean
Allan Cuthbertson . . . Capt Eric Simpson
DRAMA Edinburgh. Strict colonel takes
over lax drunkard's regiment and the
clash leads to suicide and madness.

12838
A FRENCH MISTRESS (98) (A)
Charter (BL)
P: John Boulting
D: Roy Boulting
S: (PLAY) Robert Munro (Sonnie Hale)
SC: Roy Boulting, Jeffrey Dell
Cecil Parker . . . . Mr Crane
James Robertson Justice . . Robert Martin
Ian Bannen . . . . Colin Crane
Agnes Laurent . . . . Madeleine Lefarge
Raymond Huntley . . . . . . Rev Edwin Peake
Thorley Walters . . . . Col Edmonds
Edith Sharpe . . . . Matron
Athene Seyler. . . . . Beatrice Peake
Kenneth Griffith. . . . . Mr Meade
Paul Sheridan . . . . Fraguier
COMEDY Public school headmaster
believes French teacher loved by his son
is his own bastard daughter.

SEP

12839
PICCADILLY THIRD STOP (90) (A)
Ethiro (RFD)
P: Norman Williams
D: Wolf Rilla
S: Leigh Vance
Terence Morgan . . . . Dominic Colpoys-Owen

Yoko Tani . . . . Seraphina Yokami
Mai Zetterling . . . . Christine Preedy
William Hartnell . . . . Colonel
John Crawford . . . . Joe Preedy
Dennis Price . . . . Edward
Ann Lynn . . . . Mouse
Charles Kay . . . . Toddy
Douglas Robinson . . . . . . Albert
Gillian Maude . . . . Mother
CRIME Playboy's gang rob Eastern
embassy by breaking through old underground
station.

12840
THERE WAS A CROOKED MAN (107) (U)
Knightsbridge (UA) *reissue:* 1961
P: Albert Fennell, John Bryan
D: Stuart Burge
S: (STORY) James Bridie
(THE ODD LEGEND OF SCHULTZ)
SC: Reuben Ship
Norman Wisdom . . . . Davy Cooper
Alfred Marks . . . . Adolf Carter
Andrew Cruickshank . . . . . Mayor McKillip
Reginald Beckwith . . . . Mr Foster
Susannah York . . . . Ellen Foster
Ronald Fraser . . . . Gen Cummings
Timothy Bateson . . . . Flash Dan
Brian Oulton . . . . Ashton
Redmond Phillips . . . . Padre
Percy Herbert . . . . Green
COMEDY Ex-safecracker's gang poses
as US Army to thwart mayor's share swindle.

12841
THE CRIMINAL (97) (X) USA: THE CON-
CRETE JUNGLE
Merton Park (AA)
P: Jack Greenwood
D: Joseph Losey
S: Jimmy Sangster
SC: Alun Owen
Stanley Baker . . . . Johnny Bannion
Margit Saad . . . . Suzanne
Sam Wanamaker . . . . Mike Carter
Gregoire Aslan . . . . Frank Saffron
Jill Bennett . . . . Maggie
Laurence Naismith . . . . Town
Noel Willman . . . . Governor
Patrick Magee . . . . Barrows
Edward Judd . . . .
Derek Francis . . . . Priest
Kenneth J. Warren . . . . Clobber
Patrick Wymark . . . . Sol
Rupert Davies . . . . Edwards
CRIME Gang help jailed leader escape
to locate buried loot.

12842
WATCH YOUR STERN (88) (U)
GHW Productions (AA)
P: Peter Rogers
D: Gerald Thomas
S: (PLAY) Earle Couttie (SOMETHING ABOUT
A SAILOR)
SC: Alan Hackney, Vivian A. Cox
Kenneth Connor . . . . O/S Blissworth
Eric Barker . . . . Capt David Foster
Leslie Phillips . . . . . . Lt/Cdr Bill Fanshawe
Joan Sims . . . . Ann Foster
Noel Purcell . . . . Admiral Pettigrew
Hattie Jacques . . . . Agatha Potter
Sidney James . . . . CPO Mundy
Spike Milligan . . . . Dockyard Matey
Eric Sykes . . . . Dockyard Matey
David Lodge . . . . Sgt
Victor Maddern . . . . Sailor
COMEDY Steward fools admiral by posing
as inventor of homing torpedo.

12843
CLUE OF THE TWISTED CANDLE (61) (U)
Merton Park (AA)
P: Jack Greenwood
D: Allan Davis
S: (NOVEL) Edgar Wallace
SC: Philip Mackie
Bernard Lee . . . . Supt Meredith
David Knight . . . . Lexman/Griswold
Colette Wilde . . . . Grace
Francis de Wolff . . . . Karadis
Richard Caldicott . . . . Fisher
Stanley Morgan . . . . Anson
Richard Vernon . . . . Viney
Gladys Henson . . . . Landlady
Christine Shaw . . . . Belinda Holland
CRIME Supt proves framed man broke jail
to kill Greek blackmailer.

12844
FOXHOLE IN CAIRO (80) (A)
Omnia (Britannia)
P: Steven Pallos, Donald Taylor
D: John Moxey
S: (NOVEL) Leonard Moseley
(THE CAT AND THE MICE)
SC: Leonard Moseley, Donald Taylor
James Robertson Justice . . Capt Robertson
Adrian Hoven . . . . John Eppler
Gloria Mestre . . . . Amina
Albert Lieven . . . . Rommel
Nial MacGinnis . . . . Radek
Robert Urquhart . . . . Maj Wilson
Peter Van Eyck . . . . Count Almaszy
Niall MacGinnis . . . . Radek
Fenella Fielding . . . . Yvette
John Westbrook . . . . Roger
Lee Montague . . . . Aberle
Henry Oscar . . . . Col Zeltinger
Howard Marion Crawford . . . . Major
WAR Cairo. Captain foils German spy
and saves Jewish underground girl.

12845
THE CITY OF THE DEAD (78) (X)
USA: HORROR HOTEL
Vulcan (Britannia) *reissue:* 1964 (RFI)
P: Donald Taylor, Milton Subotsky
D: John Moxey
S: Milton Subotsky
SC: George Baxt
Christopher Lee . . . . Prof Driscoll
Dennis Lotis . . . . Richard Barlow
Betta StJohn . . . . Patricia Russell
Patricia Jessel . . . . Elizabeth Selwyn
Venetia Stevenson . . . . Nan Barlow
Valentine Dyall . . . . Jethrow Keane
Norman MacOwan . . . . Rev Russell
Tom Naylor . . . . Bill Maitland
HORROR Massachusetts. Girl student
sacrificed by 250-year old witch.

12846
OCTOBER MOTH (54) (A)
Independent Artists (RFD)
P: Arthur Alcott
D:S: John Kruse
Lee Patterson . . . . Finlay
Lana Morris . . . . Molly
Peter Dyneley . . . . Tom
Robert Cawdron . . . . PC
Sheila Raynor . . . . The Woman
DRAMA Farm girl tries to convince mad
brother that crashed motorist is not
their dead mother.

12847
THE SIEGE OF SIDNEY STREET (94) *scope*
(A)
Mid-Century (RFI)

P: Robert S.Baker, Monty Berman
D: Robert S.Baker
S: Jimmy Sangster, Alexander Baron
Donald Sinden . . . . Insp Mannering
Nicole Berger . . . . Sara
Kieron Moore . . . . Yaska
Peter Wyngarde . . . . Peter the Painter
Godfrey Quigley . . . . Blakey
Leonard Sachs . . . . Svaars
Tutte Lemkow . . . . Dmitrieff
George Pastell . . . . Brodsky
Angela Newman . . . . Nina
Jimmy Sangster . . . . . . Winston Churchill
CRIME 1911. Inspector poses as crook to
catch anarchist gang.

OCT

12848
SURPRISE PACKAGE (99) (U)
Donen Enterprises (Col)
P:D: Stanley Donen
S: (NOVEL) Art Buchwald
(A GIFT FROM THE BOYS)
SC: Harry Kurnitz
Yul Brynner . . . . Nico March
Mitzi Gaynor . . . . Gabby Rogers
Noel Coward . . . . King Pavel
Bill Nagy . . . . Johnny Stettina
Eric Pohlmann . . . . Stefan Miralis
George Coulouris . . . . Dr Hugo Panzer
Mân Mountain Dean . . . . . Igor Trofim
Warren Mitchell . . . . Kilmasis
Guy Deghy . . . . Tibor Smolny
Lyndon Brook . . . . Stavrin
COMEDY Greek island. Deported American
crime boss tries to steal exiled king's
crown jewels.

12849
NOT A HOPE IN HELL (77) (U)
Parkside (Archway)
P: Roger Proudlock
D: Maclean Rogers
S: Raymond Drewe
Richard Murcoch . . . . Bertie
Sandra Dorne . . . . Diana Melton
Jon Pertwee . . . . Dan
Judith Furze . . . . Miss Applejohn
Tim Turner . . . . Cy Hallam
Humphrey Lestocq . . . . . . Cricklegate
Claude Hulbert . . . . PC Salter
Stuart Saunders . . . . Bulstrode
Zoreen Ismael . . . . Jean
COMEDY Female customs officer, US excise
agent and TV star try to catch smugglers
at seaside village.

12850
TOO HOT TO HANDLE (100) *eastman* (X)
Wigmore (WPD)
P: Selim Cattan, Ronald Rietti
D: Terence Young
S: Harry Lee
SC: Herbert Kretzmer
Jayne Mansfield . . . . Midnight Franklin
Leo Genn . . . . Johnny Solo
Carl Boehm . . . . Robert Jouvel
Danik Patisson . . . . Lilliane Decker
Christopher Lee . . . . Novak
Kai Fischer . . . . Cynthia
Patrick Holt . . . . Insp West
Martin Boddey . . . . Mr Arpels
Sheldon Lawrence . . . . . . .Diamonds Dinelli
Barbara Windsor . . . . Ponytail
Tom Bowman . . . . Flash Gordon
CRIME Blackmailed owner of Soho strip
club involved in death of German refugee
stripper.

12851
BEAT GIRL (85) (X)
Willoughby (Renown)
P: George Willoughby
D: Edmond T. Greville
S: Dail Ambler
David Farrar . . . . Paul Linden
Noelle Adam . . . . Nichole Linden
Christopher Lee . . . . Kenny
Adam Faith . . . . Dave
Gillian Hills . . . . Jennifer Linden
Shirley Ann Field . . . . Dodo
Peter McEnery . . . . Tony
Claire Gordon . . . . Honey
Nigel Green . . . . Simon
DRAMA Architect's teenage daughter
becomes stripper after learning her mother's
past.

12852
CROSSROADS TO CRIME (57) (U)
AP Films (AA)
P: Gerry Anderson, John Read
D: Gerry Anderson
S: Alun Falconer
Anthony Oliver . . . . Don Ross
Patricia Heneghan . . . . Joan Ross
Miriam Karlin . . . . Connie Williams
George Murcell . . . . Diamond
Ferdy Mayne . . . . Miles
David Graham . . . . Johnny
Arthur Rigby . . . . Sgt Pearson
Victor Maddern . . . . Len
CRIME Policeman pretends to take bribe
to catch lorry hijackers.

12853
THE TWO FACES OF DR JEKYLL (88)
tech/scope (X) USA: HOUSE OF FRIGHT
Hammer (Col)
P: Michael Carreras
D: Terence Fisher
S: (NOVEL) Robert Louis Stevenson
(DR JEKYLL AND MR HYDE)
SC: Wolf Mankowitz
Paul Massie . . . . Henry Jekyll
Dawn Addams . . . . Kitty Jekyll
Christopher Lee . . . . Paul Allen
David Kossoff . . . . Ernest Litauer
France de Wolff . . . . Inspector
Norma Marla . . . . Maria
Joy Webster . . . . Sphinx Girl
Magda Miller . . . . Sphinx Girl
William Kendall . . . . Clubman
Joe Robinson . . . . Corinthian
HORROR 1874. Old doctor discovers
drug that changes him into murderous
young sadist.

12854
THE UNSTOPPABLE MAN (68) (U)
Argo (AA)
P: Jack Lamont, John Pellatt
D: Terry Bishop
S: (NOVEL) Michael Gilbert
(AMATEUR IN VIOLENCE)
SC: Alun Falconer, P. Manning O'Brine
Terry Bishop
Cameron Mitchell . . . . James Kennedy
Marius Goring . . . . Insp Hazelrigg
Harry H. Corbett . . . . Feist
Lois Maxwell . . . . Helen Kennedy
Denis Gilmore . . . . Jimmy Kennedy
Humphrey Lestocq . . . . Sgt Plummer
Ann Sears . . . . Pat Delaney
Timothy Bateson . . . . Rocky
Kenneth Cope . . . . Benny
Tony Hawes . . . . TV Interviewer
CRIME American industrialist saves
kidnapped son without police help.

12855
THE MILLIONAIRESS (90) *eastman/scope* (U)
Anatole de Grunwald (20)
P: Dmitri de Grunwald, Pierre Rouve
D: Anthony Asquith
S: (PLAY) George Bernard Shaw
SC: Wolf Mankowitz, Riccardo Aragno
Sophia Loren . . . . Epifania Parerga
Peter Sellers . . . . . Dr Ahmed el Kabir/Parerga
Alastair Sim . . . . Julius Sagamore
Vittorio de Sica . . . . Joe
Dennis Price . . . . Dr Adrian Bland
Gary Raymond . . . . Alastair
Alfie Bass . . . , ... Fish Curer
Miriam Karlin . . . . Maria
Noel Purcell . . . . Professor
Virginia Vernon . . . . Polly Smith
Pauline Jameson . . . . . . Muriel Pilkington
COMEDY Millionairess cannot marry Indian
doctor until she has earned a living for three
months.

12856
THE GENTLE TRAP (59) (A)
Butcher's Films
P: Jack Parsons
D: Charles Saunders
S: Guido Coen
SC: Brock Williams, Alan Osborne
Spencer Teakle . . . . Johnny Ryan
Felicity Young . . . . Jean
Dorinda Stevens . . . . Mary
Martin Benson . . . . Ricky Barnes
Dawn Brooks . . . . Sylvia
Alan Edwards . . . . Al Jenkins
Hugh Latimer . . . . Vic Carter
CRIME Girl helps thief hide from nightclub
owner and police.

NOV

12857
SATURDAY NIGHT AND SUNDAY MORNING
(89) (X)
Woodfall (Bry)
P: Harry Saltzman, Tony Richardson
D: Karel Reisz
S: (NOVEL) Alan Sillitoe
SC: Alan Sillitoe
Albert Finney . . . . Arthur Seaton
Shirley Anne Field . . . . . . Doreen Gretton
Rachel Roberts . . . . Brenda
Hylda Baker . . . . Aunt Ada
Norman Rossington . . . . . . Bert
Bryan Pringle . . . . Jack
Edna Morris . . . . Mrs Bull
Avis Bunnage . . . . Woman
Frank Pettitt . . . . Mr Seaton
Elsie Wagstaffe . . . . Mrs Seaton
Robert Cawdron . . . . Robboe
Colin Blakeley . . . . Loudmouth
DRAMA Nottingham. Factory hand
impregnates workmate's wife, seduces
girl, and decides to marry her. (BFA 1960:
Best British Film, Best Actress).

12858
THE SPIDER'S WEB (89) (U) *tech*
Danziger (UA)
P: Edward J & Harry Lee Danziger
D: Godfrey Grayson
S: (PLAY) Agatha Christie
SC: Albert G. Miller, Eldon Howard
Glynis Johns . . . . . Clarissa Hailsham-Brown
John Justin . . . . . Henry Hailsham-Brown
Jack Hulbert . . . . Sir Rowland Delahaye
Cicely Courtneidge . . . . . . Miss Peake
Ronald Howard . . . . Jeremy
David Nixon . . . . Elgin
Wendy Turner . . . . Pippa

Basil Dignam . . . . Hugo
Joan Sterndale-Bennett . . . Mrs Elgin
Ferdy Mayne . . . . Oliver
Peter Butterworth . . . . . . Insp Lord
CRIME Guardian helps diplomat's wife
hide corpse of step-daughter's father.

12859
THE NIGHT WE GOT THE BIRD (82) (A)
Rix-Conyers (BL)
P: Brian Rix, Darcy Conyers
D: Darcy Conyers
S: (PLAY) Basil Thomas (THE LOVE BIRDS)
SC: Ray Cooney, Tony Hilton, Darcy Conyers
Brian Rix . . . . Bertie Skidmore
Dora Bryan . . . . Julie Skidmore
Ronald Shiner . . . . Cecil Gibson
Leo Franklyn . . . . Victor
Irene Handl . . . . Ma
Liz Fraser . . . . Fay
John Slater . . . . Wolfie Green
Reginald Beckwith . . . . Chippendale Charlie
Robertson Hare . . . . Dr Vincent
John le Mesurier . . . . Clerk
Terry Scott . . . . PC Lovejoy
Kynaston Reeves. . . . . Mr Warre-Monger
Vera Pearce . . . . Aunt
COMEDY Antiquary's search for wife's
first husband, reincarnated as parrot.

12860
LINDA (61) (A)
Independent Artists (Bryanston)
P: Arthur Alcott
D: Don Sharp
S: Bill MacIlwraith
Carol White . . . . Linda
Alan Rothwell . . . . Phil
Cavan Malone . . . . Chief
Edward Cast . . . . Vicar
Vivienne Lacey . . . . Rosie
Lois Dane . . . . Clara
Keith Faulkner . . . . Joe
DRAMA Jealous teenager helps tough's
gang fight rivals at church social.

12861
MAN IN THE MOON (99) (U)
Excalibur-AFM (RFD)
P: Michael Relph
D: Basil Dearden
S: Bryan Forbes, Michael Relph
Kenneth More . . . . William Blood
Shirley Anne Field . . . . Polly
Michael Hordern . . . . Dr Davidson
Charles Gray . . . . Leo
John Glyn-Jones . . . . Dr Wilmot
John Phillips . . . . Prof Stephens
Norman Bird . . . . Herbert
Noel Purcell . . . . Prospector
Bernard Horsfall . . . . Rex
Newton Blick . . . . Dr Hollis
Lionel Gamlin . . . . Doctor
COMEDY Healthy bachelor trained to be
first man to fly to moon, lands in Australia.

12862
MARRIAGE OF CONVENIENCE (58) (U)
Merton Park (AA)
P: Jack Greenwood
D: Clive Donner
S: (NOVEL) Edgar Wallace
(THE THREE OAK MYSTERY)
SC: Robert Stewart
John Cairney . . . . Larry Wilson
Harry H. Corbett . . . . . Insp Jock Bruce
Jennifer Daniel . . . . Barbara Blair
Russell Waters . . . . Sam Spencer
Trevor Maskell . . . . Sgt Collins
Trevor Reid . . . . Supt Carver

John Van Eyssen . . . . John Mandle
Moira Redmond . . . . Tina
Patricia Burke . . . . Woman
CRIME Robber breaks jail and finds
his ex-partner married to the inspector
who arrested him.

12863
VISA TO CANTON (75) *tech* (U) USA:
PASSPORT TO CHINA
Swallow-Hammer (Col)
P:D: Michael Carreras
S: Gordon Wellesley
Richard Basehart . . . . Don Benton
Lisa Gastoni . . . . Lola Sanchez
Athene Seyler . . . . Mao Tai Tai
Eric Pohlmann . . . . Ivano Kang
Marne Maitland . . . . Han Po
Bernard Cribbins . . . . Periera
Alan Gifford . . . . Orme
Bert Kwouk . . . . Jimmy
CRIME China. Girl helps American travel
agent clear his half-brother from charge
famed by communists.

12864
THE HOUSE IN MARSH ROAD (70) (A)
Eternal (GN)
P: Maurice J. Wilson
D: Montgomery Tully
S: (NOVEL) Laurence Meynell
SC: Maurice J. Wilson
Tony Wright . . . . David Linton
Patricia Dainton . . . . Jean Linton
Sandra Dorne . . . . Valerie Stockley
Derek Aylward . . . . Richard Foster
Sam Kydd . . . . Lumley
Llewellyn Rees . . . . Webster
Anita Sharp Bolster . . . . . . Mrs O'Brien
Roddy Hughes . . . . Daniels
Olive Sloane . . . . Mrs Morris
FANTASY Poltergeist stops book critic
and mistress from killing his wife.

12865
A CHRISTMAS CAROL (28) (U)
Alpha (AA)
P: D: Robert Hartford-Davis
S: (NOVEL) Charles Dickens
John Hayter
Stewart Brown
Gordon Mulholland
FANTASY Period. Old miser reformed
by ghosts of past and future.

12866
THE BATTLE OF NEW ORLEANS (3) (U)
Biographic (Connoisseur)
P:D: Bob Godfrey
S: (SONG) Jimmy Driftwood
SC: Bob Godfrey, Bruce Lacey, Joe McGrath
Bob Godfrey
Bruce Lacey
Joe McGrath
COMEDY Musicians fight slapstick battle
on mud flats to record by Lonnie Donegan.

12867
THE 3 WORLDS OF GULLIVER (98) (U)
eastman
Morningside (Col)
P: Charles Schneer
D: Jack Sher
S: (NOVEL) Jonathan Swift (GULLIVER'S
TRAVELS)
SC: Jack Sher, Arthur Ross
Kerwin Mathews . . . . . Dr Lemuel Gulliver
Jo Morrow . . . . Gwendolyn
June Thorburn . . . . Elizabeth
Lee Patterson . . . . Reldresal
Gregoire Aslan . . . . . . King Brobdingnag

Basil Sydney . . . . Emperor of Lilliput
Sherri Alberoni . . . . Glumdalclitch
Charles Lloyd Pack . . . . Makovan
Martin Benson . . . . Flimnap
Mary Ellis . . . . Queen Brobdingnag
Peter Bull. . . . . Lord Bermogg
FANTASY 18th C. Shipwrecked doctor's
adventures in lands inhabited by six-inch
people and forty-foot giants.

12868
ROCKETS IN THE DUNES (57) (U)
Anvil (CFF)
P: Ralph May
D: William C. Hammond
S: (NOVEL) Lois Lamplugh
SC: Gerard Bryant
Gena Yates . . . . Sandra
Heather Lyons . . . . Celia
Gordon Adam . . . . Bruce
James Luck. . . . . Ned
Peter Wood . . . . Andy
Christopher Witty . . . . Joey
Fiona Davie . . . . Betty
Hilary Mason . . . . Mrs Allen
John Lawrence . . . . Mr Allen
CHILDREN Devon. Village children scheme
to prevent army from holding manoeuvres
on their beach.

12869
CIRCLE OF DECEPTION (100) *scope* (A)
20th Century Fox
P: Tom Morahan
D: Jack Lee
S: (NOVEL) Alec Waugh
SC: Nigel Balchin, Robert Musel
Bradford Dillman . . . . Paul Raine
Suzy Parker . . . . Lucy Bowen
Harry Andrews . . . . Capt Rawson
Robert Stephens . . . . Capt Stein
John Welsh . . . . Maj Taylor
Paul Rogers . . . . Maj Spence
Duncan Lamont . . . . Ballard
Michael Ripper . . . . Chauvel
A.J.Brown . . . . Frank Bowen
Martin Boddey . . . . Henry Crow
Charles Lloyd Pack . . . . Lohman
Meier Tzelniker . . . . Barman
WAR 1944. Agent trained and sent to help
Maquis not knowing his information is false
to mislead the enemy.

DEC
12870
NO KIDDING (86) (U) USA: BEWARE OF
CHILDREN
GHW Productions (AA)
P: Peter Rogers
D: Gerald Thomas
S: (NOVEL) Verily Anderson
(BEWARE OF CHILDREN)
SC: Norman Hudis, Robin Estridge
Leslie Phillips . . . . David Robinson
Geraldine McEwan . . . Catherine Robinson
Julia Lockwood . . . . Vanilla
Noel Purcell . . . . Tandy
Irene Handl . . . . Mrs Spicer
Joan Hickson . . . . Cook
June Jago . . . . Matron
Cyril Raymond . . . . Col Matthews
Esma Cannon . . . . District Nurse
Alan Gifford . . . . Edgar Treadgold
Sydney Tafler . . . . Rockbottom
Eric Pohlmann . . . . King
Patricia Jessel . . . . Queen
Joy Shelton . . . . Mrs Rockbottom
Christopher Witty . . . . Richard Robinson
Martin Stephens . . . . Angus

COMEDY Couple inherit old house and
turn it into holiday home for deprived
children of the rich.

12871
THE MAN WHO WAS NOBODY (58) (U)
Merton Park (AA)
P: Jack Greenwood
D: Montgomery Tully
S: (NOVEL) Edgar Wallace
SC: James Eastwood
Hazel Court . . . . Marjorie Stedman
John Crawford . . . South Africa Smith
Lisa Daniely . . . . Alma Weston
Paul Eddington . . . . Franz Reuter
Robert Dorning . . . . Vance
Kevin Stoney . . . . Joe
Jack Watson . . . . Inspector
Vanda Godsell . . . . Mrs Ferber
CRIME Girl tec helps man unmask gambler
as killer of jewel-thief brother.

12872
THE MALPAS MYSTERY (69) (U)
Independent Artists-Langton (AA)
P: Julian Wintle, Leslie Parkyn
D: Sidney Hayers
S: (NOVEL) Edgar Wallace
(FACE IN THE NIGHT)
SC: Paul Tabori, Gordon Wellesley
Maureen Swanson . . . . Audrey Bedford
Allan Cuthbertson . . . . Lacy Marshall
Geoffrey Keen . . . . Torrington
Sandra Dorne . . . . Dora
Ronald Howard . . . . Insp Dick Shannon
Alan Tilvern . . . . Gordon Seager
Leslie French . . . . Wilkins
Catherine Feller . . . . Ginette
CRIME Mistress of "faceless" crook poses
as long-lost daughter of rich ex-convict.

12873
EVIDENCE IN CONCRETE (30) (U)
Merton Park (AA)
P: Jack Greenwood
D: Gordon Hales
S: James Eastwood
N: Edgar Lustgarten
Russell Napier . . . . Supt Duggan
Howard Pays . . . .
Jill Hyem . . . .
Derek Sydney . . . .
CRIME Police connect girl's death with
hijacking of whiskey lorry.

12874
SUSPECT (81) (A)
Charter (BL)
P: John Boulting
D: Roy Boulting
S: (NOVEL) Nigel Balchin
SC: Nigel Balchin, Roy Boulting, Jeffrey Dell
Tony Britton . . . . Bob Marriott
Peter Cushing . . . . Prof Sewell
Virginia Maskell . . . . Lucy Byrne
Ian Bannen . . . . Alan Andrews
Raymond Huntley . . . . . . Sir George Gatling
Donald Pleasence . . . . Brown
Thorley Walters . . . . Mr Prince
Kenneth Griffith . . . . Dr Schole
Spike Milligan . . . . Arthur
DRAMA Foreign agents almost trick
scientist into publishing his plague researches
against orders.

12875
THE PURE HELL OF ST TRINIAN'S (94) (U)
Vale-Tudor (BL)
P: Frank Launder, Sidney Gilliat
D: Frank Launder.
S: (CARTOONS) Ronald Searle

SC: Frank Launder, Sidney Gilliat, Val
Valentine
Cecil Parker . . . . Prof Canford
George Cole . . . . Flash Harry
Joyce Grenfell . . . . Sgt Ruby Gates
Eric Barker . . . . Culpepper-Brown
Thorley Walters . . . . Butters
Irene Handl . . . . Miss Harker-Packer
Dennis Price . . . . Gore-Blackwood
Sidney James . . . . Alphonse O'Reilly
Liz Fraser . . . . Miss Partridge
Lloyd Lamble . . . . Supt Kemp-Bird
Nicholas Phipps . . . . Major
Raymond Huntley . . . . Judge
Elwyn Brook-Jones . . . . . . Emir
John le Mesurier . . . . Minister
Lisa Lee . . . . Miss Brenner
COMEDY Crooked schoolteacher sells
sixth-form girls to Baghdad Emir.

12876
SWORD OF SHERWOOD FOREST (80)
tech/scope (U)
Hammer-Yeoman (Col)
P: Richard Greene, Sidney Cole
D: Terence Fisher
S: Alan Hackney
Richard Greene . . . . Robin Hood
Peter Cushing . . . . Sheriff of Nottingham
Niall MacGinnis . . . . Friar Tuck
Richard Pasco . . . . Earl of Newark
Jack Gwillim . . . . Archbishop Hubert
Sarah Branch . . . . . Lady Marian Fitzwater
Dennis Lotis . . . . Alan-a-Dale
Nigel Green . . . . Little John
Vanda Godsell . . . . Prioress
Derren Nesbitt . . . . Martin
Oliver Reed . . . . Melton
ADVANTURE Period. Outlaw thwarts
sheriff's plot to overthrow Archbishop of
Canterbury.

12877
FEET OF CLAY (55)
Danziger (UA)
P: Brian Taylor
D: Frank Marshall
S: Mark Grantham
Vincent Ball . . . . David Kyle
Wendy Williams . . . . Fay
Hilda Fenemore . . . . Mrs Clarke
Robert Cawdron . . . . Saunders
Brian Smith . . . . Jimmy
Angela Douglas . . . . Diana
Jack Melford . . . . Soames
CRIME Solicitor unmasks probation officer
behind dope ring.

12878
A TASTE OF MONEY (71) *tech*
Danziger (UA)
P: Brian Taylor
D: Max Varnel
S: Mark Grantham
Jean Cadell . . . . Miss Brill
Dick Emery . . . . Morrissey
Pete Murray . . . . Dave
Ralph Michael . . . . Supt White
Donald Eccles . . . . Joe
C. Denier Warren . . . . Tyler
Robert Raglan . . . . Simpson
Christina Gregg . . . . Ruth White
COMEDY Retiring cashier organises gang to
rob her insurance firm.

12879
COMPELLED (56)
Danziger (UA)
P: Brian Taylor
D: Ramsey Herrington

S: Mark Grantham
Ronald Howard . . . . Paul Adams
Beth Rogan . . . . Carol
John Gabriel . . . . Fenton
Richard Shaw . . . . Jug
Jack Melford . . . . Grimes
Mark Singleton . . . . Derek
Colin Tapley . . . . Inspector
CRIME Ex-convict engineer blackmailed into
helping jewel robbers.

12880
THE BULLDOG BREED (98)
Rank (RFD)
P: Hugh Stewart
D: Robert Asher
S: Jack Davies
SC: Jack Davies, Henry Blyth, Norman Wisdom
Norman Wisdom . . . . Norman Puckle
Ian Hunter . . . . Admiral Blyth
David Lodge . . . . CPO Knowles
Robert Urquhart . . . . Cdr Clayton
Edward Chapman . . . . Philpotts
Eddie Byrne . . . . PO Filkins
Peter Jones . . . . Instructor
Liz Fraser . . . . Naafi Girl
John le Mesurier . . . . Prosecution
Terence Alexander . . . . Defence
Sydney Tafler . . . . Owner
COMEDY Love-crossed sailor, trained to be first
first man to fly to moon, lands on Pacific isle.

12881
THE WORLD OF SUZIE WONG (126) tech (A)
Paramount British
P: Ray Stark, Hugh Perceval
D: Richard Quine
S: (NOVEL) Richard Mason
(PLAY) Paul Osborn
SC: John Patrick
William Holden . . . . Robert Lomax
Nancy Kwan . . . . Suzie Wong
Sylvia Syms . . . . Kay O'Neill
Michael Wilding . . . . Ben
Laurence Naismith . . . . O'Neill
Jacqui Chan . . . . Gwenny Lee
Yvonne Shima . . . . Minnie Ho
Andy Ho . . . . Ah Tong
Bernard Cribbins . . . . Otis
Lionel Blair . . . . Dancer
ROMANCE Hong Kong. Poor American
artist lives with Chinese prostitute and her baby.

12882
THE HANDS OF ORLAC (95) (A) bilingual
Pendennis—Riviera International (Britannia)
P: Steven Pallos, Fonald Taylor
D: Edmond T. Greville
S: (NOVEL) Maurice Renard
(LES MAINS D'ORLAC)
SC: John Baines, Edmond T. Greville,
Donald Taylor
Mel Ferrer . . . . Steven Orlac
Christopher Lee . . . . Nero
Dany Carrel . . . . Li-Lang
Lucile Saint-Simon . . . . Louise Cochrane
Donald Wolfit . . . . Prof Volcheff
Donald Pleasence . . . . Coates
Felix Aylmer . . . . Dr Cochrane
Basil Sydney . . . . Seidleman
Peter Reynolds . . . . Felix
Campbell Singer . . . . Insp Henderson
Mireille Perrey . . . . Mme Aliberti
HORROR France. Pianist thinks he is
possessed when a strangler's hands are grafted
on to his arms.

12883
HAND IN HAND (78) (U)
Helen Winston (WPD)
P: Helen Winston
D: Philip Leacock
S: Sidney Harmon, Leopold Atlas
SC: Diana Morgan
John Gregson . . . . Father Timothy
Sybil Thorndike . . . . Lady Caroline
Finlay Currie . . . . Mr Pritchard
Loretta Parry . . . . Rachel Mathias
Philip Needs . . . . Michael O'Malley
Miriam Karlin . . . . Mrs Mathias
Derek Sydney . . . . Mr Mathias
Kathleen Byron . . . . Mrs O'Malley
Martin Laurence . . . . Cantor
DRAMA Jewish girl and Roman Catholic boy
visit each other's churches.

12884
ESCORT FOR HIRE (66) tech (A)
Danziger (MGM)
P: Brian Taylor
D: Godfrey Grayson
S: Mark Grantham
June Thorburn . . . . Terry
Peter Murray . . . . Buzz
Noel Trevarthan . . . . Steve
Jan Holden . . . . Elizabeth

Peter Butterworth . . . . Insp Bruce
Mary Laura Wood . . . . Barbara
Derek Blomfield . . . . Jack
Jill Melford . . . . Nadia
Patricia Plunkett . . . . Eldon Baker
Guy Middleton . . . . Arthur
CRIME Unemployed actor turns escort and is
framed for death of rich client.

12885
A STORY OF DAVID (104) eastman (U)
Scoton—Mardeb (BL)
P: George Pitcher
D: Bob McNaught
S: Gerry Day, Terence Maple
Jeff Chandler . . . . David
Basil Sydney . . . . Saul
Peter Arne . . . . Doeg
David Knight . . . . Johnathan
Barbara Shelley . . . . Abigail
Donald Pleasence . . . . Nabal
Robert Brown . . . . Jashobeam
Richard O'Sullivan . . . . Abiathar
David Davies . . . . Abner
Martin Wyldeck . . . . Hezro
John van Eyssen . . . . Joab
Angela Browne . . . . Michal
Zena Marshall . . . . Naomi
Charles Carson . . . . Ahimelech
HISTORY Jealous King's son helps outlawed
shepherd fight Philistines.

12886
THE TELL—TALE HEART (78) (X)
Danziger (WPD) reissue: 1972
P: Brian Taylor
D: Ernest Morris
S: (STORY) Edgar Allan Poe
SC: Brian Clemens, Eldon Howard
Laurence Payne . . . . .Edgar Allan Poe
Adrienne Corri . . . . Betty Clare
Dermot Walsh . . . . Carl Loomis
Selma Vas Diaz . . . . Mrs Vine
John Scott . . . . Inspector
John Martin . . . . Sgt
Annette Carell . . . . Landlady
Yvonne Buckingham . . . . . . Mina
HORROR Paris, 1840. Author dreams he kills
his rival for a florist and is driven mad by his
heartbeat.

1961

JAN

12887
TICKET TO PARADISE (61) (U)
Bayford Films (Eros)
P: Charles A. Leeds, Francis Searle
D: Francis Searle
S: Max Kester
SC: Brock Williams

Emrys Jones	Jack Watson
Patricia Dainton	Mary Rillston
Vanda Hudson	Gina
Denis Shaw	Giuseppe
Claire Gordon	Sybil
Maureen Davis	Betty
Raymond Rollett	Higginbottom

ROMANCE Italy. Travel agent and tourist fall in love, each thinking the other is rich.

12888
HIS AND HERS (90) (U)
Sabre (Eros)
P: Hal E. Chester, John D. Merriman
D: Brian Desmond Hurst
S: Jan & Mark Lowell
SC: Stanley Mann

Terry-Thomas	Reggie Blake
Janette Scott	Fran Blake
Wilfrid Hyde White	Charles Dunton
Nicole Maurey	Simone Rolfe
Kenneth Connor	Harold
Joan Sims	Hortense
Colin Gordon	Announcer
Kenneth Williams	PC
Meier Tzelniker	Felix McGregor
Joan Hickson	Phoebe
Oliver Reed	Poet
Dorinda Stevens	Dora

COMEDY Bedouin influence on travel writer upsets his wife and publisher.

12889
THE SINGER NOT THE SONG (132)
colour/scope (U)
Rank (RFD)
P: Roy Baker, Jack Hanbury
D: Roy Baker
S: (NOVEL) Audrey Erskine Lindop
SC: Nigel Balchin

Dirk Bogarde	Anacleto Comachi
John Mills	Father Keogh
Mylene Demongeot	Locha
Laurence Naismith	Old Uncle
John Bentley	Police Capt
Leslie French	Father Gomez
Eric Pohlmann	Presidente
Nyall Florenz	Vito
Roger Delgardo	De Cortinez
Laurence Payne	Pablo
Lee Montague	Pepe

WESTERN Mexico. Bandit kills villagers alphabetically to spite an Irish priest who loves landowner's daughter.

12890
THE GIRL ON THE BOAT (91) (U)
Knightsbridge (UA)
P: John Bryan
D: Henry Kaplan
S: (NOVEL) P.G. Wodehouse
SC: Reuben Ship

Norman Wisdom	Sam
Millicent Martin	Billie Bennett
Richard Briers	Eustace Hignett
Sheila Hancock	Jane
Bernard Cribbins	Peters
Athene Seyler	Mrs Hignett
Philip Locke	Bream Mortimer
Noel Willman	Webster

Ronald Fraser	Colonel
Reginald Beckwith	Barman
Timothy Bateson	Purser
Dick Bentley	American
Peter Bull	Blacksmith

COMEDY 1920. Lecturer's nephew rents her cottage to his cousin's ex-fiancee.

12891
NO LOVE FOR JOHNNIE (111) scope (X)
Five Star (RFD)
P: Betty E. Box
D: Ralph Thomas
S: (NOVEL) Wilfred Feinburgh
SC: Nicholas Phipps, Mordecai Richler

Peter Finch	Johnnie Byrne
Stanley Holloway	Fred Andrews
Mary Peach	Pauline West
Donald Pleasence	Roger Renfrew
Billie Whitelaw	Mary
Dennis Price	Flagg
Hugh Burden	Tim Maxwell
Rosalie Crutchley	Alice Byrne
Michael Goodliffe	Dr.West
Mervyn Johns	Charlie Young
Geoffrey Keen	Prime Minister
Paul Rogers	Sydney Johnson
Peter Barkworth	Henderson
Fenella Fielding	Sheilah
Gladys Henson	Constituent

DRAMA Labour MP is deserted by his communist wife and falls for young model.
(BFA 1961: Best Actor)

12892
ECHO OF BARBARA (58) (A)
Independent Artists (RFD)
P: Arthur Alcott
D: Sidney Hayers
S: (NOVEL) Jonathan Burke
SC: John Kruse

Mervyn Johns	Sam Roscoe
Maureen Connell	Paula Brown
Paul Stassino	Caledonia
Ronald Hines	Mike Roscoe
Tom Bell	Ben
Brian Peck	Ted
Eddie Leslie	Aide
Beatrice Varley	Mrs Roscoe

CRIME Wastrell has stripper pose as his sister to wrest hidden loot from his ex-convict father.

12893
THE SUNDOWNERS (124) tech (U)
Warner Brothers (WPD)
P: Gerry Blattner
D: Fred Zinnemann
S: (NOVEL) Jon Cleary
SC: Isobel Lennart

Deborah Kerr	Ida Carmody
Robert Mitchum	Paddy Carmody
Peter Ustinov	Venneker
Glynis Johns	Mrs Firth
Dina Merrill	Jean Halstead
Chips Rafferty	Quinlan
Michael Anderson jr	Sean Carmody
Lola Brooks	Liz
Wylie Watson	Herb Johnson
John Meillon	Bluey
Ronald Fraser	Ocker
Ewen Solon	Halstead
Dick Bentley	Evan Evans
Mervyn Johns	Jack Patchogue

ADVENTURE Australia, 1920. Itinerant sheep drover resists his wife's pressure to settle down.

12894
THE TRUNK (72) (A)
Donwin (Col)
P: Lawrence Huntington

D:SC: Donovan Winter	
S: Edward & Valerie Abraham	
Phil Carey	Stephen Dorning
Julia Arnall	Lisa Maitland
Dermot Walsh	Henry Maitland
Vera Day	Diane
Peter Swanwick	Nicholas Steiner
John Atkinson	Matt
Betty le Beau	Maria
Tony Quinn	Porter

CRIME Blackmailer frames girl for murder of her husband's mistress.

12895
OFFBEAT (72) (A)
Northiam (BL)
P: E.M. Smedley Aston
D: Cliff Owen
S: Peter Barnes

William Sylvester	Steve Layton
Mai Zetterling	Ruth Lombard
Anthony Dawson	James Dawson
John Meillon	Johnny Remick
John Phillips	Supt Gault
Victor Brooks	Insp Adams
Joseph Furst	Paul Varna
Neil McCarthy	Leo Farrell
Ronald Adam	J.B. Wykeham

CRIME MI5 agent poses as bank robber to join gang of gem thieves and decides to stay crooked.

12896
THE LONG AND THE SHORT AND THE TALL (110) (X)
Michael Balcon (WPD)
P: Hal Mason
D: Leslie Norman
S: (PLAY) Willis Hall
SC: Willis Hall, Wolf Mankowitz

Richard Todd	Sgt Mitchem
Laurence Harvey	Pte Bamforth
Richard Harris	Cpl Johnstone
David McCallum	Pte Whittaker
Ronald Fraser	Cpl Macleish
John Meillon	Pte Smith
John Rees	Pte Evans
Kenji Takaki	Tojo

WAR Malaya. Loudmouthed private tries to prevent sonic warfare patrol from shooting captured Japanese soldier.

12897
SWISS FAMILY ROBINSON (126)
tech/scope (U) reissue: 1972
Walt Disney
P: William H. Anderson
D: Ken Annakin
S: (NOVEL) Johann Wyss
SC: Lowell S. Hawley

John Mills	Mr Robinson
Dorothy McGuire	Mrs Robinson
James MacArthur	Fritz Robinson
Janet Munro	Roberta
Sessue Hayakawa	Pirate Chief
Tommy Kirk	Ernst Robinson
Kevin Corcoran	Francis Robertson
Cecil Parker	Captain
Andy Ho	Pirate
Milton Reid	Pirate
Larry Taylor	Pirate

ADVENTURE Tobago, period. Shipwrecked emigrants save captain's grand-daughter from pirates.(Top Moneymaker: 1961)

12898
THE BREAKING POINT (59) (U)
Butcher's Films
P:SC: Peter Lambert
D: Lance Comfort

S':(NOVEL) Laurence Meynell
Peter Reynolds . . . . Eric Winlatter
Dermot Walsh . . . . Robert Wade
Joanna Dunham . . . . Cherry Winlatter
Lisa Gastoni . . . . Eva
Jack Allen . . . . Ernest Winlatter
Brian Cobby . . . . Peter de Savory
Arnold Diamond . . . . Telling
CRIME Printer's son turns traitor to help
communists stop shipment fo foreign currency.

12899
DOCTOR BLOOD'S COFFIN (91) *eastman* (X)
Caralan—Dador (UA)
P: David E. Rose, George Fowler
D: Sidney J. Furie
S: Jerry Juran
SC: James Kelly, Peter Miller
Kieron Moore . . . . Dr Peter Blood
Hazel Court . . . . Linda Parker
Ian Hunter . . . . Dr Blood
Kenneth C. Lawson . . . . . . Morton
Fred Johnson . . . . Tregaye
Paul Hardtmuth . . . . Professor
Paul Stockman . . . . Steve Parker
Andy Alston . . . . Beale
HORROR Cornwall. Doctor revives nurse's
dead husband by inserting living heart.

12900
THE FULL TREATMENT (109) *scope* (X)
Falcon—Hilary—Hammer (Col)
P: D: Val Guest
S: (NOVEL) Ronald Scott Thorne
SC: Val Guest, Ronald Scott Thorne
Claude Dauphin . . . . David Prade
Diane Cilento . . . . Denise Colby
Ronald Lewis . . . . Alan Colby
Francoise Rosay . . . . Mme Prade
Bernard Braden . . . . Harry Stonehouse
Katya Douglas . . . . Connie
Anne Tirard . . . . Nicole
Barbara Chilcott . . . . Baroness de la Vaillon
Edwin Styles . . . . Dr Roberts
George Merritt . . . . Dr Manfield
CRIME Riviera. Pscychiatrist makes racing
driver think he strangled his Italian wife.

12901
THE GRASS IS GREENER (104) *tech/scope* (A)
Grandon (UI)
P:D: Stanley Donen
S: (PLAY) Hugh & Margaret Williams
SC: Hugh & Margaret Williams
Cary Grant . . . . Victor Rhyall
Deborah Kerr . . . . Hilary Rhyall
Robert Mitchum . . . . Charles Delacro
Jean Simmons . . . . Hattie Durrant
Moray Watson . . . . Sellers
COMEDY Earl wins back his wife by contriving
duel with her millionaire lover.

12902
SHOOT TO KILL (64) (U)
Border (NR)
P: O. Negus Fancey
D:S: Michael Winner
Dermot Walsh . . . . Mike Roberts
Joy Webster . . . . Lee Fisher
John East . . . . Boris Altovitch
Frank Hawkins . . . . Neale Patterson
Zoreen Ismael . . . . Anna
Theodore Wilhelm . . . . Nicholi
Victor Beaumont . . . . Nauman
Ronald Adam . . . . Wood
CRIME Geneva. Reporters save atomic secrets
from communist agents.

12903
THE REBEL (105)tech(U)
ABPC (WPD)
P: W.A. Whittaker
D: Robert Day
S: Tony Hancock, Alan Simpson, Ray Galton
SC: Alan Simpson, Ray Galton
Tony Hancock . . . . Anthony Hancock
George Sanders . . . . Sir Charles Brouard
Paul Massie . . . . Paul
Margit Saad . . . . Margot Carreras
Gregoire Aslan . . . . Carreras
Dennis Price . . . . Jim Smith
Irene Handl . . . . Mrs Crevatte
Mervyn Johns . . . . Manager
John le Mesurier . . . . Office Manager
Liz Fraser . . . . Waitress
Nanette Newman . . . . Josey
Peter Bull . . . . Dubois
COMEDY Clerk goes to Paris to become painter
and achieves fame on another's work.

12904
THE MARK (127) *scope* (X)
Stross (20)
P: Sidney Buchman, Raymond Stross
D: Guy Green
S: (NOVEL) Charles Israel
SC: Sidney Buchman, Stanley Mann
Maria Schell . . . . Ruth
Stuart Whitman . . . . Jim Fuller
Rod Steiger . . . . Dr McNally
Brenda de Banzie . . . . Mrs Cartwright
Maurice Denham . . . . Arnold
Donald Wolfit . . . . Clive
Paul Rogers . . . . Milne
Donald Houston . . . . Austin
Amanda Black . . . . Janie
Russell Napier . . . . Inspector
Marie Devereux . . . . Ellen
CRIME Reporter exposes widow's lover as man
convicted of attempted sexual assault on small
girl.

12905
THE HELLFIRE CLUB (93) *eastman/scope* (A)
New World (RFI)
P: Robert S. Baker, Monty Berman
D: Robert S. Baker
S: Jimmy Sangster
SC: Jimmy Sangster, Leon Griffiths
Keith Michell . . . . Jason
Adrienne Corri . . . . Lady Isobel
Peter Arne . . . . Thomas
Kai Fischer . . . . Yvonne
Peter Cushing . . . . Merryweather
Bill Owen . . . . Martin
Miles Malleson . . . . Judge
David Lodge . . . . Timothy
Martin Stephens . . . . Jason (child)
Andrew Faulds . . . . Lord Netherden
Francis Matthews . . . . Sir Hugh
Jean Lodge . . . . Lady Netherden
Desmond Walter Ellis . . . . Lord Chorley
ADVENTURE 1752 Circus acrobat saves
childhood sweetheart and ousts usurping cousin

12906
KONGA (90) *eastman* (A)
Merton Park (AA)
P: Herman Cohen
D: John Lemont
S: Aben Kandel, Herman Cohen
Michael Gough . . . . Dr Charles Decker
Margo Johns . . . . Margaret
Jess Conrad . . . . Bob Kenton
Claire Gordon . . . . Sandra Banks

Austin Trevor . . . . Dean Foster
Jack Watson . . . . Supt Brown
George Pastell . . . . Prof Tagore
Vanda Godsell . . . . Mrs Kenton
Stanley Morgan . . . . Insp Lawson
Leonard Sachs . . . . Father
HORROR Botanist's serum from carnivorous
plant changes chimpanzee into giant gorilla.

12907
THE SILENT WEAPON (28) (U)
Merton Park (AA)
P: Jack Greenwood
D: Peter Duffell
S: James Eastwood
N: Edgar Lustgarten
Geoffrey Keen . . . . Supt Duggan
Stanley Morgan . . . . Sgt Dobbs
Norma Parnell . . . . Joan Drew
CRIME Actress and man dope greyhounds and
kill trainer with boomerang.

12908
THE CLUE OF THE NEW PIN (58) (U)
Merton Park (AA)
P: Jack Greenwood
D: Allan Davis
S: (NOVEL) Edgar Wallace
SC: Philip Mackie
Paul Daneman . . . . Rex Lander
Bernard Archard . . . . Supt Carver
James Villiers . . . . Tab Holland
Catherine Woodville . . . . . Jaen Ardfern
Clive Morton . . . . Ramsey Brown
Wolfe Morris . . . . Yeh Ling
David Horne . . . . John Trasmere
Leslie Sands . . . . Sgt Harris
Ruth Kettlewell . . . . Mrs Rushby
CRIME TV interviewer saves girl from man who
killed his rich uncle and blackmailer.

12909
THE GRAND JUNCTION CASE (30) (U)
Merton Park (AA)
P: Jack Greenwood
D: Peter Duffell
S: James Eastwood
N: Edgar Lustgarten
Russell Napier . . . . Supt Duggan
Howard Pays . . . .
Tommy Godfrey . . . . .
CRIME Supt travels to continent to solve death
of woman whose limbs were found in canal.

12910
FIVE GOLDEN HOURS (90) (U)
Anglofilm (Col)
P: Mario Zampi, Fabio Jegher
D: Mario Zampi
S: Hans Wilhelm
Ernie Kovaks . . . . Aldo Bondi
Cyd Charisse . . . . Baronessa Sandra
George Sanders . . . . Bing
Kay Hammond . . . . Martha
Dennis Price . . . . Raphael
Clelia Matania . . . . Rosalia
Reginald Beckwith . . . . . . Brother Geronimo
Finlay Currie . . . . Father Superior
Martin Benson . . . . Enrico
Ron Moody . . . . Gabriele
Sidney Tafler . . . . Alfredo
John le Mesurier . . . . Director
COMEDY Italy. Pall bearer uses time lapse
between Rome and New York to swindle rich
widows.

12911
DURING ONE NIGHT (80) (X)
Galaworldfilm (Gala)

P: Kenneth Rive, Sidney J. Furie
D:S: Sidney J. Furie
Don Borisenko	David
Susan Hampshire	Jean
Sean Sullivan	Major
Joy Webster	Prostitute
Graydon Gould	Mike
Tom Busby	Sam
Alan Gibson	Harry
Jackie Collins	Girl

DRAMA 1943. Country girl helps USAAF deserter discover his impotence is imaginary.

12912
FURY AT SMUGGLER'S BAY (96) (U)
eastman/scope
Mijo (RFI)
P: Joe Vegoda, Michael Green, John Gilling
D:S: John Gilling
Peter Cushing	Squire Trevenyan
John Fraser	Chris Trevenyan
Bernard Lee	Black John
Michele Mercier	Louise Lejeune
June Thorburn	Jenny Trevenyan
William Franklyn	Captain
Liz Fraser	Betty
Miles Malleson	Duke of Avon
George Coulouris	Francoise Lejeune
Katherine Kath	Mama
Jouma	Jouma

ADVENURE Cornwall, 1790. Squire's son joins highwayman against blackmailing smuggler.

12913
DOUBLE BUNK (92) (A)
Fanfare (Bry)
P: George H. Brown
D:S: C.M. Pennington-Richards
Ian Carmichael	Jack Goddard
Janette Scott	Peggy Deeley
Sidney James	Sid Randall
Liz Fraser	Sandra
Dennis Price	Leonard Watson
Noel Purcell	O'Malley
Naunton Wayne	Officer
Reginald Beckwith	Alfred Harper
Irene Handl	Mrs Harper
Miles Malleson	Rev Thomas
Gerald Campion	Charlie
Terry Scott	Policeman
Gladys Henson	Mme de Sola
Michael Shepley	Granville-Carter
Graham Stark	Flower Man

COMEDY Honeymooners in houseboat and rich yachtsman race from Calais.

12914
THE WIND OF CHANGE (64) (A)
Cresswell (Bry)
P: John Dark
D: Vernon Sewell
S: Alexander Dore, John McLaren
Donald Pleasence	Pop
Johnny Briggs	Frank
Ann Lynn	Josie
Hilda Fenemore	Gladys
Glyn Houston	Sgt Parker
Norman Gunn	Ron
Bunny May	Smithy
David Hemmings	Ginger

CRIME Teenager's gang beat Negro to death and slash his own sister.

12915
STRIP TEASE MURDER (66) (X)
Danziger (Par)
P: Ralph Ingram, John Elton
D: Ernest Morris
S: Paul Tabori

John Hewer	Bert Black
Ann Lynn	Rita
Jean Muir	Diana
Kenneth J. Warren	Branco
Carl Duering	Rocco
Michael Peake	Martin
Wanda Hudson	Angelina
Leon Cortez	Lou

CRIME Strip club compere proves his wife was electrocuted in mistake for crook's blackmailing girlfriend.

12916
THE DAY THE SKY FELL IN (15) (X)
Seven (Compton)
P:D: Barry Shawzin
S: (STORY) Frederic Brown
SC: Barry Shawzin, Bob Kesten
Roger Delgado	Dr. Niemand
Terence Knapp	Harry Niemann
John Stevenson Lang	Adam Martin

DRAMA Stranger pleads with scientist not to develop super weapon.

12917
DRUMS (22) (U)
Amity (Astral)
P: D: Hans G. Casparius
S: James McFarlan
Brian Dent	Mr. Fuller
Peter Tory	Paul Fuller
Jan Bullock	Doctor
Vicky Wolf	Nurse
Penny Pennyman	Penny

DRAMA Sick Drummer persuades son to abandon horn for the drums.

12918
ONE MORE RIVER (21) (U)
Brason & Hoy (Compton)
P: John Brason
N: Guy Kingsley Poynter
DRAMA Drunken idlers cheat sailor who helps them deliver boat to its owner.

12919
THE DAY (10) (U)
Finch Enterprises (Contemporary)
P:D:S: Peter Finch, Yolande Turner
Antonio	

DRAMA Ibiza. Boy travels to town to fetch father's relatives to see new baby.

12920
JOHAN SEBASTIAN BACH (28) (U)
Cross Channel
D: Philip Wrestler
Karel Stepanek	Johan Sebastian Bach
Geoffrey Hibbert	
Wallas Eaton	

HISTORY Composer influences King of Prussia's attitude to music.

12921
FREDERIC CHOPIN (29) (U)
Cross Channel
D: Philip Wrestler
Alan Wheatley	Frederic Chopin
Mary Ellis	
Rosalie Crutchley	
Ferdy Mayne	

HISTORY Majorca, 1838. Chopin and George Sand become involved with locals.

12922
PARTNERS IN CRIME (54) (U)
Merton Park (AA)
P: Jack Greenwood
D: Peter Duffell

S: (NOVEL) Edgar Wallace (THE MAN WHO KNEW)
SC: Robert Stewart
Bernard Lee	Insp Mann
John Van Eyssen	Merrill
Moira Redmond	Freda Strickland
Gordon Boyd	Rex Holland
Ernest Clark	Ashton
Ruth Meyers	Mary Nuttall
Stanley Morgan	Sgt Rutledge
Victor Platt	Harold Strickland Strickland
Richard Shaw	Bill Cross

CRIME Police trace gun to company director who paid employee to shoot his partner.

12923
CARRY ON REGARDLESS (93) (U)
GHW (AA)
P: Peter Rogers
D: Gerald Thomas
S: Norman Hudis
Sidney James	Bert Handy
Kenneth Connor	Sam Twist
Charles Hawtrey	Gabriel Dimple
Joan Sims	Lily Duveen
Kenneth Williams	Francis Courtenay
Bill Owen	Mike Weston
Liz Fraser	Delia King
Terence Longdon	Montgomery Infield-Hopping
Hattie Jacques	Sister
Esma Cannon	Miss Cooling
Sydney Tafler	Manager
Julia Arnall	Trudi Trelawney
Terence Alexander	Trevor Trelawney
Stanley Unwin	Himself
Joan Hickson	Matron
Fenella Fielding	Penny Panting
Jerry Desmonde	Martin Paul
Eric Pohlmann	Sinister Man
Freddie Mills	Lefty Vincent

COMEDY Episodic misadventures of "Helping Hands" agency.

12924
MR TOPAZE (97) *eastman/scope* (U)
USA: I LIKE MONEY
Anatole de Grunwald (20)
P: Pierre Rouve, Dimitri de Grunwald
D: Peter Sellers
S: (PLAY) Marcel Pagnol (TOPAZE)
SC: Pierre Rouve
Peter Sellers	Albert Topaze
Nadia Gray	Suzy Courtais
Herbert Lom	Castel Benac
Leo McKern	Muche
John Neville	Roger de Beauville Beauville
Martita Hunt	Baroness
Billie Whitelaw	Ere
Michael Gough	Tamise
Joan Sims	Colette
John le Measurier	Blackmailer
Pauline Shepherd	Lilette
Michael Sellers	Gaston

COMEDY France. Poor teacher, sacked for honesty, becomes rich crook.

12925
RAG DOLL (67) (A)
Blakeley's Films (Butcher)
P: Tom Blakeley
D: Lance Comfort
S: Brock Williams
SC: Brock Williams, Derry Quinn
Jess Conrad	Shane
Hermione Baddeley	Princess

Kenneth Griffith . . . . Wilson
Christina Gregg . . . . Carol
Patrick Magee . . . . Flynn
Patrick Jordan . . . . Wills
Michael Wynne . . . . Bellamy
Frank Forsyth . . . . Supt
CRIME Cafe owner's teenage stepdaughter
falls for singing burglar.

APR

12926
A WEEKEND WITH LULU (89) (A)
Hammer (Col)
P:SC: Ted Lloyd
D: John Paddy Carstairs
S: Ted Lloyd, Val Valentine
Bob Monkhouse . . . . Fred
Leslie Phillips . . . . Tim
Alfred Marks . . . . Comte de Grenoble
Shirley Eaton . . . . Deidre Proudfoot
Irene Handl . . . . Florence Proudfoot
Eugene Deckers . . . . Insp Larue
Sidney James . . . . Cafe Patron
Kenneth Connor . . . . Tourist
Sydney Tafler . . . . Station Master
Russ Conway . . . . Pianist
Graham Stark . . . . Chiron
Harold Berens . . . . Card Seller
Tutte Lemkow . . . . Leon
Heidi Erich . . . . Lulubelle
COMEDY Friends in a caravan accidentally
ferried to France.

12927
TASTE OF FEAR (82) (X)
USA: SCREAM OF FEAR
Hammer (Col)
P:SC: Jimmy Sangster
D: Seth Holt
Susan Strasberg . . . . Penny Appleby
Ronald Lewis . . . . Bob
Ann Todd . . . . Jane Appleby
Christopher Lee . . . . Dr Gerrard
Leonard Sachs . . . . Spratt
Anne Blake . . . . Marie
John Serret . . . . Insp Legrand
Fred Johnson . . . . Father
CRIME France. Chauffeur helps widow drive
crippled stepdaughter mad with her father's
corpse.

12928
THE MISSING NOTE (56) (U)
Walton (CFF)
P: Henry Passmore
D: Michael Brandt
S: Frank Wells
SC: Mary Cathcart Borer
Heather Bennett . . . . Joan
Hennie Scott . . . . Tom
John Moulder-Brown . . . . . . Willie
Toke Townley . . . . Mr Parker
Vivian Lacey . . . . Suzie
Tommy Godfrey . . . . Sam
Edgar Driver . . . . Mr. Newbolt
Patricia Leslie . . . . Mrs. Harris
RSM Brittain . . . . Commissionaire
CHILDREN Children search for old piano in
which a thief has hidden jewels.

12929
FOUR WINDS ISLAND (serial) (U)
Merton Park (CFF)
P: Frank A. Hoare
D:SC: David Villiers
S: (NOVEL) Vega Stewart SC: Lindsay Galloway
Amanda Coxell . . . . Mary Lockwood
Annette Robertson . . . . Leila
Iain Gregory . . . . George

John Pike . . . . Bob
Robert Langley . . . . Johnny
Pauline Letts . . . . Mrs Ruddock
Michael Peake . . . . Garro
Tom Bowman . . . . Buck
Nora Gordon . . . . Mrs. Bennett
Hilda Fenemore . . . . Jessie

12930
1—SHADOWS IN THE WOOD (16)

12931
2—THE LOCKWOOD JEWELS (15)

12932
3—THE RIDDLE OF JACOB'S REACH (14)

12933
4—THE CLUE TO THE JEWELS (13)

12934
5—FORTUNE IN THE SAND (16)

12935
6—BUCK SHOWS HIS HAND (15)

12936
7—HELL'S GATE (14)

12937
8—THE LAST FIGHT (16)

CHILDREN Scillies. Children help island
heiress thwart housekeeper and Australian
seeking uranium

12938
LISTEN TO MY MUSIC (9) (U)
Carisbrooke (AA)
P:D: Robert Henryson
Ted Heath and his Band
MUSICAL

12939
CUBAN MELODY (9) (U)
Carisbrooke (AA)
P:D: Robert Henryson
Hermanos Deniz Cuban Rhythm Band
MUSICAL

12940
TED HEATH AND HIS MUSIC (9) (U)
Carisbrooke (AA)
P:D: Robert Henryson
MUSICAL

12941
CUBAN RHYTHM (9) (U)
Carisbrooke (AA)
P:D: Robert Henryson
Hermanos Deniz Cuban Rhythm Band
MUSICAL

12942
THE TONY KINSEY QUARTET (9) (U)
Carisbrooke (AA)
P:D: Robert Henryson
MUSICAL

12943
TWO LIVING ONE DEAD (92)
Swan Productions (BL)
P: Karl E. Mosley, Teddy Baird
D: Anthony Asquith
S: (NOVEL) Sigurd Christianssen
SC: Lindsey Galloway
Virginia McKenna . . . . Helen Berger
Bill Travers . . . . Anderson
Patrick McGoohan . . . . Berger
Alf Kjellin . . . . Rogers
Dorothy Alison . . . . Esther Kester
Noel Willman . . . . Insp Johnson

Pauline Jameson . . . . Miss Larsen
Peter Vaughan . . . . John Kester
Derek Francis . . . . Broms
Michael Crawford . . . . Nils
John Moulder Brown . . . . . . Rolf Berger
CRIME Sweden. Post office clerk called a
coward for handing cash to robbers.

12944
THE GREENGAGE SUMMER (99) eastman (A)
USA: LOSS OF INNOCENCE
PKH Pictures (Col)
P: Victor Saville, Edward Small
D: Lewis Gilbert
S: (NOVEL) Rumer Godden
SC: Howard Koch
Kenneth More . . . . Eliot
Danielle Darrieux . . . . Mme Zizi
Susannah York . . . . Joss
Claude Nollier . . . . Mme Corbet
Maurice Denham . . . . Mr Bullock
Jane Asher . . . . Elizabeth
Elizabeth Dear . . . . Vicky
Richard Williams . . . . Willmouse
David Saire . . . . Paul
Raymond Gerome . . . . Renard
Andre Maranne . . . . Dufour
Harold Kasket . . . . Prideaux
Jacques Brunuis . . . . Joubert
Joy Shelton . . . . Mrs. Grey
Balbina . . . . Mauricette
Bessie Love . . . . Tourist
ROMANCE France. Stranded teenager falls
for hotelier's lover and unwittingly causes his
arrest for gem theft.

12945
SO EVIL SO YOUNG (77) tech (A)
Danziger (UA)
P: Brian Taylor
D: Godfrey Grayson
S: Mark Grantham
Jill Ireland . . . . Ann
Ellen Pollock . . . . Miss Smith
John Charlesworth . . . . Tom
Jocelyn Britton . . . . Lucy
Joan Haythorne . . . . Matron
John Longden . . . . Turner
Sheila Whittingham . . . . Mary
Bernice Swanson . . . . Claire
Colin Tapley . . . . Inspector
CRIME Framed girl escapes from reformatory
to prove she is not robber.

12946
VERY IMPORTANT PERSON (98) (U)
Independent Artists (RFD)
P: Julian Wintle, Leslie Parkyn
D: Ken Annakin
S: Jack Davies
James Robertson Justice . . . Sir Ernest Pease
Leslie Phillips . . . . Jimmy Cooper
Stanley Baxter . . . . Everett/Maj Stampfel
Eric Sykes . . . . Willoughby
Richard Wattis . . . . Woodcock
Godfrey Winn . . . . Himself
Colin Gordon . . . . Briggs
Jeremy Lloyd . . . . Bonzo Baines
John le Mesurier . . . . Piggott
Peter Myers . . . . Shaw
Norman Bird . . . . Travers
Ronnie Stevens . . . . Hankley
Joan Haythorne . . . . Miss Rogers
Ronald Leigh Hunt . . . . Clynes
Vincent Ball . . . . Higgins
COMEDY Germany. POW poses as his double,
a Nazi commandant, to help radar scientist
escape.

12947
THE CURSE OF THE WEREWOLF (88) *tech*
(X)
Hotspur — Hammer (UI)
P:SC: Anthony Hinds
D: Terence Fisher
S: (NOVEL) Guy Endore (THE WEREWOLF OF PARIS)

Clifford Evans	Don Alfredo Carido
Oliver Reed	Leon
Yvonne Romain	Jailer's Daughter
Catherine Feller	Christina Fernando
Anthony Dawson	Marques Siniestro
Anne Blake	Rosa Valiente
Warren Mitchell	Pepe Valiente
Michael Ripper	Drunk
Peter Sallis	Don Enrique
Ewen Solon	Don Fernando
Hira Talfrey	Teresa
Richard Wordsworth	Beggar
Justin Walters	Leon (child)

HORROR Spain, period. Professor adopts deaf mute's bastard who grows up to be lycanthropic.

12948
THE SHADOW OF THE CAT 979) (X)
BHP Films (UI)
P: Jon Penington
D: John Gilling
S: George Baxt

Andre Morell	Walter Venable
Barbara Shelley	Beth
William Lucas	Jacob
Freda Jackson	Clara
Conrad Phillips	Michael Latimer
Catherine Lacey	Ella Venable
Richard Warner	Edgar
Vanda Godsell	Louise
Alan Wheatley	Insp Rowles
Andrew Crawford	Andrew
Kynaston Reeves	Grandfather
Henry Kendall	Doctor

CRIME Murdered woman's pet cat seems to cause deaths of her will-seeking relatives.

12949
NEARLY A NASTY ACCIDENT (91) (U)
Marlow (Britannia)
P: Bertram Ostrer
D: Don Chaffey
S: (PLAY) David Stringer, David Carr (TOUCH WOOD)
SC: Jack Davies, Hugh Woodhouse

Jimmy Edwards	G/C Kingsley
Kenneth Connor	AC2 Alexander Wood
Shirley Eaton	Cpl Jean Briggs
Ronnie Stevens	F/L Pocock
Richard Wattis	Wagstaffe
Jon Pertwee	Gen Birkenstraw
Eric Barker	Minister
Joyce Carey	Lady Trowborough
Peter Jones	F/L Winters
Terry Scott	Sam Stokes
Jack Watling	F/L Grogan
Joe Baker	Watkins
Jack Douglas	Balmer
Cyril Chamberlain	W/O Breech

COMEDY Group Captain tries to get rid of accident-prone airman.

12950
PAYROLL (105) (A)
Lynx — Independent Artists (AA)
P: Norman Priggen
D: Sidney Hayers
S: (NOVEL) Derek Bickerton
SC: George Baxt

Michael Craig	Johnny Mellors
Francoise Prevost	Katie Pearson

Billie Whitelaw	Jackie Parker
William Lucas	Dennis Pearson
Kenneth Griffith	Monty
Tom Bell	Blackie
Edward Cast	Sgt Mark Bradden
Andrew Faulds	Insp Carberry
Barry Keegan	Bert Langridge
William Peacock	Harry Parker
Joan Rice	Madge Moore
Vanda Godsell	Doll

CRIME Newcastle. Armoured van driver's widow tracks gang that stole £100,000.

12951
HOUSE OF MYSTERY (56) (A)
Independent Artists (AA)
P: Julian Wintle, Leslie Parkyn
D:SC: Vernon Sewell
S: (PLAY) Pierre Mills, C. Vylars (L'ANGOISSE)

Jane Hylton	Stella Lemming
Peter Dyneley	Mark Lemming
Nanette Newman	Joan Trevor
Maurice Kaufmann	Henry Trevor
Colin Gordon	Burdon
Molly Urquhart	Mrs. Bucknall
John Merivale	Clive
Colette Wilde	Wife

FANTASY Ghost tells couple how medium uncovered murder of previous tenants.

12952
THE GREEN HELMET (88) (U)
MGM British
P: Charles Francis Vetter
D: Michael Forlong
S: (NOVEL) Jon Cleary
SC: Jon Cleary

Bill Travers	Greg Rafferty
Ed Begley	Bartell
Sidney James	Richie Launder
Nancy Walters	Diane Bartell
Ursula Jeans	Mrs. Rafferty
Megs Jenkins	Kitty Launder
Sean Kelly	Taz Rafferty
Tutte Lemkow	Carlo Zaraga
Ferdy Mayne	Rossano
Jack Brabham	Himself

SPORT Italy. Driver wins Mille Miglia despite losing nerve after causing mechanic's death.

MAY

12953
THE NAKED EDGE (99) (A)
Glass-Seltzer (UA)
P: Marlon Brando sr, George Glass, Walter Seltzer
D: Michael Anderson
S: (NOVEL) Max Ehrlich (FIRST TRAIN TO BABYLON)
SC: Joseph Stefano

Gary Cooper	George Radcliffe
Deborah Kerr	Martha Radcliffe
Eric Portman	Jeremy Clay
Diane Cilento	Mrs. Heath
Hermione Gingold	Lily Harris
Peter Cushing	Wrack
Michael Wilding	Morris Brooke
Ronald Howard	Claridge
Ray McAnally	Ronald Heath
Sandor Eles	Manfridi
Wilfrid Lawson	Pom
Helen Cherry	Miss Osborne
Joyce Carey	Victoria Hicks
Diane Clare	Betty

CRIME Delayed blackmail letter causes wife to suspect rich husband of killing employer.

12954
THE SNAKE WOMAN (68) (X)
Caralan & Dador (UA)
P: David E. Rose, George Fowler
D: Sidney J. Furie
S: Orville Hampton

John McCarthy	Charles Prentice
Susan Travers	Atheris
Geoffrey Danton	Col Wynborn
Arnold Marle	Dr Murton
Elsie Wagstaffe	Aggie
John Cazabon	Dr Adderson
Frances Bennett	Polly
Hugh Moxey	Inspector

HORROR Northumberland, 1910. Doctor cures mad wife with venom injection which causes their daughter to change into snake.

12955
THE MONSTER OF HIGHGATE PONDS (59) (U)
Halas & Batchelor (CFF)
P: John Halas
D: Alberto Cavalcanti
S: Joy Batchelor
SC: Mary Cathcart Borer

Roy Vincente	The Monster
Ronald Howard	Uncle Dick
Rachel Clay	Sophie
Michael Wade	David
Terry Raven	Chris
Frederick Piper	Sam
Michael Balfour	Bert
Beryl Cooke	Miss Haggerty

CHILDREN Children hatch Malayan monster and save it from circus showmen.

12956
HUNTED IN HOLLAND (61) *eastman* (U)
Wessex (CFF)
P: Ian Dalrymple
D: Derek Williams
S: Ian Dalrymple, Derek Williams

Sean Scully	Tim
Jacques Verbrugge	Piet
Sandra Spurr	Aanike
Thom Kelling	Van Kelling

CHILDREN Holland. British boy and Dutch children capture diamond thieves.

12957
MACBETH (108) *tech* (U)
Grand Prize (BL)
P: Sidney Kaufman, Phil C. Samuel
D: George Schaefer
S: (PLAY) William Shakespeare

Maurice Evans	Macbeth
Judith Anderson	Lady Macbeth
Michael Hordern	Banquo
Ian Bannen	Macduff
Felix Aylmer	Doctor
Malcolm Keen	Duncan
Megs Jenkins	Gentlewoman
Jeremy Brett	Malcolm
Barry Warren	Donalbain
Charles Carson	Caithness
George Rose	Porter
Valerie Taylor	First Witch
Anita Sharp Bolster	Second Witch
April Olrich	Third Witch

DRAMA Scotland, period. Thane's wife urges him to murder his way to the throne.

12958
THE GUNS OF NAVARONE
tech/scope (A)
Open Road (Col) *reissue:* 1965
P: Carl Foreman, Cecil F. Ford
D: J. Lee-Thompson

S: (NOVEL) Alistair Maclean
SC: Carl Foreman
Gregory Peck . . . . Mallory
David Niven . . . . Cpl Miller
Anthony Quinn . . . . Andrea
Stanley Baker . . . . Brown
Anthony Quayle . . . . Maj Franklin
James Darren . . . . Pappadimos
Irene Papas . . . . Maria
Gia Scala . . . . Anna
James Robertson Justice . . . Jensen
Richard Harris . . . . Barnsby
Bryan Forbes . . . . Cohn
Allan Cuthbertson . . . . Baker
Michael Trubshawe . . . . Weaver
Percy Herbert . . . . Grogan
Albert Lieven . . . . Commandant
Norman Wooland . . . . Group Captain
WAR Greece, 1943. Army Group destroys
radar-controlled guns which overlook a vital
channel. (Best Special Effects, 1961)

12959
SPARE THE ROD (93) (A)
Weyland (Bry)
P: Victor Lyndon, Jock Jacobson
D: Leslie Norman
S: (NOVEL) Michael Croft
SC: John Cresswell
Max Bygraves . . . . John Saunders
Donald Pleasence . . . . Mr Jenkins
Geoffrey Keen . . . . Arthur Gregory
Betty McDowall . . . . Ann Collins
Peter Reynolds . . . . Alec Murray
Jean Anderson . . . . Mrs. Pond
Eleanor Summerfield . . . . . . Mrs. Harkness
Mary Merrall . . . . Miss Fogg
Richard O'Sullivan . . . . Fred Harkness
Claire Marshall . . . . Margaret
Jeremy Bulloch . . . . Angell
Aubrey Woods . . . . Mr Bickerstaff
DRAMA Idealistic teacher tries to educate
rebellious East End children.

12960
THE IMPERSONATOR (64) (A)
Herald (Bry)
P: Anthony Perry
D: Alfred Shaughnessy
S: Alfred Shaughnessy, Kenneth Cavender
John Crawford . . . . Jimmy Bradford
Jane Griffiths . . . . Ann Loring
Patricia Burke . . . . Mrs. Lloyd
John Salew . . . . Harry Walker
John Dare . . . . Tommy Lloyd
Yvonne Ball . . . . Principal Boy
CRIME Schoolmistress clears suspected US
Army sgt by unmasking pantomime dame as
widow's killer.

12961
HIGHWAY TO BATTLE (71) (U)
Danziger (Par)
P: Edward J. & Harry Lee Danziger
D: Ernest Morris
S: Joseph Pole
SC: Brian Clemens, Eldon Hayward
Gerard Heinz . . . . Constantin
Margaret Tyzack . . . . Hilda
Ferdy Mayne . . . . Zeigler
Dawn Berrington . . . . Gerda
Peter Reynolds . . . . Jarvost
Vincent Ball . . . . Ransome
George Mikell . . . . Brauwitz
John Gabriel . . . . Carl
DRAMA 1936. German ambassador persuades
fugitive that suicide is preferable to capture
by Nazis.

12962
SOME LIKE IT COOL (61) *eastman* (A)
SF Films
P: B.C. Fancey, Adrienne Fancey
D:S: Michael Winner
Julie Wilson . . . . Julie
Thalia Vickers . . . . Jill Clark
Mark Roland . . . . Roger
Brian Jackson . . . . Mike Hall
Wendy Smith . . . . Joy
Douglas Muir . . . . Col Willoughby-Muir
NUDIST Devon. Nudist converts newlywed
husband and her parents.

12963
OLD MAC (53) (U)
Border (Carlyle)
P: O. Negus Fancey
D: Michael Winner
S: Richard Bayley
Charles Lamb . . . . Father
Vi Stevens . . . . Mother
Corona Academy children
ANIMAL Children save dog from tramp and
hide it from their parents.

12964
DON'T BOTHER TO KNOCK (89)
tech/scope (A)
Haileywood (WPD)
P: Richard Todd, Frank Godwin
D: Cyril Frankel
S: (NOVEL) Clifford Hanley
SC: Denis Cannan, Frederic Gotfurt,
Frederick Raphael
Richard Todd . . . . Bill Ferguson
Nicole Maurey . . . . Lucille
Elke Sommer . . . . Ingrid
Judith Anderson . . . . Maggie Shoemaker
June Thorburn . . . . Stella
Rik Battaglia . . . . Giulio
Dawn Beret . . . . Harry
Scot Finch . . . . Perry
Eleanor Summerfield . . . . . Mother
John le Mesurier . . . . Father
Colin Gordon . . . . Rolsom
Kenneth Fortescue . . . . Ian
Ronald Fraser . . . . Fred
John Laurie . . . . Taxi-driver
COMEDY Edinburgh. Travel agent's
European girl-friends all arrive together.

12965
THE SECRET PARTNER (91) (A)
MGM British
P: Michael Relph
D: Basil Dearden
S: David Pursell, Jack Seddon
Stewart Granger . . . . John Brett
Haya Harareet . . . . Nicole Brett
Bernard Lee . . . . Supt Hanbury
Hugh Burden . . . . Charles Standish
Lee Montague . . . . Insp Henderson
Melissa Stribling . . . . Helen Standish
Conrad Phillips . . . . Alan Richford
John Lee . . . . Clive Lang
Norman Bird . . . . Ralph Beldon
Peter Illing . . . . Strakarios
CRIME Blackmailed executive excapes arrest
to prove he did not rob company safe.

JUN

12966
THE NEVER NEVER MURDER (30) (U)
Merton Park (AA)
P: Jack Greenwood
D: Peter Duffell
S: James Eastwood
N: Edgar Lustgarten
Russell Napier . . . . Supt Duggan
Genine Graham . . . .
Maurice Good . . . .
Harriette Johns . . . .
CRIME Woman's corpse found in
demolished building leads to capture of
hire-purchase swindler.

12967
WINGS OF DEATH (29) (U)
Merton Park (AA)
P: Jack Greenwood
D: Allan Davis
S: James Eastwood
N: Edgar Lustgarten
Harry H. Corbett . . . . Supt Hammond
Shelagh Fraser . . . . Diane Wilton
Simon Lack . . . .
CRIME Pilot's wife and lover plant bomb in
husband's plane.

12968
THE SQUARE MILE MURDER (28) (U)
Merton Park (AA)
P: Jack Greenwood
D: Allan Davis
S: James Eastwood
N: Edgar Lustgarten
John Welsh . . . . Supt Hicks
Delphi Lawrence . . . .
Stanley Morgan . . . .
CRIME Lipstick leads to capture of woman
safecracker.

12969
THE FOURTH SQUARE (57) (U)
Merton Park (AA)
P: Jack Greenwood
D: Allan Davis
S: (NOVEL) Edgar Wallace (FOUR SQUARE
JANE)
SC: James Eastwood
Conrad Phillips . . . . Bill Lawrence
Natasha Parry . . . . Sandra Martin
Delphi Lawrence . . . . Nina Stewart
Paul Daneman . . . . Henry Adams
Miriam Karlin . . . . Josetta Alvarez
Jacqueline Jones . . . . Marie Labonne
Anthony Newlands . . . . Tom Alvarez
Basil Dignam . . . . Insp Forbes
Harold Kasket . . . . Philippe
CRIME Lawyer unmasks playboy's ex-wife as
gem thief and killer of shipowner's press
officer.

12970
DENTIST ON THE JOB (88) (A) USA: GET
ON WITH IT!
Ostrer (AA)
P: Bertram M. Ostrer
D: C.M. Pennington-Richards
S: Hazel Adair, Hugh Woodhouse, Bob
Monkhouse
Bob Monkhouse . . . . David Cookson
Kenneth Connor . . . . Sam Field
Shirley Eaton . . . . Jill Venner
Eric Barker . . . . Col Proudfoot/The Dea
Richard Wattis . . . . Macreedy
Ronnie Stevens . . . . Brian Dexter
Reginald Beckwith . . . . Duff
Charles Hawtrey . . . . Roper
Graham Stark . . . . Man
Charlotte Mitchell . . . . Mrs Burke
Jeremy Hawk . . . . Prof Lovitt
David Horne . . . . Southbound
Ian Whittaker . . . . Fuller
Patrick Holt . . . . Newsreader
Michael Miles . . . . Himself
Keith Fordyce . . . . Himself
COMEDY Dentists invent toothpaste and
plant advertising jingle in space satellite.

12971
THE MAN IN THE BACK SEAT (57) (A)
Independent Artists (AA)
P: Julian Wintle, Leslie Parkyn
D: Vernon Sewell
S: Malcolm Hulke, Eric Paice
Derren Nesbitt ; . . . . Tony
Keith Faulkner . . . . Frank
Carol White . . . . Jean
Harry Locke . . . . Joe Carter
CRIME Robber goes mad trying to dispose
of dying bookmaker.

12972
FLAME IN THE STREETS (93) *deluxe/scope*
(A)
Rank-Somerset (RFD)
P: Roy Baker, Jack Hanbury
D: Roy Baker
S: (PLAY) Ted Willis (HOT SUMMER NIGHT)
SC: Ted Willis
John Mills . . . . Jacko Palmer
Sylvia Syms . . . . Kathie Palmer
Brenda de Banzie . . . . Nell Palmer
Earl Cameron . . . . Gabriel Gomez
Johnny Sekka . . . . Peter Lincoln
Ann Lynn . . . . Judy Gomez
Wilfred Brambell . . . . Mr. Palmer
Meredith Edwards . . . . Harry Mitchell
Newton Blick . . . . Visser
Glyn Houston . . . . Hugh Davies
Cyril Chamberlain . . . . James Dowell
DRAMA Union supporter of Negro labour
learns his daughter loves Jamaican.

12973
TARNISHED HEROES (75) (U)
Danziger (WPD)
P: Brian Taylor
D: Ernest Morris
S: Brian Clemens
Dermot Walsh . . . . Maj Roy Bell
Anton Rodgers . . . . Don Conyers
Patrick McAlinney . . . . Reilly
Richard Carpenter . . . . Freddy
Maurice Kaufmann . . . . Tom Mason
Max Butterfield . . . . Tony
Brian Peck . . . . Bernie White
Sheila Whittingham . . . . . . Josette
WAR Major and defaulters destroy bridge and
hold beseiged church.

12974
THE MIDDLE COURSE (60) (U)
Danziger (UA)
P: Brian Taylor
D: Montgomery Tully
S: Brian Clemens
Vincent Ball . . . . Cliff Wilton
Lisa Daniely . . . . Anna
Peter Illing . . . . Gromik
Roland Bartrop . . . . Paul
Marne Maitland . . . . Renard
Robert Rietty . . . . Jacques
Andre Maranne . . . . Franz
Yvonne Andre . . . . Martine
WAR France. Canadian pilot crashes and helps
villagers resist the enemy.

12975
THREE ON A SPREE (91) (U)
Caralan & Dador (UA)
P: David E. Rose, George Fowler
D: Sidney J. Furie
S: (PLAY) Winchell Smith, Byron Ongley
(NOVEL) George Barr McCutcheon
(BREWSTER'S MILLIONS)
SC: Siegfried Herzig, Charles Rogers, Wilkie
Mahoney, James Kolly, Peter Miller

Jack Watling . . . . Michael Brewster
Carole Lesley . . . . Susan
John Slater . . . . Sid Johnson
Colin Gordon . . . . Mitchell
Libby Morris . . . . Trixie
Cardew Robinson . . . . Micki
Julian Orchard . . . . Walker
Ernest Clark . . . . Col Drew
Ronald Adam . . . . Judge
June Cunningham . . . . Rosie
COMEDY Clerk must spend £1,000,000 to
inherit £8,000,000.

12976
MARY HAD A LITTLE (84) (X)
Caralan & Dador (UA)
P: David E. Rose, George Fowler
D: Edward Buzzell
S: (PLAY) Arthur Herzog, Muriel Herman,
Al Rosen
SC: Robert E. Kent, Jameson Brewer
Agnes Laurent . . . . Mary Kirk
Hazel Court . . . . Laurel Clive
Jack Watling . . . . Scott Raymond
John Bentley . . . . Dr Malcolm Nettel
Michael Ward . . . . Hunter
Clifford Mollison . . . . Watkins
John Maxim . . . . Burley Shaveley
Terry Scott . . . . Police Sgt
Sidney Vivian . . . . Grimmick
Patricia Marmont . . . . Angie
COMEDY Actress feigns pregnancy to help
producer win bet from hypnotist.

12977
OUT OF THE SHADOW (61) (U)
Border (NR)
P: O. Negus-Fancey
D:S: Michael Winner
Terence Longdon . . . . Mark Kingston
Donald Gray . . . . Insp Wills
Diane Clare . . . . Mary Johnson
Robertson Hare . . . . Ronald Fortescue
Dermot Walsh . . . . Professor Taylor
Felicity Young . . . . Waitress
CRIME Cambridge. Reporter proves
brother's suicide was murder.

12978
GREYFRIARS BOBBY (91) (U) *tech*
Walt Disney
P: Hugh Attwooll
D: Don Chaffey
S: (NOVEL) Eleanor Atkinson
SC: Robert Westerby
Donald Crisp . . . . John Brown
Laurence Naismith . . . . Mr. Traill
Alexander Mackenzie . . . . . . Old Jock
Kay Walsh . . . . Mrs. Brown
Andrew Cruickshank . . . . . . Lord Provost
Gordon Jackson . . . . Farmer
Freda Jackson . . . . Caretaker
Duncan Macrae . . . . Maclean
Vincent Winter . . . . Tammy
Rosalie Crutchley . . . . Farmer's Wife
DRAMA Edinburgh, period. Skye terrier
keeps vigil over old shepherd's grave and is
given freedom of city.

12979
THE HORSEMASTERS (87) *tech* (U)
Walt Disney
P: Hugh Attwooll
D: William Fairchild
S: Ted Willis
Tony Britton . . . . Maj Brooke
Janet Munro . . . . Janet Hale
John Fraser . . . . David Lawson
Tommy Kirk . . . . Danny Grant

Annette Funicello . . . . Dinah Wilcox
Donald Pleasence . . . . Major Pinski
Harry Lockart . . . . Vincenzo Lalli
Millicent Martin . . . . Joan Finley
Colin Gordon . . . . Folliot
Anthony Nicholls . . . . Cole
Penelope Horner . . . . Penny Sutcliffe
ADVENTURE Cosmopolitan teenagers spend
16 weeks at Major's riding school.

12980
THE BOY WHO STOLE A MILLION (81) (U)
Fanfare (Bry)
P: George H. Brown
D: Charles Crichton
S: Neils West Larsen, Antonio de Leon
SC: Charles Crichton, John Eldridge
Virgilio Texera . . . . Miguel
Marianne Benet . . . . Maria
Maurice Reyna . . . . Paco
Harold Kasket . . . . Luis
Curt Christian . . . . Currito
George Coulouris . . . . Manager
Bill Nagy . . . . Police Chief
Warren Mitchell . . . . Pedro
Edwin Richfield . . . . Commissionaire
Tutte Lemkow . . . . Mateo
Andrea Malandrinos . . . . Shoemaker
COMEDY Spain. Pageboy robs bank of
million pesetas to repair his father's taxi.

JUL

12981
FOLLOW THAT MAN (84) (U)
Epiney (UA)
P: Jerry Epstein, Charles Leeds
D:S: Jerry Epstein
Sydney Chaplin . . . . Eddie Miller
Dawn Addams . . . . Janet Clark
Elspeth March . . . . Astrid Larsen
Joan Heal . . . . Harriet
Peter Bull . . . . Gustav
Jack Melford . . . . Lars Toren
Nicholas Tanner . . . . Olaf
May Hallatt . . . . Nannie
Garry Colleano . . . . Axelrod
COMEDY Swedish widow loves crook posing
as her long-lost son.

12982
TRANSATLANTIC (63) (U)
Danziger (UA)
P: Brian Taylor
D: Ernest Morris
S: Brian Clemens, James Eastwood
Pete Murray . . . . Robert Stanton
June Thorburn . . . . Judy
Malou Pantera . . . . Gina
Bill Nagy . . . . Fabroni
Neil Hallatt . . . . Evans
Jack Melford . . . . Capt Brady
Sheldon Lawrence . . . . Capt Ives
Robert Ayres . . . . Hotchkiss
Anthony Oliver . . . . Wentworth
CRIME FBI agent and dead pilot's sister track
diamond thieves who destroyed plane with
time bomb.

12983
A QUESTION OF SUSPENSE (62) (A)
Bill & Michael Luckwell (Col)
P: Bill Luckwell, Jock Macgregor
D: Max Varnel
S: (NOVEL) Roy Vickers
SC: Lawrence Huntington
Peter Reynolds . . . . Tellman Drew
Noelle Middleton . . . . Rose Marples
Yvonne Buckingham . . . . . Jean Forbes
Norman Rodway . . . . Frank Brigstock

James Neylin . . . . Insp Hunter
Pauline Delany . . . . Mrs Barlow
Anne Mulvey . . . . Sally
CRIME Girl's revenge on tycoon who killed her lover.

12984
THE TREASURE OF MONTE CRISTO (95)
eastman/scope (U) USA: THE SECRET OF MONTE CRISTO
Mid Century (RFI)
P: Robert S. Baker, Monty Berman
D: Robert S. Baker
S: Leon Griffiths
Rory Calhoun . . . . Capt Adam Corbett
Patricia Bredin . . . . Pauline Jackson
John Gregson . . . . Renato
Peter Arne . . . . Count Boldoni
Gionna Maria Canale . . . . . Lucetta
Sam Kydd . . . . Albert
Ian Hunter . . . . Col Jackson
David Davies . . . . Van Ryman
Francis Mathews . . . . Auclair
Tutte Lemkow . . . . Gino
C.Denier Warren . . . . Proprietor
ADVENTURE Italy, 1815. Captain seeking treasure saves colonel's daughter from count.

12985
WATCH IT SAILOR! (81) (U)
Cormorant-Hammer (Col)
P: Maurice Cowan
D: Wolf Rilla
S: (PLAY) Falkland Cary, Philip King
SC: Falkland Cary, Philip King
Dennis Price . . . . Lt/Cdr Hardcastle
Marjorie Rhodes . . . . Emma Hornett
Irene Handl . . . . Edie Hornett
Liz Fraser . . . . Daphne
Vera Day . . . . Shirley Hornett
John Meillon . . . . Albert Tufnell
Cyril Smith . . . . Henry Hornett
Miriam Karlin . . . . Mrs Lack
Graham Stark . . . . Carnoustie Bligh
Frankie Howerd . . . . Organist
Bobby Howes . . . . Drunk
Brian Reece . . . . Solicitor
Renee Houston . . . . Mrs Mottram
Arthur Howard . . . . Vicar
COMEDY Mother-in-law trouble and paternity problems on eve of sailor's wedding.

12986
THE FRIGHTENED CITY (97) (A)
Zodiac (AA) *reissue:* 1964 (11 mins cut)
P: John Lemont, Leigh Vance
D: John Lemont
S: John Lemont, Leigh Vance
SC: Leigh Vance
Herbert Lom . . . . Waldo Zhernikov
John Gregson . . . . Insp Sayers
Sean Connery . . . . Paddy Damion
Alfred Marks . . . . Harry Foulcher
Yvonne Romain . . . . Anya
David Davies . . . . Alf Peters
Olive McFarland . . . . Sadie
Kenneth Griffith . . . . Wally
George Pastell . . . . Sanchietti
Frederick Piper . . . . Sgt Ogle
Patrick Holt . . . . Supt Carter
Bruce Seton . . . . Commissioner
Norrie Paramor . . . . Pianist
CRIME Accountant organises six gangs into protection racket.

12987
MAN AT THE CARLTON TOWER (57) (U)
Merton Park (AA)

P: Jack Greenwood
D: Robert Tronson
S: (NOVEL) Edgar Wallace (THE MAN AT THE CARLTON)
SC: Philip Mackie
Maxine Audley . . . . Lydia Daney
Lee Montague . . . . Tim Jordan
Allan Cuthbertson . . . . Supt Cowley
Terence Alexander . . . . Johnny Time
Alfred Burke . . . . Harry Stone
Nigel Green . . . . Lew Daney
Nyree Dawn Porter . . . . . . Mary Greer
Geoffrey Frederick . . . . Sgt Pepper
CRIME Ex-policeman tracks down Rhodesian jewel robber who killed constable.

12988
WHISTLE DOWN THE WIND (99) (U)
AFM-Beaver (RFD)
P: Richard Attenborough
D: Bryan Forbes
S: (NOVEL) Mary Hayley Bell
SC: Keith Waterhouse, Willis Hall
Hayley Mills . . . . Kathy Bustock
Bernard Lee . . . . Mr. Bustock
Alan Bates . . . . Arthur Blakey
Norman Bird . . . . Eddie
Elsie Wagstaffe . . . . Auntie Dorothy
Diane Holgate . . . . Nan Bostock
Alan Barnes . . . . Charles Bostock
Hamilton Dyce . . . . Reeves
Diane Clare . . . . Miss Lodge
Patricia Heneghan . . . . SA Girl
Roy Holder . . . . Jackie
DRAMA Lancs. Widowed farmer's children shelter fugitive murderer in the belief that he is Jesus.

12989
THE LONG SHADOW (64) (U)
Argo (RFD)
P: Jack O. Lamont, John Pellatt
D: Peter Maxwell
S: Paddy Manning O'Brine
John Crawford . . . . Kelly
Susan Hampshire . . . . Gunilla
Willoughby Goddard . . . . . Schober
Humphrey Lestocq . . . . Bannister
Rory O'Brine . . . . Ruchi Korbanyi
Anne Castaldini . . . . Magda
Margaret Robertson . . . . . . Mother
William Nagy . . . . Garity
Lilly Kann . . . . Old Lady
CRIME Vienna, 1956. American reporter saves Hungarian rebel's child and Swedish nurse from Nazis working for the Russians.

AUG

12990
INFORMATION RECEIVED (77) (A)
United Co-Production (RFD)
P: John Clein, George Maynard
D: Robert Lynn
S; Berkeley Mather
SC: Paul Ryder
Sabina Sesselman . . . . Sabina Farlow
William Sylvester . . . . Rick Hogan
Hermione Baddeley . . . . . . Maudie
Edward Underdown . . . . . . Drake
Robert Raglan . . . . Supt Jeffcoate
Walter Brown . . . . Farlow
Frank Hawkins . . . . Sgt Jarvis
David Courtney . . . . Mark
CRIME American poses as jailed safecracker to help police catch gang.

12991
NO, MY DARLING DAUGHTER (96) (U)
Rank-Five Star (RFD)

P: Betty E. Box
D; Ralph Thomas
S: (PLAY) Harold Brooke, Kay Bannerman (HANDFUL OF TANSY)
SC: Frank Harvey
Michael Redgrave . . . . Sir Matthew Carr
Michael Craig . . . . Thomas Barclay
Roger Livesey . . . . Gen Henry Barclay
Rod Fulton . . . . Cornelius Allingham
Juliet Mills . . . . Tansy Carr
Renee Houston . . . . Miss Yardley
Joan Sims . . . . Typist
Peter Barkworth . . . . Charles
David Lodge . . . . Flanigan
Victor Brooks . . . . PC
Terry Scott . . . . PC
COMEDY General's son rescues tycoon's daughter from supposed elopement with American.

12992
VICTIM (100) (X)
Parkway (RFD)
P: Michael Relph
D: Basil Dearden
S: Janet Green, John McCormick
Dirk Bogarde . . . . Melville Farr
Sylvia Syms . . . . Laura Farr
Dennis Price . . . . Calloway
Nigel Stock . . . . Phip
Peter McEnery . . . . Jack Barrett
Donald Churchill . . . . Eddy Stone
Anthony Nicholls . . . . Lord Fullbrook
Hilton Edwards . . . . P.H.
Norman Bird . . . . Harold Doe
Derren Nesbitt . . . . Sandy Youth
Alan McNaughton . . . . Scott Hankin
Noel Howlett . . . . William Patterson
Charles Lloyd Pack . . . . . . Henry
John Barrie . . . . Insp Harris
CRIME Homosexually inclined barrister tracks down blackmailers despite threat to his marriage and career.

12993
MURDER IN EDEN (64) (U)
Bill & Michael Luckwell (RED)
P: Bill Luckwell, John Macgregor
D: Max Varnel
S: John Haggarty
SC: H.E. Burden
Ray McAnally . . . . Insp Sharkey
Catherine Feller . . . . Genevieve Beaujean
Yvonne Buckingham . . . . . . Vicky Woolf
Norman Rodway . . . . Michael Lucas
Mark Singleton . . . . Arnold Woolf
Jack Aranson . . . . Bill Robson
Robert Lepler . . . . Max Aaronson
CRIME Inspector unmasks killer behind fake painting plot.

12994
THE KITCHEN (74) (X)
ACT Films (BL)
P: Ralph Bond, Sidney Cole
D: James Hill
S: (PLAY) Arnold Wesker
SC: Sidney Cole
Carl Mohner . . . . Peter
Mary Yeomans . . . . Monica
Eric Pohlmann . . . . Mr Marango
Tom Bell . . . . Paul
Martin Boddey . . . . Max
Sean Lynch . . . . Dimitri
Frank Atkinson . . . . Alfred
Howard Greene . . . . Raymond
Brian Phelan . . . . Kevin
Frank Pettitt . . . . Frank
Charles Lloyd Pack . . . . . . Chef
DRAMA German cook's love for married waitress drives him berserk.

12995
TWO WIVES AT ONE WEDDING (66) (U)
Danziger (Par)
P: Brian Taylor
D: Montgomery Tully
S: Brian Clemens, Eldon Howard
Gordon Jackson . . . . Tom
Christina Gregg . . . . Janet
Lisa Daniely . . . . Annette
Andre Maranne . . . . Paul
Humphrey Lestocq . . . . . . Mark
Viola Keats . . . . Mrs Ervine
Douglas Ives . . . . Jessop
John Serret . . . . Larouche
CRIME Doctor weds socialite and is
blackmailed by French girl who claims
to be his wife.

12996
THE VISIT (35) (U)
BFI (Contemporary)
P: Jack Gold, John Hall
D:S: Jack Gold
Alice Spaul . . . . Alice
Eunice Phelps . . . . Mother
George Wood . . . . Father
David Copsey . . . . Kennie
Ann Corby . . . . Fiancee
DRAMA Middle-aged spinster, living with her
parents, is visited by a relative with his fiancee.

12997
WHAT A CARVE UP! (88) (U)
New World (RFI)
P: Robert S. Baker, Monty Berman
D: Pat Jackson
S: (NOVEL) Frank King (THE GHOUL)
SC: Ray Cooney, Tony Hilton
Sidney James . . . . Syd Butler
Kenneth Connor . . . . Ernie Broughton
Shirley Eaton . . . . Linda Dickson
Dennis Price . . . . Guy Broughton
Donald Pleasence . . . . Everett Sloane
Michael Gough . . . . Fisk
Valerie Taylor . . . . Janet Broughton
Emma Cannon . . . . Aunt Emily
Michael Gwynn . . . . Malcolm Broughton
Philip O'Flynn . . . . Gabriel Broughton
George Woodbridge . . . . . Dr Edward Broughton
Adam Faith . . . . Himself
COMEDY Yorks. Rich madman fakes his own
death to kill off his relatives.

12998
RAISING THE WIND (91) *eastman* (U)
GHW Productions (AA)
P: Peter Rogers
D: Gerald Thomas
S: Bruce Montgomery
James Robertson Justice . . . Sir Benjamin
Leslie Phillips . . . . Mervyn
Paul Massie . . . . Malcolm
Kenneth Williams . . . . Harold
Sidney James . . . . Sid
Liz Frazer . . . . Miranda
Eric Barker . . . . Morgan Rutherford
Jennifer Jayne . . . . Jill
Jimmy Thompson . . . . Alex
Esma Cannon . . . . Mrs Deevens
Geoffrey Keen . . . . Sir John
Jill Ireland . . . . Janet
David Lodge . . . . Taxi-driver
Lance Percival . . . . Harry
Dorinda Stevens . . . . Doris
COMEDY Episodic misadventures of music
academy students

12999
CLUE OF THE SILVER KEY (59) (U)
Merton Park (AA)

P: Jack Greenwood
D: Gerard Glaister
S: (NOVEL) Edgar Wallace
SC: Philip Mackie
Bernard Lee . . . . Supt Meredith
Lyndon Brook . . . . Gerry Dornford
Finlay Currie . . . . Harvey Lane
Jennifer Daniel . . . . Mary Lane
Patrick Cargill . . . . Binny
Derrick Sherwin . . . . Quigley
Anthony Sharp . . . . Mike Hennessey
Stanley Morgan . . . . Sgt Anson
Sam Kydd . . . . Tickler
CRIME Luminous key exposes murderer of
miserly moneylender.

13000
MURDER SHE SAID (86) (U)
MGM British
P: George H. Brown
D: George Pollock
S: (NOVEL) Agatha Christie (4.50 FROM
PADDINGTON)
SC: David Pursall, Jack Seddons, David Osborn
Margaret Rutherford . . . . . Jane Marple
Arthur Kennedy . . . . Dr Quimper
Muriel Pavlow . . . . Emma Ackenthorpe
James Robertson Justice . . Ackenthorpe
Thorley Walters . . . . Cedric Ackenthorpe
Charles Tingwell . . . . Insp Craddock
Conrad Philips . . . . Brian Eastley
Joan Hickson . . . . Mrs Kidder
Stringer Davis . . . . Mr Stringer
Ronnie Raymond . . . . Alexander Eastley
Peter Butterworth . . . . Conductor
Richard Briers . . . . 'Mrs Binster'
CRIME Spinster poses as maidservant to
unmask killer of French girl.

SEPT

13001
A MATTER OF WHO (92) (A)
Foray Films (MGM)
P: Walter Shanson, Milton Homes
D: Don Chaffey
S: Patricia Lee, Paul Dickson
SC: Patricia Lee, Milton Holmes
Terry Thomas . . . . Archibald Bannister
Sonja Ziemann . . . . Michele Cooper
Alex Nicol . . . . Edward Kennedy
Richard Briers . . . . Jamieson
Honor Blackman . . . . Sister Bryan
Carol White . . . . Beryl
Guy Deghy . . . . Nick Ivanovitch
Clive Morton . . . . Hatfield
Martin Benson . . . . Rahman
Geoffrey Keen . . . . Foster
Vincent Ball . . . . Dr Blake
Andrew Faulds . . . . Ralph
COMEDY American oil expert thwarts
millionaire's intrigue while virus
investigator tracks smallpox source.

13002
ATTEMPT TO KILL (57) (U)
Merton Park (AA)
P: Jack Greenwood
D: Royston Morley
S: (NOVEL) Edgar Wallace (THE LONE
HOUSE MYSTERY)
SC: Richard Harris
Derek Farr . . . . Insp Minter
Tony Wright . . . . Gerry Hamilton
Richard Pearson . . . . Frank Weyman
Freda Jackson . . . . Mrs Weyman
Patricia Mort . . . . Elisabeth Gray
J.G. Devlin . . . . Elliott
Clifford Earl . . . . Sgt Bennett
Denis Holmes . . . . Fraser
CRIME Confidence tricksters scheme to kill
business man.

13003
ON THE FIDDLE (97) (A)
S. Benjamin Fisz (AA)
P: Ben Arbeid
D: Cyril Frankel
S: (NOVEL) R.F. Delderfield (STOP AT A
WINNER)
SC: Harold Buchman, R.F. Delderfield
Alfred Lynch . . . . Horace Pope
Sean Connery . . . . Pedlar Pascoe
Cecil Parker . . . . G/C Bascombe
Wilfrid Hyde White . . . . Trowbridge
Stanley Holloway . . . . Cooksley
Kathleen Harrison . . . . Mrs Cooksley
Alan King . . . . T/Sgt Buzzer
Eleanor Summerfield . . . . Flora McNaughton
Eric Barker . . . . Doctor
Terence Longdon . . . . Air Gunner
Ann Beach . . . . Iris
Miriam Karlin . . . . Sgt
Beatrix Lehmann . . . . Lady Edith
Patsy Rowlands . . . . Waaf
John le Mesurier . . . . Hixon
Bill Owen . . . . Cpl Gittens
Harry Locke . . . . F/Sgt Huxtable
Victor Maddern . . . . Airman
Graham Stark . . . . Sgt Ellis
COMEDY 1941. Episodic misadventures of
cockney spiv and simple gipsy in the RAF.

13004
MEET MISTER BEAT (32) (U)
GIB Films (AA)
P: David Cumming
D: Ivan Barnett
S: David Cumming, Derek Collyer
David Cumming . . . . Elroy Flicker
Dominic Le Foe . . . . Agent
Mary Gillingham . . . . Girl
COMEDY Roadsweeper becomes pop singer
and is cheated by agent.

13005
THE TERROR OF THE TONGS (79) (X)
eastman
Merlin-Hammer (Col)
P: Kenneth Hyman
D: Anthony Bushell
S: Jimmy Sangster
Christopher Lee . . . . Chung King
Yvonne Monlaur . . . . Lee
Geoffrey Toone . . . . Capt Jackson
Marne Maitland . . . . Beggar
Brian Worth . . . . Harcourt
Ewen Solon . . . . Tang How
Roger Delgado . . . . Wang How
Richard Leech . . . . Insp Dean
Charles Lloyd Pack . . . . Doctor
Marie Burke . . . . Maya
CRIME Hong Kong, 1910. Slave girl helps
seaman unmask Englishman behind gang of
opium-running white slavers.

13006
A TASTE OF HONEY (X) (100)
Woodfall (Bry)
S: (PLAY) Shelagh Delaney
SC: Shelagh Delaney, Tony Richardson
SC: Shelagh Delaney, Tony Richardson
Rita Tushingham . . . . Jo
Dora Bryan . . . . Helen
Robert Stephens . . . . Peter
Murray Melvin . . . . Geoffrey
Paul Danquah . . . . Jimmy
David Boliver . . . . Bert
Moira Kaye . . . . Doris
ROMANCE Salford. Widow's teenage
daughter is seduced by Negro sailor and
looked after by a homosexual. (BFA 1961:
Best British Film, Actress, Screenplay.)

13007
DANGEROUS AFTERNOON (62) (U)
Theatrecraft (Bry)
P: Guido Coen
D: Charles Saunders
S: (PLAY) Gerald Anstruther
SC: Brandon Fleming
Ruth Dunning . . . . Miss Frost
Nora Nicholson . . . . Mrs Sprule
Joanna Dunham . . . . Freda
Howard Pays . . . . Jack Loring
May Hallett . . . . Miss Burge
Gwenda Wilson . . . . Miss Berry
Ian Colin . . . . Rev Everard Porson
Gladys Henson . . . . Miss Cassell
Barbara Everest . . . . Mrs Judson
CRIME Escaped convict runs home for female
ex-convicts and poisons blackmailer.

13008
INVASION QUARTET (87) (U)
MGM British
P: Ronald Kinnoch
D: Jay Lewis
S: Norman Collins
SC: Jack Trevor Storey, John Briley
Bill Travers . . . . Freddie
Spike Milligan . . . . Godfrey
Gregoire Aslan . . . . Debrie
John le Mesurier . . . . Colonel
Eric Sykes . . . . Conductor
Maurice Denham . . . . Dr Barker
Millicent Martin . . . . Kay
Thorley Walters . . . . Cummings
John Wood . . . . Duty Officer
Cyril Luckham . . . . Col Harbottle
Thelma Ruby . . . . Matron
COMEDY 1942. Home Guard colonel and army
hospital patients spike gun on French coast.

13009
THE THIRD ALIBI (68) (A)
Eternal (GN)
P: Maurice J. Wilson
D: Montgomery Tully
S: (PLAY) Pip & Jane Baker (MOMENT OF
BLINDNESS)
SC: Maurice J. Wilson
Laurence Payne . . . . Norman Martell
Patricia Dainton . . . . Helen Martell
Jane Griffiths . . . . Peggy Hill
Edward Underdown . . . . . . Dr Murdoch
John Arnatt . . . . Supt Ross
Humphrey Lestocq . . . . . . Producer
Lucy Griffiths . . . . Miss Potter
Cleo Laine . . . . Singer
CRIME Composer and pregnant mistress plot
to kill his incurable wife, her sister.

OCT

13010
NOTHING BARRED (83) (U)
Rix-Conyers Enterprises (BL)
P: Brian Rix, Darcy Conyers
D: Darcy Conyers
S: John Chapman
Brian Rix . . . . Wilfred Sapling
Leo Franklin . . . . Barger
Naunton Wayne . . . . Lord Whitebait
Charles Heslop . . . . Spankforth
Ann Firbank . . . . Lady Katherine
John Slater . . . . Warder Lockitt
Vera Pearce . . . . Lady Millicent
Arnold Bell . . . . Governor
Alexander Gauge . . . . Policeman
Jack Watling . . . . Peter Brewster
Irene Handl . . . . Elsie
Bernard Cribbins . . . .
Wally Patch . . . . Newspaperman

Wilfrid Lawson . . . . Albert
Terry Scott . . . . Policeman
Henry Kendall . . . . Parson
Duke of Bedford . . . . Convict
COMEDY Plumber, mistaken for cat-burglar,
helps broke Lord steal his own painting.

13011
GORGO (77) *tech* (X)
King Brothers (BL)
P: Frank & Maurice King
D: Eugene Lourie
S: Eugene Lourie, Daniel Hyatt
SC: John Loring, Daniel Hyatt
Bill Travers . . . . Joe Ryan
William Sylvester . . . . . . Sam Slade
Vincent Winter . . . . Sean
Bruce Seton . . . . Prof Flaherty
Joseph O'Conor . . . . Prof Hendricks
Martin Benson . . . . Dorkin
Barry Keegan . . . . Mate
Dervis Ward . . . . Bosun
HORROR Prehistoric monster destroys London
to save her offspring from exhibition.

13012
THE LAST RHINO (56) (U) *eastman*
World Safari (CFF)
P: Henry Geddes, Johnnie Coquillon
D:S: Henry Geddes
David Ellis . . . . David
Susan Millar-Smith . . . . . . Susan
Tom Samuels . . . . Warden
Tony Blane . . . . Commissioner
John Taylor . . . . Pilot
Shabani Hamisi . . . . Shabani
Mlonga Muli . . . . Baaba
CHILDREN Kenya. Game warden's children
save wounded rhinoceros from tribe of hunters.

13013
THE QUEEN'S GUARDS (110) *tech/scope* (U)
Imperial (20)
P: Michael Powell, Sydney Streeter.
D: Michael Powell
S: Simon Harcourt-Smith
SC: Roger Milner
Daniel Massey . . . . John Fellowes
Raymond Massey . . . . Capt Fellowes
Robert Stephens . . . . Henry Wynne Walton
Jack Watson . . . . Sgt Johnson
Peter Myers . . . . Gordon Davidson
                                  Davidson
Jess Conrad . . . . Dankworth
Ursula Jeans . . . . Mrs Fellowes
Ian Hunter . . . . Dobbie
Jack Watling . . . . Capt Shergold
Andrew Crawford . . . . Biggs
Duncan Lamont . . . . Wilkes
Laurence Payne . . . . Farinda
Judith Stott . . . . Ruth
Elizabeth Shepherd . . . . . . Susan
Nigel Green . . . . Abu Sidbar
Rene Cutforth . . . . Commentator
WAR Crippled ex-officer's son learns truth of
his brother's death in action and fights Arab
rebels.

13014
WHAT A WHOPPER! (89) (U)
Viscount (RFI)
P: Teddy Joseph
D: Gilbert Gunn
S: Trevor Peacock, Jeremy Lloyd
SC: Terry Nation
Adam Faith . . . . Tony Blake
Sidney James . . . . Harry
Carole Lesley . . . . Charlie Pinner
Terence Longdon . . . . Vernon
Marie France . . . . Marie

Clive Dunn . . . . Mr Slate
Freddie Frinton . . . . Gilbert Pinner
Charles Hawtrey . . . . Arnold
Spike Milligan . . . . Tramp
Wilfred Brambell . . . . Postie
Fabia Drake . . . . Mrs Pinner
Harold Berens . . . . Sammy
Terry Scott . . . . Policeman
Fyfe Robertson . . . . Himself
COMEDY Broke author seeks publicity with
home-made Loch Ness Monster.

13015
JUNGLE STREET (82) (A)
Theatrecraft (RFI)
P: Guido Coen
D: Charles Saunders
S: Guido Coen
SC: Alexander Dore
David McCallum . . . . Terry Collins
Kenneth Cope . . . . Johnny
Jill Ireland . . . . Sue
Brian Weske . . . . Joe Lucas
Vanda Hudson . . . . Lucy Bell
Edna Dore . . . . Mrs Collins
Thomas Gallagher . . . . Collins
Howard Pays . . . . Sgt Pelling
Joy Webster . . . . Rene
Martin Sterndale . . . . Insp Bowden
John Chandos . . . . Jacko Fielding
Meier Tzelniker . . . . Rose
CRIME Fugitive killer and ex-convict rob
strip club safe.

13016
OVER THE ODDS (65) (A)
Jermyn (RFD)
P: Alec Snowden
D: Michael Forlong
S: (PLAY) Rex Howard Arundel
SC: Ernest Player
Marjorie Rhodes . . . . Bridget Stone
Glenn Melvyn . . . . George Summers
Thora Hird . . . . Mrs Carter
Esma Cannon . . . . Alice
Cyril Smith . . . . Sam
Wilfrid Lawson . . . . Willie Summers
Frances Cuka . . . . Hilda
COMEDY Divorced bookie marries and
bribes his father to marry his ex-mother-in-law.

13017
PIT OF DARKNESS (76) (U)
Butcher's Films
P:D:SC: Lance Comfort
S: (NOVEL) Hugh McCutcheon (TO DUSTY
DEATH)
William Franklyn . . . . Richard Logan
Moira Redmond . . . . Julie Logan
Bruno Barnabe . . . . Maxie
Leonard Sachs . . . . Conrad
Nigel Green . . . . Jonathan
Bruce Beeby . . . . Mayhew
Humphrey Lestocq . . . . . . Bill
Anthony Booth . . . . Ted Mellis
Nanette Newman . . . . Mary
CRIME Wife helps amnesiac safe-designer
recall how jewel robbers tricked him into
breaking safe.

13018
MAN DETAINED (59) (U)
Merton Park (AA)
P: Jack Greenwood
D: Robert Tronson
S: (NOVEL) Edgar Wallace (A DEBT
DISCHARGED)
SC: Richard Harris
Bernard Archard . . . . Insp Verity
Elvi Hale . . . . Kay Simpson

Paul Stassino . . . . James Helder
Michael Coles . . . . Frank Murray
Ann Sears . . . . Stella Maple
Victor Platt . . . . Thomas Maple
Patrick Jordan . . . . Brand
Jean Aubrey . . . . Gillian Murray
CRIME Police use burglar who stole counterfeit money to trap photographer's killer and save kidnapped secretary.

13019
JOHNNY NOBODY (88) *scope* (U)
Viceroy (Col)
P: John R. Sloan
D: Nigel Patrick
S: (STORY) Albert Z. Carr (THE TRIAL OF JOHNNY NOBODY)
SC: Patrick Kirwan
Nigel Patrick . . . . Father Carey
Yvonne Mitchell . . . . Miss Floyd
Aldo Ray . . . . Johnny Nobody
William Bendix . . . . Mulcahy
Cyril Cusack . . . . Prosecution
Bernie Winters . . . . Photographer
Niall MacGinnis . . . . Defence
Noel Purcell . . . . Brother Timothy
Eddie Byrne . . . . Landlord
Jimmy O'Dea . . . . Postman
John Welsh . . . . Judge
Michael Brennan . . . . Supt Lynch
Joe Lynch; Michael O'Duffy; Dominic Behan
CRIME Ireland. Priest proves fanatic explorer was not divinely impelled to shoot drunken author.

NOV
13020
THE HELLIONS (80) *tech/scope* (A)
Irving Allen-Jamie Uys GW Film (Col)
P: Harold Huth
D: Ken Annakin
S: Harold Swanton
SC Harold Swanton, Patrick Kirwan, Harold Huth
Richard Todd . . . . Sam Hargis
Jamie Uys . . . . Ernie Dobbs
Anne Aubrey . . . . Priss Dobbs
Marty Wilde . . . . John Billings
James Booth . . . . Jubal Billings
Lionel Jeffries . . . . Luke Billings
Ronald Fraser . . . . Frank
Zena Walker . . . . Julie
Al Mulock . . . . Mark Billings
Colin Blakelock . . . . .Matthew Billings
ADVENTURE South Africa, 1860. Police sergeant eventually rouses settlers against vicious outlaw and his sons.

13021
NUDES OF THE WORLD (65) *eastman* (A)
Miracle-Searchlight (Miracle)
P: Harry Green
D: Arnold Louis Miller
Vivienne Raimon . . . . Carol
Monique Ammon . . . . Monique
Antony Dell . . . . Ron
Colin Goddard . . . . Peter
Geoffrey Denton . . . . Lord Greystone
Sue Chang . . . . Sue
NUDIST Beauty queen runs nudist camp in Lord's grounds and appeases postmistress with fete for crippled daughter.

13022
NAKED AS NATURE INTENDED (65) *eastman* (A)
Markten-Compass (Compton)
P:D: Harrison Marks
S: Harrison Marks, Gerald Holgate

N: Guy Kingsley Poynter
Pamela Green . . . . Pamela
Jackie Salt . . . . Jackie
Petrina Forsyth . . . . Petrina
Bridget Leonard . . . . Bridget
Angela Jones . . . . Angela
Stuart Samuels . . . . Clerk/Pianist/
                                  Waiter/
                                  Fisherman/
                                  Boatman
NUDIST Cornwall. Secretary, dancer and salesgirl on motoring holiday join nudist camp.

13023
THE DAY THE EARTH CAUGHT FIRE (99) (X)
Melina (Pax)
P: Val Guest, Frank Sherwin Green
D: Val Guest
S: Wolf Mankowitz, Val Guest
Janet Munro . . . . Jeannie
Leo McKern . . . . Bill Maguire
Edward Judd . . . . Peter Stenning
Michael Goodliffe . . . . Jacko
Bernard Braden . . . . Davis
Reginald Beckwith . . . . . . Harry
Gene Anderson . . . . May
Rene Asherson . . . . Angela
Arthur Christiansen . . . . . . Jefferson
Austin Trevor . . . . Sir John Kelly
Edward Underdown . . . . . . Sanderson
FANTASY Reporter discovers that simultaneous American and Russian nuclear bomb tests have shifted earth's axis.

13024
IN THE DOGHOUSE (93) (U)
Rank (RFD)
P: Hugh Stewart
D: Darcy Conyers
S: (NOVEL) Alex Duncan (IT'S A VET'S LIFE)
SC: Michael Pertwee
Leslie Phillips . . . . Jimmy Fox-Upton
                                  Upton
Peggy Cummins . . . . Sally Huxley
Hattie Jacques . . . . Insp Gudgeon
James Booth . . . . Bob Skeffington
Dick Bentley . . . . Peddle
Colin Gordon . . . . Dean
Joan Heal . . . . Mrs Peddle
Esma Cannon . . . . Mrs Raikes
Fenella Fielding . . . . Miss Fordyce
Richard Goolden . . . . Ribart
Joan Hickson . . . . Miss Gibbs
Vida Hope . . . . Mrs Crabtree
Kynaston Reeves . . . . Col
COMEDY Stage star helps vetinary surgeon thwart his rival's horse-exporting racket.

13025
PETTICOAT PIRATES (87) *tech/scope* (U)
ABPC (WPD)
P: Gordon L.T. Scott
D: David Macdonald
S: T.J. Morrison
SC: Lew Schwartz, Charlie Drake
Charlie Drake . . . . Charlie
Anne Heywood . . . . Ann Stephens
Cecil Parker . . . . C-in-C
John Turner . . . . Capt Michael Patterson
Maxine Audley . . . . Superintendent
Thorley Walters . . . . Lt Jerome Robertson
Eleanor Summerfield . . . . . . Mabel
Victor Maddern . . . . Nixon
Lionel Murton . . . . Admiral
Kenneth Fortescue . . . . Paul Turner
Dilys Laye . . . . Sue

Murray Melvin . . . . Kenneth
COMEDY WRNS sieze frigate, causing captive stoker to pose as one of them.

13026
THE INNOCENTS (99) (X) *scope*
Achilles (20)
P: Albert Fennell, Jack Clayton
D: Jack Clayton
S: (STORY) Henry James (THE TURN OF THE SCREW)
SC: William Archibald, Truman Capote, John Mortimer
Deborah Kerr . . . . Miss Giddens
Michael Redgrave . . . . Uncle
Peter Wyngarde . . . . Quint
Megs Jenkins . . . . Mrs Grose
Pamela Franklin . . . . Flora
Martin Stephens . . . . Miles
Clytie Jessop . . . . Miss Jessel
Isla Cameron . . . . Anna
FANTASY Spinster governess fights spirits of dead predecessor and her lover for the souls of two orphan children.

DEC

13027
ENTER INSPECTOR DUVAL (64) (U)
Bill & Michael Luckwell (Col)
P: Bill Luckwell, Jock MacGregor
D: Max Varnel
S: Jacques Monteux
SC: J. Henry Piperno
Anton Diffring . . . . Insp Duval
Diane Hart . . . . Jackie
Mark Singleton . . . . Insp Wilson
Charles Mitchell . . . . Brossier
Aiden Grennell . . . . Mark Sinclair
Susan Hallinan . . . . Doreen
Charles Roberts . . . . Charley
CRIME French inspector "helps" Scotland Yard track jewel thief who killed socialite.

13028
NEVER BACK LOSERS (61) (U)
Merton Park (AA)
P: Jack Greenwood
D: Robert Tronson
S: (NOVEL) Edgar Wallace (THE GREEN RIBBON)
SC: Lukas Heller
Jack Hedley . . . . Jim Matthews
Jacqueline Ellis . . . . Marion Palmer
Patrick Magee . . . . Ben Black
Richard Warner . . . . Crabtree
Derek Francis . . . . R.R. Harris
Austin Trevor . . . . Col Warburton
Harry Locke . . . . Burnside
Larry Martyn . . . . Clive Parker
CRIME Insurance investigator uncovers gambling ring behind death of jockey.

13029
THE SINISTER MAN (60) (U)
Merton Park (AA)
P: Jack Greenwood
D: Clive Donner
S: (NOVEL) Edgar Wallace
SC: Robert Stewart
John Bentley . . . . Supt Wills
Patrick Allen . . . . Dr Nelson Pollard
Jacqueline Ellis . . . . Elsa Marlowe
John Glyn-Jones . . . . Dr Maurice Tarn
Eric Young . . . . Johnny Choto
Arnold Lee . . . . Soyoki
Brian McDermott . . . . Sgt Stillman
Gerald Andersen . . . . Maj Paul Amery
Yvonne Buckingham . . . . Miss Russell

CRIME Girl helps supt convict American doctor and Oriental ambassador for murder of archaeologist.

13030
THE YOUNG ONES (108) *tech/scope* (U)
ABPC-Elstree (WPD)
P: Kenneth Harper
D: Sidney J. Furie
S: Peter Myers, Ronald Cass

Cliff Richard	Nicky Bal
Robert Morley	Hamilton Black
Carole Gray	Toni
Teddy Green	Chris
Richard O'Sullivan	Ernest
Melvyn Hayes	Jimmy
Annette Robertson	Barbara
Robertson Hare	Chauffeur
Sonya Cordeau	Dorinda

The Shadows
MUSICAL Teenager stages show in old theatre to save youth club from his father, a property tycoon. (Top Moneymaker: 1962)

13031
PART-TIME WIFE (70) (A)
Danziger (BL)
P: Brian Taylor
D: Max Varnel
S: H.M. McCormack

Anton Rodgers	Tom
Nyree Dawn Porter	Jenny
Kenneth J. Warren	Drew
Henry McCarthy	Whitworth
Mark Singleton	Detective
Susan Richards	Miss Aukland
Raymond Rollett	Barnsdale
June Cunningham	Blonde

COMEDY Insurance salesman lends wife to carhire manager to impress rich uncle and finds he is a thief.

13032
THE PURSUERS (63) (A)
Danziger (Col)
P: Philip Elton, Ralph Goddard
D: Godfrey Grayson
S: Brian Clemens, David Nicholl

Cyril Shaps	Karl Luther
Francis Matthews	David Nelson
Susan Denny	Jenny Walmer
Sheldon Lawrence	Rico
George Murcell	Freddy
John Gabriel	Wally
Tony Doonan	Wilmo
Steve Plytas	Petersen

CRIME Investigator tracks concentration camp chief to flat of nightclub singer.

13033
CASH ON DEMAND (66) (U)
Hammer-Woodpecker (Col)
P: Michael Carreras
D: Quentin Lawrence
S: (TV PLAY) Jacques Gillies (THE GOLD INSIDE)
SC: David T. Chantler, Lewis Greifer

Peter Cushing	Fordyce
Andre Morell	Hepburn
Richard Vernon	Pearson
Barry Lowe	Harvill
Norman Bird	Sanderson
Edith Sharpe	Miss Pringle
Charles Morgan	Collins
Kevin Stoney	Insp Mason

CRIME Bank manager forced to help robber to save kidnapped wife and son.

13034
THE COURT MARTIAL OF MAJOR KELLER (69) (A)
Danziger (WPD)
P: Brian Taylor
D: Ernest Morris
S: Brian Clemens

Laurence Payne	Maj Keller
Susan Stephen	Laura Winch
Ralph Michael	Col Winch
Richard Caldicott	Harrison
Basil Dignam	Morrell
Austin Trevor	Power
Simon Lack	Wilson
Jack McNaughton	Miller
Hugh Cross	Capt Cuby
Humphrey Lestocq	Lt Cameron

Peter Sinclair .... Sgt
WAR Major proves he shot CO for deserting to enemy.

13035
BOMB IN THE HIGH STREET (60) (U)
Foxwarren-Elthea (RFD)
P: Ethel Linder Reiner, T.B.R. Zichy, Henry Passmore
D: Terence Bishop, Peter Bezencenet
S: Benjamin Simcoe

Ronald Howard	Capt Manning
Terry Palmer	Mike
Suzanne Leigh	Jackie
Jack Allen	Supt Haley
Peter Gilmore	Shorty
Russell Waters	Trent
Maurice Good	Feeney
Geoffrey Bayldon	Clay
Jack Lambert	Sgt
Humphrey Lestocq	Reporter

CRIME Eloping teenagers foil gang posing as bomb disposal squad to raid bank.

13036
THE JOHNNY LEYTON TOUCH (10) (U)
Viscount Films (RFI)
MUSICAL Songs

13037
LIGHT IN THE PIAZZA (101) (A) *metro/ scope*
MGM British
P: Arthur Freed
D: Guy Green
S: Elizabeth Spencer
SC: Julius J. Epstein

Olivia de Haviland	Margaret Johnson
Rossano Brazzi	Signor Naccarelli
Yvette Mimieux	Clara Johnson
George Hamilton	Fabrizio Naccarelli
Barry Sullivan	Noel Johnson
Nancy Nevinson	Signora Naccarelli
Isabel Dean	Ann Hawtree
Moultrie Kelsall	Minister

ROMANCE Florence. American industrialist fails to prevent wife from allowing mentally deficient daughter to marry.

1962

JAN

13038
ONLY TWO CAN PLAY (106) (X)
Vale (BL)
P: Frank Launder, Sidney Gilliat
D: Sidney Gilliat
S: (NOVEL) Kingsley Amis (THAT UNCERTAIN FEELING)
SC: Bryan Forbes

Peter Sellers	John Lewis
Mai Zetterling	Liz Gruffyd-Williams
Virginia Maskell	Jean Lewis
Richard Attenborough	Probert
Kenneth Griffith	Jenkins
Raymond Huntley	Vernon Gruffyd-Williams
Maudie Edwards	Mrs Davies
David Davies	Beynon
Meredith Edwards	Clergyman
John le Mesurier	Salter
Frederick Piper	Mr Davies
Graham Stark	Hyman
E. Eynon Evans	Town Clerk

COMEDY Wales. Married librarian tries an affair with rich man's wife.

13039
HAIR OF THE DOG (66) (U)
Parroch (RFD)
P: C. Jack Parsons
D: Terry Bishop
S: John O'Gorman
SC: Tony Hawes

Reginald Beckwith	Fred Tickle
Dorinda Stevens	Ann Tickle
John le Mesurier	Sir Mortimer Gallant
Brian Oulton	Gregory Willett
Alison Bayley	Violet Tickle
Harold Goodwin	Percy
Barbara Windsor	Elsie Grumble
Stanley Morgan	Jim Lester
Stanley Unwin	Vicar
Keith Smith	Interviewer
Tony Hawes	Mr Rembrandt

COMEDY Commissionaire causes strike at razor blade factory when he refuses to shave his beard.

13040
FREEDOM TO DIE (61) (A)
Bayford (Butcher)
P: Charles A. Leeds
D: Francis Searle
S: Arthur la Bern

Paul Maxwell	Craig Owen
Felicity Young	Linda
Bruce Seton	Felix
Kay Callard	Coral
T.P. McKenna	Mike
Laurie Leigh	Julie
Charlie Byrne	Happy Joe

CRIME Robber breaks jail and forces his partner's adopted daughter to surrender safe deposit key.

13041
THE VALIANT (90) (A) bilingual
BHP-Euro International (UA)
P: Jon Penington
D: Roy Baker
S: (PLAY) Robert Mallet (L'EQUIPAGE AU COMPLET)
SC: Willis Hall, Keith Waterhouse

John Mills	Capt Morgan
Ettore Manni	Luigi Durand de la Penne
Roberto Risso	Emilio Bianchi
Robert Shaw	Lt Field
Liam Redmond	Surg/Cdr Reilly
Laurence Naismith	Admiral
Ralph Michael	Cdr Clark
Colin Douglas	Gnrs Mate
John Meillon	Bedford
Moray Watson	Turbull
Dinsdale Landen	Norris
Patrick Barr	Rev Ellis

WAR Alexandria, 1941. Battleship captain tries to force captured Italian frogmen to reveal time-fuse mine.

13042
RETURN OF A STRANGER (63) (A)
Danziger (WPD)
P: Brian Taylor
D: Max Varnel
S: Brian Clemens

John Ireland	Ray Reed
Susan Stephen	Pam Reed
Cyril Shaps	Homer Trent
Timothy Beaton	Tommy Reed
Patrick McAlinney	Whittaker
Kevin Stoney	Wayne
Ian Fleming	Meecham
Raymond Rollett	Somerset
Frederick Piper	Fred

CRIME Ex-convict plots to kill husband of schoolgirl he assaulted.

13043
STORK TALK (97) (A)
Unifilms
P: Lionel Clyne, Bruce Newbery
D: Michael Forlong
S: (PLAY) Gloria Russell (THE NIGHT LIFE OF A VIRILE POTATO)
SC: Donald Ford, Peter Rosser, William Hepper

Tony Britton	Dr Paul Vernon
Anne Heywood	Lisa Vernon
John Turner	Dr Robert Sterne
Nicole Perrault	Tina Monet
Daphne Anderson	Dr Mary Willis
Marie Kean	Mrs Webster
Gladys Henson	Matron
John Sharp	Papa Pierre

COMEDY Gynaecologist fathers twins by his intellectual wife and his French maid.

13044
THE BARBER OF STAMFORD HILL (64) (U)
Ben Arbeid (BL)
D: Casper Wrede
S: (TV PLAY) Ronald Harwood
SC: Ronald Harwood

John Bennett	Mr Figg
Megs Jenkins	Mrs Werner
Maxwell Shaw	Dober
David Franks	Lennie Werner
John Graham	Mr Lister
Trevor Peacock	Willy
Judi Bloom	Marilyn Werner

DRAMA Jewish barber considers marrying widow with two children, but returns to his dumb friend.

13045
THE SPANISH SWORD (62) (U)
Danziger (UA)
P: Brian Taylor
D: Ernest Morris
S: Brian Clemens

Ronald Howard	Sir Richard Clovell
June Thorburn	Lady Eleanor
Nigel Green	Baron Breaute
Trader Faulkner	Philip
Derrick Sherwin	Edmund
Robin Hunter	Thomas of Exeter
Sheila Whittingham	Frances
Barry Shawzin	Redbeard

ADVENTURE 1264. Knight thwarts baron's treason against Henry III and regains stolen treasure.

13046
THREE SPARE WIVES (70) (U)
Danziger (UA)
P: Ralph Goddard
D: Ernest Morris
S: (PLAY) Talbot Rothwell
SC: Eldon Howard

Robin Hunter	George Pittock
Susan Stephen	Susan Pittock
John Hewer	Rupert Duff-Cooper
Barbara Leake	Mrs Hornsby
Ferdy Mayne	Hazim Bey
Gale Sheridan	O'Hara
Dani Seper	Blini
Golda Casimir	Fatima

COMEDY Married man has trouble with Foreign Office when he inherits uncle's three Eastern wives.

13047
A FILM FOR MARIA (17) (U)
Circuits Management Association (CFF)
P: Fred Murray
D:S: Jack Smith
CHILDREN Saturday Morning Cinema Club children catch burglar.

13048
THE SILENT INVASION (70) (U)
Danziger (Planet)
P: John Draper
D: Max Varnel
S: Brian Clemens

Eric Flynn	Erik von Strafen
Petra Davies	Maria
Francis de Wolff	Emile
Martin Benson	Borge
Jan Conrad	Sgt-Major
Noel Dyson	Mme Veroux
Andre Maranne	Argen
Melvyn Hayes	Jean
C. Denier Warren	Gillie

WAR France. Saboteur's sister loves German captain and saves him from Resistance.

13049
CROSSTRAP (61) (A)
Newbery Clyne Avon (Unifilms)
P: Michael Deeley, George Mills
D: Robert Hartford-Davis
S: (NOVEL) John Newton Chance
SC: Philip Wrestler

Laurence Payne	Duke
Jill Adams	Sally
Gary Cockrell	Geoff
Zena Marshall	Rina
Bill Nagy	Gaunt
Robert Cawdron	Joe
Larry Taylor	Peron

CRIME Author and wife find their holiday bungalow occupied by thieves and besieged by a rival gang.

FEB

13050
ALL NIGHT LONG (95) (A)
Rank (RFD)
P: Bob Roberts, Michael Relph
D: Basil Dearden
S: Nel King, Peter Achilles

Patrick McGoohan	Johnny Cousin
Keith Michell	Cass Michaels
Betsy Blair	Emily
Paul Harris	Aurelius Rex
Marti Stevens	Delia Lane
Richard Attenborough	Rod Hamilton
Bernard Braden	Berger
Maria Velasco	Benny
Harry Towb	Phales

Dave Brubeck; Johnny Dankworth; Charles Mingus; Tubby Hayes; Keith Christie; Ray

Dempsey; Geoffrey Holder
MUSICAL Drummer's faked recording almost causes jazzman to strangle his singing wife.

13051
THE PIPER'S TUNE (62) (U)
ACT Films (CFF)
P: Robert Dunbar
D: Muriel Box
S: Frank Wells
SC: Michael Barnes
Mavis Ranson . . . . Anna
Roberta Tovey . . . . Suzy
Angela White . . . . Maria
Malcolm Ranson . . . . Thomas
Brian Wills . . . .'. . . Paul
Graham Wills . . . . Peter
Christopher Rhodes . . . . Captain
Frederick Piper . . . . Gonzales
CHILDREN Spain, period. Children fleeing from Napoleon's army betrayed by spy posing as doctor.

13052
FATE TAKES A HAND (72) (A)
Danziger (MGM)
P: Brian Taylor
D: Max Varnel
S: Brian Clemens
Ronald Howard . . . . Tony
Christina Gregg . . . . Karon
Basil Dignam . . . . Wheeler
Jack Watson . . . . Bulldog
Peter Butterworth . . . . Ronnie
Mary Laura Wood . . . . Sandra
Noel Trevarthen . . . . Bob
Sheila Whittingham . . . . . . Jenny
Valentine Dyall . . . . Wilson
DRAMA GPO man and girl reporter deliver letters stolen 15 years ago.

13053
GO TO BLAZES (84) tech/scope (U)
ABPC (WPD)
P: Kenneth Harper
D: Michael Truman
S: Peter Myers, Ronald Cass
SC: Patrick Campbell, Vivienne Knight
Dave King . . . . Bernard
Robert Morley . . . . Arson Eddie
Daniel Massey . . . . Harry
Dennis Price . . . . Withers
Coral Browne . . . . Colette
Norman Rossington . . . . Alfie
Maggie Smith . . . . Chantal
Miles Malleson . . . . Salesman
Finlay Currie . . . . Judge
James Hayter . . . . Smoker
Wilfrid Lawson . . . . Scrap Dealer
John Welsh . . . . Fire Officer
David Lodge . . . . Sergeant
John le Mesurier . . . . Fisherman
Kynaston Reeves . . . . Clubman
COMEDY Arsonist helps ex-convicts pose as firemen to rob bank.

13054
HMS DEFIANT (101) (A) tech/scope
USA: DAMN THE DEFIANT
GW Films (Col)
P: John Brabourne
D: Lewis Gilbert
S: (NOVEL) Frank Tilsey (MUTINY)
SC: Nigel Kneale, Edmund North
Alec Guinness . . . . Capt Crawford
Dirk Bogarde . . . . Lt Scott-Paget
Anthony Quayle . . . . Vizard
Tom Bell . . . . Evans
Maurice Denham . . . . Mt Goss

Walter Fitzgerald . . . . Admiral Jackson
Victor Maddern . . . . Dawlish
Murray Melvin . . . . Percival Wagstaffe
Nigel Stock . . . . Kilpatrick
Johnny Briggs . . . . Wheatley
David Robinson . . . . Harvey Crawford
Joy Shelton . . . . Mrs Crawford
ADVENTURE 1797. Sadistic lieut's treatment of his captain's son and crew leads to mutiny.

13055
CRAZY DAYS (34) (U)
Doverton (Planet)
P: Henry E. Fisher
D:S: James M. Anderson
N: Hughie Green
COMPILATION Extracts from early films, mostly American.

13056
KIL 1 (61) (A)
Searchlight (Eagle)
P: Stanley Long, Arnold Miller
D: Arnold Louis Miller
S: Bob Kesten
Ronald Howard . . . . Insp Gordon
Jess Conrad . . . . Ted-O
Peter Gray . . . . Hon John
David Graham . . . . Belda
Melody O'Brian . . . . Marlene
Peter Hagen . . . . Sgt Phelan
Lawrence Taylor . . . . Sammy
CRIME Insp traces dud cheques to dead car-breaker, and the teenager who killed him.

13057
THE GOLDEN RABBIT (64) (U)
Argo (RFD)
P: Jack Lamont, Barry Delmaine
D: David MacDonald
S: Dick Sharples, Gerald Kelsey
Timothy Bateson . . . . Henry Tucker
Maureen Beck . . . . Sally
Willoughby Goddard . . . . . . Clitheroe
Dick Bentley . . . . Insp Jackson
John Sharp . . . . Peebles
Humphrey Lestocq . . . .
Ronald Adam . . . .
Kenneth Fortescue . . . . Det Wilson
Raymond Rollett . . . . Manager
COMEDY Business men kidnap girl to obtain bank clerk's formula for making gold.

13058
SEVEN KEYS (57) (U)
Independent Artists (AA)
P: Julian Wintle, Leslie Parkyn
D: Pat Jackson
S: Jack Davies, Henry Blyth
Jeannie Carson . . . . Shirley Steele
Alan Dobie . . . . Russell
Delphi Lawrence . . . . Natalie Worth
John Carson . . . . Norman
John Lee . . . . Jefferson
Anthony Nicholls . . . . Governor
Robertson Hare . . . . Mr Piggott
Fabia Drake . . . . Mrs Piggott
Alan White . . . .'. . Warder
Colin Gordon . . . . Mr Barber
Peter Barkworth . . . . Estate Agent
CRIME Ex-convict's search for dead cell-mate's hidden loot.

13059
POSTMAN'S KNOCK (87) (U)
MGM British
P: Ronald Kinnoch
D: Robert Lynn
S: Jack Trevor Story

SC: Jack Trevor Story, John Briley, Spike Milligan, George Barclay.
Spike Milligan . . . . Harold Petts
Barbara Shelley . . . . Jean
John Wood . . . . PC Woods
Miles Malleson . . . . Psychiatrist
Ronald Adam . . . . Fordyce
Wilfrid Lawson . . . . Postman Lawson
Archie Duncan . . . . Inspector
Warren Mitchell . . . . Rupert
Lance Percival . . . . Joe
Arthur Mullard . . . . Sam
Mario Fabrizi . . . . Villager
COMEDY Efficient village postman transferred to London thwarts thieves posing as postmen.

13060
THE DEVIL NEVER SLEEPS (120) (A)
deluxe/scope
20th Century Fox
P: Leo McCarey, Cecil F. Ford
D: Leo McCarey
S: (NOVEL) Pearl S. Buck
SC: Leo McCarey, Claude Binyon
William Holden . . . . Father O'Banion
Clifton Webb . . . . Father Bovard
France Nuyen . . . . Siu-Lan
Weaver Lee . . . . Ho-San
Athene Seyler . . . . Sister Agnes
Martin Benson . . . . Kuznietsky
Edith Sharpe . . . . Sister Theresa
Robert Lee . . . . Chung Ren
Marie Yang . . . . Mother
Andy Ho . . . . Father
Bert Kwouk . . . . Ah Wang
WAR China, 1948. Communist colonel reforms after raping girl and helps catholic missionaries flee.

13061
TWICE ROUND THE DAFFODILS (89) (A)
GWH Productions (AA)
P: Peter Rogers
D: Gerald Thomas
S: (PLAY) Patrick Cargill, Jack Beale (RING FOR CATTY)
SC: Norman Hudis
Juliet Mills . . . . Catty
Donald Sinden . . . . Ian Richards
Donald Houston . . . . John Rhodes
Kenneth Williams . . . . Harry Halfpenny
Ronald Lewis . . . . Bob White
Andrew Ray . . . . Chris Walker
Joan Sims . . . . Harriet Halfpenny
Jill Ireland . . . . Janet
Lance Percival . . . . George Logg
Sheila Hancock . . . . Dora
Nanette Newman . . . . Joyce
Renee Houston . . . . Matron
Amanda Reiss . . . . Dorothy
Mary Powell . . . . Mrs Rhodes
Barbara Roscoe . . . . Mary
COMEDY Episodic misadventures in male TB sanatorium.

13062
CANDIDATE FOR MURDER (60) (A)
Merton Park (AA)
P: Jack Greenwood
D: David Villiers
S: (STORY) Edgar Wallace (THE BEST LAID PLANS OF A MAN IN LOVE)
SC: Lukas Heller
Michael Gough . . . . Donald Edwards
Erika Remberg . . . . Helena Edwards
Hans Borsody . . . . Kersten
John Justin . . . . Robert Vaughan
Paul Whitsun-Jones . . . . Phillips
Vanda Godsell . . . . Betty Conlon

Jerold Wells . . . . Inspector
Annika Wills . . . . Jacqueline
CRIME Madman hires German to kill actress
wife and shoots him when he reneges.

13063
BACKFIRE! (59) (U)
Merton Park (AA)
P: Jack Greenwood
D: Paul Almond
S: (NOVEL) Edgar Wallace
SC: Robert Stewart
Alfred Burke . . . . Mitchell Logan
Zena Marshall . . . . Pauline Logan
Oliver Johnston . . . . Bernard Curzon
Noel Trevarthen . . . . Jack Bryce
Suzanne Neve . . . . Shirley Curzon
Derek Francis . . . . Arthur Tilsley
John Cazabon . . . . Willy Kyser
Madeleine Christie . . . . Hannah Chenko
CRIME Insurance investigator saves dead
cosmetician's daughter from fir-raising partner.

13064
THE SHARE OUT (61) (U)
Merton Park (AA)
P: Jack Greenwood
D: Gerald Glaister
S: (NOVEL) Edgar Wallace (JACK O'
JUDGEMENT)
SC: Philip Mackie
Bernard Lee . . . . Supt Meredith
Alexander Knox . . . . Col Calderwood
Moira Redmond . . . . Diana Marsh
William Russell . . . . Mike Stafford
Richard Vernon . . . . John Crewe
Richard Warner . . . . Mark Speller
John Gabriel . . . . Monet
Jack Rodney . . . . Gregory
CRIME Tec joins colonel's gang to unmask
him as blackmailer, and kills him to steal his
diamonds.

13065
FLAT TWO (60) (U)
Merton Park (AA)
P: Jack Greenwood
D: Alan Cooke
S: (NOVEL) Edgar Wallace
SC: Lindsay Galloway
John le Mesurier . . . . Warden
Jack Watling . . . . Frank Leamington
Bernard Archard . . . . Insp Trainer
Barry Keegan . . . . Charles Berry
Ann Bell . . . . Susan
Campbell . . . . Hurley Brown
Charles Lloyd Pack . . . . Miller
David Bauer . . . . Emil Louba
CRIME Barrister defending architect is
forced to admit that he himself killed gambler.

13066
THE ROMAN SPRING OF MRS STONE (103)
tech (X)
AA-Seven Arts (WPD)
P: Louis de Rochement, Lothar Wolff
D: Jose Quintero
S: (NOVEL) Tennessee Williams
SC: Gavin Lambert, Jan Read
Vivien Leigh . . . . Karen Stone
Warren Beatty . . . . Paolo di Leo
Lotte Lenya . . . . Contessa Gonzales
Jill St John . . . . Barbara Bingham
Coral Browne . . . . Meg
Jeremy Spenser . . . . Young Man
Ernest Thesiger . . . . Stefano
Paul Stassino . . . . Barber
Bessie Love . . . . Bunny
John Phillips . . . . Tom Stone

Viola Keats . . . . Julia
Peter Dyneley . . . . Greener
Warren Mitchell . . . . Giorgio
Carl Jaffe . . . . Baron
Cleo Laine . . . . Singer
ROMANCE Rome. Rich widowed American
actress falls in love with gigolo who prefers
younger starlet.

MAR

13067
THE BATTLEAXE (66) (U)
Danziger (Par)
P: John Ingram
D: Godfrey Grayson
S: M.M. McCormack
Jill Ireland . . . . Audrey Page
Francis Matthews . . . . Tony Evers
Joan Haythorne . . . . Mrs Page
Michael Beint . . . . Dodson
Olaf Pooley . . . .
Richard Caldicott . . . .
Juliette Manet . . . .
COMEDY Playboy sues socialite for breach
of promise and proves her mother responsible.

13068
DESIGN FOR LOVING (68) (U)
Danziger (Col)
P: John Ingram
D: Godfrey Grayson
S: Mark Grantham
June Thorburn . . . . Barbara Winters
Pete Murray . . . . Lord Stanford
Soraya Rafat . . . . Irene
James Maxwell . . . . Joe
June Cunningham . . . . Alice
Prudence Hyman . . . . Lady Bayliss
Michael Balfour . . . . Bernie
Edward Palmer . . . . Graves
Humphrey Lestocq . . . . Manager
Mary Malcolm . . . . Commere
COMEDY Fashion executive makes artistic
beatnik her chief designer.

13069
VILLAGE OF DAUGHTERS (86) (U)
MGM British
P: George H. Brown
D; George Pollock
S: David Pursall, Jack Seddon
Eric Sykes . . . . Herbert Harris
Scilla Gabel . . . . Angelina Vimercati
Gregoire Aslan . . . . Gastoni
Yvonne Romain . . . . Annunziata Gastoni
John le Mesurier . . . . Don Calogero
Erich Pohlmann . . . . Marcio
Warren Mitchell . . . . Puccelli
Ina de la Haye . . . . Maria Gastoni
Peter Illing . . . . Alfredo Predati
Mario Fabrizi . . . . Antonio Durigo
Graham Stark . . . . Postman
Monty Landis . . . . Faccino
Jill Carson . . . . Lucia Puccelli
Talitha Pol . . . . Gioia Spartaco
COMEDY Sicily. Villagers mistake British
salesman for rich emigrant seeking wife.

13070
OPERATION SNATCH (87) (A)
Keep (RFI)
P: Jules Buck
D: Robert Day
S: Paul Mills
SC: Alan Hackney, John Warren, Len Heath
Terry Thomas . . . . Lt Piggy Wigg
George Sanders . . . . Maj Hobson
Lionel Jeffries . . . . Evans
Jackie Lane . . . . Bianca Tabori

Lee Montague . . . . Miklos Tabori
Michael Trubshawe . . . . Col Marston
James Villiers . . . . Lt Keen
Dinsdale Landen . . . . Capt Whittington
Jeremy Lloyd . . . . Capt James
John Meillon . . . . MO
Gerard Heinz . . . . Col Waldock
Mario Fabrizi . . . . Tall Man
Graham Stark . . . . Soldier
COMEDY Gibraltar. Inept lieut and batman
kidnap ape from German circus to save island
ape colony.

13071
A PAIR OF BRIEFS (90) (A)
Rank (RFD)
P: Betty E. Box
D: Ralph Thomas
S: (PLAY) Harold Brooke, Kay Bannerman
(HOW SAY YOU)
SC: Nicholas Phipps
Michael Craig . . . . Tony Stevens
Mary Peach . . . . Francis Pilbright
Brenda de Banzie . . . . Gladys Pudney
James Robertson Justice . . . Mr Justice Hadden
Roland Culver . . . . Sir John Pilbright
Liz Fraser . . . . Pearly Girl
Ron Moody . . . . Sid Pudney
Jameson Clark . . . . George Lockwood
Charles Heslop . . . . Peebles
Bill Kerr . . . . Victor
Nicholas Phipps . . . . Peter Sutcliffe
Joan Sims . . . . Beryl
Graham Stark . . . . Policeman
Ronnie Stevens . . . . Detective
COMEDY Inept lawyers fall in love while
opposing each other in a case for restitution
of conjugal rights.

13072
THE LAMP IN ASSASSIN MEWS (65) (A)
Danziger (UA)
P: Brian Taylor
D: Godfrey Grayson
S: M.M. McCormack
Francis Matthews . . . . Jack
Lisa Daniely . . . . Mary Clarke
Ian Fleming . . . . Albert Potts
Amy Dalby . . . . Victoria Potts
Ann Sears . . . . Ruth
Anne Lawson . . . . Ella
Derek Tansey . . . . Jarvis
Ann Lancaster . . . . Mrs Dowling
Colin Tapley . . . . Inspector
COMEDY Old couple try to kill councillor
who wants to remove their lamp.

13073
EMERGENCY (63) (U)
Butcher's Films
P:D: Francis Searle
S: Lewis Gilbert, Vernon Harris
SC: Don Nicholl, James O'Connolly
Glyn Houston . . . . Insp Harris
Zena Walker . . . . Joan Bell
Dermot Walsh . . . . John Bell
Colin Tapley . . . . Dr Lloyd
Garard Green . . . . Prof Graham
Anthony Dawes . . . . Sgt Phillips
Edward Ogden . . . . Tommy Day
Helen Forrest . . . . Mrs Day
DRAMA Police seek rare blood from
murderer, footballer and traitor.

13074
THE BREAK (76) (A)
Blakeley's Films (Planet)
P: Tom Blakeley
D: Lance Comfort

S: Pip & Jane Baker
Tony Britton . . . . Greg Parker
William Lucas . . . . Jacko Thomas
Eddie Byrne . . . . Judd Tredegar
Robert Urquhart . . . . Pearson
Sonia Dresdel . . . . Sarah
Edwin Richfield . . . . Moses
Gene Anderson . . . . Jean Tredegar
Christian Gregg . . . . Sue Thomas
CRIME Devon. Guests at smuggler's farm include detective, novelist, fugitive robber, and his sister.

13075
THE GENTLE TERROR (67) (U)
Danziger (UA)
P: Brian Taylor
D: Frank Marshall
S: M.M. McCormack
Terence Alexander . . . . David
Angela Douglas . . . . Nancy
Jill Hyem . . . . Daphne
Laidman Browne . . . . Byrne
Malcolm Webster . . . . Ian
Patrick McAlinney . . . . Sam
Victor Spinetti . . . . Joe
Jack Melford . . . . Insp Miles
COMEDY Shy clerk, suspected of embezzling £5000, catches bank robber who gave it to him.

13076
PLAY IT COOL (81) (U)
Independent Artists-Lynx (AA)
P: Dennis Holt
D: Michael Winner
S: Jack Henry
Billy Fury . . . . Billy Universe
Michael Anderson . . . . Alvin
Dennis Price . . . . Sir Charles Bryant
Richard Wattis . . . . Nervous Man
Anna Palk . . . . Ann Bryant
Maurice Kaufmann . . . . . . Larry Granger
Peter Barkworth . . . . Skinner
Bernie Winters . . . . Sydney Norman
Keith Hamshere . . . . Ringading
Helen Shapiro; Bobby Vee; Danny Williams; Shane Fenton; Jimmy Crawford; Lionel Blair
MUSICAL Teenage singer saves heiress from eloping with rival.

APR
13077
SHE ALWAYS GETS THEIR MAN (61)
Danziger (UA)
P: John Ingram
D: Godfrey Grayson
S: Mark Grantham
Terence Alexander . . . . Bob Conley
Ann Sears . . . . Betty Tate
Sally Smith . . . . Sally
William Fox . . . . Waling
Avril Edgar . . . . Sylvia
Bernice Swanson . . . . May
Gale Sheridan . . . . Phyllis
Michael Balfour . . . . Runkle
COMEDY Hostel girls hire actor to pose as millionaire to foil gold-digging girl.

13078
THE DEVIL'S DAFFODIL (86) bilingual
Omnia-Rialto (Britannia)
P: Steven Pallos, Donald Taylor
D: Akos Rathony
S: (NOVEL) Edgar Wallace (THE DAFFODIL MYSTERY)
SC: Donald Taylor, Basil Dawson
Christopher Lee . . . . Ling Chu

Marius Goring . . . . Oliver Milburgh
Albert Lieven . . . . Raymond Lyne
Penelope Horner . . . . Anne Rider
Ingrid Van Bergen . . . . Gloria
William Lucas . . . . Jack Tarling
Jan Hendricks . . . . Charles
Colin Jeavons . . . . Peter Keene
Peter Illing . . . . Jan Putek
Walter Gotell . . . . Supt Whiteside
Lance Percival . . . . Gendarme
Irene Prador . . . . Maisie
CRIME Airways investigator and Chinese detective track down maniacal heroin smuggler.

13079
THE PAINTED SMILE (60)
Blakeley's Films-Doverton (Planet)
P: Tom Blakeley
D: Lance Comfort
S: Brock Williams
SC: Pip & Jane Baker
Liz Fraser . . . . Jo Lake
Kenneth Griffith . . . . Kleinie
Craig Douglas . . . . Singer
Peter Reynolds . . . . Mark
Tony Wickert . . . . Tom
Nanette Newman . . . . Mary
Harold Berens . . . . Mikhala
CRIME Fugitive tracks confidence trickster to prove he did not kill her partner.

13080
CARRY ON CRUISING (89) (U) *eastman*
GHW Productions (AA)
P: Peter Rogers
D: Gerald Thomas
S: Eric Barker
SC: Norman Hudis
Sidney James . . . . Capt Wellington Crowther
Kenneth Williams . . . . . Leonard Marjoribanks
Kenneth Connor . . . . Arthur Binn
Liz Fraser . . . . Gladys Trimble
Dilys Laye . . . . Flo Castle
Esma Cannon . . . . Bridget MadderJey
Lance Percival . . . . Wilfred Haines
Jimmy Thompson . . . . Sam Turner
Vincent Ball . . . . Jenkins
Cyril Chamberlain . . . . Tom Tree
COMEDY Episodic misadventures of captain and his new crew on Mediterranean cruise.

13081
THE PRINCE AND THE PAUPER (93) (U)
tech
Walt Disney
P: Hugh Attwooll
D: Don Chaffey
S: (NOVEL) Mark Twain
SC: Jack Whittingham
Guy Williams . . . . Miles Hendon
Laurence Naismith . . . . Hertford
Donald Houston . . . . John Canty
Sean Scully . . . . Prince Edward/ Tom Canty
Niall MacGinnis . . . . Father Andrew
Geoffrey Keen . . . . Yokel
Walter Hudd . . . . Archbishop
Paul Rogers . . . . Henry VIII
Dorothy Alison . . . . Mrs Canty
Jane Asher . . . . Lady Jane Grey
Peter Butterworth . . . . Will
Reginald Beckwith . . . . Landlord
ADVENTURE 1547. Prince changes places with beggar's son and becomes involved with thieves.

13082
WALTZ OF THE TOREADORS (102) (X)
eastman

Independent Artists (RFD)
P: Peter de Sarigny
D: John Guillermin
S: (PLAY) Jean Anouilh
SC: Wolf Mankowitz
Peter Sellers . . . . Gen Leo Fitzjohn
Dany Robin . . . . Ghislaine
John Fraser . . . . Robert
Cyril Cusack . . . . Dr Grogan
Margaret Leighton . . . . Emily Fitzjohn
Raymond Huntley . . . . . . Court President
Jean Anderson . . . . Agnes
Cardew Robinson . . . . Midgeley
Vanda Godsell . . . . Mrs Bulstrode
John le Mesurier . . . . Vicar
Prunella Scales . . . . Estella
Denise Coffey . . . . Sidonia
Guy Middleton . . . . Huntsman
Humphrey Lestocq . . . . . . Huntsman
COMEDY 1905. Retired General tries to leave invalid wife for his French mistress but lets her wed his bastard son.

13083
NIGHT OF THE EAGLE (87) (X) USA: BURN WITCH BURN
Independent Artists (AA)
P: Albert Fennell
D: Sidney Hayers
S: (NOVEL) Fritz Leiber jr (CONJURE WIFE)
SC: Charles Beaumont, Richard Matheson, George Baxt
Peter Wyngarde . . . . Norman Taylor
Janet Blair . . . . Tansy Taylor
Margaret Johnston . . . . Flora Carr
Anthony Nicholls . . . . Harvey Sawtelle
Colin Gordon . . . . Prof Lindsay Carr
Kathleen Byron . . . . Evelyn Sawtelle
Reginald Beckwith . . . . . . Harold Gunnison
Jessica Dunning . . . . Hilda Gunnison
Norman Bird . . . . Doctor
Judith Stott . . . . Margaret Abbott
Bill Mitchell . . . . Fred Jennings
HORROR Jealous cripple uses black magic to animate stone eagle to kill medical professor and wife.

13084
A KIND OF LOVING (112) (X)
Vic Films (AA)
P: Joseph Janni
D: John Schlesinger
S: (NOVEL) Stan Barstow
SC: Willis Hall, Keith Waterhouse
Alan Bates . . . . Vic Brown
June Ritchie . . . . Ingrid Rothwell
Thora Hird . . . . Mrs Rothwell
Bert Palmer . . . . Mr Brown
Pat Keen . . . . Christine
James Bolam . . . . Jeff
Jack Smethurst . . . . Conroy
Gwen Nelson . . . . Mrs Brown
John Ronane . . . . Draughtsman
David Mahlowe . . . . David
Patsy Rowlands . . . . Dorothy
Michael Deacon . . . . Les
Jerry Desmonde . . . . TV Compere
DRAMA Northern factory draughtsman weds girl he impregnates and they live with her possessive mother.

13085
SHE'LL HAVE TO GO (90) (U)
Asher Brothers (AA)
P: Jack & Robert Asher
D: Robert Asher
S: (PLAY) Ian Stuart Black (WE MUST KILL TONI)
SC: John Waterhouse

Bob Monkhouse . . . . Francis Oberon
Alfred Marks . . . . Douglas Oberon
Hattie Jacques . . . . Miss Richards
Anna Karina . . . . Toni Oberon
Dennis Lotis . . . . Gilbert
Clive Dunn . . . . Chemist
Peter Butterworth . . . . Doctor
Graham Stark . . . . Arnold
Hugh Lloyd . . . . MacDonald
Harry Locke . . . . Station Master
COMEDY Broke brothers scheme to marry or
murder their Corsican cousin.

13086
NUMBER SIX (59) (U)
Merton Park (AA)
P: Jack Greenwood
D: Robert Tronson
S: (NOVEL) Edgar Wallace
SC: Philip Mackie
Ivan Desny . . . . Charles Valentine
Nadja Regin . . . . Nadia Leiven
Michael Goodliffe . . . . Supt Hallett
Brian Bedford . . . . Jimmy Gale
Joyce Blair . . . . Carol Clyde
Leonard Sachs . . . . Welland
Michael Shaw . . . . Luigi Pirani
Harold Goodwin . . . . Smith
CRIME Secret agent foils crook's scheme to
rob heiress.

13087
IT'S TRAD, DAD! (73) (U)
Amicus (Col)
P:S: Milton Subotsky
D: Dick Lester
Helen Shapiro . . . . Helen
Craig Douglas . . . . Craig
Felix Felton . . . . Mayor
Timothy Bateson . . . . Coffee Shop Owner
Frank Thornton . . . . TV Director
Bruce Lacey . . . . Gardener
Hugh Lloyd . . . . Usher
Ronnie Stevens . . . . TV Director
Arthur Mullard . . . . Police Chief
Mario Fabrizi . . . . Customer
Chubby Checker; John Leyton; Gene Vincent;
Brook Brothers; Gary (US) Bonds; Gene
McDaniels; Del Shannon; Chris Barber and his
Band; Ottillie Patterson; Acker Bilk and his
Band; Kenny Ball and his Jazzmen; Terry
Lightfoot and his Band; Bob Wallis and his
Jazzmen; Temperance Seven; David Jacobs;
Pete Murray; Alan Freeman
MUSICAL Teenagers win over pompous
mayor by staging jazz festival.

13088
THE ROAD TO HONG KONG (91) (U)
Melnor (UA) reissue: 1964
P: Melvin Frank
D: Norman Panama
S: Norman Panama, Melvin Frank
Bing Crosby . . . . Harry Turner
Bob Hope . . . . Chester Babcock
Joan Collins . . . . Diane
Dorothy Lamour . . . . Herself
Robert Morley . . . . The Leader
Walter Gotell . . . . Dr Zorbb
Felix Aylmer . . . . Grand Lama
Alan Gifford . . . . Official
Peter Sellers . . . . Indian Doctor
David Niven . . . . Lama
Jerry Colonna . . . . Man
Dave King . . . . Chinaman
Frank Sinatra . . . . Astronaut
Dean Martin . . . . Astronaut
COMEDY China. Crook seeks rocket fuel
formula memorised by salesman.

13089
REACH FOR GLORY (86) (X)
Blazer (Gala)
P: John Kohn, Jud Kinberg
D: Philip Leacock
S: (NOVEL) John Rae (THE CUSTARD
BOYS)
SC: John Rae, John Kohn, Jud Kinberg
Harry Andrews . . . . Capt Curlew
Kay Walsh . . . . Mrs Curlew
Michael Anderson jr . . . . Lewis Craig
Oliver Grimm . . . . Mark Stein
Martin Tomlinson . . . . John Curlew
Alexis Kanner . . . . Stephen
Michael Trubshawe . . . . Maj Burton
George Pravda . . . . Stein
Richard Vernon . . . . Dr Alrich
Peter Furnell . . . . Arthur Chettle
James Luck . . . . Michael Freen
Allan Jeayes . . . . Crabtree
DRAMA 1942. Unfit soldier's evacuated son
joins boys in persecuting Austrian refugee.
(UN Award: 1962)

13090
MRS GIBBONS' BOYS (82) (A) scope
Byron (BL)
P: Harry Halstead
D: Max Varnel
S: (PLAY) Will Glickman, Joseph Stein
SC: Max Varnel, Peter Blackmore
Kathleen Harrison . . . . Mrs Gibbons
Lionel Jeffries . . . . Lester Martins
Diana Dors . . . . Myra
John le Mesurier . . . . Coles
Frederick Bartman . . . . Mike Gibbons
David Lodge . . . . Frank Gibbons
Dick Emery . . . . Woodrow
Eric Pohlmann . . . . Morelli
Milo O'Shea . . . . Horse
Peter Hempson . . . . Ronnie
COMEDY Escaped convicts almost ruin their
widowed mother's romance.

13091
CROOKS ANONYMOUS (88) (U)
Independent Artists (AA)
P: Julian Wintle, Leslie Parkyn
D: Ken Annakin
S: Jack Davies, Henry Blyth
Leslie Phillips . . . . Dandy Forsdyke
Stanley Baxter . . . . R.S. Widdowes
Wilfrid Hyde White . . . . Montague
Julie Christie . . . . Babette
James Robertson Justice . . . . Sir Harvey
                                    Russellrod
Michael Medwin . . . . Ronnie
Pauline Jameson . . . . Prunella
Robertson Hare . . . . Grimsdale
Raymond Huntley . . . . Wagstaffe
Harry Fowler . . . . Woods
Charles Lloyd Pack . . . . Fletcher
Arthur Mullard . . . . Grogan
Joyce Blair . . . . Carol
Colin Gordon . . . . Drunk
Dick Emery . . . . Cundall
COMEDY Thief joins ex-convict's
organisation for reform but backslides.

13092
THE POT CARRIERS (84) (A)
ABPC (WPD)
P: Gordon L.T. Scott
D: Peter Graham Scott
S: (TV PLAY) Mike Watts
SC: Mike Watts, T.J. Morrison
Ronald Fraser . . . . Redband
Paul Massie . . . . James Rainbow
Carole Lesley . . . . Wendy
Dennis Price . . . . Smooth-tongue

Paul Rogers . . . . Governor
Davy Kaye . . . . Mouse
Eddie Byrne . . . . Chief Bailey
Alfred Burke . . . . Lang
Vanda Godsell . . . . Redbeard's Wife
Campbell Singer . . . . PO Mott
Patrick McAlliney . . . . Dillon
David Ensor . . . . Judge
COMEDY Young prisoner takes blame for
old lag when his plot to steal ham goes wrong.

13093
GAOLBREAK (61) (U)
Butcher's Films
P: Francis Searle, Ronald Liles
D: Francis Searle
S: A.R. Rawlinson
Peter Reynolds . . . . Eddie Wallis
Avice Landone . . . . Mrs Wallis
David Kernan . . . . Len Rogerson
Carol White . . . . Carol Marshall
David Gregory . . . . Ron Wallis
John Blythe . . . . Slim
Robert Desmond . . . . Page
Geoffrey Hibbert . . . . Dr Cambus
CRIME Crooked newsagent's son helps brother
break jail to rob auctioneer's safe.

13094
BEHAVE YOURSELF (29) (U)
Harold Baim (UA)
D:S: Michael Winner
Dennis Price
Jack Jackson
Pete Murray
Glen Mason
Harold Berens
Bernice Swanson
Alexandra Sinclair
COMEDY Correct behaviour and manners
humourously illustrated.

MAY

13095
THE TRAITORS (69) (A)
Ello (RFD)
P:SC: James O'Connolly
D: Robert Tronson
S: J.P. O'Connolly, J. Levy
Patrick Allen . . . . John Lane
James Maxwell . . . . Ray Ellis
Ewan, Roberts . . . . Col Burlington
Jacqueline Ellis . . . . Mary
Zena Walker . . . . Annette Lane
Jeffrey Segal . . . . Dr Lindt
Harold Goodwin . . . . Edwards
CRIME Agent and NATO man uncover
communist spy ring behind death of
scientist.

13096
TERM OF TRIAL (130) (X)
Remus-Romulus (WPD)
P: James Woolf
D:SC: Peter Glenville
S: (NOVEL) James Barlow
Laurence Olivier . . . . Graham Weir
Simone Signoret . . . . Anne Weir
Sarah Miles . . . . Shirley Taylor
Hugh Griffith . . . . O'Hara
Terence Stamp . . . . Mitchell
Roland Culver . . . . Trowman
Frank Pettingell . . . . Ferguson
Thora Hird . . . . Mrs Taylor
Norman Bird . . . . Mr Taylor
Dudley Foster . . . . Sgt Kiernan
Newton Blick . . . . Prosecutor
Allan Cuthbertson . . . . Sylvan-Jones
Nicholas Hannen . . . . Sharp

Lloyd Lamble . . . . Insp Ullyatt
Vanda Godsell . . . . Mrs Thompson
Earl Cameron . . . . Chard
DRAMA Teenager charges teacher with
assault when he rejects her advances.

13097
THE QUARE FELLOW (90) (X)
Liger (Bry)
P: Anthony Havelock-Allan
D: Arthur Dreifuss
S: (PLAY) Brendan Behan
SC: Arthur Dreifuss, Jacqueline Sundstrom
Patrick McGoohan . . . . . . Thomas Crimmin
Sylvia Syms . . . . Kathleen
Walter Macken . . . . Warder Regan
Harry Brogan . . . . Dunlavin
Dermot Kelly . . . . Donelly
Hilton Edwards . . . . Holy Healy
Marie Kean . . . . Mrs O'Hara
Pauline Delany . . . . Mickser's Wife
Philip O'Flynn . . . . Governor
Arthur O'Sullivan . . . . Himself
John Welsh . . . . Carroll
Jack Cunningham . . . . Chief Warder
Norman Rodway . . . . Lavery
CRIME Dublin. New warder comes to
oppose hanging after learning why
condemned man killed his brother.

13098
STRONGROOM (80) (A)
Theatrecraft (Bry)
P: Guido Coen
D: Vernon Sewell
S: Richard Harris
SC: Richard Harris, Max Marquis
Derren Nesbitt . . . . Griff
Colin Gordon . . . . Spencer
Ann Lynn . . . . Rose Taylor
Keith Faulkner . . . . Len
Morgan Sheppard . . . . Alec
Hilda Fenemore . . . . Charlady
Diana Chesney . . . . Charlady
Jack Stewart . . . . Sgt McIntyre
Colin Tapley . . . . Haynes
Ian Colin . . . . Creighton
CRIME Car breakers rob bank at Easter
and lock the manager and his secretary in
airtight vault.

13099
TWO AND TWO MAKE SIX (89) (A)
Prometheus (Bry)
P: Monja Danischewsky, Norman Priggen
D: Freddie Francis
S: Monja Danischewsky
George Chakaris . . . . Larry Curado
Janette Scott . . . . Irene
Alfred Lynch . . . . Tom
Jackie Lane . . . . Julie
Athene Seyler . . . . Aunt Phoebe
Bernard Braden . . . . Sgt Sokolow
Malcolm Keen . . . . Harry Stoneham
Ambrosine Philpotts . . . . . Lady Smith Adams
Jack Mac Gowran . . . . Porter
Robert Ayres . . . . Col Thompson
Edward Evans . . . . Mack
Gary Cockrill . . . . Leo Kober
COMEDY USAAF deserter and another
motorcyclist unknowingly exchange their
girl pillion riders.

13100
THE PIRATES OF BLOOD RIVER (84) (U)
eastman/scope
Hammer (Col)
P: Anthony Nelson Keys
D: John Gilling
S: Jimmy Sangster

SC: John Gilling, John Hunter
Kerwin Matthews . . . . Jonathan Standing
Christopher Lee . . . . la Roche
Glenn Corbett . . . . Henry
Peter Arne . . . . Hench
Marla Landi . . . . Bess
Oliver Reed . . . . Brocaire
Andrew Keir . . . . Jason Standing
Michael Ripper . . . . Mac
David Lodge . . . . Smith
Marie Devereux . . . . Maggie
ADVENTURE Period. Pirate forces fugitive
to help him raid Huguenot settlement.

13101
THE DURANT AFFAIR (73) (U)
Danziger (Par)
P: Philip Elton
D: Godfrey Grayson
S: Eldon Howard
Jane Griffiths . . . . Mary Grant
Conrad Phillips . . . . Julian Armour
Nigel Green . . . . Sir Patrick
Francis de Wolff . . . .
Richard Caldicott . . . .
Simon Lack . . . . Roland Farley
Ann Lancaster . . . .
Katharine Pate . . . . Ethel Durant
DRAMA Solicitor persuades bastard spinster
to contest her mother's will.

13102
WHAT EVERY WOMAN WANTS (69) (U)
Danziger (UA)
P: Brian Taylor
D: Ernest Morris
S: M.M. McCormack
William Fox . . . . Philip Goodwin
Hy Hazell . . . . Jean Goodwin
Dennis Lotis . . . . Tom Yardley
Elizabeth Shepherd . . . . . . Sue Goodwin
Guy Middleton . . . . George Barker
Andrew Faulds . . . . Derek Chadwick
Patsy Smart . . . . Hilda
Ian Fleming . . . . Nelson
George Merritt . . . . Maxwell
COMEDY Wife and daughter scheme to
change the characters of their husbands,
marriage counsellor and reporter.

13103
WORLD WITHOUT SHAME (71) (A) *eastman*
Mistral (Gala)
P: Russell Gay
D:S: Donovan Winter
Yvonne Martel
Larry Bowen
Diane Valerie
Jean Robert
Laurel Grey
Laura Beaumont
NUDIST Pools winners live naked on
Mediterranean island.

13104
AMBUSH IN LEOPARD STREET (60) (A)
Bill & Michael Luckwell (Col)
P: Bill Luckwell, Jock MacGregor
D: J. Henry Piperno
S: Bernard Spicer
SC: Bernard Spicer, Ahmed Faroughy
James Kenney . . . . Johnny
Michael Brennan . . . . Harry
Bruce Seton . . . . Nimmo
Norman Rodway . . . . Kegs
Jean Harvey . . . . Jean
Pauline Delany . . . . Cath
Marie Conmee . . . . Myra
CRIME Retired crook's plan to ambush
diamond consignment goes wrong.

13105
TWO LETTER ALIBI (60) (A)
Playpont (BL)
P: E.M. Smedley Aston
D: Robert Lynn
S: (NOVEL) Andrew Garve (DEATH AND
THE SKY ABOVE)
SC: Roger Marshall
Peter Williams . . . . Charles
Petra Davies . . . . Kathy
Ursula Howells . . . . Louise
Ronald Adam . . . . Sir John Fawcett
Bernard Archard . . . . Duke
Stratford Johns . . . . Bates
Peter Howell . . . . Carlton
CRIME TV star proves her convicted lover
did not kill his alcoholic wife.

13106
NIGHT WITHOUT PITY (56) (A)
Parroch (GEF)
P: Jack Parsons
D: Theodore Zichy
S: Aubrey Cash
Sarah Lawson . . . . Diana Martin
Neil McCallum . . . . O'Brien
Alan Edwards . . . . Randall
Dorinda Stevens . . . . Girl Friend
Michael Browning . . . . Philip
Patrick Newell . . . . Doctor
Beatrice Varley . . . . Mother
John Moulder Brown . . . . . Geoffrey Martin
Brian Weske . . . . Arthur
Vanda Godsell . . . . Tart
CRIME Crook holds woman and child
captive while his partner robs her husband's
factory.

13107
THE INSPECTOR (111) (A) *deluxe/scope*
Red Lion (20)
P: Mark Robson, Bob McNaught
D: Philip Dunne
S: (NOVEL) Jan de Hartog
SC: Nelson Gidding
Stephen Boyd . . . . Peter Jongman
Dolores Hart . . . . Lisa Held
Leo McKern . . . . Brandt
Hugh Griffith . . . . Van der Pink
Harry Andrews . . . . Ayoob
Donald Pleasence . . . . Sgt Wolters
Robert Stephens . . . . Dickens
Marius Goring . . . . Thorens
Finlay Currie . . . . De Kooi
Harold Goldblatt . . . . Dr Mitropoulos
Neil McCallum . . . . Browne
Geoffrey Keen . . . . Bartels
Jean Anderson . . . . Mrs Jongman
Tibby Brittain . . . . MP Sergeant
ADVENTURE 1946. Dutch inspector
smuggles Jewess from Holland to Palestine,
via Tangier.

JUN

13108
THE PHANTOM OF THE OPERA (84) (A)
eastman
Hammer-Laverstock (U)
P:SC: Anthony Hinds
D: Terence Fisher
S: (NOVEL) Gaston Leroux
Herbert Lom . . . . Prof Petrie
Heather Sears . . . . Christine Charles
Thorley Walters . . . . Lattimer
Michael Gough . . . . Lord Ambrose d'Arcy
Edward de Souza . . . . Harry Hunter
Miles Malleson . . . . Cabby
Miriam Karlin . . . . Charwoman
Marne Maitland . . . . Xavier

Harold Goodwin . . . . Bill
Martin Miller . . . . Rossi
John Harvey . . . . Vickers
Ian Wilson . . . . Dwarf
Renee Houston . . . . Mrs Tucker
HORROR Burned composer, cheated by Lord, trains girl to sing in his opera.

13109
CAPTAIN CLEGG (82) (A) *tech* USA: NIGHT CREATURES
Hammer-Merlin-Major (UI)
P: John Temple-Smith
D: Peter Graham Scott
S: (NOVEL) Russell Thorndike (DR SYN)
SC: Barbara S. Harper, Anthony Hinds
Peter Cushing . . . . Dr Blyss
Yvonne Romain . . . . Imogene
Patrick Allen . . . . Capt Collier
Oliver Reed . . . . Harry Crabtree
Michael Ripper . . . . Mipps
Martin Benson . . . . Rash
David Lodge . . . . Bosun
Daphne Anderson . . . . Mrs Rash
Derek Francis . . . . Squire
Milton Reid . . . . Mulatto
ADVENTURE Dymchurch, 1792. Captain unmasks vicar as the 'dead' pirate leader of smugglers who pose as ghosts.

13110
GANG WAR (65) (A)
Danziger (UA)
P: Brian Langslow
D: Frank Marshall
S: Mark Grantham
Sean Kelly . . . . Insp Bob Craig
Eira Heath . . . . Maria Alexis
David Davies . . . . Jim Alexis
Sean Sullivan . . . . Al Hodges
John Gabriel . . . . Doc Tobin
Mark Singleton . . . . Tony Danton
Colin Tapley . . . . Paul Alexis
Leon Cortez . . . . Grimes
CRIME Club owner and Chicago crook kill rival gangster's brother in an effort to take over jukebox racket.

13111
SERENA (62) (U)
Butcher's Films
P: John I. Phillips
D: Peter Maxwell
S: Edward & Valerie Abraham
SC: Edward Abrahams, Reginald Hearne
Patrick Holt . . . . Insp Gregory
Emrys Jones . . . . Howard Rogers
Honor Blackman . . . . Ann Rogers
Bruce Beeby . . . . Sgt Conway
John Horsley . . . . Mr Fisher
Robert Perceval . . . . Bank Manager
Wally Patch . . . . Barman
CRIME Inspector proves artist's model shot his wife and is posing as her.

13112
A PRIZE OF ARMS (105) (A)
Inter-State   (Bry)
P: George Maynard
D: Cliff Owen
S: Nicholas Roeg, Kevin Kavanagh
SC: Paul Ryder
Stanley Baker . . . . Turpin
Helmut Schmidt . . . . Swavek
Tom Bell . . . . Fenner
John Phillips . . . . Col Fowler
Patrick Magee . . . . RSM Hicks
John Westbrook . . . . Capt Stafford
Kenneth Mackintosh . . . . . Capt Nicholson

Jack May . . . . MO
Frank Gatliff . . . . Maj Palmer
Michael Ripper . . . . Cpl Freeman
John Rees . . . . Sgt Jones
CRIME Sussex. Crooks pose as soldiers to steal £250,000 from army camp.

13113
MYSTERIOUS ISLAND (100) (U) *tech*
Ameran (Col)
P: Charles H. Schneer
D: Cy Endfield
S: (NOVEL) Jules Verne
SC: John Prebble, Daniel Ullman, Crane Wilbur
Michael Craig . . . . Capt Cyrus Harding
Joan Greenwood . . . . Lady Mary Fairchild
Michael Callan . . . . Herbert Brown
Gary Merrill . . . . Gideon Spillett
Herbert Lom . . . . Capt Nemo
Beth Rogan . . . . Elena
Percy Herbert . . . . Sgt Pencroft
Dan Jackson . . . . Neb
Nigel Green . . . . Tom
FANTASY 1865. Union Army prisoners of war escape by balloon to Pacific island where an inventor has created monsters.

13114
THE WEBSTER BOY (83) (A)
Emmet Dalton (RFI)
D: Don Chaffey
S: Leo Marks
SC: Ted Allan
John Cassavetes . . . . Vance Miller
Elizabeth Sellars . . . . Margaret Webster
David Farrar . . . . Paul Webster
Niall MacGinnis . . . . Headmaster
Geoffrey Bayldon . . . . Charles Jamison
Richard O'Sullivan . . . . Jimmy Webster
Karl Lanchbury . . . . Michael Johnson
John Bull . . . . Alfred Baxter
Norman Rodway . . . . Donald Saunders
Seymour Cassel Vic
DRAMA Sadistic schoolteacher persecutes boy he suspects to be an ex-convict's son.

13115
TIARA TAHITI (100) (A) *eastman*
Rank (RFD)
P: Ivan Foxwell
D: William T. Kotcheff
S: (NOVEL) Geoffrey Cotterell
SC: Geoffrey Cotterell, Ivan Foxwell, Mordecai Richler
James Mason . . . . Capt Brett Aimsley
John Mills . . . . Lt-col Clifford
Claude Dauphin . . . . Henri Farengue
Herbert Lom . . . . Chong Sing
Rosenda Monteros . . . . Belle Annie
Jacques Marin . . . . Desmoulins
Libby Morris . . . . Adele Franklin
Madge Ryan . . . . Millie Brooks
Gary Cockrell . . . . Joey
Peter Barkworth . . . . Lt David Harper
DRAMA Tahiti. Beachcomber causes deportation of tycoon who cashiered him during war.

13116
SHE KNOWS Y'KNOW (72) (A)
Eternal (GN)
P: Maurice J. Wilson
D: Montgomery Tully
S: (PLAY) Kate Sullivan (THE RELUCTANT GRANDMOTHER)
SC: Montgomery Tully, Maurice J. Wilson
Hylda Baker . . . . Hylda Worswick
Cyril Smith . . . . Joe Worswick

Joe Gibbons . . . . Charlie Todger
Peter Myers . . . . Leslie Worswick
Linda Castle . . . . Marilyn Smallhope
Tim Connor . . . . Terry Roy
Neil Wilson . . . . Clarence Smallhope
Joan Sanderson . . . . .Euphemia Smallhope
COMEDY Lancs. Student's mother tries to make her lodger take blame for flirt's pregnancy.

13117
GUNS OF DARKNESS (102) (A)
Cavalcade-Concorde (WPD)
P: Ben Kadish, Thomas Clyde
D: Anthony Asquith
S: (NOVEL) Francis Clifford (ACT OF MERCY)
SC: John Mortimer
Leslie Caron . . . . Claire Jordan
David Niven . . . . Tom Jordan
James Robertson Justice . . . Hugo Bryant
David Opatoshu . . . . Rivera
Richard Pearson . . . . Bastian
Eleanor Summerfield . . . . . . Mrs Bastian
Derek Godfrey . . . . Hernandez
Ian Hunter . . . . Dr Swann
Sandor Eles . . . . Lt Gomez
ADVENTURE South America..Pacifist planter and pregnant wife help wounded president escape revolutionaries.

JUL

13118
LIFE FOR RUTH (91) (A) USA: WALK IN THE SHADOW
AFM (RFD)
P: Michael Relph
D: Basil Dearden
S: Janet Green, John McCormack
Michael Craig . . . . John Harris
Patrick McGoohan . . . . Dr Jim Brown
Janet Munro . . . . Pat Harris
Paul Rogers . . . . Hart Davis
Malcolm Keen . . . . Mr Harris
Norman Wooland . . . . Crown Counsel
Megs Jenkins . . . . Mrs Gordon
John Barrie . . . . Mr Gordon
Walter Hudd . . . . Judge
Leslie Sands . . . . Clyde
Michael Aldridge . . . . Howard
Lynne Taylor . . . . Ruth Harris
Basil Dignam . . . . Mapleton
Frank Finlay . . . . Father
Maureen Pryor . . . . Mother
DRAMA Durham. Agnostic doctor prosecutes religious miner for refusing blood transfusion for his dying daughter.

13119
FLIGHT FROM SINGAPORE (74) (U)
President (Par)
P: James Mellor
D:S: Dudley Birch
Patrick Allan . . . . John Scott
Patrick Holt . . . . S/L Hill
William Abney . . . . F/L Bob Elliott
Harry Fowler . . . . Sgt Brooks
Denis Holmes . . . . Smithy
Jane Jordan Rogers . . . . Cleo
Rosemary Dorken . . . . Joan Elliott
ADVENTURE Malaya Pilots crash in jungle while transporting blood.

13120
THE DAY OF THE TRIFFIDS (94) (X)
eastman/scope
Security (RFD)
P: Philip Yordan, George Pitcher

D: Steve Sekeley
S: (NOVEL) John Wyndham
SC: Philip Yordan

Howard Keel	Bill Masen
Nicole Maurey	Christine Durrant
Janette Scott	Karen Goodwin
Kieron Moore	Tom Goodwin
Mervyn Johns	Mr Coker
Alison Leggatt	Mrs Coker
Janina Faye	Susan
Geoffrey Matthews	Luis de la Vega
Gilgi Hauser	Teresa de la Vega
Carol Ann Ford	Bettina

HORROR Meteorites blind populations of London, Paris and Spain, activating giant mobile plants.

13121
THE AMOROUS PRAWN (89) (U)
Covent Garden (BL)
P: Leslie Gilliat
D: Anthony Kimmins
S: (PLAY) Anthony Kimmins
SC: Anthony Kimmins, Nicholas Phipps

Ian Carmichael	Cpl Sidney Green
Joan Greenwood	Lady Fitzadam
Cecil Parker	Gen Fitzadam
Dennis Price	Prawn
Robert Beatty	Larry Hoffman
Finlay Currie	Lochaye
Liz Fraser	Susie Tidmarsh
Robert Nichols	Sam Goulansky
Bridget Armstrong	Biddy O'Hara
Harry Locke	Albert Huggins
Derek Nimmo	Willie Maltravers
RSM Brittain	Sgt
Sandra Dorne	Dusty Babs

COMEDY Scotland. Absent general's wife poses as widow and his staff pose as servants to board American lodgers.

13122
TIME TO REMEMBER (58) (U)
Merton Park (AA)
P: Jack Greenwood
D: Charles Jarrett
S: (NOVEL) Edgar Wallace (THE MAN WHO BOUGHT LONDON)
SC: Arthur la Bern

Yvonne Monlaur	Suzanne
Harry H. Corbett	Jack Burgess
Robert Rietty	Victor
Ernest Clark	Cracknell
David Lodge	Jumbo Johnson
Ray Barrett	Sammy
Genine Graham	Mrs Johnson
Patricia Mort	Vera
Jack Watson	Insp Bolam

CRIME Estate agent finds gem-thief's cache, sought by his wife and associates.

13123
LOLITA (153) (X)
AA-Seven Arts-Anya-Transworld (MGM
P: James B. Harris
D: Stanley Kubrick
S: (NOVEL) Vladimir Nabokov
SC: Vladimir Nabokov

James Mason	Humbert Humbert Humbert
Shelley Winters	Charlotte Haze
Sue Lyon	Lolita Haze
Peter Sellers	Clare Quilty
Gary Cockrell	Dick
Jerry Stovin	John Farlow
Diana Decker	Jean Farlow
Lois Maxwell	Mary Lore
Cec Linder	Physician
Bill Greene	Swine
Shirley Douglas	Mrs Starch
Marianne Stone	Vivian Darkbloom

Marion Mathie	Miss Lebone
James Dyrenforth	Beale

DRAMA Ohio. Lecturer weds widow, elopes with her teenage daughter, and shoots pursuant playwright.

13124 THE PLAYBOY OF THE WESTERN WORLD (100) (U) *eastman*
FourProvinces (BL)
P: Michael Killanin, Brendan Smith, Denis O'Dell
D:SC: Brian Desmond Hurst
S: (PLAY) John Millington Synge

Siobhan McKenna	Pegeen Mike
Gary Raymond	Christy Mahan
Elspeth March	Widow Quin
Liam Redmond	Michael James
Niall McGinnis	Old Mahon
John Welsh	Philly Cullen
Michael O'Briain	Shawn Keogh
Brendan Cauldwell	Jimmy Farrell

COMEDY Kerry. Innkeeper's daughter falls for man who thinks he has killed his Tyrannical father.

13125
SOME PEOPLE (93) (A) *eastman*
Vic Films (AA)
P: James Archibald
D: Clive Donner
S: John Eldridge

Kenneth More	Mr Smith
Ray Brooks	Johnnie
Annika Wills	Anne Smith
Michael Gwynn	Vicar
Cyril Luckham	Magistrate
David Andrews	Bill
Angela Douglas	Terry
Harry H. Corbett	Father
Fanny Corby	Mother
David Hemmings	Bert
Timothy Nightingale	Tim
Frankie Dymon jr	Jimmy

MUSICAL Choirmaster reforms teenagers with "Duke of Edinburgh Award Scheme".

13126
DER ROSENKAVALIER (192) (U) *eastman*
Poetic-Rank (RFD)
P:D: Paul Czinner
S: (OPERA) Hugo von Hofmannsthal, Richard Strauss

Elisabeth Schwarzkopf	Princess von Werdenberg
Sena Jurinac	Octavian
Anneliese Rothenberger	Sophie
Otto Edelmann	Baron von Lerchenau
Erich Kunz	Herr von Faninal
Judith Hellwig	Duenna
Renato Ercolani	Valzacchi
Hilde Rossel-Majdan	Annina
Alois Pernerstorfer	Commissary

MUSICAL Salzberg Festival performance of the opera.

13127
THE LION (96) *deluxe/scope* (U)
20th Century Fox
P: Samuel G. Engel
D: Jack Cardiff
S: (NOVEL) Joseph Kessel
SC: Irene & Louis Kamp

William Holden	Robert Hayward
Trevor Howard	John Bullitt
Capucine	Christine Bullitt
Pamela Franklin	Tina
Makara Kwaiha Ramadhani	Bogo
Zakee	Ol' Kalu
Paul Oduor	Oriunga

ADVENTURE Kenya. Game warden loses wife to her first husband after shooting daughter's pet lion.

13128
I THANK A FOOL (100) (A) *metro/scope*
MGM British
P: Anatole de Grunwald
D: Robert Stevens
S: (NOVEL) Audrey Erskine Lindop
SC: Karl Tunberg

Susan Hayward	Christine Allison
Peter Finch	Stephen Dane
Diane Cilento	Liane Dane
Cyril Cusack	Capt Ferris
Kieron Moore	Roscoe
Athene Seyler	Aunt Heather
Richard Wattis	Ebblington
Brenda de Banzie	Nurse Drew
J.G. Devlin	Coroner
Clive Morton	Judge
Miriam Karlin	Woman
Laurence Naismith	O'Grady

CRIME Ireland. Ex-doctor suspects prosecutor of engineering death of his insane wife.

13129
JIGSAW (108) (A) *scope*
Figaro (Britannia)
P: Val Guest, Frank Sherwin Green
D: SC: Val Guest
S: (NOVEL) Hilary Waugh (SLEEP LONG MY LOVE)

Jack Warner	Insp Fellows
Ronald Lewis	Sgt Wilks
Yolande Donlan	Jean Sherman
Michael Goodliffe	Clive Burchard
John le Mesurier	Mr Simpson
Moira Redmond	Joan Simpson
Brian Oulton	Frank Restlin
Ray Barrett	Sgt Gorman
John Barron	Ray Tenby
Graham Payn	Mr Blake
Norman Chappell	Andy Roach

CRIME Brighton. Police track down married man who murdered his mistress.

AUG

13130
DEAD MAN'S EVIDENCE (67) (U)
Bayford-RCH (BL)
P: Francis Searle, Ryck Rydon
D: Francis Searle
S: Arthur la Bern
SC: Arthur la Bern, Gordon Wellesley

Conrad Phillips	David Baxter
Jane Griffiths	Linda Howard
Veronica Hurst	Gay Clifford
Ryck Rydon	Fallon
Alex Mackintosh	Paul Kay
Godfrey Quigley	Insp O'Brian
Bruce Seton	Col Somerset

CRIME Ireland. Secret agent investigating death of frogman is exposed as traitor.

13131
MIX ME A PERSON (116) (X)
Wessex (BL)
P: Victor Saville, Sergei Nolbandov
D: Leslie Norman
S: (NOVEL) Jack Trevor Story
SC: Ian Dalrymple, Roy Kerridge

Anne Baxter	Dr Anne Dyson
Adam Faith	Harry Jukes
Donald Sinden	Philip Bellamy QC
Topsy Jane	Mona
Walter Brown	Max Taplow
Carol Ann Ford	Jenny
Jock Mac Gowran	Terence
Glyn Houston	Sam
Dilys Hamlett	Doris
Alfred Burke	Lumley
Meredith Edwards	Johnson

David Kernan . . . .   Socko
CRIME Barrister's psychiatrist wife proves
convicted teenager did not kill policeman.

13132
THE DAMNED (96) (X) *scope* USA: THESE
ARE THE DAMNED
Hammer-Swallow (Col)
P: Anthony Hinds
D: Joseph Losey
S: (NOVEL) H.L. Lawrence (THE CHILDREN
OF LIGHT)
SC: Evan Jones
Macdonald Carey . . . .   Simon Wells
Shirley Ann Field . . . .   Joan
Viveca Lindfors . . . .   Freya Nielsen
Alexander Knox . . . .   Prof Bernard
Oliver Reed . . . .   King
Walter Gotell . . . .   Maj Holland
Brian Oulton . . . .   Mr Dingle
Kenneth Cope . . . .   Sid
James Villiers . . . .   Capt Gregory
Barbara Everest . . . .   Miss Lamont
FANTASY Weymouth. American tourist
and teenage thug's sister try to free imprisoned
group of radioactive children.

13133
BAND OF THIEVES (69) (U)
Filmvale (RFD)
P: Lance Comfort, Bill Chalmers, Harold
Shampan
D: Peter Bezencenet
S: Harold Shampan
SC: Lyn Fairhurst
Acker Bilk . . . .   Himself
Jimmy Thompson . . . . . .   Hon Derek Delaney
Jennifer Jayne . . . .   Anne
Geoffrey Sumner . . . .   Governor
Maudie Edwards . . . .   Duchess of
                                     Hartlepoole
Chairman Innes . . . .   Mrs Van Der Ness
Arthur Mullard . . . .   Getaway
Michael Peake . . . .   Warder
Colin Smith . . . .   Flash
Norrie Paramor; Peter Haigh; Carol Deene
MUSICAL Ex-convicts form jazz band and
commit robberies during tour.

13134
THE BOYS (123) (A) *scope*
Galaworldfilm-Atlas (Gala)
P: Kenneth Rive, Sidney J. Furie
D: Sidney J. Furie
S: Stuart Douglass
Richard Todd . . . .   Victor Webster
Robert Morley . . . .   Montgomery
Felix Aylmer . . . .   Judge
Dudley Sutton . . . .   Stan Coulter
Jess Conrad . . . .   Barney Lee
Ronald Lacey . . . .   Billy Herne
Tony Garnett . . . .   Ginger Thompson
Wilfrid Bramble . . . .   Robert Brewer
Allan Cuthbertson . . . .   Randolph St John
Wensley Pithey . . . .   Mr Coulter
Colin Gordon . . . .   Gordon Lonsdale
Kenneth J. Warren . . . .   George Tanner
Betty Marsden . . . .   Mrs Herne
Patrick Magee . . . .   Mr Lee
Roy Kinnear . . . .   Charles Salmon
CRIME Four teenagers, tried for killing old
garage-man, are eventually proved guilty.

13135
TARZAN GOES TO INDIA (87) (U) *tech/
scope*
Solar (MGM)
P: Sy Weintraub
D: John Guillermin
S: (CHARACTERS) Edgar Rice Burroughs

SC: Robert Hardy Andrews, John Gruillermin
Jock Mahoney . . . .   Tarzan
Mark Dana . . . .   O'Hara
Jai . . . .   Jai
Simi . . . .   Princess Kamara
Leo Gordon . . . .   Bryce
Feroz Khan . . . .   Rama
Murad . . . .   Maharajah
ADVENTURE India. Tarzan thwarts engineers
and saves wild elephant herd from drowning.

13136
BILLY BUDD (125) (U) *scope*
Anglo-Allied (RFD)
P: Millard Kaufman, Ronald Lubin
D: Peter Ustinov
S: (NOVEL) Herman Melville (BILLY BUDD
FORETOPMAN) (PLAY) Louis Coxe, Robert
Chapman.
SC: Peter Ustinov, Robert Rossen
Robert Ryan . . . .   John Claggart
Peter Ustinov . . . .   Edward Fairfax Vere
                                     Vere
Melvyn Douglas . . . .   The Dansker
Terence Stamp . . . .   Billy Budd
Paul Rogers . . . .   Philip Seymour
John Neville . . . .   John Ratcliffe
David McCallum . . . .   Wyatt
Ronald Lewis . . . .   Jenkins
Niall McGinnis . . . .   Capt Graveling
Lee Montague . . . .   Squeak
Thomas Heathcote . . . .   Payne
Ray McAnally . . . .   O'Daniel
Robert Brown . . . .   Talbot
John Meillon . . . .   Kincaid
DRAMA 1797. Man-o-war captain court-
martials impressed sailor for killing sadistic
master-at-arms.

13137
MANOLIS (52) (U)
Witanhurst (Bargate)
P:D: Paul H. Crosfield
S: Rex Berry
Michali Maridalis . . . .   Manolis
Paul Homer . . . .   Puppet Man
DRAMA Greece. Teenager becomes gang's
scapegoat but is saved from drowning and
reformed by puppeteer.

SEPT

13138
LIVE NOW — PAY LATER (104) (X)
Woodlands (RFI)
P: Jack Hanbury
D: Jay Lewis
S: (NOVEL) Jack Lindsay (ALL ON THE
NEVER-NEVER)
SC: Jack Trevor Story
Ian Hendry . . . .   Albert Argyle
June Ritchie . . . .   Treasure
John Gregson . . . .   Callendar
Liz Fraser . . . .   Joyce Corby
Geoffrey Keen . . . .   Reggie Corby
Jeannette Sterke . . . .   Grace
Thelma Ruby . . . .   Hetty
Andrew Cruickshank . . . . .   Vicar
Ronald Howard . . . .   Cedric Mason
Judith Furse . . . .   Mrs Ackroyd
Monty Landis . . . .   Arnold
William Kendall . . . .   Maj Simpkins
Nyree Dawn Porter . . . .   Majorie Mason
Harold Berens . . . .   Solly Cowell
John Wood . . . .   Curate
Peter Butterworth . . . .   Fred
COMEDY Credit store tallyman deserts
pregnant mistress and is promoted after
blackmailing estate agent.

13139
IN SEARCH OF THE CASTAWAYS (100) (U)
tech
Walt Disney
P: Hugh Attwooll
D: Robert Stevenson
S: (NOVEL) Jules Verne (CAPTAIN GRANT'S
CHILDREN)
SC: Lowell S. Hawley
Maurice Chevalier . . . .   Jacques Paganel
Hayley Mills . . . .   Mary Grant
George Sanders . . . .   Thomas Ayrton
Wilfrid Hyde White . . . .   Lord Glenarvan
Michael Anderson . . . .   John Glenarvan
Keith Hamshere . . . .   Robert Grant
Antonio Cifariello . . . .   Thalcave
Wilfrid Brambell . . . .   Bill Gaye
Jack Gwillim . . . .   Capt Grant
Ronald Fraser . . . .   Guard
Inia te Wiata . . . .   Chief
ADVENTURE Period. Prof helps children
search South America and New Zealand for
their father, a mutiny victim.

13140
DANGER BY MY SIDE (63) (A)
Butcher's Films
P: John I. Phillips
D: Charles Saunders
S: Ronald C. Liles, Aubrey Cash
Anthony Oliver . . . .   Insp Willoughby
Maureen Connell . . . .   Lynne
Alan Tilvern . . . .   Venning
Bill Nagy . . . .   Sam Warren
Sonya Cordeau . . . .   Francine Dumont
Tom Naylor . . . .   Sgt Roberts
CRIME Girl works in nightclub to prove
owner killed her detective brother.

13141
KILL OR CURE (88) (U)
MGM British
P: George Brown, Lawrence Bachmann
D: George Pollock
S: David Pursall, Jack Seddon
Terry-Thomas . . . .   J. Barker-Rynde
Eric Sykes . . . .   Rumbelow
Dennis Price . . . .   Dr Crossley
Lionel Jeffries . . . .   Insp Hook
Moira Redmond . . . .   Frances Reitman
Katya Douglas . . . .   Rita Fallows
David Lodge . . . .   Richards
Ronnie Barker . . . .   Burton
Hazel Terry . . . .   Mrs Crossley
Harry Locke . . . .   Fred Higgins
Derren Nesbitt . . . .   Roger
Arthur Howard . . . .   Clerk
Peter Butterworth . . . .   Barman
Anna Russell . . . .   Margaret Clifford
COMEDY Tec and PT instructor solve
poisoning of rich widow at health hotel.

13142
LOCKER 69 (56) (U)
Merton Park (AA)
P: Jack Greenwood
D: Norman Harrison
S: (STORY) Edgar Wallace
SC: Richard Harris
Eddie Byrne . . . .   Simon York
Paul Daneman . . . .   Frank Griffiths
Walter Brown . . . .   Craig
Penelope Horner . . . .   Julie Denver
Edward Underdown . . . . . .   Bennett Sanders
Clarissa Stolz . . . .   Eva Terila
John Carson . . . .   Miguel Terila
John Glyn-Jones . . . .   Insp Roon
CRIME Private tec solves murder of his
employer and the loss of papers from safe
deposit.

13143
TOMORROW AT TEN (80) (A)
Blakeley's Films (Planet)
P: Tom Blakeley
D: Lance Comfort
S: Peter Millar, James Kelly
John Gregson . . . . Insp Parnell
Robert Shaw . . . . Marlow
Alec Clunes . . . . Anthony Chester
Alan Wheatley . . . . Bewley
Kenneth Cope . . . . Sgt Grey
Helen Cherry . . . . Robbie
William Hartnell . . . . Freddy
Betty McDowell . . . . Mrs Parnell
Ernest Clark . . . . Dr Towers
Renee Houston . . . . Mrs Maddox
CRIME Rich man kills kidnapper before
learning the whereabouts of his small son and
time bomb.

13144
THE WAR LOVER (105) (X)
Columbia British
P: Arthur Hornblow jr
D: Philip Leacock
S: (NOVEL) John Hersey
SC: Howard Koch
Steve McQueen . . . . Buzz Rickson
Robert Wagner . . . . Ed Bolland
Shirley Ann Field . . . . Daphne
Gary Cockrell . . . . Lynch
Michael Crawford . . . . Junior Sailen
Bill Edwards . . . . Brindt
Chuck Julian . . . . Lamb
Jerry Stovin . . . . Emmett
Edward Bishop . . . . Vogt
Richard Leech . . . . Murika
Bernard Braden . . . . Randall
Sean Kelly . . . . Woodman
Neil McCallum . . . . Sully
WAR 1943. USAAF Flying Fortress captain
learns the meaning of war after trying to
seduce his co-pilot's sweetheart.

13145
MASTERS OF VENUS (serial) (U)
Wallace (CFF)
P: A. Frank Bundy
D: Ernest Morris
S: H.B. Gregory
SC: Michael Barnes, Mary Cathcart Borer
Norman Wooland . . . . Dr Ballantyne
Amanda Coxell . . . . Pat Ballantyne
Robin Stewart . . . . Jim Ballantyne
Robin Hunter . . . . Peter
Patrick Kavanagh . . . . Mike
Arnold Diamond . . . . Imos
George Pastell . . . . Kallas
Ferdy Mayne . . . . Votan
Jackie Martin . . . . Borlas

13146
1—SABOTAGE (16)

13147
2—LOST IN SPACE (16)

13148
3—THE MEN WITH SIX FINGERS (15)

13149
4—THE THING IN THE CRATER (16)

13150
5—PRISONERS OF VENUS (17)

13151
6—THE KILLER VIRUS (15)

13152
7—KILL ON SIGHT (15)

13153
8—ATTACK (18)

CHILDREN Scientist's children thwart
saboteurs and travel by rocket to Venus,
where they help leader thwart rebels.

13154
THE LONELINESS OF THE LONG
DISTANCE RUNNER (104) (X)
Woodfall (Bry)
P: Tony Richardson, Michael Holden
D: Tony Richardson
S: (STORY) Alan Sillitoe
SC: Alan Sillitoe
Michael Redgrave . . . . Governor
Tom Courtenay . . . . Colin Smith
Avis Bunnage . . . . Mrs Smith
James Bolam . . . . Mike
Dervis Ward . . . . Detective
Topsy Jane . . . . Audrey
Alec McCowen . . . . Brown
Joe Robinson . . . . Roach
Julia Foster . . . . Gladys
James Cairncross . . . . Jones
Philip Martin . . . . Stacey
Peter Madden . . . . Mr Smith
CRIME Rebellious teenager, sent to Borstal
for robbery, purposely loses cross-country
race.

13155
PLAYBACK (62) (A)
Merton Park (AA)
P: Jack Greenwood
D: Quentin Lawrence
S: (STORY) Edgar Wallace
SC: Robert Stewart
Margit Saad . . . . Lisa Shillack
Barry Foster . . . . Dave Hollis
Victor Platt . . . . Insp Gorman
Dinsdale Landen . . . . Joe Ross
George Pravda . . . . Simon Shillack
Nigel Green . . . . Ralph Monk
Jerold Wells . . . . Insp Parkes
CRIME Woman persuades indebted
policeman to shoot her rich husband.

13156
THE DOCK BRIEF (88) (U)
Anatole de Grunwald (MGM)
P: Dimitri de Grunwald
D: James Hill
S: (PLAY) John Mortimer
SC: Pierre Rouve
Peter Sellers . . . . Morgenhall
Richard Attenborough . . . . . Fowle
Beryl Reid . . . . Doris Fowle
David Lodge . . . . Bateson
Frank Pettingell . . . . Tuppy Morgan
Eric Woodburn . . . . Judge Banter
Frank Thornton . . . . Photographer
Tristram Jellinek . . . . Perkins
COMEDY Barrister's imaginary defence of
wife-killer succeeds where the real thing fails.

13157
VENGEANCE (83) (A)
Stross-CCC (Garrick)
P: Raymond Stross, Artur Brauner
D: Freddie Francis
S: (NOVEL) Curt Siodmak (DONOVAN'S
BRAIN)
SC: Robert Stewart, Philip Mackie, John Kruse
Anne Heywood . . . . Anna Holt
Peter Van Eyck . . . . Dr Peter Corrie
Cecil Parker . . . . Stevenson
Bernard Lee . . . . Frank Shears
Maxine Audley . . . . Marion Fane
Jeremy Spenser . . . . Martin Holt
Ellen Schwiers . . . . Ella
Siegfried Lowitz . . . . Walters
Miles Malleson . . . . Dr Miller
Jack McGowran . . . . Furber
George A. Cooper . . . . Gabler
Allan Cuthbertson . . . . Dr Silva
Kenneth Kendall . . . . Newscaster
FANTASY Dead tycoon's living brain
hypnotises doctor into tracing his murderer.

13158
THE DEVIL'S AGENT (77) (A)
Emmet Dalton (BL)
P: Victor Lyndon
D: John Paddy Carstairs
S: (NOVEL) Hans Habe
SC: Robert Westerby
Peter Van Eyck . . . . George Droste
Macdonald Carey . . . . Mr Smith
Marianne Koch . . . . Nora Gulden
Christopher Lee . . . . Baron von Staub
Billie Whitelaw . . . . Piroska
Albert Lieven . . . .
David Knight . . . . Father Zombary
Marius Goring . . . . Gen Greenhahn
Helen Cherry . . . . .Countess Cosimano
Colin Gordon . . . . Count Dezsepalvy
Niall McGinnis . . . . Paul Vass
Eric Pohlmann . . . . Bloch
Peter Vaughan . . . . Police Chief
Michael Brennan . . . . Horvat
CRIME 1950. Viennese wine salesman, pawn
of Soviet agents, becomes spy for American
Intelligence.

13159
THE PLAIN MAN'S GUIDE TO
ADVERTISING (20) (U)
Biographic Four (BL)
P:D: Bob Godfrey
S: Colin Pearson
N: David de Keyser, Dick Emery, Vernon
Grieves
Ron Brody . . . . The Plain Man
Bruce Lacey . . . .
Johnny Vyvyan . . . .
Sheena Marshe . . . .
Andrea Lawrence . . . .
Blanche Moore . . . .
COMEDY Satire on cinema and tv
advertising techniques.

13160
THE PIT (25) (X)
BFI
P:D:SC: Edward Abrahams
S: (STORY) Edgar Allan Poe (THE PIT AND
THE PENDULUM)
Brian Peck . . . . The Victim
Bert Betts . . . . The Inquisitor
HORROR Spain, period. Inquisitor tortures
his victim.

13161
OUT OF THE FOG (68) (A)
Eternal Films (GN)
P: Maurice J. Wilson
D:S: Montgomery Tully
David Sumner . . . . George Mallon
Susan Travers . . . . June Lock
John Arnatt . . . . Supt Chadwick
James Hayter . . . . Daniels
Jack Watson . . . . Sgt Tracey
Olga Lindo . . . . Mrs Mallon
Renee Houston . . . . Ma
George Woodbridge . . . . Chopper
Anthony Oliver . . . . Chaplain
CRIME POW decoys ex-convict suspected of
killing girls when the moon is full.

13162
SOLO FOR SPARROW (56) (U)
Merton Park (AA)
P: Jack Greenwood
D: Gordon Flemyng
S: (NOVEL) Edgar Wallace (THE GUNNER)
SC: Roger Marshall

Anthony Newlands	Reynolds
Glyn Houston	Insp Sparrow
Nadja Regin	Mrs Reynolds
Michael Coles	Pin Norman
Allan Cuthbertson	Supt Symington
Ken Wayne	Baker
Jerry Stovin	Lewis
Jack May	Insp Hudson
Murray Melvin	Larkin
Michael Caine	Paddy Mooney
Nancy O'Neil	Miss Martin

CRIME Insp takes leave to prove jeweller is behind a murder and is saved from being kidnapped.

13163
DR NO (105) (A) tech
Eon (UA) reissue: 1965
P: Harry Saltzman, Albert Broccoli
D: Terence Young
S: (NOVEL) Ian Fleming
SC: Richard Maibaum, Johanna Harwood, Barkley Mather

Sean Connery	James Bond
Ursula Andress	Honey
Joseph Wiseman	Dr No
Jack Lord	Felix Leiter
Bernard Lee	M
Anthony Dawson	Prof Dent
Zena Marshall	Miss Taro
John Kitzmiller	Quarrel
Eunice Gayson	Sylvia
Lois Maxwell	Miss Moneypenny
Lester Prendergast	Pussfeller

CRIME Jamaica. Secret agent destroys mad doctor's island nuclear lab.

OCT

13164
THE WILD AND THE WILLING (112) (X)
Rank (RFD)
P: Betty E. Box
D: Ralph Thomas
S: (PLAY) Laurence Dobie, Robert Sloman (THE TINKER)
SC: Nicholas Phipps, Mordecai Richler

Virginia Maskell	Virginia Chown
Paul Rogers	Prof Chown
Ian McShane	Harry Brown
Samantha Eggar	Josie
Catherine Woodville	Sarah
David Sumner	John
John Hurt	Phil
John Standing	Arthur
Johnny Briggs	Dai
Johnny Sekka	Reggie
Jeremy Brett	Gilby
John Barrie	Mr Corbett
Megs Jenkins	Mrs Corbett
Victor Brooks	Fire Chief

DRAMA Scholarship student has affair with his tutor's wife and causes friend's death.

13165
DON'T TALK TO STRANGE MEN (65) (A)
Derick Williams (Bry)
P: Derick Williams
D: Pat Jackson
S: Gwen Cherrell

Christina Gregg	Jean Painter
Cyril Raymond	Mr Painter
Gillian Lind	Mrs Painter
Conrad Phillips	Ron
Janina Faye	Ann Painter
Dandy Nicholls	Molly
Gwen Nelson	Mrs Mason

CRIME Country girl saved from keeping blind date with sex maniac.

13166
THE PASSWORD IS COURAGE (116) (U) scope
MGM British
P: Andrew Stone, Virginia Stone
D: Andrew Stone
S: (BOOK) John Castle
SC: Andrew Stone

Dirk Bogards	Charles Coward
Maria Perschy	Irena
Alfred Lynch	Billy Pope
Nigel Stock	Cole
Reginald Beckwith	Unteroffizier
Richard Marner	Schmidt
Ed Devereaux	Aussie
Lewis Flander	Pringle
George Mikell	Necke
Richard Carpenter	Robinson
Colin Blakeley	Goon

WAR 1940-44. True exploits sergeant-major who escapes from several prison camps.

13167
A GUY CALLED CAESAR (62) (U)
Bill & Michael Luckwell (Col)
P: Bill Luckwell, Umesh Mallik
D: Frank Marshall
S: Umesh Mallik
SC: Umesh Mallik, Tom Burdon

Conrad Phillips	Tony
George Moon	Maurice
Phillip O'Flynn	Tex
Maureen Toal	Lena
Desmond Perry	Harry
Peter Maycock	Ron

CRIME Policeman poses as crook to join gang of jewel thieves and unmask their leader.

13168
THE MAN WHO FINALLY DIED (100) (A) scope
White Cross (Magna)
P: Norman Williams
D: Quentin Lawrence
S: Lewis Greifer
SC: Lewis Greifer, Louis Marks

Stanley Baker	Joe Newman
Peter Cushing	Dr von Brecht
Mai Zetterling	Lisa
Eric Portman	Insp Hofmeister
Georgina Ward	Maria
Niall MacGinnis	Brenner
Nigel Green	Hirsch
Barbara Everest	Martha
Harold Scott	Professor

CRIME Bavaria. Man investigating death of German father uncovers Communist plot to kidnap scientist.

13169
MANIAC (96) (X) scope
Hammer (Col)
P-S: Jimmy Sangster
D: Michael Carreras

Kerwin Matthews	Geoff Farrell
Nadia Gray	Eve Beynat
Donald Houston	Georges Beynat
Liliane Brousse	Annette Beynat
George Pastell	Insp Etienne
Arnold Diamond	Janiello

Norman Bird	Salon
Justine Lord	Grace
Jerold Wells	Gilles

CRIME France. Girl's stepmother involves tourist in the murder of her mad husband.

13170
THE MAIN ATTRACTION (90) (A) metro/scope
Seven Arts (MGM)
P: Abe Steinberg, John Patrick
D: Daniel Petrie
S: John Patrick

Nancy Kwan	Tessa
Pat Boone	Eddie
Mai Zetterling	Gina
Yvonne Mitchell	Elea
Keiron Moore	Ricco
John le Mesurier	Bozo
Carl Duering	Driver
Warren Mitchell	Proprietor
Lionel Murton	Burton

Lionel Blair; Rios Brothers; Bill Picton
DRAMA Italy; Fugitive singer who thinks he killed clown, is trapped in avalanche with bareback-rider.

13171
PRIVATE POTTER (89) (U)
Ben Arbeid (MGM)
P: Ben Arbeid
D: Casper Wrede
S: (TV PLAY) Ronald Harwood
SC: Ronald Harwood, Casper Wrede

Tom Courtenay	Pte Potter
Mogens Wieth	Yannis
Ronald Fraser	Doctor
James Maxwell	Lt-Col Gunyon
Ralph Michael	Padre
Brewster Mason	Brigadier
Eric Thompson	Capt Knowles
John Graham	Maj Sims
Frank Finlay	Capt Patterson

WAR Cyprus. Soldier cries out at vision of God and spoils an army operation.

13172
THE PRIMITIVES (70) (U)
Border (RFD)
P: O. Negus-Fancey
D: Alfred Travers
S: Alfred Travers, Moris Farhi

Jan Holden	Cheta
Bill Edwards	Peter
Rio Fanning	John
George Mikell	Claude
Terence Fallon	Sgt Henry
Derek Ware	Philip
Peter Hughes	Insp Wills

CRIME Girl dancer and her partners don disguises to rob jewellers.

13173
THE PUNCH AND JUDY MAN (90) (U)
MacConkey (WPD)
P: Gordon L.T. Scott
D: Jeremy Summers
S: Tony Hancock
SC: Tony Hancock, Phillip Oakes

Tony Hancock	Wally Pinner
Sylvia Syms	Delia Pinner
Ronald Fraser	Mayor Palmer
Barbara Murray	Lady Jane Caterham
John le Mesurier	Charles the Sandman
Hugh Lloyd	Edward Cox
Mario Fabrizi	Nevil Shanks
Pauline Jameson	Mayoress
Norman Bird	Committee Man
Walter Hudd	Clergyman

Eddie Byrne . . . . Assistant
Peter Myers . . . . Escort
Hattie Jacques . . . . .Dolly Zarathusa
COMEDY Seaside entertainer, married to
social climber, spoils mayor's celebration
cabaret.

13174
GIRL ON APPROVAL (75) (A)
Eyeline (Bry)
P: Anthony Perry, Harold Orton
D: Charles Frend
S: Kathleen White
SC: Kathleen White, Kenneth Cavander
Rachel Roberts . . . . Anne Howland
James Maxwell . . . . John Howland
Annette Whitley . . . . Sheila
Ellen McIntosh . . . . Mary Gardner
John Dare . . . . Stephen Howland
Michael Clarke . . . . William Howland
Pauline Letts . . . . Mrs Cox
DRAMA Imprisoned woman's teenage daughter
eventually settles down with her foster parents.

13175
DEATH TRAP (56) (U)
Merton Park (AA)
P: Jack Greenwood
D: John Moxey
S: (NOVEL) Edgar Wallace
SC: John Roddick
Albert Lieven . . . . Paul Heindrick
Barbara Shelley . . . . Jean Anscombe
John Meillon . . . . Ross Williams
Mercy Haystead . . . . Carol Halston
Kenneth Cope . . . . Derek Maitland
Leslie Sands . . . . Insp Simons
Richard Bird . . . . Ted Cupps
Gladys Henson . . . . Housekeeper
Barbara Windsor . . . . Babs Newton
CRIME Financier unmasked as killer
responsible for suicide of model's sister.

NOV
13176
NIGHT CARGOES (serial) (U)
Film Producers Guild (CFF)
P: Cecil Musk
D: Ernest Morris
S: Angela Ainley Jeans
SC: David Villers, Molly Border, Cecil Musk
Waveney Lee . . . . Nell
Hugh Jones . . . . Richard Merivale
Stephen Marriott . . . . Mr Cooper
Pauline Letts . . . . Mrs Cooper
Ian Curry . . . . Mr Howard
Neil Wilson . . . . Cobbler

13177
1—THE WOUNDED STRANGER (15)
2—
13178
2—THE SMUGGLER'S PONY (15)

13179
3—THE SECRET PANEL (15)

13180
4—THE MYSTERY OF THE RUINED ABBEY
(15)

13181
5—TRAPPED IN THE TUNNEL (15)

13182
6—RICHARD KNOWS TOO MUCH (15)

13183
7—THE ESCAPE IN THE COACH (15)

13184
8—THE LAST CARGO (15)

CHILDREN Devon, 1725. Children help rich
orphan expose his adoptive parents as leaders
of smuggling gang.

13185
MY BARE LADY (59) (A) *eastman*
Meadway-Notram Sewil (Compton)
P: Dick Randall, Phineas Lonestar jr
D: Arthur Knight
S: Jervis Macarthur
Julie Martin . . . . Tina Murray
Carl Conway . . . . Pat Kneely
Nina Huntredos . . . . Mrs Darwell
Kenneth McLelland . . . . Mr O'Hanrahan
Chantal Delors . . . .
Gilly Gerard . . . .
Jack Taylor . . . .
NUDIST. Orpington. American war hero
converts tourist to naturism.

13186
THE IRON MAIDEN (97) (U) *eastman*
GHW Productions (AA)
P: Peter Rogers
D: Gerald Thomas
S: Harold Brooks, Kay Bannerman
SC: Vivian Cox, Leslie Bricusse
Michael Craig . . . . Jack Hopkins
Anne Helm . . . . Kathy Fisher
Jeff Donnell . . . . Mrs Fisher
Alan Hale jr . . . . Paul Fisher
Noel Purcell . . . . .Admiral Trevelyan
Cecil Parker . . . . Sir Giles Trent
Roland Culver . . . . Lord Upshott
Joan Sims . . . . Mrs Fred
John Standing . . . . Humphrey
Brian Oulton . . . . Vicar
Sam Kydd . . . . Fred
Judith Furse . . . . Mrs Webb
Duke of Bedford; Raymond Glendenning
COMEDY Aircraft designer's vintage traction
engine helps him win American contract.

13187
THE GUILTY PARTY (32) (A)
Merton Park (AA)
P: Jack Greenwood
D: Lionel Harris
S: James Eastwood
N: Edgar Lustgarten
Zena Marshall . . . . Thelma Sinclair
Anthony Jacobs . . . . Edward Sinclair
Derek Francis . . . . Henry Dobbs
Jack Gwillim . . . . Mr Jepp
Wensley Pithey . . . . Mr Robbins
Jean Lodge . . . . Madge Petworth
DRAMA Broke man makes wife vamp financier
and sues her when she becomes pregnant.

13188
A WOMAN'S PRIVILEGE (29) (U)
Merton Park (AA)
P: Jack Greenwood
D: Anthony Bushell
S: James Eastwood
Bernard Archard . . . . Joe Ashton
Ann Lynn . . . . Shirley Fawsett
Patrick Wymark . . . . Mr Godfrey
Ernest Clark . . . . Mr Hayes
Noel Hood . . . . Mrs Peters
Gerald Cross . . . . Judge
DRAMA Old man sells his garage to marry
and sues for breach of promise when his
fiancee breaks engagement.

13189
THE WRONG ARM OF THE LAW (94) (U)
Romulus-Robert Velaise (BL)
P: Aubrey Baring, E.M. Smedley Aston
D; Cliff Owen
S: Ivor Jay, William Whistance Smith
SC: Ray Galton, Alan Simpson, John
Antrobus, John Warren, Len Heath
Peter Sellers . . . . Pearly Gates
Lionel Jeffries . . . . Insp Parker
Bernard Cribbins . . . . Nervous O'Toole
Davy Kaye . . . . Trainer King
Nanette Newman . . . . Valerie
Bill Kerr . . . . Jack Coomes
John le Mesurier . . . . Asst Commissioner
Dennis Price . . . . Educated Ernest
Irene Browne . . . . Dowager
Martin Boddey . . . . Supt Forrest
Arthur Mullard . . . . Brassknuckles
Ed Devereaux . . . . Bluey May
Reg Lye . . . . Reg Denton
Dermot Kelly . . . . Misery Martin
Graham Stark . . . . Sid Cooper
Vanda Godsell . . . . Annette
Dick Emery . . . . Man
COMEDY Cockney crook posing as French
couturier helps police catch gang posing as
police.

13190
LAWRENCE OF ARABIA (222) *tech/scope* (A)
Horizon (Col)
P: Sam Spiegel
D: David Lean
S: (BOOK) T.E. Lawrence (THE SEVEN
PILLARS OF WISDOM)
SC: Robert Bolt
Peter O'Toole . . . . T.E. Lawrence
Alec Guinness . . . . Prince Feisal
Anthony Quinn . . . . Auda Abu Tayi
Jack Hawkins . . . . Gen Allenby
Jose Ferrer . . . . Turkish Bey
Anthony Quayle . . . . Col Brighton
Claude Rains . . . . Mr Dryden
Arthur Kennedy . . . . Jackson Bentley
Omar Sharif . . . . Sherif Ali
Donald Wolfit . . . . Gen Murray
I.S. Johar . . . . Gasim
Zia Mohyeddin . . . . Tafas
Michel Ray . . . . Farraj
Howard Marion Crawford . . MO
Hugh Miller . . . . Col
HISTORY Arabia, 1915. British lieut helps
unify the Arabs in their revolt against Turkey.
(AA 1962: Best Film; Best Director; Best
Photography; Best Music; Best Art Direction;
Best Sound; Best Editing. BFA 1962: Best
Film; Best British Film; Best Screenplay;
Best Actor.)

13191
THE MIND BENDERS (113) (X)
Novus (AA)
P: Michael Relph
D: Basil Dearden
S: James Kennaway
Dirk Bogarde . . . . Dr Henry Longman
Mary Ure . . . . .Oonagh Longman
John Clements . . . . Maj Hall
Michael Bryant . . . . Dr Tate
Wendy Craig . . . . Annabelle
Harold Goldblatt . . . . Prof Sharpey
Geoffrey Keen . . . . Calder
Terry Palmer . . . . Norman
Norman Bird . . . . Aubrey
DRAMA Oxford. Security officer
brainwashes physiologist into mistrusting
his pregnant wife.

13192
STRANGLEHOLD (73) (A)
Argo (RFD)
P: Jack Lamont, David Henley
D: Lawrence Huntington
S: Guy Elmes
SC: Guy Elmes, Joy Garrison
Macdonald Carey . . . . Bill Morrison
Barbara Shelley . . . . Chris Morrison
Philip Friend . . . . Steffan
Nadja Regin Lilli
Leonard Sachs . . . . The Dutchman
Mark Loerering . . . . Jimmy Morrison
Susan Shaw . . . . Actress
Josephine Brown . . . . Grace
CRIME Film star believes he killed an
actress who poisoned herself.

13193
THE L-SHAPED ROOM (142) (X)
Romulus (BL)
P: James Woolf, Richard Attenborough
D:SC: Bryan Forbes
S: (NOVEL) Lynne Reid Banks
Leslie Caron . . . . Jane Fosset
Tom Bell . . . . Toby
Bernard Lee . . . . Charlie
Brock Peters . . . . Johnny
Cicely Courtneidge . . . . . . Mavis
Patricia Phoenix . . . . Sonia
Emlyn Williams . . . . Dr Weaver
Avis Bunnage . . . . Doris
Nanette Newman . . . . Girl
Harry Locke . . . . Newsagent
DRAMA Author loves French girl until he
discovers she is pregnant.
(BFA: 1962, Best Actress.)

DEC
13194
WE JOINED THE NAVY (109) (U) *eastman/*
scope
Dial (WPD)
P: Daniel M. Angel, Vivian A. Cox
D: Wendy Toye
S: (NOVEL) John Winton
SC: Arthur Dales
Kenneth More . . . . LtCdr Badger
Lloyd Nolan . . . . Admiral Ryan
Joan O'Brien . . . . Carol Blair
Mischa Auer . . . . Colonel President
Jeremy Lloyd . . . . Dewberry
Dinsdale Landen . . . . Bowles
Derek Fowlds . . . . Carson
Denise Warren . . . . Collette
John le Mesurier . . . . Dewberry
Laurence Naismith . . . . Admiral Balke
Andrew Cruickshank . . . . . Admiral Filmer
Walter Fitzgerald . . . . Admiral Thomas
Esma Cannon . . . . Consul's Wife
Kenneth Griffith . . . . Orator
Dirk Bogarde; Sidney James; Michael Bentine
COMEDY Mediterranean. British liason officer
helps American navy rescue hostage from
revolution.

13195
BREATH OF LIFE (67) (A)
Norcon (BL)
P: Norman Cohen, Bill Luckwell
D:S: J. Henry Piperno
George Moon . . . . Freddie
Larry Martyn . . . . Tony
April Wilding . . . . Monica
Barry Halliday . . . . Spud
Vivienne Lacy . . . . Marilyn
Hugh Halliday . . . . Harry

Gabrielle Blunt . . . . Winnie
CRIME Mechanic saves life of baby, who when
grown, involves his children in bank robbery.

13196
DR CRIPPEN (98) (X)
Torchlight (WPD)
P: John Clein *
D: Robert Lynn
S: Leigh Vance
Donald Pleasence . . . . Dr Crippen
Coral Browne . . . . Belle Crippen
Samantha Eggar . . . . Ethel le Neve
Donald Wolfit . . . . R.D. Muir
James Robertson Justice. . . Capt Kendall
Geoffrey Toone . . . . Mr Tobin
Oliver Johnston . . . . Lord Chief Justice
Elspeth March . . . . Mrs Jackson
Olga Lindo . . . . Clara Arditti
Paul Carpenter . . . . Bruce Martin
John Arnatt . . . . Insp Dew
Edward Underdown . . . . . . Governor
Basil Henson . . . . Paul Arditti
HISTORY American doctor kills drunken
wife and tries to escape America with his
mistress posing as his son.

13197
I COULD GO ON SINGING (100) (U)
eastman/scope
Barbican (UA)
P: Stuart Millar, Lawrence Turman
D: Ronald Neame
S: Robert Dozier
SC: Mayo Simon
Judy Garland . . . . Jenny Bowman
Dirk Bogarde . . . . David Donne
Jack Klugman . . . . George Kogan
Aline McMahon . . . . Ida
Gregory Phillips . . . . Matt
Pauline Jameson . . . . Miss Plimpton
Russell Waters . . . . Reynolds
DRAMA American singer takes to drink when
her bastard son opts to stay with his surgeon
father.

13198
THE FUR COLLAR (71) (U)
Albatross (RFD)
P:D:S: Lawrence Huntington
John Bentley . . . . Mike Andrews
Martin Benson . . . . Insp Legrain
Philip Friend . . . . Eddie Morgan
Nadja Regin . . . . Marie Lejeune
Balbina . . . . Jacqueline Legrain
Hector Ross . . . . Roger Harding
Gordon Sterne . . . . Duclos
Guy Middleton . . . . Resident
Brian Nissen . . . . Carl Jorgensen
CRIME Paris. Reporter feigns death to trap
fugitive and uncover spy ring.

13199
NIGHT OF THE PROWLER (60) (U)
Butcher's Films
P: John I. Phillips
D: Francis Searle
S: Paul Erickson
Patrick Holt . . . . Robert Langton
Colette Wilde . . . . Marie Langton
Bill Nagy . . . . Paul Conrad
Mitzi Rogers . . . . Jacky Reed
John Horsley . . . . Insp Cameron
Benny Lee . . . . Benny
Marianne Stone . . . . Mrs Cross
Mark Singleton . . . . Anders
Anthony Wager . . . . Sgt Baker
CRIME Executive frames ex-embezzler for
murder to gain control of car company.

13200
STATION SIX-SAHARA (101) (X)
CCC-Artur Brauner (BL)
P: Gene Gutowski, Victor Lyndon
D: Seth Holt
S: (PLAY) Jacques Maret (MEN WITHOUT
A PAST)
SC: Bryan Forbes, Bryan Clemens
Carroll Baker . . . . Catherine
Ian Bannen . . . . Fletcher
Denholm Elliott . . . . Macey
Peter van Eyck . . . . Kramer
Jorg Felmy . . . . Martin
Mario Adorf . . . . Santos
Biff McGuire . . . . Jimmy
DRAMA Sahara. Injured man tries to kill his
ex-wife at remote pipe-line station.

13201
FOUR HITS AND A MISTER (14) (U)
eastman
Parkside (BL)
P: Jacques de Lane Lea
D: Douglas Hickox
S: Peter Leslie
Acker Bilk and his Band
Boscoe Holder
MUSICAL

13202
THE FAST LADY (95) (A) *eastman*
Independent Artists (RFD)
P: Julian Wintle, Leslie Parkyn
D: Ken Annakin
S: (STORY) Keble Howard
SC: Jack Davies, Henry Blyth
James Robertson Justice . . Charles Chingford
Leslie Phillips . . . . Freddy Fox
Stanley Baxter . . . . Murdoch Troon
Kathleen Harrison . . . . Mrs Staggers
Julie Christie . . . . Claire Chingford
Eric Barker . . . . Wentworth
Allan Cuthbertson . . . . Bodley
Oliver Johnston . . . . Bulmer
Esma Cannon . . . . Lady
Dick Emery . . . . Shingler
Derek Guyler . . . . Dr Blake
Victor Brooks . . . . Policeman
Terence Alexander . . . . Policeman
Danny Green . . . . Bandit
Eddie Gray; Fred Emney; Frankie Howerd;
Raymond Baxter; Graham Hill
COMEDY Scots learner-driver wins
magistrate's daughter after using vintage
car to catch bank robbers.

13203
THE KISS OF THE VAMPIRE (87) (X)
eastman USA: KISS OF EVIL
Hammer-Universal (UI)
P:SC: Anthony Hinds
D: Don Sharp
S: (SCREENPLAY) Edgar G Ulmer, Peter Ruric
(THE BLACK CAT)
Clifford Evans . . . . Prof Zimmer
Edward de Souza . . . . Gerald Harcourt
Noel Willman . . . . Dr Ravna
Jennifer Daniel . . . . Marianne Harcourt

Barry Warren . . . . Carl Ravna
Brian Oulton . . . . Disciple
Noel Howlett . . . . Father Xavier
Jacqueline Wallis . . . . Sabena Ravna
Peter Madden . . . . Bruno
Isobel Black . . . . Tanya
HORROR Bavaria, 1910. Professor conjures
bats to save honeymooners from vampire
doctor's cult. (Additional seq. shot in USA)

13204
MOMENT OF DECISION (30) (U)
Merton Park (AA)
P: Jack Greenwood
D: John Knight
S: James Eastwood
N: Edgar Lustgarten
Ray Barrett . . . . Bert West
Pat Healy . . . . Mary West
Marjy Lawrence . . . . Sally Mason
Viola Keats . . . . Mrs Davies
Tim Hudson . . . . Dudley Chelsham
Norman Claridge . . . . Judge
CRIME Childless wife steals baby and her
faithless husband holds it to ransom.

13205
ON THE BEAT (105) (U)
Rank (RFD)
P: Hugh Stewart
D: Robert Asher
S: Jack Davies, Norman Wisdom, Eddie
Leslie
Norman Wisdom . . . . Norman Pitkin/
Guilio Napolitani
Jennifer Jayne . . . . Rosanna
Raymond Huntley . . . . . . Sir Ronald Ackroyd

David Lodge . . . . Supt Hobson
Esma Cannon . . . . Mrs Stammers
Eric Barker . . . . Doctor
Eleanor Summerfield . . . . . Sgt Wilkins
Ronnie Stevens . . . . Oberon
Terence Alexander . . . . Supt Belcher
Maurice Kaufmann . . . . Vince
Dilys Laye . . . . Woman
COMEDY Scotland Yard enlists sacked
car cleaner to catch his double, an
Italian jewel thief.

13206
TOUCH OF DEATH (58) (U)
Helion (Planet)
P: Lewis Linzee
D: Lance Comfort
S: Aubrey Cash, Wilfred Josephs
SC: Lyn Fairhurst
William Lucas . . . . Pete Mellor
David Sumner . . . . Len Williams
Ray Barrett . . . . Maxwell
Jan Waters . . . . Jackie
Frank Coda . . . . Sgt Byrne
Roberta Tovey . . . . Pam
Geoffrey Denton . . . . Baxter
CRIME Crooks steal poisoned money and
force girl to shelter them in her houseboat.

13207
THE WAR GAME (15) (U)
Mai Zetterling (BL)
P:D: Mai Zetterling
S: Mai Zetterling, David Hughes
Ian Ellis . . . . Boy
Joseph Robinson . . . . Boy
DRAMA Small boy chases another through
block of flats and onto roof.

13208
LUNCH HOUR (64)
Eyeline (Bry)
P: John Mortimer, Harold Orton, Alfred
Shaughnessy
D: James Hill
S: (PLAY) John Mortimer
SC: John Mortimer
Shirley Anne Field . . . . Girl
Robert Stephens . . . . Man
Kay Walsh . . . . Manageress
Hazel Hughes . . . . Aunty
Michael Robbins . . . . Harris
Nigel Davenport . . . . Manager
Neil Culleton . . . . Ronnie
Sandra Leo . . . . Susan
Vi Stephens . . . . Waitress
COMEDY Junior executive's hotel
rendezvous with designer goes awry.

1963

JAN

13209
CAIRO (91) (A)
MGM
P: Lawrence P. Bachmann, Ronald Kinnoch
D: Wolf Rilla
S: (NOVEL) W.R.Burnett
(THE ASPHALT JUNGLE)
SC: Joanne Court
George Sanders . . . . Maj Pickering
Richard Johnson . . . . Ali
Faten Hamama . . . . Amina
John Meillon . . . . Willy
Eric Pohlmann . . . . Nicodemus
Walter Rilla . . . . Kuchuk
Ahmed Mazhar . . . . Kerim
Mona . . . . Bamba
CRIME Cairo. Major's gang steals Tut-ankh-
Amun jewels from museum.

13210
COME FLY WITH ME (109) (U) *metro/scope*
MGM British
P: Anatole de Grunwald
D: Henry Levin
S: (NOVEL) Bernard Glemser (GIRL ON A
WING)
SC: William Roberts
Dolores Hart . . . . Donna Stuart
Hugh O'Brian . . . . Ray Winsley
Karl Boehm . . . . Franz von Elzingen
Pamela Tiffin . . . . Carol Brewster
Karl Malden . . . . Walter Lucas
Lois Nettleton . . . . Hilda Bergstrom
Dawn Addams . . . . Katy Rimard
Richard Wattis . . . . Garson
Andrew Cruickshank . . . . . Cardwell
John Crawford . . . . Captain
Lois Maxwell . . . . Gwen
COMEDY Three air hostesses fall in love
between New York and Paris and are
involved in diamond smuggling in Vienna.

13211
THE COOL MIKADO (81) (U) *eastman*
Film Productions of Gilbert & Sullivan
Operas (UA)
P: Harold Baim
D: Michael Winner
S: (OPERA) W.S.Gilbert, Arthur Sullivan
(THE MIKADO)
SC: Michael Winner, Maurice Browning,
Lew Schwartz
Frankie Howerd . . . . Ko-Ko
Stubby Kaye . . .`. . Judge Mikado/Charlie
Tommy Cooper . . . . Detective
Dennis Price . . . . Ronald Fortescue
Mike & Bernie Winters . . . . . . Mike & Bernie
Lionel Blair . . . . Nanki
Kevin Scott . . . . Hank Mikado
Glenn Mason . . . . Harry
Pete Murray . . . . Man in Boudoir
Jacqueline Jones . . . . Katie Shaw
Dermot Walsh . . . . Elmer
Jill Mai Meredith . . . . Yum-Yum
Yvonne Shima . . . . Peep-Bo
Tsai Chin . . . . Pitti-Sing
The John Barry Seven
MUSICAL Tokyo. American judge's
soldier son kidnapped by gangster fiance
of Japanese girl he loves.

13212
SUMMER HOLIDAY (109) (U) *tech/scope*
Ivy (WPD)
P: Kenneth Harper
D: Peter Yates, Herbert Ross
S: Peter Myers, Ronald Cass
Cliff Richard . . . . Don

Lauri Peters . . . . Barbara
David Kossoff . . . . Magistrate
Ron Moody . . . . Orlando
The Shadows . . . . Themselves
Lionel Murton . . . . Jerry
Madge Ryan . . . . Stella
Melvyn Hayes . . . . Cyril
Una Stubbs . . . . Sandy
Teddy Green . . . . Steve
Pamela Hart . . . . Angie
Nicholas Phipps . . . . Wrightmore
MUSICAL Mechanics borrow bus to tour
Europe and give lift to runaway girl singer.

13213
NINE HOURS TO RAMA (125) (A)
deluxe/scope
Red Lion (20)
P: D: Mark Robson
S: (NOVEL) Stanley Wolpert
SC: Nelson Gidding
Horst Buccholz . . . . Naturam Godse
Jose Ferrer . . . . Gopal Das
Valerie Gearon . . . . Rani Mahta
Diane Baker . . . . Sheila
Robert Morley . . . . P.K.Mussadi
Don Borisenko . . . . Vishnu Apte
J.S.Casshyap . . . . Mahatma Ghandi
Harry Andrews . . . . Gen Singh
Jairaj . . . . Birla
David Abraham . . . . Munda
Achla Sachdev . . . . Mother
Marne Maitland . . . . Karnick
Peter Illing . . . . Ramamurtia
HISTORY India. Editor joins reactionary
group and shoots Ghandi at prayer meeting.

13214
THIS SPORTING LIFE (134) (X)
Independent Artists (RFD)
P: Albert Fennell, Karel Reisz
D: Lindsay Anderson
S: (NOVEL) David Storey
SC: David Storey
Richard Harris . . . . Frank Machin
Rachel Roberts . . . . Margaret Hammond
Alan Badel . . . . Gerald Weaver
William Hartnell . . . . Johnson
Colin Blakeley . . . . . Maurice Braithwaite
Vanda Godsell . . . . Anne Weaver
Anne Cunningham . . . . . . Judith
Jack Watson . . . . Len Miller
Arthur Lowe . . . . Charles Slomer
Harry Markham . . . . Wade
DRAMA Yorkshire miner becomes professional
rugby footballer and fails to win love of
widowed landlady. (BFA 1963: Best Actress).

13215
THE SET-UP (58) (U)
Merton Park (AA)
P: Jack Greenwood
D: Gerard Glaister
S: (STORY) Edgar Wallace
SC: Roger Marshall
Maurice Denham . . . . Theo Gaunt
John Carson . . . . Insp Jackson
Maria Corvin . . . . Nicole Romain
Brian Peck . . . . Arthur Payne
Anthony Bate . . . . Ray Underwood
John Arnatt . . . . Supt Ross
Manning Wilson . . . . Sgt Bates
Billy Milton . . . . Simpson
CRIME Ex-convict hired to steal woman's
jewels is framed for her murder.

13216
THE £20,000 KISS (57) (A)
Merton Park (AA)

P: Jack Greenwood
D: John Moxey
S: (STORY) Edgar Wallace
SC: Philip Mackie
Dawn Addams . . . . Christina Hagen
Michael Goodliffe . . . . . Sir Harold Trevitt
Richard Thorp . . . . John Durran
Anthony Newlands . . . . Leo Hagen
Alfred Burke . . . . Insp Waveney
Mia Karam . . . . Paula Blair
Ellen McIntosh . . . . Ursula Clandon
Paul Whitsun-Jones . . . . . Charles Pinder
CRIME Private tec proves QC did not
shoot blackmailing maidservant.

13217
INCIDENT AT MIDNIGHT (56) (A)
Merton Park (AA)
P: Jack Greenwood
D: Norman Harrison
S: (STORY) Edgar Wallace
SC: Arthur la Bern
Anton Diffring . . . . . Dr Erik Leichner
William Sylvester . . . . Vince Warren
Justine Lord . . . . Diane Graydon
Martin Miller . . . . Dr Schroeder
Tony Garnett . . . . Brennan
Philip Locke . . . . Foster
Sylva Langova . . . . Vivienne Leichner
Warren Mitchell . . . . Chemist
Jacqueline Jones . . . . Vanessa Palmer
CRIME Girl tec poses as drug-thief's
contact to catch ex-Nazi trafficker.

13218
THE HORSE WITHOUT A HEAD (89) (U)
tech
Walt Disney
P: Hugh Attwooll
D: Don Chaffey
S: (NOVEL) Paul Berna
(A HUNDRED MILLION FRANCS)
SC: T.E.B.Clarke
Jean-Pierre Aumont . . . . . . Insp Sinet
Herbert Lom . . . . Schiapa
Leo McKern . . . . Roublot
Pamela Franklin . . . . Marion
Vincent Winter . . . . Fernand
Lee Montague . . . . Mallart
Denis Gilmore . . . . Tatave
Sean Keir . . . . Bonbon
Loretta Parry . . . . Melie
Michael Gwynn . . . . Jerome
Peter Butterworth . . . . Zigon
Jenny Laird . . . . Mme Fabert
Maureen Pryor . . . . Mme Douin
COMEDY France. Children and dogs catch
gang of train-robbers who hide loot in old
toy factory.

13219
THE MOUSE ON THE MOON (85) (U)
eastman
Walter Shenson (UA) *reissue:* 1965
P: Walter Shenson
D: Richard Lester
S: (NOVEL) Leonard Wibberley
SC: Michael Pertwee
Margaret Rutherford. . Grand Duchess Gloriana
Bernard Cribbins . . . . .Vincent Mountjoy
Ron Moody . . . . Mountjoy
David Kossoff . . . . Prof Kokintz
Terry-Thomas . . . . Spender
June Ritchie . . . . Cynthia
John le Mesurier . . . . British Delegate
John Phillips . . . . Bracewell
Eric Barker . . . . Member
Roddy McMillan . . . . Benter
Tom Aldredge . . . . Wendover

Michael Trubshawe . . . . Aide
Peter Sallis . . . .: Russian Delegate
Clive Dunn . . . . Bandleader
Hugh Lloyd . . . . Plumber
John Bluthal . . . . Max Von Neidel
Robin Bailey . . . . Member
Mario Fabrizi . . . . Mario
Graham Stark . . . . Guardsman
Allan Cuthbertson . . . . Simon
Frankie Howerd . . . . Fenwickian
FANTASY First rocket to reach moon is
from bankrupt Duchy, powered by explosive
wine.

13220
NURSE ON WHEELS (86) (U)
GHW Productions (AA)
P: Peter Rogers
D: Gerald Thomas
S: (NOVEL) Joanna Jones
(NURSE IS A NEIGHBOUR)
SC: Norman Hudis
Juliet Mills . . . . Joanna Jones
Ronald Lewis . . . . Henry Edwards
Joan Sims . . . . Deborah Walcott
Noel Purcell . . . . Abel Worthy
Esma Cannon . . . . Mrs Jones
Raymond Huntley . . . . Vicar
Athene Seyler . . . . Miss Farthingale
Norman Rossington . . . . . . George Judd
Ronald Howard . . . . Dr Harold Golfrey
Joan Hickson . . . . Mrs Wood
Renee Houston . . . . Mrs Beacon
Jim Dale . . . . Tim Taylor
George Woodbridge . . . . . . Mr Beacon
David Horne . . . . Dr Golfrey
COMEDY New District Nurse loves farmer
who wants to evict caravan couple.

13221
THE KING'S BREAKFAST (28) (U) eastman
Francis-Montagu
P: James Archibald
D: SC: Wendy Toye
S: (POEM) A.A.Milne
N: Maurice Denham
Maurice Denham . . . . King
Micha Auer . . . . Master of Musick
Reginald Beckwith . . . . . . Magician
Robert Flemyng . . . . Chamberlain
Lally Bowers . . . . Queen
Warren Mitchell . . . . Instructor
Maryon Lane . . . . Dairymaid
Una Stubbs . . . . Tweeny
Richard Hearne . . . . Footman
Edgar Driver . . . . Edgar
MUSICAL Cow tries to talk king out of
having butter with his breakfast.

13222
PARANOIAC (80) (X) scope
Hammer (UI)
P: Anthony Hinds
D: Freddie Francis
S: Jimmy Sangster
Janette Scott . . . . Eleanor Ashby
Oliver Reed . . . . Simon Ashby
Liliane Brousse . . . . Francoise
Sheila Burrell . . . . Harriet
Maurice Denham . . . . John Kosset
Alexander Davion . . . . Tony Ashby
John Bonney . . . . Keith Kosset
John Stuart . . . . Williams
Colin Tapley . . . . Vicar
Harold Lang . . . . RAF Type
CRIME Man posing as girl's dead brother
saves her from her mad, murderous brother.

13223
SPARROWS CAN'T SING (94) (A)
Carthage (Elstree)

P: Donald Taylor
D: Joan Littlewood
S: (PLAY) Stephen Lewis
(SPARRERS CAN'T SING)
SC: Stephen Lewis, Joan Littlewood
James Booth . . . . Charlie Gooding
Barbara Windsor . . . . Maggie Gooding
Roy Kinnear . . . . Fred Gooding
George Sewell . . . . Bert
Avis Bunnage . . . . Bridgie Gooding
Barbara Ferris . . . . Nellie Gooding
Murray Melvin . . . . Georgie
Griffith Davies . . . . Chunky
Fanny Carby Lil
Arthur Mullard . . . . Ted
Brian Murphy . . . . Jack
Stephen Lewis . . . . Caretaker
Wally Patch . . . . Watchman
Harry H. Corbett . . . . Greengrocer
Queenie Watts . . . . Queenie
COMEDY Cockney seaman wins wife and
baby back from bus driver.

13224
THAT KIND OF GIRL (77) (X)
Tekli (Compton)
P: Robert Hartford-Davis
D: Gerald O'Hara
S: Jan Read
Margaret-Rose Keil . . . . Eva
David Weston . . . . Keith Murray
Linda Marlowe . . . . Janet Bates
Peter Burton . . . . Elliot Collier
Frank Jarvis . . . . Max
Sylvia Kay . . . . Mrs Millar
David Davenport . . . . Mr Millar
Stephen Stocker . . . . Nicolas
Charles Houston . . . . Ted
Max Faulkner . . . . Johnson
John Wood . . . . Doctor
DRAMA Austrian 'au pair' girl's love affairs
result in pregnancy and venereal disease.

FEB

13225
BITTER HARVEST (96) (X) eastman
Independent Artists (RFD)
P: Albert Fennell
D: Peter Graham Scott
S: (NOVEL) Patrick Hamilton
(THE STREET HAS A THOUSAND SKIES)
SC: Ted Willis
Janet Munro . . . . Jennie Jones
John Stride . . . . Bob Williams
Alan Badel . . . . Karl Denny
Anne Cunningham . . . . Ella
Norman Bird . . . . Mr Pitt
Terence Alexander . . . . Andy
Daphne Anderson . . . . Nancy Medwin
May Hallatt . . . . Aunt Sarah
Mary Merrall . . . . Aunt Louise
Colin Gordon . . . . Charles
Barbara Ferris . . . . Violet
Allan Cuthbertson . . . . Mr Eccles
Vanda Godsell . . . . Mrs Pitt
William Lucas . . . . David Medwin
Thora Hird . . . . Mrs Jessup
Jane Hylton . . . . Actress
DRAMA Welsh girl, lured by soap commercial
becomes impresario's mistress and kills herself.

13226
CALCULATED RISK (72) (A)
McLeod (Bry)
P: William McLeod
D: Norman Harrison
S: Edwin Richfield
William Lucas . . . . Steve
John Rutland . . . . Kip
Dilys Watling . . . . Julie

Warren Mitchell . . . . Simmie
Shay Gorman . . . . Dodo
Terence Cooper . . . . Nodge
David Brierly . . . . Ron
CRIME Gang set off unexploded bomb while
breaking into bank vault through cellars.

13227
THE SMALL WORLD OF SAMMY LEE (107)
(X)
Elgin (Bry-Seven Arts)
P: Ken Hughes, Frank Godwin
D: Ken Hughes
S: (TV PLAY) Ken Hughes (SAMMY)
SC: Ken Hughes
Anthony Newley . . . . Sammy Lee
Robert Stephens . . . . Gerry
Wilfrid Brambell . . . . Harry
Miriam Karlin . . . . Milly
Julia Foster . . . . Patsy
Kenneth J. Warren . . . . Fred
Warren Mitchell . . . . Lou
Colin Clive Bowler . . . . Johnny
Toni Palmer . . . . Joan
Harry Locke . . . . Stage Manager
Cyril Shaps . . . . Morrie
Roy Kinnear . . . . Lucky Dave
Alfred Burke . . . . Big Eddie
June Cunningham . . . . Rita
DRAMA Soho strip club compere tries
to raise £300 to pay gambling debt.

13228
DOOMSDAY AT ELEVEN (56) (U)
Parroch (GEF)
P: C. Jack Parsons
D: Theodore Zichy
SC: Paul Tabori, Gordon Wellesley
Carl Jaffe. . . . . Stefan
Stanley Morgan . . . . Wylie
Alan Heywood . . . . Peter Godwin
Derrick de Marney . . . . . Judge Alderbrook
Jennifer Wright . . . . . . Angela Alderbrook
Delia Corrie . . . . Eve Lake
Alan Edwards . . . . Wilson
Geoffrey Dunn . . . . Jeremiah
DRAMA Injured officer and volunteers
dismantle time bomb planted in maternity
home.

13229
SUDDENLY IT'S JAZZ (14) (U)
Goldray Motion Picture Corp (BL)
D: Jeremy Summers
Dick Charlesworth and his City Gents
MUSICAL

13230
THE LEATHER BOYS (108) (X) scope
Raymond Stross (Garrick)
D: Sidney J. Furie
S: (NOVEL) Eliot George
SC: Gillian Freeman
Rita Tushingham . . . . Dot
Dudley Sutton . . . . Pete
Gladys Henson . . . . Gran
Colin Campbell . . . . Reggie
Avice Landone . . . . Reggie's Mother
Lockwood West . . . . Reggie's Father
Betty Marsden . . . . Dot's Mother
Martin Matthews . . . . Uncle Arthur
Johnny Briggs . . . . Boyfriend
James Chase . . . . Les
Geoffrey Dunn . . . . Mr Lunnis
Dandy Nichols . . . . Mrs Stanley
DRAMA Teenager marries schoolgirl and
leaves her for fellow motor-cycle enthusiast.

13231
IMPACT (61) (U)
Butcher's Films

P: John I. Phillips
D: Peter Maxwell
S: Peter Maxwell, Conrad Phillips
Conrad Phillips . . . . Jack Moir
George Pastell . . . . The Duke
Ballard Berkeley . . . . Bill Mackenzie
Linda Marlowe . . . . Diana
Richard Klee . . . . Wally
Anita West . . . . Melanie
John Rees . . . . Charlie
CRIME Reporter traps club owner who
framed him for train robbery.

13232
JASON AND THE ARGONAUTS (103) (U)
tech
Morningside-Worldwide (Col)
P: Charles H. Schneer
D: Don Chaffey
S: Jan Read, Beverley Cross
Todd Armstrong . . . . Jason
Nancy Kovack . . . . Medea
Gary Raymond . . . . Acastus
Laurence Naismith . . . . Argus
Niall MacGinnis . . . . Zeus
Michael Gwynn . . . . Hermes
Douglas Wilmer . . . . Pelias
Jack Gwillim . . . . Aeetes
Honor Blackman . . . . Hera
Andrew Faulds . . . . Phalerus
John Crawford . . . . Polydeuces
Nigel Green . . . . Hercules
FANTASY Greece. Usurped king's son's
adventures in search of golden fleece.

13233
JUST FOR FUN (85) (U)
Amicus (Col)
P: Milton Subotsky
D: Gordon Flemyng
S: Milton Subotsky
Mark Wynter . . . . Mark
Cherry Roland . . . . Cherry
Irene Handl . . . . Housewife
Hugh Lloyd . . . . Plumber
Dick Emery . . . . Jury Panel
Mario Fabrizi . . . . Diner
Richard Vernon . . . . Prime Minister
Reginald Beckwith . . . . Leader of Opposition
Jeremy Lloyd . . . . PM's Son
Harry Fowler . . . . Interviewer
John Wood . . . . Official
Bobby Vee; Joe Brown; Karl Denver;
Jet Harris; Tony Meehan; Ketty Lester;
The Crickets: Freddy Cannon; Johnny Tillotson;
The Springfields; The Spotnicks; The Tornados;
Kenny Lynch; Louise Cordet; Cloda
Rogers; The Vernon Girls; Brian Poole and
the Tremeloes; The Breakaways; Sounds Inc;
David Jacobs; Alan Freeman; Jimmy Savile
MUSICAL Teenagers are given the vote,
promote a Teenage Party, and take over the
country.

13234
ON THE RUN (59) (U)
Merton Park (AA)
P: Jack Greenwood
D: Robert Tronson
S: (STORY) Edgar Wallace
SC: Richard Harris
Emrys Jones . . . . Frank Stewart
Sarah Lawson . . . . Helen Carr
Patrick Barr . . . . Sgt Brent
Delphi Lawrence . . . . Yvonne
Kevin Stoney . . . . Wally Lucas
William Abney . . . . Jock McKay
Katy Wild . . . . Jean Stuart
Philip Locke . . . . David Hughes
CRIME Bookie helps convict break jail
to uncover hidden bonds.

13235
TAKE OFF YOUR CLOTHES AND LIVE (64)
(A) *eastman/scope*
Miracle-Searchlight (Miracle)
P: Arnold Miller, Stanley Long
D: Arnold Louis Miller
Ian Michael . . . . Tony
Gino Nennan . . . . John
Jenny Lane . . . . Lee
Maureen Haydon . . . . June
Susan Irwin-Clark . . . . Carol
Terry Lee . . . . Ingrid
Margaret Collins . . . . Mandy
Angela Lowe . . . . Pat
NUDIST Cannes. Nine girls and male
hosts spend naked holiday searching for
treasure.

MAR

13236
THE BAY OF SAINT MICHEL (73) (U)
Trionyx (RFD)
P:D: John Ainsworth
S: Christopher Davis
Keenan Wynn . . . . Nick Rawlings
Mai Zetterling . . . . Helene Bretton
Ronald Howard . . . . Bill Webb
Rona Anderson . . . . Pru Lawson
Trader Faulkner . . . . Dave Newton
Edward Underdown . . . . . Col Harvey
Michael Peake . . . . Capt Starkey
Rudolph Offenbach . . . . . . Father Laurent
ADVENTURE Normandy. Commander
reforms commando unit to seek Nazi
General's hidden loot.

13237
CALL ME BWANA (93) (U) *eastman*
Eon (RFD)
P: Harry Saltzman, Albert Broccoli
D: Gordon Douglas
S: Nate Monaster, Johanna Harwood
Bob Hope . . . . Matt Merryweather
Anita Ekberg . . . . Luba
Edie Adams . . . . Frederica Larsen
Lionel Jeffries . . . . Dr Ezra Mungo
Percy Herbert . . . . Henchman
Paul Carpenter . . . . Col Spencer
Orlando Martins . . . . Chief
Al Mulock . . . . Henchman
Peter Dyneley . . . . Williams
COMEDY Africa. Girl spy tries to stop
travel book writer from locating American
space capsule.

13238
IT'S ALL HAPPENING (101) (U) *eastman*
KNP Productions (Magna)
P: Norman Williams
D: Don Sharp
S: Leigh Vance
Tommy Steele . . . . Billy Bowles
Michael Medwin . . . . Max Catlin
Angela Douglas . . . . Julie
Jean Harvey . . . . Delia
Walter Hudd . . . . J.B.Magdeburg
Bernard Bresslaw . . . . Parsons
John Tate . . . . Julian Singleton
Richard Goolden . . . . Lord Sweatstone
John Barry; Clyde Valley Stompers;
Russ Conway; Carol Deene; Shane Fenton;
Dick Kallman; Johnny de Little; Geoff Love;
Marion Ryan; Danny Williams; George
Mitchell Show; Tony Mercer; John Boulter
MUSICAL Record company talent scout
stages show for orphanage.

13239
JUST ONE MORE TIME (13) (U)
Francis Megahy (NR)
D:S: Francis Megahy

Charles Gale . . . . The Man
COMEDY Bayswater. Adventures of
young philanderer living on his wits.

13240
RETURN TO SENDER (61) (A)
Merton Park (AA)
P: Jack Greenwood
D: Gordon Hales
S: (STORY) Edgar Wallace
SC: John Roddick
Nigel Davenport . . . . Dino Steffano
Yvonne Romain . . . . Lisa
Geoffrey Keen . . . . Robert Lindley
William Russell . . . . Mike Cochrane
Jennifer Daniel . . . . Beth Lindley
Paul Williamson . . . . Tony Shaw
John Horsley . . . . Supt Gilchrist
Richard Bird . . . . Fox
CRIME Crooked speculator hires man to
compromise his prosecutor.

13241
RICOCHET (64) (A)
Merton Park (AA)
P: Jack Greenwood
D: John Moxey
S: (STORY) Edgar Wallace
(ANGEL OF TERROR)
SC: Roger Marshall
Maxine Audley . . . . Yvonne Phipps
Richard Leech . . . . Alan Phipps
Alex Scott . . . . John Brodie
Dudley Foster . . . . Peter Dexter
Patrick Magee . . . . Insp Cummins
Frederick Piper . . . . Siddall
June Murphy . . . . Judy
Virginia Wetherell . . . . Brenda
CRIME Solicitor causes rich wife to
shoot her lover and is blackmailed.

13242
TWO LEFT FEET (93) (X)
Roy Baker (BL)
P: Leslie Gilliat
D: Roy Baker
S: (NOVEL) David Leslie
(IN MY SOLITUDE)
SC: Roy Baker, John Hopkins
Michael Crawford . . . . Alan Crabbe
Nyree Dawn Porter . . . . . . Eileen
Julia Foster . . . . Beth Crowley
David Hemmings . . . . Brian
Bernard Lee . . . . Mr Crabbe
David Lodge . . . . Bill
Michael Craze . . . . Ronnie
Dilys Watling . . . . Mavis
Cyril Chamberlain . . . . Miles
Michael Ripper . . . . Uncle Reg
Bob Wallis and his Storyville Jazzmen
COMEDY Teenager's affair with older
waitress causes fight with her fiance.

13243
IN THE COOL OF THE DAY (91) (A)
metro/scope
MGM British
P: John Houseman
D: Robert Stevens
S:(NOVEL) Susan Ertz
SC: Meade Roberts
Peter Finch . . . . Murray Logan
Jane Fonda . . . . Christine Bonner
Angela Lansbury . . . . Sybil Logan
Arthur Hill . . . . Sam Bonner
Constance Cummings . . . . . Mrs Gellert
Alexander Knox . . . . Frederick Bonner
Nigel Davenport . . . . Len
John le Mesurier . . . . Doctor
Alec McCowen . . . . Bayliss
Valerie Taylor . . . . Lily Kendrick
ROMANCE Greece. American publisher's
wife loves his married British partner.

13244
SAMMY GOING SOUTH (128) (U)
eastman/scope/trilingual USA: A BOY
TEN FEET TALL
Greatshows (Bry-Seven Arts)
P: Michael Balcon, Hal Mason
D: Alexander Mackendrick
S: (NOVEL) W.H.Canway
SC: Denis Cannan
Edward G. Robinson . . .   Cocky Wainwright
Constance Cummings. . Gloria van Imhoff
Harry H. Corbett . . . .   Lem
Paul Stassino. . . Spyros Dracondopolous
Fergus McClelland . . . . . .   Sammy Hartland
Zia Mohyeddin . . . .   Syrian
Orlando Martins . . . .   Abu Lubaba
John Turner . . . .   Heneker
Zena Walker . . . .   Aunt Jane
Jack Gwillim . . . .   Commissioner
ADVENTURE Africa, 1956. Ten year-old
orphan travels from Port Said to Durban
encountering blind peddlar, diamond
smuggler, etc. (RFP: 1963).

13245
THE HAUNTING (112) (X) *scope*
Argyle Enterprises (MGM)
P:D: Robert Wise
S: (NOVEL) Shirley Jackson
(THE HAUNTING OF HILL HOUSE)
SC: Nelson Gidding
Julie Harris . . . . Eleanor Vance
Claire Bloom . . . .   Theodora
Richard Johnson . . . .   Dr John Markway
Russ Tamblyn . . . .   Luke Sanderson
Lois Maxwell . . . .   Grace Markway
Fay Compton . . . .   Mrs Sanderson
Valentine Dyall . . . .   Mr Dudley
Rosalie Crutchley . . . .   Mrs Dudley
Diane Clare . . . .   Carrie Fredericks
Ronald Adam . . . .   Eldridge Harper
Freda Knorr . . . .   Mrs Crain
FANTASY New England. Professor, spinster,
lesbian and heir seek evil spirit of ninety
year-old house.

APR

13246
THE DOUBLE (56) (U)
Merton Park (AA)
P: Jack Greenwood
D: Lionel Harris
S: (NOVEL) Edgar Wallace
SC: Lindsay Galloway, John Roddick
Jeannette Sterke . . . .   Mary Winston
Alan McNaughton . . . .   John Cleeve
Robert Brown . . . .   Richard Harrison
Jane Griffiths . . . .   Jane Winston
Basil Henson . . . .   Derreck Alwyn
Anne Lawson . . . .   Sally Carter
Diane Clare . . . .   Selena Osmond
Llewellyn Rees . . . .   Bradshaw
Hamilton Dyce . . . .   Insp Ames
CRIME Girl proves paralysed amnesiac is
heir to estate usurped by the man he
believes he murdered.

13247
EVES ON SKIS (34) *eastman* (A)
Michael Keatering (Gala)
P:D: Michael Keatering
Elizabeth
Karl
Karen
Jill
Herbert
NUDIST Teenage London girl spends
naturist holiday in the Austrian Alps.

13248
THE FLOOD (59) (U)
AB-Pathe (CFF)
P: Terry Ashwood
D: Frederic Goode
S: Frank Wells
SC: Jean Scott Rogers
Waveney Lee . . . . . Clarissa Weathersfield
Christopher Ellis . . . .   Robin
Frank Knight . . . .   Reg
Jonathan Bergman . . . .   Bill Brasted
Ian Ellis . . . .   Charles
Leslie Hart . . . .   Ernie
Richard Leech . . . .
Daphne Anderson . . . .
Russell Waters . . . .
CHILDREN East Anglia. Six farm children
rescued from flood.

13249
THE RESCUE SQUAD (54) (U)
World Wide (CFF)
P: Hindle Edgar
D: Colin Bell
S: Frank Wells
SC: Mary Cathcart Borer
Christopher Brett . . . .   Bill
Shirley Joy . . . .   Ann
Malcolm Knight . . . .   Tom
Gareth Tandy . . . .   Charlie
Linda Leo . . . .   Carol
Danny Grove . . . .   Joe
Renee Houston . . . .   Mrs Manse
Leslie French . . . .   Mr Manse
Michael Balfour . . . .   Barrow-boy
Peter Butterworth . . . .   Mr Maggs
CHILDREN Children trapped in ruined
tower while searching for lost toy plane.

13250
WINGS OF MYSTERY (55) (U)
Rayant (CFF)
P: Anthony Gilkison
D: SC: Gilbert Gunn
S: H.K. Lewenhak
Judy Geeson . . . .   Jane
Hennis Scott . . . .   Don
Patrick Jordan . . . .   McCarthy
Francesca Bertorelli . . . . .   Yvette
Graham Aza . . . .   Antoine
Anthony Jacobs . . . .   Agent
John Gabriel . . . .   Father
Richard Carpenter . . . .   Ted
Arnold Ridley . . . .   Mr Bell
CHILDREN Children fly to Belgium to
thwart researcher who stole secret steel
alloy.

13251
HEAVENS ABOVE ! (118) (A)
Charter (BL-Romulus)
P: Roy Boulting
D: John Boulting
S: Malcolm Muggeridge
SC: John Boulting, Frank Harvey
Peter Sellers . . . .   Rev John Aspinall
Cecil Parker . . . .   Archdeacon Aspinall
Isabel Jeans . . . .   Lady Despard
Eric Sykes . . . .   Harry Smith
Bernard Miles . . . .   Simpson
Ian Carmichael . . . .   Rev John Smallwood
Irene Handl . . . .   Rene Smith
Brock Peters . . . .   Matthew
Miriam Karlin . . . .   Winnie Smith
Joan Miller . . . . Mrs Smith-Gould
Miles Malleson . . . .   Rockerby
Eric Barker . . . .   Bank Manager
William Hartnell . . . .   Maj Fowler
Roy Kinnear . . . .   Fred Smith
Joan Hickson . . . . , ...   Housewife
Kenneth Griffith . . . . . .   Rev Owen Thomas
Mark Eden . . . . . .   Sir Geoffrey Despard
Colin Gordon . . . .   Prime Minister
Thorley Walters . . . .   Executive
Conrad Phillips . . . .   PRO
Malcolm Muggeridge; Franklyn Engelman;
Tim Brinton; Ludovic Kennedy
COMEDY Prison chaplain, mistakenly
appointed to village church, causes chaos
with his Christian charity.

13252
LANCELOT AND GUINEVERE (117)
eastman/scope
Emblem (UI)
P: Cornel Wilde, Bernard Luber
D: Cornel Wilde
S: Richard Schayer, Jefferson Pascal
Cornel Wilde . . . .   Sir Lancelot
Jean Wallace . . . .   Princess Guinevere
Brian Aherne . . . .   King Arthur
George Baker . . . .   Sir Gawaine
Adrienne Corri . . . .   Lady Vivian
Michael Meacham . . . .   Sir Modred
Iain Gregory . . . .   Sir Tors
Archie Duncan . . . .   Sir Lamorak
Mark Dignam . . . .   Merlin
John Barrie . . . .   Sir Bedivere
Richard Thorp . . . .   Sir Gareth
Reginald Beckwith . . . .   Sir Dagonet
Joseph Tomelty . . . .   Sir Kaye
Walter Gotell . . . .   Sir Cedric
John Longden . . . .   King Leodogran
Graham Stark . . . .   Rian
HISTORY Knight saves beloved Queen
from stake and foils King's bastard son.

13253
MURDER AT THE GALLOP (81) (U)
MGM British
P: Lawrence P. Bachmann, George Brown
D: George Pollock
S: (NOVEL) Agatha Christie
(AFTER THE FUNERAL)
SC: James P. Cavanagh
Margaret Rutherford . . . . .   Miss Marple
Robert Morley . . . .   Hector Enderby
Flora Robson . . . . Miss Gilchrist
Charles Tingwell . . . .   Insp Craddock
Katya Douglas . . . .   Rosamund Shane
Stringer Davis . . . .   Mr Stringer
Duncan Lamont . . . .   Hillman
James Villiers . . . .   Michael Shane
Robert Urquhart . . . . . .   George Crossfield
CRIME Spinster solves murder of cat-hating
recluse and his sister.

13254
MYSTERY SUBMARINE (92) (U)
Bertram Ostrer (Britannia)
P: Bertram Ostrer
D: C.M.Pennington-Richards
S: (PLAY) Jon Manchip White
SC: Jon Manchip White, Hugh Woodhouse,
Bertram Ostrer
Edward Judd . . . . Lt-Cdr Tarlton
James Robertson Justice . Rear-Admiral Rainbird
Laurence Payne . . . .   Lt Seaton
Joachim Fuchsberger . . . .   Cdr Scheffler
Arthur O'Sullivan . . . . Mike Fitzgerald
Albert Lieven . . . . .   Capt von Neymarck
Robert Flemyng . . Admiral Sir James Carver
Richard Carpenter . . . .   Lt Hoskins
Richard Thorp . . . .   Lt Chatterton
Jeremy Hawk . . . .   Admiral Saintsbury
Robert Brown . . . .   Coxswain Drage
Frederick Jaeger . . . .   Lt Henze
Leslie Randall . . . .   Donnithorne
WAR British sailors man captured German
U-boat to locate wolfpack rendezvous.

13255
THE VERY EDGE (89) (A)
Raymond Stross (Garrick)
P: Raymond Stross
D: Cyril Frankel
S: Vivian Cox, Leslie Bricusse,
Raymond Stross
SC: Elizabeth Jane Howard
Richard Todd . . . . Geoffrey Lawrence
Anne Heywood . . . . Tracey Lawrence
Nicole Maurey . . . . Helen
Jack Hedley . . . . McInnes
Barbara Mullen . . . . Dr Shaw
Jeremy Brett . . . . Mullen
Maurice Denham . . . . Crawford
William Lucas . . . . Insp Davies
Gwen Watford . . . . Sister Holden
Patrick Magee . . . . Simmonds
DRAMA Architect's ex-model wife mis-
carries after being attacked, and becomes
frigid.

13256
THE SCARLET BLADE (82) (U) *tech/scope*
Hammer (WPD)
P: Anthony Nelson Keys
D: S: John Gilling
Lionel Jeffries . . . . Col Judd
Oliver Reed . . . . Capt Sylvester
Jack Hedley . . . . Edward Beverley
June Thorburn . . . . Clare Judd
Duncan Lamont . . . . Maj Bell
Suzan Farmer . . . . Constance Beverley
Michael Ripper . . . . Pablo
Charles Houston . . . . Drury
Harold Goldblatt . . . . Jacob
Robert Rietty . . . . Charles I
ADVENTURE 1648. Ironside colonel's
Royalist daughter loves rebel, and is
loved by her father's aide.

13257
THE OLD DARK HOUSE (86) (X) *tech*
Hammer-Castle (Col)
P: William Castle, Anthony Hinds
D: William Castle
S: (NOVEL) J.B.Priestley (BENIGHTED)
SC: Robert Dillon
Robert Morley . . . . Roderick Femm
Janette Scott . . . . Cecily Femm
Joyce Grenfell . . . . Agatha Femm
Tom Poston . . . . Tom Penderel
Mervyn Johns . . . . Potiphar Femm
Fenella Fielding . . . . Morgana Femm
Peter Bull . . . . `Casper Femm/Jasper Femm
Danny Green . . . . Morgan Femm
COMEDY Dartmoor. American salesman
solves the murder of eccentric family of
legatees.

MAY

13258
ECHO OF DIANA (61) (U)
Butcher's Films
P: John I. Phillips
D: Ernest Morris
S: Reginald Hearne
Vincent Ball . . . . Bill Vernon
Betty McDowall . . . . Joan Scott
Geoffrey Toone . . . . Col Justin
Clare Owen . . . . Pam Jennings
Peter Illing . . . . Kovali
Raymond Adamson . . . . . George
Marianne Stone . . . . Miss Green
CRIME Reporters uncover spy ring behind
death of woman's husband.

13259
80,000 SUSPECTS (113) (A) *scope*
Rank (RFD)
P: Val Guest, Frank Sherwin Green
D: SC: Val Guest
S: (NOVEL) Elleston Trevor
(THE PILLARS OF MIDNIGHT)
Claire Bloom . . . . Julie Monks
Richard Johnson . . . . Steven Monks
Yolande Donlan . . . . Ruth Preston
Cyril Cusack . . . . Father Maguire
Michael Goodliffe . . . . . . Clifford Preston
Mervyn Johns . . . . Buckridge
Kay Walsh . . . . Matron
Norman Bird . . . . Mr Davis
Basil Dignam . . . . MO
Andrew Crawford . . . . Dr Ruddling
Ray Barrett . . . . Insp Bennett
Norman Chappell . . . . Welford
Arthur Christiansen . . . . . . Mr Gracey
Vanda Godsell . . . . Mrs Davis
Ursula Howells . . . . Joanna Druten
DRAMA Bath. Hospital doctor fights
smallpox epidemic, tracing outbreak to his
colleague's unfaithful wife.

13260
HIDE AND SEEK (90) (U)
Spectrum (Albion)
P: Hal E. Chester
D: Cy Endfield
S: (NOVEL) Harold Greene
SC: Robert Foshko, David Stone
Ian Carmichael . . . . David Garrett
Janet Munro . . . . Maggie
Hugh Griffith . . . . Wilkins
Curt Jurgens . . . . Hubert Marek
Kieron Moore . . . . Paul
George Pravda . . . . Melnicker
Edward Chapman . . . . McPherson
Kynaston Reeves . . . . Hunter
Esma Cannon . . . . Tea Lady
Derek Tansey . . . . Charles
Frederick Peisley . . . . Cottrell
Lance Percival . . . . Idiot
CRIME Communist agent stages disappear-
ance of chess player as trap to capture professor
of nuclear physics.

13261
MASTER SPY (74) (U)
Eternal (GN)
P: Maurice J. Wilson
D: Montgomery Tully
S: (STORY) Gerald Anstruther, Paul White
(THEY ALSO SERVE)
SC: Maurice J. Wilson, Montgomery Tully
Stephen Murray . . . . Boris Turgenev
June Thorburn . . . . Leila
Alan Wheatley . . . . Paul Skelton
John Carson . . . . Richard Colman
John Brown . . . . John Baxter
Jack Watson . . . . Capt Foster
Ernest Clark . . . . Dr Pembury
Marne Maitland . . . . Dr Asafu
Ellen Pollock . . . . Dr Morrell
CRIME Russian scientist's assistant
suspects he is a spy, but he is working for
British intelligence.

13262
THE RUNNING MAN (113) (A) *eastman/scope*
Peet Productions (Col)
P: Carol Reed, John R. Sloan
D: Carol Reed
S: (NOVEL) Shelley Smith
(THE BALLAD OF THE RUNNING MAN)
SC: John Mortimer

Laurence Harvey . . . . Rex Black
Lee Remick . . . . Stella Black
Alan Bates . . . . Stephen Maddox
Felix Aylmer . . . . Parson
Eleanor Summerfield . . . . . Hilda Tanner
Colin Gordon . . . . Solicitor
Allan Cuthbertson . . . . Jenkins
Harold Goldblatt . . . . Tom Webster
Noel Purcell . . . . Miles Bleeker
Ramsey Ames . . . . Madge Penderby
Fernando Rey . . . . Police Official
Fortunio Bonanova . . . . . . Bank Official
John Meillon . . . . Jim Jerome
CRIME Spain. Insurance agent on holiday
loves wife of pilot who faked his own
death to defraud company.

13263
TAKE ME OVER (60) (U)
McLeod (Col)
P: William McLeod
D: Robert Lynn
S: Dail Ambler
Temperance Seven . . . . . The Twenties Group
John Paul . . . . Campbell Carter
John Rutland . . . . Sid Light
Diane Aubrey . . . . Carole Carter
Mark Burns . . . . Bill Light
Mildred Mayne . . . . Typist
Totti Truman-Taylor . . . . . Woman
MUSICAL Hotel builder schemes to purchase
coffee bar and antique shop.

13264
THE VIPS (119) (A) *metro/scope*
MGM British
P: Anatole de Grunwald
D: Anthony Asquith
S: Terence Rattigan
Elizabeth Taylor . . . . Frances Andros
Richard Burton . . . . Paul Andros
Louis Jourdan . . . . Marc Champselle
Elsa Martinelli . . . . Gloria Gritti
Margaret Rutherford . . . . Duchess of Brighton
Maggie Smith . . . . Miss Mead
Rod Taylor . . . . Les Mangrum
Orson Welles . . . . Max Buda
Linda Christian . . . . Miriam Marshall
Dennis Price . . . . Cdr Millbank
Richard Wattis . . . . Sanders
Ronald Fraser . . . . Joslin
David Frost . . . . Reporter
Robert Cooke . . . . John Coburn
Joan Benham . . . . Miss Potter
Michael Hordern . . . . Director
Lance Percival . . . . Official
DRAMA Various passengers for New York
forced to stay the night at London Airport
hotel, due to fog. (AA 1963: Best Supporting
Actress).

13265
THE STOLEN HOURS (97) (U)
Barbican-Mirisch (UA)
P: Stuart Millar, Lawrence Turman
D: Daniel M. Petrie
S: (PLAY) George Emerson Brewer,
Bertram Bloch (DARK VICTORY)
SC: Jessamyn West
Susan Hayward . . . . Laura Pember
Michael Craig . . . . John Carmody
Diane Baker . . . . Ellen Pember
Edward Judd . . . . Mike Bannerman
Paul Rogers . . . . Eric Mackenzie
Robert Bacon . . . . Peter
Paul Stassino . . . . Palporto
Jerry Desmonde . . . . Colonel

Ellen McIntosh . . . . Miss Kendall
Peter Madden . . . . Reynolds
Chet Baker
ROMANCE On the eve of her marriage to a
surgeon a woman learns she has one year to
live.

13266
THE SWITCH (69) (U)
Philip Ridgeway (RFD)
P: Philip Ridgeway, Lance Comfort
D: Peter Maxwell
S: Philip Ridgeway
SC: Philip Ridgeway, Colin Fraser
Anthony Steel . . . . Bill Craddock
Zena Marshall . . . . Caroline Markham
Conrad Phillips . . . . John Curry
Dermot Walsh . . . . Insp Tomlinson
Susan Shaw . . . . Search Officer
Dawn Beret . . . . Janice Lampton
Jerry Desmonde . . . . Customs Chief
Arnold Diamond . . . . Jean Lecraze
CRIME Customs officer saves girl kidnapped
by watch smugglers.

13267
THE RIVALS (56) (U)
Merton Park (AA)
P: Jack Greenwood
D: Max Varnel
S: (NOVEL) Edgar Wallace
(ELEGANT EDWARD)
SC: John Roddick
Jack Gwillim . . . . Rolf Neilson
Erica Rogers . . . . Kim Harris
Brian Smith . . . . Steve Houston
Tony Garnett . . . . Jimmy Vosier
Barry Linehan . . . . Paul Kenyon
Murray Hayne . . . . Alex Nichols
Howard Greene . . . . Eddy McQuire
Philip Latham . . . . Lawrence
CRIME Car thieves scheme to obtain ransom
money for Swedish millionaire's kidnapped
daughter.

JUN

13268
BILLY LIAR ! (98) (A) *scope*
Vic-Waterhall (AA)
P: Joseph Janni
D: John Schlesinger
S: (NOVEL) Keith Waterhouse
(PLAY) Keith Waterhouse, Willis Hall
SC: Keith Waterhouse, Willis Hall
Tom Courtenay . . . . Billy Fisher
Julie Christie . . . . Liz
Wilfred Pickles . . . . Geoffrey Fisher
Mona Washbourne . . . . Alice Fisher
Ethel Griffies . . . . Florence
Finlay Currie . . . . Duxbury
Gwendolyn Watts . . . . Rita
Helen Fraser . . . . Barbara
Leslie Randall . . . . Danny Boone
Rodney Bewes . . . . Arthur Crabtree
George Innes . . . . Eric Stamp
Patrick Barr . . . . Insp Macdonald
Godfrey Winn . . . . Himself
COMEDY Undertaker's imaginative clerk,
engaged to two girls, hopes to write scripts
for a TV comic.

13269
BLAZE OF GLORY (57) (U)
Argo (GEF)
P: Jack O. Lamont, David Henley
D: Robert Lynn
S: Paddy Manning O'Brine
SC: Paddy Manning O'Brine, Joy Garrison

Gary Cockrell . . . . Johnny de Bois
Geoffrey Toone . . . . Roche
Ljubica Jovil . . . . Yvette
Marian Spencer . . . . Grandmother
WAR Soldier, trapped with dying CO,
finds he has shot his own brother.

13270
CALL ME A CAB (91) (U) retitled:
CARRY ON CABBY
Adder (AA)
P: Peter Rogers
D: Gerald Thomas
S: Sidney Green, Richard Hills
SC: Talbot Rothwell
Sidney James . . . . Charlie Hawkins
Hattie Jacques . . . . Peggy Hawkins
Kenneth Connor . . . . Ted
Charles Hawtrey . . . . Pintpot
Esma Cannon . . . . Flo
Liz Fraser . . . . Sally
Bill Owen . . . . Smiley
Milo O'Shea . . . . Len
Judith Furse . . . . Battleaxe
Ambrosine Philpotts . . . . . . Lady
Renee Houston . . . . Molly
Jim Dale . . . . Man
Cyril Chamberlain . . . . Sarge
COMEDY Taxi owner's neglected wife
secretly runs taxi service driven by pretty
girls.

13271
THE CRACKSMAN (112) (U) *tech/scope*
ABPC (WPD)
P: W.A. Whittaker
D: Peter Graham Scott
S: Lew Schwarz
SC: Lew Schwarz, Charlie Drake, Mike Watts
Charlie Drake . . . . Ernest Wright
George Sanders . . . . The Guvnor
Dennis Price . .` . . . . Grantley
Nyree Dawn Porter . . . . . . Muriel
Finlay Currie . . . . Feathers
Eddie Byrne . . . . Domino
Percy Herbert . . . . Nosher
Geoffrey Keen . . . . Magistrate
George A. Cooper . . . . Fred
Norman Bird . . . . PC
COMEDY Rival gangs combine to force
jailbird locksmith to steal gems from
museum.

13272
WEST 11 (93) (X)
Dial Films (WPD)
P: Daniel M. Angel
D: Michael Winner
S: (NOVEL) Laura Del Rivo
(THE FURNISHED ROOM)
SC: Keith Waterhouse, Willis Hall
Alfred Lynch . . . . Joe Beckett
Kathleen Breck . . . . Ilsa Barnes
Eric Portman. . . . . Richard Dyce
Diana Dors . . . . Georgia
Kathleen Harrison . . . . Mrs Beckett
Finlay Currie . . . . Cash
Freda Jackson . . . . Mrs Hartley
Peter Reynolds . . . . Jacko
Harold Lang . . . . Silent
Marie Ney . . . . Mildred Dyce
Sean Kelly . . . . Larry
Patrick Wymark . . . . Father Hogan
Ken Collyer and his Band; Tony Kinsey and his
Band
CRIME Notting Hill. Ex-officer hires
shiftless drifter to kill his rich aunt.

13273
THE WORLD TEN TIMES OVER (93) (X)
Cyclops (WPD)
P: Michael Luke
D: Wolf Rilla
S: Wolf Rilla
Sylvia Syms . . . . Billa
Edward Judd . . . . Bob Shelbourne
June Ritchie . . . . Ginnie
William Hartnell . . . . Dad
Sarah Lawson . . . . Elizabeth Shelbourne
Francis de Wolff . . . . Shelbourne
Davy Kaye . . . . Compere
Linda Marlowe . . . . Penny
Jack Gwillim . . . . Bolton
DRAMA Club hostess loved by tycoon's
married son, finds happiness with her
pregnant room-mate.

13274
DOCTOR IN DISTRESS (112) (A) *eastman*
Rank (RFD)
P: Betty E. Box
D: Ralph Thomas
S: (CHARACTERS) Richard Gordon
SC: Nicholas Phipps, Ronald Scott Thorn
Dirk Bogarde . . . . Simon Sparrow
Samantha Eggar . . . . Delia
James Robertson Justice . .Sir Lancelot Spratt
Mylene Demongeot . . . . . . Sonja
Donald Houston . . . . Maj Ffrench
Barbara Murray . . . . Iris
Dennis Price . . . . Blacker
Leo McKern . . . . Heilbronn
Jessie Evans . . . . Mrs Parry
Ann Lynn . . . . Mrs Whittaker
Fenella Fielding . . . . Passenger
Jill Adams . . . . Genevieve
Michael Flanders . . . . Bradby
Frank Finlay . . . . Corsetiere
Reginald Beckwith . . . . Meyer
Bill Kerr . . . . Sailor
Ronnie Stevens . . . . Manager
Peter Butterworth . . . . Driver
COMEDY Hospital doctor helps surgeon woo
his physiotherapist.

13275
THE MARKED ONE (65) (A)
Planet
P: Tom Blakeley
D: Francis Searle
S: Paul Erickson
William Lucas . . . . Don Mason
Zena Walker . . . . Kay Mason
Patrick Jordan . . . . Insp Mayne
Laurie Leigh . . . . Maisie
David Gregory . . . . Ed Jones
Edward Ogden . . . . Nevil
Arthur Lovegrove . . . . Benson
Brian Nissen . . . . Charles Warren
CRIME Ex-convict truck driver traces
counterfeit plates to save kidnapped child.

13276
TOM JONES (128) (X) *eastman*
Woodfall (UA) *reissue:* 1966
P:D: Tony Richardson
S: (NOVEL) Henry Fielding
SC: John Osborne
N: Michael MacLiammoir
Albert Finney . . . . Tom Jones
Susannah York . . . . Sophie Western
Hugh Griffith . . . . Squire Western
Edith Evans . . . . Miss Western
Joan Greenwood . . . . Lady Bellaston
Diane Cilento . . . . Molly Seagrim
George Devine . . . . Squire Allworthy

David Tomlinson . . . . Lord Fellamar
Rosalind Atkinson . . . . Mrs Millar
George A. Cooper . . . . Fitzpatrick
Angela Baddeley . . . . Mrs Wilkins
Joyce Redman . . . . Mrs Waters
Rosalind Knight . . . . . . Mrs Fitzpatrick
David Warner . . . . Blifil
Freda Jackson . . . . Mrs Seagrim
Rachel Kempson . . . . . . Bridget Allworthy
Wilfrid Lawson . . . . Black George
Peter Bull . . . . Thwackum
Jack McGowran . . . . Partridge
Patsy Rowlands . . . . Honour
Avis Bunnage . . . . Landlady
COMEDY Somerset, 18th C. Amorous
escapades of a bastard who loves the
daughter of his adoptive father. (AA 1963:
Best Film; Best Director; Best Screenplay;
Best Score; BFA 1963: Best Film; Best
British Film; Best Screenplay).

13277
LADIES WHO DO (85) (U)
Fanfare (Bry)
P: George H. Brown
D: C.M.Pennington-Richards
S: John Bignell
SC: Michael Pertwee
Peggy Mount . . . . Mrs Cragg
Robert Morley . . . . Col Whitforth
Harry H. Corbett . . . . James Ryder
Miriam Karlin . . . . Mrs Higgins
Avril Edgar . . . . Emily Parrish
Dandy Nichols . . . . Mrs Merriweather
Jon Pertwee . . . . Mr Tait
Nigel Davenport . . . . Mr Strang
Graham Stark . . . . Foreman
Ron Moody . . . . Inspector
Cardew Robinson . . . . Chauffeur
John Laurie . . . . Dr MacGregor
Arthur Howard . . . . Chauffeur
Carol White . . . . Sandra
COMEDY Charladies form company with
ex-colonel to exploit tips found in property
dealer's waste-baskets.

13278
GIRL IN THE HEADLINES (93) (A)
Viewfinder (Bry)
P: John Davis
D: Michael Truman
S: (NOVEL) Laurence Payne
(THE NOSE ON MY FACE)
SC: Vivienne Knight, Patrick Campbell
Ian Hendry . . . . Insp Birkett
Ronald Fraser . . . . Sgt Saunders
Margaret Johnston . . . . . . Mrs Gray
Natasha Parry . . . . Perlita Barker
Jeremy Brett . . . . Jordon Barker
Kieron Moore . . . . Herter
Peter Arne . . . . Hammond Barker
Jane Asher . . . . Lindy Birkett
Rosalie Crutchley . . . . Maud Klein
Robert Harris . . . . William Lamotte
Duncan Macrae . . . . Barney
Zena Walker . . . . Mildred Birkett
Marie Burke . . . . Mme Lavalle
Patrick Holt . . . . Warbrook
CRIME Inspector investigates death of
model and uncovers drug ring.

13279
A PLACE TO GO (86) (A)
Excalibur (Bry)
P: Michael Relph
D: Basil Dearden
S: (NOVEL) Michael Fisher
(BETHNAL GREEN)
SC: Michael Relph, Clive Exton

Rita Tushingham . . . . Cat
Mike Sarne . . . . Ricky Flint
Bernard Lee . . . . Matt Flint
Doris Hare . . . . Lil Flint
John Slater . . . . Jack Ellerman
Barbara Ferris . . . . Betsy
David Andrews . . . . Jim
William Marlowe . . . . Charlie Batey
Roy Kinnear . . . . Bunting
Michael Wynne . . . . Pug
Jerry Verno . . . . Nobby Knowles
CRIME Bethnal Green. Unemployed docker's
son steals brother-in-law's lorry to help
rob factory.

13280
THE SIEGE OF THE SAXONS (85) (U) *tech*
Ameran (Col)
P: Jud Kinberg
D: Nathan Juran
S: Jud Kinberg, John Kohn
Janette Scott . . . . Katherine
Ronald Lewis . . . . Robert Marshall
Ronald Howard . . . . . . Edmund of Cornwall
John Laurie . . . . Merlin
Mark Dignam . . . . King Arthur
Jerome Willis . . . . Limping Man
Francis de Wolff . . . . Blacksmith
Charles Lloyd Pack . . . . . . Doctor
Richard Clarke . . . . Prince
ADVENTURE Period. Outlaw and princess
thwart knight who killed king.

JUL

13281
THE CARETAKER (105) (A)
Caretaker (BL)
P: Michael Birkett
D: Clive Donner
S: (PLAY) Harold Pinter
SC: Harold Pinter
Alan Bates . . . . Mick
Donald Pleasence . . . . Davis
Robert Shaw . . . . Aston
DRAMA Tramp torn between builder and
his brother who both wish him to take care
of their house.

13282
MODERN RHYTHM (11) (U)
Carisbrooke (GN)
P:D: Robert Henryson
Hermanos Deniz Cuban Rhythm Band
Tony Kinsey
Ted Heath and his Band
MUSICAL

13283
TAMAHINE (95) (A) *tech/scope*
ABPC (WPD)
P: John Bryan
D: Philip Leacock
S: (NOVEL) Thelma Nicklaus
SC: Dennis Cannan
Nancy Kwan . . . . Tamahine
John Fraser . . . . Richard Poole
Dennis Price . . . . Charles Poole
Coral Browne . . . . Mme Becque
Dick Bentley . . . . Storekeeper
Derek Nimmo . . . . Clove
Justine Lord . . . . Diana Poole
James Fox . . . . Oliver
Michael Gough . . . . Cartwright
Allan Cuthbertson . . . . . . Housemaster
Howard Marion Crawford . . Housemaster
COMEDY Polynesian halfcaste stays with
public school headmaster and eventually
marries his son.

13284
SHADOW OF FEAR (60) (U)
Butcher's Films
P: John I. Phillips
D: Ernest Morris
S: (NOVEL) T.F.Fotherby
(DECOY BE DAMNED)
SC: Ronald Liles, James O'Connolly
Paul Maxwell . . . . Bill Martin
Clare Owen . . . . Barbara
Anita West . . . . Ruth
Alan Tilvern . . . . Warner
John Arnatt . . . . Sharp
Eric Pohlman . . . . Spiroulos
Reginald Marsh . . . . Oliver
John Sutton . . . . Halliday
Colin Tapley . . . . John Bowen
CRIME Couple let themselves be kidnapped
to help M15 capture gang of espionage
agents.

13285
WHAT A CRAZY WORLD (88) (A) *scope*
Capricorn (WPD)
P:D: Michael Carreras
S: (PLAY) Alan Klein
SC: Alan Klein, Michael Carreras
Joe Brown . . . . Alf Hitchens
Susan Maugham . . . . Marilyn
Marty Wilde . . . . Herbie Shadbolt
Harry H. Corbett . . . . Sam Hitchens
Avis Bunnage . . . . Mary Hitchens
Michael Ripper . . . . . . Salesman/clerk/
attendant/cafe man/passenger/
doorman/cleaner/park keeper/
client.
Grazina Frame . . . . Doris Hitchens
Monty Landis . . . . Solly Gold
Michael Goodman . . . . . . Joey Hitchens
Fanny Carby . . . . Dolly
Bill Fraser . . . . Milligan
Alan Klein . . . . Jervis
The Bruvvers; Freddie and the Dreamers;
The Happy Wanderers; Tricky Dicky
MUSICAL East End layabout writes popular
song. (Includes extract from THE CURSE
OF FRANKENSTEIN).

13286
THE YELLOW TEDDYBEARS (85) (X)
Tekli (Compton)
P: Robert Hartford-Davis, Nat Miller
D: Robert Hartford-Davis
S: Donald Ford, Derek Ford
Jacqueline Ellis . . . . Anne Mason
Annette Whiteley . . . . Linda Donoghue
Iain Gregory . . . . Kinky Karson
Douglas Sheldon . . . . Mike Griffin
Georgina Patterson . . . . . . Pat Long
Raymond Huntley . . . . Halburton
Jill Adams . . . . June Wilson
Victor Brooks . . . . Mr Donoghue
John Bonney . . . . Paul
John Glyn Jones . . . . Benny Wintle
Harriette Johns . . . . Lady Gregg
The Embers
DRAMA Schoolgirl joins non-virgins' club,
becomes pregnant, and tries to have abortion.

13287
A MATTER OF CHOICE (79) (A)
Holmwood (Bry)
P: George Maynard
D: Vernon Sewell
S: Vernon Sewell, Derren Nesbitt
SC: Paul Ryder
Anthony Steel . . . . John Crighton
Jeanne Moody . . . . Lisa Grant
Ballard Berkeley . . . . Charles Grant

Malcolm Gerard . . . . Mike
Michael Davis . . . . Tony
Penny Morell . . . . Jackie
Lisa Peake . . . . Jane
James Bree . . . . Alfred
George Moon . . . . Spiek
CRIME Youths accidentally kill married
woman's diabetic lover.

13288
THE GIRL HUNTERS (103) (A) *colorama/
scope*
Present Day-Fellane (20)
P: Robert Fellows, Charles Reynolds
D: Roy Rowland
S: (NOVEL) Mickey Spillane
SC: Mickey Spillane, Roy Rowland, Robert
Fellows
Mickey Spillane . . . . Mike Hammer
Shirley Eaton . . . . Laura Knapp
Lloyd Nolan . . . . Art Rickaby
Scott Peters . . . . Capt Pat Chambers
Hy Gardner . . . . Himself
Guy Kingsley Poynter . . . . Dr Larry Snyder
James Dyrenforth . . . . . . Bayliss Henry
Charles Farrell . . . . Joe Grissi
Kim Tracy . . . . Nurse
Benny Lee . . . . Nat Drutman
Murray Kash . . . . Richie Cole
Bill Nagy . . . . Georgie
Larry Cross . . . . Red Markham
CRIME New York. Private tec seeking 'dead'
secretary unmasks Communists behind
senator's death.

13289
THE EYES OF ANNIE JONES (71) (A)
Parroch-McCallum-API (RFD)
P: Jack Parsons, Neil McCallum
D: Reginald le Borg
S: Henry Slesar
SC: Louis Vittes
Richard Conte . . . . David Wheeler
Francesca Annis . . . . Annie Jones
Joyce Carey . . . . Aunt Helen
Myrtle Reed . . . . Caroline Wheeler
Shay Gorman . . . . Lucas
Jean Lodge . . . . Geraldine Wheeler
Victor Brooks . . . . Sgt Henry
Mark Dignam . . . . Frobisher
Max Bacon . . . . Hoskins
CRIME Orphan's extra-sensory perception
reveals mill-owner's murderer as her
brother's hireling.

13290
TO HAVE AND TO HOLD (71) (A)
Merton Park (AA)
P: Jack Greenwood
D: Herbert Wise
S: (STORY) Edgar Wallace
(THE BREAKING POINT)
SC: John Sansom
Ray Barrett . . . . Henry Fraser
Katharine Blake . . . . Claudia Lyon
Nigel Stock . . . . George Lyon
William Hartnell . . . . Insp Roberts
Patricia Bredin . . . . Lucy
Noel Trevarthen . . . . Blake
Richard Clarke . . . . Charles Wagner
CRIME Police sgt loves woman who
involves him in plan to kill her husband
for insurance.

13291
LIVE IT UP (74) (U) USA: SING AND SWING
Three Kings (RFD)
P:D: Lance Comfort
S: Harold Shampan
SC: Lyn Fairhurst

David Hemmings . . . . Dave Martin
Heinz Burt . . . . Ron
Joan Newell . . . . Margaret Martin
Veronica Hurst . . . . Kay
Ed Devereaux . . . . Herbert Martin
Jennifer Moss . . . . Jill
John Pike . . . . Phil
Steven Marriott . . . . Ricky
Penny Lambirth . . . . Barbara
Kenny Ball and his Jazzmen; Gene Vincent;
Patsy Ann Noble; Kim Roberts;
The Outlaws; Sounds Incorporated; Andy Cavell
and the Saints; Nancy Spain; Peter Haigh;
Peter Noble
MUSICAL Post Office messenger forms
beat group and stars in musical film.

13292
TREASURE IN MALTA (U) eastman
Anvil (CFF)
P: Ralph N. May
D: Derek Williams
S: (NOVEL) David Scott Daniell (BY JIMINY)
SC: Anne Barrett, Mary Cathcart Borer

Mario Debono . . . . Jiminy
Aidan Mompalao de Piro . . . . Tom
Charles Thake . . . . Dr Trevor
Mary Lu Ripard . . . . Suki
Guido Saliba . . . . Maxim
Vanni Riolo . . . . Scabio

13293
1: KIDNAPPED (16)

13294
2: BY JIMINY ! (15)

13295
3: CARNIVAL (15)

13296
4: ESCAPE TO GOZO (15)

13297
5: AT THE VILLA ROSA (16)

13298
6: THE TOMB OF CALYPSO (15)

CHILDREN Malta. Peanut vendor helps
archaeologist's children save golden
statue from crooks.

13299
TOWERS OPEN FIRE (11) (A)
Antony Balch (Connoisseur)
P:D: Antony Balch
S: William Burroughs
William Burroughs
Alexander Trocchi
David Jacobs
Brion Gysin
Ian Sommerville
Bachoo Sen
Liam O'Leary
John Gillett
FANTASY Shuffled images and sound
concerning drugs, masturbation, homosexuality
and violence.

AUG
13300
UNEARTHLY STRANGER (75) (A)
Independent Artists (AA)
P: Albert Fennell
D: John Krish
S: Rex Carlton
John Neville . . . . Dr Mark Davidson
Gabriella Licudi . . . . Julie Davidson

Philip Stone . . . . . Prof John Lancaster
Patrick Newell . . . . Maj Clarke
Jean Marsh . . . . Miss Ballard
Warren Mitchell . . . . Dr Munro
FANTASY Scientist working on time/space
formula finds his wife is from another
planet.

13301
FAREWELL PERFORMANCE (73) (A)
Sevenay (RFD)
P: J.P. O'Connolly
D: Robert Tronson
S: Aileen Burke, Leone Stuart, James
O'Connolly
David Kernan . . . . Ray Baron
Delphi Lawrence . . . . Janice Marlon
Frederick Jaeger . . . . Paul Warner
Derek Francis . . . . Supt Raven
Alfred Burke . . . . Marlon
John Kelland . . . . Mitch
Toni Gilpin . . . . Carol
James Copeland . . . . Andrews
Ron Parry . . . . Dennis
The Tornadoes; Heinz; Tommy Devel &
Partner; Chad Carson
MUSICAL Animal trainer's wife unmasks
poisoner of her lover, a pop singer.

13302
THE CHALK GARDEN (106) (U) *tech*
Quota Rentals (UI)
P: Ross Hunter
D: Ronald Neame
S: (PLAY) Enid Bagnold
SC: John Michael Hayes
Deborah Kerr . . . . Miss Madrigal
Hayley Mills . . . . Laurel
John Mills . . . . Maitland
Edith Evans . . . . Mrs StMaugham
Felix Aylmer . . . . Judge McWhirrey
Elizabeth Sellars . . . . Olivia
Lally Bowers . . . . Anna
Toke Townley . . . . Shopkeeper
Tonie MacMillan . . . . Mrs Williams
DRAMA Sussex. Governess realises her
employer is trying to keep her wild
granddaughter from her widowed mother.

SEP
13303
THE CHIMNEY SWEEPS (45) (U)
Compass-Pyewacket (Compton)
P: Harrison Marks, Derek Horne
D: Dudley Birch
S: Jim McDonald, Harrison Marks
Harrison Marks . . . . Sweep
Stuart Samuels . . . . Sweep
Pamela Green . . . . Maid
Joan Hurley . . . . Lady
Billy Maxam . . . . Gangster
Johnny Franks . . . . Gangster
Jerry Lorden . . . . Caretaker
Del Watson . . . . Postman
Diz Disley . . . . Conductor
COMEDY Sweeps wreck old lady's flat and
capture jewel thieves.

13304
THE INFORMERS (105) (X)
Rank (RFD)
P: William MacQuitty
D: Ken Annakin
S: (NOVEL) Douglas Warner
(DEATH OF A SNOUT)
SC: Alun Falconer, Paul Durst
Nigel Patrick . . . . Insp Johnnoe
Margaret Whiting . . . . Maisie

Harry Andrews . . . . Supt Bestwick
Colin Blakeley . . . . Charlie Ruskin
Catherine Woodville . . . . . . Mary Johnnoe
Derren Nesbitt . . . . Bertie Hoyle
Frank Finlay . . . . Leon Sale
Roy Kinnear . . . . Shorty
Allan Cuthbertson . . . . Smythe
Michael Coles . . . . Ben
John Cowley . . . . Jim Ruskin
Kenneth J. Warren . . . . . . Lou Walters
CRIME Inspector traces bank robber who
framed him for taking bribe after killing
informer.

13305
THE PARTNER (58) (U)
Merton Park (AA)
P: Jack Greenwood
D: Gerard Glaister
S: (STORY) Edgar Wallace
(A MILLION DOLLAR STORY)
SC: John Roddick
Yoko Tani . . . . Lin Siyan
Guy Doleman . . . . Wayne Douglas
Ewan Roberts . . . . Insp Simons
Mark Eden . . . . Richard Webb
Anthony Booth . . . . Buddy Forrester
Helen Lindsay . . . . Helen Douglas
Noel Johnson . . . . Charles Briers
Denis Holmes . . . . Sgt Rigby
CRIME Inspector solves murder of film
director's accountant.

13306
POSITION OF TRUST (32) (A)
Merton Park (AA)
P: Jack Greenwood
D: Lionel Harris
S: James Eastwood
Derrick Sherwin . . . . . . Simon Dennington
Imogen Hassall . . . . Yvonne Purvis
Edward Atienza . . . . William Purvis
Peter Barkworth . . . . Robbins
Cyril Luckham . . . . Lawson
Geoffrey Chater . . . . Soames
Kenneth Mackintosh . . . . . . Bank Manager
CRIME Detective blackmails industrialist's
son who has affair with his butler's French wife.

13307
THE DEVIL DOLL (80) (X)
Galaworldfilm-Gordon (Gala)
P: Kenneth Rive, Richard Gordon, Lindsay
Shonteff
D: Lindsay Shonteff
S: Frederick E. Smith
SC: George Barclay, Lance Z.Hargreaves
William Sylvester . . . . Mark English
Bryant Halliday . . . . The Great Vorelli
Yvonne Romain . . . . Marian
Sandra Dorne . . . .
Nora Nicholson . . . . Aunt Eva
Karel Stepanek . . . . Dr Heller
Francis de Wolff . . . . Kr Keisling
Philip Ray . . . . Uncle Walter
Alan Gifford . . . . Bob Garrett
Heidi Erich . . . . Grace
HORROR Hypnotist transfers soul of
American reporter's fiancee to his ventriloquial
dummy.

13308
LORD OF THE FLIES (91) (X)
Allen-Hodgdon-Two Arts (BL)
P: Al Hine, Lewis Allen
D: SC: Peter Brook
S: (NOVEL) William Golding
James Aubrey . . . . Ralph
Tom Chapin . . . . Jack

Hugh Edwards . . . . Piggy
Roger Elwin . . . . Roger
Tom Gaman . . . . Simon
Surtees Twins . . . . Sam & Eric
DRAMA 40 schoolboys, stranded on
uninhabited tropical island, revert to
primitive savagery.

13309
AN EVENING WITH THE ROYAL BALLET
(85) (U) tech
BHE
P: Anthony Havelock-Allan
D: Anthony Asquith, Anthony Havelock-Allan
S: (BALLETS) Maurice Ravel (LA VALSE)
R. Drigo, L. Minkus (LE CORSAIRE)
Frederick Chopin (LES SYPHIDES)
Piotr Techaikovsky (AURORA'S WEDDING)
Margot Fonteyn   Rudolph Nureyev
David Blair   Antoinette Sibley
Graham Usher   Merle Park
MUSICAL Ballets filmed at Royal Opera
House, Covent Garden.

13310
PANIC (69) (A)
Ingram (Bry)
P: Guido Coen
D: SC: John Gilling
S: Guido Coen, John Gilling
Janine Gray . . . . Janine Heining
Glyn Houston . . . . Mike
Dyson Lovell . . . . Johnnie Cobb
Duncan Lamont . . . . Insp Saunders
Stanley Meadows . . . . Tom
Brian Weske . . . . Ben
Charles Houston . . . . Louis Cobb
Philip Ray . . . . Jessop
Marne Maitland . . . . Lantern
John Horsley . . . . Insp Malcolm
Dermot Kelly . . . . Murphy
Paul Carpenter . . . . Commentator
CRIME Ex-boxer saves Swiss girl with
amnesia from trumpeter who used her in
diamond robbery.

13311
THE PARTY'S OVER (94) (X)
Tricastle (Monarch)
P: Anthony Perry, Jules Buck, Jack
Hawkins
D: Guy Hamilton
S: Marc Behm
Oliver Reed . . . . Moise
Ann Lynn . . . . Libby
Clifford David . . . . Carson
Louise Sorel . . . . Melina
Eddie Albert . . . . Ben
Catherine Woodville . . . . . Nina
Maurice Browning . . . . Tutzi
Jonathan Burn . . . . Phil
Roddy Maude-Roxby . . . . . Hector
Mildred Mayne . . . . Countess
Mike Pratt . . . . Geronimo
DRAMA Fiance of American industrialist's
daughter learns she died during drunken
party and was then violated.

13312
THE UNDESIRABLE NEIGHBOUR (29) (A)
Merton Park (AA)
P: Jack Greenwood
D: Gordon Hales
S: James Eastwood
N: Edgar Lustgarten
Vanda Godsell . . . . Agnes Chester
Bridget Armstrong . . . . . . Anna Bosworth
Anthony Newlands . . . . Strang
Ronald Hatton . . . . Peter Bosworth

Dorinda Stevens . . . . Mary Bennett
Howard Pays . . . . Harry Finch
CRIME Newlyweds bring slander action
against gossiping neighbour.

13313
WALK A TIGHTROPE (78) (A)
Parroch-McCallum (BL)
P: Jack Parsons
D: Frank Nesbitt
S: Manny Rubin
SC: Neil McCallum
Dan Duryea . . . . Lutcher
Patricia Owens . . . . Ellen
Terence Cooper . . . . Jason
Richard Leech . . . . Doug
Neil McCallum . . . . Counsel
Trevor Reid . . . . Insp McMitchell
A.J.Brown . . . . Magistrate
CRIME Mad killer claims woman hired him
to shoot her husband.

13314
HEADS I WIN (23) (U)
Rora Films (NR)
P: Georges Robin, Ousama Rawi
D:S: Georges Robin
N: Brendan Collins
Brendan Collins . . . . The Boy
Daniele Noel . . . . The Girl
ROMANCE Lonely teenager shows French
girl around London.

OCT

13315
FROM RUSSIA WITH LOVE (116) (A) tech
Eon Productions (UA) reissue: 1965
P: Harry Saltzman, Albert R.Broccoli
D: Terence Young
S: (NOVEL) Ian Fleming
SC: Richard Maibaum, Joanna Harwood
Sean Connery . . . . James Bond
Daniela Bianchi . . . . Tatiana Romanova
Pedro Armendariz . . . . Kerim Bey
Lotte Lenya . . . . Rosa Klebb
Robert Shaw . . . . Red Grant
Bernard Lee . . . . M
Eunice Gayson . . . . Sylvia
Walter Gotell . . . . Morzeny
Francis de Wolff . . . . Vavra
George Pastell . . . . Conductor
Nadja Regin . . . . Girl
Lois Maxwell . . . . Miss Moneypenny
CRIME Istanbul. British agent saves a
Russian girl from international crooks. (Top Moneymaker: 1963;
BFA 1963: Best colour ph.)

13316
THE SERVANT (115) (X)
Springbok (Elstree)
P: Joseph Losey, Norman Priggen
D: Joseph Losey
S: (NOVEL) Robin Maugham
SC: Harold Pinter
Dirk Bogarde . . . . Barrett
Sarah Miles . . . . Vera
Wendy Craig . . . . Susan
James Fox . . . . Tony
Catherine Lacey . . . . Lady Mounset
Richard Vernon . . . . Lord Mounset
Brian Phelan . . . . Irishman
Dorothy Bromiley . . . . Girl
Hazel Terry . . . . Woman in Hat
Alison Seebohm . . . . Girl in Pub
Philippa Hare . . . . Girl in Bedroom
Patrick Magee . . . . Bishop
Alun Owen . . . . Curate
Harold Pinter . . . . Society Man

DRAMA Manservant gains control of his young employer by having his mistress seduce him. (BFA 1963: Best Actor; Best B/W Pho.)

13317
THE INVISIBLE ASSET (31) (U)
Merton Park (AA)
P: Jack Greenwood
D: Norman Harrison
S: James Eastwood

Kenneth J. Warren	Sam Warren
Ronald Leigh-Hunt	Jimmy Donovan
Annette Carrell	Joyce Warren
Philip Latham	Official Receiver
Gabriella Licudi	Beryl
John Wentworth	Registrar

CRIME Bankrupt restaurateur's embezzlement scheme foiled by unloved wife.

13318
CHILDREN OF THE DAMNED (88) (X)
MGM British
P: Lawrence P. Bachmann, Ben Arbeid
D: Anton M. Leader
S: (NOVEL) John Wyndham
(THE MIDWICH CUCKOOS)
SC: John Briley

Ian Hendry	Dr Tom Lewellin
Alan Badel	Dr David Neville
Barbara Ferris	Susan Elliott
Alfred Burke	Colin Webster
Sheila Allen	Diana Looran
Ralph Michael	Defence Minister
Martin Miller	Prof Gruber
Harold Goldblatt	Harib
Clive Powell	Paul
Lee Yoke-Moon	Mi Ling

FANTASY Six children with supernatural powers killed to save humanity.

13319
NOTHING BUT THE BEST (99) (A) *eastman*
Domino (AA)
P: David Deutsch
D: Clive Donner
S: (STORY) Stanley Ellin
(THE BEST OF EVERYTHING)
SC: Frederick Raphael

Alan Bates	Jimmy Brewster
Denholm Elliott	Charlie Prince
Harry Andrews	Horton
Millicent Martin	Ann Horton
Pauline Delany	Mrs March
Godfrey Quigley	Coates
Alison Leggatt	Mrs Brewster
Lucinda Curtis	Nadine
Nigel Stock	Ferris
James Villiers	Hugh
Avice Landon	Mrs Horton
William Rushton	Gerry
Bernard Levin	Himself

COMEDY Estate agent adopts upper class scapegrace to help him marry his boss's daughter, then kills him.

13320
NIGHTMARE (82) (X) *scope*
Hammer-Universal (UI)
P:S: Jimmy Sangster
D: Freddie Francis

David Knight	Henry Baxter
Moira Redmond	Grace Maddox
Jennie Linden	Janet
Brenda Bruce	Mary Lewis
George A. Cooper	John
Irene Richmond	Mrs Gibbs
John Welsh	Doctor
Timothy Bateson	Barman

Clytie Jessop	Woman in White
Isla Cameron	Mother

CRIME Guardian conspires with nurse to drive his ward insane enough to kill his wife.

13321
A STITCH IN TIME (94) (U)
Rank (RFD)
P: Hugh Stewart
D: Robert Asher
S: Jack Davies, Norman Wisdom, Henry Blyth, Eddie Leslie

Norman Wisdom	Norman Pitkin
Edward Chapman	Grimsdale
Jeannette Sterke	Janet Haskell
Jerry Desmonde	Sir Hector
Jill Melford	Lady Brinkley
Glyn Houston	Welsh
Hazel Hughes	Matron
Patsy Rowlands	Amy
Peter Jones	Russell
Ernest Clark	Prof Crankshaw
Vera Day	Betty
Francis Matthews	Benson
John Blythe	Dale

COMEDY Butcher's assistant poses as ambulance man to visit sick orphan.

13322
THE VICTORS (175) (X) *scope*
Open Road-Highroad (Col)
P:D:SC: Carl Foreman
S: (NOVEL) Alexander Baron
(THE HUMAN KIND)

Vincent Edwards	Baker
Albert Finney	Russian Soldier
George Hamilton	Trower
Melina Mercouri	Magda
Jeanne Moreau	French Woman
George Peppard	Chase
Maurice Ronet	French Lieutenant
Rosanna Schiaffino	Maria
Romy Schneider	Regine
Elke Sommer	Helga
Eli Wallach	Craig
Michael Callan	Eldridge
Peter Fonda	Weaver
James Mitchum	Grogan
Senta Berger	Trudi
Joel Flateau	Jean-Pierre
Albert Lieven	Metzger
Mervyn Johns	Dennis

WAR American infantry squad fights its way from Italy to Berlin.

13323
MAN IN THE MIDDLE (94) (A) *scope*
Pennebaker-Belmont (20)
P: Walter Seltzer
D: Guy Hamilton
S: (NOVEL) Howard Fast
(THE WINSTON AFFAIR)
SC: Keith Waterhouse, Willis Hall

Robert Mitchum	Lt/Col Barney Adams
France Nuyen	Kate Davray
Barry Sullivan	Gen Kempton
Trevor Howard	Maj Kensington
Keenan Wynn	Lt Kingston
Sam Wanamaker	Maj Kaufmann
Alexander Knox	Col Burton
Gary Cockrell	Lt Morse
Robert Nicholls	Lt Bender
Michael Goodliffe	Col Shaw
Errol John	Sgt Jackson
Paul Maxwell	Maj Smith
Lionel Murton	Capt Gunther
Russell Napier	Col Thompson
Edward Underdown	Maj Wycliff

Howard Marion Crawford	Maj Poole

CRIME India, 1943. Defending officer proves American lieut who murdered British sgt is a psychopath.

NOV

13324
THE COMEDY MAN (92) (X)
Grayfilms-Consantfilms (BL)
P: Jon Penington
D: Alvin Rakoff
S: (NOVEL) Douglas Hayes
SC: Peter Yeldham

Kenneth More	Chick Byrd
Cecil Parker	Rutherford
Dennis Price	Tommy Morris
Edmund Purdom	Julian
Billie Whitelaw	Judy
Angela Douglas	Fay
Norman Rossington	Theodore
Frank Finlay	Prout
Alan Dobie	Jack Lavery
J.G.Devlin	Sloppitt
Valerie & Leila Croft	Yvonne & Pauline
Gerald Campion	Gerry
Freddie Mills	Indian Chief
Jill Adams	Jan Kennedy

DRAMA Middle-aged provincial repertory actor finds TV fame advertising deodorant.

13325
BLIND CORNER (80) (A)
Blakeley's Films (Mancunian)
P: Tom Blakeley
D: Lance Comfort
S: Vivian Kemble
SC: James Kelly, Peter Miller

William Sylvester	Paul Gregory
Barbara Shelley	Anne Gregory
Elizabeth Shepherd	Joan Marshall
Alexander Davion	Rickie Seldon
Mark Eden	Mike Williams
Ronnie Carroll	Ronnie
Barry Aldis	Compere
Edward Evans	Chauffeur
Frank Forsyth	Policeman

CRIME Woman persuades artist lover to kill her husband, a blind composer of pop music.

13326
THE SIX-SIDED TRIANGLE (30) (U)
Milesian (BL)
P:D:S: Christopher Miles

Sarah Miles	Wife
Nicol Williamson	Lover
Bill Meilen	Husband

COMEDY The eternal triangle as filmed in America, England, Japan, Italy, Sweden and France.

13327
ACCIDENTAL DEATH (57) (U)
Merton Park (AA)
P: Jack Greenwood
D: Geoffrey Nethercott
S: (STORY) Edgar Wallace
(JACK O' JUDGEMENT)
SC: Arthur La Bern

John Carson	Paul Lanson
Jacqueline Ellis	Henriette
Derrick Sherwin	Alan
Richard Vernon	Johnnie Paxton
Jean Lodge	Brenda
Gerald Case	Inspector
Jacqueline Lacey	Milly

CRIME Man plots to kill French girl's benefactor for wartime treachery.

13328
THIS IS MY STREET (94) (A)
Adder (AA)
P: Peter Rogers, Jack Hanbury
D: Sidney Hayers
S: (NOVEL) Nan Maynard
SC: Bill MacIlwraith
Ian Hendry . . . . Harry King
June Ritchie . . . . Margery Graham
Avice Landone . . . . Lily
Meredith Edwards . . . . Steve
Madge Ryan . . . . Kitty
John Hurt . . . . Charlie
Annette Andre . . . . Jinny
Philippa Gail . . . . Maureen
Mike Pratt . . . . Sid Graham
Tom Adams . . . . Paul
Hilda Fenemore . . . . Doris
John Bluthal . . . . Joe
DRAMA Battersea. Married woman has
affair with mother's shiftless lodger, who
prefers her affianced sister.

13329
STRICTLY FOR THE BIRDS (63) (A)
Independent Artists (RFD)
P: E. Smedley Aston
D: Vernon Sewell
S: Tony Hawes
Tony Tanner . . . . Terry Blessing
Joan Sims . . . . Peggy Blessing
Graham Stark . . . . Hartley
Jeanne Moody . . . . Claire
Alan Baulch . . . . Alfie
Toni Palmer . . . . Bridget
Valerie Walsh . . . . Maxine
Carol Cleveland . . . . Sandra
Bernard Goldman . . . . Mendoza
Murray Kash . . . . Mario
Tony Hawes . . . . Joe
COMEDY Soho. Gambling layabout has
lucky day but loses winnings to crooked blonde.

13330
A JOLLY BAD FELLOW (96) (A)
Tower (Pax)
P: Steven Pallos, Donald Taylor, Michael
Balcon
D: Don Chaffey
S: (NOVEL) C.E.Vulliamy
(DON AMONG THE DEAD MEN)
SC: Robert Hamer, Donald Taylor
Leo McKern . . . . . Prof Bowles-Ottery
Janet Munro . . . . Delia
Maxine Audley . . . Clarinda Bowles-Ottery
Dennis Price . . . . Jack Hughes
Miles Malleson . . . . Dr Woolley
Duncan MacRae . . . . Dr Brass
Mervyn Johns . . . . Willie Pugh-Smith
George Benson . . . . Insp Butts
Ralph Michael . . . . Supt Rastleigh
Patricia Jessel . . . . Mrs Pugh-Smith
Alan Wheatley . . . . Epicene
Wally Patch . . . . Landlord
Mark Dignam . . . . Master
Dinsdale Landen . . . . Fred
Cliff Michelmore . . . . Himself
COMEDY Philandering university chemist
uses his non-detectable poison to murder
his way to professorship.

13331
TAKE SIX (16) (U) *eastman*
Parkside (BL)
P: Jacques De Lane Lea
D: Douglas Hickox
N: Kent Walton
Eden Kane   Steve Perry

Alan Klein   Vince Hill
Julie Samuel   Boscoe Holder
Shane Fenton   The Viscounts
MUSICAL Disc jockey introduces six top
tunes from 1962 'Cinebox' films.

13332
NEVER PUT IT IN WRITING (90) (U)
Seven Arts-Andrew & Virginia Stone (MGM)
P: Andrew Stone, Virginia Stone
D: S: Andrew Stone
Pat Boone . . . . Stephen Cole
Milo O'Shea . . . . Danny O'Toole
Fidelma Murphy . . . . . . Katie O'Connell
Reginald Beckwith . . . . . . Lombardi
John le Mesurier . . . . Adams
Sarah Ballantine . . . . Secretary
Colin Blakeley . . . . Oscar
Ed Devereaux . . . . Pringle
Harry Brogan . . . . Breeden
COMEDY Ireland. Promoted insurance
executive tries to get his abusive letter to
employer back from the postal authorities.

13333
FATHER CAME TOO (93) (A) *eastman*
Independent Artists (RFD)
P: Julian Wintle, Leslie Parkyn
D: Peter Graham Scott
S: (NOVEL) Hazel Adair, Henry Blyth
James Robertson Justice . Sir Beverley Grant
Leslie Phillips . . . . Roddy Chipfield
Stanley Baxter . . . . Dexter Munro
Sally Smith . . . . Juliet Munro
Eric Barker . . . . Gallagher
Terry Scott . . . . Executioner
Hugh Lloyd . . . . . . Mary Queen of Scots
Fred Emney . . . . . . Sir Francis Drake
Kenneth Cope . . . . Ron
Peter Jones . . . . Charles II
Ronnie Barker . . . . Josh
Timothy Bateson . . . . Wally
James Villiers . . . . Benzil Bulstrode
Raymond Huntley . . . . . . Mr Wedgewood
COMEDY Actor-manager's daughter and
newlywed husband try to set up home in
old cottage.

13334
CROOKS IN CLOISTERS (97) (U) *tech/scope*
ABPC (WPD)
P: Gordon L.T.Scott
D: Jeremy Summers
S: Mike Watts
SC: Mike Watts, T.J.Morrison
Ronald Fraser . . . . Walt
Barbara Windsor . . . . Bikini
Gregoire Aslan . . . . Lorenzo
Bernard Cribbins . . . . Squirts
Davy Kaye . . . . Specs
Wilfrid Brambell . . . . Phineas
Mervyn Hayes . . . . Willy
Joseph O'Connor . . . . . Father Septimus
Corin Redgrave . . . . Brother Lucius
Francesca Annis . . . . June
Patricia Laffan . . . . Lady Florence
Arnold Ridley . . . . Newsagent
Max Bacon . . . . Bookmaker
Karen Kaufman . . . . Strip Girl
COMEDY Cornwall. Forgers and receivers
posing as monks are reformed by country
life.

DEC

13335
DR SYN - ALIAS THE SCARECROW (98) (U)
tech
Walt Disney
P: William Anderson

D: James Neilson
S: (NOVEL) Russell Thorndike, William
Buchanan (CHRISTOPHER SYN)
SC: Robert Westerby
Patrick McGoohan . . . . Dr Syn
George Cole . . . . Sexton Mipps
Tony Britton . . . . Simon Bates
Michael Hordern . . . . . . Sir Thomas Banks
Geoffrey Keen . . . . Gen Pugh
Kay Walsh . . . . Mrs Waggett
Eric Pohlmann . . . . George III
Patrick Wymark . . . . Joe Ransley
Alan Dobie . . . . Fragg
Sean Scully . . . . John Banks
Eric Flynn . . . . Phillip Brackenbury
David Buck . . . . Harry Banks
Richard O'Sullivan . . . . George Ransley
ADVENTURE Dymchurch, 1775. Village
vicar secretly leads smugglers, foils traitor,
and rescues fugitives.

13336
DR STRANGELOVE; OR, HOW I LEARNED
TO STOP WORRYING AND LOVE THE
BOMB (94) (A)
Hawk (Col)
P:D: Stanley Kubrick
S: (NOVEL) Peter George (RED ALERT)
SC: Stanley Kubrick, Peter George, Terry
Southern
Peter Sellers . . . . . Dr Strangelove/GC Lionel
                            Mandrake/President Muffley
George C. Scott . . . Gen 'Buck' Turgidson
Sterling Hayden . . . . Gen Jack D. Ripper
Keenan Wynn . . . . Col 'Bat' Guano
Slim Pickens . . . . Maj T.J. 'King' Kong
Tracy Reed . . . . Miss Scott
Peter Bull . . . . .Ambassador de Sadesky
James Earl Jones . . . . Lt Lothar Zogg
Jack Creley . . . . Mr Staines
Frank Berry . . . . Lt H.R.Dietrich
Glenn Beck . . . . Lt W.D.Kivel
Shane Rimmer . . . . . . Capt G.A.'Ace' Owens
Paul Tamarin . . . . Lt B.Goldberg
Gordon Tanner . . . . Gen Faceman
FANTASY USAAF commander suspects
Russia of poisoning water and launches an
H-Bomb attack. (BFA 1964: Best Film;
Best British Film; UN Award; Best Art Dir.)

13337
IT'S ALL OVER TOWN (55) (A) *eastman*
Delmore (BL)
P: Ben Nisbet, Jacques De Lane Lea
D: Douglas Hickox
S: Stewart Farrar
SC: Stewart Farrar, Lance Percival,
William Rushton
Lance Percival . . . . Richard Abel
William Rushton . . . . Fat Friend
Frankie Vaughan; Mr Acker Bilk and the
Paramount Jazz Band; The Springfields;
The Bachelors; The Hollies; April Olrich;
Jan & Kelly; Caroline Maudling; Cloda Rogers;
Ingrid Anthofer; Ivor Cutler; Paul Raymond
Bunnies; Wayne Gibson
MUSICAL Theatre electrician and friend
dream of visiting London shows.

13338
ZULU (135) *tech/scope* (U)
Diamond (Par)
P: Stanley Baker, Cy Endfield
D: Cy Endfield
S: (ARTICLE) John Prebble
SC: John Prebble, Cy Endfield
N: Richard Burton
Stanley Baker . . . . Lt John Chard
Jack Hawkins . . . . Rev Otto Witt

Ulla Jacobsson . . . . Margaretta Witt
James Booth . . . . Pte Henry Hook
Michael Caine . . . . Lt Gonville Bromhead
Nigel Green. . . . . Col-Sgt Bourne
Ivor Emmanuel . . . . Pte Owen
Paul Daneman . . . . Sgt Maxfield
Glynn Edwards . . . . Cpl Allen
Neil McCarthy . . . . Pte Thomas
David Kernan . . . . Pte Hitch
Gary Bond . . . . Pte Cole
Patrick Magee . . . . Surgeon Reynolds
Chief Buthelezi . . . . Cetewayo
WAR Natal, 1879. 105 British soldiers
defend Rorke's Drift against 4,000 Zulus.

13339
CARRY ON JACK (91) (A) *tech*
Anglo-Amalgamated (AA)
P: Peter Rogers
D: Gerald Thomas
S: Talbot Rothwell
Kenneth Williams . . . . Capt Fearless
Bernard Cribbins . . . . . . Albert Poop-Decker
Juliet Mills . . . . Sally
Charles Hawtrey . . . . Walter Sweetley
Donald Houston . . . . . . Lt Jonathan Howett
Cecil Parker . . . . First Sea Lord
Percy Herbert . . . . Bosun Angel
Jim Dale . . . . Carrier
Patrick Cargill . . . . Don Luis
Ed Devereaux . . . . Hook
Peter Gilmore . . . . Roger Patch
George Woodbridge . . . . . . Ned
Jimmy Thompson . . . . Lord Nelson
Anton Rodgers . . . . Hardy
COMEDY 1805. New midshipman press-
ganged aboard his own frigate, and girl
posing as him, foil mutineers, and pirates.

13340
FIVE TO ONE (56) (A)
Merton Park (AA)
P: Jack Greenwood
D: Gordon Flemyng
S: (STORY) Edgar Wallace
(THIEF IN THE NIGHT)
SC: Roger Marshall
Lee Montague . . . . Larry Hart
Ingrid Hafner . . . . Pat Dunn
John Thaw . . . . Alan Roper
Brian McDermott . . . . John Lea
Ewan Roberts . . . . Deighton
Heller Toren . . . . Mai Hart
Jack Watson . . . . Insp Davis
Richard Clarke . . . . Lucas
CRIME Gang's plot to rob bookmaker's
betting shop goes wrong.

13341
THE HI-JACKERS (69) (A)
Butcher's Films
P: John I. Phillips
D:S: Jim O'Connolly
Anthony Booth . . . . . . Terry McKinley
Jacqueline Ellis . . . . Shirley
Derek Francis . . . . Jack Carter
Patrick Cargill . . . . Insp Grayson
Glynn Edwards . . . . Bluey
David Gregory . . . . Pete
Harold Goodwin . . . . Scouse
Arthur English . . . . Bert
Anthony Wager . . . . Smithy
CRIME Divorcee helps haulage contractor
expose his partner as member of hijacking
gang.

13342
RING OF SPIES (90) (A)
British Lion
P: Leslie Gilliat

D: Robert Tronson
S: Frank Launder, Peter Barnes
Bernard Lee . . . . Henry Houghton
William Sylvester . . . . . . Gordon Lonsdale
Margaret Tyzack . . . . Elizabeth Gee
David Kossoff . . . . Peter Kroger
Nancy Nevinson . . . . Helen Kroger
Thorley Walters . . . . Cdr Winters
Patrick Barr . . . . Capt Warner
Hector Ross . . . . Supt Woods
Newton Blick . . . . PO Meadows
Gillian Lewis . . . . Marjorie Shaw
Brian Nissen . . . . Lt Downes
HISTORY Portland. Warrant Officer joins
spy ring and steals files from Underwater
Weapons Establishment.

13343
THE YOUNG DETECTIVES (serial) (U)
Littleton Park (CFF)
P: Ronald Spencer
D: Gilbert Gunn
S: Roy Brown
SC: Michael Barnes
Neil McCarthy . . . . Hammer Harris
Jonathan Collins . . . . Johnny
Graham Ashley . . . . Chuck
Alexander Riley . . . . Dicky Buntly
Michael Redfern . . . . Goldie
Darryl Reed . . . . Moggs
Roy Purcell . . . . Sgt Royce
Neil Wilson . . . . Supt Trumper
Grace Denbeigh-Russell . . . Mrs Griffiths
Cardew Robinson . . . . Skinny
Sam Kydd . . . . Driver

13344
1: KIDNAPPED (14)

13345
2: THE SEARCHERS (14)

13346
3: IN DEEP WATER (15)

13347
4: TRAPPED (15)

13348
5: THE RUNAWAY CART (15)

13349
6: THE HOSTAGE (15)

13350
7: WHEN THIEVES FALL OUT (15)

13351
8: THE LAST ROUND (15)
CHILDREN Boy and gang rescue three-year
old brother from kidnap by jewellery
hi-jackers.

13352
HOT ENOUGH FOR JUNE (98) (A)
eastman USA: AGENT 8¾
Rank (RFD)
P: Betty E. Box
D: Ralph Thomas
S: (NOVEL) Lionel Davidson
(NIGHT OF WENCESLAS)
SC: Lukas Heller
Dirk Bogarde . . . . Nicholas Whistler
Sylvia Koscina . . . . Vlasta Simenova
Robert Morley . . . . Col Cunliffe
Leo McKern . . . . Simenova
Roger Delgado . . . . Josef
John le Mesurier . . . . Roger Allsop
Richard Pasco . . . . Plakov
Eric Pohlmann . . . . Galushka
Richard Vernon . . . . Roddinghead

Amanda Grinling . . . . Secretary
Noel Harrison . . . . Johnnie
Derek Nimmo . . . . Fred
George Pravda . . . . Pavelko
Frank Finlay . . . . Janitor
Norman Bird . . . . Clerk
COMEDY Secret service fool unemployed
author into thinking he is being sent
to Prague on goodwill errand.

13353
PSYCHE 59 (94) (X)
Troy-Schenck (Col)
P: Philip Hazelton
D: Alexander Singer
S: (NOVEL) Francoise de Ligneris
SC: Julian Halevy
Patricia Neal . . . . Allison Crawford
Curt Jurgens . . . . Eric Crawford
Samantha Eggar . . . . Robin
Ian Bannen . . . . Paul
Beatrix Lehmann . . . . Grandmother
Elspeth March . . . . Mme Valadier
Sandra Lee . . . . Susan
Peter Porteous . . . .
Gladys Spencer . . . .
DRAMA Woman is psychosomatically blind
because her husband seduced her divorced
sister.

13354
CLASH ·· BY NIGHT (75) (A)
USA: ESCAPE BY NIGHT
Eternal (GN)
P: Maurice J. Wilson
D: Montgomery Tully
S: (NOVEL) Rupert Croft-Cooke
SC: Maurice J. Wilson, Montgomery Tully
Terence Longdon . . . . Martin Lord
Jennifer Jayne . . . . Nita Lord
Harry Fowler . . . . Doug Roberts
Peter Sallis . . . . Victor Lush
Alan Wheatley . . . . . Ronald Grey-Simmons
Vanda Godsell . . . . . . Mrs Grey-Simmons
Arthur Lovegrove . . . . Ernie Peel
Hilda Fenemore . . . . Mrs Peel
Mark Dignam . . . . Sydney Selweyn
CRIME Crooks capture busload of prisoners
to free convict.

13355
THE WILD AFFAIR (88) (A)
Seven Arts (Bry)
P: Richard Patterson
D:SC: John Krish
S: (NOVEL) William Sansom
(THE LAST HOURS OF SANDRA LEE)
Nancy Kwan . . . . Marjorie Lee
Terry-Thomas . . . . Godfrey Deane
Jimmy Logan . . . . Craig
Bud Flanagan . . . . Sgt Bletch
Gladys Morgan . . . . Mrs Tovey
Betty Marsden . . . . Mavis Cook
Paul Whitsun-Jones . . . . . . Tiny Hearst
Victor Spinetti . . . . Quentin
Joyce Blair . . . . Monica
Donald Churchill . . . . Andy
David Sumner . . . . Ralph
Diane Aubrey . . . . Jill
Bernard Adams . . . . Bone
Bessie Love . . . . Mrs Lee
COMEDY Bride-to-be has final fling at
office Christmas party.

13356
DEATH DRUMS ALONG THE RIVER (83) (U)
tech/scope
Big Ben-Hallam (Planet)
P: Harry Alan Towers
D: Lawrence Huntington

S: (NOVEL) Edgar Wallace
(SANDERS OF THE RIVER)
SC: Harry Alan Towers, Nicolas Roeg,
Kevin Kavanagh, Lawrence Huntington
Richard Todd . . . .   Insp Harry Sanders
Marianne Koch . . . .   Dr Inge Jung
Albert Lieven . . . .   Dr Weiss
Vivi Bach . . . .   Marlene
Walter Rilla . . . .   Dr Schneider
Jeremy Lloyd . . . .   Hamilton
Robert Arden . . . .   Hunter
Bill Brewer . . . .   Pearson
CRIME Africa. Inspector investigating
murder in hospital finds hidden diamond mine.

13357
THE RELUCTANT NUDIST (47) (A) *eastman*
Avon Overseas (Gala)
D: Stanley Pelc
S: S.M.C.Mitchell
Annette Briand . . . .   Sandy
Jeremy Howes . . . .   David
Vivienne Taylor . . . .   Bridget
Peter Benison . . . .   Allan
John Atkinson . . . .   Detective
Mary Chapman . . . .   Mrs Schofield
Bertha Russell . . . .   Mrs Dearlove
NUDIST Spielplatz. Jealous girl discovers
boyfriend is nudist and is converted.

13358
THE SILENT PLAYGROUND (75) (U)
Focus (Pax-BL)
P: George Mills, Esther Kiss
D:S: Stanley Goulder
Bernard Archard . . . .   Insp Duffy
Jean Anderson . . . .   Mrs Lacey
Roland Curram . . . .   Simon Lacey
Ellen McIntosh . . . .   Mavis Nugent
John Ronane . . . .   Alan
Desmond Llewelyn . . . .   Dr Green
Rowena Gregory . . . .   Jane Wilson
Basil Beale . . . .   Sgt Clark
DRAMA Mental hospital out-patient
unwittingly gives barbiturates to children.

1964

JAN

13359
BECKET (149) (A) *tech/scope*
Keep-Paramount (Par)
P: Hal Wallis
D: Peter Glenville
S: (PLAY) Jean Anouilh
SC: Edward Anhalt
Richard Burton . . . . Thomas Becket
Peter O'Toole . . . . Henry II
John Gielgud . . . . Louis VII
Donald Wolfit . . . . Bishop Folliot
Martita Hunt . . . . Queen Matilda
Pamela Brown . . . . Queen Eleanor
Sian Phillips . . . . Gwendolen
Paolo Stoppa. . . . . Pope Alexander II
Gino Cervi . . . . Cardinal Zambelli
David Weston . . . . Brother John
Percy Herbert . . . . Baron
Nial McGinnis . . . . Baron
Felix Aylmer . . . . Archbishop of Canterbury
John Phillips . . . . . Bishop of Winchester
Frank Pettingell . . . . Bishop of York
Wilfrid Lawson . . . . Soldier
Graham Stark . . . . Secretary
HISTORY 1170. Norman king appoints
Saxon friend Chancellor of England and
causes his murder. (AA 1964: Best Screenplay;
BFA 1964: Best Colour Pho, art dir.)

13360
BEWARE OF THE DOG (serial) (U)
Mandarin (CFF)
P: Donald Wynne
D: Phil Ford
S: Paul Tabori, Gordon Wellesley
Sean Bury . . . . David Woodley
Janette Lynn . . . . Betty Woodley
Amanda Humby . . . . Susie
John Moulder-Brown . . . . Michael
Rodney Goodall . . . . Alastair
Jane Barratt . . . . Mary Woodley
Charles Tingwell . . . . John Woodley
Maurice Hedley . . . . Maj Craddock
Michael Balfour . . . . Buller
Mary Merrall . . . . Mrs Rushington

13361
1: DANGER, KEEP OUT ! (17)

13362
2: THE DOG CATCHERS (16)

13363
3: THE RESCUE (15)

13364
4: THE FUGITIVES (18)

13365
5: THE DOG PRISON (14)

13366
6: THE BATTLE (16)
CHILDREN Sussex. Children save great
dane from dog-stealing major.

13367
SEVENTY DEADLY PILLS (55) (U)
Derick Williams (CFF)
P: Derick Williams
D: SC: Pat Jackson
S: Frank Wells
Gareth Robinson . . . . Brian
Len Jones . . . . Phil Streaker
John Ross . . . . Rusty
Sally Thomsett . . . . Gerty
Linda Hansen . . . . Nellie
Ronnie Johnson . . . . Dickie Goodwin
Edward Cast . . . . PC Weaver
Leslie Dwyer . . . . PC Robinson

Warren Mitchell . . . . Lofty
Timothy Bateson . . . . Goldstone
Ronald Leigh-Hunt . . . . . . Sgt
Newton Blick . . . . Sgt
Ian Fleming . . . . Doctor
CHILDREN Police search for children who
have mistaken stolen poison pills for sweets.

13368
DOWNFALL (59) (A)
Merton Park (AA)
P: Jack Greenwood
D: John Moxey
S: (STORY) Edgar Wallace
SC: Robert Stewart
Maurice Denham . . . . . Sir Harold Crossley
Nadja Regin . . . . Suzanne Crossley
T.P. McKenna . . . . Martin Somers
Peter Barkworth . . . . Tom Cotterell
Ellen McINtosh . . . . Jane Meldrum
Iris Russell . . . . Mrs Webster
Victor Brooks . . . . Insp Royd
G.H.Mulcaster . . . . Elderly Man
CRIME Lawyer acquits murderer, hires
him as chauffeur, and schemes to have him
shoot faithless wife.

13369
THE LONG SHIPS (124) (A) *tech/scope*
Warwick-Avala (Col)
P: Irving Allen, Denis O'Dell
D: Jack Cardiff
S: (NOVEL) Franz G. Bengtsson
SC: Berkley Mather, Beverley Cross
Richard Widmark . . . . Rolfe
Sidney Poitier . . . . El Mansuh
Russ Tamblyn . . . . Orm
Rosanna Schiaffino . . . . .. Aminah
Oscar Homolka . . . . Krok
Edward Judd . . . . Sven
Lionel Jeffries . . . . Aziz
Beba Loncar . . . . Gerda
Clifford Evans . . . . King Harald
Gordon Jackson . . . . Vahlin
Paul Stassino . . . . Raschid
Colin Blakeley . . . . Rhykka
Jeanne Moody . . . . Ylva
David Lodge . . . . Olla
ADVENTURE Viking steals king's funeral
ship to save golden bell from Moorish prince.

13370
SATURDAY NIGHT OUT (96) (X)
Compton-Tekli (Compton)
P: Tony Tenser, Michael Klinger
D: Robert Hartford-Davis
S: Donald Ford, Derek Ford
Heather Sears . . . . Penny
Bernard Lee . . . . George Hudson
Erika Remberg . . . . Wanda
John Bonney . . . . Lee
Francesca Annis . . . . Jean
Colin Campbell . . . . Jamie
David Lodge . . . . Arthur
Caroline Mortimer . . . . Marlene
Vera Day . . . . Arline
Inigo Jackson . . . . Harry
Nigel Green . . . . Paddy
Derek Bond . . . . Paul
Patricia Hayes . . . .
Freddie Mills . . . . Joe
Toni Gilpin . . . . Margaret
The Searchers
DRAMA Five seamen and widowed
passenger spend fourteen-hour leave in
London.

13371
THE DEVIL-SHIP PIRATES (86) (U)
tech/scope
Hammer (WPD)

P: Anthony Nelson-Keys
D: Don Sharp
S: Jimmy Sangster
Christopher Lee . . . . Capt Robeles
Andrew Keir . . . . Tom
John Cairney . . . . Harry
Michael Ripper . . . . Pepe
Duncan Lamont . . . . Bosun
Ernest Clark . . . . Sir Basil Smeeton
Barry Warren . . . . Manuel
Natasha Pyne . . . . Jane
Suzan Farmer . . . . Angela
Annette Whiteley . . . . Meg
Charles Houston . . . . Antonio
ADVENTURE Cornwall. Spanish captain
captures girl to force villagers to repair
crippled ship.

13372
NIGHT MUST FALL (105) (X)
MGM British
P: Lawrence P. Bachmann, Albert Finney,
Karel Reisz
D: Karel Reisz
S: (PLAY) Emlyn Williams
SC: Clive Exton
Albert Finney . . . . Danny
Susan Hampshire . . . . Olivia Bramson
Mona Washbourne . . . . Mrs Bramson
Sheila Hancock . . . . Dora
Michael Medwin . . . . Derek
Joe Gladwyn . . . . Dodge
Martin Wyldeck . . . . Insp Willet
John Gill . . . . Foster
CRIME Widow's charming handyman is
psychopathic axe-murderer.

13373
SEANCE ON A WET AFTERNOON (116) (A)
AFM-Beaver (RFD)
P: Richard Attenborough, Bryan Forbes
D:SC: Bryan Forbes
S: (NOVEL) Mark McShane
Kim Stanley . . . . Myra Savage
Richard Attenborough . . . . Billy Savage
Nanette Newman . . . . Mrs Clayton
Patrick Magee . . . . Supt Walsh
Mark Eden. . . . . Charles Clayton
Gerald Sim . . . . Sgt Beedle
Marian Spencer . . . . Mrs Wintry
Lionel Gamlin . . . . Man
Judith Donner . . . . Amanda Clayton
Arnold Bell . . . . Mr Weaver
DRAMA Medium's husband kidnaps
industrialist's child so she can "divine"
her whereabouts. (BFA 1964: Best Actor.)

13374
THE THREE LIVES OF THOMASINA
(97) (U) *tech*
Walt Disney
P: Hugh Attwooll
D: Don Chaffey
S: (NOVEL) Paul Gallico (THOMASINA)
SC: Robert Westerby
Patrick McGoohan . . . . . . Andrew McDhui
Susan Hampshire . . . . Lori MacGregor
Karen Dotrice . . . . Mary McDhui
Vincent Winter . . . . Hughie Stirling
Denis Gilmore . . . . Jamie McNab
Laurence Naismith . . . . Rev Angus Peddie
Finlay Currie . . . . Grandpa Stirling
Wilfrid Brambell . . . . . . Willie Bannock
Jean Anderson . . . . Mrs MacKenzie
Francis de Wolff . . . . Targu
Oliver Johnston . . . . Mr Dobbie
Elspeth March . . . . .Thomasina (voice)
DRAMA Scotland, 1912. "Witch girl's"
love cures injured cat of widowed veterinary's
daughter.

13375-13398

13375
WOMAN OF STRAW (117) (A) *eastman*
Novus (UA)
P: Michael Relph
D: Basil Dearden
S: (NOVEL) Catherine Arley
SC: Robert Muller, Stanley Mann,
Michael Relph

Gina Lollobrigida	Maria
Sean Connery	Anthony Richmond
Ralph Richardson	Charles Richmond
Alexander Knox	Lomer
Johnny Sekka	Thomas
Laurence Hardy	Baines
Peter Madden	Captain
Danny Daniels.	Fenton
Andre Morell	Judge
Edward Underdown	Executive
George Curzon	Executive

CRIME Negro servant saves Italian nurse
from conviction for murder of her paralysed
husband by his nephew.

13376
THE HORROR OF IT ALL (75) (A)
Lippert (20)
P: Robert L. Lippert
D: Terence Fisher
S: Roy Russell

Pat Boone	Jack Robinson
Erica Rogers	Cynthia
Dennis Price	Cornwallis
Andree Melly	Natalia
Valentine Dyall	Reginald
Jack Bligh	Percival
Erik Chitty	Grandpapa
Archie Duncan	Muldoon

COMEDY American discovers his fiancee's
family are maniacs and zombies.

13377
CATACOMBS (84) (X) USA: THE WOMAN
WHO WOULDN'T DIE
Parroch-McCallum
P: Jack Parsons, Neil McCallum
D: Gordon Hessler
S: (NOVEL) Jay Bennett
SC: Daniel Mainwaring

Gary Merrill	Raymond Garth
Jane Merrow	Alice Taylor
Georgina Cookson	Ellen Garth
Neil McCallum	Dick Corbett
Rachel Thomas	Christine
Jack Train	Solicitor
Frederick Piper	Inspector

CRIME Blackmailed secretary helps American
kill his wife to marry her niece.

FEB

13378
GIRL WITH GREEN EYES (91) (X)
Woodfall (UA)
P: Tony Richardson, Oscar Lewenstein
D: Desmond Davis
S: (NOVEL) Edna O'Brien (THE LONELY
GIRL)
SC: Edna O'Brien

Peter Finch	Eugene Galliard
Rita Tushingham	Kate Brady
Lynn Redgrave	Baba
Marie Kean	Josie Hannigan
Arthur O'Sullivan	James Brady
Julian Glover	Malachai Sullivan
T.P. McKenna	Priest
Lislott Goettinger	Joanna
Eileen Crowe	Mrs Byrne
Harry Brogan	Jack Holland
Patrick Laffan	Bertie Counihan

ROMANCE Dublin. Farmer's daughter
lives with married, middle-aged writer, but
eventually leaves him.

13379
GO KART GO ! (55) (U)
Fanfare (CFF)
P: George H. Brown
D: Jan Darnley-Smith
S: Frank Wells
SC: Michael Barnes

Dennis Waterman	Jimpy
Jimmy Capehorn	Squarehead
Frazer Hines	Harry
Pauline Challenor	Patchy
Melanie Garland	Squirt
Robert Ferguson	Stiggy
John Moulder Brown	Spuggy
Graham Stark	Policeman
Campbell Singer	Policeman
Wilfrid Brambell	Junkman
Cardew Robinson	Postman
Gladys Henson	Housewife
Alan White	Father
Harry Locke	Father

CHILDREN Harrow. Children build
motorised gocart and win race against
rivals.

13380
THE VERDICT (55) (U)
Merton Park (AA)
P: Jack Greenwood
D: David Eady
S: (STORY) Edgar Wallace (THE BIG FOUR)
SC: Arthur la Bern

Cec Linder	Joe Armstrong
Zena Marshall	Carola
Nigel Davenport	Larry Mason
Paul Stassino	Danny Thorne
Derek Francis	Supt Brett
John Bryan	Prendergast
Derek Partridge	Peter
Glyn Jones	Harry
Dorinda Stevens	Molly

CRIME Jailed American killer has partner
rig jury but is blackmailed and double-crossed.

13381
IT'S A BARE, BARE WORLD (33) (A)
eastman
Antler (SF)
P: A.M.B. Fancey
D: W.Lang

Vicki Kennedy	Vicki
Carol Haynes	Carol
Vera Novak	Vera
Denise Martin	Denise
Angela Jones	Angela
Leslie Bainbridge	Leslie

NUDIST Windsor. Girls persuade friend
to join nudist camp.

13382
THE SYSTEM (90) (X) USA: THE GIRL
GETTERS
Kenneth Shipman (Bry)
P: Kenneth Shipman
D: Michael Winner
S: Peter Draper

Oliver Reed	Tinker
Jane Merrow	Nicola
Barbara Ferris	Suzy
Harry Andrews	Larsey
Julia Foster	Lorna
Andrew Ray	Willy
John Alderton	Nidge
Ann Lynn	Ella
Iain Gregory	Sammy
John Porter Davison	Grib
Colin Clive Bowler	Sneakers
Guy Doleman	Philip

ROMANCE Torbay. Beach photographer
sleeps with rich holiday-maker and falls
in love with her.

13383
MURDER MOST FOUL (90) (A)
MGM British
P: Lawrence P. Bachmann, Ben Arbeid
D: George Pollock
S: (NOVEL) Agatha Christie
(MRS McGINTY'S DEAD)
SC: David Pursall, Jack Seddon

Margaret Rutherford	Miss Marple
Ron Moody	H. Driffold Cosgood
Dennis Price	Harris Tumbrill
Terry Scott	PC Wells
Charles Tingwell	Insp Craddock
Andrew Cruickshank	Justice Crosby
Megs Jenkins	Mrs Thomas
Ralph Michael	Ralph Summers
James Bolam	Bill Hanson
Stringer Davis	Mr Stringer
Francesca Annis	Sheila Howard

CRIME Lady juror joins repertory company
to uncover actress's murderer.

13384
THE THIRD SECRET (103) (A) *scope*
Hubris (20)
P: Robert L. Joseph, Hugh Perceval
D: Charles Crichton
S: Robert L. Joseph

Stephen Boyd	Alex Stedman
Jack Hawkins	Sir Frederick Belline
Richard Attenborough . . .	Alfred Price-Gorham
Diane Cilento	Anne Tanner
Pamela Franklin	Catherine Whitset
Paul Rogers	Dr Milton Gillen
Alan Webb	Alden Hoving
Rachel Kempson	Mildred Hoving
Pater Sallis	Lawrence Jacks
Patience Collier	Mrs Pelton
Freda Jackson	Mrs Bales
Judi Dench	Miss Humphries
Peter Copley	Dr Leo Whitset
Nigel Davenport	Lew Harding
Charles Lloyd Pack	Dermot McHenry

CRIME TV star discovers his psychiatrist
was killed by his young daughter.

MAR

13385
WHERE HAS POOR MICKEY GONE ? (59) (X)
Ledeck-Indigo (Compton)
P:D: Gerry Levy
S: Peter Marcus

Warren Mitchell	Emilio Dinelli
John Malcolm	Mick
Raymond Armstrong	Ginger
John Challis	Tim
Christopher Robbie	Kip
Karol Hagar	Girl
Joseph Cook	Boy

FANTASY Italian carnival magician,
persecuted by hooligans, causes three of
them to vanish.

13386
THE 7TH DAWN (123) (A) *tech*
Holdean (UA)
P: Charles K. Feldman, Karl Tunberg
D: Lewis Gilbert
S: (NOVEL) Michael Keon
(THE DURIAN TREE)
SC: Karl Tunberg

William Holden	Ferris
Susannah York	Candace Trumpey
Capucine	Dhana Mercer
Tetsuro Tamba	Ng
Michael Goodliffe	Trumpey
Allan Cuthbertson	Cavendish
Maurice Denham	Tarlton
Sidney Tafler	CPO
Buelah Quo	Ah Ming

Hugh Robinson . . . . Judge
ADVENTURE Malaya, 1950. Rubber planter
saves British Resident's daughter from
terrorist who frames his native mistress.

13387
WITCHCRAFT (80) (X)
Parroch-McCallum (20)
P: Robert L. Lippert, C.Jack Parsons,
Neil McCallum
D: Don Sharp
S: Harry Spalding
Lon Chaney . . . . Morgan Whitlock
Jack Hedley . . . . Bill Lanier
Jill Dixon . . . . Tracy Lanier
Marie Ney . . . . Malvina Lanier
Viola Keats . . . . Helen Lanier
Yvette Rees . . . . Vanessa Whitlock
David Weston . . . . Todd Lanier
Diane Clare . . . . Amy Whitlock
Victor Brooks . . . . Insp Baldwin
HORROR 300-year old witch helps
coven leader kidnap builder's wife to
thwart his plan to develop cemetery.

13388
THE BOY AND THE PELICAN (18) (U)
Wessex (BL)
P: Arden Winch
D: Geoffrey Gurrin
ANIMAL Greek island. Pampered pelican
is jealous of small boy.

APR
13389
THE BARGEE (106) (A) *tech/scope*
Galton-Simpson (WPD)
P: W.A.Whittaker
D: Duncan Wood
S: Ray Galton, Alan Simpson
Harry H. Corbett . . . . Hemel Pike
Hugh Griffith . . . . Joe Turnbull
Eric Sykes . . . . The Mariner
Julia Foster . . . . Christine Turnbull
Ronnie Barker . . . . Ronnie
Eric Barker . . . . Foreman
Miriam Karlin . . . . Nellie
Derek Nimmo . . . . Dr Scott
Norman Bird . . . . Supervisor
Richard Briers . . . . Tomkins
George A. Cooper . . . . Official
Grazina Frame . . . . Girl
Brian Wilde . . . . Policeman
Wally Patch . . . . Bargee
Godfrey Winn . . . . Announcer
COMEDY Amorous canal bargee impregnates
lock-keeper's daughter and marries her.

13390
THE EVIL OF FRANKENSTEIN (84) (X)
eastman
Hammer-Universal (UI)
P:SC: Anthony Hinds
D: Freddie Francis
S: (CHARACTERS) Mary Shelley
(FRANKENSTEIN)
Peter Cushing . . . . Baron Frankenstein
Peter Woodthorpe . . . . Prof Zoltan
Duncan Lamont . . . . . . Chief of Police
Sandor Elles . . . . Hans
Kiwi Kingston . . . . The Creature
Katy Wild . . . . Beggar Girl
David Hutcheson . . . . Burgomaster
James Maxwell . . . . Priest
Howard Goorney . . . . Drunk
Caron Gardner . . . . . Burgomaster's Wife
Tony Arpino . . . . Bodysnatcher
HORROR Bavaria, period. Baron revives
frozen monster with aid of fairground
hypnotist, who uses it as an intrument of
revenge. (Additional seq shot in USA).

13391
THE CURSE OF THE MUMMY'S TOMB (80)
(X) *tech/scope*
Hammer-Swallow (Col)
P:D: Michael Carreras
S: Henry Younger
Terence Morgan . . . . Adam Beauchamp (Be)
Ronald Howard . . . . John Bray
Fred Clark . . . . Alexander King
Jeanne Roland . . . . Annette Dubois
George Pastell . . . . Hashmi Bey
Jack Gwilim . . . . . Sir Giles Dalrymple
John Paul . . . . Insp Mackenzie
Dickie Owen . . . . Ra-Antep the Mummy
Jill Mai Meredith . . . . Jenny
Michael Ripper . . . . Achmed
Harold Goodwin . . . . Fred
HORROR 1900. Egyptian prince, cursed
to eternal life, revives 3000-year old
mummy to kill desecrators of tomb.

13392
THE BEAUTY JUNGLE (114) (A) *eastman/
scope* USA: CONTEST GIRL
Rank (RFD)
P:D: Val Guest
S: Val Guest, Robert Muller
Ian Hendry . . . . Don Mackenzie
Janette Scott . . . . Shirley Freeman
Ronald Fraser. . . . . Walter Carey
Edmund Purdom . . . . Rex Carrick
Jean Claudio . . . . Roger Armand
Kay Walsh . . . . Mrs Freeman
Norman Bird . . . . Mr Freeman
Janina Faye . . . . Elaine Freeman
Tommy Trinder . . . . Charlie Dorton
David Weston . . . . Harry
Francis Matthews . . . . Taylor
Jerry Desmonde . . . . Organiser
Jacqueline Jones . . . . Jean Watson
Paul Carpenter . . . . Tourist
Eve Eden . . . . Angela
Sidney James; Joe Brown; Stirling Moss;
Duchess of Bedford; Lionel Blair; Norman
Hartnell; Linda Christian
DRAMA Reporter helps Bristol typist
become professional beauty contest winner.

13393
BOY WITH A FLUTE (30) (U)
Grand National
P:D:S: Montgomery Tully
Freda Jackson . . . . Anne Winters
Ursula Jeans . . . . Dorothy Winters
Andree Melly . . . . Caroline Naser
Bill Nagy . . . . Conrad Barstow
Richard Bidlake . . . . Charles
Ernest Clark . . . . Sir George Noble
Guy Doleman . . . . Supt Fitch
Gerard Heinz . . . . Duclos
CRIME Widow's sister thwarts collector's
scheme to substitute copy for painting.

13394
FRENCH DRESSING (86) (A) *scope*
Kenwood (WPD)
P: Kenneth Harper
D: Ken Russell
S: Peter Myers, Ronald Cass
SC: Peter Myers, Ronald Cass, Peter Brett,
Johnny Speight
James Booth . . . . Jim
Roy Kinnear . . . . Henry
Marisa Mell . . . . Francoise Fayol
Alita Naughton . . . . Judy
Bryan Pringle . . . . Mayor
Robert Robinson . . . . Himself
Sandor Eles . . . . Vladek
Norman Pitt . . . . Mayor
Henry McCarthy . . . . Mayor

COMEDY Deckchair attendant and girl
reporter stage film festival to popularise
moribund resort.

13395
WE SHALL SEE (61) (A)
Merton Park (AA)
P: Jack Greenwood
D: Quentin Lawrence
S: (NOVEL) Edgar Wallace
SC: Donal Giltinan
Maurice Kaufmann . . . . . . Evan Collins
Faith Brook . . . . Alva Collins
Alec Mango . . . . Ludo
Alex McIntosh . . . . Greg Thomas
Hugh Paddick . . . . Connell
Talitha Pol . . . . Jirina
Bridget Armstrong . . . . . . Rosemary Layton
William Abney . . . . Shaw
CRIME Airline pilot's psychopathic wife
apparently murdered by bees.

13396
633 SQUADRON (94) (A) *scope/tech*
Mirisch (UA)
P: Lewis J. Rachmil, Cecil F.Ford
D: Walter E. Grauman
S: (NOVEL) Frederick E. Smith
SC: James Clavell, Howard Koch
Cliff Robertson . . . . WC Roy Grant
George Chakiris . . . . Lt Erik Bergman
Maria Perschy . . . . Hilde Bergman
Harry Andrews . . . Air Vice Marshal Davis
Donald Houston . . . . . . GC Tom Barrett
Michael Goodliffe . . . . . . SL Bill Adams
Angus Lennie . . . . FL Hoppy Hopkinson
John Meillon . . . . FL Gillibrand
Scot Finch . . . . FL Bissel
John Bonney . . . . FL Scott
Suzan Farmer . . . . Mary
Barbara Archer . . . . Rosie
WAR 1944, Norway. Resistance leader
tortured into betraying Mosquito air
attack on V2 factory.

13397
OF HUMAN BONDAGE (99) (X)
Seven Arts (MGM)
P: James Woolf
D: Ken Hughes, Henry Hathaway
S: (NOVEL) Somerset Maugham
SC: Bryan Forbes
Kim Novak . . . . Mildred Rogers
Laurence Harvey . . . . Philip Carey
Robert Morley . . . . Dr Jacobs
Siobhan McKenna . . . . . . Nora Nesbitt
Roger Livesey . . . . Thorpe Athelney
Jack Hedley . . . . Griffiths
Nanette Newman . . . . Sally Athelney
Ronald Lacey . . . . Matthews
David Morris . . . . Young Philip
ROMANCE 1910. Clubfooted medical
student loves cockney waitress who is
deserted by husband and turns prostitute.

13398
HYSTERIA (85) (X)
Hammer (MGM)
P:S: Jimmy Sangster
D: Freddie Francis
Robert Webber . . . . Christopher Smith
Leila Goldoni . . . . Denise James
Anthony Newlands . . . . . . Dr Keller
Jennifer Jayne . . . . Gina
Maurice Denham . . . . Hemmings
Peter Woodthorpe . . . . . . Marcus Allan
Sandra Boize . . . . English Girl
Sue Lloyd . . . . French Girl
CRIME Amnesiac American's hallucinations
induced by woman to frame him for
killing his doctor's wife.

MAY

13399
THE MASQUE OF THE RED DEATH (84) (X)
tech
Anglo-Amalgamated-Alta Vista (AA)
P: George Willoughby
D: Roger Corman
S: (STORIES) Edgar Allan Poe
(THE MASQUE OF THE RED DEATH;
HOPFROG)
SC: Charles Beaumont, R. Wright Campbell
Vincent Price . . . . Prince Prospero
Hazel Court . . . . Juliana
Jane Asher . . . . Francesca
David Weston . . . . Gino
Nigel Green . . . . Ludovico
Patrick Magee . . . . Alfredo
Paul Whitsun-Jones . . . . . . Scarlatti
John Westbrook . . . . Man in Red
Skip Martin . . . . Hoptoad
Gay Brown . . . . Senora Escobar
Julian Burton . . . . Senor Veronese
Doreen Dawn . . . . Anna-Marie
Verina Greenlaw . . . . Esmeralda
FANTASY Italy, 12th C. Devil-worshipping
Prince prevented from corrupting young
girl by personified plague.

13400
PETER STUDIES FORM (27) (A) *eastman*
Film Facilities (Gala)
P:D:S: Stan Strangeway
N: Anthony Oliver
Peter Benison . . . . Peter
Sophie Dawn . . . . Gina
Mollie Peters . . . . Mollie
Kay Fitzsimmons . . . . Kay
Wendy Luton . . . . Wendy
Ann Driver . . . . Ann
NUDIST Man tries to emulate artistic
friends and finds forte in trick photography.

13401
EAST OF SUDAN (85) (U) *tech/scope*
Ameran (Col)
P: Charles H. Schneer, Nathan Juran
D: Nathan Juran
S: Jud Kinberg
Anthony Quayle . . . . Richard Baker
Sylvia Syms . . . . Margaret Woodville
Derek Fowldes . . . . Murchison
Jenny Agutter . . . . Asua
Johnny Sekka . . . . Kimrasi
Joseph Layode . . . . Gondoko
Harold Coyne . . . . Maj Harris
Derek Blomfield . . . . Major
ADVENTURE India, period. Trooper helps
governess and native charge escape from
beseiged outpost.

13402
FIRST MEN IN THE MOON (103) (U)
tech/scope
Ameran (Col)
P: Charles H. Schneer, Ray Harryhausen
D: Nathan Juran
S: (NOVEL) H.G.Wells
SC: Nigel Kneale, Jan Read
Edward Judd . . . . : . . Arnold Bedford
Martha Hyer . . . . Kate Callender
Lionel Jeffries . . . . Prof Cavor
Peter Finch . . . . Bailiff
Erik Chitty . . . . Gibbs
Betty McDowall . . . . Maggie
Miles Malleson . . . . Registrar
Gladys Henson . . . . Matron
Lawrence Herder . . . . Glushkov
Marne Maitland . . . . Dr Tok
Hugh McDermott . . . . Challis

Paul Carpenter . . . . Announcer
Huw Thomas . . . . Announcer
FANTASY UN astronauts discover that
English professor reached moon in 1899.

13403
THE PEACHES (15) (A)
BFI (BL)
P:D: Michael Gill
S: Yvonne Gilan
N: Peter Ustinov
Juliet Harmer . . . . The Girl
Tom Adams . . . . The Man
COMEDY Intelligent beauty with passion
for peaches finally finds love.

13404
STOPOVER FOREVER (59) (A)
A.B.Pathe (WPD)
P: Terry Ashwood
D: Frederic Goode
S: David Osborne
Ann Bell . . . . Sue Chambers
Anthony Bate . . . . Trevor Graham
Conrad Phillips . . . . Eric Cunningham
Bruce Boa . . . . Freddie
Julian Sherrier . . . . Capt Carlos Mordente
Britta von Krogh . . . . Jane Watson
CRIME Sicily. Air hostess tries to learn
who killed colleague in mistake for her.

13405
THE EARTH DIES SCREAMING (62) (A)
Lippert (20)
P: Robert L. Lippert, C.Jack Parsons
D: Terence Fisher
S: Henry Cross
Willard Parker . . . . Jeff Nolan
Virginia Field . . . . Peggy Taggett
Dennis Price . . . . Quinn Taggett
Thorley Walters . . . . Edgar Otis
Vanda Godsell . . . . Violet Courtland
David Spenser . . . . Mel
Anna Palk . . . . Lorna
FANTASY Robots from space kill humans
and revive corpses as mindless slaves.

JUN

13406
CARRY ON SPYING (87) (A)
Adder (AA)
P: Peter Rogers
D: Gerald Thomas
S: Sid Colin, Talbot Rothwell
Kenneth Williams . . . . . . Desmond Simkins
Barbara Windsor . . . . Daphne Honeybutt
Bernard Cribbins . . . . Harold Crump
Charles Hawtrey . . . . Charlie Bind
Eric Barker . . . . Chief
Dilys Laye . . . . Lila
Jim Dale . . . . Carstairs
Richard Wattis . . . . Cobley
Eric Pohlman . . . . Emil Fauzak
Victor Maddern . . . . Milchmann
Judith Furse . . . . Dr Crow
John Bluthal . . . . Headwaiter
Renee Houston . . . . Madame
COMEDY Four trainee agents trail spies
to Vienna and Algiers to foil bisexual
mastermind seeking formula.

13407
WHO WAS MADDOX ? (62) (U)
Merton (AA)
P: Jack Greenwood
D: Geoffrey Nethercott
S: (STORY) Edgar Wallace
(THE UNDISCLOSED CLIENT)
SC: Roger Marshall

Bernard Lee . . . . Supt Meredith
Jack Watling . . . . Jack Heath
Suzanne Lloyd . . . . Diane Heath
Finlay Currie . . . . Alec Campbell
Richard Gale . . . . Maddox
James Bree . . . . Reynolds
Dora Reisser . . . . Anne Wilding
Christa Bergmann . . . . Greta
Billy Milton . . . . Chandler
CRIME Supt exposes blackmailer behind
murder of publisher's chairman.

13408
A HARD DAY'S NIGHT (98) (U)
Proscenium (UA)
P: Walter Shenson
D: Richard Lester
S: Alun Owen
John Lennon . . . . John
Paul McCartney . . . . Paul
George Harrison . . . . George
Ringo Starr . . . . Ringo
Wilfrid Brambell . . . . . . John McCartney
Norman Rossington . . . . . Norm
Victor Spinetti . . . . TV Director
John Junkin . . . . Shake
Deryck Guyler . . . . Sgt
Anna Quayle . . . . Millie
Kenneth Haigh . . . . TV Producer
Richard Vernon . . . . Passenger
Lionel Blair
MUSICAL "The Beatles"'s drummer almost
misses TV show, thanks to colleague's
Irish grandfather.

13409
THE MOON-SPINNERS (119) (U) *tech*
Walt Disney
P: Bill Anderson, Hugh Attwooll
D: James Neilson
S: (NOVEL) Mary Stewart
SC: Michael Dyne
Hayley Mills . . . . Nikky Ferris
Eli Wallach . . . . Stratos
Peter McEnery . . . . Mark Canford
Joan Greenwood . . . . Frances Ferris
Irene Papas . . . . Sophia
Pola Negri . . . . Mme Habib
John le Mesurier . . . . Anthony Gamble
Sheila Hancock . . . . Cynthia Gamble
Michael Davis . . . . Alexis
Paul Stassino . . . . Lambis
Andre Morell . . . . Capt
George Pastell . . . . Lt
CRIME Crete. Girl on holiday helps
sacked bank clerk foil jewel-robbing
hotel keeper.

13410
WONDERFUL LIFE (113) (U) *tech/scope*
Ivy (Elstree)
P: Kenneth Harper
D: Sidney J. Furie
S: Peter Myers, Ronald Cass
Cliff Richard . . . . Johnnie
Walter Slezak . . . . Lloyd Davis
Susan Hampshire . . . . Jenny
The Shadows . . . . Mood Musicians
Melvyn Hayes . . . . Jerry
Richard O'Sullivan . . . . . . Edward
Una Stubbs . . . . Barbara
Derek Bond . . . . Douglas Leslie
Gerald Harper . . . Sheik/Scotsman/Harold
MUSICAL Canary Isle. Stranded musicians
secretly make musical version of veteran
director's comeback film.

13411
JUST FOR YOU (64) (U) *eastman*
Delmore (BL)

P: Ben Nisbet, Jacques De Lane Lea
D: Douglas Hickox
S: Douglas Hickox, Jacques De Lane Lea
SC: David Edwards

Sam Costa	The Applejacks
Al Saxon	A Band of Angels
The Orchids	The Bachelors
Doug Sheldon	Caroline Lee
Roy Sone	Judy Jason
Peter & Gordon	Freddie and the Dreamers
Millie	Jackie and the Raindrops
Mark Wynter	Johnny B. Great
The Warriors	Louise Cordet
The Merseybeats	

MUSICAL Disc-jockey in electronic push-button bed is entertained by pop singers.

13412
THE BLACK TORMENT (85) (X) *eastman*
Compton-Tekli (Compton)
P: Tony Tenser, Michael Klinger, Robert Hartford-Davis
D: Robert Hartford-Davis
S: Donald Ford, Derek Ford

Heather Sears ...	Lady Elizabeth Fordyke
John Turner	Sir Richard Fordyke
Ann Lynn	Diane
Peter Arne	Seymour
Norman Bird	Harris
Raymond Huntley	Col Wentworth
Annette Whiteley	Mary
Joseph Tomelty	Sir Giles Fordyke
Patrick Troughton	Ostler
Francis de Wolff	Black John

CRIME 1780. Sister of nobleman's dead wife uses his mad twin to drive him insane.

13413
THE SICILIANS (69) (U)
Butcher's Films
P: John I. Phillips, Ronald Liles
D: Ernest Morris
S: Ronald Liles, Reginald Hearne

Robert Hutton	Calvin Adams
Reginald Marsh	Insp Webb
Ursula Howells	Mme Perrault
Alex Scott	Henri Perrault
Susan Denny	Carole Linden
Robert Ayres	Angela di Marco
Eric Pohlmann	Insp Bressin
Patricia Hayes	Passenger
Warren Mitchell	O'Leary
Murray Kash	George Baxter

CRIME Paris. Dancer helps American Embassy man seek kidnapped son of acquitted Mafia gangster.

13414
MISTER MOSES (116) (U) *tech/scope*
Frank Ross-Talbot (UA)
P: Frank Ross
D: Ronald Neame
S: (NOVEL) Max Catto
SC: Charles Beaumont, Monja Danischewsky

Robert Mitchum	Joe Moses
Carroll Baker	Julie Anderson
Ian Bannen	Robert
Alexander Knox	Rev Anderson
Raymond St Jacques	Ubi
Orlando Martins	Chief
Reginald Beckwith	Parkhurst

ADVENTURE Africa. Diamond smuggler and missionary's daughter lead tribe to safety despite witch doctor's son.

13415
THE PUMPKIN EATER (118) (X)
Romulus (Col)
P: James Woolf

D: Jack Clayton
S: (NOVEL) Penelope Mortimer
SC: Harold Pinter

Anne Bancroft	Jo Armitage
Peter Finch	Jake Armitage
James Mason	Bob Conway
Cedric Hardwicke	James
Richard Johnson	Giles
Maggie Smith	Philpot
Eric Porter	Psychiatrist
Rosalind Atkinson	Mrs James
Frances White	Dinah
Alan Webb	Mr Armitage
Cyril Luckham	Doctor
Janine Gray	Beth Conway
Frank Sanguineau	King of Israel
Anthony Nicholls	Surgeon

DRAMA Mother of seven children marries for third time, breaks down, is sterilised, and leaves unfaithful husband. (BFA 1964: Best Actress, Best B/W Pho.)

13416
A SHOT IN THE DARK (103) (A) *deluxe/scope*
Mirisch-Geoffrey (UA)
P:D: Blake Edwards
S: (PLAYS) Harry Kurnitz, Marcel Archard
SC: Blake Edwards, William Peter Blatty

Peter Sellers ...	Insp Jacques Clouseau
Elke Sommer	Maria Gambelli
George Sanders	Benjamin Ballon
Herbert Lom	Chief Insp Charles Dreyfus
Tracy Reed	Dominique Ballon
Graham Stark	Hercule Lajoy
Moira Redmond	Susanne
Vanda Godsell	Mme Lafarge
Maurice Kaufmann	Pierre
Ann Lynn	Dudu
David Lodge	Georges
Andre Maranne	Francois
Martin Benson	Maurice
Reginald Beckwith	Receptionist
Bryan Forbes	Turk Thrust

COMEDY Paris. Surete inspector proves rich man's maid did not shoot her lover.

JUL

13417
GUNS AT BATASI (103) (A) *scope*
20th Century Fox
P: George Brown
D: John Guillermin
S: (NOVEL) Robert Hollis
(SIEGE OF BATTERSEA)
SC: Robert Hollis, Leo Marks, Marshall Pugh, C.M.Pennington-Richards

Richard Attenborough	RSM Lauderdale
Flora Robson	Miss Barker-Wise
John Leyton	Pte Charlie Wilkes
Jack Hawkins	Lt Col John Deal
Mia Farrow	Karen Ericson
Cecil Parker	Sir William Fletcher
Errol John	Lt Boniface
Graham Stark	Dodger
Earl Cameron	Capt Abraham
John Meillon	Digger
Percy Herbert	Ben
David Lodge	Muscles
Patrick Holt	Captain

WAR Africa. Regimental sergeant-major defends mess against rebels who are duly recognised in Britain as the new government

13418
MURDER AHOY (93)
MGM British
P: Lawrence P. Bachmann
D: George Pollock

S: (CHARACTERS) Agatha Christie
SC: David Pursall, Jack Seddon

Margaret Rutherford	Miss Marple
Lionel Jeffries ...	Capt Sidney Rhumstone
Charles Tingwell	Insp Craddock
William Mervyn	Cdr Breeze-Connington
Joan Benham	Alice Fanbraid
Stringer Davis	Mr Stringer
Nicholas Parsons	Dr Crump
Henry Oscar	Lord Rudkin
Miles Malleson	Bishop
Derek Nimmo	Lt Humbert

CRIME Lady tec investigates deaths of trustees of cadet training ship for wayward teenagers.

13419
RATTLE OF A SIMPLE MAN (95) (X)
Martello (WPD)
P: Sydney Box, William Gell
D: Muriel Box
S: (PLAY) Charles Dyer
SC: Charles Dyer

Harry H. Corbett	Percy Winthram
Diane Cilento	Cyrenne
Michael Medwin	Ginger
Thora Hird	Mrs Winthram
Charles Dyer	Chalky
Hugh Futcher	Ozzie
Carole Gray	Nurse
Brian Wilde	Fred
Barbara Archer	Iris
David Saire	Mario
Alexander Davion	Ricardo
Marie Burke	Mama

COMEDY Manchester football fan falls for Soho prostitute.

13420
THE GORGON (83) (X) *tech*
Hammer (Col)
P: Anthony Nelson Keys
D: Terence Fisher
S: J. Llewellyn Devine
SC: John Gilling

Peter Cushing	Dr Namaroff
Christopher Lee	Prof Carl Meister
Richard Pasco	Paul Heitz
Barbara Shelley.	Carla Hoffman
Michael Goodliffe	Prof Heitz
Patrick Troughton	Kanof
Joseph O'Conor	Coroner
Prudence Hyman	Chatelaine
Jack Watson	Ratoff
Redmond Phillips	Hans
Jeremy Longhurst	Bruno Heitz

HORROR Austria, 1910. Student investigating father's petrification loves nurse possessed by spirit of Megaera.

13421
SWINGING U.K. (28) (U) *eastman*
Harold Baim (UA)
D: Frank Gilpin

Brian Poole and the Tremeloes	
Millie	The Merseybeats
The Cockneys	The Wackers
The Four Pennies	The Migil Five
Brian Matthew	Kent Walton
Alan Freeman	

MUSICAL Three disc-jockeys introduce popular singers. (Released in USA as part of GO GO BIG BEAT)

13422
U.K.SWINGS AGAIN (27) (U) *eastman*
Harold Baim (UA)
D: Frank Gilpin
Brian Poole and the Tremeloes

The Hollies   The Swinging Blue Jeans
Lulu and the Luvvers
The Applejacks   The Animals
The Tornadoes   Brian Matthew
Kent Walton   Alan Freeman
MUSICAL Three disc-jockeys introduce
popular singers. (Released in USA as
part of GO GO BIG BEAT)

13423
NIGHT TRAIN TO PARIS (64) (U)
Lippert (20)
P: Robert L. Lippert, Jack Parsons
D: Robert Douglas
SC: Henry Cross
Leslie Nielsen . . . . Alan Holiday
Alizia Gur . . . . Catherine Carrel
Dorinda Stevens . . . . Olive Davies
Eric Pohlmann . . . . Krogh
Edina Ronay . . . . Julie
Andre Maranne . . . . Louis Vernay
Cyril Raymond . . . . Insp Fleming
Hugh Latimer . . . . Jules Lemoine
CRIME Girl helps ex-OSS agent save
tape recording from spies.

AUG

13424
GOLDFINGER (109) (A) *tech*
Eon-Danjaq SA (UA)
P: Harry Saltzman, Albert Broccoli
D: Guy Hamilton
S: (NOVEL) Ian Fleming
SC: Richard Maibaum, Paul Dehn
Sean Connery . . . . James Bond
Honor Blackman . . . . Pussy Galore
Gert Frobe . . . . Auric Goldfinger
Shirley Eaton . . . . Jill Masterson
Tania Mallet . . . . Tilly Masterson
Harold Sakata . . . . Odd Job
Bernard Lee . . . . M
Martin Benson . . . . Solo
Cec Linder . . . . Felix Leiter
Austin Willis . . . . Simmons
Lois Maxwell . . . . Miss Moneypenny
Bill Nagy . . . . Midnight
Nadja Regin . . . . Bonita
CRIME Secret Agent and girl thwart
a communist plan to explode an atomic
device in Fort Knox. (Top Moneymaker,
1964. AA 1964: Best Sound)

13425
SMOKESCREEN (66) (U)
Butcher's Films
P: John I. Phillips
D:S; Jim O'Connolly
Peter Vaughan . . . . Ropey Roper
John Carson . . . . Trevor Baylis
Yvonne Romain . . . . Janet Dexter
Gerald Flood . . . . Graham Turner
Glynn Edwards . . . . Insp Wright
John Glyn Jones . . . . Player
Sam Kydd . . . . Waiter
Deryck Guyler . . . . Porter
CRIME Brighton. Insurance investigator
proves car accident victim was murdered.

13426
ONE WAY PENDULUM (85) (U)
Woodfall (UA)
P: Oscar Lewenstein, Michael Deeley
D: Peter Yates
S: (PLAY) N.F. Simpson
SC: N.F. Simpson
Eric Sykes . . . . Arthur Groomkirby
George Cole . . . . Defence Counsel/Friend

Julia Foster . . . . Sylvia Groomkirby
Jonathan Miller . . . . Kirby Groomkirby
Peggy Mount . . . . Mrs Gantry
Alison Leggat . . . . Mabel Groomkirby
Mona Washbourne . . . . . . Aunt Mildred
Douglas Wilmer . . . . Judge/Maintenance Man
Glyn Houston . . . . Insp Barnes
Graham Crowden . . . . . . Prosecution/Caretaker
Tommy Bruce . . . . Cormless (voice)
Kenneth Farrindon . . . . . . Stan
Walter Horsbrugh . . . . . . Clerk/Assistant
Frederick Piper . . . . Usher/Clerk
COMEDY Suburban family's hobbies include
do-it-yourself Old Bailey and training weighing
machines to sing.

13427
FIVE HAVE A MYSTERY TO SOLVE (U)
(serial)
Rayant) (CFF)
P: John Durst
D: Ernest Morris
S: (NOVEL) Enid Blyton
SC: Michael Barnes
David Palmer . . . . Julian
Darryl Read . . . . Dick
Amanda Coxell . . . . George
Paula Boyd . . . . Ann
Michael Wennick . . . . Wilfred
Keith Pyott . . . . Sir Hugo Blaize
Michael Balfour . . . .
Robin Hunter . . . .
Diane Powell . . . .
Grace Arnold . . . .
Howard Douglas . . . .

13428
1—WHISPERING ISLAND (16)

13429
2—THE HUNT IN THE WOODS (16)

13430
+—THE CASTAWAYS (16)

13431
4—THE SECRET DOOR (16)

13432
5—THE CRUSADER'S TREASURE (16)

13433
6—HIGH TIDE (16)

CHILDREN Children and orphan animal-lover
foil gamekeepers' scheme to steal eccentric's
striped rabbits and treasure.

13434
DEVILS OF DARKNESS (90) (X) *eastman*
Planet
P: Tom Blakeley
D: Lance Comfort
S: Lyn Fairhurst
William Sylvester . . . . Paul Baxter
Hubert Noel . . . . Count Sinistre
Tracy Reed . . . . Karen
Carole Gray . . . . Tania
Diana Decker . . . . Madeleine Braun
Rona Anderson . . . . .Anne Forrest
Peter Illing . . . . Insp Malin
Gerard Heinz. . . . . Bouvier
Victor Brooks . . . . Insp Hardwicke
Avril Angers . . . . Midge
Julie Mendes . . . . Dancer
HORROR Writer exposes French count as
400-year old vampire who sacrifices girls to
keep young.

13435
DOWN BOY! (26) (U)
Norcon (BL)
P:D: Norman Cohen
S: Norman Cohen, Malcolm Yaffe
N: Kenneth Horne
Milo O'Shea . . . . The Man
COMEDY Humorous analysis of the dog.

SEPT
13436
RHYTHM 'N' GREENS (32) (U) *tech*
Interstate-AB Pathe (WPD)
P: Terry Ashwood
D:S: Christopher Miles
N: Robert Morley
Hank B. Marvin . . . .
Brian Bennett . . . .
Bruce Welch . . . .
John Rostill . . . .
Joan Palethorpe . . . .
Sally Bradley . . . .
Audrey Bayley . . . .
Wendy Barry . . . .
MUSICAL "The Shadows" illustrate English
history from Stone Age to date.

13437
KING AND COUNTRY (88) (A)
BHE (WPD)
P: Daniel Angel, Norman Priggen, Joseph
Losey
D: Joseph Losey
S: (PLAY) John Wilson (HAMP)/(NOVEL)
James Lansdale Hodson (RETURN TO THE
WOOD)
SC: Evan Jones
Dirk Bogarde . . . . Capt Hargreaves
Tom Courtney . . . . Pte Hamp
Leo McKern . . . . Capt O'Sullivan
Barry Foster . . . . Lt Webb
James Villiers . . . . Capt Midgeley
Peter Copley . . . . Colonel
Barry Justice . . . . Lt Prescott
Vivan Matalon . . . . Padre
Jeremy Spenser . . . . Sparrow
James Hunter . . . . Sykes
David Cook . . . . Wilson
WAR Passchendaele, 1917. Captain defends
deserter at his court-martial but he is
sentenced to death.

13438
THE SOLDIER'S TALE (52) (U) *tech*
Ipsilon (BHE)
P: Leonard Cassini, Dennis Miller
D:SC: Michael Birkett
S: (OPERA) Igor Stravinski, C.F. Ramuz
Robert Helpmann . . . . The Devil
Brian Phelan . . . . The Soldier
Svetlana Beriosova . . . . . . The Princess
MUSICAL Soldier exchanges violin for
Devil's book of riches, but regrets it when he
falls in love with princess.

13439
IT HAPPENED HERE (99) (A)
Rath (UA)
P:D:S: Kevin Brownlow, Andrew Mollo
SC: Kevin Brownlow, Andrew Mollo, Dinah
Brooke, Jonathan Ingram
N: John Snagge, Alvar Liddell, Frank Phillips,
Michael Mellinger
Pauline Murray . . . . Pauline Murray
Sebastian Shaw . . . . .Dr Richard Fletcher
Nicolette Bernard . . . . IA Commandant
Bart Allison . . . . Skipworth

Stella Kemball . . . . Nurse Drayton
Fiona Leland . . . . Mrs Fletcher
Frank Bennett . . . . Group Leader
John Herrington . . . . Dr Westerman
Reginald Marsh . . . . MO
Bertha Russell . . . . Matron
Honor Fearson . . . . Honor Hutton
Ralph Wilson . . . . Dr Walton
FANTASY 1940. After Germany wins war,
Welsh nurse comes to London and joins Nazi
party.

13440
ACT OF MURDER (62) (A)
Merton Park (AA)
P: Jack Greenwood
D: Alan Bridges
S: Lewis Davidson
John Carson . . . . Tim Ford
Anthony Bate . . . . Ralph Longman
Justine Lord . . . . Anne Longman
Duncan Lewis . . . . Will Peterson
Richard Burrell . . . . John Quick
Dandy Nichols . . . . Maud Peterson
Sheena Marshe . . . . Pauline
Norman Scace . . . . Watson
CRIME Actor uses crook's plot to steal
antiques to lure his ex-mistress from her
husband.

13441
MODS AND ROCKERS (28) (U) *eastman*
USA: GO GO BIG BEAT
Kenneth Hume (AA)
P: Kenneth Hume, Larry Parnes
D: Kenneth Hume
S: Peter Darrell
Western Theatre Ballet Company
The Cheynes
MUSICAL Mod girl takes up with Rocker boy,
causing fight in vicar's youth club. (Released in
USA combined with SWINGING UK AND UK
SWINGS AGAIN.)

13442
FACE OF A STRANGER (56) (A)
Merton Park (AA)
P: Jack Greenwood
D: John Moxey
S: (NOVEL) Edgar Wallace
SC: John Sansom
Jeremy Kemp . . . . Vince Howard
Bernard Archard . . . . Michael Forrest
Rosemary Leach . . . . Mary Bell
Philip Locke . . . . John Bell
Elizabeth Begley . . . . . .
Jean Marsh . . . .
Mike Pratt . . . .
Keith Smith . . . .
CRIME Ex-convict poses as his cell mate to live
with his blind wife and find hidden loot.

OCT

13443
EVERY DAY'S A HOLIDAY (94) (U)
tech/scope
USA: SEASIDE SWINGERS
Fitzroy—Maycroft (GN)
P: Maurice J. Wilson, Ronald J. Khan
D: James Hill
S: Anthony Marriott
SC: Anthony Marriott, James Hill, Jeri Matos
John Leyton . . . . Gerry Pullman
Mike Sarne . . . . Timothy Gilpin
Freddie and the Dreamers . . . The Chefs
Ron Moody . . . . Prof. Bastinado
Liz Fraser . . . . Miss Slightly
Grazina Frame . . . . Christina Barrington de Witt
The Baker Twins . . . . Susan and Jennifer

Nicholas Parsons . . . . Julian Goddard
Richard O'Sullivan . . . . Jimmy
Michael Ripper . . . . Mr Pullman
Hazel Hughes . . . . Mrs Barrington de Witt
Charles Lloyd Pack . . . . Mr Close
The Mojos; The Leroys; Gillian Lynne Dancers
MUSICAL Teenagers working in holiday camp
win TV talent contest.

13444
THE TOMB OF LIGEIA (81) (X) *eastman/scope*

Alta Vista (AA)
P: Roger Corman, Pat Green
D: Roger Corman
S: (STORY) Edgar Allan Poe (LIGEIA)
SC: Robert Towne
Vincent Price . . . . Verden Fell
Elizabeth Shepherd . . . . . Lady Rowena/
                                    Ligeia Fell
John Westbrook . . . . Christopher Gough
Derek Francis . . . . Lord Trevanion
Oliver Johnston . . . . Kenrick
Richard Vernon . . . . Dr Vivian
Frank Thornton . . . . Peperel
Ronald Adam . . . . Parson
HORROR 1821. Lady marries widower and is
almost killed by spirit of his dead wife
inhabiting black cat.

13445
BALLAD IN BLUE (88) (U)
Alsa (WPD)
P: Alexander Salkind, Miguel Salkind,
Herman Blaser
D: Paul Henreid
S: Paul Henreid, Burton Wohl
SC: Burton Wohl
Ray Charles . . . . Himself
Tom Bell . . . . Steve Collins
Mary Peach . . . . Peggy Harrison
Dawn Addams . . . . Gina Graham
Betty McDowall . . . . Mrs Babbage
Lucy Appleby . . . . Margaret
Piers Bishop . . . . David Harrison
Joe Adams . . . . Fred
Robert Lee Ross . . . . Duke Wade
The Raelets
MUSICAL Paris. Blind Negro singer helps
widow's blind son and her romance with
poor composer.

13446
VICTIM FIVE (88) (U) *tech/scope*
USA: CODE SEVEN, VICTIM FIVE
Towers of London (BL)
P: Harry Alan Towers, Skip Steloff
D: Robert Lynn
S: Peter Welbeck
SC: Peter Yeldham
Lex Barker . . . . Steve Martin
Ronald Fraser . . . . Insp Lean
Ann Smyrner . . . . Helga
Veronique Vendell . . . . Gina
Walter Rilla . . . . Wexler
Dietmar Schonherr . . . . Paul
Gert Van den Bergh . . . . . . Vanberger
Howard Davies . . . . Rawling
Percy Sief . . . . Anderson
CRIME Cape Town. Millionaire hires American
detective to solve murder of his valet.

13447
EAGLE ROCK (62) (U) *eastman*
World Safari (CFF)
P:D:SC: Henry Geddes
S: Mary Cathcart Borer
Pip Rolls . . . . Mark
Christine Thomas . . . . Jean
Stephen Morris . . . . Gavin
Bryan Marsh . . . . Mr MacGregor
Jim Cameron . . . . Mr McTavish

(spoken by John Laurie)
Tony Paul . . . . Tony
Colin Neal . . . . Hugh
Nicholas Young . . . . Trevor
CHILDREN Lake District. Dungeon Ghyll
Adventure School pupil rescued after climbing
for eagles' eggs.

13448
ALLEZ FRANCE (92) (U) *eastman/bilingual*
USA: THE COUNTERFEIT CONSTABLE
Seven Arts—Film D'Art—Arthur Lesser—
CICC (Gala)
P: Hal Mason, Henri Diamant-Berger,
Maurice Hartwig
D: Robert Dhery
S: Robert Dhery, Pierre Tcherina
Robert Dhery . . . . Henri
Colette Brosset . . . . Yvette
Diana Dors . . . . Herself
Ronald Fraser . . . . Chief Constable
Pierre Olaf . . . . Operator
Bernard Cribbins . . . . PC 202
Robert Rollis . . . . Desk Sgt
Ferdy Mayne . . . . Agent
Henri Genes . . . . Friend
Catherine Sola . . . . Sister
Richard Vernon . . . .
Percy Herbert . . . .
COMEDY French football fan, mistaken for
PC, saves film star from crooks.

NOV

13449
FERRY CROSS THE MERSEY (85) (U)
Suba (UA)
P: Brian Epstein, Michael Holden
D: Jeremy Summers
S: Tony Warren
Gerry Marsden . . . . Gerry
The Pacemakers . . . . Fred, Chad and Les
Cilla Black . . . . Herself
Julie Samuel . . . . Dodie Dawson
Eric Barker . . . . Col Dawson
Deryck Guyler . . . . Trasler
George A. Cooper . . . . Mr Lumsden
Patricia Lawrence . . . . Miss Kneave
Mona Washbourne . . . . Aunt Lil
Mischa de la Motte . . . . . . Butler
T.P. McKenna . . . . Hanson
The Fourmost
Jimmy Savile
Earl Royce and the Olympics
The Blackwells
The Black Knights
MUSICAL Liverpool. Art student's group find
lost instruments in time to win European Beat
Contest.

13450
CARRY ON CLEO (92) (A) *eastman*
Adder (AA)
P: Peter Rogers
D: Gerald Thomas
S: (PLAYS) William Shakespeare (JULIUS
CAESAR; ANTHONY AND CLEOPATRA)
SC: Talbot Rothwell
N: E.V.H. Emmett
Sidney James . . . . Mark Anthony
Kenneth Williams . . . . Julius Caesar
Kenneth Connor . . . . Hengist Pod
Charles Hawtrey . . . . Seneca
Joan Sims . . . . Calpurnia
Jim Dale . . . . Horsa
Amanda Barrie . . . . Cleopatra
Victor Maddern . . . . Sgt-Major
Julie Stevens . . . . Gloria
Sheila Hancock . . . . Senna Pod
Jon Pertwee . . . . Soothsayer

Francis de Wolff .... Agrippa
Michael Ward .... Archimedes
Brian Oulton .... Brutus
Warren Mitchell .... Spencius
COMEDY Rome, 50 BC. British slaves save
Caesar from assassination by ambitious
soldier and Queen of Egypt.

13451
SCENE NUN, TAKE ONE (26) (A)
Mithras (Col)
P: Tim Pitt Miller, Maurice Hatton
D: Maurice Hatton
S: Maurice Hatton, Michael Wood
Susannah York .... The Actress
COMEDY Film actress dressed as nun has
various adventures.

13452
THE YELLOW ROLLS ROYCE (122) (A)
metro/scope
Anatole de Grunwald (MGM)
P: Anatole de Grunwald
D: Anthony Asquith
S: Terence Rattigan
England
Rex Harrison .... Marquis of Frinton
Jeanne Moreau .... Marchioness Eloise
Edmund Purdom .... John Fane
Moira Lister .... Lady Angela St Simeon
Isa Miranda .... Duchesse d' Angouleme
Roland Culver .... Norwood
Michael Hordern .... Harmsworth
Lance Percival .... Assistant
Gregoire Aslan .... Ambassador
Jacques Brunius .... Duc de d'Angouleme
Italy
Shirley MacLaine .... Mae Jenkins
Alain Delon .... Stefano
George C. Scott .... Paolo Maltese
Art Carney .... Joey
Riccardo Garrone .... Bomba
Yugoslavia
Ingrid Bergman .... Gerda Millett
Omar Sharif .... Davich
Joyce Grenfell .... Hortense Astor
Wally Cox .... Ferguson
Guy Deghy .... Mayor
DRAMA 3 stories centreing on car: Nobility
in Ascot week; gangster's moll and gigolo;
American socialite escapes Germans.

13453
THE HIGH BRIGHT SUN (114) (A) *tech*
USA: McGUIRE GO HOME !
Rank (RFD)
P: Betty E. Box
D: Ralph Thomas
S: (NOVEL) Ian Stuart Black
SC: Ian Stuart Black, Bryan Forbes
Dirk Bogarde .... Maj McGuire
George Chakiris .... Haghios
Susan Strasberg .... Juno Kozani
Denholm Elliott .... Baker
Gregoire Aslan .... Gen Skyros
Colin Campbell .... Emile Andros
Joseph Fuerst .... Dr Andros
Nigel Stock .... Col Park
Katherine Kath .... Mrs Andros
George Pastell .... Prinos
Paul Stassino .... Alkis
WAR Cyprus, 1957. British intelligence
officer seeking guerilla leader loves American
archaeologist.

13454
DR TERROR'S HOUSE OF HORRORS (98)
(X) *tech/scope*
Amicus (RFI)
P: Milton Subotsky, Max Rosenberg
D: Freddie Francis

SC: Milton Subotsky
Peter Cushing .... Dr Sandor Schreck
Christopher Lee .... Franklyn Marsh
Roy Castle .... Biff Bailey
Max Adrian .... Dr Blake
Michael Gough .... Eric Landor
Neil McCallum .... Jim Dawson
Ann Bell .... Ann Rogers
Jennifer Jayne .... Nicolle
Bernard Lee .... Hopkins
Alan Freeman .... Bill Rogers
Peter Madden .... Caleb
Kenny Lynch .... Sammy Coin
Jeremy Kemp .... Drake
Donald Sutherland .... Bob Carroll
Harold Lang .... Shine
Ursula Howells .... Deirdre Biddulph
Edward Underdown ...... Tod
Russ Henderson Steel Band
Tubby Hayes Quintet
HORROR Death personified predicts deaths of
five train passengers, by werewolf, creeping vine,
voodoo, severed hand and vampire.

13455
NEVER MENTION MURDER (56) (U)
Merton Park (AA)
P: Jack Greenwood
D: John Nelson Burton
S: (STORY) Edgar Wallace
SC: Robert Banks Stewart
Maxine Audley .... Liz Teasdale
Dudley Foster .... Philip Teasdale
Michael Coles .... Tony Sorbo
Pauline Yates .... Zita Sorbo
Brian Haines .... Felix Carstairs
Peter Butterworth .... Porter
Philip Stone .... Inspector
CRIME Surgeon poisons and tries to operate on
wife's lover.

13456
THE MAIN CHANCE (61) (U)
Merton Park (AA)
P: Jack Greenwood
D: John Knight
S: (NOVEL) Edgar Wallace
SC: Richard Harris
Gregoire Aslan .... Potter
Edward de Souza .... Michael Blake
Tracy Reed .... Christine
Stanley Meadows .... Joe Hayes
Jack Smethurst .... Ross
Bernard Stone .... Miller
Will Stampe .... Carter
Joyce Barbour .... Mme Rozanne
CRIME Pilot tries to steal crook's diamonds,
but they are stolen by his mistress.

13457
THE TRUTH ABOUT SPRING (102) (U) *tech*
Quota Rentals (UI)
P: Alan Brown
D: Richard Thorpe
S: (NOVEL) Henry deVere Stacpoole(SATAN)
SC: James Lee Barrett
Hayley Mills .... Spring Tyler
John Mills .... Tommy Tyler
James MacArthur .... William Ashton
Lionel Jeffries .... Cark
David Tomlinson .... Skelton
Harry Andrews .... Sellers
Niall McGinnis .... Cleary
Lionel Murton .... Simmons
ADVENTURE Caribbean. Millionaire's son and
tomboy save beachcomber father's treasure map
from pirates.

13458
TRAITOR'S GATE (80) (A)
Summit (Col)

P: Ted Lloyd
D: Freddie Francis
S: (NOVEL) Edgar Wallace
SC: John Samson
Albert Lieven .... Trayne
Gary Raymond .. Graham/Lt Dick Lee-Carnby
Margot Trooger .... Dinah
Catherina Von Schell ..... Hope
Eddie Arent .... Hector
Klaus Kinski .... Kinski
Anthony James .... John
Tim Barrett .:......... Lloyd
Heinz Bernard .... Martin
Dave Birks .... Spider
Edward Underdown .... Insp Gray
Alec Ross .... Sgt Carter
Julie Mendez .... Stripper
CRIME Executive robs Tower of London by
replacing an officer with his convict double.

13459
DEAD END CREEK (serial) (U)
Anvil (CFF)
P: Ralph N. May
D: Pat Jackson
S: Alec Grieve
SC: Pat Jackson, Michael Barnes
Len Jones .... Len
Sally Thomsett .... Jane
Nicholas Bonham .... Peter Mills
John Welsh .... Paddy
David Hutcheson .... Fixer
Robin Chapman .... Nick
Roger Avon .... Uncle Bob
Moira Lynd .... Auntie
George Woodbridge ..... Sir Robert Darby
Fabia Drake .... Lady Darby

13460
1—HIGHWAY ROBBERY (14)

13461
2—MYSTERY AT THE FORGE (15)

13462
3—THE NIGHT PROWLER (16)

13463
4—THE MYSTERIOUS STRANGER (18)

13464
5—ALL AT SEA (16)

13465
6—CATCH AS CATCH CAN (15)
CHILDREN Farmer's niece and nephew
unmask gang of bullion robbers.

13466
THE RUNAWAY (62) (U)
Luckwell (Col)
P: Bill Luckwell, David Vigo
D: Tony Young
S: John Perceval
SC: John Perceval, John Gerrard Sharp
Greta Gynt .... Anita Peshkin
Alex Gallier .... Andrian Peshkin
Paul Williamson .... Thomas
Michael Trubshawe .... Sir Roger Clements
Tony Quinn .... Prof Hawkley
Wendy Varnals .... Tania
Denis Shaw .... Agent
CRIME MI5 agent saves Polish chemist and
synthetic ballistic chemical from Russian spies.

DEC

13467
A HOME OF YOUR OWN (42) (U)
Dormar (BL)
P: Bob Kellett
D: Jay Lewis

S: Jay Lewis, John Whyte
Bernard Cribbins	Stone Mason
Bill Fraser	Workman
Fred Emney	Mayor
Harry Locke	Gas Foreman
Peter Butterworth	Carpenter
George Benson	Watchman
Ronnie Barker	Cement Mixer
Ronnie Stevens	Architecht
Tony Tanner	Driver
Douglas Ives	Foreman
Richard Briers	Husband
Aubrey Woods	Water Official
Gerald Campion	Glazier
Jack Melford	Engineer
Thorley Walters	Estate Agent

COMEDY "Silent" slapstick misadventures of builders erecting block of flats.

13468
VALLEY OF THE KINGS (serial) (U) *eastman*
AB—Pathe (CFF)
P: Terry Ashwood
D: Frederic Goode
S: Jean Scott Rogers
Kenneth Nash	Peter Marsh
Elizabeth White	Carol Marsh
J. Peter Graeffe	Geoff Lowe
M. Salah El Din	Ramzi
Ray Barrett	Mr Marsh
Gwen Watford	Mrs Marsh
Ahmed Luxor	Ali
Mohammed Abaza	Yussef

13469
1— JACKALS IN THE DESERT (16)

13470
2— THE TRAITOR'S BAIT (18)

13471
3— LOST IN LUXOR (16)

13472
4— THE LAND OF THE DEAD (17)

13473
5— LOST IN A SANDSTORM (16)

13474
6— ORDEAL IN THE DESERT (18)
CHILDREN Egypt. Archaeologist's children thwart youth's plan to upset father's treasure hunt.

13475
MASQUERADE (102) (U) *eastman*
Novus (UA)
P: Michael Relph
D: Basil Dearden
S: (NOVEL) Victor Canning (CASTLE MINERVA)
SC: Michael Relph, William Goldman
Cliff Robertson	David Frazer
Jack Hawkins	Col Drexel
Marisa Mell	Sophie
Michel Piccoli	Sarrassin
Bill Fraser	Dunwoody
Christopher Witty	Prince Jamil
Tutte Lemkow	Paviot
Charles Gray	Benson
John le Mesurier	Sir Robert
Roger Delgardo	Ahmed Ben Faid
Felix Aylmer	Henrickson
Keith Pyott	Gustave
Jose Burgos	El Mono
James Mossman	Himself

CRIME Spain. American helps colonel abduct Arab boy prince.

13476
THE SECRET OF BLOOD ISLAND (84) (X) *eastman*
Hammer (UI)
P: Anthony Nelson Keys
D: Quentin Lawrence
S: John Gilling
Jack Hedley	Sgt Crewe
Barbara Shelley	Elaine
Patrick Wymark	Maj Jocomo
Charles Tingwell	Maj Dryden
Bill Owen	Bludgin
Peter Welch	Richardson
Lee Montague	Levy
Edwin Richfield	O'Reilly
Michael Ripper	Lt Tojoko
Philip Latham	Capt Drake
Glyn Houston	Berry

WAR Malaya. POWs shelter girl secret agent and help her escape from Japanese.

13477
DAYLIGHT ROBBERY (57) (U)
Viewfinder (CFF)
P: John Davis
D: Michael Truman
S: Frank Wells
SC: Dermot Quinn
Trudy Moors	Trudy
Janet Hannington	Janet
Kirk Martin	Kirk
Darryl Read	Darryl
Douglas Robinson	Gangster
John Trenaman	Gangster
Janet Munro	
Zena Walker	
Patricia Burke	
James Villiers	
Norman Rossington	
Gordon Jackson	
Ronald Fraser	

CHILDREN Children locked in store for weekend thwart bank robbers.

13478
COAST OF SKELETONS (91) (U) *tech/scope*
Towers of London (BL)
P: Harry Alan Towers, Oliver A. Unger
D: Robert Lynn
S: (NOVEL) Edgar Wallace (SANDERS OF THE RIVER)
SC: Anthony Scott Veitch, Peter Welbeck
Richard Todd	Harry Sanders
Dale Robertson	A.J. Magnus
Heinz Drache	Janny von Koltze
Marianne Koch	Helga
Elga Andersen	Elizabeth von Koltze
Derek Nimmo	Tom Hamilton
Gabriel Bayman	Charlie Singer
George Leech	Carlo Seton
Gordon Mulholland	Mr Spyker

ADVENTURE Africa. Insurance agent investigates scuttling of American tycoon's diamond dredger and search for sunken gold.

13479
MOZAMBIQUE (97) (U) *tech/scope*
Towers of London (BL)
P: Harry Alan Towers
D: Robert Lynn
S: Peter Welbeck
SC: Peter Yeldham
Steve Cochran	Brad Webster
Hildegarde Nef	Ilona Valdez
Paul Hubschmid	Insp Commarro
Vivvi Bach	Christina
Martin Benson	Da Silva
Dietmar Schonherr	Henderson
George Leech	Carl

Vic Perry	Himself

CRIME American pilot and Scandinavian girl help police solve murder of crook and theft of briefcase.

13480
THE CROOKED ROAD (92) (A)
Argo—Triglav—Trident (Gala)
P: Jack O. Lamont, David Henley
D: Don Chaffey
S: (NOVEL) Morris L. West (THE BIG STORY)
SC: Don Chaffey, J. Garrison
Robert Ryan	Richard Ashley
Stewart Granger	Duke of Orgagna
Nadia Gray	Cosima
Catherine Woodville	Elena
Marius Goring	Harlequin
George Coulouris	Carlos
Robert Rietty	Police Chief

CRIME Balkans. Duke poisons reporter to prevent his exposure as ambezzler of aid funds.

13481
THE UNCLE (87) (U)
Play—Pix (BL)
P: Leonard Davis, Robert Goldston
D: Desmond Davis
S: (NOVEL) Margaret Abrams
SC: Margaret Abrams, Desmond Davis
Rupert Davies	David
Brenda Bruce	Addie
Maurice Denham	Mr Ream
Christopher Ariss	Tom
Robert Duncan	Gus
William Marlowe	Wayne
Ann Lynn	Sally
Barbara Leake	Emma
Helen Fraser	Mary Neame
John Moulder Brown	Jamie

COMEDY 7—year boy has his nephew of the same age spend holiday with him.

13482
THE MEETING (10) (A)
Mamoun Hassan (Bargate)
D:S: Mamoun Hassan
Cleo Bowan	Girl
John Stokes	Man

DRAMA Girl waits for brief glimpse of her captive lover.

13483
FROZEN ALIVE (63) (A) bilingual
Alfa-Créole (Butcher)
P: Arthur Brauner, Ronald Rietti
D: Bernard Knowles
S: Evelyn Frazer
Mark Stevens	Frank
Marianne Koch	Helen
Delphi Lawrence	Joan
Joachim Hansen	Tony
Walter Rilla	Sir Keith
Wolfgang Lukschy	Insp Prentow
Helmuth Weiss	Chairman
John Longden	Prof Hubbard

HORROR Deep-frozen scientist suspected of murdering his wife.

13484
TROUBLED WATERS
Parroch—McCallum (BL)
P: C. Jack Parsons
D: Stanley Goulder
S: Al Rosen
SC: Al Rosen, Tudor Gates
Tab Hunter	
Zena Walker	
Andy Myers	
Michael Goodliffe	

DRAMA Jealous man suspects his son is illegitimate.

1965

JAN

13485
YOUNG CASSIDY (110) (A) *tech*
Sextant (MGM)
P: Robert D. Graff, Robert Emmett Ginna
D: Jack Cardiff, John Ford
S: (BOOK) Sean O'Casey
(MIRROR IN MY HOUSE)
SC: John Whiting
Rod Taylor . . . . Johnny Cassidy
Maggie Smith . . . . Nora
Julie Christie . . . . Daisy Battles
Edith Evans . . . . Lady Gregory
Michael Redgrave . . . . W.B. Yeats
Flora Robson . . . . Mrs Cassidy
Jack Macgowran . . . . Archie
Pauline Delany . . . . Bessie Ballynoy
Philip O'Flynn . . . . Mick Mullen
T.P. McKenna . . . . Tom
Sian Phillips . . . . Ella
Julie Ross . . . . Sara
Robin Sumner . . . . Michael
Donal Donnelly . . . . Undertaker
HISTORY Dublin, 1911. Biography of
idealist who becomes successful playwright
but loses his wife and friends.

13486
LORD JIM (154) (U) *tech/scope*
Columbia—Keep (Col)
P:D:SC: Richard Brooks
S: (NOVEL) Joseph Conrad
Peter O'Toole . . . . Lord Jim
James Mason . . . . Gentleman Brown
Curt Jurgens . . . . Cornelius
Eli Wallach . . . . General
Jack Hawkins . . . . Marlow
Paul Lukas . . . . Stein
Daliah Lavi . . . . Jewel
Akim Tamiroff . . . . Schomberg
Ichizo Itami . . . . Waris
Christian Marquand . . . . . . Officer
Andrew Keir . . . . Brierly
Jack MacGowran . . . . Robinson
Noel Purcell . . . . Capt Chester
Walter Gotell . . . . Capt of Patna
ADVENTURE Malaya, 1900. Merchant Navy
officer redeems cowardice in shipwreck by
leading natives against warlord. (RFP: 1965)

13487
POP GEAR (68) (U) *tech/scope*
USA: GO GO MANIA
A.B. Pathe (WPD)
P: Harry Field
D: Frederic Goode
S: Roger Dunton
Matt Monroe
The Animals
The Rockin' Berries
The Nashville Teens
Billy J. Kramer and the Dakotas
The Fourmost
Sounds Incorporated
Spancer Davis Group
The Beatles
Susan Maugham
The Honeycombs
Herman's Hermits
The Four Pennies
Tommy Quickly and the Remo Four
Peter and Gordon
Billie Davis
Jimmy Savile
MUSICAL Disc jockey comperes performances
of popular songs of 1964.

13488
REPULSION (104) (X)
Tekli (Compton)
P: Gene Gutowski
D:S: Roman Polanski
SC: Roman Polanski, Gerard Brach,
David Stone
Catherine Deneuve . . . . Carol Ledoux
Ian Hendry . . . . Michael
John Fraser . . . . Colin
Patrick Wymark . . . . Landlord
Yvonne Furneaux . . . . Helen Ledoux
Renee Houston . . . . Miss Balch
Valerie Taylor . . . . Mme Denise
James Villiers . . . . John
Helen Fraser . . . . Bridget
Hugh Futcher . . . . Reggie
Mike Pratt . . . . Workman
CRIME Belgian manicurist, revolted by sex,
kills admirer and landlord.

13489
GONKS GO BEAT (92) (U) *eastman*
Titan (AA)
P:S: Peter Newbrook, Robert Hartford-Davis
D: Robert Hartford-Davis
SC: Jimmy Watson
Kenneth Connor . . . . Wilco Roger
Frank Thornton . . . . Mr A&R
Barbara Brown . . . . Helen
Iain Gregory . . . . Steve
Terry Scott . . . . PM
Pamela Donald . . . . Tutor
Reginald Beckwith . . . . Professor
Jerry Desmonde . . . . Great Galaxian
The Long & The Short
The Nashville Teens
Lulu & The Luvvers
The Troles
Ray Lewis & The Trekkers
The Vacqueros
The Graham Bond Organisation
Elaine & Derek
Alan David
MUSICAL Ambassador from space uses love to
promote peace between Balladisle and Beatland.

13490
THE MOOD MAN (22) (U) *eastman*
Harold (UA)
D: Frank Gilpin
Joe Loss and his Orchestra
MUSICAL Dance band plays various numbers.

13491
I'VE GOTTA HORSE (92) (U) *tech/scope*
Windmill (WPD)
P: Larry Parnes, Kenneth Hume
D: Kenneth Hume
S: Kenneth Hume, Larry Parnes
SC: Ronald Wolfe, Ronald Chesney
Billy Fury . . . . Billy
Michael Medwin . . . . Hymie Campbell
Amanda Barrie . . . . Jo
The Bachelors . . . . Themselves
Bill Fraser . . . . Mr Bartholomew
Jon Pertwee . . . . Costumier
Fred Emney . . . . Lord Bentley
Leslie Dwyer . . . . Bert
Peter Gilmore . . . . Jock
Marjorie Rhodes . . . . Mrs Bartholomew
Cal McCord . . . . Whitney
The Gamblers
MUSICAL Pop singer almost misses show
watching pet racehorse in the Derby.

13492
THREE HATS FOR LISA (99) *eastman*
Seven Hills (AA)
P: Jack Hanbury
D: Sidney Hayers
S: Leslie Bricusse
SC: Leslie Bricusse, Talbot Rothwell
Joe Brown . . . . Johnny Howjego
Sophie Hardy . . . . Lisa Milan
Sidney James . . . . Sid Marks
Una Stubbs . . . . Flora
Dave Nelson . . . . Sammy
Peter Bowles . . . . Pepper
Seymour Green . . . . Signor Molfino
Josephine Blake . . . . Miss Penny
Jeremy Lloyd . . . . Officer
Michael Brennan . . . . Sergeant
Eric Barker . . . . Sergeant
MUSICAL Bermondsey docker and taxi driver
help Italian film star steal bowler, busby, and
policeman's helmet.

13493
THE CURSE OF THE FLY (86) (X) *scope*
Lippert (20)
P: Robert L. Lippert, C. Jack Parsons
D: Don Sharp
S: (STORY) George Langelaan (THE FLY)
SC: Harry Spalding
Brian Donlevy . . . . Henri Delambre
George Baker . . . . Martin Delambre
Carole Gray . . . . Patricia Stanley
Yvette Rees . . . . Wan
Michael Graham . . . . Albert Delambre
Rachel Kempson . . . . Mme Fournier
Bert Kwouk . . . . Tai
Jeremy Wilkins . . . . Insp Ranet
Charles Carson . . . . Insp Charas
Stan Simmons . . . . Creature
HORROR Montreal. Asylum escapee weds
Canadian whose father's fourth-dimensional
invention creates monstrosities.

FEB

13494
BE MY GUEST (82) (U)
Three Kings-Harold Shampan Filmusic (RFD)
P:D: Lance Comfort
S: Lyn Fairhurst
David Hemmings . . . . Dave Martin
Avril Angers . . . . Mrs Pucil
Joyce Blair . . . . Wanda
Andrea Monet . . . . Erica Page
David Healy . . . . Milton Bass
Ivor Salter . . . . Herbert Martin
Diana King . . . . Margaret Martin
John Pike . . . . Phil
Stephen Marriott . . . . Ricky
Tony Wager . . . . Artie Clough
Jerry Lee Lewis
Nashville Teens
Zephyrs
Kenny and the Wranglers
Niteshades
Plebs
MUSICAL Brighton. Teenage reporter exposes
producer's attempt to rig beat group contest.

.13495
THE INTELLIGENCE MEN (104) (U) *eastman*
USA: SPYLARKS
Rank (RFD)
P: Hugh Stewart
D: Robert Asher
S: Peter Blackmore
SC: Sid Green, Dick Hills

Eric Morecambe . . . . Eric
Ernie Wise . . . . Ernie Sage
William Franklyn . . . . Col Grant
April Olrich . . . . Mme Petrovna
Gloria Paul . . . . Gina Carlotti
Richard Vernon . . . . Sir Edward Seabrook
David Lodge . . . . Stage-manager
Jacqueline Jones . . . . Karin
Terence Alexander . . . . Reed
Francis Matthews . . . . Thomas
Warren Mitchell . . . . Prozoroff
Brian Oulton . . . . Man
Peter Bull . . . . Phillippe
Joe Melia . . . . Conductor
Sid Green & Dick Hills . . . . Customers
COMEDY Coffee-bar waiter helps MI5 agent
save Russian ballerina from assassination.

13496
SHE (105) (U) *tech/scope*
Hammer (WPD)
P: Michael Carreras
D: Robert Day
S: (NOVEL) H. Rider Haggard
SC: David Chantler
Ursula Andress . . . . Ayesha
Peter Cushing . . . . Maj Horace Holly
Bernard Cribbins . . . . Job
John Richardson . . . . Leo Vincey
Rosenda Monteros . . . . Ustane
Christopher Lee . . . . Billali
Andre Morell . . . . Haumeid
John Maxim . . . . Captain
FANTASY Egypt, 1918. Officer is reincarnated
lover of 2000—year old white queen.

13497
FLEDGLINGS (72) (X)
Unlimited (Contemporary)
P:D:S: Norman Thaddeus Vane
Julia White . . . . Julia
Mike Ross . . . . Mike
Iain Quarrier . . . . Iain
Victor Lowndes . . . . Reev Passmore
DRAMA Chelsea. Men persuade model to give
herself to American producer in return for
finance for their film.

13498
THE IPCRESS FILE (109) (A) *tech/scope*
Lowndes—Steven (RFD)
P: Charles Kasher, Harry Saltzman
D: Sidney J. Furie
S: (NOVEL) Len Deighton
SC: Bill Cannaway, James Doran
Michael Caine . . . . Harry Palmer
Nigel Green . . . . Dalby
Guy Doleman . . . . Major Ross
Sue Lloyd . . . . Jean
Gordon Jackson . . . . Jock Carswell
Frank Gatliff . . . . Bluejay
Aubrey Richards . . . . Radcliffe
Freda Bamford . . . . Alice
Thomas Baptiste . . . . Barney
Peter Ashmore . . . . Sir Robert
Oliver Macgreevy . . . . Housemartin
CRIME Intelligence man unmasks his superior
as the traitor behind the kidnapping of a
scientist.
(BFA 1965:Best British Film, Colour, Pho,
Art Dir.)

13499
THE LITTLE ONES (66) (A)
Goldhawk (Col)
P: Freddie Robertson
D:S: Jim O'Connolly
Dudley Foster . . . . Insp Carter
Derek Francis . . . . Paddy

Kim Smith . . . . Ted
Carl Gonzales . . . . Jackie
Peter Thomas . . . . Father
Jean Marlow . . . . Mother
Derek Newark . . . . Sgt Wilson
Cyril Shaps . . . . Welfare Officer
John Chandos . . . . Lord Brantley
Diane Aubrey . . . . Peggy
DRAMA Police pursue boy and halfcaste
friend to Liverpool when they run away from
cruel parents.

13500
PERSONAL AND CONFIDENTIAL (30) (U)
Merton Park (AA)
P: Jack Greenwood
D: Geoffrey Nethercott
S: James Eastwood
Ellen McIntosh . . . . Marion Corbet
Robert Cartland . . . . Ronald Chadwell
Harry Littlewood . . . . Gibbs
Howard Lang . . . . Abbott
David Morell . . . . Wilson
Geoffrey Toone . . . . . . Sir Joseph Kenton
Billy Milton . . . . Lane
Genine Graham . . . . Betty Hill
CRIME Cabinet minister's assistant framed for
betraying secrets to her lover.

13501
THE HILL (123) (X)
Seven Arts (MGM)
P: Kenneth Hyman
D: Sidney Lumet
S: (PLAY) Ray Rigby, R.S.Allen
SC: Ray Rigby
Sean Connery . . . . Joe Roberts
Harry Andrews . . . . RSM Bert Wilson
Ian Bannen . . . . Sgt Charlie Harris
Alfred Lynch . . . . George Stevens
Ossie Davis . . . . Jacko King
Roy Kinnear . . . . Monty Bartlett
Jack Watson . . . . Jock McGrath
Ian Hendry . . . . Sgt Williams
Michael Redgrave . . . . MO
Norman Bird . . . . Commandant
Neil McCallum . . . . Sgt Burton
Howard Goorney . . . . Walters
WAR Africa, 1942. Prisoners at military
detention camp kill sadistic sergeant who
caused comrade's death.

13502
THE HIDDEN FACE (28) (A)
Merton Park (AA)
P: Jack Greenwood
D: Patrick Dromgoole
S: James Eastwood
Christine Finn . . . . Jane Penshurst
Richard Butler . . . . William Milsom
Alex Macintosh . . . . Crispin
Robert James . . . . Durrant
Vernon Dobtcheff . . . . Strang
Jill Dixon . . . . Anne Milsom
Gretchen Franklin . . . . Rose Jenkins
CRIME Authoress exposes MP who kills
himself, and is herself exposed as his bastard.

13503
THE AMOROUS ADVENTURES OF MOLL
FLANDERS (122) (X) *tech/scope*
Wichester (Par)
P: Marcel Hellman
D: Terence Young
S: (NOVELS) Daniel Defoe (MOLL
FLANDERS; ROXANA; THE LIFE OF
JACK SHEPPARD)
SC: Dennis Cannan, Roland Kibbee
Kim Novak . . . . Moll Flanders

Richard Johnson . . . . Jemmy
Angela Lansbury . . . . Lady Blystone
Vittorio de Sica . . . . Count
Leo McKern . . . . Squint
George Sanders . . . . Banker
Lilli Palmer . . . . Dutchy
Hugh Griffith . . . . Governor
Daniel Massey . . . . Elder Brother
Cecil Parker . . . . Mayor
Roger Livesey . . . . Parson
Jess Conrad . . . . Mohock
Richard Wattis . . . . Jeweller
Derren Nesbitt . . . . Younger Brother
Anthony Dawson . . . . Officer
David Hutcheson . . . . Nobleman
David Lodge . . . . Captain
Mary Merrall . . . . Lady
Reginald Beckwith . . . . Doctor
Liam Redmond . . . . Captain
Peter Butterworth . . . . Grunt
Bernard Lee . . . . Landlord
COMEDY 18th C. Lady's widowed maid weds
banker but leaves him for beloved highwayman.

13504
SPACEFLIGHT IC—1 (63) (A)
Lippert (20)
P: Robert L. Lippert, Jack Parsons
D: Bernard Knowles
S: Harry Spalding
Bill Williams . . . . Mead Ralston
Kathleen Breck . . . . Kate Saunders
John Cairney . . . . Steven Thomas
Donald Churchill . . . . Carl Walcott
Jeremy Longhurst . . . . John Saunders
Linda Marlowe . . . . Helen Thomas
Margo Mayne . . . . Joyce Walcott
Norma West . . . . Jan Ralston
FANTASY 2000. Illness of doctor's wife
causes mutiny on space flight.

13505
ONE MAN BAND (9) (U)
Bob Godfrey (Rom)
D: Bob Godfrey
Bruce Lacey . . . . The Band
COMEDY One man plays many musical
instruments.

MAR

13506
FANATIC (96) (X)
USA: DIE DIE MY DARLING
Hammer—Seven Arts (Col)
P: Anthony Hinds
D: Silvio Narizzano
S: (NOVEL) Anne Balisdell (NIGHTMARE)
SC: Richard Matheson
Tallulah Bankhead . . . . Mrs Trefoile
Stefanie Powers . . . . Patricia Carroll
Peter Vaughan . . . . Harry
Maurice Kaufmann . . . . Alan Glentower
Yootha Joyce . . . . Anna
Donald Sutherland . . . . Joseph
Gwendolyn Watts . . . . Gloria
Robert Dorning . . . . Ormsby
Philip Gilbert . . . . Oscar
CRIME Widowed religious fanatic captures
and tries to kill her dead son's American
fiancee.

13507
JOEY BOY (91) (A)
Temgrange (BL)
P: Frank Launder, Sidney Gilliat,
Leslie Gilliat
D: Frank Launder
S: (NOVEL) Eddie Chapman

SC: Frank Launder, Mike Watts
Harry H. Corbett . . . . Joey Boy Thompson
Stanley Baxter . . Benny the Kid Lindowski
Bill Fraser . . . . Sgt Dobbs
Percy Herbert . . . . Mad George Long
Lance Percival . . . . Clarence Doubleday
Reg Varney . . . . Rabbit Malone
Moira Lister . . . . Lady Thameridge
Derek Nimmo . . . . Lt Hope
Thorley Walters . . . . Colonel
John Arnatt . . . . Brig Chapman
Eric Pohlmann . . . . Farmer
John Phillips . . . . Insp Morgan
Lloyd Lamble . . . . . Sir John Averycorn
Edward Chapman . . . . Tom Hobson
Norman Rossington . . . . . . Corporal
RSM Brittain . . . . Sergeant
COMEDY 1941. Black marketeers, forced to join army, run various rackets.

13508
THE LEGEND OF YOUNG DICK TURPIN (83) (U) *tech*
Walt Disney
P: Bill Anderson, Hugh Attwooll
D: James Neilson
S: Robert Westerby
David Weston . . . . Dick Turpin
Bernard Lee . . . . Jeremiah
George Cole . . . . Mr Evans
Maurice Denham . . . . Mr Fielding
William Franklyn . . . . Tom King
Leonard Whiting . . . . Jimmy the Dip
Roger Booth . . . . Lord Calmsden
William Mervyn . . . . Justice Humphries
Colin Blakeley . . . . Gamekeeper
Richard Pearson . . . . Bailiff
Harry Locke . . . . Jailer
Gladys Henson . . . . Blind Annie
ADVENTURE Period. Young poacher, persecuted by gambling lord, turns highwayman and robs him.

13509
A HIGH WIND IN JAMAICA (103) (A)
deluxe/scope
20th Century Fox
P: John Croydon
D: Alexander Mackendrick
S: (NOVEL) Richard Hughes
SC: Stanley Mann, Ronald Harwood, Debnis Cannan
Anthony Quinn . . . . Capt Chavez
James Coburn . . . . Zac
Dennis Price . . . . Mathias
Lila Kedrova . . . . Rosa
Gert Frobe . . . . Capt Vandervort
Benito Carruthers . . . . Alberto
Kenneth J. Warren . . . . . . Capt Marpole
Nigel Davenport . . . . Mr Thornton
Isabel Dean . . . . Mrs Thornton
Deborah Baxter . . . . Emily Thornton
Viviane Ventura . . . . Margaret Fernandez
Martin Amis . . . . John Thornton
Roberta Tovey . . . . Rachel Thornton
Jeffrey Chandler . . . . Edward Thornton
Karen Flack . . . . Laura Thornton
Dan Jackson . . . . Big One
ADVENTURE 1890, Jamaica. Homeless children returning to England are captured by pirates.

13510
OPERATION CROSSBOW (116) (A)
metro/scope
USA: THE GREAT SPY MISSION
P: Carlo Ponti
D: Michael Anderson
S: Duilio Coletti, Vittoriano Petrilli

SC: Richard Imrie, Derry Quinn, Ray Digby
Sophia Loren . . . . Nora
George Peppard . . . . Lt John Curtis
Trevor Howard . . . . Prof Lindemann
John Mills . . . . Gen Boyd
Richard Johnson . . . . Duncan Sandys
Tom Courtenay . . . . Robert Henshaw
Jeremy Kemp . . . . Phil Bradley
Anthony Quayle . . . . Bamford
Lilli Palmer . . . . Frieda
Paul Henreid . . . . Gen Ziemann
Helmut Dantine . . . . Gen Linz
Richard Todd . . . . WC Kendall
Sylvia Syms . . . . Constance Babington Smith
John Fraser . . . . FL Kenny
Barbara Rutting . . . . Hanna Reitsch
Patrick Wymark . . . . Winston Churchill
Richard Wattis . . . . Charles Sims
Maurice Denham . . . . . .
WAR 1942. Allied officers posing as German scientists sent to Holland to sabotage V2 rocket.

13511
RUNAWAY RAILWAY (55) (U)
Fanfare (CFF)
P: George H. Brown
D: Jan Darnley-Smith
S: Henry Geddes
SC: Michael Barnes
John Moulder-Brown . . . . . Charlie
Kevin Bennett . . . . Arthur
Leonard Brockwell . . . . . . John
Roberta Tovey . . . . Carole
Sydney Tafler . . . . Mr Jones
Ronnie Barker . . . . Mr Galore
Graham Stark . . . . Grample
Hugh Lloyd . . . . Disposals Man
CHILDREN Children thwart closure of local line and foil mail van robbers posing as enthusiasts.

13512
24 HOURS TO KILL (83) (U) *tech/scope*
Grixflag (WPD)
P: Bernard Coote, Harry Alan Towers
D: Peter Bezencenet
S: Peter Welbeck
SC: Peter Yeldham
Lex Barker . . . . Jamie
Mickey Rooney . . . . Norman Jones
Michael Medwin . . . . Tommy
Wolfgang Lukschy . . . . Kurt
Helga Somerfield . . . . Louise
France Anglade . . . . Francoise
Helga Lehner . . . . Helga
Walter Slezak . . . . Malouj
CRIME Beirut. Airline pilots save hostess from kidnap by gold smugglers.

APR

13513
THOSE MAGNIFICENT MEN IN THEIR FLYING MACHINES; OR, HOW I FLEW FROM LONDON TO PARIS IN 25 HRS AND 11 MINUTES (132) *tech/scope* (U)
20th Century Fox
P: Stan Margulies
D: Ken Annakin
S: Jack Davies, Ken Annakin
N: James Robertson Justice
Sarah Miles . . . . Patricia Rawnsley
Stuart Whitman . . . . Orvil Newton
James Fox . . . . Richard Mays
Alberto Sordi . . . . Emilio Ponticelli
Robert Morley . . . . Lord Rawnsley
Gert Frobe . . . . Col Von Holstein
Jean-Pierre Cassel . . . . Pierre DuBois

Irina Demick . . . . . Brigitte/Ingrid/Marlene/
Francois/Yvette/Betty
Eric Sykes . . . . Courtney
Terry-Thomas . . . . Sir Percy Ware-Armitage
Benny Hill . . . . Perkins
Yujiro Ishihara . . . . Yamamoto
Flora Robson . . . . Mother Superior
Red Skelton . . . . Neanderthal Man
Karl Michael Vogler . . . . Capt Rumplestrasse
Sam Wanamaker . . . . George Gruber
Tony Hancock . . . . Harry Popperwell
Eric Barker . . . . Postman
Fred Emney . . . . Colonel Willie
Davy Kaye . . . . Jean
Norman Rossington . . . . . . Asst Fire Chief
Graham Stark . . . . Fireman
William Rushton . . . . Gascoyne Tremayne
Gordon Jackson . . . . McDougal
Zena Marshall . . . . Sophia Ponticelli
Maurice Denham . . . . Skipper
John le Mesurier . . . . Painter
Cicely Courtneidge . . . . Muriel
Millicent Martin . . . . Stewardess
COMEDY 1910. Guards officer and American, rivals for press Lord's daughter, compete in London-Paris air race. (BFA 1965: Best costumes.)

13514
THE BATTLE OF THE VILLA FIORITA (105) (U)
tech/scope
Warner Brothers (WPD)
P:D:SC: Delmer Daves
S: (NOVEL) Rumer Godden
Maureen O'Hara . . . . Moira Clavering
Rossano Brazzi . . . . Lorenzo Tassara
Richard Todd . . . . Darrell Clavering
Phyllis Calvert . . . . Margot
Martin Stephens . . . . Michael Clavering
Elizabeth Dear . . . . Debby Clavering
Olivia Hussey . . . . Donna Tassara
Maxine Audley . . . . Charmian
Ursula Jeans . . . . Lady Anthea
Ettore Manni . . . . Father Rossi
Richard Wattis . . . . Travel Agent
Finlay Currie . . . . MC
Clelia Matania . . . . Celestina
ROMANCE Milan. Rich pianist's daughter helps English girls win their mother back from her father.

13515
THE BIG JOB (88) (U)
Adder (AA)
P: Peter Rogers
D: Gerald Thomas
S: John Antrobus
SC: Talbot Rothwell
Sidney James . . . . George Brain
Sylvia Syms . . . . Myrtle Robbins
Dick Emery . . . . Fred 'Booky' Binns
Joan Sims . . . . Mildred Gamely
Lance Percival . . . . Tim 'Dipper' Day
Jim Dale . . . . Harold
Edina Ronay . . . . Sally Gamely
Deryck Guyler . . . . Sgt
Reginald Beckwith . . . . Registrar
David Horne . . . . Judge
COMEDY Bank robbers leave jail to find tree concealing their loot is now in a police station yard.

13516
YOU MUST BE JOKING ! (100) (U)
Ameran (Col)
P: Charles H. Schneer
D: Michael Winner
S: Michael Winner, Alan Hackney
SC: Alan Hackney
Michael Callan . . . . Lt Tim Morton

Lionel Jeffries . . . . Sgt-Maj McGregor
Denholm Elliott . . . . Capt Tabasco
Wilfrid Hyde White . . . . Gen Lockwood
Bernard Cribbins . . . . Sgt Clegg
James Robertson Justice . . Librarian
Leslie Phillips . . . . Husband
Gabriella Licudi . . . . Annabelle
Patricia Viterbo . . . . Sylvie Tarnet
Terry-Thomas . . . . Maj Foskett
Lee Montague . . . . Sgt Mansfield
Irene Handl . . . . Woman
Richard Wattis . . . . Parkins
Norman Vaughan . . . . Norman Stone
Miles Malleson . . . . Man
Tracy Reed . . . . Poppy
James Villiers . . . . Bill Simpson
Ronald Howard . . . . Cecil
David Jacobs . . . . Himself
COMEDY Soldiers must find six 'British
symbols' within 48 hours.

13517
GAME FOR THREE LOSERS (55) (A)
Merton Park (AA)
P: Jack Greenwood
D: Gerry O'Hara
S: (NOVEL) Edgar Lustgarten
SC: Roger Marshall
Michael Gough . . . . Robert Hilary
Mark Eden . . . . Oliver Marchant
Toby Robins . . . . Frances Challinor
Rachel Gurney . . . . Adele
Allan Cuthbertson . . . . Garsden
Al Mulock . . . . Nick
Roger Hammond . . . . Peter Fletcher
Lockwood West . . . . Justice Tree
Mark Dignam . . . . Attorney General
Catherine Wilmer . . . . Miss Stewart
Anne Pichon . . . . Miss Fawcett
Leslie Sarony . . . . Harley
CRIME MP ruined when he prosecutes
blackmailer who accuses him of seducing
his secretary.

13518
CATCH US IF YOU CAN (91) (U)
USA: HAVING A WILD WEEKEND
Bruton (AA)
P: David Deutsch
D: John Boorman
S: Peter Nichols
Dave Clark . . . . Steve
Barbara Ferris . . . . Dinah
Lenny Davidson . . . . Lenny
Rick Huxley . . . . Rick
Mike Smith . . . . Mike
Denis Payton . . . . Denis
David Lodge . . . . Louis
Robin Bailey . . . . Guy
Yootha Joyce . . . . Nan
David de Keyser . . . . Zissell
Robert Lang . . . . Whiting
Clive Swift . . . . Duffle
Ronald Lacey . . . . Beatnik
MUSICAL Stunt man and poster girl's flight
from exploitation is turned into publicity stunt.

13519
THE BRIGAND OF KANDAHAR (81) (U)
tech/scope
Hammer (WPD)
P: Anthony Nelson Keys
D:S: John Gilling
Ronald Lewis . . . . Lt Case
Oliver Reed . . . . Eli Khan
Duncan Lamont . . . . Col Drewe
Yvonne Romain . . . . Ratina
Catherine Woodville . . . . . . Elsa Connolly
Glyn Houston . . . . Marriott

Sean Lynch . . . . Rattu
Walter Brown . . . . Hitala
Inigo Jackson . . . . Capt Boyd
Jeremy Burnham . . . . Capt Connelly
ADVENTURE Bengal, period. Halfcaste lieut,
unjustly discharged, leads rebels against English.

MAY

13520
THE KNACK . . . and how to get it (84) (X)
Woodfall (UA)
P: Oscar Lewenstein
D: Richard Lester
S: (PLAY) Ann Jellicoe
SC: Charles Wood, Richard Lester
Rita Tushingham . . . . Nancy Jones
Ray Brooks . . . . Tolen
Michael Crawford . . . . Colin
Donal Donnelly . . . . Tom
John Bluthal . . . . Father
Wensley Pithey . . . . Teacher
William Dexter . . . . Owner
Charles Dyer . . . . Man in Booth
Peter Copley . . . . Picture Owner
Dandy Nichols . . . . Landlady
Timothy Bateson . . . . Junkman
George Chisholm . . . . Porter
Bruce Lacey . . . . Assistant
Charles Wood . . . . Soldier
COMEDY Shy teacher learns lodger's knack
with girls and wins young provincial away
from him.

13521
THE PLEASURE GIRLS (88) (X)
Tekli (Compton)
P: Harry Fine
D:S: Gerry O'Hara
Ian McShane . . . . Keith Dexter
Francesca Annis . . . . Sally Feathers
Klaus Kinski . . . . Nikko
Mark Eden . . . . Prinny
Tony Tanner . . . . Paddy
Suzanna Leigh . . . . Dee
Rosemary Nichols . . . . Marion
Anneke Wills . . . . Angela
Coleen Fitzpatrick . . . . Cobber
DRAMA Several affairs of model girl and girls
with whom she shares house.

13522
CURSE OF SIMBA (61) (A)
USA: CURSE OF THE VOODOO
Galaworldfilm—Gordon (Gala)
P: Kenneth Rive
D: Lindsay Shonteff
S: Tony O'Grady
SC: Tony O'Grady, Leigh Vance
Bryant Halliday . . . . Mike Stacey
Dennis Price . . . . Maj Lomas
Lisa Daniely . . . . Janet Stacey
Mary Kerridge . . . . Mother
Ronald Leigh Hunt . . . . Doctor
Jean Lodge . . . . Mrs Lomas
Dennis Alaba Peters . . . . . . Saidi
Tony Thawnton . . . . Radlett
Andy Myers . . . . Tommy Stacey
Beryl Cunningham
Bobby Breen Quintet
HORROR Africa. Big game hunter cursed and
suffers when voodoo chief tortures his bearer.

13523
THE BEDFORD INCIDENT (102) (A)
Bedford (Col)
P: James B. Harris, Richard Widmark
D: James B. Harris
S: (NOVEL) Mark Rascovich
SC: James Poe

Richard Widmark . . . . . . Capt Eric Finland
Sidney Poitier . . . . Ben Munceford
James MacArthur . . . . Ensign Ralston
Martin Balsam . . . . Lt-Cdr Chester Potter
Wally Cox . . . . Sonar man
Eric Portman . . . . Cdr Wolfgang Schrepke
Michael Kane . . . . Cdr Allison
Phil Brown . . . . CMM McKinley
Gary Cockrell . . . . Lt Bascombe
Brian Davis . . . . Lt Beckman
WAR Greenland. USN destroyer's tough
captain causes sinking of Russian submarine,
and his own ship.

13524
WHERE THE SPIES ARE (113) (A)
metro/scope
Val Guest (MGM)
P: Val Guest, Steven Pallos
D: Val Guest
S: (NOVEL) James Leasor (PASSPORT TO
OBLIVION)
SC: Val Guest, Wolf Mankowitz, James Leasor
David Niven . . . . Dr Jason Love
Francoise Dorleac . . . . Vikki
Cyril Cusack . . . . Rosser
John le Mesurier . . . . Macgillivray
Nigel Davenport . . . . Parkington
Eric Pohlmann . . . . Farouk
Paul Stassino . . . . Simmias
Ronald Radd . . . . Stanislaus
Noel Harrison . . . . Jackson
George Pravda . . . . Agent
CRIME Beirut. English GP foils Russian
assassination of prince.

13525
FOUR IN THE MORNING (94) (X)
West One
P: John Morris
D:S: Anthony Simmons
Ann Lynn . . . . Girl
Judi Dench . . . . Wife
Norman Rodway . . . . Husband
Brian Phelan . . . . Boy
Joe Melia . . . . Friend
DRAMA Man picks up singer, young mother
waits for husband, and girl drowns in river.

13526
JOEY AND SAM (20) (U)
Benco
P:D:S: Roy Benson
CHILDREN Adventures of small boy and dog
in the East End.

JUN

13527
DR WHO AND THE DALEKS (83) (U)
tech/scope
Aaru (RFI)
P: Milton Subotsky, Max J. Rosenberg
D: Gordon Fleming
S: (TV SERIAL) Terry Nation (DR WHO)
SC: Milton Subotsky
Peter Cushing . . . . Dr Who
Roy Castle . . . . Ian
Jennie Linden . . . . Barbara
Roberta Tovey . . . . Susan
Barrie Ingham . . . . Alydon
Michael Coles . . . . Ganatus
Geoffrey Toone . . . . Temmosus
Mark Peterson . . . . Elydon
John Bown . . . . Antodus
Yvonne Antrobus . . . . Dyoni
FANTASY Time travellers lead peaceful
race against robot-like creatures.

13528
ROTTEN TO THE CORE (88) (A) scope
Tudor (BL)

P: Roy Boulting
D: John Boulting
S: John Warren, Len Heath
SC: John Warren, Len Heath, Jeffrey Dell, Roy Boulting
Anton Rodgers . . . Randolph Berkeley-Greene
Eric Sykes . . . . William Hunt
Charlotte Rampling . . . . . . Sara Capel
Ian Bannen . . . . Lt Percy Vine
Avis Bunnage . . . . Countess
Dudley Sutton . . . . Jelly Knight
Kenneth Griffith . . . . Lenny the Dip
James Beckett . . . . Scapa Flood
Thorley Walters . . . . Insp Preston
Victor Maddern . . . . Anxious O'Toole
Peter Vaughan . . . . Sir Henry
Raymond Huntley . . . . Governor
Ian Wilson . . . . Chopper Parsons
Kenneth Dight . . . . Dirty Bertie
Barbara Everest . . . . Mrs Dick
Cameron Hall . . . . Admiral
Basil Dignam . . . . General
COMEDY Gang boss dons disguises to steal army payroll.

13529
HOW TO UNDRESS IN PUBLIC WITHOUT UNDUE EMBARRASSMENT (50) (X)
Welbeck (Monarch)
P:D:S: Bob Compton-Bennett
N: Fenella Fielding
Jon Pertwee . . . .
Kenneth Connor . . . .
Zelma Malik . . . .
Reginald Beckwith . . . . . .
Christine Child . . . .
COMEDY History of public undressing, including extracts from earlier films.

13530
THE CITY UNDER THE SEA (84) (U) USA: WARGODS OF THE DEEP *eastman/scope*
AIP-Bruton (AA)
P: George Willoughby, Daniel Haller
D: Jacques Tourneur
S: (POEM) Edgar Allan Poe (CITY IN THE SEA)
SC: Charles Bennett, Louis M. Heyward, David Whittaker
Vincent Price . . . . . .Sir Hugh Tregathion
David Tomlinson . . . Harold Tufnell-Jones
Tab Hunter . . . . Ben Harris
Susan Hart . . . . Jill Tregellis
John le Mesurier . . . . . . Rev Jonathan Ives
Henry Oscar . . . . Mumford
Derek Newark . . . . Dan
Roy Patrick . . . . Simon
Anthony Selby . . . . George
FANTASY Cornwall, 1903. 100-year old smuggler ruling undersea city kidnaps American girl who resembles his wife.

13531
MONSTER OF TERROR (78) (X) USA: DIE MONSTER DIE *pathe/scope*
AIP—Alta Vista (AA)
P: Pat Green
D: Daniel Haller
S: (NOVEL) H.P. Lovecraft (COLOUR OUT OF SPACE)
SC: Jerry Sohl
Boris Karloff . . . . Nahum Witley
Nick Adams . . . . Stephen Reinhart
Freda Jackson . . . . Letitia Witley
Suzan Farmer . . . . Susan Witley
Terence de Marney . . . . Merwyn
Patrick Magee . . . . Dr Henderson
Paul Farrell . . . . Jason

George Moon . . . . Taximan
Gretchen Franklin . . . . Miss Bailey
Billy Milton . . . . Henry
HORROR Cripple used radioactive meteorite to develop plant and insect mutations.

JUL

13532
CUP FEVER (53) (U)
Century (CFF)
P: Roy Simpson
D:S: David Bracknell
Bernard Cribbins . . . . Policeman
David Lodge . . . . Mr Bates
Dermot Kelly . . . . Bodger
Norman Rossington . . . . Driver
Sonia Graham . . . . Mrs Davis
Johnny Wade . . . . Milkman
Denis Gilmore . . . . Skipper
Susan George . . . . Vicky
Jim Morgan . . . . Rocket
Raymond Davis . . . . Denis
Matt Busby; Manchester United Football Team
CHILDREN Manchester. Policeman and footballers help children's team thwarts unscrupulous councillor.

13533
SAN FERRY ANN (55) (U)
Dormar (BL)
P: John G. Berry, Bob Kellett
D: Jeremy Summers
S: Bob Kellett
Wilfrid Brambell . . . . Grandad
David Lodge . . . . Dad
Ron Moody . . . . German
Joan Sims . . . . Mum
Graham Stark . . . . Gendarme
Ronnie Stevens . . . . Hiker
Barbara Windsor . . . . Hiker
Rodney Bewes . . . . Loverboy
Catherine Feller . . . . Lovergirl
Lynn Carol . . . . Grandma
Warren Mitchell . . . . Maitre d'Hotel
Aubrey Woods . . . . Immigration Officer
Hugh Paddick . . . . Traveller
Joan Sterndale Bennett . . . Madame
COMEDY 'Silent' misadventures of British holidaymakers in France.

13534
DARLING . . . (127) (X)
Vic-Appia (AA)
P: Joseph Janni
D: John Schlesinger
S: Frederic Raphael, John Schlesinger, Joseph Janni
SC: Frederic Raphael
Dirk Bogarde . . . . Robert Gold
Laurence Harvey . . . . Miles Brand
Julie Christie . . . . Diana Scott
Jose-Luis de Villalonga . . . . Prince Cesare
Roland Curram . . . . Malcolm
Alex Scott . . . . Sean Martin
Basil Henson . . . . Alec Prosser-Jones
Helen Lindsay . . . . Felicity Prosser-Jones
Tyler Butterworth . . . .William Prosser-Jones
Pauline Yates . . . . Estelle Gold
Hugo Dyson . . . . Matthew Southgate
DRAMA Model marries young, lives with married journalist, has an abortion, becomes depraved, and weds widowed Italian count.
(BFA 1965: Best Actress, Actor, Screenplay, Art Dir; AA1965: Best Actress, Screenplay, Costumes)

13535
THE FACE OF FU MANCHU (94) (U) tech/scope
Hallam (WPD)

P: Harry Alan Towers, Oliver Unger
D: Don Sharp
S: (CHARACTERS) Sax Rohmer
SC: Peter Welbeck
Christopher Lee . . . . Fu Manchu
Nigel Green . . . . Nayland Smith
Joachim Fuchsberger . . . . . . Carl Jansen
Karin Dor . . . . Maria Muller
Tsai Chin . . . . Lin Tang
James Robertson Justice . . . . Sir Charles
Howard Marion Crawford . . Dr Petrie
Walter Rilla . . . . Prof Ernst Muller
Harry Brogan . . . . Prof Gaskell
Poulet Tu . . . . Lotus
Peter Mossbacher . . . . Hanumon
Edwin Richfield . . . . Mandarin
CRIME 1925. Chinese crook kidnaps German biochemist and daughter to distil poison from Tibetan poppies.

13536
THE RETURN OF MR MOTO (71) (A)
Lippert (20)
P: Robert L. Lippert, Jack Parsons
D: Ernest Morris
S: (CHARACTERS) John P. Marquand
SC: Fred Eggers, Randall Hood
Henry Silva . . . . Mr Moto
Terence Longdon . . . . . . Jonathan Westering
Suzanne Lloyd . . . . Maxine Powell
Martin Wyldeck . . . . Dargo
Marne Maitland . . . . Wasir Hussein
Harold Kasket . . . . Shahrdar
Henry Gilbert . . . . David Lennox
Brian Coburn . . . . Magda
Stanley Morgan . . . . Insp Halliday
CRIME Interpol agent foils ex-Nazi's syndicate seeking to sabotage Middle East oil concession.

13537
TEN LITTLE INDIANS (91) (A)
Tenlit (WPD)
P: Harry Alan Towers, Harry M. Popkin
D: George Pollock
S: (NOVEL) Agatha Christie (TEN LITTLE NIGGERS)
SC. Peter Yeldham, Peter Welbeck
Hugh O'Brian . . . . Hugh Lombard
Shirley Eaton . . . . Ann Clyde
Fabian . . . . Mike Raven
Leo Genn . . . . Gen Mandrake
Stanley Holloway . . . . William Blore
Marianne Hoppe . . . . Frau Grohmann
Wilfrid Hyde White . . . . Judge Cannon
Daliah Lavi . . . . Ilona Bergen
Dennis Price . . . . Dr Armstrong
Mario Adorf . . . . Herr Grohmann
CRIME Austrian Alps. Eight undetected murderers invited to isolated house and killed by their unknown host.

13538
HELP! (92) (U) *eastman*
Walter Shenson-Subafilms (UA)
P: Walter Shenson
D: Richard Lester
S: Marc Behm
SC: Marc Behm, Charles Wood
John Lennon . . . . John
Paul McCartney . . . . Paul
Ringo Starr . . . . Ringo
George Harrison . . . . George
Leo McKern . . . . Clang
Eleanor Bron . . . . Ahme
Victor Spinetti . . . . Prof Foot
Roy Kinnear . . . . Algernon
John Bluthal . . . . Bhuta
Patrick Cargill . . . . Supt
Alfie Bass . . . . Doorman

Warren Mitchell . . . . Abdul
Peter Copley . . . . Jeweller
Bruce Lacey . . . . Lawnmower
MUSICAL Indians pursue "The Beatles" to
sacrifice their drummer to a goddess. (Top
Moneymaker: 1965).

13539
LICENSED TO KILL (97) (A) *eastman*
USA: THE SECOND BEST SECRET AGENT
IN THE WHOLE WIDE WORLD
Alistair (GEFD)
P: S.H.J. Ward
D: Lindsay Shonteff
S: Lindsay Shonteff, Howard Griffiths
Tom Adams . . . . Charles Vine
Karel Stepanek . . . . Henrik Jacobsen
Veronica Hurst . . . . Julia Lindberg
Peter Bull . . . . Masterman
John Arnatt . . . . Rockwell
Francis de Wolff . . . . Walter Pickering
Felix Felton . . . . Tetchkinov
George Pastell . . . . Commissar
Judy Huxtable . . . . computer Girl
Billy Milton . . . . Wilson
Tony Wall . . . . Sadistikov
Stuart Saunders . . . . Inspector
CRIME Secret agent thwarts spies seeking
scientist's anti-gravity machine.

13540
THE NANNY (91) (X)
Hammer-Seven Arts (WPD)
P:SC: Jimmy Sangster
D: Seth Holt
S: (NOVEL) Evelyn Piper
Bette Davis . . . . Nanny
Wendy Craig . . . . Virginia Fane
Jill Bennett . . . . Penelope Fane
James Villiers . . . . Bill Fane
William Dix . . . . Joey Fane
Pamela Franklin . . . . Bobby
Jack Watling . . . . Dr Medman
Maurice Denham . . . . Dr Beamaster
Alfred Burke . . . . Dr Wills
Nora Gordon . . . . Mrs Griggs
CRIME Parents do not believe their ten year old
son's story that his nurse is trying to kill him.

13541
CHANGE PARTNERS (63) (A)
Merton Park (AA)
P: Jack Greenwood
D: Robert Lynn
S: Donal Giltinian
Zena Walker . . . . Anna Arkwright
Kenneth Cope . . . . Joe Trent
Basil Henson . . . . Ricky Gallen
Anthony Dawson . . . . Ben Arkwright
Jane Barrett . . . . Betty Gallen
Pamela Ann Davey . . . . . . Jean
Peter Bathurst . . . . McIvor
Josephine Pritchard . . . . . . Sally Morrison
CRIME Alcoholic's wife helps partner kill him
and his own wife.

13542
THE SKULL (83) (X) *tech/scope*
Amicus (Par)
P: Milton Subotsky, Max Rosenberg
D: Freddie Francis
S: (STORY) Robert Bloch (THE SKULL OF
THE MARQUIS DE SADE)
SC: Milton Subotsky
Peter Cushing . . . . Prof Christopher Maitland
Patrick Wymark . . . . Marco
Christopher Lee . . . . . Sir Matthew Phillips
Jill Bennett . . . . Jane Maitland
Nigel Green . . . . Wilson
Michael Gough . . . . Auctioneer

George Coulouris . . . . Dr Londe
Patrick Magee . . . . Dr
Peter Woodthorpe . . . . Travers
April Olrich . . . . Girl
HORROR Prof falls under influence of evil
spirit inhabiting skull.

13543
OUR LOVE IS SLIPPING AWAY (8) *color*
Searchlight (Monarch)
D: Arnold Louis Miller
The Ivy League
MUSICAL

AUG

13544
MISTER LEWIS (16) (U)
Malcolm Craddock (Balch)
D:S: Malcolm Craddock
Jonathan Burn . . . . Mr Lewis
COMEDY Clerk kills fellow lodger for
occupying bathroom too long.

13545
THE HEROES OF TELEMARK (131) (U)
eastman/scope
Benton (RFD)
P: S. Benjamin Fisz
D: Anthony Mann
S: (BOOKS) Knut Haukelid (SKIES AGAINST
THE ATOM) John Drummond (BUT FOR
THESE MEN)
SC: Ivan Moffat, Ben Barzman
Kirk Douglas . . . . Dr Rolf Pedersen
Richard Harris . . . . Knut Straud
Ulla Jacobsson . . . . Anna
Michael Redgrave . . . . Uncle
David Weston . . . . Arne
Anton Diffring . . . . Maj Frick
Eric Porter . . . . Terboven
Mervyn Johns . . . . Col Wilkinson
Jennifer Hilary . . . . Sigrid
Roy Dotrice . . . . Jenson
Barry Jones . . . . Prof Logan
Ralph Michael . . . . Nilssen
Geoffrey Keen . . . . Gen Bolts
Maurice Denham . . . . Doctor
David Davies . . . . Captain
Karel Stepanek . . . . Hartmuller
George Murcell . . . . Sturmfuhrer
Gerard Heinz . . . . Erhardt
WAR Norway, 1942. Resistance workers foil
German plan to move heavy water plant to
Berlin.

13546
BUNNY LAKE IS MISSING (107) *scope* (X)
Wheel (Col)
P:D: Otto Preminger
S: (NOVEL) Evelyn Piper
SC: John Mortimer, Penelope Mortimer
Laurence Olivier . . . . Supt Newhouse
Carol Lynley . . . . Ann Lake
Keir Dullea . . . . Steven Lake
Noel Coward . . . . Horatio Wilson
Martita Hunt . . . . Ada Ford
Anna Massey . . . . Elvira Smollett
Clive Revill . . . . Sgt Andrews
Lucie Mannheim . . . . Cook
Finlay Currie . . . . Dollmaker
Adrienne Corri . . . . Dorothy
Megs Jenkins . . . . Sister
Delphi Lawrence . . . . Mother
Jill Melford . . . . Teacher
Richard Wattis . . . . Clerk
Victor Maddern . . . . Taxidriver
Percy Herbert . . . . PC
Fred Emney . . . . Man
The Zombies; Tim Brinton
CRIME Inspector helps American search for
his unmarried sister's missing daughter.

13547
THE ALPHABET MURDERS (90) (U)
MGM British
P: Lawrence P. Bachmann
D: Frank Tashlin
S: (NOVEL) Agatha Christie (THE ABC
MURDERS)
SC: David Pursall, Jack Seddon
Tony Randall . . . . Hercule Poirot
Anita Ekberg . . . . Amanda Beatrice Cross
Robert Morley . . . . Capt Hastings
Maurice Denham . . . . Insp Japp
Guy Rolfe . . . . Duncan Doncaster
Sheila Allen . . . . Lady Diane
James Villiers . . . . Franklin
Julian Glover . . . . Don Fortune
Grazina Frame . . . . Betty Barnard
Clive Morton X
Cyril Luckham . . . . Sir Carmichael Clarke
Richard Wattis . . . . Wolf
Austin Trevor . . . . Judson
Margaret Rutherford . . . . . . Miss Marple
COMEDY French tec prevents poison dart killer
from murdering his way through alphabet.

13548
THE MURDER GAME (76) (A)
Lippert (20)
P: C. Jack Parsons
D: Sidney Salkow
S: Irving Yergin
SC: Harry Spalding
Marla Landi . . . . Marie Aldrich
Trader Faulkner . . . . Chris Aldrich
Ken Scott . . . . Steve Baldwin
Conrad Phillips . . . . Peter Shanley
Gerald Sim . . . . Larry Landstrom
Duncan Lamont . . . . Insp Telford
Rosamund Greenwood . . . . . Mrs Potter
Victor Brooks . . . . Rev Francis Hood
Ballard Berkeley . . . . Sir Colin Chalmers
Clement Freud . . . . Croupier
CRIME Indured engineer, suspecting wife and
her blackmailing husband of planning his murder,
frames them for his own.

13549
STRANGLER'S WEB (55) (A)
Merton Park (AA)
P: Jack Greenwood
D: John Moxey
S: George Baxt
John Stratton . . . . Lewis Preston
Pauline Munro . . . . Melanie
Griffith Jones . . . . Jackson Delacourt
Gerald Harper . . . . Insp Murray
Maurice Hedley . . . . Amos Colfax
Michael Balfour . . . . John Vichelski
Pauline Boty . . . . Nell Pretty
Patricia Burke . . . . Norma Brent
CRIME Solicitor suspects disfigured actor of
strangling his bigamous wife.

SEP

13550
THE LIFT (90) (X)
Libra (NR)
P: Julius Rascheff
D:S: Burt Krancer
Helen Ryan . . . . Margot Maxwell
Alastair Williamson . . . . Mr Maxwell
Holly Doone . . . . Jane Maxwell
Job Stewart . . . . Joe
Shirley Rogers . . . . Fanny
DRAMA Ambitious youth has affairs with
millionaire's two daughters.

13551
DRACULA — PRINCE OF DARKNESS (90)
(X) *tech/scope*

Hammer (WPD)
P: Anthony Nelson Keys
D: Terence Fisher
S: (CHARACTERS) Bram Stoker (DRACULA)
SC: John Sansom, Anthony Hinds

Christopher Lee	Count Dracula
Barbara Shelley	Helen Kent
Andrew Keir	Father Sandor
Francis Matthews	Charles Kent
Suzan Farmer	Diana Kent
Charles Tingwell	Alan Kent
Thorley Walters	Ludwig
Walter Brown	Brother Mark
Philip Latham	Klove
George Woodbridge	Landlord

HORROR Carpathia, 19thC. Butler uses tourist's blood to revive his vampiric master.

13552
UP JUMPED A SWAGMAN (88) (U)
tech/scope
Ivy (Elstree)
P: Andrew Mitchell
D: Christopher Miles
S: Lewis Greifer

Frank Ifield	Dave Kelly
Annette Andre	Patsy
Ronald Radd	Harry King
Richard Wattis	Lever
Suzy Kendall	Melissa Smythe-Fury
Donal Donnelly	Bockeye
Bryan Moseley	Jojo
Martin Miller	Herman
Harvey Spencer	Luigi
Carl Jaffe	Analyst
Cyril Shaps	Phil Myers

MUSICAL Clothes dealer uses Australian singer's flat to rob jeweller.

13553
SKY WEST AND CROOKED (102) (A) *eastman*
USA: GIPSY GIRL
John Mills (RFD)
P: Jack Hanbury
D: John Mills
S: (NOVEL) John Prebble (BATS WITH BABY FACES)
SC: John Prebble, Mary Hayley Bell

Hayley Mills	Brydie White
Ian McShane	Roibin
Laurence Naismith	Edwin Dacres
Geoffrey Bayldon	Rev Philip Moss
Annette Crosbie	Mrs Whyte
Norman Bird	Cheeseman
Hamilton Dyce	Bill Slim
Pauline Jameson	Mrs Moss
Rachel Thomas	Grandma
Judith Furse	Mrs Rigby

DRAMA Mentally-retarded teenager falls in love with gypsy.

13554
RETURN FROM THE ASHES (104) *scope*
Mirisch (UA)
P: Lewis J. Rachmil, J. Lee Thomspon
D: J. Lee Thompson
S: (NOVEL) Hubert Monteilhe
SC: Julius J. Epstein, Charles Blair

Maximilian Schell	Stanislaus Pilgrin
Samatha Eggar	Fabi
Ingrid Thulin	Dr Michele Wolf
Herbert Lom	Dr Charles Bovard
Talitha Pol	Claudine
Vladek Sheybal	Manager
Jacques Brunius	Detective
Andre Maranne	Detective
Yvonne Andre	Woman
John Serret	Man

CRIME Paris. Polish chess player and step-daughter plot to murder his wife for her inheritance.

13555
THE SECRET OF MY SUCCESS (96) metro/scope (A)
MGM British
P: Andrew & Virginia Stone
D:SC: Andrew Stone

Shirley Jones	Marigold Marado
Stella Stevens	Violet Lawson
Honor Blackman	Baroness von Lukenberg
James Booth	Arthur Tate
Lionel Jeffries	Inspector Hobart/Baron von Lukenberg/President Esteda/Earl of Aldershot
Amy Dalby	Mrs Tate
Joan Hickson	Mrs Pringle
Robert Barnete	Col Armandez

COMEDY Policeman's rise to success by proving murderous females innocent.

OCT
13556
A STUDY IN TERROR (95) (X) *eastman*
USA: FOG
Compton-Tekli-Sir Nigel (Compton)
P: Herman Cohen, Henry E. Lester
D: James Hill
S: (CHARACTERS) Arthur Conan Doyle
SC: Donald Ford, Derek Ford

John Neville	Sherlock Holmes
Donald Houston	Dr John Watson
John Fraser	Lord Edward Carfax
Anthony Quayle	Dr Murray
Barbara Windsor	Annie Chapman
Robert Morley	Mycroft Holmes
Cecil Parker	Prime Minister
Georgia Brown	Singer
Barry Jones	Duke of Shires
Adrienne Corri	Angela Osborne
Frank Finlay	Insp Lestrade
Judi Dench	Sally
Charles Regnier	Joseph Beck
Dudley Foster	Home Secretary
Peter Carsten	Max Steiner
Terry Downes	Chunky

CRIME 1880. Detective unmasks Jack the Ripper, murderer of Whitechapel Prostitutes.

13557
THE EARLY BIRD (98) (U) *eastman*
Rank (RFD)
P. Hugh Stewart
D: Robert Asher
S: Jack Davies, Norman Wisdom, Eddie Leslie, Henry Blyth

Norman Wisdom	Norman Pitkin
Edward Chapman	Grimsdale
Jerry Desmonde	Hunter
Paddie O'Neil	Mrs Hoskins
Bryan Pringle	Austin
Richard Vernon	Sir Roger
John le Mesurier	Col Foster
Penny Morell	Miss Curry
Frank Thornton	Doctor
Harry Locke	Commissionaire

COMEDY Milkman and small dairy owner fight large combine.

13558
HE WHO RIDES A TIGER (103) (A)
David Newman (BL)
P: David Newman
D: Charles Crichton
S: Trevor Peacock

Tom Bell	Peter Rayston
Judi Dench	Joanne
Paul Rogers	Supt Taylor
Kay Walsh	Mrs Woodley
Ray McAnally	Orphanage Supt
Jeremy Spenser	The Panda
Peter Madden	Peepers Woodley

Inigo Jackson	Sgt Scott
Annette Andre	Julie
Edina Ronay	Anna
Ralph Michael	Carter
Naomi Chance	Lady Cleveland
The Rapiers	

CRIME Unmarried mother working in orphanage learns the man she loves is a burglar.

13559
DEAD MAN'S CHEST (59) (U)
Merton Park (AA)
P: Jack Greenwood
D: Patrick Dromgoole
S: Donal Giltinian

John Thaw	David Jones
Ann Firbank	Mildred Jones
John Meillon	Johnnie Gordon
John Collin	Insp Briggs
Peter Bowles	Joe
John Abineri	Arthur
Arthur Brough	Groves
Graham Crowden	Murchie

CRIME Reporter fakes colleague's murder to expose weakness of circumstantial evidence.

13560
CARRY ON COWBOY (95) (A) *eastman*
Adder (AA)
P: Peter Rogers
D: Gerald Thomas
S: Talbot Rothwell

Sidney James	Rumpo Kid
Kenneth Williams	Judge Burke
Jim Dale	Marshal P. Knutt
Charles Hawtrey	Big Heap
Joan Sims	Belle
Angela Douglas	Annie Oakley
Percy Herbert	Charlie
Bernard Bresslaw	Little Heap
Davy Kaye	Josh
Peter Butterworth	Doc
Sydney Bromley	Sam
Jon Pertwee	Sheriff Oakley
Edina Ronay	Dolores

COMEDY America, period. Girl helps sanitary engineer thwart outlaw who shot her father.

13561
RASPUTIN THE MAD MONK (91) (A)
deluxe/scope
Hammer Seven Arts (WPD)
P: Anthony Nelson Keys
D: Don Sharp
S: Anthony Hinds

Christopher Lee	Rasputin
Barbara Shelley	Sonia
Richard Pasco	Dr Zargo
Francis Matthews	Ivan
Suzan Farmer	Venessa
Dinsdale Landen	Peter
Renee Asherson	Tsarina
Joss Ackland	Bishop
Robert Duncan	Tsarvitch
John Bailey	Physician

HISTORY Russia, 1905. Ex-monk uses hypnotism to attain power at court.

13562
INVASION (82) (U)
Merton Park (AA)
P: Jack Greenwood
D: Alan Bridges
S: Robert Holmes
SC: Roger Marshall

Edward Judd	Dr Vernon
Yoko Tani	Lystrian Leader
Valerie Gearon	Dr Claire Harlan
Lyndon Brook	Brian Carter
Tsai Chin	Nurse Lim
Eric Young	Lystrian Man

Barrie Ingham . . . . Maj Muncaster
Glyn Houston . . . . Sgt Draycott
Anthony Sharp . . . . Lawrence Blackburn
Jean Lodge . . . . Barbara Gough
Peter Sinclair . . . . Old Joe
FANTASY People from another planet crash near
hospital and their prisoner escapes.

13563
CUCKOO PATROL (76) (U)
Eternal (GN)
P: Maurice J. Wilson
D: Duncan Wood
S: Freddie and the Dreamers
SC: Lew Schwarz
Freddie and the Dreamers . . Themselves
Kenneth Connor . . . . Willoughby Wick
Victor Maddern . . . . Dicko
John le Mesurier . . . . Gibbs
Arthur Mullard . . . . Yossle
Ernest Clark . . . . Marshall
Basil Dignam . . . . Snodgrass
Michael Brennan . . . . Superman
Peggy Ann Clifford . . . . . Scout Mistress
Jack Lambert . . . . Inspector
Vic Wise . . . . Moley
COMEDY Misadventures of Boy Scouts at
summer camp involving wrestlers, Girl Guides,
and thieves.

NOV
13564
SANDS OF THE KALAHARI (119) (A)
eastman/scope
Pendennis (Par-Embassy)
P: Joseph E. Levine, Cy Endfield, Stanley Baker
D:SC: Cy Endfield
S: (NOVEL) William Mulvihill
Stanley Baker . . . . Bain
Stuart Whitman . . . . O'Brien
Susannah York . . . . Grace
Harry Andrews . . . . Grimmelman
Theodore Bikel . . . . Dr Bondarahkai
Nigel Davenport . . . . Sturdevant
Barry Lowe . . . . Detjens
ADVENTURE Africa. Private plane carrying
English woman, alcoholic, Lebanese doctor,
German, and gunman crashes near baboon
colony.

13565
DATELINE DIAMONDS (70) (U)
Viscount (RFD)
P: Harold Shampan, Harry Benn
D: Jeremy Summers
S: Harold Shampan
SC: Tudor Gates
William Lucas . . . . Maj Fairclough
Kenneth Cope . . . . Lester Benson
George Mikell . . . . Paul Verlekt
Conrad Phillips. . . . . Tom Jenkins
Patsy Rowlands . . . . Mrs Edgecomb
Burnell Tucker . . . . Dale Meredith
Anna Carteret . . . . Gay Jenkins
Vanda Godsell . . . . Mrs Jenkins
Gertan Klauber . . . . Meyerhof
The Small Faces; The Chantelles; Kiki Dee;
Mark Richardson; Kenny Everett.
MUSICAL Cashiered explosives expert blackmails
pop group manager into using pirate radio ship to
smuggle stolen gems.

13566
LIFE AT THE TOP (117) (X)
Romulus (Col)
P: James Woolf, William Kirby
D: Ted Kotcheff
S: (NOVEL) John Braine
SC: Mordecai Richler
Laurence Harvey . . . . Joe Lampton

Jean Simmons . . . . Susan Lampton
Honor Blackman . . . . Norah Hauxley
Michael Craig . . . . Mark
Donald Wolfit . . . . Abe Brown
Robert Morley . . . . Tiffield
Margaret Johnston . . . . Sybil
Allan Cuthbertson . . . . George Aisgill
Ambrosine Philpotts . . . . . . Mrs Brown
Nigel Davenport . . . . Mortram
George A. Cooper . . . . Graffham
Paul Whitsun Jones . . . . Keatley
Ian Shand . . . . Ralph Hethersett
DRAMA Mill-owner's son-in-law elected to local
council has affair with tv star.

13567
THE SPY WHO CAME IN FROM THE COLD
(112) (A)
Salem (Par)
P:D: Martin Ritt
S: (NOVEL) John le Carre
SC: Paul Dehn, Guy Trosper
Richard Burton . . . . Alec Leamas
Claire Bloom . . . . Nan Perry
Oskar Werner . . . . Fiedler
Sam Wanamaker . . . . Peters
Peter Van Eyck . . . . Hans-Dieter Mundt
George Voskovec . . . . Defence Attorney
Rupert Davies . . . . Smiley
Cyril Cusack . . . . Control
Michael Hordern . . . . Ashe
Robert Hardy . . . . Carlton
Bernard Lee . . . . Patmore
Beatrix Lehmann . . . . President
Esmond Knight . . . . Judge
Niall McGinnis. . . . . Guard
Warren Mitchell . . . . Zanfrello
Kathy Keeton . . . . Stripper
CRIME Berlin. British spy poses as traitor to
foil Communist agent. (BFA 1966: Best British
Film, Actor, B & W Pho, B & W Art Dir.)

13568
DOCTOR IN CLOVER (101) (A) eastman
Rank (RFD)
P: Betty E. Box
D: Ralph Thomas
S: (NOVEL) Richard Gordon
SC: Jack Davies
Leslie Phillips . . . . Dr Gaston Grimsdyke
James Robertson Justice . Sir Lancelot Spratt
Shirley Anne Field . . . . Nurse Bancroft
John Fraser . . . . Dr Miles Grimsdyke
Joan Sims . . . . Matron Sweet
Arthur Haynes . . . . Tarquin Wendover
Elizabeth Ercy . . . . Jeannine
Fenella Fielding . . . . Tatiana Rubikov
Jeremy Lloyd . . . . Lambert Symington
Noel Purcell . . . . O'Malley
Robert Hutton . . . . Rock Stewart
Eric Barker . . . . Prof Halfbeck
Terry Scott . . . . Robert
Alfie Bass . . . . Fleming
Norman Vaughan . . . . TV Commentator
Ronnie Stevens . . . . TV Producer
Suzan Farmer . . . . Nurse Holiday
Bill Kerr . . . . Digger
Roddy Maude-Roxby . . . . . Tristram
COMEDY Philandering doctor on hospital
refresher course falls for French physiotherapist.

13569
OTHELLO (166) (A) tech/scope
BHE (Eagle)
P: Anthony Havelock-Allan, John Brabourne
D: Stuart Burge
S: (PLAY) William Shakespeare
Laurence Olivier . . . . Othello
Maggie Smith . . . . Desdemona

Joyce Redman . . . . Emilia
Frank Finlay . . . . Iago
Derek Jacobi . . . . Cassio
Robert Lang . . . . Roderigo
Kenneth Mackintosh . . . . . . Lodovico
Anthony Nicholls . . . . Brabantio
Sheila Reid . . . . Bianca
Michael Turner . . . . Gratiano
Edward Hardwicke . . . . Montano
Harry Lomax . . . . Duke
Roy Holder . . . . Clown
DRAMA Venice, period. Jealous Moor strangles
wife (National Theatre stage production).

13570
BORN FREE (95) (U) tech/scope
Open Road-Atlas-Highroad (Col)
P: Carl Foreman, Sam Jaffe, Paul Radin
D: James Hill
S: (BOOKS) Joy Adamson
SC: Gerald L.C.Copley
Virginia McKenna . . . . Joy Adamson
Bill Travers . . . . George Adamson
Geoffrey Keen . . . . Comm Kendall
Peter Luckoye . . . . Nuru
Omar Chambati . . . . Makkede
Bill Godden . . . . Sam
Bryan Epsom . . . . Baker
Robert Cheetham . . . . Ken
Robert Young . . . . James
HISTORY Kenya. Game warden and wife rear
lion cub and then train her to return to the
wild (RFP: 1966; AA1966: Best Song, Score).

13571
1812 (18) (U) eastman
Film Facilities (Col)
P:D:SC: Stan Strangeway
S: (MUSIC) Peter Tchaikovsky
Eva Brett . . . . Girl
MUSICAL Napoleon's Russian campaign
reenacted with toy soldiers.

13572
EMMA (13) (U)
Midas (Border)
P:D:S: Anthony Perry
DRAMA Small girl's games in Highgate
cemetery.

13573
THE LIQUIDATOR (104) (A) metro/scope
Leslie Elliott (MGM)
P: Jon Pennington
D: Jack Cardiff
S: (NOVEL) John Gardner
SC: Peter Yeldham
Rod Taylor . . . . Boysie Oakes
Trevor Howard .. . . Col Mostyn
Jill St John . . . . Iris Mackintosh
Wilfrid Hyde White . . . . Chief
Akim Tamiroff . . . . Sheriek
David Tomlinson . . . . Quadrant
Eric Sykes . . . . Griffen
Gabriella Licudi . . . . Corale
John le Mesurier . . . . Chekhov
Derek Nimmo . . . . Fly
Jeremy Lloyd . . . . Man
Jennifer Jayne . . . . Janice Benedict
Betty McDowell . . . . Frances Anne
Colin Gordon . . . . Vicar
Richard Wattis . . . . Instructor
Tony Wright . . . . Control
CRIME Reluctant agent foils spy plot to assassinate
Duke of Edinburgh.

13574
THE MARCH OF THE MOVIES (73) (U)
New Realm
P:D: E.J. Fancey

S: Lottie Teasdale
N: Ben Lyon
COMPILATION History of films, mostly
American.

13575
PASSAGE OF LOVE (91) (A) retitled:
I WAS HAPPY HERE
USA: TIME LOST AND TIME REMEMBERED
Partisan (RFD)
P: Roy Millichip
D: Desmond Davis
S: (STORY) Edna O'Brien (A WOMAN BY
THE SEASIDE)
SC: Edna O'Brien, Desmond Davis
Sarah Miles . . . . Cass Langdon
Cyril Cusack . . . . Hogan
Julian Glover . . . . Dr Matthew Langdon
Sean Caffrey . . . . Colin Foley
Marie Kean . . . . Barkeeper
Eve Belton . . . . Kate
Cardew Robinson . . . . Gravedigger
ROMANCE Ireland. Girl leaves her husband and
tries to take up with her affianced ex-sweetheart.

13576
SLAG'S PLACE (27) (U)
David Naden (Amanda)
P: Jane Wood
D:S: David Naden, Gwyneth Furdivall
CHILDREN Purfleet. Children explore deserted
house by river.

13577
PROMISE HER ANYTHING (97) (A) *tech*
Seven Arts (Par)
P: Stanley Rubin
D: Arthur Hiller
S: Arne Sultan, Marvin Worth
SC: William Peter Blatty
Warren Beatty . . . . Harley Rummell
Leslie Caron . . . . Michele O'Brien
Bob Cummings . . . . Dr Philip Brock
Hermione Gingold . . . . Mrs Luce
Keenan Wynn . . . . Angelo Carelli
Lionel Stander . . . . Sam
Cathleen Nesbitt . . . . Mrs Brock
Asa Maynor . . . . Rusty
Michael Bradley . . . . John Thomas
Bessie Love . . . . Woman

Warren Mitchell . . . . Panellist
Sydney Tafler . . . . Panellist
Margaret Nolan . . . . Stripper
Vivienne Ventura . . . . Stripper
Ferdy Mayne . . . . Fettucini
George Moon . . . . Dancer
Michael Chaplin . . . . Beatnick
COMEDY Greenwich Village. Strip movie maker
loves French window who loves pediatrician who
hates babies.

DEC
13578
THUNDERBALL (130) (A) *tech/scope*
Eon (UA)
P: Kevin McClory
D: Terence Young
S: (NOVEL) Ian Fleming (STORY) Ian Fleming,
Kevin McClory, Jack Whittingham
SC: Richard Maibaum, John Hopkins
Sean Connery . . . . James Bond
Claudine Auger . . . . Domino
Adolfo Celi . . . . Emilio Largo
Luciana Paluzzi . . . . Fiona
Rik Van Nutter . . . . Felix Leiter
Bernard Lee . . . . M
Martine Beswick . . . . Paula
Guy Doleman . . . . Count Lippe
Molly Peters . . . . Patricia
Desmond Llewellyn . . . . . . Q
Lois Maxwell . . . . Miss Moneypenny
Roland Culver . . . . Foreign Secretary
Earl Cameron . . . . Pinder
Paul Stassino . . . . Palazzi
Reginald Beckwith . . . . Kenniston
CRIME Spy and frogmen thwart a crime
syndicate's plan to steal atom bombs and hold
cities to ransom. (AA 1965: Best Special Effects;
Top Moneymaker 1966).

13579
THE PLAGUE OF THE ZOMBIES (91) (X) *tech*
Hammer (WPD)
P: Anthony Nelson Keys
D: John Gilling
S: Peter Bryan
Andre Morell . . . . Sir James Forbes
Diana Clare . . . . Sylvia Forbes
John Carson . . . . Clive Hamilton
Alex Davion . . . . Denver

Jacqueline Pearce . . . . Alice Tompson
Brook Williams . . . . Dr Peter Tompson
Michael Ripper . . . . Sgt Swift
Marcus Hammond . . . . Martinus
Dennis Chinnery . . . . PC Christian
Roy Royston . . . . Vicar
HORROR Cornwall, 1860. Professor thwarts squire
using voodoo to revive corpses to work his tin
mine.

13580
THE REPTILE (91) (X) *tech*
Hammer (WPD)
P: Anthony Nelson Keys
D: John Gilling
S: Anthony Hinds
Noel Willman . . . . Dr Franklyn
Ray Barrett . . . . Harry Spalding
Jennifer Daniel . . . . Valerie Spalding
Jacqueline Pearce . . . . Anna Franklyn
Michael Ripper . . . . Tom Bailey
John Laurie . . . . Mad Peter
Marne Maitland . . . . Malay
David Baron . . . . Charles Spalding
Charles Lloyd Pack . . . . Vicar
HORROR Cornwall. Malayan sect causes
doctor's daughter to change into snake.

13581
THE NIGHT CALLER (84) (X) USA: BLOOD
BEAST FROM OUTER SPACE
New Art-Armitage (Butcher)
P: John Phillips, Ronald Liles
D: John Gilling
S: (NOVEL) Frank Crisp (THE NIGHT CALLERS)
SC: Jim O'Connolly
John Saxon . . . . Jack Costain
Maurice Denham . . . . Prof Morley
Patricia Haines . . . . Ann Barlow
Alfred Burke . . . . Supt Hartley
John Carson . . . . Major ·
Jack Watson . . . . Sgt Hawkins
Stanley Meadows . . . . Grant
Warren Mitchell . . . . Lilburn
Ballard Barkeley . . . . Cdr Savage
Anthony Wager . . . . Pte Higgins
Robert Crewdson . . . . Medra
FANTASY Alien from Ganymede abducts girls
for genetic purposes.

1966

JAN

13582
MORGAN—A SUITABLE CASE FOR
TREATMENT (97) (A)
Quintra (BL)
P: Leon Clore
D: Karel Reisz
S: (TV PLAY) David Mercer
SC: David Mercer

Vanessa Redgrave	Leonie Delt
David Warner	Morgan Delt
Robert Stephens	Charles Napier
Irene Handl	Mrs Delt
Bernard Bresslaw	PC
Arthur Mullard	Wally
Newton Blick	Mr Henderson
Nan Munro	Mrs Henderson
Graham Crowden	Counsel
John Rae	Judge

COMEDY Artist's crazy schemes to stop rich
wife's marriage to staid art dealer. (BFA 1966:
Best Screenplay, Best Editing.).

13583
THE SPECIALIST (20) (U)
Heald-Samson (Ritz)
D: James Hill
S: (NOVEL) Charles Sale

Bernard Miles
Colin Ellis
Douglas Milvain
Sheila Shand
Golda Casimir
Jimmy Gardner

COMEDY Country carpenter specialises in
building outdoors WCs.

13584
CIRCUS OF FEAR (83) (A) *eastman*
USA: PSYCHO-CIRCUS
Circus-David Henley (AA)
P: Harry Alan Towers
D: John Moxey
S: Peter Welbeck

Christopher Lee	Gregor
Leo Genn	Insp Elliott
Anthony Newlands	Barberini
Heinz Drache	Carl
Eddi Arent	Eddie
Klaus Kinski	Manfred
Margaret Lee	Gina
Suzy Kendall	Natasha
Cecil Parker	Sir John
Victor Maddern	Mason
Maurice Kaufmann	Mario
Skip Martin	Mr Big

CRIME Inspector unmasks killer behind series
of circus murders.

13585
THEATRE OF DEATH (91) (X) *tech/scope*
Pennea (LIP)
P: William Gell, Michael Smedley-Aston
D: Samuel Gallu
S: Ellis Kadison
SC: Ellis Kadison, Roger Marshall

Christopher Lee	Philippe Darvas
Lelia Goldoni	Dani Cirreaux
Julian Glover	Charles Marquis
Evelyn Laye	Mme Angele
Jenny Till	Nicole Chapel
Ivor Dean	Insp Michaeud

HORROR Paris. Surgeon helps police unmask
necrophiliac vampire.

13586
NAKED EVIL (79) (A)
Gibraltar (Col)
P: Steven Pallos

D:SC: Stanley Goulder
S: (PLAY) Jon Manchip White (THE OBI)

Anthony Ainley	Dick Alderson
Basil Dignam	Benson
Suzanne Neve	Janet
Richard Coleman	Hollis
Ronald Bridges	Wilkins
George A. Saunders	Danny
Pearl Prescod	Landlady
Carmen Munroe	Beverley
Brylo Ford	Amazon
Dan Jackson	Lloyd

FANTASY Murdered Jamaican voodoo
practicioner takes over secretary of student's
hostel.

FEB

13587
THE GREAT ST TRINIAN'S TRAIN
ROBBERY (94) (U) *eastman*
Braywild (BL)
P: Leslie Gilliat
D: Frank Launder, Sidney Gilliat
S: (CARTOONS) Ronald Searle
SC: Frank Launder, Ivor Herbert

Frankie Howard	Alphonse Askett
Dora Bryan	Amber Spottiswoode
George Cole	Flash Harry
Reg Varney	Gilbert
Raymond Huntley	Minister
Richard Wattis	Bassett
Portland Mason	Georgina
Terry Scott	
Eric Barker	Culpepper Brown
Godfrey Winn	Truelove
Desmond Walter-Ellis	Leonard Edwards
Colin Gordon	Noakes
Barbara Couper	Mabel Radnage
Elspeth Duxbury	Veronica Bledlow
George Benson	Gore-Blackwood
Carole Ann Ford	Albertine
Arthur Mullard	Big Jim
Stratford Johns	Voice

COMEDY Train robbers hide loot in old mansion
which is taken over by girls' school.

13588
THAT RIVIERA TOUCH (98) (U) *eastman*
Rank (RFD)
P: Hugh Stewart
D: Cliff Owen
S: Peter Blackmore
SC: S.C. Green, R.M. Hills

Eric Morecambe	Eric
Ernie Wise	Ernie
Suzanne Lloyd	Claudette
Paul Stassino	Le Pirate
Armand Mestral	Insp Duval
George Eugeniou	Marcel
George Pastell	Ali
Peter Jeffrey	Mauron
Gerald Lawson	Coco
Michael Forrest	Pierre
Paul Danquah	Hassim

COMEDY France. Girl reforms and helps
holiday-makers thwart jewel thieves.

13589
CUL-DE-SAC (111) (X)
Compton-Tekli (Compton)
P: Sam Waynberg, Gene Gutowski
D: Roman Polanski
S: Roman Polanski, Gerard Brach

Donald Pleasence	George
Francoise Dorleac	Teresa
Lionel Stander	Richard
Jack MacGowran	Albert
Iain Quarrier	Christopher
Renee Houston	Mother

Geoffrey Sumner	Father
Robert Dorning	Mr Fairweather
Marie Kean	Marion Fairweather
William Franklyn	Cecil

COMEDY Northumberland. Wounded robbers shelter
in castle occupied by artist and French wife.

13590
ISLAND OF TERROR (89) (X) *eastman*
Planet
P: Tom Blakeley
D: Terence Fisher
S: Edward Andrew Mann, Alan Ramsen

Peter Cushing	Dr Brian Stanley
Edward Judd	Dr David West
Carole Gray	Toni Merrill
Eddie Byrne	Dr Landers
Sam Kydd	PC Harriss
Niall MacGinnis	Campbell
James Caffrey	Argyle
Liam Gaffney	Bellows
Roger Heathcote	Dunley
Peter Forbes Robertson	Dr Phillips

HORROR Ireland. Dr seeking cancer cure
creates silicon-based life form that eats bones.

13591
ARABESQUE (105) (A) *tech/scope*
Donen-Enterprises (RFD)
P:D: Stanley Donen
S: (NOVEL) Gordon Cotler (THE CIPHER)
SC: Julian Mitchell, Stanley Price, Pierre
Marton

Gregory Peck	David Pollock
Sophia Loren	Yasmin Azir
Alan Badel	Nejim Beshraavi
Keiron Moore	Yussef Kassim
Carl Duering	Hassan Jena
John Merivale	Sloane
Duncan Lamont	Webster
George Coulouris	Ragheeb
Ernest Clark	Beauchamp
Harold Kasket	Mohammed Lufti

CRIME Oil magnate's mistress helps American
professor foil assassination of Middle East Prime
Minister. (BFA 1966: Best colour pho.)

13592
DEATH IS A WOMAN (81) (X) *tech*
AB-Pathe (WPD)
P: Harry Field
D: Frederic Goode
S: Wally Bosco

Patsy Ann Noble	Francesca
Mark Burns	Dennis
Shaun Curry	Joe
Wanda Ventham	Priscilla
Terence de Marney	Jacomini
Caron Gardner	Mary
William Dexter	Malc
Anita Harris	Herself

CRIME Malta. Agent proves girl killed
nightclub partners for heroin.

13593
THE IDOL (111) (X)
Embassy (WPD)
P: Leonard Lightstone
D: Daniel Petrie
S: Ugo Liberatore
SC: Millard Lampell

Jennifer Jones	Carol
Michael Parks	Marco
John Leyton	Timothy
Jennifer Hilary	Sarah
Guy Doleman	Martin Livesey
Natasha Pyne	Rosalind
Jack Watson	Inspector
Jeremy Bulloch	Lewis

Gordon Gostelow . . . .   Simon
Priscilla Morgan . . . . .Rosie
Edna Morris . . . .   Mrs Muller
Renee Houston . . . .   Woman
DRAMA American art student has affair with
widow and is killed by her son.

13594
THE PSYCHOPATH (83) (X) tech/scope
Amicus (Par)
P: Max Rosenburg, Milton Subotsky
D: Freddie Francis
S: Robert Bloch
Patrick Wymark . . . .   Insp Holloway
Margaret Johnston . . . .   Mrs Von Sturm
John Standing . . . .   Mark von Sturm
Alexander Knox . . . .   Frank Saville
Judy Huxtable . . . .   Louise Saville
Don Borisenko . . . .   Donald Loftis
Thorley Walters . . . .   Martin Rolfe
Robert Crewdson . . . .   Victor Ledoux
Colin Gordon . . . .   Dr Glyn
Frank Forsyth . . . .   Tucker
CRIME Doll-addicted German woman kills mem-
bers of Allied Commission who condemned her
husband.

13595
MR BROWN COMES DOWN THE HILL (88) (A)
Westminster (MRA)
P:D:SC: Henry Cass
D: (PLAY) Peter Howard
Eric Flynn . . . .   Mr Brown
Mark Heath . . . .   Black Man
Lillias Walker . . . .   Harlot
John Richmond . . . .   Bishop
Richard Warner . . . .   Doctor
Bryan Coleman . . . .   Bishop
Alan White . . . .   Andy
Donald Simpson . . . .   Bishop
RELIGION Negro, prostitute and bishop find faith
through a strange preacher who is killed by
betrayers.

13596
THE NATIONAL YOUTH ORCHESTRA OF
GREAT BRITAIN (10) (U) eastman
Anvil (RFD)
MUSICAL Young people's orchestra plays a
Dvorak overture.

13597
ROUND THE BEND (30) (U) eastman
Border Films (NR)
P:D: O. Negus-Fancey
S: Barry Cryer
N: Bernard Cribbens
Bernard Bresslaw . . . .   Driver
Barry Cryer . . . .   Instructor
COMEDY Man fails driving test and becomes
stock car racer.

13598
FISH AND MILLIGAN (16) (U)
Clarens (NR)
P: Andrew McCall
D:S: Christopher Mason
Spike Milligan . . . .   Fisherman
Arthur Mullard . . . .   Everyone Else
COMEDY Episodic mishaps of a determined
fisherman.
MAR

13599
STOP THE WORLD I WANT TO GET OFF
(100) (A) tech
WB (WPD)
P: Bill Sargent

D: Philip Saville
S: (PLAY) Anthony Newley, Leslie Bricusse
SC: Anthony Newley, Leslie Bricusse, David
Donable, Al Ham, Marilyn Bergman, Alan
Bergman
Tony Tanner . . . .   Littlechap
Millicent Martin . . . . .Evie;Anya;Ara;Ginnie
Leila Croft . . . .   Susan
Valerie Croft . . . .   Jane
Neil Hawley . . . .   Little Littlechap
MUSICAL Teaboy rises to peerage and has
various affairs on the way.

13600
ALFIE (114) (X) tech/scope
Sheldrake (Par)
P:D: Lewis Gilbert
S: (TV PLAY) Bill Naughton
SC: Bill Naughton
Michael Caine . . . .   Alfie
Shelley Winters . . . .   Ruby
Millicent Martin . . . .   Siddie
Julia Foster . . . .   Gilda
Jane Asher . . . .   Annie
Shirley Anne Field . . . .   Carla
Vivien Merchant . . . .   Lily
Eleanor Bron . . . .   Doctor
Denholm Elliot . . . .   Abortionist
Alfie Bass . . . .   Harry
Graham Stark . . . .   Humphrey
Murray Melvin . . . .   Nat
Sydney Tafler . . . .   Frank
COMEDY Cockney has affairs with various
girls, all of whom leave him.

13601
DAVEY JONES' LOCKER (60) (U) eastman
AB—Pathe (CFF)
P: Lionel Hoare
D: Frederic Goode
S: Wally Boscoe
Anthony Bate . . . . . . .Lt-Cdr Jim Matthews
Susan George . . . .   Susan Haddock
Michael Wennink . . . .   Spike Haddock
Stephen Craig . . . .   Derek Matthews
Vanessa Page . . . .   Vanessa
Penelope Wansbury . . . .   Penny
Adrian Ellyl-Soler   Vic
CHILDREN Malta. Boy discovers sunken
treasure while learning to skindive.

13602
L'ART POUR L'ART (ART FOR ART'S SAKE)
(6) (U) colour
Bob Godfrey (Curzon)
D: Bob Godfrey
S: Colin Pearson
Bob Godfrey . . . .   Pop
Bruce Lacey . . . .   Dotty
Johnny Vyvyan . . . .   Porno
Jill Bruce . . . .   Girl
COMEDY Pop artist, pointilliste and
pornographer battle over model in a marsh.

13603
A PENNY FOR YOUR THOUGHTS; OR,
BIRDS, DOLLS AND SCRATCH —
ENGLISH STYLE (40) (X)
Donwin (Gala)
P:D:S: Donovan Winter
Yvonne Antrobus . . . .   Carol Cleveland
Miranda Connell . . . .   Venetia Cunninghame
Celestine Randall . . . .   Tracy Rogers
Sheila White . . . .   Annette Whiteley
Susan Worth . . . .   Jennifer Wood
Jill Mai Meredith . . . .   Girl
COMEDY Talk between girls in ladies' public
toilet.

13604
THE PROJECTED MAN (90) (X) eastman/scope
MLC (Compton)
P: John Croydon. Maurice Foster
D: Ian Curteis
S: Frank Quattrocchi
SC: John C. Cooper, Peter Bryan
Bryant Halliday . . . .   Prof Steiner
Mary Peach . . . .   Dr Pat Hill
Norman Wooland . . . .   Dr Blanchard
Ronald Allen . . . .   Christopher Mitchell
Derek Farr . . . .   Insp Davis
Tracey Crisp . . . .   Sheila Anderson
Derrick de Marney . . . .   Latham
Gerard Heinz . . . .   Prof Lembach
Sam Kydd . . . .   Harry
HORROR Professor researching into laser
projection becomes murderous monster.

13605
ROAD TO SAINT TROPEZ (31) (A)
eastman/scope
Script and Play (20)
P:D:S: Michael Sarne
N: Fenella Fielding
Melissa Stribling . . . .   Woman
Udo Kier . . . .   Boy
Gabriella Licudi . . . .   Girl
COMEDY France. Woman tourist has affair
with hitch-hiker.

13606
KHARTOUM (128) (U) tech/scope
Julian Blaustein (UA)
P: Julian Blaustein
D: Basil Dearden, Eliot Elisofen, Yakima Canutt
S: Robert Ardrey
Charlton Heston . . . . . .   Gen Charles Gordon
Laurence Olivier . . . .   The Mahdi
Richard Johnson . . . .   Col J.D.H. Stewart
Ralph Richardson . . . .   Mr Gladstone
Alexander Knox . . . . . .   Sir Evelyn Baring
Johnny Sekka . . . .   Khaleel
Nigel Green . . . .   Gen Wolseley
Michael Hordern . . . .   Lord Granville
Zia Mohyeddin . . . .   Zobeir Pasha
Hugh Williams . . . .   Lord Hartington
Douglas Wilmer . . . .   Khalifa Abdullah
Edward Underdown . . . . . .   Col Hicks
Alec Mango . . . .   Bordeini Bey
Jerome Willis . . . .   Frank Power
Peter Arne . . . .   Major Kitchener
Marne Maitland . . . .   Sheikh Osman
Leila . . . .   Dancer
Ronald Leigh-Hunt . . . . . .   Lord Northbrook
Ralph Michael . . . .   Sir Charles Dilke
HISTORY Sudan, 1883. British general
refuses to leave city beseiged by Arabs.

13607
SLAVE GIRLS (95) (A) tech/scope
USA: PREHISTORIC WOMEN
Hammer (WPD)
P:D:S: Michael Carreras
Martine Beswick . . . .   Kari
Edina Ronay . . . .   Saria
Michael Latimer . . . .   David Marchant
Stephanie Randall . . . .   Amyak
Carol White . . . .   Gido
Alexandra Stevenson . . . . .   Luri
Yvonne Horner . . . .   Amazon
Sydney Bromley . . . .   Ullo
Robert Raglan . . . .   Col Hammett
FANTASY Africa, period. Hunter is enslaved
by tribe of Amazons.

13608
HOTEL PARADISO (99) (A) metro/scope
MGM Pictures

P:D: Peter Glenville
S: (PLAY) Georges Feydeau, Maurice Desvallieres (L'HOTEL DU LIBRE ECHANGE)
SC: Peter Glenville, Jean-Claude Carriere
Alec Guiness . . . . Benedict Boniface
Gina Lollobrigida . . . . Marcelle Cot
Robert Morley . . . . Henri Cot
Peggy Mount . . . . Angelique Boniface
Akim Tamiroff . . . . Anniello
Marie Bell . . . . La Grande Antoinette
Derek Fowldes . . . . Maxime
Douglas Byng . . . . Martin
Robertson Hare . . . . Duke
Ann Beach . . . . Victoire
Leonard Rossiter . . . . Inspector
Peter Glenville . . . . Georges Feydeau
COMEDY Paris, 1910. Comprising complications of couples at a disreputable hotel.

13609
THE WAR GAME (50) (X)
BBC (BFI)
P:D:S: Peter Watkins
N: Michael Aspel, Dick Graham
WAR Fictional documentary of future atomic war, made for TV but shown only in cinemas.
(AA 1966: Best Doc; BFA 1966: Best Short; UN Award.)

APR
13610
MODESTY BLAISE (119) (A) tech
Modesty Blaise (20)
P: Joseph Janni, Norman Priggen, Michael Birkett
D: Joseph Losey
S: (COMIC STRIP) Peter O'Donnell, Jim Holdaway
SC: Evan Jones
Monica Vitti . . . . Modesty Blaise
Terence Stamp . . . . Willie Garvin
Dirk Bogarde . . . . Gabriel
Harry Andrews . . . . Sir Gerald Tarrant
Michael Craig . . . . Paul Hagan
Clive Revill . . . McWhirter/Sheikh Abu Tahir
Scilla Gabel . . . . Melina
Tina Marquand . . . . Nicole
Rosella Falk . . . . Mrs Fothergill
Joe Melia . . . . Crevier
Lex Schoorel . . . . Walter
Alexander Knox . . . . Minister
CRIME Girl secret agent thwarts master crook and delivers diamonds to sheikh.

13611
OUR MAN IN MARRAKESH (94) (U) eastman
USA: BANG BANG YOU'RE DEAD
Marrakesh—Towers of London (AA)
P: Harry Alan Towers
D: Don Sharp
S: Peter Yeldham
Tony Randall . . . . Andrew Jessel
Senta Berger . . . . Kyra Stanovy
Herbert Lom . . . . Narim Casimir
Wilfrid Hyde White . . . . . Arthur Fairbrother
Terry-Thomas . . . . El Caid
Gregoire Aslan . . . . Achmed
John le Mesurier . . . . George C. Lilleywhite
Klaus Kinski . . . . Jonquil
Margaret Lee . . . . Samia Voss
Keith Peacock . . . . Philippe
COMEDY Morocco. American tourist and girl secret agent, framed for murder, thwart crook.

13612
THE WRONG BOX (110) (U) tech
Salamander (Col)
P: Bryan Forbes, Larry Gelbart,

Bert Shevelove
D: Bryan Forbes
S: (NOVEL) Robert Louis Stevenson, Lloyd Osbourne
SC: Larry Gelbart, Bert Shevelove
John Mills . . . . Masterman Finsbury
Ralph Richardson . . . . Joseph Finsbury
Michael Caine . . . . Michael Finsbury
Peter Cook . . . . Morris Finsbury
Dudley Moore . . . . John Finsbury
Nanette Newman . . . . Julia Finsbury
Tony Hancock . . . . Detective
Peter Sellers . . . . Dr Pratt
Cicely Courtneidge . . . . Maj Martha
Wilfred Lawson . . . . Peacock
Thorley Walters . . . . Mountaineer
Peter Graves . . . . Officer
Irene Handl . . . . Mrs Hackett
Norman Bird . . . . Clergyman
John le Mesurier . . . . Dr Slattery
Norman Rossington . . . . Rough
Diane Clare . . . . Mercy
Tutte Lemkow . . . . . Bournemouth Strangler
Nicholas Parsons . . . . OC
Avis Burrage . . . . Queen Victoria
Valentine Dyall . . . . . Oliver Pike Harmsworth
Andre Morell . . . . Servant
Temperance Seven . . . . The Band
COMEDY 1890. Brothers try to secure £100,000 Tontine shared by aged uncles.
(BFA 1966: Best Costumes.)

13613
RUN WITH THE WIND (95) (X)
(GEFD)
P: James Ward
D: Lindsay Shonteff
S: Jeremy Craig Dryden
Francesca Annis . . . . Jean Parker
Sean Caffrey . . . . Frank Hiller
Shawn Phillips . . . . Paul Walton
Jack Smethurst . . . . Bernie
George Pastell . . . . Lennie
Sheena Campbell . . . . Sue
Mark York . . . . Tony
Leslie Lawton . . . . Steve
Hedgehoppers Anonymous
DRAMA Girl leaves boxer for folk singer, returns to him, and is rejected.

13614
CARRY ON SCREAMING (97) (A) eastman
Ethiro (AA)
P: Peter Rogers
D: Gerald Thomas
S: Talbot Rothwell
Harry H. Corbett . . . . Sgt Bung
Kenneth Williams . . . . Dr Watt
Jim Dale . . . . Albert Potter
Charles Hawtrey . . . . Dan Dann
Fenella Fielding . . . . Valeria Watt
Joan Sims . . . . Emily Bung
Angela Douglas . . . . Doris Mann
Peter Butterworth . . . . Slobotham
Bernard Bresslaw . . . . Sockett
Jon Pertwee . . . . Fettle
Tom Clegg . . . . Odbodd
Billy Cornelius . . . . Odbodd jr
Denis Blake . . . . Rubbatiti
COMEDY Period. Tec investigates revived corpse and his vampiric sister who vitrify girls for window-dummies.

13615
OPERATION THIRD FORM (58) (U)
World Wide (CFF)
P: Hindle Edgar
D: David Eady
S: Hindle Edgar, David Eady

SC: Michael Barnes
John Moulder Brown . . . . . Dick
Kevin Bennett . . . . Tom
Sidney Bromley . . . . Paddy
Derren Nesbitt . . . . Skinner
Michael Crockett . . . . Alan
Ronnie Caryl . . . . Brian
Roberta Tovey . . . . Jill
George Roderick . . . . Boss
CHILDREN Suspected boy's classmates track down thieves who stole bell.

13616
THE SANDWICH MAN (95) (U) eastman
Titan (RFD)
P: Peter Newbrook
D: Robert Hartford-Davis
S: Robert Hartford-Davis, Michael Bentine
Michael Bentine . . . . Horace Quilby
Dora Bryan . . . . Mrs DeVere
Harry H. Corbett . . . . . . Stage-doorkeeper
Bernard Cribbins . . . . Photographer
Diana Dors . . . . .Billingsgate Woman
Ian Hendry . . . . Motorcycle Cop
Stanley Holloway . . . . Coach
Wilfrid Hyde White . . . . . Lord Uffingham
Michael Medwin . . . . Sewer Man
Ron Moody . . . . Coach
Anna Quayle . . . . Billingsgate Woman
Terry-Thomas . . . . Scoutmaster
Norman Wisdom . . . . .Father O'Malley
Donald Wolfit . . . . Manager
Tracey Crisp . . . . Girl in Mac
Suzy Kendall . . . . Sue
Alfie Bass . . . . Yachtsman
Earl Cameron . . . . Conductor
Max Bacon . . . . Chef
Michael Chaplin . . . . Artist
Fred Emney . . . . . . .Sir Arthur Moleskin
Sid & Max Harrison . . . . Zoo Men
Peter Jones . . . . Escapologist
John le Mesurier . . . . Sandwich Man
Tony Tanner . . . . Ferryman
Peter Arne . . . . Gentleman
Warren Mitchell . . . . Gypsy Syd
COMEDY Adventures of sandwich-board man during one day in London.

13617
SECRETS OF A WINDMILL GIRL (86) (X) eastman
Searchlight—Markten (Compton)
P: Arnold Miller, Stanley Long
D:S: Arnold Louis Miller
April Wilding . . . . Linda Gray
Pauline Collins . . . . Pat Lord
Renee Houston . . . . Dresser
Derek Bond . . . . Insp Thomas
Harry Fowler . . . . Larry
Howard Marion Crawford . . Producer
Peter Swanick . . . . Len Mason
Martin Jarvis . . . . Mike
Leon Cortez . . . . Agent
Dana Gillespie; George Rutland; Deirdre O'Dea; Sadie Eddon; Pat Patterson; Jill Millard
CRIME Revue singer tells how friend became drunken stripper and died after multiple rape.

13618
THEY'RE A WEIRD MOB (112) (U) eastman
Williamson—Powell International (RFD)
P:D: Michael Powell
S: (BOOK) Nino Culotta
SC: Richard Imrie
Walter Chiari . . . . Nino Culotta
Clare Dunne . . . . Kay Kelly
Chips Rafferty . . . . Harry Kelly
Alida Chelli . . . . Giuliana
Ed Devereaux . . . . Joe

Slim de Gray . . . . Pat
John Meillon . . . . Dennis
Charles Little . . . . Jimmy
Muriel Steinbeck . . . . Mrs Kelly
Gloria Dawn . . . . Mrs Chapman
COMEDY Sydney. Italian immigrant becomes
builder and falls for girl his cousin cheated.
(Made in Australia)

13619
THE TRAP (106) (A) *eastman/scope*
Parallel (RFD)
P: George H. Brown
D: Sidney Hayers
S: David Osborn
Rita Tushingham . . . . Eve
Oliver Reed . . . . Jean La Bete
Rex Sevenoaks . . . . Trader
Barbara Chilcott . . . . Wife
Linda Goranson . . . . Daughter
Blain Fairman . . . . Clerk
Walter Marsh . . . . Preacher
Jo Golland . . . . Baptiste
ADVENTURE British Columbia, 1850. Fur
trapper buys dumb orphan from trader's wife.

MAY

13620
THE BLUE MAX (155) (A) *deluxe/scope*
20th Century—Fox
P: Elmo Williams, Christian Ferry
D: John Guillermin
S: (NOVEL) Jack D. Hunter
SC: David Pursall, Jack Seddon, Gerald Hanley,
Ben Barzman, Basilio Franchina
George Peppard . . . . Bruno Stachel
James Mason . . . . . . Count von Klugermann
Ursula Andress . . . . Countess Kaeti
Jeremy Kemp . . . . . . Willi von Klugermann
Karl Michael Vogler . . . . . Heidemann
Loni von Friedl . . . . Elfie Heidmann
Anton Diffring . . . . Holbach
Carl Schell . . . . Baron von Richthofen
Peter Woodthorpe . . . . Rupp
Harry Towb . . . . Kettering
Derek Newark . . . . Ziegel
Derren Nesbitt . . . . Fabian
Friedrich Ledebur . . . . . . Von Lenndorf
WAR Germany, 1918. Unpopular fighter
pilot's ambition to win medal causes his
downfall. (BFA 1966: Best colour Art Dir.)

13621
SONGS OF SCOTLAND (15) (U) *color*
International Film Associates (Hillcrest)
D: Laurence Henson, Edward McConnell
MUSICAL Scottish ballads and folk songs.

13622
A FUNNY THING HAPPENED ON THE WAY
TO THE FORUM (98) *deluxe*
Quadrangle (UA)
P: Melvin Frank
D: Richard Lester
S: (PLAY) Burt Shevelove, Larry Gelbart
SC: Melvin Frank, Michael Pertwee
Zero Mostel . . . . Pseudolus
Phil Silvers . . . . Lycus
Jack Gilford . . . . Hysterium
Buster Keaton . . . . Erronius
Michael Crawford . . . . Hero
Michael Hordern . . . . Senex
Annette Andre . . . . Philia
Patricia Jessel . . . . Domina
Leon Greene . . . . Miles Gloriosus
Inga Neilsen . . . . Gymnasia
Myrna White . . . . Vibrata
Pamela Brown . . . . Priestess
Jennifer & Susan Baker . . . . Geminae

Beatrix Lehmann . . . . Mother
Alfie Bass . . . . Gatekeeper
Roy Kinnear . . . . Instructor
COMEDY Rome, 100. Slave seeks freedom by
arranging affair between his master's son and
soldier's betrothed. (AA 1966: Best Score
Adaptation; Made in Spain.)

13623
GEORGY GIRL (99) (X)
Everglades (Col)
P: Otto Plaschkes, Robert Goldston
D: Silvio Narizzano
S: (NOVEL) Margaret Forster
SC: Margaret Forster, Peter Nichols
James Mason . . . . James Leamington
Alan Bates . . . . Jos
Lynn Redgrave . . . . Georgy
Charlotte Rampling . . . . Meredith
Bill Owen . . . . Ted
Rachel Kempson . . . . Ellen
Clare Kelly . . . . Doris
Denise Coffey . . . . Peg
Dorothy Alison . . . . Health Visitor
Peggy Thorp-Bates . . . . Sister
Dandy Nichols . . . . Nurse
ROMANCE Girl seduced by her roomate's
lover while she is away having his baby.

13624
ROMEO AND JULIET (126) (U) *eastman*
Poetic (RFD)
P:D: Paul Czinner
S: (PLAY) William Shakespeare (BALLET)
Kenneth MacMillan, Serge Prokoviev
Margot Fonteyn . . . . Juliet
Rudolph Nureyev . . . . Romeo
David Blair . . . . Mercutio
Desmond Doyle . . . . Tybalt
Julia Farron . . . . Lady Capulet
Michael Somes . . . . Lord Capulet
Anthony Dowell . . . . Benvolio
Derek Rencher . . . . Paris
Leslie Edwards . . . . Prince Escalus
Georgina Parkinson . . . . Rosaline
Gerd Larsen . . . . Nurse
Ronald Hynd . . . . Friar Laurence
Christopher Newton . . . . . . Lord Montague
Betty Kavanagh . . . . Lady Montague
MUSICAL Royal Ballet production.

JUNE

13625
CITY OF FEAR (75) (A)
Towers of London (Planet)
P: Harry Alan Towers
D: Peter Bezencenet
S: Peter Welbeck
SC: Peter Welbeck, Max Bourne
Terry Moore . . . . Suzan
Albert Lieven . . . . Paul
Marisa Mell . . . . Ilona
Paul Maxwell . . . . Mike Foster
Pinkas Braun . . . . Ferenc
Zsu Zsu Banki . . . . Magda
Maria Takacs . . . . Marika
CRIME Hungary. Canadian reporter and
American fashion expert smuggle scientist and
daughter across border.

13626
DALEKS—INVASION EARTH 2150 AD
(84) (U) *tech/scope*
Aaru (BL)
P: Max Rosenberg, Milton Subotsky,
Joe Vegoda
D: Gordon Flemyng
S: (TV SERIAL) Terry Nation

SC: Milton Subotsky, David Whittaker
Peter Cushing . . . . Dr Who
Bernard Cribbins . . . . Tom Campbell
Ray Brooks . . . . David
Jill Curzon . . . . Louise
Roberta Tovey . . . . Susan
Andrew Keir . . . . Wyler
Godfrey Quigley . . . . Dortmun
Roger Avon . . . . Wells
Keith Marsh . . . . Conway
Geoffrey Cheshire . . . . Roboman
Steve Peters . . . . Leader Roboman
Robert Jewell . . . . Leader Dalek
FANTASY Dr and PC travel forward in time to
save Earth from being used as space ship by
extraterrestials.

13627
JUST LIKE A WOMAN (89) (A) *eastman*
Dormar (Monarch)
P: Bob Kellett
D:S: Robert Fuest
Wendy Craig . . . . Scilla McKenzie
Francis Matthews . . . . Lewis McKenzie
John Wood . . . . John
Dennis Price . . . . Salesman
Peter Jones . . . . Saul Alexander
Miriam Karlin . . . . Ellen Newman
Clive Dunn . . . . Von Fischer
Ray Barrett . . . . Australian
Sheila Staefel . . . . Isolde
Barry Fantoni . . . . Elijah Stark
Bob Godfrey . . . . Assistant
Mark Murphy . . . . Himself
COMEDY TV director's wife leaves him and
has weird house designed by ex-Nazi.

JULY

13628
KALEIDOSCOPE (103) (U) *tech/scope*
Winkast (WPD)
P: Elliott Kastner, Jerry Gershwin
D: Jack Smight
S: Robert & Jane Howard-Carrington
Warren Beatty . . . . Barney Lincoln
Susannah York . . . . Angel McGinnis
Clive Revill . . . . Insp Manny McGlinnis
Eric Porter . . . . Harry Dominion
Murray Melvin . . . . Aimes
George Sewell . . . . Billy
Stanley Meadows . . . . Captain
John Junkin . . . . Evelyn
Yootha Joyce . . . . Receptionist
George Murcell . . . . Johnny
CRIME American playboy caught using
crooked cards helps a tec catch a drug smuggler.

13629
THE CHRISTMAS TREE (59) (U)
Augusta (CFF)
P:S: Ed Harper
D: James Clark
SC: James Clark, Michael Barnes
William Burleigh . . . . Gary
Anthony Honour . . . . Sam
Kate Nicholls . . . . Jane
Anthony Baird . . . . Father
Doreen Keogh . . . . Mother
Brian Blessed . . . . Policeman
Sydney Bromley . . . . Motorist
Oliver McGreevy . . . . Baldy
CHILDREN Adventures of three children
taking a Christmas tree across London to a
hospital.

13630
THE PRETTY THINGS (14) (U)
West Associates (Amanda)
P: Anthony West

D: Anthony West, Caterina Arvat
S: Caterina Arvat
The Pretty Things
MUSICAL "Midnight to Six"; "Can't Stand
the Pain"; "Me Needing You".

13631
FRAGMENT (11) (A)
Mantic (Contemporary)
ROMANCE Girl's first love encounter causes
consideration of suicide.

13632
MADEMOISELLE (103) (X) *scope/bilingual*
Woodfall—Procinex (UA)
P: Oscar Lewenstein
D: Tony Richardson
S: Jean Genet
Jeanne Moreau .... Mademoiselle
Ettore Manni .... Manou
Keith Skinner .... Bruno
Umberto Orsini .... Antonio
Jane Berretta .... Annette
Mony Reh .... Vievotte
Georges Douking .... Priest
Rosine Luguet .... Lisa
Gabriel Gobin .... Sgt
Pierre Collet .... Marcel
DRAMA France. Villagers blame Italian
woodcutter for disasters perpetrated by
spinster teacher.(BFA 1967: Best costumes.)

13633
STRANGLER'S WEB (55) (A)
Merton Park (AA)
P: Jack Greenwood
D: John Moxey
S: George Baxt
John Stratton .... Lewis Preston
Pauline Munro .... Melanie
Griffith Jones .... Jackson Delacorte
Gerald Harper .... Insp Murray
Maurice Hedley .... Amos Colfax
Michael Balfour .... John Vichelski
Pauline Boty .... Nell Pretty
Patricia Burke .... Norma Brent
Barry Jackson .... Morton Bray
Marianne Stone .... Alicia Preston
CRIME Solicitor uncovers strangler of ex-
actress.

13634
EYE OF THE DEVIL (90) (X)
Filmways—MGM (MGM)
P: Martin Ransohoff, John Calley
D: J. Lee Thompson
S: (NOVEL) Philip Loraine (DAY OF THE
ARROW)
SC: Robin Estridge, Denis Murphy
Deborah Kerr ... Catherine de Montfaucon
David Niven .... Philippe de Montfaucon
Donald Pleasence .... Pere Dominic
Edward Mulhare ...... Jean-Claude Ibert
Flora Robson .... Countess Estelle
Emlyn Williams ...... Alain de Montfaucon
Sharon Tate .... Odile
David Hemmings ...... Christian de Caray
John le Mesurier .... Dr Monnet
Suky Appleby .... Antoinette
Donald Bisset .... Rennard
HORROR France. Vineyard owner sacrifices
himself to pre-Christian cult to save his grapes.

AUG
13635
THE BRIDES OF FU MANCHU (91) (U)
eastman
Fu Manchu—Seven Arts—Constantin (AA)
P: Harry Alan Towers

D: Don Sharp
S: (CHARACTERS) Sax Rohmer
SC: Peter Welbeck
Christopher Lee .... Dr Fu Manchu
Douglas Wilmer ...... Nayland Smith
Marie Versini , ... Marie Lentz
Heinz Drache .... Franz Baumer
Howard Marion Crawford .. Dr Petrie
Tsai Chin .... Lin Tang
Kenneth Fortescue .... Sgt Spicer
Joseph Furst .... Otto Lentz
Carole Gray ....,....... Michele
Harald Leipnitz .... Nikki Sheldon
Rupert Davies .... Merlin
CRIME 1925. German helps detective foil
Chinese crook's vaporising ray beamed from
Africa.

13636
FAHRENHEIT 451 (112) (A) *tech*
Vineyard—Anglo—Enterprise—Universal (RFD)
P: Lewis M. Allen
D: Francois Truffaut
S: (NOVEL) Ray Bradbury
SC: Francois Truffaut, Jean-Louis Richard,
David Rudkin, Helen Scott
Oskar Werner .... Montag
Julie Christie .... Linda/Clarisse
Cyril Cusack .... Captain
Anton Diffring .... Fabian
Jeremy Spenser .... Man with Apple
Ann Bell .... Doris
Caroline Hunt .... Helen
Anna Palk .... Jackie
Alex Scott .... Life of Henry Brulard
Dennis Gilmore .... Martian Chronicles
Fred & Frank Cox .... Pride & Prejudice
Michael Balfour ...... Machiavelli's Prince
Judith Drynan .... Plato's Dialogues
David Glover .... Pickwick Papers
Yvonne Blake .... Jewish Question
John Rae .... Weir of Hermiston
Gillian Aldam .... Judoka Woman
FANTASY Future. Book burner discovers
value of literature but is betrayed by his wife.

13637
THE YELLOW HAT (77) (U) *eastman*
Margot Dagmar (Monarch)
P: David Henley
D: Honoria Plesch
S: Dai Noel
SC: Dai Noel. Honoria Plesch, M.A.F. Stevens
Valentine Palmer .... Tony
Frances Barlow .... Sally
Toni Palmer .... Christine
Tommy Bruce .... Harry
Eleanor Summerfield ..... Lady Xenia
Pierre Dduan .... Raoul
John Slater .... Slack
Salina Jones .... Patsy
Derek Nimmo .... Douglas
Canna Kendal .... Hortense
Elspeth Duxbury .... Customer
Fugere
Centre de Danse Classique Dancers
Harlequin Ballet Trust
MUSICAL Travels of new hat borrowed by
milliner's assistant.

13638
WHO KILLED THE CAT? (76) (U)
Eternal (GN)
P: Maurice J. Wilson
D: Montgomery Tully
S: (PLAY) Arnold Ridley, Mary Cathcart Borer
(TABITHA)
SC: Maurice J. Wilson, Montgomery Tully
Mary Merrall .... Janet Bowering

Ellen Pollock .... Ruth Prendergast
Amy Dalby .... Lavinia Goldsworthy
Mervyn Johns .... Henry Fawcett
Vanda Godsell ...... .Eleanor Trellington
Conrad Phillips .... Insp Bruton
Natasha Pyne .... Mary Trellington
Ronald Adam .... Gregory
Gregory Phillips .... Peter Parsons
CRIME Old spinsters suspected of poisoning
vicious landlady.

13639
JEMIMA AND JOHNNY (30) (U)
Vukani Ventures-Derrick Knight (Monarch)
P: Robert Angel
D:S: Lionel Ngakane
Nicolette Robinson .... Jemima
Patrick Hatfield .... Johnny
Thomas Baptiste ...... Jemima's Father
Myrtle Robinson ...... Jemima's Mother
Brian Phelan .... Johnny's Father
Dorothy Bromiley ...... Johnny's Mother
DRAMA Search for Jamaican girl and white boy in
ruined house.

13640
AMBUSH AT DEVIL'S GAP (U) serial
Rayant (CFF)
P: John Durst
D: David Eastman
S: David & Kerry Eastman
Chris Barrington .... Tommy Seldon
Sue Sylvaine .... Sue Seldon
Stephen Brown .... Mokey Seldon
Jacqueline Mitchell ...... Meg McAllister
Hugh Latimer .... Laker
Jack Rodney .... Spider
Eric Woodburn .... Prof Jennings
Dean Gardner .... Jamie McAllister
Duncan McIntyre .... Sgt McBain

13641
1: STRANGERS IN THE SNOW (15)

13642
2: THE SECRET OF THE CASTLE (17)

13643
3: THE ARREST (16)

13644 .
4: TRAPPED (16)

13645
5: NO ESCAPE (16)

13646
6: AMBUSH (15)
CHILDREN Scotland. Children thwart crooks
after a prof's metal that generates electricity
under light.

SEP

13647
COMPANY OF FOOLS (33) (U) *eastman*
Merton Park (AA)
P: Jack Greenwood
D: Peter Duffell
S: James Eastwood
N: Edgar Lustgarten
Barrie Ingham .... Maj MacDonald
Jacqueline Jones .... Liz Jason
Maurice Kaufmann .... Kasabis
Garfield Morgan .... Jason
Barry Keegan .... Webb
Frank Williams .... Price
CRIME Ex-major poses as sheik to ruin
financier who ruined him.

13648
THE FIGHTING PRINCE OF DONEGAL (104)
(U) *tech*

Walt Disney
P: Bill Anderson
D: Michael O'Herlihy
S: (NOVEL) Robert T. Reilly (RED HUGH PRINCE OF DONEGAL)
SC: Robert Westerby

Peter McEnery	Red Hugh
Susan Hampshire	Kathleen MacSweeney
Tom Adams	Henry O'Neill
Gordon Jackson	Capt Leeds
Andrew Keir	Lord MacSweeney
Norman Wooland	Sir John Perrott
Richard Leech	Phelim O'Toole
Peter Jeffery	Sgt
Marie Kean	Mother
Bill Owen	Powell

ADVENTURE Ireland. Prince escapes capture and leads united clans to save his sweetheart.

13649
PRESS FOR TIME (102) (U) *eastman*
Ivy (RFD)
P: Robert Hartford-Davis, Peter Newbrook
D: Robert Asher
S: (NOVEL) Mangus McGill (YEA YEA YEA)
SC: Norman Wisdom, Eddie Leslie

Norman Wisdom	Norman Shields/Sir Wilfred Shields/Emily
Derek Bond	Maj Bartlett
Angela Browne	Eleanor
Derek Francis	Alderman Corcoran
Noel Dyson	Mrs Corcoran
Frances White	Liz Corcoran
Peter Jones	Willoughby
David Lodge	Ross
Tracey Crisp	Ruby Fairchild
Allan Cuthbertson	Ballard
Hazel Coppin	Granny Fork
Stanley Unwin	Nottage

COMEDY PM's grandson becomes reporter on seaside newspaper.

13650
THE QUILLER MEMORANDUM (103) (A) *eastman/scope*
Ivan Foxwell-Carthay (RFD)
P: Ivan Foxwell, Sydney Streeter
D: Michael Anderson
S: (NOVEL) Elleston Trevor (THE BERLIN MEMORANDUM)
SC: Harold Pinter

George Segal	Quiller
Alec Guinness	Pol
Max von Sydow	Oktober
Senta Berger	Inge
George Sanders	Gibbs
Robert Helpmann	Weng
Robert Felmyng	Rushington
Peter Carsten	Hengel
Edith Schneider	Headmistress
Gunter Meisner	Hassler

CRIME Berlin. Schoolmistress helps British agent thwart neo-Nazi organisation.

13651
WHERE THE BULLETS FLY (90) (A) *eastman*
Puck (GEF)
P: S.J.H. Ward
D: John Gilling
S: Michael Pittock

Tom Adams	Charles Vine
Dawn Addams	Fiz
Sidney James	Mortician
Wilfred Brambell	Guard
Joe Baker	Minister
Tim Barrett	Seraph
Michael Ripper	Angel
John Arnott	Rockwell

Ronald Leigh-Hunt	Thursby
Marcus Hammond	O'Neill
Michael Ward	Michael
Heidi Erich	Carruthers
Suzan Farmer	Caron
Garry Marsh	Major

COMEDY Secret agent saves nuclear power unit for aircraft from the Russians.

13652
ZABAGLIONE (14) (U) *color*
Dais Films (Planet)
P: Malcolm Haslan
D: Georges Robin

Leslie Phillips	The Man
Daniele Noel	The Girl

COMEDY Man follows girl from night club but only to return her lost medallion.

13653
THE GHOST GOES GEAR (41) (U) *tech*
AB-Pathe (WPD)
P: Harry Field
D: Hugh Gladwish
S: Hugh Gladwish, Roger Dunton

Spencer Davis Group	Themselves
Stevie Winwood	Himself
Nicholas Parsons	Algernon Rowthorpe-Plumley
Sheila White	Polly
Lorne Gibson	The Ghost
Arthur Howard	Vicar
Joan Ingram	Lady Rowthorpe
Tony Sympson	Lord Plumley
Jack Haig	Edwards
Huw Thomas	Newscaster

Acker Bilk and the Paramount Jazz Band, Lorne Gibson Trio; The M6; St. Louis Union; Dave Berry; Three Bells.
MUSICAL Stately, haunted home saved by pop music festival.

13654
THE HAND OF NIGHT (73) (X) *tech*
AB-Pathe (WPD)
P: Harry Field
D: Frederic Goode
S: Bruce Stewart

William Sylvester	Paul Carver
Diane Clare	Chantal
Alizia Gur	Marisa
Edward Underdown	Gunther
Terence de Marney	Omar
William Dexter	Leclerc
Sylivia Marriott	Mrs Petty
Avril Sadler	Mrs Carver

Boscoe Holder Dancers
HORROR Morocco. Explorer ensnared by vampire princess.

13655
THE HAUNTED MAN (26) (U) *eastman*
Merton Park (AA)
P: Jack Greenwood
D: Stanley Willis
S: James Eastwood
N: Edgar Lustgarten

Keith Barron	Mark Godfrey
James Ellis	Bill Kenton
Alexandra Bastedo	Laura
Isobel Black	Bridget
John Gabriel	Defence
Tenniel Evans	Prosecution
John Boxer	Jeweller

CRIME Injured actor's search for smash-and-grab thieves.

13656
THE FAMILY WAY (114) (X) *eastman*
Janbox (BL)
P: John Boulting
D: Roy Boulting
S: (PLAY) Bill Naughton (ALL IN GOOD TIME)
SC: Bill Naughton, Roy Boulting, Jeffrey Dell

Hayley Mills	Jenny Piper
John Mills	Ezra Fitton
Hywel Bennett	Arthur Fitton
Marjorie Rhodes	Lucy Fitton
Avril Angers	Liz Piper
Liz Fraser	Molly Thompson
Wilfred Pickles	Uncle Fred
John Comer	Leslie Piper
Barry Foster	Joe Thompson
Murray Head	Geoffrey Fitton
Colin Gordon	Mr Hutton
Robin Parkinson	Mr Phillips
Andrew Bradford	Eddie
Harry Locke	Stubbs
Thorley Walters	Vicar

COMEDY Circumstances conspire to prevent couple from consummating marriage.

13657
FINDERS KEEPERS (94) (U) *eastman*
Interstate-Ivy (UA)
P:S: George H. Brown
D: Sidney Hayers
SC: Michael Pertwee

Cliff Richard	Cliff
The Shadows	Themselves
Robert Morley	Col Riberts
Peggy Mount	Mrs Bragg
Viviane Ventura	Emilia
Graham Stark	Burke
John le Mesurier	Mr X
Robert Hutton	Commander
Ellen Pollock	Grandma
Ernest Clark	Air Marshal
Ronnie Brody	Drunk

MUSICAL Spain. Singers thwart hotelier's plan to steal American bomb for foreign spy.

13658
ONE MILLION YEARS BC (100) (A) *tech*
Hammer (WPD)
P:SC: Michael Carreras
D: Don Chaffey
S: Mickell Novak, George Baker, Joseph Frickert

Raquel Welch	Loana
John Richardson	Tumak
Percy Herbert	Sakana
Robert Brown	Akhoba
Martine Beswick	Nupondi
Jean Wladon	Ahot
Lisa Thomas	Sura
Malaya Nappi	Tohana
William Lyon Brown	Payto

FANTASY Stone age leader's banished son loves girl from peaceful tribe.

13659
THE WITCHES (91) (X) *tech*
Hammer -Seven Arts (WPD)
P: Anthony Nelson Keys
D: Cyril Frankel
S: (NOVEL) Peter Curtis (THE DEVIL'S OWN)
SC: Nigel Kneale

Joan Fontaine	Gwen Mayfield
Alex McCowen	Alan Bax
Kay Walsh	Stephanie Bax
Gwen Ffrangcon-Davies	Granny Rigg
Ingrid Brett	Linda Rigg

Martin Stephens . . . . Ronnie Dowsett
Duncan Lamont . . . . Bob Curd
Leonard Rossiter . . . . Dr Wallis
Michele Dotrice . . . . Valerie
CRIME Headmistress saves pupil from being sacrificed by employer's witch-cult.

13660
THE DEADLY AFFAIR (107) (X) *tech*
Sidney Lumet (Col)
D: Sidney Lumet
S: (NOVEL) John Le Carre (CALL FOR THE DEAD)
SC: Paul Dehn
James Mason . . . . Charles Dobbs
Simone Signoret . . . . Elsa Fennan
Maximilian Schell . . . . Dieter Frey
Harriet Andersson . . . . Anna Dobbs
Harry Andrews . . . . Insp Mendel
Kenneth Haigh . . . . Bill Appleby
Roy Kinnear . . . . Adam Scarr
Max Adrian . . . . Adviser
Lynn Redgrave . . . . Virgin
Robert Fleming . . . . Samuel Fennan
Corin Redgrave . . . . Director
Les White . . . . Harek
June Murphy . . . . Witch
Sheraton Blount . . . . Eunice Scarr
David Warner . . . . Edward II
Michael Bryant . . . . Gaveston
Stanley Lebor . . . . Lancaster
Paul Hardwick . . . . Mortimer
CRIME Spy resigns to investigate apparent suicide of Foreign Office official.

13661
FUNERAL IN BERLIN (102) (A) *tech/scope*
Lowndes (Par)
P: Harry Saltzman, Charles Kasher
D: Guy Hamilton
S: (NOVEL) Len Deighton
SC: Evan Jones
Michael Caine . . . . Harry Palmer
Paul Hubschmid . . . . Johnny Vulkan
Oscar Homolka . . . . Col Stok
Eva Rienzi . . . . Samatha Steel
Guy Doleman . . . . Ross
Rachel Gurney . . . . Mrs Ross
Hugh Burden . . . . Hallam
Thomas Holtzmann . . . . . . Reinhart
Gunter Meisner . . . . Kreutzmann
Heinz Schubert . . . . Aaron Levine
Wolfgang Volz . . . . Werner
Klaus Jepsen . . . . Otto Rukel
CRIME Russian spy's apparent defection is involved with search for stolen Jewish fortune.

13662
INFAMOUS CONDUCT (30) (A) *eastman*
Merton Park (AA)
P: Jack Greenwood
D: Richard Martin
S: James Eastwood
N: Ernest Lustgarten
Dermot Walsh . . . . Anthony Searle
Bridget Armstrong . . . . Janet Davis
Richard Warner . . . . Prosecution
Ewen Solon . . . . Dixon
Terry Wale . . . . Riki
Norman Scace . . . . Defence
Nancy Nevinson . . . . Maggie Searle
CRIME Struck-off surgeon falls for artist and becomes involved with criminals.

13663
MISS MACTAGGART WON'T LIE DOWN (28) (U)
Chairene (Monarch)
P:D: Francis Searle
S: Elwyn Ambrose

Barbara Mullen . . . . Jean Mactaggart
Eric Woodburn . . . . Morrison
Andrew Downie . . . . Sgt McLeod
Pat Mason . . . . Mrs Murray
Katherine Page . . . . Postmistress
Jack Lambert . . . . Lord Longbrae
COMEDY Proclaimed dead in error for her sister, spinster commits crimes to regain her identity.

13664
THE FROZEN DEAD (95) (X) *eastman*
Seven Arts-Goldstar (WPD)
P: Robert Goldstein, Herbert J. Leder
D:S: Herbert J. Leder
Dana Andrews . . . . Dr Norberg
Anna Palk . . . . Jean
Philip Gilbert . . . . Dr Ted Roberts
Karel Stepanek . . . . Gen Lubeck
Kathleen Breck . . . . Elsa
Alan Tilvern . . . . Karl Essen
Tom Chatto . . . . Insp Witt
Basil Henson . . . . Capt Tirpitz
HORROR. Decapitated girl's living head thwarts scientist's experiment with deep-frozen Nazis.

13665
THE JOKERS (94) (U) *tech*
Adastra-Gildor-Scimitar (RFD)
P: Maurice Foster, Ben Arbeid
D:S: Michael Winner
SC: Dick Clement, Ian La Frenais
Michael Crawford . . . . Michael Tremayne
Oliver Reed . . . . David Tremayne
Harry Andrews . . . . Marryatt
James Donald . . . . Col Gurney-Simms
Daniel Massey . . . . Riggs
Michael Hordern . . . . Sir Matthew
Gabriella Licudi . . . . Eve
Lotte Tarp . . . . Inge
Frank Finlay . . . . Man
Warren Mitchell . . . . Lennie
Rachel Kempson . . . . Mrs Tremayne
Peter Graves . . . . Mr Tremayne
Ingrid Brett . . . . Sarah
Brian Wilde . . . . Catchpole
Edward Fox . . . . Lieut Sprague
Michael Goodliffe . . . . Lt Col Paling
William Mervyn . . . . Uncle Edward
William Kendall . . . . Maj Gen Jeffcock
Freda Jackson . . . . Mrs Pervis
COMEDY Brother failures conspire to steal Crown Jewels.

13666
TO SIR, WITH LOVE (105) (A) *tech*
Columbia British (Col)
P: John R. Sloan, James Clavell
D:SC: James Clavell
S: (NOVEL) E.R. Braithwaite
Sidney Poitier . . . . Mark Thackeray
Christian Roberts . . . . Denham
Judy Geeson . . . . Pamela Dare
Suzy Kendall . . . . Gillian Blanchard
Lulu . . . . , . . . , ... Barbara Pegg
Faith Brook . . . . Mrs Evans
Geoffrey Bayldon . . . . Weston
Edward Burnham . . . . Florian
Gareth Robinson . . . . Tich
Graham Charles . . . . Fernman
Patricia Routledge . . . . Clinty
Fiona Duncan . . . . Miss Phillips
Adrienne Posta . . . . Moira Jackson
Ann Bell . . . . Mrs Dare
DRAMA British Guianan teacher wins respect of East End pupils.

13667
THE WHISPERERS (106) (A)
Seven Pines (UA)
P: Michael Laughlin, Ronald Shedlo
D:SC: Bryan Forbes

S: (NOVEL) Robert Nicholson
Edith Evans . . . . Maggie Ross
Eric Portman . . . . Archie Ross
Avis Bunnage . . . . Mrs Noonan
Nanette Newman . . . . Girl
Gerald Sim . . . . Mr Conrad
Ronald Fraser . . . . Charlie Ross
Leonard Rossiter . . . . Official
Kenneth Griffith . . . . Mr Weaver
Harry Baird . . . . Earl
Margaret Tyzack . . . . Almoner
Clare Kelly . . . . Prostitute
Robin Bailey . . . . Psychiatrist
Max Bacon . . . . Mr Fish
Sarah Forbes . . . . Maggie (child)
DRAMA Lonely old pensioner robbed of her son's stolen loot. (BFA 1967: Best Actress, B/W Pho.)

NOV

13668
A COUNTESS FROM HONG KONG (120) (A) *tech*
Universal Pictures (RFD)
P: Jerome Epstein, Charles Chaplin
D:S: Charles Chaplin
Marlon Brando . . . . Ogden
Sophia Loren . . . . Natascha
Sydney Chaplin . . . . Harvey
Tippi Hedren . . . . Martha
Patrick Cargill . . . . Hudson
Margaret Rutherford . . . . . . Miss Gaulswallow
Bill Nagy . . . . Crawford
Dilys Laye . . . . Saleswoman
Charles Chaplin . . . . Steward
COMEDY American ambassador hides Russian emigre countess in his liner cabin.

13669
DEADLIER THAN THE MALE (98) (X) *tech/scope*
Santor (RFD)
P: Betty Box, Sydney Box, Bruce Newbery
D: Ralph Thomas
S: (CHARACTERS) "Sapper"
SC: Jimmy Sangster, David Osborn, Liz Charles-Williams
Richard Johnson . . . . Hugh Drummond
Elke Sommer . . . . Irma Eckman
Sylvia Koscina . . . . Penelope
Nigel Green . . . . Carl Petersen
Suzanna Leigh . . . . Grace
Steve Carlson . . . . Robert Drummond
Virginia North . . . . Brenda
Zia Mohyeddin . . . . King Fedra
Justine Lord . . . . Miss Ashenden
Leonard Rossiter . . . . Bridgenorth
Laurence Naismith . . . . Sir John Bledlow
CRIME Adventurer thwarts international crook's plan to kill king for oil.

13670
THUNDERBIRDS ARE GO (94) (U) *tech/scope*
Animated Pictures (UA)
P:S: Gerry & Sylvia Anderson
D: David Lane
VOICES:
Sylvia Anderson . . . . Lady Penelope
Ray Barrett . . . . John Tracy/Controller
Peter Dyneley . . . . Jeff Tracy
David Graham . . . . . . Gordon Tracy/Parker/Brains
Shane Rimmer . . . . Scott Tracy
Jeremy Wilkin . . . . . . Virgil Tracey/President
Matt Zimmerman . . . . Alan Tracy/Messenger
Bob Monkhouse . . . . Brad Newman
Neil McCallum . . . . Dr Pierce
Charles Tingwell . . . . . . Dr Grant/PRO/Man
FANTASY 2000. International Rescue save first Martian exploration ship from crashing. (Puppet film).

13671
G.G. PASSION (25) (A)
Cadre (Tenser)
P: Gene Gutowski
D: David Bailey
S: Gerard Brach
Eric Swayne .... G.G. Passion
Chrissie Shrimpton .... Girl Friend
Rory Davis .... Judge
Janice Hayes .... Girl
FANTASY Middle-aged people condemn, pursue and execute teenage singer.

13672
THE SPY WITH A COLD NOSE (93) (U)
eastman
Associated London-Embassy (Par)
P: Leonard Lightstone
D: Daniel Petrie
S: Ray Galton, Alan Simpson
Laurence Harvey .... Francis Trevellyan
Lionel Jeffries .... Stanley Farquhar
Daliah Lavi .... Princess Natasha Romanova
Eric Sykes .... Wrigley
Eric Portman .... Ambassador
Denholm Elliott .... Pond-Jones
Colin Blakeley .... Russian PM
Robert Fleming .... Director M15
June Whitfield .... Elsie Farquhar
Paul Ford .... General
Bernard Archard .... Russian Chief
Robin Bailey .... Man
Nai Bonet .... Belly-dancer
RSM Ronald Brittain ...... Commissionaire
COMEDY Russian Princess helps spy get radio-bugged bulldog back from Moscow.

13673
IT (97) (X) *eastman*
Seven Arts-Goldstar (WPD)
P: Robert Goldstein, Herbert J. Leger
D:SC: Herbert J. Leger
Roddy McDowall .... Arthur Pimm
Jill Haworth .... Ellen Groves
Paul Maxwell .... Tim Perkins
Noel Trevarthen .... Insp White
Ian McCulloch .... Assistant Insp
Ernest Clark .... Harold Groves
Aubrey Richards .... Prof Weal
Oliver Johnson .... Trimingham
Allan Sellers .... The Golem
HORROR Museum curator revives ancient statue and uses it to wreak havoc on London.

13674
THE PERSECUTION AND ASSASSINATION OF JEAN–PAUL MARAT AS PERFORMED BY THE INMATES OF THE ASYLUM OF CHARENTON UNDER THE DIRECTION OF THE MARQUIS DE SADE (116) (X) *deluxe*
Marat-Sade (UA)
P: Michael Birkett
D: Peter Brook
S: (PLAY) Peter Weiss
SC: Adrian Mitchell
Patrick Magee .... Marquis de Sade
Ian Richardson .... Jean-Paul Marat
Glenda Jackson .... Charlotte Corday
Michael Williams .... Herald

Clifford Rose .... Coulmier
Freddie Jones .... Cucurucu
Hugh Sullivan .... Kokol
Morgan Sheppard .... Mad Animal
Jonathan Burn .... Polpoch
Jeanette Landis .... Rossignol
Robert Lloyd .... Jacques Roux
John Steiner .... Duperret
DRAMA Charenton, 1808. Asylum inmates perform play about assassination of Marat. (Longest title).

DEC

13675
DROP DEAD DARLING (100) (X) *tech/scope*
USA: ARRIVEDERCI BABY
Seven Arts (Par)
P:D: Ken Hughes
S: (NOVEL) Richard Deeming (THE CAREFUL MAN)
SC: Ken Hughes, Ronald Harwood
Tony Curtis .... Nick Johnson
Rosanna Schiaffino .... Francesca
Lionel Jeffries .... Parker
Zsa-Zsa Gabor .... Gigi
Nancy Kwan .... Baby
Fenella Fielding .... Fenella
Anna Quayle .... Aunt Miriam
Warren Mitchell ... Comte de Rienzi/Maximilian
Mischa Auer .... Romeo
Noel Purcell .... Capt Flannery
Alan Gifford .... Officer
COMEDY Conman kills wives for their money and finds his latest wife plans to kill him.

13676
THE NIGHT OF THE GENERALS (147) (A)
tech/scope
Horizon-Filmsonor (Col)
P: Sam Spiegel
D: Anatole Litvak
S: (NOVEL) Hans Helmut Kirst (STORY)
James Hadley Chase
SC: Joseph Kessel, Paul Dehn
Peter O'Toole .... Gen Tanz
Omar Sharif .... Maj Grau
Tom Courtenay .... Cpl Curt Hartmann
Christopher Plummer ... Field-Marshal Rommel
Donald Pleasence .... Gen Kahlenberge
Joanna Pettet .... Ulrike von Seydlitz-Gabler
Philippe Noiret .... Insp Morand
Juliette Greco .... Juliette
Charles Gray ..... Gen von Seydlitz-Gabler
Coral Browne .... Eleanor
John Gregson .... Col Sandauer
Nigel Stock .... Otto
Yves Brainville .... Liesowski
Gerard Buhr .... von Stauffenberg
Gordon Jackson .... Capt Engel
Patrick Allen .... Col Mannheim
Harry Andrews .... Governor
WAR Paris, 1944. German intelligence officer proves General involved in plot to kill Hitler murders prostitutes.

13677
DON'T LOSE YOUR HEAD (90) (A) *eastman*
Eastman
Adder (RFD)

P: Peter Rogers
D: Gerald Thomas
S: Talbot Rothwell
Sidney James .... Sir Rodney Ffing
Kenneth Williams .... Citizen Camembert
Jim Dale .... Lord Darcy
Charles Hawtrey .... Duke de Pommfrit
Joan Sims .... Desiree Dubarry
Dany Robin .... Jacqueline
Peter Butterworth .... Citizen Bidet
Peter Gilmore .... Robespierre
Michael Ward .... Henri
Leon Greene .... Malabonce
Diana Macnamara .... Princess Stephanie
COMEDY Paris, 1789. English nobles don disguises to save aristocrats from guillotine.

13678
A MAN FOR ALL SEASONS (120)(U) tech
Highroad (Col)
P: Fred Zinneman, Wilton N. Graf
D: Fred Zinneman
S: (PLAY) Robert Bolt
SC: Robert Bolt
Paul Scofield .... Sir Thomas More
Wendy Hiller .... Alice More
Leo McKern .... Thomas Cromwell
Robert Shaw .... Henry VIII
Orson Welles .... Cardinal Wolsey
Susannah York .... Margaret More
Nigel Davenport .... Duke of Norfolk
John Hurt .... Richard Rich
Corin Redgrave .... William Roper
Colin Blakeley .... Matthew
Vanessa Redgrave .... Anne Boleyn
HISTORY 1582. Henry VIII tries to force Catholic councillor's consent to divorce.
(AA 1966: Best Film, Director, Actor, Screenplay, Colour Pho, Costumes BFA 1967: Best Film, Best British Film, Actor, Screenplay Colour Pho, Art Dir, Costumes).

13679
MAROC 7 (91) (A) *eastman/scope*
Cyclone (RFD)
P: John Gale, Leslie Phillips, Martin C. Chute
D: Gerry O'Hara
S: David Osborn
Gene Barry .... Simon Grant
Elsa Martinelli .... Claudia
Leslie Phillips .... Raymond Lowe
Cyd Charisse .... Louise Henderson
Denholm Elliott .... Insp Barrada
Alexandra Stewart .... Michele Craig
Eric Parker .... Prof Bannen
Angela Douglas .... Freddie
Tracey Reed .... Vivienne
Maggie London .... Suzie
Lionel Blair .... Receptionist
Paul Danquah .... Policeman
CRIME Morocco. Fashion magazine editress plots to steal ancient medal.

13680
TROUBLE WITH JUNIA (18) (U)
Woodhouse (Saxon)
P:D:S: Barbara Woodhouse
Junia
CHILDREN Pensioner wins Great Dane which catches thief.

1967

JAN

13681
ACCIDENT (105) (A) *eastman*
Royal Avenue Chelsea (LIP)
P: Joseph Losey, Norman Priggen
D: Joseph Losey
S: (NOVEL) Nicholas Mosley
SC: Harold Pinter
Dirk Bogarde . . . . Stephen
Stanley Baker . . . . Charley
Jacqueline Sassard . . . . Anna
Delphine Seyrig . . . . Francesca
Alexander Knox . . . . Provost
Michael York . . . . William
Vivien Merchant . . . . Rosalind
Harold Pinter . . . . Bell
Ann Firbank . . . . Laura
Brian Phelan . . . . Sgt
Freddie Jones . . . . Frantic Man
Nicholas Mosley . . . . Don
DRAMA Oxford. Married tutors have affairs with
rich student's Austrian fiancee.

13682
BLOW-UP (111) (X) *eastman*
Bridge (MGM)
P: Pierre Rouve, Carlo Ponti
D: Michaelangelo Antonioni
S: (STORY) Julio Cortazar
SC: Michelangelo Antonioni, Tonino Guerra,
Edward Bond
Vanessa Redgrave . . . . Jane
David Hemmings . . . . Thomas
Sarah Miles . . . . Patricia
Peter Bowles . . . . Ron
John Castle . . . . Painter
Jane Birkin . . . . Girl
Gillian Hills . . . . Girl
Harry Hutchinson . . . . Dealer
Verushka . . . . Model
Julian Chagrin . . . . Mime
The Yardbirds
CRIME Fashion photographer accidentally
photographs murder.

13683
THE MAGNIFICENT TWO (100) (U)
eastman
Rank (RFD)
P: Hugh Stewart
D: Cliff Owen
S: Peter Blackmore
SC: S.C. Green, R.M. Hills, Michael Pertwee
Eric Morecambe . . . . Eric
Ernie Wise . . . . Ernie
Margit Saad . . . . Carla
Virgilio Teixeira . . . . Carllo
Cecil Parker . . . . Ambassador
Isobel Black . . . . Juanita
Martin Benson . . . . President Diaz
Michael Godfrey . . . . Manuelo
Sue Sylvaine . . . . Carmelita
Andreas Malandrinos . . . . . Juan
Victor Maddern . . . . Assassin
COMEDY South America. Salesman, double
for dead revolutionary, becomes president.

13684
SON OF THE SAHARA (U) *eastman*
AB-Pathe (CFF)
P: Harry Field, Lionel Hoare
D: Frederick Goode
S: (NOVEL) Kelman D. Frost
SC: Henry Geddes, Roger Dunton
Darryl Read . . . . Abu
Kit Williams . . . . Yusef
Ria Mills . . . . Selima
Michael Wennink . . . . Musa
Bernard Archard . . . . Bu Kader

Terence deMarney . . . . Ibrahim
William Dexter . . . . Sidi Faisal
John Stuart . . . . Caid

13685
1—THE GUN RUNNERS (15)

13686
2—THE CONSPIRATORS (15)

13687
3—TRAPPED (15)

13688
4—THE VALLEY OF GHOSTS (15)

13689
5—THE LAST HOPE (15)

13690
6—COUNTER PLOT (15)

13691
7—AMBUSH (15)

13692
8—GHOST ARMY (15)
CHILDREN Morocco. Stable boy thwarts
rebellion led by Caid's cousin.

FEB

13693
CASINO ROYALE (131) (U) *tech/scope*
Famous Artists (Col)
P: Charles K. Feldman, Jerry Bresler
D: John Huston, Ken Hughes, Val Guest,
Robert Parrish, Joe McGrath, Richard
Talmadge, Anthony Squire
S: (NOVEL) Ian Fleming
SC: Wolf Mankowitz, John Law, Michael
Sayers
Peter Sellers . . . . Evelyn Tremble
Ursula Andress . . . . Vesper Lynd
David Niven . . . . Sir James Bond
Orson Welles . . . . Le Chiffre
Joanna Pettet . . . . Mata Bond
Dahlia Lavi . . . . Detainer
Woody Allen . . . . Jimmy Bond
Deborah Kerr . . . . Mimi
William Holden . . . . Ransome
Charles Boyer . . . . Le Grand
John Huston . . . . M
Kurt Kasznar . . . . Smernov
George Raft . . . . Himself
Jean-Pierre Belmondo . . . . . Legionnaire
Terence Cooper . . . . Cooper
Barbara Bouchet . . . . Moneypenny
Angela Scoular . . . . Buttercup
Tracey Crisp . . . . Heather
Elaine Taylor . . . . Peg
Gabriella Licudi . . . . Eliza
Anna Quayle . . . . Frau Hoffner
Derek Nimmo . . . . Hadley
Peter O'Toole . . . . Piper
Stirling Moss . . . . Driver
Colin Gordon . . . . Director
Bernard Cribbins . . . . Taxi driver
Duncan Macrae . . . . Insp Mathis
Richard Wattis . . . . Officer
Valentine Dyall . . . . Dr Noah (voice)
COMEDY Agent emerges from retirement and
uses baccarat expert to foil SMERSH.

13694
THE DOUBLE MAN (105) (U) *tech*
Albion (WPD)
P: Hal E. Chester
D: Franklin J. Schaffner
S: (NOVEL) Henry S. Maxfield (LEGACY FOR
A SPY)
SC: Frank Tarloff, Alfred Hayes

Yul Brynner . . . . .Dan Slater/Kalmar
Britt Ekland . . . . Gina
Clive Revill . . . . Frank Wheatley
Anton Diffring . . . . Berthold
Moira Lister . . . . Mrs Carrington
Lloyd Nolan . . . . Edwards
George Mikell . . . . Max Gruner
Brandon Brady . . . . Gregori
Julia Arnall . . . . Anna
Kenneth J. Warren . . . . Police Chief
Franklin J. Schaffner . . . . . Man
CRIME Austria. Communists kill CIA agent's
son in order to kill him and substitute double.

13695
THE MIKADO (122) (U) *tech*
BHE (Eagle)
P: Anthony Havelock-Allan, John Brabourne
D: Stuart Burge
S: (OPERA) W.S. Gilbert, Arthur Sullivan
Donald Adams . . . . The Mikado
Philip Potter . . . . Nanki-Poo
John Reed . . . . Ko-Ko
Kenneth Sandford . . . . Pooh-Bah
Valerie Masterson . . . . Yum-Yum
Peggy Ann Jones . . . . Pitti-Sing
Christene Palmer . . . . Katisha
Thomas Lawler . . . . Pish-Tush
Pauline Wales . . . . Peep-Bo
George Cook . . . . Go-To
D'Oyly Carte Opera Co Chorus
MUSICAL Japan. Mikado's son poses as
poor minstrel to woo executioner's ward.

13696
FRANKENSTEIN CREATED WOMAN (86)
(X) *tech*
Hammer (WPD)
P: Anthony Nelson Keys
D: Terence Fisher
S: (CHARACTERS) Mary Shelley
SC: Anthony Hinds
Peter Cushing . . . . Baron Frankenstein
Susan Denberg . . . . Christine Kleve
Thorley Walters . . . . Dr Hertz
Robert Morris . . . . Hans
Duncan Lamont . . . . Prisoner
Peter Blythe . . . . Anton
Barry Warren . . . . Karl
Derek Fowlds . . . . Johann
Alan MacNaughton . . . . Kleve
Peter Madden . . . . Police Chief
Philip Ray . . . . Mayor
HORROR Austria, period. Baron revives
cripple girl's corpse with soul of guillotined
sweetheart.

13697
JULES VERNE'S ROCKET TO THE MOON
(101) (U) *eastman/scope*
USA THOSE FANTASTIC FLYING FOOLS
Jules Verne (AA)
P: Harry Alan Towers
D: Don Sharp
S: (NOVEL) Jules Verne
SC: Peter Welbeck, Dave Freeman
Burl Ives . . . . Phineas T. Barnum
Troy Donahue . . . . .Gaylord Sullivan
Gert Frobe . . . . Prof Von Bulow
Terry•Thomas . . .Sir Harry Washington-Smythe
Hermione Gingold . . . . Angelica
Daliah Lavi . . . . Madelaine
Lionel Jeffries . . . . .Sir Charles Dillworthy
Dennis Price . . . . Duke of Barset
Stratford Johns . . . . Warrant Officer
Graham Stark . . . . Grundle
Jimmy Clitheroe . . . . Gen Tom Thumb
Edward De Souza . . . . Henry
Joan Sterndale Bennett . . . . Queen Victoria

Allan Cuthbertson . . . . . . Inspector
COMEDY American showman and lord finance
rocket to send midget to moon.

13698
PRIVILEGE (103) (A) *tech*
World Film Services-Memorial Enterprises (UI)
P: John Heyman
D: Peter Watkins
S: Johnny Speight
SC: Norman Bogner, Peter Watkins
Paul Jones . . . . Steve Shorter
Jean Shrimpton . . . . Vanessa Ritchie
Mark London . . . . Alvin Kirsch
Max Bacon . . . . Julie Jordan
Jeremy Child . . . . Martin Crossley
William Job . . . . Andrew Butler
James Cossins . . . . Tatham
Frederick Danner . . . . Hooper
Victor Henry . . . . Freddie K
Arthur Pentelow . . . . Stanley
FANTASY Church and government use pop
singer's power to control nation's youth.

13699
THE SHUTTERED ROOM (99) (X) *tech*
Seven Arts-Troy-Schenck (WPD)
P: Philip Hazleton
D: David Greene
S: (NOVEL) H.P. Lovecraft, August Derleth
SC: D.B. Ledrov, Nat Tanchuck
Gig Young . . . . Mike Kelton
Carol Lynley . . . . . . .Susannah Kelton/Sarah
Oliver Reed . . . . Ethan
Flora Robson . . . . Aunt Agatha
William Devlin . . . . Zebulon Whateley
Bernard Kay . . . . Tait
Judith Arthy . . . . Emma
Robert Cawdron . . . . Luther Whateley
Celia Hewitt . . . . Aunt Sarah
HORROR New England. Girl discovers millhouse
ghost to be her own disfigured, demented sister.

13700
THE SORCERORS (85) (X) *eastman*
Global-Tigon-Curtwel (Tigon)
P: Arnold Miller, Patrick Curtis, Tony Tenser
D: Michael Reeves
S: John Burke
SC: Michael Reeves, Tom Baker
Boris Karloff . . . . Prof Monserrat
Catherine Lacey . . . . . . .Estelle Monserrat
Ian Ogilvy . . . . Mike
Elizabeth Ercy . . . . Nicole
Victor Henry . . . . Alan
Susan George . . . . Audrey
Dani Sheridan . . . . Laura
Ivor Dean . . . . Insp Matalon
Peter Fraser . . . . Detective
FANTASY Hypnotist and his wife use a youth
to experience crime and murder.

13701
STRANGER IN THE HOUSE (104) (X) *eastman*
De Grunwald (RFD)
P: Dimitri De Grunwald,
D:SC: Pierre Rouve
S: (NOVEL) Georges Simenon (LES INCONNUS
DANS LA MAISON)
James Mason . . . . John Sawyer
Geraldine Chaplin . . . . Angela Sawyer
Bobby Darin . . . . Barney Teale
Paul Bertoya . . . . .Jo Christophorides
Ian Ogilvy . . . . Desmond Flower
Bryan Stanton . . . . Peter Hawkins
Pippa Steel . . . . Sue Phillips
Clive Morton . . . . Col Flower
James Hayter . . . . Harry Hawkins
Megs Jenkins . . . . .Mrs Christophorides
Marjie Lawrence . . . . Brenda

Moira Lister . . . . Mrs Flower
Lisa Daniely . . . . Diana
CRIME Winchester. Drunken ex-barrister defends
his daughter's Cypriot lover on charge of murdering
American steward.

13702
CALAMITY THE COW (59) (U)
Island-Shepperton (CFF)
P: Ian Dalrymple
D: David Eastman
S: David Eastman, Kerry Eastman
John Moulder-Brown . . . . . . Rob Grant
Elizabeth Dear . . . . Jo Grant
Stephen Brown . . . . Tim Lucas
Philip Collins . . . . Mike Lucas
Josephine Gillick . . . . Beth Lucas
Grant Taylor . . . . Mr Grant
Honor Shepherd . . . . Mrs Grant
Alastair Hunter . . . . Kincaid
Desmond Carrington . . . . . Uncle Jim
CHILDREN Children groom ill-treated cow
for dairy show and save her from rustlers.

13703
DANCE OF THE VAMPIRES (107) (X) *metro/
scope* USA: THE FEARLESS VAMPIRE
KILLERS
Cadre-Filmways (MGM)
P; Martin Ransohoff, Gene Gutowski
D: Roman Polanski
S: Gerard Brach, Roman Polanski
Jack MacGowran . . . . Prof Abronsius
Roman Polanski . . . . Alfred
Alfie Bass . . . . Shagal
Jessie Robins . . . . Mrs Shagal
Sharon Tate . . . . Sarah Shagal
Ferdy Mayne . . . . Count VonKrolock
Iain Quarrier . . . . Herbert Von Krolock
Terry Downes . . . . Koukol
Fiona Lewis . . . . Maid
Ronald Lacey . . . . Idiot
Sydney Bromley . . . . Driver
Andreas Malandrinos . . . . . Woodcutter
HORROR Transylvania, period. Professor
rescues innkeeper's daughter from vampire,
but too late.

13704
THE TERRONAUTS (75) (U) *pathe*
Anglo-Embassy-Amicus (Avoc-Embassy)
P: Milton Subotsky, Max Rosenberg
D: Montgomery Tully
S: (NOVEL) Murray Leinster (THE WAILING
ASTEROID)
SC: John Brunner
Simon Oates . . . . Dr Joe Burke
Zena Marshall . . . . Sandy Lund
Charles Hawtrey . . . . Yellowlees
Patricia Hayes . . . . Mrs Jones
Shirley Meadows . . . . Ben Keller
Max Adrian . . . . Dr Henry Shore
Frank Barry . . . . Burke (child)
Richard Carpenter . . . . Danny
Leonard Cracknell . . . . . .Nick/Frank Forsyth/
                                    Uncle
Robert Jewell . . . . Robot Operator
FANTASY Robot abducts astronomer to alien
asteroid.

MAR

13705
THE BOBO (103) (A) *tech*
Gina (WPD)
P: Elliott Kastner, Jerry Gershwin
D: Robert Parrish
S: (NOVEL) Burt Cole (OLIMPIA); (PLAY)
David R. Schwartz
SC: David R. Schwartz
Peter Sellers . . . . Juan Bautista

Britt Ekland . . . . Olimpia Segura
Rossano Brazzi . . . . Carlos Matabosch
Adolfo Celi . . . . Francisco Carbonell
Hattie Jacques . . . . Trinity Martinez
Ferdy Mayne . . . . Silvestre Flores
Kenneth Griffith . . . . Pepe Gamazo
Alfredo Lettieri . . . . Eugenio Gomez
John Wells . . . . .Pompadour Major
Marne Maitland . . . . Luis Castillo
La Chana and Los Tarantos
COMEDY Spain. Unsuccessful bullfighter poses as
count's aide to seduce rich girl and become a singer

13706
DANNY THE DRAGON (U)
Ansus (CFF)
P: Frank Godwin
D: C.M. Pennington-Richards
S: Henry Geddes
SC: C.M. Pennington-Richards, Michael Barnes
Sally Thomsett . . . . Jean
Christopher Cooper . . . . Peter
Jack Wild . . . . Gavin
Peter Butterworth . . . . Farmer
Frank Thornton . . . . Sgt Bull
Patrick Newell . . . . Potter
Jack le White . . . . Danny
Kenneth Connor . . . . Danny's Voice

13707
1—THE INVISIBLE SPACE BUBBLE (16)

13708
2—STRANGER FROM DRAGONARA (16)

13709
3—DANNICAFORILITHERMIDOR (17)

13710
3—THE TENT WITH FOUR LEGS (14)

13711
5—DRAGON HUNT (15)

13712
6—DANNY GETS JET PROPELLED (15)

13713
7—THE RUNAWAY BUBBLE (16)

13714
8—POTTER IN PURSUIT (16)

13715
9—IN SEARCH OF ZOOMITE (17)
13716
10—DRAGON TRAP (17)
CHILDREN Three children help extra-terrestial
recover his invisible vehicle.

13717
FLASH THE SHEEPDOG (58) (U) *eastman*
International Film Associates (CFF)
P: J.B. Holmes
D:SC: Laurence Henson
S: (NOVEL) Kathleen Fidler
Earl Younger . . . . Tom Stokes
Ross Campbell . . . . Dougie
Alex Allan . . . . Andra
Victor Carin . . . . Uncle John
Margaret Greig . . . . Elspeth
David Hanley . . . . Ian
John Short . . . . Jimmie
Marjorie Thomson . . . . . . Aunt Meg
CHILDREN Scotland. English orphan
trains his uncle's sheepdog to win trials.

13718
MISTER TEN PERCENT (84) (U) *tech/scope*
ABPC (WPD)
P: W.A.Whittaker
D: Peter Graham Scott
S: Mira Avrech

SC: Norman Hudis, Charlie Drake

Charlie Drake	Percy Pointer
Derek Nimmo	Tony
Wanda Ventham	Kathy
John Le Mesurier	Jocelyn Macauley
Anthony Nicholls	Casey
Noel Dyson	Mrs Gorman
John Hewer	Townsend
Anthony Gardner	Claude Crepe
Ronald Radd	Publicist
John Laurie	Scotsman
Annette Andre	Muriel
Justine Lord	Lady Dorothea
George Baker	Lord Edward
Joyce Blair	Lady Dorothea
Una Stubbs	Lady Dorothea

COMEDY Builder's drama becomes hit as comedy.

13719
THE MUMMY'S SHROUD (84) (X) *tech*
Hammer (WPD)
P: Anthony Nelson Keys
D: SC: John Gilling
S: Anthony Hinds

Andre Morell	Sir Basil Walden
John Phillips	Stanley Preston
David Buck	Paul Preston
Elizabeth Sellars	Barbara Preston
Catherine Lacey	Haiti
Maggie Kimberley	Claire
Michael Ripper	Longbarrow
Roger Delgado	Hasmid Ali
Tim Barrett	Harry
Richard Warner	Insp Barrani
Dickie Owen	Prem
Bruno Barnabe	Pharaoh
Eddie Powell	Mummy

HORROR Egypt, 1920. Ancient mummy revived to murder archaeologists.

13720
RIVER RIVALS (U) *eastman*
Century (CFF)
P: Roy Simpson
D: Harry Booth
S: Harry Booth, Michael Barnes

Renee Houston	Mrs Fredericks
Brian Haines	Mr Craig
Darryl Read	Ricky Holmes
Sally Thomsett	Penny Holmes
Cordel Leigh	Tich Holmes
Philip Meredith	Mike Craig
Rufus Frampton	Pete Craig
Julie Booth	Molly Craig
Dick Emery	
Rona Anderson	

13721
1: THE GOLDEN DRAGON (13)

13722
2: THE BLOCKADE RUNNERS (13)

13723
3: NIGHT RAIDERS (14)

13724
4: OPERATION AIRLIFT (14)

13725
5: MISSION ACCOMPLISHED (13)

13726
6: SHIPWRECK (15)

13727
7: THE DRAGON'S SECRET (19)
CHILDREN Children build boat to enter race and help widowed houseboat owner.

13728
THE LONG DUEL (115) (U) *tech/scope*
Rank (RFD)
P:D: Ken Annakin
S: Ranveer Singh
SC: Ernest Bornemann, Peter Yeldham, Geoffrey Orme

Yul Brynner	Sultan
Trevor Howard	Freddy Young
Harry Andrews	Supt Stafford
Andrew Keir	Gungaram
Charlotte Rampling	Jane Stafford
Virginia North	Champa
Laurence Naismith	McDougal
Maurice Denham	Governor
Imogen Hassall	Tara
Zorah Segal	Devi
Paul Hardwick	Jamadar
Norman Florence	Nathu
Antonio Ruiz	Munnu
Kurt Christian	Babu
Terence Alexander	Major

ADVENTURE India, 1920. British police officer tries to capture tribal leader without too much bloodshed.

13729
THE VIKING QUEEN (91) (A) *tech*
Hammer (WPD)
P:S: John Temple-Smith
D: Don Chaffey
SC: Clarke Reynolds

Don Murray	Justinian
Carita	Salina
Donald Houston	Maelgan
Andrew Keir	Octavian
Patrick Troughton	Tristram
Adrienne Corri	Beatrice
Niall MacGinnis	Tiberion
Wilfrid Lawson	King Priam
Nicola Paget	Talia
Percy Herbert	Catus
Denis Shaw	Osiris

ADVENTURE Britain, 100. Queen of Iceni tribe's love for Roman Governor causes Druids to revolt.

13730
ULYSSES (132) (X)
Ulysses (BL)
P:D: Joseph Strick
S: (NOVEL) James Joyce
SC: Joseph Strick, Fred Haines

Milo O'Shea	Leopold Bloom
Barbara Jefford	Molly Bloom
Maurice Roeves	Stephen Dedalus
T.P.McKenna	Buck Mulligan
Anna Manahan	Bella Cohen
Maureen Potter	Josie Breen
Martin Dempsey	Simon Dedalus
Graham Lines	Haines
Joe Lynch	Blazes Boylan
Fionnuala Flanagan	Gerty MacDowell
Maire Hastings	Mary Driscoll
Geoffrey Golden	Citizen
Dave Kelly	Garrett Deasy
Maureen Toal	Zoe Higgins
O.Z. Whitehead	Alexander J. Dowie

DRAMA Dublin, 1904. Day in the life of Jewish salesman whose wife loves boxing promoter.

13731
COUNTDOWN TO DANGER (63) (U) *eastman*
Wallace (CFF)
P: A. Frank Bundy
D:S: Peter Seabourne

David MacAlister	Mike
Paul Martin	Tony

Angela Lee	Sandie
Penny Spencer	Sue
Richard Coleman	Capt Wright
Lane Meddick	Sgt Thompson
Frank Williams	Harry

CHILDREN Alderney. Bomb disposal officer helps trapped boy dismantle German mine.

13732
GO WITH MATT MUNRO (25) (U) eastman
AB-Pathe
P: Harry Field
D: Bertram Tyrer
Matt Munro
Roy Castle
Marian Montgomery
MUSICAL Pop singer tours Rome.

13733
PAYMENT IN KIND (30) (A) *eastman*
Merton Park (AA)
P: Jack Greenwood
D: Peter Duffell
S: John Roddick, Peter Duffell
N: Edgar Lustgarten

Justine Lord	Paula Morgan
Derrick Sherwin	Andrews
Maxine Audley	Counsel
Brian Haines	John Morgan
Gwen Cherrill	Mrs Ferguson
Peter Bathurst	Ferguson
Henry McGee	Jeweller

CRIME Indebted wife kills her lustful blackmailer.

APR

13734
MINI WEEKEND (79) (X)
Global-Tigon (Tigon)
P: Tony Tenser
D: Georges Robin
S: Georges Robin, Tony Tenser

Anthony Trent	Tom
Veronica Lang	Jenny
Anna Palk	Girl in Tiles
Liza Rogers	Sandra
Connie Fraser	Mother
Karen Leslie	Girl in Pub
Nina Dwyer	Girl on Bus
Valerie Stanton	Girl in Shop
Eve Aubrey	Hag
Vicky Hodge	Girl in Dream

FANTASY Man lives dream life with pretty girls he sees in street.

13735
THE DEADLY BEES (123) (X) *tech*
Amicus (Par)
P: Max J. Rosenberg, Milton Subotsky
D: Freddie Francis
S: (NOVEL) H.F.Heard
(A TASTE FOR HONEY)
SC: Robert Bloch, Anthony Marriott

Suzanna Leigh	Vicky Robbins
Frank Finlay	Manfred
Guy Doleman	Ralph Hargrove
Catherine Finn	Mary Hargrove
John Harvey	Thompson
Michael Ripper	Dave Hawkins
Tim Barrett	Harcourt
Katy Wild	Doris
Michael Gwynn	Dr Lang

HORROR Recuperating singer discovers islander has developed killer bees.

13736
FIVE GOLDEN DRAGONS (70) (A)
tech/scope

Blansfilm (AA)
P: Harry Alan Towers
D: Jeremy Summers
S: Peter Welbeck

Robert Cummings	Bob Mitchell
Rupert Davies	Comm Sanders
Margaret Lee	Magda
Maria Perschy	Margret
Klaus Kinsky	Gert
Maria Rohm	Ingrid
Brian Donlevy	Dragon
Dan Duryea	Dragon
Christopher Lee	Dragon
George Raft	Dragon

CRIME Hong Kong. American playboy poses as masked gang-leader to thwart crime organisation.

13737
HOW I WON THE WAR (110) (X) *eastman*
Petersham (UA)
P: Richard Lester, Denis O'Dell
D: Richard Lester
S: (NOVEL) Patrick Ryan
SC: Charles Wood

Michael Crawford	Lt Ernest Goodbody
John Lennon	Gripweed
Roy Kinnear	Clapper
Lee Montague	Sgt Transom
Jack MacGowran	Juniper
Michael Hordern	Grapple
Jack Hedley	Melancholy Musketeer
Karl Michael Vogler	Odlebog
Ronald Lacey	Spool
James Cossins	Drogue
Alexander Knox	General
Robert Hardy	General
Sheila Hancock	Friend
Bryan Pringle	Reporter
Fanny Carby	Mrs Clapper
Dandy Nichols	Old Lady
John Junkin	Large Child

COMEDY Egypt, 1943. Officer sets up cricket pitch to impress VIP.

13738
THE MAN OUTSIDE (98) (A) *tech/scope*
Trio-Group W (LIP)
P: William Gell
D: Samuel Gallu
S: (NOVEL) Gene Stackleborg
(DOUBLE AGENT)
SC: Samuel Gallu, Julian Bond, Roger Marshall

Van Heflin	Bill Maclean
Heidelinde Weis	Kay Sebastian
Pinkas Braun	Rafe Machek
Peter Vaughan	Nicolai Volkov
Charles Gray	Charles Griddon
Paul Maxwell	Judson Murphy
Ronnie Barker	George Venaxas
Linda Marlowe	Dorothy
Gary Cockrell	Brune Parry
Bill Nagy	Morehouse
Larry Cross	Austen
Willoughby Gray	Inspector
Carole Ann Ford	Cindy

CRIME Ex-CIA agent, framed for murder by Russians, saves kidnapped girl.

MAY

13739
AFRICA — TEXAS STYLE (109) (U) *eastman*
Vantors (Par)
P: Ivan Tors, Andrew Marton
D: Andrew Marton
S: Andy White

Hugh O'Brian	Jim Sinclair
John Mills	W/C Howard Hayes

Nigel Green	Karl Bekker
Tom Nardini	John Henry
Adrienne Corri	Fay Carter
Ronald Howard	Hugo Copp
Charles Malinda	Sampson
Honey Wamala	Mr Oyondi
Charles Hayes	Veterinary
Stephen Kikumu	Peter
Hayley Mills	Girl

ADVENTURE Kenya. English settler and Texas cowboys start wild game ranch despite villainous cattle rancher.

13740
THE PLANK (54) (U) *tech*
Associated London (RFD)
P: Beryl Vertue, Jon Penington
D:S: Eric Sykes

Tommy Cooper	Larger Workman
Eric Sykes	Smaller Workman
Jimmy Edwards	Policeman
Roy Castle	Garbage Man
Graham Stark	Van Driver
Stratford Johns	Sergeant
Jimmy Tarbuck	Barman
Jim Dale	Painter
Hattie Jacques	Woman
Dermot Kelley	Concertina Man
Libby Morris	Tourist
Rex Garner	Tourist
John Junkin	Truck Driver
Dave Freeman	Cement Mixer
Johnny Speight	Chauffeur
Kenny Lynch	Garbage Driver
Howard Douglas	Old Man

COMEDY Misadventures of two builders taking plank to house.

13741
SAILOR FROM GIBRALTAR (91) (X)
Woodfall (UA)
P: Oscar Lewenstein, Neil Hartley
D: Tony Richardson
S: (NOVEL) Marguerite Duras
(LE MARIN DE GIBRALTAR)
SC: Tony Richardson, Christopher Isherwood, Don Magner

Jeanne Moreau	Anna
Ian Bannen	Alan
Vanessa Redgrave	Sheila
Hugh Griffith	Llewellyn
Orson Welles	Louis
Zia Mohyeddin	Noori
Umberto Orsini	Vendor
Erminio Spalla	Eolo
Eleanor Brown	Carla
Arnoldo Foa	Man
John Hurt	John

ROMANCE Italy. Clerk on holiday abandons his mistress for a rich Frenchwoman.

13742
THE TRYGON FACTOR (87) (X) *tech*
Rialto-Preben Philipsen (RFD)
P: Ian Warren, Brian Taylor
D: Cyril Frankel
S: Derry Quinn, Stanley Munro

Stewart Granger	Supt Cooper-Smith
Susan Hampshire	Trudy Emberday
Cathleen Nesbitt	Livia Emberday
James Culliford	Luke Emberday
Brigitte Horney	Sister General
Robert Morley	Hubert Hamlyn
Sophie Hardy	Sophie
James Robertson Justice	Sir John
Colin Gordon	Dice
Eddi Arent	Emil Clossen
Diane Clare	Sister Clare
Allan Cuthbertson	Thompson

CRIME Rich woman's gang steals million in gold and melts it in her convent.

13743
TWO FOR THE ROAD (111) (A) *deluxe/scope*
Stanley Donen (20)
P:D: Stanley Donen
S: Frederic Raphael

Audrey Hepburn	Joanna Wallace
Albert Finney	Mark Wallace
Eleanor Bron	Cathy Manchester
William Daniels	Howard Manchester
Claude Dauphin	Maurice Dalbret
Nadia Gray	Francoise Dalbret
Georges Descrieres	David
Gabrielle Middleton	Ruth Manchester
Jacqueline Bisset	Jackie
Judy Cornwell	Pat
Irene Hilda	Yvonne de Florac
Roger Dann	Comte de Florac
Libby Morris	American
Yves Barsac	Inspector

COMEDY France. Architect and wife recall the past during motoring holiday.

13744
YOU ONLY LIVE TWICE (116) (A) *tech/scope*
Eon-Danjaq (UA)
P: Harry Saltzman, Albert R. Broccoli
D: Lewis Gilbert
S: (NOVEL) Ian Fleming
SC: Roald Dahl, Harry Jack Bloom

Sean Connery	James Bond
Akiko Wakabayashi	Aki
Tetsuro Tamba	Tiger Tanaka
Mie Hama	Kissy Suzuki
Teru Shimada	Osata
Karin Dor	Helga Brandt
Lois Maxwell	Miss Moneypenny
Desmond Llewelyn	Q
Bernard Lee	M
Charles Gray	Henderson
Tsai Chin	Girl
Donald Pleasence	Ernst Blofeld
Alexander Knox	President
Robert Hutton	Aide

CRIME Japan. Secret agent feigns death to thwart SPECTRE'S seizure of space capsules. (Top Moneymaker 1967).

13745
THE LAST SAFARI (110) (U) *tech*
Paramount (Par)
P:D: Henry Hathaway
S: (NOVEL) Gerald Hanley
(GILLIGAN'S LAST ELEPHANT)
SC: John Gay

Kaz Garas	Casey
Stewart Granger	Miles Gilchrist
Gabriella Licudi	Grant
Johnny Sekka	Jama
Liam Redmond	Alec Beaumont
Eugene Deckers	Leader
David Munya	Chongu
John De Villiers	Rich
Jean Parnell	Mrs Beaumont
John Sutton	Harry

Masai Tribe Wakamba Tribal Dancers
ADVENTURE Africa. Rich tourist and hunter go on elephant safari.

13746
NIGHT OF THE BIG HEAT (94) (X) *eastman*
Planet
P: Tom Blakeley
D: Terence Fisher
S: (NOVEL) John Lymington
SC: Ronald Liles, Pip & Jane Baker

Christopher Lee	Hanson
Peter Cushing	Dr Stone
Patrick Allen	Jeff Callum
Sarah Lawson	Frankie Callum
Jane Merrow	Angela Roberts

William Lucas . . . . Ken Stanley
Kenneth Cope . . . . Tinker Mason
Jack Bligh . . . . Ben Siddle
Thomas Heathcote . . . . Bob Hayward
Sidney Bromley . . . . Tramp
Percy Herbert. . . . . Gerald Foster
HORROR Fara. Alien invaders cause island's
temperature to rise.

13747
THEY CAME FROM BEYOND SPACE (85) (A)
eastman
Anglo Embassy-Amicus (Planet)
P: Max Rosenberg, Milton Subotsky
D: Freddie Francis
S: (NOVEL) Joseph Millard
(THE GODS HATE KANSAS)
SC: Milton Subotsky
Robert Hutton . . . . Dr Curtis Temple
Jennifer Jayne . . . . Lee Mason
Zia Mohyeddin . . . . Farge
Bernard Kay . . . . Richard Arden
Michael Gough . . . . Monj
Geoffrey Wallace . . . . Mullane
Luanshiya Greer . . . . Attendant
John Harvey . . . . Bill Trethowan
Kenneth Kendall . . . . TV Commentator
FANTASY Cornwall. Alien intellects
cause plague and transfer victims to the
moon.

13748
TORTURE GARDEN (93) (X) *tech*
Amicus (Col)
P: Max Rosenberg, Milton Subotsky
D: Freddie Francis
S: (STORIES) Robert Bloch
SC: Robert Bloch
Jack Palance . . . . Ronald Wyatt
Burgess Meredith . . . . Dr Diabolo
Beverly Adams . . . . Carla Hayes
Michael Bryant . . . . Colin Williams
Peter Cushing . . . . Canning
Maurice Denham . . . . Uncle
Robert Hutton . . . . Paul
Barbara Ewing . . . . . . Dorothy Endicott
Michael Ripper . . . . Gordon Roberts
David Bauer . . . . Charles
Nicole Shelby . . . . Millie
Bernard Kay . . . . Dr Heim
John Phillips . . . . Storm
Niall MacGinnis . . . . Doctor
HORROR Satan as fairground barker
predicts five fantastic futures.

13749
SUMURU (95) (A) *tech/scope* USA: THE
1,000,000 EYES OF SUMURU
Sumuru (AA)
P: Harry Alan Towers
D: Lindsay Shonteff
S: (NOVEL) Sax Rohmer
SC: Peter Welbeck
Frankie Avalon . . . . Tommy Carter
Geroge Nader . . . . Nick West
Shirley Eaton . . . . Sumuru
Wilfrid Hyde White . . . . . . Col Baisbrook
Klaus Kinski . . . . President Boong
Patti Chandler . . . . Louise
Salli Sachse . . . . Mikki
Ursula Rank . . . . Erna
Krista Nell . . . . Zoe
Maria Rohm . . . . Helga
Paul Chang . . . . Insp Koo
CRIME Hong Kong. Americans save
Oriental President from assassination.

13750
VENGEANCE OF FU MANCHU (89) (A)
eastman
Babasdave (AA)

P: Harry Alan Towers
D: Jeremy Summers
S: (CHARACTERS) Sax Rohmer
SC: Peter Welbeck
Christopher Lee . . . . Fu Manchu
Douglas Wilmer . . . . Nayland Smith
Tony Ferrer . . . . Insp Ramos
Tsai Chin . . . . Lin Tang
Wolfgang Kieling . . . . Dr Lieberson
Susanne Roquette . . . . . . Maria Lieberson
Howard Marion Crawford . . . .Dr Petrie
Noel Trevarthen . . . . Mark Weston
Horst Frank . . . . Rudy Moss
Peter Carsten . . . . Kurt Heller
Maria Rohm . . . . Ingrid
CRIME Chinese crook bent on forming
international crime ring, creates double
of British detective.

13751
THE COMMUTER (16) (U)
Norland (Contemporary)
P:D:S: Tom Misha Norland
FANTASY Commuter uses dress dummy
to turn illusions into reality.

13752
THE CROWNING GIFT (50) (U) *eastman*
Religious Films (RFD)
P: Lord Rank, R.N.F.Evans
D: Norman Walker
S: Lawrence Barratt
Michael Gwynn . . . . Jesus Christ
RELIGION Business man recalls sergeant's
sacrifice in POW camp.

JUN

13753
FATHOM (99) (U) *deluxe/scope*
20th Century-Fox (20)
P: John Kohn
D: Leslie Martinson
S: (NOVEL) Larry Forrester
SC: Lorenzo Semple jr
Tony Franciosa. . . . . . Peter Merriweather
Raquel Welch . . . . Fathom Harvill
Ronald Fraser . . . . Douglas Campbell
Richard Briers. . . . . Timothy
Greta Chi . . . . Jo-May Soon
Tom Adams . . . . Mike
Clive Revill. . . . . Serapkin
Elizabeth Ercy . . . . Ulla
Ann Lancaster . . . . Mrs Trivers
Tutte Lemkow. . . . . Mehmed
Reg Lye . . . . Mr Trivers
ADVENTURE Malaga. Crooks hoodwink
American parachutist into thinking
she is helping NATO recover stolen figurine.

13754
THE NAKED RUNNER (102) (U) *tech/scope*
Artanis (WPD)
P: Brad Dexter
D: Sidney J. Furie
S: (NOVEL) Francis Clifford
SC: Stanley Mann
Frank Sinatra . . . . Sam Laker
Peter Vaughan . . . . Martin Slattery
Derren Nesbitt . . . . Col Hartmann
Nadia Gray . . . . Karen Gisevius
Toby Robins . . . . Ruth
Inger Stratton . . . . Anna
Cyril Luckham . . . . Minister
Edward Fox . . . . Ritchie Jackson
Michael Newport . . . . Patrick Laker
CRIME Leipzig. Intelligence chief forces
ex-agent to kill escaped spy.

13755
TRIPLE CROSS (140) (A) *eastman/bilingual*
Cineurop (AA)
P: Fred Feldkamp, Jacques-Paul Bertrand
D: Terence Young
S: (BOOK) Frank Owen
(THE EDDIE CHAPMAN STORY)
SC: Rene Hardy, William Marchant
Christopher Plummer . . . . . Eddie Chapman
Yul Brynner . . . . Col Baron von Grunen
Romy Schneider . . . . Countess
Gert Frobe . . . . Col Steinhanger
Trevor Howard . . . . Civilian
Claudine Auger . . . . Paulette
Harry Meyen . . . . Lt Keller
Georges Lycan . . . . Leo
Gil Barber . . . . Bergman
Jean-Claude Bercq . . . . . . Maj von Leeb
Francis de Wolff . . . . Col-General
WAR True story of crook who wins pardon
by pretending to spy for Germany.

13756
THE GHOST OF MONK'S ISLAND (U) *eastman*
Countrywide (CFF)
P:S: Michael C. Fairall
D: Jeremy Summers
SC: Jeremy Summers, Anthony Marriott,
Michael Barnes
Pierre Bedenes . . . . Skinny Robinson
Lucinda Jackson . . . . Jane Robinson
Peter Bartlett . . . . Andy Robinson
Robert Bartlett . . . . . . Jamie Robinson
Beryl Cooke . . . . Aunt Edna
Conrad Phillips . . . . Eli Oakes
Ivor Salter . . . . Jacob Finch
Jerold Wells . . . . Convict

13757
1: UNHAPPY BIRTHDAY (14)

13758
2: THE MYSTERIOUS ISLAND (13)

13759
3: S.O.S. (13)

13760
4: FIGHT FOR SURVIVAL (15)

13761
5: THE TUNNEL (16)

13762
6: CAPTURED (12)

13763
7: ORDEAL BY FIRE (12)
CHILDREN Holiday children catch escaped
convict.

13764
I'LL NEVER FORGET WHAT'S 'IS NAME
(97) (X) *tech*
Scimitar-Universal (RFD)
P:D: Michael Winner
S: Peter Draper
Orson Welles . . . . Jonathan Lute
Oliver Reed . . . . Andrew Quint
Carol White . . . . Georgina
Harry Andrews . . . . Gerald Sater
Michael Hordern . . . . Headmaster
Wendy Craig . . . . Louise Quint
Marianne Faithfull . . . . . . Josie
Norman Rodway . . . . Nicholas
Frank Finlay . . . . Chaplain
Harvey Hall . . . . Macabee
Ann Lynn . . . . Carla
Lyn Ashley . . . . Susannah
Peter Graves . . . . Bankman

Mark Eden . . . . Kellaway
COMEDY Advertising expert quits to make
an honest career in literature.

13765
THE PENTHOUSE (96) (X) *eastman*
Tahiti (Par)
P: Michael Klinger, Guido Coen
D: SC: Peter Collinson
S: (PLAY) C. Scott Forbes
(THE METER MAN)
Suzy Kendall . . . . Barbara
Terence Morgan . . . . Bruce
Tony Beckley . . . . Tom
Norman Rodway . . . . Dick
Martine Beswick . . . . Harry
DRAMA Men hold married man and mistress
captive in unfinished apartment.

13766
PRETTY POLLY (102) (A) *tech/scope*
George-Granat-Universal (RFD)
P: George W. George, Frank Granat
D: Guy Green
S: (STORY) Noel Coward
SC: Keith Waterhouse, Willis Hall
Hayley Mills . . . . Polly Barlow
Trevor Howard . . . . Robert Hook
Shashi Kapoor . . . . Amaz
Brenda de Banzie . . . . Mrs Innes-Hook
Dick Patterson . . . . Rick Preston
Kalen Liu . . . . Lorelei
Peter Bayliss . . . . Critch
Patricia Routledge . . . . Miss Gudgeon
Dorothy Alison . . . . Mrs Barlow
ROMANCE Singapore. Meek girl transforms
herself when her rich aunt dies.

13767
HEROSTRATUS (142) (X) *eastman*
"i" Films-BFI (BFI-ICA)
P: Don Levy, James Quinn
D: SC: Don Levy
S: Don Levy, Alan Daiches
Michael Gothard . . . . Max
Gabriella Licudi . . . . Clio
Peter Stephens . . . . Farson
Antony Paul . . . . Pointer
Mona Chin . . . . Sandy
Malcolm Muggeridge . . . . . Himself
DRAMA Unsuccessful poet offers his
suicide to an advertiser, but changes his
mind after seduction.

JUL
13768
A CHALLENGE FOR ROBIN HOOD (96) (U)
tech
Hammer-7 Arts (WPD)
P: Clifford Parkes
D: C.M. Pennington Richards
S: Peter Bryan
Barrie Ingham . . . . Robin Hood
James Hayter . . . . Friar Tuck
Leon Greene . . . . Little John
Gay Hamilton . . . . Lady Marian Fitzwarren
Peter Blythe . . . . Roger de Courtenay
Jenny Till . . . . Lady Marian
John Arnatt . . . . . Sheriff of Nottingham
Eric Flynn . . . . Alan-a-Dale
Alfie Bass . . . . Merchant
Reg Lye . . . . Much
William Squire . . . Sir John de Courtenay
Douglas Mitchell . . . . Will Scarlett
ADVENTURE Period. Outlawed heir proves
he did not kill cousin.

13769
CHARLIE BUBBLES (89) (X) *tech*
Memorial Enterprises-Universal (RFD)

P: Michael Medwin
D: Albert Finney
S: Shelagh Delaney
Albert Finney . . . . Charlie Bubbles
Billie Whitelaw . . . . Lottie
Colin Blakeley . . . . Smokey Pickles
Liza Minnelli . . . . Eliza
Timothy Garland . . . . Jack
Richard Pearson . . . . Accountant
John Ronane . . . . Gerry
Nicholas Phipps . . . . Agent
Peter Sallis . . . . Lawyer
Charles Lamb . . . . Noseworthy
Diana Coupland . . . . Maud
COMEDY Successful writer's return home
to the North is less successful. (BFA 1968:
Best Supporting Actress).

13770
COUNTDOWN TO DANGER (63) (U) *eastman*
Wallace (CFF)
P: A. Frank Bundy
D:S: Peter Seabourne
David Macalister . . . . Mike
Paul Martin . . . . Tony
Angela Lee . . . . Sandie
Penny Spencer . . . . Sue
Richard Coleman . . . . Capt Wright
Lane Meddick . . . . Sgt Thompson
Frank Williams . . . . Harry
CHILDREN Alderney. Holiday boy trapped
in store of German mines.

13771
THE DIRTY DOZEN (140) (X) *metro/scope*
MKH Productions (MGM)
P: Kenneth Hyman
D: Robert Aldrich
S: (NOVEL) E.M.Nathanson
SC: Nunnally Johnson, Lukas Heller
Lee Marvin . . . . Maj Reisman
Ernest Borgnine . . . . Gen Warden
Charles Bronson . . . . . Joseph Wladislaw
John Cassavetes . . . . Victor Franko
Richard Jaekel . . . . Sgt Bowren
Robert Ryan . . . . Col Everett Dasher-Breed
Telly Savalas . . . . Archer Maggott
Donald Sutherland . . . . . . Vernon Pinkley
George Kennedy . . . Maj Max Armbruster
Jim Brown . . . . Robert Jefferson
Trini Lopez . . . . Pedro Jiminez
Ralph Meeker . . . . . Capt Stuart Kinder
Clint Walker . . . . Samson Posey
Robert Webber . . . . Gen Denton
Tom Busby . . . . Milo Vladek
Ben Carruthers . . . . Glenn Gilpin
Al Mancini . . . . Tassos Bravos
George Roubicek . . . . Pte Gardner
Dora Reisser . . . . Girl
WAR 1944. Twelve American soldier
prisoners trained to destroy French
chateau. (AA 1967: Best Sound Effects).

13772
DOCTOR FAUSTUS (93) (X) *tech*
Oxford University-Nassau-Venfilms (Col)
P: Richard Burton, Richard McWhorter
D: Richard Burton, Nevill Coghill
S: (PLAY) Christopher Marlowe
(THE TRAGICAL HISTORY OF DR
FAUSTUS)
SC: Nevill Coghill
Richard Burton . . . . Dr Faustus
Elizabeth Taylor . . . . Helen of Troy
Andreas Teuber . . . . Mephistopheles
Ian Marter . . . . Emperor
Elizabeth O'Donovan . . . . Empress
David McIntosh . . . . Lucifer
Jeremy Eccles . . . . Beelzebub
Ram Chopra . . . . Valdes

Richard Carwardine . . . . . . Cornelius
Hugh Williams . . . . Scholar
Nevill Coghill . . . . Professor
Ambrose Coghill . . . . Avarice
Bridget Coghill . . . . Gluttony
FANTASY Period. Scholar sells his soul
to the Devil in exchange for Helen of Troy.

13773
DUTCHMAN (56) (X)
Persson-Kaitlin-Dutchman (Planet)
P: Gene Persson
D: Anthony Harvey
S: (PLAY) Leroi Jones
SC: Leroi Jones
Shirley Knight . . . . Lula
Al Freeman jr . . . . Clay
Robert Calvert . . . .
Frank Lieberman . . . .
Howard Bennett . . . .
Sandy McDonald . . . .
Denis Peters . . . .
DRAMA New York. Slut seduces a Negro
in the subway, then kills him.

13774
OUR MOTHER'S HOUSE (105) (X) *metro*
Heron-Filmways (MGM)
P: Martin Ransohoff, Jack Clayton
D: Jack Clayton
S: (NOVEL) Julian Gloag
SC: Jeremy Brooks, Haya Harareet
Dirk Bogarde . . . . Charlie Hook
Margaret Brooks . . . . Elsa Hook
Pamela Franklin . . . . Diana Hook
Louis Sheldon Williams . . . Hubert Hook
John Gugolka . . . . Dunstan Hook
Mark Lester . . . . Jiminee Hook
Sarah Nicholls . . . . Gerty Hook
Gustav Henry . . . . Willy Hook
Yootha Joyce . . . . Mrs Quayle
Claire Davidson . . . . Miss Bailey
Anthony Nicholls . . . . Mr Halbert
Edina Ronay . . . . Doreen
DRAMA Frightened of being sent to an
orphanage, seven children bury their dead
mother.

13775
THE DAY THE FISH CAME OUT (109) (A)
bilingual/ *deluxe*
Cacoyannis (20)
P:D:S: Michael Cacoyannis
Tom Courtenay . . . . Navigator
Colin Blakeley . . . . Pilot
Sam Wanamaker . . . . Elias
Candice Bergen . . . . Electra
Ian Ogilvy . . . . Peter
Patricia Burke . . . . Mrs Mavroyannis
Dimitris Nicolaides . . . . Dentist
Tom Klunis . . . . Mr French
Nicos Alexious . . . . Goatherd
Costas Papaconstantinou . . . Manolias
FANTASY Greece, 1972. Islanders search
for lost box containing radio-active objects.

AUG
13776
THE ANNIVERSARY (95)(X) *tech*
Hammer (WPD)
P:SC: Jimmy Sangster
D: Roy Ward Baker
S: (PLAY) Bill MacIlwraith
Bette Davis . . . . Mrs Taggart
Sheila Hancock . . . . Karen Taggart
Jack Hedley . . . . Terry Taggart
James Cossins . . . . Henry Taggart
Elaine Taylor . . . . Shirley Blair
Christian Roberts . . . . Tom Taggart

Timothy Bateson . . . . Mr Bird
DRAMA One-eyed widow's determination to keep her sons together.

13777
FOLLOW THAT CAMEL (95) (A) *eastman*
Adder (RFD)
P: Peter Rogers
D: Gerald Thomas
S: Talbot Rothwell
Phil Silvers . . . . Sgt Nocker
Jim Dale . . . . Bertram Oliphant West
Peter Butterworth . . . . Simpson
Charles Hawtrey . . . . Capt Le Pice
Kenneth Williams . . . . . . Commandant Burger
Anita Harris . . . . Corktip
Joan Sims . . . . Zigzig
Bernard Bresslaw . . . . Abdul Abulbul
Angela Douglas . . . . . Lady Jane Ponsonby
John Bluthal . . . . Cpl Clotski
William Mervyn . . . . Ponsonby
COMEDY Disgraced socialite joins Foreign Legion and saves fort from Arabs.

13778
ROBBERY (114) (U) *eastman*
Oakhurst (Par)
P: Michael Deeley, Stanley Baker
D: Peter Yates
S: Peter Yates, Edward Boyd, George Markstein
Stanley Baker . . . . Paul Clifton
James Booth . . . . Insp Langdon
Frank Finlay . . . . Robinson
Joanne Pettet . . . . Kate Clifton
Barry Foster . . . . Frank
William Marlowe . . . . Dave
Clinton Greyn . . . . Jack
George Sewell . . . . Ben
Michael McStay . . . . Don
Patrick Jordan . . . . Freddy
CRIME Ex-convict organises jewel theft to finance mail train robbery.

13779
SOME MAY LIVE (89) (A) *tech*
RKO-Krasne-Foundation (Butcher)
P: Philip Krasne, Clive Sharp
D: Vernon Sewell
S: David T. Chantler
Joseph Cotten . . . . Col Woodward
Martha Hyer . . . . Kate Meredith
Peter Cushing . . . . John Meredith
John Ronane . . . . Capt Elliott Thomas
David Spenser . . . . Insp Sung
Alec Mango . . . . Ducrai
Walter Brown . . . . Maj Matthews
Kim Smith . . . . Allan Meredith
WAR Saigon. Girl in code department learns her husband is Communist agent.

SEP

13780
OUCH ! (27) (U) *eastman*
Cabal (Monarch)
P: Robert Angell, Roger Hancock
D: Gerard Bryant
S: Anthony Marriott, Alistair Foot
Peter Butterworth . . . . Jonah Whale
Dennis Castle . . . . Shopkeeper
Bob Todd . . . . Policeman
Ian Wilson . . . . Outfitters Man
Totti Truman Taylor . . . . . Auntie
Erik Chitty . . . . Vicar
Garry Marsh . . . . Father
Johnny Wade . . . . Bridegroom
Dilys Watling . . . . Bride
Bill Shine . . . . Father
Michael Ward . . . . Photographer

Tutte Lemkow . . . . Waiter
COMEDY Accident-prone best man causes chaos at wedding.

13781
BERSERK (96) (X) *tech*
Herman Cohen (Col)
P: Herman Cohen
D: Jim O'Connolly
S: Aben Kandel, Herman Cohen
Joan Crawford . . . . Monica Rivers
Ty Hardin . . . . Frank Hawkins
Diana Dors . . . . Matilda
Michael Gough . . . . Dorando
Judy Geeson . . . . Angela Rivers
Robert Hardy . . . . Supt Brooks
Geoffrey Keen . . . . Comm Dalby
Sydney Tafler . . . . Harrison Liston
George Claydon . . . . Bruno
Ambrosine Philpotts . . . . . Miss Burrows
Ted Lune . . . . Skeleton
Billy Smart's Circus
CRIME Circus owner's teenage daughter kills her mother's lovers.

13782
FAR FROM THE MADDING CROWD (168) (U) *tech/scope*
Appia-Vic (WPD)
P: Joseph Janni
D: John Schlesinger
S: (NOVEL) Thomas Hardy
SC: Frederic Raphael
Julie Christie . . . . Bathsheba Everdene
Terence Stamp . . . . Sgt Troy
Peter Finch . . . . William Boldwood
Alan Bates . . . . Gabriel Oak
Fiona Walker . . . . Liddy
Prunella Ransome . . . . Fanny Robin
Alison Leggatt . . . . Mrs Hurst
Paul Dawkins . . . . Henery Fray
Julian Somers . . . . Jan Coggan
Freddie Jones . . . . Cainy Ball
Brian Rawlinson . . . . Matthew Moon
Denise Coffey . . . . Soberness
DRAMA Period. Girl inherits farm but marries wastrel soldier.

13783
QUATERMASS AND THE PIT (97) (X) *tech*
USA: 5,000,000 YEARS TO EARTH
Hammer (WPD)
P: Anthony Nelson Keys
D: Roy Ward Baker
S: (TV SERIAL) Nigel Kneale
SC: Nigel Kneale
James Donald . . . . Dr Matthew Roney
Andrew Keir . . . . Prof Bernard Quatermass
Barbara Shelley . . . . Barbara Judd
Julian Glover . . . . Col Breen
Duncan Lamont . . . . Sladden
Bryan Marshall . . . . Capt Potter
Peter Copley . . . . Howell
Edwin Richfield . . . . Minister
Grant Taylor . . . . Sgt Ellis
Maurice Good . . . . Sgt Cleghorn
Sheila Staefel . . . . Journalist
Thomas Heathcote . . . . . . Vicar
HORROR Ancient spaceship unearthed in London Tube excavations.

13784
30 IS A DANGEROUS AGE, CYNTHIA (84) (U) *tech*
Walter Shenson (Col)
P: Walter Shenson
D: Joseph McGrath
S: Dudley Moore, Joseph McGrath, John Wells
Dudley Moore . . . . Rupert Street
Eddie Foy jr . . . . Oscar

Suzy Kendall . . . . Louise
John Bird . . . . Herbert Greenslade
Harry Towb . . . . Mr Woolley
Duncan MacRae . . . . Jock McCue
John Wells . . . . Hon Gavin Hopton
Patricia Routledge . . . . . . Mrs Woolley
Jonathan Routh . . . . . . Capt Gore-Taylor
Ted Dicks . . . . Horst Cohen jr
Clive Dunn . . . . Doctor
Derek Farr . . . . TV Announcer
Michael MacLiammoir . . . Storyteller
COMEDY Night club pianist determines to marry art student within six weeks.

13785
TWO WEEKS IN SEPTEMBER (95) (X) *eastman/scope/bilingual*
Francos-Quadrangle-Pomereu-Kenwood (RFD)
P: Francis Cosne, Kenneth Harper
D: Serge Bourguignon
S: Vahe Katcha, Pascal Jardin, Serge Bourguignon
SC: Sean Graham
Brigitte Bardot . . . . Cecile
Laurent Terzieff . . . . Vincent
Jean Rochefort . . . . Philippe
James Robertson Justice . . McClintock
Michael Sarne . . . . Dickinson
Georgina Ward . . . . Patricia
Carl Lebel. . . . . Monique
ROMANCE French model in London has affair with suitor.

13786
UP THE JUNCTION (119) (X) *tech/scope*
BHE-Collinson-Cresto (Par)
P: Anthony Havelock-Allan, John Brabourne
D: Peter Collinson
S: (BOOK) Nell Dunn
SC: Roger Smith
Suzy Kendall . . . . Polly
Dennis Waterman . . . . Peter
Liz Fraser . . . . Mrs McCarthy
Maureen Lipman . . . . Sylvie
Adrienne Posta. . . . . Rube
Michael Gothard . . . . Terry
Alfie Bass . . . . Charlie
Hylda Baker . . . . Winny
Linda Cole . . . . Pauline
Barbara Archer . . . . May
Susan George . . . . Joyce
Queenie Watts . . . . Mrs Hardy
The Delacardos
DRAMA Chelsea girl sets up home in Battersea to discover life. (Top Moneymaker: 1968):

OCT

13787
BATTLE BENEATH THE EARTH (91) (U) *tech*
Reynolds-Vetter (MGM)
P: Charles Vetter, Charles Reynolds
D: Montgomery Tully
S: Lance Z. Hargreaves
Kerwin Matthews . . . . . . Cdr Jonathan Shaw
Viviane Ventura . . . . Tila Yung
Robert Ayres . . . . Admiral Hillebrand
Peter Arne . . . . Arnold Kramer
Al Mulock . . . . Sgt Marvin Mulberry
Martin Benson . . . . Gen Chan Lu
Peter Elliott . . . . Kengh Lee
Earl Cameron . . . . Sgt Seth Hawkins
Peter Brandon . . . . Maj Frank Cannon
Edward Bishop . . . . Lt-Cdr Vance Cassidy
Bill Nagy . . . . Col Talbot Wilson
Sarah Brackett . . . . Meg Webson
Carl Jaffe . . . . Dr Galissi
Bessie Love . . . . Matron
FANTASY Los Alamos. Red Chinese use laser borer to penetrate USA.

13788
BEDAZZLED (103) (A) *deluxe/scope*
Donen Enterprises (20)
P:D: Stanley Donen
S: Peter Cook, Dudley Moore
SC: Peter Cook
Peter Cook . . . . George Spiggott
Dudley Moore . . . . Stanley Moon
Raquel Welch . . . . Lilian Lust
Eleanor Bron . . . . Margaret Spencer
Michael Bates . . . . Insp Clarke
Bernard Spear . . . . Irving Moses
Parnell McGarry . . . . Gluttony
Howard Goorney . . . . Sloth
Alba . . . . Vanity
Barry Humphries . . . . Envy
Daniele Noel . . . . Avarice
Robert Russell . . . . Anger
Michael Trubshawe . . . . . . Lord Dowdy
FANTASY Cafe cook granted seven wishes
in exchange for his soul.

13789
BILLION DOLLAR BRAIN (111) (A) *tech/scope*
Lowndes (UA)
P: Andre de Toth, Harry Saltzman
D: Ken Russell
S: (NOVEL) Len Deighton
SC: John McGrath
Michael Caine . . . . Harry Palmer
Karl Malden . . . . Leo Newbegin
Francoise Dorleac . . . . Anys
Oscar Homolka . . . . Col Stok
Ed Begley . . . . Gen Midwinter
Guy Doleman . . . . Col Ross
Vladek Scheybal . . . . Dr Eiwort
Milo Sperber . . . . Basil
Mark Elwes. . . . . Birkinshaw
CRIME Finland. Ex-agent blackmailed into
thwarting general's private virus war on Russia.

13790
DANGER ROUTE (92) (A) *deluxe*
Amicus (UA)
P: Max Rosenberg, Milton Subotsky
D: Seth Holt
S: (NOVEL) Andrew York
(THE ELIMINATOR)
SC: Meade Roberts, Robert Stewart
Richard Johnson . . . . Jones Wilde
Carol Lynley . . . . Jocelyn
Barbar Bouchet . . . . Mari
Sylvia Syms . . . . Barbara Canning
Gordon Jackson . . . . Stern
Diana Dors . . . . Rhoda Gooderich
Maurice Denham . . . . . . Peter Ravenspur
Sam Wanamaker . . . . Lucinda
David Bauer . . . . Bennett
Robin Bailey . . . . Parsons
Leslie Sands . . . . Man
CRIME Dorset. Secret agent ordered to kill
defected Czech scientist.

13791
GREAT CATHERINE (98) (U) *tech*
Keep (WPD)
P: Jules Buck
D: Gordon Flemyng
S: (PLAY) George Bernard Shaw
SC: Hugh Leonard
Peter O'Toole . . . . . . Capt Charles Edstaston
Jeanne Moreau. . . . . . Catherine the Great
Zero Mostel . . . . Prince Patiomkin
Jack Hawkins . . . . Sir George Gorse
Akim Tamiroff . . . . Sergeant
Marie Lohr . . . . Lady Gorse
Marie Kean . . . . Princess Dashkoff
Kenneth Griffith . . . . Naryshkin

Angela Scoular . . . . Claire
Kate O'Mara . . . . Varinka
Les Seidl . . . . Grand Duchess
Claire Gordon . . . . Elizabeth Vokonska
HISTORY Russia, period. Dragoon captain's
amorous excursions with Empress.

13792
HALF A SIXPENCE (146) (U) *tech/scope*
Ameran (Par)
P: John Dark, Charles H. Schneer, George
Sidney
D: George Sidney
S: (NOVEL) H.G.Wells (KIPPS)
SC: Beverley Cross
Tommy Steele . . . . Arthur Kipps
Julia Foster . . . . Ann
Cyril Ritchard . . . . Harry Chitterlow
Penelope Horner . . . . . Helen Walsingham
Elaine Taylor . . . . Kate
Grover Dale . . . . Pearce
Hilton Edwards . . . . Shalford
Julia Sutton . . . . Flo
Leslie Meadows . . . . Buggins
Sheila Falconer . . . . Victoria
Pamela Brown . . . . Mrs Walsingham
James Villiers . . . . Hubert Walsingham
Allan Cuthbertson . . . . Wilkins
MUSICAL Period. Orphan clerk inherits
fortune and tries to crash society.

13793
I LIKE BIRDS (43) (A) *eastman*
USA: HOT GIRLS FOR MEN ONLY (61)
Pete Walker (Border)
P:D:S: Peter Walker
David Kernan . . . . Freddie Horne
Andrea Allen . . . . Rosalie
Derek Aylward . . . . Miles Fanthorpe
Tom Gill . . . . Father
Mai Bacon . . . . Mother
John Cazabon . . . . Lamphrey Gussett
Monika Dietrich . . . . Janet
Jill Field . . . . Gunella
NUDIST Puritan magazine publisher
actually edits sexy magazine. (US version
includes 18 mins additional sequences).

13794
POOR COW (101) (X) *eastman*
Fenchurch-Vic (AA)
P: Joseph Janni
D: Kenneth Loach
S: (NOVEL) Nell Dunn
SC: Nell Dunn, Kenneth Loach
Carol White . . . . Joy
Terence Stamp . . . . Dave
John Bindon . . . . Tom
Kate Williams . . . . Beryl
Queenie Watts . . . . Aunt Emm
Geraldine Sherman . . . . . . Trixie
Ellis Dale . . . . Solicitor
Gerald Young . . . . Judge
Gladys Dawson . . . . Bet
DRAMA Thief's young wife moves in
with his mate while he is in jail.

13795
SEBASTIAN (100) (A) *eastman*
Maccius (Par)
P: Herbert Brodkin, Michael Powell
D: David Greene
S: Leo Marks
SC: Gerald Vaughan-Hughes
Dirk Bogarde . . . . Sebastian
Susannah York . . . . Becky Howard
Lilli Palmer . . . . Elsa Shahn
John Gielgud . . . . Intelligence Head
Janet Munro . . . . Carol

Margaret Johnston . . . . Miss Elliott
Nigel Davenport . . . . Gen Phillips
Ronald Fraser . . . . Toby
John Ronane . . . . Jameson
Susan Whitman . . . . Tilly
Ann Beach . . . . Pamela
Alan Freeman . . . . TV Disc jockey
CRIME Oxford professor joins secret
service as code expert.

13796
SMASHING TIME (96) (A) *eastman*
Partisan (Par)
P: Carlo Ponti
D: Desmond Davis
S: George Melly
Lynn Redgrave . . . . Yvonne
Rita Tushingham. . . . . Brenda
Anna Quayle . . . . Charlotte Brilling
Michael York . . . . Tom Wabe
Ian Carmichael . . . . Bobby Mome-Rath
Irene Handl. . . . . Mrs Gimble
Jeremy Lloyd . . . . Jeremy Tove
Toni Palmer . . . . Toni
Peter Jones . . . . Dominic
Arthur Mullard . . . . Boss
Ronnie Stevens . . . . Waiter
Murray Melvin . . . . Exquisite
Bruce Lacey . . . . Clive Sword
Cardew Robinson . . . . Vicar
David Lodge . . . . Caretaker
Veronica Carlson . . . . Girl
COMEDY Slapstick misadventures of two
Northern girls in London.

13797
A TWIST OF SAND (91) (A) *deluxe*
Christina (UA)
P: Fred Engel
D: Don Chaffey
S: (NOVEL) Geoffrey Jenkins
SC: Marvin H. Albert
Richard Johnson . . . . Geoffrey Peace
Honor Blackman . . . . Julie Chambois
Jeremy Kemp . . . . Harry Riker
Peter Vaughan . . . . Johann
Roy Dotrice . . . . David Carland
James Falkland . . . . Lieut
Guy Doleman . . . . Cdr
Clifford Evans . . . . Admiral Tringham
ADVENTURE Africa. Contraband runners
seek hidden diamonds.

13798
GIVE A DOG A BONE (77) (U) *tech*
Westminster (MRA)
P:D:SC: Henry Cass
S: (PLAY) Peter Howard
Ronnie Stevens . . . . Ringo
Robert Davies . . . . Micky Merry
Ivor Danvers . . . . Mr Space
Richard Warner . . . . Rat King
Bryan Coleman . . . . Lord Swill
Len Maley. . . . . Pa Merry
Patricia O'Callaghan. . . . . . Ma Merry
MUSICAL Boy and dog save world from
rat who turns humans into animals.

13799
THE VULTURE (91) (X)
Homeric-Iliad-Film Financial (Par)
P: Jack O. Lamont, Lawrence Huntington
D: S: Lawrence Huntington
Robert Hutton . . . . Eric Lutyens
Akim Tamiroff . . . . Prof Koniglich
Broderick Crawford . . . . . . Brian Stroud
Diane Clare . . . . Trudy Lutyens
Philip Friend . . . . Vicar
Annette Carell . . . . Ellen West
Patrick Holt . . . . Jarvis
Edward Caddick. . . . . Sexton

Gordon Sterne . . . . Edward Stroud
Monty Landis . . . . Driver
HORROR Cornwall. Professor's nuclear
experiment combines him with dead vulture.

13800
THE INN WAY OUT (30) (A)
Minotaur
D: Anthony Short
Hugh Burden . . . . Husband
COMEDY Henpeck escapes into alcohol.

NOV

13801
CARRY ON DOCTOR (94) (A) *eastman*
Adder (RFD)
P: Peter Rogers
D: Gerald Thomas
S: Talbot Rothwell
Frankie Howerd . . . . Francis Bigger
Sidney James . . . . Charlie Roper
Kenneth Williams . . . . Dr Tinkle
Charles Hawtrey . . . . Mr Barron
Jim Dale . . . . Dr Kilmore
Barbara Windsor . . . . Sandra May
Joan Sims . . . . Chloe Gibson
Hattie Jacques . . . . Matron
Anita Harris . . . . Nurse Clarke
Bernard Bresslaw . . . . Ken Biddle
Peter Butterworth . . . . Mr Smith
Dilys Laye . . . . Mavis Winkle
Derek Francis . . . . Sir Edmund Burke
COMEDY Hospital misadventures of
charlatan who thinks he has but one week to
live.

13802
DEADFALL (120) (X) *deluxe*
Salamanda (20)
P: Paul Monash
D:SC: Bryan Forbes
S: (NOVEL) Desmond Cory
Michael Caine . . . . Henry Clarke
Giovanna Ralli . . . . Fe Moreau
Eric Portman . . . . Richard Moreau
Nanette Newman . . . . Girl
David Buck . . . . Salinas
Carlos Pierre . . . . Antonio
Leonard Rossiter . . . . Fillmore
Emilio Rodriguez . . . . Insp Ballastero
Vladek Shaybal . . . . Dr Delgado
Carmen Dene . . . . Masseuse
John Barry . . . . Conductor
CRIME Jewel thief falls in love with
wife of French homosexual crook.

13803
THE HUNCH (56) (U) *eastman*
Anvil (CFF)
P: J.B. Holmes
D:S: Sarah Erukkar
Alex Norton . . . . Ian
Gordon Robb . . . . Harry
Amanda Jones . . . . Janet
Ross Campbell . . . . Saul
John Bannerman . . . . Grandad
Douglas Murchie . . . . Skipper
Bill McCabe . . . . Mate
Ian Dewar . . . . Pat McAinch
CHILDREN Wick. Trawler captain's
children try to salvage cruiser.

13804
INTERLUDE (113) (A) *tech*
Domino (Col)
P: David Deutsch
D: Kevin Billington
S: Lee Langley, Hugh Leonard
Oskar Werner . . . . Stefan Zelter

Barbara Ferris . . . . Sally
Virginia Maskell . . . . Antonia Zelter
Donald Sutherland . . . . Lawrence
Nora Swinburne . . . . Mary
Alan Webb . . . . Andrew
Bernard Kay . . . . George Selworth
Geraldine Sherman . . . . Natalie
John Cleese . . . . TV PR Man
Humphrey Burton . . . . TV Director
ROMANCE Girl reporter has affair with
married conductor.

DEC

13805
THE CUT-UPS (19) (U)
Antony Balch
P:D:S: Antony Balch
William Burroughs
Brion Gysin
TRICK Four sequences intercut to produce
fragmented film.

13806
HERE WE GO ROUND THE MULBERRY
BUSH (96) (X) *tech reissue:* 1972
Giant (UA)
P: Clive Donner, Larry Kramer
D: Clive Donner
S: (NOVEL) Hunter Davies
SC: Hunter Davies, Larry Kramer
Barry Evans . . . . Jamie McGregor
Judy Geeson . . . . Mary Gloucester
Angela Scoular . . . . Caroline Beauchamp
Sheila White . . . . Paula
Adrienne Posta . . . . Linda
Vanessa Howard . . . . Audrey
Diane Keen . . . . Claire
Moyra Fraser . . . . Mrs McGregor
Maxine Audley . . . . Mrs Beauchamp
Denholm Elliott . . . . Mr Beauchamp
Nicky Henson . . . . Craig Foster
Angela Pleasence . . . . Girl
Spencer Davis Group
MUSICAL Sixth-form schoolboy's attempts
to lose his virginity.

13807
PROMENADE (38) (A) *eastman*
Donwin (20)
P:D:S: Donovan Winter
Robert Morris . . . . Don
Kate O'Mara . . . . Laura
Richard Leech
Margo Cunningham
ROMANCE Brighton. Painter reunites with
his married mistress.

13808
THE PRIVATE RIGHT (86) (X)
Onyx (LIP)
P:D:S: Michael Papas
Dimitris Andreas. . . . . Minos Elias
George Kafkaris . . . . Tassos Phantis
Tamara Hinchco. . . . . Girl
Cristos Demetriou. . . . . . . Kypros
Charlotte Selwyn . . . . Waitress
Seraphim Nicola . . . . Rebel
John Brogan . . . . Interrogator
WAR Tortured patriot comes from Cyprus
to seek his betrayer.

13809
THE SKY BIKE (62) (U) *eastman*
Eyeline (CFF)
P: Harold Orton
D: S: Charles Frend
Spencer Shires . . . . Tom Smith
Liam Redmond . . . . Mr Lovejoy
Ian Ellis . . . . Porker

William Lucas . . . . Mr Smith
Ellen McIntosh . . . . Mrs Smith
Della Rands . . . . Daphne
John Howard . . . . Jack
Bill Shine . . . . Wingco
David Lodge . . . . Guard
Harry Locke . . . . Owner
CHILDREN Boy pedals inventor's flying
bicycle to win contest.

13810
WORK IS A FOUR LETTER WORD (3) (U)
tech
Cavalcade-Universal (RFD)
P: Thomas Clyde
D: Peter Hall
S: (PLAY) Henry Livings (EH?)
SC: Jeremy Brooks
David Warner . . . . Val Brose
Cilla Black . . . . Betty Dorrick
Elizabeth Spriggs . . . . Mrs Murray
Zia Mohyeddin . . . . Dr Narayana
Joe Gladwyn . . . . Pa Brose
Julie May . . . . Mrs Dorrick
Alan Howard . . . . Rev Mort
Jan Holden . . . . Mrs Price
COMEDY The future. Power station attendant
grows hallucinogenic mushrooms.

13811
ASSIGNMENT K (97) (U) *tech/scope*
Mazurka-Gildor (Col)
P: Ben Arbeid, Maurice Foster
D: Val Guest
S: (NOVEL) Hartley Howard (DEPARTMENT
K)
SC: Val Guest, Bill Strutton, Maurice Foster
Stephen Boyd . . . . Philip Scott
Camilla Sparv. . . . . Toni Peters
Leo McKern . . . . Smith
Robert Hoffmann . . . . Paul Spiegler
Michael Redgrave . . . . Harris
Jan Werich . . . . Dr Spiegler
Jeremy Kemp . . . . Hall
Jane Merrow . . . . Martine
Vivi Bach . . . . Erika Herschel
David Healy . . . . David
Geoffrey Bayldon . . . . Boffin
Carl Mohner . . . . Inspector
Werner Peters . . . . Kramer
Ursula Howells . . . . Estelle
Friedrich von Ledebur . . . . Proprietor
CRIME Secret agent posing as toy tycoon
loves girl in employ of German agents.

13812
TALK OF THE DEVIL (27) (U) *eastman*
Chairene (Monarch)
P:D: Francis Searle
Tim Barrett. . . . . Stephen Wallace
Suzan Farmer . . . . Wendy
Hugh Latimer . . . . Nick Beelzebub
Victor Maddern . . . . Cinders
Robert Gallico . . . . Harvey
FANTASY Henpeck changes places with
the Devil

13813
ALBERT CARTER Q.O.S.O.(27) (U) *eastman*
Dormar (Par)
P: Malcolm Heyworth
D: Ian Brims
S: Ian Brims, Eric Idle
Roy Kinnear . . . . Albert Carter
COMEDY Road sweeper saves the Queen's
corgi.

13814
BENEFIT OF THE DOUBT (70) (X) *eastman*
Lorrimer-Saga

P: Peter Whitehead, Carol Weisweiller
D: Peter Whitehead
S: (PLAY) Denis Cannan (US)
Eric Allan . . . .
Mary Allen . . . .
Hugh Armstrong. . . . .
Roger Brierley . . . .
Ian Hogg . . . .
Glenda Jackson . . . .
Joanne Lindsay. . . . .
Pauline Munro . . . .
Mike Pratt . . . .
DRAMA Excerpts from Royal Shakespeare Company stage production.

13815
THE WHITE BUS (41) (A) *eastman*
Holly (UA)
P: Oscar Lewenstein, Lindsay Anderson
D: Lindsay Anderson
S: (STORY) Shelagh Delaney
SC: Shelagh Delaney
Patricia Healey . . . .　The Girl
Arthur Lowe. . . . .　The Mayor
John Sharp . . . .　Mace Bearer
Julie Perry . . . .　Conductress
Anthony Hopkins . . . .　Brechtian
Victor Henry . . . .　Man
Fanny Carby . . . .　Woman
Stephen Moore . . . .　Young Man
DRAMA Northern girl returns home and takes guided tour.

13816
RED AND BLUE (35) (A) *eastman*
Holly (UA)
P: Oscar Lewenstein, Lindsay Anderson
D: S: Tony Richardson
Vanessa Redgrave . . . .　Jacky
John Bird . . . .　Man on Train
Gary Raymond. . . . .　Songwriter
William Sylvester . . . .　Trumpeter
Michael York . . . .　Acrobat

Douglas Fairbanks jr . . . . .　Millionaire
ROMANCE Paris. Cabaret singer recalls her various affairs.

13817
TWO A PENNY (98) (A) *eastman*
World Wide-Burbank (WW)
P: Frank R. Jacobson
D: James F. Collier
S: Stella Linden
Cliff Richard . . . .　Jamie Hopkins
Dora Bryan . . . .　Ruby Hopkins
Ann Holloway . . . .　Carol Turner
Avril Angers . . . .　Mrs Burry
Geoffrey Bayldon. . . . .　Alec Fitch
Peter Barkworth. . . . .　Vicar
Donald Bisset . . . .　Dr Berman
Edward Evans . . . .　Jenkins
Mona Washbourne . . . .　Mrs Duckett
Earl Cameron . . . .　Verger
Billy Graham . . . .　Himself
RELIGION Drug pusher reformed by Billy Graham.

13818
HELL IS EMPTY (109) (A) *eastman/bilingual*
Dominion (RFD)
P: Michael Eland
D: John Ainsworth, Bernard Knowles
S: (NOVEL) J.F.Straker
SC: John Ainsworth, Bernard Knowles, John Fowler
Martine Carol. . . . .　Martine Grant
Anthony Steel. . . . .　Maj Morton
James Robertson Justice . . .　Angus McGee
Shirley Anne Field . . . . . .　Shirley McGee
Isa Miranda . . . .　Isa Grant
Carl Mohner . . . .　Carl Schultz
Jess Conrad . . . .　Jess Shepherd
Anthony Dawson . . . .　Paul Grant
Catherine von Schell. . . . . .　Catherine Grant
Irene von Meyendorff. . . . .　Helen McGee
Patricia Viterbo . . . .　Patricia

Anna Gael . . . .　Anna
Eugene Deckers . . . .　Counsel
Sheila Burrell . . . .　Judge
CRIME Prague. Robber gang hides out in island mansion.

13819
OEDIPUS THE KING (97) (A) *tech*
Crossroads-Universal (RFD)
P: Michael Luke
D: Philip Saville
S: (PLAY) Sophocles; Paul Roche
SC: Michael Luke, Philip Saville
Christopher Plummer. . . . .　Oedipus
Lilli Palmer . . . .　Jocasta
Richard Johnson . . . .　Creon
Orson Welles . . . .　Tiresias
Cyril Cusack . . . .　Messenger
Roger Livesey . . . .　Shepherd
Donald Sutherland . . . . . .　Chorus
Alexis Matheakis . . . .　Official
Friedrich Ledebur . . . .　King Laius
Oenone Luke . . . .　Atigone
DRAMA Thebes. Oracle predicts city will not be saved from plague until king's murderer is punished.

13820
THE SPARE TYRES (27) (U) *eastman*
Sandpiper (Monarch)
P: Kenneth Cowan
D: Michael J. Lane
S: Donald Churchill
Terence Alexander . . . .　Dennis Colville
Judy Franklin . . . .　Audrey Colville
Kenneth Cowan . . . .　Leonard Dawkins
Julia Jones . . . .　Monica Dawkins
Marika Morley . . . .　Gina
Frank Finlay . . . .　Foreman
Donald Churchill . . . .　Milkman
Pauline Yates . . . .　Doreen
COMEDY Husband tries to get rid of two old tyres.

1968

JAN

13821
ATTACK ON THE IRON COAST (90) (U) *deluxe*
Mirisch (UA)
P: Irving Temaner
D: Paul Wendkos
S: John Champion
SC: Herman Hoffmann

Lloyd Bridges	Maj James Wilson
Andrew Keir	Capt Owen Franklin
Mark Eden	Lt-Cdr Donald Kimberley
Sue Lloyd	Sue Wilson
Maurice Denham	Sir Frederick Grafton
Glyn Owen	Lt Forrester
Howard Pays	Lt Graham
George Mikell	Capt Strasser
Simon Prebble	Lt Smythe
Ernest Clark	AVM Woodbridge
Walter Gotell	Von Horst

WAR Canadian commando leads mission against German naval base on French coast.

13822
THE BLOOD BEAST TERROR (88) (X) *eastman*
Tigon British (Tigon)
P: Tony Tenser, Arnold Miller
D: Vernon Sewell
S: Peter Bryan

Peter Cushing	Insp Quennell
Robert Flemyng	Prof Mallinger
Wanda Ventham	Clare Mallinger
Vanessa Howard	Meg Quennell
Roy Hudd	Morgue Attendant
David Griffin	William
Kevin Stoney	Grainger
Glynn Edwards	Sgt Allan
John Paul	Warrander
Russell Napier	Landlord

HORROR Entomologist's daughter metamorphoses into giant deathshead moth.

13823
HER PRIVATE HELL (84) (X)
Piccadilly (RSE)
P: Bachoo Sen
D: Norman J. Warren
S: Glynn Christian

Lucia Modunio	Marisa
Terry Skelton	Bernie
Pearl Catlin	Margaret
Daniel Ollier	Matt
Jeanette Wild	Paula
Mary Land	Sally
Robert Crewdson	Neville

DRAMA Fashion model falls for pornographic photographer.

13824
A GHOST OF A CHANCE (51) (U) *eastman*
Fanfare (CFF)
P: George H. Brown
D: Jan Darnley-Smith
S: Ed Harper
SC: Patricia Latham

Jimmy Edwards	Sir Jocelyn
Patricia Hayes	Miss Woollie
Graham Stark	Thomas Dogood
Bernard Cribbins	Ron
Terry Scott	Mr Perry
Ronnie Barker	Mr Prendergast
Stephen Brown	Mike
Mark Ward	John
Cheryl Vigden	Jane
John Bluthal	Assistant

CHILDREN Ghosts of Roundhead and Cavalier help children save an old manor from destruction.

13825
AMSTERDAM AFFAIR (91) (A) *eastman*
Trio-Group W (LIP)
P: William Gell, Howard Barnes
D: Gerry O'Hara
S: (NOVEL) Nicolas Freeling
(LOVE IN AMSTERDAM)
SC: Edmund Ward

Wolfgang Kieling	Insp Van Der Valk
William Marlowe	Martin Ray
Catherine Von Schell	Sophie Ray
Pamela Ann Davy	Elsa de Charmoy
Josef Dubin-Behrman	Eric de Charmoy
Will Van Selst	Policeman
Lo Van Hensbergen	Magistrate
Guido de Moor	Piet Ulbricht

CRIME Amsterdam. Inspector proves novelist did not kill mistress.

13826
THE MERCENARIES (100) (X) *metro/scope*
Englund Enterprises (MGM)
P: George Englund
D: Jack Cardiff
S: (NOVEL) Wilbur Smith
(DARK OF THE SUN)
SC: Quentin Werty, Adrian Spies

Rod Taylor	Bruce Curry
Yvette Mimieux	Claire
Peter Carsten	Henlein
Jim Brown	Ruffo
Kenneth More	Dr Wreid
Andre Morell	Bussier
Oliver Despax	Surrier
Guy Deghy	Delage
Bloke Modisane	Kataki
Alan Gifford	Jansen
Murray Kash	Cochrane

WAR Congo, 1960. Mercenaries try to rescue beseiged whites from Simba rebels.

13827
THUNDERBIRD 6 (90) *tech/scope*
A.P.Films-Century 21 (UA)
P:S: Gerry & Sylvia Anderson
D: David Lane
VOICES:

Peter Dyneley	Jeff Tracy
Christine Finn	Tin-Tin
Keith Alexander	Black Phantom/John Tracy
Jeremy Wilkin	Virgil Tracy/Hogarth
Gary Files	Foster/Lane
John Carson	Foster 2
Sylvia Anderson	Lady Penelope
David Graham	Brains/Gordon/Parker
Matt Zimmerman	Alan Tracy
Geoffrey Keen	Controller
Shane Rimmer	Scott Tracy

FANTASY 2100 AD: Rescue organisation saves new skyship from pirate. (Puppet film).

FEB

13828
CORRUPTION (91) (X) *tech*
Titan (Col)
P: Peter Newbrook
D: Robert Hartford-Davis
S: Donald & Derek Ford

Peter Cushing	Sir John Rowan
Sue Lloyd	Lynn Nolan
Noel Trevarthen	Dr Stephen Harris
Kate O'Mara	Val Nolan
David Lodge	Groper
Anthony Booth	Mike Orme
Wendy Varnals	Terry
Vanessa Howard	Kate

HORROR Surgeon combines gland injections and laser to restore disfigured faces.

13829
DECLINE AND FALL. . .OF A BIRD-WATCHER ! (113) (A) *deluxe*
Foxwell Entertainments (20)
P: Ivan Foxwell
D: John Krish
S: (NOVEL) Evelyn Waugh
(DECLINE AND FALL)
SC: Ivan Foxwell, Alan Hackney, Hugh Whitemore

Robin Phillips	Paul Pennyfeather
Genevieve Page	Margot Beste-Chetwynde
Donald Wolfit	Dr Fagan
Colin Blakeley	Philbrick
Robert Harris	Prendergast
Leo McKern	Capt Grimes
Patience Collier	Flossie Fagan
David McAlister	Peter Beste-Chetwynde
Michael Elwyn	Alastair Digby-Vane-Trump-ington
Felix Aylmer	Judge
Griffith Jones	Home Secretary
Donald Sinden	Governor
Paul Rogers	Warder
Duncan Lamont	Inspector
Patrick Magee	Lunatic
Joan Sterndale Bennett	Lady Circumference
Kenneth Griffith	Church
Jack Watson	Warder

COMEDY Expelled divinity student's adventures as teacher, tutor, and white slaver.

13830
INSPECTOR CLOUSEAU (105) (U) *eastman/scope*
Mirisch (UA)
P: Lewis J. Rachmil
D: Bud Yorkin
S: (CHARACTER) Blake Edwards, Maurice Richlin
SC: Tom & Frank Waldman

Alan Arkin	Insp Jacques Clouseau
Delia Boccardo	Lisa Morrel
Frank Finlay	Supt Weaver
Patrick Cargill	Sir Charles Braithwaite
Beryl Reid	Mrs Weaver
Barry Foster	Addison Steele
Clive Francis	Clyde Hargreaves
John Bindon	Bull Parker
Michael Ripper	Frey
Tutte Lemkow	Frenchy LeBec
Anthony Ainley	Bomber LeBec
Wallas Eaton	Hoeffler
Eric Pohlmann	Bergesch

COMEDY Gang use 13 masks of French detective to rob Swiss banks.

13831
ROMEO AND JULIET (152) (A) *tech*
BHE-Verona-De Laurentiis (Par)
P: Anthony Havelock-Allan, John Brabourne
D: Franco Zeffirelli
S: (PLAY) William Shakespeare
SC: Franco Brusati, Masolino D'Amico
N: Laurence Olivier

Leonard Whiting	Romeo
Olivia Hussey	Juliet
Milo O'Shea	Friar Laurence
Michael York	Tybalt
John McEnery	Mercutio
Pat Heywood	Nurse
Natasha Parry	Lady Capulet
Paul Hardwick	Lord Capulet
Robert Stephens	Prince of Verona
Keith Skinner	Balthazar
Roberto Bisacco	Count Paris
Bruce Robinson	Benvolio

ROMANCE Italy, period. Children of feuding families fall in love. (RFP: 1968; AA 1968: Best Costumes; BFA 1968: Best Costumes).

13832
THE WINTER'S TALE (151) (U) *eastman*
Cressida-Hurst Park (WPD)
P: Peter Snell
D: Frank Dunlop
S: (PLAY) William Shakespeare

Laurence Harvey	Leontes
Jane Asher	Perdita
Diana Churchill	Paulina
Moira Redmond	Hermione
Jim Dale	Autolycus
Esmond Knight	Camillo
Richard Gale	Polixenes
David Weston	Florizel/Archidamas
John Gray	Clown
Monica Maughan	Lady

DRAMA Film record of 'Pop Theatre' production at Edinburgh Festival, 1966.

13833
THE MAGNIFICENT SIX AND ½ (U) *eastman*
Century (CFF)
P: Roy Simpson
D: Harry Booth
S: Henry Geddes
SC: Harry Booth, Glyn Jones

Len Jones	Steve
Ian Ellis	Dumbo
Brinsley Forde	Toby
Suzanne Togni	Liz
Lionel Hawkes	Stodger
Kim Tallmadge	Peewee
Michael Audreson	Whizz
Eddie Malin	Old Tom
Charmian Innes	Nanny
Deryck Guyler	Warden

13834
1: GHOSTS AND GHOULIES (19)

13835
2: WHEN KNIGHTS WERE BOLD (15)

13836
3: BILLY THE KID (16)

13837
4: KON TIKI KIDS (15)

13838
5: BOB A JOB (14)

13839
6: PEE WEE'S PIANOLA (14)
CHILDREN Comedy series about gang of children.

13840
THE GREAT PONY RAID (58) (U) *eastman*
AB-Pathe (CFF)
P: Lionel Hoare
D: Frederic Goode
S: Wally Bosco
SC: Wallace Bosco, Geoffrey Hayes

Edward Underdown	Snowy
Michael Brennan	Butch
Christian Comber	Tom
Tina Paget Brown	Joan
Andrew Purcell	Jim
Shelley Crowhurst	Angela
Tim Killinback	Joe
Patrick Barr	Col Gore

CHILDREN Dartmoor. Children foil gang of pony rustlers.

13841
TELL ME LIES (116) (X) *eastman*
Ronorus (London Continental)
P: Peter Sykes, Peter Brook
D: SC: Peter Brook
S: (PLAY) Dennis Cannan (US)

Mark Jones	Mark
Pauline Munro	Pauline
Eric Allan	
Mary Allen	
Ian Hogg	
Glenda Jackson	
Joanne Lindsay	
Hugh Sullivan	
Kingsley Amis	
Peggy Ashcroft	
James Cameron	
Stokeley Carmichael	
Tom Driberg	
Paul Scofield	
Patrick Wymark	

DRAMA Young couple seek truth about Vietnam war.

MAR

13842
PRUDENCE AND THE PILL (92) (X) *deluxe*
Prudence (20)
P: Kenneth Harper, Ronald Kahn
D: Fielder Cook, Ronald Neame
S: (NOVEL) Hugh Mills
SC: Hugh Mills

Deborah Kerr	Prudence Hardcastle
David Niven	Gerald Hardcastle
Robert Coote	Henry Hardcastle
Irina Demick	Elizabeth
Joyce Redman	Grace Hardcastle
Judy Geeson	Geraldine Hardcastle
Keith Michell	Dr Alan Hewitt
Edith Evans	Lady Roberta Bates
David Dundas	Tony Bates
Vickery Turner	Rose
Hugh Armstrong	Ted
Peter Butterworth	Chemist
Moyra Fraser	Woman

COMEDY Teenager switches aspirin for mother's birth control pills.

13843
THE STRANGE AFFAIR (106) (X) *tech/scope*
Paramount (Par)
P: Howard Harrison, Stanley Mann
D: David Greene
S: (NOVEL) Bernard Toms
SC: Stanley Mann

Michael York	Peter Strange
Jeremy Kemp	Sgt Pierce
Susan George	Fred March
Jack Watson	Quince
George A. Cooper	Supt Kingley
Artro Morris	Insp Evans
Barry Fantoni	Charley Small
Nigel Davenport	Defence Counsel
Madge Ryan	Aunt Mary
George Benson	Uncle Bertrand
Terence de Marney	Mahon
John E. Paul and the Blue Mountain Boys	

CRIME Det-sgt blackmails police recruit into helping convict drug peddlers.

13844
THE TOUCHABLES (94) (X) *deluxe*
Film Designs (20)
P: John Bryan
D:S: Robert Freeman
SC: David & Donald Cammell, Ian La Frenais

Judy Huxtable	Sadie
Esther Anderson	Melanie
Marilyn Rickard	Busbee
Kathy Simmonds	Samson
David Anthony	Christian
Ricki Starr	Ricki
James Villiers	Twyning
John Ronane	Kasher
Harry Baird	Lillywhite
Joan Bakewell	Interviewer
William Dexter	Quayle

DRAMA Four girls kidnap pop singer and compete for his favours.

13845
THE VENGEANCE OF SHE (101) (A) *tech*
Hammer (WPD)
P: Aida Young
D: Cliff Owen
S: (CHARACTERS) Sir H. Rider Haggard
SC: Peter O'Donnell

John Richardson	Killikrates
Olinka Berova	Carol
Edward Judd	Philip Smith
Colin Blakeley	George Carter
Derek Godfrey	Men-Hari
Jill Melford	Sheila Carter
George Sewell	Harry Walker
Andre Morell	Kassim
Noel Willman	Za-Tor
Daniele Noel	Sharna
Gerald Lawson	Seer

FANTASY Africa. High Priest hypnotises girl into believing she is reincarnation of Ayesha.

13846
THE BEE GEES (6) (U) *eastman*
Associated London
The Bee Gees
MUSICAL

13847
2001: A SPACE ODYSSEY (141) (A)
metro/scope
Hawk-MGM (MGM)
P:D: Stanley Kubrick
S: (STORY) Arthur C. Clarke
(THE SENTINEL)
SC: Stanley Kubrick, Arthur C.Clarke

Keir Dullea	David Bowman
Gary Lockwood	Frank Poole
William Sylvester	Dr Heywood Floyd
Daniel Richter	Moonwatcher
Douglas Rain	Hal 9000 (voice)
Leonard Rossiter	Smyslov
Margaret Tyzack	Elena
Robert Beatty	Halvorsen
Sean Sullivan	Michaels
Frank Miller	Controller

FANTASY 2001. Astronaut, marooned by computer, travels through star-gate in space. (AA 1968: Best Special Effects; BFA 1968: Best Pho, Art Dir, Sound).

13848
INADMISSIBLE EVIDENCE (96) (X)
Woodfall (Par)
P: Ronald Kinnoch
D: Anthony Page
S: (PLAY) John Osborne
SC: John Osborne

Nicol Williamson	Bill Maitland
Eleanor Fazan	Anna Maitland
Jill Bennett	Liz Eaves
Peter Sallis	Hudson
David Valla	Jones
Eileen Atkins	Shirley
Ingrid Brett	Jane
Gillian Hills	Joy
Isobel Dean	Mrs Garnsey
Claire Kelly	Mrs Anderson

John Normington .... Maples
Patsy Huxter .... Hilda Maples
Hilary Hardiman .... Wendy Watson
Lindsay Anderson ...... Barrister
Lee .... Stripper
DRAMA Married solicitor has affairs with two women.

APR

13849
THE BOFORS GUN (105) (X) *tech*
Everglades-Universal (RFD)
P: Robert A. Goldston, Otto Platchkes
D: Jack Gold
S: (PLAY) John McGrath (EVENTS WHILE GUARDING THE BOFORS GUN)
SC: John McGrath
Nicol Williamson ...... Gunner O'Rourke
Ian Holm .... Gunner Flynn
David Warner .... Lance Bdr Evans
Richard O'Callaghan ...... Rowe
Barry Jackson .... Shone
Donald Gee .... Crawley
John Thaw .... Featherstone
Peter Vaughan .... Sgt Walker
Gareth Forwood .... Lt Pickering
Barbara Jefford .... NAAFI Girl
DRAMA Germany, 1954. Guard commander covers up for suicidal Irishman. (BFA 1968: Best Supporting Actor).

13850
THE BIG SWITCH (81) (X) *eastman*
retitled: STRIP POKER
Pete Walker (Miracle)
P:D:S: Pete Walker
Sebastian Breaks .... John Carter
Virginia Weatherell ...... Karen
Erika Raffael .... Samantha
Jack Allen .... Hornsby-Smith
Derek Aylward .... Carl Mendez
Douglas Blackwell ...... Bruno
Julie Shaw .... Cathy
Jane Howard .... Jane
Roy Stone .... Al
Brian Weske .... Mike
Tracey Yorke .... Stripper
Lena Ellis .... Stripper
CRIME Plot to kill playboy and have gangster take his place.

13851
THE CHARGE OF THE LIGHT BRIGADE (141) (A) *deluxe/scope*
Woodfall (UA)
P: Neil Hartley
D: Tony Richardson
S: Charles Wood, John Osborne
Trevor Howard .... Lord Cardigan
Vanessa Redgrave .... Clarissa Codrington
John Gielgud .... Lord Raglan
Harry Andrews .... Lord Lucan
Jill Bennett .... Mrs Duberly
David Hemmings .... Capt Nolan
Peter Bowles .... Duberly
Mark Burns .... Capt Morris
Howard Marion Crawford ... Sir George Brown
Mark Dignam .... Airey
Alan Dobie .... Mogg
T.P. McKenna .... William Russell
Corin Redgrave .... Featherstonehaugh
Norman Rossington ...... Corbett
Helen Cherry .... Lady Scarlett
Andrew Faulds .... Quaker
Rachel Kempson ...... Mrs Codrington
Donald Wolfit .... Macbeth
HISTORY 1854, Crimea. Events climaxing in battle of Balaclava.

13852
THE DEVIL RIDES OUT (95) (X) *tech*
USA: THE DEVIL'S BRIDE
Hammer (WPD)
P: Anthony Nelson Keys
D: Terence Fisher
S: (NOVEL) Dennis Wheatley
SC: Richard Matheson
Christopher Lee .... Duc de Richleau
Charles Gray .... Mocata
Nike Arrighi .... Tanith
Leon Greene .... Rex Van Ryn
Patrick Mower .... Simon Aron
Gwen Ffrangcon-Davies.. Countess D'Urfe
Sarah Lawson .... Marie Eaton
Paul Eddington .... Richard Eaton
Rosalyn Landor .... Peggy Eaton
Russell Waters .... Malin
FANTASY Period. Duc uses magic to combat Satanist who conjures forth Angel of Death.

13853
A DANDY IN ASPIC (107) (A) *tech/scope*
Columbia British (Col)
P: Anthony Mann, Leslie Gilliat
D: Anthony Mann, Laurence Harvey
S: (NOVEL) Derek Marlowe
SC: Derek Marlowe
Laurence Harvey ...... Alexander Eberlin
Tom Courtenay .... Gatiss
Mia Farrow .... Caroline
Lionel Stander .... Sobakevich
Harry Andrews .... Fraser
Peter Cook .... Prentiss
Per Oscarsson .... Pavel
Barbara Murray .... Heather Vogler
Norman Bird .... Copperfield
John Bird .... Henderson
Michael Trubshawe...... Flowers
Richard O'Sullivan ...... Nevil
Michael Pratt .... Greff
CRIME Russian agent posing as British agent is ordered to kill himself.

13854
HAMMERHEAD (99) (A) *tech*
Irving Allen (Col)
D: David Miller
S: (NOVEL) James Briley
SC: William Bast, Herbert Baker, John Briley
Vince Edwards .... Charles Hood
Judy Geeson .... Sue Trenton
Peter Vaughan .... Hammerhead
Diana Dors .... Kit
Michael Bates ..... Andreas/Sir Richard
Beverly Adams .... Ivory
Patrick Cargill .... Condor
Patrick Holt .... Huntzinger
William Mervyn .... Perrin
Douglas Wilmer .... Vendriani
Tracy Reed .... Miss Hull
Kenneth Cope .... Motorcyclist
Kathleen Byron .... Lady Calvert
Jack Woolgar .... Tookey Tate
Veronica Carlson ...... Ulla
CRIME US agent thwarts master crook's plan to kidnap NATO delegate.

13855
OLIVER ! (146) (U) *tech/scope*
Warwick-Romulus (Col)
P: John Woolf
D: Carol Reed
S: (NOVEL) Charles Dickens (OLIVER TWIST); (PLAY) Lionel Bart
SC: Vernon Harris
Ron Moody .... Fagin
Shani Wallis .... Nancy
Oliver Reed .... Bill Sikes

Harry Secombe .... Mr Bumble
Hugh Griffith .... Magistrate
Jack Wild .... Artful Dodger
Clive Moss .... Charlie Bates
Mark Lester .... Oliver Twist
Peggy Mount .... Widow Corney
Leonard Rossiter ...... Mr Sowerberry
Joseph O'Conor .... Mr Brownlow
Hylda Baker .... Mrs Sowerberry
Sheila White .... Bet
Kenneth Cranham .... Noah Claypole
Megs Jenkins .... Mrs Bedwin
James Hayter .... Jessop
Fred Emney .... Chairman
MUSICAL Period. Runaway foundling becomes pawn of pickpocket. (AA 1968: Best Film, Director, Screenplay, Pho, Art Dir, Sound, Score. Top Moneymaker 1969).

13856
PETULIA (105) (X) *tech*
Petersham (WPD)
P: Raymond Wagner
D: Richard Lester
S: (NOVEL) John Haase (ME AND THE ARCH KOOK PETULIA)
SC: Lawrence B. Marcus, Barbara Turner
Julie Christie .... Petulia Danner
George C. Scott .... Archie Bollen
Richard Chamberlain ..... David Danner
Arthur Hill .... Barney
Shirley Knight .... Polo
Pippa Scott .... May
Kathleen Widdoes .... Wilma
Roger Bowen .... Warren
Richard Dysart .... Receptionist
Nat Esformes .... Mr Mendoza
Maria Val .... Mrs Mendoza
Joseph Cotten .... Mr Danner
The Grateful Dead, Big Brother and the Holding Company, the Committee, the ATC Company
DRAMA San Francisco. Girl's unhappy marriage to immature playboy.

13857
SALT & PEPPER (101) (A) *deluxe*
Chrislaw-Trace-Mark (UA)
P: Peter Lawford, Sammy Davis jr, Milton Ebbins
D: Richard Donner
S: Michael Pertwee
Sammy Davis jr .... Charles Salt
Peter Lawford .... Christopher Pepper
Michael Bates .... Insp Crabbe
Ilona Rodgers .... Marianne Renaud
John Le Mesurier .... Col Woodstock
Graham Stark .... Sgt Walters
Ernest Clark .... Col Balsom
Jeanne Roland .... Mai Ling
Robertson Hare .... Dove
William Mervyn ...... Prime Minister
Michael Trubshawe ...... First Lord
Beth Rogan .... Greta
COMEDY Nightclub owners thwart plot to take over Britain by hijacking Polaris submarine.

13858
WITCHFINDER GENERAL (87) (X) *eastman*
USA: THE CONQUEROR WORM
AIP-Tigon (Tigon)
P: Tony Tenser, Arnold Miller, Louis M. Heyward
D: Michael Reeves
S: (NOVEL) Ronald Bassett
SC: Michael Reeves, Tom Baker, Louis M. Heyward
Vincent Price .... Matthew Hopkins

Ian Ogilvy . . . . Richard Marshall
Rupert Davies . . . . John Lowes
Patrick Wymark . . . . Oliver Cromwell
Wilfrid Brambell . . . . Master Coach
Robert Russell . . . . John Stearne
Nicky Henson . . . . Trooper Swallow
Hilary Dwyer . . . . Sara
Tony Selby . . . . Salter
Michael Beint . . . . Capt Gordon
Peter Haigh . . . . Magistrate
HISTORY 1645. Lawyer uses torture to
obtain confessions to witchcraft.

MAY

13859
THE COMMITTEE (58) (A)
Craytic (Planet)
P: Max Steuer
D: Peter Sykes
S: (STORY) Max Steuer
SC: Max Steuer, Peter Sykes
Paul Jones . . . . Central Figure
Tom Kempinski . . . . Victim
Robert Lloyd . . . . Director
Pauline Munro . . . . Girl
Jimmy Gardner . . . . Boss
The Crazy World of Arthur Brown
FANTASY Murderous hitch-hiker summoned
by strange committee.

13860
DUFFY (101) tech
Columbia British (Col)
P: Martin Manulis
D: Robert Parrish
S: Donald Cammell, Harry Joe Brown jr
James Coburn . . . . Duffy
James Mason . . . . Charles Calvert
James Fox . . . . Stefane Calvert
Susannah York . . . . Segolene
John Alderton . . . . Antony Calvert
Guy Deghy . . . . Capt Schoeller
Carl During . . . . Bonivet
Tutte Lemkow . . . . Spaniard
Marne Maitland . . . . Abdul
Andre Maranne . . . . Insp Garain
Barry Shawzin . . . . Bakirgian
CRIME Tangier. Brothers hire hippy
to help them rob their rich father.

13861
THE LOST CONTINENT (98) (X) tech
Hammer (WPD)
P: Anthony Hinds, Michael Carreras
D: Michael Carreras
S: (NOVEL) Dennis Wheatley
(UNCHARTED SEAS)
SC: Michael Nash
Eric Porter . . . . Capt Lansen
Hildegarde Neff . . . . Eva
Suzanna Leigh . . . . Unita
Tony Beckley . . . . Harry Tyler
Nigel Stock . . . . Webster
Neil McCallum . . . . Hemmings
Benito Carruthers . . . . Ricaldi
Jimmy Hanley . . . . Pat
James Cossins . . . . Chief
Dana Gillespie . . . . Sarah
Victor Maddern . . . . Mate
Michael Ripper . . . . Sea Lawyer
Darryl Read . . . . El Diabolo
FANTASY Tramp steamer drifts into
seaweed land of monsters.

13862
THE FACE OF EVE (94) (U) eastman/bilingual
Udastex-Hispamer (WPD)
P: Harry Alan Towers
D: Jeremy Summers, Robert Lynn

S: Peter Welbeck
Robert Walker . . . . Mike Yates
Celeste Yarnall . . . . Eve
Herbert Lom . . . . Diego
Christopher Lee . . . . Col Stuart
Jean Cafferel . . . . Jose
Rosenda Monteros . . . . . . Pili
Fred Clarke . . . . Burke
Maria Rohm . . . . Anna
ADVENTURE Amazon. Explorer's lost
granddaughter leads expedition to Inca
treasure.

13863
ONLY WHEN I LARF (103) (A) eastman
Beecord (Par)
P: Len Deighton, Brian Duffy
D: Basil Dearden
S: (NOVEL) Len Deighton
SC: John Salmon
Richard Attenborough . . . . Silas
David Hemmings . . . . Bob
Alexandra Stewart . . . . Liz
Nicholas Pennell . . . . Spencer
Melissa Stribling . . . . Diana
Terence Alexander . . . . Gee Gee Gray
Edric Connor . . . . Awana
Clifton Jones . . . . Gen Sakut
Calvin Lockhart . . . . Ali Lin
David Healy . . . . Jones
CRIME Three tricksters plot to swindle
tycoon.

JUN

13864
CURSE OF THE CRIMSON ALTAR (89) (X)
eastman USA: CRIMSON CULT
Tigon British-AIP (Tigon)
P: Tony Tenser, Louis M. Heyward
D: Vernon Sewell
S: Mervyn Haisman, Henry Lincoln,
Gerry Levy
Boris Karloff . . . . Prof Marsh
Christopher Lee . . . . J.D.Morley
Mark Eden . . . . Robert Manning
Virginia Wetherell . . . . Eve
Barbara Steele . . . . Lavinia
Rupert Davies . . . . Vicar
Michael Gough . . . . Elder
Rosemarie Reede . . . . Esther
Derek Tansley . . . . Judge
Denys Peek . . . . Peter Manning
Millicent Scott . . . . Stripper
HORROR Witch reincarnated as man
murders accusers' descendants.

13865
A LITTLE OF WHAT YOU FANCY (75) (U)
eastman
Border (Border)
P: O. Negus-Fancey
D: Robert Webb
S: Ray Mackender
Mark Eden   Helen Shapiro
Barry Cryer   Sheila Bernette
Sidney Bromley   Mary King
Terry Day   John Rutland
MUSICAL History of Music Hall.

13866
THE MINI AFFAIR (84) (A) tech/scope
United Screen Arts
D: Robert Amram
Georgie Fame . . . .
Rosemary Nicols . . . .
John Clive . . . .
Bernard Archard . . . .
Lucille Soong. . . . .
Rick Dane . . . .

Gretchen Regan . . . .
Madeleine Smith. . . . .
DRAMA

13867
GATES TO PARADISE (89) tech/scope
Jointex
P: Sam Waynberg
D: Andrzej Wajda
S: (NOVEL) Jerzy Andrzejewski
SC: Jerzy Andrzejewski, Donald Kravanth
Lionel Stander . . . . Monk
Ferdy Mayne . . . . Count Ludovic
Matthieu Carriere . . . . Alexis
Pauline Challoner . . . . Blanche
John Fordyce . . . . Jacob
Jenny Agutter . . . . Maud
HISTORY 13th C. Monk accompanies
children on crusade from France to
Jerusalem.

13868
THE GREEN SHOES (27) (A) eastman
Isleworth (Par)
P: Ralph Solomons
D: Ian Brims
S: Ivor Jay
George Cole . . . .
Donald Webster. . . . .
Tom Macaulay . . . .
Fred Davis . . . .
CRIME Police track killer of a girl
wearing green shoes.

JUL

13869
THE BLISS OF MRS BLOSSOM (93) (A) tech
Paramount
P: Josef Shaftel
D: Joseph McGrath
S: (PLAY) Alec Coppel
SC: Alec Coppel, Denis Norden
Shirley Maclaine . . . . Harriet Blossom
Richard Attenborough . . . . . Robert Blossom
James Booth . . . . Ambrose Tuttle
Freddie Jones . . . . Sgt Dylan
William Rushton . . . . Assistant
Bob Monkhouse . . . . Dr Taylor
Patricia Routledge . . . . Miss Reece
John Bluthal . . . . Judge
Harry Towb . . . . Doctor
Barry Humphries . . . . Dealer
Clive Dunn . . . . Man
COMEDY Bra manufacturer's wife keeps
her lover in the attic.

13870
THE BURNING (30) (U)
Memorial Enterprises (BFI)
P:D: Stephen Frears
S: (STORY) Roland Starke (THE DAY)
SC: Roland Starke
Gwen Ffrangcon-Davies . . . Gran
Mark Baillie . . . . Child
Isabel Muller . . . . Cook
Maxine Day . . . . Nurse
Cosmo Pieterse . . . . Chauffeur
DRAMA South Africa. Grandmother
visits sister's farm during uprising.

13871
CARRY ON . . . UP THE KHYBER (88) (A)
eastman
Adder (RFD)
P: Peter Rogers
D: Gerald Thomas
S: Talbot Rothwell
Sidney James . . . . Sir Sidney Ruff-Diamond
Kenneth Williams . . . . Khasi of Kalabar
Charles Hawtrey . . . . . . Pte James Widdle

Roy Castle . . . . Capt Keene
Joan Sims . . . . Lady Ruff-Diamond
Bernard Bresslaw . . . . Bungdit Din
Peter Butterworth . . . . Missionary
Terry Scott . . . . Sgt-Maj MacNutt
Angela Douglas . . . . Princess Jelhi
Cardew Robinson . . . . Fakir
Julian Holloway . . . . Maj Shorthouse
Leon Thau . . . . Stinghi
Alexandra Dane . . . . Busti
COMEDY India, 1895. Native leader threatens uprising on learning Scottish soldiers wear pants under their kilts.

13872
GIRL ON A MOTORCYCLE (91) (X) *tech/ bilingual*
Midatlantic-Ares (BL)
P: William Sassoon
D: Jack Cardiff
S: (NOVEL) Andre Pieyre de Mandiargues (LA MOTOCYCLETTE)
SC: Ronald Duncan
Marianne Faithfull . . . . Rebecca
Alain Delon . . . . Daniel
Roger Mutton . . . . Raymond
Marius Goring . . . . Father
Catherine Jourdan . . . . Catherine
Jean Leduc . . . . Jean
Jacques Marin . . . . Attendant
John G. Heller . . . . Customs Officer
ROMANCE Alsace. French teacher's wife recalls her affair during fatal ride to lover.

13873
HOT MILLIONS (106) (U) *metro*
MGM British-Milberg (MGM)
P: Mildred Freed Alberg
D: Eric Till
S: Ira Wallach, Peter Ustinov
Peter Ustinov . . . . Marcus Pendleton
Maggie Smith . . . . Patty
Karl Malden . . . . Klemper
Bob Newhart . . . . Gnatpole
Robert Morley . . . . Caesar Smith
Cesar Romero . . . . Customs Officer
Melinda May . . . . Nurse
Ann Lancaster . . . . Landlady
Margaret Courtenay . . . . . . Mrs Hubbard
Lynda Baron . . . . Louise
Billy Milton . . . . Agent
Peter Jones . . . . Governor
COMEDY Embezzler poses as computer expert to set up elaborate swindle.

13874
PROJECT Z (U) *eastman*
Lion Pacesetter (CFF)
P:D:S: Ronald Spencer
SC: Michael Barnes
Annabel Littledale . . . . . . Pam
Michael Howe . . . . Alan
Michael Crockett . . . . Colin
Roy Purcell . . . . Knight
Neil McCarthy . . . . MacNab
Michael Murray . . . . Peters
Desmond Jordan . . . . Griffiths

13875
1: AFRICAN LANDFALL (14)

13876
2: ESPIONAGE (15)

13877
3: THE RUNAWAY TRUCK (13)

13878
4: SANDSTORM (13)

13879
5: SHARPSHOOTERS OF THE DESERT (14)

13880
6: DOUBLE DOUBLE CROSS (14)

13881
7: TRAPPED IN THE TOMBS (14)

13882
8: THE DESERTED VILLAGE (14)
CHILDREN Tunisia. Holiday children thwart a spy's theft of experimental truck.

AUG

13883
THE BLOOD OF FU MANCHU (91) (A) *eastman*
Udastex (AA)
P: Harry Alan Towers
D: Jesus Franco
S: (CHARACTERS) Sax Rohmer
SC: Peter Welbeck
Christopher Lee . . . . Fu Manchu
Gotz George . . . . Carl Janson
Richard Greene . . . . Nayland Smith
Howard Marion Crawford . . Dr Petrie
Tsai Chin . . . . Lin Tang
Maria Rohm . . . . Ursula
Richard Palacios . . . . Sancho Lopez
Shirley Eaton . . . . Black Widow
Frances Kahn . . . . Carmen
CRIME South America. Chinese crook blinds his enemies with poisoned kiss.

13884
THE SYNDICATE (106) (A) *tech*
AB-Pathe (WPD)
P: Harry Field
D: Frederic Goode
S: (NOVEL) Denys Rhodes
SC: Geoffrey Hayes
William Sylvester . . . . Burt Hickey
June Ritchie . . . . Mari Brant
Robert Urquhart . . . . George Brant
Christian Doermer . . . . . . Kurt Hohmann
John Bennett . . . . Dr Singh
John De Villers . . . . Schultz
Omari Suleman . . . . Kamahru
ADVENTURE Kenya. Search for uranium deposit by rival factions.

13885
NOBODY RUNS FOREVER (101) (A) *eastman*
Selmur-Rank (RFD)
P: Selig J. Seligman, Betty E. Box
D: Ralph Thomas
S: (NOVEL) Jon Cleary (THE HIGH COMMISSIONER)
SC: Wilfred Greatorex
Rod Taylor . . . . Scobie Malone
Christopher Plummer . . . Sir James Quentin
Lilli Palmer . . . . Sheila Quentin
Camilla Sparv . . . . Lisa Pretorius
Daliah Lavi . . . . Maria Cholon
Clive Revill . . . . Joseph
Franchot Tone . . . . . . Ambassador Townsend
Leo McKern . . . . . . Premier of NSW
Lee Montague . . . . Denzil
Calvin Lockhart . . . . Jamaica
Derren Nesbitt . . . . Pallain
Edric Connor . . . . Julius
Russell Napier . . . . Leeds
Charles Tingwell . . . . Jackaroo
CRIME Australian detective unmasks killer of High Commissioner's first wife.

13886
DON'T RAISE THE BRIDGE, LOWER THE RIVER (100) (U) *tech*

Walter Shenson (Col)
P: Walter Shenson
D: Jerry Paris
S: (NOVEL) Max Wilk
SC: Max Wilk
Jerry Lewis . . . . George Lester
Terry-Thomas . . . . H. William Homer
Jacqueline Pearce . . . . Pamela Lester
Bernard Cribbins . . . . Fred Davies
Patricia Routledge . . . . . . Lucille Beatty
Nicholas Parsons . . . . Dudley Heath
Michael Bates . . . . Dr Spink
John Bluthal . . . . Dr Pinto
Sandra Caron . . . . Nurse
Colin Gordon . . . . Hartford
Pippa Benedict . . . . Fern Averback
Harold Goodwin . . . . . . Six-eyes Wiener
Alexandra Dane . . . . Masseuse
Nike Arrighi . . . . Waitress
Jerry Paris . . . . Umpire
COMEDY Man steals electronic oil drill from his wife's lover, to sell to Arab sheik.

13887
ESCAPE FROM THE SEA (57) (U) *eastman*
Wallace (CFF)
P: A. Frank Bundy
D: SC: Peter Seabourne
S: Frank Wells
Paul Martin . . . . Mat
Simon Milton . . . . Chris Oakley
Nicky Broadway . . . . Robbie
Alison Glennie . . . . Jane Oakley
Larry Hamilton . . . . Pen
Fabienne Symons . . . . Meg
Peggy Sinclair . . . . Mrs Oakley
CPO Fairfield . . . . CPO Scott
CHILDREN Cornwall. Coastguards rescue marooned children.

SEP

13888
BABY LOVE (93) (X) *eastman*
Avton (Avco Embassy)
P: Michael Klinger, Guido Coen
D: Alastair Reid
S: (NOVEL) Tina Chad Christian
SC: Alastair Reid, Guido Coen, Michael Klinger
Ann Lynn . . . . Amy Quayle
Keith Barron . . . . Robert Quayle
Linda Hayden . . . . Luci
Diana Dors . . . . Liz
Derek Lamden . . . . Nicholas Quayle
Patience Collier . . . . Mrs Carmichael
Dick Emery . . . . Harry Pearson
Sheila Staefel . . . . Tessa Pearson
Sally Stephens . . . . Margo Pearson
Timothy Carlton . . . . Jeremy
Christopher Witty . . . . . . Jonathan
DRAMA Suicide's teenage bastard seduces mother's ex-lover, his son and his wife.

13889
MAYERLING (141) (A) *eastman/scope bilingual*
Corona-Winchester (WPD)
P: Eugene Tucherer, Marcel Hellman
D: Terence Young
S: (NOVEL) Claude Anet; (NOVEL) Michael Arnold (THE ARCHDUKE)
SC: Terence Young, Denis Cannan
Omar Sharif . . . . Crown Prince Rudolf
Catherine Deneuve . . . . . . Maria Vetsera
James Mason . . . . . Emperor Franz-Josef
Ava Gardner . . . . Empress Elizabeth
James Robertson Justice . Prince Edward
Genevieve Page . . . . Countess Larisch

Andrea Parisy . . . . Princess Stephanie
Ivan Desny . . . . Count Josef Hoyos
Charles Millot . . . . Count Taafe
Maurice Teynac . . . . Moritz Szeps
Fabienne Dali . . . . Mizzi Kaspar
HISTORY Vienna, 1888. Hapsburg Emperor interferes with son's love for commoner.

13890
A MIDSUMMER NIGHT'S DREAM (124) (U)
eastman
Royal Shakespeare Enterprises-Filmways (Eagle)
P: Martin Ransohoff, Michael Birkett
D: Peter Hall
S: (PLAY) William Shakespeare
Derek Godfrey . . . . Theseus
Barbara Jefford . . . . Hippolyta
Hugh Sullivan . . . . Philostrate
Nicholas Selby . . . . Egeus
David Warner . . . . Lysander
Michael Jayston . . . . Demetrius
Diana Rigg . . . . Helena
Helen Mirren . . . . Hermia
Ian Richardson . . . . Oberon
Judi Dench . . . . Titania
Ian Holm . . . . Puck
Paul Rogers . . . . Bottom
Sebastian Shaw . . . . Quince
Bill Travers . . . . Snout
FANTASY Athens, period. Lovers' lives complicated by fairies.

13891
NEGATIVES (98) (X) *eastman*
Kettledrum-Narrizzano (Crispin)
P: Judd Bernard
D: Peter Medak
S: (NOVEL) Peter Everett
SC: Peter Everett, Roger Lowry
Peter McEnery . . . . Theo
Diane Cilento . . . . Reingard
Glenda Jackson . . . . Vivien
Maurice Denham . . . . Father
Steven Lewis . . . . Dealer
Norman Rossington . . . . . . Auctioneer
Billy Russell . . . . Old Man
DRAMA Antique shop owner and wife play strange games.

13892
WONDERWALL (92) (X) *eastman*
Alan Clore-Compton (Cinecenta)
P: Andrew Braunsberg
D: Joe Massot
S: Gerard Brach
SC: G. Cain
Jack MacGowran . . . . Oscar Collins
Jane Birkin . . . . Penny
Irene Handl . . . . Mrs Peurofoy
Richard Wattis . . . . Perkins
Iain Quarrier . . . . Man
Beatrix Lehmann . . . . Mother
Brian Walsh . . . . Photographer
Sean Lynch . . . . Riley
Bea Duffell . . . . Mrs Charmer
DRAMA Voyeur watches model through crack in his wall.

13893
HEADLINE HUNTERS (60) (U) *eastman*
Ansus (CFF)
P: Frank Godwin
D: Jonathan Ingrams
S: Geoffrey Bond
SC: Jonathan Ingrams, C.M.Pennington Richards
Leonard Brockwell . . . . Terry Hunter
Susan Payne . . . . Joan Hunter
Stephen Garlick . . . . Peter Hunter

Jeffrey Chandler . . . . Alec
Bill Owen . . . . Henry
Reginald Marsh . . . . Bagshot
Keith Smith . . . . Fustwick
Glyn Houston . . . . Gresham
David Lodge . . . . Harry
Dermot Kelly . . . . Ernie
CHILDREN Children run newspaper while father is ill.

13894
THE OTHER PEOPLE (X) *eastman*
Telstar-Oakhurst (Par)
P: Michael Deeley, Harry Field
D: David Hart
S: David Hart, Michael Joseph
Peter McEnery . . . .
John McEnery; . . . .
Olga Georges-Picot . . . . . .
Bruce Robinson . . . .
DRAMA Middle-aged pornographer and daughter.

13895
GOLD IS WHERE YOU FIND IT (27) (U)
eastman
Chairene (Mon)
P:D: Francis Searle
Eddie Byrne . . . . Tyg McMahon
Dermot Kelly . . . . Mad Mike
Sam Kydd . . . . Pader Murphy
Pat McAlliney . . . . Billy Ryan
Barry Keegan . . . . Steve Lenihan
Barbara Berkery . . . . Molly Ryan
Patrick Jordan . . . . Insp O'Regan
COMEDY Ireland. Drunk millionaire's lost nuggets start a gold rush.

OCT

13896
STOP ! (32) (A)
Oracle (Continental Art)
P:D:S: Mark Petersen
CRIME Assassin uncovers the background of his victim.

13897
BOOM ! (113) (X) *tech/scope*
World Film Services-Moon Lake (RFD)
P: John Heyman, Norman Priggen
D: Joseph Losey
S: (PLAY) Tennessee Williams
(THE MILK TRAIN DOESN'T STOP HERE ANY MORE)
SC: Tennessee Williams
Elizabeth Taylor . . . . Flora Goforth
Richard Burton . . . . Chris Flanders
Noel Coward . . . . Witch of Capri
Joanna Shimkus . . . . Blackie Black
Michael Dunn . . . . Rudy
Romolo Valli . . . . Dr Lullo
Veronica Wells . . . . Simonetta
Fernando Piazza . . . . Giulio
Howard Taylor . . . . Journalist
DRAMA Mediterranean island. Much-widowed millionairess dies after last affair with poet.

13898
CHITTY CHITTY BANG BANG (145) (U)
tech/scope
Warfield-DFI (UA)
P: Albert R. Broccoli
D: Ken Hughes
S: (NOVEL) Ian Fleming
SC: Roald Dahl, Ken Hughes
Dick Van Dyke . . . . . Caractacus Potts
Sally Ann Howes . . . . . . Truly Scrumptious
Lionel Jeffries . . . . Grandpa Potts
Gert Frobe . . . . Baron Bomburst

Anna Quayle . . . . . . Baroness Bomburst
Benny Hill . . . . Toymaker
James Robertson Justice . Lord Scrumptious
Robert Helpmann . . . . Child Catcher
Heather Ripley . . . . Jemina Potts
Adrian Hall . . . . Jeremy Potts
Barbara Windsor . . . . Blonde
Davy Kaye . . . . Admiral
Stanley Unwin . . . . Chancellor
Peter Arne . . . . Captain
Victor Maddern . . . . Junkman
Totti Truman Taylor . . . . . Duchess
Max Bacon . . . . Orchestra Leader
Felix Felton . . . . Minister
Richard Wattis . . . . Secretary
Max Wall . . . . Inventor
MUSICAL Whistling-sweet inventor tells his children story of flying car.

13899
DRACULA HAS RISEN FROM THE GRAVE
(92) (X) *tech*
Hammer (WPD)
P: Aida Young
D: Freddie Francis
S: (CHARACTER) Bram Stoker (DRACULA)
SC: Anthony Hinds
Christopher Lee . . . . Count Dracula
Rupert Davies . . . . Monsignor
Veronica Carlson . . . . Maria
Barbara Ewing . . . . Zena
Barry Andrews . . . . Paul
Ewan Hooper . . . . Priest
Marion Mathie . . . . Anna
Michael Ripper . . . . Max
George A. Cooper . . . . Landlord
HORROR Transylvania, period. Revived vampire enslaves church man's niece.

13900
THE LION IN WINTER (134) (A) *eastman/scope*
Haworth (Avco Embassy)
P: Martin Poll
D: Anthony Harvey
S:(PLAY) James Goldman
SC: James Goldman
Peter O'Toole . . . . Henry II
Katharine Hepburn . . . . . . Queen Eleanor
Jane Merrow . . . . Princess Alais
John Castle . . . . Prince Geoffrey
Anthony Hopkins . . . . Prince Richard
Nigel Terry . . . . Prince John
Timothy Dalton . . . . King Philip
Nigel Stock . . . . William Marshall
O.Z. Whitehead . . . . Bishop of Durham
Kenneth Griffith . . . . Player
HISTORY 1183. Complicated schemings of English King and French wife over the marriages of their sons. (AA 1968: Best Actress, Score. BFA 1968: Best Actress, (Music)

13901
OTLEY (91) (A) *tech*
Open Road-Curtis (Col)
P: Carl Foreman, Bruce Cohn Curtis
D: Dick Clement
S: (NOVEL) Martin Waddell
SC: Ian La Frenais, Dick Clement
Tom Courtenay . . . Gerald Arthur Otley
Romy Schneider . . . . Imogen
Alan Badel . . . . Sir Alec Hadrian
James Villiers . . . . Hendrickson
Leonard Rossiter . . . . Johnston
James Bolam . . . . Albert
Fiona Lewis . . . . Lin
Freddie Jones . . . . Philip Proudfoot
James Cossins . . . . Jeffcock
James Maxwell . . . . Rollo
Ronald Lacey . . . . Curtis
Barry Fantoni . . . . Larry

Pete Murray, Jimmy Young, The Herd
COMEDY Man framed for murder gets
involved with espionage groups.

13902
SECRET CEREMONY (109) (X) *eastman*
Universal-World-Paul Heller (RFD)
P: John Heyman, Norman Priggen
D: Joseph Losey
S: (STORY) Marco Denevi
SC: George Tabori
Elizabeth Taylor . . . .   Leonora
Mia Farrow . . . .   Cenci
Robert Mitchum . . . .   Albert
Pamela Brown . . . .   Aunt Hilda
Peggy Ashcroft . . . .   Aunt Hanna
DRAMA Prostitute mothers a seemingly-
innocent girl.

13903
SHALAKO (113) (A) *tech/scope*
Kingston-De Grunwald (WPD)
P: Euan Lloyd
D: Edward Dmytryk
S: (NOVEL) Louis L'Amour
SC: J.J. Griffith, Hal Hopper, Scot Finch
Sean Connery . . . .   Shalako
Brigitte Bardot . . . .   Irina Lazaar
Stephen Boyd . . . .   Bosky Fulton
Jack Hawkins . . . .   Sir Charles Daggett
Peter Van Eyck . . . Frederick von Halstaat
Honor Blackman . . . .   Lady Daggett
Woody Strode . . . .   Chato
Eric Sykes . . . .   Mako
Alexander Knox . . . .   Henry Clarke
Valerie French . . . .   Elena Clarke
Donald Barry . . . .   Buffalo
Rodd Redwing . . . .   Father
Chief Elmer Smith . . . .   Loco
WESTERN New Mexico, 1880. Ex-cavalry officer
leads European tourists to safety from Apaches.

13904
TWISTED NERVE (118) (X) *eastman*
Charter (BL)
P: John Boulting, George W. George,
Frank Granat
D: Roy Boulting
S: Roger Marshall, Jeremy Scott
SC: Leo Marks, Roy Boulting
Hayley Mills . . . .   Susan Harper
Hywel Bennett . . . .   Martin Durnley
Billie Whitelaw . . . .   Joan Harper
Phyllis Calvert . . . .   Enid Durnley
Frank Finlay . . : . . . .   Eric Durnley
Barry Foster . . . .   Gerry Henderson
Salmaan Peer . . . .   Shashi Kadir
Gretchen Franklin . . . .   Clarkie
Christian Roberts . . . .   Philip Harvey
Thorley Walters . . . .   Sir John Forrester
Timothy West . . . .   Supt Dakin
Russell Napier . . . .   Prof Fuller
CRIME Mongol child's brother becomes
homicidal maniac.

13905
THE LONG DAY'S DYING (95) (X) *tech/scope*
Junction (Par)
P: Michael Deeley, Harry Fine
D: Peter Collinson
S: (NOVEL) Alan White
SC: Charles Wood
David Hemmings . . . .   John
Tom Bell . . . .   Tom
Tony Beckley . . . .   Cliff
Alan Dobie . . . .   Helmut
WAR Three paratroopers capture German
and all die returning to base.

13906
BEDTIME (27) (A) scope
Viewpoint (Gala)

P: Peter Griffiths
D: John Irvin
S: Michael Hastings
Imogen Hassall . . . .   Woman
Michael Latimer . . . .   Man
ROMANCE Couple make love and converse.

13907
MRS BROWN YOU'VE GOT A LOVELY
DAUGHTER (95) (U) metro/*scope*
Ivorygate (MGM)
P: Allen Klein
D: Saul Swimmer
S: Thaddeus Vane
Peter Noone . . . .   Herman Tulley
Karl Green . . . .   Karl
Keith Hopwood . . . .   Keith
Derek Leckenby . . . .   Derek
Barry Whitwam . . . .   Barry
Stanley Holloway . . . .   Mr Brown
Mona Washbourne . . . .   Mrs Brown
Lance Percival . . . .   Percy
Marjorie Rhodes . . . .   Grandma
Sheila White . . . .   Tulip
Sarah Caldwell . . . .   Judy
Avis Bunnage . . . .   Mother
John Sharp . . . .   Oakshott
Nat Jackley . . . .   Singer
Billy Milton . . . .   Landlord
Dermot Kelly . . . .   Conman
Margery Manners . . . .   Singer
MUSICAL Manchester youths form pop
group to enter their greyhound in race.

NOV

13908
THE BIG CATCH (55) (U) *eastman*
International Film Associates (CFF)
P: Laurence Henson, Edward McConnell
D: Laurence Henson
S: Laurence Henson, Charles Gormley
David Gallacher . . . .   Ewan Cameron
Ronald Sinclair . . . . .Lindsay Murray
Andrew Byatt . . . .   Anderson
Simon Orr . . . .   Ian
Murray Forbes . . . .   Graham
James Copeland . . . .   Mr Cameron
Michael O'Halloran . . . . . .   Campbell Murray
Willie Joss . . . .   Willie John
CHILDREN Scots children rescue boy
cut off by tide.

13909
THE FILE OF THE GOLDEN GOOSE (109)
(A) *deluxe*
Theme-Caralan-Dador (UA)
P: David E. Rose
D: Sam Wanamaker
S: John C. Higgins
SC: John C.Higgins, James B. Gordon
Yul Brynner . . . .   Peter Novak
Charles Gray . . . .   Nick Harrison
Edward Woodward . . . . . .   Peter Thompson
John Barrie . . . .   Sloane
Bernard Archard . . . .   Collins
Ivor Dean . . . .   Reynolds
Anthony Jacobs . . . .   Firenos
Adrienne Corri . . . .   Tina Dell
Karel Stepanek . . . .   Mieller
Walter Gotell . . . .   Leeds
Hugh McDermott . . . .   Moss
CRIME American agent and Yard man pose
as gangsters to catch counterfeiters.

13910
LES BICYCLETTES DE BELSIZE (29) (U)
eastman
Delmore-Illustra (BL)
P: Jacques De Lane Lea
D: Douglas Hickox

S: Bernie Cooper, Francis Megahy
SC: Michael Newling
Judy Huxtable . . . .   Julie
Anthony May . . . .   Steve
Leslie Goddard . . . .   Kate
Barney Reisz. . . . .   Boy
MUSICAL Hampstead. Shop owner falls
for fashion model.

13911
THE LIMBO LINE (99) (U) *eastman*
Trio-Group W (LIP)
P: William Gell, Howard Barnes
D: Samuel Gallu
S: (NOVEL) Victor Canning
SC: Donald James
Craig Stevens . . . .   Manston
Kate O'Mara . . . .   Irina
Vladek Sheybal . . . .   Oleg
Eugene Deckers . . . .   Cadillet
Moira Redmond . . . .   Ludmilla
Yolande Turner . . . .   Pauline
Jean Marsh . . . .   Dilys
Rosemary Rogers . . . .   Joan Halst
Norman Bird . . . .   Chivers
Robert Urquhart . . . .   Hardwick
Ferdy Mayne . . . .   Sutcliffe
Joan Benham . . . .   Lady Faraday
CRIME Intelligence agent saves
Russian ballerina from kidnappers.

13912
LIONHEART (57) (U) *eastman*
Forlong (CFF)
P:D: Michael Forlong
S: (NOVEL) Alexander Fullerton
SC: Michael Forlong, Alexander Fullerton
James Forlong . . . .   Andrew Fowler
Louise Rush . . . .   Belinda
Ian Jessup . . . .   Robert
Robert Dean . . . .   Father
Pauline Yates . . . .   Mother
Joe Brown . . . .   Pte Worms
Ben Aris . . . .   Capt Harris
Wilfred Brambell . . . .   Dignett
Jimmy Edwards . . . .   Butcher
Irene Handl   Lil
Leslie Dwyer . . . .   Carpenter
CHILDREN Tonbridge. Boy makes pet of
escaped circus lion.

13913
PLAY DIRTY (117) (X) *tech/scope*
Lowndes (UA)
P: Harry Saltzman
D: Andre De Toth
S: George Marton
SC: Lotte Colin, Melvin Bragg
Michael Caine . . . .   Capt Douglas
Nigel Davenport . . . .   Cyril Leech
Nigel Green . . . .   Col Masters
Harry Andrews . . . .   Brig Blore
Bernard Archard . . . .   Col Homerton
Daniel Pilon . . . .   Capt Attwood
Aly Ben Ayed . . . .   Sadok
Takis Emmanouel . . . .   Kostas Manou
Enrique Avila . . . .   Kafkarides
Patrick Jordan . . . .   Maj Watkins
WAR Africa. Company of ex-criminals destroy
German oil depot.

13914
HOSTILE WITNESS (101) (U) *deluxe*
Caralan-Dador (UA)
P: David E. Rose
D: Ray Milland
S: (PLAY) Jack Roffey
SC: Jack Roffey
Ray Milland . . . .   Simon Crawford QC

Sylvia Sims . . . . Sheila Larkin
Felix Aylmer . . . . Mr Justice Osborne
Raymond Huntley . . . . John Naylor
Geoffrey Lumsden . . . . . Maj Hugh Maitland
Norman Barrs . . . . Charles Milburn
Percy Marmont . . . . Sir Matthew Gregory
Dulcie Bowman . . . . Lady Gregory
Ewan Roberts . . . . Hamish Gillespie
Richard Hurndall . . . . Insp Elsy
Ronald Leigh-Hunt . . . . Dr Wimbourne
CRIME Barrister framed for killing man who
ran over his daughter.

13915
DIAMONDS FOR BREAKFAST (102) (A)
eastman
Bridge (Par)
P: Selig J. Seligman, Carlo Ponti, Pierre Rouve
D: Christopher Morahan
S: Pierre Rouve, Ronald Harwood, N.F.
Simpson
Marcello Mastroianni . . . . . Grand Duke Nicholas
Rita Tushingham . . . . Bridget Rafferty
Elaine Taylor . . . . Victoria
Maggie Blye . . . . Honey
Francisca Tu . . . . Jeanne Silkfingers
The Karlins . . . . Triplets
Warren Mitchell . . . . Popov
Nora Nicholson . . . . Anastasia Petrovna
Bryan Pringle . . . . Sergeant
Leonard Rossiter . . . . Insp Dudley
Bill Fraser . . . . Bookseller
David Horne . . . . Duke of Windemere
Charles Lloyd Pack . . . . . . Butler
COMEDY Russian Duke recruits girl gang to steal
back family jewels.

DEC
13916
ALL NEAT IN BLACK STOCKINGS (99) (X)
eastman
Miron (AA)
P: Leon Clore, John Arnold
D: Christopher Morahan
S: (NOVEL) Jane Gaskell
SC: Jane Gaskell, Hugh Whitemore
Victor Henry . . . . Ginger
Susan George . . . . Jill
Jack Shepherd . . . . Dwyer
Clare Kelly . . . . Mother
Anna Cropper . . . . Sis
Harry Towb . . . . Issur
Vanessa Forsyth . . . . Carole
Terence de Marney . . . . Gunge
Jasmina Hamzavi . . . . Babette
Nita Lorraine . . . . Jocasta
DRAMA Window cleaner takes care of sick
man's house, and fills it with friends and
relations.

13917
IF . . . (111) (X) *eastman*
Memorial Enterprises (Par)
P: Michael Medwin, Lindsay Anderson
D: Lindsay Anderson
S: David Sherwin, John Howlett
SC: David Sherwin
Malcolm McDowell . . . . Mick Travers
David Wood . . . . Johnny
Richard Warwick . . . . Wallace
Robert Swann . . . . Rowntree
Christine Noonan . . . . Girl
Hugh Thomas . . . . Denson
Rupert Webster . . . . Bobby Phillips
Peter Jeffrey . . . . Headmaster
Anthony Nicholls . . . . Gen Denson
Arthur Lowe . . . . Mr Kemp
Mona Washbourne . . . . Matron
Mary McLeod . . . . Mrs Kemp

Geoffrey Chater . . . . Chaplain
Ben Aris . . . . John Thomas
DRAMA Senior schoolboys lead murderous
rebellion.

13918
TILL DEATH US DO PART (100) (A)
eastman
Associated London (BL)
P: Beryl Vertue, Jon Pennington
D: Norman Cohen
S: (TV SERIES) Johnny Speight
SC: Johnny Speight
Warren Mitchell . . . . Alf Garnett
Dandy Nichols . . . . Else Garnett
Anthony Booth . . . . Mike
Una Stubbs . . . . Rita Garnett
Liam Redmond . . . . Father
Bill Maynard . . . . Bert
Brian Blessed . . . . Sergeant
Sam Kydd . . . . Man
COMEDY Wapping, 1939. Life in war and
peace with cockney family.

13919
WHERE EAGLES DARE (155) (A) *metro/
scope*
Winkast (MGM)
P: Jerry Gershwin, Elliott Kastner
D: Brian G. Hutton, Yakima Canutt
S: (NOVEL) Alistair Maclean
SC: Alistair MacLean
Richard Burton . . . . . . Maj John Smith
Clint Eastwood . . . . Lt Morris Schaffer
Mary Ure . . . . Mary Ellison
Patrick Wymark . . . . Col Turner
Michael Hordern . . . . Admiral Rolland
Donald Houston . . . . Christiansen
Peter Barkworth . . . . Berkeley
Robert Beatty . . . . Cartwright Jones
William Squire . . . . Thomas
Derren Nesbitt . . . . . . Major Von Hapen
Anton Diffring . . . . Col Kramer
Brook Williams . . . . Sgt Harrod
Neil McCarthy . . . . MacPherson
Ferdy Mayne . . . . Rosemeyer
Ingrid Pitt . . . . Heidi
WAR Bavaria. Seven soldiers parachute into
Alps to rescue captured officer.

13920
SEPARATION (93) (X) *eastman*
Bond (LIP)
P:D: Jack Bond
S: Jane Dewar
Jane Arden . . . . Jane
David De Keyser . . . . Husband
Ann Lynn . . . . Woman
Ian Quarrier . . . . Lover
Terence De Marney . . . . Man
FANTASY Dreams of woman separated from
her husband.

13921
JOANNA (122) (X) *deluxe/scope*
Laughlin (20)
P: Michael Laughlin
D:S: Michael Sarne
Genevieve Waite . . . . Joanna
Christian Doermer . . . . Hendrik Casson
Calvin Lockhart . . . . Gordon
Donald Sutherland . . . . . Lord Peter Sanderson
Glenna Forster-Jones . . . . . Beryl
David Scheuer . . . . Dominic Endersley
Marda Vanne . . . . Granny
Geoffrey Morris . . . . Father
Michele Cooke . . . . Margot
Manning Wilson . . . . Inspector
Jenny Hanley . . . . Woman
DRAMA Country art student's promiscuous
career in London and Tangier.

13922
DANCE OF THE HANDS (15) (U) *eastman*
Monarch (LIP)
MUSICAL Hands wearing white gloves enact
six stories.

13923
THE MAGUS (116) (X) *deluxe/scope*
Blazer (20)
P: John Kohn, Jud Kinberg
D: Guy Green
S: (NOVEL) John Fowles
SC: John Fowles
Michael Caine . . . . Nicholas Urfe
Anthony Quinn . . . . Maurice Conchis
Candice Bergen . . . . . . Lily (Julie Holmes)
Anna Karina . . . . Anne
Paul Stassino . . . . Meli
Julian Glover . . . . Anton
Takis Emmanuel . . . . Kapetan
George Pastell . . . . Priest
Danielle Noel . . . . Soula
Andreas Malandrinos . . . . . Goathead
Corin Redgrave . . . . Capt Wimmel
DRAMA Greece. English teacher gets involved
with psychiatrist's dramatised charades to cure
schizophrenics.

13924
CRY WOLF (58) (U) *eastman*
Damor Leaderfilm (CFF)
P: Michael Truman
D:S: John Davis
SC: Derry Quinn
Antony Kemp . . . . Tony
Mary Burleigh . . . . Mary
Martin Beuamont . . . . Martin
Judy Cornwell . . . . Stella
Eileen Moore . . . . Muriel Walker
Maurice Kaufmann . . . . Jim Walker
John Trenaman . . . . Ben
Alfred Bell . . . . Insp Blake
Pat Coombs . . . . Mrs Blades
Wilfrid Brambell . . . . Delivery Man
Adrienne Corri . . . . Woman
Ian Hendry . . . .
Janet Munro . . . .
CHILDREN Imaginative boy not believed when
he uncovers plot to kidnap Prime Minister.

13925
SUBTERFUGE (86) (AA) *eastman*
Intertel-VTR (RFD)
P: Trevor Wallace, Peter Snell
D: Peter Graham Scott
S: David Whittaker
Gene Barry . . . . Donovan
Joan Collins . . . . Anne Langley
Richard Todd . . . . Col Victor Redmayne
Tom Adams . . . . Peter Langley
Suzanna Leigh . . . . Donetta
Michael Rennie . . . . Goldsmith
Marius Goring . . . . Shevick
Scott Forbes . . . . Pannell
Colin Gordon . . . . Kitteridge
Guy Deghy . . . . Dr Lundgren
CRIME CIA agent discovers British colleague is
a traitor.

13926
POPDOWN (98) (A) *eastman*
Premar (NR)
P:D:S: Fred Marshall
Diane Keen . . . . Miss 1970
Jane Bates . . . . Aries
Zoot Money . . . . Sagittarius
Carol Rachell . . . . Miss Withit
Debbie Slater . . . . Girl
Bill Aron . . . . Host
Nicole Yarna . . . . Body

Fred Marshall . . . . Boy
Margaret Evans . . . . Nude
Brenton Wood; Treasure Chest; Don Partridge;
Tony Hicks; Kevin & Gary; Dantalion's Chariot;
Blossom Toes; Hetty Schneider Quartet; Julie
Driscoll; The Brian Auger Trinity.
MUSICAL Extra-terrestrials observe teenage
music scene.

13927
ONE PLUS ONE (109) (X) *eastman* retitled:

SYMPATHY FOR THE DEVIL
Cupid (Connoisseur)
P: Eleni Collard, Michael Pearson, Iain
Quarrier
D:S: Jean-Luc Godard
N: Sean Lynch
Mick Jagger . . . . Himself
The Rolling Stones . . . . Themselves
Anne Wiazemsky . . . . Eve Democracy
Iain Quarrier

Frankie Dymon Jr
Danny Daniels
Illario Pedro
Roy Stewart
Nike Arrighi
Francoise Pascal
Joanna David
FANTASY Intercut episodes concerning
Bolivian revolutionary in hiding, pop group,
Black Power militants, etc.

1969

JAN

13928
THE ADDING MACHINE (99) (A) *tech*
Associated London-Universal (RFD)
P:D:SC: Jerome Epstein
S: (PLAY) Elmer Rice

Phyllis Diller	Mrs Zero
Milo O'Shea	Mr Zero
Billie Whitelaw	Daisy
Sidney Chaplin	Lt Charles
Julian Glover	Shrdlu
Raymond Huntley	Smithers
Phil Brown	Ben
Libby Morris	Ethel
Hugh McDermott	Harry
Paddie O'Neil	Mabel
Carol Cleveland	Judy
C. Denier Warren	Foreman
Tommy Duggan	Judge
Cal McCord	Tenant

FANTASY Book-keeper kills boss when replaced by machine, and goes to an automated heaven.

13929
CAN HEIRONYMUS MERKIN EVER FORGET MERCY HUMPPE AND FIND TRUE HAPPINESS? (117) (X) *tech*
Taralex-Universal (RFD)
P:D:S: Anthony Newley
SC: Anthony Newley, Herman Raucher

Anthony Newley	Heironymus Merkin
Joan Collins	Polyester
Milton Berle	Good Time Eddie Filth
George Jessel	Presence
Stubby Kaye	Writer
Bruce Forsyth	Uncle Limelight
Patricia Hayes	Grandma
Victor Spinetti	Sharpnose
Connie Kreski	Mercy Humppe
Judy Cornwell	Filigree Fondle
Sally Douglas	Automation.Bunny
Desmond Walter Ellis	Philip Bluster
Gilly Grant	Maidenhead Fern
Rosalind Knight	Penelope
Tara Newley	Tumbelina
Alexander Newley	Thaxted
Yolanda	Trampolena Whambang
Robert Hutton	Insurance Agent
Muriel Young	Liz Harper

MUSICAL Showbiz life of a performer.

13930
CARRY ON CAMPING (88) (A) *eastman*
Adder (RFD)
P: Peter Rogers
D: Gerald Thomas
S: Talbot Rothwell

Sidney James	Sid Boggle
Kenneth Williams	Dr Soper
Joan Sims	Joan Fussey
Charles Hawtrey	Charlie Muggins
Bernard Bresslaw	Bernie Lugg
Terry Scott	Peter Potter
Barbara Windsor	Babs
Hattie Jacques	Miss Haggerd
Peter Butterworth	Joshua Fiddler
Julian Holloway	Jim Tanner
Betty Marsden	Harriet Potter
Dilys Laye	Anthea Meeks
Trisha Noble	Sally

COMEDY Devon. Misadventures in holiday camp.

13931
HANNIBAL BROOKS (102) (U) *deluxe*
Scimitar (UA)
P:D: Michael Winner
S: Michael Winner, Tom Wright
SC: Dick Clement, Ian Le Frenais

Oliver Reed	Brooks
Michael J. Pollard	Packy
Wolfgang Preiss	Col von Haller
Helmut Lohner	Willi
Karin Baal	Vronia
Peter Karsten	Kurt
Ralf Wolter	Dr Mendel
James Donald	Padre

WAR British POW escapes to Switzerland with bombed-out elephant.

13932
MOSQUITO SQUADRON (90) (U) *deluxe*
Oakmont (UA)
P: Lewis J. Rachmil
D: Boris Sagal
S: Donald Sanford, Joyce Perry

David McCallum	SL Quint Munroe
Suzanne Neve	Beth Scott
David Buck	SL David Scott
David Dundas	FL Douglas Shelton
Dinsdale Landen	WC Penrose
Charles Gray	Air Comm Hufford
Michael Anthony	Father Bellague
Vladek Sheybal	Lt Shack
Gordon Sterne	Leader
Robert Urquhart	Maj Kemble
Nicky Henson	Wiley Bunce

WAR 1944. RAF attack rocket base in France using bouncing bombs.

13933
THE PRIME OF MISS JEAN BRODIE (116) (X) *deluxe*
20th Century Fox (20)
P: Robert Fryer
D: Ronald Neame
S: (NOVEL) Muriel Spark
SC: Jay Presson Allen

Maggie Smith	Jean Brodie
Robert Stephens	Teddy Lloyd
Pamela Franklin	Sandy
Gordon Jackson	Gordon Lowther
Celia Johnson	Miss Mackay
Diane Grayson	Jenny
Jane Carr	Mary McGregor
Shirley Steedman	Monica
Lavinia Lang	Emily Carstairs
Isla Cameron	Miss McKenzie
Rona Anderson	Miss Lockhart
Molly Weir	Allison Kerr

DRAMA Edinburgh, 1930. Spinster school-teacher's influence on her girls. RFP: 1969; AA1969: Best Actress; BFA 1969: Best Actress, Supporting Actress).

13934
UP IN THE AIR (55) (U) *eastman*
Fanfare (CFF)
P: George H. Brown
D: Jan Darnley Smith
S: Wally Bosco
SC: Wally Bosco, Jan Darnley Smith

Gary Smith	Freddie
Jon Pertwee	Figworthy
Felix Felton	Sir Humphrey
Mark Colleano	Moriarty
Susan Payne	Mary
Gary Warren	Hubert
Julian Close	Ben
Earl Younger	Rollo Sadby
Brenda Cowling	Lady Pennyweight
Leslie Dwyer	Driver

CHILDREN Period. Boarding school pupils escape from tyrannical teacher.

13935
SOME GIRLS DO (93) (A) *eastman*
Ashdown (RFD)

P: Betty E. Box
D: Ralph Thomas
S: (CHARACTER) Sapper
SC: David Osborn, Liz Charles-Williams

Richard Johnson	Hugh Drummond
Daliah Lavi	Baroness Helga Hagen
Beba Loncar	Pandora
James Villiers	Carl Petersen
Sydney Rome	Flicky
Ronnie Stevens	Peregrine Carruthers
Robert Morley	Miss Mary
Maurice Denham	Mortimer
Vanessa Howard	Robot 7
Florence Desmond	Lady Manderley
Adrienne Posta	Daily
Nicholas Phipps	Lord Dunberry
Virigina North	Robot 9

CRIME Secret agent thwarts master criminal's infrasonic wave device.

13936
SUBMARINE X-1 (90) (U) *eastman*
Mirisch (UA)
P: Irving Temaner, John C. Champion
D: William Graham
S: John C. Champion, Edmund North
SC: Donald Sanford, Guy Elmes

James Caan	Lt Cdr John Bolton
Norman Bowler	Sub Lt Pennington
David Sumner	Lt Davies
Brian Grellis	CPO Barquist
Paul Young	Quentin
John Kelland	Sub Lt Keith Willis
Kenneth Farrington	PO Boker Knowles
William Dysart	Lt Gogan
Rupert Davies	Vice Admiral Redmayne
George Pravda	Capt Erlich

WAR Midge submarine team attack German battleship in Norway.

13937
THE IMAGE (14) (A)
Border Films
P: O. Negus-Fancey
D:S: Michael Armstrong

David Bowie	The Artist
Michael Byrne	The Boy

FANTASY Artist is haunted by the face of a boy he paints.

13938
STRANGE TALES (11) (U)
John Dooley (NR)
P:D:S: John Dooley
DRAMA "The story of Pat Quin".

FEB

13939
ISADORA (138) (A) *eastman/scope*
Universal (RFD)
P: Robert Hakim, Raymond Hakim
D: Karel Reisz
S: (BOOKS) Isadora Duncan (MY LIFE)
Sewell Stokes (ISADORA DUNCAN, AN INTIMATE PORTRAIT)
SC: Melvyn Bragg, Clive Exton, Margaret Drabble

Vanessa Redgrave	Isadore Duncan
James Fox	Gordon Craig
Jason Robards	Paris Singer
Ivan Tchenko	Sergei Essenin
John Fraser	Roger
Bessie Love	Mrs Duncan
Cynthia Harris	Mary Desti
Libby Glenn	Elizabeth Duncan
Tony Vogel	Raymond Duncan
Wallas Eaton	Archer
John Quentin	Pim
Nicholas Pennell	Bedford

Ronnie Gilbert . . . . Miss Chase
Alan Gifford . . . . Manager
HISTORY Life and loves of dancer from San
Francisco.

13940
RING OF BRIGHT WATER (107) (U) *tech*
Brightwater-Palomar (RFD)
P: Joseph Strick
D: Jack Couffer
S: (BOOK) Gavin Maxwell
SC: Jack Couffer, Bill Travers
Bill Travers . . . . Graham Merrill
Virginia McKenna . . . . Mary MacKenzie
Peter Jeffrey . . . . Colin Clifford
Roddy McMillan . . . . Driver
Jameson Clark . . . . Storekeeper
Jean Taylor-Smith . . . . Sarah Chambers
Helena Gloag . . . . Flora Elrich
W.H.D. Joss . . . . Lighthouse Keeper
Archie Duncan . . . . Roadmender
Kevin Collins . . . . Fisherman
ANIMAL. Scotland. Civil servant raises wild otter.

13941
SINFUL DAVEY (95) (A) *eastman/scope*
Mirisch-Webb (UA)
P: Walter Mirisch, William Graf
D: John Huston
S: (BOOK) David Haggart (THE LIFE OF
DAVID HAGGART)
SC: James Haggart
John Hurt . . . . David Haggart
Pamela Franklin . . . . Annie
Nigel Davenport . . . . Richardson
Ronald Fraser . . . . MacNab
Robert Morley . . . . Duke of Argyll
Maxine Audley . . . . Duchess of Argyll
Fionnuala Flanagan . . . . . . Daughter
Fidela Murphy . . . . Jean Carlisle
Noel Purcell . . . . Jock
Francis de Wolff . . . . Friend
Donal McCann . . . Sir James Campbell
Eddie Byrne . . . . Yorkshire Bill
Niall McGinnis . . . . Boots Simpson
CRIME Scotland, 1821. True story of army
deserter turned highwayman.

13942
THREE INTO TWO WON'T GO (94) (X) *tech*
Universal (RFD)
P: Julian Blaustein
D: Peter Hall
S: (NOVEL) Andrea Newman
SC: Edna O'Brien
Rod Steiger . . . . Steve Howard
Claire Bloom . . . . Frances Howard
Judy Geeson . . . . Ella Patterson
Peggy Ashcroft . . . . Belle
Paul Rogers . . . . Jack
Lynn Farleigh . . . . Janet
Elizabeth Spriggs . . . . Marcia
Sheila Allen . . . . Beth
DRAMA Triangle between sales executive,
schoolteacher wife and pregant teenager.

13943
WHAT'S GOOD FOR THE GOOSE (104) (A)
eastman
Tigon British (Tigon)
P: Tony Tenser, Norman Wisdom
D:S: Menahem Golan
SC: Menahem Golan, Christopher Gilmore
Norman Wisdom . . . . Timothy Bartlett
Sally Geeson . . . . Nikki
Sally Bazely . . . . Margaret Bartlett
Sarah Atkinson . . . . Meg
Derek Francis . . . . Harrington
Terence Alexander . . . . Frisby

Paul Whitsun-Jones . . : . . . . Clark
David Lodge . . . . Porter
Karl Lanchbury . . . . Pete
George Meaton . . . . Speaker
The Pretty Things
COMEDY Assistant bank manager at conference
gets involved with teenagers.

13944
WHERE'S JACK? (119) (U) *eastman*
Heathfield-Oakhurst (Par)
P: Michael Deeley, Stanley Baker
D: James Clavell
S: Rafe Newhouse, David Newhouse
Tommy Steele . . . . Jack Sheppard
Stanley Baker . . . . Jonathan Wild
Fiona Lewis . . . . Edgworth Bess
Alan Badel . . . . Lord Chancellor
Dudley Foster . . . . Blueskin
Noel Purcell . . . . Leatherchest
William Marlowe . . . . Tom Sheppard
Sue Lloyd . . . . Lady Darlington
Harold Kasket . . . . King
Cardew Robinson . . . . Lord Mayor
Esmond Knight . . . . Singer
Eddie Byrne . . . . Rev Wagstaff
George Woodbridge . . . . Hangman
Cecil Nash . . . . Storyteller
HISTORY 18th C. Adventures of highwayman
working for thief-taker.

13945
THE WINDOW CLEANER (35) (X) *eastman*
Border
P: O. Negus-Fancey
D:S: Malcolm Leigh
Donald Sumpter . . . . David
Edina Ronay . . . . Sharon
Ann Lancaster . . . . Mother
Jennifer Hill . . . . Secretary
Peggy Aitchison . . . . Landlady
Fred Griffiths . . . . Foreman
DRAMA Mother-ridden window-cleaner finds
new courage after seduction.

13946
TWENTY—NINE (26) (X) *eastman*
Shillingford-Lambe-Plantaganet (Monarch)
P: Peter Shillingford, John Lambe
D:S: Brian Cummins
Alexis Kanner . . . . Graham Baird
Susan Hunt . . . . Priscilla
Robert Lang . . . . Peter
Justine Lord . . . . Dee Baird
Peter Sanders . . . . Butler
Yootha Joyce . . . . Prostitute
DRAMA Husband thinks he killed prostitute
after drug party.

13947
LOVING FEELING (82) (X) *eastman/scope*
Piccadilly (RSE)
P: Bachoo Sen
D: Norman J. Warren
S: Robert Hewison, Bachoo Sen, Norman J.
Warren
Simon Brent . . . . Steve Day
Georgina Ward . . . . Suzanne Day
Paula Patterson . . . . Carol Taylor
John Railton . . . . Scott Fisher
Francoise Pascal . . . . Model
Heather Kyd . . . . Christine Johnson
Peter Dixon . . . . Philip Peterson
Carol Cunningham . . . . Jane Butler
Sonya Benjamin . . . . Belly Dancer
DRAMA Affairs of a married disc jockey.

13948
NORTHWEST CONFIDENTIAL (11) (A) colour
Maya (Cinecenta)
CRIME Story of a robbery.

MAR

13949
THE ASSASSINATION BUREAU (110) (A) *tech*
Heathfield (Par)
P: Michael Relph
D: Basil Dearden
S: (NOVEL) Jack London, Robert Fish
SC: Michael Relph, Wolf Mankowitz
Oliver Reed . . . . Ivan Dragomiloff
Diana Rigg . . . . Sonya Winter
Telly Savalas . . . . Lord Bostwick
Curd Jurgens . . . . General von Pinck
Philippe Noiret . . . . Lucoville
Warren Mitchell . . . . Weiss
Beryl Reid . . . . Mme Otero
Clive Revill . . . . Cesare Spado
Vernon Dobtcheff . . . . Muntzov
Annabella Incontrera . . . . . . Eleanora
Kenneth Griffith . . . . Popescu
Jess Conrad . . . . Angelo
George Colouris . . . . Peasant
Ralph Michael . . . . Editor
Katherine Kath . . . . Mme Lucoville
Eugene Deckers . . . . Clerk
Olaf Pooley . . . . Cashier
William Kendall . . . . Client
CRIME 1906. Heir to assassination
organisation foils plan to bomb peace
conference.

13950
THE BODY STEALERS (91) (A) *eastman*
Tigon British-Sagittarius (Tigon)
P: Tony Tenser
D: Gerry Levy
S: Michael St Clair, Peter Marcus
George Sanders . . . . Gen Armstrong
Maurice Evans . . . . Dr Matthews
Patrick Allen . . . . Bob Megan
Neil Connery . . . . Jim Radford
Hilary Dwyer . . . . Julie Slade
Robert Flemyng . . . . WC Baldwin
Lorna Wilde . . . . Lorna
Allan Cuthberton . . . . Hindsmith
Michael Culver . . . . Lt Bailes
Sally Faulkner . . . . Joanna
Shelagh Fraser . . . . Mrs Thatcher
FANTASY Ex-USAF investigator finds space
aliens cause parachutists to vanish.

13951
DOPPELGANGER (101) (A): *tech* USA: THE
FAR SIDE OF THE SUN
Century 21 (RFD)
P:S:Gerry Anderson, Sylvia Anderson
D: Robert Parrish
SC: Gerry Anderson, Sylvia Anderson, Donald
James
Ian Hendry . . . . John Kane
Roy Thinnes . . . . Col Glenn Ross
Lynn Loring . . . . Sharon Ross
Loni von Friedl . . . . Lise
Herbert Lom . . . . Dr Hassler
George Sewell . . . . Mark Neuman
Franco Derosa . . . . Paulo Landi
Edward Bishop . . . . David Poulson
FANTASY Astronaut crashes on mirror planet on
far side of sun.

13952
HAPPY DEATHDAY (89) (A) *tech*
Westminster-MRA (MRA)
P: Louis Fleming, Donald Loughman
D:SC: Henry Cass
S: (PLAY) Peter Howard
Cyril Luckham . . . . Josiah Swinyard
Harry Baird . . . . .Dr John Sylvester
Clement McCallin . . . . . . Prof Esteban Zoltan
Yvonne Antrobus . . . . Jetta Zoltan

Bryan Coleman . . . . Dr Oliver Tarquin
Harriette Johns . . . . Rebecca Zoltan
John Comer . . . . Briggs
RELIGION Dying man's scientific son-in-law
reforms after pregnant daughter's suicide.

13953
LOCK UP YOUR DAUGHTERS! (103) (X)
tech
Domino (Col)
P: David Deutsch
D: Peter Coe
S: (PLAYS) Henry Fielding (RAPE UPON
RAPE): John Vanbrugh (THE RELAPSE);
Bernard Miles, Laurie Johnson, Lionel Bart
(LOCK UP YOUR DAUGHTERS)
SC: Keith Waterhouse, Willis Hall
Christopher Plummer . . . . . Lord Foppington
Susannah York . . . . Hilaret
Glynis Johns . . . . Mrs Squeezum
Ian Bannen . . . . Ramble
Tom Bell . . . . Shaftoe
Elaine Taylor . . . . Cloris
Jim Dale . . . . Lusty
Kathleen Harrison . . . . Lady Clumsey
Roy Kinnear . . . . Sir Tunbelly Clumsey
Georgia Brun . . . . Nell
Vanessa Howard . . . . Hoyden Clumsey
Roy Dotrice . . . . Gossip
Fenella Fielding . . . . Lady Eager
Paul Dawkins . . . . Lord Eager
Peter Bayliss . . . . Justice Squeezum
Richard Wordsworth . . . . . . Cupler
Peter Bull . . . . Bull
Wallas Eaton . . . . Staff
Arthur Mullard . . . . Watchman
Fred Emney . . . . Earl of Ware
COMEDY 18th C. Complicated love affairs of
three lusty sailors.

13954
OH! WHAT A LOVELY WAR (144) (A)
tech/scope
Accord (Par)
P: Brian Duffy, Richard Attenborough
D: Richard Attenborough
S: (PLAYS) Charles Chilton (THE LONG LONG
TRAIL); Joan Littlewood (OH WHAT A LOVELY
WAR)
SC: Len Deighton
Dirk Bogarde . . . . Stephen
Phyllis Calvert . . . . Lady Haig
Jean-Pierre Cassel . . . . Colonel
John Clements . . . . Gen Von Moltke
John Gielgud . . . . Count Berchtold
Jack Hawkins . . . . Franz Josef
Kenneth More . . . . Kaiser Wilhelm II
Laurence Olivier . . . . Sir John French
Michael Redgrave . . . . Sir Henry Wilson
Vanessa Redgrave . . . . Sylvia Pankhurst
Ralph Richardson . . . . Sir Edward Grey
Maggie Smith . . . . Singer
Susannah York . . . . Eleanor
John Mills . . . . Sir Douglas Haig
Vincent Ball . . . . Soldier
Pia Colombo . . . . Estaminet Singer
Paul Daneman . . . . Tsar Nicholas II
Isabel Dean . . . . Lady
Christian Doermer . . . . Fritz
Robert Flemyng . . . . Officer
Meriel Forbes . . . . Lady Grey
Ian Holm . . . . Poincare
David Lodge . . . . Sergeant
Joe Melia . . . . Photographer
Guy Middleton . . . . Sir William Robertson
Juliet Mills . . . . Nurse
Nanette Newman . . . . Nurse
Cecil Parker . . . . Sir John
Natasha Parry . . . . Lady

Gerald Sim . . . . Chaplain
Thorley Walters . . . . Officer
Wendy Allnutt . . . . Flo Smith
Colin Farrell . . . . Harry Smith
Malcolm McFee . . . . Freddie Smith
Corin Redgrave . . . . Bertie Smith
Paul Shelley . . . . Jack Smith
Angela Thorne . . . . Betty Smith
Clifford Mollison . . . . Heckler
MUSICAL 1914-1918. History of the Great War
in song and symbolism. (BFA 1969: Best
Supporting Actor, Photography, Art Dir,
Costumes, Sound: UN Award).

13955
ON THE RUN (56) (U) *eastman*
Derick Williams (CFF)
P: Derick Williams
D:SC: Pat Jackson
S: (NOVEL) Nina Bawden
Dennis Conoley . . . . Ben Mallory
Robert Kennedy . . . . Thomas Okapi
Tracey Collins Lil
Gordon Jackson . . . . Mr Mallory
Bari Johnson . . . . Uncle Joseph
John Hollis . . . . Baldy
Olwen Brooks . . . . Miss Fisher
Dan Jackson . . . . Chief Okapi
Harry Locke . . . . Removal Man
CHILDREN Cockney children save African
chief's son from kidnappers.

13956
DARLING, DO YOU LOVE ME? (3) (A)
BFI-Robert Whittaker (Connoisseur)
P: Bob Whittaker
D: Bob Whittaker, Martin Sharp
S: Martin Sharp
Germaine Greer . . . . Woman
Alistair Burg . . . . Man
COMEDY Large lady kills mild man with her
demanding love.

APR
13957
THE BED SITTING ROOM (91) (X) *deluxe*
Oscar Lewenstein (UA)
P:D: Richard Lester
S: (PLAY) Spike Milligan, John Antrobus
SC: John Antrobus
Ralph Richardson . . . . Lord Fortnum
Rita Tushingham . . . . Penelope
Michael Hordern . . . . Capt Bules Martin
Arthur Lowe . . . . Father
Mona Washbourne . . . . mother
Richard Warwick . . . . Alan
Peter Cook . . . . Inspector
Dudley Moore . . . . Sergeant
Spike Milligan . . . . Mate
Roy Kinnear . . . . Plastic Mac Man
Marty Feldman . . . . . . National Health Service
Frank Thornton . . . . Newscaster
Dandy Nichols . . . . Ethel Shroake
Harry Secombe . . . . Shelter Man
Ronald Fraser . . . . Field Marshal/Sgt
Jimmy Edwards . . . . Nigel
Ron Brody . . . . Dwarf
FANTASY Metamorphosis of group of
survivors of nuclear war.

13958
CROOKS AND CORONETS (106) (U) *tech*
Cohen-Seven Arts (WPD)
P: Herman Cohen
D:S: Jim O'Connolly
Telly Savalas . . . . Herbie Hassler
Edith Evans . . . . Lady Sophie Fitzmore
Warren Oates . . . . Marty Miller

Nicky Henson . . . . . . Lord Freddie Fitzmore
Cesar Romero . . . . Nick Marco
Harry H. Corbett . . . . Frank Finley
Vickery Turner . . . . Annie
Arthur Mullard . . . . Perce
Frank Thornton . . . . Cyril
Thorley Walters . . . . Hubbard
Hattie Jacques . . . . Mabel
Clive Dunn . . . . Basil
Leslie Dwyer . . . . Henry
David Lodge . . . . Policeman
COMEDY American gangster attempts to rob
Lady's stately home.

13959
CROSSPLOT (96) (A) *eastman*
Tribune (UA)
P: Robert S. Baker
D: Alvin Rakoff
S: Leigh Vance
SC: Leigh Vance, John Kruse
Roger Moore . . . . Gary Fenn
Martha Hyer . . . . Jo Grinling
Claudie Lange . . . . Marla Kogash
Alexis Kanner . . . . Tarquin
Francis Matthews . . . . Ruddock
Bernard Lee . . . . Chilmore
Derek Francis . . . . Sir Charles Moberley
Ursula Howells . . . . Maggi Thwaites
Veronica Carlson . . . . Dinah
Dudley Sutton . . . . Warren
Tim Preece . . . . Sebastian
CRIME Advertising man and model thwart plot to
assassinate African statesman.

13960
SCHOOL FOR SEX (80) (X) *eastman*
Eastman
Pete Walker (Miracle)
P:D:S: Pete Walker
Derek Aylward . . . . Giles Wingate
Rose Alba . . . . Duchess of Burwash
Hugh Latimer . . . . Berridge
Nosher Powell . . . . Hector
Bob Andrews . . . . Sgt Braithewaite
Vic Wise . . . . Horace Clapp
Wilfred Babbage . . . . Judge
Robert Dorning . . . . Official
Dennis Castle . . . . Col Roberts
Edgar K. Bruce . . . . Fred
Julie May . . . . Ethel
Cathy Howard . . . . Sue Randall
Gilly Grant . . . . Stripper
COMEDY Much-married embezzler trains girls
to fleece rich men.

13961
BEFORE WINTER COMES (107) (A) *tech*
Windward (Col)
P: Robert Emmett Ginna
D: J. Lee Thompson
S: (STORY) Frederick L. Keefe
SC: Andrew Sinclair
David Niven . . . . Maj Giles Burnside
Topol . . . . Janovic
Anna Karina . . . . Maria
John Hurt . . . . Lt Francis Pilkington
Ori Levy . . . . Capt Kamenev
Anthony Quayle . . . . Brig Bewley
John Collin . . . . Sgt Woody
George Innes . . . . Bill
Hugh Futcher . . . . Joe
Tony Selby . . . . Ted
Colin Spaull . . . . Alf
Karel Stepanek . . . . Count Kerassy
Guy Deghy . . . . Kovacs
WAR Austria, 1945, Russian deserter helps British
major run transit camp for displaced persons.

13962
THE ASSISTANT (37) (AA) colour
Armada (BL)
P:D:S: John Dooley
SC: John Pitt
Richard Poore .... Jimmy
Susan Drury .... Model
Tom Georgeson ....
Tessa Roberts ....
FANTASY Photographer's assistant dreams of loving model.

MAY

13963
FRANKENSTEIN MUST BE DESTROYED(97) (X) *tech*
Hammer (WPD)
P: Anthony Nelson Keys
D: Terence Fisher
S: Mary Shelley
(FRANKENSTEIN)
SC: Anthony Nelson Keys, Bert Batt
S: Anthony Nelson Keys, Bert Batt
Peter Cushing .... Baron Frankenstein
Veronica Carlson .... Anna Spengler
Simon Ward .... Dr Karl Holst
Freddie Jones .... Prof Richter
Thorley Walters .... Insp Frisch
Maxine Audley .... Ella Brandt
George Pravda .... Dr Brandt
Geoffrey Bayldon .... Doctor
Colette O'Neil .... Madwoman
Peter Copley .... Principal
HORROR Dr transplants mad colleague's brain into professor.

13964
KES(113) (U) *tech*
Woodfall-Kestrel (UA)
P: Tony Garnett
D: Ken Loach
S: (NOVEL) Barry Hines (KESTREL FOR A KNAVE)
SC: Barry Hines, Ken Loach
David Bradley .... Billy Casper
Lynne Perrie .... Mrs Casper
Freddie Fletcher .... Jud
Colin Welland .... Farthing
Brian Glover .... Sugden
Bob Bowes .... Gryce
Robert Naylor .... MacDowall
Trevor Hesketh .... Crossley
Geoffrey Banks .... Teacher
Eric Bolderson .... Farmer
Joey Kaye .... Entertainer
ANIMAL Northern boy raises fledgling kestrel and trains it. (BFA 1970: Best Supporting Actor).

13965
TASTE OF EXCITEMENT (99) (X) *eastman*
Trio-Group W (Crispin)
P: William Gell, George Willoughby
D: Don Sharp
S: (NOVEL) Ben Healey (WAITING FOR A TIGER)
SC: Brian Carton, Don Sharp
Eva Rienzi .... Jane Kerrell
David Buck .... Paul Hedley
Peter Vaughan .... Insp Malling
Paul Hubschmid .... Hans Beiber
Sophie Hardy .... Michela
Kay Walsh .... Miss Barrow
Francis Matthews .... Mr Breese
Peter Bowles .... Alfredo Guardi
George Pravda .... Dr Forla
CRIME France. Painter saves girl involved in plan to murder traitor.

13966
THE VIRGIN SOLDIERS (96) (X) *tech*
Columbia British
P: Carl Foreman, Leslie Gilliat, Ned Sherrin
D: John Dexter
S: (NOVEL) Leslie Thomas
SC: John Hopkins, John McGrath, Ian La Fresnais
Lynn Redgrave .... Phillipa Raskin
Hywel Bennett .... Pte Brigg
Nigel Davenport .... Sgt Driscoll
Nigel Patrick .... RSM Raskin
Rachel Kempson .... Mrs Raskin
Jack Shepherd .... Sgt Wellbeloved
Michael Gwynn ......Lt Col Bromley-Pickering
Tsai Chin .... Juicy Lucy
Christopher Timothy ...... Cpl Brook
Don Hawkins .... Tasker
Geoffrey Hughes .... Lantry
Roy Holder .... Fenwick
Jolyon Jackley ....LCpl Gravy Browning
WAR Singapore, 1950. National Serviceman's exploits with guerilas and sgt's daughter.

13967
THE VIOLENT ENEMY (94) (U) *eastman*
Trio Films-Group W (Monarch)
P: William Gell, Wilfred Eades
D: Don Sharp
S: (NOVEL) Hugh Marlowe (A CANDLE FOR THE DEAD)
SC: Edmund Ward
Tom Bell .... Sean Rogan
Susan Hampshire .... Hannah Costello
Ed Begley .... Colum O'More
Jon Laurimore .... Austin
Michael Standing .... Fletcher
Noel Purcell ....John Michael Leary
Philip O'Flynn .... Insp Sullivan
CRIME Ireland. Escaped Republican prisoner tries to stop patriotic crooks from dynamiting power station.

13968
THE SOUTHERN STAR (105)(U) *tech/scope/bilingual*
Columbia British -Euro France-Capitole (Col)
P: Roger Duchet
D: Sidney Hayers
S: (NOVEL) Jules Verne
SC: David Pursall, John Seddon
George Segal .... Dan Rockland
Ursula Andress .... Erica Kramer
Orson Welles .... Plankett
Ian Hendy .... Karl Ludwig
Michel Constantin .... Jose
Harry Andrews .... Kramer
Johnny Sekka .... Matakit
Georges Geret .... Andre
Sylvain .... Louis
National Ballet of Senegal
ADVENTURE Africa, 1912. American finds huge diamond and is accused of stealing it.

JUN

13969
ALFRED THE GREAT (122) (A)
metro/scope
Bernard Smith-MGM British (MGM)
P: Bernard Smith, James R.Webb
D: Clive Donner
S: James R. Webb
SC: James R. Webb, Ken Taylor
David Hemmings .... Alfred
Michael York .... Guthrum
Prunella Ransome .... Aelhswith
Colin Blakeley .... Asher
Julian Glover .... Athelstan
Ian McKellen .... Roger
Alan Dobie .... Etherlred
Peter Vaughan .... Budrud
Julian Chagrin .... Ivar
Barry Jackson .... Wulfstan
Vivien Merchant .... Freda
Christopher Timothy ...... Cedric
Michael Billington .... Offa
HISTORY 871. Christian King battles Danes and unites England.

13970
THE BEST HOUSE IN LONDON (96) (X) *eastman*
Bridge-Carlo Ponti (MGM)
P: Philip Breen, Kurt Unger
D: Philip Saville
S: Denis Norden
David Hemmings . . . .Walter Leybourne/Benjamin Oakes
Joanna Pettet .... Josephine Pacefoot
George Sanders .... Sir Francis Leybourne
Dany Robin .... Babette
Warren Mitchell .... Count Pandolfo
John Bird .... Home Secretary
William Rushton .... Sylvester Wall
Bill Fraser .... Insp Macpherson
Maurice Denham .... Editor
Wolfe Morris .... Attache
Martita Hunt .... Headmistress
Arnold Diamond .... Charles Dickens
Hugh Burden .... Lord Tennyson
John De Marco .... Oscar Wilde
George Reynolds .... Lord Alfred Douglas
Jan Holden .... Lady Dilke
Mike Lennox .... Algernon Swinburne
Arthur Howard .... Mr Fortnum
Clement Freud .... Mr Mason
Neal Arden .... Dr Livinstone
Walter Brown .... Mr Barrett
Suzanne Hunt .... Elizabeth Barrett
Betty Marsden .... Felicity
COMEDY 19th C. Prostitute rehabilitator inherits her uncle's brothel.

13971
CARRY ON AGAIN, DOCTOR (89) (A) *eastman*
Eastman
Adder-Ethiro (RFD)
P: Peter Rogers
D: Gerald Thomas
S: Talbot Rothwell
Kenneth Williams .... Frederick Carver
Jim Dale .... Dr James Nookey
Sidney James .... Gladstone Screwer
Joan Sims .... Ellen Moore
Charles Hawtrey ....Dr Ernest Stoppidge
Barbara Windsor .... Goldie Locks
Hattie Jacques .... Matron
Patsy Rowlands .... Miss Fosdick
Lucy Griffiths .... Old Lady
Ann Lancaster .... Miss Armitage
Shakira Baksh .... Scrubba
Harry Locke .... Porter
Wilfrid Brambell .... Mr Pullen
Peter Butterworth .... Patient
COMEDY Surgeon sets up slimming clinic with island orderly's patent potion.

13972
MONTE CARLO OR BUST! (125) (U) *tech/scope/bilingual*
Dino De Laurentiis-Marianne (Par)
P:D: Ken Annakin
S: Ken Annakin, Jack Davies
Bourvil .... M. Dupont
Lando Buzznca .... Marcello

Walter Chiari . . . . Angelo
Peter Cook . . . . Maj Dawlish
Tony Curtis . . . . Chester Schofield
Mireille Darc . . . . Marie-Claude
Marie Dubois . . . . Pascale
Gert Frobe . . . . Willi Schickel
Susan Hampshire . . . . Betty
Jack Hawkins . . . . Count Levinovitch
Nicoletta Machiavelli . . . . . Dominique
Dudley Moore . . . . Lt Barrington
Peer Schmidt . . . . Otto
Eric Sykes . . . . Perkins
Terry Thomas . . . . . .Sir Cuthbert Ware-Armitage
Hattie Jacques . . . . Journalist
Derren Nesbitt . . . . Waleska
Nicholas Phipps . . . . Golfer
William Rushton . . . . Official
Richard Wattis . . . . Secretary
COMEDY Slapstick misadventures during 1500-
mile race to Monte Carlo.

13973
THE NINE AGES OF NAKEDNESS (95) (X)
eastman
Token (Orb)
P: Harry Reuben
D:S: George Harrison Marks
N: Charles Gray
George Harrison Marks . . . . Harrison Marks
Max Wall . . . . Witchfinder
Max Bacon . . . .
Julian Orchard . . . .
Cardew Robinson . . . .
Big. Bruno Elrington . . . . . .
June Palmer . . . .
Oliver McGreavey . . . .
Rita Webb . . . .
COMEDY Photographer recounts ancestors'
problems with naked ladies.

13974
99 WOMEN (90) (X) *eastman/trilingual*
Hesperia-Corona-Towers of London-Cine-
produzione (CUE)
P: Harry Alan Towers
D: Jesus Franco
S: Peter Welbeck, Carlo Fadda, Millo Cuccia,
Jesus Franco
Maria Schell . . . . Leonie
Mercedes McCambridge . . . . Thelma
Herbert Lom . . . . Governor
Maria Rohm . . . . Marie
Rosalba Neri 76
Valentine Godoy 81
Elisa Montes 99
Luciana Paluzzi . . . . Natalie
CRIME Panama. Women prisoners suffer
under cruel wardress and lecherous governor.

13975
THE SMASHING BIRD I USED TO KNOW (95)
(X) *eastman*
Lucinda-Titan International (GN)
P: Peter Newbrook
D: Robert Hartford-Davis
S: John Peacock
Madeline Hinde . . . . Nicki Johnson
Renee Asherson . . . . Anne Johnson
Dennis Waterman . . . . Peter Lang
Patrick Mower . . . . Harry Spenton
Faith Brook . . . . Dr Sands
Maureen Lipman . . . . Sarah
Janina Faye . . . . Susan
Derek Fowlds . . . . Geoffrey
Colette O'Neil . . . . Miss Waldron
Megs Jenkins . . . . Matron
Cleo Sylvestre . . . . Carlien
David Lodge . . . . Richard Johnson
CRIME Teenager stabs her widowed mother's
lover and escapes from remand home.

13976
GUNS IN THE HEATHER (90) (U) *tech*
Walt Disney
P: Ron Miller
D: Robert Butler
S: (NOVEL) Lockhart Amerman
SC: Herman Groves, Charles Frend
Glenn Corbett . . . . Tom Evans
Alfred Burke . . . . Kersner
Kurt Russell . . . . Rich Evans
Patrick Dawson . . . . Sean O'Connor
Patrick Barr . . . . Lord Boyne
Hugh McDermott . . . . Carleton
Patrick Westwood . . . . Levick
Eddie Byrne . . . . Bailey
Godfrey Quigley . . . . Meister
CRIME Ireland. American boys save defected
scientist from Russians.

13977
THE ITALIAN JOB (100) (U) *eastman/scope*
Oakhurst-Paramount (Par)
P: Michael Deeley
D: Peter Collinson
S; Troy Kennedy Martin
Michael Caine . . . . Charlie Croker
Noel Coward . . . . Mr Bridger
Benny Hill . . . . Prof Simon Peach
Raf Vallone . . . . Altabani
Tony Beckley . . . . Camp Freddie
Rossano Brazzi . . . . Beckerman
Maggie Blythe . . . . Lorna
Irene Handl . . . . Miss Peach
John Le Mesurier . . . . Governor
Fred Emney . . . . Birkenshaw
Graham Payn . . . . Keats
Robert Rietty . . . . Police Chief
Simon Dee . . . . Shirtmaker
Henry McGee . . . . Tailor
CRIME Turin. Crook inherits plan to steal
four million dollars in gold.

13978
RUN WILD, RUN FREE (98) (U) *tech*
Irving Allen (Col)
P: Andrew Donally, John Danischewsky
D: Richard C. Sarafian
S: (NOVEL) David Rook (THE WHITE COLT)
SC: David Rook
John Mills . . . . Moorman
Mark Lester . . . . Philip Ransome
Sylvia Sims . . . . Ellen Ransome
Gordon Jackson . . . . James Ransome
Bernard Miles . . . . Reg
Fiona Fullerton . . . . Diana
ANIMAL Dartmoor. Mute boy trains kestrel
and saves wild pony.

13979
THE TAKING MOOD (33) (U)
Greenpark (Saxon)
P:D: Derek Williams
COMEDY Two fishermen compete for a bet.

13980
THE INTREPID MR TWIGG (36) (U) colour
Talus International (BL)
P: Alistair Foot, Anthony Marriott
D: Freddie Francis
S: Keith Williams
Roy Castle . . . . Mr Twigg
Clovissa Newcombe . . . . Girl
Jack Haig . . . . Garage Owner
Clayton & Walker . . . . Crooks
Peter Frazer . . . . Driver
Peter Elliott . . . . Chemist
Dennis Ramsden . . . . Policeman
Jackie Toye . . . . Nurse
COMEDY "Silent" misadventures of an
accident-prone motorist.

13981
BATTLE OF BRITAIN (131) (U) *tech/scope*
Spitfire (UA)
P: Harry Saltzman, S. Benjamin Fisz
D: Guy Hamilton
S: (BOOK) Derek Wood, Derek Dempster
(THE NARROW MARGIN)
SC: James Kennaway, Wilfred Greatorex
Laurence Olivier . . . . . .ACM Sir Hugh Dowding
Robert Shaw . . . . SL Skipper
Christopher Plummer . . . . . SL Colin Harvey
Susannah York . . . . .SO Maggie Harvey
Ian McShane . . . . Sgt Andy
Michael Caine . . . . SL Canfield
Kenneth More . . . . GC Baker
Trevor Howard . . . . AVM Keith Park
Patrick Wymark . . AVM Trafford Leigh-Mallory
Ralph Richardson . . . . Minister
Curd Jurgens . . . . Baron von Richter
Harry Andrews . . . . Civil Servant
Michael Redgrave . . . . AVM Evill
Nigel Patrick . . . . GC Hope
Michael Bates . . . . WO Warrick
Isla Blair . . . . Mrs Andy
Robert Flemyng . . . . WC Willoughby
Barry Foster . . . . SL Edwards
Duncan Lamont . . . . F Sgt Arthur
Sarah Lawson . . . . Mrs Skipper
Nicholas Pennell . . . . Simon
Peter Hager . . . . Kesselring
Hein Reiss . . . . Goering
Rolf Stiefel . . . . Hitler
WAR 1940. True story of the RAF's air battle
with the Luftwaffe. (Top Moneymaker: 1970).

13982
CAPTAIN NEMO AND THE UNDERWATER
CITY (106) (U) *metro/scope*
Omnia (MGM)
P: Steven Pallos, Bertram Ostrer
D: James Hill
S: (CHARACTERS) Jules Verne
SC: Pip Baker, Jane Baker, R. Wright Campbell
Robert Ryan . . . . Captain Nemo
Chuck Connors . . . . Robert Frazer
Nanette Newman . . . . Helena
John Turner . . . . Joab
Luciana Paluzzi . . . . Mala
Bill Fraser . . . . Barnaby
Kenneth Connor . . . . Swallow
Allan Cuthbertson . . . . Lomax
Christopher Hartsone . . . . . . Philip
FANTASY 19th C. Shipwreck survivors taken
by submarine to domed undersea city.

13983
THE HAUNTED HOUSE OF HORROR (92)
(X) *eastman*
Tigon British-AIP (Tigon)
P: Tony Tenser
D: Michael Armstrong
S: Michael Armstrong, Peter Marcus
Frankie Avalon . . . . Chris
Jill Hayworth . . . . Sheila
Dennis Price . . . . Inspector
Mark Wynter . . . . Gary
Julian Barnes . . . . Richard
Richard O'Sullivan . . . . Peter
Gina Warwick . . . . Sylvia
Robin Stewart . . . . Henry
Carol Dilworth . . . . Dorothy
Veronica Doran . . . . Madge
Clifford Earl . . . . Sgt
Jan Holden . . . . Peggy
Robert Raglan . . . . Chief Insp
HORROR Teenagers exploring haunted
house realise one of their number is
psychopathic killer.

13984
THE MIND OF MR SOAMES (98) (AA) *tech*
Amicus (Col)
P: Max Rosenberg, Milton Subotsky
D: Alan Cooke
S: (NOVEL) Charles Eric Maine
SC: John Hale, Edward Simpson
Terence Stamp . . . . John Soames
Robert Vaughan . . . . Dr Michael Bergen
Nigel Davenport . . . . Dr Maitland
Donal Donnelly . . . . Dr Allen
Christian Roberts . . . . Thomas Fleming
Vickery Turner . . . . Naomi
Scott Forbes . . . . Richard
Judy Parfitt . . . . Jenny
Norman Jones . . . . Davis
Dan Jackson . . . . Nicholls
Joe McPartland . . . . Insp Moore
DRAMA Surgery frees 30-year old man from
lifetime in synoptic coma.

13985
THE MOST DANGEROUS MAN IN THE WORLD
(99) (A) *deluxe/scope*
Apjac (20)
P: Mort Abrahams
D: J. Lee Thompson
S: (NOVEL) Jay Richard Kennedy (THE
CHAIRMAN)
SC: Ben Maddow
Gregory Peck . . . . Dr John Hathaway
Anne Heywood . . . . Kay Hanna
Arthur Hill . . . . Lt-Gen Shelby
Conrad Yama . . . . Chairman
Francisca Tu . . . . Soong Chu
Keye Luke . . . . Prof Soong Li
Alan Dobie . . . . AC Benson
Zienia Merton . . . . Ting Ling
Bert Kwouk . . . . Chang Shou
Alan White . . . . Col Gardner
ADVENTURE Nobel prizewinner obtains
enzyme formula from China.

AUG

13986
ALL AT SEA (60) (U) *eastman*
Anvil (CFF)
P: Hugh Stewart
D: Ken Fairbairn
S: Patricia Latham
Gary Smith . . . . Steve
Steven Mallett . . . . Ian
Stephen Childs . . . . Douglas
Norman Bird . . . . Mr Danvers
Sara Nicholls . . . . Vicky
Lee Chamberlain . . . . Jim
Ali Soussi . . . . Hello
Peter Copley . . . . Mr Gordon
Joan Sterndale-Bennett . . . . Miss Fisby
Simon Lack . . . . Mr Parker
CHILDREN Boys on holiday cruise catch
painting thief in Tangier.

13987
GOODBYE, MR CHIPS (147) (U) *metro/scope*
MGM-Keep-Apjac (MGM)
P: Arthur P. Jacobs
D: Herbert Ross
S: (NOVEL) James Hilton
SC: Terence Rattigan
Peter O'Toole . . . . Arthur Chipping
Petula Clark . . . . Katherine Bridges
Michael Redgrave . . . . Headmaster
George Baker . . . . Lord Sutterwick
Michael Bryant . . . . Max Staefel
Jack Hedley . . . . William Baxter
Sian Phillips . . . . Ursula Mossbank
Alison Leggatt . . . . Wife

Clinton Greyn . . . . Bill Calbury
Michael Culver . . . . Johnny Longbridge
Barbara Couper . . . . Mrs Paunceforth
Elspeth March . . . . Mrs Summersthwaite
Clive Morton . . . . Gen Paunceforth
Michael Ridgeway . . . . David
MUSICAL 1924. Life of devoted schoolmaster
who weds singer.

13988
MOON ZERO TWO (100) (U) *tech*
Hammer (WPD)
P:SC: Michael Carreras
D: Roy Ward Baker
S: Gavin Lyall, Frank Hardman, Martin
Davison
James Olson . . . . Bill Kemp
Catherina von Schell . . . . Clementine Taplin
Warren Mitchell . . . . JJ Hubbard
Adrienne Corri . . . . Liz Murphy
Ori Levy . . . . Karminski
Dudley Foster . . . . Whitsun
Bernard Bresslaw . . . . Harry
Neil McCallum . . . . Captain
Joby Blanshard . . . . Smith
Michael Ripper . . . . Player
FANTASY 2021. Ferry-rocket pilot saves
sapphire asteroid from magnate.

13989
THE OBLONG BOX (91) (X) *eastman*
AIP (WPD)
P: Louis M. Heyward, Gordon Hessler
D: Gordon Hessler
S: (STORY) Edgar Allan Poe
SC: Lawrence Huntington, Christopher Wicking
Vincent Price . . . . Julian Markham
Christopher Lee . . . . Dr Neuhartt
Alastair Williamson . . . . . Sir Edward Markham
Hilary Dwyer . . . . Elizabeth
Peter Arne . . . . Samuel Trench
Harry Baird . . . . N'Galo
Carl Rigg . . . . Mark Norton
Maxwell Shaw . . . . Tom Hackett
Michael Balfour . . . . Ruddock
Rupert Davies . . . . Joshua Kemp
Sally Geeson . . . . Sally Baxter
HORROR 19th C. Madman, disfigured by witch
doctor's curse, escapes burial alive and goes on
masked rampage.

13990
THE DANCE OF DEATH (149) (A) *tech*
BHE-National Theatre (Par)
P: John Brabourne
D: David Giles
S: (PLAY) August Strindberg
SC: C.D. Locock
Laurence Olivier . . . . Edgar
Geraldine McEwan . . . . Alice
Carolyn Jones . . . . Jenny
Maggie Riley . . . . Kristin
Robert Lang . . . . Kurt
Jeanne Watts . . . . Old Woman
Janina Faye . . . . Judith
Malcolm Reynolds . . . . Allan
Peter Penry-Jones . . . . Lieut
DRAMA Sweden. Sick captain ruins his wife's
cousin, but their children fall in love.

13991
COME BACK PETER (74) (X) *eastman*
Donwin (RSE)
P:D:S: Donovan Winter
Christopher Matthews . . . . . Peter
Erika Bergmann . . . . Lisa
Penny Riley . . . . Sue
Yolanda Turner . . . . . Mrs Beaufort-Smith
Maddy Smith . . . . Miss Beaufort-Smith

Valerie St Helene . . . . Cleo
Annabel Leventon . . . . Creampuff
Nicole Paget . . . . Jenny
Mary & Madeleine Collinson
ROMANCE Butcher's assistant has love affairs
with several girls.

13992
SUSPENDED FORTH (33) (U)
Horoscope
P: Paul Sidey
D: James Horwitz
S: James Horwitz, Paul Sidey
DRAMA Expatriate American agrees to deliver
package to France.

SEP

13993
CRESCENDO (95) (X) *tech*
Hammer (WPD)
P: Michael Carreras
D: Alan Gibson
S: Alfred Shaughnessy
SC: Alfred Shaughnessy, Jimmy Sangster
Stephanie Powers . . . . Susan Roberts
James Olson . . . . Georges/Jacques
Margaretta Scott . . . . Danielle Ryman
Jane Lapotaire . . . . Lilliane
Joss Ackland . . . . Carter
Kirsten Betts . . . . Catherine
CRIME France. Girl discovers heroin-addicted
son of composer's widow has murderous, mad
twin.

13994
HAMLET (117) (U) *tech*
Woodfall (Col)
P: Leslie Linder, Martin Ransohoff
D: Tony Richardson
S: (PLAY) William Shakespeare
Nicol Williamson . . . . Hamlet
Judy Parfitt . . . . Gertrude
Anthony Hopkins . . . . Claudus
Marianne Faithfull . . . . Ophelia
Mark Dignam . . . . Polonius
Michael Pennington . . . . . . Laertes
Gordon Jackson . . . . Horatio
Ben Aris . . . . Rosencrantz
Clive Graham . . . . Guildenstern
Peter Gale . . . . Osric
Roger Livesey . . . . Lucianus/Gravedigger
DRAMA Denmark. Prince inspired to avenge
the murder of his father.

13995
I START COUNTING (105) (AA) *deluxe*
Triumvirate (UA)
P: Stanley Jaffe, David Greene
D: David Greene
S: (NOVEL) Audrey Erskine Lindop
SC: Richard Harris
Jenny Agutter . . . . Wynne
Bryan Marshall . . . . George
Clare Sutcliffe . . . . Corinne
Simon Ward . . . . Conductor
Gregory Phillips . . . . Len
Lana Morris . . . . Leonie
Billy Russell . . . . Grandad
Madge Ryan . . . . Mother
Michael Feast . . . . Jim
Fay Compton . . . . Mrs Bennett
CRIME Midlands. Teenager suspects foster
brother is sex killer.

13996
THE MAGNIFICENT 6 AND ½ (U) *eastman* (seria
Century (CFF)
P; Roy Simpson
D: Harry Booth

S: Yvonne Richards, Glyn Jones, Wally Bosco,
Don Nichol, Michael Barnes
Robin Davies . . . . Steve
Ian Ellis . . . . Dumbo
Brinsley Forde . . . . Toby
Suzanne Togni . . . . Liz
Lionel Hawkes . . . . Stodger
Kim Talmadge . . . . Peewee
Michael Audreson . . . . Whizz
Cardew Robinson . . . . Painter
Bill Maynard . . . . Magician
Denis Shaw . . . . Ice-cream Man
Sheila Hancock . . . . Woman

13997
1: PEEWEE HAD A LITTLE APE (20)

13998
2: A GOOD DEED IN TIME (17)

13999
3: THE MAGICIAN (19)

14000
4: A LAD IN THE LAMP (15)

14001
5: IT'S NOT CRICKET (14)

14002
6: THE ASTRONOUGHTS (19)
CHILDREN Slapstick misadventures of gang of
kids.

14003
LAUGHTER IN THE DARK (104) (X) *deluxe/
bilingual*
Woodfall-Winkast-Marceau (UA)
P: Neil Hartley
D: Tony Richardson
S: (NOVEL) Vladimir Nabokov
SC: Edward Bond
Nicol Williamson . . . . Sir Edward More
Anna Karina . . . . Margot
Jean-Claude Drouot . . . . Herve Tourace
Peter Bowles . . . . Paul
Sian Phillips . . . . Lady Elizabeth More
Sebastian Breaks . . . . Brian
Kate O'Toole . . . . Amelia More
Edward Gardner . . . . Chauffeur
Sheila Burrell . . . . Miss Porley
Willoughby Goddard . . . . . . Colonel
Basil Dignam . . . . Dealer
DRAMA Art dealer's infatuation with
usherette who is his associate's mistress.

14004
THE LOOKING GLASS WAR (107) (A) *tech/
scope*
Frankovich (Col)
P: M.J. Frankovich, John Box
D:SC: Frank R. Pierson
S:(NOVEL) John Le Carre
Christopher Jones . . . . Leiser
Pia Degermark . . . . Girl
Ralph Richardson . . . . Leclerc
Anthony Hopkins . . . . John Avery
Paul Rogers . . . . Haldane
Susan George . . . . Susan
Ray McAnally . . . . Starr
Robert Urquhart . . . . Johnson
Maxine Audley . . . . Babs Leclerc
Anna Massey . . . . Sarah
Frederick Jaeger . . . . Capt Lansen
Paul Maxwell . . . . CIA Man
Vivien Pickles . . . . Carol
WAR Polish refugee trained and sent to
Germany to locate film of Russian missile site.

14005
A NICE GIRL LIKE ME (91) (A) *eastman*
Anglo Embassy-Partisan (Avco Embassy)
P: Leonard Lightstone, Roy Millichip
D: Desmond Davis
S: Anne Piper, Desmond Davis
Barbara Ferris . . . . Candida
Harry Andrews . . . . Savage
Gladys Cooper . . . . Aunt Mary
Bill Hinnant . . . . Ed
James Villiers . . . . Freddie
Joyce Carey . . . . Aunt Celia
Christopher Guinee . . . . Pierre
Fabia Drake . . . . Miss Grimsby
Irene Prador . . . . Mme Dupont
Erik Chitty . . . . Vicar
Totti Truman Taylor . . . . . . Miss Carter
Ann Lancaster . . . . Miss Garland
Douglas Wilmer . . . . Doctor
ROMANCE Orphaned teenager has babies by
two men and adopts a third.

14006
A TOUCH OF LOVE (107) (A) *eastman*
Amicus-Palomar (BL)
P: Max Rosenberg, Milton Subotsky
D: Waris Hussein
S: (NOVEL) Margaret Drabble (THE MILLSTONE)
SC: Margaret Drabble
Sandy Dennis . . . . Rosamund Stacey
Ian McKellen . . . . George Stacey
Michael Coles . . . . Joe
John Standing . . . . Roger
Eleanor Bron . . . . Lydia
Deborah Stanford . . . . Beatrice
Roger Hammond . . . . Mike
Margaret Denham . . . . Dr Prothero
Rachel Kempson . . . . Sister Harvey
DRAMA Research graduate bears bastard baby
requiring heart operation.

14007
TWINKY (98) (A) *tech*
World Film Services (RFD)
P: John Heyman, Clive Sharp
D: Richard Donner
S: Norman Thaddeus Vane
Charles Bronson . . . . Scot Wardman
Susan George . . . . Twinky Londonderry
Trevor Howard . . . . Grandfather
Michael Craig . . . . Daddy
Honor Blackman . . . . Mummy
Lionel Jeffries . . . . Creighton
Elspeth March . . . . Secretary
Eric Chitty . . . . Client
Cathy Jose . . . . Felicity
Robert Morley . . . . Judge Roxburgh
Jack Hawkins . . . . Judge Millington-Draper
Jimmy Tarbuck . . . . Comic
Norman Vaughan . . . . Comic
Orson Bean . . . . Hal
Eric Barker . . . . Clerk
ROMANCE Middleaged American novelist
weds teenager and takes her to New York.

14008
WOMEN IN LOVE (130) (X) *deluxe*
Brandywine (UA)
P:SC: Larry Kramer
D: Ken Russell
S: (NOVEL) D.H. Lawrence
Alan Bates . . . . Rupert Birkin
Oliver Reed . . . . Gerard Crich
Glenda Jackson . . . . Gudrun Brangwen
Jennie Linden . . . . Ursula Brangwen
Eleanor Bron . . . . Hermione Roddice
Michael Gough . . . . Tom Brangwen
Norman Shebbeare . . . . Anna Brangwen

Alan Webb . . . . Thomas Crich
Catherine Wilmer . . . . Mrs Crich
Sarah Nicholls . . . . Winifred Crich
Sharon Gurney . . . . Laura Crich
Christopher Gable . . . . Lupton
Nike Arrighi . . . . Contessa
DRAMA Love affairs of emancipated artist and
her sister with mineowner's son and school
inspector. (AA1970: Best Actress).

14009
CONNECTING ROOMS (102) (AA) *tech*
Telstar-Three Capitols-De Grunwald (London
Screen)
P: Harry Field, Jack Smith, Arthur S. Cooper
D:SC: Franklin Gollings
S: (PLAY) Marion Hart (THE CELLIST)
Bette Davis . . . . Wanda Fleming
Michael Redgrave . . . . James Wallraven
Alexis Kanner . . . . Mickey Hollister
Kay Walsh . . . . Mrs Brent
Gabrielle Drake . . . . Jean
Leo Genn . . . . Dr Norman
Olga Georges-Picot . . . . Claudia Fouchet
Richard Wyler . . . . Dick Grayson
Brian Wilde . . . . Ellerman
John Woodnutt . . . . Doctor
Tony Hughes . . . . Lew
Eyes of Blue; The Ladybirds
ROMANCE Sacked schoolmaster loves cellist
involved with aspiring pop writer.

14010
THE MADWOMAN OF CHAILLOT (142) (U)
tech/scope
CUE (WPD)
P: Henry Weinstein, Ely Landau
D: Bryan Forbes, John Huston
S: (PLAY) Jean Giraudoux (LA FOLLE DE
CHAILLOT)
SC: Edward Anhalt
Katharine Hepburn . . . . Countess Aurelia
Charles Boyer . . . . Broker
Claude Dauphin . . . . Dr Jadin
Edith Evans . . . . Josephine
John Gavin . . . . Reverend
Paul Henreid . . . . General
Oscar Homolka . . . . Commissar
Margaret Leighton . . . . Constance
Giulietta Masina . . . . Gabrielle
Nanette Newman . . . . Irma
Richard Chamberlain . . . . . Roderick
Yul Brynner . . . . Chairman
Donald Pleasence . . . . Prospector
Danny Kaye . . . . Ragpicker
Fernand Graavey . . . . Sergeant
Gordon Heath . . . . Folksinger
DRAMA Paris. Eccentric countess foils
conspiracy to drill for oil.

OCT

14011
CLEGG (87) (X) *tech/scope*
Sutton-Shonteff (Tigon)
P: Herbert Alpert, Lewis Force
D: Lindsay Shonteff
S: Lewis J. Hagleton
Gilbert Wynne . . . . Harry Clegg
Garry Hope . . . . Francis Wildman
Gilly Grant . . . . Suzy the Slag
Norman Claridge . . . . Lord Cruik Shank
A.J. Brown . . . . Joseph Valentine
Michael Nightingale . . . . Col Sullivan
Noel Davis . . . . Manager
Ronald Leigh Hunt . . . . Insp Kert
Jenny Robbins . . . . Shirley
CRIME Tec discovers man behind murders
committed by man-hating whore.

14012
DEATH MAY BE YOUR SANTA CLAUS (50)
(X) *tech/scope*
Space-Soul-Creative Enterprises (Amanda)
P:D:S: Frankie Dymon Jr
Ken Gajadhar . . . . Raymond
Donnah Dolce . . . . White Girl
Merdel Jordine . . . . Georgina
The Second Hand
FANTASY Hallucinations of Negro who loves
both black and white girls.

14013
THE ROYAL HUNT OF THE SUN (121) (U) *tech*
Royal-Benmar-Security (RFD)
P: Eugene Frenke, Philip Yordan
D: Irving Lerner
S: (PLAY) Peter Shaffer
SC: Philip Yordan
Robert Shaw . . . . Francisco Pizarro
Christopher Plummer . . . . . Atahuallpa
Nigel Davenport . . . . De Soto
Michael Craig . . . . Estete
Leonard Whiting . . . . Young Martin
Andrew Keir . . . . Valverde
James Donald . . . . King Carlos V
William Marlowe . . . . . `. . . Candia
Percy Herbert . . . . Diego
Alexander Davion . . . . De Nizza
HISTORY Peru. Spanish General poses as god to
impress Inca God-King.

14014
ARTHUR ARTHUR *eastman*
Gallu
P: E.M. Smedley Aston
D: Samuel Gallu
S: Julian Symonds, Beverley Cross, John
Esmonds, Bob Larbey
Shelley Winters . . . .
Donald Pleasence . . . .
Terry Thomas . . . .
Tammy Grimes . . . .
COMEDY

NOV

14015
IN SEARCH OF GREGORY (90) (X)
tech/bilingual
Vic-Vera (RFD)
P: Joseph Janni, Daniele Senatore
D: Peter Wood
S: Tonino Guerra, Lucile Laks
Julie Christie . . . . Catherine Morelli
Michael Sarrazin . . . . Gregory
John Hurt . . . . Daniel Morelli
Adolfo Celi . . . . Max Morelli
Paola Pitagora . . . . Nicole
Roland Culver . . . . Wardle
Tony Selby . . . . Taxidriver
Ernesto Pagano . . . . Priest
ROMANCE Geneva. Girl's fascination for poet
she has never met leads her into affair with autoball
player.

14016
MISTER JERICO (85) (U) *eastman*
Incorporated Television (RFD)
P: Julian Wintle
D: Sidney Hayers
S: Philip Levene
Patrick MacNee . . . . Dudley Jerico
Connie Stevens . . . . Susan
Herbert Lom . . . . Victor Rosso
Marty Allen . . . . Wally
Leonardo Pieroni . . . . Angelo
Bruce Boa . . . . Nolan
Joanne Dainton . . . . Merle
COMEDY Con-man steals diamond to sell as
twin to his rival, but finds it is fake.

14017
THE SEA GULL (141) (A) *tech*
Sidney Lumet (WPD)
P:D: Sidney Lumet
S: (PLAY) Anton Chekhov
SC: Moura Budberg
James Mason . . . . Trigorin
Vanessa Redgrave . . . . Nina
Simone Signoret . . . . Arkadina
David Warner . . . . Konstantin
Harry Andrews . . . . Sorin
Ronald Radd . . . . Shamraev
Eileen Herlie . . . . Polina
Kathleen Widdoes . . . . Masha
Denholm Elliott . . . . Dorn
Alfred Lynch . . . . Medvedenko
DRAMA Russia, 19th C. Actress's playwright son
loves girl who loves his mother's lover.

14018
IT ALL GOES TO SHOW (28) (U) *eastman*
Bayford (Crispin)
P: John Hogarth
D: Francis Searle
Arthur Lowe . . . . Henry Parker
Bill Maynard . . . . Mike Sago
Tim Barrett . . . . Rev Blunt
Sheila Keith . . . . Mrs Parker
Valerie Van Ost . . . . Angela
COMEDY Attempts to brighten up seaside shows
offend local councillors.

14019
IT'S THE ONLY WAY TO GO (28) (U)
eastman
Hallelujah (Gala)
D: Ray Austin
Dave King . . . . The Man
COMEDY Old man dies watching a striptease.

14020
THE SANDAL (29)(X) colour
Rosalba (Eagle)
D: Ray Austin
Anna Matisse . . . . The Woman
Lionel Blair . . . .
FANTASY Drugged mother's dream saves her
from suicide.

14021
THE UNDERTAKERS (29) (U) colour
Chilton (Par)
P: Peter Andrews, Malcolm Heyworth
D: Brian Cummins
S: Mike Sharland, Philippe le Bars
Bernard Cribbins . . . . Mr Rigor
Wilfrid Brambell . . . . Mr Mortis
Michael Balfour
John Bluthal
Clive Dunn
Ray Ellington
Kenny Everett
Benny Lee
John Le Mesurier
Spike Milligan
Johnny Speight
June Whitfield
COMEDY Day in the life of two inept
undertakers.

DEC

14022
DAVID COPPERFIELD (118) (U) *tech*
Omnibus (20)
P: Frederick H. Brogger
D: Delbert Mann
S: (NOVEL) Charles Dickens
SC: Jack Pulman
Richard Attenborough . . . . Mr Tungay
Cyril Cusack . . . . Barkis
Edith Evans . . . . Betsy Trotwood

Pamela Franklin . . . . Dora
Susan Hampshire . . . . Agnes Wickfield
Wendy Hiller . . . . Mrs Micawber
Ron Moody . . . . Uriah Heep
Lawrence Olivier . . . . Mr Creakle
Robin Phillips . . . . David Copperfield
Michael Redgrave . . . . Mr Peggotty
Ralph Richardson . . . . Mr Micawber
Emlyn Williams . . . . Mr Dick
Isobel Black . . . . Clara Copperfield
Sinead Cusack . . . . Emily
James Donald . . . . Mr Murdstone
James Hayter . . . . Porter
Megs Jenkins . . . . Clara Peggotty
Anna Massey . . . . Jane Murdstone
Nicholas Pennell . . . . Traddles
Corin Redgrave . . . . Steerforth
Liam Redmond . . . . Quinion
DRAMA Young man recalls his boyhood days
and youthful adventures

14023
THE MAGIC CHRISTIAN (95) (A) *tech*
Grand (CUE)
P: Henry Weinstein, Anthony Unger
D: Joseph McGrath
S: (NOVEL) Terry Southern
SC: Terry Southern, Joseph McGrath, Peter
Sellers, Graham Chapman, John Cleese
Peter Sellers . . . . Sir Guy Grand
Ringo Starr . . . . Youngman Grand
Richard Attenborough . . . . . Coach
Laurence Harvey . . . . Hamlet
Christopher Lee . . . . Dracula
Spike Milligan . . . . Warden
Yul Brynner . . . . Lady Singer
Roman Polanski . . . . Listener
Raquel Welch . . . . Slave Driver
Isabel Jeans . . . . Sister
Wilfrid Hyde White . . . . Captain
Terence Alexander . . . . Mad Major
Patrick Cargill . . . . Auctioneer
Clive Dunn . . . . Sommelier
Fred Emney . . . . Fitzgibbon
Peter Graves . . . . Lord
Patrick Holt . . . . Duke
Hattie Jacques . . . . Ginger Horton
John Le Mesurier . . . . Sir John
Ferdy Mayne . . . . Edouard
Guy Middleton . . . . Duke of Mantisbriar
Dennis Price . . . . Winthrop
Graham Stark . . . . Waiter
Edward Underdown . . . . . . Prince Henry
Michael Aspel; Michael Barratt; Harry Carpenter;
W. Barrington Dalby; John Snagge; Alan Whicker
COMEDY Rich joker adopts grown man and
they spend their fortune on elaborate hoaxes.

14024
THE PROMISE (98) (U) *eastman*
Howard & Wyndham (CUE)
P: Henry T. Weinstein, Anthony B. Unger
D:SC: Michael Hayes
S: (PLAY) Aleksei Arbuzov
John Castle . . . . . Marat Yestignyev
Ian McKellen . . . . Leonidik
Susan Macready . . . . Like Vasilyevna
Mary Jones . . . . Mother
David Nettheim . . . . Stepfather
David Garfield . . . . Soldier
Christopher Banks . . . . Neighbour
Donald Bain . . . . Actor
DRAMA Russia, 1942. Poet and engineer both
love homeless girl.

14025
A PROMISE OF BED (83) (X) *eastman*
Dorak (Miracle)
P: Stanley Long
D:S: Derek Ford
Victor Spinetti . . . . George

Vanessa Howard . . . . Barbara
Dennis Waterman . . . . Photographer
Vanda Hudson . . . . Susan Stress
John Bird . . . . Driver
COMEDY Three stories with erotic overtones.

14026
SANDY THE SEAL (70) (U) *tech/scope*
Towers of London (Tigon)
P: Oliver Unger, Harry Alan Towers
D: Robert Lynn
S: Peter Welbeck
Heinz Drache . . . . Jan Van Heerden
Marianne Koch . . . . Karen Van Heerden
David Richards . . . . David
Anne Mervis . . . . Anne
Bill Brewer . . . . Loewenstein
Gabriel Bayman . . . . Lofty
Gert Van Den Berg . . . . . . Jacobson
ANIMAL Children raise baby seal and foil
poachers.

14027
ON HER MAJESTY'S SECRET SERVICE (140)
(A) *tech/scope*
Eon-Danilaq (UA)
P: Harry Satlzman, Albert R. Broccoli
D: Peter Hunt
S: (NOVEL) Ian Fleming
SC: Richard Maibaum
George Lazenby . . . . James Bond
Diana Rigg . . . . Tracy Draco
Telly Savalas . . . . Ernst Stavros Blofeld
Ilse Steppat . . . . Irma Bunt
Gabriele Ferzetti . . . . Marc Ange Draco
Yuri Borienko . . . . Grunther
Bernard Horsfall . . . . Campbell
George Baker . . . . Sir Hilary Bray
Bernard Lee . . . . M
Lois Maxwell . . . . Miss Moneypenny
Desmond Llewellyn . . . . . . Q
Angela Scoular . . . . Ruby
Catherina Von Schell . . . . . Nancy
Julie Ege . . . . Girl
Jenny Hanley . . . . Girl
Brian Worth . . . . Manuel
Bessie Love . . . . Guest
CRIME Agent foils master crook's plot for
bacteriological destruction of plant and animal
life.

14028
MUMSY, NANNY, SONNY & GIRLY (102)
(X) *eastman*
Brigitte-Fitzroy-Francis (CIRO)
P: Ronald J. Kahn
D: Freddie Francis
S: (PLAY) Maisie Mosco
SC: Brien Comport
Michael Bryant . . . . New Friend
Ursula Howells . . . . Mumsy
Patricia Heywood . . . . Nanny
Howard Trevor . . . . Sonny
Vanessa Howard . . . . Girly
Robert Swann . . . . Soldier
Imogen Hassall . . . . Girlfriend
Michael Ripper . . . . Attendant
CRIME Murderous teenagers kidnap drunk to
play games with.

14029
HELL BOATS (95) (A) *tech*
Mirisch-Oakmont (UA)
P: Lewis J. Rachmil
D: Paul Wendkos
S: S.S. Schweitzer
SC: Anthony Spinner, Donald Ford, Derek
Ford
James Franciscus . . . . . . Lt Cdr Tom Jeffords
Elizabeth Shepherd . . . . . . Alison Ashurst

Ronald Allen . . . . Cdr Roger Ashurst
Reuven Bar-Yotam . . . . Yacov
Inigo Jackson . . . . Stanhope
Mark Hawkins . . . . .Barlow
Drewe Henley . . . . Johnson
Magda Konopka . . . . Lucianna
Takis Emmanuel . . . . Salvatore
WAR 1942. American cdr in Royal Navy uses
captured E-Boat to destroy German base in
Sicily.

14030
TAKE A GIRL LIKE YOU (101) (X) *tech*
Albion (Col)
P: Hal E. Chester
D: Jonathan Miller
S: (NOVEL) Kingsley Amis
SC: George Melly
Hayley Mills . . . . Jenny Bunn
Oliver Reed . . . . Patrick Standish
Noel Harrison . . . . Julian
Sheila Hancock . . . . Martha Thompson
John Bird . . . . Dick Thompson
Aimi MacDonald . . . . Wendy
Reonoald Lacey . . . . Graham
Geraldine Sherman . . . . Anna
COMEDY Country virgin eventually yields after
sundry men attempt to seduce her.

14031
ZETA ONE (82) (X) *eastman*
Tigon British (Tigon)
P: Tony Tenser, George Maynard
D: Michael Cort
S: Michael Cort, Alastair McKenzie
Robin Hawdon . . . . James Word
Yutte Stensgaard . . . . Ann Olsen
James Robertson Justice . . . . .Maj Bourdon
Charles Hawtrey . . . . Swyne
Lionel Murton . . . . W
Dawn Addams . . . . Zeta
Anna Gael . . . . Clotho
Brigitte Skay . . . . Lachesis
Valerie Leon . . . . Atropos
Carol-Anne Hawkins . . . . . . Zara
Wendy Lingham . . . . Edwina Strain
Yolande Del Mar . . . . Stripper
FANTASY Agent and stripper versus extra-
terrestrial superwomen.

14032
COUNTRY DANCE (112) (X) *metro*
Windward-Keep-MGM British (MGM-EMI)
P: Robert Emmett Ginna
D: J. Lee Thompson
S: (NOVEL) James Kennaway (HOUSEHOLD
GHOSTS)
SC: James Kennaway
Peter O'Toole . . . . Sir Charles Ferguson
Susannah York . . . . Hilary
Michael Craig . . . . Douglas Dow
Harry Andrews . . . . Brig Crieff
Cyril Cusack . . . . Dr Maitland
Judy Cornwell . . . . Rosie
Brian Blessed . . . . Jock Baird
Robert Urquhart . . . . Auctioneer
Mark Malicz . . . . Benny the Pole
Lennox Milne . . . . Miss Mailer
Jean Anderson . . . . Matron
Peter Reeves . . . . Alex Smart
DRAMA Perth. Man eventually reunited with his
wife whose brother is an incestuous alcoholic.

14033
BACHELOR OF ARTS (31) (U) *colour*
Cresswell (Par)
P: John Dark
D: Harry Booth
S: Michael Bentine
SC: Michael Bentine, Harry Booth

Michael Bentine . . . . Miklos Durti
Norman Vaughan
Melvyn Hayes
Johnny Briggs
George Moon
Una Stubbs
David Lodge
George Woodbridge
COMEDY Foreign artist causes chaos during
a weekend in Britain.

14034
THE WAITERS (30) (U) *colour*
Fanfare (Par)
P: George H. Brown
D: Jan Darnley-Smith
S: Benny Hill
Benny Hill
David Battley
Arthur Hewlett
Pamela Cundell
James Ottaway
Jan Butlin
COMEDY Slapstick mishaps of clumsy waiters
at an elegant party.

14035
THE GAMES (96) (U) *deluxe/scope*
20th Century-Fox (20)
P: Lester Linsk
D: Michael Winner
S: (NOVEL) Hugh Atkinson
SC: Erich Segal
Michael Crawford . . . . Harry Hayes
Stanley Baker . . . . Bill Oliver
Ryan O'Neal . . . . Scott Reynolds
Charles Aznavour . . . . Pavel Vendek
Jeremy Kemp . . . . Jim Harcourt
Elaine Taylor . . . . Christine
Athol Compton . . . . Sunny Pintubi
Fritz Wepper . . . . Kovanda
Kent Smith . . . . Kaverley
Sam Elliott . . . . Richie Robinson
Reg Lye . . . . Charlie Gilmour
Mona Washbourne . . . . Mrs Hayes
June Jago . . . . .Mae Harcourt
Karel Stepanek . . . . Kubitsek
SPORT. Rome. Four runners from four
countries race in the Olympics.

14036
PADDY (87) (X) *pathe*
Dun Laoghaire (20)
P: Tamara Asseyev
D: Daniel Haller
S: (NOVEL) Lee Dunne (GOODBYE TO THE
HILL)
SC: Lee Dunne
Des Cave . . . . Paddy Maguire
Milo O'Shea . . . . Harry Redmond
Dearbhla Cave . . . . Paddy Maguire
Maureen Toal . . . . Claire Kearney
Peggy Cass . . . . Irenee
Judy Cornwell . . . . Breeda
Maire O'Donnell . . . . Mrs Maguire
Ita Darcy . . . . Josie Maguire
Dominic Roche . . . . Duncan Stuart
DRAMA Dublin. Romantic adventures of an
ex-butcher boy.

14037
SCREAM AND SCREAM AGAIN (95) (X)
eastman
Amicus—AIP (WPD)
P: Louis Heyward, Max Rosenberg,
Milton Subotsky
D: Gordon Hessler
S: (NOVEL) Peter Saxon
(THE DISORIENTATED MAN)
SC: Christopher Wicking
Vincent Price . . . . Dr Browning

Christopher Lee . . . . Fremont
Peter Cushing . . . . Maj Heinrich
Afred Marks . . . . Supt Bellaver
Anthony Newlands . . . . Ludwig
Peter Sallis . . . . Schweitz
David Lodge . . . . Insp Strickland
Uta Levka . . . . Jane
Christopher Matthews . . . . . David Sorel
Judy Bloom . . . . Helen Bradford
Clifford Earl . . . . Sgt Jimmy Joyce
HORROR Doctor creates composite humans
from amputated limbs.

14038
ALL THE RIGHT NOISES (91) (AA) *eastman*
Trigon (20)

P: Max L. Raab, John Quested, Si Litvinoff
D:S: Gerry O'Hara
Tom Bell . . . . Len Lewin
Olivia Hussey . . . . Val
Judy Carne . . . . Joy Lewin
John Standing . . . . Bernie
Edward Higgins . . . . Ted
Chloe Franks . . . . Jenny Lewin
Gareth Wright . . . . Ian
Gordon Griffith . . . . Terry
Robert Keegan . . . . Mr Lewin
Lesley-Ann Down . . . . Laura
Yootha Joyce . . . . Mrs Bird
Paul Whitsun-Jones . . . . Performer
Nicolette Roeg . . . . Performer
ROMANCE Married electrician has an affair
with a teenage chorus girl.

14039
MISCHIEF (57) (U) *eastman*
Shand (CFF)
P: Ian Shand, Jack Grossman
D: Ian Shand
S: Jack Grossman
Paul Fraser . . . . Davy
Iain Burton . . . . Harry
Adrienne Byrne . . . . Jenny
Michael Newport . . . . Sam
Gina Malcolm . . . . Pat Crawford
Gerald Sim . . . . Jim
Colin Gordon . . . . Mr Crawford
Bill Owen . . . . Quarryman
CHILDREN Wales. Ex-circus pony throws girl
but helps boy to save her.

1970

JAN

14040
THE ADVENTURES OF GERARD (91) (A)
deluxe/bilingual
Sir Nigel Films (UA)
P: Henry Lester, Gene Gutowski
D: Jerzy Skolimowski
S: (STORIES) Arthur Conan Doyle
(THE EXPLOITS OF BRIGADIER GERARD)
SC: H.A.L. Craig, Henry Lester, Gene Gutowski, Jerzy Skolimowski
Peter McEnery . . . . .Col Etienne Gerard
Claudia Cardinale . . . . Countess Teresa
Eli Wallach . . . . Napoleon Bounaparte
Jack Hawkins . . . . Millefleurs
Mark Burns . . . . Col Russell
Norman Rossington . . . . . . Sgt Papilette
John Neville . . . . Duke of Wellington
Paolo Stoppa . . . . Count of Morales
Ivan Desny . . . . Gen Lasalle
HISTORY Spain, 1808. Love and war adventures of boastful hussar during Napoleon's Peninsula campaign.

14041
ALL THE WAY UP (97) (A) *tech*
Granada (AA)
P:SC: Philip Mackie
D: James MacTaggart
S:(PLAY) David Turner (SEMI—DETACHED)
Warren Mitchell . . . . Fred Midway
Pat Heywood . . . . Hilda Midway
Elaine Taylor . . . . Eileen Midway
Kenneth Cranham . . . . Tom Midway
Vanessa Howard . . . . Avril Hadfield
Richard Briers . . . . Nigel Hadfield
Adrienne Posta . . . . Daphne Dunmore
Bill Fraser . . . . Arnold Makepiece
Terence Alexander . . . . Bob Chickman
Maggie McGrath . . . . Mrs Chickman
Clifford Parrish . . . . Mr Hadfield
Lally Bowers . . . . Mrs Hadfield
Janet Monta . . . . Stripper
COMEDY Insurance man and family scheme to rise in social scale.

14042
THE BIRTHDAY PARTY (124) (X) *tech*
Palomar—Amerbroco (Connoisseur)
P: Edgar Scherick, Max Rosenberg, Milton Subotsky
D: William Friedkin
S:(PLAY) Harold Pinter
SC: Harold Pinter
Robert Shaw . . . . Stanley Webber
Patrick Magee . . . . Shamus McCann
Dandy Nichols . . . . Meg Bowles
Sydner Tafler . . . . Nat Goldberg
Moultrie Kelsall . . . . Petey Bowles
Helen Fraser . . . . Lulu
DRAMA Strangers at seaside hold menacing party for pianist.

14043
CARRY ON UP THE JUNGLE (89) (A) *eastman*
Adder—Ethiro (RFD)
P: Peter Rogers
D: Gerald Thomas
S: Talbot Rothwell
Frankie Howard . . . . Prof Inigo Tinkle
Sidney James . . . . Bill Boosey
Charles Hawtrey . . . . Tonka (Sir Walter Bagley)
Joan Sims . . . . Lady Evelyn Bagley
Terry Scott . . . . Jungle Boy
Kenneth Connor . . . . Claude Chumley
Bernard Bresslaw . . . . Upsidasi
Jacki Piper . . . . June
Reuben Martin . . . . Gorilla
Valerie Leon . . . . Leda
COMEDY 1900. Expedition seeking rare bird captured by tribe of girls.

14044
1917 (34) (X) *tech*
Tigon British (Tigon)
P: Tony Tenser
D:SC: Stephen Weeks
S: (PLAY) Derek Banham (THE GAP)
Timothy Bateson . . . . Willi Falk
David Leland . . . . Felix
Geoffrey Davis . . . . Gessel
Anthony Trent . . . . Colman
Richardson Morgan . . . . . . Penfold
Christopher Hancock . . . . . Cox
Edward Caddick . . . . Whittaker
WAR France, 1917. Eager British soldier shoots German soldier.

14045
ONE BRIEF SUMMER (86) (AA) *eastman*
Twickenham Film Associates (20)
P: Michael Green, Guido Coen
D: John Mackenzie
S: (PLAY) Harry Tierney (VALKYRIE'S ARMOUR)
SC: Harrye Tierney, Guido Coen, Wendy Marshall Wendy Marshall
Felicity Gibson . . . . Susan Long
Clifford Evans . . . . Mark Stevens
Jennifer Hilary . . . . Jennifer Stevens
Jan Holden . . . . Elizabeth
Peter Egan . . . . Bill Denton
Fanny Carby . . . . Mrs Shaw
Richard Vernon . . . . Hayward
Helen Lindsay . . . . Mrs Hayward
Basil Moss . . . . John Robertson
DRAMA Kent. Girl tries to stop her father from marrying her friend.

14046
SPRING AND PORT WINE (101) (A) *tech*
Memorial Enterprises (WPD)
P: Roy Baird, Michael Medwin
D: Peter Hammond
S: (PLAY) Bill Naughton
SC: Bill Naughton
James Mason . . . . Rafe Crompton
Susan George . . . . Hilda Crompton
Diana Coupland . . . . Daisy Crompton
Rodney Bewes . . . . Harold Crompton
Hannah Gordon . . . . Florence Crompton
Len Jones . . . . Wilfred Crompton
Keith Buckley . . . . Arthur Gasket
Adrienne Posta . . . . Betty Duckworth
Avril Edgar . . . . .Betsy Jane Duckworth
Frank Windsor . . . . Ned Duckworth
Arthur Lowe . . . . Mr Aspinall
Marjorie Rhodes . . . . Mrs Gaskett
Bernard Bresslaw . . . . Driver
DRAMA Bolton. Mill engineer's wife pawns his new coat to pay her pregnant daughter's fare to London.

14047
THE RECKONING (111) (X) *tech*
Columbia British (Col)
P: Ronald Shedlo
D: Jack Gold
S: (NOVEL) Patrick Hall (THE HARP THAT ONCE)
SC: John McGrath
Nicol Williamson . . . . Michael Marler
Rachel Roberts . . . . Joyce Eglington
Paul Rogers . . . . Hazlitt
Zena Walker . . . . Hilda Greening
Ann Bell . . . . Rosemary Marler
Gwen Nelson . . . . Mrs Marler
Christine Hargreaves . . . . . Kath
Thomas Kempinski . . . . Brunzy
J.G. Devlin . . . . Cocky Burke
Peter Sallis . . . . Keresley

DRAMA Liverpool. Irish businessman beats up teenagers who killed his father, and discredits his boss.

14048
PRAISE MARX AND PASS THE AMMUNITION (90) (X) *eastman*
Mithras (Mithras)
P:D:SC: Maurice Hatton
S: Maurice Hatton, Michael Wood
John Thaw . . . . Dom
Edina Ronay . . . . Lucy
Louis Mahoney . . . . Julius
Anthony Villaroel . . . . Arthur
Helen Fleming . . . . Clara
David David . . . . Lal
Tanya . . . . Girl
DRAMA Communist tries to bring about revolution.

FEB

14049
ENTERTAINING MR SLOANE (94) (X) *tech*
Canterbury (WPD)
P: Douglas Kentish
D: Douglas Hickox
S: (PLAY) Joe Orton
SC: Clive Exton
Beryl Reid . . . . Kath
Harry Andrews . . . . Ed
Peter McEnery . . . . Mr Sloane
Alan Webb . . . . Dada Kemp
COMEDY Woman and her homosexual brother both marry the lodger who murdered their father.

14050
EVERY HOME SHOULD HAVE ONE (94) (X) *eastman*
Example (BL)
P: Ned Sherrin
D: Jim Clark
S: Milton Shulman, Herbert Kretzmer
SC: Marty Feldman, Barry Took, Denis Norden
Marty Feldman . . . . Teddy
Shelley Berman . . . . Nat Kaplan
Judy Cornwell . . . . Liz
Julie Ege . . . . .Inga Giltenberg
Patrick Cargill . . . . Wallace Trufitt
Jack Watson . . . . McLaughlin
Patience Collier . . . . Mrs Levin
Penelope Keith . . . . . . Lotte von Gelbstein
Dinsdale Landen . . . . Rev Mellish
John McKelvey . . . . Col Belper
Sarah Badel . . . . Joanna Snow
Dave Dee . . . . Ern
Hy Hazell . . . . Mrs Kaplan
Judy Huxtable . . . . Dracula's Victim
John Wells . . . . Tolworth
COMEDY Advertising man dreams up erotic schemes to exploit frozen porridge.

14051
FUTTOCKS END (49) (A) *eastman*
Paradine—Gannet (BL)
P:D: Bob Kellett
S: Ronnie Barker
Michael Hordern . . . . Butler
Ronnie Barker . . . . Gen Futtock
Roger Livesey . . . . Artist
Julian Orchard . . . . Twit
Kika Markham . . . . Niece
Mary Merrall . . . . Aunt
Hilary Pritchard . . . . Bird
Richard O'Sullivan . . . . Boots
COMEDY "Silent" misadventures at weekend houseparty.

14052
RHUBARB (37) (U) *tech*
Avalon (WPD)

P: Jon Penington
D:SC: Eric Sykes
Harry Secombe . . . . Vicar
Eric Sykes . . . . Inspector
Jimmy Edwards . . . . Constable
Hattie Jacques . . . . Nurse
Gordon Rollings . . . . Dentist
Graham Stark . . . . Pro
Kenneth Connor . . . . Mower
Johnny Speight . . . . Man
COMEDY Slapstick golf match between vicar
and police inspector.

14053
JULIUS CAESAR (116) (U) *tech/scope*
CUE
P: Henry Weinstein, Anthony Unger
D: Stuart Burge
S: (PLAY) William Shakespeare
SC: Robert Furnival
Charlton Heston . . . . Mark Antony
Jason Robarts . . . . Brutus
John Gielgud . . . . Julius Caesar
Richard Johnson . . . . Cassius
Robert Vaughan . . . . Casca
Richard Chamberlain . . . . . Octavius Caesar
Diana Rigg . . . . Portia
Jill Bennett . . . . Calpurnia
Christopher Lee . . . . Artemidorus
Alan Browning . . . . Marullus
Norman Bowler . . . . Titinius
Andrew Crawford . . . . Volumnius
David Dodimead . . . . Lepidus
Michael Gough . . . . Metellus Cimber
Andre Morell . . . . Cicero
HISTORY Rome. Senators conspire to kill
Caesar.

14054
THE MAN WHO HAUNTED HIMSELF (94)
(A) *tech*
Excalibur (WPD)
P: Michael Relph
D: Basil Dearden
S: (NOVEL) Anthony Armstrong (THE CASE
OF MR PELHAM)
SC: Michael Relph, Basil Dearden
Roger Moore . . . . Harold Pelham
Hildegarde Neff . . . . Eve Pelham
Olga Georges-Picot . . . . Julie
Anton Rogers . . . . Tony Alexander
Freddie Jones . . . . Dr Harris
Thorley Walters . . . . Bellamy
John Carson . . . . Ashton
John Welsh . . . . Sir Charles Freeman
Edward Chapman . . . . Barton
Laurence Hardy . . . . Mason
Charles Lloyd Pack . . . . Jameson
Anthony Nicholls . . . . . Sir Arthur Richardson
FANTASY Extrovert double, released by
operation, takes over executive's life.

14055
TASTE THE BLOOD OF DRACULA (95) (X)
tech
Hammer (WPD)
P: Aida Young
D: Peter Sasdy
S: (CHARACTER) Bram Stoker
SC: Anthony Hinds
Christopher Lee . . . . Count Dracula
Geoffrey Keen . . . . William Hargood
Gwen Watford . . . . Martha Hargood
Linda Hayden . . . . Alice Hargood
Peter Sallis . . . . Samuel Paxton
Anthony Corlan . . . . Paul Paxton
Isla Blair . . . . Lucy Paxton
John Carson . . . . Jonathon Secker
Martin Jarvis . . . . Jeremy Secker

Ralph Bates . . . . Lord Courtley
Roy Kinnear . . . . Weller
Michael Ripper . . . . Cob
HORROR Vampire, revived in England,
avenges himself on three families.

14056
ANNE OF THE THOUSAND DAYS (146) (A)
tech/scope
Universal (RFD)
P: Hal B. Wallis
D: Charles Jarrott
S: (PLAY) Maxwell Anderson
SC: John Hale, Bridget Boland
Richard Burton . . . . Henry VIII
Genevieve Bujold . . . . Anne Boleyn
Irene Papas . . . . Queen Katherine
Anthony Quayle . . . . Cardinal Wolsey
John Colicos . . . . Thomas Cromwell
Michael Hordern . . . . Thomas Boleyn
Katherine Blake . . . . Elizabeth Boleyn
Valerie Gearon . . . . Mary Boleyn
Michael Johnson . . . . George Boleyn
Peter Jeffrey . . . . Norfolk
Joseph O'Conor . . . . Fisher
William Squire . . . . Thomas More
Esmond Knight . . . . Mendoza
Brook Williams . . . . Brereton
Nora Swinburne . . . . Lady Kingston
Gary Bond . . . . Smeaton
Lesley Paterson . . . . Jane Seymour
Kynaston Reeves . . . . Willoughby
HISTORY 1526. King Henry VIII divorces his
queen and marries young Anne Boleyn.
(AA 1969: Best Costumes: RFP: 1970)

MAR

14057
HOFFMAN (113) (X) *tech*
Longstone (WPD)
P: Ben Arbeid
D: Alvin Rakoff
S: (NOVEL) Ernest Gebler
SC: Ernest Gebler
Peter Sellers . . . . Benjamin Hoffman
Sinead Cusack . . . . Janet Smith
Jeremy Bulloch . . . . Tom Mitchell
Ruth Dunning . . . . Mrs Mitchell
COMEDY Middle-aged man blackmails
teenager into spending week with him.

14058
LEO THE LAST (104) (X) *deluxe*
Char—Wink—Boor—Calisbury (UA)
P: Irwin Winkler, Robert Chartoff
D: John Boorman
S: (PLAY) George Tabori (THE PRINCE)
SC: William Stair, John Boorman
Marcello Mastroianni . . . . . . Leo
Billie Whitelaw . . . . Margaret
Calvin Lockhart . . . . Roscoe
Glenna Forster Jones . . . . . . Salambo
Graham Crowden . . . . Max
Gwen Ffrangcon-Davies . . . Hilda
David De Keyser . . . . David
Vladek Shaybal . . . . Laszlo
Keefe West . . . . Jasper
Kenneth J. Warren . . . . Kowalski
DRAMA Convalescing prince protects Negro
slumdwellers.

14059
NIGHT AFTER NIGHT AFTER NIGHT (88)
(X) *eastman*
Dudley Birch (Butcher)
P: James Mellor
D: Lewis J. Force
S: Dail Ambler
Jack May . . . . Judge Charles Lomax

Justine Lord . . . . Helena Lomax
Gilbert Wynne . . . . Insp Bill Rowan
Linda Marlowe . . . . Jenny Rowan
Terry Scully . . . . Carter
Donald Sumpter . . . . Pete Laver
Peter Forbes-Robertson . . . . Powell
Jacqueline Clark . . . . Josie Leach
Jack Smethurst . . . . Chief Inspector
April Harlow . . . . Stripper
CRIME Inspector convicts teenager of murder,
then finds judge is the killer.

14060
THE LAST SHOT YOU HEAR (91) (X)
Lippert (20)
P: Robert Lippert, Jack Parsons
D: Gordon Hessler
S: (PLAY) William Fairchild (THE SOUND OF
MURDER)
SC: Tim Shields
Hugh Marlowe . . . . Charles Nordeck
Zena Walker . . . . Eileen
Patricia Haines . . . . Anne Nordeck
William Dysart . . . . Peter Marriott
Thorley Walters . . . . Gen Jowett
Lionel Murton . . . . Rubens
Helen Horton . . . . Dodie Rubens
John Nettleton . . . . Nash
John Wentworth . . . . Chambers
CRIME Lovers' plot to murder marriage
counsellor backfires.

14061
THE LAST GRENADE (93) (A) *eastman/scope*
Lockmore—Cinerama—de Grunwald (CIRO)
P: Josef Shaftel
D: Gordon Flemyng
S: (NOVEL) John Sherlock (THE ORDEAL OF
MAJOR GRIGSBY)
SC: Kenneth Ware, James Mitchell, John Sherlock
Stanley Baker . . . . Maj Harry Grigsby
Alex Cord . . . . Kip Thompson
Honor Blackman . . . . Katherine Whiteley
Richard Attenborough . Gen Charles Whiteley
Rafer Johnson . . . . Joe Jackson
Andrew Keir . . . . Gordon Mackenzie
Ray Brooks . . . . Lt David Coulson
Julian Glover . . . . Andy Royale
John Thaw . . . . , Terry Mitchell
Philip Latham . . . . Adams
Pamela Stanley . . . . Wife
WAR Hong Kong. Major tracks down friend
who betrayed him in the Congo.

14062
SECRETS OF SEX (91) (X) *eastman*
Noteworthy (Balch)
P: Richard Gordon, Anthony Balch
D: Anthony Balch
S: (STORY) Alfred Mazure
SC: Martin Locke, John Eliot, Maureen Owen,
Elliott Stein, Anthony Balch
Richard Schulman . . . . Judge
Janet Spearman . . . . Wife
Dorothy Grumbar . . . . Photographer
Anthony Rowlands . . . . Model
George Herbert . . . . Steward
Kenneth Benda . . . . Sacha Seremona
Yvonne Quenet . . . . Mary-Clare
Reid Anderson . . . . Dr Rilke
Cathy Howard . . . . Burglar
Mike Britton . . . . Burgled man
Maria Frost . . . . Lindy Leigh
Peter Carlisle . . . . Col X
Sue Bond . . . . Callgirl
Elliott Stein . . . . Strange Man
FANTASY Mummified Arabian recounts strange
sex stories.

14063
MY LOVER, MY SON (95) (X) *metro*
Sagittarius—MGM British (MGM)
P: Wilbur Stark
D: John Newland
S: (NOVEL) Edward Grierson (REPUTATION FOR A SONG); (STORY) Wilbur Stark (SECOND LEVEL)
SC: William Marchant, Jenni Hall, Brian Degas, Tudor Gates
Romy Schneider . . . . Francesca Anderson
Donald Houston . . . . Robert
Dennis Waterman . . . . James Anderson
Patricia Brake . . . . Julie
Peter Sallis . . . . Sidney Brent
William Dexter . . . . Parks
Alexandra Bastedo . . . . Cicely Clarkson
Mark Hawkins . . . . Macer
Maggie Wright . . . . Prostitute
Janet Brown . . . . Mrs Woods
Tom Chatto . . . . Mr Woods
Michael Forrest . . . . Insp Chidley
Arthur Howard . . . . Judge
DRAMA Rich man's second wife has an incestuous love for her son.

14064
SOME WILL, SOME WON'T (90) (U) *tech*
Transocean (WPD)
P: Giulio Zampi
D: Duncan Wood
S: (SCREENPLAY) Jack Davies, Michael Pertwee (LAUGHTER IN PARADISE)
SC: Lew Schwartz
Ronnie Corbett . . . . Herbert Russell
Thora Hird . . . . Agnes Russell
Michael Hordern . . . . Denniston Russell
Leslie Phillips . . . . Simon Russell
Barbara Murray . . . . Lucille
Wilfrid Brambell . . . . Henry Russell
Dennis Price . . . . Benson
James Robertson Justice .Sir Charles Robson
Sheila Steafel . . . . Sheila Wilcott
Eleanor Summerfield . . . . . Elizabeth Robson
Arthur Lowe . . . . Sgt
COMEDY Heirs must fulfil uncharacteristic conditions to inherit fortune.

14065
LOVE IS A SPLENDID ILLUSION (86) (X) *tech*
Piccadilly (RSE)
P: Bachoo Sen
D: Tom Clegg
S: David Baker, Bachoo Sen
Simon Brent . . . . Christian Dubarry
Andree Flamand . . . . Michele Howard
Lisa Collings . . . . Amanda Dubarry
Peter Hughes . . . . Maurice Howard
Mark Kingston . . . . Bernard Collins
Fiona Curzon . . . . Liz
Maxine Casson . . . . Debbie
Anna Matisse . . . . Sophie
Carl Ferber . . . . Jason
Nancy Nevinson . . . . Mother
DRAMA Italy. Designer discovers his mistress had been mistress of an associate.

14066
THE NUTCRACKER SUITE (9) (U) *colour*
Carlyle
D: Robert Webb
S: (MUSIC) Tchaikowsky
Belinda Wright
Jelco Yuresha
MUSICAL Pas de Deux and Coda from the ballet.

APR
14067
BRONCO BULLFROG (86) (AA)
Maya (BL)

P: Andrew StJohn
D:S: Barney Platts-Mills
Del Walker . . . . Del Quant
Anne Gooding . . . . Irene Richardson
Sam Shepherd . . . . Jo Saville
Roy Haywood . . . . Roy
Freda Shepherd . . . . Mrs Richardson
Dick Philpott . . . . Quant
Chris Shepherd . . . . Chris
Stuart Stones . . . . Sgt Johnson
Geoff Wincott . . . . Geoff
DRAMA East End teenagers get involved with Borstal escapee.

14068
WITH LOVE IN MIND (49) (U) *tech/scope*
Cecil-Wright Topping (AEMI)
P: Michael Topping
D: Robin Cecil-Wright
S: N.J. Crisp
SC: N.J. Crisp, N.L. Hoey
Keith Baxter . . . . Tony Preston
Shirley Ann Field . . . . Jane
Eva Wishaw . . . . Carolyn
Carl Schell . . . . Max
ROMANCE Mexico. Affairs of fashion photographer.

14069
THE WALKING STICK (101) (A) *metro/scope*
Winkast—Gershwin—Kastner (MGM)
P: Alan Ladd jr
D: Eric Till
S: (NOVEL) Winston Graham
SC: George Bluestone
David Hemmings . . . . Leigh Hartley
Samantha Eggar . . . . Deborah Dainton
Emlyn Williams . . . . Jack Foil
Phyllis Calvert . . . . Erica Dainton
Ferdy Mayne . . . . Douglas Dainton
Francesca Annis . . . . Arabella Dainton
Bridget Turner . . . . Sarah Dainton
Dudley Sutton . . . . Ted Sandymount
John Woodvine . . . . Bertie Irons
David Saville . . . . David Talbot
Basil Henson . . . . Insp Malcolm
Anthony Nicholls . . . . Lewis Maude
CRIME Crippled girl deceived into assisting in antique robbery.

MAY
14070
CROMWELL (140) (U) *tech/scope*
Irving Allen (Col)
P: Irving Allen
D:S: Ken Hughes
SC: Ken Hughes, Ronald Harwood
Richard Harris . . . . Oliver Cromwell
Alec Guinness . . . . Charles I
Robert Morley . . . . Earl of Manchester
Dorothy Tutin . . . . Queen Henrietta Maria
Frank Finlay . . . . John Carter
Timothy Dalton . . . . Prince Rupert
Patrick Wymark . . . . Earl of Stafford
Patrick Magee . . . . Hugh Peters
Nigel Stock . . . . Sir Edward Hyde
Charles Gray . . . . Lord Essex
Michael Jayston . . . . Henry Ireton
Richard Cornish . . . . Oliver Cromwell II
Anna Cropper . . . . Ruth Carter
Michael Goodliffe . . . . . . Solicitor General
Patrick Holt . . . . Capt Lundsford
Stratford Johns . . . . Pres Bradshaw
Geoffrey Keen . . . . John Pym
Zena Walker . . . . Mrs Cromwell
George Merritt . . . . William
HISTORY Puritan leads Parliament and people against King (AA1970: Best Costumes).

14071
DOCTOR IN TROUBLE (90) (AA) *tech*
Welbeck-Rank (RFD)
P: Betty Box
D: Ralph Thomas
S: (NOVEL) Richard Gordon (DOCTOR ON TOAST)
SC: Jack Davies
Leslie Phillips . . . . Dr Simon Burke
Harry Secombe . . . . Llewellyn Wendover
Angela Scoular . . . . Ophelia O'Brien
Irene Handl . . . . Mrs Dailey
Simon Dee . . . . Basil Beauchamp
Robert Morley . . . . Capt George Spratt
Freddie Jones . . . . Master at Arms
James Robertson Justice . . Sir Lancelot Spratt
Joan Sims . . . . Russian Captain
John Le Mesurier . . . . Purser
Graham Stark . . . . Satterjee
Janet Mahoney . . . . Dawn Dailey
Graham Chapman . . . . Roddy
Fred Emney . . . . Sir Thomas Relph
Jimmy Thompson . . . . Doctor
COMEDY Doctor stows away on ship and is made to work as captain's steward.

14072
THE HORROR OF FRANKENSTEIN (95) (X) *tech*
EMI-Hammer(MGM-EMI)
P:D: Jimmy Sangster
S: (NOVEL) Mary Shelley (FRANKENSTEIN)
SC: Jimmy Sangster, Jeremy Burnham
Ralph Bates . . . . Victor Frankenstein
Kate O'Mara . . . . Alys
Veronica Carlson . . . . Elizabeth
Dennis Price . . . . Graverobber
Joan Rice . . . . Wife
Bernard Archard . . . . Father
Graham James . . . . Wilhelm
Dave Prowse . . . . Monster
HORROR Period. Science student creates life in the form of a monster.

14073
LOOT (101) (X) *eastman*
Performing Arts (BL)
P: Arthur Lewis
D: Silvio Narizzano
S: (PLAY) Joe Orton
SC: Ray Galton, Alan Simpson
Richard Attenborough . . . . . . Truscott
Lee Remick . . . . Fay
Hywel Bennett . . . . Dennis
Milo O'Shea . . . . McLeavy
Roy Holder . . . . Hal McLeavy
Dick Emery . . . . Bateman
Joe Lynch . . . . .Father O'Shaughnessy
John Cater . . . . Meadows
Aburey Woods . . . . Undertaker
Robert Raglan . . . . Doctor
COMEDY Man robs bank and hides loot in his mother's coffin.

14074
NED KELLY (103) (A) *tech*
Woodfall (UA)
P: Neil Hartley
D: Tony Richardson
S: Tony Richardson, Ian Jones
Mick Jagger . . . . Ned Kelly
Allen Bickford . . . . Dan Kelly
Geoff Gilmour . . . . Steve Hart
Mark McManus . . . . Joe Byrne
Serge Lazareff . . . . Wild Wright
Peter Sumner . . . . Tom Lloyd
Ken Shorter . . . . Aaron Sherritt
James Elliott . . . . Pat O'Donnell
Clarissa Kaye . . . . Mrs Kelly
Diana Craig . . . . Maggie Kelly

Susan Lloyd . . . . Kate Kelly
Alexi Long . . . . Grace Kelly
Bruce Barry . . . . George King
Janne Wesley . . . . Caithlyn
HISTORY Australia. Adventures with music of
teenage outlaw and gang.

14075
THE RISE AND RISE OF MICHAEL RIMMER
(94) (AA) *tech*
David Paradine-WB Seven Arts (WB)
P: David Forst, Harry Fine
D: Kevin Billington
S: Peter Cook, John Cleese, Graham
Chapman, Kevin Billington
Peter Cook . . . . Michael Rimmer
Denholm Elliott . . . . Peter Niss
Ronald Fraser . . . . Tom Hutchinson
Vanessa Howard . . . . Patricia Cartwright
Arthur Lowe . . . . Ferret
George A. Cooper . . . . Blackett
Harold Pinter . . . . Steven Hench
James Cossins . . . . Crodder
Roland Culver . . . . Sir Eric Bentley
Dudley Foster . . . . Federman
Dennis Price . . . . Fairburn
Ronnie Corbett . . . . Interviewer
John Cleese . . . . Plumer
Diana Coupland . . . . Mrs Spimm
Nicholas Phipps . . . . Snaggot
Desmond Walter-Ellis . . . . . Buffery
Norman Bird . . . . Alderman Poot
Graham Chapman . . . . Fromage
Elspeth March . . . . Mrs Ferret
Norman Rossington . . . . . . Guide
Percy Edwards . . . . Bird Impersonator
COMEDY Advertising man manoeuvres his way to
Presidency.

14076
THE ENGAGEMENT (44) (U) *tech*
Memorial Enterprises (A-EMI)
P: David Barber
D: Paul Joyce
S: Tom Stoppard
David Warner . . . . Dominic Boot
George Innes . . . . Lemon
Michael Bates . . . . Cartwright
Juliet Harmer . . . . Vivian
Paul Curran . . . . Father
Barbara Couper . . . . Mother
Gillian Raine . . . . Miss Bligh
Norman Rossington . . . . Albert
Peter Copley . . . . Manager
Diane Aubrey . . . . Nurse
COMEDY Young man attempts to raise
money to pay taxi fare.

14077
THE ENIGMA VARIATIONS (34) (U) *colour*
Archibald Associates (Argo)
P:D: James Archibald
S: (BALLET) Frederick Ashton, Edward Elgar
Svetlana Beriozova
MUSICAL Ballet.

JUN

14078
CRY OF THE BANSHEE (87) (X) *colour*
AIP (MGM-EMI)
P: Louis M. Heyward, Gordon Hessler
D: Gordon Hessler
S: Tim Kelly
SC: Tim Kelly, Christopher Wicking
Vincent Price . . . . . . Lord Edward Whitman
Elizabeth Bergner . . . . Cona
Essy Persson . . . . Lady Patricia
Patrick Mower . . . . Roderick
Hugh Griffith . . . . Mickey

Hilary Dwyer . . . . Maureen
Sally Geeson . . . . Sarah
Pamela Fairbrother . . . . Margaret
Marshall Jones . . . . Father Tom
Carl Rigg . . . . Harry Whitman
Robert Hutton . . . . Guest
HORROR 16th C. Lover of lord's daughter is
monster conjured up by witch.

14079
EYEWITNESS (91) (A) *tech*
Irving Allen-ABP (MGM—EMI)
P: Paul Maslansky
D: John Hough
S: (NOVEL) Mark Hebden
SC: Ronald Harwood
Mark Lester . . . . Timothy
Lionel Jeffries . . . . Colonel
Susan George . . . . Pippa
Tony Bonner . . . . Tom
Jeremy Kemp . . . . Galleria
Peter Vaughan . . . . Paul
Peter Bowles . . . . Victor
Betty Marsden . . . . Mme Robiac
Antony Stamboulieh . . . . . . Tacherie
CRIME Mediterranean island boy with vivid
imagination is sole witness to assassination.

14080
GOODBYE GEMINI (89) (X) *eastman*
Josef Shaftel (CIRO)
P: Josef Shaftel, Peter Snell
D: Alan Gibson
S: (NOVEL) Jenni Hall (ASK AGAMEMNON)
SC: Edmund Ward
Judy Geeson . . . . Jacki Dewar
Martin Potter . . . . Julian Dewar
Michael Redgrave . . . . .James Harrington-Smith
Alexis Kanner . . . . Clive Landseer
Mike Pratt . . . . Rod Barstowe
Marion Diamond . . . . . . Denise Pryce-Fletcher
Freddie Jones . . . . David Curry
Terry Scully . . . . Nigel Garfield
Peter Jeffrey . . . . Insp Kingsley
CRIME Adolescent twins get involved in
blackmail, homosexuality and murder.

14081
GROUPIE GIRL (87) (X) *eastman*
Salon (Eagle)
P: Barry Jacobs, Stanley Long
D: Derek Ford
S: Derek Ford, Suzanne Mercer
Esme Johns . . . . Sally
Billy Boyle . . . . Wes
Donald Sumpter . . . . Steve
Richard Shaw . . . . Morrie
Neil Hallett . . . . Sgt
Charles Finch . . . . Handler
Eliza Terry . . . . Mooncake
The Sweaty Betty; The Orange Butterfly
DRAMA Girl runs away from home to live
with drug-taking pop groups.

14082
THE VIRGIN AND THE GYPSY (95)(AA)
colour
Kenwood (London Screenplays)
P: Dmitri De Grunwald, Kenneth Harper
D: Christopher Miles
S: (NOVEL) D.H. Lawrence
SC: Alan Plater
Joanna Shimkus . . . . Yvette Saywell
Franco Nero . . . . Gypsy
Honor Blackman . . . . Mrs Fawcett
Mark Burns . . . . Maj Eastwood
Maurice Denham . . . . . . Rector Arthur Saywell
Fay Compton . . . . Grandma
Kay Walsh . . . . Aunt Cissie
Harriet Harper . . . . Lucille Saywell

Norman Bird . . . . Uncle Fred
Imogen Hassall . . . . Gypsy's Wife
Roy Holder . . . . Bob
ROMANCE Rector's daughter becomes
infatuated with amoral gypsy.

14083
MAN OF VIOLENCE (107) (X) *eastman*
retitled: THE SEX RACKETEERS
Peter Walker (Miracle)
P:D: Peter Walker
S: Pete Walker, Brian Comport
Michael Latimer . . . . Moon
Luan Peters . . . . Angel
Derek Aylward . . . . Nixon
Maurice Kaufmann . . . . Charles Grayson
Derek Francis . . . . Sam Bryant
Kenneth Hendel . . . . Hunt
George Belbin . . . . Burgess
Erika Raffael . . . . Goose
Virginia Wetherell . . . . Gale
Andreas Malandrinos . . . . . Pergolesi
CRIME Loan operator investigating property
enterprises gets involved in theft of Arab
bullion.

14084
DAY OF REST (25) (U) *colour*
Signal (Col)
D: James Clark
Avis Bunnage
Roy Holder
Lee Montagu
Joe Gladwyn
COMEDY Northern suburban family spend
typical Sunday.

14085
AND SOON THE DARKNESS (99) (AA) *tech*
Associated British (WPD)
P: Albert Fennell, Brian Clemens
D: Robert Fuest
S: Brian Clemens, Terry Nation
Pamela Franklin . . . . Jane
Michele Dotrice . . . . Cathy
Sandor Eles . . . . Paul
John Nettleton . . . . Gendarme
Clare Kelly . . . . Schoolmistress
Hana-Maria Pravda . . . . Mme Lassal
John Franklyn . . . . Man
CRIME France. Nurses on cycling holiday get
involved with sexual murderer.

14086
MONIQUE (87) (X) *eastman*
Tigon British (Tigon)
P: Tony Tenser, Michael Style
D:S: John Bown
Sibylla Kay . . . . Monique
Joan Alcorn . . . . Jean
David Sumner . . . . Bill
Jacob Fitz-Jones . . . . Edward
Nicola Bown . . . . Susan
Davilia O'Connor . . . . Harriet
Carolanne Hawkins . . . . Girl
ROMANCE French au pair girl has sexual
adventures with both husband and wife.

14087
COLOSSEUM AND JUICY LUCY (33) (U)
tech
Oakhurst Enterprises (WPD)
P: Stanley Baker, Timothy Burrill
D: Tony Palmer
Colosseum
Juicy Lucy
MUSICAL Pop concert with effects.

14088
THE EXECUTIONER (111) (AA) *tech/scope*
Ameran (Col)
P: Charles H. Schneer
D: Sam Wanamaker
S: Gordon McDonell
SC: Jack Pulman
George Peppard . . . . John Shay
Joan Collins . . . . Sarah Booth
Judy Geeson . . . . Polly Bendel
Oscar Homolka . . . . Racovsky
Charles Gray . . . . Vaughan Jones
Nigel Patrick . . . . Col Scott
Keith Michell . . . . Adam Booth
George Baker . . . . Philip Crawford
Alexander Scourby . . . . Prof Parker
Peter Bull . . . . Butterfield
Peter Dyneley . . . . Balkov
CRIME British spy investigates complex web of counter espionage.

JUL

14089
SIMON, SIMON (30) (U) *eastman*
Denouement Shillingford-Hemdale (Tigon)
P: Peter Shillingford
D:S: Graham Stark
Graham Stark . . . . Workman
John Junkin . . . . Workman
Julia Foster . . . . Typist
Norman Rossington . . . . Fireman
Kenneth Earl
Paul Whitsun-Jones
Peter Sellers
Michael Caine
Eric Morecambe
Ernie Wise
Bernie Winters
Bob Monkhouse
COMEDY Miscellaneous misadventures of workman driving hydraulic platform truck.

14090
WALK A CROOKED PATH (88) (AA) *eastman*
Hanover (Butcher)
P:D: John Brason
S: Barry Perowne
Tenniel Evans . . . . John Hemming
Faith Brook . . . . Elizabeth Hemming
Christopher Coll . . . . Bill Colman
Patricia Haines . . . . Nancy Colman
Clive Endersby . . . . Philip Dreaper
Georgina Simpson . . . . Elaine
Margery Mason . . . . Mildred
Georgina Cookson . . . . Imogen
Peter Copley . . . . Dr Oberon
Paul Dawkins . . . . Inspector
Barry Perowne . . . . Unwins
CRIME Boy's charge of homosexual assault is plot to drive teacher's wife to suicide.

14091
THE WIFE SWAPPERS (86) (X) *eastman*
Salon (Eagle)
P: Barry Jacobs, Stanley Long
D: Derek Ford
S: Derek Ford, Stanley Long
James Donnelly . . . . Paul
Larry Taylor . . . . Leonard
Valerie St John . . . . Ellen
Denys Hawthorne . . . . Cliff
Bunty Garland . . . . Sheila
Sandra Satchwith . . . . Carol
Fiona Fraser . . . . Marion
Joan Hayward . . . . Jean
DRAMA Episodic dramatisations of sexual case-histories.

14092
KING LEAR (136) (A)
Filmways-Lanterna-Athena (Col)
P: Michael Birkett, Sam Lomberg, Mogens Skot-Hansen
D:SC: Peter Brook
S: (PLAY) William Shakespeare
Paul Scofield . . . . King Lear
Irene Worth . . . . Goneril
Alan Webb . . . . Duke of Gloucester
Cyril Cusack . . . . Duke of Albany
Tom Fleming . . . . Earl of Kent
Jack MacGowran . . . . Fool
Susan Engel . . . . Regan
Patrick Magee . . . . Duke of Cornwall
Robert Lloyd . . . . Edgar
Soeren Elung-Jensen . . . . . . Duke of Burgundy
Barry Stanton . . . . Oswald
Anne-Lise Gabold . . . . Cordelia
HISTORY Period. Mad King's conflict with his daughters (Made in Denmark).

14093
QUACKSER FORTUNE HAS A COUSIN IN THE BRONX (90) *eastman*
UMC (Scotia-Barber)
P: Sidney Glazier, John Cushingham, Mel Howard
D: Waris Hussein
S: Gabriel Walsh
Gene Wilder . . . . Quackser Fortune
Margot Kidder . . . . Zazl Pierce
Eileen Colgan . . . . Betsy Bourke
Seamus Ford . . . . Mr Fortune
May Ollis . . . . Mrs Fortune
Liz Davis . . . . Kathleen Fortune
Caroline Tully . . . . Vera Fortune
Paul Murphy . . . . Damien
David Kelly . . . . Tom Maguire
ROMANCE Dublin. Manure collector's affair with American student.

14094
THE BEAST IN THE CELLAR (87) (X) *eastman*
Tigon-Leander (Tigon)
P: Tony Tenser, Graham Harris
D:S: James Kelly
Beryl Reid . . . . Ellie Ballantyne
Flora Robson . . . . Joyce Ballantyne
Tessa Wyatt . . . . Joanna Sutherland
John Hamill . . . . Cpl Alan Marlow
T.P. McKenna . . . . Supt Paddick
David Dodimead . . . . Dr Spencer
Christopher Chittell . . . . . . Baker
Peter Craze . . . . Roy
John Kelland . . . . Sgt Young
Vernon Dobtcheff . . . . . . Sir Bernard Newsmith
Dafydd Harvard . . . . Stephen Ballantyne
HORROR Lancashire. Spinster sisters keep mad brother bricked up in cellar.

AUG

14095
THE VAMPIRE LOVERS (91) (X) *tech*
Hammer-AIP (MGM—EMI)
P: Harry Fine, Michael Style
D: Roy Ward Baker
S: (STORY) Sheridan Le Fanu (CARMILLA)
SC: Tudor Gates, Harry Fine, Michael Style
Ingrid Pitt . . . Carmilla/Mircalla/Marcilla Karnstein
Peter Cushing . . . . General Spielsdorf
George Cole . . . . Morton
Dawn Addams . . . . Countess
Kate O'Mara . . . . Governess
Pippa Steele . . . . Laura
Madeleine Smith . . . . Emma
Douglas Wilmer . . . . Baron Hartog
Jon Finch . . . . Carl

Ferdy Mayne . . . . Doctor
Kirsten Betts . . . . Vampire
John Forbes Robertson . . . . Man in Black
HORROR Europe, period. Lesbian vampire returns to enslave sundry girls.

14096
WHEN DINOSAURS RULED THE EARTH (100) (A) *tech*
Hammer (WB)
P: Aida Young
D:SC: Val Guest
S: J.B. Ballard
Victoria Vetri . . . . Sanna
Robin Hawdon . . . . Tara
Patrick Allen . . . . Kingsor
Drewe Henley . . . . Khaku
Sean Caffrey . . . . Kane
Magda Konopka . . . . Ulido
Imogen Hassall . . . . Ayak
Patrick Holt . . . . Ammon
Jan Rossini . . . . Rock Girl
Carol-Anne Hawkins . . . . . . Yanni
FANTASY Girl of prehistoric Rock Tribe is adopted by dinosaur and observes origin of the moon.

14097
TOOMORROW (95) (A) *tech/scope*
Lowndes-Sweet Music (RFD)
P: Harry Saltzman, Don Kirschner
D:S: Val Guest
Olivia Newton-John . . . . Olivia
Benny Thomas . . . . Benny
Vic Cooper Vic
Karl Chambers . . . . Karl
Roy Dotrice . . . . John Williams
Imogen Hassall . . . . Amy
Tracey Crisp . . . . Suzanne Gilmore
Margaret Nolan . . . . Johnson
Roy Marsden . . . . Alpha
Carl Rigg . . . . Matthew
Maria O'Brien . . . . Francoise
Student Henry; Sam Apple Pie
MUSICAL Teenage pop group kidnapped by aliens who want the secret of their special sound.

14098
THE PERFUMED GARDEN (14) (X) *eastman*
Mira (Eagle)
P: Ray Austin, Maggie Fitzgibbon, Michael Pratt
D:SC: Ray Austin
S: (BOOK) Anon.
Chitra Noegy . . . . Woman
Saeed Jaffrey . . . . Man
NUDIST Representation of Persian love manual.

14099
TROG (93) (AA) *tech*
Herman Cohen (WB)
P: Herman Cohen
D: Freddie Francis
S: Peter Bryan, John Gilling
SC: Aben Kandel
Joan Crawford . . . . Dr Brockton
Michael Gough . . . . Sam Murdock
Joe Cornelius . . . . Trog
Kim Braden . . . . Ann Brockton
David Griffith . . . . Malcolm Travers
Bernard Kay . . . . Insp Greenham
John Hamill . . . . Cliff
Thorley Walters . . . . Magistrate
Jack May . . . . Dr Selbourne
Geoffrey Case . . . . Bill
Robert Hutton . . . . Dr Richard Warren
Simon Lack . . . . Col Vickers
HORROR Anthropologist captures a primitive man, who escapes and abducts a child.

SEP

14100 *
CARRY ON LOVING (88) (A) *eastman*
Adder-G.T. (RFD)
P: Peter Rogers
D: Gerald Thomas
S: Talbot Rothwell

Sidney James	Sidney Bliss
Kenneth Williams	Percival Snooper
Charles Hawtrey	James Bedsop
Joan Sims	Esme Crowfoot
Hattie Jacques	Sophie
Terry Scott	Terence Philpot
Richard O'Callaghan	Bertie Muffet
Bernard Bresslaw	Gripper Burke
Jacki Piper	Sally Martin
Imogen Hassall	Jenny Grubb
Patsy Rowlands	Miss Dempsey
Bill Maynard	Mr Dreery
Sonny Farrar	Violinist
Lauri Lupino Lane	Husband
Kenny Lynch	Conductor

COMEDY Miscellaneous misadventures of marriage agency clients.

14101
THE PRIVATE LIFE OF SHERLOCK HOLMES (125) (A) *deluxe/scope*
Mirisch-Phalanx-Sir Nigel (UA)
P:D: Billy Wilder
S: (CHARACTERS) Arthur Conan Doyle
SC: Billy Wilder, I.A.L. Diamond

Robert Stephens	Sherlock Holmes
Colin Blakeley	Dr John H. Watson
Irene Handl	Mrs Hudson
Christopher Lee	Mycroft Holmes
Tamara Toumanova	Petrova
Genevieve Page	Gabrielle Valladon
Clive Revill	Rogozhin
Catherine Lacey	Old Lady
Stanley Holloway	Gravedigger
Mollie Maureen	Queen Victoria
Peter Madden	Von Tirpitz

CRIME 19th C. Detective gets involved with secret submarine tests.

14102
THE SCARS OF DRACULA (96) (X) *tech*
Hammer-EMI (MGM—EMI)
P: Aida Young
D: Roy Ward Baker
S: (CHARACTERS) Bram Stoker
SC: Anthony Hinds

Christopher Lee	Count Dracula
Dennis Waterman	Simon
Jenny Hanley	Sarah Framsen
Christopher Matthews	Paul
Patrick Troughton	Klove
Michael Gwynn	Priest
Wendy Hamilton	Julie
Anouskha Hempel	Tania
Delia Lindsay	Alice
Bob Todd	Burgomaster

HORROR Vampire's crippled servant helps young people escape.

14103
FRAGMENT OF FEAR (95) (AA) *tech*
Columbia British (Col)
P: John R. Sloan
D: Richard C. Sarafian
S: (NOVEL) John Bingham
SC: Paul Dehn

David Hemmings	Tim Brett
Gayle Hunnicutt	Juliet Bristow
Flora Robson	Lucy Dawson
Wilfrid Hyde White	Mr Copsey
Daniel Massey	Maj Ricketts
Roland Culver	Mr Vellacot

Adolfo Celi	Bardoni
Mona Washbourne	Mrs Gray
Mary Wimbush	Bunface
Glynn Edwards	Supt
Derek Newark	Sgt Matthews
Arthur Lowe	Mr Nugent
Yootha Joyce	Mrs Ward-Cadbury
Bernard Archard	Priest

CRIME Young writer goes mad trying to solve aunt's murder.

14104
PERFECT FRIDAY (95) (AA) *eastman*
Sunnymede-De Grunwald (London Screenplays)
P: Jack Smith
D: Peter Hall
S: C. Scott Forbes
SC: C. Scott Forbes, Anthony Greville-Bell

Ursula Andress	Lady Britt Dorset
Stanley Baker	Mr Graham
David Warner	Lord Nicholas Dorset
Patience Collier	Nanny
T.P. McKenna	Smith
David Waller	Williams
Joan Benham	Miss Welsh
Julian Orchard	Thompson
Trisha Mortimer	Janet
Ann Tirard	Miss Marsh
Carleton Hobbs	Peer

CRIME Manager, infatuated with Lady, robs his bank of £300,000.

14105
THE BUTTERCUP CHAIN (95) (X) *tech/scope*
Columbia British
P: Leslie Gilliat, John Whitney, Philip Waddilove
D: Robert Ellis Miller
S: (NOVEL) Janice Elliott
SC: Peter Draper

Hywel Bennett	France
Leigh Taylor-Hunt	Manny
Jane Asher	Margaret
Sven-Bertil Taube	Fred
Clive Revill	George
Roy Dotrice	Martin Carr-Gibbons
Michael Elphick	Chauffeur
Jonathan Burn	Alberto
Susan Baker	Kate
Jennifer Baker	Ursula

ROMANCE Children of twin sisters have love affairs with Swede and American.

14106
CRIME DOESN'T PAY (24) (U)
Anvil (CFF)
Compiler: Gordon Shadrick
N: David Lodge
CHILDREN Compilation of extracts from Headline Hunters, The Christmas Tree, Operation Third Form, The Runaway Railway.

14107
DON'T MAKE ME LAUGH (21) (U)
Anvil (CFF)
Compiler: Gordon Shadrick
N: Richard Attenborough
CHILDREN Compilation of extracts from The Rescue Squad, Ali and the Camel, The Salvage Gang, Go Kart Go, Danny the Dragon, A Ghost of a Chance, Peewee's Pianola.

14108
THE MAN WHO HAD POWER OVER WOMEN (90) (X) *eastman*
Kettledrum-Rodlor (Avco Embassy)
P: Leonard Lightstone, Judd Bernard
D: John Krish
S: (NOVEL) Gordon Williams
SC: Allan Scott, Chris Bryant

Rod Taylor	Peter Reaney
Carol White	Jody Pringle
James Booth	Val Pringle
Penelope Horner	Angela Reaney
Charles Korvin	Alfred Felix
Alexandra Stewart	Frances
Keith Barron	Jake Braid
Clive Francis	Barry Black
Marie-France Boyer	Maggie
Magali Noel	Mrs Franchetti
Jimmy Jewel	Mr Pringle

DRAMA PR man's eventual disgust with amoral associates.

14109
THREE SISTERS (165) (U) *eastman*
Alan Clore (BL)
P: Alan Clore, John Goldstone
D: Laurence Olivier
S: (PLAY) Anton Chekhov
SC: Moura Budberg

Jeanne Watts	Olga Prosorov
Joan Plowright	Masha Prosorov
Louise Purnell	Irina Prosorov
Derek Jacobi	Andrei Prosorov
Alan Bates	Col Vershinin
Laurence Olivier	Dr Chebutikin
Kenneth Mackintosh	Kulighin
Sheila Reid	Natasha
Ronald Pickup	Baron Tusenbach
Frank Wylie	Maj Vassili Solloni
Daphne Heard	Anfissa

DRAMA Russia, 1900. Lives and loves of three orphaned sisters.

14110
SAY HELLO TO YESTERDAY (92) (AA) *eastman*
Shaftel (CIRO)
P: Josef Shaftel
D: Alvin Rakoff
S: Alvin Rakoff, Ray Matthew
SC: Alvin Rakoff, Peter King

Jean Simmons	Woman
Leonard Whiting	Boy
Evelyn Laye	Mother
John Lee	Husband
Jack Woolgar	Father
Constance Chapman	Mother
Gwen Nelson	Char
Richard Pescud	Official
Laraine Humphreys	Teenager
Ben Aris	Floorwalker
Nora Nicholson	Lady

ROMANCE Middle-aged housewife has affair with persistent teenager.

OCT

14111
FIGURES IN A LANDSCAPE (11) (AA) *tech/scope*
Cinecrest-Cinema Center (20)
P: Sir William Piggott-Brown
D: Joseph Losey
S: (NOVEL) Barry England
SC: Robert Shaw

Robert Shaw	MacConnachie
Malcolm McDowell	Ansell
Henry Woolf	Pilot
Christopher Malcolm	Observer
Andrew Bradford	Soldier
Roger Lloyd Pack	Soldier

WAR Two escapees pursued by helicopter.

14112
THE HOUSE THAT DRIPPED BLOOD (102) (X) *eastman*
Amicus (Cinerama)
P: Max Rosenberg, Milton Subotsky
D: Peter Duffell

S: (STORIES) Robert Bloch, (METHOD FOR MURDER; WAXWORKS; SWEETS TO THE SWEET; THE CLOAK)
SC: Robert Bloch

John Bennett	Insp Holloway
John Bryans	Stoker
Denholm Elliott	Charles Hillyer
Joanna Dunham	Alice Hillyer
Tom Adams	Dominick
Peter Cushing	Philip Grayson
Joss Ackland	Rogers
Christopher Lee	John Reid
Nyree Dawn Porter	Ann
Chloe Franks	Jane Reid
Jon Pertwee	Paul Anderson
Ingrid Pitt	Carla Lind

HORROR Estate agent narrates tales of murder, waxworks, witchcraft and vampires.

14113
PERCY (103) (X) *tech*
Welbeck-Anglo-EMI (MGM-EMI)
P: Betty Box
D: Ralph Thomas
S: (NOVEL) Raymond Hitchcock
SC: Hugh Leonard, Terence Feely

Hywel Bennett	Edwin Anthony
Denholm Elliott	Emmanuel Whitbread
Elke Sommer	Helga
Britt Ekland	Dorothy Chiltern-Barlow
Cyd Hayman	Moira Warrington
Janet Key	Hazel
Tracey Crisp	Miss Elder
Antonia Ellis	Rita La Rousse
Tracy Reed	Mrs Penney
Patrick Mower	James Vaile
Adrienne Posta	Maggie Hyde
Julia Foster	Marilyn
Arthur English	MC
Margaretta Scott	Mother

COMEDY Man tries to find donor of his transplanted penis.

14114
PERFORMANCE (105) (X) *tech*
Goodtimes Enterprises (WB)
P: Sanford Lieberson
D: Donald Cammell, Nicolas Roeg
S: Donald Cammell

James Fox	Chas Devlin
Mick Jagger	Turner
Anita Pallenberg	Pherber
Michele Breton	Lucy
Ann Sidney	Dana
John Bindon	Moody
Stanley Meadows	Rosebloom
Allan Cuthbertson	Lawyer
Antony Morton	Dennis
Johnny Shannon	Harry Flowers

CRIME Killer on the run shelters in retired pop star's house.

14115
PERMISSIVE (75) (X) *eastman*
Shonteff (Tigon)
P: Jack Shulton
D: Lindsay Shonteff
S: Jeremy Craig Dryden

Maggie Stride	Suzy
Gay Singleton	Fiona
Gilbert Wynne	Jimmy
Alan Gorrie	Lee
Robert Daubigny	Hippie
Forever More	Group

DRAMA Teenage girl lives with pop groups.

14116
SCROOGE (118) (U) *tech/scope*
Waterbury (20)
P: Leslie Bricusse, Robert Solo
D: Ronald Neame

S: (NOVEL) Charles Dickens (A CHRISTMAS CAROL)
SC: Leslie Bricusse

Albert Finney	Ebenezer Scrooge
Alec Guinness	Jacob Marley
Edith Evans	Christmas Past
Kenneth More	Christmas Present
Michael Medwin	Nephew
Laurence Naismith	Fezziwig
David Collings	Bob Cratchit
Anton Rodgers	Tom Jenkins
Suzanne Neve	Isabel
Frances Cuka	Mrs Cratchit
Derek Francis	Gentleman
Roy Kinnear	Gentleman
Mary Peach	Wife
Paddy Stone	Christmas Yet to Come
Kay Walsh	Mrs Fezziwig
Gordon Jackson	Friend
Richard Beaumont	Tiny Tim

MUSICAL Mean man reformed after visits from Past, Present and Future.

14117
10 RILLINGTON PLACE (111) (X) *eastman*
Genesis-Filmways-Columbia (Col)
P: Martin Ransohoff, Leslie Linder
D: Richard Fleischer
S: (BOOK) Ludovic Kennedy
SC: Clive Exton

Richard Attenborough	John Reginald Christie
Judy Geeson	Beryl Evans
John Hurt	Timothy John Evans
Pat Heywood	Mrs Christie
Isobel Black	Alice
Phyllis MacMahon	Muriel Eady
Geoffrey Chater	Christmas Humphries
Robert Hardy	Morris
Andre Morell	Judge
Bernard Lee	Insp J
Robert Keegan	Insp K
David Jackson	Constable C
Edward Evans	Insp A
Sam Kydd	Roberts

HISTORY Reconstruction of 1954 murder case.

14118
MISS MAGNIFICAT (28)
Syntax (Gala)
DRAMA Girl thinks she is pregnant and considers abortion.

14119
A HOLE LOT OF TROUBLE (27) (A) *eastman*
Chairene (Mon)
P: Francis Searle, John Hogarth
D: Francis Searle

Arthur Lowe	Whitehouse
Victor Maddern	Percy
Tim Barrett	Longbottom
Bill Maynard	Bill
Georgina Simpson	Carol
Brian Weske	Digby
Leslie Dwyer	Evangelist
Benny Lee	Bert
Neal Arden	Man

COMEDY Trouble revolving around workmen digging a hole.

14120
THE MACKENZIE BREAK (106) (AA) *deluxe*
Brighton (UA)
P: Jules Levy, Arthur Gardner, Arnold Laven
D: Lamont Johnson
S: (NOVEL) Sidney Shelley
SC: William Norton

Brian Keith	Capt Jack Connor
Helmut Griem	Kapt Schluetter
Ian Hendry	Maj Perry
Jack Watson	Gen Kerr
Patrick O'Connell	Sgt Cox

Caroline Mortimer	Sgt Bell
Horst Janson	Neuchl
Michael Sheard	Unger
Jon Abineri	Kranz
Eric Allan	Hochbauer
Tom Kempinski	Schmidt
Noel Purcell	Captain

WAR U-Boat officers escape from POW camp in Scotland.

14121
NO BLADE OF GRASS (96) (AA) *metro/scope*
Symbol (MGM)
P:D: Cornel Wilde
S: (NOVEL) John Christopher (DEATH OF GRASS)
SC: Sean Forestal, Jefferson Pascal

Nigel Davenport	John Custance
Jean Wallace	Ann Custance
Anthony May	Andrew Pirrie
John Hamill	Roger Burnham
Lynne Frederick	Mary Custance
Patrick Holt	David Custance
Wendy Richmond	Clara
Anthony Sharp	Sir Charles Bremmer
George Coulouris	Sturdevant

14122
SWEET AND SEXY (79) (X) *eastman*
Liongrange (Miracle)
P: Ray Selfe
D: Anthony Sloman
S: Andrew Best
SC: Andrew Best, Anthony Sloman

Quinn O'Hara	Sarah
Susanne Rogers	Julie
Robert Case	Ted Hawkins
Rose Alba	Landlady
Cathy Howard	Olivia
Jason Twelvetrees	Bert
Max Burns	Tony
Raymond Cross	Dennis
Prudence Paige	Janet

Tessa Lewis; Barbara Hunter; Julie Green
DRAMA Countryman's sexual adventures in seach of his sister.

NOV

14123
BARTLEBY (79) (A) *eastman*
Pantheon (BL)
P:SC: Rodney Carr-Smith, Anthony Friedmann
D: Anthony Friedmann
S: (STORY) Herman Melville

Paul Schofield	Accountant
John McEnery	Bartleby
Thorley Walters	Colleague
Colin Jeavons	Tucker
Raymond Mason	Landlord
Charles Kinross	Tenant
Hope Jackman	Hilda
Robin Asquith	Office Boy

DRAMA Audit clerk refuses to work and lives in the office.

14124
LUST FOR A VAMPIRE (95) (X) *tech*
Hammer (MGM-EMI)
P: Harry Fine, Michael Style
D: Jimmy Sangster
S: (STORY) J. Sheridan LeFanu (CARMILLA)
SC: Tudor Gates

Ralph Bates	Giles Barton
Barbara Jefford	Countess
Suzanna Leigh	Janet
Michael Johnson	Richard Lestrange
Yutte Stensgaard	Mircalla
Mike Raven	Count Karnstein
Helen Christie	Miss Simpson
David Healy	Pelley
Michael Brennan	Landlord
Pippa Steel	Susan

Jack Melford . . . . Bishop
Erik Chitty . . . . Professor Hertz
HORROR 1830. English teacher at European castle school loves his pupil, reincarnation of a vampire.

14125
THE RAILWAY CHILDREN (108) (U) *tech*
EMI-Associated British (MGM-EMI)
P: Robert Lynn
D:SC: Lionel Jeffries
S: (NOVEL) E. Nesbit
Dinah Sheridan . . . . Mother
Bernard Cribbins . . . . Perks
William Mervyn . . . . Old Gentleman
Iain Cuthbertson . . . . Father
Jenny Agutter . . . . Bobbie
Sally Thomsett . . . . Phyllis
Peter Bromilow . . . . Doctor
Ann Lancaster . . . . Ruth
Gary Warren . . . . Peter
Gordon Whiting . . . . Russian
David Lodge . . . . Bandmaster
CHILDREN Yorkshire, period. Experiences of three children whose father is in prison.

14126
THERE'S A GIRL IN MY SOUP (96) (X) *eastman*
Charter-Ascot-Frankovich (Col)
P: John Dark, M.J. Frankovich, John Boulting
D: Roy Boulting
S: (PLAY) Terence Frisby
SC: Terence Frisby
Peter Sellers . . . . Robert Danvers
Goldie Hawn . . . . Marion
Tony Britton . . . . Andrew Hunter
Nicky Henson . . . . Jimmy
John Comer . . . . John
Diana Dors . . . . Wife
Gabrielle Drake . . . . Julia
Geraldine Sherman . . . . Caroline
Judy Campbell . . . . Lady Heather
Nicola Pagett . . . . Clare
Christopher Cazenove . . . . . Nigel
Raf de la Torre . . . . Leguestier
Thorley Walters . . . . Manager
Avril Angers . . . . Woman
Eric Barker . . . . Guest
Lance Percival . . . . Guest
COMEDY TV personality's affair with young American girl.

14127
ONE MORE TIME (93) (A) *deluxe*
Chrislaw-Trace-Mark (UA)
P: Peter Lawford, Sammy Davis, Jr
D: Jerry Lewis
S: Michael Pertwee
Sammy Davis Jr . . . . Charlie Salt
Peter Lawford . . . . . . .Chris Pepper/Lord Sydney
Maggie Wright . . . . Miss Tomkins
Leslie Sands . . . . Insp Crock
John Wood . . . . Figg
Sydney Arnold . . . . Tombs
Edward Evans . . . . Gordon
Percy Herbert . . . . Mander
Bill Maynard . . . . Jenson
Dudley Sutton . . . . Wilson
Glyn Owen . . . . Dennis
Lucille Soong . . . . Kim Lee
Anthony Nicholls . . . . Candler
Allan Cuthbertson . . . . Belton
COMEDY Nightclub owner poses as dead twin to unmask murderer.

14128
UNDERGROUND (100) (A) *deluxe*
Brighton (UA)
P: Jules Levy, Arthur Gardner, Arnold Laven

D: Arthur H. Nadel
S: Marc L. Roberts, Ron Bishop
SC: Ron Bishop, Andy Lewis
Robert Goulet . . . . Maj Joe Dawson
Daniele Gaubert . . . . Yvonne
Lawrence Dobkin . . . . Boule
Carl Duering . . . . Stryker
Joachim Hansen . . . . Hessler
Roger Delgardo . . . . Xavier
Alexander Peleg . . . . Moravin
George Pravda . . . . Menke
Leon Lissek . . . . Sgt
Sebastian Breaks . . . . Condon
Nicole Croiselle . . . . Singer
Derry Power . . . . Pommard
WAR US major escapes from mental hospital to kidnap German general.

DEC

14129
COUNTESS DRACULA (93) (X) *eastman*
Hammer (RFD)
P: Alexander Paal
D: Peter Sasdy
S: Gabriel Ronay
SC: Alexander Paal, Peter Sasdy, Jeremy Paul
Ingrid Pitt . . . . .Countess Elizabeth Nadasdy
Nigel Green . . . . Capt Dobi
Sandor Eles . . . . Imre Toth
Maurice Denham . . . . Master Fabio
Patience Collier . . . . Julia
Peter Jeffrey . . . . Capt Balogh
Lesley-Anne Down . . . . Ilona
Leon Lissek . . . . Sgt
Jessie Evans . . . . Rosa
Andrea Lawrence . . . . Zizi
Nike Arrighi . . . . Gypsy
Charles Farrell . . . . Seller
Hulya Babus . . . . Belly Dancer
HORROR Widowed Countess rejuvenates by bathing in murdered virgins' blood.

14130
GET CARTER (112) (X) *metro*
MGM British (EMG-EMI)
P: Michael Klinger
D:SC: Mike Hodges
S: (NOVEL) Ted Lewis (JACK'S RETURN HOME)
Michael Caine . . . . Jack Carter
Britt Ekland . . . . Anna Fletcher
John Osborne . . . . Cyril Kinnear
Ian Hendry . . . . Eric Paice
Bryan Mosley . . . . Cliff Brumby
Geraldine Moffatt . . . . Glenda
Dorothy White . . . . Margaret
Alun Armstrong . . . . Keith
Glynn Edwards . . . . Albert Swift
Tony Beckley . . . . Peter
George Sewell . . . . Con McCarty
Rosemarie Dunham . . . . . . Edna Garfoot
CRIME Newcastle. Racketeer's vendetta on those concerned in his brother's death.

14131
MURPHY'S WAR (106) (A) *eastman/scope*
Deeley-Yates-London Screenplays (London Screen)
P: Michael Deeley
D: Peter Yates
S:(NOVEL) Max Catto
SC: Stirling Silliphant
Peter O'Toole . . . . Murphy
Sian Phillips . . . . Dr Hayden
Philippe Noiret . . . . Louis Brezan
Horst Janson . . . . U-Boat Cdr
John Hallam . . . . Lt Ellis
Ingo Mogendorf . . . . Voght
WAR 1944, Venezuela. Merchant sailor's one-man war on the U-Boat that sank his ship.

14132
THE RAGING MOON (111) (AA) *tech*
EMI (MGM-EMI)
P: Bruce Cohn Curtis
D:SC: Bryan Forbes
S: (NOVEL) Peter Marshall
Malcolm McDowell . . . . Bruce Pritchard
Nanette Newman . . . . Jill Matthews
Georgia Brown . . . . Sarah Charles
Barry Jackson . . . . Bill Charles
Gerald Sim . . . . Rev Corbett
Michael Flanders . . . . Clarence Marlow
Margery Mason . . . . Matron
Geoffrey Whitehead . . . . . . Harold Pritchard
Jack Woolgar . . . . Mr Pritchard
Norman Bird . . . . Dr Matthews
Constance Chapman . . . . . . Mrs Matthews
Bernard Lee . . . . Uncle Bob
Brook Williams . . . . Hugh Collins
DRAMA Crippled man falls in love with polio victim who dies.

14133
RYAN'S DAUGHTER (206) (AA) *metro/scope*
Faraway (MGM-EMI)
P: Anthony Havelock-Allan
D: David Lean
S: Robert Bolt
Sarah Miles . . . . Rosy Ryan
Robert Mitchum . . . . . .Charles Shaughnessy
Trevor Howard . . . . Father Collins
Christopher Jones . . . . Randolph Droyan
John Mills . . . . Michael
Leo McKern . . . . Tom Ryan
Barry Foster . . . . Tim O'Leary
Archie O'Sullivan . . . . McCardle
Marie Kean . . . . Mrs McCardle
Barry Jackson . . . . Cpl
ROMANCE Ireland, 1916. Schoolmaster's wife loves shell-shocked Major. (AA1970: Best Supporting Actor, Best Photography).

14134
SATAN'S SKIN (93) (X) *eastman*
retitled: BLOOD ON SATAN'S CLAW
Tigon British-Chilton (Tigon)
P: Tony Tenser, Peter Andrews, Malcolm Heyworth
D: Piers Haggard
S: Robert Wynne-Simmons, Piers Haggard
Patrick Wymark . . . . Judge
Linda Hayden . . . . Angela Blake
Barry Andrews . . . . Ralph Gower
Avice Landone . . . . Isobel Banham
Simon Williams . . . . Peter Edmonton
Tamara Ustinov . . . . Rosalind
Anthony Ainley . . . . Rev Fallowfield
Howard Goorney . . . . Doctor
Robin Davies . . . . Mark Vespers
James Hayter . . . . Squire Middleton
Michele Dotrice . . . . Margaret
HORROR 1670. Village children's witch cult and clawed creature dispelled by the cross.

14135
COOL IT CAROL! (101) (X) *eastman*
Peter Walker (Miracle)
P:D: Peter Walker
S: Murray Smith
Janet Lynn . . . . Carol Thatcher
Robin Askwith . . . . Joe Sickles
Peter Elliot . . . . Philip Stanton
Jess Conrad . . . . Jonathan
Stubby Kaye . . . . Rod Strangeways
Pearl Hackney . . . . Mother
Martin Wyldeck . . . . Father
Chris Sandford . . . . David Thing
Derek Aylward . . . . Tommy Sanders
Peter Murray . . . . Himself
Eric Barker . . . . Signalman
DRAMA Country girl and lover get involved in London vice.

14136
A SEVERED HEAD (98) (X) *tech*
Winkast (Col)
P: Alan Ladd jr
D: Dick Clement
S: (NOVEL) Iris Murdoch; (PLAY) Iris
Murdoch, J.B. Priestley
SC: Frederic Raphael
Lee Remick . . . . Antonia Lynch-Gibbon
Richard Attenborough . . . . . Palmer Anderson
Ian Holm . . . . Martin Lynch-Gibbon
Claire Bloom . . . . Honor Klein
Jennie Linden . . . . George Hands
Clive Revill . . . . .Alexander Lynch-Gibbon
Ann Firbank . . . . Rosemary Lynch-Gibbon
Rosamund Greenwood . . . . Miss Seelhaft
Constance Lorne . . . . Miss Hernshaw
DRAMA Wine merchant's affair with art treacher
and his wife's affair with psychiatrist.

14137
YOU CAN'T WIN 'EM ALL (99) (A) *tech/scope*
scope
SRO (Col)
P: Gene Corman
D: Peter Collinson
S: Leo V. Gordon
Tony Curtis . . . . Adam Dyer
Charles Bronson . . . . Josh Corey
Michele Mercier . . . . Aila
Gregoire Aslan . . . . Osman Bey
Fikret Hakan . . . . Col Elci
Salih Guney . . . . Capt Enver
Patrick Magee . . . . General
Tony Bonner . . . . Reese
John Acheson . . . . Davis
John Alderson . . . . Major
Leo Gordon . . . . Bolek
ADVENTURE 1922. American ex-soldiers join
Turkish colonel in plan to hijack bullion train.

14138
GAMES THAT LOVERS PLAY (91) (X)
eastman
Border (Border)
P: O. Negus-Fancey
D:S: Malcolm Leigh
Joanna Lumley . . . . Fanny Hill
Penny Brahms . . . . .Constance Chatterley
Richard Wattis . . . . Mr Lothran
Jeremy Lloyd . . . . .Jonathan Willoughby
Diana Hart . . . . Mrs Hill
Nan Munro . . . . Lady Evelyn
John Gatrell . . . . Bishop
Charles Cullum . . . . Charles
Leigh Anthony . . . . Keeper
George Belbin . . . . Maj Thumper
June Palmer . . . . Girl
New Temperance Seven
COMEDY 1920. Brothel keepers wager their
top girls in seduction contest.

14139
THE MUSIC LOVERS (123) (X) *eastman/*
scope
Russfilms (UA)
P: Roy Baird, Ken Russell
D: Ken Russell
S: (BOOK) Catherine Drinker Bowen
Barbara von Meck (BELOVED FRIEND)
SC: Melvyn Bragg
Richard Chamberlain . . . . . Tchaikovsky
Glenda Jackson . . . . Antonia Milyukova
Max Adrian . . . . Nicholas Rubinstein
Christopher Gable . . . . .Count Anton Chiluvsky
Isabella Telezynska . . . . . Mme von Meck
Kenneth Colley . . . . Modest Tchaikovsky
Sabina Maydelle . . . . Sasha Tchaikovsky
Maureen Pryor . . . . Mme Milyukova
Andrew Faulds . . . . Davidov

James Russell . . . . Bobyek
Victoria Russell . . . . Tatiana
Alexander Russell . . . . Grandson
Georgina Parkinson . . . . . . Odile
Alain Dubreuil . . . . Prince Siegfried
HISTORY Russia, 1875. Musical biography of
Russian composer.

14140
JANE EYRE (110)(A) *eastman*
Omnibus-Sagittarius (BL)
P: Frederick H. Brogger
D: Delbert Mann
S: (NOVEL) Charlotte Bronte
SC: Jack Pulman
George C. Scott . . . . Rochester
Susannah York . . . . Jane Eyre
Ian Bannen . . . . Rev St. John Rivers
Jack Hawkins . . . . Mr Brocklehurst
Nyree Dawn Porter . . . . . . Blanche Ingram
Rachel Kempson . . . . Mrs Fairfax
Kenneth Griffith . . . . Mason
Peter Copley . . . . John
Michele Dotrice . . . . Mary Rivers
Kara Wilson . . . . Diana Rivers
Sarah Gibson . . . . Young Jane
Jean Marsh . . . . Mrs Rochester
Clive Morton . . . . Mr Eshton
Constance Cummings . . . . . Mrs Reed
Hugh Latimer . . . . Col Dent
ROMANCE Period. Orphan governess loves her
employer, then finds he has a mad wife.

14141
THE LAST VALLEY (125) (AA) *eastman/*
scope
Season-Seamaster-ABC (Cinerama)
P: Martin Baum, James Clavell
D:SC: James Clavell
S: (NOVEL) J.B. Pick
Michael Caine . . . . Captain
Omar Sharif . . . . Vogel
Florinda Bolkan . . . . Erica
Nigel Davenport . . . . Gruber
Per Oscarsson . . . . Father Sebastian
Arthur O'Connell . . . . Hoffman
Madeline Hinde . . . . Inge
Yorgo Voyagis . . . . Pirelli
Miguel Alejandro . . . . Julio
Christian Roberts . . . . Andreas
Ian Hogg . . . . Graf
Michale Gothard . . . . Hansen
Brian Blessed . . . . Korski
Irene Prador . . . . Frau Hoffman
Edward Underdown . . . . . . Priest
WAR Alps, 1641. Scholar mediates between
mercenaries and villagers.

14142
THE REVOLUTIONARY (101) (AA) *tech*
Pressman-Williams Enterprises (UA)
P: Edward Rambach Pressman
D: Paul Williams
S: (NOVEL) Hans Koningsberger
SC: Hans Koningsberger
John Voight . . . . A
Jennifer Salt . . . . Helen Peret
Seymour Cassel . . . . Leonard
Robert Duvall . . . . Despard
Collin Wilcox-Horne . . . . . . Anne
Lionel Murton . . . . Professor
Reed de Rouen . . . . Mayor
Warren Stanhope . . . . Father
Mary Barclay . . . . Mother
Richard Pendry . . . . nco
Alexandra Berlin . . . . Nurse
Julie Garfield . . . . Girl
Kenneth J. Warren . . . . Sgt
Earl Cameron . . . . Speaker
James Dyrenforth . . . . Guest

DRAMA Revolutionary student deserts
army to warn strikers, and becomes an
assassin.

14143
WUTHERING HEIGHTS (105) (A) *movielab*
AIP (Anglo-EMI)
P: Louis M. Heyward
D: Robert Fuest
S: (NOVEL) Emily Bronte
SC: Patrick Tilley
Anna Calder-Marshall . . . . .Catherine Earnshaw
Timothy Dalton . . . . Heathcliff
Julian Glover . . . . Hindley Earnshaw
Ian Ogilvy . . . . Edgar Linton
Hilary Dwyer . . . . Isabella Linton
Judy Cornwell . . . . Nellie
Hugh Griffith . . . . Dr Kenneth
Harry Andrews . . . . Mr Earnshaw
Pamela Brown . . . . Mrs Linton
James Cossins . . . . Mr Linton
Rosalie Crutchley . . . . Mrs Earnshaw
Peter Sallis . . . . Mr Sheilders
ROMANCE Yorkshire period. Girl loves gypsy
stable boy but weds rich magistrate.

14144
THE STATUE (89) (X) *eastman*
Shaftel (Cinerama)
P: Josef Shaftel, Anis Nohra
D: Rod Amateau
S: (PLAY) Alec Coppel (CHIP, CHIP, CHIP)
SC: Alec Coppel, Denis Norden
David Niven . . . . Alex Bolt
Virna Lisi . . . . Rhonda Bolt
Robert Vaughan . . . . Ray Whiteley
Anne Bell . . . . Pat Demarest
John Cleese . . . . Harry
Tim Brooke-Taylor . . . . Hillcrest
Hugh Burden . . . . Sir Geoffrey
Erik Chitty . . . . Mouser
Derek Francis . . . . Sanders
Susan Travers . . . . Mrs Southwick
Desmond Walter-Ellis . . . . . Mr Southwick
COMEDY Nobel Prize winner seeks the model
for the penis on his nude statue.

14145
EGGHEAD'S ROBOT (56) (U) *eastman*
Interfilm (CFF)
P: Cecil Musk
D: Milo Lewis
S: Leif Saxon
Keith Chegwin . . . . Egghead Wentworth
Jeffrey Chegwin . . . . Eric
Kathryn Dawe . . . . Elspeth
Roy Kinnear . . . . Park Keeper
Richard Wattis . . . . Paul Wentworth
Patricia Routledge . . . . Mrs Wentworth
CHILDREN Inventor's son uses his father's
robot as his double.

14146
SCRAMBLE (61) (U) *eastman*
Eady-Barnes (CFF)
P: Tom Lyndon-Haynes
D: David Eady
S: Michael Barnes
Ian Ramsey . . . . Jimmy Riley
Stuart Lock . . . . Colin Buxton
Stephen Mallett . . . . Brian Buxton
Lucinda Barnes . . . . Vicky
Gareth Marks . . . . Oscar Heppelwhite
Robin Askwith . . . . Lennie
Carling Paton . . . . Cliff
Alfred Marks . . . . Mr Heppelwhite
James Hayter
David Lodge
William Lucas
Graham Stark
CHILDREN Prisoner's son joins motorbike club
and foils car thieves.

14147
PUPPET ON A CHAIN (98) (AA) *tech*
Big City (Scotia-Barber)
P: Kurt Unger
D: Geoffrey Reeve, Don Sharp
S: (NOVEL) Alistair MacLean
SC: Alistair MacLean, Don Sharp, Paul
Wheeler
Sven Bertil-Taube . . . . Paul Sherman
Barbara Parkins . . . . Maggie
Alexander Knox . . . . Col De Graaf
Patrick Allen . . . . Insp Van Gelder
Vladek Sheybal . . . . Meegeren
Ania Marson . . . . Astride Lemay
Penny Casdagli . . . . Trudi
Peter Hutchins . . . . Assassin
Henni Orri . . . . Herta
Stewart Lane . . . . George Lemay
CRIME Holland. Interpol agent unmasks inspector
as heroin smuggler.

14148
CARRY ON HENRY (89) (A) *eastman*
Adder (RFD)
P: Peter Rogers
D: Gerald Thomas
S: Talbot Rothwell
Sidney James . . . . Henry VIII
Kenneth Williams . . . . Sir Thomas Cromwell
Joan Sims . . . . Marie Of Normandy
Charles Hawtrey . . . . . Sir Roger de Loggerley
Terry Scott . . . . Cardinal Wolsey
Barbara Windsor . . . . Bettina
Kenneth Connor . . . . 'Lord Hampton
Julian Holloway . . . . Sir Thomas
Julian Orchard . . . . Duc de Pincenay
Gertain Klauber . . . . Bidet
William Mervyn . . . . Physician
Bill Maynard . . . . Fawkes
Monica Dietrich . . . . Katharine Howard
Peter Butterworth . . . . Earl of Bristol
COMEDY King discovers his garlic-loving wife
is pregnant by her lover.

14149
DOCTORS WEAR SCARLET (87) (X) *eastman*
retitled: INCENSE FOR THE DAMNED
Lucinda-Titan International (GN)
P: Peter Newbrook
D: Robert Hartford-Davis
S: (NOVEL) Simon Raven
SC: Julian More
Patrick Macnee . . . . Maj Derek Longbow
Peter Cushing . . . . Dr Goodrich
Alex Davion . . . . Tony Seymour
Johnny Sekka . . . . Bob Kirby
Madeline Hinde . . . . Penelope
Patrick Mower . . . . Richard Fountain
Imogen Hassall . . . . . Chriseis Constandinidi
Edward Woodward . . . . . Holmstrom
William Mervyn . . . . Honeydew
David Lodge . . . . Colonel
HORROR Greece. Foreign Secretary's son
becomes a vampire.

14150
THE CASTLE OF FU MANCHU (92) (A)
eastman/trilingual
Terra Filmkunst-Balcazar-Towers of London
(MGM-EMI)
P: Harry Alan Towers
D: Jesus Franco
S: (CHARACTERS) Sax Rohmer
SC: Peter Welbeck
Christopher Lee . . . . Fu Manchu
Richard Greene . . . . Nayland Smith
Howard Marion Crawford . . Dr Petrie
Tsai Chin . . . . Lin Tang
Gunther Stoll . . . . Curt
Rosalba Neri . . . . Lisa

Maria Perschy . . . . Marie
Jose Manuel Martin . . . . Omar Pasha
Werner Aprelat . . . . Melnik
CRIME Chinese crook forces surgeon to trans-
plant heart of captive inventor.

14151
BLOOMFIELD (95) (U) *tech*
World Film Services-Limbridge (20)
P: John Heyman, Wolf Mankowitz
D: Richard Harris
S: Joseph Gross
SC: Wolf Mankowitz, Richard Harris
Richard Harris . . . . Eitan
Romy Schneider . . . . Nira
Kim Burfield . . . . Nimrod
Maurice Kaufmann . . . . Yasha
Yossi Yadin . . . . Weiner
Shraga Friedman . . . . Chairman
Aviva Marks . . . . Teddy
Yossi Grabber . . . . Bank Manager
David Heyman . . . . Eldad
SPORT Israel. Boy's football hero is bribed to
lose his last game.

14152
THE CORPSE (90) (X) *colour*
London Cannon-Abacus (GN)
P: Dennis Friedland, Christopher Dewey,
Gabrielle Beaumont
D: Viktors Ritelis
S: Olaf Pooley
Michael Gough . . . . Walter Eastwood
Yvonne Mitchell . . . . Edith Eastwood
Sharon Gurney . . . . Jane Eastwood
Simon Gough . . . . Rupert Eastwood
Olaf Pooley . . . . Reid
David Butler . . . . Gregson
Mary Hignett . . . . Mrs Roberts
Nicholas Jones . . . . Benjie
CRIME Richmond. Woman and daughter poison
tyrranical husband and are haunted by his corpse.

14153
A TOUCH OF THE OTHER (92) (X) *eastman*
Global (Queensway)
P: Leslie Berens, Arnold Louis Miller, Sheila
Miller
D: Arnold Louis Miller
S: Frank Wyman
Kenneth Cope . . . . Delger
Shirley-Anne Field . . . . Elaine
Helene Francois . . . . Wendy
Timothy Craven . . . . Webber
Vasco Koulolia . . . . Hughes
Noel Davis . . . . Max Ronleau
Renny Lister . . . . Sheila
Gypsy Kemp . . . . Shirley
Paul Stassino . . . . Connely
CRIME Prostitute helps detective framed for
killing his friend.

14154
THE FIRECHASERS (101) (U) *eastman*
ITC (RFD)
P: Julian Wintle
D: Sidney Hayers
S: Philip Levine
Chad Everett . . . . Quentin Barnaby
Anjanette Comer . . . . Toby Collins
Keith Barron . . . . Jim Maxwell
Joanne Dainton . . . . Valerie Chrane
Rupert Davies . . . . Prentice
James Hayter . . . . Insp Herman
Robert Flemyng . . . . Carlton
Roy Kinnear . . . . Roscoe
Allan Cuthbertson . . . . Jarvis
John Loder . . . . Routledge
CRIME Girl reporter helps insurance tec trap
arsonist behind explosive tea-makers.

14155
DIE SCREAMING, MARIANNE (104) (X)
eastman
Pete Walker (London Screen)
P:D: Pete Walker
S: Murray Smith
Susan George . . . . Marianne
Barry Evans . . . . Eli Frome
Christopher Sandford . . . . Sebastian Smith
Judy Huxtable . . . . Hildegarde
Leo Genn . . . . Judge
Kenneth Hendel . . . . Rodriguez
Anthony Sharp . . . . Registrar
Martin Wyldeck . . . . Policeman
CRIME Portugal. Blackmailer's schemes to get
money from corrupt judge's illegitimate daughter.

14156
THE GO-BETWEEN (116) (AA) *tech*
World Film Services (MGM-EMI)
P: Robert Velaise, John Heyman, Norman
Priggen
D: Joseph Losey
S: (NOVEL) L.P. Hartley
SC: Harold Pinter
Julie Christie . . . . Marion Maudsley
Alan Bates . . . . Ted Burgess
Dominic Guard . . . . Leo Colston
Margaret Leighton . . . . . . Mrs Maudsley
Michael Regrave . . . . Leo (old)
Michael Gough . . . . Mr Maudsley
Edward Fox . . . . Hugh Trimingham
Richard Gibson . . . . Marcus Maudsley
Simon Hume-Kendall . . . . . Denys
Amaryllis Garnett . . . . Kate
ROMANCE Norfolk. Boy on holiday acts as go-
between for his friend's sister and a farmer.

14157
HOVERBUG (57) (U) *eastman*
Fanfare (CFF)
P: George H. Brown
D: Jan Darnley-Smith
S: Michael Barnes
Jill Riddick . . . . Jenny Brewster
John Trayhorn . . . . Dick Brewster
Francis Attard . . . . Charlie
Gary Cann . . . . Sydney
Arthur Howard . . . . Mr Watts
Michael Balfour . . . . Father
Peter Myers . . . . Mr Brewster
Cardew Robinson . . . .
CHILDREN Inventor's super glue helps children
win home-made hovercraft race.

14158
VIRGIN WITCH (89) (X) *eastman*
Univista (Tigon)
P: Dennis Durack, Edward Brady, Ralph
Solomons
D: Ray Austin
S: (NOVEL) Klaus Vogel
SC: Klaus Vogel
Ann Michelle . . . . Christine
Vicky Michelle . . . . Betty
Keith Buckley . . . . Johnny
Patricia Haines . . . . Sybil Waite
James Chase . . . . Peter
Paula Wright . . . . Mrs Wendell
Neil Hallett . . . . Gerald Amberley
Helen Downing . . . . Abby Darke
CRIME Psychic lesbian tries to make her girl-
friend a witch.

14159
WELCOME TO THE CLUB (88) (X) *eastman*
Welcome (Col-WB)
P: Sam Lomburg, Walter Shenson
D: Walter Shenson
S: (NOVEL) Clement Biddle Wood
SC: Clement Biddle Wood

Brian Foley . . . . Andrew Oxblood
Jack Warden . . . . Gen Strapp
Lee Meredith . . . . Betsy Wholecloth
Andy Jarrell . . . . Robert E. Lee Fairfax
Kevin O'Connor . . . . Harrison W. Morve
Francesca Tu . . . . Hogan
David Toguri . . . . Hideki Ikada
Al Mancini . . . . PFC Marcantonio
Art Wallace . . . . Col Buonocuore
Lionel Murton . . . . Col Ames
Marsha Hunte . . . . Leah Wheat
COMEDY Hiroshima, 1945. US Army morale
officer's problems with visiting Negro entertainers.

14160
JUNKET 89 (56) (U) *eastman*
Balfour (CFF)
P: Carole Smith
D: Peter Plummer
S: David Ash
Stephen Brassett . . . . Junket
John Blundell . . . . O'Fred
Linda Robson . . . . Daisy
Mario Renzullo . . . . Boofles
Freddy Foote . . . . Burns
John Barrow . . . . Boston
Fanny Carby . . . . Mrs Trowser-Legge

Gary Sobers . . . . Himself
CHILDREN Schoolboy transported to island by
his teacher's invention.

14161
LOVING MEMORY (57) (-)
Scott Free-BFI-Memorial Enterprises (BFI)
P: Steve Bayley
D:S: Anthony Scott
David Pugh . . . . Young Man
Roy Evans . . . . Man
Rosamund Greenwood . . . . Woman
DRAMA Yorkshire. Old woman treats cyclist's
corpse as her late brother.

Index

Compiled by Kathleen Binns

Z